EUROPEAN COMPANY AND FINANCIAL LAW

FOURTH EDITION

EUROPEAN COMPANY AND FINANCIAL LAW

Texts and Leading Cases

FOURTH EDITION

Edited by
KLAUS HOPT
and
EDDY WYMEERSCH

Great Clarendon Street, Oxford OX2 6DP

Oxford University Press is a department of the University of Oxford.
It furthers the University's objective of excellence in research, scholarship,
and education by publishing worldwide in

Oxford New York

Auckland Cape Town Dar es Salaam Hong Kong Karachi
Kuala Lumpur Madrid Melbourne Mexico City Nairobi
New Delhi Shanghai Taipei Toronto

With offices in

Argentina Austria Brazil Chile Czech Republic France Greece
Guatemala Hungary Italy Japan Poland Portugal Singapore
South Korea Switzerland Thailand Turkey Ukraine Vietnam

Oxford is a registered trade mark of Oxford University Press
in the UK and in certain other countries

Published in the United States
by Oxford University Press Inc., New York

© K. Hopt and E. Wymeersch 2007

The moral rights of the authors have been asserted

Crown copyright material is reproduced under Class Licence
Number C01P0000148 with the permission of OPSI
and the Queen's Printer for Scotland

Database right Oxford University Press (maker)

First published 2007

All rights reserved. No part of this publication may be reproduced,
stored in a retrieval system, or transmitted, in any form or by any means,
without the prior permission in writing of Oxford University Press,
or as expressly permitted by law, or under terms agreed with the appropriate
reprographics rights organization. Enquiries concerning reproduction
outside the scope of the above should be sent to the Rights Department,
Oxford University Press, at the address above

You must not circulate this book in any other binding or cover
and you must impose the same condition on any acquirer

British Library Cataloguing in Publication Data

Data available

Library of Congress Cataloging in Publication Data

Data available

Typeset by Newgen Imaging Systems (P) Ltd., Chennai, India
Printed in Great Britain
on acid-free paper by
Antony Rowe Ltd., Chippenham

ISBN 978–0–19–922760–0

1 3 5 7 9 10 8 6 4 2

PREFACE

This is now the fourth edition of our text collection of European Union legal instruments. It contains texts and leading cases up to 15 December 2006. As with the previous editions, it deals mainly with the EU directives, regulations, recommendations, and other relevant instruments in the fields of banking, company law, and consumer protection related to financial transactions, enterprise law, insurance, and securities regulation.

The main purpose of this text collection is to offer the user a convenient, easily accessible, properly organised and updated collection of all European Instruments that have been enacted in the above-mentioned fields. Both in legal practice and academia, more and more often the need arises to consult the European directives in their latest, preferably co-ordinated version. Practitioners and researchers in these topics will find this book a particularly useful tool in obtaining rapid access to the texts and having it ready whenever needed, in daily work, in conferences and eventually in the courtroom.

The previous editions, published in 1992, 1994, and 2003, have constituted the basis for this publication, both in terms of content and format. As in the previous editions, and for the reasons stated there, tax law and antitrust rules have not been included. On the other hand, the summaries to most of the more recent European Court of Justice cases, in toto around 175, have been included either under the article of the directive to which the case specifically relates, or under the heading of the directive where the case relates to the directive in general. Some cases relating to the Treaty provisions have not been included. The references to the ECJ's cases identify the Court's authoritative interpretation of the Secondary Community Law, and inform on the policy orientations the Court has adopted. This constitutes a helpful tool in accessing the increasingly voluminous source material. By so doing, it has not been the intention to give a comprehensive overview of all ECJ cases that could be relevant for the interpretation of these directives.

Over the last three years, the number of texts has once more increased beyond any expectation. Therefore, as in the previous edition, only those instruments have been included that have been finally adopted. They now amount to over 186. Among the more than 20 instruments that have been added since the last edition, there are such important ones as those on capital requirements (Basel II) takeover bids, market abuse, transparency, prospectus and markets for financial instruments, that constitute almost a full re-regulation of the securities field. In addition, there are instruments on money laundering, several measures dealing with company law (remuneration of directors, independent directors and committees, cross-border mergers, statutory audits of annual accounts and consolidated accounts), unfair business-to-consumer commercial practices, insurance against civil liability in respect of the use of motor vehicles. For directives currently proposed by the European Commission, which are often considerably modified during the legislative process, the user is referred to the Commission's homepage.

We would like to thank Dr. Ingrid De Poorter, Doctor-Assistent and Ms. Nicolle Kransfeld, management assistant, both at the Ghent Law Faculty, without whose considerable effort and valuable and patient assistance this fourth edition could not have been realised.

Hamburg and Gent, December 2006

K. J. Hopt and E. Wymeersch

CONTENTS SUMMARY

I.	Banking Law	1
II.	Capital Movement	423
III.	Company Law	445
IV.	Consumer Protection especially related to Financial Transactions	789
V.	Enterprise Law	961
VI.	Insurance Law	1049
VII.	Securities Regulation	1399

Chronological List of Directives	1764
Alphabetical List of Cases	1783
Chronological List of Cases	1793
Correlation Table EU-Treaty—Treaty of Amsterdam	1803

CONTENTS

Part I. Banking Law

B. 1.	Council Directive 73/183/EEC of 28 June 1973 on the abolition of restrictions on freedom of establishment and freedom to provide services in respect of self-employed activities of banks and other financial institutions, OJ L 194, 16 July 1973, 1–10.[1]	1
B. 2.	First Council Directive 77/780/EEC of 12 December 1977 on the co-ordination of laws, regulations and administrative provisions relating to the taking up and pursuit of the business of credit institutions, OJ L 322, 17 December 1977, 30.[1]	2
B. 3.	Council Directive 83/350/EEC of 13 June 1983 on the supervision of credit institutions on consolidated basis, OJ L 193, 18 July 1983, 18–20.[1]	3
B. 4.	Council Directive 85/345/EEC of 8 July 1985 amending Directive 77/780/EEC on the co-ordination of laws, regulations and administrative provisions relating to the taking up and pursuit of the business of credit institutions, OJ L 183, 16 July 1985, 19–20.[1]	4
B. 5.	Council Directive 86/137/EEC of 17 April 1986 authorising certain Member States to defer further application of Directive 77/780/EEC as regards certain credit institutions, OJ L 106, 23 April 1986, 35.[1]	5
B. 6.	Council Directive 86/524/EEC of 27 October 1986 amending Directive 77/780/EEC in respect of the list of permanent exclusions of certain credit institutions, OJ L 309, 4 November 1986, 15–16.[1]	6
B. 7.	Council Directive 86/635/EEC of 8 December 1986 on the annual accounts and consolidated accounts of banks and other financial institutions, OJ L 372, 31 December 1986, 1–17.	7
B. 8.	Commission Recommendation 87/62/EEC of 22 December 1986 on monitoring and controlling large exposures of credit institutions, OJ L 33, 4 February 1987, 10–15.	26
B. 9.	Commission Recommendation 87/63/EEC of 22 December 1986 concerning the introduction of deposit-guarantee schemes in the Community, OJ L 33, 4 February 1987, 16–17.	27

---

[1] This Directive has been repealed as from 15 June 2000 by article 67 of Directive 2000/12/EC (OJ L 126, 26.5.2000, 1), reproduced infra no. B. 32, which subsequently has been repealed as from 20 July 2006 by article 158 of Directive 2006/48/EC (OJ L 177, 30.06.2006, 1) reproduced infra under no. B. 41.

B. 10.	Council Directive 89/117/EEC of 13 February 1989 on the obligations of branches established in a Member State of credit institutions and financial institutions having their head offices outside that Member State regarding the publication of annual accounting documents, OJ L 44, 16 February 1989, 40–42.	28
B. 11.	Council Directive 89/299/EEC of 17 April 1989 on the own funds of credit institutions, OJ L 124, 5 May 1989, 16–20.[I]	32
B. 12.	Second Council Directive 89/646/EEC of 15 December 1989 on the co-ordination of laws, regulations and administrative provisions relating to the taking up and pursuit of the business of credit institutions and amending Directive 77/780/EEC, OJ L 386, 30 December 1989, 1–13.[I]	33
B. 13.	Council Directive 89/647/EEC of 18 December 1989 on a solvency ratio for credit institutions, OJ L 386, 30 December 1989, 14–22.[I]	34
B. 14.	Commission Directive 91/31/EEC of 19 December 1990 adapting the technical definition of 'multilateral development banks' in Council Directive 89/647/EEC of 18 December 1989 on a solvency ratio for credit institutions, OJ L 17, 23 January 1991, 20.[I]	35
B. 15.	Council Directive 91/308/EEC of 10 June 1991 on prevention of the use of the financial system for the purpose of money laundering, OJ L 166, 28 June 1991, 77–83.[II]	36
B. 16.	Council Directive 91/633/EEC of 3 December 1991 implementing Directive 89/299/EEC on the own funds of credit institutions, OJ L 339, 11 December 1991, 33–34.[I]	38
B. 17.	Council Directive 92/16/EEC of 16 March 1992 amending Directive 89/299/EEC on the own funds of credit institutions, OJ L 75, 21 March 1992, 48–50.[I]	39
B. 18.	Council Directive 92/30/EEC of 6 April 1992 on the supervision of credit institutions on a consolidated basis, OJ L 110, 28 April 1992, 52–58.[I]	40
B. 19.	Council Directive 92/121/EEC of 21 December 1992 on the monitoring and control of large exposures of credit institutions, OJ L 29, 5 February 1993, 1–8.[I]	41
B. 20.	Council Directive 93/6/EEC of 15 March 1993 on the capital adequacy of investments firms and credit institutions, OJ L 141, 11 June 1993, 1–26.[III]	42
B. 21.	Commission Directive 94/7/EC of 15 March 1994 adapting Council Directive 89/647/EEC on a solvency ratio for credit institutions as regards the technical definition of 'multilateral development banks', OJ L 89, 6 April 1994, 17.[I]	45

[II] This Directive has been repealed as from 14 November 2004 by article 44 of Directive 2005/60/EC (OJ L 309, 25.11.2005, 15), reproduced infra under no. B. 40.

[III] This Directive has been repealed as from 20 July 2006 by article 52 of Directive 2006/49/EC (OJ L 177, 30.6.2006, 201), reproduced infra under no. B. 42.

B. 22.	European Parliament and Council Directive 94/19/EC of 30 May 1994 on deposit-guarantee schemes, OJ L 135, 31 May 1994, 5–14.	46
B. 23.	Commission Directive 95/15/EC of 31 May 1995 adapting Council Directive 89/647/EEC on a solvency ratio for credit institutions, as regards the technical definition of 'Zone A' and in respect of the weighting of asset items constituting claims carrying the explicit guarantee of the European Communities, OJ L 125, 8 June 1995, 23–24.[I]	59
B. 24.	Commission Directive 95/67/EC of 15 December 1995 making a technical amendment to Council Directive 89/647/EEC on a solvency ratio for credit institutions as regards the definition of 'multilateral development banks', OJ L 314, 28 December 1995, 72.[I]	60
B. 25.	Council Directive 96/13/EC of 11 March 1996 amending Article 2 (2) of Directive 77/780/EEC in respect of the list of permanent exclusions of certain credit institutions, OJ L 66, 16 March 1996, 15–16.[I]	61
B. 26.	European Parliament and Council Directive 96/10/EC of 21 March 1996 amending Directive 89/647/EEC as regards recognition of contractual netting by the competent authorities, OJ L 85, 3 April 1996, 17–21.[I]	62
B. 27.	Commission Interpretative Communication 97/C 209/04 of 10 July 1997 on freedom to provide services and the interest of the general good in the Second Banking Directive, OJ C 209, 10 July 1997, 6–22.	63
B. 28.	European Parliament and Council Directive 98/31/EC of 22 June 1998 amending Council Directive 93/6/EEC on the capital adequacy of investment firms and credit institutions, OJ L 204, 21 July 1998, 13–25.[III]	82
B. 29.	European Parliament and Council Directive 98/32/EC of 22 June 1998 amending, as regards in particular mortgages, Council Directive 89/647/EEC on a solvency ratio for credit institutions, OJ L 204, 21 July 1998, 26–28.[I]	85
B. 30.	European Parliament and Council Directive 98/33/EC of 22 June 1998 amending Article 12 of Council Directive 77/780/EEC on the taking up and pursuit of the business of credit institutions, Articles 2, 5, 6, 7, 8 of and Annexes II and III to Council Directive 89/647/EEC on a solvency ratio for credit institutions and Article 2 of and Annex II to Council Directive 93/6/EEC on the capital adequacy of investment firms and credit institutions, OJ L 204, 21 July 1998, 29–36.[III]	86
B. 31.	Joint Action 98/699/JHA of 3 December 1998 adopted by the Council on the basis of Article [31][IV] of the Treaty on European Union, on money laundering, the identification, tracing, freezing, seizing and confiscation of instrumentalities and the proceeds from crime, OJ L 333, 9 December 1998, 1–3.	87

[IV] The number between brackets has been changed as from 1 May 1999 by article 12 of the Treaty of Amsterdam.

B. 32.	European Parliament and Council Directive 2000/12/EC of 20 March 2000 relating to the taking up and pursuit of the business of credit institutions, OJ L 126, 26 May 2000, 1–59.^V	91
B. 33.	Commission Recommendation 2000/408/EC of 23 June 2000 concerning disclosure of information on financial instruments and other items complementing the disclosure required according to Council Directive 86/635/EEC on the annual accounts and consolidated accounts of banks and other financial institutions, OJ L 154, 27 June 2000, 36–41.	95
B. 34.	European Parliament and Council Directive 2000/28/EC of 18 September 2000 amending Directive 2000/12/EC relating to the taking up and pursuit of the business of credit institutions, OJ L 275, 27 October 2000, 37–38.^V	101
B. 35.	European Parliament and Council Directive 2000/46/EC of 18 September 2000 on the taking up, pursuit of and prudential supervision of the business of electronic money institutions, OJ L 275, 27 October 2000, 39–43.	102
B. 36.	European Parliament and Council Directive 2001/24/EC of 4 April 2001 on the reorganisation and winding up of credit institutions, OJ L 125, 5 May 2001, 15–23.	108
B. 37.	European Parliament and Council Directive 2001/97/EC of 4 December 2001 amending Council Directive 91/308/EEC on prevention of the use of the financial system for the purpose of money laundering, OJ L 344, 28 December 2001, 76–81.	120
B. 38.	European Parliament and Council Directive 2002/87/EC of 16 December 2002 on the supplementary supervision of credit institutions, insurance undertakings and investment firms in a financial conglomerate and amending Council Directives 73/239/EEC, 79/267/EEC, 92/49/EEC, 92/96/EEC, 93/6/EEC and 93/22/EEC, and Directives 98/78/EC and 2000/12/EC of the European Parliament and of the Council, OJ L 35, 11 February 2003, 1–27.	123
B. 39.	European Parliament and Council Directive 2005/1/EC of 9 March 2005 amending Council Directives 73/239/EEC, 85/611/EEC, 91/675/EEC, 92/49/EEC and 93/6/EEC and Directives 94/19/EC, 98/78/EC, 2000/12/EC, 2001/34/EC, 2002/83/EC and 2002/87/EC in order to establish a new organisational structure for financial services committees, OJ L 79, 24 March 2005, 9–17.	145
B. 40.	European Parliament and Council Directive 2005/60/EC of 26 October 2005 on the prevention of the use of the financial system for the purpose of money laundering and terrorist financing, OJ L 309, 25 November 2005, 15–36.	151

---

^V This Directive has been repealed as from 20 July 2006 by article 158 of Directive 2006/48/EC (OJ L 177, 30.6.2006, 1), reproduced infra under no. B. 41.

B. 41.	European Parliament and Council Directive 2006/48/EC of 14 June 2006 relating to the taking up and pursuit of the business of credit institutions (recast), OJ L 177, 30 June 2006, 1–200.	175
B. 42.	European Parliament and Council Directive 2006/49/EC of 14 June 2006 on the capital adequacy of investment firms and credit institutions (recast), OJ L 177, 30 June 2006, 201–255.	369

Part II. Capital Movement

C.M. 1.	EU Treaty: Chapter 4–Capital and Payments	423
C.M. 2.	Council Directive 88/361/EEC of 24 June 1988 for the implementation of Article [67][VI] of the Treaty, OJ L 178, 8 July 1988, 5–18.	431

Part III. Company Law

C. 1.	First Council Directive 68/151/EEC of 9 March 1968 on co-ordination of safeguards which, for the protection of the interests of members and others, are required by Member States of companies within the meaning of the second paragraph of Article [48][IV] of the Treaty, with a view to making such safeguards equivalent throughout the Community, OJ L 65, 14 March 1968, 8–12.	445
C. 2.	Second Council Directive 77/91/EEC of 13 December 1976 on co-ordination of safeguards which, for the protection of the interests of members and others, are required by Member States of companies within the meaning of the second paragraph of Article [48][IV] of the Treaty, in respect of the formation of public limited liability companies and the maintenance and alteration of their capital, with a view to making such safeguards equivalent, OJ L 26, 31 January 1977, 1–13.	454
C. 3.	Third Council Directive 78/855/EEC of 9 October 1978 based on Article [44][IV] (3) (g) of the Treaty concerning mergers of public limited liability companies, OJ L 295, 20 October 1978, 36–43.	476
C. 4.	Fourth Council Directive 78/660/EEC of 25 July 1978 based on Article [44][IV] (3) (g) of the Treaty on the annual accounts of certain types of companies, OJ L 222, 14 August 1978, 11–31.[II]	486
C. 5.	Sixth Council Directive 82/891/EEC of 17 December 1982 based on Article [44][IV] (3) (g) of the Treaty, concerning the division of public limited liability companies, OJ L 378, 31 December 1982, 47–54.	520
C. 6.	Seventh Council Directive 83/349/EEC of 13 June 1983 based on Article [44][IV] (3) (g) of the Treaty on Consolidated Accounts, OJ L 193, 18 June 1983, 1–17.	529

[VI] Article 67 has been repealed as from 1 May 1999 by article 12 of the Treaty of Amsterdam.

C. 7.	Eighth Council Directive 84/253/EEC of 10 April 1984 based on Article [44]^{IV} (3) (g) of the Treaty on the approval of persons responsible for carrying out the statutory audits of accounting documents, OJ L 126, 12 May 1984, 20–26.^{VII}	550
C. 8.	Council Regulation 2137/85/EEC of 25 July 1985 on the European Economic Interest Grouping (EEIG), OJ L 199, 31 July 1985, 1–9.	551
C. 9.	Eleventh Council Directive 89/666/EEC of 21 December 1989 concerning disclosure requirements in respect of branches opened in a Member State by certain types of company governed by the law of another State, OJ L 395, 30 December 1989, 36–39.	562
C. 10.	Twelfth Council Directive 89/667/EEC of 21 December 1989 on single-member private limited-liability companies, OJ L 395, 30 December 1989, 40–42.	567
C. 11.	Council Directive 90/604/EEC of 8 November 1990 amending Directive 78/660/EEC on annual accounts and Directive 83/349/EEC on consolidated accounts as concerns the exemptions for small and medium-sized companies and the publication of accounts in ecus, OJ L 317, 16 November 1990, 57–59.	570
C. 12.	Council Directive 90/605/EEC of 8 November 1990 amending Directive 78/660/EEC on annual accounts and Directive 83/349/EEC on consolidated accounts as regards the scope of those Directives, OJ L 317, 16 November 1990, 60–62.	572
C. 13.	Council Directive 92/101/EEC of 23 November 1992 for a Council Directive amending Directive 77/91/EEC on the formation of public limited-liability companies and the maintenance and alteration of their capital, OJ L 347, 28 November 1992, 64–66.	574
C. 14.	Council Directive 94/8/EC of 21 March 1994 amending Directive 78/660/EEC as regards the revision of amounts expressed in ecus, OJ L 82, 25 March 1994, 33–34.	576
C. 15.	Communication 97/C 285/10 from the Commission. Participation of European Economic Interest Groupings (EEIGs) in public contracts and programmes financed by public funds, OJ C 285, 20 September 1997, 17–24.	577
C. 16.	Council Directive 1999/60/EC of 17 June 1999 amending Directive 78/660/EEC as regards amounts expressed in ecus, OJ L 162, 26 June 1999, 65–66.	586
C. 17.	Commission Recommendation 2001/453/EC of 30 May 2001 on the recognition, measurement and disclosure of environmental issues in the annual accounts and annual reports of companies, OJ L 156, 13 June 2001, 33–42.	588

---

^{VII} This Directive has been repealed as from 29 June 2006 by article 50 of Directive 2006/43/EC (OJ L 157, 9.6.2006, 87), reproduced infra under no. C. 30.

C. 18.	European Parliament and Council Directive 2001/65/EC of 27 September 2001 amending Directives 78/660/EEC, 83/349/EEC and 86/635/EEC as regards the valuation rules for the annual and consolidated accounts of certain types of companies as well as of banks and other financial institutions, OJ L 283, 27 September 2001, 28–32.	600
C. 19.	Council Regulation 2157/2001/EC of 8 October 2001 on the statute for a European Company (SE), OJ L 294, 10 November 2001, 1–21.	603
C. 20.	Council Directive 2001/86/EC of 8 October 2001 supplementing the Statute for a European company with regard to the involvement of employees, OJ L 294, 10 November 2001, 22–32.	625
C. 21.	Commission Recommendation 2002/590/EC of 16 May 2002, Statutory Auditors' Independence in the EU: A Set of Fundamental Principles (C(2002)1873), OJ L 191, 19 July 2002, 22–57.	637
C. 22.	European Parliament and Council Regulation 1606/2002/EC of 19 July 2002 on the application of international accounting standards, OJ L 243, 11 September 2002, 1–4.	677
C. 23.	European Parliament and Council Directive 2003/51/EC of 18 June 2003 amending Directives 78/660/EEC, 83/349/EEC, 86/635/EEC and 91/674/EEC on the annual and consolidated accounts of certain types of companies, banks and other financial institutions and insurance undertakings, OJ L 178, 17 July 2003, 16–22.	683
C. 24.	European Parliament and Council Directive 2003/58/EC of 15 July 2003 amending Council Directive 68/151/EEC, as regards disclosure requirements in respect of certain types of companies, OJ L 221, 4 September 2003, 13–16.	686
C. 25.	Council Regulation 1435/2003/EC of 22 July 2003 on the Statute for a European Cooperative Society (SCE), OJ L 207, 18 August 2003, 1–24.	688
C. 26.	Council Directive 2003/72/EC of 22 July 2003 supplementing the Statute for a European Cooperative Society with regard to the involvement of employees, OJ L 207, 18 August 2003, 25–36.	715
C. 27.	Commission Recommendation 2004/913/EC of 14 December 2004 fostering an appropriate regime for the remuneration of directors of listed companies, OJ L 385, 29 December 2004, 55–59.	728
C. 28.	Commission Recommendation 2005/162/EC of 15 February 2005 on the role of non-executive or supervisory directors of listed companies and on the committees of the (supervisory) board, OJ L 52, 25 February 2005, 51–63.	734
C. 29.	European Parliament and Council Directive 2005/56/EC of 26 October 2005 on cross-border mergers of limited liability companies, OJ L 310, 25 November 2005, 1–9.	747
C. 30.	European Parliament and Council Directive 2006/43/EC of 17 May 2006 on statutory audits of annual accounts and consolidated accounts, amending	

	Council Directives 78/660/EEC and 83/349/EEC and repealing Council Directive 84/253/EEC, OJ L 157, 9 June 2006, 87–107.	757
C. 31.	European Parliament and Council Directive 2006/46/EC of 14 June 2006 amending Council Directives 78/660/EEC on the annual accounts of certain types of companies, 83/349/EEC on consolidated accounts, 86/635/EEC on the annual accounts and consolidated accounts of banks and other financial institutions and 91/674/EEC on the annual accounts and consolidated accounts of insurance undertakings, OJ L 224, 16 August 2006, 1–7.	783
C. 32.	European Parliament and Council Directive 2006/68/EC of 6 September 2006 amending Council Directive 77/91/EEC as regards the formation of public limited liability companies and the maintenance and alteration of their capital, OJ L 264, 25 September 2006, 32–36.	787

Part IV. Consumer Protection especially related to Financial Transactions

C.P. 1.	Council Directive 84/450/EEC of 10 September 1984 concerning misleading and comparative advertising, OJ L 250, 19 September 1984, 17–20.	789
C.P. 2.	Council Directive 85/374/EEC of 25 July 1985 on the approximation of the laws, regulations and administrative provisions of the Member States concerning liability for defective products, OJ L 210, 7 August 1985, 29–33.	796
C.P. 3	Council Directive 85/577/EEC of 20 December 1985 to protect the consumer in respect of contracts negotiated away from business premises, OJ L 372, 31 December 1985, 31–33.	803
C.P. 4.	Council Directive 87/102/EEC of 22 December 1986 for the approximation of the laws, regulations and administrative provisions of the Member States concerning consumer credit, OJ L 42, 12 February 1987, 48–52.	811
C.P. 5.	Commission Recommendation 87/598/EEC of 8 December 1987 on a European Code of Conduct relating to electronic payment (Relations between financial institutions, traders and service establishments, and consumers), OJ L 365, 24 December 1987, 72–76.	822
C.P. 6.	Commission Recommendation 88/590/EEC of 17 November 1988 concerning Payment Systems, and in particular the relationship between cardholder and card issuer, OJ L 317, 24 November 1988, 55–58.	825
C.P. 7.	Commission Recommendation 90/109/EEC of 14 February 1990 on the transparency of banking conditions relating to cross-border financial transactions, OJ L 67, 15 March 1990, 39–42.	830
C.P. 8.	Council Directive 90/88/EEC of 22 February 1990 amending Directive 87/102/EEC for the approximation of the laws, regulations and administrative provisions of the Member States concerning consumer credit, OJ L 61, 10 March 1990, 14–18.	834

C.P. 9.	Council Directive 93/13/EEC of 5 April 1993 on unfair terms in consumer contracts, OJ L 95, 21 April 1993, 29–34.	835
C.P. 10.	European Parliament and Council Directive 97/5/EC of 27 January 1997 on cross-border credit transfers, OJ L 43, 14 February 1997, 25–31.	842
C.P. 11.	European Parliament and Council Directive 97/7/EC of 20 May 1997 on the protection of consumers in respect of distance contracts–Statement by the Council and the Parliament re Article 6 (1)–Statement by the Commission re Article 3 (1), first indent, OJ L 144, 4 June 1997, 19–28.	849
C.P. 12.	Commission Recommendation 97/489/EC of 30 July 1997 concerning transactions by electronic payment instruments and in particular the relationship between issuer and holder, OJ L 208, 2 August 1997, 52–58.	858
C.P. 13.	European Parliament and Council Directive 97/55/EC of 6 October 1997 amending Directive 84/450/EEC concerning misleading advertising so as to include comparative advertising, OJ L 290, 23 October 1997, 18–23.	864
C.P. 14.	European Parliament and Council Directive 98/7/EC of 16 February 1998 amending Directive 87/102/EEC for the approximation of the laws, regulations and administrative provisions of the Member States concerning consumer credit, OJ L 101, 1 April 1998, 17–23.	868
C.P. 15.	European Parliament and Council Directive 98/27/EC of 19 May 1998 on injunctions for the protection of consumers' interests, OJ L 166, 11 June 1998, 51–55.	870
C.P. 16.	European Parliament and Council Directive 1999/34/EC of 10 May 1999 amending Council Directive 85/374/EEC on the approximation of the laws, regulations and administrative provisions of the Member States concerning liability for defective products, OJ L 141, 4 June 1999, 20–21.	875
C.P. 17.	European Parliament and Council Directive 1999/44/EC of 25 May 1999 on certain aspects of the sale of consumer goods and associated guarantees, OJ L 171, 7 July 1999, 12–16.	877
C.P. 18.	European Parliament and Council Directive 1999/93/EC of 13 December 1999 on a Community framework for electronic signatures, OJ L 13, 19 January 2000, 12–20.	884
C.P. 19.	European Parliament and Council Directive 2000/31/EC of 8 June 2000 on certain legal aspects of information society services, in particular electronic commerce, in the Internal Market (Directive on electronic commerce), OJ L 178, 17 July 2000, 1–16.	894
C.P. 20.	Commission Recommendation 2001/193/EC of 1 March 2001 on pre-contractual information to be given to consumers by lenders offering home loans (C(2001) 477), OJ L 69, 10 March 2001, 25–29.	912
C.P. 21.	European Parliament and Council Regulation 2560/2001/EC of 19 December 2001 on cross-border payments in euro, OJ L 344, 28 December 2001, 13–16.	917

C.P. 22. European Parliament and Council Directive 2002/65/EC of 23 September 2002 concerning the distance marketing of consumer financial services and amending Council Directive 90/619/EEC and Directives 97/7/EC and 98/27/EC, OJ L 271, 9 October 2002, 16–24. 922

C.P. 23. European Parliament and Council Regulation 2006/2004/EC of 27 October 2004 on cooperation between national authorities responsible for the enforcement of consumer protection laws (the Regulation on consumer protection cooperation), OJ L 341, 9 December 2004, 1–11. 933

C.P. 24. European Parliament and Council Directive 2005/29/EC of 11 May 2005 concerning unfair business-to-consumer commercial practices in the internal market and amending Council Directive 84/450/EEC, Directives 97/7/EC, 98/27/EC and 2002/65/EC of the European Parliament and of the Council and Regulation (EC) No 2006/2004 of the European Parliament and of the Council ('Unfair Commercial Practices Directive'), OJ L 149, 11 June 2005, 22–39. 946

Part V. Enterprise Law

E. 1. Council Directive 75/129/EEC of 17 February 1975 on the approximation of the laws of the Member States relating to collective redundancies, OJ L 48, 22 February 1975, 29–30.[VIII] 961

E. 2. [Council Directive 77/187/EEC of 14 February 1977 on the approximation of the laws of the Member States relating to the safeguarding of employees' rights in the event of transfers of undertakings, businesses or parts of undertakings or businesses],[IX] OJ L 61, 5 March 1977, 26.[X] 962

E. 3. [Council Directive 80/987/EEC of 20 October 1980 on the approximation of the laws of the Member States relating to the protection of employees in the event of the insolvency of their employer],[XI] OJ L 283, 28 October 1980, 23–27. 963

E. 4. Council Directive 92/56/EEC of 24 June 1992 amending Directive 75/129/EEC on the approximation of the laws of the Member States relating to collective redundancies, OJ L 245, 26 August 1992, 3–5.[VIII] 973

E. 5. Council Directive 94/45/EC of 22 September 1994 on the establishment of a European Works Council or a procedure in Community-scale undertakings and Community-scale groups of undertakings for the purposes of informing and consulting employees, OJ L 254, 30 September 1994, 64–72. 974

[VIII] This Directive has been repealed as from 31 August 1998 by article 8 of Directive 98/59/EC (OJ L 225, 12.8.1998, 16), reproduced infra under no. E. 8.

[IX] This title has been amended by article 1(1) of Directive 98/50/EC (OJ L 201, 17.7.1998, 88), reproduced infra under no. E. 7.

[X] This Directive has been repealed as from 11 April 2001 by article 12 of Directive 2001/23/EC (OJ L 82, 22.3.2001, 16), reproduced infra under no. E. 11.

[XI] The title has been replaced by article 1(1) of Directive 2002/74/EC (OJ L 270, 8.10.2002, 10), reproduced infra under no. E. 13.

E. 6.	Council Directive 97/74/EC of 15 December 1997 extending, to the United Kingdom of Great Britain and Northern Ireland, Directive 94/45/EC on the establishment of a European Works Council or a procedure in Community-scale undertakings and Community-scale groups of undertakings for the purposes of informing and consulting employees, OJ L 10, 16 January 1998, 22–23.	985
E. 7.	Council Directive 98/50/EC of 29 June 1998 amending Directive 77/187/EEC on the approximation of the laws of the Member States relating to the safeguarding of employees' rights in the event of transfers of undertakings, businesses or parts of businesses, OJ L 201, 17 July 1998, 88–92.	987
E. 8.	Council Directive 98/59/EC of 20 July 1998 on the approximation of the laws of the Member States relating to collective redundancies, OJ L 225, 12 August 1998, 16–21.	989
E. 9.	Council Regulation 1346/2000/EC of 29 May 2000 on insolvency proceedings, OJ L 160, 30 June 2000, 1–18.	997
E. 10.	European Parliament and Council Directive 2000/35/EC of 29 June 2000 on combating late payment in commercial transactions, OJ L 200, 8 August 2000, 35–38.	1016
E. 11.	Council Directive 2001/23/EC of 12 March 2001 on the approximation of the laws of the Member States relating to the safeguarding of employees' rights in the event of transfers of undertakings, businesses or parts of undertakings or businesses, OJ L 82, 22 March 2001, 16–20.	1022
E. 12.	European Parliament and Council Directive 2002/14/EC of 11 March 2002 establishing a general framework for informing and consulting employees in the European Community, OJ L 80, 23 March 2002, 29–33.	1040
E. 13.	European Parliament and Council Directive 2002/74/EC of 23 September 2002 amending Council Directive 80/987/EEC on the approximation of the laws of the Member States relating to the protection of employees in the event of the insolvency of their employer, OJ L 270, 8 October 2002, 10–13.	1046

Part VI. Insurance Law

I. 1.	Council Directive 64/225/EEC of 25 February 1964 on the abolition of restrictions on freedom of establishment and freedom to provide services in respect of reinsurance and retrocession, OJ L 56, 4 April 1964, 878–880.	1049
I. 2.	Council Directive 72/166/EEC of 24 April 1972 on the approximation of the laws of the Member States relating to insurance against civil liability in respect of the use of motor vehicles, and to the enforcement of the obligation to insure against such liability, OJ L 103, 2 May 1972, 1–4.	1052
I. 3.	Council Directive 73/239/EEC of 24 July 1973 on the co-ordination of laws, regulations and administrative provisions relating to the taking-up and	

	pursuit of the business of direct insurance other than life assurance (First non-life insurance Directive), OJ L 228, 16 August 1973, 3–19.	1059
I. 4.	Council Directive 73/240/EEC of 24 July 1973 abolishing restrictions on freedom of establishment in the business of direct insurance other than life assurance, OJ L 228, 16 August 1973, 20–22.	1092
I. 5.	Commission Recommendation 74/165/EEC of 6 February 1974 to the Member States concerning the application of the Council Directive of 24 April 1972 on the approximation of the laws of the Member States relating to the use of motor vehicles, and to the enforcement of the obligation to insure against such liability, OJ L 87, 30 March 1974, 12.	1095
I. 6.	Council Directive 76/580/EEC of 29 June 1976 amending Directive 73/239/EEC on the co-ordination of laws, regulations and administrative provisions relating to the taking up and pursuit of the business of direct insurance other than life assurance, OJ L 189, 11 July 1976, 13–14.	1096
I. 7.	Council Directive 77/92/EEC of 13 December 1976 on measures to facilitate the effective exercise of freedom of establishment and freedom to provide services in respect of the activities of insurance agents and brokers (ex ISIC Group 630) and, in particular, transitional measures in respect of those activities, OJ L 26, 31 January 1977, 14–19.[XII]	1097
I. 8.	Council Directive 78/473/EEC of 30 May 1978 on the co-ordination of laws, regulations and administrative provisions relating to Community co-insurance, OJ L 151, 7 June 1978, 25–28.	1098
I. 9.	Council Directive 79/267/EEC of 5 March 1979 on the co-ordination of laws, regulations and administrative provisions relating to the taking up and pursuit of the business of direct life assurance (First life assurance Directive), OJ L 63, 13 March 1979, 1–18.[XIII]	1102
I. 10.	Commission Recommendation 81/76/EEC of 8 January 1981 on accelerated settlement of claims under insurance against civil liability in respect of the use of motor vehicles, OJ L 57, 4 March 1981, 27.	1104
I. 11.	Council Directive 84/5/EEC of 30 December 1983 on the approximation of the laws of the Member States relating to insurance against civil liability in respect of the use of motor vehicles (Second motor insurance Directive), OJ L 8, 11 January 1984, 17–20.	1105
I. 12.	Council Directive 84/641/EEC of 10 December 1984 amending, particularly as regards tourist assistance, the First Directive (73/239/EEC) on the co-ordination of laws, regulations and administrative provisions relating to	

[XII] This Directive has been repealed as from 15 January 2005 by article 15 of Directive 2002/92/EC (OJ L 9, 15.01.2003, 3), reproduced infra under no. I. 34.

[XIII] This Directive has been repealed as from 19 December 2002 by Annex V, part A of Directive 2002/83/EC (OJ L 345, 19.12.2002, 1), reproduced infra under no. I. 33.

	the taking-up and pursuit of the business of direct insurance other than life assurance, OJ L 339, 27 December 1984, 21–25.	1111
I. 13.	Council Directive 87/343/EEC of 22 June 1987 amending, as regards credit insurance and suretyship insurance, First Directive 73/239/EEC on the co-ordination of laws, regulations and administrative provisions relating to the taking-up and pursuit of the business of direct insurance other than life assurance, OJ L 185, 4 July 1987, 72–76.	1114
I. 14.	Council Directive 87/344/EEC of 22 June 1987 on the co-ordination of laws, regulations and administrative provisions relating to legal expenses insurance, OJ L 185, 4 July 1987, 77–80.	1116
I. 15.	Council Directive 88/357/EEC of 22 June 1988 on the co-ordination of laws, regulations and administrative provisions relating to direct insurance other than life assurance and laying down provisions to facilitate the effective exercise of freedom to provide services and amending Directive 73/239/EEC (Second non-life insurance Directive), OJ L 172, 4 July 1988, 1–14.	1120
I. 16.	Council Directive 90/232/EEC of 14 May 1990 on the approximation of the laws of the Member States relating to insurance against civil liability in respect of the use of motor vehicles (Third motor insurance Directive), OJ L 129, 19 May 1990, 33–36.	1131
I. 17.	Council Directive 90/618/EEC of 8 November 1990 amending, particularly as regards motor vehicle liability insurance, Directive 73/239/EEC and Directive 88/357/EEC which concern the co-ordination of laws, regulations and administrative provisions relating to direct insurance other than life assurance, OJ L 330, 29 November 1990, 44–49.	1135
I. 18.	Council Directive 90/619/EEC of 8 November 1990 on the co-ordination of laws, regulations and administrative provisions relating to direct life assurance, laying down provisions to facilitate the effective exercise of freedom to provide services and amending Directive 79/267/EEC (Second life assurance Directive), OJ L 330, 29 November 1990, 50–61.[XIII]	1139
I. 19.	Council Regulation 1534/91/EEC of 31 May 1991 on the application of Article [81(3)][IV] of the Treaty to certain categories of agreements, decisions and concerted practices in the insurance sector, OJ L 143, 7 June 1991, 1–3.	1140
I. 20.	Council Regulation 2155/91/EEC of 20 June 1991 laying down particular provisions for the application of Articles 37, 39 and 40 of the Agreement between the European Economic Community and the Swiss Confederation on direct insurance other than life assurance, OJ L 205, 27 July 1991, 1.	1143
I. 21.	Council Directive 91/371/EEC of 20 June 1991 on the implementation of the Agreement between the European Economic Community and the Swiss Confederation concerning direct insurance other than life assurance, OJ L 205, 27 July 1991, 48.	1144

I. 22.	Commission Recommendation 92/48/EEC of 18 December 1991 on insurance intermediaries, OJ L 19, 28 January 1992, 32–33.	1145
I. 23.	Council Directive 91/674/EEC of 19 December 1991 on the annual accounts and consolidated accounts of insurance undertakings, OJ L 374, 31 December 1991, 7–31.	1148
I. 24.	Council Directive 91/675/EEC of 19 December 1991 setting up an [European Insurance and Occupational Pensions Committee],[XIV] OJ L 374, 31 December 1991, 32–33.	1172
I. 25.	Council Directive 92/49/EEC of 18 June 1992 on the co-ordination of laws, regulations and administrative provisions relating to direct insurance other than life assurance and amending Directives 73/239/EEC and 88/357/EEC (Third non-life insurance Directive), OJ L 228, 11 August 1992, 1–23.	1174
I. 26.	Council Directive 92/96/EEC of 10 November 1992 on the co-ordination of laws, regulations and administrative provisions relating to direct life assurance and amending Directives 79/267/EEC and 90/619/EEC (Third life assurance Directive), OJ L 360, 9 December 1992, 1–27.[XIII]	1196
I. 27.	European Parliament and Council Directive 95/26/EC of 29 June 1995 amending Directives 77/780/EEC and 89/646/EEC in the field of credit institutions, Directives 73/239/EEC and 92/49/EEC in the field of non-life insurance, Directives 79/267/EEC and 92/96/EEC in the field of life assurance, Directive 93/22/EEC in the field of investment firms and Directive 85/611/EEC in the field of undertakings for collective investment in transferable securities (UCITS), with a view to reinforcing prudential supervision, OJ L 168, 18 July 1995, 7–13.[XIII]	1198
I. 28.	[European Parliament and Council Directive 98/78/EC of 27 October 1998 on the supplementary supervision of insurance and reinsurance undertakings in an insurance or reinsurance group],[XV] OJ L 330, 5 December 1998, 1–12.	1199
I. 29.	Commission Interpretative Communication 2000/C 43/03 on freedom to provide services and the general good in the insurance sector, OJ C 43, 16 February 2000, 5–27.	1213
I. 30.	European Parliament and Council Directive 2000/26/EC of 16 May 2000 on the approximation of the laws of the Member States relating to insurance against civil liability in respect of the use of motor vehicles and amending Council Directives 73/239/EEC and 88/357/EEC (Fourth motor insurance Directive), OJ L 181, 20 July 2000, 65–74.	1241

[XIV] The title of this directive has been amended by article 5(1) of Directive 2005/1/EC (OJ L 79, 24.3.2005, 9), reproduced infra under no. B. 39.

[XV] The title of this Directive has been replaced by article 59(1) of Directive 2005/68/EC (OJ L 323, 9.12.2005), reproduced infra under no. I. 40.

I. 31.	European Parliament and Council Directive 2002/12/EC of 5 March 2002 amending Council Directive 79/267/EEC as regards the solvency margin requirements for life assurance undertakings, OJ L 77, 20 March 2002, 11–16.^{XIII}	1251
I. 32.	European Parliament and Council Directive 2002/13/EC of 5 March 2002 amending Council Directive 73/239/EEC as regards the solvency margin requirements for non-life insurance undertakings, OJ L 77, 20 March 2002, 17–22.	1252
I. 33.	European Parliament and Council Directive 2002/83/EC of 5 November 2002 concerning life assurance, OJ L 345, 19 December 2002, 1–51.	1255
I. 34.	European Parliament and Council Directive 2002/92/EC of 9 December 2002 on insurance mediation, OJ L 9, 15 January 2003, 3–10.	1314
I. 35.	European Parliament and Council Directive 2003/41/EC of 3 June 2003 on the activities and supervision of institutions for occupational retirement provision, OJ L 235, 23 September 2003, 10–21.	1325
I. 36.	Commission Decision 2003/564/EC of 28 July 2003 on the application of Council Directive 72/166/EEC relating to checks on insurance against civil liability in respect of the use of motor vehicles, OJ L 192, 31 July 2003, 23–39.	1341
I. 37.	Commission Decision 2004/6/EC of 5 November 2003 establishing the Committee of European Insurance and Occupational Pensions Supervisors, OJ L 3, 7 January 2004, 30–31.	1356
I. 38.	Commission Decision 2004/9/EC of 5 November 2003 establishing the European Insurance and Occupational Pensions Committee, OJ L 3, 7 January 2004, 34–35.	1358
I.39.	European Parliament and Council Directive 2005/14/EC of 11 May 2005 amending Council Directives 72/166/EEC, 84/5/EEC, 88/357/EEC and 90/232/EEC and Directive 2000/26/EC of the European Parliament and of the Council relating to insurance against civil liability in respect of the use of motor vehicles, OJ L 149, 11 June 2005, 14–21.	1360
I. 40.	European Parliament and Council Directive 2005/68/EC of 16 November 2005 on reinsurance and amending Council Directives 73/239/EEC, 92/49/EEC as well as Directives 98/78/EC and 2002/83/EC, OJ L 323, 9 December 2005, 1–50.	1366

Part VII. Securities Regulation

S. 1.	Commission Recommendation 77/534/EEC of 25 July 1977 concerning a European code of conduct relating to transactions in transferable securities, OJ L 212, 20 August 1977, 37–43.	1399

S. 2.	Council Directive 79/279/EEC of 5 March 1979 co-ordinating the conditions for the admission of securities to official stock exchange listing, OJ L 66, 16 March 1979, 21–32.[XVI]	1407
S. 3.	Council Directive 80/390/EEC of 17 March 1980 co-ordinating the requirements for the drawing up, scrutiny and distribution of the listing particulars to be published for the admission of securities to official stock exchange listing, OJ L 100, 17 April 1980, 1–26.[XVI]	1410
S. 4.	Council Directive 82/121/EEC of 15 February 1982 on information to be published on a regular basis by companies the shares of which have been admitted to official stock exchange listing, OJ L 48, 20 February 1982, 26–29.[XVI]	1415
S. 5.	Council Directive 82/148/EEC of 3 March 1982 amending Directive 79/279/EEC co-ordinating the conditions for the admission of securities to official stock exchange listing and Directive 80/390/EEC co-ordinating the requirements for the drawing up, scrutiny and distribution of the listing particulars to be published for the admission of securities to official stock exchange listing, OJ L 62, 5 March 1982, 22–23.[XVI]	1417
S. 6.	Council Directive 85/611/EEC of 20 December 1985 on the co-ordination of laws, regulations and administrative provisions relating to undertakings for collective investment in transferable securities (UCITS), OJ L 375, 31 December 1985, 3–18.	1418
S. 7.	Council Recommendation 85/612/EEC of 20 December 1985 concerning the second subparagraph of Article 25(1) of Directive 85/611/EEC, OJ L 375, 31 December 1985, 19.	1454
S. 8.	Council Directive 87/345/EEC of 22 June 1987 amending Directive 80/390/EEC co-ordinating the requirements for the drawing-up, scrutiny and distribution of the listing particulars to be published for the admission of securities to official stock exchange listing, OJ L 185, 4 July 1987, 81–83.[XVI]	1455
S. 9.	Council Directive 88/220/EEC of 22 March 1988 amending, as regards the investment policies of certain UCITS, Directive 85/611/EEC on the co-ordination of laws, regulations and administrative provisions relating to undertakings for collective investments in transferable securities (UCITS), OJ L 100, 19 April 1988, 31–32.	1456
S. 10.	Council Directive 88/627/EEC of 12 December 1988 on the information to be published when a major holding in a listed company is acquired or disposed of, OJ L 348, 17 December 1988, 62–65.[XVI]	1457
S. 11.	Council Directive 89/298/EEC of 17 April 1989 co-ordinating the requirements for the drawing-up, scrutiny and distribution of the prospectus	

[XVI] This Directive has been repealed as from 26 July 2001 by article 111 of Directive 2001/34/EC (OJ L 184, 6.7.2001, 1), reproduced infra under no. S. 18.

	to be published when transferable securities are offered to the public, OJ L 124, 5 May 1989, 8–15.^XVII	1459
S. 12.	Council Directive 89/592/EEC of 13 November 1989 co-ordinating regulations on insider dealing, OJ L 334, 18 November 1989, 30–32.^XVIII	1460
S. 13.	Council Directive 90/211/EEC of 23 April 1990 amending Directive 80/390/EEC in respect of the mutual recognition of public-offer prospectuses as stock exchange listing particulars, OJ L 112, 3 May 1990, 24–25.^XVI	1461
S. 14.	Council Directive 93/22/EEC of 10 May 1993 on investment services in the securities field, OJ L 141, 11 June 1993, 27–46.^XIX	1462
S. 15.	European Parliament and Council Directive 94/18/EC of 30 May 1994 amending Directive 80/390/EEC co-ordinating the requirements for the drawing up, scrutiny and distribution of the listing particulars to be published for the admission of securities to official stock-exchange listing, with regard to the obligation to publish listing particulars, OJ L 135, 31 May 1994, 1–4.^XVI	1463
S. 16.	European Parliament and Council Directive 97/9/EC of 3 March 1997 on investor-compensation schemes, OJ L 84, 26 March 1997, 22–31.	1464
S. 17.	European Parliament and Council Directive 98/26/EC of 19 May 1998 on settlement finality in payment and securities settlement systems, OJ L 166, 11 June 1998, 45–50.	1474
S. 18.	European Parliament and Council Directive 2001/34/EC of 28 May 2001 on the admission of securities to official stock exchange listing and on information to be published on those securities, OJ L 184, 6 July 2001, 1–66.	1480
S. 19.	Commission Decision 2001/527/EC of 6 June 2001 establishing the Committee of European Securities Regulators, OJ L 191, 13 July 2001, 43–44.	1516
S. 20.	Commission Decision 2001/528/EC of 6 June 2001 establishing the European Securities Committee, OJ L 191, 13 July 2001, 45–46.	1518
S. 21.	European Parliament and Council Directive 2001/107/EC of 21 January 2002 amending Council Directive 85/611/EEC on the coordination of laws, regulations and administrative provisions relating to undertakings for collective investment in transferable securities (UCITS) with a view to regulating management companies and simplified prospectuses, OJ L 41, 13 February 2002, 20–34.	1520

[XVII] This Directive has been repealed as from 1 July 2005 by article 28 of Directive 2003/71/EC (OJ L 345, 31.12.2003, 64), reproduced infra under no. S. 25.

[XVIII] This Directive has been repealed as from 12 April 2003 by article 20 of Directive 2003/6/EC (OJ L 96, 12.4.2003, 16), reproduced infra under no. S. 24.

[XIX] This Directive has been repealed as from 30 April 2006 by article 69 of Directive 2004/39/EC (OJ L 145, 30.4.2004, 1) on markets in financial instruments, reproduced infra under no. S. 29.

S. 22.	European Parliament and Council Directive 2001/108/EC of 21 January 2002 amending Council Directive 85/611/EEC on the coordination of laws, regulations and administrative provisions relating to undertakings for collective investment in transferable securities (UCITS), with regard to investments of UCITS, OJ L 41, 13 February 2002, 35–42.	1524
S. 23.	European Parliament and Council Directive 2002/47/EC of 6 June 2002 on financial collateral arrangements, OJ L 168, 27 June 2002, 43–50.	1528
S. 24.	European Parliament and Council Directive 2003/6/EC of 28 January 2003 on insider dealing and market manipulation (market abuse), OJ L 96, 12 April 2003, 16–25.	1538
S. 25.	European Parliament and Council Directive 2003/71/EC of 4 November 2003 on the prospectus to be published when securities are offered to the public or admitted to trading and amending Directive 2001/34/EC, OJ L 345, 31 December 2003, 64–89.	1552
S. 26.	Commission Directive 2003/124/EC of 22 December 2003 implementing Directive 2003/6/EC of the European Parliament and of the Council as regards the definition and public disclosure of inside information and the definition of market manipulation, OJ L 339, 24 December 2003, 70–72.	1580
S. 27.	Commission Directive 2003/125/EC of 22 December 2003 implementing Directive 2003/6/EC of the European Parliament and of the Council as regards the fair presentation of investment recommendations and the disclosure of conflicts of interest, OJ L 339, 24 December 2003, 73–77.	1584
S. 28.	European Parliament and Council Directive 2004/25/EC of 21 April 2004 on takeover bids, OJ L 142, 30 April 2004, 12–23.	1591
S. 29.	European Parliament and Council Directive 2004/39/EC of 21 April 2004 on markets in financial instruments amending Council Directives 85/611/EEC and 93/6/EEC and Directive 2000/12/EC of the European Parliament and of the Council and repealing Council Directive 93/22/EEC, OJ L 145, 30 April 2004, 1–44.	1606
S. 30.	Commission Directive 2004/72/EC of 29 April 2004 implementing Directive 2003/6/EC of the European Parliament and of the Council as regards accepting market practices, the definition of inside information in relation to derivatives on commodities, the drawing up of lists of insiders, the notification of managers' transactions and the notification of suspicious transactions, OJ L 162, 30 April 2004, 70–75.	1660
S. 31.	European Parliament and Council Directive 2004/109/EC of 15 December 2004 on the harmonisation of transparency requirements in relation to information about issuers whose securities are admitted to trading on a regulated market and amending Directive 2001/34/EC, OJ L 390, 31 December 2004, 38–57.	1667

S. 32.	European Parliament and Council Directive 2006/31/EC of 5 April 2006 amending directive on markets in financial instruments, as regards certain deadlines, OJ L 114, 27 April 2006, 60–63.	1692
S. 33.	Commission Regulation 1287/2006/EC of 10 August 2006 implementing Directive 2004/39/EC of the European Parliament and of the Council as regards record-keeping obligations for investment firms, transaction reporting, market transparency, admission of financial instruments to trading, and defined terms for the purposes of that Directive, OJ L 241, 2 September 2006, 1–25.	1695
S. 34.	Commission Directive 2006/73/EC of 10 August 2006 implementing Directive 2004/39/EC of the European Parliament and of the Council as regards organisational requirements and operating conditions for investment firms and defined terms for the purposes of that Directive, OJ L 241, 2 September 2006, 26–58.	1722

Chronological List of Directives   1764
Alphabetical List of Cases   1783
Chronological List of Cases   1793
Correlation Table EU-Treaty—Treaty of Amsterdam   1803

PART I
BANKING LAW

B. 1.

Council Directive 73/183/EEC
of 28 June 1973
on the abolition of restrictions on freedom of establishment and freedom to provide services in respect of self-employed activities of banks and other financial institutions[1]

This Directive has been repealed by article 67 of Directive 2000/12/EC, which subsequently has been repealed by article 158 of Directive 2006/48/EC (OJ L 177, 30.06.2006, 1) reproduced infra under no. B. 41.

---

[1] OJ L 194, 16.7.1973, 1–10.

B. 2.

First Council Directive 77/780/EEC
of 12 December 1977
on the co-ordination of laws, regulations and administrative provisions relating to the taking up and pursuit of the business of credit institutions[1]

This Directive has been repealed by article 67 of Directive 2000/12/EC, which subsequently has been repealed by article 158 of Directive 2006/48/EC (OJ L 177, 30.06.2006, 1) reproduced infra under no. B. 41.

---

[1] OJ L 322, 17.12.1977, 30.

B. 3.

Council Directive 83/350/EEC
of 13 June 1983
on the supervision of credit institutions on consolidated basis[1]

This Directive has been repealed as from 1 January 1993 by article 10 (1) of Directive 92/30/EEC, which has been repealed by article 67 of Directive 2000/12/EC, which subsequently has been repealed by article 158 of Directive 2006/48/EC (OJ L 177, 30.06.2006, 1) reproduced infra under no. B. 41.

---

[1] OJ L 193, 18.7.1983, 18–20.

B. 4.

Council Directive 85/345/EEC
of 8 July 1985
amending Directive 77/780/EEC on the co-ordination of laws, regulations
and administrative provisions relating to the taking up
and pursuit of the business of credit institutions[1]

This Directive has been repealed by article 67 of Directive 2000/12/EC, which subsequently has been repealed by article 158 of Directive 2006/48/EC (OJ L 177, 30.06.2006, 1) reproduced infra under no. B. 41.

---

[1] OJ L 183, 16.7.1985, 19–20.

B. 5.
Council Directive 86/137/EEC
of 17 April 1986
authorising certain Member States to defer further application of Directive 77/780/EEC as regards certain credit institutions[1]

This Directive has been repealed by article 67 of Directive 2000/12/EC, which subsequently has been repealed by article 158 of Directive 2006/48/EC (OJ L 177, 30.06.2006, 1) reproduced infra under no. B. 41.

---

[1] OJ L 106, 23.4.1986, 35.

B. 6.

Council Directive 86/524/EEC
of 27 October 1986
amending Directive 77/780/EEC in respect of the list of permanent exclusions of certain credit institutions[1]

This Directive has been repealed by article 67 of Directive 2000/12/EC, which subsequently has been repealed by article 158 of Directive 2006/48/EC (OJ L 177, 30.06.2006, 1) reproduced infra under no. B. 41.

---

[1] OJ L 309, 4.11.1986, 15–16.

B. 7.
Council Directive 86/635/EEC
of 8 December 1986
on the annual accounts and consolidated accounts of banks and other financial institutions[1]

THE COUNCIL OF THE EUROPEAN COMMUNITIES,

Having regard to the Treaty establishing the European Community, and in particular Article [44][2] (3) (g) thereof,

Having regard to the proposal from the Commission,[3]

Having regard to the opinion of the European Parliament,[4]

Having regard to the opinion of the Economic and Social Committee,[5]

Whereas Council Directive 78/660/EEC of 25 July 1978, based on Article [44][2] (3) (g) of the Treaty, on the annual accounts of certain types of companies[6] as last amended by Directive 84/569/EEC,[7] need not be applied to banks and other financial institutions, hereafter referred to as 'credit institutions', pending subsequent co-ordination; whereas in view of the central importance of these undertakings in the Community, such co-ordination is necessary;

Whereas Council Directive 83/349/EEC of 13 June 1983, based on Article [44(3)(g)][2] of the Treaty, on consolidated accounts,[8] provides for derogations for credit institutions only until expiry of the deadline imposed for the application of this Directive; whereas this Directive must therefore also include provisions specific to credit institutions in respect of consolidated accounts;

Whereas such co-ordination has also become urgent because more and more credit institutions are operating across national borders; whereas for creditors, debtors and members and for the general public improved comparability of the annual accounts and consolidated accounts of these institutions is of crucial importance;

Whereas in virtually all the Member States of the Community credit institutions within the meaning of Council Directive 77/780/EEC of 12 December 1977 on the co-ordination of laws, regulations and administrative provisions relating to the taking up and pursuit of the business of credit institutions,[9] having many different legal forms, are in competition with one another in the banking sector; whereas it therefore seems advisable not to confine co-ordination in respect of these credit institutions to the legal forms covered by Directive 78/660/EEC but rather to opt for a scope which includes all companies and firms as defined in the second paragraph of Article [48][2] of the Treaty;

Whereas as far as financial institutions are concerned the scope of this Directive should however be confined to those financial institutions taking one of the legal forms referred to in Directive 78/660/EEC; whereas financial institutions which are not subject to that Directive must automatically come under this Directive;

Whereas a link with co-ordination in respect of credit institutions is necessary because aspects of the provisions governing annual accounts and

---

[1] OJ L 372, 31.12.1986, 1–17.
[2] The number between brackets has been changed as from 1 May 1999 by article 12 of the Treaty of Amsterdam.
[3] OJ C 130, 1.6.1981, 1; OJ C 83, 24.3.1984, 6 and OJ C 351, 31.12.1985, 24.
[4] OJ C 242, 12.9.1983, 33 and OJ C 163, 10.7.1978, 60.
[5] OJ C 112, 3.5.1982, 60.
[6] OJ L 222, 14.8.1978, 11, Fourth Company Law Directive, reproduced infra under no. C. 4.
[7] OJ L 314, 4.12.1984, 28.
[8] OJ L 193, 18.7.1983, Seventh Company Law Directive, reproduced infra under no. C. 6.

[9] OJ L 322, 17.12.1977, 30, First Banking Directive, which has been repealed by Directive 2000/12/EC (OJ L 126, 26.5.2001), reproduced infra under no. B. 32.

consolidated accounts will have an impact on other areas of that co-ordination, such as authorisation requirements and the indicators used for supervisory purposes;

Whereas although, in view of the specific characteristics of credit institutions, it would appear appropriate to adopt a separate Directive on the annual accounts and consolidated accounts of such institutions, this does not imply a new set of rules separate from those under Directives 78/660/EEC and 83/349/EEC; whereas such separate rules would be neither appropriate nor consistent with the principles underlying the co-ordination of company law since, given the important role which they play in the Community economy, credit institutions cannot be excluded from a framework of rules devised for undertakings generally; whereas, for this reason, only the particular characteristics of credit institutions have been taken into account and this Directive deals only with exceptions to the rules contained in Directives 78/660/EEC and 83/349/EEC;

Whereas the structure and content of the balance sheets of credit institutions differ in each Member State; whereas this Directive must therefore prescribe the same layout, nomenclature and terminology for the balance sheets of all credit institutions in the Community; whereas derogations should be allowed if necessitated by the legal form of an institution or by the special nature of its business;

Whereas, if the annual accounts and consolidated accounts are to be comparable, a number of basic questions regarding the disclosure of various transactions in the balance sheet and off the balance sheet must be settled;

Whereas, in the interests of greater comparability, it is also necessary that the content of the various balance sheet and off-balance sheet items be determined precisely;

Whereas the same applies to the layout and definition of the items in the profit and loss account;

Whereas the comparability of figures in the balance sheet and profit and loss account also depends crucially on the values at which assets and liabilities are entered in the balance sheet;

Whereas, in view of the particular risks associated with banking and of the need to maintain confidence, provision should be made for the possibility of introducing a liabilities item in the balance sheet entitled 'Fund for general banking risks'; whereas it would appear advisable for the same reasons that the Member States be permitted, pending subsequent co-ordination, to allow credit institutions some discretion, especially in the valuation of loans and advances and of certain securities; whereas, however, in this last case the Member States should allow these same credit institutions to create the 'Fund for general banking risks' mentioned above; whereas it would also appear appropriate to permit the Member States to allow credit institutions to set off certain charges and income in the profit and loss account;

Whereas, in view of the special nature of credit institutions, certain changes are also necessary with regard to the notes on the accounts;

Whereas, in the desire to place on the same footing as many credit institutions as possible, as was the case with Directive 77/780/EEC, the relief under Directive 78/660/EEC is not provided for in the case of small and medium-sized credit institutions; whereas, nevertheless, if in the light of experience such relief were to prove necessary it would be possible to provide for it in subsequent co-ordination; whereas for the same reasons the scope allowed the Member States under Directive 83/349/EEC to exempt parent undertakings from the consolidation requirement if the undertakings to be consolidated do not together exceed a certain size has not been extended to credit institutions;

Whereas the application of the provisions on consolidated accounts to credit institutions requires certain adjustments to some of the rules applicable to all industrial and commercial companies; whereas explicit rules have been provided for in the case of mixed groups and exemption from subconsolidation may be made subject to additional conditions;

Whereas, given the scale on which banking networks extend beyond national borders and their constant development, the annual accounts and consolidated accounts of a credit institution having its head office in one Member State should be published in all the Member States in which it is established;

Whereas the examination of problems which arise in connection with the subject matter of this Directive, notably concerning its application, requires the co-operation of representatives of the Member States and the Commission in a contact committee; whereas, in order to avoid the proliferation of such committees, it is desirable that such co-operation take place in the Committee provided for in Article 52 of Directive 78/660/EEC; whereas, nevertheless, when examining problems concerning credit institutions, the Committee will have to be appropriately constituted;

Whereas, in view of the complexity of the matter, the credit institutions covered by this Directive must be allowed a longer period than usual to implement its provisions;

Whereas provision should be made for the review of certain provisions of this Directive after five years' experience of its application, in the light of the aims of greater transparency and harmonisation,

HAS ADOPTED THIS DIRECTIVE:

SECTION I

PRELIMINARY PROVISIONS AND SCOPE

Article 1

[1. Articles 2, 3, 4(1), (3) to (6), Articles 6, 7, 13, 14, 15(3) and (4), Articles 16 to 21, 29 to 35, 37 to 41, 42 first sentence, 42a to 42f, 45(1), 46(1) and (2), 46a, Articles 48 to 50, 50a, 50b, 50c, 51(1) and 51a, 56 to 59, 60a, 61 and 61a of Directive 78/660/EEC shall apply to the institutions mentioned in Article 2 of this Directive, except where this Directive provides otherwise.] However, Articles 35(3), 36, 37 and 39(1) to (4) of this Directive shall not apply with respect to assets and liabilities that are valued in accordance with Section 7a of Directive 78/660/EEC.

[2. Where reference is made in Directives 78/660/EEC and 83/349/EEC to Articles 9, 10 and 10a (balance sheet) or to Articles 22 to 26 (profit and loss account) of Directive 78/660/EEC, such references shall be deemed to be references to Articles 4 and 4a (balance sheet) or to Articles 26, 27 and 28 (profit and loss account) of this Directive.]

3. References in Directives 78/660/EEC and 83/349/EEC to Articles 31 to 42 of Directive 78/660/EEC shall be deemed to be references to those Articles, taking account of Articles 35 to 39 of this Directive.

4. Where reference is made in the aforementioned provisions of Directive 78/660/EEC to balance sheet items for which this Directive makes no equivalent provision, such references shall be deemed to be references to the items in Article 4 of this Directive which include the assets and liabilities in question.

¶ *Paragraphs 1 and 2 have been replaced by article 3(1) of Directive 2003/51/EC, reproduced infra under no. C. 23.*
¶ *The first sentence of paragraph 1 has been amended by article 3 of Directive 2006/46/EC, reproduced infra under no. C. 31.*

Article 2

1. The co-ordination measures prescribed by this Directive shall apply to

(a) credit institutions within the meaning of the first indent of Article 1 of Directive 77/780/EEC which are companies or firms as defined in the second paragraph of Article [48][2] of the Treaty;

(b) financial institutions having one of the legal forms referred to in Article 1 (1) of Directive 78/660/EEC which, on the basis of paragraph 2 of that Article, are not subject to that Directive.

For the purposes of this Directive 'credit institutions' shall also include financial institutions unless the context requires otherwise.

2. The Member States need not apply this Directive to:

(a) the credit institutions listed in Article 2 (2) of Directive 77/780/EEC;

(b) institutions of the same Member State which, as defined in Article 2 (4) (a) of Directive 77/780/EEC, are affiliated to a central body in that Member State. In that case, without prejudice to the application of this Directive to the central body, the whole constituted by the central body and its affiliated institutions must be the subject of consolidated accounts including an annual report which shall be drawn up, audited and published in accordance with this Directive;

(c) the following credit institutions:
- in Greece: ETEBA (National Investment Bank for Industrial Development) and Τραπεξα Επενδυσεων (Investment Bank);
- in Ireland: Industrial and Provident Societies;
- in the United Kingdom: Friendly Societies and Industrial and Provident Societies.

4. Without prejudice to Article 2 (3) of Directive 78/660/EEC and pending subsequent co-ordination, the Member States may:

(a) in the case of the credit institutions referred to in Article 2 (1) (a) of this Directive which are not companies of any of the types listed in Article 1 (1) of Directive 78/660/EEC, lay down rules derogating from this Directive where derogating rules are necessary because of such institutions' legal form;

(b) in the case of specialised credit institutions, lay down rules derogating from this Directive where derogating rules are necessary because of the special nature of such institutions' business.

Such derogating rules may provide only for adaptations to the layout, nomenclature, terminology and content of items in the balance sheet and the profit and loss account; they may not have the effect of permitting the institutions to which they apply to provide less information in their annual accounts than other institutions subject to this Directive.

The Member States shall inform the Commission of those credit institutions, possibly by category, within six months of the end of the period stipulated in Article 47 (2). They shall inform the Commission of the derogations laid down to that end.

These derogations shall be reviewed within 10 years of the notification of this Directive. The Commission shall, if appropriate, submit suitable proposals. It shall also submit an interim report within five years of the notification of this Directive.

Section II
General Provisions Concerning the Balance Sheet and the Profit and Loss Account

Article 3

In the case of credit institutions the possibility of combining items pursuant to Article 4 (3) (a) or (b) of Directive 78/660/EEC shall be restricted to balance sheet and profit and loss account subitems preceded by lower-case letters and shall be authorised only under the rules laid down by the Member States to that end.

Section III
Layout of the Balance Sheet

Article 4

[The Member States shall prescribe the following layout for the balance sheet. As an alternative, Member States may permit or require credit institutions to adopt the presentation of the balance sheet set out in Article 4a.]

Assets

1. Cash in hand, balances with central banks and post office banks.

2. Treasury bills and other bills eligible for refinancing with central banks:

(a) Treasury bills and similar securities

(b) Other bills eligible for refinancing with central banks (unless national law prescribes that such bills be shown under Assets items 3 and 4).

3. Loans and advances to credit institutions:

(a) repayable on demand

(b) other loans and advances.

4. Loans and advances to customers.

5. Debt securities including fixed-income securities:

(a) issued by public bodies

(b) issued by other borrowers, showing separately:
- own-debt securities (unless national law requires their deduction from liabilities).

6. Shares and other variable-yield securities.

7. Participating interests, showing separately:
– participating interests in credit institutions (unless national law requires their disclosure in the notes on the accounts).

8. Shares in affiliated undertakings, showing separately:
– shares in credit institutions (unless national law requires their disclosure in the notes on the accounts).

9. Intangible assets as described under Assets headings B and C.I of Article 9 of Directive 78/660/EEC, showing separately:
– formation expenses, as defined by national law and in so far as national law permits their being shown as an asset (unless national law requires their disclosure in the notes on the accounts)
– goodwill, to the extent that it was acquired for valuable consideration (unless national law requires its disclosure in the notes on the accounts).

10. Tangible assets as described under Assets heading C.II of Article 9 of Directive 78/660/EEC, showing separately:
– land and buildings occupied by a credit institution for its own activities (unless national law requires their disclosure in the notes on the accounts).

11. Subscribed capital unpaid, showing separately:
– called-up capital (unless national law provides for called-up capital to be included under liabilities, in which case capital called but not yet paid must be included either in this Assets item or in Assets item 14).

12. Own shares (with an indication of their nominal value or, in the absence of a nominal value, their accounting par value to the extent that national law permits their being shown in the balance sheet).

13. Other assets.

14. Subscribed capital called but not paid (unless national law requires that called-up capital be shown under Assets item 11).

15. Prepayments and accrued income.

16. Loss for the financial year (unless national law provides for its inclusion under Liabilities item 14).

Total assets

Liabilities

1. Amounts owed to credit institutions:
(a) repayable on demand
(b) with agreed maturity dates or periods of notice.

2. Amounts owed to customers:
(a) savings deposits, showing separately:
– those repayable on demand and those with agreed maturity dates or periods of notice where national law provides for such a breakdown (unless national law provides for such information to be given in the notes on the accounts)
(b) other debts
    (ba) repayable on demand
    (bb) with agreed maturity dates or periods of notice.

3. Debts evidenced by certificates:
(a) debt securities in issue
(b) others.

4. Other liabilities.

5. Accruals and deferred income.

6. [Provisions]:
(a) provisions for pensions and similar obligations
(b) provisions for taxation
(c) other provisions.

7. Profit for the financial year (unless national law provides for its inclusion under Liabilities item 14).

8. Subordinated liabilities.

9. Subscribed capital (unless national law provides for called-up capital to be shown under this item. In that case, the amounts of subscribed capital and paid-up capital must be shown separately).

10. Share premium account.

11. Reserves.

12. Revaluation reserve.

13. Profit or loss brought forward.

14. Profit or loss for the financial year (unless national law requires that this item be shown under Assets item 16 or Liabilities item 7).

Total liabilities

Off-balance sheet items

1. Contingent liabilities, showing separately:
– acceptances and endorsements;
– guarantees and assets pledged as collateral security.

2. Commitments, showing separately:
– commitments arising out of sale and repurchase transactions.

¶ *The first sentence of article 4 has been amended by article 3(2)(a) of Directive 2003/51/EC, reproduced infra under no. C. 23.*

¶ *Under Liabilities, in point 6, the title has been amended by article 3(2)(b) of Directive 2003/51/EC, reproduced infra under no. C. 23.*

[Article 4a

Instead of the presentation of balance sheet items in accordance with Article 4, Member States may permit or require credit institutions, or certain classes of credit institution, to present those items classified by their nature and in order of their relative liquidity provided that the information given is at least equivalent to that otherwise required by Article 4.]

¶ *This article has been added by article 3(3) of Directive 2003/51/EC, reproduced infra under no. C. 23.*

Article 5

The following must be shown separately as sub-items of the items in question:
– claims, whether or not evidenced by certificates, on affiliated undertakings and included in Assets items 2 to 5;
– claims, whether or not evidenced by certificates, on undertakings with which a credit institution is linked by virtue of a participating interest and included in Assets items 2 to 5;
– liabilities, whether or not evidenced by certificates, to affiliated undertakings and included in Liabilities items 1, 2, 3 and 8;
– liabilities, whether or not evidenced by certificates, to undertakings with which a credit institution is linked by virtue of a participating interest and included in Liabilities items 1, 2, 3 and 8.

Article 6

1. Subordinated assets shall be shown separately as sub-items of the items of the layout and the sub-items created in accordance with Article 5.

2. Assets, whether or not evidenced by certificates, are subordinated if, in the event of winding up or bankruptcy, they are to be repaid only after the claims of other creditors have been met.

Article 7

The Member States may permit the disclosure of the information referred to in Articles 5 and 6, duly broken down into the various relevant items, in the notes on the accounts.

Article 8

1. Assets shall be shown under the relevant balance sheet headings even where the credit institution drawing up the balance sheet has pledged them as security for its own liabilities or for those of third parties or has otherwise assigned them as security to third parties.

2. A credit institution shall not include in its balance sheet assets pledged or otherwise assigned to it as security unless such assets are in the form of cash in the hands of that credit institution.

Article 9

1. Where a loan has been granted by a syndicate consisting of a number of credit institutions, each credit institution participating in the syndicate shall disclose only that part of the total loan which it has itself funded.

2. If in the case of a syndicated loan such as described in paragraph 1 the amount of funds

guaranteed by a credit institution exceeds the amount which it has made available, any additional guarantee portion shall be shown as a contingent liability (in Off-balance sheet item 1, second indent).

Article 10

1. Funds which a credit institution administers in its own name but on behalf of third parties must be shown in the balance sheet if the credit institution acquires legal title to the assets concerned. The total amount of such assets and liabilities shall be shown separately or in the notes on the accounts, broken down according to the various Assets and Liabilities items. However, the Member States may permit the disclosure of such funds off the balance sheet provided there are special rules whereby such funds can be excluded from the assets available for distribution in the event of the winding-up of a credit institution (or similar proceedings).

2. Assets acquired in the name of and on behalf of third parties must not be shown in the balance sheet.

Article 11

Only those amounts which can at any time be withdrawn without notice or for which a maturity or period of notice of 24 hours or one working day has been agreed shall be regarded as repayable on demand.

Article 12

1. Sale and repurchase transactions shall mean transactions which involve the transfer by a credit institution or customer (the 'transferor') to another credit institution or customer (the 'transferee') of assets, for example, bills, debts or transferable securities, subject to an agreement that the same assets will subsequently be transferred back to the transferor at a specified price.

2. If the transferee undertakes to return the assets on a date specified or to be specified by the transferor, the transaction in question shall be deemed to be a genuine sale and repurchase transaction.

3. If, however, the transferee is merely entitled to return the assets at the purchase price or for a different amount agreed in advance on a date specified or to be specified, the transaction in question shall be deemed to be a sale with an option to repurchase.

4. In the case of the sale and repurchase transactions referred to in paragraph 2, the assets transferred shall continue to appear in the transferor's balance sheet; the purchase price received by the transferor shall be shown as an amount owed to the transferee. In addition, the value of the assets transferred shall be disclosed in a note in the transferor's accounts. The transferee shall not be entitled to show the assets transferred in his balance sheet; the purchase price paid by the transferee shall be shown as an amount owed by the transferor.

5. In the case of the sale and repurchase transactions referred to in paragraph 3, however, the transferor shall not be entitled to show in his balance sheet the assets transferred; those items shall be shown as assets in the transferee's balance sheet. The transferor shall enter under Off-balance sheet item 2 an amount equal to the price agreed in the event of repurchase.

6. No forward exchange transactions, options, transactions involving the issue of debt securities with a commitment to repurchase all or part of the issue before maturity of any similar transactions shall be regarded as sale and repurchase transactions within the meaning of this Article.

SECTION IV

SPECIAL PROVISIONS RELATING TO CERTAIN BALANCE SHEET ITEMS

Article 13

Assets: Item 1—Cash in hand, balances with central banks and post office banks

1. Cash in hand shall comprise legal tender including foreign notes and coins.

2. This item may include only balances with the central banks and post office banks of the country or countries in which a credit institution is

established. Such balances must be readily available at all times. Other claims on such bodies must be shown as loans and advances to credit institutions (Assets item 3) or as loans and advances to customers (Assets item 4).

Article 14

Assets: Item 2—Treasury bills and other bills eligible for refinancing with central banks

1. This item shall comprise, under (a), treasury bills and similar securities, ie treasury bills, treasury certificates and similar debt instruments issued by public bodies which are eligible for refinancing with the central banks of the country or countries in which a credit institution is established. Those debt instruments issued by public bodies which fail to meet the above condition shall be shown under Assets sub-item 5 (a).

2. This item shall comprise, under (b), bills eligible for refinancing with central banks, i.e. all bills held in portfolio that were purchased from credit institutions or from customers to the extent that they are eligible, under national law, for refinancing with the central banks of the country or countries in which a credit institution is established.

Article 15

Assets: Item 3—Loans and advances to credit institutions

1. Loans and advances to credit institutions shall comprise all loans and advances arising out of banking transactions to domestic or foreign credit institutions by the credit institution drawing up the balance sheet, regardless of their actual designations.

The only exception shall be loans and advances represented by debt securities or any other security, which must be shown under Assets item 5.

2. For the purposes of this Article credit institutions shall comprise all undertakings on the list published in the *Official Journal of the European Communities* pursuant to Article 3 (7) of Directive 77/780/EEC, as well as central banks and official domestic and international banking organisations and all private and public undertakings which are not established in the Community but which satisfy the definition in Article 1 of Directive 77/780/EEC.

Loans and advances to undertakings which do not satisfy the above conditions shall be shown under Assets item 4.

Article 16

Assets: Item 4—Loans and advances to customers

Loans and advances to customers shall comprise all types of assets in the form of claims on domestic and foreign customers other than credit institutions, regardless of their actual designations.

The only exception shall be loans and advances represented by debt securities or any other security, which must be shown under Assets item 5.

Article 17

Assets: Item 5—Debt securities including fixed-income securities

1. This item shall comprise negotiable debt securities including fixed-income securities issued by credit institutions, by other undertakings or by public bodies; such securities issued by the latter, however, shall be included only if they are not to be shown under Assets item 2.

2. Securities bearing interest rates that vary in accordance with specific factors, for example the interest rate on the inter-bank market or on the Euromarket, shall also be regarded as debt securities including fixed-income securities.

3. Only repurchased and negotiable owndebt securities may be included in sub-item 5 (b).

Article 18

Liabilities: Item 1—Amounts owed to credit institutions

1. Amounts owed to credit institutions shall include all amounts arising out of banking transactions owed to other domestic or foreign credit institutions by the credit institution drawing up the balance sheet, regardless of their actual designations.

The only exception shall be liabilities represented by debt securities or by any other security, which must be shown under Liabilities item 3.

2. For the purposes of this Article credit institutions shall comprise all undertakings on the list published in the *Official Journal of the European Communities* pursuant to Article 3 (7) of Directive 77/780/EEC, as well as central banks and official domestic and international banking organisations and all private and public undertakings which are not established in the Community but which satisfy the definition in Article 1 of Directive 77/780/EEC.

Article 19

Liabilities: Item 2—Amounts owed to customers

1. Amounts owed to customers shall include all amounts owed to creditors that are not credit institutions within the meaning of Article 18, regardless of their actual designations.

The only exception shall be liabilities represented by debt securities or by any other security, which must be shown under Liabilities item 3.

2. Only deposits which satisfy the conditions laid down in national law shall be treated as savings deposits.

3. Savings bonds shall be shown under the corresponding sub-item only if they are not represented by negotiable certificates.

Article 20

Liabilities: Item 3—Debts evidenced by certificates

1. This item shall include both debt securities and debts for which negotiable certificates have been issued, in particular deposit receipts, 'bons de caisse' and liabilities arising out of own acceptances and promissory notes.

2. Only acceptances which a credit institution has issued for its own refinancing and in respect of which it is the first party liable ('drawee') shall be treated as own acceptances.

Article 21

Liabilities: Item 8—Subordinated liabilities

Where it has been contractually agreed that, in the event of winding up or of bankruptcy, liabilities, whether or not evidenced by certificates, are to be repaid only after the claims of all other creditors have been met, the liabilities in question shall be shown under this item.

Article 22

Liabilities: Item 9—Subscribed capital

This item shall comprise all amounts, regardless of their actual designations, which, in accordance with the legal structure of the institution concerned, are regarded under national law as equity capital subscribed by the shareholders or other proprietors.

Article 23

Liabilities: Item 11—Reserves

This item shall comprise all the types of reserves listed in Article 9 of Directive 78/660/EEC under Liabilities item A.IV, as defined therein. The Member States may also prescribe other types of reserves if necessary for credit institutions the legal structures of which are not covered by Directive 78/660/EEC.

The types of reserve referred to in the first paragraph shall be shown separately, as sub-items of Liabilities item 11, in the balance sheets of the credit institutions concerned, with the exception of the revaluation reserve which shall be shown under item 12.

Article 24

Off-balance sheet: Item 1—Contingent liabilities

This item shall comprise all transactions whereby an institution has underwritten the obligations of a third party.

Notes on accounts shall state the nature and amount of any type of contingent liability which is material in relation to an institution's activities.

Liabilities arising out of the endorsement of rediscounted bills shall be included in this item only if national law does not require otherwise. The same shall apply to acceptances other than own acceptances.

Sureties and assets pledged as collateral security shall include all guarantee obligations incurred and assets pledged as collateral security on behalf of third parties, particularly in respect of sureties and irrevocable letters of credit.

Article 25

Off-balance sheet: Item 2—Commitments

This item shall include every irrevocable commitment which could give rise to a risk.

Notes on accounts shall state the nature and amount of any type of commitment which is material in relation to an institution's activities.

Commitments arising out of sale and repurchase transactions shall include commitments entered into by a credit institution in the context of sale and repurchase transactions (on the basis of firm agreements to sell with options to repurchase) within the meaning of Article 12 (3).

SECTION V

LAYOUT OF THE PROFIT AND LOSS ACCOUNT

Article 26

For the presentation of the profit and loss account, the Member States shall prescribe one or both of the layouts provided for in Articles 27 and 28. If a Member State prescribes both layouts it may allow undertakings to choose between them.

[By way of derogation from Article 2(1) of Directive 78/660/EEC, Member States may permit or require all credit institutions, or any classes of credit institution, to present a statement of their performance instead of the presentation of profit and loss items in accordance with Articles 27 or 28, provided that the information given is at least equivalent to that otherwise required by those Articles.]

¶ *The second paragraph of this article has been added by article 3(4) of Directive 2003/51/EC, reproduced infra under no. C. 23.*

Article 27

Vertical layout

1. Interest receivable and similar income, showing separately that arising from fixed-income securities.

2. Interest payable and similar charges.

3. Income from securities:
 (a) Income from shares and other variable-yield
 (b) Income from participating interests
 (c) Income from shares in affiliated undertakings.

4. Commissions receivable.

5. Commissions payable.

6. Net profit or net loss on financial operations.

7. Other operating income.

8. General administrative expenses:
 (a) Staff costs, showing separately:
 – wages and salaries
 – social security costs, with a separate indication of those relating to pensions
 (b) Other administrative expenses.

9. Value adjustments in respect of Assets items 9 and 10.

10. Other operating charges.

11. Value adjustments in respect of loans and advances and provisions for contingent liabilities and for commitments.

12. Value re-adjustments in respect of loans and advances and provisions for contingent liabilities and for commitments.

13. Value adjustments in respect of transferable securities held as financial fixed assets, participating interests and shares in affiliated undertakings.

14. Value re-adjustments in respect of transferable securities held as financial fixed assets, participating interests and shares in affiliated undertakings.

15. Tax on profit or loss on ordinary activities.

16. Profit or loss on ordinary activities after tax.

17. Extraordinary income.

18. Extraordinary charges.

19. Extraordinary profit or loss.

20. Tax on extraordinary profit or loss.

21. Extraordinary profit or loss after tax.

22. Other taxes not shown under the preceding items securities.

23. Profit or loss for the financial year.

Article 28
Horizontal layout

A. *Charges*

1. Interest payable and similar charges.

2. Commissions payable.

3. Net loss on financial operations.

4. General administrative expenses:

(a) Staff costs, showing separately:
– wages and salaries
– social security costs, with a separate indication of those relating to pensions

(b) Other administrative expenses.

5. Value adjustments in respect of Assets items 9 and 10.

6. Other operating charges.

7. Value adjustments in respect of loans and advances and provisions for contingent liabilities and for commitments.

8. Value adjustments in respect of transferable securities held as financial fixed assets, participating interests and shares in affiliated undertakings.

9. Tax on profit or loss on ordinary activities.

10. Profit or loss on ordinary activities after tax.

11. Extraordinary charges.

12. Tax on extraordinary profit or loss.

13. Extraordinary loss after tax.

14. Other taxes not shown under the preceding items.

15. Profit for the financial year.

Section VI
Special Provisions Relating to Certain Items in the Profit and Loss Account

Article 29

Article 27, items 1 and 2 (vertical layout)

Article 28, items A 1 and B 1 (horizontal layout)

Interest receivable and similar income and interest payable and similar charges

These items shall include all profits and losses arising out of banking activities, including:

(1) all income from assets entered under Assets items 1 to 5 in the balance sheet, however calculated. Such income shall also include income arising from the spreading on a time basis of the discount on assets acquired at an amount below, and liabilities contracted at an amount above, the sum payable at maturity;

(2) all charges arising out of liabilities entered under Liabilities items 1, 2, 3 and 8, however calculated. Such charges shall also include charges arising from the spreading on a time basis of the premium on assets acquired at an amount above, and liabilities contracted at an amount below, the sum payable at maturity;

(3) income and charges resulting from covered forward contracts, spread over the actual duration of the contract and similar in nature to interest;

(4) fees and commission similar in nature to interest and calculated on a time basis or by reference to the amount of the claim or liability.

Article 30

Article 27, item 3 (vertical layout)

Article 28, item B 2 (horizontal layout)

Income from shares and other variable-yield securities, from participating interests, and from shares in affiliated undertakings

This item shall comprise all dividends and other income from variable-yield securities, from participating interests and from shares in affiliated undertakings. Income from shares in investment companies shall also be included under this item.

Article 31

Article 27, items 4 and 5 (vertical layout)

Article 28, items A 2 and B 3 (horizontal layout)

Commissions receivable and commissions payable

Without prejudice to Article 29, commissions receivable shall include income in respect of all services supplied to third parties, and commissions payable shall include charges for services rendered by third parties, in particular:
– commissions for guarantees, loans administration on behalf of other lenders and securities transactions on behalf of third parties,
– commissions and other charges and income in respect of payment transactions, account administration charges and commissions for the safe custody and administration of securities,
– commissions for foreign currency transactions and for the sale and purchase of coin and precious metals on behalf of third parties,
– commissions charged for brokerage services in connection with savings and insurance contracts and loans.

Article 32

Article 27, item 6 (vertical layout)

Article 28, item A 3 or item B 4 (horizontal layout)

Net profit or net loss on financial operations

This item covers:

1. the net profit or loss on transactions in securities which are not held as financial fixed assets together with value adjustments and value re-adjustments on such securities, taking into account, where Article 36 (2) has been applied, the difference resulting from application of that article; however, in those Member States which exercise the option provided for in Article 37, these net profits or losses and value adjustments and value re-adjustments shall be included only in so far as they relate to securities included in a trading portfolio;

2. the net profit or loss on exchange activities, without prejudice to Article 29, point 3;

3. the net profits and losses on other buying and selling operations involving financial instruments, including precious metals.

Article 33

Article 27, items 11 and 12 (vertical layout)

Article 28, items A 7 and B 5 (horizontal layout)

Value adjustments in respect of loans and advances and provisions for contingent liabilities and for commitments

Value re-adjustments in respect of loans and advances and provisions for contingent liabilities and for commitments

1. These items shall include, on the one hand, charges for value adjustments in respect of loans and advances to be shown under Assets items 3 and 4 and provisions for contingent liabilities and for commitments to be shown under Off-balance sheet items 1 and 2 and, on the other hand, credits from the recovery of written-off loans and advances and amounts written back following earlier value adjustments and provisions.

2. In those Member States which exercise the option provided for in Article 37, this item shall also include the net profit or loss on transactions in securities included in Assets items 5 and 6 which are neither held as financial fixed assets as defined in Article 35 (2) nor included in a trading portfolio, together with value adjustments and value re-adjustments on such securities taking into account, where Article 36 (2) has been applied, the difference resulting from application

of that article. The nomenclature of this item shall be adapted accordingly.

3. The Member States may permit the charges and income covered by these items to be set off against each other, so that only a net item (income or charge) is shown.

4. Value adjustments in respect of loans and advances to credit institutions, to customers, to undertakings with which a credit institution is linked by virtue of participating interests and to affiliated undertakings shall be shown separately in the notes on the accounts where they are material. This provision need not be applied if a Member State permits setting-off pursuant to paragraph 3.

Article 34

Article 27, items 13 and 14 (vertical layout)

Article 28, items A 8 and B 5 (horizontal layout)

Value adjustments in respect of transferable securities held as financial fixed assets, participating interests and shares in affiliated undertakings

Value re-adjustments in respect of transferable securities held as financial fixed assets, participating interests and shares in affiliated undertakings

1. These items shall include, on the one hand, charges for value adjustments in respect of assets shown in Assets items 5 to 8 and, on the other hand, all the amounts written back following earlier value adjustments, in so far as the charges and income relate to transferable securities held as financial fixed assets as defined in Article 35 (2), participating interests and shares in affiliated undertakings.

2. The Member States may permit the charges and income covered by these items to be set off against each other, so that only a net item (income or charge) is shown.

3. Value adjustments in respect of these transferable securities, participating interests and shares in affiliated undertakings shall be shown separately in the notes on the accounts where they are material. This provision need not be applied if a Member State permits setting off pursuant to paragraph 2.

SECTION VII

VALUATION RULES

Article 35

1. Assets items 9 and 10 must always be valued as fixed assets. The assets included in other balance sheet items shall be valued as fixed assets where they are intended for use on a continuing basis in the normal course of an undertaking's activities.

2. Where reference is made to financial fixed assets in Section 7 of Directive 78/660/EEC, this term shall in the case of credit institutions be taken to mean participating interests, shares in affiliated undertakings and securities intended for use on a continuing basis in the normal course of an undertaking's activities.

3. (a) Debt securities including fixed-income securities held as financial fixed assets shall be shown in the balance sheet at purchase price. The Member States may, however, require or permit such debt securities to be shown in the balance sheet at the amount repayable at maturity;

(b) Where the purchase price of such debt securities exceeds the amount repayable at maturity the amount of the difference must be charged to the profit and loss account. The Member States may, however, require or permit the amount of the difference to be written off in instalments so that it is completely written off by the time when the debt securities are repaid. The difference must be shown separately in the balance sheet or in the notes on the accounts;

(c) Where the purchase price of such debt securities is less than the amount repayable at maturity, the Member States may require or permit the amount of the difference to be released to income in instalments over the period remaining until repayment. The difference must be shown separately in the balance sheet or in the notes on the accounts.

Article 36

1. Where transferable securities which are not held as financial fixed assets are shown in the balance sheet at purchase price, credit institutions shall disclose in the notes on their accounts the difference between the purchase price and the higher market value of the balance sheet date.

2. The Member States may, however, require or permit those transferable securities to be shown in the balance sheet at the higher market value at the balance sheet date. The difference between the purchase price and the higher market value shall be disclosed in the notes on the accounts.

Article 37

1. Article 39 of Directive 78/660/EEC shall apply to the valuation of credit institutions' loans and advances, debt securities, shares and other variable-yield securities which are not held as financial fixed assets.

2. Pending subsequent co-ordination, however, the Member States may permit:

(a) loans and advances to credit institutions and customers (Assets items 3 and 4) and debt securities, shares and other variable-yield securities included in Assets items 5 and 6 which are neither held as financial fixed assets as defined in Article 35 (2) nor included in a trading portfolio to be shown at a value lower than that which would result from the application of Article 39 (1) of Directive 78/660/EEC, where that is required by the prudence dictated by the particular risks associated with banking. Nevertheless, the difference between the two values must not be more than 4% of the total amount of the assets mentioned above after application of the aforementioned Article 39;

(b) that the lower value resulting from the application of subparagraph (a) be maintained until the credit institution decides to adjust it;

(c) where a Member State exercises the option provided for in subparagraph (a), neither Article 36 (1) of this Directive nor Article 40 (2) of Directive 78/660/EEC shall apply.

Article 38

1. Pending subsequent co-ordination, those Member States which exercise the option provided for in Article 37 must permit and those Member States which do not exercise that option may permit the introduction of a Liabilities item 6A entitled 'Fund for general banking risks'. That item shall include those amounts which a credit institution decides to put aside to cover such risks where that is required by the particular risks associated with banking.

2. The net balance of the increases and decreases of the 'Fund for general banking risks' must be shown separately in the profit and loss account.

Article 39

1. Assets and liabilities denominated in foreign currency shall be translated at the spot rate of exchange ruling on the balance sheet date. The Member States may, however, require or permit assets held as financial fixed assets and tangible and intangible assets, not covered or not specifically covered in either the spot or forward markets, to be translated at the rates ruling on the dates of their acquisition.

2. Uncompleted forward and spot exchange transactions shall be translated at the spot rates of exchange ruling on the balance sheet date.

The Member States may, however, require forward transactions to be translated at the forward rate ruling on the balance sheet date.

3. Without prejudice to Article 29 (3), the differences between the book values of the assets, liabilities and forward transactions and the amounts produced by translation in accordance with paragraphs 1 and 2 shall be shown in the profit and loss account. The Member States may, however, require or permit differences produced by translation in accordance with paragraphs 1 and 2 to be included, in whole or in part, in reserves not available for distribution, where they arise on assets held as financial fixed assets, on tangible and intangible assets and on any transactions undertaken to cover those assets.

4. The Member States may provide that positive translation differences arising out of forward transactions, assets or liabilities not covered or not specifically covered by other forward transactions, or by assets or liabilities shall not be shown in the profit and loss account.

5. If a method specified in Article 59 of Directive 78/660/EEC is used, the Member States may provide that any translation differences shall be transferred, in whole or in part, directly to reserves. Positive and negative translation differences transferred to reserves shall be shown separately in the balance sheet or in the notes on the accounts.

6. The Member States may require or permit translation differences arising on consolidation out of the retranslation of an affiliated undertaking's capital and reserves or the share of a participating interest's capital and reserves at the beginning of the accounting period to be included, in whole or in part, in consolidated reserves, together with the translation differences arising on the translation of any transactions undertaken to cover that capital and those reserves.

7. The Member States may require or permit the income and expenditure of affiliated undertakings and participating interests to be translated on consolidation at the average rates of exchange ruling during the accounting period.

Section VIII
Contents of the Notes on the Accounts

Article 40

1. Article 43 (1) of Directive 78/660/EEC shall apply, subject to Article 37 of this Directive and to the following provisions.

2. In addition to the information required under Article 43 (1) (5) of Directive 78/660/EEC, credit institutions shall disclose the following information relating to Liabilities item 8 (Subordinated liabilities):

(a) in respect of each borrowing which exceeds 10% of the total amount of the subordinated liabilities:

(i) the amount of the borrowing, the currency in which it is denominated, the rate of interest and the maturity date or the fact that it is a perpetual issue;
(ii) whether there are any circumstances in which early repayment is required;
(iii) the terms of the subordination, the existence of any provisions to convert the subordinated liability into capital or some other form of liability and the terms of any such provisions.

(b) an overall indication of the rules governing other borrowings.

3. (a) In place of the information required under Article 43 (1) (6) of Directive 78/660/EEC, credit institutions shall in the notes on their accounts state separately for each of the Assets items 3 (b) and 4 and the Liabilities items 1 (b), 2 (a), 2 (b) (bb) and 3 (b) the amounts of those loans and advances and liabilities on the basis of their remaining maturity as follows:
– not more than three months,
– more than three months but not more than one year,
– more than one year but not more than five years,
– more than five years.

For Assets item 4, loans and advances on call and at short notice must also be shown.

If loans and advances or liabilities involve payment by instalments, the remaining maturity shall be the period between the balance sheet date and the date on which each instalment falls due.

However, for five years after the date referred to in Article 47 (2) the Member States may require or permit the listing by maturity of the assets and liabilities referred to in this Article to be based on the originally agreed maturity or period of notice. In that event, where a credit institution has acquired an existing loan not evidenced by a certificate, the Member States shall require classification of that loan to be based on the remaining maturity as at the date on which it was acquired. For the purposes of this subparagraph, the originally agreed maturity for loans shall be the period between the date of first drawing and the date of repayment; the period of notice shall be deemed to be the period between the date on which notice is given and the date on which repayment is to be made; if loans and advances or liabilities are redeemable by instalments, the agreed maturity shall be the period between the date on which such loans and advances or liabilities arose and the date on which the last instalment falls due. Credit institutions shall also indicate for the balance sheet items referred to in this subparagraph what proportion of those assets and liabilities will become due within one year of the balance sheet date.

(b) Credit institutions shall, in respect of Assets item 5 (Debt securities including fixed-income securities) and Liabilities item 3 (a) (Debt securities in issue), indicate what proportion of assets and liabilities will become due within one year of the balance sheet date.

(c) The Member States may require the information referred to in subparagraphs (a) and (b) to be given in the balance sheet.

(d) Credit institutions shall give particulars of the assets which they have pledged as security for their own liabilities or for those of third parties (including contingent liabilities); the particulars should be in sufficient detail to indicate for each Liabilities item and for each Off-balance sheet item the total amount of the assets pledged as security.

4. Where credit institutions have to provide the information referred to in Article 43 (1) (7) of Directive 78/660/EEC in Off-balance sheet items, such information need not be repeated in the notes on the accounts.

5. In place of the information required under Article 43 (1) (8) of Directive 78/660/EEC, a credit institution shall indicate in the notes on its accounts the proportion of its income relating to items 1, 3, 4, 6 and 7 of Article 27 or to items B 1, B 2, B 3, B 4 and B 7 of Article 28 by geographical markets, in so far as, taking account of the manner in which the credit institution is organised, those markets differ substantially from one another. Article 45 (1) (b) of Directive 78/660/EEC shall apply.

6. The reference in Article 43 (1) (9) of Directive 78/660/EEC to Article 23 (6) of that Directive shall be deemed to be a reference to Article 27 (8) or Article 28 (A 4) of this Directive.

7. By way of derogation from Article 43 (1) (13) of Directive 78/660/EEC, credit institutions need disclose only the amounts of advances and credits granted to the members of their administrative, managerial and supervisory bodies, and the commitments entered into on their behalf by way of guarantees of any kind. That information must be given in the form of a total for each category.

Article 41

1. The information prescribed in Article 15 (3) of Directive 78/660/EEC must be given in respect of assets held as fixed assets as defined in Article 35 of this Directive. The obligation to show value adjustments separately shall not, however, apply where a Member State has permitted set-off between value adjustments pursuant to Article 34 (2) of this Directive. In that event value adjustments may be combined with other items.

2. The Member States shall require credit institutions to give the following information as well in the notes on their accounts:

(a) a breakdown of the transferable securities shown under Assets items 5 to 8 into listed and unlisted securities;

(b) a breakdown of the transferable securities shown under Assets items 5 and 6 into securities which, pursuant to Article 35, are or are not held as financial fixed assets and the criterion used to distinguish between the two categories of transferable securities;

(c) the value of leasing transactions, apportioned between the relevant balance sheet items;

(d) a breakdown of Assets item 13, Liabilities item 4, items 10 and 18 in the vertical layout or A 6 and A 11 in the horizontal layout and items 7 and 17 in the vertical layout or B 7 and B 9 in the horizontal layout in the profit and loss account into their main component amounts, where such amounts are important for the purpose of assessing the annual accounts, as well as explanations of their nature and amount;

(e) the charges paid on account of subordinated liabilities by a credit institution in the year under review;

(f) the fact that an institution provides management and agency services to third parties where the scale of business of that kind is material in relation to the institution's activities as a whole;

(g) the aggregate amounts of assets and of liabilities denominated in foreign currencies, translated into the currency in which the annual accounts are drawn up;

(h) a statement of the types of unmatured forward transactions outstanding at the balance sheet date indicating, in particular, for each type of transaction, whether they are made to a material extent for the purpose of hedging the effects of fluctuations in interest rates, exchange rates and market prices, and whether they are made to a material extent for dealing purposes. These types of transaction shall include all those in connection with which the income or expenditure is to be included in Article 27, item 6, Article 28, items A 3 or B 4 or Article 29 (3), for example, foreign currencies, precious metals, transferable securities, certificates of deposit and other assets.

Section IX
Provisions Relating to Consolidated Accounts

Article 42

1. Credit institutions shall draw up consolidated accounts and consolidated annual reports in accordance with Directive 83/349/EEC, in so far as this section does not provide otherwise.

2. Insofar as a Member State does not have recourse to Article 5 of Directive 83/349/EEC, paragraph 1 of this Article shall also apply to parent undertakings the sole object of which is to acquire holdings in subsidiary undertakings and to manage such holdings and turn them to profit, where those subsidiary undertakings are either exclusively or mainly credit institutions.

Article 43

1. Directive 83/349/EEC shall apply, subject to Article 1 of this Directive and paragraph 2 of this Article.

2. (a) Articles 4, 6, 15 and 40 of Directive 83/349/EEC shall not apply.

(b) The Member States may make application of Article 7 of Directive 83/349/EEC subject to the following additional conditions:
- the parent undertaking must have declared that it guarantees the commitments entered into by the exempted undertaking; the existence of that declaration shall be disclosed in the accounts of the exempted undertaking;
- the parent undertaking must be a credit institution within the meaning of Article 2 (1) (a) of this Directive.

(c) The information referred to in the first two indents of Article 9 (2) of Directive 83/349/EEC, namely:
- the amount of the fixed assets and
- the net turnover

shall be replaced by:
- the sum of items 1, 3, 4, 6 and 7 in Article 27 or B 1, B 2, B 3, B 4 and B 7 in Article 28 of this Directive.

(d) Where, as a result of applying Article 13 (3) (c) of Directive 83/349/EEC, a subsidiary undertaking which is a credit institution is not included in consolidated accounts but where the shares of that undertaking are temporarily held as a result of a financial assistance operation with a view to the reorganisation or rescue of the undertaking in question, the annual accounts of that undertaking shall be attached to the consolidated accounts and additional information shall be given in the notes on the accounts concerning the nature and terms of the financial assistance operation.

(e) A Member State may also apply Article 12 of Directive 83/349/EEC to two or more credit institutions which are not connected as described in Article 1 (1) or (2) of that Directive but are managed on a unified basis other than pursuant to a contract or provisions in the memorandum or articles of association.

(f) [. . .]

(g) For the purposes of the layout of consolidated accounts:
- Articles 3, 5 to 26 and 29 to 34 of this Directive shall apply;
- the reference in Article 17 of Directive 83/349/EEC to Article 15 (3) of Directive 78/660/EEC shall apply to the assets deemed to

be fixed assets pursuant to Article 35 of this Directive.

(h) Article 34 of Directive 83/349/EEC shall apply in respect of the contents of the notes on consolidated accounts, subject to Articles 40 and 41 of this Directive.

¶ *Article 43(2)(f) has been repealed by article 3(5) of Directive 2003/51/EC, reproduced infra under no. C. 23.*

Section X
Publication

Article 44

1. The duly approved annual accounts of credit institutions, together with the annual reports and the reports by the persons responsible for auditing the accounts shall be published as laid down by national law in accordance with Article 3 of Directive 68/151/EEC.[10]

National law may, however, permit the annual report not to be published as stipulated above. In that case, it shall be made available to the public at the company's registered office in the Member State concerned. It must be possible to obtain a copy of all or part of any such report on request. The price of such a copy must not exceed its administrative cost.

2. Paragraph 1 shall also apply to the duly approved consolidated accounts, the consolidated annual reports and the reports by the persons responsible for auditing the accounts.

3. However, where a credit institution which has drawn up annual accounts or consolidated accounts is not established as one of the types of company listed in Article 1 (1) of Directive 78/660/EEC and is not required by its national law to publish the documents referred to in paragraphs 1 and 2 of this Article as prescribed in Article 3 of Directive 68/151/EEC, it must at least make them available to the public at its registered office or, in the absence of a registered office, at its principal place of business. It must be possible to obtain copies of such documents on request. The prices of such copies must not exceed their administrative cost.

4. The annual accounts and consolidated accounts of a credit institution must be published in every Member State in which that credit institution has branches within the meaning of the third indent of Article 1 of Directive 77/780/EEC. Such Member States may require that those documents be published in their official languages.

5. The Member States shall provide for appropriate sanctions for failure to comply with the publication rules referred to in this Article.

Section XI
Auditing

Article 45

A Member State need not apply Article 2 (1) (b) (iii) of Directive 84/253/EEC[11] to public savings banks where the statutory auditing of the documents of those undertakings referred to in Article 1 (1) of that Directive is reserved to an existing supervisory body for those savings banks at the time of the entry into force of this Directive and where the person responsible complies at least with the conditions laid down in Articles 3 to 9 of Directive 84/253/EEC.

Section XII
Final Provisions

Article 46

The Contact Committee established in accordance with Article 52 of Directive 78/660/EEC shall, when meeting as constituted appropriately, also have the following functions:

(a) to facilitate, without prejudice to Articles [226 and 227][2] of the Treaty, harmonised application of this Directive through regular meetings dealing in particular with practical problems arising in connection with its application;

---

[10] OJ L 65, 14.3.1968, 8, First Company Law Directive, reproduced infra under no. C. 1.

[11] OJ L 126, 12.5.1984, 20, Eighth Company Law Directive, reproduced infra under no. C. 7.

(b) to advise the Commission, if necessary, on additions or amendments to this Directive.

Article 47

1. The Member States shall bring into force the laws, regulations and administrative provisions necessary for them to comply with this Directive by 31 December 1990. They shall forthwith inform the Commission thereof.

2. A Member State may provide that the provisions referred to in paragraph 1 shall first apply to annual accounts and consolidated accounts for financial years beginning on 1 January 1993 or during the calendar year 1993.

3. The Member States shall communicate to the Commission the texts of the main provisions of national law which they adopt in the field governed by this Directive.

Article 48

Five years after the date referred to in Article 47 (2), the Council, acting on a proposal from the Commission, shall examine and if need be revise all those provisions of this Directive which provide for Member State options, together with Articles 2 (1), 27, 28 and 41, in the light of the experience acquired in applying this Directive and in particular of the aims of greater transparency and harmonisation of the provisions referred to by this Directive.

Article 49

This Directive is addressed to the Member States.

B. 8.

Commission Recommendation 87/62/EEC
of 22 December 1986
on monitoring and controlling large exposures of credit institutions[1]

This Recommendation has been superseded by Directive 92/121/EEC (OJ L 29, 5.02.1993, 1), consolidated in Directive 2000/12/EC, which subsequently has been repealed by article 158 of Directive 2006/48/EC (OJ L 177, 30.06.2006, 1) reproduced infra under no. B. 41.

---

[1] OJ L 33, 4.2.1987, 10–15.

B. 9.

Commission Recommendation 87/63/EEC
of 22 December 1986
concerning the introduction of deposit-guarantee schemes in the Community[1]

This Recommendation has been superseded by Directive 94/19/EC (OJ L 135, 31.05.1994, 5), reproduced infra under no. B. 22.

---

[1] OJ L 33, 4.2.1987, 16–17.

B. 10.

Council Directive 89/117/EEC
of 13 February 1989
on the obligations of branches established in a Member State of credit institutions and financial institutions having their head offices outside that Member State regarding the publication of annual accounting documents[1]

THE COUNCIL OF THE EUROPEAN COMMUNITIES,

Having regard to the Treaty establishing the European Economic Community, and in particular Article [44][2] thereof,

Having regard to the proposal from the Commission,[3]

In co-operation with the European Parliament,[4]

Having regard to the opinion of the Economic and Social Committee,[5]

Whereas the establishment of a European internal market presupposes that the branches of credit institutions and financial institutions having their head offices in other Member States should be treated in the same way as branches of credit institutions and financial institutions having their head offices in the same Member State; whereas this means that, with regard to the publication of annual accounting documents, it is sufficient for the branches of such institutions having their head offices in other Member States to publish the annual accounting documents of their institution as a whole;

Whereas, as part of a further instrument of co-ordination of the disclosure requirements in respect of branches, provision is made for certain documents and particulars relating to branches established in a Member State which certain types of companies governed by the law of another Member State, including banks and other financial institutions, have to publish; whereas, as regards disclosure of accounting documents, reference is made to specific provisions to be laid down for banks and other financial institutions;

Whereas the present practice of some Member States of requiring the branches of credit institutions and financial institutions having their head offices outside these Member States to publish annual accounts relating to their own activities is no longer justified following the adoption of Council Directive 86/635/EEC of 8 December 1986 on the annual accounts and consolidated accounts of banks and other financial institutions;[6] whereas the publication of annual branch accounts cannot in any case provide the public, and in particular creditors, with an adequate view of the financial situation of the undertaking, since part of a whole cannot be viewed in isolation;

Whereas, on the other hand, in view of the present level of integration, the need for certain information on the activities of branches established in a Member State by credit institutions and financial institutions having their head offices outside that Member State cannot be disregarded; whereas, nevertheless, the extent of such information should be limited so as to prevent distortions of competition;

Whereas, however, this Directive affects only disclosure requirements concerning annual accounts, and does not in any way affect the obligations of branches of credit institutions and financial institutions to provide information pursuant to other requirements, deriving, for example, from social

---

[1] OJ L 44, 16.2.1989, 40–42.
[2] The number between brackets has been changed as from 1 May 1999 by article 12 of the Treaty of Amsterdam.
[3] OJ C 230, 11.9.1986, 4.
[4] OJ C 319, 30.11.1987, 64 and OJ C 290, 14.11.1988, 66.
[5] OJ C 345, 21.12.1987, 73.

[6] OJ L 372, 31.12.1986, 1, reproduced supra under no. B. 7.

legislation, with regard to employees' rights to information, host countries' rights of supervision over credit institutions or financial institutions and fiscal legislation and also for statistical purposes;

Whereas equality of competition means, with regard to the branches of credit institutions and financial institutions having their head offices in non-member countries, that such branches must, on the one hand, in publishing annual accounting documents, adhere to a standard which is the same as, or equivalent to, that of the Community, but, on the other hand, that such branches should not have to publish annual accounts relating to their own activities if they fulfil the above-mentioned condition;

Whereas the equivalence, required under this Directive, of annual accounting documents of credit institutions and financial institutions having their head offices in non-member countries may lead to problems of assessment; whereas it is therefore necessary for this and other problems in the area covered by the Directive, and in particular in its implementation, to be dealt with by representatives of the Member States and of the Commission jointly in a Contact Committee; whereas, in order to keep the number of such committees within limits, such co-operation should be carried out within the framework of the Committee set up under Article 52 of Council Directive 78/660/EEC of 25 July 1978 on the annual accounts of certain types of companies,[7] as last amended by Directive 84/569/EEC;[8] whereas, however, where problems relating to credit institutions are to be dealt with, the Committee should be appropriately constituted,

HAS ADOPTED THIS DIRECTIVE:

Article 1
Scope

1. The co-ordination measures prescribed by this Directive shall apply to branches established in a Member State by credit institutions and financial institutions within the meaning of Article 2 (1) (a) and (b) of Directive 86/635/EEC having their head offices outside that Member State. Where a credit institution or financial institution has its head office in a non-member country, this Directive shall apply in so far as the credit institution or financial institution has a legal form which is comparable to the legal forms specified in the above-mentioned Article 2 (1) (a) and (b).

2. The third indent of Article 1 of Directive 77/780/EEC[9] shall apply *mutatis mutandis* to branches of credit institutions and financial institutions covered by this Directive.

Article 2
Provisions relating to branches of credit institutions and financial institutions having their head offices in other Member States

1. Member States shall require branches of credit institutions and financial institutions having their head offices in other Member States to publish, in accordance with Article 44 of Directive 86/635/EEC, the credit institution or financial institution documents referred to therein (annual accounts, consolidated accounts, annual report, consolidated annual report, opinions of the person responsible for auditing the annual accounts and consolidated accounts).

2. Such documents must be drawn up and audited in the manner required by the law of the Member State in which the credit institution or financial institution has its head office in accordance with Directive 86/635/EEC.

3. Branches may not be required to publish annual accounts relating to their own activities.

4. Member States may, pending further co-ordination, require branches to publish the following additional information:
– the income and costs of the branch deriving from items 1, 3, 4, 6, 7, 8 and 15 of Article 27

---

[7] OJ L 222, 14.8.1978, 11, Fourth Company Directive, reproduced infra under no. C. 4.
[8] OJ L 314, 4.12.1984, 28.

[9] OJ L 322, 17.12.1977, 30, First Banking Directive, consolidated in Directive 2000/12/EC (OJ L 126, 26.5.2001, 1), reproduced infra under no. B. 32.

or from items A.4, A.9, B.l to B.4 and B.7 of Article 28 of Directive 86/635/EEC,
- the average number of staff employed by the branch,
- the total claims and liabilities attributable to the branch, broken down into those in respect of credit institutions and those in respect of customers, together with the overall amount of such claims and liabilities expressed in the currency of the Member State in which the branch is established,
- the total assets and the amounts corresponding to items 2, 3, 4, 5 and 6 of the assets, 1, 2 and 3 of the liabilities and 1 and 2 of the off-balance sheet items defined in Article 4 and parallel Articles of Directive 86/635/EEC, and, in the case of items 2, 5 and 6 of the assets, a breakdown of securities according to whether they have or have not been regarded as financial fixed assets pursuant to Article 35 of Directive 86/635/EEC.

Where such information is required, its accuracy and its accordance with the annual accounts must be checked by one or more persons authorised to audit accounts under the law of the Member State in which the branch is established.

Article 3
Provisions relating to branches of credit institutions and financial institutions having their head offices in non-member countries

1. Member States shall require branches of credit institutions and financial institutions having their head offices in non-member countries to publish the documents specified in Article 2 (1), drawn up and audited in the manner required by the law of the country of the head office, in accordance with the provisions set out therein.

2. Where such documents are in conformity with, or equivalent to, documents drawn up in accordance with Directive 86/635/EEC and the condition of reciprocity, for Community credit institutions and financial institutions, is fulfilled in the non-member country in which the head office is situated, Article 2 (3) shall apply.

3. In cases other than those referred to in paragraph 2, Member States may require the branches to publish annual accounts relating to their own activities.

4. In the cases specified in paragraphs 2 and 3, Member States may require branches to publish the information referred to in Article 2 (4) and the amount of the endowment capital.

5. Article 9 (1) and (3) of Directive 77/780/EEC shall apply by analogy to branches of credit institutions and financial institutions covered by this Directive.

Article 4
Language of publication

Member States may require that the documents provided for in this Directive be published in their official national language or languages and that translations thereof be certified.

Article 5
Work of the Contact Committee

The Contact Committee set up pursuant to Article 52 of Directive 78/660/EEC shall, when constituted appropriately, also:

(a) facilitate, without prejudice to Articles [226 and 227][2] of the Treaty, harmonised application of this Directive through regular meetings dealing, in particular, with practical problems arising in connection with its application, such as assessment of equivalence of documents, and facilitate decisions concerning the comparability and equivalence of the legal forms referred to in Article 1 (1);

(b) advise the Commission, if necessary, on additions or amendments to this Directive.

Article 6
Final provisions

1. Member States shall bring into force the laws, regulations and administrative provisions necessary to comply with this Directive not later than 1 January 1991. They shall forthwith inform the Commission thereof.

2. A Member State may provide that the provisions referred to in paragraph 1 shall apply for the

first time to annual accounts for the financial year beginning on 1 January 1993 or during the calendar year 1993.

3. Member States shall communicate to the Commission the texts of the main provisions of national law which they adopt in the field covered by this Directive.

Article 7

Five years after the date referred to in Article 6 (2), the Council, acting on a proposal from the Commission, shall examine and, upon a Commission proposal and in co-operation with the European Parliament, if need be, revise Article 2 (4), in the light of the experience acquired in applying this Directive and of the aim of eliminating the additional information referred to in Article 2 (4), taking account of the progress made in striving towards the harmonisation of the accounts of banks and other financial institutions.

Article 8

This Directive is addressed to the Member States.

B. 11.

Council Directive 89/299/EEC
of 17 April 1989
on the own funds of credit institutions[1]

This Directive has been repealed by article 67 of Directive 2000/12/EC, which subsequently has been repealed by article 158 of Directive 2006/48/EC (OJ L 177, 30.06.2006, 1) reproduced infra under no. B. 41.

---

[1] OJ L 124, 5.5.1989, 16–20.

B. 12.

Second Council Directive 89/646/EEC
of 15 December 1989
on the co-ordination of laws, regulations and administrative provisions relating to the taking up and pursuit of the business of credit institutions and amending Directive 77/780/EEC[1]

This Directive has been repealed by article 67 of Directive 2000/12/EC, which subsequently has been repealed by article 158 of Directive 2006/48/EC (OJ L 177, 30.06.2006, 1) reproduced infra under no. B. 41.

---

[1] OJ L 386, 30.12.1989, 1–13.

B. 13.

Council Directive 89/647/EEC
of 18 December 1989
on a solvency ratio for credit institutions[1]

This Directive has been repealed by article 67 of Directive 2000/12/EC, which subsequently has been repealed by article 158 of Directive 2006/48/EC (OJ L 177, 30.06.2006, 1) reproduced infra under no. B. 41.

---

[1] OJ L 386, 30.12.1989, 14–22.

B. 14.

Commission Directive 91/31/EEC
of 19 December 1990
adapting the technical definition of 'multilateral development banks' in
Council Directive 89/647/EEC of 18 December 1989 on a solvency ratio
for credit institutions[1]

This Directive has been repealed by article 67 of Directive 2000/12/EC, which subsequently has been repealed by article 158 of Directive 2006/48/EC (OJ L 177, 30.06.2006, 1) reproduced infra under no. B. 41.

---

[1] OJ L 17, 23.1.1991, 20.

B. 15.

Council Directive 91/308/EEC
of 10 June 1991
on prevention of use of the financial system for the purpose of money laundering[1]

This Directive has been repealed as from 14 November 2005 by article 44 of Directive 2005/60/EC of 26 October 2005 (OJ L 309, 25.11.2005, 15), reproduced infra under no. B. 40.

Correlation Table

Directive 91/308/EEC	Directive 2005/60/EC
Article 1(A)	Article 3(1)
Article 1(B)(1)	Article 3(2)(a)
Article 1(B)(2)	Article 3(2)(b)
Article 1(B)(3)	Article 3(2)(c)
Article 1(B)(4)	Article 3(2)(d)
Article 1(B), second paragraph	Article 3(2)(f)
Article 1(C)	Article 1(2)
Article 1(C) first point	Article 1(2)(a)
Article 1(C) second point	Article 1(2)(b)
Article 1(C) third point	Article 1(2)(c)
Article 1(C) fourth point	Article 1(2)(d)
Article 1(C), third paragraph	Article 1(3)
Article 1(C), second paragraph	Article 1(5)
Article 1(D)	Article 3(3)
Article 1(E), first paragraph	Article 3(4)
Article 1(E), second paragraph	Article 3(5)
Article 1(E), first indent	Article 3(5)(b)
Article 1(E), second indent	Article 3(5)(c)
Article 1(E), third indent	Article 3(5)(d)
Article 1(E), fourth indent	Article 3(5)(e)
Article 1(E), fifth indent, and third paragraph	Article 3(5)(f)
Article 2	Article 1(1)
Article 2a(1)	Article 2(1)(1)
Article 2a(2)	Article 2(1)(2)

---

[1] OJ L 166, 28.6.1991, 77–83.

Directive 91/308/EEC	Directive 2005/60/EC
Article 2a(3) to (7)	Article 2(1)(3)(a), (b) and (d) to (f)
Article 3(1)	Article 7(a)
Article 3(1)	Article 8(1)(a)
Article 3(1)	Article 9(1)
Article 3(2)	Article 7(b)
Article 3(3)	Article 11(5)(a)
Article 3(4)	Article 11(5)(b)
Article 3(4)	Article 11(5)(c)
Article 3(5) and (6)	Article 10
Article 3(7)	Article 7(d)
Article 3(8)	Article 7(c)
Article 3(9)	Article 11(1)
Article 3(10) and (11)	Article 13(1) and (2)
Article 4, first indent	Article 30(a)
Article 4, second indent	Article 30(b)
Article 5	Article 13(6)
Article 5	Article 20
Article 6(1) and (2)	Article 22
Article 6(3)	Article 23
Article 7	Article 24
Article 8(1)	Article 28(1)
Article 9	Article 26
Article 10	Article 25
Article 11(1)(a)	Article 34(1)
Article 11(1)(b), first sentence	Article 35(1), first paragraph
Article 11(1)(b), second sentence	Article 35(1), second paragraph
Article 11(1), second paragraph	Article 35(1), third paragraph
Article 12	Article 4
Article 14	Article 39(1)
Article 15	Article 5
Article 16	Article 45
Article 16	Article 46
Article 17	Article 42

B. 16.

Council Directive 91/633/EEC
of 3 December 1991
implementing Directive 89/299/EEC on the own funds of credit institutions[1]

This Directive has been repealed by article 67 of Directive 2000/12/EC, which subsequently has been repealed by article 158 of Directive 2006/48/EC (OJ L 177, 30.06.2006, 1) reproduced infra under no. B. 41.

---

[1] OJ L 339, 11.12.1991, 33–34.

B. 17.

Council Directive 92/16/EEC
of 16 March 1992
amending Directive 89/299/EEC on the own funds of credit institutions[1]

This Directive has been repealed by article 67 of Directive 2000/12/EC, which subsequently has been repealed by article 158 of Directive 2006/48/EC (OJ L 177, 30.06.2006, 1) reproduced infra under no. B. 41.

---

[1] OJ L 75, 21.3.1992, 48–50.

B. 18.

Council Directive 92/30/EEC
of 6 April 1992
on the supervision of credit institutions on a consolidated basis[1]

This Directive has been repealed by article 67 of Directive 2000/12/EC, which subsequently has been repealed by article 158 of Directive 2006/48/EC (OJ L 177, 30.06.2006, 1) reproduced infra under no. B. 41.

---

[1] OJ L 110, 28.4.1992, 52–58.

B. 19.

Council Directive 92/121/EEC
of 21 December 1992
on the monitoring and control of large exposures of credit institutions[1]

This Directive has been repealed by article 67 of Directive 2000/12/EC, which subsequently has been repealed by article 158 of Directive 2006/48/EC (OJ L 177, 30.06.2006, 1) reproduced infra under no. B. 41.

---

[1] OJ L 29, 5.2.1993, 1–8.

B. 20.

Council Directive 93/6/EEC
of 15 March 1993
on the capital adequacy of investments firms and credit institutions[1]

This Directive has been repealed as from 20 July 2007 by article 52 of Directive 2006/49/EC (OJ L 177, 30.6.2006, 201), reproduced infra under no. B. 42.

Correlation Table

Directive 93/6/EEC	Directive 2006/49/EC
Article 1	Article 1(1) second sentence and (2)
Article 2(1)	Article 3(1)(a)
Article 2(2)	Article 3(1)(b)
Article 2(3) (5)	Article to 3(1)(c) to (e)
Article 2(6)	Article 11
Article 2(7) and (8)	Article 3(2)
Article 2(9)	Article 40
Article 2(10)	Article 3(1)(h)
Article 2(11)	Article 3(1)(i)
Article 2(12)	Annex I(15) and (16)
Article 2(14)	Article 3(1)(j)
Article 2(15) and (16)	Article 3(1)(k) and (l)
Article 2(17)	Article 3(1)(m)
Article 2(18)	Article 3(1)(n)
Article 2(19) to (21)	Article 3(1)(o) to (q)
Article 2(22)	Annex I(4) last paragraph
Article 2(23)	Article 3(1)(r)
Article 2(24)	Article 4
Article 2(25)	Article 12 first paragraph
Article 2(26)	Article 3(1)(s)
Article 3(1) and (2)	Article 5
Article 3(3)	Article 9
Article 3(4)	Article 6
Article 3(4a)	Article 7
Article 3(4b)	Article 8
Article 3(5) to (8)	Article 10
Article 4(1) first sub-paragraph	Article 18(1) first sub-paragraph

---

[1] OJ L 141, 11.6.1993, 1–26.

Directive 93/6/EEC	Directive 2006/49/EC
Article 4(1)(i) and (ii)	Article 18(1) (a) and (b)
Article 4(6) to (8)	Article 18(2) to (4)
Article 5(1)	Article 28(1)
Article 5(2)	Article 28(2)
Article 6(2)	Article 33(3)
Article 7(3)	Article 2(2)
Article 7(3)	Article 3(3)(a) and (b)
Article 7(3)	Article 3(3)(c)
Article 7(5) and (6)	Article 23 first and second paragraph
Article 7(10)	Article 26(1)
Article 7(11) to (13)	Article 26(2) to (4)
Article 7(14) and (15)	Article 27
Article 8(1) to (4)	Article 35(1) to (4)
Article 8(5) first sentence	Article 35(5)
Article 9(1) to (3)	Article 36
Article 9(4)	Article 38
Article 10 first, second and third indents	Article 41(1)(a) to (c)
Article 10 fourth indent	Article 41(1)(f)
Article 11(2)	Article 19(2)
Article 12	Article 46
Article 15	Article 50
Annex I(1) to (4)	Annex I(1) to (4)
Annex I(5) to (7)	Annex I(5) to (7)
Annex I(8) to (10)	Annex I(9) to (11)
Annex I(12) to (14)	Annex I(12) to (14)
Annex I(15) to (39)	Annex I(17) to (41)
Annex II(1) and (2)	Annex II(1) and (2)
Annex III(1) first sub-paragraph	Annex III(1)
Annex III(2)	Annex III(2)
Annex III(3.1)	Annex III(2.1) first to third paragraphs
Annex III(3.2)	Annex III(2.1) fifth paragraph
Annex III(4) to (6)	Annex III(2.2), (3), (3.1)
Annex III(8)	Annex III(3.2)
Annex III(11)	Annex III(4)
Annex IV	Article 21
Annex V(1) first sub-paragraph	Article 13(1) first sub-paragraph
Annex V(1) second sub-paragraph and (2) to (5)	Article 13(1) second sub-paragraph and (2) to (5)
Annex V(6) and (7)	Article 14
Annex V(8)	Article 15
Annex V(9)	Article 16

Directive 93/6/EEC	Directive 2006/49/EC
Annex VI(2)	Article 29(1)(a) to (c) and next two sub-paragraphs
Annex VI(3)	Article 29(2)
Annex VI(4) and (5)	Article 30(1) and (2) first sub-paragraph
Annex VI(6) and (7)	Article 30(3) and (4)
Annex VI(8)(1), (2) first sentence, (3) to (5)	Article 31
Annex VI(8)(2) after the first sentence	Annex VI
Annex VI(9) and (10)	Article 32
Annex VII(1) to (20)	Annex IV(1) to (20)
Article 11a	Annex IV(21)
Annex VIII(1) to (13)(ii)	Annex V(1) to (12) fourth paragraph
Annex VIII(13)(iii) to (14)	Annex V(12) sixth paragraph to (13)

B. 21.

Commission Directive 94/7/EC
of 15 March 1994
adapting Council Directive 89/647/EEC on a solvency ratio for credit institutions as regards the technical definition of 'multilateral development banks'[1]

(Text with EEA relevance)

This Directive has been repealed by article 67 of Directive 2000/12/EC, which subsequently has been repealed by article 158 of Directive 2006/48/EC (OJ L 177, 30.06.2006, 1) reproduced infra under no. B. 41.

---

[1] OJ L 89, 6.4.1994, 17.

B. 22.

European Parliament and Council Directive 94/19/EC of 30 May 1994 on deposit-guarantee schemes[1]

> **CASE**
>
> Case C-222/02 Peter Paul, Cornelia Sonnen-Lütte and Christel Mörkens v Bundesrepublik Deutschland [2004] ECR I-9425
>
> Directive 94/19/EC only related to the introduction and proper functioning of the deposit-guarantee scheme. As indicated in recital 24, it does not confer on depositors a right to have the competent authorities take supervisory measures in their interest. Article 3(2) to (5) cannot be interpreted as precluding a national rule to the effect that the functions of the national authority responsible for supervising credit institutions are to be fulfilled only in the public interest, which under national law precludes individuals from claiming compensation for damage resulting from defective supervision on the part of that authority.

THE EUROPEAN PARLIAMENT AND THE COUNCIL OF THE EUROPEAN UNION,

Having regard to the Treaty establishing the European Community, and in particular the first and third sentences of Article [47][2] (2) thereof,

Having regard to the proposal from the Commission,[3]

Having regard to the opinion of the Economic and Social Committee,[4]

Acting in accordance with the procedure referred to in Article [251][2] of the Treaty,[5]

Whereas, in accordance with the objectives of the Treaty, the harmonious development of the activities of credit institutions throughout the Community should be promoted through the elimination of all restrictions on the right of establishment and the freedom to provide services, while increasing the stability of the banking system and protection for savers;

Whereas, when restrictions on the activities of credit institutions are eliminated, consideration should be given to the situation which might arise if deposits in a credit institution that has branches in other Member States become unavailable; whereas it is indispensable to ensure a harmonised minimum level of deposit protection wherever deposits are located in the Community; whereas such deposit protection is as essential as the prudential rules for the completion of the single banking market;

Whereas in the event of the closure of an insolvent credit institution the depositors at any branches situated in a Member State other than that in which the credit institution has its head office must be protected by the same guarantee scheme as the institution's other depositors;

Whereas the cost to credit institutions of participating in a guarantee scheme bears no relation to the cost that would result from a massive withdrawal of bank deposits not only from a credit institution in difficulties but also from healthy institutions following a loss of depositor confidence in the soundness of the banking system;

Whereas the action the Member States have taken in response to Commission recommendation 87/63/EEC of 22 December 1986 concerning the introduction of deposit-guarantee schemes in the

---

[1] OJ L 135, 31.5.1994, 5–14.
[2] The number between brackets has been changed as from 1 May 1999 by article 12 of the Treaty of Amsterdam.
[3] OJ C 163, 30.6.1992, 6 and OJ C 178, 30.6.1993, 14.
[4] OJ C 332, 16.12.1992, 13.
[5] OJ C 115, 26.4.1993, 96 and Decision of the European Parliament of 9 March 1994 (OJ C 91, 28.3.1994).

Community[6] has not fully achieved the desired result; whereas that situation may prove prejudicial to the proper functioning of the internal market;

Whereas the Second Council Directive 89/646/EEC of 15 December 1989 on the co-ordination of laws, regulations and administrative provisions relating to the taking up and pursuit of the business of credit institutions and amending Directive 77/780/EEC,[7] provides for a system for the single authorisation of each credit institution and its supervision by the authorities of its home Member State, which entered into force on 1 January 1993;

Whereas a branch no longer requires authorisation in any host Member State, because the single authorisation is valid throughout the Community, and its solvency will be monitored by the competent authorities of its home Member State; whereas that situation justifies covering all the branches of the same credit institution set up in the Community by means of a single guarantee scheme; whereas that scheme can only be that which exists for that category of institution in the State in which that institution's head office is situated, in particular because of the link which exists between the supervision of a branch's solvency and its membership of a deposit-guarantee scheme;

Whereas harmonisation must be confined to the main elements of deposit-guarantee schemes and, within a very short period, ensure payments under a guarantee calculated on the basis of a harmonised minimum level;

Whereas deposit-guarantee schemes must intervene as soon as deposits become unavailable;

Whereas it is appropriate to exclude from cover, in particular, the deposits made by credit institutions on their own behalf and for own account; whereas that should not prejudice the right of a guarantee scheme to take any measures necessary for the rescue of a credit institution that finds itself in difficulties,

Whereas the harmonisation of deposit-guarantee schemes within the Community does not of itself call into question the existence of systems in operation designed to protect credit institutions, in particular by ensuring their solvency and liquidity, so that deposits with such credit institutions, including their branches established in other Member States, will not become unavailable; whereas such alternative systems serving a different protective purpose may, subject to certain conditions, be deemed by the competent authorities to satisfy the objectives of this Directive; whereas it will be for those competent authorities to verify compliance with those conditions;

Whereas several Member States have deposit-protection schemes under the responsibility of professional organisations, other Member States have schemes set up and regulated on a statutory basis and some schemes, although set up on a contractual basis, are partly regulated by statute; whereas that variety of status poses a problem only with regard to compulsory membership of and exclusion from schemes; whereas it is therefore necessary to take steps to limit the powers of schemes in this area;

Whereas the retention in the Community of schemes providing cover for deposits which is higher than the harmonised minimum may, within the same territory, lead to disparities in compensation and unequal conditions of competition between national institutions and branches of institutions from other Member States; whereas, in order to counteract those disadvantages, branches should be authorised to join their host countries' schemes so that they can offer their depositors the same guarantees as are offered by the schemes of the countries in which they are located; whereas it is appropriate that after a number of years the Commission should report on the extent to which branches have made use of this option and on the difficulties which they or the guarantee schemes may have encountered in implementing these provisions; whereas it is not ruled out that home Member State schemes

---

[6] OJ L 33, 4.2.1987, 16, superseded by Directive 94/19/EC, consolidated in Directive 2000/12/EC, reproduced infra under no. B. 32.

[7] OJ L 386, 30.12.1989, 1, Second Banking Directive, reproduced supra under no. B. 12. Directive as amended by Directive 92/30/EEC (OJ L 110, 28.4.1992, 52), consolidated in Directive 2000/12/EC, reproduced infra under no. B. 32.

should themselves offer such complementary cover, subject to the conditions such schemes may lay down;

Whereas market disturbances could be caused by branches of credit institutions which offer levels of cover higher than those offered by credit institutions authorised in their host Member States; whereas it is not appropriate that the level of scope of cover offered by guarantee schemes should become an instrument of competition; whereas it is therefore necessary, at least during an initial period, to stipulate that the level and scope of cover offered by a home Member State scheme to depositors at branches located in another Member State should not exceed the maximum level and scope offered by the corresponding scheme in the host Member State; whereas possible market disturbances should be reviewed after a number of years, on the basis of the experience acquired and in the light of developments in the banking sector;

Whereas in principle this Directive requires every credit institution to join a deposit-guarantee scheme; whereas the Directives governing the admission of any credit institution which has its head office in a non-member country, and in particular the First Council Directive (77/780/EEC) of 12 December 1977 on the co-ordination of the laws, regulations and administrative provisions relating to the taking up and pursuit of the business of credit institutions[8] allow Member States to decide whether and subject to what conditions to permit the branches of such credit institutions to operate within their territories; whereas such branches will not enjoy the freedom to provide services under the second paragraph of Article [49][2] of the Treaty, nor the right of establishment in Member States other than those in which they are established; whereas, accordingly, a Member State admitting such branches should decide how to apply the principles of this Directive to such branches in accordance with Article 9 (1) of Directive 77/780/EEC and with the need to protect depositors and maintain the integrity of the financial system; whereas it is essential that depositors at such branches should be fully aware of the guarantee arrangements which affect them;

Whereas, on the one hand, the minimum guarantee level prescribed in this Directive should not leave too great a proportion of deposits without protection in the interest both of consumer protection and of the stability of the financial system; whereas, on the other hand, it would not be appropriate to impose throughout the Community a level of protection which might in certain cases have the effect of encouraging the unsound management of credit institutions; whereas the cost of funding schemes should be taken into account; whereas it would appear reasonable to set the harmonised minimum guarantee level at ECU 20 000; whereas limited transitional arrangements might be necessary to enable schemes to comply with that figure;

Whereas some Member States offer depositors cover for their deposits which is higher than the harmonised minimum guarantee level provided for in this Directive; whereas it does not seem appropriate to require that such schemes, certain of which have been introduced only recently pursuant to recommendation 87/63/EEC, be amended on this point;

Whereas a Member State must be able to exclude certain categories of specifically listed deposits or depositors, if it does not consider that they need special protection, from the guarantee afforded by deposit-guarantee schemes;

Whereas in certain Member States, in order to encourage depositors to look carefully at the quality of credit institutions, unavailable deposits are not fully reimbursed; whereas such practices should be limited in respect of deposits falling below the minimum harmonised level;

Whereas the principle of a harmonised minimum limit per depositor rather than per deposit has been retained; whereas it is therefore appropriate to take into consideration the deposits made by depositors who either are not mentioned as holders of an account or are not the sole holders; whereas the limit must therefore be applied to

---

[8] OJ L 322, 17.12.1977, 30, reproduced supra under no. B. 2. Directive as last amended by Directive 89/646/EEC (OJ L 386, 30.12.1989, 1), reproduced supra under no. B. 12, consolidated in Directive 2000/12/EC, reproduced infra under no. B. 32.

each identifiable depositor; whereas that should not apply to collective investment undertakings subject to special protection rules which do not apply to the aforementioned deposits;

Whereas information is an essential element in depositor protection and must therefore also be the subject of a minimum number of binding provisions; whereas, however, the unregulated use in advertising of references to the amount and scope of a deposit-guarantee scheme could affect the stability of the banking system or depositor confidence; whereas Member States should therefore lay down rules to limit such references;

Whereas, in specific cases, in certain Member States in which there are no deposit-guarantee schemes for certain classes of credit institutions which take only an extremely small proportion of deposits, the introduction of such a system may in some cases take longer than the time laid down for the transposition of this Directive; whereas in such cases a transitional derogation from the requirement to belong to a deposit-guarantee scheme may be justified; whereas, however, should such credit institutions operate abroad, a Member State would be entitled to require their participation in a deposit-guarantee scheme which it had set up;

Whereas it is not indispensable, in this Directive, to harmonise the methods of financing schemes guaranteeing deposits or credit institutions themselves, given, on the one hand, that the cost of financing such schemes must be borne, in principle, by credit institutions themselves and, on the other hand, that the financing capacity of such schemes must be in proportion to their liabilities; whereas this must not, however, jeopardise the stability of the banking system of the Member State concerned;

Whereas this Directive may not result in the Member States' or their competent authorities' being made liable in respect of depositors if they have ensured that one or more schemes guaranteeing deposits or credit institutions themselves and ensuring the compensation or protection of depositors under the conditions prescribed in this Directive have been introduced and officially recognised;

Whereas deposit protection is an essential element in the completion of the internal market and an indispensable supplement to the system of supervision of credit institutions on account of the solidarity it creates amongst all the institutions in a given financial market in the event of the failure of any of them,

HAVE ADOPTED THIS DIRECTIVE:

Article 1

For the purposes of this Directive:

1. *'deposit'* shall mean any credit balance which results from funds left in an account or from temporary situations deriving from normal banking transactions and which a credit institution must repay under the legal and contractual conditions applicable, and any debt evidenced by a certificate issued by a credit institution.

Shares in United Kingdom and Irish building societies apart from those of a capital nature covered in Article 2 shall be treated as deposits.

Bonds which satisfy the conditions prescribed in Article 22 (4) of Council Directive 85/611/EEC of 20 December 1985 on the co-ordination of laws, regulations and administrative provisions relating to undertakings for collective investment in transferable securities (UCITS)[9] shall not be considered deposits.

For the purpose of calculating a credit balance, Member States shall apply the rules and regulations relating to set-off and counterclaims according to the legal and contractual conditions applicable to a deposit;

2. *'joint account'* shall mean an account opened in the names of two or more persons or over which two or more persons have rights that may operate against the signature of one or more of those persons;

3. *'unavailable deposit'* shall mean a deposit that is due and payable but has not been paid

---

[9] OJ L 375, 31.12.1985, 3, reproduced infra under no. S. 6. Directive as last amended by Directive 88/220/EEC (OJ L 100, 19.4.1988, 31), reproduced infra under no. S. 10.

by a credit institution under the legal and contractual conditions applicable thereto, where either:
(i) the relevant competent authorities have determined that in their view the credit institution concerned appears to be unable for the time being, for reasons which are directly related to its financial circumstances, to repay the deposit and to have no current prospect of being able to do so.

The competent authorities shall make that determination as soon as possible and at the latest 21 days after first becoming satisfied that a credit institution has failed to repay deposits which are due and payable; or

(ii) a judicial authority has made a ruling for reasons which are directly related to the credit institution's financial circumstances which has the effect of suspending depositors' ability to make claims against it, should that occur before the aforementioned determination has been made;

4. 'credit institution' shall mean an undertaking the business of which is to receive deposits or other repayable funds from the public and to grant credits for its own account;

¶ *Compare the definition used in article 1 of Directive 77/780/EEC, First Banking Directive, consolidated in Directive 2000/12/EC, reproduced infra under no. B. 32.*

5. 'branch' shall mean a place of business which forms a legally dependent part of a credit institution and which conducts directly all or some of the operations inherent in the business of credit institutions; any number of branches set up in the same Member State by a credit institution which has its head office in another Member State shall be regarded as a single branch.

¶ *Compare the definition used in article 1 of Directive 77/780/EEC, First Banking Directive, consolidated in Directive 2000/12/EC, reproduced infra under no. B. 32, which subsequently has been repealed by article 158 of Directive 2006/48/EC (OJ L 177, 30.06.2006, 1) reproduced infra under no. B. 41.*

Article 2

The following shall be excluded from any repayment by guarantee schemes:
– subject to Article 8 (3), deposits made by other credit institutions on their own behalf and for their own account,
– all instruments which would fall within the definition of 'own funds' in Article 2 of Council Directive 89/299/EEC of 17 April 1989 on the own funds of credit institutions,[10]
– deposits arising out of transactions in connection with which there has been a criminal conviction for money laundering as defined in Article 1 of Council Directive 91/308/ EEC of 10 June 1991 on prevention of the use of the financial system for the purpose of money laundering.[11]

Article 3

1. Each Member State shall ensure that within its territory one or more deposit-guarantee schemes are introduced and officially recognised. Except in the circumstances envisaged in the second subparagraph and in paragraph 4, no credit institution authorised in that Member State pursuant to Article 3 of Directive 77/780/ EEC may take deposits unless it is a member of such a scheme.

A Member State may, however, exempt a credit institution from the obligation to belong to a deposit-guarantee scheme where that credit institution belongs to a system which protects the credit institution itself and in particular ensures its liquidity and solvency, thus guaranteeing protection for depositors at least equivalent to that provided by a deposit-guarantee scheme, and which, in the opinion of the competent authorities, fulfils the following conditions:
– the system must be in existence and have been officially recognised when this Directive is adopted,

---

[10] OJ L 124, 5.5.1989, 16, reproduced supra under no. B. 11. Directive as last amended by Directive 92/16/EEC (OJ L 75, 21.3.1992, 48), reproduced supra under no. B. 17, consolidated in Directive 2000/12/EC, reproduced infra under no. B. 32.

[11] OJ L 166, 28.6.1991, 77, reproduced supra under no. B. 15.

- the system must be designed to prevent deposits with credit institutions belonging to the system from becoming unavailable and have the resources necessary for that purpose at its disposal,
- the system must not consist of a guarantee granted to a credit institution by a Member State itself or by any of its local or regional authorities,
- the system must ensure that depositors are informed in accordance with the terms and conditions laid down in Article 9.

Those Member States which make use of this option shall inform the Commission accordingly; in particular, they shall notify the Commission of the characteristics of any such protective systems and the credit institutions covered by them and of any subsequent changes in the information supplied. The Commission shall inform the [European Banking Committee] thereof.

2. If a credit institution does not comply with the obligations incumbent on it as a member of a deposit-guarantee scheme, the competent authorities which issued its authorisation shall be notified and, in collaboration with the guarantee scheme, shall take all appropriate measures including the imposition of sanctions to ensure that the credit institution complies with its obligations.

3. If those measures fail to secure compliance on the part of the credit institution, the scheme may, where national law permits the exclusion of a member, with the express consent of the competent authorities, give not less than 12 months' notice of its intention of excluding the credit institution from membership of the scheme. Deposits made before the expiry of the notice period shall continue to be fully covered by the scheme. If, on the expiry of the notice period, the credit institution has not complied with its obligations, the guarantee scheme may, again having obtained the express consent of the competent authorities, proceed to exclusion.

4. Where national law permits, and with the express consent of the competent authorities which issued its authorisation, a credit institution excluded from a deposit-guarantee scheme may continue to take deposits if, before its exclusion, it has made alternative guarantee arrangements which ensure that depositors will enjoy a level and scope of protection at least equivalent to that offered by the officially recognised scheme.

5. If a credit institution the exclusion of which is proposed under paragraph 3 is unable to make alternative arrangements which comply with the conditions prescribed in paragraph 4, then the competent authorities which issued its authorisation shall revoke it forthwith.

¶ *The words between square brackets in article 3 (1) have been replaced by article 2 of Directive 2005/1/EC, reproduced infra under no. B. 39.*

CASE

Case C-233/94 Federal Republic of Germany v European Parliament and Council of the European Union [1997] ECR I-2405

Article 3(1) of Directive 94/19/EC, which requires all credit institutions to join a deposit-guarantee scheme, does not infringe the principle of proportionality. Having regard to the fact that in some Member States there was no deposit-guarantee scheme and to the need for the Community legislature to ensure a harmonized minimum level of deposit guarantee, wherever those deposits were located within the Community, the effect of that obligation, in so far as it makes membership compulsory for only a few credit institutions in one Member State in which there was a voluntary membership scheme, cannot be considered to be excessive. Moreover, any other approach, such as an obligation to inform customers of any such affiliation, would not have made it possible to achieve the objective of ensuring a harmonized minimum level of guarantee for all deposits.

Article 4

1. Deposit-guarantee schemes introduced and officially recognised in a Member State in accordance with Article 3 (1) shall cover the depositors at branches set up by credit institutions in other Member States.

Until 31 December 1999 neither the level nor the scope, including the percentage, of cover provided shall exceed the maximum level or scope of cover offered by the corresponding guarantee scheme within the territory of the host Member State.

Before that date, the Commission shall draw up a report on the basis of the experience acquired in applying the second subparagraph and shall consider the need to continue those arrangements. If appropriate, the Commission shall submit a proposal for a Directive to the European Parliament and the Council, with a view to the extension of their validity.

2. Where the level and/or scope, including the percentage, of cover offered by the host Member State guarantee scheme exceeds the level and/or scope of cover provided in the Member State in which a credit institution is authorised, the host Member State shall ensure that there is an officially recognised deposit-guarantee scheme within its territory which a branch may join voluntarily in order to supplement the guarantee which its depositors already enjoy by virtue of its membership of its home Member State scheme.

The scheme to be joined by the branch shall cover the category of institution to which it belongs or most closely corresponds in the host Member State.

3. Member States shall ensure that objective and generally applied conditions are established for branches' membership of a host Member State's scheme in accordance with paragraph 2. Admission shall be conditional on fulfilment of the relevant obligations of membership, including in particular payment of any contributions and other charges. Member States shall follow the guiding principles set out in Annex II in implementing this paragraph.

4. If a branch granted voluntary membership under paragraph 2 does not comply with the obligations incumbent on it as a member of a deposit-guarantee scheme, the competent authorities which issued the authorisation shall be notified and, in collaboration with the guarantee scheme, shall take all appropriate measures to ensure that the aforementioned obligations are complied with.

If those measures fail to secure the branch's compliance with the aforementioned obligations, after an appropriate period of notice of not less than 12 months the guarantee scheme may, with the consent of the competent authorities which issued the authorisation, exclude the branch. Deposits made before the date of exclusion shall continue to be covered by the voluntary scheme until the dates on which they fall due. Depositors shall be informed of the withdrawal of the supplementary cover.

5. The Commission shall report on the operation of paragraphs 2, 3 and 4 no later than 31 December 1999 and shall, if appropriate, propose amendments thereto.

Case

Case C-233/94 Federal Republic of Germany v European Parliament and Council of the European Union [1997] ECR I-2405

1. The export prohibition laid down in the second subparagraph of Article 4(1) of Directive 94/19/EC, in accordance with which the cover enjoyed by depositors in branches established by credit institutions in Member States other than those in which they are authorized may not exceed the cover offered by the corresponding guarantee scheme of the host Member State, was judged necessary by the Council and the Parliament. Those institutions took the view that the level and scope of cover offered by the guarantee scheme should not become an instrument of competition and explained that the market could be disturbed by the fact that branches of some credit institutions offer levels of cover higher than those offered by credit institutions authorized in the host Member State. Thus they correctly set out the reasons for that prohibition, which therefore infringes neither the principle of proportionality nor Articles [3(s) and 153][2] of the Treaty. Although the freedom of establishment and the freedom to provide services in the banking sector, which Directive 94/19/EC aims to promote, must be accompanied by a high level of consumer protection–the objective set out in Articles [3(s) and 153][2] of the Treaty–no provision of the Treaty obliges the Community legislature to adopt the highest level of protection which can be found in a particular Member State. It follows that a reduction in the level of protection which

may thereby result in certain cases through the application of the second sub-paragraph of Article 4(1) of Directive 94/19/EC does not call into question the general result which the Directive seeks to achieve, namely a considerable improvement in the protection of depositors within the Community, and is not therefore incompatible with the objective set out in Articles [3(s) and 153][2] of the Treaty.

Moreover, the limited review which the Court may exercise over Community legislative action in an economically complex situation has not shown that, by choosing to avoid, from the very beginning, any market disturbance, the Community institutions were not pursuing a legitimate objective or that the export prohibition was manifestly disproportionate for the credit institutions concerned.

2. The export prohibition laid down by Article 4(1), second sub-paragraph, of Directive 94/19/EC, pursuant to which the cover enjoyed by depositors in branches established by credit institutions in Member States other than those in which they are authorized may not exceed the cover offered by the corresponding guarantee scheme of the host Member State, cannot be regarded as contrary to Article [47(2)][2] of the Treaty solely on the ground that there are situations which are not to the advantage of the branches of credit institutions authorized in one particular Member State. When harmonization takes place, traders established in one Member State may lose the advantage of national legislation which was particularly favourable to them. Moreover, although it is true that the 'export prohibition' is an exception to the minimum harmonization and mutual recognition which the Directive generally seeks to achieve, the Parliament and the Council were nevertheless empowered, in view of the complexity of the matter and the differences between the legislation of the Member States, to achieve the necessary harmonization progressively. Finally, inasmuch as it was conceivable that the pursuit of banking business by branches of institutions authorized in a particular Member State would be affected by the obligation to join a guarantee scheme in another Member State, set up in accordance with Commission Recommendation 87/63/EEC concerning the introduction of deposit-guarantee schemes in the Community, Article 4(1) of Directive 94/19/EC serves to diminish that barrier and, in any event, is a much less onerous limitation than the obligation to comply with different bodies of legislation on deposit-guarantee schemes in the various host Member States.

3. Article 4(2) of Directive 94/19/EC, which requires Member States to include in their deposit-guarantee schemes the branches of credit institutions authorized in other Member States so that they supplement the guarantee already enjoyed by their depositors on account of their affiliation to the guarantee system of their home Member State, does not infringe the principle of supervision by the home Member State. The principle of home State supervision was not laid down by the Treaty; nor was it laid down by the Community legislature in the sphere of banking law with the intention of systematically subordinating to it all other rules in that sphere. The Community legislature could therefore depart from that principle, provided that the legitimate expectations of the persons concerned were not infringed. However, since the Community legislature had not yet acted in regard to the guarantee of deposits, no such legitimate expectations could exist.

4. Article 4(2) of Directive 94/19/EC, which requires Member States to include in their deposit-guarantee schemes the branches of credit institutions authorized in other Member States so that they supplement the guarantee already enjoyed by their depositors on account of their affiliation to the guarantee system of their home Member State, does not infringe the principle of proportionality.

It is clear from that provision's objective of remedying the disadvantages resulting from disparities in compensation and different conditions of competition, within the same territory, between national institutions and branches of institutions from other Member States, and from the Community legislature's wish to take into account the cost of funding guarantee schemes by setting a harmonized minimum guarantee level, that the Community legislature did not wish to impose an excessive burden on home Member States which did not yet have deposit-guarantee schemes or which had only schemes providing for a lower guarantee and that, in those circumstances, it could not require them to bear the risk associated with additional cover resulting from a political decision of a particular host Member State. It follows that any other solution, such as compulsory supplementary cover by the schemes of the home Member State, would not have enabled the intended aim to be achieved.

Moreover, since that obligation is subject to various conditions intended to ease the host Member State's task–in particular, that State may require branches wishing to join one of its guarantee schemes to pay a contribution and require the home State to provide information on those branches–it does not have the effect of causing an excessive burden for the guarantee schemes of host Member States.

Article 5

Deposits held when the authorisation of a credit institution authorised pursuant to Article 3 of Directive 77/780/EEC is withdrawn shall continue to be covered by the guarantee scheme.

Article 6

1. Member States shall check that branches established by a credit institution which has its head office outwith the Community have cover equivalent to that prescribed in this Directive.

Failing that, Member States may, subject to Article 9 (1) of Directive 77/780/EEC, stipulate that branches established by a credit institution which has its head office outwith the Community must join deposit-guarantee schemes in operation within their territories.

2. Actual and intending depositors at branches established by a credit institution which has its head office outwith the Community shall be provided by the credit institution with all relevant information concerning the guarantee arrangements which cover their deposits.

3. The information referred to in paragraph 2 shall be made available in the official language or languages of the Member State in which a branch is established in the manner prescribed by national law and shall be drafted in a clear and comprehensible form.

Article 7

1. Deposit-guarantee schemes shall stipulate that the aggregate deposits of each depositor must be covered up to ECU 20 000 in the event of deposits' being unavailable.

Until 31 December 1999 Member States in which, when this Directive is adopted, deposits are not covered up to ECU 20 000 may retain the maximum amount laid down in their guarantee schemes, provided that this amount is not less than ECU 15 000.

2. Member States may provide that certain depositors or deposits shall be excluded from guarantee or shall be granted a lower level of guarantee. Those exclusions are listed in Annex I.

3. This Article shall not preclude the retention or adoption of provisions which offer a higher or more comprehensive cover for deposits. In particular, deposit-guarantee schemes may, on social considerations, cover certain kinds of deposits in full.

4. Member States may limit the guarantee provided for in paragraph 1 or that referred to in paragraph 3 to a specified percentage of deposits. The percentage guaranteed must, however, be equal to or exceed 90% of aggregate deposits until the amount to be paid under the guarantee reaches the amount referred to in paragraph 1.

5. The amount referred to in paragraph 1 shall be reviewed periodically by the Commission at least once every five years. If appropriate, the Commission shall submit to the European Parliament and to the Council a proposal for a Directive to adjust the amount referred to in paragraph 1, taking account in particular of developments in the banking sector and the economic and monetary situation in the Community. The first review shall not take place until five years after the end of the period referred to in Article 7 (1), second subparagraph.

6. Member States shall ensure that the depositor's rights to compensation may be the subject of an action by the depositor against the deposit-guarantee scheme.

Article 8

1. The limits referred to in Article 7 (1), (3) and (4) shall apply to the aggregate deposits placed with the same credit institution irrespective of the

number of deposits, the currency and the location within the Community.

2. The share of each depositor in a joint account shall be taken into account in calculating the limits provided for in Article 7 (1), (3) and (4).

In the absence of special provisions, such an account shall be divided equally amongst the depositors.

Member States may provide that deposits in an account to which two or more persons are entitled as members of a business partnership, association or grouping of a similar nature, without legal personality, may be aggregated and treated as if made by a single depositor for the purpose of calculating the limits provided for in Article 7 (1), (3) and (4).

3. Where the depositor is not absolutely entitled to the sums held in an account, the person who is absolutely entitled shall be covered by the guarantee, provided that that person has been identified or is identifiable before the date on which the competent authorities make the determination described in Article 1 (3) (i) or the judicial authority makes the ruling described in Article 1 (3) (ii). If there are several persons who are absolutely entitled, the share of each under the arrangements subject to which the sums are managed shall be taken into account when the limits provided for in Article 7 (1), (3) and (4) are calculated.

This provision shall not apply to collective investment undertakings.

¶ *For UCITS see Directive 85/611/EEC, reproduced infra under no. S. 6.*

Article 9

1. Member States shall ensure that credit institutions make available to actual and intending depositors the information necessary for the identification of the deposit-guarantee scheme of which the institution and its branches are members within the Community or any alternative arrangement provided for in Article 3 (1), second subparagraph, or Article 3 (4). The depositors shall be informed of the provisions of the deposit-guarantee scheme or any alternative arrangement applicable, including the amount and scope of the cover offered by the guarantee scheme. That information shall be made available in a readily comprehensible manner.

Information shall also be given on request on the conditions for compensation and the formalities which must be completed to obtain compensation.

2. The information provided for in paragraph 1 shall be made available in the manner prescribed by national law in the official language or languages of the Member State in which the branch is established.

3. Member States shall establish rules limiting the use in advertising of the information referred to in paragraph 1 in order to prevent such use from affecting the stability of the banking system or depositor confidence. In particular, Member States may restrict such advertising to a factual reference to the scheme to which a credit institution belongs.

Article 10

1. Deposit-guarantee schemes shall be in a position to pay duly verified claims by depositors in respect of unavailable deposits within three months of the date on which the competent authorities make the determination described in Article 1 (3) (i) or the judicial authority makes the ruling described in Article 1 (3) (ii).

2. In wholly exceptional circumstances and in special cases a guarantee scheme may apply to the competent authorities for an extension of the time limit. No such extension shall exceed three months. The competent authorities may, at the request of the guarantee scheme, grant no more than two further extensions, neither of which shall exceed three months.

3. The time limit laid down in paragraphs 1 and 2 may not be invoked by a guarantee scheme in order to deny the benefit of guarantee to any depositor who has been unable to assert his claim to payment under a guarantee in time.

4. The documents relating to the conditions to be fulfilled and the formalities to be completed to be eligible for a payment under the guarantee referred to in paragraph 1 shall be drawn up in detail in the manner prescribed by national law in the official language or languages of the Member State in which the guaranteed deposit is located.

5. Notwithstanding the time limit laid down in paragraphs 1 and 2, where a depositor or any person entitled to or interested in sums held in an account has been charged with an offence arising out of or in relation to money laundering as defined in Article 1 of Directive 91/308/EEC, the guarantee scheme may suspend any payment pending the judgment of the court.

Article 11

Without prejudice to any other rights which they may have under national law, schemes which make payments under guarantee shall have the right of subrogation to the rights of depositors in liquidation proceedings for an amount equal to their payments.

Article 12

Notwithstanding Article 3, those institutions authorised in Spain or in Greece and listed in Annex III shall be exempt from the requirement to belong to a deposit-guarantee scheme until 31 December 1999.

Such credit institutions shall expressly alert their actual and intending depositors to the fact that they are not members of any deposit-guarantee scheme.

During that time, should any such credit institution establish or have established a branch in another Member State, that Member State may require that branch to belong to a deposit-guarantee scheme set up within its territory under conditions consonant with those prescribed in Article 4 (2), (3) and (4).

Article 13

In the list of authorised credit institutions which it is required to draw up pursuant to Article 3 (7) of Directive 77/780/EEC the Commission shall indicate the status of each credit institution with regard to this Directive.

Article 14

1. The Member States shall bring into force the laws, regulations and administrative provisions necessary for them to comply with this Directive by 1 July 1995. They shall forthwith inform the Commission thereof.

When the Member States adopt these measures they shall contain a reference to this Directive or shall be accompanied by such reference on the occasion of their official publication. The methods of making such reference shall be laid down by the Member States.

2. The Member States shall communicate to the Commission the texts of the main provisions of national law which they adopt in the field governed by this Directive.

Article 15

This Directive shall enter into force on the day of its publication in the *Official Journal of the European Communities.*

Article 16

This Directive is addressed to the Member States.

Annex I

List of exclusions referred to in Article 7 (2)

1. Deposits by financial institutions as defined in Article 1 (6) of Directive 89/646/EEC.

2. Deposits by insurance undertakings.

3. Deposits by government and central administrative authorities.

4. Deposits by provincial, regional, local and municipal authorities.

5. Deposits by collective investment undertakings.

6. Deposits by pension and retirement funds.

7. Deposits by a credit institution's own directors, managers, members personally liable, holders of at least 5% of the credit institution's capital, persons responsible for carrying out the statutory audits of the credit institution's accounting documents and depositors of similar status in other companies in the same group.

8. Deposits by close relatives and third parties acting on behalf of the depositors referred to in 7.

9. Deposits by other companies in the same group.

10. Non-nominative deposits.

11. Deposits for which the depositor has, on an individual basis, obtained from the same credit institution rates and financial concessions which have helped to aggravate its financial situation.

12. Debt securities issued by the same institution and liabilities arising out of own acceptances and promissory notes.

13. Deposits in currencies other than:
– those of the Member States,
– ecus.

14. Deposits by companies which are of such a size that they are not permitted to draw up abridged balance sheets pursuant to Article 11 of the Fourth Council Directive (78/660/EEC) of 25 July 1978 based on Article [44]² (3) (g) of the Treaty on the annual accounts of certain types of companies.[12]

Annex II

Guiding principles

Where a branch applies to join a host Member State scheme for supplementary cover, the host Member State scheme will bilaterally establish with the home Member State scheme appropriate rules and procedures for paying compensation to depositors at that branch. The following principles shall apply both to the drawing up of those procedures and in the framing of the membership conditions applicable to such a branch (as referred to in Article 4 (2)):

(a) the host Member State scheme will retain full rights to impose its objective and generally applied rules on participating credit institutions; it will be able to require the provision of relevant information and have the right to verify such information with the home Member State's competent authorities;

(b) the host Member State scheme will meet claims for supplementary compensation upon a declaration from the home Member State's

---

[12] OJ L 222, 14.8.1978, 11, reproduced infra under no. C. 4. Directive as last amended by Directive 90/605/EEC (OJ L 317, 16.11.1990, 60), reproduced infra under no. C. 12.

competent authorities that deposits are unavailable. The host Member State scheme will retain full rights to verify a depositor's entitlement according to its own standards and procedures before paying supplementary compensation;

(c) home Member State and host Member State schemes will co-operate fully with each other to ensure that depositors receive compensation promptly and in the correct amounts. In particular, they will agree on how the existence of a counterclaim which may give rise to set-off under either scheme will affect the compensation paid to the depositor by each scheme;

(d) host Member State schemes will be entitled to charge branches for supplementary cover on an appropriate basis which takes into account the guarantee funded by the home Member State scheme. To facilitate charging, the host Member State scheme will be entitled to assume that its liability will in all circumstances be limited to the excess of the guarantee it has offered over the guarantee offered by the home Member State regardless of whether the home Member State actually pays any compensation in respect of deposits held within the host Member State's territory.

Annex III

List of credit institutions mentioned in Article 12

(a) Specialised classes of Spanish institutions, the legal status of which is currently undergoing reform, authorised as
– Entidades de Financiación o Factoring,
– Sociedades de Arrendamiento Financiero,
– Sociedades de Crédito Hipotecario.

(b) The following Spanish state institutions:
– Banco de Crédito Agrícola, SA,
– Banco Hipotecario de España, SA,
– Banco de Crédito Local, SA.

(c) The following Greek credit co-operatives:
– Lamia Credit Cooperative,
– Ioannina Credit Cooperative,
– Xylocastron Credit Cooperative,

as well as those of the credit co-operatives of a similar nature listed below which are authorised or in the process of being authorised on the date of the adoption of this Directive:
– Chania Credit Cooperative,
– Iraklion Credit Cooperative,
– Magnissia Credit Cooperative,
– Larissa Credit Cooperative,
– Patras Credit Cooperative,
– Thessaloniki Credit Cooperative.

B. 23.

Commission Directive 95/15/EC
of 31 May 1995
adapting Council Directive 89/647/EEC on a solvency ratio for credit institutions, as regards the technical definition of 'Zone A' and in respect of the weighting of asset items constituting claims carrying the explicit guarantee of the European Communities[1]

This Directive has been repealed by article 67 of Directive 2000/12/EC, which subsequently has been repealed by article 158 of Directive 2006/48/EC (OJ L 177, 30.06.2006, 1) reproduced infra under no. B. 41.

---

[1] OJ L 125, 8.6.1995, 23–24.

B. 24.

Commission Directive 95/67/EC
of 15 December 1995
making a technical amendment to Council Directive 89/647/EEC on a solvency ratio for credit institutions as regards the definition of 'multilateral development banks'[1]

(Text with EEA relevance)

This Directive has been repealed by article 67 of Directive 2000/12/EC, which subsequently has been repealed by article 158 of Directive 2006/48/EC (OJ L 177, 30.06.2006, 1) reproduced infra under no. B. 41.

---

[1] OJ L 314, 28.12.1995, 72.

B. 25.

Council Directive 96/13/EC
of 11 March 1996
amending Article 2 (2) of Directive 77/780/EEC in respect of the list of permanent exclusions of certain credit institutions[1]

This Directive has been repealed by article 67 of Directive 2000/12/EC, which subsequently has been repealed by article 158 of Directive 2006/48/EC (OJ L 177, 30.06.2006, 1) reproduced infra under no. B. 41.

---

[1] OJ L 66, 16.3.1996, 15–16.

B. 26.

European Parliament and Council Directive 96/10/EC
of 21 March 1996
amending Directive 89/647/EEC as regards recognition of contractual netting by the competent authorities[1]

This Directive has been repealed by article 67 of Directive 2000/12/EC, which subsequently has been repealed by article 158 of Directive 2006/48/EC (OJ L 177, 30.06.2006, 1) reproduced infra under no. B. 41.

---

[1] OJ L 85, 3.4.1996, 17–21.

B. 27.

Commission Interpretative Communication 97/C 209/04 of 10 July 1997 on freedom to provide services and the interest of the general good in the Second Banking Directive[1]

(Text with EEA relevance)

This Communication is the product of the discussions conducted by the Commission on the questions of the freedom to provide services and the interest of the general good in the Second Banking Directive.[2]

Not only the Member States (within the Banking Advisory Committee and the Working Group on the Interpretation of the Banking Directives) but also private establishments have been involved in the discussions.

The Commission published, in the *Official Journal of the European Communities*,[3] a draft communication which marked the launch of a broad consultation. Following the publication of this Communication, the Commission received numerous contributions from all the circles concerned (Member States, professional associations, credit institutions, consumer organisations, lawyers, etc.). It also organised hearings with all the parties who had taken part in the written consultation.

The Commission came to realise in the course of this consultation that there was still some uncertainty regarding the interpretation of basic concepts such as freedom to provide services and the interest of the general good. This uncertainty is such as to deter certain credit institutions from exercising the very freedoms which the Second Directive sets out to promote and, consequently, to hamper the free movement of banking services within the European Union.

The Commission therefore deems it desirable to restate in a Communication the principles laid down by the Court of Justice and to set out its position regarding the application of those principles to the specific problems raised by the Second Banking Directive.

Its objective in publishing this Communication is to explain and clarify the Community rules. It provides all the parties concerned—national administrations, traders and consumers—with a reference document defining the legal framework within which, in the view of the Commission, banking activities benefiting from mutual recognition should be pursued.

The interpretations and ideas set out in this Communication, which are confined to problems specifically related to the Second Directive, set out to cover not all possible situations, but merely the most frequent or the most likely.

They are put forward in the light of Community policy regarding the information society, which is aimed at promoting the growth and movement of information-society services between Member States and, in particular, electronic commerce.[4]

---

[1] OJ C 209, 10.7.1997, 6–22.
[2] Second Council Directive 89/646/EEC of 15 December 1989 on the co-ordination of laws, regulations and administrative provisions relating to the taking-up and pursuit of the business of credit institutions and amending Directive 77/780/EEC (OJ L 386, 30.12.1989, 1), reproduced supra under no. B. 12, as amended by Directive 92/30/EEC (OJ L 110, 28.4.1992, 52), reproduced supra under no. B. 18, consolidated in Directive 2000/12/EC, reproduced infra under no. B. 32.
[3] OJ C 291, 4.11.1995, 7.

[4] Council Resolution on new policy priorities regarding the information society, adopted on 8 October 1996; Commission Communication to the European Council: 'Putting services to

They do not necessarily represent the views of the Member States and should not, in themselves, impose any obligation on them.

Lastly, they do not prejudice the interpretation that the Court of Justice, as the final instance responsible for interpreting the Treaty and secondary legislation, might place on the matters at issue.

Part One

Freedom to provide Services in the Second Banking Directive

Part One analyses in turn (A) the results of the consultations on the notification procedure, (B) the difficulties relating to the distinction between the freedom to provide services and the right of establishment and (C) the question of the time when an activity falling within the scope of the freedom to provide services may begin.

A. *Notification procedure*

1. Scope in terms of time

Article 20(1) of the Second Banking Directive provides that:

> 'Any credit institution wishing to exercise the freedom to provide services by carrying on its activities within the territory of another Member State for the first time shall notify the competent authorities of the home Member State of the activities on the list in the Annex which it intends to carry on.'

The procedure laid down in Article 20(1) thus concerns only those credit institutions (and their subsidiaries within the meaning of Article 18(2)) which intend to conduct for the first time an activity listed in the Annex. Article 23(2) provides for an exemption from notification for credit institutions which provided services before the provisions implementing the Directive came into force.

The Commission considers that, in order to benefit from acquired rights, a credit institution need only have provided a service at least once in the territory of a Member State (in accordance with the line of reasoning set out in section 2 below), regardless of when that was, but it must have carried on this activity lawfully within the territory of the Member State in question. It must also be able to furnish evidence of this previous activity if so requested by the competent authority of the country of origin.

The exemption is, however, restricted to the activity and Member State concerned.

The Commission considers that the lawful nature of the previous activity should be assessed at the time when this activity was being exercised and not at the time when the Second Directive entered into force. It is irrelevant, therefore, whether the host Member State's legislation changed after the activity was exercised by the credit institution. It is, of course, assumed that the institution complied with the host country's new legislation if it continued to carry on its activities there or that it ceased its activities under the freedom to provide services at that time.

2. Scope in terms of territory

(a) *Principles*

Article 20(1) of the Second Directive makes implementation of the notification procedure conditional upon the intention to carry on activities '*within the territory of another Member State*'.

It is necessary, therefore, to 'locate' the place of supply of the future banking service in order to determine whether prior notification is required.

Unlike other services, where the place of supply can give rise to no doubts (legal defence, construction of a building, etc.), the banking services listed in the Annex to the Second Directive are difficult to pin down to a specific location. They are also very different from one another and are increasingly provided in an intangible form.

---

work': CSE(96) 6 final of 27 November 1996; Communication to the European Parliament, the Council of the European Union and the Economic and Social Committee entitled 'Regulatory transparency in the single market for information society services'; Proposal for a European Parliament and Council Directive amending for the third time Directive 83/189/EEC laying down a procedure for the provision of information in the field of technical standards and regulations (COM(96) 392 final of 30 August 1996; also published in OJ C 307, 16.10.1996, 11).

The growth of distance services, particularly those using electronic means (Internet, home banking, etc.), will undoubtedly soon result in excessively strict criteria on location becoming obsolete.

The Commission has examined certain possibilities for locating the service (originator of the initiative, customer's place of residence, supplier's place of establishment, place where contracts are signed, etc.) and considers that none could satisfactorily apply to all the activities listed in the Annex.

It considers it necessary to adhere to a simple and flexible interpretation of Article 20 of the Second Directive. Accordingly, in its opinion, only activities carried on *within the territory* of another Member State should be the subject of prior notification. In order to determine where an activity was carried on, the place of provision of what may be termed the 'characteristic performance' of the service, i.e. the essential supply for which payment is due must be determined.

This line of reasoning is aimed merely at establishing whether prior notification is necessary. It does not affect the law or tax system applicable to the banking service concerned.

(b) *Application to the Second Directive*

A bank may have non-resident customers without necessarily pursuing the activities concerned *within the territory* of the Member States where the customers have their domicile.

Consequently, the fact of temporarily visiting the territory of a Member State to carry on an activity preceding (e.g. survey of property prior to granting a loan) or following (incidental activities) the essential activity does not, in the Commission's view, constitute a situation that is liable in itself to be the subject of prior notification. The same is true of any visits which a credit institution may pay to customers if such visits do not involve the provision of the characteristic performance of the service that is the subject of the contractual relationship.

Furthermore, the Commission considers that the fact of temporarily visiting the territory of a Member State in order to conclude contracts prior to the exercise of a banking activity should not be regarded as exercising the activity itself. Prior notification would not be required in such circumstances.

If, on the other hand, the institution intends to provide the characteristic performance of a banking service by sending a member of its staff or a temporarily authorised intermediary to the territory of another Member State, prior notification should be necessary.

Conversely, if the service is supplied to a beneficiary who has gone in person, for the purpose of receiving that service, to the Member State where the institution is established, prior notification should not take place. The Commission considers, in fact, that the service is not provided by the credit institution in the territory of another Member State within the meaning of Article 20 of the Second Banking Directive.

Lastly, the provision of distance banking services, for example through the Internet, should not, in the Commission's view, require prior notification, since the supplier cannot be deemed to be pursuing its activities in the customer's territory.

The Commission is aware that this solution will require a case-by-case analysis, which could prove difficult.

It is also aware that, as long as the Court has not ruled on this issue, any credit institution is at liberty to choose, for reasons of legal certainty, to make use of the notification procedures provided for in the Second Directive even if, according to the criteria proposed above, notification may not be necessary.

The fact that certain types of supplies of services do not, according to the Commission, fall within the scope of Article 20 of the Second Directive and, consequently, should not be notified does not mean that such activities are not the subject of mutual recognition and home-country control.

The Commission considers that mutual recognition of the activities contained in the Annex, accompanied by home-country control, is established by Article 18 of the Second Directive. Article 20 is merely a procedural article, of residual scope, which is merely for the use of banks wishing to operate for the first time under the freedom to provide services in another Member State.

3. Advertising and offers of services

The Commission considers that the prior existence of advertising or an offer cannot be linked with the need to comply with the notification procedure.

Such a link would be artificial in that no express provision for it is made in the Second Directive. It is not the prior offer of a service to a non-resident but merely the intention to carry on activities within the territory of another Member State that Article 20 makes conditional on notification.

Moreover, canvassing customers from a distance does not necessarily mean that an institution plans to provide services within the territory of another Member State.

Similarly, linking advertising with notification could lead to ridiculous situations in which an institution was required to notify the authorities of all the countries where its advertising might theoretically be received.

The Commission therefore considers that, for the sake of simplicity and in keeping with the Second Directive, all forms of advertising, targeted or otherwise, and all offers of a service made at a distance by any means whatsoever (e.g. post, fax, electronic mail) should be exempt from the requirement of prior notification. Only if a credit institution plans to carry on its activities *within the territory of the customer's country* under the freedom to provide services (according to the line of reasoning employed in paragraph (a)) will it be obliged to notify.

This view, which concerns only the notification requirement, does not affect the law applicable to the banking service. In accordance with the Rome Convention,[5] the existence of a specific invitation or prior advertising may, in the case of contracts concluded with consumers, have an effect on the law applicable to the contract concluded subsequently.[6]

4. Nature of the procedure

The Commission considers that the notification procedure laid down in the Second Directive pursues a simple objective of exchange of information between supervisory authorities and is not a consumer-protection measure. It should not, in the Commission's view, be considered a procedural condition affecting the validity of a banking contract.

5. Future of the procedure

As a result of the debate launched by the draft communication, the Commission realised that many interested parties were in favour of simply abolishing the notification procedure within the context of the freedom to provide services. On the other hand, some contributions stressed how useful the procedure was in checking compliance with the interest of the general good and, in particular, with consumer-protection rules.

Some of those who called for the system to be abolished considered that it was not in line with the Treaty, being a disproportionate restriction on freedom to provide services. Others drew attention to the fact that third-country banks were not covered by it. Others still considered that it was costly and unnecessary and could give rise to legal risks.

In the Commission's view, while the notification procedure should be clarified and simplified, it should be no more than a simple administrative formality permitting the notifier to benefit from considerable advantages.

It considers that the interpretations proposed above would clarify the scope of a procedure which, on account of the very growth of the cross-border supply of banking services, particularly in the context of electronic commerce, is bound to become almost obsolete. The more

---

[5] Convention on the law applicable to contractual obligations, opened for signature in Rome on 19 June 1980 and brought into force on 1 April 1991 (OJ L 266, 9.10.1980, 1). Ratified by all Member States except Sweden, Austria and Finland, who signed the Convention on 29 November 1996 and whose ratification procedures are still under way.

[6] See Part Two of this Communication.

services are provided without any physical movement, the less the notification will be used.

The Commission could, in due course, envisage proposing the abolition of the procedure altogether in the context of the freedom to provide services.

B. Freedom to provide services and Right of establishment

1. Freedom to provide services

(a) *Temporary nature*

The Treaty stipulates in the third paragraph of Article [50][7] that a person providing a service may, in order to do so, '*temporarily*' pursue his activity in the State where the service is provided. The Court considered, in a judgment of 30 November 1995,[8] that the temporary nature of the supply of services provided for by this Article:

'is to be determined in the light of its duration, regularity, periodicity and continuity.'

On the basis of this case-law, the Commission considers that, if a banking activity is exercised within a territory in a durable, frequent, regular or continuous manner by a credit institution exercising the freedom to provide services, the question must be asked whether that credit institution can still lawfully be considered to be working temporarily within the meaning of the Treaty. The question also arises whether the credit institution is not attempting to side-step the rules on establishment by unjustifiably invoking the freedom to provide services.

(b) *Preventing circumvention of the rules*

The Court has acknowledged that a Member State is entitled to take steps to prevent a service provider whose activity is entirely or mainly directed towards its territory, but who has become established in another Member State in order to circumvent the rules of professional conduct that would apply to him if he were established in the territory of the State where he entirely or mainly pursues his activities, from exercising the freedom to provide services that is enshrined in Article [49][7] of the Treaty.[9] It adds that such instances of 'circumvention' may fall within the ambit of the chapter of the Treaty on the right of establishment and not of that on the provision of services.

However, the Commission considers that a situation where a credit institution is frequently approached within its own territory by consumers residing in other Member States could not be held to constitute 'circumvention'.

2. Right of establishment

If an undertaking maintains a permanent presence in the Member State in which it provides services, it comes, in principle, under the Treaty provisions on the right of establishment.[10]

The Court has ruled that:

'A national of a Member State who pursues a professional activity on a stable and continuous basis in another Member State where he holds himself out from an established professional base to, amongst others, nationals of that State comes under the provisions of the chapter relating to the right of establishment and not those of the chapter relating to services.'[11]

However, in the same judgment, the Court ruled that a person operating under the freedom to provide services may equip himself in the host Member State with the infrastructure necessary for the purposes of performing the services in question without falling within the scope of the right of establishment.

On the basis of this case-law, an employee of a credit institution coming to work within the territory of a Member State in order to carry out a limited number of specific tasks in connection with existing customers could, therefore, have the infrastructure necessary to perform these tasks

---

[7] The number between brackets has been changed as from 1 May 1999 by article 12 of the Treaty of Amsterdam.
[8] Case C-55/94 *Gebhard* [1995] ECR I-4165.
[9] Case 205/84 *Commission v Germany* [1986] ECR 3755; Case 33/74 *Van Binsbergen* [1974] ECR 1299; Case C-148/91 *Veronica* [1993] ECR I-487; Case C-23/93 *TV 10* [1994] ECR I-4795.
[10] Case 205/84 *Commission v Germany*; see note 9.
[11] Case C-55/94 *Gebhard*; see note 8.

without the bank being deemed to be 'established' within the meaning laid down by Community law. If, on the other hand, he went beyond the bounds of these specific tasks by using that '*pied-à-terre*' to approach nationals of the host Member State, e.g. to offer them banking services as a branch would do, the bank could fall within the scope of the right of establishment.

3. 'Grey' area

It is not always easy to draw the line between the concepts of provision of services and establishment, particularly since, as the case-law of the Court indicates, one may be considered in certain circumstances to be operating in a Member State under the freedom to provide services despite having some kind of infrastructure in that Member State.

Some situations are particularly difficult to classify. This is especially true of:
– recourse to independent intermediaries; and
– electronic machines (ATMs) carrying out banking activities.

(a) *Independent intermediaries*

The problem lies in determining the extent to which a credit institution having recourse to an independent intermediary in another Member State could be deemed to be pursuing a permanent activity in that Member State.

We are concerned here with intermediaries who drum up business but are not in themselves credit institutions or investment firms, and who are not operating on their own behalf.

In its judgment of 4 December 1986,[12] the Court held that:

> 'an insurance undertaking of another Member State which maintains a permanent presence in the Member State in question comes within the scope of the provisions of the Treaty on the right of establishment, even if that presence does not take the form of a branch or agency, but consists merely of an office managed by the undertaking's own staff or by a person who is independent but authorised to act on a permanent basis for the undertaking, as will be the case with an agency.'

The Court has therefore acknowledged that an undertaking which uses an intermediary within the territory of another Member State on a permanent basis may, on account of that fact, lose its status as a service provider and fall within the scope of the provisions on the right of establishment.

The Commission, therefore, suggests the following interpretations.

Intermediaries and freedom to provide services
In the view of the Commission, if a bank uses an intermediary to provide temporarily or from time to time a banking service within the territory of a Member State, it must first give notification within the meaning of Article 20 of the Second Directive.

It considers that if, in a given country, a bank has independent intermediaries whose duties consist solely in seeking customers for it, it cannot be considered to be necessarily intending to carry on its activities, within the meaning of Article 20, in the territory of the Member State in question. Notification would not be required in that case.

On the other hand, in certain circumstances set out below, it may be considered that a bank having one or more intermediaries permanently established in a Member State does in fact come within the rules on the right of establishment.

Intermediaries and the right of establishment
In its *De Bloos* ruling of 6 October 1976,[13] the Court held that:

> 'One of the essential characteristics of the concepts of branch or agency is the fact of being subject to the direction and control of the parent body.'

It concluded that a sole concessionaire not subject to the control and direction of a company could not be regarded as a branch, agency or establishment.

---

[12] See note 9.

[13] Case 14/76 [1976] ECR 1497.

In its ruling of 18 March 1981 in *Blanckaert & Willems*,[14] the Court held that:

> 'An independent commercial agent who merely negotiates business, inasmuch as his legal status leaves him basically free to arrange his own work and decide what proportion of his time to devote to the interests of the undertaking which he agrees to represent and whom that undertaking may not prevent from representing at the same time several firms competing in the same manufacturing or marketing sector, and who, moreover, merely transmits orders to the parent undertaking without being involved in either their terms or their execution, does not have the character of a branch, agency or other establishment . . . '.

In even more pointed terms, in its Somafer ruling of 22 November 1978,[15] the Court held that:

> 'The concept of branch, agency or other establishment implies a place of business which has the appearance of permanency, such as the extension of a parent body, has a management and is materially equipped to negotiate business with third parties, so that the latter, although knowing that there will if necessary be a legal link with the parent body, the head office of which is abroad, do not have to deal directly with such parent body but may transact business at the place of business constituting the extension.'

On the basis of these precedents, the Commission considers that, for the use of an intermediary to result in a bank possibly falling within the scope of the right of establishment, three criteria must be met at one and the same time:

– the intermediary must have a permanent mandate;
– the intermediary must be subject to the management and control of the credit institution he represents. In order to ascertain whether this condition is met, it is necessary to check whether the intermediary is free to organise his own work and to decide what proportion of his time to devote to the undertaking. A final pointer is whether the intermediary can represent several firms competing to provide the service concerned or whether he is, on the contrary, bound by an exclusive agreement to one credit institution;
– the intermediary must be able to commit the credit institution. A credit institution may be committed via an intermediary even if that intermediary cannot sign contracts. For example, if the intermediary can make a complete offer on behalf of an institution but only the bank itself has the power to sign the contract, the criterion of commitment may still be met. If the credit institution can reject the proposal submitted by the intermediary and signed by the customer, the criterion of the commitment capacity is not met.

The application of these three criteria requires a detailed examination to be carried out in each specific case.

The fact that an intermediary can cause a bank to fall within the scope of the right of establishment does not, however, mean that the intermediary himself constitutes a branch. Under the Second Directive, a branch is '*a place of business which forms a legally dependent part of a credit institution (. . .)*'. Since the intermediary is assumed to be independent, he cannot constitute '*part*' of a credit institution. His business will normally be established in the form of a company having its own legal personality.

Finally, if a bank's services are marketed in another Member State through the intermediary of another bank, notification should not, logically speaking, be necessary. The fact that the intermediate bank is itself subject to supervision in the Member State where it is established should offer that Member State sufficient guarantees for it to consider notification unnecessary. If the intermediate bank is acting on its own behalf, notification should not take place, since such a situation does not fall within the scope of, the freedom to provide cross-border services.

(b) *Electronic machines*

This means fixed, ATM-type electronic machines capable of performing the banking

---

[14] Case 139/80 [1981] ECR 819.
[15] Case 33/78 [1978] ECR 2183. See also Case C-439/93 *Lloyd's Register of Shipping v Société Campenon Bernard* [1995] ECR I-961.

activities listed in the Annex to the Second Directive.[16]

Such machines may be covered by the right of establishment if they fulfil the criteria laid down by the Court of Justice (see above).

For such a machine to be capable of being treated as an establishment, therefore, it would have to have a management, which is by definition impossible unless the Court acknowledges that the concept can encompass not only human management but also electronic management.

However, such a machine is unlikely to be the only place of business of a credit institution in a Member State. It is likely to be attached, in the same country, to a branch or an agency. In that event, the machine is not an entity in its own right as it is covered by the rules governing the establishment to which it is attached.

If the machine does, however, constitute the only presence of a credit institution in a Member State, the Commission takes the view that it may be possible to treat it as a provision of services in the territory of that Member State.

The presence in the host country of a person or company responsible simply for maintaining the machine, equipping it and dealing with any technical problems encountered by users cannot rank as an establishment and does not deprive the credit institution of the right to operate under the freedom to provide services.

The Commission considers, however, that technological developments could, in the future, induce it to review its position.

If such developments were to make it possible for an institution to have only a machine in a given country which could 'act' as a branch, taking actual decisions which would completely obviate the need for the customer to have contact with the parent company, the Commission would be forced to consider an appropriate Community legal framework. The present legal framework in fact rests on mechanisms which are still based on a 'human' concept of a branch (for example, the programme of operations must contain the names of those responsible for the management of the branch). It is therefore not possible, under the existing rules, to consider machines as constituting a branch.

4. Simultaneous exercise of the freedom to provide services and the right of establishment

The Commission considers that there is nothing in the Treaty, Directives or case-law to prevent a credit institution from carrying on its activities under the freedom to provide services and, at the same time, through some form of establishment (branch or subsidiary), even if the same activities are involved.

The institution must, however, be able clearly to connect the activity to one of the two forms of operation. This connection is important from both a tax and a regulatory point of view.[17] It should be ensured that an institution is not able 'artificially' to connect its activities to the arrangements governing freedom to provide services as a way of side-stepping the legal and tax framework which would apply if the same activity were considered to be carried on by a branch or by any other form of establishment.[18]

5. Control by the host Member State of the conditions for granting a passport

The Commission interprets a recent ruling by the Court of Justice[19] to mean that the host country may not carry out checks to determine whether a credit institution intending to operate in its territory under the freedom to provide services or through a branch met the standard conditions for

---

[16] It does not mean individual, mobile data-processing equipment which can provide or receive distance banking services, eg through the internet.

[17] Consideration may, for example, be given to the importance of the connection for the purposes of determining the deposit-guarantee scheme.
[18] See footnote 9.
[19] See the judgment delivered by the Court on 10 September 1996 on a similar issue in Case C-11/95 *Commission v Belgium* [1996] ECR I-4115. The Court ruled that the receiving Member State was not authorised to monitor the application of the law of the originating Member State applying to television broadcasts and to ensure compliance with Council Directive 89/552/EEC (known as the 'TV without frontiers' Directive; OJ L 298, 17.10.1989, 23).

granting the single licence in its home country. Such checks may be carried out by the home Member State alone. It is on the responsibility of the home country that the single licence is granted, and the host country cannot question the granting of such a licence.

If the host country has reason to doubt that the standard conditions have been met, it may have recourse to Article [227][7] of the Treaty or request the Commission to take action against the home Member State for failing to meet its obligations pursuant to Article [226][7] of the Treaty.

6. Miscellaneous

In the Commission's opinion, it would very likely be contrary to Community law for a credit institution which has carried on its business under the freedom to provide services within the territory of a Member State for a given length of time to be forced by that Member State to become established as a prerequisite for the continued pursuit of its activities.

It also considers that the freedom to provide services may be exercised by a branch vis-à-vis a third Member State. In such a situation, it is necessary for the branch's home Member State to have sent notification (Article 20) to that third Member State (provided, of course, the conditions for notification are met).

C. Commencement of the provision of services

The problem lies in the interpretation of Article 20(2) of the Second Banking Directive, which merely lays down that:

> 'The competent authorities of the home Member State shall, within one month of receipt of the notification mentioned in paragraph 1, send that notification to the competent authorities of the host Member State.'

Consequently, the procedure to be followed prior to exercising the freedom to provide services differs from that applicable to the establishment of a branch, in that, for the latter arrangement, Article 19(5) provides for the '*receipt*' by the branch of a '*communication*' from the competent authorities of the host Member State or, failing that, the absence of any such communication for a period of two months as a prerequisite for the branch to commence its activities.

This triangular relationship is not provided for in the context of the freedom to provide services, for which there is a more flexible set of arrangements deliberately provided for by the Community legislature so as not to create obstacles which did not exist under the previous arrangements.

A credit institution should therefore be able to commence its activities under the freedom to provide services as soon as it has notified its intention to its own supervisory authorities, which, under Article 20(2), have one month in which to send that notification to the supervisory authorities of the host country.

In the Commission's opinion, where the host Member State requires, as a prerequisite to commencement of any activity relating to the provision of services in its territory (a procedure envisaged for the establishment of a branch), that an acknowledgement of receipt of the notification sent by the country of origin be issued, this constitutes an infringement of the Second Directive.

Part Two

The General Good in the Second Banking Directive

Part Two examines in turn the question of (A) notification of rules adopted in the interest of the general good, (B) problems connected with the application of rules adopted in the interest of the general good and (C) private international law.

A. Notification of rules adopted in the interest of the general good

In the view of the Commission, it is difficult to infer from the wording of Article 19(4) of the Second Directive that there is any obligation on the host country to inform a credit institution wishing to set up a branch in its territory of the conditions to be fulfilled in the interest of the general good. The term '*if necessary*' indicates that

Member States may exercise their discretion in this connection.

Nevertheless, the Commission considers that, in keeping with the spirit of the Second Directive, a credit institution which has let it be known, via its supervisory authority, that it wishes to set up a branch and would like to find out about the general-good rules applicable in the host country should be able to obtain the information it is seeking from that Member State.

Where the Member State responds favourably to the credit institution's request, it should, in the Commission's opinion, be bound only by an obligation as to means and not as to result. That is to say that it cannot be required to communicate all its legislation relating to the interest of the general good (only legislation applicable to banking activities) and, in any event, a text which was not communicated could still be fully relied on against the credit institution. It is inconceivable that the application of a legal provision within the territory of the Member State which adopted it should be ruled out on the ground that a prior administrative formality has not been carried out.

The Commission agrees that the optional nature of notification by the host Member State of its general-good rules may constitute an obstacle to the exercise of the right of establishment. How can a credit institution know what rules it has to observe if a Member State refuses to notify it of those rules? This situation was, moreover, almost unanimously deplored during the consultations which the Commission recently conducted with the banking sector.

The Commission will make every attempt to remedy this situation.

B. Application of rules adopted in the interest of the general good

The main purpose of the Second Banking Directive is to enable authorised credit institutions in a Member State to supply, throughout the European Union, all or some of the banking activities listed in the Annex, either by the establishment of a branch or under the freedom to provide services, on condition that such activities are covered by the authorisation (Article 18).

Community law has not, however, harmonised the content of banking activities, with a few exceptions such as some aspects of consumer credit.[20]

It is likely, therefore, that a credit institution wishing to carry on its activities in another Member State will be confronted with different rules applicable both to the service itself and to the conditions in which it may be offered and marketed. It suffices, for example, to think of the variety of national rules applicable to loans.

The sixteenth recital of the Second Directive reads:

'... the Member States must ensure that there are no obstacles to carrying on activities receiving mutual recognition in the same manner as in the home Member State, as long as the latter do not conflict with legal provisions protecting the general good in the host Member State'.

It should be pointed out that, since the recitals to a directive have legal value as an aid to interpretation, they shed light for the reader on the intentions of the Community legislature.[21]

The Commission considers that a credit institution operating in the context of mutual recognition could, therefore, be forced to bring its services into line with the legislation of the host country only if the measures relied on against it are in the interest of the general good, whether it is acting via a branch or under the freedom to provide services.

This approach is, moreover, confirmed by the Court of Justice, which has ruled that only the general-good rules can restrict or hinder the exercise of the two fundamental freedoms, namely the freedom to provide services[22] and the freedom of establishment.[23]

---

[20] Directive 87/102/EEC (OJ L 42, 12.2.1987, 48), reproduced supra under C.P. 4 as amended by Directive 90/88/EEC (OJ L 61, 10.3.1990, 14), reproduced supra under C.P. 8.
[21] See in particular Case 76/72 *Michel* [1973] ECR 457.
[22] Case C-76/90 *Säger v Dennemeyer* [1991] ECR I-4221. See the analysis contained in the Commission interpretative communication concerning the free movement of services across frontiers, OJ C 334, 9.12.1993, 3.
[23] Case C-55/94 *Gebhard*; see note 8. See also judgment in Case C-19/92 *Kraus* [1993] I-1663.

Consequently, a credit institution would be entitled to challenge, by means of a legal or administrative procedure or a complaint to the Commission, the legitimacy, with regard to Community law, of a national legal norm that is imposed upon it.

However, the Second Banking Directive does not contain any definition of 'the general good'. The reason for this is that, in non-harmonised areas, the level of general good involved depends on the assessment of the Member States and can vary substantially from one country to another according to national traditions and the objectives of the Member States.

Similarly, the Second Directive does not specify within what limits and under what conditions the host Member State may impose its general-good rules upon a Community credit institution.

It is necessary, therefore, to refer to the relevant case-law of the Court of Justice.

1. Definition of the general good

It is the Court of Justice which originated this concept. It has consistently held that:

> 'Taking into account the particular nature of certain services to be provided (. . .), specific requirements imposed on persons providing services cannot be considered incompatible with the Treaty where they have as their purpose the application of professional rules, justified by the general good (. . .).'[24]

However, the Court has never given a definition of the general good, preferring to maintain its progressive nature. It has expressed its opinion, in individual cases, on the possibility of deeming a given national measure to be aimed at achieving an imperative objective serving the general good and has specified the line of reasoning to be followed in determining whether such a measure may be enforced by one Member State against a trader from another Member State who is operating within the territory of the first in accordance with the basic freedoms provided for by the Treaty.

The Court has, however, provided much clarification regarding the measures which can be considered to be aimed at achieving an imperative objective in the general good.

Accordingly, it has consistently held that such measures must not have been the subject of prior Community harmonisation.[25]

Through its case-law, the Court has specified the areas which may be considered to be in the general good. National rules adopted in one of these areas may still, therefore, under certain circumstances outlined below, be enforced against a Community trader.

The Court has so far recognised the following objectives as being imperative reasons in the general good:[26]
– protection of the recipient of services,[27] protection of workers,[28] including social protection,[29] consumer protection,[30] preservation of the good reputation of the national financial sector,[31] prevention of fraud,[32] social order,[33] protection of intellectual property,[34] cultural policy,[35] preservation of the national historical and artistic heritage,[36] cohesion of the tax system,[37] road safety,[38] protection of creditors[39] and protection of the proper administration of justice.[40]

---

[25] Case 52/79 *Debauve* [1980] ECR 833; Case 205/84; see note 9; Case 353/89 *Mediawet* [1991] ECR I-4069.
[26] To this list must be added *a fortiori* the provisions of Article 56, ie public policy, public security and public health. 'Mandatory requirements', which are recognised by the Court in its case-law on the free movement of goods (protection of the environment, fairness of commercial transactions) can probably also be invoked in connection with services.
[27] Joined cases 110/78 and 111/78 *Van Wesemael*; see note 24.
[28] Case 279/80 *Webb* [1981] ECR 3305.
[29] Case C-272/94 *Guiot* [1996] ECR I-1905.
[30] Case 205/84 *Commission v Germany*; see note 9.
[31] Case C-384/93 *Alpine Investments BV* [1995] ECR I-1141.
[32] Case C-275/92 *Schindler* [1994] ECR I-1039.
[33] Ibid.
[34] Case 62/79 *Coditel* [1980] ECR 881.
[35] Case C-353/89 *Mediawet*; see note 25.
[36] Case C-180/89 *Commission v Italy* [1991] ECR 709.
[37] Case C-204/90, judgment of 28 January 1992, *Bachmann* [1992] ECR 249.
[38] Case 55/93 *van Schaik* [1994] ECR I-4837.
[39] Judgment delivered on 12 December 1996 in Case C-3/95 *Reisebüro Broede v Gerd Sandker* (not yet reported).
[40] Ibid.

---

[24] Joined cases 110 and 111/78 *Van Wesemael* [1979] ECR 35.

The list is open-ended and the Court reserves the right to add to it at any time.

Most of these areas can involve banking activity. For example, a national measure aimed at protecting recipients of banking services may, if it does not come within the scope of a harmonised area, be relied upon for reasons relating to the general good by a Member State vis-à-vis a Community credit institution operating within its territory in the context of mutual recognition. For this rule to be enforceable, some additional conditions must, however, be met.

2. General-good 'tests'

In its case-law, the Court has held that:

> 'National measures liable to hinder or make less attractive the exercise of fundamental freedoms guaranteed by the Treaty must fulfil four conditions: they must be applied in a non-discriminatory manner; they must be justified by imperative requirements in the general interest; they must be suitable for securing the attainment of the objective which they pursue; and they must not go beyond what is necessary in order to attain it.' [41]

It has consistently held that a rule relating to the public interest is enforceable against a person providing services only if *'that interest is not protected by the rules to which the person providing the services is subject in the Member State in which he is established'*.[42]

3. Procedures for applying the tests

If a host Member State imposes on a credit institution a national measure which does not derive from Community harmonisation and which, in the view of the credit institution, constitutes a restriction on the freedom to provide services, that institution may question the Member State's right to do so if the measure does not meet the six criteria laid down: non-discrimination, absence of prior harmonisation, existence of an imperative reason relating to the interest of the general good, non-duplication, necessity and proportionality.

Such a restriction could relate to the service itself or to the conditions on which it is offered, such as relevant advertising.[43]

In order to challenge a national measure which constitutes a restriction (e.g. a clause that must be included in every contract and is different from or unknown in the normal practice of the home Member State) that it considers unjustified, a credit institution must normally have recourse to legal procedures or inform the Commission by, for example, lodging a complaint.

In practice, various possibilities are open to it:
– in order to avoid any potential conflict, it may obviously bring all aspects of its services into line with the rules of the host country.
– if, however, it offers banking services which do not correspond exactly to the mandatory provisions of the host country, proceedings will probably be brought against it by the national authorities or one of its customers. It will then have to put forward arguments based on Community law to a tribunal or national authority in order to establish that the rule which the Member State intends to enforce against it does not comply with the conditions laid down by the Court of Justice. It will be the task of the national courts to assess the validity of the parties' arguments, possibly after referring the matter to the Court of Justice for a preliminary ruling pursuant to Article [234][7] of the Treaty.
– it can at any time inform the Commission, which may, if it considers the restrictions to be unjustified, initiate proceedings against the Member State concerned for failing to meet its obligations, in accordance with Article [226].[7] In this case, it will be up to the Commission to provide proof of the alleged failure.[44] In the final resort, it will be the task of the Court of

---

[41] Case C-55/94 *Gebhard*; see note 8.
[42] Case C-76/90 *Säger v Dennemeyer*; see note 22.

[43] Article 21(11) of the Second Banking Directive provides that *'nothing in this Article shall prevent credit institutions with head offices in other Member States from advertising their services through all available means of communication in the host Member State, subject to any rules governing the form and the content of such advertising adopted in the interest of the general good'*.
[44] Case C-157/91 *Commission v Netherlands* [1992] ECR I-5899.

Justice to decide whether or not the national measure in question passes the general-good tests.

Let us see how these six tests could be applied in practice by the Commission or a judge.

Is the measure discriminatory?
In its case-law, the Court has consistently defined discrimination as:

> 'the application of different rules to comparable situations or the application of the same rule to different situations'.[45]

Consequently, the Commission considers that, if a Member State imposes on a Community credit institution measures which it does not impose or imposes more advantageously on its own credit institutions, there will be discrimination.

If the restriction in question is discriminatory, it can, according to the case-law of the Court, be justified only on the grounds set out in Article [46][7] of the Treaty (public policy, public security and public health), subject to compliance with the principle of proportionality.[46]

The concept of public policy must, according to the Court, be understood in a very restrictive sense. Accordingly, the Court has consistently held that economic objectives cannot constitute public-policy grounds within the meaning of Article [46][7] of the Treaty.[47]

According to the Court,

> 'recourse by a national authority to the concept of public policy presupposes, in any event, the existence, in addition to the perturbation to the social order which any infringement of the law involves, of a genuine and sufficiently serious threat affecting one of the fundamental interests of society'.[48]

It is difficult to see what measures could satisfy this condition of a serious threat to society in the field of banking. It is reasonable to believe, therefore, that discriminatory measures are unlikely to be justified in the banking sector.

Does the measure fall within the scope of a harmonised area?
The Commission considers that the Harmonisation Directives define the minimum level of the general good within the Community. In its opinion, this means that a Member State could not use the general good as justification for imposing on a Community credit institution operating in its territory in the context of mutual recognition stricter rules than those laid down in the Directives.

This is true of the harmonised rules concerning the taking-up of the business and the conditions for pursuing it (own funds, minimum capital, deposit guarantee, large exposures, cover for lending and market risks, etc.).

It is also true of the harmonised rules concerning certain specific banking activities, such as those on consumer credit (indication of the annual percentage rate of charge, right of the consumer to discharge his obligations in advance of the scheduled date, etc.).[49]

Lastly, it is the case with harmonised rules concerning certain horizontal aspects of contracts (unfair terms[50]) and certain conditions relating to the contractual environment (contracts negotiated away from business premises,[51] misleading advertising).[52]

Where these harmonised rules constitute minimum provisions, however, a Member State is free to impose on its own credit institutions stricter rules than those laid down in the Directives. Reverse discrimination is not, in theory, contrary to Community law. The Court has in fact consistently ruled that it is not contrary to the principle of non-discrimination enshrined in

---

[45] See most recently Case C-107/94 *Asscher* [1996] ECR I-3089.
[46] See most recently Case C-17/92 *Federación de Distribuidores Cinematográficos* [1993] ECR I-2239.
[47] Case 352/85 *Bond van Adverteerders* [1988] ECR 2085.
[48] Case 30/77 *Bouchereau* [1977] ECR 1999.

[49] Directives 87/102/EEC and 90/88/EEC; see note 20.
[50] Directive 93/13/EEC (OJ L 95, 21.4.1993, 29), reproduced infra under no. C.P. 9.
[51] Directive 85/577/EEC (OJ L 372, 31.12.1985, 31), reproduced infra under no. C.P. 3.
[52] Directive 84/450/EEC of (OJ L 250, 19.9.1984, 17), reproduced infra under no. C.P. 1.

Community law for a Member State to treat its own nationals less favourably than other Community nationals.[53]

Should a Member State impose, for reasons which it deems to be of general good, a level of consumer protection stricter than the one set by a minimal Community provision on a Community credit institution operating on its territory, the proportionality test would, in any event, have to be satisfied.

Does the measure have a general-good objective?
Where there is no harmonisation, the Commission considers that, as the Court has consistently ruled, the restrictions imposed by a Member State are compatible with the Treaty only '*if it is established that in the field of activity concerned there are imperative reasons relating to the public interest (. . .)*'.[54]

If the rule does not fall within the scope of a harmonised area, it is necessary to examine whether it comes under one of the areas which the Court has to date considered as falling within the scope of the interest of the general good (e.g. consumer protection). If this is so, the first criterion is met, but the line of reasoning must be pursued. If this is not so, one can merely speculate as to whether the Court would recognise the area concerned as coming under the interest of the general good. It must be borne in mind that the Court has an ongoing case-law and that it reserves the right to add new areas to the existing list on the basis of individual cases.

Is the interest of the general good not already safeguarded in the country of origin?
It is necessary to examine in this connection whether the credit institution is not already subject to similar or comparable provisions aimed at safeguarding the same interest under the legislation of its Member State of origin.

Under the Second Banking Directive, this criterion could be important, particularly for the purpose of assessing the compatibility of the measures imposed by the host State in exercising its residual powers.

For example, it is necessary to examine in the context of this 'test', the extent to which certain controls required by the host State might already be carried out in the country of origin, the extent to which accounting, supervisory, statistical or financial information might already be communicated to the competent authority of the country of origin, etc.

Is the measure capable of guaranteeing that the objective will be met?
Even if a measure is presented by a host State as defending an objective conducive to the general good, one may ask whether it is really necessary in order to protect that interest.

There may be instances where a measure is not objectively necessary or is not suited to protecting the interest.

The Court of Justice assesses such circumstances and has held in certain judgments that a given rule that was justified by the host country on grounds of consumer protection was not in the end likely to provide such protection.

For example, the Court has held that, since information is one of the principal requirements of consumer protection, a Member State which imposes rules which ultimately restrict consumers' access to certain kinds of information cannot justify those rules on grounds of consumer protection.[55]

The Court, therefore, carefully examines the measure presented to it in order to ascertain whether it actually benefits the consumer[56] and whether the Member State imposing it is not underestimating the consumer's ability to judge for himself.[57] In this way, it checks whether certain measures, under cover of consumer

---

[53] Case 332/90 *Steen* [1992] ECR I-341; Joined cases C-29/94 to C-35/94 *Aubertin and others* [1995] ECR I-301. See also the judgment of 12 December 1996 in Joined cases C-320/94, C-328/94, C-329/94, C-337/94, C-338/94 and C-339/94 making the use of minimum provisions conditional upon compliance with the Treaty.
[54] Case 205/84 *Commission v Germany*; see note 9.

[55] Case C-362/88 *GB-INNO-BM* [1990] ECR I-667.
[56] See also judgment in Case C-240/95 *Schmit* [1996] ECR I-3179.
[57] See in particular Case C-470/93 *Mars* [1995] ECR I-1923. In this judgment, the Court had recourse to the concept of 'circumspect consumers'.

protection, are not actually aimed at achieving less worthy objectives connected with the protection of the national market.

Does the measure not go beyond what is necessary to achieve the objective pursued?
Finally, it is necessary to ask whether there are not less restrictive means of achieving the general-good objective pursued. This involves the application of the legal principle of the appropriateness of the response in relation to the risk.

The Court systematically examines whether the Member State did not have at its disposal measures with a less restrictive effect on trade.[58] In the context of such an examination, the Court may deduce from a comparative analysis of the legislation of the other Member States that less restrictive consumer protection measures exist.[59] However, the Court has also ruled that *'the fact that one Member State imposes less strict rules than another Member State does not mean that the latter's rules are disproportionate and hence incompatible with Community law'*.[60]

Where a national measure constituting a restriction on a credit institution benefiting from mutual recognition is justified by the host State on the ground that it protects the recipient of the service, it is essential, in checking whether the proportionality test is satisfied, to question the actual need to protect the recipient.

The Court held, in its judgment of 4 December 1986, Commission v Germany, that *'there may be cases where, because of the nature of the risk insured and of the party seeking insurance, there is no need to protect the latter by the application of the mandatory rules of his national law'*.[61] The scope of this ruling naturally goes beyond the field of insurance.

It is necessary, therefore, to give consideration, in each individual case, to the need for protection of the recipient of the banking service offered in the context of mutual recognition by examining the nature of the service and the level of sophistication of the recipient.

The Commission considers that Member States should, in imposing their general-good rules, make a distinction according to whether or not services are supplied to circumspect recipients. In other words, in order to respect the principle of proportionality, they should take account of the degree of vulnerability of the persons they are setting out to protect.

European Parliament and Council Directive 94/19/EC on deposit guarantees and, in particular, the possible exclusions for which it provides, may be taken as a basis for determining whether a recipient is circumspect.[62] The logic underlying these possible exclusions is in fact the same as that being defended in the present communication. As a guide, it may be considered that credit institutions, financial institutions, insurance undertakings, central and other government authorities, UCITS, pension funds and companies within the meaning of point 14 of Annex I to Directive 94/19/EC[63] are customers of a nature or size such that they are in a position to recognise the risks they are incurring and to commit themselves in full knowledge of the facts.

For example, business transactions of the type listed in the Annex, when carried out between professionals in the financial sector, should not be the subject of particular general-good rules imposed by the host Member State. The proportionality test would be especially difficult to satisfy in such cases.

Finally, it is necessary in certain cases to determine whether the service is supplied under the freedom to provide services or by a branch.

An assessment of the proportionality of a restriction may in fact differ depending on the mode of operation.

---

[58] See most recently Case C-101/94 *Commission v Italy ('SIM')* [1996] ECR 2691. See also Case C-384/93 *Alpine Investments*; see note 31.
[59] Case C-129/91 *Yves Rocher* [1993] ECR I-2361.
[60] Case C-384/93 *Alpine Investments*; see note 31.
[61] Case 205/84 *Commission v Germany*; see note 9.

[62] Directive 94/19/EC (OJ L 135, 31.5.1994, 5), reproduced supra under no. B. 22.
[63] Companies comprising more than 50 people with a balance-sheet total of at least ECU 2.500.000 and a net turnover of at least ECU 5.000.000. Council Directive 94/8/EC (OJ L 82, 25.3.1994, 33), reproduced supra under no. C. 7.

Accordingly, a restriction could more readily be considered to be proportionate in the case of an operator working permanently within a territory than in the case of the same operator working only temporarily.

The Court has recognised this difference by imposing a less restrictive and more 'lightweight' legal framework for suppliers of services operating in a temporary capacity than for established suppliers.

It has consistently held that a Member State:

'may not make the provision of services in its territory subject to compliance with all the conditions required for establishment and thereby deprive of all practical effectiveness the provisions of the Treaty whose object is, precisely, to guarantee the freedom to provide services.'[64]

The Court has also held that restrictions on the freedom to provide services are even less acceptable in cases where the service is supplied '*without its being necessary for the person providing it to visit the territory of the Member State where it is provided*'.[65] This clarification is particularly relevant to banking services, which are increasingly supplied without physical movement on the part of the supplier.

The Court has likewise consistently held that it does not follow from the third paragraph of Article [50][7] of the Treaty that:

'all national legislation applicable to nationals of that State and usually applied to the permanent activities of undertakings established therein may be similarly applied in its entirety to the temporary activities of undertakings which are established in other Member States.'[66]

Thus, depending on the circumstances, the same restriction applied in the interest of the general good could be adjudged proportionate in respect of a branch but disproportionate in respect of a temporary provider of services. The Commission considers, for example, that a Member State which imposes certain formalities on credit institutions (controls, registration, costs, communication of information, etc.) for reasons that purport to be in the general good should take account of the mode of operation chosen by the credit institution carrying on activities within its territory under mutual-recognition arrangements.

However, this distinction cannot be applied to consumer-protection rules (provided, of course, that they have satisfied the other tests). The level of consumer protection required must be identical, whether the service is supplied under the freedom to provide services or by way of establishment. It would be unacceptable for a consumer to be less well protected according to whether he received a service from a non-established undertaking or an established undertaking.

It may be necessary, however, to take account of the circumstances in which the service was requested. There may be situations in which the consumer has deliberately avoided the protection afforded him by his national law, particularly where he requests a service from a non-established bank without having first been canvassed in any way by that bank.

C. *Interest of the general good and private international law*

1. Principles

An examination of the compatibility with Community law of a national rule justified on general-good grounds may be carried out where a legal discrepancy caused by an absence of harmonisation creates an obstacle to the movement of banking services.

Any national rule must be compatible with Community law irrespective of the area in which it falls. In a judgment delivered on 21 March 1972, the Court ruled that:

'The effectiveness of Community law cannot vary according to the various branches of national law which it may affect'. [67]

---

[64] Case C-76/90 *Säger*; see note 22. See also Case C-198/89 *Commission v Greece* [1991] ECR I-727.
[65] Case C-76/90 *Säger*; see note 22.
[66] Case 205/84 *Commission v Germany*; see note 9. See also the judgment of 17 December 1981, Case 279/80 *Webb*; see note 28.

[67] Case 82/71 *SAIL* [1972] ECR 119. See also Case 20/92 *Hubbard* [1993] ECR I-3777.

Where necessary, Community law takes precedence, therefore, over national private law provisions.

The Court has accordingly had to check the compatibility with Community law of national provisions of civil law[68] and civil procedure.[69]

It may be stated that most contractual rules falling within the scope of civil law or procedural law (means of extinguishing obligations, limitation periods, expiry, invalidity, etc.) are unlikely to constitute barriers to the trade in banking services.

However, banking contracts do contain provisions, usually of a mandatory nature, which may well constitute rules on contractual obligations, but actually affect trade. Let us take, for example, a clause preventing any variation in a rate or relating to early repayment. The effects of such provisions may constitute a restriction if they oblige a bank to alter a service to bring it into line with the legislation of the country in which it is marketed.

The Commission considers that such provisions cannot escape the controls laid down by Community law simply on the ground that they fall within the scope of the law on contractual obligations.

In this context, a judge may be required to examine the compatibility with Community law of the results achieved by applying the rules on the choice of law governing contractual obligations contained in private international legal instruments, particularly the Rome Convention.[70]

Such choice-of-law rules do not, however, constitute restrictions in themselves. It is not, in principle, the mechanism for designating the law applicable which constitutes a barrier but the result to which it leads under substantive law.[71]

2. Link with the Rome Convention

This Convention establishes the principle of contractual freedom, which is common to all Member States.

The parties to a banking contract may, therefore, freely choose the law which is to govern the contract and the obligations which they mutually undertake to fulfil. This may be the law of the home country, the host country or even a third country, whether or not a Member of the European Union.

The Convention lays down that, where no choice is expressed by the parties, the law applicable is that of the country with which the contract is most closely connected. Under the Convention, this is presumed to be the country where the party who is to effect the performance has his habitual residence or principal or secondary place of business, depending on whether the performance is to be effected by the parent company or a branch.

In the case of a contract concluded with a consumer,[72] the Convention lays down that, where the parties do not express a choice, the law applicable is that of the country of the consumer if the contract is entered into in one of the following sets of circumstances (Article 5):
– the contract was preceded by a specific invitation addressed to the consumer in his country and he had taken in that country all the steps necessary on his part for the conclusion of the contract;
– the other party or his agent received the consumer's order in that country.

Where, however, the parties have chosen the law governing the contract, this choice must not deprive the consumer of the protection afforded him by the mandatory rules[73] of the law of the country in which he has his habitual residence if one of the sets of circumstances described above is found to prevail.

In addition, under the Convention, the '*mandatory rules*' (Article 7) and '*public policy*'

---

[68] Case C-168/91 *Konstantinidis* [1993] ECR I-1191; Case C-339/89 *Alsthom Atlantique* [1991] ECR I-107; judgment of 13 October 1993, Case C-93/92 *Motorradcenter* [1993] ECR I-5009.
[69] See in this connection Case C-398/92 *Mund & Fester* [1994] ECR I-467; Case C-43/95 *Data Delecta Aktiebolag* [1996] ECR I-4661; Case C-177/94 *Perfili* [1996] ECR I-161; see also Case 20/92 *Hubbard*; see note 67.
[70] See note 5.
[71] See, however, Case C-214/94 *Boukhalfa* [1996] ECR I-2253.

[72] Contract carried out for a purpose outside his trade or profession.
[73] Provisions which cannot be derogated from by contract.

(Article 6)[74] of Member States may be applied at the choice of the parties or, in the absence of an express choice, according to the relevant rules contained in the Convention.

On the basis of the Rome Convention, a banking contract concluded with a consumer must, therefore, observe at least the mandatory rules of the law of the consumer's country if the consumer was first canvassed in the consumer's country or if the order for the service was received there.

If, on the other hand, the banking contract is concluded not with a consumer (contract concluded between a bank and a customer acting in the course of his business), the contract will be governed by the law chosen by the parties and, in the absence of an express choice, by the law of the country where the bank has its principal or secondary place of business.

3. Precedence of Community law

The Commission considers that a further level of reasoning must be added to that deriving from the application of the Rome Convention.

Thus, in accordance with the principle of the precedence of Community law, the provisions of substantive law applicable to a banking service pursuant to the choice-of-law rules laid down in the Rome Convention (it being possible for freedom of choice to be overridden by mandatory rules, mandatory requirements and public policy) may, if they constitute a restriction, be examined in the light of the general good.

Two possible situations may be envisaged:[75]

(a) *Banking services supplied by a branch*

Article 4 of the Rome Convention lays down that the law applicable in the absence of a choice by the parties is that of the country in which the principal place of business is situated or, if the performance is to be effected through a place of business other than the principal place of business, the country in which that other place of business is situated. The Convention therefore implies that, where a service is supplied by a bank branch, the law of the country where the branch is situated is presumed to prevail in the absence of a choice by the parties concerned.[76]

In accordance with the principle of the precedence of Community law, the Commission considers that, where the legal provisions of the country of the branch constitute a restriction, they may be put to the general-good test and, if necessary, overruled.

(b) *Banking services supplied to consumers under the freedom to provide services*

According to the principle of the precedence of Community law, the application by a consumer's country of residence of its '*mandatory rules*', '*mandatory requirements*' and '*public policy*' provisions to contracts entered into by the consumer may also be put to the general-good test if a restriction results.

It is necessary, therefore, to extend the line of reasoning developed on the basis of the Rome Convention and to question whether, for example, the '*mandatory rules*' which the consumer's country intends to enforce satisfy the general-good tests. Since they are adopted with a view to protecting the consumer, there is a strong chance that these provisions of substantive law will pass the general-good test. The Court has in fact recognised that consumer protection is a general-good objective which justifies restrictions on fundamental freedoms. It cannot be assumed, however, that they will pass the general-good test in every case. It has been seen above that national rules which purport

---

[74] This concept must be understood here within its meaning under national law and private international law, which is not necessarily the meaning conferred upon it by the Court of Justice; for the latter, it is a non-economic concept, implying a serious threat to society.

[75] The Court of Justice will be responsible for interpreting the Rome Convention, particularly with a view to guaranteeing an interpretation that is compatible with Community law. However, it is not yet empowered to do so since the two protocols vesting such powers in the Court (89/128/EEC and 89/129/EEC) have not yet entered into force since not all the Member States which ratified the Rome Convention have ratified Protocol 89/129/EEC.

[76] Under normal circumstances, however, the parties to a banking contract would choose which law to apply.

to have been adopted for reasons of consumer protection may be subjected to review by the Court and possibly 'disqualified' if they are, for example, unnecessary or disproportionate.

In the context of the single market, therefore, this additional level of reasoning is essential in order to ascertain whether, in the absence of harmonisation, national measures are not being maintained, in the guise of consumer-protection measures, merely in order to restrict or to prevent banking services which are different or unfamiliar from gaining entry to national territory.

B. 28.

European Parliament and Council Directive 98/31/EC of 22 June 1998 amending Council Directive 93/6/EEC on the capital adequacy of investment firms and credit institutions[1]

THE EUROPEAN PARLIAMENT AND THE COUNCIL OF THE EUROPEAN UNION,

Having regard to the Treaty establishing the European Community, and in particular the first and third sentences of Article [47(2)][2] thereof,

Having regard to the proposal from the Commission,[3]

Having regard to the opinion of the Economic and Social Committee,[4]

Having regard to the opinion of the European Monetary Institute,[5]

Acting in accordance with the procedure laid down in Article [251][2] of the Treaty,[6]

(1) Whereas the risks associated with commodities trading and commodity derivatives are currently subject to Council Directive 89/647/EEC of 18 December 1989 on a solvency ratio for credit institutions;[7] whereas, however, the market risks associated with those positions are not captured accurately by Directive 89/647/EEC; whereas it is necessary to extend the concept of the 'trading book' to positions in commodities or commodity derivatives which are held for trading purposes and are subject mainly to market risks; whereas institutions must comply with this Directive as regards the coverage of commodity risks on their overall business; whereas the perpetration of serious fraud by certain commodity futures traders is of growing concern to the Community and a threat to the image and integrity of the futures trading business; whereas it is desirable that the Commission should consider defining an appropriate prudential framework in order to prevent these fraudulent practices in the future;

(2) Whereas Council Directive 93/6/EEC of 15 March 1993 on the capital adequacy of investment firms and credit institutions[8] lays down a standardised method for the calculation of capital requirements for market risks incurred by investment firms and credit institutions; whereas institutions have developed their own risk-management systems (internal models), designed to measure more accurately than the standardised method the market risks incurred by investment firms and credit institutions; whereas the use of more accurate methods of measuring risks should be encouraged;

(3) Whereas the use of such internal models for the purpose of calculating capital requirements requires strict internal control mechanisms and should be subject to recognition and supervision by the competent authorities; whereas the continued reliability of the results of the internal

---

[1] OJ L 204, 21.7.1998, 13–25.
[2] The number between brackets has been changed as from 1 May 1999 by article 12 of the Treaty of Amsterdam.
[3] OJ C 240, 6.8.1997, 24, and OJ C 118, 17.4.1998, 16.
[4] OJ C 19, 21.1.1998, 9.
[5] Opinion delivered on 7 October 1997.
[6] Opinion of the European Parliament of 18 December 1997 (OJ C 14, 19.1.1998), Council common position of 9 March 1998 (OJ C 135, 30.4.1998, 7) and Decision of the European Parliament of 30 April 1998 (OJ C 152, 18.5.1998). Council Decision of 19 May 1998.
[7] OJ L 386, 30.12.1989, 14, reproduced supra under no. B. 13. Directive as last amended by Directive 98/32/EC (OJ L 204, 21.7.1998, 13), consolidated in Directive 2000/12/EC, reproduced infra under no. B. 32.

[8] OJ L 141, 11.6.1993, 1, reproduced supra under no. B. 20. Directive as amended by Directive 98/33/EC (OJ L 204, 21.7.1998, 13), consolidated in Directive 2000/12/EC, reproduced infra under no. B. 32. Directive 93/6/EEC has been repealed as from 20 July 2006 by article 58 of Directive 2006/49/EC, (OJ L 177, 30.6.2006, 201), reproduced infra under no. B. 41.

model calculation should be verified by a back-testing procedure;

(4) Whereas it is appropriate that competent authorities may allow margin requirements for exchange-traded futures and options, and on a transitional basis for cleared over-the-counter derivatives of the same nature, to be used as substitutes for the capital requirement calculated for such instruments in accordance with this Directive, provided that this does not lead to a capital requirement which is lower than the capital requirement calculated according to the other methods prescribed in this Directive; whereas the application of this principle does not require that the equivalence between such margin requirements and the capital requirements calculated according to the other methods prescribed in this Directive must be continually verified by the institutions applying this principle;

(5) Whereas the rules adopted at the wider international level may, in order to encourage more sophisticated risk-management methods based on internal models, lower capital requirements for credit institutions from third countries; whereas those credit institutions compete with investment firms and credit institutions incorporated in the Member States; whereas for investment firms and credit institutions incorporated in the Member States, only an amendment of Directive 93/6/EEC can provide similar incentives for the development and use of internal models;

(6) Whereas for the purpose of calculating market-risk-capital requirements, positions in gold and gold derivatives should be treated in a similar fashion to foreign-exchange positions;

(7) Whereas the issue of subordinated debt should not automatically exclude an issuer's equity from being included in a portfolio qualifying for a 2% specific-risk weighting according to point 33 of Annex I to Directive 93/6/EEC;

(8) Whereas this Directive is in accordance with the work of an international forum of banking supervisors on the supervisory treatment of market risk and of positions in commodities and commodity derivatives;

(9) Whereas it is necessary to have a transitional capital regime on an optional basis for investment firms and credit institutions undertaking significant commodities business, having a diversified commodity portfolio and being not yet able to use models for the purpose of calculating the commodities risk capital requirement, in order to ensure a harmonious application of this Directive;

(10) Whereas this Directive is the most appropriate means of attaining the objectives sought and does not go beyond what is necessary to achieve those objectives,

HAVE ADOPTED THIS DIRECTIVE:

Article 1

[...]

¶ *This article replaces article 2, point 6(a), the introductory phrase and subpoints (i) and (ii) of point 6(b), points 15, 16, 17, first paragraph, point 18, article 4(1), first subparagraph, points (i) and (ii), article 5(2), article 7(10), the introductory part of article 7(11) and article 8(5) and inserts article 11a by Directive 93/6, reproduced supra under no. B. 20. Directive 93/6/EEC has been repealed as from 20 July 2006 by article 58 of Directive 2006/49/EC, (OJ L 177, 30.6.2006, 201), reproduced infra under no. B. 41.*

Correlation Table

Directive 98/31/EC	Directive 2006/49/EC
Article 1(1)(b)	Article 3(1)(k) and (l)
Article 1(1)(c)	Article 3(1)(m)
Article 1(1)(d)	Article 3(1)(n)
Article 1(2)	Article 18(1) (a) and (b)
Article 1(3)	Article 28(2)
Article 1(4)	Article 26(1)
Article 1(5)	Article 35(5)
Article 1(6)	Annex IV(21)
Article 1(7) and Annex 3(a)	Annex III(1)
Article 1(7) and Annex 3(b)	Annex III(2.1) first to third paragraphs
Article 1(7) and Annex 3(b)	Annex III(2.1) fifth paragraph
Article 1(7) and	Annex III(2.2),

Directive 98/31/EC	Directive 2006/49/EC
Annex 3(c)	(3), (3.1)
Article 1(7) and Annex 4(a)(b)	Article 13(1) second sub-paragraph and (2) to (5)
Article 1(7) and Annex 5	Annex IV(1) to (20)
Article 1(7) and Annex 5	Annex V(1) to (12) fourth paragraph
Article 1(7) and Annex 5	Annex V(12) sixth paragraph to (13)
Annex 4(c)	Article 14

Article 2

1. Member States shall bring into force the laws, regulations and administrative provisions necessary to comply with this Directive not later than 24 months after the date of its entry into force. They shall forthwith inform the Commission thereof.

When Member States adopt these measures, they shall contain a reference to this Directive or shall be accompanied by such reference on the occasion of their official publication. The methods of making such reference shall be laid down by Member States.

2. Member States shall communicate to the Commission the text of the main provisions of domestic law which they adopt in the field governed by this Directive.

Article 3

This Directive shall enter into force on the day of its publication in the *Official Journal of the European Communities*.

Article 4

This Directive is addressed to the Member States.

Annex

[...]

¶ *This annex amends annexes I, II, III and V and adds annexes VII and VIII to Directive 93/6/EEC, reproduced supra under no. B. 20. This Directive has been repealed as from 20 July 2006 by article 52 of Directive 2006/49/EC (OJ L 177, 30.6.2006, 201), reproduced infra under no. B. 42*

B. 29.

European Parliament and Council Directive 98/32/EC of 22 June 1998 amending, as regards in particular mortgages, Council Directive 89/647/EEC on a solvency ratio for credit institutions[1]

This Directive has been repealed by article 67 of Directive 2000/12/EC, which subsequently has been repealed by article 158 of Directive 2006/48/EC (OJ L 177, 30.06.2006, 1) reproduced infra under no. B. 41.

---

[1] OJ L 204, 21.7.1998, 26–28.

B. 30.

European Parliament and Council Directive 98/33/EC
of 22 June 1998
amending Article 12 of Council Directive 77/780/EEC on the taking up and pursuit of the business of credit institutions, Articles 2, 5, 6, 7, 8 of and Annexes II and III to Council Directive 89/647/EEC on a solvency ratio for credit institutions and Article 2 of and Annex II to Council Directive 93/6/EEC on the capital adequacy of investment firms and credit institutions[1]

This Directive has been repealed by as from 20 July 2006 by article 52 of Directive 2006/49/EC (OJ L 177, 30.6.2006, 201), reproduced infra under no. B. 42.

Correlation Table

Directive 98/33/EC	Directive 2006/49/EC
Article 3(1)	Article 3(1)(i)

---

[1] OJ L 204, 21.7.1998, 29–36.

B. 31.

(Acts pursuant to Title [VII][1] of the Treaty on European Union)

Joint Action 98/699/JHA
of 3 December 1998
adopted by the Council on the basis of Article [31][1] of the Treaty on European Union, on money laundering, the identification, tracing, freezing, seizing and confiscation of instrumentalities and the proceeds from crime[2]

THE COUNCIL OF THE EUROPEAN UNION,

Having regard to the Treaty on European Union and, in particular, Article [31][1] (b) thereof,

Having regard to the initiative of the United Kingdom,

Having regard to the action plan of the High Level Group on Organised Crime approved by the Amsterdam European Council on 16 and 17 June 1997, and in particular recommendation 26(b) on strengthening the tracing and seizure of the proceeds from crime,

Having examined the views of the European Parliament following the consultation conducted by the Presidency in accordance with Article [34][1] of the Treaty on European Union,

Having regard to the Joint Actions of 5 December 1997 establishing a mechanism for evaluating the application and implementation at national level for international undertakings in the fight against organised crime,[3] and of 19 March 1998, establishing a programme of exchanges, training and co-operation for persons responsible for action to combat organised crime (Falcone Programme),[4]

Considering the commitment of Member States of the principles of the Council of Europe Convention on Laundering, Search, Seizure and Confiscation of the Proceeds from Crime 1990,

Having regard to the proposed Joint Action on making it a criminal offence to participate in a criminal organisation in the Member States of the European Union, and in particular to the offences covered by that Joint Action,

Considering the requirements of Council Directive 91/308/EEC of 10 June 1991 on prevention of the use of the financial system for the purpose of money laundering,[5] and the 40 recommendations to combat money laundering of the Financial Action Task Force on Money Laundering (FATF) as formulated in 1996, and in particular recommendation 4 thereof,

Having regard to the Joint Action of 17 December 1996 concerning the approximation of the laws and practices of the Member States of the European Union to combat drug addiction and to prevent and combat illegal drug trafficking,[6]

Mindful of the common objective of improving co-ordination between law enforcement authorities,

Recalling the Joint Action on the creation of a European Judicial Network, adopted by the Council on 29 June 1998,[7]

Whereas the potential for disrupting criminal activity in the field of organised crime, by more effective co-operation between Member States in identifying, tracing, freezing or seizing, and

---

[1] The number between brackets has been changed as from 1 May 1999 by article 12 of the Treaty of Amsterdam.
[2] OJ L 333, 9.12.1998, 1–3.
[3] OJ L 344, 15.12.1997, 7.
[4] OJ L 99, 31.3.1998, 8.

[5] OJ L 166, 28.6.1991, 77, reproduced supra under no. B. 20.
[6] OJ L 342, 31.12.1996, 6.
[7] OJ L 191, 7.7.1998, 4.

confiscating the assets deriving from crime, is being improved;

Whereas mutually compatible practices are making co-operation at European level more efficient at identifying, tracing, freezing or seizing, and confiscating illegal assets;

Whereas recommendation No 16 of the above-mentioned action plan to combat organised crime emphasised the need to accelerate procedures for judicial co-operation in matters relating to organised crime, while considerably reducing delay in transmission and responses to requests;

Considering the Member States' adherence to the 1959 European Convention on Mutual Assistance in Criminal Matters;

In the light of the United Nations Convention against Illicit Traffic in Narcotic Drugs and Psychotropic Substances 1988 and the 1998 United Nations General Assembly Special Session on Drugs;

Recognising the achievement of the 1996 Dublin Seminar on asset confiscation in identifying obstacles to effective co-operation;

On the understanding that the forms of co-operation laid down in this Joint Action are without prejudice to other forms of bilateral or multilateral co-operation,

HAS ADOPTED THIS JOINT ACTION:

Article 1

1. In order to enhance effective action against organised crime, Member States shall ensure that no reservations are made or upheld in respect of the following Articles of the 1990 Council of Europe Convention on Laundering, Search, Seizure and Confiscation of the Proceeds from Crime (hereinafter referred to as 'the 1990 Convention'):

(a) Article 2: in so far as the offence is punishable by deprivation of liberty or a detention order of a maximum of more than one year;

(b) Article 6: in so far as serious offences are concerned. Such offences should in any event include offences which are punishable by deprivation of liberty or a detention order of a maximum of more than one year, or, as regards those States which have a minimum threshold for offences in their legal system, offences punishable by deprivation of liberty or a detention order of a minimum of more than six months.

Point (a) shall not affect reservations made with regard to the confiscation of proceeds from offences punishable under legislation on taxation.

2. Each Member State shall ensure that its legislation and procedures on the confiscation of the proceeds from crime shall also allow for the confiscation of property the value of which corresponds to such proceeds, both in purely domestic proceedings and in proceedings instituted at the request of another Member State, including requests for the enforcement of foreign confiscation orders. However, Member States may exclude the confiscation of property the value of which corresponds to the proceeds from crime in minor cases. The words 'property', 'proceeds', and 'confiscation' shall have the same meaning as in Article 1 of the 1990 Convention.

3. Each Member State shall ensure that its legislation and procedures enable it to permit the identification and tracing of suspected proceeds from crime at the request of another Member State where there are reasonable grounds to suspect that a criminal offence has been committed. Such legislation and procedures shall enable assistance to be given at the earliest possible stages in an investigation, and to that end, Member States will endeavour to restrict their use of the optional grounds for refusal in respect of other Member States under paragraphs 2 and 3 of Article 18 of the 1990 Convention.

Article 2

1. Within the framework of the functioning of the European Judicial Network, each Member State shall prepare a user-friendly guide, including information about where to obtain advice, setting out the assistance it can provide in identifying, tracing, freezing or seizing and confiscating instrumentalities and the proceeds from crime. The guide shall also include any important

restrictions on such assistance and the information which requesting States should supply.

2. The General Secretariat of the Council of the European Union shall be sent the guides referred to in paragraph 1 and shall translate them into the official languages of the institutions of the European Community. The General Secretariat shall distribute the guides to Member States, the European Judicial Network and Europol.

3. Each Member State shall ensure that the guide referred to in paragraph 1 is kept up to date and that any changes are sent to the General Secretariat of the Council for translation and distribution in accordance with paragraph 2.

Article 3

Member States shall give the same priority to all requests from other Member States which relate to asset identification, tracing, freezing or seizing, and confiscation as is given to such measures in domestic proceedings.

Article 4

1. Member States shall encourage direct contact between investigators, investigating magistrates and prosecutors of Member States making appropriate use of available co-operation arrangements, to ensure that requests for assistance through formal channels are not made unnecessarily. When a formal request is necessary, the requesting State shall ensure that it is properly prepared and meets all the requirements of the requested State.

2. Where it is not possible to execute a request for assistance in the manner expected by the requesting State, the requested State shall endeavour to satisfy the request in some alternative way, after appropriate consultation with the requesting State, while fully respecting national legislation and international obligations.

3. Member States shall submit requests for assistance as soon as the precise nature of the assistance required is identified and, where a request is marked 'urgent' or a deadline is indicated, explain the reasons for the urgency or deadline.

Article 5

1. Member States shall, where it is not contrary to their law, take all necessary steps to minimise the risk of assets being dissipated. Those steps shall include such measures as may be necessary to ensure that assets which are the subject of a request from another Member State may be frozen or seized expeditiously so that a later confiscation request is not frustrated.

2. Where, in the course of fulfilling a request for legal assistance in one area of a Member State the need arises to pursue further enquiries in another area of that Member State, the Member State shall, where it is not contrary to its law, take all possible steps to enable the necessary assistance to be rendered without the need for preparation of a further letter of request.

3. Where the execution of a request leads to the need to pursue further enquiries on a related issue, and the requesting State issues a supplementary letter of request, the requested State shall, where it is not contrary to its law, take all possible steps to expedite the execution of such a supplementary request.

Article 6

1. Member States shall ensure that arrangements are in place to acquaint their judiciary with best practice in international co-operation in the identification, tracing, freezing or seizing, and confiscation of instrumentalities and the proceeds from crime.

2. Member States shall ensure that appropriate training, reflecting best practice, is provided to all investigators, investigating magistrates, prosecutors and other officials concerned with international co-operation in asset identification, tracing, freezing or seizing and confiscation matters.

3. The Presidency and interested Member States, in co-operation as appropriate with the European Judicial Network and Europol, shall as necessary arrange seminars for officials from Member States and other practitioners involved to promote and develop best practice and to encourage compatibility of procedures.

Article 7

The Council shall, before the end of 2000, review this Joint Action in the light of the results of the operation of the Joint Action of 5 December 1997 establishing a mechanism for evaluating the application and implementation at national level of international undertakings in the fight against organised crime.

Article 8

1. Subject to paragraph 2, Member States shall take all appropriate steps to implement this Joint Action as soon as it enters into force, and shall ensure that its contents are brought to the attention of their relevant national and local authorities.

2. Appropriate proposals for the implementation of Article 1 shall be submitted by Member States within three years of the entry into force of this Joint Action for consideration by the competent authorities with a view to their adoption.

Article 9

This Joint Action shall be published in the Official Journal and shall enter into force on the day of its publication.

B. 32.

(Acts whose publication is obligatory)

European Parliament and Council Directive 2000/12/EC
of 20 March 2000
relating to the taking up and pursuit of the business of credit institutions[1]

This Directive has been repealed as from 20 July 2007 by article 158 of Directive 2006/48/EC (OJ L 177, 30.6.2006, 1), reproduced infra under no. B. 41.

Correlation Table

Directive 2000/12/EC	Directive 2006/48/EC
Article 1(1)	Article 4(1)
Article 1(1), third subparagraph	Article 107
Article 1(3), second sentence	Article 27
Article 1(10), (12) and (13)	Article 4(11) to (14)
Article 1(23)	Article 4(23)
Article 1(24)	Article 106
Article 1(25) to (27)	Article 4(45) to (47)
Article 2(3) Act of Accession	Article 2
Article 2(4)	Article 2
Article 2(5) and (6)	Article 3
Article 4	Article 6
Article 5(1) and 1 (11)	Article 9(1)
Article 5(2)	Article 9(2)
Article 5(3) to (7)	Article 10
Article 6	Article 11
Article 7	Article 12
Article 8	Article 7
Article 9	Article 8
Article 10	Article 13
Article 11	Article 14
Article 12	Article 15(1)
Article 13	Article 16
Article 14	Article 17
Article 15	Article 18
Article 16(1)	Article 19(1)

---

[1] OJ L 126, 26.5.2000, 1–59.

Directive 2000/12/EC	Directive 2006/48/EC
Article 16(3)	Article 20
Article 16(4) to (6)	Article 21
Article 17	Article 22
Article 18	Article 23
Article 19(1) to (3)	Article 24(1)
Article 19(4)	Article 24(3)
Article 19(5)	Article 25(3)
Article 19(6)	Article 24(2)
Article 20(1) to (3), first and second subparagraphs	Article 25(1) to (3)
Article 20(3), third subparagraph	Article 25(4)
Article 20(4) to (7)	Article 26
Article 21	Article 28
Article 22	Article 29
Article 22(2) to (4)	Article 30
Article 22(5)	Article 31
Article 22(6)	Article 32
Article 22(7)	Article 33
Article 22(8)	Article 34
Article 22(9)	Article 35
Article 22(10)	Article 36
Article 22(11)	Article 37
Article 24	Article 38
Article 25	Article 39(1) and (2)
Article 26	Article 40
Article 27	Article 41
Article 28	Article 42
Article 29	Article 43
Article 30(1) to (3)	Article 44
Article 30(3)	Article 46
Article 30(4)	Article 45
Article 30(5)	Article 47
Article 30(6) and (7)	Article 48
Article 30(8)	Article 49
Article 30(9), first and second subparagraphs	Article 50
Article 30(9), third subparagraph	Article 51
Article 30(10)	Article 52
Article 31	Article 53
Article 32	Article 54
Article 33	Article 55

Directive 2000/12/EC	Directive 2006/48/EC
Article 34(1)	Article 56
Article 34(2), first subparagraph; and Article 34(2), point 2, second sentence	Article 57
Article 34(3) and (4)	Article 61
Article 35	Article 63
Article 36	Article 64
Article 37	Article 65
Article 38(1) and (2)	Article 66(1) and (2)
Article 39	Article 67
Article 48(1)	Article 108
Article 48(2) to (4), second subparagraph	Article 110
Article 48(4), first subparagraph	Article 109
Article 49(1) to (5)	Article 111
Article 49(4), (6) and (7)	Article 113
Article 49(8) and (9)	Article 115
Article 49(10)	Article 116
Article 49(11)	Article 117
Article 50	Article 118
Article 51(1), (2) and (5)	Article 120
Article 51(4)	Article 121
Article 51(6)	Article 122(1) and (2)
Article 52(3)	Article 73
Article 53(1) and (2)	Article 125
Article 53(3)	Article 126
Article 53(5)	Article 128
Article 54(1)	Article 133(1)
Article 54(2) and (3)	Article 133(2) and (3)
Article 54(4), first subparagraph	Article 134(1)
Article 54(4), second subparagraph	Article 134(2)
Article 55	Article 137
Article 56(1) to (3)	Article 139
Article 56(4) to (6)	Article 140
Article 56(7)	Article 141
Article 56(8)	Article 142

Directive 2000/12/EC	Directive 2006/48/EC
Article 60(1)	Article 150
Article 60(2)	Article 151
Article 67	Article 158
Article 68	Article 159
Article 69	Article 160
Annex I	Annex I, points 1 to 14, excluding the final paragraph
Annex II	Annex II
Annex III	Annex III
Annex IV	Annex IV

B. 33.

Commission Recommendation 2000/408/EC
of 23 June 2000
concerning disclosure of information on financial instruments and other items complementing the disclosure required according to Council Directive 86/635/EEC on the annual accounts and consolidated accounts of banks and other financial institutions[1]

(notified under document number C(2000) 1372)

THE COMMISSION OF THE EUROPEAN COMMUNITIES,

Having regard to the Treaty establishing the European Community, and in particular Article 211 thereof,

Whereas:

(1) On the wider international level, banks and other undertakings are increasingly called upon to provide enhanced disclosure of their activities in financial instruments and other similar instruments.

(2) This international development towards enhanced disclosure was echoed in the European Parliament's Resolution A4-0207/95 of 22 September 1995 on financial derivative instruments.[2]

(3) Due to banks' and other financial institutions' pivotal role in financial markets and in the overall monetary and economic system, enhanced disclosure of information on activities relating to financial instruments and other similar instruments appears to be particularly desirable for these institutions.

(4) Due to the enormous increase in these institutions' activities relating to such instruments, regarding notably derivative instruments, since the time of the adoption of Council Directive 86/635/EEC,[3] disclosure of additional information complementing the limited disclosure required under that Directive is considered necessary.

(5) Disclosure of such information allows investors and market participants to take well-informed decisions, thus fostering market transparency and market discipline as a most valuable complement to prudential supervision.

(6) To this effect, meaningful and comparable qualitative and quantitative information on institutions' activities relating to financial instruments and information on the objectives and methods of risk measurement and management systems is necessary.

(7) Notwithstanding the obligation to disclose all material information, the potential usefulness of particular disclosures should be balanced against the need not to overburden financial statements with excessive disclosure and the likely cost of providing such information. The obligation to disclose information does not impose an obligation to disclose confidential or proprietary information.

(8) Given the ongoing international discussions on the methods for disclosing such information a formal amendment of Directive 86/635/EEC introducing mandatory disclosure requirements appears to be premature.

(9) It is necessary for the smooth functioning of the internal market that the accounting information published by banks and other financial

---

[1] OJ L 154, 27.6.2000, 36–41.
[2] OJ C 269, 16.10.1995, 217.
[3] OJ L 372, 31.12.1986, 1, reproduced supra under no. B. 7.

institutions remains sufficiently comparable. The Commission will therefore closely follow the effect of this recommendation on current practice in the Member States and will later, if necessary, propose further actions to ensure sufficient harmonisation in this field,

HEREBY RECOMMENDS:

1. For accounting periods commencing within 12 months from the date of this Recommendation and for all future accounting periods, information in accordance with the Annex should be disclosed by banks and financial institutions in the notes on the annual and consolidated accounts and/or in the annual report, as appropriate.

2. The Member States should take the appropriate measures to promote the application of this Recommendation, having due regard to the nature and size of particular institutions and the consequent usefulness to the market of the information provided in their accounts.

3. The Member States should notify the Commission of measures taken in compliance with this Recommendation.

Annex

1. Scope and definitions

1.1. Information on financial instruments, commodities and commodity-related derivative instruments (hereinafter: "instruments") according to this recommendation should be disclosed by banks and financial institutions (hereinafter: "institutions") which are subject of Council Directive 86/635/EEC in the notes on the annual and consolidated accounts and/or in the annual report, as appropriate.

The Appendices to this Annex set out illustrative examples of how this information might be disclosed to meet the objectives of this recommendation. These illustrative examples are not exhaustive. Other forms of disclosure, such as those based on in-house models, may also be used provided information on the basis of the models, including the reliability of information that stems from those models and whether they are recognised by the competent authorities for the purpose of calculating prudential capital requirements, is also disclosed.

1.2. A financial instrument is any contract that gives rise to both a financial asset of one party and a financial liability or equity instrument of another party. Financial instruments include both
– primary financial instruments such as receivables, payables and equity securities and
– derivative financial instruments such as options, futures, forwards, interest rate swaps and currency swaps, the value of which is derived from the price of an underlying financial instrument or a rate or an index or the price of an underlying other item.

1.3. A financial asset is any asset that is:

(a) cash;

(b) a contractual right to receive cash or another financial asset from another party;

(c) a contractual right to exchange instruments with another party under conditions that are potentially favourable; or

(d) an equity instrument of another party.

1.4. A financial liability is any liability that is a contractual obligation:

(a) to deliver cash or another financial asset to another party; or

(b) to exchange instruments with another party under conditions that are potentially unfavourable.

1.5. An equity instrument is any contract that evidences a residual interest in the assets of a party after deducting all of its liabilities.

1.6. Trading is the buying and selling of instruments with a view:
– to take advantage from variations or short term changes in market rates, indices or prices,
– to facilitate customer transactions,
– to hedge related trading positions.

Other activities are non-trading.

1.7. Fair value is the amount at which an asset could be exchanged or a liability settled in a current transaction entered into under normal terms and conditions between independent, informed and willing parties, other than in a forced or liquidation sale.

1.8. Information according to this recommendation need not concern:

(a) interests in subsidiaries;

(b) interests in associates;

(c) interests in joint ventures;

(d) employers' plans and obligations for post-employment benefits of all types, including retirement benefits;

(e) employers' obligations under employee stock option and stock purchase plans;

(f) obligations arising under insurance contracts;

(g) operating leases; take or pay contracts;

(h) own equity, own warrants and options on own shares.

2. Materiality principle

The recommendation's provisions need not be applied to immaterial items. In deciding whether instruments (either individually or in aggregate) are material, both the amount and the nature of the instruments should be taken into account.

Notwithstanding the obligation to disclose all material information, the potential usefulness of particular disclosures should be balanced against the need not to overburden financial statements with excessive disclosure and the likely cost of providing such information.

The level of detail to be disclosed should reflect the relative significance of activities, results and/or risks within the institution's overall business.

3. Qualitative disclosure

3.1 Qualitative information necessary for understanding the annual and consolidated accounts should be included in the notes to the accounts; other qualitative information should be included in either the notes to the accounts or elsewhere in the annual report.

3.2. Information should be disclosed in the annual report on the institution's risk management objectives and strategies reflecting its use of instruments within the context of its overall business objectives.

3.3. Information should be disclosed in the annual report on the policies and practice of managing the risks associated with trading and non-trading activities addressing the specific nature of the institution's exposure to, and its management of, credit risk, market risk (i.e. foreign exchange risk, interest rate risk, other price risks), liquidity risk and other risks of significance.

3.4. Information should be disclosed in the notes to the annual and consolidated accounts on all significant accounting policies relating to instruments.

4. Quantitative disclosure—principles and general information

4.1. Quantitative information necessary for the understanding of annual and consolidated accounts should be disclosed in institutions' notes to the annual and consolidated accounts. Other quantitative information should be included elsewhere in the annual report. Furthermore, the fair values of instruments held for trading, both on and off the balance sheet, should be disclosed where they differ materially from the amounts at which they are included in the accounts.

4.2. Where disclosure of quantitative information draws on institutions' internal risk management systems and the methods used within those systems (e.g. sensitivity analysis, VAR models) it is not necessary for the disclosure to be such as to disseminate information relating to those systems and methods that could be seriously prejudicial to the institution.

4.3. Appropriate analysis should be provided of trading and non-trading instruments, including information on the level of activity in the institution with respect to those instruments. The analysis should reflect in particular significant terms and conditions that may affect the amount, timing and certainty of future cash flows.

5. Quantitative disclosure—information on credit risk

5.1. Information on credit risk should be disclosed on the basis of the amount that best represents the maximum credit risk exposure at the balance sheet date (net of any netting agreements that are legally enforceable by the institution) without taking account of any collateral. Information on the maximum credit risk exposure should be complemented by information on the potential credit risk exposure taking into account collateral and other netting agreements.

If the carrying amount of an instrument represents the maximum credit risk exposure, disclosure of additional information, for the purposes of this paragraph, is not necessary.

5.2. Information should be disclosed on significant concentrations of credit risk from on- and off-balance-sheet exposures by economic sector and geographic location, for example, by different industry sectors, individual countries or groups of countries.

6. Quantitative disclosure—information on market risk

6.1. Information on market risk should be disclosed on the basis of value-at-risk, sensitivity analysis or other market price risk measure.

6.2. The different methods should be used alternatively or in combination in such a way as to provide a comprehensive picture of the institution's exposure to market risks inherent in its positions in trading and non-trading instruments. Where practicable, separate disclosures should be provided for each type of market risk.

Appendix 1

(This Appendix is purely illustrative and does not form part of the recommendation)

Information in relation to qualitative disclosure

(a) The basic features of management of risks including in particular the assessment and measurement of risk; if applicable, the internal limit system and the avoidance of undue concentrations of risk.

(b) The activities in instruments used for trading purposes.

(c) The activities in instruments used for non-trading purposes, reflecting in particular hedging policies.

(d) The activities in high-risk instruments or complex instruments such as leveraged derivative instruments.

(e) The use of collateral.

(f) The use of netting agreements.

Appendix 2

(This Appendix is purely illustrative and does not form part of the recommendation)

Disclosure of information in relation to accounting principles adopted

(a) Information on the method of applying these principles to:
– trading and non-trading instruments and their eventual reclassification,
– specific relationships between different instruments (e.g. synthetic instruments, hedging, termination of hedges, hedging by internal transactions, hedging of anticipated transactions),
– specific types of instruments or related transactions (e.g. disclosure may be necessary in particular for securitisations; repurchase and reverse repurchase agreements; in-substance defeasance), and
– primary instruments with embedded financial derivatives.

(b) The information disclosed might also include:
(i) the criteria applied for recognition and derecognition of instruments in the balance sheet;

(ii) the basis for valuation of the different types or classes of instruments at inception and subsequently;
(iii) the methods used for determining fair value of instruments (e.g. on the basis of quoted market prices, use of bid/ask/mid prices, discounted cash flow analysis, estimation techniques or some other appropriate method) including the significant assumptions made in applying these methods;
(iv) in cases where determination of fair value is based on quoted market prices the nature of the adjustments made to these prices, if any;
(v) the methods used for including in the profit and loss account gains and losses, interest and other items of income and expense associated with trading and non-trading instruments addressing in particular the recognition of income;
(vi) policies adopted in cases of hedging and termination of hedging relationships.

Appendix 3

(This Appendix is purely illustrative and does not form part of the recommendation)

Disclosure of complementary information to aid better understanding of quantitative information

Provision of complementary information on the terminology and the presentation forms used, on risk measurement methods, related assumptions and, as appropriate, other parameters can assist readers of financial statements better to understand the quantitative information supplied.

Where average values are disclosed the intervals used to arrive at those averages can also assist readers of financial statements better to understand the information supplied. If the year end figure is not representative of average values, average values can further assist understanding.

Appendix 4

(This Appendix is purely illustrative and does not form part of the recommendation)

Disclosure of quantitative information

1. Quantitative information may be disclosed in tabular form including in particular:

A. As an indication, inter alia, of the level of activity, with respect to primary instruments on the carrying amount:
(i) broken down on the vertical axis into the different classes of instruments distinguishing between assets and liabilities, and
(ii) broken down on the horizontal axis into residual maturities, with additional indication of fair value of trading totals.

B. As an indication, inter alia, of the level of activity with respect to derivative instruments, on the notional amount:
(i) broken down on the vertical axis into the different classes of derivative instruments (e.g. interest rate, foreign exchange and gold, equities, precious metals except gold, other commodities, other), further subdivided into:
   – OTC derivative instruments (with subcategories e.g. forwards, swaps, options purchased/written), and
   – exchange traded derivative instruments (with as sub-categories e.g. futures long/short, options purchased/written); and
(ii) broken down on the horizontal axis into residual maturities with additional indication of fair value of trading totals.

C. Time bands that are relevant for the information disclosed may be used, for example:
(i) not more than three months;
(ii) more than three but not more than six months;
(iii) more than six months but not more than one year;
(iv) more than one year but not more than five years;
(v) more than five years.

Subject to materiality, the time bands specified may be further broken down (e.g. ≤ one month; > one ≤ three months) or merged to larger time bands (e.g. ≤ one year; > one and ≤ five years; > five years) as appropriate.

D. As an indication, inter alia, of the level of activity in terms of fair value as opposed to the carrying amount, information may be disclosed in tabular form distinguishing between assets and liabilities
– on carrying amounts and fair values of classes of trading instruments, and

– for trading instruments, on average-of-period fair values, and:

if the determination of fair value is not possible, practicable or reliable, additional information on the principal characteristics of the instrument that may affect its fair value.

2. The above information could also be disclosed in tabular form combining the tabular formats set out above.

Appendix 5

(This Appendix is purely illustrative and does not form part of the recommendation)

Credit risk disclosure

With respect to the credit risk exposure from OTC derivative instruments, information may be disclosed in tabular form:
- broken down on the vertical axis into different degrees of credit worthiness of counterparties assessed on the basis of internal or external ratings; and
- broken down on the horizontal axis into:
- gross replacement costs,
- net replacement costs if enforceable netting agreements exist,
- potential future credit exposure.

Undertakings that calculate the credit risk of OTC derivative instruments on the basis of the original risk method may disclose only the information that is obtained by applying the said method.

Information on the potential future credit exposures may be complemented by a discussion of the related estimation techniques.

Appendix 6

(This Appendix is purely illustrative and does not form part of the recommendation)

Market risk disclosure

Information on market risk arising on instruments may be given on any of the following basis.

A. Value at risk information.

B. The potential effect on future earnings of selected hypothetical changes in market prices and rates. The hypothetical changes used should be reasonably possible during the 12 months following the date on which the annual or consolidated accounts are approved. One of these hypothetical changes might usefully include an adverse change of at least 10% in the year-end market prices or rates (unless such a change may be demonstrated not to be reasonably possible).

C. A market price measure, other than those covered by A and B provided that:
(i) the institution's management uses the model from which the measure has been derived for the purpose of managing the market price risk arising from the use of trading instruments; and
(ii) the model has been recognised for the purpose of providing capital adequacy returns to the prudential regulator.

D. An analysis of the aggregate fair values by major categories of financial assets and financial liabilities arising from trading instruments and, within those categories, by time bands according to the earlier of the period to the next interest rate repricing or the maturity date.

Time bands that are relevant for the information disclosed may be used, for example:
(i) not more than three months;
(ii) more than three but not more than six months;
(iii) more than six months but not more than one year;
(iv) more than one year but not more than five years;
(v) more than five years.

If the value at risk, sensitivity analysis or other market price risk measure figures disclosed are not typical of the figures during the financial year, then additional figures provided to put the figures at the balance sheet date in context can assist readers of financial statements to better understand the information supplied. These additional figures might be either the average values or the highest and lowest.

B. 34.

European Parliament and Council Directive 2000/28/EC of 18 September 2000 amending Directive 2000/12/EC relating to the taking up and pursuit of the business of credit institutions[1]

This Directive has been repealed as from 20 July 2006 by article 158 of Directive 2006/48/EC (OJ L 177, 30.06.2006, 1) reproduced infra under no. B. 41.

Correlation Table

Directive 2000/28/EC	Directive 2006/48/EC
Article 1(2) to (5)	Article 4(2) to (5)
Article 1(6) to (8)	Article 4(7) to (9)

---

[1] OJ L 275, 27.10.2000, 37–38.

B. 35.

European Parliament and Council Directive 2000/46/EC of 18 September 2000 on the taking up, pursuit of and prudential supervision of the business of electronic money institutions[1]

THE EUROPEAN PARLIAMENT AND THE COUNCIL OF THE EUROPEAN UNION,

Having regard to the Treaty establishing the European Community, and in particular the first and third sentences of Article 47(2) thereof,

Having regard to the proposal from the Commission,[2]

Having regard to the opinion of the Economic and Social Committee,[3]

Having regard to the opinion of the European Central Bank,[4]

Acting in accordance with the procedure laid down in Article 251 of the Treaty,[5]

Whereas:

(1) Credit institutions within the meaning of Article 1, point 1, first subparagraph (b) of Directive 2000/12/EC[6] are limited in the scope of their activities.

---

[1] OJ L 275, 27.10.2000, 39–43.
[2] OJ C 317, 15.10.1998, 7.
[3] OJ C 101, 12.4.1999, 64.
[4] OJ C 189, 6.7.1999, 7.
[5] Opinion of the European Parliament of 15 April 1999 (OJ C 219, 30.7.1999, 415), confirmed on 27 October 1999, Council Common Position of 29 November 1999 (OJ C 26, 28.1.2000, 1) and Decision of the European Parliament of 11 April 2000 (not yet published in the Official Journal). Decision of the Council of 16 June 2000.
[6] Directive 2000/12/EC of the European Parliament and of the Council of 20 March 2000 relating to the taking up and pursuit of the business of credit institutions (OJ L 126, 26.5.2000, 1), reproduced supra under no. B. 32. Directive as last amended by Directive 2000/28/EC (OJ L 275, 27.10.2000, 39), reproduced supra under no. B. 34. As from 20 July 2006 Directive 2000/12/EC has been repealed by article 158 of Directive 2006/48/EC (OJ L 177, 30.6.2006, 1), reproduced infra under no. B. 41.

(2) It is necessary to take account of the specific characteristics of these institutions and to provide the appropriate measures necessary to co-ordinate and harmonise Member States' laws, regulations and administrative provisions relating to the taking up, pursuit and prudential supervision of the business of electronic money institutions.

(3) For the purposes of this Directive, electronic money can be considered an electronic surrogate for coins and banknotes, which is stored on an electronic device such as a chip card or computer memory and which is generally intended for the purpose of effecting electronic payments of limited amounts.

(4) The approach adopted is appropriate to achieve only the essential harmonisation necessary and sufficient to secure the mutual recognition of authorisation and prudential supervision of electronic money institutions, making possible the granting of a single licence recognised throughout the Community and designed to ensure bearer confidence and the application of the principle of home Member State prudential supervision.

(5) Within the wider context of the rapidly evolving electronic commerce it is desirable to provide a regulatory framework that assists electronic money in delivering its full potential benefits and that avoids hampering technological innovation in particular. Therefore, this Directive introduces a technology-neutral legal framework that harmonises the prudential supervision of electronic money institutions to the extent necessary for ensuring their sound and prudent operation and their financial integrity in particular.

(6) Credit institutions, by virtue of point 5 of Annex I to Directive 2000/12/EC, are already allowed to issue and administer means of payment including electronic money and to carry on such activities Community-wide subject to mutual recognition and to the comprehensive prudential supervisory system applying to them in accordance with the European banking Directives.

(7) The introduction of a separate prudential supervisory regime for electronic money institutions, which, although calibrated on the prudential supervisory regime applying to other credit institutions and Directive 2000/12/EC except Title V, Chapters 2 and 3 thereof in particular, differs from that regime, is justified and desirable because the issuance of electronic money does not constitute in itself, in view of its specific character as an electronic surrogate for coins and banknotes, a deposit-taking activity pursuant to Article 3 of Directive 2000/12/EC, if the received funds are immediately exchanged for electronic money.

(8) The receipt of funds from the public in exchange for electronic money, which results in a credit balance left on account with the issuing institution, constitutes the receipt of deposits or other repayable funds for the purpose of Directive 2000/12/EC.

(9) It is necessary for electronic money to be redeemable to ensure bearer confidence. Redeemability does not imply, in itself, that the funds received in exchange for electronic money shall be regarded as deposits or other repayable funds for the purpose of Directive 2000/12/EC.

(10) Redeemability should always be understood to be at par value.

(11) In order to respond to the specific risks associated with the issuance of electronic money this prudential supervisory regime must be more targeted and, accordingly, less cumbersome than the prudential supervisory regime applying to credit institutions, notably as regards reduced initial capital requirements and the non-application of Directive 93/6/EEC[7] and Title V, Chapter 2, Sections II and III of Directive 2000/12/EC.

(12) However, it is necessary to preserve a level playing field between electronic money institutions and other credit institutions issuing electronic money and, thus, to ensure fair competition among a wider range of institutions to the benefit of bearers. This is achieved since the abovementioned less cumbersome features of the prudential supervisory regime applying to electronic money institutions are balanced by provisions that are more stringent than those applying to other credit institutions, notably as regards restrictions on the business activities which electronic money institutions may carry on and, particularly, prudent limitations of their investments aimed at ensuring that their financial liabilities related to outstanding electronic money are backed at all times by sufficiently liquid low risk assets.

(13) Pending the harmonisation of prudential supervision of outsourced activities for credit institutions it is appropriate that electronic money institutions have sound and prudent management and control procedures. With a view to the possibility of operational and other ancillary functions related to the issuance of electronic money being performed by undertakings which are not subject to prudential supervision it is essential that electronic money institutions have in place internal structures which should respond to the financial and non-financial risks to which they are exposed.

(14) The issuance of electronic money may affect the stability of the financial system and the smooth operation of payments systems. Close

---

[7] Council Directive 93/6/EEC of 15 March 1993 on the capital adequacy of investment firms and credit institutions (OJ L 141, 11.6.1993, 1), reproduced supra under no. B. 20. Directive as last amended by Directive 98/33/EC (OJ L 204, 21.7.1998, 29), consolidated in Directive 2000/12/EC, reproduced supra under no. B. 32. Directive 93/6/EEC has been repealed as from 20 July 2006 by article 52 of Directive 2006/49/EC (OJ L 177, 30.6.2006, 201), reproduced infra under no. B. 42.

co-operation in assessing the integrity of electronic money schemes is called for.

(15) It is appropriate to afford competent authorities the possibility of waiving some or all of the requirements imposed by this Directive for electronic money institutions which operate only within the territories of the respective Member States.

(16) Adoption of this Directive constitutes the most appropriate means of achieving the desired objectives. This Directive is limited to the minimum necessary to achieve these objectives and does not go beyond what is necessary for this purpose.

(17) Provision should be made for the review of this Directive in the light of experience of developments in the market and the protection of bearers of electronic money.

(18) The Banking Advisory Committee has been consulted on the adoption of this Directive,

HAVE ADOPTED THIS DIRECTIVE:

Article 1

Scope, definitions and restriction of activities

1. This Directive shall apply to electronic money institutions.

2. It shall not apply to the institutions referred to in Article 2(3) of Directive 2000/12/EC.

3. For the purposes of this Directive:

(a) "electronic money institution" shall mean an undertaking or any other legal person, other than a credit institution as defined in Article 1, point 1, first subparagraph (a) of Directive 2000/12/EC which issues means of payment in the form of electronic money;

(b) "electronic money" shall mean monetary value as represented by a claim on the issuer which is:
(i) stored on an electronic device;
(ii) issued on receipt of funds of an amount not less in value than the monetary value issued;
(iii) accepted as means of payment by undertakings other than the issuer.

4. Member States shall prohibit persons or undertakings that are not credit institutions, as defined in Article 1, point 1, first subparagraph of Directive 2000/12/EC, from carrying on the business of issuing electronic money.

5. The business activities of electronic money institutions other than the issuing of electronic money shall be restricted to:

(a) the provision of closely related financial and non-financial services such as the administering of electronic money by the performance of operational and other ancillary functions related to its issuance, and the issuing and administering of other means of payment but excluding the granting of any form of credit; and

(b) the storing of data on the electronic device on behalf of other undertakings or public institutions.

Electronic money institutions shall not have any holdings in other undertakings except where these undertakings perform operational or other ancillary functions related to electronic money issued or distributed by the institution concerned.

Article 2

Application of Banking Directives

1. Save where otherwise expressly provided for, only references to credit institutions in Directive 91/308/EEC[8] and Directive 2000/12/EC except Title V, Chapter 2 thereof shall apply to electronic money institutions.

2. Articles 5, 11, 13, 19, 20(7), 51 and 59 of Directive 2000/12/EC shall not apply. The mutual recognition arrangements provided for in Directive 2000/12/EC shall not apply to electronic money institutions' business activities other than the issuance of electronic money.

3. The receipt of funds within the meaning of Article 1(3)(b)(ii) does not constitute a deposit or other repayable funds according to Article 3 of

---

[8] Council Directive 91/308/EEC of 10 June 1991 on prevention of the use of the financial system for the purpose of money laundering (OJ L 166, 28.6.1991, 77), reproduced supra under no. B. 15.

Directive 2000/12/EC, if the funds received are immediately exchanged for electronic money.

Article 3
Redeemability

1. A bearer of electronic money may, during the period of validity, ask the issuer to redeem it at par value in coins and bank notes or by a transfer to an account free of charges other than those strictly necessary to carry out that operation.

2. The contract between the issuer and the bearer shall clearly state the conditions of redemption.

3. The contract may stipulate a minimum threshold for redemption. The threshold may not exceed EUR 10.

Article 4
Initial capital and ongoing own funds requirements

1. Electronic money institutions shall have an initial capital, as defined in Article 34(2), subparagraphs (1) and (2) of Directive 2000/12/EC, of not less than EUR 1 million. Notwithstanding paragraphs 2 and 3, their own funds, as defined in Directive 2000/12/EC, shall not fall below that amount.

2. Electronic money institutions shall have at all times own funds which are equal to or above 2% of the higher of the current amount or the average of the preceding six months' total amount of their financial liabilities related to outstanding electronic money.

3. Where an electronic money institution has not completed a six months' period of business, including the day it starts up, it shall have own funds which are equal to or above 2% of the higher of the current amount or the six months' target total amount of its financial liabilities related to outstanding electronic money. The six months' target total amount of the institution's financial liabilities related to outstanding electronic money shall be evidenced by its business plan subject to any adjustment to that plan having been required by the competent authorities.

Article 5
Limitations of investments

1. Electronic money institutions shall have investments of an amount of no less than their financial liabilities related to outstanding electronic money in the following assets only:

(a) asset items which according to Article 43(1)(a) (1), (2), (3) and (4) and Article 44(1) of Directive 2000/12/EC attract a zero credit risk weighting and which are sufficiently liquid;

(b) sight deposits held with Zone A credit institutions as defined in Directive 2000/12/EC; and

(c) debt instruments which are:
(i) sufficiently liquid;
(ii) not covered by paragraph 1(a);
(iii) recognised by competent authorities as qualifying items within the meaning of Article 2(12) of Directive 93/6/EEC; and
(iv) issued by undertakings other than undertakings which have a qualifying holding, as defined in Article 1 of Directive 2000/12/EC, in the electronic money institution concerned or which must be included in those undertakings' consolidated accounts.

2. Investments referred to in paragraph 1(b) and (c) may not exceed 20 times the own funds of the electronic money institution concerned and shall be subject to limitations which are at least as stringent as those applying to credit institutions in accordance with Title V, Chapter 2, Section III of Directive 2000/12/EC.

3. For the purpose of hedging market risks arising from the issuance of electronic money and from the investments referred to in paragraph 1, electronic money institutions may use sufficiently liquid interest-rate and foreign-exchange-related off balance-sheet items in the form of exchange-traded (i.e. not OTC) derivative instruments where they are subject to daily margin requirements or foreign exchange contracts with an original maturity of 14 calendar days or less. The use of derivative instruments according to the first sentence is permissible only if the full elimination of market risks is intended and, to the extent possible, achieved.

4. Member States shall impose appropriate limitations on the market risks electronic money

institutions may incur from the investments referred to in paragraph 1.

5. For the purpose of applying paragraph 1, assets shall be valued at the lower of cost or market value.

6. If the value of the assets referred to in paragraph 1 falls below the amount of financial liabilities related to outstanding electronic money, the competent authorities shall ensure that the electronic money institution in question takes appropriate measures to remedy that situation promptly. To this end, and for a temporary period only, the competent authorities may allow the institution's financial liabilities related to outstanding electronic money to be backed by assets other than those referred to in paragraph 1 up to an amount not exceeding the lower of 5% of these liabilities or the institution's total amount of own funds.

Article 6
Verification of specific requirements by the competent authorities

The competent authorities shall ensure that the calculations justifying compliance with Articles 4 and 5 are made, not less than twice each year, either by electronic money institutions themselves, which shall communicate them, and any component data required, to the competent authorities, or by competent authorities, using data supplied by the electronic money institutions.

Article 7
Sound and prudent operation

Electronic money institutions shall have sound and prudent management, administrative and accounting procedures and adequate internal control mechanisms. These should respond to the financial and non-financial risks to which the institution is exposed including technical and procedural risks as well as risks connected to its co-operation with any undertaking performing operational or other ancillary functions related to its business activities.

Article 8
Waiver

1. Member States may allow their competent authorities to waive the application of some or all of the provisions of this Directive and the application of Directive 2000/12/EC to electronic money institutions in cases where either:

(a) the total business activities of the type referred to in Article 1(3)(a) of this Directive of the institution generate a total amount of financial liabilities related to outstanding electronic money that normally does not exceed EUR 5 million and never exceeds EUR 6 million; or

(b) the electronic money issued by the institution is accepted as a means of payment only by any subsidiaries of the institution which perform operational or other ancillary functions related to electronic money issued or distributed by the institution, any parent undertaking of the institution or any other subsidiaries of that parent undertaking; or

(c) electronic money issued by the institution is accepted as payment only by a limited number of undertakings, which can be clearly distinguished by:
(i) their location in the same premises or other limited local area; or
(ii) their close financial or business relationship with the issuing institution, such as a common marketing or distribution scheme.

The underlying contractual arrangements must provide that the electronic storage device at the disposal of bearers for the purpose of making payments is subject to a maximum storage amount of not more than EUR 150.

2. An electronic money institution for which a waiver has been granted under paragraph 1 shall not benefit from the mutual recognition arrangements provided for in Directive 2000/12/EC.

3. Member States shall require that all electronic money institutions to which the application of this Directive and Directive 2000/12/EC has been waived report periodically on their activities including the total amount of financial liabilities related to electronic money.

Article 9
Grandfathering

Electronic money institutions subject to this Directive which have commenced their activity in accordance with the provisions in force in the Member State in which they have their head office before the date of entry into force of the provisions adopted in implementation of this Directive or the date referred to in Article 10(1), whichever date is earlier, shall be presumed to be authorised. The Member States shall oblige such electronic money institutions to submit all relevant information to the competent authorities in order to allow them to assess within six months from the date of entry into force of the provisions adopted in implementation of this Directive, whether the institutions comply with the requirements pursuant to this Directive, which measures need to be taken in order to ensure compliance, or whether a withdrawal of authorisation is appropriate. If compliance is not ensured within six months from the date referred to in Article 10(1), the electronic money institution shall not benefit from mutual recognition after that time.

Article 10
Implementation

1. Member States shall bring into force the laws, regulations and administrative provisions necessary to comply with this Directive not later than 27 April 2002. They shall immediately inform the Commission thereof.

When Member States adopt these measures, they shall contain a reference to this Directive or shall be accompanied by such reference on the occasion of their official publication. The methods of making such a reference shall be laid down by the Member States.

2. Member States shall communicate to the Commission the text of the main provisions of national law, which they adopt in the field covered by this Directive.

Article 11
Review

Not later than 27 April 2005 the Commission shall present a report to the European Parliament and the Council on the application of this Directive, in particular on:
– the measures to protect the bearers of electronic money, including the possible need to introduce a guarantee scheme,
– capital requirements,
– waivers, and
– the possible need to prohibit interest being paid on funds received in exchange for electronic money, accompanied where appropriate by a proposal for its revision.

Article 12
Entry into force

This Directive shall enter into force on the day of its publication in the *Official Journal of the European Communities*.

Article 13

This Directive is addressed to the Member States.

B. 36.

European Parliament and Council Directive 2001/24/EC of 4 April 2001 on the reorganisation and winding up of credit institutions[1]

THE EUROPEAN PARLIAMENT AND THE COUNCIL OF THE EUROPEAN UNION,

Having regard to the Treaty establishing the European Community, and in particular Article 47(2) thereof,

Having regard to the proposal from the Commission,[2]

Having regard to the opinion of the Economic and Social Committee,[3]

Having regard to the opinion of the European Monetary Institute,[4]

Acting in accordance with the procedure laid down in Article 251 of the Treaty[5]

Whereas:

(1) In accordance with the objectives of the Treaty, the harmonious and balanced development of economic activities throughout the Community should be promoted through the elimination of any obstacles to the freedom of establishment and the freedom to provide services within the Community.

(2) At the same time as those obstacles are eliminated, consideration should be given to the situation which might arise if a credit institution runs into difficulties, particularly where that institution has branches in other Member States.

(3) This Directive forms part of the Community legislative framework set up by Directive 2000/12/EC of the European Parliament and of the Council of 20 March 2000 relating to the taking up and pursuit of the business of credit institutions.[6] It follows therefrom that, while they are in operation, a credit institution and its branches form a single entity subject to the supervision of the competent authorities of the State where authorisation valid throughout the Community was granted.

(4) It would be particularly undesirable to relinquish such unity between an institution and its branches where it is necessary to adopt reorganisation measures or open winding-up proceedings.

(5) The adoption of Directive 94/19/EC of the European Parliament and of the Council of 30 May 1994 on deposit-guarantee schemes,[7] which introduced the principle of compulsory membership by credit institutions of a guarantee scheme in their home Member State, brings out even more clearly the need for mutual recognition of reorganisation measures and winding-up proceedings.

(6) The administrative or judicial authorities of the home Member State must have sole power to decide upon and to implement the reorganisation measures provided for in the law and practices in force in that Member State. Owing to the difficulty of harmonising Member States' laws and practices, it is necessary to establish mutual

---

[1] OJ L 125, 5.5.2001, 15–23.
[2] OJ C 356, 31.12.1985, 55 and OJ C 36, 8.2.1988, 1.
[3] OJ C 263, 20.10.1986, 13.
[4] OJ C 332, 30.10.1998, 13.
[5] Opinion of the European Parliament of 13 March 1987 (OJ C 99, 13.4.1987, 211), confirmed on 2 December 1993 (OJ C 342, 20.12.1993, 30), Council Common Position of 17 July 2000 (OJ C 300, 20.10.2000, 13) and Decision of the European Parliament of 16 January 2001 (OJ C 262, 18.9.2001, 40). Council Decision of 12 March 2001.

[6] OJ L 126, 26.5.2000, 1, reproduced supra under no. B. 32. Directive as amended by Directive 2000/28/EC (OJ L 275, 27.10.2000, 37), reproduced supra under no. B. 34. Directive 2000/12/EC has been repealed as from 20 July 2006 by article 158 of Directive 2006/48/EC (OJ L 177, 30.6.2006, 1), reproduced infra under no. B. 41.
[7] OJ L 135, 31.5.1994, 5, reproduced supra under no. B. 22.

recognition by the Member States of the measures taken by each of them to restore to viability the credit institutions which it has authorised.

(7) It is essential to guarantee that the reorganisation measures adopted by the administrative or judicial authorities of the home Member State and the measures adopted by persons or bodies appointed by those authorities to administer those reorganisation measures, including measures involving the possibility of a suspension of payments, suspension of enforcement measures or reduction of claims and any other measure which could affect third parties' existing rights, are effective in all Member States.

(8) Certain measures, in particular those affecting the functioning of the internal structure of credit institutions or managers' or shareholders' rights, need not be covered by this Directive to be effective in Member States insofar as, pursuant to the rules of private international law, the applicable law is that of the home State.

(9) Certain measures, in particular those connected with the continued fulfilment of conditions of authorisation, are already the subject of mutual recognition pursuant to Directive 2000/12/EC insofar as they do not affect the rights of third parties existing before their adoption.

(10) Persons participating in the operation of the internal structures of credit institutions as well as managers and shareholders of such institutions, considered in those capacities, are not to be regarded as third parties for the purposes of this Directive.

(11) It is necessary to notify third parties of the implementation of reorganisation measures in Member States where branches are situated when such measures could hinder the exercise of some of their rights.

(12) The principle of equal treatment between creditors, as regards the opportunities open to them to take action, requires the administrative or judicial authorities of the home Member State to adopt such measures as are necessary for the creditors in the host Member State to be able to exercise their rights to take action within the time limit laid down.

(13) There must be some co-ordination of the role of the administrative or judicial authorities in reorganisation measures and winding-up proceedings for branches of credit institutions having head offices outside the Community and situated in different Member States.

(14) In the absence of reorganisation measures, or in the event of such measures failing, the credit institutions in difficulty must be wound up. Provision should be made in such cases for mutual recognition of winding-up proceedings and of their effects in the Community.

(15) The important role played by the competent authorities of the home Member State before winding-up proceedings are opened may continue during the process of winding up so that these proceedings can be properly carried out.

(16) Equal treatment of creditors requires that the credit institution is wound up according to the principles of unity and universality, which require the administrative or judicial authorities of the home Member State to have sole jurisdiction and their decisions to be recognised and to be capable of producing in all the other Member States, without any formality, the effects ascribed to them by the law of the home Member State, except where this Directive provides otherwise.

(17) The exemption concerning the effects of reorganisation measures and winding-up proceedings on certain contracts and rights is limited to those effects and does not cover other questions concerning reorganisation measures and winding-up proceedings such as the lodging, verification, admission and ranking of claims concerning those contracts and rights and the rules governing the distribution of the proceeds of the realisation of the assets, which are governed by the law of the home Member State.

(18) Voluntary winding up is possible when a credit institution is solvent. The administrative or judicial authorities of the home Member State may nevertheless, where appropriate, decide on a reorganisation measure or winding-up proceedings, even after voluntary winding up has commenced.

(19) Withdrawal of authorisation to pursue the business of banking is one of the consequences

which winding up a credit institution necessarily entails. Withdrawal should not, however, prevent certain activities of the institution from continuing insofar as is necessary or appropriate for the purposes of winding up. Such a continuation of activity may nonetheless be made subject by the home Member State to the consent of, and supervision by, its competent authorities.

(20) Provision of information to known creditors on an individual basis is as essential as publication to enable them, where necessary, to lodge their claims or submit observations relating to their claims within the prescribed time limits. This should take place without discrimination against creditors domiciled in a Member State other than the home Member State, based on their place of residence or the nature of their claims. Creditors must be kept regularly informed in an appropriate manner throughout winding-up proceedings.

(21) For the sole purpose of applying the provisions of this Directive to reorganisation measures and winding-up proceedings involving branches located in the Community of a credit institution of which the head office is situated in a third country, the definitions of "home Member State", "competent authorities" and "administrative or judicial authorities" should be those of the Member State in which the branch is located.

(22) Where a credit institution which has its head office outside the Community possesses branches in more than one Member State, each branch should receive individual treatment in regard to the application of this Directive. In such a case, the administrative or judicial authorities and the competent authorities as well as the administrators and liquidators should endeavour to co-ordinate their activities.

(23) Although it is important to follow the principle that the law of the home Member State determines all the effects of reorganisation measures or winding-up proceedings, both procedural and substantive, it is also necessary to bear in mind that those effects may conflict with the rules normally applicable in the context of the economic and financial activity of the credit institution in question and its branches in other Member States. In some cases reference to the law of another Member State represents an unavoidable qualification of the principle that the law of the home Member State is to apply.

(24) That qualification is especially necessary to protect employees having a contract of employment with a credit institution, ensure the security of transactions in respect of certain types of property and protect the integrity of regulated markets functioning in accordance with the law of a Member State on which financial instruments are traded.

(25) Transactions carried out in the framework of a payment and settlement system are covered by Directive 98/26/EC of the European Parliament and of the Council of 19 May 1998 on settlement finality in payment and securities settlement systems.[8]

(26) The adoption of this Directive does not call into question the provisions of Directive 98/26/EC according to which insolvency proceedings must not have any effect on the enforceability of orders validly entered into a system, or on collateral provided for a system.

(27) Some reorganisation measures or winding-up proceedings involve the appointment of a person to administer them. The recognition of his appointment and his powers in all other Member States is therefore an essential factor in the implementation of decisions taken in the home Member State. However, the limits within which he may exercise his powers when he acts outside the home Member State should be specified.

(28) Creditors who have entered into contracts with a credit institution before a reorganisation measure is adopted or winding-up proceedings are opened should be protected against provisions relating to voidness, voidability or unenforceability laid down in the law of the home Member State, where the beneficiary of the transaction produces evidence that in the law applicable to that transaction there is no available means of contesting the act concerned in the case in point.

(29) The confidence of third-party purchasers in the content of the registers or accounts regarding certain assets entered in those registers or accounts

---

[8] OJ L 166, 11.6.1998, 45, reproduced infra under no. S. 17.

and by extension of the purchasers of immovable property should be safeguarded, even after winding-up proceedings have been opened or a reorganisation measure adopted. The only means of safeguarding that confidence is to make the validity of the purchase subject to the law of the place where the immovable asset is situated or of the State under whose authority the register or account is kept.

(30) The effects of reorganisation measures or winding-up proceedings on a lawsuit pending are governed by the law of the Member State in which the lawsuit is pending, by way of exception to the application of the lex concursus. The effects of those measures and procedures on individual enforcement actions arising from such lawsuits are governed by the legislation of the home Member State, in accordance with the general rule established by this Directive.

(31) Provision should be made for the administrative or judicial authorities in the home Member State to notify immediately the competent authorities of the host Member State of the adoption of any reorganisation measure or the opening of any winding-up proceedings, if possible before the adoption of the measure or the opening of the proceedings, or, if not, immediately afterwards.

(32) Professional secrecy as defined in Article 30 of Directive 2000/12/EC is an essential factor in all information or consultation procedures. For that reason it should be respected by all the administrative authorities taking part in such procedures, whereas the judicial authorities remain, in this respect, subject to the national provisions relating to them,

HAVE ADOPTED THIS DIRECTIVE:

TITLE I

SCOPE AND DEFINITIONS

Article 1

Scope

1. This Directive shall apply to credit institutions and their branches set up in Member States other than those in which they have their head offices, as defined in points (1) and (3) of Article 1 of Directive 2000/12/EC, subject to the conditions and exemptions laid down in Article 2(3) of that Directive.

2. The provisions of this Directive concerning the branches of a credit institution having a head office outside the Community shall apply only where that institution has branches in at least two Member States of the Community.

Article 2

Definitions

For the purposes of this Directive:
- "home Member State" shall mean the Member State of origin within the meaning of Article 1, point (6) of Directive 2000/12/EC;
- "host Member State" shall mean the host Member State within the meaning of Article 1, point (7) of Directive 2000/12/EC;
- "branch" shall mean a branch within the meaning of Article 1, point (3) of Directive 2000/12/EC;
- "competent authorities" shall mean the competent authorities within the meaning of Article 1, point (4) of Directive 2000/12/EC;
- "administrator" shall mean any person or body appointed by the administrative or judicial authorities whose task is to administer reorganisation measures;
- "administrative or judicial authorities" shall mean such administrative or judicial authorities of the Member States as are competent for the purposes of reorganisation measures or winding-up proceedings;
- "reorganisation measures" shall mean measures which are intended to preserve or restore the financial situation of a credit institution and which could affect third parties' pre-existing rights, including measures involving the possibility of a suspension of payments, suspension of enforcement measures or reduction of claims;
- "liquidator" shall mean any person or body appointed by the administrative or judicial authorities whose task is to administer winding-up proceedings;
- "winding-up proceedings" shall mean collective proceedings opened and monitored by the

administrative or judicial authorities of a Member State with the aim of realising assets under the supervision of those authorities, including where the proceedings are terminated by a composition or other, similar measure;
- "regulated market" shall mean a regulated market within the meaning of Article 1, point (13) of Directive 93/22/EEC;
- "instruments" shall mean all the instruments referred to in Section B of the Annex to Directive 93/22/EEC.

Title II
Reorganisation Measures

A. Credit institutions having their head offices within the Community

Article 3
Adoption of reorganisation measures— applicable law

1. The administrative or judicial authorities of the home Member State shall alone be empowered to decide on the implementation of one or more reorganisation measures in a credit institution, including branches established in other Member States.

2. The reorganisation measures shall be applied in accordance with the laws, regulations and procedures applicable in the home Member State, unless otherwise provided in this Directive.

They shall be fully effective in accordance with the legislation of that Member State throughout the Community without any further formalities, including as against third parties in other Member States, even where the rules of the host Member State applicable to them do not provide for such measures or make their implementation subject to conditions which are not fulfilled.

The reorganisation measures shall be effective throughout the Community once they become effective in the Member State where they have been taken.

Article 4
Information for the competent authorities of the host Member State

The administrative or judicial authorities of the home Member State shall without delay inform, by any available means, the competent authorities of the host Member State of their decision to adopt any reorganisation measure, including the practical effects which such a measure may have, if possible before it is adopted or otherwise immediately thereafter. Information shall be communicated by the competent authorities of the home Member State.

Article 5
Information for the supervisory authorities of the home Member State

Where the administrative or judicial authorities of the host Member State deem it necessary to implement within their territory one or more reorganisation measures, they shall inform the competent authorities of the home Member State accordingly. Information shall be communicated by the host Member State's competent authorities.

Article 6
Publication

1. Where implementation of the reorganisation measures decided on pursuant to Article 3(1) and (2) is likely to affect the rights of third parties in a host Member State and where an appeal may be brought in the home Member State against the decision ordering the measure, the administrative or judicial authorities of the home Member State, the administrator or any person empowered to do so in the home Member State shall publish an extract from the decision in the Official Journal of the European Communities and in two national newspapers in each host Member State, in order in particular to facilitate the exercise of the right of appeal in good time.

2. The extract from the decision provided for in paragraph 1 shall be forwarded at the earliest opportunity, by the most appropriate route, to the Office for Official Publications of the

European Communities and to the two national newspapers in each host Member State.

3. The Office for Official Publications of the European Communities shall publish the extract at the latest within twelve days of its dispatch.

4. The extract from the decision to be published shall specify, in the official language or languages of the Member States concerned, in particular the purpose and legal basis of the decision taken, the time limits for lodging appeals, specifically a clearly understandable indication of the date of expiry of the time limits, and the full address of the authorities or court competent to hear an appeal.

5. The reorganisation measures shall apply irrespective of the measures prescribed in paragraphs 1 to 3 and shall be fully effective as against creditors, unless the administrative or judicial authorities of the home Member State or the law of that State governing such measures provide otherwise.

Article 7

Duty to inform known creditors and right to lodge claims

1. Where the legislation of the home Member State requires lodgement of a claim with a view to its recognition or provides for compulsory notification of the measure to creditors who have their domiciles, normal places of residence or head offices in that State, the administrative or judicial authorities of the home Member State or the administrator shall also inform known creditors who have their domiciles, normal places of residence or head offices in other Member States, in accordance with the procedures laid down in Articles 14 and 17(1).

2. Where the legislation of the home Member State provides for the right of creditors who have their domiciles, normal places of residence or head offices in that State to lodge claims or to submit observations concerning their claims, creditors who have their domiciles, normal places of residence or head offices in other Member States shall also have that right in accordance with the procedures laid down in Article 16 and Article 17(2).

B. Credit institutions having their head offices outside the Community

Article 8

Branches of third-country credit institutions

1. The administrative or judicial authorities of the host Member State of a branch of a credit institution having its head office outside the Community shall without delay inform, by any available means, the competent authorities of the other host Member States in which the institution has set up branches which are included on the list referred to in Article 11 of Directive 2000/12/EC and published each year in the Official Journal of the European Communities, of their decision to adopt any reorganisation measure, including the practical effects which that measure may have, if possible before it is adopted or otherwise immediately thereafter. Information shall be communicated by the competent authorities of the host Member State whose administrative or judicial authorities decide to apply the measure.

2. The administrative or judicial authorities referred to in paragraph 1 shall endeavour to co-ordinate their actions.

Title III

Winding-Up Proceedings

A. Credit institutions having their head offices within the Community

Article 9

Opening of winding-up proceedings—Information to be communicated to other competent authorities

1. The administrative or judicial authorities of the home Member State which are responsible for winding up shall alone be empowered to decide on the opening of winding-up proceedings concerning a credit institution, including branches established in other Member States.

A decision to open winding-up proceedings taken by the administrative or judicial authority of the home Member State shall be recognised, without further formality, within the territory of all other Member States and shall be effective there when the decision is effective in the Member State in which the proceedings are opened.

2. The administrative or judicial authorities of the home Member State shall without delay inform, by any available means, the competent authorities of the host Member State of their decision to open winding-up proceedings, including the practical effects which such proceedings may have, if possible before they open or otherwise immediately thereafter. Information shall be communicated by the competent authorities of the home Member State.

Article 10

Law applicable

1. A credit institution shall be wound up in accordance with the laws, regulations and procedures applicable in its home Member State insofar as this Directive does not provide otherwise.

2. The law of the home Member State shall determine in particular:

(a) the goods subject to administration and the treatment of goods acquired by the credit institution after the opening of winding-up proceedings;

(b) the respective powers of the credit institution and the liquidator;

(c) the conditions under which set-offs may be invoked;

(d) the effects of winding-up proceedings on current contracts to which the credit institution is party;

(e) the effects of winding-up proceedings on proceedings brought by individual creditors, with the exception of lawsuits pending, as provided for in Article 32;

(f) the claims which are to be lodged against the credit institution and the treatment of claims arising after the opening of winding-up proceedings;

(g) the rules governing the lodging, verification and admission of claims;

(h) the rules governing the distribution of the proceeds of the realisation of assets, the ranking of claims and the rights of creditors who have obtained partial satisfaction after the opening of insolvency proceedings by virtue of a right in re or through a set-off;

(i) the conditions for, and the effects of, the closure of insolvency proceedings, in particular by composition;

(j) creditors' rights after the closure of winding-up proceedings;

(k) who is to bear the costs and expenses incurred in the winding-up proceedings;

(l) the rules relating to the voidness, voidability or unenforceability of legal acts detrimental to all the creditors.

Article 11

Consultation of competent authorities before voluntary winding up

1. The competent authorities of the home Member State shall be consulted in the most appropriate form before any voluntary winding-up decision is taken by the governing bodies of a credit institution.

2. The voluntary winding up of a credit institution shall not preclude the adoption of a reorganisation measure or the opening of winding-up proceedings.

Article 12

Withdrawal of a credit institution's authorisation

1. Where the opening of winding-up proceedings is decided on in respect of a credit institution in the absence, or following the failure, of reorganisation measures, the authorisation of the institution shall be withdrawn in accordance with, in particular, the procedure laid down in Article 22(9) of Directive 2000/12/EC.

2. The withdrawal of authorisation provided for in paragraph 1 shall not prevent the person or persons entrusted with the winding up from carrying on some of the credit institution's activities insofar as that is necessary or appropriate for the purposes of winding up.

The home Member State may provide that such activities shall be carried on with the consent, and under the supervision, of the competent authorities of that Member State.

Article 13
Publication

The liquidators or any administrative or judicial authority shall announce the decision to open winding-up proceedings through publication of an extract from the winding-up decision in the Official Journal of the European Communities and at least two national newspapers in each of the host Member States.

Article 14
Provision of information to known creditors

1. When winding-up proceedings are opened, the administrative or judicial authority of the home Member State or the liquidator shall without delay individually inform known creditors who have their domiciles, normal places of residence or head offices in other Member States, except in cases where the legislation of the home State does not require lodgement of the claim with a view to its recognition.

2. That information, provided by the dispatch of a notice, shall in particular deal with time limits, the penalties laid down in regard to those time limits, the body or authority empowered to accept the lodgement of claims or observations relating to claims and the other measures laid down. Such a notice shall also indicate whether creditors whose claims are preferential or secured in re need lodge their claims.

Article 15
Honouring of obligations

Where an obligation has been honoured for the benefit of a credit institution which is not a legal person and which is the subject of winding-up proceedings opened in another Member State, when it should have been honoured for the benefit of the liquidator in those proceedings, the person honouring the obligation shall be deemed to have discharged it if he was unaware of the opening of proceedings. Where such an obligation is honoured before the publication provided for in Article 13 has been effected, the person honouring the obligation shall be presumed, in the absence of proof to the contrary, to have been unaware of the opening of winding-up proceedings; where the obligation is honoured after the publication provided for in Article 13 has been effected, the person honouring the obligation shall be presumed, in the absence of proof to the contrary, to have been aware of the opening of proceedings.

Article 16
Right to lodge claims

1. Any creditor who has his domicile, normal place of residence or head office in a Member State other than the home Member State, including Member States' public authorities, shall have the right to lodge claims or to submit written observations relating to claims.

2. The claims of all creditors whose domiciles, normal places of residence or head offices are in Member States other than the home Member State shall be treated in the same way and accorded the same ranking as claims of an equivalent nature which may be lodged by creditors having their domiciles, normal places of residence, or head offices in the home Member State.

3. Except in cases where the law of the home Member State provides for the submission of observations relating to claims, a creditor shall send copies of supporting documents, if any, and shall indicate the nature of the claim, the date on which it arose and its amount, as well as whether he alleges preference, security in re or reservation of title in respect of the claim and what assets are covered by his security.

Article 17
Languages

1. The information provided for in Articles 13 and 14 shall be provided in the official language or one of the official languages of the home Member State. For that purpose a form shall be

used bearing, in all the official languages of the European Union, the heading "Invitation to lodge a claim. Time limits to be observed" or, where the law of the home Member State provides for the submission of observations relating to claims, the heading "Invitation to submit observations relating to a claim. Time limits to be observed".

2. Any creditor who has his domicile, normal place of residence or head office in a Member State other than the home Member State may lodge his claim or submit observations relating to his claim in the official language or one of the official languages of that other Member State. In that event, however, the lodgement of his claim or the submission of observations on his claim shall bear the heading "Lodgement of claim" or "Submission of observations relating to claims" in the official language or one of the official languages of the home Member State. In addition, he may be required to provide a translation into that language of the lodgement of claim or submission of observations relating to claims.

Article 18

Regular provision of information to creditors

Liquidators shall keep creditors regularly informed, in an appropriate manner, particularly with regard to progress in the winding up.

B. Credit institutions the head offices of which are outside the Community

Article 19

Branches of third-country credit institutions

1. The administrative or judicial authorities of the host Member State of the branch of a credit institution the head office of which is outside the Community shall without delay inform, by any available means, the competent authorities of the other host Member States in which the credit institution has set up branches on the list referred to in Article 11 of Directive 2000/12/EC and published each year in the *Official Journal of the European Communities*, of their decision to open winding-up proceedings, including the practical effects which these proceedings may have, if possible before they open or otherwise immediately thereafter. Information shall be communicated by the competent authorities of the first abovementioned host Member State.

2. Administrative or judicial authorities which decide to open proceedings to wind up a branch of a credit institution the head office of which is outside the Community shall inform the competent authorities of the other host Member States that winding-up proceedings have been opened and authorisation withdrawn. Information shall be communicated by the competent authorities in the host Member State which has decided to open the proceedings.

3. The administrative or judicial authorities referred to in paragraph 1 shall endeavour to co-ordinate their actions.

Any liquidators shall likewise endeavour to co-ordinate their actions.

Title IV

Provisions Common to Reorganisation Measures and Winding-Up Proceedings

Article 20

Effects on certain contracts and rights

The effects of a reorganisation measure or the opening of winding-up proceedings on:

(a) employment contracts and relationships shall be governed solely by the law of the Member State applicable to the employment contract;

(b) a contract conferring the right to make use of or acquire immovable property shall be governed solely by the law of the Member State within the territory of which the immovable property is situated. That law shall determine whether property is movable or immovable;

(c) rights in respect of immovable property, a ship or an aircraft subject to registration in a public register shall be governed solely by the law of the Member State under the authority of which the register is kept.

Article 21
Third parties' rights in re

1. The adoption of reorganisation measures or the opening of winding-up proceedings shall not affect the rights in re of creditors or third parties in respect of tangible or intangible, movable or immovable assets—both specific assets and collections of indefinite assets as a whole which change from time to time—belonging to the credit institution which are situated within the territory of another Member State at the time of the adoption of such measures or the opening of such proceedings.

2. The rights referred to in paragraph 1 shall in particular mean:

(a) the right to dispose of assets or have them disposed of and to obtain satisfaction from the proceeds of or income from those assets, in particular by virtue of a lien or a mortgage;

(b) the exclusive right to have a claim met, in particular a right guaranteed by a lien in respect of the claim or by assignment of the claim by way of a guarantee;

(c) the right to demand the assets from, and/or to require restitution by, anyone having possession or use of them contrary to the wishes of the party so entitled;

(d) a right in re to the beneficial use of assets.

3. The right, recorded in a public register and enforceable against third parties, under which a right in re within the meaning of paragraph 1 may be obtained, shall be considered a right in re.

4. Paragraph 1 shall not preclude the actions for voidness, voidability or unenforceability laid down in Article 10(2)(l).

Article 22
Reservation of title

1. The adoption of reorganisation measures or the opening of winding-up proceedings concerning a credit institution purchasing an asset shall not affect the seller's rights based on a reservation of title where at the time of the adoption of such measures or opening of such proceedings the asset is situated within the territory of a Member State other than the State in which the said measures were adopted or the said proceedings were opened.

2. The adoption of reorganisation measures or the opening of winding-up proceedings concerning a credit institution selling an asset, after delivery of the asset, shall not constitute grounds for rescinding or terminating the sale and shall not prevent the purchaser from acquiring title where at the time of the adoption of such measures or the opening of such proceedings the asset sold is situated within the territory of a Member State other than the State in which such measures were adopted or such proceedings were opened.

3. Paragraphs 1 and 2 shall not preclude the actions for voidness, voidability or unenforceability laid down in Article 10(2)(l).

Article 23
Set-off

1. The adoption of reorganisation measures or the opening of winding-up proceedings shall not affect the right of creditors to demand the set-off of their claims against the claims of the credit institution, where such a set-off is permitted by the law applicable to the credit institution's claim.

2. Paragraph 1 shall not preclude the actions for voidness, voidability or unenforceability laid down in Article 10(2)(l).

Article 24
Lex rei sitae

The enforcement of proprietary rights in instruments or other rights in such instruments the existence or transfer of which presupposes their recording in a register, an account or a centralised deposit system held or located in a Member State shall be governed by the law of the Member State where the register, account, or centralised deposit system in which those rights are recorded is held or located.

Article 25
Netting agreements

Netting agreements shall be governed solely by the law of the contract which governs such agreements.

Article 26
Repurchase agreements

Without prejudice to Article 24, repurchase agreements shall be governed solely by the law of the contract which governs such agreements.

Article 27
Regulated markets

Without prejudice to Article 24, transactions carried out in the context of a regulated market shall be governed solely by the law of the contract which governs such transactions.

Article 28
Proof of liquidators' appointment

1. The administrator or liquidator's appointment shall be evidenced by a certified copy of the original decision appointing him or by any other certificate issued by the administrative or judicial authority of the home Member State.

A translation into the official language or one of the official languages of the Member State within the territory of which the administrator or liquidator wishes to act may be required. No legalisation or other similar formality shall be required.

2. Administrators and liquidators shall be entitled to exercise within the territory of all the Member States all the powers which they are entitled to exercise within the territory of the home Member State. They may also appoint persons to assist or, where appropriate, represent them in the course of the reorganisation measure or winding-up proceedings, in particular in host Member States and, specifically, in order to help overcome any difficulties encountered by creditors in the host Member State.

3. In exercising his powers, an administrator or liquidator shall comply with the law of the Member States within the territory of which he wishes to take action, in particular with regard to procedures for the realisation of assets and the provision of information to employees. Those powers may not include the use of force or the right to rule on legal proceedings or disputes.

Article 29
Registration in a public register

1. The administrator, liquidator or any administrative or judicial authority of the home Member State may request that a reorganisation measure or the decision to open winding-up proceedings be registered in the land register, the trade register and any other public register kept in the other Member States.

A Member State may, however, prescribe mandatory registration. In that event, the person or authority referred to in the preceding subparagraph shall take all the measures necessary to ensure such registration.

2. The costs of registration shall be regarded as costs and expenses incurred in the proceedings.

Article 30
Detrimental acts

1. Article 10 shall not apply as regards the rules relating to the voidness, voidability or unenforceability of legal acts detrimental to the creditors as a whole, where the beneficiary of these acts provides proof that:
– the act detrimental to the creditors as a whole is subject to the law of a Member State other than the home Member State, and
– that law does not allow any means of challenging that act in the case in point.

2. Where a reorganisation measure decided on by a judicial authority provides for rules relating to the voidness, voidability or unenforceability of legal acts detrimental to the creditors as a whole performed before adoption of the measure, Article 3(2) shall not apply in the cases provided for in paragraph 1 of this Article.

Article 31
Protection of third parties

Where, by an act concluded after the adoption of a reorganisation measure or the opening of winding-up proceedings, a credit institution disposes, for consideration, of:
– an immovable asset,
– a ship or an aircraft subject to registration in a public register, or
– instruments or rights in such instruments the existence or transfer of which presupposes their being recorded in a register, an account or a centralised deposit system held or located in a Member State,

the validity of that act shall be governed by the law of the Member State within the territory of which the immovable asset is situated or under the authority of which that register, account or deposit system is kept.

Article 32
Lawsuits pending

The effects of reorganisation measures or winding-up proceedings on a pending lawsuit concerning an asset or a right of which the credit institution has been divested shall be governed solely by the law of the Member State in which the lawsuit is pending.

Article 33
Professional secrecy

All persons required to receive or divulge information in connection with the information or consultation procedures laid down in Articles 4, 5, 8, 9, 11 and 19 shall be bound by professional secrecy, in accordance with the rules and conditions laid down in Article 30 of Directive 2000/12/EC, with the exception of any judicial authorities to which existing national provisions apply.

TITLE V
FINAL PROVISIONS

Article 34
Implementation

1. Member States shall bring into force the laws, regulations and administrative provisions necessary to comply with this Directive on 5 May 2004. They shall forthwith inform the Commission thereof.

National provisions adopted in application of this Directive shall apply only to reorganisation measures or winding-up proceedings adopted or opened after the date referred to in the first subparagraph. Measures adopted or proceedings opened before that date shall continue to be governed by the law that was applicable to them at the time of adoption or opening.

2. When Member States adopt these measures, they shall contain a reference to this Directive or shall be accompanied by such reference on the occasion of their official publication. The methods of making such reference shall be laid down by Member States.

3. Member States shall communicate to the Commission the texts of the main provisions of national law which they adopt in the field governed by this Directive.

Article 35
Entry into force

This Directive shall enter into force on the date of its publication.

Article 36
Addressees

This Directive is addressed to the Member States.

B. 37.

European Parliament and Council Directive 2001/97/EC of 4 December 2001 amending Council Directive 91/308/EEC on prevention of the use of the financial system for the purpose of money laundering[1]

THE EUROPEAN PARLIAMENT AND THE COUNCIL OF THE EUROPEAN UNION,

Having regard to the Treaty establishing the European Community, and in particular Article 47(2), first and third sentences, and Article 95 thereof,

Having regard to the proposal from the Commission,[2]

Having regard to the opinion of the Economic and Social Committee,[3]

Acting in accordance with the procedure laid down in Article 251 of the Treaty,[4] in the light of the joint text approved by the Conciliation Committee on 18 September 2001,

Whereas:

(1) It is appropriate that Directive 91/308/EEC,[5] hereinafter referred to as 'the Directive', as one of the main international instruments in the fight against money laundering, should be updated in line with the conclusions of the Commission and the wishes expressed by the European Parliament and the Member States. In this way the Directive should not only reflect best international practice in this area but should also continue to set a high standard in protecting the financial sector and other vulnerable activities from the harmful effects of the proceeds of crime.

(2) The General Agreement on Trade in Services (GATS) allows Members to adopt measures necessary to protect public morals and to adopt measures for prudential reasons, including for ensuring the stability and integrity of the financial system. Such measures should not impose restrictions that go beyond what is necessary to achieve those objectives.

(3) The Directive does not establish clearly which Member State's authorities should receive suspicious transaction reports from branches of credit and financial institutions having their head office in another Member State nor which Member State's authorities are responsible for ensuring that such branches comply with the Directive. The authorities of the Member States in which the branch is located should receive such reports and exercise the above responsibilities.

(4) This allocation of responsibilities should be set out clearly in the Directive by means of an amendment to the definition of 'credit institution' and 'financial institution'.

(5) The European Parliament has expressed concerns that the activities of currency exchange offices ('bureaux de change') and money transmitters (money remittance offices) are vulnerable to money laundering. These activities should already fall within the scope of the Directive. In order to dispel any doubt in this matter the Directive should clearly confirm that these activities are covered.

(6) To ensure the fullest possible coverage of the financial sector it should also be made clear that the Directive applies to the activities of

---

[1] OJ L 344, 28.12.2001, 76–81.
[2] OJ C 177 E, 27.6.2000, 14.
[3] OJ C 75, 15.3.2000, 22.
[4] Opinion of the European Parliament of 5 July 2000 (OJ C 121, 24.4.2001, 133), Council Common Position of 30 November 2000 (OJ C 36, 2.2.2001, 24) and Decision of the European Parliament of 5 April 2001 (OJ C 21, 24.1.2002, 305). Decision of the European Parliament of 13 November 2001 and Decision of the Council of 19 November 2001.
[5] OJ L 166, 28.6.1991, 77, reproduced supra under no. B. 15.

investment firms as defined in Council Directive 93/22/EEC of 10 May 1993 on investment services in the securities field.[6]

(7) The Directive obliges Member States only to combat the laundering of the proceeds of drugs offences. There has been a trend in recent years towards a much wider definition of money laundering based on a broader range of predicate or underlying offences, as reflected for example in the 1996 revision of the 40 Recommendations of the Financial Action Task Force (FATF), the leading international body devoted to the fight against money laundering.

(8) A wider range of predicate offences facilitates suspicious transaction reporting and international cooperation in this area. Therefore, the Directive should be brought up to date in this respect.

(9) In Joint Action 98/699/JHA of 3 December 1998 adopted by the Council on money laundering, the identification, tracing, freezing, seizing and confiscation of instrumentalities and the proceeds from crime,[7] the Member States agreed to make all serious offences, as defined in the Joint Action, predicate offences for the purpose of the criminalisation of money laundering.

(10) The suppression of organised crime in particular is closely linked to measures to combat money laundering. The list of predicate offences should therefore be adapted accordingly.

(11) The Directive imposes obligations regarding in particular the reporting of suspicious transactions. It would be more appropriate and in line with the philosophy of the Action Plan to Combat Organised Crime[8] for the prohibition of money laundering under the Directive to be extended.

(12) On 21 December 1998 the Council adopted Joint Action 98/733/JHA on making it a criminal offence to participate in a criminal organisation in the Member States of the European Union.[9] This Joint Action reflects the Member States' agreement on the need for a common approach in this area.

(13) As required by the Directive, suspicious transaction reports are being made by the financial sector, and particularly by the credit institutions, in every Member State. There is evidence that the tightening of controls in the financial sector has prompted money launderers to seek alternative methods for concealing the origin of the proceeds of crime.

(14) There is a trend towards the increased use by money launderers of non-financial businesses. This is confirmed by the work of the FATF on money laundering techniques and typologies.

(15) The obligations of the Directive concerning customer identification, record keeping and the reporting of suspicious transactions should be extended to a limited number of activities and professions which have been shown to be vulnerable to money laundering.

(16) Notaries and independent legal professionals, as defined by the Member States, should be made subject to the provisions of the Directive when participating in financial or corporate transactions, including providing tax advice, where there is the greatest risk of the services of those legal professionals being misused for the purpose of laundering the proceeds of criminal activity.

(17) However, where independent members of professions providing legal advice which are legally recognised and controlled, such as lawyers, are ascertaining the legal position of a client or representing a client in legal proceedings, it would not be appropriate under the Directive to put these legal professionals in respect of these activities under an obligation to report suspicions of money laundering. There must be exemptions from any obligation to report information obtained either before, during or after judicial proceedings, or in the course of ascertaining the legal position for a client. Thus, legal advice remains subject to the obligation of professional secrecy unless the legal counsellor is taking part in money laundering activities, the legal advice is provided for money laundering purposes, or the lawyer knows that

---

[6] OJ L 141, 11.6.1993, 27. Directive as last amended by Directive 97/9/EC of the European Parliament and of the Council (OJ L 84, 26.3.1997, 22).
[7] OJ L 333, 9.12.1998, 1.
[8] OJ C 251, 15.8.1997, 1.
[9] OJ L 351, 29.12.1998, 1.

the client is seeking legal advice for money laundering purposes.

(18) Directly comparable services need to be treated in the same manner when practised by any of the professionals covered by the Directive. In order to preserve the rights laid down in the European Convention for the Protection of Human Rights and Fundamental Freedoms (ECHR) and the Treaty of the European Union, in the case of auditors, external accountants and tax advisors who, in some Member States, may defend or represent a client in the context of judicial proceedings or ascertain a client's legal position, the information they obtain in the performance of these tasks should not be subject to the reporting obligations in accordance with the Directive.

(19) The Directive makes reference to 'the authorities responsible for combating money laundering' to which reports of suspicious operations must be made on the one hand, and to authorities empowered by law or regulation to supervise the activity of any of the institutions or persons subject to this Directive ('competent authorities') on the other hand. It is understood that the Directive does not oblige Member States to create such 'competent authorities' where they do not exist, and that bar associations and other self-regulatory bodies for independent professionals do not fall under the term 'competent authorities'.

(20) In the case of notaries and independent legal professionals, Member States should be allowed, in order to take proper account of these professionals' duty of discretion owed to their clients, to nominate the bar association or other self-regulatory bodies for independent professionals as the body to which reports on possible money laundering cases may be addressed by these professionals. The rules governing the treatment of such reports and their possible onward transmission to the 'authorities responsible for combating money laundering' and in general the appropriate forms of cooperation between the bar associations or professional bodies and these authorities should be determined by the Member States,

HAVE ADOPTED THIS DIRECTIVE:

Article 1

[. . .]

¶ *Article 1 replaces articles 1, 3, 6, 7, 9, and 11, inserts article 2a, adds paragraph 2 to article 8 and a paragraph to article 10 of Directive 91/308/EEC, reproduced supra under no. B. 15. It also replaces the terms 'credit and financial institutions' in the articles 4, 5, 8, 10 and 12 of that Directive. The modifications are directly incorporated therein.*

Article 2

Within three years of the entry into force of this Directive, the Commission shall carry out a particular examination, in the context of the report provided for in Article 17 of Directive 91/308/EEC, of aspects relating to the implementation of the fifth indent of Article 1(E), the specific treatment of lawyers and other independent legal professionals, the identification of clients in non-face to face transactions and possible implications for electronic commerce.

Article 3

1. Member States shall bring into force the laws, regulations and administrative provisions necessary to comply with this Directive by 15 June 2003 at the latest. They shall forthwith inform the Commission thereof.

Where Member States adopt these measures, they shall contain a reference to this Directive or shall be accompanied by such reference on the occasion of their official publication. The methods of making such a reference shall be laid down by the Member States.

2. Member States shall communicate to the Commission the text of the main provisions of domestic law which they adopt in the field governed by this Directive.

Article 4

This Directive shall enter into force on the day of its publication in the Official Journal of the European Communities.

Article 5

This Directive is addressed to the Member States.

B. 38.

European Parliament and Council Directive 2002/87/EC of 16 December 2002 on the supplementary supervision of credit institutions, insurance undertakings and investment firms in a financial conglomerate and amending Council Directives 73/239/EEC, 79/267/EEC, 92/49/EEC, 92/96/EEC, 93/6/EEC and 93/22/EEC, and Directives 98/78/EC and 2000/12/EC of the European Parliament and of the Council[1]

THE EUROPEAN PARLIAMENT AND THE COUNCIL OF THE EUROPEAN UNION,

Having regard to the Treaty establishing the European Community, and in particular Article 47(2) thereof,

Having regard to the proposal from the Commission,[2]

Having regard to the opinion of the Economic and Social Committee,[3]

After consulting the Committee of the Regions,

Having regard to the opinion of the European Central Bank,[4]

Acting in accordance with the procedure laid down in Article 251 of the Treaty,[5]

Whereas:

(1) The current Community legislation provides for a comprehensive set of rules on the prudential supervision of credit institutions, insurance undertakings and investment firms on a stand alone basis and credit institutions, insurance undertakings and investment firms which are part of respectively a banking/investment firm group or an insurance group, i.e. groups with homogeneous financial activities.

(2) New developments in financial markets have led to the creation of financial groups which provide services and products in different sectors of the financial markets, called financial conglomerates. Until now, there has been no form of prudential supervision on a group-wide basis of credit institutions, insurance undertakings and investment firms which are part of such a conglomerate, in particular as regards the solvency position and risk concentration at the level of the conglomerate, the intra-group transactions, the internal risk management processes at conglomerate level, and the fit and proper character of the management. Some of these conglomerates are among the biggest financial groups which are active in the financial markets and provide services on a global basis. If such conglomerates, and in particular credit institutions, insurance undertakings and investment firms which are part of such a conglomerate, were to face financial difficulties, these could seriously destabilise the financial system and affect individual depositors, insurance policy holders and investors.

(3) The Commission Action Plan for Financial Services identifies a series of actions which are needed to complete the Single Market in Financial Services, and announces the development of supplementary prudential legislation for financial conglomerates which will address loopholes in the present sectoral legislation and additional prudential risks to ensure sound supervisory arrangements with regard to financial groups with cross-sectoral financial activities. Such an ambitious objective can only be attained in stages. The establishment of the supplementary supervision of credit institutions, insurance

---

[1] OJ L 35, 11.2.2003, 1–27.
[2] OJ C 213 E, 31.7.2001, 227.
[3] OJ C 36, 8.2.2002, 1.
[4] OJ C 271, 26.9.2001, 10.
[5] Opinion of the European Parliament of 14 March 2002 (not yet published in the Official Journal), Council Common Position of 12 September 2002 (OJ C 253 E, 22.10.2002, 1) and Decision of the European Parliament of 20 November 2002 (not yet published in the Official Journal).

undertakings and investment firms in a financial conglomerate is one such stage.

(4) Other international forums have also identified the need for the development of appropriate supervisory concepts with regard to financial conglomerates.

(5) In order to be effective, the supplementary supervision of credit institutions, insurance undertakings and investment firms in a financial conglomerate should be applied to all such conglomerates, the cross-sectoral financial activities of which are significant, which is the case when certain thresholds are reached, no matter how they are structured. Supplementary supervision should cover all financial activities identified by the sectoral financial legislation and all entities principally engaged in such activities should be included in the scope of the supplementary supervision, including asset management companies.

(6) Decisions not to include a particular entity in the scope of supplementary supervision should be taken, bearing in mind inter alia whether or not such entity is included in the group-wide supervision under sectoral rules.

(7) The competent authorities should be able to assess at a group-wide level the financial situation of credit institutions, insurance undertakings and investment firms which are part of a financial conglomerate, in particular as regards solvency (including the elimination of multiple gearing of own funds instruments), risk concentration and intra-group transactions.

(8) Financial conglomerates are often managed on a business-line basis which does not fully coincide with the conglomerate's legal structures. In order to take account of this trend, the requirements for management should be further extended, in particular as regards the management of the mixed financial holding company.

(9) All financial conglomerates subject to supplementary supervision should have a coordinator appointed from among the competent authorities involved.

(10) The tasks of the coordinator should not affect the tasks and responsibilities of the competent authorities as provided for by the sectoral rules.

(11) The competent authorities involved, and especially the coordinator, should have the means of obtaining from the entities within a financial conglomerate, or from other competent authorities, the information necessary for the performance of their supplementary supervision.

(12) There is a pressing need for increased collaboration between authorities responsible for the supervision of credit institutions, insurance undertakings and investment firms, including the development of ad hoc cooperation arrangements between the authorities involved in the supervision of entities belonging to the same financial conglomerate.

(13) Credit institutions, insurance undertakings and investment firms which have their head office in the Community can be part of a financial conglomerate, the head of which is outside the Community. These regulated entities should also be subject to equivalent and appropriate supplementary supervisory arrangements which achieve objectives and results similar to those pursued by the provisions of this Directive. To this end, transparency of rules and exchange of information with third-country authorities on all relevant circumstances are of great importance.

(14) Equivalent and appropriate supplementary supervisory arrangements can only be assumed to exist if the third-country supervisory authorities have agreed to cooperate with the competent authorities concerned on the means and objectives of exercising supplementary supervision of the regulated entities of a financial conglomerate.

(15) This Directive does not require the disclosure by competent authorities to a financial conglomerates committee of information which is subject to an obligation of confidentiality under this Directive or other sectoral directives.

(16) Since the objective of the proposed action, namely the establishment of rules on the supplementary supervision of credit institutions, insurance undertakings and investment firms in a financial conglomerate, cannot be sufficiently

achieved by the Member States and can therefore, by reason of the scale and the effects of the action, be better achieved at Community level, the Community may adopt measures, in accordance with the principle of subsidiarity as set out in Article 5 of the Treaty. In accordance with the principle of proportionality, as set out in that Article, this Directive does not go beyond what is necessary in order to achieve this objective. Since this Directive defines minimum standards, Member States may lay down stricter rules.

(17) This Directive respects the fundamental rights and observes the principles recognised in particular by the Charter of Fundamental Rights of the European Union.

(18) The measures necessary for the implementation of this Directive should be adopted in accordance with Council Decision 1999/468/EC of 28 June 1999 laying down the procedures for the exercise of implementing powers conferred on the Commission.[6]

(19) Technical guidance and implementing measures for the rules laid down in this Directive may from time to time be necessary to take account of new developments on financial markets. The Commission should accordingly be empowered to adopt implementing measures, provided that these do not modify the essential elements of this Directive.

(20) The existing sectoral rules for credit institutions, insurance undertakings and investment firms should be supplemented to a minimum level, in particular to avoid regulatory arbitrage between the sectoral rules and those for financial conglomerates. Therefore, First Council Directive 73/239/EEC of 24 July 1973 on the coordination of laws, regulations and administrative provisions relating to the taking up and pursuit of the business of direct insurance other than life assurance,[7] First Council Directive 79/267/EEC of 5 March 1979 on the coordination of laws, regulations and administrative provisions relating to the taking up and pursuit of the business of direct life assurance,[8] Council Directive 92/49/EEC of 18 June 1992 on the coordination of laws, regulations and administrative provisions relating to direct insurance other than life insurance (third non-life insurance Directive),[9] Council Directive 92/96/EEC of 10 November 1992 on the coordination of laws, regulations and administrative provisions relating to direct life assurance (third life insurance Directive),[10] Council Directive 93/6/EEC of 15 March 1993 on the capital adequacy of investments firms and credit institutions[11] and Council Directive 93/22/EEC of 10 May 1993 on investment services in the securities field,[12] as well as Directive 98/78/EC of the European Parliament and of the Council of 27 October 1998 on the supplementary supervision of insurance undertakings in an insurance group[13] and Directive 2000/12/EC of the European Parliament and of the Council of 20 March 2000 relating to the taking up and pursuit of the business of credit institutions[14] should be amended accordingly. The objective of further harmonisation can, however, only be achieved by stages and needs to be based on careful analysis.

---

[6] OJ L 184, 17.7.1999, 23.
[7] OJ L 228, 16.8.1973, 3, reproduced infra under no. I. 3. Directive as last amended by Directive 2002/13/EC of the European Parliament and of the Council (OJ L 77, 20.3.2002, 17), reproduced infra under no. I. 32.
[8] OJ L 63, 13.3.1979, 1, reproduced infra under no. I. 9. Directive as last amended by Directive 2002/12/EC of the European Parliament and of the Council (OJ L 77, 20.3.2002, 11), reproduced infra under no. I. 31.
[9] OJ L 228, 11.8.1992, 1, reproduced infra under no. I. 25. Directive as last amended by Directive 2000/64/EC of the European Parliament and of the Council (OJ L 290, 17.11.2000, 27).
[10] OJ L 360, 9.12.1992, 1, reproduced infra under no. I. 26. Directive as last amended by Directive 2000/64/EC.
[11] OJ L 141, 11.6.1993, 1, reproduced supra under no. B. 20. Directive as last amended by Directive 98/33/EC of the European Parliament and of the Council (OJ L 204, 21.7.1998, 29), reproduced infra under no. B. 29. Directive 93/6/EEC has been repealed as from 20 July 2006 by article 52 of Directive 2006/49/EC (OJ L 177, 30.6.2006, 201), reproduced infra under no. B. 42.
[12] OJ L 141, 11.6.1993, 27, reproduced infra under no. S. 14. Directive as last amended by Directive 2000/64/EC.
[13] OJ L 330, 5.12.1998, 1, reproduced infra under no. I. 28.
[14] OJ L 126, 26.5.2000, 1, reproduced supra under no. B. 32. Directive as last amended by Directive 2000/28/EC (OJ L 275, 27.10.2000, 37), reproduced supra under no. B. 34. Directive 2000/12/EC has been repealed as from 20 July 2006 by article 158 of Directive 2006/48/EC (OJ L 177, 30.6.2006, 1), reproduced infra under no. B. 41.

(21) In order to assess the need for and prepare any possible future harmonisation of the treatment of asset management companies under sectoral rules, the Commission should report on Member States' practices in this field,

HAVE ADOPTED THIS DIRECTIVE:

CHAPTER I
OBJECTIVE AND DEFINITIONS

Article 1
Objective

This Directive lays down rules for supplementary supervision of regulated entities which have obtained an authorisation pursuant to Article 6 of Directive 73/239/EEC, Article 6 of Directive 79/267/EEC, Article 3(1) of Directive 93/22/ EEC or Article 4 of Directive 2000/12/EC, and which are part of a financial conglomerate. It also amends the relevant sectoral rules which apply to entities regulated by the Directives referred to above.

Article 2
Definitions

For the purposes of this Directive:

1. 'credit institution' shall mean a credit institution within the meaning of the second subparagraph of Article 1(1) of Directive 2000/12/EC;

2. 'insurance undertaking' shall mean an insurance undertaking within the meaning of Article 6 of Directive 73/239/EEC, Article 6 of Directive 79/267/EEC or Article 1(b) of Directive 98/78/EC;

3. 'investment firm' shall mean an investment firm within the meaning of Article 1(2) of Directive 93/22/EEC, including the undertakings referred to in Article 2(4) of Directive 93/6/EEC;

4. 'regulated entity' shall mean a credit institution, an insurance undertaking or an investment firm;

5. 'asset management company' shall mean a management company within the meaning of Article 1a(2) of Council Directive 85/611/EEC of 20 December 1985 on the coordination of laws, regulations and administrative provisions relating to undertakings for collective investment in transferable securities (UCITS),[15] as well as an undertaking the registered office of which is outside the Community and which would require authorisation in accordance with Article 5(1) of that Directive if it had its registered office within the Community;

6. 'reinsurance undertaking' shall mean a reinsurance undertaking within the meaning of Article 1(c) of Directive 98/78/EC;

7. 'sectoral rules' shall mean the Community legislation relating to the prudential supervision of regulated entities, in particular laid down in Directives 73/239/EEC, 79/267/EEC, 98/78/EC, 93/6/EEC, 93/22/EEC and 2000/12/EC;

8. 'financial sector' shall mean a sector composed of one or more of the following entities:

(a) a credit institution, a financial institution or an ancillary banking services undertaking within the meaning of Article 1(5) and (23) of Directive 2000/12/EC (the banking sector);

(b) an insurance undertaking, a reinsurance undertaking or an insurance holding company within the meaning of Article 1(i) of Directive 98/78/EC (the insurance sector);

(c) an investment firm or a financial institution within the meaning of Article 2(7) of Directive 93/6/EEC (the investment services sector);

(d) a mixed financial holding company;

9. 'parent undertaking' shall mean a parent undertaking within the meaning of Article 1 of Seventh Council Directive 83/349/EEC of 13 June 1983 on consolidated accounts[16] and any undertaking which, in the opinion of the competent authorities, effectively exercises a dominant influence over another undertaking;

---

[15] OJ L 375, 31.12.1985, 3, reproduced infra under no. S. 6. Directive as last amended by Directive 2001/108/EC of the European Parliament and of the Council (OJ L 41, 13.2.2002, 35), reproduced infra under no. S. 22.
[16] OJ L 193, 18.7.1983, 1, reproduced infra under no. C. 6. Directive as last amended by Directive 2001/65/EC of the European Parliament and of the Council (OJ L 283, 27.10.2001, 28), reproduced infra under no. C. 18.

10. 'subsidiary undertaking' shall mean a subsidiary undertaking within the meaning of Article 1 of Directive 83/349/EEC and any undertaking over which, in the opinion of the competent authorities, a parent undertaking effectively exercises a dominant influence; all subsidiary undertakings of subsidiary undertakings shall also be considered as subsidiary undertakings of the parent undertaking;

11. 'participation' shall mean a participation within the meaning of the first sentence of Article 17 of Fourth Council Directive 78/660/EEC of 25 July 1978 on the annual accounts of certain types of companies,[17] or the direct or indirect ownership of 20% or more of the voting rights or capital of an undertaking;

12. 'group' shall mean a group of undertakings, which consists of a parent undertaking, its subsidiaries and the entities in which the parent undertaking or its subsidiaries hold a participation, as well as undertakings linked to each other by a relationship within the meaning of Article 12(1) of Directive 83/349/EEC;

13. 'close links' shall mean a situation in which two or more natural or legal persons are linked by:

(a) 'participation', which shall mean the ownership, direct or by way of control, of 20% or more of the voting rights or capital of an undertaking; or

(b) 'control', which shall mean the relationship between a parent undertaking and a subsidiary, in all the cases referred to in Article 1(1) and (2) of Directive 83/349/EEC, or a similar relationship between any natural or legal person and an undertaking; any subsidiary undertaking of a subsidiary undertaking shall also be considered a subsidiary of the parent undertaking which is at the head of those undertakings.

A situation in which two or more natural or legal persons are permanently linked to one and the same person by a control relationship shall also be regarded as constituting a close link between such persons;

14. 'financial conglomerate' shall mean a group which meets, subject to Article 3, the following conditions:

(a) a regulated entity within the meaning of Article 1 is at the head of the group or at least one of the subsidiaries in the group is a regulated entity within the meaning of Article 1;

(b) where there is a regulated entity within the meaning of Article 1 at the head of the group, it is either a parent undertaking of an entity in the financial sector, an entity which holds a participation in an entity in the financial sector, or an entity linked with an entity in the financial sector by a relationship within the meaning of Article 12(1) of Directive 83/349/EEC;

(c) where there is no regulated entity within the meaning of Article 1 at the head of the group, the group's activities mainly occur in the financial sector within the meaning of Article 3(1);

(d) at least one of the entities in the group is within the insurance sector and at least one is within the banking or investment services sector;

(e) the consolidated and/or aggregated activities of the entities in the group within the insurance sector and the consolidated and/or aggregated activities of the entities within the banking and investment services sector are both significant within the meaning of Article 3(2) or (3).

Any subgroup of a group within the meaning of point 12 which meets the criteria in this point shall be considered as a financial conglomerate;

15. 'mixed financial holding company' shall mean a parent undertaking, other than a regulated entity, which together with its subsidiaries, at least one of which is a regulated entity which has its head office in the Community, and other entities, constitutes a financial conglomerate;

16. 'competent authorities' shall mean the national authorities of the Member States which are empowered by law or regulation to supervise credit institutions, and/or insurance undertakings and/or investment firms whether on an individual or a group-wide basis;

---

[17] OJ L 222, 14.8.1978, 11, reproduced infra under no. C. 4. Directive as last amended by Directive 2001/65/EC.

17. 'relevant competent authorities' shall mean:

(a) Member States' competent authorities responsible for the sectoral group-wide supervision of any of the regulated entities in a financial conglomerate;

(b) the coordinator appointed in accordance with Article 10 if different from the authorities referred to in (a);

(c) other competent authorities concerned, where relevant, in the opinion of the authorities referred to in (a) and (b); this opinion shall especially take into account the market share of the regulated entities of the conglomerate in other Member States, in particular if it exceeds 5%, and the importance in the conglomerate of any regulated entity established in another Member State;

18. 'intra-group transactions' shall mean all transactions by which regulated entities within a financial conglomerate rely either directly or indirectly upon other undertakings within the same group or upon any natural or legal person linked to the undertakings within that group by 'close links', for the fulfilment of an obligation, whether or not contractual, and whether or not for payment;

19. 'risk concentration' shall mean all exposures with a loss potential borne by entities within a financial conglomerate, which are large enough to threaten the solvency or the financial position in general of the regulated entities in the financial conglomerate; such exposures may be caused by counterparty risk/credit risk, investment risk, insurance risk, market risk, other risks, or a combination or interaction of these risks.

Article 3

Thresholds for identifying a financial conglomerate

1. For the purposes of determining whether the activities of a group mainly occur in the financial sector, within the meaning of Article 2(14)(c), the ratio of the balance sheet total of the regulated and non-regulated financial sector entities in the group to the balance sheet total of the group as a whole should exceed 40%.

2. For the purposes of determining whether activities in different financial sectors are significant within the meaning of Article 2(14)(e), for each financial sector the average of the ratio of the balance sheet total of that financial sector to the balance sheet total of the financial sector entities in the group and the ratio of the solvency requirements of the same financial sector to the total solvency requirements of the financial sector entities in the group should exceed 10%.

For the purposes of this Directive, the smallest financial sector in a financial conglomerate is the sector with the smallest average and the most important financial sector in a financial conglomerate is the sector with the highest average. For the purposes of calculating the average and for the measurement of the smallest and the most important financial sectors, the banking sector and the investment services sector shall be considered together.

3. Cross-sectoral activities shall also be presumed to be significant within the meaning of Article 2(14)(e) if the balance sheet total of the smallest financial sector in the group exceeds EUR 6 billion. If the group does not reach the threshold referred to in paragraph 2, the relevant competent authorities may decide by common agreement not to regard the group as a financial conglomerate, or not to apply the provisions of Articles 7, 8 or 9, if they are of the opinion that the inclusion of the group in the scope of this Directive or the application of such provisions is not necessary or would be inappropriate or misleading with respect to the objectives of supplementary supervision, taking into account, for instance, the fact that:

(a) the relative size of its smallest financial sector does not exceed 5%, measured either in terms of the average referred to in paragraph 2 or in terms of the balance sheet total or the solvency requirements of such financial sector; or

(b) the market share does not exceed 5% in any Member State, measured in terms of the balance sheet total in the banking or investment services sectors and in terms of gross premiums written in the insurance sector.

Decisions taken in accordance with this paragraph shall be notified to the other competent authorities concerned.

4. For the application of paragraphs 1, 2 and 3, the relevant competent authorities may by common agreement:

(a) exclude an entity when calculating the ratios, in the cases referred to in Article 6(5);

(b) take into account compliance with the thresholds envisaged in paragraphs 1 and 2 for three consecutive years so as to avoid sudden regime shifts, and disregard such compliance if there are significant changes in the group's structure.

Where a financial conglomerate has been identified according to paragraphs 1, 2 and 3, the decisions referred to in the first subparagraph of this paragraph shall be taken on the basis of a proposal made by the coordinator of that financial conglomerate.

5. For the application of paragraphs 1 and 2, the relevant competent authorities may, in exceptional cases and by common agreement, replace the criterion based on balance sheet total with one or both of the following parameters or add one or both of these parameters, if they are of the opinion that these parameters are of particular relevance for the purposes of supplementary supervision under this Directive: income structure, off-balance-sheet activities.

6. For the application of paragraphs 1 and 2, if the ratios referred to in those paragraphs fall below 40% and 10% respectively for conglomerates already subject to supplementary supervision, a lower ratio of 35% and 8% respectively shall apply for the following three years to avoid sudden regime shifts.

Similarly, for the application of paragraph 3, if the balance sheet total of the smallest financial sector in the group falls below EUR 6 billion for conglomerates already subject to supplementary supervision, a lower figure of EUR 5 billion shall apply for the following three years to avoid sudden regime shifts.

During the period referred to in this paragraph, the coordinator may, with the agreement of the other relevant competent authorities, decide that the lower ratios or the lower amount referred to in this paragraph shall cease to apply.

7. The calculations referred to in this Article regarding the balance sheet shall be made on the basis of the aggregated balance sheet total of the entities of the group, according to their annual accounts. For the purposes of this calculation, undertakings in which a participation is held shall be taken into account as regards the amount of their balance sheet total corresponding to the aggregated proportional share held by the group. However, where consolidated accounts are available, they shall be used instead of aggregated accounts.

The solvency requirements referred to in paragraphs 2 and 3 shall be calculated in accordance with the provisions of the relevant sectoral rules.

Article 4

Identifying a financial conglomerate

1. Competent authorities which have authorised regulated entities shall, on the basis of Articles 2, 3 and 5, identify any group that falls under the scope of this Directive.

For this purpose:

– competent authorities which have authorised regulated entities in the group shall, where necessary, cooperate closely,

– if a competent authority is of the opinion that a regulated entity authorised by that competent authority is a member of a group which may be a financial conglomerate, which has not already been identified according to this Directive, the competent authority shall communicate its view to the other competent authorities concerned.

2. The coordinator appointed in accordance with Article 10 shall inform the parent undertaking at the head of a group or, in the absence of a parent undertaking, the regulated entity with the largest balance sheet total in the most important financial sector in a group, that the group has

been identified as a financial conglomerate and of the appointment of the coordinator. The coordinator shall also inform the competent authorities which have authorised regulated entities in the group and the competent authorities of the Member State in which the mixed financial holding company has its head office, as well as the Commission.

Chapter II
Supplementary Supervision

Section 1
Scope

Article 5

Scope of supplementary supervision of regulated entities referred to in Article 1

1. Without prejudice to the provisions on supervision contained in the sectoral rules, Member States shall provide for the supplementary supervision of the regulated entities referred to in Article 1, to the extent and in the manner prescribed in this Directive.

2. The following regulated entities shall be subject to supplementary supervision at the level of the financial conglomerate in accordance with Articles 6 to 17:

(a) every regulated entity which is at the head of a financial conglomerate;

(b) every regulated entity, the parent undertaking of which is a mixed financial holding company which has its head office in the Community;

(c) every regulated entity linked with another financial sector entity by a relationship within the meaning of Article 12(1) of Directive 83/349/EEC.

Where a financial conglomerate is a subgroup of another financial conglomerate which meets the requirements of the first subparagraph, Member States may apply Articles 6 to 17 to the regulated entities within the latter group only and any reference in the Directive to the terms group and financial conglomerate will then be understood as referring to that latter group.

3. Every regulated entity which is not subject to supplementary supervision in accordance with paragraph 2, the parent undertaking of which is a regulated entity or a mixed financial holding company, having its head office outside the Community, shall be subject to supplementary supervision at the level of the financial conglomerate to the extent and in the manner prescribed in Article 18.

4. Where persons hold participations or capital ties in one or more regulated entities or exercise significant influence over such entities without holding a participation or capital ties, other than the cases referred to in paragraphs 2 and 3, the relevant competent authorities shall, by common agreement and in conformity with national law, determine whether and to what extent supplementary supervision of the regulated entities is to be carried out, as if they constitute a financial conglomerate.

In order to apply such supplementary supervision, at least one of the entities must be a regulated entity as referred to in Article 1 and the conditions set out in Article 2(14)(d) and (e) must be met. The relevant competent authorities shall take their decision, taking into account the objectives of the supplementary supervision as provided for by this Directive.

For the purposes of applying the first subparagraph to 'cooperative groups', the competent authorities must take into account the public financial commitment of these groups with respect to other financial entities.

5. Without prejudice to Article 13, the exercise of supplementary supervision at the level of the financial conglomerate shall in no way imply that the competent authorities are required to play a supervisory role in relation to mixed financial holding companies, third-country regulated entities in a financial conglomerate or unregulated entities in a financial conglomerate, on a stand-alone basis.

Section 2
Financial Position

Article 6
Capital adequacy

1. Without prejudice to the sectoral rules, supplementary supervision of the capital adequacy of the regulated entities in a financial conglomerate shall be exercised in accordance with the rules laid down in Article 9(2) to (5), in Section 3 of this Chapter, and in Annex I.

2. The Member States shall require regulated entities in a financial conglomerate to ensure that own funds are available at the level of the financial conglomerate which are always at least equal to the capital adequacy requirements as calculated in accordance with Annex I.

The Member States shall also require regulated entities to have in place adequate capital adequacy policies at the level of the financial conglomerate.

The requirements referred to in the first and second subparagraphs shall be subject to supervisory overview by the coordinator in accordance with Section 3.

The coordinator shall ensure that the calculation referred to in the first subparagraph is carried out at least once a year, either by the regulated entities or by the mixed financial holding company.

The results of the calculation and the relevant data for the calculation shall be submitted to the coordinator by the regulated entity within the meaning of Article 1 which is at the head of the financial conglomerate, or, where the financial conglomerate is not headed by a regulated entity within the meaning of Article 1, by the mixed financial holding company or by the regulated entity in the financial conglomerate identified by the coordinator after consultation with the other relevant competent authorities and with the financial conglomerate.

3. For the purposes of calculating the capital adequacy requirements referred to in the first subparagraph of paragraph 2, the following entities shall be included in the scope of supplementary supervision in the manner and to the extent defined in Annex I:

(a) a credit institution, a financial institution or an ancillary banking services undertaking within the meaning of Article 1(5) and (23) of Directive 2000/12/EC;

(b) an insurance undertaking, a reinsurance undertaking or an insurance holding company within the meaning of Article 1(i) of Directive 98/78/EC;

(c) an investment firm or a financial institution within the meaning of Article 2(7) of Directive 93/6/EEC;

(d) mixed financial holding companies.

4. When calculating the supplementary capital adequacy requirements with regard to a financial conglomerate by applying method 1 (Accounting consolidation) referred to in Annex I, the own funds and the solvency requirements of the entities in the group shall be calculated by applying the corresponding sectoral rules on the form and extent of consolidation as laid down in particular in Article 54 of Directive 2000/12/EC and Annex I.1.B. of Directive 98/78/EC.

When applying methods 2 or 3 (Deduction and aggregation, Book value/Requirement deduction) referred to in Annex I, the calculation shall take account of the proportional share held by the parent undertaking or undertaking which holds a participation in another entity of the group. 'Proportional share' means the proportion of the subscribed capital which is held, directly or indirectly, by that undertaking.

5. The coordinator may decide not to include a particular entity in the scope when calculating the supplementary capital adequacy requirements in the following cases:

(a) if the entity is situated in a third country where there are legal impediments to the transfer of the necessary information, without prejudice to the sectoral rules regarding the obligation of competent authorities to refuse authorisation where the effective exercise of their supervisory functions is prevented;

(b) if the entity is of negligible interest with respect to the objectives of the supplementary supervision of regulated entities in a financial conglomerate;

(c) if the inclusion of the entity would be inappropriate or misleading with respect to the objectives of supplementary supervision.

However, if several entities are to be excluded pursuant to (b) of the first subparagraph, they must nevertheless be included when collectively they are of non-negligible interest.

In the case mentioned in (c) of the first subparagraph the coordinator shall, except in cases of urgency, consult the other relevant competent authorities before taking a decision.

When the coordinator does not include a regulated entity in the scope under one of the cases provided for in (b) and (c) of the first subparagraph, the competent authorities of the Member State in which that entity is situated may ask the entity which is at the head of the financial conglomerate for information which may facilitate their supervision of the regulated entity.

Article 7

Risk concentration

1. Without prejudice to the sectoral rules, supplementary supervision of the risk concentration of regulated entities in a financial conglomerate shall be exercised in accordance with the rules laid down in Article 9(2) to (4), in Section 3 of this Chapter and in Annex II.

2. The Member States shall require regulated entities or mixed financial holding companies to report on a regular basis and at least annually to the coordinator any significant risk concentration at the level of the financial conglomerate, in accordance with the rules laid down in this Article and in Annex II. The necessary information shall be submitted to the coordinator by the regulated entity within the meaning of Article 1 which is at the head of the financial conglomerate or, where the financial conglomerate is not headed by a regulated entity within the meaning of Article 1, by the mixed financial holding company or by the regulated entity in the financial conglomerate identified by the coordinator after consultation with the other relevant competent authorities and with the financial conglomerate.

These risk concentrations shall be subject to supervisory overview by the coordinator in accordance with Section 3.

3. Pending further coordination of Community legislation, Member States may set quantitative limits or allow their competent authorities to set quantitative limits, or take other supervisory measures which would achieve the objectives of supplementary supervision, with regard to any risk concentration at the level of a financial conglomerate.

4. Where a financial conglomerate is headed by a mixed financial holding company, the sectoral rules regarding risk concentration of the most important financial sector in the financial conglomerate, if any, shall apply to that sector as a whole, including the mixed financial holding company.

Article 8

Intra-group transactions

1. Without prejudice to the sectoral rules, supplementary supervision of intra-group transactions of regulated entities in a financial conglomerate shall be exercised in accordance with the rules laid down in Article 9(2) to (4), in Section 3 of this Chapter, and in Annex II.

2. The Member States shall require regulated entities or mixed financial holding companies to report, on a regular basis and at least annually, to the coordinator all significant intra-group transactions of regulated entities within a financial conglomerate, in accordance with the rules laid down in this Article and in Annex II. Insofar as no definition of the thresholds referred to in the last sentence of the first paragraph of Annex II has been drawn up, an intra-group transaction shall be presumed to be significant if its amount exceeds at least 5% of the total amount of capital adequacy requirements at the level of a financial conglomerate.

The necessary information shall be submitted to the coordinator by the regulated entity within the meaning of Article 1 which is at the head of the financial conglomerate or, where the financial conglomerate is not headed by a regulated entity within the meaning of Article 1, by the mixed financial holding company or by the regulated entity in the financial conglomerate identified by the coordinator after consultation with the other relevant competent authorities and with the financial conglomerate.

These intra-group transactions shall be subject to supervisory overview by the coordinator.

3. Pending further coordination of Community legislation, Member States may set quantitative limits and qualitative requirements or allow their competent authorities to set quantitative limits and qualitative requirements, or take other supervisory measures that would achieve the objectives of supplementary supervision, with regard to intra-group transactions of regulated entities within a financial conglomerate.

4. Where a financial conglomerate is headed by a mixed financial holding company, the sectoral rules regarding intra-group transactions of the most important financial sector in the financial conglomerate shall apply to that sector as a whole, including the mixed financial holding company.

Article 9

Internal control mechanisms and risk management processes

1. The Member States shall require regulated entities to have, in place at the level of the financial conglomerate, adequate risk management processes and internal control mechanisms, including sound administrative and accounting procedures.

2. The risk management processes shall include:

(a) sound governance and management with the approval and periodical review of the strategies and policies by the appropriate governing bodies at the level of the financial conglomerate with respect to all the risks they assume;

(b) adequate capital adequacy policies in order to anticipate the impact of their business strategy on risk profile and capital requirements as determined in accordance with Article 6 and Annex I;

(c) adequate procedures to ensure that their risk monitoring systems are well integrated into their organisation and that all measures are taken to ensure that the systems implemented in all the undertakings included in the scope of supplementary supervision are consistent so that the risks can be measured, monitored and controlled at the level of the financial conglomerate.

3. The internal control mechanisms shall include:

(a) adequate mechanisms as regards capital adequacy to identify and measure all material risks incurred and to appropriately relate own funds to risks;

(b) sound reporting and accounting procedures to identify, measure, monitor and control the intra-group transactions and the risk concentration.

4. The Member States shall ensure that, in all undertakings included in the scope of supplementary supervision pursuant to Article 5, there are adequate internal control mechanisms for the production of any data and information which would be relevant for the purposes of the supplementary supervision.

5. The processes and mechanisms referred to in paragraphs 1 to 4 shall be subject to supervisory overview by the coordinator.

SECTION 3

MEASURES TO FACILITATE SUPPLEMENTARY SUPERVISION

Article 10

Competent authority responsible for exercising supplementary supervision (the coordinator)

1. In order to ensure proper supplementary supervision of the regulated entities in a financial conglomerate, a single coordinator, responsible for coordination and exercise of supplementary supervision, shall be appointed from among the competent authorities of the Member States concerned, including those of the Member State in which the mixed financial holding company has its head office.

2. The appointment shall be based on the following criteria:

(a) where a financial conglomerate is headed by a regulated entity, the task of coordinator shall be exercised by the competent authority which has authorised that regulated entity pursuant to the relevant sectoral rules;

(b) where a financial conglomerate is not headed by a regulated entity, the task of coordinator shall be exercised by the competent authority identified in accordance with the following principles:

(i) where the parent of a regulated entity is a mixed financial holding company, the task of coordinator shall be exercised by the competent authority which has authorised that regulated entity pursuant to the relevant sectoral rules;

(ii) where more than one regulated entity with a head office in the Community have as their parent the same mixed financial holding company, and one of these entities has been authorised in the Member State in which the mixed financial holding company has its head office, the task of coordinator shall be exercised by the competent authority of the regulated entity authorised in that Member State.

Where more than one regulated entity, being active in different financial sectors, have been authorised in the Member State in which the mixed financial holding company has its head office, the task of coordinator shall be exercised by the competent authority of the regulated entity active in the most important financial sector.

Where the financial conglomerate is headed by more than one mixed financial holding company with a head office in different Member States and there is a regulated entity in each of these States, the task of coordinator shall be exercised by the competent authority of the regulated entity with the largest balance sheet total if these entities are in the same financial sector, or by the competent authority of the regulated entity in the most important financial sector;

(iii) where more than one regulated entity with a head office in the Community have as their parent the same mixed financial holding company and none of these entities has been authorised in the Member State in which the mixed financial holding company has its head office, the task of coordinator shall be exercised by the competent authority which authorised the regulated entity with the largest balance sheet total in the most important financial sector;

(iv) where the financial conglomerate is a group without a parent undertaking at the top, or in any other case, the task of coordinator shall be exercised by the competent authority which authorised the regulated entity with the largest balance sheet total in the most important financial sector.

3. In particular cases, the relevant competent authorities may by common agreement waive the criteria referred to in paragraph 2 if their application would be inappropriate, taking into account the structure of the conglomerate and the relative importance of its activities in different countries, and appoint a different competent authority as coordinator. In these cases, before taking their decision, the competent authorities shall give the conglomerate an opportunity to state its opinion on that decision.

Article 11

Tasks of the coordinator

1. The tasks to be carried out by the coordinator with regard to supplementary supervision shall include:

(a) coordination of the gathering and dissemination of relevant or essential information in going concern and emergency situations, including the dissemination of information which is of importance for a competent authority's supervisory task under sectoral rules;

(b) supervisory overview and assessment of the financial situation of a financial conglomerate;

(c) assessment of compliance with the rules on capital adequacy and of risk concentration and intra-group transactions as set out in Articles 6, 7 and 8;

(d) assessment of the financial conglomerate's structure, organisation and internal control system as set out in Article 9;

(e) planning and coordination of supervisory activities in going concern as well as in emergency situations, in cooperation with the relevant competent authorities involved;

(f) other tasks, measures and decisions assigned to the coordinator by this Directive or deriving from the application of this Directive.

In order to facilitate and establish supplementary supervision on a broad legal basis, the coordinator and the other relevant competent authorities, and where necessary other competent authorities concerned, shall have coordination arrangements in place. The coordination arrangements may entrust additional tasks to the coordinator and may specify the procedures for the decision-making process among the relevant competent authorities as referred to in Articles 3, 4, 5(4), 6, 12(2), 16 and 18, and for cooperation with other competent authorities.

2. The coordinator should, when it needs information which has already been given to another competent authority in accordance with the sectoral rules, contact this authority whenever possible in order to prevent duplication of reporting to the various authorities involved in supervision.

3. Without prejudice to the possibility of delegating specific supervisory competences and responsibilities as provided for by Community legislation, the presence of a coordinator entrusted with specific tasks concerning the supplementary supervision of regulated entities in a financial conglomerate shall not affect the tasks and responsibilities of the competent authorities as provided for by the sectoral rules.

Article 12

Cooperation and exchange of information between competent authorities

1. The competent authorities responsible for the supervision of regulated entities in a financial conglomerate and the competent authority appointed as the coordinator for that financial conglomerate shall cooperate closely with each other. Without prejudice to their respective responsibilities as defined under sectoral rules, these authorities, whether or not established in the same Member State, shall provide one another with any information which is essential or relevant for the exercise of the other authorities' supervisory tasks under the sectoral rules and this Directive. In this regard, the competent authorities and the coordinator shall communicate on request all relevant information and shall communicate on their own initiative all essential information.

This cooperation shall at least provide for the gathering and the exchange of information with regard to the following items:

(a) identification of the group structure of all major entities belonging to the financial conglomerate, as well as of the competent authorities of the regulated entities in the group;

(b) the financial conglomerate's strategic policies;

(c) the financial situation of the financial conglomerate, in particular on capital adequacy, intra-group transactions, risk concentration and profitability;

(d) the financial conglomerate's major shareholders and management;

(e) the organisation, risk management and internal control systems at financial conglomerate level;

(f) procedures for the collection of information from the entities in a financial conglomerate, and the verification of that information;

(g) adverse developments in regulated entities or in other entities of the financial conglomerate which could seriously affect the regulated entities;

(h) major sanctions and exceptional measures taken by competent authorities in accordance with sectoral rules or this Directive.

The competent authorities may also exchange with the following authorities such information as may be needed for the performance of their respective tasks, regarding regulated entities in a financial conglomerate, in line with the provisions laid down in the sectoral rules: central banks, the European System of Central Banks and the European Central Bank.

2. Without prejudice to their respective responsibilities as defined under sectoral rules, the

competent authorities concerned shall, prior to their decision, consult each other with regard to the following items, where these decisions are of importance for other competent authorities' supervisory tasks:

(a) changes in the shareholder, organisational or management structure of regulated entities in a financial conglomerate, which require the approval or authorisation of competent authorities;

(b) major sanctions or exceptional measures taken by competent authorities.

A competent authority may decide not to consult in cases of urgency or where such consultation may jeopardise the effectiveness of the decisions. In this case, the competent authority shall, without delay, inform the other competent authorities.

3. The coordinator may invite the competent authorities of the Member State in which a parent undertaking has its head office, and which do not themselves exercise the supplementary supervision pursuant to Article 10, to ask the parent undertaking for any information which would be relevant for the exercise of its coordination tasks as laid down in Article 11, and to transmit that information to the coordinator.

Where the information referred to in Article 14(2) has already been given to a competent authority in accordance with sectoral rules, the competent authorities responsible for exercising supplementary supervision may apply to the first-mentioned authority to obtain the information.

4. Member States shall authorise the exchange of the information between their competent authorities and between their competent authorities and other authorities, as referred to in paragraphs 1, 2 and 3. The collection or possession of information with regard to an entity within a financial conglomerate which is not a regulated entity shall not in any way imply that the competent authorities are required to play a supervisory role in relation to these entities on a stand-alone basis.

Information received in the framework of supplementary supervision, and in particular any exchange of information between competent authorities and between competent authorities and other authorities which is provided for in this Directive, shall be subject to the provisions on professional secrecy and communication of confidential information laid down in the sectoral rules.

Article 13

Management body of mixed financial holding companies

Member States shall require that persons who effectively direct the business of a mixed financial holding company are of sufficiently good repute and have sufficient experience to perform those duties.

Article 14

Access to information

1. Member States shall ensure that there are no legal impediments within their jurisdiction preventing the natural and legal persons included within the scope of supplementary supervision, whether or not a regulated entity, from exchanging amongst themselves any information which would be relevant for the purposes of supplementary supervision.

2. Member States shall provide that, when approaching the entities in a financial conglomerate, whether or not a regulated entity, either directly or indirectly, their competent authorities responsible for exercising supplementary supervision shall have access to any information which would be relevant for the purposes of supplementary supervision.

Article 15

Verification

Where, in applying this Directive, competent authorities wish in specific cases to verify the information concerning an entity, whether or not regulated, which is part of a financial conglomerate and is situated in another Member State, they shall ask the competent authorities of that other Member State to have the verification carried out.

The authorities which receive such a request shall, within the framework of their competences, act upon it either by carrying out the verification themselves, by allowing an auditor or expert to carry it out, or by allowing the authority which made the request to carry it out itself.

The competent authority which made the request may, if it so wishes, participate in the verification when it does not carry out the verification itself.

Article 16
Enforcement measures

If the regulated entities in a financial conglomerate do not comply with the requirements referred to in Articles 6 to 9 or where the requirements are met but solvency may nevertheless be jeopardised or where the intra-group transactions or the risk concentrations are a threat to the regulated entities' financial position, the necessary measures shall be required in order to rectify the situation as soon as possible:
– by the coordinator with respect to the mixed financial holding company,
– by the competent authorities with respect to the regulated entities; to that end, the coordinator shall inform those competent authorities of its findings.

Without prejudice to Article 17(2), Member States may determine what measures may be taken by their competent authorities with respect to mixed financial holding companies.

The competent authorities involved, including the coordinator, shall where appropriate coordinate their supervisory actions.

Article 17
Additional powers of the competent authorities

1. Pending further harmonisation between sectoral rules, the Member States shall provide that their competent authorities shall have the power to take any supervisory measure deemed necessary in order to avoid or to deal with the circumvention of sectoral rules by regulated entities in a financial conglomerate.

2. Without prejudice to their criminal law provisions, Member States shall ensure that penalties or measures aimed at ending observed breaches or the causes of such breaches may be imposed on mixed financial holding companies, or their effective managers, which infringe laws, regulations or administrative provisions enacted to implement this Directive. In certain cases, such measures may require the intervention of the courts. The competent authorities shall cooperate closely to ensure that such penalties or measures produce the desired results.

SECTION 4
THIRD COUNTRIES

Article 18
Parent undertakings outside the Community

1. Without prejudice to the sectoral rules, in the case referred to in Article 5(3), competent authorities shall verify whether the regulated entities, the parent undertaking of which has its head office outside the Community, are subject to supervision by a third-country competent authority, which is equivalent to that provided for by the provisions of this Directive on the supplementary supervision of regulated entities referred to in Article 5(2). The verification shall be carried out by the competent authority which would be the coordinator if the criteria set out in Article 10(2) were to apply, on the request of the parent undertaking or of any of the regulated entities authorised in the Community or on its own initiative. That competent authority shall consult the other relevant competent authorities, and shall take into account any applicable guidance prepared by the Financial Conglomerates Committee in accordance with Article 21(5). For this purpose the competent authority shall consult the Committee before taking a decision.

2. In the absence of equivalent supervision referred to in paragraph 1, Member States shall apply to the regulated entities, by analogy, the provisions concerning the supplementary supervision of regulated entities referred to in Article 5(2). As an alternative, competent authorities may apply one of the methods set out in paragraph 3.

3. Member States shall allow their competent authorities to apply other methods which ensure

appropriate supplementary supervision of the regulated entities in a financial conglomerate. These methods must be agreed by the coordinator, after consultation with the other relevant competent authorities. The competent authorities may in particular require the establishment of a mixed financial holding company which has its head office in the Community, and apply this Directive to the regulated entities in the financial conglomerate headed by that holding company. The methods must achieve the objectives of the supplementary supervision as defined in this Directive and must be notified to the other competent authorities involved and the Commission.

Article 19
Cooperation with third-country competent authorities

1. Article 25(1) and (2) of Directive 2000/12/EC and Article 10a of Directive 98/78/EC shall apply mutatis mutandis to the negotiation of agreements with one or more third countries regarding the means of exercising supplementary supervision of regulated entities in a financial conglomerate.

[2. Without prejudice to Article 300(1) and (2) of the Treaty, the Commission shall, with the assistance of the European Banking Committee, the European Insurance and Occupational Pensions Committee and the Financial Conglomerates Committee, examine the outcome of the negotiations referred to in paragraph 1 and the resulting situation.]

¶ *Paragraph 2 of this article has been amended by article 11 of Directive 2005/1/EC, reproduced infra under no. B. 39.*

Chapter III
Powers Conferred on the Commission and Committee Procedure

Article 20
Powers conferred on the Commission

1. The Commission shall adopt, in accordance with the procedure referred to in Article 21(2), the technical adaptations to be made to this Directive in the following areas:

(a) a more precise formulation of the definitions referred to in Article 2 in order to take account of developments in financial markets in the application of this Directive;

(b) a more precise formulation of the definitions referred to in Article 2 in order to ensure uniform application of this Directive in the Community;

(c) the alignment of terminology and the framing of definitions in the Directive in accordance with subsequent Community acts on regulated entities and related matters;

(d) a more precise definition of the calculation methods set out in Annex I in order to take account of developments on financial markets and prudential techniques;

(e) coordination of the provisions adopted pursuant to Articles 7 and 8 and Annex II with a view to encouraging uniform application within the Community.

2. The Commission shall inform the public of any proposal presented in accordance with this Article and will consult interested parties prior to submitting the draft measures to the Financial Conglomerates Committee referred to in Article 21.

Article 21
Committee

1. The Commission shall be assisted by a Financial Conglomerates Committee, hereinafter referred to as the 'Committee'.

2. Where reference is made to this paragraph, Articles 5 and 7 of Decision 1999/468/EC shall apply, having regard to the provisions of Article 8 thereof.

The period laid down in Article 5(6) of Decision 1999/468/EC shall be set at three months.

3. The Committee shall adopt its rules of procedure.

4. Without prejudice to the implementing measures already adopted, on the expiry of a

four-year period following the entry into force of this Directive, the application of the provisions thereof requiring the adoption of technical rules and decisions in accordance with the procedure referred to in paragraph 2 shall be suspended. On a proposal from the Commission, the European Parliament and the Council may renew the provisions concerned in accordance with the procedure laid down in Article 251 of the Treaty and, to that end, they shall review them prior to the expiry of the period referred to above.

5. The Committee may give general guidance as to whether the supplementary supervision arrangements of competent authorities in third countries are likely to achieve the objectives of the supplementary supervision as defined in this Directive, in relation to the regulated entities in a financial conglomerate, the head of which has its head office outside the Community. The Committee shall keep any such guidance under review and take into account any changes to the supplementary supervision carried out by such competent authorities.

6. The Committee shall be kept informed by Member States of the principles they apply concerning the supervision of intra-group transactions and risk concentration.

CHAPTER IV
AMENDMENTS TO EXISTING DIRECTIVES

Article 22

Amendments to Directive 73/239/EEC

[. . .]

¶ *This article inserts article 12a and adds the text between square brackets to article 16(2) to Directive 73/239/EEC, reproduced infra under no. I. 3. The modifications are directly incorporated therein.*

Article 23

Amendments to Directive 79/267/EEC

[. . .]

¶ *This article inserts article 12a and adds the text between square brackets to article 18(2) to Directive 79/267/EEC, reproduced infra under no. I. 9. The modifications are directly incorporated therein.*

Article 24

Amendments to Directive 92/49/EEC

[. . .]

¶ *This article inserts article 15 and replaces article 16(5c) to Directive 92/49/EEC, reproduced infra under no. I. 25. The modifications are directly incorporated therein.*

Article 25

Amendments to Directive 92/96/EEC

[. . .]

¶ *This article inserts paragraph 1a in article 14 and replaces article 15(5c) of Directive 92/96/EEC, reproduced infra under no. I. 26. The modifications are directly incorporated therein.*

Article 26

Amendments to Directive 93/6/EEC

[. . .]

¶ *This article replaces the first and the second indent of article 7(3) of Directive 93/6/EEC, reproduced supra under no. B. 20. This Directive has been repealed as from 20 July 2006 by article 52 of Directive 2006/49/EC (OJ L 177, 30.6.2006, 201), reproduced infra under no. B. 42.*

Correlation Table	
Directive 2002/87/EC	Directive 2006/49/EC
Article 26	Article 3(3)(a) and (b)

Article 27

Amendments to Directive 93/22/EEC

[. . .]

¶ *This article adds the text between square brackets in article 6 and replaces article 9 of Directive 93/22/EEC, reproduced infra under no. S. 14. The modifications are directly incorporated therein.*

Article 28

Amendments to Directive 98/78/EC

[. . .]

¶ *This article amends article 1 point (g), (h), (i) and (j), adds the words between brackets in article 6(3), replaces article 8(2) first subparagraph, inserts articles 10a, 10b, the words between brackets in Annex I.1.B and point 2.4a in Annex I.2 to Directive 98/78/EC, reproduced infra under no. I. 28. The modifications are directly incorporated therein.*

Article 29
Amendments to Directive 2000/12/EC

[. . .]

¶ *This article amends article 1(a), point 9 and article 1(b), points 21 and 22, adds the words between square brackets in article 12, replaces articles 16(2), 34(2), 51(3), 54 and the last sentence of article 52(2) and inserts articles 54a, 55a, 56a, the words between square brackets in article 56(7) to Directive 2000/12/EC, reproduced supra under no. B. 32. This Directive has been repealed as from 20 July 2006 by article 158 of Directive 2006/48/EC (OJ L 177, 30.6.2006, 1), reproduced infra under no. B. 41.*

Correlation Table

Directive 2002/87/EC	Directive 2006/48/EC
Article 29(1)(a)	Article 4(10)
Article 29(1)(b)	Article 4(21) and (22)
Article 29(2)	Article 15(2) and (3)
Article 29(3)	Article 19(2)
Article 29(4)(a)	Article 57
Article 29(4)(b)	Article 58
Article 29(4)(b)	Article 59
Article 29(4)(b)	Article 60
Article 29(5)	Article 122(1) and (2)
Article 29(7)(a)	Article 133(1)
Article 29(8)	Article 135
Article 29(9)	Article 138
Article 29(10)	Article 141
Article 29(11)	Article 143

CHAPTER V
ASSET MANAGEMENT COMPANIES

Article 30
Asset management companies

Pending further coordination of sectoral rules, Member States shall provide for the inclusion of asset management companies:

(a) in the scope of consolidated supervision of credit institutions and investment firms, and/or in the scope of supplementary supervision of insurance undertakings in an insurance group; and

(b) where the group is a financial conglomerate, in the scope of supplementary supervision within the meaning of this Directive.

For the application of the first paragraph, Member States shall provide, or give their competent authorities the power to decide, according to which sectoral rules (banking sector, insurance sector or investment services sector) asset management companies shall be included in the consolidated and/or supplementary supervision referred to in (a) of the first paragraph. For the purposes of this provision, the relevant sectoral rules regarding the form and extent of the inclusion of financial institutions (where asset management companies are included in the scope of consolidated supervision of credit institutions and investment firms) and of reinsurance undertakings (where asset management companies are included in the scope of supplementary supervision of insurance undertakings) shall apply mutatis mutandis to asset management companies. For the purposes of supplementary supervision referred to in (b) of the first paragraph, the asset management company shall be treated as part of whichever sector it is included in by virtue of (a) of the first paragraph.

Where an asset management company is part of a financial conglomerate, any reference to the notion of regulated entity and any reference to the notion of competent authorities and relevant competent authorities shall therefore, for the purposes of this Directive, be understood as including, respectively, asset management companies and the competent authorities responsible for the supervision of asset management companies. This applies mutatis mutandis as regards groups referred to in (a) of the first paragraph.

CHAPTER VI
TRANSITIONAL AND FINAL PROVISIONS

Article 31
Report by the Commission

1. By 11 August 2007, the Commission shall submit to the Financial Conglomerates Committee referred to in Article 21 a report on Member States' practices, and, if necessary, on the need for further harmonisation, with regard to

– the inclusion of asset management companies in group-wide supervision,

- the choice and the application of the capital adequacy methods set out in Annex I,
- the definition of significant intra-group transactions and significant risk concentration and the supervision of intra-group transactions and risk concentration referred to in Annex II, in particular regarding the introduction of quantitative limits and qualitative requirements for this purpose,
- the intervals at which financial conglomerates shall carry out the calculations of capital adequacy requirements as set out in Article 6(2) and report to the coordinator on significant risk concentration as set out in Article 7(2).

The Commission shall consult the Committee before making its proposals.

2. Within one year of agreement being reached at international level on the rules for eliminating the double gearing of own funds in financial groups, the Commission shall examine how to bring the provisions of this Directive into line with those international agreements and, if necessary, make appropriate proposals.

Article 32

Transposition

Member States shall bring into force the laws, regulations and administrative provisions necessary to comply with this Directive before 11 August 2004. They shall forthwith inform the Commission thereof.

Member States shall provide that the provisions referred to in the first subparagraph shall first apply to the supervision of accounts for the financial year beginning on 1 January 2005 or during that calendar year.

When Member States adopt these measures, they shall contain a reference to this Directive or shall be accompanied by such reference on the occasion of their official publication. The methods of making such reference shall be laid down by Member States.

Article 33

Entry into force

This Directive shall enter into force on the day of its publication in the Official Journal of the European Union.

Article 34

Addressees

This Directive is addressed to the Member States.

Annex I

Capital Adequacy

The calculation of the supplementary capital adequacy requirements of the regulated entities in a financial conglomerate referred to in Article 6(1) shall be carried out in accordance with the technical principles and one of the methods described in this Annex.

Without prejudice to the provisions of the next paragraph, Member States shall allow their competent authorities, where they assume the role of coordinator with regard to a particular financial conglomerate, to decide, after consultation with the other relevant competent authorities and the conglomerate itself, which method shall be applied by that financial conglomerate.

Member States may require that the calculation be carried out according to one particular method among those described in this Annex if a financial conglomerate is headed by a regulated entity which has been authorised in that Member State. Where a financial conglomerate is not headed by a regulated entity within the meaning of Article 1, Member States shall authorise the application of any of the methods described in this Annex, except in situations where the relevant competent authorities are located in the same Member State, in which case that Member State may require the application of one of the methods.

I. Technical principles

1. *Extent and form of the supplementary capital adequacy requirements calculation*

Whichever method is used, when the entity is a subsidiary undertaking and has a solvency deficit, or, in the case of a non-regulated financial sector entity, a notional solvency deficit, the total solvency deficit of the subsidiary has to be taken into account. Where in this case, in the opinion of the coordinator, the responsibility of the parent undertaking owning a share of the capital is limited strictly and unambiguously to that share of the capital, the coordinator may give permission for the solvency deficit of the subsidiary undertaking to be taken into account on a proportional basis.

Where there are no capital ties between entities in a financial conglomerate, the coordinator, after consultation with the other relevant competent authorities, shall determine which proportional share will have to be taken into account, bearing in mind the liability to which the existing relationship gives rise.

2. *Other technical principles*

Regardless of the method used for the calculation of the supplementary capital adequacy requirements of regulated entities in a financial conglomerate as laid down in Section II of this Annex, the coordinator, and where necessary other competent authorities concerned, shall ensure that the following principles will apply:
(i) the multiple use of elements eligible for the calculation of own funds at the level of the financial conglomerate (multiple gearing) as well as any inappropriate intra-group creation of own funds must be eliminated; in order to ensure the elimination of multiple gearing and the intra-group creation of own funds, competent authorities shall apply by analogy the relevant principles laid down in the relevant sectoral rules;

(ii) pending further harmonisation of sectoral rules, the solvency requirements for each different financial sector represented in a financial conglomerate shall be covered by own funds elements in accordance with the corresponding sectoral rules; when there is a deficit of own funds at the financial conglomerate level, only own funds elements which are eligible according to each of the sectoral rules (cross-sector capital) shall qualify for verification of compliance with the additional solvency requirements;

where sectoral rules provide for limits on the eligibility of certain own funds instruments, which would qualify as cross-sector capital, these limits would apply mutatis mutandis when calculating own funds at the level of the financial conglomerate;

when calculating own funds at the level of the financial conglomerate, competent authorities shall also take into account the effectiveness of the transferability and availability of the own funds across the different legal entities in the group, given the objectives of the capital adequacy rules;

where, in the case of a non-regulated financial sector entity, a notional solvency requirement is calculated in accordance with Section II of this Annex, notional solvency requirement means the capital requirement with which such an entity would have to comply under the relevant sectoral rules as if it were a regulated entity of that particular financial sector; in the case of asset management companies, solvency requirement means the capital requirement set out in Article 5a(1)(a) of Directive 85/611/EEC; the notional solvency requirement of a mixed financial holding company shall be calculated according to the sectoral rules of the most important financial sector in the financial conglomerate.

II. Technical calculation methods

Method 1: 'Accounting consolidation' method
The calculation of the supplementary capital adequacy requirements of the regulated entities in a financial conglomerate shall be carried out on the basis of the consolidated accounts.

The supplementary capital adequacy requirements shall be calculated as the difference between:
(i) the own funds of the financial conglomerate calculated on the basis of the consolidated position of the group; the elements eligible are those that qualify in accordance with the relevant sectoral rules;
and
(ii) the sum of the solvency requirements for each different financial sector represented in the group; the solvency requirements for each different financial sector are calculated in accordance with the corresponding sectoral rules.

The sectoral rules referred to are in particular Directives 2000/12/EC, Title V, Chapter 3, as regards credit institutions, 98/78/EC as regards insurance undertakings, and 93/6/EEC as regards credit institutions and investment firms.

In the case of non-regulated financial sector entities which are not included in the aforementioned sectoral solvency requirement calculations, a notional solvency requirement shall be calculated.

The difference shall not be negative.

Method 2: 'Deduction and aggregation' method
The calculation of the supplementary capital adequacy requirements of the regulated entities in a financial conglomerate shall be carried out on the basis of the accounts of each of the entities in the group.

The supplementary capital adequacy requirements shall be calculated as the difference between:
(i) the sum of the own funds of each regulated and non-regulated financial sector entity in the financial conglomerate; the elements eligible are those which qualify in accordance with the relevant sectoral rules;
and
(ii) the sum of
– the solvency requirements for each regulated and non-regulated financial sector entity in the group; the solvency requirements shall be calculated in accordance with the relevant sectoral rules, and
– the book value of the participations in other entities of the group.

In the case of non-regulated financial sector entities, a notional solvency requirement shall be calculated. Own funds and solvency requirements shall be taken into account for their proportional share as provided for in Article 6(4) and in accordance with Section I of this Annex.

The difference shall not be negative.

Method 3: 'Book value/Requirement deduction' method
The calculation of the supplementary capital adequacy requirements of the regulated entities in a financial conglomerate shall be carried out on the basis of the accounts of each of the entities in the group.

The supplementary capital adequacy requirements shall be calculated as the difference between:
(i) the own funds of the parent undertaking or the entity at the head of the financial conglomerate; the elements eligible are those which qualify in accordance with the relevant sectoral rules;
and
(ii) the sum of
– the solvency requirement of the parent undertaking or the head referred to in (i), and
– the higher of the book value of the former's participation in other entities in the group and these entities' solvency requirements; the solvency requirements of the latter shall be taken into account for their proportional share as provided for in Article 6(4) and in accordance with Section I of this Annex.

In the case of non-regulated financial sector entities, a notional solvency requirement shall be calculated. When valuing the elements eligible for the calculation of the supplementary capital adequacy requirements, participations may be valued by the equity method in accordance with the option set out in Article 59(2)(b) of Directive 78/660/EEC.

The difference shall not be negative.

Method 4: Combination of methods 1, 2 and 3
Competent authorities may allow a combination of methods 1, 2 and 3, or a combination of two of these methods.

Annex II

Technical application of the provisions on intra-group transactions and risk concentration

The coordinator, after consultation with the other relevant competent authorities, shall identify the type of transactions and risks regulated entities in a particular financial conglomerate shall report in accordance with the provisions of Article 7(2) and Article 8(2) on the reporting of intra-group transactions and risk concentration.

When defining or giving their opinion about the type of transactions and risks, the coordinator and the relevant competent authorities shall take into account the specific group and risk management structure of the financial conglomerate. In order to identify significant intra-group transactions and significant risk concentration to be reported in accordance with the provisions of Articles 7 and 8, the coordinator, after consultation with the other relevant competent authorities and the conglomerate itself, shall define appropriate thresholds based on regulatory own funds and/or technical provisions.

When overviewing the intra-group transactions and risk concentrations, the coordinator shall in particular monitor the possible risk of contagion in the financial conglomerate, the risk of a conflict of interests, the risk of circumvention of sectoral rules, and the level or volume of risks.

Member States may allow their competent authorities to apply at the level of the financial conglomerate the provisions of the sectoral rules on intra-group transactions and risk concentration, in particular to avoid circumvention of the sectoral rules.

B. 39.

European Parliament and Council Directive 2005/1/EC
of 9 March 2005
amending Council Directives 73/239/EEC, 85/611/EEC, 91/675/EEC, 92/49/EEC and 93/6/EEC and Directives 94/19/EC, 98/78/EC, 2000/12/EC, 2001/34/EC, 2002/83/EC and 2002/87/EC in order to establish a new organisational structure for financial services committees[1]

(Text with EEA relevance)

THE EUROPEAN PARLIAMENT AND THE COUNCIL OF THE EUROPEAN UNION,

Having regard to the Treaty establishing the European Community, and in particular Article 47(2) thereof,

Having regard to the proposal from the Commission,

Having regard to the opinion of the European Economic and Social Committee,[2]

Having consulted the Committee of the Regions,

Having regard to the opinion of the European Central Bank,[3]

Acting in accordance with the procedure laid down in Article 251 of the Treaty,[4]

Whereas:

(1) The Commission Communication of 11 May 1999 entitled 'Implementing the framework for financial markets: action plan' identifies a series of actions that are required in order to complete the single market for financial services.

(2) At its meeting in Lisbon of 23 and 24 March 2000, the European Council called for the implementation of this Action Plan by 2005.

(3) On 17 July 2000, the Council set up the Committee of Wise Men on the Regulation of European Securities Markets. In its final report, the Committee of Wise Men called for the establishment of a four-level regulatory framework in order to make the regulatory process for Community securities legislation more flexible, effective and transparent.

(4) In its Resolution on more effective securities market regulation in the European Union, the Stockholm European Council of 23 and 24 March 2001 welcomed the report of the Committee of Wise Men and called for the four-level approach to be implemented.

(5) In the light of those developments, the Commission adopted on 6 June 2001 Decisions 2001/527/EC[5] and 2001/528/EC[6] setting up, respectively, the Committee of European Securities Regulators (CESR) and the European Securities Committee (ESC).

(6) Democratic accountability and transparency must be inherent in the Lamfalussy process and its extension, which can only be sufficiently guaranteed by respecting the interinstitutional balance with regard to implementing measures.

(7) This Directive amends Council Directives 73/239/EEC of 24 July 1973 on the coordination of laws, regulations and administrative

---

[1] OJ L 79, 24.3.2005, 9–17.
[2] OJ C 112, 30.4.2004, 21.
[3] OJ C 58, 6.3.2004, 23.
[4] Opinion of the European Parliament of 31 March 2004 (not yet published in the Official Journal) and Council Decision of 11 May 2004.
[5] OJ L 191, 13.7.2001, 43, reproduced infra under no. S. 19.
[6] OJ L 191, 13.7.2001, 45, reproduced infra under no. S. 19. Decision as amended by Decision 2004/8/EC (OJ L 3, 7.1.2004, 33), reproduced infra under no. I. 37.

provisions relating to the taking up and pursuit of the business of direct insurance other than life assurance,[7] 85/611/EEC of 20 December 1985 on the coordination of laws, regulations and administrative provisions relating to undertakings for collective investment in transferable securities (UCITS),[8] 91/675/EEC of 19 December 1991 setting up an insurance committee,[9] 92/49/EEC of 18 June 1992 on the coordination of laws, regulations and administrative provisions relating to direct insurance other than life assurance (third non-life insurance Directive)[10] and 93/6/EEC of 15 March 1993 on the capital adequacy of investment firms and credit institutions[11] and Directives of the European Parliament and of the Council 94/19/EC of 30 May 1994 on deposit-guarantee schemes,[12] 98/78/EC of 27 October 1998 on the supplementary supervision of insurance undertakings in an insurance group,[13] 2000/12/EC of 20 March 2000 relating to the taking up and pursuit of the business of credit institutions,[14] 2001/34/EC of 28 May 2001 on the admission of securities to official stock exchange listing and on information to be published on those securities,[15] 2002/83/EC of 5 November 2002 concerning life assurance[16] and 2002/87/EC of 16 December 2002 on the supplementary supervision of credit institutions, insurance undertakings and investment firms in a financial conglomerate. This Directive aims only at making certain changes in the organisational structure of committees. None of the modifications are intended to extend the powers to adopt implementing measures vested in the Commission pursuant to these Directives, nor the powers vested in the Council pursuant to Directive 93/6/EEC.

(8) In its Resolution of 5 February 2002, the European Parliament endorsed the four-level approach for securities, on the basis of a solemn declaration made before Parliament the same day by the Commission and the letter of 2 October 2001 addressed by the Internal Market Commissioner to the Chairman of the Parliament's Committee on Economic and Monetary Affairs with regard to the safeguards for the European Parliament's role in this process. In its Resolution of 21 November 2002 the Parliament called for certain aspects of that approach to be extended to the banking and insurance sectors subject to a clear commitment on the part of the Council to guarantee a proper institutional balance.

(9) The commitments made by the Commission regarding securities legislation via the abovementioned declaration of 5 February 2002 and letter of 2 October 2001 should be complemented by sufficient guarantees concerning a proper institutional balance.

(10) On 3 December 2002, the Council invited the Commission to implement arrangements for the remaining financial services sectors based upon the Final Report of the Committee of Wise Men.

(11) Safeguards with respect to the extension of the four-level approach are also required because the EU institutions do not yet benefit from an extensive practical experience of the four-level

---

[7] OJ L 228, 16.8.1973, 3, reproduced infra under no. I. 3. Directive as last amended by the 2003 Act of Accession.

[8] OJ L 375, 31.12.1985, 3, reproduced infra under no S. 6. Directive as last amended by Directive 2004/39/EC of the European Parliament and of the Council (OJ L 145, 30.4.2004, 1), reproduced infra under no. S. 29.

[9] OJ L 374, 31.12.1991, 32, reproduced infra under no. I. 24. Directive as amended by Regulation (EC) No 1882/2003 of the European Parliament and of the Council (OJ L 284, 31.10.2003, 1).

[10] OJ L 228, 11.8.1992, 1, reproduced infra under no. I. 25. Directive as last amended by Directive 2002/87/EC of the European Parliament and of the Council (OJ L 35, 11.2.2003, 1), reproduced supra under no. B. 38.

[11] OJ L 141, 11.6.1993, 1, reproduced supra under no. B. 20. Directive as last amended by Directive 2004/39/EC, reproduced infra under no. S. 29. Directive 93/6/EEC has been repealed as from 20 July 2006 by article 52 of Directive 2006/49/EC (OJ L 177, 30.6.2006, 201), reproduced infra under no. B. 42.

[12] OJ L 135, 31.5.1994, 5, reproduced supra under no. B. 22. Directive as amended by the 2003 Act of Accession.

[13] OJ L 330, 5.12.1998, 1, reproduced infra under no. I. 28. Directive as amended by Directive 2002/87/EC, reproduced supra under no. B. 38.

[14] OJ L 126, 26.5.2000, 1, reproduced supra under no. B. 32. Directive as last amended by Commission Directive 2004/69/EC (OJ L 125, 28.4.2004, 44). Directive 2000/12/EC has been repealed as from 20 July 2006 by article 158 of Directive 2006/48/EC (OJ L 177, 30.6.2006, 1), reproduced infra under no. B. 41.

[15] OJ L 184, 6.7.2001, 1, reproduced infra under no. S. 18. Directive as last amended by Directive 2004/109/EC (OJ L 390, 31.12.2004, 38), reproduced infra under no. S. 31.

[16] OJ L 345, 19.12.2002, 1, reproduced infra under no. I. 33. Directive as amended by Council Directive 2004/66/EC (OJ L 168, 1.5.2004, 35).

Lamfalussy approach. Furthermore, the first and second Interim Reports of the Interinstitutional Monitoring Group monitoring the Lamfalussy process have made certain remarks and criticisms concerning the functioning of the process.

(12) The speed of adoption of legislation and the quality of legislation are fundamental objectives of the Lamfalussy process. The success of the Lamfalussy process depends more on the political will of the institutional partners to set up an appropriate framework for the adoption of the legislation than on an acceleration of the setting up of the related technical delegated provisions. In addition, an overemphasis on the speed of setting up of the delegated provisions could create significant problems with regard to the quality of those provisions.

(13) The extension of the Lamfalussy procedure is without prejudice to possible decisions regarding the organisation of supervision at a European level.

(14) For those purposes, as regards the banking sector, the role of the Banking Advisory Committee (BAC) set up by Directive 2000/12/EC should be adapted.

(15) To reflect that adapted role, the BAC should be replaced by 'the European Banking Committee'.

(16) The measures necessary for the implementation of Directive 2000/12/EC are measures of general scope and should be adopted in accordance with Article 5 of Council Decision 1999/468/EC of 28 June 1999 laying down the procedures for the exercise of implementing powers conferred on the Commission.[17]

(17) The implementing measures adopted should not modify the essential provisions of the Directives.

(18) The European Parliament should be given a period of three months from the first transmission of draft implementing measures to allow it to examine them and to give its opinion. However, in urgent and duly justified cases this period may be shortened. If, within that period, a resolution is passed by the European Parliament, the Commission will re-examine the draft measures.

(19) In exercising its implementing powers, the Commission should respect the following principles: the need to ensure confidence in financial markets among investors by promoting high standards of transparency in those markets; the need to provide investors with a wide range of competing investments and a level of disclosure and protection tailored to their circumstances; the need to ensure that independent regulatory authorities enforce the rules consistently, especially as regards the fight against economic crime; the need for high levels of transparency and consultation with all market participants and with the European Parliament and the Council; the need to encourage innovation in financial markets if they are to be dynamic and efficient; the need to ensure market integrity by close and reactive monitoring of financial innovation; the importance of reducing the cost of, and increasing access to, capital; the balance of costs and benefits to market participants on a long-term basis (including small and medium-sized businesses and small investors) in any implementing measures; the need to foster the international competitiveness of EU financial markets without prejudice to a much-needed extension of international cooperation; the need to achieve a level playing field for all market participants by establishing EU-wide regulations every time it is appropriate; the need to respect differences in national markets where these do not unduly impinge on the cohesion of the single market; and the need to ensure coherence with other Community legislation in this area, as imbalances in information and a lack of transparency may jeopardise the operation of the markets and above all harm consumers and small investors.

(20) Certain existing provisions for technical amendments to Directive 2000/12/EC need to be brought into line with Decision 1999/468/EC.

(21) In order to ensure institutional and legal consistency with the approach taken in other

---

[17] OJ L 184, 17.7.1999, 23.

Community sectors, Commission Decision 2004/10/EC[18] established the European Banking Committee in an advisory capacity to assist the Commission as regards the development of Community banking legislation. References to the advisory functions of the BAC in Directive 2000/12/EC should therefore be deleted.

(22) As regards the monitoring of observation ratios for the solvency and liquidity of credit institutions, the competencies of the BAC are no longer needed in view of the harmonisation of capital adequacy rules and of developments in the techniques used by credit institutions to measure and manage their liquidity risk.

(23) Moreover, the substantial progress made in cooperation and exchange of information between supervisory authorities, in particular through Memoranda of Understanding, has rendered superfluous the regular monitoring by the Commission of certain individual supervisory decisions and their systematic reporting to the BAC.

(24) The establishment of the European Banking Committee should not rule out other forms of cooperation between the different authorities involved in the regulation and supervision of credit institutions, in particular within the Committee of European Banking Supervisors established by Commission Decision 2004/5/EC.[19]

(25) The Insurance Committee (IC) set up under Directive 91/675/EEC is to assist the Commission in the exercise of the implementing powers granted by Directives adopted in the field of insurance, and in particular to make the technical adaptations necessary to take account of developments in the insurance sector; such measures being taken in accordance with Decision 1999/468/EC.

(26) Under Directive 91/675/EEC, the IC is also to examine any question relating to the application of Community provisions concerning the insurance sector and, in particular, to advise the Commission on proposals for legislation which the Commission intends to present to the European Parliament and to the Council.

(27) In order to build an internal market where policyholders and beneficiaries are properly protected, insurance and occupational pensions undertakings operating in the internal market under the principles of freedom of establishment and freedom to provide services are subject to specific Community legislation. To ensure the proper functioning of the internal market and maintain financial stability, that legislation should be capable of being rapidly adapted to market changes affecting those sectors, in particular with regard to financial and technical aspects.

(28) The role of the IC should therefore be adapted, and this Committee should accordingly be renamed 'the European Insurance and Occupational Pensions Committee'. However, in the occupational pensions field, the European Insurance and Occupational Pensions Committee should not address labour and social law aspects such as the organisation of occupational regimes, in particular compulsory membership and the results of collective bargaining agreements.

(29) The measures necessary for the implementation of acts covered by Directive 91/675/EEC are measures of general scope and should be adopted in accordance with Article 5 of Decision 1999/468/EC.

(30) To ensure institutional and legal consistency with the approach taken in other Community sectors, Commission Decision 2004/9/EC,[20] established the European Insurance and Occupational Pensions Committee in an advisory capacity to assist the Commission in the fields of insurance and occupational pensions. References to the advisory functions of the IC in Directive 91/675/EEC should therefore be deleted.

(31) Directive 85/611/EEC set up the UCITS Contact Committee to assist the Commission by

---

[18] OJ L 3, 7.1.2004, 36.
[19] OJ L 3, 7.1.2004, 28.

[20] OJ L 3, 7.1.2004, 34, reproduced infra under no. I. 38.

facilitating the harmonised implementation of that Directive through regular consultations, promoting consultation between Member States and advising the Commission, if necessary, on amendments to be made to that Directive.

(32) The UCITS Contact Committee also acts as a 'comitology' Committee within the meaning of Decision 1999/468/EC to assist the Commission with regard to the technical amendments to be made to Directive 85/611/EEC.

(33) On 3 December 2002, the Council invited the Commission to take steps in order to transfer to the ESC, inter alia, the function of advice to the Commission in the exercise of its implementing powers held by the UCITS Contact Committee.

(34) In order to fully implement the model set out in recent Directives in the securities field, in particular Directive 2003/6/EC of the European Parliament and of the Council of 28 January 2003 on insider dealing and market manipulation (market abuse),[21] which gives to the ESC the function to advise the Commission in the exercise of its regulatory powers, while leaving the organisation of other aspects of the ESC's work to be governed by Decision 2001/528/EC, it is necessary to delete the provisions setting up, under Article 53 of Directive 85/611/EEC, the organisation and functions of the present UCITS Contact Committee outside its 'comitology' capacity.

(35) The competences of the ESC should therefore be expressly extended beyond those already conferred upon it by Directive 2003/6/EC, to cover the functions currently laid down in Directive 85/611/EEC. The measures necessary for the implementation of the latter Directive are measures of general scope and should be adopted in accordance with Article 5 of Decision 1999/468/EC.

(36) It is accordingly necessary to amend Directives 73/239/EEC, 85/611/EEC, 91/675/EEC, 92/49/EEC, 93/6/EEC, 94/19/EC, 98/78/

---

[21] OJ L 96, 12.4.2003, 16, reproduced infra under no. S. 24.

EC, 2000/12/EC, 2001/34/EC, 2002/83/EC and 2002/87/EC,

HAVE ADOPTED THIS DIRECTIVE:

CHAPTER I—CHAPTER IV

[. . .]

¶ *This Directive modifies Council Directives 73/239/EEC (I.3.), 85/611/EEC (S.6.), 91/675/EEC (I.24.), 92/49/EEC (I.25.) and 93/6/EEC (B.20.) and Directives of the European Parliament and of the Council 94/19/EC (B.22.), 98/78/EC (I.28.), 2000/12/EC (B.32., which subsequently has been repealed as from 20 July 2006 by article 158 of Directive 2006/48/EC, reproduced infra under no. B.41)), 2001/34/EC (S.18.), 2002/83/EC (I.33.) and 2002/87/EC (B.38.). The modifications are directly incorporated therein.*

Correlation Table

Directive 2005/1/EC	Directive 2006/48/EC
Article 3(2)	Article 3(1), third subparagraph
Article 3(8)	Article 39(3)
Article 3(10)	Article 143
Article 3(10)	Article 151

CHAPTER V
FINAL PROVISIONS

Article 12
Implementing measures

1. The implementing measures adopted in accordance with the procedure referred to in Articles 5 and 7 of Decision 1999/468/EC having regard to the provisions of Article 8 thereof must not modify the essential provisions of the Directives.

2. The period laid down in Article 5(6) of Decision 1999/468/EC shall be set at three months.

3. Should the conditions established under the Treaty governing the exercise of implementing powers conferred on the Commission be modified, the Commission shall review this Directive

and, if appropriate, propose amendments. Such a review shall in any case be carried out by 31 December 2007 at the latest.

Article 13

Transposition

Member States shall bring into force the laws, regulations and administrative provisions necessary to comply with this Directive by 13 May 2005.

When Member States adopt these provisions, they shall contain a reference to this Directive or shall be accompanied by such a reference on the occasion of their official publication. The methods of making such reference shall be laid down by Member States.

Article 14

Entry into force

This Directive shall enter into force on the 20th day following its publication in the Official Journal of the European Union.

Article 15

Addressees

This Directive is addressed to the Member States.

B. 40.

European Parliament and Council Directive 2005/60/EC
of 26 October 2005
on the prevention of the use of the financial system for the purpose of money laundering and terrorist financing[1]

(Text with EEA relevance)

THE EUROPEAN PARLIAMENT AND THE COUNCIL OF THE EUROPEAN UNION,

Having regard to the Treaty establishing the European Community, and in particular Article 47(2), first and third sentences, and Article 95 thereof,

Having regard to the proposal from the Commission,

Having regard to the opinion of the European Economic and Social Committee,[2]

Having regard to the opinion of the European Central Bank,[3]

Acting in accordance with the procedure laid down in Article 251 of the Treaty,[4]

Whereas:

(1) Massive flows of dirty money can damage the stability and reputation of the financial sector and threaten the single market, and terrorism shakes the very foundations of our society. In addition to the criminal law approach, a preventive effort via the financial system can produce results.

(2) The soundness, integrity and stability of credit and financial institutions and confidence in the financial system as a whole could be seriously jeopardised by the efforts of criminals and their associates either to disguise the origin of criminal proceeds or to channel lawful or unlawful money for terrorist purposes. In order to avoid Member States' adopting measures to protect their financial systems which could be inconsistent with the functioning of the internal market and with the prescriptions of the rule of law and Community public policy, Community action in this area is necessary.

(3) In order to facilitate their criminal activities, money launderers and terrorist financers could try to take advantage of the freedom of capital movements and the freedom to supply financial services which the integrated financial area entails, if certain coordinating measures are not adopted at Community level.

(4) In order to respond to these concerns in the field of money laundering, Council Directive 91/308/EEC of 10 June 1991 on prevention of the use of the financial system for the purpose of money laundering[5] was adopted. It required Member States to prohibit money laundering and to oblige the financial sector, comprising credit institutions and a wide range of other financial institutions, to identify their customers, keep appropriate records, establish internal procedures to train staff and guard against money laundering and to report any indications of money laundering to the competent authorities.

---

[1] OJ L 309, 25.11.2005, 15–36.
[2] Opinion delivered on 11 May 2005 (not yet published in the Official Journal).
[3] OJ C 40, 17.2.2005, 9.
[4] Opinion of the European Parliament of 26 May 2005 (not yet published in the Official Journal) and Council Decision of 19 September 2005.

[5] OJ L 166, 28.6.1991, 77, reproduced supra under no. B. 15. Directive as amended by Directive 2001/97/EC of the European Parliament and of the Council (OJ L 344, 28.12.2001, 76), reproduced supra under no. B. 37.

(5) Money laundering and terrorist financing are frequently carried out in an international context. Measures adopted solely at national or even Community level, without taking account of international coordination and cooperation, would have very limited effects. The measures adopted by the Community in this field should therefore be consistent with other action undertaken in other international fora. The Community action should continue to take particular account of the Recommendations of the Financial Action Task Force (hereinafter referred to as the FATF), which constitutes the foremost international body active in the fight against money laundering and terrorist financing. Since the FATF Recommendations were substantially revised and expanded in 2003, this Directive should be in line with that new international standard.

(6) The General Agreement on Trade in Services (GATS) allows Members to adopt measures necessary to protect public morals and prevent fraud and adopt measures for prudential reasons, including for ensuring the stability and integrity of the financial system.

(7) Although initially limited to drugs offences, there has been a trend in recent years towards a much wider definition of money laundering based on a broader range of predicate offences. A wider range of predicate offences facilitates the reporting of suspicious transactions and international cooperation in this area. Therefore, the definition of serious crime should be brought into line with the definition of serious crime in Council Framework Decision 2001/500/JHA of 26 June 2001 on money laundering, the identification, tracing, freezing, seizing and confiscation of instrumentalities and the proceeds of crime.[6]

(8) Furthermore, the misuse of the financial system to channel criminal or even clean money to terrorist purposes poses a clear risk to the integrity, proper functioning, reputation and stability of the financial system. Accordingly, the preventive measures of this Directive should cover not only the manipulation of money derived from crime but also the collection of money or property for terrorist purposes.

(9) Directive 91/308/EEC, though imposing a customer identification obligation, contained relatively little detail on the relevant procedures. In view of the crucial importance of this aspect of the prevention of money laundering and terrorist financing, it is appropriate, in accordance with the new international standards, to introduce more specific and detailed provisions relating to the identification of the customer and of any beneficial owner and the verification of their identity. To that end a precise definition of 'beneficial owner' is essential. Where the individual beneficiaries of a legal entity or arrangement such as a foundation or trust are yet to be determined, and it is therefore impossible to identify an individual as the beneficial owner, it would suffice to identify the class of persons intended to be the beneficiaries of the foundation or trust. This requirement should not include the identification of the individuals within that class of persons.

(10) The institutions and persons covered by this Directive should, in conformity with this Directive, identify and verify the identity of the beneficial owner. To fulfil this requirement, it should be left to those institutions and persons whether they make use of public records of beneficial owners, ask their clients for relevant data or obtain the information otherwise, taking into account the fact that the extent of such customer due diligence measures relates to the risk of money laundering and terrorist financing, which depends on the type of customer, business relationship, product or transaction.

(11) Credit agreements in which the credit account serves exclusively to settle the loan and the repayment of the loan is effected from an account which was opened in the name of the customer with a credit institution covered by this Directive pursuant to Article 8(1)(a) to (c) should generally be considered as an example of types of less risky transactions.

(12) To the extent that the providers of the property of a legal entity or arrangement have significant control over the use of the property they should be identified as a beneficial owner.

---

[6] OJ L 182, 5.7.2001, 1.

(13) Trust relationships are widely used in commercial products as an internationally recognised feature of the comprehensively supervised wholesale financial markets. An obligation to identify the beneficial owner does not arise from the fact alone that there is a trust relationship in this particular case.

(14) This Directive should also apply to those activities of the institutions and persons covered hereunder which are performed on the Internet.

(15) As the tightening of controls in the financial sector has prompted money launderers and terrorist financers to seek alternative methods for concealing the origin of the proceeds of crime and as such channels can be used for terrorist financing, the anti-money laundering and anti-terrorist financing obligations should cover life insurance intermediaries and trust and company service providers.

(16) Entities already falling under the legal responsibility of an insurance undertaking, and therefore falling within the scope of this Directive, should not be included within the category of insurance intermediary.

(17) Acting as a company director or secretary does not of itself make someone a trust and company service provider. For that reason, the definition covers only those persons that act as a company director or secretary for a third party and by way of business.

(18) The use of large cash payments has repeatedly proven to be very vulnerable to money laundering and terrorist financing. Therefore, in those Member States that allow cash payments above the established threshold, all natural or legal persons trading in goods by way of business should be covered by this Directive when accepting such cash payments. Dealers in high-value goods, such as precious stones or metals, or works of art, and auctioneers are in any event covered by this Directive to the extent that payments to them are made in cash in an amount of EUR 15 000 or more. To ensure effective monitoring of compliance with this Directive by that potentially wide group of institutions and persons, Member States may focus their monitoring activities in particular on those natural and legal persons trading in goods that are exposed to a relatively high risk of money laundering or terrorist financing, in accordance with the principle of risk-based supervision. In view of the different situations in the various Member States, Member States may decide to adopt stricter provisions, in order to properly address the risk involved with large cash payments.

(19) Directive 91/308/EEC brought notaries and other independent legal professionals within the scope of the Community anti-money laundering regime; this coverage should be maintained unchanged in this Directive; these legal professionals, as defined by the Member States, are subject to the provisions of this Directive when participating in financial or corporate transactions, including providing tax advice, where there is the greatest risk of the services of those legal professionals being misused for the purpose of laundering the proceeds of criminal activity or for the purpose of terrorist financing.

(20) Where independent members of professions providing legal advice which are legally recognised and controlled, such as lawyers, are ascertaining the legal position of a client or representing a client in legal proceedings, it would not be appropriate under this Directive to put those legal professionals in respect of these activities under an obligation to report suspicions of money laundering or terrorist financing. There must be exemptions from any obligation to report information obtained either before, during or after judicial proceedings, or in the course of ascertaining the legal position for a client. Thus, legal advice shall remain subject to the obligation of professional secrecy unless the legal counsellor is taking part in money laundering or terrorist financing, the legal advice is provided for money laundering or terrorist financing purposes or the lawyer knows that the client is seeking legal advice for money laundering or terrorist financing purposes.

(21) Directly comparable services need to be treated in the same manner when provided by any of the professionals covered by this Directive. In order to ensure the respect of the rights laid

down in the European Convention for the Protection of Human Rights and Fundamental Freedoms and the Treaty on European Union, in the case of auditors, external accountants and tax advisors, who, in some Member States, may defend or represent a client in the context of judicial proceedings or ascertain a client's legal position, the information they obtain in the performance of those tasks should not be subject to the reporting obligations in accordance with this Directive.

(22) It should be recognised that the risk of money laundering and terrorist financing is not the same in every case. In line with a risk-based approach, the principle should be introduced into Community legislation that simplified customer due diligence is allowed in appropriate cases.

(23) The derogation concerning the identification of beneficial owners of pooled accounts held by notaries or other independent legal professionals should be without prejudice to the obligations that those notaries or other independent legal professionals have pursuant to this Directive. Those obligations include the need for such notaries or other independent legal professionals themselves to identify the beneficial owners of the pooled accounts held by them.

(24) Equally, Community legislation should recognise that certain situations present a greater risk of money laundering or terrorist financing. Although the identity and business profile of all customers should be established, there are cases where particularly rigorous customer identification and verification procedures are required.

(25) This is particularly true of business relationships with individuals holding, or having held, important public positions, particularly those from countries where corruption is widespread. Such relationships may expose the financial sector in particular to significant reputational and/or legal risks. The international effort to combat corruption also justifies the need to pay special attention to such cases and to apply the complete normal customer due diligence measures in respect of domestic politically exposed persons or enhanced customer due diligence measures in respect of politically exposed persons residing in another Member State or in a third country.

(26) Obtaining approval from senior management for establishing business relationships should not imply obtaining approval from the board of directors but from the immediate higher level of the hierarchy of the person seeking such approval.

(27) In order to avoid repeated customer identification procedures, leading to delays and inefficiency in business, it is appropriate, subject to suitable safeguards, to allow customers to be introduced whose identification has been carried out elsewhere. Where an institution or person covered by this Directive relies on a third party, the ultimate responsibility for the customer due diligence procedure remains with the institution or person to whom the customer is introduced. The third party, or introducer, also retains his own responsibility for all the requirements in this Directive, including the requirement to report suspicious transactions and maintain records, to the extent that he has a relationship with the customer that is covered by this Directive.

(28) In the case of agency or outsourcing relationships on a contractual basis between institutions or persons covered by this Directive and external natural or legal persons not covered hereby, any anti-money laundering and anti-terrorist financing obligations for those agents or outsourcing service providers as part of the institutions or persons covered by this Directive, may only arise from contract and not from this Directive. The responsibility for complying with this Directive should remain with the institution or person covered hereby.

(29) Suspicious transactions should be reported to the financial intelligence unit (FIU), which serves as a national centre for receiving, analysing and disseminating to the competent authorities suspicious transaction reports and other information regarding potential money laundering or terrorist financing. This should not compel Member States to change their existing reporting systems where the reporting is done through a public prosecutor or other law enforcement authorities, as long as the information is forwarded promptly and unfiltered to FIUs, allowing them to conduct their business properly,

including international cooperation with other FIUs.

(30) By way of derogation from the general prohibition on executing suspicious transactions, the institutions and persons covered by this Directive may execute suspicious transactions before informing the competent authorities, where refraining from the execution thereof is impossible or likely to frustrate efforts to pursue the beneficiaries of a suspected money laundering or terrorist financing operation. This, however, should be without prejudice to the international obligations accepted by the Member States to freeze without delay funds or other assets of terrorists, terrorist organisations or those who finance terrorism, in accordance with the relevant United Nations Security Council resolutions.

(31) Where a Member State decides to make use of the exemptions provided for in Article 23(2), it may allow or require the self-regulatory body representing the persons referred to therein not to transmit to the FIU any information obtained from those persons in the circumstances referred to in that Article.

(32) There has been a number of cases of employees who report their suspicions of money laundering being subjected to threats or hostile action. Although this Directive cannot interfere with Member States' judicial procedures, this is a crucial issue for the effectiveness of the anti-money laundering and anti-terrorist financing system. Member States should be aware of this problem and should do whatever they can to protect employees from such threats or hostile action.

(33) Disclosure of information as referred to in Article 28 should be in accordance with the rules on transfer of personal data to third countries as laid down in Directive 95/46/EC of the European Parliament and of the Council of 24 October 1995 on the protection of individuals with regard to the processing of personal data and on the free movement of such data.[7] Moreover, Article 28 cannot interfere with national data protection and professional secrecy legislation.

---

[7] OJ L 281, 23.11.1995, 31. Directive as amended by Regulation (EC) No 1882/2003 (OJ L 284, 31.10.2003, 1).

(34) Persons who merely convert paper documents into electronic data and are acting under a contract with a credit institution or a financial institution do not fall within the scope of this Directive, nor does any natural or legal person that provides credit or financial institutions solely with a message or other support systems for transmitting funds or with clearing and settlement systems.

(35) Money laundering and terrorist financing are international problems and the effort to combat them should be global. Where Community credit and financial institutions have branches and subsidiaries located in third countries where the legislation in this area is deficient, they should, in order to avoid the application of very different standards within an institution or group of institutions, apply the Community standard or notify the competent authorities of the home Member State if this application is impossible.

(36) It is important that credit and financial institutions should be able to respond rapidly to requests for information on whether they maintain business relationships with named persons. For the purpose of identifying such business relationships in order to be able to provide that information quickly, credit and financial institutions should have effective systems in place which are commensurate with the size and nature of their business. In particular it would be appropriate for credit institutions and larger financial institutions to have electronic systems at their disposal. This provision is of particular importance in the context of procedures leading to measures such as the freezing or seizing of assets (including terrorist assets), pursuant to applicable national or Community legislation with a view to combating terrorism.

(37) This Directive establishes detailed rules for customer due diligence, including enhanced customer due diligence for high-risk customers or business relationships, such as appropriate procedures to determine whether a person is a politically exposed person, and certain additional, more detailed requirements, such as the existence of compliance management procedures and policies. All these requirements are to be met by each of

the institutions and persons covered by this Directive, while Member States are expected to tailor the detailed implementation of those provisions to the particularities of the various professions and to the differences in scale and size of the institutions and persons covered by this Directive.

(38) In order to ensure that the institutions and others subject to Community legislation in this field remain committed, feedback should, where practicable, be made available to them on the usefulness and follow-up of the reports they present. To make this possible, and to be able to review the effectiveness of their systems to combat money laundering and terrorist financing Member States should keep and improve the relevant statistics.

(39) When registering or licensing a currency exchange office, a trust and company service provider or a casino nationally, competent authorities should ensure that the persons who effectively direct or will direct the business of such entities and the beneficial owners of such entities are fit and proper persons. The criteria for determining whether or not a person is fit and proper should be established in conformity with national law. As a minimum, such criteria should reflect the need to protect such entities from being misused by their managers or beneficial owners for criminal purposes.

(40) Taking into account the international character of money laundering and terrorist financing, coordination and cooperation between FIUs as referred to in Council Decision 2000/642/JHA of 17 October 2000 concerning arrangements for cooperation between financial intelligence units of the Member States in respect of exchanging information,[8] including the establishment of an EU FIU-net, should be encouraged to the greatest possible extent. To that end, the Commission should lend such assistance as may be needed to facilitate such coordination, including financial assistance.

(41) The importance of combating money laundering and terrorist financing should lead Member States to lay down effective, proportionate and dissuasive penalties in national law for failure to respect the national provisions adopted pursuant to this Directive. Provision should be made for penalties in respect of natural and legal persons. Since legal persons are often involved in complex money laundering or terrorist financing operations, sanctions should also be adjusted in line with the activity carried on by legal persons.

(42) Natural persons exercising any of the activities referred to in Article 2(1)(3)(a) and (b) within the structure of a legal person, but on an independent basis, should be independently responsible for compliance with the provisions of this Directive, with the exception of Article 35.

(43) Clarification of the technical aspects of the rules laid down in this Directive may be necessary to ensure an effective and sufficiently consistent implementation of this Directive, taking into account the different financial instruments, professions and risks in the different Member States and the technical developments in the fight against money laundering and terrorist financing. The Commission should accordingly be empowered to adopt implementing measures, such as certain criteria for identifying low and high risk situations in which simplified due diligence could suffice or enhanced due diligence would be appropriate, provided that they do not modify the essential elements of this Directive and provided that the Commission acts in accordance with the principles set out herein, after consulting the Committee on the Prevention of Money Laundering and Terrorist Financing.

(44) The measures necessary for the implementation of this Directive should be adopted in accordance with Council Decision 1999/468/EC of 28 June 1999 laying down the procedures for the exercise of implementing powers conferred on the Commission.[9] To that end a new Committee on the Prevention of Money Laundering and Terrorist Financing, replacing the Money Laundering Contact Committee

---

[8] OJ L 271, 24.10.2000, 4.

[9] OJ L 184, 17.7.1999, 23.

set up by Directive 91/308/EEC, should be established.

(45) In view of the very substantial amendments that would need to be made to Directive 91/308/EEC, it should be repealed for reasons of clarity.

(46) Since the objective of this Directive, namely the prevention of the use of the financial system for the purpose of money laundering and terrorist financing, cannot be sufficiently achieved by the Member States and can therefore, by reason of the scale and effects of the action, be better achieved at Community level, the Community may adopt measures, in accordance with the principle of subsidiarity as set out in Article 5 of the Treaty. In accordance with the principle of proportionality, as set out in that Article, this Directive does not go beyond what is necessary in order to achieve that objective.

(47) In exercising its implementing powers in accordance with this Directive, the Commission should respect the following principles: the need for high levels of transparency and consultation with institutions and persons covered by this Directive and with the European Parliament and the Council; the need to ensure that competent authorities will be able to ensure compliance with the rules consistently; the balance of costs and benefits to institutions and persons covered by this Directive on a long-term basis in any implementing measures; the need to respect the necessary flexibility in the application of the implementing measures in accordance with a risk-sensitive approach; the need to ensure coherence with other Community legislation in this area; the need to protect the Community, its Member States and their citizens from the consequences of money laundering and terrorist financing.

(48) This Directive respects the fundamental rights and observes the principles recognised in particular by the Charter of Fundamental Rights of the European Union. Nothing in this Directive should be interpreted or implemented in a manner that is inconsistent with the European Convention on Human Rights,

HAVE ADOPTED THIS DIRECTIVE:

Chapter I
Subject Matter, Scope and Definitions

Article 1

1. Member States shall ensure that money laundering and terrorist financing are prohibited.

2. For the purposes of this Directive, the following conduct, when committed intentionally, shall be regarded as money laundering:

(a) the conversion or transfer of property, knowing that such property is derived from criminal activity or from an act of participation in such activity, for the purpose of concealing or disguising the illicit origin of the property or of assisting any person who is involved in the commission of such activity to evade the legal consequences of his action;

(b) the concealment or disguise of the true nature, source, location, disposition, movement, rights with respect to, or ownership of property, knowing that such property is derived from criminal activity or from an act of participation in such activity;

(c) the acquisition, possession or use of property, knowing, at the time of receipt, that such property was derived from criminal activity or from an act of participation in such activity;

(d) participation in, association to commit, attempts to commit and aiding, abetting, facilitating and counselling the commission of any of the actions mentioned in the foregoing points.

3. Money laundering shall be regarded as such even where the activities which generated the property to be laundered were carried out in the territory of another Member State or in that of a third country.

4. For the purposes of this Directive, 'terrorist financing' means the provision or collection of funds, by any means, directly or indirectly, with the intention that they should be used or in the knowledge that they are to be used, in full or in part, in order to carry out any of the offences within the meaning of Articles 1 to 4 of Council

Framework Decision 2002/475/JHA of 13 June 2002 on combating terrorism.[10]

5. Knowledge, intent or purpose required as an element of the activities mentioned in paragraphs 2 and 4 may be inferred from objective factual circumstances.

Article 2

1. This Directive shall apply to:

(1) credit institutions;

(2) financial institutions;

(3) the following legal or natural persons acting in the exercise of their professional activities:

(a) auditors, external accountants and tax advisors;

(b) notaries and other independent legal professionals, when they participate, whether by acting on behalf of and for their client in any financial or real estate transaction, or by assisting in the planning or execution of transactions for their client concerning the:
 (i) buying and selling of real property or business entities;
 (ii) managing of client money, securities or other assets;
 (iii) opening or management of bank, savings or securities accounts;
 (iv) organisation of contributions necessary for the creation, operation or management of companies;
 (v) creation, operation or management of trusts, companies or similar structures;

(c) trust or company service providers not already covered under points (a) or (b);

(d) real estate agents;

(e) other natural or legal persons trading in goods, only to the extent that payments are made in cash in an amount of EUR 15 000 or more, whether the transaction is executed in a single operation or in several operations which appear to be linked;

(f) casinos.

2. Member States may decide that legal and natural persons who engage in a financial activity on an occasional or very limited basis and where there is little risk of money laundering or terrorist financing occurring do not fall within the scope of Article 3(1) or (2).

Article 3

For the purposes of this Directive the following definitions shall apply:

(1) 'credit institution' means a credit institution, as defined in the first subparagraph of Article 1(1) of Directive 2000/12/EC of the European Parliament and of the Council of 20 March 2000 relating to the taking up and pursuit of the business of credit institutions,[11] including branches within the meaning of Article 1(3) of that Directive located in the Community of credit institutions having their head offices inside or outside the Community;

(2) 'financial institution' means:

(a) an undertaking other than a credit institution which carries out one or more of the operations included in points 2 to 12 and 14 of Annex I to Directive 2000/12/EC, including the activities of currency exchange offices (bureaux de change) and of money transmission or remittance offices;

(b) an insurance company duly authorised in accordance with Directive 2002/83/EC of the European Parliament and of the Council of 5 November 2002 concerning life assurance,[12] insofar as it carries out activities covered by that Directive;

(c) an investment firm as defined in point 1 of Article 4(1) of Directive 2004/39/EC of the European Parliament and of the Council of 21 April 2004 on markets in financial instruments;[13]

---

[10] OJ L 164, 22.6.2002, 3.

[11] OJ L 126, 26.5.2000, 1, reproduced supra under no. B. 32. Directive as last amended by Directive 2005/1/EC (OJ L 79, 24.3.2005, 9), reproduced supra under no. B. 39. Directive 2000/12/EC has been repealed as from 20 July 2006 by article 158 of Directive 2006/48/EC (OJ L 177, 30.6.2006, 1), reproduced infra under no. B. 41.

[12] OJ L 345, 19.12.2002, 1, reproduced supra under no. B. 37. Directive as last amended by Directive 2005/1/EC, reproduced supra under no. B. 39.

[13] OJ L 145, 30.4.2004, 1, reproduced infra under no. S. 29.

(d) a collective investment undertaking marketing its units or shares;

(e) an insurance intermediary as defined in Article 2(5) of Directive 2002/92/EC of the European Parliament and of the Council of 9 December 2002 on insurance mediation,[14] with the exception of intermediaries as mentioned in Article 2(7) of that Directive, when they act in respect of life insurance and other investment related services;

(f) branches, when located in the Community, of financial institutions as referred to in points (a) to (e), whose head offices are inside or outside the Community;

(3) 'property' means assets of every kind, whether corporeal or incorporeal, movable or immovable, tangible or intangible, and legal documents or instruments in any form including electronic or digital, evidencing title to or an interest in such assets;

(4) 'criminal activity' means any kind of criminal involvement in the commission of a serious crime;

(5) 'serious crimes' means, at least:

(a) acts as defined in Articles 1 to 4 of Framework Decision 2002/475/JHA;

(b) any of the offences defined in Article 3(1)(a) of the 1988 United Nations Convention against Illicit Traffic in Narcotic Drugs and Psychotropic Substances;

(c) the activities of criminal organisations as defined in Article 1 of Council Joint Action 98/733/JHA of 21 December 1998 on making it a criminal offence to participate in a criminal organisation in the Member States of the European Union;[15]

(d) fraud, at least serious, as defined in Article 1(1) and Article 2 of the Convention on the Protection of the European Communities' Financial Interests;[16]

(e) corruption;

(f) all offences which are punishable by deprivation of liberty or a detention order for a maximum of more than one year or, as regards those States which have a minimum threshold for offences in their legal system, all offences punishable by deprivation of liberty or a detention order for a minimum of more than six months;

(6) 'beneficial owner' means the natural person(s) who ultimately owns or controls the customer and/or the natural person on whose behalf a transaction or activity is being conducted. The beneficial owner shall at least include:

(a) in the case of corporate entities:
(i) the natural person(s) who ultimately owns or controls a legal entity through direct or indirect ownership or control over a sufficient percentage of the shares or voting rights in that legal entity, including through bearer share holdings, other than a company listed on a regulated market that is subject to disclosure requirements consistent with Community legislation or subject to equivalent international standards; a percentage of 25% plus one share shall be deemed sufficient to meet this criterion;
(ii) the natural person(s) who otherwise exercises control over the management of a legal entity:

(b) in the case of legal entities, such as foundations, and legal arrangements, such as trusts, which administer and distribute funds:
(i) where the future beneficiaries have already been determined, the natural person(s) who is the beneficiary of 25% or more of the property of a legal arrangement or entity;
(ii) where the individuals that benefit from the legal arrangement or entity have yet to be determined, the class of persons in whose main interest the legal arrangement or entity is set up or operates;
(iii) the natural person(s) who exercises control over 25% or more of the property of a legal arrangement or entity;

(7) 'trust and company service providers' means any natural or legal person which by way of business provides any of the following services to third parties:

(a) forming companies or other legal persons;

---

[14] OJ L 9, 15.1.2003, 3, reproduced infra under no. I. 34.
[15] OJ L 351, 29.12.1998, 1.
[16] OJ C 316, 27.11.1995, 49.

(b) acting as or arranging for another person to act as a director or secretary of a company, a partner of a partnership, or a similar position in relation to other legal persons;

(c) providing a registered office, business address, correspondence or administrative address and other related services for a company, a partnership or any other legal person or arrangement;

(d) acting as or arranging for another person to act as a trustee of an express trust or a similar legal arrangement;

(e) acting as or arranging for another person to act as a nominee shareholder for another person other than a company listed on a regulated market that is subject to disclosure requirements in conformity with Community legislation or subject to equivalent international standards;

(8) 'politically exposed persons' means natural persons who are or have been entrusted with prominent public functions and immediate family members, or persons known to be close associates, of such persons;

(9) 'business relationship' means a business, professional or commercial relationship which is connected with the professional activities of the institutions and persons covered by this Directive and which is expected, at the time when the contact is established, to have an element of duration;

(10) 'shell bank' means a credit institution, or an institution engaged in equivalent activities, incorporated in a jurisdiction in which it has no physical presence, involving meaningful mind and management, and which is unaffiliated with a regulated financial group.

Article 4

1. Member States shall ensure that the provisions of this Directive are extended in whole or in part to professions and to categories of undertakings, other than the institutions and persons referred to in Article 2(1), which engage in activities which are particularly likely to be used for money laundering or terrorist financing purposes.

2. Where a Member State decides to extend the provisions of this Directive to professions and to categories of undertakings other than those referred to in Article 2(1), it shall inform the Commission thereof.

Article 5

The Member States may adopt or retain in force stricter provisions in the field covered by this Directive to prevent money laundering and terrorist financing.

CHAPTER II
CUSTOMER DUE DILIGENCE

SECTION I
GENERAL PROVISIONS

Article 6

Member States shall prohibit their credit and financial institutions from keeping anonymous accounts or anonymous pass-books. By way of derogation from Article 9(6), Member States shall in all cases require that the owners and beneficiaries of existing anonymous accounts or anonymous passbooks be made the subject of customer due diligence measures as soon as possible and in any event before such accounts or passbooks are used in any way.

Article 7

The institutions and persons covered by this Directive shall apply customer due diligence measures in the following cases:

(a) when establishing a business relationship;

(b) when carrying out occasional transactions amounting to EUR 15 000 or more, whether the transaction is carried out in a single operation or in several operations which appear to be linked;

(c) when there is a suspicion of money laundering or terrorist financing, regardless of any derogation, exemption or threshold;

(d) when there are doubts about the veracity or adequacy of previously obtained customer identification data.

Article 8

1. Customer due diligence measures shall comprise:

(a) identifying the customer and verifying the customer's identity on the basis of documents, data or information obtained from a reliable and independent source;

(b) identifying, where applicable, the beneficial owner and taking risk-based and adequate measures to verify his identity so that the institution or person covered by this Directive is satisfied that it knows who the beneficial owner is, including, as regards legal persons, trusts and similar legal arrangements, taking risk-based and adequate measures to understand the ownership and control structure of the customer;

(c) obtaining information on the purpose and intended nature of the business relationship;

(d) conducting ongoing monitoring of the business relationship including scrutiny of transactions undertaken throughout the course of that relationship to ensure that the transactions being conducted are consistent with the institution's or person's knowledge of the customer, the business and risk profile, including, where necessary, the source of funds and ensuring that the documents, data or information held are kept up-to-date.

2. The institutions and persons covered by this Directive shall apply each of the customer due diligence requirements set out in paragraph 1, but may determine the extent of such measures on a risk-sensitive basis depending on the type of customer, business relationship, product or transaction. The institutions and persons covered by this Directive shall be able to demonstrate to the competent authorities mentioned in Article 37, including self-regulatory bodies, that the extent of the measures is appropriate in view of the risks of money laundering and terrorist financing.

Article 9

1. Member States shall require that the verification of the identity of the customer and the beneficial owner takes place before the establishment of a business relationship or the carrying-out of the transaction.

2. By way of derogation from paragraph 1, Member States may allow the verification of the identity of the customer and the beneficial owner to be completed during the establishment of a business relationship if this is necessary not to interrupt the normal conduct of business and where there is little risk of money laundering or terrorist financing occurring. In such situations these procedures shall be completed as soon as practicable after the initial contact.

3. By way of derogation from paragraphs 1 and 2, Member States may, in relation to life insurance business, allow the verification of the identity of the beneficiary under the policy to take place after the business relationship has been established. In that case, verification shall take place at or before the time of payout or at or before the time the beneficiary intends to exercise rights vested under the policy.

4. By way of derogation from paragraphs 1 and 2, Member States may allow the opening of a bank account provided that there are adequate safeguards in place to ensure that transactions are not carried out by the customer or on its behalf until full compliance with the aforementioned provisions is obtained.

5. Member States shall require that, where the institution or person concerned is unable to comply with points (a), (b) and (c) of Article 8(1), it may not carry out a transaction through a bank account, establish a business relationship or carry out the transaction, or shall terminate the business relationship, and shall consider making a report to the financial intelligence unit (FIU) in accordance with Article 22 in relation to the customer.

Member States shall not be obliged to apply the previous sub-paragraph in situations when notaries, independent legal professionals, auditors, external accountants and tax advisors are in the course of ascertaining the legal position for their client or performing their task of defending or representing that client in, or concerning judicial proceedings, including advice on instituting or avoiding proceedings.

6. Member States shall require that institutions and persons covered by this Directive apply the

customer due diligence procedures not only to all new customers but also at appropriate times to existing customers on a risk-sensitive basis.

Article 10

1. Member States shall require that all casino customers be identified and their identity verified if they purchase or exchange gambling chips with a value of EUR 2 000 or more.

2. Casinos subject to State supervision shall be deemed in any event to have satisfied the customer due diligence requirements if they register, identify and verify the identity of their customers immediately on or before entry, regardless of the amount of gambling chips purchased.

SECTION 2
SIMPLIFIED CUSTOMER DUE DILIGENCE

Article 11

1. By way of derogation from Articles 7(a), (b) and (d), 8 and 9(1), the institutions and persons covered by this Directive shall not be subject to the requirements provided for in those Articles where the customer is a credit or financial institution covered by this Directive, or a credit or financial institution situated in a third country which imposes requirements equivalent to those laid down in this Directive and supervised for compliance with those requirements.

2. By way of derogation from Articles 7(a), (b) and (d), 8 and 9(1) Member States may allow the institutions and persons covered by this Directive not to apply customer due diligence in respect of:

(a) listed companies whose securities are admitted to trading on a regulated market within the meaning of Directive 2004/39/EC in one or more Member States and listed companies from third countries which are subject to disclosure requirements consistent with Community legislation;

(b) beneficial owners of pooled accounts held by notaries and other independent legal professionals from the Member States, or from third countries provided that they are subject to requirements to combat money laundering or terrorist financing consistent with international standards and are supervised for compliance with those requirements and provided that the information on the identity of the beneficial owner is available, on request, to the institutions that act as depository institutions for the pooled accounts;

(c) domestic public authorities,

or in respect of any other customer representing a low risk of money laundering or terrorist financing which meets the technical criteria established in accordance with Article 40(1)(b).

3. In the cases mentioned in paragraphs 1 and 2, institutions and persons covered by this Directive shall in any case gather sufficient information to establish if the customer qualifies for an exemption as mentioned in these paragraphs.

4. The Member States shall inform each other and the Commission of cases where they consider that a third country meets the conditions laid down in paragraphs 1 or 2 or in other situations which meet the technical criteria established in accordance with Article 40(1)(b).

5. By way of derogation from Articles 7(a), (b) and (d), 8 and 9(1), Member States may allow the institutions and persons covered by this Directive not to apply customer due diligence in respect of:

(a) life insurance policies where the annual premium is no more than EUR 1 000 or the single premium is no more than EUR 2 500;

(b) insurance policies for pension schemes if there is no surrender clause and the policy cannot be used as collateral;

(c) a pension, superannuation or similar scheme that provides retirement benefits to employees, where contributions are made by way of deduction from wages and the scheme rules do not permit the assignment of a member's interest under the scheme;

(d) electronic money, as defined in Article 1(3)(b) of Directive 2000/46/EC of the European Parliament and of the Council of 18 September 2000 on the taking up, pursuit of and prudential supervision of the business of electronic money institutions,[17] where, if the device cannot be recharged, the maximum amount stored in the device is no more than EUR 150, or where, if the device can be recharged, a limit of EUR 2 500 is imposed on the total amount transacted in a calendar year, except when an amount of EUR 1 000 or more is redeemed in that same calendar year by the bearer as referred to in Article 3 of Directive 2000/46/EC,

or in respect of any other product or transaction representing a low risk of money laundering or terrorist financing which meets the technical criteria established in accordance with Article 40(1)(b).

Article 12

Where the Commission adopts a decision pursuant to Article 40(4), the Member States shall prohibit the institutions and persons covered by this Directive from applying simplified due diligence to credit and financial institutions or listed companies from the third country concerned or other entities following from situations which meet the technical criteria established in accordance with Article 40(1)(b).

SECTION 3

ENHANCED CUSTOMER DUE DILIGENCE

Article 13

1. Member States shall require the institutions and persons covered by this Directive to apply, on a risk-sensitive basis, enhanced customer due diligence measures, in addition to the measures referred to in Articles 7, 8 and 9(6), in situations which by their nature can present a higher risk of money laundering or terrorist financing, and at least in the situations set out in paragraphs 2, 3, 4 and in other situations representing a high risk of money laundering or terrorist financing which

---

[17] OJ L 275, 27.10.2000, 39, reproduced supra under no. B. 35.

meet the technical criteria established in accordance with Article 40(1)(c).

2. Where the customer has not been physically present for identification purposes, Member States shall require those institutions and persons to take specific and adequate measures to compensate for the higher risk, for example by applying one or more of the following measures:

(a) ensuring that the customer's identity is established by additional documents, data or information;

(b) supplementary measures to verify or certify the documents supplied, or requiring confirmatory certification by a credit or financial institution covered by this Directive;

(c) ensuring that the first payment of the operations is carried out through an account opened in the customer's name with a credit institution.

3. In respect of cross-frontier correspondent banking relationships with respondent institutions from third countries, Member States shall require their credit institutions to:

(a) gather sufficient information about a respondent institution to understand fully the nature of the respondent's business and to determine from publicly available information the reputation of the institution and the quality of supervision;

(b) assess the respondent institution's anti-money laundering and anti-terrorist financing controls;

(c) obtain approval from senior management before establishing new correspondent banking relationships;

(d) document the respective responsibilities of each institution;

(e) with respect to payable-through accounts, be satisfied that the respondent credit institution has verified the identity of and performed ongoing due diligence on the customers having direct access to accounts of the correspondent and that it is able to provide relevant customer due diligence data to the correspondent institution, upon request.

4. In respect of transactions or business relationships with politically exposed persons residing in

another Member State or in a third country, Member States shall require those institutions and persons covered by this Directive to:

(a) have appropriate risk-based procedures to determine whether the customer is a politically exposed person;

(b) have senior management approval for establishing business relationships with such customers;

(c) take adequate measures to establish the source of wealth and source of funds that are involved in the business relationship or transaction;

(d) conduct enhanced ongoing monitoring of the business relationship.

5. Member States shall prohibit credit institutions from entering into or continuing a correspondent banking relationship with a shell bank and shall require that credit institutions take appropriate measures to ensure that they do not engage in or continue correspondent banking relationships with a bank that is known to permit its accounts to be used by a shell bank.

6. Member States shall ensure that the institutions and persons covered by this Directive pay special attention to any money laundering or terrorist financing threat that may arise from products or transactions that might favour anonymity, and take measures, if needed, to prevent their use for money laundering or terrorist financing purposes.

SECTION 4

PERFORMANCE BY THIRD PARTIES

Article 14

Member States may permit the institutions and persons covered by this Directive to rely on third parties to meet the requirements laid down in Article 8(1)(a) to (c). However, the ultimate responsibility for meeting those requirements shall remain with the institution or person covered by this Directive which relies on the third party.

Article 15

1. Where a Member State permits credit and financial institutions referred to in Article 2(1)(1) or (2) situated in its territory to be relied on as a third party domestically, that Member State shall in any case permit institutions and persons referred to in Article 2(1) situated in its territory to recognise and accept, in accordance with the provisions laid down in Article 14, the outcome of the customer due diligence requirements laid down in Article 8(1)(a) to (c), carried out in accordance with this Directive by an institution referred to in Article 2(1)(1) or (2) in another Member State, with the exception of currency exchange offices and money transmission or remittance offices, and meeting the requirements laid down in Articles 16 and 18, even if the documents or data on which these requirements have been based are different to those required in the Member State to which the customer is being referred.

2. Where a Member State permits currency exchange offices and money transmission or remittance offices referred to in Article 3(2)(a) situated in its territory to be relied on as a third party domestically, that Member State shall in any case permit them to recognise and accept, in accordance with Article 14, the outcome of the customer due diligence requirements laid down in Article 8(1)(a) to (c), carried out in accordance with this Directive by the same category of institution in another Member State and meeting the requirements laid down in Articles 16 and 18, even if the documents or data on which these requirements have been based are different to those required in the Member State to which the customer is being referred.

3. Where a Member State permits persons referred to in Article 2(1)(3)(a) to (c) situated in its territory to be relied on as a third party domestically, that Member State shall in any case permit them to recognise and accept, in accordance with Article 14, the outcome of the customer due diligence requirements laid down in Article 8(1)(a) to (c), carried out in accordance with this Directive by a person referred to in Article 2(1)(3)(a) to (c) in another Member State and meeting the requirements laid down in Articles 16 and 18, even if the documents or data on which these requirements have been based are different to those required in the Member State to which the customer is being referred.

Article 16

1. For the purposes of this Section, 'third parties' shall mean institutions and persons who are listed in Article 2, or equivalent institutions and persons situated in a third country, who meet the following requirements:

(a) they are subject to mandatory professional registration, recognised by law;

(b) they apply customer due diligence requirements and record keeping requirements as laid down or equivalent to those laid down in this Directive and their compliance with the requirements of this Directive is supervised in accordance with Section 2 of Chapter V, or they are situated in a third country which imposes equivalent requirements to those laid down in this Directive.

2. Member States shall inform each other and the Commission of cases where they consider that a third country meets the conditions laid down in paragraph 1(b).

Article 17

Where the Commission adopts a decision pursuant to Article 40(4), Member States shall prohibit the institutions and persons covered by this Directive from relying on third parties from the third country concerned to meet the requirements laid down in Article 8(1)(a) to (c).

Article 18

1. Third parties shall make information requested in accordance with the requirements laid down in Article 8(1)(a) to (c) immediately available to the institution or person covered by this Directive to which the customer is being referred.

2. Relevant copies of identification and verification data and other relevant documentation on the identity of the customer or the beneficial owner shall immediately be forwarded, on request, by the third party to the institution or person covered by this Directive to which the customer is being referred.

Article 19

This Section shall not apply to outsourcing or agency relation-ships where, on the basis of a contractual arrangement, the outsourcing service provider or agent is to be regarded as part of the institution or person covered by this Directive.

CHAPTER III
REPORTING OBLIGATIONS

SECTION I
GENERAL PROVISIONS

Article 20

Member States shall require that the institutions and persons covered by this Directive pay special attention to any activity which they regard as particularly likely, by its nature, to be related to money laundering or terrorist financing and in particular complex or unusually large transactions and all unusual patterns of transactions which have no apparent economic or visible lawful purpose.

Article 21

1. Each Member State shall establish a FIU in order effectively to combat money laundering and terrorist financing.

2. That FIU shall be established as a central national unit. It shall be responsible for receiving (and to the extent permitted, requesting), analysing and disseminating to the competent authorities, disclosures of information which concern potential money laundering, potential terrorist financing or are required by national legislation or regulation. It shall be provided with adequate resources in order to fulfil its tasks.

3. Member States shall ensure that the FIU has access, directly or indirectly, on a timely basis, to the financial, administrative and law enforcement information that it requires to properly fulfil its tasks.

Article 22

1. Member States shall require the institutions and persons covered by this Directive, and where applicable their directors and employees, to cooperate fully:

(a) by promptly informing the FIU, on their own initiative, where the institution or person covered by this Directive knows, suspects or has reasonable grounds to suspect that money laundering or terrorist financing is being or has been committed or attempted;

(b) by promptly furnishing the FIU, at its request, with all necessary information, in accordance with the procedures established by the applicable legislation.

2. The information referred to in paragraph 1 shall be forwarded to the FIU of the Member State in whose territory the institution or person forwarding the information is situated. The person or persons designated in accordance with the procedures provided for in Article 34 shall normally forward the information.

Article 23

1. By way of derogation from Article 22(1), Member States may, in the case of the persons referred to in Article 2(1)(3)(a) and (b), designate an appropriate self-regulatory body of the profession concerned as the authority to be informed in the first instance in place of the FIU. Without prejudice to paragraph 2, the designated self-regulatory body shall in such cases forward the information to the FIU promptly and unfiltered.

2. Member States shall not be obliged to apply the obligations laid down in Article 22(1) to notaries, independent legal professionals, auditors, external accountants and tax advisors with regard to information they receive from or obtain on one of their clients, in the course of ascertaining the legal position for their client or performing their task of defending or representing that client in, or concerning judicial proceedings, including advice on instituting or avoiding proceedings, whether such information is received or obtained before, during or after such proceedings.

Article 24

1. Member States shall require the institutions and persons covered by this Directive to refrain from carrying out transactions which they know or suspect to be related to money laundering or terrorist financing until they have completed the necessary action in accordance with Article 22(1)(a). In conformity with the legislation of the Member States, instructions may be given not to carry out the transaction.

2. Where such a transaction is suspected of giving rise to money laundering or terrorist financing and where to refrain in such manner is impossible or is likely to frustrate efforts to pursue the beneficiaries of a suspected money laundering or terrorist financing operation, the institutions and persons concerned shall inform the FIU immediately afterwards.

Article 25

1. Member States shall ensure that if, in the course of inspections carried out in the institutions and persons covered by this Directive by the competent authorities referred to in Article 37, or in any other way, those authorities discover facts that could be related to money laundering or terrorist financing, they shall promptly inform the FIU.

2. Member States shall ensure that supervisory bodies empowered by law or regulation to oversee the stock, foreign exchange and financial derivatives markets inform the FIU if they discover facts that could be related to money laundering or terrorist financing.

Article 26

The disclosure in good faith as foreseen in Articles 22(1) and 23 by an institution or person covered by this Directive or by an employee or director of such an institution or person of the information referred to in Articles 22 and 23 shall not constitute a breach of any restriction on disclosure of information imposed by contract or by any legislative, regulatory or administrative provision, and shall not involve the institution or person or its directors or employees in liability of any kind.

Article 27

Member States shall take all appropriate measures in order to protect employees of the institutions or persons covered by this Directive who report suspicions of money laundering or terrorist financing either internally or to the FIU from being exposed to threats or hostile action.

Section 2
Prohibition of Disclosure

Article 28

1. The institutions and persons covered by this Directive and their directors and employees shall not disclose to the customer concerned or to other third persons the fact that information has been transmitted in accordance with Articles 22 and 23 or that a money laundering or terrorist financing investigation is being or may be carried out.

2. The prohibition laid down in paragraph 1 shall not include disclosure to the competent authorities referred to in Article 37, including the self-regulatory bodies, or disclosure for law enforcement purposes.

3. The prohibition laid down in paragraph 1 shall not prevent disclosure between institutions from Member States, or from third countries provided that they meet the conditions laid down in Article 11(1), belonging to the same group as defined by Article 2(12) of Directive 2002/87/EC of the European Parliament and of the Council of 16 December 2002 on the supplementary supervision of credit institutions, insurance undertakings and investment firms in a financial conglomerate.[18]

4. The prohibition laid down in paragraph 1 shall not prevent disclosure between persons referred to in Article 2(1)(3)(a) and (b) from Member States, or from third countries which impose requirements equivalent to those laid down in this Directive, who perform their professional activities, whether as employees or not, within the same legal person or a network. For the purposes of this Article, a 'network' means the larger structure to which the person belongs and which shares common ownership, management or compliance control.

5. For institutions or persons referred to in Article 2(1)(1), (2) and (3)(a) and (b) in cases related to the same customer and the same transaction involving two or more institutions or persons, the prohibition laid down in paragraph 1 shall not prevent disclosure between the relevant institutions or persons provided that they are situated in a Member State, or in a third country which imposes requirements equivalent to those laid down in this Directive, and that they are from the same professional category and are subject to equivalent obligations as regards professional secrecy and personal data protection. The information exchanged shall be used exclusively for the purposes of the prevention of money laundering and terrorist financing.

6. Where the persons referred to in Article 2(1)(3)(a) and (b) seek to dissuade a client from engaging in illegal activity, this shall not constitute a disclosure within the meaning of paragraph 1.

7. The Member States shall inform each other and the Commission of cases where they consider that a third country meets the conditions laid down in paragraphs 3, 4 or 5.

Article 29

Where the Commission adopts a decision pursuant to Article 40(4), the Member States shall prohibit the disclosure between institutions and persons covered by this Directive and institutions and persons from the third country concerned.

---

[18] OJ L 35, 11.2.2003, 1, reproduced supra under no. B. 38.

Chapter IV

Record Keeping and Statistical Data

Article 30

Member States shall require the institutions and persons covered by this Directive to keep the following documents and information for use in any investigation into, or analysis of, possible money laundering or terrorist financing by the FIU or by other competent authorities in accordance with national law:

(a) in the case of customer due diligence, a copy or the references of the evidence required, for a period of at least five years after the business relationship with their customer has ended;

(b) in the case of business relationships and transactions, the supporting evidence and records, consisting of the original documents or copies admissible in court proceedings under the applicable national legislation for a period of at least five years following the carrying-out of the transactions or the end of the business relationship.

Article 31

1. Member States shall require the credit and financial institutions covered by this Directive to apply, where applicable, in their branches and majority-owned subsidiaries located in third countries measures at least equivalent to those laid down in this Directive with regard to customer due diligence and record keeping.

Where the legislation of the third country does not permit application of such equivalent measures, the Member States shall require the credit and financial institutions concerned to inform the competent authorities of the relevant home Member State accordingly.

2. Member States and the Commission shall inform each other of cases where the legislation of the third country does not permit application of the measures required under the first subparagraph of paragraph 1 and coordinated action could be taken to pursue a solution.

3. Member States shall require that, where the legislation of the third country does not permit application of the measures required under the first subparagraph of paragraph 1, credit or financial institutions take additional measures to effectively handle the risk of money laundering or terrorist financing.

Article 32

Member States shall require that their credit and financial institutions have systems in place that enable them to respond fully and rapidly to enquiries from the FIU, or from other authorities, in accordance with their national law, as to whether they maintain or have maintained during the previous five years a business relationship with specified natural or legal persons and on the nature of that relationship.

Article 33

1. Member States shall ensure that they are able to review the effectiveness of their systems to combat money laundering or terrorist financing by maintaining comprehensive statistics on matters relevant to the effectiveness of such systems.

2. Such statistics shall as a minimum cover the number of suspicious transaction reports made to the FIU, the follow-up given to these reports and indicate on an annual basis the number of cases investigated, the number of persons prosecuted, the number of persons convicted for money laundering or terrorist financing offences and how much property has been frozen, seized or confiscated.

3. Member States shall ensure that a consolidated review of these statistical reports is published.

Chapter V

Enforcement Measures

Section I

Internal Procedures, Training and Feedback

Article 34

1. Member States shall require that the institutions and persons covered by this Directive establish adequate and appropriate policies and procedures of customer due diligence, reporting, record keeping, internal control, risk assessment, risk management,

compliance management and communication in order to forestall and prevent operations related to money laundering or terrorist financing.

2. Member States shall require that credit and financial institutions covered by this Directive communicate relevant policies and procedures where applicable to branches and majority-owned subsidiaries in third countries.

Article 35

1. Member States shall require that the institutions and persons covered by this Directive take appropriate measures so that their relevant employees are aware of the provisions in force on the basis of this Directive.

These measures shall include participation of their relevant employees in special ongoing training programmes to help them recognise operations which may be related to money laundering or terrorist financing and to instruct them as to how to proceed in such cases.

Where a natural person falling within any of the categories listed in Article 2(1)(3) performs his professional activities as an employee of a legal person, the obligations in this Section shall apply to that legal person rather than to the natural person.

2. Member States shall ensure that the institutions and persons covered by this Directive have access to up-to-date information on the practices of money launderers and terrorist financers and on indications leading to the recognition of suspicious transactions.

3. Member States shall ensure that, wherever practicable, timely feedback on the effectiveness of and follow-up to reports of suspected money laundering or terrorist financing is provided.

Section 2
Supervision

Article 36

1. Member States shall provide that currency exchange offices and trust and company service providers shall be licensed or registered and casinos be licensed in order to operate their business legally. Without prejudice to future Community legislation, Member States shall provide that money transmission or remittance offices shall be licensed or registered in order to operate their business legally.

2. Member States shall require competent authorities to refuse licensing or registration of the entities referred to in paragraph 1 if they are not satisfied that the persons who effectively direct or will direct the business of such entities or the beneficial owners of such entities are fit and proper persons.

Article 37

1. Member States shall require the competent authorities at least to effectively monitor and to take the necessary measures with a view to ensuring compliance with the requirements of this Directive by all the institutions and persons covered by this Directive.

2. Member States shall ensure that the competent authorities have adequate powers, including the power to compel the production of any information that is relevant to monitoring compliance and perform checks, and have adequate resources to perform their functions.

3. In the case of credit and financial institutions and casinos, competent authorities shall have enhanced supervisory powers, notably the possibility to conduct on-site inspections.

4. In the case of the natural and legal persons referred to in Article 2(1)(3)(a) to (e), Member States may allow the functions referred to in paragraph 1 to be performed on a risk-sensitive basis.

5. In the case of the persons referred to in Article 2(1)(3)(a) and (b), Member States may allow the functions referred to in paragraph 1 to be performed by self-regulatory bodies, provided that they comply with paragraph 2.

Section 3
Cooperation

Article 38

The Commission shall lend such assistance as may be needed to facilitate coordination, including the exchange of information between FIUs within the Community.

Section 4
Penalties

Article 39

1. Member States shall ensure that natural and legal persons covered by this Directive can be held liable for infringements of the national provisions adopted pursuant to this Directive. The penalties must be effective, proportionate and dissuasive.

2. Without prejudice to the right of Member States to impose criminal penalties, Member States shall ensure, in conformity with their national law, that the appropriate administrative measures can be taken or administrative sanctions can be imposed against credit and financial institutions for infringements of the national provisions adopted pursuant to this Directive. Member States shall ensure that these measures or sanctions are effective, proportionate and dissuasive.

3. In the case of legal persons, Member States shall ensure that at least they can be held liable for infringements referred to in paragraph 1 which are committed for their benefit by any person, acting either individually or as part of an organ of the legal person, who has a leading position within the legal person, based on:

(a) a power of representation of the legal person;

(b) an authority to take decisions on behalf of the legal person, or

(c) an authority to exercise control within the legal person.

4. In addition to the cases already provided for in paragraph 3, Member States shall ensure that legal persons can be held liable where the lack of supervision or control by a person referred to in paragraph 3 has made possible the commission of the infringements referred to in paragraph 1 for the benefit of a legal person by a person under its authority.

Chapter VI
Implementing Measures

Article 40

1. In order to take account of technical developments in the fight against money laundering or terrorist financing and to ensure uniform implementation of this Directive, the Commission may, in accordance with the procedure referred to in Article 41(2), adopt the following implementing measures:

(a) clarification of the technical aspects of the definitions in Article 3(2)(a) and (d), (6), (7), (8), (9) and (10);

(b) establishment of technical criteria for assessing whether situations represent a low risk of money laundering or terrorist financing as referred to in Article 11(2) and (5);

(c) establishment of technical criteria for assessing whether situations represent a high risk of money laundering or terrorist financing as referred to in Article 13;

(d) establishment of technical criteria for assessing whether, in accordance with Article 2(2), it is justified not to apply this Directive to certain legal or natural persons carrying out a financial activity on an occasional or very limited basis.

2. In any event, the Commission shall adopt the first implementing measures to give effect to paragraphs 1(b) and 1(d) by 15 June 2006.

3. The Commission shall, in accordance with the procedure referred to in Article 41(2), adapt the amounts referred to in Articles 2(1)(3)(e), 7(b), 10(1) and 11(5)(a) and (d) taking into account Community legislation, economic developments and changes in international standards.

4. Where the Commission finds that a third country does not meet the conditions laid down in Article 11(1) or (2), Article 28(3), (4) or (5), or in the measures established in accordance with paragraph 1(b) of this Article or in Article 16(1)(b), or that the legislation of that third country does not permit application of the measures required under the first subparagraph of Article 31(1), it shall adopt a decision so stating in accordance with the procedure referred to in Article 41(2).

Article 41

1. The Commission shall be assisted by a Committee on the Prevention of Money Laundering and Terrorist Financing, hereinafter 'the Committee'.

2. Where reference is made to this paragraph, Articles 5 and 7 of Decision 1999/468/EC shall apply, having regard to the provisions of Article 8 thereof and provided that the implementing measures adopted in accordance with this procedure do not modify the essential provisions of this Directive.

The period laid down in Article 5(6) of Decision 1999/468/EC shall be set at three months.

3. The Committee shall adopt its Rules of Procedure.

4. Without prejudice to the implementing measures already adopted, the implementation of the provisions of this Directive concerning the adoption of technical rules and decisions in accordance with the procedure referred to in paragraph 2 shall be suspended four years after the entry into force of this Directive. On a proposal from the Commission, the European Parliament and the Council may renew the provisions concerned in accordance with the procedure laid down in Article 251 of the Treaty and, to that end, shall review them prior to the expiry of the four-year period.

CHAPTER VII
FINAL PROVISIONS

Article 42

By 15 December 2009, and at least at three-yearly intervals thereafter, the Commission shall draw up a report on the implementation of this Directive and submit it to the European Parliament and the Council. For the first such report, the Commission shall include a specific examination of the treatment of lawyers and other independent legal professionals.

Article 43

By 15 December 2010, the Commission shall present a report to the European Parliament and to the Council on the threshold percentages in Article 3(6), paying particular attention to the possible expediency and consequences of a reduction of the percentage in points (a)(i), (b)(i) and (b)(iii) of Article 3(6) from 25% to 20%. On the basis of the report the Commission may submit a proposal for amendments to this Directive.

Article 44

Directive 91/308/EEC is hereby repealed.

References made to the repealed Directive shall be construed as being made to this Directive and should be read in accordance with the correlation table set out in the Annex.

Article 45

1. Member States shall bring into force the laws, regulations and administrative provisions necessary to comply with this Directive by 15 December 2007. They shall forthwith communicate to the Commission the text of those provisions together with a table showing how the provisions of this Directive correspond to the national provisions adopted.

When Member States adopt those measures, they shall contain a reference to this Directive or be accompanied by such a reference on the occasion of their official publication. The methods of making such reference shall be laid down by Member States.

2. Member States shall communicate to the Commission the text of the main provisions of national law which they adopt in the field covered by this Directive.

Article 46

This Directive shall enter into force on the 20th day after its publication in the *Official Journal of the European Union*.

Article 47

This Directive is addressed to the Member States.

Annex
Correlation Table

Directive 2005/60/EC	Directive 91/308/EEC
Article 1(1)	Article 2
Article 1(2)	Article 1(C)
Article 1(2)(a)	Article 1(C) first point
Article 1(2)(b)	Article 1(C) second point
Article 1(2)(c)	Article 1(C) third point
Article 1(2)(d)	Article 1(C) fourth point
Article 1(3)	Article 1(C), third paragraph
Article 1(4)	
Article 1(5)	Article 1(C), second paragraph
Article 2(1)(1)	Article 2a(1)
Article 2(1)(2)	Article 2a(2)
Article 2(1)(3)(a), (b) and (d) to (f)	Article 2a(3) to (7)
Article 2(1)(3)(c)	
Article 2(2)	
Article 3(1)	Article 1(A)
Article 3(2)(a)	Article 1(B)(1)
Article 3(2)(b)	Article 1(B)(2)
Article 3(2)(c)	Article 1(B)(3)
Article 3(2)(d)	Article 1(B)(4)
Article 3(2)(e)	
Article 3(2)(f)	Article 1(B), second paragraph
Article 3(3)	Article 1(D)
Article 3(4)	Article 1(E), first paragraph
Article 3(5)	Article 1(E), second paragraph
Article 3(5)(a)	
Article 3(5)(b)	Article 1(E), first indent
Article 3(5)(c)	Article 1(E), second indent
Article 3(5)(d)	Article 1(E), third indent
Article 3(5)(e)	Article 1(E), fourth indent
Article 3(5)(f)	Article 1(E), fifth indent, and third paragraph
Article 3(6)	
Article 3(7)	
Article 3(8)	
Article 3(9)	
Article 3(10)	
Article 4	Article 12
Article 5	Article 15
Article 6	

Directive 2005/60/EC	Directive 91/308/EEC
Article 7(a)	Article 3(1)
Article 7(b)	Article 3(2)
Article 7(c)	Article 3(8)
Article 7(d)	Article 3(7)
Article 8(1)(a)	Article 3(1)
Article 8(1)(b) to (d)	
Article 8(2)	
Article 9(1)	Article 3(1)
Article 9(2) to (6)	
Article 10	Article 3(5) and (6)
Article 11(1)	Article 3(9)
Article 11(2)	
Article 11(3) and (4)	
Article 11(5)(a)	Article 3(3)
Article 11(5)(b)	Article 3(4)
Article 11(5)(c)	Article 3(4)
Article 11(5)(d)	
Article 12	
Article 13(1) and (2)	Article 3(10) and (11)
Article 13(3) to (5)	
Article 13(6)	Article 5
Article 14	
Article 15	
Article 16	
Article 17	
Article 18	
Article 19	
Article 20	Article 5
Article 21	
Article 22	Article 6(1) and (2)
Article 23	Article 6(3)
Article 24	Article 7
Article 25	Article 10
Article 26	Article 9
Article 27	
Article 28(1)	Article 8(1)
Article 28(2) to (7)	
Article 29	
Article 30(a)	Article 4, first indent
Article 30(b)	Article 4, second indent
Article 31	
Article 32	
Article 33	

Directive 2005/60/EC	Directive 91/308/EEC
Article 34(1)	Article 11(1) (a)
Article 34(2)	
Article 35(1), first paragraph	Article 11(1)(b), first sentence
Article 35(1), second paragraph	Article 11(1)(b) second sentence
Article 35(1), third paragraph	Article 11(1), second paragraph
Article 35(2)	
Article 35(3)	
Article 36	
Article 37	
Article 38	
Article 39(1)	Article 14
Article 39(2) to (4)	
Article 40	
Article 41	
Article 42	Article 17
Article 43	
Article 44	
Article 45	Article 16
Article 46	Article 16

B. 41.

I
(Acts whose publication is obligatory)

European Parliament and Council Directive 2006/48/EC of 14 June 2006 relating to the taking up and pursuit of the business of credit institutions (recast)[1]

(Text with EEA relevance)

CASES

I. Case C-222/02 Peter Paul, Cornelia Sonnen-Lütte and Christel Mörkens v Bundesrepublik Deutschland [2004] ECR I-9425

Directives 77/780/EEC, 89/299/EEC and 89/646/EEC, combined in Directive 2000/12/EC (which has been repealed by Directive 2006/48/EC) insofar as they contain rules on the supervision of credit institutions, do not preclude a national rule to the effect that the functions of the national authority responsible for supervising credit institutions are to be fulfilled only in the public interest, which under national law precludes individuals from claiming compensation for damage resulting from defective supervision on the part of that authority.

From the Directive's organization of such supervisory obligations or from the fact that the objectives pursued by those Directives also include the protection of depositors it does not necessarily follow that said Directives seek to confer rights on depositors in the event that their deposits are unavailable as a result of defective supervision on the part of the competent national authorities.

The liability of national authorities in respect of depositors in the event of defective supervision does not appear to be necessary to secure the objectives laid down in the Directives.

II. Case C-410/96 Criminal Proceedings Against André Ambry [1998] ECR I-7875

It is contrary to Article [49][2] of the Treaty, and to Directive 89/646/EEC[3] and Directive 92/49/EEC,[4] for national rules to require, with a view to implementing Article 7 of Directive 90/314, that, where financial security is provided by a credit institution or insurance company situated in another Member State, the guarantor must conclude an agreement with a credit institution or insurance company situated in the national territory.

That requirement has the effect, first and foremost, of restricting and discouraging financial institutions established in other Member States, inasmuch as it prevents them from offering the security required directly to the travel organizer on the same basis as a guarantor situated in the national territory. It is also likely to discourage the travel operator from approaching a financial institution situated in another Member State, since the fact that such an institution must enter into a further guarantee agreement is liable to give rise to additional costs which would normally be passed on to the travel operator. It constitutes a restriction on the

---

[1] OJ L 177, 30.6.2006, 1–200.

[2] The number between brackets has been changed as from 1 May 1999 by article 12 of the Treaty of Amsterdam.

[3] Directive 89/646/EEC on the co-ordination of laws, regulations and administrative provisions relating to the taking up and pursuit of the business of credit institutions and amending Directive 77/780/EEC, consolidated in this Directive.

[4] Directive 92/49/EC on the co-ordination of laws, regulations and administrative provisions relating to direct insurance other than life assurance and amending Directives 73/239/EC and 88/357/EC, reproduced infra under no. I. 25.

freedom to provide services which is not justified as being necessary for the protection of consumers.

III. Case C-222/95 Société Civile Immobilière Parodi v Banque H. Albert de Bary et Cie [1997] ECR I-3899

1. With regard to the period preceding the entry into force of Second Directive 89/646/EEC[3] on the co-ordination of laws, regulations and administrative provisions relating to the taking up and pursuit of the business of credit institutions, Article [49][2] of the Treaty must be construed as precluding a Member State from requiring a credit institution already authorized in another Member State to obtain an authorization in order to be able to grant a mortgage loan to a person resident within its territory, unless that authorization:
- is required of every person or company pursuing such an activity within the territory of the Member State of destination;
- is justified on grounds of public interest, such as consumer protection; and
- is objectively necessary to ensure compliance with the rules applicable in the sector under consideration and to protect the interests which those rules are intended to safeguard, and the same result cannot be achieved by less restrictive rules.

In its assessment, the national court must, in particular, draw a distinction according to the nature of the banking activity in question and the risk incurred by the person for whom the service is intended. Thus, the conclusion of a contract for a mortgage loan presents the consumer with risks that differ from those associated with the lodging of funds with a credit institution. Furthermore, the need to protect the borrower will vary according to the nature of the mortgage loans, and there may be cases where, precisely because of the nature of the loan granted and the status of the borrower, there is no need to protect the latter by the application of the mandatory rules of his national law.

2. If the requirement of authorization constitutes a restriction on the freedom to provide services, the requirement of a permanent establishment is the very negation of that freedom. It has the result of depriving Article [49][2] of the Treaty of all effectiveness, a provision whose very purpose is to abolish restrictions on the freedom to provide services of persons who are not established in the State in which the service is to be provided. In order for such a requirement to be acceptable, it must constitute a condition which is indispensable for attaining the objective pursued.

IV. Case 166/85 Criminal Proceedings Against Italo Bullo and Francesco Bonivento [1987] ECR 1583

Council Directive 77/780/EEC[5] contains no provision governing the status which is to be given to credit institutions under the national law of the Member States or the extent of any criminal liability on the part of their employees. Consequently the Directive does not detract from the Member States' power to lay down rules on the legal status of credit institutions and, in particular, does not put them under a duty to require that the duties and powers given by credit institutions to their employees should be of a private nature. The classification of employees of credit institutions as 'public officials' or as 'persons responsible for a public service' for the purposes of the application of the criminal law of a Member State is therefore not contrary to the provisions or the objective of Directive 77/780/EEC.

V. Case 300/81 Commission of the European Communities v Italian Republic [1983] ECR 449

Directive 77/780/EEC [5] is intended to reduce the discretion which the supervisory authorities of certain Member States enjoy in authorizing credit institutions.

THE EUROPEAN PARLIAMENT AND THE COUNCIL OF THE EUROPEAN UNION,

Having regard to the Treaty establishing the European Community, and in particular the first and third sentences of Article 47 (2) thereof,

Having regard to the proposal from the Commission,

Having regard to the Opinion of the European Economic and Social Committee,[6]

---

[5] First Banking Directive 77/780/EEC on the co-ordination of laws, regulations and administrative provisions relating to the taking-up and pursuit of the business of credit institutions, consolidated in this Directive.
[6] OJ C 234, 22.9.2005, 8.

Having regard to the Opinion of the European Central Bank,[7]

Acting in accordance with the procedure laid down in Article 251 of the Treaty,[8]

Whereas:

(1) Directive 2000/12/EC of the European Parliament and of the Council of 20 March 2000 relating to the taking up and pursuit of the business of credit institutions[9] has been significantly amended on several occasions. Now that new amendments are being made to the said Directive, it is desirable, in order to clarify matters, that it should be recast.

(2) In order to make it easier to take up and pursue the business of credit institutions, it is necessary to eliminate the most obstructive differences between the laws of the Member States as regards the rules to which these institutions are subject.

(3) This Directive constitutes the essential instrument for the achievement of the internal market from the point of view of both the freedom of establishment and the freedom to provide financial services, in the field of credit institutions.

(4) The Commission Communication of 11 May 1999 entitled 'Implementing the framework for financial markets: Action plan', listed a number of goals that need to be achieved in order to complete the internal market in financial services. The Lisbon European Council of 23 and 24 March 2000 set the goal of implementing the action plan by 2005. Recasting of the provisions on own funds is a key element of the action plan.

(5) Measures to coordinate credit institutions should, both in order to protect savings and to create equal conditions of competition between these institutions, apply to all of them. Due regard should however be had to the objective differences in their statutes and their proper aims as laid down by national laws.

(6) The scope of those measures should therefore be as broad as possible, covering all institutions whose business is to receive repayable funds from the public, whether in the form of deposits or in other forms such as the continuing issue of bonds and other comparable securities and to grant credits for their own account. Exceptions should be provided for in the case of certain credit institutions to which this Directive cannot apply. The provisions of this Directive should not prejudice the application of national laws which provide for special supplementary authorisations permitting credit institutions to carry on specific activities or undertake specific kinds of operations.

(7) It is appropriate to effect only the essential harmonisation necessary and sufficient to secure the mutual recognition of authorisation and of prudential supervision systems, making possible the granting of a single licence recognised throughout the Community and the application of the principle of home Member State prudential supervision. Therefore, the requirement that a programme of operations be produced should be seen merely as a factor enabling the competent authorities to decide on the basis of more precise information using objective criteria. A measure of flexibility should nonetheless be possible as regards the requirements on the legal form of credit institutions concerning the protection of banking names.

(8) Since the objectives of this Directive, namely the introduction of rules concerning the taking up and pursuit of the business of credit institutions, and their prudential supervision, cannot be sufficiently achieved by the Member States and can therefore, by reason of the scale and the effects of the proposed action, be better achieved at Community level, the Community may adopt measures, in accordance with the principle of subsidiarity as set out in Article 5 of the Treaty. In accordance with the principle of proportionality, as set out in that Article, this Directive does not

---

[7] OJ C 52, 2.3.2005, 37.
[8] Opinion of the European Parliament of 28 September 2005 (not yet published in the OJ) and Decision of the Council of 7 June 2006.
[9] OJ L 126, 26.5.2000, 1, reproduced supra under no. B. 32. Directive as last amended by Directive 2006/29/EC (OJ L 70, 9.3.2006, 50). Directive 2000/12/EC has been repealed by article 158 of this Directive.

go beyond what is necessary in order to achieve those objectives.

(9) Equivalent financial requirements for credit institutions are necessary to ensure similar safeguards for savers and fair conditions of competition between comparable groups of credit institutions. Pending further coordination, appropriate structural ratios should be formulated making it possible within the framework of cooperation between national authorities to observe, in accordance with standard methods, the position of comparable types of credit institutions. This procedure should help to bring about the gradual approximation of the systems of coefficients established and applied by the Member States. It is necessary, however to make a distinction between coefficients intended to ensure the sound management of credit institutions and those established for the purposes of economic and monetary policy.

(10) The principles of mutual recognition and home Member State supervision require that Member States' competent authorities should not grant or should withdraw an authorisation where factors such as the content of the activities programmes, the geographical distribution of activities or the activities actually carried on indicate clearly that a credit institution has opted for the legal system of one Member State for the purpose of evading the stricter standards in force in another Member State within whose territory it carries on or intends to carry on the greater Part of its activities. Where there is no such clear indication, but the majority of the total assets of the entities in a banking group are located in another Member State the competent authorities of which are responsible for exercising supervision on a consolidated basis, in the context of Articles 125 and 126 responsibility for exercising supervision on a consolidated basis should be changed only with the agreement of those competent authorities. A credit institution which is a legal person should be authorised in the Member State in which it has its registered office. A credit institution which is not a legal person should have its head office in the Member State in which it has been authorised. In addition, Member States should require that a credit institution's head office always be situated in its home Member State and that it actually operates there.

(11) The competent authorities should not authorise or continue the authorisation of a credit institution where they are liable to be prevented from effectively exercising their supervisory functions by the close links between that institution and other natural or legal persons. Credit institutions already authorised should also satisfy the competent authorities in that respect.

(12) The reference to the supervisory authorities' effective exercise of their supervisory functions covers supervision on a consolidated basis which should be exercised over a credit institution where the provisions of Community law so provide. In such cases, the authorities applied to for authorisation should be able to identify the authorities competent to exercise supervision on a consolidated basis over that credit institution.

(13) This Directive enables Member States and/or competent authorities to apply capital requirements on a solo and consolidated basis, and to disapply solo where they deem this appropriate. Solo, consolidated and cross-border consolidated supervision are useful tools in overseeing credit institutions. This Directive enables competent authorities to support cross-border institutions by facilitating cooperation between them. In particular, the competent authorities should continue to make use of Articles 42, 131 and 141 to coordinate their activities and information requests.

(14) Credit institutions authorised in their home Member States should be allowed to carry on, throughout the Community, any or all of the activities listed in Annex I by establishing branches or by providing services.

(15) The Member States may also establish stricter rules than those laid down in Article 9(1), first subparagraph, Article 9(2) and Articles 12, 19 to 21, 44 to 52, 75 and 120 to 122 for credit institutions authorised by their competent authorities. The Member States may also require that Article 123 be complied with on an individual or other basis, and that the sub-consolidation described in Article 73(2) be applied to other levels within a group.

(16) It is appropriate to extend mutual recognition to the activities listed in Annex I when they are carried on by financial institutions which are subsidiaries of credit institutions, provided that such subsidiaries are covered by the consolidated supervision of their parent undertakings and meet certain strict conditions.

(17) The host Member State should be able, in connection with the exercise of the right of establishment and the freedom to provide services, to require compliance with specific provisions of its own national laws or regulations on the Part of institutions not authorised as credit institutions in their home Member States and with regard to activities not listed in Annex I provided that, on the one hand, such provisions are compatible with Community law and are intended to protect the general good and that, on the other hand, such institutions or such activities are not subject to equivalent rules under this legislation or regulations of their home Member States.

(18) The Member States should ensure that there are no obstacles to carrying on activities receiving mutual recognition in the same manner as in the home Member State, as long as the latter do not conflict with legal provisions protecting the general good in the host Member State.

(19) The rules governing branches of credit institutions having their head office outside the Community should be analogous in all Member States. It is important to provide that such rules may not be more favourable than those for branches of institutions from another Member State. The Community should be able to conclude agreements with third countries providing for the application of rules which accord such branches the same treatment throughout its territory. The branches of credit institutions authorised in third countries should not enjoy the freedom to provide services under the second paragraph of Article 49 of the Treaty or the freedom of establishment in Member States other than those in which they are established.

(20) Agreement should be reached, on the basis of reciprocity, between the Community and third countries with a view to allowing the practical exercise of consolidated supervision over the largest possible geographical area.

(21) Responsibility for supervising the financial soundness of a credit institution, and in particular its solvency, should lay with its home Member State. The host Member State's competent authorities should be responsible for the supervision of the liquidity of the branches and monetary policies. The supervision of market risk should be the subject of close cooperation between the competent authorities of the home and host Member States.

(22) The smooth operation of the internal banking market requires not only legal rules but also close and regular cooperation and significantly enhanced convergence of regulatory and supervisory practices between the competent authorities of the Member States. To this end, in particular, consideration of problems concerning individual credit institutions and the mutual exchange of information should take place in the Committee of European Banking Supervisors set up by Commission Decision 2004/5/EC.[10] That mutual information procedure should not in any case replace bilateral cooperation. Without prejudice to their own powers of control, the competent authorities of the host Member States should be able, in an emergency, on their own initiative or following the initiative of the competent authorities of the home Member State, to verify that the activities of a credit institution established within their territories comply with the relevant laws and with the principles of sound administrative and accounting procedures and adequate internal control.

(23) It is appropriate to allow the exchange of information between the competent authorities and authorities or bodies which, by virtue of their function, help to strengthen the stability of the financial system. In order to preserve the confidential nature of the information forwarded, the list of addressees should remain within strict limits.

---

[10] OJ L 3, 7.1.2004, 28, reproduced infra under no. I. 37.

(24) Certain behaviour, such as fraud and insider offences, is liable to affect the stability, including the integrity, of the financial system, even when involving institutions other than credit institutions. It is necessary to specify the conditions under which exchange of information in such cases is authorised.

(25) Where it is stipulated that information may be disclosed only with the express agreement of the competent authorities, these should be able, where appropriate, to make their agreement subject to compliance with strict conditions.

(26) Exchanges of information between, on the one hand, the competent authorities and, on the other, central banks and other bodies with a similar function in their capacity as monetary authorities and, where appropriate, other public authorities responsible for supervising payment systems should also be authorised.

(27) For the purpose of strengthening the prudential supervision of credit institutions and the protection of clients of credit institutions, auditors should have a duty to report promptly to the competent authorities, wherever, during the performance of their tasks, they become aware of certain facts which are liable to have a serious effect on the financial situation or the administrative and accounting organisation of a credit institution. For the same reason Member States should also provide that such a duty applies in all circumstances where such facts are discovered by an auditor during the performance of his tasks in an undertaking which has close links with a credit institution. The duty of auditors to communicate, where appropriate, to the competent authorities certain facts and decisions concerning a credit institution which they discover during the performance of their tasks in a non-financial undertaking should not in itself change the nature of their tasks in that undertaking nor the manner in which they should perform those tasks in that undertaking.

(28) This Directive specifies that for certain own funds items qualifying criteria should be specified, without prejudice to the possibility of Member States to apply more stringent provisions.

(29) According to the nature of the items constituting own funds, this Directive distinguishes between on the one hand, items constituting original own funds and, on the other, those constituting additional own funds.

(30) To reflect the fact that items constituting additional own funds are not of the same nature as those constituting original own funds, the amount of the former included in own funds should not exceed the original own funds. Moreover, the amount of certain items of additional own funds included should not exceed one half of the original own funds.

(31) In order to avoid distortions of competition, public credit institutions should not include in their own funds guarantees granted them by the Member States or local authorities.

(32) Whenever in the course of supervision it is necessary to determine the amount of the consolidated own funds of a group of credit institutions, the calculation should be effected in accordance with this Directive.

(33) The precise accounting technique to be used for the calculation of own funds, their adequacy for the risk to which a credit institution is exposed, and for the assessment of the concentration of exposures should take account of the provisions of Council Directive 86/635/EEC of 8 December 1986 on the annual accounts and consolidated accounts of banks and other financial institutions,[11] which incorporates certain adaptations of the provisions of Seventh Council Directive 83/349/EEC of 13 June 1983 on consolidated accounts[12] or of Regulation (EC) No 1606/2002 of the European Parliament and of the Council of 19 July 2002 on the application of international accounting standards,[13] whichever

---

[11] OJ L 372, 31.12.1986, 1, reproduced supra under no. B. 7. Directive as last amended by Directive 2003/51/EC of the European Parliament and of the Council (OJ L 178, 17.7.2003, 16), reproduced infra under no. C. 23.
[12] OJ L 193, 18.7.1983, 1, reproduced supra under no. B. 3. Directive as last amended by Directive 2003/51/EC, reproduced infra under no. C. 23.
[13] OJ L 243, 11.9.2002, 1, reproduced infra under no. C. 22.

governs the accounting of the credit institutions under national law.

(34) Minimum capital requirements play a central role in the supervision of credit institutions and in the mutual recognition of supervisory techniques. In that respect, the provisions on minimum capital requirements should be considered in conjunction with other specific instruments also harmonising the fundamental techniques for the supervision of credit institutions.

(35) In order to prevent distortions of competition and to strengthen the banking system in the internal market, it is appropriate to lay down common minimum capital requirements.

(36) For the purposes of ensuring adequate solvency it is important to lay down minimum capital requirements which weight assets and off-balance-sheet items according to the degree of risk.

(37) On this point, on 26 June 2004 the Basel Committee on Banking Supervision adopted a framework agreement on the international convergence of capital measurement and capital requirements. The provisions in this Directive on the minimum capital requirements of credit institutions, and the minimum capital provisions in Directive 2006/49/EC of the European Parliament and of the Council of 14 June 2006 on the capital adequacy of investment firms and credit institutions,[14] form an equivalent to the provisions of the Basel framework agreement.

(38) It is essential to take account of the diversity of credit institutions in the Community by providing alternative approaches to the calculation of minimum capital requirements for credit risk incorporating different levels of risk-sensitivity and requiring different degrees of sophistication. Use of external ratings and credit institutions' own estimates of individual credit risk parameters represents a significant enhancement in the risk-sensitivity and prudential soundness of the credit risk rules. There should be appropriate incentives for credit institutions to move towards the more risk-sensitive approaches. In producing the estimates needed to apply the approaches to credit risk of this Directive, credit institutions will have to adjust their data processing needs to their clients' legitimate data protection interests as governed by the existing Community legislation on data protection, while enhancing credit risk measurement and management processes of credit institutions to make methods for determining credit institutions' regulatory own funds requirements available that reflect the sophistication of individual credit institutions' processes. The processing of data should be in accordance with the rules on transfer of personal data laid down in Directive 95/46/EC of the European Parliament and of the Council of 24 October 1995 on the protection of individuals with regard to the processing of personal data and on the free movement of such data.[15] In this regard, the processing of data in connection with the incurring and management of exposures to customers should be considered to include the development and validation of credit risk management and measurement systems. That serves not only to fulfil the legitimate interest of credit institutions but also the purpose of this Directive, to use better methods for risk measurement and management and also use them for regulatory own funds purposes.

(39) With regard to the use of both external and an institution's own estimates or internal ratings, account should be taken of the fact that, at present, only the latter are drawn up by an entity—the financial institution itself—which is subject to a Community authorisation process. In the case of external ratings use is made of the products of what are known as recognised rating agencies, which in the Community are not currently subject to an authorisation process. In view of the importance of external ratings in connection with the calculation of capital requirements under this Directive, appropriate future authorisation and supervisory process for rating agencies need to be kept under review.

(40) The minimum capital requirements should be proportionate to the risks addressed. In particular the reduction in risk levels deriving

---

[14] See page 201 of this Official Journal.

[15] OJ L 281, 23.11.1995, 31. Directive as amended by Regulation (EC) No 1882/2003 (OJ L 284, 31.10.2003, 1).

from having a large number of relatively small exposures should be reflected in the requirements.

(41) The provisions of this Directive respect the principle of proportionality, having regard in particular to the diversity in size and scale of operations and to the range of activities of credit institutions. Respect of the principle of proportionality also means that the simplest possible rating procedures, even in the Internal Ratings Based Approach ('IRB Approach'), are recognised for retail exposures.

(42) The 'evolutionary' nature of this Directive enables credit institutions to choose amongst three approaches of varying complexity. In order to allow especially small credit institutions to opt for the more risk-sensitive IRB Approach, the competent authorities should implement the provisions of Article 89(1)(a) and (b) whenever appropriate. Those provisions should be read as such that exposure classes referred to in Article 86(1)(a) and (b) include all exposures that are, directly or indirectly, put on a par with them throughout this Directive. As a general rule, the competent authorities should not discriminate between the three approaches with regard to the Supervisory Review Process, i.e. credit institutions operating according to the provisions of the Standardised Approach should not for that reason alone be supervised on a stricter basis.

(43) Increased recognition should be given to techniques of credit risk mitigation within a framework of rules designed to ensure that solvency is not undermined by undue recognition. The relevant Member States' current customary banking collateral for mitigating credit risks should wherever possible be recognised in the Standardised Approach, but also in the other approaches.

(44) In order to ensure that the risks and risk reductions arising from credit institutions' securitisation activities and investments are appropriately reflected in the minimum capital requirements of credit institutions it is necessary to include rules providing for a risk-sensitive and prudentially sound treatment of such activities and investments.

(45) Operational risk is a significant risk faced by credit institutions requiring coverage by own funds. It is essential to take account of the diversity of credit institutions in the Community by providing alternative approaches to the calculation of operational risk requirements incorporating different levels of risk-sensitivity and requiring different degrees of sophistication. There should be appropriate incentives for credit institutions to move towards the more risk-sensitive approaches. In view of the emerging state of the art for the measurement and management of operational risk the rules should be kept under review and updated as appropriate including in relation to the charges for different business lines and the recognition of risk mitigation techniques. Particular attention should be paid in this regard to taking insurance into account in the simple approaches to calculating capital requirements for operational risk.

(46) In order to ensure adequate solvency of credit institutions within a group it is essential that the minimum capital requirements apply on the basis of the consolidated financial situation of the group. In order to ensure that own funds are appropriately distributed within the group and available to protect savings where needed, the minimum capital requirements should apply to individual credit institutions within a group, unless this objective can be effectively otherwise achieved.

(47) The essential rules for monitoring large exposures of credit institutions should be harmonised. Member States should still be able to adopt provisions more stringent than those provided for by this Directive.

(48) The monitoring and control of a credit institution's exposures should be an integral Part of its supervision. Therefore, excessive concentration of exposures to a single client or group of connected clients may result in an unacceptable risk of loss. Such a situation can be considered prejudicial to the solvency of a credit institution.

(49) Since credit institutions in the internal market are engaged in direct competition, monitoring requirements should be equivalent throughout the Community.

(50) While it is appropriate to base the definition of exposures for the purposes of limits to large exposures on that provided for the purposes of minimum own funds requirements for credit risk, it is not appropriate to refer on principle to the weightings or degrees of risk. Those weightings and degrees of risk were devised for the purpose of establishing a general solvency requirement to cover the credit risk of credit institutions. In order to limit the maximum loss that a credit institution may incur through any single client or group of connected clients it is appropriate to adopt rules for the determination of large exposures which take account of the nominal value of the exposure without applying weightings or degrees of risk.

(51) While it is desirable, pending further review of the large exposures provisions, to permit the recognition of the effects of credit risk mitigation in a manner similar to that permitted for minimum capital requirement purposes in order to limit the calculation requirements, the rules on credit risk mitigation were designed in the context of the general diversified credit risk arising from exposures to a large number of counterparties. Accordingly, recognition of the effects of such techniques for the purposes of limits to large exposures designed to limit the maximum loss that may be incurred through any single client or group of connected clients should be subject to prudential safeguards.

(52) When a credit institution incurs an exposure to its own parent undertaking or to other subsidiaries of its parent undertaking, particular prudence is necessary. The management of exposures incurred by credit institutions should be carried out in a fully autonomous manner, in accordance with the principles of sound banking management, without regard to any other considerations. Where the influence exercised by persons directly or indirectly holding a qualifying participation in a credit institution is likely to operate to the detriment of the sound and prudent management of that institution, the competent authorities should take appropriate measures to put an end to that situation. In the field of large exposures, specific standards, including more stringent restrictions, should be laid down for exposures incurred by a credit institution to its own group. Such standards need not, however be applied where the parent undertaking is a financial holding company or a credit institution or where the other subsidiaries are either credit or financial institutions or undertakings offering ancillary services, provided that all such undertakings are covered by the supervision of the credit institution on a consolidated basis.

(53) Credit institutions should ensure that they have internal capital that, having regard to the risks to which they are or may be exposed, is adequate in quantity, quality and distribution. Accordingly, credit institutions should have strategies and processes in place for assessing and maintaining the adequacy of their internal capital.

(54) Competent authorities have responsibility to be satisfied that credit institutions have good organisation and adequate own funds, having regard to the risks to which the credit institutions are or might be exposed.

(55) In order for the internal banking market to operate effectively the Committee of European Banking Supervisors should contribute to the consistent application of this Directive and to the convergence of supervisory practices throughout the Community, and should report on a yearly basis to the Community institutions on progress made.

(56) For the same reason, and to ensure that Community credit institutions which are active in several Member States are not disproportionately burdened as a result of the continued responsibilities of individual Member State competent authorities for authorisation and supervision, it is essential to significantly enhance the cooperation between competent authorities. In this context, the role of the consolidating supervisor should be strengthened. The Committee of European Banking Supervisors should support and enhance such cooperation.

(57) Supervision of credit institutions on a consolidated basis aims at, in particular, protecting the interests of the depositors of credit institutions and at ensuring the stability of the financial system.

(58) In order to be effective, supervision on a consolidated basis should therefore be applied to all banking groups, including those the parent undertakings of which are not credit institutions. The competent authorities should hold the necessary legal instruments to be able to exercise such supervision.

(59) In the case of groups with diversified activities where parent undertakings control at least one credit institution subsidiary, the competent authorities should be able to assess the financial situation of a credit institution in such a group. The competent authorities should at least have the means of obtaining from all undertakings within a group the information necessary for the performance of their function. Cooperation between the authorities responsible for the supervision of different financial sectors should be established in the case of groups of undertakings carrying on a range of financial activities. Pending subsequent coordination, the Member States should be able to lay down appropriate methods of consolidation for the achievement of the objective of this Directive.

(60) The Member States should be able to refuse or withdraw banking authorisation in the case of certain group structures considered inappropriate for carrying on banking activities, in particular because such structures could not be supervised effectively. In this respect the competent authorities should have the necessary powers to ensure the sound and prudent management of credit institutions.

(61) In order for the internal banking market to operate with increasing effectiveness and for citizens of the Community to be afforded adequate levels of transparency, it is necessary that competent authorities disclose publicly and in a way which allows for meaningful comparison the manner in which this Directive is implemented.

(62) In order to strengthen market discipline and stimulate credit institutions to improve their market strategy, risk control and internal management organization, appropriate public disclosure by credit institutions should be provided for.

(63) The examination of problems connected with matters covered by this Directive, as well as by other Directives on the business of credit institutions, requires cooperation between the competent authorities and the Commission, particularly when conducted with a view to closer coordination.

(64) The measures necessary for the implementation of this Directive should be adopted in accordance with Council Decision 1999/468/EC of 28 June 1999 laying down the procedures for the exercise of implementing powers conferred on the Commission.[16]

(65) In its resolution of 5 February 2002 on the implementation of financial services legislation[17] the Parliament requested that it and the Council should have an equal role in supervising the way in which the Commission exercises its executive role in order to reflect the legislative powers of Parliament under Article 251 of the Treaty. In the solemn declaration made before the Parliament the same day by its President, the Commission supported this request. On 11 December 2002 the Commission proposed amendments to Decision 1999/468/EC, and then submitted an amended proposal on 22 April 2004. The Parliament does not consider that this proposal preserves its legislative prerogatives. In the view of the Parliament, it and the Council should have the opportunity of evaluating the conferral of implementing powers on the Commission within a determined period. It is therefore appropriate to limit the period during which the Commission may adopt implementing measures.

(66) The Parliament should be given a period of three months from the first transmission of draft amendments and implementing measures to allow it to examine them and to give its opinion. However, in urgent and duly justified cases, it should be possible to shorten this period. If, within that period, a resolution is adopted by the Parliament, the Commission should re-examine the draft amendments or measures.

(67) In order to avoid disruption to markets and to ensure continuity in overall levels of own funds it is appropriate to provide for specific transitional arrangements.

---

[16] OJ L 184, 17.7.1999, 23.
[17] OJ C 284 E, 21.11.2002, 115.

(68) In view of the risk-sensitivity of the rules relating to minimum capital requirements, it is desirable to keep under review whether these have significant effects on the economic cycle. The Commission, taking into account the contribution of the European Central Bank should report on these aspects to the European Parliament and to the Council.

(69) The arrangements necessary for the supervision of liquidity risks should also be harmonised.

(70) This Directive respects fundamental rights and observes the principles recognised in particular by the Charter of Fundamental Rights of the European Union as general principles of Community law.

(71) The obligation to transpose this Directive into national law should be confined to those provisions which represent a substantive change as compared with earlier directives. The obligation to transpose the provisions which are unchanged exists under the earlier directives.

(72) This Directive should be without prejudice to the obligations of the Member States relating to the time-limits for transposition into national law of the Directives set out in Annex XIII, Part B,

HAVE ADOPTED THIS DIRECTIVE:

Contents

Title I. Subject Matter, Scope and Definitions	186
Title II. Requirements for Access to the Taking up and Pursuit of the Business of Credit Institutions	192
Title III. Provisions Concerning the Freedom of Establishment and the Freedom to Provide Services	196
Section 1. Credit Institutions	196
Section 2. Financial Institutions	196
Section 3. Exercise of the Right of Establishment	197
Section 4. Exercise of the Freedom to Provide Services	198
Section 5. Powers of the Competent Authorities of the Host Member State	198
Title IV. Relations with Third Countries	200
Section 1. Notification in Relation to Third Countries' Undertakings and Conditions of Access to the Markets of these Countries	200
Section 2. Cooperation with Third Countries' Competent Authorities Regarding Supervision on a Consolidated Basis	200
Title V. Principles and Technical Instruments for Prudential Supervision and Disclosure	200
Chapter 1. Principles of Prudential Supervision	200
Section 1. Competence of Home and Host Member State	200
Section 2. Exchange of Information and Professional Secrecy	201
Section 3. Duty of Persons Responsible for the Legal Control of Annual and Consolidated Accounts	204
Section 4. Power of Sanction and Right to Apply to the Courts	205
Chapter 2. Technical Instruments of Prudential Supervision	205
Section 1. Own Funds	205
Section 2. Provision Against Risks	209
Subsection 1. Level of Application	209
Subsection 2. Calculation of Requirements	212
Subsection 3. Minimum Level of Own Funds	213
Section 3. Minimum Own Funds Requirements for Credit Risk	213
Subsection 1. Standardised Approach	213
Subsection 2. Internal Ratings Based Approach	216
Subsection 3. Credit Risk Mitigation	222
Subsection 4. Securitisation	223
Section 4. Minimum Own Funds Requirements for Operational Risk	224
Section 5. Large Exposures	225
Section 6. Qualifying Holdings Outside the Financial Sector	231
Chapter 3. Credit Institutions' Assessment Process	232
Chapter 4. Supervision and Disclosure by Competent Authorities	232
Section 1. Supervision	232
Section 2. Disclosure by Competent Authorities	239
Chapter 5. Disclosure by Credit Institutions	240
Title VI. Powers of Execution	241
Title VII. Transitional and Final Provisions	242
Chapter 1. Transitional Provisions	242
Chapter 2. Final Provisions	244
Annex I. List of Activities Subject to Mutual Recognition	245
Annex II. Classification of Off-Balance-Sheet Items	246
Annex III. The Treatment of Counterparty Credit Risk of Derivative Instruments, Repurchase Transactions, Securities or Commodities Lending or Borrowing Transactions, Long Settlement Transactions and Margin Lending Transactions	247
Part 1. Definitions	247
Part 2. Choice of the Method	249
Part 3. Mark-to-Market Method	250
Part 4. Original Exposure Method	251
Part 5. Standardised Method	251
Part 6. Internal Model Method	255
Part 7. Contractual Netting (Contracts for Novation and other Netting Agreements)	261
Annex IV. Types of Derivatives	263
Annex V. Technical Criteria Concerning the Organisation and Treatment of Risks	264
Annex VI. Standardised Approach	265
Part 1. Risk Weights	265
Part 2. Recognition of ECAIs and Mapping of their Credit Assessments	276
Part 3. Use of ECAIs' Credit Assessments for the Determination of Risk Weights	278
Annex VII. Internal Ratings Based Approach	279

Part 1. Risk-Weighted Exposure Amounts and Expected Loss Amounts	279
Part 2. PD, LGD, and Maturity	284
Part 3. Exposure Value	288
Part 4. Minimum Requirements for IRB Approach	290
Annex VIII. Credit Risk Mitigation	306
Part 1. Eligibility	306
Part 2. Minimum Requirements	311
Part 3. Calculating the Effects of Credit Risk Mitigation	318
Part 4. Maturity Mismatches	332
Part 5. Combinations of Credit Risk Mitigation in the Standardised Approach	333
Part 6. Basket CRM Techniques	333
Annex IX. Securitisation	334
Part 1. Definitions for the Purposes of Annex IX	334
Part 2. Minimum Requirements for Recognition of Significant Credit Risk Transfer and Calculation of Risk-Weighted Exposure Amounts and Expected Loss Amounts for Securitised Exposures	334
Part 3. External Credit Assessments	336
Part 4. Calculation	337
Annex X. Operational Risk	349
Part 1. Basic Indicator Approach	349
Part 2. Standardised Approach	350
Part 3. Advanced Measurement Approaches	353
Part 4. Combined use of Different Methodologies	356
Part 5. Loss Event Type Classification	357
Annex XI. Technical Criteria on Review and Evaluation by the Competent Authorities	357
Annex XII. Technical Criteria on Disclosure	358
Part 1. General Criteria	358
Part 2. General Requirements	358
Part 3. Qualifying Requirements for the use of Particular Instruments or Methodologies	362
Annex XIII. Part A Repealed Directives, together with their Successive Amendments (referred to in Article 158)	364
Annex XIII. Part B Deadlines for Transposition (referred to in article 158)	364
Annex XIV. Correlation Table	365

Title I

Subject Matter, Scope and Definitions

Article 1

1. This Directive lays down rules concerning the taking up and pursuit of the business of credit institutions, and their prudential supervision.

2. Article 39 and Title V, Chapter 4, Section 1 shall apply to financial holding companies and mixed-activity holding companies which have their head offices in the Community.

3. The institutions permanently excluded pursuant to Article 2, with the exception, however, of the central banks of the Member States, shall be treated as financial institutions for the purposes of Article 39 and Title V, Chapter 4, Section 1.

Article 2

This Directive shall not apply to the following:

– the central banks of Member States,
– post office giro institutions,
– in Belgium, the 'Institut de Réescompte et de Garantie/Herdiscontering- en Waarborginstituut',
– in Denmark, the 'Dansk Eksportfinansieringsfond', the 'Danmarks Skibskreditfond', the 'Dansk Landbrugs Realkreditfond', and the 'KommuneKredit',
– in Germany, the 'Kreditanstalt für Wiederaufbau', undertakings which are recognised under the 'Wohnungsgemeinnützigkeitsgesetz' as bodies of State housing policy and are not mainly engaged in banking transactions, and undertakings recognised under that law as non-profit housing undertakings,
– in Greece, the 'Ταμείο Παρακαταθηκών και Δανείων' (Tamio Parakatathikon kai Danion),
– in Spain, the 'Instituto de Crédito Oficial',
– in France, the 'Caisse des dépôts et consignations',
– in Ireland, credit unions and the friendly societies,
– in Italy, the 'Cassa depositi e prestiti',
– in Latvia, the 'krājaizdevu sabiedrības', undertakings that are recognised under the 'krājaizdevu sabiedrību likums' as cooperative undertakings rendering financial services solely to their members,
– in Lithuania, the 'kredito unijos' other than the 'Centrinė kredito unija',
– in Hungary, the 'Magyar Fejlesztési Bank Rt.' and the 'Magyar Export-Import Bank Rt.',
– in the Netherlands, the 'Nederlandse Investeringsbank voor Ontwikkelingslanden NV', the 'NV Noordelijke Ontwikkelingsmaatschappij', the 'NV Industriebank Limburgs Instituut voor Ontwikkeling en Financiering' and the 'Overijsselse Ontwikkelingsmaatschappij NV',
– in Austria, undertakings recognised as housing associations in the public interest and the 'Österreichische Kontrollbank AG',

- in Poland, the 'Spółdzielcze Kasy Oszczędnościowo—Kreditowe' and the 'Bank Gospodarstwa Krajowego',
- in Portugal, 'Caixas Económicas' existing on 1 January 1986 with the exception of those incorporated as limited companies and of the 'Caixa Económica Montepio Geral',
- in Finland, the 'Teollisen yhteistyön rahasto Oy/Fonden för industriellt samarbete AB', and the 'Finnvera Oyj/Finnvera Abp',
- in Sweden, the 'Svenska Skeppshypotekskassan',
- in the United Kingdom, the National Savings Bank, the Commonwealth Development Finance Company Ltd, the Agricultural Mortgage Corporation Ltd, the Scottish Agricultural Securities Corporation Ltd, the Crown Agents for overseas governments and administrations, credit unions and municipal banks.

Article 3

1. One or more credit institutions situated in the same Member State and which are permanently affiliated, on 15 December 1977, to a central body which supervises them and which is established in the same Member State, may be exempted from the requirements of Articles 7 and 11(1) if, no later than 15 December 1979, national law provides that:

(a) the commitments of the central body and affiliated institutions are joint and several liabilities or the commitments of its affiliated institutions are entirely guaranteed by the central body;

(b) the solvency and liquidity of the central body and of all the affiliated institutions are monitored as a whole on the basis of consolidated accounts; and

(c) the management of the central body is empowered to issue instructions to the management of the affiliated institutions.

Credit institutions operating locally which are permanently affiliated, subsequent to 15 December 1977, to a central body within the meaning of the first subparagraph, may benefit from the conditions laid down therein if they constitute normal additions to the network belonging to that central body.

In the case of credit institutions other than those which are set up in areas newly reclaimed from the sea or have resulted from scission or mergers of existing institutions dependent or answerable to the central body, the Commission, pursuant to the procedure referred to in Article 151(2) may lay down additional rules for the application of the second subparagraph including the repeal of exemptions provided for in the first subparagraph, where it is of the opinion that the affiliation of new institutions benefiting from the arrangements laid down in the second subparagraph might have an adverse effect on competition.

2. A credit institution referred to in the first subparagraph of paragraph 1, may also be exempted from the provisions of Articles 9 and 10, and also Title V, Chapter 2, Sections 2, 3, 4, 5 and 6 and Chapter 3 provided that, without prejudice to the application of those provisions to the central body, the whole as constituted by the central body together with its affiliated institutions is subject to those provisions on a consolidated basis.

In case of exemption, Articles 16, 23, 24, 25, 26(1) to (3) and 28 to 37 shall apply to the whole as constituted by the central body together with its affiliated institutions.

Article 4

For the purposes of this Directive, the following definitions shall apply:

(1) 'credit institution' means:

(a) an undertaking whose business is to receive deposits or other repayable funds from the public and to grant credits for its own account; or

(b) an electronic money institution within the meaning of Directive 2000/46/EC;[18]

(2) 'authorisation' means an instrument issued in any form by the authorities by which the right to carry on the business of a credit institution is granted;

---

[18] Directive 2000/46/EC of the European Parliament and of the Council of 18 September 2000 on the taking up, pursuit of and prudential supervision of the business of electronic money institutions (OJ L 275, 27.10.2000, 39), reproduced supra under no. B. 34.

(3) 'branch' means a place of business which forms a legally dependent Part of a credit institution and which carries out directly all or some of the transactions inherent in the business of credit institutions;

(4) 'competent authorities' means the national authorities which are empowered by law or regulation to supervise credit institutions;

(5) 'financial institution' means an undertaking other than a credit institution, the principal activity of which is to acquire holdings or to carry on one or more of the activities listed in points 2 to 12 of Annex I;

(6) 'institutions', for the purposes of Sections 2 and 3 of Title V, Chapter 2, means institutions as defined in Article 3(1)(c) of Directive 2006/49/EC;

(7) 'home Member State' means the Member State in which a credit institution has been authorised in accordance with Articles 6 to 9 and 11 to 14;

(8) 'host Member State' means the Member State in which a credit institution has a branch or in which it provides services;

(9) 'control' means the relationship between a parent undertaking and a subsidiary, as defined in Article 1 of Directive 83/349/EEC, or a similar relationship between any natural or legal person and an undertaking;

(10) 'participation' for the purposes of points (o) and (p) of Article 57, Articles 71 to 73 and Title V, Chapter 4 means participation within the meaning of the first sentence of Article 17 of Fourth Council Directive 78/660/EEC of 25 July 1978 on the annual accounts of certain types of companies,[19] or the ownership, direct or indirect, of 20% or more of the voting rights or capital of an undertaking;

(11) 'qualifying holding' means a direct or indirect holding in an undertaking which represents 10% or more of the capital or of the voting rights or which makes it possible to exercise a significant influence over the management of that undertaking;

(12) 'parent undertaking' means:

(a) a parent undertaking as defined in Articles 1 and 2 of Directive 83/349/EEC; or

(b) for the purposes of Articles 71 to 73, Title V, Chapter 2, Section 5 and Chapter 4, a parent undertaking within the meaning of Article 1(1) of Directive 83/349/EEC and any undertaking which, in the opinion of the competent authorities, effectively exercises a dominant influence over another undertaking;

(13) 'subsidiary' means:

(a) a subsidiary undertaking as defined in Articles 1 and 2 of Directive 83/349/EEC; or

(b) for the purposes of Articles 71 to 73, Title V, Chapter 2, Section 5, and Chapter 4 a subsidiary undertaking within the meaning of Article 1(1) of Directive 83/349/EEC and any undertaking over which, in the opinion of the competent authorities, a parent undertaking effectively exercises a dominant influence.

All subsidiaries of subsidiary undertakings shall also be considered subsidiaries of the undertaking that is their original parent;

(14) 'parent credit institution in a Member State' means a credit institution which has a credit institution or a financial institution as a subsidiary or which holds a participation in such an institution, and which is not itself a subsidiary of another credit institution authorised in the same Member State, or of a financial holding company set up in the same Member State;

(15) 'parent financial holding company in a Member State' means a financial holding company which is not itself a subsidiary of a credit institution authorised in the same Member State, or of a financial holding company set up in the same Member State;

(16) 'EU parent credit institution' means a parent credit institution in a Member State which is not a subsidiary of another credit

---

[19] OJ L 222, 14.8.1978, 11, reproduced infra under no. C. 4. Directive as last amended by Directive 2003/51/EC, reproduced infra under no. C. 23.

institution authorised in any Member State, or of a financial holding company set up in any Member State;

(17) 'EU parent financial holding company' means a parent financial holding company in a Member State which is not a subsidiary of a credit institution authorised in any Member State or of another financial holding company set up in any Member State;

(18) 'public sector entities' means non-commercial administrative bodies responsible to central governments, regional governments or local authorities, or authorities that in the view of the competent authorities exercise the same responsibilities as regional and local authorities, or non-commercial undertakings owned by central governments that have explicit guarantee arrangements, and may include self administered bodies governed by law that are under public supervision;

(19) 'financial holding company' means a financial institution, the subsidiary undertakings of which are either exclusively or mainly credit institutions or financial institutions, at least one of such subsidiaries being a credit institution, and which is not a mixed financial holding company within the meaning of Article 2(15) of Directive 2002/87/EC;[20]

(20) 'mixed-activity holding company' means a parent undertaking, other than a financial holding company or a credit institution or a mixed financial holding company within the meaning of Article 2(15) of Directive 2002/87/EC, the subsidiaries of which include at least one credit institution;

(21) 'ancillary services undertaking' means an undertaking the principal activity of which consists in owning or managing property, managing data-processing services, or any other similar activity which is ancillary to the principal activity of one or more credit institutions;

(22) 'operational risk' means the risk of loss resulting from inadequate or failed internal processes, people and systems or from external events, and includes legal risk;

(23) 'central banks' include the European Central Bank unless otherwise indicated;

(24) 'dilution risk' means the risk that an amount receivable is reduced through cash or non-cash credits to the obligor;

(25) 'probability of default' means the probability of default of a counterparty over a one year period;

(26) 'loss', for the purposes of Title V, Chapter 2, Section 3, means economic loss, including material discount effects, and material direct and indirect costs associated with collecting on the instrument;

(27) 'loss given default (LGD)' means the ratio of the loss on an exposure due to the default of a counterparty to the amount outstanding at default;

(28) 'conversion factor' means the ratio of the currently undrawn amount of a commitment that will be drawn and outstanding at default to the currently undrawn amount of the commitment, the extent of the commitment shall be determined by the advised limit, unless the unadvised limit is higher;

(29) 'expected loss (EL)', for the purposes of Title V, Chapter 2, Section 3, shall mean the ratio of the amount expected to be lost on an exposure from a potential default of a counterparty or dilution over a one year period to the amount outstanding at default;

(30) 'credit risk mitigation' means a technique used by a credit institution to reduce the credit risk associated with an exposure or exposures which the credit institution continues to hold;

(31) 'funded credit protection' means a technique of credit risk mitigation where the reduction of the credit risk on the exposure of a credit

---

[20] Directive 2002/87/EC of the European Parliament and of the Council of 16 December 2002 on the supplementary supervision of credit institutions, insurance undertakings and investment firms in a financial conglomerate (OJ L 35, 11.2.2003, 1), reproduced supra under no. B. 38. Directive as amended by Directive 2005/1/EC, reproduced supra under no. B. 39.

institution derives from the right of the credit institution—in the event of the default of the counterparty or on the occurrence of other specified credit events relating to the counterparty—to liquidate, or to obtain transfer or appropriation of, or to retain certain assets or amounts, or to reduce the amount of the exposure to, or to replace it with, the amount of the difference between the amount of the exposure and the amount of a claim on the credit institution;

(32) 'unfunded credit protection' means a technique of credit risk mitigation where the reduction of the credit risk on the exposure of a credit institution derives from the undertaking of a third party to pay an amount in the event of the default of the borrower or on the occurrence of other specified credit events;

(33) 'repurchase transaction' means any transaction governed by an agreement falling within the definition of 'repurchase agreement' or 'reverse repurchase agreement' as defined in Article 3(1)(m) of Directive 2006/49/EC;

(34) 'securities or commodities lending or borrowing transaction' means any transaction falling within the definition of 'securities or commodities lending' or 'securities or commodities borrowing' as defined in Article 3(1)(n) of Directive 2006/49/EC;

(35) 'cash assimilated instrument' means a certificate of deposit or other similar instrument issued by the lending credit institution;

(36) 'securitisation' means a transaction or scheme, whereby the credit risk associated with an exposure or pool of exposures is tranched, having the following characteristics:

(a) payments in the transaction or scheme are dependent upon the performance of the exposure or pool of exposures; and

(b) the subordination of tranches determines the distribution of losses during the ongoing life of the transaction or scheme;

(37) 'traditional securitisation' means a securitisation involving the economic transfer of the exposures being securitised to a securitisation special purpose entity which issues securities. This shall be accomplished by the transfer of ownership of the securitised exposures from the originator credit institution or through sub-participation. The securities issued do not represent payment obligations of the originator credit institution;

(38) 'synthetic securitisation' means a securitisation where the tranching is achieved by the use of credit derivatives or guarantees, and the pool of exposures is not removed from the balance sheet of the originator credit institution;

(39) 'tranche' means a contractually established segment of the credit risk associated with an exposure or number of exposures, where a position in the segment entails a risk of credit loss greater than or less than a position of the same amount in each other such segment, without taking account of credit protection provided by third parties directly to the holders of positions in the segment or in other segments;

(40) 'securitisation position' shall mean an exposure to a securitisation;

(41) 'originator' means either of the following:

(a) an entity which, either itself or through related entities, directly or indirectly, was involved in the original agreement which created the obligations or potential obligations of the debtor or potential debtor giving rise to the exposure being securitised; or

(b) an entity which purchases a third party's exposures onto its balance sheet and then securitises them;

(42) 'sponsor' means a credit institution other than an originator credit institution that establishes and manages an asset backed commercial paper programme or other securitisation scheme that purchases exposures from third party entities;

(43) 'credit enhancement' means a contractual arrangement whereby the credit quality of a position in a securitisation is improved in relation to what it would have been if the enhancement had not been provided, including the enhancement provided by more junior tranches in the securitisation and other types of credit protection;

(44) 'securitisation special purpose entity (SSPE)' means a corporation trust or other entity, other than a credit institution, organised for carrying

on a securitisation or securitisations, the activities of which are limited to those appropriate to accomplishing that objective, the structure of which is intended to isolate the obligations of the SSPE from those of the originator credit institution, and the holders of the beneficial interests in which have the right to pledge or exchange those interests without restriction;

(45) 'group of connected clients' means:

(a) two or more natural or legal persons who, unless it is shown otherwise, constitute a single risk because one of them, directly or indirectly, has control over the other or others; or

(b) two or more natural or legal persons between whom there is no relationship of control as set out in point (a) but who are to be regarded as constituting a single risk because they are so interconnected that, if one of them were to experience financial problems, the other or all of the others would be likely to encounter repayment difficulties;

(46) 'close links' means a situation in which two or more natural or legal persons are linked in any of the following ways:

(a) participation in the form of ownership, direct or by way of control, of 20% or more of the voting rights or capital of an undertaking;

(b) control; or

(c) the fact that both or all are permanently linked to one and the same third person by a control relationship;

(47) 'recognised exchanges' means exchanges which are recognised as such by the competent authorities and which meet the following conditions:

(a) they function regularly;

(b) they have rules, issued or approved by the appropriate authorities of the home country of the exchange, defining the conditions for the operation of the exchange, the conditions of access to the exchange as well as the conditions that shall be satisfied by a contract before it can effectively be dealt on the exchange; and

(c) they have a clearing mechanism whereby contracts listed in Annex IV are subject to daily margin requirements which, in the opinion of the competent authorities, provide appropriate protection.

CASE

Case C-366/97 Criminal Proceedings Against Massimo Romanelli and Paolo Romanelli [1999] ECR I-855

The term 'other repayable funds' in Article 3 of the Second Directive 89/646/EEC[3] which lays down a prohibition, in the case of persons or undertakings which are not credit institutions, on carrying on the business of taking deposits or other repayable funds from the public, refers not only to financial instruments which possess the intrinsic characteristic of repayability, but also to those which, although not possessing that characteristic, are the subject of a contractual agreement to repay the funds paid. It is clear from Directives 77/780/EEC[5] and 89/646/EEC that the protection of savings constitutes one of the objectives of the measures taken to co-ordinate credit institutions. According to the fourth recital in the preamble to the First Directive 77/780/EEC, those measures must apply to all credit institutions. The fifth recital adds that their scope should therefore be as broad as possible, covering all institutions whose business is to receive repayable funds from the public whether in the form of deposits or in other forms such as the continuing issue of bonds and other comparable securities.

Article 5

Member States shall prohibit persons or undertakings that are not credit institutions from carrying on the business of taking deposits or other repayable funds from the public.

The first paragraph shall not apply to the taking of deposits or other funds repayable by a Member State or by a Member State's regional or local authorities or by public international bodies of which one or more Member States are members or to cases expressly covered by national or Community legislation, provided that those activities are subject to regulations and controls intended to protect depositors and investors and applicable to those cases.

Title II

Requirements for Access to the Taking up and Pursuit of the Business of Credit Institutions

Article 6

Member States shall require credit institutions to obtain authorisation before commencing their activities. Without prejudice to Articles 7 to 12, they shall lay down the requirements for such authorisation and notify them to the Commission.

Article 7

Member States shall require applications for authorisation to be accompanied by a programme of operations setting out, inter alia, the types of business envisaged and the structural organisation of the credit institution.

Article 8

Member States may not require the application for authorisation to be examined in terms of the economic needs of the market.

Article 9

1. Without prejudice to other general conditions laid down by national law, the competent authorities shall not grant authorisation when the credit institution does not possess separate own funds or in cases where initial capital is less than EUR 5 million.

'Initial capital' shall comprise capital and reserves as referred to in Article 57(a) and (b).

Member States may decide that credit institutions which do not fulfil the requirement of separate own funds and which were in existence on 15 December 1979 may continue to carry on their business. They may exempt such credit institutions from complying with the requirement contained in the first subparagraph of Article 11(1).

2. Member States may, subject to the following conditions, grant authorisation to particular categories of credit institutions the initial capital of which is less than that specified in paragraph 1:

(a) the initial capital shall be no less than EUR 1 million;

(b) the Member States concerned shall notify the Commission of their reasons for exercising this option; and

(c) the name of each credit institution that does not have the minimum capital specified in paragraph 1 shall be annotated to that effect in the list referred to in Article 14.

Article 10

1. A credit institution's own funds may not fall below the amount of initial capital required under Article 9 at the time of its authorisation.

2. Member States may decide that credit institutions already in existence on 1 January 1993, the own funds of which do not attain the levels specified for initial capital in Article 9, may continue to carry on their activities. In that event, their own funds may not fall below the highest level reached with effect from 22 December 1989.

3. If control of a credit institution falling within the category referred to in paragraph 2 is taken by a natural or legal person other than the person who controlled the institution previously, the own funds of that credit institution shall attain at least the level specified for initial capital in Article 9.

4. In certain specific circumstances and with the consent of the competent authorities, where there is a merger of two or more credit institutions falling within the category referred to in paragraph 2, the own funds of the credit institution resulting from the merger may not fall below the total own funds of the merged credit institutions at the time of the merger, as long as the appropriate levels specified in Article 9 have not been attained.

5. If, in the cases referred to in paragraphs 1, 2 and 4, the own funds should be reduced, the competent authorities may, where the circumstances justify it, allow a credit institution a limited period in which to rectify its situation or cease its activities.

Article 11

1. The competent authorities shall grant an authorisation to the credit institution only when there are at least two persons who effectively direct the business of the credit institution.

They shall not grant authorisation if these persons are not of sufficiently good repute or lack sufficient experience to perform such duties.

2. Each Member State shall require that:

(a) any credit institution which is a legal person and which, under its national law, has a registered office shall have its head office in the same Member State as its registered office; and

(b) any other credit institution shall have its head office in the Member State which granted its authorisation and in which it actually carries on its business.

Article 12

1. The competent authorities shall not grant authorisation for the taking-up of the business of credit institutions unless they have been informed of the identities of the shareholders or members, whether direct or indirect, natural or legal persons, that have qualifying holdings, and of the amounts of those holdings.

In determining a qualifying holding in the context of this Article, the voting rights referred to in Article 92 of Directive 2001/34/EC of the European Parliament and of the Council of 28 May 2001 on the admission of securities to official stock exchange listing and on information to be published on those securities[21] shall be taken into consideration.

2. The competent authorities shall not grant authorisation if, taking into account the need to ensure the sound and prudent management of a credit institution, they are not satisfied as to the suitability of the shareholders or members.

3. Where close links exist between the credit institution and other natural or legal persons, the competent authorities shall grant authorisation only if those links do not prevent the effective exercise of their supervisory functions.

The competent authorities shall also not grant authorisation if the laws, regulations or administrative provisions of a third country governing one or more natural or legal persons with which the credit institution has close links, or difficulties involved in the enforcement of those laws, regulations or administrative provisions, prevent the effective exercise of their supervisory functions.

The competent authorities shall require credit institutions to provide them with the information they require to monitor compliance with the conditions referred to in this paragraph on a continuous basis.

Article 13

Reasons shall be given whenever a decision not to grant an authorisation is taken and the applicant shall be notified thereof within six months of receipt of the application or, should the latter be incomplete, within six months of the applicant's sending the information required for the decision. A decision shall, in any case, be taken within 12 months of the receipt of the application.

Article 14

Every authorisation shall be notified to the Commission.

The name of each credit institution to which authorisation has been granted shall be entered in a list. The Commission shall publish that list in the Official Journal of the European Union and shall keep it up to date.

Article 15

1. The competent authority shall, before granting authorisation to a credit institution, consult the competent authorities of the other Member State involved in the following cases:

(a) the credit institution concerned is a subsidiary of a credit institution authorised in another Member State;

---

[21] OJ L 184, 6.7.2001, 1, reproduced infra under no. S. 18. Directive as last amended by Directive 2005/1/EC, reproduced supra under no. B. 39.

(b) the credit institution concerned is a subsidiary of the parent undertaking of a credit institution authorised in another Member State; or

(c) the credit institution concerned is controlled by the same persons, whether natural or legal, as control a credit institution authorised in another Member State.

2. The competent authority shall, before granting authorisation to a credit institution, consult the competent authority of a Member State involved, responsible for the supervision of insurance undertakings or investment firms in the following cases:

(a) the credit institution concerned is a subsidiary of an insurance undertaking or investment firm authorised in the Community;

(b) the credit institution concerned is a subsidiary of the parent undertaking of an insurance undertaking or investment firm authorised in the Community; or

(c) the credit institution concerned is controlled by the same person, whether natural or legal, as controls an insurance undertaking or investment firm authorised in the Community.

3. The relevant competent authorities referred to in paragraphs 1 and 2 shall in particular consult each other when assessing the suitability of the shareholders and the reputation and experience of directors involved in the management of another entity of the same group. They shall exchange any information regarding the suitability of shareholders and the reputation and experience of directors which is of relevance for the granting of an authorisation as well as for the ongoing assessment of compliance with operating conditions.

Article 16

Host Member States may not require authorisation or endowment capital for branches of credit institutions authorised in other Member States. The establishment and supervision of such branches shall be effected in accordance with Articles 22, 25, 26 (1) to (3), 29 to 37 and 40.

Article 17

1. The competent authorities may withdraw the authorisation granted to a credit institution only where such an institution:

(a) does not make use of the authorisation within 12 months, expressly renounces the authorisation or has ceased to engage in business for more than six months, if the Member State concerned has made no provision for the authorisation to lapse in such cases;

(b) has obtained the authorisation through false statements or any other irregular means;

(c) no longer fulfils the conditions under which authorisation was granted;

(d) no longer possesses sufficient own funds or can no longer be relied on to fulfil its obligations towards its creditors, and in particular no longer provides security for the assets entrusted to it; or

(e) falls within one of the other cases where national law provides for withdrawal of authorisation.

2. Reasons shall be given for any withdrawal of authorisation and those concerned informed thereof. Such withdrawal shall be notified to the Commission.

Article 18

For the purposes of exercising their activities, credit institutions may, notwithstanding any provisions in the host Member State concerning the use of the words 'bank', 'savings bank' or other banking names, use throughout the territory of the Community the same name as they use in the Member State in which their head office is situated. In the event of there being any danger of confusion, the host Member State may, for the purposes of clarification, require that the name be accompanied by certain explanatory particulars.

Article 19

1. The Member States shall require any natural or legal person who proposes to hold, directly or indirectly, a qualifying holding in a credit institution first to inform the competent authorities,

telling them of the size of the intended holding. Such a person shall likewise inform the competent authorities if he proposes to increase his qualifying holding so that the proportion of the voting rights or of the capital held by him would reach or exceed 20%, 33% or 50% or so that the credit institution would become his subsidiary.

Without prejudice to paragraph 2, the competent authorities shall have a maximum of three months from the date of the notification provided for in the first and second subparagraphs to oppose such a plan if, in view of the need to ensure sound and prudent management of the credit institution, they are not satisfied as to the suitability of the person concerned. If they do not oppose the plan, they may fix a maximum period for its implementation.

2. If the person proposing to acquire the holdings referred to in paragraph 1 is a credit institution, insurance undertaking or investment firm authorised in another Member State or the parent undertaking of a credit institution, insurance undertaking or investment firm authorised in another Member State or a natural or legal person controlling a credit institution, insurance undertaking or investment firm authorised in another Member State, and if, as a result of that acquisition, the credit institution in which the acquirer proposes to hold a holding would become a subsidiary or subject to the control of the acquirer, the assessment of the acquisition shall be subject to the prior consultation provided for in Article 15.

Article 20

The Member States shall require any natural or legal person who proposes to dispose, directly or indirectly, of a qualifying holding in a credit institution first to inform the competent authorities, telling them of the size of his intended holding. Such a person shall likewise inform the competent authorities if he proposes to reduce his qualifying holding so that the proportion of the voting rights or of the capital held by him would fall below 20%, 33% or 50% or so that the credit institution would cease to be his subsidiary.

Article 21

1. Credit institutions shall, on becoming aware of any acquisitions or disposals of holdings in their capital that cause holdings to exceed or fall below one of the thresholds referred to in Article 19(1) and Article 20, inform the competent authorities of those acquisitions or disposals.

They shall also, at least once a year, inform the competent authorities of the names of shareholders and members possessing qualifying holdings and the sizes of such holdings as shown, for example, by the information received at the annual general meetings of shareholders and members or as a result of compliance with the regulations relating to companies listed on stock exchanges.

2. The Member States shall require that, where the influence exercised by the persons referred to in Article 19(1) is likely to operate to the detriment of the prudent and sound management of the institution, the competent authorities shall take appropriate measures to put an end to that situation. Such measures may consist in injunctions, sanctions against directors and managers, or the suspension of the exercise of the voting rights attaching to the shares held by the shareholders or members in question.

Similar measures shall apply to natural or legal persons who fail to comply with the obligation to provide prior information, as laid down in Article 19(1).

If a holding is acquired despite the opposition of the competent authorities, the Member States shall, regardless of any other sanctions to be adopted, provide either for exercise of the corresponding voting rights to be suspended, or for the nullity of votes cast or for the possibility of their annulment.

3. In determining a qualifying holding and other levels of holding referred to in this Article, the voting rights referred to in Article 92 of Directive 2001/34/EC shall be taken into consideration.

Article 22

1. Home Member State competent authorities shall require that every credit institution have

robust governance arrangements, which include a clear organisational structure with well defined, transparent and consistent lines of responsibility, effective processes to identify, manage, monitor and report the risks it is or might be exposed to, and adequate internal control mechanisms, including sound administrative and accounting procedures.

2. The arrangements, processes and mechanisms referred to in paragraph 1 shall be comprehensive and proportionate to the nature, scale and complexity of the credit institution's activities. The technical criteria laid down in Annex V shall be taken into account.

Title III

Provisions Concerning the Freedom of Establishment and the Freedom to Provide Services

Section 1
Credit Institutions

Article 23

The Member States shall provide that the activities listed in Annex I may be carried on within their territories, in accordance with Articles 25, 26(1) to (3), 28(1) and (2) and 29 to 37 either by the establishment of a branch or by way of the provision of services, by any credit institution authorised and supervised by the competent authorities of another Member State, provided that such activities are covered by the authorisation.

Section 2
Financial Institutions

Article 24

1. The Member States shall provide that the activities listed in Annex I may be carried on within their territories, in accordance with Articles 25, 26(1) to (3), 28(1) and (2) and 29 to 37, either by the establishment of a branch or by way of the provision of services, by any financial institution from another Member State, whether a subsidiary of a credit institution or the jointly-owned subsidiary of two or more credit institutions, the Memorandum and Articles of Association of which permit the carrying on of those activities and which fulfils each of the following conditions:

(a) the parent undertaking or undertakings shall be authorised as credit institutions in the Member State by the law of which the financial institution is governed;

(b) the activities in question shall actually be carried on within the territory of the same Member State;

(c) the parent undertaking or undertakings shall hold 90% or more of the voting rights attaching to shares in the capital of the financial institution;

(d) the parent undertaking or undertakings shall satisfy the competent authorities regarding the prudent management of the financial institution and shall have declared, with the consent of the relevant home Member State competent authorities, that they jointly and severally guarantee the commitments entered into by the financial institution; and

(e) the financial institution shall be effectively included, for the activities in question in particular, in the consolidated supervision of the parent undertaking, or of each of the parent undertakings, in accordance with Title V, Chapter 4, Section 1, in particular for the purposes of the minimum own funds requirements set out in Article 75 for the control of large exposures and for purposes of the limitation of holdings provided for in Articles 120 to 122.

Compliance with these conditions shall be verified by the competent authorities of the home Member State and the latter shall supply the financial institution with a certificate of compliance which shall form Part of the notification referred to in Articles 25 and 28.

The competent authorities of the home Member State shall ensure the supervision of the financial institution in accordance with Articles 10(1), 19 to 22, 40, 42 to 52 and 54.

2. If a financial institution as referred to in the first subparagraph of paragraph 1 ceases to fulfil any of the conditions imposed, the home Member State shall notify the competent authorities of the host Member State and the activities carried on by that financial institution in the host Member State shall become subject to the legislation of the host Member State.

3. Paragraphs 1 and 2 shall apply mutatis mutandis to subsidiaries of a financial institution as referred to in the first subparagraph of paragraph 1.

Section 3
Exercise of the Right of Establishment

Article 25

1. A credit institution wishing to establish a branch within the territory of another Member State shall notify the competent authorities of its home Member State.

2. Member States shall require every credit institution wishing to establish a branch in another Member State to provide the following information when effecting the notification referred to in paragraph 1:

(a) the Member State within the territory of which it plans to establish a branch;

(b) a programme of operations setting out, inter alia, the types of business envisaged and the structural organisation of the branch;

(c) the address in the host Member State from which documents may be obtained; and

(d) the names of those to be responsible for the management of the branch.

3. Unless the competent authorities of the home Member State have reason to doubt the adequacy of the administrative structure or the financial situation of the credit institution, taking into account the activities envisaged, they shall within three months of receipt of the information referred to in paragraph 2 communicate that information to the competent authorities of the host Member State and shall inform the credit institution accordingly.

The home Member State's competent authorities shall also communicate the amount of own funds and the sum of the capital requirements under Article 75 of the credit institution.

By way of derogation from the second subparagraph, in the case referred to in Article 24, the home Member State's competent authorities shall communicate the amount of own funds of the financial institution and the sum of the consolidated own funds and consolidated capital requirements under Article 75 of the credit institution which is its parent undertaking.

4. Where the competent authorities of the home Member State refuse to communicate the information referred to in paragraph 2 to the competent authorities of the host Member State, they shall give reasons for their refusal to the credit institution concerned within three months of receipt of all the information.

That refusal or a failure to reply, shall be subject to a right to apply to the courts in the home Member State.

Article 26

1. Before the branch of a credit institution commences its activities the competent authorities of the host Member State shall, within two months of receiving the information referred to in Article 25, prepare for the supervision of the credit institution in accordance with Section 5 and if necessary indicate the conditions under which, in the interest of the general good, those activities shall be carried on in the host Member State.

2. On receipt of a communication from the competent authorities of the host Member State, or in the event of the expiry of the period provided for in paragraph 1 without receipt of any communication from the latter, the branch may be established and may commence its activities.

3. In the event of a change in any of the particulars communicated pursuant to points (b), (c) or (d) of Article 25 (2), a credit institution shall give written notice of the change in question to the competent authorities of the home and host Member States at least one month before making the change so as to enable the competent authorities of the home Member State to take a decision pursuant to Article 25 and the competent authorities of the host Member State to take a decision on the change pursuant to paragraph 1 of this Article.

4. Branches which have commenced their activities, in accordance with the provisions in force in their host Member States, before 1 January 1993, shall be presumed to have been subject to the procedure laid down in Article 25 and in paragraphs 1 and 2 of this Article. They shall be governed, from 1 January 1993, by paragraph 3 of this Article and by Articles 23 and 43 as well as Sections 2 and 5.

Article 27

Any number of places of business set up in the same Member State by a credit institution with headquarters in another Member State shall be regarded as a single branch.

Section 4

Exercise of the Freedom to Provide Services

Article 28

1. Any credit institution wishing to exercise the freedom to provide services by carrying on its activities within the territory of another Member State for the first time shall notify the competent authorities of the home Member State, of the activities on the list in Annex I which it intends to carry on.

2. The competent authorities of the home Member State shall, within one month of receipt of the notification provided for in paragraph 1, send that notification to the competent authorities of the host Member State.

3. This Article shall not affect rights acquired by credit institutions providing services before 1 January 1993.

Section 5

Powers of the Competent Authorities of the Host Member State

Article 29

Host Member States may, for statistical purposes, require that all credit institutions having branches within their territories shall report periodically on their activities in those host Member States to the competent authorities of those host Member States.

In discharging the responsibilities imposed on them in Article 41, host Member States may require that branches of credit institutions from other Member States provide the same information as they require from national credit institutions for that purpose.

Article 30

1. Where the competent authorities of a host Member State ascertain that a credit institution having a branch or providing services within its territory is not complying with the legal provisions adopted in that State pursuant to the provisions of this Directive involving powers of the host Member State's competent authorities, those authorities shall require the credit institution concerned to put an end to that irregular situation.

2. If the credit institution concerned fails to take the necessary steps, the competent authorities of the host Member State shall inform the competent authorities of the home Member State accordingly.

The competent authorities of the home Member State shall, at the earliest opportunity, take all appropriate measures to ensure that the credit institution concerned puts an end to that irregular situation. The nature of those measures shall be communicated to the competent authorities of the host Member State.

3. If, despite the measures taken by the home Member State or because such measures prove inadequate or are not available in the Member State in question, the credit institution persists in violating the legal rules referred to in paragraph 1 in force in the host Member State, the latter State may, after informing the competent authorities of the home Member State, take appropriate measures to prevent or to punish further irregularities and, in so far as is necessary, to prevent that credit institution from initiating further transactions within its territory. The Member States shall ensure that within their territories it is possible to serve the legal documents necessary for these measures on credit institutions.

Article 31

Articles 29 and 30 shall not affect the power of host Member States to take appropriate measures to prevent or to punish irregularities committed within their territories which are contrary to the legal rules they have adopted in the interests of the general good. This shall include the possibility of preventing offending credit institutions from initiating further transactions within their territories.

Article 32

Any measure taken pursuant to Article 30(2) and (3), or Article 31 involving penalties or restrictions on the exercise of the freedom to provide services shall be properly justified and communicated to the credit institution concerned. Every such measure shall be subject to a right of appeal to the courts in the Member State in which it was taken.

Article 33

Before following the procedure provided for in Article 30, the competent authorities of the host Member State may, in emergencies, take any precautionary measures necessary to protect the interests of depositors, investors and others to whom services are provided. The Commission and the competent authorities of the other Member States concerned shall be informed of such measures at the earliest opportunity.

The Commission may, after consulting the competent authorities of the Member States concerned, decide that the Member State in question shall amend or abolish those measures.

Article 34

Host Member States may exercise the powers conferred on them under this Directive by taking appropriate measures to prevent or to punish irregularities committed within their territories. This shall include the possibility of preventing offending credit institutions from initiating further transactions within their territories.

Article 35

In the event of the withdrawal of authorisation, the competent authorities of the host Member State shall be informed and shall take appropriate measures to prevent the credit institution concerned from initiating further transactions within its territory and to safeguard the interests of depositors.

Article 36

The Member States shall inform the Commission of the number and type of cases in which there has been a refusal pursuant to Articles 25 and 26(1) to (3) or in which measures have been taken in accordance with Article 30(3).

Article 37

This Section shall not prevent credit institutions with head offices in other Member States from advertising their services through all available means of communication in the host Member State, subject to any rules governing the form and the content of such advertising adopted in the interests of the general good.

Title IV
Relations with Third Countries

Section 1
Notification in Relation to Third Countries' Undertaking and Conditions of Access to the Markets of these Countries

Article 38

1. Member States shall not apply to branches of credit institutions having their head office outside the Community, when commencing or carrying on their business, provisions which result in more favourable treatment than that accorded to branches of credit institutions having their head office in the Community.

2. The competent authorities shall notify the Commission and the European Banking Committee of all authorisations for branches granted to credit institutions having their head office outside the Community.

3. Without prejudice to paragraph 1, the Community may, through agreements concluded with one or more third countries, agree to apply provisions which accord to branches of a credit institution having its head office outside the Community identical treatment throughout the territory of the Community.

Section 2
Cooperation with Third Countries' Competent Authorities Regarding Supervision on a Consolidated Basis

Article 39

1. The Commission may submit proposals to the Council, either at the request of a Member State or on its own initiative, for the negotiation of agreements with one or more third countries regarding the means of exercising supervision on a consolidated basis over the following:

(a) credit institutions the parent undertakings of which have their head offices in a third country; or

(b) credit institutions situated in third countries the parent undertakings of which, whether credit institutions or financial holding companies, have their head offices in the Community.

2. The agreements referred to in paragraph 1 shall, in particular, seek to ensure the following:

(a) that the competent authorities of the Member States are able to obtain the information necessary for the supervision, on the basis of their consolidated financial situations, of credit institutions or financial holding companies situated in the Community and which have as subsidiaries credit institutions or financial institutions situated outside the Community, or holding participation in such institutions; and

(b) that the competent authorities of third countries are able to obtain the information necessary for the supervision of parent undertakings the head offices of which are situated within their territories and which have as subsidiaries credit institutions or financial institutions situated in one or more Member States or holding participation in such institutions.

3. Without prejudice to Article 300(1) and (2) of the Treaty, the Commission shall, with the assistance of the European Banking Committee, examine the outcome of the negotiations referred to in paragraph 1 and the resulting situation.

Title V
Principles and Technical Instruments for Prudential Supervision and Disclosure

Chapter 1
Principles of Prudential Supervision

Section 1
Competence of Home and Host Member State

Article 40

1. The prudential supervision of a credit institution, including that of the activities it carries on in

accordance with Articles 23 and 24, shall be the responsibility of the competent authorities of the home Member State, without prejudice to those provisions of this Directive which give responsibility to the competent authorities of the host Member State.

2. Paragraph 1 shall not prevent supervision on a consolidated basis pursuant to this Directive.

Article 41

Host Member States shall, pending further coordination, retain responsibility in cooperation with the competent authorities of the home Member State for the supervision of the liquidity of the branches of credit institutions.

Without prejudice to the measures necessary for the reinforcement of the European Monetary System, host Member States shall retain complete responsibility for the measures resulting from the implementation of their monetary policies.

Such measures may not provide for discriminatory or restrictive treatment based on the fact that a credit institution is authorised in another Member State.

Article 42

The competent authorities of the Member States concerned shall collaborate closely in order to supervise the activities of credit institutions operating, in particular through a branch, in one or more Member States other than that in which their head offices are situated. They shall supply one another with all information concerning the management and ownership of such credit institutions that is likely to facilitate their supervision and the examination of the conditions for their authorisation, and all information likely to facilitate the monitoring of such institutions, in particular with regard to liquidity, solvency, deposit guarantees, the limiting of large exposures, administrative and accounting procedures and internal control mechanisms.

Article 43

1. Host Member States shall provide that, where a credit institution authorised in another Member State carries on its activities through a branch, the competent authorities of the home Member State may, after having first informed the competent authorities of the host Member State, carry out themselves or through the intermediary of persons they appoint for that purpose on-the-spot verification of the information referred to in Article 42.

2. The competent authorities of the home Member State may also, for purposes of the verification of branches, have recourse to one of the other procedures laid down in Article 141.

3. Paragraphs 1 and 2 shall not affect the right of the competent authorities of the host Member State to carry out, in the discharge of their responsibilities under this Directive, on-the-spot verifications of branches established within their territory.

Section 2

Exchange of Information and Professional Secrecy

Article 44

1. Member States shall provide that all persons working for or who have worked for the competent authorities, as well as auditors or experts acting on behalf of the competent authorities, shall be bound by the obligation of professional secrecy.

No confidential information which they may receive in the course of their duties may be divulged to any person or authority whatsoever, except in summary or collective form, such that individual credit institutions cannot be identified, without prejudice to cases covered by criminal law.

Nevertheless, where a credit institution has been declared bankrupt or is being compulsorily wound up, confidential information which does not concern third parties involved in attempts to rescue that credit institution may be divulged in civil or commercial proceedings.

2. Paragraph 1 shall not prevent the competent authorities of the various Member States from

exchanging information in accordance with this Directive and with other Directives applicable to credit institutions. That information shall be subject to the conditions of professional secrecy indicated in paragraph 1.

> **CASE**
>
> **Case 110/84 Commune de Hillegom v Cornelis Hillenius [1985] ECR 3947**
>
> Article 12 (1) of Directive 77/780/EEC,[5] which states that the obligation to maintain professional secrecy imposed on persons now or in the past employed by the authorities empowered to authorize and supervise credit institutions means that the confidential information received in the course of their duties may not be divulged to any person or authority except by virtue of provisions laid down by law, also applies to statements which such persons make as witnesses in civil proceedings.
>
> Amongst the provisions laid down by law allowing confidential information to be divulged, as envisaged by article 12 (1), cited above, must be included general provisions not specifically intended to lay down exceptions to the ban on disclosing the kind of information covered by the Directive but establishing the limits which the maintenance of confidentiality places on the obligation to give evidence as a witness.
>
> When such general provisions are applied, it is for the national courts to find the balance between the interest in establishing the truth and the interest in maintaining of confidentiality certain kinds of information, especially where such information has been supplied by the competent authorities of other Member States in accordance with article 12 (2) of the Directive.

Article 45

Competent authorities receiving confidential information under Article 44 may use it only in the course of their duties and only for the following purposes:

(a) to check that the conditions governing the taking-up of the business of credit institutions are met and to facilitate monitoring, on a non-consolidated or consolidated basis, of the conduct of such business, especially with regard to the monitoring of liquidity, solvency, large exposures, and administrative and accounting procedures and internal control mechanisms;

(b) to impose penalties;

(c) in an administrative appeal against a decision of the competent authority; or

(d) in court proceedings initiated pursuant to Article 55 or to special provisions provided for in this or in other Directives adopted in the field of credit institutions.

Article 46

Member States may conclude cooperation agreements, providing for exchanges of information, with the competent authorities of third countries or with authorities or bodies of third countries as defined in Articles 47 and 48(1) only if the information disclosed is subject to guarantees of professional secrecy at least equivalent to those referred to in Article 44(1). Such exchange of information shall be for the purpose of performing the supervisory task of the authorities or bodies mentioned.

Where the information originates in another Member State, it may not be disclosed without the express agreement of the competent authorities which have disclosed it and, where appropriate, solely for the purposes for which those authorities gave their agreement.

Article 47

Articles 44(1) and 45 shall not preclude the exchange of information within a Member State, where there are two or more competent authorities in the same Member State, or between Member States, between competent authorities and the following:

(a) authorities entrusted with the public duty of supervising other financial organisations and insurance companies and the authorities responsible for the supervision of financial markets;

(b) bodies involved in the liquidation and bankruptcy of credit institutions and in other similar procedures; and

(c) persons responsible for carrying out statutory audits of the accounts of credit institutions and other financial institutions;

in the discharge of their supervisory functions.

Articles 44(1) and 45 shall not preclude the disclosure to bodies which administer deposit-guarantee schemes of information necessary to the exercise of their functions.

In both cases, the information received shall be subject to the conditions of professional secrecy specified in Article 44(1).

Article 48

1. Notwithstanding Articles 44 to 46, Member States may authorise exchange of information between the competent authorities and the following:

(a) the authorities responsible for overseeing the bodies involved in the liquidation and bankruptcy of credit institutions and in other similar procedures; and

(b) the authorities responsible for overseeing persons charged with carrying out statutory audits of the accounts of insurance undertakings, credit institutions, investment firms and other financial institutions.

In such cases, Member States shall require fulfilment of at least the following conditions:

(a) the information shall be for the purpose of performing the supervisory task referred to in the first subparagraph;

(b) information received in this context shall be subject to the conditions of professional secrecy specified in Article 44(1); and

(c) where the information originates in another Member State, it may not be disclosed without the express agreement of the competent authorities which have disclosed it and, where appropriate, solely for the purposes for which those authorities gave their agreement.

Member States shall communicate to the Commission and to the other Member States the names of the authorities which may receive information pursuant to this paragraph.

2. Notwithstanding Articles 44 to 46, Member States may, with the aim of strengthening the stability, including integrity, of the financial system, authorise the exchange of information between the competent authorities and the authorities or bodies responsible under law for the detection and investigation of breaches of company law.

In such cases Member States shall require fulfilment of at least the following conditions:

(a) the information is for the purpose of performing the task referred to in the first subparagraph;

(b) information received in this context is subject to the conditions of professional secrecy specified in Article 44(1); and

(c) where the information originates in another Member State, it may not be disclosed without the express agreement of the competent authorities which have disclosed it and, where appropriate, solely for the purposes for which those authorities gave their agreement.

Where, in a Member State, the authorities or bodies referred to in the first subparagraph perform their task of detection or investigation with the aid, in view of their specific competence, of persons appointed for that purpose and not employed in the public sector, the possibility of exchanging information provided for in the first subparagraph may be extended to such persons under the conditions specified in the second subparagraph.

In order to implement the third subparagraph, the authorities or bodies referred to in the first subparagraph shall communicate to the competent authorities which have disclosed the information, the names and precise responsibilities of the persons to whom it is to be sent.

Member States shall communicate to the Commission and to the other Member States the names of the authorities or bodies which may receive information pursuant to this Article.

The Commission shall draw up a report on the application of the provisions of this Article.

Article 49

This Section shall not prevent a competent authority from transmitting information to the following for the purposes of their tasks:

(a) central banks and other bodies with a similar function in their capacity as monetary authorities; and

(b) where appropriate, to other public authorities responsible for overseeing payment systems.

This Section shall not prevent such authorities or bodies from communicating to the competent authorities such information as they may need for the purposes of Article 45.

Information received in this context shall be subject to the conditions of professional secrecy specified in Article 44(1).

Article 50

Notwithstanding Articles 44(1) and 45, the Member States may, by virtue of provisions laid down by law, authorise the disclosure of certain information to other departments of their central government administrations responsible for legislation on the supervision of credit institutions, financial institutions, investment services and insurance companies and to inspectors acting on behalf of those departments.

However, such disclosures may be made only where necessary for reasons of prudential control.

Article 51

The Member States shall provide that information received under Articles 44(2) and 47 and information obtained by means of the on-the-spot verification referred to in Article 43(1) and (2) may never be disclosed in the cases referred to in Article 50 except with the express consent of the competent authorities which disclosed the information or of the competent authorities of the Member State in which on-the-spot verification was carried out.

Article 52

This Section shall not prevent the competent authorities of a Member State from communicating the information referred to in Articles 44 to 46 to a clearing house or other similar body recognised under national law for the provision of clearing or settlement services for one of their national markets if they consider that it is necessary to communicate the information in order to ensure the proper functioning of those bodies in relation to defaults or potential defaults by market participants. The information received in this context shall be subject to the conditions of professional secrecy specified in Article 44(1).

The Member States shall, however, ensure that information received under Article 44(2) may not be disclosed in the circumstances referred to in this Article without the express consent of the competent authorities which disclosed it.

Section 3
Duty of Persons Responsible for the Legal Control of Annual and Consolidated Accounts

Article 53

1. Member States shall provide at least that any person authorised within the meaning of Directive 84/253/EEC[22] performing in a credit institution the task described in Article 51 of Directive 78/660/EEC, Article 37 of Directive 83/349/EEC or Article 31 of Directive 85/611/EEC,[23] or any other statutory task, shall have a duty to report promptly to the competent authorities any fact or decision concerning that credit institution of which he has become aware while carrying out that task which is liable to:

(a) constitute a material breach of the laws, regulations or administrative provisions which lay down the conditions governing authorisation or

---

[22] Eighth Council Directive 84/253/EEC of 10 April 1984 on the approval of persons responsible for carrying out the statutory audits of accounting documents (OJ L 126, 12.5.1984, 20), reproduced infra under no. C. 7.

[23] Council Directive 85/611/EEC of 20 December 1985 on the coordination of laws, regulations and administrative provisions relating to undertakings for collective investment in transferable securities (UCITS) (OJ L 375, 31.12.1985, 3), reproduced infra under no. S. 6. Directive as last amended by Directive 2005/1/EC, reproduced supra under no. B. 39.

which specifically govern pursuit of the activities of credit institutions;

(b) affect the continuous functioning of the credit institution; or

(c) lead to refusal to certify the accounts or to the expression of reservations.

Member States shall provide at least that that person shall likewise have a duty to report any fact or decision of which he becomes aware in the course of carrying out a task as described in the first sub-paragraph in an undertaking having close links resulting from a control relationship with the credit institution within which he is carrying out that task.

2. The disclosure in good faith to the competent authorities, by persons authorised within the meaning of Directive 84/253/EEC, of any fact or decision referred to in paragraph 1 shall not constitute a breach of any restriction on disclosure of information imposed by contract or by any legislative, regulatory or administrative provision and shall not involve such persons in liability of any kind.

Section 4
Power of Sanction and Right to Apply to the Courts

Article 54

Without prejudice to the procedures for the withdrawal of authorisations and the provisions of criminal law, the Member States shall provide that their respective competent authorities may, as against credit institutions, or those who effectively control the business of credit institutions, which breach laws, regulations or administrative provisions concerning the supervision or pursuit of their activities, adopt or impose penalties or measures aimed specifically at ending the observed breaches or the causes of such breaches.

Article 55

Member States shall ensure that decisions taken in respect of a credit institution in pursuance of laws, regulations and administrative provisions adopted in accordance with this Directive may be subject to the right to apply to the courts. The same shall apply where no decision is taken, within six months of its submission, in respect of an application for authorisation which contains all the information required under the provisions in force.

Chapter 2
Technical Instruments of Prudential Supervision

Section 1
Own Funds

Article 56

Wherever a Member State lays down by law, regulation or administrative action a provision in implementation of Community legislation concerning the prudential supervision of an operative credit institution which uses the term or refers to the concept of own funds, it shall bring this term or concept into line with the definition given in Articles 57 to 61 and Articles 63 to 66.

Article 57

Subject to the limits imposed in Article 66, the unconsolidated own funds of credit institutions shall consist of the following items:

(a) capital within the meaning of Article 22 of Directive 86/635/EEC, in so far as it has been paid up, plus share premium accounts but excluding cumulative preferential shares;

(b) reserves within the meaning of Article 23 of Directive 86/635/EEC and profits and losses brought forward as a result of the application of the final profit or loss;

(c) funds for general banking risks within the meaning of Article 38 of Directive 86/635/EEC;

(d) revaluation reserves within the meaning of Article 33 of Directive 78/660/EEC;

(e) value adjustments within the meaning of Article 37(2) of Directive 86/635/EEC;

(f) other items within the meaning of Article 63;

(g) the commitments of the members of credit institutions set up as cooperative societies and the joint and several commitments of the borrowers of certain institutions organised as funds, as referred to in Article 64(1); and

(h) fixed-term cumulative preferential shares and subordinated loan capital as referred to in Article 64(3).

The following items shall be deducted in accordance with Article 66:

(i) own shares at book value held by a credit institution;

(j) intangible assets within the meaning of Article 4(9) ('Assets') of Directive 86/635/EEC;

(k) material losses of the current financial year;

(l) holdings in other credit and financial institutions amounting to more than 10% of their capital;

(m) subordinated claims and instruments referred to in Article 63 and Article 64(3) which a credit institution holds in respect of credit and financial institutions in which it has holdings exceeding 10% of the capital in each case;

(n) holdings in other credit and financial institutions of up to 10% of their capital, the subordinated claims and the instruments referred to in Article 63 and Article 64(3) which a credit institution holds in respect of credit and financial institutions other than those referred to in points (l) and (m) in respect of the amount of the total of such holdings, subordinated claims and instruments which exceed 10% of that credit institution's own funds calculated before the deduction of items in points (l) to (p);

(o) participations within the meaning of Article 4(10) which a credit institution holds in:

(i) insurance undertakings within the meaning of Article 6 of Directive 73/239/EEC,[24] Article 4 of Directive 2002/83/EC[25] or Article 1(b) of Directive 98/78/ EC,[26]

(ii) reinsurance undertakings within the meaning of Article 1(c) of Directive 98/78/EC, or

(iii) insurance holding companies within the meaning of Article 1(i) of Directive 98/78/EC;

(p) each of the following items which the credit institution holds in respect of the entities defined in point (o) in which it holds a participation:

(i) instruments referred to in Article 16(3) of Directive 73/239/EEC, and

(ii) instruments referred to in Article 27(3) of Directive 2002/83/EC;

(q) for credit institutions calculating risk-weighted exposure amounts under Section 3, Subsection 2, negative amounts resulting from the calculation in Annex VII, Part 1, point 36 and expected loss amounts calculated in accordance with Annex VII, Part 1 points 32 and 33; and

(r) the exposure amount of securitisation positions which receive a risk weight of 1, 250% under Annex IX, Part 4, calculated in the manner there specified.

For the purposes of point (b), the Member States may permit inclusion of interim profits before a formal decision has been taken only if these profits have been verified by persons responsible for the auditing of the accounts and if it is proved to the satisfaction of the competent authorities that the amount thereof has been evaluated in accordance with the principles set out in Directive 86/635/EEC and is net of any foreseeable charge or dividend. In the case of a credit institution which is the originator of a securitisation, net gains arising from the capitalisation of future income from the securitised assets and providing credit enhancement to positions in the securitisation shall be excluded from the item specified in point (b).

Article 58

Where shares in another credit institution, financial institution, insurance or reinsurance undertaking or insurance holding company are held

---

[24] First Council Directive 73/239/EEC of 24 July 1973 on the coordination of laws, regulations and administrative provisions relating to the taking-up and pursuit of the business of direct insurance other than life assurance (OJ L 228, 16.8.1973, 3), reproduced infra under no. I. 3. Directive as last amended by Directive 2005/1/EC, reproduced supra under no. B. 39.

[25] Directive 2002/83/EC of the European Parliament and of the Council of 5 November 2002 concerning life assurance (OJ L 345, 19.12.2002, 1), reproduced infra under no. I. 33. Directive as last amended by Directive 2005/1/EC, reproduced supra under no. B. 39.

[26] Directive 98/78/EC of the European Parliament and of the Council of 27 October 1998 on the supplementary supervision of insurance undertakings in an insurance group (OJ L 330, 5.12.1998, 1), reproduced infra under no. I. 28. Directive as last amended by Directive 2005/1/EC, reproduced supra under no. B. 39.

temporarily for the purposes of a financial assistance operation designed to reorganise and save that entity, the competent authority may waive the provisions on deduction referred to in points (l) to (p) of Article 57.

Article 59

As an alternative to the deduction of the items referred to in points (o) and (p) of Article 57, Member States may allow their credit institutions to apply mutatis mutandis methods 1, 2 or 3 of Annex I to Directive 2002/87/EC. Method 1 (accounting consolidation) may be applied only if the competent authority is confident about the level of integrated management and internal control regarding the entities which would be included in the scope of consolidation. The method chosen shall be applied in a consistent manner over time.

Article 60

Member States may provide that for the calculation of own funds on a stand-alone basis, credit institutions subject to supervision on a consolidated basis in accordance with Chapter 4, Section 1, or to supplementary supervision in accordance with Directive 2002/87/EC, need not deduct the items referred to in points (l) to (p) of Article 57 which are held in credit institutions, financial institutions, insurance or reinsurance undertakings or insurance holding companies, which are included in the scope of consolidated or supplementary supervision.

This provision shall apply to all the prudential rules harmonised by Community acts.

Article 61

The concept of own funds as defined in points (a) to (h) of Article 57 embodies a maximum number of items and amounts. The use of those items and the fixing of lower ceilings, and the deduction of items other than those listed in points (i) to (r) of Article 57 shall be left to the discretion of the Member States.

The items listed in points (a) to (e) of Article 57 shall be available to a credit institution for unrestricted and immediate use to cover risks or losses as soon as these occur. The amount shall be net of any foreseeable tax charge at the moment of its calculation or be suitably adjusted in so far as such tax charges reduce the amount up to which these items may be applied to cover risks or losses.

Article 62

Member States may report to the Commission on the progress achieved in convergence with a view to a common definition of own funds. On the basis of these reports the Commission shall, if appropriate, by 1 January 2009, submit a proposal to the European Parliament and to the Council for amendment of this Section.

Article 63

1. The concept of own funds used by a Member State may include other items provided that, whatever their legal or accounting designations might be, they have the following characteristics:

(a) they are freely available to the credit institution to cover normal banking risks where revenue or capital losses have not yet been identified;

(b) their existence is disclosed in internal accounting records; and

(c) their amount is determined by the management of the credit institution, verified by independent auditors, made known to the competent authorities and placed under the supervision of the latter.

2. Securities of indeterminate duration and other instruments that fulfil the following conditions may also be accepted as other items:

(a) they may not be reimbursed on the bearer's initiative or without the prior agreement of the competent authority;

(b) the debt agreement shall provide for the credit institution to have the option of deferring the payment of interest on the debt;

(c) the lender's claims on the credit institution shall be wholly subordinated to those of all non-subordinated creditors;

(d) the documents governing the issue of the securities shall provide for debt and unpaid interest to be such as to absorb losses, whilst leaving the credit institution in a position to continue trading; and

(e) only fully paid-up amounts shall be taken into account.

To these securities and other instruments may be added cumulative preferential shares other than those referred to in point (h) of Article 57.

3. For credit institutions calculating risk-weighted exposure amounts under Section 3, Subsection 2, positive amounts resulting from the calculation in Annex VII, Part 1, point 36, may, up to 0.6% of risk weighted exposure amounts calculated under Subsection 2, be accepted as other items. For these credit institutions value adjustments and provisions included in the calculation referred to in Annex VII, Part 1, point 36 and value adjustments and provisions for exposures referred to in point (e) of Article 57 shall not be included in own funds other than in accordance with this paragraph. For these purposes, risk weighted exposure amounts shall not include those calculated in respect of securitisation positions which have a risk weight of 1,250%.

Article 64

1. The commitments of the members of credit institutions set up as cooperative societies referred to in point (g) of Article 57, shall comprise those societies' uncalled capital, together with the legal commitments of the members of those cooperative societies to make additional non-refundable payments should the credit institution incur a loss, in which case it shall be possible to demand those payments without delay.

The joint and several commitments of borrowers in the case of credit institutions organised as funds shall be treated in the same way as the preceding items.

All such items may be included in own funds in so far as they are counted as the own funds of institutions of this category under national law.

2. Member States shall not include in the own funds of public credit institutions guarantees which they or their local authorities extend to such entities.

3. Member States or the competent authorities may include fixed-term cumulative preferential shares referred to in point (h) of Article 57 and subordinated loan capital referred to in that provision in own funds, if binding agreements exist under which, in the event of the bankruptcy or liquidation of the credit institution, they rank after the claims of all other creditors and are not to be repaid until all other debts outstanding at the time have been settled.

Subordinated loan capital shall fulfil the following additional criteria:

(a) only fully paid-up funds may be taken into account;

(b) the loans involved shall have an original maturity of at least five years, after which they may be repaid;

(c) the extent to which they may rank as own funds shall be gradually reduced during at least the last five years before the repayment date; and

(d) the loan agreement shall not include any clause providing that in specified circumstances, other than the winding-up of the credit institution, the debt shall become repayable before the agreed repayment date.

For the purposes of point (b) of the second subparagraph, if the maturity of the debt is not fixed, the loans involved shall be repayable only subject to five years' notice unless the loans are no longer considered as own funds or unless the prior consent of the competent authorities is specifically required for early repayment. The competent authorities may grant permission for the early repayment of such loans provided the request is made at the initiative of the issuer and the solvency of the credit institution in question is not affected.

4. Credit institutions shall not include in own funds either the fair value reserves related to gains or losses on cash flow hedges of financial instruments measured at amortised cost, or any gains or losses on their liabilities valued at fair value that are due to changes in the credit institutions' own credit standing.

Article 65

1. Where the calculation is to be made on a consolidated basis, the consolidated amounts relating to the items listed under Article 57 shall be used in accordance with the rules laid down in Chapter 4, Section 1. Moreover, the following may, when they are credit ('negative') items, be regarded as consolidated reserves for the calculation of own funds:

(a) any minority interests within the meaning of Article 21 of Directive 83/349/EEC, where the global integration method is used;

(b) the first consolidation difference within the meaning of Articles 19, 30 and 31 of Directive 83/349/EEC;

(c) the translation differences included in consolidated reserves in accordance with Article 39(6) of Directive 86/635/EEC; and

(d) any difference resulting from the inclusion of certain participating interests in accordance with the method prescribed in Article 33 of Directive 83/349/EEC.

2. Where the items referred to in points (a) to (d) of paragraph 1 are debit ('positive') items, they shall be deducted in the calculation of consolidated own funds.

Article 66

1. The items referred to in points (d) to (h) of Article 57, shall be subject to the following limits:

(a) the total of the items in points (d) to (h) may not exceed a maximum of 100% of the items in points (a) plus (b) and (c) minus (i) to (k); and

(b) the total of the items in points (g) to (h) may not exceed a maximum of 50% of the items in points (a) plus (b) and (c) minus (i) to (k).

2. The total of the items in points (l) to (r) of Article 57 shall be deducted half from the total of the items (a) to (c) minus (i) to (k), and half from the total of the items (d) to (h) of Article 57, after application of the limits laid down in paragraph 1 of this Article. To the extent that half of the total of the items (l) to (r) exceeds the total of the items (d) to (h) of Article 57, the excess shall be deducted from the total of the items (a) to (c) minus (i) to (k) of Article 57. Items in point (r) of Article 57 shall not be deducted if they have been included in the calculation of risk-weighted exposure amounts for the purposes of Article 75 as specified in Annex IX, Part 4.

3. For the purposes of Sections 5 and 6, the provisions laid down in this Section shall be read without taking into account the items referred to in points (q) and (r) of Article 57 and Article 63(3).

4. The competent authorities may authorise credit institutions to exceed the limits laid down in paragraph 1 in temporary and exceptional circumstances.

Article 67

Compliance with the conditions laid down in this Section shall be proved to the satisfaction of the competent authorities.

Section 2
Provision Against Risks

Subsection 1
Level of Application

Article 68

1. Credit institutions shall comply with the obligations laid down in Articles 22 and 75 and Section 5 on an individual basis.

2. Every credit institution which is neither a subsidiary in the Member State where it is authorised and supervised, nor a parent undertaking, and every credit institution not included in the consolidation pursuant to Article 73, shall comply with the obligations laid down in Articles 120 and 123 on an individual basis.

3. Every credit institution which is neither a parent undertaking, nor a subsidiary, and every credit institution not included in the consolidation pursuant to Article 73, shall comply with the obligations laid down in Chapter 5 on an individual basis.

Article 69

1. The Member States may choose not to apply Article 68(1) to any subsidiary of a credit institution, where both the subsidiary and the credit institution are subject to authorisation and supervision by the Member State concerned, and the subsidiary is included in the supervision on a consolidated basis of the credit institution which is the parent undertaking, and all of the following conditions are satisfied, in order to ensure that own funds are distributed adequately among the parent undertaking and the subsidiaries:

(a) there is no current or foreseen material practical or legal impediment to the prompt transfer of own funds or repayment of liabilities by its parent undertaking;

(b) either the parent undertaking satisfies the competent authority regarding the prudent management of the subsidiary and has declared, with the consent of the competent authority, that it guarantees the commitments entered into by the subsidiary, or the risks in the subsidiary are of negligible interest;

(c) the risk evaluation, measurement and control procedures of the parent undertaking cover the subsidiary; and

(d) the parent undertaking holds more than 50% of the voting rights attaching to shares in the capital of the subsidiary and/or has the right to appoint or remove a majority of the members of the management body of the subsidiary described in Article 11.

2. The Member States may exercise the option provided for in paragraph 1 where the parent undertaking is a financial holding company set up in the same Member State as the credit institution, provided that it is subject to the same supervision as that exercised over credit institutions, and in particular to the standards laid down in Article 71(1).

3. The Member States may choose not to apply Article 68(1) to a parent credit institution in a Member State where that credit institution is subject to authorisation and supervision by the Member State concerned, and it is included in the supervision on a consolidated basis, and all the following conditions are satisfied, in order to ensure that own funds are distributed adequately among the parent undertaking and the subsidiaries:

(a) there is no current or foreseen material practical or legal impediment to the prompt transfer of own funds or repayment of liabilities to the parent credit institution in a Member State; and

(b) the risk evaluation, measurement and control procedures relevant for consolidated supervision cover the parent credit institution in a Member State.

The competent authority which makes use of this paragraph shall inform the competent authorities of all other Member States.

4. Without prejudice to the generality of Article 144, the competent authority of the Member States exercising the discretion laid down in paragraph 3 shall publicly disclose, in the manner indicated in Article 144:

(a) criteria it applies to determine that there is no current or foreseen material practical or legal impediment to the prompt transfer of own funds or repayment of liabilities;

(b) the number of parent credit institutions which benefit from the exercise of the discretion laid down in paragraph 3 and the number of these which incorporate subsidiaries in a third country; and

(c) on an aggregate basis for the Member State:
(i) the total amount of own funds on the consolidated basis of the parent credit institution in a Member State, which benefits from the exercise of the discretion laid down in paragraph 3, which are held in subsidiaries in a third country;
(ii) the percentage of total own funds on the consolidated basis of parent credit institutions in a Member State which benefits from the exercise of the discretion laid down in paragraph 3, represented by own funds which are held in subsidiaries in a third country; and
(iii) the percentage of total minimum own funds required under Article 75 on the consolidated basis of parent credit institutions in a Member State, which benefits from the

exercise of the discretion laid down in paragraph 3, represented by own funds which are held in subsidiaries in a third country.

Article 70

1. Subject to paragraphs 2 to 4 of this Article, the competent authorities may allow on a case by case basis parent credit institutions to incorporate in the calculation of their requirement under Article 68(1) subsidiaries which meet the conditions laid down in points (c) and (d) of Article 69(1), and whose material exposures or material liabilities are to that parent credit institution.

2. The treatment in paragraph 1 shall be allowed only where the parent credit institution demonstrates fully to the competent authorities the circumstances and arrangements, including legal arrangements, by virtue of which there is no material practical or legal impediment, and none are foreseen, to the prompt transfer of own funds, or repayment of liabilities when due by the subsidiary to its parent undertaking.

3. Where a competent authority exercises the discretion laid down in paragraph 1, it shall on a regular basis and not less than once a year inform the competent authorities of all the other Member States of the use made of paragraph 1 and of the circumstances and arrangements referred to in paragraph 2. Where the subsidiary is in a third country, the competent authorities shall provide the same information to the competent authorities of that third country as well.

4. Without prejudice to the generality of Article 144, a competent authority which exercises the discretion laid down in paragraph 1 shall publicly disclose, in the manner indicated in Article 144:

(a) the criteria it applies to determine that there is no current or foreseen material practical or legal impediment to the prompt transfer of own funds or repayment of liabilities;

(b) the number of parent credit institutions which benefit from the exercise of the discretion laid down in paragraph 1 and the number of these which incorporate subsidiaries in a third country; and

(c) on an aggregate basis for the Member State:

(i) the total amount of own funds of parent credit institutions which benefit from the exercise of the discretion laid down in paragraph 1 which are held in subsidiaries in a third country;

(ii) the percentage of total own funds of parent credit institutions which benefit from the exercise of the discretion laid down in paragraph 1 represented by own funds which are held in subsidiaries in a third country; and

(iii) the percentage of total minimum own funds required under Article 75 of parent credit institutions which benefit from the exercise of the discretion laid down in paragraph 1 represented by own funds which are held in subsidiaries in a third country.

Article 71

1. Without prejudice to Articles 68 to 70, parent credit institutions in a Member State shall comply, to the extent and in the manner prescribed in Article 133, with the obligations laid down in Articles 75, 120, 123 and Section 5 on the basis of their consolidated financial situation.

2. Without prejudice to Articles 68 to 70, credit institutions controlled by a parent financial holding company in a Member State shall comply, to the extent and in the manner prescribed in Article 133, with the obligations laid down in Articles 75, 120, 123 and Section 5 on the basis of the consolidated financial situation of that financial holding company.

Where more than one credit institution is controlled by a parent financial holding company in a Member State, the first subparagraph shall apply only to the credit institution to which supervision on a consolidated basis applies in accordance with Articles 125 and 126.

Article 72

1. EU parent credit institutions shall comply with the obligations laid down in Chapter 5 on the basis of their consolidated financial situation.

Significant subsidiaries of EU parent credit institutions shall disclose the information specified in Annex XII, Part 1, point 5, on an individual or sub-consolidated basis.

2. Credit institutions controlled by an EU parent financial holding company shall comply with the obligations laid down in Chapter 5 on the basis of the consolidated financial situation of that financial holding company.

Significant subsidiaries of EU parent financial holding companies shall disclose the information specified in Annex XII, Part 1, point 5, on an individual or sub-consolidated basis. 3. The competent authorities responsible for exercising supervision on a consolidated basis pursuant to Articles 125 and 126 may decide not to apply in full or in part paragraphs 1 and 2 to the credit institutions which are included within comparable disclosures provided on a consolidated basis by a parent undertaking established in a third country.

Article 73

1. The Member States or the competent authorities responsible for exercising supervision on a consolidated basis pursuant to Articles 125 and 126 may decide in the following cases that a credit institution, financial institution or ancillary services undertaking which is a subsidiary or in which a participation is held need not be included in the consolidation:

(a) where the undertaking concerned is situated in a third country where there are legal impediments to the transfer of the necessary information;

(b) where, in the opinion of the competent authorities, the undertaking concerned is of negligible interest only with respect to the objectives of monitoring credit institutions and in any event where the balance-sheet total of the undertaking concerned is less than the smaller of the following two amounts:
(i) EUR 10 million, or
(ii) 1% of the balance-sheet total of the parent undertaking or the undertaking that holds the participation,

(c) where, in the opinion of the competent authorities responsible for exercising supervision on a consolidated basis, the consolidation of the financial situation of the undertaking concerned would be inappropriate or misleading as far as the objectives of the supervision of credit institutions are concerned.

If, in the cases referred to in point (b) of the first subparagraph, several undertakings meet the above criteria set out therein, they shall nevertheless be included in the consolidation where collectively they are of non-negligible interest with respect to the specified objectives.

2. Competent authorities shall require subsidiary credit institutions to apply the requirements laid down in Articles 75, 120 and 123 and Section 5 on a sub-consolidated basis if those credit institutions, or the parent undertaking where it is a financial holding company, have a credit institution or a financial institution or an asset management company as defined in Article 2(5) of Directive 2002/87/EC as a subsidiary in a third country, or hold a participation in such an undertaking.

3. Competent authorities shall require the parent undertakings and subsidiaries subject to this Directive to meet the obligations laid down in Article 22 on a consolidated or sub-consolidated basis, to ensure that their arrangements, processes and mechanisms are consistent and well-integrated and that any data and information relevant to the purpose of supervision can be produced.

Subsection 2
Calculation of Requirements

Article 74

1. Save where otherwise provided, the valuation of assets and off-balance-sheet items shall be effected in accordance with the accounting framework to which the credit institution is subject under Regulation (EC) No 1606/2002 and Directive 86/635/EEC.

2. Notwithstanding the requirements laid down in Articles 68 to 72, the calculations to verify the compliance of credit institutions with the obligations laid down in Article 75 shall be carried out not less than twice each year.

The credit institutions shall communicate the results and any component data required to the competent authorities.

SUBSECTION 3
MINIMUM LEVEL OF OWN FUNDS

Article 75

Without prejudice to Article 136, Member States shall require credit institutions to provide own funds which are at all times more than or equal to the sum of the following capital requirements:

(a) for credit risk and dilution risk in respect of all of their business activities with the exception of their trading book business and illiquid assets if deducted from own funds under Article 13(2)(d) of Directive 2006/49/EC, 8% of the total of their risk-weighted exposure amounts calculated in accordance with Section 3;

(b) in respect of their trading-book business, for position risk, settlement and counter-party risk and, in so far as the limits laid down in Articles 111 to 117 are authorised to be exceeded, for large exposures exceeding such limits, the capital requirements determined in accordance with Article 18 and Chapter V, Section 4 of Directive 2006/49/EC;

(c) in respect of all of their business activities, for foreign exchange risk and for commodities risk, the capital requirements determined according to Article 18 of Directive 2006/49/EC; and

(d) in respect of all of their business activities, for operational risk, the capital requirements determined in accordance with Section 4.

SECTION 3
MINIMUM OWN FUNDS REQUIREMENTS FOR CREDIT RISK

Article 76

Credit institutions shall apply either the Standardised Approach provided for in Articles 78 to 83 or, if permitted by the competent authorities in accordance with Article 84, the Internal Ratings Based Approach provided for in Articles 84 to 89 to calculate their risk-weighted exposure amounts for the purposes of Article 75(a).

Article 77

'Exposure' for the purposes of this Section means an asset or off-balance-sheet item.

SUBSECTION 1
STANDARDISED APPROACH

Article 78

1. Subject to paragraph 2, the exposure value of an asset item shall be its balance-sheet value and the exposure value of an off-balance-sheet item listed in Annex II shall be the following percentage of its value: 100% if it is a full-risk item, 50% if it is a medium-risk item, 20% if it is a medium/low-risk item, 0% if it is a low-risk item. The off-balance-sheet items referred to in the first sentence of this paragraph shall be assigned to risk categories as indicated in Annex II. In the case of a credit institution using the Financial Collateral Comprehensive Method under Annex VIII, Part 3, where an exposure takes the form of securities or commodities sold, posted or lent under a repurchase transaction or under a securities or commodities lending or borrowing transaction, and margin lending transactions the exposure value shall be increased by the volatility adjustment appropriate to such securities or commodities as prescribed in Annex VIII, Part 3, points 34 to 59.

2. The exposure value of a derivative instrument listed in Annex IV shall be determined in accordance with Annex III with the effects of contracts of novation and other netting agreements taken into account for the purposes of those methods in accordance with Annex III. The exposure value of repurchase transactions, securities or commodities lending or borrowing transactions, long settlement transactions and margin lending transactions may be determined either in accordance with Annex III or Annex VIII.

3. Where an exposure is subject to funded credit protection, the exposure value applicable to that item may be modified in accordance with Subsection 3.

4. Notwithstanding paragraph 2, the exposure value of credit risk exposures outstanding, as determined by the competent authorities, with a central counterparty shall be determined in accordance with Annex III, Part 2, point 6, provided that the central counterparty's counterparty credit risk exposures with all participants in its arrangements are fully collateralised on a daily basis.

Article 79

1. Each exposure shall be assigned to one of the following exposure classes:

(a) claims or contingent claims on central governments or central banks;

(b) claims or contingent claims on regional governments or local authorities;

(c) claims or contingent claims on administrative bodies and non-commercial undertakings;

(d) claims or contingent claims on multilateral development banks;

(e) claims or contingent claims on international organisations;

(f) claims or contingent claims on institutions;

(g) claims or contingent claims on corporates;

(h) retail claims or contingent retail claims;

(i) claims or contingent claims secured on real estate property;

(j) past due items;

(k) items belonging to regulatory high-risk categories;

(l) claims in the form of covered bonds;

(m) securitisation positions;

(n) short-term claims on institutions and corporate;

(o) claims in the form of collective investment undertakings ('CIU'); or

(p) other items.

2. To be eligible for the retail exposure class referred to in point (h) of paragraph 1, an exposure shall meet the following conditions:

(a) the exposure shall be either to an individual person or persons, or to a small or medium-sized entity;

(b) the exposure shall be one of a significant number of exposures with similar characteristics such that the risks associated with such lending are substantially reduced; and

(c) the total amount owed to the credit institution and parent undertakings and its subsidiaries, including any past due exposure, by the obligor client or group of connected clients, but excluding claims or contingent claims secured on residential real estate collateral, shall not, to the knowledge of the credit institution, exceed EUR 1 million. The credit institution shall take reasonable steps to acquire this knowledge.

Securities shall not be eligible for the retail exposure class.

3. The present value of retail minimum lease payments is eligible for the retail exposure class.

Article 80

1. To calculate risk-weighted exposure amounts, risk weights shall be applied to all exposures, unless deducted from own funds, in accordance with the provisions of Annex VI, Part 1. The application of risk weights shall be based on the exposure class to which the exposure is assigned and, to the extent specified in Annex VI, Part 1, its credit quality. Credit quality may be determined by reference to the credit assessments of External Credit Assessment Institutions ('ECAIs') in accordance with the provisions of Articles 81 to 83 or the credit assessments of Export Credit Agencies as described in Annex VI, Part 1.

2. For the purposes of applying a risk weight, as referred to in paragraph 1, the exposure value shall be multiplied by the risk weight specified or determined in accordance with this Subsection.

3. For the purposes of calculating risk-weighted exposure amounts for exposures to institutions,

Member States shall decide whether to adopt the method based on the credit quality of the central government of the jurisdiction in which the institution is incorporated or the method based on the credit quality of the counterparty institution in accordance with Annex VI.

4. Notwithstanding paragraph 1, where an exposure is subject to credit protection the risk weight applicable to that item may be modified in accordance with Subsection 3.

5. Risk-weighted exposure amounts for securitised exposures shall be calculated in accordance with Subsection 4.

6. Exposures the calculation of risk-weighted exposure amounts for which is not otherwise provided for under this Subsection shall be assigned a risk weight of 100%.

7. With the exception of exposures giving rise to liabilities in the form of the items referred to in paragraphs (a) to (h) of Article 57, competent authorities may exempt from the requirements of paragraph 1 of this Article the exposures of a credit institution to a counterparty which is its parent undertaking, its subsidiary, a subsidiary of its parent undertaking or an undertaking linked by a relationship within the meaning of Article 12(1) of Directive 83/349/EEC, provided that the following conditions are met:

(a) the counterparty is an institution or a financial holding company, financial institution, asset management company or ancillary services undertaking subject to appropriate prudential requirements;

(b) the counterparty is included in the same consolidation as the credit institution on a full basis;

(c) the counterparty is subject to the same risk evaluation, measurement and control procedures as the credit institution;

(d) the counterparty is established in the same Member State as the credit institution; and

(e) there is no current or foreseen material practical or legal impediment to the prompt transfer of own funds or repayment of liabilities from the counterparty to the credit institution.

In such a case, a risk weight of 0% shall be assigned.

8. With the exception of exposures giving rise to liabilities in the form of the items referred to in points (a) to (h) of Article 57, competent authorities may exempt from the requirements of paragraph 1 of this Article the exposures to counterparties which are members of the same institutional protection scheme as the lending credit institution, provided that the following conditions are met:

(a) the requirements set out in points (a), (d) and (e) of paragraph 7;

(b) the credit institution and the counterparty have entered into a contractual or statutory liability arrangement which protects those institutions and in particular ensures their liquidity and solvency to avoid bankruptcy in case it becomes necessary (referred to below as an institutional protection scheme);

(c) the arrangements ensure that the institutional protection scheme will be able to grant support necessary under its commitment from funds readily available to it;

(d) the institutional protection scheme disposes of suitable and uniformly stipulated systems for the monitoring and classification of risk (which gives a complete overview of the risk situations of all the individual members and the institutional protection scheme as a whole) with corresponding possibilities to take influence; those systems shall suitably monitor defaulted exposures in accordance with Annex VII, Part 4, point 44;

(e) the institutional protection scheme conducts its own risk review which is communicated to the individual members;

(f) the institutional protection scheme draws up and publishes once in a year either, a consolidated report comprising the balance sheet, the profit-and-loss account, the situation report and the risk report, concerning the institutional protection scheme as a whole, or a report comprising the aggregated balance sheet, the aggregated profit-and-loss account, the situation report and the risk report, concerning the institutional protection scheme as a whole;

(g) members of the institutional protection scheme are obliged to give advance notice of at least 24 months if they wish to end the arrangements;

(h) the multiple use of elements eligible for the calculation of own funds ('multiple gearing') as well as any inappropriate creation of own funds between the members of the institutional protection scheme shall be eliminated;

(i) the institutional protection scheme shall be based on a broad membership of credit institutions of a predominantly homogeneous business profile; and

(j) the adequacy of the systems referred to in point (d) is approved and monitored at regular intervals by the relevant competent authorities.

In such a case, a risk weight of 0% shall be assigned.

Article 81

1. An external credit assessment may be used to determine the risk weight of an exposure in accordance with Article 80 only if the ECAI which provides it has been recognised as eligible for those purposes by the competent authorities ('an eligible ECAI' for the purposes of this Subsection).

2. Competent authorities shall recognise an ECAI as eligible for the purposes of Article 80 only if they are satisfied that its assessment methodology complies with the requirements of objectivity, independence, ongoing review and transparency, and that the resulting credit assessments meet the requirements of credibility and transparency. For those purposes, the competent authorities shall take into account the technical criteria set out in Annex VI, Part 2.

3. If an ECAI has been recognised as eligible by the competent authorities of a Member State, the competent authorities of other Member States may recognise that ECAI as eligible without carrying out their own evaluation process.

4. Competent authorities shall make publicly available an explanation of the recognition process, and a list of eligible ECAIs.

Article 82

1. The competent authorities shall determine, taking into account the technical criteria set out in Annex VI, Part 2, with which of the credit quality steps set out in Part 1 of that Annex the relevant credit assessments of an eligible ECAI are to be associated. Those determinations shall be objective and consistent.

2. When the competent authorities of a Member State have made a determination under paragraph 1, the competent authorities of other Member States may recognise that determination without carrying out their own determination process.

Article 83

1. The use of ECAI credit assessments for the calculation of a credit institution's risk-weighted exposure amounts shall be consistent and in accordance with Annex VI, Part 3. Credit assessments shall not be used selectively.

2. Credit institutions shall use solicited credit assessments. However, with the permission of the relevant competent authority, they may use unsolicited assessments.

SUBSECTION 2

INTERNAL RATINGS BASED APPROACH

Article 84

1. In accordance with this Subsection, the competent authorities may permit credit institutions to calculate their risk-weighted exposure amounts using the Internal Ratings Based Approach ('IRB Approach'). Explicit permission shall be required in the case of each credit institution.

2. Permission shall be given only if the competent authority is satisfied that the credit institution's systems for the management and rating of credit risk exposures are sound and implemented with integrity and, in particular, that they meet the following standards in accordance with Annex VII, Part 4:

(a) the credit institution's rating systems provide for a meaningful assessment of obligor and transaction characteristics, a meaningful differentiation of risk and accurate and consistent quantitative estimates of risk;

(b) internal ratings and default and loss estimates used in the calculation of capital requirements and associated systems and processes play an essential role in the risk management and decision-making process, and in the credit approval, internal capital allocation and corporate governance functions of the credit institution;

(c) the credit institution has a credit risk control unit responsible for its rating systems that is appropriately independent and free from undue influence;

(d) the credit institution collects and stores all relevant data to provide effective support to its credit risk measurement and management process; and

(e) the credit institution documents its rating systems and the rationale for their design and validates its rating systems.

Where an EU parent credit institution and its subsidiaries or an EU parent financial holding company and its subsidiaries use the IRB Approach on a unified basis, the competent authorities may allow minimum requirements of Annex VII, Part 4 to be met by the parent and its subsidiaries considered together.

3. A credit institution applying for the use of the IRB Approach shall demonstrate that it has been using for the IRB exposure classes in question rating systems that were broadly in line with the minimum requirements set out in Annex VII, Part 4 for internal risk measurement and management purposes for at least three years prior to its qualification to use the IRB Approach.

4. A credit institution applying for the use of own estimates of LGDs and/or conversion factors shall demonstrate that it has been estimating and employing own estimates of LGDs and/or conversion factors in a manner that was broadly consistent with the minimum requirements for use of own estimates of those parameters set out in Annex VII, Part 4 for at least three years prior to qualification to use own estimates of LGDs and/or conversion factors.

5. If a credit institution ceases to comply with the requirements set out in this Subsection, it shall either present to the competent authority a plan for a timely return to compliance or demonstrate that the effect of non-compliance is immaterial.

6. When the IRB Approach is intended to be used by the EU parent credit institution and its subsidiaries, or by the EU parent financial holding company and its subsidiaries, the competent authorities of the different legal entities shall cooperate closely as provided for in Articles 129 to 132.

Article 85

1. Without prejudice to Article 89, credit institutions and any parent undertaking and its subsidiaries shall implement the IRB Approach for all exposures.

Subject to the approval of the competent authorities, implementation may be carried out sequentially across the different exposure classes, referred to in Article 86, within the same business unit, across different business units in the same group or for the use of own estimates of LGDs or conversion factors for the calculation of risk weights for exposures to corporates, institutions, and central governments and central banks.

In the case of the retail exposure class referred to in Article 86, implementation may be carried out sequentially across the categories of exposures to which the different correlations in Annex VII, Part 1, points 10 to 13 correspond.

2. Implementation as referred to in paragraph 1 shall be carried out within a reasonable period of time to be agreed with the competent authorities. The implementation shall be carried out subject to strict conditions determined by the competent authorities. Those conditions shall be designed to ensure that the flexibility under paragraph 1 is not used selectively with the purpose of achieving reduced minimum capital requirements in respect of those exposure classes or business units that are yet to be included in the IRB Approach or in the use of own estimates of LGDs and/or conversion factors.

3. Credit institutions using the IRB Approach for any exposure class shall at the same time use the IRB Approach for the equity exposure class.

4. Subject to paragraphs 1 to 3 of this Article and Article 89, credit institutions which have obtained permission under Article 84 to use the

IRB Approach shall not revert to the use of Subsection 1 for the calculation of risk-weighted exposure amounts except for demonstrated good cause and subject to the approval of the competent authorities.

5. Subject to paragraphs 1 and 2 of this Article and Article 89, credit institutions which have obtained permission under Article 87(9) to use own estimates of LGDs and conversion factors, shall not revert to the use of LGD values and conversion factors referred to in Article 87(8) except for demonstrated good cause and subject to the approval of the competent authorities.

Article 86

1. Each exposure shall be assigned to one of the following exposure classes:

(a) claims or contingent claims on central governments and central banks;

(b) claims or contingent claims on institutions;

(c) claims or contingent claims on corporates;

(d) retail claims or contingent retail claims;

(e) equity claims;

(f) securitisation positions; or

(g) other non credit-obligation assets.

2. The following exposures shall be treated as exposures to central governments and central banks:

(a) exposures to regional governments, local authorities or public sector entities which are treated as exposures to central governments under Subsection 1; and

(b) exposures to Multilateral Development Banks and International Organisations which attract a risk weight of 0% under Subsection 1.

3. The following exposures shall be treated as exposures to institutions:

(a) exposures to regional governments and local authorities which are not treated as exposures to central governments under Subsection 1;

(b) exposures to Public Sector Entities which are treated as exposures to institutions under Subsection 1; and

(c) exposures to Multilateral Development Banks which do not attract a 0% risk weight under Subsection 1.

4. To be eligible for the retail exposure class referred to in point (d) of paragraph 1, exposures shall meet the following criteria:

(a) they shall be either to an individual person or persons, or to a small or medium-sized entity, provided in the latter case that the total amount owed to the credit institution and parent undertakings and its subsidiaries, including any past due exposure, by the obligor client or group of connected clients, but excluding claims or contingent claims secured on residential real estate collateral, shall not, to the knowledge of the credit institution, which shall have taken reasonable steps to confirm the situation, exceed EUR 1 million;

(b) they are treated by the credit institution in its risk management consistently over time and in a similar manner;

(c) they are not managed just as individually as exposures in the corporate exposure class; and

(d) they each represent one of a significant number of similarly managed exposures.

The present value of retail minimum lease payments is eligible for the retail exposure class.

5. The following exposures shall be classed as equity exposures:

(a) non-debt exposures conveying a subordinated, residual claim on the assets or income of the issuer; and

(b) debt exposures the economic substance of which is similar to the exposures specified in point (a).

6. Within the corporate exposure class, credit institutions shall separately identify as specialised lending exposures, exposures which possess the following characteristics:

(a) the exposure is to an entity which was created specifically to finance and/or operate physical assets;

(b) the contractual arrangements give the lender a substantial degree of control over the assets and the income that they generate; and

(c) the primary source of repayment of the obligation is the income generated by the assets being financed, rather than the independent capacity of a broader commercial enterprise.

7. Any credit obligation not assigned to the exposure classes referred to in points (a), (b) and (d) to (f) of paragraph 1 shall be assigned to the exposure class referred to in point (c) of that paragraph.

8. The exposure class referred to in point (g) of paragraph 1 shall include the residual value of leased properties if not included in the lease exposure as defined in Annex VII, Part 3, paragraph 4.

9. The methodology used by the credit institution for assigning exposures to different exposure classes shall be appropriate and consistent over time.

Article 87

1. The risk-weighted exposure amounts for credit risk for exposures belonging to one of the exposure classes referred to in points (a) to (e) or (g) of Article 86(1) shall, unless deducted from own funds, be calculated in accordance with Annex VII, Part 1, points 1 to 27.

2. The risk-weighted exposure amounts for dilution risk for purchased receivables shall be calculated according to Annex VII, Part 1, point 28. Where a credit institution has full recourse in respect of purchased receivables for default risk and for dilution risk, to the seller of the purchased receivables, the provisions of Articles 87 and 88 in relation to purchased receivables need not be applied. The exposure may instead be treated as a collateralised exposure.

3. The calculation of risk-weighted exposure amounts for credit risk and dilution risk shall be based on the relevant parameters associated with the exposure in question. These shall include probability of default (PD), LGD, maturity (M) and exposure value of the exposure. PD and LGD may be considered separately or jointly, in accordance with Annex VII, Part 2.

4. Notwithstanding paragraph 3, the calculation of risk-weighted exposure amounts for credit risk for all exposures belonging to the exposure class referred to in point (e) of Article 86(1) shall be calculated in accordance with Annex VII, Part 1, points 17 to 26 subject to approval of the competent authorities. Competent authorities shall only allow a credit institution to use the approach set out in Annex VII, Part 1, points 25 and 26 if the credit institution meets the minimum requirements set out in Annex VII, Part 4, points 115 to 123.

5. Notwithstanding paragraph 3, the calculation of risk-weighted exposure amounts for credit risk for specialised lending exposures may be calculated in accordance with Annex VII, Part 1, point 6. Competent authorities shall publish guidance on how credit institutions should assign risk weights to specialised lending exposures under Annex VII, Part 1, point 6 and shall approve credit institution assignment methodologies.

6. For exposures belonging to the exposure classes referred to in points (a) to (d) of Article 86(1), credit institutions shall provide their own estimates of PDs in accordance with Article 84 and Annex VII, Part 4.

7. For exposures belonging to the exposure class referred to in point (d) of Article 86(1), credit institutions shall provide own estimates of LGDs and conversion factors in accordance with Article 84 and Annex VII, Part 4.

8. For exposures belonging to the exposure classes referred to in points (a) to (c) of Article 86(1), credit institutions shall apply the LGD values set out in Annex VII, Part 2, point 8, and the conversion factors set out in Annex VII, Part 3, point 9(a) to (d).

9. Notwithstanding paragraph 8, for all exposures belonging to the exposure classes referred to in points (a) to (c) of Article 86 (1), competent authorities may permit credit institutions to use own estimates of LGDs and conversion factors in accordance with Article 84 and Annex VII, Part 4.

10. The risk-weighted exposure amounts for securitised exposures and for exposures belonging to the exposure class referred to in point (f) of Article 86(1) shall be calculated in accordance with Subsection 4.

11. Where exposures in the form of a collective investment undertaking (CIU) meet the criteria set out in Annex VI, Part 1, points 77 and 78 and the credit institution is aware of all of the underlying exposures of the CIU, the credit institution shall look through to those underlying exposures in order to calculate risk-weighted exposure amounts and expected loss amounts in accordance with the methods set out in this Subsection.

Where the credit institution does not meet the conditions for using the methods set out in this Subsection, risk-weighted exposure amounts and expected loss amounts shall be calculated in accordance with the following approaches:

(a) for exposures belonging to the exposure class referred to in point (e) of Article 86(1), the approach set out in Annex VII, Part 1, points 19 to 21. If, for those purposes, the credit institution is unable to differentiate between private equity, exchange-traded and other equity exposures, it shall treat the exposures concerned as other equity exposures;

(b) for all other underlying exposures, the approach set out in Subsection 1, subject to the following modifications:
 (i) the exposures are assigned to the appropriate exposure class and attributed the risk weight of the credit quality step immediately above the credit quality step that would normally be assigned to the exposure, and
 (ii) exposures assigned to the higher credit quality steps, to which a risk weight of 150% would normally be attributed, are assigned a risk weight of 200%.

12. Where exposures in the form of a CIU do not meet the criteria set out in Annex VI, Part 1, points 77 and 78, or the credit institution is not aware of all of the underlying exposures of the CIU, the credit institution shall look through to the underlying exposures and calculate risk-weighted exposure amounts and expected loss amounts in accordance with the approach set out in Annex VII, Part 1, points 19 to 21. If, for those purposes, the credit institution is unable to differentiate between private equity, exchange-traded and other equity exposures, it shall treat the exposures concerned as other equity exposures. For these purposes, non equity exposures are assigned to one of the classes (private equity, exchange traded equity or other equity) set out in Annex VII, Part 1, point 19 and unknown exposures are assigned to other equity class.

Alternatively to the method described above, credit institutions may calculate themselves or may rely on a third party to calculate and report the average risk-weighted exposure amounts based on the CIU's underlying exposures in accordance with the following approaches, provided that the correctness of the calculation and the report is adequately ensured:

(a) for exposures belonging to the exposure class referred to in point (e) of Article 86(1), the approach set out in Annex VII, Part 1, points 19 to 21. If, for those purposes, the credit institution is unable to differentiate between private equity, exchange-traded and other equity exposures, it shall treat the exposures concerned as other equity exposures; or

(b) for all other underlying exposures, the approach set out in Subsection 1, subject to the following modifications:
 (i) the exposures are assigned to the appropriate exposure class and attributed the risk weight of the credit quality step immediately above the credit quality step that would normally be assigned to the exposure, and
 (ii) exposures assigned to the higher credit quality steps, to which a risk weight of 150% would normally be attributed, are assigned a risk weight of 200%.

Article 88

1. The expected loss amounts for exposures belonging to one of the exposure classes referred to in points (a) to (e) of Article 86(1) shall be calculated in accordance with the methods set out in Annex VII, Part 1, points 29 to 35.

2. The calculation of expected loss amounts in accordance with Annex VII, Part 1, points 29 to 35 shall be based on the same input figures of PD, LGD and the exposure value for each

exposure as being used for the calculation of risk-weighted exposure amounts in accordance with Article 87. For defaulted exposures, where credit institutions use own estimates of LGDs, expected loss ('EL') shall be the credit institution's best estimate of EL ('ELBE,') for the defaulted exposure, in accordance with Annex VII, Part 4, point 80.

3. The expected loss amounts for securitised exposures shall be calculated in accordance with Subsection 4.

4. The expected loss amount for exposures belonging to the exposure class referred to in point (g) of Article 86(1) shall be zero.

5. The expected loss amounts for dilution risk of purchased receivables shall be calculated in accordance with the methods set out in Annex VII, Part 1, point 35.

6. The expected loss amounts for exposures referred to in Article 87(11) and (12) shall be calculated in accordance with the methods set out in Annex VII, Part 1, points 29 to 35.

Article 89

1. Subject to the approval of the competent authorities, credit institutions permitted to use the IRB Approach in the calculation of risk-weighted exposure amounts and expected loss amounts for one or more exposure classes may apply Subsection 1 for the following:

(a) the exposure class referred to in point (a) of Article 86(1), where the number of material counterparties is limited and it would be unduly burdensome for the credit institution to implement a rating system for these counterparties;

(b) the exposure class referred to in point (b) of Article 86(1), where the number of material counterparties is limited and it would be unduly burdensome for the credit institution to implement a rating system for these counterparties;

(c) exposures in non-significant business units as well as exposure classes that are immaterial in terms of size and perceived risk profile;

(d) exposures to central governments of the home Member State and to their regional governments, local authorities and administrative bodies, provided that:

(i) there is no difference in risk between the exposures to that central government and those other exposures because of specific public arrangements, and

(ii) exposures to the central government are assigned a 0% risk weight under Subsection 1;

(e) exposures of a credit institution to a counterparty which is its parent undertaking, its subsidiary or a subsidiary of its parent undertaking provided that the counterparty is an institution or a financial holding company, financial institution, asset management company or ancillary services undertaking subject to appropriate prudential requirements or an undertaking linked by a relationship within the meaning of Article 12(1) of Directive 83/349/EEC and exposures between credit institutions which meet the requirements set out in Article 80(8);

(f) equity exposures to entities whose credit obligations qualify for a 0% risk weight under Subsection 1 (including those publicly sponsored entities where a zero risk weight can be applied);

(g) equity exposures incurred under legislative programmes to promote specified sectors of the economy that provide significant subsidies for the investment to the credit institution and involve some form of government oversight and restrictions on the equity investments. This exclusion is limited to an aggregate of 10% of original own funds plus additional own funds;

(h) the exposures identified in Annex VI, Part 1, point 40 meeting the conditions specified therein; or

(i) State and State-reinsured guarantees pursuant to Annex VIII, Part 2, point 19.

This paragraph shall not prevent the competent authorities of other Member States to allow the application of the rules of Subsection 1 for equity exposures which have been allowed for this treatment in other Member States.

2. For the purposes of paragraph 1, the equity exposure class of a credit institution shall be considered material if their aggregate value, excluding equity exposures incurred under

legislative programmes as referred to in paragraph 1, point (g), exceeds, on average over the preceding year, 10% of the credit institution's own funds. If the number of those equity exposures is less than 10 individual holdings, that threshold shall be 5% of the credit institution's own funds.

SUBSECTION 3
CREDIT RISK MITIGATION

Article 90

For the purposes of this Subsection, 'lending credit institution' shall mean the credit institution which has the exposure in question, whether or not deriving from a loan.

Article 91

Credit institutions using the Standardised Approach under Articles 78 to 83 or using the IRB Approach under Articles 84 to 89, but not using their own estimates of LGD and conversion factors under Articles 87 and 88, may recognise credit risk mitigation in accordance with this Subsection in the calculation of risk-weighted exposure amounts for the purposes of Article 75 point (a) or as relevant expected loss amounts for the purposes of the calculation referred to in point (q) of Article 57, and Article 63(3).

Article 92

1. The technique used to provide the credit protection together with the actions and steps taken and procedures and policies implemented by the lending credit institution shall be such as to result in credit protection arrangements which are legally effective and enforceable in all relevant jurisdictions.

2. The lending credit institution shall take all appropriate steps to ensure the effectiveness of the credit protection arrangement and to address related risks.

3. In the case of funded credit protection, to be eligible for recognition the assets relied upon shall be sufficiently liquid and their value over time sufficiently stable to provide appropriate certainty as to the credit protection achieved having regard to the approach used to calculate risk-weighted exposure amounts and to the degree of recognition allowed. Eligibility shall be limited to the assets set out in Annex VIII, Part 1.

4. In the case of funded credit protection, the lending credit institution shall have the right to liquidate or retain, in a timely manner, the assets from which the protection derives in the event of the default, insolvency or bankruptcy of the obligor—or other credit event set out in the transaction documentation—and, where applicable, of the custodian holding the collateral. The degree of correlation between the value of the assets relied upon for protection and the credit quality of the obligor shall not be undue.

5. In the case of unfunded credit protection, to be eligible for recognition the party giving the undertaking shall be sufficiently reliable, and the protection agreement legally effective and enforceable in the relevant jurisdictions, to provide appropriate certainty as to the credit protection achieved having regard to the approach used to calculate risk-weighted exposure amounts and to the degree of recognition allowed. Eligibility shall be limited to the protection providers and types of protection agreement set out in Annex VIII, Part 1.

6. The minimum requirements set out in Annex VIII, Part 2 shall be complied with.

Article 93

1. Where the requirements of Article 92 are met the calculation of risk-weighted exposure amounts, and, as relevant, expected loss amounts, may be modified in accordance with Annex VIII, Parts 3 to 6.

2. No exposure in respect of which credit risk mitigation is obtained shall produce a higher risk-weighted exposure amount or expected loss amount than an otherwise identical exposure in respect of which there is no credit risk mitigation.

Where the risk-weighted exposure amount already takes account of credit protection under Articles 78 to 83 or Articles 84 to 89, as relevant, the calculation of the credit protection shall not be further recognised under this Subsection.

SUBSECTION 4

SECURITISATION

Article 94

Where a credit institution uses the Standardised Approach set out in Articles 78 to 83 for the calculation of risk-weighted exposure amounts for the exposure class to which the securitised exposures would be assigned under Article 79, it shall calculate the risk-weighted exposure amount for a securitisation position in accordance with Annex IX, Part 4, points 1 to 36.

In all other cases, it shall calculate the risk-weighted exposure amount in accordance with Annex IX, Part 4, points 1 to 5 and 37 to 76.

Article 95

1. Where significant credit risk associated with securitised exposures has been transferred from the originator credit institution in accordance with the terms of Annex IX, Part 2, that credit institution may:

(a) in the case of a traditional securitisation, exclude from its calculation of risk-weighted exposure amounts, and, as relevant, expected loss amounts, the exposures which it has securitised; and

(b) in the case of a synthetic securitisation, calculate risk-weighted exposure amounts, and, as relevant, expected loss amounts, in respect of the securitised exposures in accordance with Annex IX, Part 2.

2. Where paragraph 1 applies, the originator credit institution shall calculate the risk-weighted exposure amounts prescribed in Annex IX for the positions that it may hold in the securitisation.

Where the originator credit institution fails to transfer significant credit risk in accordance with paragraph 1, it need not calculate risk-weighted exposure amounts for any positions it may have in the securitisation in question.

Article 96

1. To calculate the risk-weighted exposure amount of a securitisation position, risk weights shall be assigned to the exposure value of the position in accordance with Annex IX, based on the credit quality of the position, which may be determined by reference to an ECAI credit assessment or otherwise, as set out in Annex IX.

2. Where there is an exposure to different tranches in a securitisation, the exposure to each tranche shall be considered a separate securitisation position. The providers of credit protection to securitisation positions shall be considered to hold positions in the securitisation. Securitisation positions shall include exposures to a securitisation arising from interest rate or currency derivative contracts.

3. Where a securitisation position is subject to funded or unfunded credit protection the risk weight to be applied to that position may be modified in accordance with Articles 90 to 93, read in conjunction with Annex IX.

4. Subject to point (r) of Article 57 and Article 66(2), the risk-weighted exposure amount shall be included in the credit institution's total of risk-weighted exposure amounts for the purposes of Article 75(a).

Article 97

1. An ECAI credit assessment may be used to determine the risk weight of a securitisation position in accordance with Article 96 only if the ECAI has been recognised as eligible by the competent authorities for this purpose (hereinafter 'an eligible ECAI').

2. The competent authorities shall recognise an ECAI as eligible for the purposes of paragraph 1 only if they are satisfied as to its compliance with the requirements laid down in Article 81, taking into account the technical criteria in Annex VI, Part 2, and that it has a demonstrated ability in the area of securitisation, which may be evidenced by a strong market acceptance.

3. If an ECAI has been recognised as eligible by the competent authorities of a Member State for

the purposes of paragraph 1, the competent authorities of other Member States may recognise that ECAI as eligible for those purposes without carrying out their own evaluation process.

4. The competent authorities shall make publicly available an explanation of the recognition process and a list of eligible ECAIs.

5. To be used for the purposes of paragraph 1, a credit assessment of an eligible ECAI shall comply with the principles of credibility and transparency as elaborated in Annex IX, Part 3.

Article 98

1. For the purposes of applying risk weights to securitisation positions, the competent authorities shall determine with which of the credit quality steps set out in Annex IX the relevant credit assessments of an eligible ECAI are to be associated. Those determinations shall be objective and consistent.

2. When the competent authorities of a Member State have made a determination under paragraph 1, the competent authorities of other Member States may recognise that determination without carrying out their own determination process.

Article 99

The use of ECAI credit assessments for the calculation of a credit institution's risk-weighted exposure amounts under Article 96 shall be consistent and in accordance with Annex IX, Part 3. Credit assessments shall not be used selectively.

Article 100

1. Where there is a securitisation of revolving exposures subject to an early amortisation provision, the originator credit institution shall calculate, in accordance with Annex IX, an additional risk-weighted exposure amount in respect of the risk that the levels of credit risk to which it is exposed may increase following the operation of the early amortisation provision.

2. For those purposes, a 'revolving exposure' shall be an exposure whereby customers' outstanding balances are permitted to fluctuate based on their decisions to borrow and repay, up to an agreed limit, and an early amortisation provision shall be a contractual clause which requires, on the occurrence of defined events, investors' positions to be redeemed before the originally stated maturity of the securities issued.

Article 101

1. An originator credit institution which, in respect of a securitisation, has made use of Article 95 in the calculation of risk-weighted exposure amounts or a sponsor credit institution shall not, with a view to reducing potential or actual losses to investors, provide support to the securitisation beyond its contractual obligations.

2. If an originator credit institution or a sponsor credit institution fails to comply with paragraph 1 in respect of a securitisation, the competent authority shall require it at a minimum, to hold capital against all of the securitised exposures as if they had not been securitised. The credit institution shall disclose publicly that it has provided non-contractual support and the regulatory capital impact of having done so.

Section 4
Minimum Own Funds Requirements for Operational Risk

Article 102

1. Competent authorities shall require credit institutions to hold own funds against operational risk in accordance with the approaches set out in Articles 103, 104 and 105.

2. Without prejudice to paragraph 4, credit institutions that use the approach set out in Article 104 shall not revert to the use of the approach set out in Article 103, except for demonstrated good cause and subject to approval by the competent authorities.

3. Without prejudice to paragraph 4, credit institutions that use the approach set out in Article 105 shall not revert to the use of the approaches set out in Articles 103 or 104 except

for demonstrated good cause and subject to approval by the competent authorities.

4. Competent authorities may allow credit institutions to use a combination of approaches in accordance with Annex X, Part 4.

Article 103

The capital requirement for operational risk under the Basic Indicator Approach shall be a certain percentage of a relevant indicator, in accordance with the parameters set out in Annex X, Part 1.

Article 104

1. Under the Standardised Approach, credit institutions shall divide their activities into a number of business lines as set out in Annex X, Part 2.

2. For each business line, credit institutions shall calculate a capital requirement for operational risk as a certain percentage of a relevant indicator, in accordance with the parameters set out in Annex X, Part 2.

3. For certain business lines, the competent authorities may under certain conditions authorise a credit institution to use an alternative relevant indicator for determining its capital requirement for operational risk as set out in Annex X, Part 2, points 5 to 11.

4. The capital requirement for operational risk under the Standardised Approach shall be the sum of the capital requirements for operational risk across all individual business lines.

5. The parameters for the Standardised Approach are set out in Annex X, Part 2.

6. To qualify for use of the Standardised Approach, credit institutions shall meet the criteria set out in Annex X, Part 2.

Article 105

1. Credit institutions may use Advanced Measurement Approaches based on their own operational risk measurement systems, provided that the competent authority expressly approves the use of the models concerned for calculating the own funds requirement.

2. Credit institutions shall satisfy their competent authorities that they meet the qualifying criteria set out in Annex X, Part 3.

3. When an Advanced Measurement Approach is intended to be used by an EU parent credit institution and its subsidiaries or by the subsidiaries of an EU parent financial holding company, the competent authorities of the different legal entities shall cooperate closely as provided for in Articles 129 to 132. The application shall include the elements listed in Annex X, Part 3.

4. Where an EU parent credit institution and its subsidiaries or the subsidiaries of an EU parent financial holding company use an Advanced Measurement Approach on a unified basis, the competent authorities may allow the qualifying criteria set out in Annex X, Part 3 to be met by the parent and its subsidiaries considered together.

Section 5
Large Exposures

Article 106

1. 'Exposures', for the purposes of this Section, shall mean any asset or off-balance-sheet item referred to in Section 3, Subsection 1, without application of the risk weights or degrees of risk there provided for.

Exposures arising from the items referred to in Annex IV shall be calculated in accordance with one of the methods set out in Annex III. For the purposes of this Section, Annex III, Part 2, point 2 shall also apply.

All elements entirely covered by own funds may, with the agreement of the competent authorities, be excluded from the determination of exposures, provided that such own funds are not included in the credit institution's own funds for the purposes of Article 75 or in the calculation of other monitoring ratios provided for in this Directive and in other Community acts.

2. Exposures shall not include either of the following:

(a) in the case of foreign exchange transactions, exposures incurred in the ordinary course of settlement during the 48 hours following payment; or

(b) in the case of transactions for the purchase or sale of securities, exposures incurred in the ordinary course of settlement during the five working days following payment or delivery of the securities, whichever is the earlier.

Article 107

For the purposes of applying this Section, the term 'credit institution' shall cover the following:

(a) a credit institution, including its branches in third countries; and

(b) any private or public undertaking, including its branches, which meets the definition of 'credit institution' and has been authorised in a third country.

Article 108

A credit institution's exposure to a client or group of connected clients shall be considered a large exposure where its value is equal to or exceeds 10% of its own funds.

Article 109

The competent authorities shall require that every credit institution have sound administrative and accounting procedures and adequate internal control mechanisms for the purposes of identifying and recording all large exposures and subsequent changes to them, in accordance with this Directive, and for that of monitoring those exposures in the light of each credit institution's own exposure policies.

Article 110

1. A credit institution shall report every large exposure to the competent authorities.

Member States shall provide that reporting is to be carried out, at their discretion, in accordance with one of the following two methods:

(a) reporting of all large exposures at least once a year, combined with reporting during the year of all new large exposures and any increases in existing large exposures of at least 20% with respect to the previous communication; or

(b) reporting of all large exposures at least four times a year.

2. Except in the case of credit institutions relying on Article 114 for the recognition of collateral in calculating the value of exposures for the purposes of paragraphs 1, 2 and 3 of Article 111, exposures exempted under Article 113(3)(a) to (d) and (f) to (h) need not be reported as laid down in paragraph 1 and the reporting frequency laid down in point (b) of paragraph 1 of this Article may be reduced to twice a year for the exposures referred to in Article 113(3)(e) and (i), and in Articles 115 and 116.

Where a credit institution invokes this paragraph, it shall keep a record of the grounds advanced for at least one year after the event giving rise to the dispensation, so that the competent authorities may establish whether it is justified.

3. Member States may require credit institutions to analyse their exposures to collateral issuers for possible concentrations and where appropriate take action or report any significant findings to their competent authority.

Article 111

1. A credit institution may not incur an exposure to a client or group of connected clients the value of which exceed 25% of its own funds.

2. Where that client or group of connected clients is the parent undertaking or subsidiary of the credit institution and/or one or more subsidiaries of that parent undertaking, the percentage laid down in paragraph 1 shall be reduced to 20%. Member States may, however, exempt the exposures incurred to such clients from the 20% limit if they provide for specific monitoring of such exposures by other measures or procedures. They shall inform the Commission and the

European Banking Committee of the content of such measures or procedures.

3. A credit institution may not incur large exposures which in total exceed 800% of its own funds.

4. A credit institution shall at all times comply with the limits laid down in paragraphs 1, 2 and 3 in respect of its exposures. If in an exceptional case exposures exceed those limits, that fact shall be reported without delay to the competent authorities which may, where the circumstances warrant it, allow the credit institution a limited period of time in which to comply with the limits.

Article 112

1. For the purposes of Articles 113 to 117, the term 'guarantee' shall include credit derivatives recognised under Articles 90 to 93 other than credit linked notes.

2. Subject to paragraph 3, where, under Articles 113 to 117, the recognition of funded or unfunded credit protection may be permitted, this shall be subject to compliance with the eligibility requirements and other minimum requirements, set out under Articles 90 to 93 for the purposes of calculating risk-weighted exposure amounts under Articles 78 to 83.

3. Where a credit institution relies upon Article 114(2), the recognition of funded credit protection shall be subject to the relevant requirements under Articles 84 to 89.

Article 113

1. Member States may impose limits more stringent than those laid down in Article 111.

2. Member States may fully or partially exempt from the application of Article 111(1), (2) and (3) exposures incurred by a credit institution to its parent undertaking, to other subsidiaries of that parent undertaking or to its own subsidiaries, in so far as those undertakings are covered by the supervision on a consolidated basis to which the credit institution itself is subject, in accordance with this Directive or with equivalent standards in force in a third country.

3. Member States may fully or partially exempt the following exposures from the application of Article 111:

(a) asset items constituting claims on central governments or central banks which, unsecured, would be assigned a 0% risk weight under Articles 78 to 83;

(b) asset items constituting claims on international organisations or multilateral development banks which, unsecured, would be assigned a 0% risk weight under Articles 78 to 83;

(c) asset items constituting claims carrying the explicit guarantees of central governments, central banks, international organisations, multilateral development banks or public sector entities, where unsecured claims on the entity providing the guarantee would be assigned a 0% risk weight under Articles 78 to 83;

(d) other exposures attributable to, or guaranteed by, central governments, central banks, international organisations, multilateral development banks or public sector entities, where unsecured claims on the entity to which the exposure is attributable or by which it is guaranteed would be assigned a 0% risk weight under Articles 78 to 83;

(e) asset items constituting claims on and other exposures to central governments or central banks not mentioned in point (a) which are denominated and, where applicable, funded in the national currencies of the borrowers;

(f) asset items and other exposures secured, to the satisfaction of the competent authorities, by collateral in the form of debt securities issued by central governments or central banks, international organisations, multilateral development banks, Member States' regional governments, local authorities or public sector entities, which securities constitute claims on their issuer which would be assigned a 0% risk weighting under Articles 78 to 83;

(g) asset items and other exposures secured, to the satisfaction of the competent authorities, by collateral in the form of cash deposits placed with the lending credit institution or with a credit institution which is the parent undertaking or a subsidiary of the lending institution;

(h) asset items and other exposures secured, to the satisfaction of the competent authorities, by collateral in the form of certificates of deposit issued by the lending credit institution or by a credit institution which is the parent undertaking or a subsidiary of the lending credit institution and lodged with either of them;

(i) asset items constituting claims on and other exposures to institutions, with a maturity of one year or less, but not constituting such institutions' own funds;

(j) asset items constituting claims on and other exposures to those institutions which are not credit institutions but which fulfil the conditions referred to in Annex VI, Part 1, point 85, with a maturity of one year or less, and secured in accordance with the same point;

(k) bills of trade and other similar bills, with a maturity of one year or less, bearing the signatures of other credit institutions;

(l) covered bonds falling within the terms of Annex VI, Part 1, points 68 to 70;

(m) pending subsequent coordination, holdings in the insurance companies referred to in Article 122(1) up to 40% of the own funds of the credit institution acquiring such a holding;

(n) asset items constituting claims on regional or central credit institutions with which the lending credit institution is associated in a network in accordance with legal or statutory provisions and which are responsible, under those provisions, for cash-clearing operations within the network;

(o) exposures secured, to the satisfaction of the competent authorities, by collateral in the form of securities other than those referred to in point (f);

(p) loans secured, to the satisfaction of the competent authorities, by mortgages on residential property or by shares in Finnish residential housing companies, operating in accordance with the Finnish Housing Company Act of 1991 or subsequent equivalent legislation and leasing transactions under which the lessor retains full ownership of the residential property leased for as long as the lessee has not exercised his option to purchase, in all cases up to 50% of the value of the residential property concerned;

(q) the following, where they would receive a 50% risk weight under Articles 78 to 83, and only up to 50% of the value of the property concerned:

(i) exposures secured by mortgages on offices or other commercial premises, or by shares in Finnish housing companies, operating in accordance with the Finnish Housing Company Act of 1991 or subsequent equivalent legislation, in respect of offices or other commercial premises; and

(ii) exposures related to property leasing transactions concerning offices or other commercial premises;

for the purposes of point (ii), until 31 December 2011, the competent authorities of each Member State may allow credit institutions to recognise 100% of the value of the property concerned. At the end of this period, this treatment shall be reviewed. Member States shall inform the Commission of the use they make of this preferential treatment;

(r) 50% of the medium/low-risk off-balance-sheet items referred to in Annex II;

(s) subject to the competent authorities' agreement, guarantees other than loan guarantees which have a legal or regulatory basis and are given for their members by mutual guarantee schemes possessing the status of credit institutions, subject to a weighting of 20% of their amount; and

(t) the low-risk off-balance-sheet items referred to in Annex II, to the extent that an agreement has been concluded with the client or group of connected clients under which the exposure may be incurred only if it has been ascertained that it will not cause the limits applicable under Article 111 (1) to (3) to be exceeded.

Cash received under a credit linked note issued by the credit institution and loans and deposits of a counterparty to or with the credit institution which are subject to an on-balance sheet netting agreement recognised under Articles 90 to 93 shall be deemed to fall under point (g).

For the purposes of point (o), the securities used as collateral shall be valued at market price, have a value that exceeds the exposures guaranteed and be either traded on a stock exchange or effectively negotiable and regularly quoted on a market operated under the auspices of recognised professional operators and allowing, to the satisfaction of the competent authorities of the Member State of origin of the credit institution, for the establishment of an objective price such that the excess value of the securities may be verified at any time. The excess value required shall be 100%. It shall, however, be 150% in the case of shares and 50% in the case of debt securities issued by institutions, Member State regional governments or local authorities other than those referred to in subpoint (f), and in the case of debt securities issued by multilateral development banks other than those assigned a 0% risk weight under Articles 78 to 83. Where there is a mismatch between the maturity of the exposure and the maturity of the credit protection, the collateral shall not be recognised. Securities used as collateral may not constitute credit institutions' own funds.

For the purposes of point (p), the value of the property shall be calculated, to the satisfaction of the competent authorities, on the basis of strict valuation standards laid down by law, regulation or administrative provisions. Valuation shall be carried out at least once a year. For the purposes of point (p), residential property shall mean a residence to be occupied or let by the borrower.

Member States shall inform the Commission of any exemption granted under point (s) in order to ensure that it does not result in a distortion of competition.

Article 114

1. Subject to paragraph 3, for the purposes of calculating the value of exposures for the purposes of Article 111(1) to (3) Member States may, in respect of credit institutions using the Financial Collateral Comprehensive Method under Articles 90 to 93, in the alternative to availing of the full or partial exemptions permitted under points (f), (g), (h), and (o) of Article 113(3), permit such credit institutions to use a value lower than the value of the exposure, but no lower than the total of the fully-adjusted exposure values of their exposures to the client or group of connected clients.

For these purposes, 'fully adjusted exposure value' means that calculated under Articles 90 to 93 taking into account the credit risk mitigation, volatility adjustments, and any maturity mismatch (E^*).

Where this paragraph is applied to a credit institution, points (f), (g), (h), and (o) of Article 113(3) shall not apply to the credit institution in question.

2. Subject to paragraph 3, a credit institution permitted to use own estimates of LGDs and conversion factors for an exposure class under Articles 84 to 89 may be permitted, where it is able to the satisfaction of the competent authorities to estimate the effects of financial collateral on their exposures separately from other LGD-relevant aspects, to recognise such effects in calculating the value of exposures for the purposes of Article 111(1) to (3).

Competent authorities shall be satisfied as to the suitability of the estimates produced by the credit institution for use for the reduction of the exposure value for the purposes of compliance with the provisions of Article 111.

Where a credit institution is permitted to use its own estimates of the effects of financial collateral, it shall do so on a basis consistent with the approach adopted in the calculation of capital requirements.

Credit institutions permitted to use own estimates of LGDs and conversion factors for an exposure class under Articles 84 to 89 which do not calculate the value of their exposures using the method referred to in the first subparagraph may be permitted to use the approach set out in paragraph 1 or the exemption set out in Article 113(3)(o) for calculating the value of exposures. A credit institution shall use only one of these two methods.

3. A credit institution that is permitted to use the methods described in paragraphs 1 and 2 in calculating the value of exposures for the purposes of Article 111(1) to (3), shall conduct

periodic stress tests of their credit-risk concentrations, including in relation to the realisable value of any collateral taken.

These periodic stress tests shall address risks arising from potential changes in market conditions that could adversely impact the credit institutions' adequacy of own funds and risks arising from the realisation of collateral in stressed situations.

The credit institution shall satisfy the competent authorities that the stress tests carried out are adequate and appropriate for the assessment of such risks.

In the event that such a stress test indicates a lower realisable value of collateral taken than would be permitted to be taken into account under paragraphs 1 and 2 as appropriate, the value of collateral permitted to be recognised in calculating the value of exposures for the purposes of Article 111(1) to (3) shall be reduced accordingly.

Such credit institutions shall include the following in their strategies to address concentration risk:

(a) policies and procedures to address risks arising from maturity mismatches between exposures and any credit protection on those exposures;

(b) policies and procedures in the event that a stress test indicates a lower realisable value of collateral than taken into account under paragraphs 1 and 2; and

(c) policies and procedures relating to concentration risk arising from the application of credit risk mitigation techniques, and in particular large indirect credit exposures, for example to a single issuer of securities taken as collateral.

4. Where the effects of collateral are recognised under the terms of paragraphs 1 or 2, Member States may treat any covered Part of the exposure as having been incurred to the collateral issuer rather than to the client.

Article 115

1. For the purposes of Article 111(1) to (3), Member States may assign a weighting of 20% to asset items constituting claims on Member States' regional governments and local authorities where those claims would be assigned a 20% risk weight under Articles 78 to 83 and to other exposures to or guaranteed by such governments and authorities claims on which are assigned a 20% risk weight under Articles 78 to 83. However, Member States may reduce that rate to 0% in respect of asset items constituting claims on Member States' regional governments and local authorities where those claims would be assigned a 0% risk weight under Article 78 to 83 and to other exposures to or guaranteed by such governments and authorities claims on which are assigned a 0% risk weight under Articles 78 to 83.

2. For the purposes of Article 111(1) to (3), Member States may assign a weighting of 20% to asset items constituting claims on and other exposures to institutions with a maturity of more than one but not more than three years and a weighting of 50% to asset items constituting claims on institutions with a maturity of more than three years, provided that the latter are represented by debt instruments that were issued by a institution and that those debt instruments are, in the opinion of the competent authorities, effectively negotiable on a market made up of professional operators and are subject to daily quotation on that market, or the issue of which was authorised by the competent authorities of the Member State of origin of the issuing institutions. In no case may any of these items constitute own funds.

Article 116

By way of derogation from Article 113(3)(i) and Article 115(2), Member States may assign a weighting of 20% to asset items constituting claims on and other exposures to institutions, regardless of their maturity.

Article 117

1. Where an exposure to a client is guaranteed by a third party, or by collateral in the form of securities issued by a third party under the conditions laid down in Article 113(3)(o), Member States may:

(a) treat the exposure as having been incurred to the guarantor rather than to the client; or

(b) treat the exposure as having been incurred to the third party rather than to the client, if the exposure defined in Article 113(3)(o) is guaranteed by collateral under the conditions there laid down.

2. Where Member States apply the treatment provided for in point (a) of paragraph 1:

(a) where the guarantee is denominated in a currency different from that in which the exposure is denominated the amount of the exposure deemed to be covered will be calculated in accordance with the provisions on the treatment of currency mismatch for unfunded credit protection in Annex VIII;

(b) a mismatch between the maturity of the exposure and the maturity of the protection will be treated in accordance with the provisions on the treatment of maturity mismatch in Annex VIII; and

(c) partial coverage may be recognised in accordance with the treatment set out in Annex VIII.

Article 118

Where compliance by a credit institution on an individual or sub-consolidated basis with the obligations imposed in this Section is disapplied under Article 69(1), or the provisions of Article 70 are applied in the case of parent credit institutions in a Member State, measures must be taken to ensure the satisfactory allocation of risks within the group.

Article 119

By 31 December 2007, the Commission shall submit to the European Parliament and to the Council a report on the functioning of this Section, together with any appropriate proposals.

SECTION 6
QUALIFYING HOLDINGS OUTSIDE THE FINANCIAL SECTOR

Article 120

1. No credit institution may have a qualifying holding the amount of which exceeds 15% of its own funds in an undertaking which is neither a credit institution, nor a financial institution, nor an undertaking carrying on activities which are a direct extension of banking or concern services ancillary to banking, such as leasing, factoring, the management of unit trusts, the management of data processing services or any other similar activity.

2. The total amount of a credit institution's qualifying holdings in undertakings other than credit institutions, financial institutions or undertakings carrying on activities which are a direct extension of banking or concern services ancillary to banking, such as leasing, factoring, the management of unit trusts, the management of data processing services, or any other similar activity may not exceed 60% of its own funds.

3. The limits laid down in paragraphs 1 and 2 may be exceeded only in exceptional circumstances. In such cases, however, the competent authorities shall require a credit institution either to increase its own funds or to take other equivalent measures.

Article 121

Shares held temporarily during a financial reconstruction or rescue operation or during the normal course of underwriting or in an institution's own name on behalf of others shall not be counted as qualifying holdings for the purpose of calculating the limits laid down in Articles 120(1) and (2). Shares which are not financial fixed assets as defined in Article 35(2) of Directive 86/635/EEC shall not be included in the calculation.

Article 122

1. The Member States need not apply the limits laid down in Articles 120(1) and (2) to holdings in insurance companies as defined in Directives 73/239/EEC and 2002/83/EC, or in reinsurance companies as defined in Directive 98/78/EC.

2. The Member States may provide that the competent authorities are not to apply the limits laid down in Article 120 (1) and (2) if they provide that 100% of the amounts by which a credit institution's qualifying holdings exceed those limits shall be covered by own funds and that the

latter shall not be included in the calculation required under Article 75. If both the limits laid down in Article 120(1) and (2) are exceeded, the amount to be covered by own funds shall be the greater of the excess amounts.

CHAPTER 3

CREDIT INSTITUTIONS' ASSESSMENT PROCESS

Article 123

Credit institutions shall have in place sound, effective and complete strategies and processes to assess and maintain on an ongoing basis the amounts, types and distribution of internal capital that they consider adequate to cover the nature and level of the risks to which they are or might be exposed.

These strategies and processes shall be subject to regular internal review to ensure that they remain comprehensive and proportionate to the nature, scale and complexity of the activities of the credit institution concerned.

CHAPTER 4

SUPERVISION AND DISCLOSURE BY COMPETENT AUTHORITIES

SECTION 1
SUPERVISION

Article 124

1. Taking into account the technical criteria set out in Annex XI, the competent authorities shall review the arrangements, strategies, processes and mechanisms implemented by the credit institutions to comply with this Directive and evaluate the risks to which the credit institutions are or might be exposed.

2. The scope of the review and evaluation referred to in paragraph 1 shall be that of the requirements of this Directive.

3. On the basis of the review and evaluation referred to in paragraph 1, the competent authorities shall determine whether the arrangements, strategies, processes and mechanisms implemented by the credit institutions and the own funds held by these ensure a sound management and coverage of their risks.

4. Competent authorities shall establish the frequency and intensity of the review and evaluation referred to in paragraph 1 having regard to the size, systemic importance, nature, scale and complexity of the activities of the credit institution concerned and taking into account the principle of proportionality. The review and evaluation shall be updated at least on an annual basis.

5. The review and evaluation performed by competent authorities shall include the exposure of credit institutions to the interest rate risk arising from non-trading activities. Measures shall be required in the case of institutions whose economic value declines by more than 20% of their own funds as a result of a sudden and unexpected change in interest rates the size of which shall be prescribed by the competent authorities and shall not differ between credit institutions.

Article 125

1. Where a parent undertaking is a parent credit institution in a Member State or an EU parent credit institution, supervision on a consolidated basis shall be exercised by the competent authorities that authorised it under Article 6.

2. Where the parent of a credit institution is a parent financial holding company in a Member State or an EU parent financial holding company, supervision on a consolidated basis shall be exercised by the competent authorities that authorised that credit institution under Article 6.

Article 126

1. Where credit institutions authorised in two or more Member States have as their parent the same parent financial holding company in a Member State or the same EU parent financial holding company, supervision on a consolidated basis shall be exercised by the competent authorities of the credit institution authorised in the Member State in which the financial holding

company was set up. Where the parents of credit institutions authorised in two or more Member States comprise more than one financial holding company with head offices in different Member States and there is a credit institution in each of these States, supervision on a consolidated basis shall be exercised by the competent authority of the credit institution with the largest balance sheet total.

2. Where more than one credit institution authorised in the Community has as its parent the same financial holding company and none of these credit institutions has been authorised in the Member State in which the financial holding company was set up, supervision on a consolidated basis shall be exercised by the competent authority that authorised the credit institution with the largest balance sheet total, which shall be considered, for the purposes of this Directive, as the credit institution controlled by an EU parent financial holding company.

3. In particular cases, the competent authorities may by common agreement waive the criteria referred to in paragraphs 1 and 2 if their application would be inappropriate, taking into account the credit institutions and the relative importance of their activities in different countries, and appoint a different competent authority to exercise supervision on a consolidated basis. In these cases, before taking their decision, the competent authorities shall give the EU parent credit institution, or EU parent financial holding company, or credit institution with the largest balance sheet total, as appropriate, an opportunity to state its opinion on that decision.

4. The competent authorities shall notify the Commission of any agreement falling within paragraph 3.

Article 127

1. Member States shall adopt any measures necessary, where appropriate, to include financial holding companies in consolidated supervision. Without prejudice to Article 135, the consolidation of the financial situation of the financial holding company shall not in any way imply that the competent authorities are required to play a supervisory role in relation to the financial holding company on a stand-alone basis.

2. When the competent authorities of a Member State do not include a credit institution subsidiary in supervision on a consolidated basis under one of the cases provided for in points (b) and (c) of Article 73(1), the competent authorities of the Member State in which that credit institution subsidiary is situated may ask the parent undertaking for information which may facilitate their supervision of that credit institution.

3. Member States shall provide that their competent authorities responsible for exercising supervision on a consolidated basis may ask the subsidiaries of a credit institution or a financial holding company, which are not included within the scope of supervision on a consolidated basis for the information referred to in Article 137. In such a case, the procedures for transmitting and verifying the information laid down in that Article shall apply.

Article 128

Where Member States have more than one competent authority for the prudential supervision of credit institutions and financial institutions, Member States shall take the requisite measures to organise coordination between such authorities.

Article 129

1. In addition to the obligations imposed by the provisions of this Directive, the competent authority responsible for the exercise of supervision on a consolidated basis of EU parent credit institutions and credit institutions controlled by EU parent financial holding companies shall carry out the following tasks:

(a) coordination of the gathering and dissemination of relevant or essential information in going concern and emergency situations; and

(b) planning and coordination of supervisory activities in going concern as well as in emergency situations, including in relation to the activities in Article 124, in cooperation with the competent authorities involved.

2. In the case of applications for the permissions referred to in Articles 84(1), 87(9) and 105 and in Annex III, Part 6, respectively, submitted by an EU parent credit institution and its subsidiaries, or jointly by the subsidiaries of an EU parent financial holding company, the competent authorities shall work together, in full consultation, to decide whether or not to grant the permission sought and to determine the terms and conditions, if any, to which such permission should be subject.

An application as referred to in the first subparagraph shall be submitted only to the competent authority referred to in paragraph 1.

The competent authorities shall do everything within their power to reach a joint decision on the application within six months. This joint decision shall be set out in a document containing the fully reasoned decision which shall be provided to the applicant by the competent authority referred to in paragraph 1.

The period referred to in subparagraph 3 shall begin on the date of receipt of the complete application by the competent authority referred to in paragraph 1. The competent authority referred to in paragraph 1 shall forward the complete application to the other competent authorities without delay.

In the absence of a joint decision between the competent authorities within six months, the competent authority referred to in paragraph 1 shall make its own decision on the application. The decision shall be set out in a document containing the fully reasoned decision and shall take into account the views and reservations of the other competent authorities expressed during the six months period. The decision shall be provided to the applicant and the other competent authorities by the competent authority referred to in paragraph 1.

The decisions referred to in the third and fifth subparagraphs shall be recognised as determinative and applied by the competent authorities in the Member States concerned.

Article 130

1. Where an emergency situation arises within a banking group which potentially jeopardises the stability of the financial system in any of the Member States where entities of a group have been authorised, the competent authority responsible for the exercise of supervision on a consolidated basis shall alert as soon as is practicable, subject to Chapter 1, Section 2, the authorities referred to in Article 49(a) and Article 50. This obligation shall apply to all competent authorities identified under Articles 125 and 126 in relation to a particular group, and to the competent authority identified under Article 129(1). Where possible, the competent authority shall use existing defined channels of communication.

2. The competent authority responsible for supervision on a consolidated basis shall, when it needs information which has already been given to another competent authority, contact this authority whenever possible in order to prevent duplication of reporting to the various authorities involved in supervision.

Article 131

In order to facilitate and establish effective supervision, the competent authority responsible for supervision on a consolidated basis and the other competent authorities shall have written coordination and cooperation arrangements in place.

Under these arrangements additional tasks may be entrusted to the competent authority responsible for supervision on a consolidated basis and procedures for the decision-making process and for cooperation with other competent authorities, may be specified.

The competent authorities responsible for authorising the subsidiary of a parent undertaking which is a credit institution may, by bilateral agreement, delegate their responsibility for supervision to the competent authorities which authorised and supervise the parent undertaking so that they assume responsibility for supervising the subsidiary in accordance with this Directive. The Commission shall be kept informed of the existence and content of such agreements. It shall forward such information to the competent authorities of the other Member States and to the European Banking Committee.

Article 132

1. The competent authorities shall cooperate closely with each other. They shall provide one another with any information which is essential or relevant for the exercise of the other authorities' supervisory tasks under this Directive. In this regard, the competent authorities shall communicate on request all relevant information and shall communicate on their own initiative all essential information.

Information referred to in the first subparagraph shall be regarded as essential if it could materially influence the assessment of the financial soundness of a credit institution or financial institution in another Member State.

In particular, competent authorities responsible for consolidated supervision of EU parent credit institutions and credit institutions controlled by EU parent financial holding companies shall provide the competent authorities in other Member States who supervise subsidiaries of these parents with all relevant information. In determining the extent of relevant information, the importance of these subsidiaries within the financial system in those Member States shall be taken into account.

The essential information referred to in the first subparagraph shall include, in particular, the following items:

(a) identification of the group structure of all major credit institutions in a group, as well as of the competent authorities of the credit institutions in the group;

(b) procedures for the collection of information from the credit institutions in a group, and the verification of that information;

(c) adverse developments in credit institutions or in other entities of a group, which could seriously affect the credit institutions; and

(d) major sanctions and exceptional measures taken by competent authorities in accordance with this Directive, including the imposition of an additional capital charge under Article 136 and the imposition of any limitation on the use of the Advanced Measurement Approach for the calculation of the own funds requirements under Article 105.

2. The competent authorities responsible for the supervision of credit institutions controlled by an EU parent credit institution shall whenever possible contact the competent authority referred to in Article 129(1) when they need information regarding the implementation of approaches and methodologies set out in this Directive that may already be available to that competent authority.

3. The competent authorities concerned shall, prior to their decision, consult each other with regard to the following items, where these decisions are of importance for other competent authorities' supervisory tasks:

(a) changes in the shareholder, organisational or management structure of credit institutions in a group, which require the approval or authorisation of competent authorities; and

(b) major sanctions or exceptional measures taken by competent authorities, including the imposition of an additional capital charge under Article 136 and the imposition of any limitation on the use of the Advances Measurement Approaches for the calculation of the own funds requirements under Article 105.

For the purposes of point (b), the competent authority responsible for supervision on a consolidated basis shall always be consulted.

However, a competent authority may decide not to consult in cases of urgency or where such consultation may jeopardise the effectiveness of the decisions. In this case, the competent authority shall, without delay, inform the other competent authorities.

Article 133

1. The competent authorities responsible for supervision on a consolidated basis shall, for the purposes of supervision, require full consolidation of all the credit institutions and financial institutions which are subsidiaries of a parent undertaking.

However, the competent authorities may require only proportional consolidation where, in their opinion, the liability of a parent undertaking holding a share of the capital is limited to that share of the capital in view of the liability of the other shareholders or members whose solvency is satisfactory. The liability of the other shareholders and members shall be clearly established, if necessary by means of formal signed commitments.

In the case where undertakings are linked by a relationship within the meaning of Article 12(1) of Directive 83/349/EEC, the competent authorities shall determine how consolidation is to be carried out.

2. The competent authorities responsible for supervision on a consolidated basis shall require the proportional consolidation of participations in credit institutions and financial institutions managed by an undertaking included in the consolidation together with one or more undertakings not included in the consolidation, where those undertakings' liability is limited to the share of the capital they hold.

3. In the case of participations or capital ties other than those referred to in paragraphs 1 and 2, the competent authorities shall determine whether and how consolidation is to be carried out. In particular, they may permit or require use of the equity method. That method shall not, however, constitute inclusion of the undertakings concerned in supervision on a consolidated basis.

Article 134

1. Without prejudice to Article 133, the competent authorities shall determine whether and how consolidation is to be carried out in the following cases:

(a) where, in the opinion of the competent authorities, a credit institution exercises a significant influence over one or more credit institutions or financial institutions, but without holding a participation or other capital ties in these institutions; and

(b) where two or more credit institutions or financial institutions are placed under single management other than pursuant to a contract or clauses of their Memoranda or Articles of association.

In particular, the competent authorities may permit, or require use of, the method provided for in Article 12 of Directive 83/349/EEC. That method shall not, however, constitute inclusion of the undertakings concerned in consolidated supervision.

2. Where consolidated supervision is required pursuant to Articles 125 and 126, ancillary services undertakings and asset management companies as defined in Directive 2002/87/EC shall be included in consolidations in the cases, and in accordance with the methods, laid down in Article 133 and paragraph 1 of this Article.

Article 135

The Member States shall require that persons who effectively direct the business of a financial holding company be of sufficiently good repute and have sufficient experience to perform those duties.

Article 136

1. Competent authorities shall require any credit institution that does not meet the requirements of this Directive to take the necessary actions or steps at an early stage to address the situation.

For those purposes, the measures available to the competent authorities shall include the following:

(a) obliging credit institutions to hold own funds in excess of the minimum level laid down in Article 75;

(b) requiring the reinforcement of the arrangements, processes, mechanisms and strategies implemented to comply with Articles 22 and 123;

(c) requiring credit institutions to apply a specific provisioning policy or treatment of assets in terms of own funds requirements;

(d) restricting or limiting the business, operations or network of credit institutions; and

(e) requiring the reduction of the risk inherent in the activities, products and systems of credit institutions.

The adoption of these measures shall be subject to Chapter 1, Section 2.

2. A specific own funds requirement in excess of the minimum level laid down in Article 75 shall be imposed by the competent authorities at least on the credit institutions which do not meet the requirements laid down in Articles 22, 109 and 123, or in respect of which a negative determination has been made on the issue described in Article 124, paragraph 3, if the sole application of other measures is unlikely to improve the arrangements, processes, mechanisms and strategies sufficiently within an appropriate timeframe.

Article 137

1. Pending further coordination of consolidation methods, Member States shall provide that, where the parent undertaking of one or more credit institutions is a mixed-activity holding company, the competent authorities responsible for the authorisation and supervision of those credit institutions shall, by approaching the mixed-activity holding company and its subsidiaries either directly or via credit institution subsidiaries, require them to supply any information which would be relevant for the purpose of supervising the credit institution subsidiaries.

2. Member States shall provide that their competent authorities may carry out, or have carried out by external inspectors, on-the-spot inspections to verify information received from mixed-activity holding companies and their subsidiaries. If the mixed-activity holding company or one of its subsidiaries is an insurance undertaking, the procedure laid down in Article 140(1) may also be used. If a mixed-activity holding company or one of its subsidiaries is situated in a Member State other than that in which the credit institution subsidiary is situated, on-the-spot verification of information shall be carried out in accordance with the procedure laid down in Article 141.

Article 138

1. Without prejudice to Chapter 2, Section 5, Member States shall provide that, where the parent undertaking of one or more credit institutions is a mixed-activity holding company, the competent authorities responsible for the supervision of these credit institutions shall exercise general supervision over transactions between the credit institution and the mixed-activity holding company and its subsidiaries.

2. Competent authorities shall require credit institutions to have in place adequate risk management processes and internal control mechanisms, including sound reporting and accounting procedures, in order to identify, measure, monitor and control transactions with their parent mixed-activity holding company and its subsidiaries appropriately. Competent authorities shall require the reporting by the credit institution of any significant transaction with these entities other than the one referred to in Article 110. These procedures and significant transactions shall be subject to overview by the competent authorities. Where these intra-group transactions are a threat to a credit institution's financial position, the competent authority responsible for the supervision of the institution shall take appropriate measures.

Article 139

1. Member States shall take the necessary steps to ensure that there are no legal impediments preventing the exchange, as between undertakings included within the scope of supervision on a consolidated basis, mixed-activity holding companies and their subsidiaries, or subsidiaries of the kind covered in Article 127(3), of any information which would be relevant for the purposes of supervision in accordance with Articles 124 to 138 and this Article.

2. Where a parent undertaking and any of its subsidiaries that are credit institutions are situated in different Member States, the competent authorities of each Member State shall communicate to each other all relevant information which may allow or aid the exercise of supervision on a

consolidated basis. Where the competent authorities of the Member State in which a parent undertaking is situated do not themselves exercise supervision on a consolidated basis pursuant to Articles 125 and 126, they may be invited by the competent authorities responsible for exercising such supervision to ask the parent undertaking for any information which would be relevant for the purposes of supervision on a consolidated basis and to transmit it to these authorities.

3. Member States shall authorise the exchange between their competent authorities of the information referred to in paragraph 2, on the understanding that, in the case of financial holding companies, financial institutions or ancillary services undertakings, the collection or possession of information shall not in any way imply that the competent authorities are required to play a supervisory role in relation to those institutions or undertakings standing alone. Similarly, Member States shall authorise their competent authorities to exchange the information referred to in Article 137 on the understanding that the collection or possession of information does not in any way imply that the competent authorities play a supervisory role in relation to the mixed-activity holding company and those of its subsidiaries which are not credit institutions, or to subsidiaries of the kind covered in Article 127(3).

Article 140

1. Where a credit institution, financial holding company or a mixed-activity holding company controls one or more subsidiaries which are insurance companies or other undertakings providing investment services which are subject to authorisation, the competent authorities and the authorities entrusted with the public task of supervising insurance undertakings or those other undertakings providing investment services shall cooperate closely. Without prejudice to their respective responsibilities, those authorities shall provide one another with any information likely to simplify their task and to allow supervision of the activity and overall financial situation of the undertakings they supervise.

2. Information received, in the framework of supervision on a consolidated basis, and in particular any exchange of information between competent authorities which is provided for in this Directive, shall be subject to the obligation of professional secrecy defined in Chapter 1, Section 2.

3. The competent authorities responsible for supervision on a consolidated basis shall establish lists of the financial holding companies referred to in Article 71(2). Those lists shall be communicated to the competent authorities of the other Member States and to the Commission.

Article 141

Where, in applying this Directive, the competent authorities of one Member State wish in specific cases to verify the information concerning a credit institution, a financial holding company, a financial institution, an ancillary services undertaking, a mixed-activity holding company, a subsidiary of the kind covered in Article 137 or a subsidiary of the kind covered in Article 127(3), situated in another Member State, they shall ask the competent authorities of that other Member State to have that verification carried out. The authorities which receive such a request shall, within the framework of their competence, act upon it either by carrying out the verification themselves, by allowing the authorities who made the request to carry it out, or by allowing an auditor or expert to carry it out. The competent authority which made the request may, if it so wishes, participate in the verification when it does not carry out the verification itself.

Article 142

Without prejudice to their criminal law provisions, Member States shall ensure that penalties or measures aimed at ending observed breaches or the causes of such breaches may be imposed on financial holding companies and mixed-activity holding companies, or their effective managers, that infringe laws, regulation or administrative provisions enacted to implement Articles 124 to 141 and this Article. The competent authorities shall cooperate closely to ensure that those penalties or measures produce the desired results, especially when the central administration or main establishment of a financial holding company or of a mixed-activity holding company is not located at its head office.

Article 143

1. Where a credit institution, the parent undertaking of which is a credit institution or a financial holding company, the head office of which is in a third country, is not subject to consolidated supervision under Articles 125 and 126, the competent authorities shall verify whether the credit institution is subject to consolidated supervision by a third-country competent authority which is equivalent to that governed by the principles laid down in this Directive.

The verification shall be carried out by the competent authority which would be responsible for consolidated supervision if paragraph 3 were to apply, at the request of the parent undertaking or of any of the regulated entities authorised in the Community or on its own initiative. That competent authority shall consult the other competent authorities involved.

2. The Commission may request the European Banking Committee to give general guidance as to whether the consolidated supervision arrangements of competent authorities in third countries are likely to achieve the objectives of consolidated supervision as defined in this Chapter, in relation to credit institutions, the parent undertaking of which has its head office in a third country. The Committee shall keep any such guidance under review and take into account any changes to the consolidated supervision arrangements applied by such competent authorities.

The competent authority carrying out the verification specified in the first subparagraph of paragraph 1 shall take into account any such guidance. For this purpose the competent authority shall consult the Committee before taking a decision.

3. In the absence of such equivalent supervision, Member States shall apply the provisions of this Directive to the credit institution by analogy or shall allow their competent authorities to apply other appropriate supervisory techniques which achieve the objectives of supervision on a consolidated basis of credit institutions.

Those supervisory techniques shall, after consultation with the other competent authorities involved, be agreed upon by the competent authority which would be responsible for consolidated supervision.

Competent authorities may in particular require the establishment of a financial holding company which has its head office in the Community, and apply the provisions on consolidated supervision to the consolidated position of that financial holding company. The supervisory techniques shall be designed to achieve the objectives of consolidated supervision as defined in this Chapter and shall be notified to the other competent authorities involved and the Commission.

Section 2
Disclosure by Competent Authorities

Article 144

Competent authorities shall disclose the following information:

(a) the texts of laws, regulations, administrative rules and general guidance adopted in their Member State in the field of prudential regulation;

(b) the manner of exercise of the options and discretions available in Community legislation;

(c) the general criteria and methodologies they use in the review and evaluation referred to in Article 124; and

(d) without prejudice to the provisions laid down in Chapter 1, Section 2, aggregate statistical data on key aspects of the implementation of the prudential framework in each Member State.

The disclosures provided for in the first subparagraph shall be sufficient to enable a meaningful comparison of the approaches adopted by the competent authorities of the different Member States. The disclosures shall be published with a common format, and updated regularly. The disclosures shall be accessible at a single electronic location.

CHAPTER 5
DISCLOSURE BY CREDIT INSTITUTIONS

Article 145

1. For the purposes of this Directive, credit institutions shall publicly disclose the information laid down in Annex XII, Part 2, subject to the provisions laid down in Article 146.

2. Recognition by the competent authorities under Chapter 2, Section 3, Subsections 2 and 3 and Article 105 of the instruments and methodologies referred to in Annex XII, Part 3 shall be subject to the public disclosure by credit institutions of the information laid down therein.

3. Credit institutions shall adopt a formal policy to comply with the disclosure requirements laid down in paragraphs 1 and 2, and have policies for assessing the appropriateness of their disclosures, including their verification and frequency.

4. Credit institutions should, if requested, explain their rating decisions to SMEs and other corporate applicants for loans, providing an explanation in writing when asked. Should a voluntary undertaking by the sector in this regard prove inadequate, national measures shall be adopted. The administrative costs of the explanation have to be at an appropriate rate to the size of the loan.

Article 146

1. Notwithstanding Article 145, credit institutions may omit one or more of the disclosures listed in Annex XII, Part 2 if the information provided by such disclosures is not, in the light of the criterion specified in Annex XII, Part 1, point 1, regarded as material.

2. Notwithstanding Article 145, credit institutions may omit one or more items of information included in the disclosures listed in Annex XII, Parts 2 and 3 if those items include information which, in the light of the criteria specified in Annex XII, Part 1, points 2 and 3, is regarded as proprietary or confidential.

3. In the exceptional cases referred to in paragraph 2, the credit institution concerned shall state in its disclosures the fact that the specific items of information are not disclosed, the reason for non-disclosure, and publish more general information about the subject matter of the disclosure requirement, except where these are to be classified as proprietary or confidential under the criteria set out in Annex XII, Part 1, points 2 and 3.

Article 147

1. Credit institutions shall publish the disclosures required under Article 145 on an annual basis at a minimum. Disclosures shall be published as soon as practicable.

2. Credit institutions shall also determine whether more frequent publication than is provided for in paragraph 1 is necessary in the light of the criteria set out in Annex XII, Part 1, point 4.

Article 148

1. Credit institutions may determine the appropriate medium, location and means of verification to comply effectively with the disclosure requirements laid down in Article 145. To the degree feasible, all disclosures shall be provided in one medium or location.

2. Equivalent disclosures made by credit institutions under accounting, listing or other requirements may be deemed to constitute compliance with Article 145. If disclosures are not included in the financial statements, credit institutions shall indicate where they can be found.

Article 149

Notwithstanding Articles 146 to 148, Member States shall empower the competent authorities to require credit institutions:

(a) to make one or more of the disclosures referred to in Annex XII, Parts 2 and 3;

(b) to publish one or more disclosures more frequently than annually, and to set deadlines for publication;

(c) to use specific media and locations for disclosures other than the financial statements; and

(d) to use specific means of verification for the disclosures not covered by statutory audit.

Title VI
Powers of Execution

Article 150

1. Without prejudice, regarding own funds, to the proposal that the Commission is to submit pursuant to Article 62, the technical adjustments in the following areas shall be adopted in accordance with the procedure referred to in Article 151(2):

(a) clarification of the definitions in order to take account, in the application of this Directive, of developments on financial markets;

(b) clarification of the definitions to ensure uniform application of this Directive;

(c) the alignment of terminology on, and the framing of definitions in accordance with, subsequent acts on credit institutions and related matters;

(d) technical adjustments to the list in Article 2;

(e) alteration of the amount of initial capital prescribed in Article 9 to take account of developments in the economic and monetary field;

(f) expansion of the content of the list referred to in Articles 23 and 24 and set out in Annex I or adaptation of the terminology used in that list to take account of developments on financial markets;

(g) the areas in which the competent authorities shall exchange information as listed in Article 42;

(h) technical adjustments in Articles 56 to 67 and in Article 74 as a result of developments in accounting standards or requirements which take account of Community legislation or with regard to convergence of supervisory practices;

(i) amendment of the list of exposure classes in Articles 79 and 86 in order to take account of developments on financial markets;

(j) the amount specified in Article 79(2)(c), Article 86(4)(a), Annex VII, Part 1, point 5 and Annex VII, Part 2, point 15 to take into account the effects of inflation;

(k) the list and classification of off-balance-sheet items in Annexes II and IV and their treatment in the determination of exposure values for the purposes of Title V, Chapter 2, Section 3; or

(l) adjustment of the provisions in Annexes V to XII in order to take account of developments on financial markets (in particular new financial products) or in accounting standards or requirements which take account of Community legislation, or with regard to convergence of supervisory practice.

2. The Commission may adopt the following implementing measures in accordance with the procedure referred to in Article 151(2):

(a) specification of the size of sudden and unexpected changes in the interest rates referred to in Article 124(5);

(b) a temporary reduction in the minimum level of own funds laid down in Article 75 and/or the risk weights laid down in Title V, Chapter 2, Section 3 in order to take account of specific circumstances;

(c) without prejudice to the report referred to in Article 119, clarification of exemptions provided for in Articles 111(4), 113, 115 and 116;

(d) specification of the key aspects on which aggregate statistical data are to be disclosed under Article 144(1)(d); or

(e) specification of the format, structure, contents list and annual publication date of the disclosures provided for in Article 144.

3. None of the implementing measures enacted may change the essential provisions of this Directive.

4. Without prejudice to the implementing measures already adopted, upon expiry of a two-year period following the adoption of this Directive, and by 1 April 2008 at the latest, the application of

the provisions of this Directive requiring the adoption of technical rules, amendments and decisions in accordance with paragraph 2 shall be suspended. Acting on a proposal from the Commission and in accordance with the procedure laid down in Article 251 of the Treaty, the Parliament and the Council may renew those provisions and, to that end, shall review them prior to the expiry of the period or by the date referred to in this paragraph, whichever is the earlier.

Article 151

1. The Commission shall be assisted by the European Banking Committee established by Commission Decision 2004/10/EC.[27]

2. Where reference is made to this paragraph, the procedure laid down in Article 5 of Decision 1999/468/EC shall apply, having regard to the provisions of Article 7(3) and Article 8 thereof. The period laid down in Article 5(6) of Decision 1999/468/EC shall be three months.

3. The Committee shall adopt its Rules of Procedure.

Title VII
Transitional and Final Provisions

Chapter 1
Transitional Provisions

Article 152

1. Credit institutions calculating risk-weighted exposure amounts in accordance with Articles 84 to 89 shall during the first, second and third twelve-month periods after 31 December 2006 provide own funds which are at all times more than or equal to the amounts indicated in paragraphs 3, 4 and 5.

2. Credit institutions using the Advanced Measurement Approaches as specified in Article 105 for the calculation of their capital requirements for operational risk shall, during the second and third twelve-month periods after 31 December 2006, provide own funds which are at all times more than or equal to the amounts indicated in paragraphs 4 and 5.

3. For the first twelve-month period referred to in paragraph 1, the amount of own funds shall be 95% of the total minimum amount of own funds that would be required to be held during that period by the credit institution under Article 4 of Council Directive 93/6/EEC of 15 March 1993 on the capital adequacy of investment firms and credit institutions[28] as that Directive and Directive 2000/12/EC stood prior to 1 January 2007.

4. For the second twelve-month period referred to in paragraph 1, the amount of own funds shall be 90% of the total minimum amount of own funds that would be required to be held during that period by the credit institution under Article 4 of Directive 93/6/EEC as that Directive and Directive 2000/12/EC stood prior to 1 January 2007.

5. For the third twelve-month period referred to in paragraph 1, the amount of own funds shall be 80% of the total minimum amount of own funds that would be required to be held during that period by the credit institution under Article 4 of Directive 93/6/EEC as that Directive and Directive 2000/12/EC stood prior to 1 January 2007.

6. Compliance with the requirements of paragraphs 1 to 5 shall be on the basis of amounts of own funds fully adjusted to reflect differences in the calculation of own funds under Directive 2000/12/EC and Directive 93/6/EEC as those Directives stood prior to 1 January 2007 and the calculation of own funds under this Directive deriving from the separate treatments of expected loss and unexpected loss under Articles 84 to 89 of this Directive.

---

[27] OJ L 3, 7.1.2004, 36, reproduced infra under no. I. 37.

[28] OJ L 141, 11.6.1993, 1, reproduced supra under no. B. 7. Directive as last amended by Directive 2005/1/EC, reproduced supra under no. B. 39. Directive 93/6/EEC has been repealed as from 20 July 2006 by article 52 of Directive 2006/49/EC (OJ L 177, 30.6.2006, 201), reproduced infra under no. B. 42.

7. For the purposes of paragraphs 1 to 6 of this Article, Articles 68 to 73 shall apply.

8. Until 1 January 2008 credit institutions may treat the Articles constituting the Standardised Approach set out in Title V, Chapter 2, Section 3, Subsection 1 as being replaced by Articles 42 to 46 of Directive 2000/12/EC as those Articles stood prior to 1 January 2007.

9. Where the discretion referred to in paragraph 8 is exercised, the following shall apply concerning the provisions of Directive 2000/12/EC:

(a) the provisions of that Directive referred to in Articles 42 to 46 shall apply as they stood prior to 1 January 2007;

(b) 'risk-adjusted value' as referred to in Article 42(1) of that Directive shall mean 'risk-weighted exposure amount';

(c) the figures produced by Article 42(2) of that Directive shall be considered risk-weighted exposure amounts;

(d) 'credit derivatives' shall be included in the list of 'Full risk' items in Annex II of that Directive; and

(e) the treatment set out in Article 43(3) of that Directive shall apply to derivative instruments listed in Annex IV of that Directive whether on- or off-balance sheet and the figures produced by the treatment set out in Annex III shall be considered risk-weighted exposure amounts.

10. Where the discretion referred to in paragraph 8 is exercised, the following shall apply in relation to the treatment of exposures for which the Standardised Approach is used:

(a) Title V, Chapter 2, Section 3, Subsection 3 relating to the recognition of credit risk mitigation shall not apply;

(b) Title V, Chapter 2, Section 3, Subsection 4 concerning the treatment of securitisation may be disapplied by competent authorities.

11. Where the discretion referred to in paragraph 8 is exercised, the capital requirement for operational risk under Article 75(d) shall be reduced by the percentage representing the ratio of the value of the credit institution's exposures for which risk-weighted exposure amounts are calculated in accordance with the discretion referred to in paragraph 8 to the total value of its exposures.

12. Where a credit institution calculates risk-weighted exposure amounts for all of its exposures in accordance with the discretion referred to in paragraph 8, Articles 48 to 50 of Directive 2000/12/EC relating to large exposures may apply as they stood prior to 1 January 2007.

13. Where the discretion referred to in paragraph 8 is exercised, references to Articles 78 to 83 of this Directive shall be read as references to Articles 42 to 46 of Directive 2000/12/EC as those Articles stood prior to 1 January 2007.

14. If the discretion referred to in paragraph 8 is exercised, Articles 123, 124, 145 and 149 shall not apply before the date referred to therein.

Article 153

In the calculation of risk-weighted exposure amounts for exposures arising from property leasing transactions concerning offices or other commercial premises situated in their territory and meeting the criteria set out in Annex VI, Part 1, point 54, the competent authorities may, until 31 December 2012 allow a 50% risk weight to be assigned without the application of Annex VI, Part 1, points 55 and 56.

Until 31 December 2010, competent authorities may, for the purpose of defining the secured portion of a past due loan for the purposes of Annex VI, recognise collateral other than eligible collateral as set out under Articles 90 to 93.

In the calculation of risk-weighted exposure amounts for the purposes of Annex VI, Part 1, point 4, until 31 December 2012 the same risk weight shall be assigned in relation to exposures to Member States' central governments or central banks denominated and funded in the domestic currency of any Member State as would be applied to such exposures denominated and funded in their domestic currency.

Article 154

1. Until 31 December 2011, the competent authorities of each Member State may, for the

purposes of Annex VI, Part 1, point 61, set the number of days past due up to a figure of 180 for exposures indicated in Annex VI, Part 1, points 12 to 17 and 41 to 43, to counterparties situated in their territory, if local conditions make it appropriate. The specific number may differ across product lines.

Competent authorities which do not exercise the discretion provided for in the first subparagraph in relation to exposures to counterparties situated in their territory may set a higher number of days for exposures to counterparties situated in the territories of other Member States, the competent authorities of which have exercised that discretion. The specific number shall fall within 90 days and such figures as the other competent authorities have set for exposures to such counterparties within their territory.

2. For credit institutions applying for the use of the IRB Approach before 2010, subject to the approval of the competent authorities, the three-years' use requirement prescribed in Article 84(3) may be reduced to a period no shorter than one year until 31 December 2009.

3. For credit institutions applying for the use of own estimates of LGDs and/or conversion factors, the three year use requirement prescribed in Article 84(4) may be reduced to two years until 31 December 2008.

4. Until 31 December 2012, the competent authorities of each Member State may allow credit institutions to continue to apply to participations of the type set out in Article 57(o) acquired before 20 July 2006 the treatment set out in Article 38 of Directive 2000/12/EC as that article stood prior to 1 January 2007.

5. Until 31 December 2010 the exposure weighted average LGD for all retail exposures secured by residential properties and not benefiting from guarantees from central governments shall not be lower than 10%.

6. Until 31 December 2017, the competent authorities of the Member States may exempt from the IRB treatment certain equity exposures held by credit institutions and EU subsidiaries of credit institutions in that Member State at 31 December 2007.

The exempted position shall be measured as the number of shares as of 31 December 2007 and any additional share arising directly as a result of owning those holdings, as long as they do not increase the proportional share of ownership in a portfolio company.

If an acquisition increases the proportional share of ownership in a specific holding the exceeding Part of the holding shall not be subject to the exemption. Nor shall the exemption apply to holdings that were originally subject to the exemption, but have been sold and then bought back.

Equity exposures covered by this transitional provision shall be subject to the capital requirements calculated in accordance with Title V, Chapter 2, Section 3, Subsection 1.

7. Until 31 December 2011, for corporate exposures, the competent authorities of each Member State may set the number of days past due that all credit institutions in its jurisdiction shall abide by under the definition of 'default' set out in Annex VII, Part 4, point 44 for exposures to such counterparts situated within this Member State. The specific number shall fall within 90- up to a figure of 180 days if local conditions make it appropriate. For exposures to such counterparts situated in the territories of other Member States, the competent authorities shall set a number of days past due which is not higher than the number set by the competent authority of the respective Member State.

Article 155

Until 31 December 2012, for credit institutions the relevant indicator for the trading and sales business line of which represents at least 50% of the total of the relevant indicators for all of its business lines in accordance with Annex X, Part 2, points 1 to 4, Member States may apply a percentage of 15% to the business line 'trading and sales'.

CHAPTER 2

FINAL PROVISIONS

Article 156

The Commission, in cooperation with Member States, and taking into account the contribution of the European Central Bank, shall periodically monitor whether this Directive taken as a whole, together with Directive 2006/49/EC, has significant effects on the economic cycle and, in the light of that examination, shall consider whether any remedial measures are justified.

Based on that analysis and taking into account the contribution of the European Central Bank, the Commission shall draw up a biennial report and submit it to the European Parliament and to the Council, together with any appropriate proposals. Contributions from credit taking and credit lending parties shall be adequately acknowledged when the report is drawn up.

By 1 January 2012 the Commission shall review and report on the application of this Directive with particular attention to all aspects of Articles 68 to 73, 80(7), 80(8) and 129, and shall submit this report to the Parliament and the Council together with any appropriate proposals.

Article 157

1. By 31 December 2006 Member States shall adopt and publish the laws, regulations and administrative provisions necessary to comply with Articles 4, 22, 57, 61 to 64, 66, 68 to 106, 108, 110 to 115, 117 to 119, 123 to 127, 129 to 132, 133, 136, 144 to 149 and 152 to 155, and Annexes II, III and V to XII. They shall forthwith communicate to the Commission the text of those provisions and a correlation table between those provisions and this Directive.

Notwithstanding paragraph 3, Member States shall apply those provisions from 1 January 2007.

When Member States adopt those provisions, they shall contain a reference to this Directive or be accompanied by such a reference on the occasion of their official publication. They shall also include a statement that references in existing laws, regulations and administrative provisions to the directives repealed by this Directive shall be construed as references to this Directive. Member States shall determine how such reference is to be made and how that statement is to be formulated.

2. Member States shall communicate to the Commission the text of the main provisions of national law which they adopt in the field covered by this Directive.

3. Member States shall apply, from 1 January 2008, and no earlier, the laws regulations and administrative provisions necessary to comply with Articles 87(9) and 105.

Article 158

1. Directive 2000/12/EC as amended by the Directives set out in Annex XIII, Part A, is hereby repealed without prejudice to the obligations of the Member States concerning the deadlines for transposition of the said Directives listed in Annex XIII, Part B.

2. References to the repealed Directives shall be construed as being made to this Directive and should be read in accordance with the correlation table in Annex XIV.

Article 159

This Directive shall enter into force on the 20th day following its publication in the *Official Journal of the European Union*.

Article 160

This Directive is addressed to the Member States.

Annex I

List of Activities subject to Mutual Recognition

1. Acceptance of deposits and other repayable funds

2. Lending including, inter alia: consumer credit, mortgage credit, factoring, with or without

recourse, financing of commercial transactions (including forfeiting)

3. Financial leasing

4. Money transmission services

5. Issuing and administering means of payment (e.g. credit cards, travellers' cheques and bankers' drafts)

6. Guarantees and commitments

7. Trading for own account or for account of customers in:

(a) money market instruments (cheques, bills, certificates of deposit, etc.);

(b) foreign exchange;

(c) financial futures and options;

(d) exchange and interest-rate instruments; or

(e) transferable securities.

8. Participation in securities issues and the provision of services related to such issues

9. Advice to undertakings on capital structure, industrial strategy and related questions and advice as well as services relating to mergers and the purchase of undertakings

10. Money broking

11. Portfolio management and advice

12. Safekeeping and administration of securities

13. Credit reference services

14. Safe custody services

The services and activities provided for in Sections A and B of Annex I to Directive 2004/39/EC of the European Parliament and of the Council of 21 April 2004 on markets in financial instruments,[29] when referring to the financial instruments provided for in Section C of Annex I of that Directive, are subject to mutual recognition according to this Directive.

Annex II

Classification of Off-Balance-Sheet Items

Full risk:
- Guarantees having the character of credit substitutes,
- Credit derivatives,
- Acceptances,
- Endorsements on bills not bearing the name of another credit institution,
- Transactions with recourse,
- Irrevocable standby letters of credit having the character of credit substitutes,
- Assets purchased under outright forward purchase agreements,
- Forward forward deposits,
- The unpaid portion of partly-paid shares and securities,
- Asset sale and repurchase agreements as defined in Article 12(3) and (5) of Directive 86/635/EEC, and
- Other items also carrying full risk.

Medium risk:
- Documentary credits issued and confirmed (see also 'Medium/low risk'),
- Warranties and indemnities (including tender, performance, customs and tax bonds) and guarantees not having the character of credit substitutes,
- Irrevocable standby letters of credit not having the character of credit substitutes,
- Undrawn credit facilities (agreements to lend, purchase securities, provide guarantees or acceptance facilities) with an original maturity of more than one year,
- Note issuance facilities (NIFs) and revolving underwriting facilities (RUFs), and

---

[29] OJ L 145, 30.4.2004, 1, reproduced infra under no. S. 29. Directive as amended by Directive 2006/31/EC (OJ L 114, 27.4.2006, 60), reproduced infra under no. S. 32.

– Other items also carrying medium risk and as communicated to the Commission.

Medium/low risk:
– Documentary credits in which underlying shipment acts as collateral and other self-liquidating transactions,
– Undrawn credit facilities (agreements to lend, purchase securities, provide guarantees or acceptance facilities) with an original maturity of up to and including one year which may not be cancelled unconditionally at any time without notice or that do not effectively provide for automatic cancellation due to deterioration in a borrower's creditworthiness, and
– Other items also carrying medium/low risk and as communicated to the Commission.

Low risk:
– Undrawn credit facilities (agreements to lend, purchase securities, provide guarantees or acceptance facilities) which may be cancelled unconditionally at any time without notice, or that do effectively provide for automatic cancellation due to deterioration in a borrower's creditworthiness. Retail credit lines may be considered as unconditionally cancellable if the terms permit the credit institution to cancel them to the full extent allowable under consumer protection and related legislation, and
– Other items also carrying low risk and as communicated to the Commission.

Annex III

The Treatment of Counterparty Credit Risk of Derivative Instruments, Repurchase Transactions, Securities or Commodities Lending or Borrowing Transactions, Long Settlement Transactions and Margin Lending Transactions

PART 1

Definitions

For the purposes of this Annex the following definitions shall apply:

General terms

1. 'Counterparty Credit Risk (CCR)' means the risk that the counterparty to a transaction could default before the final settlement of the transaction's cash flows.

2. 'Central counterparty' means an entity that legally interposes itself between counterparties to contracts traded within one or more financial markets, becoming the buyer to every seller and the seller to every buyer.

Transaction types

3. 'Long Settlement Transactions' mean transactions where a counterparty undertakes to deliver a security, a commodity, or a foreign exchange amount against cash, other financial instruments, or commodities, or vice versa, at a settlement or delivery date that is contractually specified as more than the lower of the market standard for this particular transaction and five business days after the date on which the credit institution enters into the transaction.

4. 'Margin Lending Transactions' mean transactions in which a credit institution extends credit in connection with the purchase, sale, carrying or trading of securities. Margin lending transactions do not include other loans that happen to be secured by securities collateral.

Netting sets, hedging sets, and related terms

5. 'Netting Set' means a group of transactions with a single counterparty that are subject to a legally enforceable bilateral netting arrangement and for which netting is recognised under Part 7

of this Annex and Articles 90 to 93. Each transaction that is not subject to a legally enforceable bilateral netting arrangement, which is recognised under Part 7 of this Annex, should be interpreted as its own netting set for the purpose of this Annex.

6. 'Risk Position' means a risk number that is assigned to a transaction under the Standardised Method set out in Part 5 following a predetermined algorithm.

7. 'Hedging Set' means a group of risk positions from the transactions within a single netting set for which only their balance is relevant for determining the exposure value under the Standardised Method set out in Part 5.

8. 'Margin Agreement' means a contractual agreement or provisions of an agreement under which one counterparty shall supply collateral to a second counterparty when an exposure of that second counterparty to the first counterparty exceeds a specified level.

9. 'Margin Threshold' means the largest amount of an exposure that remains outstanding until one party has the right to call for collateral.

10. 'Margin Period of Risk' means the time period from the last exchange of collateral covering a netting set of transactions with a defaulting counterpart until that counterpart is closed out and the resulting market risk is re-hedged.

11. 'Effective Maturity under the Internal Model Method, for a netting set with maturity greater than one year' means the ratio of the sum of expected exposure over the life of the transactions in the netting set discounted at the risk-free rate of return divided by the sum of expected exposure over one year in a netting set discounted at the risk-free rate. This effective maturity may be adjusted to reflect rollover risk by replacing expected exposure with effective expected exposure for forecasting horizons under one year.

12. 'Cross-Product Netting' means the inclusion of transactions of different product categories within the same netting set pursuant to the Cross-Product Netting rules set out in this Annex.

13. For the purposes of Part 5, 'Current Market Value (CMV)' refers to the net market value of the portfolio of transactions within the netting set with the counterparty. Both positive and negative market values are used in computing CMV.

Distributions

14. 'Distribution of Market Values' means the forecast of the probability distribution of net market values of transactions within a netting set for some future date (the forecasting horizon), given the realised market value of those transactions up to the present time.

15. 'Distribution of Exposures' means the forecast of the probability distribution of market values that is generated by setting forecast instances of negative net market values equal to zero.

16. 'Risk-Neutral Distribution' means a distribution of market values or exposures at a future time period where the distribution is calculated using market implied values such as implied volatilities.

17. 'Actual Distribution' means a distribution of market values or exposures at a future time period where the distribution is calculated using historic or realised values such as volatilities calculated using past price or rate changes.

Exposure measures and adjustments

18. 'Current Exposure' means the larger of zero or the market value of a transaction or portfolio of transactions within a netting set with a counterparty that would be lost upon the default of the counterparty, assuming no recovery on the value of those transactions in bankruptcy.

19. 'Peak Exposure' means a high percentile of the distribution of exposures at any particular future date before the maturity date of the longest transaction in the netting set.

20. 'Expected Exposure (EE)' means the average of the distribution of exposures at any particular future date before the longest maturity transaction in the netting set matures.

21. 'Effective Expected Exposure (Effective EE) at a specific date' means the maximum expected exposure that occurs at that date or any prior date. Alternatively, it may be defined for a specific date as the greater of the expected exposure at that date, or the effective exposure at the previous date.

22. 'Expected Positive Exposure (EPE)' means the weighted average over time of expected exposures where the weights are the proportion that an individual expected exposure represents of the entire time interval. When calculating the minimum capital requirement, the average is taken over the first year or, if all the contracts within the netting set mature within less than one year, over the time period of the longest maturity contract in the netting set.

23. 'Effective Expected Positive Exposure (Effective EPE)' means the weighted average over time of effective expected exposure over the first year, or, if all the contracts within the netting set mature within less than one year, over the time period of the longest maturity contract in the netting set, where the weights are the proportion that an individual expected exposure represents of the entire time interval.

24. 'Credit Valuation Adjustment' means an adjustment to the mid-market valuation of the portfolio of transactions with a counterparty. This adjustment reflects the market value of the credit risk due to any failure to perform on contractual agreements with a counterparty. This adjustment may reflect the market value of the credit risk of the counterparty or the market value of the credit risk of both the credit institution and the counterparty.

25. 'One-Sided Credit Valuation Adjustment' means a credit valuation adjustment that reflects the market value of the credit risk of the counterparty to the credit institution, but does not reflect the market value of the credit risk of the credit institution to the counterparty.

CCR related risks

26. 'Rollover Risk' means the amount by which expected positive exposure is understated when future transactions with a counterpart are expected to be conducted on an ongoing basis. The additional exposure generated by those future transactions is not included in calculation of EPE.

27. 'General Wrong-Way Risk' arises when the PD of counterparties is positively correlated with general market risk factors.

28. 'Specific Wrong-Way Risk' arises when the exposure to a particular counterparty is positively correlated with the PD of the counterparty due to the nature of the transactions with the counterparty. A credit institution shall be considered to be exposed to Specific Wrong-Way Risk if the future exposure to a specific counterparty is expected to be high when the counterparty's PD is also high.

PART 2

Choice of the Method

1. Subject to paragraphs 2 to 7, credit institutions shall determine the exposure value for the contracts listed in Annex IV with one of the methods set out in Parts 3 to 6. Credit institutions which are not eligible for the treatment set out in Article 18(2) of Directive 2006/49/EC are not permitted to use the method set out in Part 4. To determine the exposure value for the contracts listed in point 3 of Annex IV, credit institutions are not permitted to use the method set out in Part 4.

The combined use of the methods set out in Parts 3 to 6 shall be permitted on a permanent basis within a group, but not within a single legal entity. Combined use of the methods set out in Parts 3 and 5 within a legal entity shall be permitted where one of the methods is used for the cases set out in Part 5, point 19.

2. Subject to the approval of the competent authorities, credit institutions may determine the exposure value for:
(i) the contracts listed in Annex IV,
(ii) repurchase transactions,
(iii) securities or commodities lending or borrowing transactions,

(iv) margin lending transactions, and
(v) long settlement transactions

using the Internal Model Method as set out in Part 6.

3. When a credit institution purchases credit derivative protection against a non-trading book exposure, or against a CCR exposure, it may compute its capital requirement for the hedged asset in accordance with Annex VIII, Part 3, points 83 to 92, or subject to the approval of the competent authorities, in accordance with Annex VII, Part 1, point 4 or Annex VII, Part 4, points 96 to 104. In these cases, the exposure value for CCR for these credit derivatives is set to zero.

4. The exposure value for CCR from sold credit default swaps in the non-trading book, where they are treated as credit protection provided by the credit institution and subject to a capital requirement for credit risk for the full notional amount, is set to zero.

5. Under all methods set out in Parts 3 to 6, the exposure value for a given counterparty is equal to the sum of the exposure values calculated for each netting set with that counterparty.

6. An exposure value of zero for CCR can be attributed to derivative contracts, or repurchase transactions, securities or commodities lending or borrowing transactions, long settlement transactions and margin lending transactions outstanding with a central counterparty and that have not been rejected by the central counterparty. Furthermore, an exposure value of zero can be attributed to credit risk exposures to central counterparties that result from the derivative contracts, repurchase transactions, securities or commodities lending or borrowing transactions, long settlement transactions and margin lending transactions or other exposures, as determined by the competent authorities, that the credit institution has outstanding with the central counterparty. The central counterparty CCR exposures with all participants in its arrangements shall be fully collateralised on a daily basis.

7. Exposures arising from long settlement transactions can be determined using any of the methods set out in Parts 3 to 6, regardless of the methods chosen for treating OTC derivatives and repurchase transactions, securities or commodities lending or borrowing transactions, and margin lending transactions. In calculating capital requirements for long settlement transactions, credit institutions that use the approach set out in Articles 84 to 89 may assign the risk weights under the approach set out in Articles 78 to 83 on a permanent basis and irrespective of the materiality of such positions.

8. For the methods set out in Parts 3 and 4 the competent authorities must ensure that the notional amount to be taken into account is an appropriate yardstick for the risk inherent in the contract. Where, for instance, the contract provides for a multiplication of cash flows, the notional amount must be adjusted in order to take into account the effects of the multiplication on the risk structure of that contract.

Part 3

Mark-to-Market Method

Step (a): by attaching current market values to contracts (mark-to-market), the current replacement cost of all contracts with positive values is obtained.

Step (b): to obtain a figure for potential future credit exposure, except in the case of single-currency 'floating/floating' interest rate swaps in which only the current replacement cost will be calculated, the notional principal amounts or underlying values are multiplied by the percentages in Table 1:

For the purpose of calculating the potential future credit exposure in accordance with step (b) the competent authorities may allow credit institutions to apply the percentages in Table 2 instead of those prescribed in Table 1 provided that the institutions make use of the option set out in Annex IV, point 21 to Directive 2006/49/EC for

Table 1[30, 31]

Residual maturity[32]	Interest-rate contracts	Contracts concerning foreign exchange rates and gold	Contracts concerning equities	Contracts concerning precious metals except gold	Contracts concerning commodities other than precious metals
One year or less	0%	1%	6%	7%	10%
Over one year, not exceeding five years	0.5%	5%	8%	7%	12%
Over five years	1.5%	7.5%	10%	8%	15%

Table 2

Residual maturity	Precious metals (except gold)	Base metals	Agricultural products (softs)	Other, including energy products
One year or less	2%	2.5%	3%	4%
Over one year, not exceeding five years	5%	4%	5%	6%
Over five years	7.5%	8%	9%	10%

contracts relating to commodities other than gold within the meaning of paragraph 3 of Annex IV, to this Directive:

Step (c): the sum of current replacement cost and potential future credit exposure is the exposure value.

Part 4

Original Exposure Method

Step (a): the notional principal amount of each instrument is multiplied by the percentages given in Table 3.

Step (b): the original exposure thus obtained shall be the exposure value.

---

[30] Contracts which do not fall within one of the five categories indicated in this table shall be treated as contracts concerning commodities other than precious metals.

[31] For contracts with multiple exchanges of principal, the percentages have to be multiplied by the number of remaining payments still to be made according to the contract.

[32] For contracts that are structured to settle outstanding exposure following specified payment dates and where the terms are reset such that the market value of the contract is zero on these specified dates, the residual maturity would be equal to the time until the next reset date. In the case of interest-rate contracts that meet these criteria and have a remaining maturity of over one year, the percentage shall be no lower than 0.5%.

Table 3

Original maturity[33]	Interest-rate contracts	Contracts foreign-exchange rates and gold
One year or less	0.5%	5%
Over one year, not exceeding two years	1%	5%
Additional allowance for each additional year	1%	3%

Part 5

Standardised Method

1. The Standardised Method (SM) can be used only for OTC derivatives and long settlement transactions. The exposure value shall be calculated separately for each netting set. It shall be determined net of collateral, as follows:

exposure value =

$$\beta * \max\left(CMV - CMC_j \sum_j \left|\sum_i RPT_{ij} - \sum_l RPC_{lj}\right| * CCRM_j\right)$$

---

[33] In the case of interest-rate contracts, credit institutions may, subject to the consent of their competent authorities, choose either original or residual maturity.

where:

CMV = current market value of the portfolio of transactions within the netting set with a counterparty gross of collateral, that is, where:

$$CMV = \sum_i CMV_i$$

CMV_i = the current market value of transaction i;

CMC = the current market value of the collateral assigned to the netting set, that is, where:

$$CMC = \sum_l CMC_l$$

where

CMC_l = the current market value of collateral l;

i = index designating transaction;

l = index designating collateral;

j = index designating hedging set category. These hedging sets correspond to risk factors for which risk positions of opposite sign can be offset to yield a net risk position on which the exposure measure is then based;

RPT_{ij} = risk position from transaction i with respect to hedging set j;

RPC_{lj} = risk position from collateral l with respect to hedging set j;

$CCRM_j$ = CCR Multiplier set out in Table 5 with respect to hedging set j;

β = 1.4.

Collateral received from a counterparty has a positive sign and collateral posted to a counterparty has a negative sign.

Collateral that is recognised for this method is confined to the collateral that is eligible under point 11 of Part 1 of Annex VIII to this Directive and point 9 of Annex II to Directive 2006/49/EC.

2. When an OTC derivative transaction with a linear risk profile stipulates the exchange of a financial instrument for a payment, the payment Part is referred to as the payment leg. Transactions that stipulate the exchange of payment against payment consist of two payment legs. The payment legs consist of the contractually agreed gross payments, including the notional amount of the transaction. Credit institutions may disregard the interest rate risk from payment legs with a remaining maturity of less than one year for the purposes of the following calculations. Credit institutions may treat transactions that consist of two payment legs that are denominated in the same currency, such as interest rate swaps, as a single aggregate transaction. The treatment for payment legs applies to the aggregate transaction.

3. Transactions with a linear risk profile with equities (including equity indices), gold, other precious metals or other commodities as the underlying financial instruments are mapped to a risk position in the respective equity (or equity index) or commodity (including gold and other precious metals) and an interest rate risk position for the payment leg. If the payment leg is denominated in a foreign currency, it is additionally mapped to a risk position in the respective currency.

4. Transactions with a linear risk profile with a debt instrument as the underlying instrument are mapped to an interest rate risk position for the debt instrument and another interest rate risk position for the payment leg. Transactions with a linear risk profile that stipulate the exchange of payment against payment, including foreign exchange forwards, are mapped to an interest rate risk position for each of the payment legs. If the underlying debt instrument is denominated in a foreign currency, the debt instrument is mapped to a risk position in this currency. If a payment leg is denominated in foreign currency, the payment leg is again mapped to a risk position in this currency. The exposure value assigned to a foreign exchange basis swap transaction is zero.

5. The size of a risk position from a transaction with linear risk profile is the effective notional value (market price multiplied by quantity) of the underlying financial instruments (including commodities) converted to the credit institution's domestic currency, except for debt instruments.

6. For debt instruments and for payment legs, the size of the risk position is the effective

notional value of the outstanding gross payments (including the notional amount) converted to the credit institution's domestic currency, multiplied by the modified duration of the debt instrument, or payment leg, respectively.

7. The size of a risk position from a credit default swap is the notional value of the reference debt instrument multiplied by the remaining maturity of the credit default swap.

8. The size of a risk position from an OTC derivative with a non-linear risk profile, including options and swaptions, is equal to the delta equivalent effective notional value of the financial instrument that underlies the transaction, except in the case of an underlying debt instrument.

9. The size of a risk position from an OTC derivative with a non-linear risk profile, including options and swaptions, of which the underlying is a debt instrument or a payment leg, is equal to the delta equivalent effective notional value of the financial instrument or payment leg multiplied by the modified duration of the debt instrument, or payment leg, respectively.

10. For the determination of risk positions, collateral received from a counterparty is to be treated as a claim on the counterparty under a derivative contract (long position) that is due today, while collateral posted is to be treated like an obligation to the counterparty (short position) that is due today.

11. Credit institutions may use the following formulae to determine the size and sign of a risk position:

for all instruments other than debt instruments:

effective notional value, or

delta equivalent notional value = $P_{ref} \frac{\partial V}{\partial p}$

where:

P_{ref} = price of the underlying instrument, expressed in the reference currency;

V = value of the financial instrument (in the case of an option this is the option price and in the case of a transaction with a linear risk profile this is the value of the underlying instrument itself);

p = price of the underlying instrument, expressed in the same currency as V;

for debt instruments and the payment legs of all transactions:

effective notional value multiplied by the modified duration, or

delta equivalent in notional value multiplied by the modified duration

$$\frac{\partial V}{\partial r}$$

where:

V = value of the financial instrument (in the case of an option this is the option price and in the case of a transaction with a linear risk profile this is the value of the underlying instrument itself or of the payment leg, respectively);

r = interest rate level.

If V is denominated in a currency other than the reference currency, the derivative must be converted into the reference currency by multiplication with the relevant exchange rate.

12. The risk positions are to be grouped into hedging sets. For each hedging set, the absolute value amount of the sum of the resulting risk positions is computed. This sum is termed the 'net risk position' and is represented by:

$$\left| \sum_i RPT_{ij} - \sum_l RPC_{lj} \right|$$

in the formulae set out in paragraph 1.

13. For interest rate risk positions from money deposits received from the counterparty as collateral, from payment legs and from underlying debt instruments, to which according to Table 1 of Annex I to Directive 2006/49/EC a capital charge of 1.60% or less applies, there are six hedging sets for each currency, as set out in Table 4 below. Hedging sets are defined by a combination of the criteria 'maturity' and 'referenced interest rates'.

Table 4

	Government referenced interest rates	Non-government referenced interest rates
Maturity	← 1 year	← 1 year
Maturity	>1— ← 5 years	>1— ← 5 years
Maturity	>5 years	>5 years

14. For interest rate risk positions from underlying debt instruments or payment legs for which the interest rate is linked to a reference interest rate that represents a general market interest level, the remaining maturity is the length of the time interval up to the next re-adjustment of the interest rate. In all other cases, it is the remaining life of the underlying debt instrument or in the case of a payment leg, the remaining life of the transaction.

15. There is one hedging set for each issuer of a reference debt instrument that underlies a credit default swap.

16. For interest rate risk positions from money deposits that are posted with a counterparty as collateral when that counterparty does not have debt obligations of low specific risk outstanding and from underlying debt instruments, to which according to Table 1 of Annex I to Directive 2006/49/EC a capital charge of more than 1.60% applies, there is one hedging set for each issuer. When a payment leg emulates such a debt instrument, there is also one hedging set for each issuer of the reference debt instrument. Credit institutions may assign risk positions that arise from debt instruments of a certain issuer, or from reference debt instruments of the same issuer that are emulated by payment legs, or that underlie a credit default swap, to the same hedging set.

17. Underlying financial instruments other than debt instruments shall be assigned to the same respective hedging sets only if they are identical or similar instruments. In all other cases they shall be assigned to separate hedging sets. The similarity of instruments is established as follows:
– for equities, similar instruments are those of the same issuer. An equity index is treated as a separate issuer;
– for precious metals, similar instruments are those of the same metal. A precious metal index is treated as a separate precious metal;
– for electric power, similar instruments are those delivery rights and obligations that refer to the same peak or off-peak load time interval within any 24-hour interval; and
– for commodities, similar instruments are those of the same commodity. A commodity index is treated as a separate commodity.

18. The CCR multipliers (CCRM) for the different hedging set categories are set out in Table 5 below:

Table 5

	Hedging set categories	CCRM
1.	Interest Rates	0.2%
2.	Interest Rates for risk positions from a reference debt instrument that underlies a credit default swap and to which a capital charge of 1.60%, or less, applies under Table 1 of Annex I to Directive 2006/49/EC	0.3%
3.	Interest Rates for risk positions from a debt instrument or reference debt instrument to which a capital charge of more than 1.60% applies under Table 1 of Annex I to Directive 2006/49/EC	0.6%
4.	Exchange Rates	2.5%
5.	Electric Power	4%
6.	Gold	5%
7.	Equity	7%
8.	Precious Metals (except gold)	8.5%
9.	Other Commodities (excluding precious metals and electricity power)	10%
10.	Underlying instruments of OTC derivatives that are not in any of the above categories	10%

Underlying instruments of OTC derivatives, as referred to in point 10 of Table 5, shall be assigned to separate individual hedging sets for each category of underlying instrument.

19. For transactions with a non-linear risk profile or for payment legs and transactions with debt instruments as underlying for which the credit institution cannot determine the delta or the modified duration, respectively, with an instrument model that the competent authority has approved for the purposes of determining the minimum capital requirements for market risk, the competent authority shall determine the size of the risk positions and the applicable CCRMs conservatively. Alternatively, competent authorities may require the use of the method set out in Part 3. Netting shall not be recognised (that is, the exposure value shall be determined as if there were a netting set that comprises just the individual transaction).

20. A credit institution shall have internal procedures to verify that, prior to including a transaction in a hedging set, the transaction is covered by a legally enforceable netting contract that meets the requirements set out in Part 7.

21. A credit institution that makes use of collateral to mitigate its CCR shall have internal procedures to verify that, prior to recognising the effect of collateral in its calculations, the collateral meets the legal certainty standards set out in Annex VIII.

Part 6

Internal Model Method

1. Subject to the approval of the competent authorities, a credit institution may use the Internal Model Method (IMM) to calculate the exposure value for the transactions in Part 2, paragraph 2(i), or for the transactions in Part 2, point 2(ii), (iii) and (iv), or for the transactions in Part 2, point 2(i) to (iv). In each of these cases the transactions in Part 2, point 2(v) may be included as well. Notwithstanding Part 2, point 1, second paragraph, credit institutions may choose not to apply this method to exposures that are immaterial in size and risk.

To apply the IMM, a credit institution shall meet the requirements set out in this Part.

2. Subject to the approval of the competent authorities, implementation of the IMM may be carried out sequentially across different transaction types, and during this period a credit institution may use the methods set out in Part 3 or Part 5. Notwithstanding the remainder of this Part, credit institutions shall not be required to use a specific type of model.

3. For all OTC derivative transactions and for long settlement transactions for which a credit institution has not received approval to use the IMM, the credit institution shall use the methods set out in Part 3 or Part 5. Combined use of these two methods is permitted on a permanent basis within a group. Combined use of these two methods within a legal entity is only permitted where one of the methods is used for the cases set out in Part 5, point 19.

4. Credit institutions which have obtained permission to use the IMM shall not revert to the use of the methods set out in Part 3 or Part 5 except for demonstrated good cause and subject to approval of the competent authorities. If a credit institution ceases to comply with the requirements set out in this Part, it shall either present to the competent authority a plan for a timely return to compliance or demonstrate that the effect of non-compliance is immaterial.

Exposure value

5. The exposure value shall be measured at the level of the netting set. The model shall specify the forecasting distribution for changes in the market value of the netting set attributable to changes in market variables, such as interest rates, foreign exchange rates. The model shall then compute the exposure value for the netting set at each future date given the changes in the market variables. For margined counterparties, the model may also capture future collateral movements.

6. Credit institutions may include eligible financial collateral as defined in point 11 of Part 1 of Annex VIII to this Directive and point 9 of

Annex II to Directive 2006/49/EC in their forecasting distributions for changes in the market value of the netting set, if the quantitative, qualitative and data requirements for the IMM are met for the collateral.

7. The exposure value shall be calculated as the product of α times Effective EPE, as follows:

Exposure value = α x Effective EPE

where:

alpha (α) shall be 1.4, but competent authorities may require a higher α, and Effective EPE shall be computed by estimating expected exposure (EEt) as the average exposure at future date t, where the average is taken across possible future values of relevant market risk factors. The model estimates EE at a series of future dates t1, t2, t3, etc.

8. Effective EE shall be computed recursively as:

Effective EEtk = max(Effective EEtk−1; EEtk)

where:

the current date is denoted as t0 and Effective EEt0 equals current exposure.

9. In this regard, Effective EPE is the average Effective EE during the first year of future exposure. If all contracts in the netting set mature within less than one year, EPE is the average of EE until all contracts in the netting set mature. Effective EPE is computed as a weighted average of Effective EE:

$$\text{EffectiveEPE} = \sum_{k=1}^{\min(1\ year\ maturity)} \text{EffectiveEE}^*_{lk}\, \Delta t_k$$

where:

the weights $\Delta t_k = t_k - t_{k-1}$ allow for the case when future exposure is calculated at dates that are not equally spaced over time.

10. EE or peak exposure measures shall be calculated based on a distribution of exposures that accounts for the possible non-normality of the distribution of exposures.

11. Credit institutions may use a measure that is more conservative than Éø multiplied by Effective EPE as calculated according to the equation above for every counterparty.

12. Notwithstanding point 7, competent authorities may permit credit institutions to use their own estimates of Éø, subject to a floor of 1.2, where Éø shall equal the ratio of internal capital from a full simulation of CCR exposure across counterparties (numerator) and internal capital based on EPE (denominator). In the denominator, EPE shall be used as if it were a fixed outstanding amount. Credit institutions shall demonstrate that their internal estimates of Éø capture in the numerator material sources of stochastic dependency of distribution of market values of transactions or of portfolios of transactions across counterparties. Internal estimates of Éø shall take account of the granularity of portfolios.

13. A credit institution shall ensure that the numerator and denominator of Éø are computed in a consistent fashion with respect to the modelling methodology, parameter specifications and portfolio composition. The approach used shall be based on the credit institution's internal capital approach, be well documented and be subject to independent validation. In addition, credit institutions shall review their estimates on at least a quarterly basis, and more frequently when the composition of the portfolio varies over time. Credit institutions shall also assess the model risk.

14. Where appropriate, volatilities and correlations of market risk factors used in the joint simulation of market and credit risk should be conditioned on the credit risk factor to reflect potential increases in volatility or correlation in an economic downturn.

15. If the netting set is subject to a margin agreement, credit institutions shall use one of the following EPE measures:

(a) Effective EPE without taking into account the margin agreement;

(b) the threshold, if positive, under the margin agreement plus an add-on that reflects the potential increase in exposure over the margin period of risk. The add-on is computed as the expected increase in the netting set's exposure beginning from a current exposure of zero over the margin period of risk. A floor of five business days for netting sets consisting only of repo-style transactions subject to daily remargining and daily mark-to-market, and ten business days for all other netting sets is imposed on the margin period of risk used for this purpose; or

(c) if the model captures the effects of margining when estimating EE, the model's EE measure may be used directly in the equation in point 8 subject to the approval of the competent authorities.

Minimum requirements for EPE models

16. A credit institution's EPE model shall meet the operational requirements set out in points 17 to 41.

CCR control

17. The credit institution shall have a control unit that is responsible for the design and implementation of its CCR management system, including the initial and on-going validation of the model. This unit shall control input data integrity and produce and analyse reports on the output of the credit institution's risk measurement model, including an evaluation of the relationship between measures of risk exposure and credit and trading limits. This unit shall be independent from units responsible for originating, renewing or trading exposures and free from undue influence; it shall be adequately staffed; it shall report directly to the senior management of the credit institution. The work of this unit shall be closely integrated into the day-to-day credit risk management process of the credit institution. Its output shall, accordingly, be an integral Part of the process of planning, monitoring and controlling the credit institution's credit and overall risk profile.

18. A credit institution shall have CCR management policies, processes and systems that are conceptually sound and implemented with integrity. A sound CCR management framework shall include the identification, measurement, management, approval and internal reporting of CCR.

19. A credit institution's risk management policies shall take account of market, liquidity, and legal and operational risks that can be associated with CCR. The credit institution shall not undertake business with a counterparty without assessing its creditworthiness and shall take due account of settlement and pre-settlement credit risk. These risks shall be managed as comprehensively as practicable at the counterparty level (aggregating CCR exposures with other credit exposures) and at the firm-wide level.

20. A credit institution's board of directors and senior management shall be actively involved in the CCR control process and shall regard this as an essential aspect of the business to which significant resources need to be devoted. Senior management shall be aware of the limitations and assumptions of the model used and the impact these can have on the reliability of the output. Senior management shall also consider the uncertainties of the market environment and operational issues and be aware of how these are reflected in the model.

21. The daily reports prepared on a credit institution's exposures to CCR shall be reviewed by a level of management with sufficient seniority and authority to enforce both reductions of positions taken by individual credit managers or traders and reductions in the credit institution's overall CCR exposure.

22. A credit institution's CCR management system shall be used in conjunction with internal credit and trading limits. Credit and trading limits shall be related to the credit institution's risk measurement model in a manner that is consistent over time and that is well understood by credit managers, traders and senior management.

23. A credit institution's measurement of CCR shall include measuring daily and intra-day usage of credit lines. The credit institution shall measure current exposure gross and net of collateral. At portfolio and counterparty level, the credit institution shall calculate and monitor peak exposure or PFE at the confidence interval chosen by the credit institution. The credit institution shall take account of large or concentrated positions, including by groups of related counterparties, by industry, by market, etc.

24. A credit institution shall have a routine and rigorous programme of stress testing in place as a supplement to the CCR analysis based on the day-to-day output of the credit institution's risk measurement model. The results of this stress testing shall be reviewed periodically by senior management and shall be reflected in the CCR policies and limits set by management and the board of directors. Where stress tests reveal particular vulnerability to a given set of circumstances, prompt steps shall be taken to manage those risks appropriately.

25. A credit institution shall have a routine in place for ensuring compliance with a documented set of internal policies, controls and procedures concerning the operation of the CCR management system. The credit institution's CCR management system shall be well documented and shall provide an explanation of the empirical techniques used to measure CCR.

26. A credit institution shall conduct an independent review of its CCR management system regularly through its own internal auditing process. This review shall include both the activities of the business units referred to in point 17 and of the independent CCR control unit. A review of the overall CCR management process shall take place at regular intervals and shall specifically address, at a minimum:

(a) the adequacy of the documentation of the CCR management system and process;

(b) the organisation of the CCR control unit;

(c) the integration of CCR measures into daily risk management;

(d) the approval process for risk pricing models and valuation systems used by front- and back-office personnel;

(e) the validation of any significant change in the CCR measurement process;

(f) the scope of CCR captured by the risk measurement model;

(g) the integrity of the management information system;

(h) the accuracy and completeness of CCR data;

(i) the verification of the consistency, timeliness and reliability of data sources used to run models, including the independence of such data sources;

(j) the accuracy and appropriateness of volatility and correlation assumptions;

(k) the accuracy of valuation and risk transformation calculations; and

(l) the verification of the model's accuracy through frequent back-testing.

Use test

27. The distribution of exposures generated by the model used to calculate effective EPE shall be closely integrated into the day-to-day CCR management process of the credit institution. The model's output shall accordingly play an essential role in the credit approval, CCR management, internal capital allocation and corporate governance of the credit institution.

28. A credit institution shall have a track record in the use of models that generate a distribution of exposures to CCR. Thus, the credit institution shall demonstrate that it has been using a model to calculate the distributions of exposures upon which the EPE calculation is based that meets, broadly, the minimum requirements set out in this Part for at least one year prior to approval by the competent authorities.

29. The model used to generate a distribution of exposures to CCR shall be Part of a CCR management framework that includes the identification, measurement, management, approval and internal reporting of CCR. This framework shall include the measurement of usage of credit lines (aggregating CCR exposures with other credit exposures) and internal capital allocation. In addition to EPE, a credit institution shall measure and manage current exposures. Where appropriate, the credit institution shall measure current exposure gross and net of collateral. The use test is satisfied if a credit institution uses other CCR measures, such as peak exposure or PFE, based on the distribution of exposures generated by the same model to compute EPE.

30. A credit institution shall have the systems capability to estimate EE daily if necessary, unless it demonstrates to its competent authorities that its exposures to CCR warrant less frequent

calculation. The credit institution shall compute EE along a time profile of forecasting horizons that adequately reflects the time structure of future cash flows and maturity of the contracts and in a manner that is consistent with the materiality and composition of the exposures.

31. Exposure shall be measured, monitored and controlled over the life of all contracts in the netting set (not just to the one-year horizon). The credit institution shall have procedures in place to identify and control the risks for counterparties where the exposure rises beyond the one-year horizon. The forecast increase in exposure shall be an input into the credit institution's internal capital model.

Stress testing

32. A credit institution shall have in place sound stress testing processes for use in the assessment of capital adequacy for CCR. These stress measures shall be compared with the measure of EPE and considered by the credit institution as Part of the process set out in Article 123. Stress testing shall also involve identifying possible events or future changes in economic conditions that could have unfavourable effects on a credit institution's credit exposures and an assessment of the credit institution's ability to withstand such changes.

33. The credit institution shall stress test its CCR exposures, including jointly stressing market and credit risk factors. Stress tests of CCR shall consider concentration risk (to a single counterparty or groups of counterparties), correlation risk across market and credit risk, and the risk that liquidating the counterparty's positions could move the market. Stress tests shall also consider the impact on the credit institution's own positions of such market moves and integrate that impact in its assessment of CCR.

Wrong-Way Risk

34. Credit institutions shall give due consideration to exposures that give rise to a significant degree of General Wrong-Way Risk.

35. Credit institutions shall have procedures in place to identify, monitor and control cases of Specific Wrong-Way Risk, beginning at the inception of a transaction and continuing through the life of the transaction.

Integrity of the modelling process

36. The model shall reflect transaction terms and specifications in a timely, complete, and conservative fashion. Such terms shall include at least contract notional amounts, maturity, reference assets, margining arrangements, netting arrangements. The terms and specifications shall be maintained in a database that is subject to formal and periodic audit. The process for recognising netting arrangements shall require signoff by legal staff to verify the legal enforceability of netting and be input into the database by an independent unit. The transmission of transaction terms and specifications data to the model shall also be subject to internal audit and formal reconciliation processes shall be in place between the model and source data systems to verify on an ongoing basis that transaction terms and specifications are being reflected in EPE correctly or at least conservatively.

37. The model shall employ current market data to compute current exposures. When using historical data to estimate volatility and correlations, at least three years of historical data shall be used and shall be updated quarterly or more frequently if market conditions warrant. The data shall cover a full range of economic conditions, such as a full business cycle. A unit independent from the business unit shall validate the price supplied by the business unit. The data shall be acquired independently of the lines of business, fed into the model in a timely and complete fashion, and maintained in a database subject to formal and periodic audit. A credit institution shall also have a well-developed data integrity process to clean the data of erroneous and/or anomalous observations. To the extent that the model relies on proxy market data, including, for new products, where three years of historical data may not be available, internal policies shall identify suitable proxies and the credit institution shall demonstrate empirically that the proxy provides a conservative representation of the underlying risk under adverse market conditions. If the model includes

the effect of collateral on changes in the market value of the netting set, the credit institution shall have adequate historical data to model the volatility of the collateral.

38. The model shall be subject to a validation process. The process shall be clearly articulated in credit institutions' policies and procedures. The validation process shall specify the kind of testing needed to ensure model integrity and identify conditions under which assumptions are violated and may result in an understatement of EPE. The validation process shall include a review of the comprehensiveness of the model.

39. A credit institution shall monitor the appropriate risks and have processes in place to adjust its estimation of EPE when those risks become significant. This includes the following:

(a) the credit institution shall identify and manage its exposures to specific wrong-way risk;

(b) for exposures with a rising risk profile after one year, the credit institution shall compare on a regular basis the estimate of EPE over one year with EPE over the life of the exposure; and

(c) for exposures with a residual maturity below one year, the credit institution shall compare on a regular basis the replacement cost (current exposure) and the realised exposure profile, and/or store data that would allow such a comparison.

40. A credit institution shall have internal procedures to verify that, prior to including a transaction in a netting set, the transaction is covered by a legally enforceable netting contract that meets the requirements set out in Part 7.

41. A credit institution that makes use of collateral to mitigate its CCR shall have internal procedures to verify that, prior to recognising the effect of collateral in its calculations, the collateral meets the legal certainty standards set out in Annex VIII.

Validation requirements for EPE models

42. A credit institution's EPE model shall meet the following validation requirements:

(a) the qualitative validation requirements set out in Annex V to Directive 2006/49/EC;

(b) interest rates, foreign exchange rates, equity prices, commodities, and other market risk factors shall be forecast over long time horizons for measuring CCR exposure. The performance of the forecasting model for market risk factors shall be validated over a long time horizon;

(c) the pricing models used to calculate CCR exposure for a given scenario of future shocks to market risk factors shall be tested as part of the model validation process. Pricing models for options shall account for the non-linearity of option value with respect to market risk factors;

(d) the EPE model shall capture transaction-specific information in order to aggregate exposures at the level of the netting set. A credit institution shall verify that transactions are assigned to the appropriate netting set within the model;

(e) the EPE model shall also include transaction-specific information to capture the effects of margining. It shall take into account both the current amount of margin and margin that would be passed between counterparties in the future. Such a model shall account for the nature of margin agreements (unilateral or bilateral), the frequency of margin calls, the margin period of risk, the minimum threshold of unmargined exposure the credit institution is willing to accept, and the minimum transfer amount. Such a model shall either model the mark-to-market change in the value of collateral posted or apply the rules set out in Annex VIII; and

(f) static, historical back-testing on representative counterparty portfolios shall be part of the model validation process. At regular intervals, a credit institution shall conduct such back-testing on a number of representative counterparty portfolios (actual or hypothetical). These representative portfolios shall be chosen based on their sensitivity to the material risk factors and correlations to which the credit institution is exposed.

If back-testing indicates that the model is not sufficiently accurate, the competent authorities shall revoke the model approval or impose appropriate measures to ensure that the model is improved promptly. They may also require additional own funds to be held by credit institutions pursuant to Article 136.

Part 7

Contractual Netting (Contracts for Novation and other Netting Agreements)

(a) Types of netting that competent authorities may recognise

For the purpose of this Part, 'counterparty' means any entity (including natural persons) that has the power to conclude a contractual netting agreement and 'contractual cross product netting agreement' means a written bilateral agreement between a credit institution and a counterparty which creates a single legal obligation covering all included bilateral master agreements and transactions belonging to different product categories. Contractual cross-product netting agreements do not cover netting other than on a bilateral basis.

For the purposes of cross-product netting, the following are considered different product categories:
(i) repurchase transactions, reverse repurchase transactions, securities and commodities lending and borrowing transactions,
(ii) margin lending transactions, and
(iii) the contracts listed in Annex IV.

The competent authorities may recognise as risk-reducing the following types of contractual netting:
(i) bilateral contracts for novation between a credit institution and its counterparty under which mutual claims and obligations are automatically amalgamated in such a way that this novation fixes one single net amount each time novation applies and thus creates a legally binding, single new contract extinguishing former contracts,
(ii) other bilateral agreements between a credit institution and its counterparty, and
(iii) contractual cross-product netting agreements for credit institutions that have received approval by their competent authorities to use the method set out in Part 6, for transactions falling under the scope of that method. Netting across transactions entered by members of a group is not recognised for the purposes of calculating capital requirements.

(b) Conditions for recognition

The competent authorities may recognise contractual netting as risk-reducing only under the following conditions:
(i) a credit institution must have a contractual netting agreement with its counterparty which creates a single legal obligation, covering all included transactions, such that, in the event of a counterparty's failure to perform owing to default, bankruptcy, liquidation or any other similar circumstance, the credit institution would have a claim to receive or an obligation to pay only the net sum of the positive and negative mark-to-market values of included individual transactions,
(ii) a credit institution must have made available to the competent authorities written and reasoned legal opinions to the effect that, in the event of a legal challenge, the relevant courts and administrative authorities would, in the cases described under (i), find that the credit institution's claims and obligations would be limited to the net sum, as described in (i), under:
– the law of the jurisdiction in which the counterparty is incorporated and, if a foreign branch of an undertaking is involved, also under the law of the jurisdiction in which the branch is located,
– the law that governs the individual transactions included, and
– the law that governs any contract or agreement necessary to effect the contractual netting,
(iii) a credit institution must have procedures in place to ensure that the legal validity of its contractual netting is kept under review in the light of possible changes in the relevant laws,
(iv) the credit institution maintains all required documentation in its files,
(v) the effects of netting shall be factored into the credit institution's measurement of each counterparty's aggregate credit risk exposure and the credit institution manages its CCR on such a basis, and
(vi) credit risk to each counterparty is aggregated to arrive at a single legal exposure across

transactions. This aggregation shall be factored into credit limit purposes and internal capital purposes.

The competent authorities must be satisfied, if necessary after consulting the other competent authorities concerned, that the contractual netting is legally valid under the law of each of the relevant jurisdictions. If any of the competent authorities are not satisfied in that respect, the contractual netting agreement will not be recognised as risk-reducing for either of the counterparties.

The competent authorities may accept reasoned legal opinions drawn up by types of contractual netting.

No contract containing a provision which permits a non-defaulting counterparty to make limited payments only, or no payments at all, to the estate of the defaulter, even if the defaulter is a net creditor (a 'walkaway' clause), may be recognised as risk-reducing.

In addition, for contractual cross-product netting agreements the following criteria shall be met:

(a) the net sum referred to in subpoint (b)(i) of this Part shall be the net sum of the positive and negative close out values of any included individual bilateral master agreement and of the positive and negative mark-to-market value of the individual transactions (the 'Cross-Product Net Amount');

(b) the written and reasoned legal opinions referred to in subpoint (b)(ii) of this Part shall address the validity and enforceability of the entire contractual cross-product netting agreement under its terms and the impact of the netting arrangement on the material provisions of any included individual bilateral master agreement. A legal opinion shall be generally recognised as such by the legal community in the Member State in which the credit institution is authorised or a memorandum of law that addresses all relevant issues in a reasoned manner;

(c) the credit institution shall have procedures in place under subpoint (b)(iii) of this Part to verify that any transaction which is to be included in a netting set is covered by a legal opinion; and

(d) taking into account the contractual cross-product netting agreement, the credit institution shall continue to comply with the requirements for the recognition of bilateral netting and the requirements of Articles 90 to 93 for the recognition of credit risk mitigation, as applicable, with respect to each included individual bilateral master agreement and transaction.

(c) Effects of recognition

Netting for the purposes of Parts 5 and 6 shall be recognised as set out therein.

(i) Contracts for novation

The single net amounts fixed by contracts for novation, rather than the gross amounts involved, may be weighted. Thus, in the application of Part 3, in:

– step (a): the current replacement cost, and in

– step (b): the notional principal amounts or underlying values

may be obtained taking account of the contract for novation. In the application of Part 4, in step (a) the notional principal amount may be calculated taking account of the contract for novation; the percentages of Table 3 must apply.

(ii) Other netting agreements

In application of Part 3:

– in step (a) the current replacement cost for the contracts included in a netting agreement may be obtained by taking account of the actual hypothetical net replacement cost which results from the agreement; in the case where netting leads to a net obligation for the credit institution calculating the net replacement cost, the current replacement cost is calculated as '0', and

– in step (b) the figure for potential future credit exposure for all contracts included in a netting agreement may be reduced according to the following formula:

$$PCE_{red} = 0.4 * PCE_{gross} + 0.6 * NGR * PCE_{gross}$$

where:

– PCE_{red} = the reduced figure for potential future credit exposure for all contracts with a

given counterparty included in a legally valid bilateral netting agreement
- PCEgross = the sum of the figures for potential future credit exposure for all contracts with a given counterparty which are included in a legally valid bilateral netting agreement and are calculated by multiplying their notional principal amounts by the percentages set out in Table 1
- NGR = 'net-to-gross ratio': at the discretion of the competent authorities either:
(i) separate calculation: the quotient of the net replacement cost for all contracts included in a legally valid bilateral netting agreement with a given counterparty (numerator) and the gross replacement cost for all contracts included in a legally valid bilateral netting agreement with that counterparty (denominator), or
(ii) aggregate calculation: the quotient of the sum of the net replacement cost calculated on a bilateral basis for all counterparties taking into account the contracts included in legally valid netting agreements (numerator) and the gross replacement cost for all contracts included in legally valid netting agreements (denominator).

If Member States permit credit institutions a choice of methods, the method chosen is to be used consistently.

For the calculation of the potential future credit exposure according to the above formula perfectly matching contracts included in the netting agreement may be taken into account as a single contract with a notional principal equivalent to the net receipts. Perfectly matching contracts are forward foreign-exchange contracts or similar contracts in which a notional principal is equivalent to cash flows if the cash flows fall due on the same value date and fully or partly in the same currency.

In the application of Part 4, in step (a)
- perfectly matching contracts included in the netting agreement may be taken into account as a single contract with a notional principal equivalent to the net receipts, the notional principal amounts are multiplied by the percentages given in Table 3, and
- for all other contracts included in a netting agreement, the percentages applicable may be reduced as indicated in Table 6:

Table 6

Original maturity[34]	Interest-rate contracts	Foreign-exchange contracts
One year or less	0.35%	1.50%
More than one year but not more than two years	0.75%	3.75%
Additional allowance for each additional year	0.75%	2.25%

Annex IV

Types of Derivatives

1. Interest-rate contracts:
(a) single-currency interest rate swaps;
(b) basis-swaps;
(c) forward rate agreements;
(d) interest-rate futures;
(e) interest-rate options purchased; and
(f) other contracts of similar nature.

2. Foreign-exchange contracts and contracts concerning gold:

(a) cross-currency interest-rate swaps;
(b) forward foreign-exchange contracts;
(c) currency futures;
(d) currency options purchased;
(e) other contracts of a similar nature; and
(f) contracts concerning gold of a nature similar to (a) to (e).

---

[34] In the case of interest-rate contracts, credit institutions may, subject to the consent of their competent authorities, choose either original or residual maturity.

3. Contracts of a nature similar to those in points 1(a) to (e) and 2(a) to (d) concerning other reference items or indices. This includes as a minimum all instruments specified in points 4 to 7, 9 and 10 of Section C of Annex I to Directive 2004/39/EC not otherwise included in points 1 or 2.

Annex V

Technical Criteria Concerning the Organisation and Treatment of Risks

1. Governance

1. Arrangements shall be defined by the management body described in Article 11 concerning the segregation of duties in the organisation and the prevention of conflicts of interest.

2. Treatment of Risks

2. The management body described in Article 11 shall approve and periodically review the strategies and policies for taking up, managing, monitoring and mitigating the risks the credit institution is or might be exposed to, including those posed by the macroeconomic environment in which it operates in relation to the status of the business cycle.

3. Credit and Counterparty Risk

3. Credit-granting shall be based on sound and well-defined criteria. The process for approving, amending, renewing, and re-financing credits shall be clearly established.

4. The ongoing administration and monitoring of their various credit risk-bearing portfolios and exposures, including for identifying and managing problem credits and for making adequate value adjustments and provisions, shall be operated through effective systems.

5. Diversification of credit portfolios shall be adequate given the credit institution's target markets and overall credit strategy.

4. Residual Risk

6. The risk that recognised credit risk mitigation techniques used by the credit institution prove less effective than expected shall be addressed and controlled by means of written policies and procedures.

5. Concentration Risk

7. The concentration risk arising from exposures to counterparties, groups of connected counterparties, and counterparties in the same economic sector, geographic region or from the same activity or commodity, the application of credit risk mitigation techniques, and including in particular risks associated with large indirect credit exposures (e.g. to a single collateral issuer), shall be addressed and controlled by means of written policies and procedures.

6. Securitisation Risk

8. The risks arising from securitisation transactions in relation to which the credit institutions are originator or sponsor shall be evaluated and addressed through appropriate policies and procedures, to ensure in particular that the economic substance of the transaction is fully reflected in the risk assessment and management decisions.

9. Liquidity plans to address the implications of both scheduled and early amortization shall exist at credit institutions which are originators of

7. MARKET RISK

10. Policies and processes for the measurement and management of all material sources and effects of market risks shall be implemented.

8. INTEREST RATE RISK ARISING FROM NON-TRADING ACTIVITIES

11. Systems shall be implemented to evaluate and manage the risk arising from potential changes in interest rates as they affect a credit institution's non-trading activities.

9. OPERATIONAL RISK

12. Policies and processes to evaluate and manage the exposure to operational risk, including to low-frequency high-severity events, shall be implemented. Without prejudice to the definition laid down in Article 4(22), credit institutions shall articulate what constitutes operational risk for the purposes of those policies and procedures.

13. Contingency and business continuity plans shall be in place to ensure a credit institution's ability to operate on an ongoing basis and limit losses in the event of severe business disruption.

10. LIQUIDITY RISK

14. Policies and processes for the measurement and management of their net funding position and requirements on an ongoing and forward-looking basis shall exist. Alternative scenarios shall be considered and the assumptions underpinning decisions concerning the net funding position shall be reviewed regularly.

15. Contingency plans to deal with liquidity crises shall be in place.

Annex VI

Standardised Approach

PART 1

Risk Weights

1. EXPOSURES TO CENTRAL GOVERNMENTS OR CENTRAL BANKS

1.1. Treatment

1. Without prejudice to points 2 to 7, exposures to central governments and central banks shall be assigned a 100% risk weight.

2. Subject to point 3, exposures to central governments and central banks for which a credit assessment by a nominated ECAI is available shall be assigned a risk weight according to Table 1 in accordance with the assignment by the competent authorities of the credit assessments of eligible ECAIs to six steps in a credit quality assessment scale.

3. Exposures to the European Central Bank shall be assigned a 0% risk weight.

Table 1

Credit quality step	1	2	3	4	5	6
Risk weight	0%	20%	50%	100%	100%	150%

1.2. Exposures in the national currency of the borrower

4. Exposures to Member States' central governments and central banks denominated and funded in the domestic currency of that central government and central bank shall be assigned a risk weight of 0%.

5. When the competent authorities of a third country which apply supervisory and regulatory arrangements at least equivalent to those applied in the Community assign a risk weight which is lower than that indicated in point 1 to 2 to exposures to their central government and central bank denominated and funded in the domestic currency, Member States may allow their credit institutions to risk weight such exposures in the same manner.

1.3. Use of credit assessments by Export Credit Agencies

6. Export Credit Agency credit assessments shall be recognised by the competent authorities if either of the following conditions is met:

(a) it is a consensus risk score from Export Credit Agencies participating in the OECD 'Arrangement on Guidelines for Officially Supported Export Credits'; or

(b) the Export Credit Agency publishes its credit assessments, and the Export Credit Agency subscribes to the OECD agreed methodology, and the credit assessment is associated with one of the eight minimum export insurance premiums (MEIP) that the OECD agreed methodology establishes.

7. Exposures for which a credit assessment by an Export Credit Agency is recognised for risk weighting purposes shall be assigned a risk weight according to Table 2.

2. EXPOSURES TO REGIONAL GOVERNMENTS OR LOCAL AUTHORITIES

8. Without prejudice to points 9 to 11, exposures to regional governments and local authorities shall be risk weighted as exposures to institutions. This treatment is independent of the exercise of discretion as specified in Article 80(3). The preferential treatment for short-term exposures specified in points 31, 32 and 37 shall not be applied.

9. Exposures to regional governments and local authorities shall be treated as exposures to the central government in whose jurisdiction they are established where there is no difference in risk between such exposures because of the specific revenue-raising powers of the former, and the existence of specific institutional arrangements the effect of which is to reduce their risk of default.

Competent authorities shall draw up and make public the list of the regional governments and local authorities to be risk-weighted like central governments.

10. Exposures to churches and religious communities constituted in the form of a legal person under public law shall, in so far as they raise taxes in accordance with legislation conferring on them the right to do so, be treated as exposures to regional governments and local authorities, except that point 9 shall not apply. In this case for the purposes of Article 89(1)(a), permission to apply Title V, Chapter 2, Section 3, subsection 1 shall not be excluded.

11. When competent authorities of a third country jurisdiction which apply supervisory and regulatory arrangements at least equivalent to those applied in the Community treat exposures to regional governments and local authorities as

Table 2

MEIP	0	1	2	3	4	5	6	7
Risk weight	0%	0%	20%	50%	100%	100%	150%	150%

exposures to their central government, Member States may allow their credit institutions to risk weight exposures to such regional governments and local authorities in the same manner.

3. EXPOSURES TO ADMINISTRATIVE BODIES AND NON-COMMERCIAL UNDERTAKINGS

3.1. Treatment

12. Without prejudice to points 13 to 17, exposures to administrative bodies and non-commercial undertakings shall be assigned a 100% risk weight.

3.2. Public Sector Entities

13. Without prejudice to points 14 to 17, exposures to public sector entities shall be assigned a 100% risk weight.

14. Subject to the discretion of competent authorities, exposures to public sector entities may be treated as exposures to institutions. Exercise of this discretion by competent authorities is independent of the exercise of discretion as specified in Article 80(3). The preferential treatment for short-term exposures specified in points 31, 32 and 37 shall not be applied.

15. In exceptional circumstances, exposures to public sector entities may be treated as exposures to the central government in whose jurisdiction they are established where in the opinion of the competent authorities there is no difference in risk between such exposures because of the existence of an appropriate guarantee by the central government.

16. When the discretion to treat exposures to public sector entities as exposures to institutions or as exposures to the central government in whose jurisdiction they are established is exercised by the competent authorities of one Member State, the competent authorities of another Member State shall allow their credit institutions to risk-weight exposures to such public sector entities in the same manner.

17. When competent authorities of a third country jurisdiction, which apply supervisory and regulatory arrangements at least equivalent to those applied in the Community, treat exposures to public sector entities as exposures to institutions, Member States may allow their credit institutions to risk weight exposures to such public sector entities in the same manner.

4. EXPOSURES TO MULTILATERAL DEVELOPMENT BANKS

4.1. Scope

18. For the purposes of Articles 78 to 83, the Inter-American Investment Corporation, the Black Sea Trade and Development Bank and the Central American Bank for Economic Integration are considered to be Multilateral Development Banks (MDB).

4.2. Treatment

19. Without prejudice to points 20 and 21, exposures to multilateral development banks shall be treated in the same manner as exposures to institutions in accordance with points 29 to 32. The preferential treatment for short-term exposures as specified in points 31, 32 and 37 shall not apply.

20. Exposures to the following multilateral development banks shall be assigned a 0% risk weight:

(a) the International Bank for Reconstruction and Development;

(b) the International Finance Corporation;

(c) the Inter-American Development Bank;

(d) the Asian Development Bank;

(e) the African Development Bank;

(f) the Council of Europe Development Bank;

(g) the Nordic Investment Bank;

(h) the Caribbean Development Bank;

(i) the European Bank for Reconstruction and Development;

(j) the European Investment Bank;

(k) the European Investment Fund; and

(l) the Multilateral Investment Guarantee Agency.

21. A risk weight of 20% shall be assigned to the portion of unpaid capital subscribed to the European Investment Fund.

5. Exposures to International Organisations

22. Exposures to the following international organisations shall be assigned a 0% risk weight:

(a) the European Community;

(b) the International Monetary Fund;

(c) the Bank for International Settlements.

6. Exposures to Institutions

6.1. Treatment

23. One of the two methods described in points 26 to 27 and 29 to 32 shall apply in determining the risk weights for exposures to institutions.

24. Without prejudice to the other provisions of points 23 to 39, exposures to financial institutions authorised and supervised by the competent authorities responsible for the authorisation and supervision of credit institutions and subject to prudential requirements equivalent to those applied to credit institutions shall be risk-weighted as exposures to institutions.

6.2. Risk-weight floor on exposures to unrated institutions

25. Exposures to an unrated institution shall not be assigned a risk weight lower than that applied to exposures to its central government.

6.3. Central government risk-weight based method

26. Exposures to institutions shall be assigned a risk weight according to the credit quality step to which exposures to the central government of the jurisdiction in which the institution is incorporated are assigned in accordance with Table 3.

27. For exposures to institutions incorporated in countries where the central government is unrated, the risk weight shall be not more than 100%.

28. For exposures to institutions with an original effective maturity of three months or less, the risk weight shall be 20%.

6.4. Credit assessment based method

29. Exposures to institutions with an original effective maturity of more than three months for which a credit assessment by a nominated ECAI is available shall be assigned a risk weight according to Table 4 in accordance with the assignment by the competent authorities of the credit assessments of eligible ECAIs to six steps in a credit quality assessment scale.

30. Exposures to unrated institutions shall be assigned a risk weight of 50%.

Table 3

Credit quality step to which central government is assigned	1	2	3	4	5	6
Risk weight of exposure	20%	50%	100%	100%	100%	150%

Table 4

Credit quality step	1	2	3	4	5	6
Risk weight	20%	50%	50%	100%	100%	150%

Table 5

Credit quality step	1	2	3	4	5	6
Risk weight	20%	20%	20%	50%	50%	150%

31. Exposures to an institution with an original effective maturity of three months or less for which a credit assessment by a nominated ECAI is available shall be assigned a risk weight according to Table 5 in accordance with the assignment by the competent authorities of the credit assessments of eligible ECAIs to six steps in a credit quality assessment scale:

32. Exposures to unrated institutions having an original effective maturity of three months or less shall be assigned a 20% risk weight.

6.5. Interaction with short-term credit assessments

33. If the method specified in points 29 to 32 is applied to exposures to institutions, then the interaction with specific short-term assessments shall be as follows.

34. If there is no short-term exposure assessment, the general preferential treatment for short-term exposures as specified in point 31 shall apply to all exposures to institutions of up to three months residual maturity.

35. If there is a short-term assessment and such an assessment determines the application of a more favourable or identical risk weight than the use of the general preferential treatment for short-term exposures, as specified in point 31, then the short-term assessment shall be used for that specific exposure only. Other short-term exposures shall follow the general preferential treatment for short-term exposures, as specified in point 31.

36. If there is a short-term assessment and such an assessment determines a less favourable risk weight than the use of the general preferential treatment for short-term exposures, as specified in point 31, then the general preferential treatment for short-term exposures shall not be used and all unrated short-term claims shall be assigned the same risk weight as that applied by the specific short-term assessment.

6.6. Short-term exposures in the national currency of the borrower

37. Exposures to institutions of a residual maturity of 3 months or less denominated and funded in the national currency may, subject to the discretion of the competent authority, be assigned, under both methods described in points 26 to 27 and 29 to 32, a risk weight that is one category less favourable than the preferential risk weight, as described in points 4 and 5, assigned to exposures to its central government.

38. No exposures of a residual maturity of 3 months or less denominated and funded in the national currency of the borrower shall be assigned a risk weight less than 20%.

6.7 Investments in regulatory capital instruments

39. Investments in equity or regulatory capital instruments issued by institutions shall be risk weighted at 100%, unless deducted from the own funds.

6.8 Minimum reserves required by the ECB

40. Where an exposure to an institution is in the form of minimum reserves required by the ECB or by the central bank of a Member State to be held by the credit institution, Member States may permit the assignment of the risk weight that would be assigned to exposures to the central bank of the Member State in question provided:

(a) the reserves are held in accordance with Regulation (EC) No 1745/2003 of the European

Table 6

Credit quality step	1	2	3	4	5	6
Risk weight	20%	50%	100%	100%	150%	150%

Central Bank of 12 September 2003 on the application of minimum reserves[35] or a subsequent replacement regulation or in accordance with national requirements in all material respects equivalent to that Regulation; and

(b) in the event of the bankruptcy or insolvency of the institution where the reserves are held, the reserves are fully repaid to the credit institution in a timely manner and are not made available to meet other liabilities of the institution.

7. Exposures to Corporates

7.1. Treatment

41. Exposures for which a credit assessment by a nominated ECAI is available shall be assigned a risk weight according to Table 6 in accordance with the assignment by the competent authorities of the credit assessments of eligible ECAIs to six steps in a credit quality assessment scale.

42. Exposures for which such a credit assessment is not available shall be assigned a 100% risk weight or the risk weight of its central government, whichever is the higher.

8. Retail Exposures

43. Exposures that comply with the criteria listed in Article 79(2) shall be assigned a risk weight of 75%.

9. Exposures Secured by Real Estate Property

44. Without prejudice to points 45 to 60, exposures fully secured by real estate property shall be assigned a risk weight of 100%.

---

[35] OJ L 250, 2.10.2003, 10.

9.1. Exposures secured by mortgages on residential property

45. Exposures or any part of an exposure fully and completely secured, to the satisfaction of the competent authorities, by mortgages on residential property which is or shall be occupied or let by the owner, or the beneficial owner in the case of personal investment companies, shall be assigned a risk weight of 35%.

46. Exposures fully and completely secured, to the satisfaction of the competent authorities, by shares in Finnish residential housing companies, operating in accordance with the Finnish Housing Company Act of 1991 or subsequent equivalent legislation, in respect of residential property which is or shall be occupied or let by the owner shall be assigned a risk weight of 35%.

47. Exposures to a tenant under a property leasing transaction concerning residential property under which the credit institution is the lessor and the tenant has an option to purchase, shall be assigned a risk weight of 35% provided that the competent authorities are satisfied that the exposure of the credit institution is fully and completely secured by its ownership of the property.

48. In the exercise of their judgement for the purposes of points 45 to 47, competent authorities shall be satisfied only if the following conditions are met:

(a) the value of the property does not materially depend upon the credit quality of the obligor. This requirement does not preclude situations where purely macro-economic factors affect both the value of the property and the performance of the borrower;

(b) the risk of the borrower does not materially depend upon the performance of the underlying property or project, but rather on the underlying capacity of the borrower to repay the debt from other sources. As such, repayment of the facility does not materially depend on any cash flow generated by the underlying property serving as collateral;

(c) the minimum requirements set out in Annex VIII, Part 2, point 8 and the valuation rules set out in Annex VIII, Part 3, points 62 to 65 are met; and

(d) the value of the property exceeds the exposures by a substantial margin.

49. Competent authorities may dispense with the condition contained in point 48(b) for exposures fully and completely secured by mortgages on residential property which is situated within their territory, if they have evidence that a well-developed and long-established residential real estate market is present in their territory with loss rates which are sufficiently low to justify such treatment.

50. When the discretion contained in point 49 is exercised by the competent authorities of a Member State, the competent authorities of another Member State may allow their credit institutions to assign a risk weight of 35% to such exposures fully and completely secured by mortgages on residential property.

9.2. Exposures secured by mortgages on commercial real estate

51. Subject to the discretion of the competent authorities, exposures or any part of an exposure fully and completely secured, to the satisfaction of the competent authorities, by mortgages on offices or other commercial premises situated within their territory may be assigned a risk weight of 50%.

52. Subject to the discretion of the competent authorities, exposures fully and completely secured, to the satisfaction of the competent authorities, by shares in Finnish housing companies, operating in accordance with the Finnish Housing Company Act of 1991 or subsequent equivalent legislation, in respect of offices or other commercial premises may be assigned a risk weight of 50%.

53. Subject to the discretion of the competent authorities, exposures related to property leasing transactions concerning offices or other commercial premises situated in their territories under which the credit institution is the lessor and the tenant has an option to purchase may be assigned a risk weight of 50% provided that the exposure of the credit institution is fully and completely secured to the satisfaction of the competent authorities by its ownership of the property.

54. The application of points 51 to 53 is subject to the following conditions:

(a) the value of the property must not materially depend upon the credit quality of the obligor. This requirement does not preclude situations where purely macro-economic factors affect both the value of the property and the performance of the borrower;

(b) the risk of the borrower must not materially depend upon the performance of the underlying property or project, but rather on the underlying capacity of the borrower to repay the debt from other sources. As such, repayment of the facility must not materially depend on any cash flow generated by the underlying property serving as collateral; and

(c) the minimum requirements set out in Annex VIII, Part 2, point 8, and the valuation rules set out in Annex VIII, Part 3, points 62 to 65 are met.

55. The 50% risk weight shall be assigned to the Part of the loan that does not exceed a limit calculated according to either of the following conditions:

(a) 50% of the market value of the property in question;

(b) 50% of the market value of the property or 60% of the mortgage lending value, whichever is lower, in those Member States that have laid down rigorous criteria for the assessment of the mortgage lending value in statutory or regulatory provisions.

56. A 100% risk weight shall be assigned to the Part of the loan that exceeds the limits set out in point 55.

57. When the discretion contained in points 51 to 53 is exercised by the competent authorities of one Member State, the competent authorities of another Member State may allow their credit institutions to risk weight at 50% such exposures fully and completely secured by mortgages on commercial property.

58. Competent authorities may dispense with the condition contained in point 54(b) for exposures fully and completely secured by mortgages on commercial property which is situated within their territory, if they have evidence that a well-developed and long-established commercial real estate market is present in their territory with loss-rates which do not exceed the following limits:

(a) losses stemming from lending collateralised by commercial real estate property up to 50% of the market value (or where applicable and if lower 60% of the mortgage lending value (MLV)) do not exceed 0.3% of the outstanding loans collateralised by commercial real estate property in any given year; and

(b) overall losses stemming from lending collateralised by commercial real estate property must not exceed 0.5% of the outstanding loans collateralised by commercial real estate property in any given year.

59. If either of the limits referred to in point 58 is not satisfied in a given year, the eligibility to use point 58 shall cease and the condition contained in point 54(b) shall apply until the conditions in point 58 are satisfied in a subsequent year.

60. When the discretion contained in point 58 is exercised by the competent authorities of a Member State, the competent authorities of another Member State may allow their credit institutions to assign a risk weight of 50% to such exposures fully and completely secured by mortgages on commercial property.

10. Past Due Items

61. Without prejudice to the provisions contained in points 62 to 65, the unsecured part of any item that is past due for more than 90 days and which is above a threshold defined by the competent authorities and which reflects a reasonable level of risk shall be assigned a risk weight of:

(a) 150%, if value adjustments are less than 20% of the unsecured part of the exposure gross of value adjustments; and

(b) 100%, if value adjustments are no less than 20% of the unsecured part of the exposure gross of value adjustments.

62. For the purpose of defining the secured part of the past due item, eligible collateral and guarantees shall be those eligible for credit risk mitigation purposes.

63. Nonetheless, where a past due item is fully secured by forms of collateral other then those eligible for credit risk mitigation purposes, a 100% risk weight may be assigned subject to the discretion of competent authorities based upon strict operational criteria to ensure the good quality of the collateral when value adjustments reach 15% of the exposure gross of value adjustments.

64. Exposures indicated in points 45 to 50 shall be assigned a risk weight of 100% net of value adjustments if they are past due for more than 90 days. If value adjustments are no less than 20% of the exposure gross of value adjustments, the risk weight to be assigned to the remainder of the exposure may be reduced to 50% at the discretion of competent authorities.

65. Exposures indicated in points 51 to 60 shall be assigned a risk weight of 100% if they are past due for more than 90 days.

11. Items Belonging to Regulatory High-Risk Categories

66. Subject to the discretion of competent authorities, exposures associated with particularly high risks such as investments in venture capital firms and private equity investments shall be assigned a risk weight of 150%.

67. Competent authorities may permit non past due items to be assigned a 150% risk weight according to the provisions of this Part and for

which value adjustments have been established to be assigned a risk weight of:

(a) 100%, if value adjustments are no less than 20% of the exposure value gross of value adjustments; and

(b) 50%, if value adjustments are no less than 50% of the exposure value gross of value adjustments.

12. Exposures in the Form of Covered Bonds

68. 'Covered bonds' shall mean bonds as defined in Article 22(4) of Directive 85/611/EEC and collateralised by any of the following eligible assets:

(a) exposures to or guaranteed by central governments, central banks, public sector entities, regional governments and local authorities in the EU;

(b) exposures to or guaranteed by non-EU central governments, non-EU central banks, multilateral development banks, international organisations that qualify for the credit quality step 1 as set out in this Annex, and exposures to or guaranteed by non-EU public sector entities, non-EU regional governments and non-EU local authorities that are risk weighted as exposures to institutions or central governments and central banks according to points 8, 9, 14 or 15 respectively and that qualify for the credit quality step 1 as set out in this Annex, and exposures in the sense of this point that qualify as a minimum for the credit quality step 2 as set out in this Annex, provided that they do not exceed 20% of the nominal amount of outstanding covered bonds of issuing institutions;

(c) exposures to institutions that qualify for the credit quality step 1 as set out in this Annex. The total exposure of this kind shall not exceed 15% of the nominal amount of outstanding covered bonds of the issuing credit institution. Exposures caused by transmission and management of payments of the obligors of, or liquidation proceeds in respect of, loans secured by real estate to the holders of covered bonds shall not be comprised by the 15% limit. Exposures to institutions in the EU with a maturity not exceeding 100 days shall not be comprised by the step 1 requirement but those institutions must as a minimum qualify for credit quality step 2 as set out in this Annex;

(d) loans secured by residential real estate or shares in Finnish residential housing companies as referred to in point 46 up to the lesser of the principal amount of the liens that are combined with any prior liens and 80% of the value of the pledged properties or by senior units issued by French Fonds Communs de Créances or by equivalent securitisation entities governed by the laws of a Member State securitising residential real estate exposures provided that at least 90% of the assets of such Fonds Communs de Créances or of equivalent securitisation entities governed by the laws of a Member State are composed of mortgages that are combined with any prior liens up to the lesser of the principal amounts due under the units, the principal amounts of the liens, and 80% of the value of the pledged properties and the units qualify for the credit quality step 1 as set out in this Annex where such units do not exceed 20% of the nominal amount of the outstanding issue. Exposures caused by transmission and management of payments of the obligors of, or liquidation proceeds in respect of, loans secured by pledged properties of the senior units or debt securities shall not be comprised in calculating the 90% limit;

(e) loans secured by commercial real estate or shares in Finnish housing companies as referred to in point 52 up to the lesser of the principal amount of the liens that are combined with any prior liens and 60% of the value of the pledged properties or by senior units issued by French Fonds Communs de Créances or by equivalent securitisation entities governed by the laws of a Member State securitising commercial real estate exposures provided that, at least, 90% of the assets of such Fonds Communs de Créances or of equivalent securitisation entities governed by the laws of a Member State are composed of mortgages that are combined with any prior liens up to the lesser of the principal amounts due under the units, the principal amounts of the liens, and 60% of the value of the pledged properties and the units qualify for the credit quality step 1 as set out in this Annex where such units do not exceed 20% of the nominal amount of the outstanding issue. The competent authorities may recognise loans secured by commercial real estate as eligible where the Loan to Value ratio of 60% is exceeded up to a maximum level of 70% if the value of the total assets pledged as collateral for the covered bonds exceed the nominal amount outstanding on the covered bond by at least 10%, and the bondholders' claim meets the legal certainty requirements set out in Annex VIII. The bondholders' claim must take priority over all other claims on the collateral. Exposures caused by transmission and management of payments of the obligors of, or liquidation proceeds in respect of, loans secured by pledged properties of the senior units or debt securities shall not be comprised in calculating the 90% limit; or

(f) loans secured by ships where only liens that are combined with any prior liens within 60% of the value of the pledged ship.

For these purposes 'collateralised' includes situations where the assets as described in subpoints (a) to (f) are exclusively dedicated in law to the protection of the bondholders against losses.

Until 31 December 2010 the 20% limit for senior units issued by French Fonds Communs de Créances or by equivalent securitisation entities as specified in subpoints (d) and (e) does not apply, provided that those senior units have a credit assessment by a nominated ECAI which is the most favourable category of credit assessment made by the ECAI in respect of covered bonds. Before the end of this period this derogation shall be reviewed and consequent to such review the Commission may as appropriate extend this period in accordance with the procedure referred to in Article 151(2) with or without a further review clause.

Until 31 December 2010 the figure of 60% indicated in subpoint (f) can be replaced with a figure of 70%. Before the end of this period this derogation shall be reviewed and consequent to such review the Commission may as appropriate extend this period in accordance with the procedure referred to in Article 151(2) with or without a further review clause.

69. Credit institutions shall for real estate collateralising covered bonds meet the minimum requirements set out in Annex VIII Part 2, point 8 and the valuation rules set out in Annex VIII, Part 3, points 62 to 65.

70. Notwithstanding points 68 and 69, covered bonds meeting the definition of Article 22(4) of Directive 85/611/EEC and issued before 31 December 2007 are also eligible for the preferential treatment until their maturity.

71. Covered bonds shall be assigned a risk weight on the basis of the risk weight assigned to senior unsecured exposures to the credit institution which issues them. The following correspondence between risk weights shall apply:

(a) if the exposures to the institution are assigned a risk weight of 20%, the covered bond shall be assigned a risk weight of 10%;

(b) if the exposures to the institution are assigned a risk weight of 50%, the covered bond shall be assigned a risk weight of 20%;

(c) if the exposures to the institution are assigned a risk weight of 100%, the covered bond shall be assigned a risk weight of 50%; and

(d) if the exposures to the institution are assigned a risk weight of 150%, the covered bond shall be assigned a risk weight of 100%.

13. ITEMS REPRESENTING SECURITISATION POSITIONS

72. Risk-weight exposure amounts for securitisation positions shall be determined in accordance with Articles 94 to 101.

14. SHORT-TERM EXPOSURES TO INSTITUTIONS AND CORPORATES

73. Short-term exposures to an institution or corporate for which a credit assessment by a

Table 7

Credit quality step	1	2	3	4	5	6
Risk weight	20%	50%	100%	150%	150%	150%

Table 8

Credit quality step	1	2	3	4	5	6
Risk weight	20%	50%	100%	100%	150%	150%

nominated ECAI is available shall be assigned a risk weight according to Table 7 as follows, in accordance with the mapping by the competent authorities of the credit assessments of eligible ECAIs to six steps in a credit quality assessment scale.

15. Exposures in the Form of Collective Investment Undertakings (CIUs)

74. Without prejudice to points 75 to 81, exposures in collective investment undertakings (CIUs) shall be assigned a risk weight of 100%.

75. Exposures in the form of CIUs for which a credit assessment by a nominated ECAI is available shall be assigned a risk weight according to Table 8, in accordance with the assignment by the competent authorities of the credit assessments of eligible ECAIs to six steps in a credit quality assessment scale.

76. Where competent authorities consider that a position in a CIU is associated with particularly high risks they shall require that that position is assigned a risk weight of 150%.

77. Credit institutions may determine the risk weight for a CIU as set out in points 79 to 81, if the following eligibility criteria are met:

(a) the CIU is managed by a company which is subject to supervision in a Member State or, subject to approval of the credit institution's competent authority, if:
(i) the CIU is managed by a company which is subject to supervision that is considered equivalent to that laid down in Community law; and
(ii) cooperation between competent authorities is sufficiently ensured;

(b) the CIU's prospectus or equivalent document includes:
(i) the categories of assets in which the CIU is authorised to invest; and
(ii) if investment limits apply, the relative limits and the methodologies to calculate them; and

(c) the business of the CIU is reported on at least an annual basis to enable an assessment to be made of the assets and liabilities, income and operations over the reporting period.

78. If a competent authority approves a third country CIU as eligible, as set out in point 77(a), then a competent authority in another Member State may make use of this recognition without conducting its own assessment.

79. Where the credit institution is aware of the underlying exposures of a CIU, it may look through to those underlying exposures in order to calculate an average risk weight for the CIU in accordance with the methods set out in Articles 78 to 83.

80. Where the credit institution is not aware of the underlying exposures of a CIU, it may calculate an average risk weight for the CIU in accordance with the methods set out in Articles 78 to 83 subject to the following rules: it will be assumed that the CIU first invests, to the maximum extent allowed under its mandate, in the exposure classes attracting the highest capital requirement, and then continues making investments in descending

order until the maximum total investment limit is reached.

81. Credit institutions may rely on a third party to calculate and report, in accordance with the methods set out in points 79 and 80, a risk weight for the CIU provided that the correctness of the calculation and report shall be adequately ensured.

16. Other Items

16.1. Treatment

82. Tangible assets within the meaning of Article 4(10) of Directive 86/635/EEC shall be assigned a risk weight of 100%.

83. Prepayments and accrued income for which an institution is unable to determine the counterparty in accordance with Directive 86/635/EEC, shall be assigned a risk weight of 100%.

84. Cash items in the process of collection shall be assigned a 20% risk weight. Cash in hand and equivalent cash items shall be assigned a 0% risk weight.

85. Member States may allow a risk weight of 10% for exposures to institutions specialising in the inter-bank and public-debt markets in their home Member States and subject to close supervision by the competent authorities where those asset items are fully and completely secured, to the satisfaction of the competent authorities of the home Member States, by items assigned a 0% or a 20% risk weight and recognised by the latter as constituting adequate collateral.

86. Holdings of equity and other participations, except where deducted from own funds, shall be assigned a risk weight of at least 100%.

87. Gold bullion held in own vaults or on an allocated basis to the extent backed by bullion liabilities shall be assigned a 0% risk weight.

88. In the case of asset sale and repurchase agreements and outright forward purchases, the risk weight shall be that assigned to the assets in question and not to the counterparties to the transactions.

89. Where a credit institution provides credit protection for a number of exposures under terms that the nth default among the exposures shall trigger payment and that this credit event shall terminate the contract, and where the product has an external credit assessment from an eligible ECAI, the risk weights prescribed in Articles 94 to 101 shall be assigned. If the product is not rated by an eligible ECAI, the risk weights of the exposures included in the basket will be aggregated, excluding n-1 exposures, up to a maximum of 1250% and multiplied by the nominal amount of the protection provided by the credit derivative to obtain the risk-weighted asset amount. The n-1 exposures to be excluded from the aggregation shall be determined on the basis that they shall include those exposures each of which produces a lower risk-weighted exposure amount than the risk-weighted exposure amount of any of the exposures included in the aggregation.

Part 2

Recognition of ECAIs and Mapping of their Credit Assessments

1. Methodology

1.1. Objectivity

1. Competent authorities shall verify that the methodology for assigning credit assessments is rigorous, systematic, continuous and subject to validation based on historical experience.

1.2. Independence

2. Competent authorities shall verify that the methodology is free from external political influences or constraints, and from economic pressures that may influence the credit assessment.

3. Independence of the ECAI's methodology shall be assessed by competent authorities according to factors such as the following:

(a) ownership and organisation structure of the ECAI;

(b) financial resources of the ECAI;

(c) staffing and expertise of the ECAI; and

(d) corporate governance of the ECAI.

1.3. Ongoing review

4. Competent authorities shall verify that ECAI's credit assessments are subject to ongoing review and shall be responsive to changes in the financial conditions. Such review shall take place after all significant events and at least annually.

5. Before any recognition, competent authorities shall verify that the assessment methodology for each market segment is established according to standards such as the following:

(a) the back-testing must be established for at least one year;

(b) the regularity of the review process by the ECAI must be monitored by the competent authorities; and

(c) the competent authorities must be able to receive from the ECAI the extent of its contacts with the senior management of the entities which it rates.

6. Competent authorities shall take the necessary measures to be promptly informed by ECAIs of any material changes in the methodology they use for assigning credit assessments.

1.4. Transparency and disclosure

7. Competent authorities shall take the necessary measures to assure that the principles of the methodology employed by the ECAI for the formulation of its credit assessments are publicly available as to allow all potential users to decide whether they are derived in a reasonable way.

2. INDIVIDUAL CREDIT ASSESSMENTS

2.1. Credibility and market acceptance

8. Competent authorities shall verify that ECAIs' individual credit assessments are recognised in the market as credible and reliable by the users of such credit assessments.

9. Credibility shall be assessed by competent authorities according to factors such as the following:

(a) market share of the ECAI;

(b) revenues generated by the ECAI, and more in general financial resources of the ECAI;

(c) whether there is any pricing on the basis of the rating; and

(d) at least two credit institutions use the ECAI's individual credit assessment for bond issuing and/or assessing credit risks.

2.2. Transparency and disclosure

10. Competent authorities shall verify that individual credit assessments are accessible at equivalent terms at least to all credit institutions having a legitimate interest in these individual credit assessments.

11. In particular, competent authorities shall verify that individual credit assessments are available to non-domestic parties on equivalent terms as to domestic credit institutions having a legitimate interest in these individual credit assessments.

3. 'MAPPING'

12. In order to differentiate between the relative degrees of risk expressed by each credit assessment, competent authorities shall consider quantitative factors such as the long-term default rate associated with all items assigned the same credit assessment. For recently established ECAIs and for those that have compiled only a short record of default data, competent authorities shall ask the ECAI what it believes to be the long-term default rate associated with all items assigned the same credit assessment.

13. In order to differentiate between the relative degrees of risk expressed by each credit assessment, competent authorities shall consider qualitative factors such as the pool of issuers that the ECAI covers, the range of credit assessments that the ECAI assigns, each credit assessment meaning and the ECAI's definition of default.

14. Competent authorities shall compare default rates experienced for each credit assessment of a particular ECAI and compare them with a benchmark built on the basis of default rates experienced by other ECAIs on a population of issuers that the competent authorities believes to present an equivalent level of credit risk.

15. When competent authorities believe that the default rates experienced for the credit assessment of a particular ECAI are materially and systematically higher then the benchmark, competent authorities shall assign a higher credit quality step in the credit quality assessment scale to the ECAI credit assessment.

16. When competent authorities have increased the associated risk weight for a specific credit assessment of a particular ECAI, if the ECAI demonstrates that the default rates experienced for its credit assessment are no longer materially and systematically higher than the benchmark, competent authorities may decide to restore the original credit quality step in the credit quality assessment scale for the ECAI credit assessment.

Part 3

Use of ECAIs' Credit Assessments for the Determination of Risk Weights

1. Treatment

1. A credit institution may nominate one or more eligible ECAIs to be used for the determination of risk weights to be assigned to asset and off-balance-sheet items.

2. A credit institution which decides to use the credit assessments produced by an eligible ECAI for a certain class of items must use those credit assessments consistently for all exposures belonging to that class.

3. A credit institution which decides to use the credit assessments produced by an eligible ECAI must use them in a continuous and consistent way over time.

4. A credit institution can only use ECAIs' credit assessments that take into account all amounts both in principal and in interest owed to it.

5. If only one credit assessment is available from a nominated ECAI for a rated item, that credit assessment shall be used to determine the risk weight for that item.

6. If two credit assessments are available from nominated ECAIs and the two correspond to different risk weights for a rated item, the higher risk weight shall be assigned.

7. If more than two credit assessments are available from nominated ECAIs for a rated item, the two assessments generating the two lowest risk weights shall be referred to. If the two lowest risk weights are different, the higher risk weight shall be assigned. If the two lowest risk weights are the same, that risk weight shall be assigned.

2. Issuer and Issue Credit Assessment

8. Where a credit assessment exists for a specific issuing program or facility to which the item constituting the exposure belongs, this credit assessment shall be used to determine the risk weight to be assigned to that item.

9. Where no directly applicable credit assessment exists for a certain item, but a credit assessment exists for a specific issuing program or facility to which the item constituting the exposure does not belong or a general credit assessment exists for the issuer, then that credit assessment shall be used if it produces a higher risk weight than would otherwise be the case or if it produces a lower risk weight and the exposure in question ranks pari passu or senior in all respects to the specific issuing program or facility or to senior unsecured exposures of that issuer, as relevant.

10. Points 8 and 9 are not to prevent the application of points 68 to 71 of Part 1.

11. Credit assessments for issuers within a corporate group cannot be used as credit assessment of another issuer within the same corporate group.

3. Long-Term and Short-Term Credit Assessments

12. Short-term credit assessments may only be used for short-term asset and off-balance-sheet

items constituting exposures to institutions and corporates.

13. Any short-term credit assessment shall only apply to the item the short-term credit assessment refers to, and it shall not be used to derive risk weights for any other item.

14. Notwithstanding point 13, if a short-term rated facility is assigned a 150% risk weight, then all unrated unsecured exposures on that obligor whether short-term or long-term shall also be assigned a 150% risk weight.

15. Notwithstanding point 13, if a short-term rated facility is assigned a 50% risk weight, no unrated short-term exposure shall be assigned a risk weight lower than 100%.

4. DOMESTIC AND FOREIGN CURRENCY ITEMS

16. A credit assessment that refers to an item denominated in the obligor's domestic currency cannot be used to derive a risk weight for another exposure on that same obligor that is denominated in a foreign currency.

17. Notwithstanding point 16, when an exposure arises through a credit institution's participation in a loan that has been extended by a Multilateral Development Bank whose preferred creditor status is recognised in the market, competent authorities may allow the credit assessment on the obligors' domestic currency item to be used for risk-weighting purposes.

Annex VII

Internal Ratings Based Approach

PART 1

Risk-Weighted Exposure Amounts and Expected Loss Amounts

1. CALCULATION OF RISK WEIGHTED EXPOSURE AMOUNTS FOR CREDIT RISK

1. Unless noted otherwise, the input parameters PD, LGD, and maturity value (M) shall be determined as set out in Part 2 and the exposure value shall be determined as set out in Part 3.

2. The risk-weighted exposure amount for each exposure shall be calculated in accordance with the following formulae:

1.1. Risk-weighted exposure amounts for exposures to corporates, institutions and central governments and central banks

3. Subject to points 5 to 9, the risk-weighted exposure amounts for exposures to corporates, institutions and central governments and central banks shall be calculated according to the following formulae:

Correlation (R) = $0.12 \times (1-\text{EXP}(-50*\text{PD}))/(1-\text{EXP}(-50))+0.24*[1-(1-\text{EXP}(-50*\text{PD}))/(1-\text{EXP}(-50))]$

Looptijdfactor (b) = $(0.11852-0.05478*\ln(\text{PD}))^2$

$(\text{LGD}*N[(1-R)^{-0.5}*G(\text{PD})+(R/(1-R))^{0.5}*G(0.999)]-\text{PD}*\text{LGD})*(1-1.5*b)^{-1}*(1+(M-2.5)*b)*12.5*1.06$

N(x) denotes the cumulative distribution function for a standard normal random variable (i.e. the probability that a normal random variable with mean zero and variance of one is less than or equal to x). G (Z) denotes the inverse cumulative distribution function for a standard normal random variable (i.e. the value x such that N(x) z)

For PD = 0, RW shall be 0.

For PD = 1:
- for defaulted exposures where credit institutions apply the LGD values set out in Part 2, point 8, RW shall be 0; and

– for defaulted exposures where credit institutions use own estimates of LGDs, RW shall be Max{0, 12.5 *(LGD-EL$_{BE}$)};

where ELBE shall be the credit institution's best estimate of expected loss for the defaulted exposure according to point 80 of Part 4.

Risk-weighted exposure amount = RW * exposure value.

4. The risk-weighted exposure amount for each exposure which meets the requirements set out in Annex VIII, Part 1, point 29 and Annex VIII, Part 2, point 22 may be adjusted according to the following formula:

Risk-weighted exposure amount = RW* exposure value * [(0.15 + 160 * PDpp)]

where:

PDpp = PD of the protection provider.

RW shall be calculated using the relevant risk weight formula set out in point 3 for the exposure, the PD of the obligor and the LGD of a comparable direct exposure to the protection provider. The maturity factor (b) shall be calculated using the lower of the PD of the protection provider and the PD of the obligor.

5. For exposures to companies where the total annual sales for the consolidated group of which the firm is a part is less than EUR 50 million, credit institutions may use the following correlation formula for the calculation of risk weights for corporate exposures. In this formula S is expressed as total annual sales in millions of Euros with EUR 5 million < = S < = EUR 50 million. Reported sales of less than EUR 5 million shall be treated as if they were equivalent to EUR 5 million. For purchased receivables the total annual sales shall be the weighted average by individual exposures of the pool.

Correlation (R) = 0.12 × (1−EXP (−50 * PD))/(1−EXP(−50))+0.24 * [1−(1−EXP(−50 * PD)/(1−EXP(−50))]−0.04 * (1−(S−5) / 45)

Credit institutions shall substitute total assets of the consolidated group for total annual sales when total annual sales are not a meaningful indicator of firm size and total assets are a more meaningful indicator than total annual sales.

6. For specialised lending exposures in respect of which a credit institution cannot demonstrate that its PD estimates meet the minimum requirements set out in Part 4 it shall assign risk weights to these exposures according to Table 1, as follows:

The competent authorities may authorise a credit institution generally to assign preferential risk weights of 50% to exposures in category 1, and a 70% risk weight to exposures in category 2, provided the credit institution's underwriting characteristics and other risk characteristics are substantially strong for the relevant category.

In assigning risk weights to specialised lending exposures credit institutions shall take into account the following factors: financial strength, political and legal environment, transaction and/or asset characteristics, strength of the sponsor and developer, including any public private partnership income stream, and security package.

7. For their purchased corporate receivables credit institutions shall comply with the minimum requirements set out in points 105 to 109 of Part 4. For purchased corporate receivables that comply in addition with the conditions set out in point 14, and where it would be unduly burdensome for a credit institution to use the risk quantification standards for corporate exposures as set out in Part 4 for these receivables, the risk quantification standards for retail exposures as set out in Part 4 may be used.

Table 1

Remaining Maturity	Category 1	Category 2	Category 3	Category 4	Category 5
Less than 2.5 years	50%	70%	115%	250%	0%
Equal or more than 2.5 years	70%	90%	115%	250%	0%

8. For purchased corporate receivables, refundable purchase discounts, collateral or partial guarantees that provide first-loss protection for default losses, dilution losses, or both, may be treated as first-loss positions under the IRB securitisation framework.

9. Where an institution provides credit protection for a number of exposures under terms that the nth default among the exposures shall trigger payment and that this credit event shall terminate the contract, if the product has an external credit assessment from an eligible ECAI the risk weights set out in Articles 94 to 101 will be applied. If the product is not rated by an eligible ECAI, the risk weights of the exposures included in the basket will be aggregated, excluding n-1 exposures where the sum of the expected loss amount multiplied by 12.5 and the risk-weighted exposure amount shall not exceed the nominal amount of the protection provided by the credit derivative multiplied by 12.5. The n-1 exposures to be excluded from the aggregation shall be determined on the basis that they shall include those exposures each of which produces a lower risk-weighted exposure amount than the risk-weighted exposure amount of any of the exposures included in the aggregation.

1.2. Risk-weighted exposure amounts for retail exposures

10. Subject to points 12 and 13, the risk-weighted exposure amounts for retail exposures shall be calculated according to the following formulae:

Correlation $(R) = 0.03 \times (1-EXP(-35*PD))/(1-EXP(-35))+0.16*[1-(1-EXP-35*PD)/(1-EXP(-35))]$

Risk weighted (RW)

$(LGD * N\{(1-R)^{-0.5} G(PD)+(R/(1-R))^{0.5} G(0.999)\}-PD*12.5*1.06)$

$N(x)$ denotes the cumulative distribution function for a standard normal random variable (i.e. the probability that a normal random variable with mean zero and variance of one is less than or equal to x). $G(Z)$ denotes the inverse cumulative distribution function for a standard normal random variable (i.e. the value x such that $N(x)=z$).

For $PD = 1$ (defaulted exposure), RW shall be Max $\{0, 12.5*(LGD-EL_{BE})\}$,

where EL_{BE} shall be the credit institution's best estimate of expected loss for the defaulted exposure according to point 80 of Part 4.

Risk-weighted exposure amount = RW* exposure value.

11. The risk-weighted exposure amount for each exposure to small and medium sized entities as defined in Article 86(4) which meets the requirements set out in Annex VIII, Part 1, point 29 and Annex VIII, Part 2, point 22 may be calculated according to point 4.

12. For retail exposures secured by real estate collateral a correlation (R) of 0.15 shall replace the figure produced by the correlation formula in point 10.

13. For qualifying revolving retail exposures as defined in points (a) to (e), a correlation (R) of 0.04 shall replace the figure produced by the correlation formula in point 10.

Exposures shall qualify as qualifying revolving retail exposures if they meet the following conditions:

(a) The exposures are to individuals;

(b) The exposures are revolving, unsecured, and to the extent they are not drawn immediately and unconditionally, cancellable by the credit institution. (In this context revolving exposures are defined as those where customers' outstanding balances are permitted to fluctuate based on their decisions to borrow and repay, up to a limit established by the credit institution.) Undrawn commitments may be considered as unconditionally cancellable if the terms permit the credit institution to cancel them to the full extent allowable under consumer protection and related legislation;

(c) The maximum exposure to a single individual in the sub-portfolio is EUR 100 000 or less;

(d) The credit institution can demonstrate that the use of the correlation of this point is limited to portfolios that have exhibited low volatility of loss rates, relative to their average level of loss rates, especially within the low PD bands.

Competent authorities shall review the relative volatility of loss rates across the qualifying revolving retail sub-portfolios, as well the aggregate qualifying revolving retail portfolio, and intend to share information on the typical characteristics of qualifying revolving retail loss rates across jurisdictions; and

(e) The competent authority concurs that treatment as a qualifying revolving retail exposure is consistent with the underlying risk characteristics of the sub-portfolio.

By way of derogation from point (b), competent authorities may waive the requirement that the exposure be unsecured in respect of collateralised credit facilities linked to a wage account. In this case amounts recovered from the collateral shall not be taken into account in the LGD estimate.

14. To be eligible for the retail treatment, purchased receivables shall comply with the minimum requirements set out in Part 4, points 105 to 109 and the following conditions:

(a) The credit institution has purchased the receivables from unrelated, third party sellers, and its exposure to the obligor of the receivable does not include any exposures that are directly or indirectly originated by the credit institution itself;

(b) The purchased receivables shall be generated on an arm's-length basis between the seller and the obligor. As such, inter-company accounts receivables and receivables subject to contra-accounts between firms that buy and sell to each other are ineligible;

(c) The purchasing credit institution has a claim on all proceeds from the purchased receivables or a pro-rata interest in the proceeds; and

(d) The portfolio of purchased receivables is sufficiently diversified.

15. For purchased receivables, refundable purchase discounts, collateral or partial guarantees that provide first-loss protection for default losses, dilution losses, or both, may be treated as first-loss positions under the IRB securitisation framework.

16. For hybrid pools of purchased retail receivables where purchasing credit institutions cannot separate exposures secured by real estate collateral and qualifying revolving retail exposures from other retail exposures, the retail risk weight function producing the highest capital requirements for those exposures shall apply.

1.3. Risk-weighted exposure amounts for equity exposures

17. A credit institution may employ different approaches to different portfolios where the credit institution itself uses different approaches internally. Where a credit institution uses different approaches, the credit institution shall demonstrate to the competent authorities that the choice is made consistently and is not determined by regulatory arbitrage considerations.

18. Notwithstanding point 17, competent authorities may allow the attribution of risk-weighted exposure amounts for equity exposures to ancillary services undertakings according to the treatment of other non credit-obligation assets.

1.3.1. Simple risk weight approach

19. The risk-weighted exposure amount shall be calculated according to the following formula:

Risk weight (RW) = 190% for private equity exposures in sufficiently diversified portfolios.

Risk weight (RW) = 290% for exchange traded equity exposures.

Risk weight (RW) = 370% for all other equity exposures.

Risk-weighted exposure amount = RW * exposure value.

20. Short cash positions and derivative instruments held in the non-trading book are permitted to offset long positions in the same individual stocks provided that these instruments have been explicitly designated as hedges of specific equity exposures and that they provide a hedge for at least another year. Other short positions are to be treated as if they are long positions with the relevant risk weight assigned to the absolute value of each position. In the context of maturity mismatched positions, the method is that for

corporate exposures as set out in point 16 of Annex VII, Part 2.

21. Credit institutions may recognise unfunded credit protection obtained on an equity exposure in accordance with the methods set out in Articles 90 to 93.

1.3.2. *PD/LGD approach*

22. The risk weighted exposure amounts shall be calculated according to the formulas in point 3. If credit institutions do not have sufficient information to use the definition of default set out in points 44 to 48 of Part 4, a scaling factor of 1.5 shall be assigned to the risk weights.

23. At the individual exposure level the sum of the expected loss amount multiplied by 12.5 and the risk weighted exposure amount shall not exceed the exposure value multiplied by 12.5.

24. Credit institutions may recognise unfunded credit protection obtained on an equity exposure in accordance with the methods set out in Articles 90 to 93. This shall be subject to an LGD of 90% on the exposure to the provider of the hedge. For private equity exposures in sufficiently diversified portfolios an LGD of 65% may be used. For these purposes M shall be 5 years.

1.3.3. *Internal models approach*

25. The risk weighted exposure amount shall be the potential loss on the credit institution's equity exposures as derived using internal value-at-risk models subject to the 99th percentile, one-tailed confidence interval of the difference between quarterly returns and an appropriate risk-free rate computed over a long-term sample period, multiplied by 12.5. The risk weighted exposure amounts at the individual exposure level shall not be less than the sum of minimum risk weighted exposure amounts required under the PD/LGD Approach and the corresponding expected loss amounts multiplied by 12.5 and calculated on the basis of the PD values set out in Part 2, point 24(a) and the corresponding LGD values set out in Part 2, points 25 and 26.

26. Credit institutions may recognise unfunded credit protection obtained on an equity position.

1.4. Risk-weighted exposure amounts for other non-credit obligation assets

27. The risk weighted exposure amounts shall be calculated according to the formula:

Risk-weighted exposure amount = 100% * exposure value,

except for when the exposure is a residual value in which case it should be provisioned for each year and will be calculated as follows:

1/t * 100% * exposure value,

where t is the number of years of the lease contract term.

2. CALCULATION OF RISK-WEIGHTED EXPOSURE AMOUNTS FOR DILUTION RISK OF PURCHASED RECEIVABLES

28. Risk weights for dilution risk of purchased corporate and retail receivables:

The risk weights shall be calculated according to the formula in point 3. The input parameters PD and LGD shall be determined as set out in Part 2, the exposure value shall be determined as set out in Part 3 and M shall be 1 year. If credit institutions can demonstrate to the competent authorities that dilution risk is immaterial, it need not be recognised.

3. CALCULATION OF EXPECTED LOSS AMOUNTS

29. Unless noted otherwise, the input parameters PD and LGD shall be determined as set out in Part 2 and the exposure value shall be determined as set out in Part 3.

30. The expected loss amounts for exposures to corporates, institutions, central governments and central banks and retail exposures shall be calculated according to the following formulae:

Expected loss (EL) = PD × LGD.

Expected loss amount = EL × exposure value.

For defaulted exposures (PD = 1) where credit institutions use own estimates of LGDs, EL shall

Table 2

Remaining Maturity	Category 1	Category 2	Category 3	Category 4	Category 5
Less than 2.5 years	0%	0.4%	2.8%	8%	50%
Equal or more than 2.5 years	0.4%	0.8%	2.8%	8%	50%

be ELBE, the credit institution's best estimate of expected loss for the defaulted exposure according to Part 4, point 80.

For exposures subject to the treatment set out in Part 1, point 4, EL shall be 0.

31. The EL values for specialised lending exposures where credit institutions use the methods set out in point 6 for assigning risk weights shall be assigned according to Table 2.

Where competent authorities have authorised a credit institution generally to assign preferential risk weights of 50% to exposures in category 1, and 70% to exposures in category 2, the EL value for exposures in category 1 shall be 0%, and for exposures in category 2 shall be 0.4%.

32. The expected loss amounts for equity exposures where the risk-weighted exposure amounts are calculated according to the methods set out in points 19 to 21, shall be calculated according to the following formula:

Expected loss amount = EL × exposure value

The EL values shall be the following:

Expected loss (EL) = 0.8% for private equity exposures in sufficiently diversified portfolios

Expected loss (EL) = 0.8% for exchange traded equity exposures

Expected loss (EL) = 2.4% for all other equity exposures.

33. The expected loss amounts for equity exposures where the risk weighted exposure amounts are calculated according to the methods set out in points 22 to 24 shall be calculated according to the following formulae:

Expected loss (EL) = PD × LGD and

Expected loss amount = EL × exposure value

34. The expected loss amounts for equity exposures where the risk-weighted exposure amounts are calculated according to the methods set out in points 25 to 26 shall be 0%.

35. The expected loss amounts for dilution risk of purchased receivables shall be calculated according to the following formula:

Expected loss (EL) = PD × LGD and

Expected loss amount = EL × exposure value

4. Treatment of Expected Loss Amounts

36. The expected loss amounts calculated in accordance with points 30, 31 and 35 shall be subtracted from the sum of value adjustments and provisions related to these exposures. Discounts on balance sheet exposures purchased when in default according to Part 3, point 1 shall be treated in the same manner as value adjustments. Expected loss amounts for securitised exposures and value adjustments and provisions related to these exposures shall not be included in this calculation.

Part 2

PD, LGD and Maturity

1. The input parameters PD, LGD and maturity value (M) into the calculation of risk-weighted exposure amounts and expected loss amounts specified in Part 1 shall be those estimated by the credit institution in accordance with Part 4, subject to the following provisions.

1. EXPOSURES TO CORPORATES, INSTITUTIONS AND CENTRAL GOVERNMENTS AND CENTRAL BANKS

1.1. PD

2. The PD of an exposure to a corporate or an institution shall be at least 0.03%.

3. For purchased corporate receivables in respect of which a credit institution cannot demonstrate that its PD estimates meet the minimum requirements set out in Part 4, the PDs for these exposures shall be determined according to the following methods: for senior claims on purchased corporate receivables PD shall be the credit institutions estimate of EL divided by LGD for these receivables. For subordinated claims on purchased corporate receivables PD shall be the credit institution's estimate of EL. If a credit institution is permitted to use own LGD estimates for corporate exposures and it can decompose its EL estimates for purchased corporate receivables into PDs and LGDs in a reliable manner, the PD estimate may be used.

4. The PD of obligors in default shall be 100%.

5. Credit institutions may recognise unfunded credit protection in the PD in accordance with the provisions of Articles 90 to 93. For dilution risk, however, competent authorities may recognise as eligible unfunded credit protection providers other than those indicated in Annex VIII, Part 1.

6. Credit institutions using own LGD estimates may recognise unfunded credit protection by adjusting PDs subject to point 10.

7. For dilution risk of purchased corporate receivables, PD shall be set equal to EL estimate for dilution risk. If a credit institution is permitted to use own LGD estimates for corporate exposures and it can decompose its EL estimates for dilution risk of purchased corporate receivables into PDs and LGDs in a reliable manner, the PD estimate may be used. Credit institutions may recognise unfunded credit protection in the PD in accordance with the provisions of Articles 90 to 93. Competent authorities may recognise as eligible unfunded credit protection providers other than those indicated in Annex VIII, Part 1.

If a credit institution is permitted to use own LGD estimates for dilution risk of purchased corporate receivables, it may recognise unfunded credit protection by adjusting PDs subject of point 10.

1.2. LGD

8. Credit institutions shall use the following LGD values:

(a) Senior exposures without eligible collateral: 45%;

(b) Subordinated exposures without eligible collateral: 75%;

(c) Credit institutions may recognise funded and unfunded credit protection in the LGD in accordance with Articles 90 to 93;

(d) Covered bonds as defined in Annex VI, Part 1, points 68 to 70 may be assigned an LGD value of 12.5%;

(e) For senior purchased corporate receivables exposures where a credit institution cannot demonstrate that its PD estimates meet the minimum requirements set out in Part 4: 45%;

(f) For subordinated purchased corporate receivables exposures where a credit institution cannot demonstrate that its PD estimates meet the minimum requirements set out in Part 4: 100%; and

(g) For dilution risk of purchased corporate receivables: 75%.

Until 31 December 2010, covered bonds as defined in Annex VI, Part 1, points 68 to 70 may be assigned an LGD value of 11.25% if:

– assets as set out in Annex VI, Part 1, point 68(a) to (c) collateralising the bonds all qualify for credit quality step 1 as set out in that Annex;

– where assets set out in Annex VI, Part 1, point 68(d) and (e) are used as collateral, the respective upper limits laid down in each of those points is 10% of the nominal amount of the outstanding issue;

– assets as set out in Annex VI, Part 1, point 68(f) are not used as collateral; or

– the covered bonds are the subject of a credit assessment by a nominated ECAI, and the

ECAI places them in the most favourable category of credit assessment that the ECAI could make in respect of covered bonds.

By 31 December 2010, this derogation shall be reviewed and consequent to such review the Commission may make proposals in accordance with the procedure referred to in Article 151(2).

9. Notwithstanding point 8, for dilution and default risk if a credit institution is permitted to use own LGD estimates for corporate exposures and it can decompose its EL estimates for purchased corporate receivables into PDs and LGDs in a reliable manner, the LGD estimate for purchased corporate receivables may be used.

10. Notwithstanding point 8, if a credit institution is permitted to use own LGD estimates for exposures to corporates, institutions, central governments and central banks, unfunded credit protection may be recognised by adjusting PD and/or LGD subject to minimum requirements as specified in Part 4 and approval of competent authorities. A credit institution shall not assign guaranteed exposures an adjusted PD or LGD such that the adjusted risk weight would be lower than that of a comparable, direct exposure to the guarantor.

11. Notwithstanding points 8 and 10, for the purposes of Part 1, point 4, the LGD of a comparable direct exposure to the protection provider shall either be the LGD associated with an unhedged facility to the guarantor or the unhedged facility of the obligor, depending upon whether in the event both the guarantor and obligor default during the life of the hedged transaction, available evidence and the structure of the guarantee indicate that the amount recovered would depend on the financial condition of the guarantor or obligor, respectively.

1.3. Maturity

12. Subject to point 13, credit institutions shall assign to exposures arising from repurchase transactions or securities or commodities lending or borrowing transactions a maturity value (M) of 0.5 years and to all other exposures an M of 2.5 years. Competent authorities may require all credit institutions in their jurisdiction to use M for each exposure as set out under point 13.

13. Credit institutions permitted to use own LGDs and/or own conversion factors for exposures to corporates, institutions or central governments and central banks shall calculate M for each of these exposures as set out in (a) to (e) and subject to points 14 to 16. In all cases, M shall be no greater than 5 years:

(a) For an instrument subject to a cash flow schedule, M shall be calculated according to the following formula:

$$M = \text{MAX}\{1; \text{MIN}\{\Sigma_t * CF_t / \Sigma_t CF_t, 5\}\}$$

where CF_t denotes the cash flows (principal, interest payments and fees) contractually payable by the obligor in period t;

(b) For derivatives subject to a master netting agreement, M shall be the weighted average remaining maturity of the exposure, where M shall be at least 1 year. The notional amount of each exposure shall be used for weighting the maturity;

(c) For exposures arising from fully or nearly-fully collateralised derivative instruments (listed in Annex IV) transactions and fully or nearly-fully collateralised margin lending transactions which are subject to a master netting agreement, M shall be the weighted average remaining maturity of the transactions where M shall be at least 10 days. The notional amount of each transaction shall be used for weighting the maturity;

(d) If a credit institution is permitted to use own PD estimates for purchased corporate receivables, for drawn amounts M shall equal the purchased receivables exposure weighted average maturity, where M shall be at least 90 days. This same value of M shall also be used for undrawn amounts under a committed purchase facility provided the facility contains effective covenants, early amortisation triggers, or other features that protect the purchasing credit institution against a significant deterioration in the quality of the future receivables it is required to purchase over the facility's term. Absent such effective protections, M for undrawn amounts shall be calculated as the sum of the longest-dated potential receivable under the purchase agreement and the remaining maturity of the purchase facility, where M shall be at least 90 days;

(e) For any other instrument than those mentioned in this point or when a credit institution is not in a position to calculate M as set out in (a), M shall be the maximum remaining time (in years) that the obligor is permitted to take to fully discharge its contractual obligations, where M shall be at least 1 year;

(f) For credit institutions using the Internal Model Method set out in Annex III, Part 6 to calculate the exposure values, M shall be calculated for exposures to which they apply this method and for which the maturity of the longest-dated contract contained in the netting set is greater than one year according to the following formula:

$$M = \operatorname{Min}\left(\frac{\sum_{k=1}^{tk \leq 1year} \text{Effective EE}_k \cdot \Delta t_k \cdot df_k + \sum_{tk>1year}^{maturity} EE_k \cdot \Delta t_k df_k}{\sum_{k=1}^{tk \leq 1year} \text{Effective EE}_k \cdot \Delta t_k \cdot df_k}; 5\right)$$

where:

df = the risk-free discount factor for future time period tk and the remaining symbols are defined in Annex III, Part 6.

Notwithstanding the first paragraph of point 13(f), a credit institution that uses an internal model to calculate a one-sided credit valuation adjustment (CVA) may use, subject to the approval of the competent authorities, the effective credit duration estimated by the internal model as M.

Subject to paragraph 14, for netting sets in which all contracts have an original maturity of less than one year the formula in point (a) shall apply; and

(g) for the purposes of Part 1, point 4, M shall be the effective maturity of the credit protection but at least 1 year.

14. Notwithstanding point 13(a), (b), (d) and (e), M shall be at least one-day for:
– fully or nearly-fully collateralised derivative instruments listed in Annex IV;
– fully or nearly-fully collateralised margin lending transactions; and
– repurchase transactions, securities or commodities lending or borrowing transactions

provided the documentation requires daily re-margining and daily revaluation and includes provisions that allow for the prompt liquidation or setoff of collateral in the event of default or failure to re-margin.

In addition, for other short-term exposures specified by the competent authorities which are not part of the credit institution's ongoing financing of the obligor, M shall be at least one-day. A careful review of the particular circumstances shall be made in each case.

15. The competent authorities may allow for exposures to corporates situated in the Community and having consolidated sales and consolidated assets of less than EUR 500 million the use of M as set out in point 12. Competent authorities may replace EUR 500 million total assets with EUR 1000 million total assets for corporates which primarily invest in real estate.

16. Maturity mismatches shall be treated as specified in Articles 90 to 93.

2. Retail Exposures

2.1. PD

17. The PD of an exposure shall be at least 0.03%.

18. The PD of obligors or, where an obligation approach is used, of exposures in default shall be 100%.

19. For dilution risk of purchased receivables PD shall be set equal to EL estimates for dilution risk. If a credit institution can decompose its EL estimates for dilution risk of purchased receivables into PDs and LGDs in a reliable manner, the PD estimate may be used.

20. Unfunded credit protection may be recognised as eligible by adjusting PDs subject to point 22. For dilution risk, where credit institutions do not use own estimates of LGDs, this shall be subject to compliance with Articles 90 to 93; for this purpose competent authorities may recognise as

eligible unfunded protection providers other than those indicated in Annex VIII, Part 1.

2.2. LGD

21. Credit institutions shall provide own estimates of LGDs subject to minimum requirements as specified in Part 4 and approval of competent authorities. For dilution risk of purchased receivables, an LGD value of 75% shall be used. If a credit institution can decompose its EL estimates for dilution risk of purchased receivables into PDs and LGDs in a reliable manner, the LGD estimate may be used.

22. Unfunded credit protection may be recognised as eligible by adjusting PD or LGD estimates subject to minimum requirements as specified in Part 4, points 99 to 104 and approval of competent authorities either in support of an individual exposure or a pool of exposures. A credit institution shall not assign guaranteed exposures an adjusted PD or LGD such that the adjusted risk weight would be lower than that of a comparable, direct exposure to the guarantor.

23. Notwithstanding point 22, for the purposes of Part 1, point 11 the LGD of a comparable direct exposure to the protection provider shall either be the LGD associated with an unhedged facility to the guarantor or the unhedged facility of the obligor, depending upon whether, in the event both the guarantor and obligor default during the life of the hedged transaction, available evidence and the structure of the guarantee indicate that the amount recovered would depend on the financial condition of the guarantor or obligor, respectively.

3. Equity Exposures Subject to PD/LGD Method

3.1. PD

24. PDs shall be determined according to the methods for corporate exposures.

The following minimum PDs shall apply:

(a) 0.09% for exchange traded equity exposures where the investment is part of a long-term customer relationship;

(b) 0.09% for non-exchange traded equity exposures where the returns on the investment are based on regular and periodic cash flows not derived from capital gains;

(c) 0.40% for exchange traded equity exposures including other short positions as set out in part 1, point 20; and

(d) 1.25% for all other equity exposures including other short positions as set out in Part 1, point 20.

3.2. LGD

25. Private equity exposures in sufficiently diversified portfolios may be assigned an LGD of 65%.

26. All other exposures shall be assigned an LGD of 90%.

3.3. Maturity

27. M assigned to all exposures shall be 5 years.

Part 3

Exposure Value

1. Exposures to Corporates, Institutions, Central Governments and Central Banks and Retail Exposures

1. Unless noted otherwise, the exposure value of on-balance sheet exposures shall be measured gross of value adjustments. This rule also applies to assets purchased at a price different than the amount owed. For purchased assets, the difference between the amount owed and the net value recorded on the balance sheet of credit institutions is denoted discount if the amount owed is larger, and premium if it is smaller.

2. Where credit institutions use Master netting agreements in relation to repurchase transactions or securities or commodities lending or borrowing transactions, the exposure value shall be calculated in accordance with Articles 90 to 93.

3. For on-balance sheet netting of loans and deposits, credit institutions shall apply for the calculation of the exposure value the methods set out in Articles 90 to 93.

4. The exposure value for leases shall be the discounted minimum lease payments.

'Minimum lease payments' are the payments over the lease term that the lessee is or can be required to make and any bargain option (i.e. option the exercise of which is reasonably certain). Any guaranteed residual value fulfilling the set of conditions in Annex VIII, Part 1, points 26 to 28 regarding the eligibility of protection providers as well as the minimum requirements for recognising other types of guarantees provided in Annex VIII, Part 2, points 14 to 19 should also be included in the minimum lease payments.

5. In the case of any item listed in Annex IV, the exposure value shall be determined by the methods set out in Annex III.

6. The exposure value for the calculation of risk-weighted exposure amounts of purchased receivables shall be the outstanding amount minus the capital requirements for dilution risk prior to credit risk mitigation.

7. Where an exposure takes the form of securities or commodities sold, posted or lent under repurchase transactions or securities or commodities lending or borrowing transactions, long settlement transactions and margin lending transactions, the exposure value shall be the value of the securities or commodities determined in accordance with Article 74. Where the Financial Collateral Comprehensive Method as set out under Annex VIII, Part 3 is used, the exposure value shall be increased by the volatility adjustment appropriate to such securities or commodities, as set out therein. The exposure value of repurchase transactions, securities or commodities lending or borrowing transactions, long settlement transactions and margin lending transactions may be determined either in accordance with Annex III or Annex VIII, Part 3, points 12 to 21.

8. Notwithstanding point 7, the exposure value of credit risk exposures outstanding, as determined by the competent authorities, with a central counterparty shall be determined in accordance with Annex III, Part 2, point 6, provided that the central counterparty's counterparty credit risk exposures with all participants in its arrangements are fully collateralised on a daily basis.

9. The exposure value for the following items shall be calculated as the committed but undrawn amount multiplied by a conversion factor.

Credit institutions shall use the following conversion factors:

(a) for credit lines which are uncommitted, that are unconditionally cancellable at any time by the credit institution without prior notice, or that effectively provide for automatic cancellation due to deterioration in a borrower's credit worthiness, a conversion factor of 0% shall apply. To apply a conversion factor of 0%, credit institutions shall actively monitor the financial condition of the obligor, and their internal control systems shall enable them to immediately detect a deterioration in the credit quality of the obligor. Undrawn retail credit lines may be considered as unconditionally cancellable if the terms permit the credit institution to cancel them to the full extent allowable under consumer protection and related legislation;

(b) for short-term letters of credit arising from the movement of goods, a conversion factor of 20% shall apply for both the issuing and confirming institutions;

(c) for undrawn purchase commitments for revolving purchased receivables that are unconditionally cancellable or that effectively provide for automatic cancellation at any time by the institution without prior notice, a conversion factor of 0% shall apply. To apply a conversion factor of 0%, credit institutions shall actively monitor the financial condition of the obligor, and their internal control systems shall enable them to immediately detect a deterioration in the credit quality of the obligor;

(d) for other credit lines, note issuance facilities (NIFs), and revolving underwriting facilities (RUFs), a conversion factor of 75% shall apply; and

(e) credit institutions which meet the minimum requirements for the use of own estimates of conversion factors as specified in Part 4 may use their own estimates of conversion factors across different product types as mentioned in points (a) to (d), subject to approval of the competent authorities.

10. Where a commitment refers to the extension of another commitment, the lower of the two conversion factors associated with the individual commitment shall be used.

11. For all off-balance-sheet items other than those mentioned in points 1 to 9, the exposure value shall be the following percentage of its value:
– 100% if it is a full risk item,
– 50% if it is a medium-risk item,
– 20% if it is a medium/low-risk item, and
– 0% if it is a low-risk item.

For the purposes of this point the off-balance-sheet items shall be assigned to risk categories as indicated in Annex II.

2. EQUITY EXPOSURES

12. The exposure value shall be the value presented in the financial statements. Admissible equity exposure measures are the following:

(a) For investments held at fair value with changes in value flowing directly through income and into own funds, the exposure value is the fair value presented in the balance sheet;

(b) For investments held at fair value with changes in value not flowing through income but into a tax-adjusted separate component of equity, the exposure value is the fair value presented in the balance sheet; and

(c) For investments held at cost or at the lower of cost or market, the exposure value is the cost or market value presented in the balance sheet.

3. OTHER NON-CREDIT OBLIGATION ASSETS

13. The exposure value of other non-credit obligation assets shall be the value presented in the financial statements.

PART 4

Minimum Requirements for IRB Approach

1. RATING SYSTEMS

1. A 'rating system' shall comprise all of the methods, processes, controls, data collection and IT systems that support the assessment of credit risk, the assignment of exposures to grades or pools (rating), and the quantification of default and loss estimates for a certain type of exposure.

2. If a credit institution uses multiple rating systems, the rationale for assigning an obligor or a transaction to a rating system shall be documented and applied in a manner that appropriately reflects the level of risk.

3. Assignment criteria and processes shall be periodically reviewed to determine whether they remain appropriate for the current portfolio and external conditions.

1.1. Structure of rating systems

4. Where a credit institution uses direct estimates of risk parameters these may be seen as the outputs of grades on a continuous rating scale.

1.1.1. *Exposures to corporates, institutions and central governments and central banks*

5. A rating system shall take into account obligor and transaction risk characteristics.

6. A rating system shall have an obligor rating scale which reflects exclusively quantification of the risk of obligor default. The obligor rating scale shall have a minimum of 7 grades for non-defaulted obligors and one for defaulted obligors.

7. An 'obligor grade' shall mean a risk category within a rating system's obligor rating scale, to which obligors are assigned on the basis of a specified and distinct set of rating criteria, from which estimates of PD are derived. A credit institution shall document the relationship between obligor grades in terms of the level of default risk each grade implies and the criteria used to distinguish that level of default risk.

8. Credit institutions with portfolios concentrated in a particular market segment and range of default risk shall have enough obligor grades within that range to avoid undue concentrations of obligors in a particular grade. Significant concentrations within a single grade shall be supported by convincing empirical evidence that the obligor grade covers a reasonably narrow PD band and that the default risk posed by all obligors in the grade falls within that band.

9. To qualify for recognition by the competent authorities of the use for capital requirement calculation of own estimates of LGDs, a rating system shall incorporate a distinct facility rating scale which exclusively reflects LGD related transaction characteristics.

10. A 'facility grade' shall mean a risk category within a rating system's facility scale, to which exposures are assigned on the basis of a specified and distinct set of rating criteria from which own estimates of LGDs are derived. The grade definition shall include both a description of how exposures are assigned to the grade and of the criteria used to distinguish the level of risk across grades.

11. Significant concentrations within a single facility grade shall be supported by convincing empirical evidence that the facility grade covers a reasonably narrow LGD band, respectively, and that the risk posed by all exposures in the grade falls within that band.

12. Credit institutions using the methods set out in Part 1, point 6 for assigning risk weights for specialised lending exposures are exempt from the requirement to have an obligor rating scale which reflects exclusively quantification of the risk of obligor default for these exposures. Notwithstanding point 6, these institutions shall have for these exposures at least 4 grades for non-defaulted obligors and at least one grade for defaulted obligors.

1.1.2. *Retail exposures*

13. Rating systems shall reflect both obligor and transaction risk, and shall capture all relevant obligor and transaction characteristics.

14. The level of risk differentiation shall ensure that the number of exposures in a given grade or pool is sufficient to allow for meaningful quantification and validation of the loss characteristics at the grade or pool level. The distribution of exposures and obligors across grades or pools shall be such as to avoid excessive concentrations.

15. Credit institutions shall demonstrate that the process of assigning exposures to grades or pools provides for a meaningful differentiation of risk, provides for a grouping of sufficiently homogenous exposures, and allows for accurate and consistent estimation of loss characteristics at grade or pool level. For purchased receivables the grouping shall reflect the seller's underwriting practices and the heterogeneity of its customers.

16. Credit institutions shall consider the following risk drivers when assigning exposures to grades or pools.

(a) Obligor risk characteristics;

(b) Transaction risk characteristics, including product or collateral types or both. Credit institutions shall explicitly address cases where several exposures benefit from the same collateral; and

(c) Delinquency, unless the credit institution demonstrates to its competent authority that delinquency is not a material risk drivers for the exposure.

1.2. Assignment to grades or pools

17. A credit institution shall have specific definitions, processes and criteria for assigning exposures to grades or pools within a rating system.

(a) The grade or pool definitions and criteria shall be sufficiently detailed to allow those charged with assigning ratings to consistently assign obligors or facilities posing similar risk to the same grade or pool. This consistency shall exist across lines of business, departments and geographic locations;

(b) The documentation of the rating process shall allow third parties to understand the assignments of exposures to grades or pools, to replicate grade and pool assignments and to evaluate the appropriateness of the assignments to a grade or a pool; and

(c) The criteria shall also be consistent with the credit institution's internal lending standards and its policies for handling troubled obligors and facilities.

18. A credit institution shall take all relevant information into account in assigning obligors and facilities to grades or pools. Information shall be current and shall enable the credit institution to forecast the future performance of the exposure. The less information a credit institution has, the more conservative shall be its assignments of exposures to obligor and facility grades or pools. If a credit institution uses an external rating as a primary factor determining an internal rating assignment, the credit institution shall ensure that it considers other relevant information.

1.3. Assignment of exposures

1.3.1. *Exposures to corporates, institutions and central governments and central banks*

19. Each obligor shall be assigned to an obligor grade as part of the credit approval process.

20. For those credit institutions permitted to use own estimates of LGDs and/or conversion factors, each exposure shall also be assigned to a facility grade as part of the credit approval process.

21. Credit institutions using the methods set out in Part 1, point 6 for assigning risk weights for specialised lending exposures shall assign each of these exposures to a grade in accordance with point 12.

22. Each separate legal entity to which the credit institution is exposed shall be separately rated. A credit institution shall demonstrate to its competent authority that it has acceptable policies regarding the treatment of individual obligor clients and groups of connected clients.

23. Separate exposures to the same obligor shall be assigned to the same obligor grade, irrespective of any differences in the nature of each specific transaction. Exceptions, where separate exposures are allowed to result in multiple grades for the same obligor are:

(a) country transfer risk, this being dependent on whether the exposures are denominated in local or foreign currency;

(b) where the treatment of associated guarantees to an exposure may be reflected in an adjusted assignment to an obligor grade; and

(c) where consumer protection, bank secrecy or other legislation prohibit the exchange of client data.

1.3.2. *Retail exposures*

24. Each exposure shall be assigned to a grade or a pool as part of the credit approval process.

1.3.3. *Overrides*

25. For grade and pool assignments credit institutions shall document the situations in which human judgement may override the inputs or outputs of the assignment process and the personnel responsible for approving these overrides. Credit institutions shall document these overrides and the personnel responsible. Credit institutions shall analyse the performance of the exposures whose assignments have been overridden. This analysis shall include assessment of the performance of exposures whose rating has been overridden by a particular person, accounting for all the responsible personnel.

1.4. Integrity of assignment process

1.4.1. *Exposures to corporates, institutions and central governments and central banks*

26. Assignments and periodic reviews of assignments shall be completed or approved by an independent party that does not directly benefit from decisions to extend the credit.

27. Credit institutions shall update assignments at least annually. High risk obligors and problem exposures shall be subject to more frequent review. Credit institutions shall undertake a new assignment if material information on the obligor or exposure becomes available.

28. A credit institution shall have an effective process to obtain and update relevant information on obligor characteristics that affect PDs, and on transaction characteristics that affect LGDs and/or conversion factors.

1.4.2. *Retail exposures*

29. A credit institution shall at least annually update obligor and facility assignments or review the loss characteristics and delinquency status of each identified risk pool, whichever applicable. A credit institution shall also at least annually review in a representative sample the status of individual exposures within each pool as a means of ensuring that exposures continue to be assigned to the correct pool.

1.5. Use of models

30. If a credit institution uses statistical models and other mechanical methods to assign exposures to obligors or facilities grades or pools, then:

(a) the credit institution shall demonstrate to its competent authority that the model has good predictive power and that capital requirements are not distorted as a result of its use. The input variables shall form a reasonable and effective basis for the resulting predictions. The model shall not have material biases;

(b) the credit institution shall have in place a process for vetting data inputs into the model, which includes an assessment of the accuracy, completeness and appropriateness of the data;

(c) the credit institution shall demonstrate that the data used to build the model is representative of the population of the credit institution's actual obligors or exposures;

(d) the credit institution shall have a regular cycle of model validation that includes monitoring of model performance and stability; review of model specification; and testing of model outputs against outcomes; and

(e) the credit institution shall complement the statistical model by human judgement and human oversight to review model-based assignments and to ensure that the models are used appropriately. Review procedures shall aim at finding and limiting errors associated with model weaknesses. Human judgements shall take into account all relevant information not considered by the model. The credit institution shall document how human judgement and model results are to be combined.

1.6. Documentation of rating systems

31. The credit institutions shall document the design and operational details of its rating systems. The documentation shall evidence compliance with the minimum requirements in this part, and address topics including portfolio differentiation, rating criteria, responsibilities of parties that rate obligors and exposures, frequency of assignment reviews, and management oversight of the rating process.

32. The credit institution shall document the rationale for and analysis supporting its choice of rating criteria. A credit institution shall document all major changes in the risk rating process, and such documentation shall support identification of changes made to the risk rating process subsequent to the last review by the competent authorities. The organisation of rating assignment including the rating assignment process and the internal control structure shall also be documented.

33. The credit institutions shall document the specific definitions of default and loss used internally and demonstrate consistency with the definitions set out in this Directive.

34. If the credit institution employs statistical models in the rating process, the credit institution shall document their methodologies. This material shall:

(a) provide a detailed outline of the theory, assumptions and/or mathematical and empirical basis of the assignment of estimates to grades, individual obligors, exposures, or pools, and the data source(s) used to estimate the model;

(b) establish a rigorous statistical process (including out-of-time and out-of-sample performance tests) for validating the model; and

(c) indicate any circumstances under which the model does not work effectively.

35. Use of a model obtained from a third-party vendor that claims proprietary technology is not a justification for exemption from documentation or any other of the requirements for rating systems. The burden is on the credit institution to satisfy competent authorities.

1.7. Data maintenance

36. Credit institutions shall collect and store data on aspects of their internal ratings as required under Articles 145 to 149.

1.7.1. *Exposures to corporates, institutions and central governments and central banks*

37. Credit institutions shall collect and store:

(a) complete rating histories on obligors and recognised guarantors;

(b) the dates the ratings were assigned;

(c) the key data and methodology used to derive the rating;

(d) the person responsible for the rating assignment;

(e) the identity of obligors and exposures that defaulted;

(f) the date and circumstances of such defaults; and

(g) data on the PDs and realised default rates associated with rating grades and ratings migration;

Credit institutions not using own estimates of LGDs and/or conversion factors shall collect and store data on comparisons of realised LGDs to the values as set out in Part 2, point 8 and realised conversion factors to the values as set out in Part 3, point 9.

38. Credit institutions using own estimates of LGDs and/or conversion factors shall collect and store:

(a) complete histories of data on the facility ratings and LGD and conversion factor estimates associated with each rating scale;

(b) the dates the ratings were assigned and the estimates were done;

(c) the key data and methodology used to derive the facility ratings and LGD and conversion factor estimates;

(d) the person who assigned the facility rating and the person who provided LGD and conversion factor estimates;

(e) data on the estimated and realised LGDs and conversion factors associated with each defaulted exposure;

(f) data on the LGD of the exposure before and after evaluation of the effects of a guarantee/or credit derivative, for those credit institutions that reflect the credit risk mitigating effects of guarantees or credit derivatives through LGD; and

(g) data on the components of loss for each defaulted exposure.

1.7.2. *Retail exposures*

39. Credit institutions shall collect and store:

(a) data used in the process of allocating exposures to grades or pools;

(b) data on the estimated PDs, LGDs and conversion factors associated with grades or pools of exposures;

(c) the identity of obligors and exposures that defaulted;

(d) for defaulted exposures, data on the grades or pools to which the exposure was assigned over the year prior to default and the realised outcomes on LGD and conversion factor; and

(e) data on loss rates for qualifying revolving retail exposures.

1.8. Stress tests used in assessment of capital adequacy

40. A credit institution shall have in place sound stress testing processes for use in the assessment of its capital adequacy. Stress testing shall involve identifying possible events or future changes in economic conditions that could have unfavourable effects on a credit institution's credit exposures and assessment of the credit institution's ability to withstand such changes.

41. A credit institution shall regularly perform a credit risk stress test to assess the effect of certain specific conditions on its total capital requirements for credit risk. The test shall be one chosen by the credit institution, subject to supervisory review. The test to be employed shall be meaningful and reasonably conservative, considering at

least the effect of mild recession scenarios. A credit institution shall assess migration in its ratings under the stress test scenarios. Stressed portfolios shall contain the vast majority of a credit institution's total exposure.

42. Credit institutions using the treatment set out in Part 1, point 4 shall consider as part of their stress testing framework the impact of a deterioration in the credit quality of protection providers, in particular the impact of protection providers falling outside the eligibility criteria.

2. RISK QUANTIFICATION

43. In determining the risk parameters to be associated with rating grades or pools, credit institutions shall apply the following requirements.

2.1. Definition of default

44. A 'default' shall be considered to have occurred with regard to a particular obligor when either or both of the two following events has taken place:

(a) the credit institution considers that the obligor is unlikely to pay its credit obligations to the credit institution, the parent undertaking or any of its subsidiaries in full, without recourse by the credit institution to actions such as realising security (if held);

(b) the obligor is past due more than 90 days on any material credit obligation to the credit institution, the parent undertaking or any of its subsidiaries.

For overdrafts, days past due commence once an obligor has breached an advised limit, has been advised a limit smaller than current outstandings, or has drawn credit without authorisation and the underlying amount is material.

An 'advised limit' shall mean a limit which has been brought to the knowledge of the obligor.

Days past due for credit cards commence on the minimum payment due date.

In the case of retail exposures and exposures to public sector entities (PSE) the competent authorities shall set a number of days past due as specified in point 48.

In the case of corporate exposures the competent authorities may set a number of days past due as specified in Article 154(7).

In the case of retail exposures credit institutions may apply the definition of default at a facility level.

In all cases, the exposure past due shall be above a threshold defined by the competent authorities and which reflects a reasonable level of risk.

45. Elements to be taken as indications of unlikeliness to pay shall include:

(a) The credit institution puts the credit obligation on non-accrued status,

(b) The credit institution makes a value adjustment resulting from a significant perceived decline in credit quality subsequent to the credit institution taking on the exposure,

(c) The credit institution sells the credit obligation at a material credit-related economic loss,

(d) The credit institution consents to a distressed restructuring of the credit obligation where this is likely to result in a diminished financial obligation caused by the material forgiveness, or postponement, of principal, interest or (where relevant) fees. This includes, in the case of equity exposures assessed under a PD/LGD Approach, distressed restructuring of the equity itself,

(e) The credit institution has filed for the obligor's bankruptcy or a similar order in respect of an obligor's credit obligation to the credit institution, the parent undertaking or any of its subsidiaries, and

(f) The obligor has sought or has been placed in bankruptcy or similar protection where this would avoid or delay repayment of a credit obligation to the credit institution, the parent undertaking or any of its subsidiaries.

46. Credit institutions that use external data that is not itself consistent with the definition of default, shall demonstrate to their competent authorities that appropriate adjustments have been made to achieve broad equivalence with the definition of default.

47. If the credit institution considers that a previously defaulted exposure is such that no trigger of default continues to apply, the credit institution shall rate the obligor or facility as they would for a non-defaulted exposure. Should the definition of default subsequently be triggered, another default would be deemed to have occurred.

48. For retail and PSE exposures, the competent authorities of each Member State shall set the exact number of days past due that all credit institutions in its jurisdiction shall abide by under the definition of default set out in point 44, for exposures to such counterparts situated within this Member State. The specific number shall fall within 90–180 days and may differ across product lines. For exposures to such counterparts situated in the territories of other Member States, the competent authorities shall set a number of days past due which is not higher than the number set by the competent authority of the respective Member State.

2.2. Overall requirements for estimation

49. A credit institution's own estimates of the risk parameters PD, LGD, conversion factor and EL shall incorporate all relevant data, information and methods. The estimates shall be derived using both historical experience and empirical evidence, and not based purely on judgemental considerations. The estimates shall be plausible and intuitive and shall be based on the material drivers of the respective risk parameters. The less data a credit institution has, the more conservative it shall be in its estimation.

50. The credit institution shall be able to provide a breakdown of its loss experience in terms of default frequency, LGD, conversion factor, or loss where EL estimates are used, by the factors it sees as the drivers of the respective risk parameters. The credit institution shall demonstrate that its estimates are representative of long run experience.

51. Any changes in lending practice or the process for pursuing recoveries over the observation periods referred to in points 66, 71, 82, 86, 93 and 95 shall be taken into account. A credit institution's estimates shall reflect the implications of technical advances and new data and other information, as it becomes available. Credit institutions shall review their estimates when new information comes to light but at least on an annual basis.

52. The population of exposures represented in the data used for estimation, the lending standards used when the data was generated and other relevant characteristics shall be comparable with those of the credit institution's exposures and standards. The credit institution shall also demonstrate that the economic or market conditions that underlie the data are relevant to current and foreseeable conditions. The number of exposures in the sample and the data period used for quantification shall be sufficient to provide the credit institution with confidence in the accuracy and robustness of its estimates.

53. For purchased receivables the estimates shall reflect all relevant information available to the purchasing credit institution regarding the quality of the underlying receivables, including data for similar pools provided by the seller, by the purchasing credit institution, or by external sources. The purchasing credit institution shall evaluate any data relied upon which is provided by the seller.

54. A credit institution shall add to its estimates a margin of conservatism that is related to the expected range of estimation errors. Where methods and data are less satisfactory and the expected range of errors is larger, the margin of conservatism shall be larger.

55. If credit institutions use different estimates for the calculation of risk weights and for internal purposes, it shall be documented and their reasonableness shall be demonstrated to the competent authority.

56. If credit institutions can demonstrate to their competent authorities that for data that has been collected prior to the date of implementation of this Directive appropriate adjustments have been made to achieve broad equivalence with the definitions of default or loss, competent authorities may allow the credit

institutions some flexibility in the application of the required standards for data.

57. If a credit institution uses data that is pooled across credit institutions it shall demonstrate that:

(a) the rating systems and criteria of other credit institutions in the pool are similar with its own;

(b) the pool is representative of the portfolio for which the pooled data is used; and

(c) the pooled data is used consistently over time by the credit institution for its estimates.

58. If a credit institution uses data that is pooled across credit institutions, it shall remain responsible for the integrity of its rating systems. The credit institution shall demonstrate to the competent authority that it has sufficient in-house understanding of its rating systems, including effective ability to monitor and audit the rating process.

2.2.1. *Requirements specific to PD estimation*

Exposures to corporates, institutions and central governments and central banks

59. Credit institutions shall estimate PDs by obligor grade from long run averages of one-year default rates.

60. For purchased corporate receivables credit institutions may estimate ELs by obligor grade from long run averages of one-year realised default rates.

61. If a credit institution derives long run average estimates of PDs and LGDs for purchased corporate receivables from an estimate of EL, and an appropriate estimate of PD or LGD, the process for estimating total losses shall meet the overall standards for estimation of PD and LGD set out in this part, and the outcome shall be consistent with the concept of LGD as set out in point 73.

62. Credit institutions shall use PD estimation techniques only with supporting analysis. Credit institutions shall recognise the importance of judgmental considerations in combining results of techniques and in making adjustments for limitations of techniques and information.

63. To the extent that a credit institution uses data on internal default experience for the estimation of PDs, it shall demonstrate in its analysis that the estimates are reflective of underwriting standards and of any differences in the rating system that generated the data and the current rating system. Where underwriting standards or rating systems have changed, the credit institution shall add a greater margin of conservatism in its estimate of PD.

64. To the extent that a credit institution associates or maps its internal grades to the scale used by an ECAI or similar organisations and then attributes the default rate observed for the external organisation's grades to the credit institution's grades, mappings shall be based on a comparison of internal rating criteria to the criteria used by the external organisation and on a comparison of the internal and external ratings of any common obligors. Biases or inconsistencies in the mapping approach or underlying data shall be avoided. The external organisation's criteria underlying the data used for quantification shall be oriented to default risk only and not reflect transaction characteristics. The credit institution's analysis shall include a comparison of the default definitions used, subject to the requirements in points 44 to 48. The credit institution shall document the basis for the mapping.

65. To the extent that a credit institution uses statistical default prediction models it is allowed to estimate PDs as the simple average of default-probability estimates for individual obligors in a given grade. The credit institution's use of default probability models for this purpose shall meet the standards specified in point 30.

66. Irrespective of whether a credit institution is using external, internal, or pooled data sources, or a combination of the three, for its PD estimation, the length of the underlying historical observation period used shall be at least five years for at least one source. If the available observation period spans a longer period for any source, and this data is relevant, this longer period shall be used. This point also applies to the PD/LGD Approach to

equity. Member States may allow credit institutions which are not permitted to use own estimates of LGDs or conversion factors to have, when they implement the IRB Approach, relevant data covering a period of two years. The period to be covered shall increase by one year each year until relevant data covers a period of five years.

Retail exposures

67. Credit institutions shall estimate PDs by obligor grade or pool from long run averages of one-year default rates.

68. Notwithstanding point 67, PD estimates may also be derived from realised losses and appropriate estimates of LGDs.

69. Credit institutions shall regard internal data for assigning exposures to grades or pools as the primary source of information for estimating loss characteristics. Credit institutions are permitted to use external data (including pooled data) or statistical models for quantification provided a strong link can be demonstrated between:

(a) the credit institution's process of assigning exposures to grades or pools and the process used by the external data source; and

(b) the credit institution's internal risk profile and the composition of the external data.

For purchased retail receivables, credit institutions may use external and internal reference data. Credit institutions shall use all relevant data sources as points of comparison.

70. If a credit institution derives long run average estimates of PD and LGD for retail from an estimate of total losses and an appropriate estimate of PD or LGD, the process for estimating total losses shall meet the overall standards for estimation of PD and LGD set out in this part, and the outcome shall be consistent with the concept of LGD as set out in point 73.

71. Irrespective of whether a credit institution is using external, internal or pooled data sources or a combination of the three, for their estimation of loss characteristics, the length of the underlying historical observation period used shall be at least five years for at least one source. If the available observation spans a longer period for any source, and this data is relevant, this longer period shall be used. A credit institution need not give equal importance to historic data if it can convince its competent authority that more recent data is a better predictor of loss rates. Member States may allow credit institutions to have, when they implement the IRB Approach, relevant data covering a period of two years. The period to be covered shall increase by one year each year until relevant data covers a period of five years.

72. Credit institutions shall identify and analyse expected changes of risk parameters over the life of credit exposures (seasoning effects).

2.2.2. Requirements specific to own-LGD estimates

73. Credit institutions shall estimate LGDs by facility grade or pool on the basis of the average realised LGDs by facility grade or pool using all observed defaults within the data sources (default weighted average).

74. Credit institutions shall use LGD estimates that are appropriate for an economic downturn if those are more conservative than the long-run average. To the extent a rating system is expected to deliver realised LGDs at a constant level by grade or pool over time, credit institutions shall make adjustments to their estimates of risk parameters by grade or pool to limit the capital impact of an economic downturn.

75. A credit institution shall consider the extent of any dependence between the risk of the obligor with that of the collateral or collateral provider. Cases where there is a significant degree of dependence shall be addressed in a conservative manner.

76. Currency mismatches between the underlying obligation and the collateral shall be treated conservatively in the credit institution's assessment of LGD.

77. To the extent that LGD estimates take into account the existence of collateral, these estimates shall not solely be based on the collateral's estimated market value. LGD estimates shall take

into account the effect of the potential inability of credit institutions to expeditiously gain control of their collateral and liquidate it.

78. To the extent that LGD estimates take into account the existence of collateral, credit institutions must establish internal requirements for collateral management, legal certainty and risk management that are generally consistent with those set out in Annex VIII, Part 2.

79. To the extent that a credit institution recognises collateral for determining the exposure value for counterparty credit risk according to Annex III, Part 5 or 6, any amount expected to be recovered from the collateral shall not be taken into account in the LGD estimates.

80. For the specific case of exposures already in default, the credit institution shall use the sum of its best estimate of expected loss for each exposure given current economic circumstances and exposure status and the possibility of additional unexpected losses during the recovery period.

81. To the extent that unpaid late fees have been capitalised in the credit institution's income statement, they shall be added to the credit institution's measure of exposure and loss.

Exposures to corporates, institutions and central governments and central banks

82. Estimates of LGD shall be based on data over a minimum of five years, increasing by one year each year after implementation until a minimum of seven years is reached, for at least one data source. If the available observation period spans a longer period for any source, and the data is relevant, this longer period shall be used.

Retail exposures

83. Notwithstanding point 73, LGD estimates may be derived from realised losses and appropriate estimates of PDs.

84. Notwithstanding point 89, credit institutions may reflect future drawings either in their conversion factors or in their LGD estimates.

85. For purchased retail receivables credit institutions may use external and internal reference data to estimate LGDs.

86. Estimates of LGD shall be based on data over a minimum of five years. Notwithstanding point 73, a credit institution need not give equal importance to historic data if it can demonstrate to its competent authority that more recent data is a better predictor of loss rates. Member States may allow credit institutions to have, when they implement the IRB Approach, relevant data covering a period of two years. The period to be covered shall increase by one year each year until relevant data covers a period of five years.

2.2.3. *Requirements specific to own-conversion factor estimates*

87. Credit institutions shall estimate conversion factors by facility grade or pool on the basis of the average realised conversion factors by facility grade or pool using all observed defaults within the data sources (default weighted average).

88. Credit institutions shall use conversion factor estimates that are appropriate for an economic downturn if those are more conservative than the long-run average. To the extent a rating system is expected to deliver realised conversion factors at a constant level by grade or pool over time, credit institutions shall make adjustments to their estimates of risk parameters by grade or pool to limit the capital impact of an economic downturn.

89. Credit institutions' estimates of conversion factors shall reflect the possibility of additional drawings by the obligor up to and after the time a default event is triggered.

The conversion factor estimate shall incorporate a larger margin of conservatism where a stronger positive correlation can reasonably be expected between the default frequency and the magnitude of conversion factor.

90. In arriving at estimates of conversion factors credit institutions shall consider their specific policies and strategies adopted in respect of account monitoring and payment processing. Credit institutions shall also consider their ability and willingness to prevent further drawings in circumstances short of payment default, such as covenant violations or other technical default events.

91. Credit institutions shall have adequate systems and procedures in place to monitor facility amounts, current outstandings against committed lines and changes in outstandings per obligor and per grade. The credit institution shall be able to monitor outstanding balances on a daily basis.

92. If credit institutions use different estimates of conversion factors for the calculation of risk-weighted exposure amounts and internal purposes it shall be documented and their reasonableness shall be demonstrated to the competent authority.

Exposures to corporates, institutions and central governments and central banks

93. Estimates of conversion factors shall be based on data over a minimum of five years, increasing by one year each year after implementation until a minimum of seven years is reached, for at least one data source. If the available observation period spans a longer period for any source, and the data is relevant, this longer period shall be used.

Retail exposures

94. Notwithstanding point 89, credit institutions may reflect future drawings either in their conversion factors or in their LGD estimates.

95. Estimates of conversion factors shall be based on data over a minimum of five years. Notwithstanding point 87, a credit institution need not give equal importance to historic data if it can demonstrate to its competent authority that more recent data is a better predictor of draw downs. Member States may allow credit institutions to have, when they implement the IRB Approach, relevant data covering a period of two years. The period to be covered shall increase by one year each year until relevant data covers a period of five years.

2.2.4. *Minimum requirements for assessing the effect of guarantees and credit derivatives*

Exposures to corporates, institutions and central governments and central banks where own estimates of LGD are used and retail exposures

96. The requirements in points 97 to 104 shall not apply for guarantees provided by institutions and central governments and central banks if the credit institution has received approval to apply the rules of Articles 78 to 83 for exposures to such entities. In this case the requirements of Articles 90 to 93 shall apply.

97. For retail guarantees, these requirements also apply to the assignment of exposures to grades or pools, and the estimation of PD.

Eligible guarantors and guarantees

98. Credit institutions shall have clearly specified criteria for the types of guarantors they recognise for the calculation of risk-weighted exposure amounts.

99. For recognised guarantors the same rules as for obligors as set out in points 17 to 29 shall apply.

100. The guarantee shall be evidenced in writing, non-cancellable on the part of the guarantor, in force until the obligation is satisfied in full (to the extent of the amount and tenor of the guarantee) and legally enforceable against the guarantor in a jurisdiction where the guarantor has assets to attach and enforce a judgment. Guarantees prescribing conditions under which the guarantor may not be obliged to perform (conditional guarantees) may be recognised subject to approval of competent authorities. The credit institution shall demonstrate that the assignment criteria adequately address any potential reduction in the risk mitigation effect.

Adjustment criteria

101. A credit institution shall have clearly specified criteria for adjusting grades, pools or LGD estimates, and, in the case of retail and eligible purchased receivables, the process of allocating exposures to grades or pools, to reflect the impact of guarantees for the calculation of risk-weighted exposure amounts. These criteria shall comply with the minimum requirements set out in points 17 to 29.

102. The criteria shall be plausible and intuitive. They shall address the guarantor's ability and

willingness to perform under the guarantee, the likely timing of any payments from the guarantor, the degree to which the guarantor's ability to perform under the guarantee is correlated with the obligor's ability to repay, and the extent to which residual risk to the obligor remains.

Credit derivatives

103. The minimum requirements for guarantees in this part shall apply also for single-name credit derivatives. In relation to a mismatch between the underlying obligation and the reference obligation of the credit derivative or the obligation used for determining whether a credit event has occurred, the requirements set out under Annex VIII Part 2, point 21 shall apply. For retail exposures and eligible purchased receivables, this point applies to the process of allocating exposures to grades or pools.

104. The criteria shall address the payout structure of the credit derivative and conservatively assess the impact this has on the level and timing of recoveries. The credit institution shall consider the extent to which other forms of residual risk remain.

2.2.5. Minimum requirements for purchased receivables

Legal certainty

105. The structure of the facility shall ensure that under all foreseeable circumstances the credit institution has effective ownership and control of all cash remittances from the receivables. When the obligor makes payments directly to a seller or servicer, the credit institution shall verify regularly that payments are forwarded completely and within the contractually agreed terms. 'Servicer' shall mean an entity that manages a pool of purchased receivables or the underlying credit exposures on a day-to-day basis. Credit institutions shall have procedures to ensure that ownership over the receivables and cash receipts is protected against bankruptcy stays or legal challenges that could materially delay the lender's ability to liquidate or assign the receivables or retain control over cash receipts.

Effectiveness of monitoring systems

106. The credit institution shall monitor both the quality of the purchased receivables and the financial condition of the seller and servicer. In particular:

(a) the credit institution shall assess the correlation among the quality of the purchased receivables and the financial condition of both the seller and servicer, and have in place internal policies and procedures that provide adequate safeguards to protect against any contingencies, including the assignment of an internal risk rating for each seller and servicer;

(b) the credit institution shall have clear and effective policies and procedures for determining seller and servicer eligibility. The credit institution or its agent shall conduct periodic reviews of sellers and servicers in order to verify the accuracy of reports from the seller or servicer, detect fraud or operational weaknesses, and verify the quality of the seller's credit policies and servicer's collection policies and procedures. The findings of these reviews shall be documented;

(c) the credit institution shall assess the characteristics of the purchased receivables pools, including over-advances; history of the seller's arrears, bad debts, and bad debt allowances; payment terms, and potential contra accounts;

(d) the credit institution shall have effective policies and procedures for monitoring on an aggregate basis single-obligor concentrations both within and across purchased receivables pools; and

(e) the credit institution shall ensure that it receives from the servicer timely and sufficiently detailed reports of receivables ageings and dilutions to ensure compliance with the credit institution's eligibility criteria and advancing policies governing purchased receivables, and provide an effective means with which to monitor and confirm the seller's terms of sale and dilution.

Effectiveness of work-out systems

107. The credit institution shall have systems and procedures for detecting deteriorations in the seller's financial condition and purchased receivables quality at an early stage, and for addressing emerging problems pro-actively. In particular,

the credit institution shall have clear and effective policies, procedures, and information systems to monitor covenant violations, and clear and effective policies and procedures for initiating legal actions and dealing with problem purchased receivables.

Effectiveness of systems for controlling collateral, credit availability, and cash

108. The credit institution shall have clear and effective policies and procedures governing the control of purchased receivables, credit, and cash. In particular, written internal policies shall specify all material elements of the receivables purchase programme, including the advancing rates, eligible collateral, necessary documentation, concentration limits, and the way cash receipts are to be handled. These elements shall take appropriate account of all relevant and material factors, including the seller and servicer's financial condition, risk concentrations, and trends in the quality of the purchased receivables and the seller's customer base, and internal systems shall ensure that funds are advanced only against specified supporting collateral and documentation.

Compliance with the credit institution's internal policies and procedures

109. The credit institution shall have an effective internal process for assessing compliance with all internal policies and procedures. The process shall include regular audits of all critical phases of the credit institution's receivables purchase programme, verification of the separation of duties between firstly the assessment of the seller and servicer and the assessment of the obligor and secondly between the assessment of the seller and servicer and the field audit of the seller and servicer, and evaluations of back office operations, with particular focus on qualifications, experience, staffing levels, and supporting automation systems.

3. Validation of Internal Estimates

110. Credit institutions shall have robust systems in place to validate the accuracy and consistency of rating systems, processes, and the estimation of all relevant risk parameters. A credit institution shall demonstrate to its competent authority that the internal validation process enables it to assess the performance of internal rating and risk estimation systems consistently and meaningfully.

111. Credit institutions shall regularly compare realised default rates with estimated PDs for each grade and, where realised default rates are outside the expected range for that grade, credit institutions shall specifically analyse the reasons for the deviation. Credit institutions using own estimates of LGDs and/or conversion factors shall also perform analogous analysis for these estimates. Such comparisons shall make use of historical data that covers as long a period as possible. The credit institution shall document the methods and data used in such comparisons. This analysis and documentation shall be updated at least annually.

112. Credit institutions shall also use other quantitative validation tools and comparisons with relevant external data sources. The analysis shall be based on data that is appropriate to the portfolio, are updated regularly, and cover a relevant observation period. Credit institutions' internal assessments of the performance of their rating systems shall be based on as long a period as possible.

113. The methods and data used for quantitative validation shall be consistent through time. Changes in estimation and validation methods and data (both data sources and periods covered) shall be documented.

114. Credit institutions shall have sound internal standards for situations where deviations in realised PDs, LGDs, conversion factors and total losses, where EL is used, from expectations, become significant enough to call the validity of the estimates into question. These standards shall take account of business cycles and similar systematic variability in default experience. Where realised values continue to be higher than expected values, credit institutions shall revise estimates upward to reflect their default and loss experience.

4. Calculation of Risk-Weighted Exposure Amounts for Equity Exposures Under the Internal Models Approach

4.1. Capital requirement and risk quantification

115. For the purpose of calculating capital requirements credit institutions shall meet the following standards:

(a) the estimate of potential loss shall be robust to adverse market movements relevant to the long-term risk profile of the credit institution's specific holdings. The data used to represent return distributions shall reflect the longest sample period for which data is available and meaningful in representing the risk profile of the credit institution's specific equity exposures. The data used shall be sufficient to provide conservative, statistically reliable and robust loss estimates that are not based purely on subjective or judgmental considerations. Credit institutions shall demonstrate to competent authorities that the shock employed provides a conservative estimate of potential losses over a relevant long-term market or business cycle. The credit institution shall combine empirical analysis of available data with adjustments based on a variety of factors in order to attain model outputs that achieve appropriate realism and conservatism. In constructing Value at Risk (VaR) models estimating potential quarterly losses, credit institutions may use quarterly data or convert shorter horizon period data to a quarterly equivalent using an analytically appropriate method supported by empirical evidence and through a well-developed and documented thought process and analysis. Such an approach shall be applied conservatively and consistently over time. Where only limited relevant data is available the credit institution shall add appropriate margins of conservatism;

(b) the models used shall be able to capture adequately all of the material risks embodied in equity returns including both the general market risk and specific risk exposure of the credit institution's equity portfolio. The internal models shall adequately explain historical price variation, capture both the magnitude and changes in the composition of potential concentrations, and be robust to adverse market environments. The population of risk exposures represented in the data used for estimation shall be closely matched to or at least comparable with those of the credit institution's equity exposures;

(c) the internal model shall be appropriate for the risk profile and complexity of a credit institution's equity portfolio. Where a credit institution has material holdings with values that are highly non-linear in nature the internal models shall be designed to capture appropriately the risks associated with such instruments;

(d) mapping of individual positions to proxies, market indices, and risk factors shall be plausible, intuitive, and conceptually sound;

(e) credit institutions shall demonstrate through empirical analyses the appropriateness of risk factors, including their ability to cover both general and specific risk;

(f) the estimates of the return volatility of equity exposures shall incorporate relevant and available data, information, and methods. Independently reviewed internal data or data from external sources (including pooled data) shall be used; and

(g) a rigorous and comprehensive stress-testing programme shall be in place.

4.2. Risk management process and controls

116. With regard to the development and use of internal models for capital requirement purposes, credit institutions shall establish policies, procedures, and controls to ensure the integrity of the model and modelling process. These policies, procedures, and controls shall include the following:

(a) full integration of the internal model into the overall management information systems of the credit institution and in the management of the non-trading book equity portfolio. Internal models shall be fully integrated into the credit institution's risk management infrastructure if they are particularly used in measuring and assessing equity portfolio performance (including the risk-adjusted performance), allocating economic capital to equity exposures and evaluating overall capital adequacy and the investment management process;

(b) established management systems, procedures, and control functions for ensuring the periodic and independent review of all elements of the internal modelling process, including approval of model revisions, vetting of model inputs, and review of model results, such as direct verification of risk computations. These reviews shall assess the accuracy, completeness, and appropriateness of model inputs and results and focus on both finding and limiting potential errors associated with known weaknesses and identifying unknown model weaknesses. Such reviews may be conducted by an internal independent unit, or by an independent external third party;

(c) adequate systems and procedures for monitoring investment limits and the risk exposures of equity exposures;

(d) the units responsible for the design and application of the model shall be functionally independent from the units responsible for managing individual investments; and

(e) parties responsible for any aspect of the modelling process shall be adequately qualified. Management shall allocate sufficient skilled and competent resources to the modelling function.

4.3. Validation and documentation

117. Credit institutions shall have a robust system in place to validate the accuracy and consistency of their internal models and modelling processes. All material elements of the internal models and the modelling process and validation shall be documented.

118. Credit institutions shall use the internal validation process to assess the performance of its internal models and processes in a consistent and meaningful way.

119. The methods and data used for quantitative validation shall be consistent through time. Changes in estimation and validation methods and data (both data sources and periods covered) shall be documented.

120. Credit institutions shall regularly compare actual equity returns (computed using realised and unrealised gains and losses) with modelled estimates. Such comparisons shall make use of historical data that cover as long a period as possible. The credit institution shall document the methods and data used in such comparisons. This analysis and documentation shall be updated at least annually.

121. Credit institutions shall make use of other quantitative validation tools and comparisons with external data sources. The analysis shall be based on data that is appropriate to the portfolio, is updated regularly, and covers a relevant observation period. Credit institutions' internal assessments of the performance of their models shall be based on as long a period as possible.

122. Credit institutions shall have sound internal standards for situations where comparison of actual equity returns with the models' estimates calls the validity of the estimates or of the models as such into question. These standards shall take account of business cycles and similar systematic variability in equity returns. All adjustments made to internal models in response to model reviews shall be documented and consistent with the credit institution's model review standards.

123. The internal model and the modelling process shall be documented, including the responsibilities of parties involved in the modelling, and the model approval and model review processes.

5. CORPORATE GOVERNANCE AND OVERSIGHT

5.1. Corporate governance

124. All material aspects of the rating and estimation processes shall be approved by the credit institution's management body described in Article 11 or a designated committee thereof and senior management. These parties shall possess a general understanding of the credit institution's rating systems and detailed comprehension of its associated management reports.

125. Senior management shall provide notice to the management body described in Article 11 or a designated committee thereof of material changes or exceptions from established policies

that will materially impact the operations of the credit institution's rating systems.

126. Senior management shall have a good understanding of the rating systems designs and operations. Senior management shall ensure, on an ongoing basis that the rating systems are operating properly. Senior management shall be regularly informed by the credit risk control units about the performance of the rating process, areas needing improvement, and the status of efforts to improve previously identified deficiencies

127. Internal ratings-based analysis of the credit institution's credit risk profile shall be an essential part of the management reporting to these parties. Reporting shall include at least risk profile by grade, migration across grades, estimation of the relevant parameters per grade, and comparison of realised default rates, and to the extent that own estimates are used of realised LGDs and realised conversion factors against expectations and stress-test results. Reporting frequencies shall depend on the significance and type of information and the level of the recipient.

5.2. Credit risk control

128. The credit risk control unit shall be independent from the personnel and management functions responsible for originating or renewing exposures and report directly to senior management. The unit shall be responsible for the design or selection, implementation, oversight and performance of the rating systems. It shall regularly produce and analyse reports on the output of the rating systems.

129. The areas of responsibility for the credit risk control unit(s) shall include:

(a) testing and monitoring grades and pools;

(b) production and analysis of summary reports from the credit institution's rating systems;

(c) implementing procedures to verify that grade and pool definitions are consistently applied across departments and geographic areas;

(d) reviewing and documenting any changes to the rating process, including the reasons for the changes;

(e) reviewing the rating criteria to evaluate if they remain predictive of risk. Changes to the rating process, criteria or individual rating parameters shall be documented and retained;

(f) active participation in the design or selection, implementation and validation of models used in the rating process;

(g) oversight and supervision of models used in the rating process; and

(h) ongoing review and alterations to models used in the rating process.

130. Notwithstanding point 129, credit institutions using pooled data according to points 57 and 58 may outsource the following tasks:

(a) production of information relevant to testing and monitoring grades and pools;

(b) production of summary reports from the credit institution's rating systems;

(c) production of information relevant to review of the rating criteria to evaluate if they remain predictive of risk;

(d) documentation of changes to the rating process, criteria or individual rating parameters; and

(e) production of information relevant to ongoing review and alterations to models used in the rating process.

Credit institutions making use of this point shall ensure that the competent authorities have access to all relevant information from the third party that is necessary for examining compliance with the minimum requirements and that the competent authorities may perform on-site examinations to the same extent as within the credit institution.

5.3. Internal audit

131. Internal audit or another comparable independent auditing unit shall review at least annually the credit institution's rating systems and its operations, including the operations of the credit function and the estimation of PDs, LGDs, ELs and conversion factors. Areas of review shall include adherence to all applicable minimum requirements.

Annex VIII

Credit Risk Mitigation

Part 1

Eligibility

1. This part sets out eligible forms of credit risk mitigation for the purposes of Article 92.

2. For the purposes of this Annex:

'Secured lending transaction' shall mean any transaction giving rise to an exposure secured by collateral which does not include a provision conferring upon the credit institution the right to receive margin frequently.

'Capital market-driven transaction' shall mean any transaction giving rise to an exposure secured by collateral which includes a provision conferring upon the credit institution the right to receive margin frequently.

1. Funded Credit Protection

1.1. On-balance sheet netting

3. The on-balance sheet netting of mutual claims between the credit institution and its counterparty may be recognised as eligible.

4. Without prejudice to point 5, eligibility is limited to reciprocal cash balances between the credit institution and the counterparty. Only loans and deposits of the lending credit institution may be subject to a modification of risk-weighted exposure amounts and, as relevant, expected loss amounts as a result of an on-balance sheet netting agreement.

1.2. Master netting agreements covering repurchase transactions and/or securities or commodities lending or borrowing transactions and/or other capital market-driven transactions

5. For credit institutions adopting the Financial Collateral Comprehensive Method under Part 3, the effects of bilateral netting contracts covering repurchase transactions, securities or commodities lending or borrowing transactions, and/or other capital market-driven transactions with a counterparty may be recognised. Without prejudice to Annex II to Directive 2006/49/EC to be recognised the collateral taken and securities or commodities borrowed within such agreements must comply with the eligibility requirements for collateral set out at points 7 to 11.

1.3. Collateral

6. Where the credit risk mitigation technique used relies on the right of the credit institution to liquidate or retain assets, eligibility depends upon whether risk-weighted exposure amounts, and, as relevant, expected loss amounts, are calculated under Articles 78 to 83 or Articles 84 to 89. Eligibility further depends upon whether the Financial Collateral Simple Method is used or the Financial Collateral Comprehensive Method under Part 3. In relation to repurchase transactions and securities or commodities lending or borrowing transactions, eligibility also depends upon whether the transaction is booked in the non-trading book or the trading book.

1.3.1. *Eligibility under all approaches and methods*

7. The following financial items may be recognised as eligible collateral under all approaches and methods:

(a) cash on deposit with, or cash assimilated instruments held by, the lending credit institution;

(b) debt securities issued by central governments or central banks, which securities have a credit assessment by an ECAI or export credit agency recognised as eligible for the purposes of Articles 78 to 83 which has been determined by the competent authority to be associated with credit quality step 4 or above under the rules for the risk weighting of exposures to central governments and central banks under Articles 78 to 83;

(c) debt securities issued by institutions, which securities have a credit assessment by an eligible ECAI which has been determined by the competent authority to be associated with credit quality step 3 or above under the rules for the risk weighting of exposures to credit institutions under Articles 78 to 83;

(d) debt securities issued by other entities, which securities have a credit assessment by an eligible ECAI which has been determined by the competent authority to be associated with credit quality step 3 or above under the rules for the risk weighting of exposures to corporates under Articles 78 to 83;

(e) debt securities with a short-term credit assessment by an eligible ECAI which has been determined by the competent authority to be associated with credit quality step 3 or above under the rules for the risk weighting of short term exposures under Articles 78 to 83;

(f) equities or convertible bonds that are included in a main index; and

(g) gold.

For the purposes of point (b), 'debt securities issued by central governments or central banks' shall include:

(i) debt securities issued by regional governments or local authorities, exposures to which are treated as exposures to the central government in whose jurisdiction they are established under Articles 78 to 83;

(ii) debt securities issued by public sector entities which are treated as exposures to central governments in accordance with point 15 of Part 1 of Annex VI;

(iii) debt securities issued by multilateral development banks to which a 0% risk weight is assigned under Articles 78 to 83; and

(iv) debt securities issued by international organisations which are assigned a 0% risk weight under Articles 78 to 83.

For the purposes of point (c), 'debt securities issued by institutions' include:

(i) debt securities issued by regional governments or local authorities other than those exposures to which are treated as exposures to the central government in whose jurisdiction they are established under Articles 78 to 83;

(ii) debt securities issued by public sector entities, exposures to which are treated as exposures to credit institutions under Articles 78 to 83; and

(iii) debt securities issued by multilateral development banks other than those to which a 0% risk weight is assigned under Articles 78 to 83.

8. Debt securities issued by institutions which securities do not have a credit assessment by an eligible ECAI may be recognised as eligible collateral if they fulfil the following criteria:

(a) they are listed on a recognised exchange;

(b) they qualify as senior debt;

(c) all other rated issues by the issuing institution of the same seniority have a credit assessment by an eligible ECAI which has been determined by the competent authorities to be associated with credit quality step 3 or above under the rules for the risk weighting of exposures to institutions or short term exposures under Articles 78 to 83;

(d) the lending credit institution has no information to suggest that the issue would justify a credit assessment below that indicated in (c); and

(e) the credit institution can demonstrate to the competent authorities that the market liquidity of the instrument is sufficient for these purposes.

9. Units in collective investment undertakings may be recognised as eligible collateral if the following conditions are satisfied:

(a) they have a daily public price quote; and

(b) the collective investment undertaking is limited to investing in instruments that are eligible for recognition under points 7 and 8.

The use (or potential use) by a collective investment undertaking of derivative instruments to hedge permitted investments shall not prevent units in that undertaking from being eligible.

10. In relation to points (b) to (e) of point 7, where a security has two credit assessments by eligible ECAIs, the less favourable assessment shall be deemed to apply. In cases where a security has more than two credit assessments by eligible ECAIs, the two most favourable assessments shall be deemed to apply. If the two most favourable

credit assessments are different, the less favourable of the two shall be deemed to apply.

1.3.2. *Additional eligibility under the Financial Collateral Comprehensive Method*

11. In addition to the collateral set out in points 7 to 10, where a credit institution uses the Financial Collateral Comprehensive Method under Part 3, the following financial items may be recognised as eligible collateral:

(a) equities or convertible bonds not included in a main index but traded on a recognised exchange; and

(b) units in collective investment undertakings if the following conditions are met:
(i) they have a daily public price quote; and
(ii) the collective investment undertaking is limited to investing in instruments that are eligible for recognition under point 7 and 8 and the items mentioned in point (a) of this point.

The use (or potential use) by a collective investment undertaking of derivative instruments to hedge permitted investments shall not prevent units in that undertaking from being eligible.

1.3.3. *Additional eligibility for calculations under Articles 84 to 89*

12. In addition to the collateral set out above the provisions of points 13 to 22 apply where a credit institution calculates risk-weighted exposure amounts and expected loss amounts under the approach set out in Articles 84 to 89:

(a) *Real estate collateral*

13. Residential real estate property which is or will be occupied or let by the owner, or the beneficial owner in the case of personal investment companies, and commercial real estate property, that is, offices and other commercial premises, may be recognised as eligible collateral where the following conditions are met:

(a) the value of the property does not materially depend upon the credit quality of the obligor. This requirement does not preclude situations where purely macro-economic factors affect both the value of the property and the performance of the borrower; and

(b) the risk of the borrower does not materially depend upon the performance of the underlying property or project, but rather on the underlying capacity of the borrower to repay the debt from other sources. As such, repayment of the facility does not materially depend on any cash flow generated by the underlying property serving as collateral.

14. Credit institutions may also recognise as eligible collateral shares in Finnish residential housing companies operating in accordance with the Finnish Housing Company Act of 1991 or subsequent equivalent legislation in respect of residential property which is or will be occupied or let by the owner, as residential real estate collateral, provided that these conditions are met.

15. The competent authorities may also authorise their credit institutions to recognise as eligible collateral shares in Finnish housing companies operating in accordance with the Finnish Housing Company Act of 1991 or subsequent equivalent legislation as commercial real estate collateral, provided that these conditions are met.

16. The competent authorities may waive the requirement for their credit institutions to comply with condition (b) in point 13 for exposures secured by residential real estate property situated within the territory of that Member State, if the competent authorities have evidence that the relevant market is well-developed and long-established with loss-rates which are sufficiently low to justify such action. This shall not prevent the competent authorities of a Member State, which do not use this waiver from recognising as eligible residential real estate property recognised as eligible in another Member State by virtue of the waiver. Member States shall disclose publicly the use they make of this waiver.

17. The competent authorities of the Member States may waive the requirement for their credit institutions to comply with the condition in point 13(b) for commercial real estate property situated within the territory of that Member

State, if the competent authorities have evidence that the relevant market is well-developed and long-established and that loss-rates stemming from lending secured by commercial real estate property satisfy the following conditions:

(a) losses stemming from loans collateralised by commercial real estate property up to 50% of the market value (or where applicable and if lower 60% of the mortgage-lending-value) do not exceed 0.3% of the outstanding loans collateralised by commercial real estate property in any given year; and

(b) overall losses stemming from loans collateralised by commercial real estate property do not exceed 0.5% of the outstanding loans collateralised by commercial real estate property in any given year.

18. If either of these conditions is not satisfied in a given year, the eligibility to use this treatment will cease until the conditions are satisfied in a subsequent year.

19. The competent authorities of a Member State may recognise as eligible collateral commercial real estate property recognised as eligible collateral in another Member State by virtue of the waiver provided for in point 17.

(b) *Receivables*

20. The competent authorities may recognise as eligible collateral amounts receivable linked to a commercial transaction or transactions with an original maturity of less than or equal to one year. Eligible receivables do not include those associated with securitisations, sub-participations or credit derivatives or amounts owed by affiliated parties.

(c) *Other physical collateral*

21. The competent authorities may recognise as eligible collateral physical items of a type other than those types indicated in points 13 to 19 if satisfied as to the following:

(a) the existence of liquid markets for disposal of the collateral in an expeditious and economically efficient manner; and

(b) the existence of well-established publicly available market prices for the collateral. The credit institution must be able to demonstrate that there is no evidence that the net prices it receives when collateral is realised deviate significantly from these market prices.

(d) *Leasing*

22. Subject to the provisions of Part 3, point 72, where the requirements set out in Part 2, point 11 are met, exposures arising from transactions whereby a credit institution leases property to a third party will be treated the same as loans collateralised by the type of property leased.

1.4. Other funded credit protection

1.4.1. *Cash on deposit with, or cash assimilated instruments held by, a third party institution.*

23. Cash on deposit with, or cash assimilated instruments held by, a third party institution in a non-custodial arrangement and pledged to the lending credit institution may be recognised as eligible credit protection.

1.4.2. *Life insurance policies pledged to the lending credit institution*

24. Life insurance policies pledged to the lending credit institution may be recognised as eligible credit protection.

1.4.3. *Institution instruments repurchased on request*

25. Instruments issued by third party institutions which will be repurchased by that institution on request may be recognised as eligible credit protection.

2. Unfunded Credit Protection

2.1. Eligibility of protection providers under all approaches

26. The following parties may be recognised as eligible providers of unfunded credit protection:

(a) central governments and central banks;

(b) regional governments or local authorities;

(c) multilateral development banks;

(d) international organisations exposures to which a 0% risk weight under Articles 78 to 83 is assigned;

(e) public sector entities, claims on which are treated by the competent authorities as claims on institutions or central governments under Articles 78 to 83;

(f) institutions; and

(g) other corporate entities, including parent, subsidiary and affiliate corporate entities of the credit institution, that:

(i) have a credit assessment by a recognised ECAI which has been determined by the competent authorities to be associated with credit quality step 2 or above under the rules for the risk weighting of exposures to corporates under Articles 78 to 83; and

(ii) in the case of credit institutions calculating risk-weighted exposure amounts and expected loss amounts under Articles 84 to 89, do not have a credit assessment by a recognised ECAI and are internally rated as having a PD equivalent to that associated with the credit assessments of ECAIs determined by the competent authorities to be associated with credit quality step 2 or above under the rules for the risk weighting of exposures to corporate under Articles 78 to 83.

27. Where risk-weighted exposure amounts and expected loss amounts are calculated under Articles 84 to 89, to be eligible a guarantor must be internally rated by the credit institution in accordance with the provisions of Annex VII, Part 4.

28. By way of derogation from point 26, the Member States may also recognise as eligible providers of unfunded credit protection, other financial institutions authorised and supervised by the competent authorities responsible for the authorisation and supervision of credit institutions and subject to prudential requirements equivalent to those applied to credit institutions.

2.2 Eligibility of protection providers under the IRB Approach which qualify for the treatment set out in Annex VII, Part 1, point 4

29. Institutions, insurance and reinsurance undertakings and export credit agencies which fulfil the following conditions may be recognised as eligible providers of unfunded credit protection which qualify for the treatment set out in Annex VII, Part 1, point 4:

– the protection provider has sufficient expertise in providing unfunded credit protection;

– the protection provider is regulated in a manner equivalent to the rules laid down in this Directive, or had, at the time the credit protection was provided, a credit assessment by a recognised ECAI which had been determined by the competent authorities to be associated with credit quality step 3, or above, under the rules for the risk weighting of exposures to corporate under Articles 78 to 83;

– the protection provider had, at the time the credit protection was provided, or for any period of time thereafter, an internal rating with a PD equivalent to or lower than that associated with credit quality step 2 or above under the rules for the risk weighting of exposures to corporates under Articles 78 to 83; and

– the provider has an internal rating with a PD equivalent to or lower than that associated with credit quality step 3 or above under the rules for the risk weighting of exposures to corporates under Articles 78 to 83.

For the purpose of this point, credit protection provided by export credit agencies shall not benefit from any explicit central government counter-guarantee.

3. TYPES OF CREDIT DERIVATIVES

30. The following types of credit derivatives, and instruments that may be composed of such credit

derivatives or that are economically effectively similar, may be recognised as eligible:

(a) credit default swaps;

(b) total return swaps; and

(c) credit linked notes to the extent of their cash funding.

31. Where a credit institution buys credit protection through a total return swap and records the net payments received on the swap as net income, but does not record offsetting deterioration in the value of the asset that is protected (either through reductions in fair value or by an addition to reserves), the credit protection shall not be recognised as eligible.

3.1. Internal hedges

32. When a credit institution conducts an internal hedge using a credit derivative—i.e. hedges the credit risk of an exposure in the non-trading book with a credit derivative booked in the trading book—in order for the protection to be recognised as eligible for the purposes of this Annex the credit risk transferred to the trading book shall be transferred out to a third party or parties. In such circumstances, subject to the compliance of such transfer with the requirements for the recognition of credit risk mitigation set out in this Annex, the rules set out in Parts 3 to 6 for the calculation of risk-weighted exposure amounts and expected loss amounts where unfunded credit protection is acquired shall be applied.

PART 2

Minimum Requirements

1. The credit institution must satisfy the competent authorities that it has adequate risk management processes to control those risks to which the credit institution may be exposed as a result of carrying out credit risk mitigation practices.

2. Notwithstanding the presence of credit risk mitigation taken into account for the purposes of calculating risk-weighted exposure amounts and as relevant expected loss amounts, credit institutions shall continue to undertake full credit risk assessment of the underlying exposure and be in a position to demonstrate the fulfilment of this requirement to the competent authorities. In the case of repurchase transactions and/or securities or commodities lending or borrowing transactions the underlying exposure shall, for the purposes of this point only, be deemed to be the net amount of the exposure.

1. FUNDED CREDIT PROTECTION

1.1. On-balance sheet netting agreements (other than master netting agreements covering repurchase transactions, securities or commodities lending or borrowing transactions and/or other capital marketdriven transactions)

3. For on-balance sheet netting agreements—other than master netting agreements covering repurchase transactions, securities or commodities lending or borrowing transactions and/or other capital market-driven transactions—to be recognised for the purposes of Articles 90 to 93, the following conditions shall be satisfied:

(a) they must be legally effective and enforceable in all relevant jurisdictions, including in the event of the insolvency or bankruptcy of a counterparty;

(b) the credit institution must be able to determine at any time those assets and liabilities that are subject to the on-balance sheet netting agreement;

(c) the credit institution must monitor and control the risks associated with the termination of the credit protection; and

(d) the credit institution must monitor and control the relevant exposures on a net basis.

1.2. Master netting agreements covering repurchase transactions and/or securities or commodities lending or borrowing transactions and/or other capital market driven transactions

4. For master netting agreements covering repurchase transactions and/or securities or

commodities lending or borrowing transactions and/or other capital market driven transactions to be recognised for the purposes of Articles 90 to 93, they shall:

(a) be legally effective and enforceable in all relevant jurisdictions, including in the event of the bankruptcy or insolvency of the counterparty;

(b) give the non-defaulting party the right to terminate and close-out in a timely manner all transactions under the agreement upon the event of default, including in the event of the bankruptcy or insolvency of the counterparty; and

(c) provide for the netting of gains and losses on transactions closed out under a master agreement so that a single net amount is owed by one party to the other.

5. In addition, the minimum requirements for the recognition of financial collateral under the Financial Collateral Comprehensive Method set out in point 6 shall be fulfilled.

1.3. Financial collateral

1.3.1. *Minimum requirements for the recognition of financial collateral under all Approaches and Methods*

6. For the recognition of financial collateral and gold, the following conditions shall be met.

(a) *Low correlation*

The credit quality of the obligor and the value of the collateral must not have a material positive correlation.

Securities issued by the obligor, or any related group entity, are not eligible. This notwithstanding, the obligor's own issues of covered bonds falling within the terms of Annex VI, Part 1, points 68 to 70 may be recognised as eligible when they are posted as collateral for repurchase transactions, provided that the first paragraph of this point is complied with.

(b) *Legal certainty*

Credit institutions shall fulfil any contractual and statutory requirements in respect of, and take all steps necessary to ensure, the enforceability of the collateral arrangements under the law applicable to their interest in the collateral.

Credit institutions shall have conducted sufficient legal review confirming the enforceability of the collateral arrangements in all relevant jurisdictions. They shall re-conduct such review as necessary to ensure continuing enforceability.

(c) *Operational requirements*

The collateral arrangements shall be properly documented, with a clear and robust procedure for the timely liquidation of collateral.

Credit institutions shall employ robust procedures and processes to control risks arising from the use of collateral—including risks of failed or reduced credit protection, valuation risks, risks associated with the termination of the credit protection, concentration risk arising from the use of collateral and the interaction with the credit institution's overall risk profile.

The credit institution shall have documented policies and practices concerning the types and amounts of collateral accepted.

Credit institutions shall calculate the market value of the collateral, and revalue it accordingly, with a minimum frequency of once every six months and whenever the credit institution has reason to believe that there has occurred a significant decrease in its market value.

Where the collateral is held by a third party, credit institutions must take reasonable steps to ensure that the third party segregates the collateral from its own assets.

1.3.2. *Additional minimum requirements for the recognition of financial collateral under the Financial Collateral Simple Method*

7. In addition to the requirements set out in point 6, for the recognition of financial collateral under the Financial Collateral Simple Method the residual maturity of the protection must be at least as long as the residual maturity of the exposure.

1.4. Minimum requirements for the recognition of real estate collateral

8. For the recognition of real estate collateral the following conditions shall be met.

(a) *Legal certainty*

The mortgage or charge shall be enforceable in all jurisdictions which are relevant at the time of the conclusion of the credit agreement, and the mortgage or charge shall be properly filed on a timely basis. The arrangements shall reflect a perfected lien (i.e. all legal requirements for establishing the pledge shall have been fulfilled). The protection agreement and the legal process underpinning it shall enable the credit institution to realise the value of the protection within a reasonable timeframe.

(b) *Monitoring of property values*

The value of the property shall be monitored on a frequent basis and at a minimum once every year for commercial real estate and once every three years for residential real estate. More frequent monitoring shall be carried out where the market is subject to significant changes in conditions. Statistical methods may be used to monitor the value of the property and to identify property that needs revaluation. The property valuation shall be reviewed by an independent valuer when information indicates that the value of the property may have declined materially relative to general market prices. For loans exceeding EUR 3 million or 5% of the own funds of the credit institution, the property valuation shall be reviewed by an independent valuer at least every three years.

'Independent valuer' shall mean a person who possesses the necessary qualifications, ability and experience to execute a valuation and who is independent from the credit decision process.

(c) *Documentation*

The types of residential and commercial real estate accepted by the credit institution and its lending policies in this regard shall be clearly documented.

(d) *Insurance*

The credit institution shall have procedures to monitor that the property taken as protection is adequately insured against damage.

1.5. Minimum requirements for the recognition of receivables as collateral

9. For the recognition of receivables as collateral the following conditions shall be met:

(a) *Legal certainty*

(i) The legal mechanism by which the collateral is provided shall be robust and effective and ensure that the lender has clear rights over the proceeds;

(ii) Credit institutions must take all steps necessary to fulfil local requirements in respect of the enforceability of security interest. There shall be a framework which allows the lender to have a first priority claim over the collateral subject to national discretion to allow such claims to be subject to the claims of preferential creditors provided for in legislative or implementing provisions;

(iii) Credit institutions shall have conducted sufficient legal review confirming the enforceability of the collateral arrangements in all relevant jurisdictions; and

(iv) The collateral arrangements must be properly documented, with a clear and robust procedure for the timely collection of collateral. Credit institutions' procedures shall ensure that any legal conditions required for declaring the default of the borrower and timely collection of collateral are observed. In the event of the borrower's financial distress or default, the credit institution shall have legal authority to sell or assign the receivables to other parties without consent of the receivables obligors.

(b) *Risk management*

(i) The credit institution must have a sound process for determining the credit risk associated with the receivables. Such a process shall include, among other things, analyses of the borrower's business and industry and the types of customers with whom the borrower does business. Where the credit institution relies on the borrower to ascertain the credit risk of the customers, the credit institution must review the borrower's credit practices to ascertain their soundness and credibility;

(ii) The margin between the amount of the exposure and the value of the receivables must reflect all appropriate factors, including the cost of collection, concentration within the receivables pool pledged by an individual borrower, and potential concentration risk within the credit institution's total exposures beyond that controlled by the credit institution's general methodology. The credit institution must maintain a continuous monitoring process appropriate to the receivables. Additionally, compliance with loan covenants, environmental restrictions, and other legal requirements shall be reviewed on a regular basis;

(iii) The receivables pledged by a borrower shall be diversified and not be unduly correlated with the borrower. Where there is material positive correlation, the attendant risks shall be taken into account in the setting of margins for the collateral pool as a whole;

(iv) Receivables from affiliates of the borrower (including subsidiaries and employees) shall not be recognised as risk mitigants; and

(v) The credit institution shall have a documented process for collecting receivable payments in distressed situations. The requisite facilities for collection shall be in place, even when the credit institution normally looks to the borrower for collections.

1.6. Minimum requirements for the recognition of other physical collateral

10. For the recognition of other physical collateral the following conditions shall be met:

(a) the collateral arrangement shall be legally effective and enforceable in all relevant jurisdictions and shall enable the credit institution to realise the value of the property within a reasonable timeframe;

(b) with the sole exception of permissible prior claims referred to in point 9(a)(ii), only first liens on, or charges over, collateral are permissible. As such, the credit institution shall have priority over all other lenders to the realised proceeds of the collateral;

(c) the value of the property shall be monitored on a frequent basis and at a minimum once every year. More frequent monitoring shall be required where the market is subject to significant changes in conditions;

(d) the loan agreement shall include detailed descriptions of the collateral plus detailed specifications of the manner and frequency of revaluation;

(e) the types of physical collateral accepted by the credit institution and policies and practices in respect of the appropriate amount of each type of collateral relative to the exposure amount shall be clearly documented in internal credit policies and procedures available for examination;

(f) the credit institution's credit policies with regard to the transaction structure shall address appropriate collateral requirements relative to the exposure amount, the ability to liquidate the collateral readily, the ability to establish objectively a price or market value, the frequency with which the value can readily be obtained (including a professional appraisal or valuation), and the volatility or a proxy of the volatility of the value of the collateral;

(g) both initial valuation and revaluation shall take fully into account any deterioration or obsolescence of the collateral. Particular attention must be paid in valuation and revaluation to the effects of the passage of time on fashion- or date-sensitive collateral;

(h) the credit institution must have the right to physically inspect the property. It shall have policies and procedures addressing its exercise of the right to physical inspection; and

(i) the credit institution must have procedures to monitor that the property taken as protection is adequately insured against damage.

1.7. Minimum requirements for treating lease exposures as collateralised

11. For the exposures arising from leasing transactions to be treated as collateralised by the

type of property leased, the following conditions shall be met:

(a) the conditions set out in points 8 or 10 as appropriate for the recognition as collateral of the type of property leased shall be met;

(b) there shall be robust risk management on the part of the lessor with respect to the use to which the leased asset is put, its age and the planned duration of its use, including appropriate monitoring of the value of the security;

(c) there shall be in place a robust legal framework establishing the lessor's legal ownership of the asset and its ability to exercise its rights as owner in a timely fashion; and

(d) where this has not already been ascertained in calculating the LGD level, the difference between the value of the unamortised amount and the market value of the security must not be so large as to overstate the credit risk mitigation attributed to the leased assets.

1.8. Minimum requirements for the recognition of other funded credit protection

1.8.1. *Cash on deposit with, or cash assimilated instruments held by, a third party institution*

12. To be eligible for the treatment set out at Part 3, point 79, the protection referred to in Part 1, point 23 must satisfy the following conditions:

(a) the borrower's claim against the third party institution is openly pledged or assigned to the lending credit institution and such pledge or assignment is legally effective and enforceable in all relevant jurisdictions;

(b) the third party institution is notified of the pledge or assignment;

(c) as a result of the notification, the third party institution is able to make payments solely to the lending credit institution or to other parties with the lending credit institution's consent; and

(d) the pledge or assignment is unconditional and irrevocable.

1.8.2. *Life insurance policies pledged to the lending credit institution*

13. For life insurance policies pledged to the lending credit institution to be recognised the following conditions shall be met:

(a) the company providing the life insurance may be recognised as an eligible unfunded credit protection provider under Part 1, point 26;

(b) the life insurance policy is openly pledged or assigned to the lending credit institution;

(c) the company providing the life insurance is notified of the pledge or assignment and as a result may not pay amounts payable under the contract without the consent of the lending credit institution;

(d) the declared surrender value of the policy is non-reducible;

(e) the lending credit institution must have the right to cancel the policy and receive the surrender value in a timely way in the event of the default of the borrower;

(f) the lending credit institution is informed of any non-payments under the policy by the policy-holder;

(g) the credit protection must be provided for the maturity of the loan. Where this is not possible because the insurance relationship ends before the loan relationship expires, the credit institution must ensure that the amount deriving from the insurance contract serves the credit institution as security until the end of the duration of the credit agreement; and

(h) the pledge or assignment must be legally effective and enforceable in all jurisdictions which are relevant at the time of the conclusion of the credit agreement.

2. UNFUNDED CREDIT PROTECTION AND CREDIT LINKED NOTES

2.1. Requirements common to guarantees and credit derivatives

14. Subject to point 16, for the credit protection deriving from a guarantee or credit derivative to

be recognised the following conditions shall be met:

(a) the credit protection shall be direct;

(b) the extent of the credit protection shall be clearly defined and incontrovertible;

(c) the credit protection contract shall not contain any clause, the fulfilment of which is outside the direct control of the lender, that:
  (i) would allow the protection provider unilaterally to cancel the protection;
  (ii) would increase the effective cost of protection as a result of deteriorating credit quality of the protected exposure;
  (iii) could prevent the protection provider from being obliged to pay out in a timely manner in the event that the original obligor fails to make any payments due; or
  (iv) could allow the maturity of the credit protection to be reduced by the protection provider; and

(d) it must be legally effective and enforceable in all jurisdictions which are relevant at the time of the conclusion of the credit agreement.

2.1.1. *Operational requirements*

15. The credit institution shall satisfy the competent authority that it has systems in place to manage potential concentration of risk arising from the credit institution's use of guarantees and credit derivatives. The credit institution must be able to demonstrate how its strategy in respect of its use of credit derivatives and guarantees interacts with its management of its overall risk profile.

2.2. Sovereign and other public sector counter-guarantees

16. Where an exposure is protected by a guarantee which is counter-guaranteed by a central government or central bank, a regional government or local authority, a public sector entity, claims on which are treated as claims on the central government in whose jurisdiction they are established under Articles 78 to 83, a multilateral development bank to which a 0% risk weight is assigned under or by virtue of Articles 78 to 83, or a public sector entity, claims on which are treated as claims on credit institutions under Articles 78 to 83, the exposure may be treated as protected by a guarantee provided by the entity in question, provided the following conditions are satisfied:

(a) the counter-guarantee covers all credit risk elements of the claim;

(b) both the original guarantee and the counter-guarantee meet the requirements for guarantees set out in points 14, 15 and 18, except that the counter-guarantee need not be direct; and

(c) the competent authority is satisfied that the cover is robust and that nothing in the historical evidence suggests that the coverage of the counter-guarantee is less than effectively equivalent to that of a direct guarantee by the entity in question.

17. The treatment set out in point 16 also applies to an exposure which is not counter-guaranteed by an entity listed in that point if that exposure's counter-guarantee is in turn directly guaranteed by one of the listed entities and the conditions listed in that point are satisfied.

2.3. Additional requirements for guarantees

18. For a guarantee to be recognised the following conditions shall also be met:

(a) on the qualifying default of and/or non-payment by the counterparty, the lending credit institution shall have the right to pursue, in a timely manner, the guarantor for any monies due under the claim in respect of which the protection is provided. Payment by the guarantor shall not be subject to the lending credit institution first having to pursue the obligor. In the case of unfunded credit protection covering residential mortgage loans, the requirements in point 14(c)(iii) and in the first subparagraph of this point have only to be satisfied within 24 months;

(b) the guarantee shall be an explicitly documented obligation assumed by the guarantor; and

(c) subject to the following sentence, the guarantee shall cover all types of payments the obligor is expected to make in respect of the claim. Where certain types of payment are excluded from the guarantee, the recognised value of the guarantee shall be adjusted to reflect the limited coverage.

19. In the case of guarantees provided in the context of mutual guarantee schemes recognised for these purposes by the competent authorities or provided by or counter-guaranteed by entities referred to in point 16, the requirements in point 18(a) shall be considered to be satisfied where either of the following conditions are met:

(a) the lending credit institution has the right to obtain in a timely manner a provisional payment by the guarantor calculated to represent a robust estimate of the amount of the economic loss, including losses resulting from the non-payment of interest and other types of payment which the borrower is obliged to make, likely to be incurred by the lending credit institution proportional to the coverage of the guarantee; or

(b) the lending credit institution can demonstrate that the loss-protecting effects of the guarantee, including losses resulting from the non-payment of interest and other types of payments which the borrower is obliged to make, justify such treatment.

2.4. Additional requirements for credit derivatives

20. For a credit derivative to be recognised the following conditions shall also be met:

(a) subject to point (b), the credit events specified under the credit derivative shall at a minimum include:
 (i) the failure to pay the amounts due under the terms of the underlying obligation that are in effect at the time of such failure (with a grace period that is closely in line with or shorter than the grace period in the underlying obligation);
 (ii) the bankruptcy, insolvency or inability of the obligor to pay its debts, or its failure or admission in writing of its inability generally to pay its debts as they become due, and analogous events; and
 (iii) the restructuring of the underlying obligation involving forgiveness or postponement of principal, interest or fees that results in a credit loss event (i.e. value adjustment or other similar debit to the profit and loss account);

(b) where the credit events specified under the credit derivative do not include restructuring of the underlying obligation as described in point (a)(iii), the credit protection may nonetheless be recognised subject to a reduction in the recognised value as specified in point 83 of Part 3;

(c) in the case of credit derivatives allowing for cash settlement, a robust valuation process shall be in place in order to estimate loss reliably. There shall be a clearly specified period for obtaining post-credit-event valuations of the underlying obligation;

(d) if the protection purchaser's right and ability to transfer the underlying obligation to the protection provider is required for settlement, the terms of the underlying obligation shall provide that any required consent to such transfer may not be unreasonably withheld; and

(e) the identity of the parties responsible for determining whether a credit event has occurred shall be clearly defined. This determination shall not be the sole responsibility of the protection provider. The protection buyer shall have the right/ability to inform the protection provider of the occurrence of a credit event.

21. A mismatch between the underlying obligation and the reference obligation under the credit derivative (i.e. the obligation used for the purposes of determining cash settlement value or the deliverable obligation) or between the underlying obligation and the obligation used for purposes of determining whether a credit event has occurred is permissible only if the following conditions are met:

(a) the reference obligation or the obligation used for purposes of determining whether a credit event has occurred, as the case may be, ranks pari passu with or is junior to the underlying obligation; and

(b) the underlying obligation and the reference obligation or the obligation used for purposes of determining whether a credit event has occurred, as the case may be, share the same obligor (i.e., the same legal entity) and there are in place legally enforceable cross-default or cross-acceleration clauses.

2.5. Requirements to qualify for the treatment set out in Annex VII, Part 1, point 4

22. To be eligible for the treatment set out in Annex VII, Part 1, point 4, credit protection deriving from a guarantee or credit derivative shall meet the following conditions:

(a) the underlying obligation shall be to:
- a corporate exposure as defined in Article 86, excluding insurance and reinsurance undertakings;
- an exposure to a regional government, local authority or Public Sector Entity which is not treated as an exposure to a central government or a central bank according to Article 86; or
- an exposure to a small or medium-sized entity, classified as a retail exposure according to Article 86(4);

(b) the underlying obligors shall not be members of the same group as the protection provider;

(c) the exposure shall be hedged by one of the following instruments:
- single-name unfunded credit derivatives or single-name guarantees,
- first-to-default basket products—the treatment shall be applied to the asset within the basket with the lowest risk-weighted exposure amount, or
- n^{th}-to-default basket products—the protection obtained is only eligible for consideration under this framework if eligible (n-1)th default protection has also be obtained or where (n-1) of the assets within the basket has/have already defaulted. Where this is the case the treatment shall be applied to the asset within the basket with the lowest risk-weighted exposure amount;

(d) the credit protection meets the requirements set out in points 14, 15, 18, 20 and 21;

(e) the risk weight that is associated with the exposure prior to the application of the treatment in Annex VII, Part 1, point 4, does not already factor in any aspect of the credit protection;

(f) a credit institution shall have the right and expectation to receive payment from the protection provider without having to take legal action in order to pursue the counterparty for payment. To the extent possible, a credit institution shall take steps to satisfy itself that the protection provider is willing to pay promptly should a credit event occur;

(g) the purchased credit protection shall absorb all credit losses incurred on the hedged portion of an exposure that arise due to the occurrence of credit events outlined in the contract;

(h) if the payout structure provides for physical settlement, then there shall be legal certainty with respect to the deliverability of a loan, bond, or contingent liability. If a credit institution intends to deliver an obligation other than the underlying exposure, it shall ensure that the deliverable obligation is sufficiently liquid so that the credit institution would have the ability to purchase it for delivery in accordance with the contract;

(i) the terms and conditions of credit protection arrangements shall be legally confirmed in writing by both the protection provider and the credit institution;

(j) credit institutions shall have a process in place to detect excessive correlation between the creditworthiness of a protection provider and the obligor of the underlying exposure due to their performance being dependent on common factors beyond the systematic risk factor; and

(k) in the case of protection against dilution risk, the seller of purchased receivables shall not be a member of the same group as the protection provider.

PART 3

Calculating the effects of credit risk mitigation

1. Subject to Parts 4 to 6, where the provisions in Parts 1 and 2 are satisfied, the calculation of risk-weighted exposure amounts under Articles 78 to 83 and the calculation of risk-weighted exposure amounts and expected loss amounts under

Articles 84 to 89 may be modified in accordance with the provisions of this Part.

2. Cash, securities or commodities purchased, borrowed or received under a repurchase transaction or securities or commodities lending or borrowing transaction shall be treated as collateral.

1. FUNDED CREDIT PROTECTION

1.1. Credit linked notes

3. Investments in credit linked notes issued by the lending credit institution may be treated as cash collateral.

1.2. On-balance sheet netting

4. Loans and deposits with the lending credit institution subject to on-balance sheet netting are to be treated as cash collateral.

1.3. Master netting agreements covering repurchase transactions and/or securities or commodities lending or borrowing transactions and/or other capital market-driven transactions

1.3.1. Calculation of the fully-adjusted exposure value

(a) *Using the 'Supervisory' volatility adjustments or the 'Own Estimates' volatility adjustments approaches*

5. Subject to points 12 to 21, in calculating the 'fully adjusted exposure value' (E*) for the exposures subject to an eligible master netting agreement covering repurchase transactions and/or securities or commodities lending or borrowing transactions and/or other capital market-driven transactions, the volatility adjustments to be applied shall be calculated either using the Supervisory Volatility Adjustments Approach or the Own Estimates Volatility Adjustments Approach as set out in points 30 to 61 for the Financial Collateral Comprehensive Method. For the use of the Own estimates approach, the same conditions and requirements shall apply as apply under the Financial Collateral Comprehensive Method

6. The net position in each 'type of security' or commodity shall be calculated by subtracting from the total value of the securities or commodities of that type lent, sold or provided under the master netting agreement, the total value of securities or commodities of that type borrowed, purchased or received under the agreement.

7. For the purposes of point 6, 'type of security' means securities which are issued by the same entity, have the same issue date, the same maturity and are subject to the same terms and conditions and are subject to the same liquidation periods as indicated in points 34 to 59.

8. The net position in each currency, other than the settlement currency of the master netting agreement, shall be calculated by subtracting from the total value of securities denominated in that currency lent, sold or provided under the master netting agreement added to the amount of cash in that currency lent or transferred under the agreement, the total value of securities denominated in that currency borrowed, purchased or received under the agreement added to the amount of cash in that currency borrowed or received under the agreement.

9. The volatility adjustment appropriate to a given type of security or cash position shall be applied to the absolute value of the positive or negative net position in the securities of that type.

10. The foreign exchange risk (fx) volatility adjustment shall be applied to the net positive or negative position in each currency other than the settlement currency of the master netting agreement.

11. E* shall be calculated according to the following formula:

$$E^* = \max\{0, [(\Sigma(E) - \Sigma(C)) + \Sigma|\text{nettopositie in elk effect}| \times H_{sec} + (\Sigma|E_{fx}| \times H_{fx})]\}$$

Where risk-weighted exposure amounts are calculated under Articles 78 to 83, E is the exposure value for each separate exposure under the agreement that would apply in the absence of the credit protection.

Where risk-weighted exposure amounts and expected loss amounts are calculated under Articles 84 to 89, E is the exposure value for each separate exposure under the agreement that would apply in the absence of the credit protection.

C is the value of the securities or commodities borrowed, purchased or received or the cash borrowed or received in respect of each such exposure.

S(E) is the sum of all Es under the agreement.

S(C) is the sum of all Cs under the agreement.

E_{fx} is the net position (positive or negative) in a given currency other than the settlement currency of the agreement as calculated under point 8.

H_{sec} is the volatility adjustment appropriate to a particular type of security.

H_{fx} is the foreign exchange volatility adjustment.

E* is the fully adjusted exposure value.

(b) *Using the Internal Models approach*

12. As an alternative to using the supervisory volatility adjustments approach or the Own Estimates volatility adjustments approach in calculating the fully adjusted exposure value (E*) resulting from the application of an eligible master netting agreement covering repurchase transactions, securities or commodities lending or borrowing transactions, and/or other capital market driven transactions other than derivative transactions, credit institutions may be permitted to use an internal models approach which takes into account correlation effects between security positions subject to the master netting agreement as well as the liquidity of the instruments concerned. Internal models used in this approach shall provide estimates of the potential change in value of the unsecured exposure amount (ΣE—ΣC). Subject to the approval of the competent authorities, credit institutions may also use their internal models for margin lending transactions, if the transactions are covered under a bilateral master netting agreement that meets the requirements set out in Annex III, Part 7.

13. A credit institution may choose to use an internal models approach independently of the choice it has made between Articles 78 to 83 and Articles 84 to 89 for the calculation of risk-weighted exposure amounts. However, if a credit institution seeks to use an internal models approach, it must do so for all counterparties and securities, excluding immaterial portfolios where it may use the supervisory volatility adjustments approach or the own estimates volatility adjustments approach as set out in points 5 to 11.

14. The internal models approach is available to credit institutions that have received recognition for an internal risk-management model under Annex V to Directive 2006/49/EC.

15. Credit institutions which have not received supervisory recognition for use of such a model under Directive 2006/49/EC, may apply to the competent authorities for recognition of an internal risk-measurement model for the purposes of points 12 to 21.

16. Recognition shall only be given if the competent authority is satisfied that the credit institution's risk-management system for managing the risks arising on the transactions covered by the master netting agreement is conceptually sound and implemented with integrity and that, in particular, the following qualitative standards are met:

(a) the internal risk-measurement model used for calculation of potential price volatility for the transactions is closely integrated into the daily risk-management process of the credit institution and serves as the basis for reporting risk exposures to senior management of the credit institution;

(b) the credit institution has a risk control unit that is independent from business trading units and reports directly to senior management. The unit must be responsible for designing and implementing the credit institution's risk-management system. It shall produce and analyse daily reports on the output of the risk-measurement model and on the appropriate measures to be taken in terms of position limits;

(c) the daily reports produced by the risk-control unit are reviewed by a level of management with sufficient authority to enforce reductions of positions taken and of overall risk exposure;

(d) the credit institution has sufficient staff skilled in the use of sophisticated models in the risk-control unit;

(e) the credit institution has established procedures for monitoring and ensuring compliance with a documented set of internal policies and controls concerning the overall operation of the risk-measurement system;

(f) the credit institution's models have a proven track record of reasonable accuracy in measuring risks demonstrated through the back-testing of its output using at least one year of data;

(g) the credit institution frequently conducts a rigorous programme of stress testing and the results of these tests are reviewed by senior management and reflected in the policies and limits it sets;

(h) the credit institution must conduct, as Part of its regular internal auditing process, an independent review of its risk-measurement system. This review must include both the activities of the business trading units and of the independent risk-control unit;

(i) at least once a year, the credit institution must conduct a review of its risk-management system; and

(j) the internal model shall meet the requirements set out in Annex III, Part 6, points 40 to 42.

17. The calculation of the potential change in value shall be subject to the following minimum standards:

(a) at least daily calculation of the potential change in value;

(b) a 99th percentile, one-tailed confidence interval;

(c) a 5-day equivalent liquidation period, except in the case of transactions other than securities repurchase transactions or securities lending or borrowing transactions where a 10-day equivalent liquidation period shall be used;

(d) an effective historical observation period of at least one year except where a shorter observation period is justified by a significant upsurge in price volatility; and

(e) three-monthly data set updates.

18. The competent authorities shall require that the internal risk-measurement model captures a sufficient number of risk factors in order to capture all material price risks.

19. The competent authorities may allow credit institutions to use empirical correlations within risk categories and across risk categories if they are satisfied that the credit institution's system for measuring correlations is sound and implemented with integrity.

20. The fully adjusted exposure value (E*) for credit institutions using the internal models approach shall be calculated according to the following formula:

$$E^* = \max\{0, [(\Sigma E - \Sigma C) + (\text{uitkomst van het interne model})]\}$$

Where risk-weighted exposure amounts are calculated under Articles 78 to 83, E is the exposure value for each separate exposure under the agreement that would apply in the absence of the credit protection.

Where risk-weighted exposure amounts and expected loss amounts are calculated under Articles 84 to 89, E is the exposure value for each separate exposure under the agreement that would apply in the absence of the credit protection.

C is the value of the securities borrowed, purchased or received or the cash borrowed or received in respect of each such exposure.

$\Sigma(E)$ is the sum of all Es under the agreement.

$\Sigma(C)$ is the sum of all Cs under the agreement.

21. In calculating risk-weighted exposure amounts using internal models, credit institutions shall use the previous business day's model output.

1.3.2. *Calculating risk-weighted exposure amounts and expected loss amounts for repurchase transactions and/or securities or commodities lending or borrowing transactions and/or other capital market-driven transactions covered by master netting agreements*

Standardised Approach

22. E* as calculated under points 5 to 21 shall be taken as the exposure value of the exposure to the

counterparty arising from the transactions subject to the master netting agreement for the purposes of Article 80.

IRB Approach

23. E* as calculated under points 5 to 21 shall be taken as the exposure value of the exposure to the counterparty arising from the transactions subject to the master netting agreement for the purposes of Annex VII.

1.4. Financial collateral

1.4.1. *Financial Collateral Simple Method*

24. The Financial Collateral Simple Method shall be available only where risk-weighted exposure amounts are calculated under Articles 78 to 83. A credit institution shall not use both the Financial Collateral Simple Method and the Financial Collateral Comprehensive Method.

Valuation

25. Under this method, recognised financial collateral is assigned a value equal to its market value as determined in accordance with Part 2, point 6.

Calculating risk-weighted exposure amounts

26. The risk weight that would be assigned under Articles 78 to 83 if the lender had a direct exposure to the collateral instrument shall be assigned to those portions of claims collateralised by the market value of recognised collateral. The risk weight of the collateralised portion shall be a minimum of 20% except as specified in points 27 to 29. The remainder of the exposure shall receive the risk weight that would be assigned to an unsecured exposure to the counterparty under Articles 78 to 83.

Repurchase transactions and securities lending or borrowing transactions

27. A risk weight of 0% shall be assigned to the collateralised portion of the exposure arising from transactions which fulfil the criteria enumerated in points 58 and 59. If the counterparty to the transaction is not a core market participant a risk weight of 10% shall be assigned.

OTC derivative transactions subject to daily mark-to-market

28. A risk weight of 0% shall, to the extent of the collateralisation, be assigned to the exposure values determined under Annex III for the derivative instruments listed in Annex IV and subject to daily marking-to-market, collateralised by cash or cash-assimilated instruments where there is no currency mismatch. A risk weight of 10% shall be assigned to the extent of the collateralisation to the exposure values of such transactions collateralised by debt securities issued by central governments or central banks which are assigned a 0% risk weight under Articles 78 to 83.

For the purposes of this point debt securities issued by central governments or central banks shall include:

(a) debt securities issued by regional governments or local authorities exposures to which are treated as exposures to the central government in whose jurisdiction they are established under Articles 78 to 83;

(b) debt securities issued by multilateral development banks to which a 0% risk weight is assigned under or by virtue of Articles 78 to 83; and

(c) debt securities issued by international organisations which are assigned a 0% risk weight under Articles 78 to 83.

Other transactions

29. A 0% risk weight may be assigned where the exposure and the collateral are denominated in the same currency, and either:

(a) the collateral is cash on deposit or a cash assimilated instrument; or

(b) the collateral is in the form of debt securities issued by central governments or central banks eligible for a 0% risk weight under Articles 78 to 83, and its market value has been discounted by 20%.

For the purposes of this point 'debt securities issued by central governments or central banks' shall include those indicated under point 28.

1.4.2. Financial Collateral Comprehensive Method

30. In valuing financial collateral for the purposes of the Financial Collateral Comprehensive Method, 'volatility adjustments' shall be applied to the market value of collateral, as set out in points 34 to 59 below, in order to take account of price volatility.

31. Subject to the treatment for currency mismatches in the case of OTC derivatives transactions set out in point 32, where collateral is denominated in a currency that differs from that in which the underlying exposure is denominated, an adjustment reflecting currency volatility shall be added to the volatility adjustment appropriate to the collateral as set out in points 34 to 59.

32. In the case of OTC derivatives transactions covered by netting agreements recognised by the competent authorities under Annex III, a volatility adjustment reflecting currency volatility shall be applied when there is a mismatch between the collateral currency and the settlement currency. Even in the case where multiple currencies are involved in the transactions covered by the netting agreement, only a single volatility adjustment shall be applied.

(a) *Calculating adjusted values*

33. The volatility-adjusted value of the collateral to be taken into account is calculated as follows in the case of all transactions except those transactions subject to recognised master netting agreements to which the provisions set out in points 5 to 23 are applied:

$$C_{VA} = C \times (1 - H_C - H_{FX})$$

The volatility-adjusted value of the exposure to be taken into account is calculated as follows:

$$E_{VA} = E \times (1 + H_E), \text{ and, in the case of OTC derivative transactions, } E_{VA} = E$$

The fully adjusted value of the exposure, taking into account both volatility and the risk-mitigating effects of collateral is calculated as follows:

$$E^* = \max \{0, [E_{VA} - C_{VAM}]\}$$

Where:

E is the exposure value as would be determined under Articles 78 to 83 or Articles 84 to 89 as appropriate if the exposure was not collateralised. For this purpose, for credit institutions calculating risk-weighted exposure amounts under Articles 78 to 83, the exposure value of off-balance sheet items listed in Annex II shall be 100% of its value rather than the percentages indicated in Article 78(1), and for credit institutions calculating risk-weighted exposure amounts under Articles 84 to 89, the exposure value of the items listed in Annex VII, Part 3, points 9 to 11 shall be calculated using a conversion factor of 100% rather than the conversion factors or percentages indicated in those points.

E_{VA} is the volatility-adjusted exposure amount.

C_{VA} is the volatility-adjusted value of the collateral.

C_{VAM} is C_{VA} further adjusted for any maturity mismatch in accordance with the provisions of Part 4.

H_E is the volatility adjustment appropriate to the exposure (E), as calculated under points 34 to 59.

H_C is the volatility adjustment appropriate to the collateral, as calculated under points 34 to 59.

H_{FX} is the volatility adjustment appropriate to currency mismatch, as calculated under points 34 to 59.

E* is the fully adjusted exposure value taking into account volatility and the risk-mitigating effects of the collateral.

(b) *Calculation of volatility adjustments to be applied*

34. Volatility adjustments may be calculated in two ways: the supervisory volatility adjustments approach and the own estimates of volatility adjustments approach (the 'own estimates' approach).

35. A credit institution may choose to use the supervisory volatility adjustments approach or the own estimates approach independently of the choice it has made between Articles 78 to 83 and Articles 84 to 89 for the calculation of

risk-weighted exposure amounts. However, if credit institutions seek to use the own estimates approach, they must do so for the full range of instrument types, excluding immaterial portfolios where they may use the supervisory volatility adjustments approach.

Where the collateral consists of a number of recognised items, the volatility adjustment shall be $H=\Sigma a_i H_i$,

where a_i is the proportion of an item to the collateral as a whole and H_i is the volatility adjustment applicable to that item.

(i) *Supervisory volatility adjustments*

36. The volatility adjustments to be applied under the Supervisory volatility adjustments approach (assuming daily revaluation) shall be those set out in Tables 1 to 4.

VOLATILITY ADJUSTMENTS

Table 1

Credit quality step with which the credit assessment of the debt security is associated	Residual Maturity	Volatility adjustments for debt securities issued by entities described in Part 1, point 7(b)			Volatility adjustments for debt securities issued by entities described in Part 1, point 7(c) and (d)		
		20-day liquidation period (%)	10-day liquidation period (%)	5-day liquidation period (%)	20-day liquidation period (%)	10-day liquidation period (%)	5-day liquidation period (%)
1	≤1 year	0.707	0.5	0.354	1.414	1	0.707
	>1 ≤5 years	2.828	2	1.414	5.657	4	2.828
	>5 years	5.657	4	2.828	11.314	8	5.657
2–3	≤1 year	1.414	1	0.707	2.828	2	1.414
	>1 ≤ 5 years	4.243	3	2.121	8.485	6	4.243
	>5 years	8.485	6	4.243	16.971	12	8.485
4	≤1 year	21.213	15	10.607	N/A	N/A	N/A
	>1 ≤ 5 years	21.213	15	10.607	N/A	N/A	N/A
	>5 years	21.213	15	10.607	N/A	N/A	N/A

Table 2

Credit quality step with which the credit assessment of a short term debt security is associated	Volatility adjustments for debt securities issued by entities described in Part 1, point 7(b) with short-term credit assessments			Volatility adjustments for debt securities issued by entities in Part 1, point 7(c) and (d) with short-term credit assessments		
	20-day liquidation period (%)	10-day liquidation period (%)	5-day liquidation period (%)	20-day liquidation period (%)	10-day liquidation period (%)	5-day liquidation period (%)
1	0.707	0.5	0.354	1.414	1	0.707
2–3	1.414	1	0.707	2.828	2	1.414

Table 3

Other collateral or exposure types

	20-day liquidation period (%)	10-day liquidation period (%)	5-day liquidation period (%)
Main Index Equities, Main Index Convertible Bonds	21.213	15	10.607
Other Equities or Convertible Bonds listed on a recognised exchange	35.355	25	17.678
Cash	0	0	0
Gold	21.213	15	10.607

Table 4

Volatility adjustment for currency mismatch

20-day liquidation period (%)	10-day liquidation period (%)	5-day liquidation period (%)
11.314	8	5.657

37. For secured lending transactions the liquidation period shall be 20 business days. For repurchase transactions (except insofar as such transactions involve the transfer of commodities or guaranteed rights relating to title to commodities) and securities lending or borrowing transactions the liquidation period shall be 5 business days. For other capital market-driven transactions, the liquidation period shall be 10 business days.

38. In Tables 1 to 4 and in points 39 to 41, the credit quality step with which a credit assessment of the debt security is associated is the credit quality step with which the credit assessment is determined by the competent authorities to be associated under Articles 78 to 83. For the purpose of this point, Part 1, point 10 also applies.

39. For non-eligible securities or for commodities lent or sold under repurchase transactions or securities or commodities lending or borrowing transactions, the volatility adjustment is the same as for non-main index equities listed on a recognised exchange.

40. For eligible units in collective investment undertakings the volatility adjustment is the weighted average volatility adjustments that would apply, having regard to the liquidation period of the transaction as specified in point 37, to the assets in which the fund has invested. If the assets in which the fund has invested are not known to the credit institution, the volatility adjustment is the highest volatility adjustment that would apply to any of the assets in which the fund has the right to invest.

41. For unrated debt securities issued by institutions and satisfying the eligibility criteria in Part 1, point 8 the volatility adjustments shall be the same as for securities issued by institutions or corporates with an external credit assessment associated with credit quality steps 2 or 3.

(ii) *Own estimates of volatility adjustments*

42. The competent authorities shall permit credit institutions complying with the requirements set out in points 47 to 56 to use their own volatility estimates for calculating the volatility adjustments to be applied to collateral and exposures.

43. When debt securities have a credit assessment from a recognised ECAI equivalent to investment grade or better, the competent authorities may allow credit institutions to calculate a volatility estimate for each category of security.

44. In determining relevant categories, credit institutions shall take into account the type of issuer of the security the external credit assessment of the securities, their residual maturity, and their modified duration. Volatility estimates must be representative of the securities included in the category by the credit institution.

45. For debt securities having a credit assessment from a recognised ECAI equivalent to below investment grade, and for other eligible collateral, the volatility adjustments must be calculated for each individual item.

46. Credit institutions using the own estimates approach must estimate volatility of the collateral or foreign exchange mismatch without taking into account any correlations between the unsecured exposure, collateral and/or exchange rates.

Quantitative criteria

47. In calculating the volatility adjustments, a 99th percentile one-tailed confidence interval shall be used.

48. The liquidation period shall be 20 business days for secured lending transactions; 5 business days for repurchase transactions, except insofar as such transactions involve the transfer of commodities or guaranteed rights relating to title to commodities and securities lending or borrowing transactions, and 10 business days for other capital market-driven transactions.

49. Credit institutions may use volatility adjustment numbers calculated according to shorter or longer liquidation periods, scaled up or down to the liquidation period set out in point 48 for the type of transaction in question, using the square root of time formula:

$$H_M = H_N \sqrt{T_M/T_N}$$

where T_M is the relevant liquidation period;

H_M is the volatility adjustment under T_M and

H_N is the volatility adjustment based on the liquidation period T_N.

50. Credit institutions shall take into account the illiquidity of lower-quality assets. The liquidation period shall be adjusted upwards in cases where there is doubt concerning the liquidity of the collateral. They shall also identify where historical data may understate potential volatility, e.g., a pegged currency. Such cases shall be dealt with by means of a stress scenario.

51. The historical observation period (sample period) for calculating volatility adjustments shall be a minimum length of one year. For credit institutions that use a weighting scheme or other methods for the historical observation period, the effective observation period shall be at least one year (that is, the weighted average time lag of the individual observations shall not be less than 6 months). The competent authorities may also require a credit institution to calculate its volatility adjustments using a shorter observation period if, in the competent authorities' judgement, this is justified by a significant upsurge in price volatility.

52. Credit institutions shall update their data sets at least once every three months and shall also reassess them whenever market prices are subject to material changes. This implies that volatility adjustments shall be computed at least every three months.

Qualitative criteria

53. The volatility estimates shall be used in the day-to-day risk management process of the credit institution including in relation to its internal exposure limits.

54. If the liquidation period used by the credit institution in its day-to-day risk management process is longer than that set out in this Part for the type of transaction in question, the credit institution's volatility adjustments shall be scaled up in accordance with the square root of time formula set out in point 49.

55. The credit institution shall have established procedures for monitoring and ensuring compliance with a documented set of policies and controls for the operation of its system for the estimation of volatility adjustments and for the integration of such estimations into its risk management process.

56. An independent review of the credit institution's system for the estimation of volatility adjustments shall be carried out regularly in the

credit institution's own internal auditing process. A review of the overall system for the estimation of volatility adjustments and for integration of those adjustments into the credit institution's risk management process shall take place at least once a year and shall specifically address, at a minimum:

(a) the integration of estimated volatility adjustments into daily risk management;

(b) the validation of any significant change in the process for the estimation of volatility adjustments;

(c) the verification of the consistency, timeliness and reliability of data sources used to run the system for the estimation of volatility adjustments, including the independence of such data sources; and

(d) the accuracy and appropriateness of the volatility assumptions.

(iii) *Scaling up of volatility adjustments*

57. The volatility adjustments set out in points 36 to 41 are the volatility adjustments to be applied where there is daily revaluation. Similarly, where a credit institution uses its own estimates of the volatility adjustments in accordance with points 42 to 56, these must be calculated in the first instance on the basis of daily revaluation. If the frequency of revaluation is less than daily, larger volatility adjustments shall be applied. These shall be calculated by scaling up the daily revaluation volatility adjustments, using the following 'square root of time' formula:

$$H = H_M \sqrt{\frac{N_R + (T_M - 1)}{T_M}}$$

where:

H is the volatility adjustment to be applied

H_M is the volatility adjustment where there is daily revaluation

N_R is the actual number of business days between revaluations

T_M is the liquidation period for the type of transaction in question.

(iv) *Conditions for applying a 0% volatility adjustment*

58. In relation to repurchase transactions and securities lending or borrowing transactions, where a credit institution uses the Supervisory Volatility Adjustments Approach or the Own Estimates Approach and where the conditions set out in points (a) to (h) are satisfied, credit institutions may, instead of applying the volatility adjustments calculated under points 34 to 57, apply a 0% volatility adjustment. This option is not available in respect of credit institutions using the internal models approach set out in points 12 to 21:

(a) Both the exposure and the collateral are cash or debt securities issued by central governments or central banks within the meaning of Part 1, point 7(b) and eligible for a 0% risk weight under Articles 78 to 83,

(b) Both the exposure and the collateral are denominated in the same currency,

(c) Either the maturity of the transaction is no more than one day or both the exposure and the collateral are subject to daily marking-to-market or daily remargining,

(d) It is considered that the time between the last marking-to-market before a failure to remargin by the counterparty and the liquidation of the collateral shall be no more than four business days,

(e) The transaction is settled across a settlement system proven for that type of transaction,

(f) The documentation covering the agreement is standard market documentation for repurchase transactions or securities lending or borrowing transactions in the securities concerned,

(g) The transaction is governed by documentation specifying that if the counterparty fails to satisfy an obligation to deliver cash or securities or to deliver margin or otherwise defaults, then the transaction is immediately terminable, and

(h) The counterparty is considered a 'core market participant' by the competent authorities. Core market participants shall include the following entities:

– the entities mentioned in point 7(b) of Part 1 exposures to which are assigned a 0% risk weight under Articles 78 to 83;

- institutions;
- other financial companies (including insurance companies) exposures to which are assigned a 20% risk weight under Articles 78 to 83 or which, in the case of credit institutions calculating risk-weighted exposure amounts and expected loss amounts under Articles 83 to 89, do not have a credit assessment by a recognised ECAI and are internally rated as having a PD equivalent to that associated with the credit assessments of ECAIs determined by the competent authorities to be associated with credit quality step 2 or above under the rules for the risk weighting of exposures to corporates under Articles 78 to 83
- regulated collective investment undertakings that are subject to capital or leverage requirements;
- regulated pension funds; and
- recognised clearing organisations.

59. Where a competent authority permits the treatment set out in point 58 to be applied in the case of repurchase transactions or securities lending or borrowing transactions in securities issued by its domestic government, then other competent authorities may choose to allow credit institutions incorporated in their jurisdiction to adopt the same approach to the same transactions.

(c) *Calculating risk-weighted exposure amounts and expected loss amounts*

Standardised Approach

60. E* as calculated under point 33 shall be taken as the exposure value for the purposes of Article 80. In the case of off-balance-sheet items listed in Annex II, E* shall be taken as the value at which the percentages indicated in Article 78(1) shall be applied to arrive at the exposure value.

IRB Approach

61. LGD* (the effective LGD) calculated as set out in this point shall be taken as the LGD for the purposes of Annex VII.

$LGD^* = LGD \times (E^*/E)$

where:

LGD is the LGD that would apply to the exposure under Articles 84 to 89 if the exposure was not collateralised;

E is the exposure value as described under point 33;

E* is as calculated under point 33.

1.5. Other eligible collateral for Articles 84 to 89

1.5.1. *Valuation*

(a) *Real estate collateral*

62. The property shall be valued by an independent valuer at or less than the market value. In those Member States that have laid down rigorous criteria for the assessment of the mortgage lending value in statutory or regulatory provisions the property may instead be valued by an independent valuer at or less than the mortgage lending value.

63. 'Market value' means the estimated amount for which the property should exchange on the date of valuation between a willing buyer and a willing seller in an arm's-length transaction after proper marketing wherein the parties had each acted knowledgeably, prudently and without compulsion. The market value shall be documented in a transparent and clear manner.

64. 'Mortgage lending value' means the value of the property as determined by a prudent assessment of the future marketability of the property taking into account long-term sustainable aspects of the property, the normal and local market conditions, the current use and alternative appropriate uses of the property. Speculative elements shall not be taken into account in the assessment of the mortgage lending value. The mortgage lending value shall be documented in a transparent and clear manner.

65. The value of the collateral shall be the market value or mortgage lending value reduced as appropriate to reflect the results of the monitoring required under Part 2, point 8 and to take account of the any prior claims on the property.

(b) *Receivables*

66. The value of receivables shall be the amount receivable.

Table 5

Minimum LGD for secured parts of exposures

	LGD* for senior Claims or contingent claims	LGD* for subordinated claims or contingent claims	Required minimum collateralisation level of the exposure (C*)	Required minimum level of the exposure (C**)
Receivables	35%	65%	0%	125%
Residential real estate/ commercial real estate	35%	65%	30%	140%
Other collateral	40%	70%	30%	140%

(c) *Other physical collateral*

67. The property shall be valued at its market value—that is the estimated amount for which the property would exchange on the date of valuation between a willing buyer and a willing seller in an arm's-length transaction.

1.5.2. *Calculating risk-weighted exposure amounts and expected loss amounts*

(a) *General treatment*

68. LGD* calculated as set out in points 69 to 72 shall be taken as the LGD for the purposes of Annex VII.

69. Where the ratio of the value of the collateral (C) to the exposure value (E) is below a threshold level of C* (the required minimum collateralisation level for the exposure) as laid down in Table 5, LGD* shall be the LGD laid down in Annex VII for uncollateralised exposures to the counterparty.

70. Where the ratio of the value of the collateral to the exposure value exceeds a second, higher threshold level of C** (i.e. the required level of collateralisation to receive full LGD recognition) as laid down in Table 5, LGD* shall be that prescribed in Table 5.

71. Where the required level of collateralisation C** is not achieved in respect of the exposure as a whole, the exposure shall be considered to be two exposures—that part in respect of which the required level of collateralisation C** is achieved and the remainder.

72. Table 5 sets out the applicable LGD* and required collateralisation levels for the secured parts of exposures.

By way of derogation, until 31 December 2012 the competent authorities may, subject to the levels of collateralisation indicated in Table 5:

(a) allow credit institutions to assign a 30% LGD for senior exposures in the form of Commercial Real Estate leasing;

(b) allow credit institutions to assign a 35% LGD for senior exposures in the form of equipment leasing; and

(c) allow credit institutions to assign a 30% LGD for senior exposures secured by residential or commercial real estate.

At the end of this period, this derogation shall be reviewed.

(b) *Alternative treatment for real estate collateral*

73. Subject to the requirements of this point and point 74 and as an alternative to the treatment in points 68 to 72, the competent authorities of a Member State may authorise credit institutions to assign a 50% risk weight to the part of the exposure fully collateralised by residential real estate property or commercial real estate property situated within the territory of the Member State if they have evidence that the relevant markets are well-developed and long-established with loss-rates from lending collateralised by residential real estate property or commercial real estate property respectively that do not exceed the following limits:

(a) losses stemming from lending collateralised by residential real estate property or commercial real estate property respectively up to 50% of the market value (or where applicable and if lower 60% of the mortgage-lending value) do not exceed 0.3%

of the outstanding loans collateralised by that form of real estate property in any given year; and

(b) overall losses stemming from lending collateralised by residential real estate property or commercial real estate property respectively do not exceed 0.5% of the outstanding loans collateralised by that form of real estate property in any given year.

74. If either of the conditions in point 73 is not satisfied in a given year, the eligibility to use this treatment shall cease until the conditions are satisfied in a subsequent year.

75. The competent authorities, which do not authorise the treatment in point 73, may authorise credit institutions to assign the risk weights permitted under this treatment in respect of exposures collateralised by residential real estate property of commercial real estate property respectively located in the territory of those Member States the competent authorities of which authorise this treatment subject to the same conditions as apply in that Member State.

1.6. Calculating risk-weighted exposure amounts and expected loss amounts in the case of mixed pools of collateral

76. Where risk-weighted exposure amounts and expected loss amounts are calculated under Articles 84 to 89, and an exposure is collateralised by both financial collateral and other eligible collateral, LGD*, to be taken as the LGD for the purposes of Annex VII, shall be calculated as follows.

77. The credit institution shall be required to subdivide the volatility-adjusted value of the exposure (i.e. the value after the application of the volatility adjustment as set out in point 33) into parts each covered by only one type of collateral. That is, the credit institution must divide the exposure into the part covered by eligible financial collateral, the portion covered by receivables, the portions covered by commercial real estate property collateral and/or residential real estate property collateral, the part covered by other eligible collateral, and the unsecured portion, as relevant.

78. LGD* for each part of exposure shall be calculated separately in accordance with the relevant provisions of this Annex.

1.7. Other funded credit protection

1.7.1. *Deposits with third party institutions*

79. Where the conditions set out in Part 2, point 12 are satisfied, credit protection falling within the terms of Part 1, point 23 may be treated as a guarantee by the third party institution.

1.7.2. *Life insurance policies pledged to the lending credit institution*

80. Where the conditions set out in Part 2, point 13 are satisfied, credit protection falling within the terms of Part 1, point 24 may be treated as a guarantee by the company providing the life insurance. The value of the credit protection recognised shall be the surrender value of the life insurance policy.

1.7.3. *Institution instruments repurchased on request*

81. Instruments eligible under Part 1, point 25 may be treated as a guarantee by the issuing institution.

82. The value of the credit protection recognised shall be the following:

(a) where the instrument will be repurchased at its face value, the value of the protection shall be that amount;

(b) where the instrument will be repurchased at market price, the value of the protection shall be the value of the instrument valued in the same way as the debt securities specified in Part 1, point 8.

2. UNFUNDED CREDIT PROTECTION

2.1. Valuation

83. The value of unfunded credit protection (G) shall be the amount that the protection provider has undertaken to pay in the event of the default or non-payment of the borrower or on the occurrence of other specified credit events. In the case of credit derivatives which do not include as

a credit event restructuring of the underlying obligation involving forgiveness or postponement of principal, interest or fees that result in a credit loss event (e.g. value adjustment, the making of a value adjustment or other similar debit to the profit and loss account),

(a) where the amount that the protection provider has undertaken to pay is not higher than the exposure value, the value of the credit protection calculated under the first sentence of this point shall be reduced by 40%; or

(b) where the amount that the protection provider has undertaken to pay is higher than the exposure value, the value of the credit protection shall be no higher than 60% of the exposure value.

84. Where unfunded credit protection is denominated in a currency different from that in which the exposure is denominated (a currency mismatch) the value of the credit protection shall be reduced by the application of a volatility adjustment H_{FX} as follows:

$$G^* = G \times (1-H_{FX})$$

where:

G is the nominal amount of the credit protection,

G* is G adjusted for any foreign exchange risk, and

H_{fx} is the volatility adjustment for any currency mismatch between the credit protection and the underlying obligation.

Where there is no currency mismatch

$$G^* = G$$

85. The volatility adjustments for any currency mismatch may be calculated based on the supervisory volatility adjustments approach or the own estimates approach as set out in points 34 to 57.

2.2. Calculating risk-weighted exposure amounts and expected loss amounts

2.2.1. Partial protection—tranching

86. Where the credit institution transfers a part of the risk of a loan in one or more tranches, the rules set out in Articles 94 to 101 shall apply. Materiality thresholds on payments below which no payment shall be made in the event of loss are considered to be equivalent to retained first loss positions and to give rise to a tranched transfer of risk.

2.2.2. Standardised Approach

(a) *Full protection*

87. For the purposes of Article 80, g shall be the risk weight to be assigned to an exposure which is fully protected by unfunded protection (G_A), where:

g is the risk weight of exposures to the protection provider as specified under Articles 78 to 83; and

G_A is the value of G* as calculated under point 84 further adjusted for any maturity mismatch as laid down in Part 4.

(b) *Partial protection—equal seniority*

88. Where the protected amount is less than the exposure value and the protected and unprotected parts are of equal seniority—i.e. the credit institution and the protection provider share losses on a pro-rata basis, proportional regulatory capital relief shall be afforded. For the purposes of Article 80, risk-weighted exposure amounts shall be calculated in accordance with the following formula:

$$(E-G_A) \times r + G_A \times g$$

where:

E is the exposure value;

G_A is the value of G* as calculated under point 84 further adjusted for any maturity mismatch as laid down in Part 4;

r is the risk weight of exposures to the obligor as specified under Articles 78 to 83; and

g is the risk weight of exposures to the protection provider as specified under Articles 78 to 83.

(c) *Sovereign guarantees*

89. The competent authorities may extend the treatment provided for in Annex VI, Part 1, points 4 and 5 to exposures or parts of exposures guaranteed by the central government or central bank, where the guarantee is denominated in the

domestic currency of the borrower and the exposure is funded in that currency.

2.2.3. IRB Approach

Full protection/Partial protection—equal seniority

90. For the covered portion of the exposure (based on the adjusted value of the credit protection GA), the PD for the purposes of Annex VII, Part 2 may be the PD of the protection provider, or a PD between that of the borrower and that of the guarantor if a full substitution is deemed not to be warranted. In the case of subordinated exposures and non-subordinated unfunded protection, the LGD to be applied for the purposes of Annex VII, Part 2 may be that associated with senior claims.

91. For any uncovered portion of the exposure the PD shall be that of the borrower and the LGD shall be that of the underlying exposure.

92. GA is the value of G* as calculated under point 84 further adjusted for any maturity mismatch as laid down in Part 4.

Part 4

Maturity Mismatches

1. For the purposes of calculating risk-weighted exposure amounts, a maturity mismatch occurs when the residual maturity of the credit protection is less than that of the protected exposure. Protection of less than three months residual maturity, the maturity of which is less than the maturity of the underlying exposure, shall not be recognised.

2. Where there is a maturity mismatch the credit protection shall not be recognised where:

(a) the original maturity of the protection is less than 1 year; or

(b) the exposure is a short term exposure specified by the competent authorities as being subject to a one–day floor rather than a one-year floor in respect of the maturity value (M) under Annex VII, Part 2, point 14.

1. Definition of Maturity

3. Subject to a maximum of 5 years, the effective maturity of the underlying shall be the longest possible remaining time before the obligor is scheduled to fulfil its obligations. Subject to point 4, the maturity of the credit protection shall be the time to the earliest date at which the protection may terminate or be terminated.

4. Where there is an option to terminate the protection which is at the discretion of the protection seller, the maturity of the protection shall be taken to be the time to the earliest date at which that option may be exercised. Where there is an option to terminate the protection which is at the discretion of the protection buyer and the terms of the arrangement at origination of the protection contain a positive incentive for the credit institution to call the transaction before contractual maturity, the maturity of the protection shall be taken to be the time to the earliest date at which that option may be exercised; otherwise such an option may be considered not to affect the maturity of the protection.

5. Where a credit derivative is not prevented from terminating prior to expiration of any grace period required for a default on the underlying obligation to occur as a result of a failure to pay the maturity of the protection shall be reduced by the amount of the grace period.

2. Valuation of Protection

2.1. Transactions subject to funded credit protection—Financial Collateral Simple Method

6. Where there is a mismatch between the maturity of the exposure and the maturity of the protection, the collateral shall not be recognised.

2.2. Transactions subject to funded credit protection—Financial Collateral Comprehensive Method

7. The maturity of the credit protection and that of the exposure must be reflected in the adjusted value of the collateral according to the following formula:

$$C_{VAM} = C_{VA} \times (t-t^*)/(T-t^*)$$

where:

C_{VA} is the volatility adjusted value of the collateral as specified in Part 3, point 33 or the amount of the exposure, whichever is the lowest;

t is the number of years remaining to the maturity date of the credit protection calculated in accordance with points 3 to 5, or the value of T, whichever is the lower;

T is the number of years remaining to the maturity date of the exposure calculated in accordance with points 3 to 5, or 5 years, whichever is the lower; and

t^* is 0.25.

C_{VAM} shall be taken as C_{VA} further adjusted for maturity mismatch to be included in the formula for the calculation of the fully adjusted value of the exposure (E*) set out at Part 3, point 33.

2.3. Transactions subject to unfunded credit protection

8. The maturity of the credit protection and that of the exposure must be reflected in the adjusted value of the credit protection according to the following formula

$$GA = G^* \times (t-t^*)/(T-t^*)$$

where:

G^* is the amount of the protection adjusted for any currency mismatch;

G_A is G^* adjusted for any maturity mismatch;

t is the number of years remaining to the maturity date of the credit protection calculated in accordance with points 3 to 5, or the value of T, whichever is the lower;

T is the number of years remaining to the maturity date of the exposure calculated in accordance with points 3 to 5, or 5 years, whichever is the lower; and

t^* is 0.25.

G_A is then taken as the value of the protection for the purposes of Part 3, points 83 to 92.

PART 5

Combinations of Credit Risk Mitigation in the Standardised Approach

1. In the case where a credit institution calculating risk-weighted exposure amounts under Articles 78 to 83 has more than one form of credit risk mitigation covering a single exposure (e.g. a credit institution has both collateral and a guarantee partially covering an exposure), the credit institution shall be required to subdivide the exposure into parts covered by each type of credit risk mitigation tool (e.g. a part covered by collateral and a portion covered by guarantee) and the risk-weighted exposure amount for each portion must be calculated separately in accordance with the provisions of Articles 78 to 83 and this Annex.

2. When credit protection provided by a single protection provider has differing maturities, a similar approach to that described in point 1 shall be applied.

PART 6

Basket CRM Techniques

1. FIRST-TO-DEFAULT CREDIT DERIVATIVES

1. Where a credit institution obtains credit protection for a number of exposures under terms that the first default among the exposures shall trigger payment and that this credit event shall terminate the contract, the credit institution may modify the calculation of the risk-weighted exposure amount and, as relevant, the expected loss amount of the exposure which would, in the absence of the credit protection, produce the lowest risk-weighted exposure amount under

Articles 78 to 83 or Articles 84 to 89 as appropriate in accordance with this Annex, but only if the exposure value is less than or equal to the value of the credit protection.

2. Nth-to-Default Credit Derivatives

2. Where the nth default among the exposures triggers payment under the credit protection, the credit institution purchasing the protection may only recognise the protection for the calculation of risk-weighted exposure amounts and, as relevant, expected loss amounts if protection has also been obtained for defaults 1 to n-1 or when n-1 defaults have already occurred. In such cases, the methodology shall follow that set out in point 1 for first-to-default derivatives appropriately modified for nth-to-default products.

Annex IX

Securitisation

Part 1

Definitions for the Purposes of Annex IX

1. For the purposes of this Annex:
 – 'Excess spread' means finance charge collections and other fee income received in respect of the securitised exposures net of costs and expenses;
 – 'Clean-up call option' means a contractual option for the originator to repurchase or extinguish the securitisation positions before all of the underlying exposures have been repaid, when the amount of outstanding exposures falls below a specified level;
 – 'Liquidity facility' means the securitisation position arising from a contractual agreement to provide funding to ensure timeliness of cash flows to investors;
 – 'Kirb' means 8% of the risk-weighted exposure amounts that would be calculated under Articles 84 to 89 in respect of the securitised exposures, had they not been securitised, plus the amount of expected losses associated with those exposures calculated under those Articles;
 – 'Ratings based method' means the method of calculating risk-weighted exposure amounts for securitisation positions in accordance with Part 4, points 46 to 51;
 – 'Supervisory formula method' means the method of calculating risk-weighted exposure amounts for securitisation positions in accordance with Part 4, points 52 to 54;
 – 'Unrated position' means a securitisation position which does not have an eligible credit assessment by an eligible ECAI as defined in Article 97;
 – 'Rated position' means a securitisation position which has an eligible credit assessment by an eligible ECAI as defined in Article 97; and
 – 'Asset-backed commercial paper (ABCP) programme' means a programme of securitisations the securities issued by which predominantly take the form of commercial paper with an original maturity of one year or less.

Part 2

Minimum Requirements for Recognition of Significant Credit Risk Transfer and Calculation of Risk-Weighted Exposure Amounts and Expected Loss Amounts for Securitised Exposures

1. Minimum Requirements for Recognition of Significant Credit Risk Transfer in a Traditional Securitisation

1. The originator credit institution of a traditional securitisation may exclude securitised

exposures from the calculation of risk-weighted exposure amounts and expected loss amounts if significant credit risk associated with the securitised exposures has been transferred to third parties and the transfer complies with the following conditions:

(a) The securitisation documentation reflects the economic substance of the transaction;

(b) The securitised exposures are put beyond the reach of the originator credit institution and its creditors, including in bankruptcy and receivership. This shall be supported by the opinion of qualified legal counsel;

(c) The securities issued do not represent payment obligations of the originator credit institution;

(d) The transferee is a securitisation special-purpose entity (SSPE);

(e) The originator credit institution does not maintain effective or indirect control over the transferred exposures. An originator shall be considered to have maintained effective control over the transferred exposures if it has the right to repurchase from the transferee the previously transferred exposures in order to realise their benefits or if it is obligated to re-assume transferred risk. The originator credit institution's retention of servicing rights or obligations in respect of the exposures shall not of itself constitute indirect control of the exposures;

(f) Where there is a clean-up call option, the following conditions are satisfied:
(i) The clean-up call option is exercisable at the discretion of the originator credit institution;
(ii) The clean-up call option may only be exercised when 10% or less of the original value of the exposures securitised remains unamortised; and
(iii) The clean-up call option is not structured to avoid allocating losses to credit enhancement positions or other positions held by investors and is not otherwise structured to provide credit enhancement; and

(g) The securitisation documentation does not contain clauses that
(i) other than in the case of early amortisation provisions, require positions in the securitisation to be improved by the originator credit institution including but not limited to altering the underlying credit exposures or increasing the yield payable to investors in response to a deterioration in the credit quality of the securitised exposures; or
(ii) increase the yield payable to holders of positions in the securitisation in response to a deterioration in the credit quality of the underlying pool.

2. Minimum Requirements for Recognition of Significant Credit Risk Transfer in a Synthetic Securitisation

2. An originator credit institution of a synthetic securitisation may calculate risk-weighted exposure amounts, and, as relevant, expected loss amounts, for the securitised exposures in accordance with points 3 and 4 below, if significant credit risk has been transferred to third parties either through funded or unfunded credit protection and the transfer complies with the following conditions:

(a) The securitisation documentation reflects the economic substance of the transaction;

(b) The credit protection by which the credit risk is transferred complies with the eligibility and other requirements under Articles 90 to 93 for the recognition of such credit protection. For the purposes of this point, special purpose entities shall not be recognised as eligible unfunded protection providers.

(c) The instruments used to transfer credit risk do not contain terms or conditions that:
(i) impose significant materiality thresholds below which credit protection is deemed not to be triggered if a credit event occurs;
(ii) allow for the termination of the protection due to deterioration of the credit quality of the underlying exposures;
(iii) other than in the case of early amortisation provisions, require positions in the securitisation to be improved by the originator credit institution;
(iv) increase the credit institutions' cost of credit protection or the yield payable to holders of positions in the securitisation in response to

a deterioration in the credit quality of the underlying pool; and

(d) An opinion is obtained from qualified legal counsel confirming the enforceability of the credit protection in all relevant jurisdictions.

3. Originator Credit Institutions' Calculation of Risk-Weighted Exposure Amounts for Exposures Securitised in a Synthetic Securitisation

3. In calculating risk-weighted exposure amounts for the securitised exposures, where the conditions in point 2 are met, the originator credit institution of a synthetic securitisation shall, subject to points 5 to 7, use the relevant calculation methodologies set out in Part 4 and not those set out in Articles 78 to 89. For credit institutions calculating risk-weighted exposure amounts and expected loss amounts under Articles 84 to 89, the expected loss amount in respect of such exposures shall be zero.

4. For clarity, point 3 refers to the entire pool of exposures included in the securitisation. Subject to points 5 to 7, the originator credit institution is required to calculate risk-weighted exposure amounts in respect of all tranches in the securitisation in accordance with the provisions of Part 4 including those relating to the recognition of credit risk mitigation. For example, where a tranche is transferred by means of unfunded credit protection to a third party, the risk weight of that third party shall be applied to the tranche in the calculation of the originator credit institution's risk-weighted exposure amounts.

3.1. Treatment of maturity mismatches in synthetic securitisations

5. For the purposes of calculating risk-weighted exposure amounts in accordance with point 3, any maturity mismatch between the credit protection by which the tranching is achieved and the securitised exposures shall be taken into consideration in accordance with points 6 to 7.

6. The maturity of the securitised exposures shall be taken to be the longest maturity of any of those exposures subject to a maximum of five years. The maturity of the credit protection shall be determined in accordance with Annex VIII.

7. An originator credit institution shall ignore any maturity mismatch in calculating risk-weighted exposure amounts for tranches appearing pursuant to Part 4 with a risk weighting of 1250%. For all other tranches, the maturity mismatch treatment set out in Annex VIII shall be applied in accordance with the following formula:

RW^* is $[RW(SP) \times (t-t^*)/(T-t^*)] + [RW(Ass) \times (T-t)/(T-t^*)]$

Where:

RW^* is Risk-weighted exposure amounts for the purposes of Article 75(a);

$RW(Ass)$ is Risk-weighted exposure amounts for exposures if they had not been securitised, calculated on a pro-rata basis;

$RW(SP)$ is Risk-weighted exposure amounts calculated under point 3 if there was no maturity mismatch;

T is maturity of the underlying exposures expressed in years;

t is maturity of credit protection. expressed in years; and

t^* is 0.25.

Part 3

External Credit Assessments

1. Requirements to be Met by the Credit Assessments of ECAIS

1. To be used for the purposes of calculating risk-weighted exposure amounts under Part 4, a credit assessment of an eligible ECAI shall comply with the following conditions.

(a) There shall be no mismatch between the types of payments reflected in the credit assessment and the types of payment to which the credit institution is entitled under the contract giving rise to the securitisation position in question; and

(b) The credit assessments shall be available publicly to the market. Credit assessments are considered to be publicly available only if they have been published in a publicly accessible forum and they are included in the ECAI's transition matrix. Credit assessments that are made available only to a limited number of entities shall not be considered to be publicly available.

2. USE OF CREDIT ASSESSMENTS

2. A credit institution may nominate one or more eligible ECAIs the credit assessments of which shall be used in the calculation of its risk-weighted exposure amounts under Articles 94 to 101 (a 'nominated ECAI').

3. Subject to points 5 to 7 below, a credit institution must use credit assessments from nominated ECAIs consistently in respect of its securitisation positions.

4. Subject to points 5 and 6, a credit institution may not use an ECAI's credit assessments for its positions in some tranches and another ECAI's credit assessments for its positions in other tranches within the same structure that may or may not be rated by the first ECAI.

5. Where a position has two credit assessments by nominated ECAIs, the credit institution shall use the less favourable credit assessment.

6. Where a position has more than two credit assessments by nominated ECAIs, the two most favourable credit assessments shall be used. If the two most favourable assessments are different, the least favourable of the two shall be used.

7. Where credit protection eligible under Articles 90 to 93 is provided directly to the SSPE, and that protection is reflected in the credit assessment of a position by a nominated ECAI, the risk weight associated with that credit assessment may be used. If the protection is not eligible under Articles 90 to 93, the credit assessment shall not be recognised. In the situation where the credit protection is not provided to the SSPE but rather directly to a securitisation position, the credit assessment shall not be recognised.

3. MAPPING

8. The competent authorities shall determine with which credit quality step in the tables set out in Part 4 each credit assessment of an eligible ECAI shall be associated. In doing so the competent authorities shall differentiate between the relative degrees of risk expressed by each assessment. They shall consider quantitative factors, such as default and/or loss rates, and qualitative factors such as the range of transactions assessed by the ECAI and the meaning of the credit assessment.

9. The competent authorities shall seek to ensure that securitisation positions to which the same risk weight is applied on the basis of the credit assessments of eligible ECAIs are subject to equivalent degrees of credit risk. This shall include modifying their determination as to the credit quality step with which a particular credit assessment shall be associated, as appropriate.

PART 4

Calculation

1. CALCULATION OF RISK-WEIGHTED EXPOSURE AMOUNTS

1. For the purposes of Article 96, the risk-weighted exposure amount of a securitisation position shall be calculated by applying to the exposure value of the position the relevant risk weight as set out in this Part.

2. Subject to point 3:

(a) where a credit institution calculates risk-weighted exposure amounts under points 6 to 36, the exposure value of an on-balance sheet securitisation position shall be its balance sheet value;

(b) where a credit institution calculates risk-weighted exposure amounts under points 37 to 76, the exposure value of an on-balance sheet securitisation position shall be measured gross of value adjustments; and

(c) the exposure value of an off-balance sheet securitisation position shall be its nominal value multiplied by a conversion figure as prescribed in this Annex. This conversion figure shall be 100% unless otherwise specified.

3. The exposure value of a securitisation position arising from a derivative instrument listed in Annex IV, shall be determined in accordance with Annex III.

4. Where a securitisation position is subject to funded credit protection, the exposure value of that position may be modified in accordance with and subject to the requirements in Annex VIII as further specified in this Annex.

5. Where a credit institution has two or more overlapping positions in a securitisation, it will be required to the extent that they overlap to include in its calculation of risk-weighted exposure amounts only the position or portion of a position producing the higher risk-weighted exposure amounts. For the purpose of this point 'overlapping' means that the positions, wholly or partially, represent an exposure to the same risk such that to the extent of the overlap there is a single exposure.

2. CALCULATION OF RISK-WEIGHTED EXPOSURE AMOUNTS UNDER THE STANDARDISED APPROACH

6. Subject to point 8, the risk-weighted exposure amount of a rated securitisation position shall be calculated by applying to the exposure value the risk weight associated with the credit quality step with which the credit assessment has been determined to be associated by the competent authorities in accordance with Article 98 as laid down in Tables 1 and 2.

7. Subject to points 10 to 15, the risk-weighted exposure amount of an unrated securitisation position shall be calculated by applying a risk weight of 1,250%.

Table 1 Positions other than ones with short-term credit assessments

Credit quality step	1	2	3	4	5 and below
Risk weight	20%	50%	100%	350%	1,250%

Table 2 Positions with short-term credit assessments

Credit quality step	1	2	3	All other assessments
Risk weight	20%	50%	100%	1,250%

2.1. Originator and sponsor credit institutions

8. For an originator credit institution or sponsor credit institution, the risk-weighted exposure amounts calculated in respect of its positions in a securitisation may be limited to the risk-weighted exposure amounts which would be calculated for the securitised exposures had they not been securitised subject to the presumed application of a 150% risk weight to all past due items and items belonging to 'regulatory high risk categories' amongst the securitised exposures.

2.2. Treatment of unrated positions

9. Credit institutions having an unrated securitisation position may apply the treatment set out in point 10 for calculating the risk-weighted exposure amount for that position provided the composition of the pool of exposures securitised is known at all times.

10. A credit institution may apply the weighted-average risk weight that would be applied to the securitised exposures under Articles 78 to 83 by a credit institution holding the exposures, multiplied by a concentration ratio. This concentration ratio is equal to the sum of the nominal amounts of all the tranches divided by the sum of the nominal amounts of the tranches junior to or pari passu with the tranche in which the position

is held including that tranche itself. The resulting risk weight shall not be higher than 1,250% or lower than any risk weight applicable to a rated more senior tranche. Where the credit institution is unable to determine the risk weights that would be applied to the securitised exposures under Articles 78 to 83, it shall apply a risk weight of 1,250% to the position.

2.3. Treatment of securitisation positions in a second loss tranche or better in an ABCP programme

11. Subject to the availability of a more favourable treatment by virtue of the provisions concerning liquidity facilities in points 13 to 15, a credit institution may apply to securitisation positions meeting the conditions set out in point 12 a risk weight that is the greater of 100% or the highest of the risk weights that would be applied to any of the securitised exposures under Articles 78 to 83 by a credit institution holding the exposures.

12. For the treatment set out in point 11 to be available, the securitisation position shall be:

(a) in a tranche which is economically in a second loss position or better in the securitisation and the first loss tranche must provide meaningful credit enhancement to the second loss tranche;

(b) of a quality the equivalent of investment grade or better; and

(c) held by a credit institution which does not hold a position in the first loss tranche.

2.4. Treatment of unrated liquidity facilities

2.4.1. *Eligible liquidity facilities*

13. When the following conditions are met, to determine its exposure value a conversion figure of 20% may be applied to the nominal amount of a liquidity facility with an original maturity of one year or less and a conversion figure of 50% may be applied to the nominal amount of a liquidity facility with an original maturity of more than one year:

(a) The liquidity facility documentation shall clearly identify and limit the circumstances under which the facility may be drawn;

(b) It shall not be possible for the facility to be drawn so as to provide credit support by covering losses already incurred at the time of draw—for example, by providing liquidity in respect of exposures in default at the time of draw or by acquiring assets at more than fair value;

(c) The facility shall not be used to provide permanent or regular funding for the securitisation;

(d) Repayment of draws on the facility shall not be subordinated to the claims of investors other than to claims arising in respect of interest rate or currency derivative contracts, fees or other such payments, nor be subject to waiver or deferral;

(e) It shall not be possible for the facility to be drawn after all applicable credit enhancements from which the liquidity facility would benefit are exhausted; and

(f) The facility must include a provision that results in an automatic reduction in the amount that can be drawn by the amount of exposures that are in default, where 'default' has the meaning given to it under Articles 84 to 89, or where the pool of securitised exposures consists of rated instruments, that terminates the facility if the average quality of the pool falls below investment grade.

The risk weight to be applied shall be the highest risk weight that would be applied to any of the securitised exposures under Articles 78 to 83 by a credit institution holding the exposures.

2.4.2. *Liquidity facilities that may be drawn only in the event of a general market disruption*

14. To determine its exposure value, a conversion figure of 0% may be applied to the nominal amount of a liquidity facility that may be drawn only in the event of a general market disruption (i.e. where more than one SPE across different transactions are unable to roll over maturing commercial paper and that inability is not the result of an impairment of the SPE's credit quality or of the credit quality of the securitised exposures), provided that the conditions set out in point 13 are satisfied.

2.4.3. Cash advance facilities

15. To determine its exposure value, a conversion figure of 0% may be applied to the nominal amount of a liquidity facility that is unconditionally cancellable provided that the conditions set out at point 13 are satisfied and that repayment of draws on the facility are senior to any other claims on the cash flows arising from the securitised exposures.

2.5. Additional capital requirements for securitisations of revolving exposures with early amortisation provisions

16. In addition to the risk-weighted exposure amounts calculated in respect of its securitisation positions, an originator credit institution shall calculate a risk-weighted exposure amount according to the method set out in points 17 to 33 when it sells revolving exposures into a securitisation that contains an early amortisation provision.

17. The credit institution shall calculate a risk-weighted exposure amount in respect of the sum of the originator's interest and the investors' interest.

18. For securitisation structures where the securitised exposures comprise revolving and non-revolving exposures, an originator credit institution shall apply the treatment set out in point 19 to 31 to that portion of the underlying pool containing revolving exposures.

19. For the purposes of point 16 to 31, 'originator's interest' means the exposure value of that notional part of a pool of drawn amounts sold into a securitisation, the proportion of which in relation to the amount of the total pool sold into the structure determines the proportion of the cash flows generated by principal and interest collections and other associated amounts which are not available to make payments to those having securitisation positions in the securitisation.

To qualify as such, the originator's interest may not be subordinate to the investors' interest.

'Investors' interest' means the exposure value of the remaining notional part of the pool of drawn amounts.

20. The exposure of the originator credit institution, associated with its rights in respect of the originator's interest, shall not be considered a securitisation position but as a pro rata exposure to the securitised exposures as if they had not been securitised.

2.5.1. Exemptions from early amortisation treatment

21. Originators of the following types of securitisation are exempt from the capital requirement in point 16:

(a) securitisations of revolving exposures whereby investors remain fully exposed to all future draws by borrowers so that the risk on the underlying facilities does not return to the originator credit institution even after an early amortisation event has occurred, and

(b) securitisations where any early amortisation provision is solely triggered by events not related to the performance of the securitised assets or the originator credit institution, such as material changes in tax laws or regulations.

2.5.2. Maximum capital requirement

22. For an originator credit institution subject to the capital requirement in point 16 the total of the risk-weighted exposure amounts in respect of its positions in the investors' interest and the risk-weighted exposure amounts calculated under point 16 shall be no greater than the greater of:

(a) the risk-weighted exposure amounts calculated in respect of its positions in the investors' interest; and

(b) the risk-weighted exposure amounts that would be calculated in respect of the securitised exposures by a credit institution holding the exposures as if they had not been securitised in an amount equal to the investors' interest.

23. Deduction of net gains, if any, arising from the capitalisation of future income required under Article 57, shall be treated outside the maximum amount indicated in point 22.

2.5.3. Calculation of risk-weighted exposure amounts

24. The risk-weighted exposure amount to be calculated in accordance with point 16 shall be determined by multiplying the amount of the investors' interest by the product of the appropriate conversion figure as indicated in points 26 to 33 and the weighted average risk weight that would apply to the securitised exposures if the exposures had not been securitised.

25. An early amortisation provision shall be considered to be 'controlled' where the following conditions are met:

(a) the originator credit institution has an appropriate capital/liquidity plan in place to ensure that it has sufficient capital and liquidity available in the event of an early amortisation;

(b) throughout the duration of the transaction there is pro-rata sharing between the originator's interest and the investor's interest of payments of interest and principal, expenses, losses and recoveries based on the balance of receivables outstanding at one or more reference points during each month;

(c) the amortisation period is considered sufficient for 90% of the total debt (originator's and investor's interest) outstanding at the beginning of the early amortisation period to have been repaid or recognised as in default; and

(d) the speed of repayment is no more rapid than would be achieved by straight-line amortisation over the period set out in point (c).

26. In the case of securitisations subject to an early amortisation provision of retail exposures which are uncommitted and unconditionally cancellable without prior notice, where the early amortisation is triggered by the excess spread level falling to a specified level, credit institutions shall compare the three-month average excess spread level with the excess spread levels at which excess spread is required to be trapped.

27. Where the securitisation does not require excess spread to be trapped, the trapping point is deemed to be 4.5 percentage points greater than the excess spread level at which an early amortisation is triggered.

Table 3

3 months average excess spread	Conversion figure	Conversion figure
Above level A	0%	0%
Level A	1%	5%
Level B	2%	15%
Level C	10%	50%
Level D	20%	100%
Level E	40%	100%

28. The conversion figure to be applied shall be determined by the level of the actual three month average excess spread in accordance with Table 3.

29. In Table 3, 'Level A' means levels of excess spread less than 133.33% of the trapping level of excess spread but not less than 100% of that trapping level, 'Level B' means levels of excess spread less than 100% of the trapping level of excess spread but not less than 75% of that trapping level, 'Level C' means levels of excess spread less than 75% of the trapping level of excess spread but not less than 50% of that trapping level, 'Level D' means levels of excess spread less than 50% of the trapping level of excess spread but not less than 25% of that trapping level and 'Level E' means levels of excess spread less than 25% of the trapping level of excess spread.

30. In the case of securitisations subject to an early amortisation provision of retail exposures which are uncommitted and unconditionally cancellable without prior notice and where the early amortisation is triggered by a quantitative value in respect of something other than the three months average excess spread, the competent authorities may apply a treatment which approximates closely to that prescribed in points 26 to 29 for determining the conversion figure indicated.

31. Where a competent authority intends to apply a treatment in accordance with point 30 in respect of a particular securitisation, it shall first inform the relevant competent authorities of all the other Member States. Before the application of such a treatment becomes part of the general policy approach of the competent authority to

securitisations containing early amortisation clauses of the type in question, the competent authority shall consult the relevant competent authorities of all the other Member States and take into consideration the views expressed. The views expressed in such consultation and the treatment applied shall be publicly disclosed by the competent authority in question.

32. All other securitisations subject to a controlled early amortisation provision of revolving exposures shall be subject to a conversion figure of 90%.

33. All other securitisations subject to a non-controlled early amortisation provision of revolving exposures shall be subject to a conversion figure of 100%.

2.6. Recognition of credit risk mitigation on securitisation positions

34. Where credit protection is obtained on a securitisation position, the calculation of risk-weighted exposure amounts may be modified in accordance with Annex VIII.

2.7. Reduction in risk-weighted exposure amounts

35. As provided in Article 66(2), in respect of a securitisation position in respect of which a 1250% risk weight is assigned, credit institutions may, as an alternative to including the position in their calculation of risk-weighted exposure amounts, deduct from own funds the exposure value of the position. For these purposes, the calculation of the exposure value may reflect eligible funded credit protection in a manner consistent with point 34.

36. Where a credit institution makes use of the alternative indicated in point 35, 12.5 times the amount deducted in accordance with that point shall, for the purposes of point 8, be subtracted from the amount specified in point 8 as the maximum risk-weighted exposure amount to be calculated by the credit institutions there indicated.

3. Calculation of Risk-Weighted Exposure Amounts Under the Internal Ratings based Approach

3.1. Hierarchy of methods

37. For the purposes of Article 96, the risk-weighted exposure amount of a securitisation positions shall be calculated in accordance with points 38 to 76.

38. For a rated position or a position in respect of which an inferred rating may be used, the Ratings Based Method set out in points 46 to 51 shall be used to calculate the risk-weighted exposure amount.

39. For an unrated position the Supervisory Formula Method set out in points 52 to 54 shall be used except where the Internal Assessment Approach is permitted to be used as set out in points 43 and 44.

40. A credit institution other than an originator credit institution or a sponsor credit institution may only use the Supervisory Formula Method with the approval of the competent authorities.

41. In the case of an originator or sponsor credit institution unable to calculate Kirb and which has not obtained approval to use the Internal Assessment Approach for positions in ABCP programmes, and in the case of other credit institutions where they have not obtained approval to use the Supervisory Formula Method or, for positions in ABCP programmes, the Internal Assessment Approach, a risk weight of 1250% shall be assigned to securitisation positions which are unrated and in respect of which an inferred rating may not be used.

3.1.1. Use of inferred ratings

42. When the following minimum operational requirements are satisfied, an institution shall attribute to an unrated position an inferred credit assessment equivalent to the credit assessment of those rated positions (the 'reference positions') which are the most senior positions which are in

all respects subordinate to the unrated securitisation position in question:

(a) the reference positions must be subordinate in all respects to the unrated securitisation position;

(b) the maturity of the reference positions must be equal to or longer than that of the unrated position in question; and

(c) on an ongoing basis, any inferred rating must be updated to reflect any changes in the credit assessment of the reference positions.

3.1.2. *The 'Internal Assessment Approach' for positions in ABCP programmes*

43. Subject to the approval of the competent authorities, when the following conditions are satisfied a credit institution may attribute to an unrated position in an ABCP programme a derived rating as laid down in point 44:

(a) positions in the commercial paper issued from the ABCP programme shall be rated positions;

(b) the credit institution shall satisfy the competent authorities that its internal assessment of the credit quality of the position reflects the publicly available assessment methodology of one or more eligible ECAIs, for the rating of securities backed by the exposures of the type securitised;

(c) the ECAIs, the methodology of which shall be reflected as required by point (b), shall include those ECAIs which have provided an external rating for the commercial paper issued from the ABCP programme. Quantitative elements, such as stress factors, used in assessing the position to a particular credit quality must be at least as conservative as those used in the relevant assessment methodology of the ECAIs in question;

(d) in developing its internal assessment methodology the credit institution shall take into consideration relevant published ratings methodologies of the eligible ECAIs that rate the commercial paper of the ABCP programme. This consideration shall be documented by the credit institution and updated regularly, as outlined in point (g);

(e) the credit institution's internal assessment methodology shall include rating grades. There shall be a correspondence between such rating grades and the credit assessments of eligible ECAIs. This correspondence shall be explicitly documented;

(f) the internal assessment methodology shall be used in the credit institution's internal risk management processes, including its decision making, management information and capital allocation processes;

(g) internal or external auditors, an ECAI, or the credit institution's internal credit review or risk management function shall perform regular reviews of the internal assessment process and the quality of the internal assessments of the credit quality of the credit institution's exposures to an ABCP programme. If the credit institution's internal audit, credit review, or risk management functions perform the review, then these functions shall be independent of the ABCP programme business line, as well as the customer relationship;

(h) the credit institution shall track the performance of its internal ratings over time to evaluate the performance of its internal assessment methodology and shall make adjustments, as necessary, to that methodology when the performance of the exposures routinely diverges from that indicated by the internal ratings;

(i) the ABCP programme shall incorporate underwriting standards in the form of credit and investment guidelines. In deciding on an asset purchase, the ABCP programme administrator shall consider the type of asset being purchased, the type and monetary value of the exposures arising from the provision of liquidity facilities and credit enhancements, the loss distribution, and the legal and economic isolation of the transferred assets from the entity selling the assets. A credit analysis of the asset seller's risk profile shall be performed and shall include analysis of past and expected future financial performance, current market position, expected future competitiveness, leverage, cash flow, interest coverage and debt rating. In addition, a review of the seller's underwriting standards, servicing capabilities, and collection processes shall be performed;

(j) the ABCP programme's underwriting standards shall establish minimum asset eligibility criteria that, in particular:
(i) exclude the purchase of assets that are significantly past due or defaulted;
(ii) limit excess concentration to individual obligor or geographic area; and
(iii) limits the tenor of the assets to be purchased;

(k) the ABCP programme shall have collections policies and processes that take into account the operational capability and credit quality of the servicer. The ABCP programme shall mitigate seller/servicer risk through various methods, such as triggers based on current credit quality that would preclude commingling of funds;

(l) the aggregated estimate of loss on an asset pool that the ABCP programme is considering purchasing must take into account all sources of potential risk, such as credit and dilution risk. If the seller-provided credit enhancement is sized based only on credit-related losses, then a separate reserve shall be established for dilution risk, if dilution risk is material for the particular exposure pool. In addition, in sizing the required enhancement level, the programme shall review several years of historical information, including losses, delinquencies, dilutions, and the turnover rate of the receivables; and

(m) the ABCP programme shall incorporate structural features—for example wind down triggers—into the purchase of exposures in order to mitigate potential credit deterioration of the underlying portfolio.

The requirement for the assessment methodology of the ECAI to be publicly available may be waived by the competent authorities where they are satisfied that due to the specific features of the securitisation—for example its unique structure—there is as yet no publicly available ECAI assessment methodology.

44. The unrated position shall be assigned by the credit institution to one of the rating grades described in point 43. The position shall be attributed a derived rating the same as the credit assessments corresponding to that rating grade as laid down in point 43. Where this derived rating is, at the inception of the securitisation, at the level of investment grade or better, it shall be considered the same as an eligible credit assessment by an eligible ECAI for the purposes of calculating risk-weighted exposure amounts.

3.2. Maximum risk-weighted exposure amounts

45. For an originator credit institution, a sponsor credit institution, or for other credit institutions which can calculate KIRB, the risk-weighted exposure amounts calculated in respect of its positions in a securitisation may be limited to that which would produce a capital requirement under Article 75(a) equal to the sum of 8% of the risk-weighted exposure amounts which would be produced if the securitised assets had not been securitised and were on the balance sheet of the credit institution plus the expected loss amounts of those exposures.

3.3. Ratings Based Method

46. Under the Ratings Based Method, the risk-weighted exposure amount of a rated securitisation position shall be calculated by applying to the exposure value the risk weight associated with the credit quality step with which the credit assessment has been determined to be associated by the competent authorities in accordance with Article 98, as set out in the Tables 4 and 5, multiplied by 1.06.

47. Subject to points 48 and 49, the risk weights in column A of each table shall be applied where the position is in the most senior tranche of a securitisation. When determining whether a tranche is the most senior, it is not required to take into consideration amounts due under interest rate or currency derivative contracts, fees due, or other similar payments.

48. A risk weight of 6% may be applied to a position in the most senior tranche of a securitisation where that tranche is senior in all respects to another tranche of the securitisation positions which would receive a risk weight of 7% under point 46, provided that:

(a) the competent authority is satisfied that this is justified due to the loss absorption qualities of subordinate tranches in the securitisation; and

Table 4 Positions other than ones with short-term credit assessments

Credit Quality Step (CQS)	Risk weight		
	A	B	C
CQS 1	7%	12%	20%
CQS 2	8%	15%	25%
CQS 3	10%	18%	35%
CQS 4	12%	20%	35%
CQS 5	20%	35%	35%
CQS 6	35%	50%	50%
CQS 7	60%	75%	75%
CQS 8	100%	100%	100%
CQS 9	250%	250%	250%
CQS 10	425%	425%	425%
CQS 11	650%	650%	650%
Below CQS 11	1250%	1250%	1250%

Table 5 Positions with short-term credit assessments

Credit Quality Step (CQS)	Risk weight		
	A	B	C
CQS 1	7%	12%	20%
CQS 2	12%	20%	35%
CQS 3	60%	75%	75%
All other assessments	1250%	1250%	1250%

(b) either the position has an external credit assessment which has been determined to be associated with credit quality step 1 in Table 4 or 5 or, if it is unrated, requirements (a) to (c) in point 42 are satisfied where 'reference positions' are taken to mean positions in the subordinate tranche which would receive a risk weight of 7% under point 46.

49. The risk weights in column C of each table shall be applied where the position is in a securitisation where the effective number of exposures securitised is less than six. In calculating the effective number of exposures securitised multiple exposures to one obligor must be treated as one exposure. The effective number of exposures is calculated as:

$$N = \frac{\left(\sum_i EAD_i\right)^2}{\sum_i EAD_i^2}$$

where EAD_i represents the sum of the exposure values of all exposures to the ith obligor. In the case of resecuritisation (securitisation of securitisation exposures), the credit institution must look at the number of securitisation exposures in the pool and not the number of underlying exposures in the original pools from which the underlying securitisation exposures stem. If the portfolio share associated with the largest exposure, C_1, is available, the credit institution may compute N as $1/C_1$.

50. The risk weights in Column B shall be applied to all other positions.

51. Credit risk mitigation on securitisation positions may be recognised in accordance with points 60 to 62.

3.4. Supervisory Formula Method

52. Subject to points 58 and 59, under the Supervisory Formula Method, the risk weight for a securitisation position shall be the greater of 7% or the risk weight to be applied in accordance with point 53.

53. Subject to points 58 and 59, the risk weight to be applied to the exposure amount shall be:

$12.5 \times (S[L + T] - S[L])/T$

where:

$$S[x] = \begin{cases} x & \text{when } x \leq Kirbr \\ Kirbr + K[x] - K[Kirbr] + (d \cdot Kirbr/\omega) \\ (1 - e^{\omega(Kirbr - x)/Kirbr}) & \text{when } Kirbr < x \end{cases}$$

where:

$h = (1 - Kirbr/ELGD)^N$

$c = Kirbr / (1 - h)$

$$v = \frac{(ELGD - Kirbr)Kirbr + 0.25(1 - ELGD)Kirbr}{N}$$

$$f = \left(\frac{v + Kirbr^2}{1-h} - c^2\right) + \frac{(1-Kirbr)Kirbr - v}{(1-h)\tau}$$

$$g = \frac{(1-c)c}{f} - 1$$

$$a = g \cdot c$$

$$b = g \cdot (1-c)$$

$$d = 1 - (1-h) \cdot (1 - Beta[Kirbr;a,b])$$

$$K[x] = (1-h) \cdot ((1 - Beta[x;a,b])x + Beta[x;a+1,b]c)$$

$\tau = 1\,000$, and

$\omega = 20$.

In these expressions, Beta [x; a, b] refers to the cumulative beta distribution with parameters a and b evaluated at x.

T (the thickness of the tranche in which the position is held) is measured as the ratio of (a) the nominal amount of the tranche to (b) the sum of the exposure values of the exposures that have been securitised. For the purposes of calculating T the exposure value of a derivative instrument listed in Annex IV shall, where the current replacement cost is not a positive value, be the potential future credit exposure calculated in accordance with Annex III.

Kirbr is the ratio of (a) Kirb to (b) the sum of the exposure values of the exposures that have been securitised. Kirbr is expressed in decimal form (e.g. Kirb equal to 15% of the pool would be expressed as Kirbr of 0.15).

L (the credit enhancement level) is measured as the ratio of the nominal amount of all tranches subordinate to the tranche in which the position is held to the sum of the exposure values of the exposures that have been securitised. Capitalised future income shall not be included in the measured L. Amounts due by counterparties to derivative instruments listed in Annex IV that represent tranches more junior than the tranche in question may be measured at their current replacement cost (without the potential future credit exposures) in calculating the enhancement level.

N is the effective number of exposures calculated in accordance with point 49.

ELGD, the exposure-weighted average loss-given-default, is calculated as follows:

$$ELGD = \frac{\sum_i LGD_i^* EAD_i}{\sum_i EAD_i}$$

where LGD_i represents the average LGD associated with all exposures to the ith obligor, where LGD is determined in accordance with Articles 84 to 89. In the case of resecuritisation, an LGD of 100% shall be applied to the securitised positions. When default and dilution risk for purchased receivables are treated in an aggregate manner within a securitisation (e.g. a single reserve or over-collateralisation is available to cover losses from either source), the LGDi input shall be constructed as a weighted average of the LGD for credit risk and the 75% LGD for dilution risk. The weights shall be the stand-alone capital charges for credit risk and dilution risk respectively.

Simplified inputs

If the exposure value of the largest securitised exposure, C_1, is no more than 3% of the sum of the exposure values of the securitised exposures, then, for the purposes of the Supervisory Formula Method, the credit institution may set LGD = 50% and N equal to either:

$$N = \left(C_1 C_m + \left(\frac{C_m - C_1}{m-1}\right) max\{1 - mC_1, 0\}\right)^{-1}$$

or

$$N = 1/C_1.$$

C_m is the ratio of the sum of the exposure values of the largest 'm' exposures to the sum of the exposure values of the exposures securitised. The level of 'm' may be set by the credit institution.

For securitisations involving retail exposures, the competent authorities may permit the Supervisory Formula Method to be implemented using the simplifications: h = 0 and v = 0.

54. Credit risk mitigation on securitisation positions may be recognised in accordance with points 60, 61 and 63 to 67.

3.5. Liquidity facilities

55. The provisions in points 56 to 59 apply for the purposes of determining the exposure value of an unrated securitisation position in the form of certain types of liquidity facility.

3.5.1. *Liquidity facilities only available in the event of general market disruption*

56. A conversion figure of 20% may be applied to the nominal amount of a liquidity facility that may only be drawn in the event of a general market disruption and that meets the conditions to be an 'eligible liquidity facility' set out in point 13.

3.5.2. *Cash advance facilities*

57. A conversion figure of 0% may be applied to the nominal amount of a liquidity facility that meets the conditions set out in point 15.

3.5.3. *Exceptional treatment where Kirb cannot be calculated*

58. When it is not practical for the credit institution to calculate the risk-weighted exposure amounts for the securitised exposures as if they had not been securitised, a credit institution may, on an exceptional basis and subject to the consent of the competent authorities, temporarily be allowed to apply the method set out in point 59 for the calculation of risk-weighted exposure amounts for an unrated securitisation position in the form of a liquidity facility that meets the conditions to be an 'eligible liquidity facility' set out in point 13 or that falls within the terms of point 56.

59. The highest risk weight that would be applied under Articles 78 to 83 to any of the securitised exposures, had they not been securitised, may be applied to the securitisation position represented by the liquidity facility. To determine the exposure value of the position a conversion figure of 50% may be applied to the nominal amount of the liquidity facility if the facility has an original maturity of one year or less. If the liquidity facility complies with the conditions in point 56 a conversion figure of 20% may be applied. In other cases a conversion factor of 100% shall be applied.

3.6. Recognition of credit risk mitigation in respect of securitisation positions

3.6.1. *Funded credit protection*

60. Eligible funded protection is limited to that which is eligible for the calculation of risk-weighted exposure amounts under Articles 78 to 83 as laid down under Articles 90 to 93 and recognition is subject to compliance with the relevant minimum requirements as laid down under those Articles.

3.6.2. *Unfunded credit protection*

61. Eligible unfunded credit protection and unfunded protection providers are limited to those which are eligible under Articles 90 to 93 and recognition is subject to compliance with the relevant minimum requirements laid down under those Articles.

3.6.3. *Calculation of capital requirements for securitisation positions with credit risk mitigation*

Ratings Based Method

62. Where risk-weighted exposure amounts are calculated using the Ratings Based Method, the exposure value and/or the risk-weighted exposure amount for a securitisation position in respect of which credit protection has been obtained may be modified in accordance with the provisions of Annex VIII as they apply for the calculation of risk-weighted exposure amounts under Articles 78 to 83.

Supervisory Formula Method—full credit protection

63. Where risk-weighted exposure amounts are calculated using the Supervisory Formula Method, the credit institution shall determine

the 'effective risk weight' of the position. It shall do this by dividing the risk-weighted exposure amount of the position by the exposure value of the position and multiplying the result by 100.

64. In the case of funded credit protection, the risk-weighted exposure amount of the securitisation position shall be calculated by multiplying the funded protection-adjusted exposure amount of the position (E*, as calculated under Articles 90 to 93 for the calculation of risk-weighted exposure amounts under Articles 78 to 83 taking the amount of the securitisation position to be E) by the effective risk weight.

65. In the case of unfunded credit protection, the risk-weighted exposure amount of the securitisation position shall be calculated by multiplying GA (the amount of the protection adjusted for any currency mismatch and maturity mismatch in accordance with the provisions of Annex VIII) by the risk weight of the protection provider; and adding this to the amount arrived at by multiplying the amount of the securitisation position minus GA by the effective risk weight.

Supervisory formula method—partial protection
66. If the credit risk mitigation covers the 'first loss' or losses on a proportional basis on the securitisation position, the credit institution may apply points 63 to 65.

67. In other cases, the credit institution shall treat the securitisation position as two or more positions with the uncovered portion being considered the position with the lower credit quality. For the purposes of calculating the risk-weighted exposure amount for this position, the provisions in points 52 to 54 shall apply subject to the modifications that 'T' shall be adjusted to e* in the case of funded credit protection; and to T-g in the case of unfunded credit protection, where e* denotes the ratio of E* to the total notional amount of the underlying pool, where E* is the adjusted exposure amount of the securitisation position calculated in accordance with the provisions of Annex VIII as they apply for the calculation of risk-weighted exposure amounts under Articles 78 to 83 taking the amount of the securitisation position to be E; and g is the ratio of the nominal amount of credit protection (adjusted for any currency or maturity mismatch in accordance with the provisions of Annex VIII) to the sum of the exposure amounts of the securitised exposures. In the case of unfunded credit protection the risk weight of the protection provider shall be applied to that portion of the position not falling within the adjusted value of 'T'.

3.7. Additional capital requirements for securitisations of revolving exposures with early amortisation provisions

68. In addition to the risk-weighted exposure amounts calculated in respect of its securitisation positions, an originator credit institution shall be required to calculate a risk-weighted exposure amount according to the methodology set out in points 16 to 33 when it sells revolving exposures into a securitisation that contains an early amortisation provision.

69. For the purposes of point 68, points 70 and 71 shall replace points 19 and 20.

70. For the purposes of these provisions, 'originator's interest' shall be the sum of:

(a) the exposure value of that notional part of a pool of drawn amounts sold into a securitisation, the proportion of which in relation to the amount of the total pool sold into the structure determines the proportion of the cash flows generated by principal and interest collections and other associated amounts which are not available to make payments to those having securitisation positions in the securitisation; plus

(b) the exposure value of that part of the pool of undrawn amounts of the credit lines, the drawn amounts of which have been sold into the securitisation, the proportion of which to the total amount of such undrawn amounts is the same as the proportion of the exposure value described in point (a) to the exposure value of the pool of drawn amounts sold into the securitisation.

To qualify as such, the originator's interest may not be subordinate to the investors' interest.

'Investors' interest' means the exposure value of the notional part of the pool of drawn amounts not falling within point (a) plus the exposure value of that part of the pool of undrawn amounts of credit lines, the drawn amounts of which have been sold into the securitisation, not falling within point (b).

71. The exposure of the originator credit institution associated with its rights in respect of that part of the originator's interest described in point 70(a) shall not be considered a securitisation position but as a pro rata exposure to the securitised drawn amounts exposures as if they had not been securitised in an amount equal to that described in point 70(a). The originator credit institution shall also be considered to have a pro rata exposure to the undrawn amounts of the credit lines, the drawn amounts of which have been sold into the securitisation, in an amount equal to that described in point 70(b).

3.8. Reduction in risk-weighted exposure amounts

72. The risk-weighted exposure amount of a securitisation position to which a 1250% risk weight is assigned may be reduced by 12.5 times the amount of any value adjustments made by the credit institution in respect of the securitised exposures. To the extent that value adjustments are taken account of for this purpose they shall not be taken account of for the purposes of the calculation indicated in Annex VII, Part 1, point 36.

73. The risk-weighted exposure amount of a securitisation position may be reduced by 12.5 times the amount of any value adjustments made by the credit institution in respect of the position.

74. As provided in Article 66(2), in respect of a securitisation position in respect of which a 1250% risk weight applies, credit institutions may, as an alternative to including the position in their calculation of risk-weighted exposure amounts, deduct from own funds the exposure value of the position.

75. For the purposes of point 74:

(a) the exposure value of the position may be derived from the risk-weighted exposure amounts taking into account any reductions made in accordance with points 72 and 73;

(b) the calculation of the exposure value may reflect eligible funded protection in a manner consistent with the methodology prescribed in points 60 to 67; and

(c) where the Supervisory Formula Method is used to calculate risk-weighted exposure amounts and $L \leq K_{IRBR}$ and $[L+T] > K_{IRBR}$ the position may be treated as two positions with L equal to K_{IRBR} for the more senior of the positions.

76. Where a credit institution makes use of the alternative indicated in point 74, 12.5 times the amount deducted in accordance with that point shall, for the purposes of point 45, be subtracted from the amount specified in point 45 as the maximum risk-weighted exposure amount to be calculated by the credit institutions there indicated.

Annex X

Operational Risk

Part 1

Basic Indicator Approach

1. Capital Requirement

1. Under the Basic Indicator Approach, the capital requirement for operational risk is equal to 15% of the relevant indicator defined in points 2 to 9.

2. Relevant Indicator

2. The relevant indicator is the average over three years of the sum of net interest income and net non-interest income.

3. The three-year average is calculated on the basis of the last three twelve-monthly observations at the end of the financial year. When

audited figures are not available, business estimates may be used.

4. If for any given observation, the sum of net interest income and net non-interest income is negative or equal to zero, this figure shall not be taken into account in the calculation of the three-year average. The relevant indicator shall be calculated as the sum of positive figures divided by the number of positive figures.

2.1. Credit institutions subject to Directive 86/635/EEC

5. Based on the accounting categories for the profit and loss account of credit institutions under Article 27 of Directive 86/635/EEC, the relevant indicator shall be expressed as the sum of the elements listed in Table 1. Each element shall be included in the sum with its positive or negative sign.

6. These elements may need to be adjusted to reflect the qualifications in points 7 and 8.

Table 1

1	Interest receivable and similar income
2	Interest payable and similar charges
3	Income from shares and other variable/fixed-yield securities
4	Commissions/fees receivable
5	Commissions/fees payable
6	Net profit or net loss on financial operations
7	Other operating income

2.1.1. *Qualifications*

7. The indicator shall be calculated before the deduction of any provisions and operating expenses. Operating expenses shall include fees paid for outsourcing services rendered by third parties which are not a parent or subsidiary of the credit institution or a subsidiary of a parent which is also the parent of the credit institution. Expenditure on the outsourcing of services rendered by third parties may reduce the relevant indicator if the expenditure is incurred from an undertaking subject to supervision under, or equivalent to, this Directive.

8. The following elements shall not be used in the calculation of the relevant indicator:

(a) Realised profits/losses from the sale of non-trading book items;

(b) Income from extraordinary or irregular items;

(c) Income derived from insurance.

When revaluation of trading items is part of the profit and loss statement, revaluation could be included. When Article 36 (2) of Directive 86/635/EEC is applied, revaluation booked in the profit and loss account should be included.

2.2. Credit institutions subject to a different accounting framework

9. When credit institutions are subject to an accounting framework different from the one established by Directive 86/635/EEC, they should calculate the relevant indicator on the basis of data that best reflects the definition set out in points 2 to 8.

Part 2

Standardised Approach

1. Capital Requirement

1. Under the Standardised Approach, the capital requirement for operational risk is the average over three years of the risk-weighted relevant indicators calculated each year across the business lines referred to in Table 2. In each year, a negative capital requirement in one business line, resulting from a negative relevant indicator may be imputed to the whole. However, where the aggregate capital charge across all business lines within a given year is negative, then the input to the average for that year shall be zero.

2. The three-year average is calculated on the basis of the last three twelve-monthly observations at the end of the financial year. When audited figures are not available, business estimates may be used.

Table 2

Business line	List of activities	Percentage
Corporate finance	Underwriting of financial instruments and/or placing of financial instruments on a firm commitment basis Services related to underwriting Investment advice Advice to undertakings on capital structure, industrial strategy and industrial strategy and related matters and advice and services relating to the mergers and the purchase of undertakings Investment research and financial analysis and other forms of general recommendation relating to transactions in financial instruments	18%
Trading and sales	Dealing on own account Money broking Reception and transmission of orders in relation to one or more financial instruments Execution of orders on behalf of clients Placing of financial instruments without a firm commitment basis Operation of Multilateral Trading Facilities	18%
Retail brokerage (Activities with individual physical persons or with small and medium sized entities meeting the criteria set out in Article 79 for the retail exposure class)	Reception and transmission of orders in relation to one or more financial instruments Execution of orders on behalf of clients persons Placing of financial instruments without a firm commitment basis	12%
Commercial banking funds	Acceptance of deposits and other repayable Lending Financial leasing Guarantees and commitments	15%
Retail banking (Activities with individual physical persons or with small and medium sized entities meeting the criteria set out in Article 79 for the retail exposure class)	Acceptance of deposits and other repayable Lending Financial leasing Guarantees and commitments	12%
Payment and settlement	Money transmission services, Issuing and administering means of payment	18%
Agency services	Safekeeping and administration of financial instruments for the account of clients, including custodianship and related services such as cash/collateral management	15%
Asset management	Portfolio management Managing of UCITS Other forms of asset management	12%

3. Competent authorities may authorise a credit institution to calculate its capital requirement for operational risk using an alternative standardised approach, as set out in points 5 to 11.

2. Principles for Business Line Mapping

4. Credit institutions must develop and document specific policies and criteria for mapping the relevant indicator for current business lines and activities into the standardised framework. The criteria must be reviewed and adjusted as appropriate for new or changing business activities and risks. The principles for business line mapping are:

(a) all activities must be mapped into the business lines in a mutually exclusive and jointly exhaustive manner;

(b) any activity which cannot be readily mapped into the business line framework, but which represents an ancillary function to an activity included in the framework, must be allocated to the business line it supports. If more than one business line is supported through the ancillary activity, an objective-mapping criterion must be used;

(c) if an activity cannot be mapped into a particular business line then the business line yielding the highest percentage must be used. The same business line equally applies to any associated ancillary activity;

(d) credit institutions may use internal pricing methods to allocate the relevant indicator between business lines. Costs generated in one business line which are imputable to a different business line may be reallocated to the business line to which they pertain, for instance by using a treatment based on internal transfer costs between the two business lines;

(e) the mapping of activities into business lines for operational risk capital purposes must be consistent with the categories used for credit and market risks;

(f) senior management is responsible for the mapping policy under the control of the governing bodies of the credit institution; and

(g) the mapping process to business lines must be subject to independent review.

3. Alternative Indicators for Certain Business Lines

3.1. Modalities

5. The competent authorities may authorise the credit institution to use an alternative relevant indicator for the business lines: retail banking and commercial banking.

6. For these business lines, the relevant indicator shall be a normalised income indicator equal to the three-year average of the total nominal amount of loans and advances multiplied by 0.035.

7. For the retail and/or commercial banking business lines, the loans and advances shall consist of the total drawn amounts in the corresponding credit portfolios. For the commercial banking business line, securities held in the non-trading book shall also be included.

3.2. Conditions

8. The authorisation to use alternative relevant indicators shall be subject to the conditions in points 9 to 11.

3.2.1. *General condition*

9. The credit institution meets the qualifying criteria set out in point 12.

3.2.2. *Conditions specific to retail banking and commercial banking*

10. The credit institution is overwhelmingly active in retail and/or commercial banking activities, which shall account for at least 90% of its income.

11. The credit institution is able to demonstrate to the competent authorities that a significant proportion of its retail and/or commercial banking activities comprise loans associated with a high PD, and that the alternative standardised

approach provides an improved basis for assessing the operational risk.

4. Qualifying Criteria

12. Credit institutions must meet the qualifying criteria listed below, in addition to the general risk management standards set out in Article 22 and Annex V. Satisfaction of these criteria shall be determined having regard to the size and scale of activities of the credit institution and to the principle of proportionality.

(a) Credit institutions shall have a well-documented assessment and management system for operational risk with clear responsibilities assigned for this system. They shall identify their exposures to operational risk and track relevant operational risk data, including material loss data. This system shall be subject to regular independent review.

(b) The operational risk assessment system must be closely integrated into the risk management processes of the credit institution. Its output must be an integral part of the process of monitoring and controlling the credit institution's operational risk profile.

(c) Credit institutions shall implement a system of management reporting that provides operational risk reports to relevant functions within the credit institution. Credit institutions shall have procedures for taking appropriate action according to the information within the management reports.

Part 3

Advanced Measurement Approaches

1. Qualifying Criteria

1. To be eligible for an Advanced Measurement Approach, credit institutions must satisfy the competent authorities that they meet the qualifying criteria below, in addition to the general risk management standards in Article 22 and Annex V.

1.1. Qualitative standards

2. The credit institution's internal operational risk measurement system shall be closely integrated into its day-to-day risk management processes.

3. The credit institution must have an independent risk management function for operational risk.

4. There must be regular reporting of operational risk exposures and loss experience. The credit institution shall have procedures for taking appropriate corrective action.

5. The credit institution's risk management system must be well documented. The credit institution shall have routines in place for ensuring compliance and policies for the treatment of non-compliance.

6. The operational risk management processes and measurement systems shall be subject to regular reviews performed by internal and/or external auditors.

7. The validation of the operational risk measurement system by the competent authorities shall include the following elements:

(a) verifying that the internal validation processes are operating in a satisfactory manner;

(b) making sure that data flows and processes associated with the risk measurement system are transparent and accessible.

1.2. Quantitative standards

1.2.1. *Process*

8. Credit institutions shall calculate their capital requirement as comprising both expected loss and unexpected loss, unless they can demonstrate that expected loss is adequately captured in their internal business practices. The operational risk measure must capture potentially severe tail events, achieving a soundness standard comparable to a 99.9% confidence interval over a one year period.

9. The operational risk measurement system of a credit institution must have certain key elements to meet the soundness standard set out in point 8. These elements must include the use of internal data, external data, scenario analysis and factors

reflecting the business environment and internal control systems as set out in points 13 to 24. A credit institution needs to have a well documented approach for weighting the use of these four elements in its overall operational risk measurement system.

10. The risk measurement system shall capture the major drivers of risk affecting the shape of the tail of the loss estimates.

11. Correlations in operational risk losses across individual operational risk estimates may be recognised only if credit institutions can demonstrate to the satisfaction of the competent authorities that their systems for measuring correlations are sound, implemented with integrity, and take into account the uncertainty surrounding any such correlation estimates, particularly in periods of stress. The credit institution must validate its correlation assumptions using appropriate quantitative and qualitative techniques.

12. The risk measurement system shall be internally consistent and shall avoid the multiple counting of qualitative assessments or risk mitigation techniques recognised in other areas of the capital adequacy framework.

1.2.2. *Internal data*

13. Internally generated operational risk measures shall be based on a minimum historical observation period of five years. When a credit institution first moves to an Advanced Measurement Approach, a three-year historical observation period is acceptable.

14. Credit institutions must be able to map their historical internal loss data into the business lines defined in Part 2 and into the event types defined in Part 5, and to provide these data to competent authorities upon request. There must be documented, objective criteria for allocating losses to the specified business lines and event types. The operational risk losses that are related to credit risk and have historically been included in the internal credit risk databases must be recorded in the operational risk databases and be separately identified. Such losses will not be subject to the operational risk charge, as long as they continue to be treated as credit risk for the purposes of calculating minimum capital requirements. Operational risk losses that are related to market risks shall be included in the scope of the capital requirement for operational risk.

15. The credit institution's internal loss data must be comprehensive in that it captures all material activities and exposures from all appropriate sub-systems and geographic locations. Credit institutions must be able to justify that any excluded activities or exposures, both individually and in combination, would not have a material impact on the overall risk estimates. Appropriate minimum loss thresholds for internal loss data collection must be defined.

16. Aside from information on gross loss amounts, credit institutions shall collect information about the date of the event, any recoveries of gross loss amounts, as well as some descriptive information about the drivers or causes of the loss event.

17. There shall be specific criteria for assigning loss data arising from an event in a centralised function or an activity that spans more than one business line, as well as from related events over time.

18. Credit institutions must have documented procedures for assessing the on-going relevance of historical loss data, including those situations in which judgement overrides, scaling, or other adjustments may be used, to what extent they may be used and who is authorised to make such decisions.

1.2.3. *External data*

19. The credit institution's operational risk measurement system shall use relevant external data, especially when there is reason to believe that the credit institution is exposed to infrequent, yet potentially severe, losses. A credit institution must have a systematic process for determining the situations for which external data must be used and the methodologies used to incorporate the data in its measurement system. The conditions and practices for external data use must be regularly reviewed, documented and subject to periodic independent review.

1.2.4. Scenario analysis

20. The credit institution shall use scenario analysis of expert opinion in conjunction with external data to evaluate its exposure to high severity events. Over time, such assessments need to be validated and re-assessed through comparison to actual loss experience to ensure their reasonableness.

1.2.5. Business environment and internal control factors

21. The credit institution's firm-wide risk assessment methodology must capture key business environment and internal control factors that can change its operational risk profile.

22. The choice of each factor needs to be justified as a meaningful driver of risk, based on experience and involving the expert judgement of the affected business areas.

23. The sensitivity of risk estimates to changes in the factors and the relative weighting of the various factors need to be well reasoned. In addition to capturing changes in risk due to improvements in risk controls, the framework must also capture potential increases in risk due to greater complexity of activities or increased business volume.

24. This framework must be documented and subject to independent review within the credit institution and by competent authorities. Over time, the process and the outcomes need to be validated and re-assessed through comparison to actual internal loss experience and relevant external data.

2. IMPACT OF INSURANCE AND OTHER RISK TRANSFER MECHANISMS

25. Credit institutions shall be able to recognise the impact of insurance subject to the conditions set out in points 26 to 29 and other risk transfer mechanisms where the credit institution can demonstrate to the satisfaction of the competent authorities that a noticeable risk mitigating effect is achieved.

26. The provider is authorised to provide insurance or re-insurance and the provider has a minimum claims paying ability rating by an eligible ECAI which has been determined by the competent authority to be associated with credit quality step 3 or above under the rules for the risk weighting of exposures to credit institutions under Articles 78 to 83.

27. The insurance and the credit institutions' insurance framework shall meet the following conditions:

(a) the insurance policy must have an initial term of no less than one year. For policies with a residual term of less than one year, the credit institution must make appropriate haircuts reflecting the declining residual term of the policy, up to a full 100% haircut for policies with a residual term of 90 days or less;

(b) the insurance policy has a minimum notice period for cancellation of the contract of 90 days;

(c) the insurance policy has no exclusions or limitations triggered by supervisory actions or, in the case of a failed credit institution, that preclude the credit institution receiver or liquidator, from recovering for damages suffered or expenses incurred by the credit institution, except in respect of events occurring after the initiation of receivership or liquidation proceedings in respect of the credit institution; provided that the insurance policy may exclude any fine, penalty, or punitive damages resulting from actions by the competent authorities;

(d) the risk mitigation calculations must reflect the insurance coverage in a manner that is transparent in its relationship to, and consistent with, the actual likelihood and impact of loss used in the overall determination of operational risk capital;

(e) the insurance is provided by a third party entity. In the case of insurance through captives and affiliates, the exposure has to be laid off to an independent third party entity, for example through re-insurance, that meets the eligibility criteria; and

(f) the framework for recognising insurance is well reasoned and documented.

28. The methodology for recognising insurance shall capture the following elements through discounts or haircuts in the amount of insurance recognition:

(a) the residual term of an insurance policy, where less than one year, as noted above;

(b) a policy's cancellation terms, where less than one year; and

(c) the uncertainty of payment as well as mismatches in coverage of insurance policies.

29. The capital alleviation arising from the recognition of insurance shall not exceed 20% of the capital requirement for operational risk before the recognition of risk-mitigation techniques.

3. Application to Use an Advanced Measurement Approach on a Group-Wide Basis

30. When an Advanced Measurement Approach is intended to be used by the EU parent credit institution and its subsidiaries, or by the subsidiaries of an EU parent financial holding company, the application shall include a description of the methodology used for allocating operational risk capital between the different entities of the group.

31. The application shall indicate whether and how diversification effects are intended to be factored in the risk measurement system.

Part 4

Combined Use of Different Methodologies

1. Use of an Advanced Measurement Approach in Combination With Other Approaches

1. A credit institution may use an Advanced Measurement Approach in combination with either the Basic Indicator Approach or the Standardised Approach, subject to the following conditions:

(a) all operational risks of the credit institution are captured. The competent authority shall be satisfied with the methodology used to cover different activities, geographical locations, legal structures or other relevant divisions determined on an internal basis; and

(b) the qualifying criteria set out in Parts 2 and 3 are fulfilled for the part of activities covered by the Standardised Approach and Advanced Measurement Approaches respectively.

2. On a case-by-case basis, the competent authority may impose the following additional conditions:

(a) on the date of implementation of an Advanced Measurement Approach, a significant part of the credit institution's operational risks are captured by the Advanced Measurement Approach; and

(b) the credit institution takes a commitment to roll out the Advanced Measurement Approach across a material part of its operations within a time schedule agreed with its competent authorities.

2. Combined use of the Basic Indicator Approach and of the Standardised Approach

3. A credit institution may use a combination of the Basic Indicator Approach and the Standardised Approach only in exceptional circumstances such as the recent acquisition of new business which may require a transition period for the roll out of the Standardised Approach.

4. The combined use of the Basic Indicator Approach and the Standardised Approach shall be conditional upon a commitment by the credit institution to roll out the Standardised Approach within a time schedule agreed with the competent authorities.

(b) an outline of the differences in the basis of consolidation for accounting and prudential purposes, with a brief description of the entities that are:
(i) fully consolidated;
(ii) proportionally consolidated;
(iii) deducted from own funds; or
(iv) neither consolidated nor deducted;

(c) any current or foreseen material practical or legal impediment to the prompt transfer of own funds or repayment of liabilities among the parent undertaking and its subsidiaries;

(d) the aggregate amount by which the actual own funds are less than the required minimum in all subsidiaries not included in the consolidation, and the name or names of such subsidiaries; and

(e) if applicable, the circumstance of making use of the provisions laid down in Articles 69 and 70.

3. The following information shall be disclosed by the credit institutions regarding their own funds:

(a) summary information on the terms and conditions of the main features of all own funds items and components thereof;

(b) the amount of the original own funds, with separate disclosure of all positive items and deductions;

(c) the total amount of additional own funds, and own funds as defined in Chapter IV of Directive 2006/49/EC;

(d) deductions from original and additional own funds pursuant to Article 66(2), with separate disclosure of items referred to in Article 57(q); and

(e) total eligible own funds, net of deductions and limits laid down in Article 66.

4. The following information shall be disclosed regarding the compliance by the credit institution with the requirements laid down in Articles 75 and 123:

(a) a summary of the credit institution's approach to assessing the adequacy of its internal capital to support current and future activities;

(b) for credit institutions calculating the risk-weighted exposure amounts in accordance with Articles 78 to 83, 8 per cent of the risk-weighted exposure amounts for each of the exposure classes specified in Article 79;

(c) for credit institutions calculating risk-weighted exposure amounts in accordance with Articles 84 to 89, 8 per cent of the risk-weighted exposure amounts for each of the exposure classes specified in Article 86. For the retail exposure class, this requirement applies to each of the categories of exposures to which the different correlations in Annex VII, Part 1, points 10 to 13 correspond. For the equity exposure class, this requirement applies to:
(i) each of the approaches provided in Annex VII, Part 1, points 17 to 26;
(ii) exchange traded exposures, private equity exposures in sufficiently diversified portfolios, and other exposures;
(iii) exposures subject to supervisory transition regarding capital requirements; and
(iv) exposures subject to grandfathering provisions regarding capital requirements;

(d) minimum capital requirements calculated in accordance with Article 75, points (b) and (c); and

(e) minimum capital requirements calculated in accordance with Articles 103 to 105, and disclosed separately.

5. The following information shall be disclosed regarding the credit institution's exposure to counterparty credit risk as defined in Annex III, Part 1:

(a) a discussion of the methodology used to assign internal capital and credit limits for counterparty credit exposures;

(b) a discussion of policies for securing collateral and establishing credit reserves;

(c) a discussion of policies with respect to wrong-way risk exposures;

(d) a discussion of the impact of the amount of collateral the credit institution would have to provide given a downgrade in its credit rating;

(e) gross positive fair value of contracts, netting benefits, netted current credit exposure, collateral held and net derivatives credit exposure. Net derivatives credit exposure is the credit exposure on derivatives transactions after considering both the benefits from legally enforceable netting agreements and collateral arrangements;

(f) measures for exposure value under the methods set out in Parts 3 to 6 of Annex III, whichever method is applicable;

(g) the notional value of credit derivative hedges, and the distribution of current credit exposure by types of credit exposure;

(h) credit derivative transactions (notional), segregated between use for the credit institution's own credit portfolio, as well as in its intermediation activities, including the distribution of the credit derivatives products used, broken down further by protection bought and sold within each product group; and

(i) the estimate of α if the credit institution has received the approval of the competent authorities to estimate α.

6. The following information shall be disclosed regarding the credit institution's exposure to credit risk and dilution risk:

(a) the definitions for accounting purposes of 'past due' and 'impaired';

(b) a description of the approaches and methods adopted for determining value adjustments and provisions;

(c) the total amount of exposures after accounting offsets and without taking into account the effects of credit risk mitigation, and the average amount of the exposures over the period broken down by different types of exposure classes;

(d) the geographic distribution of the exposures, broken down in significant areas by material exposure classes, and further detailed if appropriate;

(e) the distribution of the exposures by industry or counterparty type, broken down by exposure classes, and further detailed if appropriate;

(f) the residual maturity breakdown of all the exposures, broken down by exposure classes, and further detailed if appropriate;

(g) by significant industry or counterparty type, the amount of:
(i)   impaired exposures and past due exposures, provided separately;
(ii) value adjustments and provisions; and
(iii) charges for value adjustments and provisions during the period;

(h) the amount of the impaired exposures and past due exposures, provided separately, broken down by significant geographical areas including, if practical, the amounts of value adjustments and provisions related to each geographical area;

(i) the reconciliation of changes in the value adjustments and provisions for impaired exposures, shown separately. The information shall comprise:
(i)   a description of the type of value adjustments and provisions;
(ii) the opening balances;
(iii) the amounts taken against the provisions during the period;
(iv) the amounts set aside or reversed for estimated probable losses on exposures during the period, any other adjustments including those determined by exchange rate differences, business combinations, acquisitions and disposals of subsidiaries, and transfers between provisions; and
(v)   the closing balances.

Value adjustments and recoveries recorded directly to the income statement shall be disclosed separately.

7. For credit institutions calculating the risk-weighted exposure amounts in accordance with Articles 78 to 83, the following information shall be disclosed for each of the exposure classes specified in Article 79:

(a) the names of the nominated ECAIs and ECAs and the reasons for any changes;

(b) the exposure classes for which each ECAI or ECA is used;

(c) a description of the process used to transfer the issuer and issue credit assessments onto items not included in the trading book;

(d) the association of the external rating of each nominated ECAI or ECA with the credit quality steps prescribed in Annex VI, taking into account that this information needs not be disclosed if the credit institution complies with the standard association published by the competent authority; and

(e) the exposure values and the exposure values after credit risk mitigation associated with each credit quality step prescribed in Annex VI, as well as those deducted from own funds.

8. The credit institutions calculating the risk-weighted exposure amounts in accordance with Annex VII, Part 1, points 6 or 19 to 21 shall disclose the exposures assigned to each category in Table 1 in point 6 of Annex VII, Part 1, or to each risk weight mentioned in points 19 to 21 of Annex VII, Part 1.

9. The credit institutions calculating their capital requirements in accordance with Article 75, points (b) and (c) shall disclose those requirements separately for each risk referred to in those provisions.

10. The following information shall be disclosed by each credit institution which calculates its capital requirements in accordance with Annex V to Directive 2006/49/EC:

(a) for each sub-portfolio covered:
(i) the characteristics of the models used;
(ii) a description of stress testing applied to the sub-portfolio;
(iii) a description of the approaches used for back-testing and validating the accuracy and consistency of the internal models and modelling processes;

(b) the scope of acceptance by the competent authority; and

(c) a description of the extent and methodologies for compliance with the requirements set out in Annex VII, Part B to Directive 2006/49/EC.

11. The following information shall be disclosed by the credit institutions on operational risk:

(a) the approaches for the assessment of own funds requirements for operational risk that the credit institution qualifies for; and

(b) a description of the methodology set out in Article 105, if used by the credit institution, including a discussion of relevant internal and external factors considered in the credit institution's measurement approach. In the case of partial use, the scope and coverage of the different methodologies used.

12. The following information shall be disclosed regarding the exposures in equities not included in the trading book:

(a) the differentiation between exposures based on their objectives, including for capital gains relationship and strategic reasons, and an overview of the accounting techniques and valuation methodologies used, including key assumptions and practices affecting valuation and any significant changes in these practices;

(b) the balance sheet value, the fair value and, for those exchange-traded, a comparison to the market price where it is materially different from the fair value;

(c) the types, nature and amounts of exchange-traded exposures, private equity exposures in sufficiently diversified portfolios, and other exposures;

(d) the cumulative realised gains or losses arising from sales and liquidations in the period; and

(e) the total unrealised gains or losses, the total latent revaluation gains or losses, and any of these amounts included in the original or additional own funds.

13. The following information shall be disclosed by credit institutions on their exposure to interest rate risk on positions not included in the trading book:

(a) the nature of the interest rate risk and the key assumptions (including assumptions regarding loan prepayments and behaviour of non-maturity deposits), and frequency of measurement of the interest rate risk; and

(b) the variation in earnings, economic value or other relevant measure used by the management for upward and downward rate shocks according to management's method for measuring the interest rate risk, broken down by currency.

14. The credit institutions calculating risk-weighted exposure amounts in accordance with Articles 94 to 101 shall disclose the following information:

(a) a description of the credit institution's objectives in relation to securitisation activity;

(b) the roles played by the credit institution in the securitisation process;

(c) an indication of the extent of the credit institution's involvement in each of them;

(d) the approaches to calculating risk-weighted exposure amounts that the credit institution follows for its securitisation activities;

(e) a summary of the credit institution's accounting policies for securitisation activities, including:
(i) whether the transactions are treated as sales or financings;
(ii) the recognition of gains on sales;
(iii) the key assumptions for valuing retained interests; and
(iv) the treatment of synthetic securitisations if this is not covered by other accounting policies;

(f) the names of the ECAIs used for securitisations and the types of exposure for which each agency is used;

(g) the total outstanding amount of exposures securitised by the credit institution and subject to the securitisation framework (broken down into traditional and synthetic), by exposure type;

(h) for exposures securitised by the credit institution and subject to the securitisation framework, a breakdown by exposure type of the amount of impaired and past due exposures securitised, and the losses recognised by the credit institution during the period;

(i) the aggregate amount of securitisation positions retained or purchased, broken down by exposure type;

(j) the aggregate amount of securitisation positions retained or purchased, broken down into a meaningful number of risk weight bands. Positions that have been risk weighted at 1250% or deducted shall be disclosed separately;

(k) the aggregate outstanding amount of securitised revolving exposures segregated by the originator's interest and the investors' interest; and

(l) a summary of the securitisation activity in the period, including the amount of exposures securitised (by exposure type), and recognised gain or loss on sale by exposure type.

PART 3

Qualifying Requirements for the Use of Particular Instruments or Methodologies

1. The credit institutions calculating the risk-weighted exposure amounts in accordance with Articles 84 to 89 shall disclose the following information:

(a) the competent authority's acceptance of approach or approved transition;

(b) an explanation and review of:
(i) the structure of internal rating systems and relation between internal and external ratings;
(ii) the use of internal estimates other than for calculating risk-weighted exposure amounts in accordance with Articles 84 to 89;
(iii) the process for managing and recognising credit risk mitigation; and
(iv) the control mechanisms for rating systems including a description of independence, accountability, and rating systems review;

(c) a description of the internal ratings process, provided separately for the following exposure classes:
(i) central governments and central banks;
(ii) institutions;
(iii) corporate, including SMEs, specialised lending and purchased corporate receivables;
(iv) retail, for each of the categories of exposures to which the different correlations in Annex VII, Part 1, points 10 to 13 correspond; and
(v) equities;

(d) the exposure values for each of the exposure classes specified in Article 86. Exposures to central governments and central banks, institutions and corporates where credit institutions use own estimates of LGDs or conversion factors for the calculation of risk-weighted exposure amounts shall be disclosed separately from exposures for which the credit institutions do not use such estimates;

(e) for each of the exposure classes central governments and central banks, institutions, corporate and equity, and across a sufficient number of obligor grades (including default) to allow for a meaningful differentiation of credit risk, credit institutions shall disclose:

(i) the total exposures (for the exposure classes central governments and central banks, institutions and corporate, the sum of outstanding loans and exposure values for undrawn commitments; for equities, the outstanding amount);

(ii) for the credit institutions using own LGD estimates for the calculation of risk-weighted exposure amounts, the exposure-weighted average LGD in percentage;

(iii) the exposure-weighted average risk weight; and

(iv) for the credit institutions using own estimates of conversion factors for the calculation of risk-weighted exposure amounts, the amount of undrawn commitments and exposure-weighted average exposure values for each exposure class;

(f) for the retail exposure class and for each of the categories as defined under point (c)(iv), either the disclosures outlined under (e) above (if applicable, on a pooled basis), or an analysis of exposures (outstanding loans and exposure values for undrawn commitments) against a sufficient number of EL grades to allow for a meaningful differentiation of credit risk (if applicable, on a pooled basis);

(g) the actual value adjustments in the preceding period for each exposure class (for retail, for each of the categories as defined under point (c)(iv) and how they differ from past experience);

(h) a description of the factors that impacted on the loss experience in the preceding period (for example, has the credit institution experienced higher than average default rates, or higher than average LGDs and conversion factors); and

(i) the credit institution's estimates against actual outcomes over a longer period. At a minimum, this shall include information on estimates of losses against actual losses in each exposure class (for retail, for each of the categories as defined under point (c)(iv)) over a period sufficient to allow for a meaningful assessment of the performance of the internal rating processes for each exposure class (for retail for each of the categories as defined under point (c)(iv)). Where appropriate, the credit institutions shall further decompose this to provide analysis of PD and, for the credit institutions using own estimates of LGDs and/or conversion factors, LGD and conversion factor outcomes against estimates provided in the quantitative risk assessment disclosures above.

For the purposes of point (c), the description shall include the types of exposure included in the exposure class, the definitions, methods and data for estimation and validation of PD and, if applicable, LGD and conversion factors, including assumptions employed in the derivation of these variables, and the descriptions of material deviations from the definition of default as set out in Annex VII, Part 4, points 44 to 48, including the broad segments affected by such deviations.

2. The credit institutions applying credit risk mitigation techniques shall disclose the following information:

(a) the policies and processes for, and an indication of the extent to which the entity makes use of, on- and off-balance sheet netting;

(b) the policies and processes for collateral valuation and management;

(c) a description of the main types of collateral taken by the credit institution;

(d) the main types of guarantor and credit derivative counterparty and their creditworthiness;

(e) information about market or credit risk concentrations within the credit mitigation taken;

(f) for credit institutions calculating risk-weighted exposure amounts in accordance with Articles 78 to 83 or 84 to 89, but not providing own estimates of LGDs or conversion factors in respect of the exposure class, separately for each exposure class, the total exposure value (after, where applicable, on- or off-balance sheet netting) that is covered—after the application of volatility adjustments—by eligible financial collateral, and other eligible collateral; and

(g) for credit institutions calculating risk-weighted exposure amounts in accordance with Articles 78 to 83 or 84 to 89, separately for each exposure class, the total exposure (after, where applicable, on- or off-balance sheet netting) that is covered by guarantees or credit derivatives. For the equity exposure class, this requirement applies to each of the approaches provided in Annex VII, Part 1, points 17 to 26.

3. The credit institutions using the approach set out in Article 105 for the calculation of their own funds requirements for operational risk shall disclose a description of the use of insurance for the purpose of mitigating the risk.

Annex XIII

Part A

Repealed Directives together with their Successive Amendments
(referred to in Article 158)

Directive 2000/12/EC of the European Parliament and of the Council of 20 March 2000 relating to the taking up and pursuit of the business of credit institutions

Directive 2000/28/EC of the European Parliament and of the Council of 18 September 2000 amending Directive 2000/12/EC relating to the taking up and pursuit of the business of credit institutions

Directive 2002/87/EC of the European Parliament and of the Council of 16 December 2002 on the supplementary supervision of credit institutions, insurance undertakings and investment firms in a financial conglomerate and amending Council Directives 73/239/EEC, 79/267/EEC, 92/49/EEC, 92/96/EEC, 93/6/EEC and 93/22/EEC, and Directives 98/78/EC and 2000/12/EC of the European Parliament and of the Council

Only Art. 29.1(a)(b), Art. 29.2, Art. 29.4(a)(b), Art. 29.5, Art. 29.6, Art. 29.7, Art. 29.8, Art. 29.9, Art. 29.10, Art. 29.11

Directive 2004/39/EC of the European Parliament and of the Council of 21 April 2004 on markets in financial instruments amending Council Directives 85/611/EEC and 93/6/EEC and Directive 2000/12/EC of the European Parliament and of the Council and repealing Council Directive 93/22/EEC

Only Art. 68

Commission Directive 2004/69/EC of 27 April 2004 amending Directive 2000/12/EC of the European Parliament and of the Council as regards the definition of 'multilateral development banks'

Directive 2005/1/EC of the European Parliament and of the Council of 9 March 2005 amending Council Directives 73/239/EEC, 85/611/EEC, 91/675/EEC, 92/49/EEC and 93/6/EEC and Directives 94/19/EC, 98/78/EC, 2000/12/EC, 2001/34/EC, 2002/83/EC and 2002/87/EC in order to establish a new organisational structure for financial services committees

Only Art. 3

non-repealed modifications

Act of Accession 2003

Part B

Deadlines for Transposition
(Referred to in Article 158)

Directive	Deadline for transposition
Directive 2000/12/EC	—
Directive 2000/28/EC	27.4.2002
Directive 2002/87/EC	11.8.2004
Directive 2004/39/EC	30.04.2006/31.1.2007
Directive 2004/69/EC	30.6.2004
Directive 2005/1/EC	13.5.2005

Annex XIV

Correlation Table

This Directive	Directive 2000/12/EC	Directive 2000/28/EC	Directive 2002/87/EC	Directive 2004/39/EC	Directive 2005/1/EC
Article 1	Article 2(1) and (2)				
Article 2	Article 2(3)				
	Act of Accession				
Article 2	Article 2(4)				
Article 3	Article 2(5) and (6)				
Article 3(1), third subparagraph					Article 3(2)
Article 4(1)	Article 1(1)				
Article 4(2) to (5)		Article 1(2) to (5)			
Article 4(7) to (9)		Article 1(6) to (8)			
Article 4(10)			Article 29(1)(a)		
Article 4(11) to (14)	Article 1(10), (12) and (13)				
Article 4(21) and (22)			Article 29(1)(b)		
Article 4(23)	Article 1(23)				
Article 4(45) to (47)	Article 1(25) to (27)				
Article 5					
Article 6	Article 4				
Article 7	Article 8				
Article 8	Article 9				
Article 9(1)	Article 5(1) and 1 (11)				
Article 9(2)	Article 5(2)				
Article 10	Article 5(3) to (7)				
Article 11	Article 6				
Article 12	Article 7				
Article 13	Article 10				
Article 14	Article 11				
Article 15(1)	Article 12				
Article 15(2) and (3)			Article 29(2)		
Article 16	Article 13				
Article 17	Article 14				
Article 18	Article 15				
Article 19(1)	Article 16(1)				
Article 19(2)			Article 29(3)		
Article 20	Article 16(3)				
Article 21	Article 16(4) to (6)				
Article 22	Article 17				
Article 23	Article 18				
Article 24(1)	Article 19(1) to (3)				

This Directive	Directive 2000/12/EC	Directive 2000/28/EC	Directive 2002/87/EC	Directive 2004/39/EC	Directive 2005/1/EC
Article 24(2)	Article 19(6)				
Article 24(3)	Article 19(4)				
Article 25(1) to (3)	Article 20(1) to (3), first and second subparagraphs				
Article 25(3)	Article 19(5)				
Article 25(4)	Article 20(3) third subparagraph				
Article 26	Article 20(4) to (7)				
Article 27	Article 1(3), second sentence				
Article 28	Article 21				
Article 29	Article 22				
Article 30	Article 22(2) to (4)				
Article 31	Article 22(5)				
Article 32	Article 22(6)				
Article 33	Article 22(7)				
Article 34	Article 22(8)				
Article 35	Article 22(9)				
Article 36	Article 22(10)				
Article 37	Article 22(11)				
Article 38	Article 24				
Article 39(1) and (2)	Article 25				
Article 39(3)					Article 3(8)
Article 40	Article 26				
Article 41	Article 27				
Article 42	Article 28				
Article 43	Article 29				
Article 44	Article 30(1) to (3)				
Article 45	Article 30(4)				
Article 46	Article 30(3)				
Article 47	Article 30(5)				
Article 48	Article 30(6) and (7)				
Article 49	Article 30(8)				
Article 50	Article 30(9), first and second subparagraphs				
Article 51	Article 30(9), third subparagraph				
Article 52	Article 30(10)				
Article 53	Article 31				
Article 54	Article 32				

This Directive	Directive 2000/12/EC	Directive 2000/28/EC	Directive 2002/87/EC	Directive 2004/39/EC	Directive 2005/1/EC
Article 55	Article 33				
Article 56	Article 34(1)				
Article 57	Article 34(2), first subparagraph; and Article 34(2), point 2, second sentence		Article 29(4)(a)		
Article 58			Article 29(4)(b)		
Article 59			Article 29(4)(b)		
Article 60			Article 29(4)(b)		
Article 61	Article 34(3) and (4)				
Article 63	Article 35				
Article 64	Article 36				
Article 65	Article 37				
Article 66(1) and (2)	Article 38(1) and (2)				
Article 67	Article 39				
Article 73	Article 52(3)				
Article 106	Article 1(24)				
Article 107	Article 1(1), third subparagraph				
Article 108	Article 48(1)				
Article 109	Article 48(4), first subparagraph				
Article 110	Article 48(2) to (4), second subparagraph				
Article 111	Article 49(1) to (5)				
Article 113	Article 49(4), (6) and (7)				
Article 115	Article 49(8) and (9)				
Article 116	Article 49(10)				
Article 117	Article 49(11)				
Article 118	Article 50				
Article 120	Article 51(1), (2) and (5)				
Article 121	Article 51(4)				
Article 122(1) and (2)	Article 51(6)		Article 29(5)		
Article 125	Article 53(1) and (2)				
Article 126	Article 53(3)				
Article 128	Article 53(5)				
Article 133(1)	Article 54(1)		Article 29(7)(a)		

This Directive	Directive 2000/12/EC	Directive 2000/28/EC	Directive 2002/87/EC	Directive 2004/39/EC	Directive 2005/1/EC
Article 133(2) and (3)	Article 54(2) and (3)				
Article 134(1)	Article 54(4), first subparagraph				
Article 134(2)	Article 54(4), second subparagraph				
Article 135			Article 29(8)		
Article 137	Article 55				
Article 138			Article 29(9)		
Article 139	Article 56(1) to (3)				
Article 140	Article 56(4) to (6)				
Article 141	Article 56(7)		Article 29(10)		
Article 142	Article 56(8)				
Article 143			Article 29(11)		Article 3(10)
Article 150	Article 60(1)				
Article 151	Article 60(2)				Article 3(10)
Article 158	Article 67				
Article 159	Article 68				
Article 160	Article 69				
Annex I, points 1 to 14, excluding the final paragraph	Annex I				
Annex I, final paragraph				Article 68	
Annex II	Annex II				
Annex III	Annex III				
Annex IV	Annex IV				

B. 42.

European Parliament and Council Directive 2006/49/EC of 14 June 2006 on the capital adequacy of investment firms and credit institutions (recast)[1]

THE EUROPEAN PARLIAMENT AND THE COUNCIL OF THE EUROPEAN UNION,

Having regard to the Treaty establishing the European Community, and in particular Article 47(2) thereof, Having regard to the proposal from the Commission,

Having regard to the Opinion of the European Economic and Social Committee,[2]

Having regard to the Opinion of the European Central Bank,[3]

After consulting the Committee of the Regions,

Acting in accordance with the procedure laid down in Article 251 of the Treaty,[4]

Whereas:

(1) Council Directive 93/6/EEC of 15 March 1993 on the capital adequacy of investment firms and credit institutions[5] has been significantly amended on several occasions. Now that new amendments are being made to the said Directive, it is desirable, in order to clarify matters, that it should be recast.

(2) One of the objectives of Directive 2004/39/EC of the European Parliament and of the Council of 21 April 2004 on markets in financial instruments[6] is to allow investment firms authorised by the competent authorities of their home Member State and supervised by the same authorities to establish branches and provide services freely in other Member States. That Directive accordingly provides for the coordination of the rules governing the authorisation and pursuit of the business of investment firms.

(3) Directive 2004/39/EC does not, however, establish common standards for the own funds of investment firms nor indeed does it establish the amounts of the initial capital of such firms or a common framework for monitoring the risks incurred by them.

(4) It is appropriate to effect only the essential harmonisation that is necessary and sufficient to secure the mutual recognition of authorisation and of prudential supervision systems; in order to achieve mutual recognition within the framework of the internal financial market, measures should be laid down to coordinate the definition of the own funds of investment firms, the establishment of the amounts of their initial capital and the establishment of a common framework for monitoring the risks incurred by investment firms.

(5) Since the objectives of this Directive, namely the establishment of the capital adequacy requirements applying to investment firms and credit institutions, the rules for their calculation and the rules for their prudential supervision, cannot be sufficiently achieved by the Member States and can therefore, by reason of the scale and the effects of the proposed action, be better achieved at Community level, the Community may adopt measures, in accordance with the principle of subsidiarity as set out in Article 5 of the Treaty. In accordance with the principle of proportionality, as set out in that Article, this Directive does not go beyond what is necessary in order to achieve its objectives.

---

[1] OJ L 177, 30.6.2006, 201–255.
[2] OJ C 234, 22.9.2005, 8.
[3] OJ C 52, 2.3.2005, 37.
[4] Opinion of the European Parliament of 28 September 2005 (not yet published in the OJ) and Decision of the Council of 7 June 2006.
[5] OJ L 141, 11.6.1993, 1, reproduced supra under no. B. 20. Directive as last amended by Directive 2005/1/EC of the European Parliament and of the Council (OJ L 79, 24.3.2005, 9), reproduced supra under no. B. 39.
[6] OJ L 145, 30.4.2004, 1, reproduced infra under no. S. 29.

(6) It is appropriate to establish different amounts of initial capital depending on the range of activities that investment firms are authorised to undertake.

(7) Existing investment firms should be permitted, under certain conditions, to continue their business even if they do not comply with the minimum amount of initial capital fixed for new investment firms.

(8) Member States should be able to establish rules stricter than those provided for in this Directive.

(9) The smooth operation of the internal market requires not only legal rules but also close and regular cooperation and significantly enhanced convergence of regulatory and supervisory practices between the competent authorities of the Member States.

(10) The Commission Communication of 11 May 1999 entitled 'Implementing the framework for financial markets: Action Plan' listed a number of goals that need to be achieved in order to complete the internal market in financial services. The Lisbon European Council of 23 and 24 March 2000 set the goal of implementing the action plan by 2005. Recasting of the provisions on own funds is a key element of the action plan.

(11) Since investment firms face in respect of their trading book business the same risks as credit institutions, it is appropriate for the pertinent provisions of Directive 2006/48/EC of the European Parliament and of the Council of 14 June 2006 relating to the taking up and pursuit of the business of credit institutions[7] to apply equally to investment firms.

(12) The own funds of investment firms or credit institutions (hereinafter referred to collectively as 'institutions') can serve to absorb losses which are not matched by a sufficient volume of profits, to ensure the continuity of institutions and to protect investors. The own funds also serve as an important yardstick for the competent authorities, in particular for the assessment of the solvency of institutions and for other prudential purposes. Furthermore, institutions, engage in direct competition with each other in the internal market. Therefore, in order to strengthen the Community financial system and to prevent distortions of competition, it is appropriate to lay down common basic standards for own funds.

(13) For the purposes of recital (12), it is appropriate for the definition of own funds as laid down in Directive 2006/48/EC to serve as a basis, and to provide for supplementary specific rules which take into account the different scope of market risk related capital requirements.

(14) As regards credit institutions, common standards have already been established for the supervision and monitoring of different types of risks by Directive 2000/12/EC.

(15) In that respect, the provisions on minimum capital requirements should be considered in conjunction with other specific instruments which also harmonise the fundamental techniques of the supervision of institutions.

(16) It is necessary to develop common standards for market risks incurred by credit institutions and provide a complementary framework for the supervision of the risks incurred by institutions, in particular market risks, and more especially position risks, counterparty/settlement risks and foreign-exchange risks.

(17) It is necessary to provide for the concept of a 'trading book' comprising positions in securities and other financial instruments which are held for trading purposes and which are subject mainly to market risks and exposures relating to certain financial services provided to customers.

(18) With a view to reducing the administrative burden for institutions with negligible trading-book business in both absolute and relative terms, such institutions should be able to apply Directive 2006/48/EC, rather than the requirements laid down in Annexes I and II to this Directive.

(19) It is important that monitoring of settlement/delivery risks should take account of the existence of systems offering adequate protection reducing those risks.

---

[7] J L 177, 30.6. 2006, 1, reproduced supra under no. B. 41.

(20) In any case, institutions should comply with this Directive as regards the coverage of the foreign-exchange risks on their overall business. Lower capital requirements should be imposed for positions in closely correlated currencies, whether statistically confirmed or arising out of binding intergovernmental agreements.

(21) The capital requirements for commodity dealers, including those dealers currently exempt from the requirements of Directive 2004/39/EC, will be reviewed as appropriate in conjunction with the review of that exemption as set out in Article 65(3) of that Directive.

(22) The goal of liberalisation of gas and electricity markets is both economically and politically important for the Community. With this in mind, the capital requirements and other prudential rules to be applied to firms active in those markets should be proportionate and should not unduly interfere with achievement of the goal of liberalisation. This goal should, in particular, be kept in mind when the reviews referred to in recital 21 are carried out.

(23) The existence of internal systems for monitoring and controlling interest-rate risks on all business of institutions is a particularly important way of minimising such risks. Consequently, such systems should be supervised by the competent authorities.

(24) Since Directive 2006/48/EC does not establish common rules for the monitoring and control of large exposures in activities which are principally subject to market risks, it is therefore appropriate to provide for such rules.

(25) Operational risk is a significant risk faced by institutions and requires coverage by own funds. It is essential to take account of the diversity of institutions in the EU by providing alternative approaches.

(26) Directive 2006/48/EC states the principle of consolidation. It does not establish common rules for the consolidation of financial institutions which are involved in activities principally subject to market risks.

(27) In order to ensure adequate solvency of institutions within a group, it is essential that the minimum capital requirements apply on the basis of the consolidated financial situation of the group. In order to ensure that own funds are appropriately distributed within the group and are available to protect investments where needed, the minimum capital requirements should apply to individual institutions within a group, unless this objective can be effectively achieved by other means.

(28) Directive 2006/48/EC does not apply to groups which include one or more investment firms but no credit institutions. A common framework for the introduction of the supervision of investment firms on a consolidated basis should therefore be provided for.

(29) Institutions should ensure that they have internal capital which, having regard to the risks to which they are or might be exposed, is adequate in quantity, quality and distribution. Accordingly, institutions should have strategies and processes in place for assessing and maintaining the adequacy of their internal capital.

(30) Competent authorities should evaluate the adequacy of own funds of institutions, having regard to the risks to which the latter are exposed.

(31) In order for the internal banking market to operate effectively, the Committee of European Banking Supervisors should contribute to the consistent application of this Directive and to the convergence of supervisory practices throughout the Community, and should report on a yearly basis to the Community Institutions on progress made.

(32) In order for the internal market to operate with increasing effectiveness it is essential that there should be significantly enhanced convergence in the implementation and application of the provisions of harmonising Community legislation.

(33) For the same reason, and to ensure that Community institutions which are active in several Member States are not disproportionately burdened as a result of the continued responsibilities of individual Member State competent authorities for authorisation and supervision, it is essential significantly to enhance the cooperation

between competent authorities. In this context the role of the consolidating supervisor should be strengthened.

(34) In order for the internal market to operate with increasing effectiveness and for citizens of the Union to be afforded adequate levels of transparency, it is necessary that competent authorities disclose publicly and in a way which allows for meaningful comparison the manner in which the requirements of this Directive are implemented.

(35) In order to strengthen market discipline and stimulate institutions to improve their market strategy, risk control and internal management organisation, appropriate public disclosures by institutions should be provided for.

(36) The measures necessary for the implementation of this Directive should be adopted in accordance with Council Decision 1999/468/EC of 28 June 1999 laying down the procedures for the exercise of implementing powers conferred on the Commission.[8]

(37) In its Resolution of 5 February 2002 on the implementation of financial services legislation,[9] the Parliament requested that the Parliament and the Council should have an equal role in supervising the way in which the Commission exercises its executive role in order to reflect the legislative powers of Parliament under Article 251 of the Treaty. In the solemn declaration made before the Parliament the same day, by its President, the Commission supported this request. On 11 December 2002, the Commission proposed amendments to Decision 1999/468/EC and then submitted an amended proposal on 22 April 2004. The Parliament considers that this proposal does not preserve its legislative prerogatives. In the Parliament's view, the Parliament and the Council should have the opportunity of evaluating the conferral of implementing powers on the Commission within a determined period. It is therefore appropriate to limit the period during which the Commission may adopt implementing measures.

(38) The Parliament should be given a period of three months from the first transmission of draft amendments and implementing measures to allow it to examine them and to give its opinion. However, in urgent and duly justified cases, it should be possible to shorten this period. If, within that period, a resolution is adopted by the Parliament, the Commission should re-examine the draft amendments or measures.

(39) In order to avoid disruption to markets and to ensure continuity in overall levels of own funds, it is appropriate to provide for specific transitional arrangements.

(40) This Directive respects fundamental rights and observes the principles recognised in particular by the Charter of Fundamental Rights of the European Union as general principles of Community law.

(41) The obligation to transpose this Directive into national law should be confined to those provisions that represent a substantive change compared to earlier directives. The obligation to transpose the provisions that remain unchanged exists under the earlier directives.

(42) This Directive should be without prejudice to the obligations of the Member States relating to the time-limits for transposition into national law of the Directives set out in Part B of Annex VIII,

HAVE ADOPTED THIS DIRECTIVE:

CHAPTER I

SUBJECT MATTER, SCOPE AND DEFINITIONS

SECTION 1

SUBJECT MATTER AND SCOPE

Article 1

1. This Directive lays down the capital adequacy requirements applying to investment firms and credit institutions, the rules for their calculation and the rules for their prudential supervision. Member States shall apply the requirements of this Directive to investment firms and credit institutions as defined in Article 3.

---

[8] OJ L 184, 17.7.1999, 23.
[9] OJ C 284 E, 21.11.2002, 115.

2. A Member State may impose additional or more stringent requirements on those investment firms and credit institutions that it has authorised.

Article 2

1. Subject to Articles 18, 20, 22 to 32, 34 and 39 of this Directive, Articles 68 to 73 of Directive 2006/48/EC shall apply mutatis mutandis to investment firms. In applying Articles 70 to 72 of Directive 2006/48/EC to investment firms, every reference to a parent credit institution in a Member State shall be construed as a reference to a parent investment firm in a Member State and every reference to an EU parent credit institution shall be construed as a reference to an EU parent investment firm.

Where a credit institution has as a parent undertaking a parent investment firm in a Member State, only that parent investment firm shall be subject to requirements on a consolidated basis in accordance with Articles 71 to 73 of Directive 2006/48/EC.

Where an investment firm has as a parent undertaking a parent credit institution in a Member State, only that parent credit institution shall be subject to requirements on a consolidated basis in accordance with Articles 71 to 73 of Directive 2006/48/EC.

Where a financial holding company has as a subsidiary both a credit institution and an investment firm, requirements on the basis of the consolidated financial situation of the financial holding company shall apply to the credit institution.

2. When a group covered by paragraph 1 does not include a credit institution, Directive 2006/48/EC shall apply, subject to the following:

(a) every reference to credit institutions shall be construed as a reference to investment firms;

(b) in Articles 125 and 140(2) of Directive 2006/48/EC, each reference to other articles of that Directive shall be construed as a reference to Directive 2004/39/EC;

(c) for the purposes of Article 39(3) of Directive 2006/48/EC, references to the European Banking Committee shall be construed as references to the Council and the Commission; and

(d) by way of derogation from Article 140(1) of Directive 2006/48/EC, where a group does not include a credit institution, the first sentence of that Article shall be replaced by the following: 'Where an investment firm, a financial holding company or a mixed-activity holding company controls one or more subsidiaries which are insurance companies, the competent authorities and the authorities entrusted with the public task of supervising insurance undertakings shall cooperate closely'.

SECTION 2
DEFINITIONS

Article 3

1. For the purposes of this Directive the following definitions shall apply:

(a) 'credit institutions' means credit institutions as defined in Article 4(1) of Directive 2006/48/EC;

(b) 'investment firms' means institutions as defined in Article 4 (1)(1) of Directive 2004/39/EC, which are subject to the requirements imposed by that Directive, excluding:
(i) credit institutions;
(ii) local firms as defined in point (p); and
(iii) firms which are only authorised to provide the service of investment advice and/or receive and transmit orders from investors without holding money or securities belonging to their clients and which for that reason may not at any time place themselves in debt with those clients;

(c) 'institutions' means credit institutions and investment firms;

(d) 'recognised third-country investment firms' means firms meeting the following conditions:
(i) firms which, if they were established within the Community, would be covered by the definition of investment firm;
(ii) firms which are authorised in a third country; and
(iii) firms which are subject to and comply with prudential rules considered by the

competent authorities as at least as stringent as those laid down by this Directive;

(e) 'financial instruments' means any contract that gives rise to both a financial asset of one party and a financial liability or equity instrument of another party;

(f) 'parent investment firm in a Member State' means an investment firm which has an institution or financial institution as a subsidiary or which holds a participation in one or both such entities, and which is not itself a subsidiary of another institution authorised in the same Member State or of a financial holding company set up in the same Member State;

(g) 'EU parent investment firm' means a parent investment firm in a Member State which is not a subsidiary of another institution authorised in any Member State or of a financial holding company set up in any Member State;

(h) 'over-the-counter (OTC) derivative instruments' means the items falling within the list in Annex IV to Directive 2006/48/EC other than those items to which an exposure value of zero is attributed under point 6 of Part 2 of Annex III to that Directive;

(i) 'regulated market' means a market as defined in Article 4(1) (14) of Directive 2004/39/EC;

(j) 'convertible' means a security which, at the option of the holder, may be exchanged for another security;

(k) 'warrant' means a security which gives the holder the right to purchase an underlying asset at a stipulated price until or at the expiry date of the warrant and which may be settled by the delivery of the underlying itself or by cash settlement;

(l) 'stock financing' means positions where physical stock has been sold forward and the cost of funding has been locked in until the date of the forward sale;

(m) 'repurchase agreement' and 'reverse repurchase agreement' mean any agreement in which an institution or its counterparty transfers securities or commodities or guaranteed rights relating to title—to securities or commodities where that guarantee is issued by a recognised exchange which holds the rights to the securities or commodities and the agreement does not allow an institution to transfer or pledge a particular security or commodity to more than one counterparty at one time, subject to a commitment to repurchase them—or substituted securities or commodities of the same description—at a specified price on a future date specified, or to be specified, by the transferor, being a repurchase agreement for the institution selling the securities or commodities and a reverse repurchase agreement for the institution buying them;

(n) 'securities or commodities lending' and 'securities or commodities borrowing' mean any transaction in which an institution or its counterparty transfers securities or commodities against appropriate collateral, subject to a commitment that the borrower will return equivalent securities or commodities at some future date or when requested to do so by the transferor, that transaction being securities or commodities lending for the institution transferring the securities or commodities and being securities or commodities borrowing for the institution to which they are transferred;

(o) 'clearing member' means a member of the exchange or the clearing house which has a direct contractual relationship with the central counterparty (market guarantor);

(p) 'local firm' means a firm dealing for its own account on markets in financial futures or options or other derivatives and on cash markets for the sole purpose of hedging positions on derivatives markets, or dealing for the accounts of other members of those markets and being guaranteed by clearing members of the same markets, where responsibility for ensuring the performance of contracts entered into by such a firm is assumed by clearing members of the same markets;

(q) 'delta' means the expected change in an option price as a proportion of a small change in the price of the instrument underlying the option;

(r) 'own funds' means own funds as defined in Directive 2006/48/EC; and

(s) 'capital' means own funds.

For the purposes of applying supervision on a consolidated basis, the term 'investment firm' shall include third-country investment firms.

For the purposes of point (e), financial instruments shall include both primary financial instruments or cash instruments and derivative financial instruments the value of which is derived from the price of an underlying financial instrument, a rate, an index or the price of another underlying item, and include as a minimum the instruments specified in Section C of Annex I to Directive 2004/39/EC.

2. The terms 'parent undertaking', 'subsidiary undertaking', 'asset management company' and 'financial institution' shall cover undertakings defined in Article 4 of Directive 2006/48/EC.

The terms 'financial holding company', 'parent financial holding company in a Member State', 'EU parent financial holding company' and 'ancillary services undertaking' shall cover undertakings defined in Article 4 of Directive 2006/48/EC, save that every reference to credit institutions shall be read as a reference to institutions.

3. For the purposes of applying Directive 2006/48/EC to groups covered by Article 2(1) which do not include a credit institution, the following definitions shall apply:

(a) 'financial holding company' means a financial institution the subsidiary undertakings of which are either exclusively or mainly investment firms or other financial institutions, at least one of which is an investment firm, and which is not a mixed financial holding company within the meaning of Directive 2002/87/EC of the European Parliament and of the Council of 16 December 2002 on the supplementary supervision of credit institutions, insurance undertakings and investment firms in a financial conglomerate;[10]

(b) 'mixed-activity holding company' means a parent undertaking, other than a financial holding company or an investment firm or a mixed financial holding company within the meaning of Directive 2002/87/EC, the subsidiaries of which include at least one investment firm; and

(c) 'competent authorities' means the national authorities which are empowered by law or regulation to supervise investment firms.

Chapter II

Initial Capital

Article 4

For the purposes of this Directive, 'initial capital' shall be comprised of the items referred to in Article 57(a) and (b) of Directive 2006/48/EC.

Article 5

1. An investment firm that does not deal in any financial instruments for its own account or underwrite issues of financial instruments on a firm commitment basis, but which holds clients' money and/or securities and which offers one or more of the following services, shall have initial capital of EUR 125 000:

(a) the reception and transmission of investors' orders for financial instruments;

(b) the execution of investors' orders for financial instruments; or

(c) the management of individual portfolios of investments in financial instruments.

2. The competent authorities may allow an investment firm which executes investors' orders for financial instruments to hold such instruments for its own account if the following conditions are met:

(a) such positions arise only as a result of the firm's failure to match investors' orders precisely;

(b) the total market value of all such positions is subject to a ceiling of 15% of the firm's initial capital;

(c) the firm meets the requirements laid down in Articles 18, 20 and 28; and

(d) such positions are incidental and provisional in nature and strictly limited to the time required to carry out the transaction in question.

The holding of non-trading-book positions in financial instruments in order to invest own funds shall not be considered as dealing in relation to the

---

[10] OJ L 35, 11.2.2003, 1, reproduced supra under no. B. 38. Directive as amended by Directive 2005/1/EC, reproduced supra under no. B. 39.

services set out in paragraph 1 or for the purposes of paragraph 3.

3. Member States may reduce the amount referred to in paragraph 1 to EUR 50 000 where a firm is not authorised to hold clients' money or securities, to deal for its own account, or to underwrite issues on a firm commitment basis.

Article 6

Local firms shall have initial capital of EUR 50 000 insofar as they benefit from the freedom of establishment or to provide services specified in Articles 31 and 32 of Directive 2004/39/EC.

Article 7

Coverage for the firms referred to in Article 3(1)(b)(iii) shall take one of the following forms:

(a) initial capital of EUR 50 000;

(b) professional indemnity insurance covering the whole territory of the Community or some other comparable guarantee against liability arising from professional negligence, representing at least EUR 1 000 000 applying to each claim and in aggregate EUR 1 500 000 per year for all claims; or

(c) a combination of initial capital and professional indemnity insurance in a form resulting in a level of coverage equivalent to that referred to in points (a) or (b).

The amounts referred to in the first sub-paragraph shall be periodically reviewed by the Commission in order to take account of changes in the European Index of Consumer Prices as published by Eurostat, in line with and at the same time as the adjustments made under Article 4(7) of Directive 2002/92/EC of the European Parliament and of the Council of 9 December 2002 on insurance mediation.[11]

Article 8

If a firm as referred to in Article 3(1)(b)(iii) is also registered under Directive 2002/92/EC, it shall comply with Article 4(3) of that Directive and have coverage in one of the following forms:

(a) initial capital of EUR 25 000;

(b) professional indemnity insurance covering the whole territory of the Community or some other comparable guarantee against liability arising from professional negligence, representing at least EUR 500 000 applying to each claim and in aggregate EUR 750 000 per year for all claims; or

(c) a combination of initial capital and professional indemnity insurance in a form resulting in a level of coverage equivalent to that referred to in points (a) or (b).

Article 9

All investment firms other than those referred to in Articles 5 to 8 shall have initial capital of EUR 730 000.

Article 10

1. By way of derogation from Articles 5(1), 5(3), 6 and 9, Member States may continue an authorisation of investment firms and firms covered by Article 6 which was in existence before 31 December 1995, the own funds of which firms or investment firms are less than the initial capital levels specified for them in Articles 5(1), 5(3), 6 and 9.

The own funds of such firms or investment firms shall not fall below the highest reference level calculated after the date of notification contained in Directive 93/6/EEC. That reference level shall be the average daily level of own funds calculated over a six month period preceding the date of calculation. It shall be calculated every six months in respect of the corresponding preceding period.

2. If control of a firm covered by paragraph 1 is taken by a natural or legal person other than the person who controlled it previously, the own funds of that firm shall attain at least the level specified for them in Articles 5(1), 5(3), 6 and 9, except in the case of a first transfer by inheritance made after 31 December 1995, subject to the competent authorities' approval and for a period

---

[11] OJ L 9, 15.1.2003, 3, reproduced infra under no. I. 34.

of not more than 10 years from the date of that transfer.

3. In certain specific circumstances, and with the approval of the competent authorities, in the event of a merger of two or more investment firms and/or firms covered by Article 6, the own funds of the firm produced by the merger need not attain the level specified in Articles 5(1), 5(3), 6 and 9. Nevertheless, during any period when the level specified in Articles 5(1), 5(3), 6 and 9 has not been attained, the own funds of the new firm may not fall below the merged firms' total own funds at the time of the merger.

4. The own funds of investment firms and firms covered by Article 6 may not fall below the level specified in Articles 5(1), 5 (3), 6 and 9 and paragraphs 1 and 3 of this Article.

In the event that the own funds of such firms and investment firms fall below that level, the competent authorities may, where the circumstances justify it, allow such firms a limited period in which to rectify their situations or cease their activities.

Chapter III
Trading Book

Article 11

1. The trading book of an institution shall consist of all positions in financial instruments and commodities held either with trading intent or in order to hedge other elements of the trading book and which are either free of any restrictive covenants on their tradability or able to be hedged.

2. Positions held with trading intent are those held intentionally for short-term resale and/or with the intention of benefiting from actual or expected short-term price differences between buying and selling prices or from other price or interest rate variations. The term "positions" shall include proprietary positions and positions arising from client servicing and market making.

3. Trading intent shall be evidenced on the basis of the strategies, policies and procedures set up by the institution to manage the position or portfolio in accordance with Part A of Annex VII.

4. Institutions shall establish and maintain systems and controls to manage their trading book in accordance with Parts B and D of Annex VII.

5. Internal hedges may be included in the trading book, in which case Part C of Annex VII shall apply.

Chapter IV
Own Funds

Article 12

'Original own funds' means the sum of points (a) to (c), less the sum of points (i) to (k) of Article 57 of Directive 2006/48/EC.

The Commission shall, by 1 January 2009, submit an appropriate proposal to the European Parliament and to the Council for amendment of this Chapter.

Article 13

1. Subject to paragraphs 2 to 5 of this Article and Articles 14 to 17, the own funds of investment firms and credit institutions shall be determined in accordance with Directive 2006/48/EC.

In addition, the first subparagraph applies to investment firms which do not have one of the legal forms referred to in Article 1(1) of the Fourth Council Directive 78/660/EEC of 25 July 1978 based on Article 54(3) of the Treaty on the annual accounts of certain types of companies.[12]

2. By way of derogation from paragraph 1, the competent authorities may permit those institutions which are obliged to meet the capital requirements calculated in accordance with Articles 21 and 28 to 32 and Annexes I and III to VI to use, for that purpose only, an alternative determination of own funds. No part of the own

---

[12] OJ L 222, 14.8.1978, 11, reproduced infra under no. C. 4. Directive as last amended by Directive 2003/51/EC of the European Parliament and of the Council (OJ L 178, 17.7.2003, 16), reproduced infra under no. C. 23.

funds used for that purpose may be used simultaneously to meet other capital requirements.

Such an alternative determination shall be the sum of the items set out in points (a) to (c) of this subparagraph, minus the item set out in point (d), with the deduction of that last item being left to the discretion of the competent authorities:

(a) own funds as defined in Directive 2006/48/EC, excluding only points (l) to (p) of Article 57 of that Directive for those investment firms which are required to deduct item (d) of this paragraph from the total of items (a) to (c);

(b) an institution's net trading-book profits net of any foreseeable charges or dividends, less net losses on its other business, provided that none of those amounts has already been included in item (a) of this paragraph as one of the items set out in points (b) or (k) of Article 57 of Directive 2006/48/EC;

(c) subordinated loan capital and/or the items referred to in paragraph 5 of this Article, subject to the conditions set out in paragraphs 3 and 4 of this Article and in Article 14; and

(d) illiquid assets as specified in Article 15.

3. The subordinated loan capital referred to in point (c) of the second subparagraph of paragraph 2 shall have an initial maturity of at least two years. It shall be fully paid up and the loan agreement shall not include any clause providing that in specified circumstances, other than the winding up of the institution, the debt will become repayable before the agreed repayment date, unless the competent authorities approve the repayment. Neither the principal nor the interest on such subordinated loan capital may be repaid if such repayment would mean that the own funds of the institution in question would then amount to less than 100% of that institution's overall capital requirements.

In addition, an institution shall notify the competent authorities of all repayments on such subordinated loan capital as soon as its own funds fall below 120% of its overall capital requirements.

4. The subordinated loan capital referred to in point (c) of the second subparagraph of paragraph 2 may not exceed a maximum of 150% of the original own funds left to meet the requirements calculated in accordance with Articles 21 and 28 to 32 and Annexes I to VI and may approach that maximum only in particular circumstances acceptable to the competent authorities.

5. The competent authorities may permit institutions to replace the subordinated loan capital referred to in point (c) of the second subparagraph of paragraph 2 with points (d) to (h) of Article 57 of Directive 2006/48/EC.

Article 14

1. The competent authorities may permit investment firms to exceed the ceiling for subordinated loan capital set out in Article 13(4) if they judge it prudentially adequate and provided that the total of such subordinated loan capital and the items referred to in Article 13(5) does not exceed 200% of the original own funds left to meet the requirements calculated in accordance with Articles 21 and 28 to 32 and Annexes I and III to VI, or 250% of the same amount where investment firms deduct the item set out in Article 13(2)(d) when calculating own funds.

2. The competent authorities may permit the ceiling for subordinated loan capital set out in Article 13(4) to be exceeded by a credit institution if they judge it prudentially adequate and provided that the total of such subordinated loan capital and points (d) to (h) of Article 57 of Directive 2006/48/EC does not exceed 250% of the original own funds left to meet the requirements calculated in accordance with Articles 28 to 32 and Annexes I and III to VI to this Directive.

Article 15

Illiquid assets as referred to in point (d) of the second subparagraph of Article 13(2) shall include the following:

(a) tangible fixed assets, except to the extent that land and buildings may be allowed to count against the loans which they are securing;

(b) holdings in, including subordinated claims on, credit or financial institutions which may be included in the own funds of those institutions, unless they have been deducted under points (l) to (p) of Article 57 of Directive 2006/48/EC or under Article 16(d) of this Directive;

(c) holdings and other investments in undertakings other than credit or financial institutions, which are not readily marketable;

(d) deficiencies in subsidiaries;

(e) deposits made, other than those which are available for repayment within 90 days, and also excluding payments in connection with margined futures or options contracts;

(f) loans and other amounts due, other than those due to be repaid within 90 days; and

(g) physical stocks, unless they are already subject to capital requirements at least as stringent as those set out in Articles 18 and 20.

For the purposes of point (b), where shares in a credit or financial institution are held temporarily for the purpose of a financial assistance operation designed to reorganise and save that institution, the competent authorities may waive the application of this Article. They may also waive it in respect of those shares which are included in an investment firm's trading book.

Article 16

Investment firms included in a group which has been granted the waiver provided for in Article 22 shall calculate their own funds in accordance with Articles 13 to 15, subject to the following:

(a) the illiquid assets referred to in Article 13(2)(d) shall be deducted;

(b) the exclusion referred to in point (a) of Article 13(2) shall not cover those components of points (l) to (p) of Article 57 of Directive 2006/48/EC which an investment firm holds in respect of undertakings included in the scope of consolidation as defined in Article 2(1) of this Directive;

(c) the limits referred to in points (a) and (b) of Article 66(1) of Directive 2006/48/EC shall be calculated with reference to the original own funds less the components of points (l) to (p) of Article 57 of that Directive as referred to in point (b) of this Article which are elements of the original own funds of those undertakings; and

(d) the components of points (l) to (p) of Article 57 of Directive 2006/48/EC referred to in point (c) of this Article shall be deducted from the original own funds rather than from the total of all items as laid down in Article 66(2) of that Directive for the purposes in particular of Articles 13(4), 13(5) and 14 of this Directive.

Article 17

1. Where an institution calculates risk-weighted exposure amounts for the purposes of Annex II to this Directive in accordance with Articles 84 to 89 of Directive 2006/48/EC, then for the purposes of the calculation provided for in point 4 of Part 1 of Annex VII to Directive 2006/48/EC, the following shall apply:

(a) value adjustments made to take account of the credit quality of the counterparty may be included in the sum of value adjustments and provisions made for the exposures indicated in Annex II; and

(b) subject to the approval of the competent authorities, if the credit risk of the counterparty is adequately taken into account in the valuation of a position included in the trading book, the expected loss amount for the counterparty risk exposure shall be zero.

For the purposes of point (a), for such institutions, such value adjustments shall not be included in own funds other than in accordance with the provisions of this paragraph.

2. For the purposes of this Article, Article 153 and 154 of Directive 2006/48/EC shall apply.

CHAPTER V

SECTION 1

PROVISIONS AGAINST RISKS

Article 18

1. Institutions shall have own funds which are always more than or equal to the sum of the following:

(a) the capital requirements, calculated in accordance with the methods and options laid down in

Articles 28 to 32 and Annexes I, II and VI and, as appropriate, Annex V, for their trading-book business; and

(b) the capital requirements, calculated in accordance with the methods and options laid down in Annexes III and IV and, as appropriate, Annex V, for all of their business activities.

2. By way of derogation from paragraph 1, the competent authorities may allow institutions to calculate the capital requirements for their trading-book business in accordance with Article 75(a) of Directive 2006/48/EC and points 6, 7, and 9 of Annex II to this Directive, where the size of the trading-book business meets the following requirements:

(a) the trading-book business of such institutions does not normally exceed 5% of their total business;

(b) their total trading-book positions do not normally exceed EUR 15 million; and

(c) the trading-book business of such institutions never exceeds 6% of their total business and their total trading-book positions never exceed EUR 20 million.

3. In order to calculate the proportion that trading-book business bears to total business for the purposes of points (a) and (c) of paragraph 2, the competent authorities may refer either to the size of the combined on- and off-balance-sheet business, to the profit and loss account or to the own funds of the institutions in question, or to a combination of those measures. When the size of on- and off-balance-sheet business is assessed, debt instruments shall be valued at their market prices or their principal values, equities at their market prices and derivatives according to the nominal or market values of the instruments underlying them. Long positions and short positions shall be summed regardless of their signs.

4. If an institution should happen for more than a short period to exceed either or both of the limits imposed in paragraph 2(a) and (b) or either or both of the limits imposed in paragraph 2(c), it shall be required to meet the requirements imposed in paragraph 1(a) in respect of its trading-book business and to notify the competent authority thereof.

Article 19

1. For the purposes of point 14 of Annex I, subject to the discretion of the national authorities, a 0% weighting can be assigned to debt securities issued by the entities listed in Table 1 of Annex I, where these debt securities are denominated and funded in domestic currency.

2. By way of derogation from points 13 and 14 of Annex I, Member States may set a specific risk requirement for any bonds falling within points 68 to 70 of Part 1 of Annex VI to Directive 2006/48/EC which shall be equal to the specific risk requirement for a qualifying item with the same residual maturity as such bonds and reduced in accordance with the percentages given in point 71 of Part 1 to Annex VI to that Directive.

3. If, as set out in point 52 of Annex I, a competent authority approves a third country's collective investment undertaking (CIU) as eligible, a competent authority in another Member State may make use of this approval without conducting its own assessment.

Article 20

1. Subject to paragraphs 2, 3 and 4 of this Article, and Article 34 of this Directive, the requirements in Article 75 of Directive 2006/48/EC shall apply to investment firms.

2. By way of derogation from paragraph 1, competent authorities may allow investment firms that are not authorised to provide the investment services listed in points 3 and 6 of Section A of Annex I to Directive 2004/39/EC to provide own funds which are always more than or equal to the higher of the following:

(a) the sum of the capital requirements contained in points (a) to (c) of Article 75 of Directive 2006/48/EC; and

(b) the amount laid down in Article 21 of this Directive.

3. By way of derogation from paragraph 1, competent authorities may allow investment firms which hold initial capital as set out in Article 9, but which fall within the following categories, to provide own funds which are always more than or equal to the sum of the capital requirements calculated in accordance with the requirements contained in points (a) to (c) of Article 75 of Directive 2006/48/EC and the amount laid down in Article 21 of this Directive:

(a) investment firms that deal on own account only for the purpose of fulfilling or executing a client order or for the purpose of gaining entrance to a clearing and settlement system or a recognised exchange when acting in an agency capacity or executing a client order; and

(b) investment firms:
(i) that do not hold client money or securities;
(ii) that undertake only dealing on own account;
(iii) that have no external customers;
(iv) the execution and settlement of whose transactions takes place under the responsibility of a clearing institution and are guaranteed by that clearing institution.

4. Investment firms referred to in paragraphs 2 and 3 shall remain subject to all other provisions regarding operational risk set out in Annex V of Directive 2006/48/EC.

5. Article 21 shall apply only to investment firms to which paragraphs (2) or (3) or Article 46 apply and in the manner specified therein.

Article 21

Investment firms shall be required to hold own funds equivalent to one quarter of their preceding year's fixed overheads.

The competent authorities may adjust that requirement in the event of a material change in a firm's business since the preceding year.

Where a firm has not completed a year's business, starting from the day it starts up, the requirement shall be a quarter of the fixed overheads projected in its business plan, unless an adjustment to that plan is required by the competent authorities.

SECTION 2
APPLICATION OF REQUIREMENTS ON A CONSOLIDATED BASIS

Article 22

1. The competent authorities required or mandated to exercise supervision of groups covered by Article 2 on a consolidated basis may waive, on a case-by-case basis, the application of capital requirements on a consolidated basis provided that:

(a) each EU investment firm in such a group uses the calculation of own funds set out in Article 16;

(b) all investment firms in such a group fall within the categories in Article 20(2) and (3);

(c) each EU investment firm in such a group meets the requirements imposed in Articles 18 and 20 on an individual basis and at the same time deducts from its own funds any contingent liability in favour of investment firms, financial institutions, asset management companies and ancillary services undertakings, which would otherwise be consolidated; and

(d) any financial holding company which is the parent financial holding company in a Member State of any investment firm in such a group holds at least as much capital, defined here as the sum of points (a) to (h) of Article 57 of Directive 2006/48/EC, as the sum of the full book value of any holdings, subordinated claims and instruments as referred to in Article 57 of that Directive in investment firms, financial institutions, asset management companies and ancillary services undertakings which would otherwise be consolidated, and the total amount of any contingent liability in favour of investment firms, financial institutions, asset management companies and ancillary services undertakings which would otherwise be consolidated.

Where the criteria in the first subparagraph are met, each EU investment firm shall have in place systems to monitor and control the sources of capital and funding of all financial holding companies, investment firms, financial institutions, asset management companies and ancillary services undertakings within the group.

2. By way of derogation from paragraph 1, competent authorities may permit financial holding companies which are the parent financial holding company in a Member State of an investment firm in such a group to use a value lower than the value calculated under paragraph 1(d), but no lower than the sum of the requirements imposed in Articles 18 and 20 on an individual basis to investment firms, financial institutions, asset management companies and ancillary services undertakings which would otherwise be consolidated and the total amount of any contingent liability in favour of investment firms, financial institutions, asset management companies and ancillary services undertakings which would otherwise be consolidated. For the purposes of this paragraph, the capital requirement for investment undertakings of third countries, financial institutions, asset management companies and ancillary services undertakings is a notional capital requirement.

Article 23

The competent authorities shall require investment firms in a group which has been granted the waiver provided for in Article 22 to notify them of the risks which could undermine their financial positions, including those associated with the composition and sources of their capital and funding. If the competent authorities then consider that the financial positions of those investment firms is not adequately protected, they shall require them to take measures including, if necessary, limitations on the transfer of capital from such firms to group entities.

Where the competent authorities waive the obligation of supervision on a consolidated basis provided for in Article 22, they shall take other appropriate measures to monitor the risks, namely large exposures, of the whole group, including any undertakings not located in a Member State.

Where the competent authorities waive the application of capital requirements on a consolidated basis provided for in Article 22, the requirements of Article 123 and Chapter 5 of Title V of Directive 2006/48/EC shall apply on an individual basis, and the requirements of Article 124 of that Directive shall apply to the supervision of investment firms on an individual basis.

Article 24

1. By way of derogation from Article 2(2), competent authorities may exempt investment firms from the consolidated capital requirement established in that Article, provided that all the investment firms in the group are covered by Article 20(2) and the group does not include credit institutions.

2. Where the requirements of paragraph 1 are met, a parent investment firm in a Member State shall be required to provide own funds at a consolidated level which are always more than or equal to the higher of the following two amounts, calculated on the basis of the parent investment firm's consolidated financial position and in compliance with Section 3 of this Chapter:

(a) the sum of the capital requirements contained in points (a) to (c) of Article 75 of Directive 2006/48/EC; and

(b) the amount prescribed in Article 21 of this Directive.

3. Where the requirements of paragraph 1 are met, an investment firm controlled by a financial holding company shall be required to provide own funds at a consolidated level which are always more than or equal to the higher of the following two amounts, calculated on the basis of the financial holding company's consolidated financial position and in compliance with Section 3 of this Chapter:

(a) the sum of the capital requirements contained in points (a) to (c) of Article 75 of Directive 2006/48/EC; and

(b) the amount prescribed in Article 21 of this Directive.

Article 25

By way of derogation from Article 2(2), competent authorities may exempt investment firms from the consolidated capital requirement established in that Article, provided that all the investment firms in the group fall within the investment firms referred to in Article 20(2) and (3), and the group does not include credit institutions.

Where the requirements of the first paragraph are met, a parent investment firm in a Member State shall be required to provide own funds at a consolidated level which are always more than or equal to the sum of the requirements contained in points (a) to (c) of Article 75 of Directive 2006/48/EC and the amount prescribed in Article 21 of this Directive, calculated on the basis of the parent investment firm's consolidated financial position and in compliance with Section 3 of this Chapter.

Where the requirements of the first paragraph are met, an investment firm controlled by a financial holding company shall be required to provide own funds at a consolidated level which are always more than or equal to the sum of the requirements contained in points (a) to (c) of Article 75 of Directive 2006/48/EC and the amount prescribed in Article 21 of this Directive, calculated on the basis of the financial holding company's consolidated financial position and in compliance with Section 3 of this Chapter.

SECTION 3
CALCULATION OF CONSOLIDATED REQUIREMENTS

Article 26

1. Where the waiver provided for in Article 22 is not exercised, the competent authorities may, for the purpose of calculating the capital requirements set out in Annexes I and V and the exposures to clients set out in Articles 28 to 32 and Annex VI on a consolidated basis, permit positions in the trading book of one institution to offset positions in the trading book of another institution according to the rules set out in Articles 28 to 32 Annexes I, V and VI.

In addition, the competent authorities may allow foreign-exchange positions in one institution to offset foreign-exchange positions in another institution in accordance with the rules set out in Annex III and/or Annex V. They may also allow commodities positions in one institution to offset commodities positions in another institution in accordance with the rules set out in Annex IV and/or Annex V.

2. The competent authorities may permit offsetting of the trading book and of the foreign-exchange and commodities positions, respectively, of undertakings located in third countries, subject to the simultaneous fulfilment of the following conditions:

(a) such undertakings have been authorised in a third country and either satisfy the definition of credit institution set out in Article 4(1) of Directive 2006/48/EC or are recognised third-country investment firms;

(b) such undertakings comply, on an individual basis, with capital adequacy rules equivalent to those laid down in this Directive; and

(c) no regulations exist in the third countries in question which might significantly affect the transfer of funds within the group.

3. The competent authorities may also allow the offsetting provided for in paragraph 1 between institutions within a group that have been authorised in the Member State in question, provided that:

(a) there is a satisfactory allocation of capital within the group; and

(b) the regulatory, legal or contractual framework in which the institutions operate is such as to guarantee mutual financial support within the group.

4. Furthermore, the competent authorities may allow the offsetting provided for in paragraph 1 between institutions within a group that fulfil the conditions imposed in paragraph 3 and any institution included in the same group which has been authorised in another Member State provided that that institution is obliged to fulfil the capital requirements imposed in Articles 18, 20 and 28 on an individual basis.

Article 27

1. In the calculation of own funds on a consolidated basis Article 65 of Directive 2006/48/EC shall apply.

2. The competent authorities responsible for exercising supervision on a consolidated basis may recognise the validity of the specific own-funds definitions applicable to the institutions concerned under Chapter IV in the calculation of their consolidated own funds.

SECTION 4
MONITORING AND CONTROL OF LARGE EXPOSURES

Article 28

1. Institutions shall monitor and control their large exposures in accordance with Articles 106 to 118 of Directive 2006/48/EC.

2. By way of derogation from paragraph 1, institutions which calculate the capital requirements for their trading-book business in accordance with Annexes I and II, and, as appropriate, Annex V to this Directive, shall monitor and control their large exposures in accordance with Articles 106 to 118 of Directive 2006/48/EC subject to the amendments laid down in Articles 29 to 32 of this Directive.

3. By 31 December 2007, the Commission shall submit to the European Parliament and to the Council a report on the functioning of this Section, together with any appropriate proposals.

Article 29

1. The exposures to individual clients which arise on the trading book shall be calculated by summing the following items:

(a) the excess—where positive—of an institution's long positions over its short positions in all the financial instruments issued by the client in question, the net position in each of the different instruments being calculated according to the methods laid down in Annex I;

(b) the net exposure, in the case of the underwriting of a debt or an equity instrument; and

(c) the exposures due to the transactions, agreements and contracts referred to in Annex II with the client in question, such exposures being calculated in the manner laid down in that Annex, for the calculation of exposure values.

For the purposes of point (b), the net exposure is calculated by deducting those underwriting positions which are subscribed or sub-underwritten by third parties on the basis of a formal agreement reduced by the factors set out in point 41 of Annex I.

For the purposes of point (b), pending further coordination, the competent authorities shall require institutions to set up systems to monitor and control their underwriting exposures between the time of the initial commitment and working day one in the light of the nature of the risks incurred in the markets in question.

For the purposes of point (c), Articles 84 to 89 of Directive 2006/48/EC shall be excluded from the reference in point 6 of Annex II to this Directive.

2. The exposures to groups of connected clients on the trading book shall be calculated by summing the exposures to individual clients in a group, as calculated in paragraph 1.

Article 30

1. The overall exposures to individual clients or groups of connected clients shall be calculated by summing the exposures which arise on the trading book and the exposures which arise on the non-trading book, taking into account Article 112 to 117 of Directive 2006/48/EC.

In order to calculate the exposure which arises on the non-trading book, institutions shall take the exposure arising from assets which are deducted from their own funds by virtue of point (d) of the second subparagraph of Article 13(2) to be zero.

2. Institutions' overall exposures to individual clients and groups of connected clients calculated in accordance with paragraph 4 shall be reported in accordance with Article 110 of Directive 2006/48/EC.

Other than in relation to repurchase transactions, securities or commodities lending or borrowing transactions, the calculation of large exposures to individual clients and groups of connected clients for reporting purposes shall not include the recognition of credit risk mitigation.

3. The sum of the exposures to an individual client or group of connected clients in paragraph 1 shall be limited in accordance with Articles 111 to 117 of Directive 2006/48/EC.

4. By derogation from paragraph 3 competent authorities may allow assets constituting claims and other exposures on recognised third-country investment firms and recognised clearing houses and exchanges in financial instruments to be subject to the same treatment accorded to those on institutions laid out in Articles 113(3)(i), 115(2) and 116 of Directive 2006/48/EC.

Article 31

The competent authorities may authorise the limits laid down in Articles 111 to 117 of Directive 2006/48/EC to be exceeded if the following conditions are met:

(a) the exposure on the non-trading book to the client or group of clients in question does not exceed the limits laid down in Articles 111 to 117 of Directive 2006/48/EC, those limits being calculated with reference to own funds as specified in that Directive, so that the excess arises entirely on the trading book;

(b) the institution meets an additional capital requirement on the excess in respect of the limits laid down in Article 111(1) and (2) of Directive 2006/48/EC, that additional capital requirement being calculated in accordance with Annex VI to that Directive;

(c) where 10 days or less has elapsed since the excess occurred, the trading-book exposure to the client or group of connected clients in question shall not exceed 500% of the institution's own funds;

(d) any excesses that have persisted for more than 10 days must not, in aggregate, exceed 600% of the institution's own funds; and

(e) institutions shall report to the competent authorities every three months all cases where the limits laid down in Article 111(1) and (2) of Directive 2006/48/EC have been exceeded during the preceding three months.

In relation to point (e), in each case in which the limits have been exceeded the amount of the excess and the name of the client concerned shall be reported.

Article 32

1. The competent authorities shall establish procedures to prevent institutions from deliberately avoiding the additional capital requirements that they would otherwise incur, on exposures exceeding the limits laid down in Article 111(1) and (2) of Directive 2006/48/EC once those exposures have been maintained for more than 10 days, by means of temporarily transferring the exposures in question to another company, whether within the same group or not, and/or by undertaking artificial transactions to close out the exposure during the 10-day period and create a new exposure.

The competent authorities shall notify the Council and the Commission of those procedures.

Institutions shall maintain systems which ensure that any transfer which has the effect referred to in the first subparagraph is immediately reported to the competent authorities.

2. The competent authorities may permit institutions which are allowed to use the alternative determination of own funds under Article 13(2) to use that determination for the purposes of Articles 30(2), 30(3) and 31 provided that the institutions concerned are required to meet all of the obligations set out in Articles 110 to 117 of Directive 2006/48/EC, in respect of the exposures which arise outside their trading books by using own funds as defined in that Directive.

SECTION 5

VALUATION OF POSITIONS FOR REPORTING PURPOSES

Article 33

1. All trading-book positions shall be subject to prudent valuation rules as specified in Annex VII,

Part B. These rules shall require institutions to ensure that the value applied to each of its trading-book positions appropriately reflects the current market value. The former value shall contain an appropriate degree of certainty having regard to the dynamic nature of trading-book positions, the demands of prudential soundness and the mode of operation and purpose of capital requirements in respect of trading-book positions.

2. Trading-book positions shall be re-valued at least daily.

3. In the absence of readily available market prices, the competent authorities may waive the requirement imposed in paragraphs 1 and 2 and shall require institutions to use alternative methods of valuation provided that those methods are sufficiently prudent and have been approved by competent authorities.

Section 6
Risk Management and Capital Assessment

Article 34

Competent authorities shall require that every investment firm, as well as meeting the requirements set out in Article 13 of Directive 2004/39/EC, shall meet the requirements set out in Articles 22 and 123 of Directive 2006/48/EC, subject to the provisions on level of application set out in Articles 68 to 73 of that Directive.

Section 7
Reporting Requirements

Article 35

1. Member States shall require that investment firms and credit institutions provide the competent authorities of their home Member States with all the information necessary for the assessment of their compliance with the rules adopted in accordance with this Directive. Member States shall also ensure that internal control mechanisms and administrative and accounting procedures of the institutions permit the verification of their compliance with such rules at all times.

2. Investment firms shall report to the competent authorities in the manner specified by the latter at least once every month in the case of firms covered by Article 9, at least once every three months in the case of firms covered by Article 5(1) and at least once every six months in the case of firms covered by Article 5(3).

3. Notwithstanding paragraph 2, investment firms covered by Articles 5(1) and 9 shall be required to provide the information on a consolidated or sub-consolidated basis only once every six months.

4. Credit institutions shall be obliged to report in the manner specified by the competent authorities as often as they are obliged to report under Directive 2006/48/EC.

5. The competent authorities shall oblige institutions to report to them immediately any case in which their counter parties in repurchase and reverse repurchase agreements or securities and commodities-lending and securities and commodities-borrowing transactions default on their obligations.

Chapter VI
Section 1
Competent Authorities

Article 36

1. Member States shall designate the authorities which are competent to carry out the duties provided for in this Directive. They shall inform the Commission thereof, indicating any division of duties.

2. The competent authorities shall be public authorities or bodies officially recognized by national law or by public authorities as part of the supervisory system in operation in the Member State concerned.

3. The competent authorities shall be granted all the powers necessary for the performance of their

tasks, and in particular that of overseeing the constitution of trading books.

Section 2
Supervision

Article 37

1. Chapter 4 of Title V of Directive 2006/48/EC shall apply mutatis mutandis to the supervision of investment firms in accordance with the following:

(a) references to Article 6 of Directive 2006/48/EC shall be construed as references to Article 5 of Directive 2004/39/EC;

(b) references to Article 22 and 123 of Directive 2006/48/EC shall be construed s references to Article 34 of this Directive; and

(c) references to Articles 44 to 52 of Directive 2006/48/EC shall be construed as references to Articles 54 and 58 of Directive 2004/39/EC.

Where an EU parent financial holding company has as subsidiary both a credit institution and an investment firm, Title V, Chapter 4 of Directive 2006/48/EC shall apply to the supervision of institutions as if references to credit institutions were to institutions.

2. Article 129(2) of Directive 2006/48/EC shall also apply to the recognition of internal models of institutions under Annex V to this Directive where the application is submitted by an EU parent credit institution and its subsidiaries or an EU parent investment firm and its subsidiaries, or jointly by the subsidiaries of an EU parent financial holding company.

The period for the recognition referred to in the first sub-paragraph shall be six months.

Article 38

1. The competent authorities of the Member States shall cooperate closely in the performance of the duties provided for in this Directive, particularly where investment services are provided on the basis of the freedom to provide services or through the establishment of branches.

The competent authorities shall on request supply one another with all information likely to facilitate the supervision of the capital adequacy of institutions, in particular the verification of their compliance with the rules laid down in this Directive.

2. Any exchange of information between competent authorities which is provided for in this Directive shall be subject to the following obligations of professional secrecy:

(a) for investment firms, those imposed in Article 54 and 58 of Directive 2004/39/EC; and

(b) for credit institutions, those imposed in Articles 44 to 52 of Directive 2006/48/EC.

Chapter VII
Disclosure

Article 39

The requirements set out in Title V, Chapter 5 of Directive 2006/48/EC shall apply to investment firms.

Chapter VIII
Section 1

Article 40

For the purposes of the calculation of minimum capital requirements for counterparty risk under this Directive, and for the calculation of minimum capital requirements for credit risk under Directive 2006/48/EC, and without prejudice to the provisions of Part 2, point 6 of Annex III to that Directive, exposures to recognised third-country investment firms and exposures to recognised clearing houses and exchanges shall be treated as exposures to institutions.

Section 2
Powers of Execution

Article 41

1. The Commission shall decide on any technical adaptations in the following areas in accordance

with the procedure referred to in Article 42(2):

(a) clarification of the definitions in Article 3 in order to ensure uniform application of this Directive;

(b) clarification of the definitions in Article 3 to take account of developments on financial markets;

(c) adjustment of the amounts of initial capital prescribed in Articles 5 to 9 and the amount referred to in Article 18(2) to take account of developments in the economic and monetary field;

(d) adjustment of the categories of investment firms in Article 20(2) and (3) to take account of developments on financial markets;

(e) clarification of the requirement laid down in Article 21 to ensure uniform application of this Directive;

(f) alignment of terminology on and the framing of definitions in accordance with subsequent acts on institutions and related matters;

(g) adjustment of the technical provisions in Annexes I to VII as a result of developments on financial markets, risk measurement, accounting standards or requirements which take account of Community legislation or which have regard to convergence of supervisory practices; or

(h) technical adaptations to take account of the outcome of the review referred to in Article 65(3) of Directive 2004/39/EC.

2. None of the implementing measures enacted may change the essential provisions of this Directive

Article 42

1. The Commission shall be assisted by the European Banking Committee established by Commission Decision 2004/10/EC[13] of 5 November 2003 (hereinafter referred to as "the Committee").

2. Where reference is made to this paragraph, the procedure laid down in Article 5 of Decision 1999/468/EC shall apply, having regard to the provisions of Article 7(3) and 8 thereof.

The period laid down in Article 5(6) of Decision 1999/468/EC shall be three months.

3. Without prejudice to the implementing measures already adopted, upon expiry of a two-year period following the adoption of this Directive, and by 1 April 2008, the application of the provisions of this Directive requiring the adoption of technical rules, amendments and decisions in accordance with paragraph 2 shall be suspended. Acting on a proposal from the Commission and in accordance with the procedure laid down in Article 251 of the Treaty, the Parliament and the Council may renew those provisions and, to that end, shall review them prior to the expiry of the period or by the date referred to in this paragraph, whichever is the earlier.

4. The Committee shall adopt its Rules of Procedure

Section 3
Transitional Provisions

Article 43

Article 152(1) to (7) of Directive 2006/48/EC shall apply, in accordance with Article 2 and Chapter V, Sections 2 and 3 of this Directive, to investment firms calculating risk-weighted exposure amounts, for the purposes of Annex II to this Directive, in accordance with Articles 84 to 89 of Directive 2006/48/EC, or using the Advanced Measurement Approach as specified in Article 105 of that Directive for the calculation of their capital requirements for operational risk.

Article 44

Until 31 December 2012, for investment firms the relevant indicator for the trading and sales business line of which represents at least 50% of the total of relevant indicators for all of their business lines calculated in accordance with Article 20 of this Directive and points 1 to 4 of Part 2 of Annex X to Directive 2006/48/EC, Member

---

[13] OJ L 3, 7.1.2004, 36, reproduced infra under no. I. 37.

States may apply a percentage of 15% to the business line 'trading and sales'.

Article 45

1. Competent authorities may permit investment firms to exceed the limits concerning large exposures set out in Article 111 of Directive 2006/48/EC. Investment firms need not include any excesses in their calculation of capital requirements exceeding such limits, as set out in Article 75(b) of that Directive. This discretion is available until 31 December 2010 or the date of entry into force of any modifications consequent to the treatment of large exposures pursuant to Article 119 of Directive 2006/48/EC, whichever is the earlier. For this discretion to be exercised, the following conditions shall be met:

(a) the investment firm provides investment services or investment activities related to the financial instruments listed in points 5, 6, 7, 9 and 10 of Section C of Annex I to Directive 2004/39/EC;

(b) the investment firm does not provide such investment services or undertake such investment activities for, or on behalf of, retail clients;

(c) breaches of the limits referred to in the introductory part of this paragraph arise in connection with exposures resulting from contracts that are financial instruments as listed in point (a) and relate to commodities or underlyings within the meaning of point 10 of Section C of Annex I to Directive 2004/39/EC (MiFID) and are calculated in accordance with Annexes III and IV of Directive 2006/48/EC, or in connection with exposures resulting from contracts concerning the delivery of commodities or emission allowances; and

(d) the investment firm has a documented strategy for managing and, in particular, for controlling and limiting risks arising from the concentration of exposures. The investment firm shall inform the competent authorities of this strategy and all material changes to it without delay. The investment firm shall make appropriate arrangements to ensure a continuous monitoring of the creditworthiness of borrowers, according to their impact on concentration risk.

These arrangements shall enable the investment firm to react adequately and sufficiently promptly to any deterioration in that creditworthiness.

2. Where an investment firm exceeds the internal limits set according to the strategy referred to in point (d) of paragraph 1, it shall notify the competent authority without delay of the size and nature of the excess and of the counterparty.

Article 46

By way of derogation from Article 20(1), until 31 December 2011 competent authorities may choose, on a case-by-case basis, not to apply the capital requirements arising from point (d) of Article 75 of Directive 2006/48/EC in respect of investment firms to which Article 20(2) and (3) do not apply, whose total trading-book positions never exceed EUR 50 million and whose average number of relevant employees during the financial year does not exceed 100.

Instead, the capital requirement in relation to those investment firms shall be at least the lower of:

(a) the capital requirements arising from point (d) of Article 75 of Directive 2006/48/EC; and

(b) 12/88 of the higher of the following:
(i) the sum of the capital requirements contained in points (a) to (c) of Article 75 of Directive 2006/48/EC; and
(ii) the amount laid down in Article 21 of this Directive, notwithstanding Article 20(5).

If point (b) applies, an incremental increase shall be applied on at least an annual basis.

Applying this derogation shall not result in a reduction in the overall level of capital requirements for an investment firm, in comparison to the requirements as at 31 December 2006, unless such a reduction is prudentially justified by a reduction in the size of the investment firm's business.

Article 47

Until 31 December 2009 or any earlier date specified by the competent authorities on a case-by-case basis, institutions that have received specific risk model recognition prior to 1 January 2007 in accordance with point 1 of Annex V may, for that existing recognition, treat points 4 and 8 of Annex V to Directive 93/6/EEC as those points stood prior to 1 January 2007.

Article 48

1. The provisions on capital requirements as laid down in this Directive and Directive 2006/48/EC shall not apply to investment firms whose main business consists exclusively of the provision of investment services or activities in relation to the financial instruments set out in points 5, 6, 7, 9 and 10 of Section C of Annex I to Directive 2004/39/EC and to whom Directive 93/22/EEC[14] did not apply on 31 December 2006. This exemption is available until 31 December 2010 or the date of entry into force of any modifications pursuant to paragraphs 2 and 3, whichever is the earlier.

2. As part of the review required by Article 65(3) of Directive 2004/39/EC, the Commission shall, on the basis of public consultations and in the light of discussions with the competent authorities, report to the Parliament and the Council on:

(a) an appropriate regime for the prudential supervision of investment firms whose main business consists exclusively of the provision of investment services or activities in relation to the commodity derivatives or derivatives contracts set out in points 5, 6, 7, 9 and 10 of Section C of Annex I to Directive 2004/39/EC; and

(b) the desirability of amending Directive 2004/39/EC to create a further category of investment firm whose main business consists exclusively of the provision of investment services or activities in relation to the financial instruments set out in points 5, 6, 7, 9 and 10 of Section C of Annex I to Directive 2004/39/EC relating to energy supplies (including electricity, coal, gas and oil).

3. On the basis of the report referred to in paragraph 2, the Commission may submit proposals for amendments to this Directive and to Directive 2006/48/EC

SECTION 4
FINAL PROVISIONS

Article 49

1. Member States shall adopt and publish, by 31 December 2006, the laws, regulations and administrative provisions necessary to comply with Articles 2, 3, 11, 13, 17, 18, 19, 20, 22, 23, 24, 25, 29, 30, 33, 34, 35, 37, 39, 40, 41, 43, 44, 50 and the Annexes I, II, III, V, VII. They shall forthwith communicate to the Commission the text of those provisions and a correlation table between those provisions and this Directive.

They shall apply those provisions from 1 January 2007.

When Member States adopt those measures, they shall contain a reference to this Directive or be accompanied by such a reference on the occasion of their official publication. They shall also include a statement that references in existing laws, regulations and administrative provisions to the directives repealed by this Directive shall be construed as references to this Directive.

2. Member States shall communicate to the Commission the text of the main provisions of national law which they adopt in the field covered by this Directive.

Article 50

1. Article 152(8) to (14) of Directive 2006/48/EC shall apply mutatis mutandis for the purposes of this Directive subject to the following provisions which shall apply where the discretion referred to in Article 152(8) of Directive 2006/48/EC is exercised:

(a) references in point 7 of Annex II to this Directive to Directive 2006/48/EC shall be read as references to Directive 2000/12/EC as that Directive stood prior to 1 January 2007; and

---

[14] Council Directive 93/22/EEC of 10 May 1993 on investment services in the securities field (OJ L 141, 11.6.1993, 27), reproduced infra under no. S. 14. Directive as last amended by Directive 2002/87/EC, reproduced supra under no. B. 38.

(b) point 4 of Annex II to this Directive shall apply as it stood prior to 1 January 2007.

2. Article 157(3) of Directive 2006/48/EC shall apply mutatis mutandis for the purposes of Articles 18 and 20 of this Directive.

Article 51

By 1 January 2011, the Commission shall review and report on the application of this Directive and submit its report to the Parliament and the Council together with any appropriate proposals for amendment.

Article 52

Directive 93/6/EEC, as amended by the Directives listed in Annex VIII, Part A, is repealed, without prejudice to the obligations of the Member States relating to the time-limits for transposition into national law of the Directives set out in Annex VIII, Part B.

References made to the repealed directives shall be construed as being made to this Directive and should be read in accordance with the correspondence table set out in Annex IX.

Article 53

This Directive shall enter into force on the twentieth day following that of its publication in the Official Journal of the European Union.

Article 54

This Directive is addressed to the Member States.

Annex I

Calculating Capital Requirements for Position Risk

GENERAL PROVISIONS

Netting

1. The excess of an institution's long (short) positions over its short (long) positions in the same equity, debt and convertible issues and identical financial futures, options, warrants and covered warrants shall be its net position in each of those different instruments. In calculating the net position the competent authorities shall allow positions in derivative instruments to be treated, as laid down in points 4 to 7, as positions in the underlying (or notional) security or securities. Institutions' holdings of their own debt instruments shall be disregarded in calculating specific risk under point 14.

2. No netting shall be allowed between a convertible and an offsetting position in the instrument underlying it, unless the competent authorities adopt an approach under which the likelihood of a particular convertible's being converted is taken into account or have a capital requirement to cover any loss which conversion might entail.

3. All net positions, irrespective of their signs, must be converted on a daily basis into the institution's reporting currency at the prevailing spot exchange rate before their aggregation.

Particular instruments

4. Interest-rate futures, forward-rate agreements (FRAs) and forward commitments to buy or sell debt instruments shall be treated as combinations of long and short positions. Thus a long interest-rate futures position shall be treated as a combination of a borrowing maturing on the delivery date of the futures contract and a holding of an asset with maturity date equal to that of the instrument or notional position underlying the futures contract in question. Similarly a sold FRA will be treated as a long position with a maturity date equal to the settlement date plus the contract period, and a short position with maturity equal to the settlement date. Both the borrowing and the asset holding shall be included in the first category set out in Table 1 in point 14 in order to calculate the capital required against specific risk

for interest-rate futures and FRAs. A forward commitment to buy a debt instrument shall be treated as a combination of a borrowing maturing on the delivery date and a long (spot) position in the debt instrument itself. The borrowing shall be included in the first category set out in Table 1 in point 14 for purposes of specific risk, and the debt instrument under whichever column is appropriate for it in the same table.

The competent authorities may allow the capital requirement for an exchange-traded future to be equal to the margin required by the exchange if they are fully satisfied that it provides an accurate measure of the risk associated with the future and that it is at least equal to the capital requirement for a future that would result from a calculation made using the method set out in this Annex or applying the internal models method described in Annex V. The competent authorities may also allow the capital requirement for an OTC derivatives contract of the type referred to in this point cleared by a clearing house recognised by them to be equal to the margin required by the clearing house if they are fully satisfied that it provides an accurate measure of the risk associated with the derivatives contract and that it is at least equal to the capital requirement for the contract in question that would result from a calculation made using the method set out in the this Annex or applying the internal models method described in Annex V.

For the purposes of this point, 'long position' means a position in which an institution has fixed the interest rate it will receive at some time in the future, and "short position" means a position in which it has fixed the interest rate it will pay at some time in the future.

5. Options on interest rates, debt instruments, equities, equity indices, financial futures, swaps and foreign currencies shall be treated as if they were positions equal in value to the amount of the underlying instrument to which the option refers, multiplied by its delta for the purposes of this Annex. The latter positions may be netted off against any offsetting positions in the identical underlying securities or derivatives. The delta used shall be that of the exchange concerned, that calculated by the competent authorities or, where that is not available or for OTC options, that calculated by the institution itself, subject to the competent authorities being satisfied that the model used by the institution is reasonable.

However, the competent authorities may also prescribe that institutions calculate their deltas using a methodology specified by the competent authorities.

Other risks, apart from the delta risk, associated with options shall be safeguarded against. The competent authorities may allow the requirement against a written exchange-traded option to be equal to the margin required by the exchange if they are fully satisfied that it provides an accurate measure of the risk associated with the option and that it is at least equal to the capital requirement against an option that would result from a calculation made using the method set out in the remainder of this Annex or applying the internal models method described in Annex V. The competent authorities may also allow the capital requirement for an OTC option cleared by a clearing house recognised by them to be equal to the margin required by the clearing house if they are fully satisfied that it provides an accurate measure of the risk associated with the option and that it is at least equal to the capital requirement for an OTC option that would result from a calculation made using the method set out in the remainder of this Annex or applying the internal models method described in Annex V. In addition they may allow the requirement on a bought exchange-traded or OTC option to be the same as that for the instrument underlying it, subject to the constraint that the resulting requirement does not exceed the market value of the option. The requirement against a written OTC option shall be set in relation to the instrument underlying it.

6. Warrants relating to debt instruments and equities shall be treated in the same way as options under point 5.

7. Swaps shall be treated for interest-rate risk purposes on the same basis as on-balance-sheet instruments. Thus, an interest-rate swap under

which an institution receives floating-rate interest and pays fixed-rate interest shall be treated as equivalent to a long position in a floating-rate instrument of maturity equivalent to the period until the next interest fixing and a short position in a fixed-rate instrument with the same maturity as the swap itself.

A. Treatment of the Protection Seller

8. When calculating the capital requirement for market risk of the party who assumes the credit risk (the 'protection seller'), unless specified differently, the notional amount of the credit derivative contract must be used. For the purpose of calculating the specific risk charge, other than for total return swaps, the maturity of the credit derivative contract is applicable instead of the maturity of the obligation. Positions are determined as follows:

(i) A total return swap creates a long position in the general market risk of the reference obligation and a short position in the general market risk of a government bond with a maturity equivalent to the period until the next interest fixing and which is assigned a 0% risk weight under Annex VI of Directive 2006/48/EC. It also creates a long position in the specific risk of the reference obligation.

(ii) A credit default swap does not create a position for general market risk. For the purposes of specific risk, the institution must record a synthetic long position in an obligation of the reference entity, unless the derivative is rated externally and meets the conditions for a qualifying debt item, in which case a long position in the derivative is recorded. If premium or interest payments are due under the product, these cash flows must be represented as notional positions in government bonds.

(iii) A single name credit linked note creates a long position in the general market risk of the note itself, as an interest rate product. For the purpose of specific risk, a synthetic long position is created in an obligation of the reference entity. An additional long position is created in the issuer of the note. Where the credit linked note has an external rating and meets the conditions for a qualifying debt item, a single long position with the specific risk of the note need only be recorded.

(iv) In addition to a long position in the specific risk of the issuer of the note, a multiple name credit linked note providing proportional protection creates a position in each reference entity, with the total notional amount of the contract assigned across the positions according to the proportion of the total notional amount that each exposure to a reference entity represents. Where more than one obligation of a reference entity can be selected, the obligation with the highest risk weighting determines the specific risk.

Where a multiple name credit linked note has an external rating and meets the conditions for a qualifying debt item, a single long position with the specific risk of the note need only be recorded.

(v) A first-asset-to-default credit derivative creates a position for the notional amount in an obligation of each reference entity. If the size of the maximum credit event payment is lower than the capital requirement under the method in the first sentence of this point, the maximum payment amount may be taken as the capital requirement for specific risk.

A second-asset-to-default credit derivative creates a position for the notional amount in an obligation of each reference entity less one (that with the lowest specific risk capital requirement). If the size of the maximum credit event payment is lower than the capital requirement under the method in the first sentence of this point, this amount may be taken as the capital requirement for specific risk.

If a first- or second-asset-to-default derivative is externally rated and meets the conditions for a qualifying debt item, then the protection seller need only calculate one specific risk charge reflecting the rating of the derivative.

B. Treatment of the Protection Buyer

For the party who transfers credit risk (the 'protection buyer'), the positions are determined as the mirror image of the protection seller, with the exception of a credit linked note (which entails no short position in the issuer). If at a given moment there is a call option in combination with a step-up, such moment is treated as the maturity of the protection. In the case of nth to default credit derivatives, protection buyers are allowed to off-set specific risk for n-1 of the underlyings (i.e., the n-1 assets with the lowest specific risk charge).

9. Institutions which mark-to-market and manage the interest-rate risk on the derivative instruments covered in points 4 to 7 on a discounted-cash-flow basis may use sensitivity models to calculate the positions referred to in those points and may use them for any bond which is amortised over its residual life rather than via one final repayment of principal. Both the model and its use by the institution must be approved by the competent authorities. These models should generate positions which have the same sensitivity to interest-rate changes as the underlying cash flows. This sensitivity must be assessed with reference to independent movements in sample rates across the yield curve, with at least one sensitivity point in each of the maturity bands set out in Table 2 of point 20. The positions shall be included in the calculation of capital requirements according to the provisions laid down in points 17 to 32.

10. For the party who transfers credit risk (the 'protection buyer'), the positions are determined as the mirror image of the protection seller, with the exception of a credit linked note (which entails no short position in the issuer). If at a given moment there is a call option in combination with a step-up, such moment is treated as the maturity of the protection. In the case of nth to default credit derivatives, protection buyers are allowed to off-set specific risk for n-1 of the underlyings (i.e., the n-1 assets with the lowest specific risk charge).

(a) the positions are of the same value and denominated in the same currency;

(b) the reference rate (for floating-rate positions) or coupon (for fixed-rate positions) is closely matched; and

(c) the next interest-fixing date or, for fixed coupon positions, residual maturity corresponds with the following limits:
(i) less than one month hence: same day;
(ii) between one month and one year hence: within seven days; and
(iii) over one year hence: within 30 days.

11. The transferor of securities or guaranteed rights relating to title to securities in a repurchase agreement and the lender of securities in a securities lending shall include these securities in the calculation of its capital requirement under this Annex provided that such securities meet the criteria laid down in Article 11.

Specific and general risks

12. The position risk on a traded debt instrument or equity (or debt or equity derivative) shall be divided into two components in order to calculate the capital required against it. The first shall be its specific-risk component—this is the risk of a price change in the instrument concerned due to factors related to its issuer or, in the case of a derivative, the issuer of the underlying instrument. The second component shall cover its general risk—this is the risk of a price change in the instrument due (in the case of a traded debt instrument or debt derivative) to a change in the level of interest rates or (in the case of an equity or equity derivative) to a broad equity-market movement unrelated to any specific attributes of individual securities.

Traded Debt Instruments

13. Net positions shall be classified according to the currency in which they are denominated and shall calculate the capital requirement for general and specific risk in each individual currency separately.

Specific risk

14. The institution shall assign its net positions in the trading book, as calculated in accordance

with point 1 to the appropriate categories in Table 1 on the basis of their issuer/obligor, external or internal credit assessment, and residual maturity, and then multiply them by the weightings shown in that table. It shall sum its weighted positions (regardless of whether they are long or short) in order to calculate its capital requirement against specific risk.

For institutions which apply the rules for the risk weighting of exposures under Articles 84 to 89 of Directive 2006/48/EC, to qualify for a credit quality step the obligor of the exposure shall have an internal rating with a PD equivalent to or lower than that associated with the appropriate credit quality step under the rules for the risk weighting of exposures to corporates under Articles 78 to 83 of that Directive.

Instruments issued by a non-qualifying issuer shall receive a specific risk capital charge of 8% or 12% according to Table 1. Competent authorities may require institutions to apply a higher specific risk charge to such instruments and/or to disallow offsetting for the purposes of defining the extent of general market risk between such instruments and any other debt instruments.

Table 1

Categories	Specific risk capital charge
Debt securities issued or guaranteed by central governments, issued by central banks, international organisations, multilateral development banks or Member States' regional government or local authorities which would qualify for credit quality step 1 or which would receive a 0% risk weight under the rules for the risk weighting of exposures under Articles 78 to 83 of Directive 2006/48/EC.	0%
Debt securities issued or guaranteed by central governments, issued by central banks, international organisations, multilateral development banks or Member States' regional governments or local authorities which would qualify for credit quality step 2 or 3 under the rules for the risk weighting of exposures under Articles 78 to 83 of Directive 2006/48/EC, and debt securities issued or guaranteed by institutions which would qualify for credit quality step 1 or 2 under the rules for the risk weighting of exposures under Articles 78 to 83 of Directive 2006/48/EC, and debt securities issued or guaranteed by institutions which would qualify for credit quality step 3 under the rules for the risk weighting of exposures under point 28, Part 1 of Annex VI to Directive 2006/48/EC, and debt securities issued or guaranteed by corporates which would qualify for credit quality step 1 or 2 under the rules for the risk weighting of exposures under Articles 78 to 83 of Directive 2006/48/EC. Other qualifying items as defined in point 15.	0.25% (residual term to final maturity 6 months or less) 1.00% (residual term to final maturity greater than 6 and up to and including 24 months) 1.60% (residual term to final maturity exceeding 24 months)
Debt securities issued or guaranteed by central governments, issued by central banks, international organisations, multilateral development banks or Member States' regional governments or local authorities or institutions which would qualify for credit quality step 4 or 5 under the rules for the risk weighting of exposures under Articles 78 to 83 of Directive 2006/48/EC, and debt securities issued or guaranteed by institutions which would qualify for credit quality step 3 under the rules for the risk weighting of exposures under point 26 of Part 1 of Annex VI to Directive 2006/48/EC, and debt securities issued or guaranteed by corporates which would qualify for credit quality step 3 or 4 under the rules for the risk weighting of exposures under Articles 78 to 83 of Directive 2006/48/EC. Exposures for which a credit assessment by a nominated ECAI is not available.	8.00%
Debt securities issued or guaranteed by central governments, issued by central banks, international organisations, multilateral development banks or Member States' regional governments or local authorities or institutions which would qualify for credit quality step 6 under the rules for the risk weighting of exposures under Articles 78 to 83 of Directive 2006/48/EC, and debt securities issued or guaranteed by corporates which would qualify for credit quality step 5 or 6 under the rules for the risk weighting of exposures under Articles 78 to 83 of Directive 2006/48/EC.	12.00%

Securitisation exposures that would be subject to a deduction treatment as set out in Article 66(2) of Directive 2006/48/EC, or risk-weighted at 1,250% as set out in Part 4 of Annex IX to that Directive, shall be subject to a capital charge that is no less than that set out under those treatments. Unrated liquidity facilities shall be subject to a capital charge that is no less than that set out in Part 4 of Annex IX to Directive 2006/48/EC.

15. For the purposes of point 14 qualifying items shall include:

(a) long and short positions in assets qualifying for a credit quality step corresponding at least to investment grade in the mapping process described in Title V, Chapter 2, Section 3, Sub-section 1 of Directive 2006/48/EC;

(b) long and short positions in assets which, because of the solvency of the issuer, have a PD which is not higher than that of the assets referred to under (a), under the approach described in Title V, Chapter 2, Section 3, Sub-section 2 of Directive 2006/48/EC;

(c) long and short positions in assets for which a credit assessment by a nominated external credit assessment institution is not available and which meet the following conditions:

(i) they are considered by the institutions concerned to be sufficiently liquid;

(ii) their investment quality is, according to the institution's own discretion, at least equivalent to that of the assets referred to under point (a); and

(iii) they are listed on at least one regulated market in a Member State or on a stock exchange in a third country provided that the exchange is recognised by the competent authorities of the relevant Member State;

(d) long and short positions in assets issued by institutions subject to the capital adequacy requirements set out in Directive 2006/48/EC which are considered by the institutions concerned to be sufficiently liquid and whose investment quality is, according to the institution's own discretion, at least equivalent to that of the assets referred to under point (a); and

(e) securities issued by institutions that are deemed to be of equivalent, or higher, credit quality than those associated with credit quality step 2 under the rules for the risk weighting of exposures to institutions set out in Articles 78 to 83 of Directive 2006/48/EC and that are subject to supervisory and regulatory arrangements comparable to those under this Directive.

The manner in which the debt instruments are assessed shall be subject to scrutiny by the competent authorities, which shall overturn the judgment of the institution if they consider that the instruments concerned are subject to too high a degree of specific risk to be qualifying items.

16. The competent authorities shall require the institution to apply the maximum weighting shown in Table 1 to point 14 to instruments that show a particular risk because of the insufficient solvency of the issuer.

General risk

(a) *Maturity-based*

17. The procedure for calculating capital requirements against general risk involves two basic steps. First, all positions shall be weighted according to maturity (as explained in point 18), in order to compute the amount of capital required against them. Second, allowance shall be made for this requirement to be reduced when a weighted position is held alongside an opposite weighted position within the same maturity band. A reduction in the requirement shall also be allowed when the opposite weighted positions fall into different maturity bands, with the size of this reduction depending both on whether the two positions fall into the same zone, or not, and on the particular zones they fall into. There are three zones (groups of maturity bands) altogether.

18. The institution shall assign its net positions to the appropriate maturity bands in column 2 or 3, as appropriate, in Table 2 in point 20. It shall do so on the basis of residual maturity in the case of fixed-rate instruments and on the basis of the period until the interest rate is next set in the case of instruments on which the interest rate is variable before final maturity. It shall also distinguish between debt instruments with a coupon of 3%

or more and those with a coupon of less than 3% and thus allocate them to column 2 or column 3 in Table 2. It shall then multiply each of them by the weighing for the maturity band in question in column 4 in Table 2.

19. It shall then work out the sum of the weighted long positions and the sum of the weighted short positions in each maturity band. The amount of the former which are matched by the latter in a given maturity band shall be the matched weighted position in that band, while the residual long or short position shall be the unmatched weighted position for the same band. The total of the matched weighted positions in all bands shall then be calculated.

20. The institution shall compute the totals of the unmatched weighted long positions for the bands included in each of the zones in Table 2 in order to derive the unmatched weighted long position for each zone. Similarly, the sum of the unmatched weighted short positions for each band in a particular zone shall be summed to compute the unmatched weighted short position for that zone. That part of the unmatched weighted long position for a given zone that is matched by the unmatched weighted short position for the same zone shall be the matched weighted position for that zone. That part of the unmatched weighted long or unmatched weighted short position for a zone that cannot be thus matched shall be the unmatched weighted position for that zone.

21. The amount of the unmatched weighted long (short) position in zone one which is matched by the unmatched weighted short (long) position in zone two shall then be computed. This shall be referred to in point 25 as the matched weighted position between zones one and two. The same calculation shall then be undertaken with regard to that part of the unmatched weighted position in zone two which is left over and the unmatched weighted position in zone three in order to calculate the matched weighted position between zones two and three.

22. The institution may, if it wishes, reverse the order in point 21 so as to calculate the matched weighted position between zones two and three before calculating that position between zones one and two.

Table 2

Zone	Maturity band		Weighting (in%)	Assumed interest rate change (in%)
	Coupon of 3% or more	Coupon of less than 3%		
One	$0 \leq 1$ month	$0 \leq 1$ month	0.00	—
	$>1 \leq 3$ months	$>1 \leq 3$ months	0.20	1.00
	$>3 \leq 6$ months	$>3 \leq 6$ months	0.40	1.00
	$>6 \leq 12$ months	$>6 \leq 12$ months	0.70	1.00
Two	$>1 \leq 2$ years	$>1.0 \leq 1.9$ years	1.25	0.90
	$>2 \leq 3$ years	$>1.9 \leq 2.8$ years	1.75	0.80
	$>3 \leq 4$ years	$>2.8 \leq 3.6$ years	2.25	0.75
Three	$>4 \leq 5$ years	$>3.6 \leq 4.3$ years	2.75	0.75
	$>5 \leq 7$ years	$>4.3 \leq 5.7$ years	3.25	0.70
	$>7 \leq 10$ years	$>5.7 \leq 7.3$ years	3.75	0.65
	$>10 \leq 15$ years	$>7.3 \leq 9.3$ years	4.50	0.60
	$>15 \leq 20$ years	$>9.3 \leq 10.6$ years	5.25	0.60
	>20 years	$>10.6 \leq 12.0$ years	6.00	0.60
		$>12.0 \leq 20.0$ years	8.00	0.60
		>20 years	12.50	0.60

23. The remainder of the unmatched weighted position in zone one shall then be matched with what remains of that for zone three after the latter's matching with zone two in order to derive the matched weighted position between zones one and three.

24. Residual positions, following the three separate matching calculations in points 21, 22 and 23, shall be summed.

25. The institution's capital requirement shall be calculated as the sum of:

(a) 10% of the sum of the matched weighted positions in all maturity bands;

(b) 40% of the matched weighted position in zone one;

(c) 30% of the matched weighted position in zone two;

(d) 30% of the matched weighted position in zone three;

(e) 40% of the matched weighted position between zones one and two and between zones two and three (see point 21);

(f) 150% of the matched weighted position between zones one and three; and

(g) 100% of the residual unmatched weighted positions.

(b) *Duration-based*

26. The competent authorities may allow institutions in general or on an individual basis to use a system for calculating the capital requirement for the general risk on traded debt instruments which reflects duration, instead of the system set out in points 17 to 25, provided that the institution does so on a consistent basis.

27. Under a system referred to in point 26 the institution shall take the market value of each fixed-rate debt instrument and thence calculate its yield to maturity, which is implied discount rate for that instrument. In the case of floating-rate instruments, the institution shall take the market value of each instrument and thence calculate its yield on the assumption that the principal is due when the interest rate can next be changed.

28. The institution shall then calculate the modified duration of each debt instrument on the basis of the following formula: modified duration = ((duration (D))/(1 + r)), where:

$$D = ((\Sigma_t = 1^m ((tC_t)/((1+r)^t)))/\Sigma_t = 1^m ((C_t)/((1+r)^t)))$$

where:

R = yield to maturity (see point 25),

Ct = cash payment in time t,

M = total maturity (see point 25).

29. The institution shall then allocate each debt instrument to the appropriate zone in Table 3. It shall do so on the basis of the modified duration of each instrument.

30. The institution shall then calculate the duration-weighted position for each instrument by multiplying its market price by its modified duration and by the assumed interest-rate change for an instrument with that particular modified duration (see column 3 in Table 3).

31. The institution shall calculate its duration-weighted long and its duration-weighted short positions within each zone. The amount of the former which are matched by the latter within each zone shall be the matched duration-weighted position for that zone.

The institution shall then calculate the unmatched duration-weighted positions for each zone. It shall then follow the procedures laid down for unmatched weighted positions in points 21 to 24.

32. The institution's capital requirement shall then be calculated as the sum of:

(a) 2% of the matched duration-weighted position for each zone;

(b) 40% of the matched duration-weighted positions between zones one and two and between zones two and three;

(c) 150% of the matched duration-weighted position between zones one and three; and

Table 3

Zone	Modified duration (in years)	Assumed interest (change in%)
One	$>0 \leq 1.0$	1.0
Two	$>1.0 \leq 3.6$	0.85
Three	>3.6	0.7

(d) 100% of the residual unmatched duration-weighted positions.

EQUITIES

33. The institution shall sum all its net long positions and all its net short positions in accordance with point 1. The sum of the two figures shall be its overall gross position. The difference between them shall be its overall net position.

Specific risk

34. The institution shall sum all its net long positions and all its net short positions in accordance with point 1. It shall multiply its overall gross position by 4% in order to calculate its capital requirement against specific risk.

35. By derogation from point 34, the competent authorities may allow the capital requirement against specific risk to be 2% rather than 4% for those portfolios of equities that an institution holds which meet the following conditions:

(a) the equities shall not be those of issuers which have issued only traded debt instruments that currently attract an 8% or 12% requirement in Table 1 to point 14 or that attract a lower requirement only because they are guaranteed or secured;

(b) the equities must be adjudged highly liquid by the competent authorities according to objective criteria; and

(c) no individual position shall comprise more than 5% of the value of the institution's whole equity portfolio.

For the purpose of point (c), the competent authorities may authorise individual positions of up to 10% provided that the total of such positions does not exceed 50% of the portfolio.

General risk

36. Its capital requirement against general risk shall be its overall net position multiplied by 8%.

Stock-index futures

37. Stock-index futures, the delta-weighted equivalents of options in stock-index futures and stock indices collectively referred to hereafter as "stock-index futures", may be broken down into positions in each of their constituent equities. These positions may be treated as underlying positions in the equities in question, and may, subject to the approval of the competent authorities, be netted against opposite positions in the underlying equities themselves.

38. The competent authorities shall ensure that any institution which has netted off its positions in one or more of the equities constituting a stock-index future against one or more positions in the stock-index future itself has adequate capital to cover the risk of loss caused by the future's values not moving fully in line with that of its constituent equities; they shall also do this when an institution holds opposite positions in stock-index futures which are not identical in respect of either their maturity or their composition or both.

39. By derogation from points 37 and 38, stock-index futures which are exchange traded and—in the opinion of the competent authorities—represent broadly diversified indices shall attract a capital requirement against general risk of 8%, but no capital requirement against specific risk. Such stock-index futures shall be included in the calculation of the overall net position in point 33, but disregarded in the calculation of the overall gross position in the same point.

40. If a stock-index future is not broken down into its underlying positions, it shall be treated as if it were an individual equity. However, the specific risk on this individual equity can be ignored if the stock-index future in question is exchange traded and, in the opinion of the competent authorities, represents a broadly diversified index.

UNDERWRITING

41. In the case of the underwriting of debt and equity instruments, the competent authorities may allow an institution to use the following procedure in calculating its capital requirements. Firstly, it shall calculate the net positions by deducting the underwriting positions which are subscribed or sub-underwritten by third parties

Table 4

working day 0:	100%
working day 1:	90%
working days 2 to 3:	75%
working day 4:	50%
working day 5:	25%
after working day 5:	0%

on the basis of formal agreements. Secondly, it shall reduce the net positions by the reduction factors in Table 4.

'Working day zero' shall be the working day on which the institution becomes unconditionally committed to accepting a known quantity of securities at an agreed price.

Thirdly, it shall calculate its capital requirements using the reduced underwriting positions.

The competent authorities shall ensure that the institution holds sufficient capital against the risk of loss which exists between the time of the initial commitment and working day 1.

Specific Risk Capital Charges for Trading Book Positions Hedged by Credit Derivatives

42. An allowance shall be given for protection provided by credit derivatives, in accordance with the principles set out in points 43 to 46.

43. Full allowance shall be given when the value of two legs always move in the opposite direction and broadly to the same extent. This will be the case in the following situations:

(a) the two legs consist of completely identical instruments; or

(b) a long cash position is hedged by a total rate of return swap (or vice versa) and there is an exact match between the reference obligation and the underlying exposure (i.e., the cash position). The maturity of the swap itself may be different from that of the underlying exposure.

In these situations, a specific risk capital charge should not be applied to either side of the position.

44. An 80% offset will be applied when the value of two legs always move in the opposite direction and where there is an exact match in terms of the reference obligation, the maturity of both the reference obligation and the credit derivative, and the currency of the underlying exposure. In addition, key features of the credit derivative contract should not cause the price movement of the credit derivative to materially deviate from the price movements of the cash position. To the extent that the transaction transfers risk, an 80% specific risk offset will be applied to the side of the transaction with the higher capital charge, while the specific risk requirements on the other side shall be zero.

45. Partial allowance shall be given when the value of two legs usually move in the opposite direction. This would be the case in the following situations:

(a) the position falls under point 43(b) but there is an asset mismatch between the reference obligation and the underlying exposure. However, the positions meet the following requirements:
 (i) the reference obligation ranks pari passu with or is junior to the underlying obligation; and
 (ii) the underlying obligation and reference obligation share the same obligor and have legally enforceable cross-default or cross-acceleration clauses;

(b) the position falls under point 43(a) or point 44 but there is a currency or maturity mismatch between the credit protection and the underlying asset (currency mismatches should be included in the normal reporting foreign exchange risk under Annex III); or

(c) the position falls under point 44 but there is an asset mismatch between the cash position and the credit derivative. However, the underlying asset is included in the (deliverable) obligations in the credit derivative documentation.

In each of those situations, rather than adding the specific risk capital requirements for each side of the transaction, only the higher of the two capital requirements shall apply.

46. In all situations not falling under points 43 to 45, a specific risk capital charge will be assessed against both sides of the positions.

Capital charges for CIUs in the trading book

47. The capital requirements for positions in CIUs which meet the conditions specified in Article 11 for a trading book capital treatment shall be calculated in accordance with the methods set out in points 48 to 56.

48. Without prejudice to other provisions in this section, positions in CIUs shall be subject to a capital requirement for position risk (specific and general) of 32%. Without prejudice to the provisions of the fourth paragraph of point 2.1 of Annex III or the sixth paragraph of point 12 of Annex V (commodity risk) taken together with the fourth paragraph of point 2.1 of Annex III, where the modified gold treatment set out in those points is used, positions in CIUs shall be subject to a capital requirement for position risk (specific and general) and foreign-exchange risk of no more than 40%.

49. Institutions may determine the capital requirement for positions in CIUs which meet the criteria set out in point 51, by the methods set out in points 53 to 56.

50. Unless noted otherwise, no netting is permitted between the underlying investments of a CIU and other positions held by the institution.

GENERAL CRITERIA

51. The general eligibility criteria for using the methods in points 53 to 56, for CIUs issued by companies supervised or incorporated within the Community are that:

(a) the CIU's prospectus or equivalent document shall include:
(i) the categories of assets the CIU is authorised to invest in;
(ii) if investment limits apply, the relative limits and the methodologies to calculate them;
(iii) if leverage is allowed, the maximum level of leverage; and
(iv) if investment in OTC financial derivatives or repo-style transactions are allowed, a policy to limit counterparty risk arising from these transactions;

(b) the business of the CIU shall be reported in half-yearly and annual reports to enable an assessment to be made of the assets and liabilities, income and operations over the reporting period;

(c) the units/shares of the CIU are redeemable in cash, out of the undertaking's assets, on a daily basis at the request of the unit holder;

(d) investments in the CIU shall be segregated from the assets of the CIU manager; and

(e) there shall be adequate risk assessment of the CIU, by the investing institution.

52. Third country CIUs may be eligible if the requirements in points (a) to (e) of point 51 are met, subject to the approval of the institution's competent authority.

SPECIFIC METHODS

53. Where the institution is aware of the underlying investments of the CIU on a daily basis, the institution may look through to those underlying investments in order to calculate the capital requirements for position risk (general and specific) for those positions in accordance with the methods set out in this Annex or, if permission has been granted, in accordance with the methods set out in Annex V. Under this approach, positions in CIUs shall be treated as positions in the underlying investments of the CIU. Netting is permitted between positions in the underlying investments of the CIU and other positions held by the institution, as long as the institution holds a sufficient quantity of units to allow for redemption/creation in exchange for the underlying investments.

54. Institutions may calculate the capital requirements for position risk (general and specific) for positions in CIUs in accordance with the methods set out in this Annex or, if permission has been granted, in accordance with the methods set out in Annex V, to assumed positions representing those necessary to replicate the composition and performance of the externally generated index or fixed basket of equities or debt securities referred to in (a), subject to the following conditions

(a) the purpose of the CIU's mandate is to replicate the composition and performance of an externally generated index or fixed basket of equities or debt securities; and

(b) a minimum correlation of 0.9 between daily price movements of the CIU and the index or basket of equities or debt securities it tracks can be clearly established over a minimum period of six months. "Correlation" in this context means the correlation coefficient between daily returns on the CIU and the index or basket of equities or debt securities it tracks.

55. Where the institution is not aware of the underlying investments of the CIU on a daily basis, the institution may calculate the capital requirements for position risk (general and specific) in accordance with the methods set out in this Annex, subject to the following conditions:

(a) it will be assumed that the CIU first invests to the maximum extent allowed under its mandate in the asset classes attracting the highest capital requirement for position risk (general and specific), and then continues making investments in descending order until the maximum total investment limit is reached. The position in the CIU will be treated as a direct holding in the assumed position;

(b) institutions shall take account of the maximum indirect exposure that they could achieve by taking leveraged positions through the CIU when calculating their capital requirement for position risk, by proportionally increasing the position in the CIU up to the maximum exposure to the underlying investment items resulting from the mandate; and

(c) should the capital requirement for position risk (general and specific) according to this point exceed that set out in point 48, the capital requirement shall be capped at that level.

56. Institutions may rely on a third party to calculate and report capital requirements for position risk (general and specific) for positions in CIUs falling under points 53 and 55, in accordance with the methods set out in this Annex, provided that the correctness of the calculation and the report is adequately ensured.

Annex II

Calculating Capital Requiremetns for Settlement and Counterparty Credit Risk

Settlement/Delivery Risk

1. In the case of transactions in which debt instruments, equities, foreign currencies and commodities (excluding repurchase and reverse repurchase agreements and securities or commodities lending and securities or commodities borrowing) are unsettled after their due delivery dates, an institution must calculate the price difference to which it is exposed. This is the difference between the agreed settlement price for the debt instrument, equity, foreign currency or commodity in question and its current market value, where the difference could involve a loss for the institution. It must multiply this difference by the appropriate factor in column A of Table 1 in order to calculate its capital requirement.

Free Deliveries

2. An institution shall be required to hold own funds, as set out in Table 2, if:

(a) it has paid for securities, foreign currencies or commodities before receiving them or it has delivered securities, foreign currencies or

Table 1

Number of working days after due settlement date	(%)
5–15	8
16–30	50
31–45	75
46 or more	100

Table 2 Capital treatment for free deliveries

Transaction Type	Up to first contractual payment or delivery leg	From first contractual payment or delivery leg up to four days after second contractual payment or delivery leg	From 5 business days post second contractual payment or delivery leg until extinction of the transaction
Free delivery	No capital charge	Treat as an exposure	Deduct value transferred plus current positive exposure from own funds

commodities before receiving payment for them; and

(b) in the case of cross border transactions, one day or more has elapsed since it made that payment or delivery.

3. In applying a risk weight to free delivery exposures treated according to column 3 of Table 2, institutions using the approach set out in Articles 84 to 89 of Directive 2006/48/EC, may assign PDs to counterparties, for which they have no other non-trading book exposure, on the basis of the counterparty's external rating. Institutions using own estimates of loss given defaults ('LGDs') may apply the LGD set out in point 8 of Part 2 of Annex VII to Directive 2006/48/EC to free delivery exposures treated according to column 3 of Table 2 provided that they apply it to all such exposures. Alternatively, institutions using the approach set out in Articles 84 to 89 of Directive 2006/48/EC may apply the risk weights, as set out in Articles 78 to 83 of that Directive provided that they apply them to all such exposures or may apply a 100% risk weight to all such exposures.

If the amount of positive exposure resulting from free delivery transactions is not material, institutions may apply a risk weight of 100% to these exposures.

4. In cases of a system wide failure of a settlement or clearing system, competent authorities may waive the capital requirements calculated as set out in points 1 and 2 until the situation is rectified. In this case, the failure of a counterparty to settle a trade shall not be deemed a default for purposes of credit risk.

COUNTERPARTY CREDIT RISK (CCR)

5. An institution shall be required to hold capital against the CCR arising from exposures due to the following:

(a) OTC derivative instruments and credit derivatives;

(b) repurchase agreements, reverse repurchase agreements, securities or commodities lending or borrowing transactions based on securities or commodities included in the trading book;

(c) margin lending transactions based on securities or commodities; and

(d) long settlement transactions.

6. Subject to the provisions of points 7 to 10, exposure values and risk-weighted exposure amounts for such exposures shall be calculated in accordance with the provisions of Section 3 of Chapter 2 of Title V of Directive 2006/48/EC with references to 'credit institutions' in that Section interpreted as references to 'institutions', references to 'parent credit institutions' interpreted as references to 'parent institutions', and with concomitant terms interpreted accordingly.

7. For the purposes of point 6:

Annex IV to Directive 2006/48/EC shall be considered to be amended to include point 8 of Section C of Annex I to Directive 2004/39/EC;

Annex III to Directive 2006/48/EC shall be considered to be amended to include, after the footnotes of Table 1, the following text:

'To obtain a figure for potential future credit exposure in the case of total return swap credit

derivatives and credit default swap credit derivatives, the nominal amount of the instrument is multiplied by the following percentages:
- where the reference obligation is one that if it gave rise to a direct exposure of the institution it would be a qualifying item for the purposes of Annex I: 5%; and
- where the reference obligation is one that if it gave rise to a direct exposure of the institution it would not be a qualifying item for the purposes of Annex I: 10%.

However, in the case of a credit default swap, an institution the exposure of which arising from the swap represents a long position in the underlying shall be permitted to use a figure of 0% for potential future credit exposure, unless the credit default swap is subject to closeout upon the insolvency of the entity the exposure of which arising from the swap represents a short position in the underlying, even though the underlying has not defaulted.'

Where the credit derivative provides protection in relation to 'nth to default' amongst a number of underlying obligations, which of the percentage figures prescribed above is to be applied is determined by the obligation with the nth lowest credit quality determined by whether it is one that if incurred by the institution would be a qualifying item for the purposes of Annex I.

8. For the purposes of point 6, in calculating risk-weighted exposure amounts institutions shall not be permitted to use the Financial Collateral Simple Method, set out in points 24 to 29, Part 3, Annex VIII to Directive 2006/48/EC, for the recognition of the effects of financial collateral.

9. For the purposes of point 6, in the case of repurchase transactions and securities or commodities lending or borrowing transactions booked in the trading book, all financial instruments and commodities that are eligible to be included in the trading book may be recognised as eligible collateral. For exposures due to OTC derivative instruments booked in the trading book, commodities that are eligible to be included in the trading book may also be recognised as eligible collateral. For the purposes of calculating volatility adjustments where such financial instruments or commodities which are not eligible under Annex VIII of Directive 2006/48/EC are lent, sold or provided, or borrowed, purchased or received by way of collateral or otherwise under such a transaction, and the institution is using the Supervisory Volatility adjustments approach under Part 3 of Annex VIII to that Directive, such instruments and commodities shall be treated in the same way as non-main index equities listed on a recognised exchange.

Where institutions are using the Own Estimates of Volatility adjustments approach under Part 3 of Annex VIII to Directive 2006/48/EC in respect of financial instruments or commodities which are not eligible under Annex VIII of that Directive, volatility adjustments must be calculated for each individual item. Where institutions are using the Internal Models Approach defined in Part 3 of Annex VIII to Directive 2006/48/EC, they may also apply this approach in the trading book.

10. For the purposes of point 6, in relation to the recognition of master netting agreements covering repurchase transactions and/or securities or commodities lending or borrowing transactions and/or other capital market-driven transactions netting across positions in the trading book and the non-trading book will only be recognised when the netted transactions fulfil the following conditions:

(a) all transactions are marked-to-market daily; and

(b) any items borrowed, purchased or received under the transactions may be recognised as eligible financial collateral under Title V, Chapter 2, Section 3, Subsection 3 of Directive 2006/48/EC without the application of point 9 of this Annex.

11. Where a credit derivative included in the trading book forms part of an internal hedge and the credit protection is recognised under Directive 2006/48/EC, there shall be deemed not to be counterparty risk arising from the position in the credit derivative.

12. The capital requirement shall be 8% of the total risk-weighted exposure amounts.

Annex III

Calculating Capital Requirements for Foreign-Exchange Risk

1. If the sum of an institution's overall net foreign-exchange position and its net gold position, calculated in accordance with the procedure set out in point 2, exceeds 2% of its total own funds, it shall multiply the sum of its net foreign-exchange position and its net gold position by 8% in order to calculate its own-funds requirement against foreign-exchange risk.

2. A two-stage calculation shall be used for capital requirements for foreign-exchange risk.

2.1. Firstly, the institution's net open position in each currency (including the reporting currency) and in gold shall be calculated.

This net open position shall consist of the sum of the following elements (positive or negative):

(a) the net spot position (i.e. all asset items less all liability items, including accrued interest, in the currency in question or, for gold, the net spot position in gold);

(b) the net forward position (i.e. all amounts to be received less all amounts to be paid under forward exchange and gold transactions, including currency and gold futures and the principal on currency swaps not included in the spot position);

(c) irrevocable guarantees (and similar instruments) that are certain to be called and likely to be irrecoverable;

(d) net future income/expenses not yet accrued but already fully hedged (at the discretion of the reporting institution and with the prior consent of the competent authorities, net future income/expenses not yet entered in accounting records but already fully hedged by forward foreign-exchange transactions may be included here). Such discretion must be exercised on a consistent basis;

(e) the net delta (or delta-based) equivalent of the total book of foreign-currency and gold options; and

(f) the market value of other (i.e. non-foreign-currency and non-gold) options.

Any positions which an institution has deliberately taken in order to hedge against the adverse effect of the exchange rate on its capital ratio may be excluded from the calculation of net open currency positions. Such positions should be of a non-trading or structural nature and their exclusion, and any variation of the terms of their exclusion, shall require the consent of the competent authorities. The same treatment subject to the same conditions as above may be applied to positions which an institution has which relate to items that are already deducted in the calculation of own funds.

For the purposes of the calculation referred to in the first paragraph, in respect of CIUs the actual foreign-exchange positions of the CIU shall be taken into account. Institutions may rely on third party reporting of the foreign-exchange positions in the CIU, where the correctness of this report is adequately ensured. If an institution is not aware of the foreign-exchange positions in a CIU, it shall be assumed that the CIU is invested up to the maximum extent allowed under the CIU's mandate in foreign exchange and institutions shall, for trading book positions, take account of the maximum indirect exposure that they could achieve by taking leveraged positions through the CIU when calculating their capital requirement for foreign-exchange risk. This shall be done by proportionally increasing the position in the CIU up to the maximum exposure to the underlying investment items resulting from the investment mandate. The assumed position of the CIU in foreign exchange shall be treated as a separate currency according to the treatment of investments in gold, subject to the modification that, if the direction of the CIU's investment is available, the total long position may be added to the total long open foreign exchange position and the total short position may be added to the total short open foreign exchange position. There would be no netting allowed between such positions prior to the calculation.

The competent authorities shall have the discretion to allow institutions to use the net present value when calculating the net open position in each currency and in gold.

2.2. Secondly, net short and long positions in each currency other than the reporting currency and the net long or short position in gold shall be converted at spot rates into the reporting currency. They shall then be summed separately to form the total of the net short positions and the total of the net long positions respectively. The higher of these two totals shall be the institution's overall net foreign-exchange position.

3. By derogation from points 1 and 2 and pending further coordination, the competent authorities may prescribe or allow institutions to use the following procedures for the purposes of this Annex.

3.1. The competent authorities may allow institutions to provide lower capital requirements against positions in closely correlated currencies than those which would result from applying points 1 and 2 to them. The competent authorities may deem a pair of currencies to be closely correlated only if the likelihood of a loss—calculated on the basis of daily exchange-rate data for the preceding three or five years—occurring on equal and opposite positions in such currencies over the following 10 working days, which is 4% or less of the value of the matched position in question (valued in terms of the reporting currency) has a probability of at least 99%, when an observation period of three years is used, or 95%, when an observation period of five years is used.

The own-funds requirement on the matched position in two closely correlated currencies shall be 4% multiplied by the value of the matched position. The capital requirement on unmatched positions in closely correlated currencies, and all positions in other currencies, shall be 8%, multiplied by the higher of the sum of the net short or the net long positions in those currencies after the removal of matched positions in closely correlated currencies.

3.2. The competent authorities may allow institutions to remove positions in any currency which is subject to a legally binding intergovernmental agreement to limit its variation relative to other currencies covered by the same agreement from whichever of the methods described in points 1, 2 and 3.1 that they apply. Institutions shall calculate their matched positions in such currencies and subject them to a capital requirement no lower than half of the maximum permissible variation laid down in the intergovernmental agreement in question in respect of the currencies concerned. Unmatched positions in those currencies shall be treated in the same way as other currencies.

By derogation from the first paragraph, the competent authorities may allow the capital requirement on the matched positions in currencies of Member States participating in the second stage of the economic and monetary union to be 1.6%, multiplied by the value of such matched positions.

4. Net positions in composite currencies may be broken down into the component currencies according to the quotas in force.

Annex IV

Calculating Capital Requirements for Commodities Risk

1. Each position in commodities or commodity derivatives shall be expressed in terms of the standard unit of measurement. The spot price in each commodity shall be expressed in the reporting currency.

2. Positions in gold or gold derivatives shall be considered as being subject to foreign-exchange risk and treated according to Annex III or Annex V, as appropriate, for the purpose of calculating market risk.

3. For the purposes of this Annex, positions which are purely stock financing may be excluded from the commodities risk calculation only.

4. The interest-rate and foreign-exchange risks not covered by other provisions of this Annex shall be included in the calculation of general risk for traded debt instruments and in the calculation of foreign-exchange risk.

5. When the short position falls due before the long position, institutions shall also guard against the risk of a shortage of liquidity which may exist in some markets.

6. For the purpose of point 19, the excess of an institution's long (short) positions over its short (long) positions in the same commodity and identical commodity futures, options and warrants shall be its net position in each commodity.

The competent authorities shall allow positions in derivative instruments to be treated, as laid down in points 8, 9 and 10, as positions in the underlying commodity.

7. The competent authorities may regard the following positions as positions in the same commodity:

(a) positions in different sub-categories of commodities in cases where the sub-categories are deliverable against each other; and

(b) positions in similar commodities if they are close substitutes and if a minimum correlation of 0.9 between price movements can be clearly established over a minimum period of one year.

Particular instruments

8. Commodity futures and forward commitments to buy or sell individual commodities shall be incorporated in the measurement system as notional amounts in terms of the standard unit of measurement and assigned a maturity with reference to expiry date.

The competent authorities may allow the capital requirement for an exchange-traded future to be equal to the margin required by the exchange if they are fully satisfied that it provides an accurate measure of the risk associated with the future and that it is at least equal to the capital requirement for a future that would result from a calculation made using the method set out in the remainder of this Annex or applying the internal models method described in Annex V.

The competent authorities may also allow the capital requirement for an OTC commodity derivatives contract of the type referred to in this point cleared by a clearing house recognised by them to be equal to the margin required by the clearing house if they are fully satisfied that it provides an accurate measure of the risk associated with the derivatives contract and that it is at least equal to the capital requirement for the contract in question that would result from a calculation made using the method set out in the remainder of this Annex or applying the internal models method described in Annex V.

9. Commodity swaps where one side of the transaction is a fixed price and the other the current market price shall be incorporated into the maturity ladder approach, as set out in points 13 to 18, as a series of positions equal to the notional amount of the contract, with one position corresponding with each payment on the swap and slotted into the maturity ladder set out in Table 1 to point 13. The positions would be long positions if the institution is paying a fixed price and receiving a floating price and short positions if the institution is receiving a fixed price and paying a floating price.

Commodity swaps where the sides of the transaction are in different commodities are to be reported in the relevant reporting ladder for the maturity ladder approach.

10. Options on commodities or on commodity derivatives shall be treated as if they were positions equal in value to the amount of the underlying to which the option refers, multiplied by its delta for the purposes of this Annex. The latter positions may be netted off against any offsetting positions in the identical underlying commodity or commodity derivative. The delta used shall be that of the exchange concerned, that calculated by the competent authorities or, where none of those is available, or for OTC options, that calculated by the institution itself, subject to the competent authorities being satisfied that the model used by the institution is reasonable.

However, the competent authorities may also prescribe that institutions calculate their deltas using a methodology specified by the competent authorities.

Other risks, apart from the delta risk, associated with commodity options shall be safeguarded against.

The competent authorities may allow the requirement for a written exchange-traded commodity option to be equal to the margin required by the exchange if they are fully satisfied that it provides an accurate measure of the risk associated with the option and that it is at least equal to the capital requirement against an option that would result from a calculation made using the method set out in the remainder of this Annex or applying the internal models method described in Annex V.

The competent authorities may also allow the capital requirement for an OTC commodity option cleared by a clearing house recognised by them to be equal to the margin required by the clearing house if they are fully satisfied that it provides an accurate measure of the risk associated with the option and that it is at least equal to the capital requirement for an OTC option that would result from a calculation made using the method set out in the remainder of this Annex or applying the internal models method described in Annex V.

In addition they may allow the requirement on a bought exchange-traded or OTC commodity option to be the same as that for the commodity underlying it, subject to the constraint that the resulting requirement does not exceed the market value of the option. The requirement for a written OTC option shall be set in relation to the commodity underlying it.

11. Warrants relating to commodities shall be treated in the same way as commodity options referred to in point 10.

12. The transferor of commodities or guaranteed rights relating to title to commodities in a repurchase agreement and the lender of commodities in a commodities lending agreement shall include such commodities in the calculation of its capital requirement under this Annex.

(a) *Maturity ladder approach*

13. The institution shall use a separate maturity ladder in line with Table 1 for each commodity.

Table 1

Maturity band (1)	Spread rate (in%) (2)
$0 \leq 1$ month	1.50
$>1 \leq 3$ months	1.50
$>3 \leq 6$ months	1.50
$>6 \leq 12$ months	1.50
$>1 \leq 2$ years	1.50
$>2 \leq 3$ years	1.50
>3 years	1.50

All positions in that commodity and all positions which are regarded as positions in the same commodity pursuant to point 7 shall be assigned to the appropriate maturity bands. Physical stocks shall be assigned to the first maturity band.

14. Competent authorities may allow positions which are, or are regarded pursuant to point 7 as, positions in the same commodity to be offset and assigned to the appropriate maturity bands on a net basis for the following:

(a) positions in contracts maturing on the same date; and

(b) positions in contracts maturing within 10 days of each other if the contracts are traded on markets which have daily delivery dates.

15. The institution shall then calculate the sum of the long positions and the sum of the short positions in each maturity band. The amount of the former (latter) which are matched by the latter (former) in a given maturity band shall be the matched positions in that band, while the residual long or short position shall be the unmatched position for the same band.

16. That part of the unmatched long (short) position for a given maturity band that is matched by the unmatched short (long) position for a maturity band further out shall be the matched position between two maturity bands. That part of the unmatched long or unmatched short position that cannot be thus matched shall be the unmatched position.

17. The institution's capital requirement for each commodity shall be calculated on the basis

Table 2

	Precious metals (except gold)	Base metals	Agricultural products (softs)	Other, including energy products
Spread rate (%)	1.0	1.2	1.5	1.5
Carry rate (%)	0.3	0.5	0.6	0.6
Outright rate (%)	8	10	12	15

of the relevant maturity ladder as the sum of the following:

(a) the sum of the matched long and short positions, multiplied by the appropriate spread rate as indicated in the second column of Table 1 to point 13 for each maturity band and by the spot price for the commodity;

(b) the matched position between two maturity bands for each maturity band into which an unmatched position is carried forward, multiplied by 0.6% (carry rate) and by the spot price for the commodity; and

(c) the residual unmatched positions, multiplied by 15% (outright rate) and by the spot price for the commodity.

18. The institution's overall capital requirement for commodities risk shall be calculated as the sum of the capital requirements calculated for each commodity according to point 17.

(b) *Simplified approach*

19. The institution's capital requirement for each commodity shall be calculated as the sum of:

(a) 15% of the net position, long or short, multiplied by the spot price for the commodity; and

(b) 3% of the gross position, long plus short, multiplied by the spot price for the commodity.

20. The institution's overall capital requirement for commodities risk shall be calculated as the sum of the capital requirements calculated for each commodity according to point 19.

(c) *Extended Maturity ladder approach*

21. Competent authorities may authorise institutions to use the minimum spread, carry and outright rates set out in the following table (Table 2) instead of those indicated in points 13, 14, 17 and 18 provided that the institutions, in the opinion of their competent authorities:

(a) undertake significant commodities business;

(b) have a diversified commodities portfolio; and

(c) are not yet in a position to use internal models for the purpose of calculating the capital requirement on commodities risk in accordance with Annex V.

Annex V

Use of Internal Models to Calculate Capital Requirements

1. The competent authorities may, subject to the conditions laid down in this Annex, allow institutions to calculate their capital requirements for position risk, foreign-exchange risk and/or commodities risk using their own internal risk-management models instead of or in combination with the methods described in Annexes I, III and IV. Explicit recognition by the competent authorities of the use of models for supervisory capital purposes shall be required in each case.

2. Recognition shall only be given if the competent authority is satisfied that the institution's risk-management system is conceptually sound and implemented with integrity and that, in particular, the following qualitative standards are met:

(a) the internal risk-measurement model is closely integrated into the daily risk-management process of the institution and serves as the basis for reporting risk exposures to senior management of the institution;

(b) the institution has a risk control unit that is independent from business trading units and reports directly to senior management. The unit must be responsible for designing and implementing the institution's risk-management system. It shall produce and analyse daily reports on the output of the risk-measurement model and on the appropriate measures to be taken in terms of trading limits. The unit shall also conduct the initial and on-going validation of the internal model;

(c) the institution's board of directors and senior management are actively involved in the risk-control process and the daily reports produced by the risk-control unit are reviewed by a level of management with sufficient authority to enforce both reductions of positions taken by individual traders as well as in the institution's overall risk exposure;

(d) the institution has sufficient numbers of staff skilled in the use of sophisticated models in the trading, risk-control, audit and back-office areas;

(e) the institution has established procedures for monitoring and ensuring compliance with a documented set of internal policies and controls concerning the overall operation of the risk-measurement system;

(f) the institution's model has a proven track record of reasonable accuracy in measuring risks;

(g) the institution frequently conducts a rigorous programme of stress testing and the results of these tests are reviewed by senior management and reflected in the policies and limits it sets. This process shall particularly address illiquidity of markets in stressed market conditions, concentration risk, one way markets, event and jump-to-default risks, non-linearity of products, deep out-of-the-money positions, positions subject to the gapping of prices and other risks that may not be captured appropriately in the internal models. The shocks applied shall reflect the nature of the portfolios and the time it could take to hedge out or manage risks under severe market conditions; and

(h) the institution must conduct, as part of its regular internal auditing process, an independent review of its risk-measurement system.

The review referred to in point (h) of the first paragraph shall include both the activities of the business trading units and of the independent risk-control unit. At least once a year, the institution must conduct a review of its overall risk-management process.

The review shall consider the following:

(a) the adequacy of the documentation of the risk-management system and process and the organisation of the risk-control unit;

(b) the integration of market risk measures into daily risk management and the integrity of the management information system;

(c) the process the institution employs for approving risk-pricing models and valuation systems that are used by front- and back-office personnel;

(d) the scope of market risks captured by the risk-measurement model and the validation of any significant changes in the risk-measurement process;

(e) the accuracy and completeness of position data, the accuracy and appropriateness of volatility and correlation assumptions, and the accuracy of valuation and risk sensitivity calculations;

(f) the verification process the institution employs to evaluate the consistency, timeliness and reliability of data sources used to run internal models, including the independence of such data sources; and

(g) the verification process the institution uses to evaluate back-testing that is conducted to assess the models' accuracy.

3. Institutions shall have processes in place to ensure that their internal models have been adequately validated by suitably qualified parties independent of the development process to ensure that they are conceptually sound and adequately capture all material risks. The validation shall be conducted when the internal model is initially developed and when any significant changes are made to the internal model.

The validation shall also be conducted on a periodic basis but especially where there have been any significant structural changes in the market or changes to the composition of the portfolio which might lead to the internal model no longer being adequate. As techniques and best practices evolve, institutions shall avail themselves of these advances. Internal model validation shall not be limited to back-testing, but shall, at a minimum, also include the following:

(a) tests to demonstrate that any assumptions made within the internal model are appropriate and do not underestimate or overestimate the risk;

(b) in addition to the regulatory back-testing programmes, institutions shall carry out their own internal model validation tests in relation to the risks and structures of their portfolios; and

(c) the use of hypothetical portfolios to ensure that the internal model is able to account for particular structural features that may arise, for example material basis risks and concentration risk.

4. The institution shall monitor the accuracy and performance of its model by conducting a back-testing programme. The back-testing has to provide for each business day a comparison of the one-day value-at-risk measure generated by the institution's model for the portfolio's end-of-day positions to the one-day change of the portfolio's value by the end of the subsequent business day.

Competent authorities shall examine the institution's capability to perform back-testing on both actual and hypothetical changes in the portfolio's value. Back-testing on hypothetical changes in the portfolio's value is based on a comparison between the portfolio's end-of-day value and, assuming unchanged positions, its value at the end of the subsequent day. Competent authorities shall require institutions to take appropriate measures to improve their back-testing programme if deemed deficient. Competent authorities may require institutions to perform back-testing on either hypothetical (using changes in portfolio value that would occur were end-of-day positions to remain unchanged), or actual trading (excluding fees, commissions, and net interest income) outcomes, or both.

5. For the purpose of calculating capital requirements for specific risk associated with traded debt and equity positions, the competent authorities may recognise the use of an institution's internal model if, in addition to compliance with the conditions in the remainder of this Annex, the internal model meets the following conditions:

(a) it explains the historical price variation in the portfolio;

(b) it captures concentration in terms of magnitude and changes of composition of the portfolio;

(c) it is robust to an adverse environment;

(d) it is validated through back-testing aimed at assessing whether specific risk is being accurately captured. If competent authorities allow this back-testing to be performed on the basis of relevant sub-portfolios, these must be chosen in a consistent manner;

(e) it captures name-related basis risk, that is institutions shall demonstrate that the internal model is sensitive to material idiosyncratic differences between similar but not identical positions; and

(f) it captures event risk.

The institution shall also meet the following conditions:

– where an institution is subject to event risk that is not reflected in its value-at-risk measure, because it is beyond the 10-day holding period and 99 per cent confidence interval (low probability and high severity events), the institution shall ensure that the impact of such events is factored in to its internal capital assessment; and

– the institution's internal model shall conservatively assess the risk arising from less liquid positions and positions with limited price transparency under realistic market scenarios. In addition, the internal model shall meet minimum data standards. Proxies shall be appropriately conservative and may be used only where available data is insufficient or is not reflective of the true volatility of a position or portfolio.

Further, as techniques and best practices evolve, institutions shall avail themselves of these advances.

In addition, the institution shall have an approach in place to capture, in the calculation of its capital requirements, the default risk of its trading book positions that is incremental to the default risk captured by the value-at-risk measure as specified in the previous requirements of this point. To avoid double counting, an institution may, when calculating its incremental default risk charge, take into account the extent to which default risk has already been incorporated into the value-at-risk measure, especially for risk positions that could and would be closed within 10 days in the event of adverse market conditions or other indications of deterioration in the credit environment. Where an institution captures its incremental default risk through a surcharge, it shall have in place methodologies for validating the measure.

The institution shall demonstrate that its approach meets soundness standards comparable to the approach set out in Articles 84 to 89 of Directive 2006/48/EC, under the assumption of a constant level of risk, and adjusted where appropriate to reflect the impact of liquidity, concentrations, hedging and optionality.

An institution that does not capture the incremental default risk through an internally developed approach shall calculate the surcharge through an approach consistent with either the approach set out in Articles 78 to 83 of Directive 2006/48/EC or the approach set out in Articles 84 to 89 of that Directive.

With respect to cash or synthetic securitisation exposures that would be subject to a deduction treatment under the treatment set out in Article 66(2) of Directive 2006/48/EC, or risk-weighted at 1,250% as set out in Part 4 of Annex IX to that Directive, these positions shall be subject to a capital charge that is no less than set forth under that treatment. Institutions that are dealers in these exposures may apply a different treatment where they can demonstrate to their competent authorities, in addition to trading intent, that a liquid two-way market exists for the securitisation exposures or, in the case of synthetic securitisations that rely solely on credit derivatives, for the securitisation exposures themselves or all their constituent risk components. For the purposes of this section a two-way market is deemed to exist where there are independent good faith offers to buy and sell so that a price reasonably related to the last sales price or current good faith competitive bid and offer quotations can be determined within one day and settled at such a price within a relatively short time conforming to trade custom. For an institution to apply a different treatment, it shall have sufficient market data to ensure that it fully captures the concentrated default risk of these exposures in its internal approach for measuring the incremental default risk in accordance with the standards set out above.

6. Institutions using internal models which are not recognised in accordance with point 4 shall be subject to a separate capital charge for specific risk as calculated according to Annex I.

7. For the purposes of point 9(b), the results of the institution's own calculation shall be scaled up by a multiplication factor of at least 3.

8. The multiplication factor shall be increased by a plus-factor of between 0 and 1 in accordance with Table 1, depending on the number of overshootings for the most recent 250 business days as evidenced by the institution's back-testing. Competent authorities shall require the institutions to calculate overshootings consistently on the basis of back-testing either on actual or on hypothetical changes in the portfolio's value. An overshooting is a one-day change in the portfolio's value that exceeds the related one-day value-at-risk measure generated by the institution's model. For the purpose of determining the plus-factor the number of overshootings shall be assessed at least quarterly.

The competent authorities may, in individual cases and owing to an exceptional situation, waive the requirement to increase the multiplication factor by the 'plus-factor' in accordance with Table 1, if the institution has demonstrated to the satisfaction of the competent authorities that such an increase is unjustified and that the model is basically sound.

If numerous overshootings indicate that the model is not sufficiently accurate, the competent authorities shall revoke the model's recognition or impose appropriate measures to ensure that the model is improved promptly.

Table 1

Number of overshootings	Plus-factor
Fewer than 5	0.00
5	0.40
6	0.50
7	0.65
8	0.75
9	0.85
10 or more	1.00

In order to allow competent authorities to monitor the appropriateness of the plus-factor on an ongoing basis, institutions shall notify promptly, and in any case no later than within five working days, the competent authorities of overshootings that result from their back-testing programme and that would according to the above table imply an increase of a plus-factor.

9. Each institution must meet a capital requirement expressed as the higher of:

(a) its previous day's value-at-risk measure according to the parameters specified in this Annex plus, where appropriate, the incremental default risk charge required under point 5; or

(b) an average of the daily value-at-risk measures on each of the preceding 60 business days, multiplied by the factor mentioned in point 7, adjusted by the factor referred to in point 8 plus, where appropriate, the incremental default risk charge required under point 5.

10. The calculation of the value-at-risk measure shall be subject to the following minimum standards:

(a) at least daily calculation of the value-at-risk measure;

(b) a 99th percentile, one-tailed confidence interval;

(c) a 10-day equivalent holding period;

(d) an effective historical observation period of at least one year except where a shorter observation period is justified by a significant upsurge in price volatility; and

(e) three-monthly data set updates.

11. The competent authorities shall require that the model captures accurately all the material price risks of options or option-like positions and that any other risks not captured by the model are covered adequately by own funds.

12. The risk-measurement model shall capture a sufficient number of risk factors, depending on the level of activity of the institution in the respective markets and in particular the following.

Interest rate risk

The risk-measurement system shall incorporate a set of risk factors corresponding to the interest rates in each currency in which the institution has interest rate sensitive on- or off-balance sheet positions. The institution shall model the yield curves using one of the generally accepted approaches. For material exposures to interest-rate risk in the major currencies and markets, the yield curve shall be divided into a minimum of six maturity segments, to capture the variations of volatility of rates along the yield curve. The risk-measurement system must also capture the risk of less than perfectly correlated movements between different yield curves.

Foreign-exchange risk

The risk-measurement system shall incorporate risk factors corresponding to gold and to the individual foreign currencies in which the institution's positions are denominated.

For CIUs the actual foreign exchange positions of the CIU shall be taken into account. Institutions may rely on third party reporting of the foreign exchange position of the CIU, where the correctness of this report is adequately ensured. If an institution is not aware of the foreign exchange positions of a CIU, this position should be carved out and treated in accordance with the fourth paragraph of point 2.1 of Annex III.

Equity risk

The risk-measurement system shall use a separate risk factor at least for each of the equity markets in which the institution holds significant positions.

Commodity risk

The risk-measurement system shall use a separate risk factor at least for each commodity in which the institution holds significant positions. The risk-measurement system must also capture the risk of less than perfectly correlated movements between similar, but not identical, commodities and the exposure to changes in forward prices arising from maturity mismatches. It shall also take account of market characteristics, notably delivery dates and the scope provided to traders to close out positions.

13. The competent authorities may allow institutions to use empirical correlations within risk categories and across risk categories if they are satisfied that the institution's system for measuring correlations is sound and implemented with integrity.

Annex VI

Calculating Capital Requirements for Large Exposures

1. The excess referred to in Article 31(b) shall be calculated by selecting those components of the total trading exposure to the client or group of clients in question which attract the highest specific-risk requirements in Annex I and/or requirements in Annex II, the sum of which equals the amount of the excess referred to in Article 31(a).

2. Where the excess has not persisted for more than 10 days, the additional capital requirement shall be 200% of the requirements referred to in point 1, on these components.

3. As from 10 days after the excess has occurred, the components of the excess, selected in accordance with point 1, shall be allocated to the appropriate line in column 1 of Table 1 in ascending order of specific-risk requirements in Annex I and/or requirements in Annex II. The additional capital requirement shall be equal to the sum of the specific-risk requirements in Annex I and/or the Annex II requirements on these components, multiplied by the corresponding factor in column 2 of Table 1.

Table 1

Excess over the limits (on the basis of a percentage of own funds)	Factors
Up to 40%	200%
From 40% to 60%	300%
From 60% to 80%	400%
From 80% to 100%	500%
From 100% to 250%	600%
Over 250%	900%

Annex VII

Trading

Part A

Trading Intent

1. Positions/portfolios held with trading intent shall comply with the following requirements:

(a) there must be a clearly documented trading strategy for the position/instrument or portfolios, approved by senior management, which shall include expected holding horizon;

(b) there must be clearly defined policies and procedures for the active management of the position, which shall include the following:
  (i) positions entered into on a trading desk;
  (ii) position limits are set and monitored for appropriateness;

(iii) dealers have the autonomy to enter into/manage the position within agreed limits and according to the approved strategy;
(iv) positions are reported to senior management as an integral part of the institution's risk management process; and
(v) positions are actively monitored with reference to market information sources and an assessment made of the marketability or hedge-ability of the position or its component risks, including the assessment of, the quality and availability of market inputs to the valuation process, level of market turnover, sizes of positions traded in the market; and

(c) there must be clearly defined policy and procedures to monitor the position against the institution's trading strategy including the monitoring of turnover and stale positions in the institution's trading book.

Part B
Systems and Controls

1. Institutions shall establish and maintain systems and controls sufficient to provide prudent and reliable valuation estimates.

2. Systems and controls shall include at least the following elements:

(a) documented policies and procedures for the process of valuation. This includes clearly defined responsibilities of the various areas involved in the determination of the valuation, sources of market information and review of their appropriateness, frequency of independent valuation, timing of closing prices, procedures for adjusting valuations, month end and ad-hoc verification procedures; and

(b) reporting lines for the department accountable for the valuation process that are clear and independent of the front office.

The reporting line shall ultimately be to a main board executive director.

Prudent Valuation Methods
3. Marking to market is the at least daily valuation of positions at readily available close out prices that are sourced independently. Examples include exchange prices, screen prices, or quotes from several independent reputable brokers.

4. When marking to market, the more prudent side of bid/offer shall be used unless the institution is a significant market maker in the particular type of financial instrument or commodity in question and it can close out at mid market.

5. Where marking to market is not possible, institutions must mark to model their positions/portfolios before applying trading book capital treatment. Marking to model is defined as any valuation which has to be benchmarked, extrapolated or otherwise calculated from a market input.

6. The following requirements must be complied with when marking to model:

(a) senior management shall be aware of the elements of the trading book which are subject to mark to model and shall understand the materiality of the uncertainty this creates in the reporting of the risk/performance of the business;

(b) market inputs shall be sourced, where possible, in line with market prices, and the appropriateness of the market inputs of the particular position being valued and the parameters of the model shall be assessed on a frequent basis;

(c) where available, valuation methodologies which are accepted market practice for particular financial instruments or commodities shall be used;

(d) where the model is developed by the institution itself, it shall be based on appropriate assumptions, which have been assessed and challenged by suitably qualified parties independent of the development process;

(e) there shall be formal change control procedures in place and a secure copy of the model shall be held and periodically used to check valuations;

(f) risk management shall be aware of the weaknesses of the models used and how best to reflect those in the valuation output; and

(g) the model shall be subject to periodic review to determine the accuracy of its performance (e.g. assessing the continued appropriateness of assumptions, analysis of profit and loss versus risk factors, comparison of actual close out values to model outputs).

For the purposes of point (d), the model shall be developed or approved independently of the front office and shall be independently tested, including validation of the mathematics, assumptions and software implementation.

7. Independent price verification should be performed in addition to daily marking to market or marking to model. This is the process by which market prices or model inputs are regularly verified for accuracy and independence. While daily marking to market may be performed by dealers, verification of market prices and model inputs should be performed by a unit independent of the dealing room, at least monthly (or, depending on the nature of the market/trading activity, more frequently). Where independent pricing sources are not available or pricing sources are more subjective, prudent measures such as valuation adjustments may be appropriate.

Valuation adjustments or reserves
8. Institutions shall establish and maintain procedures for considering valuation adjustments/reserves.

General standards
9. The competent authorities shall require the following valuation adjustments/reserves to be formally considered: unearned credit spreads, close-out costs, operational risks, early termination, investing and funding costs, future administrative costs and, where relevant, model risk.

Standards for less liquid positions
10. Less liquid positions could arise from both market events and institution-related situations e.g. concentrated positions and/or stale positions.

11. Institutions shall consider several factors when determining whether a valuation reserve is necessary for less liquid positions. These factors include the amount of time it would take to hedge out the position/risks within the position, the volatility and average of bid/offer spreads, the availability of market quotes (number and identity of market makers) and the volatility and average of trading volumes, market concentrations, the ageing of positions, the extent to which valuation relies on marking to model, and the impact of other model risks.

12. When using third party valuations or marking to model, institutions shall consider whether to apply a valuation adjustment. In addition, institutions shall consider the need for establishing reserves for less liquid positions and on an ongoing basis review their continued suitability.

13. When valuation adjustments/reserves give rise to material losses of the current financial year, these shall be deducted from an institution's original own funds according to point (k) of Article 57 of Directive 2006/48/EC

14. Other profits/losses originating from valuation adjustments/reserves shall be included in the calculation of 'net trading book profits' mentioned in point (b) of Article 13(2) and be added to/deducted from the additional own funds eligible to cover market risk requirements according to such provisions.

15. Valuation adjustments/reserves which exceed those made under the accounting framework to which the institution is subject shall be treated in accordance with point 13 if they give rise to material losses, or point 14 otherwise.

Part C
Internal Hedges

1. An internal hedge is a position that materially or completely offsets the component risk element of a non-trading book position or a set of positions. Positions arising from internal hedges are eligible for trading book capital treatment, provided that they are held with trading intent and that the general criteria on trading intent and prudent valuation specified in Parts A and B are met. In particular:

(a) internal hedges shall not be primarily intended to avoid or reduce capital requirements;

(b) internal hedges shall be properly documented and subject to particular internal approval and audit procedures;

(c) the internal transaction shall be dealt with at market conditions;

(d) the bulk of the market risk that is generated by the internal hedge shall be dynamically managed in the trading book within the authorised limits; and

(e) internal transactions shall be carefully monitored.

Monitoring must be ensured by adequate procedures.

2. The treatment referred to in point 1 applies without prejudice to the capital requirements applicable to the 'non-trading book leg' of the internal hedge.

3. Notwithstanding points 1 and 2, when an institution hedges a non-trading book credit risk exposure using a credit derivative booked in its trading book (using an internal hedge), the non-trading book exposure is not deemed to be hedged for the purposes of calculating capital requirements unless the institution purchases from an eligible third party protection provider a credit derivative meeting the requirements set out in point 19 of Part 2 of Annex VIII to Directive 2006/48/EC with regard to the non-trading book exposure. Where such third party protection is purchased and is recognised as a hedge of a non-trading book exposure for the purposes of calculating capital requirements, neither the internal nor external credit derivative hedge shall be included in the trading book for the purposes of calculating capital requirements.

Part D

Inclusion in the Trading Book

1. Institutions shall have clearly defined policies and procedures for determining which position to include in the trading book for the purposes of calculating their capital requirements, consistent with the criteria set out in Article 11 and taking into account the institution's risk management capabilities and practices. Compliance with these policies and procedures shall be fully documented and subject to periodic internal audit.

2. Institutions shall have clearly defined policies and procedures for overall management of the trading book. At a minimum these policies and procedures shall address:

(a) the activities the institution considers to be trading and as constituting part of the trading book for capital requirement purposes;

(b) the extent to which a position can be marked to market daily by reference to an active, liquid two-way market;

(c) for positions that are marked to model, the extent to which the institution can:
  (i) identify all material risks of the position;
  (ii) hedge all material risks of the position with instruments for which an active, liquid two-way market exists; and
  (iii) derive reliable estimates for the key assumptions and parameters used in the model;

(d) the extent to which the institution can, and is required to, generate valuations for the position that can be validated externally in a consistent manner;

(e) the extent to which legal restrictions or other operational requirements would impede the institution's ability to effect a liquidation or hedge of the position in the short term;

(f) the extent to which the institution can, and is required to, actively risk manage the position within its trading operation; and

(g) the extent to which the institution may transfer risk or positions between the non-trading and trading books and the criteria for such transfers.

3. Competent authorities may allow institutions to treat positions that are holdings in the trading book as set out in Article 57(l), (m) and (n) of Directive 2006/48/EC as equity or debt instruments, as appropriate, where an institution demonstrates that it is an active market maker in these positions. In this case, the institution shall have adequate systems and controls surrounding the trading of eligible own funds instruments.

4. Term trading-related repo-style transactions that an institution accounts for in its non-trading book may be included in the trading book for capital requirement purposes so long as all such repo-style transactions are included. For this

purpose, trading-related repo-style transactions are defined as those that meet the requirements of Article 11(2) and of Annex VII, Part A, and both legs are in the form of either cash or securities includable in the trading book. Regardless of where they are booked, all repo-style transactions are subject to a non-trading book counterparty credit risk charge.

Annex VIII

Repealed Directives

Part A
Repealed Directives Together with their Successive Amendments

(referred to in Article 52)

Council Directive 93/6/EEC of 15 March 1993 on the capital adequacy of investments firms and credit institutions

Directive 98/31/EC of the European Parliament and of the Council of 22 June 1998 amending Council Directive 93/6/EEC on the capital adequacy of investment firms and credit institutions

Directive 98/33/EC of the European Parliament and of the Council of 22 June 1998 amending Article 12 of Council Directive 77/780/EEC on the taking up and pursuit of the business of credit institutions, Articles 2, 5, 6, 7, 8 of and Annexes II and III to Council Directive 89/647/EEC on a solvency ratio for credit institutions and Article 2 of and Annex II to Council Directive 93/6/EEC on the capital adequacy of investment firms and credit institutions

Directive 2002/87/EC of the European Parliament and of the Council of 16 December 2002 on the supplementary supervision of credit institutions, insurance undertakings and investment firms in a financial conglomerate and amending Council Directives 73/239/EEC, 79/267/EEC, 92/49/EEC, 92/96/EEC, 93/6/EEC and 93/22/EEC, and Directives 98/78/EC and 2000/12/EC of the European Parliament and of the Council:

Only Article 26

Directive 2004/39/EC of the European Parliament and of the Council of 21 April 2004 on markets in financial instruments amending Council Directives 85/611/EEC and 93/6/EEC and Directive 2000/12/EC of the European Parliament and of the Council and repealing Council Directive 93/22/EEC:

Only Article 67

Part B
Deadlines for Transposition

(referred to in Article 52)

Directive	Deadline for transposition
Council Directive 93/6/EEC	1.7.1995
Directive 98/31/EC	21.7.2000
Directive 98/33/EC	21.7.2000
Directive 2002/87/EC	11.8.2004
Directive 2004/39/EC	30.4.2006/31.1.2007
Directive 2005/1/EC	13.5.2005

Annex IX

Correlation Table

This Directive	Directive 93/6/EEC	Directive 98/31/EC	Directive 98/33/EC	Directive 2002/87/EC	Directive 2004/39/EC
Article 1(1) first sentence					
Article 1(1) second sentence and (2)	Article 1				
Article 2(1)					
Article 2(2)	Article 7(3)				
Article 3(1)(a)	Article 2(1)				
Article 3(1)(b)	Article 2(2)			Article 67(1)	
Article 3(1)(c) to (e)	Article 2(3) to (5)				
Article 3(1)(f) and (g)					
Article 3(1)(h)	Article 2(10)				
Article 3(1)(i)	Article 2(11)		Article 3(1)		
Article 3(1)(j)	Article 2(14)				
Article 3(1)(k) and (l)	Article 2(15) and (16)	Article 1(1)(b)			
Article 3(1)(m)	Article 2(17)	Article 1(1)(c)			
Article 3(1)(n)	Article 2(18)	Article 1(1)(d)			
Article 3(1)(o) to (q)	Article 2(19) to (21)				
Article 3(1)(r)	Article 2(23)				
Article 3(1)(s)	Article 2(26)				
Article 3(2)	Article 2(7) and (8)				
Article 3(3)(a) and (b)	Article 7(3)		Article 26		
Article 3(3)(c)	Article 7(3)				
Article 4	Article 2(24)				
Article 5	Article 3(1) and (2)				
Article 6	Article 3(4)			Article 67(2)	
Article 7	Article 3(4a)			Article 67(3)	
Article 8	Article 3(4b)			Article 67(3)	
Article 9	Article 3(3)				
Article 10	Article 3(5) to (8)				
Article 11	Article 2(6)				
Article 12 first paragraph	Article 2(25)				
Article 12 second paragraph					
Article 13(1) first sub-paragraph	Annex V(1) first sub-paragraph				
Article 13(1) second sub-paragraph and (2) to (5)	Annex V(1) second sub-paragraph and (2) to (5)		Article 1(7) and Annex 4(a)(b)		
Article 14	Annex V(6) and (7)	Annex 4(c)			

This Directive	Directive 93/6/EEC	Directive 98/31/EC	Directive 98/33/EC	Directive 2002/87/EC	Directive 2004/39/EC
Article 15	Annex V(8)				
Article 16	Annex V(9)				
Article 17					
Article 18(1) first sub-paragraph	Article 4(1) first sub-paragraph				
Article 18(1) (a) and (b)	Article 4(1)(i) and (ii)	Article 1(2)			
Article 18(2) to (4)	Article 4(6) to (8)				
Article 19(1)					
Article 19(2)	Article 11(2)				
Article 19(3)					
Article 20					
Article 21	Annex IV				
Article 22					
Article 23 first and second paragraph	Article 7(5) and (6)				
Article 23 third paragraph					
Article 24					
Article 25					
Article 26(1)	Article 7(10)	Article 1(4)			
Article 26(2) to (4)	Article 7(11) to (13)				
Article 27	Article 7(14) and (15)				
Article 28(1)	Article 5(1)				
Article 28(2)	Article 5(2)	Article 1(3)			
Article 28(3)					
Article 29(1)(a) to (c) and next two sub-paragraphs	Annex VI(2)				
Article 29(1) last sub-paragraph					
Article 29(2)	Annex VI(3)				
Article 30(1) and (2) first sub-paragraph	Annex VI(4) and (5)				
Article 30(2) second sub-paragraph					
Article 30(3) and (4)	Annex VI(6) and (7)				
Article 31	Annex VI(8)(1), (2) first sentence, (3) to (5)				
Article 32	Annex VI(9) and (10)				
Article 33(1) and (2)					
Article 33(3)	Article 6(2)				
Article 34					
Article 35(1) to (4)	Article 8(1) to (4)				

This Directive	Directive 93/6/EEC	Directive 98/31/EC	Directive 98/33/EC	Directive 2002/87/EC	Directive 2004/39/EC
Article 35(5)	Article 8(5) first sentence	Article 1(5)			
Article 36	Article 9(1) to (3)				
Article 37					
Article 38	Article 9(4)				
Article 39					
Article 40	Article 2(9)				
Article 41(1)(a) to (c)	Article 10 first, second and third indents				
Article 41(1) (d) and (e)					
Article 41(1)(f)	Article 10 fourth indent				
Article 41(1)(g)					
Article 42					
Article 43					
Article 44					
Article 45					
Article 46	Article 12				
Article 47					
Article 48					
Article 49					
Article 50	Article 15				
Annex I(1) to (4)	Annex I(1) to (4)				
Annex I(4) last paragraph	Article 2(22)				
Annex I(5) to (7)	Annex I(5) to (7)				
Annex I(8)					
Annex I(9) to (11)	Annex I(8) to (10)				
Annex I(12) to (14)	Annex I(12) to (14)				
Annex I(15) and (16)	Article 2(12)				
Annex I(17) to (41)	Annex I(15) to (39)				
Annex I(42) to (56)					
Annex II(1) and (2)	Annex II(1) and (2)				
Annex II(3) to (10)					
Annex III(1)	Annex III(1) first sub-paragraph	Article 1(7) and Annex 3(a)			
Annex III(2)	Annex III(2)				
Annex III(2.1) first to third paragraphs	Annex III(3.1)	Article 1(7) and Annex 3(b)			
Annex III(2.1) fourth paragraph					
Annex III(2.1) fifth paragraph	Annex III(3.2)	Article 1(7) and Annex 3(b)			

This Directive	Directive 93/6/EEC	Directive 98/31/EC	Directive 98/33/EC	Directive 2002/87/EC	Directive 2004/39/EC
Annex III(2.2), (3), (3.1)	Annex III(4) to (6)	Article 1(7) and Annex 3(c)			
Annex III(3.2)	Annex III(8)				
Annex III(4)	Annex III(11)				
Annex IV(1) to (20)	Annex VII(1) to (20)	Article 1(7) and Annex 5			
Annex IV(21)	Article 11a	Article 1(6)			
Annex V(1) to (12) fourth paragraph	Annex VIII(1) to (13)(ii)	Article 1(7) and Annex 5			
Annex V(12) fifth paragraph					
Annex V(12) sixth paragraph to (13)	Annex VIII(13) (iii) to (14)	Article 1(7) and Annex 5			
Annex VI	Annex VI(8)(2) after the first sentence				
Annex VII					
Annex VIII					
Annex IX					

Part II
CAPITAL MOVEMENT

C.M. 1.
EU Treaty: Chapter 4—Capital and Payments

Article 56 (ex Article 73b)

1. Within the framework of the provisions set out in this chapter, all restrictions on the movement of capital between Member States and between Member States and third countries shall be prohibited.

2. Within the framework of the provisions set out in this Chapter, all restrictions on payments between Member States and between Member States and third countries shall be prohibited.

Cases

I. Case C-174/04 Commission of the European Communities v Italian Republic [2005] ECR I-4933

A national decree that provides for the automatic suspension of voting rights attached to holdings exceeding 2 per cent of the capital of undertakings operating in the electricity and gas sectors, where such holdings are acquired by public undertakings that are not quoted on regulated financial markets and hold a dominant position, are not compatible with the rules on freedom of capital as it would have the effect of dissuading public undertakings established in other Member States, in particular, from acquiring shares in said undertakings. Such acquisitions fall under the capital movement rules and this would imply the possibility of participating effectively in the management and control of a company.

The Treaty provisions on the free moment of capital do not draw a distinction between private undertakings and public undertakings or between undertakings that hold a dominant position and those that do not. The limitation of voting rights, allowed according to Directive 2004/39/EC serve the purpose of allowing securities to be listed on a stock exchange. It was enacted on the basis of the rules on freedom of establishment, and serving a different purpose it cannot be invoked in the context of freedom of capital movements.

II. Case C-319/02 Petri Manninen [2004] ECR I-7477

Articles 56 EC and 58 EC preclude legislation whereby the entitlement of a person fully taxable in one Member State to a tax credit in relation to dividends paid to him by limited companies is excluded where those companies are not established in that State.

III. Case C-483/99 Commission of the European Communities v French Republic [2002] ECR I-4781; see also Case C-367/98 Commission of the European Communities v Portuguese Republic [2002] ECR I-4731

The French Republic has failed to comply with its obligations under Article 73b of the EC Treaty (now Article 56 EC) by maintaining in force Article 2(1) and (3) of Decree No 93–1298 of 13 December 1993 vesting in the State a 'golden share' in Société Nationale Elf-Aquitaine, according to which the following rights attach to the 'golden share' held by the French Republic in that company:

(a) any direct or indirect shareholding by a natural or legal person, acting alone or in conjunction with others, which exceeds the ceiling of one-tenth, one-fifth or one-third of the capital of, or voting rights in, the company must first be approved by the Minister for Economic Affairs;

(b) the right to oppose any decision to transfer or use as security the assets listed in the annex to the Decree—the assets in question being the majority of the capital of four subsidiaries of that company, namely Elf-Aquitaine Production, Elf-Antar France, Elf-Gabon SA, and Elf-Congo SA.

IV. Case C-464/98 Westdeutsche Landesbank Girozentrale v Friedrich Stefan and Republik Österreich [2001] ECR I-0173

1. Article [56][1] EC is to be construed as precluding the application of national rules such as those at issue in the main proceedings, requiring a mortgage securing a debt payable in the currency of another Member State to be registered in the national currency.

2. Article [56][1] of the Treaty is to be construed as meaning that it did not apply in Austria prior to the date of accession of the Republic of Austria to the European Union.

3. Article [56][1] of the Treaty is to be construed as incapable of remedying, with effect from the entry into force of the EC Treaty in Austria, a mortgage registration which, under the relevant national law, is vitiated from the outset by absolute and incurable nullity such as to render that registration non-existent.

V. Case C-35/98 Staatssecretaris van Financiën v B.G.M. Verkooijen [2000] ECR I-4071

Article 1(1) of Council Directive 88/361/EEC[2] of 24 June 1988 for the implementation of Article [67][3] of the Treaty precludes a legislative provision of a Member State which, like the one at issue in the main proceedings, makes the grant of an exemption from the income tax payable on dividends paid to natural persons who are shareholders subject to the condition that those dividends are paid by a company whose seat is in that Member State.

The position is not in any way changed by the fact that the taxpayer applying for such a tax exemption is an ordinary shareholder or an employee who holds shares giving rise to the payment of dividends under an employees' savings plan.

VI. Case C-412/97 ED Srl v Italo Fenocchio [1999] ECR I-3845

Like Article 106 of the EEC Treaty (subsequently Article [73h][4] of the EC Treaty, and repealed by the Treaty of Amsterdam), Article [56(2)][1] EC is intended to enable a person liable to pay a sum of money in the context of a supply of goods or services to discharge that contractual obligation voluntarily without undue restriction and to enable the creditor freely to receive such a payment. However, that provision is not applicable to the procedural rules which govern an action by a creditor seeking payment of a sum of money from a recalcitrant debtor.

Accordingly, a national procedural provision which excludes recourse to the special procedure for a summary payment order in cases where the order would have to be served on the debtor in another Member State does not constitute a restriction on the freedom to make payments.

VII. Case C-222/97 Manfred Trummer and Peter Mayer [1999] ECR I-1661

1. It is apparent from the nomenclature in respect of movements of capital annexed to Directive 88/361/EEC for the implementation of Article [67][3] of the Treaty[2]—which, despite the fact that the Directive was adopted on the basis of Articles 69 and 70(1) of the EEC Treaty, still has the same indicative value as it did before Articles 67 to 73 of the EEC Treaty were replaced by Article [56][1] et seq. of the EC Treaty—that both the liquidation of an investment in real property (Point II of the nomenclature) and the grant of sureties, other guarantees and rights of pledge (Point IX of the nomenclature) constitute movements of capital within the meaning of Article [56].[1] Since a mortgage is inextricably linked to the liquidation of an investment in real property, and since, as the classic

---

[1] The number between brackets has been changed as from 1 May 1999 by article 12 of the Treaty of Amsterdam.
[2] Council Directive 88/361/EEC of 24 June 1988 for the implementation of article 67 if the Treaty (OJ L 178, 8.7.1988, 5–18), reproduced infra under no. C.M. 2.
[3] Article 67 has been repealed as from 1 May 1999, by article 12 of the Treaty of Amsterdam.

[4] Article 73h has been repealed as from 1 May 1999 by article 12 of the Treaty of Amsterdam.

method of securing a loan linked to a sale of real property, it constitutes an 'other guarantee', it is covered by Article [56][1] of the Treaty, prohibiting restrictions on the movement of capital between Member States and between Member States and third countries.

2. Article [56][1] of the Treaty precludes the application of national rules requiring a mortgage securing a debt payable in the currency of another Member State to be registered in the national currency, since it cannot be registered for an amount greater than the corresponding value of that debt in the national currency as at the date of the application for registration. Such rules must be regarded as a restriction on the movement of capital, since their effect is to weaken the link between the debt to be secured, payable in the currency of another Member State, and the mortgage, whose value may, as a result of subsequent currency exchange fluctuations, come to be lower than that of the debt to be secured. This can only reduce the effectiveness of such a security, and thus its attractiveness. Consequently, those rules are liable to dissuade the parties concerned from denominating a debt in the currency of another Member State, thus depriving them of a right, which constitutes a component element of the free movement of capital and payments. Moreover, the obligation imposed by the rules at issue, requiring recourse to the national currency for the purposes of creating a mortgage, cannot be justified by any overriding factor designed, in the public interest, to ensure the foreseeability and transparency of the mortgage system. Although a Member State is entitled in that connection to take the necessary measures to ensure that the mortgage system clearly and transparently prescribes the respective rights of mortgagees inter se, as well as the rights of mortgagees as a whole vis-à-vis other creditors, the rules at issue enable lower-ranking creditors to establish the precise amount of prior-ranking debts, and thus to assess the value of the security offered to them, only at the price of a lack of security for creditors whose debts are denominated in foreign currencies.

VIII. Case C-439/97 Sandoz GmbH v Finanzlandesdirektion für Wien, Niederösterreich und Burgenland [1999] ECR I-7041

1. Articles [56 (1) and 58(1) (b) and (3)][1] of the Treaty are to be interpreted as not precluding the levying of duty, under the legislation of a Member State, on loan agreements, including those entered into in another Member State, payable by all natural and legal persons resident in that State who enter into such a contract, irrespective of the nationality of the contracting parties or of the place where the loan is contracted.

Although, in depriving residents of a Member State of the possibility of benefiting from the absence of taxation which may be associated with loans obtained outside the national territory, such legislation is likely to deter them from obtaining loans from persons established in other Member States and therefore constitutes a restriction on the movement of capital, it is intended to ensure equality of tax treatment of borrowers by preventing taxable persons from evading the requirements of domestic tax legislation and is therefore essential in order to prevent infringements of national tax law and regulations.

2. Articles [56(1) EC and 58(1)(b)][1] of the Treaty preclude legislation of a Member State which provides that, where a natural or legal person resident in that State concludes outside the national territory a loan agreement which is not set down in a written instrument and not recorded by an entry in the borrower's books and accounts, he is liable to pay stamp duty, whereas, in the case of a loan entered into in that Member State such duty is not payable even if the agreement is not set down in a written instrument. Such legislation, which discriminates according to the place where the loan is contracted, is likely to deter residents from contracting loans with persons established in other Member States and therefore constitutes a restriction on the movement of capital. It cannot be justified by the need to ensure equal tax treatment of residents, since the discrimination entailed as between residents runs counter to that objective; nor can it be justified in terms of the objective of preventing fraud by borrowers who are resident in that State.

IX. Case C-302/97 Klaus Konle v Republik Österreich [1999] ECR I-3099

1. National legislation on the acquisition of land must comply with the provisions of the Treaty on freedom of establishment for nationals of Member States and the free movement of capital. As is apparent from Article [44(3)(e)][1] of the Treaty, the right to acquire, use or dispose of immovable property on the territory of another Member State is the necessary corollary of freedom of establishment. Capital movements include investments in

immovable property on the territory of a Member State by non-residents, as is clear from the nomenclature of capital movements set out in Annex I to Directive 88/361/EEC for the implementation of Article [67][3] of the Treaty.

2. The concept of 'existing legislation' within the meaning of Article 70 of the 1994 Act of Accession—a provision which permits Austria to maintain its existing legislation regarding secondary residences for five years from the date of accession—is based on a factual criterion, so that its application does not require an assessment of the validity in domestic law of the national provisions at issue. Thus, any rule regarding secondary residences which was in force in the Republic of Austria at the date of accession is, in principle, covered by the derogation laid down in Article 70 of the Act of Accession. It would be otherwise if that rule were withdrawn from the domestic legal system by a decision by the constitutional court of the Member State concerned subsequent to the date of accession but with retroactive effect from before that date, thereby eliminating the provision in question as regards the past, it being for the courts of that Member State to assess the temporal effects of declarations of unconstitutionality made by the constitutional court of that State.

3. Article [56][1] of the Treaty and Article 70 of the 1994 Act of Accession do not preclude a scheme for acquiring land such as that introduced by the Tiroler Grundverkehrsgesetz 1993 (Tyrol Law on the Transfer of Land), exempting only Austrian nationals from having to obtain authorization before acquiring a plot of land which is built on and thus from having to demonstrate, to that end, that the planned acquisition will not be used to establish a secondary residence. Although that legislation creates a discriminatory restriction against nationals of other Member States in respect of capital movements between Member States, that is authorized by the Act of Accession, which allows Austria to maintain its existing legislation regarding secondary residences for five years from the date of accession.

4. Article [56][1] of the Treaty and Article 70 of the 1994 Act of Accession preclude a scheme for acquiring land such as that introduced by the Tiroler Grundverkehrsgesetz 1996 (Tyrol Law on the Transfer of Land), which places all prospective acquirers of land under an obligation to apply for administrative authorisation prior to the acquisition of such property. As regards Article [56],[1] such a requirement entails, by its very purpose, a restriction on the free movement of capital and constitutes a restrictive measure which can be justified only if it meets a town and country planning objective such as maintaining, in the general interest, a permanent population and an economic activity independent of the tourist sector in certain regions, provided that it is not applied in a discriminatory manner and that the same result cannot be achieved by other less restrictive procedures. That is not the position, however, given the risk of discrimination inherent in a system of prior authorization for the acquisition of land and the other possibilities at the disposal of the Member State concerned for ensuring compliance with its town and country planning guidelines. As regards the purported justification based on Article 70 of the Act of Accession, which enables Austria to maintain its existing legislation regarding secondary residences for five years from the date of accession, the relevant provisions of the 1996 law cannot be covered by the derogation provided for by that provision. Although no measure adopted after the date of accession is, by that fact alone, automatically excluded from the derogation—for example, it is covered by the derogation if, in substance, it is identical to the previous legislation or limited to reducing or eliminating an obstacle to the exercise of Community rights and freedoms in the earlier legislation—legislation such as that at issue, which is based on an approach which differs from that of the previous law and establishes new procedures, cannot be treated as legislation existing at the time of accession.

X. Case C-410/96 Criminal Proceedings Against André Ambry [1998] ECR I-7875

See supra under no. B. 28 and infra under no. I. 26.

XI. Joined cases C-163/94, C-165/94 and C-250/94 Criminal Proceedings Against Lucas Emilio Sanz de Lera, Raimundo Díaz Jiménez and Figen Kapanoglu [1995] ECR I-4821

Articles [56(1) and 58(1)(b)][1] of the Treaty, which prohibit restrictions on movements of capital between Member States and between Member States and non-Member countries, on the one hand, and authorizing Member States to take all requisite measures to prevent infringements of national law and regulations, on the other, preclude national rules which make the export of coins, banknotes or bearer cheques generally subject to prior authorization but do not by contrast preclude a transaction of that nature being made conditional on a prior declaration.

Although the measures authorized by Article [58(1)(b)][1] include those designed to ensure effective fiscal supervision and to prevent illegal activities such as tax evasion, money laundering, drug trafficking, and terrorism, the requirement of an authorization is not necessary for those purposes, which may be achieved by measures less restrictive of the free movement of capital. It is sufficient, rather than requiring an authorization, which has the effect of subjecting the free movement of capital to the discretion of the administrative authorities and is thus capable of making that freedom illusory, to set up an adequate system requiring a declaration indicating the nature of the operation envisaged and the identity of the declarant, which would require the competent authorities to proceed with a rapid examination of the declaration and enable them, if necessary, to carry out in due time the investigations found to be necessary to determine whether capital was being unlawfully transferred and to impose the requisite penalties if national legislation was being contravened, a course which would not suspend the operation concerned but would nevertheless enable the national authorities to carry out, in order to uphold public policy, effective supervision to prevent infringements of national law and regulations.

Moreover, rules requiring an authorization as a general principle do not fall within the scope of Article [57(1)][1] of the Treaty, which authorizes, subject to certain conditions, restrictions on movements of capital between Member States and non-Member countries where they involve direct investment, establishment, the provision of financial services or the admission of securities to capital markets because, on the one hand, the physical export of means of payment cannot itself be regarded as a capital movement of that kind, and on the other hand the rules apply to all exports of means of payment, including those which do not, in the non-Member countries, involve such operations.

Article [56(1)],[1] in conjunction with Articles [57 and 58(1)(b)],[1] may be relied on before national courts and may render inapplicable national rules inconsistent therewith.

XII. Case C-484/93 Peter Svensson and Lena Gustavsson v Ministre du Logement et de l'Urbanisme [1995] ECR I-3955

1. It is not compatible with Article [67][3] of the Treaty for a Member State to make the grant of a housing benefit, in particular an interest rate subsidy, subject to the requirement that the loans intended to finance the construction, acquisition, or improvement of the housing which is to benefit from the subsidy have been obtained from a credit institution approved in that Member State, which implies that it must be established there.

Such a requirement is liable to dissuade borrowers from approaching banks established in another Member State and therefore constitutes an obstacle to liberalized movement of capital, which includes bank loans.

2. It is not compatible with Article [49][1] of the Treaty for a Member State to make the grant of a housing benefit, in particular an interest rate subsidy, subject to the requirement that the loans intended to finance the construction, acquisition, or improvement of the housing which is to benefit from the subsidy have been obtained from a credit institution approved in that Member State, which implies that it must be established there.

That requirement leads in the case of services such as the provision of building loans by banks to discrimination against providers of such services established in other Member States, which is prohibited by that article and is not justified under the derogations authorized by Article [46][1] of the Treaty, which do not include economic aims, or by the need to maintain the integrity of the national fiscal regime, since there is no direct link between the grant of the interest rate subsidy to borrowers on the one hand and its financing by means of the profit tax on financial establishments on the other.

XIII. Joined cases C-358/93 and C-416/93 Criminal Proceedings Against Aldo Bordessa and Vicente Marí Mellado and Concepción Barbero Maestre [1995] ECR I-361

Rules which make the export of coins, banknotes or bearer cheques conditional upon a prior declaration or an administrative authorization and make that requirement subject to criminal penalties do not fall within the scope of Articles [28][1] and [49][1] of the Treaty.

It is clear from the system of the Treaty that the physical transfer of assets falls not under those articles but under Article [67][3] and Directive 88/361/EEC implementing that provision and, even if it were established that such a transfer constituted a payment connected with trade in goods or services, the transaction would be governed not by Articles [28][1] and [49][1] but by Article 106 of the Treaty.

2. Directive 88/361/EEC for the implementation of Article [67][3] of the Treaty[2] and in particular Article 1 thereof, requiring Member States to abolish restrictions on movements of capital, and Article 4, authorizing them to take all requisite measures to prevent infringements of their national laws and regulations, preclude the export of coins, bank notes, or bearer cheques being made conditional on prior authorization but do not by contrast preclude a transaction of that nature being made conditional on a prior declaration.

Although Article 4 applies not only to measures to prevent infringements in the field of taxation and for the prudential supervision of financial institutions, but also to those designed to prevent illegal activities of comparable seriousness, such as money laundering, drug trafficking, or terrorism, the requirement of authorization cannot be regarded as a requisite measure within the meaning of that provision, because it would cause the exercise of the free movement of capital to be subject to the discretion of the administrative authorities and thus be such as to render that freedom illusory. A prior declaration, on the other hand, may constitute a requisite measure within that meaning since, unlike prior authorization, it does not entail suspension of the transaction in question but does still allow the national authorities to exercise effective supervision in order to prevent infringements of their laws and regulations.

The provisions mentioned above may be relied on before national courts and render inapplicable national rules which conflict with them.

XIV. Case 308/86 Criminal Proceedings Against R Lambert [1988] ECR 4369

1. As Community law now stands, rules which require exporters to have foreign currency payable in respect of their sales paid through a bank and to exchange such currency on the regulated foreign exchange market and which as a result prohibit them from taking payments in bank notes, are not a barrier to the liberalization of payments connected with the movement of goods which is incompatible with Article [107][1] of the EEC Treaty.

2. Rules such as those at issue, even if they give rise to unequal treatment vis-à-vis exporters established in other Member States, do not involve discrimination contrary to Article [7][5] of the Treaty since the legislation at issue applies to all persons concerned on the basis of objective criteria and without regard to their nationality.

XV. Case 157/85 Luigi Brugnoni and Roberto Ruffinengo v Cassa di Risparmio di Genova e Imperia [1986] ECR 2013

The compulsory deposit of securities issued or payable abroad with an approved bank or a foreign bank chosen by an approved bank may not be required by a Member State, in the context of the liberalization of capital movements provided for in Article 2 and list B of the first Council Directive for the implementation of Article [67][2] of the Treaty unless such a requirement is indispensable for monitoring compliance with the conditions laid down by the legislation of that Member State in conformity with the Community law.

XVI. Joined cases 286/82 and 26/83 Graziana Luisi and Guiseppe Carbone v Ministero del Tesoro [1984] ECR 377

The general scheme of the Treaty shows, and a comparison between Articles [67][2] and [107][1] confirms, that the current payments covered by Article [106][1] are transfers of foreign exchange with constitute the consideration within the context of an underlying transaction, whilst the movements of capital covered by Article [67][2] are financial operations essentially concerned with the investment of the funds in question rather than remuneration for a service. For that reason movements of capital may themselves give rise to current payments, as is implied by Articles [67(2)][3] and [107(1)].[1]

The physical transfer of bank notes may not therefore be classified as a movement of capital where the transfer in question corresponds to an obligation to pay arising from a transaction involving the movement of goods or services.

XVII. Case 7/78 Regina v Ernest George Thompson, Brian Albert Johnson and Colin Alex Norman Woodiwiss [1978] ECR 2247

1. In the system of the EEC Treaty means of payment are not to be considered as goods falling within the terms of Articles [28 to 31][1] of the Treaty. These provisions do not therefore apply to (a) silver alloy coins which are legal tender in a Member State, or (b) gold coins such as krugerrands which

---

[5] Article 7 has been repealed as from 1 May 1999 by article 12 of the Treaty of Amsterdam.

are produced in a non-Member country but which circulate freely within a Member State.

2. A ban on the export from a Member State of silver alloy coins, which have been but are no longer legal tender in that State and the melting down or destruction whereof on national territory is forbidden, which has been adopted with a view to preventing such melting down or destruction in another Member State, is justified on grounds of public policy within the meaning of Article [30][1] of the Treaty because it stems from the need to protect the right to mint coinage which is traditionally regarded as involving the fundamental interests of the state.

Article 57 (ex Article 73c)

1. The provisions of Article [46][1] shall be without prejudice to the application to third countries of any restrictions which exist on 31 December 1993 under national or Community law adopted in respect of the movement of capital to or from third countries involving direct investment—including in real estate—establishment, the provision of financial services or the admission of securities to capital markets.

2. Whilst endeavouring to achieve the objective of free movement of capital between Member States and third countries to the greatest extent possible and without prejudice to the other Chapters of this Treaty, the Council may, acting by a qualified majority on a proposal from the Commission, adopt measures on the movement of capital to or from third countries involving direct investment—including investment in real estate—establishment, the provision of financial services or the admission of securities to capital markets. Unanimity shall be required for measures under this paragraph which constitute a step back in Community law as regards the liberalisation of the movement of capital to or from third countries.

Article 58 (ex Article 73d)

1. The provisions of Article [46][1] shall be without prejudice to the right of Member States:

(a) to apply the relevant provisions of their tax law which distinguish between taxpayers who are not in the same situation with regard to their place of residence or with regard to the place where their capital is invested;

(b) to take all requisite measures to prevent infringements of national law and regulations, in particular in the field of taxation and the prudential supervision of financial institutions, or to lay down procedures for the declaration of capital movements for purposes of administrative or statistical information, or to take measures which are justified on grounds of public policy or public security.

2. The provisions of this Chapter shall be without prejudice to the applicability of restrictions on the right of establishment which are compatible with this Treaty.

3. The measures and procedures referred to in paragraphs 1 and 2 shall not constitute a means of arbitrary discrimination or a disguised restriction on the free movement of capital and payments as defined in Article [46].[1]

Cases

I. Case C-503/99 Commission of the European Communities v Kingdom of Belgium [2002] ECR I-4809

The free movement of capital, as a fundamental principle of the Treaty, may be restricted only by national rules which are justified by reasons referred to in Article 73d(1) of the Treaty or by overriding requirements of the general interest and which are applicable to all persons and undertakings pursuing an activity in the territory of the host Member State. Furthermore, in order to be so justified, the national legislation must be suitable for securing the objective which it pursues and must not go beyond what is necessary in order to attain it, so as to accord with the principle of proportionality. The safeguarding of energy supplies in the event of a crisis, falls undeniably within the ambit of a legitimate public interest. Public security is one of the grounds of justification referred to in Article 73d(1)(b) of the Treaty. Public security may be relied on only if there is a genuine and sufficiently serious threat to a fundamental interest of society. It is necessary, therefore, to ascertain whether the legislation in issue enables the Member State concerned to ensure a minimum level of energy supplies in the event of a genuine and serious threat, and whether or not it goes beyond what is necessary for that purpose.

II. Case C-54/99 Association Eglise de Scientologie de Paris and Scientology International Reserves Trust v The Prime Minister [2000] ECR I-1335

Article [58(1)(b)][1] EC must be interpreted as precluding a system of prior authorization for direct foreign investments which confines itself to defining in general terms the affected investments as being investments that are such as to represent a threat to public policy and public security, with the result that the persons concerned are unable to ascertain the specific circumstances in which prior authorization is required.

III. Case C-118/96 Jessica Safir v Skattemyndigheten i Dalarnas Län, formerly Skattemyndigheten i Kopparbergs Län [1998] ECR I-1897

Although direct taxation does not as such fall within the purview of the Community, the powers retained by the Member States must nevertheless be exercised consistently with Community law.

As regards freedom to provide services, Article [49][1] of the Treaty precludes the application of legislation in a Member State which provides for different tax regimes for capital life assurance policies, depending on whether they are taken out with companies established in that Member State or with companies established elsewhere, where that legislation contains a number of elements liable to dissuade individuals from taking out capital life assurance with companies established in other Member States and liable to dissuade those insurance companies from offering their services on the market in that Member State.

IV. Cases C-163/94, C-165/94 and C-250/94 Criminal Proceedings Against Lucas Emilio Sanz de Lera, Raimundo Díaz Jiménez and Figen Kapanoglu [1995] ECR I-4821

See supra under Article 56.

V. Joined cases C-358/93 and C-416/93 Criminal Proceedings Against Aldo Bordessa and Vicente Marí Mellado and Concepción Barbero Maestre [1995] ECR I-361

See supra under Article 56.

Article 59 (ex Article 73f)

Where, in exceptional circumstances, movements of capital to or from third countries cause, or threaten to cause, serious difficulties for the operation of economic and monetary union, the Council, acting by a qualified majority on a proposal from the Commission and after consulting the ECB, may take safeguard measures with regard to third countries for a period not exceeding six months if such measures are strictly necessary.

Article 60 (ex Article 73g)

1. If, in the cases envisaged in Article 301, action by the Community is deemed necessary, the Council may, in accordance with the procedure provided for in Article 301, take the necessary urgent measures on the movement of capital and on payments as regards the third countries concerned.

2. Without prejudice to Article 297 and as long as the Council has not taken measures pursuant to paragraph 1, a Member State may, for serious political reasons and on grounds of urgency, take unilateral measures against a third country with regard to capital movements and payments. The Commission and the other Member States shall be informed of such measures by the date of their entry into force at the latest.

The Council may, acting by a qualified majority on a proposal from the Commission, decide that the Member State concerned shall amend or abolish such measures. The President of the Council shall inform the European Parliament of any such decision taken by the Council.

C.M. 2.

Council Directive 88/361/EEC
of 24 June 1988
for the implementation of Article [67][1] of the Treaty[2]

¶ *This Directive has largely been superseded by Chapter 4 (articles 56 to 60) of the Treaty establishing the European Community. Article 67 has been repealed as from 1 May 1999, by article 12 of the Treaty of Amsterdam.*

THE COUNCIL OF THE EUROPEAN COMMUNITIES,

Having regard to the Treaty establishing the European Economic Community, and in particular Articles [69 and 70 (1)][3] thereof,

Having regard to the proposal from the Commission, submitted following consultation with the Monetary Committee,[4]

Having regard to the opinion of the European Parliament,[5]

Whereas Article [18][2] of the Treaty stipulates that the internal market shall comprise an area without internal frontiers in which the free movement of capital is ensured, without prejudice to the other provisions of the Treaty;

Whereas Member States should be able to take the requisite measures to regulate bank liquidity; whereas these measures should be restricted to this purpose;

Whereas Member States should, if necessary, be able to take measures to restrict, temporarily and within the framework of appropriate Community procedures, short-term capital movements which, even where there is no appreciable divergence in economic fundamentals, might seriously disrupt the conduct of their monetary and exchange rate policies;

Whereas, in the interests of transparency, it is advisable to indicate the scope, in accordance with the arrangements laid down in this Directive, of the transitional measures adopted for the benefit of the Kingdom of Spain and the Portuguese Republic by the 1985 Act of Accession in the field of capital movements;

Whereas the Kingdom of Spain and the Portuguese Republic may, under the terms of Articles 61 to 66 and 222 to 232 respectively of the 1985 Act of Accession, postpone the liberalisation of certain capital movements in derogation from the obligations set out in the First Council Directive of 11 May 1960 for the implementation of Article [67][1] of the Treaty[6] as last amended by Directive 86/566/EEC;[7] whereas Directive 86/566/EEC also provides for transitional arrangements to be applied for the benefit of those two Member States in respect of their obligations to liberalise capital movements; whereas it is appropriate for those two Member States to be able to postpone the application of the new liberalisation obligations resulting from this Directive;

Whereas the Hellenic Republic and Ireland are faced, albeit to differing degrees, with difficult balance-of-payments situations and high levels of external indebtedness; whereas the immediate and complete liberalisation of capital movements by those two Member States would make it more difficult for them to continue to apply the measures they have taken to improve their external positions and to reinforce the capacity of their financial systems to adapt to the

---

[1] Article 67 has been repealed as from 1 May 1999, by article 12 of the Treaty of Amsterdam.
[2] OJ L 178, 8.7.1988, 5–18.
[3] Articles 69 and 70 (1) have been repealed as from 1 May 1999 by article 12 of the Treaty of Amsterdam.
[4] OJ C 26, 1.2.1988, 1.
[5] Opinion delivered on 17 June 1988.
[6] OJ 43, 12.7.1960, 921.
[7] OJ L 332, 26.11.1986, 22, as amended by Directive 63/21/EEC of 18 December 1963, OJ L 9, 22.1.1963, 62; by Directive 85/583/EEC, of 20 December 1985, OJ L 372, 31.12.1985, 39; and by Directive 86/566/EEC, of 17 November 1986, OJ L 332, 26.11.1986, 22.

requirements of an integrated financial market in the Community; whereas it is appropriate, in accordance with Article [20][2] of the Treaty, to grant to those two Member States, in the light of their specific circumstances, further time in which to comply with the obligations arising from this Directive;

Whereas, since the full liberalisation of capital movements could in some Member States, and especially in border areas, contribute to difficulties in the market for secondary residences; whereas existing national legislation regulating these purchases should not be affected by the entry into effect of this Directive;

Whereas advantage should be taken of the period adopted for bringing this Directive into effect in order to enable the Commission to submit proposals designed to eliminate or reduce risks of distortion, tax evasion and tax avoidance resulting from the diversity of national systems for taxation and to permit the Council to take a position on such proposals;

Whereas, in accordance with Article [70 (1)][2] of the Treaty, the Community shall endeavour to attain the highest possible degree of liberalisation in respect of the movement of capital between its residents and those of third countries;

Whereas large-scale short-term capital movements to or from third countries may seriously disturb the monetary or financial situation of Member States or cause serious stresses on the exchange markets; whereas such developments may prove harmful for the cohesion of the European Monetary System, for the smooth operation of the internal market and for the progressive achievement of economic and monetary union; whereas it is therefore appropriate to create the requisite conditions for concerted action by Member States should this prove necessary;

Whereas this Directive replaces Council Directive 72/156/EEC of 21 March 1972 on regulating international capital flows and neutralising their undesirable effects on domestic liquidity;[8]

whereas Directive 72/156/EEC should accordingly be repealed,

HAS ADOPTED THIS DIRECTIVE:

Article 1

1. Without prejudice to the following provisions Member States shall abolish restrictions on movements of capital taking place between persons resident in Member States. To facilitate application of this Directive, capital movements shall be classified in accordance with the Nomenclature in Annex I.

2. Transfers in respect of capital movements shall be made on the same exchange rate conditions as those governing payments relating to current transactions.

Article 2

Member States shall notify the Committee of Governors of the Central Banks, the Monetary Committee and the Commission, by the date of their entry into force at the latest, of measures to regulate bank liquidity which have a specific impact on capital transactions carried out by credit institutions with non-residents.

Such measures shall be confined to what is necessary for the purposes of domestic monetary regulation. The Monetary Committee and the Committee of Governors of the Central Banks shall provide the Commission with opinions on this subject.

Article 3

1. Where short-term capital movements of exceptional magnitude impose severe strains on foreign-exchange markets and lead to serious disturbances in the conduct of a Member State's monetary and exchange rate policies, being reflected in particular in substantial variations in domestic liquidity, the Commission may, after consulting the Monetary Committee and the Committee of Governors of the Central Banks, authorise that Member State to take, in respect of the capital movements listed in Annex II,

---

[8] OJ L 91, 18.4.1972, 13.

protective measures the conditions and details of which the Commission shall determine.

2. The Member State concerned may itself take the protective measures referred to above, on grounds of urgency, should these measures be necessary. The Commission and the other Member States shall be informed of such measures by the date of their entry into force at the latest. The Commission, after consulting the Monetary Committee and the Committee of Governors of the Central Banks, shall decide whether the Member State concerned may continue to apply these measures or whether it should amend or abolish them.

3. The decisions taken by the Commission under paragraphs 1 and 2 may be revoked or amended by the Council acting by a qualified majority.

4. The period of application of protective measures taken pursuant to this Article shall not exceed six months.

5. Before 31 December 1992, the Council shall examine, on the basis of a report from the Commission, after delivery of an opinion by the Monetary Committee and the Committee of Governors of the Central Banks, whether the provisions of this Article remain appropriate, as regards their principle and details, to the requirements which they were intended to satisfy.

Article 4

This Directive shall be without prejudice to the right of Member States to take all requisite measures to prevent infringements of their laws and regulations, *inter alia* in the field of taxation and prudential supervision of financial institutions, or to lay down procedures for the declaration of capital movements for purposes of administrative or statistical information.

Application of those measures and procedures may not have the effect of impeding capital movements carried out in accordance with Community law.

Article 5

For the Kingdom of Spain and the Portuguese Republic, the scope, in accordance with the Nomenclature of capital movements contained in Annex I, of the provisions of the 1985 Act of Accession in the field of capital movements shall be as indicated in Annex III.

Article 6

1. Member States shall take the measures necessary to comply with this Directive no later than 1 July 1990. They shall forthwith inform the Commission thereof. They shall also make known, by the date of their entry into force at the latest, any new measure or any amendment made to the provisions governing the capital movements listed in Annex I.

2. The Kingdom of Spain and the Portuguese Republic, without prejudice for these two Member States to Articles 61 to 66 and 222 to 232 of the 1985 Act of Accession, and the Hellenic Republic and Ireland may temporarily continue to apply restrictions to the capital movements listed in Annex IV, subject to the conditions and time limits laid down in that Annex.

If, before expiry of the time limit set for the liberalisation of the capital movements referred to in Lists III and IV of Annex IV, the Portuguese Republic or the Hellenic Republic considers that it is unable to proceed with liberalisation, in particular because of difficulties as regards its balance of payments or because the national financial system is insufficiently adapted, the Commission, at the request of one or other of these Member States, shall in collaboration with the Monetary Committee, review the economic and financial situation of the Member State concerned. On the basis of the outcome of this review, the Commission shall propose to the Council an extension of the time limit set for liberalisation of all or part of the capital movements referred to. This extension may not exceed three years. The Council shall act in accordance with the procedure laid down in Article [69]² of the Treaty.

3. The Kingdom of Belgium and the Grand Duchy of Luxembourg may temporarily continue to operate the dual exchange market under the conditions and for the periods laid down in Annex V.

4. Existing national legislation regulating purchases of secondary residences may be upheld until the Council adopts further provisions in this area in accordance with Article [69]² of the Treaty. This provision does not affect the applicability of other provisions of Community law.

5. The Commission shall submit to the Council, by 31 December 1988, proposals aimed at eliminating or reducing risks of distortion, tax evasion and tax avoidance linked to the diversity of national systems for the taxation of savings and for controlling the application of these systems.

The Council shall take a position on these Commission proposals by 30 June 1989. Any tax provisions of a Community nature shall, in accordance with the Treaty, be adopted unanimously.

Article 7

1. In their treatment of transfers in respect of movements of capital to or from third countries, the Member States shall endeavour to attain the same degree of liberalisation as that which applies to operations with residents of other Member States, subject to the other provisions of this Directive.

The provisions of the preceding subparagraph shall not prejudice the application to third countries of domestic rules or Community law, particularly any reciprocal conditions, concerning operations involving establishment, the provisions of financial services and the admission of securities to capital markets.

2. Where large-scale short-term capital movements to or from third countries seriously disturb the domestic or external monetary or financial situation of the Member States, or of a number of them, or cause serious strains in exchange relations within the Community or between the Community and third countries, Member States shall consult with one another on any measure to be taken to counteract such difficulties. This consultation shall take place within the Committee of Governors of the Central Banks and the Monetary Committee on the initiative of the Commission or of any Member State.

Article 8

At least once a year the Monetary Committee shall examine the situation regarding free movement of capital as it results from the application of this Directive. The examination shall cover measures concerning the domestic regulation of credit and financial and monetary markets which could have a specific impact on international capital movements and on all other aspects of this Directive. The Committee shall report to the Commission on the outcome of this examination.

Article 9

The First Directive of 11 May 1960 and Directive 72/156/EEC shall be repealed with effect from 1 July 1990.

Article 10

This Directive is addressed to the Member States.

Annex I

Nomenclature of the capital movements referred to in Article 1 of the Directive

In this Nomenclature, capital movements are classified according to the economic nature of the - assets and liabilities they concern, denominated either in national currency or in foreign exchange.

The capital movements listed in this Nomenclature are taken to cover:
– all the operations necessary for the purposes of capital movements: conclusion and

performance of the transaction and related transfers. The transaction is generally between residents of different Member States although some capital movements are carried out by a single person for his own account (e.g. transfers of assets belonging to emigrants),

— operations carried out by any natural or legal person[a] including operations in respect of the assets or liabilities of Member States or of other public administrations and agencies, subject to the provisions of Article [68 (3)][2] of the Treaty,

— access for the economic operator to all the financial techniques available on the market approached for the purpose of carrying out the operation in question. For example, the concept of acquisition of securities and other financial instruments covers not only spot transactions but also all the dealing techniques available: forward transactions, transactions carrying an option or warrant, swaps against other assets, etc. Similarly, the concept of operations in current and deposit accounts with financial institutions, includes not only the opening and placing of funds on accounts but also forward foreign exchange transactions, irrespective of whether these are intended to cover an exchange risk or to take an open foreign exchange position,

— operations to liquidate or assign assets built up, repatriation of the proceeds of liquidation thereof or immediate use of such proceeds within the limits of Community obligations,

— operations to repay credits or loans.

This Nomenclature is not an exhaustive list for the notion of capital movements—whence a heading XIII—F. 'Other capital movements—Miscellaneous'. It should not therefore be interpreted as restricting the scope of the principle of full liberalisation of capital movements as referred to in Article 1 of the Directive.

---

[a] See explanatory notes below.

I—DIRECT INVESTMENTS[a]

1. Establishment and extension of branches or new undertakings belonging solely to the person providing the capital, and the acquisition in full of existing undertakings.

2. Participation in new or existing undertaking with a view to establishing or maintaining lasting economic links.

3. Long-term loans with a view to establishing or maintaining lasting economic links.

4. Reinvestment of profits with a view to maintaining lasting economic links.

A *Direct investments on national territory by non-residents*[a]

B *Direct investments abroad by residents*[a]

II—INVESTMENTS IN REAL ESTATE (not included under I)[a]

A *Investments in real estate on national territory by non-residents*

B *Investments in real estate abroad by residents*

III—OPERATIONS IN SECURITIES NORMALLY DEALT IN ON THE CAPITAL MARKET (not included under I, IV and V)

(a) *Shares and other securities of a participating nature*[a]

(b) *Bonds*[a]

A *Transactions in securities on the capital market*

1. Acquisition by non-residents of domestic securities dealt in on a stock exchange.[a]

2. Acquisition by residents of foreign securities dealt in on a stock exchange.

3. Acquisition by non-residents of domestic securities not dealt in on a stock exchange.[a]

4. Acquisition by residents of foreign securities not dealt in on a stock exchange.

B *Admission of securities to the capital market*[a]

(i) Introduction on a stock exchange.[a]
(ii) Issue and placing on a capital market.[a]

1. Admission of domestic securities to a foreign capital market.

2. Administration of foreign securities to the domestic capital market.

IV—Operations in Units of Collective Investment Undertakings[a]

(a) Units of undertakings for collective investment in securities normally dealt in on the capital market (shares, other equities and bonds).

(b) Units of undertakings for collective investment in securities or instruments normally dealt in on the money market.

(c) Units of undertakings for collective investment in other assets.

A *Transactions in units of collective investment undertakings*

1. Acquisition by non-residents of units of national undertakings dealt in on a stock exchange.

2. Acquisition by residents of units of foreign undertakings dealt in on a stock exchange.

3. Acquisition by non-residents of units of national undertakings not dealt in on a stock exchange.

4. Acquisition by residents of units of foreign undertakings not dealt in on a stock exchange.

B *Administration of units of collective investment undertakings to the capital market*

(i) Introduction on a stock exchange.
(ii) Issue and placing on a capital market.

1. Admission of units of national collective investment undertakings to a foreign capital market.

2. Admission of units of foreign collective investment undertakings to the domestic capital market.

V—Operations in Securities and Other Instruments Normally Dealt in on the Money Market[a]

A *Transactions in securities and other instruments on the money market*

1. Acquisition by non-residents of domestic money market securities and instruments.

2. Acquisition by residents of foreign money market securities and instruments.

B *Admission of securities and other instruments to the money market*

(i) Introduction on a recognised money market.[a]
(ii) Issue and placing on a recognised money market.

1. Admission of domestic securities and instruments to a foreign money market.

2. Admission of foreign securities and instruments to the domestic money market.

VI—Operations in Current and Deposit Accounts with Financial Institutions[a]

A *Operations carried out by non-residents with domestic financial institutions*

B *Operations carried out by residents with foreign financial institutions*

VII—Credits Related to Commercial Transactions or to the Provision of Services in which a Resident is Participating[a]

1. Short-term (less than one year).

2. Medium-term (from one to five years).

3. Long-term (five years or more).

A *Credits granted by non-residents to residents*

B *Credits granted by residents to non-residents*

---

[a] See explanatory notes below.

VIII—Financial Loans and Credits (not included under I, VII and XI)[a]

1. Short-term (less than one year).
2. Medium-term (from one to five years).
3. Long-term (five years or more).

A *Loans and credits granted by non-residents to residents*

B *Loans and credits granted by residents to non-residents*

IX—Sureties, Other Guarantees and Rights of Pledge

A *Granted by non-residents to residents*
B *Granted by residents to non-residents*

X—Transfers in Performance of Insurance Contracts

A *Premiums and payments in respect of life assurance*

1. Contracts concluded between domestic life assurance companies and non-residents.
2. Contracts concluded between foreign life assurance companies and residents.

B *Premiums and payments in respect of credit insurance*

1. Contracts concluded between domestic credit insurance companies and non-residents.
2. Contracts concluded between foreign credit insurance companies and residents.

C *Other transfers of capital in respect of insurance contracts*

XI—Personal Capital Movements

A *Loans*
B *Gifts and endowments*
C *Dowries*

D *Inheritances and legacies*
E *Settlement of debts by immigrants in their previous country of residence*
F *Transfers of assets constituted by residents, in the event of emigration, at the time of their installation or during their period of stay abroad*
G *Transfers, during their period of stay, of immigrants' savings to their previous country of residence*

XII—Physical Import and Export of Financial Assets

A *Securities*
B *Means of payment of every kind*

XIII—Other Capital Movements

A *Death duties*
B *Damages (where these can be considered as capital)*
C *Refunds in the case of cancellation of contracts and refunds of uncalled-for payments (where these can be considered as capital)*
D *Authors' royalties: patents, designs, trademarks and inventions (assignments and transfers arising out of such assignments)*
E *Transfers of the monies required for the provision of services (not included under VI)*
F *Miscellaneous*

Explanatory Notes

For the purposes of this Nomenclature and the Directive only, the following expressions have the meanings assigned to them respectively:

Direct investments

Investments of all kinds by natural persons or commercial, industrial or financial undertakings, and which serve to establish or to maintain lasting and direct links between the person providing the capital and the entrepreneur to whom or the undertaking to which the capital is made available in order to carry on an economic activity. This concept must therefore be understood in its widest sense.

The undertakings mentioned under I-1 of the Nomenclature include legally independent undertakings (wholly-owned subsidiaries) and branches.

As regards those undertakings mentioned under I-2 of the Nomenclature which have the status of companies limited by shares, there is participation in the nature of direct investment where the block of shares held by a natural person of another undertaking or any other holder enables the shareholder, either pursuant to the provisions of national laws relating to companies limited by shares or otherwise, to participate effectively in the management of the company or in its control.

Long-term loans of a participating nature, mentioned under I-3 of the Nomenclature, means loans for a period of more than five years which are made for the purpose of establishing or maintaining lasting economic links. The main examples that may be cited are loans granted by a company to its subsidiaries or to companies in which it has a share and loans linked with a profit-sharing arrangement. Loans granted by financial institutions with a view to establishing or maintaining lasting economic links are also included under this heading.

Investments in real estate

Purchases of buildings and land and the construction of buildings by private persons for gain or personal use. This category also includes rights of usufruct, easements and building rights.

Introduction on a stock exchange or on a recognised money market

Access—in accordance with a specified procedure—for securities and other negotiable instruments to dealings, whether controlled officially or unofficially, on an officially recognised stock exchange or in an officially recognised segment of the money market.

Securities dealt in on a stock exchange (quoted or unquoted)

Securities the dealings in which are controlled by regulations, the prices for which are regularly published, either by official stock exchanges (quoted securities) or by other bodies attached to a stock exchange—e.g. committees of banks (unquoted securities).

Issue of securities and other negotiable instruments

Sale by way of an offer to the public.

Placing of securities and other negotiable instruments

The direct sale of securities by the issuer or by the consortium which the issuer has instructed to sell them, with no offer being made to the public.

Domestic or foreign securities and other instruments

Securities according to the country in which the issuer has his principal place of business. Acquisition by residents of domestic securities and other instruments issued on a foreign market ranks as the acquisition of foreign securities.

Shares and other securities of a participating nature

Including rights to subscribe to new issues of shares.

Bonds

Negotiable securities with a maturity of two years or more from issue for which the interest rate and the terms for the repayment of the principal and the payment of interest are determined at the time of issue.

Collective investment undertakings

Undertakings:
- the object of which is the collective investment in transferable securities or other assets of the capital they raise and which operate on the principle of risk-spreading, and
- the units of which are, at the request of holders, under the legal, contractual or statutory conditions governing them, repurchased or redeemed, directly or indirectly, out of those undertakings' assets. Action taken by a collective investment undertaking to ensure that the stock exchange value of its units does not significantly vary from their net asset value shall be regarded as equivalent to such repurchase or redemption.

Such undertakings may be constituted according to law either under the law of contract (as common funds managed by management companies) or trust law (as unit trusts) or under statute (as investment companies).

For the purposes of the Directive, 'common funds' shall also include unit trusts.

Securities and other instruments normally dealt in on the money market

Treasury bills and other negotiable bills, certificates of deposit, bankers' acceptances, commercial paper and other like instruments.

Credits related to commercial transactions or to the provision of services.

Contractual trade credits (advances or payments by instalment in respect of work in progress or on order and extended payment terms, whether or not involving subscription to a commercial bill) and their financing by credits provided by credit institutions. This category also includes factoring operations.

Financial loans and credits

Financing of every kind granted by financial institutions, including financing related to commercial transactions or to the provision of services in which no resident is participating.

This category also includes mortgage loans, consumer credit and financial leasing, as well as back-up facilities and other note-issuance facilities.

Residents or non-residents

Natural and legal persons according to the definitions laid down in the exchange control regulations in force in each Member State.

Proceeds of liquidation (of investments, securities, etc.)

Proceeds of sale including any capital appreciation, amount of repayments, proceeds of execution of judgments, etc.

Natural or legal persons

As defined by the national rules.

Financial institutions

Banks, savings banks and institutions specialising in the provision of short-term, medium-term and long-term credit, and insurance companies, building societies, investment companies and other institutions of like character.

Credit institutions

Banks, savings banks and institutions specialising in the provision of short-term, medium-term and long-term credit.

Annex II

List of operations referred to in Article 3 of the Directive

Nature of operation	Heading
Operations in securities and other instruments normally dealt in on the money market	V
Operations in current and deposit accounts with financial institutions	IV
Operations in units of collective investment undertakings – undertakings for investment in securities or instruments normally dealt in on the money market	IV-A and B (c)
Financial loans and credits – short-term	VIII-A and B-1
Personal capital movements – loans	XI-A
Physical import and export of financial assets – securities normally dealt in on the money market – means of payment	XII
Other capital movements: Miscellaneous – short-term operations similar to those listed above	XIII-F

The restrictions which Member States may apply to the capital movements listed above must be defined and applied in such a way as to cause the least possible hindrance to the free movement of persons, goods and services.

Annex III

Referred to in Article 5 of the Directive

Scope of the provisions of the 1985 Act of Accession relating to capital movements, in accordance with the Nomenclature of capital movements set out in Annex I to the Directive

Articles of the Act of Accession (dates of expiry of transitional provisions)	Nature of operation	Heading
(a) Provisions concerning the Kingdom of Spain		
Article 62 (31.2.1990)	Direct investments abroad by residents	I-B
Article 63 (31.2.1990)	Investments in real estate abroad by residents	II-B
Article 64 (31.12.1988)	Operations in securities normally dealt in on the capital market – Acquisition by residents of foreign securities dealt in on a stock exchange	III-A-2

Articles of the Act of Accession (dates of expiry of transitional provisions)	Nature of operation	Heading
	– excluding bonds issued on a foreign market and denominated in national currency	
	Operations in units of collective investment undertakings – Acquisition by residents of units of collective investment undertakings dealt in on a stock exchange – excluding units of undertakings taking the form of common funds	IV-A-2

(b) Provisions concerning the Portuguese Republic

Articles of the Act of Accession (dates of expiry of transitional provisions)	Nature of operation	Heading
Article 222 (31.12.1989)	Direct investments on national territory by non-residents	I-A
Article 224 (31.12.1992)	Direct investments abroad by residents	II-B
Articles 225 and 226 (31.12.1990)	Investments in real estate on national territory by non-residents Investments in real estate abroad by residents	II-A II-B
Article 227 (31.12.1992) Article 228 (31.12.1990)	Personal capital movements (i) for the purpose of applying the higher amounts specified in Article 228 (2): – Dowries – Inheritances and legacies – Transfers of assets built up by residents in case of emigration at the time of their installation or during their period of stay abroad (ii) for the purpose of applying the lower amounts specified in Article 228 (2): – Gifts and endowments – Settlement of debts by immigrants in their previous country of residence – Transfers of immigrants' savings to their previous country of residence during their period of stay	 XI-C XI-D XI-F XI-F XI-B XI-E XI-G
Article (31.12.1990)	Operations in securities normally dealt in on the capital market – Acquisition by residents of foreign securities dealt in on a stock exchange – excluding bonds issued on a foreign market and denominated in national currency	III-A-2
	Operations in units of collective investment undertakings – Acquisition by residents of units of foreign collective investment undertakings dealt in on a stock exchange – excluding units of undertakings taking the form of common funds	IV-A-2

Annex IV

Referred to in Article 6 (2) of the Directive

I. The Portuguese Republic may continue to apply or reintroduce, until 31 December 1990 restrictions existing on the date of notification of the Directive on capital movements given in List I below:

List I

Nature of operation	Heading
Operations in units of collective investment undertakings	
– Acquisition by residents of units of foreign collective investment undertakings dealt in on a stock exchange	IV-A-2 (a)
– undertakings subject to Directive 85/611/EEC[1] and taking the form of common funds	
– Acquisition by residents of units of foreign collective investment undertakings not dealt in on a stock exchange	IV-A-4 (a)
– undertakings subject to Directive 85/611/EEC[1]	

[1] Council Directive 85/611/EEC on the co-ordination of laws, regulations and administrative provisions relating to undertakings for collective investment in transferable securities (UCITS) (OJ L 375, 31.12.1985, 3), reproduced infra under no. S.6.

II. The Kingdom of Spain and the Portuguese Republic may continue to apply or reintroduce, until 31 December 1990 and 31 December 1992 respectively, restrictions existing on the date of notification of the Directive on capital movements given in List II below:

List II

Nature of operation	Heading
Operations in securities normally dealt in on the capital market	
– Acquisition by residents of foreign securities dealt in on a stock exchange	III-A-2 (b)
– bonds issued on a foreign market and denominated in national currency	
– Acquisition by residents (non-residents) of foreign (domestic) securities not dealt in on a stock exchange	III-A-3 and 4
– Admission of securities to the capital market	III-B-1 and 2
– where they are dealt in on or in the process of introduction to a stock exchange in a Member State	
Operations in units of collective investment undertakings	
– Acquisition by residents of units of foreign collective investment undertakings dealt in on a stock exchange	IV-A-2
– undertakings not subject to Directive 85/611/EEC[1] and taking the form of common funds	
– Acquisition by residents (non-residents) of units of foreign (domestic) collective investment undertakings not dealt in on a stock exchange	IV-A-3 and 4
– undertakings not subject to Directive 85/611/EEC[1] and the sole object of which is the acquisition of assets that have been liberalised	

List II

Nature of operation	Heading
– Admission to the capital market of units of collective investment of undertakings – undertakings subject to Directive 85/611/EEC[1]	IV-B-1 and 2(a)
– Credits related to commercial transactions or to the provision of services in which a resident is participating – Long-term credits	VII-A and B-3

[1] See footnote to List I.

III. The Hellenic Republic, the Kingdom of Spain, Ireland and the Portuguese Republic may, until 31 December 1992, continue to apply or reintroduce restrictions existing at the date of notification of the Directive on capital movements given in List III below.

List III

Nature of operation	Heading
Operations in securities dealt in on the capital market – Admission of securities to the capital market – where they are not dealt in on or in the process of introduction to a stock exchange in a Member State	III-B-1 and 2
Operations in units of collective investment undertakings – Admission to the capital market of units of collective investment of undertakings – undertakings not subject to Directive 85/611/EEC[1] and the sole object of which is the acquisition of assets that have been liberalised	IV-B-1 and 2
Financial loans and credits – medium-term and long-term	VIII-A, B-2 and 3

[1] See footnote to List I.

IV. The Hellenic Republic, the Kingdom of Spain, Ireland and the Portuguese Republic may, until 31 December 1992, defer liberalisation of the capital movements given in List IV below:

List IV

Nature of operation	Heading
Operations in securities and other instruments normally dealt in on the money market	V
Operations in current and deposit accounts with financial institutions	VI
Operations in units of collective investment undertakings – undertakings for investment in securities or instruments normally dealt in on the money market	IV-A and B (c)
Financial loans and credits – short term	VIII-A and B-1
Personal and capital movements – loans	XI-A
Physical import and export of financial assets – securities normally dealt in on the money market – means of payment	XII
Other capital movements: Miscellaneous	XIII-F

Annex V

Since the dual exchange market system, as operated by the Kingdom of Belgium and the Grand Duchy of Luxembourg, has not had the effect of restricting capital movements but nevertheless constitutes an anomaly in the EMS and should therefore be brought to an end in the interests of effective implementation of the Directive and with a view to strengthening the European Monetary System, these two Member States undertake to abolish it by 31 December 1992. They also undertake to administer the system, until such time as it is abolished, on the basis of procedures which will still ensure the de facto free movement of capital on such conditions that the exchange rates ruling on the two markets show no appreciable and lasting differences.

¶ *The dual market system was in fact abolished in February 1990.*

Part III

Company Law

C.1.

**First Council Directive 68/151/EEC
of 9 March 1968
on co-ordination of safeguards which, for the protection of the interests of members
and others, are required by Member States of companies within the meaning of the
second paragraph of Article [48][1] of the Treaty, with a view to making such safeguards
equivalent throughout the Community[2]**

THE COUNCIL OF THE EUROPEAN COMMUNITIES,

Having regard to the Treaty establishing the European Economic Community, and in particular Article [44][1] (3) (g) thereof;

Having regard to the General Programme for the abolition of restrictions on freedom of establishment, and in particular Title VI thereof;

Having regard to the proposal from the Commission;[3]

Having regard to the Opinion of the European Parliament;[4]

Having regard to the Opinion of the Economic and Social Committee;[5]

Whereas the co-ordination provided for in Article 54 (3) (g) and in the General Programme for the abolition of restrictions on freedom of establishment is a matter of urgency, especially in regard to companies limited by shares or otherwise having limited liability, since the activities of such companies often extend beyond the frontiers of national territories;

Whereas the co-ordination of national provisions concerning disclosure, the validity of obligations entered into by, and the nullity of, such companies is of special importance, particularly for the purpose of protecting the interests of third parties;

Whereas in these matters Community provisions must be adopted in respect of such companies simultaneously, since the only safeguards they offer to third parties are their assets;

Whereas the basic documents of the company should be disclosed in order that third parties may be able to ascertain their contents and other information concerning the company, especially particulars of the persons who are authorised to bind the company;

Whereas the protection of third parties must be ensured by provisions which restrict to the greatest possible extent the grounds on which obligations entered into in the name of the company are not valid;

Whereas it is necessary, in order to ensure certainty in the law as regards relations between the company and third parties, and also between

---

[1] The number between brackets has been changed as from 1 May 1999 by article 12 of the Treaty of Amsterdam.
[2] OJ L 65, 14.3.1968, 8–12.
[3] OJ 2, 15.1.1962, 36/62.
[4] OJ 96, 28.5.1966, 1519/66.
[5] OJ 194, 27.11.1964, 3248/64.

members, to limit the cases in which nullity can arise and the retroactive effect of a declaration of nullity, and to fix a short time limit within which third parties may enter objection to any such declaration;

HAS ADOPTED THIS DIRECTIVE:

Article 1

The co-ordination measures prescribed by this Directive shall apply to the laws, regulations and administrative provisions of the Member States relating to the following types of company:
- In Germany:
  die Aktiengesellschaft, die Kommanditgesellschaft auf Aktien, die Gesellschaft mit beschränkter Haftung;
- In Belgium:
  de naamloze vennootschap / la société anonyme, de commanditaire vennootschap op aandelen/ la société en commandite par actions, de personenvennootschap met beperkte aansprakelijkheid/la société à responsabilité limitée;
- [In France:
  la société anonyme, la société en commandite par actions, la société à responsabilité limitée, la société par actions simplifiée];
- In Italy:
  società per azioni, società in accomandita per azioni, società a responsabilità limitata;
- In Luxembourg:
  la société anonyme, la société en commandite par actions, la société à responsabilité limitée;
- [In the Netherlands:
  de naamloze vennootschap, de besloten vennootschap met beperkte aansprakelijkheid];
- [In the United Kingdom:
  companies incorporated with limited liability];
- [In Ireland:
  companies incorporated with limited liability];
- [In Denmark:
  aktieselskab; kommanditaktieselskab, anpartsselskab];
- [In Greece:
  ανωνυμη εταιρια, εταιρια περιωρισμε–ϖης ευθυνης, ετερορρυθμη κατα μετοχεςεταιρια];
- [In Spain:
  la sociedad anonima, la sociedad comanditaria por acciones, la sociedad de responsabilidad limitada];
- [In Portugal:
  a sociedade anonima de responsabilidade limitada, a sociedade em comandita por acçoes, a sociedade por quotas de responsabilidade limitada];
- [In Austria:
  die Aktiengesellschaft, die Gesellschaft mit beschränkter Haftung];
- [In Finland:
  yksityinen osakeyhtiö/privat aktiebolag, julkinen osakeyhtiö/publikt aktiebolag];
- [In Sweden:
  aktiebolag];
- [In the Czech Republic:
  společnost s ručením omezeným, akciová společnost];
- [In Estonia:
  aktsiaselts, osaühing];
- [In Cyprus:
  Δημόσιες εταιρείες περιορισμένης ευθύνης με μετοχές ή με εγγύηση, ιδιωτικές εταιρείες περιορισμένης ευθύνης με μετοχές ή με εγγύηση];
- [In Latvia:
  akciju sabiedrība, sabiedrība ar ierobežotu atbildību, komandītsabiedrība];
- [In Lithuania:
  akcinė bendrovė, uždaroji akcinė bendrovė];
- [In Hungary:
  részvénytársaság, korlátolt felelősségű társaság];
- [In Malta:
  kumpanija pubblika/public limited liability company, kumpanija privata/private limited liability company];
- [In Poland:
  spółka z ograniczoną odpowiedzialnością, spółka komandytowoakcyjna, spółka akcyjna];
- [In Slovenia:
  delniška družba, družba z omejeno odgovornostjo, komaditna delniška družba];
- [In Slovakia:
  akciová spoločnosť, spoločnosť s ručením obmedzeným].

¶ *This Directive has been rendered applicable to Denmark, Ireland and the UK by Annex I(III), litera H(1) of the Act of Accession (OJ L 304, 30.10.1978); to Greece by the Act of*

Accession of the Hellenic Republic, Annex I, (III)(c)(1) (OJ L 291, 19.11.1979); to Spain and Portugal by the Act of Accession of the Kingdom of Spain and the Portuguese Republic, Annex I, (II)(d)(1) (OJ L 302, 15.11.1985); to Austria, Sweden and Finland by the Act of Accession of Austria, Finland and Sweden, Annex I, (XI)(A)(1) (OJ C 241, 29.8.1994) and to Poland, Czech Republic, Slovenia, Slovakia, Estonia, Lithuania, Latvia, Cyprus, Hungary and Malta by the Act concerning the conditions of accession of the Czech Republic, the Republic of Estonia, the Republic of Cyprus, the Republic of Latvia, the Republic of Lithuania, the Republic of Hungary, the Republic of Malta, the Republic of Poland, the Republic of Slovenia and the Slovak Republic and the adjustments to the Treaties on which the European Union is founded, Annex II, (4)(a)(1) (OJ L 236, 23.9.2003).

¶ *For France, the Netherlands, Denmark, and Finland, this article has been amended by article 1 of Directive 2003/58/EC, reproduced infra under no. C. 24.*

Section I
Disclosure

Article 2

1. Member States shall take the measures required to ensure compulsory disclosure by companies of at least the following documents and particulars:

(a) The instrument of constitution, and the statutes if they are contained in a separate instrument;

(b) Any amendments to the instruments mentioned in (a), including any extension of the duration of the company;

(c) After every amendment of the instrument of constitution or of the statutes, the complete text of the instrument or statutes as amended to date;

(d) The appointment, termination of office and particulars of the persons who either as a body constituted pursuant to law or as members of any such body:
 (i) are authorised to represent the company in dealings with third parties and in legal proceedings;
 (ii) take part in the administration, supervision or control of the company.

It must appear from the disclosure whether the persons authorised to represent the company may do so alone or must act jointly;

(e) At least once a year, the amount of the capital subscribed, where the instrument of constitution or the statutes mention an authorised capital, unless any increase in the capital subscribed necessitates an amendment of the statutes;

[(f) The accounting documents for each financial year, which are required to be published in accordance with Council Directives 78/660/EEC,[6] 83/349/EEC,[7] 86/635/EEC[8] and 91/674/EEC[9];

(g) Any transfer of the seat of the company;

(h) The winding up of the company;

(i) Any declaration of nullity of the company by the courts;

(j) The appointment of liquidators, particulars concerning them, and their respective powers, unless such powers are expressly and exclusively derived from law or from the statutes of the company;

(k) The termination of the liquidation and, in Member States where striking off the register entails legal consequences, the fact of any such striking off.

2. [. . .]

¶ *Article 2(1)(f) has been replaced by article 1(2)(a) of Directive 2003/58/EC, reproduced infra under no. C. 24.*
¶ *Article 2(2) has been deleted by article 1(2)(b) of Directive 2003/58/EC, reproduced infra under no. C. 24.*

[Article 3

1. In each Member State, a file shall be opened in a central register, commercial register or companies register, for each of the companies registered therein.

2. All documents and particulars which must be disclosed pursuant to Article 2 shall be kept in the file, or entered in the register; the subject matter of the entries in the register must in every case appear in the file.

---

[6] OJ L 222, 14.8.1978, 11, reproduced infra under no. C. 4. Directive as last amended by Council Directive 2003/38/EC (OJ L 120, 15.5.2003, 22).

[7] OJ L 193, 18.7.1983, 1, reproduced infra under no. C. 6. Directive as last amended by Directive 2003/51/EC (OJ L 178, 17.7.2003, 16), reproduced infra under no. C. 23.

[8] OJ L 372, 31.12.1986, 1, reproduced supra under no. B. 7. Directive as last amended by Directive 2003/51/EC, reproduced infra under no. C. 23.

[9] OJ L 374, 31.12.1991, 7, reproduced infra under no. I. 23.

Member States shall ensure that, by 1 January 2007, the filing by companies, as well as by other persons and bodies required to make or assist in making notifications, of all documents and particulars which must be disclosed pursuant to Article 2 will be possible by electronic means. In addition, Member States may require all, or certain categories of, companies to file all, or certain types of, such documents and particulars by electronic means.

All documents and particulars referred to in Article 2 which are filed as from 1 January 2007 at the latest, whether by paper means or by electronic means, must be kept in the file, or entered in the register, in electronic form. To this end, Member States shall ensure that all such documents and particulars which are filed by paper means as from 1 January 2007 at the latest are converted by the register to electronic form.

The documents and particulars referred to in Article 2 that have been filed by paper means up to 31 December 2006 shall not be required to be converted automatically into electronic form by the register. Member States shall nevertheless ensure that they are converted into electronic form by the register upon receipt of an application for disclosure by electronic means submitted in accordance with the rules adopted to give effect to paragraph 3.

3. A copy of the whole or any part of the documents or particulars referred to in Article 2 must be obtainable on application. As from 1 January 2007 at the latest, applications may be submitted to the register by paper means or by electronic means as the applicant chooses.

As from a date to be chosen by each Member State, which shall be no later than 1 January 2007, copies as referred to in the first subparagraph must be obtainable from the register by paper means or by electronic means as the applicant chooses. This shall apply in the case of all documents and particulars, irrespective of whether they were filed before or after the chosen date. However, Member States may decide that all, or certain types of, documents and particulars filed by paper means on or before a date which may not be later than 31 December 2006 shall not be obtainable from the register by electronic means if a specified period has elapsed between the date of filing and the date of the application submitted to the register. Such specified period may not be less than 10 years.

The price of obtaining a copy of the whole or any part of the documents or particulars referred to in Article 2, whether by paper means or by electronic means, shall not exceed the administrative cost thereof.

Paper copies supplied shall be certified as 'true copies', unless the applicant dispenses with such certification. Electronic copies supplied shall not be certified as 'true copies', unless the applicant explicitly requests such a certification.

Member States shall take the necessary measures to ensure that certification of electronic copies guarantees both the authenticity of their origin and the integrity of their contents, by means at least of an advanced electronic signature within the meaning of Article 2(2) of Directive 1999/93/EC of the European Parliament and of the Council of 13 December 1999 on a Community framework for electronic signatures.[10]

4. Disclosure of the documents and particulars referred to in paragraph 2 shall be effected by publication in the national gazette appointed for that purpose by the Member State, either of the full text or of a partial text, or by means of a reference to the document which has been deposited in the file or entered in the register. The national gazette appointed for that purpose may be kept in electronic form.

Member States may decide to replace publication in the national gazette with equally effective means, which shall entail at least the use of a system whereby the information disclosed can be accessed in chronological order through a central electronic platform.

5. The documents and particulars may be relied on by the company as against third parties only after they have been disclosed in accordance with

---

[10] OJ L 13, 19.1.2000, 12, reproduced infra under no. C.P. 18.

paragraph 4, unless the company proves that the third parties had knowledge thereof.

However, with regard to transactions taking place before the 16th day following the disclosure, the documents and particulars shall not be relied on as against third parties who prove that it was impossible for them to have had knowledge thereof.

6. Member States shall take the necessary measures to avoid any discrepancy between what is disclosed in accordance with paragraph 4 and what appears in the register or file.

However, in cases of discrepancy, the text disclosed in accordance with paragraph 4 may not be relied on as against third parties; such third parties may nevertheless rely thereon, unless the company proves that they had knowledge of the texts deposited in the file or entered in the register.

7. Third parties may, moreover, always rely on any documents and particulars in respect of which the disclosure formalities have not yet been completed, save where non-disclosure causes them not to have effect.

8. For the purposes of this Article, 'by electronic means' shall mean that the information is sent initially and received at its destination by means of electronic equipment for the processing (including digital compression) and storage of data, and entirely transmitted, conveyed and received in a manner to be determined by Member States by wire, by radio, by optical means or by other electromagnetic means.]

¶ *Article 3 has been replaced by article 1(3) of Directive 2003/58/EC, reproduced infra under no. C. 24.*

[Article 3a

1. Documents and particulars which must be disclosed pursuant to Article 2 shall be drawn up and filed in one of the languages permitted by the language rules applicable in the Member State in which the file referred to in Article 3(1) is opened.

2. In addition to the mandatory disclosure referred to in Article 3, Member States shall allow documents and particulars referred to in Article 2 to be disclosed voluntarily in accordance with Article 3 in any official language(s) of the Community.

Member States may prescribe that the translation of such documents and particulars be certified.

Member States shall take the necessary measures to facilitate access by third parties to the translations voluntarily disclosed.

3. In addition to the mandatory disclosure referred to in Article 3, and to the voluntary disclosure provided for under paragraph 2 of this Article, Member States may allow the documents and particulars concerned to be disclosed, in accordance with Article 3, in any other language(s).

Member States may stipulate that the translation of such documents and particulars be certified.

4. In cases of discrepancy between the documents and particulars disclosed in the official languages of the register and the translation voluntarily disclosed, the latter may not be relied upon as against third parties. Third parties may nevertheless rely on the translations voluntarily disclosed, unless the company proves that the third parties had knowledge of the version which was the subject of the mandatory disclosure.]

¶ *Article 3a has been inserted by article 1(4) of Directive 2003/58/EC, reproduced infra under no. C. 24.*

[Article 4

Member States shall stipulate that letters and order forms, whether they are in paper form or use any other medium, shall state the following particulars:

(a) the information necessary to identify the register in which the file mentioned in Article 3 is kept, together with the number of the company in that register;

(b) the legal form of the company, the location of its registered office and, where appropriate, the fact that the company is being wound up.

Where, in these documents, mention is made of the capital of the company, the reference shall be to the capital subscribed and paid up.

Member States shall prescribe that company websites shall contain at least the particulars mentioned in the first paragraph and, if applicable, the reference to the capital subscribed and paid up.]

¶ *Article 4 has been replaced by article 1(5) of Directive 2003/58/EC, reproduced infra under no. C. 24.*

Article 5

Each Member State shall determine by which persons the disclosure formalities are to be carried out.

[*Article 6*

Member States shall provide for appropriate penalties at least in the case of:

(a) failure to disclose accounting documents as required by Article 2 (1) (f);

(b) omission from commercial documents of from any company website of the compulsory particulars provided for in Article 4.]

¶ *Article 6 has been replaced by article 1(6) of Directive 2003/58/EC, reproduced infra under no. C. 24.*

Cases

I. Joined cases C-387/02, C-391/02 and C-403/02 Criminal Proceedings Against Silvio Berlusconi, Sergio Adelchi and Marcello Dell'Utri and others [2005] ECR I-3565

Article 6 of the first directive indicates that the requirement to provide for appropriate penalties is to be understood as covering not only the case of the absence of any disclosure of annual accounts but also the case of the disclosure of annual accounts which have not been drawn up in accordance with the rules prescribed by the Fourth Companies Directive in regard to the content of such accounts. Due to its formulation, the same provision cannot be held to apply to the case of non-compliance with the 7th Directive on Consolidated Accounts.

Based on both Article 5 of the Treaty and Article 6 of the first directive, the requirement implies that penalties, for offences resulting from false

accounting, be appropriate and ensure in particular that infringements of Community law are penalized under conditions, both procedural and substantive, which are analogous to those applicable to infringements of national law of a similar nature and importance and which, in any event, make the penalty effective, proportionate, and dissuasive.

The principle of the retroactive application of the more lenient penalty forms part of the constitutional traditions common to the Member States and ought to be applied even if the provision entered into force only after the commission of the acts underlying the prosecutions. The question whether the penalty provision is compatible with the first directive is moot as this amounts to the authorities relying on a directive to impose obligations to an individual: a directive cannot, of itself and independently of a national law adopted by a Member State for its implementation, have the effect of determining or aggravating the criminal liability of persons who act in contravention of the provisions of that directive.

II. Case C-97/96 Verband Deutscher Daihatsu-Händler eV v Daihatsu Deutschland GmbH [1997] ECR I-6843

Article 6 of the First Council Directive 68/151/EEC, must be interpreted as precluding the legislation of a Member State from restricting to members or creditors of a company, the central works council or the company's works council the right to apply for imposition of the penalty provided for by the law of that Member State in the event of failure by a company to fulfil the obligations regarding disclosure of annual accounts laid down by the First Directive 68/151.

Section II
Validity of Obligations Entered into by a Company

Article 7

If, before a company being formed has acquired legal personality, action has been carried out in its name and the company does not assume the obligations arising from such action, the persons who acted shall, without limit, be jointly and severally liable therefore, unless otherwise agreed.

> **CASE**
>
> Case 136/87 Ubbink Isolatie BV v Dak- en Wandtechniek [1988] ECR 4665
>
> See infra under Article 11 of this Directive.

Article 8

Completion of the formalities of disclosure of the particulars concerning the persons who, as an organ of the company, are authorised to represent it shall constitute a bar to any irregularity in their appointment being relied upon as against third parties unless the company proves that such third parties had knowledge thereof.

Article 9

1. Acts done by the organs of the company shall be binding upon it even if those acts are not within the objects of the company, unless such acts exceed the powers that the law confers or allows to be conferred on those organs.

However, Member States may provide that the company shall not be bound where such acts are outside the objects of the company, if it proves that the third party knew that the act was outside those objects or could not in view of the circumstances have been unaware of it; disclosure of the statutes shall not of itself be sufficient proof thereof.

2. The limits on the powers of the organs of the company, arising under the statutes or from a decision of the competent organs, may never be relied on as against third parties, even if they have been disclosed.

3. If the national law provides that authority to represent a company may, in derogation from the legal rules governing the subject, be conferred by the statutes on a single person or on several persons acting jointly, that law may provide that such a provision in the statutes may be relied on as against third parties on condition that it relates to the general power of representation; the question whether such a provision in the statutes can be relied on as against third parties shall be governed by Article 3.

> **CASE**
>
> Case C-104/96 Coöperatieve Rabobank 'Vecht en Plassengebied' BA v Erik Aarnoud Minderhoud [1997] ECR I-7211
>
> The rules governing the enforceability as against third parties of acts done by members of company organs in circumstances where there is a conflict of interests with the company fall outside the normative framework of the First Council Directive 68/151/EEC and are matters for the national legislature.

SECTION III
NULLITY OF THE COMPANY

Article 10

In all Member States whose laws do not provide for preventive control, administrative or judicial, at the time of formation of a company, the instrument of constitution, the company statutes and any amendments to those documents shall be drawn up and certified in due legal form.

Article 11

The laws of the Member States may not provide for the nullity of companies otherwise than in accordance with the following provisions:

1. Nullity must be ordered by decision of a court of law;

2. Nullity may be ordered only on the following grounds:

(a) that no instrument of constitution was executed or that the rules of preventive control or the requisite legal formalities were not complied with;

(b) that the objects of the company are unlawful or contrary to public policy;

(c) that the instrument of constitution or the statutes do not state the name of the company, the amount of the individual subscriptions of capital, the total amount of the capital subscribed or the objects of the company;

(d) failure to comply with the provisions of the national law concerning the minimum amount of capital to be paid up;

(e) the incapacity of all the founder members;

(f) that, contrary to the national law governing the company, the number of founder members is less than two.

Apart from the foregoing grounds of nullity, a company shall not be subject to any cause of non-existence, nullity absolute, nullity relative or declaration of nullity.

¶ *See also the Twelfth Company Directive on single-member private limited-liability companies, reproduced infra under no. C. 10.*

Cases

I. Case C-106/89 Marleasing SA v La Comercial Internacional de Alimentacion SA [1990] ECR I-4135

A national court hearing a case which falls within the scope of Directive 68/151/EEC, is required to interpret its national law in the light of the purpose and the wording of that directive in order to preclude a declaration of nullity of a public limited company on a ground other than those listed in Article 11 of the Directive. Those grounds must themselves be strictly interpreted, in the light of that purpose, so as to ensure that nullity on the ground that the objects of the company are unlawful or contrary to public policy must be understood as referring exclusively to the objects of the company as described in the instrument of incorporation or the articles of association.

II. Case 136/87 Ubbink Isolatie BV v Daken Wandtechniek BV [1988] ECR 4665

Section I of the First Company Directive provides for formalities in regard to disclosure intended to provide third parties with prior information on the essential features of companies within the meaning of the said directive. Third parties may thus legitimately rely on the information available concerning such a company, but only if that information has been disclosed in the manner provided for. Consequently, the rules concerning the nullity of companies laid down in Section III of the First Directive apply only where third parties have been led to believe by the information published in accordance with Section I that a company within the meaning of the First Directive exists. They do not apply where the acts in question were performed in the name of a private limited liability company whose existence is not confirmed by the public register because the formalities for incorporation required by national law have not been completed. However, in so far as acts performed in the name of a limited liability company not yet incorporated are regarded by the applicable national law as having been performed in the name of a company being formed within the meaning of Article 7 of the Directive, it is for the national law in question to provide, in accordance with that provision, that the persons who perform them are to be jointly and severally liable.

Article 12

1. The question whether a decision of nullity pronounced by a court of law may be relied on as against third parties shall be governed by Article 3. Where the national law entitles a third party to challenge the decision, he may do so only within six months of public notice of the decision of the court being given.

2. Nullity shall entail the winding up of the company, as may dissolution.

3. Nullity shall not of itself affect the validity of any commitments entered into by or with the company, without prejudice to the consequences of the company's being wound up.

4. The laws of each Member State may make provision for the consequences of nullity as between members of the company.

5. Holders of shares in the capital shall remain obliged to pay up the capital agreed to be subscribed by them but which has not been paid up, to the extent that commitments entered into with creditors so require.

Section IV
General Provisions

Article 13

Member States shall put into force, within eighteen months following notification of this Directive, all amendments to their laws, regulations or administrative provisions required in order to comply with provisions of this Directive and shall forthwith inform the Commission thereof.

The obligation of disclosure provided for in Article 2 (1) (f) shall not enter into force until thirty months after notification of this Directive in respect of *naamloze vennootschappen* under Netherlands law other than those referred to in the present Article 42 (c) of the Netherlands Commercial Code.

Member States may provide that initial disclosure of the full text of the statutes as amended since the formation of the company shall not be required until the statutes are next amended or until 31 December 1970, whichever shall be the earlier.

Member States shall ensure that they communicate to the Commission the text of the main provisions of national law which they adopt in the field covered by this Directive.

Article 14

This Directive is addressed to the Member States.

C.2.

Second Council Directive 77/91/EEC
of 13 December 1976
on co-ordination of safeguards which, for the protection of the interests of members and others, are required by Member States of companies within the meaning of the second paragraph of Article [48][1] of the Treaty, in respect of the formation of public limited liability companies and the maintenance and alteration of their capital, with a view to making such safeguards equivalent[2]

THE COUNCIL OF THE EUROPEAN COMMUNITIES,

Having regard to the Treaty establishing the European Economic Community, and in particular Article [54][1] (3) (g) thereof,

Having regard to the proposals from the Commission,

Having regard to the opinion of the European Parliament,[3]

Having regard to the opinion of the Economic and Social Committee,[4]

Whereas the co-ordination proved for in Article [44][1] (3) (g) and in the General Programme for the abolition of restrictions on freedom of establishment, which was begun by Directive 68/151/EEC,[5] is especially important in relation to public limited liability companies, because their activities predominate in the economy of the Member States and frequently extend beyond their national boundaries;

Whereas in order to ensure minimum equivalent protection for both shareholders and creditors of public limited liability companies, the co-ordination of national provisions relating to their formation and to the maintenance, increase or reduction of their capital is particularly important;

Whereas in the territory of the Community, the statutes or instrument of incorporation of a public limited liability company must make it possible for any interested person to acquaint himself with the basic particulars of the company, including the exact composition of its capital;

Whereas Community provisions could be adopted for maintaining the capital, which constitutes the creditors' security, in particular by prohibiting any reduction thereof by distribution to shareholders where the latter are not entitled to it and by imposing limits on the company's right to acquire its own shares;

Whereas it is necessary, having regard to the objectives of Article [44][1] (3) (g), that the Member States' laws relating to the increase or reduction of capital ensure that the principles of equal treatment of shareholders in the same position and of protection of creditors whose claims exist prior to the decision on reduction are observed and harmonised,

HAS ADOPTED THIS DIRECTIVE:

Article 1

1. The co-ordination measures prescribed by this Directive shall apply to the provisions laid down by law, regulation or administrative action in Member States relating to the following types of company:
— *in Belgium:*
    la société anonyme/de naamloze vennootschap;
— *in Denmark:*
    aktieselskabet;

---

[1] The number between brackets has been changed as from 1 May 1999 by article 12 of the Treaty of Amsterdam.
[2] OJ L 26, 31.1.1977, 1–13.
[3] OJ C 114, 11.11.1971, 18.
[4] OJ C 88, 6.9.1971, 1.
[5] OJ L 65, 14.3.1968, 8, reproduced supra under no. C. 1.

– *in France:*
   la société anonyme;
– *in Germany:*
   die Aktiengesellschaft;
[– *in Greece:*
   η ανωνμη εταιρια];
– *in Ireland:*
   the public company limited by shares, the public company limited by guarantee and having a share capital;
– *in Italy:*
   la società per azioni;
– *in Luxembourg:*
   la société anonyme;
– *in the Netherlands:*
   de naamloze vennootschap;
[– *in Portugal:*
   a sociedade anonima de responsabilidade limitada];
– *in Spain:*
   la sociedad anonima];
– *in the United Kingdom:*
   the public company limited by shares, the public company limited by guarantee and having a share capital;
[– *in Austria:*
   die Aktiengesellschaft];
[– *in Finland:*
   osakeyhtiö —aktiebolag];
[– *in Sverige:*
   aktiebolag];
[– *in the Czech Republic:*
   akciová společnost];
[– *in Estonia:*
   aktsiaselts];
[– *in Cyprus:*
   Δημόσιες εταιρείες περιορισμένης ευθύνης με μετοχές, δημόσιες εταιρείες περιορισμένης ευθύνης με εγγύηση που διαθέτουν μετοχικό κεφάλαιο];
[– *in Latvia:*
   akciju sabiedrība];
[– *in Lithuania:*
   akcinė bendrovė];
[– *in Hungary:*
   nyilvánosan múködö részvenytársaság];
[– *in Malta:*
   kumpanija pubblika—public limited liability company];
[– *in Poland:*
   spólka akcyjna];
[– *in Slovenia:*
   delniška družba];
[– *in Slovakia*:
   akciová spoločnost].

The name for any company of the above types shall comprise or be accompanied by a description which is distinct from the description required of other types of companies.

2. The Member States may decide not to apply this Directive to investment companies with variable capital and to co-operatives incorporated as one of the types of company listed in paragraph 1. In so far as the laws of the Member States make use of this option, they shall require such companies to include the words 'investment company with variable capital' or 'co-operative' in all documents indicated in Article 4 of Directive 68/151/EEC.

The expression 'investment company with variable capital', within the meaning of this Directive, means only those companies:
– the exclusive object of which is to invest their funds in various stocks and shares, land or other assets with the sole aim of spreading investment risks and giving their shareholders the benefit of the results of the management of their assets,
– which offer their own shares for subscription by the public, and
– the statutes of which provide that, within the limits of a minimum and maximum capital, they may at any time issue, redeem or resell their shares.

¶ *This Directive has been rendered applicable to Greece by the Act of Accession of the Hellenic Republic, Annex I (III)(c)(2) (OJ L 291, 19.11.1979), to Spain and Portugal by the Act of Accession of the Kingdom of Spain and the Portuguese Republic, Annex I, (II)(d)(2) (OJ L 302, 15.11. 1985), to Austria, Sweden, and Finland by the Act of Accession of Austria, Sweden, and Finland (OJ C 241, 29.8.1994, 21), adapted by Council Decision 91/1/EC, Euratom, ECSC (OJ L 1, 1.1.1995, 1), and to the Czech Republic, Estonia, Cyprus, Latvia, Hungary, Malta, Poland, Slovenia, and Slovakia by the Act concerning the conditions of accession of the Czech Republic, the Republic of Estonia, the Republic of Cyprus, the Republic of Latvia, the Republic of Hungary, the Republic of Malta, the Republic of Poland, the Republic of Slovenia, and the Slovak Republic and the adjustments to the Treaties on which the European Union is founded (OJ L 236, 23.9.2003, 33).*

¶ *'Investment companies': compare Directive 85/611/EEC of 20 December 1985 (UCITS), reproduced infra under no. S. 6.*

¶ *The 21st indent of article 1(1) has been replaced by article 1 of Directive 2006/68/EC, reproduced infra under no. C. 32.*

Article 2

The statutes or the instrument of incorporation of the company shall always give at least the following information:

(a) the type and name of the company;

(b) the objects of the company;

(c) – when the company has no authorised capital, the amount of the subscribed capital,
 – when the company has an authorised capital, the amount thereof and also the amount of the capital subscribed at the time the company is incorporated or is authorised to commence business, and at the time of any change in the authorised capital, without prejudice to Article 2 (1) (e) of Directive 68/151/EEC;

(d) in so far as they are not legally determined, the rules governing the number of and the procedure for appointing members of the bodies responsible for representing the company with regard to third parties, administration, management, supervision or control of the company and the allocation of powers among those bodies;

(e) the duration of the company, except where this is indefinite.

¶ *Representation: see article 9 of Directive 68/151/EEC, First Company Directive, reproduced supra under no. C. 1.*

Article 3

The following information at least must appear in either the statutes or the instrument of incorporation or a separate document published in accordance with the procedure laid down in the laws of each Member State in accordance with Article 3 of Directive 68/151/EEC:

(a) the registered office;

(b) the nominal value of the shares subscribed and, at least once a year, the number thereof;

(c) the number of shares subscribed without stating the nominal value, where such shares may be issued under national law;

(d) the special conditions if any limiting the transfer of shares;

(e) where there are several classes of shares, the information under (b), (c) and (d) for each class and the rights attaching to the shares of each class;

(f) whether the shares are registered or bearer, where national law provides for both types, and any provisions relating to the conversion of such shares unless the procedure is laid down by law;

(g) the amount of the subscribed capital paid up at the time the company is incorporated or is authorised to commence business;

(h) the nominal value of the shares or, where there is not nominal value, the number of shares issued for a consideration other than in cash, together with the nature of the consideration and the name of the person providing this consideration;

(i) the identity of the natural or legal persons or companies or firms by whom or in whose name the statutes or the instrument of incorporation, or where the company was not formed at the same time, the drafts of these documents, have been signed;

(j) the total amount, or at least an estimate, of all the costs payable by the company or chargeable to it by reason of its formation and, where appropriate, before the company is authorised to commence business;

(k) any special advantage granted, at the time the company is formed or up to the time it receives authorisation to commence business, to anyone who has taken part in the formation of the company or in transactions leading to the grant of such authorisation.

Article 4

1. Where the laws of a Member State prescribe that a company may not commence business without authorisation, they shall also make provision for responsibility for liabilities incurred by or on behalf of the company during the period before such authorisation is granted or refused.

2. Paragraph 1 shall not apply to liabilities under contracts concluded by the company conditionally upon its being granted authorisation to commence business.

¶ *See also article 7 of Directive 68/151/EEC, First Company Directive, reproduced supra under no C. 1.*

Article 5

1. Where the laws of a Member State require a company to be formed by more than one member, the fact that all the shares are held by one person or that the number of members has fallen below the legal minimum after incorporation of the company shall not lead to the automatic dissolution of the company.

2. If in the cases referred to in paragraph 1, the laws of a Member State permit the company to be wound up by order of the court, the judge having jurisdiction must be able to give the company sufficient time to regularise its position.

3. Where such a winding up order is made the company shall enter into liquidation.

¶ *See also the Twelfth Company Directive (89/667/EEC) on single-member private limited-liability companies, reproduced infra under no. C. 10.*

Article 6

1. The laws of the Member States shall require that, in order that a company may be incorporated or obtain authorisation to commence business, a minimum capital shall be subscribed the amount of which shall be not less than 25.000 European units of account.

The European unit of account shall be that defined by Commission Decision 3289/75/ECSC.[6] The equivalent in national currency shall be calculated initially at the rate applicable on the date of adoption of this Directive.

2. If the equivalent of the European unit of account in national currency is altered so that the value of the minimum capital in national currency remains less than 22.500 European units of account for a period of one year, the Commission shall inform the Member State concerned that it must amend its legislation to comply with paragraph 1 within 12 months following the expiry of that period. However, the Member State may provide that the amended legislation shall not apply to companies already in existence until 18 months after its entry into force.

3. Every five years the Council, acting on a proposal from the Commission, shall examine and, if need be, revise the amounts expressed in this article in European units of account in the light of economic and monetary trends in the Community and of the tendency towards allowing only large and medium-sized undertakings to opt for the types of company listed in Article 1.

¶ *According to Regulation 3308/80/EEC (OJ L 345, 20.12.1980, 1) the 'Unit of account' has been replaced by the 'European currency unit' or 'ECU'. No revisions of the minimum amount of the capital have been made.*

Cases

I. Case C-167/01 Kamer van Koophandel en Fabrieken voor Amsterdam v Inspire Art Ltd [2003] ECR I-10155

It is contrary to Articles 43 and 48 EC to impose on a company formed in accordance with the law of another Member State, and qualified as pseudo-foreign, certain requirements in respect of company formation relating to minimum capital and directors' liability. The reasons for which the company was formed in that other Member State, and the fact that it carries on its activities exclusively or almost exclusively in the Member State of establishment, do not deprive it of the right to invoke the freedom of establishment guaranteed by the EC Treaty, save where the existence of an abuse is established on a case-by-case basis.

II. Case C-208/00 Überseering BV v Nordic Construction Company Baumanagement GmbH (NCC) [2002] ECR I-9919

1. Where a company formed in accordance with the law of a Member State ('A') in which it has its registered office is deemed, under the law of another Member State ('B'), to have moved its actual centre of administration to Member State B, Articles 43 EC and 48 EC preclude Member State

---

[6] OJ L 327, 19.12.1975, 4.

B from denying the company legal capacity and, consequently, the capacity to bring legal proceedings before its national courts for the purpose of enforcing rights under a contract with a company established in Member State B.

2. Where a company formed in accordance with the law of a Member State ('A') in which it has its registered office exercises its freedom of establishment in another Member State ('B'), Articles 43 EC and 48 EC require Member State B to recognize the legal capacity and, consequently, the capacity to be a party to legal proceedings which the company enjoys under the law of its State of incorporation ('A').

III. Case C-212/97 Centros Ltd v Erhvervs- og Selskabsstyrelsen [1999] ECR I-1459

It is contrary to Articles [43 and 48][1] of the Treaty for a Member State to refuse to register a branch of a company formed in accordance with the law of another Member State in which it has its registered office but in which it conducts no business where the branch is intended to enable the company in question to carry on its entire business in the State in which that branch is to be created, while avoiding the need to form a company there, thus evading application of the rules governing the formation of companies which, in that State, are more restrictive as regards the paying up of a minimum share capital. Given that the right to form a company in accordance with the law of a Member State and to set up branches in other Member States is inherent in the exercise, in a single market, of the freedom of establishment guaranteed by the Treaty, the fact that a national of a Member State who wishes to set up a company chooses to form it in the Member State whose rules of company law seem to him the least restrictive and to set up branches in other Member States cannot, in itself, constitute an abuse of the right of establishment.

That interpretation does not, however, prevent the authorities of the Member State concerned from adopting any appropriate measure for preventing or penalizing fraud, either in relation to the company itself, if need be in cooperation with the Member State in which it was formed, or in relation to its members, where it has been established that they are in fact attempting, by means of the formation of a company, to evade their obligations towards private or public creditors established in the territory of the Member State concerned.

See also on the related subject of cross-border establishment:

IV. Case 81/87 The Queen v HM Treasury and Commissioners of Inland Revenue, ex parte Daily Mail and General Trust plc [1988] ECR 5483

The Treaty regards the differences in national legislation concerning the connecting factor required of companies incorporated thereunder and the question whether—and if so how—the registered office or real head office of a company incorporated under national law may be transferred from one Member State to another as problems which are not resolved by the rules concerning the right of establishment but must be dealt with by future legislation or conventions, which have not yet been adopted or concluded. Therefore, in the present state of Community law, Articles 52 and 58 of the Treaty, properly construed, confer no right on a company incorporated under the legislation of a Member State and having its registered office there to transfer its central management and control to another Member State.

Article 7

The subscribed capital may be formed only of assets capable of economic assessment. However, an undertaking to perform work or supply services may not form part of these assets.

Article 8

1. Shares may not be issued at a price lower than their nominal value, or, where there is no nominal value, their accountable par.

2. However, Member States may allow those who undertake to place shares in the exercise of their profession to pay less than the total price of the shares for which they subscribe in the course of this transaction.

Article 9

1. Shares issued for a consideration must be paid up at the time the company is incorporated or is authorised to commence business at not less than 25% of their nominal value or, in the absence of a nominal value, their accountable par.

2. However, where shares are issued for a consideration other than in cash at the time the company is incorporated or is authorised to commence business, the consideration must be transferred in full within five years of that time.

Article 10

1. A report on any consideration other than in cash shall be drawn up before the company is incorporated or is authorised to commence business, by one or more independent experts appointed or approved by an administrative or judicial authority. Such experts may be natural persons as well as legal persons and companies or firms under the laws of each Member State.

2. The experts' report shall contain at least a description of each of the assets comprising the consideration as well as of the methods of valuation used and shall state whether the values arrived at by the application of these methods correspond at least to the number and nominal value or, where there is no nominal value, to the accountable par and, where appropriate, to the premium on the shares to be issued for them.

3. The experts' report shall be published in the manner laid down by the laws of each Member State, in accordance with Article 3 of Directive 68/151/EEC.

4. Member States may decide not to apply this article where 90% of the nominal value, or where there is no nominal value, of the accountable par, of all the shares is issued to one or more companies for a consideration other than in cash, and where the following requirements are met:

(a) with regard to the company in receipt of such consideration, the persons referred to in Article 3 (i) have agreed to dispense with the experts' report;

(b) such agreement has been published as provided for in paragraph 3;

(c) the companies furnishing such consideration have reserves which may not be distributed under the law or the statutes and which are at least equal to the nominal value or, where there is no nominal value, the accountable par of the shares issued for consideration other than in cash;

(d) the companies furnishing such consideration guarantee, up to an amount equal to that indicated in paragraph (c), the debts of the recipient company arising between the time the shares are issued for a consideration other than in cash and one year after the publication of that company's annual accounts for the financial year during which such consideration was furnished. Any transfer of these shares is prohibited within this period;

(e) the guarantee referred to in (d) has been published as provided for in paragraph 3;

(f) the companies furnishing such consideration shall place a sum equal to that indicated in (c) into a reserve which may not be distributed until three years after publication of the annual accounts of the recipient company for the financial year during which such consideration was furnished or, if necessary, until such later date as all claims relating to the guarantee referred to in (d) which are submitted during this period have been settled.

[Article 10a

1. Member States may decide not to apply Article 10(1), (2) and (3) where, upon a decision of the administrative or management body, transferable securities as defined in point 18 of Article 4(1) of Directive 2004/39/EC of the European Parliament and of the Council of 21 April 2004 on markets in financial instruments[7] or money-market instruments as defined in point 19 of Article 4(1) of that Directive are contributed as consideration other than in cash, and those securities or money-market instruments are valued at the weighted average price at which they have been traded on one or more regulated market(s) as defined in point 14 of Article 4(1) of that Directive during a sufficient period, to be determined by national law, preceding the effective date of the contribution of the respective consideration other than in cash.

---

[7] OJ L 145, 30.4.2004, 1, reproduced infra under no. S. 29. Directive as last amended by Directive 2006/31/EC (OJ L 114, 27.4.2006, 60), reproduced infra under no. S. 32.

However, where that price has been affected by exceptional circumstances that would significantly change the value of the asset at the effective date of its contribution, including situations where the market for such transferable securities or money-market instruments has become illiquid, a revaluation shall be carried out on the initiative and under the responsibility of the administrative or management body.

For the purposes of the aforementioned revaluation, Article 10(1), (2) and (3) shall apply.

2. Member States may decide not to apply Article 10(1), (2) and (3) where, upon a decision of the administrative or management body, assets, other than the transferable securities and money-market instruments referred to in paragraph 1, are contributed as consideration other than in cash which have already been subject to a fair value opinion by a recognised independent expert and where the following conditions are fulfilled:

(a) the fair value is determined for a date not more than 6 months before the effective date of the asset contribution;

(b) the valuation has been performed in accordance with generally accepted valuation standards and principles in the Member State, which are applicable to the kind of assets to be contributed.

In the case of new qualifying circumstances that would significantly change the fair value of the asset at the effective date of its contribution, a revaluation shall be carried out on the initiative and under the responsibility of the administrative or management body. For the purposes of the aforementioned revaluation, Article 10(1), (2) and (3) shall apply.

In the absence of such a revaluation, one or more shareholders holding an aggregate percentage of at least 5% of the company's subscribed capital on the day the decision on the increase in the capital is taken may demand a valuation by an independent expert, in which case Article 10(1), (2) and (3) shall apply. Such shareholder(s) may submit a demand up until the effective date of the asset contribution, provided that, at the date of the demand, the shareholder(s) in question still hold(s) an aggregate percentage of at least 5% of the company's subscribed capital, as it was on the day the decision on the increase in the capital was taken.

3. Member States may decide not to apply Article 10(1), (2) and (3) where, upon a decision of the administrative or management body, assets, other than the transferable securities and money-market instruments referred to in paragraph 1, are contributed as consideration other than in cash whose fair value is derived by individual asset from the statutory accounts of the previous financial year provided that the statutory accounts have been subject to an audit in accordance with Directive 2006/43/EC of the European Parliament and of the Council of 17 May 2006 on statutory audits of annual accounts and consolidated accounts.[8]

The second and third subparagraphs of paragraph 2 shall apply mutatis mutandis.

Article 10b

1. Where consideration other than in cash as referred to in Article 10a occurs without an expert's report as referred to in Article 10(1), (2) and (3), in addition to the requirements set out in point (h) of Article 3 and within one month after the effective date of the asset contribution, a declaration containing the following shall be published:

(a) a description of the consideration other than in cash at issue;

(b) its value, the source of this valuation and, where appropriate, the method of valuation;

(c) a statement whether the value arrived at corresponds at least to the number, to the nominal value or, where there is no nominal value, the accountable par and, where appropriate, to the premium on the shares to be issued for such consideration;

(d) a statement that no new qualifying circumstances with regard to the original valuation have occurred.

---

[8] OJ L 157, 9.6.2006, 87, reproduced infra under no. C. 30.

That publication shall be effected in the manner laid down by the laws of each Member State in accordance with Article 3 of Directive 68/151/EEC.

2. Where consideration other than in cash is proposed to be made without an expert's report as referred to in Article 10(1), (2) and (3) in relation to an increase in the capital proposed to be made under Article 25(2), an announcement containing the date when the decision on the increase was taken and the information listed in paragraph 1 shall be published, in the manner laid down by the laws of each Member State in accordance with Article 3 of Directive 68/151/EEC, before the contribution of the asset as consideration other than in cash is to become effective. In that event, the declaration pursuant to paragraph 1 shall be limited to the statement that no new qualifying circumstances have occurred since the aforementioned announcement was published.

3. Each Member State shall provide for adequate safeguards ensuring compliance with the procedure set out in Article 10a and in this Article where a contribution for a consideration other than in cash is made without an expert's report as referred to in Article 10(1), (2) and (3).]

¶ *Articles 10a and 10b have been added by article 1(2) of Directive 2006/68/EC, reproduced infra under no. C. 32.*

Article 11

1. If, before the expiry of a time limit laid down by national law of at least two years from the time the company is incorporated or is authorised to commence business, the company acquires any asset belonging to a person or company or firm referred to in Article 3 (i) for a consideration of not less than one-tenth of the subscribed capital, the acquisition shall be examined and details of it published in the manner provided for in [Article 10(1), (2) and (3)] and it shall be submitted for the approval of the general meeting. [Articles 10a and 10b shall apply *mutatis mutandis*.]

Member States may also require these provisions to be applied when the assets belong to a shareholder or to any other person.

2. Paragraph 1 shall not apply to acquisitions effected in the normal course of the company's business, to acquisitions effected at the instance or under the supervision of an administrative or judicial authority, or to stock exchange acquisitions.

¶ *The words between square brackets in paragraph 1 have been replaced by article 1(3) of Directive 2006/68/EC, reproduced infra under no. C. 32.*

Article 12

Subject to the provisions relating to the reduction of subscribed capital, the shareholders may not be released from the obligation to pay up their contributions.

Article 13

Pending co-ordination of national laws at a subsequent date, Member States shall adopt the measures necessary to require provision of at least the same safeguards as are laid down in Articles 2 to 12 in the event of the conversion of another type of company into a public limited liability company.

Article 14

Articles 2 to 13 shall not prejudice the provisions of Member States on competence and procedure relating to the modification of the statutes or of the instrument of incorporation.

Article 15

1. (a) Except for cases of reductions of subscribed capital, no distribution to shareholders may be made when on the closing date of the last financial year the net assets as set out in the company's annual accounts are, or following such a distribution would become, lower than the amount of the subscribed capital plus those reserves which may not be distributed under the law or the statutes.

(b) Where the uncalled part of the subscribed capital is not included in the assets shown in the balance sheet, this amount shall be deducted from the amount of subscribed capital referred to in paragraph (a).

(c) The amount of a distribution to shareholders may not exceed the amount of the profits at the end of the last financial year plus any profits brought forward and sums drawn from reserves available for this purpose, less any losses brought forward and sums placed to reserve in accordance with the law or the statutes.

(d) The expression 'distribution' used in sub-paragraphs (a) and (c) includes in particular the payment of dividends and of interest relating to shares.

2. When the laws of a Member State allow the payment of interim dividends, the following conditions at least shall apply:

(a) interim accounts shall be drawn up showing that the funds available for distribution are sufficient,

(b) the amount to be distributed may not exceed the total profits made since the end of the last financial year for which the annual accounts have been drawn up, plus any profits brought forward and sums drawn from reserves available for this purpose, less losses brought forward and sums to be placed to reserve pursuant to the requirements of the law or the statutes.

3. Paragraphs 1 and 2 shall not affect the provisions of the Member States as regards increases in subscribed capital by capitalisation of reserves.

4. The laws of a Member State may provide for derogations from paragraph (1) (a) in the case of investment companies with fixed capital.

The expression 'investment company with fixed capital', within the meaning of this paragraph means only those companies:
– the exclusive object of which is to invest their funds in various stocks and shares, land or other assets with the sole aim of spreading investment risks and giving their shareholders the benefit of the results of the management of their assets, and
– which offer their own shares for subscription by the public.

In so far as the laws of Member States make use of this option they shall:

(a) require such companies to include the expression 'investment company' in all documents indicated in Article 4 of Directive 68/151/EEC;

(b) not permit any such company whose net assets fall below the amount specified in paragraph 1 (a) to make a distribution to shareholders when on the closing date of the last financial year company's total assets as set out in the annual accounts are, or following such distribution would become, less than one-and-a-half times the amount of the company's total liabilities to creditors as set out in the annual accounts;

(c) require any such company which makes a distribution when its net assets fall below the amount specified in paragraph 1 (a) to include in its annual accounts a note to that effect.

Article 16

Any distribution made contrary to Article 15 must be returned by shareholders who have received it if the company proves that these shareholders knew of the irregularity of the distributions made to them, or could not in view of the circumstances have been unaware of it.

Article 17

1. In the case of a serious loss of the subscribed capital, a general meeting of shareholders must be called within the period laid down by the laws of the Member States, to consider whether the company should be wound up or any other measures taken.

2. The amount of a loss deemed to be serious within the meaning of paragraph 1 may not be set by the laws of Member States at a figure higher than half the subscribed capital.

Article 18

1. The shares of a company may not be subscribed for by the company itself.

2. If the shares of a company have been subscribed for by a person acting in his own name, but on behalf of the company, the subscriber shall be deemed to have subscribed for them for his own account.

3. The persons or companies or firms referred to in Article 8 (i) or, in cases of an increase in subscribed capital, the members of the administrative or management body shall be liable to pay

for shares subscribed in contravention of this article.

However, the laws of a Member State may provide that any such person may be released from his obligation if he proves that no fault is attributable to him personally.

Article 19

[1. Without prejudice to the principle of equal treatment of all shareholders who are in the same position, and to Directive 2003/6/EC of the European Parliament and of the Council of 28 January 2003 on insider dealing and market manipulation (market abuse),[9] Member States may permit a company to acquire its own shares, either itself or through a person acting in his own name but on the company's behalf. To the extent that the acquisitions are permitted, Member States shall make such acquisitions subject to the following conditions:

(a) authorisation shall be given by the general meeting, which shall determine the terms and conditions of such acquisitions, and, in particular, the maximum number of shares to be acquired, the duration of the period for which the authorisation is given, the maximum length of which shall be determined by national law without, however, exceeding 5 years, and, in the case of acquisition for value, the maximum and minimum consideration. Members of the administrative or management body shall satisfy themselves that, at the time when each authorised acquisition is effected, the conditions referred to in points (b) and (c) are respected;

(b) the acquisitions, including shares previously acquired by the company and held by it, and shares acquired by a person acting in his own name but on the company's behalf, may not have the effect of reducing the net assets below the amount mentioned in points (a) and (b) of Article 15(1);

(c) only fully paid-up shares may be included in the transaction.

---

[9] OJ L 96, 12.4.2003, 16, reproduced infra under no. S. 24.

Furthermore, Member States may subject acquisitions within the meaning of the first subparagraph to any of the following conditions:

(i) that the nominal value or, in the absence thereof, the accountable par of the acquired shares, including shares previously acquired by the company and held by it, and shares acquired by a person acting in his own name but on the company's behalf, may not exceed a limit to be determined by Member States. This limit may not be lower than 10% of the subscribed capital;

(ii) that the power of the company to acquire its own shares within the meaning of the first subparagraph, the maximum number of shares to be acquired, the duration of the period for which the power is given and the maximum or minimum consideration are laid down in the statutes or in the instrument of incorporation of the company;

(iii) that the company complies with appropriate reporting and notification requirements;

(iv) that certain companies, as determined by Member States, may be required to cancel the acquired shares provided that an amount equal to the nominal value of the shares cancelled must be included in a reserve which cannot be distributed to the shareholders, except in the event of a reduction in the subscribed capital. This reserve may be used only for the purposes of increasing the subscribed capital by the capitalisation of reserves;

(v) that the acquisition shall not prejudice the satisfaction of creditors' claims.]

2. The laws of a Member State may provide for derogations from the first sentence of paragraph 1 (a) where the acquisition of a company's own shares is necessary to prevent serious and imminent harm to the company. In such a case, the next general meeting must be informed by the administrative or management body of the reasons for and nature of the acquisitions effected, of the number and nominal value or, in the absence of a nominal value, the accountable par, of the shares acquired, of the proportion of the subscribed capital which they represent, and of the consideration for these shares.

3. Member States may decide not to apply the first sentence of paragraph 1 (a) to shares acquired by either the company itself or by a person acting in his own name but on the company's behalf, for distribution to that company's employees or to the employees of an associate company. Such shares must be distributed within 12 months of their acquisition.

¶ *Paragraph 1 has been replaced by article 1(4) of Directive 2006/68/EC, reproduced infra under no. C. 32.*

Article 20

1. Member States may decide not to apply Article 19 to:

(a) shares acquired in carrying out a decision to reduce capital, or in the circumstances referred to in Article 39;

(b) shares acquired as a result of a universal transfer of assets;

(c) fully paid-up shares acquired free of charge, or by banks and other financial institutions as purchasing commission;

(d) shares acquired by virtue of a legal obligation or resulting from a court ruling for the protection of minority shareholders in the event, particularly, of a merger, a change in the company's object or form, transfer abroad of the registered office, or the introduction of restrictions on the transfer of shares;

(e) shares acquired from a shareholder in the event of failure to pay them up;

(f) shares acquired in order to indemnify minority shareholders in associated companies;

(g) fully paid-up shares acquired under a sale enforced by a court order for the payment of a debt owed to the company by the owner of the shares;

(h) fully paid-up shares issued by an investment company with fixed capital, as defined in the second subparagraph of Article 15 (4), and acquired at the investor's request by that company or by an associate company. Article 15 (4) (a) shall apply. These acquisitions may not have the effect of reducing the net assets below the amount of the subscribed capital plus any reserves the distribution of which is forbidden by law.

2. Shares acquired in the cases listed in paragraph 1 (b) to (g) above must, however, be disposed of within not more than three years of their acquisition unless the nominal value or, in the absence of a nominal value, the accountable par of the shares acquired, including shares which the company may have acquired through a person acting in his own name but, on the company's behalf, does not exceed 10% of the subscribed capital.

3. If the shares are not disposed of within the period laid down in paragraph 2, they must be cancelled. The laws of a Member State may make this cancellation subject to a corresponding reduction in the subscribed capital. Such a reduction must be prescribed where the acquisition of shares to be cancelled results in the net assets having fallen below the amount specified in [points (a) and (b) of Article 15(1)].

¶ *The words between square brackets in paragraph 3 have been replaced by article 1(5) of Directive 2006/68/EC, reproduced infra under no. C. 32.*

Article 21

Shares acquired in contravention of Articles 19 and 20 shall be disposed of within one year of their acquisition. Should they not be disposed of within that period, Article 20 (3) shall apply.

Article 22

1. Where the laws of a Member State permit a company to acquire its own shares, either itself or through a person acting in his own name but on the company's behalf, they shall make the holding of these shares at all times subject to at least the following conditions:

(a) among the rights attaching to the shares, the right to vote attaching to the company's own shares shall in any event be suspended;

(b) if the shares are included among the assets shown in the balance sheet, a reserve of the same amount, unavailable for distribution, shall be included among the liabilities.

2. Where the laws of a Member State permit a company to acquire its own shares, either itself or through a person acting in his own name but on

the company's behalf, they shall require the annual report to state at least:

(a) the reasons for acquisitions made during the financial year;

(b) the number and nominal value or, in the absence of a nominal value, the accountable par of the shares acquired and disposed of during the financial year and the proportion of the subscribed capital which they represent;

(c) in the case of acquisition or disposal for a value, the consideration for the shares;

(d) the number and nominal value or, in the absence of a nominal value, the accountable par of all the shares acquired and held by the company and the proportion of the subscribed capital which they represent.

Article 23

[1. Where Member States permit a company to, either directly or indirectly, advance funds or make loans or provide security, with a view to the acquisition of its shares by a third party, they shall make such transactions subject to the conditions set out in the second, third, fourth and fifth subparagraphs.

The transactions shall take place under the responsibility of the administrative or management body at fair market conditions, especially with regard to interest received by the company and with regard to security provided to the company for the loans and advances referred to in the first subparagraph. The credit standing of the third party or, in the case of multiparty transactions, of each counterparty thereto shall have been duly investigated.

The transactions shall be submitted by the administrative or management body to the general meeting for prior approval, whereby the general meeting shall act in accordance with the rules for a quorum and a majority laid down in Article 40. The administrative or management body shall present a written report to the general meeting, indicating the reasons for the transaction, the interest of the company in entering into such a transaction, the conditions on which the transaction is entered into, the risks involved in the transaction for the liquidity and solvency of the company and the price at which the third party is to acquire the shares. This report shall be submitted to the register for publication in accordance with Article 3 of Directive 68/151/EEC.

The aggregate financial assistance granted to third parties shall at no time result in the reduction of the net assets below the amount specified in points (a) and (b) of Article 15(1), taking into account also any reduction of the net assets that may have occurred through the acquisition, by the company or on behalf of the company, of its own shares in accordance with Article 19(1). The company shall include, among the liabilities in the balance sheet, a reserve, unavailable for distribution, of the amount of the aggregate financial assistance.

Where a third party by means of financial assistance from a company acquires that company's own shares within the meaning of Article 19(1) or subscribes for shares issued in the course of an increase in the subscribed capital, such acquisition or subscription shall be made at a fair price.]

2. Paragraph 1 shall not apply to transactions concluded by banks and other financial institutions in the normal course of business, nor to transactions effected with a view to the acquisition of shares by or for the company's employees or the employees of an associate company. However, these transactions may not have the effect of reducing the net assets below the amount specified in Article 15 (1) (a).

3. Paragraph 1 shall not apply to transactions effected with a view to acquisition of shares as described in article 20 (1) (h).

¶ *Paragraph 1 has been replaced by article 1 of Directive 2006/68/EC, reproduced infra under no. C. 32.*

[Article 23a

In cases where individual members of the administrative or management body of the company being party to a transaction referred to in Article 23(1), or of the administrative or management body of a parent undertaking within the meaning of Article 1 of Council Directive 83/349/EEC of

13 June 1983 on consolidated accounts[10] or such parent undertaking itself, or individuals acting in their own name, but on behalf of the members of such bodies or on behalf of such undertaking, are counterparties to such a transaction, Member States shall ensure through adequate safeguards that such transaction does not conflict with the company's best interests.]

¶ *Article 23a has been inserted by article 1(7) of Directive 2006/68/EC, reproduced infra under no. C. 32.*

Article 24

1. The acceptance of the company's own shares as security, either by the company itself or through a person acting in his own name but on the company's behalf, shall be treated as an acquisition for the purposes of Articles 19, 20 (1), 22 and 28.

2. The Member States may decide not to apply paragraph 1 to transactions concluded by banks and other financial institutions in the normal course of business.

Article 24a

1. [(a) The subscription, acquisition or holding of shares in a public limited-liability company by another company within the meaning of Article 1 of Directive 68/151/EEC in which the public limited-liability company directly or indirectly holds a majority of the voting rights or on which it can directly or indirectly exercise a dominant influence shall be regarded as having been effected by the public limited-liability company itself;

(b) subparagraph (a) shall also apply where the other company is governed by the law of a third country and has a legal form comparable to those listed in Article 1 of Directive 68/151/EEC.

2. However, where the public limited-liability company holds a majority of the voting rights indirectly or can exercise a dominant influence indirectly, Member States need not apply paragraph 1 if they provide for the suspension of the voting rights attached to the shares in the public limited-liability company held by the other company.

3. In the absence of co-ordination of national legislation on groups of companies, Member States may:

(a) define the cases in which a public limited-liability company shall be regarded as being able to exercise a dominant influence on another company; if a Member State exercises this option, its national law must in any event provide that a dominant influence can be exercised if a public limited-liability company:

– has the right to appoint or dismiss a majority of the members of the administrative organ, of the management organ or of the supervisory organ, and is at the same time a shareholder or member of the other company or

– is a shareholder or member of the other company and has sole control of a majority of the voting rights of its shareholders or members under an agreement concluded with other shareholders or members of that company.

Member States shall not be obliged to make provision for any cases other than those referred to in the first and second indents;

(b) define the cases in which a public limited-liability company shall be regarded as indirectly holding voting rights or as able indirectly to exercise a dominant influence;

(c) specify the circumstances in which a public limited-liability company shall be regarded as holding voting rights.

4. (a) Member States need not apply paragraph 1 where the subscription, acquisition or holding is effected on behalf of a person other than the person subscribing, acquiring or holding the shares, who is neither the public limited-liability company referred to in paragraph 1 nor another company in which the public limited-liability company directly or indirectly holds a majority of the voting rights or on which it can directly or indirectly exercise a dominant influence.

(b) Member States need not apply paragraph 1 where the subscription, acquisition or holding is effected by the other company in its capacity and

---

[10] OJ L 193, 18.7.1983, 1, reproduced infra under no. C. 6. Directive as last amended by Directive 2006/43/EC, reproduced infra under no. C. 30.

in the context of its activities as a professional dealer in securities, provided that it is a member of a stock exchange situated or operating within a Member State, or is approved or supervised by an authority of a Member State competent to supervise professional dealers in securities which, within the meaning of this Directive, may include credit institutions.

5. Member States need not apply paragraph 1 where shares in a public limited-liability company held by another company were acquired before the relationship between the two companies corresponded to the criteria laid down in paragraph 1.

However, the voting rights attached to those shares shall be suspended and the shares shall be taken into account when it is determined whether the condition laid down in Article 19 (1) (b) is fulfilled.

6. Member States need not apply Article 20 (2) or (3) or Article 21 where shares in a public limited-liability company are acquired by another company on condition that they provide for:

(a) the suspension of the voting rights attached to the shares in the public limited-liability company held by the other company, and

(b) the members of the administrative or the management organ of the public limited-liability company to be obliged to buy back from the other company the shares referred to in Article 20 (2) and (3) and Article 21 at the price at which the other company acquired them; this sanction shall be inapplicable only where the members of the administrative or the management organ of the public limited-liability company prove that that company played no part whatsoever in the subscription for or acquisition of the shares in question.]

¶ *'Dominant influence': see article 1 of the Seventh Company Directive, reproduced infra under no. C. 6.*
¶ *This article has been inserted by article 1 of Directive 92/101/EEC, reproduced infra under no. C. 13. The date of entry into force of this provision shall be no later than 1 January 1995. For the transitional arrangements see article 2 of the abovementioned directive.*

Article 25

1. Any increase in capital must be decided upon by the general meeting. Both this decision and the increase in the subscribed capital shall be published in the manner laid down by the laws of each Member State, in accordance with Article 3 of Directive 68/151/EEC.

2. Nevertheless, the statutes or instrument of incorporation or the general meeting, the decision of which must be published in accordance with the rules referred to in paragraph 1, may authorise an increase in the subscribed capital up to a maximum amount which they shall fix with due regard for any maximum amount provided for by law. Where appropriate, the increase in the subscribed capital shall be decided on within the limits of the amount fixed, by the company body empowered to do so. The power of such body in this respect shall be for a maximum period of five years and may be renewed one or more times by the general meeting, each time for a period not exceeding five years.

3. Where there are several classes of shares, the decision by the general meeting concerning the increase in capital referred to in paragraph 1 or the authorisation to increase the capital referred to in paragraph 2, shall be subject to a separate vote at least for each class of shareholder whose rights are affected by the transaction.

4. This article shall apply to the issue of all securities which are convertible into shares or which carry the right to subscribe for shares, but not to the conversion of such securities, nor to the exercise of the right to subscribe.

CASES

I. Case C-373/97 Dionysios Diamantis v Elliniko Dimosio (Greek State) and Organismos Ikonomikis Anasygkrotisis Epicheiriseon AE (OAE) [2000] ECR I-1705

Community law does not preclude national courts from applying a provision of national law which enables them to determine whether a right deriving from a Community law provision is being abused. However, in making that determination, it is not permissible to deem a shareholder relying on Article 25(1) of the Second Directive 77/91/EEC, to be abusing his rights under that provision merely because he is a minority shareholder of a company subject to reorganization measures, or has benefited from reorganization of the company, or has not exercised his right of pre-emption, or was among the shareholders who asked for the company to be placed under the scheme applicable to companies in serious difficulties, or has allowed a certain period of time to elapse before bringing his action. In contrast, Community law does not preclude national courts from applying the provision of national law concerned if, of the remedies available for a situation that has arisen in breach of that provision, a shareholder has chosen a remedy that will cause such serious damage to the legitimate interests of others that it appears manifestly disproportionate.

II. Case C-367/96 Alexandros Kefalas and others v Elliniko Dimosio (Greek State) and Organismos Oikonomikis Anasygkrotisis Epicheiriseon AE (OAE) [1998] ECR I-2843

1. Community law cannot be relied on for abusive or fraudulent ends. Consequently, Community law does not preclude the application by national courts of a provision of national law in order to assess whether a right arising from a provision of Community law is being exercised abusively. However, the application of such a national rule must not prejudice the full effect and uniform application of Community law in the Member States. In particular, it is not open to national courts, when assessing the exercise of a right arising from a provision of Community law, to alter the scope of that provision or to compromise the objectives pursued by it.

2. A shareholder relying on Article 25(1) of the Second Directive 77/91 on company law cannot be deemed to be abusing the right conferred on him by that provision merely because the increase in capital by administrative decision which he contests resolved the financial difficulties threatening the existence of the company concerned and clearly ensured to his economic benefit, or because he did not exercise his preferential right under Article 29(1) of that directive to acquire new shares issued on the increase of capital at issue. First, the decision-making power of the general meeting provided for in Article 25(1) applies even where the company is experiencing serious financial difficulties. Secondly, by exercising his preferential right, the shareholder would have shown his willingness to assist in the implementation of the decision to increase the capital without the approval of the general meeting, whereas he is in fact contesting that very decision on the basis of Article 25(1) of the Second Directive.

III. Case C-441/93 Panagis Pafitis and others v Trapeza Kentrikis Ellados AE and others [1996] ECR I-1347

The Second Directive 77/91, and in particular Articles 25 and 29 thereof, must be interpreted as applying to banks constituted in the form of limited liability companies. The criterion adopted by the Community legislature to define the scope of the Second Directive is that of the legal form of the company, irrespective of its business.

Article 25 of the directive, pursuant to which any increase in capital must be decided on by the general meeting, precludes national legislation under which the capital of a bank constituted in the form of a public limited liability company which, as a result of its debt burden, is in exceptional circumstances may be increased by an administrative measure, without a resolution of the general meeting. Although the directive does not preclude the taking of execution measures intended to put an end to the company's existence and, in particular, does not preclude liquidation measures placing the company under compulsory administration with a view to safeguarding the rights of creditors, it continues to apply where ordinary reorganization measures are taken in order to ensure the survival of the company, even if those measures mean that the shareholders and the normal organs of the company are temporarily divested of their powers.

Since the application of a rule of national law such as that prohibiting the abusive exercise of rights must not detract from the full effect and uniform application of Community law in the Member States, an action by a shareholder on the basis of Article 25 cannot, without the scope of that provision being changed, be deemed to be abusive merely because he is a minority shareholder of a company subject to reorganization measures or has benefited from the reorganization of the company.

Publication in daily newspapers of an offer of subscription in connection with an increase of capital does not constitute information given in writing to the holders of registered shares within the meaning of the third sentence of Article 29(3) of the directive where the national legislation does not provide for publication in the national gazette appointed for that purpose.

IV. Joined cases C-134/91 and C-135/91 Kerafina-Keramische und Finanz Holding AG and Vioktimatiki AEVE v Hellenic Republic and Organismos Oikonomikis Anasygkrotissis Epicheirisseon AE [1992] ECR I-5699

1. Article 25(1) of the Second Directive 77/91, may be relied upon by individuals against the public authorities before national courts.

Article 25 in conjunction with Article 41(1) of that directive must be interpreted as meaning that they preclude national rules which, in order to ensure the survival and continued operation of undertakings which are of particular economic and social importance for society as a whole and are in exceptional circumstances by reason of their excessive debt burden, provide for the adoption by administrative act of a decision to increase the company capital, without prejudice to the right of pre-emption of the original shareholders when the new shares are issued.

2. The discretion conferred on the Commission by Article [88][1] of the Treaty in the field of State aid does not permit the Commission to authorize Member States to derogate from provisions of Community law other than those relating to the application of Article [87(l)][1] of the Treaty. Consequently, a decision adopted by the Commission under Article [88][1] cannot be interpreted as authorizing the Member State to whom it is addressed to maintain in force, even if only provisionally, a national provision which is contrary to the Second Directive 77/91 on company law.

V. Case C-381/89 Syndesmos Melon tis Eleftheras Evangelikis Ekklissias and others v Greek State and others [1992] ECR I-2111

Articles 25(1) and 29(1) of the Second Directive (77/91/EEC) may be relied upon by individuals against the public authorities before the national courts. Those provisions are to be interpreted as precluding the application of rules which, being designed to ensure the rationalisation and continued trading of undertakings that are of particular importance to the economy of a Member State and are in an exceptional situation because of their debts, allow an increase of capital to be decided upon by administrative measure, without any resolution being passed by the general meeting, and enable a decision to be taken, by administrative measure, that new shares are to be allotted without being offered on a pre-emptive basis to the shareholders in proportion to the capital represented by their shares.

VI. Joined cases C-19/90 and C-20/90 Marina Karella and Nicolas Karellas v Minister for Industry, Energy and Technology and Organismos Anasygkrotiseos Epicheiriseon AE [1991] ECR I-2691

Article 25 of the Second Council Directive 77/91/EEC may be relied upon by individuals against the public authorities before national courts.

By providing that any increase in capital must be decided upon by the general meeting, Article 25(1) lays down provisions which appear, as far as their subject-matter is concerned, to be unconditional and sufficiently precise for them to be held to have direct effect.

Article 25 in conjunction with Article 41(1) of that directive must be interpreted as meaning that they preclude national rules which, in order to ensure the survival and continued operation of undertakings which are of particular economic and social importance for society as a whole and are in exceptional circumstances by reason of their excessive debt burden, provide for the adoption by administrative act of a decision to increase the company capital, without prejudice to the right of pre-emption of the original shareholders when the new shares are issued. In that regard, it is irrelevant that those rules provide that the shares so created may, in the context of a policy of encouraging shareholding by private individuals, be transferred to employees of the company or other groups of private individuals as long as that possibility has not crystallized.

Article 26

Shares issued for a consideration, in the course of an increase in subscribed capital, must be paid up to at least 25% of their nominal value or, in the absence of a nominal value, of their accountable par.

Where provision is made for an issue premium, it must be paid in full.

Article 27

1. Where shares are issued for a consideration other than in cash in the course of an increase in the subscribed capital the consideration must be transferred in full within a period of five years from the decision to increase the subscribed capital.

2. The consideration referred to in paragraph 1 shall be the subject of a report drawn up before the increase in capital is made by one or more experts who are independent of the company and appointed or approved by an administrative or judicial authority. Such experts may be natural persons as well as legal persons and companies and firms under the laws of each Member State.

[Article 10(2) and (3) and Articles 10a and 10b shall apply.]

3. Member States may decide not to apply paragraph 2 in the event of an increase in subscribed capital made in order to give effect to a merger or a public offer for the purchase or exchange of shares and to pay the shareholders of the company which is being absorbed or which is the object of the public offer for the purchase or exchange of shares.

4. Member States may decide not to apply paragraph 2 if all the shares issued in the course of an increase in subscribed capital are issued for a consideration other than in cash to one or more companies, on condition that all the shareholders in the company which receive the consideration have agreed not to have an experts' report drawn up and that the requirements of Article 10 (4) (b) to (f) are met.

¶ *The second subparagraph of article 27(2) has been replaced by article 1(8) of Directive 2006/68/EC, reproduced infra under no. C. 32.*

Article 28

Where an increase in capital is not fully subscribed, the capital will be increased by the amount of the subscriptions received only if the conditions of the issue so provide.

Article 29

1. Whenever the capital is increased by consideration in cash, the shares must be offered on a pre-emptive basis to shareholders in proportion to the capital represented by their shares.

2. The laws of a Member State:

(a) need not apply paragraph 1 above to shares which carry a limited right to participate in distributions within the meaning of Article 15 and/or in the company's assets in the event of liquidation; or

(b) may permit, where the subscribed capital of a company having several classes of shares carrying different rights with regard to voting, or participation in distributions within the meaning of Article 15 or in assets in the event of liquidation, is increased by issuing new shares in only one of these classes, the right of pre-emption of shareholders of the other classes to be exercised only after the exercise of this right by the shareholders of the class in which the new shares are being issued.

3. Any offer of subscription on a pre-emptive basis and the period within which this right must be exercised shall be published in the national gazette appointed in accordance with Directive 68/151/EEC. However, the laws of a Member State need not provide for such publication where all a company's shares are registered. In such case, all the company's shareholders must be informed in writing. The right of pre-emption must be exercised within a period which shall not be less than 14 days from the date of publication of the offer or from the date of dispatch of the letters to the shareholders.

4. The right of pre-emption may not be restricted or withdrawn by the statutes or instrument of incorporation. This may, however, be done by decision of the general meeting. The administrative or management body shall be

required to present to such a meeting a written report indicating the reasons for restriction or withdrawal of the right of pre-emption, and justifying the proposed issue price. The general meeting shall act in accordance with the rules for a quorum and a majority laid down in Article 40. Its decision shall be published in the manner laid down by the laws of each Member State, in accordance with Article 3 of Directive 68/151/EEC.

5. The laws of a Member State may provide that the statutes, the instrument of incorporation or the general meeting, acting in accordance with the rules for a quorum, a majority and publication set out in paragraph (4), may give the power to restrict or withdraw the right of pre-emption to the company body which is empowered to decide on an increase in subscribed capital within the limits of the authorised capital. This power may not be granted for a longer period than the power for which provision is made in Article 25 (2).

6. Paragraphs 1 to 5 shall apply to the issue of all securities which are convertible into shares or which carry the right to subscribe for shares, but not to the conversion of such securities, nor to the exercise of the right to subscribe.

7. The right of pre-emption is not excluded for the purposes of paragraphs 4 and 5 where, in accordance with the decision to increase the subscribed capital, shares are issued to banks or other financial institutions with a view to their being offered to shareholders of the company in accordance with paragraphs 1 and 3.

CASES

I. Case C-367/96 Dionysios Diamantis v Elliniko Dimosio (Greek State) and Organismos Ikonomikis Anasygkrotisis Epicheiriseon AE (OAE) [2000] ECR I-1705

See supra under Article 25 of this Directive.

II. Case C-42/95 Siemens AG v Henry Nold [1996] ECR I-6017

The Second Council Directive 77/91/EEC, in particular Article 29(1) and (4), does not preclude a Member State's domestic law from granting a right of pre-emption to shareholders in the event of an increase in capital by consideration in kind and from subjecting the legality of a decision withdrawing that right of pre-emption to a substantive review which secures a higher level of protection for shareholders than that required by Article 29(4) of the directive in the case of contributions in cash.

The fact that that provision does not refer to increases in capital by consideration in kind does not mean that the conclusion can be drawn that the Community legislator elected to restrict the shareholders' right of pre-emption to increases in capital by consideration in cash, thereby precluding Member States from extending it also to increases in capital by consideration in kind. On the contrary, since the Second Directive merely prescribes a right of pre-emption in the event of increases in capital by consideration in cash, whilst refraining from laying down rules on the complex situation–unknown in most Member States–where the right of pre-emption is exercised in the event of increases in capital by consideration in kind, it left Member States at liberty to provide or not to provide for a right of pre-emption in the latter case. In addition, a national rule extending the principle that shareholders should have a right of pre-emption to increases in capital by consideration in kind, while providing for the possibility of restricting or withdrawing that right in certain circumstances, is consistent with one of the aims of the Second Directive, namely that of ensuring more effective protection for shareholders.

III. Case C-441/93 Panagis Pafitis and others v Trapeza Kentrikis Ellados AE and others [1996] ECR I-1347

See supra under Article 25 of this Directive.

IV. Case C-381/89 Syndesmos Melon tis Eleftheras Evangelikis Ekklissias and others v Greek State and others [1992] ECR I-2111

See supra under Article 25 of this Directive.

Article 30

Any reduction in the subscribed capital, except under a court order, must be subject at least to a decision of the general meeting acting in accordance with the rules for a quorum and a majority laid down in Article 40 without prejudice to Articles 36 and 37. Such decision shall be published in the manner laid down by the laws of each Member State in accordance with Article 8 of Directive 68/151/EEC.

The notice convening the meeting must specify at least the purpose of the reduction and the way in which it is to be carried out.

Article 31

Where there are several classes of shares, the decision by the general meeting concerning a reduction in the subscribed capital shall be subject to a separate vote, at least for each class of shareholders whose rights are affected by the transaction.

Article 32

[1. In the event of a reduction in the subscribed capital, at least the creditors whose claims antedate the publication of the decision on the reduction shall at least have the right to obtain security for claims which have not fallen due by the date of that publication. Member States may not set aside such a right unless the creditor has adequate safeguards, or unless such safeguards are not necessary having regard to the assets of the company.

Member States shall lay down the conditions for the exercise of the right provided for in the first subparagraph. In any event, Member States shall ensure that the creditors are authorised to apply to the appropriate administrative or judicial authority for adequate safeguards provided that they can credibly demonstrate that due to the reduction in the subscribed capital the satisfaction of their claims is at stake, and that no adequate safeguards have been obtained from the company.]

2. The laws of the Member States shall also stipulate at least that the reduction shall be void or that no payment may be made for the benefit of the shareholders, until the creditors have obtained satisfaction or a court has decided that their application should not be acceded to.

3. This article shall apply where the reduction in the subscribed capital is brought about by the total or partial waiving of the payment of the balance of the shareholders' contributions.

¶ *Paragraph 1 has been replaced by article 1(9) of Directive 2006/68/EC, reproduced infra under no. C. 32.*

Article 33

1. Member States need not apply Article 32 to a reduction in the subscribed capital whose purpose is to offset losses incurred or to include sums of money in a reserve provided that, following this operation, the amount of such reserve is not more than 10% of the reduced subscribed capital. Except in the event of a reduction in the subscribed capital, this reserve may not be distributed to shareholders; it may be used only for offsetting losses incurred or for increasing the subscribed capital by the capitalisation of such reserve, in so far as the Member States permit such an operation.

2. In the cases referred to in paragraph 1 the laws of the Member States must at least provide for the measures necessary to ensure that the amounts deriving from the reduction of subscribed capital may not be used for making payments or distributions to shareholders or discharging shareholders from the obligation to make their contributions.

Article 34

The subscribed capital may not be reduced to an amount less than the minimum capital laid down in accordance with Article 6. However, Member States may permit such a reduction if they also provide that the decision to reduce the subscribed capital may take effect only when the subscribed capital is increased to an amount at least equal to the prescribed minimum.

Article 35

Where the laws of a Member State authorise total or partial redemption of the subscribed capital without reduction of the latter, they shall at least require that the following conditions are observed:

(a) where the statutes or instrument of incorporation provide for redemption, the latter shall be decided on by the general meeting voting at least under the usual conditions of quorum and majority. Where the statutes or instrument of incorporation do not provide for redemption, the latter shall be decided upon by the general meeting acting at least under the conditions of quorum and majority laid down in Article 40. The decision must be published in the manner prescribed by the laws of each Member State, in accordance with Article 3 of Directive 68/151/EEC;

(b) only sums which are available for distribution within the meaning of Article 15 (1) may be used for redemption purposes;

(c) shareholders whose shares are redeemed shall retain their rights in the company, with the exception of their rights to the repayment of their investment and participation in the distribution of an initial dividend on unredeemed shares.

Article 36

1. Where the laws of a Member State may allow companies to reduce their subscribed capital by compulsory withdrawal of shares, they shall require that at least the following conditions are observed:

(a) compulsory withdrawal must be prescribed or authorised by the statutes or instrument of incorporation before subscription of the shares which are to be withdrawn are subscribed for;

(b) where the compulsory withdrawal is merely authorised by the statutes or instrument of incorporation, it shall be decided upon by the general meeting unless it has been unanimously approved by the shareholders concerned;

(c) the company body deciding on the compulsory withdrawal shall fix the terms and manner thereof, where they have not already been fixed by the statutes or instrument of incorporation;

(d) Article 32 shall apply except in the case of fully paid-up shares which are made available to the company free of charge or are withdrawn using sums available for distribution in accordance with Article 15 (1); in these cases, an amount equal to the nominal value or, in the absence thereof, to the accountable par of all the withdrawn shares must be included in a reserve. Except in the event of a reduction in the subscribed capital this reserve may not be distributed to shareholders. It can be used only for offsetting losses incurred or for increasing the subscribed capital by the capitalisation of such reserve, in so far as Member States permit such an operation;

(e) the decision on compulsory withdrawal shall be published in the manner laid down by the laws of each Member State in accordance with Article 3 of Directive 68/151/EEC.

2. Articles 30 (1), 31, 33 and 40 shall not apply to the cases to which paragraph 1 refers.

Article 37

1. In case of a reduction in the subscribed capital by the withdrawal of shares acquired by the company itself or by a person acting in his own name but on behalf of the company, the withdrawal must always be decided on by the general meeting.

2. Article 32 shall apply unless the shares are fully paid up and are acquired free of charge or using sums available for distribution in accordance with Article 15 (1); in these cases an amount equal to the nominal value or, in the absence thereof, to the accountable par of all the shares withdrawn must be included in a reserve. Except in the event of a reduction in the subscribed capital, this reserve may not be distributed to shareholders. It may be used only for offsetting losses incurred or for increasing the subscribed capital by the capitalisation of such reserve, in so far as the Member States permit such an operation.

3. Articles 31, 33 and 40 shall not apply to the cases to which paragraph 1 refers.

Article 38

In the cases covered by Articles 35, 36 (1) (b) and 37 (1), when there are several classes of shares, the decision by the general meeting concerning redemption of the subscribed capital or its reduction by withdrawal of shares shall be subject to a separate vote, at least for each class of shareholders whose rights are affected by the transaction.

Article 39

Where the laws of a Member State authorise companies to issue redeemable shares, they shall require that the following conditions, at least, are complied with for the redemption of such shares:

(a) redemption must be authorised by the company's statutes or instrument of incorporation before the redeemable shares are subscribed for;

(b) the shares must be fully paid up;

(c) the terms and the manner of redemption must be laid down in the company's statutes or instrument of incorporation;

(d) redemption can be only effected by using sums available for distribution in accordance with Article 15 (1) or the proceeds of a new issue made with a view to effecting such redemption;

(e) an amount equal to the nominal value or, in the absence thereof, to the accountable par of all the redeemed shares must be included in a reserve which cannot be distributed to the shareholders, except in the event of a reduction in the subscribed capital; it may be used only for the purpose of increasing the subscribed capital by the capitalisation of reserves;

(f) subparagraph (c) shall not apply to redemption using the proceeds of a new issue made with a view to effecting such redemption;

(g) where provision is made for the payment of a premium to shareholders in consequence of a redemption, the premium may be paid only from sums available for distribution in accordance with Article 15 (1) or from a reserve other than that referred to in (e) which may not be distributed to shareholders except in the event of a reduction in the subscribed capital; this reserve may be used only for the purposes of increasing the subscribed capital by the capitalisation of reserves or for covering the costs referred to in Article 3 (j) or the cost of issuing shares or debentures or for the payment of a premium to holders of redeemable shares or debentures;

(h) notification of redemption shall be published in the manner laid down by the laws of each Member State in accordance with Article 3 of Directive 68/151/EEC.

Article 40

1. The laws of the Member States shall provide that the decisions referred to in Articles 29 (4) and (5), 30, 31, 35 and 38 must be taken at least by a majority of not less than two-thirds of the votes attaching to the securities or the subscribed capital represented.

2. The laws of the Member States may, however, lay down that a simple majority of the votes specified in paragraph 1 is sufficient when at least half the subscribed capital is represented.

Article 41

[1. Member States may derogate from Article 9(1), the first sentence of point (a) of Article 19(1), and Articles 25, 26 and 29 to the extent that such derogations are necessary for the adoption or application of provisions designed to encourage the participation of employees, or other groups of persons defined by national law, in the capital of undertakings.]

2. Member States may decide not to apply Article 19 (1) (a), first sentence, and Articles 30, 31, 36, 37, 38 and 39 to companies incorporated under a special law which issue both capital shares and workers' shares, the latter being issued to the company's employees as a body, who are represented at general meetings of shareholders by delegates having the right to vote.

¶ *Paragraph 1 has been replaced by article 1(10) of Directive 2006/68/EC, reproduced infra under no. C. 32.*

Cases

I. Joined cases C-134/91 and C-135/91 Kerafina-Keramische und Finanz Holding AG and Vioktimatiki AEVE v Hellenic Republic and Organismos Oikonomikis Anasygkrotissis Epicheirisseon AE [1992] ECR I-5699

See supra under Article 25 of this Directive.

> II. Joined cases C-19/90 and C-20/90
> Marina Karella and Nicolas Karellas v
> Minister for Industry, Energy and
> Technology and Organismos
> Anasygkrotiseos Epicheiriseon AE [1991]
> ECR I-2691
>
> See supra under Article 25 of this Directive.

Article 42

For the purposes of the implementation of this Directive, the laws of the Member States shall ensure equal treatment to all shareholders who are in the same position.

¶ *Article 42 embodies the fundamental precept of equal treatment of shareholders who are in the same position but limits the principle to the application of the rules contained in the Directive. Compare, for a similar, but more general formulation, limited to stock exchange listed companies: Directive 79/279/EEC of 5 March 1979, schedule C, point 2a, reproduced infra under no. S. 2.*

Article 43

1. Member States shall bring into force the laws, regulations and administrative provisions needed in order to comply with this Directive within two years of its notification. They shall forthwith inform the Commission thereof.

2. Member States may decide not to apply Article 3 (g), (i), (j) and (k) to companies already in existence at the date of entry into force of the provisions referred to in paragraph 1.

They may provide that the other provisions of this Directive shall not apply to such companies until 18 months after that date.

However, this time limit may be three years in the case of Articles 6 and 9 and five years in the case of unregistered companies in the United Kingdom and Ireland.

3. Member States shall ensure that they communicate to the Commission the text of the main provisions of national law which they adopt in the field covered by this Directive.

Article 44

This Directive is addressed to the Member States.

C.3.
Third Council Directive 78/855/EEC of 9 October 1978 based on Article [44][1] (3) (g) of the Treaty concerning mergers of public limited liability companies[2]

CASE

Case C-411/03 Sevic Systems AG [2005] I-10805

The right of establishment covers all measures which permit or even merely facilitate access to another Member State and the pursuit of an economic activity in that State by allowing the persons concerned to participate in the economic life of the country effectively and under the same conditions as national operators. Cross-border merger operations, like other company transformation operations, respond to the need for cooperation and consolidation between companies established in different Member States. They constitute particular methods of exercise of the freedom of establishment, important for the proper functioning of the internal market. When a national companies act establishes a difference in treatment between companies according to the internal or cross-border nature of the merger, this is likely to deter the exercise of the freedom of establishment laid down by the Treaty. Member States may maintain restrictions to the free establishment in the public interest, such as protection of the interests of creditors, minority shareholders and employees (see Case C-208/00 *Überseering* [2002] ECR I-9919, paragraph 92), and the preservation of the effectiveness of fiscal supervision and the fairness of commercial transactions (see Case C-167/01 *Inspire Art* [2003] ECR I-10155, paragraph 132). However, by refusing to register in the commercial register a merger between a company established in one Member State and one established in another Member State in general terms even if the interests mentioned general good interests are not threatened goes beyond what is necessary to protect those interests.

The existence of harmonization provisions such as laid down in the Third and Sixth Directives cannot be made a precondition for the implementation of the freedom of establishment laid down by Articles 43 EC and 48 EC.

THE COUNCIL OF THE EUROPEAN COMMUNITIES,

Having regard to the Treaty establishing the European Economic Community, and in particular Article [44][1] (3) (g) thereof,

Having regard to the proposal from the Commission,[3]

Having regard to the opinion of the European Parliament,[4]

Having regard to the opinion of the Economic and Social Committee,[5]

Whereas the co-ordination provided for in Article 54 (3) (g) and in the general programme for the abolition of restrictions on freedom of establishment[6] was begun with Directive 68/151/EEC;[7]

---

[1] The number between brackets has been changed as from 1 May 1999 by article 12 of the Treaty of Amsterdam.
[2] OJ L 295, 20.10.1978, 36–43.

[3] OJ C 89, 14.7.1970, 20.
[4] OJ C 129, 11.12.1972, 50; OJ C 95, 28. 4.1975, 12.
[5] OJ C 88, 6.9.1971, 18.
[6] OJ 2, 15.1.1962, 36/62.
[7] OJ L 65, 14.3.1968, 8, First Company Directive, reproduced supra under no. C. 1.

Whereas this co-ordination was continued as regards the formation of public limited liability companies and the maintenance and alteration of their capital with Directive 77/91/EEC,[8] and as regards the annual accounts of certain types of companies with Directive 78/660/EEC;[9]

Whereas the protection of the interests of members and third parties requires that the laws of the Member States relating to mergers of public limited liability companies be co-ordinated and that provision for mergers should be made in the laws of all the Member States;

Whereas in the context of such co-ordination it is particularly important that the shareholders of merging companies be kept adequately informed in as objective a manner as possible and that their rights be suitably protected;

Whereas the protection of employees' rights in the event of transfers of undertakings, businesses or parts of businesses is at present regulated by Directive 77/187/EEC;[10]

Whereas creditors, including debenture holders, and persons having other claims on the merging companies must be protected so that the merger does not adversely affect their interests;

Whereas the disclosure requirements of Directive 68/151/EEC must be extended to include mergers so that third parties are kept adequately informed;

Whereas the safeguards afforded to members and third parties in connection with mergers must be extended to cover certain legal practices which in important respects are similar to merger, so that the obligation to provide such protection cannot be evaded;

Whereas to ensure certainty in the law as regards relations between the companies concerned, between them and third parties, and between the members, the cases in which nullity can arise must be limited by providing that defects be remedied wherever that is possible and by restricting the period within which nullification proceedings may be commenced,

HAS ADOPTED THIS DIRECTIVE:

Article 1
Scope

1. The co-ordination measures laid down by this Directive shall apply to the laws, regulations and administrative provisions of the Member States relating to the following types of company:
– *in Germany:*
  die Aktiengesellschaft,
– *in Belgium:*
  la société anonyme/de naamloze vennootschap,
– *in Denmark:*
  aktieselskaber,
– *in France:*
  la société anonyme,
[– *in Greece:*
  η ανωνυμη εταιρια,]
– *in Ireland:*
  public companies limited by shares, and public companies limited by guarantee having a share capital,
– *in Italy:*
  la società per azioni,
– *in Luxembourg:*
  la société anonyme,
– *in the Netherlands:*
  de naamloze vennootschap,
[– *in Portugal:*
  a sociedade anonima de responsabilidade limitada,
– *in Spain:*
  la sociedad anonima,]
– *in the United Kingdom:*
  public companies limited by shares, and public companies limited by guarantee having a share capital.
[– *in Austria:*
  die Aktiengesellschaft];
[– *in Finland:*
  osakeyhtiö—aktiebolag];
[– *in Sverige:*
  aktiebolag];

---

[8] OJ L 26, 31.1.1977, 1, Second Company Directive, reproduced supra under no. C. 2.
[9] OJ L 222, 14.8.1978, 11, Fourth Company Directive, reproduced infra under no. C. 4.
[10] OJ L 61, 5.3.1977, 26, reproduced infra under no. E. 2.

[– in the Czech Republic:
akciová společnost];
[– in Estonia:
aktsiaselts];
[– in Cyprus:
Δημόσιες εταιρείες περιορισμένης ευθύνης με μετοχές, δημόσιες εταιρείες περιορισμένης ευθύνης με εγγύηση που διαθέτουν μετοχικό κεφάλαιο];
[– in Latvia:
akciju sabiedrība];
[– in Lithuania:
akcinė bendrovė];
[– in Hungary:
részvénytársaság];
[– in Malta:
kumpanija pubblika—public limited liability company];
[– in Poland:
spólka akcyjna];
[– in Slovenia:
delniška družba];
[– in Slovakia:
akciová spoločnost].

2. The Member States need not apply this Directive to co-operatives incorporated as one of the types of company listed in paragraph 1. In so far as the laws of the Member States make use of this option, they shall require such companies to include the word 'co-operative' in all the documents referred to in Article 4 of Directive 68/151/EEC.

3. The Member States need not apply this Directive in cases where the company or companies which are being acquired or will cease to exist are the subject of bankruptcy proceedings, proceedings relating to the winding-up of insolvent companies, judicial arrangements, compositions and analogous proceedings.

¶ *This Directive has been rendered applicable to Greece by the Act of Accession of the Hellenic Republic, Annex I (III)(c)(2) (OJ L 291, 19.11.1979), to Spain and Portugal by the Act of Accession of the Kingdom of Spain and the Portuguese Republic, Annex I, (II)(d)(2) (OJ L 302, 15.11. 1985), to Austria, Sweden, and Finland by the Act of Accession of Austria, Sweden, and Finland (OJ C 241, 29.8.1994, 21), adapted by Council Decision 91/1/EC, Euratom, ECSC (OJ L 1, 1.1.1995, 1), and to the Czech Republic, Estonia, Cyprus, Latvia, Hungary, Malta, Poland, Slovenia, and Slovakia by the Act concerning the conditions of accession of the Czech Republic, the Republic of Estonia, the Republic of Cyprus, the Republic of Latvia, the Republic of Hungary, the Republic of Malta, the Republic of Poland, the Republic of Slovenia, and the Slovak Republic and the adjustments to the Treaties on which the European Union is founded (OJ L 236, 23.9.2003, 33).*

¶ *Compare also Sixth Company Directive 82/891/EEC, reproduced infra under no. C. 5.*

Chapter I

Regulation of Merger by the Acquisition of One or More Companies by Another and of Merger by the Formation of a New Company

Article 2

The Member States shall, as regards companies governed by their national laws, make provision for rules governing merger by the acquisition of one or more companies by another and merger by the formation of a new company.

Article 3

1. For the purposes of this Directive, 'merger by acquisition' shall mean the operation whereby one or more companies are wound up without going into liquidation and transfer to another all their assets and liabilities in exchange for the issue to the shareholders of the company or companies being acquired of shares in the acquiring company and a cash payment, if any, not exceeding 10% of the nominal value of the shares so issued or, where they have no nominal value, of their accounting par value.

2. A Member State's laws may provide that merger by acquisition may also be effected where one or more of the companies being acquired is in liquidation, provided that this option is restricted to companies which have not yet begun to distribute their assets to their shareholders.

Article 4

1. For the purposes of this Directive, 'merger by the formation of a new company' shall mean the operation whereby several companies are wound up without going into liquidation and transfer to a company that they set up all their assets and liabilities in exchange for the issue to their shareholders of shares in the new company and a cash payment,

if any, not exceeding 10% of the nominal value of the shares so issued or, where they have no nominal value, of their accounting par value.

2. A Member State's laws may provide that merger by the formation of a new company may also be effected where one or more of the companies which are ceasing to exist is in liquidation, provided that this option is restricted to companies which have not yet begun to distribute their assets to their shareholders.

CHAPTER II
MERGER BY ACQUISITION

Article 5

1. The administrative or management bodies of the merging companies shall draw up draft terms of merger in writing.

2. Draft terms of merger shall specify at least:

(a) the type, name and registered office of each of the merging companies;

(b) the share exchange ratio and the amount of any cash payment;

(c) the terms relating to the allotment of shares in the acquiring company;

(d) the date from which the holding of such shares entitles the holders to participate in profits and any special conditions affecting that entitlement;

(e) the date from which the transactions of the company being acquired shall be treated for accounting purposes as being those of the acquiring company;

(f) the rights conferred by the acquiring company on the holders of shares to which special rights are attached and the holders of securities other than shares, or the measures proposed concerning them;

(g) any special advantage granted to the experts referred to in Article 10 (1) and members of the merging companies' administrative, management, supervisory or controlling bodies.

Article 6

Draft terms of merger must be published in the manner prescribed by the laws of each Member State in accordance with Article 3 of Directive 68/151/EEC, for each of the merging companies, at least one month before the date fixed for the general meeting which is to decide thereon.

Article 7

1. A merger shall require at least the approval of the general meeting of each of the merging companies. The laws of the Member States shall provide that this decision shall require a majority of not less than two thirds of the votes attaching either to the shares or to the subscribed capital represented.

The laws of a Member State may, however, provide that a simple majority of the votes specified in the first subparagraph shall be sufficient when at least half of the subscribed capital is represented. Moreover, where appropriate, the rules governing alterations to the memorandum and articles of association shall apply.

2. Where there is more than one class of shares, the decision concerning a merger shall be subject to a separate vote by at least each class of shareholders whose rights are affected by the transaction.

3. The decision shall cover both the approval of the draft terms of merger and any alterations to the memorandum and articles of association necessitated by the merger.

Article 8

The laws of a Member State need not require approval of the merger by the general meeting of the acquiring company if the following conditions are fulfilled:

(a) the publication provided for in Article 6 must be effected, for the acquiring company, at least one month before the date fixed for the general meeting of the company or companies being acquired which are to decide on the draft terms of merger;

(b) at least one month before the date specified in (a), all shareholders of the acquiring company must be entitled to inspect the documents specified in Article 11 (1) at the registered office of the acquiring company;

(c) one or more shareholders of the acquiring company holding a minimum percentage of the subscribed capital must be entitled to require that a general meeting of the acquiring company be called to decide whether to approve the merger. This minimum percentage may not be fixed at more than 5%. The Member States may, however, provide for the exclusion of non-voting shares from this calculation.

Article 9

The administration or management bodies of each of the merging companies shall draw up a detailed written report explaining the draft terms of merger and setting out the legal and economic grounds for them, in particular the share exchange ratio.

The report shall also describe any special valuation difficulties which have arisen.

Article 10

1. One or more experts, acting on behalf of each of the merging companies but independent of them, appointed or approved by a judicial or administrative authority, shall examine the draft terms of merger and draw up a written report to the shareholders. However, the laws of a Member State may provide for the appointment of one or more independent experts for all the merging companies, if such appointment is made by a judicial or administrative authority at the joint request of those companies. Such experts may, depending on the laws of each Member State, be natural or legal persons or companies or firms.

2. In the report mentioned in paragraph 1 the experts must in any case state whether in their opinion the share exchange ratio is fair and reasonable. Their statement must at least:

(a) indicate the method or methods used to arrive at the share exchange ratio proposed;

(b) state whether such method or methods are adequate in the case in question, indicate the values arrived at using each such method and give an opinion on the relative importance attributed to such methods in arriving at the value decided.

The report shall also describe any special valuation difficulties which have arisen.

3. Each expert shall be entitled to obtain from the merging companies all relevant information and documents and to carry out all necessary investigations.

¶ *Compare article 27 of Second Company Directive 77/91/EEC, reproduced supra under no. C. 2.*

Article 11

1. All shareholders shall be entitled to inspect at least the following documents at the registered office at least one month before the date fixed for the general meeting which is to decide on the draft terms of merger:

(a) the draft terms of merger;

(b) the annual accounts and annual reports of the merging companies for the preceding three financial years;

(c) an accounting statement drawn up as at a date which must not be earlier than the first day of the third month preceding the date of the draft terms of merger, if the latest annual accounts relate to a financial year which ended more than six months before that date;

(d) the reports of the administrative or management bodies of the merging companies provided for in Article 9;

(e) the reports provided for in Article 10.

2. The accounting statement provided for in paragraph 1 (c) shall be drawn up using the same methods and the same layout as the last annual balance sheet.

However, the laws of a Member State may provide that:

(a) it shall not be necessary to take a fresh physical inventory;

(b) the valuations shown in the last balance sheet shall be altered only to reflect entries in the books of account; the following shall nevertheless be taken into account:
– interim depreciation and provisions,
– material changes in actual value not shown in the books.

3. Every shareholder shall be entitled to obtain, on request and free of charge, full or, if so desired,

partial copies of the documents referred to in paragraph 1.

Article 12

Protection of the rights of the employees of each of the merging companies shall be regulated in accordance with Directive 77/187/EEC.

Article 13

1. The laws of the Member States must provide for an adequate system of protection of the interests of creditors of the merging companies whose claims antedate the publication of the draft terms of merger and have not fallen due at the time of such publication.

2. To this end, the laws of the Member States shall at least provide that such creditors shall be entitled to obtain adequate safeguards where the financial situation of the merging companies makes such protection necessary and where those creditors do not already have such safeguards.

3. Such protection may be different for the creditors of the acquiring company and for those of the company being acquired.

Article 14

Without prejudice to the rules governing the collective exercise of their rights, Article 13 shall apply to the debenture holders of the merging companies, except where the merger has been approved by a meeting of the debenture holders, if such a meeting is provided for under national laws, or by the debenture holders individually.

Holders of securities, other than shares, to which special rights are attached, must be given rights in the acquiring company at least equivalent to those they possessed in the company being acquired, unless the alteration of those rights has been approved by a meeting of the holders of such securities, if such a meeting is provided for under national laws, or by the holders of those securities individually, or unless the holders are entitled to have their securities repurchased by the acquiring company.

Article 15

Holders of securities, other than shares, to which special rights are attached, must be given rights in the acquiring company at least equivalent to those they possessed in the company being acquired, unless the alteration of those rights has been approved by a meeting of the holders of such securities, if such a meeting is provided for under national laws, or by the holders of those securities individually, or unless the holders are entitled to have their securities repurchased by the acquiring company.

Article 16

1. Where the laws of a Member State do not provide for judicial or administrative preventive supervision of the legality of mergers, or where such supervision does not extend to all the legal acts required for a merger, the minutes of the general meetings which decide on the merger and, where appropriate, the merger contract subsequent to such general meetings shall be drawn up and certified in due legal form. In cases where the merger need not be approved by the general meetings of all the merging companies, the draft terms of merger must be drawn up and certified in due legal form.

2. The notary or the authority competent to draw up and certify the document in due legal form must check and certify the existence and validity of the legal acts and formalities required of the company for which he or it is acting and of the draft terms of merger.

Article 17

The laws of the Member States shall determine the date on which a merger takes effect.

Article 18

1. A merger must be publicised in the manner prescribed by the laws of each Member State, in accordance with Article 3 of Directive 68/151/EEC, in respect of each of the merging companies.

2. The acquiring company may itself carry out the publication formalities relating to the company or companies being acquired.

Article 19

1. A merger shall have the following consequences *ipso jure* and simultaneously:

(a) the transfer, both as between the company being acquired and the acquiring company and as regards third parties, to the acquiring company of all the assets and liabilities of the company being acquired;

(b) the shareholders of the company being acquired become shareholders of the acquiring company;

(c) the company being acquired ceases to exist.

2. No shares in the acquiring company shall be exchanged for shares in the company being acquired held either:

(a) by the acquiring company itself or through a person acting in his own name but on its behalf; or

(b) by the company being acquired itself or through a person acting in his own name but on its behalf.

3. The foregoing shall not affect the laws of Member States which require the completion of special formalities for the transfer of certain assets, rights and obligations by the acquired company to be effective as against third parties. The acquiring company may carry out these formalities itself; however, the laws of the Member States may permit the company being acquired to continue to carry out these formalities for a limited period which cannot, save in exceptional cases, be fixed at more than six months from the date on which the merger takes effect.

Article 20

The laws of the Member States shall at least lay down rules governing the civil liability towards the shareholders of the company being acquired of the members of the administrative or management bodies of that company in respect of misconduct on the part of members of those bodies in preparing and implementing the merger.

Article 21

The laws of the Member States shall at least lay down rules governing the civil liability towards the shareholders of the company being acquired of the experts responsible for drawing up on behalf of that company the report referred to in Article 10 (1) in respect of misconduct on the part of those experts in the performance of their duties.

Article 22

1. The laws of the Member States may lay down nullity rules for mergers in accordance with the following conditions only:

(a) nullity must be ordered in a court judgment;

(b) mergers which have taken effect pursuant to Article 17 may be declared void only if there has been no judicial or administrative preventive supervision of their legality, or if they have not been drawn up and certified in due legal form, or if it is shown that the decision of the general meeting is void or voidable under national law;

(c) nullification proceedings may not be initiated more than six months after the date on which the merger becomes effective as against the person alleging nullity or if the situation has been rectified;

(d) where it is possible to remedy a defect liable to render a merger void, the competent court shall grant the companies involved a period of time within which to rectify the situation;

(e) a judgment declaring a merger void shall be published in the manner prescribed by the laws of each Member State in accordance with Article 3 of Directive 68/151/EEC;

(f) where the laws of a Member State permit a third party to challenge such a judgment, he may do so only within six months of publication of the judgment in the manner prescribed by Directive 68/151/EEC;

(g) a judgment declaring a merger void shall not of itself affect the validity of obligations owed by or in relation to the acquiring company which arose before the judgment was published and after the date referred to in Article 17;

(h) companies which have been parties to a merger shall be jointly and severally liable in respect of the obligations of the acquiring company referred to in (g).

2. By way of derogation from paragraph 1 (a), the laws of a Member State may also provide for the nullity of a merger to be ordered by an administrative authority if an appeal against such a decision lies to a court. Subparagraphs (b), (d), (e), (f), (g) and (h) shall apply by analogy to the administrative authority. Such nullification proceedings may not be initiated more than six months after the date referred to in Article 17.

3. The foregoing shall not affect the laws of the Member States on the nullity of a merger pronounced following any supervision other than judicial or administrative preventive supervision of legality.

Chapter III

Merger by Formation of a New Company

Article 23

1. Articles 5, 6, 7 and 9 to 22 shall apply, without prejudice to Articles 11 and 12 of Directive 68/151/EEC, to merger by formation of a new company. For this purpose, 'merging companies' and 'company being acquired' shall mean the companies which will cease to exist, and 'acquiring company' shall mean the new company.

2. Article 5 (2) (a) shall also apply to the new company.

3. The draft terms of merger and, if they are contained in a separate document, the memorandum or draft memorandum of association and the articles or draft articles of association of the new company shall be approved at a general meeting of each of the companies that will cease to exist.

4. The Member States need not apply to the formation of a new company the rules governing the verification of any consideration other than cash which are laid down in Article 10 of Directive 77/91/EEC.

Chapter IV

Acquisition of One Company by Another Which Holds 90% or More of its Shares

Article 24

The Member States shall make provision, in respect of companies governed by their laws, for the operation whereby one or more companies are wound up without going into liquidation and transfer all their assets and liabilities to another company which is the holder of all their shares and other securities conferring the right to vote at general meetings. Such operations shall be regulated by the provisions of Chapter II, with the exception of Articles 5 (2) (b), (c) and (d), 9, 10, 11 (1) (d) and (e), 19 (1) (b), 20 and 21.

Article 25

The Member States need not apply Article 7 to the operations specified in Article 24 if the following conditions at least are fulfilled:

(a) the publication provided for in Article 6 must be effected, as regards each company involved in the operation, at least one month before the operation takes effect;

(b) at least one month before the operation takes effect, all shareholders of the acquiring company must be entitled to inspect the documents specified in Article 11 (1) (a), (b) and (c) at the company's registered office. Article 11 (2) and (3) must apply;

(c) Article 8 (c) must apply.

Article 26

The Member States may apply Articles 24 and 25 to operations whereby one or more companies are wound up without going into liquidation and transfer all their assets and liabilities to another company, if all the shares and other securities specified in Article 24 of the company or companies being acquired are held by the acquiring company and/or by persons holding those shares and securities in their own names but on behalf of that company.

Article 27

In cases of merger where one or more companies are acquired by another company which holds 90% or more, but not all, of the shares and other securities of each of those companies the holding of which confers the right to vote at general meetings, the Member States need not require approval of the merger by the general meeting of the acquiring company, provided that the following conditions at least are fulfilled:

(a) the publication provided for in Article 6 must be effected, as regards the acquiring company, at least one month before the date fixed for the general meeting of the company or companies being acquired which is to decide on the draft terms of merger;

(b) at least one month before the date specified in (a), all shareholders of the acquiring company must be entitled to inspect the documents specified in Article 11 (1) (a), (b) and (c) at the company's registered office. Article 11 (2) and (3) must apply;

(c) Article 8 (c) must apply.

Article 28

The Member States need not apply Articles 9 to 11 to a merger within the meaning of Article 27 if the following conditions at least are fulfilled:

(a) the minority shareholders of the company being acquired must be entitled to have their shares acquired by the acquiring company;

(b) if they exercise that right, they must be entitled to receive consideration corresponding to the value of their shares;

(c) in the event of disagreement regarding such consideration, it must be possible for the value of the consideration to be determined by a court.

Article 29

The Member States may apply Articles 27 and 28 to operations whereby one or more companies are wound up without going into liquidation and transfer all their assets and liabilities to another company if 90% or more, but not all, of the shares and other securities referred to in Article 27 of the company or companies being acquired are held by that acquiring company and/or by persons holding those shares and securities in their own names but on behalf of that company.

CHAPTER V

OTHER OPERATIONS TREATED AS MERGERS

Article 30

Where in the case of one of the operations referred to in Article 2 the laws of a Member State permit a cash payment to exceed 10%, Chapters II and III and Articles 27, 28 and 29 shall apply.

Article 31

Where the laws of a Member State permit one of the operations referred to in Articles 2, 24 and 30, without all of the transferring companies thereby ceasing to exist, Chapter II, except for Article 19 (1) (c), Chapter III or Chapter IV shall apply as appropriate.

CHAPTER VI

FINAL PROVISIONS

Article 32

1. The Member States shall bring into force the laws, regulations and administrative provisions necessary for them to comply with this Directive within three years of its notification. They shall forthwith inform the Commission thereof.

2. However, provision may be made for a delay of five years from the entry into force of the provisions referred to in paragraph 1 for the application of those provisions to unregistered companies in the United Kingdom and Ireland.

3. The Member States need not apply Articles 13, 14 and 15 as regards the holders of convertible debentures and other convertible securities

if, at the time when the laws, regulations and administrative provisions referred to in paragraph 1 come into force, the position of these holders in the event of a merger has previously been determined by the conditions of issue.

4. The Member States need not apply this Directive to mergers or to operations treated as mergers for the preparation or execution of which an act or formality required by national law has already been completed when the provisions referred to in paragraph 1 enter into force.

Article 33

This Directive is addressed to the Member States.

C.4.

Fourth Council Directive 78/660/EEC of 25 July 1978 based on Article [44]¹ (3) (g) of the Treaty on the annual accounts of certain types of companies²

THE COUNCIL OF THE EUROPEAN COMMUNITIES,

Having regard to the Treaty establishing the European Economic Community, and in particular Article [44]¹ (3) (g) thereof,

Having regard to the proposal from the Commission,

Having regard to the opinion of the European Parliament,³

Having regard to the opinion of the Economic and Social Committee,⁴

Whereas the co-ordination of national provisions concerning the presentation and content of annual accounts and annual reports, the valuation methods used therein and their publication in respect of certain companies with limited liability is of special importance for the protection of members and third parties;

Whereas simultaneous co-ordination is necessary in these fields for these forms of company because, on the one hand, these companies' activities frequently extend beyond the frontiers of their national territories and, on the other, they offer no safeguards to third parties beyond the amounts of their net assets; whereas, moreover, the necessity for and the urgency of such co-ordination have been recognised and confirmed by Article 2 (1) (f) of Directive 68/151/EEC;⁵

Whereas it is necessary, moreover, to establish in the Community minimum equivalent legal requirements as regards the extent of the financial information that should be made available to the public by companies that are in competition with one another;

Whereas annual accounts must give a true and fair view of a company's assets and liabilities, financial position and profit or loss; whereas to this end a mandatory layout must be prescribed for the balance sheet and the profit and loss account and whereas the minimum content of the notes on the accounts and the annual report must be laid down; whereas, however, derogations may be granted for certain companies of minor economic or social importance;

Whereas the different methods for the valuation of assets and liabilities must be co-ordinated to the extent necessary to ensure that annual accounts disclose comparable and equivalent information;

Whereas the annual accounts of all companies to which this Directive applies must be published in accordance with Directive 68/151/EEC; whereas, however, certain derogations may likewise be granted in this area for small and medium-sized companies;

Whereas annual accounts must be audited by authorised persons whose minimum qualifications will be the subject of subsequent co-ordination; whereas only small companies may be relieved of this audit obligation;

Whereas, when a company belongs to a group, it is desirable that group accounts giving a true and fair view of the activities of the group as a whole be published; whereas, however, pending the

---

¹ The number between brackets has been changed as from 1 May 1999 by article 12 of the Treaty of Amsterdam.
² OJ L 222, 14.8.1978, 11–31.
³ OJ C 129, 11.12.1972, 38.
⁴ OJ C 39, 7.6.1973, 31.
⁵ OJ L 65, 14.3.1968, 8, First Company Directive, reproduced supra under no. C. 1.

entry into force of a Council Directive on consolidated accounts, derogations from certain provisions of this Directive are necessary;

Whereas, in order to meet the difficulties arising from the present position regarding legislation in certain Member States, the period allowed for the implementation of certain provisions of this Directive must be longer than the period generally laid down in such cases,

HAS ADOPTED THIS DIRECTIVE:

Article 1

1. The co-ordination measures prescribed by this Directive shall apply to the laws, regulations and administrative provisions of the Member States relating to the following types of companies:
- in Germany:
  die Aktiengesellschaft, die Kommanditgesellschaft auf Aktien, die Gesellschaft mit beschränkter Haftung;
- in Belgium:
  la société anonyme/de naamloze vennootschap, la société en commandite par actions/de commanditaire vennootschap op aandelen, la société de personnes à responsabilité limitée/de personenvennootschap met beperkte aansprakelijkheid;
- in Denmark:
  aktieselskaber, kommanditaktieselskaber, anpartsselskaber;
- in France:
  la société anonyme, la société en commandite par actions, la société à responsabilité limitée;
[– in Greece:
  η ανώνυμη εταιρία, η εταιρία περιωρισμένης ευθύνης, η ετερόρρυθμη κατά μετοχές εταιρία;]
- in Ireland:
  public companies limited by shares or by guarantee, private companies limited by shares or by guarantee;
- in Italy:
  la società per azioni, la società in accomandita per azioni, la società a responsabilità limitata;
- in Luxembourg:
  la société anonyme, la société en commandite par actions, la société à responsabilité limitée;
- in the Netherlands:
  de naamloze vennootschap, de besloten vennootschap met beperkte aansprakelijkheid;
[– in Portugal:
  a sociedade anonima de responsabilidade limitada, a sociedade em comandita por acçoes, a sociedade por quotas de responsabilidade limitada;]
[– in Spain:
  la sociedad anonima, la sociedad comanditaria por acciones, la sociedad de responsabilidad limitada;]
- in the United Kingdom:
  public companies limited by shares, or by guarantee, private companies limited by shares or by guarantee;
[– in Austria:
  die Aktiengesellschaft, die Gesellschaft mit beschränkter Haftung];
[– in Finland:
  osakeyhtiö/aktiebolag];
[– in Sweden:
  aktiebolag];
[– in the Czech Republic:
  společnost s ručením omezeným, akciová společnost];
[– in Estonia:
  aktsiaselts, osaühing];
[– in Cyprus:
  Δημόσιες εταιρείες περιορισμένης ευθύνης με μετοχές δ με εγγύηση, ιδιωτικές εταιρείες περιορισμένης ευθύνης με μετοχές ή με εγγύηση];
[– in Latvia:
  akciju sabiedrība, sabiedrība ar ierobežotu atbildību];
[– in Lithuania:
  akcinės bendrovės, uždarosios akcinės bendrovės];
[– in Hungary:
  részvénytársaság, korlátolt felelösségü társaság];
[– in Malta:
  kumpanija pubblika—public limited liability company, kumpannija privata—private limited liability company,
  soėjeta in akkomandita bil-kapital maqsum f'azzjonijiet—partnership en commandite with the capital divided into shares];

[– in Poland:
spółka akcyjna, spółka z ograniczoną odpowiedzialnością, spółka komandytowo-akcyjna];
[– in Slovenia:
delniška družba, družba z omejeno odgovornostjo, komanditna delniška družba];
[– in Slovakia:
akciová spoločnosť, spoločnosť s ručením obmedzenym].

[The co-ordination measures prescribed by this Directive shall also apply to the Member States' laws, regulations and administrative provisions relating to the following types of company:

(a) in Germany:
die offene Handelsgesellschaft, die Kommanditgesellschaft;

(b) in Belgium:
la société en nom collectif/de vennootschap onder firma, la société en commandite simple/de gewone commanditaire vennootschap;

(c) in Denmark:
interessentskaber, kommanditselskaber;

(d) in France:
la société en nom collectif, la société en commandite simple;

(e) in Greece:
η ομόρρυθμος εταιρία, η ετερόρρυθμος εταιρία;

(f) in Spain:
sociedad colectiva, sociedad en comandita simple;

(g) in Ireland:
partnerships, limited partnerships, unlimited companies;

(h) in Italy:
la società in nome collettivo, la società in accomandita semplice;

(i) in Luxembourg:
la société en nom collectif, la société en commandite simple;

(j) in the Netherlands:
de vennootschap onder firma, de commanditaire vennootschap;

(k) in Portugal:
sociedade em nome colectivo, sociedade em comandita simples;

(l) in the United Kingdom:
partnerships, limited partnerships, unlimited companies,

where all members having unlimited liability are companies of the types set out in the first subparagraph or companies which are not governed by the laws of a Member State but which have a legal form comparable to those referred to in Directive 68/151/EEC.

This Directive shall also apply to the types of companies or firms referred to in the second subparagraph where all members having unlimited liability are themselves companies of the types set out in that or the first subparagraph.]

2. Pending subsequent co-ordination, the Member States need not apply the provisions of this Directive to banks and other financial institutions or to insurance companies.

¶ *This Directive has been rendered applicable to Greece by the Act of Accession of the Hellenic Republic, Annex I (III)(c)(2) (OJ L 291, 19.11.1979), to Spain and Portugal by the Act of Accession of the Kingdom of Spain and the Portuguese Republic, Annex I, (II)(d)(2) (OJ L 302, 15.11. 1985), to Austria, Sweden, and Finland by the Act of Accession of Austria, Sweden, and Finland (OJ C 241, 29.8.1994, 21), adapted by Council Decision 91/1/EC, Euratom, ECSC (OJ L 1, 1.1.1995, 1), and to the Czech Republic, Estonia, Cyprus, Latvia, Hungary, Malta, Poland, Slovenia, and Slovakia by the Act concerning the conditions of accession of the Czech Republic, the Republic of Estonia, the Republic of Cyprus, the Republic of Latvia, the Republic of Hungary, the Republic of Malta, the Republic of Poland, the Republic of Slovenia, and the Slovak Republic and the adjustments to the Treaties on which the European Union is founded (OJ L 236, 23.9.2003, 33).*

¶ *The subparagraphs between brackets in article 1(1) have been added by article 1(1) of Directive 90/605/EEC, reproduced infra under no. C. 12. Member States may provide that these provisions shall first apply to the annual accounts and consolidated accounts for financial years beginning on 1 January 1995 or during the 1995 calendar year.*

¶ *Directive 86/635/EEC of 8 December 1986, reproduced supra under no. B. 7, contains specific rules applicable to the annual accounts and the consolidated annual accounts of credit institutions.*

¶ *Directive 91/674/EEC of 19 December 1991, reproduced infra under no. I. 23, contains specific rules applicable to the annual accounts and the consolidated annual accounts of insurance undertakings.*

SECTION 1

GENERAL PROVISIONS

Article 2

1. The annual accounts shall comprise the balance sheet, the profit and loss account and the

notes on the accounts. These documents shall constitute a composite whole.

[Member States may permit or require the inclusion of other statements in the annual accounts in addition to the documents referred to in the first subparagraph.]

2. They shall be drawn up clearly and in accordance with the provisions of this Directive.

3. The annual accounts shall give a true and fair view of the company's assets, liabilities, financial position and profit or loss.

4. Where the application of the provisions of this Directive would not be sufficient to give a true and fair view within the meaning of paragraph 3, additional information must be given.

5. Where in exceptional cases the application of a provision of this Directive is incompatible with the obligation laid down in paragraph 3, that provision must be departed from in order to give a true and fair view within the meaning of paragraph 3. Any such departure must be disclosed in the notes on the accounts together with an explanation of the reasons for it and a statement of its effect on the assets, liabilities, financial position and profit or loss. The Member States may define the exceptional cases in question and lay down the relevant special rules.

6. The Member States may authorise or require the disclosure in the annual accounts of other information as well as that which must be disclosed in accordance with this Directive.

¶ *The second subparagraph of article 2(1) has been added by article 1(1) of Directive 2003/51/EC, reproduced infra under no. C. 23.*

SECTION 2

GENERAL PROVISIONS CONCERNING THE BALANCE SHEET AND THE PROFIT AND LOSS ACCOUNT

Article 3

The layout of the balance sheet and of the profit and loss account, particularly as regards the form adopted for their presentation, may not be changed from one financial year to the next. Departures from this principle shall be permitted in exceptional cases. Any such departure must be disclosed in the notes on the accounts together with an explanation of the reasons therefor.

Article 4

1. In the balance sheet and in the profit and loss account the items prescribed in Articles 9, 10 and 23 to 26 must be shown separately in the order indicated. A more detailed subdivision of the items shall be authorised provided that the layouts are complied with. New items may be added provided that their contents are not covered by any of the items prescribed by the layouts. Such subdivision or new items may be required by the Member States.

2. The layout, nomenclature and terminology of items in the balance sheet and profit and loss account that are preceded by Arabic numerals must be adapted where the special nature of an undertaking so requires. Such adaptations may be required by the Member States of undertakings forming part of a particular economic sector.

3. The balance sheet and profit and loss account items that are preceded by Arabic numerals may be combined where:

(a) they are immaterial in amount for the purposes of Article 2 (3); or

(b) such combination makes for greater clarity, provided that the items so combined are dealt with separately in the notes on the accounts. Such combination may be required by the Member States.

4. In respect of each balance sheet and profit and loss account item the figure relating to the corresponding item for the preceding financial year must be shown. The Member States may provide that, where these figures are not comparable, the figure for the preceding financial year must be adjusted. In any case, non-comparability and any adjustment of the figures must be disclosed in the notes on the accounts, with relevant comments.

5. Save where there is a corresponding item for the preceding financial year within the meaning of paragraph 4, a balance sheet or profit and loss account item for which there is no amount shall not be shown.

[6. Member States may permit or require the presentation of amounts within items in the profit and loss account and balance sheet to have regard to the substance of the reported transaction or arrangement. Such permission or requirement may be restricted to certain classes of company and/or to consolidated accounts as defined in the Seventh Council Directive 83/349/EEC of 13 June 1983 on consolidated accounts.[6]]

¶ *Article 4(6) has been added by article 1(2) of Directive 2003/51/EC, reproduced infra under no. C. 23.*

Article 5

1. By way of derogation from Article 4 (1) and (2), the Member States may prescribe special layouts for the annual accounts of investment companies and of financial holding companies provided that these layouts give a view of these companies equivalent to that provided for in Article 2 (3).

2. For the purposes of this Directive, 'investment companies' shall mean only:

(a) those companies the sole object of which is to invest their funds in various securities, real property and other assets with the sole aim of spreading investment risks and giving their shareholders the benefit of the results of the management of their assets;

(b) those companies associated with investment companies with fixed capital if the sole object of the companies so associated is to acquire fully paid shares issued by those investment companies without prejudice to the provisions of Article 20 (l) (h) of Directive 77/91/EEC.[7]

3. For the purposes of this Directive, 'financial holding companies' shall mean only those companies the sole object of which is to acquire holdings in other undertakings, and to manage such holdings and turn them to profit, without involving themselves directly or indirectly in the management of those undertakings, the aforegoing without prejudice to their rights as shareholders. The limitations imposed on the activities of these companies must be such that compliance with them can be supervised by an administrative or judicial authority.

¶ *For the application of the rules on consolidated accounts on a 'financial holding company', see article 5 of Directive 83/349/EEC, Seventh Company Directive, reproduced infra under no. C. 6.*

Article 6

The Member States may authorise or require adaptation of the layout of the balance sheet and profit and loss account in order to include the appropriation of profit or the treatment of loss.

Article 7

Any set-off between asset and liability items, or between income and expenditure items, shall be prohibited.

SECTION 3
LAYOUT OF THE BALANCE SHEET

Article 8

For the presentation of the balance sheet, the Member States shall prescribe one or both of the layouts prescribed by Articles 9 and 10. If a Member State prescribes both, it may allow companies to choose between them.

[Member States may permit or require companies to adopt the presentation of the balance sheet set out in Article 10a as an alternative to the layouts otherwise prescribed or permitted.]

¶ *The second paragraph of article 8 has been added by article 1(3) of Directive 2003/51/EC, reproduced infra under no. C. 23.*

Article 9

Assets

A. *Subscribed capital unpaid*

of which there has been called

(unless national law provides that called-up capital be shown under 'Liabilities'. In that case, the part of the capital called but not yet paid must appear as an asset either under A or under D (II) (5)).

---

[6] OJ L 193, 18.7.1983, 1, reproduced infra under no. C. 6. Directive as last amended by Directive 2001/65/EC of the European Parliament and of the Council (OJ L 283, 27.10.2001, 28), reproduced infra under no. C. 18.

[7] OJ L 26, 31.1.1977, 1, Second Company Directive, reproduced supra under no. C. 2.

B. *Formation expenses*

as defined by national law, and in so far as national law permits their being shown as an asset. National law may also provide for formation expenses to be shown as the first item under 'Intangible assets'.

C. *Fixed assets*

I. *Intangible assets*

1. Costs of research and development, in so far as national law permits their being shown as assets.

2. Concessions, patents, licences, trade marks and similar rights and assets, if they were:

(a) acquired for valuable consideration and need not be shown under C (I) (3); or

(b) created by the undertaking itself, in so far as national law permits their being shown as assets.

3. Goodwill, to the extent that it was acquired for valuable consideration.

4. Payments on account.

II. *Tangible assets*

1. Land and buildings.

2. Plant and machinery.

3. Other fixtures and fittings, tools and equipment.

4. Payments on account and tangible assets in course of construction.

III. *Financial assets*

1. Shares in affiliated undertakings.

2. Loans to affiliated undertakings.

3. Participating interests.

4. Loans to undertakings with which the company is linked by virtue of participating interests.

5. Investments held as fixed assets.

6. Other loans.

7. Own shares (with an indication of their nominal value or, in the absence of a nominal value, their accounting par value) to the extent that national law permits their being shown in the balance sheet.

D. *Current assets*

I. *Stocks*

1. Raw materials and consumables.

2. Work in progress.

3. Finished goods and goods for resale.

4. Payments on account.

II. *Debtors*

(Amounts becoming due and payable after more than one year must be shown separately for each item.)

1. Trade debtors.

2. Amounts owed by affiliated undertakings.

3. Amounts owed by undertakings with which the company is linked by virtue of participating interests.

4. Other debtors.

5. Subscribed capital called but not paid (unless national law provides that called-up capital be shown as an asset under A).

6. Prepayments and accrued income (unless national law provides for such items to be shown as an asset under E).

III. *Investments*

1. Shares in affiliated undertakings.

2. Own shares (with an indication of their nominal value or, in the absence of a nominal value, their accounting par value) to the extent that national law permits their being shown in the balance sheet.

3. Other investments.

IV. *Cash at bank and in hand*

E. *Prepayments and accrued income*

(unless national law provides for such items to be shown as an asset under D (II) (6)).

F. *Loss for the financial year*

(unless national law provides for it to be shown under A (VI) under 'Liabilities').

Liabilities

A. *Capital and reserves*

I. *Subscribed capital*
(unless national law provides for called-up capital to be shown under this item. In that case, the amounts of subscribed capital and paid-up capital must be shown separately).

II. *Share premium account*

III. *Revaluation reserve*

1. Legal reserve, in so far as national law requires such a reserve.

2. Reserve for own shares, in so far as national law requires such a reserve, without prejudice to Article 22 (1) (b) of Directive 77/91/EEC.

3. Reserves provided for by the articles of association.

4. Other reserves.

V. *Profit or loss brought forward*

VI. *Profit or loss for the financial year*
(unless national law requires that this item be shown under F under 'Assets' or under E under 'Liabilities').

B. *[Provisions]*

1. Provisions for pensions and similar obligations.

2. Provisions for taxation.

3. Other provisions.

C. *Creditors*
(Amounts becoming due and payable within one year and amounts becoming due and payable after more than one year must be shown separately for each item and for the aggregate of these items.)

1. Debenture loans, showing convertible loans separately.

2. Amounts owed to credit institutions.

3. Payments received on account of orders in so far as they are not shown separately as deductions from stocks.

4. Trade creditors.

5. Bills of exchange payable.

6. Amounts owed to affiliated undertakings.

7. Amounts owed to undertakings with which the company is linked by virtue of participating interests.

8. Other creditors including tax and social security.

9. Accruals and deferred income (unless national law provides for such items to be shown under D under 'Liabilities').

D. *Accruals and deferred income*
(unless national law provides for such items to be shown under C (9) under 'Liabilities').

E. *Profit for the financial year*
(unless national law provides for it to be shown under A (VI) under 'Liabilities').

¶ *In article 9, under 'Liabilities', in point B, the title has been amended by article 1(4) of Directive 2003/51/EC, reproduced infra under no. C. 23.*

Article 10

A. *Subscribed capital unpaid*
of which there has been called

(unless national law provides that called-up capital be shown under L. In that case, the part of the capital called but not yet paid must appear either under A or under D (II) (5)).

B. *Formation expenses*
as defined by national law, and in so far as national law permits their being shown as an asset. National law may also provide for formation expenses to be shown as the first item under 'Intangible assets'.

C. *Fixed assets*

I. *Intangible assets*

1. Costs of research and development, in so far as national law permits their being shown as assets.

2. Concessions, patents, licences, trade marks and similar rights and assets, if they were:

(a) acquired for valuable consideration and need not be shown under C (I) (3); or

(b) created by the undertaking itself, in so far as national law permits their being shown as assets.

3. Goodwill, to the extent that it was acquired for valuable consideration.

4. Payments on account.

II. *Tangible assets*
1. Land and buildings.

2. Plant and machinery.

3. Other fixtures and fittings, tools and equipment.

4. Payments on account and tangible assets in course of construction.

III. *Financial assets*
1. Shares in affiliated undertakings.

2. Loans to affiliated undertakings.

3. Participating interests.

4. Loans to undertakings with which the company is linked by virtue of participating interests.

5. Investments held as fixed assets.

6. Other loans.

7. Own shares (with an indication of their nominal value or, in the absence of a nominal value, their accounting par value) to the extent that national law permits their being shown in the balance sheet.

D. *Current assets*
I. *Stocks*
1. Raw materials and consumables.

2. Work in progress.

3. Finished goods and goods for resale.

4. Payments on account.

II. *Debtors*
(Amounts becoming due and payable after more than one year must be shown separately for each item.)

1. Trade debtors.

2. Amounts owed by affiliated undertakings.

3. Amounts owed by undertakings with which the company is linked by virtue of participating interests.

4. Other debtors.

5. Subscribed capital called but not paid (unless national law provides that called-up capital be shown under A).

6. Prepayments and accrued income (unless national law provides that such items be shown under E).

III. *Investments*
1. Shares in affiliated undertakings.

2. Own shares (with an indication of their nominal value or, in the absence of a nominal value, their accounting par value) to the extent that national law permits their being shown in the balance sheet.

3. Other investments.

IV. *Cash at bank and in hand*

E. *Prepayments and accrued income*
(unless national law provides for such items to be shown under D (II) (6)).

F. *Creditors: amounts becoming due and payable within one year*

1. Debenture loans, showing convertible loans separately.

2. Amounts owed to credit institutions.

3. Payments received on account of orders in so far as they are not shown separately as deductions from stocks.

4. Trade creditors.

5. Bills of exchange payable.

6. Amounts owed to affiliated undertakings.

7. Amounts owed to undertakings with which the company is linked by virtue of participating interests.

8. Other creditors including tax and social security.

9. Accruals and deferred income (unless national law provides for such items to be shown under K).

G. *Net current assets/liabilities*

(taking into account prepayments and accrued income when shown under E and accruals and deferred income when shown under K).

H. *Total assets less current liabilities*

I. *Creditors: amounts becoming due and payable after more than one year*

1. Debenture loans, showing convertible loans separately.

2. Amounts owed to credit institutions.

3. Payments received on account of orders in so far as they are not shown separately as deductions from stocks.

4. Trade creditors.

5. Bills of exchange payable.

6. Amounts owed to affiliated undertakings.

7. Amounts owed to undertakings with which the company is linked by virtue of participating interests.

8. Other creditors including tax and social security.

9. Accruals and deferred income (unless national law provides for such items to be shown under K).

J. *[Provisions]*

1. Provisions for pensions and similar obligations.

2. Provisions for taxation.

3. Other provisions.

K. *Accruals and deferred income*

(unless national law provides for such items to be shown under F (9) or I (9) or both).

L. *Capital and reserves*

I. *Subscribed capital*

(unless national law provides for called-up capital to be shown under this item. In that case, the amounts of subscribed capital and paid-up capital must be shown separately).

II. *Share premium account*

III. *Revaluation reserve*

IV. *Reserves*

1. Legal reserve, in so far as national law requires such a reserve.

2. Reserve for own shares, in so far as national law requires such a reserve, without prejudice to Article 22 (1) (b) of Directive 77/91/EEC.

3. Reserves provided for by the articles of association.

4. Other reserves.

V. *Profit or loss brought forward*

VI. *Profit or loss for the financial year*

¶ *In article 10, point J, the title has been amended by article 1(5) of Directive 2003/51/EC, reproduced infra under no. C. 23.*

[Article 10a

Instead of the presentation of balance sheet items in accordance with Articles 9 and 10, Member States may permit or require companies, or certain classes of company, to present those items on the basis of a distinction between current and non-current items provided that the information given is at least equivalent to that otherwise required by Articles 9 and 10.]

¶ *Article 10a has been added by article 1(6) of Directive 2003/51/EC, reproduced infra under no. C. 23.*

Article 11

The Member States may permit companies which on their balance sheet dates do not exceed the limits of two of the three following criteria:
– balance sheet total: [EUR 4.400.000],
– net turnover: [EUR 8.800.000],
– average number of employees during the financial year: 50

to draw up abridged balance sheets showing only those items preceded by letters and roman numerals in Articles 9 and 10, disclosing separately the information required in brackets in D (II) under 'Assets' and C under 'Liabilities' in Article 9 and in D (II) in Article 10, but in total for each.

[Member States may waive the application of Article 15 (3) (a) and (4) to the abridged balance sheet.]

In the case of those Member States which have not adopted the euro, the amount in national currency equivalent to the amounts specified in the first paragraph shall be that obtained by applying the exchange rate published in the *Official Journal of the European Union* on the date of the entry into force of [any Directive setting those amounts].

¶ *The amounts between square brackets repeatedly have been modified by article 1 of Directive 84/569/EEC of 27 November 1984, by article 1 of Directive 90/604/EEC, reproduced infra under no. C. 11, which constitutes the second five-yearly revision, by article 1 of Directive 94/8/EC, which constitutes the third five-yearly revision (see article 53(2) of Directive 78/660/EEC), reproduced infra under no. C. 14, by article 1(1) of Directive 1999/60/EC, which constitutes the third five-yearly revision (see article 53(2) of Directive 78/660/EEC), reproduced infra under no. C. 16, by article 1(1) of Directive 2003/38/EC, which constitutes the last five-yearly revision and subsequently been amended by article 1(1) of Directive 2006/46/EC, reproduced infra under no. C. 31.*

¶ *The first paragraph between square brackets has been added by article 1 of Directive 90/604/EEC, reproduced infra under no. C. 11. Member States may provide that these provisions shall first apply to the annual accounts and consolidated accounts for financial years beginning on 1 January 1995 or during the 1995 calendar year.*

¶ *The second paragraph between square brackets has been inserted by article 1(1) of Directive 2003/38/EC (OJ L 120, 15.5.2003, 22).*

¶ *The words between square brackets in the third paragraph of this article have been amended by article 1(2) of Directive 2006/46/EC, reproduced infra under no. C. 31.*

Article 12

1. Where on its balance sheet date, a company exceeds or ceases to exceed the limits of two of the three criteria indicated in Article 11, that fact shall affect the application of the derogation provided for in that Article only if it occurs in two consecutive financial years.

2. For the purposes of translation into national currencies, the amounts in European units of account specified in Article 11 may be increased by not more than 10%.

3. The balance sheet total referred to in Article 11 shall consist of the assets in A to E under 'Assets' in the layout prescribed in Article 9 or those in A to E in the layout prescribed in Article 10.

Article 13

1. Where an asset or liability relates to more than one layout item, its relationship to other items must be disclosed either under the item where it appears or in the notes on the accounts, if such disclosure is essential to the comprehension of the annual accounts.

2. Own shares and shares in affiliated undertakings may be shown only under the items prescribed for that purpose.

Article 14

All commitments by way of guarantee of any kind must, if there is no obligation to show them as liabilities, be clearly set out at the foot of the balance sheet or in the notes on the accounts, and a distinction made between the various types of guarantee which national law recognises; specific disclosure must be made of any valuable security which has been provided. Commitments of this kind existing in respect of affiliated undertakings must be shown separately.

CASE

Case C-306/99 Banque Internationale pour l'Afrique Occidentale SA (BIAO) v Finanzamt für Großunternehmen in Hamburg [2003] ECR I-1

1. The Fourth Directive 78/660/EEC does not preclude a provision intended to cover possible losses or debts arising from a commitment appearing at the foot of the balance sheet pursuant to Article 14 of that directive from being entered on the liabilities side of the balance sheet pursuant to Article 20(1), provided that the loss or debt in question may be characterised as 'likely or certain' at the balance sheet date. Article 31(1)(e) of that directive does not exclude the possibility that, in order to ensure compliance with the principle of prudence and the principle that a true and fair view of the assets and liabilities be given, the most appropriate method of valuation might be to carry out a globalized assessment of all the relevant factors.

2. In circumstances such as those in point in the main proceedings, repayment of a loan, which takes place after the balance sheet date (that being the relevant date for valuing balance sheet items), does not constitute a fact necessitating retrospective revaluation of a provision relating to that loan entered on the liabilities side of the balance sheet. However, compliance with the principle that a true and fair view of the assets and liabilities be given requires that mention should be made in the annual accounts of the disappearance of the risk covered by that provision.

Section 4

Special Provisions Relating to Certain Balance Sheet Items

Article 15

1. Whether particular assets are to be shown as fixed assets or current assets shall depend upon the purpose for which they are intended.

2. Fixed assets shall comprise those assets which are intended for use on a continuing basis for the purposes of the undertaking's activities.

3. (a) Movements in the various fixed asset items shall be shown in the balance sheet or in the notes on the accounts. To this end there shall be shown separately, starting with the purchase price or production cost, for each fixed asset item, on the one hand, the additions, disposals and transfers during the financial year and, on the other, the cumulative value adjustments at the balance sheet date and the rectifications made during the financial year to the value adjustments of previous financial years. Value adjustments shall be shown either in the balance sheet, as clear deductions from the relevant items, or in the notes on the accounts.

(b) If, when annual accounts are drawn up in accordance with this Directive for the first time, the purchase price or production cost of a fixed asset cannot be determined without undue expense or delay, the residual value at the beginning of the financial year may be treated as the purchase price or production cost. Any application of this provision must be disclosed in the notes on the accounts.

(c) Where Article 33 is applied, the movements in the various fixed asset items referred to in subparagraph (a) of this paragraph shall be shown starting with the purchase price or production cost resulting from revaluation.

4. Paragraph 3 (a) and (b) shall apply to the presentation of 'Formation expenses'.

Article 16

Rights to immovables and other similar rights as defined by national law must be shown under 'Land and buildings'.

Article 17

For the purposes of this Directive, 'participating interest' shall mean rights in the capital of other undertakings, whether or not represented by certificates, which, by creating a durable link with those undertakings, are intended to contribute to the company's activities. The holding of part of the capital of another company shall be presumed to constitute a participating interest where it exceeds a percentage fixed by the Member States which may not exceed 20%.

Article 18

Expenditure incurred during the financial year but relating to a subsequent financial year, together with any income which, though relating to the financial year in question, is not due until after its expiry must be shown under 'Prepayments and accrued income'. The Member States may, however, provide that such income shall be included in 'Debtors'. Where such income is material, it must be disclosed in the notes on the accounts.

Article 19

Value adjustments shall comprise all adjustments intended to take account of reductions in the values of individual assets established at the balance sheet date whether that reduction is final or not.

Article 20

[1. Provisions are intended to cover liabilities the nature of which is clearly defined and which at the date of the balance sheet are either likely to be incurred, or certain to be incurred but uncertain as to amount or as to the date on which they will arise.]

2. The Member States may also authorise the creation of provisions intended to cover charges which have their origin in the financial year under review or in a previous financial year, the nature of which is clearly defined and which at the date of the balance sheet are either likely to be incurred, or certain to be incurred but uncertain as to amount or as to the date on which they will arise.

[3. Provisions may not be used to adjust the values of assets.]

¶ *Paragraphs 1 and 3 of article 20 have been replaced by article 1(7) of Directive 2003/51/EC, reproduced infra under no. C. 23.*

CASES

I. Case C-275/97 DE + ES Bauunternehmung GmbH v Finanzamt Bergheim [1999] ECR I-5331

Under Article 20(1) of the Fourth Directive (78/660) based on Article [44(3)(g)][1] of the Treaty on the annual accounts of certain types of companies, which lays down the obligation to enter provisions for liabilities and charges in the accounts under 'Liabilities', provisions for potential warranty liabilities must be entered under 'Liabilities' provided that those liabilities constitute charges the nature of which is clearly defined and which are likely to be incurred but in respect of which the amount or the date on which they will arise is uncertain. Provisions for potential warranty liabilities must therefore be entered as liabilities arising in law before the date of the balance sheet but whose effects will not become apparent until after that date. Any other interpretation of the above provision would mean that such potential debts would not be shown in the balance sheet. This would lead to an overestimate of the assets, which would be incompatible not only with the principle of making valuations on a prudent basis, but also with the principle of the 'true and fair view', compliance with which is the primary objective of the Directive.

II. Case 161/78 Advokatrådet Comme Mandataire pour P. Conradsen A/S v Ministère des Impôts et Accises [1979] ECR I-2221

The principle laid down in Article 5(1)(a) of Directive No 69/335[8] that the charging of capital duty on the actual value of the assets at the time at which they were contributed and not on the basis of their book value cannot be affected by the fact that Article 9 (liabilities b.2) of Council Directive No 78/660 based on Article [44(3)(g)][1] of the Treaty on the annual accounts of certain types of companies provides for 'provisions for taxation' to be entered under liabilities as 'provisions for liabilities and charges'. That directive pursues an objective which differs considerably from that of Directive No 69/335: it does not aim at harmonizing taxation of the raising of capital, but, as provided for in Article [44(3)(g)][1] of the Treaty, is among the measures which, in the context of the right of establishment aim at 'co-ordinating to the necessary extent the safeguards which, for the protection of the interests of members and others, are required by Member States of companies or firms within the meaning of the second paragraph of Article [48][1] with a view to making such safeguards equivalent throughout the community'.

In these circumstances, although entering 'provisions for taxation' under liabilities fulfils the requirements for the presentation by companies of their balance sheets, in accord with the interests of the members and of third parties, it does not imply that such an entry may affect the value of capital which has been raised and is liable to the capital duty introduced by Directive No 69/335. although Article 20 (1) of Directive No 78/660 does not rule out the possibility that provisions for liabilities and charges are intended to cover losses or debts the nature of which is clearly defined and which at the date of the balance sheet are either likely to be incurred, or certain to be incurred but uncertain as to amount or as to the date on which they will arise, paragraph (3) of the very same article states that the said provisions 'may not be used to adjust the values of assets', and thus makes it clear that entering these provisions in the accounts relates to the requirements for the presentation of the balance sheets of certain types of companies but cannot in fact alter the basis for the assessment of a tax such as capital duty which in substance is based on the actual value of the assets.

Article 21

Income receivable before the balance sheet date but relating to a subsequent financial year, together with any charges which, though relating to the financial year in question, will be paid only in the course of a subsequent financial year, must be shown under 'Accruals and deferred income'. The Member States may, however, provide that such charges shall be included in 'Creditors'. Where such charges are material, they must be disclosed in the notes on the accounts.

---

[8] OJ L 269, 28.10.1969, 12.

Section 5

Layout of the Profit and Loss Account

Article 22

For the presentation of the profit and loss account, the Member States shall prescribe one or more of the layouts provided for in Articles 23 to 26. If a Member State prescribes more than one layout, it may allow companies to choose from among them.

[By way of derogation from Article 2(1), Member States may permit or require all companies, or any classes of company, to present a statement of their performance instead of the presentation of profit and loss items in accordance with Articles 23 to 26, provided that the information given is at least equivalent to that otherwise required by those Articles.]

¶ *The second paragraph of article 22 has been added by article 1(8) of Directive 2003/51/EC, reproduced infra under no. C. 23.*

Article 23

1. Net turnover.

2. Variation in stocks of finished goods and in work in progress.

3. Work performed by the undertaking for its own purposes and capitalised.

4. Other operating income.

5. (a) Raw materials and consumables;

(b) Other external charges.

6. Staff costs:

(a) wages and salaries;

(b) social security costs, with a separate indication of those relating to pensions.

7. (a) Value adjustments in respect of formation expenses and of tangible and intangible fixed assets;

(b) Value adjustments in respect of current assets, to the extent that they exceed the amount of value adjustments which are normal in the undertaking concerned.

8. Other operating charges.

9. Income from participating interests, with a separate indication of that derived from affiliated undertakings.

10. Income from other investments and loans forming part of the fixed assets, with a separate indication of that derived from affiliated undertakings.

11. Other interest receivable and similar income, with a separate indication of that derived from affiliated undertakings.

12. Value adjustments in respect of financial assets and of investments held as current assets.

13. Interest payable and similar charges, with a separate indication of those concerning affiliated undertakings.

14. Tax on profit or loss on ordinary activities.

15. Profit or loss on ordinary activities after taxation.

16. Extraordinary income.

17. Extraordinary charges.

18. Extraordinary profit or loss.

19. Tax on extraordinary profit or loss.

20. Other taxes not shown under the above items.

21. Profit or loss for the financial year.

Article 24

A. *Charges*

1. Reduction in stocks of finished goods and in work in progress:

2. (a) raw materials and consumables;

(b) other external charges.

3. Staff costs:

(a) wages and salaries;

(b) social security costs, with a separate indication of those relating to pensions.

4. (a) Value adjustments in respect of formation expenses and of tangible and intangible fixed assets;

(b) Value adjustments in respect of current assets, to the extent that they exceed the amount of value adjustments which are normal in the undertaking concerned.

5. Other operating charges.

6. Value adjustments in respect of financial assets and of investments held as current assets.

7. Interest payable and similar charges, with a separate indication of those concerning affiliated undertakings.

8. Tax on profit or loss on ordinary activities.

9. Profit or loss on ordinary activities after taxation.

10. Extraordinary charges.

11. Tax on extraordinary profit or loss.

12. Other taxes not shown under the above items.

13. Profit or loss for the financial year.

B. *Income*

1. Net turnover.

2. Increase in stocks of finished goods and in work in progress.

3. Work performed by the undertaking for its own purposes and capitalised.

4. Other operating income.

5. Income from participating interests, with a separate indication of that derived from affiliated undertakings.

6. Income from other investments and loans forming part of the fixed assets, with a separate indication of that derived from affiliated undertakings.

7. Other interest receivable and similar income, with a separate indication of that derived from affiliated undertakings.

8. Profit or loss on ordinary activities after taxation.

9. Extraordinary income.

10. Profit or loss for the financial year.

Article 25

1. Net turnover.

2. Cost of sales (including value adjustments).

3. Gross profit or loss.

4. Distribution costs (including value adjustments).

5. Administrative expenses (including value adjustments).

6. Other operating income.

7. Income from participating interests, with a separate indication of that derived from affiliated undertakings.

8. Income from other investments and loans forming part of the fixed assets, with a separate indication of that derived from affiliated undertakings.

9. Other interest receivable and similar income, with a separate indication of that derived from affiliated undertakings.

10. Value adjustments in respect of financial assets and of investments held as current assets.

11. Interest payable and similar charges, with a separate indication of those concerning affiliated undertakings.

12. Tax on profit or loss on ordinary activities.

13. Profit or loss on ordinary activities after taxation.

14. Extraordinary income.

15. Extraordinary charges.

16. Extraordinary profit or loss.

17. Tax on extraordinary profit or loss.

18. Other taxes not shown under the above items.

19. Profit or loss for the financial year.

Article 26

A. *Charges*

1. Cost of sales (including value adjustments).

2. Distribution costs (including value adjustments).

3. Administrative expenses (including value adjustments).

4. Value adjustments in respect of financial assets and of investments held as current assets.

5. Interest payable and similar charges, with a separate indication of those concerning affiliated undertakings.

6. Tax on profit or loss on ordinary activities.

7. Profit or loss on ordinary activities after taxation.

8. Extraordinary charges.

9. Tax on extraordinary profit or loss.

10. Other taxes not shown under the above items.

11. Profit or loss for the financial year.

B. *Income*

1. Net turnover.

2. Other operating income.

3. Income from participating interests, with a separate indication of that derived from affiliated undertakings.

4. Income from other investments and loans forming part of the fixed assets, with a separate indication of that derived from affiliated undertakings.

5. Other interest receivable and similar income, with a separate indication of that derived from affiliated undertakings.

6. Profit or loss on ordinary activities after taxation.

7. Extraordinary income.

8. Profit or loss for the financial year.

Article 27

The Member States may permit companies which on their balance sheet dates do not exceed the limits of two of the three following criteria:
– balance sheet total: [EUR 17.500.000],
– net turnover: [EUR 35.000.000],
– average number of employees during the financial year: 250

to adopt layouts different from those prescribed in Articles 23 to 26 within the following limits:

(a) in Article 23: 1 to 5 inclusive may be combined under one item called 'Gross profit or loss';

(b) in Article 24: A (1), A (2) and B (1) to E (4) inclusive may be combined under one item called 'Gross profit or loss';

(c) in Article 25: (1), (2), (3) and (6) may be combined under one item called 'Gross profit or loss';

(d) in Article 26, A (1), B (1) and B (2) may be combined under one item called 'Gross profit or loss'.

Article 12 shall apply.

[In the case of those Member States which have not adopted the euro, the amount in national currency equivalent to the amounts specified in the first paragraph shall be that obtained by applying the exchange rate published in the *Official Journal of the European Union* on the date of the entry into force of any Directive setting those amounts.]

¶ *The amounts between square brackets have been modified by article 1 of Directive 84/569/EEC of 27 November 1984, by article 2 of Directive 90/604/EEC, reproduced infra under no. C. 11, which constitutes the second five-yearly revision, by article 1 of Directive 94/8/EC, reproduced infra under no. C. 14, which constitutes the third five-yearly revision (see article 53(2)), by article 1(2) of Directive 1999/60/EC, reproduced infra under no. C. 16, which constitutes the fourth five-yearly revision (see article 53(2) of Directive 78/660/EEC), by article 1(2) of Directive 2003/38/EC (OJ L 120, 15.5.2003), which constitutes the last five-yearly revision and subsequently have been amended by article 1(3) of Directive 2006/46/EC, reproduced infra under no. C. 31.*

¶ *The paragraph between square brackets has been inserted by article 1(2) of Directive 2003/38/EC (OJ L 120, 15.5.2003).*

¶ *The words between square brackets in the third paragraph of this article have been amended by article 1(4) of Directive 2006/46/EC, reproduced infra under no. C. 31.*

Section 6

Special Provisions Relating to Certain Items in the Profit and Loss Account

Article 28

The net turnover shall comprise the amounts derived from the sale of products and the provision of services falling within the company's ordinary activities, after deduction of sales rebates and of value added tax and other taxes directly linked to the turnover.

Article 29

1. Income and charges that arise otherwise than in the course of the company's ordinary activities must be shown under 'Extraordinary Income and extraordinary charges'.

2. Unless the income and charges referred to in paragraph 1 are immaterial for the assessment of the results, explanations of their amount and nature must be given in the notes on the accounts. The same shall apply to income and charges relating to another financial year.

Article 30

The Member States may permit taxes on the profit or loss on ordinary activities and taxes on the extraordinary profit or loss to be shown in total as one item in the profit and loss account before 'Other taxes not shown under the above items'. In that case, 'Profit or loss on ordinary activities after taxation' shall be omitted from the layouts prescribed in Articles 23 to 26.

Where this derogation is applied, companies must disclose in the notes on the accounts the extent to which the taxes on the profit or loss affect the profit or loss on ordinary activities and the 'Extraordinary profit or loss'.

Section 7
Valuation Rules

Article 31

1. The Member States shall ensure that the items shown in the annual accounts are valued in accordance with the following general principles:

(a) the company must be presumed to be carrying on its business as a going concern;

(b) the methods of valuation must be applied consistently from one financial year to another;

(c) valuation must be made on a prudent basis, and in particular:

    (aa) only profits made at the balance sheet date may be included,

    [(bb) account must be taken of all liabilities arising in the course of the financial year concerned or of a previous one, even if such liabilities become apparent only between the date of the balance sheet and the date on which it is drawn up,]

    (cc) account must be taken of all depreciation, whether the result of the financial year is a loss or a profit;

(d) account must be taken of income and charges relating to the financial year, irrespective of the date of receipt or payment of such income or charges;

(e) the components of asset and liability items must be valued separately;

(f) the opening balance sheet for each financial year must correspond to the closing balance sheet for the preceding financial year.

[(1a) In addition to those amounts recorded pursuant to paragraph (1)(c)(bb), Member States may permit or require account to be taken of all foreseeable liabilities and potential losses arising in the course of the financial year concerned or of a previous one, even if such liabilities or losses become apparent only between the date of the balance sheet and the date on which it is drawn up.]

2. Departures from these general principles shall be permitted in exceptional cases. Any such departures must be disclosed in the notes on the accounts and the reasons for them given together with an assessment of their effect on the assets, liabilities, financial position and profit or loss.

¶ *Paragraph 1(c), point (bb) has been replaced by article 1(9)(a) of Directive 2003/51/EC, reproduced infra under no. C. 23.*

¶ *Paragraph (1a) has been added by article 1(9)(b) of Directive 2003/51/EC, reproduced infra under no. C. 23.*

Cases

I. Case C-275/97 DE + ES
Bauunternehmung GmbH v Finanzamt Bergheim [1999] ECR I-5331

Article 31(2) of the Fourth Directive (78/660) based on Article [44(3)(g)][1] of the Treaty on the annual accounts of certain types of companies permits, 'in exceptional cases', departure from the principle that the components of asset and liability items are to be evaluated separately. Since the expression 'in exceptional cases' must be interpreted in the light of the Directive's aim—that the annual accounts of the companies concerned must give a true and fair view of their assets, of their financial position and of their profit or loss—the cases envisaged are those in which separate valuation would not give the truest and fairest possible view of the actual financial position of the company concerned. It follows that a single provision for all such liabilities should be made where a global valuation is the most appropriate way of ensuring that the expenditure to be shown under 'Liabilities' represents a true and fair view of its amount.

In the absence of Community rules specifically applying to the method and criteria for evaluating provisions for charges and liabilities which, by virtue of the Fourth Directive (78/660) based on Article [44(3)(g)][1] of the Treaty on the annual accounts of certain types of companies, must be entered under 'Liabilities' in the company's balance sheet, those provisions should be determined under the conditions laid down by the national legislation of the various Member States, provided, however, that the annual accounts give a true and fair view of the assets, financial position and the profit or loss of the company and that the provisions do not exceed in amount the sums which are necessary.

II. Case C-234/94 Waltraud Tomberger v Gebrüder von der Wettern GmbH [1996] ECR I-3133

In order to coordinate the content of annual accounts, the Fourth Directive 78/660 lays down the principle of the 'true and fair view', compliance with which is the primary objective of that directive. Application of that principle must, as far as possible, be guided by the general principles contained in Article 31 of the directive, particularly in Article 31(1)(c), (aa) and (bb), and (d). It is clear from those provisions that taking account of all elements which actually relate to the financial year in question ensures observance of the principle of a true and fair view. Where one company (the parent company) is the sole shareholder in another company (the subsidiary), and controls it, under national law, the parent company and the subsidiary form a group, the financial years of the two companies coincide, the subsidiary's annual accounts for the financial year in question were adopted by the general meeting before completion of the audit of the parent company's annual accounts for that year, the subsidiary's annual accounts for the financial year in question, as adopted by its general meeting, show that on the subsidiary's balance sheet date namely the last day of that financial year the subsidiary appropriated profits to the parent company, and the national court is satisfied that the subsidiary's annual accounts for the financial year in question give a true and fair view of its assets and liabilities, financial position and profit or loss, it is not contrary to the rule laid down in Article 31(1)(c)(aa) of the directive according to which, for the purpose of valuing the items shown in the annual accounts, only profits made at the balance sheet date may be included for the national court to consider that the profits in question must be entered in the parent company's balance sheet for the financial year in respect of which they were appropriated by the subsidiary.

Article 32

The items shown in the annual accounts shall be valued in accordance with Articles 34 to 42, which are based on the principle of purchase price or production cost.

Article 33

1. The Member States may declare to the Commission that they reserve the power, by way of derogation from Article 32 and pending subsequent co-ordination, to permit or require in respect of all companies or any classes of companies:

(a) valuation by the replacement value method for tangible fixed assets with limited useful economic lives and for stocks;

(b) valuation by methods other than that provided for in (a) which are designed to take account of inflation for the items shown in annual accounts, including capital and reserves;

[(c) revaluation of fixed assets.]

Where national law provides for valuation methods as indicated in (a), (b) and (c), it must define their content and limits and the rules for their application.

The application of any such method, the balance sheet and profit and loss account items concerned and the method by which the values shown are calculated shall be disclosed in the notes on the accounts.

2. (a) Where paragraph 1 is applied, the amount of the difference between valuation by the method used and valuation in accordance with the general rule laid down in Article 32 must be entered in the revaluation reserve under 'Liabilities'. The treatment of this item for taxation purposes must be explained either in the balance sheet or in the notes on the accounts.

For purposes of the application of the last subparagraph of paragraph 1, companies shall, whenever the amount of the reserve has been changed in the course of the financial year, publish in the notes on the accounts *inter alia* a table showing:
- the amount of the revaluation reserve at the beginning of the financial year,
- the revaluation differences transferred to the revaluation reserve during the financial year,
- the amounts capitalised or otherwise transferred from the revaluation reserve during the financial year, the nature of any such transfer being disclosed,
- the amount of the revaluation reserve at the end of the financial year.

(b) The revaluation reserve may be capitalised in whole or in part at any time.

(c) The revaluation reserve must be reduced to the extent that the amounts transferred thereto are no longer necessary for the implementation of the valuation method used and the achievement of its purpose.

The Member States may lay down rules governing the application of the revaluation reserve, provided that transfers to the profit and loss account from the revaluation reserve may be made only to the extent that the amounts transferred have been entered as charges in the profit and loss account or reflect increases in value which have been actually realised. These amounts must be disclosed separately in the profit and loss account. No part of the revaluation reserve may be distributed, either directly or indirectly, unless it represents gains actually realised.

(d) Save as provided under (b) and (c) the revaluation reserve may not be reduced.

3. Value adjustments shall be calculated each year on the basis of the value adopted for the financial year in question, save that by way of derogation from Articles 4 and 22, the Member States may permit or require that only the amount of the value adjustments arising as a result of the application of the general rule laid down in Article 32 be shown under the relevant items in the layouts prescribed in Articles 23 to 26 and that the difference arising as a result of the valuation method adopted under this Article be shown separately in the layouts. Furthermore, Articles 34 to 42 shall apply *mutatis mutandis*.

4. Where paragraph 1 is applied, the following must be disclosed, either in the balance sheet or in the notes on the accounts, separately for each balance sheet item as provided for in the layouts prescribed in Articles 9 and 10, except for stocks, either:

(a) the amount at the balance sheet date of the valuation made in accordance with the general rule laid down in Article 32 and the amount of the cumulative value adjustments; or

(b) the amount at the balance sheet date of the difference between the valuation made in accordance with this Article and that resulting from the application of Article 32 and, where appropriate, the cumulative amount of the additional value adjustments.

5. Without prejudice to Article 52 the Council shall, on a proposal from the Commission and within seven years of the notification of this Directive, examine and, where necessary, amend this Article in the light of economic and monetary trends in the Community.

¶ *Article 33(1)(c) has been replaced by article 1(10) of Directive 2003/51/EC, reproduced infra under no. C. 23.*

Article 34

1. (a) Where national law authorises the inclusion of formation expenses under 'Assets', they must be written off within a maximum period of five years.

(b) In so far as formation expenses have not been completely written off, no distribution of profits shall take place unless the amount of the reserves available for distribution and profits brought forward is at least equal to that of the expenses not written off.

2. The amounts entered under 'Formation expenses' must be explained in the notes on the accounts.

Article 35

1. (a) Fixed assets must be valued at purchase price or production cost, without prejudice to (b) and (c) below.

(b) The purchase price or production cost of fixed assets with limited useful economic lives *must be reduced by value adjustments* calculated to write off the value of such assets systematically over their useful economic lives.

(c) (aa) Value adjustments may be made in respect of financial fixed assets, so that they are valued at the lower figure to be attributed to them at the balance sheet date.

(bb) Value adjustments must be made in respect of fixed assets, whether their useful economic lives are limited or not, so that they are valued at the lower figure to be attributed to them at the balance sheet date if it is expected that the reduction in their value will be permanent.

(cc) The value adjustments referred to in (aa) and (bb) must be charged to the profit and loss account and disclosed separately—in the notes on the accounts if they have not been shown separately in the profit and loss account.

(dd) Valuation at the lower of the values provided for in (aa) and (bb) may not be continued if the reasons for which the value adjustments were made have ceased to apply.

(d) If fixed assets are the subject of exceptional value adjustments for taxation purposes alone, the amount of the adjustments and the reasons for making them shall be indicated in the notes on the accounts.

2. The purchase price shall be calculated by adding to the price paid the expenses incidental thereto.

3. (a) The production cost shall be calculated by adding to the purchasing price of the raw materials and consumables the costs directly attributable to the product in question.

(b) A reasonable proportion of the costs which are only indirectly attributable to the product in question may be added into the production costs to the extent that they relate to the period of production.

4. Interest on capital borrowed to finance the production of fixed assets may be included in the production costs to the extent that it relates to the period of production. In that event, the inclusion of such interest under 'Assets' must be disclosed in the notes on the accounts.

Article 36

By way of derogation from Article 35 (1) (c) (cc), the Member States may allow investment companies within the meaning of Article 5 (2) to set off value adjustments to investments directly against 'Capital and reserves'. The amounts in question must be shown separately under 'Liabilities' in the balance sheet.

Article 37

1. Article 34 shall apply to costs of research and development. In exceptional cases, however, the Member States may permit derogations from Article 34 (1) (a). In that case, they may also provide for derogations from Article 34 (1) (b). Such derogations and the reasons for them must be disclosed in the notes on the accounts.

2. Article 34 (1) (a) shall apply to goodwill. The Member States may, however, permit companies to write goodwill off systematically over a limited period exceeding five years provided that this period does not exceed the useful economic life of the asset and is disclosed in the notes on the accounts together with the supporting reasons therefore.

Article 38

Tangible fixed assets, raw materials and consumables which are constantly being replaced and the overall value of which is of secondary importance to the undertaking may be shown under 'Assets' at a fixed quantity and value, if the quantity, value and composition thereof do not vary materially.

Article 39

1. (a) Current assets must be valued at purchase price or production cost, without prejudice to (b) and (c) below.

(b) Value adjustments shall be made in respect of current assets with a view to showing them at the lower market value or, in particular circumstances, another lower value to be attributed to them at the balance sheet date.

(c) The Member States may permit exceptional value adjustments where, on the basis of a reasonable commercial assessment, these are necessary if the valuation of these items is not to be modified in the near future because of fluctuations in value. The amount of these value adjustments must be disclosed separately in the profit and loss account or in the notes on the accounts.

(d) Valuation at the lower value provided for in (b) and (c) may not be continued—if the reasons for which the value adjustments were made have ceased to apply.

(e) If current assets are the subject of exceptional value adjustments for taxation purposes alone, the amount of the adjustments and the reasons for making them must be disclosed in the notes on the accounts.

2. The definitions of purchase price and of production cost given in Article 35 (2) and (3) shall apply. The Member States may also apply Article 35 (4). Distribution costs may not be included in production costs.

Article 40

1. The Member States may permit the purchase price or production cost of stocks of goods of the same category and all fungible items including investments to be calculated either on the basis of weighted average prices or by the 'first in, first out' (FIFO) method, the 'last in, first out' (LIFO) method, or some similar method.

2. Where the value shown in the balance sheet, following application of the methods of calculation specified in paragraph 1, differs materially, at the balance sheet date, from the value on the basis of the last known market value prior to the balance sheet date, the amount of that difference must be disclosed in total by category in the notes on the accounts.

Article 41

1. Where the amount repayable on account of any debt is greater than the amount received, the difference may be shown as an asset. It must be shown separately in the balance sheet or in the notes on the accounts.

2. The amount of this difference must be written off by a reasonable amount each year and completely written off no later than the time of repayment of the debt.

Article 42

[Provisions may not exceed in amount the sums which are necessary.]

The provisions shown in the balance sheet under 'Other provisions' must be disclosed in the notes on the accounts if they are material.

¶ *The first paragraph of article 42 has been replaced by article 1(11) of Directive 2003/51/EC, reproduced infra under no. C. 23.*

[SECTION 7A

VALUATION AT FAIR VALUE

Article 42a

1. By way of derogation from Article 32 and subject to the conditions set out in paragraphs 2 to 4 of this Article, Member States shall permit or require in respect of all companies or any classes of companies valuation at fair value of financial instruments, including derivatives.

Such permission or requirement may be restricted to consolidated accounts as defined in Directive 83/349/EEC.

2. For the purpose of this Directive commodity-based contracts that give either contracting party the right to settle in cash or some other financial instrument shall be considered to be derivative financial instruments, except when:

(a) they were entered into and continue to meet the company's expected purchase, sale or usage requirements;

(b) they were designated for such purpose at their inception; and

(c) they are expected to be settled by delivery of the commodity.

3. Paragraph 1 shall apply only to liabilities that are:

(a) held as part of a trading portfolio; or

(b) derivative financial instruments.

4. Valuation according to paragraph 1 shall not apply:

(a) to non-derivative financial instruments held to maturity;

(b) to loans and receivables originated by the company and not held for trading purposes; and

(c) to interests in subsidiaries, associated undertakings and joint ventures, equity instruments issued by the company, contracts for contingent consideration in a business combination as well as other financial instruments with such special characteristics that the instruments, according to what is generally accepted, should be accounted for differently from other financial instruments.

5. By way of derogation from Article 32, Member States may in respect of any assets and liabilities which qualify as hedged items under a fair value hedge accounting system, or identified portions of such assets or liabilities, permit valuation at the specific amount required under that system.

5a. By way of derogation from the provisions of paragraphs 3 and 4, Member States may, in accordance with international accounting standards as adopted by Commission Regulation (EC) No 1725/2003 of 29 September 2003 adopting certain international accounting standards in accordance with Regulation (EC) No 1606/2002 of the European Parliament and of the Council,[9] as amended until 5 September 2006, permit or require valuation of financial instruments, together with the associated disclosure requirements which are provided for in international accounting standards adopted in accordance with Regulation (EC) No 1606/2002 of the European Parliament and of the Council of 19 July 2002 on the application of international accounting standards.[10]]

¶ *Paragraph 5a has been added by article 1(5) of Directive 2006/46/EC, reproduced infra under no. C. 31.*

Article 42b

1. The fair value referred to in Article 42a shall be determined by reference to:

(a) a market value, for those financial instruments for which a reliable market can readily be identified. Where a market value is not readily identifiable for an instrument but can be identified for its components or for a similar instrument, the market value may be derived from that of its components or of the similar instrument; or

(b) a value resulting from generally accepted valuation models and techniques, for those instruments for which a reliable market cannot be readily identified. Such valuation models and techniques shall ensure a reasonable approximation of the market value.

2. Those financial instruments that cannot be measured reliably by any of the methods described in paragraph 1, shall be measured in accordance with Articles 34 to 42.

Article 42c

1. Notwithstanding Article 31(1)(c), where a financial instrument is valued in accordance with Article 42b, a change in the value shall be included in the profit and loss account. However,

---

[9] OJ L 261, 13.10.2003, 1. Regulation as last amended by Regulation (EC) No 108/2006 (OJ L 24, 27.1.2006, 1).
[10] OJ L 243, 11.9.2002, 1, reproduced infra under no. C. 22.

such a change shall be included directly in equity, in a fair value reserve, where:

(a) the instrument accounted for is a hedging instrument under a system of hedge accounting that allows some or all of the change in value not to be shown in the profit and loss account; or

(b) the change in value relates to an exchange difference arising on a monetary item that forms part of a company's net investment in a foreign entity.

2. Member States may permit or require a change in the value on an available for sale financial asset, other than a derivative financial instrument, to be included directly in equity, in the fair value reserve.

3. The fair value reserve shall be adjusted when amounts shown therein are no longer necessary for the implementation of paragraphs 1 and 2.

Article 42d

Where valuation at fair value of financial instruments has been applied, the notes on the accounts shall disclose:

(a) the significant assumptions underlying the valuation models and techniques where fair values have been determined in accordance with Article 42b(1)(b);

(b) per category of financial instruments, the fair value, the changes in value included directly in the profit and loss account as well as changes included in the fair value reserve;

(c) for each class of derivative financial instruments, information about the extent and the nature of the instruments, including significant terms and conditions that may affect the amount, timing and certainty of future cash flows; and

(d) a table showing movements in the fair value reserve during the financial year.]

[*Article 42e*

By way of derogation from Article 32, Member States may permit or require in respect of all companies or any classes of company the valuation of specified categories of assets other than financial instruments at amounts determined by reference to fair value.

Such permission or requirement may be restricted to consolidated accounts as defined in Directive 83/349/EEC.

Article 42f

Notwithstanding Article 31(1)(c), Member States may permit or require in respect of all companies or any classes of company that, where an asset is valued in accordance with Article 42e, a change in the value is included in the profit and loss account.]

¶ *Section 7a has been added by article 1(1) of Directive 2001/65/EC, reproduced infra under no. C. 18.*
¶ *Articles 42e and 42f have been added by article 1(12) of Directive 2003/51/EC, reproduced infra under no. C. 23.*

SECTION 8

CONTENTS OF THE NOTES ON THE ACCOUNTS

Article 43

1. In addition to the information required under other provisions of this Directive, the notes on the accounts must set out information in respect of the following matters at least:

(1) the valuation methods applied to the various items in the annual accounts, and the methods employed in calculating the value adjustments. For items included in the annual accounts which are or were originally expressed in foreign currency, the bases of conversion used to express them in local currency must be disclosed;

(2) the name and registered office of each of the undertakings in which the company, either itself or through a person acting in his own name but on the company's behalf, holds at least a percentage of the capital which the Member States cannot fix at more than 20%, showing the proportion of the capital held, the amount of capital and reserves, and the profit or loss for the latest financial year of the undertaking concerned for which accounts have been adopted. This information may be omitted where for the purposes of Article 2 (3) it is of negligible importance only.

The information concerning capital and reserves and the profit or loss may also be omitted where the undertaking concerned does not publish its balance sheet and less than 50% of its capital is held (directly or indirectly) by the company;

[the name, the head or registered office and the legal form of each of the undertakings of which the company or firm is a member having unlimited liability. This information may be omitted where for the purposes of Article 2 (3) it is of negligible importance only;]

(3) the number and the nominal value or, in the absence of a nominal value, the accounting par value of the shares subscribed during the financial year within the limits of an authorised capital, without prejudice as far as the amount of this capital is concerned to Article 2 (1) (e) of Directive 68/151/EEC or to Article 2 (c) of Directive 77/91/EEC;

(4) where there is more than one class of shares, the number and the nominal value or, in the absence of a nominal value, the accounting par value for each class;

(5) the existence of any participation certificates, convertible debentures or similar securities or rights, with an indication of their number and the rights they confer;

(6) amounts owed by the company becoming due and payable after more than five years as well as the company's entire debts covered by valuable security furnished by the company with an indication of the nature and form of the security. This information must be disclosed separately for each creditors item, as provided for in the layouts prescribed in [Articles 9, 10 and 10a];

(7) the total amount of any financial commitments that are not included in the balance sheet, in so far as this information is of assistance in assessing the financial position. Any commitments concerning pensions and affiliated undertakings must be disclosed separately;

[(7a) the nature and business purpose of the company's arrangements that are not included in the balance sheet and the financial impact on the company of those arrangements, provided that the risks or benefits arising from such arrangements are material and in so far as the disclosure of such risks or benefits is necessary for assessing the financial position of the company.

Member States may permit the companies referred to in Article 27 to limit the information required to be disclosed by this point to the nature and business purpose of such arrangements;]

[(7b) transactions which have been entered into with related parties by the company, including the amount of such transactions, the nature of the related party relationship and other information about the transactions necessary for an understanding of the financial position of the company, if such transactions are material and have not been concluded under normal market conditions. Information about individual transactions may be aggregated according to their nature except where separate information is necessary for an understanding of the effects of related party transactions on the financial position of the company.

Member States may permit the companies referred to in Article 27 to omit the disclosures prescribed in this point unless those companies are of a type referred to in Article 1(1) of Directive 77/91/EEC, in which case Member States may limit disclosure to, as a minimum, 'transactions entered into directly or indirectly between':

(i) the company and its major shareholders, and

(ii) the company and the members of the administrative, management and supervisory bodies.

Member States may exempt transactions entered into between two or more members of a group provided that subsidiaries which are party to the transaction are wholly owned by such a member.

'Related party' has the same meaning as in international accounting standards adopted in accordance with Regulation (EC) No 1606/2002.]

(8) the net turnover within the meaning of Article 28, broken down by categories of activity and into geographical markets in so far as, taking account of the manner in which the sale of products and the provision of services falling within

the company's ordinary activities are organised, these categories and markets differ substantially from one another;

(9) the average number of persons employed during the financial year, broken down by categories and, if they are not disclosed separately in the profit and loss account, the staff costs relating to the financial year, broken down as provided for in Article 23 (6);

(10) the extent to which the calculation of the profit or loss for the financial year has been affected by a valuation of the items which, by way of derogation from the principles enunciated in [Articles 31 and 34 to 42c], was made in the financial year in question or in an earlier financial year with a view to obtaining tax relief. Where the influence of such a valuation on future tax charges is material, details must be disclosed;

(11) the difference between the tax charged for the financial year and for earlier financial years and the amount of tax payable in respect of those years, provided that this difference is material for purposes of future taxation. This amount may also be disclosed in the balance sheet as a cumulative amount under a separate item with an appropriate heading;

(12) the amount of the emoluments granted in respect of the financial year to the members of the administrative, managerial and supervisory bodies by reason of their responsibilities, and any commitments arising or entered into in respect of retirement pensions for former members of those bodies, with an indication of the total for each category;

(13) the amount of advances and credits granted to the members of the administrative, managerial and supervisory bodies, with indications of the interest rates, main conditions and any amounts repaid, as well as commitments entered into on their behalf by way of guarantees of any kind, with an indication of the total for each category.

[(14) where valuation at fair value of financial instruments has not been applied in accordance with Section 7a:

(a) for each class of derivative financial instruments:

(i) the fair value of the instruments, if such a value can be determined by any of the methods prescribed in Article 42b(1);
(ii) information about the extent and the nature of the instruments; and

(b) for financial fixed assets covered by Article 42a, carried at an amount in excess of their fair value and without use being made of the option to make a value adjustment in accordance with Article 35(1)(c)(aa):

(i) the book value and the fair value of either the individual assets or appropriate groupings of those individual assets;
(ii) the reasons for not reducing the book value, including the nature of the evidence that provides the basis for the belief that the book value will be recovered.]

[(15) separately, the total fees for the financial year charged by the statutory auditor or audit firm for the statutory audit of annual accounts, the total fees charged for other assurance services, the total fees charged for tax advisory services and the total fees charged for other non-audit services.

Member States may provide that this requirement shall not apply where the company is included within the consolidated accounts required to be drawn up under Article 1 of Directive 83/349/EEC, provided that such information is given in the notes to the consolidated accounts.]

2. Pending subsequent co-ordination, the Member States need not apply paragraph 1 (2) to financial holding companies within the meaning of Article 5 (3).

[3. Member States may waive the requirement to provide the information referred to in paragraph 1 point 12 where such information makes it possible to identify the position of a specific member of such a body.]

¶ *The subparagraph to paragraph 1(2) has been added by article 1(2) of Directive 90/605/EEC, reproduced infra under no. C. 12. Member States may provide that these provisions shall first apply to the annual accounts and consolidated accounts for financial years beginning on 1 January 1995 or during the 1995 calendar year.*

¶ *The reference between the square brackets in paragraph (1)(6) has been amended by article 1(13) of Directive 2003/51/EC, reproduced infra under no. C. 23.*

¶ Points (7a) and (7b) of article 43 (1) have been added by article 1(5) of Directive 2006/46/EC, reproduced infra under no. C. 31.
¶ The reference between the square brackets in point 10 has been amended by article 1(2)(a) of Directive 2001/65/EC, reproduced infra under no. C. 18.
¶ Point 14 has been added by article 1(2)(b) of Directive 2001/65/EC, reproduced infra under no. C. 18.
¶ Point 15 has been added by article 49(1) of Directive 2006/43/EC, reproduced infra under no. C. 30.
¶ Paragraph 3 has been added by article 4 of Directive 90/604/EEC, reproduced infra under no. C. 11. Member States may provide that these provisions shall first apply to the annual accounts and consolidated accounts for financial years beginning on 1 January 1995 or during the 1995 calendar year.

[Article 44

[1. Member States may permit the companies referred to in Article 11 to draw up abridged notes on their accounts without the information required in Article 43(1)(5) to (12), (14)(a) and (15). However, the notes must disclose the information specified in Article 43(1)(6) in total for all the items concerned.]

2. Member States may also permit the companies referred to in paragraph 1 to be exempted from the obligation to disclose in the notes on their accounts the information prescribed in Article 15 (3) (a) and (4), Articles 18, 21 and 29 (2), the second subparagraph of Article 30, Article 34 (2), Article 40 (2) and the second subparagraph of Article 42.

3. Article 12 shall apply.]

¶ This article has been replaced by article 5 of Directive 90/604/EEC, reproduced infra under no. C. 11. Member States may provide that these provisions shall first apply to the annual accounts and consolidated accounts for financial years beginning on 1 January 1995 or during the 1995 calendar year.
¶ Article 44(1) has been replaced by article 1(3) of Directive 2001/65/EC, reproduced infra under no. C. 18. It subsequently has been replaced by article 49(b) of Directive 2006/43/EC, reproduced infra under no. C. 30.

Article 45

1. The Member States may allow the disclosures prescribed in Article 43 (1) (2):

(a) to take the form of a statement deposited in accordance with Article 3 (1) and (2) of Directive 68/151/EEC; this must be disclosed in the notes on the accounts;

(b) to be omitted when their nature is such that they would be seriously prejudicial to any of the undertakings to which Article 43 (1) (2) relates. The Member States may make such omissions subject to prior administrative or judicial authorisation. Any such omission must be disclosed in the notes on the accounts.

[2. Paragraph 1(b) shall also apply to the information specified in Article 43(1)(8).

The Member States may permit the companies referred to in Article 27 to omit disclosure of the information specified in Article 43(1)(8). The Member States may also permit the companies referred to in Article 27 to omit disclosure of the information specified in Article 43(1)(15), provided that such information is delivered to the public oversight system referred to in Article 32 of Directive 2006/43/EC of the European Parliament and of the Council of 17 May 2006 on statutory audit of annual accounts and consolidated accounts[11] when requested by such a public oversight system.]

¶ Article 45(2) has been replaced by article 49(c) of Directive 2006/43/EC, reproduced infra under no. C. 30.

SECTION 9
CONTENTS OF THE ANNUAL REPORT

Article 46

[1. (a) The annual report shall include at least a fair review of the development and performance of the company's business and of its position, together with a description of the principal risks and uncertainties that it faces.

The review shall be a balanced and comprehensive analysis of the development and performance of the company's business and of its position, consistent with the size and complexity of the business;

(b) To the extent necessary for an understanding of the company's development, performance or position, the analysis shall include both financial and, where appropriate, non-financial key performance indicators relevant to the particular business, including information relating to environmental and employee matters;

---

[11] OJ L 157, 9.6.2006, 87.

(c) In providing its analysis, the annual report shall, where appropriate, include references to and additional explanations of amounts reported in the annual accounts.]

2. The report shall also give an indication of:

(a) any important events that have occurred since the end of the financial year;

(b) the company's likely future development;

(c) activities in the field of research and development;

(d) the information concerning acquisitions of own shares prescribed by Article 22 (2) of Directive 77/91/EEC;

[(e) the existence of branches of the company.]

[(f) in relation to the company's use of financial instruments and where material for the assessment of its assets, liabilities, financial position and profit or loss,
– the company's financial risk management objectives and policies, including its policy for hedging each major type of forecasted transaction for which hedge accounting is used, and
– the company's exposure to price risk, credit risk, liquidity risk and cash flow risk.]

[3. Member States may waive the obligation on companies covered by Article 11 to prepare annual reports, provided that the information referred to in Article 22 (2) of Directive 77/91/EEC concerning the acquisition by a company of its own shares is given in the notes to their accounts.]

[4. Member States may choose to exempt companies covered by Article 27 from the obligation in paragraph 1(b) above in so far as it relates to non-financial information.]

¶ *Paragraph 1 has been replaced by article 1(14)(a) of Directive 2003/51/EC, reproduced infra under no. C. 23.*
¶ *Paragraph 2, litera (e) has been introduced by article 11 of Directive 89/666/EEC, Eleventh Company Directive, reproduced infra under no. C. 9; the modification shall apply for the first time to annual accounts for the financial year beginning on 1 January 1993 or during 1993.*
¶ *Paragraph 2(f) has been added by article 1(4) of Directive 2001/65/EEC, reproduced infra under no. C. 18.*
¶ *Paragraph 3 has been added by article 6 of Directive 90/604/EEC, reproduced infra under no. C. 11. Member States may provide that these provisions shall first apply to the annual accounts and consolidated accounts for financial years beginning on 1 January 1995 or during the 1995 calendar year.*

¶ *Paragraph 4 has been added by article 1(14)(b) of Directive 2003/51/EC, reproduced infra under no. C. 23.*

[*Article 46a*]

1. A company whose securities are admitted to trading on a regulated market within the meaning of Article 4(1), point (14) of Directive 2004/39/EC of the European Parliament and of the Council of 21 April 2004 on markets in financial instruments[12] shall include a corporate governance statement in its annual report. That statement shall be included as a specific section of the annual report and shall contain at least the following information:

(a) a reference to:
(i) the corporate governance code to which the company is subject,
and/or
(ii) the corporate governance code which the company may have voluntarily decided to apply,
and/or
(iii) all relevant information about the corporate governance practices applied beyond the requirements under national law.

Where points (i) and (ii) apply, the company shall also indicate where the relevant texts are publicly available; where point (iii) applies, the company shall make its corporate governance practices publicly available;

(b) to the extent to which a company, in accordance with national law, departs from a corporate governance code referred to under points (a)(i) or (ii), an explanation by the company as to which parts of the corporate governance code it departs from and the reasons for doing so. Where the company has decided not to apply any provisions of a corporate governance code referred to under points (a)(i) or (ii), it shall explain its reasons for doing so;

(c) a description of the main features of the company's internal control and risk management systems in relation to the financial reporting process;

(d) the information required by Article 10(1), points (c), (d), (f), (h) and (i) of Directive 2004/25/EC of the European Parliament and of

[12] OJ L 145, 30.4.2004, 1, reproduced infra under no. S. 29.

the Council of 21 April 2004 on takeover bids,[13] where the company is subject to that Directive;

(e) unless the information is already fully provided for in national laws or regulations, the operation of the shareholder meeting and its key powers, and a description of shareholders' rights and how they can be exercised;

(f) the composition and operation of the administrative, management and supervisory bodies and their committees.

2. Member States may permit the information required by this Article to be set out in a separate report published together with the annual report in the manner set out in Article 47 or by means of a reference in the annual report where such document is publicly available on the company's website. In the event of a separate report, the corporate governance statement may contain a reference to the annual report where the information required in paragraph 1, point (d) is made available. Article 51(1), second subparagraph shall apply to the provisions of paragraph 1, points (c) and (d) of this Article. For the remaining information, the statutory auditor shall check that the corporate governance statement has been produced.

3. Member States may exempt companies which have only issued securities other than shares admitted to trading on a regulated market, within the meaning of Article 4(1), point (14) of Directive 2004/39/EC, from the application of the provisions of paragraph 1, points (a), (b), (e) and (f), unless such companies have issued shares which are traded in a multilateral trading facility, within the meaning of Article 4(1), point (15) of Directive 2004/39/EC.]

¶ *Article 46a has been added by article 1(7) of Directive 2006/46/EC, reproduced infra under no. C. 31.*

Section 10
Publication

Article 47

[1. The annual accounts, duly approved, and the annual report, together with the opinion submitted by the person responsible for auditing the accounts, shall be published as laid down by the laws of each Member State in accordance with Article 3 of Directive 68/151/EEC.

The laws of a Member State may, however, permit the annual report not to be published as stipulated above. In that case, it shall be made available to the public at the company's registered office in the Member State concerned. [It must be possible to obtain a copy of all or part of any such report upon request. The price of such a copy must not exceed its administrative cost.]

[1a. The Member State of a company or firm referred to in Article 1 (1), second and third subparagraphs (entity concerned) may exempt that entity from publishing its accounts in accordance with Article 3 of Directive 68/151/EEC, provided that those accounts are available to the public at its head office, where:

(a) all the members having unlimited liability of the entity concerned are the companies referred to in the first subparagraph of Article 1 (1) governed by the laws of Member States other than the Member State whose law governs that entity and none of those companies publishes the accounts of the entity concerned with its own accounts; or

(b) all the members having unlimited liability are companies which are not governed by the laws of a Member State but which have a legal form comparable to those referred to in Directive 68/151/EEC.

Copies of the accounts must be obtainable upon request. The price of such a copy may not exceed its administrative cost. Appropriate sanctions must be provided for failure to comply with the publication obligation imposed in this paragraph.]

2. By way of derogation from paragraph 1, the Member States may permit the companies referred to in Article 11 to publish:

(a) abridged balance sheets showing only those items preceded by letters and roman numerals in Articles 9 and 10, disclosing separately the information required in brackets in D (II) under 'Assets' and C under 'Liabilities' in Article 9 and in D (II) in Article 10, but in total for all the items concerned; and

---

[13] OJ L 142, 30.4.2004, 12, reproduced infra under no. S. 28.

[(b) abridged notes on their accounts in accordance with Article 44].

Article 12 shall apply.

In addition, the Member States may relieve such companies from the obligation to publish their profit and loss accounts and annual reports and the opinions of the persons responsible for auditing the accounts.

3. The Member States may permit the companies mentioned in Article 27 to publish:

(a) abridged balance sheets showing only those items preceded by letters and roman numerals in Articles 9 and 10 disclosing separately, either in the balance sheet or in the notes on the accounts:
– C (I) (3), C (II) (1), (2), (3) and (4), C (III) (1), (2), (3), (4) and (7), D (II) (2), (3) and (6) and D (III) (1) and (2) under 'Assets' and C (1), (2), (6), (7) and (9) under 'Liabilities' in Article 9,
– C (I) (3), C (II) (1), (2), (3) and (4), C (III) (1), (2), (3), (4) and (7), D (II) (2), (3) and (6), D (III) (1) and (2), F (1), (2), (6), (7) and (9) and (I) (1), (2), (6), (7) and (9) in Article 10,
– the information required in brackets in D (II) under 'Assets' and C under 'Liabilities' in Article 9, in total for all the items concerned and separately for D (II) (2) and (3) under 'Assets' and C (1), (2), (6), (7) and (9) under 'Liabilities',
– the information required in brackets in D (II) in Article 10, in total for all the items concerned, and separately for D (II) (2) and (3);

(b) abridged notes on their accounts without the information required in Article 43 (1) (5), (6), (8), (10) and (11). However, the notes on the accounts must give the information specified in Article 43 (1) (6) in total for all the items concerned.

This paragraph shall be without prejudice to paragraph 1 in so far as it relates to the profit and loss account, the annual report and the opinion of the person responsible for auditing the accounts.

Article 12 shall apply.

¶ *Paragraph 1 has been modified by article 38 of Directive 83/349/EEC, Seventh Company Directive, reproduced infra under no. C. 6.*
¶ *Paragraph 1a has been inserted by article 1(3) of Directive 90/605/EEC, reproduced infra under no. C. 12. Member States may provide that these provisions shall first apply to the annual accounts and consolidated accounts for financial years beginning on 1 January 1995 or during the 1995 calendar year.*
¶ *Paragraph 2(b) has been modified by article 7 of Directive 90/604/EEC, reproduced infra under no. C. 11. Member States may provide that these provisions shall first apply to the annual accounts and consolidated accounts for financial years beginning on 1 January 1995 or during the 1995 calendar year.*

Article 48

Whenever the annual accounts and the annual report are published in full, they must be reproduced in the form and text on the basis of which the person responsible for auditing the accounts has drawn up his opinion. They must be accompanied by the full text of his report.

[. . .]

¶ *The third sentence has been deleted by article 1(15) of Directive 2003/51/EC, reproduced infra under no. C. 23.*

Article 49

If the annual accounts are not published in full, it must be indicated that the version published is abridged and reference must be made to the register in which the accounts have been filed in accordance with Article 47 (1). Where such filing has not yet been effected, the fact must be disclosed. [The report of the person or persons responsible for auditing the annual accounts (hereinafter: the statutory auditors) shall not accompany this publication, but it shall be disclosed whether an unqualified, qualified or adverse audit opinion was expressed, or whether the statutory auditors were unable to express an audit opinion. It shall also be disclosed whether the report of the statutory auditors included a reference to any matters to which the statutory auditors drew attention by way of emphasis without qualifying the audit opinion.]

¶ *The third sentence has been replaced by article 1(16) of Directive 2003/51/EC, reproduced infra under no. C. 23.*

Article 50

The following must be published together with the annual accounts, and in like manner:
– the proposed appropriation of the profit or treatment of the loss,
– the appropriation of the profit or treatment of the loss,

where these items do not appear in the annual accounts.

[*Article 50a*]

Annual accounts may be published in the currency in which they were drawn up and in ecus, translated at the exchange rate prevailing on the balance sheet date. That rate shall be disclosed in the notes on the accounts.]

¶ *This article has been inserted by article 8 of Directive 90/604/EEC, reproduced infra under no. C. 11. Member States may provide that these provisions shall first apply to the annual accounts and consolidated accounts for financial years beginning on 1 January 1995 or during the 1995 calendar year.*

[SECTION 10A

DUTY AND LIABILITY FOR DRAWING UP AND PUBLISHING THE ANNUAL ACCOUNTS AND THE ANNUAL REPORT

Article 50b

Member States shall ensure that the members of the administrative, management and supervisory bodies of the company have collectively the duty to ensure that the annual accounts, the annual report and, when provided separately, the corporate governance statement to be provided pursuant to Article 46a are drawn up and published in accordance with the requirements of this Directive and, where applicable, in accordance with the international accounting standards adopted in accordance with Regulation (EC) No 1606/2002. Such bodies shall act within the competences assigned to them by national law.

Article 50c

Member States shall ensure that their laws, regulations and administrative provisions on liability apply to the members of the administrative, management and supervisory bodies referred to in Article 50b, at least towards the company, for breach of the duty referred to in Article 50b.]

¶ *Section 10A has been added by article 1(8) of Directive 2006/46/EC, reproduced infra under no. C. 31.*

SECTION 11

AUDITING

Article 51

[1. The annual accounts of companies shall be audited by one or more persons approved by Member States to carry out statutory audits on the basis of the Eighth Council Directive 84/253/EEC of 10 April 1984 on the approval of persons responsible for carrying out the statutory audits of accounting documents.[14]

The statutory auditors shall also express an opinion concerning the consistency or otherwise of the annual report with the annual accounts for the same financial year.]

2. The Member States may relieve the companies referred to in Article 11 from the obligation imposed by paragraph 1.

Article 12 shall apply.

3. Where the exemption provided for in paragraph 2 is granted the Member States shall introduce appropriate sanctions into their laws for cases in which the annual accounts or the annual reports of such companies are not drawn up in accordance with the requirements of this Directive.

¶ *Article 51(1) has been replaced by article 1(17) of Directive 2003/51/EC, reproduced infra under no. C. 23.*

[*Article 51a*

1. The report of the statutory auditors shall include:

(a) an introduction which shall at least identify the annual accounts that are the subject of the statutory audit, together with the financial reporting framework that has been applied in their preparation;

(b) a description of the scope of the statutory audit which shall at least identify the auditing standards in accordance with which the statutory audit was conducted;

(c) an audit opinion which shall state clearly the opinion of the statutory auditors as to whether the annual accounts give a true and fair view in accordance with the relevant financial reporting framework and, where appropriate, whether the annual accounts comply with statutory requirements; the audit opinion shall be either unqualified, qualified, an adverse opinion or, if the statutory auditors are

---

[14] OJ L 126, 12.5.1984, 20, reproduced infra under no. C. 7, which has been repealed as from 29 June 2006 by article 50 of Directive 2006/43/EC, reproduced infra under no. C. 30.

unable to express an audit opinion, a disclaimer of opinion;

(d) a reference to any matters to which the statutory auditors draw attention by way of emphasis without qualifying the audit opinion;

(e) an opinion concerning the consistency or otherwise of the annual report with the annual accounts for the same financial year.

2. The report shall be signed and dated by the statutory auditors.]

¶ *This article has been added by article 1(18) of Directive 2003/51/EC, reproduced infra under no. C. 23.*

Section 12

Final Provisions

Article 52

1. A Contact Committee shall be set up under the auspices of the Commission. Its function shall be:

(a) to facilitate, without prejudice to the provisions of Articles [226 and 227][1] of the Treaty, harmonised application of this Directive through regular meetings dealing in particular with practical problems arising in connection with its application;

(b) to advise the Commission, if necessary, on additions or amendments to this Directive.

2. The Contact Committee shall be composed of representatives of the Member States and representatives of the Commission. The chairman shall be a representative of the Commission. The Commission shall provide the secretariat.

3. The Committee shall be convened by the chairman either on his own initiative or at the request of one of its members.

¶ *See for an extension of its functions also article 5 of Directive 89/117/EEC, superseded by Directive 94/19/EC, reproduced supra under no. B. 22; article 17 of the Eleventh Company Directive 89/666/EEC, reproduced infra under no. C. 9; and article 69 of Directive 91/674/EEC, reproduced infra under no. I. 23.*

Article 53

1. [. . .].

2. Every five years the Council, acting on a proposal from the Commission, shall examine and, if need be, revise the amounts expressed in European units of account in this Directive, in the light of economic and monetary trends in the Community.

¶ *Paragraph 1 of this article has been repealed by article 1(20) of Directive 2003/51/EC, reproduced infra under no. C. 23.*

[Article 53a

Member States shall not make available the exemptions set out in Articles 11, 27, 43(1), points (7a) and (7b), 46, 47 and 51 in the case of companies whose securities are admitted to trading on a regulated market within the meaning of Article 4(1), point (14) of Directive 2004/39/EC.]

¶ *This article has been inserted by article 1(20) of Directive 2003/51/EC, reproduced infra under no. C. 23 and amended by article 1(9) of Directive 2006/46/EC, reproduced infra under no. C. 31.*

Article 54

[. . .]

¶ *This article has been repealed by article 12 of Directive 89/666/EEC, Eleventh Company Directive, reproduced infra under no. C. 11.*

Article 55

1. The Member States shall bring into force the laws, regulations and administrative provisions necessary for them to comply with this Directive within two years of its notification. They shall forthwith inform the Commission thereof.

2. The Member States may stipulate that the provisions referred to in paragraph 1 shall not apply until 18 months after the end of the period provided for in that paragraph.

That period of 18 months may, however, be five years:

(a) in the case of unregistered companies in the United Kingdom and Ireland;

(b) for purposes of the application of Articles 9 and 10 and Articles 23 to 26 concerning the layouts for the balance sheet and the profit and loss account, where a Member State has brought other layouts for these documents into force not more than three years before the notification of this Directive;

(c) for purposes of the application of this Directive as regards the calculation and disclosure in balance sheets of depreciation relating to assets covered by the asset items mentioned in Article 9, C (II) (2) and (3), and Article 10, C (II) (2) and (3);

(d) for purposes of the application of Article 47 (1) of this Directive except as regards companies already under an obligation of publication under Article 2 (1) (f) of Directive 68/151/EEC. In this case the second subparagraph of Article 47 (1) of this Directive shall apply to the annual accounts and to the opinion drawn up by the person responsible for auditing the accounts;

(e) for purposes of the application of Article 51 (1) of this Directive.

Furthermore, this period of 18 months may be extended to eight years for companies the principal object of which is shipping and which are already in existence on the entry into force of the provisions referred to in paragraph 1.

3. The Member States shall ensure that they communicate to the Commission the texts of the main provisions of national law which they adopt in the field covered by this Directive.

[Article 56

1. The obligation to show in annual accounts the items prescribed by [Articles 9, 10, 10a] and 23 to 26 which relate to affiliated undertakings, as defined by Article 41 of Directive 83/349/EEC, and the obligation to provide information concerning these undertakings in accordance with Articles 13 (2), and 14 and point 7 of Article 43 (1) shall enter into force on the date fixed in Article 49 (2) of that Directive.

2. The notes on the accounts must also disclose:

(a) the name and registered office of the undertaking which draws up the consolidated accounts of the largest body of undertakings of which the company forms part as a subsidiary undertaking;

(b) the name and registered office of the undertaking which draws up the consolidated accounts of the smallest body of undertakings of which the company forms part as a subsidiary undertaking

and which is also included in the body of undertakings referred to in (a) above;

(c) the place where copies of the consolidated accounts referred to in (a) and (b) above may be obtained provided that they are available.]

¶ *This article has been replaced by article 42 of Directive 83/349/EEC, Seventh Company Directive, reproduced infra under no. C. 6.*

¶ *The reference between square brackets in paragraph 1 of this article has been amended by article 1(21) of Directive 2003/51/EC, reproduced infra under no. C. 23.*

[Article 57

Notwithstanding the provisions of Directives 68/151/EEC and 77/91/EEC, a Member State need not apply the provisions of this Directive concerning the content, auditing and publication of annual accounts to companies governed by their national laws which are subsidiary undertakings, as defined in Directive 83/349/EEC, where the following conditions are fulfilled:

(a) the parent undertaking must be subject to the laws of a Member State;

(b) all shareholders or members of the subsidiary undertaking must have declared their agreement to the exemption from such obligation; this declaration must be made in respect of every financial year;

(c) the parent undertaking must have declared that it guarantees the commitments entered into by the subsidiary undertaking;

(d) the declarations referred to in (b) and (c) must be published by the subsidiary undertaking as laid down by the laws of the Member State in accordance with Article 3 of Directive 68/151/EEC;

(e) the subsidiary undertaking must be included in the consolidated accounts drawn up by the parent undertaking in accordance with Directive 83/349/EEC;

(f) the above exemption must be disclosed in the notes on the consolidated accounts drawn up by the parent undertaking;

(g) the consolidated accounts referred to in (e), the consolidated annual report, and the report by the person responsible for auditing those accounts must be published for the subsidiary undertaking as laid down by the laws of the Member State in accordance with Article 3 of Directive 68/151/EEC.]

¶ *This article has been replaced by article 43 of Directive 83/349/EEC, Seventh Company Directive, reproduced infra under no. C. 6.*

[Article 57a

1. Member States may require the companies referred to in the first subparagraph of Article 1 (1) governed by their law, which are members having unlimited liability of any of the companies and firms listed in Article 1 (1), second and third subparagraphs (entity concerned), to draw up, have audited and publish, with their own accounts, the accounts of the entity concerned in conformity with the provisions of this Directive.

In this case, the requirements of this Directive do not apply to the entity concerned.

2. Member States need not apply the requirements of this Directive to the entity concerned where:

(a) the accounts of this entity are drawn up, audited and published in conformity with the provisions of this Directive by a company which is a member having unlimited liability of the entity and is governed by the law of another Member State;

(b) the entity concerned is included in consolidated accounts drawn up, audited and published in accordance with Directive 83/349/EEC by a member having unlimited liability or where the entity concerned is included in the consolidated accounts of a larger body of undertakings drawn up, audited and published in conformity with Council Directive 83/349/EEC by a parent undertaking governed by the law of a Member State. The exemption must be disclosed in the notes on the consolidated accounts.

3. In these cases, the entity concerned must reveal to whomsoever so requests the name of the entity publishing the accounts.]

¶ *This article has been inserted by article 1(4) of Directive 90/605/EEC, reproduced infra under no. C. 12. Member States may provide that these provisions shall first apply to the annual accounts and consolidated accounts for financial years beginning on 1 January 1995 or during the 1995 calendar year.*

[Article 58

A Member State need not apply the provisions of this Directive concerning the auditing and publication of the profit and loss account to companies governed by their national laws which are parent undertakings for the purposes of Directive 83/349/EEC where the following conditions are fulfilled:

(a) the parent undertaking must draw up consolidated accounts in accordance with Directive 83/349/EEC and be included in the consolidated accounts;

(b) the above exemption must be disclosed in the notes on the annual accounts of the parent undertaking;

(c) the above exemption must he disclosed in the notes on the consolidated accounts drawn up by the parent undertaking;

(d) the profit or loss of the parent company, determined in accordance with this Directive, must be shown in the balance sheet of the parent company.]

¶ *This article has been replaced by article 44 of Directive 83/349/EEC, Seventh Company Directive, reproduced infra under no. C. 6.*

[Article 59

1. A Member State may require or permit that participating interests, as defined in Article 17, in the capital of undertakings over the operating and financial policies of which significant influence is exercised, be shown in the balance sheet in accordance with paragraphs 2 to 9 below, as sub-items of the items 'shares in affiliated undertakings' or 'participating interests', as the case may be. An undertaking shall be presumed to exercise a significant influence over another undertaking where it has 20% or more of the shareholders' or members' voting rights in that undertaking. Article 2 of Directive 83/349/EEC shall apply.

2. When this Article is first applied to a participating interest covered by paragraph 1, it shall be shown in the balance sheet either:

(a) at its book value calculated in accordance with [Section 7 or 7a]. The difference between that value and the amount corresponding to the proportion of capital and reserves represented by the participating interest shall be disclosed separately in the balance sheet or in the notes on the accounts. That difference shall be calculated as at the date as at which the method is applied for the first time; or

(b) at the amount corresponding to the proportion of the capital and reserves represented by the participating interest. The difference between that amount and the book value calculated in accordance with [Section 7 or 7a] shall be disclosed separately in the balance sheet or in the notes on the accounts. That difference shall be calculated as at the date as at which the method is applied for the first time.

(c) A Member State may prescribe the application of one or other of the above paragraphs. The balance sheet or the notes on the accounts must indicate whether (a) or (b) above has been used.

(d) In addition, when applying (a) and (b) above, a Member State may require or permit calculation of the difference as at the date of acquisition of the participating interest referred to in paragraph 1 or, where the acquisition took place in two or more stages, as at the date as at which the holding became a participating interest within the meaning of paragraph 1 above.

3. Where the assets or liabilities of an undertaking in which a participating interest within the meaning of paragraph 1 above is held have been valued by methods other than those used by the company drawing up the annual accounts, they may, for the purpose of calculating the difference referred to in paragraph 2 (a) or (b) above, be revalued by the methods used by the company drawing up the annual accounts. Disclosure must be made in the notes on the accounts where such revaluation has not been carried out. A Member State may require such revaluation.

4. The book value referred to in paragraph 2 (a) above, or the amount corresponding to the proportion of capital and reserves referred to in paragraph 2 (b) above, shall be increased or reduced by the amount of the variation which has taken place during the financial year in the proportion of capital and reserves represented by that participating interest; it shall be reduced by the amount of the dividends relating to the participating interest.

5. In so far as a positive difference covered by paragraph 2 (a) or (b) above cannot be related to any category of asset or liability, it shall be dealt with in accordance with the rules applicable to the item 'goodwill'.

6. (a) The proportion of the profit or loss attributable to participating interests within the meaning of paragraph 1 above shall be shown in the profit and loss account as a separate item with an appropriate heading.

(b) Where that amount exceeds the amount of dividends already received or the payment of which can be claimed, the amount of the difference must be placed in a reserve which cannot be distributed to shareholders.

(c) A Member State may require or permit that the proportion of the profit or loss attributable to the participating interests referred to in paragraph 1 above be shown in the profit and loss account only to the extent of the amount corresponding to dividends already received or the payment of which can be claimed.

7. The eliminations referred to in Article 26 (1) (c) of Directive 83/349/EEC shall be effected in so far as the facts are known or can be ascertained. Article 26 (2) and (3) of that Directive shall apply.

8. Where an undertaking in which a participating interest within the meaning of paragraph 1 above is held draws up consolidated accounts, the foregoing paragraphs shall apply to the capital and reserves shown in such consolidated accounts.

9. This Article need not be applied where a participating interest as defined in paragraph 1 is not material for the purposes of Article 2 (3).]

¶ *This article has been replaced by article 45 of Directive 83/349/EEC, Seventh Company Directive, reproduced infra under no. C. 6.*
¶ *The words between square brackets in paragraph 2(a) and (b) have been changed by article 1(5) of Directive 2001/65/EEC, reproduced infra under no. C. 18.*

Article 60

Pending subsequent co-ordination, the Member States may prescribe that investments in which investment companies within the meaning of Article 5 (2) have invested their funds shall be valued [on the basis of their fair value.]

In that case, the Member States may also waive the obligation on investment companies with variable capital to show separately the value adjustments referred to in Article 36.

¶ *The words between square brackets in paragraph 1 have been amended by article 1(22) of Directive 2003/51/EC, reproduced infra under no. C. 23.*

[Article 60a

Member States shall lay down the rules on penalties applicable to infringements of the national provisions adopted pursuant to this Directive and shall take all the measures necessary to ensure that they are implemented. The penalties provided for must be effective, proportionate and dissuasive.]

¶ *Article 60a has been added by article 1(10) of Directive 2006/46/EC, reproduced infra under no. C. 31.*

[Article 61

A Member State need not apply the provisions of point 2 of Article 43 (1) of this Directive concerning the amount of capital and reserves and profits and losses of the undertakings concerned to companies governed by their national laws which are parent undertakings for the purposes of profits and losses of the undertakings concerned to companies governed by their national laws which are parent undertakings for the purposes of Directive 83/349/EEC:

(a) where the undertakings concerned are included in consolidated accounts drawn up by that parent undertaking, or in the consolidated accounts of a larger body of undertakings as referred to in Article 7 (2) of Directive 83/349/EEC; or

(b) where the holdings in the undertakings concerned have been dealt with by the parent undertaking in its annual accounts in accordance with Article 59, or in the consolidated accounts drawn up by that parent undertaking in accordance with Article 33 of Directive 83/349/EEC.]

¶ *This article has been replaced by article 46 of Directive 83/349/EEC, Seventh Company Directive, reproduced infra under no. C. 6.*

[Article 61a

Not later than 1 July 2007, the Commission shall review the provisions in Articles 42a to 42f, Article 43(1)(10) and (14), Article 44(1), Article 46(2)(f) and Article 59(2)(a) and (b) in the light of the experience acquired in applying provisions on fair value accounting, with particular regard to IAS 39 as endorsed in accordance with Regulation (EC) No 1606/2002, and taking account of international developments in the field of accounting and, if appropriate, submit a proposal to the European Parliament and the Council with a view to amending the abovementioned Articles.]

¶ *This article has been inserted by article 1(6) of Directive 2001/65/EEC, reproduced infra under no. C. 18, and amended by article 1(11) of Directive 2006/48/EC, reproduced infra under no. C. 31.*

Article 62

This Directive is addressed to the Member States.

C.5.

Sixth Council Directive 82/891/EEC
of 17 December 1982
based on Article [44]¹ (3) (g) of the Treaty, concerning
the division of public limited liability companies²

THE COUNCIL OF THE EUROPEAN COMMUNITIES,

Having regard to the Treaty establishing the European Economic Community, and in particular Article [44(3)(g)]¹ thereof,

Having regard to the proposal from the Commission,³

Having regard to the opinion of the European Parliament,⁴

Having regard to the opinion of the Economic and Social Committee,⁵

Whereas the co-ordination provided for in Article 54 (3) (g) and in the general programme for the abolition of restrictions on freedom of establishment⁶ was begun with Directive 68/151/EEC;⁷

Whereas that co-ordination was continued as regards the formation of public limited liability companies and the maintenance and alteration of their capital with Directive 77/91/EEC,⁸ as regards the annual accounts of certain types of companies with Directive 78/660/EEC,⁹ and as regards mergers of public limited liability companies with Directive 78/855/EEC;¹⁰

Whereas Directive 78/855/EEC dealt only with mergers of public limited liability companies and certain operations treated as mergers; whereas, however, the Commission proposal also covered division operations; whereas the opinions of the European Parliament and of the Economic and Social Committee were in favour of the regulation of such operation;

Whereas, because of the similarities which exist between merger and division operations, the risk of the guarantees given with regard to mergers by Directive 78/855/EEC being circumvented can be avoided only if provision is made for equivalent protection in the event of division;

Whereas the protection of the interests of members and third parties requires that the laws of the Member States relating to divisions of public limited liability companies be co-ordinated where the Member States permit such operations;

Whereas, in the context of such co-ordination, it is particularly important that the shareholders of the companies involved in a division be kept adequately informed in as objective a manner as possible and that their rights be suitably protected;

Whereas the protection of employees' rights in the event of transfers of undertakings, businesses or parts of businesses is at present regulated by Directive 77/187/EEC;¹¹

Whereas creditors, including debenture holders, and persons having other claims on the companies involved in a division, must be protected so that the division does not adversely affect their interests;

---

¹ The number between brackets has been changed as from 1 May 1999 by article 12 of the Treaty of Amsterdam.
² OJ L 378, 31.12.1982, 47–54.
³ OJ C 89, 14.7.1970, 20.
⁴ OJ C 129, 11.12.1972, 50 and OJ C 95, 28.4.1975, 12.
⁵ OJ C 88, 6.9.1971, 18.
⁶ OJ 2, 15.1.1962, 36–62.
⁷ OJ L 65, 14.3.1968, 8, First Company Directive, reproduced supra under no. C. 1.
⁸ OJ L 26, 31.1.1977, 1, Second Company Directive, reproduced supra under no. C. 2.
⁹ OJ L 222, 14.8.1978, 11, Fourth Company Directive, reproduced supra under no. C. 4.
¹⁰ OJ L 295, 20.10.1978, 36, Third Company Directive, reproduced supra under no. C. 3.
¹¹ OJ L 61, 5.3.1977, 26, reproduced infra under no. E. 2.

Whereas the disclosure requirements of Directive 68/151/EEC must be extended to include divisions so that third parties are kept adequately informed;

Whereas the safeguards afforded to members and third parties in connection with divisions must be extended to cover certain legal practices which in important respects are similar to division, so that the obligation to provide such protection cannot be evaded;

Whereas to ensure certainty in the law as regards relations between the companies involved in the division, between them and third parties, and between the members, the cases in which nullity can arise must be limited by providing that defects be remedied wherever that is possible and by restricting the period within which nullification proceedings may be commenced,

HAS ADOPTED THIS DIRECTIVE:

Article 1

1. Where Member States permit the companies referred to in Article 1 (1) of Directive 78/855/EEC coming under their laws to carry out division operations by acquisition as defined in Article 2 of this Directive, they shall subject those operations to the provisions of Chapter I of this Directive.

2. Where Member States permit the companies referred to in paragraph 1 to carry out division operations by the formation of new companies as defined in Article 21, they shall subject those operations to the provisions of Chapter II of this Directive.

3. Where Member States permit the companies referred to in paragraph 1 to carry out operations, whereby a division by acquisition as defined in Article 2 (1) is combined with a division by the formation of one or more new companies as defined in Article 21 (1), they shall subject operation to the provisions of Chapter I and Article 22.

4. Article 1 (2) and (3) of Directive 78/855/EEC shall apply.

CHAPTER I
DIVISION BY ACQUISITION

Article 2

1. For the purposes of this Directive, 'division by acquisition' shall mean the operation whereby, after being wound up without going into liquidation, a company transfers to more than one company all its assets and liabilities in exchange for the allocation to the shareholders of the company being divided of shares in the companies receiving contributions as a result of the division (hereinafter referred to as 'recipient companies') and possibly a cash payment not exceeding 10% of the nominal value of the shares allocated or, where they have no nominal value, of their accounting par value.

2. Article 3 (2) of Directive 78/855/EEC shall apply.

3. In so far as this Directive refers to Directive 78/855/EEC, the expression 'merging companies' shall mean 'the companies involved in a division' the expression 'company being acquired' shall mean 'the company being divided', the expression 'acquiring company' shall mean 'each of the recipient companies' and the expression 'draft terms of merger' shall mean 'draft terms of division'.

Article 3

1. The administrative or management bodies of the companies involved in a division shall draw up draft terms of division in writing.

2. Draft terms of division shall specify at least:

(a) the type, name and registered office of each of the companies involved in the division;

(b) the share exchange ratio and the amount of any cash payment;

(c) the terms relating to the allotment of shares in the recipient companies;

(d) the date from which the holding of such shares entitles the holders to participate in profits and any special conditions affecting that entitlement;

(e) the date from which the transactions of the company being divided shall be treated for accounting purposes as being those of one or other of the recipient companies;

(f) the rights conferred by the recipient companies on the holders of shares to which special rights are attached and the holders of securities other than shares, or the measures proposed concerning them;

(g) any special advantage granted to the experts referred to in Article 8 (1) and members of the administrative, management, supervisory or controlling bodies of the companies involved in the division;

(h) the precise description and allocation of the assets and liabilities to be transferred to each of the recipient companies;

(i) the allocation to the shareholders of the company being divided of shares in the recipient companies and the criterion upon which such allocation is based.

3. (a) Where an asset is not allocated by the draft terms of division and where the interpretation of these terms does not make a decision on its allocation possible, the asset or the consideration therefore shall be allocated to all the recipient companies in proportion to the share of the net assets allocated to each of those companies under the draft terms of division.

(b) Where a liability is not allocated by the draft terms of division and where the interpretation of these terms does not make a decision on its allocation possible, each of the recipient companies shall be jointly and severally liable for it. Member States may provide that such joint and several liability be limited to the net assets allocated to each company.

Article 4

Draft terms of division must be published in the manner prescribed by the laws of each Member State in accordance with Article 3 of Directive 68/151/EEC for each of the companies involved in a division, at least one month before the date of the general meeting which is to decide thereon.

Article 5

1. A division shall require at least the approval of a general meeting of each company involved in the division. Article 7 of Directive 78/855/EEC shall apply with regard to the majority required for such decisions, their scope and the need for separate votes.

2. Where shares in the recipient companies are allocated to the share holders of the company being divided otherwise than in proportion to their rights in the capital of that company, Member States may provide that the minority shareholders of that company may exercise the right to have their shares purchased. In such case, they shall be entitled to receive consideration corresponding to the value of their shares. In the event of a dispute concerning such consideration, it must be possible for the consideration to be determined by a court.

Article 6

The laws of a Member State need not require approval of a division by a general meeting of a recipient company if the following conditions are fulfilled:

(a) the publication provided for in Article 4 must be effected, for each recipient company, at least one month before the date fixed for the general meeting of the company being divided which is to decide on the draft terms of division;

(b) at least one month before the date specified in point (a), all share holders of each recipient company must be entitled to inspect the documents specified in Article 9 (1) at the registered office of that company;

(c) one or more shareholders of any recipient company holding a minimum percentage of the subscribed capital must be entitled to require that a general meeting of such recipient company be called to decide whether to approve the division. This minimum percentage may not be fixed at more than 5%. Member States may, however, provide for the exclusion of non voting shares from this calculation.

Article 7

1. This administration or management bodies of each of the companies involved in the division shall draw up a detailed written report explaining the draft terms of division and setting out the

legal and economic grounds for them, in particular the share exchange ratio and the criterion determining the allocation of shares.

2. The report shall also describe any special valuation difficulties which have arisen.

It shall disclose the preparation of the report on the consideration other than in cash referred to in Article 27 (2) of Directive 77/91/EEC for recipient companies and the register where that report must be lodged.

3. The administrative or management bodies of a company being divided must inform the general meeting of that company and the administrative or management bodies of the recipient companies so that they can inform their respective general meetings of any material change in the assets and liabilities between the date of preparation of the draft terms of division and the date of the general meeting of the company being divided which is to decide on the draft terms of division.

Article 8

1. One or more experts acting on behalf of each of the companies involved in the division but independent of them, appointed or approved by a judicial or administrative authority, shall examine the draft terms of division and draw up a written report to the shareholders. However, the laws of a Member State may provide for the appointment of one or more independent experts for all of the companies involved in a division if such appointment is made by a judicial or administrative authority at the joint request of those companies. Such experts may, depending on the laws of each Member State, be natural or legal persons or companies or firms.

2. Article 10 (2) and (3) of Directive 78/855/EEC shall apply.

3. Member States may provide that the report on the consideration other than in cash referred to in Article 27 (2) of Directive 77/91/EEC and the report on the draft terms of division drawn up in accordance with paragraph 1 shall be drawn up by the same expert or experts.

Article 9

1. All shareholders shall be entitled to inspect at least the following documents at the registered office at least one month before the date of the general meeting which is to decide on the draft terms of division:

(a) the draft terms of division;

(b) the annual accounts and annual reports of the companies involved in the division for the preceding three financial years;

(c) an accounting statement drawn up as at a date which must not be earlier than the first day of the third month preceding the date of the draft terms of division, if the latest annual accounts relate to a financial year which ended more than six months before that date;

(d) the reports of the administrative or management bodies of the companies involved in the division provided for in Article 7 (1);

(e) the reports provided for in Article 8.

2. The accounting statement provided for in paragraph 1 (c) shall be drawn up using the same methods and the same layout as the last annual balance sheet.

However, the laws of a Member State may provide that:

(a) it shall not be necessary to take a fresh physical inventory;

(b) the valuations shown in the last balance sheet shall be altered only to reflect entries in the books of account; the following shall nevertheless be taken into account:
– interim depreciation and provisions,
– material changes in actual value not shown in the books.

3. Every shareholder shall be entitled to obtain, on request and free of charge, full or, if so desired, partial copies of the documents referred to in paragraph 1.

Article 10

Member States may permit the non-application of Articles 7 and 8 (1) and (2), and of Article 9 (1) (c), (d) and (e) if all the shareholders and the holders of other securities giving the right to vote of the companies involved in a division have so agreed.

Article 11

Protection of the rights of the employees of each of the companies involved in a division shall be regulated in accordance with Directive 77/187/EEC.

Article 12

1. The laws of Member States must provide for an adequate system of protection for the interests of the creditors of the companies involved in a division whose claims antedate publication of the draft terms of division and have not yet fallen due at the time of such publication.

2. To that end, the laws of Member States shall at least provide that such creditors shall be entitled to obtain adequate safeguards where the financial situation of the company being divided and that of the company to which the obligation will be transferred in accordance with the draft terms of division make such protection necessary and where those creditors do not already have such safeguards.

3. In so far as a creditor of the company to which the obligation has been transferred in accordance with the draft terms of division has not obtained satisfaction, the recipient companies shall be jointly and severally liable for that obligation. Member States may limit that liability to the net assets allocated to each of those companies other than the one to which the obligation has been transferred. However, they need not apply this paragraph where the division operation is subject to the supervision of a judicial authority in accordance with Article 23 and a majority in number representing three-fourths in value of the creditors or any class of creditors of the company being divided have agreed to forego such joint and several liability at a meeting held pursuant to Article 23 (1) (c).

4. Article 13 (3) of Directive 78/855/EEC shall apply.

5. Without prejudice to the rules governing the collective exercise of their rights, paragraphs 1 to 4 shall apply to the debenture holders of the companies involved in the division except where the division has been approved by a meeting of the debenture holders, if such a meeting is provided for under national laws, or by the debenture holders individually.

6. Member States may provide that the recipient companies shall be jointly and severally liable for the obligations of the company being divided. In such case they need not apply the foregoing paragraphs.

7. Where a Member State combines the system of creditor protection set out in paragraph 1 to 5 with the joint and several liability of the recipient companies as referred to in paragraph 6, it may limit such joint and several liability to the net assets allocated to each of those companies.

Article 13

Holders of securities, other than shares, to which special rights are attached, must be given rights in the recipient companies against which such securities may be invoked in accordance with the draft terms of division, at least equivalent to the rights they possessed in the company being divided, unless the alteration of those rights has been approved by a meeting of the holders of such securities, if such a meeting is provided for under national laws, or by the holders of those securities individually, or unless the holders are entitled to have their securities repurchased.

Article 14

Where the laws of a Member State do not provide for judicial or administrative preventive supervision of the legality of divisions or where such supervision does not extend to all the legal acts required for a division, Article 16 of Directive 78/855/EEC shall apply.

Article 15

The laws of Member States shall determine the date on which a division takes effect.

Article 16

1. A division must be published in the manner prescribed by the laws of each Member State in accordance with Article 3 of Directive 68/151/EEC in respect of each of the companies involved in a division.

2. Any recipient company may itself carry out the publication formalities relating to the company being divided.

Article 17

1. A division shall have the following consequences *ipso jure* and simultaneously:

(a) the transfer, both as between the company being divided and the recipient companies and as regards third parties, to each of the recipient companies of all the assets and liabilities of the company being divided; such transfer shall take effect with the assets and liabilities being divided in accordance with the allocation laid down in the draft terms of division or in Article 3 (3);

(b) the shareholders of the company being divided become shareholders of one or more of the recipient companies in accordance with the allocation laid down in the draft terms of division;

(c) the company being divided ceases to exist.

2. No shares in a recipient company shall be exchanged for shares held in the company being divided either:

(a) by that recipient company itself or by a person acting in his own name but on its behalf; or

(b) by the company being divided itself or by a person acting in his own name but on its behalf.

3. The foregoing shall not affect the laws of Member States which require the completion of special formalities for the transfer of certain assets, rights and obligations by a company being divided to be effective as against third parties. The recipient company or companies to which such assets, rights or obligations are transferred in accordance with the draft terms of division or with Article 3 (3) may carry out these formalities themselves; however, the laws of Member States may permit a company being divided to continue to carry out these formalities for a limited period which may not, save in exceptional circumstances, be fixed at more than six months from the date on which the division takes effect.

Article 18

The laws of Member States shall at least lay down rules governing the civil liability of members of the administrative or management bodies of a company being divided towards the shareholders of that company in respect of misconduct on the part of members of those bodies in preparing and implementing the division and the civil liability of the experts responsible for drawing up for that company the report provided for in Article 8 in respect of misconduct on the part of those experts in the performance of their duties.

Article 19

1. The laws of Member States may lay down nullity rules for divisions in accordance with the following conditions only:

(a) nullity must be ordered in a court judgment;

(b) divisions which have taken effect pursuant to Article 15 may be declared void only if there has been no judicial or administrative preventive supervision of their legality, or if they have not been drawn up and certified in due legal form, or if it is shown that the decision of the general meeting is void or voidable under national law;

(c) nullification proceedings may not be initiated more than six months after the date on which the division becomes effective as against the person alleging nullity or if the situation has been rectified;

(d) where it is possible to remedy a defect liable to render a division void, the competent court shall grant the companies involved a period of time within which to rectify the situation;

(e) a judgment declaring a division void shall be published in the manner prescribed by the laws of each Member State in accordance with Article 3 of Directive 68/151/EEC;

(f) where the laws of a Member State permit a third party to challenge such a judgment, he may do so only within six months of publication of the judgment in the manner prescribed by Directive 68/151/EEC;

(g) a judgment declaring a division void shall not of itself affect the validity of obligations owed by or in relation to the recipient companies which arose before the judgment was published and after the date referred to in Article 15;

(h) each of the recipient companies shall be liable for its obligations arising after the date on which the division took effect and before the date on which the decision pronouncing the nullity of the division was published. The company being divided shall also be liable for such obligations; Member States may provide that this liability be limited to the share of net assets transferred to the recipient company on whose account such obligations arose.

2. By way of derogation from paragraph 1 (a), the laws of a Member State may also provide for the nullity of a division to be ordered by an administrative authority if an appeal against such a decision lies to a court. Subparagraphs (b), (d), (e), (f), (g), and (h) shall apply by analogy to the administrative authority. Such nullification proceedings may not be initiated more than six months after the date referred to in Article 15.

3. The foregoing shall not affect the laws of the Member States on the nullity of a division pronounced following any supervision of legality.

Article 20

Without prejudice to Article 6, Member States need not require the division to be approved by the general meeting of the company being divided where the recipient companies together hold all the shares of the company being divided and all other securities conferring the right to vote at general meetings of the company being divided, and the following conditions, at least, are fulfilled:

(a) each of the companies involved in the operation must carry out the publication provided for in Article 4 at least one month before the operation takes effect;

(b) at least one month before the operation takes effect, all shareholders of companies involved in the operation must be entitled to inspect the documents specified in Article 9 (1), at their company's registered office. Article 9 (2) and (3) shall also apply;

(c) one or more shareholders of the company being divided holding a minimum percentage of the subscribed capital must be entitled to require that a general meeting of the company being divided be called to decide whether to approve the division. This minimum percentage may not be fixed at more than 5%. Member States may, however, provide for the exclusion of non voting shares from this calculation;

(d) where a general meeting of the company being divided, required for the approval of the division, is not summoned, the information provided for by Article 7 (3) covers any material change in the asset and liabilities after the date of preparation of the draft terms of division.

Chapter II

Division by the Formation of New Companies

Article 21

1. For the purposes of this Directive, 'division by the formation of new companies' means the operation whereby, after being wound up without going into liquidation, a company transfers to more than one newly-formed company all its assets and liabilities in exchange for the allocation to the shareholders of the company being divided of shares in the recipient companies, and possibly a cash payment not exceeding 10% of the nominal value of the shares allocated or, where they have no nominal value, of their accounting par value.

2. Article 4 (2) of Directive 78/855/EEC shall apply.

Article 22

1. Articles 3, 4, 5 and 7, 8 (1) and (2) and 9 to 19 of this Directive shall apply, without prejudice to Articles 11 and 12 of Directive 68/151/EEC, to division by the formation of new companies.

For this purpose, the expression 'companies involved in a division' shall refer to the company being divided and the expression 'recipient companies' shall refer to each of the new companies.

2. In addition to the information specified in Article 3 (2), the draft terms of division shall indicate the form, name and registered office of each of the new companies.

3. The draft terms of division and, if they are contained in a separate document, the memorandum or draft memorandum of association and the articles or draft articles of association of each of the new companies shall be approved at a general meeting of the company being divided.

4. Member States may provide that the report on the consideration other than in cash as referred to in Article 10 of Directive 77/91/EEC and the report on the draft terms of division as referred to in Article 8 (1) shall be drawn up by the same expert or experts.

5. Member States may provide that neither Article 8, nor Article 9 as regards the expert's report, shall apply where the shares in each of the new companies are allocated to the shareholders of the company being divided in proportion to their rights in the capital of that company.

Chapter III

Division under the Supervision of a Judicial Authority

Article 23

1. Member States may apply paragraph 2 where division operations are subject to the supervision of a judicial authority having the power:

(a) to call a general meeting of the shareholders of the company being divided in order to decide upon the division;

(b) to ensure that the shareholders of each of the companies involved in a division have received or can obtain at least the documents referred to in Article 9 in time to examine them before the date of the general meeting of their company called to decide upon the division. Where a Member State makes use of the option provided for in Article 6 the period must be long enough for the shareholders of the recipient companies to be able to exercise the rights conferred on them by that Article;

(c) to call any meeting of creditors of each of the companies involved in a division in order to decide upon the division;

(d) to ensure that the creditors of each of the companies involved in a division have received or can obtain at least the draft terms of division in time to examine them before the date referred to in (b);

(e) to approve the draft terms of division.

2. Where the judicial authority establishes that the conditions referred to in paragraph 1 (b) and (d) have been fulfilled and that no prejudice would be caused to shareholders or creditors, it may relieve the companies involved in the division from applying:

(a) Article 4, on condition that the adequate system of protection of the interest of the creditors referred to in Article 12 (1) covers all claims regardless of their date;

(b) the conditions referred to in Article 6 (a) and (b) where a Member State makes use of the option provided for in Article 6;

(c) Article 9, as regards the period and the manner prescribed for the inspection of the documents referred to therein.

Chapter IV

Other Operations Treated as Divisions

Article 24

Where, in the case of one of the operations specified in Article 1, the laws of a Member State permit the cash payment to exceed 10%, Chapters I, II and III shall apply.

Article 25

Where the laws of a Member State permit one of the operations specified in Article 1 without the company being divided ceasing to exist, Chapters I, II and III shall apply, except for Article 17 (1) (c).

Chapter V

Final Provisions

Article 26

1. The Member States shall bring into force before 1 January 1986, the laws, regulations and administrative provisions necessary for them to comply with this Directive provided that on that date they permit the operations to which this Directive applies. They shall immediately inform the Commission thereof.

2. Where, after the date mentioned in paragraph 1, a Member State permits division operations, it shall bring into force the provisions mentioned in that paragraph on the date on which it permits such operations. It shall immediately inform the Commission thereof.

3. However, provision may be made for a period of five years from the entry into force of the provisions referred to in paragraph 1 for the application of those provisions to unregistered companies in the United Kingdom and Ireland.

4. Member States need not apply Articles 12 and 13 as regards the holders of convertible debentures and other securities convertible into shares if, at the time when the provisions referred to in paragraph 1 or 2 come into force, the position of these holders in the event of a division has previously been determined by the conditions of issue.

5. Member States need not apply this Directive to divisions or to operations treated as divisions for the preparation or execution of which an act or formality required by national law has already been completed when the provisions referred to in paragraph 1 or 2 enter into force.

Article 27

This Directive is addressed to the Member States.

C. 6.

Seventh Council Directive 83/349/EEC of 13 June 1983 based on Article [44][1] (3) (g) of the Treaty on Consolidated Accounts[2]

THE COUNCIL OF THE EUROPEAN COMMUNITIES,

Having regard to the Treaty establishing the European Economic Community, and in particular Article [44(3)(g)][1] thereof,

Having regard to the proposal from the Commission,[3]

Having regard to the opinion of the European Parliament,[4]

Having regard to the opinion of the Economic and Social Committee,[5]

Whereas on 25 July 1978 the Council adopted Directive 78/660/EEC[6] on the co-ordination of national legislation governing the annual accounts of certain types of companies; whereas many companies are members of bodies of undertakings; whereas consolidated accounts must be drawn up so that financial information concerning such bodies of undertakings may be conveyed to members and third parties; whereas national legislation governing consolidated accounts must therefore be co-ordinated in order to achieve the objectives of comparability and equivalence in the information which companies must publish within the Community;

Whereas, in the determination of the conditions for consolidation, account must be taken not only of cases in which the power of control is based on a majority of voting rights but also of those in which it is based on agreements, where these are permitted; whereas, furthermore, Member States in which the possibility occurs must be permitted to cover cases in which in certain circumstances control has been effectively exercised on the basis of a minority holding; whereas the Member States must be permitted to cover the case of bodies of undertakings in which the undertakings exist on an equal footing with each other;

Whereas the aim of co-ordinating the legislation governing consolidated accounts is to protect the interests subsisting in companies with share capital; whereas such protection implies the principle of the preparation of consolidated accounts where such a company is a member of a body of undertakings, and that such accounts must be drawn up at least where such a company is a parent undertaking; whereas, furthermore, the cause of full information also requires that a subsidiary undertaking which is itself a parent undertaking draw up consolidated accounts; whereas, nevertheless, such a parent undertaking may, and, in certain circumstances, must be exempted from the obligation to draw up such consolidated accounts provided that its members and third parties are sufficiently protected;

Whereas, for bodies of undertakings not exceeding a certain size, exemption from the obligation to prepare consolidated accounts may be justified; whereas, accordingly, maximum limits must be set for such exemptions; whereas it follows therefrom that the Member States may either provide that it is sufficient to exceed the limit of one only of the three criteria for the exemption not to apply or adopt limits lower than those prescribed in the Directive;

Whereas consolidated accounts must give a true and fair view of the assets and liabilities, the financial position and the profit and loss of all the

---

[1] The number between brackets has been changed as from 1 May 1999 by article 12 of the Treaty of Amsterdam.
[2] OJ L 193, 18.6.1983, 1–17.
[3] OJ C 121, 2.6.1976, 2.
[4] OJ C 163, 10.7.1978, 60.
[5] OJ C 75, 26.3.1977, 5.
[6] OJ L 222, 14.8.1978, 11, Fourth Company Directive, reproduced supra under no. C. 4.

undertakings consolidated taken as a whole; whereas, therefore, consolidation should in principle include all of those undertakings; whereas such consolidation requires the full incorporation of the assets and liabilities and of the income and expenditure of those undertakings and the separate disclosure of the interests of persons outwith such bodies; whereas, however, the necessary corrections must be made to eliminate the effects of the financial relations between the undertakings consolidated;

Whereas a number of principles relating to the preparation of consolidated accounts and valuation in the context of such accounts must be laid down in order to ensure that items are disclosed consistently, and may readily be compared not only as regards the methods used in their valuation but also as regards the periods covered by the accounts;

Whereas participating interests in the capital of undertakings over which undertakings included in a consolidation exercise significant influence must be included in consolidated accounts by means of the equity method;

Whereas the notes on consolidated accounts must give details of the undertakings to be consolidated;

Whereas certain derogations originally provided for on a transitional basis in Directive 78/660/ EEC may be continued subject to review at a later date,

HAS ADOPTED THIS DIRECTIVE:

Section 1
Conditions for the Preparation of Consolidated Accounts

Article 1

1. A Member State shall require any undertaking governed by its national law to draw up consolidated accounts and a consolidated annual report if that undertaking (a parent undertaking):

(a) has a majority of the shareholders' or members' voting rights in another undertaking (a subsidiary undertaking); or

(b) has the right to appoint or remove a majority of the members of the administrative, management or supervisory body of another undertaking (a subsidiary undertaking) and is at the same time a shareholder in or member of that undertaking; or

(c) has the right to exercise a dominant influence over an undertaking (a subsidiary undertaking) of which it is a shareholder or member, pursuant to a contract entered into with that undertaking or to a provision in its memorandum or articles of association, where the law governing that subsidiary undertaking permits its being subject to such contracts or provisions. A Member State need not prescribe that a parent undertaking must be a shareholder in or member of its subsidiary undertaking. Those Member States the laws of which do not provide for such contracts or clauses shall not be required to apply this provision; or

(d) is a shareholder in or member of an undertaking, and:

(aa) a majority of the members of the administrative, management or supervisory bodies of that undertaking (a subsidiary undertaking) who have held office during the financial year, during the preceding financial year and up to the time when the consolidated accounts are drawn up, have been appointed, solely as a result of the exercise of its voting rights; or

(bb) controls alone, pursuant to an agreement with other shareholders in or members of that undertaking (a subsidiary undertaking), a majority of shareholders' or members' voting rights in that undertaking. The Member States may introduce more detailed provisions concerning the form and contents of such agreements.

The Member States shall prescribe at least the arrangements referred to in (bb) above.

They may make the application of (aa) above dependent upon the holding's representing 20% or more of the shareholders' or members' voting rights.

However, (aa) above shall not apply where another undertaking has the rights referred to in subparagraphs (a), (b) or (c) above with regard to that subsidiary undertaking.

[2. Apart from the cases mentioned in paragraph 1 the Member States may require any undertaking governed by their national law to draw up consolidated accounts and a consolidated annual report if:

(a) that undertaking (a parent undertaking) has the power to exercise, or actually exercises, dominant influence or control over another undertaking (the subsidiary undertaking); or

(b) that undertaking (a parent undertaking) and another undertaking (the subsidiary undertaking) are managed on a unified basis by the parent undertaking.]

¶ *Paragraph 2 of this article has been amended by article 2(1) of Directive 2003/51/EC, reproduced infra under no. C. 23.*

Article 2

1. For the purposes of Article 1 (1) (a), (b) and (d), the voting rights and the rights of appointment and removal of any other subsidiary undertaking as well as those of any person acting in his own name but on behalf of the parent undertaking or of another subsidiary undertaking must be added to those of the parent undertaking.

2. For the purposes of Article 1 (1) (a), (b) and (d), the rights mentioned in paragraph (1) above must be reduced by the rights:

(a) attaching to shares held on behalf of a person who is neither the parent undertaking nor a subsidiary thereof, or

(b) attaching to shares held by way of security, provided that the rights in question are exercised in accordance with the instructions received, or held in connection with the granting of loans as part of normal business activities, provided that the voting rights are exercised in the interests of the person providing the security.

3. For the purposes of Article 1 (1) (a) and (d), the total of the shareholders' or members' voting rights in the subsidiary undertaking must be reduced by the voting rights attaching to the shares held by that undertaking itself by a subsidiary undertaking of that undertaking or by a person acting in his own name but on behalf of those undertakings.

Article 3

1. Without prejudice to [Articles 13 and 15], a parent undertaking and all of its subsidiary undertakings shall be undertakings to be consolidated regardless of where the registered offices of such subsidiary undertakings are situated.

2. For the purposes of paragraph (1) above, any subsidiary undertaking of a subsidiary undertaking shall be considered a subsidiary undertaking of the parent undertaking which is the parent of the undertakings to be consolidated.

¶ *The reference in paragraph 1 has been replaced by article 2(2) of Directive 2003/51/EC, reproduced infra under no. C. 23.*

Article 4

1. For the purposes of this Directive, a parent undertaking and all of its subsidiary undertakings shall be undertakings to be consolidated where either the parent undertaking or one or more subsidiary undertakings is established as one of the following types of company:

(a) *in Germany:*
die Aktiengesellschaft, die Kommanditgesellschaft auf Aktien, die Gesellschaft mit beschränkter Haftung;

(b) *in Belgium:*
la société anonyme / de naamloze ven nootschap—la société en commandite par actions/de commanditaire vennootschap op aandelen—la société de personnes à responsabilité limitée/de personenvennootschap met beperkte aansprakelijkheid;

(c) *in Denmark:*
aktieselskaber, kommanditaktieselskaber, anpartsselskaber;

(d) *in France:*
la société anonyme, la société en commandite par actions, la société à responsabilité limitée;

(e) *in Greece:*
η ανωνυμη εταιρια, η εταιρια περιωρισμενης ευθυνης, η ετερορρυθμη κατα μετοχες εταιρια;

(f) *in Ireland:*
public companies limited by shares or by guarantee, private companies limited by shares or by guarantee;

(g) *in Italy:*
la società per azioni, la società in accomandita per azioni, la società a responsabilità limitata;

(h) *in Luxembourg:*
la société anonyme, la société en commandite par actions, la société à responsabilité limitée;

(i) *in the Netherlands:*
de naamloze vennootschap, de besloten vennootschap met beperkte aansprakelijkheid;

(j) *in the United Kingdom:*
public companies limited by shares or by guarantee, private companies limited by shares or by guarantee;

[(k) *in Spain:*
la sociedad anonima, la sociedad comanditaria por acciones, la sociedad de responsabilidad limitada;

(l) *in Portugal:*
a sociedade anonima de responsabilidade limitada, a sociedade em comandita por acçoes, a sociedade por quotas de responsabilidade limitada.]

[(m) *in Austria:*
die Aktiengesellschaft, die Gesellschaft mit beschränkter Haftung];

[(n) *in Finland:*
osakeyhtiö / aktiebolag];

[(o) *in Sweden:*
aktiebolag];

[(p) *in the Czech Republic:*
společnost s ručením omezenym, akciová společnost];

[(q) *in Estonia:*
aktsiaselts, osaühing];

[(r) *in Cyprus:*
Δημόσιες εταιρείες περιορισμένης ευθύνης με μετοχές, ή με εγγύηση, ιδιωτικές εταιρείες περιορισμένης ευθύνης με με τοχές ή με εγγύηση];

[(s) *in Latvia:*
akciju sabiedrība, sabiedrība ar ierobežotu atbildību];

[(t) *in Lithuania:*
akcinės bendrovės, uždarosios akcinėsbendrov ės];

[(u) *in Hungary:*
részvénytársaság, korlátolt felelösségű társaság];

[(v) *in Malta:*
kumpanija pubblika—public limited liability company, kumpannija privata—private limited liability company,

soċjeta in akkomandita bil-kapital maqsum f'azzjonijiet—partnership en commandite with the capital divided into shares];

[(w) *in Poland:*
spółka akcyjna, spółka z ograniczoną odpowiedzialnolcią, spółka komandytowo-akcyjna];

[(x) *in Slovenia:*
delniška družba, družba z omejeno odgovornostjo, komanditna delniška družba];

[(y) *in Slovakia:*
akciová spoločnost', spoločnost' s ručením obmedzenym.]

[The first subparagraph shall also apply where either the parent undertaking or one or more subsidiary undertakings is constituted as one of the types of company mentioned in Article 1 (1), second or third subparagraph of Directive 78/660/EEC.]

[2. The Member States may, however, grant exemption from the obligation imposed in Article 1 (1) where the parent undertaking is not constituted as one of the types of company mentioned in Article 4 (1) of this Directive or in Article 1 (1), second or third subparagraph of Directive 78/660/EEC.]

¶ *This Directive has been rendered applicable to Greece by the Act of Accession of the Hellenic Republic, Annex I(III)(c)(2) (OJ L 291, 19.11.1979), to Spain and Portugal by the Act of Accession of the Kingdom of Spain and the Portuguese Republic, Annex I(II)(d)(2) (OJ L 302, 15.11. 1985), to Austria, Sweden, and Finland by the Act of Accession of Austria, Sweden, and Finland (OJ C 241, 29.8.1994, 21), adapted by Council Decision 91/1/EC, Euratom, ECSC (OJ L 1, 1.1.1995, 1), and to the Czech Republic, Estonia, Cyprus, Latvia, Hungary, Malta, Poland, Slovenia, and Slovakia by the Act concerning the conditions of accession of the Czech Republic, the Republic of Estonia, the Republic of Cyprus, the Republic of Latvia, the Republic of Hungary, the Republic of Malta, the Republic of Poland, the Republic of Slovenia, and the Slovak Republic and the adjustments to the Treaties on which the European Union is founded (OJ L 236, 23.9.2003, 33).*

¶ *The second subparagraph of paragraph 1 has been inserted by article 2(1) and paragraph 2 has been replaced by article 2(2) of Directive 90/605/EEC, reproduced infra under no. C. 12. Member States may provide that these provisions shall first apply to the annual accounts and consolidated accounts for financial years beginning on 1 January 1995 or during the 1995 calendar year.*

Article 5

1. A Member State may grant exemption from the obligation imposed in Article 1 (1) where the parent undertaking is a financial holding company as defined in Article 5 (3) of Directive 78/660/EEC, and:

(a) it has not intervened during the financial year, directly or indirectly, in the management of a subsidiary undertaking;

(b) it has not exercised the voting rights attaching to its participating interest in respect of the appointment of a member of a subsidiary undertaking's administrative, management or supervisory bodies during the financial year or the five preceding financial years or, where the exercise of voting rights was necessary for the operation of the administrative, management or supervisory bodies of the subsidiary undertaking, no shareholder in or member of the parent undertaking with majority voting rights or member of the administrative, management or supervisory bodies of that understanding or of a member thereof with majority voting rights is a member of the administrative, management or supervisory bodies of the subsidiary undertaking and the members of those bodies so appointed have fulfilled their functions without any interference or influence on the part of the parent undertaking or of any of its subsidiary undertakings;

(c) it has made loans only to undertakings in which it holds participating interests. Where such loans have been made to other parties, they must have been repaid by the end of the previous financial year; and

(d) the exemption is granted by an administrative authority after fulfilment of the above conditions has been checked.

2. (a) Where a financial holding company has been exempted, Article 43 (2) of Directive 78/660/EEC shall not apply to its annual accounts with respect to any majority holdings in subsidiary undertakings as from the date provided for in Article 49 (2).

(b) The disclosures in respect of such majority holdings provided for in point 2 of Article 43 (1) of Directive 78/660/EEC may be omitted when their nature is such that they would be seriously prejudicial to the company, to its shareholders or members or to one of its subsidiaries. A Member State may make such omissions subject to prior administrative or judicial authorisation. Any such omission must be disclosed in the notes on the accounts.

Article 6

1. Without prejudice to Articles 4 (2) and 5, a Member State may provide for an exemption from the obligation imposed in Article 1 (1) if as at the balance sheet date of a parent undertaking the undertakings to be consolidated do not together, on the basis of their latest annual accounts, exceed the limits of two of the three criteria laid down in Article 27 of Directive 78/660/EEC.

2. A Member State may require or permit that the set-off referred to in Article 19 (1) and the elimination referred to in Article 26 (1) (a) and (b) be not effected when the aforementioned limits are calculated. In that case, the limits for the balance sheet total and net turnover criteria shall be increased by 20%.

3. Article 12 of Directive 78/660/EEC shall apply to the above criteria.

[4. This Article shall not apply where one of the undertakings to be consolidated is a company whose securities are admitted to trading on a regulated market of any Member State within the meaning of Article 1(13) of Council Directive 93/22/EEC of 10 May 1993 on investment services in the securities field.[7]]

5. [. . .]

¶ *Paragraph 4 of this article has been replaced by article 2(3)(a) of Directive 2003/51/EC, reproduced infra under no. C. 23.*
¶ *Paragraph 5 of this article has been repealed by article 2(3)(b) of Directive 2003/51/EC, reproduced infra under no. C. 23.*

---

[7] OJ L 141, 11.6.1993, 27, reproduced infra under no. S. 14. Directive as last amended by Directive 2002/87/EC of the European Parliament and of the Council (OJ L 35, 11.2.2003, 1), reproduced supra under no. B. 38.

Article 7

1. Notwithstanding Articles 4 (2), 5 and 6, a Member State shall exempt from the obligation imposed in Article 1 (1) any parent undertaking governed by its national law which is also a subsidiary undertaking if its own parent undertaking is governed by the law of a Member State in the following two cases:

(a) where that parent undertaking holds all of the shares in the exempted undertaking. The shares in that undertaking held by members of its administrative, management or supervisory bodies pursuant to an obligation in law or in the memorandum or articles of association shall be ignored for this purpose; or

(b) where that parent undertaking holds 90% or more of the shares in the exempted undertaking and the remaining shareholders in or members of that undertaking have approved the exemption.

[. . .]

2. Exemption shall be conditional upon compliance with all of the following conditions:

(a) the exempted undertaking and, without prejudice to [Articles 13 and 15], all of its subsidiary undertakings must be consolidated in the accounts of a larger body of undertakings, the parent undertaking of which is governed by the law of a Member State;

(b) (aa) the consolidated accounts referred to in (a) above and the consolidated annual report of the larger body of undertakings must be drawn up by the parent undertaking of that body and audited, according to the law of the Member State by which the parent undertaking of that larger body of undertakings is governed, in accordance with this Directive;

(bb) the consolidated accounts referred to in (a) above and the consolidated annual report referred to in (aa) above, the report by the person responsible for auditing those accounts and, where appropriate, the appendix referred to in Article 9 must be published for the exempted undertaking in the manner prescribed by the law of the Member State governing that undertaking in accordance with Article 38. That Member State may require that those documents be published in its official language and that the translation be certified;

(c) the notes on the annual accounts of the exempted undertaking must disclose:

(aa) the name and registered office of the parent undertaking that draws up the consolidated accounts referred to in (a) above; and

(bb) the exemption from the obligation to draw up consolidated accounts and a consolidated annual report.

[3. This Article shall not apply to companies whose securities are admitted to trading on a regulated market of any Member State within the meaning of Article 1(13) of Directive 93/22/EEC.]

¶ *The second sentence of paragraph 1(b) has been deleted, the reference in paragraph 2(a) and paragraph 3 has been replaced by article 2(4) of Directive 2003/51/EC, reproduced infra under no. C. 23.*

Article 8

1. In cases not covered by Article 7 (1), a Member State may, without prejudice to Articles 4 (2), 5 and 6, exempt from the obligation imposed in Article 1 (1) any parent undertaking governed by its national law which is also a subsidiary undertaking, the parent undertaking of which is governed by the law of a Member State, provided that all the conditions set out in Article 7 (2) are fulfilled and that the shareholders in or members of the exempted undertaking who own a minimum proportion of the subscribed capital of that undertaking have not requested the preparation of consolidated accounts at least six months before the end of the financial year. The Member States may fix that proportion at not more than 10% for public limited liability companies and for limited partnerships with share capital, and at not more than 20% for undertakings of other types.

2. A Member State may not make it a condition for this exemption that the parent undertaking which prepared the consolidated accounts

described in Article 7 (2) (a) must also be governed by its national law.

3. A Member State may not make exemption subject to conditions concerning the preparation and auditing of the consolidated accounts referred to in Article 7 (2) (a).

Article 9

1. A Member State may make the exemptions provided for in Articles 7 and 8 dependent upon the disclosure of additional information, in accordance with this Directive, in the consolidated accounts referred to in Article 7 (2) (a), or in an appendix thereto, if that information is required of undertakings governed by the national law of that Member State which are obliged to prepare consolidated accounts and are in the same circumstances.

2. A Member State may also make exemption dependent upon the disclosure, in the notes on the consolidated accounts referred to in Article 7 (2) (a), or in the annual accounts of the exempted undertaking, of all or some of the following information regarding the body of undertakings, the parent undertaking of which is exempting from the obligation to draw up consolidated accounts:
– the amount of the fixed assets,
– the net turnover,
– the profit or loss for the financial year and the amount of the capital and reserves,
– the average number of persons employed during the financial year.

Article 10

Articles 7 to 9 shall not affect any Member State's legislation on the drawing up of consolidated accounts or consolidated annual reports in so far as those documents are required:
– for the information of employees or their representatives, or
– by an administrative or judicial authority for its own purposes.

Article 11

1. Without prejudice to Articles 4 (2), 5 and 6, a Member State may exempt from the obligation imposed in Article 1 (1) any parent undertaking governed by its national law which is also a subsidiary undertaking of a parent undertaking not governed by the law of a Member State, if all of the following conditions are fulfilled:

(a) the exempted undertaking and, without prejudice to [Articles 13 and 15,] all of its subsidiary undertakings must be consolidated in the accounts of a larger body of undertakings;

(b) the consolidated accounts referred to in (a) above and, where appropriate, the consolidated annual report must be drawn up in accordance with this Directive or in a manner equivalent to consolidated accounts and consolidated annual reports drawn up in accordance with this Directive;

(c) the consolidated accounts referred to in (a) above must have been audited by one or more persons authorised to audit accounts under the national law governing the undertaking which drew them up.

2. Articles 7 (2) (b) (bb) and (c) and 8 to 10 shall apply.

3. A Member State may provide for exemptions under this Article only if it provides for the same exemptions under Articles 7 to 10.

¶ *The reference between square brackets in paragraph 1(a) of this article has been amended by article 2(5) of Directive 2003/51/EC, reproduced infra under no. C. 23.*

Article 12

1. Without prejudice to Articles 1 to 10, a Member State may require any undertaking governed by its national law to draw up consolidated accounts and a consolidated annual report if:

(a) that undertaking and one or more other undertakings with which it is not connected, as described in Article 1 (1) or (2), are managed on a unified basis pursuant to a contract concluded with that undertaking or provisions in the memorandum or articles of association of those undertakings; or

(b) the administrative, management or supervisory bodies of that undertaking and of one or more other undertakings with which it is not connected, as described in Article 1 (1) or (2), consist for the major part of the same persons in office during the financial year and until the consolidated accounts are drawn up.

2. Where paragraph (1) above is applied, undertakings related as defined in that paragraph together with all of their subsidiary undertakings shall be undertakings to be consolidated, as defined in this Directive, where one or more of those undertakings is established as one of the types of company listed in Article 4.

3. Articles 3, 4 (2), 5, 6, 13 to 28, 29 (1), (3), (4) and (5), 30 to 38 and 39 (2) shall apply to the consolidated accounts and the consolidated annual report covered by this Article, references to parent undertakings being understood to refer to all the undertakings specified in paragraph 1 above. Without prejudice to Article 19 (2), however, the items 'capital', 'share premium account', 'revaluation reserve', 'reserves', 'profit or loss brought forward', and 'profit or loss for the financial year' to be included in the consolidated accounts shall be the aggregate amounts attributable to each of the undertakings specified in paragraph 1.

Article 13

1. An undertaking need not be included in consolidated accounts where it is not material for the purposes of Article 16 (3).

2. Where two or more undertakings satisfy the requirements of paragraph 1 above, they must nevertheless be included in consolidated accounts if, as a whole, they are material for the purposes of Article 16 (3).

3. In addition, an undertaking need not be included in consolidated accounts where:

(a) severe long-term restrictions substantially hinder:
    (aa) the parent undertaking in the exercise of its rights over the assets or management of that undertaking; or
    (bb) the exercise of unified management of that undertaking where it is in one of the relationships defined in Article 12 (1); or

(b) the information necessary for the preparation of consolidated accounts in accordance with this Directive cannot be obtained without disproportionate expense or undue delay; or

(c) the shares of that undertaking are held exclusively with a view to their subsequent resale.

Article 14

[. . .]

¶ *This article has been repealed by article 2(6) of Directive 2003/51/EC, reproduced infra under no. C. 23.*

Article 15

1. A Member State may, for the purposes of Article 16 (3), permit the omission from consolidated accounts of any parent undertaking not carrying on any industrial or commercial activity which holds shares in a subsidiary undertaking on the basis of a joint arrangement with one or more undertakings not included, in the consolidated accounts.

2. The annual accounts of the parent undertaking shall be attached to the consolidated accounts.

3. Where use is made of this derogation, either Article 59 of Directive 78/660/EEC shall apply to the parent undertaking's annual accounts or the information which would have resulted from its application must be given in the notes on those accounts.

Section 2

The Preparation of Consolidated Accounts

Article 16

1. Consolidated accounts shall comprise the consolidated balance sheet, the consolidated profits-and-loss account and the notes on the accounts. These documents shall constitute a composite whole.

[Member States may permit or require the inclusion of other statements in the consolidated accounts in addition to the documents referred to in the first subparagraph.]

2. Consolidated accounts shall be drawn up clearly and in accordance with this Directive.

3. Consolidated accounts shall give a true and fair view of the assets, liabilities, financial position and profit or loss of the undertakings included therein taken as a whole.

4. Where the application of the provisions of this Directive would not be sufficient to give a true and fair view within the meaning of paragraph 3 above, additional information must be given.

5. Where, in exceptional cases, the application of a provision of Articles 17 to 35 and 39 is incompatible with the obligation imposed in paragraph 3 above, that provision must be departed from in order to give a true and fair view within the meaning of paragraph 3. Any such departure must be disclosed in the notes on the accounts together with an explanation of the reasons for it and a statement of its effect on the assets, liabilities, financial position and profit or loss. The Member States may define the exceptional cases in question and lay down the relevant special rules.

6. A Member State may require or permit the disclosure in the consolidated accounts of other information as well as that which must be disclosed in accordance with this Directive.

¶ *The second subparagraph to paragraph 1 of this article has been added by article 2(7) of Directive 2003/51/EC, reproduced infra under no. C. 23.*

Article 17

1. [Articles 3 to 10a,] 13 to 26 and 28 to 30 of Directive 78/660/EEC shall apply in respect of the layout of consolidated accounts, without prejudice to the provisions of this Directive and taking account of the essential adjustments resulting from the particular characteristics of consolidated accounts as compared with annual accounts.

2. Where there are special circumstances which would entail undue expense a Member State may permit stocks to be combined in the consolidated accounts.

¶ *The reference in paragraph 1 of this article has been amended by article 2(8) of Directive 2003/51/EC, reproduced infra under no. C. 23.*

Article 18

The assets and liabilities of undertakings included in a consolidation shall be incorporated in full in the consolidated balance sheet.

Article 19

1. The book values of shares in the capital of undertakings included in a consolidation shall be set-off against the proportion which they represent of the capital and reserves of those undertakings:

(a) That set-off shall be effected on the basis of book values as at the date as at which such undertakings are included in the consolidations for the first time. Differences arising from such set-offs shall as far as possible be entered directly against those items in the consolidated balance sheet which have values above or below their book values.

(b) A Member State may require or permit set-offs on the basis of the values of identifiable assets and liabilities as at the date of acquisition of the shares or, in the event of acquisition in two or more stages, as at the date on which the undertaking became a subsidiary.

(c) Any difference remaining after the application of (a) or resulting from the application of (b) shall be shown as a separate item in the consolidated balance sheet with an appropriate heading. That item, the methods used and any significant changes in relation to the preceding financial year must be explained in the notes on the accounts. Where the offsetting of positive and negative differences is authorised by a Member State, a breakdown of such differences must also be given in the notes on the accounts.

2. However, paragraph 1 above shall not apply to shares in the capital of the parent undertaking held either by that undertaking itself or by another undertaking included in the consolidation. In the consolidated accounts such shares shall be treated as own shares in accordance with Directive 78/660/EEC.

Article 20

1. A Member State may require or permit the book values of shares held in the capital of an

undertaking included in the consolidation to be set-off against the corresponding percentage of capital only, provided that:

(a) the shares held represent at least 90% of the nominal value or, in the absence of a nominal value, of the accounting par value of the shares of that undertaking other than shares of the kind described in Article 29 (2) (a) of Directive 77/91/EEC;[8]

(b) the proportion referred to in (a) above has been attained pursuant to an arrangement providing for the issue of shares by an undertaking included in the consolidation; and

(c) the arrangement referred to in (b) above did not include a cash payment exceeding 10% of the nominal value or, in the absence of a nominal value, of the accounting par value of the shares issued.

2. Any difference arising under paragraph 1 above shall be added to or deducted from consolidated reserves as appropriate.

3. The application of the method described in paragraph 1 above, the resulting movement in reserves and the names and registered offices of the undertakings concerned shall be disclosed in the notes on the accounts.

Article 21

The amount attributable to shares in subsidiary undertakings included in the consolidation held by persons other than the undertakings included in the consolidation shall be shown in the consolidated balance sheet as a separate item with an appropriate heading.

Article 22

The income and expenditure of undertakings included in a consolidation shall be incorporated in full in the consolidated profit-and-loss account.

Article 23

The amount of any profit or loss attributable to shares in subsidiary undertakings included in the consolidation held by persons other than the undertakings included in the consolidation shall be shown in the consolidated profit-and-loss account as a separate item with an appropriate heading.

Article 24

Consolidated accounts shall be drawn up in accordance with the principles enunciated in Articles 25 to 28.

Article 25

1. The methods of consolidation must be applied consistently from one financial year to another.

2. Derogations from the provisions of paragraph 1 above shall be permitted in exceptional cases. Any such derogations must be disclosed in the notes on the accounts and the reasons for them given together with an assessment of their effect on the assets, liabilities, financial position and profit or loss of the undertakings included in the consolidation taken as a whole.

Article 26

1. Consolidated accounts shall show the assets, liabilities, financial positions and profits or losses of the undertakings included in a consolidation as if the latter were a single undertaking. In particular:

(a) debts and claims between the undertakings included in a consolidation shall be eliminated from the consolidated accounts;

(b) income and expenditure relating to transactions between the undertakings included in a consolidation shall be eliminated from the consolidated accounts;

(c) where profits and losses resulting from transactions between the undertakings included in a consolidation are included in the book values of assets, they shall be eliminated from the consolidated accounts. Pending subsequent co-ordination, however, a Member State may allow the eliminations mentioned above to be effected in proportion to the percentage of the capital held by the

---

[8] OJ L 26, 31.1.1977, 1, Second Company Directive, reproduced supra under no. C. 2.

parent undertaking in each of the subsidiary undertakings included in the consolidation.

2. A Member State may permit derogations from the provisions of paragraph 1 (c) above where a transaction has been concluded according to normal market conditions and where the elimination of the profit or loss would entail undue expense. Any such derogations must be disclosed and where the effect on the assets, liabilities, financial position and profit or loss of the undertakings, included in the consolidation, taken as a whole, is material, that fact must be disclosed in the notes on the consolidated accounts.

3. Derogations from the provisions of paragraph 1 (a), (b) or (c) above shall be permitted where the amounts concerned are not material for the purposes of Article 16 (3).

Article 27

1. Consolidated accounts must be drawn up as at the same date as the annual accounts of the parent undertaking.

2. A Member State may, however, require or permit consolidated accounts to be drawn up as at another date in order to take account of the balance sheet dates of the largest number or the most important of the undertakings included in the consolidation. Where use is made of this derogation that fact shall be disclosed in the notes on the consolidated accounts together with the reasons therefor. In addition, account must be taken or disclosure made of important events concerning the assets and liabilities, the financial position or the profit or loss of an undertaking included in a consolidation which have occurred between that undertaking's balance sheet date and the consolidated balance sheet date.

3. Where an undertaking's balance sheet date precedes the consolidated balance sheet date by more than three months, that undertaking shall be consolidated on the basis of interim accounts drawn up as at the consolidated balance sheet date.

Article 28

If the composition of the undertakings included in a consolidation has changed significantly in the course of a financial year, the consolidated accounts must include information which makes the comparison of successive sets of consolidated accounts meaningful. Where such a change is a major one, a Member State may require or permit this obligation to be fulfilled by the preparation of an adjusted opening balance sheet and an adjusted profit-and-loss account.

Article 29

[1. Assets and liabilities to be included in consolidated accounts shall be valued according to uniform methods and in accordance with Sections 7 and 7a and Article 60 of Directive 78/660/EEC.]

2. (a) An undertaking which draws up consolidated accounts must apply the same methods of valuation as in its annual accounts. However, a Member State may require or permit the use in consolidated accounts of other methods of valuation in accordance with the abovementioned Articles of Directive 78/660/EEC.

(b) Where use is made of this derogation that fact shall be disclosed in the notes on the consolidated accounts and the reasons therefore given.

3. Where assets and liabilities to be included in consolidated accounts have been valued by undertakings included in the consolidation by methods differing from those used for the consolidation, they must be revalued in accordance with the methods used for the consolidation, unless the results of such revaluation are not material for the purposes of Article 16 (3). Departures from this principle shall be permitted in exceptional cases. Any such departures shall be disclosed in the notes on the consolidated accounts and the reasons for them given.

4. Account shall be taken in the consolidated balance sheet and in the consolidated profit-and-loss account of any difference arising on consolidation between the tax chargeable for the financial year and for preceding financial years and the amount of tax paid or payable in respect of those years, provided that it is probable that an actual charge to tax will arise within the foreseeable future for one of the undertakings included in the consolidation.

5. Where assets to be included in consolidated accounts have been the subject of exceptional value adjustments solely for tax purposes, they shall be incorporated in the consolidated accounts only after those adjustments have been eliminated. A Member State may, however, require or permit that such assets be incorporated in the consolidated accounts without the elimination of the adjustments, provided that their amounts, together with the reasons for them, are disclosed in the notes on the consolidated accounts.

¶ *Paragraph 1 has been replaced by article 2(1) of Directive 2001/65/EC, reproduced infra under no. C. 18.*

Article 30

1. A separate item as defined in Article 19 (1) (c) which corresponds to a positive consolidation difference shall be dealt with in accordance with the rules laid down in Directive 78/660/EEC for the item 'goodwill'.

2. A Member State may permit a positive consolidation difference to be immediately and clearly deducted from reserves.

Article 31

An amount shown as a separate item, as defined in Article 19 (1) (c), which corresponds to a negative consolidation difference may be transferred to the consolidated profit-and-loss account only:

(a) where that difference corresponds to the expectation at the date of acquisition of unfavourable future results in that undertaking, or to the expectation of costs which that undertaking would incur, in so far as such an expectation materialises; or

(b) in so far as such a difference corresponds to a realised gain.

Article 32

1. Where an undertaking included in a consolidation manages another undertaking jointly with one or more undertakings not included in that consolidation, a Member State may require or permit the inclusion of that other undertaking in the consolidated accounts in proportion to the rights in its capital held by the undertaking included in the consolidation.

2. Articles 13 to 31 shall apply mutatis mutandis to the proportional consolidation referred to in paragraph 1 above.

3. Where this Article is applied, Article 33 shall not apply if the undertaking proportionally consolidated is an associated undertaking as defined in Article 33.

Article 33

1. Where an undertaking included in a consolidation exercises a significant influence over the operating and financial policy of an undertaking not included in the consolidation (an associated undertaking) in which it holds a participating interest, as defined in Article 17 of Directive 78/660/EEC, that participating interest shall be shown in the consolidated balance sheet as a separate item with an appropriate heading. An undertaking shall be presumed to exercise a significant influence over another undertaking where it has 20% or more of the shareholders' or members' voting rights in that undertaking. Article 2 shall apply.

2. When this Article is applied for the first time to a participating interest covered by paragraph 1 above, that participating interest shall be shown in the consolidated balance sheet either:

(a) at its book value calculated in accordance with the valuation rules laid down in Directive 78/660/EEC. The difference between that value and the amount corresponding to the proportion of capital and reserves represented by that participating interest shall be disclosed separately in the consolidated balance sheet or in the notes on the accounts. That difference shall be calculated as at the date as at which that method is used for the first time; or

(b) at an amount corresponding to the proportion of the associated undertaking's capital and reserves represented by that participating interest. The difference between that amount and the book value calculated in accordance with the valuation rules laid down in Directive 78/660/EEC shall be disclosed separately in the consolidated balance sheet or in the notes on the accounts. That difference shall be calculated as at the date as at which that method is used for the first time.

(c) A Member State may prescribe the application of one or other of (a) and (b) above. The consolidated balance sheet or the notes on the accounts must indicate whether (a) or (b) has been used.

(d) In addition, for the purposes of (a) and (b) above, a Member State may require or permit the calculation of the difference as at the date of acquisition of the shares or, where they were acquired in two or more stages, as at the date on which the undertaking became an associated undertaking.

3. Where an associated undertaking's assets or liabilities have been valued by methods other than those used for consolidation in accordance with Article 29 (2), they may, for the purpose of calculating the difference referred to in paragraph 2 (a) or (b) above, be revalued by the methods used for consolidation. Where such revaluation has not been carried out that fact must be disclosed in the notes on the accounts. A Member State may require such revaluation.

4. The book value referred to in paragraph 2 (a) above, or the amount corresponding to the proportion of the associated undertaking's capital and reserves referred to in paragraph 2 (b) above, shall be increased or reduced by the amount of any variation which has taken place during the financial year in the proportion of the associated undertaking's capital and reserves represented by that participating interest; it shall be reduced by the amount of the dividends relating to that participating interest.

5. In so far as the positive difference referred to in paragraph 2 (a) or (b) above cannot be related to any category of assets or liabilities it shall be dealt with in accordance with Articles 30 and 39 (3).

6. The proportion of the profit or loss of the associated undertakings attributable to such participating interests shall be shown in the consolidated profit-and-loss account as a separate item under an appropriate heading.

7. The eliminations referred to in Article 26 (1) (c) shall be effected in so far as the facts are known or can be ascertained. Article 26 (2) and (3) shall apply.

8. Where an associated undertaking draws up consolidated accounts, the foregoing provisions shall apply to the capital and reserves shown in such consolidated accounts.

9. This Article need not be applied where the participating interest in the capital of the associated undertaking is not material for the purposes of Article 16 (3).

Article 34

In addition to the information required under other provisions of this Directive the notes on the accounts must set out information in respect of the following matters at least:

1. The valuation methods applied to the various items in the consolidated accounts, and the methods employed in calculating the value adjustments. For items included in the consolidated accounts which are or were originally expressed in foreign currency the bases of conversion used to express them in the currency in which the consolidated accounts are drawn up must be disclosed.

2. (a) The names and registered offices of the undertakings included in the consolidation; the proportion of the capital held in undertakings included in the consolidation, other than the parent undertaking, by the undertakings included in the consolidation or by persons acting in their own names but on behalf of those undertakings; which of the conditions referred to in Articles 1 and 12 (1) following application of Article 2 has formed the basis on which the consolidation has been carried out. The latter disclosure may, however, be omitted where consolidation has been carried out on the basis of Article 1 (1) (a) and where the proportion of the capital and the proportion of the voting rights held are the same.

(b) The same information must be given in respect of undertakings excluded from a consolidation pursuant to [Article 13 and] an explanation must be given for the exclusion of the undertakings referred to in Article 13.

3. (a) The names and registered offices of undertakings associated with an undertaking included in the consolidation as described in Article 33 (1) and the proportion of their capital held by undertakings included in the consolidation or by persons acting in their own names but on behalf of those undertakings.

(b) The same information must be given in respect of the associated undertakings referred to in Article 33 (9), together with the reasons for applying that provision.

4. The names and registered offices of undertakings proportionally consolidated pursuant to Article 32, the factors on which joint management is based, and the proportion of their capital held by the undertakings included in the consolidation or by persons acting in their own names but on behalf of those undertakings.

5. The name and registered office of each of the undertakings, other than those referred to in paragraphs 2, 3 and 4 above, in which undertakings included in the consolidation [. . .], either themselves or through persons acting in their own names but on behalf of those undertakings, hold at least a percentage of the capital which the Member States cannot fix at more than 20%, showing the proportion of the capital held, the amount of the capital and reserves, and the profit or loss for the latest financial year of the undertaking concerned for which accounts have been adopted. This information may be omitted where, for the purposes of Article 16 (3), it is of negligible importance only. The information concerning capital and reserve and the profit or loss may also be omitted where the undertaking concerned does not publish its balance sheet and where less than 50% of its capital is held (directly or indirectly) by the above-mentioned undertakings.

6. The total amount shown as owed in the consolidated balance sheet and becoming due and payable after more than five years, as well as the total amount shown as owed in the consolidated balance sheet and covered by valuable security furnished by undertakings included in the consolidation, with an indication of the nature and form of the security.

7. The total amount of any financial commitments that are not included in the consolidated balance sheet, in so far as this information is of assistance in assessing the financial position of the undertakings included in the consolidation taken as a whole. Any commitments concerning pensions and affiliated undertakings which are not included in the consolidation must be disclosed separately.

[(7a) The nature and business purpose of any arrangements that are not included in the consolidated balance sheet, and the financial impact of those arrangements, provided that the risks or benefits arising from such arrangements are material and in so far as the disclosure of such risks or benefits is necessary for assessing the financial position of the undertakings included in the consolidation taken as a whole.

(7b) The transactions, save for intra-group transactions, entered into by the parent undertaking, or by other undertakings included in the consolidation, with related parties, including the amounts of such transactions, the nature of the related party relationship as well as other information about the transactions necessary for an understanding of the financial position of the undertakings included in the consolidation taken as a whole, if such transactions are material and have not been concluded under normal market conditions. Information about individual transactions may be aggregated according to their nature except where separate information is necessary for an understanding of the effects of the related party transactions on the financial position of the undertakings included in the consolidation taken as a whole.]

8. The consolidated net turnover as defined in Article 28 of Directive 78/660/EEC, broken down by categories of activity and into geographical markets in so far as, taking account of the manner in which the sale of products and the provision of services falling within the ordinary activities of the undertakings included in the consolidation taken as a whole are organised, these categories and markets differ substantially from one another.

9. (a) The average number of persons employed during the financial year by undertakings included in the consolidation broken down by categories and, if they are not disclosed separately in the consolidated profit-and-loss account, the staff costs relating to the financial year.

(b) The average number of persons employed during the financial year by undertakings to which Article 32 has been applied shall be disclosed separately.

10. The extent to which the calculation of the consolidated profit or loss for the financial year has been affected by a valuation of the items which, by way of derogation from the principles enunciated in [Articles 31 and 34 to 42c] of Directive 78/660/EEC and in Article 29 (5) of this Directive, was made in the financial year in question or in an earlier financial year with a view to obtaining tax relief. Where the influence of such a valuation on the future tax charges of the undertakings included in the consolidation taken as a whole is material, details must be disclosed.

11. The difference between the tax charged to the consolidated profit-and-loss account for the financial year and to those for earlier financial years and the amount of tax payable in respect of those years, provided that this difference is material for the purposes of future taxation. This amount may also be disclosed in the balance sheet as a cumulative amount under a separate item with an appropriate heading.

12. The amount of the emoluments granted in respect of the financial year to the members of the administrative, managerial and supervisory bodies of the parent undertaking by reason of their responsibilities in the parent undertaking and its subsidiary undertakings, and any commitments arising or entered into under the same conditions in respect of retirement pension for former members of those bodies, with an indication of the total for each category. A Member State may require that emoluments granted by reason of responsibilities assumed in undertakings linked as described in Article 32 or 33 shall also be included with the information specified in the first sentence.

13. The amount of advances and credits granted to the members of the administrative, managerial and supervisory bodies of the parent undertaking by that undertaking or by one of its subsidiary undertakings, with indications of the interest rates, main conditions and any amounts repaid, as well as commitments entered into on their behalf by way of guarantee of any kind with an indication of the total for each category. A Member State may require that advances and credits granted by undertakings linked as described in Article 32 or 33 shall also be included with the information specified in the first sentence.

[14. Where valuation at fair value of financial instruments has been applied in accordance with Section 7a of Directive 78/660/EEC:

(a) the significant assumptions underlying the valuation models and techniques where fair values have been determined in accordance with Article 42b(1)(b) of that Directive;

(b) per category of financial instruments, the fair value, the changes in value included directly in the profit-and-loss account as well as, in accordance with Article 42c of that Directive, changes included in the fair value reserve;

(c) for each class of derivative financial instruments, information about the extent and the nature of the instruments, including significant terms and conditions that may affect the amount, timing and certainty of future cash flows; and

(d) a table showing movements in the fair value reserve during the financial year.

15. Where valuation at fair value of financial instruments has not been applied in accordance with Section 7a of Directive 78/660/EEC:

(a) for each class of derivative instruments:
(i) the fair value of the instruments, if such a value can be determined by any of the methods prescribed in Article 42b(1) of that Directive;
(ii) information about the extent and the nature of the instruments; and

(b) for financial fixed assets covered by Article 42a of that Directive, carried at an amount in

excess of their fair value and without use being made of the option to make a value adjustment in accordance with Article 35(1)(c)(aa) of that Directive:
(i) the book value and the fair value of either the individual assets or appropriate groupings of those individual assets;
(ii) the reasons for not reducing the book value, including the nature of the evidence that provides the basis for the belief that the book value will be recovered.]

[(16) Separately, the total fees for the financial year charged by the statutory auditor or audit firm for the statutory audit of the consolidated accounts, the total fees charged for other assurance services, the total fees charged for tax advisory services and the total fees charged for other non-audit services.]

¶ *The reference between square brackets in points (2)(b) of this article have been amended by article 2(9)(a) of Directive 2003/51/EC, reproduced infra under no. C. 23.*
¶ *The reference between square brackets in point (5) of this article have been deleted by article 2(9)(b) of Directive 2003/51/EC, reproduced infra under no. C. 23.*
¶ *Points 7a and 7b have been added by article 2(1) of Directive 2006/46/EC, reproduced infra under no. C. 31.*
¶ *The references between square brackets in point 10 have been replaced by article 2(2)(a) of Directive 2001/65/EC, reproduced infra under no. C. 18.*
¶ *Paragraphs 14 and 15 have been added by article 2(2)(b) of Directive 2001/65/EC, reproduced infra under no. C. 18.*
¶ *Paragraph 16 has been added by article 49(2) of Directive 2006/43/EC, reproduced infra under no. C. 30.*

Article 35

1. A Member State may allow the disclosures prescribed in Article 34 (2), (3), (4) and (5):

(a) to take the form of a statement deposited in accordance with Article 3 (1) and (2) of Directive 68/151/EEC; this must be disclosed in the notes on the accounts;

(b) to be omitted when their nature is such that they would be seriously prejudicial to any of the undertakings affected by these provisions. A Member State may make such omissions subject to prior administrative or judicial authorisation. Any such omission must be disclosed in the notes on the accounts.

2. Paragraph (1) (b) shall also apply to the information prescribed in Article 34 (8).

Section 3
The Consolidated Annual Report

Article 36

[1. The consolidated annual report shall include at least a fair review of the development and performance of the business and of the position of the undertakings included in the consolidation taken as a whole, together with a description of the principal risks and uncertainties that they face.

The review shall be a balanced and comprehensive analysis of the development and performance of the business and of the position of the undertakings included in the consolidation taken as a whole, consistent with the size and complexity of the business. To the extent necessary for an understanding of such development, performance or position, the analysis shall include both financial and, where appropriate, non-financial key performance indicators relevant to the particular business, including information relating to environmental and employee matters.

In providing its analysis, the consolidated annual report shall, where appropriate, provide references to and additional explanations of amounts reported in the consolidated accounts.]

2. In respect of those undertakings, the report shall also give an indication of:

(a) any important events that have occurred since the end of the financial year;

(b) the likely future development of those undertakings taken as a whole;

(c) the activities of those undertakings taken as a whole in the field of research and development;

(d) the number and nominal value or, in the absence of a nominal value, the accounting par value of all of the parent undertaking's shares held by that undertaking itself, by subsidiary undertakings of that undertaking or by a person acting in his own name but on behalf of those undertakings. A Member State may require or permit the disclosure of these particulars in the notes on the accounts;

[(e) in relation to the use by the undertakings of financial instruments and, where material for the

assessment of assets, liabilities, financial position and profit or loss,
– the financial risk management objectives and policies of the undertakings, including their policies for hedging each major type of forecasted transaction for which hedge accounting is used, and
– the exposure to price risk, credit risk, liquidity risk and cash flow risk;]

[(f) a description of the main features of the group's internal control and risk management systems in relation to the process for preparing consolidated accounts, where an undertaking has its securities admitted to trading on a regulated market within the meaning of Article 4(1), point (14) of Directive 2004/39/EC of the European Parliament and of the Council of 21 April 2004 on markets in financial instruments.[9] In the event that the consolidated annual report and the annual report are presented as a single report, this information must be included in the section of the report containing the corporate governance statement as provided for by Article 46a of Directive 78/660/EEC.

If a Member State permits the information required by paragraph 1 of Article 46a of Directive 78/660/EEC to be set out in a separate report published together with the annual report in the manner prescribed by Article 47 of that Directive, the information provided under the first subparagraph shall also form part of that separate report. Article 37(1), second subparagraph of this Directive shall apply.]

[3. Where a consolidated annual report is required in addition to an annual report, the two reports may be presented as a single report. In preparing such a single report, it may be appropriate to give greater emphasis to those matters which are significant to the undertakings included in the consolidation taken as a whole.]

¶ *Paragraph 1 of this article has been replaced by article 2(10)(a) of Directive 2003/51/EC, reproduced infra under no. C. 23.*

¶ *Paragraph 2(e) has been added by article 2(2)(b) of Directive 2001/65/EC, reproduced infra under no. C. 18.*
¶ *Paragraph 2(f) has been added by article 2(2) of Directive 2006/46/EC, reproduced infra under no. C. 31.*
¶ *Paragraph 3 of this article has been added by article 2(10)(b) of Directive 2003/51/EC, reproduced infra under no. C. 23.*

[SECTION 3A

DUTY AND LIABILITY FOR DRAWING UP AND PUBLISHING THE CONSOLIDATED ACCOUNTS AND THE CONSOLIDATED ANNUAL REPORT

Article 36a

Member States shall ensure that the members of the administrative, management and supervisory bodies of undertakings drawing up the consolidated accounts and the consolidated annual report have collectively the duty to ensure that the consolidated accounts, the consolidated annual report and, when provided separately, the corporate governance statement to be provided pursuant to Article 46a of Directive 78/660/EEC are drawn up and published in accordance with the requirements of this Directive and, where applicable, in accordance with the international accounting standards adopted in accordance with Regulation (EC) No 1606/2002 of the European Parliament and of the Council of 19 July 2002 on the application of international accounting standards.[10] Such bodies shall act within the competences assigned to them by national law.

Article 36b

Member States shall ensure that their laws, regulations and administrative provisions on liability apply to the members of the administrative, management and supervisory bodies referred to in Article 36a, at least towards the undertaking drawing up the consolidated accounts, for breach of the duty referred to in Article 36a.]

¶ *Section 3A has been inserted by article 2(3) of Directive 2006/46/EC, reproduced infra under no. C. 31.*

---

[9] OJ L 145, 30.4.2004, 1, reproduced infra under no. S. 29.

[10] OJ L 243, 11.9.2002, 1, reproduced infra under no. C. 22.

Section 4
The Auditing of Consolidated Accounts

[Article 37]

1. The consolidated accounts of companies shall be audited by one or more persons approved by the Member State whose laws govern the parent undertaking to carry out statutory audits on the basis of the Eighth Council Directive 84/253/EEC of 10 April 1984 on the approval of persons responsible for carrying out the statutory audits of accounting documents.[11]

The person or persons responsible for auditing the consolidated accounts (hereinafter: the statutory auditors) shall also express an opinion concerning the consistency or otherwise of the consolidated annual report with the consolidated accounts for the same financial year.

2. The report of the statutory auditors shall include:

(a) an introduction which shall at least identify the consolidated accounts which are the subject of the statutory audit, together with the financial reporting framework that has been applied in their preparation;

(b) a description of the scope of the statutory audit which shall at least identify the auditing standards in accordance with which the statutory audit was conducted;

(c) an audit opinion which shall state clearly the opinion of the statutory auditors as to whether the consolidated accounts give a true and fair view in accordance with the relevant financial reporting framework and, where appropriate, whether the consolidated accounts comply with statutory requirements; the audit opinion shall be either unqualified, qualified, an adverse opinion or, if the statutory auditors are unable to express an audit opinion, a disclaimer of opinion;

(d) a reference to any matters to which the statutory auditors draw attention by way of emphasis without qualifying the audit opinion;

(e) an opinion concerning the consistency or otherwise of the consolidated annual report with the consolidated accounts for the same financial year.

3. The report shall be signed and dated by the statutory auditors.

4. Where the annual accounts of the parent undertaking are attached to the consolidated accounts, the report of the statutory auditors required by this Article may be combined with any report of the statutory auditors on the annual accounts of the parent undertaking required by Article 51 of Directive 78/660/EEC.]

¶ *This article has been replaced by article 2(11) of Directive 2003/51/EC, reproduced infra under no. C. 23.*

Section 5
The Publication of Consolidated Accounts

Article 38

1. Consolidated accounts, duly approved, and the consolidated annual report, together with the opinion submitted by the person responsible for auditing the consolidated accounts, shall be published for the undertaking which drew up the consolidated accounts as laid down by the laws of the Member State which govern it in accordance with Article 3 of Directive 68/151/EEC.

2. The second subparagraph of Article 47 (1) of Directive 78/660/EEC shall apply with respect to the consolidated annual report.

3. [. . .]

4. However, where the undertaking which drew up the consolidated accounts is not established as one of the types of company listed in Article 4 and is not required by its national law to publish the documents referred to in paragraph 1 in the same manner as prescribed in Article 3 of Directive 68/151/EEC, it must at least make them available to the public at its head office. It must be possible to obtain a copy of such documents upon request. The price of such a copy must not exceed its administrative cost.

5. Articles 48 and 49 of Directive 78/660/EEC shall apply.

---

[11] OJ L 126, 12.5.1984, 20, reproduced infra under no. C. 7, which has been repealed as from 29 June 2006 by article 50 of Directive 2006/43/EC, reproduced infra under no. C. 30.

6. The Member States shall provide for appropriate sanctions for failure to comply with the publication obligations imposed in this Article.

[7. Paragraphs 2 and 3 shall not be applied in respect of companies whose securities are admitted to trading on a regulated market of any Member State within the meaning of Article 1(13) of Directive 93/22/EEC.]

¶ *Paragraph 3 modifies article 47 of Directive 78/660/EEC, Fourth Company Directive, reproduced supra under no. C. 4. The modification is directly incorporated therein.*
¶ *Paragraph 7 of this article has been added by article 2(12) of Directive 2003/51/EC, reproduced infra under no. C. 23.*

[*Article 38a*

Consolidated accounts may be published in the currency in which they were drawn up and in ecus, translated at the exchange rate prevailing on the consolidated balance sheet date. That rate shall be disclosed in the notes on the accounts.]

¶ *This article has been inserted by article 9 of Directive 90/604/EEC, reproduced infra under no. C. 11. Member States may provide that these provisions shall first apply to the annual accounts and consolidated accounts for financial years beginning on 1 January 1995 or during the 1995 calendar year.*

Section 6
Transitional and Final Provisions

Article 39

1. When, for the first time, consolidated accounts are drawn up in accordance with this Directive for a body of undertakings which was already connected, as described in Article 1 (1), before application of the provisions referred to in Article 49 (1), a Member State may require or permit that, for the purposes of Article 19 (1), account be taken of the book value of a holding and the proportion of the capital and reserves that it represents as at a date before or the same as that of the first consolidation.

2. Paragraph 1 above shall apply *mutatis mutandis* to the valuation for the purposes of Article 33 (2) of a holding, or of the proportion of capital and reserves that it represents, in the capital of an undertaking associated with an undertaking included in the consolidation, and to the proportional consolidation referred to in Article 32.

3. Where the separate item defined in Article 19 (1) corresponds to a positive consolidation difference which arose before the date of the first consolidated accounts drawn up in accordance with this Directive, a Member State may:

(a) for the purposes of Article 30 (1), permit the calculation of the limited period of more than five years provided for in Article 37 (2) of Directive 78/660/EEC as from the date of the first consolidated accounts drawn up in accordance with this Directive; and

(b) for the purposes of Article 30 (2), permit the deduction to be made from reserves as at the date of the first consolidated accounts drawn up in accordance with this Directive.

Article 40

1. Until expiry of the deadline imposed for the application in national law of the Directives supplementing Directive 78/660/EEC as regards the harmonisation of the rules governing the annual accounts of banks and other financial institutions and insurance undertakings, a Member State may derogate from the provisions of this Directive concerning the layout of consolidated accounts, the methods of valuing the items included in those accounts and the information to be given in the notes on the accounts:

(a) with regard to any undertaking to be consolidated which is a bank, another financial institution or an insurance undertaking;

(b) where the undertakings to be consolidated comprise principally banks, financial institutions or insurance undertakings.

They may also derogate from Article 6, but only in so far as the limits and criteria to be applied to the above undertakings are concerned.

2. In so far as a Member State has not required all undertakings which are banks, other financial institutions or insurance undertakings to draw up consolidated accounts before implementation of the provisions referred to in Article 49 (1), it may, until its national law implements one of the

Directives mentioned in paragraph 1 above, but not in respect of financial years ending after 1993:

(a) suspend the application of the obligation imposed in Article 1 (1) with respect to any of the above undertakings which is a parent undertaking. That fact must be disclosed in the annual accounts of the parent undertaking and the information prescribed in point 2 of Article 43 (1) of Directive 78/660/EEC must be given for all subsidiary undertakings;

(b) where consolidated accounts are drawn up and without prejudice to Article 33, permit the omission from the consolidation of any of the above undertakings which is a subsidiary undertaking. The information prescribed in Article 34 (2) must be given in the notes on the accounts in respect of any such subsidiary undertaking.

3. In the cases referred to in paragraph 2 (b) above, the annual or consolidated accounts of the subsidiary undertaking must, in so far as their publication is compulsory, be attached to the consolidated accounts or, in the absence of consolidated accounts, to the annual accounts of the parent undertaking or be made available to the public. In the latter case it must be possible to obtain a copy of such documents upon request. The price of such a copy must not exceed its administrative cost.

Article 41

1. Undertakings which are connected as described in Article 1 (1) (a), (b) and (d) (bb), and those other undertakings which are similarly connected with one of the aforementioned undertakings, shall be affiliated undertakings for the purposes of this Directive and of Directive 78/660/EEC.

[1a. 'Related party' has the same meaning as in international accounting standards adopted in accordance with Regulation (EC) No 1606/ 2002.]

2. Where a Member State prescribes the preparation of consolidated accounts pursuant to Article 1 (1) (c), (d), (aa) or (2) or Article 12 (1), the undertakings which are connected as described in those Articles and those other undertakings which are connected similarly, or are connected as described in paragraph 1 above to one of the aforementioned undertakings, shall be affiliated undertakings as defined in paragraph 1.

3. Even where a Member State does not prescribe the preparation of consolidated accounts pursuant to Article 1 (c), (d) (aa) or (2) or Article 12 (1), it may apply paragraph 2 of this Article.

4. Articles 2 and 3 (2) shall apply.

5. When a Member State applies Article 4 (2), it may exclude from the application of paragraph 1 above affiliated undertakings which are parent undertakings and which by virtue of their legal form are not required by that Member State to draw up consolidated accounts in accordance with the provisions of this Directive, as well as parent undertakings with a similar legal form.

¶ *Paragraph 1a has been inserted by article 2(4) of Directive 2006/46/EC, reproduced infra under no. C. 31.*

Articles 42 to 46

[. . .]

¶ *These articles amend articles 56, 57, 58, 59 and 61 of Directive 78/660/EEC, the Fourth Company Directive, reproduced supra under no. C. 4. The modifications are directly incorporated therein.*

Article 47

The Contact Committee set up pursuant to Article 52 of Directive 78/660/EEC shall also:

(a) facilitate, without prejudice to Articles [226 and 227][1] of the Treaty, harmonised application of this Directive through regular meetings dealing, in particular, with practical problems arising in connection with its application;

(b) advise the Commission, if necessary, on additions or amendments to this Directive.

Article 48

[Member States shall lay down the rules on penalties applicable to infringements of the national provisions adopted pursuant to this Directive and shall take all the measures necessary to ensure that they are implemented. The penalties provided for must be effective, proportionate and dissuasive.]

¶ *This article has been repealed by article 12 of Directive 89/666/EEC, Eleventh Company Directive, reproduced infra under no. C. 11 and subsequently been inserted by article 2(5) of Directive 2006/46/EC, reproduced infra under no. C. 31.*

Article 49

1. The Member States shall bring into force the laws, regulations and administrative provisions necessary for them to comply with this Directive before 1 January 1988. They shall forthwith inform the Commission thereof.

2. A Member State may provide that the provisions referred to in paragraph 1 above shall first apply to consolidated accounts for financial years beginning on 1 January 1990 or during the calendar year 1990.

3. The Member States shall ensure that they communicate to the Commission the texts of the main provisions of national law which they adopt in the field covered by this Directive.

Article 50

1. Five years after the date referred to in Article 49 (2), the Council acting on a proposal from the Commission, shall examine and if need be revise Articles 1 (1) (d) (second subparagraph), 4 (2), 5, 6, 7 (1), 12, 43 and 44 in the light of the experience acquired in applying this Directive, the aims of this Directive and the economic and monetary situation at the time.

2. Paragraph (1) above shall not affect Article 53 (2) of Directive 78/660/EEC.

[Article 50a

Not later than 1 January 2007, the Commission shall review the provisions in Article 29(1), Article 34(10), (14)and (15) and Article 36(2)(e) in the light of the experience acquired in applying provisions on fair value accounting and taking account of international developments in the field of accounting and, if appropriate, submit a proposal to the European Parliament and the Council with a view to amending the abovementioned Articles.]

¶ *This article has been inserted by article 2(4) of Directive 2001/65/EC, reproduced infra under no. C. 18.*

Article 51

This Directive is addressed to the Member States.

C. 7.

**Eighth Council Directive 84/253/EEC
of 10 April 1984
based on Article [44][1] (3) (g) of the Treaty on the approval of persons responsible for carrying out the statutory audits of accounting documents[2]**

This Directive has been repealed as from 29 June 2006 by article 50 of Directive 2006/43/EC, reproduced infra under no. C. 30.[3] References to the repealed Directive shall be construed as references to the Directive.

---

[1] The number between brackets has been changed as from 1 May 1999 by article 12 of the Treaty of Amsterdam.
[2] OJ L 126, 12.5.1984, 20–26.
[3] Entry into force of Directive 2006/43/EC: 6 June 2006

C. 8.

Council Regulation 2137/85/EEC
of 25 July 1985
on the European Economic Interest Grouping (EEIG)[1]

THE COUNCIL OF THE EUROPEAN COMMUNITIES,

Having regard to the Treaty establishing the European Economic Community, and in particular Article [308][2] thereof,

Having regard to the proposal from the Commission,[3]

Having regard to the opinion of the European Parliament,[4]

Having regard to the opinion of the Economic and Social Committee,[5]

Whereas a harmonious development of economic activities and a continuous and balanced expansion throughout the Community depend on the establishment and smooth functioning of a common market offering conditions analogous to those of a national market; whereas to bring about this single market and to increase its unity a legal framework which facilitates the adaptation of their activities to the economic conditions of the Community should be created for natural persons, companies, firms and other legal bodies in particular; whereas to that end it is necessary that those natural persons, companies, firms and other legal bodies should be able to co-operate effectively across frontiers;

Whereas co-operation of this nature can encounter legal, fiscal or psychological difficulties; whereas the creation of an appropriate Community legal instrument in the form of a European Economic Interest Grouping would contribute to the achievement of the abovementioned objectives and therefore proves necessary;

Whereas the Treaty does not provide the necessary powers for the creation of such a legal instrument;

Whereas a grouping's ability to adapt to economic conditions must be guaranteed by the considerable freedom for its members in their contractual relations and the internal organisation of the grouping;

Whereas a grouping differs from a firm or company principally in its purpose, which is only to facilitate or develop the economic activities of its members to enable them to improve their own results; whereas, by reason of that ancillary nature, a grouping's activities must be related to the economic activities of its members but not replace them so that, to that extent, for example, a grouping may not itself, with regard to third parties, practise a profession, the concept of economic activities being interpreted in the widest sense;

Whereas access to grouping form must be made as widely available as possible to natural persons, companies, firms and other legal bodies, in keeping with the aims of this Regulation; whereas this Regulation shall not, however, prejudice the application at national level of legal rules and/or ethical codes concerning the conditions for the pursuit of business and professional activities;

Whereas this Regulation does not itself confer on any person the right to participate in a grouping, even where the conditions it lays down are fulfilled;

Whereas the power provided by this Regulation to prohibit or restrict participation in grouping on grounds of public interest is without prejudice to the laws of Member States which govern the

---

[1] OJ L 199, 31.7.1985, 1–9.
[2] The number between brackets has been changed as from 1 May 1999 by article 12 of the Treaty of Amsterdam.
[3] OJ C 14, 15.2.1974, 30 and OJ C 130, 28.4.1978, 14.
[4] OJ C 163, 11.7.1977, 17.
[5] OJ C 108, 15.5.1975, 46.

pursuit of activities and which may provide further prohibitions or restrictions or otherwise control or supervise participation in a grouping by any natural person, company, firm or other legal body or any class of them;

Whereas, to enable a grouping to achieve its purpose, it should be endowed with legal capacity and provision should be made for it to be represented *vis-à-vis* third parties by an organ legally separate from its membership;

Whereas the protection of third parties requires widespread publicity; whereas the members of a grouping have unlimited joint and several liability for the grouping's debts and other liabilities, including those relating to tax or social security, without, however, that principle's affecting the freedom to exclude or restrict the liability of one or more of its members in respect of a particular debt or other liability by means of a specific contract between the grouping and a third party;

Whereas matters relating to the status or capacity of natural persons and to the capacity of legal persons are governed by national law;

Whereas the grounds for winding up which are peculiar to the grouping should be specific while referring to national law for its liquidation and the conclusion thereof;

Whereas groupings are subject to national laws relating to insolvency and cessation of payments; whereas such laws may provide other grounds for the winding up of groupings;

Whereas this Regulation provides that the profits or losses resulting from the activities of a grouping shall be taxable only in the hands of its members; whereas it is understood that otherwise national tax laws apply, particularly as regards the apportionment of profits, tax procedures and any obligations imposed by national tax law;

Whereas in matters not covered by this Regulation the laws of the Member States and Community law are applicable, for example with regard to:
– social and labour laws,
– competition law,
– intellectual property law;

Whereas the activities of groupings are subject to the provisions of Member States' laws on the pursuit and supervision of activities; whereas in the event of abuse or circumvention of the laws of a Member State by a grouping or its members that Member State may impose appropriate sanctions;

Whereas the Member States are free to apply or to adopt any laws, regulations or administrative measures which do not conflict with the scope or objectives of this Regulation;

Whereas this Regulation must enter into force immediately in its entirety; whereas the implementation of some provisions must nevertheless be deferred in order to allow the Member States first to set up the necessary machinery for the registration of groupings in their territories and the disclosure of certain matters relating to groupings; whereas, with effect from the date of implementation of this Regulation, groupings set up may operate without territorial restrictions,

HAS ADOPTED THIS REGULATION:

Article 1

1. European Economic Interest Groupings shall be formed upon the terms, in the manner and with the effects laid down in this Regulation.

Accordingly, parties intending to form a grouping must conclude a contract and have the registration provided for in Article 6 carried out.

2. A grouping so formed shall, from the date of its registration as provided for in Article 6, have the capacity, in its own name, to have rights and obligations of all kinds, to make contracts or accomplish other legal acts, and to sue and be sued.

3. The Member States shall determine whether or not groupings registered at their registries, pursuant to Article 6, have legal personality.

Article 2

1. Subject to the provisions of this Regulation, the law applicable, on the one hand, to the contract for the formation of a grouping, except as regards matters relating to the status or capacity

of natural persons and to the capacity of legal persons and, on the other hand, to the internal organisation of a grouping shall be the internal law of the State in which the official address is situated, as laid down in the contract for the formation of the grouping.

2. Where a State comprises several territorial units, each of which has its own rules of law applicable to the matters referred to in paragraph 1, each territorial unit shall be considered as a State for the purposes of identifying the law applicable under this Article.

Article 3

1. The purpose of a grouping shall be to facilitate or develop the economic activities of its members and to improve or increase the results of those activities; its purpose is not to make profits for itself.

Its activity shall be related to the economic activities of its members and must not be more than ancillary to those activities.

2. Consequently, a grouping may not:

(a) exercise, directly or indirectly, a power of management or supervision over its members' own activities or over the activities of another undertaking, in particular in the fields of personnel, finance and investment;

(b) directly or indirectly, on any basis whatsoever, hold shares of any kind in a member undertaking; the holding of shares in another undertaking shall be possible only in so far as it is necessary for the achievement of the grouping's objects and if it is done on its members' behalf;

(c) employ more than 500 persons;

(d) be used by a company to make a loan to a director of a company, or any person connected with him, when the making of such loans is restricted or controlled under the Member States' laws governing companies. Nor must a grouping be used for the transfer of any property between a company and a director, or any person connected with him, except to the extent allowed by the Member States' laws governing companies. For the purposes of this provision the making of a loan includes entering into any transaction or arrangement of similar effect, and property includes moveable and immovable property;

(e) be a member of another European Economic Interest Grouping.

Article 4

1. Only the following may be members of a grouping:

(a) companies or firms within the meaning of the second paragraph of Article [48][2] of the Treaty and other legal bodies governed by public or private law, which have been formed in accordance with the law of a Member State and which have their registered or statutory office and central administration in the Community; where, under the law of a Member State, a company, firm or other legal body is not obliged to have a registered or statutory office, it shall be sufficient for such a company, firm or other legal body to have its central administration in the Community;

(b) natural persons who carry on any industrial, commercial, craft or agricultural activity or who provide professional or other services in the Community.

2. A grouping must comprise at least:

(a) two companies, firms or other legal bodies, within the meaning of paragraph 1, which have their central administrations in different Member States, or

(b) two natural persons, within the meaning of paragraph 1, who carry on their principal activities in different Member States, or

(c) a company, firm or other legal body within the meaning of paragraph 1 and a natural person, of which the first has its central administration in one Member State and the second carries on his principal activity in another Member State.

3. A Member State may provide that groupings registered at its registries in accordance with Article 6 may have no more than 20 members. For this purpose, that Member State may provide that, in accordance with its laws, each member of a legal body formed under its laws, other than a

registered company, shall be treated as a separate member of a grouping.

4. Any Member State may, on grounds of that State's public interest, prohibit or restrict participation in groupings by certain classes of natural persons, companies, firms, or other legal bodies.

¶ *Art. [48]² of the Treaty:*
'Companies or firms formed in accordance with the law of a Member State and having their registered office, central administration or principal place of business within the community shall, for the purposes of this Chapter, be treated in the same way as natural persons who are nationals of Member States.
"Companies or firms" means companies or firms constituted under civil or commercial law, including co-operative societies, and other legal persons governed by public or private law, save for those which are non-profit-making.'

Article 5

A contract for the formation of a grouping shall include at least:

(a) the name of the grouping preceded or followed either by the words 'European Economic Interest Grouping' or by the initials 'EEIG', unless those words or initials already form part of the name;

(b) the official address of the grouping;

(c) the objects for which the grouping is formed;

(d) the name, business name, legal form, permanent address or registered office and the number and place of registration, if any, of each member of the grouping;

(e) the duration of the grouping, except where this is indefinite.

CASE

Case C-402/96 European Information Technology Observatory, Europäische Wirtschaftliche Interessenvereinigung [1997] ECR I-7515

Article 5(a) of Council Regulation 2137/85/EEC of 25 July 1985 on the European Economic Interest Grouping (EEIG) is to be interpreted as meaning that the business name of an EEIG must include the words 'European Economic Interest Grouping' or the initials 'EEIG', whilst the other elements to be included may be imposed by the provisions of internal law applicable in the Member State in which the grouping has its official address.

Article 6

A grouping shall be registered in the State in which it has its official address, at the registry designated pursuant to Article 39 (1).

Article 7

A contract for the formation of a grouping shall be filed at the registry referred to in Article 6.

The following documents and particulars must also be filed at that registry:

(a) any amendment to the contract for the formation of a grouping, including any change in the composition of a grouping;

(b) notice of the setting up or closure of any establishment of the grouping;

(c) any judicial decision establishing or declaring the nullity of a grouping, in accordance with Article 15;

(d) notice of the appointment of the manager or managers of a grouping, their names and any other identification particulars required by the law of the Member State in which the register is kept, notification that they may act alone or must act jointly, and the termination of any manager's appointment;

(e) notice of a member's assignment of his participation in a grouping or a proportion thereof, in accordance with Article 22 (1);

(f) any decision by members ordering or establishing the winding up of a grouping, in accordance with Article 31, or any judicial decision ordering such winding up, in accordance with Articles 31 or 32;

(g) notice of the appointment of the liquidator or liquidators of a grouping, as referred to in Article 35, their names and any other identification particulars required by the law of the Member State in which the register is kept, and the termination of any liquidator's appointment;

(h) notice of the conclusion of a grouping's liquidation, as referred to in Article 35 (2);

(i) any proposal to transfer the official address, as referred to in Article 14 (1);

(j) any clause exempting a new member from the payment of debts and other liabilities which originated prior to his admission, in accordance with Article 26 (2).

Article 8

The following must be published, as laid down in Article 39, in the gazette referred to in paragraph 1 of that Article:

(a) the particulars which must be included in the contract for the formation of a grouping, pursuant to Article 5, and any amendments thereto;

(b) the number, date and place of registration as well as notice of the termination of that registration;

(c) the documents and particulars referred to in Article 7 (b) to (j).

The particulars referred to in (a) and (b) must be published in full. The documents and particulars referred to in (c) may be published either in full or in extract form or by means of a reference to their filing at the registry, in accordance with the national legislation applicable.

Article 9

1. The documents and particulars which must be published pursuant to this Regulation may be relied on by a grouping as against third parties under the conditions laid down by the national law applicable pursuant to Article 3 (5) and (7) of Council Directive 68/151/EEC of 9 March 1968 on co-ordination of safeguards which, for the protection of the interests of members and others, are required by Member States of companies within the meaning of the second paragraph of Article [48][1] of the Treaty, with a view to making such safeguards equivalent throughout the Community.

2. If activities have been carried on on behalf of a grouping before its registration in accordance with Article 6 and if the grouping does not, after its registration, assume the obligations arising out of such activities, the natural persons, companies, firms or other legal bodies which carried on those activities shall bear unlimited joint and several liability for them.

Article 10

Any grouping establishment situated in a Member State other than that in which the official address is situated shall be registered in that State. For the purpose of such registration, a grouping shall file, at the appropriate registry in that Member State, copies of the documents which must be filed at the registry of the Member State in which the official address is situated, together, if necessary, with a translation which conforms with the practice of the registry where the establishment is registered.

Article 11

Notice that a grouping has been formed or that the liquidation of a grouping has been concluded stating the number, date and place of registration and the date, place and title of publication, shall be given in the *Official Journal of the European Communities* after it has been published in the gazette referred to in Article 39 (1).

Article 12

The official address referred to in the contract for the formation of a grouping must be situated in the Community.

The official address must be fixed either:

(a) where the grouping has its central administration, or

(b) where one of the members of the grouping has its central administration or, in the case of a natural person, his principal activity, provided that the grouping carries on an activity there.

Article 13

The official address of a grouping may be transferred within the Community.

When such a transfer does not result in a change in the law applicable pursuant to Article 2, the decision to transfer shall be taken in accordance with the conditions laid down in the contract for the formation of the grouping.

Article 14

1. When the transfer of the official address results in a change in the law applicable pursuant to Article 2, a transfer proposal must be drawn up, filed and published in accordance with the conditions laid down in Articles 7 and 8.

No decision to transfer may be taken for two months after publication of the proposal. Any such decision must be taken by the members of the grouping unanimously. The transfer shall take effect on the date on which the grouping is registered, in accordance with Article 6, at the registry for the new official address. That registration may not be effected until evidence has been produced that the proposal to transfer the official address has been published.

2. The termination of a grouping's registration at the registry for its old official address may not be effected until evidence has been produced that the grouping has been registered at the registry for its new official address.

3. Upon publication of a grouping's new registration the new official address may be relied on as against third parties in accordance with the conditions referred to in Article 9 (1); however, as long as the termination of the grouping's registration at the registry for the old official address has not been published, third parties may continue to rely on the old official address unless the grouping proves that such third parties were aware of the new official address.

4. The laws of a Member State may provide that, as regards groupings registered under Article 6 in that Member State, the transfer of an official address which would result in a change of the law applicable shall not take effect if, within the two-month period referred to in paragraph 1, a competent authority in that Member State opposes it. Such opposition may be based only on grounds of public interest. Review by a judicial authority must be possible.

Article 15

1. Where the law applicable to a grouping by virtue of Article 2 provides for the nullity of that grouping, such nullity must be established or declared by judicial decision. However the court to which the matter is referred must, where it is possible for the affairs of the grouping to be put in order, allow time to permit that to be done.

2. The nullity of a grouping shall entail its liquidation in accordance with the conditions laid down in Article 35.

3. A decision establishing or declaring the nullity of a grouping may be relied on as against third parties in accordance with the conditions laid down in Article 9 (1).

Such a decision shall not of itself affect the validity of liabilities, owed by or to a grouping which originated before it could be relied on as against third parties in accordance with the conditions laid down in the previous subparagraph.

Article 16

1. The organs of a grouping shall be the members acting collectively and the manager or managers.

A contract for the formation of a grouping may provide for other organs; if it does it shall determine their powers.

2. The members of a grouping, acting as a body, may take any decision for the purpose of achieving the objects of the grouping.

Article 17

1. Each member shall have one vote. The contract for the formation of a grouping may, however, give more than one vote to certain members, provided that no one member holds a majority of the votes.

2. A unanimous decision by the members shall be required to:

(a) alter the objects of a grouping;

(b) alter the number of votes allotted to each member;

(c) alter the conditions for the taking of decisions;

(d) extend the duration of a grouping beyond any period fixed in the contract for the formation of the grouping;

(e) alter the contribution by every member or by some members to the grouping's financing;

(f) alter any other obligation of a member, unless otherwise provided by the contract for the formation of the grouping;

(g) make any alteration to the contract for the formation of the grouping not covered by this paragraph, unless otherwise provided by that contract.

3. Except where this Regulation provides that decisions must be taken unanimously, the contract for the formation of a grouping may prescribe the conditions for a quorum and for a majority, in accordance with which the decisions, or some of them, shall be taken. Unless otherwise provided for by the contract, decisions shall be taken unanimously.

4. On the initiative of a manager or at the request of a member, the manager or managers must arrange for the members to be consulted so that the latter can take a decision.

Article 18

Each member shall be entitled to obtain information from the manager or managers concerning the grouping's business and to inspect the grouping's books and business records.

Article 19

1. A grouping shall be managed by one or more natural persons appointed in the contract for the formation of the grouping or by decision of the members.

No person may be a manager of a grouping if:
— by virtue of the law applicable to him, or
— by virtue of the internal law of the State in which the grouping has its official address, or
— following a judicial or administrative decision made or recognised in a Member State

he may not belong to the administrative or management body of a company, may not manage an undertaking or may not act as manager of a European Economic Interest Grouping.

2. A Member State may, in the case of groupings registered at their registries pursuant to Article 6, provide that legal persons may be managers on condition that such legal persons designate one or more natural persons, whose particulars shall be the subject of the filing provisions of Article 7 (d) to represent them.

If a Member State exercises this option, it must provide that the representative or representatives shall be liable as if they were themselves managers of the groupings concerned.

The restrictions imposed in paragraph 1 shall also apply to those representatives.

3. The contract for the formation of a grouping or, failing that, a unanimous decision by the members shall determine the conditions for the appointment and removal of the manager or managers and shall lay down their powers.

Article 20

1. Only the manager or, where there are two or more, each of the managers shall represent a grouping in respect of dealings with third parties.

Each of the managers shall bind the grouping as regards third parties when he acts on behalf of the grouping, even where his acts do not fall within the objects of the grouping unless the grouping proves that the third party knew or could not, under the circumstances, have been unaware that the act fell outside the objects of the grouping; publication of the particulars referred to in Article 5 (c) shall not of itself be proof thereof.

No limitation on the powers of the manager or managers, whether deriving from the contract for the formation of the grouping or from a decision by the members, may be relied on as against third parties even if it is published.

2. The contract for the formation of the grouping may provide that the grouping shall be validly bound only by two or more managers acting jointly. Such a clause may be relied on as against third parties in accordance with the conditions referred to in Article 9 (1) only if it is published in accordance with Article 8.

Article 21

1. The profits resulting from a grouping's activities shall be deemed to be the profits of the members and shall be apportioned among them in the proportions laid down in the contract for the formation of the grouping or, in the absence of any such provision, in equal shares.

2. The members of a grouping shall contribute to the payment of the amount by which expenditure exceeds income in the proportions laid down in the contract for the formation of the grouping or, in the absence of any such provision, in equal shares.

Article 22

1. Any member of a grouping may assign his participation in the grouping, or a proportion thereof, either to another member or to a third party; the assignment shall not take effect without the unanimous authorisation of the other members.

2. A member of a grouping may use his participation in the grouping as security only after the other members have given their unanimous authorisation, unless otherwise laid down in the contract for the formation of the grouping. The holder of the security may not at any time become a member of the grouping by virtue of that security.

Article 23

No grouping may invite investment by the public.

Article 24

1. The members of a grouping shall have unlimited joint and several liability for its debts and other liabilities of whatever nature. National law shall determine the consequences of such liability.

2. Creditors may not proceed against a member for payment in respect of debts and other liabilities, in accordance with the conditions laid down in paragraph 1, before the liquidation of a grouping is concluded, unless they have first requested the grouping to pay and payment has not been made within an appropriate period.

Article 25

Letters, order forms and similar documents must indicate legibly:

(a) the name of the grouping preceded or followed either by the words 'European Economic Interest Grouping' or by the initials 'EEIG', unless those words or initials already occur in the name;

(b) the location of the registry referred to in Article 6, in which the grouping is registered, together with the number of the grouping's entry at the registry;

(c) the grouping's official address;

(d) where applicable, that the managers must act jointly;

(e) where applicable, that the grouping is in liquidation, pursuant to Articles 15, 31, 32 or 36.

Every establishment of a grouping, when registered in accordance with Article 10, must give the above particulars, together with those relating to its own registration, on the documents referred to in the first paragraph of this Article uttered by it.

Article 26

1. A decision to admit new members shall be taken unanimously by the members of the grouping.

2. Every new member shall be liable, in accordance with the conditions laid down in Article 24, for the grouping's debts and other liabilities, including those arising out of the grouping's activities before his admission.

He may, however, be exempted by a clause in the contract for the formation of the grouping or in the instrument of admission from the payment of debts and other liabilities which originated before his admission. Such a clause may be relied on as against third parties, under the conditions referred to in Article 9 (1), only if it is published in accordance with Article 8.

Article 27

1. A member of a grouping may withdraw in accordance with the conditions laid down in the

contract for the formation of a grouping or, in the absence of such conditions, with the unanimous agreement of the other members.

Any member of a grouping may, in addition, withdraw on just and proper grounds.

2. Any member of a grouping may be expelled for the reasons listed in the contract for the formation of the grouping and, in any case, if he seriously fails in his obligations or if he causes or threatens to cause serious disruption in the operation of the grouping.

Such expulsion may occur only by the decision of a court to which joint application has been made by a majority of the other members, unless otherwise provided by the contract for the formation of a grouping.

Article 28

1. A member of a grouping shall cease to belong to it on death or when he no longer complies with the conditions laid down in Article 4 (1).

In addition, a Member State may provide, for the purposes of its liquidation, winding up, insolvency or cessation of payments laws, that a member shall cease to be a member of any grouping at the moment determined by those laws.

2. In the event of the death of a natural person who is a member of a grouping, no person may become a member in his place except under the conditions laid down in the contract for the formation of the grouping or, failing that, with the unanimous agreement of the remaining members.

Article 29

As soon as a member ceases to belong to a grouping, the manager or managers must inform the other members of that fact; they must also take the steps required as listed in Articles 7 and 8. In addition, any person concerned may take those steps.

Article 30

Except where the contract for the formation of a grouping provides otherwise and without prejudice to the rights acquired by a person under Articles 22 (1) or 28 (2), a grouping shall continue to exist for the remaining members after a member has ceased to belong to it, in accordance with the conditions laid down in the contract for the formation of the grouping or determined by unanimous decision of the members in question.

Article 31

1. A grouping may be wound up by a decision of its members ordering its winding up. Such a decision shall be taken unanimously, unless otherwise laid down in the contract for the formation of the grouping.

2. A grouping must be wound up by a decision of its members:

(a) noting the expiry of the period fixed in the contract for the formation of the grouping or the existence of any other cause for winding up provided for in the contract, or

(b) noting the accomplishment of the grouping's purpose or the impossibility of pursuing it further.

Where, three months after one of the situations referred to in the first subparagraph has occurred, a members' decision establishing the winding up of the grouping has not been taken, any member may petition the court to order winding up.

3. A grouping must also be wound up by a decision of its members or of the remaining member when the conditions laid down in Article 4 (2) are no longer fulfilled.

4. After a grouping has been wound up by decision of its members, the manager or managers must take the steps required as listed in Articles 7 and 8. In addition, any person concerned may take those steps.

Article 32

1. On application by any person concerned or by a competent authority, in the event of the infringement of Articles 3, 12 or 31 (3), the court must order a grouping to be wound up, unless its affairs can be and are put in order before the court has delivered a substantive ruling.

2. On applications by a member, the court may order a grouping to be wound up on just and proper grounds.

3. A Member State may provide that the court may, on application by a competent authority, order the winding up of a grouping which has its official address in the State to which that authority belongs, wherever the grouping acts in contravention of that State's public interest, if the law of that State provides for such a possibility in respect of registered companies or other legal bodies subject to it.

Article 33

When a member ceases to belong to a grouping for any reason other than the assignment of his rights in accordance with the conditions laid down in Article 22 (1), the value of his rights and obligations shall be determined taking into account the assets and liabilities of the grouping as they stand when he ceases to belong to it.

The value of the rights and obligations of a departing member may not be fixed in advance.

Article 34

Without prejudice to Article 37 (1), any member who ceases to belong to a grouping shall remain answerable, in accordance with the conditions laid down in Article 24, for the debts and other liabilities arising out of the grouping's activities before he ceased to be a member.

Article 35

1. The winding up of a grouping shall entail its liquidation.

2. The liquidation of a grouping and the conclusion of its liquidation shall be governed by national law.

3. A grouping shall retain its capacity, within the meaning of Article 1 (2), until its liquidation is concluded.

4. The liquidator or liquidators shall take the steps required as listed in Articles 7 and 8.

Article 36

Groupings shall be subject to national laws governing insolvency and cessation of payments. The commencement of proceedings against a grouping on grounds of its insolvency or cessation of payments shall not by itself cause the commencement of such proceedings against its members.

Article 37

1. A period of limitation of five years after the publication, pursuant to Article 8, of notice of a member's ceasing to belong to a grouping shall be substituted for any longer period which may be laid down by the relevant national law for actions against that member in connection with debts and other liabilities arising out of the grouping's activities before he ceased to be a member.

2. A period of limitation of five years after the publication, pursuant to Article 8, of notice of the conclusion of the liquidation of a grouping shall be substituted for any longer period which may be laid down by the relevant national law for actions against a member of the grouping in connection with debts and other liabilities arising out of the grouping's activities.

Article 38

Where a grouping carries on any activity in a Member State in contravention of that State's public interest, a competent authority of that State may prohibit that activity. Review of that competent authority's decision by a judicial authority shall be possible.

Article 39

1. The Member States shall designate the registry or registries responsible for effecting the registration referred to in Articles 6 and 10 and shall lay down the rules governing registration. They shall prescribe the conditions under which the documents referred to in Articles 7 and 10 shall be filed. They shall ensure that the documents and particulars referred to in Article 8 are published in the appropriate official gazette of the Member State in which the grouping has its official

address, and may prescribe the manner of publication of the documents and particulars referred to in Article 8 (c).

The Member States shall also ensure that anyone may, at the appropriate registry pursuant to Article 6 or, where appropriate, Article 10, inspect the documents referred to in Article 7 and obtain, even by post, full or partial copies thereof.

The Member States may provide for the payment of fees in connection with the operations referred to in the preceding subparagraphs; those fees may not, however, exceed the administrative cost thereof.

2. The Member States shall ensure that the information to be published in the *Official Journal of the European Communities* pursuant to Article 11 is forwarded to the Office for Official Publications of the European Communities within one month of its publication in the official gazette referred to in paragraph 1.

3. The Member States shall provide for appropriate penalties in the event of failure to comply with the provisions of Articles 7, 8 and 10 on disclosure and in the event of failure to comply with Article 25.

Article 40

The profits or losses resulting from the activities of a grouping shall be taxable in the hands of its members.

Article 41

1. The Member States shall take the measures required by virtue of Article 39 before 1 July 1989. They shall immediately communicate them to the Commission.

2. For information purposes, the Member States shall inform the Commission of the classes of natural persons, companies, firms and other legal bodies which they prohibit from participating in groupings pursuant to Article 4 (4). The Commission shall inform the other Member States.

Article 42

1. Upon the adoption of this Regulation, a Contact Committee shall be set up under the auspices of the Commission. Its function shall be:

(a) to facilitate, without prejudice to Articles [226 and 227][2] of the Treaty, application of this Regulation through regular consultation dealing in particular with practical problems arising in connection with its application;

(b) to advise the Commission, if necessary, on additions or amendments to this Regulation.

2. The Contact Committee shall be composed of representatives of the Member States and representatives of the Commission. The chairman shall be a representative of the Commission. The Commission shall provide the secretariat.

3. The Contact Committee shall be convened by its chairman either on his own initiative or at the request of one of its members.

Article 43

This Regulation shall enter into force on the third day following its publication in the *Official Journal of the European Communities.*

It shall apply from 1 July 1989, with the exception of Articles 39, 41 and 42 which shall apply as from the entry into force of the Regulation.

This Regulation shall be binding in its entirety and directly applicable in all Member States.

C. 9.

Eleventh Council Directive 89/666/EEC of 21 December 1989 concerning disclosure requirements in respect of branches opened in a Member State by certain types of company governed by the law of another State[1]

THE COUNCIL OF THE EUROPEAN COMMUNITIES,

Having regard to the Treaty establishing the European Economic Community, and in particular Article [44][2] thereof,

Having regard to the proposal from the Commission,[3]

In co-operation with the European Parliament,[4]

Having regard to the opinion of the Economic and Social Committee,[5]

Whereas in order to facilitate the exercise of the freedom of establishment in respect of companies covered by Article [48][2] of the Treaty, Article [44(3)(g)][2] and the general programme on the elimination of restrictions on the freedom of establishment require co-ordination of the safeguards required of companies and firms in the Member States for the protection of the interests of members and others;

Whereas hitherto this co-ordination has been effected in respect of disclosure by the adoption of the First Directive 68/151/EEC[6] covering companies with share capital, as last amended by the 1985 Act of Accession; whereas it was continued in the field of accounting by the Fourth Directive 78/660/EEC[7] on the annual accounts of certain types of companies, as last amended by the 1985 Act of Accession, the Seventh Directive 83/349/EEC[8] on consolidated accounts, as amended by the 1985 Act of Accession, and the Eighth Directive 84/253/EEC[9] on the persons responsible for carrying out the statutory audits of accounting documents;

Whereas these Directives apply to companies as such but do not cover their branches; whereas the opening of a branch, like the creation of a subsidiary, is one of the possibilities currently open to companies in the exercise of their right of establishment in another Member State;

Whereas in respect of branches the lack of co-ordination, in particular concerning disclosure, gives rise to some disparities, in the protection of shareholders and third parties, between companies which operate in other Member States by opening branches and those which operate there by creating subsidiaries;

Whereas in this field the differences in the laws of the Member States may interfere with the exercise of the right of establishment; whereas it is therefore necessary to eliminate such differences in order to safeguard, inter alia, the exercise of that right;

Whereas to ensure the protection of persons who deal with companies through the intermediary of branches, measures in respect of disclosure are required in the Member State in which a branch is situated; whereas, in certain respects, the economic and social influence of a branch may be comparable to that of a subsidiary company, so

---

[1] OJ L 395, 30.12.1989, 36–39.
[2] The number between brackets has been changed as from 1 May 1999 by article 12 of the Treaty of Amsterdam.
[3] OJ C 105, 21.4.1988, 6.
[4] OJ C 345, 21.12.1987, 76 and OJ C 256, 9.10.1989, 27.
[5] OJ C 319, 30.11.1987, 61.
[6] OJ L 65, 14.3.1968, 8, First Company Directive, reproduced supra under no. C. 1.
[7] OJ L 222, 14.8.1978, 11, Fourth Company Directive, reproduced supra under no. C. 4.

[8] OJ L 193, 18.7.1983, 1–17, Seventh Company Directive, reproduced supra under no. C. 6.
[9] OJ L 126, 12.5.1984, 20, Eighth Company Directive, reproduced supra under no. C. 7, which has been repealed as from 29 June 2006 by article 50 of Directive 2006/43/EC, reproduced infra under no. C. 30.

that there is public interest in disclosure of the company at the branch; whereas to effect such disclosure it is necessary to make use of the procedure already instituted for companies with share capital within the Community;

Whereas such disclosure relates to a range of important documents and particulars and amendments thereto;

Whereas such disclosure, with the exception of the powers of representation, the name and legal form and the winding-up of the company and the insolvency proceedings to which it is subject, may be confined to information concerning a branch itself together with a reference to the register of the company of which that branch is part, since under existing Community rules all information covering the company as such is available in that register;

Whereas national provisions in respect of the disclosure of accounting documents relating to a branch can no longer be justified following the co-ordination of national law in respect of the drawing up, audit and disclosure of companies' accounting documents; whereas it is accordingly sufficient to disclose, in the register of the branch, the accounting documents as audited and disclosed by the company;

Whereas letters and order forms used by a branch must give at least the same information as letters and order forms used by the company, and state the register in which the branch is entered;

Whereas to ensure that the purposes of this Directive are fully realised and to avoid any discrimination on the basis of a company's country of origin, this Directive must also cover branches opened by companies governed by the law of non-member countries and set up in legal forms comparable to companies to which Directive 68/151/EEC applies; whereas for these branches it is necessary to apply certain provisions different from those that apply to the branches of companies governed by the law of other Member States since the Directives referred to above do not apply to companies from non-member countries;

Whereas this Directive in no way affects the disclosure requirements for branches under other provisions of, for example, employment law on workers' rights to information and tax law, or for statistical purposes;

HAS ADOPTED THIS DIRECTIVE:

SECTION 1

BRANCHES OF COMPANIES FROM OTHER MEMBER STATES

Article 1

1. Documents and particulars relating to a branch opened in a Member State by a company which is governed by the law of another Member State and to which Directive 68/151/EEC applies shall be disclosed pursuant to the law of the Member State of the branch, in accordance with Article 3 of that Directive.

2. Where disclosure requirements in respect of the branch differ from those in respect of the company, the branch's disclosure requirements shall take precedence with regard to transactions carried out with the branch.

Article 2

1. The compulsory disclosure provided for in Article 1 shall cover the following documents and particulars only:

(a) the address of the branch;

(b) the activities of the branch;

(c) the register in which the company file mentioned in Article 3 of Council Directive 68/151/EEC is kept, together with the registration number in that register;

(d) the name and legal form of the company and the name of the branch if that is different from the name of the company;

(e) the appointment, termination of office and particulars of the persons who are authorised to represent the company in dealings with third parties and in legal proceedings,

– as a company organ constituted pursuant to law or as members of any such organ, in accordance with the disclosure by the company as provided for in Article 2 (1) (d) of Directive 68/151/EEC;

– as permanent representatives of the company for the activities of the branch, with an indication of the extent of their powers;

(f) the winding-up of the company, the appointment of liquidators, particulars concerning them and their powers and the termination of the liquidation in accordance with disclosure by the company as provided for in Article 2 (1) (h), (j) and (k) of Directive 68/151/EEC;

– insolvency proceedings, arrangements, compositions, or any analogous proceedings to which the company is subject;

(g) the accounting documents in accordance with Article 3;

(h) the closure of the branch.

2. The Member State in which the branch has been opened may provide for the disclosure, as referred to in Article 1, of

(a) the signature of the persons referred to in paragraph 1 (e) and (f) of this Article;

(b) the instruments of constitution and the memorandum and articles of association if they are contained in a separate instrument in accordance with Article 2 (1) (a), (b) and (c) of Directive 68/151/EEC, together with amendments to those documents;

(c) an attestation from the register referred to in paragraph 1 (c) of this Article relating to the existence of the company;

(d) an indication of the securities on the company's property situated in that Member State, provided such disclosure relates to the validity of those securities.

CASE

Case C-167/01 Kamer van Koophandel en Fabrieken voor Amsterdam v Inspire Art Ltd [2003] ECR I-10155

It is contrary to Article 2 for national legislation to impose on the branch of a company formed in accordance with the laws of another Member State disclosure obligations not provided for by that directive.

Article 3

The compulsory disclosure provided for by Article 2 (1) (g) shall be limited to the accounting documents of the company as drawn up, audited and disclosed pursuant to the law of the Member State by which the company is governed in accordance with Directives 78/660/EEC, 83/349/EEC and 84/253/EEC.

Article 4

The Member State in which the branch has been opened may stipulate that the documents referred to in Article 2 (2) (b) and Article 3 must be published in another official language of the Community and that the translation of such documents must be certified.

Article 5

Where a company has opened more than one branch in a Member State, the disclosure referred to in Article 2 (2) (b) and Article 3 may be made in the register of the branch of the company's choice.

In this case, compulsory disclosure by the other branches shall cover the particulars of the branch register of which disclosure was made, together with the number of that branch in that register.

Article 6

The Member States shall prescribe that letters and order forms used by a branch shall state, in addition to the information prescribed by Article 4 of Directive 68/151/EEC, the register in which the file in respect of the branch is kept together with the number of the branch in that register.

SECTION 2

BRANCHES OF COMPANIES FROM THIRD COUNTRIES

Article 7

1. Documents and particulars concerning a branch opened in a Member State by a company which is not governed by the law of a Member State but which is of a legal form comparable with the types of company to which Directive 68/151/EEC applies shall be disclosed in accordance with the law of the Member State of the branch as laid down in Article 3 of that Directive.

2. Article 1 (2) shall apply.

Article 8

The compulsory disclosure provided for in Article 7 shall cover at least the following documents and particulars:

(a) the address of the branch;

(b) the activities of the branch;

(c) the law of the State by which the company is governed;

(d) where that law so provides, the register in which the company is entered and the registration number of the company in that register;

(e) the instruments of constitution, and memorandum and articles of association if they are contained in a separate instrument, with all amendments to these documents;

(f) the legal form of the company, its principal place of business and its object and, at least annually, the amount of subscribed capital if these particulars are not given in the documents referred to in subparagraph (e);

(g) the name of the company and the name of the branch if that is different from the name of the company;

(h) the appointment, termination of office and particulars of the persons who are authorised to represent the company in dealings with third parties and in legal proceedings:

– as a company organ constituted pursuant to law or as members of any such organ,

– as permanent representatives of the company for the activities of the branch.

The extent of the powers of the persons authorised to represent the company must be stated, together with whether they may do so alone or must act jointly;

(i) – the winding-up of the company and the appointment of liquidators, particulars concerning them and their powers and the termination of the liquidation;

– insolvency proceedings, arrangements, compositions or any analogous proceedings to which the company is subject;

(j) the accounting documents in accordance with Article 7;

(k) the closure of the branch.

Article 9

1. The compulsory disclosure provided for by Article 8 (l) (j) shall apply to the accounting documents of the company as drawn up, audited and disclosed pursuant to the law of the State that governs the company. Where they are not drawn up in accordance with or in a manner equivalent to Directives 78/660/EEC and 83/349/EEC, Member States may require that accounting documents relating to the activities of the branch be drawn up and disclosed.

2. Articles 4 and 5 shall apply.

Article 10

The Member States shall prescribe that letters and order forms used by a branch state the register in which the file in respect of the branch is kept together with the number of the branch in that register. Where the law of the State by which the company is governed requires entry in a register, the register in which the company is entered, and the registration number of the company in that register must also be stated.

SECTION 3

INDICATION OF BRANCHES IN THE COMPANY'S ANNUAL REPORT

Article 11

[. . .]

¶ *This article modifies article 46(2) of Directive 78/660/EEC, Fourth Company Directive, reproduced supra under no. C. 4. The modification is directly incorporated therein.*

SECTION 4

TRANSNATIONAL AND FINAL PROVISIONS

Article 12

The Member States shall provide for appropriate penalties in the event of failure to disclose the matters set out in Articles 1, 2, 3, 7, 8 and 9 and of omission from letters and order forms of the compulsory particulars provided for in Articles 6 and 10.

Article 13

Each Member State shall determine who shall carry out the disclosure formalities provided for in this Directive.

Article 14

1. Articles 3 and 9 shall not apply to branches opened by credit institutions and financial institutions covered by Directive 89/117/EEC.[10]

2. Pending subsequent co-ordination, the Member States need not apply Articles 3 and 9 to branches opened by insurance companies.

Article 15

[...]

¶ *This article modifies Directive 78/660/EEC, Fourth Company Directive, reproduced supra under no. C. 4 amended by Directive 92/101/EEC, reproduced infra under no. C. 13 and Directive 83/349/EEC, Seventh Company Directive, reproduced supra under no. C. 6. The modifications are directly incorporated therein.*

Article 16

1. Member States shall adopt the laws, regulations and administrative provisions necessary to comply with this Directive not later than 1 January 1992. They shall forthwith inform the Commission thereof.

2. Member States shall stipulate that the provisions referred to in paragraph 1 shall apply from 1 January 1993 and, with regard to accounting documents, shall apply for the first time to annual accounts for the financial year beginning on 1 January 1993 or during 1993.

3. Member States shall communicate to the Commission the texts of the provisions of national law that they adopt in the field covered by this Directive.

Article 17

The Contact Committee set up pursuant to Article 52 of Directive 78/660/EEC shall also:

(a) facilitate, without prejudice to Articles [226 and 227][2] of the Treaty, the harmonised application of this Directive, through regular meetings dealing, in particular, with practical problems arising in connection with its application;

(b) advise the Commission, if necessary, on any additions or amendments to this Directive.

Article 18

This Directive is addressed to the Member States.

---

[10] OJ L 44, 16.2.1989, 40, reproduced supra under no. B. 10.

C. 10.

Twelfth Council Directive 89/667/EEC
of 21 December 1989
on single-member private limited-liability companies[1]

THE COUNCIL OF THE EUROPEAN COMMUNITIES,

Having regard to the Treaty establishing the European Economic Community, and in particular Article [44][2] thereof,

Having regard to the proposal from the Commission,[3]

In co-operation with the European Parliament,[4]

Having regard to the opinion of the Economic and Social Committee,[5]

Whereas certain safeguards which, for the protection of the interests of members and others, are required by Member States of companies and firms within the meaning of the second paragraph of Article [48][2] of the Treaty should be co-ordinated with a view to making such safeguards equivalent throughout the Community;

Whereas, in this field, Directives 68/151/EEC[6] and 78/660/EEC[7] as last amended by the Act of Accession of Spain and Portugal, and Directive 83/349/EEC,[8] as amended by the Act of Accession of Spain and Portugal, on disclosure, the validity of commitments, nullity, annual accounts and consolidated accounts, apply to all share capital companies; whereas Directives 77/91/EEC[9] and 78/855/EEC,[10] as last amended by the Act of Accession of Spain and Portugal, and Directive 82/891/EEC[11] on formation and capital, mergers and divisions apply only to public limited-liability companies;

Whereas the small and medium-sized enterprises (SME) action programme[12] was approved by the Council in its Resolution of 3 November 1986;

Whereas reforms in the legislation of certain Member States in the last few years, permitting single-member private limited-liability companies, have created divergences between the laws of the Member States;

Whereas it is important to provide a legal instrument allowing the limitation of liability of the individual entrepreneur throughout the Community, without prejudice to the laws of the Member States which, in exceptional circumstances, require that entrepreneur to be liable for the obligations of his undertaking;

Whereas a private limited-liability company may be a single-member company from the time of its formation, or may become one because its shares have come to be held by a single shareholder; whereas, pending the co-ordination of national provisions on the laws relating to groups, Member States may lay down certain special provisions and penalties for cases where a natural person is the sole member of several companies or where a single-member company or any other legal person is the sole member of a company;

---

[1] OJ L 395, 30.12.1989, 40–42.
[2] The number between brackets has been changed as from 1 May 1999 by article 12 of the Treaty of Amsterdam.
[3] OJ C 173, 2.7.1988, 10; see also the re-examined proposal for a Council Directive on company law concerning single-member private limited companies, 90/C 30/06, OJ C 30, 8.2.1990, 91–92.
[4] OJ C 96, 17.4.1989, 92 and OJ C 291, 20.11.1989, 53.
[5] OJ C 318, 12.12.1988, 9.
[6] OJ L 65, 14.3.1968, 8, First Company Directive, reproduced supra under no. C. 1.
[7] OJ L 222, 14.8.1978, 11, Fourth Company Directive, reproduced supra under no. C. 4.
[8] OJ L 193, 18.7.1983, Seventh Company Directive, reproduced supra under no. C. 6.
[9] OJ L 26, 31.1.1977, Second Company Directive, reproduced supra under no. C. 2.
[10] OJ L 295, 20.10.1978, Third Company Directive, reproduced supra under no. C. 3.
[11] OJ L 378, 31.12.1982, 47, Sixth Company Directive, reproduced supra under no. C. 5.
[12] OJ C 287, 14.11.1986, 1.

whereas the sole aim of this provision is to take account of the differences which currently exist in certain national laws; whereas, for that purpose, Member States may in specific cases lay down restrictions on the use of single-member companies or remove the limits on the liabilities of sole members; whereas Member States are free to lay down rules to cover the risks that single-member companies may present as a consequence of having single members, particularly to ensure that the subscribed capital is paid;

Whereas the fact that all the shares have come to be held by a single shareholder and the identity of the single member must be disclosed by an entry in a register accessible to the public;

Whereas decisions taken by the sole member in his capacity as general meeting must be recorded in writing;

Whereas contracts between a sole member and his company as represented by him must likewise be recorded in writing, insofar as such contracts do not relate to current operations concluded under normal conditions,

HAS ADOPTED THIS DIRECTIVE:

Article 1

The co-ordination measures prescribed by this Directive shall apply to the laws, regulations and administrative provisions of the Member States relating to the following types of company:
– *in Germany:*
Gesellschaft mit beschränkter Haftung,

– *in Belgium:*
Société privée à responsabilité limitée/de besloten vennootschap met beperkte aansprakelijkheid,

– *in Denmark:*
Anpartsselskaber,

– *in Spain:*
Sociedad de responsabilidad limitada,

– *in France:*
Société à responsabilité limitée,

– *in Greece:*
η εταιρεία περιορισμένης ευθύνης,

– *in Ireland:*
Private company limited by shares or by guarantee,

– *in Italy:*
Società a responsabilità limitata,

– *in Luxembourg:*
Société à responsabilité limitée,

– *in the Netherlands:*
Besloten vennootschap met beperkte aansprakelijkheid,

– *in Portugal:*
Sociedade por quotas,

– *in the United Kingdom:*
Private company limited by shares or by guarantee,

[– *in Austria:*
Aktiengesellschaft, Gesellschaft mit beschränkter Haftung],

[– *in Finland:*
Osakeyhtiö/aktiebolag],

[– *in Sweden:*
Aktiebolag],

[– *in the Czech Republic:*
Společnost s ručením omezenym],

[– *in Estonia:*
Aktsiaselts, osaühing],

[– *in Cyprus:*
Ιδιωτική εταιρεία περιορισμένης ευθύνης με μετοχές ή με εγγύηση],

[– *in Latvia:*
Sabiedrība ar ierobežotu atbildību],

[– *in Lithuania:*
Uždaroji akcinė bendrovė],

[– *in Hungary:*
Korlátolt felelősségű társaság, részvénytársaság],

[– *in Malta:*
Kumpanija privata—Private limited liability company],

[– *in Poland:*
Spółka z ograniczoną odpowiedzialnością],

[– *in Slovenia:*
Družba z omejeno odgovornostjo],

[– *in Slovakia:*
Spoločnosť; s ručením obmedzenym],

¶ *This Directive has been rendered applicable to Austria, Sweden, and Finland by the Act of Accession of Austria, Sweden, and Finland by the Act of Accession of Austria, Sweden, and Finland (OJ C 241, 29.8.1994, 21) adapted by Council Decision 91/1/EC, Euratom, ECSL (OJ L 1, 1.1.1995, 1) and to the Czech Republic, to Estonia, to Cyprus, to Latvia, to Lithuania,* to Hungary, to Malta, to Holland, to Slovenia, and to Slovakia by the Act concerning the conditions of accession of the Czech Republic, the Republic of Estonia, the Republic of Cyprus, the Republic of Latvia, the Republic of Lithuania, the Republic of Hungary, the Republic of Malta, the Republic of Poland, the Republic of Slovenia, and the Slovak Republic and the adjustments to the Treaties on which the European Union is founded (OJ L 236, 23.9.2003, 33).

Article 2

1. A company may have a sole member when it is formed and also when all its shares come to be held by a single person (single-member company).

2. Member States may, pending co-ordination of national laws relating to groups, lay down special provisions or sanctions for cases where:

(a) a natural person is the sole member of several companies;

(b) a single-member company or any other legal person is the sole member of a company.

Article 3

Where a company becomes a single-member company because all its shares come to be held by a single person, that fact, together with the identity of the sole member, must either be recorded in the file or entered in the register within the meaning of Article 3 (1) and (2) of Directive 68/151/EEC or be entered in a register kept by the company and accessible to the public.

Article 4

1. The sole member shall exercise the powers of the general meeting of the company.

2. Decisions taken by the sole member in the field referred to in paragraph 1 shall be recorded in minutes or drawn up in writing.

Article 5

1. Contracts between the sole member and his company as represented by him shall be recorded in minutes or drawn up in writing.

2. Member States need not apply paragraph 1 to current operations concluded under normal conditions.

Article 6

Where a Member State allows single-member companies as defined by Article 2 (1) in the case of public limited companies as well, this Directive shall apply.

Article 7

A Member State need not allow the formation of single-member companies where its legislation provides that an individual entrepreneur may set up an undertaking the liability of which is limited to a sum devoted to a stated activity, on condition that safeguards are laid down for such undertakings which are equivalent to those imposed by this Directive or by any other Community provisions applicable to the companies referred to in Article 1.

Article 8

1. Member States shall bring into force the laws, regulations and administrative provisions necessary to comply with this Directive by 1 January 1992. They shall inform the Commission thereof.

2. Member States may provide that, in the case of companies already in existence on 1 January 1992, this Directive shall not apply until 1 January 1993.

3. Member States shall communicate to the Commission the texts of the main provisions of national law that they adopt in the field covered by this Directive.

Article 9

This Directive is addressed to the Member States.

C. 11.

Council Directive 90/604/EEC
of 8 November 1990
amending Directive 78/660/EEC on annual accounts and Directive 83/349/EEC on consolidated accounts as concerns the exemptions for small and medium-sized companies and the publication of accounts in ecus[1]

THE COUNCIL OF THE EUROPEAN COMMUNITIES,

Having regard to the Treaty establishing the European Economic Community, and in particular Article [44][2] thereof,

Having regard to the proposal from the Commission,[3]

In co-operation with the European Parliament,[4]

Having regard to the opinion of the Economic and Social Committee,[5]

Whereas the harmonisation of the national provisions concerning the presentation and content of annual accounts and of the annual report, the valuation methods and the publication of these documents as concerns, in particular, public and private limited liability companies was the subject of Directive 78/660/EEC,[6] as last amended by the Act of Accession of Spain and Portugal;

Whereas the administrative procedures imposed on small and medium-sized undertakings should be simplified in accordance with the Council resolution of 3 November 1986 on the action programme for small and medium-sized undertakings (SMUs)[7] and the Council resolution of 30 June 1988 on the improvement of the business environment and action to promote the development of enterprises, especially small and medium-sized enterprises in the Community,[8] which calls more especially for a substantial simplification of the obligations arising from Directive 78/660/EEC;

Whereas, on the basis of Article 53 (2) of Directive 78/660/EEC, it is appropriate that a second review of the thresholds defining small and medium-sized undertakings should be carried out;

Whereas the derogations as regards establishment, audit and publication of accounts that Member States may provide for under Directive 78/660/EEC should be increased as far as small companies are concerned;

Whereas Member States should be afforded the possibility of allowing companies not to include in the notes to the accounts certain information concerning remuneration granted to members of the company's administrative or management body where such information enables the position of a given member of such bodies to be identified;

Whereas it is also appropriate to enable Member States to render less stringent the obligations imposed on small companies as regards the drawing up and publication of the notes to the accounts; whereas Member States should be able to exempt such companies from the obligation to supply, in the notes to the accounts, certain data which may be deemed of less importance for small companies; whereas, with the same interests in view, Member States should have the possibility of exempting such companies from the obligation to draw up an annual report providing they include,

---

[1] OJ L 317, 16.11.90, 57–59.
[2] The number between brackets has been changed as from 1 May 1999 by article 12 of the Treaty of Amsterdam.
[3] OJ C 287, 11.11.1986, 5; OJ C 318, 20.12.1989, 12.
[4] OJ C 158, 26.6.1989, 257 and OJ C 295, 26.11.1990, 80.
[5] OJ C 139, 5.6.1989, 42.
[6] OJ L 222, 14.8.1978, 11, Fourth Company Directive, reproduced supra under no. C. 4.
[7] OJ C 287, 14.11.1986, 1.

[8] OJ C 197, 27.7.1988, 6.

in the notes to the accounts, the data referred to in Article 22 (2) of Directive 77/91/EEC[9] concerning the acquisition of own shares;

Whereas it is important to promote European monetary integration by allowing companies, at least, to publish their accounts in ecus; whereas this is simply an additional facility which does not change the position of companies which can at present already draw up and publish accounts in ecus; whereas, on this point, the provisions of Directives 78/660/EEC and 83/349/EEC,[10] as amended by the Act of Accession of Spain and Portugal should be clarified by obliging companies which have recourse to this facility to indicate the conversion rate used in the notes to the accounts,

HAS ADOPTED THIS DIRECTIVE:

Articles 1 to 9

[. . .]

¶ *These articles modify Directive 78/660/EEC, Fourth Company Directive, reproduced supra under no. C. 4. and Directive 83/349/EEC, Seventh Company Directive, reproduced supra under no. C. 6. The modifications are directly incorporated therein.*

Article 10

1. Member States shall bring into force the laws, regulations and administrative provisions necessary for them to comply with this Directive by 1 January 1993. They shall forthwith inform the Commission thereof.

2. Member States may provide that this Directive shall only apply for the first time to accounts for the financial year beginning on 1 January 1995 or during the calendar year 1995.

3. Member States shall communicate to the Commission the texts of the main provisions of national law that they adopt in the field covered by this Directive.

Article 11

This Directive is addressed to the Member States.

---

[9] OJ L 26, 31.1.1977, 1, Second Company Directive, reproduced supra under no. C. 2.
[10] OJ L 193, 18.7.1983, 1, Seventh Company Directive, reproduced supra under no. C. 6.

C. 12.

Council Directive 90/605/EEC
of 8 November 1990
amending Directive 78/660/EEC on annual accounts and Directive 83/349/EEC on consolidated accounts as regards the scope of those Directives[1]

THE COUNCIL OF THE EUROPEAN COMMUNITIES,

Having regard to the Treaty establishing the European Economic Community, and in particular Article [44][2] thereof,

Having regard to the proposal from the Commission,[3]

In co-operation with the European Parliament,[4]

Having regard to the opinion of the Economic and Social Committee,[5]

Whereas Directive 78/660/EEC,[6] as last amended by Directive 90/604/EEC,[7] applies to the annual accounts of public and private limited liability companies in particular because those types of company offer no safeguards to third parties beyond the amounts of their net assets;

Whereas, in accordance with Directive 83/349/EEC,[8] as last amended by Directive 90/604/EEC, Member States need require only companies covered by Directive 78/660/EEC to draw up consolidated accounts;

Whereas, within the Community, there is a substantial and constantly growing number of partnerships and limited partnerships all of the fully liable members of which are constituted either as public or as private limited liability companies;

Whereas these fully liable members may also be companies, which do not fall within the law of a Member State but which have, a legal status comparable to that referred to in Directive 68/151/EEC;[9]

Whereas it would run counter to the spirit and aims of those Directives to allow such partnerships and partnerships with limited liability not to be subject to Community rules;

Whereas the provisions covering the scope of the two Directives in question should therefore be explicitly supplemented;

Whereas it is of importance that the name, head office and legal status of any undertaking of which a limited liability company is a fully liable member should be indicated in the notes to the accounts of such member;

Whereas the obligation to draw up, publish and to have audited the accounts of partnerships and limited liability partnerships may also be imposed on the fully liable member; whereas it should also be possible to include these companies in consolidated accounts, drawn up by such member or established at a higher level;

Whereas some of the partnerships covered by this Directive are not subject, in the Member State where they have their head office, to entry in a register, which makes it difficult to apply accounting obligations to them; whereas, in particular in these cases, special rules are necessary according to whether the fully liable members are undertakings which fall within the law of the same Member State, another Member State or a third country,

---

[1] OJ L 317, 16.11.90, 60–62.
[2] The number between brackets has been changed as from 1 May 1999 by article 12 of the Treaty of Amsterdam.
[3] OJ C 144, 11.6.1986, 10.
[4] OJ C 125, 11.5.1987, 140.
[5] OJ C 328, 22.12.1986, 43.
[6] OJ L 222, 14.8.1978, 11, Fourth Company Directive, reproduced supra under no. C. 4.
[7] OJ L 317, 16.11.90, 57, reproduced supra under no. C. 11.
[8] OJ L 193, 18.7.1983, 1, Seventh Company Directive, reproduced supra under no. C. 6.

[9] OJ L 65, 14.3.1968, 8, First Company Directive, reproduced supra under no. C. 1.

HAS ADOPTED THIS DIRECTIVE:

Articles 1 to 2

[...]

¶ *These articles modify Directive 78/660/EEC, Fourth Company Directive, reproduced supra under no. C. 4. and Directive 83/349/EEC, Seventh Company Directive, reproduced supra under no. C. 6. The modifications are directly incorporated therein.*

Article 3

1. Member States shall bring into force the laws, regulations and administrative provisions necessary for them to comply with this Directive before 1 January 1993. They shall forthwith inform the Commission thereof.

2. Member States may provide that the provisions referred to in paragraph 1 shall first apply to the annual accounts and consolidated accounts for financial years beginning on 1 January 1995 or during the 1995 calendar year.

3. The Member States shall communicate to the Commission the texts of the main provisions of national law that they adopt in the field covered by this Directive.

Article 4

This Directive is addressed to the Member States.

C. 13.

Council Directive 92/101/EEC
of 23 November 1992
amending Directive 77/91/EEC on the formation of public limited-liability companies and the maintenance and alteration of their capital[1]

THE COUNCIL OF THE EUROPEAN COMMUNITIES,

Having regard to the Treaty establishing the European Economic Community, and in particular Article [44][2] thereof,

Having regard to the proposal from the Commission,[3]

In co-operation with the European Parliament,[4]

Having regard to the opinion of the Economic and Social Committee,[5]

Whereas in order to maintain the subscribed capital and ensure equal treatment of shareholders, Directive 77/91/EEC[6] restricts a public limited-liability company's right to acquire its own shares;

Whereas the restrictions on a company's acquisition of its own shares apply not only to acquisitions made by a company itself but also to those made by any person acting in his own name but on the company's behalf;

Whereas in order to prevent a public limited-liability company from using another company in which it holds a majority of the voting rights or on which it can exercise a dominant influence to make such acquisitions without complying with the restrictions imposed in that respect, the arrangements governing a company's acquisition of its own shares should be extended to cover the most important and most frequent cases of the acquisition of shares by such other companies; whereas those arrangements should be extended to cover subscription for shares in the public limited-liability company;

Whereas in order to prevent the circumvention of Directive 77/91/EEC companies governed by Directive 68/151/EEC[7] and companies governed by the laws of third countries and having comparable legal forms should also be covered;

Whereas, where the relationship between a public limited-liability company and another company such as referred to in the third recital is only indirect, it would appear to be justified to relax the provisions applicable when that relationship is direct by providing for the suspension of voting rights as a minimum measure for the purpose of achieving the aims of this Directive;

Whereas, where a Member State provides for a system of penalties equivalent to those laid down in Directive 77/91/EEC and for the suspension of voting rights, it may be considered that such legislation already meets the objectives of this Directive;

Whereas, furthermore, it is justifiable to exempt cases in which the specific nature of a professional activity rules out the possibility that the objectives of this Directive may be endangered;

Whereas, in order to avoid the disturbance of a Member State's financial market as a result of that country's economic structure and excessively abrupt consequences as regards the rules for self-regulation, provision should be made for an appropriate adaptation period,

---

[1] OJ L 347, 28.11.1992, 64–66.
[2] The number between brackets has been changed as from 1 May 1999 by article 12 of the Treaty of Amsterdam.
[3] OJ C 8, 12.1.1991, 5 and OJ C 317, 7.12.1992, 13.
[4] OJ C 240, 16.9.1991, 103 and OJ C 175, 11.7.1992, 1.
[5] OJ C 269, 14.10.1991, 21.
[6] OJ L 26, 31.1.1977, 1, Second Company Directive, reproduced supra under no. C. 2.

[7] OJ L 65, 14.3.1968, 8, First Company Directive, reproduced supra under no. C. 1.

HAS ADOPTED THIS DIRECTIVE:

Article 1

[. . .]

¶ *This article inserts article 24a in Directive 77/91/EEC, Second Company Directive, reproduced supra under no. C. 2. The modifications are directly incorporated therein.*

Article 2

1. Member States need not apply Article 24a of Directive 77/91/EEC to shares acquired before the date referred to in Article 3 (2).

However, the voting rights attached to those shares shall be suspended and the shares shall be taken into account when it is determined whether the condition laid down in Article 19 (1) (b) of the same Directive is fulfilled.

2. In order to avoid disturbance of the financial market, the Kingdom of Belgium may postpone the suspension of such voting rights until 1 January 1998 on condition that:
– they are attached to shares acquired before the notification of this Directive, and
– for all companies the relationship of which with a public limited-liability company meets the criteria laid down in Article 24a (1) of Directive 77/91/EEC, they do not exceed 10% of the voting rights attached to the shares in the public limited-liability company.

Article 3

1. Member States shall adopt before 1 January 1994 the laws, regulations and administrative provisions necessary to comply with this Directive. They shall forthwith inform the Commission thereof.

2. The date of entry into force which Member States shall lay down for those provisions shall be no later than 1 January 1995.

3. Member States shall communicate to the Commission the texts of the main provisions of national law that they adopt in the field covered by this Directive.

4. When Member States adopt these measures, they shall include a reference to this Directive or shall be accompanied by such a reference at the time of their official publication. The manner in which such a reference is to be made shall be laid down by the Member States.

Article 4

This Directive is addressed to the Member States.

C. 14.

Council Directive 94/8/EC
of 21 March 1994
amending Directive 78/660/EEC as regards the revision of amounts expressed in ecus[1]

This Directive has been directly incorporated in the Fourth Company Directive 78/660/EEC (OJ L 222, 14.08.1978, 11), reproduced under no. C. 4. Therefore it will not be reproduced.

---

[1] OJ L 82, 25.3.1994, 33–34.

C. 15.

Communication 97/C 285/10 from the Commission
Participation of European Economic Interest Groupings (EEIGs) in public contracts and programmes financed by public funds[1]

INTRODUCTION

In its communication of 10 July 1996 on the integrated programme for small and medium-sized enterprises (SMEs) and the craft sector,[2] the Commission decided to issue a communication on measures designed to ensure that the European Economic Interest Grouping (EEIG) can tender on an equal footing for public contracts and can participate fully in programmes financed by public funds. In this way, better use can be made of the EEIG as a means of enabling SMEs to combine their resources.

The European Economic Interest Grouping was established by Council Regulation 2137/85/EEC of 25 July 1985 on the European Economic Interest Grouping (referred to below as 'the Regulation').[3]

The creation at Community level of a legal instrument for facilitating transnational co-operation between firms is an important element in the completion of the internal market.

The EEIG is currently the only legal vehicle for co-operation that is directly connected with the Community system, and it thus constitutes a key element in European co-operation, particularly for SMEs wishing to participate in European-scale projects. More than 800 groupings are currently developing economic activities in a wide range of sectors. This is an encouraging figure given that the first EEIGs could only be set up from 1 July 1989, the date on which the Regulation came into force.

However, a recent conference organised by the Commission[4] showed that optimum use is not yet being made of the EEIG by firms wishing to co-operate at transnational level, particularly where they hope to participate in public contracts and programmes financed by public funds.

This communication describes the EEIG and clarifies some of its characteristics and the way in which it operates so as to ensure that it can tender for public contracts and participate in programmes financed by public funds on an equal footing with other firms. This clarification should ultimately lead to better use of the EEIG by firms, particularly SMEs. The Commission has pointed out on a number of occasions that the access of SMEs to public contracts, the rules governing which are frequently applied in programmes financed by public funds, is a means of speeding up completion of the internal market and regional economic development.[5]

From a wider viewpoint, the Commission intends to encourage EEIG participation in such contracts and programmes; the EEIG represents considerable progress for all Community firms in that it enables them to organise their co-operation within a transnational structure that guarantees its members' freedom to pursue their own activities.

---

[1] OJ C 285, 20.9.1997, 17–24.
[2] COM (96) 329 final.
[3] OJ L 199, 31.7.1985, 1, reproduced supra under no. C. 8.

[4] The 1996 'Regie' conference held on 25 and 26 March 1996 to review six years of experience of the EEIG.
[5] See Commission notice C (88) 2510 to the Member States on monitoring compliance with public procurement rules in the case of projects and programmes financed by the Structural Funds and financial instruments (OJ C 22, 28.1.1989, 3). See also the following Commission communications: 'Promoting SME participation in public procurement in the Community', COM (90) 166 of 7 May 1990; 'SME participation in public procurement in the Community', SEC (92) 722 final of 1 June 1992.

I. Definition of the EEIG

The EEIG is a flexible and light structure that enables its members to interlink some of their economic activities while retaining their economic and legal independence.

The formation of an EEIG gives rise to an independent legal entity with legal capacity whose purpose is to facilitate or develop its members' economic activities and to improve or increase the results of those activities.

This definition shows that the objective pursued by those who conceived this instrument is to promote transnational co-operation between firms at European level through the development of a common activity that is ancillary to their own activities.

The EEIG is similar to a partnership (or 'société en nom collectif', 'offene Handelsgesellschaft') in that, for example, its members have unlimited joint and several liability for its debts (see point II.5). However, the EEIG has features which are peculiar to more structured forms of companies: for example, it has the capacity to act in its own name through managers who can be appointed independently of their status as members[6] on the basis of a rule which applies generally to limited companies (see point II.2).

II. Characteristics of the EEIG

1. *Community nature of the EEIG*

EEIGs are connected with the Community legal system. Their formation and legal existence can therefore come about only on the terms, in the manner and with the effects laid down by Community law, even if that law refers back to national laws in certain respects.

The EEIG's legal neutrality places its members on an equal footing, which is very important for overcoming members' fears that one of them may be more favourably placed because it is operating in a more familiar legal environment.

2. *The EEIG's legal capacity and its members' autonomy*

The EEIG has full and independent legal capacity that differentiates it from purely contractual forms of co-operation. In particular, the fact that it has its own organs gives it a much greater power to negotiate and represent its members than each of those members could exercise individually. The EEIG has the capacity to act in its own name through managers who can be appointed independently of their status as grouping members and whose representative powers are directly based on the rules applicable to limited companies. This feature is important for the EEIG's participation in public contracts and programmes financed by public funds because it enables its members to present a united front when negotiating contracts and seeking loans or financial guarantees directly linked to public contracts.[7]

3. *The ancillary nature of an EEIG's activity*

An EEIG differs from a company principally in its aim, which is to facilitate or develop the economic activities of its members in order to enable them to increase their own profits. A company, by contrast, generally aims to make profits for itself.

Owing to its ancillary nature, the grouping's activity must be connected with its members' economic activities and not replace them.

However, the formation of an EEIG should establish a legal framework that facilitates the adaptation of its members' activities to the economic conditions of the market.[8]

The ancillary nature of the EEIG's activity should not therefore be regarded as an operational limitation that confines the grouping to a subsidiary or minor role.

Notwithstanding the ancillary nature of its activities, a grouping can be regarded as being capable

---

[6] Article 19 of the Regulation.

[7] Article 1 (2) of the Regulation.
[8] First recital of the Regulation.

of carrying out any of the functions which may fall to any other form of grouping participating in a public contract or in a programme financed by public funds.

In this context, the EEIG can have different functions: it can be used simply as a framework for co-ordinating and organising its members' activities or it can conclude in its own name and execute contracts awarded by the public authorities or under programmes financed by public funds.

In particular, the Regulation does not prohibit the EEIG from completely but temporarily taking over some of its members' activities. This matter was clarified by the Commission in 1991 when it stated: 'there is nothing to prevent an EEIG carrying on some of the activities of its members for a limited period, for the purposes of performing site work, for example'.[9]

4. *Structural aspects of the EEIG: stability and flexibility*

The Regulation guarantees a grouping's ability to adapt to economic conditions through the considerable freedom its members have in their contractual relations and the internal organisation of the grouping.[10]

This flexibility is reflected both in the formation and duration of the EEIG and in the arrangements governing its financing or operation.

The formalities involved in the formation of an EEIG are very simple, being limited to the conclusion of a written contract (the notarial procedure is not required) and the filing of the contract at the registry in the Member State in which the official address is situated.

Furthermore, the EEIG can be formed for an indefinite or a limited period. This flexibility of formation makes the grouping a particularly suitable instrument for projects with a limited life, such as feasibility studies or the carrying out of work.

The very wide access to the EEIG form enables it to respond effectively, where necessary, to any change in the conditions of co-operation. This openness is made unequivocally clear in the sixth recital of the Regulation, which states that 'access to grouping form must be made as widely available as possible to natural persons, companies, firms and other legal bodies, in keeping with the aims of the Regulation'.[11]

The flexibility which an EEIG's members enjoy regarding its financing is also very attractive to firms. Capital is not required when it is formed. This flexibility is very important and distinguishes the formation of an EEIG from that of a company, where large sums of money may be tied up for a given period. In the case of a grouping, by contrast, intermediate stages are possible which permit optimum use to be made of the funds that will subsequently be released.

It is important to point out that all types of contribution are possible: contributions in cash, in kind or even in industrial property (technological knowledge, patents, commercial or trade relationships, etc.).

The EEIG may even function in some cases through the payment of regular contributions or through funds being made available on current account.

Furthermore, although the Regulation prohibits an EEIG from inviting investment by the public, it is permitted to borrow from a bank.[12]

The flexibility of operation of an EEIG is further reflected in its ability to transfer its official address from one Member State to another while retaining its legal personality or capacity. Such an operation cannot therefore be regarded as the winding-up of the grouping or be taxed as such.

The Regulation broadly leaves it to an EEIG's members to organise relations between themselves.

---

[9] Answer given by Mr Bangemann on behalf of the Commission to Written Question No 1587/91 (OJ C 323, 13.12.1991, 32 and 33).
[10] Fourth recital of the Regulation.
[11] See also Article 4 of the Regulation.
[12] Article 23 of the Regulation.

However, it also includes certain peremptory and non-peremptory arrangements in the interests of third parties but also in those of the members themselves, enabling the latter to gauge the extent of their personal commitment.[13]

Certain major decisions affecting the operation and composition of the grouping must be adopted unanimously. These include modification of the grouping's aims, changes in the number of votes allotted to each member, alteration of the conditions under which decisions are taken, amendment of the members' or some members' contributions to the grouping's financing, transfer of the grouping's official address where that transfer involves a change in the law applicable to the grouping, and authorisation for a member to assign all or part of its rights.

The winding-up of a grouping requires a unanimous decision, unless the contract for the formation of the grouping provides otherwise.

It should be added that, if the contract for the formation of the grouping contains no provision governing the collective decision taking, the unanimity rule applies in all cases.[14]

The Regulation also imposes fairly strict conditions on the admission and withdrawal of members of the grouping. These rules confirm the very marked *intuitu personae* nature of the relationships between members. The admission of new members thus requires a unanimous decision of the grouping's members. A member's withdrawal from the grouping is possible under the conditions laid down in the contract for the formation of the grouping or, in the absence of such conditions, with the unanimous agreement of the other members.[15]

The Regulation subjects assignment of participations in the grouping to the unanimous authorisation of the other members. In the absence of any clause in the contract for the formation of the grouping concerning the provision of guarantees in respect of a member's participation, such an operation can be carried out only with the unanimous agreement of the other members.[16]

The Regulation therefore reduces the risk of structural change within a grouping by imposing effective controls on the admission and withdrawal of members.

Such control is important as a means of reassuring an EEIG's potential co-contracting parties, in particular banks and insurance companies from which credit or guarantees may be sought in connection with a grouping's participation in public contracts, or the authorities from whom funding is requested in connection with programmes.

5. *Unlimited joint and several liability of members*

Independently of the credit and guarantees that may be granted to the EEIG depending on its members' financial position, maximum effective protection is provided for third parties entering into a business relationship with the grouping.

The Regulation establishes the principle that the members of a grouping have unlimited joint and several liability for its debts.[17]

The EEIG may enter into commitments in its own name that have financial implications. It will of course be required to meet the cost from its own assets. Where payment has not been made within an appropriate period by the grouping itself, its members have unlimited joint and several liability for debts of any kind it may have. This personal commitment of the members is the natural counterweight to the contractual freedom underlying the EEIG and to the lack of a capital requirement.

In addition, former members of an EEIG remain answerable for five years following their withdrawal for the debts and other liabilities arising

---

[13] Article 17 of the Regulation.
[14] Article 17 (3) of the Regulation.
[15] Articles 26 (1) and 27 (1) of the Regulation.
A member may withdraw at any time on just and proper grounds without having to obtain the unanimous agreement of the other members (second paragraph of Article 27 (1)).

[16] Article 22 of the Regulation.
[17] Article 24 of the Regulation.

out of the grouping's activities during the period they were members.[18] The unlimited joint and several liability of the grouping's members constitutes a fundamental guarantee that makes it easier for third parties to enter into a business relationship with the EEIG, to insure it or lend to it in the light of the financial position of one or more of its members.

This rule demonstrates, particularly in the case of an EEIG formed without capital, that the combined financial standing of its members and the guarantees they may provide should be taken into account where a grouping tenders for a contract or applies for funding or credit.

III. EEIG participation in public procurement

(a) *General considerations*

The Community Directives on public procurement require compliance, throughout the European Union, with certain minimum conditions of information and procedures for the award of public supply contracts by, on the one hand, public authorities ('traditional sectors' Directives) and, on the other hand, by the entities operating in the water, energy, transport and telecommunications sectors (the 'special sectors' Directives). This legal framework is supplemented by certain rules on the legal remedies available when it is necessary to settle disputes between firms and contracting bodies. These rules together constitute what are commonly referred to as the Procurement Directives.[19]

Although they differ on a number of points, the two groups of Directives ban discrimination, provide for transparent candidate selection and contract award procedures, based on objective criteria that must be known in advance and compliance with the rules applicable in the technical field.

As regards the participation of EEIGs in public procurement, it is important to note that the Community Directives in this area do not contain any provisions that could impede such participation. On the contrary, all the Procurement Directives provide for the possibility of groupings participating in contracts without requiring them to have a specific legal form when they have been awarded a contract by the contracting authorities or contracting body.[20]

The ancillary nature of the activity of an EEIG should not be an obstacle to its participation in public procurement. In this connection, the Court of Justice recently stated that 'not only a natural or legal person who will himself carry out the works but also a person who will have the contract carried out through agencies or branches or will have recourse to technicians or outside technical divisions, or even a group of undertakings, whatever its legal form, may seek to be awarded public works contracts'.[21] An EEIG may therefore participate in and perform a public works contract.

(b) *Consolidated assessment of public procurement contract participation criteria*

In the abovementioned judgment, the Court establishes the principle of a consolidated

---

[18] Articles 34 and 37(1) of the Regulation.
[19] Council Directive 93/36/EEC of 14 June 1993 co-ordinating procedures for the award of public supply contracts (OJ L 199, 9.8.1993); Council Directive 93/37/EEC of 14 June 1993 concerning the co-ordination of procedures for the award of public works contracts (OJ L 199, 9.8.1993); Council Directive 92/50/EEC of 18 June 1992 relating to the co-ordination of procedures for the award of public service contracts (OJ L 209, 24.7.1992); Council Directive 89/665/EEC of 21 December 1989 on the co-ordination of the laws, regulations and administrative provisions relating to the application of review procedures to the award of public supply and public works contracts (OJ L 395, 30.12.1989); Council Directive 93/38/EEC of 14 June 1993 co-ordinating the procurement procedures of entities operating in the water, energy, transport and telecommunications sectors (OJ L 199,

9.8.1993); Council Directive 92/13/EEC of 25 February 1992 on the co-ordination of the laws, regulations and administrative provisions relating to the application of the Community rules on the procurement procedures of entities operating in the water, energy, transport and telecommunications sectors (OJ L 76, 23.3.1992).

[20] Article 18 of Directive 93/36/EEC, Article 21 of Directive 93/37/EEC, Article 26 of Directive 92/50/EEC and Article 33 of Directive 93/38/EEC.
[21] Judgment in Case C-389/92, Ballast Nedam Groep NVC v. Belgische Staat [1994] ECR I-1306, point 13. This judgment is currently the subject of a reference for a preliminary ruling (Case C-5/97).

assessment of the resources and capacities of all the members of a group of enterprises when one of the firms in the group participates in a public procurement contract, provided that the latter actually has available to it the resources and capacities of the other members of the group which are necessary for carrying out the contract.

In applying the reasoning of the Court to an EEIG, a contracting body should, when selecting tenderers or candidates for a public procurement contract, apply the assessment criteria laid down by the Directives taking account not only of the capacities of the EEIG itself but also of those of its members.

On the basis of the Procurement Directives, any contractor wishing to take part in a public procurement contract may be requested to prove his identity or his economic and financial standing or his technical capacity[22] (qualitative selection criteria). If the EEIG does not itself, as an independent legal entity, satisfy these selection criteria, the principle of consolidated assessment requires account to be taken of the capacities of its members. This means that:

– where all the members of the EEIG are firms satisfying the selection criteria, an EEIG may not be required to satisfy these conditions as well,
– on the other hand, if the members of an EEIG do not all satisfy the selection criteria, the members that will in practice perform the contract must satisfy the conditions imposed by the contracting authority,
– lastly, if none of the members of an EEIG satisfy the conditions imposed by the contracting authority, the EEIG may not be used as a means of avoiding the conditions,
– national law governing the registration and authorisation of contractors as a condition of their participation in public contracts should not impede the participation of EEIGs in such contracts. Where national law makes EEIGs' participation conditional on their registration or authorisation, it should either permit EEIGs to be registered or authorised as such or provide for an exception to enable them to participate in public contracts without being registered or authorised.

IV. EEIG participation in programmes financed by public funds

The particular features of an EEIG should enable it to take part fully in programmes financed by public funds. These features are analysed below.

1. *Transnational character of the EEIG*

A number of Community support programmes require projects to be submitted by several partners belonging to different Member States. An example is provided by Article 2 (b), second tiret, of Council Decision 94/763/EC of 21 November 1994 concerning the rules for the participation of undertakings, research centres and universities in research, technological development and demonstration activities of the European Community.[23]

Within the meaning of that Article, Community contributions may benefit only activities carried out 'by at least two legal entities. Such entities must not be affiliated and must be established in different Member States, or in at least one Member State and one State associated with the programme'.

Cross-border co-operation is also an objective of operational Community initiative programmes financed by the Structural Funds. This is true of Interreg II,[24] one of whose objectives is to promote regional cross-border co-operation, Leader II, which also subsidises (part C) transnational rural development co-operation projects,[25] or

---

[22] Articles 21 to 25 of Directive 93/36/EEC, Articles 25 to 29 of Directive 93/37/EEC, Articles 30 to 35 of Directive 92/50/EEC. See also Articles 30 to 32 of Directive 93/38/EC.

[23] OJ L 306, 30.11.1994, 8.

[24] See Commission notice to the Member States laying down guidelines for operational programmes which Member States are invited to establish in the framework of a Community initiative concerning border developments, cross-border co-operation and selected energy networks (Interreg II) (OJ C 180, 1.7.1994, 60).

[25] See notice to the Member States laying down guidelines for global grants or integrated operational programmes for which Member States are invited to submit applications for assistance in the framework of a Community initiative for rural development, Leader II (OJ C 180, 1.7.1994, 48).

Regis II, which encourages transnational co-operation between the most remote regions of the Community.[26]

As an EEIG must necessarily comprise at least two partners from two different Member States,[27] it is inherently transnational, and the EEIG can therefore be considered as a 'consortium'. This is why EEIGs are always entitled to apply to participate in Community programmes, including those that require the participation of legal entities in several Member States.

Members of an EEIG cannot therefore be required to submit tenders in parallel with that submitted by the grouping itself.

With this in mind, the Commission intends to add to its official lists of approved contractors and to the forms to be completed as part of the tender procedure, in addition to the 15 existing categories for classifying national participants, a new purely European category, called 'EUR'. EEIGs will be classified automatically in this category because of their transnational character.

2. *The presence of several independent operators*

The members of an EEIG retain full legal and economic independence in the running of their affairs. EEIGs should therefore be able to participate fully in programmes that require at least two separate legal entities to submit a joint project. One example is the Council Decision of 23 November 1994 adopting a specific programme for research and technological development, including demonstration in the field of non-nuclear energy (1994 to 1998).[28]

The Decision groups together most of the activities of the Thermie programme relating to the technical demonstration of projects. Its Annex III provides that Community funding for co-operative research projects, involving normally at least four non-affiliated SMEs from at least two different Member States, will cover 50% of the cost of research.

This means that EEIGs should participate in the programmes on an equal footing with the other eligible firms, as the grouping must comprise at least two members from two different Member States who remain economically and legally independent throughout their co-operation.[29]

An EEIG must therefore be able to participate on its own in programmes, even in those that explicitly require several independent partners. In that case, members of an EEIG should not be required to submit individual proposals in parallel with that made by the grouping itself.

3. *Creating synergy*

In certain cases, the selection of proposals takes account of the effective capacity of the proposed action to create synergy between various categories of participants.[30] Such programmes call for the participation of newly formed co-operative structures. In this context, ad hoc consortia should not be preferred to recently formed EEIGs without a detailed investigation of their characteristics and capacities.

V. Access of EEIGs to credit

Access to credit is essential to most economic operators. However, it is not always easy for firms to obtain external financing, especially in the case of SMEs that could be regarded as high-risk borrowers.

That is why the grouping together of firms within an EEIG can be a major advantage in discussions with credit institutions.

The Commission wishes to clarify and specify certain questions concerning EEIGs' access to

---

[26] See notice to the Member States laying down guidelines for operational programmes that Member States are invited to establish in the framework of a Community initiative concerning the most remote regions, Regis II (OJ C 180, 1.7.1994, 44).
[27] See Article 4 (2) of Regulation 2137/85/EEC.
[28] OJ L 334, 22.12.1994, 87.

[29] See Articles 3 and 4 of Regulation 2137/85/EEC.
[30] See Article 4 of Decision 94/763/EC.

credit in order to avoid any risk of discriminating between EEIGs and other forms of national enterprises better known to economic operators.

1. Guarantees

Despite the considerable degree of freedom and operational autonomy retained by members of an EEIG, their unlimited joint and several liability can make it much easier to obtain credit and strengthen the negotiating powers of its members.

The creditors of an EEIG, in particular banks and other financial institutions, can make a claim on the personal assets of members in respect of debts incurred by the grouping and not settled by it in good time.

A requirement that each member of an EEIG should provide a personal guarantee would add considerably to the cost of a loan and so should not be imposed in practice, as members are already liable to pay the debts of the grouping from their personal assets.

An EEIG thus provides a means of increasing the borrowing potential of its members while generally reducing the cost of a loan.

2. Managerial competences

The legal autonomy of an EEIG also enables it to act as a single interlocutor with financial institutions, as the manager or managers represent the grouping in negotiations.

Direct negotiation with each member of the grouping and its financial partners is therefore not necessary.

3. Evidence of financial soundness

An EEIG, like any other loan applicant, must be able to prove its creditworthiness.

Like the procedures described in Chapter III on public procurement, credit institutions should be able to carry out an overall assessment of the solvency of groupings on the basis of the financial status of their members.

Consolidation of the assets of an EEIG and of its members would facilitate the necessary assessments by the financial institutions.

The drawing-up by an EEIG of a balance sheet and a consolidated profit-and-loss account could considerably facilitate the assessment.

In addition, an EEIG that has equity capital, which is not compulsory within the meaning of Regulation 2137/85/EEC, offers security to all creditors dealing with a grouping.

An EEIG with its own equity thus has a significant competitive edge and could be included as one of the elements of assessment referred to above.

Without equity capital, the financial viability of the member or members established in the State where the credit institution is located will clearly be a decisive factor in obtaining a loan or guarantee.

Creditors of an EEIG can avoid time-consuming procedures for the recovery of sums due from abroad, the principle of members' unlimited joint and several liability allowing them to select the member they will have recourse against in the event of default of the grouping itself.

VI. Conclusion

The EEIG is currently the only vehicle offering firms a framework for co-operation directly attached to the Community legal order. For that reason, and in order to facilitate its use, the Commission will continue to monitor application of Regulation 2137/85/EEC closely.

In a constantly changing market, the EEIG offers businesses in the Community, especially SMEs, the opportunity to develop their potential in projects with a Community dimension. SMEs are now recognised as firms that play a crucial part in achieving the objectives of growth, competitiveness and employment that are part of the priorities of the European Union.[31] The Regie project thus represents a good means of promoting the use of the EEIG among SMEs.

---

[31] See the Commission communication on an integrated programme for small and medium-sized enterprises and the craft sector, COM (96) 329 final of 10 July 1996.

See also: 'Maximum enhancement of the employment, growth and competitive potential of European SMEs', Council Decision 97/15/EC of 9 December 1996 on a third multiannual programme for SMEs in the European Union (1997 to 2000), OJ L 6, 10.1.1997, 25.

The Commission considers it essential that all the actors concerned by the use of EEIGs, firms or bodies concluding contracts with a grouping, should be fully aware of its characteristics and potential.

This Communication is intended to provide the clarifications which should remove all uncertainty still preventing maximum use of the EEIG in public procurement, access to credit with which it is directly linked, and programmes financed by public funds.

C. 16.

Council Directive 1999/60/EC
of 17 June 1999
amending Directive 78/660/EEC as regards amounts expressed in ecus[1]

THE COUNCIL OF THE EUROPEAN UNION,

Having regard to the Treaty establishing the European Community,

Having regard to the Fourth Council Directive 78/660/EEC of 25 July 1978 based on Article 44(3)(g) of the Treaty on the annual accounts of certain types of companies,[2] and in particular Article 53(2) thereof,

Having regard to the proposal from the Commission.

(1) Whereas Articles 11 and 27 of Directive 78/660/EEC and, by way of reference, Article 6 of Directive 83/349/EEC[3] and Articles 20 and 21 of Directive 84/253/EEC[4] contain thresholds expressed in ecus for the balance sheet total and the net turnover within which Member States may grant derogations from the said Directives;

(2) Whereas, in accordance with Article 53(2) of Directive 78/660/EEC, every five years the Council, acting on a proposal from the Commission, is to examine and, if need be, revise the amounts expressed in ecus in that Directive, in the light of economic and monetary trends in the Community;

(3) Whereas to date the Council, in accordance with Article 53(2) of Directive 78/660/EEC, has on three occasions revised the amounts expressed in ecus by means of Directives 84/569/EEC,[5] 90/604/EEC[6] and 94/8/EC;[7]

(4) Whereas the fourth five-year period following the adoption of Directive 78/660/EEC on 25 July 1978 ended on 24 July 1998 and a review of those amounts is thus justified;

(5) Whereas, over the last five years, the ecu has lost part of its value, measured in real terms; whereas, on the basis of the economic and monetary trends in the Community, an increase in the amounts expressed in ecus is necessary;

(6) Whereas Council Regulation 974/98/EC of 3 May 1998 on the introduction of the euro,[8] provides that as from 1 January 1999, the currency of participating Member States shall be the euro and that the euro shall be substituted for the currency of each participating Member State at the fixed conversion rate; whereas Council Regulation 1103/97/EC of 17 June 1997 on certain provisions relating to the introduction of the euro[9] provides that during the transitional period (1 January 1999 to 31 December 2001) the euro is to be divided into national currency units according to the conversion rates; whereas it is therefore appropriate that amounts in this Directive be expressed in euro; whereas amounts in euro appearing in this Directive are to be converted into the national currency units of Member States adopting the euro according to the conversion rates; whereas amounts in euros appearing in this Directive are to be converted into the national currency of Member States not adopting the euro according to the

---

[1] OJ L 162, 26.06.1999, 65–66.
[2] OJ L 222, 14.8.1978, 11, Fourth Company Directive, reproduced supra under no. C. 4. Directive as last amended by Directive 94/8/EC (OJ L 82, 25.3.1994, 33), reproduced supra under no. C. 14.
[3] OJ L 193, 18.7.1983, 1.
[4] OJ L 126, 12.5.1984, 20, Eight Company Directive, reproduced supra under no. C. 7, which has been repealed as from 29 June 2006 by article 50 of Directive 2006/43/EC, reproduced infra under no. C. 30.

[5] OJ L 314, 4.12.1984, 28.
[6] OJ L 317, 16.11.1990, 57, reproduced supra under no. C. 11.
[7] OJ L 82, 25.3.1994, 33, reproduced supra under no. C. 14.
[8] OJ L 139, 11.5.1998, 1.
[9] OJ L 162, 19.6.1997, 1.

exchange rate published in the *Official Journal of the European Communities* of 4 January 1999,

HAS ADOPTED THIS DIRECTIVE:

Article 1

1. […]

2. […]

3. The revision of the amounts referred to in paragraphs 1 and 2 shall constitute the fourth five-yearly revision provided for in Article 53(2) of Directive 78/660/EEC.

¶ *Article 1, points (1) and (2) amend articles 11 and 27 of Directive 78/660/EEC, reproduced supra under no C. 4. The modifications are directly incorporated therein.*

Article 2

For Member States not adopting the euro, the equivalent amount in national currency shall be that obtained by applying the exchange rate published in the *Official Journal of the European Communities* published on 4 January 1999.

Article 3

1. Those Member States that intend to make use of the option provided for in Articles 11 and 27 of Directive 78/660/EEC, as amended by this Directive, shall bring into force the measures necessary for them to comply with this Directive at any time after its publication. They shall forthwith inform the Commission thereof.

2. When Member States adopt these measures, they shall contain a reference to this Directive or shall be accompanied by such reference on the occasion of their official publication. The methods of making such reference shall be laid down by Member States.

3. Member States shall communicate to the Commission the texts of the main provisions of national law that they adopt in the field governed by this Directive.

Article 4

This Directive shall enter into force on the date of its publication in the *Official Journal of the European Communities*.

Article 5

This Directive is addressed to the Member States.

C. 17.

Commission Recommendation 2001/453/EC
of 30 May 2001
on the recognition, measurement and disclosure of environmental issues in the annual accounts and annual reports of companies[1]

(notified under document number C (2001) 1495)

THE COMMISSION OF THE EUROPEAN COMMUNITIES,

Having regard to the Treaty establishing the European Community and in particular Article 211 EC,

Having regard to the fourth Council Directive 78/660/EEC of 25 July 1978 based on Article 54(3)(g) of the Treaty on the annual accounts of certain types of companies,[2] as last amended by Directive 1999/60/EC,[3]

Having regard to the seventh Council Directive 83/349/EEC of 13 June 1983 based on Article 54(3)(g) of the Treaty on consolidated accounts,[4] as last amended by Directive 90/605/EEC,[5]

Whereas:

(1) In 1992 the Commission published its fifth action programme on the environment 'Towards sustainability' (COM(92)23).[6] Among a range of proposals in the area of environmental protection, it provides for a Community initiative in the area of accounting. This initiative should relate primarily to the ways and means used by companies to report on financial aspects relating to the environment. An enhanced attention to financial aspects could contribute to achieving the goals of the programme; ensuring that environmental expenditures and risks are taken into account could increase the company's awareness of environmental issues. In 2001 the Commission has adopted a communication concerning the sixth action plan for the environment (COM (2001)31 final of 24 January 2001).

(2) The Amsterdam Treaty recognised that a key element for promoting sustainable development (Article 6 of the EC Treaty) is the principle of the integration of environmental requirements into other policies. In view of this objective, the Cardiff European Council endorsed a strategy for the integration of environmental objectives into all Community policies and actions. This strategy was confirmed and further developed by the Vienna European Council that invited the Internal Market Council to consider how such integration could be achieved in this particular domain.

(3) In 1999 the Commission adopted a communication on the single market and the environment (COM(99)263 of 8 June 1999) which is intended to contribute to making environmental and single market policies mutually supportive and reinforcing, whilst at the same time developing synergies between them. This Communication identifies specific single market policy areas in which the Commission will strive for a closer integration with environmental policy, and lays down a series of further measures, among which to issue a recommendation on environmental issues in financial reporting. Such

---

[1] OJ L 156, 13.6.2001, 33–42.
[2] OJ L 222, 14.8.1978, 11, Fourth Company Directive, reproduced supra under no. C. 4.
[3] OJ L 162, 26.6.1999, 65, reproduced supra under no. C. 16.
[4] OJ L 193, 18.7.1983, 1, Seventh Company Directive, reproduced supra under no. C. 6.
[5] OJ L 317, 16.11.1990, 60, reproduced supra under no. C. 12.
[6] OJ C 138, 17.5.1993. Programme as last revised by the European Parliament and the Council by Decision No 2179/98/EC of 24.9.1998 (OJ L 275, 10.10.1998).

recommendation is also a direct follow-up of the November 1995 Accounting advisory forum paper on environmental issues in financial reporting (Document XV/6004/94).

(4) The lack of explicit rules has contributed to a situation where different stakeholders, including regulatory authorities, investors, financial analysts and the public in general may consider the environmental information disclosed by companies to be either inadequate or unreliable. Investors need to know how companies deal with environmental issues. Regulatory authorities have an interest in monitoring the application of environmental regulations and the associated costs.

Nonetheless, voluntary disclosure of environmental data in the annual accounts and annual reports of companies is still running at low levels, even though it is often perceived that enterprises face increasing environmental costs for pollution prevention and clean-up equipment and for waste clean-up and monitoring systems, in particular those enterprises operating in sectors that have significant impacts on the environment.

(5) In the absence of harmonised authoritative guidelines in relation to environmental issues and financial reporting, comparability between companies becomes difficult. When companies do disclose environmental information it is often the case that the value of the information is seriously handicapped by the absence of a common and recognised set of disclosures that includes the necessary definitions and concepts with regard to environmental issues. The information is often disclosed in a variety of non-harmonised ways among companies and/or reporting periods, rather than being presented in an integrated and consistent manner throughout the annual accounts and the annual report.

(6) The costs of collecting and reporting environmental data and the sensitiveness or confidentiality that might be associated, in certain cases, with such information are frequently regarded as deterrent factors for disclosure of environmental information in the financial statements of companies. Nevertheless, these arguments do not eliminate the need to stimulate the provision of environmental information. Users of financial statements need information about the impact of environmental risks and liabilities on the financial position of the company, and about the company's attitude towards the environment and the enterprise's environmental performance to the extent that they may have consequences on the financial health of the company.

(7) While the European legislative framework for financial reporting does not explicitly address environmental issues, the general principles and provisions laid down in the Fourth and Seventh Company Directives apply (Directives 78/660/EEC and 83/349/EEC, respectively).

(8) As part of its 1995 accounting strategy[7] the Commission seeks to integrate European harmonisation in the accounting field within the broader context of international accounting harmonisation. Consequently, the Commission has lent its support to the work of the International Accounting Standards Committee (IASC) which, in turn, set as its objective the development of a core set of high quality international accounting standards (IASs). The Commission is committed to work towards maintaining consistency between the European Union financial reporting, framework and international accounting standards developed by the IASC.

(9) The IASC has published several international accounting standards that lay down provisions and accounting principles that are relevant when dealing with environmental issues. Nevertheless, there is little guidance directly related to such matters and no specific international accounting standard solely focused on environmental issues.

(10) The recommendation has been prepared with a view to support policies linked to the single market and to contribute to ensuring that users of financial statements receive meaningful and comparable information with regard to environmental issues, thereby reinforcing the Community initiatives in the area of environmental protection. The Commission is of the

---

[7] Accounting harmonisation: A new strategy vis-à-vis international harmonisation. Communication from the Commission (COM(95)508), 14 November 1995.

opinion that there is a justified need to facilitate further harmonisation on what to disclose in the annual accounts and annual reports of enterprises in the European Union as far as environmental matters are concerned. The quantity, transparency and comparability of environmental data flowing through the annual accounts and annual reports of companies must also be increased. In order to achieve these objectives, and given the increasing importance attached to environmental issues in the European Union, the Commission aims at clarifying existing rules and providing more specific guidance on the subjects of recognition, measurement and disclosure of environmental issues in the annual accounts and annual reports of companies.

(11) The recommendation recognises that there has been a gradual development of separate environmental reports, particularly by companies that operate in sectors with significant environmental impacts. It is not a purpose of this recommendation to identify the reasons underlying this trend. However, this recommendation recognises that different groups of stakeholders have different information needs or rank them differently. Separate environmental reports satisfy the information needs of stakeholder groups that are only partially met by the information provided in the annual accounts and annual reports of enterprises. Therefore, the aim should be to make separate environmental reports and the annual accounts and annual reports more consistent, cohesive and closely associated. The purpose of this recommendation is to promote this aim by ensuring that environmental disclosures are incorporated in the annual accounts and annual reports in a way that complements the more detailed and wide-ranging separate environmental reports.

(12) Appropriate disclosures are considered a key factor that facilitates transparency of information disclosures are appropriate where they affect the user's understanding of the financial statements. This recommendation is not intended to establish unjustified burdensome obligations on the preparers of financial statements. The recommendation aims at providing comprehensive guidance in the area of disclosure, and identifies relevant disclosures that allow for comparability and consistency of the environmental information presented. This is particularly the case for the disclosure in the notes to the accounts of environmental expenditures either charged to the profit and loss account or capitalised, as well as the expenditures incurred as a result of fines and penalties for non-compliance with environmental regulations and compensations to third parties, paragraph 6 of section 4 of the Annex to this recommendation. The disclosure in the annual report of appropriate information with regard to environmental performance, where relevant to the financial performance or position of the enterprise or its development, is specifically addressed in paragraph 2 of section 4 of the Annex to this recommendation.

(13) For the recommendations on disclosures to be effective they need to be supplemented with workable definitions of the concepts covered. In order to meet this objective the recommendation includes a section on definitions.

(14) The recommendation aims to present guidance on the application of the provisions of the fourth and seventh Directives (Directives 78/660/EEC and 83/349/EEC, respectively) with respect to environmental issues. Therefore, certain accounting treatments with regard to environmental issues are recommended in order to enhance the provision of more meaningful information by the preparers of the financial statements. While encouraging particular solutions, this approach is not aimed at eliminating the possibility of applying alternative treatments where permitted by the Directives. In the light of this, account is also taken of the Commission's 1997 interpretative communication concerning certain Articles of the fourth and seventh Directives on accounting[8] and of the November 1995 Accounting advisory forum paper on environmental issues in financial reporting (Document XV/6004/94).

(15) The recommendation takes as a source of reference several international accounting

---

[8] OJ C 143, of 21.1.1998.

standards (IAS) that have been published by the International Accounting Standards Committee (IASC) which are of specific relevance to environmental issues, in particular IAS 36 on impairment of assets, IAS 37 on provisions, contingent liabilities and contingent assets and IAS 38 on intangible assets. The provisions contained in this recommendation are intended to be consistent with these International Accounting Standards, unless stated otherwise.

(16) The recommendation is also influenced by a statement of position on Accounting and financial reporting for environmental costs and liabilities prepared by the United Nations Working Group on International Standards of Accounting and Reporting.[9]

(17) As described in recitals 14 to 16 above, in response to the need to integrate environmental considerations into financial reporting, some guidelines have been developed at Community and international level. This recommendation builds upon such developments and at the same time seeks to provide a suitable Community framework for further improvements. The Commission believes that to meet the objectives of the recommendation, action by Member States is necessary. The Commission encourages and leaves scope to Member States for measures at national level. Moreover, discussions on ways to improve the present situation are likely to continue at international level,

HEREBY RECOMMENDS:

That the Member States:

1. Ensure that for accounting periods commencing within 12 months from the date of adoption of this recommendation and for all future accounting periods, companies covered by the fourth and seventh Company Directives (Directives 78/660/EEC and 83/349/EEC respectively) apply the provisions contained in the Annex to this recommendation in the preparation of the annual and consolidated accounts and the annual report and consolidated annual report.

2. Take the appropriate measures to promote the application of this recommendation.

3. Notify the Commission of the measures taken.

Annex

1. SCOPE

1. The recommendation is limited to information provided in the annual and consolidated accounts and in the annual reports and consolidated annual reports of companies with regard to environmental issues. It does not deal with special purpose reporting, such as environmental reports, except where it is considered appropriate to relate annual accounts, annual reports and separate environmental reports with a view to making their information content consistent.

2. The recommendation covers requirements for recognition, measurement and disclosure of environmental expenditures, environmental liabilities and risks and related assets that arise from transactions and events that affect, or are likely to affect, the financial position and results of the reporting entity.

3. The recommendation also identifies the type of environmental information that is appropriate to be disclosed in the annual and consolidated accounts and/or the annual and consolidated annual report with regard to the company's attitude towards the environment and the enterprise's environmental performance, to the extent that they may have consequences on the financial position of the company. The recommendation applies to both individual accounts and consolidated accounts. In the case of consolidated accounts, disclosures should be related to the

---

[9] ISAR—Td/B/COM.2/ISAR/3, 12 March 1998.

group. The requirements for recognition and measurement should be consistently applied to all consolidated entities.

4. The recommendation applies to all companies covered by the fourth and seventh Company Directives, having due regard to the exemptions that Member States are permitted to introduce for small and medium-sized companies in accordance with Articles 11 and 27 of the fourth Directive.

5. Although the specific accounting requirements for banks, other financial institutions and insurance companies are dealt with in separate directives,[10] this recommendation also applies to banks, other financial institutions and insurance companies, as the financial implications of environmental issues are not different for these types of companies.

2. DEFINITIONS

1. For the purposes of this recommendation the term environment refers to the natural physical surroundings and includes air, water, land, flora, fauna and non-renewable resources such as fossil fuels and minerals.

2. Environmental expenditure includes the costs of steps taken by an undertaking or on its behalf by others to prevent, reduce or repair damage to the environment that results from its operating activities. These costs include, amongst others, the disposal and avoidance of waste, the protection of soil and of surface water and groundwater, the protection of clean air and climate, noise reduction, and the protection of biodiversity and landscape. Only additional identifiable costs that are primarily intended to prevent, reduce or repair damage to the environment should be included. Costs that may influence favourably the environment but whose primary purpose is to respond to other needs, for instance to increase profitability, health and safety at the workplace, safe use of the company's products or production efficiency, should be excluded. Where it is not possible to isolate separately the amount of the additional costs from other costs in which it may be integrated, it can be estimated in so far as the resulting amount fulfils the condition to be primarily intended to prevent, reduce or repair damage to the environment.

3. Costs incurred as a result of fines, or penalties for non-compliance with environmental regulation, and compensation to third parties as a result of loss or injury caused by past environmental pollution are excluded from this definition, as discussed in paragraph 6(f) of section 4 of this Annex. Whilst related to the impact of the company's operations on the environment, these costs do not prevent, reduce or repair damage to the environment.

4. Furthermore, the Statistical Office of the European Union (Eurostat) has produced a series of detailed definitions of expenditures by environmental domain, which are included in the implementation documents of the Council Regulation (EC, Euratom) No 58/97 of 20 December 1996 concerning structural business statistics.[11] These definitions, subject to regular updating, are the basis for statistical reporting requirements on environmental protection expenditures in the European Union. When using the general definition in paragraph 2, it is recommended that companies take into consideration these detailed definitions for making the disclosures for environmental expenditures stated in section 4 of this Annex to the extent that they are consistent with the recognition and measurement requirements stated in section 3.

---

[10] Council Directive of 8 December (86/635/EEC) on the annual accounts and consolidated accounts of banks and other financial institutions (OJ L 372, 31.12.1986, 1 to 17), reproduced supra under no. B. 7; Council Directive of 19 December 1991 (91/674/EEC) on the annual and consolidated accounts of insurance undertakings (OJ L 374, 31.12.1991, 7 to 31), reproduced infra under no. I. 23.

[11] OJ L 14, 17.1.1997, 1. See also implementation document ENV/96/10c. The European Classification of Environmental Protection Activities (CEPA) distinguishes between the following environmental domains: waste management; protection of ambient air and climate; waste water management; protection of soil and groundwater; protection of biodiversity and landscape; other environmental protection activities.

3. Recognition and Measurement

Recognition of environmental liabilities

1. An environmental liability is recognised when it is probable that an outflow of resources embodying economic benefits will result from the settlement of a present obligation of an environmental nature that arose from past events, and the amount at which the settlement will take place can be measured reliably. The nature of this obligation must be clearly defined and may be of two types:
– legal or contractual: the enterprise has a legal or contractual obligation to prevent, reduce or repair environmental damage, or
– constructive: a constructive obligation arises from the enterprise's own actions when the enterprise has committed itself to prevent, reduce or repair environmental damage and has no discretion to avoid such action because, on the basis of published statements of policy or intention or by an established pattern of past practice of the enterprise, the enterprise has indicated to third parties that it will accept the responsibility to prevent, reduce or repair environmental damage.

2. Past or current industry practice result in a constructive obligation for the enterprise only to the extent that management has no discretion to avoid action. It will only occur when the enterprise has accepted the responsibility to prevent, reduce or repair environmental damage by a published specific statement or by an established pattern of past practice.

3. Environmental damage which may be related to the enterprise or may have been caused by the enterprise but for which there is no legal, contractual or constructive obligation to rectify the damage's extent, does not qualify to be recognised as an environmental liability in the enterprise's annual accounts in accordance with paragraphs 1 and 2. This does not prejudice the application of the criteria set out in paragraph 5 for contingent environmental liabilities.

4. An environmental liability is recognised when a reliable estimate of the costs derived from the obligation can be made. If, at the date of the balance sheet, there is an obligation the nature of which is clearly defined and which is likely to give rise to an outflow of resources embodying economic benefits, but uncertain as to the amount or as to the date, then a provision should be recognised, provided that a reliable estimate can be made of the amount of the obligation. This treatment is in accordance with Articles 20(1)[12] and 31(1)(bb) of the fourth Directive. Uncertainties as to the date or as to the amount relate, for example, to evolving clean-up technologies and the extent and nature of the clean up required. In the rare circumstances where a reliable estimate of the costs is not possible, the liability should not be recognised. It should be regarded as a contingent liability, as mentioned in paragraph 26.

Contingent environmental liabilities

5. A contingent liability should not be recognised in the balance sheet. If there is a possibility, which is less than probable, that the damage has to be rectified in the future but the obligation has yet to be confirmed by the occurrence of an uncertain event, a contingent liability should be disclosed in the notes to the annual accounts. If it is a remote possibility that the enterprise will have to incur an environmental expenditure or such expenditure will not be material, disclosure of such contingent liability is not required.

Offsetting of liabilities and expected recoveries

6. Where the enterprise expects that some or all of the expenditures related to an environmental liability will be reimbursed from another party, the reimbursement should be recognised only when it is virtually certain that it will be received if the enterprise settles the obligation.

---

[12] Where, in accordance with paragraph 20 of the Commission's 1998 interpretative communication concerning certain Articles of the fourth and seventh Council Directives on accounting, Member States have implemented the option contained in Article 20(2) of the fourth Directive, it is also applicable to environmental charges.

7. An expected recovery from a third party should not be offset against the environmental liability. It should be separately shown as an asset in the balance sheet, at an amount that does not exceed the amount of the related provision. It can be offset against the environmental liability only when there is a legal right for such netting that the enterprise intends to use. When, on the basis of this provision, netting is appropriate, the full amount of the liability and the expected reimbursement should be disclosed in the notes.

8. Expected proceeds from the sale of related property should not be offset against an environmental liability or taken into account in measuring a provision, even if such expected disposal is closely linked to the event giving rise to the provision.

9. Normally the enterprise is liable for the whole environmental liability. If not, only the enterprise's portion would be recorded as an environmental liability.

Recognition of environmental expenditure

10. Environmental expenditures should be recognised as an expense in the period in which they are incurred unless they meet the criteria to be recognised as an asset set out in paragraph 12.

11. Environmental expenditures that relate to damage that has occurred in a prior period do not qualify as prior period adjustments but should be expensed in the current period, i.e. the period in which they are recognised.

Capitalisation of environmental expenditure

12. Environmental expenditure may be capitalised if it has been incurred to prevent or reduce future damage or conserve resources, brings future economic benefits and satisfies the condition laid down in Article 15(2) of the fourth Directive.

13. Environmental expenditures incurred to prevent or reduce future damage or conserve resources can only qualify for recognition as an asset if, in accordance with Article 15(2) of the fourth Directive, they are intended for use on a continuing basis for the purpose of the undertaking's activities and if, in addition, one of the following criteria is met:

(a) the costs relate to anticipated economic benefits that are expected to flow to the enterprise and extend the life, increase the capacity or improve the safety or efficiency of other assets owned by the enterprise (in excess of their originally assessed standard of performance); or

(b) the costs reduce or prevent environmental contamination that is likely to occur as a result of future operations of the enterprise.

14. If the criteria for recognition as an asset laid down in paragraphs 12 and 13 have not been met, environmental expenditure should be charged to the profit and loss account as incurred. If they have been met, environmental expenditure should be capitalised and amortised to the profit and loss account over the current and appropriate future periods, i.e. systematically over their expected useful economic life.

15. Environmental expenditure should not be capitalised but charged to the profit and loss account if it does not give rise to future economic benefits. This situation occurs when environmental expenditure relates to past or current activities and to the restoration of the environment to its pre-contamination state (e.g. treatment of waste, clean-up costs relating to current operating activities, clean up of damage incurred in prior periods, environmental administration costs or environmental audits).

16. Items such as plant and machinery may be acquired for environmental reasons, for example, technical installations for pollution control or pollution prevention in order to comply with environmental laws or regulations. If they meet the criteria for recognition as an asset laid down in paragraphs 12 and 13, they must be capitalised.

17. There are cases when no anticipated future economic benefits result from the environmental expenditure itself, but rather future benefits are received from another asset that is used in the enterprise's operations. When the environmental expenditure that is recognised as an asset is related to another existing asset, it should be included as an integral part of that asset, and should not be recognised separately.

18. There can be rights or items of a similar nature acquired in connection with the impact of the operations of the enterprise on the environment (for example patents, licences, pollution permits, and emission rights). If, in accordance with Articles 9(C)(I)(2)(a) and 10(C)(I)(2)(a) of the fourth Directive, they have been acquired for valuable consideration and, in addition, they meet the criteria for recognition as an asset laid down in paragraphs 12 and 13, they must be capitalised and amortised systematically over their expected useful economic lives. If not, they should be charged to the profit and loss account as incurred.

Asset impairment

19. Environmental developments or factors may cause an existing fixed asset to be impaired, for example in the case of site contamination. A value adjustment should be made if the amount recoverable from the use of the site has declined below its carrying amount. This situation should, in the context of Article 35(1)(c)(bb) of the fourth Directive, be regarded as permanent. The amount of this value adjustment should be charged to the profit and loss account. In accordance with Article 20(3) of the fourth Directive, provisions for liabilities and charges, as defined in paragraph 4, cannot be set against the values of assets.

20. Where in accordance with paragraph 17, environmental expenditure is recognised as an integral part of another asset, the combined asset should at each balance sheet date be tested for its recoverability and, where appropriate, written down to its recoverable amount.

21. If the carrying amount of an asset already takes account of a loss in economic benefits because of environmental reasons, the subsequent expenditure to restore the future economic benefits to its original standard of performance can be capitalised, to the extent that the resulting carrying amount does not exceed the recoverable amount of the asset.

Measurement of environmental liabilities

22. An environmental liability is recognised, when a reliable estimate of the expenditure to settle the obligation can be made.

23. The amount of the liability should be the best estimate of the expenditure required to settle the present obligation at the balance sheet date, based on the existing situation and taking into account future developments both technical and in legislation, in so far as their occurrence is probable to occur.

24. The amount should be an estimate of the full amount of the liability irrespective of the date on which the activity is ceased or the liability is due to be settled. A gradual build-up of the full amount of the liability over the period of the enterprise's operations is allowed under Article 20(1) of the fourth Directive.

25. In estimating the amount of an environmental liability, the following rules apply. If the liability being measured involves different possible outcomes, according to paragraph 23, the best estimate should be accounted for. In the extremely rare cases where it is not possible to determine the best estimate of the liability with sufficient reliability, that liability should be regarded as a contingent liability and, therefore, its existence should be disclosed in the notes to the annual accounts. In addition, disclosure should be given of the reasons why no reliable estimate should be made.

26. Furthermore, for measuring the amount of an environmental liability, the following should be taken into consideration:
– incremental direct costs of the remedial effort,
– cost of compensation and benefits for those employees who are expected to devote a significant amount of time directly to the restoration effort,
– post-remedial monitoring requirements,
– advances in technology, so long as it is probable that the governmental authority will approve the technology.

Provisions for site-restoration and dismantling costs

27. Expenditure relating to site restoration, removal of accumulated waste by-product, closure or removal of fixed assets, that the company is under obligation to incur, should be recognised in accordance with the criteria laid down in paragraphs 1 to 4. If these criteria are met, the

obligation to incur the future expenditure must be accounted for as an environmental liability.

28. In accordance with paragraph 24, this environmental liability for site restoration, removal or closure should be recognised at the date that the company's operations start and consequently the obligation arises. The recognition of this liability should not be delayed until the activity is completed or the site is closed. Where this liability is recognised, the estimated expenditure is included as part of the cost of the related asset that has to be dismantled and removed. This capitalised expenditure is then depreciated as part of the depreciable amount of the related asset. Additional damage could be caused during operations; the company's obligation to restore it arises when this environmental damage occurs.

29. In accordance with International Accounting Standard 37, paragraph 14, in the case of site-restoration and dismantling costs of long-term operations, the accounting treatment laid down in paragraph 28 is the preferred approach. This accounting treatment is anyway allowed on the basis of Article 20(1) of the fourth Directive together with the gradual build-up of a provision for such costs, which is the other option. The enterprise may recognise long-term decommissioning costs over the period relating to the operations. In each reporting period a portion of the costs is charged as an expense, with the resulting balance shown as a separate liability.

Discounting of long-term environmental liabilities

30. For environmental liabilities that will not be settled in the near future, measuring them at present value (i.e. discounting) is allowed, but not required,[13] if the obligation and the amount and timing of the payments are fixed or can be reliably determined. Measuring at current cost (i.e. non-discounting estimated cost) is also acceptable. However, where the effect of the time value of money is material, it is a more appropriate treatment to measure environmental liabilities at present value.

31. The method chosen should be disclosed in the notes. The expected cost to be incurred should be based on a site-specific plan for the clean-up and/or remedial treatment of the contamination. The amount and timing of the payments should be based on objective and verifiable information.

32. The undiscounted estimated cash flows should be the estimated amounts expected to be paid at the dates of settlement (including estimates of inflation) and should be computed using explicit assumptions derived from the clean-up and/or remedial plan, such that a knowledgeable party could review the computation and concur with the estimated cash flows.

33. If an enterprise uses discounting in the measurement of its environmental liabilities this should be applied on a consistent basis. Any asset, relating to the recovery of a portion or all of a liability that is measured on a discounted basis, should also be discounted. In addition, if liabilities are measured on a discounted basis, the recoverable amount of assets should also be measured on the basis of discounted cash flows.

34. Measuring at present value requires the determination of a discount rate and information about the factors that may affect the timing and the amount of the estimated cash flows required. Moreover, the amount of the liability should be reviewed each year and adjusted for any change in the assumptions.

4. DISCLOSURES

1. Environmental issues should be disclosed to the extent that they are material to the financial performance or the financial position of the reporting entity. Depending upon the item, disclosures should be included in the annual and consolidated annual report or in the notes to the annual and consolidated accounts. Paragraphs 2,

---

[13] International accounting standard 37, paragraph 45, requires discounting where the effect of the time value of money is material.

5 and 6 deal with the disclosure of items in the annual and consolidated annual report, or in the notes. Paragraphs 3 and 4 deal with the presentation of items on the face of the balance sheet.

Disclosure in the annual and consolidated annual report

2. On the basis of the provisions laid down in Article 46(1) and (2) of the fourth Directive and Article 36(1) and (2) of the seventh Directive on the contents of the annual and consolidated annual report of companies, where environmental issues are relevant to the financial performance and position of the undertaking or its development, the annual report should include a description of the respective issues and the undertaking's response thereto. This information must provide a fair review of the development of the undertaking's business and position to the extent that environmental issues can directly affect it. For this purpose, the following disclosures are recommended:

(a) the policy and programmes that have been adopted by the enterprise in respect of environmental protection measures, particularly in respect of pollution prevention. It is relevant for users of the annual report to be able to ascertain to what extent environmental protection is an integral part of the company's policies and activities. Where applicable, this may include reference to the adoption of an environmental protection system and required compliance with a given set of associated standards or certifications;

(b) the improvements that have been made in key areas of environmental protection. This information is particularly useful if, in an objective and transparent manner, it provides a record of the performance of the enterprise with respect to a given quantified objective (for example emissions over the past five years) and reasons as to why significant differences may have arisen;

(c) the extent to which environmental protection measures, owing to present legislation or resulting from change in future legal requirements that have been substantially enacted, have been implemented or are in process of implementation;

(d) where appropriate and relevant to the nature and size of the business operations of the company and to the types of environmental issues relevant to the enterprise, information on the environmental performance of the enterprise: such as energy use, materials use, water use, emissions, waste disposals;

This information could usefully be provided by means of quantitative eco-efficiency indicators and, where relevant, detailed by business segment. It is particularly relevant to provide quantitative data, in absolute terms, for emissions and consumption of energy, water and materials[14] for the reporting period together with comparative data for the previous reporting period. These figures should preferably be expressed in physical units rather than in monetary terms; moreover, for a better understanding of their relative significance and evolution, figures in monetary terms could be put in relation with items shown on the balance sheet or the profit and loss account;

(e) if the company issues a separate environmental report that contains more detailed or additional quantitative or qualitative environmental information, a reference to this report. If the environmental report contains the information mentioned in (d), a summary description of the issue and an indication that further relevant information can be found in the environmental report could also be made. Information provided in a separate environmental report should be consistent with any related information in the annual report and annual accounts of the enterprise. If the environmental report has been subject to an external verification process, this should be stated in the annual report. It is relevant to inform users of the annual report as to whether or not the environmental report contains objective, externally verifiable data.

The scope and boundaries of the reporting entity should preferably be the same in both the annual report and the separate environmental report. If not, they should be clearly stated in the

---

[14] The European Commission is one of the partners in the 'Eco-efficiency indicators and reporting' project being developed by the World Business Council of Sustainable Development. This project aims at developing standardised eco-efficiency indicators, of which the 'core indicators' are intended to be relevant to all enterprises.

environmental report so that it can be identified to what extent it corresponds to the entity reporting in the annual report. Furthermore, the reporting date and period of the separate environmental report should also preferably be the same as that of the annual report.

Disclosure in the balance sheet

3. Provisions should be shown in the balance sheet under the caption 'Other provisions'. In accordance with Article 4 of the fourth Directive, a more detailed subdivision of the items prescribed in Articles 9, 10 and 23 to 26 for the layout of the balance sheet and the profit and loss account is permitted provided that the layouts are complied with. Member States may require such subdivisions.

4. If material, it is more appropriate to show environmental liabilities separately on the face of the balance sheet. Otherwise, if material, they should be separately disclosed in the notes on the accounts, in accordance with Article 42 of the fourth Directive and Article 29(1) of the seventh Directive.

Disclosure in the notes to the annual and consolidated accounts

5. In conformity with the provisions of the fourth and seventh Directives, the following information should be disclosed in the notes:

(a) description of the valuation methods applied, and the methods applied in calculating the value adjustments, on environmental issues as part of the disclosure required by Article 43(1)(1) of the fourth Directive and Article 34(1) of the seventh Directive;

(b) extraordinary environmental expenditures charged to the profit and loss account, in accordance with Article 29 of the fourth Directive and Article 17 of the seventh Directive;

(c) disclosure and details of the caption 'Other provisions', if not disclosed on the face of the balance sheet, in line with paragraph 4;

(d) contingent environmental liabilities, in conformity with Article 43(1)(7) of the fourth Directive and Article 34(7) of the seventh Directive, including narrative information in sufficient detail, so that the nature of the contingency can be understood. If significant measurement uncertainties make it impossible to estimate the amount of an environmental liability, this fact together with the reasons therefor should be disclosed along with, where possible, the range of possible outcomes.

6. In addition to the requirements of the fourth and seventh Directives, the following disclosures should be provided in the notes:

(a) for each material environmental liability, a description of its nature and an indication of the timing and terms of settlement. An explanation of the damage and of the laws or regulations that require its remediation and the restoring or preventive steps being taken or proposed. Where the nature and conditions of the items are sufficiently similar this information could be disclosed in an aggregated manner. If the amount of costs is estimated based on a range of amounts, a description of how the estimate was arrived at, with an indication of any expected changes in the law or to existing technology that are reflected in the amounts provided for;

(b) where the present value method has been used and the effect of discounting is material, the undiscounted amount of the liability and the discount rate used should be disclosed;

(c) in the case of long-term site-restoration, decommissioning and dismantling costs, the accounting policy. Where the company uses a gradual build-up of a provision under paragraph 29 of section 3, the amount of the full provision that would be required to cover all such long-term costs. The provisions 6(d) and 6(e), with regard to disclosure of environmental expenditure charged to the profit and loss account and environmental expenditure capitalised, should also be taken into consideration;

(d) the amount of environmental expenditure charged to the profit and loss account and the basis on which such amounts are calculated. Where relevant, a subdivision of the items the enterprise has identified as environmental expenditure, in a manner that is appropriate to the nature and size of the business operations of the company and to the types of environmental issues relevant to the enterprise. To the extent that it is possible and relevant, a breakdown of the expenditure by environmental domain as referred to in paragraph 4 of section 2 is appropriate;

(e) to the extent that it can be reliably estimated, the amount of environmental expenditure capitalised during the reporting period. If applicable, it should also be disclosed what part of the amount concerned relates to expenditure aimed at removing pollutants after their creation, and what part represents the additional expenditure to adapt the installation or the production process in order to generate less pollution (i.e. that relates to technologies or practices for pollution prevention). To the extent that is possible and relevant, a breakdown of capitalised expenditure by environmental domain as referred to in paragraph 4 of section 2 is appropriate;

(f) where significant, costs incurred as a result of fines and penalties for non-compliance with environmental regulations, and compensations paid to third parties, for example as a result of loss or injury caused by past environmental pollution, should be disclosed separately, if not already separately disclosed as extraordinary items. Whilst related to the impact of the company's operation on the environment, these costs do not prevent, reduce or repair damage to the environment, therefore separate disclosure from environmental expenditures is appropriate;

(g) government incentives related to environmental protection received or entitled to by the company. The terms of each item concerned, or where similar a summary of the conditions. The accounting treatment adopted should also be disclosed.

C. 18.

European Parliament and Council Directive 2001/65/EC of 27 September 2001 amending Directives 78/660/EEC, 83/349/EEC and 86/635/EEC as regards the valuation rules for the annual and consolidated accounts of certain types of companies as well as of banks and other financial institutions[1]

THE EUROPEAN PARLIAMENT AND THE COUNCIL OF THE EUROPEAN UNION,

Having regard to the Treaty establishing the European Community, and in particular Article 44(2)(g),

Having regard to the proposal from the Commission,[2]

Having regard to the opinion of the Economic and Social Committee,[3]

Acting in accordance with the procedure laid down in Article 251 of the Treaty,[4]

Whereas:

(1) Article 32 of the Fourth Council Directive 78/660/EEC of 25 July 1978 on the annual accounts of certain types of companies[5] requires the items shown in the annual accounts to be valued on the basis of the principle of purchase price or production cost.

(2) Article 33 of Directive 78/660/EEC authorises Member States to permit or require companies to revalue certain assets, to value certain assets at replacement cost or to apply other methods that take into account the effects of inflation on the items shown in the annual accounts.

(3) Article 29 of the Seventh Council Directive 83/349/EEC of 13 June 1983 on consolidated accounts[6] requires assets and liabilities to be included in consolidated accounts to be valued in accordance with Articles 31 to 42 and Article 60 of Directive 78/660/EEC.

(4) Article 1 of Council Directive 86/635/EEC of 8 December 1986 on the annual accounts and consolidated accounts of banks and other financial institutions[7] requires assets and liabilities to be valued in accordance with Articles 31 to 42 of Directive 78/660/EEC, except when Directive 86/635/EEC provides otherwise.

(5) The annual and consolidated accounts of insurance undertakings are prepared in accordance with Council Directive 91/674/EEC of 19 December 1991 on the annual accounts and consolidated accounts of insurance undertakings.[8] The amendments to Directives 78/660/EEC and 83/349/EEC do not concern the provisions of Directive 91/674/EEC, but the Commission may bring forward similar proposals to amend that Directive after having consulted the relevant advisory committee.

(6) The dynamic nature of international financial markets has resulted in the widespread use of not only traditional primary financial instruments such as shares and bonds, but also various forms of derivative financial instruments such as futures, options, forward contracts and swaps.

(7) Leading accounting standard setters in the world are moving away from the historical cost

---

[1] OJ L 283, 27.9.2001, 28–32.
[2] OJ C 311, 31.10.2000, 1.
[3] OJ C 268, 19.9.2000, 1.
[4] Opinion of the European Parliament of 15 May 2001 (OJ C 34, 7.2.2002, 91) and Council Decision of 30 May 2001.
[5] OJ L 222, 14.8.1978, 11, reproduced supra under no. C. 4. Directive as last amended by Directive 1999/60/EC (OJ L 162, 26.6.1999, 65), reproduced supra under no. C. 16.

[6] OJ L 193, 18.7.1983, 1, reproduced supra under no. C. 6. Directive as last amended by the 1994 Act of Accession.
[7] OJ L 372, 31.12.1986, 1, reproduced supra under no. B. 7.
[8] OJ L 374, 31.12.1991, 7, reproduced infra under no. I. 23.

model for the valuation of these financial instruments towards a model of fair value accounting.

(8) The Communication of the Commission on Accounting harmonisation: a new strategy vis-à-vis international harmonisation called for the European Union to work to maintain consistency between Community accounting directives and developments in international accounting standard setting, in particular within the International Accounting Standards Committee (IASC).

(9) In order to maintain such consistency between internationally recognised accounting standards and Directives 78/660/EEC, 83/349/ EEC and 86/635/EEC, it is necessary to amend these Directives in order to allow for certain financial assets and liabilities to be valued at fair value. This will enable European companies to report inconformity with current international developments.

(10) This amendment to Directives 78/660/EEC, 83/349/EEC and 86/635/EEC is in line with the Commission's communication to the European Parliament and the Council of 13 June 2000 on the EU financial reporting strategy which proposes the use of recognised international accounting standards for the preparation of consolidated financial statements by listed companies. The purpose of this amendment is to allow the application of the international accounting standard dealing with the recognition and measurement of financial instruments.

(11) Comparability of financial information throughout the Community makes it necessary to require Member States to introduce a system of fair value accounting for certain financial instruments. Member States should permit the adoption of that system by all companies or any classes of companies subject to the Directives 78/660/EEC, 83/349/EEC and 86/635/EEC in respect of both the annual and consolidated accounts or in respect of consolidated accounts only. Further, Member States should be permitted to require the adoption of that system in respect of all companies or any classes of companies for both the annual and consolidated accounts or for the consolidated accounts only.

(12) Fair value accounting should only be possible for those items where there is a well-developed international consensus that fair value accounting is appropriate. The current consensus is that fair value accounting should not be applied to all financial assets and liabilities, for instance not to most of those relating to the banking book.

(13) The notes on the accounts should include certain information concerning financial instruments in the balance sheet, which have been measured at fair value. The annual report should give an indication of the company's risk management objectives and policies in relation to its use of financial instruments.

(14) Derivative financial instruments can have a significant impact on the financial position of companies. Disclosures on derivative financial instruments and their fair value are considered appropriate even if the company does not use fair value accounting. In order to limit the administrative burden for small companies, Member States should be allowed to exempt small companies from this disclosure requirement.

(15) Accounting for financial instruments is a fast evolving area of financial reporting which necessitates a review by the Commission based on the experiences of Member States with fair value accounting in practice,

HAVE ADOPTED THIS DIRECTIVE:

Article 1

[. . .]

¶ *Article 1 inserts section 7a and article 61a and amends articles 43(1), 44(1), 46(2) and 59(2) of Directive 78/660/EEC, reproduced supra under no. C. 4. The modifications are directly incorporated therein.*

Article 2

[. . .]

¶ *Article 2 amends articles 29(1), 34 and inserts article 36(2)(e) and article 50a to Directive 83/349/EEC, reproduced supra under no. C. 6. The modifications are directly incorporated therein.*

Article 3

[. . .]

¶ *Article 3 replaces article 1(1) of Directive 86/635/EEC, reproduced supra under no. B. 7. The modifications are directly incorporated therein.*

Article 4

1. Member States shall bring into force the laws, regulations and administrative provisions necessary for them to comply with this Directive before 1 January 2004. They shall forthwith inform the Commission thereof.

When Member States adopt these provisions, they shall contain a reference to this Directive or shall be accompanied by such reference on the occasion of their official publication. The methods for making such reference shall be laid down by Member States.

2. Member States shall communicate to the Commission the main provisions of domestic law, which they adopt in the field governed by this Directive.

Article 5

This Directive is addressed to the Member States.

C. 19.

Council Regulation 2157/2001/EC
of 8 October 2001
on the statute for a European Company (SE)[1]

THE COUNCIL OF THE EUROPEAN UNION,

Having regard to the Treaty establishing the European Community, and in particular Article 308 thereof,

Having regard to the proposal from the Commission,[2]

Having regard to the opinion of the European Parliament,[3]

Having regard to the opinion of the Economic and Social Committee,[4]

Whereas:

(1) The completion of the internal market and the improvement it brings about in the economic and social situation throughout the Community mean not only that barriers to trade must be removed, but also that the structures of production must be adapted to the Community dimension. For that purpose it is essential that companies the business of which is not limited to satisfying purely local needs should be able to plan and carry out the reorganisation of their business on a Community scale.

(2) Such reorganisation presupposes that existing companies from different Member States are given the option of combining their potential by means of mergers. Such operations can be carried out only with due regard to the rules of competition laid down in the Treaty.

(3) Restructuring and cooperation operations involving companies from different Member States give rise to legal and psychological difficulties and tax problems. The approximation of Member States' company law by means of Directives based on Article 44 of the Treaty can overcome some of those difficulties. Such approximation does not, however, release companies governed by different legal systems from the obligation to choose a form of company governed by a particular national law.

(4) The legal framework within which business must be carried on in the Community is still based largely on national laws and therefore no longer corresponds to the economic framework within which it must develop if the objectives set out in Article 18 of the Treaty are to be achieved. That situation forms a considerable obstacle to the creation of groups of companies from different Member States.

(5) Member States are obliged to ensure that the provisions applicable to European companies under this Regulation do not result either in discrimination arising out of unjustified different treatment of European companies compared with public limited-liability companies or in disproportionate restrictions on the formation of a European company or on the transfer of its registered office.

(6) It is essential to ensure as far as possible that the economic unit and the legal unit of business in the Community coincide. For that purpose, provision should be made for the creation, side by side with companies governed by a particular national law, of companies formed and carrying on business under the law created by a Community Regulation directly applicable in all Member States.

(7) The provisions of such a Regulation will permit the creation and management of companies with a European dimension, free from the obstacles arising from the disparity and the limited territorial application of national company law.

---

[1] OJ L 294, 10.11.2001, 1–21.
[2] OJ C 263, 16.10.1989, 41 and OJ C 176, 8.7.1991, 1.
[3] Opinion of 4 September 2001 (OJ C 72, 21.3.2002, 59).
[4] OJ C 124, 21.5.1990, 34.

(8) The Statute for a European public limited-liability company (hereinafter referred to as 'SE') is among the measures to be adopted by the Council before 1992 listed in the Commission's White Paper on completing the internal market, approved by the European Council that met in Milan in June 1985. The European Council that met in Brussels in 1987 expressed the wish to see such a Statute created swiftly.

(9) Since the Commission's submission in 1970 of a proposal for a Regulation on the Statute for a European public limited-liability company, amended in 1975, work on the approximation of national company law has made substantial progress, so that on those points where the functioning of an SE does not need uniform Community rules reference may be made to the law governing public limited-liability companies in the Member State where it has its registered office.

(10) Without prejudice to any economic needs that may arise in the future, if the essential objective of legal rules governing SEs is to be attained, it must be possible at least to create such a company as a means both of enabling companies from different Member States to merge or to create a holding company and of enabling companies and other legal persons carrying on economic activities and governed by the laws of different Member States to form joint subsidiaries.

(11) In the same context it should be possible for a public limited-liability company with a registered office and head office within the Community to transform itself into an SE without going into liquidation, provided it has a subsidiary in a Member State other than that of its registered office.

(12) National provisions applying to public limited-liability companies that offer their securities to the public and to securities transactions should also apply where an SE is formed by means of an offer of securities to the public and to SEs wishing to utilise such financial instruments.

(13) The SE itself must take the form of a company with share capital, that being the form most suited, in terms of both financing and management, to the needs of a company carrying on business on a European scale. In order to ensure that such companies are of reasonable size, a minimum amount of capital should be set so that they have sufficient assets without making it difficult for small and medium-sized undertakings to form SEs.

(14) An SE must be efficiently managed and properly supervised. It must be borne in mind that there are at present in the Community two different systems for the administration of public limited-liability companies. Although an SE should be allowed to choose between the two systems, the respective responsibilities of those responsible for management and those responsible for supervision should be clearly defined.

(15) Under the rules and general principles of private international law, where one undertaking controls another governed by a different legal system, its ensuing rights and obligations as regards the protection of minority shareholders and third parties are governed by the law governing the controlled undertaking, without prejudice to the obligations imposed on the controlling undertaking by its own law, for example the requirement to prepare consolidated accounts.

(16) Without prejudice to the consequences of any subsequent coordination of the laws of the Member States, specific rules for SEs are not at present required in this field. The rules and general principles of private international law should therefore be applied both where an SE exercises control and where it is the controlled company.

(17) The rule thus applicable where an SE is controlled by another undertaking should be specified, and for this purpose reference should be made to the law governing public limited-liability companies in the Member State in which the SE has its registered office.

(18) Each Member State must be required to apply the sanctions applicable to public limited-liability companies governed by its law in respect of infringements of this Regulation.

(19) The rules on the involvement of employees in the European company are laid down in Directive 2001/86/EC,[5] and those provisions

---

[5] OJ L294, 10.11.2001, 22.

thus form an indissociable complement to this Regulation and must be applied concomitantly.

(20) This Regulation does not cover other areas of law such as taxation, competition, intellectual property or insolvency. The provisions of the Member States' law and of Community law are therefore applicable in the above areas and in other areas not covered by this Regulation.

(21) Directive 2001/86/EC is designed to ensure that employees have a right of involvement in issues and decisions affecting the life of their SE. Other social and labour legislation questions, in particular the right of employees to information and consultation as regulated in the Member States, are governed by the national provisions applicable, under the same conditions, to public limited-liability companies.

(22) The entry into force of this Regulation must be deferred so that each Member State may incorporate into its national law the provisions of Directive 2001/86/EC and set up in advance the necessary machinery for the formation and operation of SEs with registered offices within its territory, so that the Regulation and the Directive may be applied concomitantly.

(23) A company the head office of which is not in the Community should be allowed to participate in the formation of an SE provided that company is formed under the law of a Member State, has its registered office in that Member State and has a real and continuous link with a Member State's economy according to the principles established in the 1962 General Programme for the abolition of restrictions on freedom of establishment. Such a link exists in particular if a company has an establishment in that Member State and conducts operations therefrom.

(24) The SE should be enabled to transfer its registered office to another Member State. Adequate protection of the interests of minority shareholders who oppose the transfer, of creditors and of holders of other rights should be proportionate. Such transfer should not affect the rights originating before the transfer.

(25) This Regulation is without prejudice to any provision which may be inserted in the 1968 Brussels Convention or in any text adopted by Member States or by the Council to replace such Convention, relating to the rules of jurisdiction applicable in the case of transfer of the registered offices of a public limited-liability company from one Member State to another.

(26) Activities by financial institutions are regulated by specific directives and the national law implementing those directives and additional national rules regulating those activities apply in full to an SE.

(27) In view of the specific Community character of an SE, the 'real seat' arrangement adopted by this Regulation in respect of SEs is without prejudice to Member States' laws and does not pre-empt any choices to be made for other Community texts on company law.

(28) The Treaty does not provide, for the adoption of this Regulation, powers of action other than those of Article 308 thereof.

(29) Since the objectives of the intended action, as outlined above, cannot be adequately attained by the Member States in as much as a European public limited-liability company is being established at European level and can therefore, because of the scale and impact of such company, be better attained at Community level, the Community may take measures in accordance with the principle of subsidiarity enshrined in Article 5 of the Treaty. In accordance with the principle of proportionality as set out in the said Article, this Regulation does not go beyond what is necessary to attain these objectives,

HAS ADOPTED THIS REGULATION:

TITLE I

GENERAL PROVISIONS

Article 1

1. A company may be set up within the territory of the Community in the form of a European public limited-liability company (Societas Europaea or SE) on the conditions and in the manner laid down in this Regulation.

2. The capital of an SE shall be divided into shares. No shareholder shall be liable for more than the amount he has subscribed.

3. An SE shall have legal personality.

4. Employee involvement in an SE shall be governed by the provisions of Directive 2001/86/EC.

Article 2

1. Public limited-liability companies such as referred to in Annex I, formed under the law of a Member State, with registered offices and head offices within the Community may form an SE by means of a merger provided that at least two of them are governed by the law of different Member States.

2. Public and private limited-liability companies such as referred to in Annex II, formed under the law of a Member State, with registered offices and head offices within the Community may promote the formation of a holding SE provided that each of at least two of them:

(a) is governed by the law of a different Member State, or

(b) has for at least two years had a subsidiary company governed by the law of another Member State or a branch situated in another Member State.

3. Companies and firms within the meaning of the second paragraph of Article 48 of the Treaty and other legal bodies governed by public or private law, formed under the law of a Member State, with registered offices and head offices within the Community may form a subsidiary SE by subscribing for its shares, provided that each of at least two of them:

(a) is governed by the law of a different Member State, or

(b) has for at least two years had a subsidiary company governed by the law of another Member State or a branch situated in another Member State.

4. A public limited-liability company, formed under the law of a Member State, which has its registered office and head office within the Community may be transformed into an SE if for at least two years it has had a subsidiary company governed by the law of another Member State.

5. A Member State may provide that a company the head office of which is not in the Community may participate in the formation of an SE provided that company is formed under the law of a Member State, has its registered office in that Member State and has a real and continuous link with a Member State's economy.

Article 3

1. For the purposes of Article 2(1), (2) and (3), an SE shall be regarded as a public limited-liability company governed by the law of the Member State in which it has its registered office.

2. An SE may itself set up one or more subsidiaries in the form of SEs. The provisions of the law of the Member State in which a subsidiary SE has its registered office that require a public limited-liability company to have more than one shareholder shall not apply in the case of the subsidiary SE. The provisions of national law implementing the twelfth Council Company Law Directive (89/667/EEC) of 21 December 1989 on single-member private limited-liability companies[6] shall apply to SEs mutatis mutandis.

Article 4

1. The capital of an SE shall be expressed in euro.

2. The subscribed capital shall not be less than EUR 120000.

3. The laws of a Member State requiring a greater subscribed capital for companies carrying on certain types of activity shall apply to SEs with registered offices in that Member State.

Article 5

Subject to Article 4(1) and (2), the capital of an SE, its maintenance and changes thereto,

---

[6] OJ L 395, 30.12.1989, 40, Twelfth Company Law Directive, reproduced supra under no. C. 10. Directive as last amended by the 1994 Act of Accession.

together with its shares, bonds and other similar securities shall be governed by the provisions which would apply to a public limited-liability company with a registered office in the Member State in which the SE is registered.

Article 6

For the purposes of this Regulation, 'the statutes of the SE' shall mean both the instrument of incorporation and, where they are the subject of a separate document, the statutes of the SE.

Article 7

The registered office of an SE shall be located within the Community, in the same Member State as its head office. A Member State may in addition impose on SEs registered in its territory the obligation of locating their head office and their registered office in the same place.

Article 8

1. The registered office of an SE may be transferred to another Member State in accordance with paragraphs 2 to 13. Such a transfer shall not result in the winding up of the SE or in the creation of a new legal person.

2. The management or administrative organ shall draw up a transfer proposal and publicise it in accordance with Article 13, without prejudice to any additional forms of publication provided for by the Member State of the registered office. That proposal shall state the current name, registered office and number of the SE and shall cover:

(a) the proposed registered office of the SE;

(b) the proposed statutes of the SE including, where appropriate, its new name;

(c) any implication the transfer may have on employees' involvement;

(d) the proposed transfer timetable;

(e) any rights provided for the protection of shareholders and/or creditors.

3. The management or administrative organ shall draw up a report explaining and justifying the legal and economic aspects of the transfer and explaining the implications of the transfer for shareholders, creditors and employees.

4. An SE's shareholders and creditors shall be entitled, at least one month before the general meeting called upon to decide on the transfer, to examine at the SE's registered office the transfer proposal and the report drawn up pursuant to paragraph 3 and, on request, to obtain copies of those documents free of charge.

5. A Member State may, in the case of SEs registered within its territory, adopt provisions designed to ensure appropriate protection for minority shareholders who oppose a transfer.

6. No decision to transfer may be taken for two months after publication of the proposal. Such a decision shall be taken as laid down in Article 59.

7. Before the competent authority issues the certificate mentioned in paragraph 8, the SE shall satisfy it that, in respect of any liabilities arising prior to the publication of the transfer proposal, the interests of creditors and holders of other rights in respect of the SE (including those of public bodies) have been adequately protected in accordance with requirements laid down by the Member State where the SE has its registered office prior to the transfer.

A Member State may extend the application of the first subparagraph to liabilities that arise (or may arise) prior to the transfer.

The first and second subparagraphs shall be without prejudice to the application to SEs of the national legislation of Member States concerning the satisfaction or securing of payments to public bodies.

8. In the Member State in which an SE has its registered office the court, notary or other competent authority shall issue a certificate attesting to the completion of the acts and formalities to be accomplished before the transfer.

9. The new registration may not be effected until the certificate referred to in paragraph 8 has been submitted, and evidence produced that the formalities required for registration in the country of the new registered office have been completed.

10. The transfer of an SE's registered office and the consequent amendment of its statutes shall take effect on the date on which the SE is registered, in accordance with Article 12, in the register for its new registered office.

11. When the SE's new registration has been effected, the registry for its new registration shall notify the registry for its old registration. Deletion of the old registration shall be effected on receipt of that notification, but not before.

12. The new registration and the deletion of the old registration shall be publicised in the Member States concerned in accordance with Article 13.

13. On publication of an SE's new registration, the new registered office may be relied on as against third parties. However, as long as the deletion of the SE's registration from the register for its previous registered office has not been publicised, third parties may continue to rely on the previous registered office unless the SE proves that such third parties were aware of the new registered office.

14. The laws of a Member State may provide that, as regards SEs registered in that Member State, the transfer of a registered office which would result in a change of the law applicable shall not take effect if any of that Member State's competent authorities opposes it within the two-month period referred to in paragraph 6. Such opposition may be based only on grounds of public interest.

Where an SE is supervised by a national financial supervisory authority according to Community directives the right to oppose the change of registered office applies to this authority as well.

Review by a judicial authority shall be possible
15. An SE may not transfer its registered office if proceedings for winding up, liquidation, insolvency or suspension of payments or other similar proceedings have been brought against it.

16. An SE which has transferred its registered office to another Member State shall be considered, in respect of any cause of action arising prior to the transfer as determined in paragraph 10, as having its registered office in the Member States where the SE was registered prior to the transfer, even if the SE is sued after the transfer.

Article 9

1. An SE shall be governed:
(a) by this Regulation,
(b) where expressly authorised by this Regulation, by the provisions of its statutes
or
(c) in the case of matters not regulated by this Regulation or, where matters are partly regulated by it, of those aspects not covered by it, by:
(i) the provisions of laws adopted by Member States in implementation of Community measures relating specifically to SEs;
(ii) the provisions of Member States' laws which would apply to a public limited-liability company formed in accordance with the law of the Member State in which the SE has its registered office;
(iii) the provisions of its statutes, in the same way as for a public limited-liability company formed in accordance with the law of the Member State in which the SE has its registered office.

2. The provisions of laws adopted by Member States specifically for the SE must be in accordance with Directives applicable to public limited-liability companies referred to in Annex I.

3. If the nature of the business carried out by an SE is regulated by specific provisions of national laws, those laws shall apply in full to the SE.

Article 10

Subject to this Regulation, an SE shall be treated in every Member State as if it were a public limited-liability company formed in accordance with the law of the Member State in which it has its registered office.

Article 11

1. The name of an SE shall be preceded or followed by the abbreviation SE.

2. Only SEs may include the abbreviation SE in their name.

3. Nevertheless, companies, firms and other legal entities registered in a Member State before the date of entry into force of this Regulation in the names of which the abbreviation SE appears shall not be required to alter their names.

Article 12

1. Every SE shall be registered in the Member State in which it has its registered office in a register designated by the law of that Member State in accordance with Article 3 of the first Council Directive (68/151/EEC) of 9 March 1968 on coordination of safeguards which, for the protection of the interests of members and others, are required by Member States of companies within the meaning of the second paragraph of Article 58 of the Treaty, with a view to making such safeguards equivalent throughout the Community.[7]

2. An SE may not be registered unless an agreement on arrangements for employee involvement pursuant to Article 4 of Directive 2001/86/EC has been concluded, or a decision pursuant to Article 3(6) of the Directive has been taken, or the period for negotiations pursuant to Article 5 of the Directive has expired without an agreement having been concluded.

3. In order for an SE to be registered in a Member State which has made use of the option referred to in Article 7(3) of Directive 2001/86/EC, either an agreement pursuant to Article 4 of the Directive must have been concluded on the arrangements for employee involvement, including participation, or none of the participating companies must have been governed by participation rules prior to the registration of the SE.

4. The statutes of the SE must not conflict at any time with the arrangements for employee involvement which have been so determined. Where new such arrangements determined pursuant to the Directive conflict with the existing statutes, the statutes shall to the extent necessary be amended.

In this case, a Member State may provide that the management organ or the administrative organ of the SE shall be entitled to proceed to amend the statutes without any further decision from the general shareholders' meeting.

Article 13

Publication of the documents and particulars concerning an SE which must be publicised under this Regulation shall be effected in the manner laid down in the laws of the Member State in which the SE has its registered office in accordance with Directive 68/151/EEC.

Article 14

1. Notice of an SE's registration and of the deletion of such a registration shall be published for information purposes in the Official Journal of the European Communities after publication in accordance with Article 13. That notice shall state the name, number, date and place of registration of the SE, the date and place of publication and the title of publication, the registered office of the SE and its sector of activity.

2. Where the registered office of an SE is transferred in accordance with Article 8, notice shall be published giving the information provided for in paragraph 1, together with that relating to the new registration.

3. The particulars referred to in paragraph 1 shall be forwarded to the Office for Official Publications of the European Communities within one month of the publication referred to in Article 13.

TITLE II
FORMATION

SECTION 1
GENERAL

Article 15

1. Subject to this Regulation, the formation of an SE shall be governed by the law applicable to

---

[7] OJ L 65, 14.3.1968, 8, First Company Law Directive, reproduced supra under no. C. 1. Directive as last amended by the 1994 Act of Accession.

public limited-liability companies in the Member State in which the SE establishes its registered office.

2. The registration of an SE shall be publicised in accordance with Article 13.

Article 16

1. An SE shall acquire legal personality on the date on which it is registered in the register referred to in Article 12.

2. If acts have been performed in an SE's name before its registration in accordance with Article 12 and the SE does not assume the obligations arising out of such acts after its registration, the natural persons, companies, firms or other legal entities which performed those acts shall be jointly and severally liable therefor, without limit, in the absence of agreement to the contrary.

SECTION 2

FORMATION BY MERGER

Article 17

1. An SE may be formed by means of a merger in accordance with Article 2(1).

2. Such a merger may be carried out in accordance with:

(a) the procedure for merger by acquisition laid down in Article 3(1) of the third Council Directive (78/855/EEC) of 9 October 1978 based on Article 54(3)(g) of the Treaty concerning mergers of public limited-liability companies[8] or

(b) the procedure for merger by the formation of a new company laid down in Article 4(1) of the said Directive.

In the case of a merger by acquisition, the acquiring company shall take the form of an SE when the merger takes place. In the case of a merger by the formation of a new company, the SE shall be the newly formed company.

---

[8] OJ L 295, 20.10.1978, 36, Third Company Law Directive, reproduced supra under no. C. 3. Directive as last amended by the 1994 Act of Accession.

Article 18

For matters not covered by this section or, where a matter is partly covered by it, for aspects not covered by it, each company involved in the formation of an SE by merger shall be governed by the provisions of the law of the Member State to which it is subject that apply to mergers of public limited-liability companies in accordance with Directive 78/855/EEC.

Article 19

The laws of a Member State may provide that a company governed by the law of that Member State may not take part in the formation of an SE by merger if any of that Member State's competent authorities opposes it before the issue of the certificate referred to in Article 25(2).

Such opposition may be based only on grounds of public interest. Review by a judicial authority shall be possible.

Article 20

1. The management or administrative organs of merging companies shall draw up draft terms of merger. The draft terms of merger shall include the following particulars:

(a) the name and registered office of each of the merging companies together with those proposed for the SE;

(b) the share-exchange ratio and the amount of any compensation;

(c) the terms for the allotment of shares in the SE;

(d) the date from which the holding of shares in the SE will entitle the holders to share in profits and any special conditions affecting that entitlement;

(e) the date from which the transactions of the merging companies will be treated for accounting purposes as being those of the SE;

(f) the rights conferred by the SE on the holders of shares to which special rights are attached and on the holders of securities other than shares, or the measures proposed concerning them;

(g) any special advantage granted to the experts who examine the draft terms of merger or to members of the administrative, management, supervisory or controlling organs of the merging companies;

(h) the statutes of the SE;

(i) information on the procedures by which arrangements for employee involvement are determined pursuant to Directive 2001/86/EC.

2. The merging companies may include further items in the draft terms of merger.

Article 21

For each of the merging companies and subject to the additional requirements imposed by the Member State to which the company concerned is subject, the following particulars shall be published in the national gazette of that Member State:

(a) the type, name and registered office of every merging company;

(b) the register in which the documents referred to in Article 3(2) of Directive 68/151/EEC are filed in respect of each merging company, and the number of the entry in that register;

(c) an indication of the arrangements made in accordance with Article 24 for the exercise of the rights of the creditors of the company in question and the address at which complete information on those arrangements may be obtained free of charge;

(d) an indication of the arrangements made in accordance with Article 24 for the exercise of the rights of minority shareholders of the company in question and the address at which complete information on those arrangements may be obtained free of charge;

(e) the name and registered office proposed for the SE.

Article 22

As an alternative to experts operating on behalf of each of the merging companies, one or more independent experts as defined in Article 10 of Directive 78/855/EEC, appointed for those purposes at the joint request of the companies by a judicial or administrative authority in the Member State of one of the merging companies or of the proposed SE, may examine the draft terms of merger and draw up a single report to all the shareholders.

The experts shall have the right to request from each of the merging companies any information they consider necessary to enable them to complete their function.

Article 23

1. The general meeting of each of the merging companies shall approve the draft terms of merger.

2. Employee involvement in the SE shall be decided pursuant to Directive 2001/86/EC. The general meetings of each of the merging companies may reserve the right to make registration of the SE conditional upon its express ratification of the arrangements so decided.

Article 24

1. The law of the Member State governing each merging company shall apply as in the case of a merger of public limited-liability companies, taking into account the cross-border nature of the merger, with regard to the protection of the interests of:

(a) creditors of the merging companies;

(b) holders of bonds of the merging companies;

(c) holders of securities, other than shares, which carry special rights in the merging companies.

2. A Member State may, in the case of the merging companies governed by its law, adopt provisions designed to ensure appropriate protection for minority shareholders who have opposed the merger.

Article 25

1. The legality of a merger shall be scrutinised, as regards the part of the procedure concerning each merging company, in accordance with the law on mergers of public limited-liability companies of the Member State to which the merging company is subject.

2. In each Member State concerned the court, notary or other competent authority shall issue a certificate conclusively attesting to the completion of the pre-merger acts and formalities.

3. If the law of a Member State to which a merging company is subject provides for a procedure to scrutinise and amend the share-exchange ratio, or a procedure to compensate minority shareholders, without preventing the registration of the merger, such procedures shall only apply if the other merging companies situated in Member States which do not provide for such procedure explicitly accept, when approving the draft terms of the merger in accordance with Article 23(1), the possibility for the shareholders of that merging company to have recourse to such procedure. In such cases, the court, notary or other competent authorities may issue the certificate referred to in paragraph 2 even if such a procedure has been commenced. The certificate must, however, indicate that the procedure is pending. The decision in the procedure shall be binding on the acquiring company and all its shareholders.

Article 26

1. The legality of a merger shall be scrutinised, as regards the part of the procedure concerning the completion of the merger and the formation of the SE, by the court, notary or other authority competent in the Member State of the proposed registered office of the SE to scrutinise that aspect of the legality of mergers of public limited-liability companies.

2. To that end each merging company shall submit to the competent authority the certificate referred to in Article 25(2) within six months of its issue together with a copy of the draft terms of merger approved by that company.

3. The authority referred to in paragraph 1 shall in particular ensure that the merging companies have approved draft terms of merger in the same terms and that arrangements for employee involvement have been determined pursuant to Directive 2001/86/EC.

4. That authority shall also satisfy itself that the SE has been formed in accordance with the requirements of the law of the Member State in which it has its registered office in accordance with Article 15.

Article 27

1. A merger and the simultaneous formation of an SE shall take effect on the date on which the SE is registered in accordance with Article 12.

2. The SE may not be registered until the formalities provided for in Articles 25 and 26 have been completed.

Article 28

For each of the merging companies the completion of the merger shall be publicised as laid down by the law of each Member State in accordance with Article 3 of Directive 68/151/EEC.

Article 29

1. A merger carried out as laid down in Article 17(2)(a) shall have the following consequences ipso jure and simultaneously:

(a) all the assets and liabilities of each company being acquired are transferred to the acquiring company;

(b) the shareholders of the company being acquired become shareholders of the acquiring company;

(c) the company being acquired ceases to exist;

(d) the acquiring company adopts the form of an SE.

2. A merger carried out as laid down in Article 17(2)(b) shall have the following consequences ipso jure and simultaneously:

(a) all the assets and liabilities of the merging companies are transferred to the SE;

(b) the shareholders of the merging companies become shareholders of the SE;

(c) the merging companies cease to exist.

3. Where, in the case of a merger of public limited-liability companies, the law of a Member State requires the completion of any special formalities before the transfer of certain assets, rights and obligations by the merging companies

becomes effective against third parties, those formalities shall apply and shall be carried out either by the merging companies or by the SE following its registration.

4. The rights and obligations of the participating companies on terms and conditions of employment arising from national law, practice and individual employment contracts or employment relationships and existing at the date of the registration shall, by reason of such registration be transferred to the SE upon its registration.

Article 30

A merger as provided for in Article 2(1) may not be declared null and void once the SE has been registered.

The absence of scrutiny of the legality of the merger pursuant to Articles 25 and 26 may be included among the grounds for the winding-up of the SE.

Article 31

1. Where a merger within the meaning of Article 17(2)(a) is carried out by a company which holds all the shares and other securities conferring the right to vote at general meetings of another company, neither Article 20(1)(b), (c) and (d), Article 29(1)(b) nor Article 22 shall apply. National law governing each merging company and mergers of public limited-liability companies in accordance with Article 24 of Directive 78/855/EEC shall nevertheless apply.

2. Where a merger by acquisition is carried out by a company which holds 90 % or more but not all of the shares and other securities conferring the right to vote at general meetings of another company, reports by the management or administrative body, reports by an independent expert or experts and the documents necessary for scrutiny shall be required only to the extent that the national law governing either the acquiring company or the company being acquired so requires.

Member States may, however, provide that this paragraph may apply where a company holds shares conferring 90% or more but not all of the voting rights.

SECTION 3
FORMATION OF A HOLDING SE

Article 32

1. A holding SE may be formed in accordance with Article 2(2).

A company promoting the formation of a holding SE in accordance with Article 2(2) shall continue to exist.

2. The management or administrative organs of the companies which promote such an operation shall draw up, in the same terms, draft terms for the formation of the holding SE. The draft terms shall include a report explaining and justifying the legal and economic aspects of the formation and indicating the implications for the shareholders and for the employees of the adoption of the form of a holding SE. The draft terms shall also set out the particulars provided for in Article 20(1)(a), (b), (c), (f), (g), (h) and (i) and shall fix the minimum proportion of the shares in each of the companies promoting the operation which the shareholders must contribute to the formation of the holding SE. That proportion shall be shares conferring more than 50% of the permanent voting rights.

3. For each of the companies promoting the operation, the draft terms for the formation of the holding SE shall be publicised in the manner laid down in each Member State's national law in accordance with Article 3 of Directive 68/151/EEC at least one month before the date of the general meeting called to decide thereon.

4. One or more experts independent of the companies promoting the operation, appointed or approved by a judicial or administrative authority in the Member State to which each company is subject in accordance with national provisions adopted in implementation of Directive 78/855/EEC, shall examine the draft terms of formation drawn up in accordance with paragraph 2 and draw up a written report for the shareholders of each company. By agreement

between the companies promoting the operation, a single written report may be drawn up for the shareholders of all the companies by one or more independent experts, appointed or approved by a judicial or administrative authority in the Member State to which one of the companies promoting the operation or the proposed SE is subject in accordance with national provisions adopted in implementation of Directive 78/855/EEC.

5. The report shall indicate any particular difficulties of valuation and state whether the proposed share-exchange ratio is fair and reasonable, indicating the methods used to arrive at it and whether such methods are adequate in the case in question.

6. The general meeting of each company promoting the operation shall approve the draft terms of formation of the holding SE.

Employee involvement in the holding SE shall be decided pursuant to Directive 2001/86/EC. The general meetings of each company promoting the operation may reserve the right to make registration of the holding SE conditional upon its express ratification of the arrangements so decided.

7. These provisions shall apply mutatis mutandis to private limited-liability companies.

Article 33

1. The shareholders of the companies promoting such an operation shall have a period of three months in which to inform the promoting companies whether they intend to contribute their shares to the formation of the holding SE. That period shall begin on the date upon which the terms for the formation of the holding SE have been finally determined in accordance with Article 32.

2. The holding SE shall be formed only if, within the period referred to in paragraph 1, the shareholders of the companies promoting the operation have assigned the minimum proportion of shares in each company in accordance with the draft terms of formation and if all the other conditions are fulfilled.

3. If the conditions for the formation of the holding SE are all fulfilled in accordance with paragraph 2, that fact shall, in respect of each of the promoting companies, be publicised in the manner laid down in the national law governing each of those companies adopted in implementation of Article 3 of Directive 68/151/EEC.

Shareholders of the companies promoting the operation who have not indicated whether they intend to make their shares available to the promoting companies for the purpose of forming the holding SE within the period referred to in paragraph 1 shall have a further month in which to do so.

4. Shareholders who have contributed their securities to the formation of the SE shall receive shares in the holding SE.

5. The holding SE may not be registered until it is shown that the formalities referred to in Article 32 have been completed and that the conditions referred to in paragraph 2 have been fulfilled.

Article 34

A Member State may, in the case of companies promoting such an operation, adopt provisions designed to ensure protection for minority shareholders who oppose the operation, creditors and employees.

SECTION 4

FORMATION OF A SUBSIDIARY SE

Article 35

An SE may be formed in accordance with Article 2(3).

Article 36

Companies, firms and other legal entities participating in such an operation shall be subject to the provisions governing their participation in the formation of a subsidiary in the form of a public limited-liability company under national law.

SECTION 5
CONVERSION OF AN EXISTING PUBLIC LIMITED-LIABILITY COMPANY INTO AN SE

Article 37

1. An SE may be formed in accordance with Article 2(4).

2. Without prejudice to Article 12 the conversion of a public limited-liability company into an SE shall not result in the winding up of the company or in the creation of a new legal person.

3. The registered office may not be transferred from one Member State to another pursuant to Article 8 at the same time as the conversion is effected.

4. The management or administrative organ of the company in question shall draw up draft terms of conversion and a report explaining and justifying the legal and economic aspects of the conversion and indicating the implications for the shareholders and for the employees of the adoption of the form of an SE.

5. The draft terms of conversion shall be publicised in the manner laid down in each Member State's law in accordance with Article 3 of Directive 68/151/EEC at least one month before the general meeting called upon to decide thereon.

6. Before the general meeting referred to in paragraph 7 one or more independent experts appointed or approved, in accordance with the national provisions adopted in implementation of Article 10 of Directive 78/855/EEC, by a judicial or administrative authority in the Member State to which the company being converted into an SE is subject shall certify in compliance with Directive 77/91/EEC[9] mutatis mutandis that the company has net assets at least equivalent to its capital plus those reserves which must not be distributed under the law or the Statutes.

7. The general meeting of the company in question shall approve the draft terms of conversion together with the statutes of the SE. The decision of the general meeting shall be passed as laid down in the provisions of national law adopted in implementation of Article 7 of Directive 78/855/EEC.

8. Member States may condition a conversion to a favourable vote of a qualified majority or unanimity in the organ of the company to be converted within which employee participation is organised.

9. The rights and obligations of the company to be converted on terms and conditions of employment arising from national law, practice and individual employment contracts or employment relationships and existing at the date of the registration shall, by reason of such registration be transferred to the SE.

TITLE III
STRUCTURE OF THE SE

Article 38

Under the conditions laid down by this Regulation an SE shall comprise:

(a) a general meeting of shareholders and

(b) either a supervisory organ and a management organ (two-tier system) or an administrative organ (one-tier system) depending on the form adopted in the statutes.

SECTION 1
TWO-TIER SYSTEM

Article 39

1. The management organ shall be responsible for managing the SE. A Member State may provide that a managing director or managing directors shall be responsible for the current

---

[9] Second Council Directive 77/91/EEC of 13 December 1976 on coordination of safeguards which, for the protection of the interests of members and others, are required by Member States of companies within the meaning of the second paragraph of Article 58 of the Treaty, in respect of the formation of public limited liability companies and the maintenance and alteration of their capital, with a view to making such safeguards equivalent (OJ L 26, 31.1.1977, 1, reproduced supra under no. C. 2). Directive as last amended by the 1994 Act of Accession.

management under the same conditions as for public limited-liability companies that have registered offices within that Member State's territory.

2. The member or members of the management organ shall be appointed and removed by the supervisory organ.

A Member State may, however, require or permit the statutes to provide that the member or members of the management organ shall be appointed and removed by the general meeting under the same conditions as for public limited-liability companies that have registered offices within its territory.

3. No person may at the same time be a member of both the management organ and the supervisory organ of the same SE. The supervisory organ may, however, nominate one of its members to act as a member of the management organ in the event of a vacancy. During such a period the functions of the person concerned as a member of the supervisory organ shall be suspended. A Member State may impose a time limit on such a period.

4. The number of members of the management organ or the rules for determining it shall be laid down in the SE's statutes. A Member State may, however, fix a minimum and/or a maximum number.

5. Where no provision is made for a two-tier system in relation to public limited-liability companies with registered offices within its territory, a Member State may adopt the appropriate measures in relation to SEs.

Article 40

1. The supervisory organ shall supervise the work of the management organ. It may not itself exercise the power to manage the SE.

2. The members of the supervisory organ shall be appointed by the general meeting. The members of the first supervisory organ may, however, be appointed by the statutes. This shall apply without prejudice to Article 47(4) or to any employee participation arrangements determined pursuant to Directive 2001/86/EC.

3. The number of members of the supervisory organ or the rules for determining it shall be laid down in the statutes. A Member State may, however, stipulate the number of members of the supervisory organ for SEs registered within its territory or a minimum and/or a maximum number.

Article 41

1. The management organ shall report to the supervisory organ at least once every three months on the progress and foreseeable development of the SE's business.

2. In addition to the regular information referred to in paragraph 1, the management organ shall promptly pass the supervisory organ any information on events likely to have an appreciable effect on the SE.

3. The supervisory organ may require the management organ to provide information of any kind which it needs to exercise supervision in accordance with Article 40(1). A Member State may provide that each member of the supervisory organ also be entitled to this facility.

4. The supervisory organ may undertake or arrange for any investigations necessary for the performance of its duties.

5. Each member of the supervisory organ shall be entitled to examine all information submitted to it.

Article 42

The supervisory organ shall elect a chairman from among its members. If half of the members are appointed by employees, only a member appointed by the general meeting of shareholders may be elected chairman.

Section 2
The One-Tier System

Article 43

1. The administrative organ shall manage the SE. A Member State may provide that a managing

director or managing directors shall be responsible for the day-to-day management under the same conditions as for public limited-liability companies that have registered offices within that Member State's territory.

2. The number of members of the administrative organ or the rules for determining it shall be laid down in the SE's statutes. A Member State may, however, set a minimum and, where necessary, a maximum number of members.

The administrative organ shall, however, consist of at least three members where employee participation is regulated in accordance with Directive 2001/86/EC.

3. The member or members of the administrative organ shall be appointed by the general meeting.

The members of the first administrative organ may, however, be appointed by the statutes. This shall apply without prejudice to Article 47(4) or to any employee participation arrangements determined pursuant to Directive 2001/86/EC.

4. Where no provision is made for a one-tier system in relation to public limited-liability companies with registered offices within its territory, a Member State may adopt the appropriate measures in relation to SEs.

Article 44

1. The administrative organ shall meet at least once every three months at intervals laid down by the statutes to discuss the progress and foreseeable development of the SE's business.

2. Each member of the administrative organ shall be entitled to examine all information submitted to it.

Article 45

The administrative organ shall elect a chairman from among its members. If half of the members are appointed by employees, only a member appointed by the general meeting of shareholders may be elected chairman.

SECTION 3

RULES COMMON TO THE ONE-TIER AND TWO-TIER SYSTEMS

Article 46

1. Members of company organs shall be appointed for a period laid down in the statutes not exceeding six years.

2. Subject to any restrictions laid down in the statutes, members may be reappointed once or more than once for the period determined in accordance with paragraph 1.

Article 47

1. An SE's statutes may permit a company or other legal entity to be a member of one of its organs, provided that the law applicable to public limited-liability companies in the Member State in which the SE's registered office is situated does not provide otherwise.

That company or other legal entity shall designate a natural person to exercise its functions on the organ in question.

2. No person may be a member of any SE organ or a representative of a member within the meaning of paragraph 1 who:

(a) is disqualified, under the law of the Member State in which the SE's registered office is situated, from serving on the corresponding organ of a public limited-liability company governed by the law of that Member State, or

(b) is disqualified from serving on the corresponding organ of a public limited-liability company governed by the law of a Member State owing to a judicial or administrative decision delivered in a Member State.

3. An SE's statutes may, in accordance with the law applicable to public limited-liability companies in the Member State in which the SE's registered office is situated, lay down special conditions of eligibility for members representing the shareholders.

4. This Regulation shall not affect national law permitting a minority of shareholders or other

persons or authorities to appoint some of the members of a company organ.

Article 48

1. An SE's statutes shall list the categories of transactions which require authorisation of the management organ by the supervisory organ in the two-tier system or an express decision by the administrative organ in the one-tier system.

A Member State may, however, provide that in the two-tier system the supervisory organ may itself make certain categories of transactions subject to authorisation.

2. A Member State may determine the categories of transactions which must at least be indicated in the statutes of SEs registered within its territory.

Article 49

The members of an SE's organs shall be under a duty, even after they have ceased to hold office, not to divulge any information which they have concerning the SE the disclosure of which might be prejudicial to the company's interests, except where such disclosure is required or permitted under national law provisions applicable to public limited-liability companies or is in the public interest.

Article 50

1. Unless otherwise provided by this Regulation or the statutes, the internal rules relating to quorums and decision-taking in SE organs shall be as follows:

(a) quorum: at least half of the members must be present or represented;

(b) decision-taking: a majority of the members present or represented.

2. Where there is no relevant provision in the statutes, the chairman of each organ shall have a casting vote in the event of a tie. There shall be no provision to the contrary in the statutes, however, where half of the supervisory organ consists of employees' representatives.

3. Where employee participation is provided for in accordance with Directive 2001/86/EC, a Member State may provide that the supervisory organ's quorum and decision-making shall, by way of derogation from the provisions referred to in paragraphs 1 and 2, be subject to the rules applicable, under the same conditions, to public limited-liability companies governed by the law of the Member State concerned.

Article 51

Members of an SE's management, supervisory and administrative organs shall be liable, in accordance with the provisions applicable to public limited-liability companies in the Member State in which the SE's registered office is situated, for loss or damage sustained by the SE following any breach on their part of the legal, statutory or other obligations inherent in their duties.

SECTION 4
GENERAL MEETING

Article 52

The general meeting shall decide on matters for which it is given sole responsibility by:

(a) this Regulation or

(b) the legislation of the Member State in which the SE's registered office is situated adopted in implementation of Directive 2001/86/EC.

Furthermore, the general meeting shall decide on matters for which responsibility is given to the general meeting of a public limited-liability company governed by the law of the Member State in which the SE's registered office is situated, either by the law of that Member State or by the SE's statutes in accordance with that law.

Article 53

Without prejudice to the rules laid down in this section, the organisation and conduct of general meetings together with voting procedures shall be governed by the law applicable to public limited-liability companies in the Member State in which the SE's registered office is situated.

Article 54

1. An SE shall hold a general meeting at least once each calendar year, within six months of the end of its financial year, unless the law of the Member State in which the SE's registered office is situated applicable to public limited-liability companies carrying on the same type of activity as the SE provides for more frequent meetings. A Member State may, however, provide that the first general meeting may be held at any time in the 18 months following an SE's incorporation.

2. General meetings may be convened at any time by the management organ, the administrative organ, the supervisory organ or any other organ or competent authority in accordance with the national law applicable to public limited-liability companies in the Member State in which the SE's registered office is situated.

Article 55

1. One or more shareholders who together hold at least 10% of an SE's subscribed capital may request the SE to convene a general meeting and draw up the agenda therefor; the SE's statutes or national legislation may provide for a smaller proportion under the same conditions as those applicable to public limited-liability companies.

2. The request that a general meeting be convened shall state the items to be put on the agenda.

3. If, following a request made under paragraph 1, a general meeting is not held in due time and, in any event, within two months, the competent judicial or administrative authority within the jurisdiction of which the SE's registered office is situated may order that a general meeting be convened within a given period or authorise either the shareholders who have requested it or their representatives to convene a general meeting. This shall be without prejudice to any national provisions which allow the shareholders themselves to convene general meetings.

Article 56

One or more shareholders who together hold at least 10% of an SE's subscribed capital may request that one or more additional items be put on the agenda of any general meeting. The procedures and time limits applicable to such requests shall be laid down by the national law of the Member State in which the SE's registered office is situated or, failing that, by the SE's statutes. The above proportion may be reduced by the statutes or by the law of the Member State in which the SE's registered office is situated under the same conditions as are applicable to public limited-liability companies.

Article 57

Save where this Regulation or, failing that, the law applicable to public limited-liability companies in the Member State in which an SE's registered office is situated requires a larger majority, the general meeting's decisions shall be taken by a majority of the votes validly cast.

Article 58

The votes cast shall not include votes attaching to shares in respect of which the shareholder has not taken part in the vote or has abstained or has returned a blank or spoilt ballot paper.

Article 59

1. Amendment of an SE's statutes shall require a decision by the general meeting taken by a majority which may not be less than two thirds of the votes cast, unless the law applicable to public limited-liability companies in the Member State in which an SE's registered office is situated requires or permits a larger majority.

2. A Member State may, however, provide that where at least half of an SE's subscribed capital is represented, a simple majority of the votes referred to in paragraph 1 shall suffice.

3. Amendments to an SE's statutes shall be publicised in accordance with Article 13.

Article 60

1. Where an SE has two or more classes of shares, every decision by the general meeting shall be subject to a separate vote by each class of shareholders whose class rights are affected thereby.

2. Where a decision by the general meeting requires the majority of votes specified in Article 59(1) or (2), that majority shall also be required for the separate vote by each class of shareholders whose class rights are affected by the decision.

Title IV

Annual Accounts and Consolidated Accounts

Article 61

Subject to Article 62 an SE shall be governed by the rules applicable to public limited-liability companies under the law of the Member State in which its registered office is situated as regards the preparation of its annual and, where appropriate, consolidated accounts including the accompanying annual report and the auditing and publication of those accounts.

Article 62

1. An SE which is a credit or financial institution shall be governed by the rules laid down in the national law of the Member State in which its registered office is situated in implementation of Directive 2000/12/EC of the European Parliament and of the Council of 20 March 2000 relating to the taking up and pursuit of the business of credit institutions[10] as regards the preparation of its annual and, where appropriate, consolidated accounts, including the accompanying annual report and the auditing and publication of those accounts.

2. An SE which is an insurance undertaking shall be governed by the rules laid down in the national law of the Member State in which its registered office is situated in implementation of Council Directive 91/674/EEC of 19 December 1991 on the annual accounts and consolidated accounts of insurance undertakings[11] as regards the preparation of its annual and, where appropriate, consolidated accounts including the accompanying annual report and the auditing and publication of those accounts.

Title V

Winding Up, Liquidation, Insolvency and Cessation of Payments

Article 63

As regards winding up, liquidation, insolvency, cessation of payments and similar procedures, an SE shall be governed by the legal provisions which would apply to a public limited-liability company formed in accordance with the law of the Member State in which its registered office is situated, including provisions relating to decision-making by the general meeting.

Article 64

1. When an SE no longer complies with the requirement laid down in Article 7, the Member State in which the SE's registered office is situated shall take appropriate measures to oblige the SE to regularise its position within a specified period either:

(a) by re-establishing its head office in the Member State in which its registered office is situated or

(b) by transferring the registered office by means of the procedure laid down in Article 8.

2. The Member State in which the SE's registered office is situated shall put in place the measures necessary to ensure that an SE which fails to regularise its position in accordance with paragraph 1 is liquidated.

---

[10] OJ L 126, 26.5.2000, 1, reproduced supra under no. B. 32.

[11] OJ L 374, 31.12.1991, 7, reproduced infra under no. I. 23.

3. The Member State in which the SE's registered office is situated shall set up a judicial remedy with regard to any established infringement of Article 7. That remedy shall have a suspensory effect on the procedures laid down in paragraphs 1 and 2.

4. Where it is established on the initiative of either the authorities or any interested party that an SE has its head office within the territory of a Member State in breach of Article 7, the authorities of that Member State shall immediately inform the Member State in which the SE's registered office is situated.

Article 65

Without prejudice to provisions of national law requiring additional publication, the initiation and termination of winding up, liquidation, insolvency or cessation of payment procedures and any decision to continue operating shall be publicised in accordance with Article 13.

Article 66

1. An SE may be converted into a public limited-liability company governed by the law of the Member State in which its registered office is situated. No decision on conversion may be taken before two years have elapsed since its registration or before the first two sets of annual accounts have been approved.

2. The conversion of an SE into a public limited-liability company shall not result in the winding up of the company or in the creation of a new legal person.

3. The management or administrative organ of the SE shall draw up draft terms of conversion and a report explaining and justifying the legal and economic aspects of the conversion and indicating the implications of the adoption of the public limited-liability company for the shareholders and for the employees.

4. The draft terms of conversion shall be publicised in the manner laid down in each Member State's law in accordance with Article 3 of Directive 68/151/EEC at least one month before the general meeting called to decide thereon.

5. Before the general meeting referred to in paragraph 6, one or more independent experts appointed or approved, in accordance with the national provisions adopted in implementation of Article 10 of Directive 78/855/EEC, by a judicial or administrative authority in the Member State to which the SE being converted into a public limited-liability company is subject shall certify that the company has assets at least equivalent to its capital.

6. The general meeting of the SE shall approve the draft terms of conversion together with the statutes of the public limited-liability company. The decision of the general meeting shall be passed as laid down in the provisions of national law adopted in implementation of Article 7 of Directive 78/855/EEC.

Title VI
Additional and Transitional Provisions

Article 67

1. If and so long as the third phase of economic and monetary union (EMU) does not apply to it each Member State may make SEs with registered offices within its territory subject to the same provisions as apply to public limited-liability companies covered by its legislation as regards the expression of their capital. An SE may, in any case, express its capital in euro as well. In that event the national currency/euro conversion rate shall be that for the last day of the month preceding that of the formation of the SE.

2. If and so long as the third phase of EMU does not apply to the Member State in which an SE has its registered office, the SE may, however, prepare and publish its annual and, where appropriate, consolidated accounts in euro. The Member State may require that the SE's annual and, where appropriate, consolidated accounts be prepared and published in the national currency under the same conditions as those laid down for public limited-liability companies governed by the law of that Member State. This shall not

prejudge the additional possibility for an SE of publishing its annual and, where appropriate, consolidated accounts in euro in accordance with Council Directive 90/604/EEC of 8 November 1990 amending Directive 78/60/EEC on annual accounts and Directive 83/349/EEC on consolidated accounts as concerns the exemptions for small and medium-sized companies and the publication of accounts in ecu.[12]

Title VII
Final Provisions

Article 68

1. The Member States shall make such provision as is appropriate to ensure the effective application of this Regulation.

2. Each Member State shall designate the competent authorities within the meaning of Articles 8, 25, 26, 54, 55 and 64. It shall inform the Commission and the other Member States accordingly.

Article 69

Five years at the latest after the entry into force of this Regulation, the Commission shall forward to the Council and the European Parliament a report on the application of the Regulation and proposals for amendments, where appropriate. The report shall, in particular, analyse the appropriateness of:

(a) allowing the location of an SE's head office and registered office in different Member States;

(b) broadening the concept of merger in Article 17(2) in order to admit also other types of merger than those defined in Articles 3(1) and 4(1) of Directive 78/855/EEC;

(c) revising the jurisdiction clause in Article 8(16) in the light of any provision which may have been inserted in the 1968 Brussels Convention or in any text adopted by Member States or by the Council to replace such Convention;

(d) allowing provisions in the statutes of an SE adopted by a Member State in execution of authorisations given to the Member States by this Regulation or laws adopted to ensure the effective application of this Regulation in respect to the SE which deviate from or are complementary to these laws, even when such provisions would not be authorised in the statutes of a public limited-liability company having its registered office in the Member State.

Article 70

This Regulation shall enter into force on 8 October 2004.

This Regulation shall be binding in its entirety and directly applicable in all Member States.

Annex I

Public limited-liability companies referred to in Article 2(1)

BELGIUM:
la société anonyme / de naamloze vennootschap

DENMARK:
aktieselskaber

GERMANY:
die Aktiengesellschaft

GREECE:
ανωνυμη εταιρεία

SPAIN:
la sociedad anónima

FRANCE:
la société anonyme

---

[12] OJ L 317, 16.11.1990, 57, reproduced supra under no. C. 11.

IRELAND:
public companies limited by shares
public companies limited by guarantee having a share capital

ITALY:
società per azioni

LUXEMBOURG:
la société anonyme

NETHERLANDS:
de naamloze vennootschap

AUSTRIA:
die Aktiengesellschaft

PORTUGAL:
a sociedade anónima de responsabilidade limitada

FINLAND:
julkinen osakeyhtiö / publikt aktiebolag

SWEDEN:
publikt aktiebolag

UNITED KINGDOM:
public companies limited by shares
public companies limited by guarantee having a share capital

[CZECH REPUBLIC:
akciová společnost]

[ESTONIA:
aksiaselts]

[CYPRUS:
Δημόσια Εταιρεία περιορισμένης ευθύνης με μετοχές, Δημόσια Εταιρεία περιορισμένης ευθύνης με εγγύηση]

[LATVIA:
akciju sabiedrība]

[LITHUANIA:
akcinės bendrovės]

[HUNGARY:
részvénytársaság]

[MALTA:
kumpaniji pubbliċi/public limited liability companies]

[POLAND:
spółka akcyjna]

[SLOVENIA:
delniška družba]

[SLOVAKIA:
akciová spoločnos]

¶ *Annex I has been changed by Council Regulation (EC) No. 885/2004 of 26 April 2004 (OJ L 168, 1.5.2004, 1).*

Annex II

Public and private limited-liability companies referred to in Article 2(2)

BELGIUM:
la société anonyme/de naamloze vennootschap,
la société privée à responsabilité limitée/besloten vennootschap met beperkte aansprakelijkheid

DENMARK:
aktieselskaber,
anpartsselskaber

GERMANY:
die Aktiengesellschaft,
die Gesellschaft mit beschränkter Haftung

GREECE:
ανωνυμη εταιρια
εταιρια περιορισμενης ευθυνης

SPAIN:
la sociedad anónima,
la sociedad de responsabilidad limitada

FRANCE:
la société anonyme,
la société à responsabilité limitée

IRELAND:
public companies limited by shares,
public companies limited by guarantee having a share capital,
private companies limited by shares,
private companies limited by guarantee having a share capital

ITALY:
società per azioni,
società a responsabilità limitata

LUXEMBOURG:
la société anonyme,
la société à responsabilité limitée

NETHERLANDS:
de naamloze vennootschap,
de besloten vennootschap met beperkte aansprakelijkheid

AUSTRIA:
die Aktiengesellschaft,
die Gesellschaft mit beschränkter Haftung

PORTUGAL:
a sociedade anónima de responsabilidade limitada,
a sociedade por quotas de responsabilidade limitada

FINLAND:
osakeyhtiö
aktiebolag

SWEDEN:
aktiebolag

UNITED KINGDOM:
public companies limited by shares,
public companies limited by guarantee having a share capital,
private companies limited by shares,
private companies limited by guarantee having a share capital

[CZECH REPUBLIC:
akciová společnost,
společnost s ručením omezenym]

[ESTONIA:
aktsiaselts ja osaühing]

[CYPRUS:
Δημόσια εταιρεία περιορισμένης ευθύνης με μετοχές, δημόσια Εταιρεία περιορισμένης ευθύνης με εγγύηση, ιδιωτική εταιρεία]

[LATVIA:
akciju sabiedrība,
un sabiedrība ar ierobežotu atbildību]

[LITHUANIA:
akcinės bendrovės,
uždarosios akcinės bendrovės]

[HUNGARY:
részvénytársaság,
korlátolt felelősségű társaság]

[MALTA:
kumpaniji pubbliċi/public limited liability companies
kumpaniji privati/private limited liability companies]

[POLAND:
spółka akcyjna,
spółka z ograniczoną odpowiedzialnością]

[SLOVENIA:
delniška družba,
družba z omejeno odgovornostjo]

[SLOVAKIA:
akciová spoločnos',
spoločnost's ručením obmedzenym]

¶ *Annex II has been changed by Council Regulation (EC) No. 885/2004 of 26 April 2004 (OJ L 168, 1.5.2004, 1).*

C. 20.

Council Directive 2001/86/EC
of 8 October 2001
supplementing the Statute for a European company with regard to the involvement of employees[1]

THE COUNCIL OF THE EUROPEAN UNION,

Having regard to the Treaty establishing the European Community, and in particular Article 308 thereof,

Having regard to the amended proposal from the Commission,[2]

Having regard to the opinion of the European Parliament,[3]

Having regard to the opinion of the Economic and Social Committee,[4]

Whereas:

(1) In order to attain the objectives of the Treaty, Council Regulation 2157/2001/EC[5] establishes a Statute for a European company (SE).

(2) That Regulation aims at creating a uniform legal framework within which companies from different Member States should be able to plan and carry out the reorganisation of their business on a Community scale.

(3) In order to promote the social objectives of the Community, special provisions have to be set, notably in the field of employee involvement, aimed at ensuring that the establishment of an SE does not entail the disappearance or reduction of practices of employee involvement existing within the companies participating in the establishment of an SE. This objective should be pursued through the establishment of a set of rules in this field, supplementing the provisions of the Regulation.

(4) Since the objectives of the proposed action, as outlined above, cannot be sufficiently achieved by the Member States, in that the object is to establish a set of rules on employee involvement applicable to the SE, and can therefore, by reason of the scale and impact of the proposed action, be better achieved at Community level, the Community may adopt measures, in accordance with the principle of subsidiarity as set out in Article 5 of the Treaty. In accordance with the principle of proportionality, as set out in that Article, this Directive does not go beyond what is necessary to achieve these objectives.

(5) The great diversity of rules and practices existing in the Member States as regards the manner in which employees' representatives are involved in decision-making within companies makes it inadvisable to set up a single European model of employee involvement applicable to the SE.

(6) Information and consultation procedures at transnational level should nevertheless be ensured in all cases of creation of an SE.

(7) If and when participation rights exist within one or more companies establishing an SE, they should be preserved through their transfer to the SE, once established, unless the parties decide otherwise.

(8) The concrete procedures of employee transnational information and consultation, as well as, if applicable, participation, to apply to each SE should be defined primarily by means of an agreement between the parties concerned or, in the absence thereof, through the application of a set of subsidiary rules.

(9) Member States should still have the option of not applying the standard rules relating to participation in the case of a merger, given the

---

[1] OJ L 294, 10.11.2001, 22–32.
[2] OJ C 138, 29.5.1991, 8.
[3] OJ C 342, 20.12.1993, 15.
[4] OJ C 124, 21.5.1990, 34.
[5] OJ L 294, 10.11.2001, 1–21, reproduced supra under no. C. 19.

diversity of national systems for employee involvement. Existing systems and practices of participation where appropriate at the level of participating companies must in that case be maintained by adapting registration rules.

(10) The voting rules within the special body representing the employees for negotiation purposes, in particular when concluding agreements providing for a level of participation lower than the one existing within one or more of the participating companies, should be proportionate to the risk of disappearance or reduction of existing systems and practices of participation. That risk is greater in the case of an SE established by way of transformation or merger than by way of creating a holding company or a common subsidiary.

(11) In the absence of an agreement subsequent to the negotiation between employees' representatives and the competent organs of the participating companies, provision should be made for certain standard requirements to apply to the SE, once it is established. These standard requirements should ensure effective practices of transnational information and consultation of employees, as well as their participation in the relevant organs of the SE if and when such participation existed before its establishment within the participating companies.

(12) Provision should be made for the employees' representatives acting within the framework of the Directive to enjoy, when exercising their functions, protection and guarantees which are similar to those provided to employees' representatives by the legislation and/or practice of the country of employment. They should not be subject to any discrimination as a result of the lawful exercise of their activities and should enjoy adequate protection as regards dismissal and other sanctions.

(13) The confidentiality of sensitive information should be preserved even after the expiry of the employees' representatives terms of office and provision should be made to allow the competent organ of the SE to withhold information which would seriously harm, if subject to public disclosure, the functioning of the SE.

(14) Where an SE and its subsidiaries and establishments are subject to Council Directive 94/45/EC of 22 September 1994 on the establishment of a European Works Council or a procedure in Community-scale undertakings and Community-scale groups of undertakings for the purposes of informing and consulting employees,[6] the provisions of that Directive and the provision transposing it into national legislation should not apply to it nor to its subsidiaries and establishments, unless the special negotiating body decides not to open negotiations or to terminate negotiations already opened.

(15) This Directive should not affect other existing rights regarding involvement and need not affect other existing representation structures, provided for by Community and national laws and practices.

(16) Member States should take appropriate measures in the event of failure to comply with the obligations laid down in this Directive.

(17) The Treaty has not provided the necessary powers for the Community to adopt the proposed Directive, other than those provided for in Article 308.

(18) It is a fundamental principle and stated aim of this Directive to secure employees' acquired rights as regards involvement in company decisions. Employee rights in force before the establishment of SEs should provide the basis for employee rights of involvement in the SE (the 'before and after' principle). Consequently, that approach should apply not only to the initial establishment of an SE but also to structural changes in an existing SE and to the companies affected by structural change processes.

(19) Member States should be able to provide that representatives of trade unions may be members of a special negotiating body regardless of whether they are employees of a company participating in the establishment of an SE.

---

[6] OJ L 254, 30.9.1994, 64, reproduced infra under no. E. 5. Directive as last amended by Directive 97/74/EC (OJ L 10, 16.1.1998, 22), reproduced infra under no. E. 6.

Member States should in this context in particular be able to introduce this right in cases where trade union representatives have the right to be members of, and to vote in, supervisory or administrative company organs in accordance with national legislation.

(20) In several Member States, employee involvement and other areas of industrial relations are based on both national legislation and practice which in this context is understood also to cover collective agreements at various national, sectoral and/or company levels,

HAS ADOPTED THIS DIRECTIVE:

SECTION I

GENERAL

Article 1

Objective

1. This Directive governs the involvement of employees in the affairs of European public limited-liability companies (Societas Europaea, hereinafter referred to as 'SE'), as referred to in Regulation 2157/2001/EC.

2. To this end, arrangements for the involvement of employees shall be established in every SE in accordance with the negotiating procedure referred to in Articles 3 to 6 or, under the circumstances specified in Article 7, in accordance with the Annex.

Article 2

Definitions

For the purposes of this Directive:

(a) 'SE' means any company established in accordance with Regulation 2157/2001/EC;

(b) 'participating companies' means the companies directly participating in the establishing of an SE;

(c) 'subsidiary' of a company means an undertaking over which that company exercises a dominant influence defined in accordance with Article 3(2) to (7) of Directive 94/45/EC;

(d) 'concerned subsidiary or establishment' means a subsidiary or establishment of a participating company which is proposed to become a subsidiary or establishment of the SE upon its formation;

(e) 'employees' representatives' means the employees' representatives provided for by national law and/or practice;

(f) 'representative body' means the body representative of the employees set up by the agreements referred to in Article 4 or in accordance with the provisions of the Annex, with the purpose of informing and consulting the employees of an SE and its subsidiaries and establishments situated in the Community and, where applicable, of exercising participation rights in relation to the SE;

(g) 'special negotiating body' means the body established in accordance with Article 3 to negotiate with the competent body of the participating companies regarding the establishment of arrangements for the involvement of employees within the SE;

(h) 'involvement of employees' means any mechanism, including information, consultation and participation, through which employees' representatives may exercise an influence on decisions to be taken within the company;

(i) 'information' means the informing of the body representative of the employees and/or employees' representatives by the competent organ of the SE on questions which concern the SE itself and any of its subsidiaries or establishments situated in another Member State or which exceed the powers of the decision-making organs in a single Member State at a time, in a manner and with a content which allows the employees' representatives to undertake an in-depth assessment of the possible impact and, where appropriate, prepare consultations with the competent organ of the SE;

(j) 'consultation' means the establishment of dialogue and exchange of views between the body representative of the employees and/or the employees' representatives and the competent organ of the SE, at a time, in a manner and with a content which allows the employees' representatives, on the basis of information provided, to express an opinion on measures envisaged by the competent organ which may be taken into account in the decision-making process within the SE;

(k) 'participation' means the influence of the body representative of the employees and/or the employees' representatives in the affairs of a company by way of:
- the right to elect or appoint some of the members of the company's supervisory or administrative organ, or
- the right to recommend and/or oppose the appointment of some or all of the members of the company's supervisory or administrative organ.

Section II
Negotiating Procedure

Article 3
Creation of a special negotiating body

1. Where the management or administrative organs of the participating companies draw up a plan for the establishment of an SE, they shall as soon as possible after publishing the draft terms of merger or creating a holding company or after agreeing a plan to form a subsidiary or to transform into an SE, take the necessary steps, including providing information about the identity of the participating companies, concerned subsidiaries or establishments, and the number of their employees, to start negotiations with the representatives of the companies' employees on arrangements for the involvement of employees in the SE.

2. For this purpose, a special negotiating body representative of the employees of the participating companies and concerned subsidiaries or establishments shall be created in accordance with the following provisions:

(a) in electing or appointing members of the special negotiating body, it must be ensured:
(i) that these members are elected or appointed in proportion to the number of employees employed in each Member State by the participating companies and concerned subsidiaries or establishments, by allocating in respect of a Member State one seat per portion of employees employed in that Member State which equals 10%, or a fraction thereof, of the number of employees employed by the participating companies and concerned subsidiaries or establishments in all the Member States taken together;

(ii) that in the case of an SE formed by way of merger, there are such further additional members from each Member State as may be necessary in order to ensure that the special negotiating body includes at least one member representing each participating company which is registered and has employees in that Member State and which it is proposed will cease to exist as a separate legal entity following the registration of the SE, in so far as:
- the number of such additional members does not exceed 20% of the number of members designated by virtue of point (i), and
- the composition of the special negotiating body does not entail a double representation of the employees concerned.

If the number of such companies is higher than the number of additional seats available pursuant to the first subparagraph, these additional seats shall be allocated to companies in different Member States by decreasing order of the number of employees they employ;

(b) Member States shall determine the method to be used for the election or appointment of the members of the special negotiating body who are to be elected or appointed in their territories. They shall take the necessary measures to ensure that, as far as possible, such members shall include at least one member representing each participating company which has employees in the Member State concerned. Such measures must not increase the overall number of members.

Member States may provide that such members may include representatives of trade unions whether or not they are employees of a participating company or concerned subsidiary or establishment.

Without prejudice to national legislation and/or practice laying down thresholds for the establishing of a representative body, Member States shall provide that employees in undertakings or establishments in which there are no employees' representatives through no fault of their own have the right to elect or appoint members of the special negotiating body.

3. The special negotiating body and the competent organs of the participating companies shall determine, by written agreement, arrangements for the involvement of employees within the SE.

To this end, the competent organs of the participating companies shall inform the special negotiating body of the plan and the actual process of establishing the SE, up to its registration.

4. Subject to paragraph 6, the special negotiating body shall take decisions by an absolute majority of its members, provided that such a majority also represents an absolute majority of the employees. Each member shall have one vote. However, should the result of the negotiations lead to a reduction of participation rights, the majority required for a decision to approve such an agreement shall be the votes of two thirds of the members of the special negotiating body representing at least two thirds of the employees, including the votes of members representing employees employed in at least two Member States,
– in the case of an SE to be established by way of merger, if participation covers at least 25% of the overall number of employees of the participating companies, or
– in the case of an SE to be established by way of creating a holding company or forming a subsidiary, if participation covers at least 50% of the overall number of employees of the participating companies.

Reduction of participation rights means a proportion of members of the organs of the SE within the meaning of Article 2(k), which is lower than the highest proportion existing within the participating companies.

5. For the purpose of the negotiations, the special negotiating body may request experts of its choice, for example representatives of appropriate Community level trade union organisations, to assist it with its work. Such experts may be present at negotiation meetings in an advisory capacity at the request of the special negotiating body, where appropriate to promote coherence and consistency at Community level. The special negotiating body may decide to inform the representatives of appropriate external organisations, including trade unions, of the start of the negotiations.

6. The special negotiating body may decide by the majority set out below not to open negotiations or to terminate negotiations already opened, and to rely on the rules on information and consultation of employees in force in the Member States where the SE has employees. Such a decision shall stop the procedure to conclude the agreement referred to in Article 4. Where such a decision has been taken, none of the provisions of the Annex shall apply.

The majority required to decide not to open or to terminate negotiations shall be the votes of two thirds of the members representing at least two thirds of the employees, including the votes of members representing employees employed in at least two Member States.

In the case of an SE established by way of transformation, this paragraph shall not apply if there is participation in the company to be transformed.

The special negotiating body shall be reconvened on the written request of at least 10% of the employees of the SE, its subsidiaries and establishments, or their representatives, at the earliest two years after the abovementioned decision, unless the parties agree to negotiations being reopened sooner. If the special negotiating body decides to reopen negotiations with the management but no agreement is reached as a result of those negotiations, none of the provisions of the Annex shall apply.

7. Any expenses relating to the functioning of the special negotiating body and, in general, to negotiations shall be borne by the participating companies so as to enable the special negotiating body to carry out its task in an appropriate manner.

In compliance with this principle, Member States may lay down budgetary rules regarding the operation of the special negotiating body. They may in particular limit the funding to cover one expert only.

Article 4
Content of the agreement

1. The competent organs of the participating companies and the special negotiating body shall negotiate in a spirit of cooperation with a view to reaching an agreement on arrangements for the involvement of the employees within the SE.

2. Without prejudice to the autonomy of the parties, and subject to paragraph 4, the agreement referred to in paragraph 1 between the competent organs of the participating companies and the special negotiating body shall specify:

(a) the scope of the agreement;

(b) the composition, number of members and allocation of seats on the representative body which will be the discussion partner of the competent organ of the SE in connection with arrangements for the information and consultation of the employees of the SE and its subsidiaries and establishments;

(c) the functions and the procedure for the information and consultation of the representative body;

(d) the frequency of meetings of the representative body;

(e) the financial and material resources to be allocated to the representative body;

(f) if, during negotiations, the parties decide to establish one or more information and consultation procedures instead of a representative body, the arrangements for implementing those procedures;

(g) if, during negotiations, the parties decide to establish arrangements for participation, the substance of those arrangements including (if applicable) the number of members in the SE's administrative or supervisory body which the employees will be entitled to elect, appoint, recommend or oppose, the procedures as to how these members may be elected, appointed, recommended or opposed by the employees, and their rights;

(h) the date of entry into force of the agreement and its duration, cases where the agreement should be renegotiated and the procedure for its renegotiation.

3. The agreement shall not, unless provision is made otherwise therein, be subject to the standard rules referred to in the Annex.

4. Without prejudice to Article 13(3)(a), in the case of an SE established by means of transformation, the agreement shall provide for at least the same level of all elements of employee involvement as the ones existing within the company to be transformed into an SE.

Article 5
Duration of negotiations

1. Negotiations shall commence as soon as the special negotiating body is established and may continue for six months thereafter.

2. The parties may decide, by joint agreement, to extend negotiations beyond the period referred to in paragraph 1, up to a total of one year from the establishment of the special negotiating body.

Article 6
Legislation applicable to the negotiation procedure

Except where otherwise provided in this Directive, the legislation applicable to the negotiation procedure provided for in Articles 3 to 5 shall be the legislation of the Member State in which the registered office of the SE is to be situated.

Article 7
Standard rules

1. In order to achieve the objective described in Article 1, Member States shall, without prejudice to paragraph 3 below, lay down standard rules on employee involvement which must satisfy the provisions set out in the Annex.

The standard rules as laid down by the legislation of the Member State in which the registered office of the SE is to be situated shall apply from the date of the registration of the SE where either:

(a) the parties so agree; or

(b) by the deadline laid down in Article 5, no agreement has been concluded, and:
- the competent organ of each of the participating companies decides to accept the application of the standard rules in relation to the SE and so to continue with its registration of the SE, and
- the special negotiating body has not taken the decision provided in Article 3(6).

2. Moreover, the standard rules fixed by the national legislation of the Member State of registration in accordance with part 3 of the Annex shall apply only:

(a) in the case of an SE established by transformation, if the rules of a Member State relating to employee participation in the administrative or supervisory body applied to a company transformed into an SE;

(b) in the case of an SE established by merger:
- if, before registration of the SE, one or more forms of participation applied in one or more of the participating companies covering at least 25% of the total number of employees in all the participating companies, or
- if, before registration of the SE, one or more forms of participation applied in one or more of the participating companies covering less than 25% of the total number of employees in all the participating companies and if the special negotiating body so decides,

(c) in the case of an SE established by setting up a holding company or establishing a subsidiary:
- if, before registration of the SE, one or more forms of participation applied in one or more of the participating companies covering at least 50% of the total number of employees in all the participating companies; or
- if, before registration of the SE, one or more forms of participation applied in one or more of the participating companies covering less than 50% of the total number of employees in all the participating companies and if the special negotiating body so decides.

If there was more than one form of participation within the various participating companies, the special negotiating body shall decide which of those forms must be established in the SE. Member States may fix the rules which are applicable in the absence of any decision on the matter for an SE registered in their territory. The special negotiating body shall inform the competent organs of the participating companies of any decisions taken pursuant to this paragraph.

3. Member States may provide that the reference provisions in part 3 of the Annex shall not apply in the case provided for in point (b) of paragraph 2.

SECTION III

MISCELLANEOUS PROVISIONS

Article 8

Reservation and confidentiality

1. Member States shall provide that members of the special negotiating body or the representative body, and experts who assist them, are not authorised to reveal any information which has been given to them in confidence.

The same shall apply to employees' representatives in the context of an information and consultation procedure.

This obligation shall continue to apply, wherever the persons referred to may be, even after the expiry of their terms of office.

2. Each Member State shall provide, in specific cases and under the conditions and limits laid down by national legislation, that the supervisory or administrative organ of an SE or of a participating company established in its territory is not obliged to transmit information where its nature is such that, according to objective criteria, to do so would seriously harm the functioning of the SE (or, as the case may be, the participating company) or its subsidiaries and establishments or would be prejudicial to them.

A Member State may make such dispensation subject to prior administrative or judicial authorisation.

3. Each Member State may lay down particular provisions for SEs in its territory which pursue directly and essentially the aim of ideological guidance with respect to information and the expression of opinions, on condition that, on the date of adoption of this Directive, such provisions already exist in the national legislation.

4. In applying paragraphs 1, 2 and 3, Member States shall make provision for administrative or judicial appeal procedures which the employees' representatives may initiate when the supervisory or administrative organ of an SE or participating company demands confidentiality or does not give information.

Such procedures may include arrangements designed to protect the confidentiality of the information in question.

Article 9

Operation of the representative body and procedure for the information and consultation of employees

The competent organ of the SE and the representative body shall work together in a spirit of cooperation with due regard for their reciprocal rights and obligations.

The same shall apply to cooperation between the supervisory or administrative organ of the SE and the employees' representatives in conjunction with a procedure for the information and consultation of employees.

Article 10

Protection of employees' representatives

The members of the special negotiating body, the members of the representative body, any employees' representatives exercising functions under the information and consultation procedure and any employees' representatives in the supervisory or administrative organ of an SE who are employees of the SE, its subsidiaries or establishments or of a participating company shall, in the exercise of their functions, enjoy the same protection and guarantees provided for employees' representatives by the national legislation and/or practice in force in their country of employment.

This shall apply in particular to attendance at meetings of the special negotiating body or representative body, any other meeting under the agreement referred to in Article 4(2)(f) or any meeting of the administrative or supervisory organ, and to the payment of wages for members employed by a participating company or the SE or its subsidiaries or establishments during a period of absence necessary for the performance of their duties.

Article 11

Misuse of procedures

Member States shall take appropriate measures in conformity with Community law with a view to preventing the misuse of an SE for the purpose of depriving employees of rights to employee involvement or withholding such rights.

Article 12

Compliance with this Directive

1. Each Member State shall ensure that the management of establishments of an SE and the supervisory or administrative organs of subsidiaries and of participating companies which are situated within its territory and the employees' representatives or, as the case may be, the employees themselves abide by the obligations laid down by this Directive, regardless of whether or not the SE has its registered office within its territory.

2. Member States shall provide for appropriate measures in the event of failure to comply with this Directive; in particular they shall ensure that administrative or legal procedures are available to enable the obligations deriving from this Directive to be enforced.

Article 13

Link between this Directive and other provisions

1. Where an SE is a Community-scale undertaking or a controlling undertaking of a Community-scale

group of undertakings within the meaning of Directive 94/45/EC or of Directive 97/74/EC[7] extending the said Directive to the United Kingdom, the provisions of these Directives and the provisions transposing them into national legislation shall not apply to them or to their subsidiaries.

However, where the special negotiating body decides in accordance with Article 3(6) not to open negotiations or to terminate negotiations already opened, Directive 94/45/EC or Directive 97/74/EC and the provisions transposing them into national legislation shall apply.

2. Provisions on the participation of employees in company bodies provided for by national legislation and/or practice, other than those implementing this Directive, shall not apply to companies established in accordance with Regulation 2157/2001/EC and covered by this Directive.

3. This Directive shall not prejudice:

(a) the existing rights to involvement of employees provided for by national legislation and/or practice in the Member States as enjoyed by employees of the SE and its subsidiaries and establishments, other than participation in the bodies of the SE;

(b) the provisions on participation in the bodies laid down by national legislation and/or practice applicable to the subsidiaries of the SE.

4. In order to preserve the rights referred to in paragraph 3, Member States may take the necessary measures to guarantee that the structures of employee representation in participating companies which will cease to exist as separate legal entities are maintained after the registration of the SE.

Article 14
Final provisions

1. Member States shall adopt the laws, regulations and administrative provisions necessary to comply with this Directive no later than 8 October 2004, or shall ensure by that date at the latest that management and labour introduce the required provisions by way of agreement, the Member States being obliged to take all necessary steps enabling them at all times to guarantee the results imposed by this Directive. They shall forthwith inform the Commission thereof.

2. When Member States adopt these measures, they shall contain a reference to this Directive or shall be accompanied by such reference on the occasion of their official publication. The methods of making such reference shall be laid down by the Member States.

Article 15
Review by the Commission

No later than 8 October 2007, the Commission shall, in consultation with the Member States and with management and labour at Community level, review the procedures for applying this Directive, with a view to proposing suitable amendments to the Council where necessary.

Article 16
Entry into force

This Directive shall enter into force on the day of its publication in the Official Journal of the European Communities.

Article 17
Addressees

This Directive is addressed to the Member States.

---

[7] OJ L 10, 16.1.1998, 22, reproduced infra under no. E. 6.

Annex

Standard Rules

(referred to in Article 7)

Part 1: Composition of the body representative of the employees

In order to achieve the objective described in Article 1, and in the cases referred to in Article 7, a representative body shall be set up in accordance with the following rules.

(a) The representative body shall be composed of employees of the SE and its subsidiaries and establishments elected or appointed from their number by the employees' representatives or, in the absence thereof, by the entire body of employees.

(b) The election or appointment of members of the representative body shall be carried out in accordance with national legislation and/or practice.

Member States shall lay down rules to ensure that the number of members of, and allocation of seats on, the representative body shall be adapted to take account of changes occurring within the SE and its subsidiaries and establishments.

(c) Where its size so warrants, the representative body shall elect a select committee from among its members, comprising at most three members.

(d) The representative body shall adopt its rules of procedure.

(e) The members of the representative body are elected or appointed in proportion to the number of employees employed in each Member State by the participating companies and concerned subsidiaries or establishments, by allocating in respect of a Member State one seat per portion of employees employed in that Member State which equals 10%, or a fraction thereof, of the number of employees employed by the participating companies and concerned subsidiaries or establishments in all the Member States taken together.

(f) The competent organ of the SE shall be informed of the composition of the representative body.

(g) Four years after the representative body is established, it shall examine whether to open negotiations for the conclusion of the agreement referred to in Articles 4 and 7 or to continue to apply the standard rules adopted in accordance with this Annex.

Articles 3(4) to (7) and 4 to 6 shall apply, mutatis mutandis, if a decision has been taken to negotiate an agreement according to Article 4, in which case the term 'special negotiating body' shall be replaced by 'representative body'. Where, by the deadline by which the negotiations come to an end, no agreement has been concluded, the arrangements initially adopted in accordance with the standard rules shall continue to apply.

Part 2: Standard rules for information and consultation

The competence and powers of the representative body set up in an SE shall be governed by the following rules.

(a) The competence of the representative body shall be limited to questions which concern the SE itself and any of its subsidiaries or establishments situated in another Member State or which exceed the powers of the decision-making organs in a single Member State.

(b) Without prejudice to meetings held pursuant to point (c), the representative body shall have the right to be informed and consulted and, for that purpose, to meet with the competent organ of the SE at least once a year, on the basis of regular reports drawn up by the competent organ, on the progress of the business of the SE and its prospects. The local managements shall be informed accordingly.

The competent organ of the SE shall provide the representative body with the agenda for meetings of the administrative, or, where appropriate, the management and supervisory organ, and with copies of all documents submitted to the general meeting of its shareholders.

The meeting shall relate in particular to the structure, economic and financial situation, the probable development of the business and of production and sales, the situation and probable trend of employment, investments, and substantial changes concerning organisation, introduction of new working methods or production processes, transfers of production, mergers, cut-backs or closures of undertakings, establishments or important parts thereof, and collective redundancies.

(c) Where there are exceptional circumstances affecting the employees' interests to a considerable extent, particularly in the event of relocations, transfers, the closure of establishments or undertakings or collective redundancies, the representative body shall have the right to be informed. The representative body or, where it so decides, in particular for reasons of urgency, the select committee, shall have the right to meet at its request the competent organ of the SE or any more appropriate level of management within the SE having its own powers of decision, so as to be informed and consulted on measures significantly affecting employees' interests.

Where the competent organ decides not to act in accordance with the opinion expressed by the representative body, this body shall have the right to a further meeting with the competent organ of the SE with a view to seeking agreement.

In the case of a meeting organised with the select committee, those members of the representative body who represent employees who are directly concerned by the measures in question shall also have the right to participate.

The meetings referred to above shall not affect the prerogatives of the competent organ.

(d) Member States may lay down rules on the chairing of information and consultation meetings.

Before any meeting with the competent organ of the SE, the representative body or the select committee, where necessary enlarged in accordance with the third subparagraph of paragraph (c), shall be entitled to meet without the representatives of the competent organ being present.

(e) Without prejudice to Article 8, the members of the representative body shall inform the representatives of the employees of the SE and of its subsidiaries and establishments of the content and outcome of the information and consultation procedures.

(f) The representative body or the select committee may be assisted by experts of its choice.

(g) In so far as this is necessary for the fulfilment of their tasks, the members of the representative body shall be entitled to time off for training without loss of wages.

(h) The costs of the representative body shall be borne by the SE, which shall provide the body's members with the financial and material resources needed to enable them to perform their duties in an appropriate manner.

In particular, the SE shall, unless otherwise agreed, bear the cost of organising meetings and providing interpretation facilities and the accommodation and travelling expenses of members of the representative body and the select committee.

In compliance with these principles, the Member States may lay down budgetary rules regarding the operation of the representative body. They may in particular limit funding to cover one expert only.

Part 3: Standard rules for participation

Employee participation in an SE shall be governed by the following provisions

(a) In the case of an SE established by transformation, if the rules of a Member State relating to employee participation in the administrative or supervisory body applied before registration, all aspects of employee participation shall continue to apply to the SE. Point (b) shall apply mutatis mutandis to that end.

(b) In other cases of the establishing of an SE, the employees of the SE, its subsidiaries and establishments and/or their representative body shall have the right to elect, appoint, recommend or oppose the appointment of a number of members of the administrative or supervisory body of the SE equal to the highest proportion in force in the participating companies concerned before registration of the SE.

If none of the participating companies was governed by participation rules before registration of the SE, the latter shall not be required to establish provisions for employee participation.

The representative body shall decide on the allocation of seats within the administrative or supervisory body among the members representing the employees from the various Member States or on the way in which the SE's employees may recommend or oppose the appointment of the members of these bodies according to the proportion of the SE's employees in each Member State.

If the employees of one or more Member States are not covered by this proportional criterion, the representative body shall appoint a member from one of those Member States, in particular the Member State of the SE's registered office where that is appropriate. Each Member State may determine the allocation of the seats it is given within the administrative or supervisory body.

Every member of the administrative body or, where appropriate, the supervisory body of the SE who has been elected, appointed or recommended by the representative body or, depending on the circumstances, by the employees shall be a full member with the same rights and obligations as the members representing the shareholders, including the right to vote.

C. 21.

Commission Recommendation 2002/590/EC
of 16 May 2002
Statutory Auditors' Independence in the EU: A Set of Fundamental Principles
(notified under document number C(2002) 1873)[1]

(Text with EEA relevance)

THE COMMISSION OF THE EUROPEAN COMMUNITIES,

Having regard to the Treaty establishing the European Community, and in particular Article 211, second indent thereof,

Whereas:

(1) The independence of statutory auditors is fundamental to the public confidence in the reliability of statutory auditors' reports. It adds credibility to published financial information and value to investors, creditors, employees and other stakeholders in EU companies. This is particularly the case in companies which are public interest entities (e.g., listed companies, credit institutions, insurance companies, UCITS and investment firms).

(2) Independence is also the profession's main means of demonstrating to the public and regulators that statutory auditors and audit firms are performing their task at a level that meets established ethical principles, in particular those of integrity and objectivity.

(3) Council Directive 84/253/EEC[2] on 'the approval of persons responsible for carrying out the statutory audits of accounting documents' establishes the minimum qualifications required of persons who are allowed to carry out statutory audits.

(4) Articles 24 and 25 of this Directive require EU Member States to prescribe that statutory auditors do not carry out statutory audits, either in their own right or on behalf of an audit firm, if they are not independent. Article 26 of the Directive requires Member States to ensure that statutory auditors are liable to appropriate sanctions when they do not carry out a statutory audit in an independent manner. Furthermore, Article 27 of the Directive requires Member States to ensure, at a minimum, that the members and shareholders of an audit firm do not intervene in the conduct of statutory audits in any way which jeopardises the independence of the natural persons performing the statutory audit on behalf of that audit firm. This requirement also applies to those members of the administration, management and supervisory body of the audit firm who are not personally approved as statutory auditors.

(5) Member States' national rules on statutory auditors' independence currently differ in several respects such as: the scope of persons to whom independence rules should apply, both within an audit firm and outside the firm; the kind of financial, business or other relationships that a statutory auditor, an audit firm or an individual within the firm may have with an audit client; the type of non-audit services that can and cannot be provided to an audit client; and the safeguards which need to be put in place. This situation makes it difficult to provide investors and other stakeholders in EU companies with a uniformly high level of assurance that statutory auditors perform their audit work independently throughout the EU.

(6) At present there is no internationally accepted ethics standard for statutory auditors' independence that could be used as a benchmark for national independence rules throughout the EU.

---

[1] OJ L 191, 19.7.2002, 22–57.
[2] OJ L 126, 12.5.1984, 20, reproduced supra under no. C. 7, which has been repealed as from 29 June 2006 by article 50 of Directive 2006/43/EC, reproduced infra under no. C. 30.

(7) The issue of statutory auditors' independence was addressed by the Commission's 1996 Green Paper[3] on 'The Role, Position and Liability of the Statutory Auditor in the EU' that received the support of the Council, the Economic and Social Committee and the European Parliament. As a result of the Commission's 1998 Communication 'The Statutory Audit in the European Union, the way forward'[4] the EU Committee on Auditing was created. This Committee established statutory auditors' independence as one of their priorities. Finally, the Commission's Communication 'EU Financial Reporting Strategy: the way forward'[5] underlines the importance of a statutory audit carried out to uniformly high levels across the EU, including a common approach to professional ethics standards.

(8) The scope of this initiative on statutory auditors' independence applies to the EU statutory audit profession as a whole. It aims at setting a benchmark for Member States' requirements on statutory auditors' independence throughout the EU.

(9) Agreement was reached in the Committee on Auditing that each Member State should provide statutory auditors, regulators and the interested public with a common understanding of the independence requirement by the application of fundamental principles. This will bring about consistency in interpreting and addressing facts and circumstances which threaten a statutory auditor's independence throughout the EU. The existence of such principles should also help to provide a level playing field for the provision of statutory audit services within the single market. The principles should be comprehensive, rigorous, robust, enforceable and reasonable. They should be consistently interpreted and applied by professional bodies, supervisors and regulators, as well as by statutory auditors, their clients and other interested parties.

(10) Agreement was also reached in the Committee on Auditing to build on this initiative in order to develop common independence standards. This will contribute to the creation of a single EU capital market as outlined by the Financial Services Action Plan(5) and endorsed by the Stockholm European Council.[6] However, whilst work to achieve harmonisation continues, the setting of national independence rules that are complementary to EU fundamental principles is to be left to the discretion of Member States. Such rules would apply in particular to statutory audits of companies operating in regulated industries. Member States may also decide to require the application of the same independence standards to unlisted companies as applicable to listed companies.

(11) A principles-based approach to statutory auditors' independence is preferable to one based on detailed rules because it creates a robust structure within which statutory auditors have to justify their actions. It also provides the audit profession and its regulators with the flexibility to react promptly and effectively to new developments in business and in the audit environment. At the same time, it avoids the highly legalistic and rigid approach to what is and is not permitted which can arise in a rules-based regime. A principles-based approach can cater for the almost infinite variations in individual circumstances that arise in practice and in the different legal environments throughout the EU. Consequently, a principles-based approach will better serve the needs of European capital markets, as well as those of SMEs.

(12) The benefits of safeguarding the statutory auditors' independence include efficiencies and other positive effects that, ultimately, contribute to the overall efficiency of the capital markets. On the other hand, maintaining statutory auditor independence creates a variety of additional costs that have to be borne by various parties. These include the costs that are related to developing, maintaining, and enforcing safeguards to independence. When seeking to impose a certain safeguard on statutory auditors, Member States

---

[3] OJ C 321, 28.10.1996, 1.
[4] OJ C 143, 8.5.1998, 12.
[5] COM (2000) 359, 13.6.2000.

[6] Presidency Conclusions, Stockholm European Council, 23 and 24 March 2001.

and regulators need to take into account the anticipated costs and benefits in particular circumstances. For example, a particular safeguard may bring substantial public benefits at a modest cost when applied to the audits of public interest entities. But if applied to the audit of a small company with relatively little public interest, the same safeguard may result in costs that are disproportionate to the associated benefits to the users of this company's financial statements.

(13) Establishing fundamental principles is not in itself sufficient to ensure public confidence that the EU statutory auditor applies proper standards of integrity and independence. Appropriate systems of quality assurance are necessary in order to check that the principles are properly applied by EU statutory auditors. In this regard the Commission Recommendation on 'Quality Assurance for the Statutory Auditor in the EU'[7] provides for external quality reviews of statutory auditors, including a review of compliance with independence standards. Such quality assurance systems are subject to public oversight.

(14) This Recommendation is an important step towards assuring audit quality. Further steps may be necessary. The Commission intends to come forward with a broader strategy on auditing which will address issues such as the use of International Standards on Auditing (ISAs), the establishment of a public oversight on the audit profession and the role of audit committees.

(15) This Recommendation emphasises the responsibility of the audit profession to uphold auditor independence. If this Recommendation does not bring about the desired harmonisation, the Commission will review the situation three years after the adoption of this Recommendation taking into account international developments. This review will specifically address the question to what extent this Recommendation has had an impact on auditor independence where auditors have provided non-audit services to audit clients.

(16) There is general agreement in the EU Committee on Auditing and in the Contact Committee on the Accounting Directives on the fundamental principles of this Recommendation.

(17) This Recommendation provides a framework within which all of the general issues of statutory auditors' independence are considered. Its Section A sets out the overarching independence requirements for statutory auditors and discusses the scope of persons to whom independence rules should apply. Section B then reviews a range of specific circumstances in which threats to independence could arise and provides guidance on the measures a statutory auditor should take to mitigate such threats in relation to a particular statutory audit. It is to be noted that Section B is not intended to provide an exhaustive list of all the circumstances where threats to auditor independence might arise, but that statutory auditors should be alert to any such threat and take whatever action is necessary in accordance with the principles and guidance in this Recommendation. The basic principles in Section A and the essential safeguards that are provided in Section B for specific circumstances are supported by an annex, which provides related explanations and guidance. Important terms are defined in the Appendix,

HEREBY RECOMMENDS:

That rules, standards and/or regulation on statutory auditors' independence in the Member States of the European Union should implement the following set of fundamental principles:

A. FRAMEWORK

When carrying out a Statutory Audit,[8] a Statutory Auditor[9] must be independent from his Audit Client,[10] both in mind and in appearance. A statutory auditor should not carry out a Statutory Audit if there are any financial, business, employment or

---

[7] C (2000) 3304, 15.11.2000.

[8] Defined in the glossary.
[9] Defined in the glossary. The term 'statutory auditor' refers to all natural or legal persons, or other types of company, firm or partnership who, in accordance with the provisions of the 8th Company Law Directive (84/253/EEC), are approved by the authorities of the Member States to carry out Statutory Audits.
[10] Defined in the glossary.

other relationships between the statutory auditor and his client (including certain non-audit services provided to the audit client) that a reasonable and informed third party would conclude compromise the statutory auditor's independence.

1. Objectivity, integrity and independence

1. Objectivity and professional integrity should be the overriding principles underlying a statutory auditor's audit opinion on financial statements. The main way in which the Statutory Auditor can demonstrate to the public that a Statutory Audit is performed in accordance with these principles is by acting, and being seen to act, independently.

2. Objectivity (as a state of mind) cannot be subjected to external verification, and integrity cannot be evaluated in advance.

3. Principles and rules on statutory auditors' independence should allow a reasonable and informed third party to evaluate the procedures and actions taken by a Statutory Auditor to avoid or resolve facts and circumstances that pose threats or risks to his objectivity.

2. Responsibility and scope

1. It is the responsibility of the Statutory Auditor to ensure that the requirement for statutory auditors' independence is complied with.

2. The independence requirement applies to:

(a) the Statutory Auditor himself; and

(b) those who are in a position to influence the outcome of the Statutory Audit.

3. Those in a position to influence the outcome of the Statutory Audit are:

(a) all persons who are directly involved in the Statutory Audit (the Engagement Team[11]), including

(i) the Audit Partners,[12] audit managers and audit staff (the Audit Team[13]);

(ii) professional personnel from other disciplines involved in the audit engagement (e.g., lawyers, actuaries, taxation specialists, IT-specialists, treasury management specialists);

(iii) those who provide quality control or direct oversight of the audit engagement;

(b) all persons, who form part of the Chain of Command[14] for the Statutory Audit within the Audit Firm[15] or within a Network[16] of which the firm is a member;

(c) all persons within the Audit Firm or its Network who, due to any other circumstances, may be in a position to exert influence on the Statutory Audit.

3. Independence threats and risk

1. Statutory auditors' independence can be affected by different types of threats, including self-interest, self-review, advocacy, familiarity or trust, and intimidation.

2. The level of risk that a Statutory Auditor's independence might be compromised will be determined by reference to the significance of these threats, either individually or in combination, and their impact on the Statutory Auditor's independence. This determination will need to consider the specific circumstances that relate to the Statutory Audit concerned.

3. A Statutory Auditor's independence risk assessment should have due regard to both:

(a) the services provided to the Audit Client in recent years and the relationships that existed with that Audit Client before the appointment as Statutory Auditor; and

(b) the services provided to, and the relationships that exist with, the Audit Client during the course of the Statutory Audit.

4. Systems of safeguards

1. Different types of safeguards—including prohibitions, restrictions, other policies and

---

[11] Defined in the glossary.
[12] Defined in the glossary.
[13] Defined in the glossary.
[14] Defined in the glossary.
[15] Defined in the glossary.
[16] Defined in the glossary.

procedures, and disclosures—have to be established in order to mitigate or eliminate threats to statutory auditors' independence (see A. 3).

2. The existence and the effectiveness of various safeguards affect the level of independence risk.

4.1. *Audited entities' safeguards*

4.1.1. Governance structure's impact on independence risk assessment

The Statutory Auditor should consider whether the governance structure of the audited entity provides safeguards to mitigate threats to his independence and how these safeguards are operated. Such safeguards include:

1. the appointment of the Statutory Auditor by persons other than the audited entity's management; and

2. oversight and communications within the audited entity regarding the Statutory Audit and other services provided to it by the Audit Firm or its Network.

4.1.2. Involvement of the Governance Body

1. Where a Public Interest Entity has a Governance Body (see A. 4.1.1), the Statutory Auditor should at least annually:

(a) disclose to the Governance Body, in writing:
(i) the total amount of fees that he, the Audit Firm and its Network members have charged to the Audit Client and its Affiliates for the provision of services during the reporting period. This total amount should be broken down into four broad categories of services: Statutory audit services; further assurance services;[17] tax advisory services; and other non-audit services. The category of other non-audit services should be further broken down into subcategories so far as items in them differ substantially from one another. This break-down into subcategories should at least provide information on fees for the provision of financial information technology, internal audit, valuation, litigation and recruitment services. For each (sub-)category of service, the amounts charged and contracted for, as well as existing proposals or bids for future services contracts should be separately analysed;
(ii) details of all relationships between himself, the Audit Firm and its Network member firms, and the Audit Client and its Affiliates[18] that he believes may reasonably be thought to bear on his independence and objectivity; and
(iii) the related safeguards that are in place;

(b) confirm in writing that, in his professional judgement, the Statutory Auditor is independent within the meaning of regulatory and professional requirements and the objectivity of the Statutory Auditor is not compromised, or otherwise declare that he has concerns that his independence and objectivity may be compromised; and

(c) seek to discuss these matters with the Governance Body of the Audit Client.

2. Where Audit Clients other than Public Interest Entities have a Governance Body, the Statutory Auditor should consider whether similar measures are appropriate.

4.2. *Quality assurance*

Quality assurance systems which meet the minimum requirements of the Commission Recommendation on 'Quality Assurance for the Statutory Audit in the EU'[19] are required mechanisms contributing to safeguard statutory auditors' compliance with the independence requirement at a Member State level.

4.3. *The Statutory Auditor's overall safeguards*

4.3.1. Ownership of and control over Audit Firms

If the Statutory Auditor is an Audit Firm, at least the majority of the firm's voting rights (50% plus one vote) must be held by persons who are

---

[17] Defined in the glossary.
[18] Defined in the glossary.
[19] C (2000) 3304, 15.11.2000.

authorised to perform Statutory Audits within the European Union (statutory auditors[20]). The Statutory Auditor's legal statutes should contain provisions to ensure that a non-auditor owner could not gain control over the Audit Firm.[21]

4.3.2. The Audit Firm's internal safeguarding system

1. A Statutory Auditor should set up and maintain a safeguarding system that is an integral part of his firm-wide management and internal control structure.

2. The functioning of such a system should be documented so that it can be subject to quality assurance systems (see A. 4.2).

3. Generally, the safeguarding system of an Audit Firm would include:

(a) written independence policies which address current independence standards, threats to independence, and the safeguards related thereto;

(b) active and timely communication of the policies, and any changes to them, to each Partner, manager and employee, including regular training and education thereon;

(c) appropriate procedures to be applied by Partners, managers and employees in order to meet independence standards, both on a regular basis and in response to particular circumstances;

(d) designation of top-level audit professionals (Partners) responsible for updating the policies, timely communication of those updates, and overseeing the adequate functioning of the safeguarding system;

(e) documentation for each Audit Client that summarises the conclusions that have been drawn from the assessment of threats to the Statutory Auditor's independence and the related evaluation of the independence risk. This should include the reasoning for these conclusions. If significant threats are noted, the documentation should include a summary of the steps that were, or are to be, taken to avoid or negate the independence risk, or at least reduce it to an appropriate level; and

(f) internal monitoring of compliance with safeguarding policies.

5. Public disclosure of fees

1. Where a Statutory Auditor or, if the Statutory Auditor is a natural person, a firm of which he is a member or Partner has received fees from an Audit Client for (audit and non-audit) services provided during the client's reporting period, all these fees should be publicly and appropriately disclosed.

2. Member States or their regulatory bodies should require this disclosure to the extent that an Audit Client's audited financial statements have to be published in accordance with their national law.

3. The total fee income should be broken down by four categories: statutory audit services; further assurance services; tax advisory services; and other non-audit services. The fees for other non-audit services should be further broken down into sub-categories so far as items in them differ substantially from one another. This break-down into subcategories should at least provide information on fees for the provision of financial information technology, internal audit, valuation, litigation and recruitment services. In respect of each (sub-)category item, the figure relating to the corresponding (sub-)category item for the preceding reporting period should be shown as well. Furthermore, a percentage break-down for the (sub-)categories should be provided.

4. Where a Statutory Audit of consolidated financial statements is concerned, the fees received by the Statutory Auditor and his Network members for the services they provided to the Audit Client and its consolidated entities should be disclosed accordingly.

---

[20] For the purpose of this section in particular, the term 'statutory auditors' refers to all natural or legal persons, or other types of company, firm or partnership who, in accordance with the provisions of the 8th Company Law Directive (84/253/EEC), reproduced supra under no. C.7., are approved by the authorities of the Member States to carry out Statutory Audits.

[21] This paragraph does not apply to an Audit Firm for which the relevant Member State, in accordance with Article 2.1 (ii) 2nd phrase of the 8th Directive, does not require a majority of voting rights to be held by statutory auditors, and of which all the shares are registered and can be transferred only with the agreement of the firm and/or with the approval of the national authority competent for the approval of statutory auditors.

B. Specific Circumstances

1. Financial interests

1. An actual or impending, direct or indirect financial interest in the Audit Client or its Affiliates, including any derivative directly related thereto, may threaten the Statutory Auditor's independence, if it is held by the Statutory Auditor or any other person being in a position to influence the outcome of the Statutory Audit (any person within the scope of A. 2).

The Statutory Auditor has to assess the significance of any such threat, identify whether any safeguards would mitigate the independence risk it presents, and take any action necessary. This may include refusal of, or resignation from, the audit engagement or exclusion of the relevant person from the Audit Team. Where applicable, and especially with regard to Public Interest Entity clients, the Statutory Auditor should seek to involve the Governance Body in this process.

2. Financial interest in the Audit Client or its Affiliates will be incompatible with the Statutory Auditor's independence, if:

(a) the Statutory Auditor, the Audit Firm, or any member of the Engagement Team or the Chain of Command, or any Partner of the firm or its Network who is working in an 'Office'[22] which participates in a significant proportion of an audit engagement, holds
 (i) any direct financial interest in the Audit Client; or
 (ii) any indirect financial interest in the Audit Client which is significant to either party; or
 (iii) any (direct or indirect) financial interest in the client's Affiliates which is significant to either party;

(b) any other person within the scope of A. 2, holds any (direct or indirect) financial interest in the Audit Client or its Affiliates which is significant to either party.

Accordingly, the persons concerned should not hold any such financial interests. Where such an interest is acquired as a result of an external event (e.g. inheritance, gift, merger of firms or companies) it must be disposed of as soon as practicable, but no later than one month after the person has knowledge of, and the right to dispose of, the financial interest. In the meantime, additional safeguards are needed to preserve the Statutory Auditor's independence. These could include a secondary review of the relevant person's audit work or exclusion of the relevant person from any substantive decision making concerning the Statutory Audit of the client.

3. The Statutory Auditor's independence may also be threatened by an apparently insignificant financial interest in an Audit Client or its Affiliates. The level of threat will be higher, and likely to be unacceptable, if the interest is neither acquired or held on standard commercial terms nor negotiated on an arm's length basis. It is the responsibility of the Statutory Auditor to assess the level of risk that such an interest presents and to ensure that any necessary mitigating action is taken.

2. Business relationships

1. Business relationships between the Statutory Auditor, the Audit Firm or any other person being in a position to influence the outcome of the Statutory Audit (any person within the scope of A. 2) on the one hand, and the Audit Client, its Affiliates, or its management on the other hand, may cause self-interest, advocacy or intimidation threats to the Statutory Auditor's independence.

2. Business relationships, or commitments to establish such relationships, should be prohibited unless the relationship is in the normal course of business and insignificant in terms of the threat it poses to the independence of the Statutory Auditor.

Where applicable, and especially with regard to Public Interest Entity clients, the Statutory Auditor should seek to discuss with the Governance Body of the Audit Client any cases where doubt arises whether or not a business relationship is in the normal course of business and insignificant in relation to his independence.

---

[22] Defined in the glossary.

3. Paragraphs 1 and 2 above do not apply to the provision of statutory audit services. However, neither the Audit Firm nor any of its Network member firms should provide statutory audit services to:

(a) any owner of the Audit Firm; or

(b) an Affiliate of such an owner where the owner may be in a position to influence any decision-making of the Audit Firm which affects its statutory audit function; or

(c) an entity where any individual who has a supervisory or managerial role in that entity may be in a position to influence any decision-making of the Audit Firm which affects its statutory audit function.[23]

3. Employment with the Audit Client

1. Dual employment of any individual who is in a position to influence the outcome of the Statutory Audit both in the Audit Firm (a person within the scope of A. 2) and in the Audit Client or its Affiliates should be prohibited. Loan staff assignments[24] to an Audit Client or any of its Affiliates are also regarded as dual employment relationships. Where an Audit Firm's employee has worked with an Audit Client under a loan staff assignment and is to be assigned to the audit Engagement Team of that client's Statutory Audit, this individual should not be given audit responsibility for any function or activity that he was required to perform or supervise during the former loan staff assignment (see also B. 5 below).

2. Where a member of the Engagement Team is to leave the Audit Firm and join an Audit Client, policies and procedures of the Audit Firm (see A. 4.3) should provide:

(a) a requirement that members of any Engagement Team immediately notify the Audit Firm of any situation involving their potential employment with the Audit Client;

(b) the immediate removal of any such Engagement Team member from the audit engagement; and

(c) an immediate review of the audit work performed by the resigning or former Engagement Team member in the current and/or (where appropriate) the most recent audit. This review should be performed by a more senior audit professional. If the individual joining the client is an Audit Partner or the Engagement Partner, the review should be performed by an Audit Partner who was not involved in the audit engagement. (Where, due to its size, the Audit Firm does not have a Partner who was not involved in the audit engagement, it may seek either a review by another statutory auditor or advice from its professional regulatory body.)

3. Where a former Engagement Team member or an individual within the Chain of Command has joined an Audit Client, policies and procedures of the Audit Firm should ensure that there remain no significant connections between itself and the individual. This includes:

(a) regardless of whether the individual was previously involved in the audit engagement, that all capital balances and similar financial interests must be fully settled (including retirement benefits) unless these are made in accordance with pre-determined arrangements that cannot be influenced by any remaining connections between the individual and the Audit Firm;

(b) that the individual does not participate or appear to participate further in the Audit Firm's business or professional activities.

4. A Key Audit Partner leaving the audit firm to join the audit client for a Key Management Position,[25] would be perceived to cause an unacceptably high level of independence risk.

---

[23] Paragraph 3 lit. (a) and (b) do not apply to an Audit Firm for which the relevant Member State, in accordance with Article 2.1 (ii) 2nd phrase of the 8th Directive, does not require a majority of voting rights to be held by statutory auditors, and of which all the shares are registered and can be transferred only with the agreement of the firm and/or with the approval of the national authority competent for the approval of statutory auditors; provided that an Audit Client of such an Audit Firm is not in a position to influence any decision making of the firm which affects its statutory audit function.

[24] An individual who is engaged under a loan staff agreement, works under the direct supervision of the client and does not originate any accounting transaction or prepare original data that is not subject to review and approval by the client.

[25] Defined in the glossary.

Therefore, a period of at least two years should have elapsed before a Key Audit Partner can take up a Key Management Position.

4. Managerial or supervisory role in Audit Client

1. An individual who is in a position to influence the outcome of the Statutory Audit (a person within the scope of A. 2) should not be a member of any management body (e.g. board of directors) or supervisory body (e.g. audit committee or supervisory board) of an Audit Client. Also, he should not be a member of such a body in an entity which holds directly or indirectly more than 20% of the voting rights in the client, or in which the client holds directly or indirectly more than 20% of the voting rights.

2. When a former member of the Engagement Team takes a managerial or supervisory role in an Audit Client, B. 3(3) and (4) will apply.

5. Establishing employment with Audit Firm

Where a director or manager of the Audit Client has joined the Audit Firm, this person should not become a member of the Engagement Team at any time in the two year period after leaving the Audit Client. If the person is a member of the Chain of Command, he should not take part in any substantive decisions concerning an audit engagement with this client or with one of its Affiliates at any time in the two year period after leaving the Audit Client. This requirement also applies to a former employee of the Audit Client unless the responsibilities he held and the tasks he performed at the Audit Client were insignificant in relation to the statutory audit function.

6. Family and other personal relationships

1. An individual who is a Statutory Auditor should not accept an audit engagement if one of his close family members:

(a) holds a senior management position with the Audit Client;

(b) is in a position to exert direct influence on the preparation of the Audit Client's accounting records or financial statements;

(c) has a financial interest in the Audit Client (see B. 1) unless it is insignificant; or

(d) has a business relationship with the Audit Client (see B. 2) unless it is in the normal course of business and insignificant in terms of the threat it poses to the independence of the Statutory Auditor.

2. Within an Audit Firm or Network an individual should not be assigned to the Engagement Team if one of his close family members meets any of the criteria under (1)(a) to (d) above, nor should an Audit Partner who is working in an 'Office' where any of the other Partners in it has a close family member who meets these criteria.

Appropriate safeguards should ensure that a member of the Chain of Command does not participate in any decisions that directly relate to the audit engagement if one of his close family members meets any of the criteria under (1)(a) to (d) above, or if he is working in an 'Office' where any of the Partners in it has a close family member who meets these criteria.

3. The Statutory Auditor should consider whether he or any other individual in the Engagement Team or Chain of Command, or any person working in an 'Office' which includes himself or such an individual, has any other close personal relationships where similar safeguards would be needed.

4. Assessment of the facts of a relevant individual's close personal relationship should be based upon the knowledge of the Statutory Auditor and the individual concerned. The individual should be responsible for disclosing to the Statutory Auditor any fact and circumstance which might require safeguards to mitigate an unacceptable level of independence risk.

7. Non-audit services

7.1. *General*

1. Where a Statutory Auditor, an Audit Firm or one of its Network member firms provides

services other than statutory audit work (non-audit services) to an Audit Client or to one of its Affiliates, the overall safeguarding system (A 4.3) of the Statutory Auditor has to ensure that:

(a) the individuals employed by either the Audit Firm or its Network member firm neither take any decision nor take part in any decision-making on behalf of the Audit Client or one of its Affiliates, or its management while providing a non-audit service; and

(b) where an independence risk remains due to specific threats which may result from the nature of a non-audit service, this risk is reduced to an acceptable level.

2. Even if not involved in the decision-making of the Audit Client or any of its Affiliates, the Statutory Auditor should consider, amongst others, which of the following safeguards in particular may mitigate a remaining independence threat:

(a) arrangements to reduce the risk of self-review by compartmentalising responsibilities and knowledge in specific non-audit engagements;

(b) routine notification of any audit and non-audit engagement to those in the Audit Firm or Network who are responsible for safeguarding independence, including oversight of ongoing activities;

(c) secondary reviews of the Statutory Audit by an Audit Partner who is not involved in the provision of any services to the Audit Client or to one of its Affiliates; or

(d) external review by another statutory auditor or advice by the professional regulatory body.

3. Where applicable, and especially with regard to Public Interest Entity clients, the Statutory Auditor should seek to discuss the provision of non-audit services to an Audit Client or to one of its Affiliates with the client's Governance Body (see A. 4.1.2).

7.2. *Examples—analysis of specific situations*

7.2.1. Preparing accounting records and financial statements

1. A self-review threat exists whenever a Statutory Auditor, an Audit Firm, an entity within a Network of firms or a Partner, manager or employee thereof participates in the preparation of the Audit Client's accounting records or financial statements. The significance of the threat depends upon the spectrum of these persons' involvement in the preparation process and upon the level of public interest.

2. The significance of the self-review threat is always considered too high to allow a participation in the preparation process unless the assistance provided is solely of a technical or mechanical nature or the advice given is only of an informative nature.

3. However, where Statutory Audits of Public Interest Entity clients are concerned, the provision of any such assistance other than that which is within the statutory audit mandate would be perceived to cause an unacceptably high level of independence risk, and should therefore be prohibited.

7.2.2. Design and implementation of financial information technology systems

1. The provision of services by the Statutory Auditor, the Audit Firm or an entity within its Network to an Audit Client that involve the design and implementation of financial information technology systems (FITS) used to generate information forming part of the Audit Client's financial statements may give rise to a self-review threat.

2. The significance of the self-review threat is considered too high to permit a Statutory Auditor, an Audit Firm or one of its group member firms to provide such FITS services unless:

(a) the Audit Client's management acknowledges in writing that they take responsibility for the overall system of internal control;

(b) the Statutory Auditor has satisfied himself that the Audit Client's management is not relying on the FITS work as the primary basis for determining the adequacy of its internal controls and financial reporting systems;

(c) in the case of a FITS design project, the service provided involves design to specifications set by the Audit Client's management; and

(d) the FITS services do not constitute a 'turn key' project (i.e., a project that consists of software design, hardware configuration and the implementation of both), unless the Audit Client or its management explicitly confirms in the written acknowledgement required under (a) that they take responsibility for
(i) the design, implementation and evaluation process, including any decision thereon; and
(ii) the operation of the system, including the data used or generated by the system.

These provisions shall not limit the services a Statutory Auditor, an Audit Firm or a member of its Network performs in connection with the assessment, design, and implementation of internal accounting controls and risk management controls, provided these persons do not act as an employee or perform management functions.

3. In cases not prohibited under (2) the Statutory Auditor should consider whether additional safeguards are needed to mitigate a remaining self-review threat. In particular whether services that involve the design and implementation of financial information technology systems should only be provided by an expert team with different personnel (including engagement partner) and different reporting lines to those of the audit Engagement Team.

7.2.3. Valuation services

1. A self-review threat exists whenever a Statutory Auditor, an Audit Firm, an entity within a Network or a Partner, manager or employee thereof provides the Audit Client with valuation services that result in the preparation of a valuation that is to be incorporated into the client's financial statements.

2. The significance of the self-review threat is considered too high to allow the provision of valuation services which lead to the valuation of amounts that are material in relation to the financial statements and where the valuation involves a significant degree of subjectivity inherent in the item concerned.

3. In cases not prohibited under (2) the Statutory Auditor should consider whether additional safeguards are needed to mitigate a remaining self-review threat. In particular, where a valuation service should only be provided by an expert team with different personnel (including engagement partner) and different reporting lines to those of the audit Engagement Team.

7.2.4. Participation in the Audit Client's internal audit

1. Self-review threats may arise in certain circumstances where a Statutory Auditor, an Audit Firm or an entity within a Network provides internal audit services to an Audit Client.

2. To mitigate self-review threats when involved in an Audit Client's internal audit task, the Statutory Auditor should:

(a) satisfy himself that the Audit Client's management or Governance Body is at all times responsible for
(i) the overall system of internal control (i.e., the establishment and maintenance of internal controls, including the day to day controls and processes in relation to the authorisation, execution and recording of accounting transactions);
(ii) determining the scope, risk and frequency of the internal audit procedures to be performed; and
(iii) considering and acting on the findings and recommendations provided by internal audit or during the course of a Statutory Audit.

If the Statutory Auditor is not satisfied that this is the case, neither he, nor the Audit Firm nor any entity within its Network should participate in the Audit Client's internal audit.

(b) not accept the outcomes of internal auditing processes for statutory audit purposes without adequate review. This will include a subsequent reassessment of the relevant statutory audit work by an Audit Partner who is involved neither in the Statutory Audit nor in the internal audit engagement.

7.2.5. Acting for the Audit Client in the resolution of litigation

1. An advocacy threat exists whenever a Statutory Auditor, an Audit Firm, an entity

within a Network or a Partner, manager or employee thereof acts for the Audit Client in the resolution of a dispute or litigation. A self-review threat may also arise where such a service includes the estimation of the Audit Client's chances in the resolution of litigation, and thereby affects the amounts to be reflected in the financial statements.

2. The significance of both the advocacy and the self-review threat is considered too high to allow a Statutory Auditor, an Audit Firm, an entity within a Network or a partner, manager or employee thereof to act for an Audit Client in the resolution of litigation which involves matters that would reasonably be expected to have a material impact on the client's financial statements and a significant degree of subjectivity inherent to the case concerned.

3. In cases not prohibited under (2) the Statutory Auditor should consider whether additional safeguards are needed to mitigate a remaining advocacy threat. This could include using personnel (including engagement Partner) who are not connected with the audit Engagement Team and who have different reporting lines.

7.2.6. Recruiting senior management

1. Where a Statutory Auditor, an Audit Firm, an entity within a Network or a Partner, manager or employee thereof is involved in the recruitment of senior or key staff for the Audit Client, different kinds of threats to independence may arise. These can include self-interest, trust or intimidation threats.

2. Before accepting any engagement to assist in the recruitment of senior or key staff, the Statutory Auditor should assess the current and future threats to his independence which may arise. He should then consider appropriate safeguards to mitigate such threats.

3. When recruiting staff to key financial and administrative posts, the significance of the threats to the Statutory Auditor's independence is very high. As such, the Statutory Auditor should carefully consider whether there might be circumstances where even the provision of a list of potential candidates for such posts may cause an unacceptable level of independence risk. Where Statutory Audits of Public Interest Entities are concerned the independence risk would be perceived to be too high to allow the provision of such a short-list.

4. In any case, the decision as to who should be engaged should always be taken by the Audit Client.

8. Audit and non-audit fees

8.1. *Contingent fees*

1. Fee arrangements for audit engagements in which the amount of the remuneration is contingent upon the results of the service provided raise self-interest and advocacy threats which are considered to bear an unacceptable level of independence risk. It is therefore required that:

(a) audit engagements should never be accepted on a contingent fee basis; and

(b) in order to avoid any appearance of contingency, the basis for the calculation of the audit fees must be agreed each year in advance. This should include scope for variation so as to take account of unexpected factors in the work.

2. Threats to independence may also arise from contingent fee arrangements for non-audit services which the Statutory Auditor, the Audit Firm or an entity within its Network provides to an Audit Client or to one of its Affiliates. The Statutory Auditor's safeguarding system (see A. 4.3.2) should therefore ensure that:

(a) such an arrangement is never concluded without first assessing the independence risk it might create and ensuring that appropriate safeguards are available to reduce this risk to an acceptable level; and

(b) unless the Statutory Auditor is satisfied that there are appropriate safeguards in place to overcome the independence threats, either the non-audit engagement must be refused or the Statutory Auditor must resign from the Statutory Audit to allow the acceptance of the non-audit work.

8.2. Relationship between total fees and total revenue

1. The rendering of any (audit and non-audit) services by a Statutory Auditor, an Audit Firm or a Network to one Audit Client or its Affiliates should not be allowed to create a financial dependency on that Audit Client or client group, either in fact or in appearance.

2. A financial dependency is considered to exist when the total (audit and non-audit) fees that an Audit Firm, or a Network receives or will receive from one Audit Client and its Affiliates make up an unduly high percentage of the total revenues in each year over a five-year period.

3. The Statutory Auditor should also consider whether there are certain fee relationships with one Audit Client and its Affiliates which may appear to create a financial dependency in respect of a person who is in a position to influence the outcome of the Statutory Audit (any person within the scope of A. 2).

4. In any case, the Statutory Auditor, the Audit Firm or the Network should be able to demonstrate that no financial dependency exists in relation to a particular Audit Client or its Affiliates.

8.3. Overdue fees

Where fees for audit or other work become significantly overdue and the sum outstanding, or that sum together with fees for current assignments could be regarded as a significant loan (see also B. 2), the self-interest threat to independence is considered to be so significant that a Statutory Auditor should not accept reappointment or, where appropriate and practicable, should resign from the current audit engagement. The situation should be reviewed by a Partner not involved in the provision of any services to the client. Where such a review cannot be performed, the situation should be subjected to an external review by another statutory auditor. Alternatively, advice should be sought from a professional regulatory body.

8.4. Pricing

A Statutory Auditor must be able to demonstrate that the fee for an audit engagement is adequate to cover the assignment of appropriate time and qualified staff to the task and compliance with all auditing standards, guidelines and quality control procedures. He should also be able to demonstrate that the resources allocated are at least those which would be allocated to other work of a similar nature.

9. Litigation

1. Both a self-interest and an advocacy threat may arise where litigation takes place, or appears likely to take place, between the Statutory Auditor, the Audit Firm or any other person being in a position to influence the outcome of the Statutory Audit (any person within the scope of A. 2) and an Audit Client or its Affiliates. All of the audit and non-audit services provided to the client have to be considered in order to assess these threats.

2. Where the Statutory Auditor sees that such a threat my arise, he should discuss the case with the Audit Client's Governance Body or, where such a body does not exist, with his professional regulatory body. The threats to the Statutory Auditor's independence are likely to become significant where there is a serious likelihood of litigation which is material to any of the parties involved, or of litigation which calls into question a prior Statutory Audit, or where material litigation is in progress. The Statutory Auditor should cease to act as soon as such circumstances become evident, subject to the requirements of national law.

10. Senior personnel acting for a long period of time

1. Trust or familiarity threats may arise where certain members of the Engagement Team work regularly and for a long period of time on an Audit Client engagement, particularly where Public Interest Entity Audit Clients are concerned.

2. To mitigate these threats, where the audit of a Public Interest Entity is concerned, the Statutory Auditor is required:

(a) as a minimum to replace the Key Audit Partners[26] of the Engagement Team (including

---

[26] Defined in the glossary.

the Engagement Partner) within 7 years of appointment to the Engagement Team. The replaced Key Audit Partners should not be allowed to return to the Audit Client engagement until at least a two years period has elapsed since the date of their replacement; and

(b) to consider the independence risk which may arise in relation to the prolonged involvement of other Engagement Team members, and to adopt appropriate safeguards to reduce it to an acceptable level.

3. Where Audit Clients other than Public Interest Entities are concerned, it is preferable that the procedures set out at (2) above should also apply. However, where the Audit Firm is unable to provide for rotation of Key Audit Partners, the Statutory Auditor should determine what other safeguards should be adopted to reduce the independence risk to an acceptable level.

This Recommendation is addressed to the Member States.

Annex

The following comments provide additional guidance for the interpretation of the fundamental set of principles set out in the Recommendation.

A. Framework

The basic test for the effectiveness of the approach adopted by a Statutory Auditor to mitigate threats and risks to his independence in respect of a particular audit engagement is whether a reasonable and informed third party, knowing all the relevant facts and circumstances about a particular audit engagement, will conclude that the Statutory Auditor is exercising objective and impartial judgement on all issues brought to his attention.

The Statutory Auditor should have a clear understanding of what is meant by objectivity, which is a state of mind, and independence as a matter of both fact and appearance. Accordingly, when addressing the issue of whether he can conduct an objective and independent audit, he should consider a wide range of factors and issues. These should include: the range of persons, besides himself, who may influence the result of the audit in question; whether there are any existing or potential threats or risks which a reasonable and informed third party might regard as compromising his independence; and what system of safeguards would eliminate or mitigate any such threat or risk and demonstrate his independence. In some cases, the only safeguard certain to demonstrate his independence will be to decline certain relationships with the audit client.

1. Objectivity, integrity, and independence

Public understanding of the ethical requirements that apply to statutory auditors is a prerequisite for the public confidence in the public interest role of statutory audits, the reliability of audited financial statements, and the ability of the audit profession to play its proper part in the audit process. This also includes an understanding of the ways in which compliance with such requirements can be monitored. It is therefore important that there should be a common understanding of what is meant by the 'statutory auditor's independence requirement',[27] how it relates to the ethical requirements of 'objectivity' and 'integrity',[28] and

---

[27] See Article 24 of the 8th Company Law Directive (reproduced supra under no. C. 7, which has been repealed as from 29 June 2006 by article 50 of Directive 2006/43/EC, reproduced infra under no. C. 30) which requires Member States to prescribe that statutory auditors have to be independent in accordance with the law of the Member State which requires the Statutory Audit.

[28] See also Article 23 of the 8th Company Law Directive (reproduced supra under no. C. 7, which has been repealed as from 29 June 2006 by article 50 of Directive 2006/43/EC, reproduced infra under no. C. 30) which requires Member States to prescribe that statutory auditors shall carry out Statutory Audits with professional integrity.

how, and to what extent, compliance with these requirements can be objectively assessed.

The ultimate goal of the Statutory Audit is to express an objective audit opinion. The main means by which the Statutory Auditor demonstrates that he can express such an opinion is by demonstrating that he performs the audit process in an objective manner. To achieve this he must act with fairness, intellectual honesty, integrity (which implies fair dealing and truthfulness) and without any conflict of interest which might compromise his independence.

Neither objectivity nor integrity can easily be tested or subjected to external verification. As such, the Member States and the audit profession have developed rules and guidance that both uphold the pre-eminence of these principles and clarify the ethical responsibilities of statutory auditors.

The requirement that a Statutory Auditor should be independent addresses both:
— independence of mind, i.e. the state of mind which has regard to all considerations relevant to the task in hand, but no others; and
— independence in appearance, i.e. the avoidance of facts and circumstances which are so significant that a reasonable and informed third party would question the Statutory Auditor's ability to act objectively.

The concept of statutory auditor independence requires a test which looks first at the relevant circumstances in which the Statutory Auditor finds himself, especially at any relationship or interest which has any relevance to his task.

Independence is not an absolute standard which Statutory Auditors must attain, free from all economic, financial and other relationships that could appear to entail dependence of any kind. Such a state is manifestly impossible as everyone has some dependency or relationship with another person.

Nevertheless, it is possible objectively to test a Statutory Auditor's compliance with the concept of independence through a monitoring process: This would look first at the relevant circumstances in which the Statutory Auditor finds himself, and especially at any relationship or interest that he may have with respect to his task. Secondly, it would look at whether such an interest or relationship would cause a reasonable and informed third party, knowing all these circumstances, to conclude that the Statutory Auditor is independent, i.e. is capable of exercising objective and impartial judgement on all issues encompassed within the statutory audit engagement. In this sense, independence could be seen as a proxy for integrity and objectivity and be verified by a reasonable and informed third party.

2. Responsibility and scope

Responsibility

It is the responsibility of statutory auditors, whether natural or legal persons, generally to comply with national law and national professional rules in respect of Statutory Audits. This includes rules on independence.

In the case of a particular Statutory Audit, it is the appointed Statutory Auditor who is responsible for ensuring that the requirement for statutory auditors' independence is complied with. This requirement applies not only to himself and to the organisational entity forming the Audit Firm (assuming it is not the same legal person as the Statutory Auditor), but also to any other person who is in a position to influence the outcome of the Statutory Audit.

A Statutory Auditor, or—if the Statutory Auditor is an individual—the Audit Firm that carries out the audit work, should have adequate systems to take all reasonable steps to ensure that individuals within the firm comply with its independence policies and procedures (see also A. 4.3). These systems could encompass, among others, such matters as internal organisation, employment contracts and sanctions.

If a Statutory Auditor is a member of a Network, he should take all reasonable measures to ensure that, in as far as they are in a position to exert influence on the Statutory Audit, the entities within this Network, their owners, shareholders, partners, managers and employees all comply with the independence rules that apply in the

jurisdiction where the audit opinion is to be issued. This could, for example, be achieved by:
– contractual agreements which allow the Statutory Auditor to impose independence rules on his Network member firms, their Partners,[29] managers and employees with regard to his particular Audit Clients, including inter-firm quality review procedures, and external quality assurance access;
– providing his Network member firms with regular information on Audit Clients, and requiring these firms to provide regular information on their own business and financial relationships with such clients. This two-way flow of information is necessary to identify all relationships that his network member firms may have with an Audit Client and its Affiliates that might be affected by the Statutory Auditor's independence policies;
– obligatory intra-firm consultation procedures in any case where there are doubts as to whether the Statutory Auditor's independence could be compromised by his Audit Client's relationship with one of the Network member firms.

These instruments may also be appropriate to safeguard independence in situations where sub-contractors or agents of the Statutory Auditor or the Audit Firm are involved in the audit, other than its Network member firms.

For any particular audit engagement where the Statutory Auditor is an Audit Firm, the responsibility for determining the scope of persons to whom the independence requirement applies, and what instruments and rules it may be appropriate to apply to them, generally lies with the audit Engagement Partner.[30] This individual will need to exercise adequate professional judgement in order to fulfil this task since it is his responsibility to assess whether or not the independence requirement is complied with. He should also be informed of any audit and non-audit relationship which the Statutory Auditor, the Audit Firm or the Network has with the client (see also 'Audit Firm's Independence Policies' under A. 4.3.2).

Determination of the scope

A Statutory Auditor must recognise that threats to his independence may arise not only from his own relationships with the Audit Client but also from other direct or indirect relationships with other individuals and firms within his practice and in the audit environment. The Statutory Auditor has to assess actual and potential threats arising from client relationships with the natural and legal persons within the Engagement Team, within the Audit Firm and any Network of which it is a member. He also has to consider relationships with other persons, such as sub-contractors or agents for the Audit Firm or the Audit Client, including those engaged on non-audit matters, with relationships to another. In summary, he has to identify any person who is in a position to influence the outcome of the Statutory Audit.

When considering the range of persons to whom independence requirements should apply, the Statutory Auditor must be sensitive to a variety of factors. These can include the size and legal and organisational structure of the Audit Client, the size, structure and internal organisation of the Audit Firm and of any of the Networks of which it is a member. The Statutory Auditor should also consider the volume and nature of services provided to the Audit Client by the Audit Firm or any of its Network member firms.

For example, for a small Audit Firm of four or five Partners which is the Statutory Auditor to a company with three branches all in the same Member State, the independence rules would usually apply to:
– the Engagement Partner, the Audit Team, and any Partner in their Chain of Command;
– any Partner with responsibility for non-audit services to the same client; and
– any other person within the firm who is, or might be seen to be, in a position to influence the outcome of the Statutory Audit.

However, when the Statutory Auditor of a medium-sized multinational company is one firm in a Network, the scope of the rules might extend to:
– the Engagement Partner and Audit Team in the Statutory Auditor;

---

[29] Defined in the glossary.
[30] Defined in the glossary.

– any Partner and Audit Team member in the same firm or in another firm in the Network who participates in the audit of the client's overseas entities, including any in centralised services or specialist discipline units which contribute to such work;
– any Partner in the same firm or in another firm in the Network who participates in the provision non-audit services to the client;
– any Partner in the Chain of Command (either in the jurisdiction where the audit opinion is to be delivered or in an overseas country where audit or non-audit work is done for the Audit Client); and
– any other person within the firm or another firm in the Network who is in a position to influence the outcome of the Statutory Audit.

In either case, the independence requirements apply equally to everyone falling within their scope; the difference lies in the number of people the Statutory Auditor may need to consider for inclusion within it.

Persons other than members of the Engagement Team or the Chain of Command

The Statutory Auditor should give further consideration to other persons who, even if they are not part of the Engagement Team or the Chain of Command, might influence the outcome of the Statutory Audit. These might include:
– owners or shareholders of the Audit Firm with potential influence by virtue of the significance of their voting rights. Where, for example, there are only a few owners or shareholders of an Audit Firm, every owner or shareholder might be considered as being in a position to influence the outcome of the Statutory Audit;
– individuals who have supervisory or direct management responsibility for the audit function at successive levels in any location where members of the Audit Team are employed;
– other audit and non-audit Partners with potential influence by virtue of their working relationship with a member of the Audit Team. Depending on factors such as the size and the internal organisation of an office, practice unit, Audit Firm, or even Network, all Partners of such an entity might be considered as being in a position to influence the outcome of the Statutory Audit.

The Statutory Auditor must also consider whether there might be persons outside the Audit Firm or its Network who, due to their relationship with persons within the firm or group, have or appear to have an ability to influence the outcome of the Statutory Audit. Examples might include:
– family members or other close personal contacts of members of the Engagement Team or Chain of Command who hold significant financial interests in the Audit Client or who hold a key position with the client or an entity with significant interests in it (see B. 6); or
– individuals or entities with financially significant commercial relationships with either the Statutory Auditor and his firm or the Audit Client. These could include major suppliers, customers or contractors.

The Statutory Auditor will need to identify those individuals in the Audit Firm or the Network whose involvement in the audit engagement might be affected by such an external influence, either in fact or in appearance, taking into account the fact that he would not be able to impose his independence rules on persons outside the Audit Firm or its Network.

3. Independence threats and risk

In order to avoid or resolve facts and circumstances that might compromise a Statutory Auditor's independence, it is essential firstly to identify the threats to independence which arise in specific circumstances. Secondly, one must evaluate their significance so as to determine the level of risk that a Statutory Auditor's independence may be compromised.

The more clearly a Statutory Auditor is able to identify the nature of the threats, the more clearly he can judge the level of risk to his independence that they create. Based on their general nature the following types of threats to independence have been recognised:
– Self-interest threat: the Statutory Auditor's independence may be threatened by a financial

or other self-interest conflict (e.g., direct or indirect financial interest in the client, over-dependence on the client's audit or non-audit fees, the desire to collect outstanding fees, fear of losing the client);
- Self-review threat: relates to the difficulty of maintaining objectivity in conducting self-review procedures (e.g., when taking decisions, or taking part in decisions, that should be taken wholly by the Audit Client's management; or when any product or judgement of a previous audit or non-audit assignment performed by the Statutory Auditor or his firm needs to be challenged or re-evaluated to reach a conclusion on the current audit);
- Advocacy threat: the Statutory Auditor's independence may be threatened if the Statutory Auditor becomes an advocate for, or against, his client's position in any adversarial proceedings or situations (e.g. dealing in or promoting shares or securities in the client; acting as an advocate on behalf of the client in litigation; when the client litigates against the auditor);
- Familiarity or trust threat: a risk that the Statutory Auditor may be over-influenced by the client's personality and qualities, and consequently become too sympathetic to the client's interest through, for example, too long and too close relationships with client personnel, which may result in excessive trust in the client and insufficient objective testing of his representations;
- Intimidation threat: covers the possibility that the auditor may be deterred from acting objectively by threats or by fear of, for example, an influential or overbearing client.

The significance of a particular threat depends on a variety of (quantifiable and non-quantifiable) factors such as its force, the status of the person(s) involved, the nature of the matter causing the threat, and the overall audit environment. When evaluating the significance of a threat the Statutory Auditor also has to consider that different kinds of threats may arise in one set of circumstances. With regard to one certain set of circumstances a threat can be considered significant if, considering all of its quantitative and qualitative aspects, both alone and in combination with others, it increases the level of independence risk to an unacceptably high level.

4. Systems of safeguards

Where threats to statutory auditors' independence exist, the Statutory Auditor should always consider and document whether safeguards are appropriately applied to negate or reduce the significance of threats to acceptable levels. The safeguards to be recognised relate to different responsibilities in the audit environment, including the governance structure of the Audit Client (see A. 4.1), the entire system of self-regulation, public regulation and oversight of the audit profession including disciplinary sanctions (see A. 4.2), and the Statutory Auditor's system of internal quality control (see A. 4.3).

Level of independence risk

The level of independence risk can be expressed as a point on a continuum that ranges from 'no independence risk' to 'maximum independence risk.' Although it cannot be measured precisely, the level of independence risk for any specific activity, relationship, or other circumstance that may pose a threat to a Statutory Auditor's independence can be described as being within, or at one of the endpoints, on the independence risk continuum.

The Statutory Auditor and any other person involved in a decision concerning the independence of the Statutory Auditor in relation to his client (e.g., regulatory bodies, other statutory auditors who are consulted for advice) need to evaluate the acceptability of the level of independence risk that arises from specific activities, relationships, and other circumstances. That evaluation requires these independence decision makers to judge whether existing safeguards eliminate or adequately mitigate threats to independence posed by those activities, relationships, or other circumstances. If they do not, a further decision has to be made on which additional safeguard (including prohibition) or combination of safeguards would reduce independence risk, and the corresponding likelihood of compromised objectivity, to an acceptably low level.

4.1. Audited entities' safeguards

4.1.1. Governance structure's impact on independence risk assessment

When analysing governance responsibilities in the Audit Client which may help to safeguard its Statutory Auditor's independence, it is appropriate to differentiate between the governance structure of a Public Interest Entity client[31] and that of an Audit Client with relatively little public interest. This differentiation is relevant both to the corporate governance task, which is to particularly protect actual and potential investors, and to the appearance of the Statutory Auditor's independence.

Audit Clients of public interest

With regard to the appearance of independence in relation to a Public Interest Entity[32] client, the Statutory Auditor has to consider the whole variety of possible perceptions of the national, regional or even international public. In this respect corporate governance plays an important role in safeguarding statutory auditors' independence.

Statutory auditors are formally appointed by a majority vote of the shareholders at the Annual General Meeting. Shareholders often appoint the Statutory Auditors recommended to them by management. This is particularly the case if no additional approval is required by any Governance Body[33] of the Audit Client other than management (e.g. supervisory board, non-executive directors, audit committee) or by any regulatory body (e.g. regulatory authority of a certain industry).[34] This does not necessarily protect the interests of minority shareholders or potential investors, nor does it contribute to the safeguarding of statutory auditors' independence.

Accordingly, governance structures within an entity being audited should ensure that the appointment of the Statutory Auditor is made in the interests of its shareholders, and that during the engagement the Statutory Auditor performs his work in the same interests. If, for example, a supervisory board or an audit committee is to be effective in accomplishing its task of over-seeing the financial reporting process, it must rely in part on the work, guidance and judgement of the Statutory Auditor. Integral to this reliance is the requirement that the Statutory Auditor performs his service independently.

In order to determine the significance of a threat to independence and to evaluate the level of the independence risk (see A. 3 and A. 4), the Statutory Auditor should carefully consider whether the audited entity's governance structure provides an appropriate infrastructure to generally safeguard its statutory auditor's independence. The analysis of such an infrastructure may include issues such as:

– the involvement of a Governance Body in the Statutory Auditor's appointment (e.g., formal approval of management's recommendation only or. active participation in negotiations with the potential Statutory Auditor);
– the duration of the Statutory Auditor's appointment (one audit vs. long-term contract);
– the involvement of a Governance Body in commissioning non-audit services from the Statutory Auditor, the Audit Firm or from any entity within the Network of which it is a member (e.g., no involvement or active participation when negotiating significant engagements);
– the existence of oversight and communications regarding the Statutory Audit and other services provided to the audited entity by the Statutory Auditor, the Audit Firm or its Network, and the frequency of such communications with the Statutory Auditor.

Other Audit Clients

When auditing clients other than Public Interest Entities, the Statutory Auditor should still analyse whether the governance infrastructure of the Audit Client provides general safeguards to

---

[31] Defined in the glossary.
[32] Defined in the glossary.
[33] Defined in the glossary.
[34] In some jurisdictions the national law provides for certain types of companies, such as cooperatives or associations, to have their financial statements audited by a particular Statutory Auditor who is assigned by virtue of the law governing these companies, and not appointed by any management body or Governance Body. Statutory Auditors of this kind of entities may consider this circumstance as a general safeguard contributing to mitigate a certain kind of self-interest threats to independence.

his independence. Where the client has no Governance Body, the Statutory Auditor should analyse whether the Audit Client's management policies provide safeguards to his independence and whether there are specific threats which could be addressed by appropriate policies within the entity. Such policies might include internal procedures for objective choice in commissioning non-audit services. The Statutory Auditor should also consider the quality and quantity of staff in the Audit Client. This may be particularly relevant when assessing the risk of taking managerial decisions on behalf of the client. For example, where the client has an insufficient number of staff, the Statutory Auditor may find himself taking such decisions without meaning to.

4.1.2. Involvement of the Governance Body

As stated under A. 4.1.1, to some extent it is the responsibility of the Audit Client to safeguard the independence of its Statutory Auditor. Discussions between the Statutory Auditor and the Governance Body of the client are the main means to establish a link between the Statutory Auditor's own safeguards and those of the Audit Client. To protect himself and to allow the quality assurance regime (see A. 4.2) to verify his compliance with this requirement, whenever deemed necessary, but at least annually the Statutory Auditor should initiate the process by writing to the Audit Client to invite him to discuss these issues.

Disclosure of fees

The disclosure to the Governance Body of fee relationships between the Statutory Auditor, the Audit Firm and its Network members and the Audit Client and its Affiliates will help the Governance Body to evaluate the impact of these relationships on the Statutory Auditor's independence. If necessary, the Governance Body may require additional measures to safeguard the independence of the Statutory Auditor. In this regard, the disclosure should be made on a regular basis, but at least annually, before the audit engagement is accepted or renewed. In addition, the disclosure should be more detailed and wider than required for publication purposes (see A. 5). In particular, it should extend to the amounts charged and contracted for, to the value of outstanding service contracts or arrangements, to current proposals or bids for future service engagements, and to compensation received or expected from contingent fee arrangements on non-audit services (see B. 8.1), each broken down by type of service.

4.2. *Quality assurance*

To ensure that Statutory Auditors comply with professional standards, including the independence requirement, a control or enforcement system is needed. Safeguards and procedures to be considered include the effectiveness of the overall control environment. This starts with a professional approach towards matters of quality and ethics and takes account of the levels of assurance provided by a regularly monitored and evidenced control system. One way to enforce independence requirements is the Member State system for quality assurance on Statutory Audits. The Commission Recommendation on 'Quality Assurance for the Statutory Audit in the EU' recommends that Statutory Auditors' compliance with ethical principles and rules, including independence rules, should be subjected to quality review procedures. As the recommended systems of quality assurance include public oversight, they are also able to address the public perception of independence issues.

4.3. *The Statutory Auditor's overall safeguards*

4.3.1. Ownership of and control over Audit Firms

Need to safeguard control over the Audit Firm

For an Audit Firm to be authorised to carry out Statutory Audits, Article 2.1 b) ii) of the 8th Company Law Directive requires the majority of the Audit Firm's voting rights to be held by statutory auditors. These persons must be approved by a competent authority of any of the EU Member States, i.e., natural persons or firms who satisfy at least the minimum conditions of that Directive.

Without any further restrictions, this would allow Audit Firms to raise capital on capital markets by either private or public offerings. Some

Member States regard such funding as raising serious concerns about statutory auditor independence. As a result, they have imposed more restrictive rules on the ownership of Audit Firms (e.g. allowing a maximum of 25% ownership by individuals who are not statutory auditors, or restricting minority ownership to members of certain regulated professions only).

There is a concern as to whether holding majority voting rights is sufficient to ensure that statutory auditors control the firm. For example, if one non-auditor held 49% of the voting rights and the other 51% were divided amongst a number of statutory auditors, the non-auditor owner could have effective control of the Audit Firm. In this respect, careful attention should be paid to the resulting threats to statutory auditors' independence. Consideration should also be given to the safeguards needed to avoid such situations. These might include, for example, limiting the voting rights of a single non-auditor owner to 5% or 10% of the whole. Where only a few statutory auditors hold the majority of the voting rights in an Audit Firm, it may be appropriate to allow certain individuals to hold a higher proportion than this. In particular, this may be appropriate if these individuals are members of a regulated profession (e.g., lawyers, notaries), or other persons (e.g., management or other professional consultants) whose professional activities rest with the Audit Firm or with one of its Network members.

The risks that relationships between the Statutory Auditor, the Audit Firm and a non-auditor owner of the Audit Firm and an Audit Client might compromise the Statutory Auditor's independence should be addressed by reference to A. 2, which sets out the scope of persons to which the independence requirement applies, and B. 1 and B. 2, which consider the financial and/or business links which may exist between them.

4.3.2. The Audit Firm's internal safeguarding system

As far as the Statutory Auditor is concerned, he has to comply with independence standards, regardless of whether those are imposed by law or regulators, or by professional bodies as part of a self-regulatory regime, or adopted voluntarily by the Audit Firm as part of its own policies. In order to ensure his compliance the Statutory Auditor needs to set up a system of related safeguards, or—if the Statutory Auditor and the Audit Firm are not identical legal persons—at least require the Audit Firm to do so.

Audit Firm's independence policies

An Audit Firm should develop independence policies covering activities that are acceptable and not acceptable when performed for Audit Clients or their Affiliates.

Regardless of the way in which detailed independence standards are developed, the objective is to enforce appropriate implementation and maintenance of Statutory Auditors' safeguards and to encourage their continuous improvement. Accordingly, an Audit Firm's independence policies should be flexible enough to allow for their regular update. Such an update could arise due to changing circumstances and facts or when independence standards themselves change due to a change in public expectations.

The design and documentation of the Audit Firm's independence policies should reflect the immediate practice environment (e.g., size and organisational structure of the Audit Firm). It should also reflect the audit environment (e.g., client and business portfolio of the Audit Firm and others outside the Audit Firm who are involved in the Audit Firm's assignments).

An Audit Firm must have appropriate policies and procedures in place to ensure that the relevant Engagement Partner is notified of any other relationship which exists between the firm and its Network member firms, and the Audit Client and its Affiliates. This includes the requirement that the Engagement Partner has to be consulted prior to acceptance of any assignment from the Audit Client or its Affiliates. It is then the responsibility of the Engagement Partner to assess whether any such relationship may reasonably be thought to affect the independence of the Statutory Auditor. For practical reasons, particularly with regard to group audit situations, this assessment may be partially delegated to other Audit Partners. For example, an Audit Partner of the Audit Team in a particular country should be notified of, and should assess the impact of, all (existing and potential) relationships in that country. However, the Engagement Partner should always be involved in the independence risk assessment of any significant relationship. In cases where the Audit Client has a Governance Body (see A. 4.1), it will be appropriate to involve that body in the process of assessing the independence risk.

Where persons other than the Audit Firm, its Partners, managers and employees are involved with the Audit Client or in the audit assignment (e.g., subcontracted specialists, Network member firms), the Audit Firm's independence policies should also address requirements and consultation processes needed to prevent these persons from causing an unacceptable level of independence risk for the Statutory Auditor.

In order to ensure that its Partners, managers and employees comply with its independence policies, the Audit Firm will need to communicate its policies appropriately, and to train these individuals on a regular basis. This should also include informing them about sanctions for independence policy violations.

Procedures to be applied

In accordance with the independence policies adopted by an Audit Firm and depending on its size, the procedures to be applied by Partners, managers and employees may vary. For a small Audit Firm it might be appropriate to consider its independence only on a case by case basis, and then to decide on certain procedures to mitigate the independence risk. However, for a large Audit Firm it might be necessary to establish routine procedures in order to detect even hypothetical threats to the Statutory Auditor's independence. For example, to detect a self-interest threat resulting from financial or business relationships, it might be necessary for such an Audit Firm to maintain a regularly updated database (e.g., restricted entity list). Such a database could provide all Partners, managers and employees with information on all Audit Clients that may give rise to a self-interest threat if they fulfil certain criteria. This database should be available to anyone within the Audit Firm who may be in a position to influence the outcome of any Statutory Audit. The operation of this safeguarding system will require these individuals to regularly provide the Audit Firm with certain personal and client information.

Depending on its size and structure, it might also be appropriate for an Audit Firm or Network to establish internal procedures to ensure that there is appropriate consultation across the firm or Network about any client where the significance of an independence threat is unclear. This consultation would involve experienced Partners who are not involved in the Audit Client's affairs and who are not impacted by the independence threat in question.

Documentation of independence assessment

The main purpose of the Statutory Auditor's documentation of his independence assessment on a certain Audit Client is to provide evidence that he performed his assessment properly. It is appropriate for such documentation to be included in the audit files.

Internal monitoring of compliance

The monitoring of compliance with the Audit Firm's independence policies should be an integral function of the Audit Firm's quality review structure. Large Audit Firms may designate this task to quality control specialists, or even independence specialists. This may not be appropriate for small and medium sized Audit Firms which generally only assess their independence on a case by case basis. However, such firms should at least have their individuals' compliance reviewed by a Partner who is not a member of the particular Engagement Team. In the case of sole practitioners and of small partnerships where either all Partners are in the Engagement Team or the involvement of any other Partner outside the Engagement Team would increase the level of independence risk (e.g., when this Partner provides significant non-audit services to the Audit Client), the Statutory Auditor should either seek advice from his professional regulatory body or ask for a review by another statutory auditor.

5. Public Disclosure of Fees

A Statutory Auditor should be able to demonstrate that his independence has not been compromised by providing non-audit services to an Audit Client for which the remuneration he receives is disproportionate to the fees he was paid for the Statutory Audit. This should also be in the interest of the relevant Audit Client (see also A. 4.1.2), since it will add credibility to its published financial information. Public disclosure requirements imposed by Member States through national law or their relevant regulatory bodies should enable a reasonable and informed third party to take a view on the extent of any imbalance between statutory audit and other fees. To assist such assessment, the fees received for other than statutory audit services should be broken down into three broad categories (further assurance, tax advisory and other non-audit services) reflecting the different kinds of services which may have been provided. Regarding the category other non-audit services, at least the minimum information about the provision of financial information technology, internal audit, valuation, litigation and recruitment services should be given. It may also be appropriate to identify particular engagements which make up a significant proportion of a particular (sub-)category.

B. SPECIFIC CIRCUMSTANCES

1. Financial Interests

The term 'financial interest' would usually comprise the whole variety of financial interests that the Statutory Auditor himself, his Audit Firm or any other person within the scope of section A. 2 may have in an Audit Client or in any Affiliate of the client. The term includes 'direct' and 'indirect' financial interests such as
– direct or indirect shareholding in the Audit Client or its Affiliates,
– holding or dealing in securities of the Audit Client or its Affiliates,
– accepting pension rights or other benefits from the Audit Client or its Affiliates.

Commitments to hold financial interests (e.g., contractual agreements to acquire a financial interest) and derivatives which are directly related to financial interests (e.g., stock options, futures, etc.) should be dealt with in the same way as would an already existing financial interest.

Direct financial interests

When a person who is directly involved in the conduct of the statutory audit (the Statutory Auditor, the Audit Firm, an individual in the Engagement Team or within the Chain of Command) holds a direct financial interest in the Audit Client, such as shares, bonds, notes, options, or other securities, the significance of the self-interest threat is considered to be too high to enable any safeguards to reduce the Statutory Auditor's independence risk to an acceptable level.

In such a case the Statutory Auditor either has to withdraw from the engagement or, if an individual of the Audit Firm holds the direct financial interest, has to exclude this individual from the engagement.

Where a direct financial interest in the Audit Client is held by a Partner of the Audit Firm or its Network who works in an 'Office' the perception of self-interest is considered as being too high to allow this situation to be maintained.

Indirect financial interests

The term 'indirect financial interest' refers to situations where, for example, a person within the scope of A. 2 has investments in non-client entities that have an investment in the Audit Client, or in companies in which an Audit Client also has invested.

A person within the scope of A. 2 should not hold such an indirect financial interest where the self-interest threat resulting from this financial involvement is significant. This is particularly the case when an indirect shareholding in the Audit Client allows or appears to allow that person to influence management decisions of the Audit Client (e.g., by significant indirect voting rights), or when the direct shareholder due to any circumstance could or appears to be able to influence the outcome of the Statutory Audit. In addition, an unacceptable level of independence risk can also arise in situations where the Statutory Auditor or any other person within the scope of A. 2 serves as a voting trustee of a trust or executor of an estate containing securities of an Audit Client. However, this will only be the case when there are no appropriate safeguards to mitigate this risk such as supervision and control by beneficiaries, governmental authorities or courts.

On the other hand, the potential self-interest threat to the Statutory Auditor's independence may be regarded as insignificant to the independence risk if, for example, when holding indirect financial interests in the Audit Client
– the financial interest is directly held by an investment fund, pension fund, UCITS or an equivalent investment vehicle, and
– the person holding the indirect interest is not directly involved in the audit of the fund manager, nor able to influence the individual investment decisions of the fund manager.

External events

If a financial interest is acquired as a result of an external event (e.g. inheritance, gift, merger of firms or companies) and a further holding of that interest would create a significant threat to the Statutory Auditor's independence, it must be disposed of as soon as practicable, but no later than one month after the person has knowledge of and the right to dispose of the financial interest. Where the interest is in a listed company and has been acquired by way of inheritance, for example, the shares should be sold within a month after having both the knowledge of the inheritance and the right to sell the shares in accordance with applicable stock exchange regulations that govern the disposal or sale of shares by those with insider knowledge.

Until the financial interest is disposed of, additional safeguards are needed to preserve the Statutory Auditor's independence. For example, where a Statutory Auditor becomes aware that a member of the Engagement Team has acquired shares in a client as the result of inheritance, that individual should not continue to be a member of the Engagement Team until the shares have been sold. He should also be excluded from any substantive decision making concerning the Statutory Audit of the client until the shares have been sold.

Inadvertent violations

There will be occasions where the Statutory Auditor becomes aware that an individual in his Audit Firm inadvertently holds a financial interest in an Audit Client or in one of its Affiliates which, in general, would be regarded as a violation of independence requirements. Such inadvertent violations will not compromise the Statutory Auditor's independence with respect to an Audit Client, provided that the Statutory Auditor
– has established procedures that require all professional personnel to report promptly any breaches of the independence rules resulting from the purchase, inheritance or other acquisition of a financial interest in an Audit Client by such individuals (see also A. 4.3.2);
– promptly notifies the individual to dispose of the financial interest at the earliest opportunity after the inadvertent violation is identified; and
– takes particular care when reviewing the relevant audit work of this individual.

Where it proves impossible to compel the individual to dispose of the financial interest, the individual should be removed from the Engagement Team. Where an individual other than a member of the Engagement Team inadvertently holds a financial interest that may compromise the Statutory Auditor's independence, this individual should be excluded from any substantive decision making concerning the Statutory Audit of the client.

Whatever financial involvement exists, it is primarily the Statutory Auditor's safeguarding system (see A. 4.3) which should provide evidence that the threats to independence have been identified and investigated. Where appropriate, the evidence should also refer to the involvement of the client's Governance Body in this process. In addition, wherever a decision has been taken about whether or not the threats are significant, the reasons behind that decision should be recorded.

2. Business relationships

Business relationships

Business relationships are relationships that involve a commercial or financial common interest between the Statutory Auditor, the Audit Firm or any other person being in a position to influence the outcome of the Statutory Audit (any person within the scope of A. 2) on the one hand and the Audit Client, an Affiliate of the client, or the management thereof on the other. The following are examples of such relationships that would, if significant to the auditor or conducted outside the normal course of business, cause a self-interest, advocacy or intimidation threat:

– having a financial interest in a joint venture with the Audit Client, or with an owner, managing director or other individual who performs senior management functions of that client;
– having a financial interest in a non-audit client that has an investor or investee relationship with the Audit Client;
– giving a loan to the Audit Client or guarantees for the Audit Client's risks;
– accepting a loan from an Audit Client or having borrowings guaranteed by the Audit Client;
– providing services to a managing director or another individual performing a senior management function of the Audit Client in respect of the personal interest of such individual;
– receiving services from the Audit Client or its Affiliates which concern underwriting, offering, marketing or selling of securities issued by the audit firm or one of its group member firms.

Commitments to establish such relationships should be dealt with in the same way as an already established relationship.

In the normal course of business

In the normal course of its business, a Statutory Auditor may not only provide audit or non-audit services to the Audit Client or to its Affiliates, but may also purchase goods or services from these entities. Examples could include insurance and bank services, commercial loan agreements, the purchase of office equipment, EDP software, or company cars. If these transactions are performed at arm's length (as between third parties), they generally do not threaten the Statutory Auditor's independence (e.g. purchase of goods which are offered under normal wholesale discount terms, and are available to the whole of the client's other customers). However, the Statutory Auditor should carefully consider the risk that even an arm's length transaction could reach a magnitude which threatens his independence by creating financial dependencies, either in fact or at least in appearance.

Accepting any goods or services on favourable terms from an Audit Client is not considered to be within the normal course of business, unless the value of any benefit is insignificant.

Significance of independence risk

Whether a business relationship should be regarded as a significant threat to the Statutory Auditor's independence depends on whether a reasonable and informed third party would assume that such a relationship could have an influence on the outcome of the Statutory Audit. Objective criteria are therefore needed in order to evaluate the significance of a relationship to the Statutory Auditor, as well as to the Audit Client. With regard to the financial statements and the audit task, the relationship should not result in the Statutory Auditor, the Audit Firm or one of its Network members being able to influence management decisions of the Audit Client. Conversely, the relationship should not enable the Audit Client, or one of its Affiliates to influence the outcome of the Statutory Audit, either in fact or in appearance.

Whatever business relationship exists, it is primarily the Statutory Auditor's safeguarding system (see A. 4.3) which should provide evidence that the threats to independence have been identified and investigated. Where appropriate, the evidence should also refer to the involvement of the client's Governance Body in this process. In addition, wherever a decision has been taken about whether or not the threats are significant, the reasons behind that decision should be recorded.

Provision of statutory audit services

The threat to independence is considered too high to permit a Statutory Auditor, an Audit Firm or any member of its Network to provide statutory audit services to an owner of the Audit Firm. The provision of audit services to an Affiliate of such an owner is also considered incompatible with the independence requirement when that owner is, or appears to be, in a position to influence any decision-making of the Audit Firm that impacts on its statutory audit function. Such an influence may arise, for example, due to the percentage of the voting rights that the owner holds in the Audit Firm. It could also arise due to the nature of the position held by the owner or one of the owner's representatives in the Audit Firm. A position of potential concern might include a director or senior manager of the owner being a member of the Audit Firm's supervisory board. Furthermore, the Statutory Auditor should also consider whether the provision of audit services to those clients could compromise his independence where the clients officers, directors or shareholders either hold a significant amount of voting rights of the Audit Firm or, otherwise, are, or appear to be, in a position to influence the firm's decision-making with regard to its statutory audit function.

3. Employment with the audit client

Dual employment and loan staff agreements

The risk to the Statutory Auditor's independence is considered too high to permit a person within the scope of A. 2 who is employed by the Audit Firm and/or its Network member firm to also be employed by the Audit Client and/or one of its Affiliates. The Statutory Auditor's policies and procedures (see A. 4.3.2) should provide for adequate measures to identify any instance of such dual employment.

The Statutory Auditor should also carefully consider those situations where an individual employed by the Audit Firm or a Network member firm works under any loan staff agreement with the Audit Client or one of its Affiliates. A loan staff agreement means an engagement where an employee of the Audit Firm or Network works under the direct supervision of the client and does not originate any accounting transaction or prepare original data that is not subject to review and approval by the client. Such an assignment may be acceptable, provided that the individual does not take a position where he can influence the outcome of the Statutory Audit. If an individual is to be assigned to the Engagement Team having completed such a loan staff engagement, he should not be given audit responsibility for any function or activity that he was required to perform or supervise during the former loan staff assignment (see also B. 5 below).

Engagement team member joining the Audit Client

The overall safeguarding system of the Audit Firm (see A. 4.3) should include policies and procedures that can be adapted to suit the specific circumstances. These will, for example, depend upon a number of factors such as:

– the position of the departing individual at the Audit Firm (e.g. Partner vs. senior or other professional),
– the circumstances which lead to the departure (e.g. retirement, termination, voluntary withdrawal),
– the position the departing individual is taking at the client (e.g., managerial position vs. position with insignificant influence on the financial statements),
– the length of time that has passed since the individual left the Audit Firm, and
– the length of time that has elapsed since the departing individual performed services related to the audit engagement.

Second Partner's review

In cases, where the individual leaving the Audit Firm was an Engagement or Audit Partner, the required review by another Audit Partner should also consider the risk that the former partner might have been influenced by the client during the previous audit. In addition, the former partner may have established close relationships with other Audit Team members which might threaten the independence of those staying on the Audit Team. Finally, the former partner could use his knowledge of the current audit approach and testing strategy to circumvent the audit designs.

It might be appropriate for a small Audit Firm which is not able to perform a second Partner's review either to have a similar review performed by another statutory auditor or, at least, to seek advice from its professional regulatory authority.

4. Managerial or supervisory role in Audit Client

The acceptance of a managerial or supervisory role in an Audit Client is not the only potential concern with regard to intimidation and self-review threats. Such threats can also arise when an individual within the scope of A.2 becomes a member of a managerial or supervisory body of an entity that is not an Audit Client (non-client entity), but is either in a position to influence the Audit Client or to be influenced by the Audit Client. In these cases, the level of independence risk is unacceptably high. The acceptance of such positions should therefore be prohibited.

Where national law requires members of the audit profession to undertake supervisory roles in certain companies, safeguards must ensure that such professionals do not have any responsibility with regard to the Engagement Team.

B.4 (2) recognises that a former member of an Engagement Team who leaves the Audit Firm, whether to retire or to take up a post with a non-client entity, might be invited to take a non-executive post on a management or supervisory body of the Audit Client. In such cases, the Audit Firm will need to ensure that the requirements of B. 3(3) and (4) are met.

5. Establishing employment with Audit Firm

When a director or manager of an Audit Client joins the Audit Firm, the self-review threat is considered as too high to be mitigated by any safeguard other than the prohibition of such a person from becoming a member of the Engagement Team or from taking part in any substantive decisions concerning the client's audit for a two-year period. Where a former employee of the Audit Client joins the Audit Firm, the significance of the self-review threat will relate to the responsibilities and tasks this employee had at the Audit Client and those he is going to take at the Audit Firm. For example, if the former employee prepared accounts or valued elements of the financial statements, the same safeguards would apply as for a director or manager; on the other hand, when the former employee held, for example, a non-management position in a branch of the Audit Client, the self-review threat may be mitigated if his activities as a member of the Engagement Team do not relate to that branch.

6. Family and other personal relationships

The Statutory Auditor must be able to assess the risk to his independence when he or any member of the audit Engagement Team or the Chain of Command, or any Partner in an 'Office' which includes himself or such an individual, has any close family member or any other close personal relationship with anyone who meets the criteria under 1(a) to (d). His consideration of the facts should be based on his knowledge of the circumstances of all relevant individuals within the Audit Firm or its Network. Policies and procedures should be in place that require such individuals to disclose to the best of their knowledge, on which the Statutory Auditor would then rely, any fact or circumstance which need to be taken into account. The Statutory Auditor should evaluate all such information, determine whether any of the criteria are met and take any necessary mitigating action within a reasonable period of time. This might include refusal of the engagement, or exclusion of an individual from the Engagement Team or the 'Office'.

The Audit Firm's policies and procedures should make it clear that it is the responsibility of individuals in the Engagement Team or Chain of Command or 'Office' to assess to the best of their knowledge who are, or might appear to be, their close family members and close non-family contacts. They should disclose any relevant facts or circumstances in respect of a particular Audit

Client to the Audit Partner in charge of the engagement.

Close family members

The term 'close family member' normally refers to parents, siblings, spouses or cohabitants, children and other dependants. Depending on the different cultural and social environments in which the audit takes place, the term may extend to other family members who may have less immediate but not necessarily less close relationships with the relevant individual. These could include former spouses or cohabitants and the spouses and children of family members.

Close non-family relationships

Close relationships other than family ones are hard to define, but could include a relationship with any person other than a family member which entails frequent or regular social contact.

Inadvertent violations

There will be occasions where the Statutory Auditor becomes aware that an individual in his Audit Firm inadvertently has not reported to the firm a family or other personal relationship with an Audit Client which, in general, would be regarded as a violation of independence requirements. Such inadvertent violations will not compromise the Statutory Auditor's independence with respect to an Audit Client, provided that the Statutory Auditor
- has established procedures that require all professional personnel to report promptly any breaches of the independence rules resulting from changes in their family or other personal relationships, the acceptance of an audit sensitive position by their close family members or other close persons (i.e., those falling within the scope of (1)(a) and (1)(b) above), or the purchase, inheritance or other acquisition of a significant financial interest in an Audit Client by such family members or persons;
- promptly removes the individual from the Engagement Team, or if the individual is not a member of the Engagement Team, excludes him from substantive decisions concerning the Statutory Audit of the relevant client. In the case of a significant financial interest, he should notify the individual to ensure that the financial interest is disposed of at the earliest opportunity after the inadvertent violation is identified; and
- takes particular care when reviewing the relevant audit work of this individual.

7. Non-audit services

7.1. *General*

Independence from Audit Client's decision-making

The self-review threat is always considered too high to allow the provision of any services other than statutory audit work that involves the Statutory Auditor in any decision-making of either the Audit Client, any of its Affiliates, or the management of such an entity. Therefore, if the Statutory Auditor or a member within his Network intends to provide non-audit services to an Audit Client or to one of its Affiliates, the Statutory Auditor has to ensure that any individual acting for or on behalf of the Audit Firm or its Network member does not take any decision for, nor take part in any decision-making on behalf of, the Audit Client, any of its Affiliates or the management of such an entity.

Any advice or assistance related to any service provided by the Statutory Auditor or the Audit Firm should give the Audit Client, a client's Affiliate or the management of such an entity the opportunity to decide between reasonable alternatives. This does not prevent the Statutory Auditor, Audit Firm or one of its Network members from making recommendations to the Audit Client. However, such advice should be justified by objective and transparent analyses in the expectation that the Audit Client will review the recommendations before reaching any decision. If the Audit Client is seeking advice where, due to legal or regulatory provisions, only one solution is available, the Statutory Auditor should ensure that his documentation refers to these provisions (e.g. quotes the relevant law, includes advice from external professionals).

7.2. *Examples—analysis of specific situations*

Business and financial markets are evolving continuously and information technologies are changing rapidly. These developments have significant consequences for management and control. With this state of change, it is not possible to draw up a comprehensive list of all those situations where the provision of non-audit services to an Audit Client would create a significant threat to statutory auditors' independence. Neither is it possible to list the different safeguards which may exist to mitigate such threats. The examples which follow describe specific situations that could compromise a Statutory Auditor's independence. They also discuss the safeguards which may be appropriate to reduce the independence risk to an acceptable level in each circumstance. In practice, the Statutory Auditor will need to assess the implications of similar, but different circumstances, and to consider what safeguards would satisfactorily address the independence risk in the judgement of an informed third party.

7.2.1. Preparing accounting records and financial statements

Spectrum of involvement in the preparation process

There is a spectrum of involvement by the Statutory Auditor (including his Audit Firm, Network member firms, or any employees thereof) in the preparation of accounting records and financial statements. At one end of the spectrum, the Statutory Auditor may prepare prime accounting records, do the bookkeeping and prepare the financial statements, as well as performing the Statutory Audit of these financial statements. In other cases, the Statutory Auditor helps his Audit Client in the preparation of the financial statements on the basis of the trial balance, assisting his Audit Client in the calculation of the closing entries (calculation of accruals, bad debts, depreciation, etc.). At the other end of the spectrum, the Statutory Auditor does not participate in any part of the preparation process. Even in the latter case, the Statutory Auditor who detects shortcomings in the Audit Client's proposed disclosures will normally suggest and draft the amendments required. This is part of the Statutory Audit mandate and should not be considered as the provision of a non-audit service. While management always has responsibility for the presentation of the financial statements, the end result is that it is uncommon for a set of financial statements to appear where the Statutory Auditor has had no hand whatsoever in the presentation or drafting.

Nature of assistance and advice

The Audit Client and its management must be responsible for the financial statements and for maintaining accounting records. The Statutory Auditor's safeguards must at least ensure that, when providing bookkeeping-related assistance, the accounting entries and any underlying assumptions (e.g. for valuation purposes) are originated by the client. In addition, the Statutory Auditor should not be involved in the decision-making of the Audit Client or its management in respect of the entries or assumptions.

The Statutory Auditor's assistance should therefore be limited to carrying out technical or mechanical tasks and to providing advisory information on alternative standards and methodologies which the Audit Client might wish to apply.

Examples of assistance which compromise independence include the following:

– determining or changing journal entries, or the classifications for accounts or transactions, or other accounting records without obtaining the client's approval;
– authorising or approving transactions; or
– preparing source documents or originating data (including decisions on valuation assumptions), or making changes to such documents or data.

Examples of assistance which would not necessarily compromise independence could include:

– performing mechanical bookkeeping tasks, such as recording transactions for which the Audit Client's management has determined the appropriate account classification; posting coded transactions to a client's general ledger; posting client-approved entries to a client's trial balance; or providing certain data-processing services;
– informing the client about applicable accounting standards or valuation methodologies for the client to decide which should be adopted.

Level of public interest

The self-review threat that arises when a Statutory Auditor assists in the preparation of the accounting records or financial statements of a Public Interest Entity is perceived to be so high that it cannot be mitigated by safeguards other than the prohibition of any such assistance that goes beyond the statutory audit mandate (i.e., any assistance other than the suggestion and drafting of amendments during the due course of the Statutory Audit, after having detected shortcomings in the Audit Client's proposed disclosures).

In any case, where the Statutory Auditor is asked to participate in the preparation of an Audit Client's accounting records or financial statements, he should carefully consider the public perception in relation to his task. This may depend on the size and structure of the Audit Client as well as on the business environment in which this client operates at either a local, regional or national level. Where the threat is perceived to reach a level that would cause the public to question his independence, the Statutory Auditor should not accept the engagement.

Emergency situations

In emergency cases, a Statutory Auditor may participate in the preparation process to an extent which would not be acceptable under normal circumstances (see (2) and (3) above). This might arise when, due to external and unforeseeable events, the Statutory Auditor is the only person with the resources and necessary knowledge of the Audit Client's systems and procedures to assist the client in the timely preparation of its accounts and financial statements. A situation could be considered an emergency where the Statutory Auditor's refusal to provide these services would result in a severe burden for the Audit Client (e.g., withdrawal of credit lines), or would even threaten its going concern status.

In such an emergency situation, however, the Statutory Auditor should take no part in any final decisions and should seek the client's approvals wherever possible. He should also consider additional safeguards that would allow him to minimise the level of risk to his independence. Where appropriate, he should seek to discuss the situation with the Audit Client's Governance Body and ensure that the services he provided and the reasons for this are summarised in the financial statements.

Statutory audits on consolidated financial statements of Public Interest Entities

When the consolidated financial statements of a Public Interest Entity client are subject to a Statutory Audit, there might be situations where it is impractical for a subsidiary of such an Audit Client to make arrangements in accordance with (3) above. As a result, it is possible that its local auditor will have to participate in the preparation of financial statements that are to be included in the Audit Client's consolidated financial statements. Under such circumstances, the self-review threat from the perspective of the Statutory Auditor of the Public Interest Entity client, is generally not considered to be significant, provided that the bookkeeping-related assistance is solely of a technical or mechanical nature or the advice is only of an informative nature (see (2) above), that the financial statements of such subsidiaries are not material to the Audit Client's consolidated financial statements (neither separately nor in total), and that the fees the Audit Firm and its Network members receive for all such services collectively are insignificant in relation to the consolidated audit fee.

7.2.2. Design and implementation of financial information technology systems

Financial information

Statutory audit work includes the testing of those hardware and software systems that are used by the Audit Client to generate the financial information which is to be disclosed in its financial statements. Where a Statutory Auditor (including his Audit Firm, Network member firms, or any employees thereof) is involved in the design and implementation of such a financial information technology system (FITS), a self-review threat may arise. In this respect, financial information does not only include those figures which are directly disclosed in the financial statements, but also comprises any other valuation or physical data to which the financial statements' disclosures relate. Such information is generated by either integrated IT-systems or a variety of stand-alone systems (e.g., systems for bookkeeping, cost-accounting, payroll, or cash management as well as those systems which may only provide physical numbers, such as some warehousing and production control systems, etc.).

Spectrum of involvement

There is a spectrum of involvement by the Statutory Auditor in the design and implementation of FIT-systems:

At one end of the spectrum, there are engagements where the Statutory Auditor takes on a management role or responsibilities for the FIT-systems design and implementation project as a whole, or for the operation of the FIT-system and the data it uses or generates. Such an engagement would clearly result in an unacceptable level of independence risk.

In other cases, the Statutory Auditor must carefully assess the independence risk which might arise from his involvement in systems design and implementation for the Audit Client, particularly if there are public interest implications. In all cases he should consider whether there are appropriate safeguards to reduce the independence risk to an acceptable level. For example, the level of risk may be acceptable where the Statutory Auditor's role is to provide advice to a consortium retained by the Audit Client to design and/or implement a project. Similarly, there is little risk in the case of a smaller company client, where the Statutory Auditor is asked to tailor a standard, off-the-shelf accounting system to meet the needs of that client's business. However, independence risk may be perceived to be unacceptably high in the case of a design project for a large company or Public Interest Entity client.

At the other end of the spectrum, the Statutory Auditor might be engaged to provide his Audit Client with a review of alternative systems. Based on this review the client himself decides which system to install. The provision of such a service would generally not compromise the Statutory Auditor's independence, provided that cost and benefits of the systems reviewed are properly documented and discussed with the Audit Client. However, his independence will be compromised if the Statutory Auditor has a significant financial interest (see B.1) or a significant business relationship (see B.2) with any of the systems suppliers.

7.2.3. Valuation services

Valuation services

A valuation comprises the making of assumptions with regard to future developments, the application of certain methodologies and techniques, and the combination of both in order to compute a certain value, or a range of values, for an asset, a liability or for a business as a whole. The underlying assumptions of such a valuation may relate to interpretations of the present or expectations of the future, including both general developments and the consequences of certain actions taken or planned by the Audit Client or anybody within its close business environment.

Engagements to review or to issue an opinion on the valuation work performed by others (e.g. engagements under Articles 10 and 27 of the 2nd Company Law Directive (77/91/EEC), Articles 10 and 23 of the 3rd Company Law Directive (78/855/EEC), or under Article 8 of the 6th Company Law Directive (82/891/EEC)), or to collect and verify data to be used in a valuation performed by others (e.g., typical 'due diligence' work in connection with the sale or purchase of a business), are not regarded as valuation services under this principle.

Materiality and subjectivity

Valuation services leading to the valuation of amounts which neither separately nor in the aggregate are material in relation to the financial statements are not considered to create a significant threat to independence.

The underlying assumptions of a valuation and the methodologies to be applied are always the responsibility of the Audit Client or its management. Therefore, as part of its decision-making process, the Audit Client or its management has generally to determine the underlying assumptions of the valuation, and to decide on the methodology to be applied for the computation of the value. This is of particular importance when the valuation to be performed requires a significant degree of subjectivity, either in relation to the underlying assumptions or regarding the differences in applicable methodologies.

However, with regard to certain routine valuations, the degree of subjectivity inherent in the item concerned may be insignificant. This is the case when the underlying assumptions are determined by law (e.g., tax rates, depreciation rates for tax purposes), other regulations (e.g., provision to use certain interest rates), or are widely accepted within the Audit Client's business sector, and when the techniques and methodologies to be used are based on general accepted standards, or even prescribed by laws and regulations. In such circumstances, the result of a valuation performed by an informed third party, even if not identical, is unlikely to be materially different. The provision of such valuation services might therefore not compromise a statutory auditor's independence, even if the value itself could be regarded as material to the financial statements, provided that the Audit Client or its management has at least approved all significant matters of judgement.

Additional safeguards

Some valuation services involve an insignificant degree of subjectivity. These could include those requiring the application of standard techniques or methodologies or where the service is a review of the valuation methods used by a third party, but where the resulting valuation is material in relation to the financial statements. In these cases, the Statutory Auditor should consider whether there remains a self-review threat which should be mitigated by additional safeguards. It may be appropriate to address such a threat by setting up a valuation service team separate from the Engagement Team, with different reporting lines for both.

7.2.4. Participation in the Audit Client's internal audit

Internal Audit is an important element of an entity's internal control system. In companies, particularly small and medium sized ones, which cannot afford an internal audit department or where such a department lacks certain facilities (e.g., access to specialists in information technology or treasury management), participation by the Statutory Auditor in the internal audit may strengthen management control capacities.

However, self-review threats can arise if, for example, there is not a clear separation between the management and control of the internal audit and the internal audit activities themselves, or if the Statutory Auditor's evaluation of his Audit Client's internal control system determines the kind and volume of his subsequent statutory audit procedures. To avoid such threats, the Statutory Auditor, the Audit Firm or its Network member must be able to show that it is not involved in management and control of the internal audit. Furthermore, in his capacity as the statutory auditor of the client's financial statements the Statutory Auditor must be able to demonstrate that he has taken appropriate steps to have the results of the internal audit work reviewed and has not placed undue reliance on these results in establishing the nature, timing and extent of his statutory audit work. In order to ensure that the Audit Firm's statutory audit work meets required auditing standards and that the Statutory Auditor's independence is not compromised, an appropriate review of these matters should be performed by an Audit Partner who has not been involved in either the Statutory Audit or any of the internal audit engagements which may impact the financial statements.

In companies where the internal audit department reports to a Governance Body rather than to management itself, the internal audit function performs a role that is complementary to the statutory audit function. It can therefore be seen as a separate element of the corporate governance framework. If the Statutory Auditor is asked to perform internal audit work in these circumstances, he must still be able to demonstrate that he has adequately assessed any threats to his independence, and has applied any necessary safeguards.

7.2.5. Acting for the Audit Client in the resolution of litigation

Advocacy and self-review threats

In certain circumstances the Statutory Auditor, the Audit Firm, an entity within a Network or a Partner, manager or employee thereof will assist the Audit Client in the resolution of a dispute or litigation.

A Statutory Auditor who acts for the Audit Client in the resolution of a dispute or litigation is generally perceived to take on an advocacy role which is incompatible with the responsibility of a Statutory Auditor to give an objective opinion on the financial statements. This advocacy threat is accompanied by a self-review threat when the assistance in the resolution of litigation also requires the Statutory Auditor to estimate chances of his Audit Client succeeding in the action if this could affect amounts to be reflected in the financial statements. A Statutory Auditor who is involved in the resolution of litigation has therefore to consider the significance of both the advocacy threat and the self-review threat.

The advocacy threat is increased when the Statutory Auditor, the Audit Firm or a Network member firm takes an active role on behalf of the Audit Client to resolve disputes or litigation. It is less likely that this threat will become significant, when the Statutory Auditor is only required to give evidence to a court or tribunal in a case in which the client is involved.

Even when taking a relatively active role on behalf of the client, there can be other specific situations which are generally not seen to compromise a Statutory Auditor's independence. Such situations could include the representation of an Audit Client before the court or the tax administration in a case of tax litigation. They could also include advising the client and defending a particular accounting treatment in a situation where a Member State's authority, securities regulator or review panel, or any other similar European or international body investigates the Audit Client's financial statements. However, whatever the circumstances, the Statutory Auditor should analyse the specific situation and his particular involvement to carefully assess whether or not there is a significant risk to his independence.

Materiality and subjectivity

The provision of legal services to an Audit Client in connection with the resolution of a dispute or litigation does not usually create a significant threat to independence when these services involve matters that are not expected by a reasonable and informed third party to have any material impact on the financial statements.

Acting as an advocate of the Audit Client is inherently subjective, but the degree of subjectivity varies depending upon the nature of the legal proceedings. During the course of an audit, the Statutory Auditor usually has the choice either to evaluate the outcome of a legal proceeding himself, or to rely on a confirmation provided by an external lawyer engaged by the client. The degree of subjectivity in both cases is governed by factors such as the competence of the lawyer, his compliance with ethical rules of the lawyers' profession, and the given evidence, rather than whether or not the lawyer is an employee of the Audit Firm or of a third party law firm.

With respect to legal situations where the outcome of legal proceedings can be reasonably estimated on given evidence, the estimation of amounts affected by litigation should not lead to material differences between services provided by the Audit Firm or a third party law firm (e.g., litigation regarding employment contracts with staff, or certain tax proceedings).

On the other hand, there might be situations that involve significant inherent subjectivity. There may also be situations where it is impossible to evaluate evidence in an objective manner due to the nature of the business relationship between the Statutory Auditor and the Audit Client (e.g., personal involvement of former or present management, non-executive directors, or shareholders). In such cases, the Statutory Auditor should ensure that he is not involved in the Audit Client's actions in the resolution of litigation, except in minor cases where the matter concerned would not reasonably be expected to have a material impact on the financial statements.

Additional safeguards

In circumstances not covered under (2), the Statutory Auditor should consider whether there remain threats to independence which have to be mitigated by additional safeguards. It might be appropriate to avoid the audit Engagement Team being involved in the litigation process by setting up different engagement teams with different reporting lines for the Statutory Audit and the legal services related to the litigation.

7.2.6. Recruiting senior management

A Statutory Auditor who is asked to assist an Audit Client to recruit senior or key staff should first assess the threats to his independence which might arise from, for example, the role of the person to be recruited and the nature of the assistance sought. The need for careful assessment is highest where the person recruited is likely to have a significant role in the client's financial management processes and hence to have regular contact with the Statutory Auditor. However, threats such as self-interest and familiarity may arise from other appointments too.

With regard to the nature of the assistance sought, an example of an acceptable service might include reviewing the professional qualifications of a number of applicants and giving an objective opinion on their suitability for a post. Another acceptable service might include the provision of a short-list of candidates for interview, provided that it has been drawn up using criteria specified by the client, rather than on the Statutory Auditor's own judgement. In both cases, care would be needed to ensure that any opinion given about the candidates did not pre-empt the Audit Client's decision. If the Statutory Auditor concludes that he cannot give the assistance requested without directly or indirectly participating in the Audit Client's decision as to who should be appointed, he should decline to provide it.

8. Audit and non-audit fees

8.1. Contingent fees

Audit fee arrangements

Statutory audit work performed in the public interest is inherently unsuitable for fee arrangements where the Statutory Auditor's remuneration depends on either any performance figure of the Audit Client or the outcome of the audit itself. Audit fees that are fixed by any court or governmental body do not constitute contingent fees.

Non-audit fee arrangements

Self-interest, self-review and advocacy threats to a Statutory Auditor's independence also arise when the fee for a non-audit engagement is dependent upon a contingent event. This applies to all contingent arrangements between the Statutory Auditor, the Audit Firm or an entity within its Network, and the Audit Client or any of its Affiliates. Dependency on a contingent event means, for example, that the fee depends in some way on the progress or outcome of the project or the attainment of a particular performance figure by the Audit Client (or its Affiliate).

In assessing the extent to which contingent fee arrangements pose a threat to statutory auditor independence, and the availability of suitable safeguards, the Statutory Auditor should consider amongst other factors: the relationship between the activity for which the contingent fee is to be paid, and the conduct of any current or future audit; the range of possible fee amounts; and the basis on which the fee is to be calculated.

In performing this assessment, the Statutory Auditor should consider, inter alia, whether the amount of the contingent fee is directly determined by reference to an asset or transaction value (e.g., percentage of acquisition price) or a financial condition (e.g., growth in market capitalisation) the measurement of which will be subsequently exposed to an audit examination and whether this increases the self-interest threat to unacceptable levels. On the other hand, independence threats will generally not arise in situations where there is no direct link between the basis of the contingent fee (e.g., the starting salary of a new employee when a recruitment service is provided) and a significant aspect of the audit engagement. Where a Governance Body exists, the Statutory Auditor should disclose contingent fee arrangements to that body in accordance with the principles set out under Section A. 4.1.2.

8.2. Relationship between total fees and total revenue

Excessive dependence on audit and non-audit fees from one Audit Client or one client group clearly gives rise to a self-interest threat to the Statutory Auditor's independence. The Statutory Auditor or the Audit Firm has not only to avoid the existence of such a financial dependency, but also has to consider carefully whether the appearance of such a dependency might create a significant threat to independence.

Appearance of financial dependency

The Statutory Auditor, the Audit Firm or a Network might be perceived to be financially dependent on a single Audit Client or client group when the total audit and non-audit fee that it receives, or expects to receive, from that client or client group exceeds a critical percentage of its total income. The public perception of this critical percentage will depend upon different factors within the audit environment. For example, the level might be different depending on the size of the firm, whether it is well established or newly created, whether it operates locally, nationally or internationally, and on the general business situation in markets in which it is operating.

These circumstances have to be carefully considered by the Statutory Auditor when he assesses the significance of the self-interest threat to his appearance of independence. An analysis should be performed of all fees received for audit and non-audit services from a particular client or client group compared to the firm's or Network's total income, as well as of the relevant amounts that are expected to be received during the current firm's or Network's reporting period. If this analysis indicates a level of dependency and a need for safeguards, an Audit Partner who has not been engaged in any of the audit or non-audit work for the client should carry out a review of the significant audit and non-audit work done for the client and advise as necessary. The review should also take into consideration any audit and non-audit work that has been contracted or is the subject of an outstanding proposal. Where doubts remain, or where, because of the size of the firm, no such partner is available, the Statutory Auditor should seek the advice of his professional regulatory body or a review by another statutory auditor.

Certain other fee relationships

The Statutory Auditor should also consider whether there are, or appear to be, other types of fee relationships between a single Audit Client or client group and himself or the Audit Firm that may cause a self-interest threat. For example, an Audit Partner within an office or branch might be perceived to be dependent on fees from a certain Audit Client, if most of that office's services are provided to that Audit Client, or if the same individual is responsible for selling both audit and non-audit engagements to the Audit Client. To mitigate such self-interest threats, an Audit Firm may reconsider its organisational structures and the responsibilities of certain individuals, or, where applicable, discuss the way services are provided and charged with the Audit Client's Governance Body.

Independence may particularly be compromised when significant fees are generated from the provision of non-audit services to an Audit Client or its Affiliates. The Statutory Auditor should therefore assess this risk to his independence. In particular, he should consider the nature of the non-audit services provided, the different fees generated from the statutory audit engagement and the non-audit engagements, and their respective relationship to the total fees received by the Audit Firm or Network. If the analysis indicates the need for safeguards, particularly when the non-audit fees exceed the audit fees, an Audit Partner who is not involved in any of the audit and non-audit engagements should carry out a review of the work done for the client and advise as necessary.

8.3. *Overdue fees*

Unpaid fees for audit or other work could appear to be in effect a loan from the Statutory Auditor to the Audit Client. This could threaten the Statutory Auditor's independence by creating a mutual financial interest with the Audit Client. In such circumstances, a Statutory Auditor must assess the level of the threat and take any action that may be necessary. This could include disclosing the extent of the potential mutual interest to all relevant third parties. Where the Statutory

Auditor is an Audit Firm, the circumstances may be reviewed by another Audit Partner who has not been involved in the provision of any services to the Audit Client. In the case of a sole practitioner, or a small partnership where all the Audit Partners have been involved with the Audit Client, the Statutory Auditor should either seek advice from his professional regulatory body or ask for a review by another statutory auditor.

8.4. *Pricing*

A Statutory Auditor must be able to demonstrate that the fee he charges for any audit engagement is reasonable, particularly if it is significantly lower than that charged by a predecessor or quoted by other firms bidding for the engagement. He must also be able to demonstrate that a quoted audit fee is not dependent on the expected provision of non-audit services, and that a client has not been misled as to the basis on which future audit and non-audit fees would be charged when negotiating the current audit fees. The Statutory Auditor should have policies and procedures in place to be able to demonstrate that his fees meet these requirements. Where Statutory Audits of Public Interest Entities are concerned, the Statutory Auditor should seek to discuss the basis for calculating the audit fee with the Governance Body.

9. Litigation

Whilst it is not possible to specify precisely for all cases the point at which it would become improper for a statutory auditor to continue as Statutory Auditor of an Audit Client, the following criteria should be considered:
– if an Audit Client alleges deficiencies in statutory audit work, and the Statutory Auditor concludes that it is probable that a claim will be filed, the Statutory Auditor should first discuss the basis of the allegations with the Governance Body of the Audit Client or, where such body does not exist, with his professional regulatory body. If this confirms the judgement that it is probable that a claim will be filed, then—subject to local legal requirements—the Statutory Auditor should resign;

– if the Statutory Auditor alleges fraud or deceit by current management of an Audit Client, the level of independence risk and the decision as to whether or not he should resign also depends on safeguards such as discussion of all relevant aspects with the Governance Body of the client, or, where such a body does not exist, with the Statutory Auditor's professional regulatory body. (In some countries, however, the national law safeguards the independence of the Statutory Auditor in cases of alleged fraud by requiring the Statutory Auditor to report the detected fraud to a national authority and to continue his audit work on behalf of that authority which represents the national public interest. In any case the Statutory Auditor should consider seeking legal advice, giving due consideration to his responsibility to the public interest.);

– threatened or actual litigation relating to non-audit services for an amount not material to the Statutory Auditor or to the Audit Client (for example, claims out of disputes over billing for services, results of consultancy services) would not compromise the Statutory Auditor's independence.

10. Senior personnel acting for a long period of time

To mitigate a familiarity or trust threat to the independence of a Statutory Auditor who is engaged to audit an Audit Client of public interest, the requirement to replace the Engagement Partner and the other Key Audit Partners of the Engagement Team within a reasonable period of time cannot be replaced by other safeguards.

The Statutory Auditor should also consider the independence risk arising from the prolonged involvement of other members of the Engagement Team, including the senior staff engaged on audits of entities which are consolidated into an Audit Client's consolidated financial statements, and from the composition of the team itself. He should apply safeguards, such as rotation and measures under the Audit Firm's quality assurance scheme, to seek to ensure that the engagement may be properly continued without compromising his independence.

There might be situations, where due to the size of the Audit Firm internal rotation of the Engagement Partner and other Key Audit Partners is not possible or may not constitute an appropriate safeguard. For example, in the case of a sole practitioner's practice, or where the day to day relationship between a limited number of Audit Partners is too close. In such situations, the Statutory Auditor should ensure that other safeguards are put in place within a reasonable period of time. Such safeguards could include having the relevant audit engagement covered by an external quality review, or, as a minimum, seeking the advice of his professional regulatory body. If no suitable safeguards can be identified, the Statutory Auditor should consider whether it is appropriate to continue the audit engagement.

When any member of an Engagement Team is replaced because of time served on a particular audit, or because of a related familiarity or trust threat, that individual should not be re-assigned to the team until at least two years have elapsed since his replacement.

Appendix

Glossary

Affiliate	(a) of an Audit Firm: an undertaking within the meaning of Article 41 (1), (2) and (3) of the 7th Company Law Directive (83/349/EEC);
	(b) of an Audit Client: an undertaking within the meaning of Article 41 (1), (2) and (3) of the 7th Company Law Directive (83/349/EEC) that together with the Audit Client is required to be included by consolidation in consolidated accounts prepared in accordance with the 7th Directive, or—in those cases where the 7th Company Law Directive does not apply—would be required to be included by consolidation were the requirements of that Directive to apply.
	Without prejudice to (a) and (b) the term 'Affiliate' will include any undertaking, regardless of its legal form, which is connected to another by means of common ownership, control or management.
Assurance Service	Engagement of a statutory auditor to evaluate or measure a subject matter that is the responsibility of another party against identified suitable criteria, and to express a conclusion that provides the audit client with a level of assurance about that subject matter.
Audit Client	The company or firm whose annual accounts are subject to Statutory Audit, or the parent undertaking in the meaning of Article 1 of the 7th Company Law Directive (83/349/EEC) whose consolidated accounts are subject to Statutory Audit.
Audit Firm	The organisational—generally legal—entity that performs a Statutory Audit (e.g., a sole practitioner's practice, a partnership or a company of professional accountants). The Audit Firm and the Statutory Auditor who is appointed for the Statutory Audit might be identical legal persons, but need not be (e.g., where an individual who is a member of a partnership practice is appointed as the Statutory Auditor, the partnership as such forms the Audit Firm).

Audit Partner	An audit professional within an Audit Firm or Network who himself is an approved person in the meaning of Article 2(1) of the 8th Company Law Directive (= statutory auditor) and, as an individual, takes on ultimate responsibilities for the audit work performed during a Statutory Audit; he, generally, is authorised to sign audit reports on behalf of the Audit Firm which is the Statutory Auditor. He may also be a shareholder/owner or principal of the Audit Firm.
Audit Team	All audit professionals who, regardless of their legal relationship with the Statutory Auditor or Audit Firm, are assigned to a particular Statutory Audit engagement in order to perform the audit task, such as Audit Partner(s), audit manager(s) and audit staff.
Chain of Command	Comprises all those persons who have a direct supervisory, management, compensation or other oversight responsibility over either any Audit Partner of the Audit Team or over the conduct of the Statutory Audit at office, country, regional or global levels. This includes all Partners, principals and shareholders who may prepare, review or directly influence the performance appraisal of any Audit Partner of the Audit Team or otherwise determine their compensation as a result of their involvement with the audit engagement.
Engagement Partner	The Audit Partner who has ultimate responsibilities for the Statutory Audit of a particular Audit Client, who co-ordinates the work of the Audit Team and that of professional personnel from other disciplines involved, ensures that this work is subject to quality control, and, if applicable, co-ordinates all statutory audit activities of a Network which relate to a Statutory Audit, particularly on consolidated accounts where different Audit Partners have different responsibilities for the audits of the entities to be consolidated.
Engagement Team	All persons who, regardless of their legal relationship with the Statutory Auditor or Audit Firm, are directly involved in the acceptance and performance of a particular Statutory Audit. This includes the Audit Team, employed or subcontracted professional personnel from other disciplines involved in the audit engagement (e.g., lawyers, actuaries, taxation specialists, IT-specialists, treasury management specialists), and those who provide quality control or direct oversight of the audit engagement.
Governance Body	A body or a group of persons which is embedded in the Audit Client's corporate governance structure to exercise oversight over management as a fiduciary for investors and, if required by national law, for other stakeholders such as employees, and which consists of or, at least, includes individuals other than management, such as a supervisory board, an audit committee, or a group of non-executive directors or external board members.
Key Audit Partner	An Audit Partner of the Engagement Team (including the Engagement Partner) who is at group level responsible for reporting on significant matters, such as on significant subsidiaries or divisions of the Audit Client, or on significant risk factors that relate to the Statutory Audit of that client.

Key Management Position	Any position at the Audit Client which involves the responsibility for fundamental management decisions at the Audit Client, e.g. a CEO or CFO. This management responsibility should also provide influence on the accounting policies and the preparation of the financial statements of the Audit Client. A Key Management Position also comprises contractual and factual arrangements which by substance allow an individual to participate in exercising this management function in a different way, e.g. via a consulting contract.
Network	Includes the Audit Firm which performs the Statutory Audit, together with its Affiliates and any other entity controlled by the Audit Firm or under common control, ownership or management or otherwise affiliated or associated with the Audit Firm through the use of a common name or through the sharing of significant common professional resources.
'Office'	The term 'Office' means a distinct sub-group of an Audit Firm or Network, whether distinguished along geographical or practice lines, in which a Key Audit Partner primarily practises.
	A main criterion for identifying this sub-group should be the close working relationship between its members (e.g. working on the same kind of subjects or clients). In particular, it should be taken into account, that such working relationships are more and more evolving by means of a 'virtual' office, due to technical developments and the increasing multinational activities of Audit Clients.
	In the case of smaller partnerships, the 'Office' may encompass the whole firm, in which case all of the Partners and employees will be subject to the relevant requirements.
Partner	A professional within an Audit Firm or Network who, as an individual, takes on ultimate responsibilities for the work performed during an (audit or non-audit) engagement; he, generally, is authorised to sign on behalf of the Audit Firm, and may also be a shareholder/owner or principal of the Audit Firm.
Public Interest Entities	Entities which are of significant public interest because of their business, their size, their number of employees or their corporate status is such that they have a wide range of stakeholders. Examples of such entities might include credit institutions, insurance companies, investment firms, UCITS[1], pension firms and listed companies.
Statutory Audit	The audit service which is provided by an approved person in the meaning of Article 2(1) of the 8th Company Law Directive (= statutory auditor) when
	(a) carrying out an audit of the annual accounts of a company or firm and verifying that the annual report is consistent with those annual accounts in so far as such an audit and such a verification is required by Community law; or
	(b) carrying out an audit of the consolidated accounts of a body of undertakings and verifying that the consolidated annual report is consistent with those consolidated accounts in so far as such an audit and such a verification is required by Community law.

	For the purpose of this Recommendation, the term 'statutory audit' would also include an attest service which, dependent on national law, is provided by a statutory auditor when companies are required to have financial reporting information other than the above (e.g. companies' interim financial accounts and reports) reviewed by a Statutory Auditor who has to give an opinion on this information.
Statutory Auditor	The approved person in the meaning of Article 2(1) of the 8th Company Law Directive (= statutory auditor) who, either being a natural or a legal person, is appointed for a certain Statutory Audit engagement by means of national law and—as a consequence—in whose name the audit report is signed.

(¹) Undertakings for Collective Investment in Transferable Securities.

C. 22.

European Parliament and Council Regulation 1606/2002/EC of 19 July 2002 on the application of international accounting standards[1]

THE EUROPEAN PARLIAMENT AND THE COUNCIL OF THE EUROPEAN UNION,

Having regard to the Treaty establishing the European Community, and in particular Article 95(1) thereof,

Having regard to the proposal from the Commission,[2]

Having regard to the opinion of the Economic and Social Committee,[3]

Acting in accordance with the procedure laid down in Article 251 of the Treaty,[4]

Whereas:

(1) The Lisbon European Council of 23 and 24 March 2000 emphasised the need to accelerate completion of the internal market for financial services, set the deadline of 2005 to implement the Commission's Financial Services Action Plan and urged that steps be taken to enhance the comparability of financial statements prepared by publicly traded companies.

(2) In order to contribute to a better functioning of the internal market, publicly traded companies must be required to apply a single set of high quality international accounting standards for the preparation of their consolidated financial statements. Furthermore, it is important that the financial reporting standards applied by Community companies participating in financial markets are accepted internationally and are truly global standards. This implies an increasing convergence of accounting standards currently used internationally with the ultimate objective of achieving a single set of global accounting standards.

(3) Council Directive 78/660/EEC of 25 July 1978 on the annual accounts of certain types of companies,[5] Council Directive 83/349/EEC of 13 June 1983 on consolidated accounts,[6] Council Directive 86/635/EEC of 8 December 1986 on the annual accounts and consolidated accounts of banks and other financial institutions[7] and Council Directive 91/674/EEC of 19 December 1991 on the annual accounts and consolidated accounts of insurance companies[8] are also addressed to publicly traded Community companies. The reporting requirements set out in these Directives cannot ensure the high level of transparency and comparability of financial reporting from all publicly traded Community companies which is a necessary condition for building an integrated capital market which operates effectively, smoothly and efficiently. It is therefore necessary to supplement the legal framework applicable to publicly traded companies.

(4) This Regulation aims at contributing to the efficient and cost-effective functioning of the capital market. The protection of investors and the maintenance of confidence in the financial markets is also an important aspect of the

---

[1] OJ L 243, 11.9.2002, 1–4.
[2] OJ C 154 E, 29.5.2001, 285.
[3] OJ C 260, 17.9.2001, 86.
[4] Opinion of the European Parliament of 12 March 2002 (OJ C 47, 27.2.2003, 62) and Decision of the Council of 7 June 2002.

[5] OJ L 222, 14.8.1978, 11, reproduced supra under no. C. 4. Directive as last amended by European Parliament and Council Directive 2001/65/EC (OJ L 283, 27.10.2001, 28), reproduced supra under no. C. 18.
[6] OJ L 193, 18.7.1983, 1, reproduced supra under no. C. 6. Directive as last amended by European Parliament and Council Directive 2001/65/EC, reproduced supra under no. C. 18.
[7] OJ L 372, 31.12.1986, 1, reproduced supra under no. B. 7. Directive as last amended by European Parliament and Council Directive 2001/65/EC, reproduced supra under no. C. 18.
[8] OJ L 374, 31.12.1991, 7, reproduced infra under no. I. 23.

completion of the internal market in this area. This Regulation reinforces the freedom of movement of capital in the internal market and helps to enable Community companies to compete on an equal footing for financial resources available in the Community capital markets, as well as in world capital markets.

(5) It is important for the competitiveness of Community capital markets to achieve convergence of the standards used in Europe for preparing financial statements, with international accounting standards that can be used globally, for cross-border transactions or listing anywhere in the world.

(6) On 13 June 2000, the Commission published its Communication on 'EU Financial Reporting Strategy: the way forward' in which it was proposed that all publicly traded Community companies prepare their consolidated financial statements in accordance with one single set of accounting standards, namely International Accounting Standards (IAS), at the latest by 2005.

(7) International Accounting Standards (IASs) are developed by the International Accounting Standards Committee (IASC), whose purpose is to develop a single set of global accounting standards. Further to the restructuring of the IASC, the new Board on 1 April 2001, as one of its first decisions, renamed the IASC as the International Accounting Standards Board (IASB) and, as far as future international accounting standards are concerned, renamed IAS as International Financial Reporting Standards (IFRS). These standards should, wherever possible and provided that they ensure a high degree of transparency and comparability for financial reporting in the Community, be made obligatory for use by all publicly traded Community companies.

(8) The measures necessary for the implementation of this Regulation should be adopted in accordance with Council Decision 1999/468/EC of 28 June 1999 laying down the procedures for the exercise of implementing powers conferred on the Commission[9] and with due regard to the declaration made by the Commission in the European Parliament on 5 February 2002 concerning the implementation of financial services legislation.

(9) To adopt an international accounting standard for application in the Community, it is necessary firstly that it meets the basic requirement of the aforementioned Council Directives, that is to say that its application results in a true and fair view of the financial position and performance of an enterprise—this principle being considered in the light of the said Council Directives without implying a strict conformity with each and every provision of those Directives; secondly that, in accordance with the conclusions of the Council of 17 July 2000, it is conducive to the European public good and lastly that it meets basic criteria as to the quality of information required for financial statements to be useful to users.

(10) An accounting technical committee should provide support and expertise to the Commission in the assessment of international accounting standards.

(11) The endorsement mechanism should act expeditiously on proposed international accounting standards and also be a means to deliberate, reflect and exchange information on international accounting standards among the main parties concerned, in particular national accounting standard setters, supervisors in the fields of securities, banking and insurance, central banks including the ECB, the accounting profession and users and preparers of accounts. The mechanism should be a means to foster common understanding of adopted international accounting standards in the Community.

(12) In accordance with the principle of proportionality, the measures provided for in this Regulation, in requiring that a single set of international accounting standards be applied to publicly traded companies, are necessary to achieve the objective of contributing to the efficient and cost-effective functioning of Community capital markets and thereby to the completion of the internal market.

(13) In accordance with the same principle, it is necessary, as regards annual accounts, to leave to

---

[9] OJ L 184, 17.7.1999, 23.

Member States the option to permit or require publicly traded companies to prepare them in conformity with international accounting standards adopted in accordance with the procedure laid down in this Regulation. Member States may decide as well to extend this permission or this requirement to other companies as regards the preparation of their consolidated accounts and/or their annual accounts.

(14) In order to facilitate an exchange of views and to allow Member States to coordinate their positions, the Commission should periodically inform the accounting regulatory committee about active projects, discussion papers, point outlines and exposure drafts issued by the IASB and about the consequential technical work of the accounting technical committee. It is also important that the accounting regulatory committee is informed at an early stage if the Commission intends not to propose to adopt an international accounting standard.

(15) In its deliberations on and in elaborating positions to be taken on documents and papers issued by the IASB in the process of developing international accounting standards (IFRS and SIC-IFRIC), the Commission should take into account the importance of avoiding competitive disadvantages for European companies operating in the global marketplace, and, to the maximum possible extent, the views expressed by the delegations in the Accounting Regulatory Committee. The Commission will be represented in constituent bodies of the IASB.

(16) A proper and rigorous enforcement regime is key to underpinning investors' confidence in financial markets. Member States, by virtue of Article 10 of the Treaty, are required to take appropriate measures to ensure compliance with international accounting standards. The Commission intends to liaise with Member States, notably through the Committee of European Securities Regulators (CESR), to develop a common approach to enforcement.

(17) Further, it is necessary to allow Member States to defer the application of certain provisions until 2007 for those companies publicly traded both in the Community and on a regulated third-country market which are already applying another set of internationally accepted standards as the primary basis for their consolidated accounts as well as for companies which have only publicly traded debt securities. It is nonetheless crucial that by 2007 at the latest a single set of global international accounting standards, the IAS, apply to all Community companies publicly traded on a Community regulated market.

(18) In order to allow Member States and companies to carry out the necessary adaptations to make the application of international accounting standards possible, it is necessary to apply certain provisions only in 2005. Appropriate provisions should be put in place for the first-time application of IAS by companies as a result of the entry into force of the present regulation. Such provisions should be drawn up at international level in order to ensure international recognition of the solutions adopted,

HAVE ADOPTED THIS REGULATION:

Article 1
Aim

This Regulation has as its objective the adoption and use of international accounting standards in the Community with a view to harmonising the financial information presented by the companies referred to in Article 4 in order to ensure a high degree of transparency and comparability of financial statements and hence an efficient functioning of the Community capital market and of the Internal Market.

Article 2
Definitions

For the purpose of this Regulation, 'international accounting standards' shall mean International Accounting Standards (IAS), International Financial Reporting Standards (IFRS) and related Interpretations (SIC-IFRIC interpretations), subsequent amendments to those standards and related interpretations, future standards and related interpretations issued or adopted by the International Accounting Standards Board (IASB).

Article 3

Adoption and use of international accounting standards

1. In accordance with the procedure laid down in Article 6(2), the Commission shall decide on the applicability within the Community of international accounting standards.

2. The international accounting standards can only be adopted if:
– they are not contrary to the principle set out in Article 2(3) of Directive 78/660/EEC and in Article 16(3) of Directive 83/349/EEC and are conducive to the European public good, and
– they meet the criteria of understandability, relevance, reliability and comparability required of the financial information needed for making economic decisions and assessing the stewardship of management.

3. At the latest by 31 December 2002, the Commission shall, in accordance with the procedure laid down in Article 6(2), decide on the applicability within the Community of the international accounting standards in existence upon entry into force of this Regulation.

4. Adopted international accounting standards shall be published in full in each of the official languages of the Community, as a Commission Regulation, in the Official Journal of the European Communities.

Article 4

Consolidated accounts of publicly traded companies

For each financial year starting on or after 1 January 2005, companies governed by the law of a Member State shall prepare their consolidated accounts in conformity with the international accounting standards adopted in accordance with the procedure laid down in Article 6(2) if, at their balance sheet date, their securities are admitted to trading on a regulated market of any Member State within the meaning of Article 1(13) of Council Directive 93/22/EEC of 10 May 1993 on investment services in the securities field.[10]

Article 5

Options in respect of annual accounts and of non-publicly traded companies

Member States may permit or require:

(a) the companies referred to in Article 4 to prepare their annual accounts,

(b) companies other than those referred to in Article 4 to prepare their consolidated accounts and/or their annual accounts,

in conformity with the international accounting standards adopted in accordance with the procedure laid down in Article 6(2).

Article 6

Committee procedure

1. The Commission shall be assisted by an accounting regulatory committee hereinafter referred to as 'the Committee'.

2. Where reference is made to this paragraph, Articles 5 and 7 of Decision 1999/468/EC shall apply, having regard to the provisions of Article 8 thereof.

The period laid down in Article 5(6) of Decision 1999/468/EC shall be set at three months.

3. The Committee shall adopt its rules of procedure.

Article 7

Reporting and coordination

1. The Commission shall liaise on a regular basis with the Committee about the status of active IASB projects and any related documents issued by the IASB in order to coordinate positions and to facilitate discussions concerning the adoption

---

[10] OJ L 141, 11.6.1993, 27, reproduced infra under no. S. 14. Directive as last amended by European Parliament and Council Directive 2000/64/EC (OJ L 290, 17.11.2000, 27).

of standards that might result from these projects and documents.

2. The Commission shall duly report to the Committee in a timely manner if it intends not to propose the adoption of a standard.

Article 8
Notification

Where Member States take measures by virtue of Article 5, they shall immediately communicate these to the Commission and to other Member States.

Article 9
Transitional provisions

By way of derogation from Article 4, Member States may provide that the requirements of Article 4 shall only apply for each financial year starting on or after January 2007 to those companies:

(a) whose debt securities only are admitted on a regulated market of any Member State within the meaning of Article 1(13) of Directive 93/22/EEC; or

(b) whose securities are admitted to public trading in a non-member State and which, for that purpose, have been using internationally accepted standards since a financial year that started prior to the publication of this Regulation in the Official Journal of the European Communities.

Article 10
Information and review

The Commission shall review the operation of this Regulation and report thereon to the European Parliament and to the Council by 1 July 2007 at the latest.

Article 11
Entry into force

This Regulation shall enter into force on the third day following that of its publication in the Official Journal of the European Communities.

This Regulation shall be binding in its entirety and directly applicable in all Member States.

¶ *List of endorsed Accounting Standards:*
1. Commission Regulation (EC) No 1329/2006 of 8 September 2006 amending Regulation (EC) No 1725/2003 adopting certain international accounting standards in accordance with Regulation (EC) No 1606/2002 of the European Parliament and of the Council as regards the International Financial Reporting Interpretations Committee's (IFRIC's) Interpretations 8 and 9 (OJ L 247, 9.9.2006, 3–9).
2. Commission Regulation (EC) No 708/2006 of 8 May 2006 amending Regulation (EC) No 1725/2003 adopting certain international accounting standards in accordance with Regulation (EC) No 1606/2002 of the European Parliament and of the Council as regards International Accounting Standard (IAS) 21 and International Financial Reporting Interpretations Committee's (IFRIC) Interpretation 7 (OJ L 122, 9.5.2006, 19).
3. Commission Regulation (EC) No 108/2006 of 27 January 2006 amending Regulation (EC) No 1725/2003 adopting certain international accounting standards in accordance with Regulation (EC) No 1606/2002 of the European Parliament and of the Council, as regards IFRS 1, 4, 6 and 7, IAS 1, 14, 17, 32, 33, and 39, IFRIC Interpretation 6 (OJ L 24, 27.1.2006, 1)
4. Commission Regulation (EC) No 2106/2005 of 21 December 2005 amending Regulation (EC) No 1725/2003 adopting certain international accounting standards in accordance with Regulation (EC) No 1606/2002 of the European Parliament and of the Council, as regards International Accounting Standard (IAS) 39 (OJ L 337, 22.12.2005, 16).
5. Commission Regulation (EC) No 1910/2005 of 8 October 2005 amending Regulation (EC) No 1725/2003 adopting certain international accounting standards in accordance with Regulation (EC) No 1606/2002 of the European Parliament and of the Council, as regards International Financial Reporting Standard 1 and 6, IASs 1, 16, 19, 24, 38, and 39, International Financial Reporting Interpretations Committee's Interpretations 4 and 5 (OJ L 305, 24.11.2005, 16).
6. Commission Regulation (EC) No 1864/2005 of 15 November 2005 in accordance with Regulation (EC) No 1606/2002 of the European Parliament and of the Council, as regards International Financial Reporting Standard No 1 and International Accounting Standards Nos 32 and 39 (OJ L 299, 16.11.2005, 45).
7. Commission Regulation (EC) No 1751/2005 of 25 October 2005 amending Regulation (EC) No 1725/2003 adopting certain international accounting standards in accordance with Regulation (EC) No 1606/2002 of the European Parliament and of the Council, as regards IFRS 1, IAS 39 and SIC 12 (OJ L 282, 26.10.2005, 3).
8. Commission Regulation of 8 July 2005 amending Regulation (EC) 1725/2003 adopting certain international accounting standards in accordance with Regulation (EC) 1606/2002 of the European Parliament and of the Council (OJ L 175, 8.7.2005, 3).
9. Commission Regulation (EC) 211/2005 of 4 February 2005 amending Regulation (EC) 1725/2003 adopting certain international accounting standards in accordance with Regulation (EC) 1606/2002 of the European Parliament and of the Council (OJ L 41, 11.2.2005, 1).
10. Commission Regulation (EC) 2238/2004 of 29 December 2004 amending Regulation (EC) 1725/2003 adopting

certain international accounting standards in accordance with Regulation (EC) 1606/2002 of the European Parliament and of the Council (OJ L 394, 31.12.2004, 1).

11. Commission Regulation (EC) 2237/2004 of 29 December 2004 amending Regulation (EC) 1725/2003 adopting certain international accounting standards in accordance with Regulation (EC) 1606/2002 of the European Parliament and of the Council (OJ L 393, 31.12.2004, 1).

12. Commission Regulation (EC) 2236/2004 of 29 December 2004 amending Regulation (EC) 1725/2003 adopting certain international accounting standards in accordance with Regulation (EC) 1606/2002 of the European Parliament and of the Council (OJ L 392, 31.12.2004, 1).

13. Commission Regulation (EC) 2086/2004 of 19 November 2004 amending Regulation (EC) 1725/2003 adopting certain international accounting standards in accordance with Regulation (EC) 1606/2002 of the European Parliament and of the Council (OJ L 363, 9.12.2004, 1).

14. Commission Regulation (EC) 707/2004 of 6 April 2004 amending Regulation (EC) 1725/2003 adopting certain international accounting standards in accordance with Regulation (EC) 1606/2002 of the European Parliament and of the Council (OJ L 111, 17.4.2004, 3).

C. 23.

European Parliament and Council Directive 2003/51/EC of 18 June 2003 amending Directives 78/660/EEC, 83/349/EEC, 86/635/EEC and 91/674/EEC on the annual and consolidated accounts of certain types of companies, banks and other financial institutions and insurance undertakings[1]

(Text with EEA relevance)

THE EUROPEAN PARLIAMENT AND THE COUNCIL OF THE EUROPEAN UNION,

Having regard to the Treaty establishing the European Community, and in particular Article 44(1) thereof,

Having regard to the proposal from the Commission,[2]

Having regard to the opinion of the European Economic and Social Committee,[3]

Acting in accordance with the procedure laid down in Article 251 of the Treaty,[4]

Whereas:

(1) The Lisbon European Council of 23–24 March 2000 emphasised the need to accelerate completion of the internal market for financial services, set the deadline of 2005 for implementation of the Commission's Financial Services Action Plan and urged that steps be taken to enhance the comparability of financial statements prepared by Community companies whose securities are admitted to trading on a regulated market (hereinafter: listed companies).

(2) On 13 June 2000, the Commission published its Communication entitled 'EU Financial Reporting Strategy: The Way Forward' in which it was proposed that all listed companies prepare their consolidated accounts in accordance with one single set of accounting standards, namely International Accounting Standards (IAS), at the latest by 2005.

(3) Regulation (EC) No 1606/2002 of the European Parliament and of the Council of 19 July 2002 on the application of international accounting standards[5] (hereinafter: the IAS Regulation) introduced the requirement that, from 2005 onwards, all listed companies prepare their consolidated accounts in accordance with IAS adopted for application within the Community. It also provided an option for Member States to permit or require the application of adopted IAS in the preparation of annual accounts and to permit or require the application of adopted IAS by unlisted companies.

(4) The IAS Regulation provides that, to adopt an international accounting standard for its application in the Community, it is necessary that it meets the basic requirement of the Fourth Council Directive 78/660/EEC of 25 July 1978 on the annual accounts of certain types of companies[6] and of the Seventh Council Directive 83/349/EEC of 13 June 1983 on consolidated accounts,[7] that is to say that its application results

---

[1] OJ L 178, 17.7.2003, 16–22.
[2] OJ C 227 E, 24.9.2002, 336.
[3] OJ C 85, 8.4.2003, 140.
[4] Opinion of the European Parliament of 14 January 2003 (not yet published in the Official Journal), and Council Decision of 6 May 2003.

[5] OJ L 243, 11.9.2002, 1, reproduced supra under no. C. 22.
[6] OJ L 222, 14.8.1978, 11, reproduced supra under no. C. 4. Directive as last amended by Directive 2001/65/EC of the European Parliament and of the Council (OJ L 283, 27.10.2001, 28), reproduced supra under no. C. 18.
[7] OJ L 193, 18.7.1983, 1, reproduced supra under no. C. 6. Directive as last amended by Directive 2001/65/EC, reproduced supra under no. C. 18.

in a true and fair view of the financial position and performance of an enterprise—this principle being considered in the light of the said Directives without implying a strict conformity with each and every provision of those Directives.

(5) As the annual and consolidated accounts of undertakings covered by Directives 78/660/EEC and 83/349/EEC which are not prepared in accordance with the IAS Regulation will continue to have those Directives as the primary source of their Community accounting requirements, it is important that a level playing field exists between Community companies which apply IAS and those which do not.

(6) For the purposes both of the adoption of IAS and the application of Directives 78/660/EEC and 83/349/EEC, it is desirable that those Directives reflect developments in international accounting. In this respect, the Communication of the Commission entitled 'Accounting Harmonisation: A New Strategy vis-à-vis International Harmonisation' called for the European Union to work to maintain consistency between Community Accounting Directives and developments in international accounting standard setting, in particular within the International Accounting Standards Committee (IASC).

(7) Member States should be able to modify the presentation of the profit and loss account and balance sheet in accordance with international developments, as expressed through standards issued by the International Accounting Standards Board (IASB).

(8) Member States should be able to permit or require the application of revaluations and of fair value in accordance with international developments, as expressed through standards issued by the IASB.

(9) The annual report and the consolidated annual report are important elements of financial reporting. Enhancement, in line with current best practice, of the existing requirement for these to present a fair review of the development of the business and of its position, in a manner consistent with the size and complexity of the business, is necessary to promote greater consistency and give additional guidance concerning the information a 'fair review' is expected to contain. The information should not be restricted to the financial aspects of the company's business. It is expected that, where appropriate, this should lead to an analysis of environmental and social aspects necessary for an understanding of the company's development, performance or position. This is consistent also with Commission Recommendation 2001/453/EC of 30 May 2001 on the recognition, measurement and disclosure of environmental issues in the annual accounts and annual reports of companies.[8] However, taking into account the evolving nature of this area of financial reporting and having regard to the potential burden placed on undertakings below certain sizes, Member States may choose to waive the obligation to provide non-financial information in the case of the annual report of such undertakings.

(10) Differences in the preparation and presentation of the audit report reduce comparability and detract from the user's understanding of this vital aspect of financial reporting. Increased consistency should be achieved by amendments, consistent with current international best practice, to the specific requirements concerning the format and content of an audit report. The fundamental requirement that an audit opinion states whether the annual or consolidated accounts give a true and fair view in accordance with the relevant financial reporting framework does not represent a restriction of the scope of that opinion but clarifies the context in which it is expressed.

(11) Directives 78/660/EEC and 83/349/EEC should accordingly be amended. Furthermore, it is also necessary to amend Council Directive 86/635/EEC of 8 December 1986 on the annual accounts and consolidated accounts of banks and other financial institutions.[9]

(12) The IASB is developing and refining the accounting standards applicable to insurance activities.

---

[8] OJ L 156, 13.6.2001, 33, reproduced supra under no. C. 17.
[9] OJ L 372, 31.12.1986, 1, reproduced supra under no. B. 7. Directive as last amended by Directive 2001/65/EC, reproduced supra under no. C. 18.

(13) Insurance undertakings should also be allowed to use fair-value accounting as expressed through appropriate standards issued by the IASB.

(14) Consequently Council Directive 91/674/EEC of 19 December 1991 on the annual accounts and consolidated accounts of insurance undertakings[10] should be amended.

(15) These amendments will remove all inconsistencies between Directives 78/660/EEC, 83/349/EEC, 86/635/ EEC and 91/674/EEC on the one hand and IAS in existence at 1 May 2002, on the other,

HAVE ADOPTED THIS DIRECTIVE:

[. . .]

¶ *This Directive modifies Directive 78/660/EEC, reproduced supra under no. C. 4., Directive 83/349/EEC reproduced supra under no. C. 6., Directive 86/635/EEC, reproduced supra under no. B. 7. and Directive 91/674/EEC, reproduced infra under no. I. 23. The modifications are directly incorporated therein.*

---

[10] OJ L 374, 31.12.1991, 7, reproduced infra under no. I. 23.

C. 24.

European Parliament and Council Directive 2003/58/EC
of 15 July 2003
amending Council Directive 68/151/EEC, as regards disclosure requirements in respect of certain types of companies[1]

THE EUROPEAN PARLIAMENT AND THE COUNCIL OF THE EUROPEAN UNION,

Having regard to the Treaty establishing the European Community and in particular Article 44(2)(g) thereof,

Having regard to the proposal from the Commission,[2]

Having regard to the opinion of the European Economic and Social Committee,[3]

Acting in accordance with the procedure referred to in Article 251 of the Treaty,[4]

Whereas:

(1) The First Council Directive 68/151/EEC of 9 March 1968 on coordination of safeguards which, for the protection of the interests of members and others, are required by Member States of companies within the meaning of the second paragraph of Article 58 of the Treaty, with a view to making such safeguards equivalent throughout the Community[5] governs compulsory disclosure of a series of documents and particulars by limited liability companies.

(2) In the context of the fourth phase of the Simplification of the Legislation on the Internal Market process (SLIM), launched by the Commission in October 1998, a Company Law Working Group issued in September 1999 a Report on the simplification of the First and Second Company Law Directives which contained certain recommendations.

(3) The modernisation of Directive 68/151/EEC along the lines set out in those recommendations should not only help to meet the important objective of making company information more easily and rapidly accessible by interested parties, but should also simplify significantly the disclosure formalities imposed upon companies.

(4) The list of companies covered by Directive 68/151/EEC should be updated to take account of the new types of companies created or the types of companies abolished at national level since the adoption of that Directive.

(5) Several Directives have been adopted since 1968 with the aim of harmonising the requirements applicable to the accounting documents which must be prepared by companies, namely the Fourth Council Directive 78/660/EEC of 25 July 1978 on the annual accounts of certain types of companies,[6] the Seventh Council Directive 83/349/EEC of 13 June 1983 on consolidated accounts,[7] Council Directive 86/635/EEC of 8 December 1986 on the annual accounts and consolidated accounts of banks and other financial institutions[8] and Council Directive 91/674/EEC of 19 December 1991 on the annual accounts and consolidated accounts of insurance undertakings.[9]

---

[1] OJ L 221, 4.9.2003, 13–16.
[2] OJ C 227 E, 24.9.2002, 377.
[3] OJ C 85, 8.4.2003, 13.
[4] Opinion of the European Parliament of 12 March 2003 (not yet published in the Official Journal) and Council Decision of 11 June 2003.
[5] OJ L 65, 14.3.1968, 8, reproduced supra under no. C.1. Directive as last amended by the 1994 Act of Accession.

[6] OJ L 222, 14.8.1978, 11, reproduced supra under no. C. 4. Directive as last amended by Council Directive 2003/38/EC (OJ L 120, 15.5.2003, 22).
[7] OJ L 193, 18.7.1983, 1, reproduced supra under no. C. 6. Directive as last amended by Directive 2003/51/EC (OJ L 178, 17.7.2003, 16), reproduced supra under no. C. 23.
[8] OJ L 372, 31.12.1986, 1, reproduced supra under no. B. 7. Directive as last amended by Directive 2003/51/EC, reproduced supra under no. C. 23.
[9] OJ L 374, 31.12.1991, 7, reproduced infra under no. I. 23.

The references in Directive 68/151/EEC to the accounting documents which are required to be published in accordance with those Directives should be amended accordingly.

(6) In the context of the modernisation pursued, and without prejudice to substantive requisites and formalities established by the national law of the Member States, companies should be able to choose to file their compulsory documents and particulars by paper means or by electronic means.

(7) Interested parties should be able to obtain from the register a copy of such documents and particulars by paper means as well as by electronic means.

(8) Member States should be allowed to decide to keep the national gazette, appointed for publication of compulsory documents and particulars, in paper form or electronic form, or to provide for disclosure by equally effective means.

(9) Cross-border access to company information should be improved by allowing, in addition to the mandatory disclosure made in one of the languages permitted in the company's Member State, voluntary registration in additional languages of the required documents and particulars. Third parties acting in good faith should be able to rely on these translations.

(10) It is appropriate to clarify that the statement of the compulsory particulars set out in Article 4 of Directive 68/151/EEC should be included in all company letters and order forms, whether they are in paper form or use any other medium. In the light of technological developments, it is also appropriate to provide that these statements be placed on any company website.

(11) Directive 68/151/EEC should be amended accordingly,

HAVE ADOPTED THIS DIRECTIVE:

[. . .]

¶ *This Directive modifies Directive 68/151/EC, reproduced supra under no. C. 1. The modifications are directly incorporated therein.*

C. 25.

Council Regulation 1435/2003/EC
of 22 July 2003
on the Statute for a European Cooperative Society (SCE)[1]

THE COUNCIL OF THE EUROPEAN UNION,

Having regard to the Treaty establishing the European Community, and in particular Article 308 thereof,

Having regard to the proposal from the Commission,[2]

Having regard to the opinion of the European Parliament,[3]

Having regard to the opinion of the European Economic and Social Committee,[4]

Whereas:

(1) The European Parliament adopted resolutions on 13 April 1983 on cooperatives in the European Community,[5] on 9 July 1987 on the contribution of cooperatives to regional development,[6] on 26 May 1989 on the role of women in cooperatives and local employment initiatives,[7] on 11 February 1994 on the contribution of cooperatives to regional development[8] and on 18 September 1998 on the role of cooperatives in the growth of women's employment.[9]

(2) The completion of the internal market and the improvement it brings about in the economic and social situation throughout the Community mean not only that barriers to trade should be removed, but also that the structures of production should be adapted to the Community dimension. For that purpose it is essential that companies of all types the business of which is not limited to satisfying purely local needs should be able to plan and carry out the reorganisation of their business on a Community scale.

(3) The legal framework within which business should be carried on in the Community is still based largely on national laws and therefore does not correspond to the economic framework within which it should develop if the objectives set out in Article 18 of the Treaty are to be achieved. That situation forms a considerable obstacle to the creation of groups of companies from different Member States.

(4) The Council has adopted Regulation (EC) No 2157/2001[10] establishing the legal form of the European Company (SE) according to the general principles of the public limited-liability company. This is not an instrument which is suited to the specific features of cooperatives.

(5) The European Economic Interest Grouping (EEIG), as provided for in Regulation (EEC) No 2137/85,[11] allows undertakings to promote certain of their activities in common, while nevertheless preserving their independence, but does not meet the specific requirements of cooperative enterprise.

(6) The Community, anxious to ensure equal terms of competition and to contribute to its economic development, should provide cooperatives, which are a form of organisation generally recognised in all Member States, with adequate legal instruments capable of facilitating the development of their cross-border activities. The United Nations has encouraged all governments

---

[1] OJ L 207, 18.8.2003, 1–24.
[2] OJ C 99, 21.4.1992, 17 and OJ C 236, 31.8.1993, 17.
[3] OJ C 42, 15.2.1993, 75 and opinion delivered on 14 May 2003 (not yet published in the Official Journal).
[4] OJ C 223, 31.8.1992, 42.
[5] OJ C 128, 16.5.1983, 51.
[6] OJ C 246, 14.9.1987, 94.
[7] OJ C 158, 26.6.1989, 380.
[8] OJ C 61, 28.2.1994, 231.
[9] OJ C 313, 12.10.1998, 234.

[10] OJ L 294, 10.11.2001, 1, reproduced supra under no. C. 19.
[11] OJ L 199, 31.7.1985, 1, reproduced supra under no. C. 8.

to ensure a supportive environment in which cooperatives can participate on an equal footing with other forms of enterprise.[12]

(7) Cooperatives are primarily groups of persons or legal entities with particular operating principles that are different from those of other economic agents. These include the principles of democratic structure and control and the distribution of the net profit for the financial year on an equitable basis.

(8) These particular principles include notably the principle of the primacy of the individual which is reflected in the specific rules on membership, resignation and expulsion, where the 'one man, one vote' rule is laid down and the right to vote is vested in the individual, with the implication that members cannot exercise any rights over the assets of the cooperative.

(9) Cooperatives have a share capital and their members may be either individuals or enterprises. These members may consist wholly or partly of customers, employees or suppliers. Where a cooperative is constituted of members who are themselves cooperative enterprises, it is known as a 'secondary' or 'second-degree' cooperative. In some circumstances cooperatives may also have among their members a specified proportion of investor members who do not use their services, or of third parties who benefit by their activities or carry out work on their behalf.

(10) A European cooperative society (hereinafter referred to as 'SCE') should have as its principal object the satisfaction of its members' needs and/or the development of their economic and/or social activities, in compliance with the following principles:
– its activities should be conducted for the mutual benefit of the members so that each member benefits from the activities of the SCE in accordance with his/her participation,
– members of the SCE should also be customers, employees or suppliers or should be otherwise involved in the activities of the SCE,

– control should be vested equally in members, although weighted voting may be allowed, in order to reflect each member's contribution to the SCE,
– there should be limited interest on loan and share capital,
– profits should be distributed according to business done with the SCE or retained to meet the needs of members,
– there should be no artificial restrictions on membership,
– net assets and reserves should be distributed on winding-up according to the principle of disinterested distribution, that is to say to another cooperative body pursuing similar aims or general interest purposes.

(11) Cross-border cooperation between cooperatives in the Community is currently hampered by legal and administrative difficulties which should be eliminated in a market without frontiers.

(12) The introduction of a European legal form for cooperatives, based on common principles but taking account of their specific features, should enable them to operate outside their own national borders in all or part of the territory of the Community.

(13) The essential aim of this Regulation is to enable the establishment of an SCE by physical persons resident in different Member States or legal entities established under the laws of different Member States. It will also make possible the establishment of an SCE by merger of two existing cooperatives, or by conversion of a national cooperative into the new form without first being wound up, where that cooperative has its registered office and head office within one Member State and an establishment or subsidiary in another Member State.

(14) In view of the specific Community character of an SCE, the 'real seat' arrangement adopted by this Regulation in respect of SCEs is without prejudice to Member States' laws and does not pre-empt the choices to be made for other Community texts on company law.

(15) References to capital in this Regulation should comprise solely the subscribed capital.

---

[12] Resolution adopted by the General Assembly of the 88th plenary meeting of the United Nations, 19 December 2001 (A/RES/56/114).

This should not affect any undistributed joint assets/equity capital in the SCE.

(16) This Regulation does not cover other areas of law such as taxation, competition, intellectual property or insolvency. The provisions of the Member States' law and of Community law are therefore applicable in the above areas and in other areas not covered by this Regulation.

(17) The rules on the involvement of employees in the European cooperative society are laid down in Directive 2003/72/EC,[13] and those provisions thus form an indissociable complement to this Regulation and are to be applied concomitantly.

(18) Work on the approximation of national company law has made substantial progress so that certain provisions adopted by the Member State where the SCE has its registered office for the purpose of implementing directives on companies may be referred to by analogy for the SCE in areas where the functioning of the cooperative does not require uniform Community rules, such provisions being appropriate to the arrangements governing the SCE, especially:
- first Council Directive 68/151/EEC of 9 March 1968 on coordination of safeguards which, for the protection of the interests of members and others, are required by Member States of companies within the meaning of the second paragraph of Article 48 of the Treaty, with a view to making such safeguards equivalent throughout the Community,[14]
- fourth Council Directive 78/660/EEC of 25 July 1978 on the annual accounts of certain types of companies,[15]
- seventh Council Directive 83/349/EEC of 13 June 1983 on consolidated accounts,[16]
- eighth Council Directive 84/253/EEC of 10 April 1984 on the approval of persons responsible for carrying out the statutory audits of accounting documents,[17]
- Eleventh Council Directive 89/666/EEC of 21 December 1989 concerning disclosure requirements in respect of branches opened in a Member State by certain types of company governed by the law of another State.[18]

(19) Activities in the field of financial services in particular in so far as they concern credit establishments and insurance undertakings have been the subject of legislative measures pursuant to the following Directives:
- Council Directive 86/635/EEC of 8 December 1986 on the annual accounts and consolidated accounts of banks and other financial institutions,[19]
- Council Directive 92/49/EEC on the coordination of laws, regulations and administrative provisions relating to direct insurance other than life assurance (third non-life insurance Directive).[20]

(20) This form of organisation should be optional,

HAS ADOPTED THIS REGULATION:

CHAPTER I

GENERAL PROVISIONS

Article 1

Form of the SCE

1. A cooperative society may be set up within the territory of the Community in the form of a European Cooperative Society (SCE) on the conditions and in the manner laid down in this Regulation.

---

[13] OJ L 207, 28.8.2003, 25, reproduced infra under no. C. 26.
[14] OJ L 65, 14.3.1968, 8, reproduced supra under no. C. 1. Directive as last amended by the 1994 Act of Accession.
[15] OJ L 222, 14.8.1978, 11, reproduced supra under no. C. 4. Directive as last amended by Directive 2001/65/EC (OJ L 283, 27.10.2001, 28), reproduced supra under no. C. 18.
[16] OJ L 193, 18.7.1983, 1, reproduced supra under no. C. 6. Directive as last amended by Directive 2001/65/EC, reproduced supra under no. C. 18.

[17] OJ L 126, 12.5.1984, 20, reproduced supra under no. C. 7, which has been repealed as from 29 June 2006 by article 50 of Directive 2006/43/EC, reproduced infra under no. C. 30.
[18] OJ L 395, 30.12.1989, 36, reproduced supra under no. C. 9.
[19] OJ L 372, 31.12.1986, reproduced supra under no. B. 7. Directive as last amended by Directive 2001/65/EC, reproduced supra under no. C. 18.
[20] OJ L 228, 11.8.1992, 1, reproduced infra under no. I. 25. Directive as last amended by Directive 2002/13/EC (OJ L 77, 20.3.2002, 17), reproduced infra under no. I. 32.

2. The subscribed capital of an SCE shall be divided into shares.

The number of members and the capital of an SCE shall be variable.

Unless otherwise provided by the statutes of the SCE when that SCE is formed, no member shall be liable for more than the amount he/she has subscribed. Where the members of the SCE have limited liability, the name of the SCE shall end in 'limited'.

3. An SCE shall have as its principal object the satisfaction of its members' needs and/or the development of their economic and social activities, in particular through the conclusion of agreements with them to supply goods or services or to execute work of the kind that the SCE carries out or commissions. An SCE may also have as its object the satisfaction of its members' needs by promoting, in the manner set forth above, their participation in economic activities, in one or more SCEs and/or national cooperatives. An SCE may conduct its activities through a subsidiary.

4. An SCE may not extend the benefits of its activities to non-members or allow them to participate in its business, except where its statutes provide otherwise.

5. An SCE shall have legal personality.

6. Employee involvement in an SCE shall be governed by the provisions of Directive 2003/72/EC.

Article 2

Formation

1. An SCE may be formed as follows:
- by five or more natural persons resident in at least two Member States,
- by five or more natural persons and companies and firms within the meaning of the second paragraph of Article 48 of the Treaty and other legal bodies governed by public or private law, formed under the law of a Member State, resident in, or governed by the law of, at least two different Member States,
- by companies and firms within the meaning of the second paragraph of Article 48 of the Treaty and other legal bodies governed by public or private law formed under the law of a Member State which are governed by the law of at least two different Member States,
- by a merger between cooperatives formed under the law of a Member State with registered offices and head offices within the Community, provided that at least two of them are governed by the law of different Member States,
- by conversion of a cooperative formed under the law of a Member State, which has its registered office and head office within the Community if for at least two years it has had an establishment or subsidiary governed by the law of another Member State.

2. A Member State may provide that a legal body the head office of which is not in the Community may participate in the formation of an SCE provided that legal body is formed under the law of a Member State, has its registered office in that Member State and has a real and continuous link with a Member State's economy.

Article 3

Minimum capital

1. The capital of an SCE shall be expressed in the national currency. An SCE whose registered office is outside the Euro-area may also express its capital in euro.

2. The subscribed capital shall not be less than EUR 30000.

3. The laws of the Member State requiring a greater subscribed capital for legal bodies carrying on certain types of activity shall apply to SCEs with registered offices in that Member State.

4. The statutes shall lay down a sum below which subscribed capital may not be allowed to fall as a result of repayment of the shares of members who cease to belong to the SCE. This sum may not be less than the amount laid down in paragraph 2. The date laid down in Article 16 by which members who cease to belong to the SCE are entitled to repayment shall be suspended as long as repayment would result in subscribed capital falling below the set limit.

5. The capital may be increased by successive subscriptions by members or on the admission of new members, and it may be reduced by the total or partial repayment of subscriptions, subject to paragraph 4.

Variations in the amount of the capital shall not require amendment of the statutes or disclosure.

Article 4
Capital of the SCE

1. The subscribed capital of an SCE shall be represented by the members' shares, expressed in the national currency. An SCE whose registered office is outside of the Euro-area may also express its shares in euro. More than one class of shares may be issued.

The statutes may provide that different classes of shares shall confer different entitlements with regard to the distribution of surpluses. Shares conferring the same entitlements shall constitute one class.

2. The capital may be formed only of assets capable of economic assessment. Members' shares may not be issued for an undertaking to perform work or supply services.

3. Shares shall be held by named persons. The nominal value of shares in a single class shall be identical. It shall be laid down in the statutes. Shares may not be issued at a price lower than their nominal value.

4. Shares issued for cash shall be paid for on the day of the subscription to not less than 25% of their nominal value. The balance shall be paid within five years unless the statutes provide for a shorter period.

5. Shares issued otherwise than for cash shall be fully paid for at the time of subscription.

6. The law applicable to public limited-liability companies in the Member State where the SCE has its registered office, concerning the appointment of experts and the valuation of any consideration other than cash, shall apply by analogy to the SCE.

7. The statutes shall lay down the minimum number of shares which must be subscribed for in order to qualify for membership. If they stipulate that the majority at general meetings shall be constituted by members who are natural persons and if they lay down a subscription requirement for members wishing to take part in the activities of the SCE, they may not make membership subject to subscription for more than one share.

8. When it considers the accounts for the financial year, the annual general meeting shall by resolution record the amount of the capital at the end of the financial year and the variation by reference to the preceding financial year.

At the proposal of the administrative or management organ, the subscribed capital may be increased by the capitalisation of all or part of the reserves available for distribution, following a decision of the general meeting, in accordance with the quorum and majority requirements for an amendment of the statutes. New shares shall be awarded to members in proportion to their shares in the previous capital.

9. The nominal value of shares may be increased by consolidating the shares issued. Where such an increase necessitates a call for supplementary payments from the members under provisions laid down in the statutes, the decision shall be taken by the general meeting in accordance with the quorum and majority requirements for the amendment of the statutes.

10. The nominal value of shares may be reduced by subdividing the shares issued.

11. In accordance with the statutes and with the agreement either of the general meeting or of the management or administrative organ, shares may be assigned or sold to a member or to anyone acquiring membership.

12. An SCE may not subscribe for its own shares, purchase them or accept them as security, either directly or through a person acting in his/her own name but on behalf of the SCE.

An SCE's shares may, however, be accepted as security in the ordinary transactions of SCE credit institutions.

Article 5
Statutes

1. For the purposes of this Regulation, 'the statutes of an SCE' shall mean both the instrument of incorporation and, when they are the subject of a separate document, the statutes of the SCE.

2. The founder members shall draw up the statutes of the SCE in accordance with the provisions for the formation of cooperative societies laid down by the law of the Member State in which the SCE has its registered office. The statutes shall be in writing and signed by the founder members.

3. The law for the precautionary supervision applicable in the Member State in which the SCE has its registered office to public limited-liability companies during the phase of the constitution shall apply by analogy to the control of the constitution of the SCE.

4. The statutes of the SCE shall include at least:
– the name of the SCE, preceded or followed by the abbreviation 'SCE' and, where appropriate, the word 'limited',
– a statement of the objects,
– the names of the natural persons and the names of the entities which are founder members of the SCE, indicating their objects and registered offices in the latter case,
– the address of the SCE's registered office,
– the conditions and procedures for the admission, expulsion and resignation of members,
– the rights and obligations of members, and the different categories of member, if any, and the rights and obligations of members in each category,
– the nominal value of the subscribed shares, the amount of the subscribed capital, and an indication that the capital is variable,
– specific rules concerning the amount to be allocated from the surplus, where appropriate, to the legal reserve,
– the powers and responsibilities of the members of each of the governing organs,
– provisions governing the appointment and removal of the members of the governing organs,
– the majority and quorum requirements,
– the duration of the existence of the society, where this is of limited duration.

Article 6
Registered office

The registered office of an SCE shall be located within the Community, in the same Member State as its head office. A Member State may, in addition, impose on SCEs registered in its territory the obligation of locating the head office and the registered office in the same place.

Article 7
Transfer of registered office

1. The registered office of an SCE may be transferred to another Member State in accordance with paragraphs 2 to 16. Such transfer shall not result in the winding-up of the SCE or in the creation of a new legal person.

2. The management or administrative organ shall draw up a transfer proposal and publicise it in accordance with Article 12, without prejudice to any additional forms of publication provided for by the Member State of the registered office. That proposal shall state the current name, the registered office and number of the SCE and shall cover:

(a) the proposed registered office of the SCE;

(b) the proposed statutes of the SCE including, where appropriate, its new name;

(c) the proposed timetable for the transfer;

(d) any implication the transfer may have on employees' involvement;

(e) any rights provided for the protection of members, creditors and holders of other rights.

3. The management or administrative organ shall draw up a report explaining and justifying the legal and economic aspects as well as the employment effects of the transfer and explaining the implications of the transfer for members, creditors, employees and holders of other rights.

4. An SCE's members, creditors and the holders of other rights, and any other body which

according to national law can exercise this right, shall be entitled, at least one month before the general meeting called upon to decide on the transfer, to examine, at the SCE's registered office, the transfer proposal and the report drawn up pursuant to paragraph 3 and, on request, to obtain copies of these documents free of charge.

5. Any member who opposed the transfer decision at the general meeting or at a sectorial or section meeting may tender his/her resignation within two months of the general meeting's decision. Membership shall terminate at the end of the financial year in which the resignation was tendered; the transfer shall not take effect in respect of that member. Resignation shall entitle the member to repayment of shares on the conditions laid down in Articles 4(4) and 16.

6. No decision to transfer may be taken for two months after publication of the proposal. Such a decision shall be taken as laid down in Article 62(4).

7. Before the competent authority issues the certificate mentioned in paragraph 8, the SCE shall satisfy it that, in respect of any liabilities arising prior to the publication of the transfer proposal, the interests of creditors and holders of other rights in respect of the SCE (including those of public bodies) have been adequately protected in accordance with requirements laid down by the Member State where the SCE has its registered office prior to the transfer.

A Member State may extend the application of the first subparagraph to liabilities that arise, or may arise, prior to the transfer.

The first and second subparagraphs shall apply without prejudice to the application to SCEs of the national legislation of Member States concerning the satisfaction or securing of payments to public bodies.

8. In the Member State in which the SCE has its registered office, the court, notary or other competent authority shall issue a certificate attesting to the completion of the acts and formalities to be accomplished before the transfer.

9. The new registration may not be effected until the certificate referred to in paragraph 8 has been submitted and evidence has been produced that the formalities required for registration in the country of the new registered office have been completed.

10. The transfer of an SCE's registered office and the consequent amendment of its statutes shall take effect on the date on which the SCE is registered in accordance with Article 11(1) in the register for its new registered office.

11. When the SCE's new registration has been effected, the registry for its new registration shall notify the register for its old registration. Deletion of the old registration shall be effected on receipt of that notification, but not before.

12. The new registration and the deletion of the old registration shall be publicised in the Member States concerned, in accordance with Article 12.

13. On publication of an SCE's new registration, the new registered office may be relied on as against third parties. However, as long as the deletion of the SCE's registration from the register of its previous registered office has not been publicised, third parties may continue to rely on the previous registered office unless the SCE proves that such third parties were aware of the new registered office.

14. The laws of a Member State may provide that, as regards SCEs registered in that Member State, the transfer of a registered office which would result in a change of the law applicable shall not take effect if any of that Member State's competent authorities opposes it within the two-month period referred to in paragraph 6. Such opposition may be based only on grounds of public interest.

Where an SCE is supervised by a national financial supervisory authority according to Community directives, the right to oppose the change of registered office applies to this authority as well.

Review by a judicial authority shall be possible

15. An SCE may not transfer its registered office if proceedings for winding-up, including voluntary winding-up, liquidation, insolvency or suspension of payments or other similar proceedings have been brought against it.

16. An SCE which has transferred its registered office to another Member State shall be considered, in respect of any course of action arising prior to the transfer as determined in paragraph 10, as having its registered office in the Member State where the SCE was registered prior to the transfer, even if the SCE is sued after the transfer.

Article 8
Law applicable

1. An SCE shall be governed:

(a) by this Regulation;

(b) where expressly authorised by this Regulation, by the provisions of its statutes;

(c) in the case of matters not regulated by this Regulation or, where matters are partly regulated by it, of those aspects not covered by it, by:
(i) the laws adopted by Member States in the implementation of Community measures relating specifically to SCEs;
(ii) the laws of Member States which would apply to a cooperative formed in accordance with the law of the Member State in which the SCE has its registered office;
(iii) the provisions of its statutes, in the same way as for a cooperative formed in accordance with the law of the Member State in which the SCE has its registered office.

2. If national law provides for specific rules and/or restrictions related to the nature of business carried out by an SCE, or for forms of control by a supervisory authority, that law shall apply in full to the SCE.

Article 9
Principle of non-discrimination

Subject to this Regulation, an SCE shall be treated in every Member State as if it were a cooperative, formed in accordance with the law of the Member State in which it has its registered office.

Article 10
Particulars to be stated in the documents

1. The law applicable, in the Member State where the SCE has its registered office, to public limited-liability companies regulating the content of the letters and documents sent to third parties shall apply by analogy to that SCE. The name of the SCE shall be preceded or followed by the abbreviation 'SCE' and, where appropriate, by the word 'limited'.

2. Only SCEs may include the acronym 'SCE' before or after their name in order to determine their legal form.

3. Nevertheless, companies, firms and other legal entities registered in a Member State before the date of entry into force of this Regulation in the names of which the acronym 'SCE' appears shall not be required to alter their names.

Article 11
Registration and disclosure requirements

1. Every SCE shall be registered in the Member State in which it has its registered office in a register designated by the law of that Member State in accordance with the law applicable to public limited-liability companies.

2. An SCE may not be registered unless an agreement on arrangements for employee involvement pursuant to Article 4 of Directive 2003/72/EC has been concluded, or a decision pursuant to Article 3(6) of the Directive has been taken, or the period for negotiations pursuant to Article 5 of the Directive has expired without an agreement having been concluded.

3. In order for an SCE established by way of merger to be registered in a Member State which has made use of the option referred to in Article 7(3) of Directive 2003/72/EC, either an agreement pursuant to Article 4 of the Directive must have been concluded on the arrangements for employee involvement, including participation, or none of the participating cooperatives must have been governed by participation rules before registration of the SCE.

4. The statutes of the SCE must not conflict at any time with the arrangements for employee involvement which have been so determined. Where such new arrangements determined pursuant to Directive 2003/72/EC conflict with the existing statutes, the statutes shall be amended to the extent necessary.

In this case, a Member State may provide that the management organ or the administrative organ of the SCE shall be entitled to amend the statutes without any further decision from the general meeting.

5. The law applicable, in the Member State where the SCE has its registered office, to public limited-liability companies concerning disclosure requirements of documents and particulars shall apply by analogy to that SCE.

Article 12
Publication of documents in the Member States

1. Publication of documents and particulars concerning an SCE which must be made public under this Regulation shall be effected in the manner laid down in the laws of the Member State applicable to public limited-liability companies in which the SCE has its registered office.

2. The national rules adopted pursuant to Directive 89/666/EEC shall apply to branches of an SCE opened in a Member State other than that in which it has its registered office. However, Member States may provide for derogations from the national provisions implementing that Directive to take account of the specific features of cooperatives.

Article 13
Notice in the Official Journal of the European Union

1. Notice of an SCE's registration and of the deletion of such a registration shall be published for information purposes in the Official Journal of the European Union after publication in accordance with Article 12. That notice shall state the name, number, date and place of registration of the SCE, the date and place of publication and the title of publication, the registered office of the SCE and its sector of activity.

2. Where the registered office of an SCE is transferred in accordance with Article 7, notice shall be published giving the information provided for in paragraph 1, together with that relating to the new registration.

3. The particulars referred to in paragraph 1 shall be forwarded to the Office for Official Publications of the European Communities within one month of the publication referred to in Article 12(1).

Article 14
Acquisition of membership

1. Without prejudice to Article 33(1)(b) the acquisition of membership of an SCE shall be subject to the approval of the management or administrative organ. Candidates refused membership may appeal to the general meeting held following the application for membership.

Where the laws of the Member State of the SCE's registered office so permit, the statutes may provide that persons who do not expect to use or produce the SCE's goods and services may be admitted as investor (non-user) members. The acquisition of such membership shall be subject to approval by the general meeting or any other organ delegated to give approval by the general meeting or the statutes.

Members who are legal bodies shall be deemed to be users by virtue of the fact that they represent their own members provided that their members who are natural persons are users.

Unless the statutes provide otherwise, membership of an SCE may be acquired by natural persons or legal bodies.

2. The statutes may make admission subject to other conditions, in particular:
– subscription of a minimum amount of capital,
– conditions related to the objects of the SCE.

3. Where provided for in the statutes, applications for a supplementary stake in the capital may be addressed to members.

4. An alphabetical index of all members shall be kept at the registered office of the SCE, showing their addresses and the number and class, if

appropriate, of the shares they hold. Any party having a direct legitimate interest may inspect the index on request, and may obtain a copy of the whole or any part at a price not exceeding the administrative cost thereof.

5. Any transaction which affects the manner in which the capital is ascribed or allotted, or increased or reduced, shall be entered on the index of members provided for in paragraph 4 no later than the month following that in which the change occurs.

6. The transactions referred to in paragraph 5 shall not take effect with respect to the SCE or third parties having a direct legitimate interest until they are entered on the index referred to in paragraph 4.

7. Members shall on request be given a written statement certifying that the change has been entered.

Article 15
Loss of membership

1. Membership shall be lost:
– upon resignation,
– upon expulsion, where the member commits a serious breach of his/her obligations or acts contrary to the interests of the SCE,
– where authorised by the statutes, upon the transfer of all shares held to a member or a natural person or legal entity which has acquired membership,
– upon winding-up in the case of a member that is not a natural person,
– upon bankruptcy,
– upon death,
– in any other situation provided for in the statutes or in the legislation on cooperatives of the Member State in which the SCE has its registered office.

2. Any minority member who opposed an amendment to the statutes at the general meeting whereby:
(i) new obligations in respect of payments or other services were introduced; or
(ii) existing obligations for members were substantially extended; or
(iii) the period of notice for resignation from the SCE was extended to more than five years;

may tender his/her resignation within two months of the general meeting's decision.

Membership shall terminate at the end of the current financial year in the cases referred to in points (i) and (ii) of the first subparagraph and at the end of the period of notice which applied before the statutes were amended in the case referred to in point (iii) thereof. The amendment to the statutes shall not take effect in respect of that member. Resignation shall entitle the member to repayment of shares on the conditions laid down in Articles 3(4) and 16.

3. The decision to expel a member shall be taken by the administrative or management organ, after the member has been heard. The member may appeal against such a decision to the general meeting.

Article 16
Financial entitlements of members in the event of resignation or expulsion

1. Except where shares are transferred and subject to Article 3, loss of membership shall entitle the member to repayment of his/her part of the subscribed capital, reduced in proportion to any losses charged against the SCE's capital.

2. The amounts deducted under paragraph 1 shall be calculated by reference to the balance sheet for the financial year in which the entitlement to repayment arose.

3. The statutes shall lay down the procedures and conditions for exercising the right to resign and lay down the time within which repayment shall be made, which may not exceed three years. In any event, the SCE shall not be obliged to make the repayment less than six months after approval of the balance sheet issued following the loss of membership.

4. Paragraphs 1, 2 and 3 shall apply also where only a part of a member's shareholding is to be repaid.

Chapter II
Formation

Section 1
General

Article 17
Law applicable during formation

1. Subject to this Regulation, the formation of an SCE shall be governed by the law applicable to cooperatives in the Member State in which the SCE establishes its registered office.

2. The registration of an SCE shall be made public in accordance with Article 12.

Article 18
Acquisition of legal personality

1. An SCE shall acquire legal personality on the day of its registration in the Member State in which it has its registered office, in the register designated by that State in accordance with Article 11(1).

2. If acts are performed in an SCE's name before its registration in accordance with Article 11 and the SCE does not assume the obligations arising out of such acts after its registration, the natural persons, companies, firms or other legal entities which performed those acts shall be jointly and severally liable therefor, without limit in the absence of agreement to the contrary.

Section 2
Formation by Merger

Article 19
Procedures for formation by merger

An SCE may be formed by means of a merger carried out in accordance with:

– the procedure for merger by acquisition,
– the procedure for merger by the formation of a new legal person.

In the case of a merger by acquisition, the acquiring cooperative shall take the form of an SCE when the merger takes place. In the case of a merger by the formation of a new legal person, the latter shall take the form of an SCE.

Article 20
Law applicable in the case of merger

For matters not covered by this section or, where a matter is partly covered by it, for aspects not covered by it, each cooperative involved in the formation of an SCE by merger shall be governed by the provisions of the law of the Member State to which it is subject that apply to mergers of cooperatives and, failing that, the provisions applicable to internal mergers of public limited-liability companies under the law of that State.

Article 21
Grounds for opposition to a merger

The laws of a Member State may provide that a cooperative governed by the law of that Member State may not take part in the formation of an SCE by merger if any of that Member State's competent authorities opposes it before the issue of the certificate referred to in Article 29(2).

Such opposition may be based only on grounds of public interest. Review by a judicial authority shall be possible.

Article 22
Conditions of merger

1. The management or administrative organ of merging cooperatives shall draw up draft terms of merger. The draft terms of merger shall include the following particulars:

(a) the name and registered office of each of the merging cooperatives together with those proposed for the SCE;

(b) the share-exchange ratio of the subscribed capital and the amount of any cash payment. If there are no shares, a precise division of the assets and its equivalent value in shares;

(c) the terms for the allotment of shares in the SCE;

(d) the date from which the holding of shares in the SCE will entitle the holders to share in surplus and any special conditions affecting that entitlement;

(e) the date from which the transactions of the merging cooperatives will be treated for accounting purposes as being those of the SCE;

(f) the special conditions or advantages attached to debentures or securities other than shares which, according to Article 66, do not confer the status of member;

(g) the rights conferred by the SCE on the holders of shares to which special rights are attached and on the holders of securities other than shares, or the measures proposed concerning them;

(h) the forms of protection of the rights of creditors of the merging cooperatives;

(i) any special advantage granted to the experts who examine the draft terms of merger or to members of the administrative, management, supervisory or controlling organs of the merging cooperatives;

(j) the statutes of the SCE;

(k) information on the procedures by which arrangements for employee involvement are determined pursuant to Directive 2003/72/EC.

2. The merging cooperatives may include further items in the draft terms of merger.

3. The law applicable to public limited-liability companies concerning the draft terms of a merger shall apply by analogy to the cross-border merger of cooperatives for the creation of an SCE.

Article 23
Explanation and justification of the terms of merger

The administrative or management organs of each merging cooperative shall draw up a detailed written report explaining and justifying the draft terms of merger from a legal and economic viewpoint and in particular the share-exchange ratio. The report shall also indicate any special valuation difficulties.

Article 24
Publication

1. The law applicable to public limited-liability companies concerning the disclosure requirements of the draft terms of mergers shall apply by analogy to each of the merging cooperatives, subject to the additional requirements imposed by the Member State to which the cooperative concerned is subject.

2. Publication of the draft terms of merger in the national gazette shall, however, include the following particulars for each of the merging cooperatives:

(a) the type, name and registered office of each merging cooperative;

(b) the address of the place or of the register in which the statutes and all other documents and particulars are filed in respect of each merging cooperative, and the number of the entry in that register;

(c) an indication of the arrangements made in accordance with Article 28 for the exercise of the rights of the creditors of the cooperative in question and the address at which complete information on those arrangements may be obtained free of charge;

(d) an indication of the arrangements made in accordance with Article 28 for the exercise of the rights of members of the cooperative in question and the address at which complete information on those arrangements may be obtained free of charge;

(e) the name and registered office proposed for the SCE;

(f) the conditions determining the date on which the merger will take effect pursuant to Article 31.

Article 25
Disclosure requirements

1. Any member shall be entitled, at least one month before the date of the general meeting required to decide on the merger, to inspect at the registered office the following documents:

(a) the draft terms of merger mentioned in Article 22;

(b) the annual accounts and management reports of the merging cooperatives for the three preceding financial years;

(c) an accounting statement drafted in accordance with the provisions applicable to the internal mergers of public limited-liability companies, to the extent that such a statement is required by these provisions;

(d) the experts' report on the value of shares to be distributed in exchange for the assets for the merging cooperatives or the share exchange ratio as provided for in Article 26;

(e) the report from the cooperative's administrative or management organs as provided for in Article 23.

2. A full copy of the documents referred to in paragraph 1 or, if he/she so wishes, an extract, may be obtained by any member on request and free of charge.

Article 26
Report of independent experts

1. For each merging cooperative, one or more independent experts, appointed by that cooperative in accordance with the provisions of Article 4(6), shall examine the draft terms of merger and draw up a written report for the members.

2. A single report for all merging cooperatives may be drawn up where this is permitted by the laws of the Member States to which the cooperatives are subject.

3. The law applicable to the mergers of public limited-liability companies concerning the rights and obligations of experts shall apply by analogy to the merger of cooperatives.

Article 27
Approval of the terms of merger

1. The general meeting of each of the merging cooperatives shall approve the draft terms of the merger.

2. Employee involvement in the SCE shall be decided upon pursuant to Directive 2003/72/EC. The general meetings of each of the merging cooperatives may reserve the right to make registration of the SCE conditional upon its express ratification of the arrangements so decided.

Article 28
Laws applicable to formation by merger

1. The law of the Member State governing each merging cooperative shall apply as in the case of a merger of public limited-liability companies, taking into account the cross-border nature of the merger, with regard to the protection of the interests of:
– creditors of the merging cooperatives,
– holders of bonds in the merging cooperatives.

2. A Member State may, in the case of the merging cooperatives governed by its law, adopt provisions designed to ensure appropriate protection for members who have opposed the merger.

Article 29
Scrutiny of merger procedure

1. The legality of a merger shall be scrutinised, as regards the part of the procedure concerning each merging cooperative, in accordance with the law of the Member State to which the merging cooperative is subject that apply to mergers of cooperatives and, failing that, the provisions applicable to internal mergers of public limited companies under the law of that State.

2. In each Member State concerned the court, notary or other competent authority shall issue a certificate attesting to the completion of the pre-merger acts and formalities.

3. If the law of a Member State to which a merging cooperative is subject provides for a procedure to scrutinise and amend the share-exchange ratio, or a procedure to compensate minority members, without preventing the registration of the merger, such procedures shall apply only if the other merging cooperatives situated in Member States which do not provide for such procedure explicitly accept, when approving the draft terms of the merger in accordance with Article 27(1), the possibility for the members of

that merging cooperative to have recourse to such procedure. In such cases, the court, notary or other competent authorities may issue the certificate referred to in paragraph 2 even if such a procedure has been started. The certificate must, however, indicate that the procedure is pending. The decision in the procedure shall be binding on the acquiring cooperative and all its members.

Article 30
Scrutiny of legality of merger

1. The legality of a merger shall be scrutinised, as regards the part of the procedure concerning the completion of the merger and the formation of the SCE, by the court, notary or other competent authority in the Member State of the proposed registered office of the SCE able to scrutinise that aspect of the legality of mergers of cooperatives and, failing that, mergers of public limited-liability companies.

2. To that end, each merging cooperative shall submit to the competent authority the certificate referred to in Article 29(2) within six months of its issue together with a copy of the draft terms of merger approved by that cooperative.

3. The authority referred to in paragraph 1 shall in particular ensure that the merging cooperatives have approved draft terms of merger in the same terms and that arrangements for employee involvement have been determined pursuant to Directive 2003/72/EC.

4. The said authority shall also satisfy itself that the SCE has been formed in accordance with the requirements of the law of the Member State in which it has its registered office.

Article 31
Registration of merger

1. A merger and the simultaneous formation of an SCE shall take effect on the date on which the SCE is registered in accordance with Article 11(1).

2. The SCE may not be registered until all the formalities provided for in Articles 29 and 30 have been completed.

Article 32
Publication

For each of the merging cooperatives the completion of the merger shall be made public as laid down by the law of the Member State concerned in accordance with the laws governing mergers of public companies limited by shares.

Article 33
Consequences of merger

1. A merger carried out as laid down in the first indent of the first subparagraph of Article 19 shall have the following consequences ipso jure and simultaneously:

(a) all the assets and liabilities of each cooperative being acquired are transferred to the acquiring legal person;

(b) the members of each cooperative being acquired become members of the acquiring legal person;

(c) the cooperatives being acquired cease to exist;

(d) the acquiring legal person assumes the form of an SCE.

2. A merger carried out as laid down in the second indent of the first subparagraph of Article 19 shall have the following consequences ipso jure and simultaneously:

(a) all the assets and liabilities of the merging cooperatives are transferred to the SCE;

(b) the members of the merging cooperatives become members of the SCE;

(c) the merging cooperatives cease to exist.

3. Where, in the case of a merger of cooperatives, the law of a Member State requires the completion of any special formalities before the transfer of certain assets, rights and obligations by the merging cooperatives becomes effective against third parties, those formalities shall apply and shall be carried out either by the merging cooperatives or by the SCE following its registration.

4. The rights and obligations of the participating cooperatives in relation to both individual and collective terms and conditions of employment arising from national law, practice and individual

employment contracts or employment relationships and existing at the date of the registration shall, by reason of such registration be transferred to the SCE.

The first subparagraph shall not apply to the right of workers' representatives to participate in general or section or sectorial meetings provided for in Article 59(4).

5. When the merger has been registered, the SCE shall immediately inform the members of the cooperative being acquired of the fact that they have been entered in the register of members and of the number of their shares.

Article 34
Legality of the merger

1. A merger as provided for in the fourth indent of Article 2(1) may not be declared null and void once the SCE has been registered.

2. The absence of scrutiny of the legality of the merger pursuant to Articles 29 and 30 shall constitute one of the grounds for the winding-up of the SCE, in accordance with the provisions of Article 74.

Section 3
Conversion of an Existing Cooperative into an SCE

Article 35
Procedures for formation by conversion

1. Without prejudice to Article 11, the conversion of a cooperative into an SCE shall not result in the winding-up of the cooperative or in the creation of a new legal person.

2. The registered office may not be transferred from one Member State to another pursuant to Article 7 at the same time as the conversion is effected.

3. The administrative or management organ of the cooperative in question shall draw up draft terms of conversion and a report explaining and justifying the legal and economic aspects as well as the employment effects of the conversion and indicating the implications for members and employees of the adoption of the form of an SCE.

4. The draft terms of conversion shall be made public in the manner laid down in each Member State's law at least one month before the general meeting called upon to decide thereon.

5. Before the general meeting referred to in paragraph 6, one or more independent experts appointed or approved, in accordance with the national provisions, by a judicial or administrative authority in the Member State to which the cooperative being converted into an SCE is subject shall certify mutatis mutandis that the rules of Article 22(1)(b) are respected.

6. The general meeting of the cooperative in question shall approve the draft terms of conversion together with the statutes of the SCE.

7. Member States may make a conversion conditional on a favourable vote of a qualified majority or unanimity in the controlling organ of the cooperative to be converted within which employee participation is organised.

8. The rights and obligations of the cooperative to be converted on both individual and collective terms and conditions of employment arising from national law, practice and individual employment contracts or employment relationships and existing at the date of the registration shall, by reason of such registration, be transferred to the SCE.

Chapter III
Structure of the SCE

Article 36
Structure of organs

Under the conditions laid down by this Regulation an SCE shall comprise:

(a) a general meeting; and

(b) either a supervisory organ and a management organ (two-tier system) or an administrative organ (one-tier system) depending on the form adopted in the statutes.

Section 1
Two-Tier System

Article 37
Functions of the management organ; appointment of members

1. The management organ shall be responsible for managing the SCE and shall represent it in dealings with third parties and in legal proceedings. A Member State may provide that a managing director is responsible for the current management under the same conditions as for cooperatives that have registered offices within that Member State's territory.

2. The member or members of the management organ shall be appointed and removed by the supervisory organ.

However, a Member State may require or permit the statutes to provide that the member or members of the management organ are appointed and removed by the general meeting under the same conditions as for cooperatives that have registered offices within its territory.

3. No person may at the same time be a member of the management organ and of the supervisory organ of an SCE. The supervisory organ may, however, nominate one of its members to exercise the function of member of the management organ in the event of a vacancy. During such period, the functions of the person concerned as member of the supervisory organ shall be suspended. A Member State may impose a time limit on such a period.

4. The number of members of the management organ or the rules for determining it shall be laid down in the SCE's statutes. However, a Member State may fix a minimum and/or maximum number.

5. Where no provision is made for a two-tier system in relation to cooperatives with registered offices within its territory, a Member State may adopt the appropriate measures in relation to SCEs.

Article 38
Chairmanship and the calling of meetings of the management organ

1. The management organ shall elect a chairman from among its members, in accordance with the statutes.

2. The chairman shall call a meeting of the management organ under the conditions laid down in the statutes, either on his own initiative or at the request of any member. Any such request shall indicate the reasons for calling the meeting. If no action has been taken in respect of such a request within 15 days, the meeting of the management organ may be called by the member(s) who made the request.

Article 39
Functions of the supervisory organ; appointment of members

1. The supervisory organ shall supervise the duties performed by the management organ. It may not itself exercise the power to manage the SCE. The supervisory organ may not represent the SCE in dealings with third parties. It shall represent the SCE in dealings with the management organ, or its members, in respect of litigation or the conclusion of contracts.

2. The members of the supervisory organ shall be appointed and removed by the general meeting. The members of the first supervisory organ may, however, be appointed in the statutes. This shall apply without prejudice to any employee participation arrangements determined pursuant to Directive 2003/72/EC.

3. Of the members of the supervisory organ, not more than one quarter of the posts available may be filled by non-user members.

4. The statutes shall lay down the number of members of the supervisory organ or the rules for determining it. A Member State may, however, stipulate the number of members or the composition of the supervisory organ for SCEs having their registered office in its territory or a minimum and/or a maximum number.

Article 40
Right to information

1. The management organ shall report to the supervisory organ at least once every three months on the progress and foreseeable developments of the SCE's business, taking account of any information relating to undertakings controlled by the SCE that may significantly affect the progress of the SCE's business.

2. In addition to the regular information referred to in paragraph 1, the management organ shall promptly communicate to the supervisory organ any information on events likely to have an appreciable effect on the SCE.

3. The supervisory organ may require the management organ to provide information of any kind, which it needs to exercise supervision in accordance with Article 39(1). A Member State may provide that each member of the supervisory organ also be entitled to this facility.

4. The supervisory organ may undertake or arrange for any investigations necessary for the performance of its duties.

5. Each member of the supervisory organ shall be entitled to examine all information submitted to it.

Article 41
Chairmanship and the calling of meetings of the supervisory organ

1. The supervisory organ shall elect a chairman from among its members. If half of the members are appointed by employees, only a member appointed by the general meeting may be elected chairman.

2. The chairman shall call a meeting of the supervisory organ under the conditions laid down in the statutes, either on his/her own initiative, or at the request of at least one third of its members, or at the request of the management organ. The request shall indicate the reasons for calling the meeting. If no action has been taken in respect of such a request within 15 days, the meeting of the supervisory organ may be called by those who made the request.

SECTION 2
THE ONE-TIER SYSTEM

Article 42
Functions of the administrative organ; appointment of members

1. The administrative organ shall manage the SCE and shall represent it in dealings with third parties and in legal proceedings. A Member State may provide that a managing director shall be responsible for the current management under the same conditions as for cooperatives that have registered offices within that Member State's territory.

2. The number of members of the administrative organ or the rules for determining it shall be laid down in the statutes of the SCE. However, a Member State may set a minimum and, where necessary, a maximum number of members. Of the members of the administrative organ, not more than one quarter of the posts available may be filled by non-user members.

The administrative organ shall, however, consist of at least three members where employee participation is regulated in accordance with Directive 2003/72/EC.

3. The members of the administrative organ, and, where the statutes so provide, their alternate members, shall be appointed by the general meeting. The members of the first administrative organ may, however, be appointed by the statutes. This shall apply without prejudice to any employee participation arrangements determined pursuant to Directive 2003/72/EC.

4. Where no provision is made for a one-tier system in relation to cooperatives with registered offices within its territory, a Member State may adopt the appropriate measures in relation to SCEs.

Article 43
Intervals between meetings and the right to information

1. The administrative organ shall meet at least once every three months, at intervals laid down in the statutes, to discuss the progress of and foreseeable development of the SCE's business,

taking account, where appropriate, of any information relating to undertakings controlled by the SCE that may significantly affect the progress of the SCE's business.

2. Each member of the administrative organ shall be entitled to examine all reports, documents and information submitted to it.

Article 44
Chairmanship and the calling of meetings of the administrative organ

1. The administrative organ shall elect a chairman from among its members. If half of the members are appointed by employees, only a member appointed by the general meeting may be elected chairman.

2. The chairman shall call a meeting of the administrative organ under the conditions laid down in the statutes, either on his/her own initiative or at the request of at least one third of its members. The request must indicate the reasons for calling the meeting. If no action has been taken in respect of such a request within 15 days, the meeting of the administrative organ may be called by those who made the request.

SECTION 3
RULES COMMON TO THE ONE-TIER AND TWO-TIER SYSTEMS

Article 45
Term of office

1. Members of SCE organs shall be appointed for a period laid down in the statutes not exceeding six years.

2. Subject to any restrictions laid down in the statutes, members may be re-appointed once or more than once for the period determined in accordance with paragraph 1.

Article 46
Conditions of membership

1. An SCE's statutes may permit a company within the meaning of Article 48 of the Treaty to be a member of one of its organs, provided that the law applicable to cooperatives in the Member State in which the SCE's registered office is situated does not provide otherwise.

That company shall designate a natural person as its representative to exercise its functions on the organ in question. The representative shall be subject to the same conditions and obligations as if he/she were personally a member of the organ.

2. No person may be a member of any SCE organ or a representative of a member within the meaning of paragraph 1 who:
– is disqualified, under the law of the Member State in which the SCE's registered office is situated, from serving on the corresponding organ of a cooperative governed by the law of that State, or
– is disqualified from serving on the corresponding organ of a cooperative governed by the law of a Member State owing to a judicial or administrative decision delivered in a Member State.

3. An SCE's statutes may, in accordance with the law applicable to cooperatives in the Member State, lay down special conditions of eligibility for members representing the administrative organ.

Article 47
Power of representation and liability of the SCE

1. Where the authority to represent the SCE in dealings with third parties, in accordance with Articles 37(1) and 42(1), is conferred on two or more members, those members shall exercise that authority collectively, unless the law of the Member State in which the SCE's registered office is situated allows the statutes to provide otherwise, in which case such a clause may be relied upon against third parties where it has been disclosed in accordance with Articles 11(5) and 12.

2. Acts performed by an SCE's organs shall bind the SCE vis-à-vis third parties, even where the acts in question are not in accordance with the objects of the SCE, providing they do not exceed the powers conferred on them by the law of the Member State in which the SCE has its registered

office or which that law allows to be conferred on them.

Member States may, however, provide that the SCE shall not be bound where such acts are outside the objects of the SCE, if it proves that the third party knew that the act was outside those objects or could not in the circumstances have been unaware of it; disclosure of the statutes shall not of itself be sufficient proof thereof.

3. The limits on the powers of the organs of the SCE, arising under the statutes or from a decision of the competent organs, may never be relied on as against third parties, even if they have been disclosed.

4. A Member State may stipulate that the power to represent the SCE may be conferred by the statutes on a single person or on several persons acting jointly. Such legislation may stipulate that this provision of the statutes may be relied on as against third parties provided that it concerns the general power of representation. Whether or not such a provision may be relied on as against third parties shall be governed by the provisions of Article 12.

Article 48
Operations requiring authorisation

1. An SCE's statutes shall list the categories of transactions requiring:
 – under the two-tier system, authorisation from the supervisory organ or the general meeting to the management organ,
 – under the one-tier system, an express decision adopted by the administrative organ or authorisation from the general meeting.

2. Paragraph 1 shall apply without prejudice to Article 47.

3. However, a Member State may determine the minimum categories of transactions and the organ which shall give the authorisation which must feature in the statutes of SCEs registered in its territory and/or provide that, under the two-tier system, the supervisory organ may itself determine which categories of transactions are to be subject to authorisation.

Article 49
Confidentiality

The members of an SCE's organs shall be under a duty, even after they have ceased to hold office, not to divulge any information which they have concerning the SCE the disclosure of which might be prejudicial to the cooperative's interests or those of its members, except where such disclosure is required or permitted under national law provisions applicable to cooperatives or companies or is in the public interest.

Article 50
Conduct of the business of organs

1. Unless otherwise provided by this Regulation or the statutes, the internal rules relating to quorums and decision-taking in SCE organs shall be as follows:

(a) quorum: at least half of the members with voting rights must be present or represented;

(b) decision-taking: a majority of the members with voting rights present or represented. Members who are absent may take part in decisions by authorising another member of the organ or the alternate members who were appointed at the same time to represent them.

2. Where there is no relevant provision in the statutes, the chairman of each organ shall have a casting vote in the event of a tie. There shall be no provision to the contrary in the statutes, however, where half of the supervisory organ consists of employees' representatives.

3. Where employee participation is provided for in accordance with Directive 2003/72/EC, a Member State may provide that the supervisory organ's quorum and decision-making shall, by way of derogation from the provisions referred to in paragraphs 1 and 2, be subject to the rules applicable, under the same conditions, to cooperatives governed by the law of the Member State concerned.

Article 51
Civil liability

Members of management, supervisory and administrative organs shall be liable, in accordance with the provisions applicable to cooperatives in the Member State in which the SCE's registered office is situated, for loss or damage sustained by the SCE following any breach on their part of the legal, statutory or other obligations inherent in their duties.

SECTION 4
GENERAL MEETING

Article 52
Competence

The general meeting shall decide on matters for which it is given sole responsibility by:

(a) this Regulation; or

(b) the legislation of the Member State in which the SCE's registered office is situated, adopted under Directive 2003/72/EC.

Furthermore, the general meeting shall decide on matters for which responsibility is given to the general meeting of a cooperative governed by the law of the Member State in which the SCE's registered office is situated, either by the law of that Member State or by the SCE's statutes in accordance with that law.

Article 53
Conduct of general meetings

Without prejudice to the rules laid down in this section, the organisation and conduct of general meetings together with voting procedures shall be governed by the law applicable to cooperatives in the Member State in which the SCE's registered office is situated.

Article 54
Holding of general meetings

1. An SCE shall hold a general meeting at least once each calendar year, within six months of the end of its financial year, unless the law of the Member State in which the SCE's registered office is situated applicable to cooperatives carrying on the same type of activity as the SCE provides for more frequent meetings. A Member State may, however, provide that the first general meeting may be held at any time in the 18 months following an SCE's incorporation.

2. General meetings may be convened at any time by the management organ or the administrative organ, the supervisory organ or any other organ or competent authority in accordance with the national law applicable to cooperatives in the Member State in which the SCE's registered office is situated. The management organ shall be bound to convene a general meeting at the request of the supervisory organ.

3. The agenda for the general meeting held after the end of the financial year shall include at least the approval of the annual accounts and the allocation of profits.

4. The general meeting may in the course of a meeting decide that a further meeting be convened and set the date and the agenda.

Article 55
Meeting called by a minority of members

Members of the SCE who together number more than 5000, or who have at least 10% of the total number of the votes, may require the SCE to convene a general meeting and may draw up its agenda. The above proportions may be reduced by the statutes.

Article 56
Notice of meeting

1. A general meeting shall be convened by a notice in writing sent by any available means to every person entitled to attend the SCE's general meeting in accordance with Article 58(1) and (2) and the provisions of the statutes. That notice may be given by publication in the official internal publication of the SCE.

2. The notice calling a general meeting shall give at least the following particulars:
– the name and registered office of the SCE,
– the venue, date and time of the meeting,
– where appropriate, the type of general meeting,

– the agenda, indicating the subjects to be discussed and the proposals for decisions.

3. The period between the date of dispatch of the notice referred to in paragraph 1 and the date of the opening of the general meeting shall be at least 30 days. It may, however, be reduced to 15 days in urgent cases. Where Article 61(4) is applied, relating to quorum requirements, the time between a first and second meeting convened to consider the same agenda may be reduced according to the law of the Member State in which the SCE has its registered office.

Article 57
Additions to the agenda

Members of the SCE who together number more than 5000, or who have at least 10% of the total number of the votes, may require that one or more additional items be put on the agenda of any general meeting. The above proportions may be reduced by the statutes.

Article 58
Attendance and proxies

1. Every member shall be entitled to speak and vote at general meetings on the points that are included in the agenda.

2. Members of the SCE's organs and holders of securities other than shares and debentures within the meaning of Article 64 and, if the statutes allow, any other person entitled to do so under the law of the State in which the SCE's registered office is situated may attend a general meeting without voting rights.

3. A person entitled to vote shall be entitled to appoint a proxy to represent him/her at a general meeting in accordance with procedures laid down in the statutes.

The statutes shall lay down the maximum number of persons for whom a proxy may act.

4. The statutes may permit postal voting or electronic voting, in which case they shall lay down the necessary procedures.

Article 59
Voting rights

1. Each member of an SCE shall have one vote, regardless of the number of shares he holds.

2. If the law of the Member State in which the SCE has its registered office so permits, the statutes may provide for a member to have a number of votes determined by his/her participation in the cooperative activity other than by way of capital contribution. This attribution shall not exceed five votes per member or 30% of total voting rights, whichever is the lower.

If the law of the Member State in which the SCE has its registered office so permits, SCEs involved in financial or insurance activities may provide in their statutes for the number of votes to be determined by the members' participation in the cooperative activity including participation in the capital of the SCE. This attribution shall not exceed five votes per member or 20% of total voting rights, whichever is the lower.

In SCEs the majority of members of which are cooperatives, if the law of the Member State in which the SCE has its registered office so permits, the statutes may provide for the number of votes to be determined in accordance with the members' participation in the cooperative activity including participation in the capital of the SCE and/or by the number of members of each comprising entity.

3. As regards voting rights which the statutes may allocate to non-user (investor) members, the SCE shall be governed by the law of the Member State in which the SCE has its registered office. Nevertheless, non-user (investor) members may not together have voting rights amounting to more than 25% of total voting rights.

4. If, on the entry into force of this Regulation, the law of the Member State where an SCE has its registered office so permits, the statutes of that SCE may provide for the participation of employees' representatives in the general meetings or in the section or sectorial meetings, provided that the employees' representatives do not together control more than 15% of total voting

rights. Such rights shall cease to apply as soon as the registered office of the SCE is transferred to a Member State whose law does not provide for such participation.

Article 60
Right to information

1. Every member who so requests at a general meeting shall be entitled to obtain information from the management or administrative organ on the affairs of the SCE arising from items on which the general meeting may take a decision in accordance with Article 61(1). In so far as possible, information shall be provided at the general meeting in question.

2. The management or administrative organ may refuse to supply such information only where:
– it would be likely to be seriously prejudicial to the SCE,
– its disclosure would be incompatible with a legal obligation of confidentiality.

3. A member refused information may require that his/her question and the grounds for refusal be entered in the minutes of the general meeting.

4. Within the 10 days preceding the general meeting required to decide on the end of the financial year, members may examine the balance sheet, the profit-and-loss account and the notes thereon, the management report, the conclusion of the audit of the accounts by the person responsible and, where a parent company within the meaning of Directive 83/349/EEC is concerned, the consolidated accounts.

Article 61
Decisions

1. A general meeting may pass resolutions on items on its agenda. A general meeting may also deliberate and pass resolutions concerning items placed on the agenda of the meeting by a minority of members in accordance with Article 57.

2. A general meeting shall act by majority of the votes validly cast by the members present or represented.

3. The statutes shall lay down the quorum and majority requirements which are to apply to general meetings.

Where the statutes provide for the possibility of an SCE to admit investor (non-user) members, or to allocate votes according to capital contribution in SCEs involved in financial or insurance activities, the statutes shall also lay down special quorum requirements with relation to members other than investor (non-user) members or members that have voting rights according to capital contribution in SCEs involved in financial or insurance activities. Member States shall be free to set the minimum level of such special quorum requirements for those SCEs having their registered office in their territory.

4. A general meeting may amend the statutes the first time it is convened only if the members present or represented make up at least half of the total number of members on the date the general meeting is convened, and the second time it is convened on the same agenda no quorum shall be necessary.

In the cases referred to in the first subparagraph, at least two thirds of the votes cast validly must be cast in favour, unless the law applicable to cooperatives in the Member State in which the SCE's registered office is situated requires a greater majority.

Article 62
Minutes

1. Minutes shall be drawn up for every general meeting. The minutes shall include at least the following particulars:
– the venue and date of the meeting,
– the resolutions passed,
– the result of the voting.

2. The attendance list, the documents relating to the convening of the general meeting and the reports submitted to the members on the items on the agenda shall be annexed to the minutes.

3. The minutes and the documents annexed thereto shall be preserved for at least five years. A copy of the minutes and the documents annexed

thereto may be obtained by any member upon request against defrayal of the administrative cost.

4. The minutes shall be signed by the chairman of the meeting.

Article 63

Sectorial or section meetings

1. Where the SCE undertakes different activities or activities in more than one territorial unit, or has several establishments or more than 500 members, its statutes may provide for sectorial or section meetings, if permitted by the relevant Member State legislation. The statutes shall establish the division in sectors or sections and the number of delegates thereof.

2. The sectorial or section meetings shall elect their delegates for a maximum period of four years, unless early revocation takes place. Delegates so elected shall constitute the general meeting of the SCE and shall represent therein their sector or section to which they shall report on the outcome of the general meeting. The provisions of Section 4 of Chapter III shall be applied to the workings of the sectorial and section meetings.

Chapter IV

Issue of Shares Conferring Special Advantage

Article 64

Securities other than shares and debentures conferring special advantages

1. An SCE's statutes may provide for the issue of securities other than shares, or debentures the holders of which are to have no voting rights. These may be subscribed for by members or by non-members. Their acquisition does not confer the status of member. The statutes shall also lay down the procedure for redemption.

2. Holders of securities or debentures referred to in paragraph 1 may be given special advantages in accordance with the statutes or the conditions laid down when they are issued.

3. The total nominal value of securities or debentures referred to in paragraph 1 held may not exceed the figure laid down in the statutes.

4. Without prejudice to the right to attend the general meeting provided for in Article 58(2), the statutes may provide for special meetings of holders of securities or debentures referred to in paragraph 1. Before any decision of the general meeting is taken relating to the rights and interests of such holders, a special meeting may state its opinion, which shall be brought to the attention of the general meeting by the representatives which the special meeting appoints.

The opinion referred to in the first subparagraph shall be recorded in the minutes of the general meeting.

Chapter V

Allocation of Profits

Article 65

Legal reserve

1. Without prejudice to mandatory provisions of national laws, the statutes shall lay down rules for the allocation of the surplus for each financial year.

2. Where there is such a surplus, the statutes shall require the establishment of a legal reserve funded out of the surplus before any other allocation.

Until such time as the legal reserve is equal to the capital referred to in Article 3(2), the amount allocated to it may not be less than 15% of the surplus for the financial year after deduction of any losses carried over.

3. Members leaving the SCE shall have no claim against the sums thus allocated to the legal reserve.

Article 66

Dividend

The statutes may provide for the payment of a dividend to members in proportion to their business with the SCE, or the services they have performed for it.

Article 67
Allocation of available surplus

1. The balance of the surplus after deduction of the allocation to the legal reserve, of any sums paid out in dividends and of any losses carried over, with the addition of any surpluses carried over and of any sums drawn from the reserves, shall constitute the profits available for distribution.

2. The general meeting which considers the accounts for the financial year may allocate the surplus in the order and proportions laid down in the statutes, and in particular:
– carry them forward,
– appropriate them to any legal or statutory reserve fund,
– provide a return on paid-up capital and quasi-equity, payment being made in cash or shares.

3. The statutes may also prohibit any distribution.

CHAPTER VI
ANNUAL ACCOUNTS AND CONSOLIDATED ACCOUNTS

Article 68
Preparation of annual accounts and consolidated accounts

1. For the purposes of drawing up its annual accounts and its consolidated accounts if any, including the annual report accompanying them and their auditing and publication, an SCE shall be subject to the legal provisions adopted in the Member State in which it has its registered office in implementation of Directives 78/660/EEC and 83/349/EEC. However, Member States may provide for amendments to the national provisions implementing those Directives to take account of the specific features of cooperatives.

2. Where an SCE is not subject, under the law of the Member State in which the SCE has its registered office, to a publication requirement such as provided for in Article 3 of Directive 68/151/EEC, the SCE must at least make the documents relating to annual accounts available to the public at its registered office. Copies of those documents must be obtainable on request. The price charged for such copies shall not exceed their administrative cost.

3. An SCE must draw up its annual accounts and its consolidated accounts if any in the national currency. An SCE whose registered office is outside the euro area may also express its annual accounts and, where appropriate, consolidated accounts, in euro. In that event, the bases of conversion used to express in euro those items included in the accounts which are or were originally expressed in another currency shall be disclosed in the notes on the accounts.

Article 69
Accounts of SCEs with credit or financial activities

1. An SCE which is a credit or financial institution shall be governed by the rules laid down in the national law of the Member State in which its registered office is situated under directives relating to the taking up and pursuit of the business of credit institutions as regards the preparation of its annual and, where appropriate, consolidated accounts, including the accompanying annual report and the auditing and publication of those accounts.

2. An SCE which is an insurance undertaking shall be governed by the rules laid down in the national law of the Member State in which its registered office is situated under directives as regards the preparation of its annual and, where appropriate, consolidated accounts including the accompanying annual report and the auditing and publication of those accounts.

Article 70
Auditing

The statutory audit of an SCE's annual accounts and its consolidated accounts if any shall be carried out by one or more persons authorised to do so in the Member State in which the SCE has its registered office in accordance with the measures adopted in that State pursuant to Directives 84/253/EEC and 89/48/EEC.

Article 71
System of auditing

Where the law of a Member State requires all cooperatives, or a certain type of them, covered by the law of that State to join a legally authorised external body and to submit to a specific system of auditing carried out by that body, the arrangements shall automatically apply to an SCE with its registered office in that Member State provided that this body meets the requirements of Directive 84/253/EEC.

Chapter VII
Winding-up; Liquidation; Insolvency and Cessation of Payments

Article 72
Winding-up, insolvency and similar procedures

As regards winding-up, liquidation, insolvency, cessation of payments and similar procedures, an SCE shall be governed by the legal provisions which would apply to a cooperative formed in accordance with the law of the Member State in which its registered office is situated, including provisions relating to decision-making by the general meeting.

Article 73
Winding-up by the court or other competent authority of the Member State where the SCE has its registered office

1. On an application by any person with a legitimate interest or any competent authority, the court or any competent administrative authority of the Member State where the SCE has its registered office shall order the SCE to be wound up where it finds that there has been a breach of Article 2(1) and/or Article 3(2) and in the cases covered by Article 34.

The court or the competent administrative authority may allow the SCE time to rectify the situation. If it fails to do so within the time allowed, the court or the competent administrative authority shall order it to be wound up.

2. When an SCE no longer complies with the requirement laid down in Article 6, the Member State in which the SCE's registered office is situated shall take appropriate measures to oblige the SCE to regularise its situation within a specified period either:
– by re-establishing its head office in the Member State in which its registered office is situated, or
– by transferring the registered office by means of the procedure laid down in Article 7.

3. The Member State in which the SCE's registered office is situated shall put in place the measures necessary to ensure that an SCE which fails to regularise its position in accordance with paragraph 2 is liquidated.

4. The Member State in which the SCE's registered office is situated shall seek judicial or other appropriate remedy with regard to any established infringement of Article 6. That remedy shall have suspensory effect on the procedures laid down in paragraphs 2 and 3.

5. Where it is established on the initiative of either the authorities or any interested party that an SCE has its head office within the territory of a Member State in breach of Article 6, the authorities of that Member State shall immediately inform the Member State in which the SCE's registered office is situated.

Article 74
Publication of winding-up

Without prejudice to provisions of national law requiring additional publication, the initiation and termination of winding-up including voluntary winding-up, liquidation, insolvency or suspension of payment procedures and any decision to continue operating shall be publicised in accordance with Article 12.

Article 75
Distribution

Net assets shall be distributed in accordance with the principle of disinterested distribution, or, where permitted by the law of the Member State in which the SCE has its registered office, in accordance with an alternative arrangement set out in the statutes of the SCE. For the purposes of this Article, net assets shall comprise residual assets after payment of all amounts due to creditors and reimbursement of members' capital contributions.

Article 76
Conversion into a cooperative

1. An SCE may be converted into a cooperative governed by the law of the Member State in which its registered office is situated. No decision on conversion may be taken before two years have elapsed since its registration or before the first two sets of annual accounts have been approved.

2. The conversion of an SCE into a cooperative shall not result in winding-up or in the creation of a new legal person.

3. The management or administrative organ of the SCE shall draw up draft terms of conversion and a report explaining and justifying the legal and economic aspects as well as the employment effects of the conversion and indicating the implications of the adoption of the cooperative form for members and holders of shares referred to in Article 14 and for employees.

4. The draft terms of conversion shall be made public in the manner laid down in each Member State's law at least one month before the general meeting called to decide on conversion.

5. Before the general meeting referred to in paragraph 6, one or more independent experts appointed or approved, in accordance with the national provisions, by a judicial or administrative authority in the Member State to which the SCE being converted into a cooperative is subject, shall certify that the latter has assets at least equivalent to its capital.

6. The general meeting of the SCE shall approve the draft terms of conversion together with the statutes of the cooperative. The decision of the general meeting shall be passed as laid down in the provisions of national law.

Chapter VIII
Additional and Transitional Provisions

Article 77
Economic and monetary union

1. If and so long as the third phase of EMU does not apply to it, each Member State may make SCEs with registered offices within its territory subject to the same provisions as apply to cooperatives or public limited-liability companies covered by its legislation as regards the expression of their capital. An SCE may, in any case, express its capital in euro as well. In that event the national currency/euro conversion rate shall be that for the last day of the month preceding that of the formation of the SCE.

2. If and so long as the third phase of EMU does not apply to the Member State in which an SCE has its registered office, the SCE may, however, prepare and publish its annual and, where appropriate, consolidated accounts in euro. The Member State may require that the SCE's annual and, where appropriate, consolidated accounts be prepared and published in the national currency under the same conditions as those laid down for cooperatives and public limited-liability companies governed by the law of that Member State. This shall not prejudge the additional possibility for an SCE of publishing its annual and, where appropriate, consolidated accounts in euro in accordance with Council Directive 90/604/EEC of 8 November 1990 amending Directive 78/660/EEC on annual accounts and Directive 83/349/EEC on consolidated accounts as

concerns the exemptions for small and medium-sized companies and the publication of accounts in ecu.[21]

Chapter IX
Final Provisions

Article 78
National implementing rules

1. Member States shall make such provision as is appropriate to ensure the effective application of this Regulation.

2. Each Member State shall designate the competent authorities within the meaning of Articles 7, 21, 29, 30, 54 and 73. It shall inform the Commission and the other Member States accordingly.

Article 79
Review of the regulation

Five years at the latest after the entry into force of this Regulation, the Commission shall forward to the European Parliament and to the Council a report on the application of the Regulation and proposals for amendments, where appropriate. The report shall, in particular, analyse the appropriateness of:

(a) allowing the location of an SCE's head office and registered office in different Member States;

(b) allowing provisions in the statutes of an SCE adopted by a Member State in execution of authorisations given to the Member States by this Regulation or laws adopted to ensure the effective application of this Regulation with regard to the SCE which deviate from, or are complementary to, these laws, even when such provisions would not be authorised in the statutes of a cooperative having its registered office in the Member State;

(c) allowing provisions which enable the SCE to split into two or more national cooperatives;

(d) allowing for specific legal remedies in the case of fraud or error during the registration of an SCE established by way of merger.

Article 80
Entry into force

This Regulation shall enter into force on the third day following its publication in the *Official Journal of the European Union*.

It shall apply from 18 August 2006.

This Regulation shall be binding in its entirety and directly applicable in all Member States.

---

[21] OJ L 317, 16.11.1990, 57, reproduced supra under no. C. 11.

C. 26.

Council Directive 2003/72/EC
of 22 July 2003
supplementing the Statute for a European Cooperative Society with regard to the involvement of employees[1]

THE COUNCIL OF THE EUROPEAN UNION,

Having regard to the Treaty establishing the European Community, and in particular Article 308 thereof,

Having regard to the proposal from the Commission,[2]

Having regard to the opinion of the European Parliament,[3]

Having regard to the opinion of the European Economic and Social Committee,[4]

Whereas:

(1) In order to attain the objectives of the Treaty, Council Regulation (EC) No 1435/2003[5] establishes a Statute for a European Cooperative Society (SCE).

(2) That Regulation aims at creating a uniform legal framework within which cooperatives and other entities and natural persons from different Member States should be able to plan and carry out the reorganisation of their business in cooperative form on a Community scale.

(3) In order to promote the social objectives of the Community, special provisions have to be set, notably in the field of employee involvement, aimed at ensuring that the establishment of an SCE does not entail the disappearance or reduction of practices of employee involvement existing within the entities participating in the establishment of an SCE. This objective should be pursued through the establishment of a set of rules in this field, supplementing the provisions of Regulation (EC) No 1435/2003.

(4) Since the objectives of the proposed action, as outlined above, cannot be sufficiently achieved by the Member States, in that the object is to establish a set of rules on employee-involvement applicable to the SCE, and can therefore, by reason of the scale and impact of the proposed action, be better achieved at Community level, the Community may adopt measures, in accordance with the principle of subsidiarity as set out in Article 5 of the Treaty. In accordance with the principle of proportionality, as set out in that Article, this Directive does not go beyond what is necessary to achieve these objectives.

(5) The great diversity of rules and practices existing in the Member States as regards the manner in which employees' representatives are involved in decision-making within cooperatives makes it inadvisable to set up a single European model of employee involvement applicable to the SCE.

(6) Information and consultation procedures at transnational level should be ensured in all cases of creation of an SCE, with the necessary adaptation for SCEs formed ex novo where this is justified by their size, as measured in terms of employment.

(7) If participation rights exist within one or more entities establishing an SCE, they should in principle be preserved through their transfer to the SCE, once established, unless the parties decide otherwise.

(8) The concrete procedures of employee transnational information and consultation, as well as, if applicable, participation, to apply to

---

[1] OJ L 207, 18.8.2003, 25–36.
[2] OJ C 236, 31.8.1993, 36.
[3] OJ C 42, 15.2.1993, 75.
[4] OJ C 223, 31.8.1992, 42.
[5] OJ L 207, 18.8.2003, 1, reproduced supra under no. C. 25.

each SCE should be defined primarily by means of an agreement between the parties concerned or, in the absence thereof, through the application of a set of subsidiary rules.

(9) Member States should still have the option of not applying the standard rules relating to participation in the case of a merger, given the diversity of national systems for employee involvement. Existing systems and practices of participation where appropriate at the level of participating entities must in that case be maintained by adapting registration rules.

(10) The voting rules within the special body representing the employees for negotiation purposes, in particular when concluding agreements providing for a level of participation lower than the one existing within one or more of the participating entities, should be proportionate to the risk of disappearance or reduction of existing systems and practices of participation. That risk is greater in the case of an SCE established by way of transformation or merger than by way of creating an ex novo SCE.

(11) In the absence of an agreement subsequent to the negotiation between employees' representatives and the competent organs of the participating entities, provision should be made for certain standard rules to apply to the SCE, once it is established. These standard rules should ensure effective practices of transnational information and consultation of employees, as well as their participation in the relevant organs of the SCE if such participation existed before its establishment within the participating entities.

(12) When application of the abovementioned procedures to the entities participating in the ex novo SCE cannot be justified because of their small size as measured in terms of employment, the SCE should be subject to the national rules on the involvement of employees in force in the Member State where it establishes its registered office, or in the Member States where it has subsidiaries or establishments. This should be without prejudice to the obligation placed on an SCE already established to implement these procedures if a significant number of employees so requests.

(13) Specific provisions should apply to employee participation in general meetings, in so far as national laws so allow. The application of these provisions does not preclude the application of other forms of participation, as provided for in this Directive.

(14) Member States should ensure through appropriate provisions that, in the case of structural changes following the creation of an SCE, the arrangements for the involvement of employees can, where appropriate, be renegotiated.

(15) Provision should be made for the employees' representatives acting within the framework of this Directive to enjoy, when exercising their functions, the same protection and guarantees as those provided for employees' representatives by the legislation and/or practice of the country of employment. They should not be subject to any discrimination, including harassment, as a result of the lawful exercise of their activities and should enjoy adequate protection as regards dismissal and other sanctions.

(16) The confidentiality of sensitive information should be preserved even after the expiry of the terms of office of the employees' representatives, and provision should be made to allow the competent organ of the SCE to withhold information which would seriously harm, if subject to public disclosure, the functioning of the SCE.

(17) Where an SCE and its subsidiaries and establishments are subject to Council Directive 94/45/EC of 22 September 1994 on the establishment of a European Works Council or a procedure in Community-scale undertakings and Community-scale groups of undertakings for the purposes of informing and consulting employees,[6] the provisions of that Directive and the provisions transposing it into national legislation should not apply to it nor to its subsidiaries and establishments, unless the special negotiating body decides not to open negotiations or to terminate negotiations already opened.

---

[6] OJ L 254, 30.9.1994, 64, reproduced infra under no. E. 5. Directive as amended by Directive 97/74/EC (OJ L 10, 16.1.1998, 22), reproduced infra under no. E. 6.

(18) This Directive should not affect other existing rights regarding involvement and need not affect other existing representation structures, provided for by Community and national laws and practices.

(19) Member States should take appropriate measures in the event of failure to comply with the obligations laid down in this Directive.

(20) The Treaty has not provided the necessary powers for the Community to adopt this Directive, other than those provided for in Article 308.

(21) It is a fundamental principle and stated aim of this Directive to secure employees' acquired rights as regards involvement in company decisions. Employee rights in force before the establishment of SCEs should provide the basis for employee rights of involvement in the SCE (the 'before and after' principle). Consequently, that approach should apply not only to the initial establishment of an SCE but also to structural changes in an existing SCE and to the entities affected by structural change processes. Therefore, where the registered office of an SCE is transferred from one Member State to another, at least the same level of employee involvement rights should continue to apply. Further, if the threshold concerning employee involvement is reached or exceeded after the registration of an SCE, these rights should apply in the same manner in which they would have applied, had the threshold been reached or exceeded before registration.

(22) Member States may provide that representatives of trade unions may be members of a special negotiating body regardless of whether they are employees of an entity participating in the establishment of an SCE. Member States should in this context in particular be able to introduce this right in cases where trade union representatives have the right to be members of, and to vote in, supervisory or administrative company organs in accordance with national legislation.

(23) In several Member States, employee involvement and other areas of industrial relations are based on both national legislation and practice which in this context is understood also to cover collective agreements at various national, sectorial and/or company levels,

HAS ADOPTED THIS DIRECTIVE:

Section I
General

Article 1
Objective

1. This Directive governs the involvement of employees in the affairs of European Cooperative Societies (hereinafter referred to as SCEs), as referred to in Regulation (EC) No 1435/2003.

2. To this end, arrangements for the involvement of employees shall be established in every SCE in accordance with the negotiating procedure referred to in Articles 3 to 6 or, under the circumstances specified in Articles 7 and 8, in accordance with the Annex.

Article 2
Definitions

For the purposes of this Directive:

(a) 'SCE' means any cooperative society established in accordance with Regulation (EC) No 1435/2003;

(b) 'participating legal entities' means companies and firms within the meaning of the second paragraph of Article 48 of the Treaty, including cooperatives, as well as legal bodies formed under, and governed by, the law of a Member State, directly participating in the establishing of an SCE;

(c) 'subsidiary' of a participating legal entity or of an SCE means an undertaking over which that legal entity or SCE exercises a dominant influence defined in accordance with Article 3(2) to (7) of Directive 94/45/EC;

(d) 'concerned subsidiary or establishment' means a subsidiary or establishment of a participating legal entity which is proposed to become a subsidiary or establishment of the SCE upon its formation;

(e) 'employees' representatives' means the employees' representatives provided for by national law and/or practice;

(f) 'representative body' means the body representative of the employees set up by the agreements referred to in Article 4 or in accordance with the provisions of the Annex, with the purpose of informing and consulting the employees of an SCE and its subsidiaries and establishments situated in the Community and, where applicable, of exercising participation rights in relation to the SCE;

(g) 'special negotiating body' means the body established in accordance with Article 3 to negotiate with the competent organ of the participating legal entities regarding the establishment of arrangements for the involvement of employees within the SCE;

(h) 'involvement of employees' means any mechanism, including information, consultation and participation, through which employees' representatives may exercise an influence on decisions to be taken within an undertaking;

(i) 'information' means the informing of the body representative of the employees and/or the employees' representatives by the competent organ of the SCE on questions which concern the SCE itself and any of its subsidiaries or establishments situated in another Member State or which exceed the powers of the decision-making organs in a single Member State at a time, in a manner and with a content which allows the employees' representatives to undertake an in-depth assessment of the possible impact and, where appropriate, prepare consultations with the competent organ of the SCE;

(j) 'consultation' means the establishment of dialogue and exchange of views between the body representative of the employees and/or the employees' representatives and the competent organ of the SCE, at a time, in a manner and with a content which allows the employees' representatives, on the basis of information provided, to express an opinion on measures envisaged by the competent organ which may be taken into account in the decision-making process within the SCE;

(k) 'participation' means the influence of the body representative of the employees and/or the employees' representatives in the affairs of a legal entity by way of:
– the right to elect or appoint some of the members of the legal entity's supervisory or administrative organ, or
– the right to recommend and/or oppose the appointment of some or all of the members of the legal entity's supervisory or administrative organ.

Section II
Negotiating Procedure Applicable to SCEs Established by at Least Two Legal Entities or by Transformation

Article 3
Creation of a special negotiating body

1. Where the management or administrative organs of participating legal entities draw up a plan for the establishment of an SCE, they shall as soon as possible take the necessary steps, including providing information on the identity of the participating legal entities and subsidiaries or establishments, as well as the number of their employees, to start negotiations with the representatives of the legal entities' employees on arrangements for the involvement of employees in the SCE.

2. For this purpose, a special negotiating body representative of the employees of the participating legal entities and concerned subsidiaries or establishments shall be created in accordance with the following provisions:

(a) in electing or appointing members of the special negotiating body, it shall be ensured:
(i) that such members are elected or appointed in proportion to the number of employees employed in each Member State by the participating legal entities and concerned subsidiaries or establishments, by allocating in respect of a Member State one seat per each portion of employees employed in that Member State which equals 10%, or a fraction thereof, of the number of employees employed in all the Member States taken together;
(ii) that in the case of an SCE formed by way of merger, there are such further additional

members from each Member State as may be necessary in order to ensure that the special negotiating body includes at least one member representing each participating cooperative which is registered and has employees in that Member State and which it is proposed will cease to exist as a separate legal entity following the registration of the SCE, insofar as:
– the number of such additional members does not exceed 20% of the number of members designated by virtue of point (i); and
– the composition of the special negotiating body does not entail a double representation of the employees concerned.

If the number of such cooperatives is higher than the number of additional seats available pursuant to the first subparagraph, these additional seats shall be allocated to cooperatives in different Member States by decreasing order of the number of employees they employ.

(b) Member States shall determine the method to be used for the election or appointment of the members of the special negotiating body who are to be elected or appointed in their territories. They shall take the necessary measures to ensure that, as far as possible, such members shall include at least one member representing each participating legal entity which has employees in the Member State concerned. Such measures must not increase the overall number of members. The methods used to nominate, appoint or elect employee representatives should seek to promote gender balance.

Member States may provide that such members may include representatives of trade unions whether or not they are employees of a participating legal entity or concerned subsidiary or establishment.

Without prejudice to national legislation and/or practice laying down thresholds for the establishing of a representative body, Member States shall provide that employees in undertakings or establishments in which there are no employees' representatives through no fault of their own have the right to elect or appoint members of the special negotiating body.

3. The special negotiating body and the competent organs of the participating legal entities shall determine, by written agreement, arrangements for the involvement of employees within the SCE.

To this end, the competent organs of the participating legal entities shall inform the special negotiating body of the plan and the actual process of establishing the SCE, up to its registration.

4. Subject to paragraph 6, the special negotiating body shall take decisions by an absolute majority of its members, provided that such a majority also represents an absolute majority of the employees. Each member shall have one vote. However, should the result of the negotiations lead to a reduction of participation rights, the majority required for a decision to approve such an agreement shall be the votes of two thirds of the members of the special negotiating body representing at least two thirds of the employees, including the votes of members representing employees employed in at least two Member States,
– in the case of an SCE to be established by way of merger, if participation covers at least 25% of the overall number of employees of the participating cooperatives, or
– in the case of an SCE to be established by any other way, if participation covers at least 50% of the overall number of employees of the participating legal entities.

Reduction of participation rights means a proportion of members of the organs of the SCE within the meaning of Article 2(k), which is lower than the highest proportion existing within the participating legal entities.

5. For the purpose of the negotiations, the special negotiating body may request experts of its choice, for example representatives of appropriate Community level trade union organisations, to assist it with its work. Such experts may be present at negotiation meetings in an advisory capacity at the request of the special negotiating body, where appropriate to promote coherence and consistency at Community level. The special negotiating body may decide to inform the representatives of appropriate external organisations, including trade unions, of the start of the negotiations.

6. The special negotiating body may decide by the majority set out in the second subparagraph not to open negotiations or to terminate negotiations already opened, and to rely on the rules on information and consultation of employees in force in the Member States where the SCE has employees. Such a decision shall stop the procedure to conclude the agreement referred to in Article 4. Where such a decision has been taken, none of the provisions of the Annex shall apply.

The majority required to decide not to open or to terminate negotiations shall be the votes of two thirds of the members representing at least two thirds of the employees, including the votes of members representing employees employed in at least two Member States.

In the case of an SCE established by way of transformation, this paragraph shall not apply if there is participation in the cooperative to be transformed.

The special negotiating body shall be reconvened at the written request of at least 10% of the employees of the SCE, its subsidiaries and establishments, or their representatives, at the earliest two years after the abovementioned decision, unless the parties agree to negotiations being reopened sooner. If the special negotiating body decides to reopen negotiations with the management but no agreement is reached as a result of those negotiations, none of the provisions of the Annex shall apply.

7. Any expenses relating to the functioning of the special negotiating body and, in general, to negotiations shall be borne by the participating legal entities so as to enable the special negotiating body to carry out its task in an appropriate manner.

In compliance with this principle, Member States may lay down budgetary rules regarding the operation of the special negotiating body. They may in particular limit the funding to cover one expert only.

Article 4

Content of the agreement

1. The competent organs of the participating legal entities and the special negotiating body shall negotiate in a spirit of cooperation with a view to reaching an agreement on arrangements for the involvement of the employees within the SCE.

2. Without prejudice to the autonomy of the parties, and subject to paragraph 4, the agreement referred to in paragraph 1 between the competent organs of the participating legal entities and the special negotiating body shall specify:

(a) the scope of the agreement;

(b) the composition, number of members and allocation of seats on the representative body which will be the discussion partner of the competent organ of the SCE in connection with arrangements for the information and consultation of the employees of the SCE and its subsidiaries and establishments;

(c) the functions and the procedure for the information and consultation of the representative body;

(d) the frequency of meetings of the representative body;

(e) the financial and material resources to be allocated to the representative body;

(f) if, during negotiations, the parties decide to establish one or more information and consultation procedures instead of a representative body, the arrangements for implementing those procedures;

(g) if, during negotiations, the parties decide to establish arrangements for participation, the substance of those arrangements including (if applicable) the number of members in the SCE's administrative or supervisory body which the employees will be entitled to elect, appoint, recommend or oppose, the procedures as to how these members may be elected, appointed, recommended or opposed by the employees, and their rights;

(h) the date of entry into force of the agreement and its duration, cases where the agreement should be renegotiated and the procedure for its renegotiation, including, where appropriate, in the event of structural changes in the SCE and its subsidiaries and establishments which occur after the creation of the SCE.

3. The agreement shall not, unless provision is made otherwise therein, be subject to the standard rules referred to in the Annex.

4. Without prejudice to Article 15(3)(a), in the case of an SCE established by means of transformation, the agreement shall provide for at least the same level of all elements of employee involvement as the ones existing within the cooperative to be transformed into an SCE.

5. The agreement may specify the arrangements for the entitlement of employees to participate in the general meetings or in the section or sectorial meetings in accordance with Article 9 of this Directive and Article 59(4) of Regulation (EC) No 1435/2003.

Article 5
Duration of negotiations

1. Negotiations shall commence as soon as the special negotiating body is established and may continue for six months thereafter.

2. The parties may decide, by joint agreement, to extend negotiations beyond the period referred to in paragraph 1, up to a total of one year from the establishment of the special negotiating body.

Article 6
Legislation applicable to the negotiation procedure

Except where otherwise provided in this Directive, the legislation applicable to the negotiation procedure provided for in Articles 3, 4 and 5 shall be the legislation of the Member State in which the registered office of the SCE is to be situated.

Article 7
Standard rules

1. In order to achieve the objective described in Article 1, Member States shall lay down standard rules on employee involvement which must satisfy the provisions set out in the Annex.

The standard rules as laid down by the legislation of the Member State in which the registered office of the SCE is to be situated shall apply from the date of the registration of the SCE where either:

(a) the parties so agree; or

(b) by the deadline laid down in Article 5, no agreement has been concluded, and:
– the competent organ of each of the participating legal entities decides to accept the application of the standard rules in relation to the SCE and so to continue with its registration of the SCE, and
– the special negotiating body has not taken the decision provided in Article 3(6).

2. Moreover, the standard rules fixed by the national legislation of the Member State of registration in accordance with part 3 of the Annex shall apply only:

(a) in the case of an SCE established by transformation, if the rules of a Member State relating to employee participation in the administrative or supervisory body applied to a cooperative transformed into an SCE;

(b) in the case of an SCE established by merger:
– if, before registration of the SCE, one or more forms of participation applied in one or more of the participating cooperatives covering at least 25% of the total number of employees employed by them, or
– if, before registration of the SCE, one or more forms of participation applied in one or more of the participating cooperatives covering less than 25% of the total number of employees employed by them and if the special negotiating body so decides;

(c) in the case of an SCE established by any other way;
– if, before registration of the SCE, one or more forms of participation applied in one or more of the participating legal entities covering at least 50% of the total number of employees employed by them; or
– if, before registration of the SCE, one or more forms of participation applied in one or more of the participating legal entities covering less than 50% of the total number of employees employed by them and if the special negotiating body so decides.

If there was more than one form of participation within the various participating legal entities, the special negotiating body shall decide which of those forms must be established in the SCE.

Member States may fix the rules which are applicable in the absence of any decision on the matter for an SCE registered in their territory. The special negotiating body shall inform the competent organs of the participating legal entities of any decisions taken pursuant to this paragraph.

3. Member States may lay down that the standard rules referred to in Part 3 of the Annex shall not apply in the case provided for in paragraph 2(b).

3. If, after the registration of an SCE referred to in paragraph 2, at least one third of the total number of employees of the SCE and its subsidiaries and establishments in at least two different Member States so requests, or if the total number of employees reaches or exceeds 50 employees in at least two Member States, the provisions of Articles 3 to 7 shall be applied, mutatis mutandis. In this case, the words 'participating legal entities' and 'concerned subsidiaries or establishments' shall be replaced by the words 'SCE' and 'subsidiaries or establishments of the SCE' respectively.

Section III

Rules Applicable to SCEs Established Exclusively by Natural Persons or by a Single Legal Entity and Natural Persons

Article 8

1. In the case of an SCE established exclusively by natural persons or by a single legal entity and natural persons, which together employ at least 50 employees in at least two Member States, the provisions of Articles 3 to 7 shall apply.

2. In the case of an SCE established exclusively by natural persons or by a single legal entity and natural persons, which together employ fewer than 50 employees, or employ 50 or more employees in only one Member State, employee involvement shall be governed by the following:
– in the SCE itself, the provisions of the Member State of the SCE's registered office, which are applicable to other entities of the same type, shall apply,
– in its subsidiaries and establishments, the provisions of the Member State where they are situated, and which are applicable to other entities of the same type, shall apply.

In the case of transfer from one Member State to another of the registered office of an SCE governed by participation, at least the same level of employee participation rights shall continue to apply.

Section IV

Participation in the General Meeting or Section or Sectorial Meeting

Article 9

Subject to the limits laid down in Article 59(4) of Regulation (EC) No 1435/2003, the employees of the SCE and/or their representatives will be entitled to participate in the general meeting or, if it exists, in the section or sectorial meeting, with the right to vote, in the following circumstances:

1. when the parties so decide in the agreement referred to in Article 4, or

2. when a cooperative governed by such a system transforms itself into an SCE, or

3. when, in the case of an SCE established by means other than transformation, a participating cooperative was governed by such a system and:
(i) the parties cannot reach agreement, as referred to in Article 4, by the deadline laid down in Article 5; and
(ii) Article 7(1)(b) and Part 3 of the Annex apply; and
(iii) the participating cooperative governed by such a system has the highest proportion of participation, within the meaning of Article 2(k), in force in the participating cooperatives concerned before registration of the SCE.

Section V
Miscellaneous Provisions

Article 10
Reservation and confidentiality

1. Member States shall provide that members of the special negotiating body or the representative body, and experts who assist them, are not authorised to reveal any information which has been given to them in confidence.

The same shall apply to employees' representatives in the context of an information and consultation procedure.

This obligation shall continue to apply, wherever the persons referred to may be, even after the expiry of their terms of office.

2. Each Member State shall provide, in specific cases and under the conditions and limits laid down by national legislation, that the supervisory or administrative organ of an SCE or of a participating legal entity established in its territory is not obliged to transmit information where its nature is such that, according to objective criteria, to do so would seriously harm the functioning of the SCE (or, as the case may be, a participating legal entity) or its subsidiaries and establishments or would be prejudicial to them.

A Member State may make such dispensation subject to prior administrative or judicial authorisation.

3. Each Member State may lay down particular provisions for SCEs in its territory which pursue directly and essentially the aim of ideological guidance with respect to information and the expression of opinions, on condition that, on the date of adoption of this Directive, such provisions already exist in the national legislation.

4. In applying paragraphs 1, 2 and 3, Member States shall make provision for administrative or judicial appeal procedures which the employees' representatives may initiate when the supervisory or administrative organ of an SCE or of a participating legal entity demands confidentiality or does not give information.

Such procedures may include arrangements designed to protect the confidentiality of the information in question.

Article 11
Operation of the representative body and procedure for the information and consultation of employees

The competent organ of the SCE and the representative body shall work together in a spirit of cooperation with due regard for their reciprocal rights and obligations.

The same shall apply to cooperation between the supervisory or administrative organ of the SCE and the employees' representatives in conjunction with a procedure for the information and consultation of employees.

Article 12
Protection of employees' representatives

The members of the special negotiating body, the members of the representative body, any employees' representatives exercising functions under the information and consultation procedure and any employees' representatives in the supervisory or administrative organ of an SCE who are employees of the SCE, its subsidiaries or establishments or of a participating legal entity shall, in the exercise of their functions, enjoy the same protection and guarantees provided for employees' representatives by the national legislation and/or practice in force in their country of employment.

This shall apply in particular to attendance at meetings of the special negotiating body or representative body, any other meeting under the agreement referred to in Article 4(2)(f) or any meeting of the administrative or supervisory organ, and to the payment of wages for members employed by a participating legal entity or the SCE or its subsidiaries or establishments during a period of absence necessary for the performance of their duties.

Article 13
Misuse of procedures

Member States shall take appropriate measures in conformity with Community law with a view to preventing the misuse of an SCE for the purpose of depriving employees of rights to employee involvement or withholding such rights.

Article 14
Compliance with this Directive

1. Each Member State shall ensure that the management of establishments of an SCE and the supervisory or administrative organs of subsidiaries and of participating legal entities which are situated within its territory and the employees' representatives or, as the case may be, the employees themselves abide by the obligations laid down by this Directive, regardless of whether or not the SCE has its registered office within its territory.

2. Member States shall provide for appropriate measures in the event of failure to comply with this Directive; in particular they shall ensure that administrative or legal procedures are available to enable the obligations deriving from this Directive to be enforced.

Article 15
Link between this Directive and other provisions

1. Where an SCE is a Community-scale undertaking or a controlling undertaking of a Community-scale group of undertakings within the meaning of Directive 94/45/EC or of Council Directive 97/74/EC of 15 December 1997 extending the said Directive to the United Kingdom,[7] the provisions of these Directives and the provisions transposing them into national legislation shall not apply to them or to their subsidiaries.

However, where the special negotiating body decides in accordance with Article 3(6) not to open negotiations or to terminate negotiations already opened, Directive 94/45/EC or Directive 97/74/EC and the provisions transposing them into national legislation shall apply.

2. Provisions on the participation of employees in company bodies provided for by national legislation and/or practice, other than those implementing this Directive, shall not apply to the SCEs to which Articles 3 to 7 apply.

3. This Directive shall not prejudice:

(a) the existing rights to involvement of employees provided for by national legislation and/or practice in the Member States as enjoyed by employees of the SCE and its subsidiaries and establishments, other than participation in the bodies of the SCE;

(b) the provisions on participation in the bodies laid down by national legislation and/or practice applicable to the subsidiaries of the SCE or to SCEs to which Articles 3 to 7 do not apply.

4. In order to preserve the rights referred to in paragraph 3, Member States may take the necessary measures to guarantee that the structures of employee representation in participating legal entities which will cease to exist as separate legal entities are maintained after the registration of the SCE.

Article 16
Final provisions

1. Member States shall adopt the laws, regulations and administrative provisions necessary to comply with this Directive no later than 18 August 2006, or shall ensure by that date at the latest that management and labour introduce the required provisions by way of agreement, the Member States being obliged to take all necessary steps enabling them at all times to guarantee the results imposed by this Directive. They shall forthwith inform the Commission thereof.

2. When Member States adopt these measures, they shall contain a reference to this Directive or shall be accompanied by such reference on the occasion of their official publication.

---

[7] OJ L 10, 16.1.1998, 22, reproduced infra under no. E. 6.

Article 17
Review by the Commission

Not later than 18 August 2009, the Commission shall, in consultation with the Member States and with management and labour at Community level, review the application of applying this Directive, with a view to proposing suitable amendments to the Council where necessary.

The methods of making such reference shall be laid down by the Member States.

Article 18
Entry into force

This Directive shall enter into force on the date of its publication in the Official Journal of the European Union.

Article 19
Addressees

This Directive is addressed to the Member States.

Annex

Standard Rules

(referred to in Articles 7 and 8)

Part 1: Composition of the body representative of the employees

In order to achieve the objective described in Article 1, and in the cases referred to in Article 7, a representative body shall be set up in accordance with the following rules:

(a) The representative body shall be composed of employees of the SCE and its subsidiaries and establishments elected or appointed from their number by the employees' representatives or, in the absence thereof, by the entire body of employees.

(b) The election or appointment of members of the representative body shall be carried out in accordance with national legislation and/or practice.

Member States shall lay down rules to ensure that the number of members of, and allocation of seats on, the representative body shall be adapted to take account of changes occurring within the SCE and its subsidiaries and establishments. The methods used to nominate, appoint or elect employee representatives should seek to promote gender balance.

(c) Where its size so warrants, the representative body shall elect a select committee from among its members, comprising at most three members.

(d) The representative body shall adopt its rules of procedure.

(e) The members of the representative body are elected or appointed in proportion to the number of employees employed in each Member State by the SCE and its subsidiaries or establishments, by allocating in respect of a Member State one seat per each portion of employees employed in that Member State which equals 10%, or a fraction thereof, of the number of employees employed by them in all the Member States taken together.

(f) The competent organ of the SCE shall be informed of the composition of the representative body.

(g) Not later than four years after its establishment, the representative body shall examine whether to open negotiations for the conclusion of the agreement referred to in Articles 4 and 7 or to continue to apply the standard rules adopted in accordance with this Annex.

Article 3(4) to (7) and Articles 4, 5 and 6 shall apply, mutatis mutandis, if a decision has been taken to negotiate an agreement according to Article 4, in which case the term 'special negotiating body' shall be replaced by 'representative body'. Where, by the deadline by which the negotiations come to an end, no agreement has been concluded, the arrangements initially adopted in accordance with the standard rules shall continue to apply.

Part 2: Standard rules for information and consultation

The competence and powers of the representative body set up in an SCE shall be governed by the following rules:

(a) The competence of the representative body shall be limited to questions which concern the SCE itself and any of its subsidiaries or establishments situated in another Member State or which exceed the powers of the decision-making organs in a single Member State.

(b) Without prejudice to meetings held pursuant to paragraph (c), the representative body shall have the right to be informed and consulted and, for that purpose, to meet with the competent organ of the SCE at least once a year, on the basis of regular reports drawn up by the competent organ, on the progress of the business of the SCE and its prospects. The local managements shall be informed accordingly.

The competent organ of the SCE shall provide the representative body with the agenda for meetings of the administrative, or, where appropriate, the management and supervisory organ, and with copies of all documents submitted to the general meeting of its members.

The meeting shall relate in particular to the structure, economic and financial situation, the probable development of the business and of production and sales, initiatives with regard to corporate social responsibility, the situation and probable trend of employment, investments, and substantial changes concerning organisation, the introduction of new working methods or production processes, transfers of production, mergers, cut-backs or closures of undertakings, establishments or important parts thereof, and collective redundancies.

(c) Where there are exceptional circumstances affecting the employees' interests to a considerable extent, particularly in the event of relocations, transfers, the closure of establishments or undertakings or collective redundancies, the representative body shall have the right to be informed. The representative body or, where it so decides, in particular for reasons of urgency, the select committee, shall have the right to meet at its request, the competent organ of the SCE or any more appropriate level of management within the SCE having its own powers of decision, so as to be informed and consulted on measures significantly affecting employees' interests.

Where the competent organ decides not to act in accordance with the opinion expressed by the representative body, this body shall have the right to a further meeting with the competent organ of the SCE with a view to seeking agreement.

In the case of a meeting organised with the select committee, those members of the representative body who represent employees who are directly concerned by the measures in question shall also have the right to participate.

The meetings referred to above shall not affect the prerogatives of the competent organ.

(d) Member States may lay down rules on the chairing of information and consultation meetings.

Before any meeting with the competent organ of the SCE, the representative body or the select committee, where necessary enlarged in accordance with the third subparagraph of paragraph (c), shall be entitled to meet without the representatives of the competent organ being present.

(e) Without prejudice to Article 10, the members of the representative body shall inform the representatives of the employees of the SCE and of its subsidiaries and establishments of the content and outcome of the information and consultation procedures.

(f) The representative body or the select committee may be assisted by experts of its choice.

(g) In so far as this is necessary for the fulfilment of their tasks, the members of the representative body shall be entitled to time off for training without loss of wages.

(h) The costs of the representative body shall be borne by the SCE, which shall provide the body's members with the financial and material resources needed to enable them to perform their duties in an appropriate manner.

In particular, the SCE shall, unless otherwise agreed, bear the cost of organising meetings and providing interpretation facilities and the accommodation and travelling expenses of members of the representative body and the select committee.

In compliance with these principles, the Member States may lay down budgetary rules regarding the operation of the representative body. They may in particular limit funding to cover one expert only.

Part 3: Standard rules for participation

Employee participation in an SCE shall be governed by the following provisions:

(a) In the case of an SCE established by transformation, if the rules of a Member State relating to employee participation in the administrative or supervisory body applied before registration, all aspects of employee participation shall continue to apply to the SCE. Paragraph (b) shall apply mutatis mutandis to that end.

(b) In other cases where an SCE is established, the employees of the SCE, its subsidiaries and establishments and/or their representative body shall have the right to elect, appoint, recommend or oppose the appointment of a number of members of the administrative or supervisory body of the SCE equal to the highest proportion in force in the participating companies concerned before registration of the SCE.

(c) If none of the participating legal entities was governed by participation rules before registration of the SCE, the latter shall not be required to establish provisions for employee participation.

(d) The representative body shall decide on the allocation of seats within the administrative or supervisory body among the members representing the employees from the various Member States or on the way in which the SCE's employees may recommend or oppose the appointment of the members of these bodies according to the proportion of the SCE's employees in each Member State. If the employees of one or more Member States are not covered by this proportional criterion, the representative body shall appoint a member from one of those Member States, in particular the Member State of the SCE's registered office where that is appropriate. Each Member State may determine the allocation of the seats it is given within the administrative or supervisory body.

(e) Every member of the administrative body or, where appropriate, the supervisory body of the SCE who has been elected, appointed or recommended by the representative body or, depending on the circumstances, by the employees shall be a full member with the same rights and obligations as the members representing the members of the cooperative, including the right to vote.

C. 27.

Commission Recommendation 2004/913/EC
of 14 December 2004
fostering an appropriate regime for the remuneration of directors of listed companies[1]

(Text with EEA relevance)

THE COMMISSION OF THE EUROPEAN COMMUNITIES,

Having regard to the Treaty establishing the European Community, and in particular the second indent of Article 211 thereof,

Whereas:

(1) In May 2003, the Commission adopted a Communication on 'Modernising Company Law and enhancing Corporate Governance in the European Union—A plan to move forward'.[2] Among a range of proposals to strengthen shareholders' rights and modernise the board of directors, it provides for an initiative aimed at encouraging an appropriate regulatory regime for directors' remuneration in the Member States.

(2) The form, structure and level of directors' remuneration are matters falling within the competence of companies and their shareholders. This should facilitate the recruitment and retention of directors having the qualities required to run a company. However, remuneration is one of the key areas where executive directors may have a conflict of interest and where due account should be taken of the interests of shareholders. Remuneration systems should therefore be subjected to appropriate governance controls, based on adequate information rights. In this respect, it is important to respect fully the diversity of corporate governance systems within the Community, which reflect different Member States' views about the roles of corporations and of bodies responsible for the determination of policy on the remuneration of directors, and the remuneration of individual directors.

(3) The disclosure of accurate and timely information by the issuers of securities builds sustained investor confidence and constitutes an important tool for promoting sound corporate governance throughout the Community. To that end, it is important that listed companies display appropriate transparency in dealings with investors, so as to enable them to express their views.

(4) When implementing this Recommendation, Member States should consider the specificities of collective investment undertakings of the corporate type and should prevent the various types of collective investment undertaking from being subjected, unnecessarily, to unequal treatment. As regards collective investment undertakings as defined in Council Directive 85/611/EEC of 20 December 1985 on the coordination of laws, regulations and administrative provisions relating to undertakings for collective investment in transferable securities (UCITS),[3] that Directive already provides for a set of specific governance mechanisms. However, in order to prevent the unnecessarily unequal treatment of those collective investment undertakings of the corporate type not subject to harmonisation at Community level, Member States should take into account whether and to what extent these non-harmonised collective investment undertakings are subject to equivalent governance mechanisms.

---

[1] OJ L 385, 29.12.2004, 55–59.
[2] COM(2003) 284 final.
[3] OJ L 375, 31.12.1985, 3, reproduced infra under no. S. 6. Directive as last amended by Directive 2004/39/EC of the European Parliament and of the Council (OJ L 145, 30.4.2004, 1), reproduced infra under no. S. 29.

(5) Shareholders should be provided with a clear and comprehensive overview of the company's remuneration policy. Such disclosure would enable shareholders to assess a company's approach to remuneration and strengthen a company's accountability to shareholders. It should include elements related to compensation. This should not, however, oblige the company to disclose any information of a commercially sensitive nature which could be detrimental to the company's strategic position.

(6) Adequate transparency should also be ensured in the policy regarding directors' contracts. This should include the disclosure of information on issues such as notice periods and termination payments under such contracts which are directly linked to directors' remuneration.

(7) In order to give shareholders an effective chance to express their views and an opportunity to debate the remuneration policy on the basis of a comprehensive disclosure, without having to initiate the process of tabling a shareholders' resolution, the remuneration policy should be an explicit item on the agenda of the annual general meeting.

(8) In order to increase accountability, the remuneration policy should be submitted to the annual general meeting for a vote. The vote at that meeting could be advisory, so that the rights of the relevant bodies responsible for directors' remuneration would not be altered. An advisory vote would not entail any obligation either to amend directors' contractual entitlements or to amend the remuneration policy.

(9) Shareholders should also be provided with the information on the basis of which they can hold individual directors accountable for the remuneration they earn or have earned. Disclosure of the remuneration of individual directors of the company, executive and non-executive or supervisory directors, in the preceding financial year is therefore important to help them appreciate the remuneration in the light of the overall performance of the company.

(10) Variable remuneration schemes under which directors are remunerated in shares, share options or any other right to acquire shares or to be remunerated on the basis of share price movements, and any substantial change in such schemes, should be subject to the prior approval of the annual general meeting. The approval should relate to the scheme of remuneration and the rules applied to establish the individual remuneration under the scheme but not to the individual remuneration of directors under the scheme.

(11) In view of the importance attached to the question of remuneration of directors it is appropriate to monitor the implementation of this Recommendation and in case of insufficient implementation to consider further measures,

HEREBY RECOMMENDS:

SECTION I

SCOPE AND DEFINITIONS

1. Scope

1.1. Member States should take all appropriate measures to ensure that listed companies having their registered office in their territory have regard to this Recommendation. They should however duly consider the specific features of collective investment undertakings of the corporate type under the scope of Directive 85/611/EEC. Member States should also consider the specific features of collective investment undertakings of the corporate type which are not subject to that Directive and whose sole purpose is the investment of money raised from investors in a diversified range of assets and which do not seek to take legal or managerial control over any of the issuers of its underlying investments.

1.2. Member States should also take all appropriate measures to ensure that listed companies which are not incorporated in one of the Member States but which have their primary listing on a regulated market established in their territory have regard to the provisions of this Recommendation.

1.3. Member States should ensure that this Recommendation applies to the remuneration of the chief executive officers in circumstances where they are not members of the administrative, managerial and supervisory bodies of a listed company.

2. Definitions for the purposes of this recommendation

2.1. 'Director', means any member of the administrative, managerial or supervisory bodies of a listed company.

2.2. 'Listed company', means a company whose securities are admitted to trading on a regulated market within the meaning of Directive 2004/39/EC in one or more Member States.

Section II
Remuneration Policy

3. Disclosure of the policy on directors' remuneration

3.1. Each listed company should disclose a statement of the remuneration policy of the company (the remuneration statement). It should be part of an independent remuneration report and/or be included in the annual accounts and annual report or in the notes to the annual accounts of the company. The remuneration statement should also be posted on the listed company's website.

3.2. The remuneration statement should mainly focus on the company's policy on directors' remuneration for the following financial year and, if appropriate, the subsequent years. It should also contain an overview of the manner in which the remuneration policy has been implemented in the previous financial year. Particular emphasis should be laid on any significant changes in the listed company's remuneration policy as compared to the previous financial year.

3.3. The remuneration statement should set out at least the following information:

(a) explanation of the relative importance of the variable and non-variable components of directors' remuneration;

(b) sufficient information on the performance criteria on which any entitlement to share options, shares or variable components of remuneration is based;

(c) sufficient information on the linkage between remuneration and performance;

(d) the main parameters and rationale for any annual bonus scheme and any other non-cash benefits;

(e) a description of the main characteristics of supplementary pension or early retirement schemes for directors.

The disclosure of that information in the remuneration statement should nevertheless not entail the disclosure of information of a commercially sensitive nature.

3.4. The remuneration statement should also summarise and explain the listed company's policy with regard to the terms of the contracts of executive directors. This should include, *inter alia*, information on the duration of contracts with executive directors, the applicable notice periods and details of provisions for termination payments and other payments linked to early termination under contracts for executive directors.

3.5. Information concerning the preparatory and decision-making process used for determining the listed company's remuneration policy for directors should also be disclosed. This should include information, if applicable, about the mandate and composition of a remuneration committee, the names of external consultants whose services have been used in determination of the remuneration policy, and the role of the shareholders' annual general meeting

4. Shareholders' vote

4.1. Without prejudice to the role and organisation of the relevant bodies responsible for setting directors' remunerations, the remuneration policy and any significant change to the remuneration policy should be an explicit item on the agenda of the annual general meeting.

4.2. Without prejudice to the role and organisation of the relevant bodies responsible for setting directors' remunerations, the remuneration statement should be submitted to the annual general meeting of shareholders for a vote. The vote may be either mandatory or advisory.

Member States may, however, provide that such a vote will be held only if shareholders representing at least 25% of the total number of votes held by shareholders present or represented at the annual general meeting request it. This should nevertheless be without prejudice to the right for shareholders to table a resolution in accordance with national provisions.

4.3. The listed company should inform shareholders entitled to receive notice of the meeting of the intention to table a resolution approving the remuneration statement at the annual general meeting.

Section III
Remuneration of Individual Directors

5. Disclosure of the remuneration of individual directors

5.1. The total remuneration and other benefits granted to individual directors over the relevant financial year should be disclosed in detail in the annual accounts or in the notes to the annual accounts or, where applicable, in the remuneration report.

5.2. The annual accounts or the notes to the annual accounts or, where applicable, the remuneration report should show at least the information listed in points 5.3. to 5.6. for each person who has served as a director of the listed company at any time during the relevant financial year.

5.3. As regards the remuneration and/or emoluments, the following information should be presented:

(a) the total amount of salary paid or due to the director for the services performed under the relevant financial year, including where appropriate the attendance fees fixed by the annual general shareholders meeting;

(b) the remuneration and advantages received from any undertaking belonging to the same group;

(c) remuneration paid in the form of profit sharing and/or bonus payments and the reasons why such bonus payments and/or profit sharing were granted;

(d) where such payment is legally allowed, any significant additional remuneration paid to directors for special services outside the scope of the usual functions of a director;

(e) the compensation paid to or receivable by each former executive director in connection with the termination of his activities during that financial year;

(f) total estimated value of non-cash benefits considered as remuneration, other than the items covered in points (a) to (e).

5.4. As regards shares and/or rights to acquire share options and/or all other share-incentive schemes, the following information should be presented:

(a) the number of share options offered or shares granted by the company during the relevant financial year and their conditions of application;

(b) the number of share options exercised during the relevant financial year and, for each of them, the number of shares involved and the exercise price or the value of the interest in the share incentive scheme at the end of the financial year;

(c) the number of share options unexercised at the end of the financial year; their exercise price, the exercise date and the main conditions for the exercise of the rights;

(d) any change in the terms and conditions of existing share options occurring during the financial year.

5.5. As regards supplementary pension schemes, the following information should be presented:

(a) when the pension scheme is a defined-benefit scheme, changes in the director's accrued benefits under that scheme during the relevant financial year;

(b) when the scheme is a defined-contribution scheme, details of the contributions paid or payable by the listed company in respect of that director during the relevant financial year.

5.6. If it is permissible under national law or under the Articles of Association of the listed company to make such payments, amounts should be shown which the company, or any subsidiary or company included in the company's consolidated annual accounts, has paid by way of loans, advance payments and guarantees to each person who has served as a director at any time during the relevant financial year, including the amount outstanding and the interest rate.

Section IV
Share-Based Remuneration

6. Shareholders' approval

6.1. Schemes under which directors are remunerated in shares, share options or any other right to acquire shares or to be remunerated on the basis of share price movements should be subject to the prior approval of shareholders by way of a resolution at the annual general meeting prior to their adoption. The approval should relate to the scheme in itself and not to the grant of such share-based benefits under that scheme to individual directors.

6.2. Approval by the annual general meeting should be obtained for the following:

(a) grant of share-based schemes, including share options, to directors;

(b) the determination of their maximum number and the main conditions of the granting process;

(c) the term within which options can be exercised;

(d) the conditions for any subsequent change in the exercise price of the options, if this is appropriate and legally permissible;

(e) any other long term incentive schemes for which directors are eligible and which is not offered under similar terms to all other employees.

6.3. The annual general meeting should also set the deadline within which the body responsible for directors' remuneration may award these types of compensation to individual directors.

6.4. Any substantial change in the terms and conditions of the schemes should also be subject to the approval of shareholders by way of a resolution at the annual general meeting prior to their adoption. In those cases, shareholders should be informed of the full terms of the proposed changes and should be given an explanation of the effect of the proposed changes.

6.5. If such arrangement is permissible under national law or under the Articles of Association of the listed company, any discounted option arrangement under which any rights are granted to subscribe to shares at a price lower than the market value of the share on the date when the price is determined, or the average of the market values over a number of days preceding the date when the exercise price is determined, should also receive the approval of shareholders.

6.6. Points 6.1. to 6.4. should not apply to schemes in which participation is offered on similar terms to employees of the listed company or any of its subsidiary undertaking whose employees are eligible to participate in the scheme and which has been approved by the annual general meeting.

Section V
Information and Final Provisions

7. Information

7.1. Prior to the annual general meeting where a draft resolution is tabled in accordance with point 6.1. and in accordance with national law and/or the Articles of Association of the listed company, an information notice concerning the resolution should be made available to shareholders.

The notice should contain the full text of the share-based remuneration schemes or a description of their principal terms, and the names of the participants in the schemes. It should also set out the relationship of the schemes with the overall directors' remuneration policy.

The draft resolution should clearly refer either to the scheme itself or to the summary of its principal terms.

7.2. Information should also be made available to shareholders about how the company intends to provide for the shares needed to meet its obligations under incentive schemes. In particular it should be clearly stated whether the company intends to purchase the necessary shares in the market, whether it holds them in treasury, or whether it will issue new shares.

7.3. This information should also provide an overview of the costs of the scheme to the company in view of the intended application.

7.4. Such information should be posted on the listed company's website.

8. Final Provisions

8.1. Member States are invited to take the necessary measures to promote the application of this Recommendation by 30 June 2006 and are invited to notify the Commission of measures taken in accordance with this Recommendation in order to allow the Commission to monitor closely the situation and, on this basis, to assess the need for further measures.

8.2. This Recommendation is addressed to the Member States.

C. 28.

Commission Recommendation 2005/162/EC of 15 February 2005 on the role of non-executive or supervisory directors of listed companies and on the committees of the (supervisory) board[1]

(Text with EEA relevance)

THE COMMISSION OF THE EUROPEAN COMMUNITIES,

Having regard to the Treaty establishing the European Community, and in particular the second indent of Article 211 thereof,

Whereas:

(1) In a Communication adopted on 21 May 2003, the Commission presented its Action Plan 'Modernising Company Law and Enhancing Corporate Governance in the European Union— A Plan to Move Forward'.[2] The main objectives of the Action Plan are to strengthen shareholders' rights and protection for employees, creditors and the other parties with which companies deal, while adapting company law and corporate governance rules appropriately for different categories of company, and to foster the efficiency and competitiveness of businesses, with special attention to some specific cross-border issues.

(2) In its Resolution of 21 April 2004, the European Parliament welcomed the Action Plan and expressed strong support for most of the initiatives announced. The European Parliament called on the Commission to propose rules to eliminate and prevent conflicts of interest, and stressed in particular the need for listed companies to have an audit committee, whose functions should include overseeing the external auditor's independence, objectivity and effectiveness.

(3) Non-executive or supervisory directors are recruited by companies for a variety of purposes. Of particular importance is their role in overseeing executive or managing directors and dealing with situations involving conflicts of interests. It is vital to foster that role in order to restore confidence in financial markets. Member States should therefore be invited to adopt measures which would be applicable to listed companies, defined as companies whose securities are admitted to trading on a regulated market in the Community. When implementing this Recommendation, Member States should consider the specificities of collective investment undertakings of the corporate type and prevent the various types of collective investment undertaking from being subjected, unnecessarily, to unequal treatment. As regards collective investment undertakings as defined in Council Directive 85/611/EEC of 20 December 1985 on the coordination of laws, regulations and administrative provisions relating to undertakings for collective investment in transferable securities (UCITS),[3] that Directive already provides for a set of specific governance mechanisms. However, in order to prevent the unnecessarily unequal treatment of those collective investment undertakings of the corporate type not subject to harmonisation at Community level, Member States should take into account whether and to

---

[1] OJ L 52, 25.2.2005, 51–63.
[2] COM(2003) 284 final.

[3] OJ L 375, 31.12.1985, 3, reproduced infra under no. S. 6. Directive as last amended by Directive 2004/39/EC of the European Parliament and of the Council (OJ L 145, 30.4.2004, 1), reproduced infra under no. S. 29.

what extent these non-harmonised collective investment undertakings are subject to equivalent governance mechanisms.

(4) In view of the complexity of many of the issues at stake, the adoption of detailed binding rules is not necessarily the most desirable and efficient way of achieving the objectives pursued. Many corporate governance codes adopted in Member States tend to rely on disclosure to encourage compliance, based on the 'comply or explain' approach: companies are invited to disclose whether they comply with the code and to explain any material departures from it. This approach enables companies to reflect sector- and enterprise-specific requirements, and the markets to assess the explanations and justifications provided. With a view to fostering the role of non-executive or supervisory directors, it is therefore appropriate that all Member States be invited to take the steps necessary to introduce at national level a set of provisions based on the principles set out in this Recommendation, to be used by listed companies either on the basis of the 'comply or explain' approach or pursuant to legislation.

(5) If Member States decide to use the 'comply or explain' approach (whereby companies are required to explain their practices by reference to a set of designated best practice recommendations), they should be free to do so on the basis of relevant recommendations developed by market participants.

(6) Any measures adopted by Member States in line with this Recommendation should aim fundamentally at improving the corporate governance of listed companies. Since that objective is relevant to the protection of investors, actual or potential, in all companies listed in the Community, whether or not they are incorporated in one of the Member States, the measures should also cover companies incorporated in third countries but listed in the Community.

(7) The presence of independent representatives on the board, capable of challenging the decisions of management, is widely considered as a means of protecting the interests of shareholders and other stakeholders. In companies with a dispersed ownership, the primary concern is how to make managers accountable to weak shareholders. In companies with controlling shareholders, the focus is more on how to make sure that the company will be run in a way that sufficiently takes into account the interests of minority shareholders. Ensuring adequate protection for third parties is relevant in both cases. Whatever the formal board structure of a company, the management function should therefore be subject to an effective and sufficiently independent supervisory function. Independence should be understood as the absence of any material conflict of interest; in this context, proper attention should be paid namely to any threats which might arise from the fact that a representative on the board has close ties with a competitor of the company.

(8) In order to ensure that the management function will be submitted to an effective and sufficiently independent supervisory function, the (supervisory) board should comprise a sufficient number of committed non-executive or supervisory directors, who play no role in the management of the company or its group and who are independent in that they are free of any material conflict of interest. In view of the different legal systems existing in Member States, the proportion of (supervisory) board members to be made up of independent directors should not be defined precisely at Community level.

(9) The supervisory role of non-executive or supervisory directors is commonly perceived as crucial in three areas, where the potential for conflict of interest of management is particularly high, especially when such matters are not a direct responsibility for shareholders: nomination of directors, remuneration of directors, and audit. It is therefore appropriate to foster the role of non-executive or supervisory directors in these areas and to encourage the creation within the (supervisory) board of committees responsible respectively for nomination, remuneration and audit.

(10) In principle, and without prejudice to the powers of the general meeting, only the (supervisory) board as a whole has statutory decision-making authority and, as a collegiate body, is collectively accountable for the performance of

its duties. The (supervisory) board has the power to determine the number and structure of the committees which it deems to be appropriate to facilitate its own work, but these committees are in principle not to be a substitute for the (supervisory) board itself. As a general rule, therefore, the nomination, remuneration and audit committees should make recommendations aimed at preparing the decisions to be taken by the (supervisory) board. However, the (supervisory) board should not be precluded from delegating part of its decision-making powers to committees when it considers it appropriate and when this is permissible under national law, even though the (supervisory) board remains fully responsible for the decisions taken in its field of competence.

(11) Since the identification of candidates to fill unitary or dual board vacancies raises issues relevant to the selection of non-executive or supervisory directors who are to oversee management or relevant to the continuation in office of management, the nomination committee should be composed mainly of independent non-executive or supervisory directors. That would leave room on the nomination committee for non-executive or supervisory directors who do not meet the independence criteria. It would also leave room for executive/managing directors (in companies where the nomination committee is created within the unitary board and as long as executive/managing directors do not form a majority on that committee).

(12) Given the different approaches in the Member States with respect to the bodies responsible for appointing and removing directors, the role of a nomination committee created within the (supervisory) board should essentially be to make sure that, where the (supervisory) board plays a role in the appointment and removal process (either through a power to table proposals or to make decisions, as defined by national law), this role is performed in as objective and professional a way as possible. The nomination committee should therefore essentially make recommendations to the (supervisory) board with respect to the appointment and removal of directors by the body competent under national company law.

(13) In the area of remuneration, corporate governance code adopted in Member States tend to focus primarily on the remuneration of executive or managing directors, since the potential for abuse and conflicts of interest is essentially located there. Many codes also recognise that some consideration should be given at board level to the remuneration policy for senior management. Finally, the issue of stock options is granted special attention. Given the different approaches in the Member States with respect to the bodies responsible for setting the remuneration of directors, the role of a remuneration committee created within the (supervisory) board should essentially be to make sure that, where the (supervisory) board plays a role in the remuneration setting process (either through a power to table proposals or to make decisions, as defined by national law), this role is performed in as objective and professional a way as possible. The remuneration committee should therefore essentially make recommendations to the (supervisory) board with respect to those remuneration issues for decision by the body competent under national company law.

(14) Two key responsibilities of the (supervisory) board seem to ensure that the financial reports and other related information disseminated by the company present an accurate and complete picture of the company's position and to monitor the procedures established for the evaluation and management of risks. In this context, most corporate governance codes assign to the audit committee an essential role in assisting the (supervisory) board to fulfil these duties. In some Member States, such responsibilities are attributed, wholly or partly, to corporate bodies external to the (supervisory) board. It is therefore appropriate to provide that an audit committee created within the (supervisory) board should, as a general rule, make recommendations to the (supervisory) board with respect to those audit issues, and that such functions may be performed by other structures—external to the (supervisory) board—which would be equally effective.

(15) In order for non-executive or supervisory directors to play an effective role, they should have the right background and sufficient time for

the job. In addition, a sufficient number of them should meet appropriate independence criteria. Before the appointment of non-executive or supervisory directors, adequate information should be provided on these issues and that information should be updated with sufficient frequency.

(16) With respect to the qualifications of directors, most corporate governance codes insist on the need to have qualified individuals on the board, but at the same time recognise that the definition of what constitutes proper qualifications should be left to the company itself, because such qualifications will depend, *inter alia*, on its activities, size and environment and because they should be met by the board as a whole. There is nevertheless one issue which usually raises particular concern, namely the need for particular competence in the audit committee where some specific knowledge is deemed to be indispensable. The (supervisory) board should therefore determine the desired composition of the audit committee and evaluate it periodically, devoting specific attention to the experience necessary in that committee.

(17) With respect to the commitment of directors, most corporate governance codes seek to make sure that directors devote sufficient time to their duties. Some of these codes limit the number of directorships that may be held in other companies: the positions of chairman or of executive or managing director are usually recognised as more demanding than those of non-executive or supervisory director, but the precise numbers of other directorships acceptable vary widely. However, the involvement required from a director may vary widely depending on the company and its environment; in such a situation, each director should undertake to strike a proper balance between his various engagements.

(18) Generally, corporate governance codes adopted in the Member States recognise the need for a significant proportion of non-executive or supervisory directors to be independent, that is to say, free of any material conflict of interest. Independence is most often understood as the absence of close ties with management, controlling shareholders or the company itself. In the absence of any common understanding of what independence precisely entails, it is appropriate to provide a general statement describing what the general objective is. Provision should also be made to cover a (non-exhaustive) number of situations, involving the relationships or circumstances usually recognised as likely to generate a material conflict of interest, which Member States must duly consider when introducing at national level the criteria to be used by the (supervisory) board. The determination of what constitutes independence should principally be an issue for the (supervisory) board itself to determine. When the (supervisory) board applies the independence criteria, it should focus on substance rather than form.

(19) In view of the importance attaching to the role of non-executive or supervisory directors with respect to the restoration of confidence, and more generally to the development of sound corporate governance practices, the steps taken for the implementation of this Recommendation in Member States should be monitored closely,

HEREBY RECOMMENDS:

Section I
Scope and Definitions

1. Scope

1.1. Member States are invited to take the steps necessary to introduce, at national level, a set of provisions concerning the role of non-executive or supervisory directors and the committees of the (supervisory) board to be used by listed companies, either through a 'comply or explain' approach or through legislation, and with the instruments best suited to their legal environment.

They should take due account of the specificities of collective investment undertakings of the corporate type, as covered by Directive 85/611/EEC. Member States should also consider the specificities of collective investment undertakings of the corporate type which are not covered by that Directive and the sole purpose of which is to invest money raised from investors in a diversified range of assets and which do not seek to take legal or management control over any of the issuers of their underlying investments.

1.2. If Member States decide to use the 'comply or explain' approach, whereby companies are required to explain their practices by reference to a set of designated best practice recommendations, they should require companies to specify annually the recommendations with which they have not complied (and, in the case of recommendations whose requirements are of a continuing nature, for what part of the accounting period such non-compliance occurred), and explain in a substantial and specific manner the extent of, and the reasons for, any material non-compliance.

1.3. In their consideration of the principles set out in this Recommendation, Member States should, in particular, take into account the following:

1.3.1. the functions and characteristics assigned by Member States to any of the committees created within the (supervisory) board and proposed in this Recommendation should duly take into account the rights and duties of relevant corporate bodies as defined under national law;

1.3.2. Member States should be allowed to choose, in whole or in part, between the creation within the (supervisory) board of any of the committees with the characteristics advocated in this Recommendation, and the use of other structures—external to the (supervisory) board—or procedures. Such structures or procedures, which could be either mandatory for companies under national law or best practice recommended at national level through a 'comply or explain' approach, should be functionally equivalent and equally effective.

1.4. With respect to listed companies incorporated in one of the Member States, the set of provisions to be introduced by Member States should cover at least those listed companies which are incorporated within their territory.

With respect to listed companies not incorporated in one of the Member States, the set of provisions to be introduced by Member States should cover at least those listed companies which have their primary listing on a regulated market established in their territory.

2. Definitions for the purposes of this recommendation

2.1. 'Listed companies' means companies whose securities are admitted to trading on a regulated market, within the meaning of Directive 2004/39/EC, in one or more Member States.

2.2. 'Director' means any member of any administrative, managerial or supervisory body of a company.

2.3. 'Executive director' means any member of the administrative body (unitary board) who is engaged in the daily management of the company.

2.4. 'Non-executive director' means any member of the administrative body (unitary board) of a company other than an executive director.

2.5. 'Managing director' means any member of the managerial body (dual board) of a company.

2.6. 'Supervisory director' means any member of the supervisory body (dual board) of a company.

SECTION II

PRESENCE AND ROLE OF NON-EXECUTIVE OR SUPERVISORY DIRECTORS ON (SUPERVISORY) BOARDS

3. Presence of non-executive or supervisory directors

3.1. The administrative, managerial and supervisory bodies should include in total an appropriate balance of executive/managing and non-executive/supervisory directors such that no individual or small group of individuals can dominate decision-making on the part of these bodies.

3.2. The present or past executive responsibilities of the (supervisory) board's chairman should not stand in the way of his ability to exercise objective supervision. On a unitary board, one way to ensure this is that the roles of chairman and chief executive are separate; in the case of unitary and dual boards, one option may be that the chief executive does not immediately become the chairman of the (supervisory) board. In cases where a company chooses to combine the roles of chairman and chief executive or to immediately appoint as chairman of the (supervisory) board the former chief executive, this should be accompanied with information on any safeguards put in place.

4. Number of independent directors

A sufficient number of independent non-executive or supervisory directors should be elected to the (supervisory) board of companies to ensure that any material conflict of interest involving directors will be properly dealt with.

5. Organisation in board committees

Boards should be organised in such a way that a sufficient number of independent non-executive or supervisory directors play an effective role in key areas where the potential for conflict of interest is particularly high. To this end, but subject to point 7, nomination, remuneration and audit committees should be created within the (supervisory) board, where that board plays a role in the areas of nomination, remuneration and audit under national law, taking into account Annex I.

6. Role of the committees vis-à-vis the (supervisory) board

6.1. The nomination, remuneration and audit committees should make recommendations aimed at preparing the decisions to be taken by the (supervisory) board itself. The primary purpose of the committees should be to increase the efficiency of the (supervisory) board by making sure that decisions are based on due consideration, and to help organise its work with a view to ensuring that the decisions it takes are free of material conflicts of interest. The creation of the committees is not intended, in principle, to remove the matters considered from the purview of the (supervisory) board itself, which remains fully responsible for the decisions taken in its field of competence.

6.2. The terms of reference of any committee created should be drawn up by the (supervisory) board. Where permissible under national law, any delegation of decision-making power should be explicitly declared, properly described and made public in a fully transparent way.

7. Flexibility in setting up the committees

7.1. Companies should make sure that the functions assigned to the nomination, remuneration and audit committees are carried out. However, companies may group the functions as they see fit and create fewer than three committees. In such a situation, companies should give a clear explanation both of the reasons why they have chosen an alternative approach and how the approach chosen meets the objective set for the three separate committees.

7.2. In companies where the (supervisory) board is small, the functions assigned to the three committees may be performed by the (supervisory) board as a whole, provided that it meets the composition requirements advocated for the committees and that adequate information is provided in this respect. In such a situation, the national provisions relating to board committees (in particular with respect to their role, operation, and transparency) should apply, where relevant, to the (supervisory) board as a whole.

8. Evaluation of the (supervisory) board

Every year, the (supervisory) board should carry out an evaluation of its performance. This should encompass an assessment of its membership, organisation and operation as a group, an evaluation of the competence and effectiveness of each board member and of the board committees, and an assessment of how well the board has performed against any performance objectives which have been set.

9. Transparency and communication

9.1. The (supervisory) board should make public at least once a year (as part of the information disclosed by the company annually on its corporate governance structures and practices) adequate information about its internal organisation and the procedures applicable to its activities, including an indication of the extent to which the self-evaluation performed by the (supervisory) board has led to any material change.

9.2. The (supervisory) board should ensure that shareholders are properly informed as regards the affairs of the company, its strategic approach, and the management of risks and conflicts of interest. The roles of directors regarding communication and engagement with shareholders should be clearly delineated.

Section III
Profile of Non-Executive or Supervisory Directors

10. Appointment and removal

Non-executive or supervisory directors should be appointed for specified terms subject to individual re-election, at maximum intervals to be determined at national level with a view to enabling both the necessary development of experience and sufficiently frequent reconfirmation of their position. It should also be possible to remove them, but their removal should not be easier than for an executive or managing director.

11. Qualifications

11.1. In order to maintain a proper balance in terms of the qualifications possessed by its members, the (supervisory) board should determine its desired composition in relation to the company's structure and activities, and evaluate it periodically. The (supervisory) board should ensure that it is composed of members who, as a whole, have the required diversity of knowledge, judgement and experience to complete their tasks properly.

11.2. The members of the audit committee, should, collectively, have a recent and relevant background in and experience of finance and accounting for listed companies appropriate to the company's activities.

11.3. All new members of the (supervisory) board should be offered a tailored induction programme covering to the extent necessary their responsibilities and the company's organisation and activities. The (supervisory) board should conduct an annual review to identify areas where directors need to update their skills and knowledge.

11.4. When the appointment of a director is proposed, disclosure should be made of his particular competences which are relevant to his service on the (supervisory) board. To enable markets and the public to assess whether these competences remain appropriate over time, the (supervisory) board should disclose every year a profile of the board's composition and information on the particular competences of individual directors which are relevant to their service on the (supervisory) board.

12. Commitment

12.1. Each director should devote to his duties the necessary time and attention, and should undertake to limit the number of his other professional commitments (in particular any directorships held in other companies) to such an extent that the proper performance of his duties is assured.

12.2. Where the appointment of a director is proposed, his other significant professional commitments should be disclosed. The board should be informed of subsequent changes. Every year, the board should collect data on such commitments, and make the information available in its annual report.

13. Independence

13.1. A director should be considered to be independent only if he is free of any business, family or other relationship, with the company, its controlling shareholder or the management of either, that creates a conflict of interest such as to impair his judgement.

13.2. A number of criteria for assessment of the independence of directors should be adopted at national level, taking into account the guidance set out in Annex II, which identifies a number of situations reflecting the relationships or circumstances usually recognised as likely to generate material conflict of interest. The determination of what constitutes independence is fundamentally an issue for the (supervisory) board itself to determine. The (supervisory) board may consider that, although a particular director meets all the criteria laid down at national level for assessment of the independence of directors, he cannot be considered independent owing to the specific circumstances of the person or the company, and the converse also applies.

13.3. Proper information should be disclosed on the conclusions reached by the (supervisory) board in its determination of whether a particular director should be regarded as independent.

13.3.1. When the appointment of a non-executive or supervisory director is proposed, the company should disclose whether it considers him to be independent; if one or more of the criteria laid down at national level for assessment of independence of directors is not met, the company should disclose its reasons for nevertheless considering that director to be independent. Companies should also disclose annually which directors they consider to be independent.

13.3.2. If one or more of the criteria laid down at national level for assessment of independence of directors has not been met throughout the year, the company should disclose its reasons for considering that director to be independent. To ensure the accuracy of the information provided on the independence of directors, the company should require the independent directors to have their independence periodically re-confirmed.

Section IV
Final Provisions

14. Follow-up

Member States are invited to take the necessary measures to promote the application, by 30 June 2006, of the principles set out in this Recommendation and to notify the Commission of the measures taken in accordance with this Recommendation, in order to enable the Commission to monitor closely the situation and, on that basis, to assess the need for further measures.

15. Addressees

This Recommendation is addressed to the Member States.

Annex I
Committees of the (supervisory) board

1. Common Features

1.1. *Size*

When committees are created within the (supervisory) board, they should normally be composed of at least three members. In companies with small (supervisory) boards, they could exceptionally be composed of two members only.

1.2. *Composition*

Chairmanship and membership of the committees should be decided with due regard to the need to ensure that committee membership is refreshed and that undue reliance is not placed on particular individuals.

1.3. *Terms of reference*

The exact mandate of each committee created should be described in the terms of reference drawn up by the (supervisory) board.

1.4. *Available resources*

Companies should ensure that committees are provided with sufficient resources to discharge their duties, which includes the right to obtain—in particular from officers of the company—all the necessary information or to seek independent professional advice on issues falling in their area of competence.

1.5. Attendance at committee meetings

With a view to ensuring the autonomy and objectivity of the committees, directors other than the committee members should normally be entitled to attend its meetings only at the invitation of the committee. The committee may invite or require certain officers or experts to attend.

1.6. Transparency

1. Committees should discharge their duties within the set terms of reference, and ensure that they regularly report to the (supervisory) board about their activities and results.

2. The terms of reference set for any committee created, explaining its role and any authority delegated to it by the (supervisory) board where permissible under national law, should be made public at least once a year (as part of the information disclosed by the company annually on its corporate governance structures and practices). Companies should also make public annually a statement by existing committees about their membership, the number of their meetings and attendance over the year, and their main activities. In particular, the audit committee should confirm that it is satisfied with the independence of the audit process and describe briefly the steps it has taken to reach this conclusion.

3. The chairman of each committee should be able to communicate directly with shareholders. The circumstances in which this should happen should be spelled out in the committee's terms of reference.

2. The Nomination Committee

2.1. Creation and composition

1. Where, under national law, the (supervisory) board is playing a role, either by making decisions itself or by making proposals for consideration by another corporate body, in the process for appointment and/or removal of directors, a nomination committee should be set up within the (supervisory) board.

2. The nomination committee should be composed of at least a majority of independent non-executive or supervisory directors. When a company deems it appropriate for the nomination committee to comprise a minority of non-independent members, the Chief Executive Officer could be a member of such a committee.

2.2. Role

1. The nomination committee should at least:
– identify and recommend, for the approval of the (supervisory) board, candidates to fill board vacancies as and when they arise. In doing so, the nomination committee should evaluate the balance of skills, knowledge and experience on the board, prepare a description of the roles and capabilities required for a particular appointment, and assess the time commitment expected,
– periodically assess the structure, size, composition and performance of the unitary or dual board, and make recommendations to the (supervisory) board with regard to any changes,
– periodically assess the skills, knowledge and experience of individual directors, and report on this to the (supervisory) board,
– properly consider issues related to succession planning.

2. In addition, the nomination committee should review the policy of the (management) board for selection and appointment of senior management.

2.3. Operation

1. The nomination committee should consider proposals made by relevant parties, including management and shareholders.[4] In particular, the

---

[4] When proposals are submitted by shareholders for the consideration of the nomination committee and the latter decides not to recommend these candidates for the approval of the (supervisory) board, this does not prevent shareholders from proposing the same candidates directly to the general meeting when they have the right to table draft resolutions to this effect under national law.

Chief Executive Officer should be adequately consulted by, and entitled to submit proposals to the nomination committee, especially when dealing with issues related to executive/managing directors or senior management.

2. In performing its duties, the nomination committee should be able to use any forms of resources it deems appropriate, including external advice or advertising, and should receive appropriate funding from the company to this effect.

3. The Remuneration Committee

3.1. *Creation and composition*

1. Where, under national law, the (supervisory) board is playing a role, either by making decisions itself or by making proposals for consideration by another corporate body, in the process for setting remuneration of directors, a remuneration committee should be set up within the (supervisory) board.

2. The remuneration committee should be composed exclusively of non-executive or supervisory directors. At least a majority of its members should be independent.

3.2. *Role*

1. With respect to executive or managing directors, the committee should at least:
– make proposals, for the approval of the (supervisory) board, on the remuneration policy for executive or managing directors. Such policy should address all forms of compensation, including in particular the fixed remuneration, performance-related remuneration schemes, pension arrangements, and termination payments. Proposals related to performance-related remuneration schemes should be accompanied with recommendations on the related objectives and evaluation criteria, with a view to properly aligning the pay of executive or managing directors with the long-term interests of the shareholders and the objectives set by the (supervisory) board for the company,
– make proposals to the (supervisory) board on the individual remuneration to be attributed to executive or managing directors, ensuring that they are consistent with the remuneration policy adopted by the company and the evaluation of the performance of the directors concerned. In doing so, the committee should be properly informed as to the total compensation obtained by the directors from other companies affiliated to the group,
– make proposals to the (supervisory) board on suitable forms of contract for executive or managing directors,
– assist the (supervisory) board in overseeing the process whereby the company complies with existing provisions regarding disclosure of remuneration-related items (in particular the remuneration policy applied and the individual remuneration attributed to directors).

2. With respect to senior management (as defined by the (supervisory) board), the committee should at least:
– make general recommendations to the executive or managing directors on the level and structure of remuneration for senior management,
– monitor the level and structure of remuneration for senior management, on the basis of adequate information provided by executive or managing directors.

3. With respect to stock options and other share-based incentives which may be granted to directors, managers, or other employees, the committee should at least:
– debate the general policy regarding the granting of such schemes, in particular stock options, and make any related proposals to the (supervisory) board,
– review the information provided on this topic in the annual report and to the shareholders meeting where relevant,
– make proposals to the (supervisory) board concerning the choice between granting options to subscribe shares or granting options to purchase shares, specifying the reasons for its choice as well as the consequences that this choice has.

3.3. *Operation*

1. The remuneration committee should consult at least the chairman and/or chief executive about

their views relating to the remuneration of other executive or managing directors.

2. The remuneration committee should be able to avail itself of consultants, with a view to obtaining the necessary information on market standards for remuneration systems. The committee should be responsible for establishing the selection criteria, selecting, appointing and setting the terms of reference for any remuneration consultants who advise the committee, and should receive appropriate funding from the company to this effect.

4. The Audit Committee

4.1. *Composition*

The audit committee should be composed exclusively of non-executive or supervisory directors. At least a majority of its members should be independent.

4.2. *Role*

1. With respect to the internal policies and procedures adopted by the company, the audit committee should assist the (supervisory) board to at least:
– monitor the integrity of the financial information provided by the company, in particular by reviewing the relevance and consistency of the accounting methods used by the company and its group (including the criteria for the consolidation of the accounts of companies in the group),
– review at least annually the internal control and risk management systems, with a view to ensuring that the main risks (including those related to compliance with existing legislation and regulations) are properly identified, managed and disclosed,
– ensure the effectiveness of the internal audit function, in particular by making recommendations on the selection, appointment, reappointment and removal of the head of the internal audit department and on the department's budget, and by monitoring the responsiveness of management to its findings and recommendations. If the company does not have an internal audit function, the need for one should be reviewed at least annually.

2. With respect to the external auditor engaged by the company, the audit committee should at least:
– make recommendations to the (supervisory) board in relation to the selection, appointment, reappointment and removal of the external auditor by the body competent under national company law, and to the terms and conditions of his engagement,
– monitor the external auditor's independence and objectivity, in particular by reviewing the audit firm's compliance with applicable guidance relating to the rotation of audit partners, the level of fees paid by the company, and other related regulatory requirements,
– keep the nature and extent of non-audit services under review, based inter alia on disclosure by the external auditor of all fees paid by the company and its group to the audit firm and network, with a view to preventing any material conflicts of interest from arising. The committee should set and apply a formal policy specifying, in accordance with the principles and guidance provided in Commission Recommendation 2002/590/EC,[5] the types of non-audit services which are (a) excluded, (b) permissible after review by the committee, and (c) permissible without referral to the committee,
– review the effectiveness of the external audit process, and the responsiveness of management to the recommendations made in the external auditor's management letter,
– investigate the issues giving rise to any resignation of the external auditor, and make recommendations as to any required action.

4.3. *Operation*

1. The company should provide an induction programme for new audit committee members, and subsequent relevant training on an ongoing and timely basis. All committee members should be provided in particular with full information

---

[5] OJ L 191, 19.7.2002, 22, reproduced supra under no. C. 21.

relating to the company's specific accounting, financial and operational features.

2. The management should inform the audit committee of the methods used to account for significant and unusual transactions where the accounting treatment may be open to different approaches. In this respect, particular attention should be paid to both the existence of, and the justification for, any activity carried out by the company in offshore centres and/or through special purpose vehicles.

3. The audit committee shall decide whether and, if so, when the chief executive officer or chairman of the managing board, the chief financial officer (or senior employees responsible for finance, accounting, and treasury matters), the internal auditor and the external auditor, should attend its meetings. The committee should be entitled to meet with any relevant person outside the presence of executive or managing directors, if it so wishes.

4. The internal and external auditors should, in addition to maintaining an effective working relationship with management, be guaranteed free access to the (supervisory) board. To this effect, the audit committee shall act as the principal contact point for the internal and external auditors.

5. The audit committee should be informed of the internal auditor's work programme, and receive internal audit reports or a periodic summary.

6. The audit committee should be informed of the external auditor's work programme, and should obtain a report by the external auditor describing all relationships between the independent auditor and the company and its group. The committee should obtain timely information about any issues arising from the audit.

7. The audit committee should be free to obtain advice and assistance from outside legal, accounting or other advisors as it deems necessary to carry out its duties, and should receive appropriate funding from the company to this effect.

8. The audit committee should review the process whereby the company complies with existing provisions regarding the possibility for employees to report alleged significant irregularities in the company, by way of complaints or through anonymous submissions, normally to an independent director, and should ensure that arrangements are in place for the proportionate and independent investigation of such matters and for appropriate follow-up action.

9. The audit committee should report to the (supervisory) board on its activities at least once every six months, at the time the yearly and half-yearly statements are approved.

Annex II

Profile of independent non-executive or supervisory directors

1. It is not possible to list comprehensively all threats to directors' independence; the relationships or circumstances which may appear relevant to its determination may vary to a certain extent across Member States and companies, and best practices in this respect may evolve over time. However, a number of situations are frequently recognised as relevant in helping the (supervisory) board to determine whether a non-executive or supervisory director may be regarded as independent, even though it is widely understood that assessment of the independence of any particular director should be based on substance rather than form. In this context, a number of criteria, to be used by the (supervisory) board, should be adopted at national level. Such criteria, which should be tailored to the national context, should be based on due consideration of at least the following situations:

(a) not to be an executive or managing director of the company or an associated company, and not having been in such a position for the previous five years;

(b) not to be an employee of the company or an associated company, and not having been in such a position for the previous three years, except when the non-executive or supervisory director does not belong to senior management and has been elected to the (supervisory) board in the context of a system of workers' representation recognised by law and providing for adequate protection against abusive dismissal and other forms of unfair treatment;

(c) not to receive, or have received, significant additional remuneration from the company or an associated company apart from a fee received as non-executive or supervisory director. Such additional remuneration covers in particular any participation in a share option or any other performance-related pay scheme; it does not cover the receipt of fixed amounts of compensation under a retirement plan (including deferred compensation) for prior service with the company (provided that such compensation is not contingent in any way on continued service);

(d) not to be or to represent in any way the controlling shareholder(s) (control being determined by reference to the cases mentioned in Article 1(1) of Council Directive 83/349/EEC[6]);

(e) not to have, or have had within the last year, a significant business relationship with the company or an associated company, either directly or as a partner, shareholder, director or senior employee of a body having such a relationship. Business relationships include the situation of a significant supplier of goods or services (including financial, legal, advisory or consulting services), of a significant customer, and of organisations that receive significant contributions from the company or its group;

(f) not to be, or have been within the last three years, partner or employee of the present or former external auditor of the company or an associated company;

(g) not to be executive or managing director in another company in which an executive or managing director of the company is non-executive or supervisory director, and not to have other significant links with executive directors of the company through involvement in other companies or bodies;

(h) not to have served on the (supervisory) board as a non-executive or supervisory director for more than three terms (or, alternatively, more than 12 years where national law provides for normal terms of a very small length);

(i) not to be a close family member of an executive or managing director, or of persons in the situations referred to in points (a) to (h);

2. The independent director undertakes (a) to maintain in all circumstances his independence of analysis, decision and action, (b) not to seek or accept any unreasonable advantages that could be considered as compromising his independence, and (c) to clearly express his opposition in the event that he finds that a decision of the (supervisory) board may harm the company. When the (supervisory) board has made decisions about which an independent non-executive or supervisory director has serious reservations, he should draw all the appropriate consequences from this. If he were to resign, he should explain his reasons in a letter to the board or the audit committee, and, where appropriate, to any relevant body external to the company.

---

[6] OJ L 193, 18.7.1983, 1, reproduced supra under no. C. 6. Directive as last amended by Directive 2003/51/EC of the European Parliament and of the Council (OJ L 178, 17.7.2003, 16), reproduced supra under no. C. 23.

C. 29.

European Parliament and Council Directive 2005/56/EC of 26 October 2005 on cross-border mergers of limited liability companies[1]

(Text with EEA relevance)

THE EUROPEAN PARLIAMENT AND THE COUNCIL OF THE EUROPEAN UNION,

Having regard to the Treaty establishing the European Community, and in particular Article 44 thereof,

Having regard to the proposal from the Commission,

Having regard to the opinion of the European Economic and Social Committee,[2]

Acting in accordance with the procedure laid down in Article 251 of the Treaty,[3]

Whereas:

(1) There is a need for cooperation and consolidation between limited liability companies from different Member States. However, as regards cross-border mergers of limited liability companies, they encounter many legislative and administrative difficulties in the Community. It is therefore necessary, with a view to the completion and functioning of the single market, to lay down Community provisions to facilitate the carrying out of cross-border mergers between various types of limited liability company governed by the laws of different Member States.

(2) This Directive facilitates the cross-border merger of limited liability companies as defined herein. The laws of the Member States are to allow the cross-border merger of a national limited liability company with a limited liability company from another Member State if the national law of the relevant Member States permits mergers between such types of company.

(3) In order to facilitate cross-border merger operations, it should be laid down that, unless this Directive provides otherwise, each company taking part in a cross-border merger, and each third party concerned, remains subject to the provisions and formalities of the national law which would be applicable in the case of a national merger. None of the provisions and formalities of national law, to which reference is made in this Directive, should introduce restrictions on freedom of establishment or on the free movement of capital save where these can be justified in accordance with the case-law of the Court of Justice and in particular by requirements of the general interest and are both necessary for, and proportionate to, the attainment of such overriding requirements.

(4) The common draft terms of the cross-border merger are to be drawn up in the same terms for each of the companies concerned in the various Member States. The minimum content of such common draft terms should therefore be specified, while leaving the companies free to agree on other items.

(5) In order to protect the interests of members and others, both the common draft terms of cross-border mergers and the completion of the cross-border merger are to be publicised for each merging company via an entry in the appropriate public register.

---

[1] OJ L 310, 25.11.2005, 1–9.
[2] OJ C 117, 30.4.2004, 43.
[3] Opinion of the European Parliament of 10 May 2005 (not yet published in the Official Journal) and Council Decision of 19 September 2005.

(6) The laws of all the Member States should provide for the drawing-up at national level of a report on the common draft terms of the cross-border merger by one or more experts on behalf of each of the companies that are merging. In order to limit experts' costs connected with cross-border mergers, provision should be made for the possibility of drawing up a single report intended for all members of companies taking part in a cross-border merger operation. The common draft terms of the cross-border merger are to be approved by the general meeting of each of those companies.

(7) In order to facilitate cross-border merger operations, it should be provided that monitoring of the completion and legality of the decision-making process in each merging company should be carried out by the national authority having jurisdiction over each of those companies, whereas monitoring of the completion and legality of the cross-border merger should be carried out by the national authority having jurisdiction over the company resulting from the cross-border merger. The national authority in question may be a court, a notary or any other competent authority appointed by the Member State concerned. The national law determining the date on which the cross-border merger takes effect, this being the law to which the company resulting from the cross-border merger is subject, should also be specified.

(8) In order to protect the interests of members and others, the legal effects of the cross-border merger, distinguishing as to whether the company resulting from the cross-border merger is an acquiring company or a new company, should be specified. In the interests of legal certainty, it should no longer be possible, after the date on which a cross-border merger takes effect, to declare the merger null and void.

(9) This Directive is without prejudice to the application of the legislation on the control of concentrations between undertakings, both at Community level, by Regulation (EC) No 139/2004,[4] and at the level of Member States.

(10) This Directive does not affect Community legislation regulating credit intermediaries and other financial undertakings and national rules made or introduced pursuant to such Community legislation.

(11) This Directive is without prejudice to a Member State's legislation demanding information on the place of central administration or the principal place of business proposed for the company resulting from the cross-border merger.

(12) Employees' rights other than rights of participation should remain subject to the national provisions referred to in Council Directive 98/59/EC of 20 July 1998 on collective redundancies,[5] Council Directive 2001/23/EC of 12 March 2001 on the safeguarding of employees' rights in the event of transfers of undertakings, businesses or parts of undertakings or businesses,[6] Directive 2002/14/EC of the European Parliament and of the Council of 11 March 2002 establishing a general framework for informing and consulting employees in the European Community[7] and Council Directive 94/45/EC of 22 September 1994 on the establishment of a European Works Council or a procedure in Community-scale undertakings and Community-scale groups of undertakings for the purposes of informing and consulting employees.[8]

(13) If employees have participation rights in one of the merging companies under the circumstances set out in this Directive and, if the national law of the Member State in which the company resulting from the cross-border merger has its registered office does not provide for the same level of participation as operated in the relevant merging companies, including in committees of the supervisory board that have decision-making powers, or does not provide for the same entitlement to exercise rights for employees of establishments resulting from the cross-border merger, the participation of employees in the company resulting

---

[4] Council Regulation (EC) No 139/2004 of 20 January 2004 on the control of concentrations between undertakings (the EC Merger Regulation) (OJ L 24, 29.1.2004, 1).

[5] OJ L 225, 12.8.1998, 16, reproduced infra under no. E. 8.
[6] OJ L 82, 22.3.2001, 16, reproduced infra under no. E. 11.
[7] OJ L 80, 23.3.2002, 29, reproduced infra under no. E. 12.
[8] OJ L 254, 30.9.1994, 64, reproduced infra under no. E. 5. Directive as amended by Directive 97/74/EC (OJ L 10, 16.1.1998, p. 22), reproduced infra under no. E. 6.

from the cross-border merger and their involvement in the definition of such rights are to be regulated. To that end, the principles and procedures provided for in Council Regulation (EC) No 2157/2001 of 8 October 2001 on the Statute for a European company (SE)[9] and in Council Directive 2001/86/EC of 8 October 2001 supplementing the Statute for a European company with regard to the involvement of employees,[10] are to be taken as a basis, subject, however, to modifications that are deemed necessary because the resulting company will be subject to the national laws of the Member State where it has its registered office. A prompt start to negotiations under Article 16 of this Directive, with a view to not unnecessarily delaying mergers, may be ensured by Member States in accordance with Article 3(2)(b) of Directive 2001/86/EC.

(14) For the purpose of determining the level of employee participation operated in the relevant merging companies, account should also be taken of the proportion of employee representatives amongst the members of the management group, which covers the profit units of the companies, subject to employee participation.

(15) Since the objective of the proposed action, namely laying down rules with common features applicable at transnational level, cannot be sufficiently achieved by the Member States and can therefore, by reason of the scale and impact of the proposed action, be better achieved at Community level, the Community may adopt measures in accordance with the principle of subsidiarity as set out in Article 5 of the Treaty. In accordance with the principle of proportionality as set out in that Article, this Directive does not go beyond what is necessary to achieve that objective.

(16) In accordance with paragraph 34 of the Interinstitutional Agreement on better lawmaking,[11] Member States should be encouraged to draw up, for themselves and in the interest of the Community, their own tables which will, as far as possible, illustrate the correlation between this Directive and the transposition measures and to make them public,

HAVE ADOPTED THIS DIRECTIVE:

Article 1
Scope

This Directive shall apply to mergers of limited liability companies formed in accordance with the law of a Member State and having their registered office, central administration or principal place of business within the Community, provided at least two of them are governed by the laws of different Member States (hereinafter referred to as cross-border mergers).

Article 2
Definitions

For the purposes of this Directive:

1. 'limited liability company', hereinafter referred to as 'company', means:

(a) a company as referred to in Article 1 of Directive 68/151/EEC,[12] or

(b) a company with share capital and having legal personality, possessing separate assets which alone serve to cover its debts and subject under the national law governing it to conditions concerning guarantees such as are provided for by Directive 68/151/EEC for the protection of the interests of members and others;

2. 'merger' means an operation whereby:

(a) one or more companies, on being dissolved without going into liquidation, transfer all their assets and liabilities to another existing company, the acquiring company, in exchange for the issue

---

[9] OJ L 294, 10.11.2001, 1, reproduced supra under no. C. 19. Regulation as amended by Regulation (EC) No 885/2004 (OJ L 168, 1.5.2004, 1).
[10] OJ L 294, 10.11.2001, 22, reproduced supra under no. C. 20.
[11] OJ C 321, 31.12.2003, 1.

[12] First Council Directive 68/151/EEC of 9 March 1968 on coordination of safeguards which, for the protection of the interests of members and others, are required by Member States of companies within the meaning of the second paragraph of Article 58 of the Treaty, with a view to making such safeguards equivalent throughout the Community (OJ L 65, 14.3.1968, 8), reproduced supra under no. C. 1. Directive as last amended by the 2003 Act of Accession.

to their members of securities or shares representing the capital of that other company and, if applicable, a cash payment not exceeding 10% of the nominal value, or, in the absence of a nominal value, of the accounting par value of those securities or shares; or

(b) two or more companies, on being dissolved without going into liquidation, transfer all their assets and liabilities to a company that they form, the new company, in exchange for the issue to their members of securities or shares representing the capital of that new company and, if applicable, a cash payment not exceeding 10% of the nominal value, or in the absence of a nominal value, of the accounting par value of those securities or shares; or

(c) a company, on being dissolved without going into liquidation, transfers all its assets and liabilities to the company holding all the securities or shares representing its capital.

Article 3

Further provisions concerning the scope

1. Notwithstanding Article 2(2), this Directive shall also apply to cross-border mergers where the law of at least one of the Member States concerned allows the cash payment referred to in points (a) and (b) of Article 2(2) to exceed 10% of the nominal value, or, in the absence of a nominal value, of the accounting par value of the securities or shares representing the capital of the company resulting from the cross-border merger.

2. Member States may decide not to apply this Directive to cross-border mergers involving a cooperative society even in the cases where the latter would fall within the definition of 'limited liability company' as laid down in Article 2(1).

3. This Directive shall not apply to cross-border mergers involving a company the object of which is the collective investment of capital provided by the public, which operates on the principle of risk-spreading and the units of which are, at the holders' request, repurchased or redeemed, directly or indirectly, out of the assets of that company. Action taken by such a company to ensure that the stock exchange value of its units does not vary significantly from its net asset value shall be regarded as equivalent to such repurchase or redemption.

Article 4

Conditions relating to cross-border mergers

1. Save as otherwise provided in this Directive,

(a) cross-border mergers shall only be possible between types of companies which may merge under the national law of the relevant Member States, and

(b) a company taking part in a cross-border merger shall comply with the provisions and formalities of the national law to which it is subject. The laws of a Member State enabling its national authorities to oppose a given internal merger on grounds of public interest shall also be applicable to a cross-border merger where at least one of the merging companies is subject to the law of that Member State. This provision shall not apply to the extent that Article 21 of Regulation (EC) No 139/2004 is applicable.

2. The provisions and formalities referred to in paragraph 1 (b) shall, in particular, include those concerning the decisionmaking process relating to the merger and, taking into account the cross-border nature of the merger, the protection of creditors of the merging companies, debenture holders and the holders of securities or shares, as well as of employees as regards rights other than those governed by Article 16. A Member State may, in the case of companies participating in a cross-border merger and governed by its law, adopt provisions designed to ensure appropriate protection for minority members who have opposed the cross-border merger.

Article 5

Common draft terms of cross-border mergers

The management or administrative organ of each of the merging companies shall draw up the common draft terms of cross-border merger. The common draft terms of cross-border merger shall include at least the following particulars:

(a) the form, name and registered office of the merging companies and those proposed for the company resulting from the cross-border merger;

(b) the ratio applicable to the exchange of securities or shares representing the company capital and the amount of any cash payment;

(c) the terms for the allotment of securities or shares representing the capital of the company resulting from the cross-border merger;

(d) the likely repercussions of the cross-border merger on employment;

(e) the date from which the holding of such securities or shares representing the company capital will entitle the holders to share in profits and any special conditions affecting that entitlement;

(f) the date from which the transactions of the merging companies will be treated for accounting purposes as being those of the company resulting from the cross-border merger;

(g) the rights conferred by the company resulting from the cross-border merger on members enjoying special rights or on holders of securities other than shares representing the company capital, or the measures proposed concerning them;

(h) any special advantages granted to the experts who examine the draft terms of the cross-border merger or to members of the administrative, management, supervisory or controlling organs of the merging companies;

(i) the statutes of the company resulting from the cross-border merger;

(j) where appropriate, information on the procedures by which arrangements for the involvement of employees in the definition of their rights to participation in the company resulting from the cross-border merger are determined pursuant to Article 16;

(k) information on the evaluation of the assets and liabilities which are transferred to the company resulting from the cross-border merger;

(l) dates of the merging companies' accounts used to establish the conditions of the cross-border merger.

Article 6

Publication

1. The common draft terms of the cross-border merger shall be published in the manner prescribed by the laws of each Member State in accordance with Article 3 of Directive 68/151/EEC for each of the merging companies at least one month before the date of the general meeting which is to decide thereon.

2. For each of the merging companies and subject to the additional requirements imposed by the Member State to which the company concerned is subject, the following particulars shall be published in the national gazette of that Member State:

(a) the type, name and registered office of every merging company;

(b) the register in which the documents referred to in Article 3(2) of Directive 68/151/EEC are filed in respect of each merging company, and the number of the entry in that register;

(c) an indication, for each of the merging companies, of the arrangements made for the exercise of the rights of creditors and of any minority members of the merging companies and the address at which complete information on those arrangements may be obtained free of charge.

Article 7

Report of the management or administrative organ

The management or administrative organ of each of the merging companies shall draw up a report intended for the members explaining and justifying the legal and economic aspects of the cross-border merger and explaining the implications of the cross-border merger for members, creditors and employees.

The report shall be made available to the members and to the representatives of the employees or, where there are no such representatives, to the employees themselves, not less than one month before the date of the general meeting referred to in Article 9.

Where the management or administrative organ of any of the merging companies receives, in good time, an opinion from the representatives of their employees, as provided for under national law, that opinion shall be appended to the report.

Article 8

Independent expert report

1. An independent expert report intended for members and made available not less than one month before the date of the general meeting referred to in Article 9 shall be drawn up for each merging company. Depending on the law of each Member State, such experts may be natural persons or legal persons.

2. As an alternative to experts operating on behalf of each of the merging companies, one or more independent experts, appointed for that purpose at the joint request of the companies by a judicial or administrative authority in the Member State of one of the merging companies or of the company resulting from the cross-border merger or approved by such an authority, may examine the common draft terms of cross-border merger and draw up a single written report to all the members.

3. The expert report shall include at least the particulars provided for by Article 10(2) of Council Directive 78/855/EEC of 9 October 1978 concerning mergers of public limited liability companies.[13] The experts shall be entitled to secure from each of the merging companies all information they consider necessary for the discharge of their duties.

4. Neither an examination of the common draft terms of cross-border merger by independent experts nor an expert report shall be required if all the members of each of the companies involved in the cross-border merger have so agreed.

Article 9

Approval by the general meeting

1. After taking note of the reports referred to in Articles 7 and 8, the general meeting of each of the merging companies shall decide on the approval of the common draft terms of cross-border merger.

2. The general meeting of each of the merging companies may reserve the right to make implementation of the cross-border merger conditional on express ratification by it of the arrangements decided on with respect to the participation of employees in the company resulting from the cross-border merger.

3. The laws of a Member State need not require approval of the merger by the general meeting of the acquiring company if the conditions laid down in Article 8 of Directive 78/855/EEC are fulfilled.

Article 10

Pre-merger certificate

1. Each Member State shall designate the court, notary or other authority competent to scrutinise the legality of the cross-border merger as regards that part of the procedure which concerns each merging company subject to its national law.

2. In each Member State concerned the authority referred to in paragraph 1 shall issue, without delay to each merging company subject to that State's national law, a certificate conclusively attesting to the proper completion of the pre-merger acts and formalities.

3. If the law of a Member State to which a merging company is subject provides for a procedure to scrutinise and amend the ratio applicable to the exchange of securities or shares, or a procedure to compensate minority members, without preventing the registration of the cross-border merger, such procedure shall only apply if the other merging companies situated in Member States which do not provide for such procedure explicitly accept, when approving the draft terms of the cross-border merger in accordance with Article 9(1), the possibility for the members of that merging company to have recourse to such procedure, to be initiated before the court having jurisdiction over that merging company. In such cases, the authority referred to in paragraph 1 may issue the certificate referred to in paragraph 2 even if such procedure has commenced. The certificate must, however, indicate that the procedure is pending. The decision in the procedure shall be binding on the company resulting from the cross-border merger and all its members.

---

[13] OJ L 295, 20.10.1978, 36, reproduced supra under no. C. 3. Directive as last amended by the 2003 Act of Accession.

Article 11
Scrutiny of the legality of the cross-border merger

1. Each Member State shall designate the court, notary or other authority competent to scrutinise the legality of the cross-border merger as regards that part of the procedure which concerns the completion of the cross-border merger and, where appropriate, the formation of a new company resulting from the cross-border merger where the company created by the cross-border merger is subject to its national law. The said authority shall in particular ensure that the merging companies have approved the common draft terms of cross-border merger in the same terms and, where appropriate, that arrangements for employee participation have been determined in accordance with Article 16.

2. To that end each merging company shall submit to the authority referred to in paragraph 1 the certificate referred to in Article 10(2) within six months of its issue together with the common draft terms of cross-border merger approved by the general meeting referred to in Article 9.

Article 12
Entry into effect of the cross-border merger

The law of the Member State to whose jurisdiction the company resulting from the cross-border merger is subject shall determine the date on which the cross-border merger takes effect. That date must be after the scrutiny referred to in Article 11 has been carried out.

Article 13
Registration

The law of each of the Member States to whose jurisdiction the merging companies were subject shall determine, with respect to the territory of that State, the arrangements, in accordance with Article 3 of Directive 68/151/EEC, for publicising completion of the cross-border merger in the public register in which each of the companies is required to file documents.

The registry for the registration of the company resulting from the cross-border merger shall notify, without delay, the registry in which each of the companies was required to file documents that the cross-border merger has taken effect. Deletion of the old registration, if applicable, shall be effected on receipt of that notification, but not before.

Article 14
Consequences of the cross-border merger

1. A cross-border merger carried out as laid down in points (a) and (c) of Article 2(2) shall, from the date referred to in Article 12, have the following consequences:

(a) all the assets and liabilities of the company being acquired shall be transferred to the acquiring company;

(b) the members of the company being acquired shall become members of the acquiring company;

(c) the company being acquired shall cease to exist.

2. A cross-border merger carried out as laid down in point (b) of Article 2(2) shall, from the date referred to in Article 12, have the following consequences:

(a) all the assets and liabilities of the merging companies shall be transferred to the new company;

(b) the members of the merging companies shall become members of the new company;

(c) the merging companies shall cease to exist.

3. Where, in the case of a cross-border merger of companies covered by this Directive, the laws of the Member States require the completion of special formalities before the transfer of certain assets, rights and obligations by the merging companies becomes effective against third parties, those formalities shall be carried out by the company resulting from the cross-border merger.

4. The rights and obligations of the merging companies arising from contracts of employment or from employment relationships and existing at the date on which the cross-border merger takes effect shall, by reason of that cross-border merger taking

effect, be transferred to the company resulting from the cross-border merger on the date on which the cross-border merger takes effect.

5. No shares in the acquiring company shall be exchanged for shares in the company being acquired held either:

(a) by the acquiring company itself or through a person acting in his or her own name but on its behalf;

(b) by the company being acquired itself or through a person acting in his or her own name but on its behalf.

Article 15

Simplified formalities

1. Where a cross-border merger by acquisition is carried out by a company which holds all the shares and other securities conferring the right to vote at general meetings of the company or companies being acquired:
– Articles 5, points (b), (c) and (e), 8 and 14(1), point (b) shall not apply,
– Article 9(1) shall not apply to the company or companies being acquired.

2. Where a cross-border merger by acquisition is carried out by a company which holds 90% or more but not all of the shares and other securities conferring the right to vote at general meetings of the company or companies being acquired, reports by an independent expert or experts and the documents necessary for scrutiny shall be required only to the extent that the national law governing either the acquiring company or the company being acquired so requires.

Article 16

Employee participation

1. Without prejudice to paragraph 2, the company resulting from the cross-border merger shall be subject to the rules in force concerning employee participation, if any, in the Member State where it has its registered office.

2. However, the rules in force concerning employee participation, if any, in the Member State where the company resulting from the cross-border merger has its registered office shall not apply, where at least one of the merging companies has, in the six months before the publication of the draft terms of the cross-border merger as referred to in Article 6, an average number of employees that exceeds 500 and is operating under an employee participation system within the meaning of Article 2(k) of Directive 2001/86/EC, or where the national law applicable to the company resulting from the cross-border merger does not

(a) provide for at least the same level of employee participation as operated in the relevant merging companies, measured by reference to the proportion of employee representatives amongst the members of the administrative or supervisory organ or their committees or of the management group which covers the profit units of the company, subject to employee representation, or

(b) provide for employees of establishments of the company resulting from the cross-border merger that are situated in other Member States the same entitlement to exercise participation rights as is enjoyed by those employees employed in the Member State where the company resulting from the cross-border merger has its registered office.

3. In the cases referred to in paragraph 2, the participation of employees in the company resulting from the cross-border merger and their involvement in the definition of such rights shall be regulated by the Member States, mutatis mutandis and subject to paragraphs 4 to 7 below, in accordance with the principles and procedures laid down in Article 12(2), (3) and (4) of Regulation (EC) No 2157/2001 and the following provisions of Directive 2001/86/EC:

(a) Article 3(1), (2) and (3), (4) first subparagraph, first indent, and second subparagraph, (5) and (7);

(b) Article 4(1), (2), points (a), (g) and (h), and (3);

(c) Article 5;

(d) Article 6;

(e) Article 7(1), (2) first subparagraph, point (b), and second subparagraph, and (3). However, for the purposes of this Directive, the percentages required by Article 7(2), first subparagraph, point (b) of Directive 2001/86/EC for the application of the standard rules contained in part 3 of the Annex to that Directive shall be raised from 25 to 33 1/3%;

(f) Articles 8, 10 and 12;

(g) Article 13(4);

(h) part 3 of the Annex, point (b).

4. When regulating the principles and procedures referred to in paragraph 3, Member States:

(a) shall confer on the relevant organs of the merging companies the right to choose without any prior negotiation to be directly subject to the standard rules for participation referred to in paragraph 3(h), as laid down by the legislation of the Member State in which the company resulting from the cross-border merger is to have its registered office, and to abide by those rules from the date of registration;

(b) shall confer on the special negotiating body the right to decide, by a majority of two thirds of its members representing at least two thirds of the employees, including the votes of members representing employees in at least two different Member States, not to open negotiations or to terminate negotiations already opened and to rely on the rules on participation in force in the Member State where the registered office of the company resulting from the cross-border merger will be situated;

(c) may, in the case where, following prior negotiations, standard rules for participation apply and notwithstanding these rules, determine to limit the proportion of employee representatives in the administrative organ of the company resulting from the cross-border merger. However, if in one of the merging companies employee representatives constituted at least one third of the administrative or supervisory board, the limitation may never result in a lower proportion of employee representatives in the administrative organ than one third.

5. The extension of participation rights to employees of the company resulting from the cross-border merger employed in other Member States, referred to in paragraph 2(b), shall not entail any obligation for Member States which choose to do so to take those employees into account when calculating the size of workforce thresholds giving rise to participation rights under national law.

6. When at least one of the merging companies is operating under an employee participation system and the company resulting from the cross-border merger is to be governed by such a system in accordance with the rules referred to in paragraph 2, that company shall be obliged to take a legal form allowing for the exercise of participation rights.

7. When the company resulting from the cross-border merger is operating under an employee participation system, that company shall be obliged to take measures to ensure that employees' participation rights are protected in the event of subsequent domestic mergers for a period of three years after the cross-border merger has taken effect, by applying mutatis mutandis the rules laid down in this Article.

Article 17
Validity

A cross-border merger which has taken effect as provided for in Article 12 may not be declared null and void.

Article 18
Review

Five years after the date laid down in the first paragraph of Article 19, the Commission shall review this Directive in the light of the experience acquired in applying it and, if necessary, propose its amendment.

Article 19
Transposition

Member States shall bring into force the laws, regulations and administrative provisions necessary to comply with this Directive by 15 December 2007.

When Member States adopt these measures, they shall contain a reference to this Directive or shall be accompanied by such reference on the occasion of their official publication. The methods of making such reference shall be laid down by Member States.

Article 20

Entry into force

This Directive shall enter into force on the 20th day following its publication in the Official Journal of the European Union.

Article 21

Addressees

This Directive is addressed to the Member States.

C. 30.

European Parliament and Council Directive 2006/43/EC
of 17 May 2006
on statutory audits of annual accounts and consolidated accounts, amending Council Directives 78/660/EEC and 83/349/EEC and repealing Council Directive 84/253/EEC[1]

(Text with EEA relevance)

Case

Case C-106/91 Claus Ramrath v Ministre de la Justice, and l'Institut des Réviseurs d'Entreprises [1992] ECR I-3351

1. The Treaty provisions on the right of establishment preclude a Member State from prohibiting a person from becoming established in its territory and practising as an auditor there on the grounds that that person is established and authorized to practise in another Member State.

2. Articles [39 and 49][1] of the Treaty do not preclude a Member State from making practice as an auditor within its territory by a person who is already authorized to practise as an auditor in another Member State subject to conditions which are objectively necessary for ensuring compliance with the rules of professional practice and which relate to a permanent infrastructure for carrying out the work, actual presence in that Member State and supervision of compliance with the rules of professional conduct, unless compliance with such rules and conditions is already ensured through an auditor, whether a natural or legal person, who is established and authorized in that State's territory and in whose service the person who intends to practise as an auditor is employed for the duration of the work.

THE EUROPEAN PARLIAMENT AND THE COUNCIL OF THE EUROPEAN UNION,

Having regard to the Treaty establishing the European Community, and in particular Article 44(2)(g) thereof,

Having regard to the proposal from the Commission,

Having regard to the Opinion of the European Economic and Social Committee,[2]

Acting in accordance with the procedure laid down in Article 251 of the Treaty,[3]

Whereas:

(1) Currently, the Fourth Council Directive 78/660/EEC of 25 July 1978 on the annual accounts of certain types of companies,[4] the Seventh Council Directive 83/349/EEC of 13 June 1983 on consolidated accounts,[5] Council Directive 86/635/EEC of 8 December 1986 on the annual accounts and consolidated accounts of banks and other financial institutions[6] and Council Directive 91/674/EEC of 19 December

---

[1] OJ L 157, 9.6.2006, 87–107.

[2] OJ C 157, 28.6.2005, 115.
[3] Opinion of the European Parliament of 28 September 2005 (not yet published in the Official Journal) and Council Decision of 25 April 2006.
[4] OJ L 222, 14.8.1978, 11, reproduced supra under no. C. 4. Directive as last amended by Directive 2003/51/EC of the European Parliament and of the Council (OJ L 178, 17.7.2003, 16), reproduced supra under no. C. 23.
[5] OJ L 193, 18.7.1983, 1, reproduced supra under no. C. 6. Directive as last amended by Directive 2003/51/EC, reproduced supra under no. C. 23.
[6] OJ L 372, 31.12.1986, 1, reproduced supra under no. B. 7. Directive as last amended by Directive 2003/51/EC, reproduced supra under no. C. 23.

1991 on the annual accounts and consolidated accounts of insurance undertakings[7] require that the annual accounts or consolidated accounts be audited by one or more persons entitled to carry out such audits.

(2) The conditions for the approval of persons responsible for carrying out the statutory audit were laid down in the Eighth Council Directive 84/253/EEC of 10 April 1984 on the approval of persons responsible for carrying out the statutory audits of accounting documents.[8]

(3) The lack of a harmonised approach to statutory auditing in the Community was the reason why the Commission proposed, in its 1998 Communication on the statutory audit in the European Union: the way forward,[9] the creation of a Committee on Auditing which could develop further action in close cooperation with the accounting profession and Member States.

(4) On the basis of the work of that Committee, on 15 November 2000 the Commission issued a Recommendation on quality assurance for the statutory audit in the European Union: minimum requirements[10] and on 16 May 2002 a Recommendation on Statutory Auditors' Independence in the EU: A Set of Fundamental Principles.[11]

(5) This Directive aims at high-level—though not full—harmonisation of statutory audit requirements. A Member State requiring statutory audit may impose more stringent requirements, unless otherwise provided for by this Directive.

(6) Audit qualifications obtained by statutory auditors on the basis of this Directive should be considered equivalent. It should therefore no longer be possible for Member States to insist that a majority of the voting rights in an audit firm must be held by locally approved auditors or that a majority of the members of the administrative or management body of an audit firm must be locally approved.

(7) The statutory audit requires adequate knowledge of matters such as company law, fiscal law and social law. Such knowledge should be tested before a statutory auditor from another Member State can be approved.

(8) In order to protect third parties, all approved auditors and audit firms should be entered in a register which is accessible to the public and which contains basic information concerning statutory auditors and audit firms.

(9) Statutory auditors should adhere to the highest ethical standards. They should therefore be subject to professional ethics, covering at least their public-interest function, their integrity and objectivity and their professional competence and due care. The public-interest function of statutory auditors means that a broader community of people and institutions rely on the quality of a statutory auditor's work. Good audit quality contributes to the orderly functioning of markets by enhancing the integrity and efficiency of financial statements. The Commission may adopt implementing measures on professional ethics as minimum standards. When doing so, it might consider the principles contained in the International Federation of Accountants (IFAC) Code of Ethics.

(10) It is important that statutory auditors and audit firms respect the privacy of their clients. They should therefore be bound by strict rules on confidentiality and professional secrecy which, however, should not impede proper enforcement of this Directive. Those confidentiality rules should also apply to any statutory auditor or audit firm which has ceased to be involved in a specific audit task.

(11) Statutory auditors and audit firms should be independent when carrying out statutory audits. They may inform the audited entity of matters arising from the audit, but should abstain from the internal decision processes of the audited

---

[7] OJ L 374, 31.12.1991, 7, reproduced infra under no. I. 23. Directive as amended by Directive 2003/51/EC, reproduced supra under no. C. 23.
[8] OJ L 126, 12.5.1984, 20, reproduced supra under no. C. 7, which has been repealed as from 29 June 2006 by article 50 of this Directive.
[9] OJ C 143, 8.5.1998, 12.
[10] OJ L 91, 31.3.2001, 91.
[11] OJ L 191, 19.7.2002, 22, reproduced supra under no. C. 21.

entity. If they find themselves in a situation where the significance of the threats to their independence, even after application of safeguards to mitigate those threats, is too high, they should resign or abstain from the audit engagement. The conclusion that there is a relationship which compromises the auditor's independence may be different as regards the relationship between the auditor and the audited entity from that in respect of the relationship between the network and the audited entity. Where a cooperative within the meaning of Article 2(14), or a similar entity as referred to in Article 45 of Directive 86/635/EEC, is required or permitted under national provisions to be a member of a non-profit-making auditing entity, an objective, reasonable and informed party would not conclude that the membership-based relationship compromises the statutory auditor's independence, provided that when such an auditing entity is conducting a statutory audit of one of its members, the principles of independence are applied to the auditors carrying out the audit and those persons who may be in a position to exert influence on the statutory audit. Examples of threats to the independence of a statutory auditor or audit firm are a direct or indirect financial interest in the audited entity and the provision of additional non-audit services. Also, the level of fees received from one audited entity and/or the structure of the fees can threaten the independence of a statutory auditor or audit firm. Types of safeguards to be applied to mitigate or eliminate those threats include prohibitions, restrictions, other policies and procedures, and disclosure. Statutory auditors and audit firms should refuse to undertake any additional non-audit service that compromises their independence. The Commission may adopt implementing measures on independence as minimum standards. In doing so, the Commission might take into consideration the principles contained in the above-mentioned Recommendation of 16 May 2002. In order to determine the independence of auditors, the concept of a 'network' in which auditors operate needs to be clear. In this regard, various circumstances have to be taken into account, such as instances where a structure could be defined as a network because it is aimed at profit- or cost-sharing. The criteria for demonstrating that there is a network should be judged and weighed on the basis of all factual circumstances available, such as whether there are common usual clients.

(12) In cases of self-review or self-interest, where appropriate to safeguard the statutory auditor's or audit firm's independence, it should be for the Member State rather than the statutory auditor or the audit firm to decide whether the statutory auditor or audit firm should resign or abstain from an audit engagement with regard to its audit clients. However, this should not lead to a situation where Member States have a general duty to prevent statutory auditors or audit firms from providing non-audit services to their audit clients. For the purposes of determining whether it is appropriate, in cases of self-interest or self-review, that a statutory auditor or audit firm should not carry out statutory audits, so as to safeguard the statutory auditor's or audit firm's independence, the factors to be taken into account should include the question whether or not the audited public-interest entity has issued transferable securities admitted to trading on a regulated market within the meaning of point 14 of Article 4(1) of Directive 2004/39/EC of the European Parliament and of the Council of 21 April 2004 on markets in financial instruments.[12]

(13) It is important to ensure consistently high quality in all statutory audits required by Community law. All statutory audits should therefore be carried out on the basis of international auditing standards. Measures implementing those standards in the Community should be adopted in accordance with Council Decision 1999/468/EC of 28 June 1999 laying down the procedures for the exercise of implementing powers conferred on the Commission.[13] A technical committee or group on auditing should assist the Commission in the assessment of the technical soundness of all the international auditing standards, and should also involve the system of public oversight bodies of the Member States. In order to achieve a maximum degree of harmonisation, Member States should be allowed

---

[12] OJ L 145, 30.4.2004, 1, reproduced infra under no. S. 29.
[13] OJ L 184, 17.7.1999, 23.

to impose additional national audit procedures or requirements only if these stem from specific national legal requirements relating to the scope of the statutory audit of annual or consolidated accounts, meaning that those requirements have not been covered by the adopted international auditing standards. Member States could maintain those additional audit procedures until the audit procedures or requirements have been covered by subsequently adopted international auditing standards. If, however, the adopted international auditing standards contain audit procedures the performance of which would create a specific legal conflict with national law stemming from specific national requirements related to the scope of the statutory audit, Member States may carve out the conflicting part of the international auditing standard as long as those conflicts exist, provided the measures referred to in Article 26(3) are applied. Any addition or carving out by Member States should add a high level of credibility to the annual accounts of companies and be conducive to the public good. The above implies that Member States may, for example, require an additional auditor's report to the supervisory board or prescribe other reporting and audit requirements based on national corporate governance rules.

(14) For the Commission to adopt an international auditing standard for application in the Community, it must be generally accepted internationally and have been developed with full participation of all interested parties following an open and transparent procedure, add to the credibility and quality of annual accounts and consolidated accounts and be conducive to the European public good. The need for the adoption of an International Auditing Practice Statement as part of a standard should be assessed in accordance with Decision 1999/468/EC on a case-by-case basis. The Commission should ensure that before the start of the adoption process a review is conducted in order to verify whether those requirements have been met and report to members of the Committee set up under this Directive on the outcome of the review.

(15) In the case of consolidated accounts, it is important that there be a clear definition of responsibilities as between the statutory auditors who audit components of the group. For this purpose, the group auditor should bear full responsibility for the audit report.

(16) In order to increase comparability between companies applying the same accounting standards, and to enhance public confidence in the audit function, the Commission may adopt a common audit report for the audit of annual accounts or consolidated accounts prepared on the basis of approved international accounting standards, unless an appropriate standard for such a report has been adopted at Community level.

(17) Regular inspections are a good means of achieving a consistently high quality in statutory audits. Statutory auditors and audit firms should therefore be subject to a system of quality assurance that is organised in a manner which is independent from the reviewed statutory auditors and audit firms. For the application of Article 29 on quality assurance systems, Member States may decide that if individual auditors have a common quality assurance policy, only the requirements for audit firms need to be considered. Member States may organise the system of quality assurance in such a manner that each individual auditor is to be subject to a quality assurance review at least every six years. In this respect, the funding for the quality assurance system should be free from undue influence. The Commission should have the competence to adopt implementing measures in matters relevant to the organisation of quality assurance systems, and in respect of its funding, in cases where public confidence in the quality assurance system is seriously compromised. The public oversight systems of Member States should be encouraged to find a coordinated approach to the carrying-out of quality assurance reviews with a view to avoiding the imposition of unnecessary burdens on the parties concerned.

(18) Investigations and appropriate penalties help to prevent and correct inadequate execution of a statutory audit.

(19) Statutory auditors and audit firms are responsible for carrying out their work with due care and thus should be liable for the financial

damage caused by a lack of the care owed. However, the auditors' and audit firms' ability to obtain professional indemnity insurance cover may be affected by whether they are subject to unlimited financial liability. For its part, the Commission intends examining these issues, taking into account the fact that liability regimes of the Member States may vary considerably.

(20) Member States should organise an effective system of public oversight for statutory auditors and audit firms on the basis of home country control. The regulatory arrangements for public oversight should make possible effective cooperation at Community level in respect of the Member States' oversight activities. The public oversight system should be governed by non-practitioners who are knowledgeable in the areas relevant to statutory audit. These non-practitioners may be specialists who have never been linked with the audit profession or former practitioners who have left the profession. Member States may, however, allow a minority of practitioners to be involved in the governance of the public oversight system. Competent authorities of Member States should cooperate with each other whenever necessary for the purpose of carrying out their oversight duties on statutory auditors or audit firms approved by them. Such cooperation can make an important contribution to ensuring consistently high quality in the statutory audit in the Community. Since it is necessary to ensure effective cooperation and coordination at European level among competent authorities designated by Member States, the designation of one entity, responsible for ensuring cooperation, should be without prejudice to the ability of each single authority to cooperate directly with the other competent authorities of the Member States.

(21) In order to ensure compliance with Article 32(3) on principles of public oversight, a non-practitioner is deemed to be knowledgeable in the areas relevant to the statutory audit either because of his or her past professional skill or, alternatively, because he or she has knowledge of at least one of the subjects listed in Article 8.

(22) The statutory auditor or audit firm should be appointed by the general meeting of shareholders or members of the audited entity. In order to protect the independence of the auditor it is important that dismissal should be possible only where there are proper grounds and if those grounds are communicated to the authority or authorities responsible for public oversight.

(23) Since public-interest entities have a higher visibility and are economically more important, stricter requirements should apply in the case of a statutory audit of their annual or consolidated accounts.

(24) Audit committees and an effective internal control system help to minimise financial, operational and compliance risks, and enhance the quality of financial reporting. Member States might have regard to the Commission Recommendation of 15 February 2005 on the role of non-executive or supervisory directors of listed companies and on the committees of the (supervisory) board,[14] which sets out how audit committees should be established and function. Member States may determine that the functions assigned to the audit committee or a body performing equivalent functions may be performed by the administrative or supervisory body as a whole. With regard to the duties of the audit committee under Article 41, the statutory auditor or audit firm should in no way be subordinated to the committee.

(25) Member States may also decide to exempt public-interest entities which are collective investment undertakings whose transferable securities are admitted to trading on a regulated market from the requirement to have an audit committee. This option takes into account the fact that where a collective investment undertaking functions merely for the purpose of pooling assets, the employment of an audit committee will not always be appropriate. The financial reporting and related risks are not comparable to those of other public-interest entities. In addition, undertakings for collective investment in transferable securities (UCITS) and their management companies operate in a strictly defined regulatory environment and are subject to

---

[14] OJ L 52, 25.2.2005, 51, reproduced supra under no. C. 28.

specific governance mechanisms such as controls exercised by their depositary. For those collective investment undertakings which are not harmonized by Directive 85/611/EEC[15] but are subject to equivalent safeguards as provided for by that Directive, Member States should, in this particular case, be allowed to provide for equal treatment with Community-harmonised collective investment undertakings.

(26) In order to reinforce the independence of auditors of public-interest entities, the key audit partner(s) auditing such entities should rotate. To organise such rotation, Member States should require a change of key audit partner(s) dealing with an audited entity, while allowing the audit firm with which the key audit partner(s) is/are associated to continue being the statutory auditor of such entity. Where a Member State considers it appropriate in order to attain the objectives pursued, that Member State might, alternatively, require a change of audit firm, without prejudice to Article 42(2).

(27) The interrelation of capital markets underlines the need also to ensure high-quality work performed by auditors from third countries in relation to the Community capital market. The auditors concerned should therefore be registered so as to make them subject to quality assurance reviews and to the system of investigations and penalties. Derogations on the basis of reciprocity should be possible subject to an equivalence testing to be performed by the Commission in cooperation with Member States. In any case, an entity which has issued transferable securities on a regulated market within the meaning of point 14 of Article 4(1) of Directive 2004/39/EC should always be audited by an auditor either registered in a Member State or overseen by competent authorities of the third country from which the auditor comes from, provided that the said third country is acknowledged by the Commission or a Member State as meeting the requirements equivalent to Community requirements in the field of principles of oversight, quality assurance systems and systems of investigations and penalties, and that the basis of this arrangement is reciprocity. While one Member State may consider a third country's quality assurance system equivalent, other Member States should not be bound to accept that assessment, nor should the Commission's decision be pre-empted thereby.

(28) The complexity of international group audits requires good cooperation between the competent authorities of Member States and those of third countries. Member States should therefore ensure that competent authorities of third countries can have access to audit working papers and other documents through the national competent authorities. In order to protect the rights of the parties concerned and at the same time facilitate access to those papers and documents, Member States should be allowed to grant direct access to the competent authorities of third countries, subject to the agreement of the national competent authority. One of the relevant criteria for the granting of access is whether the competent authorities in third countries meet requirements which the Commission has declared adequate. Pending such a decision by the Commission, and without prejudice thereto, Member States may assess whether the requirements are adequate.

(29) Disclosure of information as referred to in Articles 36 and 47 should be in accordance with the rules on the transfer of personal data to third countries as laid down in Directive 95/46/EC of the European Parliament and of the Council of 24 October 1995 on the protection of individuals with regard to the processing of personal data and on the free movement of such data.[16]

(30) The measures necessary for the implementation of this Directive should be adopted in accordance with Decision 1999/468/EC and

---

[15] Council Directive 85/611/EEC of 20 December 1985 on the coordination of laws, regulations and administrative provisions relating to undertakings for collective investment in transferable securities (UCITS) (OJ L 375, 31.12.1985, 3), reproduced infra under no. S. 6. Directive as last amended by Directive 2005/1/EC of the European Parliament and of the Council (OJ L 79, 24.3.2005, 9), reproduced supra under no. B. 39.

[16] OJ L 281, 23.11.1995, 31. Directive as amended by Regulation (EC) No 1882/2003 (OJ L 284, 31.10.2003, 1).

with due regard to the declaration made by the Commission in the European Parliament on 5 February 2002 concerning the implementation of financial services legislation.

(31) The European Parliament should be given a period of three months from the first transmission of draft amendments and implementing measures to allow it to examine them and to give its opinion. However, in urgent and duly justified cases, it should be possible to shorten that period. If, within that period, a resolution is adopted by the European Parliament, the Commission should re-examine the draft amendments or measures.

(32) Since the objectives of this Directive—namely requiring the application of a single set of international auditing standards, the updating of the educational requirements, the definition of professional ethics and the technical implementation of the cooperation between competent authorities of Member States and between those authorities and the authorities of third countries, in order further to enhance and harmonise the quality of statutory audit in the Community and to facilitate cooperation between Member States and with third countries so as to strengthen confidence in the statutory audit—cannot be sufficiently achieved by the Member States and can therefore, by reason of the scale and effects of this Directive, be better achieved at Community level, the Community may adopt measures, in accordance with the principle of subsidiarity as set out in Article 5 of the Treaty. In accordance with the principle of proportionality, as set out in that Article, this Directive does not go beyond what is necessary in order to achieve those objectives.

(33) With a view to rendering the relationship between the statutory auditor or audit firm and the audited entity more transparent, Directives 78/660/EEC and 83/349/EEC should be amended so as to require disclosure of the audit fee and the fee paid for non-audit services in the notes to the annual accounts and the consolidated accounts.

(34) Directive 84/253/EEC should be repealed because it lacks a comprehensive set of rules to ensure an appropriate audit infrastructure, such as public oversight, disciplinary systems and systems of quality assurance, and because it does not provide specifically for regulatory cooperation between Member States and third countries. In order to ensure legal certainty, there is a clear need to indicate that statutory auditors and audit firms that have been approved under Directive 84/253/EEC are considered as approved under this Directive,

HAVE ADOPTED THIS DIRECTIVE:

Chapter I
Subject Matter and Definitions

Article 1
Subject matter

This Directive establishes rules concerning the statutory audit of annual and consolidated accounts.

Article 2
Definitions

For the purpose of this Directive, the following definitions shall apply:

1) 'statutory audit' means an audit of annual accounts or consolidated accounts insofar as required by Community law;

2) 'statutory auditor' means a natural person who is approved in accordance with this Directive by the competent authorities of a Member State to carry out statutory audits;

3) 'audit firm' means a legal person or any other entity, regardless of its legal form, that is approved in accordance with this Directive by the competent authorities of a Member State to carry out statutory audits;

4) 'third-country audit entity' means an entity, regardless of its legal form, which carries out audits of the annual or consolidated accounts of a company incorporated in a third country;

5) 'third-country auditor' means a natural person who carries out audits of the annual or

consolidated accounts of a company incorporated in a third country;

6) 'group auditor' means the statutory auditor(s) or audit firm(s) carrying out the statutory audit of consolidated accounts;

7) 'network' means the larger structure:
– which is aimed at cooperation and to which a statutory auditor or an audit firm belongs, and
– which is clearly aimed at profit- or cost-sharing or shares common ownership, control or management, common quality-control policies and procedures, a common business strategy, the use of a common brand-name or a significant part of professional resources;

8) 'affiliate of an audit firm' means any undertaking, regardless of its legal form, which is connected to an audit firm by means of common ownership, control or management;

9) 'audit report' means the report referred to in Article 51a of Directive 78/660/EEC and Article 37 of Directive 83/349/EEC issued by the statutory auditor or audit firm;

10) 'competent authorities' means the authorities or bodies designated by law that are in charge of the regulation and/or oversight of statutory auditors and audit firms or of specific aspects thereof; the reference to 'competent authority' in a specific article means a reference to the authority or body(ies) responsible for the functions referred to in that Article;

11) 'international auditing standards' means International Standards on Auditing (ISA) and related Statements and Standards, insofar as relevant to the statutory audit;

12) 'international accounting standards' means International Accounting Standards (IAS), International Financial Reporting Standards (IFRS) and related Interpretations (SIC-IFRIC interpretations), subsequent amendments to those standards and related interpretations, and future standards and related interpretations issued or adopted by the International Accounting Standards Board (IASB);

13) 'public-interest entities' means entities governed by the law of a Member State whose transferable securities are admitted to trading on a regulated market of any Member State within the meaning of point 14 of Article 4(1) of Directive 2004/39/EC, credit institutions as defined in point 1 of Article 1 of Directive 2000/12/EC of the European Parliament and of the Council of 20 March 2000 relating to the taking up and pursuit of the business of credit institutions[17] and insurance undertakings within the meaning of Article 2(1) of Directive 91/674/EEC. Member States may also designate other entities as public-interest entities, for instance entities that are of significant public relevance because of the nature of their business, their size or the number of their employees;

14) 'cooperative' means a European Cooperative Society as defined in Article 1 of Council Regulation (EC) No 1435/2003 of 22 July 2003 on the Statute for a European Cooperative Society (SCE),[18] or any other cooperative for which a statutory audit is required under Community law, such as credit institutions as defined in point 1 of Article 1 of Directive 2000/12/EC and insurance undertakings within the meaning of Article 2(1) of Directive 91/674/EEC;

15) 'non-practitioner' means any natural person who, for at least three years before his or her involvement in the governance of the public oversight system, has not carried out statutory audits, has not held voting rights in an audit firm, has not been a member of the administrative or management body of an audit firm and has not been employed by, or otherwise associated with, an audit firm;

16) 'key audit partner(s)' mean(s):

(a) the statutory auditor(s) designated by an audit firm for a particular audit engagement as being primarily responsible for carrying out the statutory audit on behalf of the audit firm; or

---

[17] OJ L 126, 26.5.2000, 1, reproduced supra under no. B. 32. Directive as last amended by Directive 2006/29/EC (OJ L 70, 9.3.2006, 50). Directive 2000/12/EC has been repealed as from 20 July 2006 by article 158 of Directive 2006/48/EC (OJ L 177, 30.6.1), reproduced supra under no. B. 41.

[18] OJ L 207, 18.8.2003, 1, reproduced supra under no. C. 25.

(b) in the case of a group audit, at least the statutory auditor(s) designated by an audit firm as being primarily responsible for carrying out the statutory audit at the level of the group and the statutory auditor(s) designated as being primarily responsible at the level of material subsidiaries; or

(c) the statutory auditor(s) who sign(s) the audit report.

Chapter II
Approval, Continuing Education and Mutual Recognition

Article 3
Approval of statutory auditors and audit firms

1. A statutory audit shall be carried out only by statutory auditors or audit firms which are approved by the Member State requiring the statutory audit.

2. Each Member State shall designate competent authorities which shall be responsible for approving statutory auditors and audit firms.

The competent authorities may be professional associations, provided that they are subject to a system of public oversight as provided for in Chapter VIII.

3. Without prejudice to Article 11, the competent authorities of the Member States may approve as statutory auditors only natural persons who satisfy at least the conditions laid down in Articles 4 and 6 to 10.

4. The competent authorities of the Member States may approve as audit firms only those entities which satisfy the following conditions:

(a) the natural persons who carry out statutory audits on behalf of an audit firm must satisfy at least the conditions imposed by Articles 4 and 6 to 12 and must be approved as statutory auditors in the Member State concerned;

(b) a majority of the voting rights in an entity must be held by audit firms which are approved in any Member State or by natural persons who satisfy at least the conditions imposed by Articles 4 and 6 to 12. Member States may provide that such natural persons must also have been approved in another Member State. For the purpose of the statutory audit of cooperatives and similar entities as referred to in Article 45 of Directive 86/635/EEC, Member States may establish other specific provisions in relation to voting rights;

(c) a majority—up to a maximum of 75%—of the members of the administrative or management body of the entity must be audit firms which are approved in any Member State or natural persons who satisfy at least the conditions imposed by Articles 4 and 6 to 12. Member States may provide that such natural persons must also have been approved in another Member State. Where such a body has no more than two members, one of those members must satisfy at least the conditions in this point;

(d) the firm must satisfy the condition imposed by Article 4.

Member States may set additional conditions only in relation to point (c). Such conditions shall be proportionate to the objectives pursued and shall not go beyond what is strictly necessary.

Article 4
Good repute

The competent authorities of a Member State may grant approval only to natural persons or firms of good repute.

Article 5
Withdrawal of approval

1. Approval of a statutory auditor or an audit firm shall be withdrawn if the good repute of that person or firm has been seriously compromised. Member States may, however, provide for a reasonable period of time for the purpose of meeting the requirements of good repute.

2. Approval of an audit firm shall be withdrawn if any of the conditions imposed in Article 3(4), points (b) and (c) is no longer fulfilled. Member States may, however, provide for a reasonable period of time for the purpose of fulfilling those conditions.

3. Where the approval of a statutory auditor or of an audit firm is withdrawn for any reason, the competent authority of the Member State where the approval is withdrawn shall communicate that fact and the reasons for the withdrawal to the relevant competent authorities of Member States where the statutory auditor or audit firm is also approved which are entered in the first-named Member State's register in accordance with Article 16(1), point (c).

Article 6
Educational qualifications

Without prejudice to Article 11, a natural person may be approved to carry out a statutory audit only after having attained university entrance or equivalent level, then completed a course of theoretical instruction, undergone practical training and passed an examination of professional competence of university final or equivalent examination level, organised or recognised by the Member State concerned.

Article 7
Examination of professional competence

The examination of professional competence referred to in Article 6 shall guarantee the necessary level of theoretical knowledge of subjects relevant to statutory audit and the ability to apply such knowledge in practice. Part at least of that examination shall be written.

Article 8
Test of theoretical knowledge

1. The test of theoretical knowledge included in the examination shall cover the following subjects in particular:

(a) general accounting theory and principles,

(b) legal requirements and standards relating to the preparation of annual and consolidated accounts,

(c) international accounting standards,

(d) financial analysis,

(e) cost and management accounting,

(f) risk management and internal control,

(g) auditing and professional skills,

(h) legal requirements and professional standards relating to statutory audit and statutory auditors,

(i) international auditing standards,

(j) professional ethics and independence.

2. It shall also cover at least the following subjects insofar as they are relevant to auditing:

(a) company law and corporate governance,

(b) the law of insolvency and similar procedures,

(c) tax law,

(d) civil and commercial law,

(e) social security law and employment law,

(f) information technology and computer systems,

(g) business, general and financial economics,

(h) mathematics and statistics,

(i) basic principles of the financial management of undertakings.

3. The Commission may, in accordance with the procedure referred to in Article 48(2), adapt the list of subjects to be included in the test of theoretical knowledge referred to in paragraph 1. When adopting those implementing measures the Commission shall take into account developments in auditing and the audit profession.

Article 9
Exemptions

1. By way of derogation from Articles 7 and 8, a Member State may provide that a person who has passed a university or equivalent examination or holds a university degree or equivalent qualification in one or more of the subjects referred to in Article 8 may be exempted from the test of theoretical knowledge in the subjects covered by that examination or degree.

2. By way of derogation from Article 7, a Member State may provide that a holder of a university degree or equivalent qualification in

one or more of the subjects referred to in Article 8 may be exempted from the test of the ability to apply in practice his or her theoretical knowledge of such subjects if he or she has received practical training in those subjects attested by an examination or diploma recognised by the State.

Article 10
Practical training

1. In order to ensure the ability to apply theoretical knowledge in practice, a test of which is included in the examination, a trainee shall complete a minimum of three years' practical training in, inter alia, the auditing of annual accounts, consolidated accounts or similar financial statements. At least two thirds of such practical training shall be completed with a statutory auditor or audit firm approved in any Member State.

2. Member States shall ensure that all training is carried out with persons providing adequate guarantees regarding their ability to provide practical training.

Article 11
Qualification through long-term practical experience

A Member State may approve a person who does not satisfy the conditions laid down in Article 6 as a statutory auditor, if he or she can show either:

(a) that he or she has, for 15 years, engaged in professional activities which have enabled him or her to acquire sufficient experience in the fields of finance, law and accountancy, and has passed the examination of professional competence referred to in Article 7, or

(b) that he or she has, for seven years, engaged in professional activities in those fields and has, in addition, undergone the practical training referred to in Article 10 and passed the examination of professional competence referred to in Article 7.

CASE

Case C-255/01 Panagiotis Markopoulos and Others v Ypourgos Anaptyxis and others [2004] ECR I-9077

Article 11 of the Eighth Directive enables a host Member State to approve, for the purpose of carrying out the statutory auditing of accounting documents, professional persons already approved in another Member State, without requiring them to pass an examination of professional competence, if the competent authorities of the host Member State consider their qualifications to be equivalent to those required under the national legislation of the host Member State, in accordance with the directive.

If a comparative examination of diplomas results in the finding that the knowledge and qualifications certified by the foreign diploma correspond to those required by the national provisions, the Member State must recognize that diploma as fulfilling the requirements laid down by its national provisions. If, on the other hand, the comparison reveals that the knowledge and qualifications certified by the foreign diploma and those required by the national provisions correspond only in part, the host Member State is entitled to require the person concerned to show that he or she has acquired the knowledge and qualifications which are lacking. In such a case, it will be for the competent national authorities to assess whether the knowledge acquired in the host Member State, either during a course of study or by way of practical experience, is sufficient in order to prove possession of the knowledge which is lacking.

In those circumstances, it must be concluded that Article 15 of the Eighth Directive permits the Member States to approve persons who meet the conditions laid down in that article, namely, persons who have the qualifications in the Member State concerned to carry out the statutory auditing of the documents referred to in Article 1(1) of that documents referred to in Article 1(1) of that directive and who did so until the date fixed in Article 15, without their being required first to have passed an examination of professional competence.

Article 12
Combination of practical training and theoretical instruction

1. Member States may provide that periods of theoretical instruction in the fields referred to in Article 8 shall count towards the periods of professional activity referred to in Article 11, provided that such instruction is attested by an examination recognised by the State. Such instruction shall not last less than one year, nor may it reduce the period of professional activity by more than four years.

2. The period of professional activity and practical training shall not be shorter than the course of theoretical instruction together with the practical training required in Article 10.

Article 13
Continuing education

Member States shall ensure that statutory auditors are required to take part in appropriate programmes of continuing education in order to maintain their theoretical knowledge, professional skills and values at a sufficiently high level, and that failure to respect the continuing education requirements is subject to appropriate penalties as referred to in Article 30.

Article 14
Approval of statutory auditors from other Member States

The competent authorities of the Member States shall establish procedures for the approval of statutory auditors who have been approved in other Member States. Those procedures shall not go beyond a requirement to pass an aptitude test in accordance with Article 4 of Council Directive 89/48/EEC of 21 December 1988 on a general system for the recognition of higher-education diplomas awarded on completion of professional education and training of at least three years' duration.[19] The aptitude test, which shall be conducted in one of the languages permitted by the language rules applicable in the Member State concerned, shall cover only the statutory auditor's adequate knowledge of the laws and regulations of that Member State insofar as relevant to statutory audits.

CHAPTER III
REGISTRATION

Article 15
Public register

1. Each Member State shall ensure that statutory auditors and audit firms are entered in a public register in accordance with Articles 16 and 17. In exceptional circumstances, Member States may disapply the requirements laid down in this Article and Article 16 regarding disclosure only to the extent necessary to mitigate an imminent and significant threat to the personal security of any person.

2. Member States shall ensure that each statutory auditor and audit firm is identified in the public register by an individual number. Registration information shall be stored in the register in electronic form and shall be electronically accessible to the public.

3. The public register shall also contain the name and address of the competent authorities responsible for approval as referred to in Article 3, for quality assurance as referred to in Article 29, for investigations and penalties on statutory auditors and audit firms as referred to in Article 30, and for public oversight as referred to in Article 32.

4. Member States shall ensure that the public register is fully operational by 29 June 2009.

---

[19] OJ L 19, 24.1.1989, 16. Directive as amended by Directive 2001/19/EC of the European Parliament and of the Council (OJ L 206, 31.7.2001, 1).

Article 16
Registration of statutory auditors

1. As regards statutory auditors, the public register shall contain at least the following information:

(a) name, address and registration number;

(b) if applicable, the name, address, website address and registration number of the audit firm(s) by which the statutory auditor is employed, or with whom he or she is associated as a partner or otherwise;

(c) all other registration(s) as statutory auditor with the competent authorities of other Member States and as auditor with third countries, including the name(s) of the registration authority(ies), and, if applicable, the registration number(s).

2. Third-country auditors registered in accordance with Article 45 shall be clearly indicated in the register as such and not as statutory auditors.

Article 17
Registration of audit firms

1. As regards audit firms, the public register shall contain at least the following information:

(a) name, address and registration number;

(b) legal form;

(c) contact information, the primary contact person and, where applicable, the website address;

(d) address of each office in the Member State;

(e) name and registration number of all statutory auditors employed by or associated as partners or otherwise with the audit firm;

(f) names and business addresses of all owners and shareholders;

(g) names and business addresses of all members of the administrative or management body;

(h) if applicable, the membership of a network and a list of the names and addresses of member firms and affiliates or an indication of the place where such information is publicly available;

(i) all other registration(s) as audit firm with the competent authorities of other Member States and as audit entity with third countries, including the name(s) of the registration authority(ies), and, if applicable, the registration number(s).

2. Third-country audit entities registered in accordance with Article 45 shall be clearly indicated in the register as such and not as audit firms.

Article 18
Updating of registration information

Member States shall ensure that statutory auditors and audit firms notify the competent authorities in charge of the public register without undue delay of any change of information contained in the public register. The register shall be updated without undue delay after notification.

Article 19
Responsibility for registration information

The information provided to the relevant competent authorities in accordance with Articles 16, 17 and 18 shall be signed by the statutory auditor or audit firm. Where the competent authority provides for the information to be made available electronically, that can, for example, be done by means of an electronic signature as defined in point 1 of Article 2 of Directive 1999/93/EC of the European Parliament and of the Council of 13 December 1999 on a Community framework for electronic signatures.[20]

Article 20
Language

1. The information entered in the public register shall be drawn up in one of the languages permitted by the language rules applicable in the Member State concerned.

2. Member States may additionally allow the information to be entered in the public register in any other official language(s) of the Community. Member States may require the translation of the information to be certified.

---

[20] OJ L 13, 19.1.2000, 12, reproduced infra under no. C.P. 18.

In all cases, the Member State concerned shall ensure that the register indicates whether or not the translation is certified.

Chapter IV
Professional Ethics, Independence, Objectivity, Confidentiality and Professional Secrecy

Article 21
Professional ethics

1. Member States shall ensure that all statutory auditors and audit firms are subject to principles of professional ethics, covering at least their public-interest function, their integrity and objectivity and their professional competence and due care.

2. In order to ensure confidence in the audit function and to ensure uniform application of paragraph 1 of this Article, the Commission may, in accordance with the procedure referred to in Article 48(2), adopt principle-based implementing measures governing professional ethics.

Article 22
Independence and objectivity

1. Member States shall ensure that when carrying out a statutory audit, the statutory auditor and/or the audit firm is independent of the audited entity and is not involved in the decision-taking of the audited entity.

2. Member States shall ensure that a statutory auditor or an audit firm shall not carry out a statutory audit if there is any direct or indirect financial, business, employment or other relationship—including the provision of additional non-audit services—between the statutory auditor, audit firm or network and the audited entity from which an objective, reasonable and informed third party would conclude that the statutory auditor's or audit firm's independence is compromised. If the statutory auditor's or audit firm's independence is affected by threats, such as self-review, self-interest, advocacy, familiarity or trust or intimidation, the statutory auditor or audit firm must apply safeguards in order to mitigate those threats. If the significance of the threats compared to the safeguards applied is such that his, her or its independence is compromised, the statutory auditor or audit firm shall not carry out the statutory audit.

Member States shall in addition ensure that, where statutory audits of public-interest entities are concerned and where appropriate to safeguard the statutory auditor's or audit firm's independence, a statutory auditor or an audit firm shall not carry out a statutory audit in cases of self-review or self-interest.

3. Member States shall ensure that a statutory auditor or audit firm documents in the audit working papers all significant threats to his, her or its independence as well as the safeguards applied to mitigate those threats.

4. In order to ensure confidence in the audit function and to ensure uniform application of paragraphs 1 and 2 of this Article, the Commission may, in accordance with the procedure referred to in Article 48(2), adopt principle-based implementing measures concerning:

(a) the threats and safeguards referred to in paragraph 2;

(b) the situations in which the significance of the threats, as referred to in paragraph 2, is such that the independence of the statutory auditor or audit firm is compromised;

(c) the cases of self-review and self-interest referred to in the second subparagraph of paragraph 2, in which statutory audits may or may not be carried out.

Article 23
Confidentiality and professional secrecy

1. Member States shall ensure that all information and documents to which a statutory auditor or audit firm has access when carrying out a statutory audit are protected by adequate rules on confidentiality and professional secrecy.

2. Confidentiality and professional secrecy rules relating to statutory auditors or audit firms shall

not impede enforcement of the provisions of this Directive.

3. Where a statutory auditor or audit firm is replaced by another statutory auditor or audit firm, the former statutory auditor or audit firm shall provide the incoming statutory auditor or audit firm with access to all relevant information concerning the audited entity.

4. A statutory auditor or audit firm who has ceased to be engaged in a particular audit assignment and a former statutory auditor or audit firm shall remain subject to the provisions of paragraphs 1 and 2 with respect to that audit assignment.

Article 24
Independence and objectivity of the statutory auditors carrying out the statutory audit on behalf of audit firms

Member States shall ensure that the owners or shareholders of an audit firm as well as the members of the administrative, management and supervisory bodies of such a firm, or of an affiliated firm, do not intervene in the execution of a statutory audit in any way which jeopardises the independence and objectivity of the statutory auditor who carries out the statutory audit on behalf of the audit firm.

Article 25
Audit fees

Member States shall ensure that adequate rules are in place which provide that fees for statutory audits:

(a) are not influenced or determined by the provision of additional services to the audited entity;

(b) cannot be based on any form of contingency.

CHAPTER V
AUDITING STANDARDS AND AUDIT REPORTING

Article 26
Auditing standards

1. Member States shall require statutory auditors and audit firms to carry out statutory audits in compliance with international auditing standards adopted by the Commission in accordance with the procedure referred to in Article 48(2). Member States may apply a national auditing standard as long as the Commission has not adopted an international auditing standard covering the same subject-matter. Adopted international auditing standards shall be published in full in each of the official languages of the Community in the Official Journal of the European Union.

2. The Commission may decide, in accordance with the procedure referred to in Article 48(2), on the applicability of international auditing standards within the Community. The Commission shall adopt international auditing standards for application in the Community only if they:

(a) have been developed with proper due process, public oversight and transparency, and are generally accepted internationally;

(b) contribute a high level of credibility and quality to the annual or consolidated accounts in conformity with the principles set out in Article 2(3) of Directive 78/660/EEC and in Article 16(3) of Directive 83/349/EEC; and

(c) are conducive to the European public good.

3. Member States may impose audit procedures or requirements in addition to—or, in exceptional cases, by carving out parts of—the international auditing standards only if these stem from specific national legal requirements relating to the scope of statutory audits. Member States shall ensure that these audit procedures or requirements comply with the provisions laid down in points (b) and (c) of paragraph 2 and shall communicate them to the Commission and Member States before their adoption. In the exceptional case of the carving out of parts of an international auditing standard, Member States shall communicate their specific national legal requirements, as well as the grounds for maintaining them, to the Commission and the other Member States at least six months before their national adoption or, in the case of requirements already existing at the time of adoption of an international auditing standard, at the latest within three months of the

adoption of the relevant international auditing standard.

4. Member States may impose additional requirements relating to the statutory audits of annual and consolidated accounts for a period expiring on 29 June 2010.

Article 27
Statutory audits of consolidated accounts

Member States shall ensure that in the case of a statutory audit of the consolidated accounts of a group of undertakings:

(a) the group auditor bears the full responsibility for the audit report in relation with the consolidated accounts;

(b) the group auditor carries out a review and maintains documentation of his or her review of the audit work performed by third-country auditor(s), statutory auditor(s), third-country audit entity(ies) or audit firm(s) for the purpose of the group audit. The documentation retained by the group auditor shall be such as enables the relevant competent authority to review the work of the group auditor properly;

(c) when a component of a group of undertakings is audited by auditor(s) or audit entity(ies) from a third country that has no working arrangement as referred to in Article 47, the group auditor is responsible for ensuring proper delivery, when requested, to the public oversight authorities of the documentation of the audit work performed by the third-country auditor(s) or audit entity(ies), including the working papers relevant to the group audit. To ensure such delivery, the group auditor shall retain a copy of such documentation, or alternatively agree with the third-country auditor(s) or audit entity(ies) his proper and unrestricted access upon request, or take any other appropriate action. If legal or other impediments prevent audit working papers from being passed from a third country to the group auditor, the documentation retained by the group auditor shall include evidence that he or she has undertaken the appropriate procedures in order to gain access to the audit documentation, and in the case of impediments other than legal ones arising from country legislation, evidence supporting such an impediment.

Article 28
Audit reporting

1. Where an audit firm carries out the statutory audit, the audit report shall be signed by at least the statutory auditor(s) carrying out the statutory audit on behalf of the audit firm. In exceptional circumstances Member States may provide that this signature need not be disclosed to the public if such disclosure could lead to an imminent and significant threat to the personal security of any person. In any case the name(s) of the person(s) involved shall be known to the relevant competent authorities.

2. Notwithstanding Article 51a(1) of Directive 78/660/EEC, if the Commission has not adopted a common standard for audit reports in accordance with Article 26(1) of this Directive, it may, in accordance with the procedure referred to in Article 48(2) of this Directive, adopt a common standard for audit reports for annual or consolidated accounts which have been prepared in accordance with approved international accounting standards, in order to enhance public confidence in the audit function.

CHAPTER VI
QUALITY ASSURANCE

Article 29
Quality assurance systems

1. Each Member State shall ensure that all statutory auditors and audit firms are subject to a system of quality assurance which meets at least the following criteria:

(a) the quality assurance system shall be organised in such a manner that it is independent of the reviewed statutory auditors and audit firms and subject to public oversight as provided for in Chapter VIII;

(b) the funding for the quality assurance system shall be secure and free from any possible undue influence by statutory auditors or audit firms;

(c) the quality assurance system shall have adequate resources;

(d) the persons who carry out quality assurance reviews shall have appropriate professional education and relevant experience in statutory audit and financial reporting combined with specific training on quality assurance reviews;

(e) the selection of reviewers for specific quality assurance review assignments shall be effected in accordance with an objective procedure designed to ensure that there are no conflicts of interest between the reviewers and the statutory auditor or audit firm under review;

(f) the scope of the quality assurance review, supported by adequate testing of selected audit files, shall include an assessment of compliance with applicable auditing standards and independence requirements, of the quantity and quality of resources spent, of the audit fees charged and of the internal quality control system of the audit firm;

(g) the quality assurance review shall be the subject of a report which shall contain the main conclusions of the quality assurance review;

(h) quality assurance reviews shall take place at least every six years;

(i) the overall results of the quality assurance system shall be published annually;

(j) recommendations of quality reviews shall be followed up by the statutory auditor or audit firm within a reasonable period.

If the recommendations referred to in point (j) are not followed up, the statutory auditor or audit firm shall, if applicable, be subject to the system of disciplinary actions or penalties referred to in Article 30.

2. The Commission may, in accordance with the procedure referred to in Article 48(2), adopt implementing measures in order to enhance public confidence in the audit function and to ensure uniform application of points (a), (b) and (e) to (j) of paragraph 1.

Chapter VII
Investigations and Penalties

Article 30
Systems of investigations and penalties

1. Member States shall ensure that there are effective systems of investigations and penalties to detect, correct and prevent inadequate execution of the statutory audit.

2. Without prejudice to Member States' civil liability regimes, Member States shall provide for effective, proportionate and dissuasive penalties in respect of statutory auditors and audit firms, where statutory audits are not carried out in conformity with the provisions adopted in the implementation of this Directive.

3. Member States shall provide that measures taken and penalties imposed on statutory auditors and audit firms are appropriately disclosed to the public. Penalties shall include the possibility of the withdrawal of approval.

Article 31
Auditors' liability

Before 1 January 2007 the Commission shall present a report on the impact of the current national liability rules for the carrying out of statutory audits on European capital markets and on the insurance conditions for statutory auditors and audit firms, including an objective analysis of the limitations of financial liability. The Commission shall, where appropriate, carry out a public consultation. In the light of that report, the Commission shall, if it considers it appropriate, submit recommendations to the Member States.

Chapter VIII
Public Oversight and Regulatory Arrangements between Member States

Article 32
Principles of public oversight

1. Member States shall organise an effective system of public oversight for statutory auditors

and audit firms based on the principles set out in paragraphs 2 to 7.

2. All statutory auditors and audit firms shall be subject to public oversight.

3. The system of public oversight shall be governed by non-practitioners who are knowledgeable in the areas relevant to statutory audit. Member States may, however, allow a minority of practitioners to be involved in the governance of the public oversight system. Persons involved in the governance of the public oversight system shall be selected in accordance with an independent and transparent nomination procedure.

4. The system of public oversight shall have the ultimate responsibility for the oversight of:

(a) the approval and registration of statutory auditors and audit firms,

(b) the adoption of standards on professional ethics, internal quality control of audit firms and auditing, and

(c) continuing education, quality assurance and investigative and disciplinary systems.

5. The system of public oversight shall have the right, where necessary, to conduct investigations in relation to statutory auditors and audit firms and the right to take appropriate action.

6. The system of public oversight shall be transparent. This shall include the publication of annual work programmes and activity reports.

7. The system of public oversight shall be adequately funded. The funding for the public oversight system shall be secure and free from any undue influence by statutory auditors or audit firms.

Article 33

Cooperation between public oversight systems at Community level

Member States shall ensure that regulatory arrangements for public oversight systems permit effective cooperation at Community level in respect of Member States' oversight activities. To that end, each Member State shall make one entity specifically responsible for ensuring that cooperation.

Article 34

Mutual recognition of regulatory arrangements between Member States

1. Regulatory arrangements of Member States shall respect the principle of home-country regulation and oversight by the Member State in which the statutory auditor or audit firm is approved and the audited entity has its registered office.

2. In the case of a statutory audit of consolidated accounts, the Member State requiring the statutory audit of the consolidated accounts may not impose additional requirements in relation to the statutory audit concerning registration, quality assurance review, auditing standards, professional ethics and independence on a statutory auditor or audit firm carrying out a statutory audit of a subsidiary established in another Member State.

3. In the case of a company whose securities are traded on a regulated market in a Member State other than that in which that company has its registered office, the Member State in which the securities are traded may not impose any additional requirements in relation to the statutory audit concerning registration, quality assurance review, auditing standards, professional ethics and independence on a statutory auditor or audit firm carrying out the statutory audit of the annual or consolidated accounts of that company.

Article 35

Designation of competent authorities

1. Member States shall designate one or more competent authorities for the purposes of the tasks provided for in this Directive. Member States shall inform the Commission of their designation.

2. The competent authorities shall be organised in such a manner that conflicts of interests are avoided.

Article 36
Professional secrecy and regulatory cooperation between Member States

1. The competent authorities of Member States responsible for approval, registration, quality assurance, inspection and discipline shall cooperate with each other whenever necessary for the purpose of carrying out their respective responsibilities under this Directive. The competent authorities in a Member State responsible for approval, registration, quality assurance, inspection and discipline shall render assistance to competent authorities in other Member States. In particular, competent authorities shall exchange information and cooperate in investigations related to the carrying-out of statutory audits.

2. The obligation of professional secrecy shall apply to all persons who are employed or who have been employed by competent authorities. Information covered by professional secrecy may not be disclosed to any other person or authority except by virtue of the laws, regulations or administrative procedures of a Member State.

3. Paragraph 2 shall not prevent competent authorities from exchanging confidential information. Information thus exchanged shall be covered by the obligation of professional secrecy, to which persons employed or formerly employed by competent authorities are subject.

4. Competent authorities shall, on request, and without undue delay, supply any information required for the purpose referred to in paragraph 1. Where necessary, the competent authorities receiving any such request shall, without undue delay, take the necessary measures to gather the required information. Information thus supplied shall be covered by the obligation of professional secrecy to which the persons employed or formerly employed by the competent authorities that received the information are subject.

If the requested competent authority is not able to supply the required information without undue delay, it shall notify the requesting competent authority of the reasons therefor.

The competent authorities may refuse to act on a request for information where:

(a) supplying information might adversely affect the sovereignty, security or public order of the requested Member State or breach national security rules; or

(b) judicial proceedings have already been initiated in respect of the same actions and against the same statutory auditors or audit firms before the authorities of the requested Member State; or

(c) final judgment has already been passed in respect of the same actions and on the same statutory auditors or audit firms by the competent authorities of the requested Member State.

Without prejudice to the obligations to which they are subject in judicial proceedings, competent authorities which receive information pursuant to paragraph 1 may use it only for the exercise of their functions within the scope of this Directive and in the context of administrative or judicial proceedings specifically related to the exercise of those functions.

5. Where a competent authority concludes that activities contrary to the provisions of this Directive are being or have been carried out on the territory of another Member State, it shall notify the competent authority of the other Member State of that conclusion in as specific a manner as possible. The competent authority of the other Member State shall take appropriate action. It shall inform the notifying competent authority of the outcome and, to the extent possible, of significant interim developments.

6. A competent authority of one Member State may also request that an investigation be carried out by the competent authority of another Member State on the latter's territory.

It may further request that some of its own personnel be allowed to accompany the personnel of the competent authority of that other Member State in the course of the investigation.

The investigation shall be subject throughout to the overall control of the Member State on whose territory it is conducted.

The competent authorities may refuse to act on a request for an investigation to be carried out as provided for in the first subparagraph, or on a request for its personnel to be accompanied by personnel of a competent authority of another Member State as provided for in the second subparagraph, where:

(a) such an investigation might adversely affect the sovereignty, security or public order of the requested Member State; or

(b) judicial proceedings have already been initiated in respect of the same actions and against the same persons before the authorities of the requested Member State; or

(c) final judgment has already been passed in respect of the same actions on such persons by the competent authorities of the requested Member State.

7. In accordance with the procedure referred to in Article 48(2) the Commission may adopt implementing measures in order to facilitate cooperation between competent authorities on the procedures for the exchange of information and modalities for cross-border investigations provided for in paragraphs 2 to 4 of this Article.

Chapter IX
Appointment and Dismissal

Article 37
Appointment of statutory auditors or audit firms

1. The statutory auditor or audit firm shall be appointed by the general meeting of shareholders or members of the audited entity.

2. Member States may allow alternative systems or modalities for the appointment of the statutory auditor or audit firm, provided that those systems or modalities are designed to ensure the independence of the statutory auditor or audit firm from the executive members of the administrative body or from the managerial body of the audited entity.

Article 38
Dismissal and resignation of statutory auditors or audit firms

1. Member States shall ensure that statutory auditors or audit firms may be dismissed only where there are proper grounds. Divergence of opinions on accounting treatments or audit procedures shall not be proper grounds for dismissal.

2. Member States shall ensure that the audited entity and the statutory auditor or audit firm inform the authority or authorities responsible for public oversight concerning the dismissal or resignation of the statutory auditor or audit firm during the term of appointment and give an adequate explanation of the reasons therefore.

Chapter X
Special Provisions for the Statutory Audits of Public-Interest Entities

Article 39
Application to non-listed public-interest entities

Member States may exempt public-interest entities which have not issued transferable securities admitted to trading on a regulated market within the meaning of point 14 of Article 4(1) of Directive 2004/39/EC and their statutory auditor(s) or audit firm(s) from one or more of the requirements in this Chapter.

Article 40
Transparency report

1. Member States shall ensure that statutory auditors and audit firms that carry out statutory audit(s) of public-interest entities publish on their websites, within three months of the end of each financial year, annual transparency reports that include at least the following:

(a) a description of the legal structure and ownership;

(b) where the audit firm belongs to a network, a description of the network and the legal and structural arrangements in the network;

(c) a description of the governance structure of the audit firm;

(d) a description of the internal quality control system of the audit firm and a statement by the administrative or management body on the effectiveness of its functioning;

(e) an indication of when the last quality assurance review referred to in Article 29 took place;

(f) a list of public-interest entities for which the audit firm has carried out statutory audits during the preceding financial year;

(g) a statement concerning the audit firm's independence practices which also confirms that an internal review of independence compliance has been conducted;

(h) a statement on the policy followed by the audit firm concerning the continuing education of statutory auditors referred to in Article 13;

(i) financial information showing the importance of the audit firm, such as the total turnover divided into fees from the statutory audit of annual and consolidated accounts, and fees charged for other assurance services, tax advisory services and other non-audit services;

(j) information concerning the basis for the partners' remuneration.

Member States may in exceptional circumstances disapply the requirement in point (f) to the extent necessary to mitigate an imminent and significant threat to the personal security of any person.

2. The transparency report shall be signed by the statutory auditor or audit firm, as the case may be. This can be done, for example, by means of an electronic signature as defined in Article 2(1) of Directive 1999/93/EC.

Article 41

Audit committee

1. Each public-interest entity shall have an audit committee. The Member State shall determine whether audit committees are to be composed of non-executive members of the administrative body and/or members of the supervisory body of the audited entity and/or members appointed by the general meeting of shareholders of the audited entity. At least one member of the audit committee shall be independent and shall have competence in accounting and/or auditing.

In public-interest entities which meet the criteria of Article 2(1), point (f) of Directive 2003/71/EC,[21] Member States may permit the functions assigned to the audit committee to be performed by the administrative or supervisory body as a whole, provided at least that when the chairman of such a body is an executive member, he or she is not the chairman of the audit committee.

2. Without prejudice to the responsibility of the members of the administrative, management or supervisory bodies, or of other members who are appointed by the general meeting of shareholders of the audited entity, the audit committee shall inter alia:

(a) monitor the financial reporting process;

(b) monitor the effectiveness of the company's internal control, internal audit where applicable, and risk management systems;

(c) monitor the statutory audit of the annual and consolidated accounts;

(d) review and monitor the independence of the statutory auditor or audit firm, and in particular the provision of additional services to the audited entity.

3. In a public-interest entity, the proposal of the administrative or supervisory body for the appointment of a statutory auditor or audit firm shall be based on a recommendation made by the audit committee.

4. The statutory auditor or audit firm shall report to the audit committee on key matters arising from the statutory audit, and in particular on material weaknesses in internal control in relation to the financial reporting process.

---

[21] Directive 2003/71/EC of the European Parliament and of the Council of 4 November 2003 on the prospectus to be published when securities are offered to the public or admitted to trading (OJ L 345, 31.12.2003, 64), reproduced infra under no. S. 25.

5. Member States may allow or decide that the provisions laid down in paragraphs 1 to 4 shall not apply to any public-interest entity that has a body performing equivalent functions to an audit committee, established and functioning according to provisions in place in the Member State in which the entity to be audited is registered. In such a case the entity shall disclose which body carries out these functions and how it is composed.

6. Member States may exempt from the obligation to have an audit committee:

(a) any public-interest entity which is a subsidiary undertaking within the meaning of Article 1 of Directive 83/349/EEC if the entity complies with the requirements in paragraphs 1 to 4 of this Article at group level;

(b) any public-interest entity which is a collective investment undertaking as defined in Article 1(2) of Directive 85/611/EEC. Member States may also exempt public-interest entities the sole object of which is the collective investment of capital provided by the public, which operate on the principle of risk spreading and which do not seek to take legal or management control over any of the issuers of its underlying investments, provided that those collective investment undertakings are authorised and subject to supervision by competent authorities and that they have a depositary exercising functions equivalent to those under Directive 85/611/EEC;

(c) any public-interest entity the sole business of which is to act as issuer of asset-backed securities as defined in Article 2(5) of Commission Regulation (EC) No 809/2004 of 29 April 2004 implementing Directive 2003/71/EC.[22] In such instances, the Member State shall require the entity to explain to the public the reasons for which it considers it not appropriate to have either an audit committee or an administrative or supervisory body entrusted to carry out the functions of an audit committee;

(d) any credit institution within the meaning of Article 1(1) of Directive 2000/12/EC whose shares are not admitted to trading on a regulated market of any Member State within the meaning of point 14 of Article 4(1) of Directive 2004/39/EC and which has, in a continuous or repeated manner, issued only debt securities, provided that the total nominal amount of all such debt securities remains below EUR 100 000 000 and that it has not published a prospectus under Directive 2003/71/EC.

Article 42
Independence

1. In addition to the provisions laid down in Articles 22 and 24, Member States shall ensure that statutory auditors or audit firms that carry out the statutory audit of a public-interest entity:

(a) confirm annually in writing to the audit committee their independence from the audited public-interest entity;

(b) disclose annually to the audit committee any additional services provided to the audited entity; and

(c) discuss with the audit committee the threats to their independence and the safeguards applied to mitigate those threats as documented by them pursuant to Article 22(3).

2. Member States shall ensure that the key audit partner(s) responsible for carrying out a statutory audit rotate(s) from the audit engagement within a maximum period of seven years from the date of appointment and is/are allowed to participate in the audit of the audited entity again after a period of at least two years.

3. The statutory auditor or the key audit partner who carries out a statutory audit on behalf of an audit firm shall not be allowed to take up a key management position in the audited entity before a period of at least two years has elapsed since he or she resigned as a statutory auditor or key audit partner from the audit engagement.

Article 43
Quality assurance

The quality assurance review referred to in Article 29 shall be carried out at least every three years for

---

[22] OJ L 149, 30.4.2004, 1.

statutory auditors or audit firms that carry out statutory audits of public-interest entities.

Chapter XI
International Aspects

Article 44
Approval of auditors from third countries

1. Subject to reciprocity, the competent authorities of a Member State may approve a third-country auditor as statutory auditor if that person has furnished proof that he or she complies with requirements equivalent to those laid down in Articles 4 and 6 to 13.

2. The competent authorities of a Member State shall, before granting approval to a third-country auditor who meets the requirements of paragraph 1, apply the requirements laid down in Article 14.

Article 45
Registration and oversight of third-country auditors and audit entities

1. The competent authorities of a Member State shall, in accordance with Articles 15 to 17, register every third-country auditor and audit entity that provides an audit report concerning the annual or consolidated accounts of a company incorporated outwith the Community whose transferable securities are admitted to trading on a regulated market of that Member State within the meaning of point 14 of Article 4(1) of Directive 2004/39/EC, except when the company is an issuer exclusively of debt securities admitted to trading on a regulated market in a Member State within the meaning of Article 2(1)(b) of Directive 2004/109/EC,[23] the denomination per unit of which is at least EUR 50 000 or, in case of debt securities denominated in another currency, equivalent, at the date of issue, to at least EUR 50 000.

2. Articles 18 and 19 shall apply.

3. Member States shall subject registered third-country auditors and audit entities to their systems of oversight, their quality assurance systems and their systems of investigation and penalties. A Member State may exempt a registered third-country auditor or audit entity from being subject to its quality assurance system if another Member State's or third country's system of quality assurance that has been assessed as equivalent in accordance with Article 46 has carried out a quality review of the third-country auditor or audit entity concerned during the previous three years.

4. Without prejudice to Article 46, audit reports concerning annual accounts or consolidated accounts referred to in paragraph 1 of this Article issued by third-country auditors or audit entities that are not registered in the Member State shall have no legal effect in that Member State.

5. A Member State may register a third-country audit entity only if:

(a) it meets requirements which are equivalent to those laid down in Article 3(3);

(b) the majority of the members of the administrative or management body of the third-country audit entity meet requirements which are equivalent to those laid down in Articles 4 to 10;

(c) the third-country auditor carrying out the audit on behalf of the third-country audit entity meets requirements which are equivalent to those laid down in Articles 4 to 10;

(d) the audits of the annual or consolidated accounts referred to in paragraph 1 are carried out in accordance with international auditing standards as referred to in Article 26, as well as the requirements laid down in Articles 22, 24 and 25, or with equivalent standards and requirements;

(e) it publishes on its website an annual transparency report which includes the information referred to in Article 40 or it complies with equivalent disclosure requirements.

---

[23] Directive 2004/109/EC of the European Parliament and of the Council of 15 December 2004 on the harmonisation of transparency requirements in relation to information about issuers whose securities are admitted to trading on a regulated market (OJ L 390, 31.12.2004, 38), reproduced infra under no. S. 31.

6. In order to ensure uniform application of paragraph 5, point (d), the equivalence referred to therein shall be assessed by the Commission in cooperation with Member States and shall be decided upon by the Commission in accordance with the procedure referred to in Article 48(2). Pending such a decision by the Commission, Member States may assess the equivalence referred to in paragraph 5, point (d) as long as the Commission has not taken any decision.

Article 46
Derogation in the case of equivalence

1. Member States may disapply or modify the requirements in Article 45(1) and (3) on the basis of reciprocity only if the third-country auditors or audit entities are subject to systems of public oversight, quality assurance and investigations and penalties in the third country that meet requirements equivalent to those of Articles 29, 30 and 32.

2. In order to ensure uniform application of paragraph 1 of this Article, the equivalence referred to therein shall be assessed by the Commission in cooperation with Member States and shall be decided upon by the Commission in accordance with the procedure referred to in Article 48(2). Member States may assess the equivalence referred to in paragraph 1 of this Article or rely on the assessments carried out by other Member States as long as the Commission has not taken any decision. If the Commission decides that the requirement of equivalence referred to in paragraph 1 of this Article is not complied with, it may allow the auditors and audit entities concerned to continue their audit activities in accordance with the relevant Member State's requirements during an appropriate transitional period.

3. Member States shall communicate to the Commission:

(a) their assessments of the equivalence referred to in paragraph 2; and

(b) the main elements of their cooperative arrangements with third-country systems of public oversight, quality assurance and investigations and penalties, on the basis of paragraph 1.

Article 47
Cooperation with competent authorities from third countries

1. Member States may allow the transfer to the competent authorities of a third country of audit working papers or other documents held by statutory auditors or audit firms approved by them, provided that:

(a) those audit working papers or other documents relate to audits of companies which have issued securities in that third country or which form part of a group issuing statutory consolidated accounts in that third country;

(b) the transfer takes place via the home competent authorities to the competent authorities of that third country and at their request;

(c) the competent authorities of the third country concerned meet requirements which have been declared adequate in accordance with paragraph 3;

(d) there are working arrangements on the basis of reciprocity agreed between the competent authorities concerned;

(e) the transfer of personal data to the third country is in accordance with Chapter IV of Directive 95/46/EC.

2. The working arrangements referred to in paragraph 1, point (d) shall ensure that:

(a) justification as to the purpose of the request for audit working papers and other documents is provided by the competent authorities;

(b) the persons employed or formerly employed by the competent authorities of the third country that receive the information are subject to obligations of professional secrecy;

(c) the competent authorities of the third country may use audit working papers and other documents only for the exercise of their functions of public oversight, quality assurance and investigations that meet requirements equivalent to those of Articles 29, 30 and 32;

(d) the request from a competent authority of a third country for audit working papers or other documents held by a statutory auditor or audit firm can be refused:

– where the provision of those working papers or documents would adversely affect the

sovereignty, security or public order of the Community or of the requested Member State; or
- where judicial proceedings have already been initiated in respect of the same actions and against the same persons before the authorities of the requested Member State.

3. The adequacy referred to in paragraph 1, point (c) shall be decided upon by the Commission in accordance with the procedure referred to in Article 48(2) in order to facilitate cooperation between competent authorities. The assessment of adequacy shall be carried out in cooperation with Member States and be based on the requirements of Article 36 or essentially equivalent functional results. Member States shall take the measures necessary to comply with the Commission's decision.

4. In exceptional cases and by way of derogation from paragraph 1, Member States may allow statutory auditors and audit firms approved by them to transfer audit working papers and other documents directly to the competent authorities of a third country, provided that:

(a) investigations have been initiated by the competent authorities in that third country;

(b) the transfer does not conflict with the obligations with which statutory auditors and audit firms are required to comply in relation to the transfer of audit working papers and other documents to their home competent authority;

(c) there are working arrangements with the competent authorities of that third country that allow the competent authorities in the Member State reciprocal direct access to audit working papers and other documents of that third-country's audit entities;

(d) the requesting competent authority of the third country informs in advance the home competent authority of the statutory auditor or audit firm of each direct request for information, indicating the reasons therefor;

(e) the conditions referred to in paragraph 2 are respected.

5. The Commission may, in accordance with the procedure referred to in Article 48(2), specify the exceptional cases referred to in paragraph 4 of this Article in order to facilitate cooperation between competent authorities and to ensure the uniform application of paragraph 4 of this Article.

6. Member States shall communicate to the Commission the working arrangements referred to in paragraphs 1 and 4.

Chapter XII
Transitional and Final Provisions

Article 48
Committee procedure

1. The Commission shall be assisted by a committee (hereinafter referred to as 'the Committee').

2. Where reference is made to this paragraph Articles 5 and 7 of Decision 1999/468/EC shall apply, having regard to the provisions of Article 8 thereof.

The period laid down in Article 5(6) of Decision 1999/468/EC shall be set at three months.

3. The Committee shall adopt its Rules of Procedure.

4. Without prejudice to the implementing measures already adopted, and except for the provisions laid down in Article 26, upon expiry of a two-year period following the adoption of this Directive and on 1 April 2008 at the latest, the application of its provisions requiring the adoption of technical rules, amendments and decisions in accordance with paragraph 2 shall be suspended. Acting on a proposal from the Commission, the European Parliament and the Council may renew the provisions concerned in accordance with the procedure laid down in Article 251 of the Treaty and to that end they shall review them prior to the expiry of the period or date referred to above.

Article 49
Amendment of Directive 78/660/EEC and Directive 83/349/EEC

[. . .]

¶ *Article 49 adds article 43(1)(15), replaces article 44(1) and article 45(2) of Directive 78/660/EEC, reproduced supra under no. C. 4 and adds article 34(16) of Directive 83/349/EEC, reproduced supra under no. C.6. The modifications are directly incorporated therein.*

Article 50
Repeal of Directive 84/253/EEC

[. . .]

¶ *Article 50 repeals Directive 84/253/EC, reproduced supra under no. C. 7, with effect from 29 June 2006. References to the repealed Directive shall be construed as references to this Directive.*

Article 51
Transitional provision

Statutory auditors or audit firms that are approved by the competent authorities of the Member States in accordance with Directive 84/253/EEC before the entry into force of the provisions referred to in Article 53(1) shall be considered as having been approved in accordance with this Directive.

Article 52
Minimum harmonisation

Member States requiring statutory audit may impose more stringent requirements, unless otherwise provided for by this Directive.

Article 53
Transposition

1. Before 29 June 2008 Member States shall adopt and publish the provisions necessary to comply with this Directive. They shall forthwith inform the Commission thereof.

2. When Member States adopt those provisions, they shall contain a reference to this Directive or be accompanied by such a reference on the occasion of their official publication. The methods of making such reference shall be laid down by Member States.

3. Member States shall communicate to the Commission the texts of the main provisions of national law which they adopt in the field covered by this Directive.

Article 54
Entry into force

This Directive shall enter into force on the 20th day following its publication in the Official Journal of the European Union.

Article 55
Addressees

This Directive is addressed to the Member States.

C. 31.

European Parliament and Council Directive 2006/46/EC
of 14 June 2006
amending Council Directives 78/660/EEC on the annual accounts of certain types of companies, 83/349/EEC on consolidated accounts, 86/635/EEC on the annual accounts and consolidated accounts of banks and other financial institutions and 91/674/EEC on the annual accounts and consolidated accounts of insurance undertakings[1]

(Text with EEA relevance)

THE EUROPEAN PARLIAMENT AND THE COUNCIL OF THE EUROPEAN UNION,

Having regard to the Treaty establishing the European Community, and in particular Article 44(1) thereof,

Having regard to the proposal from the Commission,

Having regard to the opinion of the European Economic and Social Committee,[2]

Acting in accordance with the procedure laid down in Article 251 of the Treaty,[3]

Whereas:

(1) On 21 May 2003, the Commission adopted an Action Plan announcing measures to modernise company law and enhance corporate governance in the Community. As a short-term priority, the Community was to confirm the collective responsibility of board members, increase transparency in transactions with related parties and off-balance-sheet arrangements and improve disclosure about corporate governance practices applied in a company.

(2) Pursuant to that Action Plan, members of the administrative, management and supervisory bodies of a company were, as a minimum requirement, to be collectively responsible towards the company for drawing up and publishing annual accounts and annual reports. The same approach was also to apply to members of the administrative, management and supervisory bodies of undertakings drawing up consolidated accounts. Those bodies act within the competences assigned to them by national law. This should not prevent Member States from going further and providing for direct responsibility towards shareholders or even other stakeholders. On the other hand, Member States were to refrain from opting for a system of responsibility limited to individual board members. However, this should not preclude the ability of courts or other enforcement bodies in the Member States to impose penalties on an individual board member.

(3) Liability for drawing up and publishing annual accounts and consolidated accounts as well as annual reports and consolidated annual reports is based on national law. Appropriate liability rules, as laid down by each Member State under its national law or regulations, should be applicable to members of the administrative, management and supervisory bodies. Member States should remain free to determine the extent of the liability.

(4) In order to promote credible financial reporting processes across the European Union, members of the company body that is responsible for the preparation of the company's financial reports should have the duty to ensure that the financial information included in a company's

---

[1] OJ L 224, 16.8.2006, 1–7.
[2] OJ C 294, 25.11.2005, 4.
[3] Opinion of the European Parliament of 15 December 2005 (not yet published in the Official Journal) and Council Decision of 22 May 2006.

annual accounts and annual reports gives a true and fair view.

(5) On 27 September 2004 the Commission adopted a Communication on preventing and combating financial and corporate malpractice outlining 'inter alia' the Commission policy initiatives regarding internal control in companies and responsibility of board members.

(6) At present Fourth Council Directive 78/660/EEC[4] and Seventh Council Directive 83/349/EEC[5] only provide for disclosure of transactions between a company and the company's affiliated undertakings. With the objective of bringing companies whose securities are not admitted to trading on a regulated market closer to companies applying the international accounting standards for their consolidated accounts, disclosure should be extended to cover other types of related parties, such as key management members and spouses of board members, but only where such transactions are material and not carried out at arm's length. Disclosure of material transactions with related parties that are not carried out under normal market conditions can assist users of annual accounts to assess the financial position of the company as well as, when the company belongs to a group, the financial situation of the group as a whole. Intra-group related party transactions should be eliminated in the preparation of consolidated financial statements.

(7) Definitions of a related party as set out in the international accounting standards adopted by the Commission in accordance with Regulation (EC) No 1606/2002 of the European Parliament and of the Council of 19 July 2002 on the application of international accounting standards[6] should apply to Directives 78/660/EEC and 83/349/EEC.

(8) Off-balance-sheet arrangements may expose a company to risks and benefits which are material for an assessment of the financial position of the company and, when the company belongs to a group, the financial position of the group as a whole.

(9) Such off-balance-sheet arrangements could be any transactions or agreements which companies may have with entities, even unincorporated ones, that are not included in the balance sheet. Such off-balance-sheet arrangements may be associated with the creation or use of one or more Special Purpose Entities (SPEs) and offshore activities designed to address, inter alia, economic, legal, tax or accounting objectives. Examples of such off-balance-sheet arrangements include risk and benefit-sharing arrangements or obligations arising from a contract such as debt factoring, combined sale and repurchase agreements, consignment stock arrangements, take or pay arrangements, securitisation arranged through separate companies and unincorporated entities, pledged assets, operating leasing arrangements, outsourcing and the like. Appropriate disclosure of the material risks and benefits of such arrangements that are not included in the balance sheet should be set out in the notes to the accounts or the consolidated accounts.

(10) Companies whose securities are admitted to trading on a regulated market and which have their registered office in the Community should be obliged to disclose an annual corporate governance statement as a specific and clearly identifiable section of the annual report. That statement should at least provide shareholders with easily accessible key information about the corporate governance practices actually applied, including a description of the main features of any existing risk management systems and internal controls in relation to the financial reporting process. The corporate governance statement should make clear whether the company applies any provisions on corporate governance other than those provided for in national law, regardless of whether those provisions are directly laid down in a corporate governance code to which the company is subject or in any corporate governance code which the company may have decided to apply. Furthermore, where relevant, companies may also provide an analysis of environmental and social aspects necessary for an understanding of

---

[4] OJ L 222, 14.8.1978, 11, reproduced supra under no. C. 4. Directive as last amended by Directive 2006/43/EC of the European Parliament and of the Council (OJ L 157, 9.6.2006, 87).
[5] OJ L 193, 18.7.1983, 1, reproduced supra under no. C. 6. Directive as last amended by Directive 2006/43/EC.
[6] OJ L 243, 11.9.2002, 1, reproduced supra under no. C. 22.

the company's development, performance and position. There is no need to impose the requirement of a separate corporate governance statement on undertakings drawing up a consolidated annual report. However, the information concerning the group's risk management system and internal control system should be presented.

(11) The various measures adopted under this Directive should not necessarily apply to the same types of companies or undertakings. Member States should be able to exempt small companies, as described in Article 11 of Directive 78/660/EEC, from the requirements concerning related parties and off-balance-sheet arrangements under this Directive. Companies which already disclose information about transactions with related parties in their accounts pursuant to international accounting standards as adopted in the European Union should not be required to disclose further information under this Directive, as the application of the international accounting standards already results in a true and fair view of such a company. The provisions of this Directive concerning the corporate governance statement should apply to all companies, including banks, insurance and reinsurance undertakings and companies which have issued securities other than shares admitted to trading on a regulated market insofar as they are not exempted by Member States. The provisions of this Directive concerning duties and liabilities of board members as well as penalties should apply to all companies to which Council Directives 78/660/EEC, 86/635/EEC[7] and 91/674/EEC[8] apply and to all undertakings which draw up consolidated accounts in accordance with Directive 83/349/EEC.

(12) At present Directive 78/660/EEC makes provision for examination every five years of, inter alia, the maximum thresholds for balance sheet and net turnover which Member States may apply in determining which companies may be exempted from certain disclosure requirements. In addition to those five-yearly examinations, an additional one-off increase in those balance sheet and net turnover thresholds may also be appropriate. There is no obligation on Member States to make use of those increased thresholds.

(13) Since the objectives of this Directive, namely facilitating cross-border investments and improving EU-wide comparability and public confidence in financial statements and reports through enhanced and consistent specific disclosures, cannot be sufficiently achieved by the Member States and can therefore, by reason of the scale and the effects of this Directive, be better achieved at Community level, the Community may adopt measures, in accordance with the principle of subsidiarity as set out in Article 5 of the Treaty. In accordance with the principle of proportionality, as set out in that Article, this Directive does not go beyond what is necessary in order to achieve those objectives.

(14) This Directive respects the fundamental rights and observes the principles recognised in particular by the Charter of the Fundamental Rights of the European Union.

(15) In accordance with paragraph 34 of the Interinstitutional agreement on better lawmaking,[9] Member States are encouraged to draw up, for themselves and in the interests of the Community, their own tables illustrating, as far as possible, the correlation between this Directive and the transposition measures, and to make them public.

(16) Directives 78/660/EEC, 83/349/EEC, 86/635/EEC and 91/674/EEC should therefore be amended accordingly,

HAVE ADOPTED THIS DIRECTIVE:

Article 1–Article 4

[ ]

---

[7] OJ L 372, 31.12.1986, 1, reproduced supra under no. B. 7. Directive as last amended by Directive 2003/51/EC of the European Parliament and of the Council (OJ L 178, 17.7.2003, 16), reproduced supra under no. C. 23.

[8] OJ L 374, 31.12.1991, 7, reproduced infra under no. I. 23. Directive as amended by Directive 2003/51/EC, reproduced supra under no. C. 23.

¶ *Articles 1 to 4 modify Directive 78/660/EEC, reproduced supra under no. C. 4, Directive 83/349/EEC, reproduced supra under*

[9] OJ C 321, 31.12.2003, 1.

no. C. 6., Directive 83/635/EEC, reproduced supra under no. B. 7. and Directive 91/674/EEC, reproduced infra under I. 23. The modifications are directly incorporated therein.

Article 5

Transposition

1. Member States shall bring into force the laws, regulations and administrative provisions necessary to comply with this Directive by 5 September 2008 at the latest.

When Member States adopt these measures, they shall contain a reference to this Directive or shall be accompanied by such a reference on the occasion of their official publication. The methods of making such reference shall be laid down by Member States.

2. Member States shall communicate to the Commission the text of the main provisions of national law which they adopt in the field covered by this Directive.

Article 6

Entry into force

This Directive shall enter into force on the 20th day following its publication in the Official Journal of the European Union.

Article 7

Addressees

This Directive is addressed to the Member States.

C. 32.

European Parliament and Council Directive 2006/68/EC of 6 September 2006 amending Council Directive 77/91/EEC as regards the formation of public limited liability companies and the maintenance and alteration of their capital[1]

(Text with EEA relevance)

THE EUROPEAN PARLIAMENT AND THE COUNCIL OF THE EUROPEAN UNION,

Having regard to the Treaty establishing the European Community, and in particular Article 44(1) thereof,

Having regard to the proposal from the Commission,

Having regard to the Opinion of the European Economic and Social Committee,[2]

Acting in accordance with the procedure laid down in Article 251 of the Treaty,[3]

Whereas:

(1) The Second Council Directive 77/91/EEC of 13 December 1976 on coordination of safeguards which, for the protection of the interests of members and others, are required by Member States of companies within the meaning of the second paragraph of Article 58 of the Treaty, in respect of the formation of public limited liability companies and the maintenance and alteration of their capital, with a view to making such safeguards equivalent,[4] sets out the requirements for several capital-related measures taken by such companies.

(2) In its Communication of 21 May 2003 to the Council and the European Parliament entitled 'Modernising Company Law and Enhancing Corporate Governance in the European Union—A Plan to Move Forward' the Commission draws the conclusion that a simplification and modernisation of Directive 77/91/EEC would significantly contribute to the promotion of business efficiency and competitiveness without reducing the protection offered to shareholders and creditors. Those objectives have the first priority but do not affect the need to proceed without delay to a general examination of the feasibility of alternatives to the capital maintenance regime which would adequately protect the interests of creditors and shareholders of a public limited liability company.

(3) Member States should be able to permit public limited liability companies to allot shares for consideration other than in cash without requiring them to obtain a special expert valuation in cases in which there is a clear point of reference for the valuation of such consideration. Nonetheless, the right of minority shareholders to require such valuation should be guaranteed.

(4) Public limited liability companies should be allowed to acquire their own shares up to the limit of the company's distributable reserves and the period for which such an acquisition may be authorised by the general meeting should be increased so as to enhance flexibility and reduce the administrative burden for companies which have to react promptly to market developments affecting the price of their shares.

(5) Member States should be able to permit public limited liability companies to grant financial assistance with a view to the acquisition of their

---

[1] OJ L 264, 25.9.2006, 32–36.
[2] OJ C 294, 25.11.2005, 1.
[3] Opinion of the European Parliament of 14 March 2006 (not yet published in the Official Journal) and Council decision of 24 July 2006.
[4] OJ L 26, 31.1.1977, 1, reproduced infra under no. I. 7. Directive as last amended by the 2003 Act of Accession.

shares by a third party up to the limit of the company's distributable reserves so as to increase flexibility with regard to changes in the ownership structure of the share capital of companies. This possibility should be subject to safeguards, having regard to this Directive's objective of protecting both shareholders and third parties.

(6) In order to enhance standardised creditor protection in all Member States, creditors should be able to resort, under certain conditions, to judicial or administrative proceedings where their claims are at stake as a consequence of a reduction in the capital of a public limited liability company.

(7) In order to ensure that market abuse is prevented, the Member States should take into account, for the purpose of implementation of this Directive, the provisions of Directive 2003/6/EC of the European Parliament and of the Council of 28 January 2003 on insider dealing and market manipulation (market abuse),[5] Commission Regulation (EC) No 2273/2003 of 22 December 2003 implementing Directive 2003/6/EC of the European Parliament and of the Council as regards exemptions for buy-back programmes and stabilisation of financial instruments[6] and Commission Directive 2004/72/EC of 29 April 2004 implementing Directive 2003/6/EC of the European Parliament and of the Council as regards accepted market practices, the definition of inside information in relation to derivatives on commodities, the drawing up of lists of insiders, the notification of managers' transactions and the notification of suspicious transactions.[7]

(8) Directive 77/91/EEC should therefore be amended accordingly.

(9) In accordance with point 34 of the Interinstitutional Agreement on better lawmaking,[8] Member States are encouraged to draw up, for themselves and in the interest of the Community, their own tables illustrating, as far as possible, the correlation between this Directive and the transposition measures, and to make them public,

HAVE ADOPTED THIS DIRECTIVE:

Article 1

[. . .]

¶ *Article 1 amends articles 1(1), 21st indent, 11(1), first subparagraph, 19, paragraph 1, 20(3), 23, paragraph 1, 27(2), second subparagraph, 32, paragraph 1 and 41, paragraph 1 and inserts articles 10a, 10b and 23a in Directive 77/91/EEC, reproduced supra under no. C. 2. The modifications are directly incorporated therein.*

Article 2

1. Member States shall bring into force the laws, regulations and administrative provisions necessary to comply with this Directive by 15 April 2008.[9]

When Member States adopt these measures, they shall contain a reference to this Directive or shall be accompanied by such reference on the occasion of their official publication. The methods of making such reference shall be laid down by Member States.

2. Member States shall communicate to the Commission the texts of the main provisions of national law which they adopt in the field covered by this Directive.

Article 3

This Directive shall enter into force on the 20th day following that of its publication in the *Official Journal of the European Union*.

Article 4

This Directive is addressed to the Member States.

---

[5] OJ L 96, 12.4.2003, 16, reproduced infra under no. S. 24.
[6] OJ L 336, 23.12.2003, 33.
[7] OJ L 162, 30.4.2004, 70, reproduced infra under no. S. 30.
[8] OJ C 321, 31.12.2003, 1.

[9] Eighteen months following the date of entry into force of this Directive.

Part IV
CONSUMER PROTECTION ESPECIALLY RELATED TO FINANCIAL TRANSACTIONS

C.P. 1.

[Council Directive 84/450/EEC
of 10 September 1984
concerning misleading and comparative advertising][1]

¶ *The title of this Directive has been replaced by article 1(1) of Directive 97/55/EC, reproduced infra under no. C.P. 13.*

THE COUNCIL OF THE EUROPEAN COMMUNITIES,

Having regard to the Treaty establishing the European Economic Community, and in particular Article [94][2] thereof,

Having regard to the proposal from the Commission,[3]

Having regard to the opinion of the European Parliament,[4]

Having regard to the opinion of the Economic and Social Committee,[5]

Whereas the laws against misleading advertising now in force in the Member States differ widely, whereas, since advertising reaches beyond the frontiers of individual Member States, it has a direct effect on the establishment and the functioning of the common market;

Whereas misleading advertising can lead to distortion of competition within the common market;

Whereas advertising, whether or not it induces a contract, affects the economic welfare of consumers;

Whereas misleading advertising may cause a consumer to take decisions prejudicial to him when acquiring goods or other property, or using services, and the differences between the laws of the Member States not only lead, in many cases, to inadequate levels of consumer protection but also hinder the execution of advertising campaigns beyond national boundaries and thus affect the free circulation of goods and provision of services;

Whereas the second programme of the European Economic Community for a consumer protection and information policy provides for appropriate action for the protection of consumers against misleading and unfair advertising;

Whereas it is in the interest of the public in general, as well as that of consumers and all those who, in competition with one another, carry on a trade, business, craft or profession, in the common market, to harmonise in the first instance national provisions against misleading advertising and that, at a second stage, unfair advertising and, as far as necessary, comparative advertising should be dealt with, on the basis of appropriate Commission proposals;

---

[1] OJ L 250, 19.9.1984, 17–20.
[2] The number between brackets has been changed as from 1 May 1999 by article 12 of the Treaty of Amsterdam.
[3] OJ C 140, 5.6.1979, 23.
[4] OJ C 171, 9.7.1979, 43.
[5] OJ C 133, 3.6.1981, 1.

Whereas minimum and objective criteria for determining whether advertising is misleading should be established for this purpose;

Whereas the laws to be adopted by Member States against misleading advertising must be adequate and effective;

Whereas persons or organisations regarded under national law as having a legitimate interest in the matter must have facilities for initiating proceedings against misleading advertising, either before a court or before an administrative authority which is competent to decide upon complaints or to initiate appropriate legal proceedings;

Whereas it should be for each Member State to decide whether to enable the courts or administrative authorities to require prior recourse to other established means of dealing with the complaint;

Whereas the courts or administrative authorities must have powers enabling them to order or obtain the cessation of misleading advertising;

Whereas in certain cases it may be desirable to prohibit misleading advertising even before it is published; whereas, however, this in no way implies that Member States are under an obligation to introduce rules requiring the systematic prior vetting of advertising;

Whereas provision should be made for accelerated procedures under which measures with interim or definitive effect can be taken;

Whereas it may be desirable to order the publication of decisions made by courts or administrative authorities or of corrective statements in order to eliminate any continuing effects of misleading advertising;

Whereas administrative authorities must be impartial and the exercise of their powers must be subject to judicial review;

Whereas the voluntary control exercised by self-regulatory bodies to eliminate misleading advertising may avoid recourse to administrative or judicial action and ought therefore to be encouraged;

Whereas the advertiser should be able to prove, by appropriate means, the material accuracy of the factual claims he makes in his advertising, and may in appropriate cases be required to do so by the court or administrative authority;

Whereas this Directive must not preclude Member States from retaining or adopting provisions with a view to ensuring more extensive protection of consumers, persons carrying on a trade, business, craft or profession, and the general public,

HAS ADOPTED THIS DIRECTIVE:

[Article 1

The purpose of this Directive is to protect traders against misleading advertising and the unfair consequences thereof and to lay down the conditions under which comparative advertising is permitted.]

¶ *Article 1 has been replaced by article 14(1) of Directive 2005/29/EC, reproduced infra under no. C.P. 24.*

Article 2

For the purpose of this Directive:

1. 'advertising' means the making of a representation in any form in connection with a trade, business, craft or profession in order to promote the supply of goods or services, including immovable property, rights and obligations;

2. 'misleading advertising' means any advertising which in any way, including its presentation, deceives or is likely to deceive the persons to whom it is addressed or whom it reaches and which, by reason of its deceptive nature, is likely to affect their economic behaviour or which, for those reasons, injures or is likely to injure a competitor;

[2a 'comparative advertising' means any advertising that explicitly or by implication identifies a competitor or goods or services offered by a competitor;]

[3. 'trader' means any natural or legal person who is acting for purposes relating to his trade, craft, business or profession and any one acting in the name of or on behalf of a trader;]

[4. 'code owner' means any entity, including a trader or group of traders, which is responsible for the formulation and revision of a code of conduct and/or for monitoring compliance with the code by those who have undertaken to be bound by it.]

¶ *Point 2a has been inserted by article 1(3) of Directive 97/55/EC, reproduced infra under no. C.P. 13.*
¶ *Point 3 of this article has been replaced by article 14(2) of Directive 2005/29/EC, reproduced infra under no. C.P. 24.*
¶ *Point 4 of this article has been added by article 14(2) of Directive 2005/29/EC, reproduced infra under no. C.P. 24.*

CASE

Case C-373/90 Criminal Proceedings Against X [1992] ECR I-0131

Directive 84/450/EEC does not preclude motor vehicles from being advertised as new, less expensive and guaranteed by the manufacturer when the vehicles concerned have been registered solely for the purpose of importation, have never been on the road and are sold in a Member State at a price lower than that charged by dealers established in that Member State because they are equipped with fewer accessories.

Article 3

In determining whether advertising is misleading, account shall be taken of all its features, and in particular of any information it contains concerning:

(a) the characteristics of goods or services, such as their availability, nature, execution, composition method and date of manufacture or provision fitness for purpose, uses, quantity, specification, geographical or commercial origin or the results to be expected from their use, or the results and material features of tests or checks carried out on the goods or services;

(b) the price or the manner in which the price is calculated, and the conditions on which the goods are supplied or the services provided;

(c) the nature, attributes and rights of the advertiser, such as his identity and assets, his qualifications and ownership of industrial, commercial or intellectual property rights or his awards and distinctions.

CASES

I. Case C-59/05 Siemens AG v VIPA Gesellschaft für Visualisierung und Prozeßautomatisierung mbH [2006] ECR I-02147

Article 3a(1)(g) of Council Directive 84/450/EEC must be interpreted as meaning that by using in its catalogues the core element of a manufacturer's distinguishing mark which is known in specialist circles, a competing supplier does not take unfair advantage of the reputation of that distinguishing mark.

II. Case C-44/01 Pippig Augenoptik GmbH & Co KG v Hartlauer Handelsgesellschaft mbH en Verlassenschaft nach dem verstorbenen Franz Josef Hartlauer [2003] ECR I-3095

1. Article 7(2) of Council Directive 84/450/EEC precludes the application to comparative advertising of stricter national provisions on protection against misleading advertising as far as the form and content of the comparison is concerned, without there being any need to establish distinctions between the various elements of the comparison, that is to say statements concerning the advertiser's offer, statements concerning the competitor's offer and the relationship between those offers.

2. Article 3a(1)(a) of Directive 84/450/EEC must be interpreted as meaning that, whereas the advertiser is in principle free to state or not to state the brand name of rival products in comparative advertising, it is for the national court to verify whether, in particular circumstances, characterized by the importance of the brand in the buyer's choice and by a major difference between the respective brand names of the compared products in terms of how well known they are, omission of the better-known brand name is capable of being misleading.

3. Article 3a(1) of Directive 84/450/EEC, does not preclude compared products from being purchased through different distribution channels.

4. Article 3a(1) of Directive 84/450/EEC, does not preclude an advertiser from carrying out a test purchase with a competitor before his own offer has even commenced, where the conditions for the lawfulness of comparative advertising set out therein are complied with.

5. A price comparison does not entail the discrediting of a competitor, within the meaning of Article 3a(1)(e) of Directive 84/450/EEC, either on the grounds that the difference in price between the products compared is greater than the average price difference or by reason of the number of comparisons made. Article 3a(1)(e) of Directive 84/450/EEC, does not prevent comparative advertising, in addition to citing the competitor's name, from reproducing its logo and a picture of its shop front, if that advertising complies with the conditions for lawfulness laid down by Community law.

III. Case C-112/99 Toshiba Europe GmbH v Katun Germany GmbH [2001] ECR I-7945

1. On a proper construction of Articles 2(2a) and 3a(1)(c) the indication, in the catalogue of a supplier of spare parts and consumable items suitable for the products of an equipment manufacturer, of product numbers (OEM numbers) by which the equipment manufacturer designates the spare parts and consumable items which he himself sells may constitute comparative advertising which objectively compares one or more material, relevant, verifiable and representative features of goods.

2. On a proper construction of Article 3a(1)(g) where product numbers (OEM numbers) of an equipment manufacturer are, as such, distinguishing marks within the meaning of that provision, their use in the catalogues of a competing supplier enables him to take unfair advantage of the reputation attached to those marks only if the effect of the reference to them is to create, in the mind of the persons at whom the advertising is directed, an association between the manufacturer whose products are identified and the competing supplier, in that those persons associate the reputation of the manufacturer's products with the products of the competing supplier. In order to determine whether that condition is satisfied, account should be taken of the overall presentation of the advertising at issue and the type of persons for whom the advertising is intended.

[Article 3a

1. Comparative advertising shall, as far as the comparison is concerned, be permitted when the following conditions are met:

(a) it is not misleading within the meaning of Articles 2(2), 3 and 7(1) of this Directive or Articles 6 and 7 of Directive 2005/29/EC of the European Parliament and of the Council of 11 May 2005 concerning unfair business-to-consumer commercial practices in the internal market ([6]);

(b) it compares goods or services meeting the same needs or intended for the same purpose;

(c) it objectively compares one or more material, relevant, verifiable and representative features of those goods and services, which may include price;

(d) it does not discredit or denigrate the trade marks, trade names, other distinguishing marks, goods, services, activities, or circumstances of a competitor;

(e) for products with designation of origin, it relates in each case to products with the same designation;

(f) it does not take unfair advantage of the reputation of a trade mark, trade name or other distinguishing marks of a competitor or of the designation of origin of competing products;

(g) it does not present goods or services as imitations or replicas of goods or services bearing a protected trade mark or trade name;

(h) it does not create confusion among traders, between the advertiser and a competitor or between the advertiser's trade marks, trade names, other distinguishing marks, goods or services and those of a competitor.]

¶ *Article 3a has been added by article 1(4) of Directive 97/55/EC, reproduced infra under no. C.P. 13, and has subsequently been replaced by article 14(3) of Directive 2005/29/EC, reproduced infra under no. C.P. 24.*

Article 4

[1. Member States shall ensure that adequate and effective means exist to combat misleading advertising in order to enforce compliance with the provisions on comparative advertising in the interest of traders and competitors. Such means shall include legal provisions under which persons or organisations regarded under national law

---

[6] OJ L 149, 11.6.2005, 22, reproduced infra under no. C.P. 24.

as having a legitimate interest in combating misleading advertising or regulating comparative advertising may:

(a) take legal action against such advertising;

or

(b) bring such advertising before an administrative authority competent either to decide on complaints or to initiate appropriate legal proceedings.

It shall be for each Member State to decide which of these facilities shall be available and whether to enable the courts or administrative authorities to require prior recourse to other established means of dealing with complaints, including those referred to in Article 5.

It shall be for each Member State to decide:

(a) whether these legal facilities may be directed separately or jointly against a number of traders from the same economic sector;

and

(b) whether these legal facilities may be directed against a code owner where the relevant code promotes non-compliance with legal requirements.]

2. Under the legal provisions referred to in paragraph 1, Member States shall confer upon the courts or administrative authorities powers enabling them, in cases where they deem such measures to be necessary taking into account all the interests involved and in particular the public interest:

[– to order the cessation of, or to institute appropriate legal proceedings for an order for the cessation of, misleading advertising or unpermitted comparative advertising, or

– if the misleading advertising or unpermitted comparative advertising has not yet been published but publication is imminent, to order the prohibition of, or to institute appropriate legal proceedings for an order for the prohibition of, such publication,]

– if misleading advertising has not yet been published but publication is imminent, to order the prohibition of, or to institute appropriate legal proceedings for an order for the prohibition of, such publication, even without proof of actual loss or damage or of intention or negligence on the part of the advertiser.

Member States shall also make provision for the measures referred to in the first sub-paragraph to be taken under an accelerated procedure:

– either with interim effect, or

– with definitive effect, on the understanding that it is for each Member State to decide which of the two options to select.

[Furthermore, Member States may confer upon the courts or administrative authorities powers enabling them, with a view to eliminating the continuing effects of misleading advertising or unpermitted comparative advertising, the cessation of which has been ordered by a final decision]

– to require publication of that decision in full or in part and in such form as they deem adequate,

– to require in addition the publication of a corrective statement.

3. The administrative authorities referred to in paragraph 1 must:

(a) be composed so as not to cast doubt on their impartiality;

(b) have adequate powers, where they decide on complaints, to monitor and enforce the observance of their decisions effectively;

(c) normally give reasons for their decisions.

Where the powers referred to in paragraph 2 are exercised exclusively by an administrative authority, reasons for its decisions shall always be given. Furthermore in this case, provision must be made for procedures whereby improper or unreasonable exercise of its powers by the administrative authority or improper or unreasonable failure to exercise the said powers can be the subject of judicial review.

This Directive does not exclude the voluntary control of misleading advertising by self-regulatory bodies and recourse to such bodies by the persons or organisations referred to in Article 4 if proceedings before such bodies are in addition to the court or administrative proceedings referred to in that Article.

¶ *Article 4(1) has been replaced by article 14(4) of Directive 2005/29/EC, reproduced infra under no. C.P. 24.*

¶ The first and the second indent of the first subparagraph of article 4(2) have been amended by article 1(6)(a) of Directive 97/55/EC, reproduced infra under no. C.P. 13.

¶ The introductory wording to the third subparagraph of article 4(2) has been replaced by article 1(6)(b) of Directive 97/55 EC, reproduced infra under no. C.P. 13.

CASE

Joined cases C-34/95, C-35/95 and C-36/95 Konsumentombudsmannen (KO) v De Agostini (Svenska) Förlag AB (C-34/95) and TV-Shop i Sverige AB (C-35/95 and C-36/95) [1997] ECR I-3843

Directive 89/552/EEC, on the coordination of certain provisions laid down by law, regulation or administrative action in Member States concerning the pursuit of television broadcasting activities, does not preclude a Member State from taking, pursuant to general legislation on protection of consumers against misleading advertising, measures such as prohibitions and injunctions against an advertiser in relation to television advertising broadcast from another Member State, provided that those measures do not prevent the retransmission, as such, in its territory of television broadcasts coming from that other Member State. Although the directive provides that the Member States are to ensure freedom of reception and are not to impede retransmission on their territory of television broadcasts coming from other Member States on grounds relating to television advertising and sponsorship, it does not have the effect of excluding completely and automatically the application of rules other than those specifically concerning the broadcasting and distribution of programmes and, in particular, of national rules which have the general aim of consumer protection, provided that they do not involve secondary control of television broadcasts in addition to the control which the broadcasting Member State must carry out. Moreover, Directive 84/450/EEC which provides in particular in Article 4(1) that Member States are to ensure that adequate and effective means exist for the control of misleading advertising in the interests of consumers as well as competitors and the general public, could be robbed of its substance in the field of television advertising if the receiving Member State were deprived of all possibility of adopting measures against an advertiser and this would be in contradiction with the express intention of the Community legislature.

[*Article 5*

This Directive does not exclude the voluntary control, which Member States may encourage, of misleading or comparative advertising by self-regulatory bodies and recourse before such bodies are in addition to the court of administrative proceedings referred to in that Article.]

¶ Article 5 has been replaced by article 1(7) of Directive 97/55/EC, reproduced infra under no. C.P. 13.

Article 6

Member States shall confer upon the courts or administrative authorities powers enabling them in the civil or administrative proceedings provided for in Article 4:

[(a) to require the advertiser to furnish evidence as to the accuracy of factual claims in advertising if, taking into account the legitimate interest of the advertiser and any other party to the proceedings, such a requirement appears appropriate on the basis of the circumstances of the particular case and in the case of comparative advertising to require the advertiser to furnish such evidence in a short period of time; and]

(b) to consider factual claims as inaccurate if the evidence demanded in accordance with (a) is not furnished or is deemed insufficient by the court or administrative authority.

¶ Article 6(a) has been replaced by article 1(8) of Directive 97/55/EC, reproduced infra under no. C.P. 13.

[*Article 7*

[1. This Directive shall not preclude Member States from retaining or adopting provisions with a view to ensuring more extensive protection, with regard to misleading advertising, for traders and competitors.]

2. Paragraph 1 shall not apply to comparative advertising as far as the comparison is concerned.

3. The provisions of this Directive shall apply without prejudice to Community provisions on advertising for specific products and/or services or to restrictions or prohibitions on advertising in particular media.

4. The provisions of this Directive concerning comparative advertising shall not oblige Member States which, in compliance with the provisions of the Treaty, maintain or introduce advertising bans regarding certain goods or services, whether imposed directly or by a body or organisation responsible, under the law of the Member States, for regulating the exercise of a commercial, industrial, craft or professional activity, to permit comparative advertising regarding those goods or services. Where these bans are limited to particular media, the Directive shall apply to the media not covered by these bans.

5. Nothing in this Directive shall prevent Member States from, in compliance with the provisions of the Treaty, maintaining or introducing bans or limitations on the use of comparisons in the advertising of professional services, whether imposed directly or by a body or organisation responsible, under the law of the Member States, for regulating the exercise of a professional activity.]

¶ *Article 7 has been replaced by article 1(9) of Directive 97/55/EC, reproduced infra under no. C.P. 13.*
¶ *The first paragraph of this article has been replaced by article 14(5) of Directive 2005/29/EC, reproduced infra under no. C.P. 24.*

> CASE
>
> Case C-44/01 Pippig Augenoptik GmbH & Co KG v Hartlauer Handelsgesellschaft mbH en Verlassenschaft nach dem verstorbenen Franz Josef Hartlauer [2003] ECR I-3095
>
> See infra under Article 3 of this Directive.

Article 8

Member States shall bring into force the measures necessary to comply with this Directive by 1 October 1986 at the latest. They shall forthwith inform the Commission thereof.

Member States shall communicate to the Commission the text of all provisions of national law that they adopt in the field covered by this Directive.

Article 9

This Directive is addressed to the Member States.

C.P. 2.

Council Directive 85/374/EEC
of 25 July 1985
on the approximation of the laws, regulations and administrative provisions of the Member States concerning liability for defective products[1]

THE COUNCIL OF THE EUROPEAN COMMUNITIES,

Having regard to the treaty establishing the European Economic Community, and in particular Article [94][2] thereof,

Having regard to the proposal from the Commission,

Having regard to the opinion of the European Parliament,

Having regard to the opinion of the Economic and Social Committee,

Whereas approximation of the laws of the Member States concerning the liability of the producer for damage caused by the defectiveness of his products is necessary because the existing divergences may distort competition and affect the movement of goods within the common market and entail a differing degree of protection of the consumer against damage caused by a defective product to his health or property;

Whereas liability without fault on the part of the producer is the sole means of adequately solving the problem, peculiar to our age of increasing technicality, of a fair apportionment of the risks inherent in modern technological production;

Whereas liability without fault should apply only to movables which have been industrially produced; whereas, as a result, it is appropriate to exclude liability for agricultural products and game, except where they have *undergone* a processing of an industrial nature which could cause a defect in *these* products; whereas the liability provided for in this Directive should also apply to movables which are used in the construction of immovables or are installed in immovables;

Whereas protection of the consumer requires that all producers involved in the production process should be made liable, in so far as their finished product, component part or any raw material supplied by them was defective; whereas, for the same reason, liability should extend to importers of products into the Community and to persons who present themselves as producers by affixing their name, trade mark or other distinguishing feature or who supply a product the producer of which cannot be identified;

Whereas, in situations where several persons are liable for the same damage, the protection of the consumer requires that the injured person should be able to claim full compensation for the damage from any one of them;

Whereas, to protect the physical well-being and property of the consumer, the defectiveness of the product should be determined by reference not to its fitness for use but to the lack of the safety which the public at large is entitled to expect; whereas the safety is assessed by excluding any misuse of the product not reasonable under the circumstances;

Whereas a fair apportionment of risk between the injured person and the producer implies that the producer should be able to free himself from liability if he furnishes proof as to the existence of certain exonerating circumstances;

Whereas the protection of the consumer requires that the liability of the producer remains unaffected by acts or omissions of other persons

---

[1] OJ L 210, 7.8.1985, 29–33.
[2] The number between brackets has been changed as from 1 May 1999 by article 12 of the Treaty of Amsterdam.

having contributed to cause the damage; whereas, however, the contributory negligence of the injured person may be taken into account to reduce or disallow such liability;

Whereas the protection of the consumer requires compensation for death and personal injury as well as compensation for damage to property; whereas the latter should nevertheless be limited to goods for private use or consumption and be subject to a deduction of a lower threshold of a fixed amount in order to avoid litigation in an excessive number of cases; whereas this directive should not prejudice compensation for pain and suffering and other non-material damages payable, where appropriate, under the law applicable to the case;

Whereas a uniform period of limitation for the bringing of action for compensation is in the interests both of the injured person and of the producer;

Whereas products age in the course of time, higher safety standards are developed and the state of science and technology progresses; whereas, therefore, it would not be reasonable to make the producer liable for an unlimited period for the defectiveness of his product; whereas, therefore, liability should expire after a reasonable length of time, without prejudice to claims pending at law;

Whereas, to achieve effective protection of consumers, no contractual derogation should be permitted as regards the liability of the producer in relation to the injured person;

Whereas under the legal systems of the Member States an injured party may have a claim for damages based on grounds of contractual liability or on grounds of non-contractual liability other than that provided for in this directive; in so far as these provisions also serve to attain the objective of effective protection of consumers, they should remain unaffected by this Directive; whereas, in so far as effective protection of consumers in the sector of pharmaceutical products is already also attained in a Member State under a special liability system, claims based on this system should similarly remain possible;

Whereas, to the extent that liability for nuclear injury or damage is already covered in all Member States by adequate special rules, it has been possible to exclude damage of this type from the scope of this directive;

Whereas, since the exclusion of primary agricultural products and game from the scope of this Directive may be felt, in certain Member States, in view of what is expected for the protection of consumers, to restrict unduly such protection, it should be possible for a Member State to extend liability to such products;

Whereas, for similar reasons, the possibility offered to a producer to free himself from liability if he proves that the state of scientific and technical knowledge at the time when he put the product into circulation was not such as to enable the existence of a defect to be discovered may be felt in certain Member States to restrict unduly the protection of the consumer; whereas it should therefore be possible for a Member State to maintain in its legislation or to provide by new legislation that this exonerating circumstance is not admitted; whereas, in the case of new legislation, making use of this derogation should, however, be subject to a Community stand-still procedure, in order to raise, if possible, the level of protection in a uniform manner throughout the community;

Whereas, taking into account the legal traditions in most of the Member States, it is inappropriate to set any financial ceiling on the producer's liability without fault, whereas, in so far as there are, however, differing traditions, it seems possible to admit that a Member State may derogate from the principle of unlimited liability by providing a limit for the total liability of the producer for damage resulting from a death or personal injury and caused by identical items with the same defect, provided that his limit is established at a level sufficiently high to guarantee adequate protection of the consumer and the correct functioning of the common market;

Whereas the harmonisation resulting from this cannot be total at the present stage, but opens the way towards greater harmonisation; whereas it is therefore necessary that the Council receive at regular intervals reports from the Commission on the application of this Directive, accompanied, as the case may be, by appropriate proposals;

Whereas it is particularly important in this respect that a re-examination be carried out of those parts of the Directive relating to the derogations open to the Member States, at the expiry of a period of sufficient length or gather practical experience on the effects of these derogations on the protection of consumers and on the functioning of the common market,

HAS ADOPTED THIS DIRECTIVE:

Article 1

The producer shall be liable for damage caused by a defect in his product.

[Article 2

For the purpose of this Directive 'product' means all movables even if incorporated into another movable or into an immovable. 'Product' includes electricity.]

¶ *Article 2 has been amended by article 1 of Directive 1999/34/EC, reproduced infra under no. C.P. 16.*

Article 3

1. 'Producer' means the manufacturer of a finished product, the producer of any raw material or the manufacturer of a component part and any person who, by putting his name, trade mark or other distinguishing feature on the product presents himself as its producer.

2. Without prejudice to the liability of the producer, any person who imports into the Community a product of sale, hire, leasing or any form of distribution in the course of his business shall be deemed to be a producer within the meaning of this Directive and shall be responsible as a producer.

3. Where the producer of the product cannot be identified, each supplier of the product shall be treated as its producer unless he informs the injured person, within a reasonable time, of the identity of the producer or of the person who supplied him with the product. The same shall apply in the case of an imported product, if this product does not indicate the identity of the importer referred to in paragraph 2, even if the name of the producer is indicated.

CASE

Case C-402/03 SkovÆg v Bilka Lavprisvarehus A/S and Bilka Lavprisvarehus A/S v Jette Mikkelsen and Michael Due Nielsen [2006] ECR I-199

Council Directive 85/374/EEC must be interpreted as:
– precluding a national rule under which the supplier is answerable, beyond the cases listed exhaustively in Article 3(3) of the Directive, for the no-fault liability which the Directive establishes and imposes on the producer;
– not precluding a national rule under which the supplier is answerable without restriction for the producer's fault-based liability.

The injured person shall be required to prove the damage, the defect and the causal relationship between defect and damage.

Article 5

Where, as a result of the provisions of this Directive, two or more persons are liable for the same damage, they shall be liable jointly and severally, without prejudice to the provision of national law concerning the rights of contribution or recourse.

Article 6

1. A product is defective when it does not provide the safety which a person is entitled to expect, taking all circumstances into account, including:

(a) the presentation of the product;

(b) the use to which it could reasonably be expected that the product would be put;

(c) the time when the product was put into circulation.

2. A product shall not be considered defective for the sole reason that a better product is subsequently put into circulation.

Article 7

The producer shall not be liable as a result of this directive if he proves:

(a) that he did not put the product into circulation; or

(b) that, having regard to the circumstances, it is probable that the defect which caused the damage did not exist at the time when the product was put into circulation by him or that this defect came into being afterwards; or

(c) that the product was neither manufactured by him for sale or any form of distribution for economic purpose nor manufactured or distributed by him in the course of his business; or

(d) that the defect is due to compliance of the product with mandatory regulations issued by the public authorities; or

(e) that the state of scientific and technical knowledge at the time when he put the product into circulation was not such as to enable the existence of the defect to be discovered, or in the case of a manufacturer of a component that the defect is attributable to the design of the product in which the component has been fitted or to the instructions given by the manufacturer of the product.

CASES

I. Case C-203/99 Henning Veedfald v Århus Amtskommune [2001] ECR I-3569

1. Article 7(a) of Council Directive 85/374/EEC of 25 July 1985 is to be interpreted as meaning that a defective product is put into circulation when it is used during the provision of a specific medical service, consisting in preparing a human organ for transplantation, and the damage caused to the organ results from that preparatory treatment.

2. Article 7(c) of Directive 85/374/EEC is to be interpreted as meaning that the exemption from liability where an activity has no economic or business purpose does not extend to the case of a defective product which has been manufactured and used in the course of a specific medical service which is financed entirely from public funds and for which the patient is not required to pay any consideration.

II. Case C-300/95 Commission of the European Communities v United Kingdom of Great Britain and Northern Ireland [1997] ECR I-2649

In order for a producer to incur liability for defective products under Directive 85/374/EEC, the victim does not have to prove that the producer was at fault; however, in accordance with the principle of fair apportionment of risk between the injured person and the producer set forth in the seventh recital in the preamble to the directive, the producer has a defence if he can prove certain facts exonerating him from liability, including 'that the state of scientific and technical knowledge at the time when he put the product into circulation was not such as to enable the existence of the defect to be discovered'. Whilst the producer has to prove that the objective state of scientific and technical knowledge, including the most advanced level of such knowledge, without any restriction as to the industrial sector concerned, was not such as to enable the existence of the defect to be discovered, in order for the relevant knowledge to be successfully pleaded as against the producer, that knowledge must have been accessible at the time when the product in question was put into circulation. A national implementing provision to the effect that the producer has a defence if he can prove that the state of such knowledge was 'not such that a producer of products of the same description as the product in question might be expected to have discovered the defect if it had existed in his products while they were under his control' is not manifestly contrary to that Community rule. The argument that such national provision permits account to be taken of the subjective knowledge of a producer taking reasonable care, having regard to the standard precautions taken in the industrial sector in question, selectively stresses particular terms used in the provision without demonstrating that the general legal context of the provision at issue fails effectively to secure full application of the directive.

Article 8

1. Without prejudice to the provisions of national law concerning the right of contribution or recourse, the liability of the producer shall not be reduced when the damage is caused both by a

defect in product and by the act or omission of a third party.

2. The liability of the producer may be reduced or disallowed when, having regard to all the circumstances, the damage is caused both by a defect in the product and by the fault of the injured person or any person for whom the injured person is responsible.

Article 9

For the purpose of Article 1, 'damage' means:

(a) damage caused by death or by personal injuries;

(b) damage to, or destruction of, any item of property other than the defective product itself, with a lower threshold of 500 ECU, provided that the item of property:
(i) is of a type ordinarily intended for private use or consumption
and
(ii) was used by the injured person mainly for his own private use or consumption.

This Article shall be without prejudice to national provisions relating to non-material damage.

CASE

Case C-203/99 Henning Veedfald v Århus Amtskommune [2001] ECR I-3569

1. Article 9 of Directive 85/374/EEC is to be interpreted as meaning that, save for non-material damage whose reparation is governed solely by national law and the exclusions detailed in that article as regards damage to an item of property, a Member State may not restrict the types of material damage, resulting from death or from personal injury, or from damage to or destruction of an item of property, which are to be made good.

2. The national court is required, under Directive 85/374/EEC, to examine under which head the circumstances of the case are to be categorized, namely whether the case concerns damage covered either by point (a) or by point (b) of the first paragraph of Article 9 or non-material damage which may possibly be covered by national law. The national court may, however, not decline to award

---

any damages at all under the Directive on the ground that, where the other conditions of liability are fulfilled, the damage incurred is not such as to fall under any of the foregoing heads.

Article 10

1. Member States shall provide in their legislation that a limitation period of three years shall apply to proceedings for the recovery of damages as provided for in this Directive. The limitation period shall begin to run from the day on which the plaintiff became aware, or should reasonably have become aware, of the damage, the defect and the identity of the producer.

2. The laws of Member States regulating suspension or interruption of the limitation period shall not be affected by the Directive.

Article 11

Member States shall provide in their legislation that the rights conferred upon the injured person pursuant to this Directive shall be extinguished upon the expiry of a period of 10 years from the date on which the producer put into circulation the actual product which caused the damage, unless the injured person has in the meantime instituted proceedings against the producer.

CASE

Case C-127/04 Declan O'Byrne v Sanofi Pasteur MSD Ltd and Sanofi Pasteur SA [2006] ECR I-1313

1. Article 11 of Council Directive 85/374/EEC is to be interpreted as meaning that a product is put into circulation when it is taken out of the manufacturing process operated by the producer and enters a marketing process in the form in which it is offered to the public in order to be used or consumed.

2. When an action is brought against a company mistakenly considered to be the producer of a product whereas, in reality, it was manufactured by

another company, it is as a rule for national law to determine the conditions in accordance with which one party may be substituted for another in the context of such an action. A national court examining the conditions governing such a substitution must, however, ensure that due regard is had to the personal scope of Directive 85/374/EEC as established by Articles 1 and 3 thereof.

Article 12

The liability of the producer arising from this Directive may not, in relation to the injured person, be limited or excluded by a provision limiting his liability or exempting him from liability.

Article 13

This Directive shall not affect any rights, which an injured person may have according to the rules of the law of contractual or non-contractual liability or a special liability system existing at the moment when this Directive is notified.

CASE

Case C-183/00 María Victoria González Sánchez v Medicina Asturiana SA [2002] ECR I-3901

Article 13 must be interpreted as meaning that the rights conferred under the legislation of a Member State on the victims of damage caused by a defective product under a general system of liability having the same basis as that put in place by the Directive may be limited or restricted as a result of the Directive's transposition into the domestic law of that State.

Article 14

This Directive shall not apply to injury or damage arising from nuclear accidents and covered by international conventions ratified by the Member States.

Article 15

1. Each Member State may:

(a) [. . .]

(b) by way of derogation from Article 7 (e), maintain or, subject to the procedure set out in paragraph 2 of this Article, provide in this legislation that the producer shall be liable even if he proves that the state of scientific and technical knowledge at the time when he put the product into circulation was not such as to enable the existence of a defect to be discovered.

2. A Member State wishing to introduce the measure specified in paragraph 1 (b) shall communicate the test of the proposed measure to the Commission. The Commission shall inform the other Member States thereof.

The Member State concerned shall hold the proposed measure in abeyance for nine months after the Commission is informed and provided that in the meantime the Commission has not submitted to the Council a proposal amending this Directive on the relevant matter. However, if within three months of receiving the said information, the Commission does not advise the Member State concerned that it intends submitting such a proposal to the Council, the Member State may take the proposed measure immediately.

If the Commission does submit to the Council such a proposal amending this Directive within the aforementioned nine months, the Member State concerned shall hold the proposed measure in abeyance for a further period of 18 months from the date on which the proposal is submitted.

3. Ten years after the date of notification of this Directive, the Commission shall submit to the Council a report on the effect that rulings by the courts as to the application of Article 7 (e) and of paragraph 1 (b) of this Article have on the consumer market. In the light of this report the Council, acting on a proposal from the Commission and pursuant to the terms of Article [94][2] of the Treaty, shall decide whether to repeal Article 7 (e).

¶ *Article 15, paragraph 1(a) has been deleted by article 1 of Directive 1999/34/EC, reproduced infra under no. C.P. 16.*

Article 16

1. Any Member State may provide that a producer's total liability for damage resulting from a death or personal injury and caused by identical items with the same defect shall be limited to an amount which may not be less than 70 million ECU.

2. Ten years after the date of notification of this Directive, the Commission shall submit to the Council a report on the effect on consumer protection and the functioning of the common market of the implementation of the financial limit on liability by those Member States that have used the option provided for in paragraph 1. In the light of this report the Council, acting on a proposal from the Commission and pursuant to the terms of Article [94][2] of the Treaty, shall decide whether to repeal paragraph 1.

Article 17

This Directive shall not apply to products put into circulation before the date on which the provisions referred to in Article 19 enter into force.

Article 18

1. For the purposes of this Directive, the ECU shall be that defined by Regulation 3180/78,[3] as amended by Regulation 2626/84.[4] The equivalent in national currency shall initially be calculated at the rate obtaining on the date of adoption of this Directive.

---

[3] OJ L 379, 30.12.1978, 1.
[4] OJ L 247, 16.9.1984, 1.

2. Every five years the Council, acting on a proposal from the Commission, shall examine and, if need be, revise the amounts in this Directive, in the light of economic and monetary trends in the Community.

Article 19

1. Member States shall bring into force, not later than three years from the date of notification of this Directive, the laws, regulations and administrative provisions necessary to comply with this Directive. They shall forthwith inform the Commission thereof. (This Directive was notified to the Member States on 30 July 1985.)

2. The procedure set out in Article 15 (2) shall apply from the date of notification of this Directive.

Article 20

Member States shall communicate to the Commission the texts of the main provisions of national law that they subsequently adopt in the field governed by this Directive.

Article 21

Every five years the Commission shall present a report to the Council on the application of this Directive and, if necessary, shall submit appropriate proposals to it.

Article 22

This Directive is addressed to the Member States.

C.P. 3.

Council Directive 85/577/EEC of 20 December 1985 to protect the consumer in respect of contracts negotiated away from business premises[1]

CASES

I. Case C-481/99 Georg Heininger et Helga Heininger v Bayerische Hypo-und Vereinsbank AG [2001] ECR I-9945

Council Directive 85/577/EEC is to be interpreted as applying to a loan agreement which is secured by means of a 'Grundschuld' (charge on the property) in the same amount as the loan, with the result that the right of cancellation provided for in Article 5 of that directive is available to a consumer who has entered into a contract of that type in one of the cases specified in Article 1.

II. Case C-45/96 Bayerische Hypotheken-und Wechselbank AG v Edgard Dietzinger [1998] ECR I-1199

On a proper construction of the first indent of Article 2 of Directive 85/577/EEC to protect the consumer in respect of contracts negotiated away from business premises, which defines a 'consumer' for the purposes of the directive, a contract of guarantee concluded by a natural person who is not acting in the course of his trade or profession does not come within the scope of the directive where it guarantees repayment of a debt contracted by another person who, for his part, is acting within the course of his trade or profession.

In that connection, although it cannot be excluded that the directive applies to a contract of guarantee, it is apparent from the wording of Article 1 thereof and from the ancillary nature of guarantees that the directive covers only a guarantee ancillary to a contract whereby, in the context of 'doorstep selling', a consumer assumes obligations towards the trader with a view to obtaining goods or services from him. Furthermore, since the directive is designed to protect only consumers, a guarantee comes within the scope of the directive only where, in accordance with the first indent of Article 2, the guarantor has entered into a commitment for a purpose which can be regarded as unconnected with his trade or profession.

III. Case 384/93/EEC Alpine Investments BV v Minister van Financiën [1995] ECR I-1141

1. The prior existence of relations between a provider and an identifiable recipient of services is not a condition for application of the provisions on the freedom to provide services. On a proper construction, therefore, Article [49][2] of the Treaty applies to offers of services that a provider makes by telephone to potential recipients established in other Member States.

2. On a proper construction, Article [49][2] of the Treaty applies to services that a provider supplies without moving from the Member State in which he is established to recipients established in other Member States.

3. Article [49][2] of the Treaty covers not only restrictions laid down by the State of destination but also those laid down by the State of origin, even if they are generally applicable measures, are not discriminatory and neither their object nor their effect is to put the national market at an advantage over providers of services from other Member States.

4. A prohibition against telephoning potential clients in another Member State without their prior consent can constitute a restriction on freedom to provide services since it deprives the operators concerned of a rapid and direct technique for marketing and contacting clients.

5. It is a restriction on freedom to provide services for a Member State to prohibit financial intermediaries established there from contacting potential clients in

---

[1] OJ L 372, 31.12.1985, 31–33.

[2] The number between brackets has been changed as from 1 May 1999 by article 12 of the Treaty of Amsterdam.

another Member State by telephone without their prior consent to offer them services linked to investment in commodities futures, but the restriction is justified by the imperative reason of public interest consisting in maintaining the good reputation of the national financial sector. The smooth operation of financial markets is largely contingent on the confidence they inspire in investors, which depends in particular on the existence of professional regulations serving to ensure the competence and trustworthiness of financial intermediaries. By protecting investors from a method of canvassing which generally catches them unawares, the prohibition of cold calling on a market as speculative as that in commodities futures seeks to secure the integrity of the national financial sector. Since the Member State from which the unsolicited telephone call is made is best placed to regulate the canvassing of potential clients who are in another Member State, it cannot be complained that the former Member State does not leave that task to the Member State of the recipient. Moreover, the restriction at issue cannot be considered excessive since it is limited to the sector in which abuses have been found and to only one of the possible methods of approaching clients.

THE COUNCIL OF THE EUROPEAN COMMUNITIES,

Having regard to the proposal from the Commission,[3]

Having regard to the opinion of the European Parliament,[4]

Having regard to the opinion of the Economic and Social Committee,[5]

Whereas it is a common form of commercial practice in the Member States for the conclusion of a contract or a unilateral engagement between a trader and consumer to be made away from the business premises of the trader, and whereas such contracts and engagements are the subject of legislation which differs from one Member State to another;

Whereas any disparity between such legislation may directly affect the functioning of the common market; whereas it is therefore necessary to approximate laws in this field;

Whereas the preliminary programme of the European Economic Community for a consumer protection and information policy[6] provides *inter alia* under paragraphs 24 and 25, that appropriate measures be taken to protect consumers against unfair commercial practices in respect of doorstep selling; whereas the second programme of the European Economic Community for a consumer protection and information policy[7] confirmed that the action and priorities defined in the preliminary programme would be pursued;

Whereas the special feature of contracts concluded away from the business premises of the trader is that as a rule it is the trader who initiates the contract negotiations, for which the consumer is unprepared or which he does not expect; whereas the consumer is often unable to compare the quality and price of the offer with other offers; whereas this surprise element generally exists not only in contracts made at the doorstep but also in other forms of contract concluded by the trader away from his business premises;

Whereas the consumer should be given a right of cancellation over a period of at least seven days in order to enable him to assess the obligations arising under the contract;

Whereas appropriate measures should be taken to ensure that the consumer is informed in writing of this period for reflection;

Whereas the freedom of Member States to maintain or introduce a total or partial prohibition on the conclusion of contracts away from business premises, inasmuch as they consider this to be in the interest of consumers, must not be affected;

HAS ADOPTED THIS DIRECTIVE:

Article 1

1. This Directive shall apply to contracts, under which a trader supplies goods or

---

[3] OJ C 22, 22.1.1977, 6 and OJ C 127, 1.6.1978, 8.
[4] OJ C 241, 10.10.1977, 26.
[5] OJ C 180, 28.7.1977, 39.

[6] OJ C 92, 25.4.1975, 2.
[7] OJ C 133, 3.6.1981, 1.

services to a consumer and which are concluded:
– during an excursion organised by the trader away from his business premises,
– or during a visit by a trader
(i) to the consumer's home or to that of another consumer;
(ii) to the consumer's place of work
where the visit does not take place at the express request of the consumer.

2. This Directive shall also apply to contracts for the supply of goods or services other than those concerning which the consumer requested the visit of the trader, provided that when he requested the visit the consumer did not know, or could not reasonably have known, that the supply of those other goods or services formed part of the trader's commercial or professional activities.

3. This Directive shall also apply to contracts in respect of which an offer was made by the consumer under conditions similar to those described in paragraph 1 or paragraph 2 although the consumer was not bound by that offer before its acceptance by the trader.

4. This Directive shall also apply to offers made contractually by the consumer under conditions similar to those described in paragraph 1 or paragraph 2 where the consumer is bound by his offer.

Cases

I. Case C-229/04 Crailsheimer Volksbank eG v Klaus Conrads, Frank Schulzke and Petra Schulzke-Lösche [2005] ECR I-9273

1. Articles 1 and 2 must be interpreted as meaning that when a third party intervenes in the name of or on behalf of a trader in the negotiation or conclusion of a contract, the application of the Directive cannot be made subject to the condition that the trader was or should have been aware that the contract was concluded in a doorstep-selling situation as referred to in Article 1 of the Directive.

2. Directive 85/577, and Article 5(2) thereof in particular, does not preclude:
– a requirement that a consumer who has exercised his right to cancel under the Directive must pay back the loan proceeds to the lender, even though according to the scheme drawn up for the investment the loan serves solely to finance the purchase of the immovable property and is paid directly to the vendor thereof;
– a requirement that the amount of the loan must be paid back immediately;
– national legislation which provides for an obligation on the consumer, in the event of cancellation of a secured credit agreement, not only to repay the amounts received under the agreement but also to pay to the lender interest at the market rate.

II. Case C-423/97 Travel Vac SL v Manuel José Antelm Sanchis [1999] ECR I-2195

1. Whilst it is true that time-share contracts are covered by Directive 94/47/EC on the protection of purchasers in respect of certain aspects of contracts relating to the purchase of the right to use immovable properties on a time-share basis, this does not preclude a contract having a time-share element from being covered by Directive 85/577/EEC if the conditions for the application of that directive are otherwise fulfilled.

Neither directive contains provisions ruling out the application of the other. Moreover, it would defeat the object of Directive 85/577/EEC to interpret it as meaning that the protection it provides is excluded solely because a contract generally falls under Directive 94/47/EC. Such an interpretation would deprive consumers of the protection of Directive 85/577/EEC even when the contract was concluded away from business premises.

2. A contract concluded in a situation in which a trader has invited a consumer to go in person to a specified place at a certain distance from the place where the consumer lives, and which is different from the premises where the trader usually carries on his business and is not clearly identified as premises for sales to the public, in order to present to him the products and services he is offering, must be considered to have been concluded during an excursion organized by the trader away from his business premises within the meaning of Directive 85/577/EEC.

III. Case C-91/92 Paola Faccini Dori v Recreb Srl [1994] ECR I-3325

The provisions of Article 1(1) and (2) and Article 5 of Directive 85/577/EEC, concerning protection of the consumer in respect of contracts negotiated away from business premises, are unconditional and sufficiently precise as regards determination of the persons for whose benefit they were adopted and the minimum period within which notice of cancellation must be given. Although Articles 4 and 5 of the directive allow the Member States some latitude regarding consumer protection when information on the right of cancellation is not provided by the trader and in determining the time limit and conditions for cancellation, that latitude does not make it impossible to determine minimum rights which must on any view be provided to consumers.

Article 2

For the purposes of this Directive:
– 'consumer' means a natural person who, in transactions covered by this Directive, is acting for purposes that can be regarded as outside his trade or profession;
– 'trader' means a natural or legal person who for the transaction in question, acts in his commercial or professional capacity, and anyone acting in the name or on behalf of a trader.

Cases

I. Case C-45/96 Bayerische Hypotheken- und Wechselbank AG v Edgard Dietzinger [1998] ECR I-1199

On a proper construction of the first indent of Article 2 of Directive 85/577/EEC to protect the consumer in respect of contracts negotiated away from business premises, which defines a 'consumer' for the purposes of the directive, a contract of guarantee concluded by a natural person who is not acting in the course of his trade or profession does not come within the scope of the directive where it guarantees repayment of a debt contracted by another person who, for his part, is acting within the course of his trade or profession. In that connection, although it cannot be excluded that the directive applies to a contract of guarantee, it is apparent from the wording of Article 1 thereof and from the ancillary nature of guarantees that the directive covers only a guarantee ancillary to a contract whereby, in the context of 'doorstep selling', a consumer assumes obligations towards the trader with a view to obtaining goods or services from him. Furthermore, since the directive is designed to protect only consumers, a guarantee comes within the scope of the directive only where, in accordance with the first indent of Article 2, the guarantor has entered into a commitment for a purpose which can be regarded as unconnected with his trade or profession.

II. Case C-91/92 Paola Faccini Dori v Recreb Srl [1994] ECR I-3325

See supra under Article 1 of this Directive.

III. Case C-361/89 Criminal Proceedings Against Patrice Di Pinto [1991] ECR I-1189

1. A trader canvassed with a view to the conclusion of an advertising contract concerning the sale of his business is not to be regarded as a consumer protected by Council Directive 85/577/EEC to protect the consumer in respect of contracts negotiated away from business premises. It follows from Article 2 of that directive that the criterion for the application of protection lies in the connection between the transactions which are the subject of the canvassing and the professional activity of the trader: the latter may claim that the directive is applicable only if the transaction in respect of which he has been canvassed lies outside his trade or profession. Acts which are preparatory to the sale of a business are connected with the professional activity of the trader; although such acts may bring the running of the business to an end, they are managerial acts performed for the purpose of satisfying requirements other than the family or personal requirements of the trader.

2. Directive 85/577/EEC does not preclude national legislation on canvassing from extending the protection that it affords to cover traders acting with a view to the sale of their business. Article 8 of that directive, which leaves Member States free to adopt or maintain more favourable provisions to protect consumers in the field covered by the directive, cannot be interpreted as precluding those States from adopting measures in an area with which it is not concerned, such as that of the protection of traders.

Article 3

1. The Member States may decide that this Directive shall apply only to contracts for which the payment to be made by the consumer exceeds a specified amount. This amount may not exceed 60 ECU.

The Council, acting on a proposal from the Commission, shall examine and, if necessary, revise this amount for the first time no later than four years after notification of the Directive and thereafter every two years, taking into account economic and monetary developments in the Community.

2. This Directive shall not apply to:

(a) contracts for the construction, sale and rental of immovable property or contracts concerning other rights relating to immovable property. Contracts for the supply of goods and for their incorporation in immovable property or contracts for repairing immovable property shall fall within the scope of this Directive;

(b) contracts for the supply of foodstuffs or beverages or other goods intended for current consumption in the household and supplied by regular roundsmen;

(c) contracts for the supply of goods or services, provided that all three of the following conditions are met:
 (i) the contract is concluded on the basis of a trader's catalogue which the consumer has a proper opportunity of reading in the absence of the trader's representative,
 (ii) there is intended to be continuity of contract between the trader's representative and the consumer in relation to that or any subsequent transaction,
 (iii) both the catalogue and the contract clearly inform the consumer of his right to return goods to the supplier within a period of not less than seven days of receipt or otherwise to cancel the contract within that period without obligation of any kind other than to take reasonable care of the goods;

(d) insurance contracts;

(e) contracts for securities.

3. By way of derogation from Article 1 (2), Member States may refrain from applying this Directive to contracts for the supply of goods or services having a direct connection with the goods or services concerning which the consumer requested the visit of the trader.

CASES

I. Case C-350/03 Elisabeth Schulte and Wolfgang Schulte v Deutsche Bausparkasse Badenia AG [2005] ECR I-9215

Article 3(2)(a) of Council Directive 85/577/EEC must be interpreted as excluding from the scope of the Directive contracts for the sale of immovable property even where they are merely a component of an investment scheme financed by a loan for which the negotiations prior to the conclusion of the contract were held in a doorstep-selling situation, both as regards the contract for the purchase of the immovable property and the loan agreement serving solely to finance that purchase.

II. Case C-423/97 Travel Vac SL v Manuel José Antelm Sanchis [1999] ECR I-2195

Directive 85/577/EEC to protect the consumer in respect of contracts negotiated away from business premises applies to a contract relating to the acquisition of a right to use immovable property on a time-share basis and to the provision of services whose value is higher than that of the right to use the immovable property.

Since a contract of that nature does not only concern the right to use time-share property, but also concerns the provision of separate services of a value higher than that of the right to use the property, it is not covered by Article 3(2)(a) of Directive 85/577/EEC, under which that directive does not apply to contracts for the construction, sale and rental of immovable property or contracts concerning other rights relating to immovable property.

Article 4

In the case of transactions within the scope of Article 1, traders shall be required to give consumers written notice of their right of cancellation within the period laid down in Article 5, together with the name and address of a person against whom that right may be exercised.

Such notice shall be dated and shall state particulars enabling the contract to be identified. It shall be given to the consumer:

(a) in the case of Article 1 (1), at the time of conclusion of the contract;

(b) in the case of Article 1 (2), not later than the time of conclusion of the contract;

(c) in the case of Article 1 (3) and 1(4), when the offer is made by the consumer.

Member States shall ensure that their national legislation lays down appropriate consumer protection measures in cases where the information referred to in this Article is not supplied.

Article 5

1. The consumer shall have the right to renounce the effects of his undertaking by sending notice within a period of not less than seven days from receipt by the consumer of the notice referred to in Article 4, in accordance with the procedure laid down by national law. It shall be sufficient if the notice is dispatched before the end of such period.

2. The giving of the notice shall have the effect of releasing the consumer from any obligations under the cancelled contract.

CASE

Case C-350/03 Elisabeth Schulte and Wolfgang Schulte v Deutsche Bausparkasse Badenia AG [2005] ECR I-9215

Directive 85/577/EEC does not preclude:
– a requirement that a consumer who has exercised his right to cancel under the Directive must pay back the loan proceeds to the lender, even though according to the scheme drawn up for the investment the loan serves solely to finance the purchase of the immovable property and is paid directly to the vendor thereof;
– a requirement that the amount of the loan must be paid back immediately;
– national legislation which provides for an obligation on the consumer, in the event of cancellation of a secured credit agreement, not only to repay the amounts received under the agreement but also to pay to the lender interest at the market rate.

However, in a situation where, if the bank had complied with its obligation to inform the consumer of his right of cancellation, the consumer would have been able to avoid exposure to the risks inherent in investments such as those at issue, Article 4 of Directive 85/577/EEC requires Member States to ensure that their legislation protects consumers who have been unable to avoid exposure to such risks, by adopting suitable measures to allow them to avoid bearing the consequences of the materialisation of those risks. (See also Case C-229/04 *Crailsheimer Volksbank eG v Klaus Conrads and others*, reproduced supra under Article 1 of Directive 85/577/EEC.)

CASES

I. Case C-229/04 Crailsheimer Volksbank eG v Klaus Conrads, Frank Schulzke and Petra Schulzke-Lösche [2005] ECR I-9273

Directive 85/577/EEC, and Article 5(2) thereof in particular, does not preclude:
– a requirement that a consumer who has exercised his right to cancel under the Directive must pay back the loan proceeds to the lender, even though according to the scheme drawn up for the investment the loan serves solely to finance the purchase of the immovable property and is paid directly to the vendor thereof;
– a requirement that the amount of the loan must be paid back immediately;
– national legislation which provides for an obligation on the consumer, in the event of cancellation of a secured credit agreement, not only to repay the amounts received under the agreement but also to pay to the lender interest at the market rate;

However, in a situation where, if the bank had complied with its obligation to inform the consumer of his right of cancellation, the consumer would have been able to avoid exposure to the risks inherent in investments such as those at issue in the main proceedings, Article 4 of the Directive requires Member States to ensure that their legislation protects consumers who have been unable to avoid exposure to such risks, by adopting suitable measures to allow them to avoid bearing the consequences of the materialisation of those risks.

II. Case C-481/99 Georg Heininger and Helga Heininger v Bayerische Hypo- und Vereinsbank AG [2001] ECR I-9945

Directive 85/577/EEC precludes the national legislature from imposing a time limit of one year from the conclusion of the contract within which the right of cancellation provided for in Article 5 of that directive may be exercised, where the consumer has not received the information specified in Article 4.

III. Case C-423/97 Travel Vac SL v Manuel José Antelm Sanchis [1999] ECR I-2195

1. The consumer can exercise his right under Article 5(1) of Directive 85/577/EEC where the contract has been concluded in circumstances such as those described in Article 1 of that directive, without there being any need to prove that the consumer was influenced or manipulated by the trader.

2. Directive 85/577/EEC does not preclude a Member State from adopting rules that provide that notice of renunciation of such a contract under Article 5(1) of that directive is not subject to any condition as to form. Given the objective of the directive, namely to protect the consumer, a Member State may adopt such provisions to make it easier for the consumer to exercise his right of renunciation. It cannot be inferred from Article 5(1) of the directive, which concerns the time limits within which notice of renunciation must be given, that this must be done in writing. That provision merely concerns the calculation of the minimum period of seven days where the consumer gives notice of renunciation in writing.

3. Directive 85/577/EEC to protect the consumer in respect of contracts negotiated away from business premises precludes the inclusion in a contract of a clause imposing payment by the consumer of a lump sum for damage caused to the trader for the sole reason that the consumer has exercised his right of renunciation of such a contract.

To enforce payment of such damages and interest would be tantamount to imposing a penalty on the consumer for exercising his right of renunciation, which would be contrary to the protective purpose of the directive, which is precisely to prevent the consumer from undertaking financial obligations without being prepared for them.

IV. Case C-91/92 Paola Faccini Dori v Recreb Srl [1994] ECR I-3325

See under Article 1 of this Directive.

Article 6

The consumer may not waive the rights conferred on him by this Directive.

Article 7

If the consumer exercises his right of renunciation, the legal effects of such renunciation shall be governed by national laws, particularly regarding the reimbursement of payments for goods or services provided and the return of goods received.

CASE

Case C-52/00 Commission of the European Communities v French Republic [2002] ECR I-3827

The French Republic has failed to fulfil its obligations under Articles 9(b), 3(3) and 7 of Directive 85/374/EEC
– by including damage of less than EUR 500 in Article 1386–2 of the French Civil Code;
– by providing in the first paragraph of Article 1386–7 thereof that the supplier of a defective product is to be liable in all cases and on the same basis as the producer; and
– by providing in the second paragraph of Article 1386–12 thereof that the producer must prove that he has taken appropriate steps to avert the consequences of a defective product in order to be able to rely on the grounds of exemption from liability provided for in Article 7(d) and (e).

Article 8

This Directive shall not prevent Member States from adopting or maintaining more favourable provisions to protect consumers in the field that it covers.

CASE

Case C-350/03 Elisabeth Schulte and Wolfgang Schulte v Deutsche Bausparkasse Badenia AG [2005] ECR I-9215

Directive 85/577/EEC does not preclude national rules which limit the effect of cancellation of the loan agreement to the avoidance of that agreement, even in the case of investment schemes in which the loan would not have been granted at all without the acquisition of the immovable property.

Article 9

1. Member States shall take the measures necessary to comply with this Directive within 24 months of its notification. They shall forthwith inform the Commission thereof.

2. Member States shall ensure that the texts of the main provisions of national law, which they adopt in the field covered by this Directive, are communicated to the Commission.

CASES

I. Case C-52/00 Commission of the European Communities v French Republic [2002] ECR I-3827

See infra under Article 7 of this Directive.

II. Case C-91/92 Paola Faccini Dori v Recreb Srl [1994] ECR I-3325

1. In the absence of measures transposing within the prescribed time limit Directive 85/577/EEC, concerning protection of the consumer in respect of contracts negotiated away from business premises, consumers cannot derive from the directive itself a right of cancellation as against traders with whom they have concluded a contract away from business premises or enforce such a right in a national court.

2. The Member States' obligation arising from a directive to achieve the result envisaged by the directive and their duty under Article [10][2] of the Treaty to take all appropriate measures, whether general or particular, is binding on all the authorities of the Member States, including, for matters within their jurisdiction, the courts. It follows that, when applying national law, whether adopted before or after the directive, the national court that has to interpret that law must do so, as far as possible, in the light of the wording and the purpose of the directive so as to achieve the result it has in view and thereby comply with the third paragraph of Article [249][2] of the Treaty.

3. If a Member State fails to comply with the obligation to transpose a directive which it has under the third paragraph of Article [249][2] of the Treaty and if the result prescribed by the directive cannot be achieved by way of interpretation of national law by the courts, Community law requires that Member State to make good the damage caused to individuals through failure to transpose the directive, provided that three conditions are fulfilled, namely that the result prescribed by the directive must entail the grant of rights to individuals, the content of those rights must be identifiable on the basis of the provisions of the directive and there must be a causal link between the breach of the State's obligation and the damage suffered. In those circumstances, it is for the national court to uphold the right of aggrieved persons to obtain reparation in accordance with national law on liability.

Article 10

This Directive is addressed to the Member States.

C.P. 4.

Council Directive 87/102/EEC
of 22 December 1986
for the approximation of the laws, regulations and administrative provisions of the Member States concerning consumer credit[1]

> **CASE**
>
> Case C-208/98 Berliner Kindl Brauerei AG v Andreas Siepert [2000] ECR I-1741
>
> On a proper construction of Council Directive 87/102/EEC, it does not cover a contract of guarantee for repayment of credit where neither the guarantor nor the borrower was acting in the course of his trade or profession.

THE COUNCIL OF THE EUROPEAN COMMUNITIES,

Having regard to the Treaty establishing the European Economic Community, and in particular Article [94][2] thereof,

Having regard to the proposal from the Commission,[3]

Having regard to the opinion of the European Parliament,[4]

Having regard to the opinion of the Economic and Social Committee,[5]

Whereas wide differences exist in the laws of the Member States in the field of consumer credit;

Whereas these differences of law can lead to distortions of competition between grantors of credit in the common market;

Whereas these differences limit the opportunities the consumer has to obtain credit in other Member States; whereas they affect the volume and the nature of the credit sought, and also the purchase of goods and services;

Whereas, as a result, these differences have an influence on the free movement of goods and services obtainable by consumers on credit and thus directly affect the functioning of the common market;

Whereas, given the increasing volume of credit granted in the Community to consumers, the establishment of a common market in consumer credit would benefit alike consumers, grantors of credit, manufacturers, wholesalers and retailers of goods and providers of services;

Whereas the programmes of the European Economic Community for a consumer protection and information policy[6] provide, *inter alia* that the consumer should be protected against unfair credit terms and that a harmonisation of the general conditions governing consumer credit should be undertaken as a priority;

Whereas differences of law and practice result in unequal consumer protection in the field of consumer credit from one Member State to another;

Whereas there has been much change in recent years in the types of credit available to and used by consumers; whereas new forms of consumer credit have emerged and continue to develop;

Whereas the consumer should receive adequate information on the conditions and cost of credit and on his obligations; whereas this information should include, *inter alia* the annual percentage rate of charge for credit, or, failing that, the total amount that the consumer must pay for credit;

---

[1] OJ L 42, 12.2.1987, 48–52.
[2] The number between brackets has been changed as from 1 May 1999 by article 12 of the Treaty of Amsterdam.
[3] OJ C 80, 27.3.1979, 4 and OJ C 183, 10.7.1984, 4.
[4] OJ C 242, 12.9.1983, 10.
[5] OJ C 113, 7.5.1980, 22.

[6] OJ C 92, 25.4.1975, 1 and OJ C 133, 3.6.1981, 1.

whereas, pending a decision on a Community method or methods of calculating the annual percentage rate of charge, Member States should be able to retain existing methods or practices for calculating this rate, or failing that, should establish provisions for indicating the total cost of the credit to the consumer;

Whereas the terms of credit may be disadvantageous to the consumer; whereas better protection of consumers can be achieved by adopting certain requirements which are to apply to all forms of credit;

Whereas, having regard to the character of certain credit agreements or types of transaction, these agreements or transactions should be partially or entirely excluded from the field of application of this Directive;

Whereas it should be possible for Member States, in consultation with the Commission, to exempt from the Directive certain forms of credit of a non-commercial character granted under particular conditions;

Whereas the practices existing in some Member States in respect of authentic acts drawn up before a notary or judge are such as to render the application of certain provisions of this Directive unnecessary in the case of such acts; whereas it should therefore be possible for Member States to exempt such acts from those provisions;

Whereas credit agreements for very large financial amounts tend to differ from the usual consumer credit agreements; whereas the application of the provisions of this Directive to agreements for very small amounts could create unnecessary administrative burdens both for consumers and grantors of credit; whereas therefore, agreements above or below specified financial limits should be excluded from the Directive;

Whereas the provision of information on the cost of credit in advertising and at the business premises of the creditor or credit broker can make it easier for the consumer to compare different offers;

Whereas consumer protection is further improved if credit agreements are made in writing and contain certain minimum particulars concerning the contractual terms;

Whereas, in the case of credit granted for the acquisition of goods, Member States should lay down the conditions in which goods may be repossessed, particularly if the consumer has not given his consent; whereas the account between the parties should upon repossession be made up in such manner as to ensure that the repossession does not entail any unjustified enrichment;

Whereas the consumer should be allowed to discharge his obligations before the due date; whereas the consumer should then be entitled to an equitable reduction in the total cost of the credit;

Whereas the assignment of the creditor's rights arising under a credit agreement should not be allowed to weaken the position of the consumer;

Whereas those Member States that permit consumers to use bills of exchange, promissory notes or cheques in connection with credit agreements should ensure that the consumer is suitably protected when so using such instruments;

Whereas, as regards goods or services which the consumer has contracted to acquire on credit, the consumer should, at least in the circumstances defined below, have rights *vis-à-vis* the grantor of credit which are in addition to his normal contractual rights against him and against the supplier of the goods or services; whereas the circumstances referred to above are those where the grantor of credit and the supplier of goods or services have a pre-existing agreement where under credit is made available exclusively by that grantor of credit to customers of that supplier for the purpose of enabling the consumer to acquire goods or services from the latter;

Whereas the ECU is as defined in Council Regulation No. 3180/78/EEC,[7] as last amended by Regulation No. 2626/84/EEC;[8] whereas Member States should to a limited extent be at liberty to round off the amounts in national currency resulting from the conversion of amounts of this Directive expressed in ECU; whereas the amounts in this Directive should be periodically

---

[7] OJ L 379, 30.12.1978, 1.
[8] OJ L 247, 16.9.1984, 1.

re-examined in the light of economic and monetary trends in the Community, and, if need be, revised;

Whereas suitable measures should be adopted by Member States for authorising persons offering credit or offering to arrange credit agreements or for inspecting or monitoring the activities of persons granting credit or arranging for credit to be granted or for enabling consumers to complain about credit agreements or credit conditions;

Whereas credit agreements should not derogate, to the detriment of the consumer, from the provisions adopted in implementation of this Directive or corresponding to its provisions; whereas those provisions should not be circumvented as a result of the way in which agreements are formulated;

Whereas, since this Directive provides for a certain degree of approximation of the laws, regulations and administrative provisions of the Member States concerning consumer credit and for a certain level of consumer protection, Member States should not be prevented from retaining or adopting more stringent measures to protect the consumer, with due regard for their obligations under the Treaty;

Whereas, not later than 1 January 1995, the Commission should present to the Council a report concerning the operation of this Directive,

HAS ADOPTED THIS DIRECTIVE:

Article 1

1. This Directive applies to credit agreements.

2. For the purpose of this Directive:

(a) 'consumer' means a natural person who, in transactions covered by this Directive, is acting for purposes that can be regarded as outside his trade or profession;

(b) 'creditor' means a natural or legal person who grants credit in the course of his trade, business or profession, or a group of such persons;

(c) 'credit agreement' means an agreement whereby a creditor grants or promises to grant to a consumer a credit in the form of a deferred payment, a loan or other similar financial accommodation. Agreements for the provision on a continuing basis of a service or a utility, where the consumer has the right to pay for them, for the duration of their provision, by means of instalments, are not deemed to be credit agreements for the purpose of this Directive;

[(d) 'total cost of the credit to the consumer' means all the costs, including interest and other charges, which the consumer has to pay for the credit;

(e) 'annual percentage rate of charge' means the total cost of the credit to the consumer, expressed as an annual percentage of the amount of the credit granted and calculated in accordance with Article 1a.]

¶ *Points (d) and (e) in paragraph 2 have been replaced by article 1(1) of Directive 90/88/EEC, reproduced infra under no. C.P. 8.*

[Article 1a

1. (a) The annual percentage rate of charge which shall be that rate, on an annual basis which equalises the present value of all commitments (loans, repayments and charges), future or existing, agreed by the creditor and the borrower, shall be calculated in accordance with the mathematical formula set out in Annex II.]

(b) Four examples of the method of calculation are given in Annex III, by way of illustration.

2. For the purpose of calculating the annual percentage rate of charge, the 'total cost of the credit to the consumer' as defined in Article 1 (2) (d) shall be determined, with the exception of the following charges:

(i) charges payable by the borrower for non-compliance with any of his commitments laid down in the credit agreement;

(ii) charges other than the purchase price which, in purchases of goods or services, the consumer is obliged to pay whether the transaction is paid in cash or by credit;

(iii) charges for the transfer of funds and charges for keeping an account intended to receive payments towards the reimbursement of the credit the payment of interest and other charges except where the consumer does not have reasonable freedom of choice in the matter and where such charges are abnormally high; this provision shall not, however, apply to charges for collection of such reimbursements or payments, whether made in cash or otherwise;

(iv) membership subscriptions to associations or groups and arising from agreements separate from the credit agreement, even though such subscriptions have an effect on the credit terms;

(v) charges for insurance or guarantees; included are, however, those designed to ensure payment to the creditor, in the event of the death, invalidity, illness or unemployment of the consumer, of a sum equal to or less than the total amount of the credit together with relevant interest and other charges which have to be imposed by the creditor as a condition for credit being granted.

3. [. . .]

4. (a) The annual percentage rate of charge shall be calculated at the time the credit contract is concluded, without prejudice to the provisions of Article 3 concerning advertisements and special offers.

(b) The calculation shall be made on the assumption that the credit contract is valid for the period agreed and that the creditor and the consumer fulfil their obligations under the terms and by the dates agreed.

5. [. . .]

6. In the case of credit contracts containing clauses allowing variations in the rate of interest and the amount or level of other charges contained in the annual percentage rate of charge but unquantifiable at the time when it is calculated, the annual percentage rate of charge shall be calculated on the assumption that interest and other charges remain fixed and will apply until the end of the credit contract.

7. Where necessary, the following assumptions may be made in calculating the annual percentage rate of charge:
– if the contract does not specify a credit limit, the amount of credit granted shall be equal to the amount fixed by the relevant Member State, without exceeding a figure equivalent to ECU 2.000;
– if there is no fixed timetable for repayment, and one cannot be deduced from the terms of the agreement and the means for repaying the credit granted, the duration of the credit shall be deemed to be one year;
– unless otherwise specified, where the contract provides for more than one repayment date, the credit will be made available and the repayments made at the earliest time provided for in the agreement].

¶ Article 1a has been inserted by article 1(2) of Directive 90/88/EEC, reproduced infra under no. C.P. 8.
¶ Article 1a(1)(a) has been replaced by article 1(a) of Directive 98/7/EC, reproduced infra under no. C.P. 14.
¶ Article 1a(3) has been deleted by article 1(b) of Directive 98/7/EC, reproduced infra under no. C.P. 14.
¶ Article 1a(5) has been deleted by article 1(c) of Directive 98/7/EC, reproduced infra under no. C.P. 14.

Article 2

1. This Directive shall not apply to:

(a) credit agreements or agreements promising to grant credit:
– intended primarily for the purpose of acquiring or retaining property rights in land or in an existing or projected building,
– intended for the purpose of renovating or improving a building as such;

(b) hiring agreements except where these provide that the title will pass ultimately to the hirer;

(c) credit granted or made available without payment of interest or any other charge;

(d) credit agreements under which no interest is charged provided the consumer agrees to repay the credit in a single payment;

(e) credit in the form of advances on a current account granted by a credit institution or financial institution other than on credit card accounts. Nevertheless, the provisions of Article 6 shall apply to such credits;

(f) credit agreements involving amounts less than 200 ECU or more than 20.000 ECU;

(g) credit agreements under which the consumer is required to repay the credit:
– either, within a period not exceeding three months,
– or, by a maximum number of four payments within a period not exceeding 12 months.

2. A Member State may, in consultation with the Commission, exempt from the application of this

Directive certain types of credit which fulfil the following conditions:
– they are granted at rates of charge below those prevailing in the market, and
– they are not offered to the public generally.

[3. The provisions of Article 1a and of Articles 4 to 12 shall not apply to credit agreements or agreements promising to grant credit, secured by mortgage on immovable property, insofar as these are not already excluded from the Directive under paragraph 1 (a).]

4. Member States may exempt from the provisions of Articles 6 to 12 credit agreements in the form of an authentic act signed before a notary or judge.

¶ *Subparagraph 3 has been replaced by article 1(3) of Directive 90/88/EEC, reproduced infra under no. C.P. 8.*

[*Article 3*]

Without prejudice to Council Directive 84/450/EEC of 10 September 1984 relating to the approximation of the laws, regulations and administrative provisions of the Member States concerning misleading advertising[9] and to the rules and principles applicable to unfair advertising, any advertisement, or any offer which is displayed at business premises, in which a person offers credit or offers to arrange a credit agreement and in which a rate of interest or any figures relating to the cost of the credit are indicated, shall also include a statement of the annual percentage rate of charge, by means of a representative example if no other means is practicable.]

¶ *Article 3 has been replaced by article 1(d) of Directive 98/7/EC, reproduced infra under no. C.P. 14.*

Article 4

1. Credit agreements shall be made in writing. The consumer shall receive a copy of the written agreement.

2. The written agreement shall include:

(a) a statement of the annual percentage rate of charge;

(b) a statement of the conditions under which the annual percentage rate of charge may be amended.

[(c) a statement of the amount, number and frequency or dates of the payments which the consumer must make to repay the credit, as well as of the payments for interest and other charges; the total amount of these payments should also be indicated where possible;

(d) a statement of the cost items referred to in Article 1a (2) with the exception of expenditure related to the breach of contractual obligations which were not included in the calculation of the annual percentage rate of charge but which have to be paid by the consumer in given circumstances, together with a statement identifying such circumstances. Where the exact amount of those items is known, that sum is to be indicated; if that is not the case, either a method of calculation or as accurate an estimate as possible is to be provided where possible.]

In cases where it is not possible to state the annual percentage rate of charge, the consumer shall be provided with adequate information in the written agreement. This information shall at least include the information provided for in the second indent of Article 6 (1).

3. The written agreement shall further include the other essential terms of the contract.

By way of illustration, the Annex to this Directive contains a list of terms that Member States may require to be included in the written agreement as being essential.

¶ *Points (c) and (d) have been added to paragraph 2 by article 1(4) of Directive 90/88/EEC, reproduced infra under no. C.P. 8.*

Article 5

[. . .]

¶ *This article has been deleted by article 1(5) of Directive 90/88/EEC, reproduced infra under no. C.P. 8.*

Article 6

1. Notwithstanding the exclusion provided for in Article 2 (1) (e), where there is an agreement between a credit institution or financial institution and a consumer for the granting of credit in the

---

[9] OJ L 250, 19.9.1984, 17, reproduced supra under no. C.P. 1. Directive as last amended by Directive 97/55/EC (OJ L 290, 23.10.1997, 18), reproduced infra under no. C.P. 13.

form of an advance on a current account, other than on credit card accounts, the consumer shall be informed at the time or before the agreement is concluded:
- of the credit limit, if any,
- of the annual rate of interest and the charges applicable from the time the agreement is concluded and the conditions under which these may be amended,
- of the procedure for terminating the agreement.

This information shall be confirmed in writing.

2. Furthermore, during the period of the agreement, the consumer shall be informed of any change in the annual rate of interest or in the relevant charges at the time it occurs. Such information may be given in a statement of account or in any other manner acceptable to Member States.

3. In Member States where tacitly accepted overdrafts are permissible, the Member States concerned shall ensure that the consumer is informed of the annual rate of interest and the charges applicable, and of any amendment thereof, where the overdraft extends beyond a period of three months.

Case

Case C-264/02 Cofinoga Mérignac SA and Sylvain Sachithanathan [2004] ECR I-2157

Council Directive 87/102/EEC, does not require, before each renewal, on the existing terms and conditions, of a credit agreement for a specified period entered into in the form of a credit facility that may be drawn down in instalments and is linked to a credit card, that is repayable in monthly instalments and bears an interest rate that is expressed to be variable, that the lender inform the borrower in writing of the current annual percentage rate of charge and of the conditions under which the latter may be amended.

Article 7

In the case of credit granted for the acquisition of goods, Member States shall lay down the conditions under which goods may be repossessed, in particular if the consumer has not given his consent. They shall further ensure that where the creditor recovers possession of the goods the account between the parties shall be made up so as to ensure that the repossession does not entail any unjustified enrichment.

Article 8

The consumer shall be entitled to discharge his obligations under a credit agreement before the time fixed by the agreement. In this event, in accordance with the rules laid down by the Member States, the consumer shall be entitled to an equitable reduction in the total cost of the credit.

Article 9

Where the creditor's rights under a credit agreement are assigned to a third person, the consumer shall be entitled to plead against that third person any defence which was available to him against the original creditor, including set-off where the latter is permitted in the Member State concerned.

Article 10

The Member States which, in connection with credit agreements, permit the consumer:

(a) to make payment by means of bills of exchange including promissory notes;

(b) to give security by means of bills of exchange including promissory notes and cheques,

shall ensure that the consumer is suitably protected when using these instruments in those ways.

Article 11

1. Member States shall ensure that the existence of a credit agreement shall not in any way affect the rights of the consumer against the supplier of goods or services purchased by means of such an agreement in cases where the goods or services are not supplied or are otherwise not in conformity with the contract for their supply.

2. Where

(a) in order to buy goods or obtain services the consumer enters into a credit agreement with a person other than the supplier of them;

(b) the grantor of the credit and the supplier of the goods or services have a pre-existing agreement whereunder credit is made available exclusively by that grantor of credit to customers of that supplier for the acquisition of goods or services from that supplier; and

(c) the consumer referred to in subparagraph (a) obtains his credit pursuant to that pre-existing agreement; and

(d) the goods or services covered by the credit agreement are not supplied, or are supplied only in part, or are not in conformity with the contract for supply of them; and

(e) the consumer has pursued his remedies against the supplier but has failed to obtain the satisfaction to which he is entitled,

the consumer shall have the right to pursue remedies against the grantor of credit. Member States shall determine to what extent and under what conditions these remedies shall be exercisable.

3. Paragraph 2 shall not apply where the individual transaction in question is for an amount less than the equivalent of 200 ECU.

Article 12

1. Member States shall:

(a) ensure that persons offering credit or offering to arrange credit agreements shall obtain official authorisation to do so, either specifically or as suppliers of goods and services; or

(b) ensure that persons granting credit or arranging for credit to be granted shall be subject to inspection or monitoring of their activities by an institution or official body; or

(c) promote the establishment of appropriate bodies to receive complaints concerning credit agreements or credit conditions and to provide relevant information or advice to consumers regarding them.

2. Member States may provide that the authorisation referred to in paragraph 1 (a) shall not be required where persons offering to conclude or arrange credit agreements satisfy the definition in Article 1 of the first Council Directive of 12 December 1977 on the co-ordination of laws, regulations and administrative provisions relating to the taking up and pursuit of the business of credit institutions[10] and are authorised in accordance with the provisions of that Directive.

Where persons granting credit or arranging for credit to be granted have been authorised both specifically, under the provisions of paragraph 1 (a) and also under the provisions of the aforementioned Directive, but the latter authorisation is subsequently withdrawn, the competent authority responsible for issuing the specific authorisation to grant credit under paragraph 1 (a) shall be informed and shall decide whether the persons concerned may continue to grant credit, or arrange for credit to be granted, or whether the specific authorisation granted under paragraph 1 (a) should be withdrawn.

Article 13

1. For the purposes of this Directive, the ECU shall be that defined by Regulation No. 3180/78/EEC, as amended by Regulation No. 2626/84/EEC. The equivalent in national currency shall initially be calculated at the rate obtaining on the date of adoption of this Directive.

Member States may round off the amounts in national currency resulting from the conversion of the amounts in ECU provided such rounding off does not exceed 10 ECU.

2. Every five years, and for the first time in 1995, the Council, acting on a proposal from the Commission, shall examine and if need be, revise the amounts in this Directive, in the light of economic and monetary trends in the Community.

Article 14

1. Member States shall ensure that credit agreements shall not derogate, to the detriment of the consumer, from the provisions of national law implementing or corresponding to this Directive.

2. Member States shall further ensure that the provisions, which they adopt in implementation

---

[10] OJ L 322, 17.12.1977, 30–37, First Banking Directive consolidated in Directive 2000/12/EC (OJ L 126, 26.5.2000, 1), reproduced supra under no. B. 32.

of this directive, are not circumvented as a result of the way in which agreements are formulated, in particular by the device of distributing the amount of credit over several agreements.

Article 15

This Directive shall not preclude Member States from retaining or adopting more stringent provisions to protect consumers consistent with their obligations under the Treaty.

Article 16

1. Member States shall bring into force the measures necessary to comply with this Directive not later than 1 January 1990 and shall forthwith inform the Commission thereof.
2. Member States shall communicate to the Commission the texts of the main provisions of national law that they adopt in the field covered by this Directive.

Article 17

Not later than 1 January 1995 the Commission shall present a report to the Council concerning the operation of this Directive.

Article 18

This Directive is addressed to the Member States.

Annex [I]

List of Terms referred to in Article 4(3)

1. Credit agreements for financing the supply of particular goods or services:

(i) a description of the goods or services covered by the agreement;
(ii) the cash price and the price payable under the credit agreement;
(iii) the amount of the deposit, if any, the number and amount of instalments and the dates on which they fall due, or the method of ascertaining any of the same if unknown at the time the agreement is concluded;
(iv) an indication that the consumer will be entitled, as provided in Article 8, to a reduction if he repays early;
(v) who owns the goods (if ownership does not pass immediately to the consumer) and the terms on which the consumer becomes the owner of them;
(vi) a description of the security required, if any;
(vii) the cooling-off period, if any;
(viii) an indication of the insurance(s) required, if any, and, when the choice of insurer is not left to the consumer, an indication of the cost thereof.
[(ix) the obligation on the consumer to save a certain amount of money that must be placed in a special account.]

2. Credit agreements operated by credit cards:

(i) the amount of the credit limit, if any;
(ii) the terms of repayment or the means of determining them;
(iii) the cooling-off period, if any.

3. Credit agreements operated by running account which are not otherwise covered by the Directive:

(i) the amount of the credit limit, if any, or the method of determining it;
(ii) the terms of use and repayment;
(iii) the cooling-off period, if any.

4. Other credit agreements covered by the Directive:

(i) the amount of the credit limit, if any;
(ii) an indication of the security required, if any;
(iii) the terms of repayment;
(iv) the cooling-off period, if any;
(v) an indication that the consumer will be entitled, as provided in Article 8, to a reduction if he repays early.

¶ The annex has been renumbered as Annex I by article 1(6) and (7) of Directive 90/88/EEC, reproduced infra under no. C.P. 8.
¶ Point (ix) has been added by article 1(6) of Directive 90/88/EEC, reproduced infra under no. C.P. 8.

[Annex II

The Basic Equation Expressing the Equivalence of Loans on the one hand and Repayments and Charges on the other

$$\sum_{K=1}^{K=m} \frac{A_K}{(1+i)^{t_K}} = \sum_{K'=1}^{K'=m'} \frac{A'_{K'}}{(1+i)^{t_{K'}}}$$

Meaning of letters and symbols:

K is the number of a loan

K' is the number of a repayment or a payment of charges

A_K is the amount of loan number K

Σ represents a sum

m is the number of the last loan

m' is the number of the last repayment or payment of charges

t_K is the interval, expressed in years and fractions of a year, between the date of loan No 1 and those of subsequent loans Nos 2 to m

$t_{K'}$ is the interval, expressed in years and fractions of a year, between the date of loan No 1 and those of repayments or payments of charges Nos 1 to m'

i is the percentage rate that can be calculated (either by algebra, by successive approximations, or by a computer programme) where the other terms in the equation are known from the contract or otherwise.

Remarks:

(a) The amounts paid by both parties at different times shall not necessarily be equal and shall not necessarily be paid at equal intervals.

(b) The starting date shall be that of the first loan.

(c) Intervals between dates used in the calculations shall be expressed in years or in fractions of a year. A year is presumed to have 365 days or 365.25 days or (for leap years) 366 days, 52 weeks or 12 equal months. An equal month is presumed to have 30.41666 days (i.e. 365/12).

(d) The result of the calculation shall be expressed with an accuracy of at least one decimal place. When rounding to a particular decimal place the following rule shall apply:

If the figure at the decimal place following this particular decimal place is greater than or equal to 5, the figure at this particular decimal place shall be increased by one.

(e) Member States shall provide that the methods of resolution applicable give a result equal to that of the examples presented in Annex III.]

¶ *Annex II has been replaced by article 1(e) of Directive 98/7/EC, reproduced infra under no. C.P. 14.*

[Annex III

Examples of Calculation

A. Calculation of the Annual Percentage Rate of Charge on a Calendar Basis (1 Year = 365 Days (or 366 Days for Leap Years))

First example

Sum loaned: S = ECU 1 000 on 1 January 1994.

It is repaid in a single payment of ECU 1 200 made on 1 July 1995 i.e. 1 1/2 years or 546 (= 365 + 181) days after the date of the loan.

$$1000 = \frac{1\,200}{(1+i)^{\frac{546}{365}}}$$

or:

$(1+i)^{546/365} = 1.2$

$1+i = 1.296204$

$i = 1.1296204$

This amount will be rounded to 13% (or 12,96% if an accuracy of two decimal places is preferred).

Second example

The sum loaned is S = ECU 1 000, but the creditor retains ECU 50 for administrative expenses, so that the loan is in fact ECU 950; the repayment of ECU 1 200, as in the first example, is again made on 1 July 1995.

The equation becomes:

$$950 = \frac{1\,200}{(1+i)^{\frac{546}{365}}}$$

or:

$(1+i)^{546/365} = 1.263157$
$1+i = 1.169026$
$i = 1.169026$

This amount will be rounded to 16,9%.

Third example

The sum loaned is ECU 1 000, on 1 January 1994, repayable in two amounts, each of ECU 600, paid after one and two years respectively.

The equation becomes:

$$1000 = \frac{600}{(1+i)} + \frac{600}{(1+i)^{\frac{730}{365}}} = \frac{600}{1+i} + \frac{600}{(1+i)^2}$$

It is solved by algebra and produces $i = 0.1306623$ rounded to 13.1% (or 13.07% if an accuracy of two decimal places is preferred).

Fourth example

The sum loaned is S = ECU 1 000, on 1 January 1994, and the amounts to be paid by the borrower are:

After 3 months (0.25 years/90 days):	ECU	272
After 6 months (0.5 years/181 days):	ECU	272
After 12 months (1 year/365 days):	ECU	544
Total:	ECU	1.088

The equation becomes:

$$1000 = \frac{272}{(1+i)^{\frac{90}{365}}} + \frac{272}{(1+i)^{\frac{181}{365}}} + \frac{544}{(1+i)^{\frac{365}{365}}}$$

This equation allows i to be calculated by successive approximations, which can be programmed on a pocket calculator.

The result is $i = 0.13226$ rounded to 13.2% (or 13.23% if an accuracy of two decimal places is preferred).

B. Calculation of the Annual Percentage Rate of Charge on the Basis of a Standard Year (1 Year = 365 Days or 365.25 Days, 52 Weeks, or 12 Equal Months)

First example

Sum loaned: S = ECU 1 000.

It is repaid in a single payment of ECU 1 200 made in 1.5 years (i.e. 1.5 x 365 = 547.5 days, 1.5 x 365,25 = 547.875 days, 1.5 x 366 = 549 days, 1.5 x 12 = 18 months, or 1.5 x 52 = 78 weeks) after the date of the loan.

The equation becomes:

$$1000 = \frac{1200}{(1+i)^{\frac{547.5}{365}}} = \frac{1200}{(1+i)^{\frac{547.875}{365.25}}} = \frac{1\,200}{(1+i)^{\frac{18}{12}}}$$

$$= \frac{1\,200}{(1+i)^{\frac{78}{52}}}$$

or:

$(1+i)^{1,5} = 1.2$
$1+i = 1.129243$
$i = 1.129243$

This amount will be rounded to 12.9% (or 12.92% if an accuracy of two decimal places is preferred).

Second example

The sum loaned is S = ECU 1 000, but the creditor retains ECU 50 for administrative expenses, so that the loan is in fact ECU 950; the repayment of

ECU 1 200, as in the first example, is again made 1.5 years after the date of the loan.

The equation becomes:

$$950 = \frac{1\,200}{(1+i)^{\frac{547,5}{365}}} = \frac{1\,200}{(1+i)^{\frac{547,875}{365,25}}} = \frac{1\,200}{(1+i)^{\frac{18}{12}}}$$

$$= \frac{1\,200}{(1+i)^{\frac{78}{52}}}$$

or:

$(1+i)^{1,5} = 1.200/950 = 1.263157$
$1+i = 1.168528$
$i = 1.168528$

This amount will be rounded to 16.9% (or 16.85% if an accuracy of two decimal places is preferred).

Third example

The sum loaned is ECU 1 000, repayable in two amounts, each of ECU 600, paid after one and two years respectively.

The equation becomes:

$$1000 = \frac{600}{(1+i)^{\frac{365}{365}}} + \frac{600}{(1+i)^{\frac{730}{365}}} = \frac{600}{(1+i)^{\frac{365,5}{365,25}}}$$

$$+ \frac{600}{(1+i)^{\frac{730,5}{365,25}}} = \frac{600}{(1+i)^{\frac{12}{12}}} + \frac{600}{(1+i)^{\frac{24}{12}}}$$

$$= \frac{600}{(1+i)^{\frac{52}{52}}} + \frac{600}{(1+i)^{\frac{104}{52}}} = \frac{600}{(1+i)^{1}}$$

$$+ \frac{600}{(1+i)^{2}}$$

It is solved by algebra and produces i = 0.13066 which will be rounded to 13.1% (or 13.07% if an accuracy of two decimal places is preferred).

Fourth example

The sum loaned is S = ECU 1 000 and the amounts to be paid by the borrower are:

After 3 months
(0.25 years/13weeks/
91.25 days/91.3125 days):   ECU   272

After 6 months
(0.5 years/26weeks/182.5 days/
182.625 days):   ECU   272

After 12 months
(1 year/52weeks/365 days/
365.25 days):   ECU   544

Total   ECU   1088

The equation becomes:

$$1000 = \frac{272}{(1+i)^{\frac{91,25}{365}}} + \frac{272}{(1+i)^{\frac{182,5}{365}}} + \frac{544}{(1+i)^{\frac{365}{365}}}$$

$$= \frac{272}{(1+i)^{\frac{91,3125}{365,25}}} + \frac{272}{(1+i)^{\frac{182,625}{365,25}}} + \frac{544}{(1+i)^{\frac{365,25}{365,25}}}$$

$$= \frac{272}{(1+i)^{\frac{13}{12}}} + \frac{272}{(1+i)^{\frac{6}{12}}} + \frac{544}{(1+i)^{\frac{12}{52}}}$$

$$= \frac{272}{(1+i)^{0,25}} + \frac{272}{(1+i)^{0,5}} + \frac{544}{(1+i)^{1}}$$

This equation allows i to be calculated by successive approximations, which can be programmed on a pocket calculator.

The result is $i = 0,13185$ which will be rounded to 13.2% (or 13.19% if an accuracy of two decimal places is preferred).

¶ *Annex III has been replaced by article 1(f) of Directive 98/7/EC, reproduced infra under no. C.P. 14.*

C.P. 5.

Commission Recommendation 87/598/EEC
of 8 December 1987
on a European code of conduct relating to electronic payment
(Relations between financial institutions, traders and service establishments, and consumers)[1]

THE COMMISSION OF THE EUROPEAN COMMUNITIES,

Having regard to the Treaty establishing the European Economic Community, and in particular the second indent of Article [211][2] thereof,

Whereas in the White Paper on completing the internal market the Commission undertook to formulate proposals with a view to adapting innovations and laws relating to new means of payment to the dimensions of that market;

Whereas on 12 January 1987 the Commission sent to the Council the communication 'Europe could play an ace: the new payment cards';[3]

Whereas, since there is a close link between technological development and the unification of the internal market, electronic payment should contribute to the rapid modernisation of banking services, distribution and the telecommunications and information industries;

Whereas consumers are entitled to except definite advantages from such a development;

Whereas Community action should add to this the benefit of a large market;

Whereas the development of new means of payment is to be seen in the context of the Community's financial and monetary integration and the extension of a people's Europe;

Whereas the free movement of goods and capital will be fully effective only if it enjoys the technological support provided by the new means of payment;

Whereas such means should be made available to economic partners in comparable circumstances in all Member States, although the Commission is aware that the development of payment cards (that is, payment cards incorporating a magnetic strip and/or a microcircuit) can vary in importance, depending on the Member State concerned, and that alternative forms of payment do exist;

Whereas it is necessary to co-operate in order to arrive at standards and implementing rules which will make it possible, in the interests of users in the Community, for payment systems to be compatible and complementary;

Whereas certain general principles should be established concerning fair practice in relations between financial institutions (i.e. banks and credit institutions), traders and service establishments, and cardholding consumers;

Whereas establishment of such principles will favour rapid and effective application of the new technology;

Whereas the heterogeneous, uncoordinated development of such technology should not diminish the opportunity which the technology itself affords of achieving the desired objective of compatible electronic payment systems within the Community;

Whereas compatible cards and interconnected Community networks are essential prerequisites for mutually accessible systems and harmonised rules of use;

Whereas, although it is for the banks and the other financial institutions concerned to decide to make systems compatible, the Commission is responsible for seeing that progress in this

---

[1] OJ L 365, 24.12.1987, 72–76.
[2] The number between brackets has been changed as from 1 May 1999 by article 12 of the Treaty of Amsterdam.
[3] COM (86) 754 final.

direction does not conflict with free competition within the Community market;

Whereas it is clear that to try now, at Community level, to produce a rigid, detailed definition of the operation of systems in the midst of change might result in the establishment of rules that would be rapidly overtaken by developments, even constituting obstacles to electronic development; whereas this in no way prejudices the benefits of laying down the basic principles of consumer protection in this area;

Whereas, nevertheless, it is appropriate that the Commission should see, at the present stage, that all changes in this sphere take place in accordance with the Treaty's rules and that it should seek, in the Community's interest, to establish and promote consensus as regards development of such systems;

Whereas the fact that this new technology is not being developed on a large scale in any of the Member States makes it impossible as yet to determine with any accuracy all the specific problems that are likely to arise in particular as networks are completed and arrangements for the use of the new means of payment are finalised;

Whereas, for these reasons, an instigative approach such as a code of conduct must be flexible so as to make it easier to adapt to changes in the new technology,

HEREBY RECOMMENDS

that all the economic partners concerned should comply with the provisions of the European Code of Conduct relating to electronic payment, as set out in the following.

European Code of Conduct Relating to Electronic Payment

I. Objective

1. The Code sets out the conditions that should be fulfilled if the new, electronic means of payment are to be developed for the benefit of all economic partners and are to afford:
– for consumers, security and convenience,
– for traders and issuers, greater security and productivity,
– or industry in the Community, a leading market.

2. The principles of fair practice must be observed by all those who bring card payment systems into operation or make use of them.

3. The technological development of electronic means of payment should have an eye to their European dimension: such means must be as widely interoperable as possible, to avoid having isolated systems and, hence, a partitioned market.

II. Definitions

For the purposes of this Code:

1. 'Electronic payment' means any payment transaction carried out by means of a card incorporating a magnetic strip or microcircuit used at an electronic payment terminal (EPT) or point-of-sale (POS) terminal.

The Code does not cover:
– 'company-specific' cards not covered by the above definition,
– cards serving purposes other than direct or deferred payment,
– payments by cheque with bank-card guarantee,
– payments by card using mechanical processes (invoice slips).

2. 'Issuer' means any banking or credit institution issuing a payment card for electronic use, plus any production or service undertaking which can also issue such a card.

3. 'Trader' means distributive trading or service establishment.

4. 'Consumer' means cardholder.

5. 'Interoperability' means a state of affairs whereby cards issued in one Member State and/or belonging to a given card system can be used in other Member States and/or in the networks installed by other systems. This requires that the cards and readers used in the various systems must be technologically compatible and that systems must be opened up by means of reciprocity agreements.

III. General Principles

1. Contracts

(a) Contracts concluded by issuers, or their agents, with traders and consumers shall be in writing and must be the result of a prior application. They shall set out in detail the general and specific conditions of the agreement.

(b) They shall be drawn up in the official language(s) of the Member State in which the contract is concluded.

(c) Any scale of charges must be determined in a transparent manner, taking account of actual costs and risks and without involving any restriction of competition.

(d) All conditions, provided they are in conformity with the law, shall be freely negotiable and clearly stipulated in the contract.

(e) Conditions specific to termination of a contract must be stated and brought to the notice of the parties prior to such contract being concluded.

2. Interoperability

By a given date,[4] interoperability, in the Community at any rate, should be full and complete, so that traders and consumers can join the network(s) or contract with the issuer(s) of their choice, with each terminal being able to process all cards.

3. Equipment

(a) Electronic payment terminals are required to register, control and transmit payments and may be integrated into a point-of-sale terminal.

(b) Traders must be able, if they wish, to install a single, multi-card terminal.

(c) Traders must be free to choose which point-of-sale terminal they will install. They must be at liberty either to rent or purchase such equipment, provided only that it is certified as satisfying the requirements of the whole payment system and can be used on an interoperable basis.

4. Data protection and security

(a) Electronic payments are irreversible. An order given by means of a payment card shall be irrevocable and may not be countermanded.

(b) The information transmitted, at the time of payment, to the trader's bank and subsequently to the issuer must not in any circumstances prejudice the protection of privacy. It shall be strictly limited to that normally laid down for cheques and transfers.

(c) Any problems whatsoever that arise in connection with the protection of information or with security must be openly acknowledged and cleared up at whatever stage in the contract between the parties.

(d) Contracts must not restrict traders' freedom of operation or freedom to compete.

5. Fair access to the system

(a) Irrespective of their economic size, all service establishments concerned must be allowed fair access to the system of electronic payment. A trader may be refused access for a legitimate reason only.

(b) There must be no unwarranted difference in the remuneration for services concerning transactions within one Member State and the remuneration for the same services concerning transnational transactions with other Community countries, especially in border regions.

IV. Supplementary Provisions

1. Relations between issuers and traders

(a) To promote mutual access among different card systems, contracts between card issuers and traders must contain no exclusive trading clause requiring the trader to operate only the system with which he has contracted an agreement.

(b) Contracts with traders must admit effective competition between the various issuers. Compulsory provisions must be limited strictly to technical requirements for ensuring that the system functions properly.

2. Relations between issuers and consumers

Cardholders shall take all reasonable precautions to ensure the safety of the card issued and shall observe the special conditions (loss or theft) in the contract that they have signed.

3. Relations between traders and consumers

Traders shall display, in a fully visible manner, the signs of the companies to which they are affiliated; they shall be obliged to accept such cards.

---

[4] 31 December 1992, i.e. the date by which the internal market must be complete.

C.P. 6.

Commission Recommendation 88/590/EEC
of 17 November 1988
concerning Payment Systems, and in particular the relationship between cardholder and card issuer[1]

THE COMMISSION OF THE EUROPEAN COMMUNITIES,

Having regard to the Treaty establishing the European Economic Community, and in particular the second indent of Article [211][2] thereof,

Whereas one of the main objectives of the Community is to complete not later than 1992 the internal market, of which payment systems are essential parts;

Whereas paragraph 18 of the Annex to the Council resolution of 14 April 1975 on a preliminary programme of the European Economic Community for a consumer protection and information policy,[3] indicated that the protection of the economic interests of consumers should be based on the following principles:[4]

(i) that purchasers of goods and services should be protected against standard contracts, and in particular against the exclusion of essential rights in contracts,

(ii) that the consumer should be protected against damage to his economic interests caused by unsatisfactory services, and

(iii) that the presentation and promotion of goods and services, including financial services, should not be designed to mislead, either directly or indirectly, the person to whom they are offered or by whom they have been requested; whereas paragraph 24 in the Annex to the said preliminary programme specified that the protection of the consumer against unfair commercial practices, *inter alia* as regards terms of contracts, is to be given priority treatment in implementing that programme;

Whereas the Commission's White Paper on 'Completing the Internal Market',[5] communicated to the Council in June 1985, referred in paragraph 121 to new technologies — which will transform the European marketing and distribution system and engender a need for adequate consumer protection, and further referred in paragraph 122 to electronic banking, payment cards and videotex;

Whereas the Commission's policy document entitled 'A New Impetus for Consumer Protection Policy', communicated to the Council in July 1985[6] which was the subject of a Council resolution adopted on 23 June 1986[7] referred in paragraph 34 to electronic fund transfer and announced in the timetable contained in the Annex thereto a proposal for a directive on that matter, for adoption by the Council in 1989; whereas it is appropriate to accelerate financial consumer protection in the field of payment systems and certain other services available to consumers; whereas the forms of financial service, including financial self-service, and the means of purchasing goods and services which are now in use in market places in Member States (some of them even in the homes of consumers) are furnished upon divergent terms of contract and of consumer protection from one Member State to another;

---

[1] OJ L 317, 24.11.1988, 55–58.
[2] The number between brackets has been changed as from 1 May 1999 by article 12 of the Treaty of Amsterdam.
[3] OJ C 92, 25.4.1975, 1.
[4] Confirmed in paragraph 28 of the second programme (OJ C 133, 3.6.1981, 1).
[5] COM (85) 310 final, 14.6.1985.
[6] COM (85) 314 final 27.6.1985.
[7] OJ C 167, 5.7.1986, 1.

Whereas there has been much change in recent years in the types of financial service available to and used by consumers, particularly as regards payment methods and as regards the purchasing of goods and services; whereas new forms thereof have emerged and are continuing to develop;

Whereas the various terms of contract currently used in this field in Member States are not only divergent from one to another (and indeed within any one Member State) but also in some cases disadvantageous to the consumer; whereas more effective protection of consumers can be achieved by the use of common terms which are to apply to all these forms of financial service;

Whereas the consumer should receive adequate information concerning the terms of contract, including the fees and other costs, if any, payable by the consumer for these services, and concerning his rights and obligations under the contract; whereas this information should include an unequivocal statement of the extent of the consumer's obligations as holder (hereinafter called 'contracting holder') of a card or other device enabling him to make payments in favour of third persons, as well as to perform certain financial services for himself;

Whereas the protection of the consumer as a contracting holder is further improved if such contracts are made in writing and contain certain minimum particulars concerning the contractual terms, including an indication of the period within which his operations will normally be credited, debited or invoiced;

Whereas no payment device, whether in the form of a plastic card or otherwise, should be dispatched to a member of the public except in response to an application from such person; whereas the contract concluded between that person and the issuer of the payment device should not be binding before the applicant has received the device and also knows the applicable terms of contract;

Whereas, given the nature of the technology currently used in the field of payment devices, including both the manufacture and use of them, it is essential that operations effected by means of them should be the subject of records in order that operations can be traced and errors can be rectified; whereas the contracting holder has no means of access to those records, and consequently the burden of proof to show that an operation was accurately recorded and entered into the accounts and was not affected by technical breakdown or other deficiency should lie upon the person who under a contract furnishes the payment device to him, namely the issuer;

Whereas payment instructions communicated electronically by a contracting holder should be irrevocable, so that a payment made thereby shall not be reversed; whereas the contracting holder should be supplied with a record of the operations he effects by means of a payment device;

Whereas common rules need to be specified concerning the issuer's liability for non-execution or for defective execution of a contracting holder's payment instructions and allied operations, and for transactions which have not been authorised by the contracting holder, subject always to the contracting holder's own obligations in the case of lost, stolen or copied payment devices;

Whereas common terms of contract need also to be specified concerning the consequences to the contracting holder if he loses his payment device or it is stolen from him or copied;

Whereas for the purpose of ensuring that electronic payment networks can function and payment devices be used internationally, it is necessary that certain minimum data relating to a contracting holder can be transmitted across frontiers, but subject to certain conditions;

Whereas the Commission will monitor the implementation of this recommendation, and if, after 12 months, it finds the implementation unsatisfactory, the Commission will take appropriate measures,

RECOMMENDS:

That not later than 12 months after the date hereof:

1. issuers of payment devices and system providers conduct their activities in accordance with the provisions contained in the Annex hereto;

2. Member States ensure, in order to facilitate the operations referred to in the Annex, that data relating to contracting holders may be transmitted, but that the data transmitted shall be kept:

– to the requisite minimum, and
– confidential by all persons to whose knowledge they are brought in the course of such operations.

Annex

1. This Annex applies to the following operations:
– electronic payment involving the use of a card, in particular at point of sale,
– the withdrawing of banknotes, the depositing of banknotes and cheques, and connected operations, at electronic devices such as cash dispensing machines and automated teller machines,
– non-electronic payment by card, including processes for which a signature is required and a voucher is produced, but not including cards whose sole function is to guarantee payment made by cheque,
– electronic payment effected by a member of the public without the use of a card, such as home banking.

2. For the purposes of this Annex the following definitions apply:

'Payment device': a card or some other means enabling its user to effect operations of the kind specified in paragraph 1.

'Issuer': a person who, in the course of his business, makes available to a member of the public a payment device pursuant to a contract concluded with him.

'System provider': a person who makes available a financial product under a specific trade name, and usually with a network, thus enabling payment devices to be used for the operations aforesaid.

'Contracting holder': a person who, pursuant to a contract concluded between him and an issuer, holds a payment device.

'Company-specific card': a card issued by a retailer to his client, or by a group of retailers to their clients, in order to allow or facilitate, without giving access to a bank account, payment for purchases of goods or services exclusively from the issuing retailer or retailers, or from retailers who under contract accept the card.

3.1. Each issuer shall draw up full and fair terms of contract, in writing to govern the issuing and use of the payment devices he issues.

3.2. Those terms of contract shall be expressed:
– in easily understandable words and in so clear a form that they are easy to read,
– in the language or languages which are ordinarily used for such or similar purposes in the regions where the terms of contract are offered.

3.3. The terms of contract shall specify the basis of calculation of the amount of the charges (including interest), if any, which the contracting holder must pay to the issuer.

3.4. The terms of contract shall specify:
– whether the debiting or crediting of operations will be instantaneous and, if not, the period of time within which this will be done,
– for those operations which lead to invoicing of the contracting cardholder, the period of time within which this will be done.

3.5. The terms of contract shall not be altered except by agreement between the parties; however, such agreement shall be deemed to exist where the issuer proposes an amendment to the contract terms and the contracting holder, having received notice thereof, continues to make use of the payment device.

4.1. The terms of contract shall put the contracting holder under obligation *vis-à-vis* the issuer:

(a) to take all reasonable steps to keep safe the payment device and the means (such as a personal identification number or code) which enable it to be used;

(b) to notify the issuer or a central agency without undue delay after becoming aware:
- of the loss or theft or copying of the payment device or of the means which enable it to be used;
- of the recording on the contracting holder's account of any unauthorised transaction;
- of any error or other irregularity in the maintaining of that account by the issuer.

(c) not to record on the payment device the contracting holder's personal identification number or code, if any, nor to record those things on anything which he usually keeps or carries with the payment device, particularly if they are likely to be lost or stolen or copied together;

(d) not to countermand an order that he has given by means of his payment device.

4.2. The terms of contract shall state that provided the contracting holder complies with the obligations imposed upon him pursuant to subparagraphs (a), (b) first indent, and (c) of paragraph 4.1., and otherwise does not act with extreme negligence, or fraudulently, in the circumstances in which he uses his payment device he shall not, after notification, be liable for damage arising from such use.

4.3. The terms of contract shall put the issuer under obligation *vis-à-vis* the contracting holder not to disclose the contracting holder's personal identification number or code or similar confidential data, if any, except to the contracting holder himself.

5. No payment device shall be dispatched to a member of the public except in response to an application from such person; and the contract between the issuer and the contracting holder shall be regarded as having been concluded at the time when the applicant receives the payment device and a copy of the terms of contract accepted by him.

6.1. In relation to the operations referred to in paragraph 1, issuers shall keep, or cause to be kept, internal records that are sufficiently substantial to enable operations to be traced and errors to be rectified. To this end, issuers shall make the requisite arrangements with the system providers, as necessary.

6.2. In any dispute with a contracting holder concerning an operation referred to in the first, second and fourth indents of paragraph 1 and relating to liability for an unauthorised electronic fund transfer, the burden of proof shall be upon the issuer to show that the operation was accurately recorded and accurately entered into accounts and was not affected by technical breakdown or other deficiency.

6.3. The contracting holder, if he so requests, shall be supplied with a record of each of his operations, instantaneously or shortly after he has completed it; however in the case of payment at point of sale the till receipt supplied by the retailer at the time of purchase and containing the references to the payment device shall satisfy the requirements of this provision.

7.1. Vis-à-vis a contracting holder the issuer shall be liable, subject to paragraphs 4 and 8:
- for the non-execution or defective execution of the contracting holder's operations as referred to in paragraph 1, even if an operation is initiated at electronic devices which are not under the issuer's direct or exclusive control,
- for operations not authorised by the contracting holder.

7.2. Save as stated in paragraph 7.3. the liability indicated in the paragraph 7.1. shall be limited as follows:
- in the case of non-execution or defective execution of an operation, the amount of the liability shall be limited to the amount of the unexecuted or defectively executed operation,
- in the case of an unauthorised operation, the amount of the liability shall extend to the sum required to restore the contracting holder to the position he was in before the unauthorised operation took place.

7.3. Any further financial consequences, and, in particular, questions concerning the extent of the damage for which compensation is to be paid, shall be governed by the law applicable to the contract concluded between the issuer and the contracting holder.

8.1. Each issuer shall provide means whereby his customers may at any time of the day or night notify the loss, theft or copying of their payment devices; but in the case of company-specific cards these means of notification need only be made available during the issuer's hours of business.

8.2. Once the contracting holder has notified the issuer or a central agency, as required by paragraph 4.1. (b), the contracting holder shall not thereafter be liable; but this provision shall not apply if the contracting holder acted with extreme negligence or fraudulently.

8.3. The contracting holder shall bear the loss sustained, up to the time of notification, in consequence of the loss, theft or copying of the payment device, but only up to the equivalent of 150 ecus for each event, except where he acted with extreme negligence or fraudulently.

8.4. The issuer, upon receipt of notification, shall be under obligation, even if the contracting holder acted with extreme negligence or fraudulently, to take all action open to him to stop any further use of the payment device.

C.P. 7.

Commission Recommendation 90/109/EEC
of 14 February 1990
on the transparency of banking conditions relating to cross-border financial transactions[1]

THE COMMISSION OF THE EUROPEAN COMMUNITIES,

Having regard to the Treaty establishing the European Economic Community, and in particular Article [211][2] thereof,

Whereas the removal of economic barriers within the Community and the progress achieved in the field of monetary and banking co-operation fostered by the directives adopted under the Single European Act should logically lead to an increase in purchases of goods and services in other Member States and to greater mobility for individuals, particularly workers, tourists and pensioners;

Whereas this free movement of individuals and products will increase the number of cross-border financial transactions and the number of operators carrying out such transactions;

Whereas the way in which international transfer systems operate is much more complex than the system of national transfers because one or more intermediary institutions are involved, because different clearing arrangements apply in countries not having the same currency and because an exchange transaction takes place;

Whereas, in view of this complexity, better-qualified staff and a wider range of checks are needed than in the case of national transfers; whereas this adds significantly to the cost of, and time needed for, cross-border financial transactions; whereas those undertaking such transactions should, therefore, be clearly informed in advance of the cost and time needed;

Whereas rules of conduct based on common principles of transparency and concerning the information to be supplied and the details to be indicated on the statement relating to the transfer of funds would be such as to encourage institutions undertaking cross-border financial transactions to estimate their costs more accurately and to rationalise as far as possible their methods of transfer;

Whereas, however, since customer information is linked, as regards the choice of means, to the commercial policy of banking institutions, it should not be subject to uniform and binding rules;

Whereas the introduction of reference periods is essential in order to make an assessment of the prices charged for cross-border transactions and to preserve the confidence of those effecting or receiving transfers;

Whereas certain national departments should specialise in dealing with complaints in connection with cross-border financial transactions which require special attention because institutions in more than one Member State are involved;

Whereas, although several Member States have binding legislation on the transparency of banking conditions, it does not appear expedient to ask those Member States to amend their legislation by inserting rules relating solely to cross-border transactions; whereas the same applies a fortiori to the Member States where legislation on transparency covers the entire services sector and not simply banking transactions;

Whereas there are also a number of Member States which wish to retain proven co-operation procedures in order to improve relations between financial institutions and users;

---

[1] OJ L 67, 15.3.1990, 39–42.
[2] The number between brackets has been changed as from 1 May 1999 by article 12 of the Treaty of Amsterdam.

Whereas a recommendation enabling the competent authorities to secure on a voluntary basis the co-operation of the institutions concerned is an appropriate instrument for bringing about a change of behaviour and devising new structures apt to reduce the cost of cross-border transfers under conditions of free competition,

HEREBY RECOMMENDS:

(i) that Member States ensure that institutions that undertake cross-border financial transactions within the meaning of this recommendation apply the principles set out in the Annex;

(ii) that Member States notify the Commission not later than 30 September 1990 of the names and addresses of the bodies referred to in paragraph 2 of the Sixth Principle set out in the Annex.

Annex

Principles governing the transparency of banking conditions relating to cross-border financial transactions

General

The aim of the principles set out in this recommendation is to make more transparent the information supplied, and the invoicing rules to be observed by the institutions concerned in connection with cross-border financial transactions as defined below.

The principles apply to all categories of customer of the institutions concerned, without prejudice to the possibility of allowing certain customers to benefit from more favourable banking conditions by virtue, for example, of the size of the transaction or transactions involved.

'Institutions concerned', hereafter referred to as 'institutions', means all legal persons, and in particular credit institutions and postal services, providing facilities for effecting or facilitating cross-border transfers. For the purposes of this recommendation, branches of institutions are deemed to be 'institutions'.

'Cross-border financial transactions' means transfers as defined below where the institutions of the transferor and the transferee are situated in two different Member States.

'Transfer' means the complete movement of funds denominated in ecus or in a currency that is legal tender in a Member State from a transferor to a transferee, regardless of whether the latter holds an account with an institution situated in another Member State.

'Transfer order' means the written, oral or electronic instruction given to an institution to credit to an account or to keep available for a given person a sum of money or to arrange for that instruction to be executed by another institution.

'Transferor' means the person who issues the first transfer order.

'Transferee' means the final recipient who is to receive the funds in a Member State other than that in which the first transfer order was issued either by way of an operation crediting his account or by way of a notification enabling him to obtain payment of the funds.

First principle

Each institution should bring to the attention of its customers easily understandable and readily available information concerning cross-border financial transactions.

This principle could be applied in one of the following ways:
– a notice or some other permanent form of information drawing attention to the cost of, and time needed for, all cross-border financial transactions and encouraging customers to seek further information,

- standardised information (in the form of a notice, booklet, brochure or some other appropriate means of providing information) specifying the amount or, where appropriate, percentage of commission fees and charges applied by the institution in respect of each transaction that may be invoiced either to the transferor or the transferee when a cross-border financial transaction is undertaken, as well as, if necessary, the provisions relating to the value dates;
- information of a more specific nature (in the form of a booklet, brochure or some other appropriate means of providing information) should also be given to the transferor, if he so requests, regarding the procedures applied by the institution in executing his orders, together with an estimate from intermediary banks of expected charges and time needed, having due regard to those various procedures.

Second principle

In the statement relating to a cross-border financial transaction, the institution should inform its customer in detail of the commission fees and charges it is invoicing and of the exchange rate it has applied.

This principle could be applied in the following way:

The institution concerned could clearly specify in a statement or some other document sent or handed to its customer, regardless of whether he is the transferor or the transferee:
- the exchange rate applied in converting the amount of foreign currency,
- the amount of the commission fee or fees applied or invoiced by the institution,
- the list and amount of any taxes payable,
- the nature and amount of the charges payable by the customer,
- the nature and amount of any additional invoice.

Third principle

1. Without prejudice to the possibility for the transferor to choose other ways of apportioning commission fees and charges, the transferor's institution should inform its customer when the latter gives his order:
- that the commission fees and charges it imposes for transmitting the order may either remain payable by the transferor or be invoiced to the transferee,
- that any commission fees and charges invoiced by the transferee's institution to its customer when it places the funds at his disposal may either remain payable by the latter or be invoiced to the transferor.

2. Where the transferor has specifically instructed his institution to ensure that the transferee is credited with the exact amount shown on the transfer order, it is recommended that the institution apply a method of transfer which will make it possible to achieve this result and that, before undertaking the transfer operation, it inform the transferor of the additional amount which will be invoiced to him.

However, this amount will represent only a non-binding estimate for the institution except where it applies a flat-rate calculation.

This principle could be applied by making available to the transferor who wanted the transferee to be credited with an exact amount prior information based on a flat-rate calculation or an estimate that could take account of the average of the commission fees and charges applied by institutions in the country of the transferee where information permitting a more accurate calculation was not available. If the amount estimated were smaller than the amount of commission fees and charges actually payable, the difference could be invoiced only to be transferor.

Fourth principle

1. In the absence of instructions to the contrary and except in cases of force majeure, each intermediary institution should deal with a transfer order within two working days of receipt of the funds specified in the order or should give notification of its refusal to execute the order or of any foreseeable delay to the institution issuing the order and, where different, to the transferor's institution.

2. The transferor should be able to obtain a refund of part of the costs of the transfer in the event of any delay in executing his order.

This principle could be applied in the following way:

On expiry of a period of two working days, the transferor's institution should pay the amount of the transfer order to the transferee's institution or to any intermediary institution unless the transferee's institution (or this intermediary institution) gives notification within two working days of receipt of the transfer order of its refusal to execute the order received.

Where it is not the transferee's institution and where it has not given notification of its refusal to execute an order, the recipient institution should, within that same period of two working days from receipt of the funds specified in the transfer order, issue to the transferee's institution or to another intermediary institution a new transfer order containing the instructions necessary for the transfer to proceed in the appropriate fashion.

Fifth principle

1. The transferee's institution should fulfil its obligations arising from a transfer order not later than the working day following receipt of the funds specified in the order unless the said order stipulates a later date of execution.

2. If the transferee's institution is unable to execute the order within the time indicated in paragraph 1, it should, as soon as possible, inform the institution issuing the order and, where different, the transferor's institution of the reasons for its failure to execute the order or for the delay in execution.

Sixth principle

1. Any institution participating in a cross-border financial transaction should be capable of dealing rapidly with complaints lodged by the transferor or the transferee in connection with the execution of the transaction or with the statement relating to it.

2. If no action is taken on a complaint or no answer received within three months, the complainants may refer the matter to one of the Member States' bodies competent to deal with complaints from users. The list and addresses of such national bodies should be available on request from any institution undertaking cross-border financial transactions.

One way of applying this principle would be to entrust the task of dealing with complaints to bodies independent of the parties concerned and forming part of:
– the public sector (ministerial department),
– the central bank,
– a specialist body such as the ombudsman's office,
– a contact committee comprising bank representatives and users.

C.P. 8.

Council Directive 90/88/EEC
of 22 February 1990
amending Directive 87/102/EEC for the approximation of the laws, regulations and administrative provisions of the Member States concerning consumer credit[1]

THE COUNCIL OF THE EUROPEAN COMMUNITIES,

Having regard to the Treaty establishing the European Economic Community, and in particular Article [95][2] thereof,

Having regard to the proposal from the Commission,[3]

In co-operation with the European Parliament,[4]

Having regard to the opinion of the Economic and Social Committee,[5]

Whereas Article 5 of Council Directive 87/102/EEC[6] provides for the introduction of a Community method or methods of calculating the annual percentage rate of charge for consumer credit;

Whereas it is desirable, in order to promote the establishment and functioning of the internal market and to ensure that consumers benefit from a high level of protection, that one method of calculating the said annual percentage rate of charge should be used throughout the Community;

Whereas it is desirable, with a view to introducing such a method and in accordance with the definition of the total cost of credit to the consumer, to draw up a single mathematical formula for calculating the annual percentage rate of charge and for determining credit cost items to be used in the calculation by indicating those costs which must not be taken into account;

Whereas, during a transitional period, Member States which prior to the date of notification of this Directive, apply laws which permit the use of another mathematical formula for calculating the annual percentage rate of charge may continue to apply such laws;

Whereas, before expiry of the transitional period and in the light of experience, the Council will, on the basis of a proposal from the Commission, take a decision that will make it possible to apply a single Community mathematical formula;

Whereas it is desirable, whenever necessary, to adopt certain hypotheses for calculating the annual percentage rate of charge;

Whereas by virtue of the special nature of loans guaranteed by a mortgage secured on immovable property it is desirable that such credit should continue to be partially excluded from this Directive;

Whereas the information which must be communicated to the consumer in the written contract should be amplified,

HAS ADOPTED THIS DIRECTIVE:

[. . .]

¶ *This Directive modifies Directive 87/102/EEC, reproduced supra under no. C.P. 4. and is directly incorporated therein.*

---

[1] OJ L 61, 10.3.1990, 14–18.
[2] The number between brackets has been changed as from 1 May 1999 by article 12 of the Treaty of Amsterdam.
[3] OJ C 155, 14.6.1988, 10.
[4] OJ C 96, 17.4.1989, 87 and OJ C 291, 20.11.1989, 50.
[5] OJ C 337, 31.12.1988, 1.
[6] OJ L 42, 12.2.1987, 48, reproduced supra under no. C.P. 4.

C.P. 9.

Council Directive 93/13/EEC
of 5 April 1993
on unfair terms in consumer contracts[1]

CASES

I. Case C-473/00 Cofidis SA v Jean-Louis Fredout [2002] ECR I-10875

This directive precludes a national provision which, in proceedings brought by a seller or supplier against a consumer on the basis of a contract concluded between them, prohibits the national court, on expiry of a limitation period, from finding, of its own motion or following a plea raised by the consumer, that a term of the contract is unfair.

II. Joined cases C-240/98 to C-244/98 Océano Grupo Editorial SA v Roció Murciano Quintero (C-240/98) and Salvat Editores SA v José M. Sánchez Alcón Prades (C-241/98), José Luis Copano Badillo (C-242/98), Mohammed Berroane (C-243/98) and Emilio Viñas Feliú (C-244/98) [2000] ECR I-4941

1. The protection provided for consumers by Council Directive 93/13/EEC entails the national court being able to determine of its own motion whether a term of a contract before it is unfair when making its preliminary assessment as to whether a claim should be allowed to proceed before the national courts.

2. The national court is obliged, when it applies national law provisions predating or postdating the said directive, to interpret those provisions, so far as possible, in the light of the wording and purpose of the directive. The requirement for an interpretation in conformity with the directive requires the national court, in particular, to favour the interpretation that would allow it to decline of its own motion the jurisdiction conferred on it by virtue of an unfair term.

THE COUNCIL OF THE EUROPEAN COMMUNITIES,

Having regard to the Treaty establishing the European Economic Community, and in particular Article [95][2] thereof,

Having regard to the proposal from the Commission,[3]

In co-operation with the European Parliament,[4]

Having regard to the opinion of the Economic and Social Committee,[5]

Whereas it is necessary to adopt measures with the aim of progressively establishing the internal market before 31 December 1992; whereas the internal market comprises an area without internal frontiers in which goods, persons, services and capital move freely;

Whereas the laws of Member States relating to the terms of contract between the seller of goods or supplier of services, on the one hand, and the consumer of them, on the other hand, show many disparities, with the result that the national markets for the sale of goods and services to consumers differ from each other and that distortions of competition may arise amongst the sellers and suppliers, notably when they sell and supply in other Member States;

Whereas, in particular, the laws of Member States relating to unfair terms in consumer contracts show marked divergences;

Whereas it is the responsibility of the Member States to ensure that contracts concluded with consumers do not contain unfair terms;

---

[1] OJ L 95, 21.4.1993, 29–34.
[2] The number between brackets has been changed as from 1 May 1999 by article 12 of the Treaty of Amsterdam.
[3] OJ C 73, 24.3.1992, 7.
[4] OJ C 326, 16.12.1991, 108 and OJ C 21, 25.1.1993.
[5] OJ C 159, 17.6.1991, 34.

Whereas, generally speaking, consumers do not know the rules of law which, in Member States other than their own, govern contracts for the sale of goods or services; whereas this lack of awareness may deter them from direct transactions for the purchase of goods or services in another Member State;

Whereas, in order to facilitate the establishment of the internal market and to safeguard the citizen in his role as consumer when acquiring goods and services under contracts which are governed by the laws of Member States other than his own, it is essential to remove unfair terms from those contracts;

Whereas sellers of goods and suppliers of services will thereby be helped in their task of selling goods and supplying services, both at home and throughout the internal market; whereas competition will thus be stimulated, so contributing to increased choice for Community citizens as consumers;

Whereas the two Community programmes for a consumer protection and information policy[6] underlined the importance of safeguarding consumers in the matter of unfair terms of contract; whereas this protection ought to be provided by laws and regulations which are either harmonised at Community level or adopted directly at that level;

Whereas in accordance with the principle laid down under the heading 'Protection of the economic interests of the consumers', as stated in those programmes: 'acquirers of goods and services should be protected against the abuse of power by the seller or supplier, in particular against one-sided standard contracts and the unfair exclusion of essential rights in contracts';

Whereas more effective protection of the consumer can be achieved by adopting uniform rules of law in the matter of unfair terms; whereas those rules should apply to all contracts concluded between sellers or suppliers and consumers; whereas as a result inter alia contracts relating to employment, contracts relating to succession rights, contracts relating to rights under family law and contracts relating to the incorporation and organisation of companies or partnership agreements must be excluded from this Directive;

Whereas the consumer must receive equal protection under contracts concluded by word of mouth and written contracts regardless, in the latter case, of whether the terms of the contract are contained in one or more documents;

Whereas, however, as they now stand, national laws allow only partial harmonisation to be envisaged; whereas, in particular, only contractual terms which have not been individually negotiated are covered by this Directive; whereas Member States should have the option, with due regard for the Treaty, to afford consumers a higher level of protection through national provisions that are more stringent than those of this Directive;

Whereas the statutory or regulatory provisions of the Member States which directly or indirectly determine the terms of consumer contracts are presumed not to contain unfair terms; whereas, therefore, it does not appear to be necessary to subject the terms which reflect mandatory statutory or regulatory provisions and the principles or provisions of international conventions to which the Member States or the Community are party; whereas in that respect the wording 'mandatory statutory or regulatory provisions' in Article 1 (2) also covers rules which, according to the law, shall apply between the contracting parties provided that no other arrangements have been established;

Whereas Member States must however ensure that unfair terms are not included, particularly because this Directive also applies to trades, business or professions of a public nature;

Whereas it is necessary to fix in a general way the criteria for assessing the unfair character of contract terms;

Whereas the assessment, according to the general criteria chosen, of the unfair character of terms, in particular in sale or supply activities of a public nature providing collective services which take account of solidarity among users, must be supplemented by a means of making an overall evaluation of the different interests involved;

---

[6] OJ C 92, 25.4.1975, 1 and OJ C 133, 3.6.1981, 1.

whereas this constitutes the requirement of good faith; whereas, in making an assessment of good faith, particular regard shall be had to the strength of the bargaining positions of the parties, whether the consumer had an inducement to agree to the term and whether the goods or services were sold or supplied to the special order of the consumer; whereas the requirement of good faith may be satisfied by the seller or supplier where he deals fairly and equitably with the other party whose legitimate interests he has to take into account;

Whereas, for the purposes of this Directive, the annexed list of terms can be of indicative value only and, because of the cause of the minimal character of the Directive, the scope of these terms may be the subject of amplification or more restrictive editing by the Member States in their national laws;

Whereas the nature of goods or services should have an influence on assessing the unfairness of contractual terms;

Whereas, for the purposes of this Directive, assessment of unfair character shall not be made of terms which describe the main subject matter of the contract nor the quality/price ratio of the goods or services supplied; whereas the main subject matter of the contract and the price/quality ratio may nevertheless be taken into account in assessing the fairness of other terms; whereas it follows, inter alia, that in insurance contracts, the terms which clearly define or circumscribe the insured risk and the insurer's liability shall not be subject to such assessment since these restrictions are taken into account in calculating the premium paid by the consumer;

Whereas contracts should be drafted in plain, intelligible language, the consumer should actually be given an opportunity to examine all the terms and, if in doubt, the interpretation most favourable to the consumer should prevail;

Whereas Member States should ensure that unfair terms are not used in contracts concluded with consumers by a seller or supplier and that if, nevertheless, such terms are so used, they will not bind the consumer, and the contract will continue to bind the parties upon those terms if it is capable of continuing in existence without the unfair provisions;

Whereas there is a risk that, in certain cases, the consumer may be deprived of protection under this Directive by designating the law of a non-Member country as the law applicable to the contract; whereas provisions should therefore be included in this Directive designed to avert this risk;

Whereas persons or organisations, if regarded under the law of a Member State as having a legitimate interest in the matter, must have facilities for initiating proceedings concerning terms of contract drawn up for general use in contracts concluded with consumers, and in particular unfair terms, either before a court or before an administrative authority competent to decide upon complaints or to initiate appropriate legal proceedings; whereas this possibility does not, however, entail prior verification of the general conditions obtaining in individual economic sectors;

Whereas the courts or administrative authorities of the Member States must have at their disposal adequate and effective means of preventing the continued application of unfair terms in consumer contracts,

HAS ADOPTED THIS DIRECTIVE:

Article 1

1. The purpose of this Directive is to approximate the laws, regulations and administrative provisions of the Member States relating to unfair terms in contracts concluded between a seller or supplier and a consumer.

2. The contractual terms which reflect mandatory statutory or regulatory provisions and the provisions or principles of international conventions to which the Member States or the Community are party, particularly in the transport area, shall not be subject to the provisions of this Directive.

Article 2

For the purposes of this Directive:

(a) 'unfair terms' means the contractual terms defined in Article 3;

(b) 'consumer' means any natural person who, in contracts covered by this Directive, is acting for purposes that are outside his trade, business or profession;

(c) 'seller or supplier' means any natural or legal person who, in contracts covered by this Directive, is acting for purposes relating to his trade, business or profession, whether publicly owned or privately owned.

> **CASE**
>
> Joined cases C-541/99 and C-542/99 Cape Snc v Idealservice Srl (C-541/99) and Idealservice MN RE Sas v OMAI Srl (C-542/99) [2001] ECR I-9049
>
> The term 'consumer', as defined in Article 2(b) must be interpreted as referring solely to natural persons.

Article 3

1. A contractual term which has not been individually negotiated shall be regarded as unfair if, contrary to the requirement of good faith, it causes a significant imbalance in the parties' rights and obligations arising under the contract, to the detriment of the consumer.

2. A term shall always be regarded as not individually negotiated where it has been drafted in advance and the consumer has therefore not been able to influence the substance of the term, particularly in the context of a pre-formulated standard contract.

The fact that certain aspects of a term or one specific term have been individually negotiated shall not exclude the application of this Article to the rest of a contract if an overall assessment of the contract indicates that it is nevertheless a pre-formulated standard contract.

Where any seller or supplier claims that a standard term has been individually negotiated, the burden of proof in this respect shall be incumbent on him.

3. The Annex shall contain an indicative and non-exhaustive list of the terms that may be regarded as unfair.

> **CASE**
>
> Case C-478/99 Commission of the European Communities v Kingdom of Sweden [2002] ECR I-4147
>
> As regards the annex referred to in Article 3(3) of the directive, implementation of which is the subject of this action, the annex in question is, according to the terms of Article 3(3), to contain an indicative and non-exhaustive list of terms which may be regarded as unfair. It is not disputed that a term appearing in the list need not necessarily be considered unfair and, conversely, a term that does not appear in the list may none the less be regarded as unfair.
>
> In so far as it does not limit the discretion of the national authorities to determine the unfairness of a term, the list contained in the annex to the directive does not seek to give consumers rights going beyond those that result from Articles 3 to 7 of the directive. It in no way alters the result sought by the directive which, as such, is binding on Member States. It follows that, contrary to the argument put forward by the Commission, the full effect of the directive can be ensured in a sufficiently precise and clear legal framework without the list contained in the annex to the directive forming an integral part of the provisions implementing the directive.

Article 4

1. Without prejudice to Article 7, the unfairness of a contractual term shall be assessed, taking into account the nature of the goods or services for which the contract was concluded and by referring, at the time of conclusion of the contract, to all the circumstances attending the conclusion of the contract and to all the other terms of the contract or of another contract on which it is dependent.

2. Assessment of the unfair nature of the terms shall relate neither to the definition of the main subject matter of the contract nor to the adequacy of the price and remuneration, on the one hand, as against the services or goods supplies in exchange, on the other, in so far as these terms are in plain intelligible language.

Article 5

In the case of contracts where all or certain terms offered to the consumer are in writing, these terms must always be drafted in plain, intelligible language. Where there is doubt about the meaning of a term, the interpretation most favourable to the consumer shall prevail. This rule on interpretation shall not apply in the context of the procedures laid down in Article 7 (2).

Article 6

1. Member States shall lay down that unfair terms used in a contract concluded with a consumer by a seller or supplier shall, as provided for under their national law, not be binding on the consumer and that the contract shall continue to bind the parties upon those terms if it is capable of continuing in existence without the unfair terms.

2. Member States shall take the necessary measures to ensure that the consumer does not lose the protection granted by this Directive by virtue of the choice of the law of a non-Member country as the law applicable to the contract if the latter has a close connection with the territory of the Member States.

Article 7

1. Member States shall ensure that, in the interests of consumers and of competitors, adequate and effective means exist to prevent the continued use of unfair terms in contracts concluded with consumers by sellers or suppliers.

2. The means referred to in paragraph 1 shall include provisions whereby persons or organisations, having a legitimate interest under national law in protecting consumers, may take action according to the national law concerned before the courts or before competent administrative bodies for a decision as to whether contractual terms drawn up for general use are unfair, so that they can apply appropriate and effective means to prevent the continued use of such terms.

3. With due regard for national laws, the legal remedies referred to in paragraph 2 may be directed separately or jointly against a number of sellers or suppliers from the same economic sector or their associations which use or recommend the use of the same general contractual terms or similar terms.

Article 8

Member States may adopt or retain the most stringent provisions compatible with the Treaty in the area covered by this Directive, to ensure a maximum degree of protection for the consumer.

Article 9

The Commission shall present a report to the European Parliament and to the Council concerning the application of this Directive five years at the latest after the date in Article 10 (1).

Article 10

1. Member States shall bring into force the laws, regulations and administrative provisions necessary to comply with this Directive no later than 31 December 1994. They shall forthwith inform the Commission thereof.

These provisions shall be applicable to all contracts concluded after 31 December 1994.

2. When Member States adopt these measures, they shall contain a reference to this Directive or shall be accompanied by such reference on the occasion of their official publication. The methods of making such a reference shall be laid down by the Member States.

3. Member States shall communicate the main provisions of national law that they adopt in the field covered by this Directive to the Commission.

Article 11

This Directive is addressed to the Member States.

Annex

Terms referred to in Article 3(3)

1. Terms that have the object or effect of:

(a) excluding or limiting the legal liability of a seller or supplier in the event of the death of a consumer or personal injury to the latter resulting from an act or omission of that seller or supplier;

(b) inappropriately excluding or limiting the legal rights of the consumer vis-à-vis the seller or supplier or another party in the event of total or partial non-performance or inadequate performance by the seller or supplier of any of the contractual obligations, including the option of offsetting a debt owed to the seller or supplier against any claim which the consumer may have against him;

(c) making an agreement binding on the consumer whereas provision of services by the seller or supplier is subject to a condition whose realisation depends on his own will alone;

(d) permitting the seller or supplier to retain sums paid by the consumer where the latter decides not to conclude or perform the contract, without providing for the consumer to receive compensation of an equivalent amount from the seller or supplier where the latter is the party cancelling the contract;

(e) requiring any consumer who fails to fulfil his obligation to pay a disproportionately high sum in compensation;

(f) authorising the seller or supplier to dissolve the contract on a discretionary basis where the same facility is not granted to the consumer, or permitting the seller or supplier to retain the sums paid for services not yet supplied by him where it is the seller or supplier himself who dissolves the contract;

(g) enabling the seller or supplier to terminate a contract of indeterminate duration without reasonable notice except where there are serious grounds for doing so;

(h) automatically extending a contract of fixed duration where the consumer does not indicate otherwise, when the deadline fixed for the consumer to express this desire not to extend the contract is unreasonably early;

(i) irrevocably binding the consumer to terms with which he had no real opportunity of becoming acquainted before the conclusion of the contract;

(j) enabling the seller or supplier to alter the terms of the contract unilaterally without a valid reason that is specified in the contract;

(k) enabling the seller or supplier to alter unilaterally without a valid reason any characteristics of the product or service to be provided;

(l) providing for the price of goods to be determined at the time of delivery or allowing a seller of goods or supplier of services to increase their price without in both cases giving the consumer the corresponding right to cancel the contract if the final price is too high in relation to the price agreed when the contract was concluded;

(m) giving the seller or supplier the right to determine whether the goods or services supplied are in conformity with the contract, or giving him the exclusive right to interpret any term of the contract;

(n) limiting the seller's or supplier's obligation to respect commitments undertaken by his agents or making his commitments subject to compliance with a particular formality;

(o) obliging the consumer to fulfil all his obligations where the seller or supplier does not perform his;

(p) giving the seller or supplier the possibility of transferring his rights and obligations under the contract, where this may serve to reduce the guarantees for the consumer, without the latter's agreement;

(q) excluding or hindering the consumer's right to take legal action or exercise any other legal remedy, particularly by requiring the consumer to take disputes exclusively to arbitration not covered by legal provisions, unduly restricting the evidence available to him or imposing on him a burden of proof which, according to the applicable law, should lie with another party to the contract.

2. Scope of subparagraphs (g), (j) and (l)

(a) Subparagraph (g) is without hindrance to terms by which a supplier of financial services reserves the right to terminate unilaterally a contract of indeterminate duration without notice where there is a valid reason, provided that the supplier is required to inform the other contracting party or parties thereof immediately.

(b) Subparagraph (j) is without hindrance to terms under which a supplier of financial services reserves the right to alter the rate of interest payable by the consumer or due to the latter, or the amount of other charges for financial services without notice where there is a valid reason, provided that the supplier is required to inform the other contracting party or parties thereof at the earliest opportunity and that the latter are free to dissolve the contract immediately.

Subparagraph (j) is also without hindrance to terms under which a seller or supplier reserves the right to alter unilaterally the conditions of a contract of indeterminate duration, provided that he is required to inform the consumer with reasonable notice and that the consumer is free to dissolve the contract.

(c) Subparagraphs (g), (j) and (l) do not apply to:
– transactions in transferable securities, financial instruments and other products or services where the price is linked to fluctuations in a stock exchange quotation or index or a financial market rate that the seller or supplier does not control;
– contracts for the purchase or sale of foreign currency, traveller's cheques or international money orders denominated in foreign currency;

(d) Subparagraph (l) is without hindrance to price-indexation clauses, where lawful, provided that the method by which prices vary is explicitly described.

C.P. 10.

European Parliament and Council Directive 97/5/EC of 27 January 1997 on cross-border credit transfers[1]

THE EUROPEAN PARLIAMENT AND THE COUNCIL OF THE EUROPEAN UNION,

Having regard to the Treaty establishing the European Community, and in particular Article [95][2] thereof,

Having regard to the proposal from the Commission,[3]

Having regard to the opinion of the Economic and Social Committee,[4]

Having regard to the opinion of the European Monetary Institute,

Acting in accordance with the procedure laid down in Article [251][2] of the Treaty[5] in the light of the joint text approved on 22 November 1996 by the Conciliation Committee,

(1) Whereas the volume of cross-border payments is growing steadily as completion of the internal market and progress towards full economic and monetary union lead to greater trade and movement of people within the Community; whereas cross-border credit transfers account for a substantial part of the volume and value of cross-border payments;

(2) Whereas it is essential for individuals and businesses, especially small and medium-sized enterprises, to be able to make credit transfers rapidly, reliably and cheaply from one part of the Community to another; whereas, in conformity with the Commission Notice on the application of the EC competition rules to cross-border credit transfers,[6] greater competition in the market for cross-border credit transfers should lead to improved services and reduced prices;

(3) Whereas this Directive seeks to follow up the progress made towards completion of the internal market, in particular towards liberalisation of capital movements, with a view to the implementation of economic and monetary union; whereas its provisions must apply to credit transfers in the currencies of the Member States and in ecus;

(4) Whereas the European Parliament, in its resolution of 12 February 1993,[7] called for a Council Directive to lay down rules in the area of transparency and performance of cross-border payments;

(5) Whereas the issues covered by this Directive must be dealt with separately from the systemic issues which remain under consideration within the Commission; whereas it may become necessary to make a further proposal to cover these systemic issues, particularly the problem of settlement finality;

(6) Whereas the purpose of this Directive is to improve cross-border credit transfer services and thus assist the European Monetary Institute (EMI) in its task of promoting the efficiency of cross-border payments with a view to the preparation of the third stage of economic and monetary union;

(7) Whereas, in line with the objectives set out in the second recital, this Directive should apply to any credit transfer of an amount of less than ECU 50 000;

---

[1] OJ L 43, 14.2.1997, 25–31.
[2] The number between brackets has been changed as from 1 May 1999 by article 12 of the Treaty of Amsterdam.
[3] OJ C 360, 17.12.1994, 13 and OJ C 199, 3.8.1995, 16.
[4] OJ C 236, 11.9.1995, 1.
[5] Opinion of the European Parliament of 19 May 1995 (OJ C 151, 19.6.1995, 370), Council common position of 4 December 1995 (OJ C 353, 30.12.1995, 52) and Decision of the European Parliament of 13 March 1996 (OJ C 96, 1.4.1996, 74). Decision of the Council of 19 December 1996 and Decision of the European Parliament of 16 January 1997.
[6] OJ C 251, 27.9.1995, 3.
[7] OJ C 72, 15.3.1993, 158.

(8) Whereas, having regard to the third paragraph of Article [5]² of the Treaty, and with a view to ensuring transparency, this Directive lays down the minimum requirements needed to ensure an adequate level of customer information both before and after the execution of a cross-border credit transfer; whereas these requirements include indication of the complaints and redress procedures offered to customers, together with the arrangements for access thereto; whereas this Directive lays down minimum execution requirements, in particular in terms of performance, which institutions offering cross-border credit transfer services should adhere to, including the obligation to execute a cross-border credit transfer in accordance with the customer's instructions; whereas this Directive fulfils the conditions deriving from the principles set out in Commission Recommendation 90/109/EEC of 14 February 1990 on the transparency of banking conditions relating to cross-border financial transactions;[8] whereas this Directive is without prejudice to Council Directive 91/308/EEC of 10 June 1991 on prevention of the use of the financial system for the purpose of money laundering;[9]

(9) Whereas this Directive should contribute to reducing the maximum time taken to execute a cross-border credit transfer and encourage those institutions which already take a very short time to do so to maintain that practice;

(10) Whereas the Commission, in the report it will submit to the European Parliament and the Council within two years of implementation of this Directive, should particularly examine the time-limit to be applied in the absence of a time-limit agreed between the originator and his institution, taking into account both technical developments and the situation existing in each Member State;

(11) Whereas there should be an obligation upon institutions to refund in the event of a failure to successfully complete a credit transfer; whereas the obligation to refund imposes a contingent liability on institutions which might, in the absence of any limit, have a prejudicial effect on solvency requirements; whereas that obligation to refund should therefore be applicable up to ECU 12 500;

(12) Whereas Article 8 does not affect the general provisions of national law whereby an institution has responsibility towards the originator when a cross-border credit transfer has not been completed because of an error committed by that institution;

(13) Whereas it is necessary to distinguish, among the circumstances with which institutions involved in the execution of a cross-border credit transfer may be confronted, including circumstances relating to insolvency, those caused by force majeure; whereas for that purpose the definition of force majeure given in Article 4 (6) of Directive 90/314/EEC of 13 June 1990 on package travel, package holidays and package tours[10] should be taken as a basis;

(14) Whereas there need to be adequate and effective complaints and redress procedures in the Member States for the settlement of possible disputes between customers and institutions, using existing procedures where appropriate,

HAVE ADOPTED THIS DIRECTIVE:

SECTION I

SCOPE AND DEFINITIONS

Article 1

Scope

The provisions of this Directive shall apply to cross-border credit transfers in the currencies of the Member States and the ECU up to the equivalent of ECU 50 000 ordered by persons other than those referred to in Article 2 (a), (b) and (c) and executed by credit institutions or other institutions.

---

[8] OJ L 67, 15.3.1990, 39, reproduced infra under no. C.P. 7.
[9] OJ L 166, 28.6.1991, 77, reproduced supra under no. B. 15.

[10] OJ L 158, 23.6.1990, 59.

Article 2

Definitions

For the purposes of this Directive:

(a) 'credit institution' means an institution as defined in Article 1 of Council Directive 77/780/EEC,[11] and includes branches, within the meaning of the third indent of that Article and located in the Community, of credit institutions which have their head offices outside the Community and which by way of business execute cross-border credit transfers;

(b) 'other institution' means any natural or legal person, other than a credit institution, that by way of business executes cross-border credit transfers;

(c) 'financial institution' means an institution as defined in Article 4 (1) of Council Regulation 3604/93/EC of 13 December 1993 specifying definitions for the application of the prohibition of privileged access referred to in Article [102][2] of the Treaty;[12]

(d) 'institution' means a credit institution or other institution; for the purposes of Articles 6, 7 and 8, branches of one credit institution situated in different Member States which participate in the execution of a cross-border credit transfer shall be regarded as separate institutions;

(e) 'intermediary institution' means an institution which is neither that of the originator nor that of the beneficiary and which participates in the execution of a cross-border credit transfer;

(f) 'cross-border credit transfer' means a transaction carried out on the initiative of an originator via an institution or its branch in one Member State, with a view to making available an amount of money to a beneficiary at an institution or its branch in another Member State; the originator and the beneficiary may be one and the same person;

(g) 'cross-border credit transfer order' means an unconditional instruction in any form, given directly by an originator to an institution to execute a cross-border credit transfer;

(h) 'originator' means a natural or legal person that orders the making of a cross-border credit transfer to a beneficiary;

(i) 'beneficiary' means the final recipient of a cross-border credit transfer for whom the corresponding funds are made available in an account to which he has access;

(j) 'customer' means the originator or the beneficiary, as the context may require;

(k) 'reference interest rate' means an interest rate representing compensation and established in accordance with the rules laid down by the Member State in which the establishment which must pay the compensation to the customer is situated;

(l) 'date of acceptance' means the date of fulfilment of all the conditions required by the institution as to the execution of the cross-border credit transfer order and relating to the availability of adequate financial cover and the information required to execute that order.

SECTION II

TRANSPARENCY OF CONDITIONS FOR CROSS-BORDER CREDIT TRANSFERS

Article 3

Prior information on conditions for cross-border credit transfers

The institutions shall make available to their actual and prospective customers in writing, including where appropriate by electronic means, and in a readily comprehensible form, information on conditions for cross-border credit transfers. This information shall include at least:

– indication of the time needed, when a cross-border credit transfer order given to the institution is executed, for the funds to be

---

[11] OJ L 322, 17.12.1977, 30, Fourth Company Directive, reproduced supra under no. C. 4. Directive as last amended by Directive 95/26/EC (OJ L 168, 18.7.1995, 7), reproduced infra under no. I. 27.

[12] OJ L 332, 31.12.1993, 4.

credited to the account of the beneficiary's institution; the start of that period must be clearly indicated,
– indication of the time needed, upon receipt of a cross-border credit transfer, for the funds credited to the account of the institution to be credited to the beneficiary's account,
– the manner of calculation of any commission fees and charges payable by the customer to the institution, including where appropriate the rates,
– the value date, if any, applied by the institution,
– details of the complaint and redress procedures available to the customer and arrangements for access to them,
– indication of the reference exchange rates used.

Article 4

Information subsequent to a cross-border credit transfer

The institutions shall supply their customers, unless the latter expressly forgo this, subsequent to the execution or receipt of a cross-border credit transfer, with clear information in writing, including where appropriate by electronic means, and in a readily comprehensible form. This information shall include at least:
– a reference enabling the customer to identify the cross-border credit transfer,
– the original amount of the cross-border credit transfer,
– the amount of all charges and commission fees payable by the customer,
– the value date, if any, applied by the institution.

Where the originator has specified that the charges for the cross-border credit transfer are to be wholly or partly borne by the beneficiary, the latter shall be informed thereof by his own institution.

Where any amount has been converted, the institution which converted it shall inform its customer of the exchange rate used.

SECTION III
MINIMUM OBLIGATIONS OF INSTITUTIONS IN RESPECT OF CROSS-BORDER CREDIT TRANSFERS

Article 5

Specific undertakings by the institution

Unless it does not wish to do business with that customer, an institution must at a customer's request, for a cross-border credit transfer with stated specifications, give an undertaking concerning the time needed for execution of the transfer and the commission fees and charges payable, apart from those relating to the exchange rate used.

Article 6

Obligations regarding time taken

1. The originator's institution shall execute the cross-border credit transfer in question within the time limit agreed with the originator.

Where the agreed time limit is not complied with or, in the absence of any such time limit, where, at the end of the fifth banking business day following the date of acceptance of the cross-border credit transfer order, the funds have not been credited to the account of the beneficiary's institution, the originator's institution shall compensate the originator.

Compensation shall comprise the payment of interest calculated by applying the reference rate of interest to the amount of the cross-border credit transfer for the period from:
– the end of the agreed time limit or, in the absence of any such time limit, the end of the fifth banking business day following the date of acceptance of the cross-border credit transfer order, to
– the date on which the funds are credited to the account of the beneficiary's institution.

Similarly, where non-execution of the cross-border credit transfer within the time limit agreed or, in the absence of any such time limit, before the end of the fifth banking business day following the date of acceptance of the cross-border credit transfer is attributable to an intermediary institution, that institution shall be required to compensate the originator's institution.

2. The beneficiary's institution shall make the funds resulting from the cross-border credit transfer available to the beneficiary within the time limit agreed with the beneficiary.

Where the agreed time limit is not complied with or, in the absence of any such time limit, where, at the end of the banking business day following the day on which the funds were credited to the account of the beneficiary's institution, the funds have not been credited to the beneficiary's account, the beneficiary's institution shall compensate the beneficiary.

Compensation shall comprise the payment of interest calculated by applying the reference rate of interest to the amount of the cross-border credit transfer for the period from:
– the end of the agreed time limit or, in the absence of any such time limit, the end of the banking business day following the day on which the funds were credited to the account of the beneficiary's institution, to
– the date on which the funds are credited to the beneficiary's account.

3. No compensation shall be payable pursuant to paragraphs 1 and 2 where the originator's institution or, as the case may be, the beneficiary's institution can establish that the delay is attributable to the originator or, as the case may be, the beneficiary.

4. Paragraphs 1, 2 and 3 shall be entirely without prejudice to the other rights of customers and institutions that have participated in the execution of a cross-border credit transfer order.

Article 7

Obligation to execute the cross-border transfer in accordance with instructions

1. The originator's institution, any intermediary institution and the beneficiary's institution, after the date of acceptance of the cross-border credit transfer order, shall each be obliged to execute that credit transfer for the full amount thereof unless the originator has specified that the costs of the cross-border credit transfer are to be borne wholly or partly by the beneficiary.

The first subparagraph shall be without prejudice to the possibility of the beneficiary's institution levying a charge on the beneficiary relating to the administration of his account, in accordance with the relevant rules and customs. However, such a charge may not be used by the institution to avoid the obligations imposed by the said subparagraph.

2. Without prejudice to any other claim which may be made, where the originator's institution or an intermediary institution has made a deduction from the amount of the cross-border credit transfer in breach of paragraph 1, the originator's institution shall, at the originator's request, credit, free of all deductions and at its own cost, the amount deducted to the beneficiary unless the originator requests that the amount be credited to him.

Any intermediary institution which has made a deduction in breach of paragraph 1 shall credit the amount deducted, free of all deductions and at its own cost, to the originator's institution or, if the originator's institution so requests, to the beneficiary of the cross-border credit transfer.

3. Where a breach of the duty to execute the cross-border credit transfer order in accordance with the originator's instructions has been caused by the beneficiary's institution, and without prejudice to any other claim which may be made, the beneficiary's institution shall be liable to credit to the beneficiary, at its own cost, any sum wrongly deducted.

Article 8

Obligation upon institutions to refund in the event of non-execution of transfers

1. If, after a cross-border credit transfer order has been accepted by the originator's institution, the relevant amounts are not credited to the account of the beneficiary's institution, and without prejudice to any other claim which may be made, the

originator's institution shall credit the originator, up to ECU 12 500, with the amount of the cross-border credit transfer plus:
– interest calculated by applying the reference interest rate to the amount of the cross-border credit transfer for the period between the date of the cross-border credit transfer order and the date of the credit, and
– the charges relating to the cross-border credit transfer paid by the originator.

These amounts shall be made available to the originator within fourteen banking business days following the date of his request, unless the funds corresponding to the cross-border credit transfer have in the meantime been credited to the account of the beneficiary's institution.

Such a request may not be made before expiry of the time limit agreed between the originator's institution and the originator for the execution of the cross-border credit transfer order or, in the absence of any such time limit, before expiry of the time limit laid down in the second subparagraph of Article 6 (1).

Similarly, each intermediary institution which has accepted the cross-border credit transfer order owes an obligation to refund at its own cost the amount of the credit transfer, including the related costs and interest, to the institution which instructed it to carry out the order. If the cross-border credit transfer was not completed because of errors or omissions in the instructions given by that institution, the intermediary institution shall endeavour as far as possible to refund the amount of the transfer.

2. By way of derogation from paragraph 1, if the cross-border credit transfer was not completed because of its non-execution by an intermediary institution chosen by the beneficiary's institution, the latter institution shall be obliged to make the funds available to the beneficiary up to ECU 12 500.

3. By way of derogation from paragraph 1, if the cross-border credit transfer was not completed because of an error or omission in the instructions given by the originator to his institution or because of non-execution of the cross-border credit transfer by an intermediary institution expressly chosen by the originator, the originator's institution and the other institutions involved shall endeavour as fast as possible to refund the amount of the transfer.

Where the amount has been recovered by the originator's institution, it shall be obliged to credit it to the originator. The institutions, including the originator's institution, are not obliged in this case to refund the charges and interest accruing, and can deduct the costs arising from the recovery if specified.

Article 9
Situation of force majeure

Without prejudice to the provisions of Directive 91/308/EEC, institutions participating in the execution of a cross-border credit transfer order shall be released from the obligations laid down in this Directive where they can adduce reasons of force majeure, namely abnormal and unforeseeable circumstances beyond the control of the person pleading force majeure, the consequences of which would have been unavoidable despite all efforts to the contrary, which are relevant to its provisions.

Article 10
Settlement of disputes

Member States shall ensure that there are adequate and effective complaints and redress procedures for the settlement of disputes between an originator and his institution or between a beneficiary and his institution, using existing procedures where appropriate.

Section IV
Final Provisions

Article 11
Implementation

1. Member States shall bring into force the laws, regulations and administrative provisions necessary to comply with this Directive by 14 August 1999 at the latest. They shall forthwith inform the Commission thereof.

When Member States adopt these provisions, they shall contain a reference to this Directive or shall be accompanied by such reference on the occasion of their official publication. The methods of making such reference shall be laid down by Member States.

2. Member States shall communicate to the Commission the text of the main laws, regulations or administrative provisions which they adopt in the field governed by this Directive.

Article 12

Report to the European Parliament and the Council

No later than two years after the date of implementation of this Directive, the Commission shall submit a report to the European Parliament and the Council on the application of this Directive, accompanied where appropriate by proposals for its revision.

This report shall, in the light of the situation existing in each Member State and of the technical developments that have taken place, deal particularly with the question of the time limit set in Article 6 (1).

Article 13

Entry into force

This Directive shall enter into force on the date of its publication in the Official Journal of the European Communities.

Article 14

Addressees

This Directive is addressed to the Member States.

Joint statement—by the European Parliament, the Council and the Commission

The European Parliament, the Council and the Commission note the determination of the Member States to implement the laws, regulations and administrative provisions required to comply with this Directive by 1 January 1999.

C.P. 11.

European Parliament and Council Directive 97/7/EC of 20 May 1997 on the protection of consumers in respect of distance contracts[1]

THE EUROPEAN PARLIAMENT AND THE COUNCIL OF THE EUROPEAN UNION,

Having regard to the Treaty establishing the European Community, and in particular Article [95][2] thereof,

Having regard to the proposal from the Commission,[3]

Having regard to the opinion of the Economic and Social Committee,[4]

Acting in accordance with the procedure laid down in Article [251][2] of the Treaty,[5] in the light of the joint text approved by the Conciliation Committee on 27 November 1996,

(1) Whereas, in connection with the attainment of the aims of the internal market, measures must be taken for the gradual consolidation of that market;

(2) Whereas the free movement of goods and services affects not only the business sector but also private individuals; whereas it means that consumers should be able to have access to the goods and services of another Member State on the same terms as the population of that State;

(3) Whereas, for consumers, cross-border distance selling could be one of the main tangible results of the completion of the internal market, as noted, *inter alia*, in the communication from the Commission to the Council entitled 'Towards a single market in distribution'; whereas it is essential to the smooth operation of the internal market for consumers to be able to have dealings with a business outside their country, even if it has a subsidiary in the consumer's country of residence;

(4) Whereas the introduction of new technologies is increasing the number of ways for consumers to obtain information about offers anywhere in the Community and to place orders; whereas some Member States have already taken different or diverging measures to protect consumers in respect of distance selling, which has had a detrimental effect on competition between businesses in the internal market; whereas it is therefore necessary to introduce at Community level a minimum set of common rules in this area;

(5) Whereas paragraphs 18 and 19 of the Annex to the Council resolution of 14 April 1975 on a preliminary programme of the European Economic Community for a consumer protection and information policy[6] point to the need to protect the purchasers of goods or services from demands for payment for unsolicited goods and from high-pressure selling methods;

(6) Whereas paragraph 33 of the communication from the Commission to the Council entitled 'A new impetus for consumer protection policy', which was approved by the Council resolution of 23 June 1986,[7] states that the Commission will submit proposals regarding the use of new information technologies enabling consumers to place orders with suppliers from their homes;

---

[1] OJ L 144, 4.6.1997, 19–28.
[2] The number between brackets has been changed as from 1 May 1999 by article 12 of the Treaty of Amsterdam.
[3] OJ C 156, 23. 6. 1992, 14 and OJ No C 308, 15.11.1993, 18.
[4] OJ C 19, 25. 1. 1993, 111.
[5] Opinion of the European Parliament of 26 May 1993 (OJ C 176, 28. 6. 1993, 95), Council common position of 29 June 1995 (OJ C 288, 30.10.1995, 1) and Decision of the European Parliament of 13 December 1995 (OJ C 17, 22.1.1996, 51). Decision of the European Parliament of 16 January 1997 and Council Decision of 20 January 1997.
[6] OJ C 92, 25.4.1975, 1.
[7] OJ C 167, 5.7.1986, 1.

(7) Whereas the Council resolution of 9 November 1989 on future priorities for relaunching consumer protection policy[8] calls upon the Commission to give priority to the areas referred to in the Annex to that resolution; whereas that Annex refers to new technologies involving teleshopping; whereas the Commission has responded to that resolution by adopting a three-year action plan for consumer protection policy in the European Economic Community (1990–1992); whereas that plan provides for the adoption of a Directive;

(8) Whereas the languages used for distance contracts are a matter for the Member States;

(9) Whereas contracts negotiated at a distance involve the use of one or more means of distance communication; whereas the various means of communication are used as part of an organised distance sales or service-provision scheme not involving the simultaneous presence of the supplier and the consumer; whereas the constant development of those means of communication does not allow an exhaustive list to be compiled but does require principles to be defined which are valid even for those which are not as yet in widespread use;

(10) Whereas the same transaction comprising successive operations or a series of separate operations over a period of time may give rise to different legal descriptions depending on the law of the Member States; whereas the provisions of this Directive cannot be applied differently according to the law of the Member States, subject to their recourse to Article 14; whereas, to that end, there is therefore reason to consider that there must at least be compliance with the provisions of this Directive at the time of the first of a series of successive operations or the first of a series of separate operations over a period of time which may be considered as forming a whole, whether that operation or series of operations are the subject of a single contract or successive, separate contracts;

(11) Whereas the use of means of distance communication must not lead to a reduction in the information provided to the consumer; whereas the information that is required to be sent to the consumer should therefore be determined, whatever the means of communication used; whereas the information supplied must also comply with the other relevant Community rules, in particular those in Council Directive 84/450/EEC of 10 September 1984 relating to the approximation of the laws, regulations and administrative provisions of the Member States concerning misleading advertising;[9] whereas, if exceptions are made to the obligation to provide information, it is up to the consumer, on a discretionary basis, to request certain basic information such as the identity of the supplier, the main characteristics of the goods or services and their price;

(12) Whereas in the case of communication by telephone it is appropriate that the consumer receives enough information at the beginning of the conversation to decide whether or not to continue;

(13) Whereas information disseminated by certain electronic technologies is often ephemeral in nature insofar as it is not received on a permanent medium; whereas the consumer must therefore receive written notice in good time of the information necessary for proper performance of the contract;

(14) Whereas the consumer is not able actually to see the product or ascertain the nature of the service provided before concluding the contract; whereas provision should be made, unless otherwise specified in this Directive, for a right of withdrawal from the contract; whereas, if this right is to be more than formal, the costs, if any, borne by the consumer when exercising the right of withdrawal must be limited to the direct costs for returning the goods; whereas this right of withdrawal shall be without prejudice to the consumer's rights under national laws, with particular regard to the receipt of damaged products and services or of products and services not

---

[8] OJ C 294, 22.11.1989, 1.

[9] OJ L 250, 19.9.1984, 17, reproduced supra under no. C.P. 1.

corresponding to the description given in the offer of such products or services; whereas it is for the Member States to determine the other conditions and arrangements following exercise of the right of withdrawal;

(15) Whereas it is also necessary to prescribe a time limit for performance of the contract if this is not specified at the time of ordering;

(16) Whereas the promotional technique involving the dispatch of a product or the provision of a service to the consumer in return for payment without a prior request from, or the explicit agreement of, the consumer cannot be permitted, unless a substitute product or service is involved;

(17) Whereas the principles set out in Articles 8 and 10 of the European Convention for the Protection of Human Rights and Fundamental Freedoms of 4 November 1950 apply; whereas the consumer's right to privacy, particularly as regards freedom from certain particularly intrusive means of communication, should be recognised; whereas specific limits on the use of such means should therefore be stipulated; whereas Member States should take appropriate measures to protect effectively those consumers, who do not wish to be contacted through certain means of communication, against such contacts, without prejudice to the particular safeguards available to the consumer under Community legislation concerning the protection of personal data and privacy;

(18) Whereas it is important for the minimum binding rules contained in this Directive to be supplemented where appropriate by voluntary arrangements among the traders concerned, in line with Commission recommendation 92/295/EEC of 7 April 1992 on codes of practice for the protection of consumers in respect of contracts negotiated at a distance;[10]

(19) Whereas in the interest of optimum consumer protection it is important for consumers to be satisfactorily informed of the provisions of this Directive and of codes of practice that may exist in this field;

(20) Whereas non-compliance with this Directive may harm not only consumers but also competitors; whereas provisions may therefore be laid down enabling public bodies or their representatives, or consumer organisations which, under national legislation, have a legitimate interest in consumer protection, or professional organisations which have a legitimate interest in taking action, to monitor the application thereof;

(21) Whereas it is important, with a view to consumer protection, to address the question of cross-border complaints as soon as this is feasible; whereas the Commission published on 14 February 1996 a plan of action on consumer access to justice and the settlement of consumer disputes in the internal market; whereas that plan of action includes specific initiatives to promote out-of-court procedures; whereas objective criteria (Annex II) are suggested to ensure the reliability of those procedures and provision is made for the use of standardised claims forms (Annex III);

(22) Whereas in the use of new technologies the consumer is not in control of the means of communication used; whereas it is therefore necessary to provide that the burden of proof may be on the supplier;

(23) Whereas there is a risk that, in certain cases, the consumer may be deprived of protection under this Directive through the designation of the law of a non-member country as the law applicable to the contract; whereas provisions should therefore be included in this Directive to avert that risk;

(24) Whereas a Member State may ban, in the general interest, the marketing on its territory of certain goods and services through distance contracts; whereas that ban must comply with Community rules; whereas there is already provision for such bans, notably with regard to medicinal products, under Council Directive 89/552/EEC of 3 October 1989 on the co-ordination of certain provisions laid down by law, regulation or administrative action in Member States concerning the pursuit of television broadcasting

---

[10] OJ L 156, 10.6.1992, 21.

activities[11] and Council Directive 92/28/EEC of 31 March 1992 on the advertising of medicinal products for human use,[12]

HAVE ADOPTED THIS DIRECTIVE:

Article 1
Object

The object of this Directive is to approximate the laws, regulations and administrative provisions of the Member States concerning distance contracts between consumers and suppliers.

Article 2
Definitions

For the purposes of this Directive:

(1) 'distance contract' means any contract concerning goods or services concluded between a supplier and a consumer under an organised distance sales or service-provision scheme run by the supplier, who, for the purpose of the contract, makes exclusive use of one or more means of distance communication up to and including the moment at which the contract is concluded;

(2) 'consumer' means any natural person who, in contracts covered by this Directive, is acting for purposes that are outside his trade, business or profession;

(3) 'supplier' means any natural or legal person who, in contracts covered by this Directive, is acting in his commercial or professional capacity;

(4) 'means of distance communication' means any means that, without the simultaneous physical presence of the supplier and the consumer, may be used for the conclusion of a contract between those parties. An indicative list of the means covered by this Directive is contained in Annex I;

(5) 'operator of a means of communication' means any public or private natural or legal person whose trade, business or profession involves making one or more means of distance communication available to suppliers.

Article 3
Exemptions

1. This Directive shall not apply to contracts:
[– relating to any financial service to which Directive 2002/65/EC of the European Parliament and of the Council of 23 September 2002 concerning the distance marketing of consumer financial services and amending Council Directive 90/619/EEC and Directives 97/7/EC and 98/27/EC[13] applies,]
– concluded by means of automatic vending machines or automated commercial premises,
– concluded with telecommunications operators through the use of public payphones,
– concluded for the construction and sale of immovable property or relating to other immovable property rights, except for rental,
– concluded at an auction.

2. Articles 4, 5, 6 and 7 (1) shall not apply:
– to contracts for the supply of foodstuffs, beverages or other goods intended for everyday consumption supplied to the home of the consumer, to his residence or to his workplace by regular roundsmen,
– to contracts for the provision of accommodation, transport, catering or leisure services, where the supplier undertakes, when the contract is concluded, to provide these services on a specific date or within a specific period; exceptionally, in the case of outdoor leisure events, the supplier can reserve the right not to apply Article 7 (2) in specific circumstances.

¶ *The first indent of article 3(1) has been replaced by article 18 of Directive 2002/65/EC, reproduced infra under no. C.P. 22.*

CASE

Case C-336/03 easyCar (UK) Ltd v Office of Fair Trading [2005] ECR I-1947

Article 3(2) of Directive 97/7/EC is to be interpreted as meaning that contracts for the provision of transport services includes contracts for the provision of car hire services. Car hire undertakings

---

[11] OJ L 298, 17.10.1989, 23.
[12] OJ L 113, 30.4.1992, 13.

[13] OJ L 271, 9.10.2002, 16, reproduced infra under no. C.P. 22.

must make arrangements for the performance, on the date fixed at the time of booking, of the agreed service and therefore, for that reason, suffer the same consequences in the event of cancellation as other undertakings operating in the transport sector or in the other sectors listed in Article 3(2).

pursuant to the legislation of the Member States, to give their consent, such as minors.

3. Moreover, in the case of telephone communications, the identity of the supplier and the commercial purpose of the call shall be made explicitly clear at the beginning of any conversation with the consumer.

Article 4
Prior information

1. In good time prior to the conclusion of any distance contract, the consumer shall be provided with the following information:

(a) the identity of the supplier and, in the case of contracts requiring payment in advance, his address;

(b) the main characteristics of the goods or services;

(c) the price of the goods or services including all taxes;

(d) delivery costs, where appropriate;

(e) the arrangements for payment, delivery or performance;

(f) the existence of a right of withdrawal, except in the cases referred to in Article 6 (3);

(g) the cost of using the means of distance communication, where it is calculated other than at the basic rate;

(h) the period for which the offer or the price remains valid;

(i) where appropriate, the minimum duration of the contract in the case of contracts for the supply of products or services to be performed permanently or recurrently.

2. The information referred to in paragraph 1, the commercial purpose of which must be made clear, shall be provided in a clear and comprehensible manner in any way appropriate to the means of distance communication used, with due regard, in particular, to the principles of good faith in commercial transactions, and the principles governing the protection of those who are unable,

Article 5
Written confirmation of information

1. The consumer must receive written confirmation or confirmation in another durable medium available and accessible to him of the information referred to in Article 4 (1) (a) to (f), in good time during the performance of the contract, and at the latest at the time of delivery where goods not for delivery to third parties are concerned, unless the information has already been given to the consumer prior to conclusion of the contract in writing or on another durable medium available and accessible to him.

In any event the following must be provided:

– written information on the conditions and procedures for exercising the right of withdrawal, within the meaning of Article 6, including the cases referred to in the first indent of Article 6 (3),

– the geographical address of the place of business of the supplier to which the consumer may address any complaints,

– information on after-sales services and guarantees that exist,

– the conclusion for cancelling the contract, where it is of unspecified duration or a duration exceeding one year.

2. Paragraph 1 shall not apply to services that are performed through the use of a means of distance communication, where they are supplied on only one occasion and are invoiced by the operator of the means of distance communication. Nevertheless, the consumer must in all cases be able to obtain the geographical address of the place of business of the supplier to which he may address any complaints.

Article 6
Right of withdrawal

1. For any distance contract the consumer shall have a period of at least seven working days in which to withdraw from the contract without penalty and without giving any reason. The only charge that may be made to the consumer because of the exercise of his right of withdrawal is the direct cost of returning the goods.

The period for exercise of this right shall begin:
– in the case of goods, from the day of receipt by the consumer where the obligations laid down in Article 5 have been fulfilled,
– in the case of services, from the day of conclusion of the contract or from the day on which the obligations laid down in Article 5 were fulfilled if they are fulfilled after conclusion of the contract, provided that this period does not exceed the three-month period referred to in the following subparagraph.

If the supplier has failed to fulfil the obligations laid down in Article 5, the period shall be three months. The period shall begin:
– in the case of goods, from the day of receipt by the consumer,
– in the case of services, from the day of conclusion of the contract.

If the information referred to in Article 5 is supplied within this three-month period, the seven working day period referred to in the first subparagraph shall begin as from that moment.

2. Where the right of withdrawal has been exercised by the consumer pursuant to this Article, the supplier shall be obliged to reimburse the sums paid by the consumer free of charge. The only charge that may be made to the consumer because of the exercise of his right of withdrawal is the direct cost of returning the goods. Such reimbursement must be carried out as soon as possible and in any case within 30 days.

3. Unless the parties have agreed otherwise, the consumer may not exercise the right of withdrawal provided for in paragraph 1 in respect of contracts:
– for the provision of services if performance has begun, with the consumer's agreement, before the end of the seven working day period referred to in paragraph 1,
– for the supply of goods or services the price of which is dependent on fluctuations in the financial market that cannot be controlled by the supplier,
– for the supply of goods made to the consumer's specifications or clearly personalised or which, by reason of their nature, cannot be returned or are liable to deteriorate or expire rapidly,
– for the supply of audio or video recordings or computer software which were unsealed by the consumer,
– for the supply of newspapers, periodicals and magazines,
– for gaming and lottery services.

4. The Member States shall make provision in their legislation to ensure that:
– if the price of goods or services is fully or partly covered by credit granted by the supplier, or
– if that price is fully or partly covered by credit granted to the consumer by a third party on the basis of an agreement between the third party and the supplier,

the credit agreement shall be cancelled, without any penalty, if the consumer exercises his right to withdraw from the contract in accordance with paragraph 1.

Member States shall determine the detailed rules for cancellation of the credit agreement.

Article 7
Performance

1. Unless the parties have agreed otherwise, the supplier must execute the order within a maximum of 30 days from the day following that on which the consumer forwarded his order to the supplier.

2. Where a supplier fails to perform his side of the contract on the grounds that the goods or services ordered are unavailable, the consumer must be informed of this situation and must be able to obtain a refund of any sums he has paid as soon as possible and in any case within 30 days.

3. Nevertheless, Member States may lay down that the supplier may provide the consumer with goods or services of equivalent quality and price

provided that this possibility was provided for prior to the conclusion of the contract or in the contract. The consumer shall be informed of this possibility in a clear and comprehensible manner. The cost of returning the goods following exercise of the right of withdrawal shall, in this case, be borne by the supplier, and the consumer must be informed of this. In such cases the supply of goods or services may not be deemed to constitute inertia selling within the meaning of Article 9.

Article 8
Payment by card

Member States shall ensure that appropriate measures exist to allow a consumer:
– to request cancellation of a payment where fraudulent use has been made of his payment card in connection with distance contracts covered by this Directive,
– in the event of fraudulent use, to be recredited with the sums paid or have them returned.

[Article 9
Inertia selling

Given the prohibition of inertia selling practices laid down in Directive 2005/29/EC of 11 May 2005 of the European Parliament and of the Council concerning unfair business-to-consumer commercial practices in the internal market,[14] Member States shall take the measures necessary to exempt the consumer from the provision of any consideration in cases of unsolicited supply, the absence of a response not constituting consent.]

¶ *This article has been replaced by article 15(1) of Directive 2005/29/EC, reproduced infra under no. C.P. 24.*

Article 10
Restrictions on the use of certain means of distance communication

1. Use by a supplier of the following means requires the prior consent of the consumer:
– automated calling system without human intervention (automatic calling machine),

---

[14] OJ L 149, 11.6.2005, 22, reproduced infra under no. C.P. 24.

– facsimile machine (fax).

2. Member States shall ensure that means of distance communication, other than those referred to in paragraph 1, which allow individual communications may be used only where there is no clear objection from the consumer.

Article 11
Judicial or administrative redress

1. Member States shall ensure that adequate and effective means exist to ensure compliance with this Directive in the interests of consumers.

2. The means referred to in paragraph 1 shall include provisions whereby one or more of the following bodies, as determined by national law, may take action under national law before the courts or before the competent administrative bodies to ensure that the national provisions for the implementation of this Directive are applied:

(a) public bodies or their representatives;

(b) consumer organisations having a legitimate interest in protecting consumers;

(c) professional organisations having a legitimate interest in acting.

3. (a) Member States may stipulate that the burden of proof concerning the existence of prior information, written confirmation, compliance with time limits or consumer consent can be placed on the supplier.

(b) Member States shall take the measures needed to ensure that suppliers and operators of means of communication, where they are able to do so, cease practices that do not comply with measures adopted pursuant to this Directive.

4. Member States may provide for voluntary supervision by self-regulatory bodies of compliance with the provisions of this Directive and recourse to such bodies for the settlement of disputes to be added to the means that Member States must provided to ensure compliance with the provisions of this Directive.

Article 12
Binding nature

1. The consumer may not waive the rights conferred on him by the transposition of this Directive into national law.

2. Member States shall take the measures needed to ensure that the consumer does not lose the protection granted by this Directive by virtue of the choice of the law of a non-member country as the law applicable to the contract if the latter has close connection with the territory of one or more Member States.

Article 13
Community rules

1. The provisions of this Directive shall apply insofar as there are no particular provisions in rules of Community law governing certain types of distance contracts in their entirety.

2. Where specific Community rules contain provisions governing only certain aspects of the supply of goods or provision of services, those provisions, rather than the provisions of this Directive, shall apply to these specific aspects of the distance contracts.

Article 14
Minimal clause

Member States may introduce or maintain, in the area covered by this Directive, more stringent provisions compatible with the Treaty, to ensure a higher level of consumer protection. Such provisions shall, where appropriate, include a ban, in the general interest, on the marketing of certain goods or services, particularly medicinal products, within their territory by means of distance contracts, with due regard for the Treaty.

Article 15
Implementation

1. Member States shall bring into force the laws, regulations and administrative provisions necessary to comply with this Directive no later than three years after it enters into force. They shall forthwith inform the Commission thereof.

2. When Member States adopt the measures referred to in paragraph 1, these shall contain a reference to this Directive or shall be accompanied by such reference on the occasion of their official publication. The procedure for such reference shall be laid down by Member States.

3. Member States shall communicate to the Commission the text of the provisions of national law that they adopt in the field governed by this Directive.

4. No later than four years after the entry into force of this Directive the Commission shall submit a report to the European Parliament and the Council on the implementation of this Directive, accompanied if appropriate by a proposal for the revision thereof.

Article 16
Consumer information

Member States shall take appropriate measures to inform the consumer of the national law transposing this Directive and shall encourage, where appropriate, professional organisations to inform consumers of their codes of practice.

Article 17
Complaints systems

The Commission shall study the feasibility of establishing effective means to deal with consumers' complaints in respect of distance selling. Within two years after the entry into force of this Directive the Commission shall submit a report to the European Parliament and the Council on the results of the studies, accompanied if appropriate by proposals.

Article 18

This Directive shall enter into force on the day of its publication in the *Official Journal of the European Communities*.

Article 19

This Directive is addressed to the Member States.

Annex I

Means of communication covered by Article 2 (4)

– Unaddressed printed matter
– Addressed printed matter
– Standard letter
– Press advertising with order form
– Catalogue
– Telephone with human intervention
– Telephone without human intervention (automatic calling machine, audiotext)
– Radio
– Videophone (telephone with screen)
– Videotex (microcomputer and television screen) with keyboard or touch screen
– Electronic mail
– Facsimile machine (fax)
– Television (teleshopping).

Annex II

[. . .]

¶ *Annex II has been deleted by article 18 of Directive 2002/65/EC, reproduced infra under no. C.P. 22.*

Statement by the Council and the Parliament re Article 6(1)

The Council and the Parliament note that the Commission will examine the possibility and desirability of harmonising the method of calculating the cooling-off period under existing consumer-protection legislation, notably Directive 85/577/EEC of 20 December 1985 on the protection of consumers in respect of contracts negotiated away from commercial establishments ('door-to-door sales').[15]

Statement by the Commission re Article 3(1), first indent

The Commission recognises the importance of protecting consumers in respect of distance contracts concerning financial services and has published a Green Paper entitled 'Financial services: meeting consumers' expectations'. In the light of reactions to the Green Paper the Commission will examine ways of incorporating consumer protection into the policy on financial services and the possible legislative implications and, if need be, will submit appropriate proposals.

---

[15] OJ L 372, 31.12.1985, 31, reproduced supra under no. C.P. 3.

C.P. 12.

Commission Recommendation 97/489/EC
of 30 July 1997
concerning transactions by electronic payment instruments and in particular the relationship between issuer and holder[1]

(Text with EEA relevance)

THE COMMISSION OF THE EUROPEAN COMMUNITIES,

Having regard to the Treaty establishing the European Community and in particular Article [211],[2] second indent, thereof,

(1) Whereas one of the main objectives of the Community is to ensure the full functioning of the internal market of which payment systems are essential parts; whereas transactions made by electronic payment instruments account for an increasing proportion of the volume and the value of domestic and cross-border payments; whereas, given the current context of rapid innovation and technological progress, this trend is expected to accelerate notably as a consequence of the wide array of innovative businesses, markets and trading communities engendered by electronic commerce;

(2) Whereas it is important for individuals and businesses to be able to use electronic payment instruments throughout the Community; whereas this recommendation seeks to follow up progress made towards the completion of the internal market, notably in the light of the liberalisation of capital movements, and will also contribute to the implementation of economic and monetary union;

(3) Whereas this recommendation covers transactions effected by electronic payment instruments; whereas, for the purposes of this recommendation, these include instruments allowing for (remote) access to a customer's account, notably payment cards and phone- and home-banking applications; whereas transactions by means of a payment card shall cover electronic and non-electronic payment by means of a payment card, including processes for which a signature is required and a voucher is produced; whereas, for the purposes of this recommendation, means of payment instruments also include reloadable electronic money instruments in the form of stored-value cards and electronic tokens stored on network computer memory; whereas reloadable electronic money instruments, because of their features, in particular the possible link to the holder's account, are those for which the need for customer protection is strongest; whereas, as far as electronic money instruments are concerned, coverage under this recommendation is therefore limited to instruments of the reloadable type;

(4) Whereas this recommendation is intended to contribute to the advent of the information society and, in particular, electronic commerce by promoting customer confidence in and retailer acceptance of these instruments; whereas, to this end, the Commission will also consider the possibility of modernising and updating its recommendation 87/598/EEC,[3] with a view to establishing a clear framework for the relationship between acquirers and acceptors in respect of electronic payment instruments; whereas, in line

---

[1] OJ L 208, 2.8.1997, 52–58.
[2] The number between brackets has been changed as from 1 May 1999 by article 12 of the Treaty of Amsterdam.

[3] OJ L 365, 24.12.1987, 72, reproduced supra under no. C.P. 5.

with those objectives, this recommendation sets out minimum information requirements which should be contained in the terms and conditions applied to transactions made by electronic payment instruments, as well as the minimum obligations and liabilities of the parties concerned; whereas such terms and conditions should be set out in writing, including where appropriate by electronic means, and maintain a fair balance between the interests of the parties concerned; whereas, in compliance with Council Directive 93/13/EEC of 5 April 1993 on unfair terms in consumer contracts,[4] such terms and conditions should in particular be in an understandable and comprehensible form;

(5) Whereas, with a view to ensuring transparency, this recommendation sets out the minimum requirements needed to ensure an adequate level of customer information upon conclusion of a contract as well as subsequent to transactions effected by means of a payment instrument, including information on charges, exchange rates and interest rates; whereas, for the purpose of informing the holder of the manner of calculation of the interest rate, reference is to be made to Council Directive 87/102/EEC of 22 December 1986 for the approximation of the laws, regulations and administrative provisions of the Member States concerning consumer credit,[5] as amended by Directive 90/88/EEC;[6]

(6) Whereas this recommendation sets out minimum requirements concerning the obligations and liabilities of the parties concerned; whereas information to a holder should include a clear statement of the extent of the customer's obligation as holder of an electronic payment instrument enabling him/her to make payments in favor of third persons, as well as to perform certain financial transactions for himself/herself;

(7) Whereas, to improve customers' access to redress, this recommendation calls on Member States to ensure that there are adequate and effective means for the settlement of disputes between a holder and an issuer; whereas the Commission published on 14 February 1996 a plan of action on consumer access to justice and the settlement of consumer disputes in the internal market; whereas that plan of action includes specific initiatives to promote out-of-court procedures; whereas objective criteria (Annex II) are suggested to ensure the reliability of those procedures and provision is made for the use of standardised claims forms (Annex III);

(8) Whereas this recommendation seeks to ensure a high level of consumer protection in the field of electronic payment instruments;

(9) Whereas it is essential that transactions effected by means of electronic payment instruments should be the subject of records in order that transactions can be traced and errors can be rectified; whereas the burden of proof to show that a transaction was accurately recorded and entered into the accounts and was not affected by technical breakdown or other deficiency should lie upon the issuer;

(10) Whereas, without prejudice to any rights of a holder under national law, payment instructions given by a holder in respect of transactions effected by means of an electronic payment instrument should be irrevocable, except if the amount was not determined when the order was given;

(11) Whereas rules need to be specified concerning the issuer's liability for non-execution or for defective execution of a holder's payment instructions and for transactions that have not been authorised by him/her, subject always to the holder's own obligations in the case of lost or stolen electronic payment instruments;

(12) Whereas the Commission will monitor the implementation of this Recommendation and, if it finds the implementation unsatisfactory, it intends to propose the appropriate binding legislation covering the issues dealt with in this recommendation,

---

[4] OJ L 95, 21.4.1993, 29, reproduced supra under no. C.P. 9.
[5] OJ L 42, 12.2.1987, 48, reproduced supra under no. C.P. 4.
[6] OJ L 61, 10.3.1990, 14, reproduced supra under no. C.P. 8.

HEREBY RECOMMENDS:

Section I
Scope and Definitions

Article 1
Scope

1. This Recommendation applies to the following transactions:

(a) transfers of funds, other than those ordered and executed by financial institutions, effected by means of an electronic payment instrument;

(b) cash withdrawals by means of an electronic payment instrument and the loading (and unloading) of an electronic money instrument, at devices such as cash dispensing machines and automated teller machines and at the premises of the issuer or an institution that is under contract to accept the payment instrument.

2. By way of derogation from paragraph 1, Article 4 (1), the second and third indents of Article 5 (b), Article 6, Article 7 (2) (c), (d) and the first indent of (e), Article 8 (1), (2) and (3) and Article 9 (2) do not apply to transactions effected by means of an electronic money instrument. However, where the electronic money instrument is used to load (and unload) value through remote access to the holder's account, this Recommendation is applicable in its entirety.

3. This recommendation does not apply to:

(a) payments by cheques;

(b) the guarantee function of certain cards in relation to payments by cheques.

Article 2
Definitions

For the purpose of this recommendation, the following definitions apply:

(a) 'electronic payment instrument' means an instrument enabling its holder to effect transactions of the kind specified in Article 1 (1). This covers both remote access payment instruments and electronic money instruments;

(b) 'remote access payment instrument' means an instrument enabling a holder to access funds held on his/her account at an institution, whereby payment is allowed to be made to a payee and usually requiring a personal identification code and/or any other similar proof of identity. This includes in particular payment cards (whether credit, debit, deferred debit or charge cards) and phone- and home-banking applications;

(c) 'electronic money instrument' means a reloadable payment instrument other than a remote access payment instrument, whether a stored-value card or a computer memory, on which value units are stored electronically, enabling its holder to effect transactions of the kind specified in Article 1 (1);

(d) 'financial institution' means an institution as defined in Article 4 (1) of Council Regulation 3604/93/EC;[7]

(e) 'issuer' means a person who, in the course of his business, makes available to another person a payment instrument pursuant to a contract concluded with him/her;

(f) 'holder' means a person who, pursuant to a contract concluded between him/her and an issuer, holds a payment instrument.

Section II
Transparency of Conditions For Transactions

Article 3
Minimum information contained in the terms and conditions governing the issuing and use of an electronic payment instrument

1. Upon signature of the contract or in any event in good time prior to delivering an electronic payment instrument, the issuer communicates to the holder the contractual terms and conditions (hereinafter referred to as 'the terms') governing the issue and use of that electronic payment

---

[7] OJ L 332, 31.12.1993, 4.

instrument. The terms indicate the law applicable to the contract.

2. The terms are set out in writing, including where appropriate by electronic means, in easily understandable words and in a readily comprehensive form, and are available at least in the official language or languages of the Member State in which the electronic payment instrument is offered.

3. The terms include at least:

(a) a description of the electronic payment instrument, including where appropriate the technical requirements with respect to the holder's communication equipment authorised for use, and the way in which it can be used, including the financial limits applied, if any;

(b) a description of the holder's and issuer's respective obligations and liabilities; they include a description of the reasonable steps that the holder must take to keep safe the electronic payment instrument and the means (such as a personal identification number or other code) which enable it to be used;

(c) where applicable, the normal period within which the holder's account will be debited or credited, including the value date, or, where the holder has no account with the issuer, the normal period within which he/she will be invoiced;

(d) the types of any charges payable by the holder. In particular, this includes where applicable details of the following charges:
– the amount of any initial and annual fees,
– any commission fees and charges payable by the holder to the issuer for particular types of transactions,
– any interest rate, including the manner of its calculation, which may be applied;

(e) the period of time during which a given transaction can be contested by the holder and an indication of the redress and complaints procedures available to the holder and the method of gaining access to them.

4. If the electronic payment instrument is usable for transactions abroad (outside the country of issuing/affiliation), the following information is also communicated to the holder:

(a) an indication of the amount of any fees and charges levied for foreign currency transactions, including where appropriate the rates;

(b) the reference exchange rate used for converting foreign currency transactions, including the relevant date for determining such a rate.

Article 4

Information subsequent to a transaction

1. The issuer supplies the holder with information relating to the transactions effected by means of an electronic payment instrument. This information, set out in writing, including where appropriate by electronic means, and in a readily comprehensible form, includes at least:

(a) a reference enabling the holder to identify the transaction, including, where appropriate, the information relating to the acceptor at/with which the transaction took place;

(b) the amount of the transaction debited to the holder in billing currency and, where applicable, the amount in foreign currency;

(c) the amount of any fees and charges applied for particular types of transactions.

The issuer also provides the holder with the exchange rate used for converting foreign currency transactions.

2. The issuer of an electronic money instrument provides the holder with the possibility of verifying the last five transactions executed with the instrument and the outstanding value stored thereon.

SECTION III

OBLIGATIONS AND LIABILITIES OF THE PARTIES TO A CONTRACT

Article 5

Obligations of the holder

The holder:

(a) uses the electronic payment instrument in accordance with the terms governing the issuing and use of a payment instrument; in particular, the holder takes all reasonable steps to keep safe the electronic payment instrument and the means (such as a personal identification number or other code) which enable it to be used;

(b) notifies the issuer (or the entity specified by the latter) without delay after becoming aware of:
- the loss or theft of the electronic payment instrument or of the means that enable it to be used,
- the recording on his/her account of any unauthorised transaction,
- any error or other irregularity in the maintaining of that account by the issuer;

(c) does not record his personal identification number or other code in any easily recognisable form, in particular on the electronic payment instrument or on any item that he/she keeps or carries with the electronic payment instrument;

(d) does not countermand an order that he/she has given by means of his/her electronic payment instrument, except if the amount was not determined when the order was given.

Article 6
Liabilities of the holder

1. Up to the time of notification, the holder bears the loss sustained in consequence of the loss or theft of the electronic payment instrument up to a limit, which may not exceed ECU 150, except where he/she acted with extreme negligence, in contravention of relevant provisions under Article 5 (a), (b) or (c), or fraudulently, in which case such a limit does not apply.

2. As soon as the holder has notified the issuer (or the entity specified by the latter) as required by Article 5 (b), except where he/she acted fraudulently, he/she is not thereafter liable for the loss arising in consequence of the loss or theft of his/her electronic payment instrument.

3. By derogation from paragraphs 1 and 2, the holder is not liable if the payment instrument has been used, without physical presentation or electronic identification (of the instrument itself). The use of a confidential code or any other similar proof of identity is not, by itself, sufficient to entail the holder's liability.

Article 7
Obligations of the issuer

1. The issuer may alter the terms, provided that sufficient notice of the change is given individually to the holder to enable him/her to withdraw if he/she so chooses. A period of not less than one month is specified after which time the holder is deemed to have accepted the terms if he/she has not withdrawn.

However, any significant change to the actual interest rate is not subject to the provisions of the first subparagraph and comes into effect upon the date specified in the publication of such a change. In this event, and without prejudice to the right of the holder to withdraw from the contract, the issuer informs the holder individually thereof as soon as possible.

2. The issuer:

(a) does not disclose the holder's personal identification number or other code, except to the holder;

(b) does not dispatch an unsolicited electronic payment instrument, except where it is a replacement for an electronic payment instrument already held by the holder;

(c) keeps for a sufficient period of time, internal records to enable the transactions referred to in Article 1 (1) to be traced and errors to be rectified;

(d) ensures that appropriate means are available to enable the holder to make the notification required under Article 5 (b). Where notification is made by telephone, the issuer (or the entity specified by the latter) provides the holder with the means of proof that he/she has made such a notification;

(e) proves, in any dispute with the holder concerning a transaction referred to in Article 1 (1), and without prejudice to any proof to the contrary that may be produced by the holder, that the transaction:
- was accurately recorded and entered into accounts,
- was not affected by technical breakdown or other deficiency.

Article 8
Liabilities of the issuer

1. The issuer is liable, subject to Article 5, Article 6 and Article 7 (2) (a) and (e):

(a) for the non-execution or defective execution of the holder's transactions referred to in Article 1 (1), even if a transaction is initiated at devices/terminals or through equipment which are not under the issuer's direct or exclusive control, provided that the transaction is not initiated at devices/terminals or through equipment unauthorised for use by the issuer;

(b) for transactions not authorised by the holder, as well as for any error or irregularity attributable to the issuer in the maintaining of the holder's account.

2. Without prejudice to paragraph 3, the amount of the liability indicated in paragraph 1 consists of:

(a) the amount of the unexecuted or defectively executed transaction and, if any, interest thereon;

(b) the sum required to restore the holder to the position he/she was in before the unauthorised transaction took place.

3. Any further financial consequences, and, in particular, those concerning the extent of the damage for which compensation is to be paid, are borne by the issuer in accordance with the law applicable to the contract concluded between the issuer and the holder.

4. The issuer is liable to the holder of an electronic money instrument for the lost amount of value stored on the instrument and for the defective execution of the holder's transactions, where the loss or defective execution is attributable to a malfunction of the instrument, of the device/terminal or any other equipment authorised for use, provided that the malfunction was not caused by the holder knowingly or in breach of Article 3 (3) (a).

SECTION IV
NOTIFICATION, SETTLEMENT OF DISPUTES AND FINAL PROVISION

Article 9
Notification

1. The issuer (or the entity specified by him) provides means whereby a holder may at any time of day or night notify the loss or theft of his/her electronic payment instrument.

2. The issuer (or the entity specified by him), upon receipt of notification, is under the obligation, even if the holder acted with extreme negligence or fraudulently, to take all reasonable action open to him to stop any further use of the electronic payment instrument.

Article 10
Settlement of disputes

Member States are invited to ensure that there are adequate and effective means for the settlement of disputes between a holder and an issuer.

Article 11
Final provision

Member States are invited to take the measures necessary to ensure that the issuers of electronic payment instruments conduct their activities in accordance with Articles 1 to 9 by not later than 31 December 1998.

C.P. 13.

European Parliament and Council Directive 97/55/EC of 6 October 1997 amending Directive 84/450/EEC concerning misleading advertising so as to include comparative advertising[1]

THE EUROPEAN PARLIAMENT AND THE COUNCIL OF THE EUROPEAN UNION,

Having regard to the Treaty establishing the European Community, and in particular Article [95][2] thereof,

Having regard to the proposal from the Commission,[3]

Having regard to the opinion of the Economic and Social Committee,[4]

Acting in accordance with the procedure laid down in Article [251][2] of the Treaty,[5] in the light of the joint text approved by the Conciliation Committee on 25 June 1997,

(1) Whereas one of the Community's main aims is to complete the internal market; whereas measures must be adopted to ensure the smooth running of the said market; whereas the internal market comprises an area which has no internal frontiers and in which goods, persons, services and capital can move freely;

(2) Whereas the completion of the internal market will mean an ever wider range of choice; whereas, given that consumers can and must make the best possible use of the internal market, and that advertising is a very important means of creating genuine outlets for all goods and services throughout the Community, the basic provisions governing the form and content of comparative advertising should be uniform and the conditions of the use of comparative advertising in the Member States should be harmonised; whereas if these conditions are met, this will help demonstrate objectively the merits of the various comparable products; whereas comparative advertising can also stimulate competition between suppliers of goods and services to the consumer's advantage;

(3) Whereas the laws, regulations and administrative provisions of the individual Member States concerning comparative advertising differ widely; whereas advertising reaches beyond the frontiers and is received on the territory of other Member States; whereas the acceptance or non-acceptance of comparative advertising according to the various national laws may constitute an obstacle to the free movement of goods and services and create distortions of competition; whereas, in particular, firms may be exposed to forms of advertising developed by competitors to which they cannot reply in equal measure; whereas the freedom to provide services relating to comparative advertising should be assured; whereas the Community is called on to remedy the situation;

(4) Whereas the sixth recital of Council Directive 84/450/EEC of 10 September 1984 relating to the approximation of laws, regulations and administrative provisions of the Member States concerning misleading advertising[6] states that, after the harmonisation of national provisions

---

[1] OJ L 290, 23.10.1997, 18–23.
[2] The number between brackets has been changed as from 1 May 1999 by article 12 of the Treaty of Amsterdam.
[3] OJ C 180, 11.7.1991, 14, and OJ C 136, 19.5.1994, 4.
[4] OJ C 49, 24.2.1992, 35.
[5] Opinion of the European Parliament of 18 November 1992 (OJ C 337, 21.12.1992, 142), Common Position of the Council of 19 March 1996 (OJ C 219, 27.7.1996, 14) and Decision of the European Parliament of 23 October 1996 (OJ C 347, 16.11.1996, 69). Decision of the European Parliament of 16 September 1997 and Decision of the Council of 15 September 1997.

[6] OJ L 250, 19.9.1984, 17, consolidated in Directive 2000/12/EC (OJ L 126, 26.5.2000, 1), reproduced supra under no. B. 32.

against misleading advertising, 'at a second stage . . . , as far as necessary, comparative advertising should be dealt with, on the basis of appropriate Commission proposals';

(5) Whereas point 3 (d) of the Annex to the Council Resolution of 14 April 1975 on a preliminary programme of the European Economic Community for a consumer protection and information policy[7] includes the right to information among the basic rights of consumers; whereas this right is confirmed by the Council Resolution of 19 May 1981 on a second programme of the European Economic Community for a consumer protection and information policy,[8] point 40 of the Annex, which deals specifically with consumer information; whereas comparative advertising, when it compares material, relevant, verifiable and representative features and is not misleading, may be a legitimate means of informing consumers of their advantage;

(6) Whereas it is desirable to provide a broad concept of comparative advertising to cover all modes of comparative advertising;

(7) Whereas conditions of permitted comparative advertising, as far as the comparison is concerned, should be established in order to determine which practices relating to comparative advertising may distort competition, be detrimental to competitors and have an adverse effect on consumer choice; whereas such conditions of permitted advertising should include criteria of objective comparison of the features of goods and services;

(8) Whereas the comparison of the price only of goods and services should be possible if this comparison respects certain conditions, in particular that it shall not be misleading;

(9) Whereas, in order to prevent comparative advertising being used in an anti-competitive and unfair manner, only comparisons between competing goods and services meeting the same needs or intended for the same purpose should be permitted;

(10) Whereas the international conventions on copyright as well as the national provisions on contractual and non-contractual liability shall apply when the results of comparative tests carried out by third parties are referred to or reproduced in comparative advertising;

(11) Whereas the conditions of comparative advertising should be cumulative and respected in their entirety; whereas, in accordance with the Treaty, the choice of forms and methods for the implementation of these conditions shall be left to the Member States, insofar as those forms and methods are not already determined by this Directive;

(12) Whereas these conditions should include, in particular, consideration of the provisions resulting from Council Regulation 2081/92/EEC of 14 July 1992 on the protection of geographical indications and designations of origin for agricultural products and foodstuffs,[9] and in particular Article 13 thereof, and of the other Community provisions adopted in the agricultural sphere;

(13) Whereas Article 5 of First Council Directive 89/104/EEC of 21 December 1988 to approximate the laws of the Member States relating to trade marks[10] confers exclusive rights on the proprietor of a registered trade mark, including the right to prevent all third parties from using, in the course of trade, any sign which is identical with, or similar to, the trade mark in relation to identical goods or services or even, where appropriate, other goods;

(14) Whereas it may, however, be indispensable, in order to make comparative advertising effective, to identify the goods or services of a competitor, making reference to a trade mark or trade name of which the latter is the proprietor;

(15) Whereas such use of another's trade mark, trade name or other distinguishing marks does

---

[7] OJ C 92, 25.4.1975, 1.
[8] OJ C 133, 3.6.1981, 1.
[9] OJ L 208, 24.7.1992, 1.
[10] OJ L 40, 11.2.1989, 1. Directive as last amended by Decision 92/10/EEC (OJ L 6, 11.1.1992, 35).

not breach this exclusive right in cases where it complies with the conditions laid down by this Directive, the intended target being solely to distinguish between them and thus to highlight differences objectively;

(16) Whereas provisions should be made for the legal and/or administrative means of redress mentioned in Articles 4 and 5 of Directive 84/450/EEC to be available to control comparative advertising which fails to meet the conditions laid down by this Directive; whereas according to the 16th recital of the Directive, voluntary control by self-regulatory bodies to eliminate misleading advertising may avoid recourse to administrative or juridical action and ought therefore to be encouraged; whereas Article 6 applies to unpermitted comparative advertising in the same way;

(17) Whereas national self-regulatory bodies may co-ordinate their work through associations or organisations established at Community level and *inter alia* deal with cross-border complaints;

(18) Whereas Article 7 of Directive 84/450/EEC allowing Member States to retain or adopt provisions with a view to ensuring more extensive protection for consumers, persons carrying on a trade, business, craft or profession, and the general public, should not apply to comparative advertising, given that the objective of amending the said Directive is to establish conditions under which comparative advertising is permitted;

(19) Whereas a comparison that presents goods or services as an imitation or a replica of goods or services bearing a protected trade mark or trade name shall not be considered to fulfil the conditions to be met by permitted comparative advertising;

(20) Whereas this Directive in no way affects Community provisions on advertising for specific products and/or services or restrictions or prohibitions on advertising in particular media;

(21) Whereas, if a Member State, in compliance with the provisions of the Treaty, prohibits advertising regarding certain goods or services, this ban may, whether it is imposed directly or by a body or organisation responsible under the law of that Member State for regulating the exercise of a commercial, industrial, craft or professional activity, be extended to comparative advertising;

(22) Whereas Member States shall not be obliged to permit comparative advertising for goods or services on which they, in compliance with the provisions of the Treaty, maintain or introduce bans, including bans as regards marketing methods or advertising which targets vulnerable consumer groups; whereas Member States may, in compliance with the provisions of the Treaty, maintain or introduce bans or limitations on the use of comparisons in the advertising of professional services, whether imposed directly or by a body or organisation responsible under the law of the Member States for regulating the exercise of a professional activity;

(23) Whereas regulating comparative advertising is, under the conditions set out in this Directive, necessary for the smooth running of the internal market and whereas action at Community level is therefore required; whereas the adoption of a Directive is the appropriate instrument because it lays down uniform general principles while allowing the Member States to choose the form and appropriate method by which to attain these objectives; whereas it is in accordance with the principle of subsidiarity,

HAVE ADOPTED THIS DIRECTIVE:

Article 1

[. . .]

¶ *Article 1 modifies the title, article 1, 2, 4(1), 4(2), 5, 6(a) and 7 and adds article 3a to Directive 84/450/EEC, reproduced supra under no. C.P. 1. The modifications are directly incorporated therein.*

Article 2

Complaints systems

The Commission shall study the feasibility of establishing effective means to deal with cross-border complaints in respect of comparative advertising. Within two years after the entry into force of this Directive the Commission shall submit a report to the European Parliament and the Council on the results of the studies, accompanied if appropriate by proposals.

Article 3

1. Member States shall bring into force the laws, regulations and administrative provisions necessary to comply with this Directive at the latest 30 months after its publication in the *Official Journal of the European Communities.* They shall forthwith inform the Commission thereof.

2. When Member States adopt these measures, they shall contain a reference to this Directive or shall be accompanied by such reference on the occasion of their official publication. The methods of making such reference shall be laid down by Member States.

3. Member States shall communicate to the Commission the text of the main provisions of domestic law that they adopt in the field governed by this Directive.

Article 4

This Directive is addressed to the Member States.

Commission declaration

The Commission declares that it intends to submit the report referred to in Article 2 as far as possible at the same time as the report on complaints systems provided for in Article 17 of Directive 97/7/EC on the protection of consumers in respect of distance contracts.

C.P. 14.

European Parliament and Council Directive 98/7/EC of 16 February 1998 amending Directive 87/102/EEC for the approximation of the laws, regulations and administrative provisions of the Member States concerning consumer credit[1]

THE EUROPEAN PARLIAMENT AND THE COUNCIL OF THE EUROPEAN UNION,

Having regard to the Treaty establishing the European Community, and in particular Article [95][2] thereof,

Having regard to the proposal of the Commission,[3]

Having regard to the opinion of the Economic and Social Committee,[4]

Acting in accordance with the procedure laid down in Article [251][2] of the Treaty,[5]

Whereas it is desirable, in order to promote the establishment and functioning of the internal market and to ensure that consumers benefit from a high level of protection, that a single method of calculating the annual percentage rate of charge for consumer credit should be used throughout the Community;

Whereas Article 5 of Directive 87/102/EEC[6] provides for the introduction of a Community method or methods of calculating the annual percentage rate of charge;

Whereas, in order to introduce this single method, it is desirable to draw up a single mathematical formula for calculating the annual percentage rate of charge and for determining the credit cost items to be used in the calculation by indicating those costs which must not be taken into account;

Whereas Annex II of Directive 87/102/EEC introduced a mathematical formula for the calculation of the annual percentage rate of charge and Article 1a(2) of that Directive provided for the charges to be excluded from the calculation of the 'total cost of credit to the consumer';

Whereas during a transitional period of three years from 1 January 1993, Member States which prior to 1 March 1990 applied laws which permitted the use of another mathematical formula for calculating the annual percentage rate of charge, were permitted to continue to apply such laws;

Whereas the Commission has submitted a Report to the Council which makes it possible, in the light of experience, to apply a single Community mathematical formula for calculating the annual percentage rate of charge;

Whereas, since no Member State has made use of Article 1a(3) of Directive 87/102/EEC by which certain costs were excluded from the calculation of the annual percentage rate of charge in certain Member States, it has become obsolete;

Whereas accuracy to at least one decimal place is necessary;

Whereas a year is presumed to have 365 days or 365,25 days or (for leap years) 366 days, 52 weeks or 12 equal months; whereas an equal month is presumed to have 30,41666 days;

Whereas it is desirable that consumers should be able to recognise the terms used by different

---

[1] OJ L 101, 1.4.1998, 17–23.
[2] The number between brackets has been changed as from 1 May 1999 by article 12 of the Treaty of Amsterdam.
[3] OJ C 235, 13.8.1996, 8 and OJ C 137, 3.5.1997, 9.
[4] OJ C 30, 30.1.1997, 94.
[5] Opinion of the European Parliament of 20 February 1997 (OJ C 85, 17.3.1997, 108), Council Common Position of 7 July 1997 (OJ C 284, 19.9.1997, 1) and Decision of the European Parliament of 19 November 1997. Council Decision of 18 December 1997.
[6] OJ L 42, 12.2.1987, 48, reproduced supra under no. C.P. 4. Directive as amended by Directive 90/88/EEC (OJ L 61, 10.3.1990, 14), reproduced supra under no. C.P. 8.

Member States to indicate the 'annual percentage rate of charge';

Whereas it is appropriate to study without delay to what extent a further degree of harmonisation of the cost elements of consumer credit is necessary in order to put the European consumer in a position to make a better comparison between the actual percentage rates of charges offered by institutions in the various Member States, thereby ensuring harmonious functioning of the internal market,

HAVE ADOPTED THIS DIRECTIVE:

Article 1

[. . .]

¶ *Article 1 replaces the English and the Greek language version of article 1a(1)(a), deletes article 1a(3) and 1a(5) and replaces article 3 of Directive 87/102/EEC, reproduced supra under no. C.P. 4.*

Article 2

1. Member States shall bring into force the laws, regulations and administrative provisions necessary for them to comply with this Directive no later than two years after the entry into force of this Directive. They shall inform the Commission thereof.

When Member States adopt those measures, they shall contain a reference to this Directive or shall be accompanied by such reference on the occasion of their official publication. The methods of making such reference shall be laid down by Member States.

2. The Member States shall communicate to the Commission the texts of the provisions of national law that they adopt in the field governed by this Directive.

Article 3

This Directive is addressed to the Member States.

Annex I

[. . .]

Annex II

[. . .]

¶ *Annexes I and II replace Annexes II and III of Directive 87/102/EEC, reproduced supra under no. C.P. 4. The modifications are directly incorporated therein.*

C.P. 15.

European Parliament and Council Directive 98/27/EC
of 19 May 1998
on injunctions for the protection of consumers' interests[1]

THE EUROPEAN PARLIAMENT AND THE COUNCIL OF THE EUROPEAN UNION,

Having regard to the Treaty establishing the European Community, and in particular Article [95][2] thereof,

Having regard to the proposal from the Commission,[3]

Having regard to the opinion of the Economic and Social Committee,[4]

Acting in accordance with the procedure laid down in Article [251][2] of the Treaty,[5]

(1) Whereas certain Directives, listed in the schedule annexed to this Directive, lay down rules with regard to the protection of consumers' interests;

(2) Whereas current mechanisms available both at national and at Community level for ensuring compliance with those Directives do not always allow infringements harmful to the collective interests of consumers to be terminated in good time; whereas collective interests mean interests which do not include the cumulating of interests of individuals who have been harmed by an infringement; whereas this is without prejudice to individual actions brought by individuals who have been harmed by an infringement;

(3) Whereas, as far as the purpose of bringing about the cessation of practices that are unlawful under the national provisions applicable is concerned, the effectiveness of national measures transposing the above Directives including protective measures that go beyond the level required by those Directives, provided they are compatible with the Treaty and allowed by those Directives, may be thwarted where those practices produce effects in a Member State other than that in which they originate;

(4) Whereas those difficulties can disrupt the smooth functioning of the internal market, their consequence being that it is sufficient to move the source of an unlawful practice to another country in order to place it out of reach of all forms of enforcement; whereas this constitutes a distortion of competition;

(5) Whereas those difficulties are likely to diminish consumer confidence in the internal market and may limit the scope for action by organisations representing the collective interests of consumers or independent public bodies responsible for protecting the collective interests of consumers, adversely affected by practices that infringe Community law;

(6) Whereas those practices often extend beyond the frontiers between the Member States; whereas there is an urgent need for some degree of approximation of national provisions designed to enjoin the cessation of the abovementioned unlawful practices irrespective of the country in which the unlawful practice has produced its effects; whereas, with regard to jurisdiction, this is without prejudice to the rules of private international law and the Conventions in force between Member States, while respecting the general obligations of the Member States deriving from the Treaty, in particular those related to the smooth functioning of the internal market;

---

[1] OJ L 166, 11.6.1998, 51–55.
[2] The number between brackets has been changed as from 1 May 1999 by article 12 of the Treaty of Amsterdam.
[3] OJ C 107, 13.4.1996, 3 and OJ C 80, 13.3.1997, 10.
[4] OJ C 30, 30.1.1997, 112.
[5] Opinion of the European Parliament of 14 November 1996 (OJ C 362, 2.12.1996, 236). Council common position of 30 October 1997 (OJ C 389, 22.12.1997, 51) and Decision of the European Parliament of 12 March 1998 (OJ C 104, 6.4.1998). Council Decision of 23 April 1998.

(7) Whereas the objective of the action envisaged can only be attained by the Community; whereas it is therefore incumbent on the Community to act;

(8) Whereas the third paragraph of Article [5][2] of the Treaty makes it incumbent on the Community not to go beyond what is necessary to achieve the objectives of the Treaty; whereas, in accordance with that Article, the specific features of national legal systems must be taken into account to every extent possible by leaving Member States free to choose between different options having equivalent effect; whereas the courts or administrative authorities competent to rule on the proceedings referred to in Article 2 of this Directive should have the right to examine the effects of previous decisions;

(9) Whereas one option should consist in requiring one or more independent public bodies, specifically responsible for the protection of the collective interests of consumers, to exercise the rights of action set out in this Directive; whereas another option should provide for the exercise of those rights by organisations whose purpose is to protect the collective interests of consumers, in accordance with criteria laid down by national law;

(10) Whereas Member States should be able to choose between or combine these two options in designating at national level the bodies and/or organisations qualified for the purposes of this Directive;

(11) Whereas for the purposes of intra-Community infringements the principle of mutual recognition should apply to these bodies and/or organisations; whereas the Member States should, at the request of their national entities, communicate to the Commission the name and purpose of their national entities which are qualified to bring an action in their own country according to the provisions of this Directive;

(12) Whereas it is the business of the Commission to ensure the publication of a list of these qualified entities in the *Official Journal of the European Communities*; whereas, until a statement to the contrary is published, a qualified entity is assumed to have legal capacity if its name is included in that list;

(13) Whereas Member States should be able to require that a prior consultation be undertaken by the party that intends to bring an action for an injunction, in order to give the defendant an opportunity to bring the contested infringement to an end; whereas Member States should be able to require that this prior consultation take place jointly with an independent public body designated by those Member States;

(14) Whereas, where the Member States have established that there should be prior consultation, a deadline of two weeks after the request for consultation is received should be set after which, should the cessation of the infringement not be achieved, the applicant shall be entitled to bring an action before the competent court or administrative authority without any further delay;

(15) Whereas it is appropriate that the Commission report on the functioning of this Directive and in particular on its scope and the operation of prior consultation;

(16) Whereas the application of this Directive should not prejudice the application of Community competition rules,

HAVE ADOPTED THIS DIRECTIVE:

Article 1
Scope

1. The purpose of this Directive is to approximate the laws, regulations and administrative provisions of the Member States relating to actions for an injunction referred to in Article 2 aimed at the protection of the collective interests of consumers included in the Directives listed in the Annex, with a view to ensuring the smooth functioning of the internal market.

2. For the purpose of this Directive, an infringement shall mean any act contrary to the Directives listed in the Annex as transposed into the internal legal order of the Member States that harms the collective interests referred to in paragraph 1.

Article 2

Actions for an injunction

1. Member States shall designate the courts or administrative authorities competent to rule on proceedings commenced by qualified entities within the meaning of Article 3 seeking:

(a) an order with all due expediency, where appropriate by way of summary procedure, requiring the cessation or prohibition of any infringement;

(b) where appropriate, measures such as the publication of the decision, in full or in part, in such form as deemed adequate and/or the publication of a corrective statement with a view to eliminating the continuing effects of the infringement;

(c) insofar as the legal system of the Member State concerned so permits, an order against the losing defendant for payments into the public purse or to any beneficiary designated in or under national legislation, in the event of failure to comply with the decision within a time-limit specified by the courts or administrative authorities, of a fixed amount for each day's delay or any other amount provided for in national legislation, with a view to ensuring compliance with the decisions.

2. This Directive shall be without prejudice to the rules of private international law, with respect to the applicable law, thus leading normally to the application of either the law of the Member State where the infringement originated or the law of the Member State where the infringement has its effects.

Article 3

Entities qualified to bring an action

For the purposes of this Directive, a 'qualified entity' means any body or organisation which, being properly constituted according to the law of a Member State, has a legitimate interest in ensuring that the provisions referred to in Article 1 are complied with, in particular:

(a) one or more independent public bodies, specifically responsible for protecting the interests referred to in Article 1, in Member States in which such bodies exist and/or

(b) organisations whose purpose is to protect the interests referred to in Article 1, in accordance with the criteria laid down by their national law.

Article 4

Intra-Community infringements

1. Each Member State shall take the measures necessary to ensure that, in the event of an infringement originating in that Member State, any qualified entity from another Member State where the interests protected by that qualified entity are affected by the infringement, may seize the court or administrative authority referred to in Article 2, on presentation of the list provided for in paragraph 3. The courts or administrative authorities shall accept this list as proof of the legal capacity of the qualified entity without prejudice to their right to examine whether the purpose of the qualified entity justifies its taking action in a specific case.

2. For the purposes of intra-Community infringements, and without prejudice to the rights granted to other entities under national legislation, the Member States shall, at the request of their qualified entities, communicate to the Commission that these entities are qualified to bring an action under Article 2. The Member States shall inform the Commission of the name and purpose of these qualified entities.

3. The Commission shall draw up a list of the qualified entities referred to in paragraph 2, with the specification of their purpose. This list shall be published in the *Official Journal of the European Communities*; changes to this list shall be published without delay, the updated list shall be published every six months.

Article 5

Prior consultation

1. Member States may introduce or maintain in force provisions whereby the party that intends to seek an injunction can only start this procedure after it has tried to achieve the cessation of the infringement in consultation with either the defendant or with both the defendant and a qualified entity within the meaning of Article 3(a) of the Member State in which the injunction

is sought. It shall be for the Member State to decide whether the party seeking the injunction must consult the qualified entity. If the cessation of the infringement is not achieved within two weeks after the request for consultation is received, the party concerned may bring an action for an injunction without any further delay.

2. The rules governing prior consultation adopted by Member States shall be notified to the Commission and shall be published in the *Official Journal of the European Communities*.

Article 6
Reports

1. Every three years and for the first time no later than five years after the entry into force of this Directive the Commission shall submit to the European Parliament and the Council a report on the application of this Directive.

2. In its first report the Commission shall examine in particular:
– the scope of this Directive in relation to the protection of the collective interests of persons exercising a commercial, industrial, craft or professional activity;
– the scope of this Directive as determined by the Directives listed in the Annex;
– whether the prior consultation in Article 5 has contributed to the effective protection of consumers.

Where appropriate, this report shall be accompanied by proposals with a view to amending this Directive.

Article 7
Provisions for wider action

This Directive shall not prevent Member States from adopting or maintaining in force provisions designed to grant qualified entities and any other person concerned more extensive rights to bring action at national level.

Article 8
Implementation

1. Member States shall bring into force the laws, regulations and administrative provisions necessary to comply with this Directive no later than 30 months after its entry into force. They shall immediately inform the Commission thereof.

When Member States adopt these measures, they shall contain a reference to this Directive or shall be accompanied by such reference on the occasion of their official publication. The methods of making such reference shall be adopted by Member States.

2. Member States shall communicate to the Commission the provisions of national law that they adopt in the field covered by this Directive.

Article 9
Entry into force

This Directive shall enter into force on the twentieth day following that of its publication in the *Official Journal of the European Communities*.

Article 10
Addressees

This Directive is addressed to the Member States.

Annex

List of Directives Covered by Article 1[6]

[1. Directive 2005/29/EC of the European Parliament and of the Council of 11 May 2005 concerning unfair business-to-consumer commercial practices in the internal market (OJ L 149, 11.6.2005, 22).]

2. Council Directive 85/577/EEC of 20 December 1985 to protect the consumer in respect of contracts negotiated away from business premises (OJ L 372, 31.12.1985, 31).[7]

3. Council Directive 87/102/EEC of 22 December 1986 for the approximation of the laws, regulations and administrative provisions of the Member States concerning consumer credit (OJ L 42, 12.2.1987, 48), as last amended by Directive 98/7/EC (OJ L 101, 1.4.1998, 17).

4. Council Directive 89/552/EEC of 3 October 1989 on the co-ordination of certain provisions laid down by law, regulation or administrative action in Member States concerning the pursuit of television broadcasting activities: Articles 10 to 21 (OJ L 298, 17.10.1989, 23 as amended by Directive 97/36/EC (OJ L 202, 30.7.1997, 60)).

5. Council Directive 90/314/EEC of 13 June 1990 on package travel, package holidays and package tours (OJ L 158, 23.6.1990, 59).

6. Council Directive 92/28/EEC of 31 March 1992 on the advertising of medicinal products for human use (OJ L 113, 30.4.1992, 13).

7. Council Directive 93/13/EEC of 5 April 1993 on unfair terms in consumer contracts (OJ L 95, 21.4.1993, 29).[8]

8. Directive 94/47/EC of the European Parliament and of the Council of 26 October 1994 on the protection of purchasers in respect of certain aspects of contracts relating to the purchase of the right to use immovable properties on a timeshare basis (OJ L 280, 29.10.1994, 83).

9. Directive 97/7/EC of the European Parliament and of the Council of 20 May 1997 on the protection of consumers in respect of distance contracts (OJ L 144, 4.6.1997, 19).[9]

[10. Directive 1999/44/EC of the European Parliament and of the Council of 25 May 1999 on certain aspects of the sale of consumer goods and associated guarantees (OJ L 171, 7.7.1999, 12).][10]

[11. Directive 2000/31/EC of the European Parliament and of the Council of 8 June 2000 on certain legal aspects on information society services, in particular electronic commerce, in the internal market (Directive on electronic commerce) (OJ L 178, 17.7.2000, 1).][11]

[12. Directive 2002/65/EC of the European Parliament and of the Council of 23 September 2002 concerning the distance marketing of consumer financial services and amending Council Directive 90/619/EEC and Directives 97/7/EC and 98/27/EC (OJ L 271, 9.10.2002, 16).][12]

¶ *Item 10 added by article 10 of Directive 1999/44/EC, reproduced infra under no. C.P. 17.*
¶ *Item 11 added by article 18(2) of Directive 2000/31/EC, reproduced infra under no. C.P. 19.*
¶ *Item 12 added by article 19 of Directive 2002/65/EC, reproduced supra under no. C.P. 22.*
¶ *Item 1 replaced by article 16(1) of Directive 2005/29/EC, reproduced infra under no. C.P. 24.*

---

[6] Directive Nos. 1, 6, 7 and 9 contain specific provisions on injunctive actions.
[7] Reproduced supra under no. C.P. 3.
[8] Reproduced supra under no. C.P. 9.
[9] Reproduced supra under no. C.P. 11.
[10] Reproduced infra under no. C.P. 17.
[11] Reproduced infra under no. C.P. 19.
[12] Reproduced infra under no. C.P. 22.

C.P. 16.

European Parliament and Council Directive 1999/34/EC of 10 May 1999 amending Council Directive 85/374/EEC on the approximation of the laws, regulations and administrative provisions of the Member States concerning liability for defective products[1]

THE EUROPEAN PARLIAMENT AND THE COUNCIL OF THE EUROPEAN UNION,

Having regard to the Treaty establishing the European Community, and in particular Article 95 thereof,

Having regard to the proposal from the Commission,[2]

Having regard to the opinion of the Economic and Social Committee,[3]

Acting in accordance with the procedure laid down in Article 251 of the Treaty,[4]

(1) Whereas product safety and compensation for damage caused by defective products are social imperatives which must be met within the internal market; whereas the Community has responded to those requirements by means of Directive 85/374/EEC[5] and Council Directive 92/59/EEC of 29 June 1992 on general product safety;[6]

(2) Whereas Directive 85/374/EEC established a fair apportionment of the risks inherent in a modern society in which there is a high degree of technicality; whereas that Directive therefore struck a reasonable balance between the interests involved, in particular the protection of consumer health, encouraging innovation and scientific and technological development, guaranteeing undistorted competition and facilitating trade under a harmonised system of civil liability; whereas that Directive has thus helped to raise awareness among traders of the issue of product safety and the importance accorded to it;

(3) Whereas the degree of harmonisation of Member States' laws achieved by Directive 85/374/EEC is not complete in view of the derogations provided for, in particular with regard to its scope, from which unprocessed agricultural products are excluded;

(4) Whereas the Commission monitors the implementation and effects of Directive 85/374/EEC and in particular its aspects relating to consumer protection and the functioning of the internal market, which have already been the subject of a first report; whereas, in this context, the Commission is required by Article 21 of that Directive to submit a second report on its application;

(5) Whereas including primary agricultural products within the scope of Directive 85/374/EEC would help restore consumer confidence in the safety of agricultural products; whereas such a measure would meet the requirements of a high level of consumer protection;

(6) Whereas circumstances call for Directive 85/374/EEC to be amended in order to facilitate, for the benefit of consumers, legitimate compensation for damage to health caused by defective agricultural products;

(7) Whereas this Directive has an impact on the functioning of the internal market in so far as

---

[1] OJ L 141, 4.6.1999, 20–21.
[2] OJ C 337, 7.11.1997, 54.
[3] OJ C 95, 30.3.1998, 69.
[4] Opinion of the European Parliament of 5 November 1998 (OJ C 359, 23.11.1998, 25), Council Common Position of 17 December 1998 (OJ C 49, 22.2.1999, 1) and Decision of the European Parliament of 23 March 1999 (OJ C 177, 26.6.1999, 28). Council Decision of 29 April 1999.
[5] OJ L 210, 7.8.1985, 29, reproduced supra under no. C.P. 2. Directive as amended by the 1994 Act of Accession.
[6] OJ L 228, 11.8.1992, 24.

trade in agricultural products will no longer be affected by differences between rules on producer liability;

(8) Whereas the principle of liability without fault laid down in Directive 85/374/EEC must be extended to all types of product, including agricultural products as defined by the second sentence of Article 32 of the Treaty and those listed in Annex II to the said Treaty;

¶ *According to the corrigendum, published in OJ L 283, 6.11.1999, the words between square brackets in recital 8 must be read: 'including agricultural products as defined by the second sentence of Article 32(1) of the Treaty and those listed in Annex I to the said Treaty.'*

(9) Whereas, in accordance with the principle of proportionality, it is necessary and appropriate in order to achieve the fundamental objectives of increased protection for all consumers and the proper functioning of the internal market to include agricultural products within the scope of Directive 85/374/EEC; whereas this Directive is limited to what is necessary to achieve the objectives pursued in accordance with the third paragraph of Article 5 of the Treaty,

HAVE ADOPTED THIS DIRECTIVE

[...]

¶ *This Directive amends article 2 and deletes article 15, paragraph 1(a) of Directive 85/374/EEC, reproduced supra under no. C.P. 2. The modifications are directly incorporated therein.*

C.P. 17.

European Parliament and Council Directive 1999/44/EC of 25 May 1999 on certain aspects of the sale of consumer goods and associated guarantees[1]

THE EUROPEAN PARLIAMENT AND THE COUNCIL OF THE EUROPEAN UNION,

Having regard to the Treaty establishing the European Community, and in particular Article 95 thereof,

Having regard to the proposal from the Commission,[2]

Having regard to the opinion of the Economic and Social Committee,[3]

Acting in accordance with the procedure laid down in Article 251 of the Treaty in the light of the joint text approved by the Conciliation Committee on 18 May 1999,[4]

(1) Whereas Article 153(1) and (3) of the Treaty provides that the Community should contribute to the achievement of a high level of consumer protection by the measures it adopts pursuant to Article 95 thereof;

(2) Whereas the internal market comprises an area without internal frontiers in which the free movement of goods, persons, services and capital is guaranteed; whereas free movement of goods concerns not only transactions by persons acting in the course of a business but also transactions by private individuals; whereas it implies that consumers resident in one Member State should be free to purchase goods in the territory of another Member State on the basis of a uniform minimum set of fair rules governing the sale of consumer goods;

(3) Whereas the laws of the Member States concerning the sale of consumer goods are somewhat disparate, with the result that national consumer goods markets differ from one another and that competition between sellers may be distorted;

(4) Whereas consumers who are keen to benefit from the large market by purchasing goods in Member States other than their State of residence play a fundamental role in the completion of the internal market; whereas the artificial reconstruction of frontiers and the compartmentalisation of markets should be prevented; whereas the opportunities available to consumers have been greatly broadened by new communication technologies which allow ready access to distribution systems in other Member States or in third countries; whereas, in the absence of minimum harmonisation of the rules governing the sale of consumer goods, the development of the sale of goods through the medium of new distance communication technologies risks being impeded;

(5) Whereas the creation of a common set of minimum rules of consumer law, valid no matter where goods are purchased within the Community, will strengthen consumer confidence and enable consumers to make the most of the internal market;

(6) Whereas the main difficulties encountered by consumers and the main source of disputes with sellers concern the non-conformity of goods with the contract; whereas it is therefore appropriate to approximate national legislation governing the sale of consumer goods in this respect, without however impinging on provisions and

---

[1] OJ L 171, 7.7.1999, 12–16.
[2] OJ C 307, 16.10.1996, 8 and OJ C 148, 14.5.1998, 12.
[3] OJ C 66, 3.3.1997, 5.
[4] Opinion of the European Parliament of 10 March 1998 (OJ C 104, 6.4.1998, 30), Council Common Position of 24 September 1998 (OJ C 333, 30.10.1998, 46) and Decision of the European Parliament of 17 December 1998 (OJ C 98, 9.4.1999, 226). Decision of the European Parliament of 5 May 1999. Council Decision of 17 May 1999.

principles of national law relating to contractual and non-contractual liability;

(7) Whereas the goods must, above all, conform with the contractual specifications; whereas the principle of conformity with the contract may be considered as common to the different national legal traditions; whereas in certain national legal traditions it may not be possible to rely solely on this principle to ensure a minimum level of protection for the consumer; whereas under such legal traditions, in particular, additional national provisions may be useful to ensure that the consumer is protected in cases where the parties have agreed no specific contractual terms or where the parties have concluded contractual terms or agreements which directly or indirectly waive or restrict the rights of the consumer and which, to the extent that these rights result from this Directive, are not binding on the consumer;

(8) Whereas, in order to facilitate the application of the principle of conformity with the contract, it is useful to introduce a rebuttable presumption of conformity with the contract covering the most common situations; whereas that presumption does not restrict the principle of freedom of contract; whereas, furthermore, in the absence of specific contractual terms, as well as where the minimum protection clause is applied, the elements mentioned in this presumption may be used to determine the lack of conformity of the goods with the contract; whereas the quality and performance which consumers can reasonably expect will depend *inter alia* on whether the goods are new or second-hand; whereas the elements mentioned in the presumption are cumulative; whereas, if the circumstances of the case render any particular element manifestly inappropriate, the remaining elements of the presumption nevertheless still apply;

(9) Whereas the seller should be directly liable to the consumer for the conformity of the goods with the contract; whereas this is the traditional solution enshrined in the legal orders of the Member States; whereas nevertheless the seller should be free, as provided for by national law, to pursue remedies against the producer, a previous seller in the same chain of contracts or any other intermediary, unless he has renounced that entitlement; whereas this Directive does not affect the principle of freedom of contract between the seller, the producer, a previous seller or any other intermediary; whereas the rules governing against whom and how the seller may pursue such remedies are to be determined by national law;

(10) Whereas, in the case of non-conformity of the goods with the contract, consumers should be entitled to have the goods restored to conformity with the contract free of charge, choosing either repair or replacement, or, failing this, to have the price reduced or the contract rescinded;

(11) Whereas the consumer in the first place may require the seller to repair the goods or to replace them unless those remedies are impossible or disproportionate; whereas whether a remedy is disproportionate should be determined objectively; whereas a remedy would be disproportionate if it imposed, in comparison with the other remedy, unreasonable costs; whereas, in order to determine whether the costs are unreasonable, the costs of one remedy should be significantly higher than the costs of the other remedy;

(12) Whereas in cases of a lack of conformity, the seller may always offer the consumer, by way of settlement, any available remedy; whereas it is for the consumer to decide whether to accept or reject this proposal;

(13) Whereas, in order to enable consumers to take advantage of the internal market and to buy consumer goods in another Member State, it should be recommended that, in the interests of consumers, the producers of consumer goods that are marketed in several Member States attach to the product a list with at least one contact address in every Member State where the product is marketed;

(14) Whereas the references to the time of delivery do not imply that Member States have to change their rules on the passing of the risk;

(15) Whereas Member States may provide that any reimbursement to the consumer may be reduced to take account of the use the consumer has had of the goods since they were delivered to him; whereas the detailed arrangements whereby rescission of the contract is effected may be laid down in national law;

(16) Whereas the specific nature of second-hand goods makes it generally impossible to replace them; whereas therefore the consumer's right of replacement is generally not available for these goods; whereas for such goods, Member States may enable the parties to agree a shortened period of liability;

(17) Whereas it is appropriate to limit in time the period during which the seller is liable for any lack of conformity which exists at the time of delivery of the goods; whereas Member States may also provide for a limitation on the period during which consumers can exercise their rights, provided such a period does not expire within two years from the time of delivery; whereas where, under national legislation, the time when a limitation period starts is not the time of delivery of the goods, the total duration of the limitation period provided for by national law may not be shorter than two years from the time of delivery;

(18) Whereas Member States may provide for suspension or interruption of the period during which any lack of conformity must become apparent and of the limitation period, where applicable and in accordance with their national law, in the event of repair, replacement or negotiations between seller and consumer with a view to an amicable settlement;

(19) Whereas Member States should be allowed to set a period within which the consumer must inform the seller of any lack of conformity; whereas Member States may ensure a higher level of protection for the consumer by not introducing such an obligation; whereas in any case consumers throughout the Community should have at least two months in which to inform the seller that a lack of conformity exists;

(20) Whereas Member States should guard against such a period placing at a disadvantage consumers shopping across borders; whereas all Member States should inform the Commission of their use of this provision; whereas the Commission should monitor the effect of the varied application of this provision on consumers and on the internal market; whereas information on the use made of this provision by a Member State should be available to the other Member States and to consumers and consumer organisations throughout the Community; whereas a summary of the situation in all Member States should therefore be published in the *Official Journal of the European Communities*;

(21) Whereas, for certain categories of goods, it is current practice for sellers and producers to offer guarantees on goods against any defect which becomes apparent within a certain period; whereas this practice can stimulate competition; whereas, while such guarantees are legitimate marketing tools, they should not mislead the consumer; whereas, to ensure that consumers are not misled, guarantees should contain certain information, including a statement that the guarantee does not affect the consumer's legal rights;

(22) Whereas the parties may not, by common consent, restrict or waive the rights granted to consumers, since otherwise the legal protection afforded would be thwarted; whereas this principle should apply also to clauses which imply that the consumer was aware of any lack of conformity of the consumer goods existing at the time the contract was concluded; whereas the protection granted to consumers under this Directive should not be reduced on the grounds that the law of a non-member State has been chosen as being applicable to the contract;

(23) Whereas legislation and case-law in this area in the various Member States show that there is growing concern to ensure a high level of consumer protection; whereas, in the light of this trend and the experience acquired in implementing this Directive, it may be necessary to envisage more far-reaching harmonisation, notably by providing for the producer's direct liability for defects for which he is responsible;

(24) Whereas Member States should be allowed to adopt or maintain in force more stringent provisions in the field covered by this Directive to ensure an even higher level of consumer protection;

(25) Whereas, according to the Commission recommendation of 30 March 1998 on the principles applicable to the bodies responsible for

out-of-court settlement of consumer disputes,[5] Member States can create bodies that ensure impartial and efficient handling of complaints in a national and cross-border context and which consumers can use as mediators;

(26) Whereas it is appropriate, in order to protect the collective interests of consumers, to add this Directive to the list of Directives contained in the Annex to Directive 98/27/EC of the European Parliament and of the Council of 19 May 1998 on injunctions for the protection of consumers' interests,[6]

HAVE ADOPTED THIS DIRECTIVE:

Article 1
Scope and definitions

1. The purpose of this Directive is the approximation of the laws, regulations and administrative provisions of the Member States on certain aspects of the sale of consumer goods and associated guarantees in order to ensure a uniform minimum level of consumer protection in the context of the internal market.

2. For the purposes of this Directive:

(a) *consumer*: shall mean any natural person who, in the contracts covered by this Directive, is acting for purposes which are not related to his trade, business or profession;

(b) *consumer goods*: shall mean any tangible movable item, with the exception of:
– goods sold by way of execution or otherwise by authority of law,
– water and gas where they are not put up for sale in a limited volume or set quantity,
– electricity;

(c) *seller*: shall mean any natural or legal person who, under a contract, sells consumer goods in the course of his trade, business or profession;

(d) *producer*: shall mean the manufacturer of consumer goods, the importer of consumer goods into the territory of the Community or any person purporting to be a producer by placing his name, trade mark or other distinctive sign on the consumer goods;

(e) *guarantee*: shall mean any undertaking by a seller or producer to the consumer, given without extra charge, to reimburse the price paid or to replace, repair or handle consumer goods in any way if they do not meet the specifications set out in the guarantee statement or in the relevant advertising;

(f) *repair*: shall mean, in the event of lack of conformity, bringing consumer goods into conformity with the contract of sale.

3. Member States may provide that the expression 'consumer goods' does not cover second-hand goods sold at public auction where consumers have the opportunity of attending the sale in person.

4. Contracts for the supply of consumer goods to be manufactured or produced shall also be deemed contracts of sale for the purpose of this Directive.

Article 2
Conformity with the contract

1. The seller must deliver goods to the consumer that are in conformity with the contract of sale.

2. Consumer goods are presumed to be in conformity with the contract if they:

(a) comply with the description given by the seller and possess the qualities of the goods which the seller has held out to the consumer as a sample or model;

(b) are fit for any particular purpose for which the consumer requires them and which he made known to the seller at the time of conclusion of the contract and which the seller has accepted;

(c) are fit for the purposes for which goods of the same type are normally used;

(d) show the quality and performance which are normal in goods of the same type and which the consumer can reasonably expect, given the nature of the goods and taking into account any public

---

[5] OJ L 115, 17.4.1998, 31.
[6] OJ L 166, 11.6.1998, 51, reproduced supra under no. C.P. 15.

statements on the specific characteristics of the goods made about them by the seller, the producer or his representative, particularly in advertising or on labelling.

3. There shall be deemed not to be a lack of conformity for the purposes of this Article if, at the time the contract was concluded, the consumer was aware, or could not reasonably be unaware of, the lack of conformity, or if the lack of conformity has its origin in materials supplied by the consumer.

4. The seller shall not be bound by public statements, as referred to in paragraph 2(d) if he:
– shows that he was not, and could not reasonably have been, aware of the statement in question,
– shows that by the time of conclusion of the contract the statement had been corrected, or
– shows that the decision to buy the consumer goods could not have been influenced by the statement.

5. Any lack of conformity resulting from incorrect installation of the consumer goods shall be deemed to be equivalent to lack of conformity of the goods if installation forms part of the contract of sale of the goods and the goods were installed by the seller or under his responsibility. This shall apply equally if the product, intended to be installed by the consumer, is installed by the consumer and the incorrect installation is due to a shortcoming in the installation instructions.

Article 3

Rights of the consumer

1. The seller shall be liable to the consumer for any lack of conformity that exists at the time the goods were delivered.

2. In the case of a lack of conformity, the consumer shall be entitled to have the goods brought into conformity free of charge by repair or replacement, in accordance with paragraph 3, or to have an appropriate reduction made in the price or the contract rescinded with regard to those goods, in accordance with paragraphs 5 and 6.

3. In the first place, the consumer may require the seller to repair the goods or he may require the seller to replace them, in either case free of charge, unless this is impossible or disproportionate.

A remedy shall be deemed to be disproportionate if it imposes costs on the seller that, in comparison with the alternative remedy, are unreasonable, taking into account:
– the value the goods would have if there were no lack of conformity,
– the significance of the lack of conformity, and
– whether the alternative remedy could be completed without significant inconvenience to the consumer.

Any repair or replacement shall be completed within a reasonable time and without any significant inconvenience to the consumer, taking account of the nature of the goods and the purpose for which the consumer required the goods.

4. The terms 'free of charge' in paragraphs 2 and 3 refer to the necessary costs incurred to bring the goods into conformity, particularly the cost of postage, labour and materials.

5. The consumer may require an appropriate reduction of the price or have the contract rescinded:
– if the consumer is entitled to neither repair nor replacement, or
– if the seller has not completed the remedy within a reasonable time, or
– if the seller has not completed the remedy without significant inconvenience to the consumer.

6. The consumer is not entitled to have the contract rescinded if the lack of conformity is minor.

Article 4

Right of redress

Where the final seller is liable to the consumer because of a lack of conformity resulting from an act or omission by the producer, a previous seller in the same chain of contracts or any other intermediary, the final seller shall be entitled to pursue remedies against the person or persons liable in the contractual chain. The person or persons liable against whom the final seller may pursue remedies, together with the relevant actions and conditions of exercise, shall be determined by national law.

Article 5
Time limits

1. The seller shall be held liable under Article 3 where the lack of conformity becomes apparent within two years as from delivery of the goods. If, under national legislation, the rights laid down in Article 3(2) are subject to a limitation period, that period shall not expire within a period of two years from the time of delivery.

2. Member States may provide that, in order to benefit from his rights, the consumer must inform the seller of the lack of conformity within a period of two months from the date on which he detected such lack of conformity.

Member States shall inform the Commission of their use of this paragraph. The Commission shall monitor the effect of the existence of this option for the Member States on consumers and on the internal market.

Not later than 7 January 2003, the Commission shall prepare a report on the use made by Member States of this paragraph. This report shall be published in the Official Journal of the European Communities.

3. Unless proved otherwise, any lack of conformity that becomes apparent within six months of delivery of the goods shall be presumed to have existed at the time of delivery unless this presumption is incompatible with the nature of the goods or the nature of the lack of conformity.

Article 6
Guarantees

1. A guarantee shall be legally binding on the offerer under the conditions laid down in the guarantee statement and the associated advertising.

2. The guarantee shall:
– state that the consumer has legal rights under applicable national legislation governing the sale of consumer goods and make clear that those rights are not affected by the guarantee,
– set out in plain intelligible language the contents of the guarantee and the essential particulars necessary for making claims under the guarantee, notably the duration and territorial scope of the guarantee as well as the name and address of the guarantor.

3. On request by the consumer, the guarantee shall be made available in writing or feature in another durable medium available and accessible to him.

4. Within its own territory, the Member State in which the consumer goods are marketed may, in accordance with the rules of the Treaty, provide that the guarantee be drafted in one or more languages which it shall determine from among the official languages of the Community.

5. Should a guarantee infringe the requirements of paragraphs 2, 3 or 4, the validity of this guarantee shall in no way be affected, and the consumer can still rely on the guarantee and require that it be honoured.

Article 7
Binding nature

1. Any contractual terms or agreements concluded with the seller before the lack of conformity is brought to the seller's attention which directly or indirectly waive or restrict the rights resulting from this Directive shall, as provided for by national law, not be binding on the consumer.

Member States may provide that, in the case of second-hand goods, the seller and consumer may agree contractual terms or agreements that have a shorter time period for the liability of the seller than that set down in Article 5(1). Such period may not be less than one year.

2. Member States shall take the necessary measures to ensure that consumers are not deprived of the protection afforded by this Directive as a result of opting for the law of a non-member State as the law applicable to the contract where the contract has a close connection with the territory of the Member States.

Article 8
National law and minimum protection

1. The rights resulting from this Directive shall be exercised without prejudice to other rights that the consumer may invoke under the national rules governing contractual or non-contractual liability.

2. Member States may adopt or maintain in force more stringent provisions, compatible with the Treaty in the field covered by this Directive, to ensure a higher level of consumer protection.

Article 9

Member States shall take appropriate measures to inform the consumer of the national law transposing this Directive and shall encourage, where appropriate, professional organisations to inform consumers of their rights.

Article 10

[. . .]

¶ *This article modifies the annex to Directive 98/27/EC, reproduced supra under no. C.P. 15. The modifications are directly incorporated therein.*

Article 11
Transposition

1. Member States shall bring into force the laws, regulations and administrative provisions necessary to comply with this Directive not later than 1 January 2002. They shall forthwith inform the Commission thereof.

When Member States adopt these measures, they shall contain a reference to this Directive, or shall be accompanied by such reference at the time of their official publication. The procedure for such reference shall be adopted by Member States.

2. Member States shall communicate to the Commission the provisions of national law that they adopt in the field covered by this Directive.

Article 12
Review

The Commission shall, not later than 7 July 2006, review the application of this Directive and submit to the European Parliament and the Council a report. The report shall examine, inter alia, the case for introducing the producer's direct liability and, if appropriate, shall be accompanied by proposals.

Article 13
Entry into force

This Directive shall enter into force on the day of its publication in the *Official Journal of the European Communities*.

Article 14

This Directive is addressed to the Member States.

C.P. 18.

European Parliament and Council Directive 1999/93/EC of 13 December 1999 on a Community framework for electronic signatures[1]

THE EUROPEAN PARLIAMENT AND THE COUNCIL OF THE EUROPEAN UNION,

Having regard to the Treaty establishing the European Community, and in particular Articles 47(2), 55 and 95 thereof,

Having regard to the proposal from the Commission,[2]

Having regard to the opinion of the Economic and Social Committee,[3]

Having regard to the opinion of the Committee of the Regions,[4]

Acting in accordance with the procedure laid down in Article 251 of the Treaty,[5]

Whereas:

(1) On 16 April 1997 the Commission presented to the European Parliament, the Council, the Economic and Social Committee and the Committee of the Regions a Communication on a European Initiative in Electronic Commerce;

(2) On 8 October 1997 the Commission presented to the European Parliament, the Council, the Economic and Social Committee and the Committee of the Regions a Communication on ensuring security and trust in electronic communication—towards a European framework for digital signatures and encryption;

(3) On 1 December 1997 the Council invited the Commission to submit as soon as possible a proposal for a Directive of the European Parliament and of the Council on digital signatures;

(4) Electronic communication and commerce necessitate 'electronic signatures' and related services allowing data authentication; divergent rules with respect to legal recognition of electronic signatures and the accreditation of certification-service providers in the Member States may create a significant barrier to the use of electronic communications and electronic commerce; on the other hand, a clear Community framework regarding the conditions applying to electronic signatures will strengthen confidence in, and general acceptance of, the new technologies; legislation in the Member States should not hinder the free movement of goods and services in the internal market;

(5) The interoperability of electronic-signature products should be promoted; in accordance with Article 14 of the Treaty, the internal market comprises an area without internal frontiers in which the free movement of goods is ensured; essential requirements specific to electronic-signature products must be met in order to ensure free movement within the internal market and to build trust in electronic signatures, without prejudice to Council Regulation 3381/94/EC of 19 December 1994 setting up a Community regime for the control of exports of dual-use goods[6] and Council Decision 94/942/CFSP of 19 December 1994 on the joint action adopted by the Council concerning the control of exports of dual-use goods;[7]

---

[1] OJ L 13, 19.1.2000, 12–20.
[2] OJ C 325, 23.10.1998, 5.
[3] OJ C 40, 15.2.1999, 29.
[4] OJ C 93, 6.4.1999, 33.
[5] Opinion of the European Parliament of 13 January 1999 (OJ C 104, 14.4.1999, 49), Council Common Position of 28 June 1999 (OJ C 243, 27.8.1999, 33) and Decision of the European Parliament of 27 October 1999 (OJ L 154, 5.6.2002, 51). Council Decision of 30 November 1999.

[6] OJ L 367, 31.12.1994, 1. Regulation as amended by Regulation 837/95/EC (OJ L 90, 21.4.1995, 1).
[7] OJ L 367, 31.12.1994, 8. Decision as last amended by Decision 99/193/CFSP (OJ L 73, 19.3.1999, 1).

(6) This Directive does not harmonise the provision of services with respect to the confidentiality of information where they are covered by national provisions concerned with public policy or public security;

(7) The internal market ensures the free movement of persons, as a result of which citizens and residents of the European Union increasingly need to deal with authorities in Member States other than the one in which they reside; the availability of electronic communication could be of great service in this respect;

(8) Rapid technological development and the global character of the Internet necessitate an approach which is open to various technologies and services capable of authenticating data electronically;

(9) Electronic signatures will be used in a large variety of circumstances and applications, resulting in a wide range of new services and products related to or using electronic signatures; the definition of such products and services should not be limited to the issuance and management of certificates, but should also encompass any other service and product using, or ancillary to, electronic signatures, such as registration services, time-stamping services, directory services, computing services or consultancy services related to electronic signatures;

(10) The internal market enables certification-service-providers to develop their cross-border activities with a view to increasing their competitiveness, and thus to offer consumers and businesses new opportunities to exchange information and trade electronically in a secure way, regardless of frontiers; in order to stimulate the Community-wide provision of certification services over open networks, certification-service-providers should be free to provide their services without prior authorisation; prior authorisation means not only any permission whereby the certification-service-provider concerned has to obtain a decision by national authorities before being allowed to provide its certification services, but also any other measures having the same effect;

(11) Voluntary accreditation schemes aiming at an enhanced level of service-provision may offer certification-service-providers the appropriate framework for developing further their services towards the levels of trust, security and quality demanded by the evolving market; such schemes should encourage the development of best practice among certification-service-providers; certification-service-providers should be left free to adhere to and benefit from such accreditation schemes;

(12) Certification services can be offered either by a public entity or a legal or natural person, when it is established in accordance with the national law; whereas Member States should not prohibit certification-service-providers from operating outside voluntary accreditation schemes; it should be ensured that such accreditation schemes do not reduce competition for certification services;

(13) Member States may decide how they ensure the supervision of compliance with the provisions laid down in this Directive; this Directive does not preclude the establishment of private-sector-based supervision systems; this Directive does not oblige certification-service-providers to apply to be supervised under any applicable accreditation scheme;

(14) It is important to strike a balance between consumer and business needs;

(15) Annex III covers requirements for secure signature-creation devices to ensure the functionality of advanced electronic signatures; it does not cover the entire system environment in which such devices operate; the functioning of the internal market requires the Commission and the Member States to act swiftly to enable the bodies charged with the conformity assessment of secure signature devices with Annex III to be designated; in order to meet market needs conformity assessment must be timely and efficient;

(16) This Directive contributes to the use and legal recognition of electronic signatures within the Community; a regulatory framework is not needed for electronic signatures exclusively used within systems, which are based on voluntary

agreements under private law between a specified number of participants; the freedom of parties to agree among themselves the terms and conditions under which they accept electronically signed data should be respected to the extent allowed by national law; the legal effectiveness of electronic signatures used in such systems and their admissibility as evidence in legal proceedings should be recognised;

(17) This Directive does not seek to harmonise national rules concerning contract law, particularly the formation and performance of contracts, or other formalities of a non-contractual nature concerning signatures; for this reason the provisions concerning the legal effect of electronic signatures should be without prejudice to requirements regarding form laid down in national law with regard to the conclusion of contracts or the rules determining where a contract is concluded;

(18) The storage and copying of signature-creation data could cause a threat to the legal validity of electronic signatures;

(19) Electronic signatures will be used in the public sector within national and Community administrations and in communications between such administrations and with citizens and economic operators, for example in the public procurement, taxation, social security, health and justice systems;

(20) Harmonised criteria relating to the legal effects of electronic signatures will preserve a coherent legal framework across the Community; national law lays down different requirements for the legal validity of hand-written signatures; whereas certificates can be used to confirm the identity of a person signing electronically; advanced electronic signatures based on qualified certificates aim at a higher level of security; advanced electronic signatures which are based on a qualified certificate and which are created by a secure-signature-creation device can be regarded as legally equivalent to hand-written signatures only if the requirements for hand-written signatures are fulfilled;

(21) In order to contribute to the general acceptance of electronic authentication methods it has to be ensured that electronic signatures can be used as evidence in legal proceedings in all Member States; the legal recognition of electronic signatures should be based upon objective criteria and not be linked to authorisation of the certification-service-provider involved; national law governs the legal spheres in which electronic documents and electronic signatures may be used; this Directive is without prejudice to the power of a national court to make a ruling regarding conformity with the requirements of this Directive and does not affect national rules regarding the unfettered judicial consideration of evidence;

(22) Certification-service-providers providing certification-services to the public are subject to national rules regarding liability;

(23) The development of international electronic commerce requires cross-border arrangements involving third countries; in order to ensure interoperability at a global level, agreements on multilateral rules with third countries on mutual recognition of certification services could be beneficial;

(24) In order to increase user confidence in electronic communication and electronic commerce, certification-service-providers must observe data protection legislation and individual privacy;

(25) Provisions on the use of pseudonyms in certificates should not prevent Member States from requiring identification of persons pursuant to Community or national law;

(26) The measures necessary for the implementation of this Directive are to be adopted in accordance with Council Decision 1999/468/EC of 28 June 1999 laying down the procedures for the exercise of implementing powers conferred on the Commission;[8]

(27) Two years after its implementation the Commission will carry out a review of this Directive so as, inter alia, to ensure that the advance of technology or changes in the legal environment have not created barriers to achieving the

---

[8] OJ L 184, 17.7.1999, 23.

aims stated in this Directive; it should examine the implications of associated technical areas and submit a report to the European Parliament and the Council on this subject;

(28) In accordance with the principles of subsidiarity and proportionality as set out in Article 5 of the Treaty, the objective of creating a harmonised legal framework for the provision of electronic signatures and related services cannot be sufficiently achieved by the Member States and can therefore be better achieved by the Community; this Directive does not go beyond what is necessary to achieve that objective,

HAVE ADOPTED THIS DIRECTIVE:

Article 1
Scope

The purpose of this Directive is to facilitate the use of electronic signatures and to contribute to their legal recognition. It establishes a legal framework for electronic signatures and certain certification-services in order to ensure the proper functioning of the internal market.

It does not cover aspects related to the conclusion and validity of contracts or other legal obligations where there are requirements as regards form prescribed by national or Community law nor does it affect rules and limits, contained in national or Community law, governing the use of documents.

Article 2
Definitions

For the purpose of this Directive:

1. "electronic signature" means data in electronic form which are attached to or logically associated with other electronic data and which serve as a method of authentication;

2. "advanced electronic signature" means an electronic signature that meets the following requirements:

(a) it is uniquely linked to the signatory;

(b) it is capable of identifying the signatory;

(c) it is created using means that the signatory can maintain under his sole control; and

(d) it is linked to the data to which it relates in such a manner that any subsequent change of the data is detectable;

3. "signatory" means a person who holds a signature-creation device and acts either on his own behalf or on behalf of the natural or legal person or entity he represents;

4. "signature-creation data" means unique data, such as codes or private cryptographic keys, which are used by the signatory to create an electronic signature;

5. "signature-creation device" means configured software or hardware used to implement the signature-creation data;

6. "secure-signature-creation device" means a signature-creation device that meets the requirements laid down in Annex III;

7. "signature-verification-data" means data, such as codes or public cryptographic keys, which are used for the purpose of verifying an electronic signature;

8. "signature-verification device" means configured software or hardware used to implement the signature-verification-data;

9. "certificate" means an electronic attestation that links signature-verification data to a person and confirms the identity of that person;

10. "qualified certificate" means a certificate that meets the requirements laid down in Annex I and is provided by a certification-service-provider who fulfils the requirements laid down in Annex II;

11. "certification-service-provider" means an entity or a legal or natural person who issues certificates or provides other services related to electronic signatures;

12. "electronic-signature product" means hardware or software, or relevant components thereof, which are intended to be used by a certification-service-provider for the provision of electronic-signature services or are intended to be used for the creation or verification of electronic signatures;

13. "voluntary accreditation" means any permission, setting out rights and obligations specific to

the provision of certification services, to be granted upon request by the certification-service-provider concerned, by the public or private body charged with the elaboration of, and supervision of compliance with, such rights and obligations, where the certification-service-provider is not entitled to exercise the rights stemming from the permission until it has received the decision by the body.

Article 3
Market access

1. Member States shall not make the provision of certification services subject to prior authorisation.

2. Without prejudice to the provisions of paragraph 1, Member States may introduce or maintain voluntary accreditation schemes aiming at enhanced levels of certification-service provision. All conditions related to such schemes must be objective, transparent, proportionate and non-discriminatory. Member States may not limit the number of accredited certification-service-providers for reasons that fall within the scope of this Directive.

3. Each Member State shall ensure the establishment of an appropriate system that allows for supervision of certification-service-providers that are established on its territory and issue qualified certificates to the public.

4. The conformity of secure signature-creation-devices with the requirements laid down in Annex III shall be determined by appropriate public or private bodies designated by Member States. The Commission shall, pursuant to the procedure laid down in Article 9, establish criteria for Member States to determine whether a body should be designated.

A determination of conformity with the requirements laid down in Annex III made by the bodies referred to in the first subparagraph shall be recognised by all Member States.

5. The Commission may, in accordance with the procedure laid down in Article 9, establish and publish reference numbers of generally recognised standards for electronic-signature products in the Official Journal of the European Communities. Member States shall presume that there is compliance with the requirements laid down in Annex II, point (f), and Annex III when an electronic signature product meets those standards.

6. Member States and the Commission shall work together to promote the development and use of signature-verification devices in the light of the recommendations for secure signature-verification laid down in Annex IV and in the interests of the consumer.

7. Member States may make the use of electronic signatures in the public sector subject to possible additional requirements. Such requirements shall be objective, transparent, proportionate and non-discriminatory and shall relate only to the specific characteristics of the application concerned. Such requirements may not constitute an obstacle to cross-border services for citizens.

Article 4
Internal market principles

1. Each Member State shall apply the national provisions that it adopts pursuant to this Directive to certification-service-providers established on its territory and to the services that they provide. Member States may not restrict the provision of certification-services originating in another Member State in the fields covered by this Directive.

2. Member States shall ensure that electronic-signature products that comply with this Directive are permitted to circulate freely in the internal market.

Article 5
Legal effects of electronic signatures

1. Member States shall ensure that advanced electronic signatures which are based on a qualified certificate and which are created by a secure-signature-creation device:

(a) satisfy the legal requirements of a signature in relation to data in electronic form in the same manner as a hand-written signature satisfies those requirements in relation to paper-based data; and

(b) are admissible as evidence in legal proceedings.

2. Member States shall ensure that an electronic signature is not denied legal effectiveness and admissibility as evidence in legal proceedings solely on the grounds that it is:
– in electronic form, or
– not based upon a qualified certificate, or
– not based upon a qualified certificate issued by an accredited certification-service-provider, or
– not created by a secure signature-creation device.

Article 6
Liability

1. As a minimum, Member States shall ensure that by issuing a certificate as a qualified certificate to the public or by guaranteeing such a certificate to the public a certification-service-provider is liable for damage caused to any entity or legal or natural person who reasonably relies on that certificate:

(a) as regards the accuracy at the time of issuance of all information contained in the qualified certificate and as regards the fact that the certificate contains all the details prescribed for a qualified certificate;

(b) for assurance that at the time of the issuance of the certificate, the signatory identified in the qualified certificate held the signature-creation data corresponding to the signature-verification data given or identified in the certificate;

(c) for assurance that the signature-creation data and the signature-verification data can be used in a complementary manner in cases where the certification-service-provider generates them both;

unless the certification-service-provider proves that he has not acted negligently.

2. As a minimum Member States shall ensure that a certification-service-provider who has issued a certificate as a qualified certificate to the public is liable for damage caused to any entity or legal or natural person who reasonably relies on the certificate for failure to register revocation of the certificate unless the certification-service-provider proves that he has not acted negligently.

3. Member States shall ensure that a certification-service-provider may indicate in a qualified certificate limitations on the use of that certificate, provided that the limitations are recognisable to third parties. The certification-service-provider shall not be liable for damage arising from use of a qualified certificate that exceeds the limitations placed on it.

4. Member States shall ensure that a certification-service-provider may indicate in the qualified certificate a limit on the value of transactions for which the certificate can be used, provided that the limit is recognisable to third parties. The certification-service-provider shall not be liable for damage resulting from this maximum limit being exceeded.

5. The provisions of paragraphs 1 to 4 shall be without prejudice to Council Directive 93/13/EEC of 5 April 1993 on unfair terms in consumer contracts.[9]

Article 7
International aspects

1. Member States shall ensure that certificates which are issued as qualified certificates to the public by a certification-service-provider established in a third country are recognised as legally equivalent to certificates issued by a certification-service-provider established within the Community if:

(a) the certification-service-provider fulfils the requirements laid down in this Directive and has been accredited under a voluntary accreditation scheme established in a Member State; or

(b) a certification-service-provider established within the Community which fulfils the requirements laid down in this Directive guarantees the certificate; or

(c) the certificate or the certification-service-provider is recognised under a bilateral or multilateral agreement between the Community and third countries or international organisations.

---

[9] OJ L 95, 21.4.1993, 29, reproduced supra under no. C.P. 9.

2. In order to facilitate cross-border certification services with third countries and legal recognition of advanced electronic signatures originating in third countries, the Commission shall make proposals, where appropriate, to achieve the effective implementation of standards and international agreements applicable to certification services. In particular, and where necessary, it shall submit proposals to the Council for appropriate mandates for the negotiation of bilateral and multilateral agreements with third countries and international organisations. The Council shall decide by qualified majority.

3. Whenever the Commission is informed of any difficulties encountered by Community undertakings with respect to market access in third countries, it may, if necessary, submit proposals to the Council for an appropriate mandate for the negotiation of comparable rights for Community undertakings in these third countries. The Council shall decide by qualified majority.

Measures taken pursuant to this paragraph shall be without prejudice to the obligations of the Community and of the Member States under relevant international agreements.

Article 8

Data protection

1. Member States shall ensure that certification-service-providers and national bodies responsible for accreditation or supervision comply with the requirements laid down in Directive 95/46/EC of the European Parliament and of the Council of 24 October 1995 on title protection of individuals with regard to the processing of personal data and on the free movement of such data.[10]

2. Member States shall ensure that a certification-service-provider which issues certificates to the public may collect personal data only directly from the data subject, or after the explicit consent of the data subject, and only insofar as it is necessary for the purposes of issuing and maintaining the certificate. The data may not be collected or processed for any other purposes without the explicit consent of the data subject.

3. Without prejudice to the legal effect given to pseudonyms under national law, Member States shall not prevent certification service providers from indicating in the certificate a pseudonym instead of the signatory's name.

Article 9

Committee

1. The Commission shall be assisted by an "Electronic-Signature Committee", hereinafter referred to as "the committee".

2. Where reference is made to this paragraph, Articles 4 and 7 of Decision 1999/468/EC shall apply, having regard to the provisions of Article 8 thereof.

The period laid down in Article 4(3) of Decision 1999/468/EC shall be set at three months.

3. The Committee shall adopt its own rules of procedure.

Article 10

Tasks of the committee

The committee shall clarify the requirements laid down in the Annexes of this Directive, the criteria referred to in Article 3(4) and the generally recognised standards for electronic signature products established and published pursuant to Article 3(5), in accordance with the procedure laid down in Article 9(2).

Article 11

Notification

1. Member States shall notify to the Commission and the other Member States the following:

(a) information on national voluntary accreditation schemes, including any additional requirements pursuant to Article 3(7);

(b) the names and addresses of the national bodies responsible for accreditation and supervision as well as of the bodies referred to in Article 3(4);

---

[10] OJ L 281, 23.11.1995, 31.

(c) the names and addresses of all accredited national certification service providers.

2. Any information supplied under paragraph 1 and changes in respect of that information shall be notified by the Member States as soon as possible.

Article 12
Review

1. The Commission shall review the operation of this Directive and report thereon to the European Parliament and to the Council by 19 July 2003 at the latest.

2. The review shall inter alia assess whether the scope of this Directive should be modified, taking account of technological, market and legal developments. The report shall in particular include an assessment, on the basis of experience gained, of aspects of harmonisation. The report shall be accompanied, where appropriate, by legislative proposals.

Article 13
Implementation

1. Member States shall bring into force the laws, regulations and administrative provisions necessary to comply with this Directive before 19 July 2001. They shall forthwith inform the Commission thereof.

When Member States adopt these measures, they shall contain a reference to this Directive or shall be accompanied by such a reference on the occasion of their official publication. The methods of making such reference shall be laid down by the Member States.

2. Member States shall communicate to the Commission the text of the main provisions of domestic law that they adopt in the field governed by this Directive.

Article 14
Entry into force

This Directive shall enter into force on the day of its publication in the *Official Journal of the European Communities*.

Article 15
Addressees

This Directive is addressed to the Member States.

Annex I
Requirements for qualified certificates

Qualified certificates must contain:

(a) an indication that the certificate is issued as a qualified certificate;

(b) the identification of the certification-service-provider and the State in which it is established;

(c) the name of the signatory or a pseudonym, which shall be identified as such;

(d) provision for a specific attribute of the signatory to be included if relevant, depending on the purpose for which the certificate is intended;

(e) signature-verification data that correspond to signature-creation data under the control of the signatory;

(f) an indication of the beginning and end of the period of validity of the certificate;

(g) the identity code of the certificate;

(h) the advanced electronic signature of the certification-service-provider issuing it;

(i) limitations on the scope of use of the certificate, if applicable; and

(j) limits on the value of transactions for which the certificate can be used, if applicable.

Annex II

Requirements for certification-service-providers issuing qualified certificates

Certification-service-providers must:

(a) demonstrate the reliability necessary for providing certification services;

(b) ensure the operation of a prompt and secure directory and a secure and immediate revocation service;

(c) ensure that the date and time when a certificate is issued or revoked can be determined precisely;

(d) verify, by appropriate means in accordance with national law, the identity and, if applicable, any specific attributes of the person to which a qualified certificate is issued;

(e) employ personnel who possess the expert knowledge, experience, and qualifications necessary for the services provided, in particular competence at managerial level, expertise in electronic signature technology and familiarity with proper security procedures; they must also apply administrative and management procedures which are adequate and correspond to recognised standards;

(f) use trustworthy systems and products that are protected against modification and ensure the technical and cryptographic security of the process supported by them;

(g) take measures against forgery of certificates, and, in cases where the certification-service-provider generates signature-creation data, guarantee confidentiality during the process of generating such data;

(h) maintain sufficient financial resources to operate in conformity with the requirements laid down in the Directive, in particular to bear the risk of liability for damages, for example, by obtaining appropriate insurance;

(i) record all relevant information concerning a qualified certificate for an appropriate period of time, in particular for the purpose of providing evidence of certification for the purposes of legal proceedings. Such recording may be done electronically;

(j) not store or copy signature-creation data of the person to whom the certification-service-provider provided key management services;

(k) before entering into a contractual relationship with a person seeking a certificate to support his electronic signature inform that person by a durable means of communication of the precise terms and conditions regarding the use of the certificate, including any limitations on its use, the existence of a voluntary accreditation scheme and procedures for complaints and dispute settlement. Such information, which may be transmitted electronically, must be in writing and in readily understandable language. Relevant parts of this information must also be made available on request to third parties relying on the certificate;

(l) use trustworthy systems to store certificates in a verifiable form so that:

- only authorised persons can make entries and changes,
- information can be checked for authenticity,
- certificates are publicly available for retrieval in only those cases for which the certificate-holder's consent has been obtained, and
- any technical changes compromising these security requirements are apparent to the operator.

Annex III

Requirements for secure signature-creation devices

1. Secure signature-creation devices must, by appropriate technical and procedural means, ensure at the least that:

(a) the signature-creation-data used for signature generation can practically occur only once, and that their secrecy is reasonably assured;

(b) the signature-creation-data used for signature generation cannot, with reasonable assurance, be derived and the signature is protected against forgery using currently available technology;

(c) the signature-creation-data used for signature generation can be reliably protected by the legitimate signatory against the use of others.

2. Secure signature-creation devices must not alter the data to be signed or prevent such data from being presented to the signatory prior to the signature process.

Annex IV

Recommendations for secure signature verification

During the signature-verification process it should be ensured with reasonable certainty that:

(a) the data used for verifying the signature correspond to the data displayed to the verifier;

(b) the signature is reliably verified and the result of that verification is correctly displayed;

(c) the verifier can, as necessary, reliably establish the contents of the signed data;

(d) the authenticity and validity of the certificate required at the time of signature verification are reliably verified;

(e) the result of verification and the signatory's identity are correctly displayed;

(f) the use of a pseudonym is clearly indicated; and

(g) any security-relevant changes can be detected.

C.P. 19.

(Acts whose publication is obligatory)

European Parliament and Council Directive 2000/31/EC of 8 June 2000 on certain legal aspects of information society services, in particular electronic commerce, in the Internal Market (Directive on electronic commerce)[1]

THE EUROPEAN PARLIAMENT AND THE COUNCIL OF THE EUROPEAN UNION,

Having regard to the Treaty establishing the European Community, and in particular Articles 47(2), 55 and 95 thereof,

Having regard to the proposal from the Commission,[2]

Having regard to the opinion of the Economic and Social Committee,[3]

Acting in accordance with the procedure laid down in Article 251 of the Treaty,[4]

Whereas:

(1) The European Union is seeking to forge ever closer links between the States and peoples of Europe, to ensure economic and social progress; in accordance with Article 14(2) of the Treaty, the internal market comprises an area without internal frontiers in which the free movements of goods, services and the freedom of establishment are ensured; the development of information society services within the area without internal frontiers is vital to eliminating the barriers which divide the European peoples.

(2) The development of electronic commerce within the information society offers significant employment opportunities in the Community, particularly in small and medium-sized enterprises, and will stimulate economic growth and investment in innovation by European companies, and can also enhance the competitiveness of European industry, provided that everyone has access to the Internet.

(3) Community law and the characteristics of the Community legal order are a vital asset to enable European citizens and operators to take full advantage, without consideration of borders, of the opportunities afforded by electronic commerce; this Directive therefore has the purpose of ensuring a high level of Community legal integration in order to establish a real area without internal borders for information society services.

(4) It is important to ensure that electronic commerce could fully benefit from the internal market and therefore that, as with Council Directive 89/552/EEC of 3 October 1989 on the co-ordination of certain provisions laid down by law, regulation or administrative action in Member States concerning the pursuit of television broadcasting activities,[5] a high level of Community integration is achieved.

(5) The development of information society services within the Community is hampered by a number of legal obstacles to the proper functioning of the internal market which make less attractive the exercise of the freedom of establishment and the freedom to provide services; these obstacles arise from divergences in legislation and from the legal uncertainty as to which national rules apply to such services; in the absence of co-ordination and adjustment of legislation in the relevant areas, obstacles might be justified in

---

[1] OJ L 178, 17.7.2000, 1–16.
[2] OJ C 30, 5.2.1999, 4.
[3] OJ C 169, 16.6.1999, 36.
[4] Opinion of the European Parliament of 6 May 1999 (OJ C 279, 1.10.1999, 389), Council common position of 28 February 2000 (OJ C 128, 8.5.2000, 32) and Decision of the European Parliament of 4 May 2000 (OJ C 41, 7.2.2001, 38).

[5] OJ L 298, 17.10.1989, 23. Directive as amended by Directive 97/36/EC of the European Parliament and of the Council (OJ L 202, 30.7.1997, 60).

the light of the case-law of the Court of Justice of the European Communities; legal uncertainty exists with regard to the extent to which Member States may control services originating from another Member State.

(6) In the light of Community objectives, of Articles 43 and 49 of the Treaty and of secondary Community law, these obstacles should be eliminated by co-ordinating certain national laws and by clarifying certain legal concepts at Community level to the extent necessary for the proper functioning of the internal market; by dealing only with certain specific matters which give rise to problems for the internal market, this Directive is fully consistent with the need to respect the principle of subsidiarity as set out in Article 5 of the Treaty.

(7) In order to ensure legal certainty and consumer confidence, this Directive must lay down a clear and general framework to cover certain legal aspects of electronic commerce in the internal market.

(8) The objective of this Directive is to create a legal framework to ensure the free movement of information society services between Member States and not to harmonise the field of criminal law as such.

(9) The free movement of information society services can in many cases be a specific reflection in Community law of a more general principle, namely freedom of expression as enshrined in Article 10(1) of the Convention for the Protection of Human Rights and Fundamental Freedoms, which has been ratified by all the Member States; for this reason, directives covering the supply of information society services must ensure that this activity may be engaged in freely in the light of that Article, subject only to the restrictions laid down in paragraph 2 of that Article and in Article 46(1) of the Treaty; this Directive is not intended to affect national fundamental rules and principles relating to freedom of expression.

(10) In accordance with the principle of proportionality, the measures provided for in this Directive are strictly limited to the minimum needed to achieve the objective of the proper functioning of the internal market; where action at Community level is necessary, and in order to guarantee an area which is truly without internal frontiers as far as electronic commerce is concerned, the Directive must ensure a high level of protection of objectives of general interest, in particular the protection of minors and human dignity, consumer protection and the protection of public health; according to Article 152 of the Treaty, the protection of public health is an essential component of other Community policies.

(11) This Directive is without prejudice to the level of protection for, in particular, public health and consumer interests, as established by Community acts; amongst others, Council Directive 93/13/EEC of 5 April 1993 on unfair terms in consumer contracts[6] and Directive 97/7/EC of the European Parliament and of the Council of 20 May 1997 on the protection of consumers in respect of distance contracts[7] form a vital element for protecting consumers in contractual matters; those Directives also apply in their entirety to information society services; that same Community acquis, which is fully applicable to information society services, also embraces in particular Council Directive 84/450/EEC of 10 September 1984 concerning misleading and comparative advertising,[8] Council Directive 87/102/EEC of 22 December 1986 for the approximation of the laws, regulations and administrative provisions of the Member States concerning consumer credit,[9] Council Directive 93/22/EEC of 10 May 1993 on investment services in the securities field,[10] Council Directive

---

[6] OJ L 95, 21.4.1993, 29, reproduced supra under no. C.P. 9.
[7] OJ L 144, 4.6.1999, 19, reproduced supra under no. C.P. 11.
[8] OJ L 250, 19.9.1984, 17, reproduced supra under no. C.P. 1. Directive as amended by Directive 97/55/EC of the European Parliament and of the Council (OJ L 290, 23.10.1997, 18), reproduced supra under no. C.P. 13.
[9] OJ L 42, 12.2.1987, 48, reproduced supra under no. C.P. 4. Directive as last amended by Directive 98/7/EC of the European Parliament and of the Council (OJ L 101, 1.4.1998, 17), reproduced supra under no. C.P. 14.
[10] OJ L 141, 11.6.1993, 27, reproduced infra under no. S. 14. Directive as last amended by Directive 97/9/EC of the European Parliament and of the Council (OJ L 84, 26.3.1997, 22), reproduced infra under no. S. 16.

90/314/EEC of 13 June 1990 on package travel, package holidays and package tours,[11] Directive 98/6/EC of the European Parliament and of the Council of 16 February 1998 on consumer production in the indication of prices of products offered to consumers,[12] Council Directive 92/59/EEC of 29 June 1992 on general product safety,[13] Directive 94/47/EC of the European Parliament and of the Council of 26 October 1994 on the protection of purchasers in respect of certain aspects on contracts relating to the purchase of the right to use immovable properties on a timeshare basis,[14] Directive 98/27/EC of the European Parliament and of the Council of 19 May 1998 on injunctions for the protection of consumers' interests,[15] Council Directive 85/374/EEC of 25 July 1985 on the approximation of the laws, regulations and administrative provisions concerning liability for defective products,[16] Directive 1999/44/EC of the European Parliament and of the Council of 25 May 1999 on certain aspects of the sale of consumer goods and associated guarantees,[17] the future Directive of the European Parliament and of the Council concerning the distance marketing of consumer financial services and Council Directive 92/28/EEC of 31 March 1992 on the advertising of medicinal products;[18] this Directive should be without prejudice to Directive 98/43/EC of the European Parliament and of the Council of 6 July 1998 on the approximation of the laws, regulations and administrative provisions of the Member States relating to the advertising and sponsorship of tobacco products[19] adopted within the framework of the internal market, or to directives on the protection of public health; this Directive complements information requirements established by the abovementioned Directives and in particular Directive 97/7/EC.

(12) It is necessary to exclude certain activities from the scope of this Directive, on the grounds that the freedom to provide services in these fields cannot, at this stage, be guaranteed under the Treaty or existing secondary legislation; excluding these activities does not preclude any instruments which might prove necessary for the proper functioning of the internal market; taxation, particularly value added tax imposed on a large number of the services covered by this Directive, must be excluded from the scope of this Directive.

(13) This Directive does not aim to establish rules on fiscal obligations nor does it pre-empt the drawing up of Community instruments concerning fiscal aspects of electronic commerce.

(14) The protection of individuals with regard to the processing of personal data is solely governed by Directive 95/46/EC of the European Parliament and of the Council of 24 October 1995 on the protection of individuals with regard to the processing of personal data and on the free movement of such data[20] and Directive 97/66/EC of the European Parliament and of the Council of 15 December 1997 concerning the processing of personal data and the protection of privacy in the telecommunications sector[21] which are fully applicable to information society services; these Directives already establish a Community legal framework in the field of personal data and therefore it is not necessary to cover this issue in this Directive in order to ensure the smooth functioning of the internal market, in particular the free movement of personal data between Member States; the implementation and application of this Directive should be made in full compliance with the principles relating to the protection of personal data, in particular as regards unsolicited commercial communication and the liability of intermediaries; this Directive cannot prevent the anonymous use of open networks such as the Internet.

---

[11] OJ L 158, 23.6.1990, 59.
[12] OJ L 80, 18.3.1998, 27.
[13] OJ L 228, 11.8.1992, 24.
[14] OJ L 280, 29.10.1994, 83.
[15] OJ L 166, 11.6.1998, 51, reproduced supra under no. C.P. 15. Directive as amended by Directive 1999/44/EC (OJ L 171, 7.7.1999, 12), reproduced supra under no. C.P. 17.
[16] OJ L 210, 7.8.1985, 29, reproduced supra under no. C.P. 2. Directive as amended by Directive 1999/34/EC (OJ L 141, 4.6.1999, 20), reproduced supra under no. C.P. 16.
[17] OJ L 171, 7.7.1999, 12, reproduced supra under no. C.P. 17.
[18] OJ L 113, 30.4.1992, 13.
[19] OJ L 213, 30.7.1998, 9.

[20] OJ L 281, 23.11.1995, 31.
[21] OJ L 24, 30.1.1998, 1.

(15) The confidentiality of communications is guaranteed by Article 5 Directive 97/66/EC; in accordance with that Directive, Member States must prohibit any kind of interception or surveillance of such communications by others than the senders and receivers, except when legally authorised.

(16) The exclusion of gambling activities from the scope of application of this Directive covers only games of chance, lotteries and betting transactions, which involve wagering a stake with monetary value; this does not cover promotional competitions or games where the purpose is to encourage the sale of goods or services and where payments, if they arise, serve only to acquire the promoted goods or services.

(17) The definition of information society services already exists in Community law in Directive 98/34/EC of the European Parliament and of the Council of 22 June 1998 laying down a procedure for the provision of information in the field of technical standards and regulations and of rules on information society services[22] and in Directive 98/84/EC of the European Parliament and of the Council of 20 November 1998 on the legal protection of services based on, or consisting of, conditional access;[23] this definition covers any service normally provided for remuneration, at a distance, by means of electronic equipment for the processing (including digital compression) and storage of data, and at the individual request of a recipient of a service; those services referred to in the indicative list in Annex V to Directive 98/34/EC which do not imply data processing and storage are not covered by this definition.

(18) Information society services span a wide range of economic activities which take place on-line; these activities can, in particular, consist of selling goods on-line; activities such as the delivery of goods as such or the provision of services off-line are not covered; information society services are not solely restricted to services giving rise to on-line contracting but also, in so far as they represent an economic activity, extend to services which are not remunerated by those who receive them, such as those offering on-line information or commercial communications, or those providing tools allowing for search, access and retrieval of data; information society services also include services consisting of the transmission of information via a communication network, in providing access to a communication network or in hosting information provided by a recipient of the service; television broadcasting within the meaning of Directive EEC/89/552 and radio broadcasting are not information society services because they are not provided at individual request; by contrast, services which are transmitted point to point, such as video-on-demand or the provision of commercial communications by electronic mail are information society services; the use of electronic mail or equivalent individual communications for instance by natural persons acting outside their trade, business or profession including their use for the conclusion of contracts between such persons is not an information society service; the contractual relationship between an employee and his employer is not an information society service; activities which by their very nature cannot be carried out at a distance and by electronic means, such as the statutory auditing of company accounts or medical advice requiring the physical examination of a patient are not information society services.

(19) The place at which a service provider is established should be determined in conformity with the case-law of the Court of Justice according to which the concept of establishment involves the actual pursuit of an economic activity through a fixed establishment for an indefinite period; this requirement is also fulfilled where a company is constituted for a given period; the place of establishment of a company providing services via an Internet website is not the place at which the technology supporting its website is located or the place at which its website is accessible but the place where it pursues its economic activity; in cases where a provider has several places of establishment it is important to determine from which place of establishment the service concerned is provided; in cases where it is

---

[22] OJ L 204, 21.7.1998, 37. Directive as amended by Directive 98/48/EC (OJ L 217, 5.8.1998, 18).
[23] OJ L 320, 28.11.1998, 54.

difficult to determine from which of several places of establishment a given service is provided, this is the place where the provider has the centre of his activities relating to this particular service.

(20) The definition of 'recipient of a service' covers all types of usage of information society services, both by persons who provide information on open networks such as the Internet and by persons who seek information on the Internet for private or professional reasons.

(21) The scope of the co-ordinated field is without prejudice to future Community harmonisation relating to information society services and to future legislation adopted at national level in accordance with Community law; the co-ordinated field covers only requirements relating to on-line activities such as on-line information, on-line advertising, on-line shopping, on-line contracting and does not concern Member States' legal requirements relating to goods such as safety standards, labelling obligations, or liability for goods, or Member States' requirements relating to the delivery or the transport of goods, including the distribution of medicinal products; the co-ordinated field does not cover the exercise of rights of pre-emption by public authorities concerning certain goods such as works of art.

(22) Information society services should be supervised at the source of the activity, in order to ensure an effective protection of public interest objectives; to that end, it is necessary to ensure that the competent authority provides such protection not only for the citizens of its own country but for all Community citizens; in order to improve mutual trust between Member States, it is essential to state clearly this responsibility on the part of the Member State where the services originate; moreover, in order to effectively guarantee freedom to provide services and legal certainty for suppliers and recipients of services, such information society services should in principle be subject to the law of the Member State in which the service provider is established.

(23) This Directive neither aims to establish additional rules on private international law relating to conflicts of law nor does it deal with the jurisdiction of Courts; provisions of the applicable law designated by rules of private international law must not restrict the freedom to provide information society services as established in this Directive.

(24) In the context of this Directive, notwithstanding the rule on the control at source of information society services, it is legitimate under the conditions established in this Directive for Member States to take measures to restrict the free movement of information society services.

(25) National courts, including civil courts, dealing with private law disputes can take measures to derogate from the freedom to provide information society services in conformity with conditions established in this Directive.

(26) Member States, in conformity with conditions established in this Directive, may apply their national rules on criminal law and criminal proceedings with a view to taking all investigative and other measures necessary for the detection and prosecution of criminal offences, without there being a need to notify such measures to the Commission.

(27) This Directive, together with the future Directive of the European Parliament and of the Council concerning the distance marketing of consumer financial services, contributes to the creating of a legal framework for the on-line provision of financial services; this Directive does not pre-empt future initiatives in the area of financial services in particular with regard to the harmonisation of rules of conduct in this field; the possibility for Member States, established in this Directive, under certain circumstances of restricting the freedom to provide information society services in order to protect consumers also covers measures in the area of financial services in particular measures aiming at protecting investors.

(28) The Member States' obligation not to subject access to the activity of an information society service provider to prior authorisation does not concern postal services covered by Directive 97/67/EC of the European Parliament and of the Council of 15 December 1997 on common rules for the development of the internal market of

Community postal services and the improvement of quality of service[24] consisting of the physical delivery of a printed electronic mail message and does not affect voluntary accreditation systems, in particular for providers of electronic signature certification service.

(29) Commercial communications are essential for the financing of information society services and for developing a wide variety of new, charge-free services; in the interests of consumer protection and fair trading, commercial communications, including discounts, promotional offers and promotional competitions or games, must meet a number of transparency requirements; these requirements are without prejudice to Directive 97/7/EC; this Directive should not affect existing Directives on commercial communications, in particular Directive 98/43/EC.

(30) The sending of unsolicited commercial communications by electronic mail may be undesirable for consumers and information society service providers and may disrupt the smooth functioning of interactive networks; the question of consent by recipient of certain forms of unsolicited commercial communications is not addressed by this Directive, but has already been addressed, in particular, by Directive 97/7/EC and by Directive 97/66/EC; in Member States which authorise unsolicited commercial communications by electronic mail, the setting up of appropriate industry filtering initiatives should be encouraged and facilitated; in addition it is necessary that in any event unsolicited commercial communities are clearly identifiable as such in order to improve transparency and to facilitate the functioning of such industry initiatives; unsolicited commercial communications by electronic mail should not result in additional communication costs for the recipient.

(31) Member States which allow the sending of unsolicited commercial communications by electronic mail without prior consent of the recipient by service providers established in their territory have to ensure that the service providers consult regularly and respect the opt-out registers in which natural persons not wishing to receive such commercial communications can register themselves.

(32) In order to remove barriers to the development of cross-border services within the Community which members of the regulated professions might offer on the Internet, it is necessary that compliance be guaranteed at Community level with professional rules aiming, in particular, to protect consumers or public health; codes of conduct at Community level would be the best means of determining the rules on professional ethics applicable to commercial communication; the drawing-up or, where appropriate, the adaptation of such rules should be encouraged without prejudice to the autonomy of professional bodies and associations.

(33) This Directive complements Community law and national law relating to regulated professions maintaining a coherent set of applicable rules in this field.

(34) Each Member State is to amend its legislation containing requirements, and in particular requirements as to form, which are likely to curb the use of contracts by electronic means; the examination of the legislation requiring such adjustment should be systematic and should cover all the necessary stages and acts of the contractual process, including the filing of the contract; the result of this amendment should be to make contracts concluded electronically workable; the legal effect of electronic signatures is dealt with by Directive 1999/93/EC of the European Parliament and of the Council of 13 December 1999 on a Community framework for electronic signatures;[25] the acknowledgement of receipt by a service provider may take the form of the on-line provision of the service paid for.

(35) This Directive does not affect Member States' possibility of maintaining or establishing general or specific legal requirements for contracts which can be fulfilled by electronic means, in particular requirements concerning secure electronic signatures.

---

[24] OJ L 15, 21.1.1998, 14.

[25] OJ L 13, 19.1.2000, 12, reproduced supra under no. C.P. 18.

(36) Member States may maintain restrictions for the use of electronic contracts with regard to contracts requiring by law the involvement of courts, public authorities, or professions exercising public authority; this possibility also covers contracts which require the involvement of courts, public authorities, or professions exercising public authority in order to have an effect with regard to third parties as well as contracts requiring by law certification or attestation by a notary.

(37) Member States' obligation to remove obstacles to the use of electronic contracts concerns only obstacles resulting from legal requirements and not practical obstacles resulting from the impossibility of using electronic means in certain cases.

(38) Member States' obligation to remove obstacles to the use of electronic contracts is to be implemented in conformity with legal requirements for contracts enshrined in Community law.

(39) The exceptions to the provisions concerning the contracts concluded exclusively by electronic mail or by equivalent individual communications provided for by this Directive, in relation to information to be provided and the placing of orders, should not enable, as a result, the by-passing of those provisions by providers of information society services.

(40) Both existing and emerging disparities in Member States' legislation and case-law concerning liability of service providers acting as intermediaries prevent the smooth functioning of the internal market, in particular by impairing the development of cross-border services and producing distortions of competition; service providers have a duty to act, under certain circumstances, with a view to preventing or stopping illegal activities; this Directive should constitute the appropriate basis for the development of rapid and reliable procedures for removing and disabling access to illegal information; such mechanisms could be developed on the basis of voluntary agreements between all parties concerned and should be encouraged by Member States; it is in the interest of all parties involved in the provision of information society services to adopt and implement such procedures; the provisions of this Directive relating to liability should not preclude the development and effective operation, by the different interested parties, of technical systems of protection and identification and of technical surveillance instruments made possible by digital technology within the limits laid down by Directives 95/46/EC and 97/66/EC.

(41) This Directive strikes a balance between the different interests at stake and establishes principles upon which industry agreements and standards can be based.

(42) The exemptions from liability established in this Directive cover only cases where the activity of the information society service provider is limited to the technical process of operating and giving access to a communication network over which information made available by third parties is transmitted or temporarily stored, for the sole purpose of making the transmission more efficient; this activity is of a mere technical, automatic and passive nature, which implies that the information society service provider has neither knowledge of nor control over the information which is transmitted or stored.

(43) A service provider can benefit from the exemptions for 'mere conduit' and for 'caching' when he is in no way involved with the information transmitted; this requires among other things that he does not modify the information that he transmits; this requirement does not cover manipulations of a technical nature which take place in the course of the transmission as they do not alter the integrity of the information contained in the transmission.

(44) A service provider who deliberately collaborates with one of the recipients of his service in order to undertake illegal acts goes beyond the activities of 'mere conduit' or 'caching' and as a result cannot benefit from the liability exemptions established for these activities.

(45) The limitations of the liability of intermediary service providers established in this Directive do not affect the possibility of injunctions of different kinds; such injunctions can in

particular consist of orders by courts or administrative authorities requiring the termination or prevention of any infringement, including the removal of illegal information or the disabling of access to it.

(46) In order to benefit from a limitation of liability, the provider of an information society service, consisting of the storage of information, upon obtaining actual knowledge or awareness of illegal activities has to act expeditiously to remove or to disable access to the information concerned; the removal or disabling of access has to be undertaken in the observance of the principle of freedom of expression and of procedures established for this purpose at national level; this Directive does not affect Member States' possibility of establishing specific requirements which must be fulfilled expeditiously prior to the removal or disabling of information.

(47) Member States are prevented from imposing a monitoring obligation on service providers only with respect to obligations of a general nature; this does not concern monitoring obligations in a specific case and, in particular, does not affect orders by national authorities in accordance with national legislation.

(48) This Directive does not affect the possibility for Member States of requiring service providers, who host information provided by recipients of their service, to apply duties of care, which can reasonably be expected from them and which are specified by national law, in order to detect and prevent certain types of illegal activities.

(49) Member States and the Commission are to encourage the drawing-up of codes of conduct; this is not to impair the voluntary nature of such codes and the possibility for interested parties of deciding freely whether to adhere to such codes.

(50) It is important that the proposed directive on the harmonisation of certain aspects of copyright and related rights in the information society and this Directive come into force within a similar time scale with a view to establishing a clear framework of rules relevant to the issue of liability of intermediaries for copyright and relating rights infringements at Community level.

(51) Each Member State should be required, where necessary, to amend any legislation which is liable to hamper the use of schemes for the out-of-court settlement of disputes through electronic channels; the result of this amendment must be to make the functioning of such schemes genuinely and effectively possible in law and in practice, even across borders.

(52) The effective exercise of the freedoms of the internal market makes it necessary to guarantee victims effective access to means of settling disputes; damage which may arise in connection with information society services is characterised both by its rapidity and by its geographical extent; in view of this specific character and the need to ensure that national authorities do not endanger the mutual confidence which they should have in one another, this Directive requests Member States to ensure that appropriate court actions are available; Member States should examine the need to provide access to judicial procedures by appropriate electronic means.

(53) Directive 98/27/EC, which is applicable to information society services, provides a mechanism relating to actions for an injunction aimed at the protection of the collective interests of consumers; this mechanism will contribute to the free movement of information society services by ensuring a high level of consumer protection.

(54) The sanctions provided for under this Directive are without prejudice to any other sanction or remedy provided under national law; Member States are not obliged to provide criminal sanctions for infringement of national provisions adopted pursuant to this Directive.

(55) This Directive does not affect the law applicable to contractual obligations relating to consumer contracts; accordingly, this Directive cannot have the result of depriving the consumer of the protection afforded to him by the mandatory rules relating to contractual obligations of the law of the Member State in which he has his habitual residence.

(56) As regards the derogation contained in this Directive regarding contractual obligations

concerning contracts concluded by consumers, those obligations should be interpreted as including information on the essential elements of the content of the contract, including consumer rights, which have a determining influence on the decision to contract.

(57) The Court of Justice has consistently held that a Member State retains the right to take measures against a service provider that is established in another Member State but directs all or most of his activity to the territory of the first Member State if the choice of establishment was made with a view to evading the legislation that would have applied to the provider had he been established on the territory of the first Member State.

(58) This Directive should not apply to services supplied by service providers established in a third country; in view of the global dimension of electronic commerce, it is, however, appropriate to ensure that the Community rules are consistent with international rules; this Directive is without prejudice to the results of discussions within international organisations (amongst others WTO, OECD, Uncitral) on legal issues.

(59) Despite the global nature of electronic communications, co-ordination of national regulatory measures at European Union level is necessary in order to avoid fragmentation of the internal market, and for the establishment of an appropriate European regulatory framework; such co-ordination should also contribute to the establishment of a common and strong negotiating position in international forums.

(60) In order to allow the unhampered development of electronic commerce, the legal framework must be clear and simple, predictable and consistent with the rules applicable at international level so that it does not adversely affect the competitiveness of European industry or impede innovation in that sector.

(61) If the market is actually to operate by electronic means in the context of globalisation, the European Union and the major non-European areas need to consult each other with a view to making laws and procedures compatible.

(62) Co-operation with third countries should be strengthened in the area of electronic commerce, in particular with applicant countries, the developing countries and the European Union's other trading partners.

(63) The adoption of this Directive will not prevent the Member States from taking into account the various social, societal and cultural implications which are inherent in the advent of the information society; in particular it should not hinder measures which Member States might adopt in conformity with Community law to achieve social, cultural and democratic goals taking into account their linguistic diversity, national and regional specificities as well as their cultural heritage, and to ensure and maintain public access to the widest possible range of information society services; in any case, the development of the information society is to ensure that Community citizens can have access to the cultural European heritage provided in the digital environment.

(64) Electronic communication offers the Member States an excellent means of providing public services in the cultural, educational and linguistic fields.

(65) The Council, in its resolution of 19 January 1999 on the consumer dimension of the information society,[26] stressed that the protection of consumers deserved special attention in this field; the Commission will examine the degree to which existing consumer protection rules provide insufficient protection in the context of the information society and will identify, where necessary, the deficiencies of this legislation and those issues which could require additional measures; if need be, the Commission should make specific additional proposals to resolve such deficiencies that will thereby have been identified,

HAVE ADOPTED THIS DIRECTIVE:

---

[26] OJ C 23, 28.1.1999, 1.

Chapter I
General Provisions

Article 1
Objective and scope

1. This Directive seeks to contribute to the proper functioning of the internal market by ensuring the free movement of information society services between the Member States.

2. This Directive approximates, to the extent necessary for the achievement of the objective set out in paragraph 1, certain national provisions on information society services relating to the internal market, the establishment of service providers, commercial communications, electronic contracts, the liability of intermediaries, codes of conduct, out-of-court dispute settlements, court actions and co-operation between Member States.

3. This Directive complements Community law applicable to information society services without prejudice to the level of protection for, in particular, public health and consumer interests, as established by Community acts and national legislation implementing them in so far as this does not restrict the freedom to provide information society services.

4. This Directive does not establish additional rules on private international law nor does it deal with the jurisdiction of Courts.

5. This Directive shall not apply to:

(a) the field of taxation;

(b) questions relating to information society services covered by Directives 95/46/EC and 97/66/EC;

(c) questions relating to agreements or practices governed by cartel law;

(d) the following activities of information society services:
- the activities of notaries or equivalent professions to the extent that they involve a direct and specific connection with the exercise of public authority,
- the representation of a client and defence of his interests before the courts,
- gambling activities that involve wagering a stake with monetary value in games of chance, including lotteries and betting transactions.

6. This Directive does not affect measures taken at Community or national level, in the respect of Community law, in order to promote cultural and linguistic diversity and to ensure the defence of pluralism.

Article 2
Definitions

For the purpose of this Directive, the following terms shall bear the following meanings:

(a) 'information society services': services within the meaning of Article 1(2) of Directive 98/34/EC as amended by Directive 98/48/EC;

(b) 'service provider': any natural or legal person providing an information society service;

(c) 'established service provider': a service provider who effectively pursues an economic activity using a fixed establishment for an indefinite period. The presence and use of the technical means and technologies required to provide the service do not, in themselves, constitute an establishment of the provider;

(d) 'recipient of the service': any natural or legal person who, for professional ends or otherwise, uses an information society service, in particular for the purposes of seeking information or making it accessible;

(e) 'consumer': any natural person who is acting for purposes that are outside his or her trade, business or profession;

(f) 'commercial communication': any form of communication designed to promote, directly or indirectly, the goods, services or image of a company, organisation or person pursuing a commercial, industrial or craft activity or exercising a regulated profession. The following do not in themselves constitute commercial communications:
- information allowing direct access to the activity of the company, organisation or person, in particular a domain name or an electronic-mail address,

— communications relating to the goods, services or image of the company, organisation or person compiled in an independent manner, particularly when this is without financial consideration;

(g) 'regulated profession': any profession within the meaning of either Article 1(d) of Council Directive 89/48/EEC of 21 December 1988 on a general system for the recognition of higher-education diplomas awarded on completion of professional education and training of at least three-years' duration[27] or of Article 1(f) of Council Directive 92/51/EEC of 18 June 1992 on a second general system for the recognition of professional education and training to supplement Directive 89/48/EEC;[28]

(h) 'co-ordinated field': requirements laid down in Member States' legal systems applicable to information society service providers or information society services, regardless of whether they are of a general nature or specifically designed for them.
(i) The co-ordinated field concerns requirements with which the service provider has to comply in respect of:
— the taking up of the activity of an information society service, such as requirements concerning qualifications, authorisation or notification,
— the pursuit of the activity of an information society service, such as requirements concerning the behaviour of the service provider, requirements regarding the quality or content of the service including those applicable to advertising and contracts, or requirements concerning the liability of the service provider;
(ii) The co-ordinated field does not cover requirements such as:
— requirements applicable to goods as such,
— requirements applicable to the delivery of goods,
— requirements applicable to services not provided by electronic means.

Article 3
Internal market

1. Each Member State shall ensure that the information society services provided by a service provider established on its territory comply with the national provisions applicable in the Member State in question which fall within the co-ordinated field.

2. Member States may not, for reasons falling within the co-ordinated field, restrict the freedom to provide information society services from another Member State.

3. Paragraphs 1 and 2 shall not apply to the fields referred to in the Annex.

4. Member States may take measures to derogate from paragraph 2 in respect of a given information society service if the following conditions are fulfilled:

(a) the measures shall be:
(i) necessary for one of the following reasons:
— public policy, in particular the prevention, investigation, detection and prosecution of criminal offences, including the protection of minors and the fight against any incitement to hatred on grounds of race, sex, religion or nationality, and violations of human dignity concerning individual persons,
— the protection of public health,
— public security, including the safeguarding of national security and defence,
— the protection of consumers, including investors;
(ii) taken against given information society service that prejudices the objectives referred to in point (i) or which presents a serious and grave risk of prejudice to those objectives;
(iii) proportionate to those objectives;

(b) before taking the measures in question and without prejudice to court proceedings, including preliminary proceedings and acts carried out in the framework of a criminal investigation, the Member State has:
— asked the Member State referred to in paragraph 1 to take measures and the latter did not take such measures, or they were inadequate,

---

[27] OJ L 19, 24.1.1989, 16.
[28] OJ L 209, 24.7.1992, 25. Directive as last amended by Commission Directive 97/38/EC (OJ L 184, 12.7.1997, 31).

– notified the Commission and the Member State referred to in paragraph 1 of its intention to take such measures.

5. Member States may, in the case of urgency, derogate from the conditions stipulated in paragraph 4(b). Where this is the case, the measures shall be notified in the shortest possible time to the Commission and to the Member State referred to in paragraph 1, indicating the reasons for which the Member State considers that there is urgency.

6. Without prejudice to the Member State's possibility of proceeding with the measures in question, the Commission shall examine the compatibility of the notified measures with Community law in the shortest possible time; where it comes to the conclusion that the measure is incompatible with Community law, the Commission shall ask the Member State in question to refrain from taking any proposed measures or urgently to put an end to the measures in question.

Chapter II
Principles

Section 1
Establishment and Information Requirements

Article 4
Principle excluding prior authorisation

1. Member States shall ensure that the taking up and pursuit of the activity of an information society service provider may not be made subject to prior authorisation or any other requirement having equivalent effect.

2. Paragraph 1 shall be without prejudice to authorisation schemes which are not specifically and exclusively targeted at information society services, or which are covered by Directive 97/13/EC of the European Parliament and of the Council of 10 April 1997 on a common framework for general authorisations and individual licences in the field of telecommunications services.[29]

Article 5
General information to be provided

1. In addition to other information requirements established by Community law, Member States shall ensure that the service provider shall render easily, directly and permanently accessible to the recipients of the service and competent authorities, at least the following information:

(a) the name of the service provider;

(b) the geographic address at which the service provider is established;

(c) the details of the service provider, including his electronic mail address, which allow him to be contacted rapidly and communicated with in a direct and effective manner;

(d) where the service provider is registered in a trade or similar public register, the trade register in which the service provider is entered and his registration number, or equivalent means of identification in that register;

(e) where the activity is subject to an authorisation scheme, the particulars of the relevant supervisory authority;

(f) as concerns the regulated professions:
– any professional body or similar institution with which the service provider is registered,
– the professional title and the Member State where it has been granted,
– a reference to the applicable professional rules in the Member State of establishment and the means to access them;

(g) where the service provider undertakes an activity that is subject to VAT, the identification number referred to in Article 22(1) of the sixth Council Directive 77/388/EEC of 17 May 1977 on the harmonisation of the laws of the Member States relating to turnover taxes—Common system of value added tax: uniform basis of assessment.[30]

2. In addition to other information requirements established by Community law, Member

---

[29] OJ L 117, 7.5.1997, 15.

[30] OJ L 145, 13.6.1977, 1. Directive as last amended by Directive 1999/85/EC (OJ L 277, 28.10.1999, 34).

States shall at least ensure that, where information society services refer to prices, these are to be indicated clearly and unambiguously and, in particular, must indicate whether they are inclusive of tax and delivery costs.

SECTION 2
COMMERCIAL COMMUNICATIONS

Article 6
Information to be provided

In addition to other information requirements established by Community law, Member States shall ensure that commercial communications which are part of, or constitute, an information society service comply at least with the following conditions:

(a) the commercial communication shall be clearly identifiable as such;

(b) the natural or legal person on whose behalf the commercial communication is made shall be clearly identifiable;

(c) promotional offers, such as discounts, premiums and gifts, where permitted in the Member State where the service provider is established, shall be clearly identifiable as such, and the conditions which are to be met to qualify for them shall be easily accessible and be presented clearly and unambiguously;

(d) promotional competitions or games, where permitted in the Member State where the service provider is established, shall be clearly identifiable as such, and the conditions for participation shall be easily accessible and be presented clearly and unambiguously.

Article 7
Unsolicited commercial communication

1. In addition to other requirements established by Community law, Member States that permit unsolicited commercial communication by electronic mail shall ensure that such commercial communication by a service provider established in their territory shall be identifiable clearly and unambiguously as such as soon as it is received by the recipient.

2. Without prejudice to Directive 97/7/EC and Directive 97/66/EC, Member States shall take measures to ensure that service providers undertaking unsolicited commercial communications by electronic mail consult regularly and respect the opt-out registers in which natural persons not wishing to receive such commercial communications can register themselves.

Article 8
Regulated professions

1. Member States shall ensure that the use of commercial communications which are part of, or constitute, an information society service provided by a member of a regulated profession is permitted subject to compliance with the professional rules regarding, in particular, the independence, dignity and honour of the profession, professional secrecy and fairness towards clients and other members of the profession.

2. Without prejudice to the autonomy of professional bodies and associations, Member States and the Commission shall encourage professional associations and bodies to establish codes of conduct at Community level in order to determine the types of information that can be given for the purposes of commercial communication in conformity with the rules referred to in paragraph 1.

3. When drawing up proposals for Community initiatives which may become necessary to ensure the proper functioning of the Internal Market with regard to the information referred to in paragraph 2, the Commission shall take due account of codes of conduct applicable at Community level and shall act in close co-operation with the relevant professional associations and bodies.

4. This Directive shall apply in addition to Community Directives concerning access to, and the exercise of, activities of the regulated professions.

Section 3
Contracts Concluded by Electronic Means

Article 9
Treatment of contracts

1. Member States shall ensure that their legal system allows contracts to be concluded by electronic means. Member States shall in particular ensure that the legal requirements applicable to the contractual process neither create obstacles for the use of electronic contracts nor result in such contracts being deprived of legal effectiveness and validity on account of their having been made by electronic means.

2. Member States may lay down that paragraph 1 shall not apply to all or certain contracts falling into one of the following categories:

(a) contracts that create or transfer rights in real estate, except for rental rights;

(b) contracts requiring by law the involvement of courts, public authorities or professions exercising public authority;

(c) contracts of suretyship granted and on collateral securities furnished by persons acting for purposes outside their trade, business or profession;

(d) contracts governed by family law or by the law of succession.

3. Member States shall indicate to the Commission the categories referred to in paragraph 2 to which they do not apply paragraph 1. Member States shall submit to the Commission every five years a report on the application of paragraph 2 explaining the reasons why they consider it necessary to maintain the category referred to in paragraph 2(b) to which they do not apply paragraph 1.

Article 10
Information to be provided

1. In addition to other information requirements established by Community law, Member States shall ensure, except when otherwise agreed by parties who are not consumers, that at least the following information is given by the service provider clearly, comprehensibly and unambiguously and prior to the order being placed by the recipient of the service:

(a) the different technical steps to follow to conclude the contract;

(b) whether or not the concluded contract will be filed by the service provider and whether it will be accessible;

(c) the technical means for identifying and correcting input errors prior to the placing of the order;

(d) the languages offered for the conclusion of the contract.

2. Member States shall ensure that, except when otherwise agreed by parties who are not consumers, the service provider indicates any relevant codes of conduct to which he subscribes and information on how those codes can be consulted electronically.

3. Contract terms and general conditions provided to the recipient must be made available in a way that allows him to store and reproduce them.

4. Paragraphs 1 and 2 shall not apply to contracts concluded exclusively by exchange of electronic mail or by equivalent individual communications.

Article 11
Placing of the order

1. Member States shall ensure, except when otherwise agreed by parties who are not consumers, that in cases where the recipient of the service places his order through technological means, the following principles apply:
– the service provider has to acknowledge the receipt of the recipient's order without undue delay and by electronic means,
– the order and the acknowledgement of receipt are deemed to be received when the parties to whom they are addressed are able to access them.

2. Member States shall ensure that, except when otherwise agreed by parties who are not consumers, the service provider makes available to the recipient of the service appropriate, effective and accessible technical means allowing him to identify

and correct input errors, prior to the placing of the order.

3. Paragraph 1, first indent, and paragraph 2 shall not apply to contracts concluded exclusively by exchange of electronic mail or by equivalent individual communications.

SECTION 4

LIABILITY OF INTERMEDIARY SERVICE PROVIDERS

Article 12

'Mere conduit'

1. Where an information society service is provided that consists of the transmission in a communication network of information provided by a recipient of the service, or the provision of access to a communication network, Member States shall ensure that the service provider is not liable for the information transmitted, on condition that the provider:

(a) does not initiate the transmission;

(b) does not select the receiver of the transmission; and

(c) does not select or modify the information contained in the transmission.

2. The acts of transmission and of provision of access referred to in paragraph 1 include the automatic, intermediate and transient storage of the information transmitted in so far as this takes place for the sole purpose of carrying out the transmission in the communication network, and provided that the information is not stored for any period longer than is reasonably necessary for the transmission.

3. This Article shall not affect the possibility for a court or administrative authority, in accordance with Member States' legal systems, of requiring the service provider to terminate or prevent an infringement.

Article 13

'Caching'

1. Where an information society service is provided that consists of the transmission in a communication network of information provided by a recipient of the service, Member States shall ensure that the service provider is not liable for the automatic, intermediate and temporary storage of that information, performed for the sole purpose of making more efficient the information's onward transmission to other recipients of the service upon their request, on condition that:

(a) the provider does not modify the information;

(b) the provider complies with conditions on access to the information;

(c) the provider complies with rules regarding the updating of the information, specified in a manner widely recognised and used by industry;

(d) the provider does not interfere with the lawful use of technology, widely recognised and used by industry, to obtain data on the use of the information; and

(e) the provider acts expeditiously to remove or to disable access to the information it has stored upon obtaining actual knowledge of the fact that the information at the initial source of the transmission has been removed from the network, or access to it has been disabled, or that a court or an administrative authority has ordered such removal or disablement.

2. This Article shall not affect the possibility for a court or administrative authority, in accordance with Member States' legal systems, of requiring the service provider to terminate or prevent an infringement.

Article 14

Hosting

1. Where an information society service is provided that consists of the storage of information provided by a recipient of the service, Member States shall ensure that the service provider is not liable for the information stored at the request of a recipient of the service, on condition that:

(a) the provider does not have actual knowledge of illegal activity or information and, as regards claims for damages, is not aware of facts or circumstances from which the illegal activity or information is apparent; or

(b) the provider, upon obtaining such knowledge or awareness, acts expeditiously to remove or to disable access to the information.

2. Paragraph 1 shall not apply when the recipient of the service is acting under the authority or the control of the provider.

3. This Article shall not affect the possibility for a court or administrative authority, in accordance with Member States' legal systems, of requiring the service provider to terminate or prevent an infringement, nor does it affect the possibility for Member States of establishing procedures governing the removal or disabling of access to information.

Article 15
No general obligation to monitor

1. Member States shall not impose a general obligation on providers, when providing the services covered by Articles 12, 13 and 14, to monitor the information that they transmit or store, nor a general obligation actively to seek facts or circumstances indicating illegal activity.

2. Member States may establish obligations for information society service providers promptly to inform the competent public authorities of alleged illegal activities undertaken or information provided by recipients of their service or obligations to communicate to the competent authorities, at their request, information enabling the identification of recipients of their service with whom they have storage agreements.

Chapter III
Implementation

Article 16
Codes of conduct

1. Member States and the Commission shall encourage:

(a) the drawing up of codes of conduct at Community level, by trade, professional and consumer associations or organisations, designed to contribute to the proper implementation of Articles 5 to 15;

(b) the voluntary transmission of draft codes of conduct at national or Community level to the Commission;

(c) the accessibility of these codes of conduct in the Community languages by electronic means;

(d) the communication to the Member States and the Commission, by trade, professional and consumer associations or organisations, of their assessment of the application of their codes of conduct and their impact upon practices, habits or customs relating to electronic commerce;

(e) the drawing up of codes of conduct regarding the protection of minors and human dignity.

2. Member States and the Commission shall encourage the involvement of associations or organisations representing consumers in the drafting and implementation of codes of conduct affecting their interests and drawn up in accordance with paragraph 1(a). Where appropriate, to take account of their specific needs, associations representing the visually impaired and disabled should be consulted.

Article 17
Out-of-court dispute settlement

1. Member States shall ensure that, in the event of disagreement between an information society service provider and the recipient of the service, their legislation does not hamper the use of out-of-court schemes, available under national law, for dispute settlement, including appropriate electronic means.

2. Member States shall encourage bodies responsible for the out-of-court settlement of, in particular, consumer disputes to operate in a way that provides adequate procedural guarantees for the parties concerned.

3. Member States shall encourage bodies responsible for out-of-court dispute settlement to inform the Commission of the significant decisions they take regarding information society services and to transmit any other information on the practices, usages or customs relating to electronic commerce.

Article 18
Court actions

1. Member States shall ensure that court actions available under national law concerning information society services' activities allow for the rapid adoption of measures, including interim measures, designed to terminate any alleged infringement and to prevent any further impairment of the interests involved.

2. [. . .]

¶ *This paragraph supplements point 11 with the Annex of Directive 98/27/EC, reproduced supra under no. C.P. 15. The modifications are directly incorporated therein.*

Article 19
Co-operation

1. Member States shall have adequate means of supervision and investigation necessary to implement this Directive effectively and shall ensure that service providers supply them with the requisite information.

2. Member States shall co-operate with other Member States; they shall, to that end, appoint one or several contact points, whose details they shall communicate to the other Member States and to the Commission.

3. Member States shall, as quickly as possible, and in conformity with national law, provide the assistance and information requested by other Member States or by the Commission, including by appropriate electronic means.

4. Member States shall establish contact points that shall be accessible at least by electronic means and from which recipients and service providers may:

(a) obtain general information on contractual rights and obligations as well as on the complaint and redress mechanisms available in the event of disputes, including practical aspects involved in the use of such mechanisms;

(b) obtain the details of authorities, associations or organisations from which they may obtain further information or practical assistance.

5. Member States shall encourage the communication to the Commission of any significant administrative or judicial decisions taken in their territory regarding disputes relating to information society services and practices, usages and customs relating to electronic commerce. The Commission shall communicate these decisions to the other Member States.

Article 20
Sanctions

Member States shall determine the sanctions applicable to infringements of national provisions adopted pursuant to this Directive and shall take all measures necessary to ensure that they are enforced. The sanctions they provide for shall be effective, proportionate and dissuasive.

CHAPTER IV
FINAL PROVISIONS

Article 21
Re-examination

1. Before 17 July 2003, and thereafter every two years, the Commission shall submit to the European Parliament, the Council and the Economic and Social Committee a report on the application of this Directive, accompanied, where necessary, by proposals for adapting it to legal, technical and economic developments in the field of information society services, in particular with respect to crime prevention, the protection of minors, consumer protection and to the proper functioning of the internal market.

2. In examining the need for an adaptation of this Directive, the report shall in particular analyse the need for proposals concerning the liability of providers of hyperlinks and location tool services, 'notice and take down' procedures and the attribution of liability following the taking down of content. The report shall also analyse the need for additional conditions for the exemption from liability, provided for in Articles 12 and 13, in the light of technical developments, and the

possibility of applying the internal market principles to unsolicited commercial communications by electronic mail.

Article 22
Transposition

1. Member States shall bring into force the laws, regulations and administrative provisions necessary to comply with this Directive before 17 January 2002. They shall forthwith inform the Commission thereof.

2. When Member States adopt the measures referred to in paragraph 1, these shall contain a reference to this Directive or shall be accompanied by such reference at the time of their official publication. The methods of making such reference shall be laid down by Member States.

Article 23
Entry into force

This Directive shall enter into force on the day of its publication in the *Official Journal of the European Communities*.

Article 24
Addressees

This Directive is addressed to the Member States.

Annex
Derogations from article 3

As provided for in Article 3(3), Article 3(1) and (2) do not apply to:
– copyright, neighbouring rights, rights referred to in Directive 87/54/EEC[31] and Directive 96/9/EC[32] as well as industrial property rights,
– the emission of electronic money by institutions in respect of which Member States have applied one of the derogations provided for in Article 8(1) of Directive 2000/46/EC,[33]
– Article 44(2) of Directive 85/611/EEC,[34]
– Article 30 and Title IV of Directive 92/49/EEC,[35] Title IV of Directive 92/96/EEC,[36] Articles 7 and 8 of Directive 88/357/EEC[37] and Article 4 of Directive 90/619/EEC,[38]
– the freedom of the parties to choose the law applicable to their contract,
– contractual obligations concerning consumer contracts,
– formal validity of contracts creating or transferring rights in real estate where such contracts are subject to mandatory formal requirements of the law of the Member State where the real estate is situated,
– the permissibility of unsolicited commercial communications by electronic mail.

---

[31] OJ L 24, 27.1.1987, 36.
[32] OJ L 77, 27.3.1996, 20.
[33] OJ L 275, 27.10.2000, 37, reproduced supra under no. B. 35.
[34] OJ L 375, 31.12.1985, 3, reproduced infra under no. S. 6. Directive as last amended by Directive 95/26/EC (OJ L 168, 18.7.1995, 7), reproduced infra under no. I. 27.
[35] OJ L 228, 11.8.1992, 1, reproduced infra under no. S. 26. Directive as last amended by Directive 95/26/EC, reproduced supra under no. S. 29.
[36] OJ L 360, 9.12.1992, 2, reproduced infra under no. I. 26. Directive as last amended by Directive 95/26/EC.

[37] OJ L 172, 4.7.1988, 1, Second Insurance Directive, reproduced infra under no. I. 15. Directive as last amended by Directive 92/49/EC, reproduced infra under no. S. 26.
[38] OJ L 330, 29.11.1990, 50, reproduced infra under I. 18. Directive as last amended by Directive 92/96/EC, reproduced infra under no. S. 27.

C.P. 20.

Commission Recommendation 2001/193/EC
of 1 March 2001
on pre-contractual information to be given to consumers by lenders offering home loans
(notified under document number C(2001) 477)[1]

(Text with EEA relevance)

THE COMMISSION OF THE EUROPEAN COMMUNITIES,

Having regard to the Treaty establishing the European Community, and in particular the second indent of Article 211 thereof,

Whereas:

(1) Achieving a single market for financial services offering consumers a high level of protection is a priority for the Community. Signing a home loan contract is often the most important financial commitment that a consumer enters into. Home lending is an area of financial services where consumers could gain substantial benefit from increased cross-border activity provided that adequate protective measures are in place.

(2) It is essential in that context that the pre-contractual information as to the terms and conditions on which home loans are offered throughout the Community are transparent and comparable. To that end, lenders should be invited to provide consumers with two sets of harmonised information, namely one containing general information and the other containing personalised information. The personalised information should be provided in a standard written format, known as a European Standardised Information Sheet.

(3) The elements of information—both general and personalised—to be given to consumers by lenders, have been negotiated under the auspices of the Commission by the associations and federations representing lenders, on the one hand, and consumers, on the other. These negotiations have resulted in a Voluntary Code of Conduct on pre-contractual information for home loans (the "Code"), a copy of which can be obtained from the adhering lenders. Adherence to the Code is open to all home loan lenders, regardless of whether they are members of one of the negotiating associations and federations.

(4) In certain Member States national requirements on additional pre-contractual consumer information for home loans already exist. It is desirable that these additional information elements be merged with those in the European Standardised Information Sheet and that this be done in a manner that ensures comparability across borders for the consumer at European level. Where a Member State imposes on lenders from other Member States an obligation to give additional pre-contractual information to consumers above and beyond what is set out in the Annexes, it is invited to ensure that this information is in conformity with Community law.

(5) Both domestic and cross-border home loans should be subject to this recommendation, excluding credit agreements which are covered by Council Directive 87/102/EEC of 22 December 1986 on the approximation of laws, regulations and administrative provisions of the Member States concerning consumer credit,[2] as last amended by Directive 98/7/EC of the European Parliament and of the Council.[3]

(6) The Commission will establish a central register of lenders offering home loans, indicating

---

[1] OJ L 69, 10.3.2001, 25–29.

[2] OJ L 42, 12.2.1987, 48.
[3] OJ L 101, 1.4.1998, 17

whether or not those lenders adhere to the Code, as well as the date on which those lenders notified their adherence to the Commission. The Commission will, by all appropriate means, ensure that the public at large can consult this central register.

(7) The Commission will monitor compliance with this recommendation and assess its effectiveness. The Commission will consider presenting binding legislation, should the terms of this recommendation not be fully complied with,

HEREBY RECOMMENDS:

Article 1
Scope

This recommendation covers pre-contractual consumer information for domestic and cross-border home loans.

Credit agreements covered by Directive 87/102/EEC are excluded from the scope of this recommendation.

Article 2
Definition

For the purposes of this recommendation, a home loan means a credit to a consumer for the purchase or transformation of the private immovable property he owns or aims to acquire, secured either by a mortgage on immovable property or by a surety commonly used in a Member State for that purpose.

Article 3
Principles

The lender should supply to the consumer in the course of the pre-contractual phase:

(a) general information as set out in Annex I;

(b) personalised information to be presented in a European Standardised Information Sheet as set out in Annex II.

In addition, the lender should supply to the consumer information on the identification, address and telephone number of the competent body to which the consumer can refer in the event of difficulties in relation to the application of the Code on pre-contractual information for home loans.

The final decision to accept a credit offer from a lender lies with the consumer.

Article 4
National requirements on additional pre-contractual consumer information

Should pre-existing national requirements provide that additional pre-contractual consumer information is to be given to the consumer, Member States are invited to take all necessary steps in order that this additional information may be merged with the information included in the European Standardised Information Sheet in a manner that does not impair comparability across borders.

Each Member State is moreover invited to ensure that those additional nation requirements are imposed on lenders from other Member States offering home loans in the territory of that Member State only if those additional requirements are in conformity with Community law.

In this case, the host Member State is invited to notify the requirements to the Commission so that the latter can consider them in the framework of its monitoring activity set out in Article 6.

Article 5
Establishment of a register by the Commission

The Commission will establish a central register of lenders offering home loans, indicating whether or not those lenders adhere to the Code.

Article 6
Monitoring by the Commission

The Commission will monitor compliance with this recommendation.

Two years after adoption of this recommendation, the Commission will assess its effectiveness: the assessment will be based on its own monitoring, on annual progress reports to be drawn up by the European Credit Sector Associations, and on any other information available.

Article 7

Final provision

Member States and lenders offering home loans in the Community, regardless of whether they are members of the associations and federations who negotiated the Code, are invited to comply with this recommendation by no later than 30 September 2002.

Article 8

Addressees

This recommendation is addressed to the Member States.

Annex I

Initial information about home loans should include or be accompanied by the following information in the same format as that initial information is itself provided:

A. Lender

1. Identification and address of the lender.

2. Where appropriate, identification and address of the intermediary.

B. Home loan

1. Purposes for which the home loan may be used.

2. Form of surety.

3. Description of the types of home loans available with short description of the differences between fixed and variable rate products, including related implications for the consumer.

4. Types of interest rate—fixed, variable, and combination thereof.

5. An indication of the cost of a typical home loan for the consumer.

6. A list of related cost elements, such as, administrative costs, insurance costs, legal costs, intermediaries costs.

7. The different options available for reimbursing the credit to the lender (including the number, frequency, amount of repayment instalments if any).

8. Whether there is a possibility of early repayment (if so, its conditions).

9. Whether a valuation of the property is necessary and, if so, by whom it has to be carried out.

10. General information on tax relief on home loan interest or other public subsidies prevailing, or information on where one can obtain further advice.

11. The duration of the reflection period, where relevant.

12. Confirmation that the institution subscribes to the Code, and indication that a copy of the Code is available in the institution.

Annex II

European standardised information sheet

This standardised information is an integral part of the voluntary Code of Conduct on pre-contractual information for home loans, a copy of which can be obtained from your lender.

Item	Description
Up front text	'This document does not constitute a legally binding offer.
	The figures are provided in good faith and are an accurate representation of the offer that the lender would make under current market conditions based on the information that has been provided. It should be noted, however, that the figures could fluctuate with market conditions.
	The provision of this information does not oblige the lender to grant a credit.'
1. Lender	
2. Description of product	This section should provide a brief but clear description of the product.
	It should be made clear whether it is a mortgage on a property or another commonly used surety.
	It should be made clear whether the product on offer is an interest only home loan (i.e. that it involves servicing the debt with a lump sum payment at the end) or a repayment home loan (i.e. that it involves paying interest and capital over the lifetime of the home loan).
	It should be made clear whether the home loan terms are dependent on the consumer supplying a certain amount of capital (perhaps expressed as a percentage of house value).
	Where the home loan terms are dependent on a third party guarantee, this should be clearly stated.
3. Nominal rate (indicates type of rate and duration of fixed period)	This section should provide information on the key conditions of the home loan—the interest rate. Where relevant, the description should include details of how the interest rate will vary including, for example, review periods, lock in periods and related penalty clauses, collars and caps, etc.
	The description should include: – whether or not a variable rate is indexed, and – provide details of indexation, where appropriate.
4. Annual percentage rate of charge (APRC) based on national regulation or effective rate, where relevant	Where a national figure for APCR is not set in legislation, the equivalent effective rate should be used.
5. Amount of credit advanced and currency	
6. Duration of home loan agreement	
7. Number and frequency of payments (may vary)	
8. For repayment home loan, amount of each instalment (may vary)	
9. For interest only home loan: – amount of each regular interest payment,	The lender should provide an indication, real or illustrative, of: (a) the amount of each regular payment in accordance with the frequency of the payments (see point 7);

Item	Description
– amount of each regular payment to the repayment vehicle	(b) the amount of each regular payment towards the repayment vehicle, in accordance with the frequency of the payments (see point 7).
	Where appropriate, a warning should be given that the repayment vehicle may not cover the amount borrowed.
	If the lender provides the repayment vehicle and has included this in part of the offer then it should be clear whether or not the offer is tied to the consumer's agreement on that repayment vehicle.
10. Additional non-recurring costs, where applicable	A list of initial non-recurring costs which the consumer is expected to pay upon taking out the home loan must be provided.
	Where these costs are under the direct or indirect control of the lender, an estimate of the costs should be provided.
	Where relevant, it should be made clear if the cost is to be paid regardless of the outcome of the home loan application.
	Such costs might include, for example: – administrative costs, – legal fees, – property valuation.
	Where an offer would be dependent on the consumer's receiving these services through the lender (provided this is permitted in national legislation), it should be clearly stated.
11. Additional recurrent costs (not included in point 8)	This list should include, for example: – insurance against default on payments (unemployment/death), – fire insurance, – building and contents insurance.
	Where an offer would be dependent on the consumer's receiving these services through the lender (provided this is permitted in national legislation), it should be clearly stated.
12. Early repayment	The lender should provide an indication of: – the possibility and terms of early repayment, – including indication of any charges applicable.
	Where it is not possible to stipulate the charge at this stage, an indication should be provided that a sum sufficient to recoup the lender's costs in unwinding the transaction would be payable.
13. Internal complaint schemes	Name, address and telephone number of contact point.
14. Illustrative amortisation table	The lender should provide an illustrative and summarised amortisation table which includes, at least: – monthly or quarterly payments (if it be the case) for the first year, – to be followed by yearly figures over the total duration of the loan.
	The table should contain figures on – amount of capital reimbursed, – amount of interest, – outstanding capital, – amount of each instalment, – sum of capital and interest.
	It should be clearly indicated that the table is illustrative only and contain a warning if the home loan proposed has a variable interest rate.
15. Obligation to domicile bank account and salary with lender	

C.P. 21.

European Parliament and Council Regulation 2560/2001/EC of 19 December 2001 on cross-border payments in euro[1]

THE EUROPEAN PARLIAMENT AND THE COUNCIL OF THE EUROPEAN UNION,

Having regard to the Treaty establishing the European Community, and in particular Article 95(1) thereof,

Having regard to the proposal from the Commission,[2]

Having regard to the opinion of the Economic and Social Committee,[3]

Having regard to the opinion of the European Central Bank,[4]

Acting in accordance with the procedure laid down in Article 251 of the Treaty,[5]

Whereas:

(1) Directive 97/5/EC of the European Parliament and of the Council of 27 January 1997 on cross-border credit transfers[6] sought to improve cross-border credit transfer services and notably their efficiency. The aim was to enable in particular consumers and small and medium-sized enterprises to make credit transfers rapidly, reliably and cheaply from one part of the Community to another. Such credit transfers and cross-border payments in general are still extremely expensive compared to payments at national level. It emerges from the findings of a study undertaken by the Commission and released on 20 September 2001 that consumers are given insufficient or no information on the cost of transfers, and that the average cost of cross-border credit transfers has hardly changed since 1993 when a comparable study was carried out.

(2) The Commission's Communication to the European Parliament and the Council of 31 January 2000 on Retail Payments in the Internal Market, together with the European Parliament Resolutions of 26 October 2000 on the Commission Communication and of 4 July 2001 on means to assist economic actors in switching to the euro, and the reports of the European Central Bank of September 1999 and September 2000 on improving cross-border payment services have each underlined the urgent need for effective improvements in this field.

(3) The Commission's Communication to the European Parliament, the Council, the Economic and Social Committee, the Committee of the Regions and the European Central Bank of 3 April 2001 on the preparations for the introduction of euro notes and coins announced that the Commission would consider using all the instruments at its disposal and would take all the steps necessary to ensure that the costs of cross-border transactions were brought more closely into line with the costs of domestic transactions, thus making the concept of the euro zone as a 'domestic payment area' tangible and transparently clear to citizens.

(4) Compared with the objective that was reaffirmed when euro book money was introduced, namely to achieve an, if not uniform, at least similar charge structure for the euro, there have been no significant results in terms of reducing the cost of cross-border payments compared to internal payments.

---

[1] OJ L 344, 28.12.2001, 13–16.
[2] OJ C 270 E, 25.9.2001, 270.
[3] Opinion delivered on 10 December 2001 (not yet published in the Official Journal).
[4] OJ C 308, 1.11.2001, 17.
[5] Opinion of the European Parliament of 15 November 2001 (OJ C 140, 13.6.2002, 531), Council Common Position of 7 December 2001 (OJ C 363, 19.12.2001, 1) and Decision of the European Parliament of 13 December 2001.
[6] OJ L 43, 14.2.1997, 25.

(5) The volume of cross-border payments is growing steadily as completion of the internal market takes place. In this area without borders, payments have been further facilitated by the introduction of the euro.

(6) The fact that the level of charges for cross-border payments continues to remain higher than the level of charges for internal payments is hampering cross-border trade and therefore constitutes an obstacle to the proper functioning of the internal market. This is also likely to affect confidence in the euro. Therefore, in order to facilitate the functioning of the internal market, it is necessary to ensure that charges for cross-border payments in euro are the same as charges for payments made in euro within a Member State, which will also bolster confidence in the euro.

(7) For cross-border electronic payment transactions in euro, the principle of equal charges should apply, taking account of the adjustment periods and the institutions' extra workload relating to the transition to the euro, as from 1 July 2002. In order to allow the implementation of the necessary infrastructure and conditions, a transitional period for cross-border credit transfers should apply until 1 July 2003.

(8) At present, it is not advisable to apply the principle of uniform charges for paper cheques as by nature they cannot be processed as efficiently as the other means of payment, in particular electronic payments. However, the principle of transparent charges should also apply to cheques.

(9) In order to allow a customer to assess the cost of a cross-border payment, it is necessary that he be informed of the charges applied and any modification to them. The same holds for the case that a currency other than the euro is involved in the cross-border euro-payment transaction.

(10) This Regulation does not affect the possibility for institutions to offer an all-inclusive fee for different payment services, provided that this does not discriminate between cross-border and national payments.

(11) It is also important to provide for improvements to facilitate the execution of cross-border payments by payment institutions. In this respect, standardisation should be promoted as regards, in particular, the use of the International Bank Account Number (IBAN)[7] and the Bank Identifier Code (BIC)[8] necessary for automated processing of cross-border credit transfers. The widest use of these codes is considered to be essential. In addition, other measures which entail extra costs should be removed in order to lower the charges to customers for cross-border payments.

(12) To lighten the burden on institutions that carry out cross-border payments, it is necessary to gradually remove the obligations concerning regular national declarations for the purposes of balance-of-payments statistics.

(13) In order to ensure that this Regulation is observed, the Member States should ensure that there are adequate and effective procedures for lodging complaints or appeals for settling any disputes between the originator and his institution or between the beneficiary and his institution, where applicable using existing procedures.

(14) It is desirable that not later than 1 July 2004 the Commission should present a report on the application of this Regulation.

(15) Provision should be made for a procedure whereby this Regulation can also be applied to cross-border payments made in a currency of another Member State where that Member State so decides,

HAVE ADOPTED THIS REGULATION:

Article 1

Subject matter and scope

This Regulation lays down rules on cross-border payments in euro in order to ensure that charges for those payments are the same as those for payments in euro within a Member State.

It shall apply to cross-border payments in euro up to EUR 50 000 within the Community.

---

[7] ISO Standard No 13613.
[8] ISO Standard No 9362.

This Regulation shall not apply to cross-border payments made between institutions for their own account.

Article 2
Definitions

For the purposes of this Regulation, the following definitions shall apply:

(a) 'cross-border payments' means:
(i) 'cross-border credit transfers' being transactions carried out on the initiative of an originator via an institution or its branch in one Member State, with a view to making an amount of money available to a beneficiary at an institution or its branch in another Member State; the originator and the beneficiary may be one and the same person,
(ii) 'cross-border electronic payment transactions' being:
– the cross-border transfers of funds effected by means of an electronic payment instrument, other than those ordered and executed by institutions,
– cross-border cash withdrawals by means of an electronic payment instrument and the loading (and unloading) of an electronic money instrument at cash dispensing machines and automated teller machines at the premises of the issuer or an institution under contract to accept the payment instrument,
(iii) 'cross-border cheques' being those paper cheques defined in the Geneva Convention providing uniform laws for cheques of 19 March 1931 drawn on an institution located within the Community and used for cross-border transactions within the Community;

(b) 'electronic payment instrument' means a remote access payment instrument and electronic money instrument that enables its holder to effect one or more electronic payment transactions;

(c) 'remote access payment instrument' means an instrument enabling a holder to access funds held on his/her account at an institution, whereby payment may be made to a payee and normally requires a personal identification code and/or any other similar proof of identity. The remote access payment instrument includes in particular payment cards (whether credit, debit, deferred debit or charge cards) and cards having phone- and home-banking applications. This definition does not include cross-border credit transfers;

(d) 'electronic money instrument' means a reloadable payment instrument, whether a stored-value card or a computer memory, on which value units are stored electronically;

(e) 'institution' means any natural or legal person which, by way of business, executes cross-border payments;

(f) 'charges levied' means any charge levied by an institution and directly linked to a cross-border payment transaction in euro.

Article 3
Charges for cross-border electronic payment transactions and credit transfers

1. With effect from 1 July 2002, charges levied by an institution in respect of cross-border electronic payment transactions in euro up to EUR 12 500 shall be the same as the charges levied by the same institution in respect of corresponding payments in euro transacted within the Member State in which the establishment of that institution executing the cross-border electronic payment transaction is located.

2. With effect from 1 July 2003 at the latest, charges levied by an institution in respect of cross-border credit transfers in euro up to EUR 12 500 shall be the same as the charges levied by the same institution in respect of corresponding credit transfers in euro transacted within the Member State in which the establishment of that institution executing the cross-border transfer is located.

3. With effect from 1 January 2006 the amount EUR 12 500 shall be raised to EUR 50 000.

Article 4
Transparency of charges

1. An institution shall make available to its customers in a readily comprehensible form, in writing, including, where appropriate, in accordance with national rules, by electronic means, prior

information on the charges levied for cross-border payments and for payments effected within the Member State in which its establishment is located.

Member States may stipulate that a statement warning consumers of the charges relating to the cross-border use of cheques must appear on cheque books.

2. Any modification of the charges shall be communicated in the same way as indicated in paragraph 1 in advance of the date of application.

3. Where institutions levy charges for exchanging currencies into and from euro, institutions shall provide their customers with:

(a) prior information on all the exchange charges which they propose to apply; and

(b) specific information on the various exchange charges which have been applied.

Article 5

Measures for facilitating cross-border transfers

1. An institution shall, where applicable, communicate to each customer upon request his International Bank Account Number (IBAN) and that institution's Bank Identifier Code (BIC).

2. The customer shall, upon request, communicate to the institution carrying out the transfer the IBAN of the beneficiary and the BIC of the beneficiary's institution. If the customer does not communicate the above information, additional charges may be levied on him by the institution. In this case, the institution must provide customers with information on the additional charges in accordance with Article 4.

3. With effect from 1 July 2003, institutions shall indicate on statements of account of each customer, or in an annex thereto, his IBAN and the institution's BIC.

4. For all cross-border invoicing of goods and services in the Community, a supplier who accepts payment by transfer shall communicate his IBAN and the BIC of his institution to his customers.

Article 6

Obligations of the Member States

1. Member States shall remove with effect from 1 July 2002 at the latest any national reporting obligations for cross-border payments up to EUR 12 500 for balance-of-payment statistics.

2. Member States shall remove with effect from 1 July 2002 at the latest any national obligations as to the minimum information to be provided concerning the beneficiary which prevent automation of payment execution.

Article 7

Compliance with this Regulation

Compliance with this Regulation shall be guaranteed by effective, proportionate and deterrent sanctions.

Article 8

Review clause

Not later than 1 July 2004, the Commission shall submit to the European Parliament and to the Council a report on the application of this Regulation, in particular on:

– changes in cross-border payment system infrastructures,

– the advisability of improving consumer services by strengthening the conditions of competition in the provision of cross-border payment services,

– the impact of the application of this Regulation on charges levied for payments made within a Member State,

– the advisability of increasing the amount provided for in Article 6(1) to EUR 50 000 as from 1 January 2006, taking into account any consequences for undertakings.

This report shall be accompanied, where appropriate, by proposals for amendments.

Article 9

Entry into force

This Regulation shall enter into force on the third day following that of its publication in the Official Journal of the European Communities.

This Regulation shall also apply to cross-border payments made in the currency of another Member State when the latter notifies the Commission of its decision to extend the Regulation's application to its currency. The notification shall be published in the Official Journal by the Commission.

The extension shall take effect 14 days after the said publication.

This Regulation shall be binding in its entirety and directly applicable in all Member States.

C.P. 22.

European Parliament and Council Directive 2002/65/EC of 23 September 2002 concerning the distance marketing of consumer financial services and amending Council Directive 90/619/EEC and Directives 97/7/EC and 98/27/EC[1]

THE EUROPEAN PARLIAMENT AND THE COUNCIL OF THE EUROPEAN UNION,

Having regard to the Treaty establishing the European Community, and in particular Article 47(2), Article 55 and Article 95 thereof,

Having regard to the proposal from the Commission,[2]

Having regard to the opinion of the Economic and Social Committee,[3]

Acting in accordance with the procedure laid down in Article 251 of the Treaty,[4]

Whereas:

(1) It is important, in the context of achieving the aims of the single market, to adopt measures designed to consolidate progressively this market and those measures must contribute to attaining a high level of consumer protection, in accordance with Articles 95 and 153 of the Treaty.

(2) Both for consumers and suppliers of financial services, the distance marketing of financial services will constitute one of the main tangible results of the completion of the internal market.

(3) Within the framework of the internal market, it is in the interest of consumers to have access without discrimination to the widest possible range of financial services available in the Community so that they can choose those that are best suited to their needs. In order to safeguard freedom of choice, which is an essential consumer right, a high degree of consumer protection is required in order to enhance consumer confidence in distance selling.

(4) It is essential to the smooth operation of the internal market for consumers to be able to negotiate and conclude contracts with a supplier established in other Member States, regardless of whether the supplier is also established in the Member State in which the consumer resides.

(5) Because of their intangible nature, financial services are particularly suited to distance selling and the establishment of a legal framework governing the distance marketing of financial services should increase consumer confidence in the use of new techniques for the distance marketing of financial services, such as electronic commerce.

(6) This Directive should be applied in conformity with the Treaty and with secondary law, including Directive 2000/31/EC[5] on electronic commerce, the latter being applicable solely to the transactions which it covers.

(7) This Directive aims to achieve the objectives set forth above without prejudice to Community or national law governing freedom to provide services or, where applicable, host Member State control and/or authorisation or supervision systems in the Member States where this is compatible with Community legislation.

(8) Moreover, this Directive, and in particular its provisions relating to information about any

---

[1] OJ L 271, 9.10.2002, 16–24.
[2] OJ C 385, 11.12.1998, 10 and OJ C 177 E, 27.6.2000, 21.
[3] OJ C 169, 16.6.1999, 43.
[4] Opinion of the European Parliament of 5 May 1999 (OJ C 279, 1.10.1999, 207), Council Common Position of 19 December 2001 (OJ C 58E, 5.3.2002, 32) and Decision of the European Parliament of 14 May 2002 (not yet published in the Official Journal). Council Decision of 26 June 2002 (not yet published in the Official Journal).

[5] OJ L 178, 17.7.2000, 1, reproduced supra under no. C.P. 19.

contractual clause on law applicable to the contract and/or on the competent court does not affect the applicability to the distance marketing of consumer financial services of Council Regulation 44/2001/EC of 22 December 2000 on jurisdiction and the recognition and enforcement of judgements in civil and commercial matters[6] or of the 1980 Rome Convention on the law applicable to contractual obligations.

(9) The achievement of the objectives of the Financial Services Action Plan requires a higher level of consumer protection in certain areas. This implies a greater convergence, in particular, in non harmonised collective investment funds, rules of conduct applicable to investment services and consumer credits. Pending the achievement of the above convergence, a high level of consumer protection should be maintained.

(10) Directive 97/7/EC of the European Parliament and of the Council of 20 May 1997 on the protection of consumers in respect of distance contracts,[7] lays down the main rules applicable to distance contracts for goods or services concluded between a supplier and a consumer. However, that Directive does not cover financial services.

(11) In the context of the analysis conducted by the Commission with a view to ascertaining the need for specific measures in the field of financial services, the Commission invited all the interested parties to transmit their comments, notably in connection with the preparation of its Green Paper entitled 'Financial Services—Meeting Consumers' Expectations'. The consultations in this context showed that there is a need to strengthen consumer protection in this area. The Commission therefore decided to present a specific proposal concerning the distance marketing of financial services.

(12) The adoption by the Member States of conflicting or different consumer protection rules governing the distance marketing of consumer financial services could impede the functioning of the internal market and competition between firms in the market. It is therefore necessary to enact common rules at Community level in this area, consistent with no reduction in overall consumer protection in the Member States.

(13) A high level of consumer protection should be guaranteed by this Directive, with a view to ensuring the free movement of financial services. Member States should not be able to adopt provisions other than those laid down in this Directive in the fields it harmonises, unless otherwise specifically indicated in it.

(14) This Directive covers all financial services liable to be provided at a distance. However, certain financial services are governed by specific provisions of Community legislation which continue to apply to those financial services. However, principles governing the distance marketing of such services should be laid down.

(15) Contracts negotiated at a distance involve the use of means of distance communication which are used as part of a distance sales or service-provision scheme not involving the simultaneous presence of the supplier and the consumer. The constant development of those means of communication requires principles to be defined that are valid even for those means which are not yet in widespread use. Therefore, distance contracts are those the offer, negotiation and conclusion of which are carried out at a distance.

(16) A single contract involving successive operations or separate operations of the same nature performed over time may be subject to different legal treatment in the different Member States, but it is important that this Directive be applied in the same way in all the Member States. To that end, it is appropriate that this Directive should be considered to apply to the first of a series of successive operations or separate operations of the same nature performed over time which may be considered as forming a whole, irrespective of whether that operation or series of operations is the subject of a single contract or several successive contracts.

(17) An 'initial service agreement' may be considered to be for example the opening of a bank

---

[6] OJ L 12, 16.1.2001, 1.
[7] OJ L 144, 4.6.1997, 19, reproduced supra under no. C.P. 11.

account, acquiring a credit card, concluding a portfolio management contract, and 'operations' may be considered to be for example the deposit or withdrawal of funds to or from the bank account, payment by credit card, transactions made within the framework of a portfolio management contract. Adding new elements to an initial service agreement, such as a possibility to use an electronic payment instrument together with one's existing bank account, does not constitute an 'operation' but an additional contract to which this Directive applies. The subscription to new units of the same collective investment fund is considered to be one of 'successive operations of the same nature'.

(18) By covering a service-provision scheme organised by the financial services provider, this Directive aims to exclude from its scope services provided on a strictly occasional basis and outside a commercial structure dedicated to the conclusion of distance contracts.

(19) The supplier is the person providing services at a distance. This Directive should however also apply when one of the marketing stages involves an intermediary. Having regard to the nature and degree of that involvement, the pertinent provisions of this Directive should apply to such an intermediary, irrespective of his or her legal status.

(20) Durable mediums include in particular floppy discs, CD-ROMs, DVDs and the hard drive of the consumer's computer on which the electronic mail is stored, but they do not include Internet websites unless they fulfil the criteria contained in the definition of a durable medium.

(21) The use of means of distance communications should not lead to an unwarranted restriction on the information provided to the client. In the interests of transparency this Directive lays down the requirements needed to ensure that an appropriate level of information is provided to the consumer both before and after conclusion of the contract. The consumer should receive, before conclusion of the contract, the prior information needed so as to properly appraise the financial service offered to him and hence make a well-informed choice. The supplier should specify how long his offer applies as it stands.

(22) Information items listed in this Directive cover information of a general nature applicable to all kinds of financial services. Other information requirements concerning a given financial service, such as the coverage of an insurance policy, are not solely specified in this Directive. This kind of information should be provided in accordance, where applicable, with relevant Community legislation or national legislation in conformity with Community law.

(23) With a view to optimum protection of the consumer, it is important that the consumer is adequately informed of the provisions of this Directive and of any codes of conduct existing in this area and that he has a right of withdrawal.

(24) When the right of withdrawal does not apply because the consumer has expressly requested the performance of a contract, the supplier should inform the consumer of this fact.

(25) Consumers should be protected against unsolicited services. Consumers should be exempt from any obligation in the case of unsolicited services, the absence of a reply not being construed as signifying consent on their part. However, this rule should be without prejudice to the tacit renewal of contracts validly concluded between the parties whenever the law of the Member States permits such tacit renewal.

(26) Member States should take appropriate measures to protect effectively consumers who do not wish to be contacted through certain means of communication or at certain times. This Directive should be without prejudice to the particular safeguards available to consumers under Community legislation concerning the protection of personal data and privacy.

(27) With a view to protecting consumers, there is a need for suitable and effective complaint and redress procedures in the Member States with a view to settling potential disputes between suppliers and consumers, by using, where appropriate, existing procedures.

(28) Member States should encourage public or private bodies established with a view to settling disputes out of court to cooperate in resolving cross-border disputes. Such cooperation could in

particular entail allowing consumers to submit to extra-judicial bodies in the Member State of their residence complaints concerning suppliers established in other Member States. The establishment of FIN-NET offers increased assistance to consumers when using cross-border services.

(29) This Directive is without prejudice to extension by Member States, in accordance with Community law, of the protection provided by this Directive to non-profit organisations and persons making use of financial services in order to become entrepreneurs.

(30) This Directive should also cover cases where the national legislation includes the concept of a consumer making a binding contractual statement.

(31) The provisions in this Directive on the supplier's choice of language should be without prejudice to provisions of national legislation, adopted in conformity with Community law governing the choice of language.

(32) The Community and the Member States have entered into commitments in the context of the General Agreement on Trade in Services (GATS) concerning the possibility for consumers to purchase banking and investment services abroad. The GATS entitles Member States to adopt measures for prudential reasons, including measures to protect investors, depositors, policyholders and persons to whom a financial service is owed by the supplier of the financial service. Such measures should not impose restrictions going beyond what is required to ensure the protection of consumers.

(33) In view of the adoption of this Directive, the scope of Directive 97/7/EC and Directive 98/27/EC of the European Parliament and of the Council of 19 May 1998 on injunctions for the protection of consumers' interests[8] and the scope of the cancellation period in Council Directive 90/619/EEC of 8 November 1990 on the coordination of laws, regulations and administrative provisions relating to direct life assurance, laying down provisions to facilitate the effective exercise of freedom to provide services[9] should be adapted.

(34) Since the objectives of this Directive, namely the establishment of common rules on the distance marketing of consumer financial services cannot be sufficiently achieved by the Member States and can therefore be better achieved at Community level, the Community may adopt measures, in accordance with the principles of subsidiarity as set out in Article 5 of the Treaty. In accordance with the principle of proportionality, as set out in that Article, this Directive does not go beyond what is necessary to achieve that objective,

HAVE ADOPTED THIS DIRECTIVE:

Article 1

Object and scope

1. The object of this Directive is to approximate the laws, regulations and administrative provisions of the Member States concerning the distance marketing of consumer financial services.

2. In the case of contracts for financial services comprising an initial service agreement followed by successive operations or a series of separate operations of the same nature performed over time, the provisions of this Directive shall apply only to the initial agreement.

In case there is no initial service agreement but the successive operations or the separate operations of the same nature performed over time are performed between the same contractual parties, Articles 3 and 4 apply only when the first operation is performed. Where, however, no operation of the same nature is performed for more than one year, the next operation will be deemed to be the first in a new series of operations and, accordingly, Articles 3 and 4 shall apply.

---

[8] OJ L 166, 11.6.1998, 51, reproduced supra under no. C.P. 15. Directive as last amended by Directive 2000/31/EC (OJ L 178, 17.7.2001, 1), reproduced supra under no. C.P. 19.

[9] OJ L 330, 29.11.1990, 50, reproduced infra under no. I. 18. Directive as last amended by Directive 92/96/EEC (OJ L 360, 9.12.1992, 1), reproduced infra under no. I. 26.

Article 2
Definitions

For the purposes of this Directive:

(a) 'distance contract' means any contract concerning financial services concluded between a supplier and a consumer under an organised distance sales or service-provision scheme run by the supplier, who, for the purpose of that contract, makes exclusive use of one or more means of distance communication up to and including the time at which the contract is concluded;

(b) 'financial service' means any service of a banking, credit, insurance, personal pension, investment or payment nature;

(c) 'supplier' means any natural or legal person, public or private, who, acting in his commercial or professional capacity, is the contractual provider of services subject to distance contracts;

(d) 'consumer' means any natural person who, in distance contracts covered by this Directive, is acting for purposes which are outside his trade, business or profession;

(e) 'means of distance communication' refers to any means which, without the simultaneous physical presence of the supplier and the consumer, may be used for the distance marketing of a service between those parties;

(f) 'durable medium' means any instrument which enables the consumer to store information addressed personally to him in a way accessible for future reference for a period of time adequate for the purposes of the information and which allows the unchanged reproduction of the information stored;

(g) 'operator or supplier of a means of distance communication' means any public or private, natural or legal person whose trade, business or profession involves making one or more means of distance communication available to suppliers.

Article 3
Information to the consumer prior to the conclusion of the distance contract

1. In good time before the consumer is bound by any distance contract or offer, he shall be provided with the following information concerning:

(1) the supplier

(a) the identity and the main business of the supplier, the geographical address at which the supplier is established and any other geographical address relevant for the customer's relations with the supplier;

(b) the identity of the representative of the supplier established in the consumer's Member State of residence and the geographical address relevant for the customer's relations with the representative, if such a representative exists;

(c) when the consumer's dealings are with any professional other than the supplier, the identity of this professional, the capacity in which he is acting vis-à-vis the consumer, and the geographical address relevant for the customer's relations with this professional;

(d) where the supplier is registered in a trade or similar public register, the trade register in which the supplier is entered and his registration number or an equivalent means of identification in that register;

(e) where the supplier's activity is subject to an authorisation scheme, the particulars of the relevant supervisory authority;

(2) the financial service

(a) a description of the main characteristics of the financial service;

(b) the total price to be paid by the consumer to the supplier for the financial service, including all related fees, charges and expenses, and all taxes paid via the supplier or, when an exact price cannot be indicated, the basis for the calculation of the price enabling the consumer to verify it;

(c) where relevant notice indicating that the financial service is related to instruments involving special risks related to their specific features or the operations to be executed or whose price depends on fluctuations in the financial markets outside the supplier's control and that historical performances are no indicators for future performances;

(d) notice of the possibility that other taxes and/or costs may exist that are not paid via the supplier or imposed by him;

(e) any limitations of the period for which the information provided is valid;

(f) the arrangements for payment and for performance;

(g) any specific additional cost for the consumer of using the means of distance communication, if such additional cost is charged;

(3) the distance contract

(a) the existence or absence of a right of withdrawal in accordance with Article 6 and, where the right of withdrawal exists, its duration and the conditions for exercising it, including information on the amount which the consumer may be required to pay on the basis of Article 7(1), as well as the consequences of non-exercise of that right;

(b) the minimum duration of the distance contract in the case of financial services to be performed permanently or recurrently;

(c) information on any rights the parties may have to terminate the contract early or unilaterally by virtue of the terms of the distance contract, including any penalties imposed by the contract in such cases;

(d) practical instructions for exercising the right of withdrawal indicating, inter alia, the address to which the notification of a withdrawal should be sent;

(e) the Member State or States whose laws are taken by the supplier as a basis for the establishment of relations with the consumer prior to the conclusion of the distance contract;

(f) any contractual clause on law applicable to the distance contract and/or on competent court;

(g) in which language, or languages, the contractual terms and conditions, and the prior information referred to in this Article are supplied, and furthermore in which language, or languages, the supplier, with the agreement of the consumer, undertakes to communicate during the duration of this distance contract;

(4) redress

(a) whether or not there is an out-of-court complaint and redress mechanism for the consumer that is party to the distance contract and, if so, the methods for having access to it;

(b) the existence of guarantee funds or other compensation arrangements, not covered by Directive 94/19/EC of the European Parliament and of the Council of 30 May 1994 on deposit guarantee schemes[10] and Directive 97/9/EC of the European Parliament and of the Council of 3 March 1997 on investor compensation schemes.[11]

2. The information referred to in paragraph 1, the commercial purpose of which must be made clear, shall be provided in a clear and comprehensible manner in any way appropriate to the means of distance communication used, with due regard, in particular, to the principles of good faith in commercial transactions, and the principles governing the protection of those who are unable, pursuant to the legislation of the Member States, to give their consent, such as minors.

3. In the case of voice telephony communications

(a) the identity of the supplier and the commercial purpose of the call initiated by the supplier shall be made explicitly clear at the beginning of any conversation with the consumer;

(b) subject to the explicit consent of the consumer only the following information needs to be given:

– the identity of the person in contact with the consumer and his link with the supplier,

– a description of the main characteristics of the financial service,

– the total price to be paid by the consumer to the supplier for the financial service including all taxes paid via the supplier or, when an exact price cannot be indicated, the basis for the calculation of the price enabling the consumer to verify it,

– notice of the possibility that other taxes and/or costs may exist that are not paid via the supplier or imposed by him,

– the existence or absence of a right of withdrawal in accordance with Article 6 and, where the right of withdrawal exists, its duration and the

---

[10] OJ L 135, 31.5.1994, 5, reproduced supra under no. B. 22.
[11] OJ L 84, 26.3.1997, 22, reproduced infra under no. S. 16.

conditions for exercising it, including information on the amount which the consumer may be required to pay on the basis of Article 7(1).

The supplier shall inform the consumer that other information is available on request and of what nature this information is. In any case the supplier shall provide the full information when he fulfils his obligations under Article 5.

4. Information on contractual obligations, to be communicated to the consumer during the pre-contractual phase, shall be in conformity with the contractual obligations which would result from the law presumed to be applicable to the distance contract if the latter were concluded.

Article 4

Additional information requirements

1. Where there are provisions in the Community legislation governing financial services which contain prior information requirements additional to those listed in Article 3(1), these requirements shall continue to apply.

2. Pending further harmonisation, Member States may maintain or introduce more stringent provisions on prior information requirements when the provisions are in conformity with Community law.

3. Member States shall communicate to the Commission national provisions on prior information requirements under paragraphs 1 and 2 of this Article when these requirements are additional to those listed in Article 3(1). The Commission shall take account of the communicated national provisions when drawing up the report referred to in Article 20(2).

4. The Commission shall, with a view to creating a high level of transparency by all appropriate means, ensure that information, on the national provisions communicated to it, is made available to consumers and suppliers.

Article 5

Communication of the contractual terms and conditions and of the prior information

1. The supplier shall communicate to the consumer all the contractual terms and conditions and the information referred to in Article 3(1) and Article 4 on paper or on another durable medium available and accessible to the consumer in good time before the consumer is bound by any distance contract or offer.

2. The supplier shall fulfil his obligation under paragraph 1 immediately after the conclusion of the contract, if the contract has been concluded at the consumer's request using a means of distance communication which does not enable providing the contractual terms and conditions and the information in conformity with paragraph 1.

3. At any time during the contractual relationship the consumer is entitled, at his request, to receive the contractual terms and conditions on paper. In addition, the consumer is entitled to change the means of distance communication used, unless this is incompatible with the contract concluded or the nature of the financial service provided.

Article 6

Right of withdrawal

1. The Member States shall ensure that the consumer shall have a period of 14 calendar days to withdraw from the contract without penalty and without giving any reason. However, this period shall be extended to 30 calendar days in distance contracts relating to life insurance covered by Directive 90/619/EEC and personal pension operations.

The period for withdrawal shall begin:
– either from the day of the conclusion of the distance contract, except in respect of the said life assurance, where the time limit will begin from the time when the consumer is informed that the distance contract has been concluded, or
– from the day on which the consumer receives the contractual terms and conditions and the information in accordance with Article 5(1) or (2), if that is later than the date referred to in the first indent.

Member States, in addition to the right of withdrawal, may provide that the enforceability of contracts relating to investment services is suspended for the same period provided for in this paragraph.

2. The right of withdrawal shall not apply to:

(a) financial services whose price depends on fluctuations in the financial market outside the suppliers control, which may occur during the withdrawal period, such as services related to:
– foreign exchange,
– money market instruments,
– transferable securities,
– units in collective investment undertakings,
– financial-futures contracts, including equivalent cash-settled instruments,
– forward interest-rate agreements (FRAs),
– interest-rate, currency and equity swaps,
– options to acquire or dispose of any instruments referred to in this point including equivalent cash-settled instruments. This category includes in particular options on currency and on interest rates;

(b) travel and baggage insurance policies or similar short-term insurance policies of less than one month's duration;

(c) contracts whose performance has been fully completed by both parties at the consumer's express request before the consumer exercises his right of withdrawal.

3. Member States may provide that the right of withdrawal shall not apply to:

(a) any credit intended primarily for the purpose of acquiring or retaining property rights in land or in an existing or projected building, or for the purpose of renovating or improving a building, or

(b) any credit secured either by mortgage on immovable property or by a right related to immovable property, or

(c) declarations by consumers using the services of an official, provided that the official confirms that the consumer is guaranteed the rights under Article 5(1).

This paragraph shall be without prejudice to the right to a reflection time to the benefit of the consumers that are resident in those Member States where it exists, at the time of the adoption of this Directive.

4. Member States making use of the possibility set out in paragraph 3 shall communicate it to the Commission.

5. The Commission shall make available the information communicated by Member States to the European Parliament and the Council and shall ensure that it is also available to consumers and suppliers who request it.

6. If the consumer exercises his right of withdrawal he shall, before the expiry of the relevant deadline, notify this following the practical instructions given to him in accordance with Article 3(1)(3)(d) by means which can be proved in accordance with national law. The deadline shall be deemed to have been observed if the notification, if it is on paper or on another durable medium available and accessible to the recipient, is dispatched before the deadline expires.

7. This Article does not apply to credit agreements cancelled under the conditions of Article 6(4) of Directive 97/7/EC or Article 7 of Directive 94/47/EC of the European Parliament and of the Council of 26 October 1994 on the protection of purchasers in respect of certain aspects of contracts relating to the purchase of the right to use immovable properties on a timeshare basis.[12]

If to a distance contract of a given financial service another distance contract has been attached concerning services provided by the supplier or by a third party on the basis of an agreement between the third party and the supplier, this additional distance contract shall be cancelled, without any penalty, if the consumer exercises his right of withdrawal as provided for in Article 6(1).

8. The provisions of this Article are without prejudice to the Member States' laws and regulations governing the cancellation or termination or non-enforceability of a distance contract or the right of a consumer to fulfil his contractual obligations before the time fixed in the distance contract. This applies irrespective of the conditions for and the legal effects of the winding-up of the contract.

Article 7

Payment of the service provided before withdrawal

1. When the consumer exercises his right of withdrawal under Article 6(1) he may only be

---

[12] OJ L 280, 29.10.1994, 83.

required to pay, without any undue delay, for the service actually provided by the supplier in accordance with the contract. The performance of the contract may only begin after the consumer has given his approval. The amount payable shall not:
– exceed an amount which is in proportion to the extent of the service already provided in comparison with the full coverage of the contract,
– in any case be such that it could be construed as a penalty.

2. Member States may provide that the consumer cannot be required to pay any amount when withdrawing from an insurance contract.

3. The supplier may not require the consumer to pay any amount on the basis of paragraph 1 unless he can prove that the consumer was duly informed about the amount payable, in conformity with Article 3(1)(3)(a). However, in no case may he require such payment if he has commenced the performance of the contract before the expiry of the withdrawal period provided for in Article 6(1) without the consumer's prior request.

4. The supplier shall, without any undue delay and no later than within 30 calendar days, return to the consumer any sums he has received from him in accordance with the distance contract, except for the amount referred to in paragraph 1. This period shall begin from the day on which the supplier receives the notification of withdrawal.

5. The consumer shall return to the supplier any sums and/or property he has received from the supplier without any undue delay and no later than within 30 calendar days. This period shall begin from the day on which the consumer dispatches the notification of withdrawal.

Article 8

Payment by card

Member States shall ensure that appropriate measures exist to allow a consumer:
– to request cancellation of a payment where fraudulent use has been made of his payment card in connection with distance contracts,
– in the event of such fraudulent use, to be re-credited with the sum paid or have them returned.

[*Article 9*

Given the prohibition of inertia selling practices laid down in Directive 2005/29/EC of 11 May 2005 of the European Parliament and of the Council concerning unfair business-to-consumer commercial practices in the internal market[13] and without prejudice to the provisions of Member States' legislation on the tacit renewal of distance contracts, when such rules permit tacit renewal, Member States shall take measures to exempt the consumer from any obligation in the event of unsolicited supplies, the absence of a reply not constituting consent.]

¶ *This article has been replaced by article 15(2) of Directive 2005/29/EC, reproduced infra under no. C.P. 24.*

Article 10

Unsolicited communications

1. The use by a supplier of the following distance communication techniques shall require the consumer's prior consent:

(a) automated calling systems without human intervention (automatic calling machines);

(b) fax machines.

2. Member States shall ensure that means of distance communication other than those referred to in paragraph 1, when they allow individual communications:

(a) shall not be authorised unless the consent of the consumers concerned has been obtained, or

(b) may only be used if the consumer has not expressed his manifest objection.

3. The measures referred to in paragraphs 1 and 2 shall not entail costs for consumers.

Article 11

Sanctions

Member States shall provide for appropriate sanctions in the event of the supplier's failure to comply with national provisions adopted pursuant to this Directive.

---

[13] OJ L 149, 11.6.2005, 22, reproduced infra under no. C.P. 24.

They may provide for this purpose in particular that the consumer may cancel the contract at any time, free of charge and without penalty.

These sanctions must be effective, proportional and dissuasive.

Article 12

Imperative nature of this Directive's provisions

1. Consumers may not waive the rights conferred on them by this Directive.

2. Member States shall take the measures needed to ensure that the consumer does not lose the protection granted by this Directive by virtue of the choice of the law of a non-member country as the law applicable to the contract, if this contract has a close link with the territory of one or more Member States.

Article 13

Judicial and administrative redress

1. Member States shall ensure that adequate and effective means exist to ensure compliance with this Directive in the interests of consumers.

2. The means referred to in paragraph 1 shall include provisions whereby one or more of the following bodies, as determined by national law, may take action in accordance with national law before the courts or competent administrative bodies to ensure that the national provisions for the implementation of this Directive are applied:

(a) public bodies or their representatives;

(b) consumer organisations having a legitimate interest in protecting consumers;

(c) professional organisations having a legitimate interest in acting.

3. Member States shall take the measures necessary to ensure that operators and suppliers of means of distance communication put an end to practices that have been declared to be contrary to this Directive, on the basis of a judicial decision, an administrative decision or a decision issued by a supervisory authority notified to them, where those operators or suppliers are in a position to do so.

Article 14

Out-of-court redress

1. Member States shall promote the setting up or development of adequate and effective out-of-court complaints and redress procedures for the settlement of consumer disputes concerning financial services provided at distance.

2. Member States shall, in particular, encourage the bodies responsible for out-of-court settlement of disputes to cooperate in the resolution of cross-border disputes concerning financial services provided at distance.

Article 15

Burden of proof

Without prejudice to Article 7(3), Member States may stipulate that the burden of proof in respect of the supplier's obligations to inform the consumer and the consumer's consent to conclusion of the contract and, where appropriate, its performance, can be placed on the supplier.

Any contractual term or condition providing that the burden of proof of the respect by the supplier of all or part of the obligations incumbent on him pursuant to this Directive should lie with the consumer shall be an unfair term within the meaning of Council Directive 93/13/EEC of 5 April 1993 on unfair terms in consumer contracts.[14]

Article 16

Transitional measures

Member States may impose national rules which are in conformity with this Directive on suppliers established in a Member State which has not yet transposed this Directive and whose law has no obligations corresponding to those provided for in this Directive.

Article 17

[...]

¶ *Article 17 replaces the first paragraph of article 15 of Directive 90/619/EEC, reproduced infra under no. I. 18. The modifications are directly incorporated therein.*

---

[14] OJ L 95, 21.4.1993, 29, reproduced supra under no. C.P. 9.

Article 18

[...]

¶ *Article 18 amends the first indent of article 3(1) and deletes Annex II of Directive 97/7/EC, reproduced supra under no. C.P. 11. The modifications are directly incorporated therein.*

Article 19

[...]

¶ *Article 19 adds point 11 of the Annex of Directive 98/27/EC, reproduced supra under no. C.P. 15. The modifications are directly incorporated therein.*

Article 20

Review

1. Following the implementation of this Directive, the Commission shall examine the functioning of the internal market in financial services in respect of the marketing of those services. It should seek to analyse and detail the difficulties that are, or might be faced by both consumers and suppliers, in particular arising from differences between national provisions regarding information and right of withdrawal.

2. Not later than 9 April 2006 the Commission shall report to the European Parliament and the Council on the problems facing both consumers and suppliers seeking to buy and sell financial services, and shall submit, where appropriate, proposals to amend and/or further harmonise the information and right of withdrawal provisions in Community legislation concerning financial services and/or those covered in Article 3.

Article 21

Transposition

1. Member States shall bring into force the laws, regulations and administrative provisions necessary to comply with this Directive not later than 9 October 2004. They shall forthwith inform the Commission thereof.

When Member States adopt these measures, they shall contain a reference to this Directive or shall be accompanied by such a reference on the occasion of their official publication. The methods of making such reference shall be laid down by Member States.

2. Member States shall communicate to the Commission the text of the main provisions of national law which they adopt in the field governed by this Directive together with a table showing how the provisions of this Directive correspond to the national provisions adopted.

Article 22

Entry into force

This Directive shall enter into force on the day of its publication in the Official Journal of the European Communities.

Article 23

Addressees

This Directive is addressed to the Member States.

C.P. 23.

European Parliament and Council Regulation 2006/2004/EC of 27 October 2004 on cooperation between national authorities responsible for the enforcement of consumer protection laws (the Regulation on consumer protection cooperation)[1]

(Text with EEA relevance)

THE EUROPEAN PARLIAMENT AND THE COUNCIL OF THE EUROPEAN UNION,

Having regard to the Treaty establishing the European Community, and in particular Article 95 thereof,

Having regard to the proposal from the Commission,

Having regard to the opinion of the European Economic and Social Committee,[2]

After consulting the Committee of the Regions,

Acting in accordance with the procedure laid down in Article 251 of the Treaty,[3]

Whereas:

(1) The Council Resolution of 8 July 1996 on cooperation between administrations for the enforcement of legislation on the internal market[4] acknowledged that a continuing effort is required to improve cooperation between administrations and invited the Member States and the Commission to examine as a matter of priority the possibility of reinforcing administrative cooperation in the enforcement of legislation.

(2) Existing national enforcement arrangements for the laws that protect consumers' interests are not adapted to the challenges of enforcement in the internal market and effective and efficient enforcement cooperation in these cases is not currently possible. These difficulties give rise to barriers to cooperation between public enforcement authorities to detect, investigate and bring about the cessation or prohibition of intra-Community infringements of the laws that protect consumers' interests. The resulting lack of effective enforcement in cross-border cases enables sellers and suppliers to evade enforcement attempts by relocating within the Community. This gives rise to a distortion of competition for law-abiding sellers and suppliers operating either domestically or cross-border. The difficulties of enforcement in cross-border cases also undermine the confidence of consumers in taking up cross-border offers and hence their confidence in the internal market.

(3) It is therefore appropriate to facilitate cooperation between public authorities responsible for enforcement of the laws that protect consumers' interests in dealing with intra-Community infringements, and to contribute to the smooth functioning of the internal market, the quality and consistency of enforcement of the laws that protect consumers' interests and the monitoring of the protection of consumers' economic interests.

(4) Enforcement cooperation networks exist in Community legislation, to protect consumers above and beyond their economic interests, not least where health is concerned. Best practice should be exchanged between the networks established by this Regulation and these other networks.

(5) The scope of the provisions on mutual assistance in this Regulation should be limited to intra-Community infringements of Community legislation that protects consumers' interests. The

---

[1] OJ L 341, 9.12.2004, 1–11.
[2] OJ C 108, 30.4.2004, 86.
[3] Opinion of the European Parliament of 20 April 2004 (not yet published in the Official Journal) and Council Decision of 7 October 2004.
[4] OJ C 224, 1.8.1996, 3.

effectiveness with which infringements at national level are pursued should ensure that there is no discrimination between national and intra-Community transactions. This Regulation does not affect the responsibilities of the Commission with regard to infringements of Community law by the Member States, nor does it confer on the Commission powers to stop intra-Community infringements defined in this Regulation.

(6) The protection of consumers from intra-Community infringements requires the establishment of a network of public enforcement authorities throughout the Community and these authorities require a minimum of common investigation and enforcement powers to apply this Regulation effectively and to deter sellers or suppliers from committing intra-Community infringements.

(7) The ability of competent authorities to cooperate freely on a reciprocal basis in exchanging information, detecting and investigating intra-Community infringements and taking action to bring about their cessation or prohibition is essential to guaranteeing the smooth functioning of the internal market and the protection of consumers.

(8) Competent authorities should also make use of other powers or measures granted to them at national level, including the power to initiate or refer matters for criminal prosecution, in order to bring about the cessation or prohibition of intra-Community infringements without delay as a result of a request for mutual assistance, where this is appropriate.

(9) Information exchanged between competent authorities should be subject to the strictest guarantees of confidentiality and professional secrecy in order to ensure investigations are not compromised or the reputation of sellers or suppliers unfairly harmed. Directive 95/46/EC of the European Parliament and of the Council of 24 October 1995 on the protection of individuals with regard to the processing of personal data and on the free movement of such data[5] and Regulation (EC) No 45/2001 of the European Parliament and of the Council of 18 December 2000 on the protection of individuals with regard to the processing of personal data by the Community institutions and bodies and on the free movement of such data[6] should apply in the context of this Regulation.

(10) The enforcement challenges that exist go beyond the frontiers of the European Union and the interests of Community consumers need to be protected from rogue traders based in third countries. Hence, there is a need for international agreements to be negotiated with third countries regarding mutual assistance in the enforcement of the laws that protect consumers' interests. These international agreements should be negotiated at Community level in the areas covered by this Regulation in order to ensure the optimum protection of Community consumers and the smooth functioning of enforcement cooperation with third countries.

(11) It is appropriate to coordinate at Community level the enforcement activities of the Member States in respect of intra-Community infringements in order to improve the application of this Regulation and contribute to raising the standard and consistency of enforcement.

(12) It is appropriate to coordinate at Community level the administrative cooperation activities of the Member States, in respect of their intra-Community dimension, in order to improve the application of the laws that protect consumers' interests. This role has already been demonstrated in the establishment of the European extra-judicial network.

(13) Where the coordination of the activities of the Member States under this Regulation entails Community financial support, the decision to grant such support shall be taken in accordance with the procedures set out in Decision No 20/2004/EC of the European Parliament and of the Council of 8 December 2003 establishing a general framework for financing Community actions in support of consumer policy for the

---

[5] OJ L 281, 23.11.1995, 31. Directive as amended by Regulation (EC) No 1882/2003 (OJ L 284, 31.10.2003, 1).

[6] OJ L 8, 12.1.2001, 1.

years 2004 to 2007,⁷ in particular Actions 5 and 10 set out in the Annex to that Decision and future Decisions.

(14) Consumer organisations play an essential role in terms of consumer information and education and in the protection of consumer interests, including in the settlement of disputes, and should be encouraged to cooperate with competent authorities to enhance the application of this Regulation.

(15) The measures necessary for the implementation of this Regulation should be adopted in accordance with Council Decision 1999/468/EC of 28 June 1999 laying down the procedures for the exercise of implementing powers conferred on the Commission.⁸

(16) The effective monitoring of the application of this Regulation and the effectiveness of consumer protection requires regular reports from the Member States.

(17) This Regulation respects the fundamental rights and observes the principles recognised in particular by the Charter of Fundamental Rights of the European Union.⁹ Accordingly this Regulation should be interpreted and applied with respect to those rights and principles.

(18) Since the objective of this Regulation, namely cooperation between national authorities responsible for the enforcement of consumer protection law, cannot be sufficiently achieved by the Member States because they cannot ensure cooperation and coordination by acting alone, and can therefore be better achieved at Community level, the Community may adopt measures, in accordance with the principle of subsidiarity as set out in Article 5 of the Treaty. In accordance with the principle of proportionality, as set out in that Article, this Regulation does not go beyond what is necessary in order to achieve that objective,

HAVE ADOPTED THIS REGULATION:

Chapter I
Introductory Provisions

Article 1
Objective

This Regulation lays down the conditions under which the competent authorities in the Member States designated as responsible for the enforcement of the laws that protect consumers' interests shall cooperate with each other and with the Commission in order to ensure compliance with those laws and the smooth functioning of the internal market and in order to enhance the protection of consumers' economic interests.

Article 2
Scope

1. The provisions on mutual assistance set out in Chapters II and III shall cover intra-Community infringements.

2. This Regulation shall be without prejudice to the Community rules on private international law, in particular rules related to court jurisdiction and applicable law.

3. This Regulation shall be without prejudice to the application in the Member States of measures relating to judicial cooperation in criminal and civil matters, in particular the operation of the European Judicial Network.

4. This Regulation shall be without prejudice to the fulfilment by the Member States of any additional obligations in relation to mutual assistance on the protection of the collective economic interests of consumers, including in criminal matters, ensuing from other legal acts, including bilateral or multilateral agreements.

5. This Regulation shall be without prejudice to Directive 98/27/EC of the European Parliament and of the Council of 19 May 1998 on injunctions for the protection of consumers' interests.¹⁰

---

⁷ OJ L 5, 9.1.2004, 1. Decision as amended by Decision No 786/2004/EC (OJ L 138, 30.4.2004, 7).
⁸ OJ L 184, 17.7.1999, 23.
⁹ OJ C 364, 18.12.2000, 1.

¹⁰ OJ L 166, 11.6.1998, 51, reproduced supra under no. C.P. 15. Directive as last amended by Directive 2002/65/EC

6. This Regulation shall be without prejudice to Community law relating to the internal market, in particular those provisions concerning the free movement of goods and services.

7. This Regulation shall be without prejudice to Community law relating to television broadcasting services.

Article 3
Definitions

For the purposes of this Regulation:

(a) "laws that protect consumers' interests" means the Directives as transposed into the internal legal order of the Member States and the Regulations listed in the Annex;

(b) "intra-Community infringement" means any act or omission contrary to the laws that protect consumers' interests, as defined in (a), that harms, or is likely to harm, the collective interests of consumers residing in a Member State or Member States other than the Member State where the act or omission originated or took place; or where the responsible seller or supplier is established; or where evidence or assets pertaining to the act or omission are to be found;

(c) "competent authority" means any public authority established either at national, regional or local level with specific responsibilities to enforce the laws that protect consumers' interests;

(d) "single liaison office" means the public authority in each Member State designated as responsible for coordinating the application of this Regulation within that Member State;

(e) "competent official" means an official of a competent authority designated as responsible for the application of this Regulation;

(f) "applicant authority" means the competent authority that makes a request for mutual assistance;

(g) "requested authority" means the competent authority that receives a request for mutual assistance;

(h) "seller or supplier" means any natural or legal person who, in respect of the laws that protect consumers' interests, is acting for purposes relating to his trade, business, craft or profession;

(i) "market surveillance activities" means the actions of a competent authority designed to detect whether intra-Community infringements have taken place within its territory;

(j) "consumer complaint" means a statement, supported by reasonable evidence, that a seller or supplier has committed, or is likely to commit, an infringement of the laws that protect consumers' interests;

(k) "collective interests of consumers" means the interests of a number of consumers that have been harmed or are likely to be harmed by an infringement.

Article 4
Competent authorities

1. Each Member State shall designate the competent authorities and a single liaison office responsible for the application of this Regulation.

2. Each Member State may, if necessary in order to fulfil its obligations under this Regulation, designate other public authorities. They may also designate bodies having a legitimate interest in the cessation or prohibition of intra-Community infringements in accordance with Article 8(3).

3. Each competent authority shall, without prejudice to paragraph 4, have the investigation and enforcement powers necessary for the application of this Regulation and shall exercise them in conformity with national law.

4. The competent authorities may exercise the powers referred to in paragraph 3 in conformity with national law either:

(a) directly under their own authority or under the supervision of the judicial authorities; or

(b) by application to courts competent to grant the necessary decision, including, where appropriate, by appeal, if the application to grant the necessary decision is not successful.

5. Insofar as competent authorities exercise their powers by application to the courts in accordance

---

(OJ L 271, 9.10.2002, 16), reproduced supra under no. C.P. 22.

with paragraph 4(b), those courts shall be competent to grant the necessary decisions.

6. The powers referred to in paragraph 3 shall only be exercised where there is a reasonable suspicion of an intra-Community infringement and shall include, at least, the right:

(a) to have access to any relevant document, in any form, related to the intra-Community infringement;

(b) to require the supply by any person of relevant information related to the intra-Community infringement;

(c) to carry out necessary on-site inspections;

(d) to request in writing that the seller or supplier concerned cease the intra-Community infringement;

(e) to obtain from the seller or supplier responsible for intra-Community infringements an undertaking to cease the intra-Community infringement; and, where appropriate, to publish the resulting undertaking;

(f) to require the cessation or prohibition of any intra-Community infringement and, where appropriate, to publish resulting decisions;

(g) to require the losing defendant to make payments into the public purse or to any beneficiary designated in or under national legislation, in the event of failure to comply with the decision.

7. Member States shall ensure that competent authorities have adequate resources necessary for the application of this Regulation. The competent officials shall observe professional standards and be subject to appropriate internal procedures or rules of conduct that ensure, in particular, the protection of individuals with regard to the processing of personal data, procedural fairness and the proper observance of the confidentiality and professional secrecy provisions established in Article 13.

8. Each competent authority shall make known to the general public the rights and responsibilities it has been granted under this Regulation and shall designate the competent officials.

Article 5
Lists

1. Each Member State shall communicate to the Commission and the other Member States the identities of the competent authorities, of other public authorities and bodies having a legitimate interest in the cessation or prohibition of intra-Community infringements, and of the single liaison office.

2. The Commission shall publish and update the list of single liaison offices and competent authorities in the Official Journal of the European Union.

CHAPTER II
MUTUAL ASSISTANCE

Article 6
Exchange of information on request

1. A requested authority shall, on request from an applicant authority, in accordance with Article 4, supply without delay any relevant information required to establish whether an intra-Community infringement has occurred or to establish whether there is a reasonable suspicion it may occur.

2. The requested authority shall undertake, if necessary with the assistance of other public authorities, the appropriate investigations or any other necessary or appropriate measures in accordance with Article 4, in order to gather the required information.

3. On request from the applicant authority, the requested authority may permit a competent official of the applicant authority to accompany the officials of the requested authority in the course of their investigations.

4. The measures necessary for the implementation of this Article shall be adopted in accordance with the procedure referred to in Article 19(2).

Article 7
Exchange of information without request

1. When a competent authority becomes aware of an intra-Community infringement, or reasonably suspects that such an infringement may occur, it shall notify the competent authorities of other Member States and the Commission, supplying all necessary information, without delay.

2. When a competent authority takes further enforcement measures or receives requests for mutual assistance in relation to the intra-Community infringement, it shall notify the competent authorities of other Member States and the Commission.

3. The measures necessary for the implementation of this Article shall be adopted in accordance with the procedure referred to in Article 19(2).

Article 8
Requests for enforcement measures

1. A requested authority shall, on request from an applicant authority, take all necessary enforcement measures to bring about the cessation or prohibition of the intra-Community infringement without delay.

2. In order to fulfil its obligations under paragraph 1, the requested authority shall exercise the powers set out under Article 4(6) and any additional powers granted to it under national law. The requested authority shall determine, if necessary with the assistance of other public authorities, the enforcement measures to be taken to bring about the cessation or prohibition of the intra-Community infringement in a proportionate, efficient and effective way.

3. The requested authority may also fulfil its obligations under paragraphs 1 and 2 by instructing a body designated in accordance with the second sentence of Article 4(2) as having a legitimate interest in the cessation or prohibition of intra-Community infringements to take all necessary enforcement measures available to it under national law to bring about the cessation or prohibition of the intra-Community infringement on behalf of the requested authority. In the event of a failure by that body to bring about the cessation or prohibition of the intra-Community infringement without delay, the obligations of the requested authority under paragraphs 1 and 2 shall remain.

4. The requested authority may only take the measures set out in paragraph 3 if, after consultation with the applicant authority on the use of these measures, both applicant and requested authority are in agreement that:
– use of the measures in paragraph 3 is likely to bring about the cessation or prohibition of the intra-Community infringement in at least equally efficient and effective a way as action by the requested authority,

and
– the instruction of the body designated under national law does not give rise to any disclosure to that body of information protected under Article 13.

5. If the applicant authority is of the opinion that the conditions set out under paragraph 4 are not fulfilled, it shall inform the requested authority in writing, setting out the grounds for its opinion. If the applicant authority and the requested authority are not in agreement, the requested authority may refer the matter to the Commission, which shall issue an opinion in accordance with the procedure referred to in Article 19(2).

6. The requested authority may consult the applicant authority in the course of taking the enforcement measures referred to in paragraphs 1 and 2. The requested authority shall notify without delay the applicant authority, the competent authorities of other Member States and the Commission of the measures taken and the effect thereof on the intra-Community infringement, including whether it has ceased.

7. The measures necessary for the implementation of this Article shall be adopted in accordance with the procedure referred to in Article 19(2).

Article 9
Coordination of market surveillance and enforcement activities

1. Competent authorities shall coordinate their market surveillance and enforcement activities. They shall exchange all information necessary to achieve this.

2. When competent authorities become aware that an intra-Community infringement harms the interests of consumers in more than two Member States, the competent authorities concerned shall coordinate their enforcement actions and requests for mutual assistance via the single liaison office. In particular they shall seek to conduct simultaneous investigations and enforcement measures.

3. The competent authorities shall inform the Commission in advance of this coordination and may invite the officials and other accompanying persons authorised by the Commission to participate.

4. The measures necessary for the implementation of this Article shall be adopted in accordance with the procedure referred to in Article 19(2).

Article 10
Database

1. The Commission shall maintain an electronic database in which it shall store and process the information it receives under Articles 7, 8 and 9. The database shall be made available for consultation only by the competent authorities. In relation to their responsibilities to notify information for storage in the database and the processing of personal data involved therein, the competent authorities shall be regarded as controllers in accordance with Article 2(d) of Directive 95/46/EC. In relation to its responsibilities under this Article and the processing of personal data involved therein, the Commission shall be regarded as a controller in accordance with Article 2(d) of Regulation (EC) No 45/2001.

2. Where a competent authority establishes that a notification of an intra-Community infringement made by it pursuant to Article 7 has subsequently proved to be unfounded, it shall withdraw the notification and the Commission shall without delay remove the information from the database. Where a requested authority notifies the Commission under Article 8(6) that an intra-Community infringement has ceased, the stored data relating to the intra-Community infringement shall be deleted five years after the notification.

3. The measures necessary for the implementation of this Article shall be adopted in accordance with the procedure referred to in Article 19(2).

CHAPTER III
CONDITIONS GOVERNING MUTUAL ASSISTANCE

Article 11
General responsibilities

1. Competent authorities shall fulfil their obligations under this Regulation as though acting on behalf of consumers in their own country and on their own account or at the request of another competent authority in their own country.

2. Member States shall take all necessary measures to ensure effective coordination of the application of this Regulation by the competent authorities, other public authorities, bodies having a legitimate interest in the cessation or prohibition of intra-Community infringements designated by them and the competent courts, through the single liaison office.

3. Member States shall encourage cooperation between the competent authorities and any other bodies having a legitimate interest under national law in the cessation or prohibition of intra-Community infringements to ensure that potential intra-Community infringements are notified to competent authorities without delay.

Article 12
Request for mutual assistance and information exchange procedures

1. The applicant authority shall ensure that all requests for mutual assistance contain sufficient

information to enable a requested authority to fulfil the request, including any necessary evidence obtainable only in the territory of the applicant authority.

2. Requests shall be sent by the applicant authority to the single liaison office of the requested authority, via the single liaison office of the applicant authority. Requests shall be forwarded by the single liaison office of the requested authority to the appropriate competent authority without delay.

3. Requests for assistance and all communication of information shall be made in writing using a standard form and communicated electronically via the database established in Article 10.

4. The languages used for requests and for the communication of information shall be agreed by the competent authorities in question before requests have been made. If no agreement can be reached, requests shall be communicated in the official language(s) of the Member State of the applicant authority and responses in the official language(s) of the Member State of the requested authority.

5. Information communicated as a result of a request shall be communicated directly to the applicant authority and simultaneously to the single liaison offices of the applicant and requested authorities.

6. The measures necessary for the implementation of this Article shall be adopted in accordance with the procedure referred to in Article 19(2).

Article 13

Use of information and protection of personal data and professional and commercial secrecy

1. Information communicated may only be used for the purposes of ensuring compliance with the laws that protect consumers' interests.

2. Competent authorities may invoke as evidence any information, documents, findings, statements, certified true copies or intelligence communicated, on the same basis as similar documents obtained in their own country.

3. Information communicated in any form to persons working for competent authorities, courts, other public authorities and the Commission, including information notified to the Commission and stored on the database referred to in Article 10, the disclosure of which would undermine:

– the protection of the privacy and the integrity of the individual, in particular in accordance with Community legislation regarding the protection of personal data,
– the commercial interests of a natural or legal person, including intellectual property,
– court proceedings and legal advice,
or
– the purpose of inspections or investigations,

shall be confidential and be covered by the obligation of professional secrecy, unless its disclosure is necessary to bring about the cessation or prohibition of an intra-Community infringement and the authority communicating the information consents to its disclosure.

4. For the purpose of applying this Regulation, Member States shall adopt the legislative measures necessary to restrict the rights and obligations under Articles 10, 11 and 12 of Directive 95/46/EC as necessary to safeguard the interests referred to in Article 13(1)(d) and (f) of that Directive. The Commission may restrict the rights and obligations under Articles 4(1), 11, 12(1), 13 to 17 and 37(1) of Regulation (EC) No 45/2001 where such restriction constitutes a necessary measure to safeguard the interests referred to in Article 20(1)(a) and (e) of that Regulation.

5. The measures necessary for the implementation of this Article shall be adopted in accordance with the procedure referred to in Article 19(2).

Article 14

Information exchange with third countries

1. When a competent authority receives information from an authority of a third country, it shall communicate the information to the relevant competent authorities of other Member States, insofar as it is permitted so to do by

bilateral assistance agreements with the third country and in accordance with Community legislation regarding the protection of individuals with regard to the processing of personal data.

2. Information communicated under this Regulation may also be communicated to an authority of a third country by a competent authority under a bilateral assistance agreement with the third country, provided the consent of the competent authority that originally communicated the information has been obtained and in accordance with Community legislation regarding the protection of individuals with regard to the processing of personal data.

Article 15
Conditions

1. Member States shall waive all claims for the reimbursement of expenses incurred in applying this Regulation. However, the Member State of the applicant authority shall remain liable to the Member State of the requested authority for any costs and any losses incurred as a result of measures held to be unfounded by a court as far as the substance of the intra-Community infringement is concerned.

2. A requested authority may refuse to comply with a request for enforcement measures under Article 8, following consultation with the applicant authority, if:

(a) judicial proceedings have already been initiated or final judgment has already been passed in respect of the same intra-Community infringements and against the same sellers or suppliers before the judicial authorities in the Member State of the requested or applicant authority;

(b) in its opinion, following appropriate investigation by the requested authority, no intra-Community infringement has taken place;

or

(c) in its opinion the applicant authority has not provided sufficient information in accordance with Article 12(1) except when the requested authority has already refused to comply with a request under paragraph (3)(c) in relation to the same intra-Community infringement.

3. A requested authority may refuse to comply with a request for information under Article 6 if:

(a) in its opinion, following consultation with the applicant authority, the information requested is not required by the applicant authority to establish whether an intra-Community infringement has occurred or to establish whether there is a reasonable suspicion it may occur;

(b) the applicant authority does not agree that the information is subject to the provisions on confidentiality and professional secrecy set out in Article 13(3);

or

(c) criminal investigations or judicial proceedings have already been initiated or final judgment has already been passed in respect of the same intra-Community infringements and against the same sellers or suppliers before the judicial authorities in the Member State of the requested or applicant authority.

4. A requested authority may decide not to comply with the obligations referred to in Article 7 if criminal investigations or judicial proceedings have already been initiated or final judgment has already been passed in respect of the same intra-Community infringements and against the same sellers or suppliers before the judicial authorities in the Member State of the requested or applicant authority.

5. The requested authority shall inform the applicant authority and the Commission of the grounds for refusing to comply with a request for assistance. The applicant authority may refer the matter to the Commission which shall issue an opinion, in accordance with the procedure referred to in Article 19(2).

6. The measures necessary for the implementation of this Article shall be adopted in accordance with the procedure referred to in Article 19(2).

Chapter IV
Community Activities

Article 16
Enforcement coordination

1. To the extent necessary to achieve the objectives of this Regulation, Member States shall inform each other and the Commission of their activities of Community interest in areas such as:

(a) the training of their consumer protection enforcement officials, including language training and the organisation of training seminars;

(b) the collection and classification of consumer complaints;

(c) the development of sector-specific networks of competent officials;

(d) the development of information and communication tools;

(e) the development of standards, methodologies and guidelines for consumer protection enforcement officials;

(f) the exchange of their officials.

Member States may, in cooperation with the Commission, carry out common activities in the areas referred to in (a) to (f). The Member States shall, in cooperation with the Commission, develop a common framework for the classification of consumer complaints.

2. The competent authorities may exchange competent officials in order to improve cooperation. The competent authorities shall take the necessary measures to enable exchanged competent officials to play an effective part in activities of the competent authority. To this end such officials shall be authorised to carry out the duties entrusted to them by the host competent authority in accordance with the laws of its Member State.

3. During the exchange the civil and criminal liability of the competent official shall be treated in the same way as that of the officials of the host competent authority. Exchanged competent officials shall observe professional standards and be subject to the appropriate internal rules of conduct of the host competent authority that ensure, in particular, the protection of individuals with regard to the processing of personal data, procedural fairness and the proper observance of the confidentiality and professional secrecy provisions established in Article 13.

4. The Community measures necessary for the implementation of this Article, including the arrangements for implementing common activities, shall be adopted in accordance with the procedure referred to in Article 19(2).

Article 17
Administrative cooperation

1. To the extent necessary to achieve the objectives of this Regulation, Member States shall inform each other and the Commission of their activities of Community interest in areas such as:

(a) consumer information and advice;

(b) support of the activities of consumer representatives;

(c) support of the activities of bodies responsible for the extra-judicial settlement of consumer disputes;

(d) support of consumers' access to justice;

(e) collection of statistics, the results of research or other information relating to consumer behaviour, attitudes and outcomes.

Member States may, in cooperation with the Commission, carry out common activities in the areas referred to in (a) to (e). The Member States shall, in cooperation with the Commission, develop a common framework for the activities referred to in (e).

2. The Community measures necessary for the implementation of this Article, including the arrangements for implementing common activities, shall be adopted in accordance with the procedure referred to in Article 19(2).

Article 18
International agreements

The Community shall cooperate with third countries and with the competent international organisations in the areas covered by this Regulation in order to enhance the protection of consumers' economic interests. The arrangements for cooperation, including the establishment of mutual assistance arrangements, may be the subject of agreements between the Community and the third countries concerned.

Chapter V
Final Provisions

Article 19
Committee procedure

1. The Commission shall be assisted by a Committee.

2. Where reference is made to this paragraph, Articles 5 and 7 of Decision 1999/468/EC shall apply, having regard to the provisions of Article 8 thereof.

The period laid down in Article 5(6) of Decision 1999/468/EC shall be set at three months.

3. The Committee shall adopt its Rules of Procedure.

Article 20
Committee tasks

1. The Committee may examine all matters relating to the application of this Regulation raised by its chairman, either on his own initiative or at the request of the representative of a Member State.

2. In particular, it shall examine and evaluate how the arrangements for cooperation provided for in this Regulation are working.

Article 21
Reports

1. Member States shall communicate to the Commission the text of any provisions of national law that they adopt, or of agreements other than to deal with individual cases that they conclude, on matters covered by this Regulation.

2. Every two years from the date of entry into force of this Regulation, the Member States shall report to the Commission on the application of this Regulation. The Commission shall make these reports publicly available.

3. The reports shall address:

(a) any new information about the organisation, powers, resources or responsibilities of the competent authorities;

(b) any information concerning trends, means or methods of committing intra-Community infringements, particularly those that have revealed shortcomings or lacunae in this Regulation or in the laws that protect consumers' interests;

(c) any information on enforcement techniques that have proved their effectiveness;

(d) summary statistics relating to the activities of competent authorities, such as actions under this Regulation, complaints received, enforcement actions and judgments;

(e) summaries of significant national interpretative judgments in the laws that protect consumers' interests;

(f) any other information relevant to the application of this Regulation.

4. The Commission shall submit to the European Parliament and the Council a report on the application of this Regulation on the basis of the reports of the Member States.

Article 22
Entry into force

This Regulation shall enter into force on the 20th day following its publication in the Official Journal of the European Union.

It shall apply from 29 December 2005.

The provisions on mutual assistance set out in Chapters II and III shall apply from 29 December 2006.

This Regulation shall be binding in its entirety and directly applicable in all Member States.

Annex

Directives and Regulations covered by Article 3(a)[11]

1. Council Directive 84/450/EEC of 10 September 1984 relating to the approximation of the laws, regulations and administrative provisions of the Member States concerning misleading advertising[12] (OJ L 250, 19.9.1984, p. 17). Directive as last amended by Directive 97/55/EC of the European Parliament and of the Council[13] (OJ L 290, 23.10.1997, p. 18).

2. Council Directive 85/577/EEC of 20 December 1985 to protect the consumer in respect of contracts negotiated away from business premises[14] (OJ L 372, 31.12.1985, p. 31).

3. Council Directive 87/102/EEC of 22 December 1986 for the approximation of the laws, regulations and administrative provisions of the Member States concerning consumer credit[15] (OJ L 42, 12.2.1987, p. 48). Directive as last amended by Directive 98/7/EC of the European Parliament and of the Council[16] (OJ L 101, 1.4.1998, p. 17).

4. Council Directive 89/552/EEC of 3 October 1989 on the coordination of certain provisions laid down by law, regulation or administrative action in Member States concerning the pursuit of television broadcasting activities: Articles 10 to 21 (OJ L 298, 17.10.1989, p. 23). Directive as last amended by Directive 97/36/EC of the European Parliament and of the Council (OJ L 202, 30.7.1997, p. 60).

5. Council Directive 90/314/EEC of 13 June 1990 on package travel, package holidays and package tours (OJ L 158, 23.6.1990, p. 59).

6. Council Directive 93/13/EEC of 5 April 1993 on unfair terms in consumer contracts[17] (OJ L 95, 21.4.1993, p. 29). Directive as amended by Commission Decision 2002/995/EC (OJ L 353, 30.12.2002, p. 1).

7. Directive 94/47/EC of the European Parliament and of the Council of 26 October 1994 on the protection of purchasers in respect of certain aspects of contracts relating to the purchase of the right to use immovable properties on a timeshare basis (OJ L 280, 29.10.1994, p. 83).

8. Directive 97/7/EC of the European Parliament and of the Council of 20 May 1997 on the protection of consumers in respect of distance contracts[18] (OJ L 144, 4.6.1997, p. 19). Directive as amended by Directive 2002/65/EC[19] (OJ L 271, 9.10.2002, p. 16).

9. Directive 97/55/EC of the European Parliament and of the Council of 6 October 1997 amending Directive 84/450/EEC concerning misleading advertising so as to include comparative advertising.[20]

10. Directive 98/6/EC of the European Parliament and of the Council of 16 February 1998 on consumer protection in the indication of the prices of products offered to consumers (OJ L 80, 18.3.1998, p. 27).

11. Directive 1999/44/EC of the European Parliament and of the Council of 25 May 1999 on certain aspects of the sale of consumer goods and associated guarantees[21] (OJ L 171, 7.7.1999, p. 12).

12. Directive 2000/31/EC of the European Parliament and of the Council of 8 June 2000 on certain legal aspects of information society services, in particular electronic commerce, in the Internal Market (Directive on electronic commerce)[22] (OJ L 178, 17.7.2000 p. 1).

---

[11] Directives Nos 1, 6, 8 and 13 contain specific provisions.
[12] Reproduced supra under no. C.P. 1.
[13] Reproduced supra under no. C.P. 13.
[14] Reproduced supra under no. C.P. 3.
[15] Reproduced supra under no. C.P. 4.
[16] Reproduced supra under no. C.P. 14.
[17] Reproduced supra under no. C.P. 9.
[18] Reproduced supra under no. C.P. 11.
[19] Reproduced supra under no. C.P. 22.
[20] Reproduced supra under no. C.P. 13.
[21] Reproduced supra under no. C.P. 17.
[22] Reproduced supra under no. C.P. 19.

13. Directive 2001/83/EC of the European Parliament and of the Council of 6 November 2001 on the Community code relating to medicinal products for human use: Articles 86 to 100 (OJ L 311, 28.11.2001, p. 67). Directive as last amended by Directive 2004/27/EC (OJ L 136, 30.4.2004, p. 34).

14. Directive 2002/65/EC of the European Parliament and of the Council of 23 September 2002 concerning the distance marketing of consumer financial services.[23]

15. Regulation (EC) No 261/2004 of the European Parliament and of the Council of 11 February 2004 establishing common rules on compensation and assistance to air passengers in the event of denied boarding and of cancellation or long delay of flights (OJ L 46, 17.2.2004, p. 1).

[16. Directive 2005/29/EC of the European Parliament and of the Council of 11 May 2005 concerning unfair business-to-consumer commercial practices in the internal market (OJ L 149, 11.6.2005, p. 22).]

¶ *Item 16 has been added by article 16(2) of Directive 2005/29/EC, reproduced infra under no. C.P. 24.*

---

[23] Reproduced supra under no. C.P. 22.

C.P. 24.

**European Parliament and Council Directive 2005/29/EC
of 11 May 2005
concerning unfair business-to-consumer commercial practices in the internal market and amending Council Directive 84/450/EEC, Directives 97/7/EC, 98/27/EC and 2002/65/EC of the European Parliament and of the Council and Regulation (EC) No 2006/2004 of the European Parliament and of the Council ('Unfair Commercial Practices Directive')**[1]

THE EUROPEAN PARLIAMENT AND THE COUNCIL OF THE EUROPEAN UNION,

Having regard to the Treaty establishing the European Community, and in particular Article 95 thereof,

Having regard to the proposal from the Commission,

Having regard to the opinion of the European Economic and Social Committee,[2]

Acting in accordance with the procedure laid down in Article 251 of the Treaty,[3]

Whereas:

(1) Article 153(1) and (3)(a) of the Treaty provides that the Community is to contribute to the attainment of a high level of consumer protection by the measures it adopts pursuant to Article 95 thereof.

(2) In accordance with Article 14(2) of the Treaty, the internal market comprises an area without internal frontiers in which the free movement of goods and services and freedom of establishment are ensured. The development of fair commercial practices within the area without internal frontiers is vital for the promotion of the development of cross border activities.

(3) The laws of the Member States relating to unfair commercial practices show marked differences which can generate appreciable distortions of competition and obstacles to the smooth functioning of the internal market. In the field of advertising, Council Directive 84/450/EEC of 10 September 1984 concerning misleading and comparative advertising[4] establishes minimum criteria for harmonising legislation on misleading advertising, but does not prevent the Member States from retaining or adopting measures which provide more extensive protection for consumers. As a result, Member States' provisions on misleading advertising diverge significantly.

(4) These disparities cause uncertainty as to which national rules apply to unfair commercial practices harming consumers' economic interests and create many barriers affecting business and consumers. These barriers increase the cost to business of exercising internal market freedoms, in particular when businesses wish to engage in cross border marketing, advertising campaigns and sales promotions. Such barriers also make consumers uncertain of their rights and undermine their confidence in the internal market.

(5) In the absence of uniform rules at Community level, obstacles to the free movement of services and goods across borders or the freedom of establishment could be justified in the light of the case-law of the Court of Justice of

---

[1] OJ L 149, 11.6.2005, 22–39.
[2] OJ C 108, 30.4.2004, 81.
[3] Opinion of the European Parliament of 20 April 2004 (OJ C 104 E, 30.4.2004, 260), Council Common Position of 15 November 2004 (OJ C 38 E, 15.2.2005, 1), Position of the European Parliament of 24 February 2005 (not yet published in the Official Journal) and Council Decision of 12 April 2005.

[4] OJ L 250, 19.9.1984, 17, reproduced supra under no. C.P. 1. Directive as amended by Directive 97/55/EC of the European Parliament and of the Council (OJ L 290, 23.10.1997, 8), reproduced supra under no. C.P. 13.

the European Communities as long as they seek to protect recognised public interest objectives and are proportionate to those objectives. In view of the Community's objectives, as set out in the provisions of the Treaty and in secondary Community law relating to freedom of movement, and in accordance with the Commission's policy on commercial communications as indicated in the Communication from the Commission entitled 'The follow-up to the Green Paper on Commercial Communications in the Internal Market', such obstacles should be eliminated. These obstacles can only be eliminated by establishing uniform rules at Community level which establish a high level of consumer protection and by clarifying certain legal concepts at Community level to the extent necessary for the proper functioning of the internal market and to meet the requirement of legal certainty.

(6) This Directive therefore approximates the laws of the Member States on unfair commercial practices, including unfair advertising, which directly harm consumers' economic interests and thereby indirectly harm the economic interests of legitimate competitors. In line with the principle of proportionality, this Directive protects consumers from the consequences of such unfair commercial practices where they are material but recognises that in some cases the impact on consumers may be negligible. It neither covers nor affects the national laws on unfair commercial practices which harm only competitors' economic interests or which relate to a transaction between traders; taking full account of the principle of subsidiarity, Member States will continue to be able to regulate such practices, in conformity with Community law, if they choose to do so. Nor does this Directive cover or affect the provisions of Directive 84/450/EEC on advertising which misleads business but which is not misleading for consumers and on comparative advertising. Further, this Directive does not affect accepted advertising and marketing practices, such as legitimate product placement, brand differentiation or the offering of incentives which may legitimately affect consumers' perceptions of products and influence their behaviour without impairing the consumer's ability to make an informed decision.

(7) This Directive addresses commercial practices directly related to influencing consumers' transactional decisions in relation to products. It does not address commercial practices carried out primarily for other purposes, including for example commercial communication aimed at investors, such as annual reports and corporate promotional literature. It does not address legal requirements related to taste and decency which vary widely among the Member States. Commercial practices such as, for example, commercial solicitation in the streets, may be undesirable in Member States for cultural reasons. Member States should accordingly be able to continue to ban commercial practices in their territory, in conformity with Community law, for reasons of taste and decency even where such practices do not limit consumers' freedom of choice. Full account should be taken of the context of the individual case concerned in applying this Directive, in particular the general clauses thereof.

(8) This Directive directly protects consumer economic interests from unfair business-to-consumer commercial practices. Thereby, it also indirectly protects legitimate businesses from their competitors who do not play by the rules in this Directive and thus guarantees fair competition in fields coordinated by it. It is understood that there are other commercial practices which, although not harming consumers, may hurt competitors and business customers. The Commission should carefully examine the need for Community action in the field of unfair competition beyond the remit of this Directive and, if necessary, make a legislative proposal to cover these other aspects of unfair competition.

(9) This Directive is without prejudice to individual actions brought by those who have been harmed by an unfair commercial practice. It is also without prejudice to Community and national rules on contract law, on intellectual property rights, on the health and safety aspects of products, on conditions of establishment and authorisation regimes, including those rules which, in conformity with Community law, relate to gambling activities, and to Community competition rules and the national provisions implementing them. The Member States will

thus be able to retain or introduce restrictions and prohibitions of commercial practices on grounds of the protection of the health and safety of consumers in their territory wherever the trader is based, for example in relation to alcohol, tobacco or pharmaceuticals. Financial services and immovable property, by reason of their complexity and inherent serious risks, necessitate detailed requirements, including positive obligations on traders. For this reason, in the field of financial services and immovable property, this Directive is without prejudice to the right of Member States to go beyond its provisions to protect the economic interests of consumers. It is not appropriate to regulate here the certification and indication of the standard of fineness of articles of precious metal.

(10) It is necessary to ensure that the relationship between this Directive and existing Community law is coherent, particularly where detailed provisions on unfair commercial practices apply to specific sectors. This Directive therefore amends Directive 84/450/EEC, Directive 97/7/EC of the European Parliament and of the Council of 20 May 1997 on the protection of consumers in respect of distance contracts,[5] Directive 98/27/EC of the European Parliament and of the Council of 19 May 1998 on injunctions for the protection of consumers' interests[6] and Directive 2002/65/EC of the European Parliament and of the Council of 23 September 2002 concerning the distance marketing of consumer financial services.[7] This Directive accordingly applies only in so far as there are no specific Community law provisions regulating specific aspects of unfair commercial practices, such as information requirements and rules on the way the information is presented to the consumer. It provides protection for consumers where there is no specific sectoral legislation at Community level and prohibits traders from creating a false impression of the nature of products. This is particularly important for complex products with high levels of risk to consumers, such as certain financial services products. This Directive consequently complements the Community *acquis*, which is applicable to commercial practices harming consumers' economic interests.

(11) The high level of convergence achieved by the approximation of national provisions through this Directive creates a high common level of consumer protection. This Directive establishes a single general prohibition of those unfair commercial practices distorting consumers' economic behaviour. It also sets rules on aggressive commercial practices, which are currently not regulated at Community level.

(12) Harmonisation will considerably increase legal certainty for both consumers and business. Both consumers and business will be able to rely on a single regulatory framework based on clearly defined legal concepts regulating all aspects of unfair commercial practices across the EU. The effect will be to eliminate the barriers stemming from the fragmentation of the rules on unfair commercial practices harming consumer economic interests and to enable the internal market to be achieved in this area.

(13) In order to achieve the Community's objectives through the removal of internal market barriers, it is necessary to replace Member States' existing, divergent general clauses and legal principles. The single, common general prohibition established by this Directive therefore covers unfair commercial practices distorting consumers' economic behaviour. In order to support consumer confidence the general prohibition should apply equally to unfair commercial practices which occur outside any contractual relationship between a trader and a consumer or following the conclusion of a contract and during its execution. The general prohibition is elaborated by rules on the two types of commercial practices which are by far the most common, namely misleading commercial practices and aggressive commercial practices.

---

[5] OJ L 144, 4.6.1997, 19, reproduced supra under no. C.P. 11. Directive as amended by Directive 2002/65/EC, reproduced supra under no. C.P. 22.

[6] OJ L 166, 11.6.1998, 51, reproduced supra under no. C.P. 15. Directive as last amended by Directive 2002/65/EC, reproduced supra under no. C.P. 22.

[7] OJ L 271, 9.10.2002, 16, reproduced supra under no. C.P. 22.

(14) It is desirable that misleading commercial practices cover those practices, including misleading advertising, which by deceiving the consumer prevent him from making an informed and thus efficient choice. In conformity with the laws and practices of Member States on misleading advertising, this Directive classifies misleading practices into misleading actions and misleading omissions. In respect of omissions, this Directive sets out a limited number of key items of information which the consumer needs to make an informed transactional decision. Such information will not have to be disclosed in all advertisements, but only where the trader makes an invitation to purchase, which is a concept clearly defined in this Directive. The full harmonisation approach adopted in this Directive does not preclude the Member States from specifying in national law the main characteristics of particular products such as, for example, collectors' items or electrical goods, the omission of which would be material when an invitation to purchase is made. It is not the intention of this Directive to reduce consumer choice by prohibiting the promotion of products which look similar to other products unless this similarity confuses consumers as to the commercial origin of the product and is therefore misleading. This Directive should be without prejudice to existing Community law which expressly affords Member States the choice between several regulatory options for the protection of consumers in the field of commercial practices. In particular, this Directive should be without prejudice to Article 13(3) of Directive 2002/58/EC of the European Parliament and of the Council of 12 July 2002 concerning the processing of personal data and the protection of privacy in the electronic communications sector.[8]

(15) Where Community law sets out information requirements in relation to commercial communication, advertising and marketing that information is considered as material under this Directive. Member States will be able to retain or add information requirements relating to contract law and having contract law consequences where this is allowed by the minimum clauses in the existing Community law instruments. A non-exhaustive list of such information requirements in the *acquis* is contained in Annex II. Given the full harmonisation introduced by this Directive only the information required in Community law is considered as material for the purpose of Article 7(5) thereof. Where Member States have introduced information requirements over and above what is specified in Community law, on the basis of minimum clauses, the omission of that extra information will not constitute a misleading omission under this Directive. By contrast Member States will be able, when allowed by the minimum clauses in Community law, to maintain or introduce more stringent provisions in conformity with Community law so as to ensure a higher level of protection of consumers' individual contractual rights.

(16) The provisions on aggressive commercial practices should cover those practices which significantly impair the consumer's freedom of choice. Those are practices using harassment, coercion, including the use of physical force, and undue influence.

(17) It is desirable that those commercial practices which are in all circumstances unfair be identified to provide greater legal certainty. Annex I therefore contains the full list of all such practices. These are the only commercial practices which can be deemed to be unfair without a case-by-case assessment against the provisions of Articles 5 to 9. The list may only be modified by revision of the Directive.

(18) It is appropriate to protect all consumers from unfair commercial practices; however the Court of Justice has found it necessary in adjudicating on advertising cases since the enactment of Directive 84/450/EEC to examine the effect on a notional, typical consumer. In line with the principle of proportionality, and to permit the effective application of the protections contained in it, this Directive takes as a benchmark the average consumer, who is reasonably well-informed and reasonably observant and circumspect, taking into account social, cultural and

---

[8] OJ L 201, 31.7.2002, 37.

linguistic factors, as interpreted by the Court of Justice, but also contains provisions aimed at preventing the exploitation of consumers whose characteristics make them particularly vulnerable to unfair commercial practices. Where a commercial practice is specifically aimed at a particular group of consumers, such as children, it is desirable that the impact of the commercial practice be assessed from the perspective of the average member of that group. It is therefore appropriate to include in the list of practices which are in all circumstances unfair a provision which, without imposing an outright ban on advertising directed at children, protects them from direct exhortations to purchase. The average consumer test is not a statistical test. National courts and authorities will have to exercise their own faculty of judgement, having regard to the case-law of the Court of Justice, to determine the typical reaction of the average consumer in a given case.

(19) Where certain characteristics such as age, physical or mental infirmity or credulity make consumers particularly susceptible to a commercial practice or to the underlying product and the economic behaviour only of such consumers is likely to be distorted by the practice in a way that the trader can reasonably foresee, it is appropriate to ensure that they are adequately protected by assessing the practice from the perspective of the average member of that group.

(20) It is appropriate to provide a role for codes of conduct, which enable traders to apply the principles of this Directive effectively in specific economic fields. In sectors where there are specific mandatory requirements regulating the behaviour of traders, it is appropriate that these will also provide evidence as to the requirements of professional diligence in that sector. The control exercised by code owners at national or Community level to eliminate unfair commercial practices may avoid the need for recourse to administrative or judicial action and should therefore be encouraged. With the aim of pursuing a high level of consumer protection, consumers' organisations could be informed and involved in the drafting of codes of conduct.

(21) Persons or organisations regarded under national law as having a legitimate interest in the matter must have legal remedies for initiating proceedings against unfair commercial practices, either before a court or before an administrative authority which is competent to decide upon complaints or to initiate appropriate legal proceedings. While it is for national law to determine the burden of proof, it is appropriate to enable courts and administrative authorities to require traders to produce evidence as to the accuracy of factual claims they have made.

(22) It is necessary that Member States lay down penalties for infringements of the provisions of this Directive and they must ensure that these are enforced. The penalties must be effective, proportionate and dissuasive.

(23) Since the objectives of this Directive, namely to eliminate the barriers to the functioning of the internal market represented by national laws on unfair commercial practices and to provide a high common level of consumer protection, by approximating the laws, regulations and administrative provisions of the Member States on unfair commercial practices, cannot be sufficiently achieved by the Member States and can therefore be better achieved at Community level, the Community may adopt measures, in accordance with the principle of subsidiarity as set out in Article 5 of the Treaty. In accordance with the principle of proportionality, as set out in that Article, this Directive does not go beyond what is necessary in order to eliminate the internal market barriers and achieve a high common level of consumer protection.

(24) It is appropriate to review this Directive to ensure that barriers to the internal market have been addressed and a high level of consumer protection achieved. The review could lead to a Commission proposal to amend this Directive, which may include a limited extension to the derogation in Article 3(5), and/or amendments to other consumer protection legislation reflecting the Commission's Consumer Policy Strategy commitment to review the existing *acquis* in order to achieve a high, common level of consumer protection.

(25) This Directive respects the fundamental rights and observes the principles recognised in particular by the Charter of Fundamental Rights of the European Union,

HAVE ADOPTED THIS DIRECTIVE:

Chapter 1
General Provisions

Article 1
Purpose

The purpose of this Directive is to contribute to the proper functioning of the internal market and achieve a high level of consumer protection by approximating the laws, regulations and administrative provisions of the Member States on unfair commercial practices harming consumers' economic interests.

Article 2
Definitions

For the purposes of this Directive:

(a) 'consumer' means any natural person who, in commercial practices covered by this Directive, is acting for purposes which are outside his trade, business, craft or profession;

(b) 'trader' means any natural or legal person who, in commercial practices covered by this Directive, is acting for purposes relating to his trade, business, craft or profession and anyone acting in the name of or on behalf of a trader;

(c) 'product' means any goods or service including immovable property, rights and obligations;

(d) 'business-to-consumer commercial practices' (hereinafter also referred to as commercial practices) means any act, omission, course of conduct or representation, commercial communication including advertising and marketing, by a trader, directly connected with the promotion, sale or supply of a product to consumers;

(e) 'to materially distort the economic behaviour of consumers' means using a commercial practice to appreciably impair the consumer's ability to make an informed decision, thereby causing the consumer to take a transactional decision that he would not have taken otherwise;

(f) 'code of conduct' means an agreement or set of rules not imposed by law, regulation or administrative provision of a Member State which defines the behaviour of traders who undertake to be bound by the code in relation to one or more particular commercial practices or business sectors;

(g) 'code owner' means any entity, including a trader or group of traders, which is responsible for the formulation and revision of a code of conduct and/or for monitoring compliance with the code by those who have undertaken to be bound by it;

(h) 'professional diligence' means the standard of special skill and care which a trader may reasonably be expected to exercise towards consumers, commensurate with honest market practice and/or the general principle of good faith in the trader's field of activity;

(i) 'invitation to purchase' means a commercial communication which indicates characteristics of the product and the price in a way appropriate to the means of the commercial communication used and thereby enables the consumer to make a purchase;

(j) 'undue influence' means exploiting a position of power in relation to the consumer so as to apply pressure, even without using or threatening to use physical force, in a way which significantly limits the consumer's ability to make an informed decision;

(k) 'transactional decision' means any decision taken by a consumer concerning whether, how and on what terms to purchase, make payment in whole or in part for, retain or dispose of a product or to exercise a contractual right in relation to the product, whether the consumer decides to act or to refrain from acting;

(l) 'regulated profession' means a professional activity or a group of professional activities, access to which or the pursuit of which, or one of the modes of pursuing which, is conditional, directly or indirectly, upon possession of specific professional qualifications, pursuant to laws, regulations or administrative provisions.

Article 3
Scope

1. This Directive shall apply to unfair business-to-consumer commercial practices, as laid down in Article 5, before, during and after a commercial transaction in relation to a product.

2. This Directive is without prejudice to contract law and, in particular, to the rules on the validity, formation or effect of a contract.

3. This Directive is without prejudice to Community or national rules relating to the health and safety aspects of products.

4. In the case of conflict between the provisions of this Directive and other Community rules regulating specific aspects of unfair commercial practices, the latter shall prevail and apply to those specific aspects.

5. For a period of six years from 12 June 2007, Member States shall be able to continue to apply national provisions within the field approximated by this Directive which are more restrictive or prescriptive than this Directive and which implement directives containing minimum harmonisation clauses. These measures must be essential to ensure that consumers are adequately protected against unfair commercial practices and must be proportionate to the attainment of this objective. The review referred to in Article 18 may, if considered appropriate, include a proposal to prolong this derogation for a further limited period.

6. Member States shall notify the Commission without delay of any national provisions applied on the basis of paragraph 5.

7. This Directive is without prejudice to the rules determining the jurisdiction of the courts.

8. This Directive is without prejudice to any conditions of establishment or of authorisation regimes, or to the deontological codes of conduct or other specific rules governing regulated professions in order to uphold high standards of integrity on the part of the professional, which Member States may, in conformity with Community law, impose on professionals.

9. In relation to 'financial services', as defined in Directive 2002/65/EC, and immovable property, Member States may impose requirements which are more restrictive or prescriptive than this Directive in the field which it approximates.

10. This Directive shall not apply to the application of the laws, regulations and administrative provisions of Member States relating to the certification and indication of the standard of fineness of articles of precious metal.

Article 4
Internal market

Member States shall neither restrict the freedom to provide services nor restrict the free movement of goods for reasons falling within the field approximated by this Directive.

CHAPTER 2
UNFAIR COMMERCIAL PRACTICES

Article 5
Prohibition of unfair commercial practices

1. Unfair commercial practices shall be prohibited.

2. A commercial practice shall be unfair if:

(a) it is contrary to the requirements of professional diligence,

and

(b) it materially distorts or is likely to materially distort the economic behaviour with regard to the product of the average consumer whom it reaches or to whom it is addressed, or of the average member of the group when a commercial practice is directed to a particular group of consumers.

3. Commercial practices which are likely to materially distort the economic behaviour only of a clearly identifiable group of consumers who are particularly vulnerable to the practice or the underlying product because of their mental or physical infirmity, age or credulity in a way which the trader could reasonably be expected to foresee, shall be assessed from the perspective of the average member of that group. This is without prejudice to

the common and legitimate advertising practice of making exaggerated statements or statements which are not meant to be taken literally.

4. In particular, commercial practices shall be unfair which:

(a) are misleading as set out in Articles 6 and 7, or

(b) are aggressive as set out in Articles 8 and 9.

5. Annex I contains the list of those commercial practices which shall in all circumstances be regarded as unfair. The same single list shall apply in all Member States and may only be modified by revision of this Directive.

Section 1
Misleading Commercial Practices

Article 6
Misleading actions

1. A commercial practice shall be regarded as misleading if it contains false information and is therefore untruthful or in any way, including overall presentation, deceives or is likely to deceive the average consumer, even if the information is factually correct, in relation to one or more of the following elements, and in either case causes or is likely to cause him to take a transactional decision that he would not have taken otherwise:

(a) the existence or nature of the product;

(b) the main characteristics of the product, such as its availability, benefits, risks, execution, composition, accessories, after-sale customer assistance and complaint handling, method and date of manufacture or provision, delivery, fitness for purpose, usage, quantity, specification, geographical or commercial origin or the results to be expected from its use, or the results and material features of tests or checks carried out on the product;

(c) the extent of the trader's commitments, the motives for the commercial practice and the nature of the sales process, any statement or symbol in relation to direct or indirect sponsorship or approval of the trader or the product;

(d) the price or the manner in which the price is calculated, or the existence of a specific price advantage;

(e) the need for a service, part, replacement or repair;

(f) the nature, attributes and rights of the trader or his agent, such as his identity and assets, his qualifications, status, approval, affiliation or connection and ownership of industrial, commercial or intellectual property rights or his awards and distinctions;

(g) the consumer's rights, including the right to replacement or reimbursement under Directive 1999/44/EC of the European Parliament and of the Council of 25 May 1999 on certain aspects of the sale of consumer goods and associated guarantees,[9] or the risks he may face.

2. A commercial practice shall also be regarded as misleading if, in its factual context, taking account of all its features and circumstances, it causes or is likely to cause the average consumer to take a transactional decision that he would not have taken otherwise, and it involves:

(a) any marketing of a product, including comparative advertising, which creates confusion with any products, trade marks, trade names or other distinguishing marks of a competitor;

(b) non-compliance by the trader with commitments contained in codes of conduct by which the trader has undertaken to be bound, where:
(i) the commitment is not aspirational but is firm and is capable of being verified, and
(ii) the trader indicates in a commercial practice that he is bound by the code.

Article 7
Misleading omissions

1. A commercial practice shall be regarded as misleading if, in its factual context, taking account of all its features and circumstances and

---

[9] OJ L 171, 7.7.1999, 12, reproduced supra under no. C.P. 17.

the limitations of the communication medium, it omits material information that the average consumer needs, according to the context, to take an informed transactional decision and thereby causes or is likely to cause the average consumer to take a transactional decision that he would not have taken otherwise.

2. It shall also be regarded as a misleading omission when, taking account of the matters described in paragraph 1, a trader hides or provides in an unclear, unintelligible, ambiguous or untimely manner such material information as referred to in that paragraph or fails to identify the commercial intent of the commercial practice if not already apparent from the context, and where, in either case, this causes or is likely to cause the average consumer to take a transactional decision that he would not have taken otherwise.

3. Where the medium used to communicate the commercial practice imposes limitations of space or time, these limitations and any measures taken by the trader to make the information available to consumers by other means shall be taken into account in deciding whether information has been omitted.

4. In the case of an invitation to purchase, the following information shall be regarded as material, if not already apparent from the context:

(a) the main characteristics of the product, to an extent appropriate to the medium and the product;

(b) the geographical address and the identity of the trader, such as his trading name and, where applicable, the geographical address and the identity of the trader on whose behalf he is acting;

(c) the price inclusive of taxes, or where the nature of the product means that the price cannot reasonably be calculated in advance, the manner in which the price is calculated, as well as, where appropriate, all additional freight, delivery or postal charges or, where these charges cannot reasonably be calculated in advance, the fact that such additional charges may be payable;

(d) the arrangements for payment, delivery, performance and the complaint handling policy, if they depart from the requirements of professional diligence;

(e) for products and transactions involving a right of withdrawal or cancellation, the existence of such a right.

5. Information requirements established by Community law in relation to commercial communication including advertising or marketing, a non-exhaustive list of which is contained in Annex II, shall be regarded as material.

SECTION 2
AGGRESSIVE COMMERCIAL PRACTICES

Article 8

Aggressive commercial practices

A commercial practice shall be regarded as aggressive if, in its factual context, taking account of all its features and circumstances, by harassment, coercion, including the use of physical force, or undue influence, it significantly impairs or is likely to significantly impair the average consumer's freedom of choice or conduct with regard to the product and thereby causes him or is likely to cause him to take a transactional decision that he would not have taken otherwise.

Article 9

Use of harassment, coercion and undue influence

In determining whether a commercial practice uses harassment, coercion, including the use of physical force, or undue influence, account shall be taken of:

(a) its timing, location, nature or persistence;

(b) the use of threatening or abusive language or behaviour;

(c) the exploitation by the trader of any specific misfortune or circumstance of such gravity as to impair the consumer's judgement, of which the trader is aware, to influence the consumer's decision with regard to the product;

(d) any onerous or disproportionate non-contractual barriers imposed by the trader where a consumer wishes to exercise rights under the contract, including rights to terminate a contract or to switch to another product or another trader;

(e) any threat to take any action that cannot legally be taken.

Chapter 3
Codes of Conduct

Article 10
Codes of conduct

This Directive does not exclude the control, which Member States may encourage, of unfair commercial practices by code owners and recourse to such bodies by the persons or organisations referred to in Article 11 if proceedings before such bodies are in addition to the court or administrative proceedings referred to in that Article.

Recourse to such control bodies shall never be deemed the equivalent of foregoing a means of judicial or administrative recourse as provided for in Article 11.

Chapter 4
Final Provisions

Article 11
Enforcement

1. Member States shall ensure that adequate and effective means exist to combat unfair commercial practices in order to enforce compliance with the provisions of this Directive in the interest of consumers.

Such means shall include legal provisions under which persons or organisations regarded under national law as having a legitimate interest in combating unfair commercial practices, including competitors, may:

(a) take legal action against such unfair commercial practices;

and/or

(b) bring such unfair commercial practices before an administrative authority competent either to decide on complaints or to initiate appropriate legal proceedings.

It shall be for each Member State to decide which of these facilities shall be available and whether to enable the courts or administrative authorities to require prior recourse to other established means of dealing with complaints, including those referred to in Article 10. These facilities shall be available regardless of whether the consumers affected are in the territory of the Member State where the trader is located or in another Member State.

It shall be for each Member State to decide:

(a) whether these legal facilities may be directed separately or jointly against a number of traders from the same economic sector;

and

(b) whether these legal facilities may be directed against a code owner where the relevant code promotes non-compliance with legal requirements.

2. Under the legal provisions referred to in paragraph 1, Member States shall confer upon the courts or administrative authorities powers enabling them, in cases where they deem such measures to be necessary taking into account all the interests involved and in particular the public interest:

(a) to order the cessation of, or to institute appropriate legal proceedings for an order for the cessation of, unfair commercial practices;

or

(b) if the unfair commercial practice has not yet been carried out but is imminent, to order the prohibition of the practice, or to institute appropriate legal proceedings for an order for the prohibition of the practice,

even without proof of actual loss or damage or of intention or negligence on the part of the trader.

Member States shall also make provision for the measures referred to in the first subparagraph to be taken under an accelerated procedure:

– either with interim effect,

or

– with definitive effect,

on the understanding that it is for each Member State to decide which of the two options to select.

Furthermore, Member States may confer upon the courts or administrative authorities powers enabling them, with a view to eliminating the continuing effects of unfair commercial practices the cessation of which has been ordered by a final decision:

(a) to require publication of that decision in full or in part and in such form as they deem adequate;

(b) to require in addition the publication of a corrective statement.

3. The administrative authorities referred to in paragraph 1 must:

(a) be composed so as not to cast doubt on their impartiality;

(b) have adequate powers, where they decide on complaints, to monitor and enforce the observance of their decisions effectively;

(c) normally give reasons for their decisions.

Where the powers referred to in paragraph 2 are exercised exclusively by an administrative authority, reasons for its decisions shall always be given. Furthermore, in this case, provision must be made for procedures whereby improper or unreasonable exercise of its powers by the administrative authority or improper or unreasonable failure to exercise the said powers can be the subject of judicial review.

Article 12

Courts and administrative authorities: substantiation of claims

Member States shall confer upon the courts or administrative authorities powers enabling them in the civil or administrative proceedings provided for in Article 11:

(a) to require the trader to furnish evidence as to the accuracy of factual claims in relation to a commercial practice if, taking into account the legitimate interest of the trader and any other party to the proceedings, such a requirement appears appropriate on the basis of the circumstances of the particular case; and

(b) to consider factual claims as inaccurate if the evidence demanded in accordance with (a) is not furnished or is deemed insufficient by the court or administrative authority.

Article 13

Penalties

Member States shall lay down penalties for infringements of national provisions adopted in application of this Directive and shall take all necessary measures to ensure that these are enforced. These penalties must be effective, proportionate and dissuasive.

Article 14

Amendments to Directive 84/450/EEC

[. . .]

¶ *This article replaces article 1, point 3 of article 2, article 3a, article 4(1), article 7(1) and adds point 4 to article 2 of Directive 84/450/EEC, reproduced supra under no. C.P. 1. The modifications are directly incorporated therein.*

Article 15

Amendments to Directives 97/7/EC and 2002/65/EC

[. . .]

¶ *This article replaces article 9 of Directive 97/7/EC, reproduced supra under no. C.P. 1, and replaces article 9 of Directive 2002/65/EC, reproduced supra under no. C.P. 22. The modifications are directly incorporated therein.*

Article 16

Amendments to Directive 98/27/EC and Regulation (EC) No 2006/2004

[. . .]

¶ *This article replaces point 1 of the Annex to Directive 98/27/EC, reproduced supra under no. C.P. 15, and adds point 16 in the Annex to Regulation 2006/2004/EC, reproduced supra under no. C.P. 23. The modifications are directly incorporated therein.*

Article 17

Information

Member States shall take appropriate measures to inform consumers of the national law transposing this Directive and shall, where appropriate, encourage traders and code owners to inform consumers of their codes of conduct.

Article 18
Review

1. By 12 June 2011 the Commission shall submit to the European Parliament and the Council a comprehensive report on the application of this Directive, in particular of Articles 3(9) and 4 and Annex I, on the scope for further harmonisation and simplification of Community law relating to consumer protection, and, having regard to Article 3(5), on any measures that need to be taken at Community level to ensure that appropriate levels of consumer protection are maintained. The report shall be accompanied, if necessary, by a proposal to revise this Directive or other relevant parts of Community law.

2. The European Parliament and the Council shall endeavour to act, in accordance with the Treaty, within two years of the presentation by the Commission of any proposal submitted under paragraph 1.

Article 19
Transposition

Member States shall adopt and publish the laws, regulations and administrative provisions necessary to comply with this Directive by 12 June 2007. They shall forthwith inform the Commission thereof and inform the Commission of any subsequent amendments without delay.

They shall apply those measures by 12 December 2007. When Member States adopt those measures, they shall contain a reference to this Directive or be accompanied by such a reference on the occasion of their official publication. Member States shall determine how such reference is to be made.

Article 20
Entry into force

This Directive shall enter into force on the day following its publication in the *Official Journal of the European Union*.

Article 21
Addressees

This Directive is addressed to the Member States.

Annex I

Commercial practices which are in all circumstances considered unfair

Misleading commercial practices

1. Claiming to be a signatory to a code of conduct when the trader is not.

2. Displaying a trust mark, quality mark or equivalent without having obtained the necessary authorisation.

3. Claiming that a code of conduct has an endorsement from a public or other body which it does not have.

4. Claiming that a trader (including his commercial practices) or a product has been approved, endorsed or authorised by a public or private body when he/it has not or making such a claim without complying with the terms of the approval, endorsement or authorisation.

5. Making an invitation to purchase products at a specified price without disclosing the existence of any reasonable grounds the trader may have for believing that he will not be able to offer for supply

or to procure another trader to supply, those products or equivalent products at that price for a period that is, and in quantities that are, reasonable having regard to the product, the scale of advertising of the product and the price offered (bait advertising).

6. Making an invitation to purchase products at a specified price and then:

(a) refusing to show the advertised item to consumers;

or

(b) refusing to take orders for it or deliver it within a reasonable time;

or

(c) demonstrating a defective sample of it,

with the intention of promoting a different product (bait and switch)

7. Falsely stating that a product will only be available for a very limited time, or that it will only be available on particular terms for a very limited time, in order to elicit an immediate decision and deprive consumers of sufficient opportunity or time to make an informed choice.

8. Undertaking to provide after-sales service to consumers with whom the trader has communicated prior to a transaction in a language which is not an official language of the Member State where the trader is located and then making such service available only in another language without clearly disclosing this to the consumer before the consumer is committed to the transaction.

9. Stating or otherwise creating the impression that a product can legally be sold when it cannot.

10. Presenting rights given to consumers in law as a distinctive feature of the trader's offer.

11. Using editorial content in the media to promote a product where a trader has paid for the promotion without making that clear in the content or by images or sounds clearly identifiable by the consumer (advertorial). This is without prejudice to Council Directive 89/552/EEC.[10]

12. Making a materially inaccurate claim concerning the nature and extent of the risk to the personal security of the consumer or his family if the consumer does not purchase the product.

13. Promoting a product similar to a product made by a particular manufacturer in such a manner as deliberately to mislead the consumer into believing that the product is made by that same manufacturer when it is not.

14. Establishing, operating or promoting a pyramid promotional scheme where a consumer gives consideration for the opportunity to receive compensation that is derived primarily from the introduction of other consumers into the scheme rather than from the sale or consumption of products.

15. Claiming that the trader is about to cease trading or move premises when he is not.

16. Claiming that products are able to facilitate winning in games of chance.

17. Falsely claiming that a product is able to cure illnesses, dysfunction or malformations.

18. Passing on materially inaccurate information on market conditions or on the possibility of finding the product with the intention of inducing the consumer to acquire the product at conditions less favourable than normal market conditions.

19. Claiming in a commercial practice to offer a competition or prize promotion without awarding the prizes described or a reasonable equivalent.

20. Describing a product as 'gratis', 'free', 'without charge' or similar if the consumer has to pay anything other than the unavoidable cost of responding to the commercial practice and collecting or paying for delivery of the item.

21. Including in marketing material an invoice or similar document seeking payment which gives the consumer the impression that he has already ordered the marketed product when he has not.

---

[10] Council Directive 89/552/EEC of 3 October 1989 on the coordination of certain provisions laid down by Law, Regulation or Administrative Action in Member States concerning the pursuit of television broadcasting activities (OJ L 298, 17.10.1989, 23). Directive as amended by Directive 97/36/EC of the European Parliament and of the Council (OJ L 202, 30.7.1997, 60).

22. Falsely claiming or creating the impression that the trader is not acting for purposes relating to his trade, business, craft or profession, or falsely representing oneself as a consumer.

23. Creating the false impression that after-sales service in relation to a product is available in a Member State other than the one in which the product is sold.

Aggressive commercial practices

24. Creating the impression that the consumer cannot leave the premises until a contract is formed.

25. Conducting personal visits to the consumer's home ignoring the consumer's request to leave or not to return except in circumstances and to the extent justified, under national law, to enforce a contractual obligation.

26. Making persistent and unwanted solicitations by telephone, fax, e-mail or other remote media except in circumstances and to the extent justified under national law to enforce a contractual obligation. This is without prejudice to Article 10 of Directive 97/7/EC and Directives 95/46/EC[11] and 2002/58/EC.

27. Requiring a consumer who wishes to claim on an insurance policy to produce documents which could not reasonably be considered relevant as to whether the claim was valid, or failing systematically to respond to pertinent correspondence, in order to dissuade a consumer from exercising his contractual rights.

28. Including in an advertisement a direct exhortation to children to buy advertised products or persuade their parents or other adults to buy advertised products for them. This provision is without prejudice to Article 16 of Directive 89/552/EEC on television broadcasting.

29. Demanding immediate or deferred payment for or the return or safekeeping of products supplied by the trader, but not solicited by the consumer except where the product is a substitute supplied in conformity with Article 7(3) of Directive 97/7/EC (inertia selling).

30. Explicitly informing a consumer that if he does not buy the product or service, the trader's job or livelihood will be in jeopardy.

31. Creating the false impression that the consumer has already won, will win, or will on doing a particular act win, a prize or other equivalent benefit, when in fact either:
– there is no prize or other equivalent benefit,
or
– taking any action in relation to claiming the prize or other equivalent benefit is subject to the consumer paying money or incurring a cost.

Annex II

Community law provisions setting out rules for advertising and commercial communication

Articles 4 and 5 of Directive 97/7/EC

Article 3 of Council Directive 90/314/EEC of 13 June 1990 on package travel, package holidays and package tours[12]

Article 3(3) of Directive 94/47/EC of the European Parliament and of the Council of 26 October 1994 on the protection of purchasers in respect of certain aspects of contracts relating to the purchase of a right to use immovable properties on a timeshare basis[13]

Article 3(4) of Directive 98/6/EC of the European Parliament and of the Council of 16 February 1998 on consumer protection in the

---

[11] Directive 95/46/EC of the European Parliament and of the Council of 24 October 1995 on the protection of individuals with regard to the processing of personal data and on the free movement of such data (OJ L 281, 23.11.1995, 31). Directive as amended by Regulation (EC) No 1882/2003 (OJ L 284, 31.10.2003, 1).

[12] OJ L 158, 23.6.1990, 59.

[13] OJ L 280, 29.10.1994, 83.

indication of the prices of products offered to consumers[14]

Articles 86 to 100 of Directive 2001/83/EC of the European Parliament and of the Council of 6 November 2001 on the Community code relating to medicinal products for human use[15]

Articles 5 and 6 of Directive 2000/31/EC of the European Parliament and of the Council of 8 June 2000 on certain legal aspects of information society services, in particular electronic commerce, in the Internal Market (Directive on electronic commerce)[16]

Article 1(d) of Directive 98/7/EC of the European Parliament and of the Council of 16 February 1998 amending Council Directive 87/102/EEC for the approximation of the laws, regulations and administrative provisions of the Member States concerning consumer credit[17]

Articles 3 and 4 of Directive 2002/65/EC

Article 1(9) of Directive 2001/107/EC of the European Parliament and of the Council of 21 January 2002 amending Council Directive 85/611/EEC on the coordination of laws, regulations and administrative provisions relating to undertakings for collective investment in transferable securities (UCITS) with a view to regulating management companies and simplified prospectuses[18]

Articles 12 and 13 of Directive 2002/92/EC of the European Parliament and of the Council of 9 December 2002 on insurance mediation[19]

Article 36 of Directive 2002/83/EC of the European Parliament and of the Council of 5 November 2002 concerning life assurance[20]

Article 19 of Directive 2004/39/EC of the European Parliament and of the Council of 21 April 2004 on markets in financial instruments[21]

Articles 31 and 43 of Council Directive 92/49/EEC of 18 June 1992 on the coordination of laws, regulations and administrative provisions relating to direct insurance other than life assurance[22] (third non-life insurance Directive)

Articles 5, 7 and 8 of Directive 2003/71/EC of the European Parliament and of the Council of 4 November 2003 on the prospectus to be published when securities are offered to the public or admitted to trading.[23]

---

[14] OJ L 80, 18.3.1998, 27.
[15] OJ L 311, 28.11.2001, 67. Directive as last amended by Directive 2004/27/EC (OJ L 136, 30.4.2004, 34).
[16] OJ L 178, 17.7.2000, 1, reproduced supra under no. C.P. 19.
[17] OJ L 101, 1.4.1998, 17, reproduced supra under no. C.P. 14.
[18] OJ L 41, 13.2.2002, 20, reproduced infra under no. S. 21.
[19] OJ L 9, 15.1.2003, 3, reproduced infra under no. I. 34.
[20] OJ L 345, 19.12.2002, 1, reproduced infra under no. I. 33. Directive as amended by Council Directive 2004/66/EC. (OJ L 168, 1.5.2004, 35).
[21] OJ L 145, 30.4.2004, 1, reproduced infra under no. S. 29.
[22] OJ L 228, 11.8.1992, 1 reproduced infra under no. I. 25. Directive as last amended by Directive 2002/87/EC of the European Parliament and of the Council (OJ L 35, 11.2.2003, 1), reproduced supra under no. B. 38.
[23] OJ L 345, 31.12.2003, 64, reproduced infra under no. S. 25.

PART V
ENTERPRISE LAW

E. 1.

Council Directive 75/129/EEC
of 17 February 1975
on the approximation of the laws of the Member States relating to collective redundancies[1]

This Directive has been repealed as from 31 August 1998 by article 8 of Directive 98/59/EC (OJ L 225, 12. 8. 1998, 16), reproduced infra under no. E. 8.

Correlation Table

Directive 75/129/EEC	Directive 98/59/EC
Article 1(1), first subparagraph, point (a), first indent, point 1	Article 1(1), first subparagraph, point (a)(i), first indent
Article 1(1), first subparagraph, point (a), first indent, point 2	Article 1(1), first subparagraph, point (a)(i), second indent
Article 1(1), first subparagraph, point (a), first indent, point 3	Article 1(1), first subparagraph, point (a)(i), third indent
Article 1(1), first subparagraph, point (a), second indent	Article 1(1), first subparagraph, point (a)(ii)
Article 1(1), first subparagraph, point (b)	Article 1(1), first subparagraph, point (b)
Article 1(1), second subparagraph	Article 1(1), second subparagraph
Article 1(2)	Article 1 (2)
Article 2	Article 2
Article 3	Article 3
Article 4	Article 4
Article 5	Article 5
Article 5a	Article 6
Article 6(1)	—
Article 6(2)	Article 7
Article 7	—
—	Article 8
—	Article 9
—	Article 10
—	Annex I
—	Annex II

---

[1] OJ L 48, 22.2.1975, 29–30.

E. 2.

[Council Directive 77/187/EEC
of 14 February 1977
on the approximation of the laws of the Member States relating to the safeguarding of employees' rights in the event of transfers of undertakings, businesses or parts of undertakings or businesses][1]

¶ *This title has been amended by article 1(1) of Directive 98/50/EC, reproduced infra under no. E. 7.*

This Directive has been repealed as from 11 April 2001 by article 12 of Directive 2001/23/EC (OJ L 82, 22.3.2001, 16), reproduced infra under no. E. 11.

Correlation Table

Directive 77/187/EEC	Directive 2001/23/EC
Article 1	Article 1
Article 2	Article 2
Article 3	Article 3
Article 4	Article 4
Article 4a	Article 5
Article 5	Article 6
Article 6	Article 7
Article 7	Article 8
Article 7a	Article 9
Article 7b	Article 10
Article 8	Article 11
—	Article 12
—	Article 13
—	Article 14
—	ANNEX I
—	ANNEX II

[1] OJ L 61, 5.3.1977, 26.

E. 3.

[Council Directive 80/987/EEC
of 20 October 1980
on the approximation of the laws of the Member States relating
to the protection of employees in the event of the insolvency of their employer][1]

¶ *The title has been replaced by article 1(1) of Directive 2002/74/EC, reproduced infra under no. E. 13.*

Cases

I. Case C-342/96 Kingdom of Spain v Commission of the European Communities [1999] ECR I-2459

In order to determine whether a State measure constitutes aid for the purposes of Article [87][2] of the Treaty, it is necessary to establish whether the recipient undertaking receives an economic advantage that it would not have obtained under normal market conditions. In the case of an undertaking in liquidation or in difficulties, for which public bodies have advanced sums for the payment of employees' salaries or of debts in respect of social security contributions and with which those bodies have concluded agreements under which the accumulated debts are to be rescheduled or paid by instalments in order to facilitate their repayment, account must be taken of the fact that those agreements were concluded because the undertaking was already subject to the pre-existing statutory obligation to make such payments, which means that they did not therefore create any new debts owed by the undertaking to the public authorities. The interest normally applicable to that type of debt is intended to make good the loss suffered by the creditor because of the debtor's delay in performing its obligation to pay off its debt, namely default interest. In cases where the rate of default interest applied to the debts of a public creditor is not the same as the rate charged for the debts owed to a private creditor, the latter rate ought to be charged where it is higher than the former, if the rate of default interest is not to constitute an element of State aid.

II. Case C-373/95 Federica Maso and others and Graziano Gazzetta and others v Istituto Nazionale della Previdenza Sociale (INPS) and Repubblica Italiana [1997] ECR I-4051

In making good the loss or damage sustained by employees as a result of the belated transposition of Directive 80/987/EEC on the approximation of the laws of the Member States relating to the protection of employees in the event of the insolvency of their employer, a Member State is entitled to apply retroactively to such employees belatedly adopted implementing measures, including rules against aggregation or other limitations on the liability of the guarantee institution, provided that the directive has been properly transposed. However, it is for the national court to ensure that reparation of the loss or damage sustained by the beneficiaries is adequate. Retroactive and proper application in full of the measures implementing the directive will suffice for that purpose unless the beneficiaries establish the existence of complementary loss sustained on account of the fact that they were unable to benefit at the appropriate time from the financial advantages guaranteed by the directive with the result that such loss must also be made good.

III. Joined cases C-6/90 and C-9/90 Andrea Francovich and Danila Bonifaci and others v Italian Republic [1991] ECR I-5357

1. Although the provisions of Directive 80/987/EEC on the protection of employees in the event of the insolvency of the employer are sufficiently precise and unconditional as regards the determination of the persons entitled to the guarantee and as regards the content of that guarantee, where no implementing measures are adopted by the Member State within the prescribed period the

---

[1] OJ L 283, 28.10.1980, 23–27.
[2] The number between brackets has been changed as from 1 May 1999 by article 12 of the Treaty of Amsterdam.

persons concerned cannot enforce those rights before the national courts, since the provisions of the directive do not identify the person liable to provide the guarantee and the State cannot be considered liable on the sole ground that it has failed to take transposition measures within the prescribed period.

2. The full effectiveness of Community rules would be impaired and the protection of the rights that they grant would be weakened if individuals were unable to obtain reparation when their rights are infringed by a breach of Community law for which a Member State can be held responsible. Such a possibility of reparation by the Member State is particularly indispensable where the full effectiveness of Community rules is subject to prior action on the part of the State and where, consequently, in the absence of such action, individuals cannot enforce before the national courts the rights conferred upon them by Community law. It follows that the principle whereby a State must be liable for loss and damage caused to individuals by breaches of Community law for which the State can be held responsible is inherent in the system of the Treaty. A further basis for the obligation of Member States to make good such loss and damage is to be found in Article [10]² of the Treaty, under which they are required to take all appropriate measures, whether general or particular, to ensure the implementation of Community law, and consequently to nullify the unlawful consequences of a breach of Community law.

3. Although the liability of the Member State to make good loss and damage caused to individuals by breaches of Community law for which it can be held responsible is required by Community law, the conditions under which there is a right to reparation depend on the nature of the breach of Community law giving rise to the loss and damage which have been caused. In the case of a Member State which fails to fulfil its obligation under the third paragraph of Article [249]² of the Treaty to take all the measures necessary to achieve the result prescribed by a directive the full effectiveness of that rule of Community law requires that there should be a right to reparation where three conditions are met, that is to say, first, that the result prescribed by the directive should entail the grant of rights to individuals; secondly, that it should be possible to identify the content of those rights on the basis of the provisions of the directive; and thirdly, that there should be a causal link between the breach of the State's obligation and the loss and damage suffered by the injured parties. In the absence of any Community legislation, it is in accordance with the rules of national law on liability that the State must make reparation for the consequences of the loss and damage caused. Nevertheless, the relevant substantive and procedural conditions laid down by the national law of the Member States must not be less favourable than those relating to similar domestic claims and must not be so framed as to make it virtually impossible or excessively difficult to obtain reparation.

IV. Case 22/87 Commission of the European Communities v Italian Republic [1989] ECR 143

Directive 80/987/EEC is intended to provide a minimum protection for all workers in the event of their employer's insolvency. The national legislation of a Member State does not satisfy the requirements of that directive where the guarantee which it provides is incomplete both as regards the persons covered–by reason of the fact that it applies only to certain categories of undertaking, it excludes certain categories of workers who under national law have the status of employees other than those for which a derogation is expressly authorized by the directive and it is not automatic, being subject to the fulfilment of a number of preconditions which have to be assessed case by case by the national authorities–and as regards its scope–since it does not ensure the automatic payment of benefits under statutory social security schemes where the contributions deducted at source have not been paid and it does not protect pension rights under supplementary pension schemes operating independently from the statutory social security schemes.

THE COUNCIL OF THE EUROPEAN COMMUNITIES,

Having regard to the Treaty establishing the European Economic Community, and in particular Article [94]² thereof,

Having regard to the proposal from the Commission,³

Having regard to the opinion of the European Parliament,⁴

---

³ OJ C 135, 9.6.1978, 2.
⁴ OJ C 39, 12.2.1979, 26.

Having regard to the opinion of the Economic and Social Committee,[5]

Whereas it is necessary to provide for the protection of employees in the event of the insolvency of their employer, in particular in order to guarantee payment of their outstanding claims, while taking account of the need for balanced economic and social development in the Community;

Whereas differences still remain between the Member States as regards the extent of the protection of employees in this respect; whereas efforts should be directed towards reducing these differences, which can have a direct effect on the functioning of the common market;

Whereas the approximation of laws in this field should, therefore, be promoted while the improvement within the meaning of Article [136][2] of the Treaty is maintained;

Whereas as a result of the geographical situation and the present job structure in that area, the labour market in Greenland is fundamentally different from that of the other areas of the Community;

Whereas to the extent that the Hellenic Republic is to become a member of the European Economic Community on January 1, 1981, in accordance with the Act concerning the Conditions of Accession of the Hellenic Republic and the Adjustments to the Treaties, it is appropriate to stipulate in the Annex to the Directive under the heading 'Greece', those categories of employees whose claims may be excluded in accordance with Article 1 (2) of the Directive,

HAS ADOPTED THIS DIRECTIVE:

[SECTION I
SCOPE AND DEFINITIONS

Article 1

1. This Directive shall apply to employees' claims arising from contracts of employment or employment relationships and existing against employers who are in a state of insolvency within the meaning of Article 2(1).

2. Member States may, by way of exception, exclude claims by certain categories of employee from the scope of this Directive, by virtue of the existence of other forms of guarantee if it is established that these offer the persons concerned a degree of protection equivalent to that resulting from this Directive.

3. Where such provision already applies in their national legislation, Member States may continue to exclude from the scope of this Directive:

(a) domestic servants employed by a natural person;

(b) share-fishermen.

CASES

I. Case C-442/00 Ángel Rodríguez Caballero v Fondo de Garantía Salarial (Fogasa) [2002] ECR I-11915

Claims in respect of 'salarios de tramitación' must be regarded as employees' claims arising from contracts of employment or employment relationships and relating to pay, within the meaning of Articles 1(1) and 3(1) irrespective of the procedure under which they are determined, if, according to the national legislation concerned, such claims, when recognised by judicial decision, give rise to liability on the part of the guarantee institution and if a difference in treatment of identical claims acknowledged in a conciliation procedure is not objectively justified.

II. Case C-334/92 Teodoro Wagner Miret v Fondo de Garantía Salarial [1993] ECR I-6911

Higher management staff may not be excluded from the scope of Council Directive 80/987/EEC as amended by Council Directive 87/164/EEC, where they are classified under national law as employees and they are not listed in section I of the Annex to the directive.

III. Case 53/88 Commission of the European Communities v Hellenic Republic [1990] ECR I-3917

Article 1(2) of Directive 80/987/EEC confers on the Member States the power to exclude from the

---

[5] OJ C 105, 26.4.1979, 15.

scope of the directive, by way of exception, the claims of certain categories of employee. When the exclusion is authorized by virtue of the special nature of the contract of employment or employment relationship, which exclusion is not conditional on the existence of a form of guarantee other than the one resulting from the directive, offering equivalent protection. However, when the exclusion is authorised precisely because there is such a guarantee, it is possible only if the employee enjoys protection that, while being based on a scheme whose detailed rules differ from those laid down by the directive, affords employees the essential guarantees set out therein.

Article 2

1. For the purposes of this Directive, an employer shall be deemed to be in a state of insolvency where a request has been made for the opening of collective proceedings based on insolvency of the employer, as provided for under the laws, regulations and administrative provisions of a Member State, and involving the partial or total divestment of the employer's assets and the appointment of a liquidator or a person performing a similar task, and the authority which is competent pursuant to the said provisions has:

(a) either decided to open the proceedings, or

(b) established that the employer's undertaking or business has been definitively closed down and that the available assets are insufficient to warrant the opening of the proceedings.

2. This Directive is without prejudice to national law as regards the definition of the terms 'employee', 'employer', 'pay', 'right conferring immediate entitlement' and 'right conferring prospective entitlement'.

However, the Member States may not exclude from the scope of this Directive:

(a) part-time employees within the meaning of Directive 97/81/EC;

(b) workers with a fixed-term contract within the meaning of Directive 1999/70/EC;

(c) workers with a temporary employment relationship within the meaning of Article 1(2) of Directive 91/383/EEC.

3. Member States may not set a minimum duration for the contract of employment or the employment relationship in order for workers to qualify for claims under this Directive.

4. This Directive does not prevent Member States from extending workers' protection to other situations of insolvency, for example where payments have been de facto stopped on a permanent basis, established by proceedings different from those mentioned in paragraph 1 as provided for under national law.

Such procedures shall not however create a guarantee obligation for the institutions of the other Member States in the cases referred to in Section IIIa.]

Cases

I. Case C-442/00 Ángel Rodríguez Caballero v Fondo de Garantía Salarial (Fogasa) [2002] ECR I-11915

The national court must set aside national legislation which, in breach of the principle of equality, excludes from the concept of 'pay' within the meaning of Article 2(2) of Directive 80/987/EEC claims in respect of 'salarios de tramitación' agreed in a conciliation procedure supervised and approved by a court; it must apply to members of the group disadvantaged by that discrimination the arrangements in force in respect of employees whose claims of the same type come, according to the national definition of 'pay', within the scope of that directive.

II. Case C-117/96 Danmarks Aktive Handelsrejsende, acting on behalf of Carina Mosbæk v Lønmodtagernes Garantifond [1997] ECR I-5017

Where the employer is established in a Member State other than that in which the employee resides and was employed, the guarantee institution responsible, under Article 3 of Directive 80/987/EEC is the institution of the State in which, in accordance with Article 2(1) of the directive, either it is decided to open the proceedings for the collective satisfaction of creditors' claims or it has been established that the employer's undertaking or business has been closed down.

¶ *Section I has been replaced by article 1(2) of Directive 2002/74/EC, reproduced infra under no. E. 13.*

Section II
Provisions Concerning Guarantee Institutions

[*Article 3*]

Member States shall take the measures necessary to ensure that guarantee institutions guarantee, subject to Article 4, payment of employees' outstanding claims resulting from contracts of employment or employment relationships, including, where provided for by national law, severance pay on termination of employment relationships.

The claims taken over by the guarantee institution shall be the outstanding pay claims relating to a period prior to and/or, as applicable, after a given date determined by the Member States.

Cases

I. Joined cases C-19/01, C-50/01 and C-84/01 Istituto Nazionale della Previdenza Sociale (INPS) v Alberto Barsotti and Others [2004] ECR I-2005

Article 3(1) and the first subparagraph of Article 4(3) of Council Directive 80/987/EEC are to be interpreted as meaning that they do not allow a Member State to limit the liability of the guarantee institutions to a sum which covers the basic needs of the employees concerned and from which are to be deducted payments made by the employer during the period covered by the guarantee.

II. Case C-520/03 José Vicente Olaso Valero v Fondo de Garantía Salarial (Fogasa) [2004] ECR I-12065

1. It falls to the national court to determine whether the word 'pay', as defined by national law, includes compensation for unfair dismissal. If it does, such compensation falls within the ambit of Council Directive 80/987/EEC, as it stood before it was amended by Directive 2002/74/EC.

2. Where, according to the national legislation in question, claims corresponding to compensation for unfair dismissal, awarded by judgment or administrative decision, fall within the definition of 'pay', identical claims, established in a conciliation must be regarded as employees' claims arising from contracts of employment or employment relationships and as relating to pay for the purposes of Directive 80/987/EEC. The national court must set aside domestic legislation which, in breach of the principle of equality, excludes the latter claims from the definition of 'pay' under that legislation.

III. Case C-160/01 Karen Mau v Bundesanstalt für Arbeit [2003] ECR I-4791

1. Articles 3(2) and 4(2) of Council Directive 80/987/EEC must be interpreted as precluding a provision of national law, such as Paragraph 183(1) of Sozialgesetzbuch III (German Social Code, Part III), which defines the date of the onset of the employer's insolvency as the date of the decision ruling on the request for opening of the insolvency procedure and not the date on which that request was lodged.

2. The expression 'employment relationship' within the meaning of Articles 3 and 4 of Directive 80/987/EEC, must be interpreted as excluding periods which, by their very nature, cannot give rise to outstanding salary claims. A period during which the employment relationship is suspended on account of child raising leave and, for that reason, confers no right to remuneration, is therefore excluded.

IV. Case C-442/00 Ángel Rodríguez Caballero v Fondo de Garantía Salarial (Fogasa) [2002] ECR I-11915

See supra under Article 1 of this Directive.

V. Case C-198/98 G. Everson and T.J. Barrass v Secretary of State for Trade and Industry and Bell Lines Ltd [1999] ECR I-8903

Where the employees adversely affected by the insolvency of their employer were employed in a Member State by the branch established in that State of a company incorporated under the laws of another Member State, where that company has its registered office and in which it was placed in liquidation, the competent institution, under Article 3 of Directive 80/987/EEC is that of the State within whose territory they were employed.

VI. Case C-117/96 Danmarks Aktive Handelsrejsende, acting on behalf of Carina Mosbæk v Lønmodtagernes Garantifond [1997] ECR I-5017

Where the employer is established in a Member State other than that in which the employee resides and was employed, the guarantee institution responsible, under Article 3 of Directive 80/987/EEC is the institution of the State in which, in accordance with Article 2(1) of the directive, either it is decided to open the proceedings for the collective satisfaction of creditors' claims or it has been established that the employer's undertaking or business has been closed down.

VII. Case C-373/95 Federica Maso and others and Graziano Gazzetta and others v Istituto Nazionale della Previdenza Sociale (INPS) and Repubblica Italiana [1997] ECR I-4051

The term 'onset of the employer's insolvency', which, according to Articles 3(2) and 4(2) of Directive 80/987/EEC, determines the outstanding claims which are subject to the guarantee provided for by the directive, must be interpreted as designating the date of the request that proceedings to satisfy collectively the claims of creditors be opened, since the guarantee cannot be provided prior to a decision to open such proceedings or to a finding that the business has been definitively closed down where the assets are insufficient. That interpretation takes into account both the social purpose of the directive and the need to settle precisely the reference periods to which it attaches legal effects. If the onset of the employer's insolvency were subject to fulfilment of the conditions governing the 'state of insolvency' set out in Article 2(1) of the directive, and in particular were dependent on the decision to open proceedings to satisfy collectively the claims of creditors, which may be given long after the request to open the proceedings, payment of unpaid remuneration might, given the temporal limits referred to in Article 4(2), never be guaranteed by the directive, for reasons wholly unconnected with the conduct of the employees.

VIII. Joined cases C-94/95 and C-95/95 Danila Bonifaci and others (C-94/95) and Wanda Berto and others (C-95/95) v Istituto Nazionale della Previdenza sociale [1997] ECR I-3969

The term 'onset of the employer's insolvency', which, according to Articles 3(2) and 4(2) of Directive 80/987/EEC, determines the outstanding claims which are subject to the guarantee provided for by the directive, must be interpreted as designating the date of the request that proceedings to satisfy collectively the claims of creditors be opened, since the guarantee cannot be provided prior to a decision to open such proceedings or to a finding that the business has been definitively closed down where the assets are insufficient. That interpretation takes into account both the social purpose of the directive and the need to settle precisely the reference periods to which it attaches legal effects.

If the onset of the employer's insolvency were subject to fulfilment of the conditions governing the 'state of insolvency' set out in Article 2(1) of the directive, and in particular were dependent on the date of the decision to open proceedings to satisfy collectively the claims of creditors, which may be given long after the request to open the proceedings, payment of unpaid remuneration might, given the temporal limits referred to in Article 4(2), never be guaranteed by the directive, for reasons wholly unconnected with the conduct of the employees.

IX. Case C-334/92 Teodoro Wagner Miret v Fondo de Garantía Salarial [1993] ECR I-6911

Higher management staff may not rely on Directive 80/987/EEC in order to request the payment of amounts owing to them by way of salary from the guarantee institution established by national law for the other categories of employee. Article 3(1) of the directive requires the Member States to take the measures necessary to ensure that guarantee institutions guarantee payment of employees' outstanding claims, but does not oblige them to establish a single institution for all categories of employee. In the event that, even when interpreted in the light of the aforementioned directive, national law does not enable higher management staff to obtain the benefit of the guarantees for which it provides, such staff are entitled to request the State concerned to make good the loss and damage sustained as a result of the failure to implement the directive in their respect.

Article 4

1. Member States shall have the option to limit the liability of the guarantee institutions referred to in Article 3.

2. When Member States exercise the option referred to in paragraph 1, they shall specify the length of the period for which outstanding claims

are to be met by the guarantee institution. However, this may not be shorter than a period covering the remuneration of the last three months of the employment relationship prior to and/or after the date referred to in Article 3. Member States may include this minimum period of three months in a reference period with a duration of not less than six months.

Member States having a reference period of not less than 18 months may limit the period for which outstanding claims are met by the guarantee institution to eight weeks. In this case, those periods which are most favourable to the employee are used for the calculation of the minimum period.

3. Furthermore, Member States may set ceilings on the payments made by the guarantee institution. These ceilings must not fall below a level which is socially compatible with the social objective of this Directive.

When Member States exercise this option, they shall inform the Commission of the methods used to set the ceiling.]

Cases

I. Case C-201/01 Maria Walcher v Bundesamt für Soziales und Behindertenwesen Steiermark [2003] ECR I-8827

1. Council Directive 80/987/EEC precludes a rule that an employee with a significant shareholding in the private limited company that employs him, but who does not exercise a dominant influence over that company, loses, pursuant to the Austrian case law relating to shareholder loans in lieu of capital contributions, his entitlement to the guarantee in respect of claims for outstanding pay which result from the employer's insolvency and are covered by Article 4(2) of that directive if, in the 60 days from the time he first could have become aware that the company was no longer creditworthy, he fails to make any genuine demand for payment of salary owed to him.

2. To avoid abuses a Member State is, in principle, entitled to take measures that deny such an employee an entitlement to a guarantee in respect of claims for outstanding salary arising after the date on which an employee who is not a shareholder would have resigned on the ground of non-payment of his salary, unless it is established that there has been no abusive conduct. As regards the guarantee to pay claims covered by Article 4(2) of Directive 80/987/EEC, the Member State is not entitled to assume that, as a general rule, an employee who is not a shareholder would have resigned on the ground of non-payment of his salary before his salary had been in arrears for a period of three months.

II. Case C-235/95 AGS Assedic Pas-de-Calais v François Dumon and Froment, Liquidator and Representative of Établissements Pierre Gilson [1998] ECR I-4531

Articles 4(3) and 11 of Directive 80/987/EEC do not preclude the application of national provisions setting a ceiling on the payment guarantee in respect of employees' outstanding claims, where the Member State has failed to inform the Commission of the methods used to set that ceiling. It does not follow from the second subparagraph of Article 4(3) of Directive 80/987/EEC, which requires Member States that have set a ceiling to the liability for employees' outstanding claims, as the preceding subparagraph authorizes them to do, to inform the Commission of the methods used to set that ceiling, that that duty gives rise to a Community procedure for monitoring the methods chosen by the Member State, or that Member States' exercise of the option to set a ceiling is subject to the express or implied agreement of the Commission. Moreover, neither the wording nor the purpose of the abovementioned provision provides justification for the view that Member States' non-compliance with their obligation to give prior notice in itself renders the ceilings thus adopted unlawful. Thus the purpose of the obligation to give notice laid down in the second subparagraph of Article 4(3) is simply to inform the Commission whether Member States have exercised the option referred to in the preceding subparagraph and, if so, in what manner. As for Article 11(2) of the directive, which requires Member States to communicate to the Commission the texts of the laws, regulations, and administrative provisions which they adopt in the field governed by the directive, it is clear from that provision that it concerns relations between the Member States and the Commission and confers no right upon individuals which could be infringed in the event of a breach by a Member State of the obligation to give prior notice to the Commission of the methods used to set the ceiling referred to in Article 4(3) of the directive.

III. Case C-125/97 A.G.R. Regeling v Bestuur van de Bedrijfsvereniging voor de Metaalnijverheid [1998] ECR I-4493

On a proper construction of Article 4(2) of Directive 80/987/EEC where a worker has, simultaneously, claims against his employer in respect of periods of employment before the reference period laid down in that provision and claims relating to the reference period itself, payments of wages made by the employer during the latter period must be set in priority against earlier claims. It would be contrary to the social purpose of the directive, which is to guarantee all employees a minimum level of protection, to interpret Article 4(2) in such a way that a worker in that situation is not entitled to the guarantee in respect of wages which he has in fact lost during the reference period.

IV. Case C-373/95 Federica Maso and others and Graziano Gazzetta and others v Istituto Nazionale della Previdenza Sociale (INPS) and Repubblica Italiana [1997] ECR I-4051

It follows from the purpose of the directive that the phrase 'the last three months of the contract of employment or employment relationship' used in Article 4(2) thereof must be interpreted as meaning three rolling months in that it represents a period of time between the day of the month corresponding to the event referred to in Article 4(2) of the directive and the same day in the third preceding month. Limitation of the guarantee to the last three calendar months, whatever the date on which the event referred to in Article 4(2) of the directive occurred, could have damaging consequences for the beneficiaries of the directive if the onset of the insolvency did not occur on the last day of the month.

V. Joined cases C-94/95 and C-95/95 Danila Bonifaci and others (C-94/95) and Wanda Berto and others (C-95/95) v Istituto Nazionale della Previdenza Sociale [1997] ECR I-3969

See supra under Article 3 of this Directive.

¶ *Articles 3 and 4 have been replaced by article 1(3) of Directive 2002/74/EC, reproduced infra under no. E. 13.*

Article 5

Member States shall lay down detailed rules for the organisation, financing and operation of the guarantee institutions, complying with the following principles in particular:

(a) the assets of the institutions shall be independent of the employers' operating capital and be inaccessible to proceedings for insolvency;

(b) employers shall contribute to financing, unless it is fully covered by the public authorities;

(c) the institutions' liabilities shall not depend on whether or not obligations to contribute to financing have been fulfilled.

SECTION III
PROVISIONS CONCERNING SOCIAL SECURITY

Article 6

Member States may stipulate that Articles 8, 4 and 5 shall not apply to contributions due under national statutory social security schemes or under supplementary company or inter-company pension schemes outside the national statutory social security schemes.

Article 7

Member States shall take the measures necessary to ensure that non-payment of compulsory contributions due from the employer, before the onset of his insolvency, to their insurance institutions under national statutory social security schemes does not adversely affect employees' benefit entitlement in respect of these insurance institutions inasmuch as the employees' contributions were deducted at source from the remuneration paid.

Article 8

Member States shall ensure that the necessary measures are taken to protect the interests of employees and of persons having already left the employer's undertaking or business at the date of the onset of the employer's insolvency in respect of rights conferring on them immediate or prospective entitlement to old age benefits, including survivors' benefits, under supplementary company or inter-company pension schemes outside the national statutory social security schemes.

[SECTION IIIa

PROVISIONS CONCERNING TRANSNATIONAL SITUATIONS

Article 8a

1. When an undertaking with activities in the territories of at least two Member States is in a state of insolvency within the meaning of Article 2(1), the institution responsible for meeting employees' outstanding claims shall be that in the Member State in whose territory they work or habitually work.

2. The extent of employees' rights shall be determined by the law governing the competent guarantee institution.

3. Member States shall take the measures necessary to ensure that, in the cases referred to in paragraph 1, decisions taken in the context of insolvency proceedings referred to in Article 2(1), which have been requested in another Member State, are taken into account when determining the employer's state of insolvency within the meaning of this Directive.

Article 8b

1. For the purposes of implementing Article 8a, Member States shall make provision for the sharing of relevant information between their competent administrative authorities and/or guarantee institutions mentioned in Article 3, making it possible in particular to inform the guarantee institution responsible for meeting the employees' outstanding claims.

2. Member States shall notify the Commission and the other Member States of the contact details of their competent administrative authorities and/or guarantee institutions. The Commission shall make these communications publicly accessible.]

¶ *Section IIIa has been inserted by article 1(4) of Directive 2002/74/EC, reproduced infra under no. E. 13.*

SECTION IV

GENERAL AND FINAL PROVISIONS

Article 9

This Directive shall not affect the option of Member States to apply or introduce laws, regulations or administrative provisions that are more favourable to employees.

[Implementation of this Directive shall not under any circumstances be sufficient grounds for a regression in relation to the current situation in the Member States and in relation to the general level of protection of workers in the area covered by it.]

¶ *The second paragraph has been inserted by article 1(5) of Directive 2002/74/EC, reproduced infra under no. E. 13.*

Article 10

This Directive shall not affect the option of Member States:

(a) to take the measures necessary to avoid abuses;

(b) to refuse or reduce the liability referred to in Article 3 or the guarantee obligation referred to in Article 7 if it appears that fulfilment of the obligation is unjustifiable because of the existence of special links between the employee and the employer and of common interests resulting in collusion between them.

[(c) to refuse or reduce the liability referred to in Article 3 or the guarantee obligation referred to in Article 7 in cases where the employee, on his or her own or together with his or her close relatives, was the owner of an essential part of the employer's undertaking or business and had a considerable influence on its activities.]

¶ *Article 10(c) has been inserted by article 1(6) of Directive 2002/74/EC, reproduced infra under no. E. 13.*

[Article 10a]
Member States shall notify the Commission and the other Member States of the types of national insolvency proceedings falling within the scope of this Directive, and of any amendments relating thereto. The Commission shall publish these communications in the Official Journal of the European Communities.]

¶ *Article 10a has been inserted by article 1(7) of Directive 2002/74/EC, reproduced infra under no. E. 13.*

Article 11

1. Member States shall bring into force the laws, regulations and administrative provisions necessary to comply with this Directive within 36 months of its notification. They shall forthwith inform the Commission thereof.

2. Member States shall communicate to the Commission the texts of the laws, regulations and administrative provisions that they adopt in the field governed by this Directive.

CASE

Case C-235/95 AGS Assedic Pas-de-Calais v François Dumon and Froment, Liquidator and Representative of Établissements Pierre Gilso [1998] ECR I-4531

See supra under Article 4 of this Directive.

Article 12

Within 18 months of the expiry of the period of 36 months laid down in Article 11 (1), Member States shall forward all relevant information to the Commission in order to enable it to draw up a report on the application of this Directive for submission to the Council.

Article 13

This Directive is addressed to the Member States

Annex

[. . .]

¶ *The Annex has been deleted by article 1(8) of Directive 2002/74/EC, reproduced infra under no. E. 13.*

CASE

Case C-441/99 Riksskatteverket v Soghra Gharehveran [2001] ECR I-7687

1. Point G of Section I of the Annex to Council Directive 80/987/EEC of 20 October 1980 as amended by the Act concerning the conditions of accession of the Republic of Austria, the Republic of Finland and the Kingdom of Sweden and the adjustments to the Treaties on which the European Union is founded, is to be interpreted as not allowing the Kingdom of Sweden to exclude from the group of persons covered by the wage payment guarantee provided for by the directive employees whose close relative owned, less than six months before the petition in insolvency, at least 20 per cent of the shares of the company employing them, when the employees concerned did not themselves have any share in the capital of that company.

2. Where a Member State has designated itself as liable to fulfil the obligation to meet wage and salary claims guaranteed under Directive 80/987/EEC, an employee whose spouse was owner of the company employing her is entitled to rely on the right to claim pay against the Member State concerned before a national court, notwithstanding the fact that, in breach of the directive, the legislation of that Member State expressly excludes from the group of persons covered by the guarantee employees whose close relative was owner of at least 20 per cent of the shares of the company but who did not themselves have any share in the capital of that company.

E. 4.
Council Directive 92/56/EEC
of 24 June 1992
amending Directive 75/129/EEC on the approximation of the laws of the Member States relating to collective redundancies[1]

This Directive has been repealed as from 31 August 1998 by article 8 of Directive 98/59/EC (OJ L 225, 12. 8. 1998, 16), reproduced infra under no. E. 8.

---

[1] OJ L 245, 26.8.1992, 3–5.

E. 5.

Council Directive 94/45/EC
of 22 September 1994
on the establishment of a European Works Council or a procedure in Community-scale undertakings and Community-scale groups of undertakings for the purposes of informing and consulting employees[1]

THE COUNCIL OF THE EUROPEAN UNION,

Having regard to the Agreement on social policy annexed to Protocol 14 on social policy annexed to the Treaty establishing the European Community, and in particular Article [2][2] (2) thereof,

Having regard to the proposal from the Commission,[3]

Having regard to the opinion of the Economic and Social Committee,[4]

Acting in accordance with the procedure referred to in Article [252][2] of the Treaty,[5]

Whereas, on the basis of the Protocol on Social Policy annexed to the Treaty establishing the European Community, the Kingdom of Belgium, the Kingdom of Denmark, the Federal Republic of Germany, the Hellenic Republic, the Kingdom of Spain, the French Republic, Ireland, the Italian Republic, the Grand Duchy of Luxembourg, the Kingdom of the Netherlands and the Portuguese Republic (hereinafter referred to as 'the Member States'), desirous of implementing the Social Charter of 1989, have adopted an Agreement on Social Policy;

Whereas Article [2][2] (2) of the said Agreement authorises the Council to adopt minimum requirements by means of directives;

Whereas, pursuant to Article 1 of the Agreement, one particular objective of the Community and the Member States is to promote dialogue between management and labour;

Whereas point 17 of the Community Charter of Fundamental Social Rights of Workers provides, *inter alia*, that information, consultation and participation for workers must be developed along appropriate lines, taking account of the practices in force in different Member States; whereas the Charter states that 'this shall apply especially in companies or groups of companies having establishments or companies in two or more Member States';

Whereas the Council, despite the existence of a broad consensus among the majority of Member States, was unable to act on the proposal for a Council Directive on the establishment of a European Works Council in Community-scale undertakings or groups of undertakings for the purposes of informing and consulting employees,[6] as amended on 3 December 1991;[7]

Whereas the Commission, pursuant to Article 3 (2) of the Agreement on Social Policy, has consulted management and labour at Community level on the possible direction of Community action on the information and consultation of workers in Community-scale undertakings and Community-scale groups of undertakings;

Whereas the Commission, considering after this consultation that Community action was advisable, has again consulted management and

---

[1] OJ L 254, 30.9.1994, 64–72.
[2] The number between brackets has been changed as from 1 May 1999 by article 12 of the Treaty of Amsterdam.
[3] OJ C 135, 18.5.1994, 8 and OJ No C 199, 21.7.1994, 10.
[4] Opinion delivered on 1 June 1994 (OJ C 2995, 22.10.1994, 10).
[5] Opinion of the European Parliament of 4 May 1994 (OJ C 205, 25.7.1994) and Council common position of 18 July 1994 (OJ C 244, 31.8.1994, 37).
[6] OJ C 39, 15.2.1991, 10.
[7] OJ C 336, 31.12.1991, 11.

labour on the content of the planned proposal, pursuant to Article 3 (3) of the said Agreement, and management and labour have presented their opinions to the Commission;

Whereas, following this second phase of consultation, management and labour have not informed the Commission of their wish to initiate the process which might lead to the conclusion of an agreement, as provided for in Article 4 of the Agreement;

Whereas the functioning of the internal market involves a process of concentrations of undertakings, cross-border mergers, take-overs, joint ventures and, consequently, a transnationalisation of undertakings and groups of undertakings; whereas, if economic activities are to develop in a harmonious fashion, undertakings and groups of undertakings operating in two or more Member States must inform and consult the representatives of those of their employees that are affected by their decisions;

Whereas procedures for informing and consulting employees as embodied in legislation or practice in the Member States are often not geared to the transnational structure of the entity which takes the decisions affecting those employees; whereas this may lead to the unequal treatment of employees affected by decisions within one and the same undertaking or group of undertakings;

Whereas appropriate provisions must be adopted to ensure that the employees of Community-scale undertakings are properly informed and consulted when decisions which affect them are taken in a Member State other than that in which they are employed;

Whereas, in order to guarantee that the employees of undertakings or groups of undertakings operating in two or more Member States are properly informed and consulted, it is necessary to set up European Works Councils or to create other suitable procedures for the transnational information and consultation of employees;

Whereas it is accordingly necessary to have a definition of the concept of controlling undertaking relating solely to this Directive and not prejudging definitions of the concepts of group or control which might be adopted in texts to be drafted in the future;

Whereas the mechanisms for informing and consulting employees in such undertakings or groups must encompass all of the establishments or, as the case may be, the group's undertakings located within the Member States, regardless of whether the undertaking or the group's controlling undertaking has its central management inside or outside the territory of the Member States;

Whereas, in accordance with the principle of autonomy of the parties, it is for the representatives of employees and the management of the undertaking or the group's controlling undertaking to determine by agreement the nature, composition, the function, mode of operation, procedures and financial resources of European Works Councils or other information and consultation procedures so as to suit their own particular circumstances;

Whereas, in accordance with the principle of subsidiarity, it is for the Member States to determine who the employees' representatives are and in particular to provide, if they consider appropriate, for a balanced representation of different categories of employees;

Whereas, however, provision should be made for certain subsidiary requirements to apply should the parties so decide or in the event of the central management refusing to initiate negotiations or in the absence of agreement subsequent to such negotiations;

Whereas, moreover, employees' representatives may decide not to seek the setting-up of a European Works Council or the parties concerned may decide on other procedures for the transnational information and consultation of employees;

Whereas, without prejudice to the possibility of the parties deciding otherwise, the European Works Council set up in the absence of agreement between the parties must, in order to fulfil the objective of this Directive, be kept informed and consulted on the activities of the undertaking or group of undertakings so that it may assess the possible impact on employees' interests in at least two different Member States; whereas, to that end, the undertaking or controlling undertaking must be required to communicate to the employees' appointed representatives general information concerning the interests of employees and information relating more specifically to those aspects of the activities of the undertaking or group of undertakings which affect employees' interests; whereas the European Works Council must be able to deliver an opinion at the end of that meeting;

Whereas certain decisions having a significant effect on the interests of employees must be the subject of information and consultation of the employees' appointed representatives as soon as possible;

Whereas provision should be made for the employees' representatives acting within the framework of the Directive to enjoy, when exercising their functions, the same protection and guarantees similar to those provided to employees' representatives by the legislation and/or practice of the country of employment; whereas they must not be subject to any discrimination as a result of the lawful exercise of their activities and must enjoy adequate protection as regards dismissal and other sanctions;

Whereas the information and consultation provisions laid down in this Directive must be implemented in the case of an undertaking or a group's controlling undertaking which has its central management outside the territory of the Member States by its representative agent, to be designated if necessary, in one of the Member States or, in the absence of such an agent, by the establishment or controlled undertaking employing the greatest number of employees in the Member States;

Whereas special treatment should be accorded to Community-scale undertakings and groups of undertakings in which there exists, at the time when this Directive is brought into effect, an agreement, covering the entire workforce, providing for the transnational information and consultation of employees;

Whereas the Member States must take appropriate measures in the event of failure to comply with the obligations laid down in this Directive,

HAS ADOPTED THIS DIRECTIVE:

Section I
General

Article 1
Objective

1. The purpose of this Directive is to improve the right to information and to consultation of employees in Community-scale undertakings and Community-scale groups of undertakings.

2. To that end, a European Works Council or a procedure for informing and consulting employees shall be established in every Community-scale undertaking and every Community-scale group of undertakings, where requested in the manner laid down in Article 5 (1), with the purpose of informing and consulting employees under the terms, in the manner and with the effects laid down in this Directive.

3. Notwithstanding paragraph 2, where a Community-scale group of undertakings within the meaning of Article 2 (1) (c) comprises one or more undertakings or groups of undertakings which are Community-scale undertakings or Community-scale groups of undertakings within the meaning of Article 2 (1) (a) or (c), a European Works Council shall be established at the level of the group unless the agreements referred to in Article 6 provide otherwise.

4. Unless a wider scope is provided for in the agreements referred to in Article 6, the powers and competence of European Works Councils and the scope of information and consultation procedures established to achieve the purpose specified in paragraph 1 shall, in the case of a Community-scale undertaking, cover all the establishments located within the Member States and, in the case of a Community-scale group of undertakings, all group undertakings located within the Member States.

5. Member States may provide that this Directive shall not apply to merchant navy crews.

Article 2
Definitions

1. For the purposes of this Directive:

(a) 'Community-scale undertaking' means any undertaking with at least 1 000 employees within the Member States and at least 150 employees in each of at least two Member States;

(b) 'group of undertakings' means a controlling undertaking and its controlled undertakings;

(c) 'Community-scale group of undertakings' means a group of undertakings with the following characteristics:
– at least 1 000 employees within the Member States,
– at least two group undertakings in different Member States, and
– at least one group undertaking with at least 150 employees in one Member State and at least one other group undertaking with at least 150 employees in another Member State;

(d) 'employees' representatives' means the employees' representatives provided for by national law and/or practice;

(e) 'central management' means the central management of the Community-scale undertaking or, in the case of a Community-scale group of undertakings, of the controlling undertaking;

(f) 'consultation' means the exchange of views and establishment of dialogue between employees' representatives and central management or any more appropriate level of management;

(g) 'European Works Council' means the council established in accordance with Article 1 (2) or the provisions of the Annex, with the purpose of informing and consulting employees;

(h) 'special negotiating body' means the body established in accordance with Article 5 (2) to negotiate with the central management regarding the establishment of a European Works Council or a procedure for informing and consulting employees in accordance with Article 1 (2).

2. For the purposes of this Directive, the prescribed thresholds for the size of the workforce shall be based on the average number of employees, including part-time employees, employed during the previous two years calculated according to national legislation and/or practice.

Article 3
Definition of 'controlling undertaking'

1. For the purposes of this Directive, 'controlling undertaking' means an undertaking which can exercise a dominant influence over another undertaking ('the controlled undertaking') by virtue, for example, of ownership, financial participation or the rules which govern it.

2. The ability to exercise a dominant influence shall be presumed, without prejudice to proof to the contrary, when, in relation to another undertaking directly or indirectly:

(a) holds a majority of that undertaking's subscribed capital; or

(b) controls a majority of the votes attached to that undertaking's issued share capital; or

(c) can appoint more than half of the members of that undertaking's administrative, management or supervisory body.

3. For the purposes of paragraph 2, a controlling undertaking's rights as regards voting and appointment shall include the rights of any other controlled undertaking and those of any person or body acting in his or its own name but on behalf of the controlling undertaking or of any other controlled undertaking.

4. Notwithstanding paragraphs 1 and 2, an undertaking shall not be deemed to be a 'controlling undertaking' with respect to another undertaking in which it has holdings where the former undertaking is a company referred to in Article 3 (5) (a) or (c) of Council Regulation 4064/89/EEC of 21 December 1989 on the control of concentrations between undertakings.[8]

5. A dominant influence shall not be presumed to be exercised solely by virtue of the fact that an office holder is exercising his functions, according to the law of a Member State relating to liquidation, winding up, insolvency, cessation of payments, compositions or analogous proceedings.

---

[8] OJ L 395, 30.12.1989, 1.

6. The law applicable in order to determine whether an undertaking is a 'controlling undertaking' shall be the law of the Member State that governs that undertaking.

Where the law governing that undertaking is not that of a Member State, the law applicable shall be the law of the Member State within whose territory the representative of the undertaking or, in the absence of such a representative, the central management of the group undertaking which employs the greatest number of employees is situated.

7. Where, in the case of a conflict of laws in the application of paragraph 2, two or more undertakings from a group satisfy one or more of the criteria laid down in that paragraph, the undertaking which satisfies the criterion laid down in point (c) thereof shall be regarded as the controlling undertaking, without prejudice to proof that another undertaking is able to exercise a dominant influence.

Section II
Establishment of a European Works Council or an Employee Information and Consultation Procedure

Article 4

Responsibility for the establishment of a European Works Council or an employee information and consultation procedure

1. The central management shall be responsible for creating the conditions and means necessary for the setting up of a European Works Council or an information and consultation procedure, as provided for in Article 1 (2), in a Community-scale undertaking and a Community-scale group of undertakings.

2. Where the central management is not situated in a Member State, the central management's representative agent in a Member State, to be designated if necessary, shall take on the responsibility referred to in paragraph 1.

In the absence of such a representative, the management of the establishment or group undertaking employing the greatest number of employees in any one Member State shall take on the responsibility referred to in paragraph 1.

3. For the purposes of this Directive, the representative or representatives or, in the absence of any such representatives, the management referred to in the second subparagraph of paragraph 2, shall be regarded as the central management.

> **Case**
>
> **Case C-349/01 Betriebsrat der Firma ADS Anker GmbH v ADS Anker GmbH–Reference for a Preliminary Ruling: Arbeitsgericht Bielefeld [2004] ECR I-6803**
>
> Article 4(1) and Article 11 of Council Directive 94/45/EC must be interpreted as meaning that Member States are required to impose on undertakings established within their territory and constituting the central management of a Community-scale group of undertakings for the purposes of Article 2(1)(e) and Article 3(1) of the directive, or the deemed central management under the second subparagraph of Article 4(2), the obligation to supply to another undertaking in the same group established in another Member State the information requested from it by its employees' representatives, where that information is not in the possession of that other undertaking and it is essential for opening negotiations for the setting up of a European Works Council.

Article 5

Special negotiating body

1. In order to achieve the objective in Article 1 (1), the central management shall initiate negotiations for the establishment of a European Works Council or an information and consultation procedure on its own initiative or at the written request of at least 100 employees or their representatives in at least two undertakings or establishments in at least two different Member States.

2. For this purpose, a special negotiating body shall be established in accordance with the following guidelines:

(a) The Member States shall determine the method to be used for the election or appointment of the members of the special negotiating body who are to be elected or appointed in their territories.

Member States shall provide that employees in undertakings and/or establishments in which there are no employees' representatives through no fault of their own, have the right to elect or appoint members of the special negotiating body.

The second subparagraph shall be without prejudice to national legislation and/or practice laying down thresholds for the establishment of employee representation bodies.

(b) The special negotiating body shall have a minimum of three and a maximum of [18] members.

(c) In these elections or appointments, it must be ensured:
- firstly, that each Member State in which the Community-scale undertaking has one or more establishments or in which the Community-scale group of undertakings has the controlling undertaking or one or more controlled undertakings is represented by one member,
- secondly, that there are supplementary members in proportion to the number of employees working in the establishments, the controlling undertaking or the controlled undertakings as laid down by the legislation of the Member State within the territory of which the central management is situated.

(d) The central management and local management shall be informed of the composition of the special negotiating body.

3. The special negotiating body shall have the task of determining, with the central management, by written agreement, the scope, composition, functions, and term of office of the European Works Council(s) or the arrangements for implementing a procedure for the information and consultation of employees.

4. With a view to the conclusion of an agreement in accordance with Article 6, the central management shall convene a meeting with the special negotiating body. It shall inform the local managements accordingly.

For the purpose of the negotiations, the special negotiating body may be assisted by experts of its choice.

5. The special negotiating body may decide, by at least two-thirds of the votes, not to open negotiations in accordance with paragraph 4, or to terminate the negotiations already opened.

Such a decision shall stop the procedure to conclude the agreement referred to in Article 6. Where such a decision has been taken, the provisions in the Annex shall not apply.

A new request to convene the special negotiating body may be made at the earliest two years after the abovementioned decision unless the parties concerned lay down a shorter period.

6. Any expenses relating to the negotiations referred to in paragraphs 3 and 4 shall be borne by the central management so as to enable the special negotiating body to carry out its task in an appropriate manner.

In compliance with this principle, Member States may lay down budgetary rules regarding the operation of the special negotiating body. They may in particular limit the funding to cover one expert only.

¶ *The number between the square brackets in article 5(2)(b) has been replaced by article 2 of Directive 97/74/EC, reproduced infra under no. E. 6.*

Article 6
Content of the agreement

1. The central management and the special negotiating body must negotiate in a spirit of co-operation with a view to reaching an agreement on the detailed arrangements for implementing the information and consultation of employees provided for in Article 1 (1).

2. Without prejudice to the autonomy of the parties, the agreement referred to in paragraph 1 between the central management and the special negotiating body shall determine:

(a) the undertakings of the Community-scale group of undertakings or the establishments of the Community-scale undertaking which are covered by the agreement;

(b) the composition of the European Works Council, the number of members, the allocation of seats and the term of office;

(c) the functions and the procedure for information and consultation of the European Works Council;

(d) the venue, frequency and duration of meetings of the European Works Council;

(e) the financial and material resources to be allocated to the European Works Council;

(f) the duration of the agreement and the procedure for its renegotiation.

3. The central management and the special negotiating body may decide, in writing, to establish one or more information and consultation procedures instead of a European Works Council.

The agreement must stipulate by what method the employees' representatives shall have the right to meet to discuss the information conveyed to them.

This information shall relate in particular to transnational questions that significantly affect workers' interests.

4. The agreements referred to in paragraphs 2 and 3 shall not, unless provision is made otherwise therein, be subject to the subsidiary requirements of the Annex.

5. For the purposes of concluding the agreements referred to in paragraphs 2 and 3, the special negotiating body shall act by a majority of its members.

Article 7
Subsidiary requirements

1. In order to achieve the objective in Article 1 (1), the subsidiary requirements laid down by the legislation of the Member State in which the central management is situated shall apply:
– where the central management and the special negotiating body so decide, or
– where the central management refuses to commence negotiations within six months of the request referred to in Article 5 (1), or
– where, after three years from the date of this request, they are unable to conclude an agreement as laid down in Article 6 and the special negotiating body has not taken the decision provided for in Article 5 (5).

2. The subsidiary requirements referred to in paragraph 1 as adopted in the legislation of the Member States must satisfy the provisions set out in the Annex.

Section III
Miscellaneous Provisions

Article 8
Confidential information

1. Member States shall provide that members of special negotiating bodies or of European Works Councils and any experts who assist them are not authorised to reveal any information that has expressly been provided to them in confidence.

The same shall apply to employees' representatives in the framework of an information and consultation procedure.

This obligation shall continue to apply, wherever the persons referred to in the first and second subparagraphs are, even after the expiry of their terms of office.

2. Each Member State shall provide, in specific cases and under the conditions and limits laid down by national legislation, that the central management situated in its territory is not obliged to transmit information when its nature is such that, according to objective criteria, it would seriously harm the functioning of the undertakings concerned or would be prejudicial to them.

A Member State may make such dispensation subject to prior administrative or judicial authorisation.

3. Each Member State may lay down particular provisions for the central management of undertakings in its territory which pursue directly and essentially the aim of ideological guidance with respect to information and the expression of opinions, on condition that, at the date of adoption of this Directive such particular provisions already exist in the national legislation.

Article 9

Operation of European Works Council and information and consultation procedure for workers

The central management and the European Works Council shall work in a spirit of co-operation with due regard to their reciprocal rights and obligations.

The same shall apply to co-operation between the central management and employees' representatives in the framework of an information and consultation procedure for workers.

Article 10

Protection of employees' representatives

Members of special negotiating bodies, members of European Works Councils and employees' representatives exercising their functions under the procedure referred to in Article 6 (3) shall, in the exercise of their functions, enjoy the same protection and guarantees provided for employees' representatives by the national legislation and/or practice in force in their country of employment.

This shall apply in particular to attendance at meetings of special negotiating bodies or European Works Councils or any other meetings within the framework of the agreement referred to in Article 6 (3), and the payment of wages for members who are on the staff of the Community-scale undertaking or the Community-scale group of undertakings for the period of absence necessary for the performance of their duties.

Article 11

Compliance with this Directive

1. Each Member State shall ensure that the management of establishments of a Community-scale undertaking and the management of undertakings which form part of a Community-scale group of undertakings which are situated within its territory and their employees' representatives or, as the case may be, employees abide by the obligations laid down by this Directive, regardless of whether or not the central management is situated within its territory.

2. Member States shall ensure that the information on the number of employees referred to in Article 2 (1) (a) and (c) is made available by undertakings at the request of the parties concerned by the application of this Directive.

3. Member States shall provide for appropriate measures in the event of failure to comply with this Directive; in particular, they shall ensure that adequate administrative or judicial procedures are available to enable the obligations deriving from this Directive to be enforced.

4. Where Member States apply Article 8, they shall make provision for administrative or judicial appeal procedures that the employees' representatives may initiate when the central management requires confidentiality or does not give information in accordance with that Article.

Such procedures may include procedures designed to protect the confidentiality of the information in question.

CASE

Case C-62/99 Betriebsrat der Bofrost* Josef H. Boquoi Deutschland West GmbH & Co KG v Bofrost* Josef H. Boquoi Deutschland West GmbH & Co KG [2001] ECR I-2579

1. On a proper construction of Article 11(1) and (2) of Council Directive 94/45/EC of 22 September 1994 on the establishment of a European Works Council or a procedure in Community-scale undertakings and Community-scale groups of undertakings for the purposes of informing and consulting employees, an undertaking which is part of a group of undertakings is required to supply information to the internal workers' representative bodies, even where it has not yet been established that the management to which the workers' request is addressed is the management of a controlling undertaking within a group of undertakings.

2. Where information relating to the structure or organization of a group of undertakings forms part of the information which is essential to the opening of negotiations for the setting-up of a European Works Council or for the transnational information

and consultation of employees, an undertaking within the group is required to supply the information which it possesses or is able to obtain to the internal workers' representative bodies requesting it. Communication of documents clarifying and explaining the information which is indispensable for that purpose may also be required, in so far as that communication is necessary in order that the employees concerned or their representatives may gain access to information enabling them to determine whether or not they are entitled to request the opening of negotiations.

Article 12

Link between this Directive and other provisions

1. This Directive shall apply without prejudice to measures taken pursuant to Council Directive 75/129/EEC of 17 February 1975 on the approximation of the laws of the Member States relating to collective redundancies,[9] and to Council Directive 77/187/EEC of 14 February 1977 on the approximation of the laws of the Member States relating to the safeguarding of employees' rights in the event of transfers of undertakings, businesses or parts of businesses.[10]

2. This Directive shall be without prejudice to employees' existing rights to information and consultation under national law.

Article 13

Agreements in force

1. Without prejudice to paragraph 2, the obligations arising from this Directive shall not apply to Community-scale undertakings or Community-scale groups of undertakings in which, on the date laid down in Article 14 (1) for the implementation of this Directive or the date of its transposition in the Member State in question, where this is earlier than the abovementioned date, there is already an agreement, covering the entire workforce, providing for the transnational information and consultation of employees.

2. When the agreements referred to in paragraph 1 expire, the parties to those agreements may decide jointly to renew them.

Where this is not the case, the provisions of this Directive shall apply.

Article 14

Final provisions

1. Member States shall bring into force the laws, regulations and administrative provisions necessary to comply with this Directive no later than 22 September 1996 or shall ensure by that date at the latest that management and labour introduce the required provisions by way of agreement, the Member States being obliged to take all necessary steps enabling them at all times to guarantee the results imposed by this Directive. They shall forthwith inform the Commission thereof.

2. When Member States adopt these measures, they shall contain a reference to this Directive or shall be accompanied by such reference on the occasion of their official publication. The methods of making such reference shall be laid down by Member States.

Article 15

Review by the Commission

Not later than 22 September 1999, the Commission shall, in consultation with the Member States and with management and labour at European level, review its operation and, in particular examine whether the workforce size thresholds are appropriate with a view to proposing suitable amendments to the Council, where necessary.

Article 16

This Directive is addressed to the Member States.

---

[9] OJ L 48, 22.2.1975, 29, reproduced supra under no. E. 1. Regulation as last amended by Directive 92/56/EEC (OJ L 245, 26.8.1992, 3), reproduced supra under no. E. 4.
[10] OJ L 61, 5.3.1977, 26, reproduced supra under no. E. 2.

Annex

Subsidiary Requirements

referred to in Article 7 of the Directive

1. In order to achieve the objective in Article 1 (1) of the Directive and in the cases provided for in Article 7 (1) of the Directive, the establishment, composition and competence of a European Works Council shall be governed by the following rules:

(a) The competence of the European Works Council shall be limited to information and consultation on the matters which concern the Community-scale undertaking or Community-scale group of undertakings as a whole or at least two of its establishments or group undertakings situated in different Member States.

In the case of undertakings or groups of undertakings referred to in Article 4 (2), the competence of the European Works Council shall be limited to those matters concerning all their establishments or group undertakings situated within the Member States or concerning at least two of their establishments or group undertakings situated in different Member States.

(b) The European Works Council shall be composed of employees of the Community-scale undertaking or Community-scale group of undertakings elected or appointed from their number by the employees' representatives or, in the absence thereof, by the entire body of employees.

The election or appointment of members of the European Works Council shall be carried out in accordance with national legislation and/or practice.

(c) The European Works Council shall have a minimum of three members and a maximum of 30.

Where its size so warrants, it shall elect a select committee from among its members, comprising at most three members.

It shall adopt its own rules of procedure.

(d) In the election or appointment of members of the European Works Council, it must be ensured:
– firstly, that each Member State in which the Community-scale undertaking has one or more establishments or in which the Community-scale group of undertakings has the controlling undertaking or one or more controlled undertakings is represented by one member,
– secondly, that there are supplementary members in proportion to the number of employees working in the establishments, the controlling undertaking or the controlled undertakings as laid down by the legislation of the Member State within the territory of which the central management is situated.

(e) The central management and any other more appropriate level of management shall be informed of the composition of the European Works Council.

(f) Four years after the European Works Council is established it shall examine whether to open negotiations for the conclusion of the agreement referred to in Article 6 of the Directive or to continue to apply the subsidiary requirements adopted in accordance with this Annex.

Articles 6 and 7 of the Directive shall apply, *mutatis mutandis*, if a decision has been taken to negotiate an agreement according to Article 6 of the Directive, in which case 'special negotiating body' shall be replaced by 'European Works Council'.

2. The European Works Council shall have the right to meet with the central management once a year, to be informed and consulted, on the basis of a report drawn up by the central management, on the progress of the business of the Community-scale undertaking or Community-scale group of undertakings and its prospects.

The local managements shall be informed accordingly.

The meeting shall relate in particular to the structure, economic and financial situation, the probable development of the business and of production and sales, the situation and probable trend of employment, investments, and substantial changes concerning organisation, introduction of new working methods or production processes, transfers of production, mergers, cut-backs or closures of undertakings, establishments or important parts thereof, and collective redundancies.

3. Where there are exceptional circumstances affecting the employees' interests to a considerable extent, particularly in the event of relocations, the closure of establishments or undertakings or collective redundancies, the select committee or, where no such committee exists, the European Works Council shall have the right to be informed. It shall have the right to meet, at its request, the central management, or any other more appropriate level of management within the Community-scale undertaking or group of undertakings having its own powers of decision, so as to be informed and consulted on measures significantly affecting employees' interests.

Those members of the European Works Council who have been elected or appointed by the establishments and/or undertakings which are directly concerned by the measures in question shall also have the right to participate in the meeting organised with the select committee.

This information and consultation meeting shall take place as soon as possible on the basis of a report drawn up by the central management or any other appropriate level of management of the Community scale undertaking or group of undertakings, on which an opinion may be delivered at the end of the meeting or within a reasonable time.

This meeting shall not affect the prerogatives of the central management.

4. The Member States may lay down rules on the chairing of information and consultation meetings.

Before any meeting with the central management, the European Works Council or the select committee, where necessary enlarged in accordance with the second paragraph of point 3, shall be entitled to meet without the management concerned being present.

5. Without prejudice to Article 8 of the Directive, the members of the European Works Council shall inform the representatives of the employees of the establishments or of the undertakings of a Community scale group of undertakings or, in the absence of representatives, the workforce as a whole, of the content and outcome of the information and consultation procedure carried out in accordance with this Annex.

6. The European Works Council or the select committee may be assisted by experts of its choice, in so far as this is necessary for it to carry out its tasks.

7. The operating expenses of the European Works Council shall be borne by the central management.

The central management concerned shall provide the members of the European Works Council with such financial and material resources as enable them to perform their duties in an appropriate manner.

In particular, the cost of organising meetings and arranging for interpretation facilities and the accommodation and travelling expenses of members of the European Works Council and its select committee shall be met by the central management unless otherwise agreed.

In compliance with these principles, the Member States may lay down budgetary rules regarding the operation of the European Works Council. They may in particular limit funding to cover one expert only.

E. 6.

Council Directive 97/74/EC
of 15 December 1997
extending, to the United Kingdom of Great Britain and Northern Ireland, Directive 94/45/EC on the establishment of a European Works Council or a procedure in Community-scale undertakings and Community-scale groups of undertakings for the purposes of informing and consulting employees[1]

THE COUNCIL OF THE EUROPEAN UNION,

Having regard to the Treaty establishing the European Community, and in particular Article [94][2] thereof,

Having regard to the proposal from the Commission,[3]

Having regard to the opinion of the European Parliament,[4]

Having regard to the opinion of the Economic and Social Committee,[5]

Whereas the Council, acting in accordance with the Agreement on social policy annexed to Protocol 14 to the Treaty, and in particular Article [2(2)][2] thereof, adopted Directive 94/45/EC;[6] whereas, as a result, the said Directive does not apply to the United Kingdom of Great Britain and Northern Ireland;

Whereas the Amsterdam European Council held on 16 and 17 June 1997 noted with approval the agreement of the Intergovernmental Conference to incorporate the Agreement on social policy in the Treaty and also noted that a means should be found to give legal effect to the wish of the United Kingdom of Great Britain and Northern Ireland to accept the Directives already adopted on the basis of that Agreement before the signature of the Amsterdam Treaty; whereas this Directive seeks to achieve this aim by extending Directive 94/45/EC to the United Kingdom;

Whereas the fact that Directive 94/45/EC is not applicable in the United Kingdom directly affects the functioning of the internal market; whereas implementation of the said Directive in all the Member States will improve the functioning of the internal market;

Whereas Directive 94/45/EC provides for a maximum of 17 members of the special negotiating body; whereas such a number corresponds to the 14 Member States which are party to the Agreement on social policy plus the three remaining Contracting Parties of the European Economic Area; whereas the adoption of this Directive will bring the total number of States covered by Directive 94/45/EC to 18; whereas, therefore, the abovementioned maximum should be increased to 18 so that each Member State in which the Community-scale undertaking has one or more establishments or in which the Community-scale group of undertakings has the controlling undertaking or one or more controlled undertakings is represented;

Whereas Directive 94/45/EC provides for special treatment to be accorded to Community-scale undertakings and groups of undertakings in which there is, at 22 September 1996, an agreement covering the entire workforce providing for the transnational information and consultation of employees; whereas, accordingly, Community-scale undertakings and groups of undertakings falling within the scope of that Directive solely as a result of its application to the United Kingdom should be granted similar treatment;

---

[1] OJ L 10, 16.1.1998, 22–23.
[2] The number between brackets has been changed as from 1 May 1999 by article 12 of the Treaty of Amsterdam.
[3] OJ C 335, 6. 11. 1997.
[4] OJ C 371, 8. 12. 1997.
[5] OJ C 355, 21. 11. 1997.
[6] OJ L 254, 30. 9. 1994, 64, reproduced supra under no. E. 5.

Whereas the adoption of this Directive will make Directive 94/45/EC applicable in all Member States including the United Kingdom; whereas, from the date on which this Directive enters into force, the term 'Member States' in Directive 94/45/EC should be construed as including, where appropriate, the United Kingdom;

Whereas Member States were required to bring into force the laws, regulations and administrative provisions to comply with Directive 94/45/EC no later than two years after its adoption; whereas a similar period should be granted to the United Kingdom, as well as to the other Member States, to bring into force the necessary measures to comply with this Directive,

HAS ADOPTED THIS DIRECTIVE:

Article 1

Without prejudice to Article 3, Directive 94/45/EC shall apply to the United Kingdom of Great Britain and Northern Ireland.

Article 2

[. . .]

¶ *This article amends article 5(2)(b) of Directive 94/45/EC, reproduced supra under no. E. 5. The modification is directly incorporated therein.*

Article 3

1. The obligations resulting from this Directive shall not apply to Community-scale undertakings or Community-scale groups of undertakings, which, solely by virtue of Article 1, fall within the scope of this Directive, provided that, on the date laid down in Article 4(1) or the date of its transposition in the Member State in question, where this is earlier than the said date, there is already an agreement covering the entire workforce providing for the transnational information and consultation of employees.

2. When the agreements referred to in paragraph 1 expire, the parties to those agreements may decide jointly to renew them. Where this is not the case, Directive 94/45/EC, as extended by this Directive, shall apply.

Article 4

1. Member States shall bring into force the laws, regulations and administrative provisions necessary to comply with this Directive no later than 15 December 1999 or shall ensure, by that date at the latest, that management and labour introduce the required provisions by way of agreement, the Member States being obliged to take all necessary steps enabling them at all times to guarantee the results imposed by this Directive. They shall forthwith inform the Commission thereof.

2. When Member States adopt these measures, they shall contain a reference to this Directive or shall be accompanied by such reference on the occasion of their official publication. The methods of making such reference shall be laid down by the Member States.

Article 5

This Directive is addressed to the Member States.

E. 7.

Council Directive 98/50/EC
of 29 June 1998
amending Directive 77/187/EEC on the approximation of the laws of the Member States relating to the safeguarding of employees' rights in the event of transfers of undertakings, businesses or parts of businesses[1]

THE COUNCIL OF THE EUROPEAN UNION,

Having regard to the Treaty establishing the European Community, and in particular Article [94][2] thereof,

Having regard to the proposal from the Commission,[3]

Having regard to the opinion of the European Parliament,[4]

Having regard to the opinion of the Economic and Social Committee,[5]

Having regard to the opinion of the Committee of the Regions,[6]

(1) Whereas the Community Charter of the fundamental social rights of workers adopted on 9 December 1989 ('Social Charter') states, in points 7, 17 and 18 in particular that: 'The completion of the internal market must lead to an improvement in the living and working conditions of workers in the European Community. The improvement must cover, where necessary, the development of certain aspects of employment regulations such as procedures for collective redundancies and those regarding bankruptcies. Information, consultation and participation for workers must be developed along appropriate lines, taking account of the practices in force in the various Member States. Such information, consultation and participation must be implemented in due time, particularly in connection with restructuring operations in undertakings or in cases of mergers having an impact on the employment of workers';

(2) Whereas Directive 77/187/EEC[7] promotes the harmonisation of the relevant national laws ensuring the safeguarding of the rights of employees and requiring transferors and transferees to inform and consult employees' representatives in good time;

(3) Whereas the purpose of this Directive is to amend Directive 77/187/EEC in the light of the impact of the internal market, the legislative tendencies of the Member States with regard to the rescue of undertakings in economic difficulties, the case-law of the Court of Justice of the European Communities. Council Directive 75/129/EEC of 17 February 1975 on the approximation of the laws of the Member States relating to collective redundancies[8] and the legislation already in force in most Member States;

(4) Whereas considerations of legal security and transparency require that the legal concept of transfer be clarified in the light of the case-law of the Court of Justice; whereas such clarification does not alter the scope of Directive 77/187/EEC as interpreted by the Court of Justice;

(5) Whereas those considerations also require an express provision, in the light of the case-law of the Court of Justice, that Directive 77/187/EEC should apply to private and public undertakings

---

[1] OJ L 201, 17.7.1998, 88–92.
[2] The number between brackets has been changed as from 1 May 1999 by article 12 of the Treaty of Amsterdam.
[3] OJ C 274, 1.10.1994, 10.
[4] OJ C 33, 3.2.1997, 81.
[5] OJ C 133, 31.5.1995, 13.
[6] OJ C 100, 2.4.1996, 25.

[7] OJ L 61, 5.3.1977, 26, reproduced supra under no. E. 2.
[8] OJ L 48, 22.2.1975, 29, reproduced supra under no. E. 1. Directive as amended by Directive 92/56/EEC (OJ L 245, 26.8.1992, 3), reproduced supra under no. E. 4.

carrying out economic activities, whether or not they operate for gain;

(6) Whereas it is necessary to clarify the concept of 'employee' in the light of the case-law of the Court of Justice;

(7) Whereas, with a view to ensuring the survival of insolvent undertakings, Member States should be expressly allowed not to apply Articles 3 and 4 of Directive 77/187/EEC to transfers effected in the framework of liquidation proceedings, and certain derogations from that Directive's general provisions should be permitted in the case of transfers effected in the context of insolvency proceedings;

(8) Whereas such derogations should also be allowed for one Member State, which has special procedures to promote the survival of companies, declared to be in a state of economic crisis;

(9) Whereas the circumstances in which the function and status of employee representatives are to be preserved should be clarified;

(10) Whereas, in order to ensure equal treatment for similar situations, it is necessary to ensure that the information and consultation requirements laid down in Directive 77/187/EEC are complied with irrespective of whether the decision leading to the transfer is taken by the employer or by an undertaking controlling the employer;

(11) Whereas it is appropriate to clarify that, when Member States adopt measures to ensure that the transferee is informed of all the rights and obligations to be transferred, failure to provide that information is not to affect the transfer of the rights and obligations concerned;

(12) Whereas it is necessary to clarify the circumstances in which employees must be informed where there are no employee representatives;

(13) Whereas the Social Charter recognises the importance of the fight against all forms of discrimination, especially based on sex, colour, race, opinion and creed,

HAS ADOPTED THIS DIRECTIVE:

Article 1

[. . .]

¶ *Article 1 amends the title and replaces articles 1 to 7 of Directive 77/178/EEC, reproduced supra under no. E. 2, which has been repealed as from 11 April 2001 by article 12 of Directive 2001/23/EC, reproduced infra under no. E. 11.*

Article 2

1. Member States shall bring into force the laws, regulations and administrative provisions necessary to comply with this Directive by 17 July 2001 at the latest or shall ensure that, by that date, at the latest, the employers' and employees' representatives have introduced the required provisions by means of agreement, Member States being obliged to take the necessary steps enabling them at all times to guarantee the results imposed by this Directive.

2. When Member States adopt the measures referred to in paragraph 1, they shall contain a reference to this Directive or shall be accompanied by such reference on the occasion on their official publication. The methods of making such reference shall be laid down by Member States.

Member States shall inform the Commission immediately of the measures they take to implement this Directive.

Article 3

This Directive shall enter into force on the day of its publication in the *Official Journal of the European Communities*.

Article 4

This Directive is addressed to the Member States.

E. 8.

Council Directive 98/59/EC
of 20 July 1998
on the approximation of the laws of the Member States relating to collective redundancies[1]

Case

Case C-383/92 Commission of the European Communities v United Kingdom of Great Britain and Northern Ireland [1994] ECR I-2479

1. Despite the limited character of the harmonization of rules in respect of collective redundancies which Directive 75/129/EEC was intended to bring about, national rules which, by not providing for a system for the designation of workers' representatives in an undertaking where an employer refuses to recognize such representatives, allow an employer to frustrate the protection provided by Articles 2 and 3 of Directive 75/129/EEC must be regarded as contrary to the provisions of that directive.

2. Where a Community directive does not specifically provide any penalty for an infringement or refers for that purpose to national laws, regulations and administrative provisions, Article [10][2] of the Treaty requires the Member States to take all measures necessary to guarantee the application and effectiveness of Community law. For that purpose, while the choice of penalties remains within their discretion, they must ensure in particular that infringements of Community law are penalized under conditions, both procedural and substantive, which are analogous to those applicable to infringements of national law of a similar nature and importance and which, in any event, make the penalty effective, proportionate and dissuasive.

In the case where an employee may be entitled to payment of various amounts under his contract of employment and by reason of its breach, an award which may be set off against such amounts cannot be regarded as sufficiently deterrent for an employer who, in the event of collective redundancies, fails to comply with his obligations under Directive 75/129/EEC to consult and inform his workers' representatives.

THE COUNCIL OF THE EUROPEAN UNION,

Having regard to the Treaty establishing the European Community, and in particular Article [94][2] thereof,

Having regard to the proposal from the Commission,

Having regard to the opinion of the European Parliament,[3]

Having regard to the opinion of the Economic and Social Committee,[4]

(1) Whereas for reasons of clarity and rationality Council Directive 75/129/EEC of 17 February 1975 on the approximation of the laws of the Member States relating to collective redundancies[5] should be consolidated;

(2) Whereas it is important that greater protection should be afforded to workers in the event of collective redundancies while taking into account the need for balanced economic and social development within the Community;

(3) Whereas, despite increasing convergence, differences still remain between the provisions in force in the Member States concerning the practical arrangements and procedures for such

---

[1] OJ L 225, 12.8.1998, 16–21.
[2] The number between brackets has been changed as from 1 May 1999 by article 12 of the Treaty of Amsterdam.
[3] OJ C 210, 6.7.1998.
[4] OJ C 158, 26.5.1997, 11.
[5] OJ L 48, 22.2.1975, 29, reproduced supra under no. E. 1. Directive as amended by Directive 92/56/EEC (OJ L 245, 26.8.1992, 3), reproduced supra under no. E. 4.

redundancies and the measures designed to alleviate the consequences of redundancy for workers;

(4) Whereas these differences can have a direct effect on the functioning of the internal market;

(5) Whereas the Council resolution of 21 January 1974 concerning a social action programme[6] made provision for a directive on the approximation of Member States' legislation on collective redundancies;

(6) Whereas the Community Charter of the fundamental social rights of workers, adopted at the European Council meeting held in Strasbourg on 9 December 1989 by the Heads of State or Government of 11 Member States, states, *inter alia*, in point 7, first paragraph, first sentence, and second paragraph; in point 17, first paragraph; and in point 18, third indent:

'7. The completion of the internal market must lead to an improvement in the living and working conditions of workers in the European Community (. . .).

The improvement must cover, where necessary, the development of certain aspects of employment regulations such as procedures for collective redundancies and those regarding bankruptcies.

(. . .)

17. Information, consultation and participation for workers must be developed along appropriate lines, taking account of the practices in force in the various Member States.

(. . .)

18. Such information, consultation and participation must be implemented in due time, particularly in the following cases:

(– . . .)

(– . . .)

– in cases of collective redundancy procedures;

(– . . .)';

(7) Whereas this approximation must therefore be promoted while the improvement is being maintained within the meaning of Article [136][2] of the Treaty;

(8) Whereas, in order to calculate the number of redundancies provided for in the definition of collective redundancies within the meaning of this Directive, other forms of termination of employment contracts on the initiative of the employer should be equated to redundancies, provided that there are at least five redundancies;

(9) Whereas it should be stipulated that this Directive applies in principle also to collective redundancies resulting where the establishment's activities are terminated as a result of a judicial decision;

(10) Whereas the Member States should be given the option of stipulating that workers' representatives may call on experts on grounds of the technical complexity of the matters which are likely to be the subject of the informing and consulting;

(11) Whereas it is necessary to ensure that employers' obligations as regards information, consultation and notification apply independently of whether the decision on collective redundancies emanates from the employer or from an undertaking that controls that employer;

(12) Whereas Member States should ensure that workers' representatives and/or workers have at their disposal administrative and/or judicial procedures in order to ensure that the obligations laid down in this Directive are fulfilled;

(13) Whereas this Directive must not affect the obligations of the Member States concerning the deadlines for transposition of the Directives set out in Annex I, Part B,

HAS ADOPTED THIS DIRECTIVE:

SECTION I

DEFINITIONS AND SCOPE

Article 1

1. For the purposes of this Directive:

(a) 'collective redundancies' means dismissals effected by an employer for one or more reasons

---

[6] OJ C 13, 12.2.1974, 1.

not related to the individual workers concerned where, according to the choice of the Member States, the number of redundancies is:

(i) either, over a period of 30 days:
– at least 10 in establishments normally employing more than 20 and less than 100 workers,
– at least 10% of the number of workers in establishments normally employing at least 100 but less than 300 workers,
– at least 30 in establishments normally employing 300 workers or more,

(ii) or, over a period of 90 days, at least 20, whatever the number of workers normally employed in the establishments in question;

(b) 'workers' representatives' means the workers' representatives provided for by the laws or practices of the Member States.

For the purpose of calculating the number of redundancies provided for in the first subparagraph of point (a), terminations of an employment contract which occur on the employer's initiative for one or more reasons not related to the individual workers concerned shall be assimilated to redundancies, provided that there are at least five redundancies.

2. This Directive shall not apply to:

(a) collective redundancies effected under contracts of employment concluded for limited periods of time or for specific tasks except where such redundancies take place prior to the date of expiry or the completion of such contracts;

(b) workers employed by public administrative bodies or by establishments governed by public law (or, in Member States where this concept is unknown, by equivalent bodies);

(c) the crews of seagoing vessels.

Cases

I. Case C-449/93 Rockfon A/S v Specialarbejderforbundet i Danmark [1995] ECR I-4291

1. Article 1(1)(a) of Directive 75/129/EEC, on the approximation of the laws of the Member States relating to collective redundancies, is to be interpreted as meaning that it does not preclude two or more interrelated undertakings in a group, neither or none of which has decisive influence over the other or others, from establishing a joint recruitment and dismissal department so that, in particular, dismissals on grounds of redundancy in one of the undertakings can take place only with that department's approval. The sole purpose of Directive 75/129/EEC is partial harmonization of collective redundancy procedures and its aim is not to restrict the freedom of undertakings to organize their activities and arrange their personnel departments in the way that they think best suits their needs.

2. The different language versions of a Community text must be given a uniform interpretation and, in the case of divergence between the versions, the provision in question must therefore be interpreted by reference to the purpose and general scheme of the rules of which it forms part.

3. The term 'establishment' appearing in Article 1(1)(a) of Directive 75/129/EEC on the approximation of the laws of the Member States relating to collective redundancies must be understood as meaning, depending on the circumstances, the unit to which the workers made redundant are assigned to carry out their duties. It is not essential, in order for there to be an establishment, for the unit in question to be endowed with a management which can independently effect collective redundancies. To make the definition of 'establishment', which is a concept of Community law and cannot be defined by reference to the laws of the Member States, dependent on the existence of such a management within the unit would be incompatible with the aim of the directive since that would allow companies belonging to the same group to try to make it more difficult for the directive to apply to them by conferring on a separate decision-making body the power to take decisions concerning redundancies and by this means they would be able to escape the obligation to follow certain procedures for the protection of workers, such as their right to be informed and consulted.

II. Case C-383/92 Commission of the European Communities v United Kingdom of Great Britain and Northern Ireland [1994] ECR I-2479

According to Article 1(1)(a) of Directive 75/129/EEC, the directive applies to collective redundancies in the sense of dismissals for one or more reasons not related to the individual workers concerned, including dismissals resulting from new working arrangements within an undertaking unconnected with its volume of business. Its scope cannot for that reason be limited to cases of redundancy defined as resulting from a cessation or reduction of the business of an undertaking or a decline in demand for work of a particular type.

Section II
Information and Consultation

Article 2

1. Where an employer is contemplating collective redundancies, he shall begin consultations with the workers' representatives in good time with a view to reaching an agreement.

2. These consultations shall, at least, cover ways and means of avoiding collective redundancies or reducing the number of workers affected, and of mitigating the consequences by recourse to accompanying social measures aimed, *inter alia*, at aid for redeploying or retraining workers made redundant.

Member States may provide that the workers' representatives may call on the services of experts in accordance with national legislation and/or practice.

3. To enable workers' representatives to make constructive proposals, the employers shall in good time during the course of the consultations:
(a) supply them with all relevant information and
(b) in any event notify them in writing of:
   (i) the reasons for the projected redundancies;
   (ii) the number of categories of workers to be made redundant;
   (iii) the number and categories of workers normally employed;
   (iv) the period over which the projected redundancies are to be effected;
   (v) the criteria proposed for the selection of the workers to be made redundant in so far as national legislation and/or practice confers the power therefore upon the employer;
   (vi) the method for calculating any redundancy payments other than those arising out of national legislation and/or practice.

The employer shall forward to the competent public authority a copy of, at least, the elements of the written communication that are provided for in the first subparagraph, point (b), subpoints (i) to (v).

4. The obligations laid down in paragraphs 1, 2 and 3 shall apply irrespective of whether the decision regarding collective redundancies is being taken by the employer or by an undertaking controlling the employer.

In considering alleged breaches of the information, consultation and notification requirements laid down by this Directive, account shall not be taken of any defence on the part of the employer on the ground that the necessary information has not been provided to the employer by the undertaking which took the decision leading to collective redundancies.

Cases

I. Case C-188/03 Irmtraud Junk v Wolfgang Kühnel [2005] ECR I-885

Articles 2 to 4 of Council Directive 98/59/EC must be construed as meaning that the event constituting redundancy consists in the declaration by an employer of his intention to terminate the contract of employment.

An employer is entitled to carry out collective redundancies after the conclusion of the consultation procedure provided for in Article 2 of Directive 98/59 and after notification of the projected collective redundancies as provided for in Articles 3 and 4 of that directive.

II. Case C-383/92 Commission of the European Communities v United Kingdom of Great Britain and Northern Ireland [1994] ECR I-2479

National rules which merely require an employer to consult trade union representatives about proposed dismissals, to 'consider' representations made by such representatives and, if he rejects them, to 'state his reasons', whereas Article 2(1) of the directive requires the workers' representatives to be consulted 'with a view to reaching an agreement' and Article 2(2) lays down that such consultation must 'at least, cover ways and means of avoiding collective redundancies or reducing the number of workers affected, and mitigating the consequences', fail correctly to transpose Directive 75/129/EEC.

Section III
Procedure for Collective Redundancies

Article 3

1. Employers shall notify the competent public authority in writing of any projected collective redundancies.

However, Member States may provide that in the case of planned collective redundancies arising from termination of the establishment's activities as a result of a judicial decision, the employer shall be obliged to notify the competent public authority in writing only if the latter so requests.

This notification shall contain all relevant information concerning the projected collective redundancies and the consultations with workers' representatives provided for in Article 2, and particularly the reasons for the redundancies, the number of workers to be made redundant, the number of workers normally employed and the period over which the redundancies are to be effected.

2. Employers shall forward to the workers' representatives a copy of the notification provided for in paragraph 1.

The workers' representatives may send any comments they may have to the competent public authority.

Case

Case C-250/97 Dansk Metalarbejderforbund, Acting on behalf of John Lauge and Others v Ønmodtagernes Garantifond [1998] ECR I-8737

See infra under Article 4 of this Directive.

Article 4

1. Projected collective redundancies notified to the competent public authority shall take effect not earlier than 30 days after the notification referred to in Article 3(1) without prejudice to any provisions governing individual rights with regard to notice of dismissal.

Member States may grant the competent public authority the power to reduce the period provided for in the preceding subparagraph.

2. The period provided for in paragraph 1 shall be used by the competent public authority to seek solutions to the problems raised by the projected collective redundancies.

3. Where the initial period provided for in paragraph 1 is shorter than 60 days, Member States may grant the competent public authority the power to extend the initial period to 60 days following notification where the problems raised by the projected collective redundancies are not likely to be solved within the initial period.

Member States may grant the competent public authority wider powers of extension.

The employer must be informed of the extension and the grounds for it before expiry of the initial period provided for in paragraph 1.

4. Member States need not apply this Article to collective redundancies arising from termination of the establishment's activities where this is the result of a judicial decision.

Cases

I. Case C-250/97 Dansk Metalarbejderforbund, Acting on Behalf of John Lauge and others v Ønmodtagernes Garantifond [1998] ECR I-8737

The second subparagraph of Article 3(1), and Article 4(4) of Directive 75/129/EEC on the approximation of the laws of the Member States relating to collective redundancies, as amended by Directive 92/56/EEC, must be interpreted to the effect that the derogations provided for therein do not apply to collective redundancies occurring on the same day as that on which the employer files a winding-up petition and terminates the undertaking's activities, and the competent court subsequently, and without any deferment other than that resulting from the date which it sets for the hearing, issues a winding-up order pursuant to the winding-up petition, that order taking effect for a number of purposes from the date on which the petition was filed.

II. Case 284/83 Dansk Metalarbejderforbund and Specialarbejderforbundet i Danmark v H. Nielsen & Søn, Maskinfabrik A/S (in liquidation) [1985] ECR 553

1. The termination by workers of their contract of employment following an announcement by the employer that he is suspending payment of his debts cannot be treated as dismissal by the employer for the purposes of Council Directive 75/129/EEC on the approximation of the laws of the Member States relating to collective redundancies.

2. Council Directive 75/129/EEC applies only where the employer has in fact contemplated collective redundancies or has drawn up a plan for collective redundancies. It does not apply where, because of the financial state of the undertaking, the employer ought to have contemplated collective redundancies but did not do so.

Section IV
Final Provisions

Article 5

This Directive shall not affect the right of Member States to apply or to introduce laws, regulations or administrative provisions which are more favourable to workers or to promote or to allow the application of collective agreements more favourable to workers.

Case

Case 91/81 Commission of the European Communities v Italian Republic [1982] ECR 2133

Directive 75/129/EEC, which the Council considers corresponds to the need, stated in Article [136][2] of the Treaty, to promote improved working conditions and an improved standard of living for workers, is intended to approximate the provisions laid down in this field by the Member States by law, regulation or administrative action relating to collective redundancies. The provisions of the directive are thus intended to serve to establish a common body of rules applicable in all the Member States, whilst leaving to the Member States power to apply or introduce provisions that are more favourable to workers.

Article 6

Member States shall ensure that judicial and/or administrative procedures for the enforcement of obligations under this Directive are available to the workers' representatives and/or workers.

Article 7

Member States shall forward to the Commission the text of any fundamental provisions of national law already adopted or being adopted in the area governed by this Directive.

Article 8

1. The Directives listed in Annex I, Part A, are hereby repealed without prejudice to the obligations of the Member States concerning the deadlines for transposition of the said Directive set out in Annex I, Part B.

2. References to the repealed Directives shall be construed as references to this Directive and shall be read in accordance with the correlation table in Annex II.

Article 9

This Directive shall enter into force on the 20th day following its publication in the *Official Journal of the European Communities*.

Article 10

This Directive is addressed to the Member States.

Annex I

Part A

Repealed Directives
(referred to by Article 8)

Council Directive 75/129/EEC and its following amendment:

Council Directive 92/56/EEC.

Part B

Deadlines for transposition into national law
(referred to by Article 8)

Directive	Deadline for transposition
75/129/EEC (OJ L 48, 22.2.1975, 29)	19 February 1977
92/56/EEC (OJ L 245, 26.8.1992, 3)	24 June 1994

Annex II

Correlation Table

Directive 75/129/EEC	This Directive
Article 1(1), first subparagraph, point (a), first indent, point 1	Article 1(1), first subparagraph, point (a)(i), first indent
Article 1(1), first subparagraph, point (a), first indent, point 2	Article 1(1), first subparagraph, point (a)(i), second indent
Article 1(1), first subparagraph, point (a), first indent, point 3	Article 1(1), first subparagraph, point (a)(i), third indent
Article 1(1), first subparagraph, point (a), second indent	Article 1(1), first subparagraph, point (a)(ii)
Article 1(1), first subparagraph, point (b)	Article 1(1), first subparagraph, point (b)
Article 1(1), second subparagraph	Article 1(1), second subparagraph
Article 1 (2)	Article 1 (2)
Article 2	Article 2
Article 3	Article 3
Article 4	Article 4
Article 5	Article 5

Directive 75/129/EEC	This Directive
Article 5a	Article 6
Article 6(1)	—
Article 6(2)	Article 7
Article 7	—
—	Article 8
—	Article 9
—	Article 10
—	Annex I
—	Annex II

E. 9.

Council Regulation 1346/2000/EC of 29 May 2000 on insolvency proceedings[1]

(Acts whose publication is obligatory)

THE COUNCIL OF THE EUROPEAN UNION,

Having regard to the Treaty establishing the European Community, and in particular Articles 61(c) and 67(1) thereof,

Having regard to the initiative of the Federal Republic of Germany and the Republic of Finland,

Having regard to the opinion of the European Parliament,[2]

Having regard to the opinion of the Economic and Social Committee,[3]

Whereas:

(1) The European Union has set out the aim of establishing an area of freedom, security and justice.

(2) The proper functioning of the internal market requires that cross-border insolvency proceedings should operate efficiently and effectively and this Regulation needs to be adopted in order to achieve this objective which comes within the scope of judicial co-operation in civil matters within the meaning of Article 65 of the Treaty.

(3) The activities of undertakings have more and more cross-border effects and are therefore increasingly being regulated by Community law. While the insolvency of such undertakings also affects the proper functioning of the internal market, there is a need for a Community act requiring co-ordination of the measures to be taken regarding an insolvent debtor's assets.

(4) It is necessary for the proper functioning of the internal market to avoid incentives for the parties to transfer assets or judicial proceedings from one Member State to another, seeking to obtain a more favourable legal position (forum shopping).

(5) These objectives cannot be achieved to a sufficient degree at national level and action at Community level is therefore justified.

(6) In accordance with the principle of proportionality this Regulation should be confined to provisions governing jurisdiction for opening insolvency proceedings and judgements which are delivered directly on the basis of the insolvency proceedings and are closely connected with such proceedings. In addition, this Regulation should contain provisions regarding the recognition of those judgements and the applicable law which also satisfy that principle.

(7) Insolvency proceedings relating to the winding-up of insolvent companies or other legal persons, judicial arrangements, compositions and analogous proceedings are excluded from the scope of the 1968 Brussels Convention on Jurisdiction and the Enforcement of Judgements in Civil and Commercial Matters,[4] as amended by the Conventions on Accession to this Convention.[5]

(8) In order to achieve the aim of improving the efficiency and effectiveness of insolvency

---

[1] OJ L 160, 30.6.2000, 1–18.
[2] Opinion delivered on 2 March 2000 (OJ C 346, 4.12.2000, 80).
[3] Opinion delivered on 26 January 2000 (OJ C 75, 13.3.2000, 1).
[4] OJ L 299, 31.12.1972, 32.
[5] OJ L 204, 2.8.1975, 28; OJ L 304, 30.10.1978, 1; OJ L 388, 31.12.1982, 1; OJ L 285, 3.10.1989, 1; OJ C 15, 15.1.1997, 1.

proceedings having cross-border effects, it is necessary, and appropriate, that the provisions on jurisdiction, recognition and applicable law in this area should be contained in a Community law measure which is binding and directly applicable in Member States.

(9) This Regulation should apply to insolvency proceedings, whether the debtor is a natural person or a legal person, a trader or an individual. The insolvency proceedings to which this Regulation applies are listed in the Annexes. Insolvency proceedings concerning insurance undertakings, credit institutions, investment undertakings holding funds or securities for third parties and collective investment undertakings should be excluded from the scope of this Regulation. Such undertakings should not be covered by this Regulation since they are subject to special arrangements and, to some extent, the national supervisory authorities have extremely wide-ranging powers of intervention.

(10) Insolvency proceedings do not necessarily involve the intervention of a judicial authority; the expression "court" in this Regulation should be given a broad meaning and include a person or body empowered by national law to open insolvency proceedings. In order for this Regulation to apply, proceedings (comprising acts and formalities set down in law) should not only have to comply with the provisions of this Regulation, but they should also be officially recognised and legally effective in the Member State in which the insolvency proceedings are opened and should be collective insolvency proceedings which entail the partial or total divestment of the debtor and the appointment of a liquidator.

(11) This Regulation acknowledges the fact that as a result of widely differing substantive laws it is not practical to introduce insolvency proceedings with universal scope in the entire Community. The application without exception of the law of the State of opening of proceedings would, against this background, frequently lead to difficulties. This applies, for example, to the widely differing laws on security interests to be found in the Community. Furthermore, the preferential rights enjoyed by some creditors in the insolvency proceedings are, in some cases, completely different. This Regulation should take account of this in two different ways. On the one hand, provision should be made for special rules on applicable law in the case of particularly significant rights and legal relationships (e.g. rights in rem and contracts of employment). On the other hand, national proceedings covering only assets situated in the State of opening should also be allowed alongside main insolvency proceedings with universal scope.

(12) This Regulation enables the main insolvency proceedings to be opened in the Member State where the debtor has the centre of his main interests. These proceedings have universal scope and aim at encompassing all the debtor's assets. To protect the diversity of interests, this Regulation permits secondary proceedings to be opened to run in parallel with the main proceedings. Secondary proceedings may be opened in the Member State where the debtor has an establishment. The effects of secondary proceedings are limited to the assets located in that State. Mandatory rules of co-ordination with the main proceedings satisfy the need for unity in the Community.

(13) The "centre of main interests" should correspond to the place where the debtor conducts the administration of his interests on a regular basis and is therefore ascertainable by third parties.

(14) This Regulation applies only to proceedings where the centre of the debtor's main interests is located in the Community.

(15) The rules of jurisdiction set out in this Regulation establish only international jurisdiction, that is to say, they designate the Member State the courts of which may open insolvency proceedings. Territorial jurisdiction within that Member State must be established by the national law of the Member State concerned.

(16) The court having jurisdiction to open the main insolvency proceedings should be enabled to order provisional and protective measures from the time of the request to open proceedings. Preservation measures both prior to and after the commencement of the insolvency proceedings

are very important to guarantee the effectiveness of the insolvency proceedings. In that connection this Regulation should afford different possibilities. On the one hand, the court competent for the main insolvency proceedings should be able also to order provisional protective measures covering assets situated in the territory of other Member States. On the other hand, a liquidator temporarily appointed prior to the opening of the main insolvency proceedings should be able, in the Member States in which an establishment belonging to the debtor is to be found, to apply for the preservation measures which are possible under the law of those States.

(17) Prior to the opening of the main insolvency proceedings, the right to request the opening of insolvency proceedings in the Member State where the debtor has an establishment should be limited to local creditors and creditors of the local establishment or to cases where main proceedings cannot be opened under the law of the Member State where the debtor has the centre of his main interest. The reason for this restriction is that cases where territorial insolvency proceedings are requested before the main insolvency proceedings are intended to be limited to what is absolutely necessary. If the main insolvency proceedings are opened, the territorial proceedings become secondary.

(18) Following the opening of the main insolvency proceedings, the right to request the opening of insolvency proceedings in a Member State where the debtor has an establishment is not restricted by this Regulation. The liquidator in the main proceedings or any other person empowered under the national law of that Member State may request the opening of secondary insolvency proceedings.

(19) Secondary insolvency proceedings may serve different purposes, besides the protection of local interests. Cases may arise where the estate of the debtor is too complex to administer as a unit or where differences in the legal systems concerned are so great that difficulties may arise from the extension of effects deriving from the law of the State of the opening to the other States where the assets are located. For this reason the liquidator in the main proceedings may request the opening of secondary proceedings when the efficient administration of the estate so requires.

(20) Main insolvency proceedings and secondary proceedings can, however, contribute to the effective realisation of the total assets only if all the concurrent proceedings pending are co-ordinated. The main condition here is that the various liquidators must co-operate closely, in particular by exchanging a sufficient amount of information. In order to ensure the dominant role of the main insolvency proceedings, the liquidator in such proceedings should be given several possibilities for intervening in secondary insolvency proceedings which are pending at the same time. For example, he should be able to propose a restructuring plan or composition or apply for realisation of the assets in the secondary insolvency proceedings to be suspended.

(21) Every creditor, who has his habitual residence, domicile or registered office in the Community, should have the right to lodge his claims in each of the insolvency proceedings pending in the Community relating to the debtor's assets. This should also apply to tax authorities and social insurance institutions. However, in order to ensure equal treatment of creditors, the distribution of proceeds must be co-ordinated. Every creditor should be able to keep what he has received in the course of insolvency proceedings but should be entitled only to participate in the distribution of total assets in other proceedings if creditors with the same standing have obtained the same proportion of their claims.

(22) This Regulation should provide for immediate recognition of judgments concerning the opening, conduct and closure of insolvency proceedings which come within its scope and of judgments handed down in direct connection with such insolvency proceedings. Automatic recognition should therefore mean that the effects attributed to the proceedings by the law of the State in which the proceedings were opened extend to all other Member States. Recognition of judgments delivered by the courts of the Member States should be based on the principle

of mutual trust. To that end, grounds for non-recognition should be reduced to the minimum necessary. This is also the basis on which any dispute should be resolved where the courts of two Member States both claim competence to open the main insolvency proceedings. The decision of the first court to open proceedings should be recognised in the other Member States without those Member States having the power to scrutinise the court's decision.

(23) This Regulation should set out, for the matters covered by it, uniform rules on conflict of laws which replace, within their scope of application, national rules of private international law. Unless otherwise stated, the law of the Member State of the opening of the proceedings should be applicable (lex concursus). This rule on conflict of laws should be valid both for the main proceedings and for local proceedings; the lex concursus determines all the effects of the insolvency proceedings, both procedural and substantive, on the persons and legal relations concerned. It governs all the conditions for the opening, conduct and closure of the insolvency proceedings.

(24) Automatic recognition of insolvency proceedings to which the law of the opening State normally applies may interfere with the rules under which transactions are carried out in other Member States. To protect legitimate expectations and the certainty of transactions in Member States other than that in which proceedings are opened, provisions should be made for a number of exceptions to the general rule.

(25) There is a particular need for a special reference diverging from the law of the opening State in the case of rights in rem, since these are of considerable importance for the granting of credit. The basis, validity and extent of such a right in rem should therefore normally be determined according to the lex situs and not be affected by the opening of insolvency proceedings. The proprietor of the right in rem should therefore be able to continue to assert his right to segregation or separate settlement of the collateral security. Where assets are subject to rights in rem under the lex situs in one Member State but the main proceedings are being carried out in another Member State, the liquidator in the main proceedings should be able to request the opening of secondary proceedings in the jurisdiction where the rights in rem arise if the debtor has an establishment there. If a secondary proceeding is not opened, the surplus on sale of the asset covered by rights in rem must be paid to the liquidator in the main proceedings.

(26) If a set-off is not permitted under the law of the opening State, a creditor should nevertheless be entitled to the set-off if it is possible under the law applicable to the claim of the insolvent debtor. In this way, set-off will acquire a kind of guarantee function based on legal provisions on which the creditor concerned can rely at the time when the claim arises.

(27) There is also a need for special protection in the case of payment systems and financial markets. This applies for example to the position-closing agreements and netting agreements to be found in such systems as well as to the sale of securities and to the guarantees provided for such transactions as governed in particular by Directive 98/26/EC of the European Parliament and of the Council of 19 May 1998 on settlement finality in payment and securities settlement systems.[6] For such transactions, the only law which is material should thus be that applicable to the system or market concerned. This provision is intended to prevent the possibility of mechanisms for the payment and settlement of transactions provided for in the payment and set-off systems or on the regulated financial markets of the Member States being altered in the case of insolvency of a business partner. Directive 98/26/EC contains special provisions which should take precedence over the general rules in this Regulation.

(28) In order to protect employees and jobs, the effects of insolvency proceedings on the continuation or termination of employment and on the rights and obligations of all parties to such employment must be determined by the law applicable to the agreement in accordance with the general rules on conflict of law. Any other

---

[6] OJ L 166, 11.6.1998, 45, reproduced infra under S. 17.

insolvency-law questions, such as whether the employees' claims are protected by preferential rights and what status such preferential rights may have, should be determined by the law of the opening State.

(29) For business considerations, the main content of the decision opening the proceedings should be published in the other Member States at the request of the liquidator. If there is an establishment in the Member State concerned, there may be a requirement that publication is compulsory. In neither case, however, should publication be a prior condition for recognition of the foreign proceedings.

(30) It may be the case that some of the persons concerned are not in fact aware that proceedings have been opened and act in good faith in a way that conflicts with the new situation. In order to protect such persons who make a payment to the debtor because they are unaware that foreign proceedings have been opened when they should in fact have made the payment to the foreign liquidator, it should be provided that such a payment is to have a debt-discharging effect.

(31) This Regulation should include Annexes relating to the organisation of insolvency proceedings. As these Annexes relate exclusively to the legislation of Member States, there are specific and substantiated reasons for the Council to reserve the right to amend these Annexes in order to take account of any amendments to the domestic law of the Member States.

(32) The United Kingdom and Ireland, in accordance with Article 3 of the Protocol on the position of the United Kingdom and Ireland annexed to the Treaty on European Union and the Treaty establishing the European Community, have given notice of their wish to take part in the adoption and application of this Regulation.

(33) Denmark, in accordance with Articles 1 and 2 of the Protocol on the position of Denmark annexed to the Treaty on European Union and the Treaty establishing the European Community, is not participating in the adoption of this Regulation, and is therefore not bound by it nor subject to its application,

HAS ADOPTED THIS REGULATION:

Chapter I
General Provisions

Article 1
Scope

1. This Regulation shall apply to collective insolvency proceedings which entail the partial or total divestment of a debtor and the appointment of a liquidator.

2. This Regulation shall not apply to insolvency proceedings concerning insurance undertakings, credit institutions, investment undertakings which provide services involving the holding of funds or securities for third parties, or to collective investment undertakings.

Article 2
Definitions

For the purposes of this Regulation:

(a) "insolvency proceedings" shall mean the collective proceedings referred to in Article 1(1). These proceedings are listed in Annex A;

(b) "liquidator" shall mean any person or body whose function is to administer or liquidate assets of which the debtor has been divested or to supervise the administration of his affairs. Those persons and bodies are listed in Annex C;

(c) "winding-up proceedings" shall mean insolvency proceedings within the meaning of point (a) involving realising the assets of the debtor, including where the proceedings have been closed by a composition or other measure terminating the insolvency, or closed by reason of the insufficiency of the assets. Those proceedings are listed in Annex B;

(d) "court" shall mean the judicial body or any other competent body of a Member State empowered to open insolvency proceedings or to take decisions in the course of such proceedings;

(e) "judgment" in relation to the opening of insolvency proceedings or the appointment of a liquidator shall include the decision of any court empowered to open such proceedings or to appoint a liquidator;

(f) "the time of the opening of proceedings" shall mean the time at which the judgment opening proceedings becomes effective, whether it is a final judgment or not;

(g) "the Member State in which assets are situated" shall mean, in the case of:
- tangible property, the Member State within the territory of which the property is situated,
- property and rights ownership of or entitlement to which must be entered in a public register, the Member State under the authority of which the register is kept,
- claims, the Member State within the territory of which the third party required to meet them has the centre of his main interests, as determined in Article 3(1);

(h) "establishment" shall mean any place of operations where the debtor carries out a non-transitory economic activity with human means and goods.

Article 3

International jurisdiction

1. The courts of the Member State within the territory of which the centre of a debtor's main interests is situated shall have jurisdiction to open insolvency proceedings. In the case of a company or legal person, the place of the registered office shall be presumed to be the centre of its main interests in the absence of proof to the contrary.

2. Where the centre of a debtor's main interests is situated within the territory of a Member State, the courts of another Member State shall have jurisdiction to open insolvency proceedings against that debtor only if he possesses an establishment within the territory of that other Member State. The effects of those proceedings shall be restricted to the assets of the debtor situated in the territory of the latter Member State.

3. Where insolvency proceedings have been opened under paragraph 1, any proceedings opened subsequently under paragraph 2 shall be secondary proceedings. These latter proceedings must be winding-up proceedings.

4. Territorial insolvency proceedings referred to in paragraph 2 may be opened prior to the opening of main insolvency proceedings in accordance with paragraph 1 only:

(a) where insolvency proceedings under paragraph 1 cannot be opened because of the conditions laid down by the law of the Member State within the territory of which the centre of the debtor's main interests is situated; or

(b) where the opening of territorial insolvency proceedings is requested by a creditor who has his domicile, habitual residence or registered office in the Member State within the territory of which the establishment is situated, or whose claim arises from the operation of that establishment.

Article 4

Law applicable

1. Save as otherwise provided in this Regulation, the law applicable to insolvency proceedings and their effects shall be that of the Member State within the territory of which such proceedings are opened, hereafter referred to as the "State of the opening of proceedings".

2. The law of the State of the opening of proceedings shall determine the conditions for the opening of those proceedings, their conduct and their closure. It shall determine in particular:

(a) against which debtors' insolvency proceedings may be brought on account of their capacity;

(b) the assets which form part of the estate and the treatment of assets acquired by or devolving on the debtor after the opening of the insolvency proceedings;

(c) the respective powers of the debtor and the liquidator;

(d) the conditions under which set-offs may be invoked;

(e) the effects of insolvency proceedings on current contracts to which the debtor is party;

(f) the effects of the insolvency proceedings on proceedings brought by individual creditors, with the exception of lawsuits pending;

(g) the claims which are to be lodged against the debtor's estate and the treatment of claims arising after the opening of insolvency proceedings;

(h) the rules governing the lodging, verification and admission of claims;

(i) the rules governing the distribution of proceeds from the realisation of assets, the ranking of claims and the rights of creditors who have obtained partial satisfaction after the opening of insolvency proceedings by virtue of a right in rem or through a set-off;

(j) the conditions for and the effects of closure of insolvency proceedings, in particular by composition;

(k) creditors' rights after the closure of insolvency proceedings;

(l) who is to bear the costs and expenses incurred in the insolvency proceedings;

(m) the rules relating to the voidness, voidability or unenforceability of legal acts detrimental to all the creditors.

Article 5
Third parties' rights in rem

1. The opening of insolvency proceedings shall not affect the rights in rem of creditors or third parties in respect of tangible or intangible, moveable or immovable assets—both specific assets and collections of indefinite assets as a whole which change from time to time—belonging to the debtor which are situated within the territory of another Member State at the time of the opening of proceedings.

2. The rights referred to in paragraph 1 shall in particular mean:

(a) the right to dispose of assets or have them disposed of and to obtain satisfaction from the proceeds of or income from those assets, in particular by virtue of a lien or a mortgage;

(b) the exclusive right to have a claim met, in particular a right guaranteed by a lien in respect of the claim or by assignment of the claim by way of a guarantee;

(c) the right to demand the assets from, and/or to require restitution by, anyone having possession or use of them contrary to the wishes of the party so entitled;

(d) a right in rem to the beneficial use of assets.

3. The right, recorded in a public register and enforceable against third parties, under which a right in rem within the meaning of paragraph 1 may be obtained, shall be considered a right in rem.

4. Paragraph 1 shall not preclude actions for voidness, voidability or unenforceability as referred to in Article 4(2)(m).

Article 6
Set-off

1. The opening of insolvency proceedings shall not affect the right of creditors to demand the set-off of their claims against the claims of the debtor, where such a set-off is permitted by the law applicable to the insolvent debtor's claim.

2. Paragraph 1 shall not preclude actions for voidness, voidability or unenforceability as referred to in Article 4(2)(m).

Article 7
Reservation of title

1. The opening of insolvency proceedings against the purchaser of an asset shall not affect the seller's rights based on a reservation of title where at the time of the opening of proceedings the asset is situated within the territory of a Member State other than the State of opening of proceedings.

2. The opening of insolvency proceedings against the seller of an asset, after delivery of the asset, shall not constitute grounds for rescinding or terminating the sale and shall not prevent the purchaser from acquiring title where at the time of the opening of proceedings the asset sold is situated within the territory of a Member State other than the State of the opening of proceedings.

3. Paragraphs 1 and 2 shall not preclude actions for voidness, voidability or unenforceability as referred to in Article 4(2)(m).

Article 8
Contracts relating to immovable property

The effects of insolvency proceedings on a contract conferring the right to acquire or make use of immovable property shall be governed solely by the law of the Member State within the territory of which the immovable property is situated.

Article 9
Payment systems and financial markets

1. Without prejudice to Article 5, the effects of insolvency proceedings on the rights and obligations of the parties to a payment or settlement system or to a financial market shall be governed solely by the law of the Member State applicable to that system or market.

2. Paragraph 1 shall not preclude any action for voidness, voidability or unenforceability which may be taken to set aside payments or transactions under the law applicable to the relevant payment system or financial market.

Article 10
Contracts of employment

The effects of insolvency proceedings on employment contracts and relationships shall be governed solely by the law of the Member State applicable to the contract of employment.

Article 11
Effects on rights subject to registration

The effects of insolvency proceedings on the rights of the debtor in immovable property, a ship or an aircraft subject to registration in a public register shall be determined by the law of the Member State under the authority of which the register is kept.

Article 12
Community patents and trade marks

For the purposes of this Regulation, a Community patent, a Community trade mark or any other similar right established by Community law may be included only in the proceedings referred to in Article 3(1).

Article 13
Detrimental acts

Article 4(2)(m) shall not apply where the person who benefited from an act detrimental to all the creditors provides proof that:
– the said act is subject to the law of a Member State other than that of the State of the opening of proceedings, and
– that law does not allow any means of challenging that act in the relevant case.

Article 14
Protection of third-party purchasers

Where, by an act concluded after the opening of insolvency proceedings, the debtor disposes, for consideration, of:
– an immovable asset, or
– a ship or an aircraft subject to registration in a public register, or
– securities whose existence presupposes registration in a register laid down by law,
the validity of that act shall be governed by the law of the State within the territory of which the immovable asset is situated or under the authority of which the register is kept.

Article 15
Effects of insolvency proceedings on lawsuits pending

The effects of insolvency proceedings on a lawsuit pending concerning an asset or a right of which the debtor has been divested shall be governed solely by the law of the Member State in which that lawsuit is pending.

CHAPTER II
RECOGNITION OF INSOLVENCY PROCEEDINGS

Article 16
Principle

1. Any judgment opening insolvency proceedings handed down by a court of a Member State which has jurisdiction pursuant to Article 3 shall be recognised in all the other Member States from the time that it becomes effective in the State of the opening of proceedings. This rule shall also apply where, on account of his capacity, insolvency proceedings cannot be brought against the debtor in other Member States.

2. Recognition of the proceedings referred to in Article 3(1) shall not preclude the opening of the proceedings referred to in Article 3(2) by a court

in another Member State. The latter proceedings shall be secondary insolvency proceedings within the meaning of Chapter III.

Article 17
Effects of recognition

1. The judgment opening the proceedings referred to in Article 3(1) shall, with no further formalities, produce the same effects in any other Member State as under this law of the State of the opening of proceedings, unless this Regulation provides otherwise and as long as no proceedings referred to in Article 3(2) are opened in that other Member State.

2. The effects of the proceedings referred to in Article 3(2) may not be challenged in other Member States. Any restriction of the creditors' rights, in particular a stay or discharge, shall produce effects vis-à-vis assets situated within the territory of another Member State only in the case of those creditors who have given their consent.

Article 18
Powers of the liquidator

1. The liquidator appointed by a court which has jurisdiction pursuant to Article 3(1) may exercise all the powers conferred on him by the law of the State of the opening of proceedings in another Member State, as long as no other insolvency proceedings have been opened there nor any preservation measure to the contrary has been taken there further to a request for the opening of insolvency proceedings in that State. He may in particular remove the debtor's assets from the territory of the Member State in which they are situated, subject to Articles 5 and 7.

2. The liquidator appointed by a court which has jurisdiction pursuant to Article 3(2) may in any other Member State claim through the courts or out of court that moveable property was removed from the territory of the State of the opening of proceedings to the territory of that other Member State after the opening of the insolvency proceedings. He may also bring any action to set aside which is in the interests of the creditors.

3. In exercising his powers, the liquidator shall comply with the law of the Member State within the territory of which he intends to take action, in particular with regard to procedures for the realisation of assets. Those powers may not include coercive measures or the right to rule on legal proceedings or disputes.

Article 19
Proof of the liquidator's appointment

The liquidator's appointment shall be evidenced by a certified copy of the original decision appointing him or by any other certificate issued by the court which has jurisdiction. A translation into the official language or one of the official languages of the Member State within the territory of which he intends to act may be required. No legalisation or other similar formality shall be required.

Article 20
Return and imputation

1. A creditor who, after the opening of the proceedings referred to in Article 3(1) obtains by any means, in particular through enforcement, total or partial satisfaction of his claim on the assets belonging to the debtor situated within the territory of another Member State, shall return what he has obtained to the liquidator, subject to Articles 5 and 7.

2. In order to ensure equal treatment of creditors a creditor who has, in the course of insolvency proceedings, obtained a dividend on his claim shall share in distributions made in other proceedings only where creditors of the same ranking or category have, in those other proceedings, obtained an equivalent dividend.

Article 21
Publication

1. The liquidator may request that notice of the judgment opening insolvency proceedings and, where appropriate, the decision appointing him, be published in any other Member State in accordance with the publication procedures provided for in that State. Such publication shall also specify the liquidator appointed and whether the

jurisdiction rule applied is that pursuant to Article 3(1) or Article 3(2).

2. However, any Member State within the territory of which the debtor has an establishment may require mandatory publication. In such cases, the liquidator or any authority empowered to that effect in the Member State where the proceedings referred to in Article 3(1) are opened shall take all necessary measures to ensure such publication.

Article 22
Registration in a public register

1. The liquidator may request that the judgment opening the proceedings referred to in Article 3(1) be registered in the land register, the trade register and any other public register kept in the other Member States.

2. However, any Member State may require mandatory registration. In such cases, the liquidator or any authority empowered to that effect in the Member State where the proceedings referred to in Article 3(1) have been opened shall take all necessary measures to ensure such registration.

Article 23
Costs

The costs of the publication and registration provided for in Articles 21 and 22 shall be regarded as costs and expenses incurred in the proceedings.

Article 24
Honouring of an obligation to a debtor

1. Where an obligation has been honoured in a Member State for the benefit of a debtor who is subject to insolvency proceedings opened in another Member State, when it should have been honoured for the benefit of the liquidator in those proceedings, the person honouring the obligation shall be deemed to have discharged it if he was unaware of the opening of proceedings.

2. Where such an obligation is honoured before the publication provided for in Article 21 has been effected, the person honouring the obligation shall be presumed, in the absence of proof to the contrary, to have been unaware of the opening of insolvency proceedings; where the obligation is honoured after such publication has been effected, the person honouring the obligation shall be presumed, in the absence of proof to the contrary, to have been aware of the opening of proceedings.

Article 25
Recognition and enforceability of other judgments

1. Judgments handed down by a court whose judgment concerning the opening of proceedings is recognised in accordance with Article 16 and which concern the course and closure of insolvency proceedings, and compositions approved by that court shall also be recognised with no further formalities. Such judgments shall be enforced in accordance with Articles 31 to 51, with the exception of Article 34(2), of the Brussels Convention on Jurisdiction and the Enforcement of Judgments in Civil and Commercial Matters, as amended by the Conventions of Accession to this Convention.

The first subparagraph shall also apply to judgments deriving directly from the insolvency proceedings and which are closely linked with them, even if they were handed down by another court.

The first subparagraph shall also apply to judgments relating to preservation measures taken after the request for the opening of insolvency proceedings.

2. The recognition and enforcement of judgments other than those referred to in paragraph 1 shall be governed by the Convention referred to in paragraph 1, provided that that Convention is applicable.

3. The Member States shall not be obliged to recognise or enforce a judgment referred to in paragraph 1 which might result in a limitation of personal freedom or postal secrecy.

Article 26 [7]
Public policy

Any Member State may refuse to recognise insolvency proceedings opened in another Member

---

[7] Note the Declaration by Portugal concerning the application of Articles 26 and 37 (OJ C 183, 30.6.2000, 1).

State or to enforce a judgment handed down in the context of such proceedings where the effects of such recognition or enforcement would be manifestly contrary to that State's public policy, in particular its fundamental principles or the constitutional rights and liberties of the individual.

CHAPTER III
SECONDARY INSOLVENCY PROCEEDINGS

Article 27
Opening of proceedings

The opening of the proceedings referred to in Article 3(1) by a court of a Member State and which is recognised in another Member State (main proceedings) shall permit the opening in that other Member State, a court of which has jurisdiction pursuant to Article 3(2), of secondary insolvency proceedings without the debtor's insolvency being examined in that other State. These latter proceedings must be among the proceedings listed in Annex B. Their effects shall be restricted to the assets of the debtor situated within the territory of that other Member State.

Article 28
Applicable law

Save as otherwise provided in this Regulation, the law applicable to secondary proceedings shall be that of the Member State within the territory of which the secondary proceedings are opened.

Article 29
Right to request the opening of proceedings

The opening of secondary proceedings may be requested by:

(a) the liquidator in the main proceedings;

(b) any other person or authority empowered to request the opening of insolvency proceedings under the law of the Member State within the territory of which the opening of secondary proceedings is requested.

Article 30
Advance payment of costs and expenses

Where the law of the Member State in which the opening of secondary proceedings is requested requires that the debtor's assets be sufficient to cover in whole or in part the costs and expenses of the proceedings, the court may, when it receives such a request, require the applicant to make an advance payment of costs or to provide appropriate security.

Article 31
Duty to co-operate and communicate information

1. Subject to the rules restricting the communication of information, the liquidator in the main proceedings and the liquidators in the secondary proceedings shall be duty bound to communicate information to each other. They shall immediately communicate any information which may be relevant to the other proceedings, in particular the progress made in lodging and verifying claims and all measures aimed at terminating the proceedings.

2. Subject to the rules applicable to each of the proceedings, the liquidator in the main proceedings and the liquidators in the secondary proceedings shall be duty bound to co-operate with each other.

3. The liquidator in the secondary proceedings shall give the liquidator in the main proceedings an early opportunity of submitting proposals on the liquidation or use of the assets in the secondary proceedings.

Article 32
Exercise of creditors' rights

1. Any creditor may lodge his claim in the main proceedings and in any secondary proceedings.

2. The liquidators in the main and any secondary proceedings shall lodge in other proceedings claims which have already been lodged in the proceedings for which they were appointed, provided that the interests of creditors in the latter proceedings are served thereby, subject to the right of creditors to oppose that or to withdraw

the lodgement of their claims where the law applicable so provides.

3. The liquidator in the main or secondary proceedings shall be empowered to participate in other proceedings on the same basis as a creditor, in particular by attending creditors' meetings.

Article 33
Stay of liquidation

1. The court, which opened the secondary proceedings, shall stay the process of liquidation in whole or in part on receipt of a request from the liquidator in the main proceedings, provided that in that event it may require the liquidator in the main proceedings to take any suitable measure to guarantee the interests of the creditors in the secondary proceedings and of individual classes of creditors. Such a request from the liquidator may be rejected only if it is manifestly of no interest to the creditors in the main proceedings. Such a stay of the process of liquidation may be ordered for up to three months. It may be continued or renewed for similar periods.

2. The court referred to in paragraph 1 shall terminate the stay of the process of liquidation:
– at the request of the liquidator in the main proceedings,
– of its own motion, at the request of a creditor or at the request of the liquidator in the secondary proceedings if that measure no longer appears justified, in particular, by the interests of creditors in the main proceedings or in the secondary proceedings.

Article 34
Measures ending secondary insolvency proceedings

1. Where the law applicable to secondary proceedings allows for such proceedings to be closed without liquidation by a rescue plan, a composition or a comparable measure, the liquidator in the main proceedings shall be empowered to propose such a measure himself.

Closure of the secondary proceedings by a measure referred to in the first subparagraph shall not become final without the consent of the liquidator in the main proceedings; failing his agreement, however, it may become final if the financial interests of the creditors in the main proceedings are not affected by the measure proposed.

2. Any restriction of creditors' rights arising from a measure referred to in paragraph 1 which is proposed in secondary proceedings, such as a stay of payment or discharge of debt, may not have effect in respect of the debtor's assets not covered by those proceedings without the consent of all the creditors having an interest.

3. During a stay of the process of liquidation ordered pursuant to Article 33, only the liquidator in the main proceedings or the debtor, with the former's consent, may propose measures laid down in paragraph 1 of this Article in the secondary proceedings; no other proposal for such a measure shall be put to the vote or approved.

Article 35
Assets remaining in the secondary proceedings

If by the liquidation of assets in the secondary proceedings it is possible to meet all claims allowed under those proceedings, the liquidator appointed in those proceedings shall immediately transfer any assets remaining to the liquidator in the main proceedings.

Article 36
Subsequent opening of the main proceedings

Where the proceedings referred to in Article 3(1) are opened following the opening of the proceedings referred to in Article 3(2) in another Member State, Articles 31 to 35 shall apply to those opened first, in so far as the progress of those proceedings so permits.

Article 37 [8]
Conversion of earlier proceedings

The liquidator in the main proceedings may request that proceedings listed in Annex A previously opened in another Member State be converted into winding-up proceedings if this proves to be in the interests of the creditors in the

---
[8] Note the Declaration by Portugal concerning the application of Articles 26 and 37 (OJ C 183, 30.6.2000, 1).

main proceedings. The court with jurisdiction under Article 3(2) shall order conversion into one of the proceedings listed in Annex B.

Article 38
Preservation measures

Where the court of a Member State which has jurisdiction pursuant to Article 3(1) appoints a temporary administrator in order to ensure the preservation of the debtor's assets, that temporary administrator shall be empowered to request any measures to secure and preserve any of the debtor's assets situated in another Member State, provided for under the law of that State, for the period between the request for the opening of insolvency proceedings and the judgment opening the proceedings.

CHAPTER IV
PROVISION OF INFORMATION FOR CREDITORS AND LODGEMENT OF THEIR CLAIMS

Article 39
Right to lodge claims

Any creditor who has his habitual residence, domicile or registered office in a Member State other than the State of the opening of proceedings, including the tax authorities and social security authorities of Member States, shall have the right to lodge claims in the insolvency proceedings in writing.

Article 40
Duty to inform creditors

1. As soon as insolvency proceedings are opened in a Member State, the court of that State having jurisdiction or the liquidator appointed by it shall immediately inform known creditors who have their habitual residences, domiciles or registered offices in the other Member States.

2. That information, provided by an individual notice, shall in particular include time limits, the penalties laid down in regard to those time limits, the body or authority empowered to accept the lodgement of claims and the other measures laid down. Such notice shall also indicate whether creditors whose claims are preferential or secured in rem need lodge their claims.

Article 41
Content of the lodgement of a claim

A creditor shall send copies of supporting documents, if any, and shall indicate the nature of the claim, the date on which it arose and its amount, as well as whether he alleges preference, security in rem or a reservation of title in respect of the claim and what assets are covered by the guarantee he is invoking.

Article 42
Languages

1. The information provided for in Article 40 shall be provided in the official language or one of the official languages of the State of the opening of proceedings. For that purpose a form shall be used bearing the heading "Invitation to lodge a claim. Time limits to be observed" in all the official languages of the institutions of the European Union.

2. Any creditor who has his habitual residence, domicile or registered office in a Member State other than the State of the opening of proceedings may lodge his claim in the official language or one of the official languages of that other State. In that event, however, the lodgement of his claim shall bear the heading "Lodgement of claim" in the official language or one of the official languages of the State of the opening of proceedings. In addition, he may be required to provide a translation into the official language or one of the official languages of the State of the opening of proceedings.

CHAPTER V
TRANSITIONAL AND FINAL PROVISIONS

Article 43
Applicability in time

The provisions of this Regulation shall apply only to insolvency proceedings opened after its entry into force. Acts done by a debtor before the entry into force of this Regulation shall continue to be governed by the law which was applicable to them at the time they were done.

Article 44
Relationship to Conventions

1. After its entry into force, this Regulation replaces, in respect of the matters referred to therein, in the relations between Member States, the Conventions concluded between two or more Member States, in particular:

(a) the Convention between Belgium and France on Jurisdiction and the Validity and Enforcement of Judgements, Arbitration Awards and Authentic Instruments, signed at Paris on 8 July 1899;

(b) the Convention between Belgium and Austria on Bankruptcy, Winding-up, Arrangements, Compositions and Suspension of Payments (with Additional Protocol of 13 June 1973), signed at Brussels on 16 July 1969;

(c) the Convention between Belgium and the Netherlands on Territorial Jurisdiction, Bankruptcy and the Validity and Enforcement of Judgements, Arbitration Awards and Authentic Instruments, signed at Brussels on 28 March 1925;

(d) the Treaty between Germany and Austria on Bankruptcy, Winding-up, Arrangements and Compositions, signed at Vienna on 25 May 1979;

(e) the Convention between France and Austria on Jurisdiction, Recognition and Enforcement of Judgements on Bankruptcy, signed at Vienna on 27 February 1979;

(f) the Convention between France and Italy on the Enforcement of Judgements in Civil and Commercial Matters, signed at Rome on 3 June 1930;

(g) the Convention between Italy and Austria on Bankruptcy, Winding-up, Arrangements and Compositions, signed at Rome on 12 July 1977;

(h) the Convention between the Kingdom of the Netherlands and the Federal Republic of Germany on the Mutual Recognition and Enforcement of Judgements and other Enforceable Instruments in Civil and Commercial Matters, signed at The Hague on 30 August 1962;

(i) the Convention between the United Kingdom and the Kingdom of Belgium providing for the Reciprocal Enforcement of Judgements in Civil and Commercial Matters, with Protocol, signed at Brussels on 2 May 1934;

(j) the Convention between Denmark, Finland, Norway, Sweden and Iceland on Bankruptcy, signed at Copenhagen on 7 November 1933;

(k) the European Convention on Certain International Aspects of Bankruptcy, signed at Istanbul on 5 June 1990.

2. The Conventions referred to in paragraph 1 shall continue to have effect with regard to proceedings opened before the entry into force of this Regulation.

3. This Regulation shall not apply:

(a) in any Member State, to the extent that it is irreconcilable with the obligations arising in relation to bankruptcy from a convention concluded by that State with one or more third countries before the entry into force of this Regulation;

(b) in the United Kingdom of Great Britain and Northern Ireland, to the extent that is irreconcilable with the obligations arising in relation to bankruptcy and the winding-up of insolvent companies from any arrangements with the Commonwealth existing at the time this Regulation enters into force.

Article 45
Amendment of the Annexes

The Council, acting by qualified majority on the initiative of one of its members or on a proposal from the Commission, may amend the Annexes.

Article 46
Reports

No later than 1 June 2012, and every five years thereafter, the Commission shall present to the European Parliament, the Council and the Economic and Social Committee a report on the application of this Regulation. The report shall be accompanied if need be by a proposal for adaptation of this Regulation.

Article 47

Entry into force

This Regulation shall enter into force on 31 May 2002.

This Regulation shall be binding in its entirety and directly applicable in the Member States in accordance with the Treaty establishing the European Community.

[Annex A

Insolvency proceedings referred to in Article 2(a)

BELGIË/BELGIQUE
- Het faillissement/La faillite
- Het gerechtelijk akkoord/Le concordat judiciaire
- De collectieve schuldenregeling/Le règlement collectif de dettes
- De vrijwillige vereffening/La liquidation volontaire
- De gerechtelijke vereffening/La liquidation judiciaire
- De voorlopige ontneming van beheer, bepaald in artikel 8 van de faillissementswet/Le dessaisissement provisoire, visé à l'article 8 de la loi sur les faillites

ČESKÁ REPUBLIKA
- Konkurs
- Nucené vyrovnání
- Vyrovnání

DEUTSCHLAND
- Das Konkursverfahren
- Das gerichtliche Vergleichsverfahren
- Das Gesamtvollstreckungsverfahren
- Das Insolvenzverfahren

EESTI
- Pankrotimenetlus

ΕΛΛΑΔΑ
- Η πτώχευση
- Η ειδική εκκαθάριση
- Η προσωρινή διαχείριση εταιρείας. Η διοίκηση και διαχείριση των πιστωτών
- Η υπαγωγή επιχείρησης υπό επίτροπο με σκοπό τη σύναψη συμβιβασμού με τους πιστωτές

ESPAÑA
- Concurso

FRANCE
- Sauvegarde
- Redressement judiciaire
- Liquidation judiciaire

IRELAND
- Compulsory winding-up by the court
- Bankruptcy
- The administration in bankruptcy of the estate of persons dying insolvent
- Winding-up in bankruptcy of partnerships
- Creditors' voluntary winding-up (with confirmation of a court)
- Arrangements under the control of the court which involve the vesting of all or part of the property of the debtor in the Official Assignee for realisation and distribution
- Company examinership

ITALIA
- Fallimento
- Concordato preventivo
- Liquidazione coatta amministrativa
- Amministrazione straordinaria

ΚΥΠΡΟΣ
- Υποχρεωτική εκκαθάριση απότο Δικαστήριο
- Εκούσια εκκαθάριση από πιστωτές κατόπιν Δικαστικού Διατάγματος
- Εκούσια εκκαθάριση απόμέλη
- Εκκαθάριση με την εποπτεία του Δικαστηρίου
- Πτώχευση κατόπιν Δικαστικού Διατάγματος
- Διαχείριση της περιουσίας προσώπων που απεβίωσαν αφερέγγυα

LATVIJA
- Bankrots
- Izlīgums
- Sanācija

LIETUVA
- įmonės restruktūrizavimo byla
- įmonės bankroto byla
- įmonės bankroto procesas ne teismo tvarka

LUXEMBOURG
- Faillite
- Gestion contrôlée
- Concordat préventif de faillite (par abandon d'actif)
- Régime spécial de liquidation du notariat

MAGYARORSZÁG
- Csődeljárás
- Felszámolási eljárás

MALTA
- Xoljiment
- Amministrazzjoni
- Stralċ volontarju mill-membri jew mill-kredituri
- Stralċ mill-Qorti
- Falliment f'każ ta' negozjant

NEDERLAND
- Het faillissement
- De surseance van betaling
- De schuldsaneringsregeling natuurlijke personen

ÖSTERREICH
- Das Konkursverfahren
- Das Ausgleichsverfahren

POLSKA
- Postępowanie upadłościowe
- Postępowanie układowe
- Upadłość obejmująca likwidację
- Upadłość z możliwością zawarcia układu

PORTUGAL
- O processo de insolvência
- O processo de falência
- Os processos especiais de recuperação de empresa, ou seja:
  A concordata
  A reconstituição empresarial
  A reestruturação financeira
  A gestão controlada

SLOVENIJA
- Stečajni postopek
- Skrajšani stečajni postopek
- Postopek prisilne poravnave
- Prisilna poravnava v stečaju

SLOVENSKO
- Konkurzné konanie
- Reštrukturalizačné konanie

SUOMI/FINLAND
- Konkurssi/konkurs
- Yrityssaneeraus/företagssanering

SVERIGE
- Konkurs
- Företagsrekonstruktion

UNITED KINGDOM
- Winding-up by or subject to the supervision of the court
- Creditors' voluntary winding-up (with confirmation by the court)
- Administration, including appointments made by filing prescribed documents with the court
- Voluntary arrangements under insolvency legislation
- Bankruptcy or sequestration]

¶ *Annex A has been changed by Annex I of Council Regulation (EC) No 694/2006 of 26 April 2006 amending the lists of insolvency proceedings, winding-up proceedings and liquidators in Annexes A, B and C of Regulation (EC) No 1346/2000 on insolvency proceedings (OJ L 121, 6.5.2006, 1).*

[Annex B
Winding-up proceedings referred to in Article 2(c)

BELGIË/BELGIQUE
- Het faillissement/La faillite
- De vrijwillige vereffening/La liquidation volontaire
- De gerechtelijke vereffening/La liquidation judiciaire

ČESKÁ REPUBLIKA
- Konkurs
- Nucené vyrovnání

DEUTSCHLAND
- Das Konkursverfahren
- Das Gesamtvollstreckungsverfahren
- Das Insolvenzverfahren

EESTI
- Pankrotimenetlus

ΕΛΛΑΔΑ
- Η πτώχευση
- Η ειδική εκκαθάριση

ESPAÑA
- Concurso

FRANCE
- Liquidation judiciaire

IRELAND
- Compulsory winding-up
- Bankruptcy
- The administration in bankruptcy of the estate of persons dying insolvent
- Winding-up in bankruptcy of partnerships
- Creditors' voluntary winding-up (with confirmation of a court)
- Arrangements under the control of the court which involve the vesting of all or part of the property of the debtor in the Official Assignee for realisation and distribution

ITALIA
- Fallimento
- Liquidazione coatta amministrativa
- Concordato preventivo con cessione dei beni

ΚΥΠΡΟΣ
- Υποχρεωτική εκκαθάριση από το Δικαστήριο
- Εκκαθάριση με την εποπτεία του Δικαστηρίου
- Εκούσια εκκαθάριση από πιστωτές (με την επικύρωση του Δικαστηρίου)
- Πτώχευση
- Διαχείριση της περιουσίας προσώπων που απεβίωσαν αφερέγγυα

LATVIJA
- Bankrots

LIETUVA
- įmonės bankroto byla
- įmonės bankroto procesas ne teismo tvarka

LUXEMBOURG
- Faillite
- Régime spécial de liquidation du notariat

MAGYARORSZÁG
- Felszámolási eljárás

MALTA
- Stralċ volontarju
- Stralċ mill-Qorti
- Falliment inkluż il-ħruġ ta' mandat ta' qbid mill-Kuratur f'każ ta' negozjant fallut

NEDERLAND
- Het faillissement
- De schuldsaneringsregeling natuurlijke personen

ÖSTERREICH
- Das Konkursverfahren

POLSKA
- Postępowanie upadłościowe
- Upadłość obejmująca likwidację

PORTUGAL
- O processo de insolvência
- O processo de falência

SLOVENIJA
- Stečajni postopek
- Skrajšani stečajni postopek

SLOVENSKO
- Konkurzné konanie

SUOMI/FINLAND
- Konkurssi/konkurs

SVERIGE
- Konkurs

UNITED KINGDOM
- Winding-up by or subject to the supervision of the court
- Winding-up through administration, including appointments made by filing prescribed documents with the court
- Creditors' voluntary winding-up (with confirmation by the court)
- Bankruptcy or sequestration]

¶ *Annex B has been changed by Annex I of Council Regulation (EC) No 694/2006 of 26 April 2006 amending the lists of insolvency proceedings, winding-up proceedings and liquidators in Annexes A, B and C of Regulation (EC) No 1346/2000 on insolvency proceedings (OJ L 121, 6.5.2006, 1).*

[Annex C

Liquidators referred to in Article 2(b)

BELGIË/BELGIQUE
- De curator/Le curateur
- De commissaris inzake opschorting/Le commissaire au sursis
- De schuldbemiddelaar/Le médiateur de dettes
- De vereffenaar/Le liquidateur
- De voorlopige bewindvoerder/ L'administrateur provisoire

ČESKÁ REPUBLIKA
- Správce podstaty
- Předběžny správce
- Vyrovnací správce
- Zvláštní správce
- Zástupce správce

DEUTSCHLAND
- Konkursverwalter
- Vergleichsverwalter
- Sachwalter (nach der Vergleichsordnung)
- Verwalter
- Insolvenzverwalter
- Sachwalter (nach der Insolvenzordnung)
- Treuhänder
- Vorläufiger Insolvenzverwalter

EESTI
- Pankrotihaldur
- Ajutine pankrotihaldur
- Usaldusisik

ΕΛΛΑΔΑ
- Ο σύνδικος
- Ο προσωρινός διαχειριστής. Η διοικούσα επιτροπή των πιστωτών
- Ο ειδικός εκκαθαριστής
- Ο επίτροπος

ESPAÑA
- Administradores concursales

FRANCE
- Mandataire judiciaire
- Liquidateur
- Administrateur judiciaire
- Commissaire à l'exécution du plan

IRELAND
- Liquidator
- Official Assignee
- Trustee in bankruptcy
- Provisional liquidator
- Examiner

ITALIA
- Curatore
- Commissario
- Liquidatore giudiziale

ΚΥΠΡΟΣ
- Εκκαθαριστής και προσωρινός εκκαθαριστής
- Επίσημος παραλήπτης
- Διαχειριστής της πτώχευσης
- Εξεταστής

LATVIJA
- Maksātnespējas procesa administrators

LIETUVA
- Bankrutuojančių įmonių administratorius
- Restruktūrizuojamų įmonių administratorius

LUXEMBOURG
- Le curateur
- Le commissaire
- Le liquidateur
- Le conseil de gérance de la section d'assainissement du notariat

MAGYARORSZÁG
- Vagyonfelügyelő
- Felszámoló

MALTA
- Amministratur Proviżorju
- Riċevitur Uffiċjali
- Stralċjarju
- Manager Speċjali
- Kuraturi f'każ ta' proċeduri ta' falliment

NEDERLAND
- De curator in het faillissement
- De bewindvoerder in de surseance van betaling

- De bewindvoerder in de schuldsaneringsregeling natuurlijke personen

ÖSTERREICH
- Masseverwalter
- Ausgleichsverwalter
- Sachwalter
- Treuhänder
- Besondere Verwalter
- Konkursgericht

POLSKA
- Syndyk
- Nadzorca sądowy
- Zarządca

PORTUGAL
- Administrador da insolvência
- Gestor judicial
- Liquidatário judicial
- Comissão de credores

SLOVENIJA
- Upravitelj prisilne poravnave
- Stečajni upravitelj
- Sodišče, pristojno za postopek prisilne poravnave

- Sodišče, pristojno za stečajni postopek

SLOVENSKO
- Predbežný správca
- Správca

SUOMI/FINLAND
- Pesänhoitaja/boförvaltare
- Selvittäjä/utredare

SVERIGE
- Förvaltare
- God man
- Rekonstruktör

UNITED KINGDOM
- Liquidator
- Supervisor of a voluntary arrangement
- Administrator
- Official receiver
- Trustee
- Provisional liquidator
- Judicial factor]

¶ *Annex C has been changed by Annex I of Council Regulation (EC) No 694/2006 of 26 April 2006 amending the lists of insolvency proceedings, winding-up proceedings and liquidators in Annexes A, B and C of Regulation (EC) No 1346/2000 on insolvency proceedings (OJ L 121, 6.5.2006, 1).*

E. 10.

European Parliament and Council Directive 2000/35/EC of 29 June 2000 on combating late payment in commercial transactions[1]

CASE

Case C-235/03 QDQ Media SA v Alejandro Omedas Lecha [2005] ECR I-1937

Where it is not possible on the basis of national law to include, in the calculation of the costs which an individual who owes a business debt might be ordered to pay, the expenses arising from representation by an abogado or procurador of the creditor in judicial proceedings for the recovery of that debt, Directive 2000/35/EC cannot of itself serve as the basis for the inclusion of such expenses.

THE EUROPEAN PARLIAMENT AND THE COUNCIL OF THE EUROPEAN UNION,

Having regard to the Treaty establishing the European Community, and in particular Article 95 thereof,

Having regard to the proposal from the Commission,[2]

Having regard to the opinion of the Economic and Social Committee,[3]

Acting in accordance with the procedure laid down in Article 251 of the Treaty,[4] in the light of the joint text approved by the Conciliation Committee on 4 May 2000,

Whereas:

(1) In its resolution on the integrated programme in favour of SMEs and the craft sector,[5] the European Parliament urged the Commission to submit proposals to deal with the problem of late payment.

(2) On 12 May 1995 the Commission adopted a recommendation on payment periods in commercial transactions.[6]

(3) In its resolution on the Commission recommendation on payment periods in commercial transactions,[7] the European Parliament called on the Commission to consider transforming its recommendation into a proposal for a Council directive to be submitted as soon as possible.

(4) On 29 May 1997 the Economic and Social Committee adopted an opinion on the Commission's Green Paper on Public procurement in the European Union: Exploring the way forward.[8]

(5) On 4 June 1997 the Commission published an action plan for the single market, which underlined that late payment represents an increasingly serious obstacle for the success of the single market.

(6) On 17 July 1997 the Commission published a report on late payments in commercial transactions,[9] summarising the results of an evaluation of the effects of the Commission's recommendation of 12 May 1995.

---

[1] OJ L 200, 8.8.2000, 35–38.
[2] OJ C 168, 3.6.1998, 13, and OJ C 374, 3.12.1998, 4.
[3] OJ C 407, 28.12.1998, 50.
[4] Opinion of the European Parliament of 17 September 1998 (OJ C 313, 12.10.1998, 142), Council Common Position of 29 July 1999 (OJ C 284, 6.10.1999, 1) and Decision of the European Parliament of 16 December 1999 (OJ C 296, 18.10.2000, 19). Decision of the European Parliament of 15 June 2000 and Decision of the Council of 18 May 2000.

[5] OJ C 323, 21.11.1994, 19.
[6] OJ L 127, 10.6.1995, 19.
[7] OJ C 211, 22.7.1996, 43.
[8] OJ C 287, 22.9.1997, 92.
[9] OJ C 216, 17.7.1997, 10.

(7) Heavy administrative and financial burdens are placed on businesses, particularly small and medium-sized ones, as a result of excessive payment periods and late payment. Moreover, these problems are a major cause of insolvencies threatening the survival of businesses and result in numerous job losses.

(8) In some Member States contractual payment periods differ significantly from the Community average.

(9) The differences between payment rules and practices in the Member States constitute an obstacle to the proper functioning of the internal market.

(10) This has the effect of considerably limiting commercial transactions between Member States. This is in contradiction with Article 14 of the Treaty as entrepreneurs should be able to trade throughout the internal market under conditions which ensure that transborder operations do not entail greater risks than domestic sales. Distortions of competition would ensue if substantially different rules applied to domestic and transborder operations.

(11) The most recent statistics indicate that there has been, at best, no improvement in late payments in many Member States since the adoption of the recommendation of 12 May 1995.

(12) The objective of combating late payments in the internal market cannot be sufficiently achieved by the Member States acting individually and can, therefore, be better achieved by the Community. This Directive does not go beyond what is necessary to achieve that objective. This Directive complies therefore, in its entirety, with the requirements of the principles of subsidiarity and proportionality as laid down in Article 5 of the Treaty.

(13) This Directive should be limited to payments made as remuneration for commercial transactions and does not regulate transactions with consumers, interest in connection with other payments, e.g. payments under the laws on cheques and bills of exchange, payments made as compensation for damages including payments from insurance companies.

(14) The fact that the liberal professions are covered by this Directive does not mean that Member States have to treat them as undertakings or merchants for purposes not covered by this Directive.

(15) This Directive only defines the term 'enforceable title' but does not regulate the various procedures of forced execution of such a title and the conditions under which forced execution of such a title can be stopped or suspended.

(16) Late payment constitutes a breach of contract which has been made financially attractive to debtors in most Member States by low interest rates on late payments and/or slow procedures for redress. A decisive shift, including compensation of creditors for the costs incurred, is necessary to reverse this trend and to ensure that the consequences of late payments are such as to discourage late payment.

(17) The reasonable compensation for the recovery costs has to be considered without prejudice to national provisions according to which a national judge can award to the creditor any additional damage caused by the debtor's late payment, taking also into account that such incurred costs may be already compensated for by the interest for late payment.

(18) This Directive takes into account the issue of long contractual payment periods and, in particular, the existence of certain categories of contracts where a longer payment period in combination with a restriction of freedom of contract or a higher interest rate can be justified.

(19) This Directive should prohibit abuse of freedom of contract to the disadvantage of the creditor. Where an agreement mainly serves the purpose of procuring the debtor additional liquidity at the expense of the creditor, or where the main contractor imposes on his suppliers and subcontractors terms of payment which are not justified on the grounds of the terms granted to himself, these may be considered to be factors constituting

such an abuse. This Directive does not affect national provisions relating to the way contracts are concluded or regulating the validity of contractual terms which are unfair to the debtor.

(20) The consequences of late payment can be dissuasive only if they are accompanied by procedures for redress which are rapid and effective for the creditor. In conformity with the principle of non-discrimination contained in Article 12 of the Treaty, those procedures should be available to all creditors who are established in the Community.

(21) It is desirable to ensure that creditors are in a position to exercise a retention of title on a non-discriminatory basis throughout the Community, if the retention of title clause is valid under the applicable national provisions designated by private international law.

(22) This Directive should regulate all commercial transactions irrespective of whether they are carried out between private or public undertakings or between undertakings and public authorities, having regard to the fact that the latter handle a considerable volume of payments to business. It should therefore also regulate all commercial transactions between main contractors and their suppliers and subcontractors.

(23) Article 5 of this Directive requires that the recovery procedure for unchallenged claims be completed within a short period of time in conformity with national legislation, but does not require Member States to adopt a specific procedure or to amend their existing legal procedures in a specific way,

HAVE ADOPTED THIS DIRECTIVE:

Article 1

Scope

This Directive shall apply to all payments made as remuneration for commercial transactions.

Article 2

Definitions

For the purposes of this Directive:

1. 'commercial transactions' means transactions between undertakings or between undertakings and public authorities which lead to the delivery of goods or the provision of services for remuneration;

'public authority' means any contracting authority or entity, as defined by the Public Procurement Directives (92/50/EEC,[10] 93/36/EEC,[11] 93/37/EEC[12] and 93/38/EEC[13]);

'undertaking' means any organisation acting in the course of its independent economic or professional activity, even where it is carried on by a single person;

2. 'late payment' means exceeding the contractual or statutory period of payment;

3. 'retention of title' means the contractual agreement according to which the seller retains title to the goods in question until the price has been paid in full;

4. 'interest rate applied by the European Central Bank to its main refinancing operations' means the interest rate applied to such operations in the case of fixed-rate tenders. In the event that a main refinancing operation was conducted according to a variable-rate tender procedure, this interest rate refers to the marginal interest rate which resulted from that tender. This applies both in the case of single-rate and variable-rate auctions;

5. enforceable title' means any decision, judgment or order for payment issued by a court or other competent authority, whether for immediate payment or payment by instalments, which permits the creditor to have his claim against the debtor collected by means of forced execution; it shall include a decision, judgment or order for payment that is provisionally enforceable and remains so even if the debtor appeals against it.

Article 3

Interest in case of late payment

1. Member States shall ensure that:

(a) interest in accordance with point (d) shall become payable from the day following the date

---

[10] OJ L 209, 24.7.1992, 1.
[11] OJ L 199, 9.8.1993, 1.
[12] OJ L 199, 9.8.1993, 54.
[13] OJ L 199, 9.8.1993, 84.

or the end of the period for payment fixed in the contract;

(b) if the date or period for payment is not fixed in the contract, interest shall become payable automatically without the necessity of a reminder:

  (i) 30 days following the date of receipt by the debtor of the invoice or an equivalent request for payment; or
  (ii) if the date of the receipt of the invoice or the equivalent request for payment is uncertain, 30 days after the date of receipt of the goods or services; or
  (iii) if the debtor receives the invoice or the equivalent request for payment earlier than the goods or the services, 30 days after the receipt of the goods or services; or
  (iv) if a procedure of acceptance or verification, by which the conformity of the goods or services with the contract is to be ascertained, is provided for by statute or in the contract and if the debtor receives the invoice or the equivalent request for payment earlier or on the date on which such acceptance or verification takes place, 30 days after this latter date;

(c) the creditor shall be entitled to interest for late payment to the extent that:

  (i) he has fulfilled his contractual and legal obligations; and
  (ii) he has not received the amount due on time, unless the debtor is not responsible for the delay;

(d) the level of interest for late payment ('the statutory rate'), which the debtor is obliged to pay, shall be the sum of the interest rate applied by the European Central Bank to its most recent main refinancing operation carried out before the first calendar day of the half-year in question ('the reference rate'), plus at least seven percentage points ('the margin'), unless otherwise specified in the contract. For a Member State which is not participating in the third stage of economic and monetary union, the reference rate referred to above shall be the equivalent rate set by its national central bank. In both cases, the reference rate in force on the first calendar day of the half-year in question shall apply for the following six months;

(e) unless the debtor is not responsible for the delay, the creditor shall be entitled to claim reasonable compensation from the debtor for all relevant recovery costs incurred through the latter's late payment. Such recovery costs shall respect the principles of transparency and proportionality as regards the debt in question. Member States may, while respecting the principles referred to above, fix maximum amounts as regards the recovery costs for different levels of debt.

2. For certain categories of contracts to be defined by national law, Member States may fix the period after which interest becomes payable to a maximum of 60 days provided that they either restrain the parties to the contract from exceeding this period or fix a mandatory interest rate that substantially exceeds the statutory rate.

3. Member States shall provide that an agreement on the date for payment or on the consequences of late payment which is not in line with the provisions of paragraphs 1(b) to (d) and 2 either shall not be enforceable or shall give rise to a claim for damages if, when all circumstances of the case, including good commercial practice and the nature of the product, are considered, it is grossly unfair to the creditor. In determining whether an agreement is grossly unfair to the creditor, it will be taken, *inter alia*, into account whether the debtor has any objective reason to deviate from the provisions of paragraphs 1(b) to (d) and 2. If such an agreement is determined to be grossly unfair, the statutory terms will apply, unless the national courts determine different conditions which are fair.

4. Member States shall ensure that, in the interests of creditors and of competitors, adequate and effective means exist to prevent the continued use of terms which are grossly unfair within the meaning of paragraph 3.

5. The means referred to in paragraph 4 shall include provisions whereby organisations officially recognised as, or having a legitimate interest in, representing small and medium-sized enterprises may take action according to the national law concerned before the courts or

before competent administrative bodies on the grounds that contractual terms drawn up for general use are grossly unfair within the meaning of paragraph 3, so that they can apply appropriate and effective means to prevent the continued use of such terms.

Article 4
Retention of title

1. Member States shall provide in conformity with the applicable national provisions designated by private international law that the seller retains title to goods until they are fully paid for if a retention of title clause has been expressly agreed between the buyer and the seller before the delivery of the goods.

2. Member States may adopt or retain provisions dealing with down payments already made by the debtor.

Article 5
Recovery procedures for unchallenged claims

1. Member States shall ensure that an enforceable title can be obtained, irrespective of the amount of the debt, normally within 90 calendar days of the lodging of the creditor's action or application at the court or other competent authority, provided that the debt or aspects of the procedure are not disputed. This duty shall be carried out by Member States in conformity with their respective national legislation, regulations and administrative provisions.

2. The respective national legislation, regulations and administrative provisions shall apply the same conditions for all creditors who are established in the European Community.

3. The 90 calendar day period referred to in paragraph 1 shall not include the following:
(a) periods for service of documents;
(b) any delays caused by the creditor, such as periods devoted to correcting applications.

4. This Article shall be without prejudice to the provisions of the Brussels Convention on jurisdiction and enforcement of judgements in civil and commercial matters.[14]

Article 6
Transposition

1. Member States shall bring into force the laws, regulations and administrative provisions necessary to comply with this Directive before 8 August 2002. They shall forthwith inform the Commission thereof.

When Member States adopt these measures, they shall contain a reference to this Directive or shall be accompanied by such reference on the occasion of their official publication. The methods of making such reference shall be laid down by Member States.

2. Member States may maintain or bring into force provisions which are more favourable to the creditor than the provisions necessary to comply with this Directive.

3. In transposing this Directive, Member States may exclude:

(a) debts that are subject to insolvency proceedings instituted against the debtor;

(b) contracts that have been concluded prior to 8 August 2002; and

(c) claims for interest of less than EUR 5.

4. Member States shall communicate to the Commission the text of the main provisions of national law which they adopt in the field covered by this Directive.

5. The Commission shall undertake two years after 8 August 2002 a review of, inter alia, the statutory rate, contractual payment periods and late payments, to assess the impact on commercial transactions and the operation of the legislation in practice. The results of this review and of other reviews will be made known to the European Parliament and the Council, accompanied where appropriate by proposals for improvement of this Directive.

---

[14] Consolidated version in OJ C 27, 26.1.1998, 3.

Article 7
Entry into force

This Directive shall enter into force on the day of its publication in the *Official Journal of the European Communities*.

Article 8
Addressees

This Directive is addressed to the Member States.

E. 11.

Council Directive 2001/23/EC
of 12 March 2001
on the approximation of the laws of the Member States relating to the safeguarding of employees' rights in the event of transfers of undertakings, businesses or parts of undertakings or businesses[1]

CASE

Case T-96/92 Comité Central d'Entreprise de la Société Générale des Grandes Sources and others v Commission of the European Communities [1995] ECR II-1213

A Commission decision on the compatibility with the common market of a concentration, taken pursuant to Regulation 4064/89, is of individual concern, within the meaning of the fourth paragraph of Article [230][2] of the Treaty, to the representatives, recognized in national law, of the employees of the undertakings in question, simply because that regulation—which allows the Commission to take into consideration the social effects of the concentration if they are liable to affect adversely the social objectives referred to in Article [2][2] of the Treaty—expressly mentions them among the third parties showing a sufficient interest to be heard by the Commission during the procedure for examination of the planned concentration, regardless of whether they have actually taken part in that procedure.

On the other hand, in principle and in the absence of exceptional circumstances, it is not of direct concern to them. First, a decision authorizing a concentration, after an examination from the point of view of Community competition law, does not in itself have any effect on the own rights of the representatives of the employees of the undertakings concerned, which, as provided for by the relevant provisions of Community law, will be applicable in accordance with the provisions of national law on the occasion of the transfer of the undertaking as a result of the concentration. Secondly, it does not directly affect the interests of the workers concerned, since, as follows from Directive 77/187/EEC on the safeguarding of employees' rights in the event of transfers of undertakings, the concentration cannot itself bring about a change in the employment relationship as regulated by the contract of employment and collective agreements. If measures which affect the interests of the workers are taken following the concentration, they will be taken by the undertakings concerned and their compatibility with social legislation, both Community and national, will be subject to review by the national courts.

THE COUNCIL OF THE EUROPEAN UNION,

Having regard to the Treaty establishing the European Community, and in particular Article 94 thereof,

Having regard to the proposal from the Commission,

Having regard to the opinion of the European Parliament,[3]

Having regard to the opinion of the Economic and Social Committee,[4]

Whereas:

(1) Council Directive 77/187/EEC of 14 February 1977 on the approximation of the laws of the Member States relating to the safeguarding of employees' rights in the event of transfers of undertakings, businesses or parts of undertakings

---

[1] OJ L 82, 22.3.2001, 16–20.
[2] The number between brackets has been changed as from 1 May 1999 by article 12 of the Treaty of Amsterdam.
[3] Opinion delivered on 25 October 2000 (OJ C 197, 12.7.2001, 171).
[4] OJ C 367, 20.12.2000, 21.

or businesses[5] has been substantially amended.[6] In the interests of clarity and rationality, it should therefore be codified.

(2) Economic trends are bringing in their wake, at both national and Community level, changes in the structure of undertakings, through transfers of undertakings, businesses or parts of undertakings or businesses to other employers as a result of legal transfers or mergers.

(3) It is necessary to provide for the protection of employees in the event of a change of employer, in particular, to ensure that their rights are safeguarded.

(4) Differences still remain in the Member States as regards the extent of the protection of employees in this respect and these differences should be reduced.

(5) The Community Charter of the Fundamental Social Rights of Workers adopted on 9 December 1989 ("Social Charter") states, in points 7, 17 and 18 in particular that: "The completion of the internal market must lead to an improvement in the living and working conditions of workers in the European Community. The improvement must cover, where necessary, the development of certain aspects of employment regulations such as procedures for collective redundancies and those regarding bankruptcies. Information, consultation and participation for workers must be developed along appropriate lines, taking account of the practice in force in the various Member States. Such information, consultation and participation must be implemented in due time, particularly in connection with restructuring operations in undertakings or in cases of mergers having an impact on the employment of workers".

(6) In 1977 the Council adopted Directive 77/187/EEC to promote the harmonisation of the relevant national laws ensuring the safeguarding of the rights of employees and requiring transferors and transferees to inform and consult employees' representatives in good time.

(7) That Directive was subsequently amended in the light of the impact of the internal market, the legislative tendencies of the Member States with regard to the rescue of undertakings in economic difficulties, the case-law of the Court of Justice of the European Communities, Council Directive 75/129/EEC of 17 February 1975 on the approximation of the laws of the Member States relating to collective redundancies[7] and the legislation already in force in most Member States.

(8) Considerations of legal security and transparency required that the legal concept of transfer be clarified in the light of the case-law of the Court of Justice. Such clarification has not altered the scope of Directive 77/187/EEC as interpreted by the Court of Justice.

(9) The Social Charter recognises the importance of the fight against all forms of discrimination, especially based on sex, colour, race, opinion and creed.

(10) This Directive should be without prejudice to the time limits set out in Annex I Part B within which the Member States are to comply with Directive 77/187/EEC, and the act amending it,

HAS ADOPTED THIS DIRECTIVE:

CHAPTER I
SCOPE AND DEFINITIONS

Article 1

1. (a) This Directive shall apply to any transfer of an undertaking, business, or part of an undertaking or business to another employer as a result of a legal transfer or merger.

(b) Subject to subparagraph (a) and the following provisions of this Article, there is a transfer within the meaning of this Directive where there is a transfer of an economic entity which retains its identity, meaning an organised grouping of resources which has the objective of pursuing an economic activity, whether or not that activity is central or ancillary.

---

[5] OJ L 61, 5.3.1977, 26, referred to supra under no. E. 2.
[6] See Annex I, Part A.

[7] OJ L 48, 22.2.1975, 29, reproduced supra under no. E. 1. Directive replaced by Directive 98/59/EC (OJ L 225, 12.8.1998, 16), reproduced supra under no. E. 8.

(c) This Directive shall apply to public and private undertakings engaged in economic activities whether or not they are operating for gain. An administrative reorganisation of public administrative authorities, or the transfer of administrative functions between public administrative authorities, is not a transfer within the meaning of this Directive.

2. This Directive shall apply where and in so far as the undertaking, business or part of the undertaking or business to be transferred is situated within the territorial scope of the Treaty.

3. This Directive shall not apply to seagoing vessels.

Cases

I. Joined cases C-232/04 and C-233/04 Nurten Güney-Görres and Gul Demir v Securicor Aviation (Germany) Ltd and Kötter Aviation Security GmbH & Co. KG [2005] not yet reported

Article 1 of Council Directive 2001/23/EC must be interpreted as meaning that in examining whether there is a transfer of an undertaking or business within the meaning of that article, in the context of a fresh award of a contract and having regard to all the facts, the transfer of the assets for independent commercial use is not an essential criterion for a finding that there was a transfer of those assets from the original contractor to the new contractor.

II. Case C-51/00 Temco Service Industries SA v Samir Imzilyen and others [2002] ECR I-969

Article 1(1) of Council Directive 77/187/EEC of 14 February 1977 must be interpreted as applying to a situation in which a contractor which has entrusted the contract for cleaning its premises to a first undertaking, which has that contract performed by a subcontractor, terminates that contract and enters into a new contract for the performance of the same work with a second undertaking, where the transaction does not involve any transfer of tangible or intangible assets between the first undertaking or the subcontractor and the second undertaking, but the second undertaking has taken on, under a collective labour agreement, part of the staff of the subcontractor, provided that the staff thus taken on are an essential part, in terms of their number and their skills, of the staff assigned by the subcontractor to the performance of the subcontract.

III. Case C-172/99 Oy Liikenne Ab v Pekka Liskojärvi and Pentti Juntunen [2001] ECR I-0745

1. The taking over by an undertaking of non-maritime public transport activities—such as the operation of scheduled local bus routes—previously operated by another undertaking, following a procedure for the award of a public service contract under Council Directive 92/50/EEC of 18 June 1992 relating to the co-ordination of procedures for the award of public service contracts, may fall within the material scope of Council Directive 77/187/EEC of 14 February 1977 on the approximation of the laws of the Member States relating to the safeguarding of employees' rights in the event of transfers of undertakings, businesses or parts of businesses, as set out in Article 1(1) of that directive.

2. Article 1(1) of Directive 77/187/EEC must be interpreted as meaning that

- that directive may apply where there is no direct contractual link between two undertakings which are successively awarded, following procedures for the award of public service contracts conducted in accordance with Directive 92/50/EEC, a non-maritime public transport service—such as the operation of scheduled local bus routes—by a legal person governed by public law;

- in a situation such as that in the main proceedings, Directive 77/187/EEC does not apply where there is no transfer of significant tangible assets between those two undertakings.

IV. Case C-175/99 Didier Mayeur v Association Promotion de l'Information Messine (APIM) [2000] ECR I-7755

On a proper construction of Article 1(1) of Council Directive 77/187/EEC of 14 February 1977 that directive applies where a municipality, a legal person governed by public law operating within the framework of specific rules of administrative law, takes over activities relating to publicity and information concerning the services which it offers to the public, where such activities were previously carried out, in the interests of that municipality, by a non-profit-making association which was a legal person governed by private law, provided always that the transferred entity retains its identity.

V. Case C-343/98 Renato Collino and Luisella Chiappero v Telecom Italia SpA [2000] ECR I-6659

Article 1(1) of Council Directive 77/187/EEC must be interpreted as meaning that that directive may apply to a situation in which an entity operating telecommunications services for public use and managed by a public body within the State administration is, following decisions of the public authorities, the subject of a transfer for value, in the form of an administrative concession, to a private-law company established by another public body which holds its entire capital. The persons concerned by such a transfer must, however, originally have been protected as employees under national employment law.

VI. Case C-234/98 G. C. Allen and others v Amalgamated Construction Co Ltd [1999] ECR I-8643

1. Directive 77/187/EEC can apply to a transfer between two companies in the same group. In contrast to competition law, nothing justifies a parent company's and its subsidiaries' uniform conduct on the market having greater importance in the application of the directive than the formal separation between those companies which have distinct legal personalities. That outcome, which would exclude transfers between companies in the same group from the scope of the directive, would be precisely contrary to the directive's aim, which is to ensure, so far as possible, that the rights of employees are safeguarded in the event of a change of employer by allowing them to remain in employment with the new employer on the terms and conditions agreed with the transferor.

2. Directive 77/187/EEC applies to a situation in which a company belonging to a group decides to subcontract works contracts to another company in the same group in so far as the transaction involves the transfer of an economic entity between the two companies. The term 'economic entity' refers to an organized grouping of persons and assets facilitating the exercise of an economic activity that pursues a specific objective.

VII. Joined cases C-173/96 and C-247/96 Francisca Sánchez Hidalgo and others v Asociación de Servicios Aser and Sociedad Cooperativa Minerva (C-173/96), and Horst Ziemann v Ziemann Sicherheit GmbH and Horst Bohn Sicherheitsdienst (C-247/96) [1998] ECR I-8237

Article 1(1) of Directive 77/187/EEC is to be interpreted as meaning that the directive applies to a situation in which a public body which has contracted out its home-help service for persons in need or awarded a contract for maintaining surveillance of some of its premises to a first undertaking decides, upon expiry of or after termination of that contract, to contract out the service or award the contract to a second undertaking, provided that the operation is accompanied by the transfer of an economic entity between the two undertakings. The term 'economic entity' refers to an organised grouping of persons and assets enabling an economic activity that pursues a specific objective to be exercised. The mere fact that the service successively provided by the old and the new undertaking to which the service is contracted out or the contract is awarded is similar does not justify the conclusion that a transfer of such an entity has occurred.

VIII. See also Joined cases C-127/96, C-229/96 and C-74/97 Francisco Hernández Vidal SA v Prudencia Gómez Pérez, María Gómez Pérez and Contratas y Limpiezas SL (C-127/96), Friedrich Santner v Hoechst AG (C-229/96), and Mercedes Gómez Montaña v Claro Sol SA and Red Nacional de Ferrocarriles Españoles (Renfe) (C-74/97) [1998] ECR I-8179

See commentary of the joined cases C-173/96 and C-247/96 (Leading Case VII of Article 1 of this directive).

IX. Case C-298/94 Annette Henke v Gemeinde Schierke and Verwaltungsgemeinschaft Brocken [1996] ECR I-4989

Article 1(1) of Directive 77/187/EEC must be interpreted as meaning that the concept of a 'transfer of an undertaking, business or part of a business' does not apply to the transfer of administrative functions from a municipality to a grouping constituted by a number of municipalities. The directive sets out to protect workers against the potentially unfavourable consequences for them of changes in the structure of undertakings resulting from economic trends at national and Community level, through, inter alia, transfers of undertakings, businesses or parts of businesses to other employers as a result of transfers or mergers, but does not cover the reorganization of structures of the public administration or the transfer of administrative functions between public administrative authorities.

X. Joined cases C-171/94 and C-172/94 Albert Merckx and Patrick Neuhuys v Ford Motors Company Belgium SA [1996] ECR I-1253

The decisive criterion for establishing whether there is a transfer for the purposes of Directive 77/187/EEC is whether the entity in question retains its economic identity, as indicated inter alia by the fact that its operation is actually continued or resumed. Consequently, Article 1(1) of the directive must be interpreted as applying where an undertaking holding a motor vehicle dealership for a particular territory discontinues its activities and the dealership is then transferred to another undertaking which takes on part of the staff and is recommended to customers, without any transfer of assets or direct contractual relations between the two undertakings concerned.

XI. Case C-48/94 Ledernes Hovedorganisation, Acting for Ole Rygaard v Dansk Arbejdsgiverforening, Acting for Strø Mølle Akustik A/S [1995] ECR I-2745

Article 1(1) of Directive 77/187/EEC must be interpreted as not covering the transfer by an undertaking to another undertaking of one of its building works with the view to its completion, by merely making available to the new contractor certain workers and materials for completing the work in question. The term 'transfers of undertakings' as used in that article assumes that what is transferred is a stable economic entity whose activity is not limited to performing one specific works contract. That is not the case where an undertaking transfers to another undertaking one of its building works with a view to its completion. Such a transfer could come within the terms of the directive only if it included the transfer of a body of assets enabling the activities, or certain activities, of the transferor undertaking to be carried on in a stable way.

XII. Case C-392/92 Christel Schmidt v Spar- und Leihkasse der früheren Ämter Bordesholm, Kiel und Cronshagen [1994] ECR I-1311

Article 1(1) of Council Directive 77/187/EEC is to be interpreted as covering a situation in which an undertaking entrusts by contract to another undertaking the responsibility for carrying out cleaning operations which it previously performed itself, even though, prior to the transfer, such work was carried out by a single employee. Neither the fact that such a transfer relates only to an ancillary activity of the transferor not necessarily connected with its objects, nor the fact that it is not accompanied by any transfer of tangible assets, nor the number of employees concerned is capable of exempting such an operation from the scope of the directive since the decisive criterion for establishing whether there is a transfer for the purposes of that directive is whether the business in question retains its identity, as indicated in particular by the actual continuation or resumption by the new employer of the same or similar activities.

XIII. Case C-209/91 Anne Watson Rask and Kirsten Christensen v Iss Kantineservice A/S [1992] ECR I-5755

Article 1(1) of Directive 77/187/EEC on the approximation of the laws of the Member States relating to the safeguarding of employees' rights in the event of transfers of undertakings, businesses or parts of businesses is to be interpreted as meaning that the directive may apply in a situation in which one businessman, by a contract, assigns to another businessman responsibility for running a facility for staff, which was formerly managed directly, in return for a fee and various advantages, details of which are laid down by the agreement between them.

XIV. Case C-29/91 Dr. Sophie Redmond Stichting v Hendrikus Bartol and others [1992] ECR I-3189

1. Article 1(1) of Council Directive 77/187/EEC is to be interpreted as meaning that the expression 'legal transfer' covers a situation in which a public authority decides to terminate the subsidy paid to one legal person, as a result of which the activities of that legal person are fully and definitively terminated, and to transfer it to another legal person with a similar aim.

2. The expression 'transfer of an undertaking, business or part of a business' contained in Article

1(1) of Directive 77/187/EEC refers to the case in which the entity in question has retained its identity. In order to ascertain whether or not there has been such a transfer, it is necessary to determine, having regard to all the factual circumstances characterising the operation in question, whether the functions performed are in fact carried out or resumed by the new legal person with the same or similar activities, it being understood that activities of a special nature which constitute independent functions may, where appropriate, be equated with a business or part of a business within the meaning of the directive.

XV. Case 101/87 P. Bork International A/S (in liquidation) v Foreningen af Arbejdsledere I Danmark, Acting on Behalf of Birger E. Petersen, and Jens E. Olsen and others v Junckers Industrier A/S [1988] ECR 3057

Article 1(1) of Directive 77/187/EEC is to be interpreted as meaning that the directive applies where, after giving notice bringing the lease to an end or upon termination thereof, the owner of an undertaking retakes possession of it and thereafter sells it to a third party who shortly afterwards brings it back into operation, which had ceased upon termination of the lease, with just over half of the staff that was employed in the undertaking by the former lessee, provided that the undertaking in question retains its identity.

XVI. Joined cases 144/87 and 145/87 Harry Berg and Johannes Theodorus Maria Busschers v Ivo Martin Besselsen [1988] ECR 2559

Article 1(1) of Directive 77/187/EEC must be interpreted as meaning that the directive applies both to the transfer of an undertaking pursuant to a lease-purchase agreement of the kind available under Netherlands law and to the retransfer of the undertaking upon the termination of the lease-purchase agreement by judicial decision.

XVII. Case 324/86 Foreningen af Arbejdsledere i Danmark v Daddy's Dance Hall A/S [1988] ECR 739

Article 1(1) of council directive 77/187/EEC must be interpreted as meaning that the directive applies where, upon the termination of a non-transferable lease, the owner of an undertaking leases it to a new lessee who carries on the business without interruption with the same staff, who had been given notice on the expiry of the initial lease.

XVIII. Case 287/86 Landsorganisationen i Danmark for Tjenerforbundet i Danmark v Ny Mølle Kro [1987] ECR 5465). See also Case 24/85 Jozef Maria Antonius Spijkers v Gebroeders Benedik Abattoir CV et Alfred Benedik en Zonen BV [1986] ECR 1119

1. Article 1(1) of directive 77/187/EEC is applicable where the owner of a leased undertaking takes over its operation following a breach of the lease by the lessee.

2. Article 1(1) of directive 77/187/EEC envisages the transfer of a business as a going concern. in order to ascertain whether this is the case, account must be taken of all the factual circumstances surrounding the transaction in question, including, where appropriate, the temporary closure of the undertaking and the fact that there were no employees at the time of the transfer, although these facts alone do not preclude the applicability of the directive, especially in the case of a seasonal business.

XIX. Case 105/84 Foreningen af Arbejdsledere i Danmark v A/S Danmols Inventar (in liquidation) [1985] ECR 2639

Article 1(1) of Council Directive 77/187/EEC does not apply to the transfer of an undertaking, business or part of a business where the transferor has been adjudged insolvent and the undertaking or business in question forms part of the assets of the insolvent transferor, although the Member States are at liberty to apply the principles of the directive to such a transfer on their own initiative. However, the mere fact that the transfer has occurred after the transferor has suspended payment of its debts is not sufficient to exclude the transfer from the scope of the directive.

Article 2

1. For the purposes of this Directive:

(a) "transferor" shall mean any natural or legal person who, by reason of a transfer within the meaning of Article 1(1), ceases to be the employer in respect of the undertaking, business or part of the undertaking or business;

(b) "transferee" shall mean any natural or legal person who, by reason of a transfer within the meaning of Article 1(1), becomes the employer in respect of the undertaking, business or part of the undertaking or business;

(c) "representatives of employees" and related expressions shall mean the representatives of the employees provided for by the laws or practices of the Member States;

(d) "employee" shall mean any person who, in the Member State concerned, is protected as an employee under national employment law.

2. This Directive shall be without prejudice to national law as regards the definition of contract of employment or employment relationship.

However, Member States shall not exclude from the scope of this Directive contracts of employment or employment relationships solely because:

(a) of the number of working hours performed or to be performed,

(b) they are employment relationships governed by a fixed-duration contract of employment within the meaning of Article 1(1) of Council Directive 91/383/EEC of 25 June 1991 supplementing the measures to encourage improvements in the safety and health at work of workers with a fixed-duration employment relationship or a temporary employment relationship,[8] or

(c) they are temporary employment relationships within the meaning of Article 1(2) of Directive 91/383/EEC, and the undertaking, business or part of the undertaking or business transferred is, or is part of, the temporary employment business that is the employer.

Cases

I. Case C-13/95 Ayse Süzen v Zehnacker Gebäudereinigung GmbH Krankenhausservice [1997] ECR I-1259

Article 1(1) of Directive 77/187/EEC is to be interpreted as meaning that the directive does not apply to a situation in which a person who had entrusted the cleaning of his premises to a first undertaking terminates his contract with the latter and, for the performance of similar work, enters into a new contract with a second undertaking, if there is no concomitant transfer from one undertaking to the other of significant tangible or intangible assets or taking over by the new employer of a major part of the workforce, in terms of their numbers and skills, assigned by his predecessor to the performance of the contract. The concept of transfer within the meaning of the directive relates to cases in which an economic entity—that is to say an organized grouping of persons and assets facilitating the exercise of an economic activity that pursues an objective specific to it—retains its identity following the transaction in question. In those circumstances, the mere loss of a service contract to a competitor cannot by itself indicate the existence of such a transfer. Furthermore, whilst it is conceivable that, in certain sectors in which the business is based essentially on the workforce, an economic entity is able to function without any significant tangible or intangible assets and may be constituted by a group of workers engaged in a joint activity on a permanent basis, it is necessary in addition, for there to be a transfer within the meaning of the directive, for that group to continue to exist after the taking over of an essential part of the workforce by the new awardee of the contract.

II. Case T-12/93 Comité Central d'Entreprise de la Société Anonyme Vittel and Comité d'Etablissement de Pierval and Fédération Générale Agroalimentaire v Commission of the European Communities [1995] ECR II-1247

A Commission decision on the compatibility with the common market of a concentration, taken pursuant to Regulation No 4064/89, is of individual concern, within the meaning of the fourth paragraph of Article [230][7] of the Treaty, to the representatives, recognized in national law, of the employees of the undertakings in question, simply because that regulation—which allows the Commission to take into consideration the social effects of the concentration if they are liable to affect adversely the social objectives referred to in Article [2][7] of the Treaty—expressly mentions them among the third parties showing a sufficient interest to be heard by the Commission during the procedure for examination of the planned

---

[8] OJ L 206, 29.7.1991, 19.

concentration, regardless of whether they have actually taken part in that procedure.

On the other hand, in principle and in the absence of exceptional circumstances, it is not of direct concern to them. First, a decision authorizing a concentration, after an examination from the point of view of Community competition law, even if it makes that concentration subject to the sale by one of the undertakings in question of part of its activities to a third undertaking, does not in itself have any effect on the own rights of the representatives of the employees of the undertakings concerned, which, as provided for by the relevant provisions of Community law, will be applicable in accordance with the provisions of national law on the occasion of the transfer of the undertaking as a result of the concentration. Secondly, it does not directly affect the interests of the workers concerned, since it is only indirectly that the employees' interests may be affected by a transfer of part of their undertaking, a transfer which, as follows from Directive 77/187/EEC on the safeguarding of employees' rights in the event of transfers of undertakings, cannot itself bring about a change in the employment relationship as regulated by the contract of employment and collective agreements. If measures which affect the interests of the workers are taken following the concentration, they will be taken by the undertakings concerned and their compatibility with social legislation, both Community and national, will be subject to review by the national courts.

However, since the representatives of the employees have been given procedural rights by Regulation No 4064/89 and those rights can in principle be given effect to by the Community judicature only at the stage of review of the lawfulness of the Commission's final decision, those representatives must be afforded a remedy limited to the defence of their procedural rights, and must therefore be recognized as entitled to bring proceedings against that decision for the specific purpose of having the Community judicature examine whether or not the procedural guarantees which they were entitled to assert during the administrative procedure under Article 18 of that regulation have been infringed. When that remedy is exercised, only a substantial breach of the procedural rights of the employees' representatives, as opposed to a plea based on substantive breach of the rules laid down in Regulation No 4064/89, may lead to annulment of the Commission's decision.

III. Case 105/84 Foreningen af Arbejdsledere i Danmark v A/S Danmols Inventar (in liquidation) [1985] ECR 2639

The expression 'employee' within the meaning of Directive 77/187/EEC must be interpreted as covering any person who, in the Member State concerned, is protected as an employee under national employment law. It is for the national court to establish whether that is the case.

CHAPTER II
SAFEGUARDING OF EMPLOYEES' RIGHTS

Article 3

1. The transferor's rights and obligations arising from a contract of employment or from an employment relationship existing on the date of a transfer shall, by reason of such transfer, be transferred to the transferee. Member States may provide that, after the date of transfer, the transferor and the transferee shall be jointly and severally liable in respect of obligations that arose before the date of transfer from a contract of employment or an employment relationship existing on the date of the transfer.

2. Member States may adopt appropriate measures to ensure that the transferor notifies the transferee of all the rights and obligations that will be transferred to the transferee under this Article, so far as those rights and obligations are or ought to have been known to the transferor at the time of the transfer. A failure by the transferor to notify the transferee of any such right or obligation shall not affect the transfer of that right or obligation and the rights of any employees against the transferee and/or transferor in respect of that right or obligation.

3. Following the transfer, the transferee shall continue to observe the terms and conditions agreed in any collective agreement on the same terms applicable to the transferor under that agreement, until the date of termination or expiry of the collective agreement or the entry into force or application of another collective agreement.

Member States may limit the period for observing such terms and conditions with the proviso that it shall not be less than one year.

4. (a) Unless Member States provide otherwise, paragraphs 1 and 3 shall not apply in relation to employees' rights to old-age, invalidity or survivors' benefits under supplementary company or intercompany pension schemes outside the statutory social security schemes in Member States.

(b) Even where they do not provide in accordance with subparagraph (a) that paragraphs 1 and 3 apply in relation to such rights, Member States shall adopt the measures necessary to protect the interests of employees and of persons no longer employed in the transferor's business at the time of the transfer in respect of rights conferring on them immediate or prospective entitlement to old age benefits, including survivors' benefits, under supplementary schemes referred to in subparagraph (a).

Cases

I. Case C-478/03 Celtec Ltd v John Astley and others [2005] ECR I-4389

Article 3(1) of Council Directive 77/187/EEC of 14 February 1977 must be interpreted as meaning that the date of a transfer within the meaning of that provision is the date on which responsibility as employer for carrying on the business of the unit transferred moves from the transferor to the transferee. That date is a particular point in time which cannot be postponed to another date at the will of the transferor or transferee. For the purposes of applying that provision, contracts of employment or employment relationships existing on the date of the transfer of the operative part between the transferor and the workers assigned to the undertaking transferred are deemed to be handed over, on that date, from the transferor to the transferee, regardless of what has been agreed between the parties in that respect.

II. Case C-425/02 Johanna Maria Delahaye, née Delahaye v Ministre de la Fonction Publique et de la Réforme Administrative [2004] ECR I-10823

Council Directive 77/187/EEC must be interpreted as not precluding in principle, in the event of a transfer of an undertaking from a legal person governed by private law to the State, the latter, as new employer, from reducing the amount of the remuneration of the employees concerned for the purpose of complying with the national rules in force for public employees. However, the competent authorities responsible for applying and interpreting those rules are obliged to do so as far as possible in the light of the purpose of that directive, taking into account in particular the employee's length of service, in so far as the national rules governing the position of State employees take a State employee's length of service into consideration for calculating his remuneration. If such a calculation leads to a substantial reduction in the employee's remuneration, such a reduction constitutes a substantial change in working conditions to the detriment of the employees concerned by the transfer, so that the termination of their contracts of employment for that reason must be regarded as resulting from the action of the employer, in accordance with Article 4(2) of Directive 77/187/EEC.

III. Case C-164/00 Katia Beckmann v Dynamco Whichloe Macfarlane Ltd [2002] ECR I-4893

1. Early retirement benefits and benefits intended to enhance the conditions of such retirement, paid in the event of dismissal to employees who have reached a certain age, such as the benefits at issue in the main proceedings, are not old-age, invalidity or survivors' benefits under supplementary company or inter-company pension schemes within the meaning of Article 3(3) of Council Directive 77/187/EEC.

2. On a proper construction of Article 3 of Directive 77/187/EEC, the obligations applicable in the event of the dismissal of an employee, arising from a contract of employment, an employment relationship or a collective agreement binding the transferor as regards that employee, are transferred to the transferee subject to the conditions and limitations laid down by that article, regardless of the fact that those obligations derive from statutory instruments or are implemented by such instruments and regardless of the practical arrangements adopted for such implementation.

IV. Case C-51/00 Temco Service Industries SA v Samir Imzilyen and others [2002] ECR I-969

Article 3(1) of Directive 77/187/EEC must be interpreted as meaning that it does not preclude the contract or employment relationship of a worker employed by the transferor on the date of the transfer of the undertaking within the meaning of Article 1(1) of that directive from continuing with the transferor where that worker objects to the transfer of his employment contract or employment.

V. Case C-343/98 Renato Collino and Luisella Chiappero v Telecom Italia SpA [2000] ECR I-6659

The first paragraph of Article 3(1) of Directive 77/187/EEC must be interpreted as meaning that, in calculating the rights of a financial nature attached, in the transferee's business, to employees' length of service, such as a termination payment or salary increases, the transferee must take into account the entire length of service, in both his employment and that of the transferor, of the employees transferred, in so far as his obligation to do so derives from the employment relationship between those employees and the transferor, and in accordance with the terms agreed in that relationship. Directive 77/187/EEC does not, however, preclude the transferee from altering the terms of the employment relationship where national law allows such an alteration in situations other than the transfer of an undertaking.

VI. Case C-399/96 Europièces SA v Wilfried Sanders and Automotive Industries Holding Company SA [1998] ECR I-6965

Article 3(1) of Directive 77/187/EEC does not preclude a worker employed by the transferor at the date of the transfer of an undertaking from objecting to the transfer of his contract of employment or employment relationship to the transferee, provided he decides to do so of his own accord. It is for the national court to determine whether the contract of employment proposed by the transferee involves a substantial change in working conditions to the detriment of the worker. If it does, Article 4(2) of the directive requires Member States to provide that the employer is to be considered responsible for the termination.

VII. Case C-305/94 Claude Rotsart de Hertaing v J. Benoidt SA (in liquidation) and IGC Housing Service SA [1996] ECR I-5927

Article 3(1) of Directive 77/187/EEC is to be interpreted as meaning that the contracts of employment and employment relationships existing on the date of the transfer of an undertaking between the transferor and the workers employed in the undertaking transferred are automatically transferred from the transferor to the transferee by the mere fact of the transfer of the undertaking, despite the contrary intention of the transferor or transferee and despite the latter's refusal to fulfil his obligations. In addition, the transfer of the contracts of employment and employment relationships necessarily takes place on the date of the transfer of the undertaking and cannot be postponed to another date at the will of the transferor or transferee. That all follows from the mandatory nature of the protection afforded to workers by the directive.

VIII. Joined cases C-171/94 and C-172/94 Albert Merckx and Patrick Neuhuys v Ford Motors Company Belgium SA [1996] ECR I-1253

Article 3(1) of Directive 77/187/EEC does not preclude an employee employed by the transferor at the date of a transfer of an undertaking from objecting to the transfer to the transferee of the contract of employment or the employment relationship. In such a case, it is for the Member States to determine what the fate of the contract of employment or employment relationship with the transferor should be. They may provide, in particular, that in such a case the contract of employment or employment relationship must be regarded as terminated either by the employee or by the employer. However, where the contract of employment or the employment relationship is terminated on account of a change in the level of remuneration awarded to the employee, Article 4(2) of the directive requires the Member States to provide that the employer is to be regarded as having been responsible for the termination, because the change in the level of remuneration awarded to the employee is a substantial change in working conditions within the meaning of that provision.

IX. Joined cases C-132/91, C-138/91 and C-139/91 Grigorios Katsikas v Angelos Konstantinidis and Uwe Skreb and Günter Schroll v PCO Stauereibetrieb Paetz & Co. Nachfolger GmbH [1992] ECR I-6577

Article 3(1) of Directive 77/187/EEC on the approximation of the laws of the Member States relating to the safeguarding of employees' rights in the event of transfers of undertakings is to be interpreted as not precluding an employee of the transferor on the date of the transfer of the undertaking, within the meaning of Article 1(1) of the directive, from objecting to the transfer of his contract of employment or employment relationship to the transferee. The directive does not, however, require Member States to provide that, in the event of the employee deciding of his own accord not to continue with the contract of employment or employment relationship with the transferee, the contract or relationship should be maintained with the transferor. Neither does the directive preclude this. In such a case, it is for the Member States to determine what the fate of the contract of employment or employment relationship with the transferor should be.

X. Case C-209/91 Anne Watson Rask and Kirsten Christensen v Iss Kantineservice A/S [1992] ECR I-5755

Article 3 of Directive 77/187/EEC is to be interpreted as meaning that that upon a transfer the terms and conditions of the contract of employment or employment relationship relating to wages, in particular those relating to the date of payment and the composition of wages, cannot be altered even if the total amount of the wages remains the same. The directive does not, however, preclude an alteration of the employment relationship with the new employer in so far as the applicable national law allows such an alteration to be made in situations other than the transfer of an undertaking. Furthermore, the transferee is also bound to continue to observe the terms and conditions of employment agreed in any collective agreement on the same terms applicable to the transferor under that agreement, until the date of termination or expiry of the collective agreement or the entry into force or application of another collective agreement.

XI. Case C-362/89 Giuseppe d'Urso, Adriana Ventadori and others v Ercole Marelli Elettromeccanica Generale SpA and others [1991] ECR I-4105

Article 3(1) of Directive 77/187/EEC is to be interpreted as meaning that all contracts of employment or employment relationships existing on the date of the transfer of an undertaking between the transferor and the workers employed in the undertaking transferred are automatically transferred to the transferee by the mere fact of the transfer. That transfer is binding on both the transferor and the transferee and on the employees' representatives, who may not agree different arrangements in an agreement with the transferor or the transferee and on the employees themselves, save that the employees may freely decide not to continue the employment relationship with the new employer after the transfer.

XII. Case 101/87 P. Bork International A/S, in liquidation v Foreningen af Arbejdsledere I Danmark, Acting on Behalf of Birger E. Petersen, and Jens E. Olsen and others v Junckers Industrier A/S [1988] ECR 3057

Although it is true that, unless otherwise expressly provided, Directive 77/187/EEC relating to the safeguarding of employees' rights in the event of transfers of undertakings may be relied upon solely by workers whose contract of employment or employment relationship is in existence at the time of the transfer, and that the existence or otherwise of such a contract or relationship must be assessed on the basis of national law, it is still necessary to comply with the mandatory provisions of the directive concerning the protection of employees from dismissal as a result of the transfer. Accordingly, the employees whose contract of employment or employment relationship was terminated with effect from a date prior to that of the transfer, contrary to Article 4 (1) of the directive, must be regarded as still in the employ of the undertaking on the date of the transfer, with the result, in particular, that the employer's obligations towards them are automatically transferred from the transferor to the transferee. In order to ascertain whether the employees were dismissed solely as a result of the transfer, it is necessary to take into consideration the objective circumstances in which the dismissal took place such as, in particular, the fact that it took effect on a date close to that of the transfer and that the employees in question were taken on again by the transferee.

XIII. Joined cases 144 and 145/87 Harry Berg and Johannes Theodorus Maria Busschers v Ivo Martin Besselsen [1988] ECR 2559

Article 3(1) of Directive 77/187/EEC which concerns the safeguarding of employees' rights in the event of transfers of undertakings must be interpreted as meaning that after the date of transfer, and by virtue of the transfer alone, the transferor is discharged from all obligations arising under the contract or the employment relationship, even if the workers employed in the undertaking do not consent or if they object, subject however to the power of the Member States to provide for joint liability of the transferor and the transferee after the date of transfer.

XIV. Case 324/86 Foreningen af Arbejdsledere i Danmark v Daddy's Dance Hall A/S [1988] ECR 739

An employee cannot waive the rights conferred on him by the mandatory provisions of directive 77/187/EEC even if the disadvantages resulting from his waiver are offset by such benefits that, taking the matter as a whole, he is not placed in a worse position. Nevertheless, the directive does not preclude an agreement with the new employer to alter the employment relationship, in so far as an alteration is permitted by the applicable national law in cases other than the transfer of an undertaking.

XV. Case 287/86 Landsorganisationen i Danmark for Tjenerforbundet i Danmark v Ny Mølle Kro [1987] ECR 5465

Article 3(2) of directive 77/187/EEC does not oblige the transferee to continue to observe the terms and conditions agreed in any collective agreement in respect of workers who were not employed by the undertaking at the time of the transfer.

XVI. Case 105/84 Foreningen af Arbejdsledere i Danmark v A/S Danmols Inventar (in liquidation) [1985] ECR 2639

Article 3(1) of Directive 77/187/EEC must be construed as not covering the transfer of the rights and obligations of persons who were employed by the transferor at the date of the transfer, but who, by their own decision, do not continue to work as employees of the transferee.

XVII. Case 186/83 Arie Botzen and others v Rotterdamsche Droogdok Maatschappij BV [1985] ECR 519

Article 3(1) of Directive 77/187/EEC must be interpreted as not covering the transferor's rights and obligations arising from a contract of employment or an employment relationship existing on the date of the transfer and entered into with employees who, although not employed in the transferred part of the undertaking, performed certain duties which involved the use of assets assigned to the part transferred or who, whilst being employed in an administrative department of the undertaking which has not itself been transferred, carried out certain duties for the benefit of the part transferred.

XVIII. Case 135/83 The Administrative Board of the Bedrijfsvereniging voor de Metaalindustrie en de Electrotechnische Industrie [1985] ECR 469

Article 3(1) of Directive 77/187/EEC must be interpreted as covering obligations of the transferor resulting from a contract of employment or an employment relationship and arising before the date of the transfer, subject only to the exceptions provided for in article 3(3).

XIX. Case 19/83 Knud Wendelboe and others v L.J. Music ApS (in liquidation) [1985] ECR 457

Council Directive 77/187/EEC does not require the member states to enact provisions under which the transferee of an undertaking becomes liable in respect of obligations concerning holiday pay and compensation to employees who were not employed in the undertaking on the date of the transfer.

The existence or otherwise of a contract of employment or an employment relationship on the date of the transfer, within the meaning of Article 3(1) of Directive 77/187/EEC, must be established on the basis of the rules of national law, subject however to observance of the mandatory provisions of the directive and, more particularly, Article 4(1) thereof, concerning the protection of employees against dismissal by the transferor or the transferee by reason of the transfer.

Article 4

1. The transfer of the undertaking, business or part of the undertaking or business shall not in itself constitute grounds for dismissal by the transferor or the transferee. This provision shall not stand in the way of dismissals that may take place for economic, technical or organisational reasons entailing changes in the workforce.

Member States may provide that the first subparagraph shall not apply to certain specific categories of employees who are not covered by the laws or practice of the Member States in respect of protection against dismissal.

2. If the contract of employment or the employment relationship is terminated because the transfer involves a substantial change in working conditions to the detriment of the employee, the employer shall be regarded as having been responsible for termination of the contract of employment or of the employment relationship.

Cases

I. Case C-399/96 Europièces SA v Wilfried Sanders and Automotive Industries Holding Company SA [1998] ECR I-6965

See supra under Article 3 of this Directive.

II. Case C-319/94 Jules Dethier Équipement SA v Jules Dassy and Sovam SPRL [1998] ECR I-1061

On a proper construction of Article 4(1) of Directive 77/187/EEC, which is designed to protect the rights of employees vis-à-vis the transferor as well as vis-à-vis the transferee against a dismissal whose sole justification is the transfer, both the transferor and the transferee are entitled to dismiss employees for economic, technical or organisational reasons. Employees unlawfully dismissed by the transferor shortly before the undertaking is transferred and not taken on by the transferee may claim, as against the transferee, that their dismissal was unlawful, since their contracts of employment must be regarded as still extant as against the transferee. First, employees dismissed by the transferor before the undertaking is transferred, contrary to Article 4(1) of the directive, must be regarded as still employed by the undertaking on the date of the transfer and, secondly, the rules of the directive, in particular those concerning the protection of workers against dismissal by reason of the transfer, must be considered to be mandatory, so that it is not possible to derogate from them in a manner unfavourable to employees.

III. Joined cases C-171/94 and C-172/94 Albert Merckx and Patrick Neuhuys v Ford Motors Company Belgium SA [1996] ECR I-1253

See supra under Article 3 of this Directive.

IV. Case 237/84 Commission of the European Communities v Kingdom of Belgium [1986] ECR 1247

1. Article 4(1) of Directive 77/187/EEC is designed to ensure that employees' rights are maintained by extending the protection against dismissal by the employer afforded by national law to cover the case in which a change in employer occurs upon the transfer of an undertaking.

That provision applies to any situation in which employees affected by a transfer enjoy some, albeit limited, protection against dismissal under national law, with the result that, under the directive, that protection may not be taken away from them or curtailed solely because of the transfer

2. A Member State may not restrict the scope of a directive by means of a notification, not even if made in accordance with a statement in the council minutes, since the true meaning of rules of community law can be derived only from those rules themselves, having regard to their context.

Article 5

1. Unless Member States provide otherwise, Articles 3 and 4 shall not apply to any transfer of an undertaking, business or part of an undertaking or business where the transferor is the subject of bankruptcy proceedings or any analogous insolvency proceedings which have been instituted with a view to the liquidation of the assets of the transferor and are under the supervision of a competent public authority (which may be an insolvency practitioner authorised by a competent public authority).

2. Where Articles 3 and 4 apply to a transfer during insolvency proceedings which have been opened in relation to a transferor (whether or not those proceedings have been instituted with a view to the liquidation of the assets of the transferor) and provided that such proceedings are under the supervision of a competent public authority (which may be an insolvency practitioner determined by national law) a Member State may provide that:

(a) notwithstanding Article 3(1), the transferor's debts arising from any contracts of employment or employment relationships and payable before the transfer or before the opening of the insolvency proceedings shall not be transferred to the transferee, provided that such proceedings give rise, under the law of that Member State, to protection at least equivalent to that provided for in situations covered by Council Directive 80/987/EEC of 20 October 1980 on the approximation of the laws of the Member States relating to the protection of employees in the event of the insolvency of their employer,[9] and, or alternatively, that,

(b) the transferee, transferor or person or persons exercising the transferor's functions, on the one hand, and the representatives of the employees on the other hand may agree alterations, in so far as current law or practice permits, to the employees' terms and conditions of employment designed to safeguard employment opportunities by ensuring the survival of the undertaking, business or part of the undertaking or business.

3. A Member State may apply paragraph 20(b) to any transfers where the transferor is in a situation of serious economic crisis, as defined by national law, provided that the situation is declared by a competent public authority and open to judicial supervision, on condition that such provisions already existed in national law on 17 July 1998.

The Commission shall present a report on the effects of this provision before 17 July 2003 and shall submit any appropriate proposals to the Council.

4. Member States shall take appropriate measures with a view to preventing misuse of insolvency proceedings in such a way as to deprive employees of the rights provided for in this Directive.

Cases

I. Case C-399/96 Europièces SA v Wilfried Sanders and Automotive Industries Holding Company SA [1998] ECR I-6965

Article 1(1) of Directive 77/187/EEC must be interpreted as meaning that the directive applies where a company in voluntary liquidation transfers all or part of its assets to another company from which the worker then takes his orders which the company in liquidation states are to be carried out.

II. Case C-319/94 Jules Dethier Équipement SA v Jules Dassy and Sovam SPRL [1998] ECR I-1061

On a proper construction of Article 1(1) of Directive 77/187/EEC the directive applies in the event of the transfer of an undertaking which is being wound up by the court if the undertaking continues to trade during that procedure.

III. Case C-472/93 Luigi Spano and others v Fiat Geotech SpA and Fiat Hitachi Excavators SpA [1995] ECR I-4321

Directive 77/187/EEC is applicable to the transfer of an undertaking which, under the procedure provided for by Italian Law No 675 of 12 August 1977 laying down measures for the co-ordination of industrial policy, restructuring, conversion and development in the relevant sector, has been declared to be in critical difficulties. That procedure for declaring undertakings to be in critical difficulties, far from being aimed at the liquidation of the undertaking, is on the contrary designed to promote the continuation of its business, and above all to preserve jobs, with a view to its subsequent recovery, and such a declaration is thus conditional on the submission of a recovery plan, which must include measures to resolve the employment problems.

IV. Case C-362/89 Giuseppe d'Urso, Adriana Ventadori and others v Ercole Marelli Elettromeccanica Generale SpA and others [1991] ECR I-4105

Article 1(1) of Council Directive 77/187/EEC does not apply to transfers of undertakings made as part of a creditors' arrangement procedure of the kind provided for in the Italian legislation on compulsory administrative liquidation to which the Law of 3 April 1979 on special administration for large undertakings in critical difficulties refers. However, that provision of that directive does apply when, in accordance with a body of legislation such as that governing special administration for large undertakings in critical difficulties, it has been decided that the undertaking is to continue trading for as long as that decision remains in force.

---

[9] OJ L 283, 20.10.1980, 23, referred to supra under no. E. 3.

V. Case 179/83 Industriebond FNV and Federatie Nederlandse Vakbeweging (FNV) v The Netherlands State [1985] ECR 511

Article 1(1) of Council Directive 77/187/EEC does not apply to the transfer of an undertaking, business or part of a business where the transferor has been adjudged insolvent and the undertaking or business in question forms part of the assets of the insolvent transferor, although the Member States are at liberty to apply the principles of the directive to such a transfer on their own initiative. The directive does, however, apply where an undertaking, business or part of a business is transferred to another employer in the course of a procedure such as the 'surseance van betaling' (judicial leave to suspend payment of debts) available under Netherlands law (Case 186/83 *Arie Botzen and others v Rotterdamsche Droogdok Maatschappij BV* [1985] ECR 0519). The directive does, however, apply where an undertaking, business or part of a business is transferred to another employer in the course of a procedure such as the 'surseance van betaling' (judicial leave to suspend payment of debts) available under Netherlands law.

VI. Case 135/83 The Administrative Board of the Bedrijfsvereniging voor de Metaalindustrie en de Electrotechnische Industrie [1985] ECR 469

See commentary of Case 179/83 (Leading Case V of Article 5 of this directive).

Article 6

1. If the undertaking, business or part of an undertaking or business preserves its autonomy, the status and function of the representatives or of the representation of the employees affected by the transfer shall be preserved on the same terms and subject to the same conditions as existed before the date of the transfer by virtue of law, regulation, administrative provision or agreement, provided that the conditions necessary for the constitution of the employee's representation are fulfilled.

The first subparagraph shall not supply if, under the laws, regulations, administrative provisions or practice in the Member States, or by agreement with the representatives of the employees, the conditions necessary for the reappointment of the representatives of the employees or for the reconstitution of the representation of the employees are fulfilled.

Where the transferor is the subject of bankruptcy proceedings or any analogous insolvency proceedings which have been instituted with a view to the liquidation of the assets of the transferor and are under the supervision of a competent public authority (which may be an insolvency practitioner authorised by a competent public authority), Member States may take the necessary measures to ensure that the transferred employees are properly represented until the new election or designation of representatives of the employees.

If the undertaking, business or part of an undertaking or business does not preserve its autonomy, the Member States shall take the necessary measures to ensure that the employees transferred who were represented before the transfer continue to be properly represented during the period necessary for the reconstitution or reappointment of the representation of employees in accordance with national law or practice.

2. If the term of office of the representatives of the employees affected by the transfer expires as a result of the transfer, the representatives shall continue to enjoy the protection provided by the laws, regulations, administrative provisions or practice of the Member States.

CHAPTER III

INFORMATION AND CONSULTATION

Article 7

1. The transferor and transferee shall be required to inform the representatives of their respective employees affected by the transfer of the following:
   – the date or proposed date of the transfer,
   – the reasons for the transfer,
   – the legal, economic and social implications of the transfer for the employees,
   – any measures envisaged in relation to the employees.

The transferor must give such information to the representatives of his employees in good time, before the transfer is carried out.

The transferee must give such information to the representatives of his employees in good time, and in any event before his employees are directly affected by the transfer as regards their conditions of work and employment.

2. Where the transferor or the transferee envisages measures in relation to his employees, he shall consult the representatives of these employees in good time on such measures with a view to reaching an agreement.

3. Member States whose laws, regulations or administrative provisions provide that representatives of the employees may have recourse to an arbitration board to obtain a decision on the measures to be taken in relation to employees may limit the obligations laid down in paragraphs 1 and 2 to cases where the transfer carried out gives rise to a change in the business likely to entail serious disadvantages for a considerable number of the employees.

The information and consultations shall cover at least the measures envisaged in relation to the employees.

The information must be provided and consultations take place in good time before the change in the business as referred to in the first subparagraph is effected.

4. The obligations laid down in this Article shall apply irrespective of whether the decision resulting in the transfer is taken by the employer or an undertaking controlling the employer.

In considering alleged breaches of the information and consultation requirements laid down by this Directive, the argument that such a breach occurred because the information was not provided by undertaking controlling the employer shall not be accepted as an excuse.

5. Member States may limit the obligations laid down in paragraphs 1, 2 and 3 to undertakings or businesses that, in terms of the number of employees, meet the conditions for the election or nomination of a collegiate body representing the employees.

6. Member States shall provide that, where there are no representatives of the employees in an undertaking or business through no fault of their own, the employees concerned must be informed in advance of:
– the date or proposed date of the transfer,
– the reason for the transfer,
– the legal, economic and social implications of the transfer for the employees,
– any measures envisaged in relation to the employees.

Case

Case T-12/93 Comité Central d'Entreprise de la Société Anonyme Vittel and Comité d'Etablissement de Pierval and Fédération Générale Agroalimentaire v Commission of the European Communities [1995] ECR II-1247

Although under Article 18(4) of Regulation No 4064/89 the recognised representatives of the workers of the undertakings concerned by a concentration have the right to submit observations, upon application by them, to the Commission, the Commission is not obliged to inform them of the existence of a concentration proposal notified to it by one of the undertakings concerned.

Under Article 6 of Directive 77/187/EEC it is the undertakings in question which are obliged to give information to the employees' representatives, and it is for the national authorities to ensure that that obligation is complied with.

Chapter IV
Final Provisions

Article 8

This Directive shall not affect the right of Member States to apply or introduce laws, regulations or administrative provisions which are more favourable to employees or to promote or permit collective agreements or agreements between social partners more favourable to employees.

> CASES
>
> I. Joined cases C-132/91, C-138/91 and C-139/91 Grigorios Katsikas v Angelos Konstantinidis and Uwe Skreb and Günter Schroll v PCO Stauereibetrieb Paetz & Co Nachfolger GmbH [1992] ECR I-6577
>
> The expression 'laws, regulations or administrative provisions' within the meaning of Article 7 of Council Directive 77/187/EEC must be understood as meaning the laws, regulations or administrative provisions of a Member State as they are interpreted by the courts of that State.
>
> II. Case 235/84 Commission of the European Communities v Italian Republic [1986] ECR 2291
>
> Although the Member States may leave the implementation of the social policy objectives pursued by directive 77/187/EEC in the first instance to management and labour, that does not discharge them from the obligation of ensuring, by the appropriate laws, regulations and administrative measures, that all workers in the Community are afforded the full protection provided for in the directive. The State guarantee must cover all cases where effective protection is not ensured by other means, in particular where collective agreements cover only specific economic sectors and create obligations only between members of the trade union in question and employers or undertakings bound by the agreements.

Article 9

Member States shall introduce into their national legal systems such measures as are necessary to enable all employees and representatives of employees who consider themselves wronged by failure to comply with the obligations arising from this Directive to pursue their claims by judicial process after possible recourse to other competent authorities.

Article 10

The Commission shall submit to the Council an analysis of the effect of the provisions of this Directive before 17 July 2006. It shall propose any amendment that may seem necessary.

Article 11

Member States shall communicate to the Commission the texts of the laws, regulations and administrative provisions that they adopt in the field covered by this Directive.

Article 12

Directive 77/187/EEC, as amended by the Directive referred to in Annex I, Part A, is repealed, without prejudice to the obligations of the Member States concerning the time limits for implementation set out in Annex I, Part B.

References to the repealed Directive shall be construed as references to this Directive and shall be read in accordance with the correlation table in Annex II.

Article 13

This Directive shall enter into force on the 20th day following its publication in the Official Journal of the European Communities.

> CASE
>
> Case C-336/95 Pedro Burdalo Trevejo and others v Fondo Garantía Salarial [1997] ECR I-2115
>
> Directive 77/187/EEC on the approximation of the laws of the Member States relating to the safeguarding of employees' rights in the event of transfers of undertakings, businesses or parts of businesses cannot be relied on in relation to a transfer of an undertaking which took place before the directive had begun to produce legal effects in the Member State concerned.

Article 14

This Directive is addressed to the Member States.

Annex I

Part A

Repealed Directive and its amending Directive
(referred to in Article 12)

Council Directive 77/187/EEC (OJ L 61, 5.3.1977, 26)

Council Directive 98/50/EC (OJ L 201, 17.7.1998, 88)

Part B

Deadlines for transposition into national law
(referred to in Article 12)

Directive	Deadline for transposition
77/187/EEC	16 February 1979
98/50/EC	17 July 2001

Annex II

Correlation Table

Directive 77/187/EEC	This Directive
Article 1	Article 1
Article 2	Article 2
Article 3	Article 3
Article 4	Article 4
Article 4a	Article 5
Article 5	Article 6
Article 6	Article 7
Article 7	Article 8
Article 7a	Article 9
Article 7b	Article 10
Article 8	Article 11
—	Article 12
—	Article 13
—	Article 14
—	ANNEX I
—	ANNEX II

E. 12.

European Parliament and Council Directive 2002/14/EC of 11 March 2002 establishing a general framework for informing and consulting employees in the European Community[1]

THE EUROPEAN PARLIAMENT AND THE COUNCIL OF THE EUROPEAN UNION,

Having regard to the Treaty establishing the European Community, and in particular Article 137(2) thereof,

Having regard to the proposal from the Commission,[2]

Having regard to the opinion of the Economic and Social Committee,[3]

Having regard to the opinion of the Committee of the Regions,[4]

Acting in accordance with the procedure referred to in Article 251,[5] and in the light of the joint text approved by the Conciliation Committee on 23 January 2002,

Whereas:

(1) Pursuant to Article 136 of the Treaty, a particular objective of the Community and the Member States is to promote social dialogue between management and labour.

(2) Point 17 of the Community Charter of Fundamental Social Rights of Workers provides, inter alia, that information, consultation and participation for workers must be developed along appropriate lines, taking account of the practices in force in different Member States.

(3) The Commission consulted management and labour at Community level on the possible direction of Community action on the information and consultation of employees in undertakings within the Community.

(4) Following this consultation, the Commission considered that Community action was advisable and again consulted management and labour on the contents of the planned proposal; management and labour have presented their opinions to the Commission.

(5) Having completed this second stage of consultation, management and labour have not informed the Commission of their wish to initiate the process potentially leading to the conclusion of an agreement.

(6) The existence of legal frameworks at national and Community level intended to ensure that employees are involved in the affairs of the undertaking employing them and in decisions which affect them has not always prevented serious decisions affecting employees from being taken and made public without adequate procedures having been implemented beforehand to inform and consult them.

(7) There is a need to strengthen dialogue and promote mutual trust within undertakings in order to improve risk anticipation, make work organisation more flexible and facilitate employee access to training within the undertaking while maintaining security, make employees aware of adaptation needs, increase employees' availability to undertake measures and activities to increase their employability, promote employee

---

[1] OJ L 80, 23.3.2002, 29–33.
[2] OJ C 2, 5.1.1999, 3.
[3] OJ C 258, 10.9.1999, 24.
[4] OJ C 144, 16.5.2001, 58.
[5] Opinion of the European Parliament of 14 April 1999 (OJ C 219, 30.7.1999, 223), confirmed on 16 September 1999 (OJ C 54, 25.2.2000, 55), Council Common Position of 27 July 2001 (OJ C 307, 31.10.2001, 16) and Decision of the European Parliament of 23 October 2001 (OJ C 112, 9.5.2002, 119). Decision of the European Parliament of 5 February 2002 and Decision of the Council of 18 February 2002.

involvement in the operation and future of the undertaking and increase its competitiveness.

(8) There is a need, in particular, to promote and enhance information and consultation on the situation and likely development of employment within the undertaking and, where the employer's evaluation suggests that employment within the undertaking may be under threat, the possible anticipatory measures envisaged, in particular in terms of employee training and skill development, with a view to offsetting the negative developments or their consequences and increasing the employability and adaptability of the employees likely to be affected.

(9) Timely information and consultation is a prerequisite for the success of the restructuring and adaptation of undertakings to the new conditions created by globalisation of the economy, particularly through the development of new forms of organisation of work.

(10) The Community has drawn up and implemented an employment strategy based on the concepts of "anticipation", "prevention" and "employability", which are to be incorporated as key elements into all public policies likely to benefit employment, including the policies of individual undertakings, by strengthening the social dialogue with a view to promoting change compatible with preserving the priority objective of employment.

(11) Further development of the internal market must be properly balanced, maintaining the essential values on which our societies are based and ensuring that all citizens benefit from economic development.

(12) Entry into the third stage of economic and monetary union has extended and accelerated the competitive pressures at European level. This means that more supportive measures are needed at national level.

(13) The existing legal frameworks for employee information and consultation at Community and national level tend to adopt an excessively a posteriori approach to the process of change, neglect the economic aspects of decisions taken and do not contribute either to genuine anticipation of employment developments within the undertaking or to risk prevention.

(14) All of these political, economic, social and legal developments call for changes to the existing legal framework providing for the legal and practical instruments enabling the right to be informed and consulted to be exercised.

(15) This Directive is without prejudice to national systems regarding the exercise of this right in practice where those entitled to exercise it are required to indicate their wishes collectively.

(16) This Directive is without prejudice to those systems which provide for the direct involvement of employees, as long as they are always free to exercise the right to be informed and consulted through their representatives.

(17) Since the objectives of the proposed action, as outlined above, cannot be adequately achieved by the Member States, in that the object is to establish a framework for employee information and consultation appropriate for the new European context described above, and can therefore, in view of the scale and impact of the proposed action, be better achieved at Community level, the Community may adopt measures in accordance with the principle of subsidiarity as set out in Article 5 of the Treaty. In accordance with the principle of proportionality, as set out in that Article, this Directive does not go beyond what is necessary in order to achieve these objectives.

(18) The purpose of this general framework is to establish minimum requirements applicable throughout the Community while not preventing Member States from laying down provisions more favourable to employees.

(19) The purpose of this general framework is also to avoid any administrative, financial or legal constraints which would hinder the creation and development of small and medium-sized undertakings. To this end, the scope of this Directive should be restricted, according to the choice made by Member States, to undertakings with at least 50 employees or establishments employing at least 20 employees.

(20) This takes into account and is without prejudice to other national measures and practices aimed at fostering social dialogue within companies not covered by this Directive and within public administrations.

(21) However, on a transitional basis, Member States in which there is no established statutory system of information and consultation of employees or employee representation should have the possibility of further restricting the scope of the Directive as regards the numbers of employees.

(22) A Community framework for informing and consulting employees should keep to a minimum the burden on undertakings or establishments while ensuring the effective exercise of the rights granted.

(23) The objective of this Directive is to be achieved through the establishment of a general framework comprising the principles, definitions and arrangements for information and consultation, which it will be for the Member States to comply with and adapt to their own national situation, ensuring, where appropriate, that management and labour have a leading role by allowing them to define freely, by agreement, the arrangements for informing and consulting employees which they consider to be best suited to their needs and wishes.

(24) Care should be taken to avoid affecting some specific rules in the field of employee information and consultation existing in some national laws, addressed to undertakings or establishments which pursue political, professional, organisational, religious, charitable, educational, scientific or artistic aims, as well as aims involving information and the expression of opinions.

(25) Undertakings and establishments should be protected against disclosure of certain particularly sensitive information.

(26) The employer should be allowed not to inform and consult where this would seriously damage the undertaking or the establishment or where he has to comply immediately with an order issued to him by a regulatory or supervisory body.

(27) Information and consultation imply both rights and obligations for management and labour at undertaking or establishment level.

(28) Administrative or judicial procedures, as well as sanctions that are effective, dissuasive and proportionate in relation to the seriousness of the offence, should be applicable in cases of infringement of the obligations based on this Directive.

(29) This Directive should not affect the provisions, where these are more specific, of Council Directive 98/59/EC of 20 July 1998 on the approximation of the laws of the Member States relating to collective redundancies[6] and of Council Directive 2001/23/EC of 12 March 2001 on the approximation of the laws of the Member States relating to the safeguarding of employees' rights in the event of transfers of undertakings, businesses or parts of undertakings or businesses.[7]

(30) Other rights of information and consultation, including those arising from Council Directive 94/45/EEC of 22 September 1994 on the establishment of a European Works Council or a procedure in Community-scale undertakings and Community-scale groups of undertakings for the purposes of informing and consulting employees,[8] should not be affected by this Directive.

(31) Implementation of this Directive should not be sufficient grounds for a reduction in the general level of protection of workers in the areas to which it applies,

HAVE ADOPTED THIS DIRECTIVE:

Article 1

Object and principles

1. The purpose of this Directive is to establish a general framework setting out minimum requirements for the right to information and consultation

---

[6] OJ L 225, 12.8.1998, 16, reproduced supra under no. E. 8.
[7] OJ L 82, 22.3.2001, 16, reproduced supra under no. E. 11.
[8] OJ L 254, 30.9.1994, 64, reproduced supra under no. E. 5. Directive as amended by Directive 97/74/EC (OJ L 10, 16.1.1998, 22), reproduced supra under no. E. 6.

of employees in undertakings or establishments within the Community.

2. The practical arrangements for information and consultation shall be defined and implemented in accordance with national law and industrial relations practices in individual Member States in such a way as to ensure their effectiveness.

3. When defining or implementing practical arrangements for information and consultation, the employer and the employees' representatives shall work in a spirit of cooperation and with due regard for their reciprocal rights and obligations, taking into account the interests both of the undertaking or establishment and of the employees.

Article 2
Definitions

For the purposes of this Directive:

(a) "undertaking" means a public or private undertaking carrying out an economic activity, whether or not operating for gain, which is located within the territory of the Member States;

(b) "establishment" means a unit of business defined in accordance with national law and practice, and located within the territory of a Member State, where an economic activity is carried out on an ongoing basis with human and material resources;

(c) "employer" means the natural or legal person party to employment contracts or employment relationships with employees, in accordance with national law and practice;

(d) "employee" means any person who, in the Member State concerned, is protected as an employee under national employment law and in accordance with national practice;

(e) "employees' representatives" means the employees' representatives provided for by national laws and/or practices;

(f) "information" means transmission by the employer to the employees' representatives of data in order to enable them to acquaint themselves with the subject matter and to examine it;

(g) "consultation" means the exchange of views and establishment of dialogue between the employees' representatives and the employer.

Article 3
Scope

1. This Directive shall apply, according to the choice made by Member States, to:

(a) undertakings employing at least 50 employees in any one Member State, or

(b) establishments employing at least 20 employees in any one Member State.

Member States shall determine the method for calculating the thresholds of employees employed.

2. In conformity with the principles and objectives of this Directive, Member States may lay down particular provisions applicable to undertakings or establishments which pursue directly and essentially political, professional organisational, religious, charitable, educational, scientific or artistic aims, as well as aims involving information and the expression of opinions, on condition that, at the date of entry into force of this Directive, provisions of that nature already exist in national legislation.

3. Member States may derogate from this Directive through particular provisions applicable to the crews of vessels plying the high seas.

Article 4
Practical arrangements for information and consultation

1. In accordance with the principles set out in Article 1 and without prejudice to any provisions and/or practices in force more favourable to employees, the Member States shall determine the practical arrangements for exercising the right to information and consultation at the appropriate level in accordance with this Article.

2. Information and consultation shall cover:

(a) information on the recent and probable development of the undertaking's or the establishment's activities and economic situation;

(b) information and consultation on the situation, structure and probable development of employment within the undertaking or establishment and on any anticipatory measures envisaged, in particular where there is a threat to employment;

(c) information and consultation on decisions likely to lead to substantial changes in work organisation or in contractual relations, including those covered by the Community provisions referred to in Article 9(1).

3. Information shall be given at such time, in such fashion and with such content as are appropriate to enable, in particular, employees' representatives to conduct an adequate study and, where necessary, prepare for consultation.

4. Consultation shall take place:

(a) while ensuring that the timing, method and content thereof are appropriate;

(b) at the relevant level of management and representation, depending on the subject under discussion;

(c) on the basis of information supplied by the employer in accordance with Article 2(f) and of the opinion which the employees' representatives are entitled to formulate;

(d) in such a way as to enable employees' representatives to meet the employer and obtain a response, and the reasons for that response, to any opinion they might formulate;

(e) with a view to reaching an agreement on decisions within the scope of the employer's powers referred to in paragraph 2(c).

Article 5
Information and consultation deriving from an agreement

Member States may entrust management and labour at the appropriate level, including at undertaking or establishment level, with defining freely and at any time through negotiated agreement the practical arrangements for informing and consulting employees. These agreements, and agreements existing on the date laid down in Article 11, as well as any subsequent renewals of such agreements, may establish, while respecting the principles set out in Article 1 and subject to conditions and limitations laid down by the Member States, provisions which are different from those referred to in Article 4.

Article 6
Confidential information

1. Member States shall provide that, within the conditions and limits laid down by national legislation, the employees' representatives, and any experts who assist them, are not authorised to reveal to employees or to third parties, any information which, in the legitimate interest of the undertaking or establishment, has expressly been provided to them in confidence. This obligation shall continue to apply, wherever the said representatives or experts are, even after expiry of their terms of office. However, a Member State may authorise the employees' representatives and anyone assisting them to pass on confidential information to employees and to third parties bound by an obligation of confidentiality.

2. Member States shall provide, in specific cases and within the conditions and limits laid down by national legislation, that the employer is not obliged to communicate information or undertake consultation when the nature of that information or consultation is such that, according to objective criteria, it would seriously harm the functioning of the undertaking or establishment or would be prejudicial to it.

3. Without prejudice to existing national procedures, Member States shall provide for administrative or judicial review procedures for the case where the employer requires confidentiality or does not provide the information in accordance with paragraphs 1 and 2. They may also provide for procedures intended to safeguard the confidentiality of the information in question.

Article 7
Protection of employees' representatives

Member States shall ensure that employees' representatives, when carrying out their functions, enjoy adequate protection and guarantees to enable them to perform properly the duties which have been assigned to them.

Article 8
Protection of rights

1. Member States shall provide for appropriate measures in the event of non-compliance with this Directive by the employer or the employees' representatives. In particular, they shall ensure that adequate administrative or judicial procedures are available to enable the obligations deriving from this Directive to be enforced.

2. Member States shall provide for adequate sanctions to be applicable in the event of infringement of this Directive by the employer or the employees' representatives. These sanctions must be effective, proportionate and dissuasive.

Article 9
Link between this Directive and other Community and national provisions

1. This Directive shall be without prejudice to the specific information and consultation procedures set out in Article 2 of Directive 98/59/EC and Article 7 of Directive 2001/23/EC.

2. This Directive shall be without prejudice to provisions adopted in accordance with Directives 94/45/EC and 97/74/EC.

3. This Directive shall be without prejudice to other rights to information, consultation and participation under national law.

4. Implementation of this Directive shall not be sufficient grounds for any regression in relation to the situation which already prevails in each Member State and in relation to the general level of protection of workers in the areas to which it applies.

Article 10
Transitional provisions

Notwithstanding Article 3, a Member State in which there is, at the date of entry into force of this Directive, no general, permanent and statutory system of information and consultation of employees, nor a general, permanent and statutory system of employee representation at the workplace allowing employees to be represented for that purpose, may limit the application of the national provisions implementing this Directive to:

(a) undertakings employing at least 150 employees or establishments employing at least 100 employees until 23 March 2007, and

(b) undertakings employing at least 100 employees or establishments employing at least 50 employees during the year following the date in point (a).

Article 11
Transposition

1. Member States shall adopt the laws, regulations and administrative provisions necessary to comply with this Directive not later than 23 March 2005 or shall ensure that management and labour introduce by that date the required provisions by way of agreement, the Member States being obliged to take all necessary steps enabling them to guarantee the results imposed by this Directive at all times. They shall forthwith inform the Commission thereof.

2. Where Member States adopt these measures, they shall contain a reference to this Directive or shall be accompanied by such reference on the occasion of their official publication. The methods of making such reference shall be laid down by the Member States.

Article 12
Review by the Commission

Not later than 23 March 2007, the Commission shall, in consultation with the Member States and the social partners at Community level, review the application of this Directive with a view to proposing any necessary amendments.

Article 13
Entry into force

This Directive shall enter into force on the day of its publication in the Official Journal of the European Communities.

Article 14
Addresses

This Directive is addressed to the Member States.

E. 13.

European Parliament and Council Directive 2002/74/EC of 23 September 2002 amending Council Directive 80/987/EEC on the approximation of the laws of the Member States relating to the protection of employees in the event of the insolvency of their employer[1]

(Text with EEA relevance)

THE EUROPEAN PARLIAMENT AND THE COUNCIL OF THE EUROPEAN UNION,

Having regard to the Treaty establishing the European Community, and in particular Article 137(2) thereof,

Having regard to the proposal from the Commission,[2]

Having regard to the opinion of the Economic and Social Committee,[3]

Having consulted the Committee of the Regions,

Acting in accordance with the procedure laid down in Article 251 of the Treaty,[4]

Whereas:

(1) The Community Charter of Fundamental Social Rights for Workers adopted on 9 December 1989 states, in point 7, that the completion of the internal market must lead to an improvement in the living and working conditions of workers in the European Community and that this improvement must cover, where necessary, the development of certain aspects of employment regulations such as procedures for collective redundancies and those regarding bankruptcies.

(2) Directive 80/987/EEC[5] aims to provide a minimum degree of protection for employees in the event of the insolvency of their employer. To this end, it obliges the Member States to establish a body which guarantees payment of the outstanding claims of the employees concerned.

(3) Changes in insolvency law in the Member States and the development of the internal market mean that certain provisions of that Directive must be adapted.

(4) Legal certainty and transparency also require clarification with regard to the scope and certain definitions of Directive 80/987/EEC. In particular the possible exclusions granted to the Member States should be indicated in the enacting provisions of the Directive and consequently the Annex thereto should be deleted.

(5) In order to ensure equitable protection for the employees concerned, the definition of the state of insolvency should be adapted to new legislative trends in the Member States and should also include within this concept insolvency proceedings other than liquidation. In this context, Member States should, in order to determine the liability of the guarantee institution, be able to lay down that where an insolvency situation results in several insolvency proceedings, the situation be treated as a single insolvency procedure.

(6) It should be ensured that the employees referred to in Directive 97/81/EC of 15

---

[1] OJ L 270, 8.10.2002, 10–13.
[2] OJ C 154 E, 29.5.2001, 109.
[3] OJ C 221, 7.8.2001, 110.
[4] Opinion of the European Parliament of 29 November 2001 (OJ C 153, 27.6.2002, 243), Council Common Position of 18 February 2002 (OJ C 119 E, 22.5.2002, 1) and (OJ C 119, 22.5.2002, 1) and European Parliament Decision of 14 May 2002 (not yet published in the Official Journal). Council Decision of 27 June 2002.

[5] OJ L 283, 28.10.1980, 23, reproduced supra under no. E. 3. Directive as last amended by the 1994 Act of Accession.

December 1997 concerning the Framework Agreement on part-time work concluded by UNICE, CEEP and the ETUC,[6] Council Directive 1999/70/EC of 28 June 1999 concerning the framework agreement on fixed-term work concluded by the ETUC, UNICE and CEEP[7] and Council Directive 91/383/EEC of 25 June 1991 supplementing the measures to encourage improvements in the safety and health at work of workers with a fixed-duration employment relationship or a temporary employment relationship[8] are not excluded from the scope of this Directive.

(7) In order to ensure legal certainty for employees in the event of insolvency of undertakings pursuing their activities in a number of Member States, and to strengthen workers' rights in line with the established case law of the Court of Justice, provisions should be introduced which expressly state which institution is responsible for meeting pay claims in these cases and establishes as the aim of cooperation between the competent administrative authorities of the Member States the early settlement of employees' outstanding claims. Furthermore it is necessary to ensure that the relevant arrangements are properly implemented by making provision for collaboration between the competent administrative authorities in the Member States.

(8) Member States may set limitations on the responsibility of the guarantee institutions which should be compatible with the social objective of the Directive and may take into account the different levels of claims.

(9) In order to make it easier to identify insolvency proceedings in particular in situations with a cross-border dimension, provision should be made for the Member States to notify the Commission and the other Member States about the types of insolvency proceedings which give rise to intervention by the guarantee institution.

(10) Directive 80/987/EEC should be amended accordingly.

(11) Since the objectives of the proposed action, namely the amendment of certain provisions of Directive 80/987/EEC to take account of changes in the activities of undertakings in the Community, cannot be sufficiently achieved by the Member States and can therefore be better achieved at Community level, the Community may adopt measures, in accordance with the principle of subsidiarity as set out in Article 5 of the Treaty. In accordance with the principle of proportionality, as set out in that Article, this Directive does not go beyond what is necessary in order to achieve that objective.

(12) The Commission should submit to the European Parliament and the Council a report on the implementation and application of this Directive in particular as regards the new forms of employment emerging in the Member States,

HAVE ADOPTED THIS DIRECTIVE:

Article 1

[. . .]

¶ *Article 1 amends the Title, Section I, articles 3 and 4, inserts Section IIIa, articles 9, 10 and 10a and deletes the Annex of Directive 80/987/EEC, reproduced supra under no. E. 3. The modifications are directly incorporated therein.*

Article 2

1. Member States shall bring into force the laws, regulations and administrative provisions necessary to comply with this Directive before 8 October 2005. They shall forthwith inform the Commission thereof.

They shall apply the provisions referred to in the first subparagraph to any state of insolvency of an employer occurring after the date of entry into force of those provisions.

When Member States adopt these measures, they shall contain a reference to this Directive or be accompanied by such reference on the occasion of their official publication. The methods of making such a reference shall be laid down by the Member States.

---

[6] OJ L 14, 20.1.1998, 9. Directive as last amended by Directive 98/23/EC (OJ L 131, 5.5.1998, 10).
[7] OJ L 175, 10.7.1999, 43.
[8] OJ L 206, 29.7.1991, 19.

2. Member States shall communicate to the Commission the text of the provisions of national law which they adopt in the field covered by this Directive.

Article 3

This Directive shall enter into force on the day of its publication in the Official Journal of the European Communities.

Article 4

By 8 October 2010 at the latest, the Commission shall submit to the European Parliament and the Council a report on the implementation and application of this Directive in the Member States.

Article 5

This Directive is addressed to the Member States.

Part VI

INSURANCE LAW

I. 1.

Council Directive 64/225/EEC
of 25 February 1964
on the abolition of restrictions on freedom of establishment and freedom to
provide services in respect of reinsurance and retrocession[1]

THE COUNCIL OF THE EUROPEAN ECONOMIC COMMUNITY,

Having regard to the Treaty establishing the European Economic Community, and in particular Articles [44 (2) and (3) 52 (2)][2] thereof,

Having regard to the General Programme for the abolition of restrictions on freedom of establishment,[3] and in particular Title IV A thereof,

Having regard to the General Programme for the abolition of restrictions on freedom to provide services,[4] and in particular Title V C thereof,

Having regard to the proposal from the Commission,

Having regard to the Opinion of the European Parliament,[5]

Having regard to the Opinion of the Economic and Social Committee,[6]

Whereas the General Programmes provide that all branches of reinsurance must, without distinction, be liberalised before the end of 1963 as regards both right of establishment and provision of services;

Whereas reinsurance is effected not only by undertakings specialising in reinsurance but also by so-called "mixed" undertakings, which deal both in direct insurance and in reinsurance and which should therefore be covered by measures taken in implementation of this Directive in respect of that part of their business which is concerned with reinsurance and retrocession;

Whereas, for the purposes of applying measures concerning right of establishment and freedom to provide services, companies and firms are to be treated in the same way as natural persons who are nationals of Member States, subject only to the conditions laid down in Article 58 and, where necessary, to the condition that there should exist a real and continuous link with the economy of a Member State; whereas therefore no company or firm may be required, in order to obtain the benefit of such measures, to fulfil any additional condition, and in particular no company or firm may be required to obtain any special authorisation not required of a domestic company or firm wishing to pursue a particular economic activity; whereas, however, such uniformity of treatment should not prevent Member States from requiring that a company having a share capital should operate in their countries under the description by which it is known in the law of the Member

---

[1] OJ L 56, 4.4.1964, 878–880/64.
[2] The numbers between brackets have been changed as from 1 May 1999 by article 12 of the Treaty of Amsterdam.
[3] OJ C 2, 15.1.1962, 36/62.
[4] OJ C 2, 15.1.1962, 32/62.
[5] OJ C 33, 4.3.1963, 482/63.
[6] OJ C 56, 4.4.1963, 882/64.

State under which it is constituted, and that it should indicate the amount of its subscribed capital on the business papers which it uses in the host Member State;

HAS ADOPTED THIS DIRECTIVE:

Article 1

Member States shall abolish, in respect of the natural persons and companies or firms covered by Title I of the General Programmes for the abolition of restrictions on freedom of establishment and freedom to provide services the restrictions referred to in Title III of those General Programmes affecting the right to take up and pursue the activities specified in Article 2 of this Directive.

Article 2

The provisions of this Directive shall apply:

1. to activities of self-employed persons in reinsurance and retrocession falling within Group ex 630 in Annex I to the General Programme for the abolition of restrictions on freedom of establishment;

2. in the special case of natural persons, companies or firms referred to in Article 1 which deal both in direct insurance and in reinsurance and retrocession, to that part of their activities which is concerned with reinsurance and retrocession.

Article 3

Article 1 shall apply in particular to restrictions arising out of the following provisions:

(a) with regard to freedom of establishment:
– *in the Federal Republic of Germany:*
  1. Versicherungsaufsichtsgesetz of June 6, 1931, last sentence of Article 106 (2), and Article 111 (2), whereby the Federal Minister of Economic Affairs is given discretionary powers to impose on foreign nationals conditions for taking up activities in insurance and to prohibit such nationals from pursuing such activities in the territory of the Federal Republic;
  2. Gewerbeordnung, paragraph (12), and Law of 30 January 1937, Article 292, whereby foreign companies and firms are required to obtain prior authorisation;
– *in the Kingdom of Belgium:*
  Arrêt royal No. 62 of November 16, 1939 and Arrêt ministériel of December 17, 1945, which require the possession of a carte professio[n]nelle;
– *in the French Republic:*
  1. Décret-loi of 12 November 1938, and Décret of 2 February 1939, both as amended by the Law of 8 October 1940, which require the possession of a carte d'identité de commerçant;
  2. Second paragraph of Article 2 of the Law of 15 February 1917, as amended and supplemented by Décret-loi of 30 October 1935, which requires that special authorisation be obtained;
– *in the Grand Duchy of Luxembourg:*
  Law of 2 June 1962, Articles 19 and 21 (*Mémorial A* No. 31 of June 19, 1962).
[– *in the Kingdom of Denmark:*
  Law of 23 December 1959, on the acquisition of immovable property.]

(b) with regard to freedom to provide services:
– *in the French Republic:*
  Law of 15 February 1917, as amended by *Décret-loi* of 30 October 1935, namely:
  1. the second paragraph of Article 1, which empowers the Minister of Finance to draw up a list of specified undertakings, or of undertakings of a specified country, with which no contract for reinsurance or retrocession of any risk in respect of any person, property or liability in France may be concluded;
  2. the last paragraph of Article 1, which prohibits the acceptance of reinsurance or of retrocession risks insured by the undertakings referred to in (b) (l) above;
  3. the first paragraph of Article 2, which requires that the name of the person referred to in that article must be submitted to the Minister of Finance for approval;

– *in the Republic of Italy:*
The second paragraph of Article 73 of the consolidated text approved by *Decreto* No. 449 of 13 February 1959, which empowers the Minister of Industry and Commerce to prohibit the transfer of reinsurance or retrocession risks to specified foreign undertakings which have not established legal representation in Italian territory.

[– *in the Kingdom of Denmark:*
Law of December 23, 1959, on the acquisition of immovable property.]

¶ *The words between square brackets in (a) and (b) have been inserted by the Act of Accession of the Kingdom of Denmark, Annex I(III)(G)(1) (OJ L 304, 30.10.1978).*

Article 4

Member States shall adopt the measures necessary to comply with this Directive within six months of its notification and shall forthwith inform the Commission thereof.

Article 5

This Directive is addressed to the Member States.

I. 2.

Council Directive 72/166/EEC
of 24 April 1972
on the approximation of the laws of the Member States relating to insurance against civil liability in respect of the use of motor vehicles, and to the enforcement of the obligation to insure against such liability[1]

Cases

I. Case C-451/99 Cura Anlagen GmbH v Auto Service Leasing GmbH (ASL) [2002] ECR I-3193

The provisions of the EC Treaty on the freedom to provide services (Articles 49 EC to 55 EC) preclude legislation of a Member State, such as that at issue in the main proceedings, requiring an undertaking established in that Member State which takes a lease of a vehicle registered in another Member State to register it in the first Member State in order to be able to use it there beyond a period that is so short, in this case three days, that it makes it impossible or excessively difficult to comply with the requirements imposed. The same provisions of the Treaty preclude legislation of a Member State, such as that at issue in the main proceedings, requiring an undertaking established in that Member State which takes a lease of a vehicle registered in another Member State to register it in the first Member State and imposing on it one or more of the following conditions:
- a requirement that the person in whose name the vehicle is registered in the Member State of use reside or have a place of business there, in so far as it obliges a leasing undertaking either to have a principal place of business in that Member State or to accept registration of the vehicle in the name of the lessee and the consequent limitation of its rights over the vehicle;
- a requirement to insure the vehicle with an authorised insurer in the Member State of use, if that requirement implies that the insurer must have its principal place of business in that Member State, as the home State within the meaning of the non-life insurance directives, and have 'official authorisation' there;
- a requirement of a roadworthiness test when the vehicle has already undergone such testing in the Member State where the leasing company is established, save where that requirement is aimed at verifying that the vehicle satisfies the conditions imposed on vehicles registered in the Member State of use that are not covered by the tests carried out in the Member State where the leasing company is established and/or, if the vehicle has in the meantime been used on the public highway, that its condition has not deteriorated since it was tested in that latter Member State, provided similar testing is imposed where a vehicle previously tested in the Member State of use is presented for registration in that State;
- payment, in the Member State of use, of a consumption tax the amount of which is not proportionate to the duration of the registration of the vehicle in that State.

II. Case 152/83 Marcel Demouche and others v Fonds de garantie automobile and Bureau Central Français [1987] ECR 3833

The court does not have jurisdiction under Article [234][2] of the Treaty to interpret an agreement concluded by national insurance bureaux, even though such an agreement was provided for by Directive 72/166/EEC. The part played by the agreement in question in the system introduced by the directive does not alter its nature as a measure adopted by private associations in the conclusion of which no community institution took part.

---

[1] OJ L 103, 2.5.1972, 1–4.

[2] The number between brackets has been changed as from 1 May 1999 by article 12 of the Treaty of Amsterdam.

III. Case 344/82 SA Gambetta Auto v Bureau Central Français and Fonds de Garantie Automobile [1984] ECR 591

Where a vehicle bears a properly issued registration plate it must be regarded as normally based, within the meaning of Directive 72/166/EEC, in the territory of the State of registration, even if at the material time authorisation to use the vehicle had been withdrawn.

IV. Case 90/76 S.r.l. Ufficio Henry van Ameyde v Srl Ufficio Centrale Italiano di Assistenza Assicurativa Automobilisti in Circolazione Internazionale (UCI) [1977] ECR 1091

1. Council Directive 72/166/EEC of 24 April 1972, Commission Recommendation 73/185/EEC of 15 May 1973 and Commission Decision 74/166/EEC of 6 February 1974 which seek to abolish checks on the green card at frontiers between Member States cannot be regarded as authorizing the existence of national provisions or agreements between national insurance bureaux or their members which are incompatible with the provisions of the Treaty relating to competition, the right of establishment and the freedom to provide services.

2. A national provision or an agreement between national bureaux established in the context of the green card system which declares that the national bureau bears sole responsibility for the settlement of claims for damage caused in the territory of that Member State by vehicles insured by foreign insurance companies but which still allows the national bureau or its members to rely on undertakings whose business consists solely in the settlement of accident claims on behalf of insurers in the sense of the handling and investigation of claims, is not incompatible with Article [86(1)]² of the treaty in conjunction with Articles [81 and 82].²

3. A decision or a course of conduct of a national bureau or concerted practices of its members which have the object or effect of excluding undertakings whose business consists solely in the settlement, in the restricted sense referred to above, of accident claims on behalf of insurers, may possibly fall under the prohibition of Article [82]² and, if the national bureau is in a dominant position, under the prohibition contained in Article [86]² of the Treaty in conjunction with Article [82].² It is for the national court to determine whether the conditions for the application of those prohibitions are fulfilled.

4. For discrimination to fall under the prohibitions contained in Articles [43 and 49]² it suffices that such discrimination results from rules of whatever kind which seek to govern collectively the carrying on of the business in question. In that case it is not relevant whether the discrimination originated in measures of a public authority, or on the other hand, in measures attributable to individuals.

5. Rules or conduct having the effect of reserving to the national bureau of a Member State or to its members or to insurance companies with an establishment there the final decision as to the payment of damages to victims of accidents caused in the territory of that state by vehicles normally based in another Member State are not discriminatory within the meaning of Articles [43 and 49]² of the Treaty if the exclusion of other categories of undertakings is not based on the criterion of nationality.

THE COUNCIL OF THE EUROPEAN COMMUNITIES,

Having regard to the Treaty establishing the European Economic Community, and in particular Article [94]² thereof;

Having regard to the proposal from the Commission;

Having regard to the Opinion of the European Parliament;

Having regard to the Opinion of the Economic and Social Committee,

Whereas the objective of the Treaty is to create a common market which is basically similar to a domestic market, and whereas one of the essential conditions for achieving this is to bring about the free movement of goods and persons;

Whereas the only purpose of frontier controls of compulsory insurance cover against civil liability in respect of the use of motor vehicles is to safeguard the interests of persons who may be the victims of accidents caused by such vehicles;

Whereas the existence of such frontier controls results from disparities between national requirements in this field;

Whereas these disparities are such as may impede the free movement of motor vehicles and persons within the Community; whereas, consequently, they have a direct effect on the establishment and functioning of the common market;

Whereas the Commission Recommendation of 21 June 1968, on control by customs of travellers crossing intra-Community frontiers calls upon Member States to carry out controls on travellers and their motor vehicles only under exceptional circumstances and to remove the physical barriers at customs posts;

Whereas it is desirable that the inhabitants of the Member States should become more fully aware of the reality of the common market and that to this end measures should be taken further to liberalise the rules regarding the movement of persons and motor vehicles travelling between Member States; whereas the need for such measures has been repeatedly emphasised by members of the European Parliament;

Whereas such relaxation of the rules relating to the movement of travellers constitutes another step towards the mutual opening of their markets by Member States and the creation of conditions similar to those of a domestic market;

Whereas the abolition of checks on green cards for vehicles normally based in a Member State entering the territory of another Member State can be effected by means of an agreement between the six national insurers' bureaux, whereby each national bureau would guarantee compensation in accordance with the provisions of national law in respect of any loss or injury giving entitlement to compensation caused in its territory by one of those vehicles, whether or not insured;

Whereas such a guarantee agreement presupposes that all Community motor vehicles travelling in Community territory are covered by insurance whereas the national law of each Member State should, therefore, provide for the compulsory insurance of vehicles against civil liability, the insurance to be valid throughout Community territory; whereas such national law may nevertheless provide for exemptions for certain persons and for certain types of vehicles;

Whereas the system provided for in this directive could be extended to vehicles normally based in the territory of any third country in respect of which the national bureaux of the six Member States have concluded a similar agreement;

HAS ADOPTED THIS DIRECTIVE:

Article 1

For the purposes of this directive:

1. "vehicle" means any motor vehicle intended for travel on land and propelled by mechanical power, but not running on rails, and any trailer, whether or not coupled;

2. "injured party" means any person entitled to compensation in respect of any loss or injury caused by vehicles;

3. "national insurers' bureau" means a professional organisation which is constituted in accordance with Recommendation No. 5 adopted on 25 January 1949, by the Road Transport Sub-committee of the Inland Transport Committee of the United Nations Economic Commission for Europe and which groups together insurance undertakings which, in a State, are authorised to conduct the business of motor vehicle insurance against civil liability;

4. "territory in which the vehicle is normally based" means

[– the territory of the state of which the vehicle bears a registration plate, irrespective of whether the plate is permanent or temporary, or]

– in cases where no registration is required for a type of vehicle but the vehicle bears an insurance plate, or a distinguishing sign analogous to the registration plate, the territory of the State in which the insurance plate or the sign is issued; or

– in cases where neither registration plate nor insurance plate nor distinguishing sign is

required for certain types of vehicle, the territory of the State in which the person who has custody of the vehicle is permanently resident; or
[– in cases where the vehicle does not bear any registration plate or bears a registration plate which does not correspond or no longer corresponds to the vehicle and has been involved in an accident, the territory of the State in which the accident took place, for the purpose of settling the claim as provided for in the first indent of Article 2(2) of this Directive or in Article 1(4) of Second Council Directive 84/5/EEC of 30 December 1983 on the approximation of the laws of the Member States relating to insurance against civil liability in respect of the use of motor vehicles;[3]]

5. "green card" means an international certificate of insurance issued on behalf of a national bureau in accordance with Recommendation No. 5 adopted on 25 January 1949, by the Road Transport Sub-committee of the Inland Transport Committee of the United Nations Economic Commission for Europe.

¶ *The first indent between square brackets in article 1(4) has been replaced by article 4 of the Second Motor Liability Directive 84/5/EEC, reproduced infra under no. I. 11, and subsequently been replaced by article 1(1) of Directive 2005/14/EC, reproduced infra under no. I. 39.*
¶ *The last indent between square brackets in article 1(4) has been added by article 1 of Directive 2005/14/EC, reproduced infra under no. I. 39.*

CASE

Case C-73/89 A. Fournier and others v V. van Werven, Bureau Central Français and others [1992] ECR I-5621

Article 1(4) of Directive 72/166/EEC as amended by Directive 84/5/EEC, must be interpreted as meaning that a vehicle which, on crossing the frontier, bears a registration plate that was duly issued by the authorities of a Member State but is false by reason of the fact that it is in reality the registration plate allocated to another vehicle, is to be regarded as normally based in the territory of the State which issued the plate in question.

---

[3] OJ L 8, 11.1.1984, 17, reproduced infra under no. I. 11.

This interpretation does not prejudge the question as to which of the national bureaux must, under the agreement between them, bear the burden of paying damages to the victim of a traffic accident caused by a person driving a vehicle in the circumstances described above. The agreement between national central bureaux, although using the same terms as the directive, in fact remains an instrument governed by private law the interpretation of which is a matter for the national court alone.

Article 2

[1. Member States shall refrain from making checks on insurance against civil liability in respect of vehicles normally based in the territory of another Member State and in respect of vehicles normally based in the territory of a third country entering their territory from the territory of another Member State. However, they may carry out non-systematic checks on insurance provided that they are not discriminatory and are carried out as part of a control which is not aimed exclusively at insurance verification;]

2. As regards vehicles normally based in the territory of a Member State, the provisions of this directive, with the exception of Articles 3 and 4, shall take effect:
– [after an agreement has been concluded between the nine national insurers' bureaux under the terms of which each national bureau guarantees the settlement, in accordance with the provisions of national law on compulsory insurance, of claims in respect of accidents occurring in its territory, caused by vehicles normally based in the territory of another Member State, whether or not such vehicles are insured;]
– from the date fixed by the Commission, upon its having ascertained in close co-operation with the Member States that such an agreement has been concluded;
– for the duration of that agreement.

¶ *Article 2(1) has been replaced by article 1(3) of Directive 2005/14/EC, reproduced infra under no. I. 39.*
¶ *The indent between square brackets in article 2(2) has been replaced by article 1 of Directive 72/430/EEC (OJ L 291, 28.12.1977, 162).*

Cases

I. Case C-537/03 Katja Candolin, Jari-Antero Viljaniemi, Veli-Matti Paananen v Vahinkovakuutusosakeyhtiö Pohjola, Jarno Ruokoranta [2005] ECR I-5745

Article 3(1) of the First Directive precludes an insurer from relying on statutory provisions or contractual clauses in order to refuse to compensate third-party victims of an accident caused by an insured vehicle. Article 2(1) of the Second Directive simply repeats that obligation with respect to certain provisions or clauses and makes only one exception for the case that the insurer can prove that the persons who voluntarily entered the vehicle which caused the injury knew that it was stolen. This exception must be read strictly: national rules, established on the basis of general and abstract criteria such as on the basis of the passenger's contribution to the injury or loss he has suffered, cannot extend that exception to either denying the passenger the right to be compensated or limit such a right in a disproportionate manner. The fact that the passenger concerned is the owner of the vehicle the driver of which caused the accident is irrelevant.

II. Case 116/83 Asbl Bureau Belge des Assureurs Automobiles v Adriano Fantozzi and SA Les Assurances populaires [1984] ECR 2481

Article 2 (2) of Directive 72/166/EEC must be interpreted as meaning that, with reference to the payment of compensation for damage caused in the territory of one member state of the community by a vehicle normally based in the territory of another Member State, if the driver of the vehicle obtained it by theft or duress, the national insurers' bureaux are under an obligation to settle such claims upon the terms laid down by their own national legislation.

III. Case 64/83 Bureau Central Français v Fonds de Garantie Automobile and others [1984] ECR 689

1. Where a vehicle bears a properly issued registration plate, that vehicle must be regarded as being normally based, within the meaning of Directive no 72/166/EEC, in the territory of the State in which it is registered, even if at the relevant time the authorisation to use the vehicle had been withdrawn, irrespective of the fact that the withdrawal of the authorisation renders the registration invalid or entails its revocation.

2. The expression 'provisions of national law on compulsory insurance' contained in Article 2 (2) of Council Directive 72/166/EEC must be understood as referring to the limits and conditions of civil liability applicable to compulsory insurance, provided always that the driver of the vehicle at the time at which the accident occurred is deemed to be covered by valid insurance in conformity with that legislation.

Article 3

1. Each Member State shall, subject to Article 4, take all appropriate measures to ensure that civil liability in respect of the use of vehicles normally based in its territory is covered by insurance. The extent of the liability covered and the terms and conditions of the cover shall be determined on the basis of these measures.

2. Each Member State shall take all appropriate measures to ensure that the contract of insurance also covers:
   – according to the law in force in other Member States, any loss or injury that is caused in the territory of those States;
   – any loss or injury suffered by nationals of Member States during a direct journey between two territories in which the Treaty establishing the European Economic Community is in force, if there is no national insurers' bureau responsible for the territory which is being crossed; in that case, the loss or injury shall be covered in accordance with the internal laws on compulsory insurance in force in the Member State in whose territory the vehicle is normally based.

Case

Case C-129/94 Criminal Proceedings Against Rafael Ruiz Bernáldez [1996] ECR I-1829

1. In the preliminary-ruling procedure under Article [234][2] of the Treaty, it is for the national courts alone, before which the proceedings are pending and which must assume responsibility for

the judgment to be given, to determine, having regard to the particular features of each case, both the need for a preliminary ruling to enable them to give judgment and the relevance of the questions which they refer to the court. A request for a preliminary ruling from a national court may be rejected only if it is quite obvious that the interpretation of Community law sought by that court bears no relation to the actual nature of the case or the subject matter of the main action.

2. Article 3(1) of Directive 72/166/EEC is to be interpreted as meaning that, without prejudice to the provisions of Article 2(1) of Directive 84/5/EEC on the approximation of the laws of the Member States relating to insurance against civil liability in respect of the use of motor vehicles, a compulsory insurance contract may not provide that in certain cases, in particular where the driver of the vehicle was intoxicated, the insurer is not obliged to pay compensation for the damage to property and personal injuries caused to third parties by the insured vehicle. In view of the aim of ensuring protection, stated repeatedly in all the relevant directives, Article 3(1) of Directive 72/166/EEC, as developed and supplemented by the later directives, must be interpreted as meaning that compulsory motor insurance must enable third-party victims of accidents caused by vehicles to be compensated for all the damage to property and personal injuries sustained by them, without the insurer being able to rely on statutory provisions or contractual clauses to refuse such compensation. Any other interpretation would deprive that provision of its effectiveness, since it would have the effect of allowing Member States to limit payment of compensation to third-party victims of a road-traffic accident to certain types of damage, thus bringing about disparities in the treatment of victims depending on where the accident occurred, which is precisely what the directives are intended to avoid. The compulsory insurance contract may, on the other hand, provide that in such cases the insurer is to have a right of recovery against the insured.

Article 4

A Member State may act in derogation of Article 3 in respect of:

(a) certain natural or legal persons, public or private; the list of such persons shall be drawn up by the State concerned and communicated to the other Member States and to the Commission.

[A Member State so derogating shall take the appropriate measures to ensure that compensation is paid in respect of any loss or injury caused in its territory and in the territory of other Member States by vehicles belonging to such persons.] It shall in particular designate an authority or body in the country where the loss or injury occurs responsible for compensating injured parties in accordance with the laws of that State in cases where the procedure provided for in the first indent of Article 2 (2) is not applicable. [It shall communicate to the Commission the list of persons exempt from compulsory insurance and the authorities or bodies responsible for compensation. The Commission shall publish the list.]

(b) certain types of vehicle or certain vehicles having a special plate; the list of such types or of such vehicles shall be drawn up by the State concerned and communicated to the other Member States and to the Commission.

[In that case Member States shall ensure that vehicles as mentioned in the first subparagraph of this point are treated in the same way as vehicles for which the insurance obligation provided for in Article 3(1) has not been satisfied. The compensation body of the Member State in which the accident has taken place shall then have a claim against the guarantee fund provided for in Article 1(4) of Directive 84/5/EEC in the Member State where the vehicle is normally based.

After a period of five years from the date of entry into force of Directive 2005/14/EC of the European Parliament and of the Council of 11 May 2005 amending Council Directives 72/166/EEC, 84/5/EEC, 88/357/EEC and 90/232/EEC and Directive 2000/26/EC of the European Parliament and of the Council relating to insurance against civil liability in respect of the use of motor vehicles,[4] Member States shall report to the Commission on the implementation

---

[4] OJ L 149, 11.6.2005, 14, reproduced infra under no. I. 39.

and practical application of this point. The Commission, after having examined these reports, shall, if appropriate, submit proposals on the replacement or repeal of this derogation.]

¶ *The words between square brackets in article 4(a) and (b) have been amended by article 1(3) of Directive 2005/14/EC, reproduced infra under no. I. 39.*

Article 5

Each Member State shall ensure that, where an accident is caused in its territory by a vehicle normally based in the territory of another Member State, the national insurers' bureau shall, without prejudice to the obligation referred to in the first indent of Article 2 (2), obtain information:
– as to the territory in which the vehicle is normally based, and as to its registration mark, if any;
– in so far as is possible, as to the details of the insurance of the vehicle, as they normally appear on the green card, which are in the possession of the person having custody of the vehicle, to the extent that these details are required by the Member State in whose territory the vehicle is normally based.

Each Member State shall also ensure that the bureau communicates this information to the national insurers' bureau of the State in whose territory the vehicle is normally based.

Article 6

Each Member State shall take all appropriate measures to ensure that vehicles normally based in the territory of a third country [. . .] entering the territory in which the Treaty establishing the European Economic Community is in force shall not be used in its territory unless any loss or injury caused by those vehicles is covered, in accordance with the requirements of the laws of the various Member States on compulsory insurance against civil liability in respect of the use of vehicles, throughout the territory in which the Treaty establishing the European Economic Community is in force.

¶ *The words between square brackets in article 6 have been deleted by article 1(4) of Directive 2005/14/EC, reproduced infra under no. I. 39.*

Article 7

1. Every vehicle normally based in the territory of a third country [. . .] must, before entering the territory in which the Treaty establishing the European Economic Community is in force, be provided either with a valid green card or with a certificate of frontier insurance establishing that the vehicle is insured in accordance with Article 6.

2. However, vehicles normally based in a third country shall be treated as vehicles normally based in the Community if the national bureaus of all the Member States severally guarantee, each in accordance with the provisions of its own national law on compulsory insurance, settlement of claims in respect of accidents occurring in their territory caused by such vehicles.

3. Upon having ascertained, in close co-operation with the Member States, that the obligations referred to in the preceding paragraph have been assumed, the Commission shall fix the date from which and the types of vehicles for which Member States shall no longer require production of the documents referred to in paragraph 1.

¶ *The words between square brackets in paragraph 1 of Article 7 have been deleted by article 1(4) of Directive 2005/14/EC, reproduced infra under no. I. 39.*

Article 8

Member States shall, not later than December 18, 1973, bring into force the measures necessary to comply with this directive and shall forthwith inform the Commission thereof.

Article 9

This directive is addressed to the Member States.

I. 3.

Council Directive 73/239/EEC
of 24 July 1973
on the co-ordination of laws, regulations and administrative provisions relating to the taking-up and pursuit of the business of direct insurance other than life assurance (First non-life insurance Directive)[1]

Cases

I. Case C-63/89 Les Assurances du Crédit SA and Compagnie Belge d'Assurance Crédit SA v Council of the European Communities and Commission of the European Communities [1991] ECR I-1799

The exclusion of public export credit insurance operations from the scope of Directive 73/239/EEC, introduced by that directive and maintained by Directive 87/343, is not discriminatory because it takes account of the differences resulting from the legal and factual situation existing at one stage of the process of co-ordinating the national provisions in the field of insurance. In such operations and at that stage, protection for insured and third parties, which the abovementioned directives seek to provide, is provided by the State itself, so that the obligation to provide financial guarantees, prescribed by the directive for other export credit insurance operations, is not justified.

II. Case 205/84 Commission of the European Communities v Federal Republic of Germany [1986] ECR 3755

So far as direct insurance is concerned, the protection of policy-holders and insured persons justifies in the present state of community law the application by the Member State in which the service is provided of its own legislation concerning technical reserves or provisions and the conditions of insurance, provided that the requirements of that legislation do not exceed what is necessary to ensure the protection of policy-holders and insured persons. Only the requirement of an authorisation that it is for the Member State in which the services are provided to grant and withdraw can provide an effective means of supervision and is therefore permissible. The authorisation must be granted on request to any undertaking established in another Member State that meets the conditions laid down by the legislation of the State in which the service is provided. Those conditions may not duplicate equivalent statutory conditions that have already been satisfied in the state in which the undertaking is established and the supervisory authority of the state in which the service is provided must take into account supervision and verifications that have already been carried out in the Member State of establishment.

III. Case 206/84 Commission of the European Communities v Ireland [1986] ECR 3817

See commentary of Case 205/84 (Case II of this directive).

IV. Case 252/83 Commission of the European Communities v Kingdom of Denmark [1986] ECR 3713

No provision of community law prevents a Member State from requiring insurance undertakings and their branches which are established on its territory to obtain an authorization not only in respect of business conducted on its territory but also for business conducted in other member states in the context of the provision of services. On the contrary, such a requirement does conform to the principles laid out in directive 73/239/EEC. The directive is based on the principle that the state of establishment is authorized to take into account all the business activities of undertakings constituted within its territory in order to be able to carry out an effective supervision of the conditions in which such activities are pursued.

---

[1] OJ L 228, 16.8.1973, 3–19.

THE COUNCIL OF THE EUROPEAN COMMUNITIES,

Having regard to the Treaty establishing the European Economic Community, and in particular Article [47(2)][2] thereof,

Having regard to the General Programme[3] for the abolition of restrictions on freedom of establishment, and in particular Title IV C thereof,

Having regard to the proposal from the Commission,

Having regard to the Opinion of the European Parliament,[4]

Having regard to the Opinion of the Economic and Social Committee,[5]

Whereas by virtue of the General Programme the removal of restrictions on the establishment of agencies and branches is, in the case of the direct insurance business, dependent on the co-ordination of the conditions for the taking-up and pursuit of this business; whereas such co-ordination should be effected in the first place in respect of direct insurance other than life assurance;

Whereas in order to facilitate the taking-up and pursuit of the business of insurance, it is essential to eliminate certain divergences which exist between national supervisory legislation; whereas in order to achieve this objective, and at the same time ensure adequate protection for insured and third parties in all the Member States, it is desirable to co-ordinate, in particular, the provisions relating to the financial guarantees required of insurance undertakings;

Whereas a classification of risks in the different classes of insurance is necessary in order to determine, in particular, the activities subject to a compulsory authorisation and the amount of the minimum guarantee fund fixed for the classes of insurance concerned;

Whereas it is desirable to exclude from the application of this Directive mutual associations which, by virtue of their legal status, fulfil appropriate conditions as to security and financial guarantees; whereas it is further desirable to exclude certain institutions in several Member States whose business covers a very limited sector only as is restricted by law to a specified territory or to specified persons;

Whereas the various laws contain different rules as to the simultaneous undertaking of health insurance, credit and suretyship insurance and insurance in respect of recourse against third parties and legal defence, whether with one another or with other classes of insurance; whereas continuance of this divergence after the abolition of restrictions on the right of establishment in classes other than life assurance would mean that obstacles to establishment would continue to exist; whereas a solution to this problem must be provided in subsequent co-ordination to be effected within a relatively short period of time;

Whereas it is necessary to extend supervision in each Member State to all the classes of insurance to which this Directive applies; whereas such supervision is not possible unless the undertaking of such classes of insurance is subject to an official authorisation; whereas it is therefore necessary to define the conditions for the granting or withdrawal of such authorisation; whereas provision must be made for a right to apply to the courts should an authorisation be refused or withdrawn;

Whereas it is desirable to bring the classes of insurance known as transport classes bearing Nos. 4, 5, 6, 7 and 12 in Paragraph A of the Annex, and the credit insurance classes bearing Nos. 14 and 15 in paragraph A of the Annex, under more flexible rules in view of the continual fluctuations in conditions affecting goods and credit;

Whereas the search for a common method of calculating technical reserves is at present the subject of studies at Community level, whereas it therefore appears to be desirable to reserve the attainment of co-ordination in

---

[2] The number between brackets has been changed as from 1 May 1999 by article 12 of the Treaty of Amsterdam.
[3] OJ 2, 15.1.1962, 36/62.
[4] OJ C 27, 28.3.1968, 15.
[5] OJ 158, 18.7.1967, 1.

this matter, as well as questions relating to the determination of categories of investments and the valuation of assets, for subsequent Directives;

Whereas it is necessary that insurance undertakings should possess, over and above technical reserves of sufficient amount to meet their underwriting liabilities, a supplementary reserve, to be known as the solvency margin, and represented by free assets, in order to provide against business fluctuations; whereas in order to ensure that the requirements imposed for such purposes are determined according to objective criteria, whereby undertakings of the same size are placed on an equal footing as regards competition, it is desirable to provide that such margin shall be related to the overall volume of business of the undertaking and be determined by reference to two indices of security, one based on premiums and the other on claims;

Whereas it is desirable to require a minimum guarantee fund related to the size of the risk in the classes undertaken, in order to ensure that undertakings possess adequate resources when they are set up and that in the subsequent course of business the solvency margin shall in no event fall below a minimum of security;

Whereas it is necessary to make provision for the case where the financial condition of the undertaking becomes such that it is difficult for it to meet its underwriting liabilities;

Whereas the co-ordinated rules concerning the taking-up and pursuit of the business or direct insurance within the Community should, in principle, apply to all undertakings entering the market and, consequently, also to agencies and branches where the head office of the undertaking is situated outside the Community; whereas it is nevertheless, desirable as regards the methods of supervision to make special provision with respect to such agencies or branches in view of the fact that the assets of the undertakings to which they belong are situated outside the Community;

Whereas it is, however, desirable to permit the relaxation of such special conditions, while observing the principle that such agencies and branches should not obtain more favourable treatment than undertakings within the Community;

Whereas certain transitional provisions are required in order, in particular, to permit small and medium-sized undertakings already in existence to adapt themselves to the requirements which must be imposed by the Member States in pursuance of this Directive, subject to the application of Article [53][2] of the Treaty;

Whereas it is important to guarantee the uniform application of the co-ordinated rules and to provide, in this respect, for close collaboration between the Commission and the Member States in this field.

HAS ADOPTED THIS DIRECTIVE:

Title I
General Provisions

[Article 1

1. This Directive concerns the taking-up and pursuit of the self-employed activity of direct insurance, including the provision of assistance referred to in paragraph 2, carried on by undertakings which are established in the territory of a Member State or which wish to become established there.

2. The assistance activity shall be the assistance provided for persons who get into difficulties while travelling, while away from home or while away from their permanent residence. It shall consist in undertaking, against the prior payment of a premium, to make aid immediately available to the beneficiary under an assistance contract where that person is in difficulties following the occurrence of a chance event, in the cases and under the conditions set out in the contract.

The aid may consist in the provision of benefits in cash or in kind. The provision of benefits in kind may also be effected by means of the staff and equipment of the person providing them.

The assistance activity does not cover servicing, maintenance, after sales service or the mere indication or provision of aid as an intermediary.

3. The classification by classes of the activity referred to in this Article appears in the Annex.]

¶ *This article has been replaced by article 1 of Directive 84/641/EEC, reproduced infra under no. I. 12.*

Article 2

This Directive does not apply to:

1. The following kinds of insurance:

(a) life assurance, that is to say, the branch of insurance which comprises, in particular, assurance on survival to a stipulated age only, assurance on death only, assurance on survival to a stipulated age or an earlier death, life assurance with return of premiums, tontines, marriage assurance, and birth assurance;

(b) annuities;

(c) supplementary insurance carried on by life-assurance undertakings, that is to say, insurance against personal injury including incapacity for employment, insurance against death resulting from an accident, and insurance against disability resulting from an accident or sickness, where these various kinds of insurance are underwritten in addition to life assurance;

(d) insurance forming part of a statutory system of social security;

(e) the type of insurance existing in Ireland and the United Kingdom known as "permanent health insurance not subject to cancellation".

2. The following operations:

(a) capital redemption operations, as defined by the law in each Member State;

(b) operations of provident and mutual benefit institutions whose benefits vary according to the resources available and in which the contributions of the members are determined on a flat-rate basis;

(c) operations carried out by organisations not having a legal personality with the purpose of providing mutual cover for their members without there being any payment of premiums or constitution of technical reserves;

[(d) pending further co-ordination, export credit insurance operations for the account of or guaranteed by the State, or where the State is the insurer.]

[3. The assistance activity in which liability is limited to the following operations provided in the event of an accident or breakdown involving a road vehicle that normally occurs in the territory of the Member State of the undertaking providing cover:

– an on-the-spot breakdown service for which the undertaking providing cover uses, in most circumstances, its own staff and equipment,

– the conveyance of the vehicle to the nearest or the most appropriate location at which repairs may be carried out and the possible accompaniment, normally by the same means of assistance, of the driver and passengers to the nearest location from where they may continue their journey by other means,

– if provided for by the Member State of the undertaking providing cover, the conveyance of the vehicle, possibly accompanied by the driver and passengers, to their home, point of departure or original destination within the same State.

– unless such operations are carried out by an undertaking subject to this Directive.

In the cases referred to in the first two indents, the condition that the accident or breakdown must have happened in the territory of the Member State of the undertaking providing cover

(a) shall not apply where the latter is a body of which the beneficiary is a member and the breakdown service or conveyance of the vehicle is provided simply on presentation of a membership card without any additional premium being paid, by a similar body in the country concerned on the basis of a reciprocal agreement;

(b) shall not preclude the provision of such assistance in Ireland and the United Kingdom by a single body operating in both States.

In the circumstances referred to in the third indent, where the accident or the breakdown has occurred in the territory of Ireland or, in the case of the United Kingdom, in the territory of Northern Ireland, the vehicle possibly accompanied by the driver and passengers, may be conveyed to their home, point of departure or original destination within either territory.

Moreover, the Directive does not concern assistance operations carried out on the occasion of an accident to or the breakdown of a road vehicle and consisting in conveying the vehicle which has been involved in an accident or has broken down outside the territory of the Grand Duchy of Luxembourg, possibly accompanied by the driver and passengers, to their home, where such operations are carried out by the Automobile Club of the Grand Duchy of Luxembourg.

Undertakings subject to this Directive may engage in the activity referred to under this point only if they have received authorisation for class 18 in point A of the Annex without prejudice to point C of the said Annex. In that event this Directive shall apply to the operations in question.]

¶ *Paragraph 2(d) has been modified by article 1 of Directive 87/343/EEC, reproduced infra under no. I. 13.*
¶ *Paragraph 3 has been added by article 2 of Directive 84/641/EEC, reproduced infra under no. I. 12.*

Article 3

[1. This Directive shall not apply to mutual associations which fulfil all the following conditions:

(a) the articles of association must contain provisions for calling up additional contributions or reducing their benefits;

(b) their business does not cover liability risks unless these constitute ancillary cover within the meaning of point C of the Annex or credit and suretyship risks;

(c) the annual contribution income for the activities covered by this Directive must not exceed EUR 5 million; and

(d) at least half of the contribution income from the activities covered by this Directive must come from persons who are members of the mutual association.

This Directive shall not apply to undertakings which fulfil all the following conditions:
– the undertaking does not pursue any activity falling within the scope of this Directive other than the one described in class 18 in point A of the Annex,
– this activity is carried out exclusively on a local basis and consists only of benefits in kind, and
– the total annual income collected in respect of the activity of assistance to persons who get into difficulties does not exceed EUR 200 000.

Nevertheless, the provisions of this Article shall not prevent a mutual insurance undertaking from applying, or continuing, to be licensed under this Directive.]

2. This Directive shall not, moreover, apply to mutual associations that have concluded with other associations of this nature an agreement that provides for the full reinsurance of the insurance policies issued by them or under which the concessionary undertaking is to meet the liabilities arising under such policies in the place of the ceding undertaking.

In such a case the concessionary undertaking shall be subject to the rules of this Directive.

¶ *Article 3, paragraph 1 has been replaced by article 1(1) of Directive 2002/13/EC, reproduced infra under no. I. 32.*

Article 4

This Directive shall not apply to the following institutions unless their statutes or the law are amended as regards capacity:

(a) *In Germany:*

The following institutions under public law enjoying a monopoly (Monopolanstalten):
1. Badische Gebäudeversicherungsanstalt, Karlsruhe,
2. Bayerische Landesbrandversicherungsanstalt, Munich,
3. Bayerische Landestierversicherungsanstalt, Schlachtviehversicherung, Munich,
4. Braunschweigische Landesbrandversicherungsanstalt, Brunswick,

5. Hamburger Feuerkasse, Hamburg,
6. Hessische Brandversicherungsanstalt (Hessische Brandversicherungskammer), Darmstadt,
7. Hessische Brandversicherungsanstalt, Kassel,
8. Hohenzollernische Feuerversicherungsanstalt, Sigmaringen,
9. Lippische Landesbrandversicherungsanstalt, Detmold,
10. Nassauische Brandversicherungsanstalt, Wiesbaden,
11. Oldenburgische Landesbrandkasse, Oldenburg,
12. Ostfriesische Landschaftliche Brandkasse, Aurich,
13. Feuersozietät Berlin, Berlin,
14. Württembergische Gebäudebrandversicherungsanstalt, Stuttgart.

However, territorial capacity shall not be regarded as modified in the case of a merger between such institutions which has the effect of maintaining for the benefit of the new institution the territorial capacity of the institutions which have merged, nor shall capacity as to the classes of insurance be regarded as modified if one of these institutions takes over in respect of the same territory one or more of the classes of another such institution.

The following semi-public institutions:
1. Postbeamtenkrankenkasse,
2. Krankenversorgung der Bundesbahnbeamten;

(b) *In France:*
The following institutions:
1. Caisse départementale des incendiés des Ardennes,
2. Caisse départementale des incendiés de la Côte d'Or,
3. Caisse départementale des incendiés de la Marne,
4. Caisse départementale des incendiés de la Meuse,
5. Caisse départementale des incendiés de la Somme,
6. Caisse départementale grêle du Gers,
7. Caisse départementale grêle de l'Hérault;

(c) *In Ireland:*
Voluntary Health Insurance Board;

(d) *In Italy:*
The Cassa di Previdenza per l'assicurazione degli sportivi (Sportass);

(e) *In the United Kingdom:*
The Crown Agents;

[(f) *In Denmark:*
Falcks Redningskorps A/S, Kobenhavn;]

[(g) *In Spain:*
The following institutions:
1. Comisaria de Seguro Obligatorio de Viajeros,
2. Consorcio de Compensacion de Seguros,
3. Fondo Nacional de Garantia de Riesgos de la Circulacion.]

¶ *Litera (f) has been added by article 4 of Directive 84/641/EEC, reproduced infra under no. I. 12.*
¶ *Litera (g) has been added by the Act of Accession of the Kingdom of Spain and the Portuguese Republic, Annex l(II)(c)(l)(a) (OJ L 302, 15.11.1985).*

Article 5

For the purposes of this Directive:

[(a) "Unit of account" means the European unit of account (EUA) as defined by Commission Decision 3289/75 ECSC.[6] Wherever this Directive refers to the unit of account, the conversion value in national currency to be adopted shall, as from December 31 of each year, be that of the last day of the preceding month of October for which EUA conversion values are available in all the Community currencies;]

(b) "Matching assets" means the representation of underwriting liabilities expressed in a particular currency by assets expressed or realisable in the same currency;

(c) "Localisation of assets" means the existence of assets, whether movable or immovable, within a Member State but shall not be construed as involving a requirement that movable property be deposited or that immovable property be subjected to restrictive measures such as the

---

[6] OJ L 327, 19.12.1975, 4.

registration of mortgages. Assets represented by claims against debtors shall be regarded as situated in the Member State where they are to be liquidated.

[(d) "large risks" means:
(i) risks classified under classes 4, 5, 6, 7, 11 and 12 of point A of the Annex;
(ii) risks classified under classes 14 and 15 of point A of the Annex, where the policyholder is engaged professionally in an industrial or commercial activity or in one of the liberal professions, and the risks relate to such activity;
(iii) risks classified under classes 3, 8, 9, 10, 13 and 16 of point A of the Annex] in so far as the policy-holder exceeds the limits of at least two of the following three criteria:

first stage: until December 31, 1992:
– balance-sheet total: 12,4 million ECU,
– net turnover: 24 million ECU,
– average number of employees during the financial year: 500.

second stage: from January 1, 1993:
– balance-sheet total: 6,2 million ECU,
– net turnover: 12,8 million ECU,
– average number of employees during the financial year: 250.

If the policyholder belongs to a group of undertakings for which consolidated accounts within the meaning of Directive 83/349[7] are drawn up, the criteria mentioned above shall be applied on the basis of the consolidated accounts.

Each Member State may add to the category mentioned under (iii) risks insured by professional associations, joint ventures or temporary groupings.]

¶ *Greece, Ireland, Spain, and Portugal may apply transitional arrangements regarding litera d; see article 27 of the Second Non-Life Insurance Directive 88/357/EEC, reproduced infra under no. I. 15.*
¶ *Litera (a) has been replaced by article 1 of Directive 76/580/EEC, reproduced infra under no. I. 6. However, as from 1.1.1980 the European Currency Unit or ECU replaces the European Unit of account, Regulation No 3308/80 (OJ L, 345, 20.12.1980, 1).*

[7] OJ L 193, 18.7.1983, 1–17, Seventh Company Directive, reproduced supra under no. C. 6.

¶ *Litera (d) has been added by article 5 of the Second Non-Life Insurance Directive 88/357/EEC, reproduced infra under no. I. 15.*
¶ *Point 5(d)(iii) has been subsequently modified by article 2 of Directive 90/618/EEC, reproduced infra under no. I. 17.*

Title II

Rules Applicable to Undertakings Whose Head Offices are Situated Within the Community

Section A
Conditions of Admission

[*Article 6*

The taking-up of the business of direct insurance shall be subject to prior official authorisation.

Such authorisation shall be sought from the competent authorities of the home Member State by:

(a) any undertaking that establishes its head office within the territory of that State;

(b) any undertaking which, having received the authorisation referred to in the first subparagraph, extends its business to an entire class or to other classes.]

¶ *This article has been replaced by article 4 of the Third Non-Life Insurance Directive 92/49/EEC, reproduced infra under no. I. 25.*

[*Article 7*

1. Authorisation shall be valid for the entire Community. It shall permit an undertaking to carry on business there, under either the right of establishment or the freedom to provide services.

2. Authorisation shall be granted for a particular class of insurance. It shall cover the entire class, unless the applicant wishes to cover only some of the risks pertaining to that class, as listed in point A of the Annex.

However:

(a) Member States may grant authorisation for the groups of classes listed in point B of the

Annex, attaching to them the appropriate denominations specified therein;

(b) authorisation granted for one class or a group of classes shall also be valid for the purpose of covering ancillary risks included in another class if the conditions imposed in point C of the Annex are fulfilled.]

¶ *This article has been modified by article 1(2) of Directive 87/343/EEC, reproduced infra under no. I. 13; and subsequently replaced by article 5 of the Third Non-Life Insurance Directive 92/49/EEC, reproduced infra under no. I. 25.*

[Article 8

1. The home Member State shall require every insurance undertaking for which authorisation is sought to:

(a) adopt one of the following forms:
- in the case of the Kingdom of Belgium:
  "société anonyme / naamloze vennootschap", "société en commandite par actions/ commanditaire vennootschap op aandelen", "association d'assurance mutuelle / onderlinge verzekeringsvereniging", "société coopérative/ coöperatieve vennootschap";
- in the case of the Kingdom of Denmark: "aktieselskaber", "gensidige selskaber";
- in the case of the Federal Republic of Germany:
  "Aktiengesellschaft", "Versicherungsverein auf Gegenseitigkeit", "Öffentlich-rechtliches Wettbewerbsversicherungsunternehmen";
- in the case of the French Republic:
  "société anonyme", "société d'assurance mutuelle", "institution de prévoyance régie par le code de la sécurite sociale", "institution de prévoyance régie par le code rural" and "mutuelles régies par le code de la mutualité";
- in the case of Ireland:
  incorporated companies limited by shares or by guarantee or unlimited;
- in the case of the Italian Republic:
  "società per azioni", "società cooperativa", "mutua di assicurazione";
- in the case of the Grand Duchy of Luxembourg:
  "société anonyme", "société en commandite par actions", "association d'assurances mutuelles", "société cooperative";
- in the case of the Kingdom of the Netherlands: "naamloze vennootschap", "onderlinge waarborgmaatschappij";
- in the case of the United Kingdom:
  incorporated companies limited by shares or by guarantee or unlimited, societies registered under the Industrial and Provident Societies Acts, societies registered under the Friendly Societies Acts, the association of underwriters known as Lloyd's;
- in the case of the Hellenic Republic:
  "ανωνυμη εταιρια", "αλληασψαλιστικος συνεταιπιμος"
- in the case of the Kingdom of Spain:
  "sociedad anónima", "sociedad mutua", "sociedad cooperativa";
- in the case of the Portuguese Republic:
  "sociedade anónima", "mutua de seguros".
[– in the case of the Republic of Austria:
  "Aktiengesellschaft", "Versicherungsverein auf Gegenseitigkeit";
- in the case of the Republic of Finland:
  "keskinäinen vakuutusyhtiö—ömsesidigt försäkringsbolag"—, "vakuutusosakeyhtiö— försäkringsaktiebolag"—, "vakuutusyhdistys— försäkringsförening";
- in the case of the Kingdom of Sweden:
  "försäkringsaktiebolag", "ömsesidiga försäkringsbolag", "understödsföreningar";
- in the case of the Czech Republic:
  "akciová společnost", "družstvo";
- in the case of the Republic of Estonia:
  "aktsiaselts";
- in the case of the Republic of Cyprus:
  "Εταιρεηα περιορισμένης ευθύνης με μετοχές ή εταιρεία περιορισμένης ευθύνης χωρίς μετοχικό κεφάλαιο";
- in the case of the Republic of Latvia:
  "apdrošiānšanas akciju sabiedrība", "savstarpējās apdrošināšanas kooperatīvā biedrība";
- in the case of the Republic of Lithuania:
  "akcinės bendrovės", "uždarosios akcinės bendrovės";
- in the case of the Republic of Hungary:
  "biztosító részvénytársaság", "biztosító szövetkezet", "biztosító egyesület", "külföldi székhelyű biztosító magyarországi fióktelepe";
- in the case of the Republic of Malta:
  "kumpanija pubblika", "kumpanija privata", "fergha", "Korp ta' l- Assikurazzjoni Rikonnoxxut";

— in the case of the Republic of Poland:
"spółka akcyjna", "towarzystwo ubezpieczeń wzajemnych";
— in the case of the Republic of Slovenia:
"delniška družba", "družba za vzajemno zavarovanje";
— in the case of the Slovak Republic:
"akciová spoločnosť".]

An insurance undertaking may also adopt the form of a European Company (SE) when that has been established.

Furthermore, Member States may, where appropriate, set up undertakings in any public law form provided that such bodies have as their objects insurance operations under conditions equivalent to those under which private-law undertakings operate;

(b) limit its objects to the business of insurance and operations arising directly there from, to the exclusion of all other commercial business;

(c) submit a scheme of operations in accordance with Article 9;

(d) possess the minimum guarantee fund provided for in Article 17 (2);

(e) be effectively run by persons of good repute with appropriate professional qualifications or experience.

[Moreover, where close links exist between the [insurance undertaking] and other natural or legal persons, the competent authorities shall grant authorisation only if those links do not prevent the effective exercise of their supervisory functions.

The competent authorities shall also refuse authorisation if the laws, regulations or administrative provisions of a non-member country governing one or more natural or legal persons with which the undertaking has close links, or difficulties involved in their enforcement, prevent the effective exercise of their supervisory functions.

The competent authorities shall require financial undertakings to provide them with the information they require monitoring compliance with the conditions referred to in this paragraph on a continuous basis.]

[1a. Member States shall require that the head offices of insurance undertakings be situated in the same Member State as their registered offices.]

2. An undertaking seeking authorisation to extend its business to other classes or to extend an authorisation covering only some of the risks pertaining to one class shall be required to submit a scheme of operations in accordance with Article 9.

It shall, furthermore, be required to show proof that it possesses the solvency margin provided for in Article 16 and, if with regard to such other classes Article 17 (2) requires a higher minimum guarantee fund than before, that it possesses that minimum.

3. Nothing in this Directive shall prevent Member States from maintaining in force or introducing laws, regulations or administrative provisions requiring approval of the memorandum and articles of association and communication of any other documents necessary for the normal exercise of supervision.

Member States shall not, however, adopt provisions requiring the prior approval or systematic notification of general and special policy conditions, scales of premiums and forms and other printed documents that an undertaking intends to use in its dealings with policyholders.

Member States may not retain or introduce prior notification or approval of proposed increases in premium rates except as part of general price-control systems.

Nothing in this Directive shall prevent Member States from subjecting undertakings seeking or having obtained authorisation for class 18 in point A of the Annex to checks on their direct or indirect resources in staff and equipment, including the qualification of their medical teams and the quality of the equipment available to such undertakings to meet their commitments arising out of this class of insurance.

4. The abovementioned provisions may not require that any application for authorisation be considered in the light of the economic requirements of the market.]

¶ Spain, Portugal and Greece may derogate from paragraph 3. For the transitional arrangements, see article 50 of the Third Non-Life Insurance Directive 92/49/EEC, reproduced infra under no. I. 25.

¶ This article has repeatedly been modified by the Acts of Accession of the Hellenic Republic, Annex I(III)(e)(1); by the Act of Accession of the Kingdom of Spain and the Portuguese Republic, Annex 1(II)(c)(1); by the Act of Accession of Austria, Sweden, and Finland (OJ C 241, 29.8.1994, 21), (adapted by Council Decision 95/1/EC, Euratom, ECSC, OJ L 1, 1.1.1995, 1); by the Act concerning the conditions of accession of the Czech Republic, the Republic of Latvia, the Republic of Lithuania, the Republic of Hungary, the Republic of Malta, the Republic of Poland, the Republic of Slovenia, and the Slovak Republic and the adjustments to the Treaties on which the European Union is founded (OJ L 236, 23.9.2003, 33); by article 5(4) of Directive 84/641/EEC, reproduced infra under no. I. 12. and by article 9(2) of the Second Non-Life Insurance Directive 88/357/EEC, reproduced infra under no. I. 15. It has subsequently been replaced by article 6 of the Third Non-Life Insurance Directive 92/49/EEC, reproduced infra under no. I. 25.

¶ The second, third and fourth paragraph of article 8(1) have been added by article 2(2), third indent of Directive 95/26/EC, reproduced infra under no. I. 27.

¶ The words "financial undertaking" between the square brackets in the second paragraph of article 8(1) have been replaced by article 1, second indent of Directive 95/26/EC, reproduced infra under no. I. 27.

¶ Paragraph 1(a) has been inserted by article 3(1) of Directive 95/26/EC, reproduced infra under no. I. 27.

Case

Case C-109/99 Association Basco-béarnaise des Opticiens Indépendants v Préfet des Pyrénées-Atlantiques [2000] ECR I-7247

1. Article 8(1)(b) of First Council Directive 73/239/EEC of 24 July 1973 as amended by Council Directive 92/49/EEC of 18 June 1992 on the co-ordination of laws, regulations and administrative provisions relating to direct insurance other than life assurance and amending Directives 73/239/EEC and 88/357/EEC (third non-life insurance directive), does not preclude mutual benefit societies engaged solely in insurance business from creating between themselves a body with legal personality and legal autonomy–such as an association of mutual benefit societies–which engages in commercial business, provided that the capital subscribed to that body by those societies does not exceed the value of their free assets and provided that, in each case, the society's liability is limited to the value of its capital contribution.

2. Article 8(1)(b) of Directive 73/239/EEC, as amended by Directive 92/49/EEC, is sufficiently precise and unconditional to be relied upon before the national courts as against the administrative authorities and entails the inapplicability of any rule of national law incompatible with it.

[Article 9

The scheme of operations referred to in Article 8 (1) (c) shall include particulars or proof concerning:

(a) the nature of the risks that the undertaking proposes to cover;

(b) the guiding principles as to reinsurance;

(c) the items constituting the minimum guarantee fund;

(d) estimates of the costs of setting up the administrative services and the organisation for securing business; the financial resources intended to meet those costs and, if the risks to be covered are classified in class 18 in point A of the Annex, the resources at the undertaking's disposal for the provision of the assistance promised

and, in addition, for the first three financial years:

(e) estimates of management expenses other than installation costs, in particular current general expenses and commissions;

(f) estimates of premiums or contributions and claims;

(g) a forecast balance sheet;

(h) estimates of the financial resources intended to cover underwriting liabilities and the solvency margin.]

¶ This article has repeatedly been modified by article 7 of Directive 84/641/EEC, reproduced infra under no. I. 12, and by article 9 of the Second Non-Life Insurance Directive 88/357/EEC, reproduced infra under no. I. 15. It has subsequently been replaced by article 7 of the Third Non-Life Insurance Directive 92/49/EEC, reproduced infra under no. I. 25.

[Article 10

1. An insurance undertaking that proposes to establish a branch within the territory of another Member State shall notify the competent authorities of its home Member State.

2. The Member States shall require every insurance undertaking that proposes to establish a branch within the territory of another Member State to provide the following information when effecting the notification provided for in paragraph 1:

(a) the Member State within the territory of which it proposes to establish a branch;

(b) a scheme of operations setting out, inter alia, the types of business envisaged and the structural organisation of the branch;

(c) the address in the Member State of the branch from which documents may be obtained and to which they may be delivered, it being understood that that address shall be the one to which all communications to the authorised agent are sent;

(d) the name of the branch's authorised agent, who must possess sufficient powers to bind the undertaking in relation to third parties and to represent it in relations with the authorities and courts of the Member State of the branch. With regard to Lloyd's, in the event of any litigation in the Member State of the branch arising out of underwritten commitments, the insured persons must not be treated less favourably than if the litigation had been brought against businesses of a conventional type. The authorised agent must, therefore, possess sufficient powers for proceedings to be taken against him and must in that capacity be able to bind the Lloyd's underwriters concerned.

Where the undertaking intends its branch to cover risks in class 10 of point A of the Annex, not including carrier's liability, it must produce a declaration that it has become a member of the national bureau and the national guarantee fund of the Member State of the branch.

3. Unless the competent authorities of the home Member State have reason to doubt the adequacy of the administrative structure or the financial situation of the insurance undertaking or the good repute and professional qualifications or experience of the directors or managers or the authorised agent, taking into account the business planned, they shall within three months of receiving all the information referred to in paragraph 2 communicate that information to the competent authorities of the Member State of the branch and shall inform the undertaking concerned accordingly.

The competent authorities of the home Member State shall also attest that the insurance undertaking has the minimum solvency margin calculated in accordance with Articles 16 and 17.

Where the competent authorities of the home Member State refuse to communicate the information referred to in paragraph 2 to the competent authorities of the Member State of the branch they shall give the reasons for their refusal to the undertaking concerned within three months of receiving all the information in question. That refusal or failure to act may be subject to a right to apply to the courts in the home Member State.

4. Before the branch of an insurance undertaking starts business, the competent authorities of the Member State of the branch shall, within two months of receiving the information referred to in paragraph 3, inform the competent authority of the home Member State, if appropriate, of the conditions under which, in the interest of the general good, that business must be carried on in the Member State of the branch.

5. On receiving a communication from the competent authorities of the Member State of the branch or, if no communication is received from them, on expiry of the period provided for in paragraph 4, the branch may be established and start business.

6. In the event of a change in any of the particulars communicated under paragraph 2 (b), (c) or (d), an insurance undertaking shall give written notice of the change to the competent authorities of the home Member State and of the Member State of the branch at least one month before making the change so that the competent authorities of the home Member State and the competent authorities of the Member State of the branch may fulfil their respective roles under paragraphs 3 and 4.]

¶ *This article has been modified by article 9(2) of the Second Non-Life Insurance Directive 88/357/EEC, reproduced infra under* no. I. 15; and subsequently replaced by article 32 of the Third Non-Life Insurance Directive 92/49/EEC, reproduced infra under no. I. 26.

Article 11

[...]

¶ This article has been modified by article 7 of Directive 84/641/EEC, reproduced infra under no. I. 12. and replaced by article 9(1) of the Second Non-Life Insurance Directive 88/357/EEC, reproduced infra under no. I. 15. It has been repealed by article 33 of the Third Non-Life Insurance Directive 92/49/EEC, reproduced infra under no. I. 25.

Article 12

Any decision to refuse an authorisation shall be accompanied by the precise grounds for doing so and notified to the undertaking in question.

Each Member State shall make provision for a right to apply to the courts should there be any refusal.

Such provision shall also be made with regard to the cases where the competent authorities have not dealt with an application for an authorisation upon the expiry of a period of six months from the date of its receipt.

[Article 12a

[1. The competent authorities of the other Member State involved shall be consulted prior to the granting of an authorisation to a non-life insurance undertaking, which is:

(a) a subsidiary of an insurance or reinsurance undertaking authorised in another Member State; or

(b) a subsidiary of the parent undertaking of an insurance or reinsurance undertaking authorised in another Member State; or

(c) controlled by the same person, whether natural or legal, who controls an insurance or reinsurance undertaking authorised in another Member State.

2. The competent authority of a Member State involved responsible for the supervision of credit institutions or investment firms shall be consulted prior to the granting of an authorisation to a non-life insurance undertaking which is:

(a) a subsidiary of a credit institution or investment firm authorised in the Community; or

(b) a subsidiary of the parent undertaking of a credit institution or investment firm authorised in the Community; or

(c) controlled by the same person, whether natural or legal, who controls a credit institution or investment firm authorised in the Community.]

3. The relevant competent authorities referred to in paragraphs 1 and 2 shall in particular consult each other when assessing the suitability of the shareholders and the reputation and experience of directors involved in the management of another entity of the same group. They shall inform each other of any information regarding the suitability of shareholders and the reputation and experience of directors which is of relevance to the other competent authorities involved for the granting of an authorisation as well as for the ongoing assessment of compliance with operating conditions.

¶ Article 12a has been inserted by article 22 of Directive 2002/87/EC, reproduced supra under no. B. 38.
¶ Paragraphs 1 and 2 have been inserted by article 57(1) of Directive 2005/68/EC, reproduced infra under no. I. 40.

Section B

Conditions for Exercise of Business

[Article 13

1. The financial supervision of an insurance undertaking, including that of the business it carries on either through branches or under the freedom to provide services, shall be the sole responsibility of the home Member State.

2. That financial supervision shall include verification, with respect to the insurance undertaking's entire business, of its state of solvency, of the establishment of technical provisions and of the assets covering them in accordance with the rules laid down or practices followed in the home Member State under provisions adopted at Community level.

Where the undertaking in question is authorised to cover the risks classified in class 18 in point A of the Annex, supervision shall extend to monitoring of the technical resources which the undertaking has at its disposal for the purpose of carrying out the assistance operations it has undertaken to perform, where the law of the home Member State provides for the monitoring of such resources.

[The home Member State of the insurance undertaking shall not refuse a reinsurance contract concluded by the insurance undertaking with a reinsurance undertaking authorised in accordance with Directive 2005/68/EC of the European Parliament and of the Council of 16 November 2005 on reinsurance[8] or an insurance undertaking authorised in accordance with this Directive or Directive 2002/83/EC of the European Parliament and of the Council of 5 November 2002 concerning life assurance,[9] on grounds directly related to the financial soundness of the reinsurance undertaking or the insurance undertaking.]

3. The competent authorities of the home Member State shall require every insurance undertaking to have sound administrative and accounting procedures and adequate internal control mechanisms.]

¶ *This article has been modified by article 8 of Directive 84/641/EEC, reproduced infra under no. I. 10; subsequently replaced by article 9 of the Third Non-Life Insurance Directive 92/49/EEC, reproduced infra under no. I. 25.*
¶ *The third subparagraph in article 13(2) has been inserted by article 57(2) of Directive 2005/68/EC, reproduced infra under no. I. 40.*

[Article 14

The Member State of the branch shall provide that where an insurance undertaking authorised in another Member State carries on business through a branch the competent authorities of the home Member State may, after having informed the competent authorities of the Member State of the branch, carry out themselves or through the intermediary of persons they appoint for that purpose on-the-spot verification of the information necessary to ensure the financial supervision of the undertaking. The authorities of the Member State of the branch may participate in that verification.]

¶ *This article has been replaced by article 10 of the Third Non-Life Insurance Directive 92/49/EEC, reproduced infra under no. I. 25.*

[Article 15

1. The home Member State shall require every insurance undertaking to establish adequate technical provisions in respect of its entire business.

The amount of such technical provisions shall be determined in accordance with the rules laid down in Directive 91/674/EEC.

[2. The home Member State shall require every insurance undertaking to cover the technical provisions and the equalisation reserve referred to in Article 15a of this Directive by matching assets in accordance with Article 6 of Directive 88/357/EEC. In respect of risks situated within the Community, those assets must be localised within the Community. Member States shall not require insurance undertakings to localise their assets in any particular Member State. The home Member State may, however, allow the rules on the localisation of assets to be relaxed.

3. Member States shall not retain or introduce for the establishment of technical provisions a system of gross reserving which requires pledging of assets to cover unearned premiums and outstanding claims provisions by the reinsurer, when the reinsurer is a reinsurance undertaking authorised in accordance with Directive 2005/68/EC or an insurance undertaking authorised in accordance with this Directive or Directive 2002/83/EC.

When the home Member State allows any technical provisions to be covered by claims against a reinsurer which is neither a reinsurance undertaking authorised in accordance with Directive 2005/68/EC nor an insurance undertaking authorised in accordance with this Directive or Directive 2002/83/EC, it shall set the conditions for accepting such claims.]

---

[8] OJ L 323, 9.12.2005, 1, reproduced infra under no. I. 40.
[9] OJ L 345, 19.12.2002, 1, reproduced infra under no. I. 33. Directive as last amended by Directive 2005/1/EC (OJ L 79, 24.3.2005, 9), reproduced supra under no. B. 39.

¶ This article has been replaced by article 17 of the Third Non-Life Insurance Directive 92/49/EEC, reproduced infra under no. I. 25.

¶ Paragraphs 2 and 3 have been replaced by article 57(3) of Directive 2005/68/EC, reproduced infra under no. I. 40. A Member State may postpone the application of the amended paragraph until 10 December 2008 (art. 63 of Directive 2005/68/EC).

CASE

Case C-28/03 Epikouriko
Kefalaio v Ypourgos Anaptyxis [2004]
ECR I-8533

Articles 15 and 16 of Directive 73/239/EEC and Articles 17 and 18 of Directive 79/267/EEC are designed to ensure that insurance undertakings, by establishing sufficient technical reserves, have the financial means to comply with their contractual commitments to policyholders. However, on the basis of Article 10(1) of Directive 2001/17/EC Member States may accord a priority ranking claims by employees above the insurance claims, including over the assets representing technical provisions, where the priority of the insurance claims is not limited in its scope to the assets representing those provisions.

[*Article 15a*]

1. Member States shall require every insurance undertaking with a head office within their territories which underwrites risks included in class 14 in point A of the Annex (hereinafter referred to as "credit insurance") to set up an equalisation reserve for the purpose of offsetting any technical deficit or above-average claims ration arising in that class in any financial year.

2. The equalisation reserve shall be calculated in accordance with the rules laid down by the home Member State in accordance with one of the four methods set out in point D of the Annex, which shall be regarded as equivalent.

3. Up to the amount calculated in accordance with the methods set out in point D of the Annex, the equalisation reserve shall be disregarded for the purpose of calculating the solvency margin.

4. Member States may exempt insurance undertakings with head offices within their territories from the obligation to set up equalisation reserves for credit insurance business where the premiums or contributions receivable in respect of credit insurance are less than 4% of the total premiums or contributions receivable by them and less than ECU 2.500.000.]

¶ Article 15a has been inserted by article 1(3) of Directive 87/343/EEC, reproduced infra under no. I. 13. It has subsequently been replaced by article 18 of the Third Non-Life Insurance Directive 92/49/EEC, reproduced infra under no. I. 25.

[*Article 16*]

1. Each Member State shall require of every insurance undertaking whose head office is situated in its territory an adequate available solvency margin in respect of its entire business at all times, which is at least equal to the requirements in this Directive.

2. The available solvency margin shall consist of the assets of the insurance undertaking free of any foreseeable liabilities, less any intangible items, including:

(a) the paid-up share capital or, in the case of a mutual insurance undertaking, the effective initial fund plus any members' accounts which meet all the following criteria:
  (i) the memorandum and articles of association must stipulate that payments may be made from these accounts to members only in so far as this does not cause the available solvency margin to fall below the required level, or, after the dissolution of the undertaking, if all the undertaking's other debts have been settled;
  (ii) the memorandum and articles of association must stipulate, with respect to any payments referred to in point (i) for reasons other than the individual termination of membership, that the competent authorities must be notified at least one month in advance and can prohibit the payment within that period;
  (iii) the relevant provisions of the memorandum and articles of association may be amended only after the competent authorities have declared that they have no objection to the amendment, without prejudice to the criteria stated in points (i) and (ii);

[(b) reserves (statutory and free reserves) which neither correspond to underwriting liabilities nor are classified as equalisation reserves;]

(c) the profit or loss brought forward after deduction of dividends to be paid.

The available solvency margin shall be reduced by the amount of own shares directly held by the insurance undertaking.

For those insurance undertakings which discount or reduce their technical provisions for claims outstanding to take account of investment income as permitted by Article 60(1)(g) of Council Directive 91/674/EEC of 19 December 1991 on the annual accounts and consolidated accounts of insurance undertakings,[10] the available solvency margin shall be reduced by the difference between the undiscounted technical provisions or technical provisions before deductions as disclosed in the notes on the accounts, and the discounted or technical provisions after deductions. This adjustment shall be made for all risks listed in point A of the Annex, except for risks listed under classes 1 and 2. For classes other than 1 and 2, no adjustment need be made in respect of the discounting of annuities included in technical provisions.

[The available solvency margin shall also be reduced by the following items:

(a) participations which the insurance undertaking holds in:
− insurance undertakings within the meaning of Article 6 of this Directive, Article 4 of Directive 2002/83/EC, or Article 1(b) of Directive 98/78/EC of the European Parliament and of the Council,
− reinsurance undertakings within the meaning of Article 3 of Directive 2005/68/EC or non-member country reinsurance undertakings within the meaning of Article 1(l) of Directive 98/78/EC,
− insurance holding companies within the meaning of Article 1(i) of Directive 98/78/EC,
− credit institutions and financial institutions within the meaning of Article 1(1) and (5) of Directive 2000/12/EC of the European Parliament and of the Council,
− investment firms and financial institutions within the meaning of Article 1(2) of Council Directive 93/22/EEC and of Article 2(4) and (7) of Council Directive 93/6/EEC],

(b) each of the following items which the insurance undertaking holds in respect of the entities defined in (a) in which it holds a participation:
− instruments referred to in paragraph 3,
− instruments referred to in Article 18(3) of Directive 79/267/EEC,
− subordinated claims and instruments referred to in Article 35 and Article 36(3) of Directive 2000/12/EC.

Where shares in another credit institution, investment firm, financial institution, insurance or reinsurance undertaking or insurance holding company are held temporarily for the purposes of a financial assistance operation designed to reorganise and save that entity, the competent authority may waive the provisions on deduction referred to under (a) and (b) of the fourth subparagraph.

As an alternative to the deduction of the items referred to in (a) and (b) of the fourth subparagraph which the insurance undertaking holds in credit institutions, investment firms and financial institutions, Member States may allow their insurance undertakings to apply mutatis mutandis methods 1, 2, or 3 of Annex I to Directive 2002/87/EC of the European Parliament and of the Council of 16 December 2002 on the supplementary supervision of credit institutions, insurance undertakings and investment firms in a financial conglomerate.[11]

Method 1 (Accounting consolidation) shall only be applied if the competent authority is confident about the level of integrated management and internal control regarding the entities which would be included in the scope of consolidation.

---

[10] OJ L 374, 31.12.1991, 7, reproduced infra under no. I. 23.

[11] OJ L 35, 11.2.2003, 1, reproduced supra under no. B. 38.

The method chosen shall be applied in a consistent manner over time.

Member States may provide that, for the calculation of the solvency margin as provided for by this Directive, insurance undertakings subject to supplementary supervision in accordance with Directive 98/78/EC or to supplementary supervision in accordance with Directive 2002/87/EC, need not deduct the items referred to in (a) and (b) of the fourth subparagraph which are held in credit institutions, investment firms, financial institutions, insurance or reinsurance undertakings or insurance holding companies which are included in the supplementary supervision.

For the purposes of the deduction of participations referred to in this paragraph, participation shall mean a participation within the meaning of Article 1(f) of Directive 98/78/EC.]

3. The available solvency margin may also consist of:

(a) cumulative preferential share capital and subordinated loan capital up to 50% of the lesser of the available solvency margin and the required solvency margin, no more than 25% of which shall consist of subordinated loans with a fixed maturity, or fixed-term cumulative preferential share capital, provided in the event of the bankruptcy or liquidation of the insurance undertaking, binding agreements exist under which the subordinated loan capital or preferential share capital ranks after the claims of all other creditors and is not to be repaid until all other debts outstanding at the time have been settled.

Subordinated loan capital must also fulfil the following conditions:
(i) only fully paid-up funds may be taken into account;
(ii) for loans with a fixed maturity, the original maturity must be at least five years. No later than one year before the repayment date the insurance undertaking must submit to the competent authorities for their approval a plan showing how the available solvency margin will be kept at or brought to the required level at maturity, unless the extent to which the loan may rank as a component of the available solvency margin is gradually reduced during at least the last five years before the repayment date. The competent authorities may authorise the early repayment of such loans provided application is made by the issuing insurance undertaking and its available solvency margin will not fall below the required level;
(iii) loans the maturity of which is not fixed must be repayable only subject to five years' notice unless the loans are no longer considered as a component of the available solvency margin or unless the prior consent of the competent authorities is specifically required for early repayment. In the latter event the insurance undertaking must notify the competent authorities at least six months before the date of the proposed repayment, specifying the available solvency margin and the required solvency margin both before and after that repayment. The competent authorities shall authorise repayment only if the insurance undertaking's available solvency margin will not fall below the required level;
(iv) the loan agreement must not include any clause providing that in specified circumstances, other than the winding-up of the insurance undertaking, the debt will become repayable before the agreed repayment dates;
(v) the loan agreement may be amended only after the competent authorities have declared that they have no objection to the amendment;

(b) securities with no specified maturity date and other instruments, including cumulative preferential shares other than those mentioned in point (a), up to 50% of the lesser of the available solvency margin and the required solvency margin for the total of such securities and the subordinated loan capital referred to in point (a) provided they fulfil the following:
(i) they may not be repaid on the initiative of the bearer or without the prior consent of the competent authority;
(ii) the contract of issue must enable the insurance undertaking to defer the payment of interest on the loan;

(iii) the lender's claims on the insurance undertaking must rank entirely after those of all non-subordinated creditors;

(iv) the documents governing the issue of the securities must provide for the loss-absorption capacity of the debt and unpaid interest, while enabling the insurance undertaking to continue its business;

(v) only fully paid-up amounts may be taken into account.

4. Upon application, with supporting evidence, by the undertaking to the competent authority of the home Member State and with the agreement of that competent authority, the available solvency margin may also consist of:

(a) one half of the unpaid share capital or initial fund, once the paid-up part amounts to 25% of that share capital or fund, up to 50% of the lesser of the available solvency margin and the required solvency margin;

(b) in the case of mutual or mutual-type association with variable contributions, any claim which it has against its members by way of a call for supplementary contribution, within the financial year, up to one half of the difference between the maximum contributions and the contributions actually called in, and subject to a limit of 50% of the lesser of the available solvency margin and the required solvency margin. The competent national authorities shall establish guidelines laying down the conditions under which supplementary contributions may be accepted;

(c) any hidden net reserves arising out of the valuation of assets, in so far as such hidden net reserves are not of an exceptional nature.

5. Amendments to paragraphs 2, 3 and 4 to take into account developments that justify a technical adjustment of the elements eligible for the available solvency margin, shall be adopted in accordance with the procedure laid down in Article 2 of Council Directive 91/675/EEC.[12]

¶ *Article 16 has been replaced by article 1(2) of Directive 2002/13/EC, reproduced infra under no. I. 32.*

---

[12] OJ L 374, 31.12.1991, 32, reproduced infra under no. I. 24.

¶ *Subparagraphs 4 to 9 in article 16(2) have been inserted by article 22(2) of Directive 2002/87/EC, reproduced supra under no. B. 38.*

¶ *Point (b) of the first subparagraph and the introductory wording and point (a) of the fourth subparagraph of paragraph 2 has been replaced by article 57(4) of Directive 2005/68/EC, reproduced infra under no. I. 40.*

> CASE
>
> Case C-28/03 Epikouriko Kefalaio v Ypourgos Anaptyxis [2004] ECR I-8533
>
> See supra under Article 15 of this directive.

[*Article 16a*

1. The required solvency margin shall be determined on the basis either of the annual amount of premiums or contributions, or of the average burden of claims for the past three financial years.

In the case, however, of insurance undertakings which essentially underwrite only one or more of the risks of credit, storm, hail or frost, the last seven financial years shall be taken as the reference period for the average burden of claims.

2. Subject to Article 17, the amount of the required solvency margin shall be equal to the higher of the two results as set out in paragraphs 3 and 4.

3. The premium basis shall be calculated using the higher of gross written premiums or contributions as calculated below, and gross earned premiums or contributions.

Premiums or contributions in respect of the classes 11, 12 and 13 listed in point A of the Annex shall be increased by 50%.

The premiums or contributions (inclusive of charges ancillary to premiums or contributions) due in respect of direct business in the last financial year shall be aggregated.

To this sum there shall be added the amount of premiums accepted for all reinsurance in the last financial year.

From this sum there shall then be deducted the total amount of premiums or contributions cancelled in the last financial year, as well as the total amount of taxes and levies pertaining to the premiums or contributions entering into the aggregate.

The amount so obtained shall be divided into two portions, the first portion extending up to EUR 50 million, the second comprising the excess; 18% and 16% of these portions respectively shall be calculated and added together.

[The sum so obtained shall be multiplied by the ratio existing in respect of the sum of the last three financial years between the amount of claims remaining to be borne by the undertaking after deduction of amounts recoverable under reinsurance and the gross amount of claims; that ratio may in no case be less than 50%. Upon application, with supporting evidence, by the insurance undertaking to the competent authority of the home Member State and with the agreement of that authority, amounts recoverable from special purpose vehicles referred to in Article 46 of Directive 2005/68/EC may be deducted as reinsurance.]

With the approval of the competent authorities, statistical methods may be used to allocate the premiums or contributions in respect of the classes 11, 12 and 13.

4. The claims basis shall be calculated, as follows, using in respect of the classes 11, 12 and 13 listed in point A of the Annex, claims, provisions and recoveries increased by 50%.

The amounts of claims paid in respect of direct business (without any deduction of claims borne by reinsurers and retrocessionaires) in the periods specified in paragraph 1 shall be aggregated.

To this sum there shall be added the amount of claims paid in respect of reinsurances or retrocessions accepted during the same periods and the amount of provisions for claims outstanding established at the end of the last financial year both for direct business and for reinsurance acceptances.

From this sum there shall be deducted the amount of recoveries effected during the periods specified in paragraph 1.

From the sum then remaining, there shall be deducted the amount of provisions for claims outstanding established at the commencement of the second financial year preceding the last financial year for which there are accounts, both for direct business and for reinsurance acceptances. If the period of reference established in paragraph 1 equals seven years, the amount of provisions for claims outstanding established at the commencement of the sixth financial year preceding the last financial year for which there are accounts shall be deducted.

One-third, or one-seventh, of the amount so obtained, according to the period of reference established in paragraph 1, shall be divided into two portions, the first extending up to EUR 35 million and the second comprising the excess; 26% and 23% of these portions respectively shall be calculated and added together.

[The sum so obtained shall be multiplied by the ratio existing in respect of the sum of the last three financial years between the amount of claims remaining to be borne by the undertaking after deduction of amounts recoverable under reinsurance and the gross amount of claims; that ratio may in no case be less than 50%. Upon application, with supporting evidence, by the insurance undertaking to the competent authority of the home Member State and with the agreement of that authority, amounts recoverable from special purpose vehicles referred to in Article 46 of Directive 2005/68/EC may be deducted as reinsurance.]

With the approval of the competent authorities, statistical methods may be used to allocate the claims, provisions and recoveries in respect of the classes 11, 12 and 13. In the case of the risks listed under class 18 in point A of the Annex, the amount of claims paid used to calculate the claims basis shall be the costs borne by the insurance undertaking in respect of assistance given. Such costs shall be calculated in accordance with the national provisions of the home Member State.

5. If the required solvency margin as calculated in paragraphs 2, 3 and 4 is lower than the required solvency margin of the year before, the

required solvency margin shall be at least equal to the required solvency margin of the year before multiplied by the ratio of the amount of the technical provisions for claims outstanding at the end of the last financial year and the amount of the technical provisions for claims outstanding at the beginning of the last financial year. In these calculations technical provisions shall be calculated net of reinsurance but the ratio may in no case be higher than 1.

6. The fractions applicable to the portions referred to in the sixth subparagraph of paragraph 3 and the sixth subparagraph of paragraph 4 shall each be reduced to a third in the case of health insurance practised on a similar technical basis to that of life assurance, if

(a) the premiums paid are calculated on the basis of sickness tables according to the mathematical method applied in insurance;

(b) a provision is set up for increasing age;

(c) an additional premium is collected in order to set up a safety margin of an appropriate amount;

(d) the insurance undertaking may cancel the contract before the end of the third year of insurance at the latest;

(e) the contract provides for the possibility of increasing premiums or reducing payments even for current contracts.]

¶ *Article 16a has been inserted by article 1(3) of Directive 2002/13/EC, reproduced infra under no. I. 32.*
¶ *Paragraph 3, seventh subparagraph and paragraph 4, seventh subparagraph have been replaced by article 57(5) of Directive 2005/68/EC, reproduced infra under no. I. 40.*

[Article 17

1. One third of the required solvency margin as specified in Article 16a shall constitute the guarantee fund. This fund shall consist of the items listed in Article 16(2), (3) and, with the agreement of the competent authority of the home Member State, (4)(c).

2. The guarantee fund may not be less than EUR 2 million. Where, however, all or some of the risks included in one of the classes 10 to 15 listed in point A of the Annex are covered, it shall be EUR 3 million.

Any Member State may provide for a one-fourth reduction of the minimum guarantee fund in the case of mutual associations and mutual-type associations.]

¶ *Article 17 has been replaced by article 1(4) of Directive 2002/13/EC, reproduced infra under no. I. 32.*

[Article 17a

1. The amounts in euro as laid down in Article 16a (3) and (4) and Article 17(2) shall be reviewed annually starting 20 September 2003 in order to take account of changes in the European index of consumer prices comprising all Member States as published by Eurostat.

The amounts shall be adapted automatically by increasing the base amount in euro by the percentage change in that index over the period between the entry into force of this Directive and the review date and rounded up to a multiple of EUR 100000.

If the percentage change since the last adaptation is less than 5%, no adaptation shall take place.

2. The Commission shall inform annually the European Parliament and the Council of the review and the adapted amounts referred to in paragraph 1.]

¶ *Article 17a has been inserted by article 1(5) of Directive 2002/13/EC, reproduced infra under no. I. 32.*

[Article 17b

1. Each Member State shall require that an insurance undertaking whose head office is situated within its territory and which conducts reinsurance activities establishes, in respect of its entire business, a minimum guarantee fund in accordance with Article 40 of Directive 2005/68/EC, where one of the following conditions is met:

(a) the reinsurance premiums collected exceed 10% of its total premium;

(b) the reinsurance premiums collected exceed EUR 50.000.000;

(c) the technical provisions resulting from its reinsurance acceptances exceed 10% of its total technical provisions.

2. Each Member State may choose to apply to such insurance undertakings as are referred to in paragraph 1 of this Article and whose head office is situated within its territory the provisions of Article 34 of Directive 2005/68/EC in respect of their reinsurance acceptance activities, where one of the conditions laid down in the said paragraph 1 is met.

In that case, the relevant Member State shall require that all assets employed by the insurance undertaking to cover the technical provisions corresponding to its reinsurance acceptances shall be ring-fenced, managed and organised separately from the direct insurance activities of the insurance undertaking, without any possibility of transfer. In such a case, and only as far as their reinsurance acceptance activities are concerned, insurance undertakings shall not be subject to Articles 20, 21 and 22 of Directive 92/49/EEC[13] and Annex I to Directive 88/357/EEC.

Each Member State shall ensure that their competent authorities verify the separation provided for in the second subparagraph.

3. If the Commission decides, pursuant to Article 56(c) of Directive 2005/68/EC to increase the amounts used for the calculation of the required solvency margin provided for in Article 37(3) and (4) of that Directive, each Member State shall apply to such insurance undertakings as are referred to in paragraph 1 of this Article the provisions of Articles 35 to 39 of that Directive in respect of their reinsurance acceptance activities.]

¶ *Article 17b has been inserted by article 57(6) of Directive 2005/68/EC, reproduced infra under no. I. 40.*

[*Article 18*

1. Member States shall not prescribe any rules as to the choice of the assets that need not be used as cover for the technical provisions referred to in Article 15.

---

[13] Council Directive 92/49/EEC of 18 June 1992 on the co-ordination of laws, regulations and administrative provisions relating to direct insurance other than life assurance (third non-life insurance Directive) (OJ L 228, 11.8.1992, 1), reproduced infra under no. I. 25. Directive as last amended by Directive 2005/1/EC, reproduced infra under no. B. 39.

2. Subject to Article 15 (2), Article 20 (1), (2), (3) and (5) and the last subparagraph of Article 22 (1), Member States shall not restrain the free disposal of those assets, whether movable or immovable, that form part of the assets of authorised insurance undertakings.

3. Paragraphs 1 and 2 shall not preclude any measures that Member States, while safeguarding the interests of the insured persons, are entitled to take as owners or members of or partners to the undertakings in question.]

¶ *This article has been replaced by article 26 of the Third Directive 92/49/EEC, reproduced infra under no. I. 25.*

> CASE
>
> Case C-241/97 Försäkringsaktiebolaget Skandia (publ.) [1999] ECR I-1879
>
> On a proper construction of Article 18(1) of the First Directive (73/239/EEC) as amended by Article 26 of Directive 92/49/EEC, and of Article 21(1) of the First Directive (79/267/EEC) on the co-ordination of laws, regulations and administrative provisions relating to the taking-up and pursuit of the business of direct life assurance, as amended by Article 27 of Directive 92/96/EEC–which provide that Member States must not prescribe any rules as to the choice, by insurance undertakings, of assets that need not be used as cover for the technical provisions–a rule of national law may not prohibit insurance undertakings from holding, as their free assets, shares representing more than 5 per cent of all the voting rights in a domestic or foreign public limited company without administrative authorization.
>
> It is clear from the very wording of the provisions at issue that the Member States must abstain from enacting any rules as to the choice of assets constituting the free assets of insurance undertakings, whether in relation to the quality or to the quantity of such assets.
>
> Moreover, the above provisions are sufficiently precise and unconditional to be relied upon before the national court as against the national authorities, rendering inapplicable any contrary rule of domestic law.

[*Article 19*

1. Each Member State shall require every undertaking whose head office is situated in its territory

to produce an annual account, covering all types of operation, of its financial situation, solvency and, as regards cover for risks listed under No. 18 in point A of the Annex, other resources available to them for meeting their liabilities, where its laws provide for supervision of such resources.

[1A. In respect of credit insurance, the undertaking shall make available to the supervisory authority accounts showing both the technical results and the technical reserves relating to that business.]

[2. Member States shall require insurance undertakings with head offices within their territories to render periodically the returns, together with statistical documents, which are necessary for the purposes of supervision. The competent authorities shall provide each other with any documents and information that are useful for the purposes of supervision.

3. Every Member State shall take all steps necessary to ensure that the competent authorities have the powers and means necessary for the supervision of the business of insurance undertakings with head offices within their territories, including business carried on out with those territories, in accordance with the Council Directives governing such business and for the purpose of seeing that they are implemented.

These powers and means must, in particular, enable the competent authorities to:

(a) make detailed enquiries regarding an undertaking's situation and the whole of its business, inter alia, by:
– gathering information or requiring the submission of documents concerning its insurance business,
– carrying out on-the-spot investigations at the undertaking's premises;

(b) take any measures with regard to an undertaking, its directors or managers or the persons who control it, that are appropriate and necessary to ensure that that undertaking's business continues to comply with the laws, regulations and administrative provisions with which the undertaking must comply in each Member State and in particular with the scheme of operations insofar as it remains mandatory, and to prevent or remedy any irregularities prejudicial to the interests of insured persons;

(c) ensure that those measures are carried out, if need be by enforcement and where appropriate through judicial channels.

Member States may also make provision for the competent authorities to obtain any information regarding contracts that are held by intermediaries.]

¶ *This article has been replaced by article 11 of Directive 84/641/EEC, reproduced infra under no. I. 12.*
¶ *Paragraph 1A has been inserted by article 1(7) of Directive 87/343/EEC, reproduced infra under no. I. 13.*
¶ *Paragraph 3 has been added by article 10 of the Second Non-Life Insurance Directive 88/357/EEC, reproduced infra under no. I. 15.*
¶ *Paragraphs 2 and 3 have been replaced by article 11 of the Third Non-Life Insurance Directive 92/49/EEC, reproduced infra under no. I. 25.*

[*Article 20*

1. If an undertaking does not comply with Article 15, the competent authority of its home Member State may prohibit the free disposal of its assets after having communicated its intention to the competent authorities of the Member States in which the risks are situated.

2. For the purposes of restoring the financial situation of an undertaking the solvency margin of which has fallen below the minimum required under [Article 16a], the competent authority of the home Member State shall require that a plan for the restoration of a sound financial situation be submitted for its approval.

In exceptional circumstances, if the competent authority is of the opinion that the financial situation of the undertaking will deteriorate further, it may also restrict or prohibit the free disposal of the undertaking's assets. It shall inform the authorities of other Member States within the territories of which the undertaking carries on business of any measures it has taken and the latter shall, at the request of the former, take the same measures.

3. If the solvency margin falls below the guarantee fund as defined in Article 17, the competent authority of the home Member State shall require

the undertaking to submit a short-term finance scheme for its approval.

It may also restrict or prohibit the free disposal of the undertaking's assets. It shall inform the authorities of other Member States within the territories of which the undertaking carries on business accordingly and the latter shall, at the request of the former, take the same measures.

4. The competent authorities may further take all measures necessary to safeguard the interests of insured persons in the cases provided for in paragraphs 1, 2 and 3.

5. Each Member State shall take the measures necessary to be able, in accordance with its national law, to prohibit the free disposal of assets located within its territory at the request, in the cases provided for in paragraphs 1, 2 and 3, of the undertaking's home Member State, which shall designate the assets to be covered by such measures.]

¶ *This article has been replaced by article 13 of the Third Non-Life Insurance Directive 92/49/EEC, reproduced infra under no. I. 25.*
¶ *The words between square brackets in the second paragraph of article 20 have been replaced by article 1(6) of Directive 2002/13/EC, reproduced infra under no. I. 32.*

[Article 20a

1. Member States shall ensure that the competent authorities have the power to require a financial recovery plan for those insurance undertakings where competent authorities consider that policyholders' rights are threatened. The financial recovery plan shall as a minimum include particulars or proof concerning for the next three financial years:

(a) estimates of management expenses, in particular current general expenses and commissions;

(b) a plan setting out detailed estimates of income and expenditure in respect of direct business, reinsurance acceptances and reinsurance cessions;

(c) a forecast balance sheet;

(d) estimates of the financial resources intended to cover underwriting liabilities and the required solvency margin;

(e) the overall reinsurance policy.

2. Where policyholders' rights are threatened because the financial position of the undertaking is deteriorating, Member States shall ensure that the competent authorities have the power to oblige insurance undertakings to have a higher required solvency margin, in order to ensure that the insurance undertaking is able to fulfil the solvency requirements in the near future. The level of this higher required solvency margin shall be based on the financial recovery plan referred to in paragraph 1.

3. Member States shall ensure that the competent authorities have the power to revalue downwards all elements eligible for the available solvency margin, in particular, where there has been a significant change in the market value of these elements since the end of the last financial year.

[4. Member States shall ensure that the competent authorities have the power to decrease the reduction, based on reinsurance, to the solvency margin as determined in accordance with Article 16a where:

(a) the nature or quality of reinsurance contracts has changed significantly since the last financial year;

(b) there is no, or a limited, risk transfer under the reinsurance contracts.]

5. If the competent authorities have required a financial recovery plan for the insurance undertaking in accordance with paragraph 1, they shall refrain from issuing a certificate in accordance with Article 10(3), second subparagraph of this Directive, Article 16(1)(a) of Council Directive 88/357/EEC (second non-life insurance Directive)[14] and Article 12(2) of Council Directive 92/49/EEC (third non-life insurance Directive),[15] as long as they consider that policyholders rights are threatened within the meaning of paragraph 1.]

---

[14] OJ L 172, 4.7.1988, 1, reproduced infra under no. I. 15. Directive as last amended by Directive 2000/26/EC of the European Parliament and of the Council (OJ L 181, 20.7.2000, 65), reproduced infra under no. I. 30.
[15] OJ L 228, 11.8.1992, 1, reproduced infra under no. I. 25. Directive as last amended by Directive 2000/64/EC of the European Parliament and of the Council (OJ L 290, 17.11.2000, 27).

¶ *Article 20a has been inserted in article 1(7) of Directive 2002/13/EC, reproduced infra under no. I. 32.*
¶ *Paragraph 4 has been replaced by article 57(7) of Directive 2005/68/EC, reproduced infra under no. I. 40.*

Article 21

[...]

¶ *This article has been repealed by article 21 of the Second Non-Life Insurance Directive 88/357/EEC, reproduced infra under no. I. 15.*

Section C
Withdrawal of Authorisation

[*Article 22*

1. Authorisation granted to an insurance undertaking by the competent authority of its home Member State may be withdrawn by that authority if that undertaking:

(a) does not make use of that authorisation within 12 months, expressly renounces it or ceases to carry on business for more than six months, unless the Member State concerned has made provision for authorisation to lapse in such cases;

(b) no longer fulfils the conditions for admission;

(c) has been unable, within the time allowed, to take the measures specified in the restoration plan or finance scheme referred to in Article 20;

(d) fails seriously in its obligation under the regulations to which it is subject.

In the event of the withdrawal or lapse of authorisation, the competent authority of the home Member State shall notify the competent authorities of the other Member States accordingly, and they shall take appropriate measures to prevent the undertaking from commencing new operations within their territories, under either the right of establishment or the freedom to provide services. The home Member State's competent authority shall, in conjunction with those authorities, take all measures necessary to safeguard the interests of insured persons and, in particular, shall restrict the free disposal of the undertaking's assets in accordance with Article 20 (1), (2), second subparagraph, or (3), second subparagraph.

2. Any decision to withdraw authorisation shall be supported by precise reasons and communicated to the undertaking in question.]

¶ *This article has been replaced by article 14 of the Third Non-Life Insurance Directive 92/49/EEC, reproduced infra under no. I. 25.*

Title III A

[Rules Applicable to Agencies or Branches Established Within the Community and Belonging to Undertakings whose Head Offices are Outside the Community]

¶ *The heading has been replaced by article 3 of Directive 90/618/EEC, reproduced infra under no. I. 17.*

Article 23

1. Each Member State shall make access to the business referred to in Article 1 by any undertaking whose head office is outside the Community subject to an official authorisation.

2. A Member State may grant an authorisation if the undertaking fulfils at least the following conditions:

(a) it is entitled to undertake insurance business under its national law;

(b) it establishes an agency or branch in the territory of such Member State;

(c) it undertakes to establish at the place of management of the agency or branch accounts specific to the business that it undertakes there, and to keep there all the records relating to the business transacted;

(d) it designates an authorised agent, to be approved by the competent authorities;

(e) it possesses in the country where it carries on its business assets of an amount equal to at least one-half of the minimum amount prescribed in Article 17(2), in respect of the guarantee fund, and deposits one-fourth of the minimum amount as security;

(f) it undertakes to keep a margin of solvency in accordance with the requirements referred to in Article 25;

(g) it submits a scheme of operations in accordance with the provisions of Article 11 (1) and (2).

[(h) communicate the name and the address of the claims representative appointed in each Member State other than the Member State in which the authorisation is sought if the risks to be covered are classified in class 10 of point A of the Annex, other than carrier's liability.]

¶ *Point (h) has been added by article 8(b) of Directive 2000/26/EC, reproduced infra under no. I. 30.*

Article 24

Member States shall require undertakings to establish adequate technical reserves to cover the underwriting liabilities assumed in their territories. Member States shall see that the agency or branch covers such technical reserves by means of assets that are equivalent to such reserves and are, to the extent fixed by the State in question, matching assets.

The law of the Member States shall be applicable to the calculation of technical reserves, the determination of categories of investments, and the valuation of assets.

The Member State in question shall require the assets representing the technical reserves shall be localised in its territory. Article 15 (3) shall, however, be applicable.

Article 25

1. Each Member State shall require for agencies or branches established in its territory a solvency margin consisting of assets free of all foreseeable liabilities, less any intangible items. The solvency margin shall be calculated in accordance with the provisions of Article 16 (3). However, for the purpose of calculating this margin, account shall be taken only of the premiums or contributions and claims pertaining to the business effected by the agency or branch concerned.

2. One-third of the solvency margin shall constitute the guarantee fund. The guarantee fund may not be less than one-half of the minimum required under Article 17 (2). The initial deposit lodged in accordance with Article 23 (2) (e) shall be counted towards such guarantee fund.

3. The assets representing the solvency margin must be kept within the country where the business is carried on up to the amount of the guarantee fund and the excess, within the Community.

[Article 26

1. Any undertaking that has requested or obtained authorisation from more than one Member State may apply for the following advantages that may be granted only jointly:

(a) the solvency margin referred to in Article 25 shall be calculated in relation to the entire business which it carries on within the Community; in such case, account shall be taken only of the operations effected by all the agencies or branches established within the Community for the purposes of this calculation;

(b) the deposit required under Article 23 (2) (e) shall be lodged in only one of those Member States;

(c) the assets representing the guarantee fund shall be localised in any one of the Member States in which it carries on its activities.

2. Application to benefit from the advantages provided for in paragraph 1 shall be made to the competent authorities of the Member States concerned. The application must state the authority of the Member State that in future is to supervise the solvency of the entire business of the agencies or branches established within the Community. Reasons must be given for the choice of authority made by the undertaking. The deposit shall be lodged with that Member State.

3. The advantages provided for in paragraph 1 may only be granted if the competent authorities of all Member States in which an application has been made agree to them. They shall take effect from the time when the selected supervisory authority informs the other supervisory authorities that it will supervise the state of solvency of the entire business of the agencies or branches within the Community.

The supervisory authority selected shall obtain from the other Member States the information necessary for the supervision of the overall solvency of the agencies and branches established in their territory.

4. At the request of one or more of the Member States concerned, the advantages granted under this Article shall be withdrawn simultaneously by all Member States concerned.]

¶ *This article has been replaced by article 12 of Directive 84/641/EEC, reproduced infra under no. I. 12.*

Article 27

The provisions of Articles 19 and 20 shall also apply in relation to agencies and branches of undertakings to which this Title applies.

[As regards the application of Article 20, where an undertaking qualifies for the advantages provided for in Article 26 (1), the authority responsible for verifying the solvency of agencies or branches established within the Community with respect to their entire business shall be treated in the same way as the authority of the State in the territory of which the head office of a Community undertaking is situated.]

¶ *Paragraph 2 has been replaced by article 13 of Directive 84/641/EEC, reproduced infra under no. I. 12.*

Article 28

In the case of a withdrawal of authorisation by the authority referred to in Article 26 (2), this authority shall notify the authorities of the other Member States where the undertaking operates and the latter supervisory authorities shall take the appropriate measures. If the reason for the withdrawal of the authorisation is the inadequacy of the overall state of solvency as fixed by the Member States that agreed to the request referred to in Article 26, the Member States that gave their approval shall also withdraw their authorisation.

[Article 28a

1. Under the conditions laid down by national law, each Member State shall authorise agencies and branches set up within its territory and covered by this Title to transfer all or part of their portfolios of contracts to an accepting office established in the same Member State if the competent authorities of that Member State or, if appropriate, of the Member State referred to in Article 26 certify that after taking the transfer into account the accepting office possesses the necessary solvency margin.

2. Under the conditions laid down by national law, each Member State shall authorise agencies and branches set up within its territory and covered by this Title to transfer all or part of their portfolios of contracts to an insurance undertaking with a head office in another Member State if the competent authorities of that Member State certify that after taking the transfer into account the accepting office possesses the necessary solvency margin.

3. If under the conditions laid down by national law a Member State authorises agencies and branches set up within its territory and covered by this Title to transfer all or part of their portfolios of contracts to an agency or branch covered by this Title and set up within the territory of another Member State it shall ensure that the competent authorities of the Member State of the accepting office or, if appropriate, of the Member State referred to in Article 26 certify that after taking the transfer into account the accepting office possesses the necessary solvency margin, that the law of the Member State of the accepting office permits such a transfer and that that State has agreed to the transfer.

4. In the circumstances referred to in paragraphs 1, 2 and 3 the Member State in which the transferring agency or branch is situated shall authorise the transfer after obtaining the agreement of the competent authorities of the Member State in which the risks are situated, where different from the Member State in which the transferring agency or branch is situated.

5. The competent authorities of the Member States consulted shall give their opinion or consent to the competent authorities of the home Member State of the transferring insurance undertaking within three months of receiving a request; the absence of any response from the

authorities consulted within that period shall be considered equivalent to a favourable opinion or tacit consent.

6. A transfer authorised in accordance with this Article shall be published as laid down by national law in the Member State in which the risk is situated. Such transfers shall automatically be valid against policyholders, insured persons and any other persons having rights or obligations arising out of the contracts transferred.

This provision shall not affect the Member States' right to give policyholders the option of cancelling contracts within a fixed period after a transfer.]

¶ *This article has been inserted by article 53 of the Third Non-Life Insurance Directive 92/49/EEC, reproduced infra under no. I. 25.*

Article 29

The Community may, by means of agreements concluded pursuant to the Treaty with one or more third countries, agree to the application of provisions different to those provided for in this Title, for the purpose of ensuring, under conditions of reciprocity, adequate protection for insured persons in the Member States.

Title III B

[Rules Applicable to Subsidiaries of Parent Undertakings Governed by the Laws of a Third Country and to Acquisitions of Holdings by such Parent Undertakings]

¶ *This heading has been inserted by article 3 of Directive 90/618/EEC, reproduced infra under no. I. 17.*

[Article 29a

1. The competent authorities of the Member States shall inform the Commission and the competent authorities of the other Member States:

(a) of any authorisation of a direct or indirect subsidiary, one or more of whose parent undertakings are governed by the law of a third country;

(b) whenever such a parent undertaking acquires a holding in a Community insurance undertaking which would turn the latter into its subsidiary.

2. When the authorisation referred to in paragraph 1(a) is granted to the direct or indirect subsidiary of one or more parent undertakings governed by the law of a third country, the structure of the group shall be specified in the notification which the competent authorities shall address to the Commission.]

¶ *This article has been inserted by article 4 of Directive 90/618/EEC, reproduced infra under no. I. 17, and has subsequently been replaced by article 4(1) of Directive 2005/1/EC, reproduced supra under no. B. 39.*

[Article 29b

1. Member States shall inform the Commission of any general difficulties encountered by their insurance undertakings in establishing themselves or carrying on their activities in a third country.

2. Initially not later than six months before the application of this Directive, and thereafter periodically, the Commission shall draw up a report examining the treatment accorded to Community insurance undertakings in third countries, in the terms referred to in paragraphs 3 and 4, as regards establishment and the carrying on of insurance activities, and the acquisition of holdings in third-country insurance undertakings. The Commission shall submit those reports to the Council, together with any appropriate proposals.

3. Whenever it appears to the Commission, either on the basis of the reports referred to in paragraph 2 or on the basis of other information, that a third country is not granting Community insurance undertakings effective market access comparable to that granted by the Community to insurance undertakings from that third country, the Commission may submit proposals to the Council for the appropriate mandate for negotiation with a view to obtaining comparable competitive opportunities for Community insurance undertakings. The Council shall decide by a qualified majority.

4. Whenever it appears to the Commission, either on the basis of the reports referred to in paragraph 2 or on the basis of other information, that Community insurance undertakings in a third country are not receiving national treatment offering the same competitive opportunities as are available to domestic insurance undertakings and that the conditions of effective market access are not being fulfilled, the Commission may initiate negotiations in order to remedy the situation.

[In the circumstances described in the first subparagraph, it may also be decided at any time, and in addition to initiating negotiations, in accordance with the procedure referred to in Article 5 of Decision 1999/468/EC[16] and in compliance with Article 7(3) and Article 8 thereof that the competent authorities of the Member States must limit or suspend their decisions regarding the following:

(a) requests for authorisation, whether pending at the moment of the decision or submitted thereafter;

(b) the acquisition of holdings by direct or indirect parent undertakings governed by the law of the third country in question.]

The duration of the measures referred to may not exceed three months.

Before the end of that three-month period, and in the light of the results of the negotiations, the Council may, acting on a proposal from the Commission, decide by a qualified majority that the measures shall be continued.

Such limitations or suspension may not apply to the setting up of subsidiaries by insurance undertakings or their subsidiaries duly authorised in the Community, or to the acquisition of holdings in Community insurance undertakings by such undertakings or subsidiaries

5. Whenever it appears to the Commission that one of the situations described in paragraphs 3 and 4 has arisen, the Member States shall inform it at its request:

(a) of any request for the authorisation of a direct or indirect subsidiary, one or more parent undertakings of which are governed by the laws of the third country in question;

(b) of any plans for such an undertaking to acquire a holding in a Community insurance undertaking such that the latter would become the subsidiary of the former.

This obligation to provide information shall lapse once an agreement is concluded with the third country referred to in paragraph 3 or 4 or when the measures referred to in the second and third subparagraphs of paragraph 4 cease to apply.

6. Measures taken under this Article shall comply with the Community's obligations under any international agreements, bilateral or multilateral, governing the taking-up and pursuit of the business of insurance undertakings.]

¶ *This article has been inserted by article 4 of Directive 90/618/EEC, reproduced infra under no. I. 17.*
¶ *The second subparagraph of article 29b(4) has been amended by article 4(2) of Directive 2005/1/EC, reproduced supra under no. B. 39.*

Title IV

Transitional and other Provisions

Article 30

1. Member States shall allow undertakings referred to in Title II which at the entry into force of the implementing measures to this Directive provide insurance in their territories in one or more of the classes referred to in Article 1 a period of five years, commencing with the date of notification of this Directive, in order to comply with the requirements of Articles 16 and 17.

2. Furthermore, Member States may:

(a) allow any undertakings referred to in (1), which upon the expiry of the five-year period have not fully established the margin of solvency, a further period not exceeding two years in which to do so provided that such undertakings have, in accordance with Article 20, submitted for the approval of the supervisory authority the measures which they propose to take for such purpose;

---

[16] OJ L 184, 17.7.1999, 23.

(b) exempt undertakings referred to in (1) whose annual premium or contribution income upon the expiry of the period of five years falls short of six times the amount of the minimum guarantee fund required under Article 17 (2) from the requirement to establish such minimum guarantee fund before the end of the financial year in respect of which the premium or contribution income is as much as six times such minimum guarantee fund. After considering the results of the examination provided for under Article 33, the Council shall unanimously decide, on a proposal from the Commission, when this exemption is to be abolished by Member States.

3. Undertakings desiring to extend their operations within the meaning of Article 8 (2) or Article 10 may not do so unless they comply immediately with the rules of this Directive. However, the undertakings referred to in paragraph (2) (b) which within the national territory extend their business to other classes of insurance or to other parts of such territory may be exempted for a period of ten years from the date of notification of the Directive from the requirement to constitute the minimum guarantee fund referred to in Article 17 (2).

4. An undertaking having a structure different from any of those listed in Article 8 may continue, for a period of three years from the notification of the Directive, to carry on their present business in the legal form in which they are constituted at the time of such notification. Undertakings set up in the United Kingdom "by Royal Charter" or "by private Act" or "by special public Act" may continue to carry on their business in their present form for an unlimited period. Undertakings in Belgium which, in accordance with their objects, carry on the business of intervention mortgage loans or savings operations in accordance with No. 4 of Article 15 of the provisions relating to the supervision of private savings banks, co-ordinated by the arrêté royal of June 23, 1967, may continue to undertake business for a period of three years from the date of notification of this Directive.

The Member States in question shall draw up a list of such undertakings and communicate it to the other Member States and the Commission.

5. At the request of undertakings that comply with the requirements of Articles 15, 16 and 17, Member States shall cease to apply restrictive measures such as those relating to mortgages, deposits and securities established under present regulations.

Article 31

Member States shall allow agencies or branches referred to in Title III which, at the entry into force of the implementing measures to this Directive, are undertaking one or more classes referred to in Article 1 and do not extend their business within the meaning of Article 10 (2) a maximum period of five years, from the date of notification of this Directive, in order to comply with the conditions of Article 25.

Article 32

During a period which terminates at the time of the entry into force of an agreement concluded with a third country pursuant to Article 29 and at the latest upon the expiry of a period of four years after the notification of the Directive, each Member State may retain in favour applied to them on 1 January 1973, in respect of matching assets and the localisation of technical reserves, provided that notification is given to the other Member States and the Commission and that the limits of relaxations granted pursuant to Article 15 (2) in favour of the undertakings of Member States established in its territory are not exceeded.

Title V
Final Provisions

Article 33

The Commission and the competent authorities of the Member States shall collaborate closely for the purpose of facilitating the supervision of direct insurance within the Community and of examining any difficulties that may arise in the application of this Directive.

Article 34

1. The Commission shall submit to the Council, within six years from the date of notification of

this Directive, a report on the effects of the financial requirements imposed by this Directive on the situation on the insurance markets of the Member States.

2. The Commission shall, as and when necessary, submit interim reports to the Council before the end of the transitional period provided for in Article 30 (1).

Article 35

Member States shall amend their national provisions to comply with this Directive within 18 months of its notification and shall forthwith inform the Commission thereof.

The provisions thus amended shall, subject to Articles 30, 31 and 32, be applied within 30 months from the date of notification.

Article 36

Upon notification of this Directive, Member States shall ensure that the texts of the main provisions of a legislative, regulatory or administrative nature, which they adopt in the field covered by this Directive, are communicated to the Commission.

Article 37

The Annex shall form an integral part of this Directive.

Article 38

This Directive is addressed to the Member States.

Annex

A. Classification of Risks According to Classes of Insurance

1. Accident (including industrial injury and occupational diseases)
– fixed pecuniary benefits
– benefits in the nature of indemnity
– combinations of the two
– injury to passengers

2. Sickness
– fixed pecuniary benefits
– benefits in the nature of indemnity
– combinations of the two

3. Land vehicles (other than railway rolling stock)

All damage to or loss of
– land motor vehicles
– land vehicles other than motor vehicles

4. Railway rolling stock

All damage to or loss of railway rolling stock

5. Aircraft

All damage to or loss of aircraft

6. Ships (sea, lake and river and canal vessels)

All damage to or loss of
– river and canal vessels
– lake vessels
– sea vessels

7. Goods in transit (including merchandise, baggage, and all other goods)

All damage to or loss of goods in transit or baggage, irrespective of the form of transport

8. Fire and natural forces

All damage to or loss of property (other than property included in classes 3, 4, 5, 6 and 7) due to
– fire
– explosion
– storm
– natural forces other than storm
– nuclear energy
– land subsidence

9. Other damage to property

All damage to or loss of property (other than property included, in classes 3, 4, 5, 6 and 7) due to hail or frost, and any event such as theft, other than those mentioned under 8

10. Motor vehicle liability

All liability arising out of the use of motor vehicles operating on the land (including carrier's liability)

11. Aircraft liability

All liability arising out of the use of aircraft (including carrier's liability)

12. Liability for ships (sea, lake and river and canal vessels)

All liability arising out of the use of ships, vessels or boats on the sea, lakes, rivers or canals (including carrier's liability)

13. General liability

All liability other than those forms mentioned under Nos. 10, 11 and 12.

14. Credit
– insolvency (general)
– export credit
– instalment credit
– mortgages
– agricultural credit

15. Suretyship
– suretyship (direct)
– suretyship (indirect)

16. Miscellaneous financial loss
– employment risks
– insufficiency of income (general)
– bad weather
– loss of benefits
– continuing general expenses
– unforeseen trading expenses
– loss of market value
– loss of rent or revenue
– indirect trading losses other than those mentioned above
– other financial loss (non-trading)
– other forms of financial loss

17. Legal expenses

Legal expenses and costs of litigation

[18. Assistance

Assistance for persons who get into difficulties while travelling, while away from home while away from their permanent residence.]

The risks included in a class may not be included in any other class except in the cases referred to in point C.

¶ *Class 18 has been added by article 14 of Directive 84/641/EEC, reproduced infra under no. I. 12.*

B. Description of Authorisations Granted for More Than one Class of Insurance

Where the authorisation simultaneously covers:

(a) Classes Nos. 1 and 2, it shall be named "Accident and Health Insurance";

(b) Classes Nos. I (fourth indent), 3, 7 and 10, it shall be named "Motor Insurance";

(c) Classes Nos. I (fourth indent), 4, 6, 7 and 12, it shall be named "Marine and Transport Insurance";

(d) Classes Nos. I (fourth indent), 5, 7 and 11, it shall be named "Aviation Insurance";

(e) Classes Nos. 8 and 9, it shall be named "Insurance against Fire and other Damage to Property";

(f) Classes Nos. 10, 11, 12 and 13, it shall be named "Liability Insurance";

(g) Classes Nos. 14 and 15, it shall be named "Credit and Suretyship Insurance";

(h) All classes, it shall be named at the choice of the Member State in question, which shall notify the other Member States and the Commission of its choice.

C. Ancillary Risks

An undertaking obtaining an authorisation for a principal risk belonging to one class or a group of classes may also insure risks included in another

class without an authorisation being necessary for them if they:
- are connected with the principal risk, concern the object which is covered against the principal risk, and
- are covered by the contract insuring the principal risk.

[However, the risks included in classes 14, 15 and 17 in point A may not be regarded as risks ancillary to other classes.

Nonetheless, the risk included in class 17 (legal expenses insurance) may be regarded as an ancillary risk of class 18 where the conditions laid down in the first subparagraph are fulfilled, where the main risk relates solely to the assistance provided for persons who fall into difficulties while travelling, while away from home or while away from their permanent residence.

Legal expenses insurance may also be regarded as an ancillary risk under the conditions set out in the first subparagraph where it concerns disputes or risks arising out of, or in connection with, the use of seagoing vessels.]

¶ *The second subparagraph has been replaced by article of Directive 87/344/EEC, reproduced infra under no. I. 14.*

[D. METHODS OF CALCULATING THE EQUALISATION RESERVE FOR THE CREDIT INSURANCE CLASS

Method No 1

1. In respect of the risks included in the class of insurance in point A No 14 (hereinafter referred to as "credit insurance"), the undertaking shall set up an equalisation reserve to which shall be charged any technical deficit arising in that class for a financial year.

2. Such reserve shall in each financial year receive 75% of any technical surplus arising on credit insurance business, subject to a limit of 12% of the net premiums or contributions until the reserve has reached 150% of the highest annual amount of net premiums or contributions received during the previous five financial years.

Method No 2

1. In respect of the risks included in the class of insurance listed in point A No 14 (hereinafter referred to as "credit insurance") the undertaking shall set up an equalisation reserve to which shall be charged any technical deficit arising in that class for a financial year.

2. The minimum amount of the equalisation reserve shall be 134% of the average of the premiums or contributions received annually during the previous five financial years after subtraction of the cessions and addition of the reinsurance acceptances.

3. Such reserve shall in each of the successive financial years receive 75% of any technical surplus arising in that class until the reserve is at least equal to the minimum calculated in accordance with paragraph 2.

4. Member States may lay down special rules for the calculation of the amount of the reserve and/or the amount of the annual levy in excess of the minimum amounts laid down in this Directive.

Method No 3

1. An equalisation reserve shall be formed for class 14 in point A (hereinafter referred to as "credit insurance") for the purpose of offsetting any above-average claims ratio for a financial year in that class of insurance.

2. The equalisation reserve shall be calculated on the basis of the method set out below.

All calculations shall relate to income and expenditure for the insurer's own account.

An amount in respect of any claims shortfall for each financial year shall be placed to the equalisation reserve until it has reached, or is restored to, the required amount.

There shall be deemed to be a claims shortfall if the claims ratio for a financial year is lower than the average claims ratio for the reference period. The amount in respect of the claims shortfall shall be arrived at by multiplying the difference between the two ratios by the earned premiums for the financial year.

The required amount shall be equal to six times the standard deviation of the claims ratios in the reference period from the average claims ratio, multiplied by the earned premiums for the financial year.

Where claims for any financial year are in excess, an amount in respect thereof shall be taken from the equalisation reserve. Claims shall be deemed to be in excess if the claims ratio for the financial year is higher than the average claims ratio. The amount in respect of the excess claims shall be arrived at by multiplying the difference between the two ratios by the earned premiums for the financial year.

Irrespective of claims experience, 3.5% of the required amount of the equalisation reserve shall be first placed to that reserve each financial year until its required amount has been reached or restored.

The length of the reference period shall be not less than 15 years and not more than 30 years. No equalisation reserve need be formed if no underwriting loss has been noted during the reference period.

The required amount of the equalisation reserve and the amount to be taken from it may be reduced if the average claims ratio for the reference period in conjunction with the expenses ratio show that the premiums include a safety margin.

Method No 4

1. An equalisation reserve shall be formed for class 14 in point A (hereinafter referred to as "credit insurance") for the purpose of offsetting any above-average claims ratio for a financial year in that class of insurance.

2. The equalisation reserve shall be calculated on the basis of the method set out below.

All calculations shall relate to income and expenditure for the insurer's own account.

An amount in respect of any claims shortfall for each financial year shall be placed to the equalisation reserve until it has reached the maximum required amount.

There shall be deemed to be a claims shortfall if the claims ratio for a financial year is lower than the average claims ratio for the reference period. The amount in respect of the claims shortfall shall be arrived at by multiplying the difference between the two ratios by the earned premiums for the financial year.

The maximum required amount shall be equal to six times the standard deviation of the claims ratio in the reference period from the average claims ratio, multiplied by the earned premiums for the financial year.

Where claims for any financial year are in excess, an amount in respect thereof shall be taken from the equalisation reserve until it has reached the minimum required amount. Claims shall be deemed to be in excess if the claims ratio for the financial year is higher than the average claims ratio. The amount in respect of the excess claims shall be arrived at by multiplying the difference between the two ratios by the earned premiums for the financial year.

The minimum required amount shall be equal to three times the standard deviation of the claims ratio in the reference from the average claims ratio multiplied by the earned premiums for the financial year.

The length of the reference period shall be not less than 15 years and not more than 30 years. No equalisation reserve need be formed if no underwriting loss has been noted during the reference period.

Both required amounts of the equalisation reserve and the amount to be placed to it or the amount to be taken from it may be reduced if the average claims ratio for the reference period in conjunction with the expenses ratio show that the premiums include a safety margin and that safety margin is more than one-and-a-half times the standard deviation of the claims ratio in the reference period. In such a case the amounts in question shall be multiplied by the quotient or one-and-a-half times the standard deviation and the safety margin.]

¶ *Annex D has been added by article 1(8) of Directive 87/343/EEC, reproduced infra under no. I. 13.*

CASE

Case C-349/96 Card Protection Plan Ltd (CPP) v Commissioners of Customs & Excise [1999] ECR I-0973

Article 13B(a) of the Sixth Council Directive 77/388, relating to the exemption from value added tax of insurance and reinsurance transactions, must be interpreted as meaning that a taxable person, not being an insurer, who, in the context of a block policy of which he is the holder, procures for his customers, who are the insured, insurance cover from an insurer who assumes the risk covered, performs an insurance transaction within the meaning of that provision. The term 'insurance' in that provision extends to the categories of assistance listed in the annex to the First Council Directive 73/239/EEC on the co-ordination of laws, regulations and administrative provisions relating to the taking-up and pursuit of the business of direct insurance other than life assurance.

I. 4.
Council Directive 73/240/EEC
of 24 July 1973
abolishing restrictions on freedom of establishment in the business of direct insurance other than life assurance[1]

THE COUNCIL OF THE EUROPEAN COMMUNITIES,

Having regard to the Treaty establishing the European Economic Community, and in particular Article [44(2) and (3)][2] thereof,

Having regard to the General Programme for the abolition of restrictions on freedom of establishment, and in particular Title IV C thereof,

Having regard to the proposal from the Commission,[3]

Having regard to the Opinion of the European Parliament,[4]

Having regard to the Opinion of the Economic and Social Committee,[5]

Whereas the General Programme referred to above provides for the abolition of all discriminatory treatment of the nationals of the other Member States as regards establishment in the business of direct insurance other than life assurance;

Whereas, in accordance with this General Programme, the lifting of restrictions on the setting-up of agencies and branches is, as regards direct insurance undertakings, dependent upon the co-ordination of conditions of taking up and pursuit of the business; whereas this co-ordination has been achieved for direct insurance other than life assurance, by the first Council Directive of 24 July 1973;[6]

Whereas the scope of this Directive is in all respects the same as that defined in item A of the Annex to the first Directive on co-ordination; whereas it appeared reasonable in the circumstances to exclude, for purposes of co-ordination, credit-insurance for exports;

Whereas, in accordance with the General Programme referred to above the restrictions on the right to join professional organisations must be abolished where the professional activities of the persons concerned involve the exercise of this right;

HAS ADOPTED THIS DIRECTIVE:

Article 1

Member States shall abolish, in respect of the natural persons and undertakings covered by Title I of the General Programme for the abolition of restrictions on freedom of establishment, hereinafter called "beneficiaries", the restrictions referred to in Title III of this programme affecting the right to take up and pursue self-employed activities in the classes of insurance specified in Article 1 of the first Co-ordination Directive.

By "First Co-ordination Directive" is meant the first Council Directive of July 24, 1973, on co-ordination of the laws, regulations and administrative provisions relating to the taking-up and pursuit of the business of direct insurance other than life assurance.

However, as regards credit-insurance for exports, these restrictions shall be maintained until the co-ordination programme laid down in Article 2 (2) (d), of the first Co-ordination Directive has been carried out.

---

[1] OJ L 228, 16.8.1973, 20–22.
[2] The number between brackets has been changed as from 1 May 1999 by article 12 of the Treaty of Amsterdam.
[3] OJ 2, 15.1.1962, 36/62.
[4] OJ C 27, 28.3.1968, 15.
[5] OJ 118, 20.6.1967, 2323/67.
[6] OJ L 228, 16.8.1973, 3–19, reproduced supra under no. I. 3.

Article 2

1. Member States shall in particular abolish the following restrictions:

(a) those that prevent beneficiaries from establishing themselves in the host country under the same conditions and with the same rights as nationals of that country;

(b) those existing by reason of administrative practices which result in treatment being applied to beneficiaries that is discriminatory by comparison with that applied to nationals.

2. The restrictions to be abolished shall include in particular those arising out of measures that prevent or limit the establishment of beneficiaries by the following means:

(a) In Germany:

the provisions granting the Federal Ministry of Economic Affairs the discretionary right to impose its own conditions of access to this business on foreign nationals and to prevent them from pursuing this business within the Federal Republic (Law of June 6, 1931 (VAG), Article 106 (2), No. 1, in conjunction with Article 8 (1), No. 3, Article 106 (2), last sentence, and Article 111 (2));

(b) In Belgium:

the obligation to hold a carte professionelle (Article 1 of the Law of February 19, 1965);

(c) In France:
- the need to obtain special consent (Law of 15 February 1917, as amended and supplemented by the "décret-loi" of 30 October 1935, Article 2 (2)—"décret" of 19 August 1941, as amended Articles 1 and 2—"décret" of 13 August 1947, as amended, Articles 2 and 10);
- the obligation to provide a surety-bond or special guarantees as a reciprocal requirement (Law of 15 February, 1917, amended and supplemented by the "décret-loi" of 30 October 1935, Article 2 (2)—"décret-loi" of 14 June 1938, Article 42—"décret" of 30 December 1938, as amended, Article 143—"décret" of 14 December 1966, Articles 9, 10 and 11);
- the obligation to deposit technical reserves ("décret" of 30 December 1938, as amended, Article 179—"décret" of 13 August 13 as amended, Articles 8 and 18—"décret" of 14 December 1966, Title 1.

(d) In Ireland:

the provision that, to be eligible for an insurance licence, a company must be registered under the Irish Companies Acts, two thirds of its shares must be owned by Irish citizens and the majority of the directors (other than a full-time managing director) must be Irish citizens (Insurance Act, 1936, section 12; Insurance Act, 1964, section 7).

3. The laws, regulations or administrative provisions that involve beneficiaries in the obligation to provide a deposit or special surety-bond shall not be abolished, as long as the undertakings do not fulfil the financial conditions under Articles 16 and 17 of the first Co-ordination Directive in accordance with the provisions of Article 30 (1) and (2) of the same Directive.

Article 3

1. Where a host Member State requires of its own nationals wishing to take up any activity referred to in Article 1 proof of good repute and proof of no previous bankruptcy, or proof of either of these, that State shall accept as sufficient evidence, in respect of nationals of other Member States, the production of an extract from the "judicial record" or, failing this, of an equivalent document issued by a competent judicial or administrative authority in the country of origin or the country whence the foreign national comes, showing that these requirements have been met.

2. Where the country of origin or the country whence the foreign national comes does not issue such documentary proof of good repute or documentary proof of no previous bankruptcy, such proof may be replaced by a declaration on oath—or in States where there is no provision for declaration on oath, by a solemn declaration—made by the person concerned before a competent judicial or administrative authority, or where appropriate a notary, in the country of origin or in the country whence that person comes; such authority or notary will issue a certificate attesting the authenticity of the declaration on oath or solemn

declaration. A declaration in respect of no previous bankruptcy may also be made before a competent professional or trade body in the said country.

3. Documents issued in accordance with paragraph (1) or with paragraph (2) may not be produced more than three months after their date of issue.

4. Member States shall, within the time limit laid down in Article 6, designate the authorities and bodies competent to issue these documents and shall forthwith inform the other Member States and the Commission thereof.

Article 4

1. Member States shall ensure that beneficiaries have the right to join professional or trade organisations under the same conditions and with the same rights and obligations as their own nationals.

2. The right to join professional or trade organisations shall, in the case of establishment, entail eligibility for election or appointment to high office in such organisations. However, such posts may be reserved for nationals where, in pursuance of any provision laid down by law or regulation, the organisation concerned is involved in the exercise of official authority.

3. In the Grand Duchy of Luxembourg membership of the "Chambre de commerce" shall not give beneficiaries the right to take part in the election of the administrative organs of that Chamber.

Article 5

No Member State shall grant to any of its nationals who got to another Member State for the purpose of pursuing any activity referred to in Article 1 any aid liable to distort the conditions of establishment.

Article 6

Member States shall amend their national regulations in accordance with this Directive and within 18 months of the notification of the first Co-ordination Directive and shall forthwith inform the Commission thereof. The regulations thus amended shall be implemented at the same time as the laws, regulations and administrative provisions set up in pursuance of the first Directive.

Article 7

This Directive is addressed to the Member States.

I. 5.

Commission Recommendation 74/165/EEC
of 6 February 1974
to the Member States concerning the application of the Council Directive of 24 April 1972 on the approximation of the laws of the Member States relating to the use of motor vehicles, and to the enforcement of the obligation to insure against such liability[1]

1. By virtue of Article 7 (1) of the Council Directive[2] of 24 April 1972 on the approximation of the laws of the Member States relating to the use of motor vehicles and to the enforcement of the obligation to insure against such liability, as amended by the Council Directive[3] of 19 December 1972, any vehicle normally based in the territory of a third country must be provided either with a valid green card or with a certificate of frontier insurance valid for the whole of the territory of the Community before entering that territory;

2. Now in the Member States practice differs as to the duration of contracts of insurance against civil liability in respect of the use of motor vehicles in the form of frontier insurance; it is necessary to render uniform the practice followed in the Member States as to the minimum duration of frontier insurance so as to prevent abuse, after the removal of checks at intra-Community frontiers on insurance against civil liability in respect of motor vehicles, of frontier insurance by vehicles from third countries no longer covered, after their entry into a Member State, by insurance against civil liability valid in other Member States.

3. For these reasons, and by virtue of Article [211][4] of the Treaty establishing the European Economic Community, the Commission recommends that the Member States ensure that contracts of insurance against civil liability in respect of the use of motor vehicles concluded in the form of frontier insurance shall, not later than 15 May 1974, have a minimum duration of 15 days.

---

[1] OJ L 87, 30.3.1974, 12.
[2] OJ L 103, 2.5.1972, 1, reproduced supra under no. I. 2.
[3] OJ L 291, 28.12.1972, 162. Correction in OJ L 75, 23.3.1973, 30.

[4] The number between brackets has been changed as from 1 May 1999 by article 12 of the Treaty of Amsterdam.

I. 6.

Council Directive 76/580/EEC
of 29 June 1976
amending Directive 73/239/EEC on the
co-ordination of laws and regulations and administrative provisions relating to the taking up and pursuit of the business of direct insurance other than life insurance[1]

This Directive amends the First Non-Life Insurance
Directive 73/239/EEC (OJ L 228, 16. 8. 1973), reproduced supra under no. I. 3.
The modifications are directly incorporated in the Directive.

---

[1] OJ L 189, 11.7.1976, 13–14.

I. 7.
Council Directive 77/92/EEC
of 13 December 1976
on measures to facilitate the effective exercise of freedom of establishment and freedom to provide services in respect of the activities of insurance agents and brokers (ex ISIC Group 630) and, in particular, transitional measures in respect of those activities[1]

This Directive has been repealed as from 15 January 2005 by article 15 of Directive 2002/92/EC (OJ L 9, 15.01.2003, 3), reproduced infra under no. I. 34.

---

[1] OJ L 26, 31.1.1977, 14–19.

I. 8.

Council Directive 78/473/EEC
of 30 May 1978
on the co-ordination of laws, regulations and administrative provisions relating to Community co-insurance[1]

> CASES
>
> ### I. Case 220/83 Commission of the European Communities v French Republic [1986] ECR 3663
>
> In the insurance sector in general there are imperative reasons relating to the protection of the consumer both as a policyholder and as an insured person that may justify restrictions on the freedom to provide services. In the present state of community law, in particular with regard to the coordination of the relevant national rules, the protection of that interest is not necessarily guaranteed by the rules of the state of establishment. It follows that, as regards the field of direct insurance in general, the requirement of a separate authorization granted by the authorities of the State in which the service is provided remains justified subject to certain conditions. On the other hand, the requirement of an establishment, which represents the very negation of the freedom to provide services, exceeds what is necessary to attain the objective pursued and, accordingly, that requirement is contrary to Articles [49 and 50][2] of the Treaty.
>
> As regards more specifically co-insurance, the position of the leading insurer referred to in Directive 78/473 may be clearly distinguished from that of insurers in general, and consequently neither the requirement of an establishment, nor even that of an authorization, in the state in which the service is provided may be regarded as compatible with Articles [49 and 50][2] of the EEC Treaty.
>
> ### II. Case 205/84 Commission of the European Communities v Federal Republic of Germany [1986] ECR 3755
>
> In the case of the insurance to which Directive 78/473 on co-insurance applies, not only the requirement that the leading insurer be established but also the requirement that he be authorized, which are laid down in the insurance supervision law, are contrary to Articles [49 and 50][2] of the Treaty and therefore also to the directive.
>
> ### III. Case 206/84 Commission of the European Communities v Ireland [1986] ECR 3817
>
> See commentary of Case 205/84 (Case II of this directive).

THE COUNCIL OF THE EUROPEAN COMMUNITIES,

Having regard to the Treaty establishing the European Economic Community, and in particular Articles [47 (2) and 55][2] thereof,

Having regard to the proposal from the Commission,

Having regard to the opinion of the European Parliament,[3]

Having regard to the opinion of the Economic and Social Committee,[4]

Whereas the effective pursuit of Community co-insurance business should be facilitated by a minimum of co-ordination in order to prevent distortion of competition and inequality of treatment, without affecting the freedom existing in several Member States;

Whereas such co-ordination covers only those co-insurance operations which are economically the most important, i.e. those which by reason of

---

[1] OJ L 151, 7.6.1978, 25–28.
[2] The number between brackets has been changed as from 1 May 1999 by article 12 of the Treaty of Amsterdam.
[3] OJ C 60, 13.3.1975, 16.
[4] OJ C 47, 27.2.1975, 40.

their nature or their size are liable to be covered by international co-insurance;

Whereas this Directive thus constitutes a first step towards the co-ordination of all operations which may be carried out by virtue of the freedom to provide services; whereas this co-ordination, in fact, is the object of the proposal for a second Council Directive on the co-ordination of laws, regulations and administrative provisions relating to direct insurance other than life assurance and laying down provisions to facilitate the effective exercise of freedom to provide services, which the Commission forwarded to the Council on December 30, 1975;[5]

Whereas the leading insurer is better placed than the other co-insurers to assess claims and to fix the minimum amount of reserves for outstanding claims;

Whereas work is in progress on the winding-up of insurance undertakings; whereas provision must be made at this stage to ensure that, in the event of winding-up, beneficiaries under Community co-insurance contracts enjoy equality of treatment with beneficiaries in respect of the other insurance business, irrespective of the nationality of such persons;

Whereas special co-operation should be provided for in the Community co-insurance field both between the competent supervisory authorities of the Member States and between those authorities and the Commission; whereas any practices which might indicate a misuse of the purpose of the Directive are to be examined in the course of such co-operation.

HAS ADOPTED THIS DIRECTIVE:

Title I

General Provisions

Article 1

1. This Directive shall apply to Community co-insurance operations referred to in Article 2 which relate to risks classified under point A. 4, 5, 6, 7, 8, 9, 11, 12, 13 and 16 of the Annex to the First Council Directive of 24 July 1973,[6] on the co-ordination of laws, regulations and administrative provisions relating to the taking-up and pursuit of the business of direct insurance other than life assurance, hereinafter called the "First Co-ordination Directive."

It shall not apply, however, to Community co-insurance operations covering risks classified under A. 13 that concern damage arising from nuclear sources or from medicinal products. The exclusion of insurance against damage arising from medicinal products shall be examined by the Council within five years of the notification of this Directive.

2. This Directive shall apply to risks referred to in the first subparagraph of paragraph (l), which by reason of their nature or size call for the participation of several insured for their coverage.

Any difficulties, which may arise in implementing this principle, shall be examined pursuant to Article 8.

Article 2

1. This Directive shall apply only to those Community co-insurance operations, which satisfy the following conditions:

(a) the risk, within the meaning of Article 1 (1), is covered by a single contract at an overall premium and for the same period by two or more insurance undertakings, hereinafter referred to as "co-insurers," each for its own part; one of these undertakings shall be the leading insurer;

(b) the risk is situated within the Community;

(c) for the purpose of covering this risk, the leading insurer is authorised in accordance with the conditions laid down in the First Co-ordination Directive, *i.e.* he is treated as if he were the insurer covering the whole risk;

(d) at least one of the co-insurers participates in the contract by means of a head office, agency or

---

[5] OJ C 32, 12.2.1976, 2. This proposal was adopted as the Second Non-Life Insurance Directive 88/357/EEC (OJ L 172, 4.7.1988, 1), reproduced infra under no. I. 15.

[6] OJ L 228, 16.8.1973, 3–19, First Non-Life Insurance Directive 73/239/EEC (OJ L 228, 16.8.1973, 1), reproduced supra under no. I. 3.

branch established in a Member State other than that of the leading insurer;

(e) the leading insurer fully assumes the leader's role in co-insurance practice and in particular determines the terms and conditions of insurance and rating.

2. Those co-insurance operations which do not satisfy the conditions set out in paragraph (1) or which cover risks other than those specified in Article 1 shall remain subject to the national laws operative at the time when this Directive comes into force.

Article 3

The right of undertakings which have their head office in a Member State and which are subject to and satisfy the requirements of the First Co-ordination Directive to participate in Community co-insurance may not be made subject to any provisions other than those of this Directive.

Title II
Conditions and Procedures for Community Co-insurance

Article 4

1. The amount of the technical reserves shall be determined by the different co-insurers according to the rules fixed by the Member State where they are established or, in the absence of such rules, according to customary practice in that State. However, the reserve for outstanding claims shall be at least equal to that determined by the leading insurer according to the rules or practice of that State where such insurer is established.

2. The technical reserves established by the different co-insurers shall be represented by matching assets. However, relaxation of the matching assets rule may be granted by the Member States in which the co-insurers are established in order to take account of the requirements of sound management of insurance undertakings. Such assets shall be localised either in the Member States in which the co-insurers are established or in the Member State in which the leading insurer is established, whichever the insurer chooses.

Article 5

The Member States shall ensure that co-insurers established in their territory keep statistical data showing the extent of Community co-insurance operations and the countries concerned.

Article 6

The supervisory authorities of the Member States shall co-operate closely in the implementation of this Directive and shall provide each other with all the information necessary to this end.

Article 7

In the event of an insurance undertaking being wound up, liabilities arising from participation in Community co-insurance contracts shall be met in the same way as those arising under that undertaking's other insurance contracts without distinction as to the nationality of the insured and of the beneficiaries.

Title III
Final Provisions

Article 8

The Commission and the competent authorities of the Member States shall co-operate closely for the purposes of examining any difficulties that might arise in implementing this Directive.

In the course of this co-operation they shall examine in particular any practices which might indicate that the purpose of the provisions of this Directive and in particular of Article 1 (2) and Article 2 are being misused either in that the leading insurer does not assume the leader's role in co-insurance practice or that the risks clearly do not require the participation of two or more insurers for their coverage.

Article 9

The Commission shall submit to the Council within six years of the notification of this Directive a report on the development of Community co-insurance.

Article 10

Member States shall amend their national provisions so as to comply with this Directive within 18 months of its notification and shall immediately inform the Commission thereof.

The provisions thereby amended shall be applied within 24 months of such notification.

Article 11

Upon notification of this Directive Member States shall ensure that the texts of the main provisions of laws, regulations or administrative measures, which they adopt in the field covered by this Directive, are communicated to the Commission.

Article 12

This Directive is addressed to the Member States.

I. 9.

Council Directive 79/267/EEC
of 5 March 1979
on the co-ordination of laws, regulations and administrative provisions relating to the taking up and pursuit of the business of direct life assurance
(First life assurance Directive)[1]

This Directive has been repealed as from 19 December 2002 by Annex V, part A of Directive 2002/83/EC (OJ L 345, 19.12.2002, 1), reproduced infra under no. I. 33.

Correlation Table

Directive 79/267/EEC	Directive 2002/83/EC
Article 1	Article 2
Article 2	Article 3(1) to (4)
Article 3	Article 3(5) and (6)
Article 4	Article 3(7)
Article 5(a), second sentence	Article 1(2)
Article 5(b), (c) and (d)	Article 1(1)(o), (p), (q)
Article 6	Article 4
Article 7	Article 5
Article 8(1)	Article 6(1)
Article 8(1) last three subparagraphs	Article 6(2)
Article 8(1)a	Article 6(3)
Article 8(2)	Article 6(4)
Article 8(3)	Article 6(5)
Article 8(4)	Article 6(6)
Article 9	Article 7
Article 10	Article 40
Article 12	Article 9
Article 13(1) and (2)	Article 18(1) and (2)
Article 13(3) to (7)	Article 18(4) to (7)
Article 14	Article 19
Article 15	Article 10
Article 16	Article 11
Article 17	Article 20
Article 18	Article 27
Article 19	Article 28

---

[1] OJ L 63, 13.3.1979, 1–18.

Directive 79/267/EEC	Directive 2002/83/EC
Article 20	Article 29
Article 20a	Article 30
Article 21	Article 31
Article 22(1)	Article 12
Article 23	Article 13
Article 24	Article 37
Article 24a	Article 38
Article 26	Article 39
Article 27(1) to (2)(f)	Article 51(1) to (2)(f)
Article 28	Article 54
Article 29	Article 55
Article 30	Article 56
Article 31	Article 52
Article 31a	Article 53
Article 32	Article 57
Article 32a	Article 58
Article 32b(1)	Article 59(1)
Article 32b(2)	Article 59(2)
Article 32b(3)	Article 59(3)
Article 32b(4)	Article 59(4)
Article 32b(5)	Article 59(5)
Article 32b(7)	Article 59(6)
Article 33(4)	Article 60(1)
Article 37	Article 61
Article 38	Article 62, first subparagraph
Article 39(1)	Article 68(1)
Article 39(3)	Article 68(2)
Article 41	Article 70
Annex	Annex I

I. 10.

Commission Recommendation 81/76/EEC
of 8 January 1981
on accelerated settlement of claims under insurance against civil liability in respect of the use of motor vehicles[1]

THE COMMISSION OF THE EUROPEAN COMMUNITIES,

Having regard to the Treaty establishing the European Economic Community, and in particular Article [211][2] thereof,

Whereas motor vehicles are responsible for a significant proportion of accidents occurring in the Community;

Whereas, on 7 August 1980, the Commission presented to the Council a proposal for a second Directive on the approximation of the laws of the Member States relating to insurance against civil liability in respect of the use of motor vehicles; whereas that proposal is aimed at reducing certain disparities which continue to exist between the obligatory motor vehicle civil liability insurance schemes in the different Member States, in order to ensure that motor vehicle accident victims have equivalent cover in all Member States;

Whereas, however, that proposal does not deal with the procedures used to settle claims; whereas it is not possible to establish a uniform procedure in all Member States for forwarding police reports, particularly in view of the effect in this area of principles of public policy governing the administration of justice;

Whereas the period elapsing between the occurrence of a road accident and the payment of compensation by the insurer of the person liable is occasionally extremely lengthy; whereas such lengthy periods are undoubtedly prejudicial to accident victims;

Whereas such lengthy periods are largely attributable to the slowness of the legal procedures for determining liability and fixing compensation;

Whereas procedures have been introduced in some Member States enabling the parties concerned and their insurers to obtain more rapid access to police reports containing the particulars that are essential for settling claims; whereas it is appropriate to encourage the extension of such arrangements,

HEREBY RECOMMENDS:

Article 1

The Member States shall take all the measures necessary to facilitate the communication to those concerned of police reports and other documents necessary for the payment of compensation by insurers covering against civil liability in respect of the use of motor vehicles.

Article 2

Member States shall inform the Commission of the measures they take on the basis of this recommendation.

Article 3

This recommendation is addressed to the Member States.

---

[1] OJ L 57, 4.3.1981, 27.
[2] The number between brackets has been changed as from 1 May 1999 by article 12 of the Treaty of Amsterdam.

I. 11.

Council Directive 84/5/EEC
of 30 December 1983
on the approximation of the laws of the Member States relating to insurance against civil liability in respect of the use of motor vehicles
(Second motor insurance Directive)[1]

THE COUNCIL OF THE EUROPEAN COMMUNITIES,

Having regard to the Treaty establishing the European Economic Community, and in particular Article [94][2] thereof,

Having regard to the proposal from the Commission,[3]

Having regard to the opinion of the European Parliament,[4]

Having regard to the opinion of the Economic and Social Committee,[5]

Whereas, by Council Directive 72/166/EEC,[6] as amended by Directive 72/430/EEC,[7] the Council approximated the laws of the Member States relating to insurance against civil liability in respect of the use of motor vehicles and to the enforcement of the obligation to insure against such liability;

Whereas Article 3 of Directive 72/166/EEC requires each Member State to take all appropriate measures to ensure that civil liability in respect of the use of vehicles normally based in its territory is covered by insurance; whereas the extent of the liability covered and the terms and conditions of the insurance cover are to be determined on the basis of those measures;

Whereas, however, major disparities continue to exist between the laws of the different Member States concerning the extent of this obligation of insurance cover; whereas these disparities have a direct effect upon the establishment and the operation of the common market;

Whereas, in particular, the extension of the obligation of insurance cover to include liability incurred in respect of damage to property is justified;

Whereas the amounts in respect of which insurance is compulsory must in any event guarantee victims adequate compensation irrespective of the Member State in which the accident occurred;

Whereas it is necessary to make provision for a body to guarantee that the victim will not remain without compensation where the vehicle which caused the accident is uninsured or unidentified; whereas it is important, without amending the provisions applied by the Member States with regard to the subsidiary or non-subsidiary nature of the compensation paid by that body and to the rules applicable with regard to subrogation, to provide that the victim of such an accident should be able to apply directly to that body as a first point of contact; whereas, however, Member States should be given the possibility of applying certain limited exclusions as regards the payment of compensation by that body and of providing that compensation for damage to property caused by an unidentified vehicle may be limited or excluded in view of the danger of fraud;

Whereas it is in the interest of victims that the effects of certain exclusion clauses be limited to the relationship between the insurer and the person responsible for the accident; whereas, however, in the case of vehicles stolen or obtained

---

[1] OJ L 8, 11.1.1984, 17–20.
[2] The number between brackets has been changed as from 1 May 1999 by article 12 of the Treaty of Amsterdam.
[3] OJ C 214, 21.8.1980, 9 and OJ C 78, 30.3.1982, 17.
[4] OJ C 287, 9.11.1981, 44.
[5] OJ C 138, 9.6.1981, 15.
[6] OJ L 103, 2.5.1972, 2, First Motor Liability Directive, reproduced supra under no. I. 2.
[7] OJ L 291, 28.12.1972, 162.

by violence, Member States may specify that compensation will be payable by the above-mentioned body;

Whereas in order to alleviate the financial burden on that body, Member States may make provision for the application of certain excesses where the body provides compensation for damage to property caused by uninsured vehicles or, where appropriate, vehicles stolen or obtained by violence;

Whereas the members of the family of the insured person, driver or any other person liable should be afforded protection comparable to that of other third parties, in any event in respect of their personal injuries;

Whereas the abolition of checks on insurance is conditional on the granting by the national insurers' bureau of the host country of a guarantee of compensation for damage caused by vehicles normally based in another Member State; whereas the most convenient criterion for determining whether a vehicle is normally based in a given Member State is the bearing of a registration plate of the State; whereas the first indent of Article 1 (4) of Directive 72/166/EEC should therefore be amended to that effect;

Whereas, in view of the situation in certain Member States at the outset as regards on the one hand the minimum amounts, and on the other hand the cover and the excesses applicable by the above-mentioned body in respect of damage to property, provision should be made for transitional measures concerning the gradual implementation in those Member States of the provisions of the Directive concerning minimum amounts and compensation for damage to property by that body,

HAS ADOPTED THIS DIRECTIVE:

[*Article 1*

1. The insurance referred to in Article 3(1) of Directive 72/166/EEC shall cover compulsorily both damage to property and personal injuries.

2. Without prejudice to any higher guarantees which Member States may lay down, each Member State shall require insurance to be compulsory at least in respect of the following amounts:

(a) in the case of personal injury, a minimum amount of cover of EUR 1.000.000 per victim or EUR 5.000.000 per claim, whatever the number of victims;

(b) in the case of damage to property, EUR 1.000.000 per claim, whatever the number of victims.

If necessary, Member States may establish a transitional period of up to five years from the date of implementation of Directive 2005/14/EC of the European Parliament and of the Council of 11 May 2005 amending Council Directives 72/166/EEC, 84/5/EEC, 88/357/EEC and 90/232/EEC and Directive 2000/26/EC of the European Parliament and of the Council relating to insurance against civil liability in respect of the use of motor vehicles,[8] within which to adapt their minimum amounts of cover to the amounts provided for in this paragraph.

Member States establishing such a transitional period shall inform the Commission thereof and indicate the duration of the transitional period.

Within 30 months of the date of implementation of Directive 2005/14/EC Member States shall increase guarantees to at least a half of the levels provided for in this paragraph.

3. Every five years after the entry into force of Directive 2005/14/EC or the end of any transitional period as referred to in paragraph 2, the amounts referred to in that paragraph shall be reviewed, in line with the European Index of Consumer Prices (EICP), as set out in Council Regulation (EC) No 2494/95 of 23 October 1995 concerning harmonised indices of consumer prices.[9]

The amounts shall be adjusted automatically. Such amounts shall be increased by the percent-

---

[8] OJ L 149, 11.6.2005, 14, reproduced infra under no. I. 39.
[9] OJ L 257, 27.10.1995, 1. Regulation as amended by Regulation (EC) No 1882/2003 of the European Parliament and of the Council (OJ L 284, 31.10.2003, 1).

age change indicated by the EICP for the relevant period, that is to say, the five years immediately preceding the review, and rounded up to a multiple of EUR 10.000.

The Commission shall communicate the adjusted amounts to the European Parliament and the Council and shall ensure their publication in the *Official Journal of the European Union*.

4. Each Member State shall set up or authorise a body with the task of providing compensation, at least up to the limits of the insurance obligation for damage to property or personal injuries caused by an unidentified vehicle or a vehicle for which the insurance obligation provided for in paragraph 1 has not been satisfied.

The first subparagraph shall be without prejudice to the right of the Member States to regard compensation by the body as subsidiary or non-subsidiary and the right to make provision for the settlement of claims between the body and the person or persons responsible for the accident and other insurers or social security bodies required to compensate the victim in respect of the same accident. However, Member States may not allow the body to make the payment of compensation conditional on the victim establishing in any way that the person liable is unable or refuses to pay.

5. The victim may in any event apply directly to the body which, on the basis of information provided at its request by the victim, shall be obliged to give him a reasoned reply regarding the payment of any compensation.

Member States may, however, exclude the payment of compensation by that body in respect of persons who voluntarily entered the vehicle which caused the damage or injury when the body can prove that they knew it was uninsured.

6. Member States may limit or exclude the payment of compensation by the body in the event of damage to property by an unidentified vehicle.

However, where the body has paid compensation for significant personal injuries to any victim of the same accident in which damage to property was caused by an unidentified vehicle, Member States may not exclude the payment of compensation for damage to property on the basis that the vehicle is not identified. Nevertheless, Member States may provide for an excess of not more than EUR 500 for which the victim of such damage to property may be responsible.

The conditions in which personal injuries are to be considered significant shall be determined in accordance with the legislation or administrative provisions of the Member State in which the accident takes place. In this regard, Member States may take into account, *inter alia*, whether the injury has required hospital care.

7. Each Member State shall apply its laws, regulations and administrative provisions to the payment of compensation by the body, without prejudice to any other practice which is more favourable to the victim.]

¶ *This article has been replaced by article 2 of Directive 2005/14/EC, reproduced infra under no. I. 39.*

CASES

I. Case C-63/01 Samuel Sidney Evans v Secretary of State for the Environment, Transport and the Regions and The Motor Insurers' Bureau [2003] ECR I-14447

1. Article 1(4) of Second Council Directive 84/5/EEC is to be interpreted as meaning that:
– A body may be regarded as authorized by a Member State within the meaning of that provision where its obligation to provide compensation to victims of damage or injury caused by unidentified or insufficiently insured vehicles derives from an agreement concluded between that body and a public authority of the Member State, provided that the agreement is interpreted and applied as obliging the body to provide victims with the compensation guaranteed to them by Directive 84/5/EEC and provided that victims may apply directly to that body.

– The compensation awarded for damage or injuries caused by an unidentified or insufficiently insured vehicle, paid by the body authorised for that purpose, must take account of the effluxion of time until actual payment of the sums awarded in order to guarantee adequate compensation for the victims. It is incumbent on the Member States to lay down the rules to be applied for that purpose.
– The compensation awarded for damage or injury caused by an unidentified or insufficiently insured vehicle, paid by the body authorized for that purpose, is not required to include reimbursement of the costs incurred by victims in connection with the processing of their application for compensation except to the extent to which such reimbursement is necessary to safeguard the rights derived by victims from Directive 84/5/EEC in conformity with the principles of equivalence and effectiveness. It is for the national court to consider whether that is the case under the procedural arrangements adopted in the Member State concerned.

2. It is incumbent on the national court, if examination of the existing compensation system discloses a defect in transposition of Directive 84/5/EEC and if that defect has adversely affected the victim, to determine whether the breach of that obligation of transposition is sufficiently serious.

II. Case C-348/98 Vitor Manuel Mendes Ferreira and Maria Clara Delgado Correia Ferreira v Companhia de Seguros Mundial Confiança SA [2000] ECR I-6711

Articles 1(2) and 5(3) of Directive 84/5/EEC, as amended by Annex I, Part IX F, entitled 'Insurance', of the Act concerning the conditions of accession of the Kingdom of Spain and the Portuguese Republic and the adjustments to the Treaties, preclude domestic laws laying down maximum amounts of compensation that are lower than the minimum amounts of cover laid down by those provisions where, in the absence of fault on the part of the driver of the vehicle which caused the accident, only civil liability for materialization of risk arises.

Article 2

1. Each Member State shall take the necessary measures to ensure that any statutory provision or any contractual clause contained in an insurance policy issued in accordance with Article 3 (1) of Directive 72/166/EEC, which excludes from insurance the use or driving of vehicles by:
– persons who do not have express or implied authorisation thereto, or
– persons who do not hold a licence permitting them to drive the vehicle concerned, or
– persons who are in breach of the statutory technical requirements concerning the condition and safety of the vehicle concerned,

shall, for the purposes of Article 3 (1) of Directive 72/166/EEC, be deemed to be void in respect of claims by third parties who have been victims of an accident.

However the provision or clause referred to in the first indent may be invoked against persons who voluntarily entered the vehicle that caused the damage or injury, when the insurer can prove that they knew the vehicle was stolen.

Member States shall have the option—in the case of accidents occurring on their territory—of not applying the provision in the first subparagraph if and in so far as the victim may obtain compensation for the damage suffered from a social security body.

2. In the case of vehicles stolen or obtained by violence, Member States may lay down that the body specified in Article 1 (4) will pay compensation instead of the insurer under the conditions set out in paragraph 1 of this Article; where the vehicle is normally based in another Member State, that body can make no claim against any body in that Member State.

The Member States which, in the case of vehicles stolen or obtained by violence, provide that the body referred to in Article 1 (4) shall pay compensation, may fix in respect of damage to property an excess of not more than 250 ECU for which the victim may be responsible.

> CASE
>
> **Case C-129/94 Criminal Proceedings Against Rafael Ruiz Bernáldez [1996] ECR I-1829**
>
> Article 3(1) of Directive 72/166/EEC on the approximation of the laws of the Member States relating to insurance against civil liability in respect of the use of motor vehicles, and to the enforcement of the obligation to insure against such liability, is to be interpreted as meaning that, without prejudice to the provisions of Article 2(1) of Directive 84/5/EEC on the approximation of the laws of the Member States relating to insurance against civil liability in respect of the use of motor vehicles, a compulsory insurance contract may not provide that in certain cases, in particular where the driver of the vehicle was intoxicated, the insurer is not obliged to pay compensation for the damage to property and personal injuries caused to third parties by the insured vehicle.
>
> In view of the aim of ensuring protection, stated repeatedly in all the relevant directives, Article 3(1) of Directive 72/166/EEC, as developed and supplemented by the later directives, must be interpreted as meaning that compulsory motor insurance must enable third-party victims of accidents caused by vehicles to be compensated for all the damage to property and personal injuries sustained by them, without the insurer being able to rely on statutory provisions or contractual clauses to refuse such compensation. Any other interpretation would deprive that provision of its effectiveness, since it would have the effect of allowing Member States to limit payment of compensation to third-party victims of a road-traffic accident to certain types of damage, thus bringing about disparities in the treatment of victims depending on where the accident occurred, which is precisely what the directives are intended to avoid.
>
> The compulsory insurance contract may, on the other hand, provide that in such cases the insurer is to have a right of recovery against the insured.

Article 3

The members of the family of the insured person, driver or any other person who is liable under civil law in the event of an accident, and whose liability is covered by the insurance referred to in Article 1 (1) shall not be excluded from insurance in respect of their personal injuries by virtue of that relationship.

> CASE
>
> **Case C-348/98 Vitor Manuel Mendes Ferreira and Maria Clara Delgado Correia Ferreira v Companhia de Seguros Mundial Confiança SA [2000] ECR I-6711**
>
> Article 3 of the Second Council Directive (84/5/EEC) of 30 December 1983 requires compulsory insurance against civil liability in respect of the use of motor vehicles to cover personal injuries to passengers who are members of the family of the insured person, of the driver of the vehicle or of any other person who incurs civil liability for an accident and whose liability is covered by compulsory motor-vehicle insurance, where those passengers are carried free of charge, whether or not there is any fault on the part of the driver of the vehicle which caused the accident, only if the domestic law of the Member State concerned requires such cover in respect of personal injuries caused in the same conditions to other third-party passengers.

Article 4

[...]

¶ *This article modifies article 1(4) of the First Motor Liability Directive 72/166/EEC, reproduced supra under no. I. 2. The modification is directly incorporated therein.*

Article 5

1. Member States shall amend their national provisions to comply with this Directive not later than 31 December 1987. They shall forthwith inform the Commission thereof.

2. The provisions thus amended shall be applied not later than 31 December 1988.

3. Notwithstanding paragraph 2:

(a) the Hellenic Republic shall have a period until 31 December 1995 in which to increase guarantees to the levels required by Article 1 (2).

- more than 16% not later than 31 December 1988,
- 31% not later than 31 December 1992;

(b) the other Member States shall have a period until 31 December 1990 in which to increase guarantees to the levels required by Article 1 (2). Member States that avail themselves of this option must, by the date indicated in paragraph 1, increase guarantees by at least half the difference between the guarantees in force on 1 January 1984 and the amounts laid down in Article 1 (2).

4. Notwithstanding paragraph 2:

(a) the Italian Republic may provide that the excess laid down in the fifth subparagraph of Article 1 (4) shall be 1.000 ECU until 31 December 1990;

(b) the Hellenic Republic and Ireland may provide that:
- compensation by the body referred to in Article 1 (4) for damage to property shall be excluded until 31 December 1992,
- the excess referred to in the fifth subparagraph of Article 1 (4) and the excess referred to in the second subparagraph of Article 2 (2) shall be 1.500 ECU until 31 December 1995.

CASE

Case C-348/98 Vitor Manuel Mendes Ferreira and Maria Clara Delgado Correia Ferreira v Companhia de Seguros Mundial Confiança SA [2000] ECR I-6711

See supra under Article 1 of this directive.

Article 6

1. Not later than 31 December 1989 the Commission shall present to the Council a report on the situation in the Member States benefiting from the transitional measures provided for in Article 5 (3) (a) and (4) (b) and shall, where appropriate, submit proposals to review these measures in the light of developments.

2. Not later than 31 December 1993 the Commission shall present to the Council a progress report on the implementation of this Directive and shall, where appropriate, submit proposals in particular as regards adjustment of the amounts laid down in Article 1 (2) and (4).

Article 7

This Directive is addressed to the Member States.

I. 12.

Council Directive 84/641/EEC
of 10 December 1984
amending, particularly as regards tourist assistance, the First Directive (73/239/EEC) on the co-ordination of laws, regulations and administrative provisions relating to the taking-up and pursuit of the business of direct insurance other than life assurance[1]

THE COUNCIL OF THE EUROPEAN COMMUNITIES,

Having regard to the Treaty establishing the European Economic Community, and in particular Article [47(2)][2] thereof,

Having regard to the proposal from the Commission,[3]

Having regard to the opinion of the European Parliament,[4]

Having regard to the opinion of the Economic and Social Committee,[5]

Whereas the First Council Directive (73/239/EEC) of 4 July 1973 on the co-ordination of laws, regulations and administrative provisions relating to the taking-up and pursuit of the business of direct insurance other than life assurance,[6] hereinafter referred to as the 'First Directive', as amended by Directive 76/580/EEC,[7] eliminated certain differences between the laws of Member States in order to facilitate the taking-up and pursuit of the above business;

Whereas considerable progress has been achieved in that area of business involving the provision of benefits in kind; whereas such benefits are governed by provisions that differ from one Member State to another; whereas those differences constitute a barrier to the exercise of the right of establishment;

Whereas, in order to eliminate that barrier to the right of establishment, it should be specified that an activity is not excluded from the application of the First Directive for the simple reason that it constitutes a benefit solely in kind or one for which the person providing it uses his own staff or equipment only; whereas, therefore such provision of assistance consisting in the promise of aid on the occurrence of a chance event should be covered by the above Directive, taking into account the special characteristics of such assistance;

Whereas the purpose of the inclusion, for reasons of supervision, of assistance operations in the scope of the First Directive, which does not involve the definition of these operations, is not to affect the fiscal rules applicable to them;

Whereas the sole fact of providing certain forms of assistance on the occasion of an accident or breakdown involving a road vehicle normally occurring in the territory of the Member State of the undertaking providing cover is not a reason for any person or undertaking that is not an insurance undertaking to be subject to the arrangements of the First Directive;

Whereas provision should be made for certain relaxations to the condition that the accident or breakdown must occur in the territory of the Member State of the undertaking providing cover in order to take into account either the existence of reciprocal agreements or of certain specific circumstances relating to the geographical situation or to the structure of the organisations concerned, or to the very limited economic importance of the operations referred to;

---

[1] OJ L 339, 27.12.1984, 21–25.
[2] The number between brackets has been changed as from 1 May 1999 by article 12 of the Treaty of Amsterdam.
[3] OJ C 51, 10.3.1981, 5 and OJ C 30, 4.2.1983, 6.
[4] OJ C 149, 14.6.1982, 129.
[5] OJ C 343, 31.12.1981, 9.
[6] OJ L 228, 16.8.1973, 3, First Non-Life Insurance Directive, reproduced supra under no. I. 3.
[7] OJ L 189, 13.7.1976, 13, reproduced supra under no. I. 6.

Whereas an organisation of a Member State whose main activity is to provide services on behalf of the public authorities should be excluded from the scope of the First Directive;

Whereas an undertaking offering assistance contracts must possess the means necessary for it to provide the benefits in kind which it offers within an appropriate period of time; whereas special provisions should be laid down for calculating the solvency margin and the minimum amount of the guarantee fund which such undertaking must possess;

Whereas certain transitional provisions are necessary in order to permit undertakings providing only assistance to adapt themselves to the application of the First Directive;

Whereas, having regard to special structural and geographical difficulties, it is necessary to allow a transitional period to the automobile club of a Member State for bringing itself into line with the said Directive concerning repatriation of the vehicle, possibly accompanied by the driver and passengers;

Whereas it is necessary to keep up-to-date the provisions of the First Directive concerning the legal forms which insurance undertakings may assume; whereas certain provisions of the said Directive concerning the rules applicable to agencies or branches established within the Community and belonging to undertakings whose head offices are situated outside the Community should be amended in order to make them consistent with the provisions of Directive 79/267/EEC,[8]

HAS ADOPTED THIS DIRECTIVE:

Articles 1 to 14
[...]

¶ *These articles modify the First Non-Life Insurance Directive 73/239/EEC, reproduced supra under no. I. 3. The modifications are directly incorporated therein.*

---

[8] OJ L 63, 13.3.1979, 1, First Life Assurance Directive, reproduced supra under no. I. 9.

Article 15

Any Member State may, in its territory, make the provision of assistance to persons who get into difficulties in circumstances other than those referred to in Article 1 subject to the arrangements introduced by the First Directive. If a Member State makes use of this possibility it shall, for the purposes of applying these arrangements, treat such activity as if it were listed in class 18 in point A of the Annex to the First Directive without prejudice to point C thereof.

The preceding paragraph shall in no way affect the possibilities for classification laid down in the Annex to the First Directive for activities that obviously come under other classes.

It shall not be possible to refuse authorisation to an agency or branch solely on the grounds that the activity covered by this Article is classified differently in the Member State in the territory of which the head office of the undertaking is situated.

Transitional provisions
Article 16

1. Member States may allow undertakings which, on the date of notification of this Directive, provide only assistance in their territories, a period of five years from that date in order to comply with the requirements set out in Articles 16 and 17 of the First Directive.

2. Member States may allow any undertakings referred to in paragraph 1 which, upon expiry of the five-year period, have not fully established the solvency margin, a further period not exceeding two years in which to do so provided that such undertakings have, in accordance with Article 20 of the First Directive, submitted for the approval of the supervisory authority the measures which they propose to take for that purpose.

3. Any undertaking referred to in paragraph 1 which wishes to extend its business within the meaning of Article 8 (2) or Article 10 of the First Directive may do so only on condition that it complies forthwith with that Directive.

4. Any undertaking referred to in paragraph 1 which has a form different to those referred to in Article 8 of the First Directive may continue for a period of three years from the date of notification of this Directive to carry on its existing business in the form in which it exists on that date.

5. This Article shall apply *mutatis mutandis* to undertakings formed after the date of notification of this Directive, which take over business already conducted on that date by a legally distinct body.

Article 17

Member States may allow agencies and branches referred to in Title III of the First Directive which provide only assistance in the territories of those Member States a maximum period of five years commencing on the date of notification of this Directive in order to comply with Article 25 of the First Directive, provided such agencies or branches do not extend their business within the meaning of Article 10 (2) of the First Directive.

Article 18

During a period of eight years from the date of notification of this Directive, the condition that the accident or breakdown must have happened in the territory of the Member State of the undertaking providing cover shall not apply to the operations referred to in the third indent of the first subparagraph of Article 2 (3) of the First Directive where these operations are carried out by the ELPA (Automobile and Touring Club of Greece).

Final provisions

Article 19

1. Member States shall amend their national provisions in order to comply with this Directive not later than 30 June 1987. They shall forthwith inform the Commission thereof. The provisions thus amended shall, subject to Articles 16, 17 and 18 of this Directive apply at the latest beginning on 1 January 1988.

2. Member States shall communicate to the Commission the texts of the main provisions laid down by law, regulation or administrative action that they adopt in the field governed by this Directive.

Article 20

The Commission shall report to the Council, within six years of notification of this Directive, on the difficulties arising from the application thereof, and in particular Article 15 thereof. It shall, if appropriate, submit proposals to put an end to them.

Article 21

This Directive is addressed to the Member States.

I. 13.

Council Directive 87/343/EEC
of 22 June 1987
amending, as regards credit insurance and suretyship insurance, First Directive 73/239/EEC on the co-ordination of laws, regulations and administrative provisions relating to the taking-up and pursuit of the business of direct insurance other than life assurance[1]

CASE

Case C-63/89 Les Assurances du Crédit SA and Compagnie Belge d'Assurance Crédit SA v Council of the European Communities and Commission of the European Communities [1991] ECR I-1799

The exclusion of public export credit insurance operations from the scope of Directive 73/239/EEC, introduced by that directive and maintained by Directive 87/343, is not discriminatory because it takes account of the differences resulting from the legal and factual situation existing at one stage of the process of co-ordinating the national provisions in the field of insurance. In such operations and at that stage, protection for insured and third parties, which the abovementioned directives seek to provide, is provided by the State itself, so that the obligation to provide financial guarantees, prescribed by the directive for other export credit insurance operations, is not justified.

THE COUNCIL OF THE EUROPEAN COMMUNITIES,

Having regard to the Treaty establishing the European Economic Community, and in particular Article [47(2)][2] thereof,

Having regard to the proposal from the Commission,[3]

Having regard to the opinion of the European Parliament,[4]

Having regard to the opinion of the Economic and Social Committee,[5]

Whereas First Council Directive 73/239/EEC of 24 July 1973 on the co-ordination of laws, regulations and administrative provisions relating to the taking-up and pursuit of the business of direct insurance other than life assurance,[6] as amended by Directive 76/580/EEC,[7] eliminated a number of divergencies in the laws of the Member States in order to facilitate the taking-up and pursuit of that business;

Whereas, however, Article 2 (2) (d) of the said Directive states that it does not apply, 'pending further co-ordination, which shall be implemented within four years of notification of this Directive', to 'export credit insurance operations for the account of or with the support of the State'; whereas, since the protection of insured persons normally provided by the Directive is provided by the State itself where export credit insurance operations are carried out for the account of or with the guarantee of the State, such operations should continue to be excluded from the scope of the said Directive pending further co-ordination;

Whereas Article 7 (2) (c) of the said Directive states that 'pending further co-ordination, which must be implemented within four years of notification of this Directive, the Federal Republic of Germany may maintain the provision prohibiting the simultaneous undertaking in its territory

---

[1] OJ L 185, 4.7.1987, 72–76.
[2] The number between brackets has been changed as from 1 May 1999 by article 12 of the Treaty of Amsterdam.
[3] OJ C 245, 29.9.1979, 7 and OJ C 5, 7.1.1983, 2.
[4] OJ C 291, 10.11.1980, 70.

[5] OJ C 146, 16.6.1980, 6.
[6] OJ L 228, 16.8.1973, 3, First Non-Life Insurance Directive, reproduced supra under no. I. 3.
[7] OJ L 189, 13.7.1976, 13, reproduced supra under no. I. 6.

of health insurance, credit and suretyship insurance or insurance in respect of recourse against third parties and legal defence, either with one another or with other classes'; whereas it follows from this that there are barriers to the establishment of agencies and branches; whereas the present Directive is intended to remedy this situation;

Whereas the interests of insured persons are sufficiently safeguarded, as regards suretyship insurance, by the said Directive; whereas the prohibition in the Federal Republic of Germany on the simultaneous undertaking of suretyship insurance and other classes should be lifted;

Whereas insurance undertakings whose credit insurance business amounts to more than a small proportion of their total business require an equalisation reserve which does not form part of the solvency margin; whereas that reserve should be calculated according to the methods laid down in this Directive, which are recognised as equivalent;

Whereas in view of the cyclical nature of claims in credit insurance, the latter should, for the purposes of calculating the average burden of claims within the meaning of Article 16 (2) of Directive 73/239/EEC, be treated on the same basis as insurance against storm, hail and frost risks;

Whereas the nature of the risk in credit insurance is such that undertakings that transact such business ought to form a higher guarantee fund than is at present provided for in the said Directive;

Whereas a sufficient period of time should be granted to undertakings which are required to meet that obligation;

Whereas it is unnecessary to impose this obligation on undertakings whose operations in this class of insurance do not exceed a certain volume;

Whereas, in view of the provisions of this Directive in respect of credit insurance, the maintenance by the Federal Republic of Germany of the prohibition of the simultaneous undertaking of credit insurance and other classes is no longer justified, and such prohibition should therefore be removed.

HAS ADOPTED THIS DIRECTIVE:

[...]

¶ *This Directive modifies the First Non-Life Insurance Directive 73/239/EEC, reproduced supra under no. I. 3. The modifications are directly incorporated therein.*

I. 14.

Council Directive 87/344/EEC
of 22 June 1987
on the co-ordination of laws, regulations and administrative provisions relating to legal expenses insurance[1]

THE COUNCIL OF THE EUROPEAN COMMUNITIES,

Having regard to the Treaty establishing the European Economic Community, and in particular Article [47(2)][2] thereof,

Having regard to the proposal from the Commission,[3]

Having regard to the opinion of the European Parliament,[4]

Having regard to the opinion of the Economic and Social Committee,[5]

Whereas Council Directive 73/239/EEC of 24 July 1973 on the co-ordination of laws, regulations and administrative provisions relating to the taking-up and pursuit of the business of direct insurance other than life assurance,[6] as last amended by Directive 87/343/EEC,[7] eliminated, in order to facilitate the taking-up and pursuit of such activities, certain differences existing between national laws;

Whereas, however, Article 7 (2) (c) of Directive 73/239/EEC provides that 'pending further co-ordination, which must be implemented within four years of notification of this Directive, the Federal Republic of Germany may maintain the provision prohibiting the simultaneous undertaking in its territory of health insurance, credit and suretyship insurance or insurance in respect of recourse against third parties and legal defence, either with one another or with other classes';

Whereas the present Directive provides for the co-ordination of legal expenses insurance as envisaged in Article 7 (2) (c) of Directive 73/239/EEC;

Whereas, in order to protect insured persons, steps should be taken to preclude, as far as possible, any conflict of interests between a person with legal expenses cover and his insurer arising out of the fact that the latter is covering him in respect of any other class of insurance referred to in the Annex to Directive 73/239/EEC or is covering another person and, should such a conflict arise, to enable it to be resolved;

Whereas legal expenses insurance in respect of disputes or risks arising out of, or in connection with, the use of sea-going vessels should, in view of its specific nature, be excluded from the scope of this Directive;

Whereas the activity of an insurer who provides services or bears the cost of defending the insured person in connection with a civil liability contract should also be excluded from the scope of this Directive if that activity is at the same time pursued in the insurer's own interest under such cover;

Whereas Member States should be given the option of excluding from the scope of this Directive the activity of legal expenses insurance undertaken by an assistance insurer where this activity is carried out in a Member State other than the one in which the insured person normally resides and where it forms part of a contract covering solely the assistance provided for persons who fall into difficulties while travelling,

---

[1] OJ L 185, 4.7.1987, 77–80.
[2] The number between brackets has been changed as from 1 May 1999 by article 12 of the Treaty of Amsterdam.
[3] OJ C 198, 7.8.1979, 2.
[4] OJ C 260, 12.10.1981, 78.
[5] OJ C 348, 31.12.1980, 22.
[6] OJ L 228, 16.8.1973, 3, First Non-Life Insurance Directive, reproduced supra under no. I. 3.
[7] OJ L 185, 4.7.1987, 72, reproduced supra under no. I. 13.

while away from home or while away from their permanent residence;

Whereas the system of compulsory specialisation at present applied by one Member State, namely the Federal Republic of Germany, precludes the majority of conflicts; whereas, however, it does not appear necessary, in order to obtain this result, to extend that system to the entire Community, which would require the splitting-up of composite undertakings;

Whereas the desired result can also be achieved by requiring undertakings to provide for a separate contract or a separate section of a single policy for legal expenses insurance and by obliging them either to have separate management for legal expenses insurance, or to entrust the management of claims in respect of legal expenses insurance to an undertaking having separate legal personality, or to afford the person having legal expenses cover the right to choose his lawyer from the moment that he has the right to claim from his insurer;

Whereas, whichever solution is adopted, the interest of persons having legal expenses cover shall be protected by equivalent safeguards;

Whereas the interest of persons having legal expenses cover means that the insured person must be able to choose a lawyer or other person appropriately qualified according to national law in any inquiry or proceedings and whenever a conflict of interests arises;

Whereas Member States should be given the option of exempting undertakings from the obligation to give the insured person this free choice of lawyer if the legal expenses insurance is limited to cases arising from the use of road vehicles on their territory and if other restrictive conditions are met;

Whereas, if a conflict arises between insurer and insured, it is important that it be settled in the fairest and speediest manner possible; whereas it is therefore appropriate that provision be made in legal expenses insurance policies for an arbitration procedure or a procedure offering comparable guarantees;

Whereas the second paragraph of point C of the Annex to Directive 73/239/EEC provides that the risks included in classes 14 and 15 in point A may not be regarded as risks ancillary to other classes; whereas an insurance undertaking should not be able to cover legal expenses as a risk ancillary to another risk without having obtained an authorisation in respect of the legal expenses risk; whereas, however, Member States should be given the option of regarding class 17 as a risk ancillary to class 18 in specific cases; whereas, therefore, point C of the said Annex should be amended accordingly,

HAS ADOPTED THIS DIRECTIVE:

Article 1

The purpose of this Directive is to co-ordinate the provisions laid down by law, regulation or administrative action concerning legal expenses insurance as referred to in paragraph 17 of point A of the Annex to Council Directive 73/239/EEC in order to facilitate the effective exercise of freedom of establishment and preclude as far as possible any conflict of interest arising in particular out of the fact that the insurer is covering another person or is covering a person in respect of both legal expenses and any other class in that Annex and, should such a conflict arise, to enable it to be resolved.

Article 2

1. This Directive shall apply to legal expenses insurance. Such consists in undertaking, against the payment of a premium, to bear the costs of legal proceedings and to provide other services directly linked to insurance cover, in particular with a view to:
– securing compensation for the loss, damage or injury suffered by the insured person, by settlement out of court or through civil or criminal proceedings,
– defending or representing the insured person in civil, criminal, administrative or other proceedings or in respect of any claim made against him.

This Directive shall not, however, apply to:
– legal expenses insurance where such insurance concerns disputes or risks arising out of,

or in connection with, the use of sea-going vessels,
- the activities pursued by the insurer providing civil liability cover for the purpose of defending or representing the insured person in any inquiry or proceedings if that activity is at the same time pursued in the insurer's own interest under such cover,
- where a Member State so chooses, the activity of legal expenses insurance undertaken by an assistance insurer where this activity is carried out in a Member State other than the one in which the insured person normally resides, where it forms part of a contract covering solely the assistance provided for persons who fall into difficulties while travelling, while away from home or while away from their permanent residence. In this event the contract must clearly state that the cover in question is limited to the circumstances referred to in the foregoing sentence and is ancillary to the assistance.

Article 3

1. Legal expenses cover shall be the subject of a contract separate from that drawn up for the other classes of insurance or shall be dealt with in a separate section of a single policy in which the nature of the legal expenses cover and, should the Member State so request, the amount of the relevant premium are specified.

2. Each Member State shall take the necessary measures to ensure that the undertakings established within its territory adopt, in accordance with the option imposed by the Member State, or at their own choice, if the Member State so agrees, at least one of the following solutions, which are alternatives:

(a) the undertaking shall ensure that no member of the staff who is concerned with the management of legal expenses claims or with legal advice in respect thereof carries on at the same time a similar activity
- if the undertaking is a composite one, for another class transacted by it,
- irrespective of whether the undertaking is a composite or a specialised one, in another having financial, commercial or administrative links with the first undertaking and carrying on one or more of the other classes of insurance set out in Directive 73/239/EEC;

(b) the undertaking shall entrust the management of claims in respect of legal expenses insurance to an undertaking having separate legal personality. That undertaking shall be mentioned in the separate contract or separate section referred to in paragraph 1. If the undertaking having separate legal personality has links with an undertaking which carries on one or more of the other classes of insurance referred to in point A of the Annex to Directive 73/239/EEC, members of the staff of the undertaking who are concerned with the processing of claims or with legal advice connected with such processing may not pursue the same or a similar activity in the other undertaking at the same time. In addition, Member States may impose the same requirements on the members of the management body;

(c) the undertaking shall, in the contract, afford the insured person the right to entrust the defence of his interests, from the moment that he has the right to claim from his insurer under the policy, to a lawyer of his choice or, to the extent that national law so permits, any other appropriately qualified person.

3. Whichever solution is adopted, the interest of persons having legal expenses cover shall be regarded as safeguarded in an equivalent manner under this Directive.

Article 4

1. Any contract of legal expenses insurance shall expressly recognise that:

(a) where recourse is had to a lawyer or other person appropriately qualified according to national law in order to defend, represent or serve the interests of the insured person in any inquiry or proceedings, that insured person shall be free to choose such lawyer or other person;

(b) the insured person shall be free to choose a lawyer or, if he so prefers and to the extent that national law so permits, any other appropriately qualified person, to serve his interests whenever a conflict of interests arises.

2. Lawyer means any person entitled to pursue his professional activities under one of the denominations laid down in Council Directive 77/249/EEC of 22 March 1977 to facilitate the effective exercise by lawyers of freedom to provide services.[8]

Article 5

1. Each Member State may provide exemption from the application of Article 4 (1) for legal expenses insurance if all the following conditions are fulfilled:

(a) the insurance is limited to cases arising from the use of road vehicles in the territory of the Member State concerned;

(b) the insurance is connected to a contract to provide assistance in the event of accident or breakdown involving a road vehicle;

(c) neither the legal expenses insurer nor the assistance insurer carries out any class of liability insurance;

(d) measures are taken so that the legal counsel and representation of each of the parties to a dispute is effected by completely independent lawyers when these parties are insured for legal expenses by the same insurer.

2. The exemption granted by a Member State to an undertaking pursuant to paragraph 1 shall not affect the application of Article 3 (2).

Article 6

Member States shall adopt all appropriate measures to ensure that, without prejudice to any right of appeal to a judicial body which might be provided for by national law, an arbitration or other procedure offering comparable guarantees of objectivity is provided for whereby, in the event of a difference of opinion between a legal expenses insurer and his insured, a decision can be taken on the attitude to be adopted in order to settle the dispute.

The insurance contract must mention the right of the insured person to have recourse to such a procedure.

Article 7

Whenever a conflict of interests arises or there is disagreement over the settlement of the dispute, the legal expenses insurer or, where appropriate, the claims settlement office shall inform the person insured of
– the right referred to in Article 4,
– the possibility of having recourse to the procedure referred to in Article 6.

Article 8

Member States shall abolish all provisions that prohibit an insurer from carrying out within their territory legal expenses insurance and other classes of insurance at the same time.

Article 9

[. . .]

¶ *This article modifies Annex (C), paragraph 2(2) of the First Non-Life Insurance Directive 73/239/EEC, reproduced supra under no. I. 3. The modification is directly incorporated therein.*

Article 10

Member States shall take the measures necessary to comply with this Directive by 1 January 1990. They shall forthwith inform the Commission thereof.

They shall apply these measures from 1 July 1990 at the latest.

Article 11

Following notification[9] of this Directive, Member States shall communicate to the Commission the texts of the main provisions of national law that they adopt in the field governed by this Directive.

Article 12

This Directive is addressed to the Member States.

---

[8] OJ L 78, 26.3.1977, 17.

[9] This Directive was notified to the Member States on 25 June 1987.

I. 15.

Council Directive 88/357/EEC
of 22 June 1988
on the co-ordination of laws, regulations and administrative provisions relating to direct insurance other than life assurance and laying down provisions to facilitate the effective exercise of freedom to provide services and amending Directive 73/239/EEC
(Second non-life insurance Directive)[1]

THE COUNCIL OF THE EUROPEAN COMMUNITIES,

Having regard to the Treaty establishing the European Economic Community, and in particular Articles [47 (2) and 55][2] thereof,

Having regard to the proposal from the Commission,[3]

In co-operation with the European Parliament,[4]

Having regard to the opinion of the Economic and Social Committee,[5]

Whereas it is necessary to develop the internal insurance market and, to achieve this objective, it is desirable to make it easier for insurance undertakings having their head office in the Community to provide services in the Member States, thus making it possible for policy-holders to have recourse not only to insurers established in their own country, but also to insurers which have their head office in the Community and are established in other Member States;

Whereas, pursuant to the Treaty, any discrimination with regard to freedom to provide services based on the fact that an undertaking is not established in the Member State in which the services are provided has been prohibited since the end of the transitional period; whereas this prohibition applies to services provided from any establishment in the Community, whether it is the head office of an undertaking or an agency or branch;

Whereas, for practical reasons, it is desirable to define the provision of services taking into account both the insurer's establishment and the place where the risk is situated; whereas therefore a definition of the situation of the risk should also be adopted; whereas, moreover, it is desirable to distinguish between the activity pursued by way of establishment and the activity pursued by way of freedom to provide services;

Whereas it is desirable to supplement the First Council Directive 73/239/EEC of 24 July 1973 on the co-ordination of laws, regulations and administrative provisions relating to the taking-up and pursuit of the business of direct insurance other than life assurance,[6] hereinafter referred to as the 'first Directive', as last amended by Directive 87/343/EEC,[7] in order particularly to clarify the powers and means of supervision vested in the supervisory authorities; whereas it is also desirable to lay down specific provisions regarding the taking-up, pursuit and supervision of activity by way of freedom to provide services;

Whereas policy-holders who, by virtue of their status, their size or the nature of the risk to be insured, do not require special protection in the State in which the risk is situated should be granted complete freedom to avail themselves of the widest possible insurance market; whereas,

---

[1] OJ L 172, 4.7.1988, 1–14.
[2] The numbers between brackets have been changed as from 1 May 1999 by article 12 of the Treaty of Amsterdam.
[3] OJ C 32, 12.2.1976, 2.
[4] OJ C 36, 13.2.1978, 14, OJ C 167, 27.6.1988 and OJ C 187, 18.7.1988, 94.
[5] OJ C 204, 30.8.1976, 13.

[6] OJ L 228, 16.8.1973, 3, First Non-Life Insurance Directive, reproduced supra under no. I. 3.
[7] OJ L 185, 4.7.1987, 72, reproduced supra under no. I. 13.

moreover, it is desirable to guarantee other policy-holders adequate protection;

Whereas the concern to protect policyholders and to avoid any disturbance of competition justifies co-ordinating the relaxation of the matching assets rules, provided for by the first Directive;

Whereas the provisions in force in the Member States regarding insurance contract law continue to differ; whereas the freedom to choose, as the law applicable to the contract, a law other than that of the State in which the risk is situated may be granted in certain cases, in accordance with rules taking into account specific circumstances;

Whereas the scope of this Directive should include compulsory insurance but should require the contract covering such insurance to be in conformity with the specific provisions relating to such insurance, as provided by the Member State imposing the insurance obligation;

Whereas the provisions of the first Directive on the transfer of portfolio should be reinforced and supplemented by provisions specifically covering the transfer of the portfolio of contracts concluded for the provision of services to another undertaking;

Whereas the scope of the provisions specifically concerning freedom to provide services should exclude certain risks, the application to which of the said provisions is rendered inappropriate at this stage by the specific rules adopted by the Member States' authorities, owing to the nature and social implications of such provisions; whereas, therefore, these exclusions should be re-examined after this Directive has been in force for a certain period;

Whereas, in the interests of protecting policy-holders, Member States should, at the present stage in co-ordination, be allowed the option of limiting the simultaneous pursuit of activity by way of freedom to provide services and activity by way of establishment; whereas no such limitation can be provided for where policy-holders do not require this protection;

Whereas the taking-up and pursuit of freedom to provide services should be subject to procedures guaranteeing the insurance undertaking's compliance with the provisions regarding both financial guarantees and conditions of insurance; whereas these procedures may be relaxed in cases where the activity by way of provision of services covers policy-holders who, by virtue of their status, their size or the nature of the risk to be insured, do not require special protection in the State in which the risk is situated;

Whereas it is necessary to initiate special co-operation with regard to freedom to provide services between the competent supervisory authorities of the Member States and between these authorities and the Commission; whereas provision should also be made for a system of penalties to apply where the undertaking providing the service fails to comply with the provisions of the Member State of provision of service;

Whereas, pending future co-ordination, the technical reserves should be subject to the rules and supervision of the Member State of provision of services where such provision of services involves risks in respect of which the State receiving the service wishes to provide special protection for policyholders; whereas, however, if such concern to protect the policy-holders is unjustified, the technical reserves continue to be subject to the rules and supervision of the Member State in which the insurer is established;

Whereas some Member States do not subject insurance transactions to any form of indirect taxation, while the majority apply special taxes and other forms of contribution, including surcharges intended for compensation bodies; whereas the structure and rate of these taxes and contributions vary considerably between the Member States in which they are applied; whereas it is desirable to avoid a situation where existing differences lead to disturbances of competition in insurance services between Member States; whereas, pending future harmonisation, the application of the tax system and of other forms of contributions provided for by the Member State in which the risk is situated is likely to remedy such mischief and whereas it is for the Member States to establish a method of ensuring that such taxes and contributions are collected;

Whereas it is desirable to prevent the uncoordinated application of this Directive and of Council Directive 78/473/EEC of 30 May 1978 on the co-ordination of laws, regulations and administrative provisions relating to Community co-insurance[8] from leading to the existence of three different systems in every Member State; whereas, therefore, the criteria defining 'large risks' in this Directive should also define risks likely to be covered under Community co-insurance arrangements;

Whereas it is desirable to take into account, within the meaning of Article [20][2] of the Treaty, the extent of the effort which needs to be made by certain economies showing differences in development; whereas, therefore, it is desirable to grant certain Member States transitional arrangements for the gradual application of the specific provisions of this Directive relating to freedom to provide services,

HAS ADOPTED THIS DIRECTIVE:

Title I

General Provisions

Article 1

The object of this Directive is:

(a) to supplement the first Directive 73/239/EEC;

(b) to lay down special provisions relating to freedom to provide services for the undertakings and in respect of the classes of insurance covered by that first Directive.

Article 2

For the purposes of this Directive:

(a) 'first Directive' means:

Directive 73/239/EEC;

(b) 'undertaking':

- for the purposes of applying Titles I and II, means:

---

[8] OJ L 151, 7.6.1978, 25, reproduced supra under no. I. 8.

any undertaking that has received official authorisation under Articles 6 or 23 of the first Directive;

- for the purposes of applying Title III and Title V, means:

any undertaking that has received official authorisation under Article 6 of the first Directive;

(c) 'establishment' means:

the head office, agency or branch of an undertaking, account being taken of Article 3;

(d) 'Member State where the risk is situated' means:

- the Member State in which the property is situated, where the insurance relates either to buildings or to buildings and their contents, in so far as the contents are covered by the same insurance policy,
- the Member State of registration, where the insurance relates to vehicles of any type,
- the Member State where the policy-holder took out the policy in the case of policies of a duration of four months or less covering travel or holiday risks, whatever the class concerned,
- the Member State where the policy-holder has his habitual residence or, if the policy-holder is a legal person, the Member State where the latter's establishment, to which the contract relates, is situated, in all cases not explicitly covered by the foregoing indents;

(e) 'Member State of establishment' means:

the Member State in which the establishment covering the risk is situated;

(f) 'Member State of provision of services' means:

the Member State in which the risk is situated when it is covered by an establishment situated in another Member State.

Case

Case C-191/99 Kvaerner plc v Staatssecretaris van Financiën [2001] ECR I-4447

1. Articles 2(c) and (d), final indent, and 3 of the Second Council Directive (88/357/EEC) of 22 June 1988 on the co-ordination of laws, regulations and administrative provisions relating to direct insurance other than life assurance and laying down provisions to facilitate the effective exercise of freedom to provide services and amending Directive

73/239/EEC permit a Member State to levy insurance tax on a legal person established in another Member State in respect of premiums which that legal person has paid to an insurer, also established in another Member State, to cover the business risks of its subsidiary or sub-subsidiary established in the Member State making the levy. It makes no difference if the legal person who paid the premiums and the legal person whose business risks are covered are two companies in the same group linked by a relationship other than that of parent and subsidiary company.

2. In interpreting 'policy-holder' or 'Member State in which the risk is situated' for the purposes of Article 2(d), final indent, of Directive 88/357/EEC, the way in which the premium relating to the risk insured is invoiced or paid within a group of companies is immaterial.

Article 3

For the purposes of the first Directive and of this Directive, any permanent presence of an undertaking in the territory of a Member State shall be treated in the same way as an agency or branch, even if that presence does not take the form of a branch or agency, but consists merely of an office managed by the undertaking's own staff or by a person who is independent but has permanent authority to act for the undertaking as an agency would.

Article 4

For the purposes of this Directive and the first Directive, general and special policy conditions shall not include specific conditions intended to meet, in an individual case the particular circumstances of the risk to be covered.

TITLE II

PROVISIONS SUPPLEMENTARY TO THE FIRST DIRECTIVE

Article 5

[. . .]

¶ *This article modifies article 5 of the First Non-Life Insurance Directive 73/239/EEC, reproduced supra under no. I. 3. The modification is directly incorporated therein.*

Article 6

For the purposes of applying the first subparagraph of Article 15 (2) and Article 24 of the first Directive, the Member States shall comply with Annex I to this Directive as regards the matching rules.

Article 7

1. The law applicable to contracts of insurance referred to by this Directive and covering risks situated within the Member States is determined in accordance with the following provisions:

(a) Where a policy-holder has his habitual residence or central administration within the territory of the Member State in which the risk is situated, the law applicable to the insurance contract shall be the law of that Member State. However, where the law of that Member State so allows, the parties may choose the law of another country.

(b) Where a policy-holder does not have his habitual residence or central administration in the Member State in which the risk is situated, the parties to the contract of insurance may choose to apply either the law of the Member State in which the risk is situated or the law of the country in which the policy-holder has his habitual residence or central administration.

(c) Where a policy-holder pursues a commercial or industrial activity or a liberal profession and where the contract covers two or more risks relating to these activities and situated in different Member States, the freedom of choice of the law applicable to the contract shall extend to the laws of those Member States and of the country in which the policy-holder has his habitual residence or central administration.

(d) Notwithstanding subparagraphs (b) and (c), where the Member States referred to in those subparagraphs grant greater freedom of choice of the law applicable to the contract, the parties may take advantage of this freedom.

(e) Notwithstanding subparagraphs (a), (b) and (c), when the risks covered by the contract are limited to events occurring in one Member State other than the Member State where the risk is situated, as defined in Article 2 (d), the parties may always choose the law of the former State.

[(f) In the case of the risks referred to in Article 5 (d) of Directive 73/239/EEC, the parties to the contract may choose any law.]

(g) The fact that, in the cases referred to in subparagraph (a) or (f), the parties have chosen a law shall not, where all the other elements relevant to the situation at the time of the choice are connected with one Member State only, prejudice the application of the mandatory rules of the law of that Member State, which means the rules from which the law of that Member State allows no derogation by means of a contract.

(h) The choice referred to in the preceding subparagraphs must be expressed or demonstrated with reasonable certainty by the terms of the contract or the circumstances of the case. If this is not so, or if no choice has been made, the contract shall be governed by the law of the country, from amongst those considered in the relevant subparagraphs above, with which it is most closely connected. Nevertheless, a severable part of the contract which has a closer connection with another country, from amongst those considered in the relevant subparagraphs, may by way of exception be governed by the law of that other country. The contract shall be rebuttably presumed to be most closely connected with the Member State in which the risk is situated.

(i) Where a State includes several territorial units, each of which has its own rules of law concerning contractual obligations, each unit shall be considered as a country for the purposes of identifying the law applicable under this Directive.

A Member State in which various territorial units have their own rules of law concerning contractual obligations shall not be bound to apply the provisions of this Directive to conflicts which arise between the laws of those units.

2. Nothing in this Article shall restrict the application of the rules of the law of the forum in a situation where they are mandatory, irrespective of the law otherwise applicable to the contract.

If the law of a Member State so stipulates, the mandatory rules of the law of the Member State in which the risk is situated or of the Member State imposing the obligation to take out insurance may be applied if and in so far as, under the law of those States, those rules must be applied whatever the law applicable to the contract.

Where the contract covers risks situated in more than one Member State, the contract is considered for the purposes of applying this paragraph as constituting several contracts each relating to only one Member State.

3. Subject to the preceding paragraphs, the Member States shall apply to the insurance contracts referred to by this Directive their general rules of private international law concerning contractual obligations.

¶ *Paragraph 1(f) has been replaced by article 27 of the Third Non-Life Insurance Directive 92/49/EEC, reproduced infra under no. I. 25.*

Article 8

1. Under the conditions set out in this Article, insurance undertakings may offer and conclude compulsory insurance contracts in accordance with the rules of this Directive and of the first Directive.

2. When a Member State imposes an obligation to take out insurance, the contract shall not satisfy that obligation unless it is in accordance with the specific provisions relating to that insurance laid down by that Member State.

3. When, in the case of compulsory insurance, the law of the Member State in which the risk is situated and the law of the Member State imposing the obligation to take out insurance contradict each other, the latter shall prevail.

4. [(a) Subject to subparagraph (c), the third subparagraph of Article 7 (2) shall apply where the insurance contract provides cover in two or more Member States, at least one of which makes insurance compulsory.]

(b) [. . .]

(c) A Member State may, by way of derogation from Article 7, lay down that the law applicable to a compulsory insurance contract is the law of the State that imposes the obligation to take out insurance.

(d) Where a Member State imposes compulsory insurance and the insurer must notify the competent authorities of any cessation of cover, such cessation may be invoked against injured third parties only in the circumstances laid down in the legislation of that State.

5. (a) Each Member State shall communicate to the Commission the risks against which insurance is compulsory under its legislation, stating:
– the specific legal provisions relating to that insurance,
– the particulars which must be given in the certificate which an insurer must issue to an insured person where that State requires proof that the obligation to take out insurance has been complied with. A Member State may require that those particulars include a declaration by the insurer to the effect that the contract complies with the specific provisions relating to that insurance.

(b) The Commission shall publish the particulars referred to in subparagraph (a) in the Official Journal of the European Communities.

(c) A Member State shall accept, as proof that the insurance obligation has been fulfilled, a certificate, the content of which is in conformity with the second indent of subparagraph (a).

¶ *Paragraph 4(a) has been replaced and paragraph 4(b) has been repealed by article 30(1) of the Third Non-Life Insurance Directive 92/49/EEC, reproduced infra under no. I. 25.*
¶ *See further article 30(2) of the Third Non-Life Insurance Directive 92/49/EEC, reproduced infra under no. I. 25.*

Articles 9 to 10

[. . .]

¶ *These articles modify articles 8(3), 9, 10(3), 11(1) and 19 of the First Non-Life Insurance Directive 73/239/EEC, reproduced supra under no. I. 3. The modifications are directly incorporated therein.*

Article 11

[. . .]

¶ *Paragraph 1 repeals article 21 of the First Non-Life Insurance Directive 73/239/EEC, reproduced supra under no. I. 3. The modification is directly incorporated therein.*
¶ *Paragraphs 2 to 7 have been repealed by article 12 of the Third Non-Life Insurance Directive 92/49/EEC, reproduced infra under no. I. 25.*

TITLE III

PROVISIONS PECULIAR TO THE FREEDOM TO PROVIDE SERVICES

Article 12

1. This Title shall apply where an undertaking, through an establishment situated in a Member State, covers a risk situated, within the meaning of Article 2 (d), in another Member State; the latter shall be the Member State of provision of services for the purposes of this Title.

2. This Title shall not apply to the transactions, undertakings and institutions to which the first Directive does not apply, nor to the risks to be covered by the institutions under public law referred to in Article 4 of that Directive.

[. . .]

¶ *The second and third subparagraph of paragraph 2 have been modified by article 5 of Directive 90/618/EEC, reproduced infra under no. I. 17 and subsequently repealed together with paragraph 3 by article 37 of the Third Non-Life Insurance Directive 92/49/EEC, reproduced infra under no. I. 25.*

[Article 12a

1. This Article shall apply where an undertaking, through an establishment situated in a Member State, covers a risk, other than carrier's liability, classified under class 10 of point A of the Annex to Directive 73/239/EEC which is situated in another Member State.

2. The Member State of provision of services shall require the undertaking to become a member of and participate in the financing of its national bureau and its national guarantee fund.

The undertaking shall not, however, be required to make any payment or contribution to the bureau and fund of the Member State of provision of services in respect of risks covered by way of provision of services other than one calculated on the same basis as for undertakings covering risks, other than carrier's liability, in class 10 through an establishment situated in that Member State, by reference to its premium income from that class in that Member State or the number of risks in that class covered there.

3. This Directive shall not prevent an insurance undertaking providing services from being required to comply with the rules in the Member State of provision of services concerning the cover of aggravated risks, insofar as they apply to established undertakings.

4. The Member State of provision of services shall require the undertaking to ensure that persons pursuing claims arising out of events occurring in its territory are not placed in a less favourable situation as a result of the fact that the undertaking is covering a risk, other than carrier's liability, in class 10 by way of provision of services rather than through an establishment situated in that State.

For this purpose, the Member State of provision of services shall require the undertaking to appoint a representative resident or established in its territory who shall collect all necessary information in relation to claims, and shall possess sufficient powers to represent the undertaking in relation to persons suffering damage who could pursue claims, including the payment of such claims, and to represent it or, where necessary, to have it represented before the courts and authorities of that Member State in relation to these claims.

The representative may also be required to represent the undertaking before the competent authorities of the State of provision of services with regard to checking the existence and validity of motor vehicle liability insurance policies.

[The Member State of provision of services may not require that appointee to undertake activities on behalf of the undertaking which appointed him other than those set out in the second and third subparagraphs.

The appointment of the representative shall not in itself constitute the opening of a branch or agency for the purpose of Article 6 (2) (b) of Directive 73/239/EEC and the representative shall not be an establishment within the meaning of Article 2 (c) of this Directive.]

¶ *This article has been inserted by article 6 of Directive 90/618/EEC, reproduced infra under no. I. 17.*

¶ *The fourth subparagraph of Article 12a(4) has been amended by article 3 of Directive 2005/14/EC, reproduced infra under no. I. 39.*

Article 13

[...]

¶ *This article has been repealed by article 37 of the Third Non-Life Insurance Directive 92/49/EEC, reproduced infra under no. I. 25.*

[Article 14

Any undertaking that intends to carry on business for the first time in one or more Member States under the freedom to provide services shall first inform the competent authorities of the home Member State, indicating the nature of the risks it proposes to cover.]

¶ *This article has been replaced by article 34 of the Third Non-Life Insurance Directive 92/49/EEC, reproduced infra under no. I. 25.*

Article 15

[...]

¶ *This article has been modified by article 7 of Directive 90/618/EEC, reproduced infra under no. I. 17 and subsequently repealed by article 37 of the Third Non-Life Insurance Directive 92/49/EEC, reproduced infra under no. I. 25.*

[Article 16

1. Within one month of the notification provided for in Article 14, the competent authorities of the home Member State shall communicate to the Member State or Member States within the territories of which an undertaking intends to carry on business under the freedom to provide services:

(a) a certificate attesting that the undertaking has the minimum solvency margin calculated in accordance with Articles 16 and 17 of Directive 73/239/EEC;

(b) The classes of insurance that the undertaking has been authorised to offer;

(c) The nature of the risks that the undertaking proposes to cover in the Member State of the provision of services.

At the same time, they shall inform the undertaking concerned accordingly.

Each Member State within the territory of which an undertaking intends, under the freedom to provide services, to cover risks in class 10 of point A of the Annex to Directive 73/239/EEC other than carrier's liability may require that the undertaking:
– communicate the name and address of the representative referred to in Article 12a (4) of this Directive,
– produce a declaration that the undertaking has become a member of the national bureau and national guarantee fund of the Member State of the provision of services.

2. Where the competent authorities of the home Member State do not communicate the information referred to in paragraph 1 within the period laid down, they shall give the reasons for their refusal to the undertaking within that same period. That refusal shall be subject to a right to apply to the courts in the home Member State.

3. The undertaking may start business on the certified date on which it is informed of the communication provided for in the first subparagraph of paragraph 1.]

¶ *This article has been modified by article 7 of Directive 90/618/EEC, reproduced infra under no. I. 17, and subsequently replaced by article 35 of the Third Non-Life Insurance Directive 92/49/EEC, reproduced infra under no. I. 25.*

[*Article 17*]

Any change that an undertaking intends in make to the information referred to in Article 14 shall be subject to the procedure provided for in Articles 14 and 16.]

¶ *This article has been replaced by article 36 of the Third Non-Life Insurance Directive 92/49/EEC, reproduced infra under no. I. 25.*

Articles 18 to 25

[. . .]

¶ *Articles 21 and 22 have been modified by articles 8 and 9 of Directive 90/618/EEC, reproduced infra under no. I. 17.*
¶ *Articles 18 to 25 have been repealed by article 19, 40(1), 42(1), 43(1), 44(1), 45(1) and 46(1) of the Third Non-Life Insurance Directive 92/49/EEC, reproduced infra under no. I. 25.*

Article 26

1. The risks, which may be covered by way of Community co-insurance within the meaning of Directive 78/473/EEC, shall be those defined in Article 5 (d) of the first Directive.

2. The provisions of this Directive regarding the risks defined in Article 5 (d) of the first Directive shall apply to the leading insurer.

TITLE IV

TRANSITIONAL ARRANGEMENTS

Article 27

1. Greece, Ireland, Spain and Portugal may apply the following transitional arrangements:

(i) until 31 December 1992, they may apply, to all risks, the regime other than that for risks referred to in Article 5 (d) of the first Directive,

(ii) from 1 January 1993 to 31 December 1994, the regime for large risks shall apply to risks referred to under (i) and (ii) of Article 5 (d) of the first Directive; for risks referred to under (iii) of the above-mentioned Article 5 (d), these Member States shall fix the thresholds to apply therefore;

(iii) Spain
– from 1 January 1995 to 31 December 1996, the thresholds of the first stage described in Article 5 (d) (iii) of the first Directive shall apply,
– from 1 January 1997, the thresholds of the second stage shall apply.

Portugal, Ireland and Greece
– from 1 January 1995 to 31 December 1998 the thresholds of the first stage described in Article 5 (d) (iii) of the first Directive shall apply,
– from 1 January 1999 the thresholds of the second stage shall apply.

[The derogation allowed from 1 January 1995 shall only apply to contracts covering risks classified under classes 3, 8, 9,10,13 and 16 situated exclusively in one of the four Member States benefiting from the transitional arrangements.]

2. Until 31 December 1994, Article 26 (1) of this Directive shall not apply to risks situated in the

four Member States listed in this Article. For the transitional period from 1 January 1995, the risks defined under Article 5 (d) (iii) of the first Directive situated in these Member States and capable of being covered by Community co-insurance within the meaning of Directive 78/473/EEC shall be those which exceed the thresholds referred to in paragraph 1 (iii) of this Article.

¶ *The last subparagraph of paragraph 1 has been replaced by article 10 of Directive 90/618/EEC, reproduced infra under no. I. 17.*

Title V
Final Provisions

Article 28

The Commission and the competent authorities of the Member States shall collaborate closely for the purpose of facilitating the supervision of direct insurance within the Community.

Every Member State shall inform the Commission of any major difficulties to which application of this Directive gives rise, inter alia any arising if a Member State becomes aware of an abnormal transfer of insurance business to the detriment of undertakings established in its territory and to the advantage of branches and agencies located just beyond its borders.

The Commission and the competent authorities of the Member States concerned shall examine these difficulties as quickly as possible in order to find an appropriate solution.

Where necessary, the Commission shall submit appropriate proposals to the Council.

Article 29

The Commission shall forward to the Council regular reports, the first on 1 July 1993, on the development of the market in insurance transacted under conditions of freedom to provide services.

Article 30

Where this Directive makes reference to the ECU, the exchange value in national currencies to be used with effect from 31 December of each year shall be the value which applies on the last day of the preceding October for which exchange values for the ECU are available in all Community currencies.

Article 2 of Directive 76/580/EEC[9] shall apply only to Articles 3, 16 and 17 of the first Directive.

Article 31

Every five years, the Council, acting on a proposal from the Commission, shall review and if necessary amend any amounts expressed in ECU in this Directive, taking into account changes in the economic and monetary situation of the Community.

Article 32

Member States shall amend their national provisions to comply with this Directive within 18 months of the date of its notification[10] and shall forthwith inform the Commission thereof.

The provisions amended in accordance with this Article shall be applied within 24 months of the date of the notification of the Directive.

Article 33

Upon notification of this Directive, Member States shall ensure that the texts of the main laws, regulations or administrative provisions, which they adopt in the field covered by this Directive, are communicated to the Commission.

Article 34

The Annexes shall form an integral part of this Directive.

Article 35

This Directive is addressed to the Member States.

---

[9] OJ L 189, 13.9.1976, 13, reproduced supra under no. I. 6.
[10] This Directive was notified to the Member States on 30 June 1988.

Annex I

Matching rules

The currency in which the insurer's commitments are payable shall be determined in accordance with the following rules:

1. Where the cover provided by a contract is expressed in terms of a particular currency, the insurer's commitments are considered to be payable in that currency.

2. Where the cover provided by a contract is not expressed in terms of any currency, the insurer's commitments are considered to be payable in the currency of the country in which the risk is situated. However, the insurer may choose the currency in which the premium is expressed if there are justifiable grounds for exercising such a choice.

This could be the case if, from the time the contract is entered into, it appears likely that a claim will be paid in the currency of the premium and not in the currency of the country in which the risk is situated.

3. The Member States may authorise the insurer to consider that the currency in which he must provide cover will be either that which he will use in accordance with experience acquired or, in the absence of such experience, the currency of the country in which he is established:
   - for contracts covering risks classified under classes 4, 5, 6, 7, 11, 12 and 13 (producers' liability only), and
   - for contracts covering the risks classified under other classes where, in accordance with the nature of the risks, the cover is to be provided in a currency other than that which would result from the application of the above procedures.

4. Where a claim has been reported to an insurer and is payable in a specified currency other than the currency resulting from application of the above procedures, the insurer's commitments shall be considered to be payable in that currency, and in particular the currency in which the compensation to be paid by the insurer has been determined by a court judgment or by agreement between the insurer and the insured.

5. Where a claim is assessed in a currency which is known to the insurer in advance but which is different from the currency resulting from application of the above procedures, the insurers may consider their commitments to be payable in that currency.

6. The Member States may authorise undertakings not to cover their technical reserves by matching assets if application of the above procedures would result in the undertaking—whether head office or branch—being obliged, in order to comply with the matching principle, to hold assets in a currency amounting to not more than 7% of the assets existing in other currencies.

However:

(a) in the case of technical reserve assets to be matched in Greek drachmas, Irish pounds and Portuguese escudos, this amount shall not exceed:
   - 1 million ECU during a transitional period ending 31 December 1992,
   - 2 million ECU from 1 January 1993 to 31 December 1998;

(b) in the case of technical reserve assets to be matched in Belgian francs, Luxembourg francs and Spanish pesetas, this amount shall not exceed 2 million ECU during a transitional period ending 31 December 1996.

From the end of the transitional periods defined under (a) and (b), the general regime shall apply for these currencies, unless the Council decides otherwise.

7. The Member States may choose not to require undertakings—whether head offices or

branches—to apply the matching principle where commitments are payable in a currency other than the currency of one of the Community Member States, if investments in that currency are regulated, if the currency is subject to transfer restrictions or if, for similar reasons, it is not suitable for covering technical reserves.

[8. Insurance undertakings may hold non-matching assets to cover an amount not exceeding 20% of their commitments in a particular currency.

9. A Member State may provide that when under the preceding procedures a commitment must be covered by assets expressed in a Member State's currency that requirement shall also be considered as satisfied when the assets are expressed in ecus.]

¶ *Points 8 and 9 have been replaced by article 23 of the Third Non-Life Insurance Directive 92/49/EEC, reproduced infra under no. I. 25.*

Annex 2A

Underwriting account

1. Total gross premiums earned
2. Total cost of claims
3. Commission costs
4. Gross underwriting result.

Annex 2B

Underwriting account

1. Gross premiums for the last underwriting year
2. Gross claims in the last underwriting year (including reserve at the end of underwriting year)
3. Commission costs
4. Gross underwriting result.

I. 16.

Council Directive 90/232/EEC
of 14 May 1990
on the approximation of the laws of the Member States relating to insurance against civil liability in respect of the use of motor vehicles
(Third motor insurance Directive)[1]

THE COUNCIL OF THE EUROPEAN COMMUNITIES,

Having regard to the Treaty establishing the European Economic Community, and in particular Article [95][2] thereof,

Having regard to the proposal from the Commission,[3]

In co-operation with the European Parliament,[4]

Having regard to the opinion of the Economic and Social Committee,[5]

Whereas, by Directive 72/166/EEC,[6] as last amended by Directive 84/5/EEC[7], the Council adopted provisions on the approximation of the laws of the Member States relating to insurance against civil liability in respect of the use of motor vehicles and to the enforcement of the obligation to insure against such liability;

Whereas Article 3 of Directive 72/166/EEC requires each Member State to take all appropriate measures to ensure that civil liability in respect of the use of vehicles normally based in its territory is covered by insurance; whereas the extent of the liability covered and the terms and conditions of the insurance cover should be determined on the basis of those measures;

Whereas Directive 84/5/EEC, as amended by the Act of Accession of Spain and Portugal, reduced considerably the disparities between the level and content of compulsory civil liability insurance in the Member States; whereas significant disparities still exist, however, in such insurance cover;

Whereas motor vehicle accident victims should be guaranteed comparable treatment irrespective of where in the Community accidents occur;

Whereas there are, in particular, gaps in the compulsory insurance cover of motor vehicle passengers in certain Member States; whereas, to protect this particularly vulnerable category of potential victims, such gaps should be filled;

Whereas any uncertainty concerning the application of the first indent of Article 3 (2) of Directive 72/166/EEC should be removed; whereas all compulsory motor insurance policies must cover the entire territory of the Community;

Whereas in the interests of the party insured, every insurance policy should, moreover, guarantee for a single premium, in each Member State, the cover required by its law or the cover required by the law of the Member State where the vehicle is normally based, when that cover is higher;

Whereas Article 1 (4) of Directive 84/5/EEC requires each Member State to set up or authorise a body to compensate the victims of accidents caused by uninsured or unidentified vehicles; whereas, however, the said provision is without prejudice to the right of the Member States to regard compensation by this body as subsidiary or non-subsidiary;

Whereas, however, in the case of an accident caused by an uninsured vehicle, the victim is required in certain Member States to prove that the party liable is unable or refuses to pay

---

[1] OJ L 129, 19.5.1990, 33–36.
[2] The number between brackets has been changed as from 1 May 1999 by article 12 of the Treaty of Amsterdam.
[3] OJ C 16, 20.1.1989, 12.
[4] OJ C 304, 4.12.1989, 41 and OJ C 113, 7.5.1990, 74.
[5] OJ C 159, 26.6.1989, 7.
[6] OJ L 103, 2.5.1972, 1, First Motor Liability Directive, reproduced supra under no. I. 2.
[7] OJ L 8, 11.1.1984, 17, Second Motor Liability Directive, reproduced supra under no. I. 11.

compensation before he can claim on the body; whereas this body is better placed than the victim to bring an action against the party liable; whereas, therefore, this body should be prevented from being able to require that the victim, if he is to be compensated, should establish that the party liable is unable or refuses to pay;

Whereas, in the event of a dispute between the body referred to above and a civil liability insurer as to which of them should compensate the victim of an accident, Member States, to avoid any delay in the payment of compensation to the victim, should ensure that one of these parties is designated to be responsible in the first instance for paying compensation pending resolution of the dispute;

Whereas motor vehicle accident victims sometimes have difficulties in finding out the name of the insurance undertaking covering the liability arising out of the use of a motor vehicle involved in an accident; whereas, in the interests of such victims, Member States should take the necessary measures to ensure that such information is made available promptly;

Whereas the previous two Directives on civil liability in respect of motor vehicles should, in view of all these considerations, be supplemented in a uniform manner;

Whereas such an addition, which leads to greater protection for the parties insured and for the victims of accidents, will facilitate still further the crossing of internal Community frontiers and hence the establishment and functioning of the internal market; whereas, therefore, a high level of consumer protection should be taken as a basis;

Whereas, under the terms of Article [20]² of the Treaty, account should be taken of the extent of the effort that must be made by certain economies that show differences in development; whereas certain Member States should, therefore, be granted transitional arrangements so that certain provisions of this Directive may be implemented gradually,

HAS ADOPTED THIS DIRECTIVE:

Article 1

Without prejudice to the second subparagraph of Article 2 (1) of Directive 84/5/EEC, the insurance referred to in Article 3 (1) of Directive 72/166/EEC shall cover liability for personal injuries to all passengers, other than the driver, arising out of the use of a vehicle.

[Member States shall take the necessary measures to ensure that any statutory provision or any contractual clause contained in an insurance policy which excludes a passenger from such cover on the basis that he knew or should have known that the driver of the vehicle was under the influence of alcohol or of any other intoxicating agent at the time of an accident, shall be deemed to be void in respect of the claims of such passenger.]

For the purposes of this Directive, the meaning of the term 'vehicle' is as defined in Article 1 of Directive 72/166/EEC.

¶ *The second paragraph of this article has been inserted by article 4(1) of Directive 2005/14/EC, reproduced infra under no. I. 39.*

[Article 1a

The insurance referred to in Article 3(1) of Directive 72/166/EEC shall cover personal injuries and damage to property suffered by pedestrians, cyclists and other non-motorised users of the roads who, as a consequence of an accident in which a motor vehicle is involved, are entitled to compensation in accordance with national civil law. This Article shall be without prejudice either to civil liability or to the amount of damages.]

¶ *This article has been inserted by article 4(2) of Directive 2005/14/EC, reproduced infra under no. I. 39.*

Article 2

Member States shall take the necessary steps to ensure that all compulsory insurance policies against civil liability arising out of the use of vehicles:

[– cover, on the basis of a single premium and during the whole term of the contract, the

entire territory of the Community, including for any period in which the vehicle remains in other Member States during the term of the contract] and
– guarantee, on the basis of the same single premium, in each Member State, the cover required by its law or the cover required by the law of the Member State where the vehicle is normally based when that cover is higher.

¶ *The first indent of this article has been replaced by article 4(3) of Directive 2005/14/EC, reproduced infra under no. I. 39.*

Article 3

[. . .]

¶ *This article modifies article 1(4) of the Second Motor Liability Directive 84/5/EEC, reproduced supra under no. I. 11. The modification is directly incorporated therein.*

Article 4

In the event of a dispute between the body referred to in Article 1 (4) of Directive 84/5/EEC and the civil liability insurer as to which must compensate the victim, the Member States shall take the appropriate measures so that one of these parties is designated to be responsible in the first instance for paying compensation to the victim without delay.

If it is ultimately decided that the other party should have paid all or part of the compensation, that other party shall reimburse accordingly the party that has paid.

[Article 4a

1. By way of derogation from the second indent of Article 2(d) of Directive 88/357/EEC,[8] where a vehicle is dispatched from one Member State to another, the Member State where the risk is situated shall be considered to be the Member State of destination, immediately upon acceptance of delivery by the purchaser for a period of thirty days, even though the vehicle has not formally been registered in the Member State of destination.

2. In the event that the vehicle is involved in an accident during the period mentioned in paragraph 1 of this Article while being uninsured, the body referred to in Article 1(4) of Directive 84/5/EEC in the Member State of destination shall be liable for the compensation provided for in Article 1 of the said Directive.

Article 4b

Member States shall ensure that the policyholder has the right to request at any time a statement relating to the third party liability claims involving the vehicle or vehicles covered by the insurance contract at least during the preceding five years of the contractual relationship, or to the absence of such claims. The insurance undertaking, or a body which may have been appointed by a Member State to provide compulsory insurance or to supply such statements, shall provide this statement to the policyholder within 15 days of the request.

Article 4c

Insurance undertakings shall not rely on excesses against the injured party to an accident as far as the insurance referred to in Article 3(1) of Directive 72/166/EEC is concerned.

Article 4d

Member States shall ensure that injured parties to accidents caused by a vehicle covered by insurance as referred to in Article 3(1) of Directive 72/166/EEC enjoy a direct right of action against the insurance undertaking covering the person responsible against civil liability.

Article 4e

Member States shall establish the procedure provided for in Article 4(6) of Directive

---

[8] Second Council Directive 88/357/EEC of 22 June 1988 on the coordination of laws, regulations and administrative provisions relating to direct insurance other than life assurance and laying down provisions to facilitate the effective exercise of freedom to provide services (OJ L 172, 4.7.1988, 1), reproduced supra under no. I. 15. Directive as last amended by Directive 2000/26/EC of the European Parliament and of the Council (OJ L 181, 20.7.2000, 65), reproduced infra under no. I. 30.

2000/26/EC(⁹) for the settlement of claims arising from any accident caused by a vehicle covered by insurance as referred to in Article 3(1) of Directive 72/166/EEC.

In the case of accidents which may be settled by the system of national insurers' bureaux provided for in Article 2(2) of Directive 72/166/EEC, Member States shall establish the same procedure as in Article 4(6) of Directive 2000/26/EC. For the purpose of applying this procedure, any reference to insurance undertaking shall be understood as a reference to national insurers' bureaux as defined in Article 1, point 3 of Directive 72/166/EEC.]

¶ *Articles 4a, 4b, 4c, 4d and 4e have been inserted by article 4(4) of Directive 2005/14/EC, reproduced infra under no. I. 39.*

Article 5

[1. Member States shall ensure that, without prejudice to their obligations under Directive 2000/26/EC, the information centres established or approved in accordance with Article 5 of that Directive, provide the information specified in that Article to any party involved in any traffic accident caused by a vehicle covered by insurance as referred to in Article 3(1) of Directive 72/166/EEC.]

2. Not later than 31 December 1995, the Commission shall present to the European Parliament and the Council a report on the implementation of paragraph 1 of this Article.

Where necessary, the Commission shall submit appropriate proposals to the Council.

¶ *Article 5(1) has been replaced by article 4(5) of Directive 2005/14/EC, reproduced infra under no. I. 39.*

Article 6

1. Member States shall take the measures necessary to comply with this Directive not later than 31 December 1992. They shall forthwith inform the Commission thereof.

2. By way of exception from paragraph 1:
– the Hellenic Republic, the Kingdom of Spain and the Portuguese Republic have until 31 December 1995 to comply with Articles 1 and 2,
– Ireland shall have until 31 December 1998 to comply with Article 1 as regards pillion passengers of motorcycles and until 31 December 1995 to comply with Article 1 as regards other vehicles and to comply with Article 2.

Article 7

This Directive is addressed to the Member States.

---

⁹ Directive 2000/26/EC of the European Parliament and of the Council of 16 May 2000 on the approximation of the laws of the Member States relating to insurance against civil liability in respect of the use of motor vehicles (fourth motor insurance Directive) (OJ L 181, 20.7.2000, 65), reproduced infra under no. I. 30.

I. 17.

Council Directive 90/618/EEC
of 8 November 1990
amending, particularly as regards motor vehicle liability insurance, Directive 73/239/EEC and Directive 88/357/EEC, which concern the co-ordination of laws, regulations and administrative provisions relating to direct insurance other than life assurance[1]

THE COUNCIL OF THE EUROPEAN COMMUNITIES,

Having regard to the Treaty establishing the European Economic Community, and in particular Articles [47 (2) and 55][2] thereof,

Having regard to the proposal from the Commission,[3]

In co-operation with the European Parliament,[4]

Having regard to the opinion of the Economic and Social Committee,[5]

Whereas in order to develop the internal insurance market, the Council adopted on 24 July 1973 Directive 73/239/EEC on the co-ordination of laws, regulations and administrative provisions relating to the taking-up and pursuit of the business of direct insurance other than life assurance[6] (also referred to as the 'First Directive') and on 22 June 1988 Directive 88/357/EEC on the co-ordination of laws, regulations and administrative provisions relating to direct insurance other than life assurance and laying down provisions to facilitate the effective exercise of freedom to provide services and amending Directive 73/239/EEC[7] (also referred to as the 'Second Directive');

Whereas Directive 88/357/EEC made it easier for insurance undertakings having their head office in the Community to provide services in the Member States, thus making it possible for policyholders to have recourse not only to insurers established in their own country, but also to insurers who have their head office in the Community and are established in other Member States;

Whereas the scope of the provisions of Directive 88/357/EEC specifically concerning freedom to provide services excluded certain risks, the application to which of the said provisions was rendered inappropriate at that stage by the specific rules adopted by the Member States' authorities, owing to the nature and social implications of such provisions; whereas those exclusions were to be re-examined after that Directive had been implemented for a certain period;

Whereas one of the exclusions concerned motor vehicle liability insurance, other than carrier's liability;

Whereas, however, when the abovementioned Directive was adopted the Commission gave an undertaking to present to the Council as soon as possible a proposal concerning freedom to provide services in the area of insurance against civil liability in respect of the use of motor vehicles (other than carrier's liability);

Whereas, subject to the provisions of the said Directive concerning compulsory insurance, it is appropriate to provide for the possibility of large risk treatment, within the meaning of Article 5 of the said Directive, for the said insurance class of motor vehicle liability;

---

[1] OJ L 330, 29.11.1990, 44–49.
[2] The numbers between brackets have been changed as from 1 May 1999 by article 12 of the Treaty of Amsterdam.
[3] OJ C 65, 15.3.1989, 6, and OJ C 180, 20.7.1990, 6.
[4] OJ C 68, 19.3.1990, 85 and OJ C 284, 12.11.1990, 70.
[5] OJ C 194, 31.7.1989, 3.
[6] OJ L 228, 16.8.1973, 3, First Non-Life Insurance Directive, reproduced supra under no. I. 3.
[7] OJ L 172, 4.7.1988, 1, Second Non-Life Insurance Directive, reproduced supra under no. I. 15.

Whereas large risk treatment should also be envisaged for insurance covering damage to or loss of land motor vehicles and land vehicles other than motor vehicles;

Whereas Directive 88/357/EEC laid down that the risks which may be covered by way of Community co-insurance within the meaning of Council Directive 78/473/EEC of 30 May 1978 on the co-ordination of laws, regulations and administrative provisions relating to Community co-insurance[8] were to be large risks as defined in Directive 88/357/EEC whereas the inclusion by the present Directive of the motor insurance classes in the large risks definition of Directive 88/357/EEC will have the effect of including those classes in the list of classes which may be covered by way of Community co-insurance;

Whereas Council Directive 72/166/EEC of 24 April 1972 on the approximation of the laws of the Member States relating to insurance against civil liability in respect of the use of motor vehicles, and to the enforcement of the obligation to insure against such liability,[9] as last amended by Directive 90/232/EEC[10] built on the green card system and the agreements between the national motor insurers' bureaux in order to enable green card checks to be abolished;

Whereas it is desirable, however, to grant Member States transitional arrangements for the gradual application of the specific provisions of this Directive relating to large risk treatment for the said insurance classes, including where risks are covered by co-insurance;

Whereas to ensure the continued proper functioning of the green card system and the agreements between the national motor insurers' bureaux it is appropriate to require insurance undertakings providing motor liability insurance in a Member State by way of provision of services to join and participate in the financing of the bureau of that Member State;

Whereas Council Directive 84/5/EEC of 30 December 1983 on the approximation of the laws of the Member States relating to insurance against civil liability in respect of the use of motor vehicles[11] as last amended by Directive 90/232/EEC, required the Member States to set up or authorise a body (guarantee fund) with the task of providing compensation to victims of accidents caused by uninsured or unidentified vehicles;

Whereas it is also appropriate to require insurance undertakings providing motor liability insurance in a Member State by way of provision of services to join and participate in the financing of the guarantee fund set up in that Member State;

Whereas the rules in force in some Member States concerning the cover of aggravated risks apply to all undertakings covering risks through an establishment situated there; whereas the purpose of those rules is to ensure that the compulsory nature of motor liability insurance is balanced by the possibility for motorists to obtain such insurance; whereas Member States should be permitted to apply those rules to undertakings providing services in their territories to the extent that the rules are justified in the public interest and do not exceed what is necessary to achieve the abovementioned purpose;

Whereas in the field of motor liability insurance the protection of the interests of persons suffering damage who could pursue claims in fact concerns each and everyone and that it is therefore advisable to ensure that these persons are not prejudiced or put to greater inconvenience where the motor liability insurer is operating by way of provision of services rather than by way of establishment; whereas for this purpose, and insofar as the interests of these persons are not sufficiently safeguarded by the rules applying to the supplier of services in the Member State in which it is established, it should be provided that the Member State of provision of services shall require the undertaking to appoint a representative resident

---

[8] OJ L 151, 7.6.1978, 25, reproduced supra under no. I. 8.
[9] OJ L 103, 2.5.1972, 1, First Motor Liability Directive, reproduced supra under no. I. 2.
[10] OJ L 129, 19.5.1990, 33, Third Motor Liability Directive, reproduced supra under no. I. 16.

[11] OJ L 8, 11.1.1984, 17, Second Motor Liability Directive, reproduced supra under no. I. 11.

or established in its territory to collect all necessary information in relation to claims and shall possess sufficient powers to represent the undertaking in relation to persons suffering damage who could pursue claims, including the payment of such claims, and to represent it or, where necessary, to have it represented before the courts and authorities of that Member State in relation to these claims;

Whereas this representative may also be required to represent the undertaking before the competent authorities of the Member State of provision of services in relation to the control of the existence and validity of motor vehicle liability insurance policies;

Whereas provision should be made for a flexible procedure to make it possible to assess reciprocity with third countries on a Community basis; whereas the aim of this procedure is not to close the Community's financial markets but rather, as the Community intends to keep its financial markets open to the rest of the world, to improve the liberalisation of the global financial markets in third countries; whereas, to that end, this Directive provided for procedures for negotiating with third countries and, as a last resort, for the possibility of taking measures involving the suspension of new applications for authorisation or the restriction of new authorisations,

HAS ADOPTED THIS DIRECTIVE:

Article 1

For the purposes of this Directive:

(a) 'vehicle' means a vehicle as defined in Article 1 (1) of Directive 72/166/EEC;

(b) 'bureau' means a national insurers' bureau as defined in Article 1 (3) of Directive 72/166/EEC;

(c) 'guarantee fund' means the body referred to in Article 1 (4) of Directive 84/5/EEC;

(d) 'parent undertaking' means a parent undertaking as defined in Articles 1 and 2 of Directive 83/349/EEC;[12]

---

[12] OJ L 193, 18.7.1983, 1, Seventh Company Law Directive, reproduced supra under no. C. 6.

(e) 'subsidiary' means a subsidiary undertaking as defined in Articles 1 and 2 of Directive 83/349/EEC; any subsidiary undertaking of a subsidiary undertaking shall also be regarded as a subsidiary of the parent undertaking which is at the head of those undertakings.

Articles 2 to 4

[. . .]

¶ *These articles modify the First Non-Life Insurance Directive 73/239/EEC, reproduced supra under no. I. 3. The modifications are directly incorporated therein.*

Articles 5 to 10

[. . .]

¶ *These articles modify the Second Non-Life Insurance Directive 88/357/EEC, reproduced supra under no. I. 15. The modifications are directly incorporated therein.*

Article 11

Notwithstanding Article 23 (2) of Directive 88/357/EEC, in the case of a large risk within the meaning of Article 5 (d) of Directive 73/239/EEC, classified under class 10, other than carrier's liability, the Member State of provision of services may provide that:

– the amount of the technical reserves relating to the contract concerned shall be determined, under the supervision of the authorities of that Member State, in accordance with its rules or, failing such rules, in accordance with established practice in that Member State, until the date by which the Member States must comply with a Directive co-ordinating the annual accounts of insurance undertakings,

– the covering of these reserves by equivalent and matching assets shall be under the supervision of the authorities of that Member State in accordance with its rules or practice, until the notification of a Third Directive on non-life insurance,

– the localisation of the assets referred to in the second indent shall be under the supervision of the authorities of that Member State in accordance with its rules or practice until the date by which the Member States must comply with a Third Directive on non-life insurance.

¶ *Article 23 of the Second Non-Life Insurance Directive 88/357/EEC has been repealed by article 19 of Third Non-Life Insurance Directive 92/49/EEC, reproduced infra under no. I. 25.*

Article 12

Member States shall amend their national provisions to comply with this Directive within 18 months of the date of its notification[13] and shall forthwith inform the Commission thereof.

The provisions amended pursuant to the first subparagraph shall be applied within 24 months of the date of the notification of this Directive.

Article 13

This Directive is addressed to the Member States.

---

[13] This Directive was notified to the Member States on 20 November 1990.

I. 18.

Council Directive 90/619/EEC
of 8 November 1990
on the co-ordination of laws, regulations and administrative provisions relating to direct life assurance, laying down provisions to facilitate the effective exercise of freedom to provide services and amending Directive 79/267/EEC
(Second life assurance Directive)[1]

This Directive has been repealed as from 19 December 2002 by Annex V, part A of Directive 2002/83/EC (OJ L 345, 19.12.2002, 1), reproduced infra under no. I. 33.

Correlation table

Directive 90/619/EEC	Directive 2002/83/EC
Article 2(c)	Article 1(1)(c)
Article 2(e)	Article 1(1)(g)
Article 3	Article 1(1)(b)
Article 4	Article 32
Article 11	Article 41
Article 14	Article 42
Article 15	Article 35
Article 17	Article 43
Article 28, first subparagraph	Article 62, first subparagraph
Article 28, second to fourth subparagraphs	Article 62, second to fourth subparagraphs
Article 29	Article 63
Article 31	Article 70

---

[1] OJ L 330, 29.11.1990, 50–61.

I. 19.

Council Regulation 1534/91/EEC
of 31 May 1991
on the application of Article [81(3)][1] of the Treaty to certain categories of agreements, decisions and concerted practices in the insurance sector[2]

THE COUNCIL OF THE EUROPEAN COMMUNITIES,

Having regard to the Treaty establishing the European Economic Community, and in particular Article [83][1] thereof,

Having regard to the proposal from the Commission,[3]

Having regard to the opinion of the European Parliament,[4]

Having regard to the opinion of the Economic and Social Committee,[5]

Whereas Article [81(1)][1] of the Treaty may, in accordance with Article [81(3)],[1] be declared inapplicable to categories of agreements, decisions and concerted practices when satisfy the requirements of Article [81(3)];[1]

Whereas the detailed rules for the application of Article [81(3)][1] of the Treaty must be adopted by way of a Regulation based on Article [83][1] of the Treaty;

Whereas co-operation between undertakings in the insurance sector is, to a certain extent, desirable to ensure the proper functioning of this sector and may at the same time promote consumers' interests;

Whereas the application of Council Regulation 4064/89/EEC of 21 December 1989 on the control of concentrations between undertakings[6] enables the Commission to exercise close supervision on issues arising from concentrations in all sectors, including the insurance sector;

Whereas exemptions granted under Article [81(3)][1] of the Treaty cannot themselves affect Community and national provisions safeguarding consumers' interests in this sector;

Whereas agreements, decisions and concerted practices serving such aims may, in so far as they fall within the prohibition contained in Article [81(1)][1] of the Treaty, be exempted there from under certain conditions; whereas this applies in particular to agreements, decisions and concerted practices relating to the establishment of common risk premium tariffs based on collectively ascertained statistics or the number of claims, the establishment of standard policy conditions, common coverage of certain types of risks, the settlement of claims, the testing and acceptance of security devices, and registers of, and information on, aggravated risks;

Whereas in view of the large number of notifications submitted pursuant to Council Regulation No 17 of 6 February 1962: First Regulation implementing Articles [81 and 82][1] of the Treaty,[7] as last amended by the Act of Accession of Spain and Portugal, it is desirable that in order to facilitate the Commission's task, it should be enabled to declare, by way of Regulation, that the provisions of Article [81(1)][1] of the Treaty are inapplicable to certain categories of agreements, decisions and concerted practices;

Whereas it should be laid down under which conditions the Commission, in close and constant liaison with the competent authorities of the Member States, may exercise such powers;

Whereas, in the exercise of such powers, the Commission will take account not only of the

---

[1] The number between brackets has been changed as from 1 May 1999 by article 12 of the Treaty of Amsterdam.
[2] OJ L 143, 7.6.1991, 1–3.
[3] OJ C 16, 23.1.1990, 13.
[4] OJ C 260, 15.10.1990, 57.
[5] OJ C 182, 23.7.1990, 27.
[6] OJ L 395, 30.12.1989, 1.

[7] OJ 13, 21.2.1962, 204/62.

risk of competition being eliminated in a substantial part of the relevant market and of any benefit that might be conferred on policyholders resulting from the agreements, but also of the risk which the proliferation of restrictive clauses and the operation of accommodation companies would entail for policyholders;

Whereas the keeping of registers and the handling of information on aggravated risks should be carried out subject to the proper protection of confidentiality;

Whereas, under Article 6 of Regulation No 17, the Commission may provide that a decision taken in accordance with Article [81(3)][1] of the Treaty shall apply with retroactive effect; whereas the Commission should also be able to adopt provisions to such effect in a Regulation;

Whereas, under Article 7 of Regulation No 17, agreements, decisions and concerted practices may, by decision of the Commission, be exempted from prohibition, in particular if they are modified in such manner that they satisfy the requirements of Article [81(3)][1] of the Treaty; whereas it is desirable that the Commission be enabled to grant by Regulation like exemption to such agreements, decisions and concerted practices if they are modified in such manner as to fall within a category defined in an exempting Regulation;

Whereas it cannot be ruled out that, in specific cases, the conditions set out in Article [81(3)][1] of the Treaty may not be fulfilled; whereas the Commission must have the power to regulate such cases pursuant to Regulation No 17 by way of a Decision having effect for the future,

HAS ADOPTED THIS REGULATION:

Article 1

1. Without prejudice to the application of Regulation No 17, the Commission may, by means of a Regulation and in accordance with Article [81(3)][1] of the Treaty, declare that Article [81(1)][1] shall not apply to categories of agreements between undertakings, decisions of associations of undertakings and concerted practices in the insurance sector which have as their object co-operation with respect to:

(a) the establishment of common risk premium tariffs based on collectively ascertained statistics or the number of claims;

(b) the establishment of common standard policy conditions;

(c) the common coverage of certain types of risks;

(d) the settlement of claims;

(e) the testing and acceptance of security devices;

(f) registers of, and information on, aggravated risks, provided that the keeping of these registers and the handling of this information is carried out subject to the proper protection of confidentiality.

2. The Commission Regulation referred to in paragraph 1, shall define the categories of agreements, decisions and concerted practices to which it applies and shall specify in particular:

(a) the restrictions or clauses that may, or may not, appear in the agreements, decisions and concerted practices;

(b) the clauses that must be contained in the agreements, decisions and concerted practices or the other conditions that must be satisfied.

Article 2

Any Regulation adopted pursuant to Article 1 shall be of limited duration.

It may be repealed or amended where circumstances have changed with respect to any of the facts that were essential to its being adopted; in such case, a period shall be fixed for modification of the agreements, decisions and concerted practices to which the earlier Regulation applies.

Article 3

A Regulation adopted pursuant to Article 1 may provide that it shall apply with retroactive effect to agreements, decisions and concerted practices to which, at the date of entry into force of the said Regulation, a Decision taken with retroactive effect pursuant to Article 6 of Regulation No 17 would have applied.

Article 4

1. A Regulation adopted pursuant to Article 1 may provide that the prohibition contained in Article [81(1)][1] of the Treaty shall not apply, for such period as shall be fixed in that Regulation, to agreements, decisions and concerted practices already in existence on 13 March 1962 which do not satisfy the conditions of Article [81(3)][1] where:
– within six months from the entry into force of the said Regulation, they are so modified as to satisfy the said conditions in accordance with the provisions of the said Regulation and
– the modifications are brought to the notice of the Commission within the time limit fixed by the said Regulation.

The provisions of the first subparagraph shall apply in the same way to those agreements, decisions and concerted practices existing at the date of accession of new Member States to which Article [81(1)][1] of the Treaty applies by virtue of accession and which do not satisfy the conditions of Article [81(3)].[1]

2. Paragraph 1 shall apply to agreements, decisions and concerted practices that had to be notified before 1 February 1963, in accordance with Article 5 of Regulation No 17, only where they have been so notified before that date.

Paragraph 1 shall not apply to agreements, decisions and concerted practices existing at the date of accession of new Member States to which Article [81(1)][1] of the Treaty applies by virtue of accession and which had to be notified within six months from the date of accession in accordance with Articles 5 and 25 of Regulation No 17, unless they have been so notified within the said period.

3. The benefit of provisions adopted pursuant to paragraph 1 may not be invoked in actions pending at the date of entry into force of a Regulation adopted pursuant to Article 1; neither may it be invoked as grounds for claims for damages against third parties.

Article 5

Where the Commission proposes to adopt a Regulation, it shall publish a draft thereof to enable all persons and organisations concerned to submit to it their comments within such time limit, being not less than one month, as it shall fix.

Article 6

1. The Commission shall consult the Advisory Committee on Restrictive Practices and Monopolies:

(a) before publishing a draft Regulation;

(b) before adopting a Regulation.

2. Article 10 (5) and (6) of Regulation No 17, relating to consultation of the Advisory Committee, shall apply. However, joint meetings with the Commission shall take place not earlier than one month after dispatch of the notice convening them.

Article 7

Where the Commission, either on its own initiative or at the request of a Member State or of natural or legal persons claiming a legitimate interest, finds that, in any particular case, agreements, decisions and concerted practices, to which a Regulation adopted pursuant to Article 1 applies, have nevertheless certain effects which are incompatible with the conditions laid down in Article [81(3)][1] of the Treaty, it may withdraw the benefit of application of the said regulation and take a decision in accordance with Articles 6 and 8 of Regulation No 17, without any notification under Article 4 (1) of Regulation No 17 being required.

Article 8

Not later than six years after the entry into force of the Commission Regulation provided for in Article 1, the Commission shall submit to the European Parliament and the Council a report on the functioning of this Regulation, accompanied by such proposals for amendments to this Regulation as may appear necessary in the light of experience.

This Regulation shall be binding in its entirety and directly applicable in all Member States.

I. 20.

(Acts whose publication is obligatory)

Council Regulation 2155/91/EEC
of 20 June 1991
laying down particular provisions for the application of Articles 37, 39 and 40 of the Agreement between the European Economic Community and the Swiss Confederation on direct insurance other than life assurance[1]

THE COUNCIL OF THE EUROPEAN COMMUNITIES,

Having regard to the Treaty establishing the European Economic Community, and in particular the last sentence of [Article 47 (2) and Article 308][2] thereof,

Having regard to the proposal from the Commission,[3]

In co-operation with the European Parliament,[4]

Having regard to the opinion of the Economic and Social Committee,[5]

Whereas an Agreement between the European Economic Community and the Swiss Confederation on direct insurance other than life assurance was signed at Luxembourg on 10 October 1989;

Whereas under that Agreement a Joint Committee is to be set up to administer the Agreement, ensure that it is properly implemented and take decisions in the circumstances provided for therein; whereas the Community's representatives on the Joint Committee have to be designated and particular provisions have to be adopted concerning the determination of the Community's positions in the Committee,

HAS ADOPTED THIS REGULATION:

Article 1

The Community shall be represented on the Joint Committee provided for in Article 37 of the Agreement by the Commission, assisted by representatives of the Member States.

Article 2

The Community's position in the Joint Committee shall be adopted by the Council acting by a qualified majority on a proposal from the Commission.

With regard to the adoption of decisions to be taken by the Joint Committee pursuant to Articles 37, 39 and 40 of the Agreement, the Commission shall submit proposals to the Council, which shall act by a qualified majority.

Article 3

This Regulation shall enter into force on the day following that of its publication in the *Official Journal of the European Communities*.

This Regulation shall be binding in its entirety and directly applicable in all Member States.

---

[1] OJ L 205, 27.7.1991, 1.
[2] The numbers between brackets have been changed as from 1 May 1999 by article 12 of the Treaty of Amsterdam.
[3] OJ C 53, 5.3.1990, 46.
[4] OJ C 72, 18.3.1991, 175, and Decision of 12 June 1991 (not yet published in the Official Journal).
[5] OJ C 56, 7.3.1990, 27.

I. 21.

Council Directive 91/371/EEC
of 20 June 1991
on the implementation of the Agreement between the European Economic Community and the Swiss Confederation concerning direct insurance other than life assurance[1]

THE COUNCIL OF THE EUROPEAN COMMUNITIES,

Having regard to the Treaty establishing the European Economic Community, and in particular the last sentence of [Article 47 (2) and Article 308][2] thereof,

Having regard to the proposal from the Commission,[3]

In co-operation with the European Parliament,[4]

Having regard to the opinion of the Economic and Social Committee,[5]

Whereas an Agreement between the European Economic Community and the Swiss Confederation concerning direct insurance other than life assurance was signed at Luxembourg on 10 October 1989,

Whereas one of the effects of that Agreement is to impose, in relation to insurance undertakings which have their head offices in Switzerland, legal rules different from those applicable, under Title III of Council Directive 73/239/EEC of 24 July 1973 on the co-ordination of laws, regulations and administrative provisions relating to the taking up and pursuit of the business of direct insurance other than life assurance,[6] to agencies and branches established within the Community of undertakings whose head offices are outside the Community,

Whereas the co-ordinated rules relating to the pursuit of these activities within the Community by the Swiss undertakings subject to the provisions of the said Agreement must take effect on the same date in all the Member States of the Community; whereas that Agreement will not come into force until the first day of the calendar year following the date on which the instruments of approval are exchanged,

HAS ADOPTED THIS DIRECTIVE:

Article 1

The Member States shall amend their national provisions to comply with the Agreement between the European Economic Community and the Swiss Confederation within a period of 24 months following the notification of this Directive. They shall immediately inform the Commission thereof.

When Member States adopt these measures, they shall contain a reference to this Directive or shall be accompanied by such reference on the occasion of their official publication. The methods of making such a reference shall be laid down by the Member States.

Article 2

The Member States shall specify in their national provisions that the amendments thereto made pursuant to the Agreement shall not come into force until the date on which the Agreement enters into force.

Article 3

This Directive is addressed to the Member States.

---

[1] OJ L 205, 27.7.1991, 48.
[2] The numbers between brackets have been changed as from 1 May 1999 by article 12 of the Treaty of Amsterdam.
[3] OJ C 53, 5. 3. 1990, 45.
[4] OJ C 72, 18. 3. 1991, 175, and Decision of 12 June 1991 (not yet published in the Official Journal).
[5] OJ C 56, 7. 3. 1990, 27.
[6] OJ L 228, 16. 8. 1973, 3, First Life Assurance Directive, reproduced supra under no. I. 3.

I. 22.

Commission Recommendation 92/48/EEC
of 18 December 1991
on insurance intermediaries[1]

THE COMMISSION OF THE EUROPEAN COMMUNITIES,

Having regard to the Treaty establishing the European Economic Community, and in particular Article [211][2] thereof,

Whereas insurance intermediaries are an important factor in the distribution of insurance in the Member States; whereas the creation of the internal market will entail an increasing range of products as a result of the freedom to provide services; whereas the professional competence of insurance intermediaries is an essential element for the protection of the policyholders and those seeking insurance; whereas not all Member States require for the taking-up of the activity of insurance intermediary or specific categories of intermediary general, commercial and professional knowledge and ability; whereas such knowledge is desirable in principle for all insurance intermediaries and measures for further convergence are necessary;

Whereas Council Directive 77/92/EEC[3] sets out measures, in the absence of mutual recognition of diplomas and immediate co-ordination, to facilitate the effective exercise of freedom of establishment and freedom to provide services for the taking up and pursuit of activities of insurance agent and broker; whereas these measures are of a transitional nature;

Whereas it should be left to the Member States or, in certain cases, their insurance undertakings or recognised professional organisations, in conformity with the EEC Treaty, to establish the exact level of general, commercial and professional knowledge considered appropriate to guarantee that policyholders and persons seeking insurance will be adequately informed and assisted, taking into account the type of intermediary involved;

Whereas it is desirable that where appropriate insurance intermediaries also meet professional requirements with regard to professional indemnity insurance, fitness and properness; whereas consistency should exist with Community rules imposing capital requirements on intermediaries holding clients' monies in assisting the administration and performance of insurance contracts;

Whereas it is appropriate to clarify the definition of independence of insurance brokers in view of the application of the relevant provisions of Council Directive 90/619/EEC[4] to insurance intermediaries;

Whereas competent insurance intermediaries should be registered in their Member States and such registration should be a condition for the taking-up and exercise of the activity of intermediating in insurance; whereas central registers should distinguish between dependent and independent insurance intermediaries;

Whereas a recommendation, which is not binding on the Member States to which it is addressed as to the result to be achieved but solicits their co-operation on a voluntary basis, should be an effective means of enabling them to adopt where necessary the appropriate provisions,

HEREBY RECOMMENDS:

1. that Member States ensure that insurance intermediaries established on their territory are subject to professional requirements and registration

---

[1] OJ L 19, 28.1.1992, 32–33.
[2] The number between brackets has been changed as from 1 May 1999 by article 12 of the Treaty of Amsterdam.
[3] OJ L 26, 31.1.1977, 14, reproduced supra under no. I. 7.

[4] OJ L 330, 29.11.1990, 50, Second Life Assurance Directive, reproduced supra under no. I. 18.

in accordance with the provisions contained in the attached Annex;

2. that Member States inform the Commission within 36 months of the notification of this recommendation of the texts of the main laws, regulations, administrative provisions which have been adopted or measures taken by professional organisations or insurance undertakings with respect to this recommendation and inform the Commission of any further changes in this field.

Annex

Professional requirements and registration of insurance intermediaries

Article 1
Definitions

For the purpose of this recommendation:
- 'insurance intermediary' is defined as a person taking up or pursuing an activity as defined in Article 2, paragraph 1 (a) to (c) of Directive 77/92/EEC in a self-employed capacity or as a paid employee.

Article 2
Scope

1. Subject to paragraphs 2 and 3, this recommendation shall apply to all insurance intermediaries as defined in Article 1.

2. The Member States need not apply this recommendation to persons providing insurance which does not require any general or specific knowledge and where such insurance covers the risk of loss or damage to goods supplied by that person, whose principal professional activity is other than providing advice on and selling insurance.

3. The management of an undertaking taking up and exercising the activity of insurance intermediary shall include an adequate number of persons who possess the general, commercial and professional knowledge and ability required by Article 4, paragraph 2.

Member States are recommended to further that such undertakings offer relevant basic training for their employees who are involved in mediating in insurance products.

Article 3
Independence of intermediaries

The persons defined in Article 2, paragraph 1 (a) of Directive 77/92/EEC shall disclose:
- to persons seeking insurance or reinsurance of risks, any direct legal or economic ties to an insurance undertaking or any shareholdings in or by such undertakings which could affect the complete freedom of choice of insurance undertaking, and
- to a competent body, as determined by the Member State, the spread of business with different insurance undertakings over the previous year.

Article 4
Professional competence

1. The taking up and pursuit of the activity of insurance intermediary shall be subject to the professional requirements of paragraphs 2 to 5.

2. Insurance intermediaries shall possess general, commercial and professional knowledge and ability. The Member States shall require if necessary different levels of knowledge and ability for the category of intermediary mentioned in Article 3. The level of such knowledge and ability shall be determined by the Member States.

Such levels and their practical application may also be determined and administered by professional organisations recognised by a Member State.

Subject to the supervision by Member States, such levels and their practical application may also be determined and administered by an insurance undertaking assuming responsibility and liability for the activities exercised by the category of intermediary defined in Article 2, paragraph 1 (b) of Directive 77/92/EEC.

3. An insurance intermediary shall possess professional indemnity insurance or any other comparable guarantee against liability arising from professional negligence, unless such insurance is already provided for by an insurance undertaking or other undertaking by which he is employed or for which he is empowered to act.

4. An insurance intermediary shall be of good repute. He shall not have previously been declared bankrupt, unless he has been rehabilitated in accordance with his national law.

5. Insurance intermediaries as defined in Article 2, paragraph 1 (a) of Directive 77/92/EEC, may be required to have sufficient financial capacity. The level and form of capital required shall be determined by the Member States.

Article 5

Registration

1. Insurance intermediaries that fulfil the professional requirements of Article 4, paragraphs 2 to 5, shall be registered in their Member State. Only registered persons shall be allowed to take up and pursue the activity of insurance intermediary.

2. Each Member State shall appoint a competent body to administer the register mentioned in paragraph 1. Professional organisations recognised by a Member State may also be appointed to administer the register. In the case of Article 4, paragraph 2, last subparagraph, such registers may also be administered by an insurance undertaking. Member States' competent authorities shall have access to the registers.

3. Where one central register exists, it should distinguish between independent and dependent insurance intermediaries.

4. Insurance intermediaries shall inform the public of the fact that they have been registered.

Article 6

Sanctions

1. Adequate sanctions and measures shall exist in the Member States that shall apply to any person pursuing the activity of insurance intermediary without being registered as such in a Member State.

2. Adequate sanctions and measures shall exist in the Member States against an insurance intermediary who ceases to fulfil the requirements of Article 4, paragraphs 3 to 5, including the possibility of removal from the register.

I. 23.

Council Directive 91/674/EEC
of 19 December 1991
on the annual accounts and consolidated accounts of insurance undertakings[1]

THE COUNCIL OF THE EUROPEAN COMMUNITIES,

Having regard to the Treaty establishing the European Economic Community, and in particular Article [44][2] thereof,

Having regard to the proposal from the Commission,[3]

In co-operation with the European Parliament,[4]

Having regard to the opinion of the Economic and Social Committee,[5]

Whereas Article [44(3)(g)][2] of the Treaty requires co-ordination to the necessary extent of the safeguards which, for the protection of the interests of members and others, are required by Member States of companies and firms within the meaning of the second paragraph of Article [48][2] of the Treaty, with a view to making such safeguards equivalent throughout the Community;

Whereas Council Directive 78/660/EEC of 25 July 1978 based on Article [44(3)(g)][2] of the Treaty on the annual accounts of certain types of companies,[6] as last amended by Directive 90/605/EEC[7] need not be applied to insurance companies, hereinafter referred to as 'insurance undertakings', pending further co-ordination; whereas, in view of the major importance of insurance undertakings in the Community, such co-ordination cannot be delayed any longer following the implementation of Directive 78/660/EEC;

Whereas Council Directive 83/349/EEC of 13 June 1983 based on Article [44(3)(g)][2] of the Treaty on consolidated accounts,[8] as last amended by Directive 90/605/EEC, provides for derogations for insurance undertakings only until the expiry of the deadline imposed for the application of this Directive; whereas this Directive must therefore also include provisions specific to insurance undertakings in respect of consolidated accounts;

Whereas such co-ordination is also urgently required because insurance undertakings operate across borders; whereas for creditors, debtors, members, policyholders and their advisers and for the general public, improved comparability of the annual accounts and consolidated accounts of such undertakings is of crucial importance;

Whereas in the Member States insurance undertakings of different legal forms are in competition with each other; whereas undertakings engaged in the business of direct insurance customarily engage in the business of reinsurance as well and are therefore in competition with specialist reinsurance undertakings; whereas it is therefore appropriate not to confine co-ordination to the legal forms covered by Directive 78/660/EEC, but to choose a scope that corresponds to that of Council Directive 73/239/EEC of 24 July 1973 on the co-ordination of laws, regulations and administrative provisions relating to the taking up and pursuit of the business of direct insurance other than life assurance,[9] as last amended by Directive 90/618/EEC,[10] and to that of Council

---

[1] OJ L 374, 31.12.1991, 7–31.
[2] The number between brackets has been changed as from 1 May 1999 by article 12 of the Treaty of Amsterdam.
[3] OJ C 131, 18.4.1987, 1.
[4] OJ C 96, 17.4.1989, 93; and OJ C 326, 16.12.1991.
[5] OJ C 319, 30.11.1987, 13.
[6] OJ L 222, 14.8.1978, 11, Fourth Company Law Directive, reproduced supra under no. C. 4.
[7] OJ L 317, 16.11.1990, 60, reproduced supra under no. C. 12.
[8] OJ L 193, 18.7.1983, 1, Seventh Company Law Directive, reproduced supra under no. C. 6.
[9] OJ L 228, 16.8.1973, 3, First Non-Life Insurance Directive, reproduced supra under no. I. 3.
[10] OJ L 330, 29.11.1990, 44, reproduced supra under no. I. 17.

Directive 79/267/EEC of 5 March 1979 on the co-ordination of laws, regulations and administrative provisions relating to the taking up and pursuit of the business of direct life assurance,[11] as last amended by Directive 90/619/EEC,[12] but which also includes certain undertakings that are excluded from the scope of those Directives and companies and firms which are reinsurance undertakings;

Whereas, although in view of the specific characteristics of insurance undertakings it would appear appropriate to propose a separate Directive on the annual accounts and consolidated accounts of such undertakings, that does not necessarily require the establishment of a set of standards different from those of Directive 78/660/EEC and 83/349/EEC; whereas such separate standards would be neither appropriate nor consistent with the principles underlying the co-ordination of company law since, given the important position they occupy in the Community economy, insurance undertakings cannot be excluded from a framework of rules devised for undertakings generally; whereas, for this reason, only the particular characteristics of insurance undertakings have been taken into account and this Directive deals only with derogations from the rules laid down in Directives 78/660/EEC and 83/349/EEC;

Whereas there are major differences in the structure and content of the balance sheets of insurance undertakings in different Member States; whereas this Directive must therefore lay down the same structure and the same item designations for the balance sheets of all Community insurance undertakings;

Whereas, if annual accounts and consolidated accounts are to be comparable, a number of basic questions regarding the disclosure of certain transactions in the balance sheet must be settled;

Whereas, in the interests of greater comparability, it is also necessary that the content of the various balance sheet items be determined precisely;

Whereas it may be useful to distinguish between the commitments of the insurer and those of the reinsurer by showing in the assets the reinsurer's share of technical provisions as an asset;

Whereas the structure of the profit and loss account should also be determined and certain items in it should be defined;

Whereas, given the specific nature of the insurance industry, it may be useful for unrealised gains and losses to be dealt with in the profit and loss account;

Whereas the comparability of figures in the balance sheet and profit and loss account also depends basically on the values at which assets and liabilities are shown in the balance sheet; whereas for a proper understanding of the financial situation of an insurance undertaking the current value of investments as well as their value based upon the principle of purchase price or production cost must be disclosed; whereas, however, the compulsory disclosure of the current value of investments, at least in the notes on the accounts, is prescribed solely for purposes of comparability and transparency and is not intended to lead to changes in the tax treatment of insurance undertakings;

Whereas in the calculation of life assurance provisions use may be made of actuarial methods customarily applied on the market or accepted by the insurance-monitoring authorities; whereas those methods may be implemented by any actuary or expert in accordance with the conditions which may be laid down in national law and with due regard for the actuarial principles recognised in the framework of the present and future co-ordination of the fundamental rules for the prudential and financial monitoring of direct life assurance business;

Whereas, in the calculation of the provision for claims outstanding, on the one hand, any implicit discounting or deduction should be prohibited, and, on the other hand, precise conditions for recourse to explicit discounting or deduction

---

[11] OJ L 63, 13.3.1979, 1, First Life Assurance Directive, reproduced supra under no. I. 9.
[12] OJ L 330, 29.11.1990, 50, Second Non-Life Insurance Directive, reproduced supra under no. I. 18.

should be defined, for the sake of prudence and transparency;

Whereas, in view of the special nature of insurance undertakings, certain changes are necessary with regard to the notes on annual accounts and on consolidated accounts;

Whereas, in line with the intention of covering all insurance undertakings that come within the scope of Directive 73/239/EEC and 79/267/EEC as well as certain others, derogations such as those for small and medium-sized insurance undertakings in Directive 78/660/EEC are not provided for, but certain small mutual associations which are excluded from the scope of Directives 73/239/EEC and 79/267/EEC should not be covered;

Whereas for the same reasons the scope allowed Member States pursuant to Directive 83/349/EEC to exempt parent undertakings of groups from compulsory consolidation if the undertakings to be consolidated do not together exceed a certain size has not been extended to insurance undertakings;

Whereas in view of its particular nature special provisions are needed for the association of underwriters known as Lloyd's;

Whereas the provisions of this Directive also apply to the consolidated accounts drawn up by a parent undertaking which is a financial holding company where its subsidiary undertakings are either exclusively or mainly insurance undertakings;

Whereas the examination of problems which arise in connection with this Directive, in particular regarding its application, requires co-operation by representatives of the Member States and the Commission in a contact committee; whereas, in order to avoid the proliferation of such committees, it is desirable that such co-operation take place in the committee provided for in Article 52 of Directive 78/660/EEC; whereas, however, when examining problems concerning insurance undertakings, the committee must be appropriately constituted;

Whereas, in view of the complexity of the matter, the insurance undertakings covered by this Directive must be allowed an appropriate period to implement its provisions; whereas that period must be extended to allow the necessary adjustments to be made concerning, on the one hand, the association of underwriters known as Lloyd's and, on the other, those undertakings which, when this Directive becomes applicable, show their investments at historical cost;

Whereas provision should be made for the review of certain provisions of this Directive after five years' experience of its application, in the light of the aims of greater transparency and harmonisation,

HAS ADOPTED THIS DIRECTIVE:

SECTION 1

PRELIMINARY PROVISIONS AND SCOPE

Article 1

[1. Articles 2, 3, 4(1), (3) to (6), Articles 6, 7, 13, 14, 15(3) and (4), Articles 16 to 21, 29 to 35, 37 to 41, 42, 42a to 42f, 43 (1), points 1 to 7b and 9 to 14, 45(1), 46(1) and (2), 46a, 48 to 50, 50a, 50b, 50c, 51(1), 51a, 56 to 59, 60a, 61 and 61a of Directive 78/660/EEC shall apply to the undertakings mentioned in Article 2 of this Directive, except where this Directive provides otherwise.] Articles 46, 47, 48, 51 and 53 of this Directive shall not apply in respect of assets and liabilities that are valued in accordance with Section 7a of Directive 78/660/EEC.

2. Where reference is made in Directives 78/660/EEC and 83/349/EEC to Articles 9, 10 and 10a (balance sheet) or to Articles 22 to 26 (profit and loss account) of Directive 78/660/EEC, such references shall be deemed to be references to Article 6 (balance sheet) or to Article 34 (profit and loss account) of this Directive as appropriate.]

3. References in Directives 78/660/EEC and 83/349/EEC to Articles 31 to 42 of Directive 78/660/EEC shall be deemed to be references to those Articles, taking account of Articles 45 to 62 of this Directive.

4. Where the aforementioned provisions of Directive 78/660/EEC relate to balance-sheet

items for which this Directive lays down no equivalent, they shall be deemed to be references to the items in Article 6 of this Directive where the corresponding assets and liabilities items are listed.

¶ *Paragraphs 1 and 2 of this article have been replaced by article 4(1) of Directive 2003/51/EC, reproduced supra under no. C. 23.*
¶ *The first sentence of paragraph 1 has been amended by article 4 of Directive 2006/46/EC, reproduced supra under no. C. 31.*

Article 2

1. The co-ordination measures prescribed by this Directive shall apply to companies and firms within the meaning of the second paragraph of Article [48][2] of the Treaty that are:

(a) undertakings within the meaning of Article 1 of Directive 73/239/EEC, excluding those mutual associations which are excluded from the scope of that Directive by virtue of Article 3 thereof but including those bodies referred to in Article 4 (a), (b), (c) and (e) thereof except where their activity does not consist wholly or mainly in carrying on insurance business;

(b) undertakings within the meaning of Article 1 of Directive 79/267/EEC, excluding those bodies and mutual associations referred to in Articles 2 (2) and (3) and 3 of that Directive; or

(c) undertakings carrying on reinsurance business.

In this Directive, such undertakings shall be referred to as insurance undertakings.

2. Funds of a group pension fund within the meaning of Article 1 (2) (c) and (d) of Directive 79/267/EEC which an insurance undertaking administers in its own name but on behalf of third parties must be shown in the balance sheet if the undertaking acquires legal title to the assets concerned. The total amount of such assets and liabilities shall be shown separately or in the notes on the accounts, broken down according to the various assets and liabilities items. However, the Member States may permit the disclosure of such funds as off-balance-sheet items provided there are special rules whereby such funds can be excluded from the assets available for distribution in the event of the winding up of an insurance undertaking (or similar proceedings).

Assets acquired in the name of and on behalf of third parties must not be shown in the balance sheet.

Article 3

Those provisions of this Directive that relate to life assurance shall apply *mutatis mutandis* to insurance undertakings which underwrite only health insurance and which do so exclusively or principally according to the technical principles of life assurance.

Member States may apply the first paragraph to health insurance underwritten by joint undertakings according to the technical principles of life assurance where such activity is significant.

Article 4

[1. This Directive shall apply to the association of underwriters known as Lloyd's. For the purpose of this Directive both Lloyd's and Lloyd's syndicates shall be deemed to be insurance undertakings.

2. By way of derogation from Article 65(1), Lloyd's shall prepare aggregate accounts instead of consolidated accounts required by Directive 83/349/EEC. Aggregate accounts shall be prepared by cumulation of all syndicate accounts.]

¶ *Article 4 has been replaced by article 4(2) of Directive 2003/51/EC, reproduced supra under no. C. 23.*

SECTION 2

GENERAL PROVISIONS CONCERNING THE BALANCE SHEET AND THE PROFIT AND LOSS ACCOUNT

The combination of items under the conditions laid down in Article 4 (3) (a) or (b) of Directive 78/660/EEC shall be restricted in the case of insurance undertakings,

– as regards the balance sheet, to items preceded by Arabic numerals, except for items concerning technical provisions, and

– as regards the profit and loss account, to items preceded by one or more lower-case letters, except for items 1(1) and (4) and 11(1), (5) and (6).

Combination shall be authorised only under the rules laid down by the Member States.

Section 3
Layout of the Balance Sheet

Article 6

The Member States shall prescribe the following layout for balance sheets:

Assets

A. *Subscribed capital unpaid*

showing separately called-up capital (unless national law requires called-up capital to be included under liabilities, in which case capital called but not yet paid must be included as an asset either under A or under E (IV)).

B. *Intangible assets*

as described under items B and C (I) of Article 9 of Directive 78/660/EEC, showing separately:
- formation expenses, as defined by national law and in so far as national law permits their being shown as an asset (unless national law requires their disclosure in the notes on the accounts),
- goodwill, to the extent that it was acquired for valuable consideration (unless national law requires its disclosure in the notes on the accounts).

C. *Investments*

I. Land and buildings:

showing separately land and buildings occupied by an insurance undertaking for its own activities—(unless national law requires their disclosure in the notes on the accounts).

II. Investments in affiliated undertakings and participating interests:

1. Shares in affiliated undertakings.

2. Debt securities issued by, and loans to, affiliated undertakings.

3. Participating interests.

4. Debt securities issued by, and loans to, undertakings with which an insurance undertaking is linked by virtue of a participating interest.

III. Other financial investments:

1. Shares and other variable-yield securities and units in unit trusts.

2. Debt securities and other fixed-income securities.

3. Participation in investment pools.

4. Loans guaranteed by mortgages.

5. Other loans.

6. Deposits with credit institutions.

7. Other.

IV. Deposits with ceding undertakings.

D. *Investments for the benefit of life assurance policyholders who bear the investment risk*

E. *Debtors*

(Amounts owed by:
- affiliated undertakings, and
- undertakings with which an insurance undertaking is linked by virtue of participating interests shall be shown separately, as sub-items of items I, II and III.)

I. Debtors arising out of direct insurance operations

1. Policyholders.

2. Intermediaries.

II. Debtors arising out of reinsurance operations.

III. Other debtors.

IV. Subscribed capital called but not paid (unless national law requires that capital called but not paid be shown as an asset under A).

F. *Other assets*

I. Tangible assets and stocks as listed under C (II) and D (I) in Article 9 of Directive 78/660/EEC, other than land and buildings, buildings under construction and deposits paid on land and buildings.

II. Cash at bank and in hand.

III. Own shares (with an indication of their nominal value or, in the absence of a nominal value, their accounting par value) to the extent that national law permits their being shown in the balance sheet.

IV. Other.

G. *Prepayments and accrued income*

I. Accrued interest and rent.

II. Deferred acquisition costs (distinguishing those arising in non-life insurance and life-assurance business).

III. Other prepayments and accrued income.

H. *Loss for the financial year*

(unless national law requires it to be shown as a liability under A (VI)).

Liabilities

A. *Capital and reserves*

I. Subscribed capital or equivalent funds

(unless national law requires called-up capital to be shown under this item. In that case, the amounts of subscribed capital and paid-up capital must be shown separately).

II. Share premium account.

III. Revaluation reserve.

IV. Reserve.

V. Profit or loss brought forward.

VI. Profit or loss for the financial year

(unless national law requires it to be shown as an asset under H or as a liability under 1).

B. *Subordinated liabilities*

C. *Technical provisions*

1. Provision for unearned premiums:
(a) gross amount   ....
(b) reinsurance amount (–)   ....
                                ....

2. Life assurance provision:
(a) gross amount (–)   ....
(b) reinsurance amount (–)   ....
                                ....

3. Claims outstanding:
(a) gross amount   ....
(b) reinsurance amount (–)   ....
                                ....

4. Provision for bonuses and rebates (unless shown under 2):
(a) gross amount   ....
(b) reinsurance amount (–)   ....
                                ....

5. Equalisation provision

6. Other technical provisions:
(a) gross amount   ....
(b) reinsurance amount (–)   ....
                                ....

D. *Technical provisions for life-assurance policies where the investment risk is borne by the policy holders:*
(a) gross amount   ....
(b) reinsurance amount (–)   ....
                                ....

[E. *Other provisions*]

1. Provisions for pensions and similar obligations.

2. Provisions for taxation.

3. Other provisions.

F. *Deposits received from reinsurers*

G. *Creditors*

(Amounts owed to:
– affiliated undertakings, and
– undertakings with which an insurance undertaking is linked by virtue of a participating interest shall be shown separately, as sub-items.)

I. Creditors arising out of direct insurance operations.

II. Creditors arising out of reinsurance operations.

III. Debenture loans, showing convertible loans separately.

IV. Amounts owed to credit institutions.

V. Other creditors, including tax and social security.

H. *Accruals and deferred income*

I. *Profit for the financial year*

(unless national law requires it to be shown as a liability under A (VI)).

¶ Article 6, under 'Liabilities', the title of point E has been amended by article 4(3) of Directive 2003/51/EC, reproduced supra under no. C. 23.

Article 7

Article 14 of Directive 78/660/EEC shall not apply to commitments linked to insurance activities.

Section 4
Special Provisions Relating to Certain Balance-sheet Items

Article 8

Article 15 (3) of Directive 78/660/EEC shall apply only to assets items B and C (I) and (II) as defined in Article 6 of this Directive. Any movements in these items shall be shown on the basis of the balance-sheet value at the beginning of the financial year.

Article 9

Assets: item C (III) (2)

Debt securities and other fixed-income securities

1. This item shall comprise negotiable debt securities and other fixed-income securities issued by credit institutions, by other undertakings or by public bodies, in so far as they are not covered by item C (11) (2) or (4).

2. Securities bearing interest the rate of which varies in line with specific factors, for example the interest rate on the inter-bank market or on the Euromarket, shall also be regarded as debt securities and other fixed-income securities.

Article 10

Assets: item C (III) (3)

Participation in investment pools

This item shall comprise shares held by an undertaking in joint investments constituted by several undertakings or pension funds, the management of which has been entrusted to one of those undertakings or to one of those pension funds.

Article 11

Assets: items C (III) (4) and (5)

Loans guaranteed by mortgages and other loans

Loans to policyholders for which the policy is the main security shall be included under 'Other loans' and their amount shall be disclosed in the notes on the accounts. Loans guaranteed by mortgage shall be shown as such even where they are also secured by insurance policies. Where the amount of 'Other loans' not secured by policies is material, an appropriate breakdown shall be given in the notes on the accounts.

Article 12

Assets: items C (III) (6)

Deposits with credit institutions

This item shall comprise sums the withdrawal of which is subject to a time restriction. Sums deposited with no such restriction shall be shown under F (II) even if they bear interest.

Article 13

Assets: items C (III) (7)

Other

This item shall comprise those investments that are not covered by items C (III) (1) to (6). Where the amount of such investments is significant, they must be disclosed in the notes on the accounts.

Article 14

Assets: item C (IV)

Deposits with ceding undertakings

In the balance sheet of an undertaking that accepts reinsurance this item shall comprise amounts, owed by the ceding undertakings and corresponding to guarantees, which are deposited with those ceding undertakings or with third parties or which are retained by those undertakings.

These amounts may not be combined with other amounts owed by the ceding insurer to the reinsurer or set off against amounts owed by the reinsurer to the ceding insurer.

Securities deposited with ceding undertakings or third parties which remain the property of the undertaking accepting reinsurance shall be entered in the latter's accounts as an investment, under the appropriate item.

Article 15

Assets: item D

Investments for the benefit of life assurance policyholders who bear the investment risk

In respect of life assurance this item shall comprise, on the one hand, investments the value of which is used to determine the value of or the return on policies relating to an investment fund and, on the other hand, investments serving as cover for liabilities that are determined by reference to an index. This item shall also comprise investments that are held on behalf of the members of a tontine and are intended for distribution among them.

Article 16

Assets: item F (IV)

Other

This item shall comprise those assets which are not covered by items F (I), (II) and (III). Where such assets are material, they must be disclosed in the notes on the accounts.

Article 17

Assets: item G (I)

Accrued interest and rent

This item shall comprise those items that represent interest and rent that have been earned up to the balance-sheet date but have not yet become receivable.

Article 18

Assets: item G (II)

Deferred acquisition costs

1. The costs of acquiring insurance policies shall be deferred in accordance with Article 18 of Directive 78/660/EEC in so far as such deferral is not prohibited by Member States.

2. Member States may, however, permit the deduction of acquisition costs from unearned premiums in non-life-insurance business and their deduction by an actuarial method from mathematical reserves in life-assurance business. Where this method is used, the amounts deducted from the provisions must be indicated in the notes on the accounts.

Article 19

Liabilities: item A (I)

Subscribed capital or equivalent funds

This item shall comprise all amounts, irrespective of their actual designations, which, in accordance with the legal structure of an insurance undertaking, are regarded under the national law of the Member State concerned as equity capital subscribed by the shareholders or other persons.

Article 20

Liabilities: item A (IV)

Reserves

This item shall comprise all the types of reserves listed in Article 9 of Directive 78/660/EEC under liabilities item A (IV), as defined therein. The Member States may also require other types of reserves if necessary for insurance undertakings the legal structures of which are not covered by Directive 78/660/EEC.

Reserves shall be shown separately, as sub-items of liabilities item A (IV), in the balance sheets of the insurance undertakings concerned, except for the revaluation reserve, which shall be shown as a liability under A (III).

Article 21

Liabilities: item B

Subordinated liabilities

Where it has been contractually agreed that, in the event of winding up or of bankruptcy, liabilities, whether or not represented by certificates, are to be repaid only after the claims of all other creditors have been met, the liabilities in question shall be shown under this item.

Article 22

Where a Member State permits an undertaking's balance sheet to include funds the allocation of which either to policyholders or to shareholders has not been determined by the close of the financial year, those amounts shall be shown as liabilities under an item Ba (Fund for future appropriations).

Variations in this item shall derive from an item 11 (12a) (Transfers to or from the fund for future appropriations) in the profit and loss account.

Article 23

Liabilities: item C

Technical provisions
Article 20 of Directive 78/660/EEC shall apply to technical provisions, subject to Articles 24 to 30 of this Directive.

Article 24

Liabilities: items C (1) (b), (2) (b), (3) (b), (4) (b) and (6) (b) and D (b)

Reinsurance amounts
1. The reinsurance amounts shall comprise the actual or estimated amounts that, under contractual reinsurance arrangements, are deducted from the gross amounts of technical provisions.

2. As regards the provision for unearned premiums, the reinsurance amounts shall be calculated according to the methods referred to in Article 57 or in accordance with the terms of the reinsurance policy.

3. Member States may require or permit the reinsurance amounts to be shown as assets. Where this option is exercised, those amounts shall be shown as assets under an item Da (Reinsurers' share of technical provisions), subdivided as follows:

1. Provision for unearned premiums

2. Life assurance provision

3. Claims outstanding

4. Provisions for bonuses and rebates (unless shown under 2)

5. Other technical provisions

6. Technical provisions for life assurance policies where the investment risk is borne by the policyholders.

Notwithstanding Article 5, these items shall not be combined.

Article 25

Liabilities: item C (1)

Provision for unearned premiums
The provision for unearned premiums shall comprise the amount representing that part of gross premiums written which is to be allocated to the following financial year or to subsequent financial years. In the case of life assurance Member States may, pending further harmonisation, require or permit the provision for unearned premiums to be included in item C (2).

If, pursuant to Article 26, item C (1) also includes the amount of the provision for unexpired risks, the description of the item shall be 'Provision for unearned premiums and unexpired risks'. Where the amount for unexpired risks is material, it shall be disclosed separately either in the balance sheet or in the notes on the accounts.

Article 26

Liabilities: item C (6)

Other technical provisions
This item shall comprise, inter alia, the provision for unexpired risks, i.e. the amount set aside in addition to unearned premiums in respect of risks to be borne by the insurance undertaking after the end of the financial year, in order to provide for all claims and expenses in connection with insurance contracts in force in excess of the related unearned premiums and any premiums receivable on those contracts. However, if national legislation so provides, the provision for unexpired risks may be added to the provision for unearned premiums, as defined in Article 25, and included in the amount shown under item C (1).

Where the amount of unexpired risks is significant, it shall be disclosed separately either in the balance sheet or in the notes on the accounts.

Where the option provided for in the second paragraph of Article 3 is not exercised, this item shall also include the ageing reserves.

Article 27
Liabilities: item C (2)

Life-assurance provision

The life assurance provision shall comprise the actuarially estimated value of an insurance undertaking's liabilities including bonuses already declared and after deducting the actuarial value of future premiums.

Article 28
Liabilities: item C (3)

Claims outstanding

The provision for claims outstanding shall be the total estimated ultimate cost to an insurance undertaking of settling all claims arising from events which have occurred up to the end of the financial year, whether reported or not, less amounts already paid in respect of such claims.

Article 29
Liabilities: item C (4)

Provision for bonuses and rebates

The provision for bonuses and rebates shall comprise amounts intended for policyholders or contract beneficiaries by way of bonuses and rebates as defined in Article 39 to the extent that such amounts have not been credited to policyholders or contract beneficiaries or included in an item Ba (Fund for future appropriations), as provided for in Article 22, first paragraph, or in item C (2).

Article 30
Liabilities: item C (5)

Equalisation provision

1. The equalisation provision shall comprise any amounts set aside in compliance with legal or administrative requirements to equalise fluctuations in loss ratios in future years or to provide for special risks.

2. Where, in the absence of any such legislative or administrative requirements, reserves within the meaning of Article 20 have been constituted for the same purpose, this shall be disclosed in the notes on the accounts.

Article 31
Liabilities: item D

Technical provisions for life-assurance policies where the investment risk is borne by the policy holders

This item shall comprise technical provisions constituted to cover liabilities relating to investment in the context of life assurance policies the value of or the return on which is determined by reference to investments for which the policyholder bears the risk, or by reference to an index.

Any additional technical provisions constituted to cover death risks, operating expenses or other risks (such as benefits payable at the maturity date or guaranteed surrender values) shall be shown under item C (2).

Item D shall also comprise technical provisions representing the obligations of a tontine's organiser *vis-à-vis* its members.

Article 32
Liabilities: item F

Deposits received from reinsurers

In the balance sheet of an undertaking ceding reinsurance this item shall comprise amounts deposited by or withheld from other insurance undertakings under reinsurance contracts. These amounts may not be merged with other amounts owed to or by the other undertakings in question.

Where an undertaking ceding reinsurance has received as a deposit securities that have been transferred to its ownership, this item shall comprise the amount owed by the ceding undertaking by virtue of the deposit.

SECTION 5
LAYOUT OF THE PROFIT AND LOSS ACCOUNT

Article 33

1. The Member States shall prescribe the layout shown in Article 34 for profit and loss accounts.

2. The technical account for non-life-insurance business shall be used for those classes of direct insurance that are within the scope of Directive 73/239/EEC and for the corresponding classes of reinsurance business.

3. The technical account for life-assurance business shall be used for those classes of direct insurance that are within the scope of Directive 79/267/EEC and for the corresponding classes of reinsurance business.

4. Member States may require or permit undertakings the activities of which consist wholly of reinsurance to use the technical account for non-life-insurance business for all their business. This shall also apply to undertakings underwriting direct non-life-insurance and also reinsurance.

Article 34

Profit and loss account

I. *Technical account—Non-life-insurance business*

1. Earned premiums, net of reinsurance:
   (a) gross premiums written   ....
   (b) outward reinsurance premiums (−)   ....
   (c) change in the gross provision for unearned premiums and, in so far as national legislation authorises the inclusion of this provision in liabilities item C (1), in the provision for unexpired risks (+/−)   ....
   (d) change in the provision for unearned premiums, reinsurers' share (+/−)   ....

2. Allocated investment return transferred from the non-technical account (item III (6))   ....

3. Other technical income, net of reinsurance   ....

4. Claims incurred, net of reinsurance:
   (a) claims paid
       (aa) gross amount   ....
       (bb) reinsurers' share (−)   ....
   (b) change in the provision for claims
       (aa) gross amount   ....
       (bb) reinsurers' share (−)   ....

5. Changes in other technical provisions, net of reinsurance, not shown under other headings (+/−)   ....

6. Bonuses and rebates, net of reinsurance   ....

7. Net operating expenses:
   (a) acquisition costs   ....
   (b) change in deferred acquisition costs (+/−)   ....
   (c) administrative expenses   ....
   (d) reinsurance commissions and profit participation (−)   ....

8. Other technical charges, net of reinsurance   ....

9. Change in the equalisation provision (+/−) ....

10. Sub-total (balance on the technical account for non-life-insurance business (item III 1)) ....

II. *Technical account—Life-assurance business*

1. Earned premiums, net of reinsurance:
(a) gross premiums written ....

(b) outward reinsurance premiums (−) ....

(c) change in the provision for unearned premiums, net of reinsurance (+/−) ....

2. Investment income:
(a) income from participating interests, with a separate indication of that derived from affiliated undertakings ....

(b) income from other investments, with a separate indication of that derived from affiliated undertakings
   (aa) income from land and buildings ....
   (bb) income from other investments ....

(c) value readjustments on investments ....

(d) gains on the realisation of investments ....

3. Unrealised gains on investments ....

4. Other technical income, net of reinsurance ....

5. Claims incurred, net of reinsurance:
(a) claims paid
   (aa) gross amount ....
   (bb) reinsurers' share (−) ....

(b) change in the provision for claims
   (aa) gross amount ....
   (bb) reinsurers' share (−) ....

6. Change in other technical provisions, net of reinsurance, not shown under other headings (+/−):
(a) life assurance provision, net of reinsurance
   (aa) gross amount ....
   (bb) reinsurers' share (−) ....

(b) other technical provisions, net of reinsurance ....

7. Bonuses and rebates, net of reinsurance ....

8. Net operating expenses:
(a) acquisition costs ....

(b) change in deferred acquisition costs (+/−) ....

(c) administrative expenses ....

(d) reinsurance commissions and profit participation (−) ....

9. Investment charges:
(a) investment management charges, including interest ....
(b) value adjustments on investments ....
(c) losses on the realisation of investments ....

10. Unrealised losses on investments ....

11. Other technical charges, net of reinsurance ....

12. Allocated investment return transferred to the non-technical account (-) (item III 4)) ....

13. Sub-total: (balance on the technical account—life assurance business (item III 2)) ....

III. *Non-technical account*

1. Balance on the technical account—non-life-insurance business (item I (10)) ....

2. Balance on the technical account—life-assurance business (item II (13)) ....

3. Investment income
(a) income from participating interests, with a separate indication of that derived from affiliated undertakings ....

(b) income from other investments, with a separate indication of that derived from affiliated undertakings
    (aa) income from land and buildings ....
    (bb) income from other investments ....
(c) value re-adjustments on investments ....
(d) gains on the realisation of investments ....

4. Allocated investment return transferred from the life-assurance technical account (item II (12)) ....

5. Investment charges:
(a) investment management charges, including interest ....
(b) value adjustments on investments ....
(c) losses on the realisation of investments ....

6. Allocated investment return transferred to the non-life-insurance technical account (item I (2)) ....

7. Other income ....

8. Other charges, including value adjustments ....

9. Tax on profit or loss on ordinary activities ....

10. Profit or loss on ordinary activities after tax ....

11. Extraordinary income ....
12. Extraordinary charges ....
13. Extraordinary profit or loss ....
14. Tax on extraordinary profit or loss ....
15. Other taxes not shown under the preceding items ....
16. Profit or loss for the financial year ....

Section 6

Special Provisions Relating to Certain Profit-and-Loss-Account Items

Article 35

Non-life-insurance technical account: item I (1) (a)

Life-assurance technical account: item II (1) (a)

Gross premiums written

Gross premiums written shall comprise all amounts due during the financial year in respect of insurance contracts regardless of the fact that such amounts may relate in whole or in part to a later financial year, and shall include *inter alia*:
  (i) premiums yet to be written, where the premium calculation can be done only at the end of the year:
 (ii) – single premiums, including annuity premiums,
      – in life assurance, single premiums resulting from bonus and rebate provisions in so far as they must be considered as premiums on the basis of contracts and where national legislation requires or permits their being shown under premiums;
(iii) additional premiums in the case of half-yearly, quarterly or monthly payments and additional payments from policyholders for expenses borne by the insurance undertaking;
 (iv) in the case of co-insurance, the undertaking's portion of total premiums;
  (v) reinsurance premiums due from ceding and retroceding insurance undertakings, including portfolio entries,

after deduction of:
– portfolio withdrawals credited to ceding and retroceding insurance undertakings, and
– cancellations.

The above amounts shall not include the amounts of taxes or charges levied with premiums.

Article 36

Non-life-insurance technical account: item I (1) (b)

Life-assurance technical account: item II (1) (b)

Outward reinsurance premiums

Outward reinsurance premiums shall comprise all premiums paid or payable in respect of outward reinsurance contracts entered into by an insurance undertaking. Portfolio entries payable on the conclusion or amendment of outward reinsurance contracts shall be added; portfolio withdrawals receivable must be deducted.

Article 37

Non-life-insurance technical account: items I (1) (c) and (d)

Life-assurance technical account: item II (1) (c)

Change in the provision for unearned premiums, net of reinsurance

Pending further co-ordination, Member States may, in the case of life assurance, require or permit the change in unearned premiums to be included in the change in the life assurance provision.

Article 38

Non-life-insurance technical account: item I (4)

Life-assurance technical account: item II (5)

Claims incurred, net of reinsurance

1. Claims incurred shall comprise all payments made in respect of the financial year plus the provision for claims but minus the provision for claims for the preceding financial year.

These amounts shall include annuities, surrenders, entries and withdrawals of loss provisions to and from ceding insurance undertakings and reinsurers, external and internal claims management costs and charges for claims incurred but not reported such as referred to in Article 60 (1) (b) and (2) (a).

Sums recoverable on the basis of subrogation and salvage within the meaning of Article 60 (1) (d) shall be deducted.

2. Where the difference between:
   - the loss provision made at the beginning of the year for outstanding claims incurred in previous years, and
   - the payments made during the year on account of claims incurred in previous years and the loss provision shown at the end of the year for such outstanding claims is material,

it shall be disclosed in the notes on the accounts, broken down by category and amount.

Article 39

Non-life-insurance technical account: item I (6)

Life-assurance technical account: item II (7)

Bonuses and rebates, net of reinsurance

Bonuses shall comprise all amounts chargeable for the financial year which are paid or payable to policyholders and other insured parties or provided for their benefit, including amounts used to increase technical provisions or applied to the reduction of future premiums, to the extent that such amounts represent an allocation of surplus or profit arising on business as a whole or a section of business, after deduction of amounts provided in previous years which are no longer required.

Rebates shall comprise such amounts to the extent that they represent a partial refund of premiums resulting from the experience of individual contracts.

Where material, the amount charged for bonuses and that charged for rebates shall be disclosed separately in the notes on the accounts.

Article 40

Non-life-insurance technical account: item I (7) (a)

Life-assurance technical account: item II (8) (a)

Acquisition costs

Acquisition costs shall comprise the costs arising from the conclusion of insurance contracts. They shall cover both direct costs, such as acquisition commissions or the cost of drawing up the insurance document or including the insurance contract in the portfolio, and indirect costs, such as advertising costs or the administrative expenses connected with the processing of proposals and the issuing of policies.

Member States may require policy renewal commissions to be entered in item I (7) (c) or II (8) (c).

Article 41

Non-life-insurance technical account: item I (7) (c)

Life-assurance technical account: item II (8) (c)

Administrative expenses

Administrative expenses shall include the costs arising from premium collection, portfolio administration, handling of bonuses and rebates, and inward and outward reinsurance. They shall in particular include staff costs and depreciation provisions in respect of office furniture and equipment in so far as these need not be shown under acquisition costs, claims incurred or investment charges.

Article 42

Life-insurance technical account: items II (2) and (9)

Non-technical account: items III (3) and (5)

Investment income and charges

1. All investment income and charges relating to non-life insurance shall be disclosed in the non-technical account.

2. In the case of an undertaking carrying on life-assurance business only, investment income and charges shall be disclosed in the life-assurance technical account.

3. In the case of an undertaking carrying on both life assurance and non-life-insurance business, investment income and charges shall, to the extent that they are directly connected with the carrying on of the life-assurance business, be disclosed in the life-assurance technical account.

4. Member States may require or permit the disclosure of investment income and charges according to the origin or attribution of the investments, if necessary by providing for further items in the non-life-insurance technical account, by analogy with the corresponding items in the life-assurance technical account.

Article 43

Non-life-insurance technical account: item I (2)

Life-assurance technical account: item II (2)

Non-technical account: items III (4) and (6)

Allocated investment return

1. Where part of the investment return is transferred to the non-life-insurance technical account, the transfer from the non-technical account shall be deducted from item III (6) and added to item I (2).

2. Where part of the investment return disclosed in the life-assurance technical account is transferred to the non-technical account, the amount transferred shall be deducted from item II (12) and added to item III (4).

3. Member States may lay down the procedures for and the amounts of transfers of allocated return from one part of the profit and loss account to another. The reasons for such transfers and the bases on which they are made shall be disclosed in the notes on the accounts in either event; where appropriate, a reference to the text of the relevant regulation shall suffice.

Article 44

Life-assurance technical account: items II (3) and (10)

Unrealised gains and losses on investments

1. In life assurance business Member States may permit the disclosure in full or in part in items II (3) and (10) in the profit and loss account of variations in the difference between:

– the valuation of investments at their current value or by means of one of the methods referred to in Article 33 (1) of Directive 78/660/EEC, and

– their valuation at purchase price.

In any event, Member States shall require that the amounts referred to in the first paragraph be disclosed in the aforementioned items where they relate to investments shown as assets under D.

2. Member States which require or permit the valuation of the investments shown as assets under C at their current value may, in respect of non-life-insurance, permit—the disclosure in full or in part in an item III (3a) and in an item III (5a) in the profit and loss account of the variation in the difference between the valuation of those investments at their current value and their valuation at purchase price.

SECTION 7

VALUATION RISKS

Article 45

Article 32 of Directive 78/660/EEC, under which the valuation of items shown in the annual accounts must be based on the principle of purchase price or production cost, shall apply to investment subject to Articles 46 to 49 of this Directive.

Article 46

1. Member States may require or permit the valuation of investments shown as assets under C

on the basis of their current value calculated in accordance with Articles 48 and 49.

2. The investments shown as assets under D shall be shown at their current value.

3. Where investments are shown at their purchase price, their current value shall be disclosed in the notes on the accounts.

However, Member States in which, on the date of the notification of this Directive, investments are shown at their purchase price may give undertakings the option of initially disclosing in the notes on the account the current value of investment shown as assets under C (I) no later than five years after the date referred to in Article 70 (1) and the current value of other investments no later than three years after the same date.

4. Where investments are shown at their current value, their purchase price shall be disclosed in the notes on the accounts.

5. The same valuation method shall be applied to all investments included in any item denoted by an Arabic numeral or shown as assets under C (1). [Member States may permit derogations from this requirement.]

[6. The method(s) applied to each investment item shall be stated in the notes on the accounts, together with the amounts so determined.]

¶ *The second sentence of paragraphs 5 has been added and paragraph 6 of this article has been amended by article 4(4) of Directive 2003/51/EC, reproduced supra under no. C. 23.*

[*Article 46a*

1. Where assets and liabilities are valued in accordance with Section 7a of Directive 78/660/EEC, paragraphs 2 to 6 of this Article shall apply.

2. The investments shown as assets under D shall be shown at their fair value.

3. Where investments are shown at their purchase price, their fair value shall be disclosed in the notes on the accounts.

4. Where investments are shown at their fair value, their purchase price shall be disclosed in the notes on the accounts.

5. The same valuation method shall be applied to all investments included in any item denoted by an Arabic numeral or shown as assets under C (I). Member States may permit derogations from this requirement.

6. The method(s) applied to each investment item shall be stated in the notes on the accounts, together with the amounts so determined.]

¶ *This article has been inserted by article 4(5) of Directive 2003/51/EC, reproduced supra under no. C. 23.*

Article 47

Where current value is applied to investments, Article 33 (2) and (3) of Directive 78/660/EEC shall apply, except as provided in Articles 37 and 44 of this Directive.

Article 48

1. In the case of investments other than land and buildings, current value shall mean market value, save as provided in paragraph 5.

2. Where investments are officially listed on an official stock exchange, market value shall mean the value on the balance-sheet date or, when the balance-sheet date is not a stock-exchange trading day, on the last stock-exchange trading day before that date.

3. Where a market exists for investments other than those referred to in paragraph 2, market value shall mean the average price at which such investments were traded on the balance-sheet date or, when the balance-sheet date is not a trading day, on the last trading day before that date.

4. Where on the date on which the accounts are drawn up investments such as referred to in paragraphs 2 or 3 have been sold or are to be sold within the short term, the market value shall be reduced by the actual or estimated realisation costs.

5. Except where the equity method is applied in accordance with Article 59 of Directive 78/660/EEC, all other investments shall be valued on a basis which has prudent regard to the likely realisable value.

6. In all cases the method of valuation shall be precisely described and the reason for adopting it stated in the notes on the accounts.

Article 49

1. In the case of land and buildings current value shall mean the market value on the date of valuation, where relevant reduced as provided in paragraphs 4 and 5.

2. Market value shall mean the price at which land and buildings could be sold under private contract between a willing seller and an arm's length buyer on the date of valuation, it being assumed that the property is publicly exposed to the market, that market conditions permit orderly disposal and that a normal period, having regard to the nature of the property, is available for the negotiation of the sale.

3. The market value shall be determined through the separate valuation of each land and buildings item, carried out at least every five years according to methods generally recognised or recognised by the insurance supervisory authorities. Article 35(1)(b) of Directive 78/660/EEC shall not apply.

4. Where the value of any land and buildings item has diminished since the preceding valuation under paragraph 3, an appropriate value adjustment shall be made. The lower value thus arrived at shall not be increased in subsequent balance sheets unless such increase results from a new determination of market value arrived at in accordance with paragraphs 2 and 3.

5. Where on the date on which the accounts are drawn up land and buildings have been sold or are to be sold within the short term, the value arrived at in accordance with paragraphs 2 and 4 shall be reduced by the actual or estimated realisation costs.

6. Where it is impossible to determine the market value of a land and buildings item, the value arrived at on the basis of the principle of purchase price or production cost shall be deemed to be the current value.

7. The method by which the current value of land and buildings has been arrived at and their breakdown by financial year of valuation shall be disclosed in the notes on the accounts.

Article 50

Where Article 33 of Directive 78/660/EEC is applied to insurance undertakings, it shall be so in the following manner:

(a) paragraph 1 (a) shall apply to assets shown under F (I) as defined in Article 6 of this Directive;

(b) paragraph 1 (c) shall apply to assets shown under C (I), (II), (III) and (IV) and F (I) (except for stocks) and (III) as defined in Article 6 of this Directive.

Article 51

Article 35 of Directive 78/660/EEC shall apply to insurance undertakings subject to the following provisions:

(a) it shall apply to assets shown under B and C and to fixed assets shown under F (I) as defined in Article 6 of this Directive;

(b) paragraph 1 (c) (aa) shall apply to assets shown under C (II), (III) and (IV) and F (III) as defined in Article 6 of this Directive.

Member States may require that value adjustments be made in respect of transferable securities shown as investments, so that they are shown at the lower value to be attributed to them at the balance-sheet date.

Article 52

Article 38 of Directive 78/660/EEC shall apply to assets shown under F (I) as defined in Article 6 of this Directive.

Article 53

Article 39 of Directive 78/660/EEC shall apply to assets shown under E (I), (II) and (III) and F (II) as defined in Article 6 of this Directive.

Article 54

In non-life insurance the amount of any deferred acquisition costs shall be established on a basis compatible with that used for unearned premiums.

In life assurance the calculation of the amount of any acquisition costs to be deferred may be taken into the actuarial calculation referred to in Article 59.

Article 55

1. (a) If they have not been valued at market value, debt securities and other fixed-income securities shown as assets under C (II) and (III) shall be shown in the balance sheet at purchase price. Member States may, however, require or permit such debt securities to be shown in the balance sheet at the amount repayable at maturity.

(b) Where the purchase price of the securities referred to in point (a) exceeds the amount repayable at maturity, the amount of the difference shall be charged to the profit and loss account. Member States may, however, require or permit the amount of the difference to be written off in instalments so that it is completely written off when the securities are repaid. That difference must be shown separately in the balance sheet or in the notes on the accounts.

(c) Where the purchase price of the securities referred to in point (a) is less than the amount repayable at maturity, Member States may require or permit the amount of the difference to be released to income in instalments over the period remaining until repayment. That difference must be shown separately in the balance sheet or in the notes on the accounts.

2. Where debt securities or other fixed-income securities that are not valued at market value are sold before maturity and the proceeds are used to purchase other debt securities or fixed-income securities, Member States may permit the difference between the proceeds of sale and their book value to be spread uniformly over the period remaining until the maturity of the original investment.

Article 56

Technical provisions

The amount of technical provisions must at all times be such that an undertaking can meet any liabilities arising out of insurance contracts as far as can reasonably be foreseen.

Article 57

Provision for unearned premiums

1. The provision for unearned premiums shall in principle be computed separately for each insurance contract. Member States may, however, permit the use of statistical methods, and in particular proportional and flat rate methods, where they may be expected to give approximately the same results as individual calculations.

2. In classes of insurance where the assumption of a temporal correlation between risk experience and premium is calculation of the provision irrespective of their not appropriate calculation methods shall be applied that take account of the differing pattern of risk over time.

Article 58

Provision for unexpired risks

The provision for unexpired risks referred to in Article 26 shall be computed on the basis of claims and administrative expenses likely to arise after the end of the financial year from contracts concluded before that date, in so far as their estimated value exceeds the provision for unearned premiums and any premiums receivable under those contracts.

Article 59

Life assurance provision

1. The life assurance provision shall in principle be computed separately for each life assurance contract. Member States may, however, permit the use of statistical or mathematical methods where they may be expected to give approximately the same results as individual calculations. A summary of the principal assumptions made shall be given in the notes on the accounts.

2. The computation shall be made annually by an actuary or other specialist in this field on the basis of recognised actuarial methods.

Article 60

Provisions for claims outstanding

1. Non-life insurance

(a) A provision shall in principle be computed separately for each case on the basis of the costs still expected to arise. Statistical methods may be used if they result in an adequate provision having regard to the nature of the risks; Member States may, however, make the application of such methods subject to prior approval.

(b) This provision shall also allow for claims incurred but not reported by the balance-sheet date; its amount shall be determined having regard to past experience as to the number and magnitude of claims reported after the balance-sheet date.

(c) Claims settlement costs shall be included in the calculation of the provision irrespective of their origin.

(d) Recoverable amounts arising out of the acquisition of the rights of policyholders with respect to third parties (subrogation) or of the legal ownership of insured property (salvage) shall be deducted from the provision for claims outstanding; they shall be estimated on a prudent basis. Where such amounts are material, they shall be disclosed in the notes on the accounts.

(e) By way of derogation from subparagraph (d), Member States may require or permit the disclosure of recoverable amounts as assets.

(f) Where benefits resulting from a claim must be paid in the form of annuity, the amounts to be set aside for that purpose shall be calculated by recognised actuarial methods.

(g) Implicit discounting or deductions, whether resulting from the placing of a present value on a provision for an outstanding claim which is expected to be settled later at a higher figure or otherwise effected, shall be prohibited.

Member States may permit explicit discounting or deductions to take account of investment income. No such discounting or deductions shall be permissible unless:

(i) the expected average date for the settlement of claims is at least four years after the accounting date;

(ii) the discounting or deduction is effected on a recognised prudential basis; the competent authority must be given advance notification of any change in method;

(iii) when calculating the total cost of settling claims, an undertaking takes account of all factors that could cause increases in that cost;

(iv) an undertaking has adequate data at its disposal to construct a reliable model of the rate of claims settlements;

(v) the rate of interest used for the calculation of present values does not exceed a prudent estimate of the investment income from assets invested as a provision for claims during the period necessary for the payment of such claims. Moreover, it must not exceed either of the following:

– the investment income from such assets over the preceding five years,

– the investment income from such assets during the year preceding the balance-sheet date.

When discounting or effecting deductions, an undertaking shall, in the notes on its accounts, disclose the total amount of provisions before discounting or deduction, the categories of claims which are discounted or from which deductions have been made and, for each category of claims, the methods used, in particular the rates used for the estimates referred to in the preceding subparagraph, points (iii) and (v), and the criteria adopted for estimating the period that will elapse before the claims are settled.

2. Life insurance

(a) The amount of the provision for claims shall be equal to the sums due to beneficiaries, plus the costs of settling claims. It shall include the provision for claims incurred but not reported.

(b) Member States may require the disclosure in liabilities item C (2) of the amounts referred to in (a).

Article 61

1. Pending further co-ordination, Member States may require or permit the application of the following methods where, because of the nature of the class or type of insurance in question,

information about premiums receivable, claims payable or both for the underwriting years is insufficient when the annual accounts are drawn up for accurate estimates to be made.

Method 1

The excess of the premiums written over the claims and expenses paid in respect of contracts commencing in the underwriting year shall form a technical provision which is included in the technical provision for claims outstanding shown in the balance sheet in liabilities item C (3). The provision may also be computed on the basis of a given percentage of the premiums written where such a method is appropriate for the type of risk insured. Should the need arise, the amount of this technical provision shall be increased to make it sufficient to meet present and future obligations. The technical provision constituted by this method shall be replaced by a provision for claims outstanding estimated in the usual manner as soon as sufficient information has been gathered and not later than the end of the third year following the underwriting year.

Method 2

1. The figures shown in the technical account or in certain items within it shall relate to a year that wholly or partly precedes the financial year. It must not do so by more than 12 months. The amounts of the technical provisions shown in the annual accounts shall if necessary be increased to make them sufficient to meet present and future obligations.

2. Where one of the methods described in paragraph 1 is adopted, it shall be applied systematically in successive years unless circumstances justify a change. The use of either method shall be disclosed in the notes on the accounts and the reasons given; in the event of a change in the method applied, the effect on the assets, liabilities, financial position and profit or loss shall be indicated in the notes on the accounts. Where Method 1 is used, the length of time that elapses before a provision for claims outstanding is constituted on the usual basis shall be disclosed in the notes on the accounts. Where Method 2 is used, the length of time by which the earlier year to which the figures relate precedes the financial year and the magnitude of the transactions concerned shall be disclosed in the notes on the accounts.

3. For the purposes of this Article, 'underwriting year' shall mean the financial year in which the insurance contracts in the class or type of insurance in question commenced.

Article 62

Pending further co-ordination, those Member States that require the constitution of equalisation provisions shall prescribe the valuation rules to be applied to them.

Section 8
Contents of the Notes on the Accounts

Article 63

In place of the information provided for in Article 43 (1) (8) of Directive 78/660/EEC, insurance undertakings shall provide the following particulars:

I. As regards non-life insurance, the notes on the accounts shall disclose:

1. gross premiums written;

2. gross premiums earned;

3. gross claims charges;

4. gross operating expenses;

5. the reinsurance balance.

These amounts shall be shown broken down between direct insurance and reinsurance acceptances, if reinsurance acceptances amount to 10% or more of gross premiums written, and then within direct insurance into the following groups of classes:
– accident and health,
– motor, third-party liability,
– motor, other classes,
– marine, aviation and transport,
– fire and other damage to property,
– third-party liability,
– credit and suretyship,

– legal expenses,
– assistance,
– miscellaneous.

The breakdown into groups of classes within direct insurance shall not be required where the amount of the gross premiums written in direct insurance for the group in question does not exceed ECU 10 million. However, undertakings shall in any case disclose the amounts relating to the three largest groups of classes in their business.

II. As regards the assurance, the notes on the accounts shall disclose:

1. gross premiums written, broken down between direct insurance and reinsurance acceptances, if reinsurance acceptances amount to 10% or more of gross premiums written, and then within direct insurance to indicate:

(a) (i) individual premiums;
    (ii) premiums under group contracts;
(b) (i) periodic premiums;
    (ii) single premiums;
(c) (i) premiums from non-bonus contracts;
    (ii) premiums from bonus contracts;
    (iii) premiums from contracts where the investment risk is borne by policyholders.

Disclosure of the figure relating to (a), (b) or (c) shall not be required where it does not exceed 10% of the gross premiums written in direct insurance;

2. the reinsurance balance;

III. In the case covered by Article 33 (4), gross premiums broken down between life assurance and non-life insurance.

IV. In all cases, the total gross direct insurance premiums resulting from contracts concluded by the insurance undertaking
– in the Member State of its head office,
– in the other Member States, and
– in other countries,

except that disclosure of the figure relating to the above shall not be required if they do not exceed 5% of total gross premiums.

Article 64

In the notes on their accounts insurance undertakings shall disclose the total amount of commissions for direct insurance business taken into the accounts for the financial year. This requirement shall cover commissions of any kind, and in particular acquisition, renewal, collection and portfolio management commissions.

SECTION 9

PROVISIONS RELATING TO CONSOLIDATED ACCOUNTS

Article 65

1. Insurance undertakings shall draw up consolidated accounts and consolidated annual reports in accordance with Directive 83/349/EEC, save as otherwise provided in this section.

2. In so far as a Member State does not have recourse to Article 5 of Directive 83/349/EEC, paragraph 1 shall also apply to parent undertakings, the sole or essential object of which is to acquire holdings in subsidiary undertakings and turn them to profit, where those subsidiary undertakings are either exclusively or mainly insurance undertakings.

Article 66

Directive 83/349/EEC shall apply subject to the following provisions:

1. Articles 4, 6, and 40 shall not apply;

2. the information referred to in the first and second indents of Article 9 (2), namely:
– the amount of the fixed assets, and
– the net turnover,

shall be replaced by particulars of the gross premiums written as defined in Article 35 of this Directive;

3. a Member State may also apply Article 12 of Directive 83/349/EEC to two or more insurance undertakings which are not connected as described in Article 1 (1) or (2) of the same Directive but are managed on a unified basis other than pursuant to a contract or provisions of

their memoranda or articles of association. Unified management may also consist of important and durable reinsurance links;

4. Member States may permit derogations from Article 26 (1) (c) of Directive 83/349/EEC where a transaction has been concluded according to normal market conditions and has established policyholder rights. Any such derogation shall be disclosed and where they have a material effect on the assets, liabilities, financial position and profit or loss of all the undertakings included in the consolidation that fact shall be disclosed in the notes on the consolidated accounts;

5. Article 27 (3) of Directive 83/349/EEC shall apply provided that the balance-sheet date of an undertaking included in a consolidation does not precede the consolidated balance-sheet date by more than six months;

6. Article 29 of Directive 83/349/EEC shall not apply to those liabilities items, the valuation of which by the undertakings included in a consolidation is based on the application of provisions specific to insurance undertakings or to those assets items changes in the values of which also affect or establish policyholders' rights. Where recourse is had to this derogation, the fact shall be disclosed in the notes on the consolidated accounts.

Article 67

In consolidated accounts alone Member States may require or permit all investment income and charges to be disclosed in the non-technical account, even when such income and charges are connected with life-assurance business.

Furthermore, Member States may in such cases require or permit the allocation of part of the investment return to the life-assurance technical account.

Section 10

Publication

Article 68

1. The duly approved annual accounts of insurance undertakings, together with the annual reports and the reports by the persons responsible for auditing the accounts, shall be published as laid down by the laws of each Member State in accordance with Article 3 of Directive 68/151/EEC.[13]

The laws of a Member State may, however, provide that annual reports need not be published as provided in the first subparagraph. In that event, they shall be made available to the public at the undertakings' head offices in the Member State concerned. It must be possible to obtain a copy of all or part of any such report upon request. The price of such a copy shall not exceed its administrative cost.

2. Paragraph 1 shall also apply to the duly approved consolidated accounts, the consolidated annual report and the reports by the persons responsible for auditing the accounts.

3. Where an insurance undertaking which has drawn up annual accounts or consolidated accounts is not established as one of the types of company listed in Article 1 (1) of Directive 78/660/EEC and is not required by its national law to publish the documents referred to in paragraph 1 and 2 of this Article as prescribed in Article 3 of Directive 68/151/EEC, it shall at least make them available to the public at its head office. It must be possible to obtain copies of such documents on request. The price of such copies shall not exceed their administrative cost.

4. Member States shall provide for appropriate sanctions for failure to comply with the publication rules laid down in this Article.

Section 11

Final Provisions

Article 69

The contact committee set up pursuant to Article 52 of Directive 78/660/EEC shall also, when

---

[13] OJ L 65, 14.3.1968, 8, First Company Law Directive, reproduced supra under no. C. 1.

constituted appropriately, have the following functions:

(a) to facilitate, without prejudice to Articles [226 and 227][2] of the Treaty, harmonised application of this Directive through regular meetings dealing in particular with practical problems arising in connection with its application;

(b) to advise the Commission, if the need arises, on additions or amendments to this Directive.

Article 70

1. Member States shall adopt the laws, regulations and administrative provisions necessary for them to comply with this Directive before 1 January 1994. They shall forthwith inform the Commission thereof.

When Member States adopt these measures, they shall include a reference to this Directive or be accompanied by such reference on the occasion of their official publication. The methods of making such a reference shall be laid down by the Member States.

2. Member States may provide that the provisions referred to in paragraph 1 shall first apply to annual accounts and consolidated accounts for financial years beginning on 1 January 1995 or during the calendar year 1995.

3. Member States shall communicate to the Commission the texts of the main provisions of national law, which they adopt in the field governed by this Directive.

Article 71

Five years after the date referred to in Article 70 (2) the Council, acting on a proposal from the Commission, shall examine and if need be revise all those provisions of this Directive which provide for Member State options in the light of the experience acquired in applying this Directive and in particular of the aims of greater transparency and harmonisation of the provisions referred to by this Directive.

Article 72

This Directive is addressed to the Member States.

Annex

[...]

¶ *The Annex has been repealed by article 4(6) of Directive 2003/51/EC, reproduced supra under no. C.23.*

I. 24.

Council Directive 91/675/EEC
of 19 December 1991
setting up an [European Insurance and Occupational Pensions Committee][1]

¶ *The title of this directive has been amended by article 5(1) of Directive 2005/1/EC, reproduced supra under no. B. 39.*

THE COUNCIL OF THE EUROPEAN COMMUNITIES,

Having regard to the Treaty establishing the European Economic Community, and in particular the third sentence of Article [47(2)][2] thereof,

Having regard to the proposal from the Commission,[3]

In co-operation with the European Parliament,[4]

Having regard to the opinion of the Economic and Social Committee,[5]

Whereas the Council shall confer on the Commission powers for the implementation of the rules which the Council lays down;

Whereas implementing measures are necessary for the application of Council directives on non-life insurance and life assurance; whereas, in particular, technical adaptations may from time to time be necessary to take account of developments in the insurance sector; whereas it is appropriate that these measures shall be taken in accordance with the procedure laid down in Article 2, procedure III, variant (b), of Council Decision 87/373/EEC of 13 July 1987 laying down the procedures for the exercise of implementing powers conferred on the Commission;[6]

Whereas it is necessary for this purpose to set up an Insurance Committee;

Whereas the establishment of an Insurance Committee does not rule out other forms of co-operation between authorities which supervise the taking up and pursuit of the business of insurance undertakings, and in particular co-operation within the Conference on Insurance Supervisory Authorities, which is in particular competent for the drafting of protocols implementing Community directives; whereas close co-operation between the Committee and the Conference would be particularly useful;

Whereas the examination of problems arising in non-life insurance and life assurance makes co-operation desirable between the competent authorities and the Commission; whereas it is appropriate to confer this task on the Insurance Committee; whereas it should furthermore be ensured that there is smooth co-ordination of the activities of this Committee with those of other committees of a similar nature set up by Community acts,

HAS ADOPTED THIS REGULATION:

[*Article 1*

1. The Commission shall be assisted by the European Insurance and Occupational Pensions Committee established by Commission Decision 2004/9/EC of 5 November 2003[7] (hereinafter the Committee).

2. The chairperson of the Committee of European Insurance and Occupational Pensions Supervisors established by Commission Decision 2004/6/EC[8] shall participate at the meetings of the Committee as an observer.

---

[1] OJ L 374, 31.12.1991, 32–33.
[2] The number between brackets has been changed as from 1 May 1999 by article 12 of the Treaty of Amsterdam.
[3] OJ C 230, 15.9.1990, 5.
[4] OJ C 240, 16.9.1991, 117 and OJ C 305, 25.11.1991.
[5] OJ C 102, 18.4.1991, 11.
[6] OJ L 197, 18.7.1987, 33.
[7] OJ L 3, 7.1.2004, 34.
[8] OJ L 3, 7.1.2004, 30.

3. The Committee may invite experts and observers to attend its meetings.

4. The secretariat of the Committee shall be provided by the Commission.]

¶ *This article has been replaced by article 5(2) of Directive 2005/1/EC, reproduced supra under no. B. 39.*

[Article 2

1. Where acts adopted in the field of direct non-life insurance and direct life assurance, reinsurance and occupational pensions confer on the Commission powers for the implementation of the rules which they lay down, Articles 5 and 7 of Council Decision 1999/468/EC of 28 June 1999 laying down the procedures for the exercise of implementing powers conferred on the Commission[9] shall apply, having regard to the provisions of Article 8 thereof.

The period laid down in Article 5(6) of Decision 1999/468/EC shall be set at three months.

2. The Committee shall adopt its rules of procedure.]

¶ *This article has been replaced by article 5(3) of Directive 2005/1/EC, reproduced supra under no. B. 39.*

Article 3

[. . .]

¶ *This article has been repealed by article 5(4) of Directive 2005/1/EC, reproduced supra under no. B. 39.*

Article 4

[. . .]

¶ *This article has been repealed by article 5(4) of Directive 2005/1/EC, reproduced supra under no. B. 39.*

Article 5

This Directive is addressed to the Member States.

---

[9] OJ L 184, 17.7.1999, 23.

I. 25.

Council Directive 92/49/EEC
of 18 June 1992
on the co-ordination of laws, regulations and administrative provisions relating to direct insurance other than life assurance and amending Directives 73/239/EEC and 88/357/EEC
(Third non-life insurance Directive)[1]

CASE

I. Case C-346/02 Commission of the European Communities v Grand Duchy of Luxemburg [2004] ECR I-7517

A national law that forbids to frustrate the application to the contract of the *bonus/malus* scale as set out in the law, eg on entry point and on increases in the scale, although affecting changes in the amount of premiums, does not result in the direct setting of premium rates by the State, since insurance undertakings remain free to apply or not to apply the scale, and to set the amount of the basic premium. Hence this legislation is not contrary to the principle of freedom to set rates and of elimination of prior or systematic controls on scales of premiums and insurance contracts, as established by Articles 6, 29 and 39 of Directive 92/49/EEC.

Full harmonization in the field of non-life insurance rates precluding any national measure liable to have effects on rates cannot be presumed in the absence of a clearly expressed intention to this effect on the part of the Community legislature.

II. Case C-410/96 Criminal Proceedings Against André Ambry [1998] ECR I-7875

It is contrary to Article [49][2] of the Treaty, and to Directive 89/646/EEC on the coordination of laws, regulations and administrative provisions relating to the taking up and pursuit of the business of credit institutions and amending Directive 77/780/EEC and Directive 92/49/EEC on the coordination of laws, regulations and administrative provisions relating to direct insurance other than life assurance and amending Directives 73/239/EEC and 88/357/EEC, for national rules to require, with a view to implementing Article 7 of Directive 90/314/EEC, that, where financial security is provided by a credit institution or insurance company situated in another Member State, the guarantor must conclude an agreement with a credit institution or insurance company situated in the national territory.

That requirement has the effect, first and foremost, of restricting and discouraging financial institutions established in other Member States, inasmuch as it prevents them from offering the security required directly to the travel organizer on the same basis as a guarantor situated in the national territory. It is also likely to discourage the travel operator from approaching a financial institution situated in another Member State, since the fact that such an institution must enter into a further guarantee agreement is liable to give rise to additional costs which would normally be passed on to the travel operator. It constitutes a restriction on the freedom to provide services, which is not justified as being necessary for the protection of consumers.

THE COUNCIL OF THE EUROPEAN COMMUNITIES,

Having regard to the Treaty establishing the European Economic Community, and in particular Articles [47 (2) and 55][2] thereof,

Having regard to the proposal from the Commission,[3]

In co-operation with the European Parliament,[4]

---

[1] OJ L 228, 11.8.1992, 1–23.

[2] The numbers between brackets have been changed as from 1 May 1999 by article 12 of the Treaty of Amsterdam.

[3] OJ C 244, 28.9.1990, 28 and OJ C 93, 13.4.1992, 1.

[4] OJ C 67, 16.3.1992, 98 and OJ C 150, 15.6.1992.

Having regard to the opinion of the Economic and Social Committee,[5]

1. Whereas it is necessary to complete the internal market in direct insurance other than life assurance from the point of view both of the right of establishment and of the freedom to provide services, to make it easier for insurance undertakings with head offices in the Community to cover risks situated within the Community;

2. Whereas the Second Council Directive of 22 June 1988 on the co-ordination of laws, regulations and administrative provisions relating to direct insurance other than life assurance and laying down provisions to facilitate the effective exercise of freedom to provide services and amending Directive 72/239/EEC (88/357/EEC)[6] has already contributed substantially to the achievement of the internal market in direct insurance other than life assurance by granting policyholders who, by virtue of their status, their size or the nature of the risks to be insured, do not require special protection in the Member State in which a risk is situated complete freedom to avail themselves of the widest possible insurance market;

3. Whereas Directive 88/357/EEC therefore represents an important stage in the merging of national markets into an integrated market and that stage must be supplemented by other Community instruments with a view to enabling all policyholders, irrespective of their status, their size or the nature of the risks to be insured, to have recourse to any insurer with a head office in the Community who carries on business there, under the right of establishment or the freedom to provide services, while guaranteeing them adequate protection;

4. Whereas this Directive forms part of the body of Community legislation already enacted which includes the First Council Directive of 24 July 1973 on the co-ordination of laws, regulations and administrative provisions relating to the taking up and pursuit of the business of direct insurance other than life assurance (73/239/EEC)[7] and the Council Directive of 19 December 1991 on the annual accounts and consolidated accounts of insurance undertakings (91/674/EEC);[8]

5. Whereas the approach adopted consists in bringing about such harmonisation as is essential, necessary and sufficient to achieve the mutual recognition of authorisations and prudential control systems, thereby making it possible to grant a single authorisation valid throughout the Community and apply the principle of supervision by the home Member State;

6. Whereas, as a result, the taking up and the pursuit of the business of insurance are henceforth to be subject to the grant of a single official authorisation issued by the competent authorities of the Member State in which an insurance undertaking has its head office; whereas such authorisation enables an undertaking to carry on business throughout the Community, under the right of establishment or the freedom to provide services; whereas the Member State of the branch or of the provision of services may no longer require insurance undertakings which wish to carry on insurance business there and which have already been authorised in their home Member State to seek fresh authorisation; whereas Directives 73/239/EEC and 88/357/EEC should therefore be amended along those lines;

7. Whereas the competent authorities of home Member States will henceforth be responsible for monitoring the financial health of insurance undertakings, including their state of solvency, the establishment of adequate technical provisions and the covering of those provisions by matching assets;

8. Whereas certain provisions of this Directive define minimum standards; whereas a home Member State may lay down stricter rules for insurance undertakings authorised by its own competent authorities;

---

[5] OJ C 102, 18.4.1991, 7.
[6] OJ L 172, 4.7.1988, 1, Second Non-Life Insurance Directive, reproduced supra under no. I. 15.
[7] OJ L 228, 16.8.1973, 3, First Non-Life Insurance Directive, reproduced supra under no. I. 3.
[8] OJ L 374, 31.12.1991, 7, reproduced supra under no. I. 23.

9. Whereas the competent authorities of the Member States must have at their disposal such means of supervision as are necessary to ensure the orderly pursuit of business by insurance undertakings throughout the Community whether carried on under the right of establishment or the freedom to provide services; whereas, in particular, they must be able to introduce appropriate safeguards or impose sanctions aimed at preventing irregularities and infringements of the provisions on insurance supervision;

10. Whereas the internal market comprises an area without internal frontiers and involves access to all insurance business other than life assurance throughout the Community and, hence, the possibility for any duly authorised insurer to cover any of the risks referred to in the Annex to Directive 73/239/EEC; whereas, to that end, the monopoly enjoyed by certain bodies in certain Member States in respect of the coverage of certain risks must be abolished;

11. Whereas the provisions on transfers of portfolios must be adapted to bring them into line with the single authorisation system introduced by this Directive;

12. Whereas Directive 91/674/EEC has already effected the necessary harmonisation of the Member States' rules on the technical provisions which insurers are required to establish to cover their commitments, and that harmonisation makes it possible to grant mutual recognition of those provisions;

13. Whereas the rules governing the spread, localisation and matching of the assets used to cover technical provisions must be co-ordinated in order to facilitate the mutual recognition of Member States' rules; whereas that co-ordination must take account of the measures on the liberalisation of capital movements provided for in the Council Directive of 24 June 1988 for the implementation of Article [67][9] of the Treaty (88/361/EEC)[10] and the progress made by the Community towards economic and monetary union;

14. Whereas, however, the home Member State may not require insurance undertakings to invest the assets covering their technical provisions in particular categories of assets, as such a requirement would be incompatible with the measures on the liberalisation of capital movements provided for in Directive 88/361/EEC;

15. Whereas, pending the adoption of a Directive on investment services harmonising inter alia the definition of the concept of regulated market, for the purposes of this Directive and without prejudice to such future harmonisation that concept must be defined provisionally; whereas that definition will be replaced by that harmonised at Community level which will give the home Member State of the market the responsibilities for these matters which this Directive transitionally gives to the insurance undertaking's home Member State;¶

¶ *See Directive 93/22/EEC, reproduced infra under no. S. 14.*

16. Whereas the list of items of which the solvency margin required by Directive 73/239/EEC may be made up must be supplemented to take account of new financial instruments and of the facilities granted to other financial institutions for the constitution of their own funds;

17. Whereas within the framework of an integrated insurance market policyholders who, by virtue of their status, their size or the nature of the risks to be insured, do not require special protection in the Member State in which a risk is situated should be granted complete freedom to choose the law applicable to their insurance contracts;

18. Whereas the harmonisation of insurance contract law is not a prior condition for the achievement of the internal market in insurance; whereas, therefore, the opportunity afforded to the Member States of imposing the application of their law to insurance contracts covering risks situated within their territories is likely to provide adequate safeguards for policyholders who require special protection;

---

[9] The number between brackets has been repealed as from 1 May 1999 by article 12 of the Treaty of Amsterdam.
[10] OJ L 178, 8.7.1988, 5, reproduced supra under no. C.M. 2.

19. Whereas within the framework of an internal market it is in the policyholder's interest that he should have access to the widest possible range of insurance products available in the Community so that he can choose that which is best suited to his needs; whereas it is for the Member State in which the risk is situated to ensure that there is nothing to prevent the marketing within its territory of all the insurance products offered for sale in the Community as long as they do not conflict with the legal provisions protecting the general good in force in the Member State in which the risk is situated, and insofar as the general good is not safeguarded by the rules of the home Member State, provided that such provisions must be applied without discrimination to all undertakings operating in that Member State and be objectively necessary and in proportion to the objective pursued;

20. Whereas the Member States must be able to ensure that the insurance products and contract documents used, under the right of establishment or the freedom to provide services, to cover risks situated within their territories comply with such specific legal provisions protecting the general good as are applicable; whereas the systems of supervision to be employed must meet the requirements of an integrated market but their employment may not constitute a prior condition for carrying on insurance business; whereas from this standpoint systems for the prior approval of policy conditions do not appear to be justified; whereas it is therefore necessary to provide for other systems better suited to the requirements of an internal market which enable every Member State to guarantee policyholders adequate protection;

21. Whereas if a policyholder is a natural person, he should be informed by the insurance undertaking of the law which will apply to the contract and of the arrangements for handling policyholders' complaints concerning contracts;

22. Whereas in some Member States private or voluntary health insurance serves as a partial or complete alternative to health cover provided for by the social security systems;

23. Whereas the nature and social consequences of health insurance contracts justify the competent authorities of the Member State in which a risk is situated in requiring systematic notification of the general and special policy conditions in order to verify that such contracts are a partial or complete alternative to the health cover provided by the social security system; whereas such verification must not be a prior condition for the marketing of the products; whereas the particular nature of health insurance, serving as a partial or complete alternative to the health cover provided by the social security system, distinguishes it from other classes of indemnity insurance and life assurance insofar as it is necessary to ensure that policyholders have effective access to private health cover or health cover taken out on a voluntary basis regardless of their age or risk profile;

24. Whereas to this end some Member States have adopted specific legal provisions; whereas, to protect the general good, it is possible to adopt or maintain such legal provisions in so far as they do not unduly restrict the right of establishment or the freedom to provide services, it being understood that such provisions must apply in an identical manner whatever the home Member State of the undertaking may be; whereas these legal provisions may differ in nature according to the conditions in each Member State; whereas these measures may provide for open enrolment, rating on a uniform basis according to the type of policy and lifetime cover; whereas that objective may also be achieved by requiring undertakings offering private health cover or health cover taken out on a voluntary basis to offer standard policies in line with the cover provided by statutory social security schemes at a premium rate at or below a prescribed maximum and to participate in loss compensation schemes; whereas, as a further possibility, it may be required that the technical basis of private health cover or health cover taken out on a voluntary basis be similar to that of life assurance;

25. Whereas, because of the co-ordination effected by Directive 73/239/EEC as amended by this Directive, the possibility, afforded to the Federal Republic of Germany under Article 7 (2) (c)

of the same Directive, of prohibiting the simultaneous transaction of health insurance and other classes is no longer justified and must therefore be abolished;

26. Whereas Member States may require any insurance undertakings offering compulsory insurance against accidents at work at their own risk within their territories to comply with the specific provisions laid down in their national law on such insurance; whereas; however, this requirement may not apply to the provisions concerning financial supervision, which are the exclusive responsibility of the home Member State;

27. Whereas exercise of the right of establishment requires an undertaking to maintain a permanent presence in the Member State of the branch; whereas responsibility for the specific interests of insured persons and victims in the case of third-party liability motor insurance requires adequate structures in the Member State of the branch for the collection of all the necessary information on compensation claims relating to that risk, with sufficient powers to represent the undertaking vis-à-vis injured parties who could claim compensation, including powers to pay such compensation, and to represent the undertaking or, if necessary, to arrange for it to be represented in the courts and before the competent authorities of that Member State in connection with claims for compensation;

28. Whereas within the framework of the internal market no Member State may continue to prohibit the simultaneous carrying on of insurance business within its territory under the right of establishment and the freedom to provide services; whereas the option granted to Member States in this connection by Directive 88/357/EEC should therefore be abolished;

29. Whereas provision should be made for a system of penalties to be imposed when, in the Member State in which a risk is situated, an insurance undertaking does not comply with those provisions protecting the general good that are applicable to it;

30. Whereas some Member States do not subject insurance transactions to any form of indirect taxation, while the majority apply special taxes and other forms of contribution, including surcharges intended for compensation bodies; whereas the structures and rates of such taxes and contributions vary considerably between the Member States in which they are applied; whereas it is desirable to prevent existing differences' leading to distortions of competition in insurance services between Member States; whereas, pending subsequent harmonisation, application of the tax systems and other forms of contribution provided for by the Member States in which risks are situated is likely to remedy that problem and it is for the Member States to make arrangements to ensure that such taxes and contributions are collected;

31. Whereas technical adjustments to the detailed rules laid down in this Directive may be necessary from time to time to take account of the future development of the insurance industry; whereas the Commission will make such adjustments as and when necessary, after consulting the Insurance Committee set up by Directive 91/675/EEC,[11] in the exercise of the implementing powers conferred on it by the Treaty;

32. Whereas it is necessary to adopt specific provisions intended to ensure smooth transition from the legal regime in existence when this Directive becomes applicable to the regime that it introduces, taking care not to place an additional workload on Member States' competent authorities;

33. Whereas under Article [20][2] of the Treaty account should be taken of the extent of the effort which must be made by certain economies at different stages of development; whereas, therefore, transitional arrangements should be adopted for the gradual application of this Directive by certain Member States,

HAS ADOPTED THIS DIRECTIVE:

---

[11] OJ L 374, 31.12.1991, 32, reproduced supra under no. I. 24.

TITLE I
DEFINITIONS AND SCOPE

Article 1

For the purposes of this Directive:

(a) *insurance undertaking* shall mean an undertaking that has received official authorisation in accordance with Article 6 of Directive 73/239/EEC;

(b) *branch* shall mean an agency or branch of an insurance undertaking, having regard to Article 3 of Directive 88/357/EEC;

(c) *home Member State* shall mean the Member State in which the head office of the insurance undertaking covering a risk is situated;

(d) *Member State of the branch* shall mean the Member State in which the branch covering a risk is situated;

(e) *Member State of the provision of services* shall mean the Member State in which a risk is situated, as defined in Article 2 (d) of Directive 88/357/EEC, if it is covered by an insurance undertaking or a branch situated in another Member State;

(f) *control* shall mean the relationship between a parent undertaking and a subsidiary, as defined in Article 1 of Directive 83/349/EEC,[12] or a similar relationship between any natural or legal person and an undertaking;

(g) *qualifying holding* shall mean a direct or indirect holding in an undertaking which represents 10% or more of the capital or of the voting rights or which makes it possible to exercise a significant influence over the management of the undertaking in which a holding subsists.

For the purposes of this definition, in the context of Articles 8 and 15 and of the other levels of holding referred to in Article 15, the voting rights referred to in Article 7 of Directive 88/627/EEC[13] shall be taken into account;

(h) *parent undertaking* shall mean a parent undertaking as defined in Articles 1 and 2 of Directive 83/349/EEC;

(i) *subsidiary* shall mean a subsidiary undertaking as defined in Articles 1 and 2 of Directive 83/349/EEC; any subsidiary of a subsidiary undertaking shall also be regarded as a subsidiary of the undertaking which is those undertakings' ultimate parent undertaking;

(j) *regulated market* shall mean a financial market regarded by an undertaking's home Member State as a regulated market pending the adoption of a definition in a Directive on investment services and characterised by:

– regular operation, and
– the fact that regulations issued or approved by the appropriate authorities define the conditions for the operation of the market, the conditions for access to the market and, where the Council Directive of 5 March 1979 co-ordinating the conditions for the admission of securities to official stock exchange listing (79/279/EEC)[14] applies, the conditions for admission to listing imposed in that Directive or, where that Directive does not apply, the conditions to be satisfied by a financial instrument in order to be effectively dealt in on the market.

For the purposes of this Directive, a regulated market may be situated in a Member State or in a third country. In the latter event, the market must be recognised by the home Member State and meet comparable requirements. Any financial instruments dealt in on that market must be of a quality comparable to that of the instruments dealt in on the regulated market or markets of the Member State in question;

(k) *competent authorities* shall mean the national authorities that are empowered by law or regulation to supervise insurance undertakings.

---

[12] OJ L 193, 18.7.1983, 1, Seventh Company Directive, reproduced supra under no. C. 6.

[13] OJ L 348, 17.12.1988, 62, reproduced infra under no. S. 10.

[14] OJ L 66, 13.3.1979, 21, reproduced infra under no. S. 2.

[(l) *close links* shall mean a situation in which two or more natural or legal persons are linked by:
(a) "participation", which shall mean the ownership, direct or by way of control, of 20% or more of the voting rights or capital of an undertaking or
(b) "control", which shall mean the relationship between a parent undertaking and a subsidiary, in all the cases referred to in Article 1 (1) and (2) of Directive 83/349/EEC,[15] or a similar relationship between any natural or legal person and an undertaking; any subsidiary undertaking of a subsidiary undertaking shall also be considered a subsidiary of the parent undertaking which is at the head of those undertakings.]

¶ *Point (l) has been added by article 2(1), second indent of Directive 95/26/EC, reproduced infra under no. I. 27.*

CASE

Case C-238/94 José García and others v Mutuelle de Prévoyance Sociale d'Aquitaine and others [1996] ECR I-1673

Article 2(2) of Directive 92/49/EEC on the coordination of laws, regulations and administrative provisions relating to direct insurance other than life assurance and amending Directives 73/239/EEC and 88/357/EEC is to be interpreted as meaning that social security schemes such as the French statutory social security schemes providing health and maternity insurance for the self-employed in non-agricultural trades, old-age insurance for those in skilled manual trades and old-age insurance for those in industrial and commercial trades are excluded from the scope of Directive 92/49/EEC. That provision quite clearly excludes from the scope of the directive not merely social security organizations but also the types of insurance and operations that they provide in that capacity. Furthermore, the Member States retain their powers to organize their social security systems and thus to set up compulsory schemes based on the principle of solidarity, which would be unable to survive if the directive were to be applied to them, removing the obligation to contribute.

Article 2

1. This Directive shall apply to the types of insurance and undertakings referred to in Article 1 of Directive 73/239/EEC.

2. This Directive shall apply neither to the types of insurance or operations, nor to undertakings or institutions to which Directive 73/239/EEC does not apply, nor to the bodies referred to in Article 4 of that Directive.

Article 3

Notwithstanding Article 2 (2), Member States shall take every step to ensure that monopolies in respect of the taking up of the business of certain classes of insurance, granted to bodies established within their territories and referred to in Article 4 of Directive 73/239/EEC, are abolished by 1 July 1994.

TITLE II

THE TAKING UP OF THE BUSINESS OF INSURANCE

Articles 4 to 7

[. . .]

¶ *These articles replace articles 6 to 9 of the First Non-Life Insurance Directive 73/239/EEC, reproduced supra under no. I. 3. The modifications are directly incorporated therein.*

Article 8

The competent authorities of the home Member State shall not grant an undertaking authorisation to take up the business of insurance before they have been informed of the identities of the shareholders or members, direct or indirect, whether natural or legal persons, who have qualifying holdings in that undertaking and of the amounts of those holdings.

---

[15] OJ L 193, 18. 7. 1983, 1, Seventh Company Directive, reproduced supra under no. C. 6. Directive as last amended by Directive 90/605/EEC (OJ L 317, 16.11.1990, 60), reproduced supra under no. C. 12.

The same authorities shall refuse authorisation if, taking into account the need to ensure the sound and prudent management of an insurance undertaking, they are not satisfied as to the qualifications of the shareholders or members.

TITLE III
HARMONISATION OF THE CONDITIONS GOVERNING THE BUSINESS OF INSURANCE

CHAPTER 1
Articles 9 to 11

[...]

¶ *These articles replace articles 13, 14 and 19(1) and (2) of the First Non-Life Insurance Directive 73/239/EEC, reproduced supra under no. I. 3. The modifications are directly incorporated therein.*

Article 12

1. [...]

2. Under the conditions laid down by national law, each Member State shall authorise insurance undertakings with head offices within its territory to transfer all or part of their portfolios of contracts, concluded either under the right of establishment or the freedom to provide services, to an accepting office established within the Community, if the competent authorities of the home Member State of the accepting office certify that after taking the transfer into account the latter possesses the necessary solvency margin.

3. Where a branch proposes to transfer all or part of its portfolio of contracts, concluded either under the right of establishment or the freedom to provide services, the Member State of the branch shall be consulted.

4. In the circumstances referred to in paragraphs 2 and 3, the competent authorities of the home Member State of the transferring undertaking shall authorise the transfer after obtaining the agreement of the competent authorities of the Member States in which the risks are situated.

5. The competent authorities of the Member States consulted shall give their opinion or consent to the competent authorities of the home Member State of the transferring insurance undertaking within three months of receiving a request; the absence of any response within that period from the authorities consulted shall be considered equivalent to a favourable opinion or tacit consent.

6. A transfer authorised in accordance with this Article shall be published as laid down by national law in the Member State in which the risk is situated. Such transfers shall automatically be valid against policyholders, insured persons and any other persons having rights or obligations arising out of the contracts transferred.

This provision shall not affect the Member States' rights to give policyholders the option of cancelling contracts within a fixed period after a transfer.

¶ *Paragraph 1 repeals article 11(2) to (7) of the Second Council Directive 88/357/EEC, reproduced supra under no. I. 15. The modifications are directly incorporated therein.*

Articles 13 to 14

[...]

¶ *These articles modify articles 20 and 22 of the First Non-Life Insurance Directive 73/239/EEC, reproduced supra under no. I. 3. The modifications are directly incorporated therein.*

Article 15

1. Member States shall require any natural or legal person [who proposes to acquire], directly or indirectly, a qualifying holding in an insurance undertaking first to inform the competent authorities of the home Member State, indicating the size of his intended holding. Such a person must likewise inform the competent authorities of the home Member State if he proposes to increase his qualifying holding so that the proportion of the voting rights or of the capital he holds would reach or exceed 20, 33 or 50% or so that the insurance undertaking would become his subsidiary.

The competent authorities of the home Member State shall have up to three months from the date of the notification provided for in the first subparagraph to oppose such a plan if, in view of the need to ensure sound and prudent management of the insurance undertaking in question, they are not satisfied as to the qualification of the person referred to in the first subparagraph. If they do not oppose the plan in question, they may fix a maximum period for its implementation.

[1a. If the acquirer of the holdings referred to in paragraph 1 of this Article is an insurance undertaking, a reinsurance undertaking, a credit institution or an investment firm authorised in another Member State, or the parent undertaking of such an entity, or a natural or legal person controlling such an entity, and if, as a result of that acquisition, the undertaking in which the acquirer proposes to hold a holding would become a subsidiary or subject to the control of the acquirer, the assessment of the acquisition shall be subject to the prior consultation referred to in Article 12a of Directive 73/ 239/EEC.]

2. Member States shall require any natural or legal person who proposes to dispose, directly or indirectly, of a qualifying holding in an insurance undertaking first to inform the competent authorities of the home Member State, indicating the size of his intended holding. Such a person must likewise inform the competent authorities if he proposes to reduce his qualifying holding so that the proportion of the voting rights or of the capital he holds would fall below 20, 33 or 50% or so that the insurance undertaking would cease to be his subsidiary.

3. On becoming aware of them, insurance undertakings shall inform the competent authorities of their home Member States of any acquisitions or disposals of holdings in their capital that cause holdings to exceed or fall below any of the thresholds referred to in paragraphs 1 and 2.

They shall also, at least once a year, inform them of the names of shareholders and members possessing qualifying holdings and the sizes of such holdings as shown, for example, by the information received at annual general meetings of shareholders or members or as a result of compliance with the regulations relating to companies listed on stock exchanges.

4. Member States shall require that, where the influence exercised by the persons referred to in paragraph 1 is likely to operate against the prudent and sound management of an insurance undertaking, the competent authorities of the home Member State shall take appropriate measures to put an end to that situation. Such measures may consist, for example, in injunctions, sanctions against directors and managers, or suspension of the exercise of the voting rights attaching to the shares held by the shareholders or members in question.

Similar measures shall apply to natural or legal persons failing to comply with the obligation to provide prior information imposes in paragraph 1. If a holding is acquired despite the opposition of the competent authorities, the Member States shall, regardless of any other sanctions to be adopted, provide either for exercise of the corresponding voting rights to be suspended, or for the nullity of votes cast or for the possibility of their annulment.

¶ *The words between square brackets in paragraph 1 of article 14(1) should be read as 'who proposes to hold'.*
¶ *Article 15(1a) has been inserted by article 24(1) of Directive 2002/87/EC, reproduced supra under no. B. 38.*
¶ *Article 15(1a) has been replaced by article 58(1) of Directive 2005/68/EC, reproduced infra under no. I. 40.*

Article 16

1. The Member States shall provide that all persons working or who have worked for the competent authorities, as well as auditors and experts acting on behalf of the competent authorities, shall be bound by the obligation of professional secrecy. This means that no confidential information which they may receive while performing their duties may be divulged to any person or authority whatsoever, except in summary or aggregate form, such that individual insurance undertakings cannot be identified, without prejudice to cases covered by criminal law.

Nevertheless, where an insurance undertaking has been declared bankrupt or is being compulsorily wound up, confidential information that does not concern third parties involved in attempts to rescue that undertaking may be divulged in civil or commercial proceedings.

2. Paragraph 1 shall not prevent the competent authorities of different Member States from exchanging information in accordance with the Directives applicable to insurance undertakings. Such information shall be subject to the conditions of professional secrecy laid down in paragraph 1.

[3. Member States may conclude co-operation agreements providing for exchange of information with the competent authorities of third countries or with authorities or bodies of third countries as defined in paragraphs 5 and 5a only if the information disclosed is subject to guarantees of professional secrecy at least equivalent to those referred to in this Article. Such exchange of information must be intended for the performance of the supervisory task of the authorities or bodies mentioned.

Where the information originates in another Member State, it may not be disclosed without the express agreement of the competent authorities that have disclosed it and, where appropriate, solely for the purposes for which those authorities gave their agreement.]

[4. Competent authorities receiving confidential information under paragraph 1 or 2 may use it only in the course of their duties:
– to check that the conditions governing the taking up of the business of insurance are met and to facilitate monitoring of the conduct of such business, especially with regard to the monitoring of technical provisions, solvency margins, administrative and accounting procedures and internal control mechanisms,
– to impose penalties,
– in administrative appeals against decisions of the competent authorities, or
– in court proceedings initiated under Article 53 or under special provisions provided for in this Directive and other Directives adopted in the field of insurance undertakings and reinsurance undertakings.

5. Paragraphs 1 and 4 shall not preclude the exchange of information within a Member State, where there are two or more competent authorities in the same Member State, or, between Member States, between competent authorities and:
– authorities responsible for the official supervision of credit institutions and other financial organisations and the authorities responsible for the supervision of financial markets,
– bodies involved in the liquidation and bankruptcy of insurance undertakings, reinsurance undertakings and in other similar procedures, and
– persons responsible for carrying out statutory audits of the accounts of insurance undertakings, reinsurance undertakings and other financial institutions, in the discharge of their supervisory functions, and the disclosure, to bodies which administer compulsory winding-up proceedings or guarantee funds, of information necessary to the performance of their duties. The information received by those authorities, bodies and persons shall be subject to the obligation of professional secrecy laid down in paragraph 1.]

Member States which have recourse to the option provided for in the first subparagraph shall require at least that the following conditions are met:
– this information shall be for the purpose of carrying out the overseeing or legal supervision referred to in the first subparagraph,
– information received in this context shall be subject to the conditions of professional secrecy imposed in paragraph 1,
– where the information originates in another Member State, it may not be disclosed without the express agreement of the competent authorities which have disclosed it and, where appropriate, solely for the purposes for which those authorities gave their agreement.

Member States shall communicate to the Commission and to the other Member States the names of the authorities, persons and bodies which may receive information pursuant to this paragraph.]

¶ *Paragraph 3 has been replaced by article 2 of Directive 2000/64/EC.*
¶ *Paragraphs 4, 5 and 6 have been replaced by article 58(2) of Directive 2005/68/EC, reproduced infra under no. I. 40.*

[Article 16a

1. Member States shall provide at least that:

(a) any person authorised within the meaning of Directive 84/253/EEC,[16] performing in a [insurance undertaking] the task described in Article 51 of Directive 78/660/EEC,[17] Article 37 of Directive 83/349/EEC or Article 31 of Directive 85/611/EEC or any other statutory task, shall have a duty to report promptly to the competent authorities any fact or decision concerning that undertaking of which he has become aware while carrying out that task which is liable to:

– constitute a material breach of the laws, regulations or administrative provisions which lay down the conditions governing authorisation or which specifically govern pursuit of the activities of [insurance undertaking], or
– affect the continuous functioning of the [insurance undertaking], or
– lead to refusal to certify the accounts or to the expression of reservations;

(b) that person shall likewise have a duty to report any facts and decisions of which he becomes aware in the course of carrying out a task as described in (a) in an undertaking having close links resulting from a control relationship with the [insurance undertaking] within which he is carrying out the abovementioned task.

2. The disclosure in good faith to the competent authorities, by persons authorised within the meaning of Directive 84/253/EEC, of any fact or decision referred to in paragraph 1 shall not constitute a breach of any restriction on disclosure of information imposed by contract of any legislative, regulatory or administrative provision and shall not involve such persons in liability of any kind.]

---

[16] OJ L 126, 12.5.1984, 20, Eight Company Directive, reproduced supra under no. C. 7.
[17] OJ L 222, 14.8.1978, 11, Fourth Company Directive, reproduced supra under no. C. 4. Directive as last amended by Directive 90/605/EEC (OJ L 317, 16.11.1990, 60), reproduced supra under no. C. 12.

¶ *Article 16a has been inserted by article 5 of Directive 95/26/EC, reproduced infra under no. I. 27.*
¶ *The words 'financial undertaking' between the square brackets in the first paragraph have been replaced by article 1, second indent of Directive 95/26/EC, reproduced infra under no. I. 27.*

CHAPTER 2
Articles 17 to 18

[. . .]

¶ *These articles replace articles 15 and 15a of the First Non-Life Insurance Directive 73/239/EEC, reproduced supra under no. I. 3. The modifications are directly incorporated therein.*

Article 19

[. . .]

¶ *This article repeals article 23 of the Second Non-Life Insurance Directive 88/357/EEC, reproduced supra under no. I. 15. The modification is directly incorporated therein.*

Article 20

The assets covering the technical provisions shall take account of the type of business carried on by an undertaking in such a way as to secure the safety, yield and marketability of its investments, which the undertaking shall ensure are diversified and adequately spread.

Article 21

[1. The home Member State may not authorise insurance undertakings to cover their technical provisions and equalisation reserves with any assets other than those in the following categories:]

A. *Investments*

(a) debt securities, bonds and other money and capital market instruments;

(b) loans;

(c) shares and other variable yield participations;

(d) units in undertakings for collective investment in transferable securities and other investment funds;

(e) land, buildings and immovable property rights;

B. *Debts and claims*

[(f) debts owed by reinsurers, including reinsurers shares of technical provisions, and by the special purpose vehicles referred to in Article 46 of Directive 2005/68/EC of the European Parliament and of the Council of 16 November 2005 on reinsurance;[18]]

(g) deposits with and debts owed by ceding undertakings;

(h) debts owed by policyholders and intermediaries arising out of direct and reinsurance operations;

(i) claims arising out of salvage and subrogation;

(j) tax recoveries;

(k) claims against guarantee funds;

C. *Others*

(l) tangible fixed assets, other than land and buildings, valued on the basis of prudent amortisation;

(m) cash at bank and in hand, deposits with credit institutions and any other bodies authorised to receive deposits;

(n) deferred acquisition costs;

(o) accrued interest and rent, other accrued income and prepayments;

In the case of the association of underwriters know as Lloyd's, asset categories shall also include guarantees and letters of credit issued by credit institutions within the meaning of Directive 77/780/EEC[19] or by assurance undertakings, together with verifiable sums arising out of life assurance policies, to the extent that they represent funds belonging to members.

[The inclusion of any asset or category of assets listed in the first subparagraph shall not mean that all those assets should automatically be accepted as cover for technical provisions. The home Member State shall lay down more detailed rules setting the conditions for the use of acceptable assets.]

In the determination and the application of the rules that it lays down, the home Member State shall, in particular, ensure that the following principles are complied with:

(i) assets covering technical provisions shall be valued net of any debts arising out of their acquisition;

(ii) all assets must be valued on a prudent basis, allowing for the risk of any amounts' not being realisable. In particular, tangible fixed assets other than land and buildings may be accepted as cover for technical provisions only if they are valued on the basis of prudent amortisation;

(iii) loans, whether to undertakings, to State authorities or international organisations, to local or regional authorities or to natural persons, may be accepted as cover for technical provisions only if there are sufficient guarantees as to their security, whether these are based on the status of the borrower, mortgages, bank guarantees or guarantees granted by insurance undertakings or other forms of security;

(iv) derivative instruments such as options, futures and swaps in connection with assets covering technical provisions may be used in so far as they contribute to a reduction of investment risks or facilitate efficient portfolio management. They must be valued on a prudent basis and may be taken into account in the valuation of the underlying assets;

(v) transferable securities that are not dealt in on a regulated market may be accepted as cover for technical provisions only if they can be realised in the short term;

(vi) debts owed by and claims against a third party may be accepted as cover for technical provisions only after deduction of all amounts owed to the same third party;

(vii) the value of any debts and claims accepted as cover for technical provisions must be calculated on a prudent basis, with due allowance for the risk of any amounts not being realisable. In particular, debts owed by policyholders and intermediaries arising out of insurance and reinsurance operations may be accepted only in so far as they have been outstanding for not more than three months;

(viii) where the assets held include an investment in a subsidiary undertaking which manages all or part of the insurance

---

[18] OJ L 323, 9.12.2005, 1, reproduced infra under no. I. 40.
[19] OJ L 322, 17.2.1977, 30, First Banking Directive, consolidated in Directive 2000/12/EC, reproduced supra under no. B. 32.

undertaking's investments on its behalf, the home Member State must, when applying the rules and principles laid down in this Article, take into account the underlying assets held by the subsidiary undertaking; the home Member State may treat the assets of other subsidiaries in the same way;

(ix) deferred acquisition costs may be accepted as cover for technical provisions only to the extent that that is consistent with the calculation of the technical provision for unearned premiums.

2. Notwithstanding paragraph 1, in exceptional circumstances and at an insurance undertaking's request, the home Member State may, temporarily and under a properly reasoned decision, accept other categories of assets as cover for technical provisions, subject to Article 20.

¶ *The introductory wording in paragraph 1 and point (f) of point (B) and the third subparagraph of point (C) has been replaced by article 58(3) of Directive 2005/68/EC, reproduced infra under no. I. 40.*

Article 22

[1. As regards the assets covering technical provisions and equalisation reserves, the home Member State shall require every insurance undertaking to invest no more than:]

(a) 10% of its total gross technical provisions in any one piece of land or building, or a number of pieces of land or buildings close enough to each other to be considered effectively as one investment;

(b) 5% of its total gross technical provisions in shares and other negotiable securities treated as shares, bonds, debt securities and other money and capital market instruments from the same undertaking, or in loans granted to the same borrower, taken together, the loans being loans other than those granted to a State, regional or local authority or to an international organisation of which one or more Member States are members. This limit may be raised to 10% if an undertaking does not invest more than 40% of its gross technical provisions in the loans or securities of issuing bodies and borrowers in each of which it invests more than 5% of its assets;

(c) 5% of its total gross technical provisions in unsecured loans, including 1% for any single unsecured loan, other than loans granted to credit institutions, assurance undertaking—in so far as Article 8 of Directive 73/239/EEC allows it—and investment undertakings established in a Member State;

(d) 3% of its total gross technical provisions in the form of cash in hand;

(e) 10% of its total gross technical provisions in shares, other securities treated as shares and debt securities, which are not dealt in on a regulated market.

2. The absence of a limit in paragraph 1 on investment in any particular category does not imply that assets in that category should be accepted as cover for technical provisions without limit. The home Member State shall lay down more detailed rules fixing the conditions for the use of acceptable assets. In particular it shall ensure, in the determination and the application of those rules, that the following principles are complied with:

(i) assets covering technical provisions must be diversified and spread in such a way as to ensure that there is no excessive reliance on any particular category of asset, investment market or investment;

(ii) investment in particular types of asset that show high levels of risk, whether because of the nature of the asset or the quality of the issuer, must be restricted to prudent levels;

(iii) limitations on particular categories of asset must take account of the treatment of reinsurance in the calculation of technical provisions;

(iv) where the assets held include an investment in a subsidiary undertaking which manages all or part of the insurance undertaking's investments on its behalf, the home Member State must, when applying the rules and principles laid down in this Article, take into account the underlying assets held by the subsidiary undertaking; the home Member State may treat the assets of other subsidiaries in the same way;

(v) the percentage of assets covering technical provisions that are the subject of non-liquid investments must be kept to a prudent level;
(vi) where the assets held include loans to or debt securities issued by certain credit institutions, the home Member State may, when applying the rules and principles laid down in this Article, take into account the underlying assets held by such credit institutions. This treatment may be applied only where the credit institution has its head office in a Member State, is entirely owned by that Member State and/or that State's local authorities and its business, according to its memorandum and articles of association, consists of extending, through its intermediary, loans to or guaranteed by the State or local authorities or loans to bodies closely linked to the State or to local authorities.

3. In the context of the detailed rules laying down the conditions for the use of acceptable assets, the Member State shall give more limitative treatment to:
– any loan unaccompanied by a bank guarantee, a guarantee issued by an insurance undertaking, a mortgage or any other form of security, as compared with loans accompanied by such collateral,
– UCITS not co-ordinated within the meaning of Directive 85/611/EEC[20] and other investment funds, as compared with UCITS co-ordinated within the meaning of that Directive,
– securities that are not dealt in on a regulated market, as compared with those that are,
– bonds, debt securities and other money and capital market instruments not issued by States, local or regional authorities or undertakings belonging to Zone A as defined in Directive 89/647/EEC[21] or the issuers of which are international organisations not numbering at least one Community Member State among their member, as compared with the same financial instruments issued by such bodies.

4. Member States may raise the limit laid down in paragraph 1 (b) to 40% in the case of certain debt securities when these are issued by a credit institution which has its head office in a Member State and is subject by law to special official supervision designed to protect the holders of those debt securities. In particular, sums deriving from the issue of such debt securities must be invested in accordance with the law in assets which, during the whole period of validity of the debt securities, are capable of covering claims attaching to the debt securities and which, in the event of failure of the issues, would be used on a priority basis for the reimbursement of the principal and payment of the accrued interest.

5. Member States shall not require insurance undertakings to invest in particular categories of assets.

6. Notwithstanding paragraph 1, in exceptional circumstances and at an insurance undertaking's request, the home Member State may, temporarily and under a properly reasoned decision, allow exceptions to the rules laid down in paragraph 1 (a) to (e), subject to Article 20.

¶ *The introductory wording in paragraph 1 has been replaced by article 58(4) of Directive 2005/68/EC, reproduced infra under no. I. 40.*

Article 23

[. . .]

¶ *This article replaces points 8 and 9 of Annex I to the Second Non-Life Insurance Directive 88/357/EEC, reproduced supra under no. I. 15. The modification is directly incorporated therein.*

Article 24

[. . .]

¶ *This article modifies article 16 of the First Non-Life Insurance Directive 73/239/EEC, reproduced supra under no. I. 3. The modification is directly incorporated therein.*

---

[20] OJ L 375, 31.12.1985, 3, reproduced infra under no. S. 6.
[21] OJ L 386, 30.12.1989, 14, consolidated in Directive 2000/12/EC (OJ L 126, 26.5.2000, 1), reproduced supra under no. B. 32. OJ L 360, 9.12.1992, 1–27.

Article 25

No more than three years after the date of application of this Directive the Commission shall submit a report to the Insurance Committee on the need for further harmonisation of the solvency margin.

Article 26

[...]

¶ *This article replaces article 18 of the First Non-Life Insurance Directive 73/239/EEC, reproduced supra under no. I. 3. The modification is directly incorporated therein.*

CHAPTER 3
Article 27

[...]

¶ *This article replaces article 7(1)(f) of the Second Non-Life Insurance Directive 88/357/EEC, reproduced supra under no. I. 15. The modification is directly incorporated therein.*

Article 28

The Member State in which a risk is situated shall not prevent a policyholder from concluding a contract with an insurance undertaking authorised under the conditions of Article 6 of Directive 73/239/EEC, as long as that does not conflict with legal provisions protecting the general good in the Member State in which the risk is situated.

Article 29

Member States shall not adopt provisions requiring the prior approval or systematic notification of general and special policy conditions, scales of premiums, or forms and other printed documents that an insurance undertaking intends to use in its dealings with policyholders. They may only require non-systematic notification of those policy conditions and other documents for the purpose of verifying compliance with national provisions concerning insurance contracts, and that requirement may not constitute a prior condition for an undertaking's carrying on its business.

CASE

Case C-59/01 Commission of the European Communities v Italian Republic [2003] ECR I-1759

The principle of freedom to set premiums is infringed by rate-freezing rules affecting both the fixing and the altering of the rates for insurance policies covering third-party liability.

The rules relating to premium rates at issue cannot be regarded as forming part of a general price-control system within the meaning of the third subparagraph of Article 8(3) of Directive 73/239, the second paragraph of Article 29, and Article 39(3) of Directive 92/49/EEC and they are not therefore covered by the exception provided for by those provisions, irrespective of the extent to which the various components of those rules form part of a system of increases in premium rates for the purposes of those provisions.

The general good referred to in that Article 28 cannot in any case be relied upon for the purpose of conferring legitimacy on the introduction or retention of national provisions which prejudice the principle of freedom to set rates, the exceptions to which have been specified in the harmonized rules laid down by Articles 6, 29, and 39 of the directive.

Member States may not retain or introduce prior notification or approval of proposed increases in premium rates except as part of general price-control systems.

Article 30

1. [...]

2. Notwithstanding any provision to the contrary, a Member State that makes insurance compulsory may require that the general and special conditions of the compulsory insurance be communicated to its competent authority before being circulated.

¶ *Paragraph 1 modifies article 8(4)(a) and (b) of the Second Non-Life Insurance Directive 88/357/EEC, reproduced supra under no. I. 15. The modifications are directly incorporated therein.*

Article 31

1. Before an insurance contract is concluded the insurance undertaking shall inform the policyholder of:
– the law applicable to the contract where the parties do not have a free choice, or the fact that the parties are free to choose the law applicable and, in the latter case, the law the insurer proposes to choose,
– the arrangements for handling policyholders' complaints concerning contracts including, where appropriate, the existence of a complaints body, without prejudice to the policyholder's right to take legal proceedings.

2. The obligation referred to in paragraph 1 shall apply only where the policyholder is a natural person.

3. The rules for implementing this Article shall be determined in accordance with the law of the Member State in which the risk is situated.

Title IV

Provisions Relating to Right of Establishment and the Freedom to Provide Services

Articles 32 to 33

[...]

¶ *These articles replace article 10 and repeal article 11 of the First Non-Life Insurance Directive 73/239/EEC, reproduced supra under no. I. 3. The modification is directly incorporated therein.*

Articles 34 to 37

[...]

¶ *These articles replace articles 14, 16 and 17, and repeal articles 12(2) second and third subparagraphs, 13, and 15 of the Second Non-Life Insurance Directive 88/357/EEC, reproduced supra under no. I. 15. The modifications are directly incorporated therein.*

Article 38

The competent authorities of the Member State of the branch or the Member State of the provision of services may require that the information which they are authorised under this Directive to request with regard to the business of insurance undertakings operating in the territory of that State shall be supplied to them in the official language or languages of that State.

Article 39

1. [...]

2. The Member State of the branch or of the provision of services shall not adopt provisions requiring the prior approval or systematic notification of general and special policy conditions, scales of premiums, or forms and other printed documents that an undertaking intends to use in its dealings with policyholders. It may only require an undertaking that proposes to carry on insurance business within its territory, under the right of establishment or the freedom to provide services, to effect non-systematic notification of those policy conditions and other documents for the purpose of verifying compliance with its national provisions concerning insurance contracts, and that requirement may not constitute a prior condition for an undertaking's carrying on its business;

3. The Member State of the branch or of the provision of services may not retain or introduce prior notification or approval of proposed increases in premium rates except as part of general price-control systems.

¶ *Paragraph 1 repeals article 18 of the Second Non-Life Insurance Directive 88/357/EEC, reproduced supra under no. I. 15. The modification is directly incorporated therein.*

Article 40

1. [...]

2. Any undertaking carrying on business under the right of establishment or the freedom to provide services shall submit to the competent authorities of the Member State of the branch

and/or of the Member State of the provision of services all documents requested of it for the purposes of this Article in so far as undertakings with head offices in those Member States are also obliged to do so.

3. If the competent authorities of a Member State establish that an undertaking with a branch or carrying on business under the freedom to provide services within its territory is not complying with the legal provisions applicable to it in that State, they shall require the undertaking concerned to remedy that irregular situation.

4. If the undertaking in question fails to take the necessary action, the competent authorities of the Member State concerned shall inform the competent authorities of the home Member State accordingly. The latter authorities shall, at the earliest opportunity, take all appropriate measures to ensure that the undertaking concerned remedies that irregular situation. The nature of those measures shall be communicated to the competent authorities of the Member State concerned.

5. If, despite the measures taken by the home Member State or because those measures prove inadequate or are lacking in that State, the undertaking persists in infringing the legal provisions in force in the Member State concerned, the latter may, after informing the competent authorities of the home Member State, take appropriate measures to prevent or penalise further infringements, including, in so far as is strictly necessary, preventing that undertaking from continuing to conclude new insurance contracts within its territory. Member States shall ensure that within their territories it is possible to serve the legal documents necessary for such measures on insurance undertakings.

6. Paragraphs 3, 4 and 5 shall not affect the emergency power of the Member States concerned to take appropriate measures to prevent irregularities within their territories. This shall include the possibility of preventing insurance undertakings from continuing to conclude new insurance contracts within their territories.

7. Paragraphs 3, 4 and 5 shall not affect the powers of the Member States to penalise infringements within their territories.

8. If an undertaking which has committed an infringement has an establishment or possesses property in the Member State concerned, the competent authorities of the latter may, in accordance with national law, apply the administrative penalties prescribed for that infringement by way of enforcement against that establishment or property.

9. Any measure adopted under paragraphs 4 to 8 involving penalties or restrictions on the conduct of insurance business must be properly reasoned and communicated to the undertaking concerned.

[10. Every two years, the Commission shall inform the European Insurance and Occupational Pensions Committee of the number and types of cases in which, in each Member State, authorisation has been refused under Article 10 of Directive 73/239/EEC or Article 16 of Directive 88/357/EEC as amended by this Directive or measures have been taken under paragraph 5. Member States shall co-operate with the Commission by providing it with the information required for that report.]

¶ *Paragraph 1 repeals article 19 of the Second Non-Life Insurance Directive 88/357/EEC, reproduced supra under no. I. 15. The modification is directly incorporated therein.*
¶ *Article 40(10) of this Directive has been amended by article 6 of Directive 2005/1/EC, reproduced supra under no. B. 38.*

Article 41

Nothing in this Directive shall prevent insurance undertakings with head offices in Member States from advertising their services, through all available means of communication, in the Member State of the branch or the Member State of the provision of services, subject to any rules governing the form and content of such advertising adopted in the interest of the general good.

Article 42

1. [...]

2. In the event of an insurance undertaking's being wound up, commitments arising out of contracts underwritten through a branch or under the freedom to provide services shall be met in the same way as those arising out of that undertaking's other insurance contracts, without distinction as to nationality as far as the persons insured and the beneficiaries are concerned.

¶ *Paragraph 1 repeals article 20 of the Second Non-Life Insurance Directive 88/357/EEC, reproduced supra under no. I. 15. The modification is directly incorporated therein.*

Article 43

1. [...]

2. Where insurance is offered under the right of establishment or the freedom to provide services, the policyholder shall, before any commitment is entered into, be informed of the Member State in which the head office or, where appropriate, the branch with which the contract is to be concluded is situated.

Any documents issued to the policyholder must convey the information referred to in the first subparagraph.

The obligations imposed in the first two subparagraphs shall not apply to the risks referred to in Article 5 (d) of Directive 73/239/EEC.

3. The contract or any other document granting cover, together with the insurance proposal where it is binding upon the policyholder, must state the address of the head office, or, where appropriate, of the branch of the insurance undertaking which grants the cover.

Each Member State may require that the name and address of the representative of the insurance undertaking referred to in Article 12 a (4) of Directive 88/357/EEC also appear in the documents referred to in the first subparagraph.

¶ *Paragraph 1 repeals article 21 of the Second Non-Life Insurance Directive 88/357/EEC, reproduced supra under no. I. 15. The modification is directly incorporated therein.*

Article 44

1. [...]

2. Every insurance undertaking shall inform the competent authority of its home Member State, separately in respect of transactions carried out under the right of establishment and those carried out under the freedom to provide services, of the amount of the premiums, claims and commissions, without deduction of reinsurance, by Member State and by group of classes, and also as regards class 10 of point A of the Annex to Directive 73/239/EEC, not including carrier's liability, the frequency and average cost of claims.

The groups of classes are hereby defined as follows:
– accident and sickness (classes 1 and 2),
– motor (classes 3, 7 and 10, the figures for class 10, excluding carriers' liability, being given separately),
– fire and other damage to property (classes 8 and 9),
– aviation, marine and transport (classes 4, 5, 6, 7, 11 and 12),
– general liability (class 13),
– credit and suretyship (classes 14 and 15),
– other classes (classes 16, 17 and 18).

The competent authority of the home Member State shall forward that information within a reasonable time and in aggregate form to the competent authorities of each of the Member States concerned which so request.

¶ *Paragraph 1 repeals article 22 of the Second Non-Life Insurance Directive 88/357/EEC, reproduced supra under no. I. 15. The modification is directly incorporated therein.*

Article 45

1. [...]

2. Nothing in this Directive shall affect the Member States' right to require undertakings carrying on business within their territories under the right of establishment or the freedom to provide services to join and participate, on the same terms as undertakings authorised there, in

any scheme designed to guarantee the payment of insurance claims to insured persons and injured third parties.

¶ *Paragraph 1 repeals article 24 of the Second Non-Life Insurance Directive 88/357/EEC, reproduced supra under no. I. 15. The modification is directly incorporated therein.*

Article 46

1. [...]

2. Without prejudice to any subsequent harmonisation, every insurance contract shall be subject exclusively to the indirect taxes and parafiscal charges on insurance premiums in the Member State in which the risk is situated as defined in Article 2 (d) of Directive 88/357/EEC, and also, in the case of Spain, to the surcharges legally established in favour of the Spanish 'Consorcio de Compensación de Seguros' for the performance of its functions relating to the compensation of losses arising from extraordinary events occurring in that Member State.

In derogation from the first indent of Article 2 (d) of Directive 88/357/EEC, and for the purposes of this paragraph, moveable property contained in a building situated within the territory of a Member State, except for goods in commercial transit, shall be a risk situated in that Member State, even if the building and its contents are not covered by the same insurance policy.

The law applicable to the contract under Article 7 of Directive 88/357/EEC shall not affect the fiscal arrangements applicable.

Pending future harmonisation, each Member State shall apply to those undertakings that cover risks situated within its territory its own national provisions to ensure the collection of indirect taxes and parafiscal charges due under the first subparagraph.

¶ *Paragraph 1 repeals article 25 of the Second Non-Life Insurance Directive 88/357/EEC, reproduced supra under no. I. 15. The modification is directly incorporated therein.*

Title V
Transitional Provisions

Article 47

The Federal Republic of Germany may postpone until 1 January 1996 the application of the first sentence of the second subparagraph of Article 54 (2). During that period, the provisions of the following subparagraph shall apply in the situation referred to in Article 54 (2).

When the technical basis for the calculation of premiums has been communicated to the competent authorities of the home Member State in accordance with the third sentence of the second subparagraph of Article 54 (2), those authorities shall without delay forward that information to the competent authorities of the Member State in which the risk is situated so that they may comment. If the competent authorities of the home Member State take no account of those comments, they shall inform the competent authorities of the Member State in which the risk is situated accordingly in detail and state their reasons.

Article 48

Member States may allow insurance undertakings with head offices in their territories, the buildings and land of which that cover their technical provisions exceed, at the time of the notification of this Directive, the percentage laid down in Article 22 (1) (a), a period expiring no later than 31 December 1998 within which to comply with that provision.

Article 49

The Kingdom of Denmark may postpone until 1 January 1999 the application of this Directive to compulsory insurance against accidents at work. During that period the exclusion provided for in Article 12 (2) of Directive 88/357/EEC for accidents at work shall continue to apply in the Kingdom of Denmark.

Article 50

Spain, until 31 December 1996, and Greece and Portugal, until 31 December 1998, may operate the following transitional arrangements for contracts covering risks situated exclusively in one of those Member States other than those defined in Article 5 (d) of Directive 73/239/EEC:

(a) in derogation from Article 8 (3) of Directive 73/239/EEC and from Articles 29 and 39 of this Directive, the competent authorities of the Member States in question may require the communication, before use, of general and special insurance policy conditions;

(b) the amount of the technical provisions relating to the contracts referred to in this Article shall be determined under the supervision of the Member State concerned in accordance with its own rules or, failing that, in accordance with the procedures established within its territory in accordance with this Directive. Cover of those technical provisions by equivalent and matching assets and the localisation of those assets shall be effected under the supervision of that Member State in accordance with its rules and practices adopted in accordance with this Directive.

Title VI
Final Provisions

Article 51

The following technical adjustments to be made to Directives 73/239/EEC and 88/357/EEC and to this Directive shall be adopted in accordance with the procedure laid down in Directive 91/675/EEC:
– extension of the legal forms provided for in Article 8 (1) (a) of Directive 73/239/EEC,
– amendments to the list set out in the Annex to Directive 73/239/EEC, or adaptation of the terminology used in that list to take account of the development of insurance markets,
– clarification of the items constituting the solvency margin listed in Article 16 (1) of Directive 73/239/EEC to take account of the creation of new financial instruments,

– alteration of the minimum guarantee fund provided for in Article 17 (2) of Directive 73/239/EEC to take account of economic and financial developments,
– amendments, to take account of the creation of new financial instruments, to the list of assets acceptable as cover for technical provisions set out in Article 21 of this Directive and to the rules on the spreading of investments laid down in Article 22,
– changes in the relaxations in the matching rules laid down in Annex 1 to Directive 88/357/EEC, to take account of the development of new currency-hedging instruments or progress made towards economic and monetary union,
– clarification of the definitions in order to ensure uniform application of Directives 73/239/EEC and 88/357/EEC and of this Directive throughout the Community.

Article 52

1. Branches which have started business, in accordance with the provisions in force in their Member State of establishment, before the entry into force of the provisions adopted in implementation of this Directive shall be presumed to have been subject to the procedure laid down in Article 10 (1) to (5) of Directive 73/239/EEC. They shall be governed, from the date of that entry into force, by Articles 15, 19, 20 and 22 of Directive 73/239/EEC and by Article 40 of this Directive.

2. Articles 34 and 35 shall not affect rights acquired by insurance undertakings carrying on business under the freedom to provide services before the entry into force of the provisions adopted in implementation of this Directive.

Article 53

[...]

¶ *This article inserts an article 28a in the First Non-Life Insurance Directive 73/239/EEC, reproduced supra under no. I. 3. The modification is directly incorporated therein.*

Article 54

1. Notwithstanding any provision to the contrary, a Member State in which contracts covering the risks in class 2 of point A of the Annex to Directive 73/239/EEC may serve as a partial or complete alternative to health cover provided by the statutory social security system may require that those contracts comply with the specific legal provisions adopted by that Member State to protect the general good in that class of insurance, and that the general and special conditions of that insurance be communicated to the competent authorities of that Member State before use.

2. Member States may require that the health insurance system referred to in paragraph 1 be operated on a technical basis similar to that of life assurance where:
– the premiums paid are calculated on the basis of sickness tables and other statistical data relevant to the Member State in which the risk is situated in accordance with the mathematical methods used in insurance,
– a reserve is set up for increasing age,
– the insurer may cancel the contract only within a fixed period determined by the Member State in which the risk is situated,
– the contract provides that premiums may be increased or payments reduced, even for current contracts,
– the contract provides that the policyholder may change his existing contract into a new contract complying with paragraph 1, offered by the same insurance undertaking or the same branch and taking account of his acquired rights. In particular, account must be taken of the reserve for increasing age and a new medical examination may be required only for increased cover.

In that event, the competent authorities of the Member State concerned shall publish the sickness tables and other relevant statistical data referred to in the first subparagraph and transmit them to the competent authorities of the home Member State. The premiums must be sufficient, on reasonable actuarial assumptions, for undertakings to be able to meet all their commitments having regard to all aspects of their financial situation. The home Member State shall require that the technical basis for the calculation of premiums be communicated to its competent authorities before the product is circulated. This paragraph shall also apply where existing contracts are modified.

Article 55

Member States may require that any insurance undertaking offering, at its own risk, compulsory insurance against accidents at work within their territories comply with the specific provisions of their national law concerning such insurance, except for the provisions concerning financial supervision, which shall be the exclusive responsibility of the home Member State.

Article 56

Member States shall ensure that decisions taken in respect of an insurance undertaking under laws, regulations and administrative provisions adopted in accordance with this Directive may be subject to the right to apply to the courts.

Article 57

1. The Member States shall adopt the laws, regulations and administrative provisions necessary for their compliance with this Directive not later than 31 December 1993 and bring them into force no later than 1 July 1994. They shall forthwith inform the Commission thereof.

When they adopt such measures the Member States shall include references to this Directive or shall make such references when they effect official publication. The manner in which such references are to be made shall be laid down by the Member States.

2. The Member States shall communicate to the Commission the texts of the main provisions of national law that they adopt in the field covered by this Directive.

Article 58

This Directive is addressed to the Member States.

I. 26.

Council Directive 92/96/EEC
of 10 November 1992
on the co-ordination of laws, regulations and administrative provisions relating to direct life assurance and amending Directives 79/267/EEC and 90/619/EEC
(Third life assurance Directive)[1]

This Directive has been repealed as from 19 December 2002 by Annex V, part A of Directive 2002/83/EC (OJ L 345, 19.12.2002, 1), reproduced infra under no. I. 33.

Correlation table

Directive 92/96/EEC	Directive 2002/83/EC
Article 1(a)	Article 1(1)(a)
Article 1(b)	Article 1(1)(b)
Article 1(c)	Article 1(1)(d)
Article 1(d)	Article 1(1)(e)
Article 1(e)	Article 1(1)(f)
Article 1(f) to (j)	Article 1(1)(h) to (l)
Article 1(l)	Article 1(1)(n)
Article 7	Article 8
Article 11(2) to (6)	Article 14(1) to (5)
Article 14	Article 15
Article 15(1) to (5)	Article 16(1) to (5)
Article 15(5)(a)	Article 16(6)
Article 15(5)(b)	Article 16(7)
Article 15(5)(c)	Article 16(8)
Article 15(6)	Article 16(9)
Article 15a	Article 17
Article 19	Article 21
Article 20	Article 22
Article 21(1) first subparagraph	Article 23(1)
Article 21(1) second subparagraph	Article 23(2)
Article 21(1) third subparagraph	Article 23(3) first subparagraph
Article 21(1) fourth subparagraph	Article 23(3) second subparagraph
Article 21(2)	Article 23(4)
Article 22	Article 24
Article 23	Article 25
Article 24	Article 26

---

[1] OJ L 360, 9.12.1992, 1–27.

Directive 92/96/EEC	Directive 2002/83/EC
Article 28	Article 33
Article 29	Article 34
Article 31	Article 36
Article 38	Article 44
Article 39(2)	Article 45
Article 40(2) to (10)	Article 46(1) to (9)
Article 41	Article 47
Article 42(2)	Article 48
Article 43(2)	Article 49
Article 44(2) first subparagraph	Article 50(1)
Article 44(2) second subparagraph	Article 50(2)
Article 44(2) third subparagraph	Article 50(3)
Article 47	Article 64
Article 47	Article 65
Article 48(1)	Article 66(1) second subparagraph
Article 48(2)	Article 66(2)
Article 50	Article 67
Article 51(2)	Article 70
Annex I	Annex II
Annex II	Annex III

I. 27.

European Parliament and Council Directive 95/26/EC of 29 June 1995 amending Directives 77/780/EEC and 89/646/EEC in the field of credit institutions, Directives 73/239/EEC and 92/49/EEC in the field of non-life insurance, Directives 79/267/EEC and 92/96/EEC in the field of life assurance, Directive 93/22/EEC in the field of investment firms and Directive 85/611/EEC in the field of undertakings for collective investment in transferable securities (UCITS), with a view to reinforcing prudential supervision[1]

This Directive has been repealed as from 19 December 2002 by Annex V, part A of Directive 2002/83/EC (OJ L 345, 19.12.2002, 1), reproduced infra under no. I. 33.

Correlation table	
Directive 95/26/EC	Directive 2002/83/EC
Article 2(1)	Article 1(1)(r)
Article 6(2)	Article 70

---

[1] OJ L 168, 18.7.1995, 7–13.

# I. 28.

[European Parliament and Council Directive 98/78/EC
of 27 October 1998
on the supplementary supervision of insurance and reinsurance undertakings in an insurance or reinsurance group][1]

¶ *The title of this Directive has been replaced by article 59(1) of Directive 2005/68/EC, reproduced infra under no. I. 40.*

THE EUROPEAN PARLIAMENT AND THE COUNCIL OF THE EUROPEAN UNION,

Having regard to the Treaty establishing the European Community, and in particular Article [47(2)][2] thereof,

Having regard to the proposal from the Commission,[3]

Having regard to the opinion of the Economic and Social Committee,[4]

Acting in accordance with the procedure laid down in Article [251][2] of the Treaty,[5]

(1) Whereas the first Council Directive 73/239/EEC of 24 July 1973 on the co-ordination of laws, regulations and administrative provisions relating to the taking up and pursuit of the business of direct insurance other than life assurance[6] and the first Council Directive 79/267/EEC of 5 March 1979 on the co-ordination of laws, regulations and administrative provisions relating to the taking up and pursuit of the business of direct life assurance[7] require insurance undertakings to have solvency margins;

(2) Whereas, under Council Directive 92/49/EEC of 18 June 1992 on the co-ordination of laws, regulations and administrative provisions relating to direct insurance other than life assurance and amending Directives 73/239/EEC and 88/357/EEC[8] and Council Directive 92/96/EEC of 10 November 1992 on the co-ordination of laws, regulations and administrative provisions relating to direct life assurance and amending Directives 79/267/EEC and 90/619/EEC[9] the taking up and the pursuit of the business of insurance are subject to the granting of a single official authorisation issued by the authorities of the Member State in which an insurance undertaking has its registered office (home Member State); whereas such authorisation allows an undertaking to carry on business throughout the Community, under either the right of establishment or the freedom to provide services; whereas the competent authorities of home Member States are responsible for monitoring the financial health of insurance undertakings, including their solvency;

(3) Whereas measures concerning the supplementary supervision of insurance undertakings in an insurance group should enable the authorities supervising an insurance undertaking to form a more soundly based judgement of its financial situation; whereas such supplementary supervision should take into account certain undertakings which are not at present subject to supervision under Community Directives; whereas this Directive does not in any way imply

---

[1] OJ L 330, 5.12.1998, 1–12.
[2] The number between brackets has been changed as from 1 May 1999 by article 12 of the Treaty of Amsterdam.
[3] OJ C 341, 19.12.1995, 16, and OJ C 108, 7.4.1998, 48.
[4] OJ C 174, 17.6.1996, 16.
[5] Opinion of the European Parliament of 23 October 1997 (OJ C 339, 10.11.1997, 136), Council common position of 30 March 1998 (OJ C 204, 30.6.1998, 1), Decision of the European Parliament of 16 September 1998 (OJ C 313, 12.10.1998) and Council Decision of 13 October 1998.
[6] OJ L 228, 16.8.1973, 3, First Insurance Directive, reproduced supra under no. I. 3. Directive as last amended by Directive 95/26/EC (OJ L 168, 18.7.1995, 7), reproduced supra under no. I. 27.
[7] OJ L 63, 13.3.1979, 1, reproduced supra under no. I. 9. Directive as last amended by Directive 95/26/EC, reproduced supra under no. I. 27.

[8] OJ L 228, 11.8.1992, 1, reproduced supra under no. I. 15. Directive as amended by Directive 95/26/EC, reproduced supra under no. I. 27.
[9] OJ L 360, 9.12.1992, 1, reproduced supra under no. I. 18. Directive as amended by Directive 95/26/EC, reproduced supra under no. I. 27.

that Member States are required to undertake supervision of those undertakings considered individually;

(4) Whereas insurance undertakings in a common insurance market engage in direct competition with each other and the rules concerning capital requirements must therefore be equivalent; whereas, to that end, the criteria applied to determine supplementary supervision must not be left solely to the discretion of Member States; whereas the adoption of common basic rules will be in the best interests of the Community in that it will prevent distortions of competition; whereas it is necessary to eliminate certain divergences between the laws of the Member States as regards the prudential rules to which insurance undertakings that are part of an insurance group are subject;

(5) Whereas the approach adopted consists in bringing about such harmonisation as is essential, necessary and sufficient to achieve the mutual recognition of prudential control systems in this field; whereas the aim of this Directive is in particular to protect the interests of insured persons;

(6) Whereas certain provisions of this Directive define minimum standards; whereas a home Member State may lay down stricter rules for insurance undertakings authorised by its own competent authorities;

(7) Whereas this Directive provides for the supplementary supervision of any insurance company which is a participating undertaking in at least one insurance undertaking, reinsurance undertaking or non-member-country insurance undertaking and, under different rules, for the supplementary supervision of any insurance company whose parent undertaking is an insurance holding company, a reinsurance undertaking, a non-member-country insurance undertaking or a mixed-activity insurance holding company; whereas the supervision of individual insurance undertakings by the competent authorities remains the essential principle of insurance supervision;

(8) Whereas it is necessary to calculate an adjusted solvency situation for insurance undertakings forming part of an insurance group; whereas different methods are applied by the competent authorities in the Community to take into account the effects on the financial situation of an insurance undertaking attributable to the fact that it belongs to an insurance group; whereas this Directive lays down three methods to effect that calculation; whereas the principle is accepted that these methods are prudentially equivalent;

(9) Whereas the solvency of a related subsidiary insurance undertaking of an insurance holding company, reinsurance undertaking or non-member-country insurance undertaking may be affected by the financial resources of the group of which it is a part and by the distribution of financial resources within that group; whereas the competent authorities should be provided with the means of exercising supplementary supervision and of taking appropriate measures at the level of the insurance undertaking where its solvency is or may be jeopardised;

(10) Whereas the competent authorities should have access to all the information relevant to the exercise of supplementary supervision; whereas co-operation between the authorities responsible for the supervision of insurance undertakings as well as between those authorities and the authorities responsible for the supervision of other financial sectors should be established;

(11) Whereas intra-group transactions can affect the financial position of an insurance undertaking; whereas the competent authorities should be in a position to exercise general supervision over certain types of such intra-group operations and take appropriate measures at the level of the insurance undertaking where its solvency is or may be jeopardised,

HAVE ADOPTED THIS DIRECTIVE:

Article 1
Definitions

For the purposes of this Directive:

(a) *insurance undertaking* means an undertaking which has received official authorisation in accordance with Article 6 of Directive 73/239/EEC or Article 6 of Directive 79/267/EEC;

(b) *non-member country insurance undertaking* means an undertaking which would require authorisation in accordance with Article 6 of Directive 73/239/EEC or Article 6 of Directive 79/267/EEC if it had its registered office in the Community;

[(c) *reinsurance undertaking* means an undertaking, which has received official authorisation in accordance with Article 3 of Directive 2005/68/EC of the European Parliament and of the Council of 16 November 2005 on reinsurance;[10]]

(d) *parent undertaking* means a parent undertaking within the meaning of Article 1 of Directive 83/349/EEC[11] and any undertaking which, in the opinion of the competent authorities, effectively exercises a dominant influence over another undertaking;

(e) *subsidiary undertaking* means a subsidiary undertaking within the meaning of Article 1 of Directive 83/349/EEC and any undertaking over which, in the opinion of the competent authorities, a parent undertaking effectively exercises a dominant influence. All subsidiaries of subsidiary undertakings shall also be considered subsidiaries of the parent undertaking which is at the head of those undertakings;

(f) *participation* means participation within the meaning of Article 17, first sentence, of Directive 78/660/EEC[12] or the holding, directly or indirectly, of 20% or more of the voting rights or capital of an undertaking;

[(g) *participating undertaking* shall mean an undertaking which is either a parent undertaking or other undertaking which holds a participation, or an undertaking linked with another undertaking by a relationship within the meaning of Article 12(1) of Directive 83/349/EEC;

(h) *related undertaking* shall mean either a subsidiary or other undertaking in which a participation is held, or an undertaking linked with another undertaking by a relationship within the meaning of Article 12(1) of Directive 83/349/EEC;

[(i) *insurance holding company* means a parent undertaking, the main business of which is to acquire and hold participations in subsidiary undertakings, where those subsidiary undertakings are exclusively or mainly insurance undertakings, reinsurance undertakings or non-member country insurance undertakings or non-member country reinsurance undertakings, at least one of such subsidiary undertakings being an insurance undertaking, or a reinsurance undertaking and which is not a mixed financial holding company within the meaning of Directive 2002/87/EC of the European Parliament and of the Council of 16 December 2002 on the supplementary supervision of credit institutions, insurance undertakings and investment firms in a financial conglomerate;[13]

(j) *mixed-activity insurance holding company* means a parent undertaking, other than an insurance undertaking, a non-member country insurance undertaking, a reinsurance undertaking, a non-member country reinsurance undertaking, an insurance holding company or a mixed financial holding company within the meaning of Directive 2002/87/EC, which includes at least one insurance undertaking or a reinsurance undertaking among its subsidiary undertakings;

(k) *competent authorities* means the national authorities which are empowered by law or regulation to supervise insurance undertakings or reinsurance undertakings;

(l) *non-member country reinsurance undertaking* means an undertaking which would require authorisation in accordance with Article 3 of Directive 2005/68/EC if it had its head office in the Community.]

¶ *Article 1(g)(h)(i) and (j) have been replaced by article 28(1) of Directive 2002/87/EC, reproduced supra under no. B. 38.*

---

[10] OJ L 323, 9.12.2005, 1, reproduced infra under no. I. 40.
[11] Seventh Company Directive 83/349/EEC of 13 June 1983 based on Article 54(3)(g) of the Treaty on consolidated accounts (OJ L 193, 18.7.1983, 1), reproduced supra under no. C. 6. Directive as last amended by the 1994 Act of Accession.
[12] Fourth Company Directive 78/660/EEC of 25 July 1978 based on Article 54(3)(g) of the Treaty on the annual accounts of certain types of companies (OJ L 222, 14.8.1978, 11), reproduced supra under no. C. 4. Directive as last amended by the 1994 Act of Accession.

[13] OJ L 35, 11.2.2003, p. 1, reproduced supra under no. B. 38. Directive as amended by Directive 2005/1/EC (OJ L 79, 24.3.2005, 9), reproduced supra under no. B. 39.

¶ *Article 1(c)(i)(j) and (k) have been replaced and point (l) has been added by article 59(2) of Directive 2005/68/EC, reproduced infra under no. I. 40.*

[*Article 2*

Cases of application of supplementary supervision of insurance undertakings and reinsurance undertakings

1. In addition to the provisions of Directive 73/239/ EEC, Directive 2002/83/EC of the European Parliament and of the Council of 5 November 2002 concerning life assurance[14] and Directive 2005/68/EC, which lay down the rules for the supervision of insurance undertakings and reinsurance undertakings, Member States shall provide supervision of any insurance undertaking or any reinsurance undertaking, which is a participating undertaking in at least one insurance undertaking, reinsurance undertaking, non-member-country insurance undertaking or non-member country reinsurance undertaking, shall be supplemented in the manner prescribed in Articles 5, 6, 8 and 9 of this Directive

2. Every insurance undertaking or reinsurance undertaking the parent undertaking of which is an insurance holding company, a non-member country insurance or a non-member country reinsurance undertaking shall be subject to supplementary supervision in the manner prescribed in Articles 5(2), 6, 8 and 10.

3. Every insurance undertaking or reinsurance undertaking the parent undertaking of which is a mixed-activity insurance holding company shall be subject to supplementary supervision in the manner prescribed in Articles 5(2), 6 and 8.]

¶ *Article 2 has been replaced by article 59(3) of Directive 2005/68/EC, reproduced infra under no. I. 40.*

[*Article 3*

Scope of supplementary supervision

1. The exercise of supplementary supervision in accordance with Article 2 shall in no way imply that the competent authorities are required to play a supervisory role in relation to the non-member country insurance undertaking, the non-member country reinsurance undertaking, insurance holding company or mixed-activity insurance holding company taken individually.

2. The supplementary supervision shall take into account the following undertakings referred to in Articles 5, 6, 8, 9 and 10:
– related undertakings of the insurance undertaking or of the reinsurance undertaking,
– participating undertakings in the insurance undertaking or in the reinsurance undertaking,
– related undertakings of a participating undertaking in the insurance undertaking or in the reinsurance undertaking.

3. Member States may decide not to take into account in the supplementary supervision referred to in Article 2 undertakings having their registered office in a non-member country where there are legal impediments to the transfer of the necessary information, without prejudice to the provisions of Annex I, point 2.5, and of Annex II, point 4.

Furthermore, the competent authorities responsible for exercising supplementary supervision may in the cases listed below decide on a case-by-case basis not to take an undertaking into account in the supplementary supervision referred to in Article 2:
– if the undertaking which should be included is of negligible interest with respect to the objectives of the supplementary supervision of insurance undertakings or reinsurance undertakings;
– if the inclusion of the financial situation of the undertaking would be inappropriate or misleading with respect to the objectives of the supplementary supervision of insurance undertakings or reinsurance;
– undertakings.]

¶ *Article 3 has been replaced by article 59(3) of Directive 2005/68/EC, reproduced infra under no. I. 40.*

[*Article 4*

Competent authorities for exercising supplementary supervision

1. Supplementary supervision shall be exercised by the competent authorities of the

---

[14] OJ L 345, 19.12.2002, 1, reproduced infra under no. I. 33. Directive as last amended by Directive 2005/1/EC, reproduced supra under no. B. 39.

Member State in which the insurance undertaking or the reinsurance undertaking has received official authorisation under Article 6 of Directive 73/239/EEC or Article 4 of Directive 2002/83/ EC or Article 3 of Directive 2005/68/EC.

2. Where insurance undertakings or reinsurance undertakings authorised in two or more Member States have as their parent undertaking the same insurance holding company, non-member country insurance undertaking, non-member country reinsurance undertaking or mixed-activity insurance holding company, the competent authorities of the Member States concerned may reach agreement as to which of them will be responsible for exercising supplementary supervision.

3. Where a Member State has more than one competent authority for the prudential supervision of insurance undertakings and reinsurance undertakings, such Member State shall take the requisite measures to organise coordination between those authorities.]

¶ *Article 4 has been replaced by article 59(3) of Directive 2005/68/EC, reproduced infra under no. I. 40.*

Article 5
Availability and quality of information

[1. Member States shall prescribe that the competent authorities are to require that every insurance undertaking or reinsurance undertaking subject to supplementary supervision shall have adequate internal control mechanisms in place for the production of any data and information relevant for the purposes of such supplementary supervision.]

2. Member States shall take the appropriate steps to ensure that there are no legal impediments within their jurisdiction preventing the undertakings that are subject to the supplementary supervision and their related undertakings and participating undertakings from exchanging among themselves any information relevant for the purposes of such supplementary supervision.

¶ *Paragraph 1 has been replaced by article 59(4) of Directive 2005/68/EC, reproduced infra under no. I. 40.*

[Article 6
Access to information

1. Member States shall provide that their competent authorities responsible for exercising supplementary supervision are to have access to any information which would be relevant for the purpose of supervision of an insurance undertaking or a reinsurance undertaking subject to such supplementary supervision. The competent authorities may address themselves directly to the relevant undertakings referred to in Article 3(2) to obtain the necessary information only if such information has been requested from the insurance undertaking or the reinsurance undertaking and has not been supplied by it.

2. Member States shall provide that their competent authorities may carry out within their territory, themselves or through the intermediary of persons whom they appoint for that purpose, on-the-spot verification of the information referred to in paragraph 1 at:
– the insurance undertaking subject to supplementary supervision,
– the reinsurance undertaking subject to supplementary supervision,
– subsidiary undertakings of that insurance undertaking,
– subsidiary undertakings of that reinsurance undertaking,
– parent undertakings of that insurance undertaking,
– parent undertakings of that reinsurance undertaking,
– subsidiary undertakings of a parent undertaking of that insurance undertaking,
– subsidiary undertakings of a parent undertaking of that reinsurance undertaking.

3. Where, in applying this Article, the competent authorities of one Member State wish in specific cases to verify important information concerning an undertaking situated in another Member State which is a related insurance undertaking, a related reinsurance undertaking, a subsidiary undertaking, a parent undertaking or a subsidiary of a parent undertaking of the insurance undertaking or of the reinsurance undertaking subject to supplementary supervision, they must ask the competent authorities of that

other Member State to have that verification carried out. The authorities which receive such a request must act on it within the limits of their jurisdiction by carrying out the verification themselves, by allowing the authorities making the request to carry it out or by allowing an auditor or expert to carry it out.

The competent authority which made the request may, if it so wishes, participate in the verification when it does not carry out the verification itself.]

¶ *Article 6 has been replaced by article 59(5) of Directive 2005/68/EC, reproduced infra under no. I. 40.*

[*Article 7*

Cooperation between competent authorities

1. Where insurance undertakings or reinsurance undertakings established in different Member States are directly or indirectly related or have a common participating undertaking, the competent authorities of each Member State shall communicate to one another on request all relevant information which may allow or facilitate the exercise of supervision pursuant to this Directive and shall communicate on their own initiative any information which appears to them to be essential for the other competent authorities.

2. Where an insurance undertaking or a reinsurance undertaking and either a credit institution as defined in Directive 2000/12/EC of the European Parliament and of the Council of 20 March 2000 relating to the taking up and pursuit of the business of credit institutions[15] or an investment firm as defined in Council Directive 93/22/EEC of 10 May 1993 on investment services in the securities field,[16] or both, are directly or indirectly related or have a common participating undertaking, the competent authorities and the authorities with public responsibility for the supervision of those other undertakings shall cooperate closely. Without prejudice to their respective responsibilities, those authorities shall provide one another with any information likely to simplify their task, in particular within the framework of this Directive.

3. Information received pursuant to this Directive and, in particular, any exchange of information between competent authorities which is provided for in this Directive shall be subject to the obligation of professional secrecy defined in Article 16 of Council Directive 92/49/EEC of 18 June 1992 on the coordination of laws, regulations and administrative provisions relating to direct insurance other than life assurance (third non-life insurance Directive)[17] and Article 16 of Directive 2002/83/EC and Articles 24 to 30 of Directive 2005/68/EC.]

¶ *Article 7 has been replaced by article 59(5) of Directive 2005/68/EC, reproduced infra under no. I. 40.*

[*Article 8*

Intra-group transactions

1. Member States shall provide that the competent authorities exercise general supervision over transactions between:

(a) an insurance undertaking or a reinsurance undertaking and:
   (i) a related undertaking of the insurance undertaking or of the reinsurance undertaking;
   (ii) a participating undertaking in the insurance undertaking or in the reinsurance undertaking;
   (iii) a related undertaking of a participating undertaking in the insurance undertaking or in the reinsurance undertaking;

(b) an insurance undertaking or a reinsurance undertaking and a natural person who holds a participation in:
   (i) the insurance undertaking, the reinsurance undertaking or any of its related undertakings;
   (ii) a participating undertaking in the insurance undertaking or in the reinsurance undertaking;

---

[15] OJ L 126, 26.5.2000, 1, reproduced supra under no. B. 32. Directive as last amended by Directive 2005/1/EC, reproduced supra under no. B. 39.
[16] OJ L 141, 11.6.1993, 27, reproduced infra under no. S. 14. Directive as last amended by Directive 2002/87/EC, reproduced supra under no. B. 38.

[17] OJ L 228, 11.8.1992, 1, reproduced supra under no. I. 25. Directive as last amended by Directive 2005/1/EC, reproduced supra under no. B. 39.

(iii) a related undertaking of a participating undertaking in the insurance undertaking or in the reinsurance undertaking.

These transactions concern in particular:
- loans,
- guarantees and off-balance-sheet transactions,
- elements eligible for the solvency margin,
- investments,
- reinsurance and retrocession operations,
- agreements to share costs.

2. Member States shall require insurance undertakings and reinsurance undertakings to have in place adequate risk management processes and internal control mechanisms, including sound reporting and accounting procedures, in order to identify, measure, monitor and control transactions as provided for in paragraph 1 appropriately. Member States shall also require at least annual reporting by insurance undertakings and reinsurance undertakings to the competent authorities of significant transactions. These processes and mechanisms shall be subject to overview by the competent authorities.

If, on the basis of this information, it appears that the solvency of the insurance undertaking or the reinsurance undertaking is, or may be, jeopardised, the competent authority shall take appropriate measures at the level of the insurance undertaking or of the reinsurance undertaking.]

¶ *Article 8 has been replaced by article 59(5) of Directive 2005/68/EC, reproduced infra under no. I. 40.*

Article 9
Adjusted solvency requirement

1. In the case referred to in Article 2(1), Member States shall require that an adjusted solvency calculation be carried out in accordance with Annex I.

2. Any related undertaking, participating undertaking or related undertaking of a participating undertaking shall be included in the calculation referred to in paragraph 1.

[3. If the calculation referred to in paragraph 1 demonstrates that the adjusted solvency is negative, the competent authorities shall take appropriate measures at the level of the insurance undertaking or the reinsurance undertaking in question.]

¶ *Paragraph 3 has been replaced by article 59(6) of Directive 2005/68/EC, reproduced infra under no. I. 40.*

Article 10
[Insurance holding companies, non-member country insurance undertakings and non-member country reinsurance undertakings]

1. In the case referred to in Article 2(2), Member States shall require the method of supplementary supervision to be applied in accordance with Annex II.

[2. In the case referred to in Article 2(2), the calculation shall include all related undertakings of the insurance holding company, the non-member country insurance undertaking or the non-member country reinsurance undertaking, in the manner provided for in Annex II.

3. If, on the basis of that calculation, the competent authorities conclude that the solvency of a subsidiary insurance undertaking or a reinsurance undertaking of the insurance holding company, the non-member country insurance undertaking or the non-member country reinsurance undertaking is, or may be, jeopardised, they shall take appropriate measures at the level of that insurance undertaking or reinsurance undertaking.]

¶ *The title and paragraphs 2 and 3 have been replaced by article 59(7) of Directive 2005/68/EC, reproduced infra under no. I. 40.*

[Article 10a
Cooperation with third countries' competent authorities

1. The Commission may submit proposals to the Council, either at the request of a Member State or on its own initiative, for the negotiation of agreements with one or more third countries regarding the means of exercising supplementary supervision over:

(a) insurance undertakings which have, as participating undertakings, undertakings within the meaning of Article 2 which have their head office situated in a third country; and [(b) reinsurance undertakings which have, as participating undertakings, undertakings within the meaning of Article 2 which have their head office situated in a third country;

(c) non-member country insurance undertakings or non-member country reinsurance undertakings which have, as participating undertakings, undertakings within the meaning of Article 2 which have their head office in the Community.]

[2. The agreements referred to in paragraph 1 shall in particular seek to ensure both:

(a) that the competent authorities of the Member States are able to obtain the information necessary for the supplementary supervision of insurance undertakings and reinsurance undertakings which have their head office in the Community and which have subsidiaries or hold participations in undertakings outside the Community; and

(b) that the competent authorities of third countries are able to obtain the information necessary for the supplementary supervision of insurance undertakings and reinsurance undertakings which have their head office in their territories and which have subsidiaries or hold participations in undertakings in one or more Member States.]

[3. Without prejudice to Article 300(1) and (2) of the Treaty, the Commission shall, with the assistance of the European Insurance and Occupational Pensions Committee, examine the outcome of the negotiations referred to in paragraph 1 and the resulting situation.]

¶ *Article 10a has been inserted by article 28(4) of Directive 2002/87/EC, reproduced supra under no. B. 38.*
¶ *Paragraphs 1(b) and (c) and paragraph 2 have been replaced by article 59(8) of Directive 2005/68/EC, reproduced infra under no. I. 40.*
¶ *Paragraph 3 of this article has been replaced by article 7(1) of Directive 2005/1/EC, reproduced supra under no. B. 39.*

[Article 10b

Management body of insurance holding companies

The Member States shall require that persons who effectively direct the business of an insurance holding company are of sufficiently good repute and have sufficient experience to perform these duties.]

¶ *Article 10b has been inserted by article 28(4) of Directive 2002/87/EC, reproduced infra under no. B. 38.*

Article 11

Implementation

1. Member States shall adopt not later than 5 June 2000 the laws, regulations and administrative provisions necessary to comply with this Directive. They shall immediately inform the Commission thereof.

2. Member States shall provide that the provisions referred to in paragraph 1 shall first apply to the supervision of accounts for financial years beginning on 1 January 2001 or during that calendar year.

3. When Member States adopt the measures referred to in paragraph 1, they shall contain a reference to this Directive or shall be accompanied by such reference on the occasion of their official publication. The methods of making such reference shall be laid down by Member States.

4. Member States shall communicate to the Commission the main provisions of national law that they adopt in the field covered by this Directive.

[5. Not later than 1 January 2006 the Commission shall issue a report on the application of this Directive and, if necessary, on the need for further harmonisation.]

¶ *Paragraph 5 of this article has been replaced by article 7(2) of Directive 2005/1/EC, reproduced supra under no. B. 39.*

Article 12

Entry into force

This Directive shall enter into force on the day of its publication in the Official Journal of the European Communities.

Article 13

Addressees

This Directive is addressed to the Member States.

[Annex I

Calculation of the adjusted solvency of insurance undertakings and
reinsurance undertakings

1. CHOICE OF CALCULATION METHOD AND GENERAL PRINCIPLES

A. Member States shall provide that the calculation of the adjusted solvency of insurance undertakings and reinsurance undertakings referred to in Article 2(1) shall be carried out according to one of the methods described in point 3. A Member State may, however, provide for the competent authorities to authorise or impose the application of a method set out in point 3 other than that chosen by the Member State.

B. *Proportionality*

The calculation of the adjusted solvency of an insurance undertaking or a reinsurance undertaking shall take account of the proportional share held by the participating undertaking in its related undertakings.

'Proportional share' means either, where method 1 or method 2 described in point 3 is used, the proportion of the subscribed capital that is held, directly or indirectly, by the participating undertaking or, where method 3 described in point 3 is used, the percentages used for the establishment of the consolidated accounts.

However, whichever method is used, when the related undertaking is a subsidiary undertaking and has a solvency deficit, the total solvency deficit of the subsidiary has to be taken into account.

However, where, in the opinion of the competent authorities, the responsibility of the parent undertaking owning a share of the capital is limited strictly and unambiguously to that share of the capital, such competent authorities may give permission for the solvency deficit of the subsidiary undertaking to be taken into account on a proportional basis.

Where there are no capital ties between some of the undertakings in an insurance group or a reinsurance group, the competent authority shall determine which proportional share will have to be taken account of.

C. Elimination of double use of solvency margin elements

C.1. *General treatment of solvency margin elements*

Regardless of the method used for the calculation of the adjusted solvency of an insurance undertaking or a reinsurance undertaking, the double use of elements eligible for the solvency margin among the different insurance undertakings or reinsurance undertakings taken into account in that calculation must be eliminated.

For that purpose, when calculating the adjusted solvency of an insurance undertaking or a reinsurance undertaking and where the methods described in point 3 do not provide for it, the following amounts shall be eliminated:

– the value of any asset of that insurance undertaking or reinsurance undertaking which represents the financing of elements eligible for the solvency margin of one of its related insurance undertakings or related reinsurance undertakings,

– the value of any asset of a related insurance undertaking or a related reinsurance undertaking of that insurance undertaking or reinsurance undertaking which represents the financing of elements eligible for the solvency margin of that insurance undertaking or reinsurance undertaking,

– the value of any asset of a related insurance undertaking or related reinsurance undertaking of that insurance undertaking or reinsurance undertaking which represents the financing of elements eligible for the solvency margin of any other related insurance undertaking or related reinsurance undertaking of that insurance undertaking or reinsurance undertaking.

C.2. *Treatment of certain elements*
Without prejudice to the provisions of Section C.1:
– profit reserves and future profits arising in a related life assurance undertaking or a related life reinsurance undertaking of the insurance undertaking or reinsurance undertaking for which the adjusted solvency is calculated, and
– any subscribed but not paid-up capital of a related insurance undertaking or a related reinsurance undertaking of the insurance undertaking or of reinsurance undertaking for which the adjusted solvency is calculated,

may only be included in the calculation in so far as they are eligible for covering the solvency margin requirement of that related undertaking. However, any subscribed but not paid-up capital which represents a potential obligation on the part of the participating undertaking shall be entirely excluded from the calculation.

Any subscribed but not paid-up capital of the participating insurance undertaking or the participating reinsurance undertaking which represents a potential obligation on the part of a related insurance undertaking or of a related reinsurance undertaking shall also be excluded from the calculation.

Any subscribed but not paid-up capital of a related insurance undertaking or a reinsurance undertaking which represents a potential obligation on the part of another related insurance undertaking or reinsurance undertaking of the same participating insurance undertaking or reinsurance undertaking shall be excluded from the calculation.

C.3. *Transferability*
If the competent authorities consider that certain elements eligible for the solvency margin of a related insurance undertaking or a related reinsurance undertaking other than those referred to in Section C.2 cannot effectively be made available to cover the solvency margin requirement of the participating insurance undertaking or the participating reinsurance undertaking for which the adjusted solvency is calculated, those elements may be included in the calculation only in so far as they are eligible for covering the solvency margin requirement of the related undertaking.

C.4. The sum of the elements referred to in Sections C.2 and C.3 may not exceed the solvency margin requirement of the related insurance undertaking or the related reinsurance undertaking.

D. Elimination of the intra-group creation of capital

When calculating adjusted solvency, no account shall be taken of any element eligible for the solvency margin arising out of reciprocal financing between the insurance undertaking or the reinsurance undertaking and:
– a related undertaking,
– a participating undertaking,
– another related undertaking of any of its participating undertakings.

Furthermore, no account shall be taken of any element eligible for the solvency margin of a related insurance undertaking or a related reinsurance undertaking of the insurance undertaking or reinsurance undertaking for which the adjusted solvency is calculated when the element in question arises out of reciprocal financing with any other related undertaking of that insurance undertaking or reinsurance undertaking.

In particular, reciprocal financing exists when an insurance undertaking or a reinsurance undertaking, or any of its related undertakings, holds shares in, or makes loans to, another undertaking which, directly or indirectly, holds an element eligible for the solvency margin of the first undertakings.

E. The competent authorities shall ensure that the adjusted solvency is calculated with the same frequency as that laid down by Directives 73/239/EEC, 91/674/EEC, 2002/83/EC and 2005/68/EC for calculating the solvency margin of insurance undertakings or reinsurance undertakings. The value of the assets and liabilities shall be assessed in accordance with the relevant provisions of Directives 73/239/EEC, 91/674/EEC, 2002/83/EC and 2005/68/EC.

2. Application of the Calculation Methods

2.1. Related insurance undertakings and related reinsurance undertakings

The adjusted solvency calculation shall be carried out in accordance with the general principles and methods set out in this Annex.

In the case of all methods, where the insurance undertaking or reinsurance undertaking has more than one related insurance undertaking or related reinsurance undertaking the adjusted solvency calculation shall be carried out by integrating each of these related insurance undertakings or related reinsurance undertakings.

In cases of successive participations (for example, where an insurance undertaking or a reinsurance undertaking is a participating undertaking in another insurance undertaking or reinsurance undertaking which is also a participating undertaking in an insurance undertaking or a reinsurance undertaking), the adjusted solvency calculation shall be carried out at the level of each participating insurance undertaking or reinsurance undertaking which has at least one related insurance undertaking or one related reinsurance undertaking.

Member States may waive calculation of the adjusted solvency of an insurance undertaking or a reinsurance undertaking:
– if the insurance undertaking or reinsurance undertaking is a related undertaking of another insurance undertaking or a reinsurance undertaking authorised in the same Member State, and that related undertaking is taken into account in the calculation of the adjusted solvency of the participating insurance undertaking or reinsurance undertaking, or
– if the insurance undertaking or the reinsurance undertaking is a related undertaking of an insurance holding company which has its registered office in the same Member State as the insurance undertaking or the reinsurance undertaking, and both the holding insurance company and the related insurance undertaking or the related reinsurance undertaking are taken into account in the calculation carried out.

Member States may also waive calculation of the adjusted solvency of an insurance undertaking or reinsurance undertaking if it is a related insurance undertaking or a related reinsurance undertaking of another insurance undertaking, a reinsurance undertaking or an insurance holding company which has its registered office in another Member State, and if the competent authorities of the Member States concerned have agreed to grant exercise of the supplementary supervision to the competent authority of the latter Member State.

In each case, the waiver may be granted only if the competent authorities are satisfied that the elements eligible for the solvency margins of the insurance undertakings or the reinsurance undertakings included in the calculation are adequately distributed between those undertakings.

Member States may provide that where the related insurance undertaking or the related reinsurance undertaking has its registered office in a Member State other than that of the insurance undertaking or the reinsurance undertaking for which the adjusted solvency calculation is carried out, the calculation shall take account, in respect of the related undertaking, of the solvency situation as assessed by the competent authorities of that other Member State.

2.2. Intermediate insurance holding companies

When calculating the adjusted solvency of an insurance undertaking or a reinsurance undertaking which holds a participation in a related insurance undertaking, a related reinsurance undertaking, a non-member country insurance undertaking or a non-member country reinsurance undertaking, through an insurance holding company, the situation of the intermediate insurance holding company is taken into account. For the sole purpose of that calculation, to be undertaken in accordance with the general principles and methods described in this Annex, this insurance holding company shall be treated as if it were an insurance undertaking or reinsurance undertaking subject to a zero solvency requirement and were subject to the same conditions as are laid down in Article 16 of Directive 73/239/EEC, in Article 27 of Directive 2002/83/EC or in Article 36 of Directive 2005/68/EC, in respect of elements eligible for the solvency margin.

2.3. Related non-member country insurance undertakings and related non-member country reinsurance undertakings

When calculating the adjusted solvency of an insurance undertaking or a reinsurance undertaking which is a participating undertaking in a non-member country insurance undertaking or in a non-member country reinsurance undertaking, the latter shall be treated solely for the purposes of the calculation, by analogy with a related insurance undertaking or a related reinsurance undertaking, by applying the general principles and methods described in this Annex.

However, where the non-member country in which that undertaking has its registered office makes it subject to authorisation and imposes on it a solvency requirement at least comparable to that laid down in Directives 73/239/EEC, 2002/83/EC or 2005/68/EC, taking into account the elements of cover of that requirement, Member States may provide that the calculation shall take into account, as regards that undertaking, the solvency requirement and the elements eligible to satisfy that requirement as laid down by the non-member country in question.

2.4. Related credit institutions, investment firms and financial institutions

When calculating the adjusted solvency of an insurance undertaking or reinsurance undertaking which is a participating undertaking in a credit institution, investment firm or financial institution, the rules laid down in Article 16 of Directive 73/239/EEC, in Article 27 of Directive 2002/83/EC and in Article 36 of Directive 2005/68/EC, on the deduction of such participations shall apply mutatis mutandis, as well as the provisions on the ability of Member States under certain conditions to allow alternative methods and to allow such participations not to be deducted.

2.5. Non-availability of the necessary information

Where information necessary for calculating the adjusted solvency of an insurance undertaking or reinsurance undertaking, concerning a related undertaking with its registered office in a Member State or a non-member country, is not available to the competent authorities, for whatever reason, the book value of that undertaking in the participating insurance undertaking or reinsurance undertaking shall be deducted from the elements eligible for the adjusted solvency margin. In that case, the unrealised gains connected with such participation shall not be allowed as an element eligible for the adjusted solvency margin.

3. CALCULATION METHODS

Method 1: *Deduction and aggregation method*

The adjusted solvency situation of the participating insurance undertaking or the participating reinsurance undertaking is the difference between:

(i) the sum of:
 (a) the elements eligible for the solvency margin of the participating insurance undertaking or the participating reinsurance undertaking, and
 (b) the proportional share of the participating insurance undertaking or the participating reinsurance undertaking in the elements eligible for the solvency margin of the related insurance undertaking or the related reinsurance undertaking,

and

(ii) the sum of:
 (a) the book value in the participating insurance undertaking or the participating reinsurance undertaking of the related insurance undertaking or the related reinsurance undertaking, and
 (b) the solvency requirement of the participating insurance undertaking or the participating reinsurance undertaking, and

(c) the proportional share of the solvency requirement of the related insurance undertaking or the related reinsurance undertaking.

Where the participation in the related insurance undertaking or the related reinsurance undertaking consists, wholly or in part, of an indirect ownership, then item (ii)(a) shall incorporate the value of such indirect ownership, taking into account the relevant successive interests, and items (i)(b) and (ii)(c) shall include the corresponding proportional shares of the elements eligible for the solvency margin of the related insurance undertaking or the related reinsurance undertaking.

Method 2: *Requirement deduction method*

The adjusted solvency of the participating insurance undertaking or the participating reinsurance undertaking is the difference between:

(i) the sum of the elements eligible for the solvency margin of the participating insurance undertaking or the participating reinsurance undertaking,

and

(ii) the sum of:
  (a) the solvency requirement of the participating insurance undertaking or the participating reinsurance undertaking, and
  (b) the proportional share of the solvency requirement of the related insurance undertaking or the related reinsurance undertaking.

When valuing the elements eligible for the solvency margin, participations within the meaning of this Directive are valued by the equity method, in accordance with the option set out in Article 59(2)(b) of Directive 78/660/EEC.

Method 3: *Accounting consolidation-based method*

The calculation of the adjusted solvency of the participating insurance undertaking or the participating reinsurance undertaking shall be carried out on the basis of the consolidated accounts. The adjusted solvency of the participating insurance undertaking or the participating reinsurance undertaking is the difference between the elements eligible for the solvency margin calculated on the basis of consolidated data, and:

(a) either the sum of the solvency requirement of the participating insurance undertaking or the participating reinsurance undertaking and of the proportional shares of the solvency requirements of the related insurance undertakings or the related reinsurance undertaking, based on the percentages used for the establishment of the consolidated accounts,

(b) or the solvency requirement calculated on the basis of consolidated data.

The provisions of Directives 73/239/EEC, 91/674/EEC, 2002/83/EC and 2005/68/EC shall apply for the calculation of the elements eligible for the solvency margin and of the solvency requirement based on consolidated data.

Annex II

Supplementary supervision for insurance undertakings and reinsurance undertakings that are subsidiaries of an insurance holding company, a non-member country insurance undertaking or a non-member country reinsurance undertaking

1. In the case of two or more insurance undertakings or reinsurance undertakings referred to in Article 2(2) which are the subsidiaries of an insurance holding company, a non-member country insurance undertaking or a non-member country reinsurance undertaking and which are established in different Member States, the competent authorities shall ensure that the method described in this Annex is applied in a consistent manner.

The competent authorities shall exercise the supplementary supervision with the same frequency as that laid down by Directives 73/239/EEC, 91/674/EEC, 2002/83/EC and 2005/68/EC for calculating the solvency margin of insurance undertakings and reinsurance undertakings.

2. Member States may waive the calculation provided for in this Annex with regard to an insurance undertaking or a reinsurance undertaking:
– if that insurance undertaking or reinsurance undertaking is a related undertaking of another insurance undertaking or reinsurance undertaking and if it is taken into account in the calculation provided for in this Annex carried out for that other undertaking,
– if that insurance undertaking or reinsurance undertaking and one or more other insurance undertakings or reinsurance undertakings authorised in the same Member State have as their parent undertaking the same insurance holding company, non-member country insurance undertaking, or non-member country reinsurance undertaking, and the insurance undertaking or reinsurance undertaking is taken into account in the calculation provided for in this Annex carried out for one of these other undertakings,
– if that insurance undertaking or reinsurance undertaking and one or more other insurance undertakings or reinsurance undertakings authorised in other Member States have as their parent undertaking the same insurance holding company, non-member country insurance undertaking or non-member country reinsurance undertaking, and an agreement granting exercise of the supplementary supervision covered by this Annex to the supervisory authority of another Member State has been concluded in accordance with Article 4(2).

In the case of successive participations (for example: an insurance holding company or a non-member country insurance or reinsurance undertaking, which is itself owned by another insurance holding company or a non-member country insurance or reinsurance undertaking), Member States may apply the calculations provided for in this Annex only at the level of the ultimate parent undertaking of the insurance undertaking or reinsurance undertaking which is an insurance holding company, a non-member country insurance undertaking or a non-member country reinsurance undertaking.

3. The competent authorities shall ensure that calculations analogous to those described in Annex I are carried out at the level of the insurance holding company, non-member country insurance undertaking or non-member country reinsurance undertaking.

The analogy shall consist in applying the general principles and methods described in Annex I at the level of the insurance holding company, non-member country insurance undertaking or non-member country reinsurance undertaking.

For the sole purpose of that calculation, the parent undertaking shall be treated as if it were an insurance undertaking or reinsurance undertaking subject to:
– a zero solvency requirement where it is an insurance holding company,
– a solvency requirement determined in accordance with the principles of Section 2.3 of Annex I, where it is a non-member country insurance undertaking or a non-member country reinsurance undertaking,

and is subject to the same conditions as laid down in Article 16 of Directive 73/239/EEC, in Article 27 of Directive 2002/83/EC and in Article 36 of Directive 2005/68/EC as regards the elements eligible for the solvency margin.

4. Non-availability of the necessary information

Where information necessary for the calculation provided for in this Annex, concerning a related undertaking with its registered office in a Member State or a non-member country, is not available to the competent authorities, for whatever reason, the book value of that undertaking in the participating undertaking shall be deducted from the elements eligible for the calculation provided for in this Annex. In that case, the unrealised gains connected with such participation shall not be allowed as an element eligible for the calculation.]

¶ *The Annexes I and II have been replaced by Annex II of Directive 2005/68/EC, reproduced infra under no. I. 40.*

I. 29.

Commission Interpretative Communication 2000/C 43/03 on freedom to provide services and the general good in the insurance sector[1]

The Third Council Directives 92/49/EEC and 92/96/EEC[2] completed the establishment of the single market in the insurance sector. They introduced a single system for the authorisation and financial supervision of insurance undertakings by the Member State in which they have their head office (the home Member State). Such authorisation issued by the home Member State enables an insurance undertaking to carry on its insurance business anywhere in the European Community, either on the rules on establishment, i.e. by opening agencies or branches in all the Member States, or under the rules on the freedom to provide services. Where it carries on business in another Member State, the insurance undertaking must comply with the conditions in which, for reasons of the general good, such business must be conducted in the host Member State. Under the system set up by the Directives, the financial supervision of the business carried on by the insurance undertaking, including business carried on under the rules on establishment or on the freedom to provide services, is always a matter only for that insurance undertaking's home Member State.

In the course of its contacts with numerous economic agents, the Commission has come to realise that uncertainty surrounds the interpretation of the scope of the Treaty rules and of the provisions of the Insurance Directives, in particular the basic concepts of freedom to provide services and the general good. In many cases this results in the application by the supervisory authorities of measures or penalties in respect of insurance undertakings wishing to do business in the single market or in the imposition by them of certain constraints or conditions regarding the conduct of business on their territory. The situation in which insurance undertakings find themselves is far from clear and they thus face considerable legal uncertainty, both as regards the arrangements applicable to them in the different Member States and as regards the content of the products they wish to offer. The differences of interpretation seriously undermine the workings of the machinery set up by the Third Directives and are thus likely to deter certain insurance undertakings from exercising the freedoms created by the Treaty which the Third Directives set out to promote and, hence, to restrict the free movement of insurance services in the European Union. These differences are also preventing those seeking insurance from having access to insurance undertakings elsewhere in the Community and to the range of insurance products available within the single market in order to select the one that best fits their needs in terms of cover and cost.

In its communication to the Council of 28 October 1998 on financial services[3] which was drawn up at the request of the Cardiff European Council of June 1998, the Commission identified differences in interpretation of the Community rules and the resulting legal uncertainty as one of the factors preventing the single market in financial services from functioning properly. At its meeting in Cologne on 4 June 1999, the European Council endorsed the Action Plan[4]

---

[1] OJ C 43, 16.2.2000, 5–27; see also for the Banking sector, reproduced supra under no. B. 27.
[2] Directives 92/49/EEC (OJ L 228, 11.8.1992, 1), reproduced supra under no. I. 25 and 92/96/EEC (OJ L 360, 9.12.1992, 1), reproduced supra under no. I. 26 as last amended by Directive 95/26/EEC of the European Parliament and of the Council (OJ L 168, 18.7.1995, 7), reproduced supra under no. I. 27.

[3] 'Financial services: building a framework for action' (COM(98) 625).
[4] 'Implementing the framework for financial markets: Action Plan' (COM(1999) 232, 11.5.1999).

including the proposals and priorities contained in it, which was presented by the Commission following discussions within a group of personal representatives of the finance ministers which it chaired. This Action Plan includes the adoption of a Commission interpretative communication on freedom to provide services and the general good in the insurance sector among the priority objectives for helping to ensure that the single market operates effectively.

This interpretative communication is the Commission's contribution to the discussions it has held on the problems associated in the insurance industry with the freedom to provide services (Part One) and the general good (Part Two), particularly in the light of the third Council Directive on insurance (92/49/EEC and 92/96/EEC).

The Member States (particularly within the framework of the insurance committee and the sub-group on the interpretation of insurance directives), private operators, the European Parliament and the Economic and Social Committee have been involved in these discussions.

Before adopting the Action Plan, the Commission published in the *Official Journal of the European Communities* a draft communication[5] which marked the beginning of a wide-ranging consultation process. Following publication of that communication, it received numerous contributions from all the groups concerned (Member States, professional associations representing insurers and intermediaries, insurance companies, consumer organisations, law firms, etc.). It also organised hearings with interested parties.

The Commission deems it desirable to draw attention to and to systematise the principles governing the right of establishment and the freedom to provide services, as elucidated by the Court of Justice, and to consider how they apply to the Third Insurance Directives.[6] This interpretation is based on the provisions of the Treaty, the texts of the community Insurance Directives and on the decisions of the Court of Justice, which has set out a large number of principles essential to the observance of the right of establishment and the freedom to provide services.[7]

In publishing this interpretative communication, the Commission is seeking to make transparent and to clarify the common rules which it is its task to see are observed. It is supplying all those concerned—national administrations, economic agents and consumers—with a reference tool which explains the Commission's opinion with regard to the legal framework in which insurance business may be carried on.

The interpretations and ideas set out in the present communication, which concern only the specific problems of the insurance sector[8] do not claim to cover all possible situations that can arise in the functioning of the single insurance market, but merely the most frequent or most likely.

It should be pointed out straight away that the interpretations given in the present communication do not necessarily represent the often very divergent views put forward by the Member States and should not, in themselves, impose any new obligation on them. Neither do the interpretations prejudge the Commission's subsequent interpretations of the principles of establishment and freedom to provide services with regard to the development of communication technology and its use in the insurance business. European Community policy on the information society

---

[5] OJ C 365, 3.12.1997.
[6] See in this connection the Commission interpretative communication concerning the free movement of services across frontiers (OJ C 334, 9.12.1993, 3).

[7] Where different interpretations of the Insurance Directives are possible, this document follows the interpretation which, in the opinion of the Commission, is closest to the Treaty. It should be noted in this respect that, in accordance with the Court's case law, where a text of secondary legislation can be interpreted differently, preference should be given to the interpretation which would align it with the Treaty, rather than one which would render it incompatible (see Case 205/84 *Commission v Germany* [1986] ECR 3755).
[8] As regards the banking sector, the Commission has published an interpretative communication on the freedom to provide service and the general good in the Second Banking Directive (SEC(97) 1193 final, 20.6.1997).

and electronic commerce is designed to promote the expansion of information society services and their movement between the Member States, especially electronic commerce.[9] The development of electronic commerce in the insurance and financial business should become very important and should eventually change the machinery for distributing insurance products in the European Community. The current legal framework for the single market in insurance is based on machinery where consideration has not been given to how to use this new technology for carrying out insurance business in the single market, and further work may possibly have to be carried out in the area. In this connection, the proposal for a European Parliament and Council Directive concerning the distance marketing of consumer financial services[10] will provide a proper harmonised legal framework for distance transactions carried out with consumers, thereby contributing to the growing use of new remote communication techniques, such as the Internet.

It goes without saying that the Commission's interpretations do not prejudge the interpretation that the Court of Justice of the European Communities, which is responsible in the final instance for interpreting the Treaty and secondary legislation, might place on the matters at issue.

---

[9] Council resolution on the new priorities concerning the information society, adopted on 8 October 1996; Commission communication to the European Council entitled 'Putting services to work' (CSE(96) final, 27.11.1996); Commission communication to the European Parliament, the Council and the Economic and Social Committee concerning regulatory transparency in the internal market for information society services and proposal for a European Parliament and Council Directive amending for the third time Directive 83/189/EEC laying down a procedure for the provision of information in the field of technical standards and regulations (COM(96) 392 final, 30.8.1996); proposal for a European Parliament and Council directive on certain legal aspects of electronic commerce in the internal market (COM(98) 586 final, 18.11.1998) and amended proposal (COM(1999) 427 final, 17.8.1999); and proposal for a European Parliament and Council directive on a common framework for electronic signatures (COM(98) 297 final, 13.5.1998) and amended proposal COM(1999) 195, 29.4.1999).

[10] COM(98) 468 final, 14.10.1998, and, for the amended proposal, COM(1999) 385 final, 23.7.1999.

I. Freedom to Provide Services and Right of Establishment in the Insurance Directives

A. Demarcation between the right of establishment and the freedom to provide services[11]

1. Freedom to provide services

(a) Temporary nature

Article 49 et seq. of the Treaty establish the principle of the free movement of services. The

---

[11] For the purposes of this communication, the terms 'Member States of the provision of services', 'business carried on under the freedom to provide services', 'Member State where the risk is situated', 'home Member State', 'Member State of the branch', etc. are used in accordance with the definitions given in Directives 88/357/EEC, reproduced supra under no. I. 15, 90/619/EEC, reproduced supra under no. I. 18, 92/49/EEC, reproduced supra under no. I. 25 and 92/96/EEC, reproduced supra under no. I. 26.

Member State of the provision of services: the Member State where the risk is situated pursuant to Article 2(d) of Directive 88/357/EEC, reproduced supra under no. I. 15, in cases where it is covered by an insurance undertaking or branch situated in another Member State, or the Member State of the commitment pursuant to Article 2(e) of Directive 90/619/EEC, reproduced supra under no. I. 18, in cases where the commitment is covered by an insurance undertaking or branch situated in another Member State (Article 1(e) of Directive 92/49/EEC, reproduced supra under no. I. 25 and Article 1(f) of Directive 92/96/EEC, reproduced supra under no. I. 26).

Business carried on under the freedom to provide services: the cover by an insurance undertaking operating from one Member State of a risk or commitment situated pursuant to Article 2(d) of Directive 88/357/EEC, reproduced supra under no. I. 15 or Article 2(e) of Directive 90/619/EEC, reproduced supra under no. I. 18, in another Member State.

Home Member State: the Member State in which the head office of the insurance undertaking covering the risk or the commitment is situated (Article 1(c) of Directive 92/49/EEC, reproduced supra under no. I. 25 and Article 1(d) of Directive 92/96/EEC, reproduced supra under no. I. 26).

Member State of the branch: the Member State in which the branch covering the risk or commitment is situated (Article 1(d) of Directive 92/49/EEC, reproduced supra under no. I. 25 and Article 1(e) of Directive 92/96/EEC, reproduced supra under no. I. 26).

Branch: any agency or branch of an insurance undertaking. Any permanent presence of an undertaking in the territory of a Member State is treated in the same way as an agency or branch, even if that presence does not take the form of a branch or agency but consists merely of an office managed by the undertaking's own staff or by a person who is independent but has permanent authority to act for the undertaking as an agency would (Articles 1(b) of Directive 92/49/EEC, reproduced supra under no. I. 25 and Directive 92/96/EEC, reproduced supra under no. I. 26, and Articles 3 of Directives 88/357/EEC,

principle acquired direct, unconditional effect on the expiry of the transitional period.[12] It confers on the parties concerned rights which the national authorities are required to observe and uphold, by refraining from applying any conflicting provision of national law, whether legislative or administrative, including specific, individual administrative decisions.[13]

It should be noted that, according to the decisions of the Court of Justice, the freedom to provide services may involve the movement of the provider of the service, as envisaged in the third paragraph of Article 50 of the Treaty, or the movement of the recipient of the service to the Member State of the provider; the service may, however, also be carried out without any movement, either of the supplier or of the recipient.[14] In other words, Article 49 et seq. of the Treaty apply in all cases where a person providing services offers those services in a Member State other than that in which he is established, wherever the recipients of those services may be established. It is only when all the relevant elements of the activity in question are confined within a single Member State that the provisions of the Treaty on freedom to provide services do not apply.[15]

Where business is carried on under the freedom to provide services with the provider present on the territory of the Member State of provision, the concept of the provision of services is basically distinguished from that of establishment by its temporary character, while the right of establishment presupposes a lasting presence in the host country.[16] The distinction stems from the Treaty itself, where the third paragraph of Article 50 stipulates that, in cases involving movement by the service provider to another Member State, the person providing the service may, in order to do so, 'temporarily' pursue his activity in the State where the service is provided. According to the case law of the Court of Justice, the temporary nature of the provision of services is to be assessed in the light of its duration, regularity, periodicity and continuity. The fact that the provision of services is temporary does not mean that the provider of services may not equip himself with some form of infrastructure in the host Member State in so far as such infrastructure is necessary for the purpose of performing the services in question.[17]

The Court has also stated that an activity which consists in providing on a lasting basis services from the home Member State and does not involve movement by the service provider to the Member State of provision falls within the scope of the rules on the freedom to provide services.[18]

(b) Prohibition of circumvention of national law

The Court has acknowledged that a host Member State is entitled to take steps to prevent a service provider whose activity is entirely or mainly directed towards its territory (i.e. the host Member State) from improperly exercising the freedom to provide services enshrined in Article 49 of the Treaty in order to circumvent the rules of professional conduct which would be applicable to him if he were established in the territory of that host Member State.[19] It adds that such a

---

reproduced supra under no. I. 15 and 90/619/EEC, reproduced supra under no. I. 18).

[12] 1 January 1970 (Case 205/84 *Commission v Germany* [1986] ECR 3755) or the date of accession in the case of new Member States (judgment of 29 April 1999 in Case C-224/97, *Ciola* [1999] ECR I-2517).

[13] See footnote II Case C-224/97 *Ciola*.

[14] Joined Cases 286/82 and 26/83, *Luisi and Carbone* [1984] ECR 377; Case C-76/90 *Denemayer* [1991] ECR I-195; Case C-384/93 *Alpine Investments BV* [1995] ECR I-1141.

[15] Joined Cases C-225/95, C-226/95 and C-227/95, *Kapasakalis* [1998] ECR I-4239; judgments of the Court of 26 February 1991 in three cases concerning tourist guides: C-154/89 [1991] ECR I-659, C-180/89 [1991] ECR I-709, and C-198/89 [1991] ECR I-659.

[16] Joined Cases 286/82 and 26/83, *Luisi und Carbone* [1984] ECR 377; Case C-55/94, *Gebhard* [1995] ECR I-4165,

paragraphs 25 to 27; Case C-221/89 *Factortame* [1991] ECR I-3905: 'the concept of establishment within the meaning of Article 52 [now Article 43] et seq. of the Treaty involves the actual pursuit of an economic activity through a fixed establishment in another Member State for an indefinite period' (paragraph 20).

[17] Case 55/94, *Gebhard* [1995] ECR I-4165, paragraph 27; Case C-56/96 *VT4* [1997] ECR I-3143.

[18] Case C-56/96, *VT4* [1997] ECR I-3143.

[19] Case 205/84 *Commission v Germany* [1986] ECR 3755 (see footnote 7); Case 33/74 *Van Binsbergen* [1974] ECR 1299; Case C-148/91 *Veronica* [1993] ECR I-487; Case C-23/93 *TV 10* [1994] ECR I-4795, paragraphs 56 and 68 of the Opinion of Mr Advocate-General Lenz; Case C-56/96 *VT4*

situation may fall within the ambit of the chapter on the right of establishment and not of that on the freedom to provide services.[20]

The criterion of frequency is important in order to determine whether there may be an attempt at 'circumvention' while exercising the freedom to provide services enshrined in Article 49, but it is not sufficient to define business as being carried on under the freedom to provide services (an establishment may also operate on an occasional basis).

The Commission takes the view that a situation where an insurance undertaking is frequently being approached within its own territory—for example, via electronic means of communication—by consumers residing in other Member States could not be regarded as a circumvention, unless it were demonstrated that there was an intention on the part of the provider of services to circumvent the national rules of those other Member States.

2. Right of establishment

If an undertaking carries on business in a Member State for an indefinite period via a permanent presence in that Member State, it is covered in principle by the provisions of the Treaty on the right of establishment. The Court has held that:

> 'A national of a Member State who pursues a professional activity on a stable and continuous basis in another Member State where he holds himself out from an established professional base to, amongst others, nationals of that State comes under the chapter relating to the right of establishment and not the chapter relating to services'.[21]

In *Commission v Germany*,[22] the Court held that:

> '... an insurance undertaking of another Member State which maintains a permanent presence in the Member State in question comes within the scope of the provisions of the Treaty on the right of establishment, even if that presence does not take the form of a branch or agency, but consists merely of an office managed by the undertaking's own staff or by a person who is independent but authorised to act on a permanent basis for the undertaking, as will be the case with an agency.'

The Court has therefore acknowledged that an undertaking which has recourse to an intermediary established on the territory of another Member State to carry on activities in that Member State on a stable and continuous basis may fall within the scope of the rules on the right of establishment. The Court sought in that judgment to avoid the freedom to provide services being misused in order to circumvent the rules that would apply in the host Member State if the undertaking were established there.[23]

Nevertheless, this risk of abuse has been eliminated to a significant degree in the insurance sector as a result of the harmonisation achieved since the above judgment by the Community directives concerning the conditions for taking up and carrying on insurance activities. The prudential and supervisory rules for insurance undertakings have been largely harmonised, whichever way insurance activities are carried out: by way of establishment or through the provision of services.

The Court of Justice recently acknowledged that the temporary character of the provision of services does not mean that the provider may not equip himself with some form of infrastructure (chambers, office, etc.) in the host Member State in so far as is necessary for the purposes of performing the services in question, without coming under the right of establishment.[24] In such cases

---

(see footnote 17). See also the Opinion of Mr Advocate-General Lenz in Case C-212/97 *Centros* [1999] ECR I-1459, a case concerning alleged misuse of the 'secondary' right of establishment. The Court applied its case law on circumvention developed in the context of the freedom to provide services.

[20] Case 205/84 *Commission v Germany* [1986] ECR 3755 paragraph 22; Case 33/74 *Van Binsbergen* [1974] ECR 1299, paragraph 13.

[21] Case 55/94 *Gebhard* [1995] ECR I-4165; Case C-221/89 *Factortame* [1991] ECR I-3905.

[22] Case 205/84 *Commission v Germany* [1986] ECR 3755.

[23] Case 205/84, (see footnote 12) paragraphs 21 and 22; Case C-148/91 *Veronica* (see footnote 19); Case C-56/96 *VT4* (see footnote 17) (see Opinion of Mr Advocate-General Lenz).

[24] Case C-55/94, *Gebhard* (see footnote 16). It should be pointed out that, in his Opinion on Case 205/84 *Commission v*

the temporary character of the services provided should be assessed by reference to their duration, frequency, periodicity and continuity.[25] However, the mere existence of infrastructure in a Member State does not prove straight away that the situation falls within the scope of the rules on the right of establishment.

In the light of the case law of the Court of Justice,[26] The Commission considers that the Member State of the provision of services may not treat any permanent presence of the provider of services on its territory as an establishment and subject it in any event to the rules relating to the right of establishment.

3. Grey area

It is, however, not always easy to draw the line between the two concepts of provision of services and establishment. Some situations are difficult to classify, in particular where the insurer, in order to carry on its insurance business, uses a permanent infrastructure in the Member State of provision. This arises in particular in the following cases:

(a) recourse to independent persons established in the host Member State;

(b) electronic machines carrying on insurance business.

On the strength of the Court's case law, the Commission departments propose the following interpretations:

(a) Recourse to independent persons established in the host Member State

The problem is to determine to what extent an insurance undertaking established in Member State A which has recourse to an independent person[27] established in Member State B in order to do insurance business there could be regarded as itself carrying on an insurance activity on a permanent basis in Member State B and hence be treated as an establishment of the insurance undertaking in the host Member State, instead of being regarded as carrying on an insurance activity under the rules on the freedom to provide services.

In *De Bloos*[28] the Court held that:

'One of the essential characteristics of the concepts of branch or agency is the fact of being subject to the direction and control of the parent body.'

In even more precise terms, in *Somafer*[29] the Court held that:

'The concept of branch, agency or other establishment implies a place of business which has the appearance of permanency, such as the extension of a parent body, has a management and is materially equipped to negotiate business with third parties, so that the latter, although knowing that there will if necessary be a legal link with the parent body, the head office of which is abroad, do not have to deal directly with such a parent body but may transact business at the place of business constituting the extension.'

Germany (see footnote 7), the Advocate-General stated that the appointment of an agent or representative (in the host Member State) did not in itself necessarily constitute establishment.

[25] Case C-55/94 *Gebhard* (see footnote 16).
[26] See, in particular, *Gebhard*, and *VT4* (see footnote 17).
[27] It should be pointed out straightaway that the notion of 'independent person' refers to structures (natural or legal persons) that are legally separate from the insurance undertaking they call on, irrespective of their form or designation. It is not used therefore in the more restrictive sense of Council Directive 77/92/EEC (OJ L 26, 31.1.1977), reproduced supra under no. I. 7, to distinguish between insurance agents (who act on behalf and for the account of, or solely on behalf of, one or more insurance undertakings) and insurance brokers (whose professional activity consists in particular in bringing together persons seeking insurance and insurance undertakings without being bound in the choice of the latter, with a view to covering risks to be insured, and who carry out work preparatory to the conclusion of policies of insurance and assist in the administration and performance of such policies, in particular in the event of a claim).

[28] Case 14/76 [1976] ECR 1497. It should be noted that this judgment and those cited in footnotes 28, 29 and 30 were delivered in cases concerning the interpretation of the concept of a branch in accordance with the Brussels Convention on jurisdiction and the enforcement of judgements in civil and commercial matters.

[29] Case 33/78 [1978] ECR 2183. See also Case C-439/93, *Lloyd's Register of Shipping v Société Campenon Bernard* [1995] ECR I-961.

It concluded that a sole concessionaire not subject to the control and direction of a company could not be regarded as a branch, agency or establishment.

In *Blanckart & Willems*,[30] the Court held that:

> 'An independent commercial agent who merely negotiates business, inasmuch as his legal status leaves him basically free to arrange his own work and decide what proportion of his time to devote to the interests of the undertaking which he agrees to represent and whom that undertaking may not prevent from representing at the same time several firms competing in the same manufacturing or marketing sector, and who, moreover, merely transmits orders to the parent undertaking without being involved in either their terms or their execution, does not have the character of a branch, agency or other establishment . . .'

Moreover, in his Opinion in *Shearson Lehman Hutton*[31] Mr Advocate-General Darmon stated that:

> 'The link of dependence vis-à-vis the company established in another signatory State[32] is not the determining criterion here. In our opinion, that criterion resides in the fact the secondary establishment has the power to enter into contracts with third parties.'

Lastly, in his report on the Brussels Convention, Mr Jenard notes that there is an agency or branch only 'where the foreign company is represented by a person capable of acting in a manner that is binding on it vis-à-vis third parties'.[33]

On the basis of these precedents, the Commission considers that, for the links between an independent person—such as, for example, an independent intermediary—and an insurance undertaking to be regarded as meaning that the insurance undertaking falls within the scope of the rules governing the right of establishment rather than those applicable to the freedom to provide services, the independent person must meet the following three cumulative conditions:

(i) *he must be subject to the direction and control of the insurance undertaking he represents;*
(ii) *he must be able to commit the insurance undertaking; and*
(iii) *he must have received a permanent brief.*

It is, therefore, only where the independent person acts as a genuine extension of the insurance undertaking that the insurance undertaking falls within the scope of the rules applicable to the establishment of a branch.

(i) The independent person must be subject to the direction and control of the insurance undertaking he represents

To verify if this criterion is met, a check should be made in particular to see whether, in the light of the links establishment between the insurance undertaking and the independent person, the latter has sufficient freedom to organise his activities, to decide how much time he will devote to the insurance undertaking and in particular, to represent competitors at the same time.

An exclusive brief received by an independent intermediary from a single insurer is an indication that the intermediary is subject to the direction and control of that insurer. It is nevertheless not uncommon in the insurance sector for intermediaries to represent several competing insurers at the same time. In most cases, such representation concerns different classes of insurance for different insurers.

Thus, in such cases, an intermediary who works for several insurers, only one of which has given him an exclusive brief, would be treated as a branch of that insurance undertaking to the extent that the brief places intermediary under the direction and control of that insurer. The other insurers would, on the other hand, be subject to the rules governing the freedom to provide services.

In any event, the remaining two conditions mentioned should also be satisfied in order for the intermediary to be treated as a branch of an

---

[30] Case 139/80 [1981] ECR 819.
[31] Case C-89/91 [1992] ECR I-165.
[32] The term 'signatory State' is used here because the case concerned the Brussels Convention on jurisdiction and the enforcement of judgements in civil and commercial matters.
[33] OJ C 59, 5.3.1979, 1.

insurance undertaking in the host Member State and for the activities of that insurer to be covered by the rules on establishment rather than the rules on the provision of services. The above considerations apply irrespective of whether the intermediary is a natural person or a legal person.

(ii) The independent person must commit the insurance undertaking

To determine whether this condition is satisfied, it has to be examined, in accordance with the Court's case law, whether the acts or decisions of the independent person can commit the insurance undertaking vis-à-vis third parties, who therefore do not need to deal with the insurance undertaking itself and may conclude business with the independent person.

The commitment of the insurance undertaking vis-à-vis the insured results primarily from the brief given to the independent person to conclude insurance policies with those seeking insurance on behalf and for the account of the insurance undertaking not established in the host Member State. The specific purpose of an agency or a branch is to conclude policies with third parties on behalf and for the account of the head office, which is thus directly committed, since the agency is an extension of the head office. If the independent person can, for instance, make on behalf of the insurance undertaking an offer containing all the essential of the proposed policy, but the insurance undertaking can still refuse the proposal submitted by the independent person and signed by the client, the condition of the ability to commit will not be met.

In some cases, other elements of the brief given by the insurance undertaking to an independent person may also show the intention of the insurance undertaking to be directly committed to the policyholder. For example, where the insurer has granted the intermediary the power to decide to accept and settle a claim submitted to it and the decisions taken by the intermediary bind the insurer vis-à-vis third parties. This function must, however, be distinguished from the brief given to the intermediary simple to manage files relating to claims; this may include, where appropriate, the payment of indemnities pursuant to the instructions given by the insurer himself.

(iii) The independent person must have received a permanent brief

The capacity of an independent person (e.g. an intermediary) established in the host Member State to commit an insurance undertaking must be based on a long-term, continuous brief and not a brief that is limited in time or a one-off instruction. This stable and continuous quality of the brief shows that the insurance undertaking intends to integrate into the economy of the host Member State the insurance activities which it carries on there.

In the Commission's opinion, where an insurance undertaking has recourse, in order temporarily and occasionally to carry on insurance business in another Member State, to an intermediary established in that other Member State, it falls within the scope of the rules governing the freedom to provide services.[34]

The Commission considers that an insurance undertaking that decides to transact insurance business under the freedom to provide services must be able to use certain services either upstream or downstream of the transaction in the Member State of provision. For example, an insurance undertaking should be able to use for its business under the freedom to provide services:
- a local expert to assess the risks to be covered under the freedom to provide services,
- a local expert to assess damage caused under risks covered by insurance policies negotiated under the freedom to provide services,
- canvassers who do not conclude insurance policies and whose activity is limited to sending insurance proposals received from potential policyholders to the insurance undertaking for acceptance,

---

[34] See Articles 14, 16 and 17 of Directive 88/357/EEC, reproduced supra under no. I. 15, as amended by Articles 34, 35 and 36 of Directive 92/49/EEC (non-life insurance), reproduced supra under no. I. 25, and Articles 11, 14 and 17 of Directive 88/357/EEC, reproduced supra under no. I. 15, as amended by Articles 34, 35 and 36 of Directive 92/96/EEC (life assurance), reproduced supra under no. I. 26, for the procedure relating to activities under the freedom to provide services falling within the scope of these Directives.

- local legal services, medical or actuarial services established in the Member State of provision,
- a permanent structure for collecting the premiums for insurance policies entered into under the freedom to provide services (e.g. a credit institution or a factoring company),
- a permanent structure for receiving notices of claims relating to policies concluded under the freedom to provide services for transmission to the insurance undertaking for a decision to accept or refuse each claim,
- a permanent structure for managing files relating to claims (this may include, where appropriate, the payment of indemnities pursuant to the instructions given by the insurer himself).

It should be made clear that the only brief which results in treating a permanent presence in the same way as a branch of the insurance undertaking in the Member State of provision is one which concerns the activities that are part of the undertaking's objects, i.e. the business of insurance. A brief given to persons established in another Member State to carry out activities other than insurance cannot be taken into account when assessing the arrangements for carrying on the insurance activity in the host Member State. This could be the case with a brief given to an investment company to manage the insurance undertaking's securities portfolio or with a company instructed to manage real estate which the undertaking owns in a Member State and which it uses as cover for technical provisions.

Conclusion:

The Commission takes the view that it is only where the above three conditions are met (i.e. where the independent person to the direction and control of the insurance undertaking, is able to commit the insurance undertaking and has received a permanent brief) that an insurance undertaking, using independent persons—e.g. intermediaries—permanently established in the host Member State, must be treated as if it had a branch in the host Member State, with all that this implies from the legal point of view. Accordingly, the insurance undertaking will have to follow the procedure for opening a branch laid down by Article 10 of the First Insurance Directives 73/329/EEC and 79/267/EEC, as amended by Article 32 of the Third Insurance Directives 92/49/EEC and 92/96/EEC (specifying that the activities envisaged will be carried on through an independent intermediary). In addition, the independent person's activities must be carried on with due regard for the rules on branches adopted in the interest of the general good by the host State.

The fact that these conditions may involve making the insurance undertaking subject to the right of establishment does not mean that the independent person himself constitutes a branch of the insurer. A branch is 'a place of business which forms a legally dependent part of an insurance undertaking'.[35] Since the person is assumed to be independent, he cannot be a 'part' of an insurance undertaking. This is without prejudice to compliance, where appropriate, by that independent person with the conditions governing the taking up and exercise of his professional activity in the Member State in which he is established.

(b) Electronic machines

This means fixed, ATM-type electronic machines capable of performing the insurance activities listed in the Annex to the First Directives.[36]

Such machines may be covered by the right of establishment if they fulfil the criteria laid down by the Court of Justice (see (a)).

For such a machine to be capable of being treated as an establishment, therefore, it would have to have a management, which is by definition impossible unless the Court acknowledges that the concept can encompass not only human management but also electronic management.

---

[35] See in this respect the concept of a branch given in Article 1(3) of Second Banking Directive 89/646/EEC (OJ L 386, 30.12.1989), consolidated in Directive 2000/12/EC, reproduced supra under no. B. 32 and Article 1(8) of Directive 93/22/EEC on investment services in the securities field (OJ L 141, 11.6.1993), reproduced infra under no. S. 14.

[36] It does not mean individual, mobile data-processing equipment which can provide or receive distance insurance services, e.g. through the Internet. Equipment of this kind is discussed in point 6.

However, such a machine is unlikely to be the only place of business of an insurance undertaking in a Member State. It is likely to be attached in the same country to a branch or an agency. In that event, the machine is not an entity in its own right as it is covered by the rules governing the establishment to which it is attached.

If the machine does, however, constitute the only presence of an insurance undertaking in a Member State for the type of insurance transaction in question, the Commission takes the view that it may be possible to treat it as a provision of services in the territory of that Member State. The presence in the host country of a person or company responsible simply for maintaining the machine, equipping it and dealing with any technical problems encountered by users cannot rank as an establishment of the insurance undertaking and does not prevent the activity being deemed to be carried on under the freedom to provide services.

The Commission cannot rule out the possibility that technological developments might, in the future, induce it to review its position. If such developments were to make it possible for an insurance undertaking to have only a machine in a given country which could 'act' as a branch, taking actual decisions which would completely obviate the need for the customer to have contact with the parent company, the Commission would be forced to consider an appropriate Community legal framework. The present legal framework in fact rests on mechanisms which are still based on a 'human' concept of a branch (for example, the programme of operations must contain the names of those responsible for the management of the branch). It is therefore not possible, under the existing rules, to consider machines as constituting a branch.

4. Simultaneous exercise of the freedom to provide services and the right of establishment

Since 1 July 1994, when the Third Directives 92/49/EEC and 92/96/EEC entered into force, an insurance undertaking can simultaneously carry on business in the same country under the freedom to provide services and through a form of establishment (branch), even if it is the same activity. Those Directives repealed the provisions of the Second Directives which allowed Member States to prohibit in certain cases simultaneous exercise of the freedom to provide services and the right of establishment.[37]

For the purpose of carrying on its insurance business under the freedom to provide services, the insurance undertaking can have recourse to an establishment opened in the Member State of the provision of services for support activities either upstream or downstream of the conclusion of the insurance policy (e.g. use the risk assessment services or of local legal or medical services, receipt of notices of claims relating to policies entered into under the freedom to provide services, evaluation by local services of damage caused under risks covered by such policies, information service for policyholders). The insurance undertaking must, however, be able clearly to relate the activity concerned to one of the methods of carrying on business: either the right of establishment or the freedom to provide services.

5. Monitoring by the host Member State of the conditions for granting the single licence

In the Commission's view, the Insurance Directives[38] do not allow the host Member State to carry out checks to determine whether an insurance undertaking intending to operate in its territory under the freedom to provide services or through a branch meets the standard conditions under which it was granted the single licence in its home Member State. Such checks may be carried out by the home Member State alone. It is on the responsibility of the home Member State that

---

[37] Directives 92/49/EEC (Article 37 and recital 28), reproduced supra under no. I. 25 and 92/96/EEC (Article 17 and recital 25), reproduced supra under no. I. 26.

[38] Non-life insurance: Articles 6, 7, 8 and 9 of the First Directive 73/239/EEC, reproduced supra under no. I. 3, as amended by Articles 4, 5, 6, 7 and 8 of Directive 92/49/EEC, reproduced supra under no. I. 25 and Article 3 of Directive 95/26/EEC, reproduced supra under no. I. 27. Life assurance: Articles 6, 7, 8 and 9 of the First Directive 79/267/EEC, reproduced supra under no. I. 9, as amended by Articles 3, 4, 5, 6 and 7 of Directive 92/96/EEC, reproduced supra under no. I. 26 and Article 3 of Directive 95/26/EEC, reproduced supra under no. I. 27.

the single licence is granted, and the host Member State cannot question the granting of such a licence.[39]

If the host Member State has reason to doubt compliance with the standard conditions, it may recourse to Article 227 of the Treaty or request the Commission to take action against the home Member State for failing to meet its obligations pursuant to Article 226 of the Treaty.

6. Insurance business carried on using remote means of communication, and in particular via electronic commerce

(a) The use of remote means of communication (telephone, fax, the press, etc.) and in particular electronic commerce (e.g. via the Internet) to conclude insurance policies covering a risk (or communication) situated in a Member State other than the Member State of establishment of the insurer should be regarded as insurance business carried on under the freedom to provide services motorised no movement on the part of the contracting parties.[40] In addition, most of the cases involve services provided on a lasting basis.[41] The Member State of establishment of the insurance undertaking with which a policy is concluded in this way is the Member State of establishment of the insurer that effectively comes on the insurance activity (head office or branch) and not the place where the technological means used for providing the service are located (e.g. the place where the Internet server is installed).[42]

In most cases, the initiative for the conclusion of such insurance policies via the Internet comes from the prospective policyholder, who decides to use his own equipment in order to contact, and to seek to conclude an insurance policy electronically with, an insurance undertaking willing to do business in this way.

Under the Insurance Directives, the location of the risk (or commitment) covered by the insurance policy is the key factor for determining the rules applicable to an insurance transaction. The location of the risk or commitment is furthermore itself determined according to precise criteria laid down by the Insurance Directives themselves.[43] Consequently, if an insurance transaction is to be carried out under the freedom to provide services, the risk or commitment covered by the insurance policy must be situated in a Member State other than the Member State of establishment of the insurance undertaking covering that risk or commitment.

The Commission takes the view that, in accordance with the rules as they stand, insurance activities carried on via electronic commerce (e.g. the Internet) and covering a risk located in a Member State other than that in which the insurer covering the risk is established are subject to the provisions of the Insurance Directives relating to the freedom to provide services. An insurance undertaking operating from one Member State which is prepared to conclude via the Internet insurance policies covering risks or commitments situated in other Member States should therefore follow the notification procedure for activities carried on under the freedom to provide services.[44]

---

[39] See the judgment delivered by the Court on 10 September 1996 on a similar issue in Case C-11/95 *Commission v Belgium* [1996] ECR I-4115. The Court ruled that the receiving Member State was not authorised to monitor the application of the law of the originating Member State applying to television broadcasts and to ensure compliance with Council Directive 89/552/EEC (known as the 'Television without Frontiers' Directive (OJ L 298, 17.10.1989, 23)).

[40] Joined Cases 286/82 and 26/83 *Luisi and Carbone* (see footnote 14); Case C-23/93 *TV10* (see footnote 19).

[41] See Part I.1 and footnote 18.

[42] See in this connection Article 1(c) of the amended proposal for a directive on certain legal aspects of electronic commerce in the internal market, supra; Case C-221/89 *Factortame* (see footnote 21).

[43] Non-life insurance: Article 2(d) of the Second Directive 88/357/EEC, reproduced supra under no. I. 15; life assurance: Article 2(e) of Directive 90/619/EEC, reproduced supra under no. I. 18. This is unlike the banking sector, for which the Second Banking Directive 89/646/EEC does not lay any criteria for locating banking activities carried on in the single market (see communication on the banking sector (SEC(97) 1193 final, 20.6.1997), which provides criteria for locating banking activities carried on under the freedom to provide services with a view to determining the rules applicable).

[44] See Articles 14, 16 and 17 of Directive 88/357/EEC, reproduced supra under no. I. 15, as amended by Articles 34, 35 and 36 of Directive 92/49/EEC (non-life insurance), reproduced supra under no. I. 25, and Articles 11, 14 and 17 of Directive 88/357/EEC, reproduced supra under no. I. 15, as amended by Articles 34, 35 and 36 of Directive 92/96/EEC (life assurance), reproduced supra under no. I. 26, for the

The existing legal framework governing the single insurance market rests on mechanisms which did not envisage the use of information technology for carrying on insurance business in the single market. For this reason, the Commission already stated in its communication to the Council on the Financial Services Action Plan[45] that it intended to bring out a Green Paper to examine whether the existing provisions of the directives in the field of financial services provided a regulatory framework that is propitious to the development of electronic commerce in financial services while ensuring that the interests of consumers are fully protected.

(b) On the other hand, the use of electronic commerce methods for the sole purposes of advertising, providing commercial information or enhancing awareness of the insurance undertaking cannot be regarded as an insurance activity. As stated in Section III below, the Insurance Directives do not make advertising activities in the host Member State subject to their notification procedure, only the intention to carry on an insurance activity in another Member State under the freedom to provide services.[46]

The Commission considers that it is out of the question to make such advertising and information activities subject to the notification procedure laid down by the Third Directives (Article 34 et seq.), which was designed for actual insurance activities carried on under the freedom to provide services.

7. Miscellaneous

In the Commission's opinion, it would very likely be contrary to Community law for an insurance undertaking which has carried on its business under freedom to provide services within the territory of a Member State for a given length of time to be forced by that Member State to become established as a prerequisite for the continued pursuit of its activities.

B. Nature of the procedure for notifying the opening of a branch or the intention to carry on business under the freedom to provide services

The Commission considers that the notification procedure laid down in the Third Insurance Directives (both for branches and for provision of services)[47] pursues a simple objective of exchange of information between supervisory authorities and is not a consumer protection measure. It should not, in the Commission's view, be considered a condition affecting the validity of any insurance policies concluded without the procedure having previously been followed.

It should be pointed out here that the expert group responsible for studying, as part of the third phase of the SLIM project, possible ways of simplifying Community legislation on insurance has recommended that the notification procedure for carrying on business under the freedom to provide services be retained with certain adjustments so as to enable Community insurers to respond with the necessary speed to requests they receive for insurance cover under the freedom to provide services, without any intention to evade the notification obligation.[48]

The Commission welcomes this recommendation and has undertaken to examine the rules in force with a view to making the adjustments

---

procedure relating to activities under the freedom to provide services falling within the scope of these Directives.

[45] COM(1999) 232, 11.5.1999.

[46] See Commission communication 'A European initiative in electronic commerce' (COM(97) 15 final), proposal for a European Parliament and Council Directive on certain legal aspects of electronic commerce in the internal market (COM(98) 586 final, 18.11.1998) and amended proposal (COM(1999) 427 final, 17.8.1999).

[47] See Article 10 of First Directive 73/239/EEC, reproduced supra under no. I. 3, as amended by Article 32 of Directive 92/49/EEC, reproduced supra under no. I. 25, as regards non-life insurance and Article 10 of First Directive 79/267/EEC, reproduced supra under no. I. 9, as amended by Article 32 of Directive 92/96/EEC, reproduced supra under no. I. 26, as regards life assurance for the procedure to be followed for opening a branch. See Articles 14, 16 and 17 of Directive 88/357/EEC, reproduced supra under no. I. 15, as amended by Articles 34, 35 and 36 of Directive 92/49/EEC, reproduced supra under no. I. 25, as regards non-life insurance and Articles 11, 14 and 17 of Directive 88/357/EEC, reproduced supra under no. I. 15, as amended by Articles 34, 35 and 36 of Directive 92/96/EEC, reproduced supra under no. I. 26 as regards life assurance for the procedure relating to activities under the freedom to provide services falling within the scope of these Directives.

[48] COM(1999) 88 final, 25.2.1999.

deemed necessary in order to enable any insurance undertaking in the Community to respond rapidly to requests for insurance cover under the freedom to provide services, particularly in cases where, not having given prior notification, it is requested on its own territory to conclude an insurance policy under the freedom to provide services.[49] The Commission will put forward the necessary proposals to that end.

C. Advertising insurance services

The Third Insurance Directives lay down that insurance undertakings with head offices in Member States may advertise their services, through all available means of communication, in the Member State of the branch or the Member State of the provision of services, subject to any rules governing the form and content of such advertising adopted in the interest of the general good.[50]

The Commission believes it is out of the question to make the right to advertise[51] conditional on compliance with the notification procedure laid down in Article 34 et seq. of the Third Directives for carrying on insurance business under the freedom to provide services.

Such a link would be artificial since it is not explicitly provided for by the Third Directives. Article 34 et seq. of the Third Insurance Directives make subject to the notification procedure not advertising activities in the host Member State but the intention to pursue an insurance activity under the freedom to provide services.

Similarly, to link advertising and the notification procedure for carrying on activities under the freedom to provide services could lead to anomalous situations where an insurance undertaking could find itself invited to notify the authorities of all the Member States in which its advertising could in theory be received, although the undertaking may not be planning to pursue its activities in all the Member States where such advertising is received.

The Commission believes, therefore, that, in accordance with the Third Directives, all forms of advertising by whatever means (mail, fax, electronic mail, etc.) should not be subject to the notification procedure referred to in Article 34 et seq. of the Third Directives. It is only if the insurance undertaking plans to carry on insurance activities under the freedom to provide services and only if it offers insurance products to potential clients established in another Member State that it must only comply with the notification procedure.

The above considerations concern only the problem of advertising seen from the formal angle and do not affect the right of Member States to enforce, on their territory and subject to current Community law, their general-good rules on the content of advertising, pursuant to Article 41 of the Third Directives.

II. THE GENERAL GOOD IN THE THIRD INSURANCE DIRECTIVES; APPLICABILITY OF RULES PROMOTING THE GENERAL GOOD

The Third Insurance Directives reflect the case law of the Court of Justice and contain several references to the concept of the general good, providing in particular that an insurance undertaking operating under a single licence must comply with host-country rules adopted in the interest of the general good.

Such compliance is required either in the specific context of freedom of establishment (Article 32(4) of Directives 92/49/EEC and 92/96/EEC) or indiscriminately in connection with freedom of establishment and freedom to provide services

---

[49] COM(1999) 88 final, 25.2.1999.
[50] Article 41 of the Third Non-life Directive (92/49/EEC), reproduced supra under no. I. 25, and Article 41 of the Third Life Directive (92/96/EEC), reproduced supra under no. I. 26.
[51] By advertising is meant 'the making of a representation in any form in connection with a trade, business, craft or profession in order to promote the supply of goods or services, including immovable property, rights and obligations' (Directive 84/450/EEC of 10 September 1984 on misleading advertising (OJ L 250, 19.9.1984, 17), reproduced supra under no. C. 1). See also Article 2(e) ('commercial communications') of the amended proposal for a European Parliament and Council Directive on certain legal aspects of electronic commerce in the internal market, supra.

(Articles 28 and 41 of Directives 92/49/EEC and 92/96/EEC).

1. The concept of the general good in the Third Insurance Directives

The Third Insurance Directives refer to the general good in several places:

(a) Under the procedure for setting up a branch establishment, the host Member State two months from the receipt of the file sent by the host Member State to indicate to the insurance undertaking the conditions in which, for reasons of the general good, such activities must be carried on in the Member State of the branch (Article 10 of Directives 73/239/EEC and 79/267/EEC, as amended by Article 32 of Directives 92/49/EEC and 92/96/EEC).

(b) As regards the marketing of insurance policies, the Member State of the commitment or that in which the risk is situated must allow insurance policies (non-life or life) to be concluded with insurance undertakings authorised in other Member States, whether under the rules on branches or under the freedom to provide services, on condition that such insurance policies do not conflict with the statutory provisions protecting the general good in force in the Member State of the commitment or that in which the risk is situated (Article 28 of Directives 92/49/EEC and 92/96/EEC).

(c) In the case of health insurance taken out as an alternative to the cover provided by a statutory system of social security Article 54 of the Third Non-life Directive (92/49/EEC) states that each Member State in which health insurance policies can be substituted either wholly or in part for the sickness cover provided by a statutory system of social security may require such policies to comply with the statutory provisions protecting the general good in that Member State for that class of insurance. The Member State may also require prior notification of policy conditions before such policies are marketed.[52]

(d) Lastly, an insurance undertaking authorised in its home Member State may advertise its services by any means of communication available in the Member State of the branch or the provision of services, on condition that it complies with any general-good rules on the form and content of the advertisement (Article 41 of Directives 92/49/EEC and 92/96/EEC).

The main objective of the Insurance Directives is to allow any insurance undertaking authorised in a Member State to carry on its insurance activities throughout the European Union, whether under the rules on branches or under the freedom to provide services. Their provisions apply to any insurance undertaking operating in Member States other than the home Member State under a single licence issued in the home Member State. This is because the Community legislator did not intend to differentiate between setting up a branch and provision of services.[53] The only differences introduced concern the notification procedure, which is more detailed for the establishment of a branch (Article 32 of Directives 92/49/EEC and 92/96/EEC) than for the conduct of insurance business under the freedom to provide services (Articles 34 et seq. of Directives 92/49/EEC and 92/96/EEC.[54] The 19th recital of Directive 92/49/EEC and the 20th recital of Directive 92/96/EEC state that the host Member State must:

'... ensure that there is nothing to prevent the marketing within its territory of the insurance

---

[52] It should be noted here that, where the technique of health insurance is similar to that in the field of life assurance, Article 54(2) of Directive 92/49/EEC, reproduced supra under no. I. 25, has already established the conditions that can be applied to insurers exercising such activities. As regards compulsory insurance for accidents at work, the Member States concerned may require every insurance undertaking to respect the specific provisions in their national law for such insurance, with the exception of provisions concerning financial supervision, which are the exclusive responsibility of the home Member State (Article 55 of Directive 92/49/EEC, reproduced supra under no. I. 25).

[53] It should be pointed out that the uniform application of the mutual recognition principle to both branches and service providers was not introduced for the first time by the Third Insurance Directives but appears also in the other directives relating to financial services: the Second Banking Directive 89/646/EEC (OJ L 386, 30.12.1989), as last amended by Directive 92/30/EEC (OJ L 110, 28.4.1992, 52), and Directive 93/22/EEC on investment services in the securities field (OJ L 141, 11.6.1993, 27), reproduced infra under no. S. 14. The Second Banking Directive has been consolidated in Directive 2000/12/EC, reproduced supra under no. B. 32.

[54] It should be pointed out that the principle of single authorisation and supervision by the home Member State does

products offered for sale in the Community as long as they do not conflict with the legal provisions protecting the general good in force in the Member State in which the risk is situated, and in so far as the general good is not safeguarded by the rules of the home Member State, provided that such provisions must be applied without discrimination to all undertakings operating in that Member State and be objectively necessary and in proportion to the objective pursued'.

Since the recitals of a directive have legal force as an aid to interpretation, they shed light for the reader on the intentions of the Community legislator.[55]

The Commission takes the view that an insurance undertaking operating under the arrangements laid down by the Insurance Directives could, therefore, be obliged to adapt its services to the host-country rules only if the measures enforced against it serve the general good, irrespective of whether it carries on its activities through a branch or under the freedom to provide services.

This approach is borne out by recent decisions of the Court of Justice, which held that only general-good rules can restrict or impede exercise of the two basic freedoms, namely the freedom to provide services[56] and the right of establishment.[57] However, the Insurance Directives do not contain any definition of 'the general good'.

They simply recall in their recitals the requirements imposed by the Court of Justice's case law on the concept of the general good. The reason for this is that is a judicial construction of an evolutive and open nature devised by the Court of Justice. It makes it possible to assess the conformity with Community law of a national measure that is taken in a non-harmonised area at Community level and hinders freedom of establishment and freedom to provide services. In non-harmonised areas, the level of what is regarded as the general good depends first on the assessment made by the Member States and can vary substantially from one country to another according to national traditions and the objectives of the Member States. It is necessary, therefore, to refer to the relevant case law of the Court of Justice.

2. *The concept of the general good*

(a) Case-law principles[58]

The concept of the general good is based in the Court's case law. It was developed first in the context of the free movement of services and goods and was subsequently applied to the right of establishment.[59]

However, the Court has never given a definition of 'the general good', preferring to maintain its evolving nature. It has expressed its opinion in individual cases on the possibility of deeming a given national measure to be aimed at achieving an imperative objective serving the general good and has specified the line of reasoning to be followed in determining whether such a measure may be enforced by one Member State against a trader from another Member State who is

---

not obstruct the application of other areas of the national law of the host Member State, e.g. tax law, social security law or labour law, which may accord differentiated treatment to Community firms depending on the way in which they choose to conduct their business, i.e. by way of freedom to provide services or by way of freedom of movement. In any event, the compatibility of such provisions with Community law will always be assessed on the basis of established case law criteria, especially where the general good is concerned, i.e. non-discrimination, non-duplication, necessity, proportionality, etc.

55 See in particular Case 76/72 *Michel* [1973] ECR 457 and Case C-238/94 *Garcia* [1996] ECR I-1673.

56 Case C-76/90 *Säger* [1991] ECR I-4221. See the analysis set out in the Commission interpretative communications concerning the free movement of services across frontiers (OJ C 334, 9.12.1993, 3) and concerning freedom to provide services and the interest of the general good in the Second Banking Directive (SEC(97) 1193, 26.6.1997).

57 *Gebhard*, footnote 16. See also Cases C-19/92 *Kraus* [1993] ECR I-1663 and C-212/97 *Centros* (see footnote 19).

58 The Commission's analysis may, of course, be modified to reflect changes in the Court's case law.

59 Case-55/94 *Gebhard* (see footnote 16). It is interesting to note that the judgment in *Gebhard* relates to an area (access to the profession of lawyer) in which harmonisation of the conditions for taking up and carrying on the activity is very limited in comparison with insurance. In the insurance sector, these conditions have been very extensively harmonised and the possibilities for relying on general-good rules are hence much more limited. On the other hand, with regard to the law of insurance policies, which is a field that has not been harmonised by secondary Community legislation, the discretion of the Member States is much wider. It is above all in this field that the test of the general good is likely to be applied.

operating within the territory of the former. The Court has though spelt out the strict conditions to be met by national measures which are aimed at achieving an imperative objective serving the general good if they are to be validly enforced against that trader.[60]

The Court requires that a national provision must satisfy the following requirements if it is validly to obstruct or limit exercise of the right of establishment and the freedom to provide services:
— it must come within a field which has not been harmonised,
— it must pursue an objective of the general good,
— it must be non-discriminatory,
— it must be objectively necessary,
— it must be proportionate to the objective pursued,
— it is also necessary for the general-good objective not to be safeguarded by rules to which the provider of services is already subject in the Member State where he is established.

These conditions are cumulative. A national measure which is claimed to be compatible with the principle of the freedom of movement must satisfy all the conditions. If a national measure does not meet one or other condition, it is not compatible with Community law.

The concept of general good is an exception to the fundamental principles of the Treaty with regard to free movement and must, therefore, be interpreted in a restrictive fashion so as to ensure that recourse is not had to it in an excessive or abusive manner. In the event of a dispute, the Member State imposing the restriction has anyway to show that the measure meets the aforementioned conditions.

(b) Analysis of the requirements of the concept of the general good

(a) *The measure must come within a field which has not been harmonised*

The harmonisation directives define the minimum level of the general good within the Community. Measures relating, for example, to the calculation of technical provisions and the solvency margin, the conditions for taking up insurance business, and financial and prudential supervision may no longer be covered by the general good of a Member State.

Where these harmonised rules constitute minimum provisions, a Member State is free to impose on its own insurance undertakings stricter rules than those laid down in the Directives.[61] As regards the Insurance Directives, this is the case with the provisions relating to investment rules and to the rules on the diversification of assets representing technical provisions. For this reason, the Third Insurance Directives stipulate that, in so far as certain of their provisions define minimum standards, 'a home Member State may lay down stricter rules for insurance undertakings authorised by its own competent authorities.'[62]

Should a Member State impose, for reasons which it deems to be in the interest of the general good, a level of consumer protection stricter than the one set by a minimal Community provision on a Community insurance undertaking carrying on insurance business on its territory, the proportionality test would have to be satisfied for it to comply with Community law.

(b) *The measure must pursue an objective of the general good*

The Court has so far acknowledged that, in the absence of harmonisation, the following areas

---

[60] See *Gebhard* (see footnote 16), where the Court held that '... national measures liable to hinder or make less attractive the exercise of fundamental freedoms guaranteed by the Treaty must fulfil four conditions: they must be applied in a non-discriminatory manner; they must be justified by imperative requirements in the general interest; they must be suitable for securing the attainment of the objective which they pursue; and they must not go beyond what is necessary in order to attain it.' This was subsequently confirmed by the Court in its judgments in Cases C-415/93 *Bosman* [1995] I-4921 and C-250/95 *Futura* [1997] I-2471.

[61] The *RTI* judgment of 12 December 1996 in Joined Cases C-320/94, C-328/94, C-329/94, C-337/94, C-338/94 and C-339/94 [1996] ECR I-6471, making the use of minimum provisions conditional upon compliance with the Treaty.

[62] Third Directive 92/49/EEC, reproduced supra under no. I. 25, recital 8, and Third Directive 92/96/EEC, reproduced supra under no. I. 26, recital 9.

could fall within the scope of the interest of the general good:[63]
- the professional rules designed to protect the recipient of services,[64]
- protection of workers,[65] including social protection,[66]
- consumer protection,[67]
- preservation of the good reputation of the national financial sector,[68]
- prevention of fraud,[69]
- social order,[70]
- protection of intellectual property,[71]
- preservation of the national historical and artistic heritage,[72]
- cultural policy and protection of cultural diversity in the audio-visual sector,[73]
- cohesion of the tax system,[74]
- road safety,[75]
- protection of creditors,[76]
- fairness of commercial transactions,[77]
- protection of the proper administration of justice.[78]

This list is not definitive and the Court reserves the right to add to it at any time.

(c) *The measure must be non-discriminatory*

Where the restriction in question is discriminatory, i.e. a Member State imposes on a Community insurance undertaking measures which it does not impose or imposes more advantageously on its own insurance undertakings, it can be justified only on the grounds set out in Article 46 of the Treaty (public policy, public security and public health),[79] economic grounds not forming part of the latter.[80] Furthermore, this concept must be interpreted in a very strict fashion.

In that case there is no reason to invoke the general good as justification that this national measure is compatible with the Community legal order.

It is difficult to see what measures in the field of insurance could satisfy this condition of a serious threat to society. It is reasonable to believe, therefore, that discriminatory measures are unlikely to be justified in the insurance sector.

(d) *The measure must be objectively necessary*

Even if a measure is presented by a host Member State as defending an objective conducive to the general good, one may ask whether it is really necessary in order to protect that interest.

The Court of Justice has held in a number of judgments that a given national rule that was justified by the host country as pursuing an objective conducive to the general good, in the event consumer protection, went beyond what was necessary to protect that interest.[81] It checks whether certain measures, under cover of pursuit of an objective concerned with the protection of the recipient of the service, e.g. consumers, are not actually aimed at other objectives connected with the protection of the national market.

---

[63] To this list must be added *a fortiori* the provisions of Article 46, namely public policy, public security and public health.
[64] Joined Cases 110/78 and 111/78 *Van Wesemael* [1979] ECR 35.
[65] Case 279/80 *Webb* [1981] ECR 3305.
[66] Case C-272/94 *Guiot* [1996] ECR I-1905.
[67] Case 205/84 *Commission v Germany* (see footnote 7).
[68] Case C-384/93 *Alpine Investments BV* (see footnote 14).
[69] Case C-275/92 *Schindler* [1994] ECR I-1039.
[70] Ibid.
[71] Case 62/79 *Coditel* [1980] ECR 881.
[72] Case C-180/89 *Commission v Italy* [1991] ECR I-709.
[73] Cases C-288/89 *Collectieve Antennevoorziening Gouda* [1991] ECR I-4007, C-353/89 *Commission v Netherlands* [1991] ECR I-4069 and C-148/91 *Veronica Omroep Organisatie* [1993] ECR I-487.
[74] Case C-204/90 *Bachmann* [1992] ECR I-249.
[75] Case C-55/93 *van Schaik* [1994] ECR I-4837.
[76] Judgment of 12 December 1996 in Case C-3/95 *Reisebüro Broede* [1996] ECR I-6511.
[77] *Alpine Investments BV* (see footnote 14); Case C-288/89 *Collectieve Antennevoorziening Gouda*, supra.
[78] Ibid.

[79] See Case C-17/92 *Federación de Distribuidores Cinematográficos* [1993] ECR I-2239, in which the Court indicated that the protection of cultural policy is not a justification featuring among those provided for in Article 46 of the Treaty. See Case C-224/97 *Ciola* (see footnote 12), paragraphs 16 and 17.
[80] Case 352/85 [1988] ECR 2085; Case C-17/92 [1993] ECR I-2239; Case C-484/93 *Svesson* [1995] ECR I-3955. For the Court, this concept presupposes the existence, in addition to the perturbation to the social order which any infringement of the law involves, of a genuine and sufficiently serious threat affecting one of the fundamental interests of society (Case 30/77 *Bouchereau* [1977] ECR 1999); Case C-114/97 *Commission v Spain* [1998] ECR I-6717.
[81] Case C-410/96 *Ambry* [1998] ECR I-7875; Case C-76/90 *Denemeyer* (see footnote 14); Case 205/84 *Commission v Germany* [1986] ECR 3755.

(e) *The measure must be proportionate to the objective pursued*

Finally, it is necessary to ask whether there are not less restrictive means of achieving the general-good objective pursued. The Court systematically examines whether the Member State did not have at its disposal measures with a less restrictive effect on trade.[82] In the context of such an examination, it may deduce from a comparative analysis of the legislation of the other Member States that less restrictive consumer protection measures exist.[83] However, the Court has also ruled that 'the fact that one Member State imposes less strict rules than another Member State does not mean that the latter's rules are disproportionate and hence incompatible with Community law'.[84]

Where a host Member State invokes the need to protect the recipient of the service as justification for a national measure constituting a restriction on an insurance undertaking benefiting from mutual recognition, the actual need to protect the recipient should be questioned. In *Commission v Germany* (insurance), the Court held on 4 December 1986 that 'there may be cases where, because of the nature of the risk insured and of the party seeking insurance, there is no need to protect the latter by the application of the mandatory rules of his national law.'[85]

The Insurance Directives follow this case law and already take account of the nature and specific circumstances of the party seeking insurance in order to impose certain provisions designed to ensure his protection. Take, for instance, the distinction made in non-life insurance between 'large risks' and 'mass risks'[86] or the scope of the provisions relating to the information requirements incumbent on policyholders[87] or of the right to cancel a life assurance policy.[88]

The Commission considers, therefore, that Member States should, in imposing their general-good rules, make a distinction according to whether or not services are supplied to circumspect recipients and take account of the degree of vulnerability of the persons they are setting out to protect.

For example, insurance services involving 'large risks' or sophisticated or professional policyholders (e.g. professionals in the financial sector) should not be the subject of particular general-good rules imposed by the host Member State, at least where the protection of policyholders is concerned. The proportionality test would be especially difficult to satisfy in such cases.

(f) *It is also necessary for the general-good objective not to be safeguarded by rules to which the provider of services is already subject in the Member State where he is established*

It is necessary to examine in this connection whether the insurance undertaking is not already subject to similar or comparable provisions aimed at safeguarding the same interest under the legislation of its Member State of origin.[89]

Under the Insurance Directives, this criterion could be important, particularly for the purpose of assessing the compatibility of the measures imposed by the host Member State in exercising its residual powers.

For example, it is necessary to examine in the context of this test the extent to which certain

---

[82] See most recently Case C-101/94 *Commission v Italy* ('*SIM*') [1996] ECR I-2691. See also Case C-384/93 *Alpine Investments* (see footnote 14).

[83] Case C-129/91 *Yves Rocher* [1993] ECR I-2361.

[84] Case C-384/93 *Alpine Investments* (see footnote 14).

[85] Case 205/84 *Commission v Germany* (see footnote 7).

[86] Article 5(d) of Directive 73/239/EEC, reproduced supra under no. I. 3, as amended by Directives 88/357/EEC, reproduced supra under no. I. 15, and 90/618/EEC, reproduced supra under no. I. 17.

[87] Non-life insurance: see Directive 92/49/EEC, reproduced supra under no. I. 25: Articles 31 (the precontractual information required must be supplied to policyholders who are natural persons) and 43 (restriction of such information to 'mass risks.').

[88] Only a person taking out an individual life assurance policy has the right to cancel that policy; Member States may not grant this right to policyholders not requiring such special protection on account of their status or of the circumstances in which the contract was concluded (see Article 15 of Directive 90/619/EEC, reproduced supra under no. I. 18, as amended by Article 30 of Directive 92/96/EEC, reproduced supra under no. I. 26).

[89] Case 205/84 *Commission v Germany* (see footnote 7); Case C-76/90 *Denemeyer* (see footnote 14).

controls required by the host Member State might already be carried out in the country of origin, the extent to which accounting, supervisory, statistical or financial information might already be communicated to the competent authority of the country of origin, etc.

(c) *Other considerations*

The inclusion by some Member States of whole areas of their national legislation in the list of provisions adopted in the interest of the general good could prove to constitute a misuse of the concept of general good. Several of them are tending to treat as rules adopted in the interest of the general good all their legislation on consumer protection, their tax or commercial law or their competition law. The Commission takes the view that the principles of necessity, non-duplication and proportionality mean that Member States should indicate, when new legislation is adopted or, where appropriate, when the conditions laid down in Article 32(4) of Directives 92/49/EEC and 92/96/EEC are notified, the specific provisions which could be in the interest of the general good.

Lastly, although the reasoning is identical and the questions are the same whether the insurance undertaking operates through a branch or under the freedom to provide services, the assessment of the proportionality of a restriction may, in certain cases, differ depending on the mode of operation. Since there are differences of kind between the provision of services and establishment, a restriction could more readily be considered to be proportionate in the case of an operator working permanently within a territory than in the case of the same operator working only temporarily.

The Court recognised this difference by imposing a less restrictive and more 'lightweight' legal framework for provision of services than for establishment.[90] It has likewise consistently held that it does not follow from Article 50(3) of the EC Treaty that: 'all national legislation applicable to nationals of that State and usually applied to the permanent activities of undertakings established therein may be similarly applied in its entirety to the temporary activities of undertakings which are established in other Member States.'[91]

Thus, depending on the circumstances, the same restriction applied in the interest of the general good could be judged proportionate in respect of a branch but disproportionate in respect of a provider of services. The Commission considers, for example, that a Member State which imposes certain formalities on insurance undertakings (controls, registration, costs, communication of information, etc.) for reasons that purport to be in the general good should take account of the mode of operation chosen by the insurance undertaking carrying on activities within its territory under mutual-recognition arrangements.

However, this distinction cannot be applied to consumer-protection rules (provided, of course, that they have satisfied the other tests). The level of consumer protection required must be identical, whether the service is supplied under the freedom to provide services or by way of establishment.

3. Application of these principles to the insurance sector

Having identified the main characteristics of the general good, the Commission regards it as appropriate to state its interpretation of the concept as it applies to insurance, giving a few examples of measures that a trader might encounter in exercising his right of establishment or his right to provide services. Once again it should be explained that this interpretation does not prejudge that which the Court of Justice, competent in the final analysis for interpreting the Treaty and secondary legislation, could be

---

[90] The Court has consistently made the point that a Member State 'may not make the provision of services in its territory subject to compliance with all the conditions required for establishment and thereby deprive of all practical effectiveness the provisions of the Treaty whose object is, precisely, to guarantee the freedom to provide services.' Case C-76/90 *Denemayer* (see footnote 14). See also Case C-198/89 *Commission v Greece* [1991] ECR I-735.

[91] Case 205/84 *Commission v Germany* (see footnote 7) and Case C-76/90 *Denemeyer* (see footnote 14).

asked to give of the questions raised. Such measures may concern, for instance:

(a) *prior notification of policy conditions;*

(b) *capital redemption operations of insurance undertakings;*

(c) *uniform no-claims bonus systems;*

(d) *language of the insurance policy;*

(e) *professional codes of conduct;*

(f) *maximum technical interest rates for life assurance;*

(g) *imposition of standard clauses or minimum insurance conditions;*

(h) *clauses imposing mandatory levels of excess in insurance policies;*

(i) *compulsory stipulation of a surrender value in life assurance policies;*

(j) *prohibition of cold calling;*

(k) *arrangements introduced by the host Member State for charging indirect taxes on insurance premiums for policies concluded under the freedom to provide services: appointment of a tax representative of the insurer.*

(a) *Prior notification of policy conditions*

The Third Directives expressly forbid any prior or systematic substantive control of insurance policies and policy documents,[92] irrespective of the name given by the national authorities to the system used, whether it involves the prior approval of policies and scales of premiums or their simple, systematic notification with tacit approval or with the deposit of documents before they can be used. Prior or systematic approval is henceforward authorised only in those cases explicitly provided for in the Community directives. Such is the case with compulsory insurance (e.g. compulsory third-party motor insurance[93] or health insurance which is a substitute for a statutory system of social security),[94] where Member States may require that the general conditions of that insurance be communicated before use but, under no circumstances, approved. As for life assurance, the Member State of origin may require systematic notification of the technical bases used for calculating scales of premiums and technical provisions.[95]

These specific cases apart, the Member States may use only systems of ex post, non-systematic control of insurance conditions—without, in any event, such a requirement constituting a condition which an insurance undertaking must satisfy before carrying on its business—in order to ensure that their general-good provisions concerning insurance conditions are complied with by policies marketed on their territory. Since the Community legislator has already determined the systems of substantive control that may be applied by the Member States and their conditions of application, this is an area which is already the subject of harmonisation at Community level.

Nevertheless, certain Member States continue to require prior notification of these particulars. In most cases, a sheet describing the insurance policy conditions has to be submitted. They argue that this is necessary to protect their consumers, to guarantee transparency of the products available on their national markets and to facilitate substantive control of insurance products by the supervisory authorities.

The Commission takes the view that, leaving aside the cases expressly provided for by the Third Directives, maintaining such systems of prior or systematic control of insurance policies is not consistent with the relevant provisions of the Third Insurance Directives. It also considers that Member States may not justify such requirements on grounds of the general good since the conditions set by the Court of Justice have not been met, in as much as this is an area which is already the subject of harmonisation at Community level.

---

[92] Articles 6(3), 29 and 39 of Directive 92/49/EEC, reproduced supra under no. I. 25 and Articles 5(3), 29 and 39 of Directive 92/96/EEC, reproduced supra under no. I. 26.

[93] Article 30(2) of Directive 92/49/EEC, reproduced supra under no. I. 25.

[94] Article 54(1) of Directive 92/49/EEC, reproduced supra under no. I. 25.

[95] Article 29 of Directive 92/96/EEC, reproduced supra under no. I. 26 and Article 5(3) of Directive 79/267/EEC, reproduced supra under no. I. 9.

(b) *Capital redemption operations of insurance undertakings*

'Capital redemption operations based on actuarial calculations, whereby, in return for single or periodic payments agreed in advance, commitments of specified duration and amount are undertaken' figure among the activities covered by the insurance undertaking's single licence where such operations are the result of a contract and are subject to supervision by the insurance monitoring authority in the home Member State. Such activities, like any other activity falling within the scope of the Life Directives, may be carried on anywhere in the Community, including in a Member State in which they are not authorised for local life assurance undertakings on the grounds, for instance, that in the host Member State such operations are regarded as banking operations and are therefore reserved for credit institutions.

The Commission considers, therefore, that there is no reason to prohibit the marketing of capital redemption products which fulfil the conditions of the First Life Directive 79/267/EEC, as amended by Directive 92/96/EEC, and which are marketed in a Member State by an insurer authorised in its home Member State to pursue such activities. The fact that in the host Member State such activities are not regarded as insurance activities and are not therefore permitted for insurers which have their head office there does not prevent insurers from other Member States from pursuing those activities which, having been the subject of mutual recognition between the Member States, benefit from the single licence system introduced by the Third Life Directive 92/96/EEC.[96]

In this connection, capital redemption products proposed in the host Member State by a life assurance undertaking will, as in any other life assurance activity, have to comply with the provisions in force in that Member State which are justified by reasons of the general good and relate in particular to the tax arrangements applicable to this type of product or the conditions governing advertising.

(c) *Uniform no-claims bonus systems*

In some Member States detailed national legislative instruments establish the criteria to be taken into account when calculating the premiums for third-party motor insurance. The instruments prescribe, inter alia, coefficients for the reduction/increase of premiums (no-claims bonus system). The method laid down consists in determining a compulsory scale for calculating the annual premium. The scale applies at the time the third-party motor insurance policy is concluded and/or when subsequent movements up or down the scale occur, depending on the frequency with which the insured submits a claim. As a result, the increase or reduction of the premium is not liberalised; on the contrary, it must comply with specific criteria laid down in the Member State's legislation. From the technical insurance perspective, such systems are tariff measures.

The main argument advanced in favour of such mandatory systems is that they contribute to preventing road accidents. Drivers who face an increased premium in the event of an accident will drive more carefully. It should also be pointed out that such mandatory systems foster transparency in that they allow those seeking insurance to compare and choose between different insurance products, thereby facilitating the mobility of such persons.

It should, however, be pointed out that the Third Non-life Directive 92/49/EEC introduced not only freedom as regards scales of premiums and the abolition of prior or systematic approval of scales and policies; it also introduced the concept of home-country control in the field of financial supervision of insurance undertakings.[97] The maintenance of a mandatory tariff measure is, therefore, contrary to the letter and spirit of the Third Directives. Under the circumstances, it is

---

[96] The same conclusion applies mutatis mutandis to the other operations referred to in Article 1(2) of the First Life Directive 79/267/EEC, reproduced supra under no. I. 9, and contained in points V (tontines) and VII (management of group pension funds) of the Annex to the First Directive.

[97] Articles 6(3), 29 and 39 of Directive 92/49/EEC, reproduced supra under no. I. 25 and Articles 5(3), 29 and 39 of Directive 92/96/EEC, reproduced supra under no. I. 26.

expedient to ask whether other less restrictive means could not achieve the same result while complying with the principle of tariff freedom for insurance undertakings laid down in the Third Non-life Directive. The same applies to market transparency. The Commission also takes the view that this objective can be met without the principle of tariff freedom being jeopardised, by providing for systems that do not include any tariff elements. For instance, no-claims bonus scales which dispense with coefficients for the reduction/increase of premiums and for which insurers are free to determine premium levels make it possible to guarantee market transparency and the mobility of those seeking insurance.

Nevertheless, if a Member State were to take the view that such mandatory systems were to be regarded as contractual clauses governing an insurance policy, it would in any event have to ask whether, with a view to achieving the possible objectives pursued by such a clause, there were not other less restrictive and less binding means of achieving the desired result.

The Commission considers that, in so far as mandatory no-claims bonus systems were tariff provisions, they would be contrary to the Third Directive. In the circumstances, it takes the view that the Member States cannot therefore invoke the general good in order to preserve the mandatory character of these systems since they concern rules which have already been co-ordinated at Community level.

If a mechanism for reducing/increasing premiums is not a State measure but an agreement between professionals, its conformity with Community law would have to be assessed in particular in the light of Article 81 of the EC Treaty. In this connection, the Commission would point out that Regulation 3932/92/EEC of 21 December 1992 on the application of Article [81(3)][98] of the Treaty to certain categories of agreements, decisions and concerted practices in the insurance sector[99] authorises agreements which have as their object the establishment and distribution of standard policy conditions for direct insurance only if certain requirements are met (Title III of the Regulation). The exemption thus applies, inter alia, only if the standard conditions are established and distributed with an explicit statement that they are purely illustrative and if they mention the possibility that different conditions may be agreed. It does not apply to undertakings or associations of undertakings which concert or agree among themselves, or oblige other undertakings, not to apply different conditions. Moreover, the Title of the Regulation relating to co-operation in calculating the premium (Title II) may not constitute a legal basis for a mechanism for reducing/increasing premiums.

(d) *Language of the insurance policy*

Some Member States require insurance policies taken out or performed on their territory to be drafted exclusively in their official language(s). Other languages, Community or otherwise, may be used only for simple translations, even if the contracting parties would have liked to use such languages for the original policy.

This absolute and unconditional requirement is justified by the linguistic sovereignty of the Member States, by a desire to protect consumers and by the need for any proceedings brought before local courts to be properly conducted.

It should be pointed out that the Commission is not calling into question the linguistic sovereignty of each Member State.[100]

The Commission considers in this respect that a distinction should be drawn between large industrial and commercial risks and mass risks. In the former case, consumer protection is not a valid concern. As regards mass risks and individual life assurance, provisions governing the language of an insurance policy should also take account of certain circumstances. Thus, the first thing to

---

[98] The number between brackets has been changed as from 1 May 1999 by article 12 of the Treaty of Amsterdam.
[99] OJ L 398, 31.12.1992, 7.

[100] See point 2 of the Commission communication to the Council and the European Parliament concerning language use in the information of consumers in the Community (COM(93) 456 final, 10.11.1993).

take into consideration is policies with an international dimension, i.e. those where the law applicable to the insurance policy is not the law of the Member State where the risk/commitment is situated. For instance, exemptions from the principle that a policy must be drawn up in the official language(s) of the Member State where the risk/commitment is situated should be provided for in those cases where the insured person is of foreign origin. In all, five million citizens of the European Union live in a Member State which is not their own. Such persons would probably be better protected if they could take out policies in their own language instead of that of the Member State of residence or location of the risk they seek to cover.

(e) *Professional codes of conduct*

Professional codes of conduct valid on the territory of a Member State of the European Union are, in principle, also valid with regard to foreign insurers; failure to observe them often incurs a penalty, especially of a commercial nature. Compliance with codes of conduct is justified by the signatory parties on grounds of consumer protection or contribution to market discipline.

In any event, where such codes of conduct result from agreements between undertakings or from decisions by associations of undertakings, they must comply with the competition rules laid down in Article 81 et seq. In this respect, the Commission clearly could not authorise under the competition rules agreements or decisions by associations of undertakings that would have the same effects as state measures contravening the basic freedoms spelt out in Articles 39, 43 and 49 of the Treaty.

(f) *Maximum technical interest rates for life assurance*

The Third Life Directive 92/96/EEC co-ordinated the actuarial principles governing the calculation of mathematical provisions.

As regards the definition of technical interest rates, it provides,[101] firstly, that the home Member State may set a maximum technical interest rate which the insurance undertakings it supervises must apply in order to calculate the bases for their technical provisions and, secondly, that the home Member State may require insurance undertakings with their head office on its territory to notify systematically the technical bases used to calculate scales of premiums and technical provisions.

The Commission would point out that, in view of the provisions of the Third Directive and the rules on supervision, which give exclusive competence for financial supervision to the insurance undertaking's home Member State, the branches of insurance undertakings and the insurers operating under the freedom to provide services are not bound by the provisions of the host Member State on maximum technical interest rates. Since the host Member State has no competence as regards financial supervision of an insurance undertaking duly authorised in its home Member State, it follows that it cannot impose compliance with its own prudential principles or check such compliance through substantive control of premium scales.

(g) *Imposition of standard clauses or minimum insurance conditions*

Member States which have rules laying down compulsory clauses for insurance policies give as justification the concern to protect the weaker party in the contractual relationship and to preserve the balance in the latter by imposing a given content for the rights and obligations of the parties and by a desire to protect third-party victims in the event of an accident.

As mentioned above, standard clauses may also result not from State measures but from agreements between professionals. The Commission would refer here to the observations in point (iii) above concerning application of exemption Regulation 3932/92/EEC.[102]

The Commission believes that, in any event, protection of the weaker party should be imposed

---

[101] See Article 17(1)(B) of the First Directive 79/267/EEC, reproduced supra under no. I. 9, as amended by Article 18 of the Third Directive 92/96/EEC, reproduced supra under no. I. 26.

[102] OJ L 398, 31.12.1992, 7.

only in those cases where it is objectively necessary, e.g. in insurance policies where the policyholder, by virtue of his nature or size, has a particular need of protection, in order to preserve the contractual balance. It will also be necessary to consider the proportionality of such measures and to analyse whether the inclusion in insurance policies of standard clauses laid down by the rules of a host Member State is a more difficult condition in practice for insurance undertakings from other Member States to fulfil than for insurance undertakings from the host Member State. This would be the case in particular if those insurance undertakings were deterred from prospecting a new market because they would be forced to create an entirely new insurance product in order to sell it on the market concerned instead of using an insurance product already used in their home Member State.

Similarly, the obligation to comply with standard clauses or minimum insurance conditions should not mean either that insurance policies cannot be worded differently.

(h) *Clauses imposing mandatory levels of excess in insurance policies*

One argument advanced in favour of retaining compulsory excesses is that they are supposed to protect the interest of the consumer, enabling him to take out insurance at a reasonable price. It is also argued that, without this mechanism, which obliges the insured to bear part of the cost of the claim, premiums would increase in a completely unreasonable manner because the insurer would have to act in the case of claims with a low economic cost. Yet another argument put forward is that the compulsory excess makes it possible to combat insurance fraud, which would otherwise be very frequent in the case of small claims. In such cases, the mandatory rule is designed to safeguard the profits of the insurer faced with a multitude of small claims.

These arguments show that the introduction of a compulsory excess meets a need to discipline the market so as to avoid undue competition over premiums charged by insurance undertakings. It may also be asked whether the aim of a compulsory excess is not to preserve the profits of the insurer faced with a multitude of small claims rather than to safeguard the interests of the policyholder or uphold public morality. It should be pointed out, however, that Community law excludes from reasons of the general good any consideration based on strictly economic grounds.

In addition, as with the imposition of standard clauses or minimum conditions in insurance policies, the rigid application of such rules by the host Member State may have a restrictive effect on insurance undertakings operating under the rules on establishment or under the freedom to provide services since they would be prevented from marketing insurance policies already correctly used in their home Member State without such excesses.

Lastly, while it could be admitted that the introduction of excesses reflects the choice of management method by the insurance undertaking, it still has to be examined whether the imposition of compulsory excesses through binding rules is consistent with the objectives of the Third Insurance Directives as regards policies and scales of premiums.

If the introduction of an excess or a level of excess was covered by an agreement between professionals, it could not benefit from an exemption under Regulation 3932/92/EEC,[103] which explicitly excludes any exemption for standard insurance conditions containing clauses that specify amounts of guarantee or excess.

Insurance undertakings should therefore be free to assess the advisability of including an excess in the policies which they market. Where an insurance undertaking satisfies the solvency requirements laid down by its home Member State, which has given its approval and is responsible for its financial supervision, it should be free to decide to market insurance policies, with or without excesses, in the host Member State, clearly indicating to customers that it is doing so, without being forced into this by binding national rules.

---

[103] OJ L 398, 31.12.1992, 7.

(i) *Compulsory stipulation of a surrender value in life assurance policies*

The main argument for justifying the compatibility of this requirement with the concept of the general good is that the obligation to fix a surrender value in a life assurance policy meets the interests of consumers, who would thus have the flexibility and liberty necessary in such policies, which are more often than not long-term policies, and would be able to mobilise their savings. As for the rules making it compulsory to provide in life assurance policies for the insured to receive a bonus, these are also justified by a desire to protect the economic interests of the insured.

A distinction should be made here between two main categories of life assurance. First, there are life assurance policies that contain a savings element (e.g. endowment assurance, assurance on survival to a stipulated age and annuity assurance). This element is taken into consideration in calculating the amount of the mathematical provisions which the insurer must establish. The person insured under such policies has the right to surrender the mathematical provision established. Second, there are life assurance policies that do not comprise any savings element since they are designed to cover only the risk associated with human life (e.g. assurance on death and insurance on the amount outstanding). Such insurance policies do not take account of the savings element in calculating the mathematical provision. In such cases, the insured person does not have the right to surrender the mathematical provision established. Each of these categories of life assurance corresponds to the differing objective needs of insured persons as to cover. In addition, the cost of each category reflects the different types of risk assumed by the insurer in the insurance policy.

The requirement to provide for a surrender value in any life assurance policy designed solely to cover the risk of death would necessitate inclusion in the policy of a savings element and payment of a higher insurance premium for acceptance of the risk. It could be asked whether this meets the needs of insured persons, many of whom are interested only in products covering the risk of death alone.

Although the situation in each Member State must be assessed separately, it should be pointed out that the Third Life Directive 92/96/EEC lays down, as part of the actuarial principles which the home Member State imposes on insurance undertakings for the establishment of their mathematical provisions, specific rules for policies with a guaranteed surrender value and rules for policies with bonuses. Annex II to the Third Life Directive specifies among the information to be provided in a clear and accurate manner and in writing to policyholders before the contract is concluded or during the term of the contract 'the indication of surrender and paid-up values and the extent to which they are guaranteed, and the means of calculation and distribution of bonuses'. This information is designed to allow policyholders to become aware of, and to understand, the essential characteristics of insurance products in order that they can select the product best suited to their specific needs.

There are grounds for wondering, therefore, whether a national rule of the host Member State which imposes in a general and absolute manner the obligation to provide for a surrender value or a bonus in life assurance policies marketed on its territory is objectively necessary and proportionate to the objective of protecting the economic interests of policyholders or, on the contrary, whether this objective cannot be achieved by other less restrictive means, e.g. the obligation to give detailed information to the policyholder prior to the conclusion of a policy.

(j) *Prohibition of cold calling*

The Court has already recognised the right to prohibit this marketing practice in the case of other financial products after examining a provision of Dutch law which was designed to protect the good reputation and reliability of the financial market in the Netherlands.[104] Consumer protection is also an argument that is often put forward in support of banning this marketing method. The reasoning followed by the Court in the Dutch case can also be applied to insurance products. Nevertheless, pending harmonisation

---

[104] Case C-384/93 *Alpine Investments* (see footnote 14).

in this area, one should avoid trying to establish a general rule for the compatibility of this marketing method as far as insurance products are concerned, and each case should be assessed individually.[105]

(k) *Arrangements introduced by the host Member State for charging indirect taxes on insurance premiums for policies concluded under the freedom to provide services: appointment of a tax representative of the insurer*

Under the Insurance Directives, policies concluded under the freedom to provide services are subject to indirect taxes and parafiscal charges on insurance premiums in the host Member State.[106] To this end, the host Member State applies to undertakings doing business under the freedom to provide services within its territory the national provisions for ensuring the charging of such taxes and charges. In this connection, it may require, for example, submission of an exhaustive list of policies concluded under the freedom to provide services or the appointment of a tax representative of the insurance undertaking domiciled within its territory.[107]

The requirement to appoint a tax representative of the insurer doing business under the freedom to provide services pursues an objective that is justified in the light of Community law, namely to guarantee the home Member State that its own legislation will be complied with and that the above taxes and charges will be charged. This measure might, however, impede the way in which freedom to provide services is exercised. An insurer wishing to avail himself of the right to provide services faces substantial administrative and financial costs in connection with the appointment of a tax representative established in the host Member State. Nevertheless, the practical arrangements whereby the host Member State implements this measure must comply with the criteria laid down by the Court, and in particular the requirements of necessity and proportionality.

Secondly, in the light of the foregoing considerations, the Commission takes the view that, where the host Member State does not charge any indirect taxes or parafiscal charges on insurance policies,[108] it may not legitimately require insurers wishing to operate under the freedom to provide services in areas of insurance not subject to indirect taxation to appoint a tax representative.

Thirdly, the requirement to appoint a tax representative is not one of the particulars that must be notified under the procedure laid down by the Insurance Directives in order to exercise freedom to provide services.[109] Accordingly, the Commission takes the view that the host Member State may not reject any notification made by the home Member State under the procedure for freedom to provide services on the grounds that no tax representative has been appointed in the host Member State and, in so doing, prevent access to freedom to provide services and the commencement of that activity. The tax representative should be appointed only once the activities carried on under the freedom to provide services have effectively begun, i.e. at the time the insurer writes his first insurance policy under the freedom to provide services and charging the insurance premium corresponding to that activity.[110]

---

[105] See amended proposal for a Directive concerning the distance marketing of consumer financial services (COM(1999) 375 final, 23.7.1999). Article 10(2) of the amended proposal provides for special arrangements concerning communications not solicited by consumers.

[106] Article 46 of the Third Non-life Directive 92/49/EEC, reproduced supra under no. I. 25 and Article 44 of the Third Life Directive 92/96/EEC, reproduced supra under no. I. 26.

[107] Statements entered in the record of the Council meeting at which the Third Directives were approved.

[108] This reasoning is also valid where insurance policies are zero-rated.

[109] See Articles 14, 16 and 17 of Directive 88/357/EEC, reproduced supra under no. I. 15, as amended by Articles 34, 35 and 36 of Directive 92/49/EEC, reproduced supra under no. I. 25, as regards non-life assurance and Articles 11, 14 and 17 of Directive 88/357/EEC, reproduced supra under no. I. 15, as amended by Articles 34, 35 and 36 of Directive 92/96/EEC, reproduced supra under no. I. 26, as regards life assurance.

[110] Frequently, a considerable amount of time, sometimes running into years, elapses between notification of the intention to do business under the freedom to provide services and the conclusion of the first insurance policy under that freedom. The requirement to appoint a tax representative before business has effectively begun appears disproportionate in that it obliges an insurer wishing to do business under the freedom to provide services to set up such a structure and thereby to incur such large costs that it might be deterred from availing itself of that freedom.

The Commission takes the view that, where the host Member State, with a view to ensuring compliance with its rules governing indirect taxation in respect of insurance policies and the charging of such taxes, requires any insurer wishing to do business under the freedom to provide services to appoint a tax representative established on its territory, the practical arrangements for applying this measure must comply with the requirements laid down in the case law of the Court of Justice, and in particular the requirements of proportionality and necessity, in order that such measures do not constitute a restriction that is incompatible with the conduct of insurance business under the freedom to provide services within its territory.

4. Rules relating to the law applicable to insurance contracts and the concept of the general good

The Insurance Directives[111] lay down specific rules for determining the law applicable to insurance contract covering risks situated within the European Economic Area.[112] They make it possible to define what substantive law will govern the contract. The rules apply both to insurance activities carried on under the rules on establishment and to those carried on under the freedom to provide services. The Directives also lay down provisions relating to application of the mandatory rules of the forum and of the Member State of the risk/commitment and to the public policy rules.[113]

The application, under the rules on the conflict of laws laid down by the Insurance Directives, by a Member State of its own mandatory substantive provisions and its public policy rules to insurance policies is likely, if it results in a restriction, to be examined from the viewpoint of the general good. The concept of the general good acts as a filter of national legislation. It obliges the authorities of the Member States to analyse their legislation for compliance with the Treaty's principles of free movement.

It is essential that any rule of national law, whatever the field it relates to, should be compatible with Community law. Thus, in a judgment dated 21 March 1972, the Court held that: 'The effectiveness of Community law cannot vary according to the various spheres of national law which it may affect.'[114]

Community law takes precedence therefore, if necessary, over national rules in the sphere of private law.

In particular, it has fallen to the Court to verify the compatibility with Community law of national rules of civil law,[115] civil procedure[116] and even of criminal law.[117]

Consequently, as has already been stated above, it is not sufficient that the host Member State's entire legislation on insurance contracts be immediately declared mandatory for the authorities to think that it must be observed in full.[118] Such provisions must also satisfy the requirements of the general good if the host Member State is to be able to require compliance with them by insurers operating through a branch or by way of freedom to provide services.

Since these are rules which were adopted in order to protect the consumer, there is a strong possibility that such rules of substantive law will pass the general-good test. The Court has recognised that consumer protection is an objective of the general

---

[111] As regards non-life assurance, see Articles 7 and 8 of the Second Directive 88/357/EEC, reproduced supra under no. I. 15, as amended by the Third Directive 92/49/EEC, reproduced supra under no. I. 25; as regards life assurance, see Article 4 of the Second Directive 90/619/EEC, reproduced supra under no. I. 18.

[112] It should be pointed out that the Rome Convention on the law applicable to contractual obligations (OJ L 266, 9.10.1980, 1) excludes from its scope insurance contracts covering risks situated in the territories of the Member States (Article 1(3)).

[113] Non-life insurance: Article 7(1)(h) of Second Directive 88/357/EEC, reproduced supra under no. I. 15; life assurance: Article 4(4) of Second Directive 90/619/EEC, reproduced supra under no. I. 18.

[114] Case C-82/71 *SAIL* [1972] ECR 119. See also Case C-20/92 *Hubbard* [1993] ECR I-3777.

[115] Case C-168/91 *Konstantinidis* [1993] ECR I-1191; Case C-399/89 *Alsthom Atlantique* [1991] ECR I-107; Case C-93/92 *Motorradcenter* [1993] ECR I-5009.

[116] See in this respect Case C-398/92 *Mund & Fester* [1994] ECR I-467; Case C-43/95 *Data Delecta* [1996] ECR I-4661; Case C-177/94 *Perfili* [1996] ECR I-161. See also *Hubbard* (footnote 114).

[117] Case C-348/96 [1999] ECR I-11.

[118] See point IV(3).

good which justifies restrictions of fundamental freedoms. It cannot be presumed, however, that the test will be passed. It was seen above that national laws adopted with the declared aim of protecting the consumer can be subjected to the control of the Court and, where appropriate, 'disqualified', e.g. if they are not necessary or are disproportionate.

This additional level of reasoning is therefore essential, in the context of a single market, in order to verify whether, in the absence of harmonisation, national measures are not, under the pretext of consumer protection, being maintained simply to restrict or prevent the entry of insurance services which are different or unknown on the national territory.

If a Member State could invoke non-conformity with its own legislation in the case of an insurance product marketed in another Member State in order to restrict the marketing thereof on its territory, it would be hindering competition between insurance undertakings.

5. What action is to be taken when faced with national rules regarded as being in the general good by the host Member State?

When faced with a national rule which, in his view, is an unjustified restriction of the freedom of establishment or the freedom to provide services, an economic agent (insurance undertaking, intermediary or policyholder) must normally resort to the courts or inform the Commission, e.g. by lodging a complaint.

In practice, if, for instance, an insurance undertaking believes that the rules of a Member State where it proposes to carry on business contains restrictions that cannot satisfy the tests of the general good (e.g. binding provisions which are to be included in any policy and which are unknown, or different to those, in its home Member State), various possibilities are open to it:

To avoid any potential conflict, it may of course adapt its services in all respects to the rules of the host country;

If, all the same, it offers insurance products that do not comply exactly with the binding provisions of the host country, it may well be prosecuted by the national authorities or by one of its clients. The insurance undertaking will have to assert its Community-law arguments before a national court or authority in order to establish that the rule which the Member State intends to invoke against it does not satisfy the conditions identified by the Court. It is the national court which will assess the validity of the parties' arguments, having possibly referred the matter to the Court of Justice for a preliminary ruling pursuant to Article 234 of the Treaty;

It may, at any moment, inform the Commission, which, if it thinks the restrictions are unjustified and hence contrary to Community law, could institute proceedings under Article 226 of the Treaty against the Member State concerned for failure to fulfil its obligations. In this context, it will be for the Commission to provide evidence of the alleged failure to fulfil obligations.[119] Where appropriate, it is the Court of Justice which will decide in the last instance whether the disputed national measure satisfies the tests of the general good or not.

---

[119] Case C-157/91 *Commission v Netherlands* [1992] ECR I-5899.

I. 30.

European Parliament and Council Directive 2000/26/EC of 16 May 2000 on the approximation of the laws of the Member States relating to insurance against civil liability in respect of the use of motor vehicles and amending Council Directives 73/239/EEC and 88/357/EEC (Fourth motor insurance Directive)[1]

THE EUROPEAN PARLIAMENT AND THE COUNCIL OF THE EUROPEAN UNION,

Having regard to the Treaty establishing the European Community, and in particular Articles 47(2) and 95 thereof,

Having regard to the proposal from the Commission,[2]

Having regard to the opinion of the Economic and Social Committee,[3]

Acting in accordance with the procedure laid down in Article 251 of the Treaty,[4] in the light of the joint text approved by the Conciliation Committee on 7 April 2000,

Whereas:

(1) At present, differences exist between provisions laid down by law, regulation or administrative action in the Member States relating to insurance against civil liability in respect of the use of motor vehicles and those differences constitute an obstacle to the free movement of persons and of insurance services.

(2) It is therefore necessary to approximate those provisions in order to promote the sound functioning of the single market.

(3) By Directive 72/166/EEC,[5] the Council adopted provisions on the approximation of the laws of the Member States relating to insurance against civil liability in respect of the use of motor vehicles, and to the enforcement of the obligation to insure against such liability.

(4) By Directive 88/357/EEC,[6] the Council adopted provisions on the co-ordination of laws, regulations and administrative provisions relating to direct insurance other than life assurance and laying down provisions to facilitate the effective exercise of freedom to provide services.

(5) The green card bureau system ensures the ready settlement of claims in the injured party's own country even where the other party comes from a different European country.

(6) The green card bureau system does not solve all problems of an injured party having to claim in another country against a party resident there and an insurance undertaking authorised there (foreign legal system, foreign language, unfamiliar settlement procedures and often unreasonably delayed settlement).

(7) By its Resolution of 26 October 1995 on the settlement of claims arising from traffic accidents occurring outside the claimant's country of origin,[7] the European Parliament, acting under the second paragraph of Article 192 of the Treaty,

---

[1] OJ L 181, 20.7.2000, 65–74.
[2] OJ C 343, 13.11.1997, 11 and OJ C 171, 18.6.1999, 4.
[3] OJ C 157, 25.5.1998, 6.
[4] Opinion of the European Parliament of 16 July 1998 (OJ C 292, 21.9.1998, 123), confirmed on 27 October 1999, Council Common Position of 21 May 1999 (OJ C 232, 13.8.1999, 8) and Decision of the European Parliament of 15 December 1999 (OJ C 296, 18.10.2000, 8). Decision of the Council of 2 May 2000 (OJ C 59, 23.2.2001, 6) and Decision of the European Parliament of 16 May 2000.

[5] OJ L 103, 2.5.1972, 1, reproduced supra under no. I. 2. Directive as last amended by Directive 84/5/EEC (OJ L 8, 11.1.1984, 17), reproduced supra under no. I. 11.
[6] OJ L 172, 4.7.1988, 1, reproduced supra under no. I. 15. Directive as last amended by Directive 92/49/EEC (OJ L 228, 11.8.1992, 1), reproduced supra under no. I. 25.
[7] OJ C 308, 20.11.1995, 108.

called on the Commission to submit a proposal for a European Parliament and Council Directive to solve these problems.

(8) It is in fact appropriate to supplement the arrangements established by Directives 72/166/EEC, 84/5/EEC[8] and 90/232/EEC[9] in order to guarantee injured parties suffering loss or injury as a result of a motor vehicle accident comparable treatment irrespective of where in the Community accidents occur; for accidents falling within the scope of this Directive occurring in a State other than that of the injured party's residence, there are gaps with regard to the settlement of injured parties' claims.

(9) The application of this Directive to accidents occurring in third countries covered by the green card system, affecting injured parties resident in the Community and involving vehicles insured and normally based in a Member State does not imply an extension of the compulsory territorial coverage of motor insurance as provided for in Article 3(2) of Directive 72/166/EEC.

(10) This entails giving the injured party a direct right of action against the insurance undertaking of the responsible party.

(11) One satisfactory solution might be for injured parties suffering loss or injury as a result of a motor vehicle accident falling within the scope of this Directive and occurring in a State other than that of their residence to be entitled to claim in their Member State of residence against a claims representative appointed there by the insurance undertaking of the responsible party.

(12) This solution would enable damage suffered by injured parties outside their Member State of residence to be dealt with by procedures familiar to them.

(13) This system of having claims representatives in the injured party's Member State of residence affects neither the substantive law to be applied in each individual case nor the matter of jurisdiction.

(14) The existence of a direct right of action against the insurance undertaking for the party who has suffered loss or injury is a logical supplement to the appointment of such representatives and moreover improves the legal position of injured parties of motor vehicle accidents occurring outside that party's Member State of residence.

(15) In order to fill the gaps in question, it should be provided that the Member State where the insurance undertaking is authorised should require the undertaking to appoint claims representatives resident or established in the other Member States to collect all necessary information in relation to claims resulting from such accidents and to take appropriate action to settle the claims on behalf and for the account of the insurance undertaking, including the payment of compensation therefore; claims representatives should have sufficient powers to represent the insurance undertaking in relation to persons suffering damage from such accidents, and also to represent the insurance undertaking before national authorities including, where necessary, before the courts, in so far as this is compatible with the rules of private international law on the conferral of jurisdiction.

(16) The activities of the claims representative are not sufficient in order to confer jurisdiction on the courts in the injured party's Member State of residence if the rules of private international law on the conferral of jurisdiction do not so provide.

[(16a) Under Article 11(2) read in conjunction with Article 9(1)(b) of Council Regulation (EC) No 44/2001 of 22 December 2000 on jurisdiction and the recognition and enforcement of judgments in civil and commercial matters,[10]

---

[8] Second Council Directive (84/5/EEC) of 30 December 1983 on the approximation of the laws of the Member States relating to insurance against civil liability in respect of the use of motor vehicles (OJ L 8, 11.1.1984, 17), reproduced supra under no. I. 2. Directive as last amended by Third Council Directive 90/232/EEC (OJ L 129, 19.5.1990, 33), reproduced supra under I. 16.

[9] Third Council Directive (90/232/EEC) of 14 May 1990 on the approximation of the laws of the Member States relating to insurance against civil liability in respect of the use of motor vehicles (OJ L 129, 19.5.1990, 33), reproduced supra under I. 16.

[10] OJ L 12, 16.1.2001, 1. Regulation as last amended by Regulation (EC) No 2245/2004 (OJ L 381, 28.12.2004, 10).

injured parties may bring legal proceedings against the civil liability insurance provider in the Member State in which they are domiciled.]

¶ *Recital 16a has been inserted by article 5(1) of Directive 2005/14/EC, reproduced infra under no. I. 39.*

(17) The appointment of representatives responsible for settling claims should be one of the conditions for access to and carrying on the activity of insurance listed in class 10 of point A of the Annex to Directive 73/239/EEC,[11] except for carriers' liability; that condition should therefore be covered by the single official authorisation issued by the authorities of the Member State where the insurance undertaking establishes its head office, as specified in Title II of Directive 92/49/EEC;[12] that condition should also apply to insurance undertakings having their head office outside the Community which have secured an authorisation granting them access to the activity of insurance in a Member State of the Community; Directive 73/239/EEC should be amended and supplemented accordingly.

(18) In addition to ensuring that the insurance undertaking has a representative in the State where the injured party resides, it is appropriate to guarantee the specific right of the injured party to have the claim settled promptly; it is therefore necessary to include in national law appropriate effective and systematic financial or equivalent administrative penalties—such as injunctions combined with administrative fines, reporting to supervisory authorities on a regular basis, on-the-spot checks, publications in the national official journal and in the press, suspension of the activities of the company (prohibition on the conclusion of new contracts for a certain period), designation of a special representative of the supervisory authorities responsible for monitoring that the business is run in line with insurance laws, withdrawal of the authorisation for this business line, sanctions to be imposed on directors and management staff—in the event that the insurance undertaking or its representative fails to fulfil its obligation to make an offer of compensation within a reasonable time-limit; this should not prejudice the application of any other measure—especially under supervisory law—which may be considered appropriate; however, it is a condition that liability and the damage and injury sustained should not be in dispute, so that the insurance undertaking is able to make a reasoned offer within the prescribed time-limit; the reasoned offer of compensation should be in writing and contain the grounds on the basis of which liability and damages have been assessed.

(19) In addition to those sanctions, it is appropriate to provide that interest should be payable on the amount of compensation offered by the insurance undertaking or awarded by the court to the injured party when the offer has not been made within the said prescribed time-limit; if Member States have existing national rules which cover the requirement for late-payment interest this provision could be implemented by a reference to those rules.

(20) Injured parties suffering loss or injury as a result of motor vehicle accidents sometimes have difficulty in establishing the name of the insurance undertaking providing insurance against civil liability in respect of the use of motor vehicles involved in an accident.

(21) In the interest of such injured parties, Member States should set up information centres to ensure that such information is made available promptly; those information centres should also make available to injured parties information concerning claims representatives; it is necessary that such centres should co-operate with each other and respond rapidly to requests for information about claims representatives made by centres in other Member States; it seems appropriate that such centres should collect information about the

---

[11] First Council Directive (73/239/EEC) of 24 July 1973 on the co-ordination of laws, regulations and administrative provisions relating to the taking-up and pursuit of the business of direct insurance other than life assurance (OJ L 228, 16.8.1973, 3), reproduced supra under no. I. 3. Directive as last amended by Directive 95/26/EC (OJ L 168, 18.7.1995, 7) reproduced supra under I. 27.

[12] Council Directive (92/49/EEC) of 18 June 1992 on the co-ordination of laws, regulations and administrative provisions relating to direct insurance other than life assurance and amending Directives 73/239/EEC and 88/357/EEC (third non-life insurance Directive) (OJ L 228, 11.8.1992, 1), reproduced supra under I. 25. Directive as amended by Directive 95/26/EC (OJ L 168, 18.7.1995, 7), reproduced supra under I. 27.

actual termination date of the insurance cover but not about the expiry of the original validity of the policy if the duration of the contract is extended owing to non-cancellation.

(22) Specific provision should be made with respect to vehicles (for example, government or military vehicles) which fall under the exemptions from the obligation to be insured against civil liability.

(23) The injured party may have a legitimate interest in being informed about the identity of the owner or usual driver or the registered keeper of the vehicle, for example if he can obtain compensation only from these persons because the vehicle is not duly insured or the damage exceeds the sum insured, this information should also be provided accordingly.

(24) Certain information provided, such as the name and address of the owner or usual driver of the vehicle and the number of the insurance policy or the registration number of the vehicle, constitutes personal data within the meaning of Directive 95/46/EC of the European Parliament and of the Council of 24 October 1995 on the protection of individuals with regard to the processing of personal data and on the free movement of such data;[13] the processing of such data which is required for the purposes of this Directive must therefore comply with the national measures taken pursuant to Directive 95/46/EC; the name and address of the usual driver should be communicated only if national legislation provides for such communication.

(25) It is necessary to make provision for a compensation body to which the injured party may apply where the insurance undertaking has failed to appoint a representative or is manifestly dilatory in settling a claim or where the insurance undertaking cannot be identified to guarantee that the injured party will not remain without the compensation to which he is entitled; the intervention of the compensation body should be limited to rare individual cases where the insurance undertaking has failed to comply with its duties in spite of the dissuasive effect of the potential imposition of penalties.

(26) The role played by the compensation body is that of settling the claim in respect of any loss or injury suffered by the injured party only in cases which are capable of objective determination and therefore the compensation body must limit its activity to verifying that an offer of compensation has been made in accordance with the time-limits and procedures laid down, without any assessment of the merits.

(27) Legal persons who are subrogated by law to the injured party in his claims against the person responsible for the accident or the latter's insurance undertaking (such as, for example, other insurance undertakings or social security bodies) should not be entitled to present the corresponding claim to the compensation body.

(28) The compensation body should have a right of subrogation in so far as it has compensated the injured party; in order to facilitate enforcing the compensation body's claim against the insurance undertaking where it has failed to appoint a claims representative or is manifestly dilatory in settling a claim, the body providing compensation in the injured party's State should enjoy an automatic right of reimbursement with subrogation to the rights of the injured party on the part of the corresponding body in the State where the insurance undertaking is established; the latter body is the best placed to institute proceedings for recourse against the insurance undertaking.

(29) Even though Member States may provide that the claim against the compensation body may be subsidiary, the injured person should not be obliged to present his claim to the person responsible for the accident before presenting it to the compensation body; in this case the injured party should be in at least the same position as in the case of a claim against the guarantee fund under Article 1(4) of Directive 84/5/EEC.

(30) This system can be made to function by means of an agreement between the compensation bodies established or approved by the Member States defining their functions and obligations and the procedures for reimbursement.

---

[13] OJ L 281, 23.11.1995, 31.

(31) Where it is impossible to identify the insurer of the vehicle, provision should be made so that the ultimate debtor in respect of the damages to be paid to the injured party is the guarantee fund provided for in Article 1(4) of Directive 84/5/EEC situated in the Member State where the non-insured vehicle, the use of which has caused the accident, is normally based; where it is impossible to identify the vehicle, provision must be made so that the ultimate debtor is the guarantee fund provided for in Article 1(4) of Directive 84/5/EEC situated in the Member State in which the accident occurred,

HAVE ADOPTED THIS DIRECTIVE:

Article 1
Scope

1. The objective of this Directive is to lay down special provisions applicable to injured parties entitled to compensation in respect of any loss or injury resulting from accidents occurring in a Member State other than the Member State of residence of the injured party which are caused by the use of vehicles insured and normally based in a Member State.

Without prejudice to the legislation of third countries on civil liability and private international law, this Directive shall also apply to injured parties resident in a Member State and entitled to compensation in respect of any loss or injury resulting from accidents occurring in third countries whose national insurers' bureaux as defined in Article 1(3) of Directive 72/166/EEC have joined the Green Card system whenever such accidents are caused by the use of vehicles insured and normally based in a Member State.

2. Articles 4 and 6 shall apply only in the case of accidents caused by the use of a vehicle

(a) insured through an establishment in a Member State other than the State of residence of the injured party, and

(b) normally based in a Member State other than the State of residence of the injured party.

3. Article 7 shall also apply to accidents caused by third-country vehicles covered by Articles 6 and 7 of Directive 72/166/EEC.

Article 2
Definitions

For the purpose of this Directive:

(a) 'insurance undertaking' means an undertaking that has received its official authorisation in accordance with Article 6 or Article 23(2) of Directive 73/239/EEC;

(b) 'establishment' means the head office, agency or branch of an insurance undertaking as defined in Article 2(c) of Directive 88/357/EEC;

(c) 'vehicle' means a vehicle as defined in Article 1(1) of Directive 72/166/EEC;

(d) 'injured party' means an injured party as defined in Article 1(2) of Directive 72/166/EEC;

(e) 'the Member State in which the vehicle is normally based' means the territory in which the vehicle is normally based as defined in Article 1(4) of Directive 72/166/EEC.

Article 3
Direct right of action

Each Member State shall ensure that injured parties referred to in Article 1 in accidents within the meaning of that provision enjoy a direct right of action against the insurance undertaking covering the responsible person against civil liability.

Article 4
Claims representatives

1. Each Member State shall take all measures necessary to ensure that all insurance undertakings covering the risks classified in class 10 of point A of the Annex to Directive 73/239/EEC, other than carrier's liability, appoint a claims representative in each Member State other than that in which they have received their official authorisation. The claims representative shall be responsible for handling and settling claims arising from an accident in the cases referred to in Article 1. The claims representative shall be resident or established in the Member State where he is appointed.

2. The choice of its claims representative shall be at the discretion of the insurance undertaking. The Member States may not restrict this choice.

3. The claims representative may work for one or more insurance undertakings.

4. The claims representative shall, in relation to such claims, collect all information necessary in connection with the settlement of the claims and shall take the measures necessary to negotiate a settlement of claims. The requirement of appointing a claims representative shall not preclude the right of the injured party or his insurance undertaking to institute proceedings directly against the person who caused the accident or his insurance undertaking.

5. Claims representatives shall possess sufficient powers to represent the insurance undertaking in relation to injured parties in the cases referred to in Article 1 and to meet their claims in full. They must be capable of examining cases in the official language(s) of the Member State of residence of the injured party.

6. The Member States shall create a duty, backed by appropriate, effective and systematic financial or equivalent administrative penalties, to the effect that, within three months of the date when the injured party presented his claim for compensation either directly to the insurance undertaking of the person who caused the accident or to its claims representative,

(a) the insurance undertaking of the person who caused the accident or his claims representative is required to make a reasoned offer of compensation in cases where liability is not contested and the damages have been quantified, or

(b) the insurance undertaking to whom the claim for compensation has been addressed or his claims representative is required to provide a reasoned reply to the points made in the claim in cases where liability is denied or has not been clearly determined or the damages have not been fully quantified.

Member States shall adopt provisions to ensure that where the offer is not made within the three-month time-limit, interest shall be payable on the amount of compensation offered by the insurance undertaking or awarded by the court to the injured party.

7. The Commission shall report to the European Parliament and Council on the implementation of paragraph 4, first subparagraph, and on the effectiveness of that provision as well as on the equivalence of national penalty provisions before 20 January 2006 and shall submit proposals if necessary.

[8. The appointment of a claims representative shall not in itself constitute the opening of a branch within the meaning of Article 1(b) of Directive 92/49/EEC and the claims representative shall not be considered an establishment within the meaning of Article 2(c) of Directive 88/357/EEC or:

– an establishment within the meaning of the Brussels Convention of 27 September 1968 on Jurisdiction and the Enforcement of Judgments in Civil and Commercial Matters ([14])—as far as Denmark is concerned,

– an establishment within the meaning of Regulation (EC) No 44/2001—as far as the other Member States are concerned.]

¶ *Article 4(8) has been replaced by article 5(2) of Directive 2005/14/EC, reproduced infra under no. I. 39.*

Article 5
Information centres

1. For the purposes of allowing the injured party to seek compensation, each Member State shall establish or approve an information centre responsible:

(a) for keeping a register containing the following information:

1. the registration numbers of motor vehicles normally based in the territory of the State in question;

2. (i) the numbers of the insurance policies covering the use of those vehicles for the risks classified in class 10 of point A of the Annex to Directive 73/239/EEC, other than carrier's liability, and where the period of validity of the policy has expired, also the date of termination of the insurance cover;

   (ii) [. . .]

---

[14] OJ C 27, 26.1.1998, 1 (consolidated version).

3. insurance undertakings covering the use of vehicles for the risks classified in class 10 of point A of the Annex to Directive 73/239/EEC, other than carrier's liability, and claims representatives appointed by such insurance undertakings in accordance with Article 4 whose names shall be notified to the information centre in accordance with paragraph 2 of this Article;

4. the list of vehicles which, in each Member State, benefit from the derogation from the requirement for civil liability insurance cover in accordance with Article 4(a) and (b) of Directive 72/166/EEC;

5. regarding the vehicles provided for in point (4):
   (i) the name of the authority or the body designated in accordance with the second subparagraph of Article 4(a) of Directive 72/166/EEC as responsible for compensating injured parties in the cases where the procedure provided for in the first indent of Article 2(2) of Directive 72/166/EEC is not applicable, if the vehicle benefits from the derogation provided for in Article 4(a) of Directive 72/166/EEC;
   (ii) the name of the body covering the vehicle in the Member State where it is normally based if the vehicle benefits from the derogation provided for in Article 4(b) of Directive 72/166/EEC;

(b) or for co-ordinating the compilation and dissemination of that information;

(c) and for assisting entitled persons to be apprised of the information mentioned in points (a)(1), (2), (3), (4) and (5).

The information under points (a)(1), (2) and (3) must be preserved for a period of seven years after the termination of the registration of the vehicle or the termination of the insurance contract.

2. Insurance undertakings referred to in paragraph 1(a)(3) shall notify to the information centres of all Member States the name and address of the claims representative that they have appointed in accordance with Article 4 in each of the Member States.

3. The Member States shall ensure that the injured party is entitled for a period of seven years after the accident to obtain without delay from the information centre of the Member State where he resides, the Member State where the vehicle is normally based or the Member State where the accident occurred the following information:

(a) the name and address of the insurance undertaking;

(b) the number of the insurance policy; and

(c) the name and address of the insurance undertaking's claims representative in the State of residence of the injured party.

Information centres shall co-operate with each other.

4. The information centre shall provide the injured party with the name and address of the owner or usual driver or the registered keeper of the vehicle if the injured party has a legitimate interest in obtaining this information. For the purposes of this provision, the information centre shall address itself in particular:

(a) to the insurance undertaking, or

(b) to the vehicle registration agency.

If the vehicle benefits from the derogation provided for in Article 4(a) of Directive 72/166/EEC, the information centre shall inform the injured party of the name of the authority or body designated in accordance with the second subparagraph of Article 4(a) of that Directive as responsible for compensating injured parties in cases where the procedure provided for in the first indent of Article 2(2) of that Directive is not applicable.

If the vehicle benefits from the derogation provided for in Article 4(b) of Directive 72/166/EEC, the information centre shall inform the injured party of the name of the body covering the vehicle in the country where it is normally based.

5. The processing of personal data resulting from the previous paragraphs must be carried out in accordance with national measures taken pursuant to Directive 95/46/EC.

¶ Article 5(1)(a), point 2(ii) has been repealed by article 5(2) of Directive 2005/14/EC, reproduced infra under no. I. 39.

Article 6[15]
Compensation bodies

1. Each Member State shall establish or approve a compensation body responsible for providing compensation to injured parties in the cases referred to in Article 1.

Such injured parties may present a claim to the compensation body in their Member State of residence:

(a) if, within three months of the date when the injured party presented his claim for compensation to the insurance undertaking of the vehicle the use of which caused the accident or to its claims representative, the insurance undertaking or its claims representative has not provided a reasoned reply to the points made in the claim; or

(b) if the insurance undertaking has failed to appoint a claims representative in the State of residence of the injured party in accordance with Article 4(1). In this case, injured parties may not present a claim to the compensation body if they have presented a claim for compensation directly to the insurance undertaking of the vehicle the use of which caused the accident and if they have received a reasoned reply within three months of presenting the claim.

Injured parties may not however present a claim to the compensation body if they have taken legal action directly against the insurance undertaking.

The compensation body shall take action within two months of the date when the injured party presents a claim for compensation to it but shall terminate its action if the insurance undertaking, or its claims representative, subsequently makes a reasoned reply to the claim.

The compensation body shall immediately inform:

(a) the insurance undertaking of the vehicle the use of which caused the accident or the claims representative;

(b) the compensation body in the Member State of the insurance undertaking's establishment that issued the policy;

(c) if known, the person who caused the accident,

that it has received a claim from the injured party and that it will respond to that claim within two months of the presentation of that claim.

This provision shall be without prejudice to the right of the Member States to regard compensation by that body as subsidiary or non-subsidiary and the right to make provision for the settlement of claims between that body and the person or persons who caused the accident and other insurance undertakings or social security bodies required to compensate the injured party in respect of the same accident. However, Member States may not allow the body to make the payment of compensation subject to any conditions other than those laid down in this Directive, in particular the injured party's establishing in any way that the person liable is unable or refuses to pay.

2. The compensation body, which has compensated the injured party in his Member State of residence, shall be entitled to claim reimbursement of the sum paid by way of compensation from the compensation body in the Member State of the insurance undertaking's establishment that issued the policy.

The latter body shall then be subrogated to the injured party in his rights against the person who caused the accident or his insurance undertaking in so far as the compensation body in the Member State of residence of the injured party has provided compensation for the loss or injury suffered. Each Member State is obliged to acknowledge this subrogation as provided for by any other Member State.

---

[15] Pursuant to the Commission Decision of 27 December 2002 on the application of Article 6 of the Directive 2000/26/EC of the European Parliament and of the Council of 16 May 2000 on the approximation of the laws of the Member States relating to insurance against civil liability in respect of the use of motor vehicles and amending Council Directives 73/239/EEC and 88/357/EEC (OJ L 8, 14.1.2003, 35), article 6 of this Directive has taken effect as from 20 January 2003.

3. This Article shall take effect:

(a) after an agreement has been concluded between the compensation bodies established or approved by the Member States relating to their functions and obligations and the procedures for reimbursement;

(b) from the date fixed by the Commission upon its having ascertained in close co-operation with the Member States that such an agreement has been concluded.

The Commission shall report to the European Parliament and the Council on the implementation of this Article and on its effectiveness before 20 July 2005 and shall submit proposals if necessary.

[*Article 6a*

Central body

Member States shall take all appropriate measures to facilitate the availability in due time to the victims, their insurers or their legal representatives of the basic data necessary for the settlement of claims.

This basic data shall, where appropriate, be made available in electronic form in a central repository in each Member State, and be accessible by parties involved in the case at their express request.]

¶ *Article 6a has been inserted by article 5(4) of Directive 2005/14/EC, reproduced infra under no. I. 39.*

Article 7

If it is impossible to identify the vehicle or if, within two months following the accident, it is impossible to identify the insurance undertaking, the injured party may apply for compensation from the compensation body in the Member State where he resides. The compensation shall be provided in accordance with the provisions of Article 1 of Directive 84/5/EEC. The compensation body shall then have a claim, on the conditions laid down in Article 6(2) of this Directive:

(a) where the insurance undertaking cannot be identified: against the guarantee fund provided for in Article 1(4) of Directive 84/5/EEC in the Member State where the vehicle is normally based;

(b) in the case of an unidentified vehicle: against the guarantee fund in the Member State in which the accident took place;

(c) in the case of third-country vehicles: against the guarantee fund of the Member State in which the accident took place.

Article 8

[. . .]

¶ *Article 8 amends the articles 8(1) and 23(2) of Directive 73/239/EEC, reproduced supra under no. I. 3. The modifications are directly incorporated therein.*

Article 9

[. . .]

¶ *Article 9 amends the article 12(4) of Directive 88/357/EEC, reproduced supra under no. I. 15. The modifications are directly incorporated therein.*

Article 10

Implementation

1. Member States shall adopt and publish before 20 July 2002 the laws, regulations and administrative provisions necessary to comply with this Directive. They shall forthwith inform the Commission thereof.

They shall apply these provisions before 20 January 2003.

2. When these measures are adopted by the Member States, they shall contain a reference to this Directive or be accompanied by such a reference on the occasion of their official publication. The methods of making such a reference shall be laid down by the Member States.

3. Without prejudice to paragraph 1, the Member States shall establish or approve the compensation body in accordance with Article 6(1) before 20 January 2002. If the compensation bodies have not concluded an agreement in accordance with Article 6(3) before 20 July 2002, the Commission shall propose measures designed to ensure that the provisions of Articles 6 and 7 take effect before 20 January 2003.

4. Member States may, in accordance with the Treaty, maintain or bring into force provisions that are more favourable to the injured party than the provisions necessary to comply with this Directive.

5. Member States shall communicate to the Commission the text of the main provisions of domestic law that they adopt in the field governed by this Directive.

Article 11

Entry into force

This Directive shall enter into force on the day of its publication in the Official Journal of the European Communities.

Article 12

Penalties

The Member States shall fix penalties for breaches of the national provisions that they adopt in implementation of this Directive and take the steps necessary to secure their application. The penalties shall be effective, proportional and dissuasive. The Member States shall notify these provisions to the Commission not later than 20 July 2002 and any subsequent amendments thereof as soon as possible.

Article 13

Addressees

This Directive is addressed to the Member States.

I. 31.

European Parliament and Council Directive 2002/12/EC of 5 March 2002 amending Council Directive 79/267/EEC as regards the solvency margin requirements for life assurance undertakings[1]

This Directive has been repealed as from 19 December 2002 by Annex V, part A of Directive 2002/83/EC (OJ L 345, 19.12.2002, 1), reproduced infra under no. I. 33.

Correlation table

Directive 2002/12/EC	Directive 2002/83/EC
Article 2	Article 71
Article 3(1), first subparagraph	Article 69(3)
Article 3(1), second subparagraph	Article 69(4)
Article 3(3)	Article 70
Article 3(4)	Article 69(5)

---

[1] OJ L 77, 20.3.2002, 11–16.

I. 32.

European Parliament and Council Directive 2002/13/EC of 5 March 2002 amending Council Directive 73/239/EEC as regards the solvency margin requirements for non-life insurance undertakings[1]

THE EUROPEAN PARLIAMENT AND THE COUNCIL OF THE EUROPEAN UNION,

Having regard to the Treaty establishing the European Community, and in particular Article 47(2) and Article 55 thereof,

Having regard to the proposal from the Commission,[2]

Having regard to the opinion of the Economic and Social Committee,[3]

Acting in accordance with the procedure laid down in Article 251 of the Treaty,[4]

Whereas:

(1) The financial services action plan, as endorsed by the European Council meetings in Cologne on 3 and 4 June 1999 and in Lisbon on 23 and 24 March 2000, recognises the importance of the solvency margin for insurance undertakings to protect policyholders in the single market by ensuring that insurance undertakings have adequate capital requirements in relation to the nature of their risks.

(2) First Council Directive 73/239/EEC of 24 July 1973 on the coordination of laws, regulations and administrative provisions relating to the taking up and pursuit of the business of direct insurance other than life assurance[5] requires insurance undertakings to have solvency margins.

(3) The requirement that insurance undertakings establish, over and above the technical provisions to meet their underwriting liabilities, a solvency margin to act as a buffer against adverse business fluctuations is an important element in the system of prudential supervision for the protection of insured persons and policyholders.

(4) The existing solvency margin rules as established by Directive 73/239/EEC have been substantially unchanged by subsequent Community legislation and Council Directive 92/49/EEC of 18 June 1992 on the coordination of laws, regulations and administrative provisions relating to direct insurance other than life assurance (third non-life insurance Directive)[6] required the Commission to submit a report to the Insurance Committee set up by Council Directive 91/675/EEC,[7] on the need for further harmonisation of the solvency margin.

(5) The Commission has prepared that report in the light of the recommendations of the report on the solvency of insurance undertakings prepared by the Conference of the Insurance Supervisory Authorities of the Member States of the European Union.

(6) While the report concluded that the simple, robust nature of the current system has operated satisfactorily and is based on sound principles benefiting from wide transparency, certain weaknesses have been identified in specific cases, particularly for sensitive risk profiles.

---

[1] OJ L 77, 20.3.2002, 17–22.
[2] OJ C 96 E, 27.3.2001, 129.
[3] OJ C 193, 10.7.2001, 16.
[4] Opinion of the European Parliament of 4 July 2001 (OJ C 65, 4.3.2002, 141) and Decision of the Council of 14 February 2002.
[5] OJ L 228, 16.8.1973, 3, reproduced supra under no. I. 4. Directive as last amended by Directive 2000/26/EC of the European Parliament and of the Council (OJ L 181, 20.7.2000, 65), reproduced supra under no. I. 30.
[6] OJ L 228, 11.8.1992, 1, reproduced supra under no. I. 25. Directive as last amended by Directive 2000/64/EC of European Parliament and of the Council (OJ L 290, 17.11.2000, 27).
[7] OJ L 374, 31.12.1991, 32, reproduced supra under no. I. 24.

(7) There is a need to simplify and increase the existing minimum guarantee funds, in particular as a result of inflation in claim levels and operational expenses since their original adoption. The thresholds above which the lower percentage rate applies for the determination of the solvency margin requirement on the premiums and claims basis should also be increased accordingly.

(8) To avoid major and sharp increases in the amount of the minimum guarantee funds and the thresholds in the future, a mechanism should be established providing for their increase in line with the European index of consumer prices.

(9) In specific situations where policyholders' rights are threatened, there is a need for the competent authorities to be empowered to intervene at a sufficiently early stage, but in the exercise of those powers, competent authorities should inform the insurance undertakings of the reasons motivating such supervisory action, in accordance with the principles of sound administration and due process. As long as such a situation exists, the competent authorities should be prevented from certifying that the insurance undertaking has a sufficient solvency margin.

(10) In the light of market developments in the nature of reinsurance cover purchased by primary insurers, there is a need for the competent authorities to be empowered to decrease the reduction to the solvency margin requirement in certain circumstances.

(11) Where an insurer substantially reduces or ceases the writing of new business, there is a need to establish an adequate solvency margin in respect of the residual liabilities for existing business as reflected by the level of technical provisions.

(12) For specific classes of non-life business which are subject to a particularly volatile risk profile, the existing solvency margin requirement should be substantially increased so that the required solvency margin is better matched to the true risk profile of the business.

(13) To reflect the impact of differing accounting and actuarial approaches, it is appropriate to make corresponding adjustments to the methodology for the calculation of the solvency margin requirement so that this is calculated in a coherent and consistent manner, thus placing insurance undertakings on an equal footing.

(14) This Directive should lay down minimum standards for the solvency margin requirements and home Member States should be able to lay down stricter rules for insurance undertakings authorised by their own competent authorities.

(15) Directive 73/239/EEC should be amended accordingly,

HAVE ADOPTED THIS DIRECTIVE:

Article 1

Amendments to Directive 73/239/EEC

[...]

¶ *Article 1 replaces article 3, paragraph 1 and article 16, inserts articles 16a, 17a, and 20a and amends article 20(2) of Directive 73/239/EEC, reproduced supra under no. I. 4. The modifications are directly incorporated therein.*

Article 2

Transitional period

1. Member States may allow insurance undertakings which at the entry into force of this Directive provide insurance in their territories in one or more of classes referred to in the Annex to Directive 73/239/EEC, a period of five years, commencing with the date of entry into force of this Directive, in order to comply with the requirements set out in Article 1 of this Directive.

2. Member States may allow any undertakings referred to in paragraph 1, which upon the expiry of the five-year period have not fully established the required solvency margin, a further period not exceeding two years in which to do so provided that such undertakings have, in accordance with Article 20 of Directive 73/239/EEC, submitted for the approval of the competent authorities the measures which they propose to take for such purpose.

Article 3

Transposition

1. Member States shall adopt by 20 September 2003 at the latest the laws, regulations and

administrative provisions necessary to comply with this Directive. They shall forthwith inform the Commission thereof.

When Member States adopt these measures, they shall contain a reference to this Directive or be accompanied by such a reference on the occasion of their official publication. The methods of making such a reference shall be laid down by the Member States.

2. Member States shall provide that the measures referred to in paragraph 1 shall first apply to the supervision of accounts for financial years beginning on 1 January 2004 or during that calendar year.

3. Member States shall communicate to the Commission the main provisions of national law which they adopt in the field covered by this Directive.

4. Not later than 1 January 2007 the Commission shall submit to the European Parliament and the Council a report on the application of this Directive and, if necessary, on the need for further harmonisation. The report shall indicate how Member States have made use of the possibilities in this Directive, and, in particular, whether the discretionary powers afforded to the national supervisory authorities have resulted in major supervisory differences in the single market.

Article 4

Entry into force

This Directive shall enter into force on the day of its publication in the Official Journal of the European Communities.

Article 5

Addressees

This Directive is addressed to the Member States.

I. 33.

European Parliament and Council Directive 2002/83/EC of 5 November 2002 concerning life assurance[1]

Cases

I. Case 205/84 Commission of the European Communities v Federal Republic of Germany [1986] ECR 3755

So far as direct insurance is concerned, the protection of policy-holders and insured persons justifies in the present state of community law the application by the Member State in which the service is provided of its own legislation concerning technical reserves or provisions and the conditions of insurance, provided that the requirements of that legislation do not exceed what is necessary to ensure the protection of policy-holders and insured persons. Only the requirement of an authorization, which it is for the Member State in which the services are provided to grant and withdraw, can provide an effective means of supervision and is therefore permissible. The authorization must be granted on request to any undertaking established in another Member state that meets the conditions laid down by the legislation of the state in which the service is provided. Those conditions may not duplicate equivalent statutory conditions that have already been satisfied in the state in which the undertaking is established and the supervisory authority of the state in which the service is provided must take into account supervision and verifications that have already been carried out in the Member State of establishment.

II. Case 206/84 Commission of the European Communities v Ireland [1986] ECR 3817

See commentary on Case 205/84 (Case 1 of this directive).

---

[1] OJ L 345, 19.12.2002, 1–51.

THE EUROPEAN PARLIAMENT AND THE COUNCIL OF THE EUROPEAN UNION,

Having regard to the Treaty establishing the European Community, and in particular Articles 47(2) and Article 55 thereof,

Having regard to the proposal from the Commission,[2]

Having regard to the opinion of the Economic and Social Committee,[3]

Acting in accordance with the procedure laid down in Article 251 of the Treaty,[4]

Whereas:

(1) First Council Directive 79/267/EEC of 5 March 1979 on the coordination of laws, regulations and administrative provisions relating to the taking-up and pursuit of the business of direct life assurance,[5] the second Council Directive 90/619/EEC of 8 November 1990 on the coordination of laws, regulations and administrative provisions relating to direct life assurance, laying down provisions to facilitate the effective exercise of freedom to provide services and amending Directive 79/267/EEC[6] and Council Directive 92/96/EEC of 10 November 1992 on the coordination of laws, regulations and administrative

---

[2] OJ C 365 E, 19.12.2000, 1.
[3] OJ C 123, 25.4.2001, 24.
[4] Opinion of the European Parliament of 15 March 2001 (OJ C 343, 5.12.2001, 202), Council Common Position of 27 May 2002 (OJ C 170 E, 16.7.2002, 45) and decision of the European Parliament of 25 September 2002 (not yet published in the Official Journal).
[5] OJ L 63, 13.3.1979, 1, reproduced supra under no. I. 9. Directive as last amended by Directive 2002/12/EC of the European Parliament and of the Council (OJ L 77, 20.3.2002, 11), reproduced supra under no. I. 31.
[6] OJ L 330, 29.11.1990, 50, reproduced supra under no. I. 18. Directive as amended by Directive 92/96/EEC (OJ L 360, 9.12.1992, 1), reproduced supra under no. I. 26.

provisions relating to direct life assurance and amending Directives 79/267/EEC and 90/619/EEC (third life assurance Directive)[7] have been substantially amended several times. Since further amendments are to be made, the Directives should be recast in the interests of clarity.

(2) In order to facilitate the taking-up and pursuit of the business of life assurance, it is essential to eliminate certain divergences which exist between national supervisory legislation. In order to achieve this objective and at the same time ensure adequate protection for policy holders and beneficiaries in all Member States, the provisions relating to the financial guarantees required of life assurance undertakings should be coordinated.

(3) It is necessary to complete the internal market in direct life assurance, from the point of view both of the right of establishment and of the freedom to provide services in the Member States, to make it easier for assurance undertakings with head offices in the Community to cover commitments situated within the Community and to make it possible for policy holders to have recourse not only to assurers established in their own country, but also to assurers which have their head office in the Community and are established in other Member States.

(4) Under the Treaty, any discrimination with regard to freedom to provide services based on the fact that an undertaking is not established in the Member State in which the services are provided is prohibited. That prohibition applies to services provided from any establishment in the Community, whether it be the head office of an undertaking or an agency or branch.

(5) This Directive therefore represents an important step in the merging of national markets into an integrated market and that stage must be supplemented by other Community instruments with a view to enabling all policy holders to have recourse to any assurer with a head office in the Community who carries on business there, under the right of establishment or the freedom to provide services, while guaranteeing them adequate protection.

(6) This Directive forms part of the body of Community legislation in the field of life assurance which also includes Council Directive 91/674/EEC of 19 December 1991 on the annual accounts and consolidated accounts of insurance undertakings.[8]

(7) The approach adopted consists in bringing about such harmonisation as is essential, necessary and sufficient to achieve the mutual recognition of authorisations and prudential control systems, thereby making it possible to grant a single authorisation valid throughout the Community and apply the principle of supervision by the home Member State.

(8) As a result, the taking up and the pursuit of the business of assurance are subject to the grant of a single official authorisation issued by the competent authorities of the Member State in which an assurance undertaking has its head office. Such authorisation enables an undertaking to carry on business throughout the Community, under the right of establishment or the freedom to provide services. The Member State of the branch or of the provision of services may not require assurance undertakings which wish to carry on assurance business there and which have already been authorised in their home Member State to seek fresh authorisation.

(9) The competent authorities should not authorise or continue the authorisation of an assurance undertaking where they are liable to be prevented from effectively exercising their supervisory functions by the close links between that undertaking and other natural or legal persons. Assurance undertakings already authorised must also satisfy the competent authorities in that respect.

(10) The definition of 'close links' in this Directive lays down minimum criteria and that does not prevent Member States from applying it

---

[7] OJ L 360, 9.12.1992, 1, reproduced supra under no. I. 26. Directive as amended by Directive 2000/64/EC of the European Parliament and of the Council (OJ L 290, 17.11.2000, 27).

[8] OJ L 374, 31.12.1991, 7, reproduced supra under no. I. 23.

to situations other than those envisaged by the definition.

(11) The sole fact of having acquired a significant proportion of a company's capital does not constitute participation, within the meaning of 'close links', if that holding has been acquired solely as a temporary investment which does not make it possible to exercise influence over the structure or financial policy of the undertaking.

(12) The principles of mutual recognition and of home Member State supervision require that Member States' competent authorities should not grant or should withdraw authorisation where factors such as the content of programmes of operations or the geographical distribution of the activities actually carried on indicate clearly that an assurance undertaking has opted for the legal system of one Member State for the purpose of evading the stricter standards in force in another Member State within whose territory it carries on or intends to carry on the greater part of its activities. An assurance undertaking must be authorised in the Member State in which it has its registered office. In addition, Member States must require that an assurance undertaking's head office always be situated in its home Member State and that it actually carries on its business there.

(13) For practical reasons, it is desirable to define provision of services taking into account both the assurer's establishment and the place where the commitment is to be covered. Therefore, commitment should also be defined. Moreover, it is desirable to distinguish between activities pursued by way of establishment and activities pursued by way of freedom to provide services.

(14) A classification by class of assurance is necessary in order to determine, in particular, the activities subject to compulsory authorisation.

(15) Certain mutual associations which, by virtue of their legal status, fulfil requirements as to security and other specific financial guarantees should be excluded from the scope of this Directive. Certain organisations whose activity covers only a very restricted sector and is limited by their articles of association should also be excluded.

(16) Life assurance is subject to official authorisation and supervision in each Member State. The conditions for the granting or withdrawal of such authorisation should be defined. Provision must be made for the right to apply to the courts should an authorisation be refused or withdrawn.

(17) It is desirable to clarify the powers and means of supervision vested in the competent authorities. It is also desirable to lay down specific provisions regarding the taking up, pursuit and supervision of activity by way of freedom to provide services.

(18) The competent authorities of home Member States should be responsible for monitoring the financial health of assurance undertakings, including their state of solvency, the establishment of adequate technical provisions and the covering of those provisions by matching assets.

(19) It is appropriate to provide for the possibility of exchanges of information between the competent authorities and authorities or bodies which, by virtue of their function, help to strengthen the stability of the financial system. In order to preserve the confidential nature of the information forwarded, the list of addressees must remain within strict limits.

(20) Certain behaviour, such as fraud and insider offences, is liable to affect the stability, including integrity, of the financial system, even when involving undertakings other than assurance undertakings.

(21) It is necessary to specify the conditions under which the abovementioned exchanges of information are authorised.

(22) Where it is stipulated that information may be disclosed only with the express agreement of the competent authorities, these may, where appropriate, make their agreement subject to compliance with strict conditions.

(23) Member States may conclude agreements on exchange of information with third countries provided that the information disclosed is

subject to appropriate guarantees of professional secrecy.

(24) For the purposes of strengthening the prudential supervision of assurance undertakings and protection of clients of assurance undertakings, it should be stipulated that an auditor must have a duty to report promptly to the competent authorities, wherever, as provided for by this Directive, he/she becomes aware, while carrying out his/her tasks, of certain facts which are liable to have a serious effect on the financial situation or the administrative and accounting organisation of an assurance undertaking.

(25) Having regard to the aim in view, it is desirable for Member States to provide that such a duty should apply in all circumstances where such facts are discovered by an auditor during the performance of his/her tasks in an undertaking which has close links with an assurance undertaking.

(26) The duty of auditors to communicate, where appropriate, to the competent authorities certain facts and decisions concerning an assurance undertaking which they discover during the performance of their tasks in a non-assurance undertaking does not in itself change the nature of their tasks in that undertaking nor the manner in which they must perform those tasks in that undertaking.

(27) The performance of the operations of management of group pension funds cannot under any circumstances affect the powers conferred on the respective authorities with regard to the entities holding the assets with which that management is concerned.

(28) Certain provisions of this Directive define minimum standards. A home Member State may lay down stricter rules for assurance undertakings authorised by its own competent authorities.

(29) The competent authorities of the Member States must have at their disposal such means of supervision as are necessary to ensure the orderly pursuit of business by assurance undertakings throughout the Community whether carried on under the right of establishment or the freedom to provide services. In particular, they must be able to introduce appropriate safeguards or impose sanctions aimed at preventing irregularities and infringements of the provisions on assurance supervision.

(30) The provisions on transfers of portfolios should include provisions specifically concerning the transfer to another undertaking of the portfolio of contracts concluded by way of freedom to provide services.

(31) The provisions on transfers of portfolios must be in line with the single legal authorisation system provided for in this Directive.

(32) Undertakings formed after the dates referred to in Article 18(3) should not be authorised to carry on life assurance and non-life insurance activities simultaneously. Member States should be allowed to permit undertakings which, on the relevant dates referred to in Article 18(3), carried on these activities simultaneously to continue to do so provided that separate management is adopted for each of their activities, in order that the respective interests of life policy holders and non-life policy holders are safeguarded and the minimum financial obligations in respect of one of the activities are not borne by the other activity. Member States should be given the option of requiring those existing undertakings established in their territory which carry on life assurance and non-life insurance simultaneously to put an end to this practice. Moreover, specialised undertakings should be subject to special supervision where a non-life undertaking belongs to the same financial group as a life undertaking.

(33) Nothing in this Directive prevents a composite undertaking from dividing itself into two undertakings, one active in the field of life assurance, the other in non-life insurance. In order to allow such division to take place under the best possible conditions, it is desirable to permit Member States, in accordance with Community rules of competition law, to provide for appropriate tax arrangements, in particular with regard to the capital gains such division could entail.

(34) Those Member States which so wish should be able to grant the same undertaking

authorisations for the classes referred to in Annex I and the insurance business coming under classes 1 and 2 in the Annex to Council Directive 73/239/EEC of 24 July 1973 on the coordination of laws, regulations and administrative provisions relating to the taking up and pursuit of the business of direct insurance other than life assurance.[9] That possibility may, however, be subject to certain conditions as regards compliance with accounting rules and rules on winding-up.

(35) It is necessary from the point of view of the protection of lives assured that every assurance undertaking should establish adequate technical provisions. The calculation of such provisions is based for the most part on actuarial principles. Those principles should be coordinated in order to facilitate mutual recognition of the prudential rules applicable in the various Member States.

(36) It is desirable, in the interests of prudence, to establish a minimum of coordination of rules limiting the rate of interest used in calculating the technical provisions. For the purposes of such limitation, since existing methods are all equally correct, prudential and equivalent, it seems appropriate to leave Member States a free choice as to the method to be used.

(37) The rules governing the calculation of technical provisions and the rules governing the spread, localisation and matching of the assets used to cover technical provisions must be coordinated in order to facilitate the mutual recognition of Member States' rules. That coordination must take account of the liberalisation of capital movements provided for in Article 56 of the Treaty and the progress made by the Community towards economic and monetary union.

(38) The home Member State may not require assurance undertakings to invest the assets covering their technical provisions in particular categories of assets, as such a requirement would be incompatible with the liberalisation of capital movements provided for in Article 56 of the Treaty.

(39) It is necessary that, over and above technical provisions, including mathematical provisions, of sufficient amount to meet their underwriting liabilities, assurance undertakings should possess a supplementary reserve, known as the solvency margin, represented by free assets and, with the agreement of the competent authority, by other implicit assets, which shall act as a buffer against adverse business fluctuations. This requirement is an important element of prudential supervision for the protection of insured persons and policy holders. In order to ensure that the requirements imposed for such purposes are determined according to objective criteria whereby undertakings of the same size will be placed on an equal footing as regards competition, it is desirable to provide that this margin shall be related to all the commitments of the undertaking and to the nature and gravity of the risks presented by the various activities falling within the scope of this Directive. This margin should therefore vary according to whether the risks are of investment, death or management only. It should accordingly be determined in terms of mathematical provisions and capital at risk underwritten by an undertaking, of premiums or contributions received, of provisions only or of the assets of tontines.

(40) Directive 92/96/EEC provided for a provisional definition of a regulated market, pending the adoption of a directive on investment services in the securities field, which would harmonise that concept at Community level. Council Directive 93/22/EEC of 10 May 1993 on investment services in the securities field[10] provides for a definition of regulated market, although it excludes from its scope life assurance activities. It is appropriate to apply the concept of regulated market also to life assurance activities.

(41) The list of items of which the solvency margin required by this Directive may be made

---

[9] OJ L 228, 16.8.1973, 3, reproduced supra under no. I. 3. Directive as last amended by Directive 2002/13/EC of the European Parliament and of the Council (OJ L 77, 20.3.2002, 17), reproduced supra under no. I. 3.

[10] OJ L 141, 11.6.1993, 27, reproduced infra under no. S. 14. Directive as last amended by Directive 2000/64/EC of the European Parliament and of the Council.

up takes account of new financial instruments and of the facilities granted to other financial institutions for the constitution of their own funds. In the light of market developments in the nature of reinsurance cover purchased by primary insurers, there is a need for the competent authorities to be empowered to decrease the reduction to the solvency margin requirement in certain circumstances. In order to improve the quality of the solvency margin, the possibility of including future profits in the available solvency margin should be limited and subject to conditions and should in any case cease after 2009.

(42) It is necessary to require a guarantee fund, the amount and composition of which are such as to provide an assurance that the undertakings possess adequate resources when they are set up and that in the subsequent course of business the solvency margin in no event falls below a minimum of security. The whole or a specified part of this guarantee fund must consist of explicit asset items.

(43) To avoid major and sharp increases in the amount of the minimum guarantee fund in the future, a mechanism should be established providing for its increase in line with the European index of consumer prices. This Directive should lay down minimum standards for the solvency margin requirements and home Member States should be able to lay down stricter rules for insurance undertakings authorised by their own competent authorities.

(44) The provisions in force in the Member States regarding contract law applicable to the activities referred to in this Directive differ. The harmonisation of assurance contract law is not a prior condition for the achievement of the internal market in assurance. Therefore, the opportunity afforded to the Member States of imposing the application of their law to assurance contracts covering commitments within their territories is likely to provide adequate safeguards for policy holders. The freedom to choose, as the law applicable to the contract, a law other than that of the State of the commitment may be granted in certain cases, in accordance with rules which take into account specific circumstances.

(45) For life assurance contracts the policy holder should be given the opportunity of cancelling the contract within a period of between 14 and 30 days.

(46) Within the framework of an internal market it is in the policy holder's interest that they should have access to the widest possible range of assurance products available in the Community so that they can choose that which is best suited to their needs. It is for the Member State of the commitment to ensure that there is nothing to prevent the marketing within its territory of all the assurance products offered for sale in the Community as long as they do not conflict with the legal provisions protecting the general good in force in the Member State of the commitment and in so far as the general good is not safeguarded by the rules of the home Member State, provided that such provisions must be applied without discrimination to all undertakings operating in that Member State and be objectively necessary and in proportion to the objective pursued.

(47) The Member States must be able to ensure that the assurance products and contract documents used, under the right of establishment or the freedom to provide services, to cover commitments within their territories comply with such specific legal provisions protecting the general good as are applicable. The systems of supervision to be employed must meet the requirements of an internal market but their employment may not constitute a prior condition for carrying on assurance business. From this standpoint, systems for the prior approval of policy conditions do not appear to be justified. It is therefore necessary to provide for other systems better suited to the requirements of an internal market which enable every Member State to guarantee policy holders adequate protection.

(48) It is necessary to make provision for cooperation between the competent authorities of the Member States and between those authorities and the Commission.

(49) Provision should be made for a system of penalties to be imposed when, in the Member State in which the commitment is entered into,

an assurance undertaking does not comply with those provisions protecting the general good that are applicable to it.

(50) It is necessary to provide for measures in cases where the financial position of the undertaking becomes such that it is difficult for it to meet its underwriting liabilities. In specific situations where policy holders' rights are threatened, there is a need for the competent authorities to be empowered to intervene at a sufficiently early stage, but in the exercise of those powers, competent authorities should inform the insurance undertakings of the reasons motivating such supervisory action, in accordance with the principles of sound administration and due process. As long as such a situation exists, the competent authorities should be prevented from certifying that the insurance undertaking has a sufficient solvency margin.

(51) For the purposes of implementing actuarial principles in conformity with this Directive, the home Member State may require systematic notification of the technical bases used for calculating scales of premiums and technical provisions, with such notification of technical bases excluding notification of the general and special policy conditions and the undertaking's commercial rates.

(52) In an internal market for assurance the consumer will have a wider and more varied choice of contracts. If he/she is to profit fully from this diversity and from increased competition, he/she must be provided with whatever information is necessary to enable him/her to choose the contract best suited to his/her needs. This information requirement is all the more important as the duration of commitments can be very long. The minimum provisions must therefore be coordinated in order for the consumer to receive clear and accurate information on the essential characteristics of the products proposed to him/her as well as the particulars of the bodies to which any complaints of policy holders, assured persons or beneficiaries of contracts may be addressed.

(53) Publicity for assurance products is an essential means of enabling assurance business to be carried on effectively within the Community. It is necessary to leave open to assurance undertakings the use of all normal means of advertising in the Member State of the branch or of provision of services. Member States may nevertheless require compliance with their national rules on the form and content of advertising, whether laid down pursuant to Community legislation on advertising or adopted by Member States for reasons of the general good.

(54) Within the framework of the internal market, no Member State may continue to prohibit the simultaneous carrying on of assurance business within its territory under the right of establishment and the freedom to provide services.

(55) Some Member States do not subject assurance transactions to any form of indirect taxation, while the majority apply special taxes and other forms of contribution. The structures and rates of such taxes and contributions vary considerably between the Member States in which they are applied. It is desirable to prevent existing differences leading to distortions of competition in assurance services between Member States. Pending subsequent harmonisation, application of the tax systems and other forms of contribution provided for by the Member States in which commitments entered into are likely to remedy that problem and it is for the Member States to make arrangements to ensure that such taxes and contributions are collected.

(56) It is important to introduce Community coordination on the winding-up of assurance undertakings. It is henceforth essential to provide, in the event of the winding-up of an assurance undertaking, that the system of protection in place in each Member State must guarantee equality of treatment for all assurance creditors, irrespective of nationality and of the method of entering into the commitment.

(57) The coordinated rules concerning the pursuit of the business of direct insurance within the Community should, in principle, apply to all undertakings operating on the market and, consequently, also to agencies and branches where the head office of the undertaking is situated outside the Community. As regards the methods of supervision this Directive lays down special provisions for such agencies or branches, in view

of the fact that the assets of the undertakings to which they belong are situated outside the Community.

(58) It is desirable to provide for the conclusion of reciprocal agreements with one or more third countries in order to permit the relaxation of such special conditions, while observing the principle that such agencies and branches should not obtain more favourable treatment than Community undertakings.

(59) A provision should be made for a flexible procedure to make it possible to assess reciprocity with third countries on a Community basis. The aim of this procedure is not to close the Community's financial markets but rather, as the Community intends to keep its financial markets open to the rest of the world, to improve the liberalisation of the global financial markets in other third countries. To that end, this Directive provides for procedures for negotiating with third countries. As a last resort, the possibility of taking measures involving the suspension of new applications for authorisation or the restriction of new authorisations should be provided for using the regulatory procedure under Article 5 of Council Decision 1999/468/EC.[11]

(60) This Directive should establish provisions concerning proof of good repute and no previous bankruptcy.

(61) In order to clarify the legal regime applicable to life assurance activities covered by this Directive, some provisions of Directives 79/267/EEC, 90/619/EEC and 92/96/EEC should be adapted. For that purpose some provisions concerning the establishment of the solvency margin and the rights acquired by branches of assurance undertakings established before 1 July 1994 should be amended. The content of the scheme of operation of branches of third-country undertakings to be established in the Community should also be defined.

(62) Technical adjustments to the detailed rules laid down in this Directive may be necessary from time to time to take account of the future development of the assurance industry. The Commission will make such adjustments as and when necessary, after consulting the Insurance Committee set up by Council Directive 91/675/EEC,[12] in the exercise of the implementing powers conferred on it by the Treaty. These measures being measures of general scope within the meaning of Article 2 of Decision 1999/468/EC, they should be adopted by the use of the regulatory procedure provided for in Article 5 of that Decision.

(63) Pursuant to Article 15 of the Treaty, account should be taken of the extent of the effort which must be made by certain economies at different stages of development. Therefore, transitional arrangements should be adopted for the gradual application of this Directive by certain Member States.

(64) Directives 79/267/EEC and 90/619/EEC granted special derogation with regard to some undertakings existing at the time of the adoption of these Directives. Such undertakings have thereafter modified their structure. Therefore they do not need any longer such special derogation.

(65) This Directive should not affect the obligations of Member States concerning the deadlines for transposition and for application of the Directives set out in Annex V(B),

HAVE ADOPTED THIS DIRECTIVE:

Contents

TITLE I DEFINITIONS AND SCOPE	1264
Article 1 Definitions	1264
Article 2 Scope	1265
Article 3 Activities and bodies excluded	1266
TITLE II THE TAKING-UP OF THE BUSINESS OF LIFE ASSURANCE	1267
Article 4 Principle of authorisation	1267
Article 5 Scope of authorisation	1267
Article 6 Conditions for obtaining authorisation	1267
Article 7 Scheme of operations	1269
Article 8 Shareholders and members with qualifying holdings	1269
Article 9 Refusal of authorisation	1270

---

[11] OJ L 184, 17.7.1999, 23.

[12] OJ L 374, 31.12.1991, 32, reproduced supra under no. I. 24.

I. 33. European Parliament & Council Directive 2002/83/EC of 5 Nov. 2002

[Article 9a Prior consultation with the competent authorities of other Member States]	1270
TITLE III CONDITIONS GOVERNING THE BUSINESS OF ASSURANCE	1270
Chapter 1 Principles and Methods of Financial Supervision	1270
Article 10 Competent authorities and object of supervision	1270
Article 11 Supervision of branches established in another Member State	1271
Article 12 Prohibition on compulsory ceding of part of underwriting.	1271
Article 13 Accounting, prudential and statistical information: supervisory powers	1271
Article 14 Transfer of portfolio	1272
Article 15 Qualifying holdings	1272
Article 16 Professional secrecy	1273
Article 17 Duties of auditors	1276
Article 18 Pursuit of life assurance and non-life insurance activities	1276
Article 19 Separation of life assurance and non-life insurance management	1277
Chapter 2 Rules Relating to Technical Provisions and their Representation	1278
Article 20 Establishment of technical provisions	1278
Article 21 Premiums for new business	1280
Article 22 Assets covering technical provisions	1280
Article 23 Categories of authorised assets	1280
Article 24 Rules for investment diversification	1281
Article 25 Contracts linked to UCITS or share index	1283
Article 26 Matching rules	1283
Chapter 3 Rules Relating to the Solvency Margin and to the Guarantee Fund	1283
Article 27 Available solvency margin	1283
Article 28 Required solvency margin	1287
[Article 28a Solvency Margin for assurance undertakings conducting reinsurance activities]	1288
Article 29 Guarantee fund	1288
Article 30 Review of the amount of the guarantee fund	1288
Article 31 Assets not used to cover technical provisions	1289
Chapter 4 Contract Law and Conditions of Assurance	1289
Article 32 Law applicable	1289
Article 33 General good	1289
Article 34 Rules relating to conditions of assurance and scales of premiums	1289
Article 35 Cancellation period	1290
Article 36 Information for policy holders	1290
Chapter 5 Assurance Undertakings in Difficulty or in an Irregular Situation	1290
Article 37 Assurance undertakings in difficulty	1290
Article 38 Financial recovery plan	1291
Article 39 Withdrawal of authorisation	1292
TITLE IV PROVISIONS RELATING TO RIGHT OF ESTABLISHMENT AND FREEDOM TO PROVIDE SERVICES	1292
Article 40 Conditions for branch establishment	1292
Article 41 Freedom to provide services: prior notification to the home Member State	1293
Article 42 Freedom to provide services: notification by the home Member State	1293
Article 43 Freedom to provide services: changes in the nature of commitments	1294
Article 44 Language	1294
Article 45 Rules relating to conditions of assurance and scales of premiums	1294
Article 46 Assurance undertakings not complying with the legal provisions	1294
Article 47 Advertising	1295
Article 48 Winding up	1295
Article 49 Statistical information on cross-border activities	1295
Article 50 Taxes on premiums	1295
TITLE V RULES APPLICABLE TO AGENCIES OR BRANCHES ESTABLISHED WITHIN THE COMMUNITY AND BELONGING TO UNDERTAKINGS WHOSE HEAD OFFICES ARE OUTSIDE THE COMMUNITY	1296
Article 51 Principles and conditions of authorisation	1296
Article 52 Rules applicable to branches of third-country undertakings	1296
Article 53 Transfer of portfolio	1297
Article 54 Technical provisions	1298
Article 55 Solvency margin and guarantee fund	1298
Article 56 Advantages to undertakings authorised in more than one Member State	1298
Article 57 Agreements with third countries	1299
TITLE VI RULES APPLICABLE TO SUBSIDIARIES OF PARENT UNDERTAKINGS GOVERNED BY THE LAWS OF A THIRD COUNTRY AND TO THE ACQUISITIONS OF HOLDINGS BY SUCH PARENT UNDERTAKINGS	1299
Article 58 Information from Member States to the Commission	1299
[Article 58a Information from Member States to the Commission]	1299
Article 59 Third-country treatment of Community assurance undertakings	1299
TITLE VII TRANSNATIONAL AND OTHER PROVISIONS	1300
Article 60 Derogations and abolition of restrictive measures	1300
Article 61 Proof of good repute	1301
TITLE VIII FINAL PROVISIONS	1301
Article 62 Cooperation between the Member States and the Commission	1301
Article 63 Reports on the development of the market under the freedom to provide services	1301
Article 64 Technical adjustment	1302
Article 65 Committee procedure	1302
Article 66 Rights acquired by existing branches and assurance undertakings	1302
Article 67 Right to apply to the courts	1302
Article 68 Review of amounts expressed in euro	1302
Article 69 Implementation of new provisions	1303
Article 70 Information to the Commission	1303
Article 71 Transitional period for Articles 3(6), 27, 28, 29, 30 and 38	1303
Article 72 Repealed directives and their correlation with this Directive	1303
Article 73 Entry into force	1304
Article 74 Addressees	1304
Annex I Classes of assurance	1304
Annex II Matching rules	1304
Annex III Information for policy holders	1305
Annex IV	1306
Annex V	1310
Part A Repealed directives together with their successive amendments (referred to in Article 72)	1310
Part B Deadlines for implementation (referred to in Article 72).	1310
Annex VI Correlation table	1311

Title I
Definitions and Scope

Article 1
Definitions

1. For the purposes of this Directive:

(a) 'assurance undertaking' shall mean an undertaking which has received official authorisation in accordance with Article 4;

(b) 'branch' shall mean an agency or branch of an assurance undertaking;

Any permanent presence of an undertaking in the territory of a Member State shall be treated in the same way as an agency or branch, even if that presence does not take the form of a branch or agency, but consists merely of an office managed by the undertaking's own staff or by a person who is independent but has permanent authority to act for the undertaking as an agency would;

(c) 'establishment' shall mean the head office, an agency or a branch of an undertaking;

(d) 'commitment' shall mean a commitment represented by one of the kinds of insurance or operations referred to in Article 2;

(e) 'home Member State' shall mean the Member State in which the head office of the assurance undertaking covering the commitment is situated;

(f) 'Member State of the branch' shall mean the Member State in which the branch covering the commitment is situated;

(g) 'Member State of the commitment' shall mean the Member State where the policy holder has his/her habitual residence or, if the policy holder is a legal person, the Member State where the latter's establishment, to which the contract relates, is situated;

(h) 'Member State of the provision of services' shall mean the Member State of the commitment, if the commitment is covered by an assurance undertaking or a branch situated in another Member State;

(i) 'control' shall mean the relationship between a parent undertaking and a subsidiary, as defined in Article 1 of Council Directive 83/349/EEC,[13] or a similar relationship between any natural or legal person and an undertaking;

(j) 'qualifying holding' shall mean a direct or indirect holding in an undertaking which represents 10% or more of the capital or of the voting rights or which makes it possible to exercise a significant influence over the management of the undertaking in which a holding subsists;

For the purposes of this definition, in the context of Articles 8 and 15 and of the other levels of holding referred to in Article 15, the voting rights referred to in Article 92 of Directive 2001/34/EC of the European Parliament and of the Council of 28 May 2001 on the admission of securities to official stock exchange listing and on information to be published on those securities[14] shall be taken into consideration;

(k) 'parent undertaking' shall mean a parent undertaking as defined in Articles 1 and 2 of Directive 83/349/EEC;

(l) 'subsidiary' shall mean a subsidiary undertaking as defined in Articles 1 and 2 of Directive 83/349/EEC; any subsidiary of a subsidiary undertaking shall also be regarded as a subsidiary of the undertaking which is those undertakings' ultimate parent undertaking;

(m) 'regulated market' shall mean:
– in the case of a market situated in a Member State, a regulated market as defined in Article 1(13) of Directive 93/22/EEC, and
– in the case of a market situated in a third country, a financial market recognised by the home Member State of the assurance undertaking which meets comparable requirements. Any financial instruments dealt in on that market must be of a quality comparable to that of the instruments dealt in on the regulated market or markets of the Member State in question;

(n) 'competent authorities' shall mean the national authorities which are empowered by law or regulation to supervise assurance undertakings;

---

[13] OJ L 193, 18.7.1983, 1, reproduced supra under no. C. 6. Directive as last amended by Directive 2001/65/EC of the European Parliament and of the Council (OJ L 283, 27.10.2001, 28), reproduced supra under no. C. 18.

[14] OJ L 184, 6.7.2001, 1, reproduced infra under no. S. 18.

(o) 'matching assets' shall mean the representation of underwriting liabilities which can be required to be met in a particular currency by assets expressed or realisable in the same currency;

(p) 'localisation of assets' shall mean the existence of assets, whether movable or immovable, within a Member State but shall not be construed as involving a requirement that movable assets be deposited or that immovable assets be subjected to restrictive measures such as the registration of mortgages; assets represented by claims against debtors shall be regarded as situated in the Member State where they are realisable;

(q) capital at risk shall mean the amount payable on death less the mathematical provision for the main risk;

(r) 'close' links shall mean a situation in which two or more natural or legal persons are linked by:
 (i) participation, which shall mean the ownership, direct or by way of control, of 20% or more of the voting rights or capital of an undertaking; or
 (ii) control, which shall mean the relationship between a parent undertaking and a subsidiary, in all the cases referred to in Article 1(1) and (2) of Directive 83/349/EEC, or a similar relationship between any natural or legal person and an undertaking; any subsidiary undertaking of a subsidiary undertaking shall also be considered a subsidiary of the parent undertaking which is at the head of those undertakings.

A situation in which two or more natural or legal persons are permanently linked to one and the same person by a control relationship shall also be regarded as constituting a close link between such persons.

[(s) 'reinsurance undertaking' shall mean a reinsurance undertaking within the meaning of Article 2 point (c) of Directive 2005/68/EC of the European Parliament and of the Council of 16 November 2005 on reinsurance.[15]]

---

[15] OJ L 323, 9.12.2005, 1, reproduced infra under no. I. 40.

2. Wherever this Directive refers to the euro, the conversion value in national currency to be adopted shall as from 31 December of each year be that of the last day of the preceding month of October for which euro conversion values are available in all the relevant Community currencies.

¶ *The littera (s) has been added by article 60(1) of Directive 2005/68/EC, reproduced infra under no. I. 40.*

Article 2
Scope

This Directive concerns the taking-up and pursuit of the self-employed activity of direct insurance carried on by undertakings which are established in a Member State or wish to become established there in the form of the activities defined below:

1. the following kinds of assurance where they are on a contractual basis:

(a) life assurance, that is to say, the class of assurance which comprises, in particular, assurance on survival to a stipulated age only, assurance on death only, assurance on survival to a stipulated age or on earlier death, life assurance with return of premiums, marriage assurance, birth assurance;

(b) annuities;

(c) supplementary insurance carried on by life assurance undertakings, that is to say, in particular, insurance against personal injury including incapacity for employment, insurance against death resulting from an accident and insurance against disability resulting from an accident or sickness, where these various kinds of insurance are underwritten in addition to life assurance;

(d) the type of insurance existing in Ireland and the United Kingdom known as permanent health insurance not subject to cancellation;

2. the following operations, where they are on a contractual basis, in so far as they are subject to supervision by the administrative authorities responsible for the supervision of private insurance:

(a) tontines whereby associations of subscribers are set up with a view to jointly capitalising their contributions and subsequently distributing the assets thus accumulated among the survivors or among the beneficiaries of the deceased;

(b) capital redemption operations based on actuarial calculation whereby, in return for single or periodic payments agreed in advance, commitments of specified duration and amount are undertaken;

(c) management of group pension funds, i.e. operations consisting, for the undertaking concerned, in managing the investments, and in particular the assets representing the reserves of bodies that effect payments on death or survival or in the event of discontinuance or curtailment of activity;

(d) the operations referred to in (c) where they are accompanied by insurance covering either conservation of capital or payment of a minimum interest;

(e) the operations carried out by assurance undertakings such as those referred to in Chapter 1, Title 4 of Book IV of the French 'Code des assurances'.

3. Operations relating to the length of human life which are prescribed by or provided for in social insurance legislation, when they are effected or managed at their own risk by assurance undertakings in accordance with the laws of a Member State.

Article 3

Activities and bodies excluded

This Directive shall not concern:

1. subject to the application of Article 2(1)(c), the classes designated in the Annex to Directive 73/239/EEC;

2. operations of provident and mutual-benefit institutions whose benefits vary according to the resources available and which require each of their members to contribute at the appropriate flat rate;

3. operations carried out by organisations other than undertakings referred to in Article 2, whose object is to provide benefits for employed or self-employed persons belonging to an undertaking or group of undertakings, or a trade or group of trades, in the event of death or survival or of discontinuance or curtailment of activity, whether or not the commitments arising from such operations are fully covered at all times by mathematical provisions;

4. subject to the application of Article 2(3), insurance forming part of a statutory system of social security;

5. organisations which undertake to provide benefits solely in the event of death, where the amount of such benefits does not exceed the average funeral costs for a single death or where the benefits are provided in kind;

6. mutual associations, where:
– the articles of association contain provisions for calling up additional contributions or reducing their benefits or claiming assistance from other persons who have undertaken to provide it, and
– the annual contribution income for the activities covered by this Directive does not exceed EUR 5 million for three consecutive years. If this amount is exceeded for three consecutive years this Directive shall apply with effect from the fourth year.

Nevertheless, the provisions of this paragraph shall not prevent a mutual assurance undertaking from applying, or continuing, to be licensed under this Directive;

7. the 'Versorgungsverband deutscher Wirtschaftsorganisationen' in Germany unless its statutes are amended as regards the scope of its activities;

8. the pension activities of pension insurance undertakings prescribed in the Employees. Pension Act (TEL) and other related Finnish legislation provided that:

(a) pension insurance companies which already under Finnish law are obliged to have separate accounting and management systems for their pension activities will furthermore, as from the date of accession, set up separate legal entities for carrying out these activities;

(b) the Finnish authorities shall allow in a non-discriminatory manner all nationals and companies of Member States to perform according to

Finnish legislation the activities specified in Article 2 related to this exemption whether by means of:
– ownership or participation in an existing insurance company or group,
– creation or participation of new insurance companies or groups, including pension insurance companies;

(c) the Finnish authorities will submit to the Commission for approval a report within three months from the date of accession, stating which measures have been taken to separate TEL activities from normal insurance activities carried out by Finnish insurance companies in order to conform to all the requirements of this Directive.

Title II

The Taking-up of the Business of Life Assurance

Article 4
Principle of authorisation

The taking-up of the activities covered by this Directive shall be subject to prior official authorisation.

Such authorisation shall be sought from the authorities of the home Member State by:

(a) any undertaking which establishes its head office in the territory of that State;

(b) any undertaking which, having received the authorisation required in the first subparagraph, extends its business to an entire class or to other classes.

Article 5
Scope of authorisation

1. Authorisation shall be valid for the entire Community. It shall permit an assurance undertaking to carry on business there, under either the right of establishment or freedom to provide services.

2. Authorisation shall be granted for a particular class of assurance as listed in Annex I. It shall cover the entire class, unless the applicant wishes to cover only some of the risks pertaining to that class.

The competent authorities may restrict authorisation requested for one of the classes to the operations set out in the scheme of operations referred to in Article 7.

Each Member State may grant authorisation for two or more of the classes, where its national laws permit such classes to be carried on simultaneously.

Article 6
Conditions for obtaining authorisation

1. The home Member State shall require every assurance undertaking for which authorisation is sought to:

(a) adopt one of the following forms:
– in the case of the Kingdom of Belgium: 'société anonyme/naamloze vennootschap', 'société en commandite par actions/commanditaire vennootschap op aandelen', 'association d'assurance mutuelle/onderlinge verzekeringsvereniging', 'société coopérative/coöperatieve vennootschap',
– [in the case of the Czech Republic: 'akciová společnost', 'družstvo'],
– in the case of the Kingdom of Denmark: 'aktieselskaber', 'gensidige selskaber', 'pensionskasser omfattet af lov om forsikringsvirksomhed (tværgående pensionskasser)',
– in the case of the Federal Republic of Germany: 'Aktiengesellschaft', 'Versicherungsverein auf Gegenseitigkeit', 'öffentlich-rechtliches Wettbewerbsversicherungsunternehmen',
– [in the case of the Republic of Estonia: 'aktsiaselts'],
– in the case of the French Republic: 'société anonyme', 'société d'assurance mutuelle', 'institution de prévoyance régie par le code de la sécurité sociale', 'institution de prévoyance régie par le code rural' and 'mutuelles régies par le code de la mutualité',
– in the case of Ireland: 'incorporated companies limited by shares or by guarantee or unlimited', 'societies registered under the Industrial and Provident Societies Acts' and

'societies registered under the Friendly Societies Acts,'
- in the case of the Italian Republic: 'societá per azioni', 'societá cooperativa', 'mutua di assicurazione',
- [in the case of the Republic of Cyprus: 'Εταιρεία περιορισμένης ενθύνης με μετοχές ή εταιρεία περιορισμένης ενθύνης με εγγύηση'],
- [in the case of the Republic of the Latvia: 'apdrošināšanas akciju sabiedrība', 'savstarpējās apdrošināšanas kooperatīvā biedrība'],
- [in the case of the Republic of Lithuania: 'akcinės bendrovės', 'uždarosios akcinės bendrovės'],
- in the case of the Grand Duchy of Luxembourg: 'société anonyme', 'société en commandite par actions', 'association d'assurances mutuelles', 'société coopérative',
- [in the case of the Republic of Hungary: 'biztosító részvénytársaság', 'biztosító szövetkezet', 'biztosító egyesület', 'külföldi székhelyű biztosító magyarországi fióktelepe'],
- [in the case of the Republic of Malta: 'kumpanija pubblika', 'kumpanija privata', 'fergha', 'Korp ta' l- Assikurazzjoni Rikonnoxxut'],
- in the case of the Kingdom of the Netherlands: 'naamloze vennootschap', 'onderlinge waarborgmaatschappij',
- in the case of the United Kingdom: 'incorporated companies limited by shares or by guarantee or unlimited', 'societies registered under the Industrial and Provident Societies Acts', 'societies registered or incorporated under the Friendly Societies Acts', 'the association of underwriters known as Lloyd's',
- in the case of the Hellenic Republic: 'ανωνύμη εταιρια',
- in the case of the Kingdom of Spain: 'sociedad anónima', 'sociedad mutua', 'sociedad cooperativa',
- in the case of the Republic of Austria: 'Aktiengesellschaft', 'Versicherungsverein auf Gegenseitigkeit',
- [in the case of the Republic of Poland: 'spółka akcyjna', 'towarzystwo ubezpieczeń wzajemnych'],
- in the case of the Portuguese Republic: 'sociedade anónima', 'mútua de seguros'
- [in the case of the Republic of Slovenia: 'delniška družba', 'družba za vzajemno zavarovanje'],
- [in the case of the Slovak Republic: 'akciová spoločnost'],
- in the case of the Republic of Finland: 'keskinäinen vakuutusyhtiö/ömsesidigt försäkringsbolag', 'vakuutusosakeyhtiö/försäkringsaktiebolag', 'vakuutusyhdistys/försäkringsförening',
- in the case of Kingdom of Sweden: 'försäkringsaktiebolag', 'ömsesidiga försäkringsbolag', 'understödsföreningar'.

An assurance undertaking may also adopt the form of a European company when that has been established.

Furthermore, Member States may, where appropriate, set up undertakings in any public-law form provided that such bodies have as their object insurance operations under conditions equivalent to those under which private-law undertakings operate;

(b) limit its objects to the business provided for in this Directive and operations directly arising therefrom, to the exclusion of all other commercial business;

(c) submit a scheme of operations in accordance with Article 7;

(d) possess the minimum guarantee fund provided for in Article 29(2);

(e) be effectively run by persons of good repute with appropriate professional qualifications or experience.

2. Where close links exist between the assurance undertaking and other natural or legal persons, the competent authorities shall grant authorisation only if those links do not prevent the effective exercise of their supervisory functions.

The competent authorities shall also refuse authorisation if the laws, regulations or administrative provisions of a non-member country governing one or more natural or legal persons with which the assurance undertaking has close links, or difficulties involved in their enforcement, prevent the effective exercise of their supervisory functions.

The competent authorities shall require assurance undertakings to provide them with the information they require to monitor compliance with the conditions referred to in this paragraph on a continuous basis.

3. Member States shall require that the head offices of insurance undertakings be situated in the same Member State as their registered offices.

4. An assurance undertaking seeking authorisation to extend its business to other classes or to extend an authorisation covering only some of the risks pertaining to one class shall be required to submit a scheme of operations in accordance with Article 7.

It shall, furthermore, be required to show proof that it possesses the solvency margin provided for in Article 28 and the guarantee fund referred to in Article 29(1) and (2).

5. Member States shall not adopt provisions requiring the prior approval or systematic notification of general and special policy conditions, of scales of premiums, of the technical bases, used in particular for calculating scales of premiums and technical provisions or of forms and other printed documents which an assurance undertaking intends to use in its dealings with policy holders.

Notwithstanding the first subparagraph, for the sole purpose of verifying compliance with national provisions concerning actuarial principles, the home Member State may require systematic notification of the technical bases used for calculating scales of premiums and technical provisions, without that requirement constituting a prior condition for an assurance undertaking to carry on its business.

Nothing in this Directive shall prevent Member States from maintaining in force or introducing laws, regulations or administrative provisions requiring approval of the memorandum and articles of association and the communication of any other documents necessary for the normal exercise of supervision.

Not later than 1 July 1999, the Commission shall submit a report to the Council on the implementation of this paragraph.

6. The provisions referred to in paragraphs 1 to 5 may not require that any application for authorisation be considered in the light of the economic requirements of the market.

¶ *This article has been amended by the Annex of Directive 2004/66/EC of 26 April 2004 (OJ L 168, 1.5.2004, 35).*

Article 7
Scheme of operations

The scheme of operations referred to in Article 6(1)(c) and (4) shall include particulars or evidence of:

(a) the nature of the commitments which the assurance undertaking proposes to cover;

(b) the guiding principles as to reassurance;

(c) the items constituting the minimum guarantee fund;

(d) estimates relating to the costs of setting up the administrative services and the organisation for securing business and the financial resources intended to meet those costs;

in addition, for the first three financial years:

(e) a plan setting out detailed estimates of income and expenditure in respect of direct business, reassurance acceptances and reassurance cessions;

(f) a forecast balance sheet;

(g) estimates relating to the financial resources intended to cover underwriting liabilities and the solvency margin.

Article 8
Shareholders and members with qualifying holdings

The competent authorities of the home Member State shall not grant an undertaking authorisation to take up the business of assurance before they have been informed of the identities of the shareholders or members, direct or indirect, whether natural or legal persons, who have qualifying holdings in that undertaking and of the amounts of those holdings.

The same authorities shall refuse authorisation if, taking into account the need to ensure the sound and prudent management of an assurance undertaking, they are not satisfied as to the qualifications of the shareholders or members.

Article 9

Refusal of authorisation

Any decision to refuse an authorisation shall be accompanied by the precise grounds for doing so and notified to the undertaking in question.

Each Member State shall make provision for a right to apply to the courts should there be any refusal.

Such provision shall also be made with regard to cases where the competent authorities have not dealt with an application for an authorisation upon the expiry of a period of six months from the date of its receipt.

[*Article 9a*

Prior consultation with the competent authorities of other Member States

1. The competent authorities of the other Member State involved shall be consulted prior to the granting of an authorisation to a life assurance undertaking, which is:

(a) a subsidiary of an insurance or reinsurance undertaking authorised in another Member State; or

(b) a subsidiary of the parent undertaking of an insurance or reinsurance undertaking authorised in another Member State; or

(c) controlled by the same person, whether natural or legal, who controls an insurance or reinsurance undertaking authorised in another Member State.

2. The competent authority of a Member State involved responsible for the supervision of credit institutions or investment firms shall be consulted prior to the granting of an authorisation to a life assurance undertaking which is:

(a) a subsidiary of a credit institution or investment firm authorised in the Community; or

(b) a subsidiary of the parent undertaking of a credit institution or investment firm authorised in the Community; or

(c) controlled by the same person, whether natural or legal, who controls a credit institution or investment firm authorised in the Community.

3. The relevant competent authorities referred to in paragraphs 1 and 2 shall in particular consult each other when assessing the suitability of the shareholders and the reputation and experience of directors involved in the management of another entity of the same group. They shall inform each other of any information regarding the suitability of shareholders and the reputation and experience of directors which is of relevance to the other competent authorities involved for the granting of an authorisation as well as for the ongoing assessment of compliance with operating conditions.]

¶ *Article 9a has been inserted by article 60(2) of Directive 2005/68/EC, reproduced infra under no. I. 40.*

TITLE III

CONDITIONS GOVERNING THE BUSINESS OF ASSURANCE

CHAPTER 1

PRINCIPLES AND METHODS OF FINANCIAL SUPERVISION

Article 10

Competent authorities and object of supervision

1. The financial supervision of an assurance undertaking, including that of the business it carries on either through branches or under the freedom to provide services, shall be the sole responsibility of the home Member State. If the competent authorities of the Member State of the commitment have reason to consider that the activities of

an assurance undertaking might affect its financial soundness, they shall inform the competent authorities of the undertaking's home Member State. The latter authorities shall determine whether the undertaking is complying with the prudential principles laid down in this Directive.

2. That financial supervision shall include verification, with respect to the assurance undertaking's entire business, of its state of solvency, the establishment of technical provisions, including mathematical provisions, and of the assets covering them, in accordance with the rules laid down or practices followed in the home Member State pursuant to the provisions adopted at Community level.

[The home Member State of the insurance undertaking shall not refuse a reinsurance contract concluded by the insurance undertaking with a reinsurance undertaking authorised in accordance with Directive 2005/68/EC or an insurance undertaking authorised in accordance with Directive 73/239/EEC or this Directive on grounds directly related to the financial soundness of the reinsurance undertaking or the insurance undertaking.]

3. The competent authorities of the home Member State shall require every assurance undertaking to have sound administrative and accounting procedures and adequate internal control mechanisms.

¶ *The second subparagraph has been added by article 60(3) of Directive 2005/68/EC, reproduced infra under no. I. 40.*

CASE

Case C-28/03 Epikouriko Kefalaio v Ypourgos Anaptyxis [2004] ECR I-8533

See supra under article 15 of Directive 73/239/ EEC reproduced under no. I. 3.

Article 11

Supervision of branches established in another Member State

The Member State of the branch shall provide that, where an assurance undertaking authorised in another Member State carries on business through a branch, the competent authorities of the home Member State may, after having first informed the competent authorities of the Member State of the branch, carry out themselves, or through the intermediary of persons they appoint for that purpose, on-the-spot verification of the information necessary to ensure the financial supervision of the undertaking. The authorities of the Member State of the branch may participate in that verification.

Article 12

Prohibition on compulsory ceding of part of underwriting

Member States may not require assurance undertakings to cede part of their underwriting of activities listed in Article 2 to an organisation or organisations designated by national regulations.

Article 13

Accounting, prudential and statistical information: supervisory powers

1. Each Member State shall require every assurance undertaking whose head office is situated in its territory to produce an annual account, covering all types of operation, of its financial situation and solvency.

2. Member States shall require assurance undertakings with head offices within their territories to render periodically the returns, together with statistical documents, which are necessary for the purposes of supervision. The competent authorities shall provide each other with any documents and information that are useful for the purposes of supervision.

3. Every Member State shall take all steps necessary to ensure that the competent authorities have the powers and means necessary for the supervision of the business of assurance undertakings with head offices within their territories, including business carried on outside those territories, in accordance with the Council directives governing those activities and for the purpose of seeing that they are implemented.

These powers and means must, in particular, enable the competent authorities to:

(a) make detailed enquiries regarding the assurance undertaking's situation and the whole of its business, inter alia, by:
– gathering information or requiring the submission of documents concerning its assurance business,
– carrying out on-the-spot investigations at the assurance undertaking's premises;

(b) take any measures, with regard to the assurance undertaking, its directors or managers or the persons who control it, that are appropriate and necessary to ensure that the undertaking's business continues to comply with the laws, regulations and administrative provisions with which the undertaking must comply in each Member State and in particular with the scheme of operations in so far as it remains mandatory, and to prevent or remedy any irregularities prejudicial to the interests of the assured persons;

(c) ensure that those measures are carried out, if need be by enforcement, where appropriate through judicial channels.

Member States may also make provision for the competent authorities to obtain any information regarding contracts which are held by intermediaries.

Article 14
Transfer of portfolio

1. Under the conditions laid down by national law, each Member State shall authorise assurance undertakings with head offices within its territory to transfer all or part of their portfolios of contracts, concluded under either the right of establishment or the freedom to provide services, to an accepting office established within the Community, if the competent authorities of the home Member State of the accepting office certify that after taking the transfer into account, the latter possesses the necessary solvency margin.

2. Where a branch proposes to transfer all or part of its portfolio of contracts, concluded under either the right of establishment or the freedom to provide services, the Member State of the branch shall be consulted.

3. In the circumstances referred to in paragraphs 1 and 2, the authorities of the home Member State of the transferring assurance undertaking shall authorise the transfer after obtaining the agreement of the competent authorities of the Member States of the commitment.

4. The competent authorities of the Member States consulted shall give their opinion or consent to the competent authorities of the home Member State of the transferring assurance undertaking within three months of receiving a request; the absence of any response within that period from the authorities consulted shall be considered equivalent to a favourable opinion or tacit consent.

5. A transfer authorised in accordance with this Article shall be published as laid down by national law in the Member State of the commitment. Such transfers shall automatically be valid against policy holders, the assured persons and any other person having rights or obligations arising out of the contracts transferred.

This provision shall not affect the Member States' rights to give policy holders the option of cancelling contracts within a fixed period after a transfer.

Article 15
Qualifying holdings

1. Member States shall require any natural or legal person who proposes to hold, directly or indirectly, a qualifying holding in an assurance undertaking first to inform the competent authorities of the home Member State, indicating the size of the intended holding. Such a person must likewise inform the competent authorities of the home Member State if he/she proposes to increase his/her qualifying holding so that the proportion of the voting rights or of the capital held by him/her would reach or exceed 20%, 33% or 50% or so that the assurance undertaking would become his/her subsidiary.

The competent authorities of the home Member State shall have a maximum of three months from the date of the notification provided for in the first subparagraph to oppose such a plan if, in view of the need to ensure sound and prudent management of the assurance undertaking, they are not satisfied as to the qualifications of the person referred to in the first subparagraph. If they do not oppose the plan in question they may fix a maximum period for its implementation.

[1a. If the acquirer of the holdings referred to in paragraph 1 of this Article is an insurance undertaking, a reinsurance undertaking, a credit institution or an investment firm authorised in another Member State, or the parent undertaking of such an entity, or a natural or legal person controlling such an entity, and if, as a result of that acquisition, the undertaking in which the acquirer proposes to hold a holding would become a subsidiary or subject to the control of the acquirer, the assessment of the acquisition must be subject to the prior consultation referred to in Article 9a.]

2. Member States shall require any natural or legal person who proposes to dispose, directly or indirectly, of a qualifying holding in an assurance undertaking first to inform the competent authorities of the home Member State, indicating the size of his/her intended holding. Such a person must likewise inform the competent authorities if he/she proposes to reduce his/her qualifying holding so that the proportion of the voting rights or of the capital held by him/her would fall below 20%, 33% or 50% or so that the assurance undertaking would cease to be his/her subsidiary.

3. On becoming aware of them, assurance undertakings shall inform the competent authorities of their home Member States of any acquisitions or disposals of holdings in their capital that cause holdings to exceed or fall below one of the thresholds referred to in paragraphs 1 and 2.

They shall also, at least once a year, inform them of the names of shareholders and members possessing qualifying holdings and the sizes of such holdings as shown, for example, by the information received at the annual general meetings of shareholders and members or as a result of compliance with the regulations relating to companies listed on stock exchanges.

4. Member States shall require that, if the influence exercised by the persons referred to in paragraph 1 is likely to operate to the detriment of the prudent and sound management of the assurance undertaking, the competent authorities of the home Member State shall take appropriate measures to put an end to that situation. Such measures may consist, for example, in injunctions, sanctions against directors and managers, or the suspension of the exercise of the voting rights attaching to the shares held by the shareholders or members in question.

Similar measures shall apply to natural or legal persons failing to comply with the obligation to provide prior information, as laid down in paragraph 1. If a holding is acquired despite the opposition of the competent authorities, the Member States shall, regardless of any other sanctions to be adopted, provide either for exercise of the corresponding voting rights to be suspended, or for the nullity of votes cast or for the possibility of their annulment.

¶ *Paragraph 1a has been added by article 60(4) of Directive 2005/68/EC, reproduced infra under no. I. 40.*

Article 16
Professional secrecy

1. Member States shall provide that all persons working or who have worked for the competent authorities, as well as auditors or experts acting on behalf of the competent authorities, shall be bound by the obligation of professional secrecy. This means that no confidential information which they may receive in the course of their duties may be divulged to any person or authority whatsoever, except in summary or aggregate form, such that individual assurance undertakings cannot be identified, without prejudice to cases covered by criminal law.

Nevertheless, where an assurance undertaking has been declared bankrupt or is being compulsorily wound up, confidential information which does not concern third parties involved in attempts to rescue that undertaking may be divulged in civil or commercial proceedings.

2. Paragraph 1 shall not prevent the competent authorities of the different Member States from exchanging information in accordance with the directives applicable to assurance undertakings. That information shall be subject to the conditions of professional secrecy indicated in paragraph 1.

3. Member States may conclude cooperation agreements providing for exchange of information with the competent authorities of third countries or with authorities or bodies of third countries as defined in paragraphs 5 and 6 only if the information disclosed is subject to guarantees of professional secrecy at least equivalent to those referred to in this Article. Such exchange of information must be intended for the performance of the supervisory task of the authorities or bodies mentioned.

Where the information originates in another Member State, it may not be disclosed without the express agreement of the competent authorities which have disclosed it and, where appropriate, solely for the purposes for which those authorities gave their agreement.

[4. Competent authorities receiving confidential information under paragraphs 1 or 2 may use it only in the course of their duties:
– to check that the conditions governing the taking-up of the business of assurance are met and to facilitate monitoring of the conduct of such business, especially with regard to the monitoring of technical provisions, solvency margins, administrative and accounting procedures and internal control mechanisms, or
– to impose penalties, or
– in administrative appeals against decisions of the competent authority, or
– in court proceedings initiated pursuant to Article 67 or under special provisions provided for in this Directive and other Directives adopted in the field of assurance undertakings and reinsurance undertakings.

5. Paragraphs 1 and 4 shall not preclude the exchange of information within a Member State, where there are two or more competent authorities in the same Member State, or, between Member States, between competent authorities and:
– authorities responsible for the official supervision of credit institutions and other financial organisations and the authorities responsible for the supervision of financial markets,
– bodies involved in the liquidation and bankruptcy of assurance undertakings, reinsurance undertakings and in other similar procedures, and
– persons responsible for carrying out statutory audits of the accounts of assurance undertakings, reinsurance undertakings and other financial institutions,

in the discharge of their supervisory functions, and the disclosure, to bodies which administer compulsory winding-up proceedings or guarantee funds, of information necessary to the performance of their duties. The information received by those authorities, bodies and persons shall be subject to the obligation of professional secrecy laid down in paragraph 1.

6. Notwithstanding paragraphs 1 to 4, Member States may authorise exchanges of information between the competent authorities and:
– the authorities responsible for overseeing the bodies involved in the liquidation and bankruptcy of assurance undertakings, reinsurance undertakings and other similar procedures, or
– the authorities responsible for overseeing the persons charged with carrying out statutory audits of the accounts of insurance undertakings, reinsurance undertakings, credit institutions, investment firms and other financial institutions, or
– independent actuaries of insurance undertakings and reinsurance undertakings carrying out legal supervision of those undertakings and the bodies responsible for overseeing such actuaries.

Member States which have recourse to the option provided for in the first subparagraph shall require at least that the following conditions are met:
– this information shall be for the purpose of carrying out the overseeing or legal supervision referred to in the first subparagraph,

— information received in this context shall be subject to the conditions of professional secrecy imposed in paragraph 1,
— where the information originates in another Member State, it may not be disclosed without the express agreement of the competent authorities which have disclosed it and, where appropriate, solely for the purposes for which those authorities gave their agreement.

Member States shall communicate to the Commission and to the other Member States the names of the authorities, persons and bodies which may receive information pursuant to this paragraph.]

7. Notwithstanding paragraphs 1 to 4, Member States may, with the aim of strengthening the stability, including integrity, of the financial system, authorise the exchange of information between the competent authorities and the authorities or bodies responsible under the law for the detection and investigation of breaches of company law.

Member States which have recourse to the option provided for in the first subparagraph shall require at least that the following conditions are met:
— the information shall be for the purpose of performing the task referred to in the first subparagraph,
— information received in this context shall be subject to the conditions of professional secrecy imposed in paragraph 1,
— where the information originates in another Member State, it may not be disclosed without the express agreement of the competent authorities which have disclosed it and, where appropriate, solely for the purposes for which those authorities gave their agreement.

Where, in a Member State, the authorities or bodies referred to in the first subparagraph perform their task of detection or investigation with the aid, in view of their specific competence, of persons appointed for that purpose and not employed in the public sector, the possibility of exchanging information provided for in the first subparagraph may be extended to such persons under the conditions stipulated in the second subparagraph.

In order to implement the third indent of the second subparagraph, the authorities or bodies referred to in the first subparagraph shall communicate to the competent authorities which have disclosed the information, the names and precise responsibilities of the persons to whom it is to be sent.

Member States shall communicate to the Commission and to the other Member States the names of the authorities or bodies which may receive information pursuant to this paragraph.

Before 31 December 2000, the Commission shall draw up a report on the application of this paragraph.

[8. Paragraphs 1 to 7 shall not prevent a competent authority from transmitting:
— to central banks and other bodies with a similar function in their capacity as monetary authorities,
— where appropriate, to other public authorities responsible for overseeing payment systems, information intended for the performance of their task, nor shall it prevent such authorities or bodies from communicating to the competent authorities such information as they may need for the purposes of paragraph 4. Information received in this context shall be subject to the conditions of professional secrecy imposed in this Article.]

9. In addition, notwithstanding paragraphs 1 and 4, Member States may, under provisions laid down by law, authorise the disclosure of certain information to other departments of their central government administrations responsible for legislation on the supervision of credit institutions, financial institutions, investment services and assurance undertakings and to inspectors acting on behalf of those departments.

However, such disclosures may be made only where necessary for reasons of prudential control.

However, Member States shall provide that information received under paragraphs 2 and 5 and that obtained by means of the on-the-spot verification referred to in Article 11 may never be disclosed in the cases referred to in this paragraph except with the express consent of the competent authorities which disclosed the information or of the competent authorities of the Member State in which on-the-spot verification was carried out.

¶ *Paragraphs 4, 5, 6, and 8 have been replaced by article 60(5) of Directive 2005/68/EC, reproduced infra under no. I. 40.*

Article 17
Duties of auditors

1. Member States shall provide at least that:

(a) any person authorised within the meaning of Council Directive 84/253/EEC,[16] performing in an assurance undertaking the task described in Article 51 of Council Directive 78/660/EEC,[17] Article 37 of Directive 83/349/EEC or Article 31 of Council Directive 85/611/EEC[18] or any other statutory task, shall have a duty to report promptly to the competent authorities any fact or decision concerning that undertaking of which he/she has become aware while carrying out that task which is liable to:
- constitute a material breach of the laws, regulations or administrative provisions which lay down the conditions governing authorisation or which specifically govern pursuit of the activities of assurance undertakings, or
- affect the continuous functioning of the assurance undertaking, or
- lead to refusal to certify the accounts or to the expression of reservations;

(b) that person shall likewise have a duty to report any facts and decisions of which he/she becomes aware in the course of carrying out a task as described in (a) in an undertaking having close links resulting from a control relationship with the assurance undertaking within which he/she is carrying out the abovementioned task.

---

[16] OJ L 126, 12.5.1984, 20, reproduced supra under no. C. 7.

[17] OJ L 222, 14.8.1978, 11, reproduced supra under no. C. 4. Directive as last amended by Directive 2001/65/EC of the European Parliament and of the Council (OJ L 283, 27.10.2001, 28) , reproduced supra under no. C. 18.

[18] OJ L 375, 31.12.1985, 3, reproduced infra under no. S. 6. Directive as last amended by Directive 2001/108/EC of the European Parliament and of the Council (OJ L 41, 13.2.2002, 35), reproduced infra under no. S. 22.

2. The disclosure in good faith to the competent authorities, by persons authorised within the meaning of Directive 84/253/EEC, of any fact or decision referred to in paragraph 1 shall not constitute a breach of any restriction on disclosure of information imposed by contract or by any legislative, regulatory or administrative provision and shall not involve such persons in liability of any kind.

Article 18
Pursuit of life assurance and non-life insurance activities

1. Without prejudice to paragraphs 3 and 7, no undertaking may be authorised both pursuant to this Directive and pursuant to Directive 73/239/EEC.

2. By way of derogation from paragraph 1, Member States may provide that:
- undertakings authorised pursuant to this Directive may also obtain authorisation, in accordance with Article 6 of Directive 73/239/EEC for the risks listed in classes 1 and 2 in the Annex to that Directive,
- undertakings authorised pursuant to Article 6 of Directive 73/239/EEC solely for the risks listed in classes 1 and 2 in the Annex to that Directive may obtain authorisation pursuant to this Directive.

3. Subject to paragraph 6, undertakings referred to in paragraph 2 and those which on:
- 1 January 1981 for undertakings authorised in Greece,
- 1 January 1986 for undertakings authorised in Spain and Portugal,
- [1 January 1995 for undertakings authorised in Austria, Finland and Sweden],
- [1 May 2004 for undertakings authorised in the Czech Republic, Estonia, Cyprus, Latvia, Lithuania, Hungary, Malta, Poland, Slovenia and Slovakia, and]
- 15 March 1979 for all other undertakings,

carried on simultaneously both the activities covered by this Directive and those covered by Directive 73/239/EEC may continue to carry on those activities simultaneously, provided that each activity is separately managed in accordance with Article 19 of this Directive.

4. Member States may provide that the undertakings referred to in paragraph 2 shall comply with the accounting rules governing assurance undertakings authorised pursuant to this Directive for all of their activities. Pending coordination in this respect, Member States may also provide that, with regard to rules on winding-up, activities relating to the risks listed in classes 1 and 2 in the Annex to Directive 73/239/EEC carried on by the undertakings referred to in paragraph 2 shall be governed by the rules applicable to life assurance activities.

5. Where an undertaking carrying on the activities referred to in the Annex to Directive 73/239/EEC has financial, commercial or administrative links with an assurance undertaking carrying on the activities covered by this Directive, the competent authorities of the Member States within whose territories the head offices of those undertakings are situated shall ensure that the accounts of the undertakings in question are not distorted by agreements between these undertakings or by any arrangement which could affect the apportionment of expenses and income.

6. Any Member State may require assurance undertakings whose head offices are situated in its territory to cease, within a period to be determined by the Member State concerned, the simultaneous pursuit of activities in which they were engaged on the dates referred to in paragraph 3.

7. The provisions of this Article shall be reviewed on the basis of a report from the Commission to the Council in the light of future harmonisation of the rules on winding-up, and in any case before 31 December 1999.

¶ *This article has been amended by the Annex of Directive 2004/66/EC of 26 April 2004 (OJ L 168, 1.5.2004, 35).*

Article 19

Separation of life assurance and non-life insurance management

1. The separate management referred to in Article 18(3) must be organised in such a way that the activities covered by this Directive are distinct from the activities covered by Directive 73/239/EEC in order that:
— the respective interests of life policy holders and non-life policy holders are not prejudiced and, in particular, that profits from life assurance benefit life policy holders as if the assurance undertaking only carried on the activity of life assurance,
— the minimum financial obligations, in particular solvency margins, in respect of one or other of the two activities, namely an activity under this Directive and an activity under Directive 73/239/EEC, are not borne by the other activity.

However, as long as the minimum financial obligations are fulfilled under the conditions laid down in the second indent of the first subparagraph and, provided the competent authority is informed, the undertaking may use those explicit items of the solvency margin which are still available for one or other activity.

The competent authorities shall analyse the results in both activities so as to ensure that the provisions of this paragraph are complied with.

2. (a) Accounts shall be drawn up in such a manner as to show the sources of the results for each of the two activities, life assurance and non-life insurance. To this end all income (in particular premiums, payments by re-insurers and investment income) and expenditure (in particular insurance settlements, additions to technical provisions, reinsurance premiums, operating expenses in respect of insurance business) shall be broken down according to origin. Items common to both activities shall be entered in accordance with methods of apportionment to be accepted by the competent authority.

(b) Assurance undertakings must, on the basis of the accounts, prepare a statement clearly identifying the items making up each solvency margin, in accordance with Article 27 of this Directive and Article 16(1) of Directive 73/239/EEC.

3. If one of the solvency margins is insufficient, the competent authorities shall apply to the deficient activity the measures provided for in the relevant Directive, whatever the results in the

other activity. By way of derogation from the second indent of the first subparagraph of paragraph 1, these measures may involve the authorisation of a transfer from one activity to the other.

Chapter 2
Rules Relating to Technical Provisions and their Representation

Article 20
Establishment of technical provisions

1. The home Member State shall require every assurance undertaking to establish sufficient technical provisions, including mathematical provisions, in respect of its entire business.

The amount of such technical provisions shall be determined according to the following principles.

A. (i) the amount of the technical life-assurance provisions shall be calculated by a sufficiently prudent prospective actuarial valuation, taking account of all future liabilities as determined by the policy conditions for each existing contract, including:
– all guaranteed benefits, including guaranteed surrender values,
– bonuses to which policy holders are already either collectively or individually entitled, however those bonuses are described—vested, declared or allotted,
– all options available to the policy holder under the terms of the contract,
– expenses, including commissions,

taking credit for future premiums due;

(ii) the use of a retrospective method is allowed, if it can be shown that the resulting technical provisions are not lower than would be required under a sufficiently prudent prospective calculation or if a prospective method cannot be used for the type of contract involved;

(iii) a prudent valuation is not a 'best estimate' valuation, but shall include an appropriate margin for adverse deviation of the relevant factors;

(iv) the method of valuation for the technical provisions must not only be prudent in itself, but must also be so having regard to the method of valuation for the assets covering those provisions;

(v) technical provisions shall be calculated separately for each contract. The use of appropriate approximations or generalisations is allowed, however, where they are likely to give approximately the same result as individual calculations. The principle of separate calculation shall in no way prevent the establishment of additional provisions for general risks which are not individualised;

(vi) where the surrender value of a contract is guaranteed, the amount of the mathematical provisions for the contract at any time shall be at least as great as the value guaranteed at that time;

B. the rate of interest used shall be chosen prudently. It shall be determined in accordance with the rules of the competent authority in the home Member State, applying the following principles:

(a) for all contracts, the competent authority of the assurance undertaking's home Member State shall fix one or more maximum rates of interest, in particular in accordance with the following rules:

(i) when contracts contain an interest rate guarantee, the competent authority in the home Member State shall set a single maximum rate of interest. It may differ according to the currency in which the contract is denominated, provided that it is not more than 60% of the rate on bond issues by the State in whose currency the contract is denominated. If a Member State decides, pursuant to the second sentence of the first subparagraph, to set a maximum rate of interest for contracts denominated in another Member State's currency, it shall first consult the competent authority of the Member State in whose currency the contract is denominated;

(ii) however, when the assets of the assurance undertaking are not valued at their purchase price, a Member State may stipulate that one or more maximum rates may be calculated taking into account the yield on the corresponding assets currently held, minus a prudential margin and, in particular for contracts with periodic premiums, furthermore taking into account the anticipated yield on future assets. The prudential margin and the maximum rate or rates of interest applied to the anticipated yield on future assets shall be fixed by the competent authority of the home Member State;

(b) the establishment of a maximum rate of interest shall not imply that the assurance undertaking is bound to use a rate as high as that;

(c) the home Member State may decide not to apply paragraph (a) to the following categories of contracts:
– unit-linked contracts,
– single-premium contracts for a period of up to eight years,
– without-profits contracts, and annuity contracts with no surrender value.

In the cases referred to in the second and third indents of the first subparagraph, in choosing a prudent rate of interest, account may be taken of the currency in which the contract is denominated and corresponding assets currently held and where the undertaking's assets are valued at their current value, the anticipated yield on future assets.

Under no circumstances may the rate of interest used be higher than the yield on assets as calculated in accordance with the accounting rules in the home Member State, less an appropriate deduction;

(d) the Member State shall require an assurance undertaking to set aside in its accounts a provision to meet interest-rate commitments vis-à-vis policy holders if the present or foreseeable yield on the undertaking's assets is insufficient to cover those commitments;

(e) the Commission and the competent authorities of the Member States which so request shall be notified of the maximum rates of interest set under (a);

C. the statistical elements of the valuation and the allowance for expenses used shall be chosen prudently, having regard to the State of the commitment, the type of policy and the administrative costs and commissions expected to be incurred;

D. in the case of participating contracts, the method of calculation for technical provisions may take into account, either implicitly or explicitly, future bonuses of all kinds, in a manner consistent with the other assumptions on future experience and with the current method of distribution of bonuses;

E. allowance for future expenses may be made implicitly, for instance by the use of future premiums net of management charges. However, the overall allowance, implicit or explicit, shall be not less than a prudent estimate of the relevant future expenses;

F. the method of calculation of technical provisions shall not be subject to discontinuities from year to year arising from arbitrary changes to the method or the bases of calculation and shall be such as to recognise the distribution of profits in an appropriate way over the duration of each policy.

2. Assurance undertakings shall make available to the public the bases and methods used in the calculation of the technical provisions, including provisions for bonuses.

3. The home Member State shall require every assurance undertaking to cover the technical provisions in respect of its entire business by matching assets, in accordance with Article 26. In respect of business written in the Community, these assets must be localised within the Community. Member States shall not require assurance undertakings to localise their assets in a particular Member State. The home Member State may, however, permit relaxations in the rules on the localisation of assets.

[4. Member States shall not retain or introduce for the establishment of technical provisions a system of gross reserving which requires pledging of assets to cover unearned premiums and outstanding claims provisions by the reinsurer, authorised in accordance with Directive 2005/68/EC when the reinsurer is a reinsurance undertaking or an insurance undertaking authorised in accordance with Directive 73/239/EEC or this Directive.

When the home Member State allows any technical provisions to be covered by claims against a reinsurer which is neither a reinsurance undertaking authorised in accordance with Directive 2005/68/EC nor an insurance undertaking authorised in accordance with Directive 73/239/EEC or this Directive, it shall set the conditions for accepting such claims.]

¶ *Paragraph 4 has been replaced by article 60(6) of Directive 2005/68/EC, reproduced infra under no. I. 40. A Member State may postpone the application of the amended provisions until 10 December 2008 (art. 63 of Directive 2005/68/EC).*

Article 21
Premiums for new business

Premiums for new business shall be sufficient, on reasonable actuarial assumptions, to enable assurance undertakings to meet all their commitments and, in particular, to establish adequate technical provisions.

For this purpose, all aspects of the financial situation of an assurance undertaking may be taken into account, without the input from resources other than premiums and income earned thereon being systematic and permanent in such a way that it may jeopardise the undertaking's solvency in the long term.

Article 22
Assets covering technical provisions

The assets covering the technical provisions shall take account of the type of business carried on by an assurance undertaking in such a way as to secure the safety, yield and marketability of its investments, which the undertaking shall ensure are diversified and adequately spread.

Article 23
Categories of authorised assets

1. The home Member State may not authorise assurance undertakings to cover their technical provisions with any but the following categories of assets:

A. investments

(a) debt securities, bonds and other money- and capital-market instruments;

(b) loans;

(c) shares and other variable-yield participations;

(d) units in undertakings for collective investment in transferable securities (UCITS) and other investment funds;

(e) land, buildings and immovable-property rights;

B. debts and claims

[(f) debts owed by reinsurers, including reinsurers' shares of technical provisions, and by special purpose vehicles referred to in Article 46 of Directive 2005/68/EC;]

(g) deposits with and debts owed by ceding undertakings;

(h) debts owed by policy holders and intermediaries arising out of direct and reassurance operations;

(i) advances against policies;

(j) tax recoveries;

(k) claims against guarantee funds;

C. others

(l) tangible fixed assets, other than land and buildings, valued on the basis of prudent amortisation;

(m) cash at bank and in hand, deposits with credit institutions and any other body authorised to receive deposits;

(n) deferred acquisition costs;

(o) accrued interest and rent, other accrued income and prepayments;

(p) reversionary interests.

2. In the case of the association of underwriters known as 'Lloyd's', asset categories shall also include guarantees and letters of credit issued by credit institutions within the meaning of Directive 2000/12/EC of the European Parliament and of the Council[19] or by assurance undertakings, together with verifiable sums arising out of life assurance policies, to the extent that they represent funds belonging to members.

---

[19] OJ L 126, 26.5.2000, 1, reproduced supra under no. B. 32. Directive as amended by Directive 2000/28/EC (OJ L 275, 27.10.2000, 37), reproduced supra under no. B. 34.

3. [The inclusion of any asset or category of assets listed in paragraph 1 shall not mean that all these assets should automatically be accepted as cover for technical provisions. The home Member State shall lay down more detailed rules setting the conditions for the use of acceptable assets.]

In determining and applying the rules which it lays down, the home Member State shall, in particular, ensure that the following principles are complied with:

(i) assets covering technical provisions shall be valued net of any debts arising out of their acquisition;

(ii) all assets must be valued on a prudent basis, allowing for the risk of any amounts not being realisable. In particular, tangible fixed assets other than land and buildings may be accepted as cover for technical provisions only if they are valued on the basis of prudent amortisation;

(iii) loans, whether to undertakings, to a State or international organisation, to local or regional authorities or to natural persons, may be accepted as cover for technical provisions only if there are sufficient guarantees as to their security, whether these are based on the status of the borrower, mortgages, bank guarantees or guarantees granted by assurance undertakings or other forms of security;

(iv) derivative instruments such as options, futures and swaps in connection with assets covering technical provisions may be used in so far as they contribute to a reduction of investment risks or facilitate efficient portfolio management. They must be valued on a prudent basis and may be taken into account in the valuation of the underlying assets;

(v) transferable securities which are not dealt in on a regulated market may be accepted as cover for technical provisions only if they can be realised in the short term or if they are holdings in credit institutions, in assurance undertakings, within the limits permitted by Article 6, or in investment undertakings established in a Member State;

(vi) debts owed by and claims against a third party may be accepted as cover for the technical provisions only after deduction of all amounts owed to the same third party;

(vii) the value of any debts and claims accepted as cover for technical provisions must be calculated on a prudent basis, with due allowance for the risk of any amounts not being realisable. In particular, debts owed by policy holders and intermediaries arising out of assurance and reassurance operations may be accepted only in so far as they have been outstanding for not more than three months;

(viii) where the assets held include an investment in a subsidiary undertaking which manages all or part of the assurance undertaking's investments on its behalf, the home Member State must, when applying the rules and principles laid down in this Article, take into account the underlying assets held by the subsidiary undertaking; the home Member State may treat the assets of other subsidiaries in the same way;

(ix) deferred acquisition costs may be accepted as cover for technical provisions only to the extent that this is consistent with the calculation of the mathematical provisions.

3. Notwithstanding paragraphs 1, 2 and 3, in exceptional circumstances and at an assurance undertaking's request, the home Member State may, temporarily and under a properly reasoned decision, accept other categories of assets as cover for technical provisions, subject to Article 22.

¶ *Litera (f) in paragraph 1(B) and the first subparagraph of paragraph 3 has been replaced by article 60(7) of Directive 2005/68/EC, reproduced infra under no. I. 40.*

Article 24

Rules for investment diversification

1. As regards the assets covering technical provisions, the home Member State shall require every assurance undertaking to invest no more than:

(a) 10% of its total gross technical provisions in any one piece of land or building, or a number of pieces of land or buildings close enough to each other to be considered effectively as one investment;

(b) 5% of its total gross technical provisions in shares and other negotiable securities treated as shares, bonds, debt securities and other money- and capital-market instruments from the same undertaking, or in loans granted to the same borrower, taken together, the loans being loans other than those granted to a State, regional or local authority or to an international organisation of which one or more Member States are members. This limit may be raised to 10% if an undertaking invests not more than 40% of its gross technical provisions in the loans or securities of issuing bodies and borrowers in each of which it invests more than 5% of its assets;

(c) 5% of its total gross technical provisions in unsecured loans, including 1% for any single unsecured loan, other than loans granted to credit institutions, assurance undertakings—in so far as Article 6 allows it—and investment undertakings established in a Member State. The limits may be raised to 8% and 2% respectively by a decision taken on a case-by-case basis by the competent authority of the home Member State;

(d) 3% of its total gross technical provisions in the form of cash in hand;

(e) 10% of its total gross technical provisions in shares, other securities treated as shares and debt securities which are not dealt in on a regulated market.

2. The absence of a limit in paragraph 1 on investment in any particular category does not imply that assets in that category should be accepted as cover for technical provisions without limit. The home Member State shall lay down more detailed rules fixing the conditions for the use of acceptable assets. In particular it shall ensure, in the determination and the application of those rules, that the following principles are complied with:

(i) assets covering technical provisions must be diversified and spread in such a way as to ensure that there is no excessive reliance on any particular category of asset, investment market or investment;

(ii) investment in particular types of asset which show high levels of risk, whether because of the nature of the asset or the quality of the issuer, must be restricted to prudent levels;

(iii) limitations on particular categories of asset must take account of the treatment of reassurance in the calculation of technical provisions;

(iv) where the assets held include an investment in a subsidiary undertaking which manages all or part of the assurance undertaking's investments on its behalf, the home Member State must, when applying the rules and principles laid down in this Article, take into account the underlying assets held by the subsidiary undertaking; the home Member State may treat the assets of other subsidiaries in the same way;

(v) the percentage of assets covering technical provisions which are the subject of non-liquid investments must be kept to a prudent level;

(vi) where the assets held include loans to or debt securities issued by certain credit institutions, the home Member State may, when applying the rules and principles contained in this Article, take into account the underlying assets held by such credit institutions. This treatment may be applied only where the credit institution has its head office in a Member State, is entirely owned by that Member State and/or that State's local authorities and its business, according to its memorandum and articles of association, consists of extending, through its intermediaries, loans to, or guaranteed by, States or local authorities or of loans to bodies closely linked to the State or to local authorities.

3. In the context of the detailed rules laying down the conditions for the use of acceptable assets, the Member State shall give more limitative treatment to:

– any loan unaccompanied by a bank guarantee, a guarantee issued by an assurance undertaking, a mortgage or any other form of security, as compared with loans accompanied by such collateral,

– UCITS not coordinated within the meaning of Directive 85/611/EEC and other investment funds, as compared with UCITS coordinated within the meaning of that Directive,

– securities which are not dealt in on a regulated market, as compared with those which are,

– bonds, debt securities and other money- and capital-market instruments not issued by States, local or regional authorities or undertakings belonging to zone A as defined in Directive 2000/12/EC or the issuers of which are international organisations not numbering at least one Community Member State among their members, as compared with the same financial instruments issued by such bodies.

4. Member States may raise the limit laid down in paragraph 1(b) to 40% in the case of certain debt securities when these are issued by a credit institution which has its head office in a Member State and is subject by law to special official supervision designed to protect the holders of those debt securities. In particular, sums deriving from the issue of such debt securities must be invested in accordance with the law in assets which, during the whole period of validity of the debt securities, are capable of covering claims attaching to debt securities and which, in the event of failure of the issuer, would be used on a priority basis for the reimbursement of the principal and payment of the accrued interest.

5. Member States shall not require assurance undertakings to invest in particular categories of assets.

6. Notwithstanding paragraph 1, in exceptional circumstances and at the assurance undertaking's request, the home Member State may, temporarily and under a properly reasoned decision, allow exceptions to the rules laid down in paragraph 1(a) to (e), subject to Article 22.

Article 25

Contracts linked to UCITS or share index

1. Where the benefits provided by a contract are directly linked to the value of units in an UCITS or to the value of assets contained in an internal fund held by the insurance undertaking, usually divided into units, the technical provisions in respect of those benefits must be represented as closely as possible by those units or, in the case where units are not established, by those assets.

2. Where the benefits provided by a contract are directly linked to a share index or some other reference value other than those referred to in paragraph 1, the technical provisions in respect of those benefits must be represented as closely as possible either by the units deemed to represent the reference value or, in the case where units are not established, by assets of appropriate security and marketability which correspond as closely as possible with those on which the particular reference value is based.

3. Articles 22 and 24 shall not apply to assets held to match liabilities which are directly linked to the benefits referred to in paragraphs 1 and 2. References to the technical provisions in Article 24 shall be to the technical provisions excluding those in respect of such liabilities.

4. Where the benefits referred to in paragraphs 1 and 2 include a guarantee of investment performance or some other guaranteed benefit, the corresponding additional technical provisions shall be subject to Articles 22, 23, and 24.

Article 26

Matching rules

1. For the purposes of Articles 20(3) and 54, Member States shall comply with Annex II as regards the matching rules.

2. This Article shall not apply to the commitments referred to in Article 25.

CHAPTER 3

RULES RELATING TO THE SOLVENCY MARGIN AND TO THE GUARANTEE FUND

Article 27

Available solvency margin

1. Each Member State shall require of every assurance undertaking whose head office is situated in its territory an adequate available solvency margin in respect of its entire business at all times which is at least equal to the requirements in this Directive.

2. The available solvency margin shall consist of the assets of the assurance undertaking free of any

foreseeable liabilities, less any intangible items, including:

(a) the paid-up share capital or, in the case of a mutual assurance undertaking, the effective initial fund plus any members' accounts which meet all the following criteria:

  (i) the memorandum and articles of association must stipulate that payments may be made from these accounts to members only in so far as this does not cause the available solvency margin to fall below the required level, or, after the dissolution of the undertaking, if all the undertaking's other debts have been settled;

  (ii) the memorandum and articles of association must stipulate, with respect to any payments referred to in point (i) for reasons other than the individual termination of membership, that the competent authorities must be notified at least one month in advance and can prohibit the payment within that period;

  (iii) the relevant provisions of the memorandum and articles of association may be amended only after the competent authorities have declared that they have no objection to the amendment, without prejudice to the criteria stated in points (i) and (ii);

(b) reserves (statutory and free) not corresponding to underwriting liabilities;

(c) the profit or loss brought forward after deduction of dividends to be paid;

(d) in so far as authorised under national law, profit reserves appearing in the balance sheet where they may be used to cover any losses which may arise and where they have not been made available for distribution to policy holders.

The available solvency margin shall be reduced by the amount of own shares directly held by the assurance undertaking.

[The available solvency margin shall also be reduced by the following items

(a) participations which the assurance undertaking holds, in:
– insurance undertakings within the meaning of Article 4 of this Directive, Article 6 of Directive 73/239/EEC, or Article 1(b) of Directive 98/78/EC of the European Parliament and of the Council of 27 October 1998 on the supplementary supervision of insurance undertakings in an insurance group,[20]
– reinsurance undertakings within the meaning of Article 3 of Directive 2005/68/EC or a non-member country reinsurance undertakings within the meaning of Article 1(l) of Directive 98/78/EC,
– insurance holding companies within the meaning of Article 1(i) of Directive 98/78/EC,
– credit institutions and financial institutions within the meaning of Article 1(1) and (5) of Directive 2000/12/EC of the European Parliament and of the Council of 20 March 2000 relating to the taking up and pursuit of the business of credit institutions,[21]
– investment firms and financial institutions within the meaning of Article 1(2) of Council Directive 93/22/EEC of 10 May 1993 on investment services in the securities field[22] and of Articles 2(4) and 2(7) of Council Directive 93/6/EEC of 15 March 1993 on the capital adequacy of investments firms and credit institutions;[23]

(b) each of the following items which the assurance undertaking holds in respect of the entities defined in point (a) in which it holds a participation:
– instruments referred to in paragraph 3,
– instruments referred to in Article 16(3) of Directive 73/239/EEC,
– subordinated claims and instruments referred to in Article 35 and Article 36(3) of Directive 2000/12/EC.

Where shares in another credit institution, investment firm, financial institution, insurance or reinsurance undertaking or insurance holding

---

[20] OJ L 330, 5.12.1998, 1, reproduced supra under no. I. 28. Directive as last amended by Directive 2005/1/EC (OJ L 79, 24.3.2005, 9), reproduced supra under no. B. 39.
[21] OJ L 126, 26.5.2000, 1, reproduced supra under no. B. 32. Directive as last amended by Directive 2005/1/EC, reproduced supra under no. B. 39.
[22] OJ L 141, 11.6.1993, 27, reproduced infra under no. S. 14. Directive as last amended by Directive 2002/87/EC (OJ L 35, 11.2.2003, 1), reproduced supra under no. B. 38.
[23] OJ L 141, 11.6.1993, 1, reproduced infra under no. S. 14. Directive as last amended by Directive 2005/1/EC, reproduced supra under no. B. 39.

company are held temporarily for the purposes of a financial assistance operation designed to reorganise and save that entity, the competent authority may waive the provisions on deduction referred to in points (a) and (b) of the third subparagraph.

As an alternative to the deduction of the items referred to in (a) and (b) of the third subparagraph which the insurance undertaking holds in credit institutions, investment firms and financial institutions, Member States may allow their insurance undertakings to apply mutatis mutandis methods 1, 2, or 3 of Annex I to Directive 2002/87/EC of the European Parliament and of the Council of 16 December 2002 on the supplementary supervision of credit institutions, insurance undertakings and investment firms in a financial conglomerate.[24] Method 1 (Accounting consolidation) shall only be applied if the competent authority is confident about the level of integrated management and internal control regarding the entities which would be included in the scope of consolidation. The method chosen shall be applied in a consistent manner over time.

Member States may provide that, for the calculation of the solvency margin as provided for by this Directive, insurance undertakings subject to supplementary supervision in accordance with Directive 98/78/EC or to supplementary supervision in accordance with Directive 2002/87/EC, need not deduct the items referred to in (a) and (b) of the third subparagraph of this Article which are held in credit institutions, investment firms, financial institutions, insurance or reinsurance undertakings or insurance holding companies which are included in the supplementary supervision. For the purposes of the deduction of participations referred to in this paragraph, participation shall mean a participation within the meaning of Article 1(f) of Directive 98/78/EC.]

3. The available solvency margin may also consist of:

(a) cumulative preferential share capital and subordinated loan capital up to 50% of the lesser of the available solvency margin and the required solvency margin, no more than 25% of which shall consist of subordinated loans with a fixed maturity, or fixed-term cumulative preferential share capital, provided that binding agreements exist under which, in the event of the bankruptcy or liquidation of the assurance undertaking, the subordinated loan capital or preferential share capital ranks after the claims of all other creditors and is not to be repaid until all other debts outstanding at the time have been settled.

Subordinated loan capital must also fulfil the following conditions:

(i) only fully paid-up funds may be taken into account;

(ii) for loans with a fixed maturity, the original maturity must be at least five years. No later than one year before the repayment date, the assurance undertaking must submit to the competent authorities for their approval a plan showing how the available solvency margin will be kept at or brought to the required level at maturity, unless the extent to which the loan may rank as a component of the available solvency margin is gradually reduced during at least the last five years before the repayment date. The competent authorities may authorise the early repayment of such loans provided application is made by the issuing assurance undertaking and its available solvency margin will not fall below the required level;

(iii) loans the maturity of which is not fixed must be repayable only subject to five years' notice unless the loans are no longer considered as a component of the available solvency margin or unless the prior consent of the competent authorities is specifically required for early repayment. In the latter event the assurance undertaking must notify the competent authorities at least six months before the date of the proposed repayment, specifying the available solvency margin and the required solvency margin both before and after that repayment. The competent authorities shall authorise repayment only if the assurance undertaking's available solvency margin will not fall below the required level;

---

[24] OJ L 35, 11.2.2003, 1, reproduced supra under no. B. 38. Directive as last amended by Directive 2005/1/EC, reproduced supra under no. B. 39.

(iv) the loan agreement must not include any clause providing that in specified circumstances, other than the winding-up of the assurance undertaking, the debt will become repayable before the agreed repayment dates;

(v) the loan agreement may be amended only after the competent authorities have declared that they have no objection to the amendment;

(b) securities with no specified maturity date and other instruments, including cumulative preferential shares other than those mentioned in point (a), up to 50% of the lesser of the available solvency margin and the required solvency margin for the total of such securities and the subordinated loan capital referred to in point (a) provided they fulfil the following:

(i) they may not be repaid on the initiative of the bearer or without the prior consent of the competent authority;

(ii) the contract of issue must enable the assurance undertaking to defer the payment of interest on the loan;

(iii) the lender's claims on the assurance undertaking must rank entirely after those of all non-subordinated creditors;

(iv) the documents governing the issue of the securities must provide for the loss-absorption capacity of the debt and unpaid interest, while enabling the assurance undertaking to continue its business;

(v) only fully paid-up amounts may be taken into account.

4. Upon application, with supporting evidence, by the undertaking to the competent authority of the home Member State and with the agreement of that competent authority, the available solvency margin may also consist of:

(a) until 31 December 2009 an amount equal to 50% of the undertaking's future profits, but not exceeding 25% of the lesser of the available solvency margin and the required solvency margin. The amount of the future profits shall be obtained by multiplying the estimated annual profit by a factor which represents the average period left to run on policies. The factor used may not exceed six. The estimated annual profit shall not exceed the arithmetical average of the profits made over the last five financial years in the activities listed in Article 2(1).

Competent authorities may only agree to include such an amount for the available solvency margin:

(i) when an actuarial report is submitted to the competent authorities substantiating the likelihood of emergence of these profits in the future; and

(ii) in so far as that part of future profits emerging from hidden net reserves referred to in point (c) has not already been taken into account;

(b) where Zillmerising is not practised or where, if practised, it is less than the loading for acquisition costs included in the premium, the difference between a non-Zillmerised or partially Zillmerised mathematical provision and a mathematical provision Zillmerised at a rate equal to the loading for acquisition costs included in the premium. This figure may not, however, exceed 3,5% of the sum of the differences between the relevant capital sums of life assurance activities and the mathematical provisions for all policies for which Zillmerising is possible. The difference shall be reduced by the amount of any undepreciated acquisition costs entered as an asset;

(c) any hidden net reserves arising out of the valuation of assets, in so far as such hidden net reserves are not of an exceptional nature;

(d) one half of the unpaid share capital or initial fund, once the paid-up part amounts to 25% of that share capital or fund, up to 50% of the lesser of the available and required solvency margin.

5. Amendments to paragraphs 2, 3 and 4 to take into account developments that justify a technical adjustment of the elements eligible for the available solvency margin shall be adopted in accordance with the procedure laid down in Article 65(2).

¶ *Subparagraphs 3 and following of article 27(2) have been added by article 60(8) of Directive 2005/68/EC, reproduced infra under no. I. 40.*

Article 28
Required solvency margin

1. Subject to Article 29, the required solvency margin shall be determined as laid down in paragraphs 2 to 7 according to the classes of assurance underwritten.

2. For the kinds of assurance referred to in Article 2(1)(a) and (b) other than assurances linked to investment funds and for the operations referred to in Article 2(3), the required solvency margin shall be equal to the sum of the following two results:

[(a) first result:

a 4% fraction of the mathematical provisions relating to direct business and reinsurance acceptances gross of reinsurance cessions shall be multiplied by the ratio, for the last financial year, of the total mathematical provisions net of reinsurance cessions to the gross total mathematical provisions. That ratio may in no case be less than 85%. Upon application, with supporting evidence, by the insurance undertaking to the competent authority of the home Member State and with agreement of that authority, amounts recoverable from the special purpose vehicles referred to in Article 46 of Directive 2005/68/EC may be deducted as reassurance];

[(b) second result:

for policies on which the capital at risk is not a negative figure, a 0.3% fraction of such capital underwritten by the assurance undertaking shall be multiplied by the ratio, for the last financial year, of the total capital at risk retained as the undertaking's liability after reinsurance cessions and retrocessions to the total capital at risk gross of reinsurance; that ratio may in no case be less than 50%. Upon application, with supporting evidence, by the insurance undertaking to the competent authority of the home Member State and with agreement of that authority, amounts recoverable from the special purpose vehicles referred to in Article 46 of Directive 2005/68/EC may be deducted as reassurance.]

For temporary assurance on death of a maximum term of three years the fraction shall be 0,1%. For such assurance of a term of more than three years but not more than five years the above fraction shall be 0,15%.

3. For the supplementary insurance referred to in Article 2(1)(c) the required solvency margin shall be equal to the required solvency margin for insurance undertakings as laid down in Article 16a of Directive 73/239/EEC, excluding the provisions of Article 17 of that Directive.

4. For permanent health insurance not subject to cancellation referred to in Article 2(1)(d), the required solvency margin shall be equal to:

(a) a 4% fraction of the mathematical provisions, calculated in compliance with paragraph 2(a) of this Article; plus

(b) the required solvency margin for insurance undertakings as laid down in Article 16a of Directive 73/239/EEC, excluding the provisions of Article 17 of that Directive. However, the condition contained in Article 16a(6)(b) of that Directive that a provision be set up for increasing age may be replaced by a requirement that the business be conducted on a group basis.

5. For capital redemption operations referred to in Article 2(2)(b), the required solvency margin shall be equal to a 4% fraction of the mathematical provisions calculated in compliance with paragraph 2(a) of this Article.

6. For tontines, referred to in Article 2(2)(a), the required solvency margin shall be equal to 1% of their assets.

7. For assurances covered by Article 2(1)(a) and (b) linked to investment funds and for the operations referred to in Article 2(2)(c), (d) and (e), the required solvency margin shall be equal to the sum of the following:

(a) in so far as the assurance undertaking bears an investment risk, a 4% fraction of the technical provisions, calculated in compliance with paragraph 2(a) of this Article;

(b) in so far as the undertaking bears no investment risk but the allocation to cover management expenses is fixed for a period exceeding five years, a 1% fraction of the technical provisions, calculated in compliance with paragraph 2(a) of this Article;

(c) in so far as the undertaking bears no investment risk and the allocation to cover management expenses is not fixed for a period exceeding five years, an amount equivalent to 25% of the last financial year's net administrative expenses pertaining to such business;

(d) in so far as the assurance undertaking covers a death risk, a 0.3% fraction of the capital at risk calculated in compliance with paragraph 2(b) of this Article.

¶ *Article 28(2)(a) and the first subparagraph of point (b) has been replaced by article 60(9) of Directive 2005/68/EC, reproduced infra under no. I. 40.*

[Article 28a

Solvency margin for assurance undertakings conducting reinsurance activities

1. Each Member State shall apply to insurance undertakings whose head office is situated within its territory, the provisions of Articles 35 to 39 of Directive 2005/68/EC in respect of their reinsurance acceptance activities, where one of the following conditions is met:

(a) the reinsurance premiums collected exceed 10% of their total premium;

(b) the reinsurance premiums collected exceed EUR 50,000,000;

(c) the technical provisions resulting from their reinsurance acceptances exceed 10% of their total technical provisions.

2. Each Member State may choose to apply to assurance undertakings referred to in paragraph 1 of this Article and whose head office is situated within its territory the provisions of Article 34 of Directive 2005/68/EC in respect of their reinsurance acceptance activities, where one of the conditions laid down in the said paragraph 1 is met.

In that case, the respective Member State shall require that all assets employed by the assurance undertaking to cover the technical provisions corresponding to its reinsurance acceptances shall be ring-fenced, managed and organised separately from the direct assurance activities of the assurance undertaking, without any possibility of transfer. In such a case, and only as far as their reinsurance acceptance activities are concerned, assurance undertakings shall not be subject to Articles 22 to 26.

Each Member State shall ensure that their competent authorities verify the separation provided for in the second subparagraph.]

¶ *Article 28a has been inserted by article 60(10) of Directive 2005/68/EC, reproduced infra under no. I. 40.*

Article 29

Guarantee fund

1. One third of the required solvency margin as specified in Article 28 shall constitute the guarantee fund. This fund shall consist of the items listed in Article 27(2), (3) and, with the agreement of the competent authority of the home Member State, (4)(c).

2. The guarantee fund may not be less than a minimum of EUR 3 million.

Any Member State may provide for a one-fourth reduction of the minimum guarantee fund in the case of mutual associations and mutual-type associations and tontines.

Article 30

Review of the amount of the guarantee fund

1. The amount in euro as laid down in Article 29(2) shall be reviewed annually starting on 20 September 2003, in order to take account of changes in the European index of consumer prices comprising all Member States as published by Eurostat.

The amount shall be adapted automatically, by increasing the base amount in euro by the percentage change in that index over the period between 20 March 2002 and the review date and rounded up to a multiple of EUR 100,000.

If the percentage change since the last adaptation is less than 5%, no adaptation shall take place.

2. The Commission shall inform annually the European Parliament and the Council of the review and the adapted amount referred to in paragraph 1.

Article 31
Assets not used to cover technical provisions

1. Member States shall not prescribe any rules as to the choice of the assets that need not be used as cover for the technical provisions referred to in Article 20.

2. Subject to Article 20(3), Article 37(1), (2), (3) and (5), and the second subparagraph of Article 39(1), Member States shall not restrain the free disposal of those assets, whether movable or immovable, that form part of the assets of authorised assurance undertakings.

3. Paragraphs 1 and 2 shall not preclude any measures which Member States, while safeguarding the interests of the lives assured, are entitled to take as owners or members of or partners in the assurance undertakings in question.

CASE

Case C-241/97 Försäkringsaktiebolaget Skandia (publ.) [1999] ECR I-1879

See supra under article 18 of Directive 73/239/EEC reproduced under no. I. 3.

CHAPTER 4
CONTRACT LAW AND CONDITIONS OF ASSURANCE

Article 32
Law applicable

1. The law applicable to contracts relating to the activities referred to in this Directive shall be the law of the Member State of the commitment. However, where the law of that State so allows, the parties may choose the law of another country.

2. Where the policy holder is a natural person and has his/her habitual residence in a Member State other than that of which he/she is a national, the parties may choose the law of the Member State of which he/she is a national.

3. Where a State includes several territorial units, each of which has its own rules of law concerning contractual obligations, each unit shall be considered a country for the purposes of identifying the law applicable under this Directive.

A Member State in which various territorial units have their own rules of law concerning contractual obligations shall not be bound to apply the provisions of this Directive to conflicts which arise between the laws of those units.

4. Nothing in this Article shall restrict the application of the rules of the law of the forum in a situation where they are mandatory, irrespective of the law otherwise applicable to the contract.

If the law of a Member State so stipulates, the mandatory rules of the law of the Member State of the commitment may be applied if and in so far as, under the law of that Member State, those rules must be applied whatever the law applicable to the contract.

5. Subject to paragraphs 1 to 4, the Member States shall apply to the assurance contracts referred to in this Directive their general rules of private international law concerning contractual obligations.

Article 33
General good

The Member State of the commitment shall not prevent a policy holder from concluding a contract with an assurance undertaking authorised under the conditions of Article 4 as long as that does not conflict with legal provisions protecting the general good in the Member State of the commitment.

Article 34
Rules relating to conditions of assurance and scales of premiums

Member States shall not adopt provisions requiring the prior approval or systematic notification of general and special policy conditions, scales of premiums, technical bases used in particular for calculating scales of premiums and technical provisions or forms and other printed documents which an assurance undertaking intends to use in its dealings with policy holders.

Notwithstanding the first subparagraph, for the sole purpose of verifying compliance with national provisions concerning actuarial principles, the home Member State may require systematic communication of the technical bases used in particular for calculating scales of premiums and technical provisions, without that requirement constituting a prior condition for an assurance undertaking to carry on its business.

Not later than 1 July 1999 the Commission shall submit a report to the Council on the implementation of those provisions.

Article 35

Cancellation period

1. Each Member State shall prescribe that a policy holder who concludes an individual life-assurance contract shall have a period of between 14 and 30 days from the time when he/she was informed that the contract had been concluded within which to cancel the contract.

The giving of notice of cancellation by the policy holder shall have the effect of releasing him/her from any future obligation arising from the contract.

The other legal effects and the conditions of cancellation shall be determined by the law applicable to the contract as defined in Article 32, notably as regards the arrangements for informing the policy holder that the contract has been concluded.

2. The Member States need not apply paragraph 1 to contracts of six months' duration or less, nor where, because of the status of the policy holder or the circumstances in which the contract is concluded, the policy holder does not need this special protection. Member States shall specify in their rules where paragraph 1 is not applied.

Article 36

Information for policy holders

1. Before the assurance contract is concluded, at least the information listed in Annex III(A) shall be communicated to the policy holder.

2. The policy holder shall be kept informed throughout the term of the contract of any change concerning the information listed in Annex III(B).

3. The Member State of the commitment may require assurance undertakings to furnish information in addition to that listed in Annex III only if it is necessary for a proper understanding by the policy holder of the essential elements of the commitment.

4. The detailed rules for implementing this Article and Annex III shall be laid down by the Member State of the commitment.

LEADING CASE AND COMMENTARY

Case C-386/00 Axa Royale Belge SA v Georges Ochoa and Stratégie Finance SPRL [2002] ECR I-2209

Article 31(3) of Council Directive 92/96/EEC of 10 November 1992 precludes national legislation which provides that a life-assurance proposal, or in the absence of a proposal, a life-assurance policy must inform the policy-holder that cancellation, reduction, or surrender of an existing life-assurance contract for the purpose of subscribing to another life-assurance policy is generally detrimental to the policy-holder.

Chapter 5

Assurance Undertakings in Difficulty or in an Irregular Situation

Article 37

Assurance undertakings in difficulty

1. If an assurance undertaking does not comply with Article 20, the competent authority of its home Member State may prohibit the free disposal of its assets after having communicated its intention to the competent authorities of the Member States of commitment.

2. For the purposes of restoring the financial situation of an assurance undertaking, the solvency margin of which has fallen below the minimum

required under Article 28, the competent authority of the home Member State shall require that a plan for the restoration of a sound financial position be submitted for its approval.

In exceptional circumstances, if the competent authority is of the opinion that the financial situation of the assurance undertaking will further deteriorate, it may also restrict or prohibit the free disposal of the assurance undertaking's assets. It shall inform the authorities of other Member States within the territories of which the assurance undertaking carries on business of any measures it has taken and the latter shall, at the request of the former, take the same measures.

3. If the solvency margin falls below the guarantee fund as defined in Article 29, the competent authority of the home Member State shall require the assurance undertaking to submit a short-term finance scheme for its approval.

It may also restrict or prohibit the free disposal of the assurance undertaking's assets. It shall inform the authorities of other Member States within the territories of which the assurance undertaking carries on business accordingly and the latter shall, at the request of the former, take the same measures.

[4. Member States shall ensure that the competent authorities have the power to decrease the reduction, based on reinsurance, to the solvency margin as determined in accordance with Article 28 where:

(a) the nature or quality of reinsurance contracts has changed significantly since the last financial year;

(b) there is no, or a limited, risk transfer under the reinsurance contracts.]

5. Each Member State shall take the measures necessary to be able in accordance with its national law to prohibit the free disposal of assets located within its territory at the request, in the cases provided for in paragraphs 1, 2 and 3, of the assurance undertaking's home Member State, which shall designate the assets to be covered by such measures.

¶ *Point 4 has been replaced by article 60(11) of Directive 2005/68/EC, reproduced infra under no. I. 40.*

Article 38
Financial recovery plan

1. Member States shall ensure that the competent authorities have the power to require a financial recovery plan for those insurance undertakings where competent authorities consider that policy holders' rights are threatened. The financial recovery plan must as a minimum include particulars or proof concerning for the next three financial years:

(a) estimates of management expenses, in particular current general expenses and commissions;

(b) a plan setting out detailed estimates of income and expenditure in respect of direct business, reinsurance acceptances and reinsurance cessions;

(c) a forecast balance sheet;

(d) estimates of the financial resources intended to cover underwriting liabilities and the required solvency margin;

(e) the overall reinsurance policy.

2. Where policy holders' rights are threatened because the financial position of the undertaking is deteriorating, Member States shall ensure that the competent authorities have the power to oblige insurance undertakings to have a higher required solvency margin, in order to ensure that the insurance undertaking is able to fulfil the solvency requirements in the near future. The level of this higher required solvency margin shall be based on a financial recovery plan referred to in paragraph 1.

3. Member States shall ensure that the competent authorities have the power to revalue downwards all elements eligible for the available solvency margin, in particular, where there has been a significant change in the market value of these elements since the end of the last financial year.

4. Member States shall ensure that the competent authorities have the powers to decrease the reduction, based on reinsurance, to the solvency margin as determined in accordance with Article 28 where:

(a) the nature or quality of reinsurance contracts has changed significantly since the last financial year;

(b) there is no or an insignificant risk transfer under the reinsurance contracts.

5. If the competent authorities have required a financial recovery plan for the insurance undertaking in accordance with paragraph 1, they shall refrain from issuing a certificate in accordance with Article 14(1), Article 40(3), second subparagraph, and Article 42(1)(a), as long as they consider that policy holders' rights are threatened within the meaning of paragraph 1.

Article 39
Withdrawal of authorisation

1. Authorisation granted to an assurance undertaking by the competent authority of its home Member State may be withdrawn by that authority if that undertaking:

(a) does not make use of the authorisation within 12 months, expressly renounces it or ceases to carry on business for more than six months, unless the Member State concerned has made provision for authorisation to lapse in such cases;

(b) no longer fulfils the conditions for admission;

(c) has been unable, within the time allowed, to take the measures specified in the restoration plan or finance scheme referred to in Article 37;

(d) fails seriously in its obligations under the regulations to which it is subject.

In the event of the withdrawal or lapse of the authorisation, the competent authority of the home Member State shall notify the competent authorities of the other Member States accordingly and they shall take appropriate measures to prevent the assurance undertaking from commencing new operations within their territories, under either the freedom of establishment or the freedom to provide services. The home Member State's competent authority shall, in conjunction with those authorities, take all necessary measures to safeguard the interests of the assured persons and shall restrict, in particular, the free disposal of the assets of the assurance undertaking in accordance with Article 37(1), (2), second subparagraph, and (3), second subparagraph.

2. Any decision to withdraw an authorisation shall be supported by precise reasons and notified to the assurance undertaking in question.

Title IV
Provisions Relating to Right of Establishment and Freedom to Provide Services

Article 40
Conditions for branch establishment

1. An assurance undertaking that proposes to establish a branch within the territory of another Member State shall notify the competent authorities of its home Member State.

2. The Member States shall require every assurance undertaking that proposes to establish a branch within the territory of another Member State to provide the following information when effecting the notification provided for in paragraph 1:

(a) the Member State within the territory of which it proposes to establish a branch;

(b) a scheme of operations setting out, inter alia, the types of business envisaged and the structural organisation of the branch;

(c) the address in the Member State of the branch from which documents may be obtained and to which they may be delivered, it being understood that that address shall be the one to which all communications to the authorised agent are sent;

(d) the name of the branch's authorised agent, who must possess sufficient powers to bind the assurance undertaking in relation to third parties and to represent it in relations with the authorities and courts of the Member State of the branch. With regard to Lloyd's, in the event of any litigation in the Member State of the branch arising out of underwritten commitments, the assured persons must not be treated less favourably than if the litigation had been brought against businesses of a conventional type. The authorised agent must, therefore, possess sufficient powers for proceedings to be taken against him and must in that capacity be able to bind the Lloyd's underwriters concerned.

3. Unless the competent authorities of the home Member State have reason to doubt the adequacy of the administrative structure or the financial situation of the assurance undertaking or the good repute and professional qualification or experience of the directors or managers or the authorised agent, taking into account the business planned, they shall, within three months of receiving all the information referred to in paragraph 2, communicate that information to the competent authorities of the Member State of the branch and shall inform the undertaking concerned accordingly.

The competent authorities of the home Member State shall also attest that the assurance undertaking has the minimum solvency margin calculated in accordance with Articles 28 and 29.

Where the competent authorities of the home Member State refuse to communicate the information referred to in paragraph 2 to the competent authorities of the Member State of the branch, they shall give the reasons for their refusal to the assurance undertaking concerned within three months of receiving all the information in question. That refusal or failure to act shall be subject to a right to apply to the courts in the home Member State.

4. Before the branch of an assurance undertaking starts business, the competent authorities of the Member State of the branch shall, within two months of receiving the information referred to in paragraph 3, inform the competent authority of the home Member State, if appropriate, of the conditions under which, in the interest of the general good, that business must be carried on in the Member State of the branch.

5. On receiving a communication from the competent authorities of the Member State of the branch or, if no communication is received from them, on expiry of the period provided for in paragraph 4, the branch may be established and start business.

6. In the event of a change in any of the particulars communicated under paragraph 2(b), (c) or (d), an assurance undertaking shall give written notice of the change to the competent authorities of the home Member State and of the Member State of the branch at least one month before making the change so that the competent authorities of the home Member State and the competent authorities of the Member State of the branch may fulfil their respective roles under paragraphs 3 and 4.

Article 41

Freedom to provide services: prior notification to the home Member State

Any assurance undertaking that intends to carry on business for the first time in one or more Member States under the freedom to provide services shall first inform the competent authorities of the home Member State, indicating the nature of the commitments it proposes to cover.

Article 42

Freedom to provide services: notification by the home Member State

1. Within one month of the notification provided for in Article 41, the competent authorities of the home Member State shall communicate to the Member State or Member States within the territory of which the assurance undertaking intends to carry on business by way of the freedom to provide services:

(a) a certificate attesting that the assurance undertaking has the minimum solvency margin calculated in accordance with Articles 28 and 29;

(b) the classes which the assurance undertaking has been authorised to offer;

(c) the nature of the commitments which the assurance undertaking proposes to cover in the Member State of the provision of services.

At the same time, they shall inform the assurance undertaking concerned accordingly.

2. Where the competent authorities of the home Member State do not communicate the information referred to in paragraph 1 within the period laid down, they shall give the reasons for their

refusal to the assurance undertaking within that same period. The refusal shall be subject to a right to apply to the courts in the home Member State.

3. The assurance undertaking may start business on the certified date on which it is informed of the communication provided for in the first subparagraph of paragraph 1.

Article 43
Freedom to provide services: changes in the nature of commitments

Any change which an assurance undertaking intends to make to the information referred to in Article 41 shall be subject to the procedure provided for in Articles 41 and 42.

Article 44
Language

The competent authorities of the Member State of the branch or the Member State of the provision of services may require that the information which they are authorised under this Directive to request with regard to the business of assurance undertakings operating in the territory of that State shall be supplied to them in the official language or languages of that State.

Article 45
Rules relating to conditions of assurance and scales of premiums

The Member State of the branch or of the provision of services shall not lay down provisions requiring the prior approval or systematic notification of general and special policy conditions, scales of premiums, technical bases used in particular for calculating scales of premiums and technical provisions, forms and other printed documents which an assurance undertaking intends to use in its dealings with policy holders. For the purpose of verifying compliance with national provisions concerning assurance contracts, it may require an assurance undertaking that proposes to carry on assurance business within its territory, under the right of establishment or the freedom to provide services, to effect only non-systematic notification of those policy conditions and other printed documents without that requirement constituting a prior condition for an assurance undertaking to carry on its business.

Article 46
Assurance undertakings not complying with the legal provisions

1. Any assurance undertaking carrying on business under the right of establishment or the freedom to provide services shall submit to the competent authorities of the Member State of the branch and/or of the Member State of the provision of services all documents requested of it for the purposes of this Article in so far as assurance undertakings the head office of which is in those Member States are also obliged to do so.

2. If the competent authorities of a Member State establish that an assurance undertaking with a branch or carrying on business under the freedom to provide services in its territory is not complying with the legal provisions applicable to it in that State, they shall require the assurance undertaking concerned to remedy that irregular situation.

3. If the assurance undertaking in question fails to take the necessary action, the competent authorities of the Member State concerned shall inform the competent authorities of the home Member State accordingly. The latter authorities shall, at the earliest opportunity, take all appropriate measures to ensure that the assurance undertaking concerned remedies that irregular situation. The nature of those measures shall be communicated to the competent authorities of the Member State concerned.

4. If, despite the measures taken by the home Member State or because those measures prove inadequate or are lacking in that State, the assurance undertaking persists in violating the legal provisions in force in the Member State concerned, the latter may, after informing the competent authorities of the home Member State, take appropriate measures to prevent or penalise further irregularities, including, in so far as is strictly necessary, preventing that undertaking from continuing to conclude new assurance contracts within its territory. Member States

shall ensure that in their territories it is possible to serve the legal documents necessary for such measures on assurance undertakings.

5. Paragraphs 2, 3 and 4 shall not affect the emergency power of the Member States concerned to take appropriate measures to prevent or penalise irregularities committed within their territories. This shall include the possibility of preventing assurance undertakings from continuing to conclude new assurance contracts within their territories.

6. Paragraphs 2, 3 and 4 shall not affect the power of the Member States to penalise infringements within their territories.

7. If an assurance undertaking which has committed an infringement has an establishment or possesses property in the Member State concerned, the competent authorities of the latter may, in accordance with national law, apply the administrative penalties prescribed for that infringement by way of enforcement against that establishment or property.

8. Any measure adopted under paragraphs 3 to 7 involving penalties or restrictions on the conduct of assurance business must be properly reasoned and communicated to the assurance undertaking concerned.

[9. Every two years, the Commission shall inform the European Insurance and Occupational Pensions Committee of the number and type of cases in which, in each Member State, authorisation has been refused pursuant to Articles 40 or 42 or measures have been taken under paragraph 4 of this Article. Member States shall cooperate with the Commission by providing it with the information required for that report.]

¶ *Article 46(9) has been amended by article 8(1) of Directive 2005/1/EC, reproduced supra under no. B. 39.*

Article 47
Advertising

Nothing in this Directive shall prevent assurance undertakings with head offices in other Member States from advertising their services through all available means of communication in the Member State of the branch or Member State of the provision of services, subject to any rules governing the form and content of such advertising adopted in the interest of the general good.

Article 48
Winding up

Should an assurance undertaking be wound up, commitments arising out of contracts underwritten through a branch or under the freedom to provide services shall be met in the same way as those arising out of that undertaking's other assurance contracts, without distinction as to nationality as far as the lives assured and the beneficiaries are concerned.

Article 49
Statistical information on cross-border activities

Every assurance undertaking shall inform the competent authority of its home Member State, separately in respect of transactions carried out under the right of establishment and those carried out under the freedom to provide services, of the amount of the premiums, without deduction of reassurance, by Member State and by each of classes I to IX, as defined in Annex I.

The competent authority of the home Member State shall, within a reasonable time and on an aggregate basis forward this information to the competent authorities of each of the Member States concerned which so requests.

Article 50
Taxes on premiums

1. Without prejudice to any subsequent harmonisation, every assurance contract shall be subject exclusively to the indirect taxes and parafiscal charges on assurance premiums in the Member State of the commitment, and also, with regard to Spain, to the surcharges legally established in favour of the Spanish 'Consorcio de Compensación de Seguros' for the performance of its functions relating to the compensation of losses arising from extraordinary events occurring in that Member State.

2. The law applicable to the contract pursuant to Article 32 shall not affect the fiscal arrangements applicable.

3. Pending future harmonisation, each Member State shall apply to those assurance undertakings which cover commitments situated within its territory its own national provisions for measures to ensure the collection of indirect taxes and parafiscal charges due under paragraph 1.

Title V

Rules Applicable to Agencies or Branches Established within the Community and Belonging to Undertakings Whose Head Offices are Outside the Community

Article 51

Principles and conditions of authorisation

1. Each Member State shall make access to the activities referred to in Article 2 by any undertaking whose head office is outside the Community subject to an official authorisation.

2. A Member State may grant an authorisation if the undertaking fulfils at least the following conditions:

(a) it is entitled to undertake insurance activities covered by Article 2 under its national law;

(b) it establishes an agency or branch in the territory of such Member State;

(c) it undertakes to establish at the place of management of the agency or branch accounts specific to the activity which it carries on there and to keep there all the records relating to the business transacted;

(d) it designates a general representative, to be approved by the competent authorities;

(e) it possesses in the Member State where it carries on an activity assets of an amount equal in value to at least one half of the minimum amount prescribed in Article 29(2), first sub-paragraph, in respect of the guarantee fund and deposits one quarter of the minimum amount as security;

(f) it undertakes to keep a solvency margin complying with Article 55;

(g) it submits a scheme of operations in accordance with the provisions of paragraph 3.

3. The scheme of operations of the agency or branch referred to in paragraph 2(g) shall contain the following particulars or evidence of:

(a) the nature of the commitments which the undertaking proposes to cover;

(b) the guiding principles as to reinsurance;

(c) the state of the undertaking's solvency margin and guarantee fund referred to in Article 55;

(d) estimates relating to the cost of setting up the administrative services and the organisation for securing business and the financial resources intended to meet those costs;

and, in addition shall include, for the first three financial years:

(e) a plan setting out detailed estimates of income and expenditure in respect of direct business, reinsurance acceptances and reinsurance cessions;

(f) a forecast balance sheet;

(g) estimates relating to the financial resources intended to cover underwriting liabilities and the solvency margin.

4. A Member State may require systematic notification of the technical bases used for calculating scales of premiums and technical provisions, without that requirement constituting a prior condition for an assurance undertaking to carry on its business.

Article 52

Rules applicable to branches of third-country undertakings

1. (a) Subject to point (b), agencies and branches referred to in this Title may not simultaneously carry on in a Member State the activities referred to in the Annex to Directive 73/239/EEC and those covered by this Directive.

(b) Subject to point (c), Member States may provide that agencies and branches referred to in this Title which on the relevant date referred to in Article 18(3) carried on both activities simultaneously in a Member State may continue to do so there provided that each activity is separately managed in accordance with Article 19.

(c) Any Member State which under Article 18(6) requires undertakings established in its territory to cease the simultaneous pursuit of the activities in which they were engaged on the relevant date referred to in Article 18(3) must also impose this requirement on agencies and branches referred to in this Title which are established in its territory and simultaneously carry on both activities there.

(d) Member States may provide that agencies and branches referred to in this Title whose head office simultaneously carries on both activities and which on the dates referred to in Article 18(3) carried on in the territory of a Member State solely the activity covered by this Directive may continue their activity there. If the undertaking wishes to carry on the activity referred to in Directive 73/239/EEC in that territory it may only carry on the activity covered by this Directive through a subsidiary.

2. Articles 13 and 37 shall apply mutatis mutandis to agencies and branches referred to in this title.

For the purposes of applying Article 37, the competent authority which supervises the overall solvency of agencies or branches shall be treated in the same way as the competent authority of the head-office Member State.

3. In the case of a withdrawal of authorisation by the authority referred to in Article 56(2), this authority shall notify the competent authorities of the other Member States where the undertaking operates and the latter authorities shall take the appropriate measures. If the reason for the withdrawal of authorisation is the inadequacy of the solvency margin calculated in accordance with Article 56(1)(a), the competent authorities of the other Member States concerned shall also withdraw their authorisations.

Article 53
Transfer of portfolio

1. Under the conditions laid down by national law, each Member State shall authorise agencies and branches set up within its territory and covered by this Title to transfer all or part of their portfolios of contracts to an accepting office established in the same Member State if the competent authorities of that Member State or, if appropriate, those of the Member State referred to in Article 56 certify that after taking the transfer into account the accepting office possesses the necessary solvency margin.

2. Under the conditions laid down by national law, each Member State shall authorise agencies and branches set up within its territory and covered by this Title to transfer all or part of their portfolios of contracts to an assurance undertaking with a head office in another Member State, if the competent authorities of that Member State certify that after taking the transfer into account the accepting office possesses the necessary solvency margin.

3. If under the conditions laid down by national law, a Member State authorises agencies and branches set up within its territory and covered by this Title to transfer all or part of their portfolios of contracts to an agency or branch covered by this Title and set up within the territory of another Member State, it shall ensure that the competent authorities of the Member State of the accepting office or, if appropriate, of the Member State referred to in Article 56 certify that after taking the transfer into account the accepting office possesses the necessary solvency margin, that the law of the Member State of the accepting office permits such a transfer and that the State has agreed to the transfer.

4. In the circumstances referred to in paragraphs 1, 2 and 3 the Member State in which the transferring agency or branch is situated shall authorise the transfer after obtaining the agreement of the competent authorities of the Member State of the commitment, where different from the

Member State in which the transferring agency or branch is situated.

5. The competent authorities of the Member States consulted shall give their opinion or consent to the competent authorities of the home Member State of the transferring assurance undertaking within three months of receiving a request; the absence of any response from the authorities consulted within that period shall be considered equivalent to a favourable opinion or tacit consent.

6. A transfer authorised in accordance with this Article shall be published as laid down by national law in the Member State of the commitment. Such transfers shall automatically be valid against policy holders, assured persons and any other persons having rights or obligations arising out of the contracts transferred.

This provision shall not affect the Member States' right to give policy holders the option of cancelling contracts within a fixed period after a transfer.

Article 54

Technical provisions

Member States shall require undertakings to establish provisions, referred to in Article 20, adequate to cover the underwriting liabilities assumed in their territories. Member States shall see that the agency or branch covers such provisions by means of assets which are equivalent to such provisions and matching assets in accordance with Annex II.

The law of the Member States shall be applicable to the calculation of such provisions, the determination of categories of investment and the valuation of assets, and, where appropriate, the determination of the extent to which these assets may be used for the purpose of covering such provisions.

The Member State in question shall require that the assets covering these provisions, shall be localised in its territory. Article 20(4) shall, however, apply.

Article 55

Solvency margin and guarantee fund

1. Each Member State shall require of agencies or branches set up in its territory a solvency margin consisting of the items listed in Article 27. The minimum solvency margin shall be calculated in accordance with Article 28. However, for the purpose of calculating this margin, account shall be taken only of the operations effected by the agency or branch concerned.

2. One third of the minimum solvency margin shall constitute the guarantee fund.

However, the amount of this fund may not be less than one half of the minimum required under Article 29(2) first subparagraph. The initial deposit lodged in accordance with Article 51(2)(e) shall be counted towards such guarantee fund.

The guarantee fund and the minimum of such fund shall be constituted in accordance with Article 29.

3. The assets representing the minimum solvency margin must be kept within the Member State where activities are carried on up to the amount of the guarantee fund and the excess within the Community.

Article 56

Advantages to undertakings authorised in more than one Member State

1. Any undertaking which has requested or obtained authorisation from more than one Member State may apply for the following advantages which may be granted only jointly:

(a) the solvency margin referred to in Article 55 shall be calculated in relation to the entire business which it carries on within the Community; in such case, account shall be taken only of the operations effected by all the agencies or branches established within the Community for the purposes of this calculation;

(b) the deposit required under Article 51(2)(e) shall be lodged in only one of those Member States;

(c) the assets representing the guarantee fund shall be localised in any one of the Member States in which it carries on its activities.

2. Application to benefit from the advantages provided for in paragraph 1 shall be made to the competent authorities of the Member States concerned. The application must state the authority of the Member State which in future is to supervise the solvency of the entire business of the agencies or branches established within the Community. Reasons must be given for the choice of authority made by the undertaking. The deposit shall be lodged with that Member State.

3. The advantages provided for in paragraph 1 may only be granted if the competent authorities of all Member States in which an application has been made agree to them. They shall take effect from the time when the selected competent authority informs the other competent authorities that it will supervise the state of solvency of the entire business of the agencies or branches within the Community.

The competent authority selected shall obtain from the other Member States the information necessary for the supervision of the overall solvency of the agencies and branches established in their territory.

4. At the request of one or more of the Member States concerned, the advantages granted under this Article shall be withdrawn simultaneously by all Member States concerned.

Article 57

Agreements with third countries

The Community may, by means of agreements concluded pursuant to the Treaty with one or more third countries, agree to the application of provisions different from those provided for in this Title, for the purpose of ensuring, under conditions of reciprocity, adequate protection for policy holders in the Member States.

TITLE VI

RULES APPLICABLE TO SUBSIDIARIES OF PARENT UNDERTAKINGS GOVERNED BY THE LAWS OF A THIRD COUNTRY AND TO THE ACQUISITIONS OF HOLDINGS BY SUCH PARENT UNDERTAKINGS

[Article 58

Information from Member States to the Commission

The competent authorities of the Member States shall inform the Commission and the competent authorities of the other Member States:

(a) of any authorisation of a direct or indirect subsidiary, one or more of whose parent undertakings are governed by the laws of a third country;

(b) whenever such a parent undertaking acquires a holding in a Community assurance undertaking which would turn the latter into its subsidiary.

When the authorisation referred to in point (a) is granted to the direct or indirect subsidiary of one or more parent undertakings governed by the law of third countries, the structure of the group shall be specified in the notification which the competent authorities shall address to the Commission and to the other competent authorities.]

¶ *This article has been replaced by article 8(2) of Directive 2005/1/EC, reproduced supra under no. B. 39.*

Article 59

Third-country treatment of Community assurance undertakings

1. The Member States shall inform the Commission of any general difficulties encountered by their assurance undertakings in establishing themselves or carrying on their activities in a third country.

2. Periodically, the Commission shall draw up a report examining the treatment accorded to Community assurance undertakings in third

countries, in the terms referred to in paragraphs 3 and 4, as regards establishment and the carrying-on of insurance activities, and the acquisition of holdings in third-country insurance undertakings. The Commission shall submit those reports to the Council, together with any appropriate proposals.

3. Whenever it appears to the Commission, either on the basis of the reports referred to in paragraph 2 or on the basis of other information, that a third country is not granting Community assurance undertakings effective market access comparable to that granted by the Community to insurance undertakings from that third country, the Commission may submit proposals to the Council for the appropriate mandate for negotiation with a view to obtaining comparable competitive opportunities for Community assurance undertakings. The Council shall decide by a qualified majority.

4. Whenever it appears to the Commission, either on the basis of the reports referred to in paragraph 2 or on the basis of other information, that Community assurance undertakings in a third country are not receiving national treatment offering the same competitive opportunities as are available to domestic insurance undertakings and that the conditions of effective market access are not being fulfilled, the Commission may initiate negotiations in order to remedy the situation.

In the circumstances described in the first subparagraph, it may also be decided at any time, and in addition to initiating negotiations, in accordance with the procedure laid down in Article 65(2), that the competent authorities of the Member States must limit or suspend their decisions:
– regarding requests pending at the moment of the decision or future requests for authorisations, and
– regarding the acquisition of holdings by direct or indirect parent undertakings governed by the laws of the third country in question.

The duration of the measures referred to may not exceed three months.

Before the end of that three-month period, and in the light of the results of the negotiations, the Council may, acting on a proposal from the Commission, decide by a qualified majority whether the measures shall be continued.

Such limitations or suspension may not apply to the setting up of subsidiaries by assurance undertakings or their subsidiaries duly authorised in the Community, or to the acquisition of holdings in Community assurance undertakings by such undertakings or subsidiaries.

5. Whenever it appears to the Commission that one of the situations described in paragraphs 3 and 4 has arisen, the Member States shall inform it at its request:

(a) of any request for the authorisation of a direct or indirect subsidiary one or more parent undertakings of which are governed by the laws of the third country in question;

(b) of any plans for such an undertaking to acquire a holding in a Community assurance undertaking such that the latter would become the subsidiary of the former.

This obligation to provide information shall lapse whenever an agreement is reached with the third country referred to in paragraph 3 or 4 when the measures referred to in the second and third subparagraphs of paragraph 4 cease to apply.

6. Measures taken under this Article shall comply with the Community's obligations under any international agreements, bilateral or multilateral, governing the taking up and pursuit of the business of insurance undertakings.

Title VII

Transitional and Other Provisions

Article 60

Derogations and abolition of restrictive measures

1. Undertakings set up in the United Kingdom by Royal Charter or by private Act or by special

Public Act may carry on their activity in the legal form in which they were constituted on 15 March 1979 for an unlimited period.

The United Kingdom shall draw up a list of such undertakings and communicate it to the other Member States and the Commission.

2. The societies registered in the United Kingdom under the Friendly Societies Acts may continue the activities of life assurance and savings operations which, in accordance with their objects, they were carrying on on 15 March 1979.

Article 61
Proof of good repute

1. Where a Member State requires of its own nationals proof of good repute and proof of no previous bankruptcy, or proof of either of these, that State shall accept as sufficient evidence in respect of nationals of other Member States the production of an extract from the 'judicial record' or, failing this, of an equivalent document issued by a competent judicial or administrative authority in the home Member State or the Member State from which the foreign national comes showing that these requirements have been met.

2. Where the home Member State or the Member State from which the foreign national concerned comes does not issue the document referred to in paragraph 1, it may be replaced by a declaration on oath—or in States where there is no provision for declaration on oath by a solemn declaration—made by the person concerned before a competent judicial or administrative authority or, where appropriate, a notary in the home Member State or the Member State from which that person comes; such authority or notary shall issue a certificate attesting the authenticity of the declaration on oath or solemn declaration. The declaration in respect of no previous bankruptcy may also be made before a competent professional or trade body in the said country.

3. Documents issued in accordance with paragraphs 1 and 2 must not be produced more than three months after their date of issue.

4. Member States shall designate the authorities and bodies competent to issue the documents referred to in paragraphs 1 and 2 and shall forthwith inform the other Member States and the Commission thereof.

Each Member State shall also inform the other Member States and the Commission of the authorities or bodies to which the documents referred to in this Article are to be submitted in support of an application to carry on in the territory of this Member State the activities referred to in Article 2.

Title VIII
Final Provisions

Article 62
Cooperation between the Member States and the Commission

The Commission and the competent authorities of the Member States shall collaborate closely with a view to facilitating the supervision of the kinds of insurance and the operations referred to in this Directive within the Community.

Each Member State shall inform the Commission of any major difficulties to which application of this Directive gives rise, inter alia, any arising if a Member State becomes aware of an abnormal transfer of business referred to in this Directive to the detriment of undertakings established in its territory and to the advantage of agencies and branches located just beyond its borders.

The Commission and the competent authorities of the Member States concerned shall examine such difficulties as quickly as possible in order to find an appropriate solution.

Where necessary, the Commission shall submit appropriate proposals to the Council.

Article 63
Reports on the development of the market under the freedom to provide services

The Commission shall forward to the European Parliament and to the Council regular reports, the first on 20 November 1995, on the development of the market in assurance and operations transacted under conditions of freedom to provide services.

Article 64
Technical adjustment

The following technical adjustments to be made to this Directive shall be adopted in accordance with the procedure laid down in Article 65(2):
- extension of the legal forms provided for in Article 6(1)(a),
- amendments to the list set out in Annex I, or adaptation of the terminology used in that list to take account of the development of assurance markets,
- clarification of the items constituting the solvency margin listed in Article 27 to take account of the creation of new financial instruments,
- alteration of the minimum guarantee fund provided for in Article 29(2) to take account of economic and financial developments,
- amendments, to take account of the creation of new financial instruments, to the list of assets acceptable as cover for technical provisions set out in Article 23 and to the rules on the spreading of investments laid down in Article 24,
- changes in the relaxations in the matching rules laid down in Annex II, to take account of the development of new currency-hedging instruments or progress made in economic and monetary union,
- clarification of the definitions in order to ensure uniform application of this Directive throughout the Community,
- the technical adjustments necessary to the rules for setting the maxima applicable to interest rates, pursuant to Article 20, in particular to take account of progress made in economic and monetary union.

Article 65
Committee procedure

[1. The Commission shall be assisted by the European Insurance and Occupational Pensions Committee established by Commission Decision 2004/9/EC.[25]]

2. Where reference is made to this paragraph, Articles 5 and 7 of Decision 1999/468/EC shall apply, having regard to the provisions of Article 8 thereof.

The period laid down in Article 5(6) of Decision 1999/468/EC shall be set at three months.

3. The Committee shall adopt its Rules of Procedure.

¶ *The first paragraph of this article has been amended by article 8(3) of Directive 2005/1/EC, reproduced supra under no. B. 39.*

Article 66
Rights acquired by existing branches and assurance undertakings

1. Branches which started business, in accordance with the provisions in force in the Member State of the branch, before 1 July 1994 shall be presumed to have been subject to the procedure laid down in Article 40(1) to (5).

They shall be governed, from that date by Articles 13, 20, 37, 39 and 46.

2. Articles 41 and 42 shall not affect rights acquired by assurance undertakings carrying on business under the freedom to provide services before 1 July 1994.

Article 67
Right to apply to the courts

Member States shall ensure that decisions taken in respect of an assurance undertaking under laws, regulations and administrative provisions adopted in accordance with this Directive may be subject to the right to apply to the courts.

Article 68
Review of amounts expressed in euro

1. The Commission shall submit to the Council before 15 March 1985 a report dealing with the effects of the financial requirements imposed by

---

[25] OJ L 3, 7.1.2004, 34.

this Directive on the situation in the insurance markets of the Member States.

2. The Council, acting on a proposal from the Commission, shall every two years examine and, where appropriate, revise the amounts expressed in euro in this Directive, in the light of how the Community's economic and monetary situation has evolved.

Article 69

Implementation of new provisions

1. Member States shall bring into force the laws, regulations and administrative provisions necessary to comply with Article 1(1)(m), Article 18(3), Article 51(2)(g), (3) and (4), Article 60(2) and Article 66(1) not later than 19 June 2004. They shall immediately inform the Commission thereof.

2. Member States shall bring into force the laws, regulations and administrative provisions necessary for them to comply with Article 16(3) not later than 17 November 2002. They shall forthwith inform the Commission thereof. Before this date, Member States shall apply the provision referred to in Annex IV(1).

3. Member States shall adopt by 20 September 2003 the laws, regulations and administrative provisions necessary to comply with Articles 3(6), 27, 28, 29, 30 and 38. They shall forthwith inform the Commission thereof.

Member States shall provide that the provisions referred to in the first subparagraph shall first apply to the supervision of accounts for financial years beginning on 1 January 2004 or during that calendar year. Before this date, Member States shall apply the provisions referred to in Annex IV(2) and (3).

4. When Member States adopt the measures mentioned in paragraphs (1), (2) and (3), they shall contain a reference to this Directive or be accompanied by such a reference on the occasion of their official publication. Member States shall determine how such reference is to be made.

5. Not later than 1 January 2007 the Commission shall submit to the European Parliament and to the Council a report on the application of Articles 3(6), 27, 28, 29, 30 and 38 and, if necessary, on the need for further harmonisation. The report shall indicate how Member States have made use of the possibilities under those articles and, in particular, whether the discretionary powers afforded to the national supervisory authorities have resulted in major supervisory differences in the single market.

Article 70

Information to the Commission

The Member States shall communicate to the Commission the texts of the main provisions of national law which they adopt in the field covered by this Directive.

Article 71

Transitional period for Articles 3(6), 27, 28, 29, 30 and 38

1. Member States may allow assurance undertakings which at 20 March 2002 provided assurance in their territories in one or more of classes referred to in Annex I, a period of five years, commencing on that same date, in order to comply with the requirements set out in Articles 3(6), 27, 28, 29, 30 and 38.

2. Member States may allow any undertakings referred to in paragraph 1, which upon the expiry of the five-year period have not fully established the required solvency margin, a further period not exceeding two years in which to do so provided that such undertakings have, in accordance with Article 37, submitted for the approval of the competent authorities, the measures which they propose to take for such purpose.

Article 72

Repealed directives and their correlation with this Directive

1. The Directives listed in Annex V, part A, are hereby repealed, without prejudice to the obligations of the Member States concerning the time limits for transposition and for application of the said Directives listed in Annex V, part B.

2. References to the repealed Directives shall be construed as references to this Directive and shall be read in accordance with the correlation table in Annex VI.

Article 73
Entry into force

This Directive shall enter into force on the day of its publication in the Official Journal of the European Communities.

Article 74
Addressees

This Directive is addressed to the Member States.

Annex I

Classes of assurance

I. The assurance referred to in Article 2(1)(a), (b) and (c) excluding those referred to in II and III

II. Marriage assurance, birth assurance

III. The assurance referred to in Article 2(1)(a) and (b), which are linked to investment funds

IV. Permanent health insurance, referred to in Article 2(1)(d)

V. Tontines, referred to in Article 2(2)(a)

VI. Capital redemption operations, referred to in Article 2(2)(b)

VII. Management of group pension funds, referred to in Article 2(2)(c) and (d)

VIII. The operations referred to in Article 2(2)(e)

IX. The operations referred to in Article 2(3)

Annex II

Matching rules

The currency in which the assurer's commitments are payable shall be determined in accordance with the following rules.

1. Where the cover provided by a contract is expressed in terms of a particular currency, the assurer's commitments are considered to be payable in that currency.

2. Member States may authorise assurance undertakings not to cover their technical provisions, including their mathematical provisions, by matching assets if application of the above procedures would result in the undertaking being obliged, in order to comply with the matching principle, to hold assets in a currency amounting to not more than 7% of the assets existing in other currencies.

3. Member States may choose not to require assurance undertakings to apply the matching principle where commitments are payable in a currency other than the currency of one of the Member States, if investments in that currency are regulated, if the currency is subject to transfer restrictions or if, for similar reasons, it is not suitable for covering technical provisions.

4. Assurance undertakings are authorised not to hold matching assets to cover an amount not exceeding 20% of their commitments in a particular currency.

However, total assets in all currencies combined must be at least equal to total commitments in all currencies combined.

5. Each Member State may provide that, whenever under the preceding procedures a commitment has to be covered by assets expressed in the currency of a Member State, this requirement shall also be considered to be satisfied when the assets are expressed in euro.

Annex III

Information for policy holders

The following information, which is to be communicated to the policy holder before the contract is concluded (A) or during the term of the contract (B), must be provided in a clear and accurate manner, in writing, in an official language of the Member State of the commitment.

However, such information may be in another language if the policy holder so requests and the law of the Member State so permits or the policy holder is free to choose the law applicable.

A. Before concluding the contract

Information about the assurance undertaking	Information about the commitment
(a)1 The name of the undertaking and its legal form	(a)4 Definition of each benefit and each option
(a)2 The name of the Member State in which the head office and, where appropriate, the agency or branch concluding the contract is situated	(a)5 Term of the contract
	(a)6 Means of terminating the contract
(a)3 The address of the head office and, where appropriate, of the agency or branch concluding the contract	(a)7 Means of payment of premiums and duration of payments
	(a)8 Means of calculation and distribution of bonuses
	(a)9 Indication of surrender and paid-up values and the extent to which they are guaranteed
	(a)10 Information on the premiums for each benefit, both main benefits and supplementary benefits, where appropriate
	(a)11 For unit-linked policies, definition of the units to which the benefits are linked
	(a)12 Indication of the nature of the underlying assets for unit-linked policies
	(a)13 Arrangements for application of the cooling-off period
	(a)14 General information on the tax arrangements applicable to the type of policy
	(a)15 The arrangements for handling complaints concerning contracts by policy holders, lives assured or beneficiaries under contracts including, where appropriate, the existence of a complaints body, without prejudice to the right to take legal proceedings
	(a)16 Law applicable to the contract where the parties do not have a free choice or, where the parties are free to choose the law applicable, the law the assurer proposes to choose

B. During the term of the contract	
Information about the assurance undertaking	Information about the commitment
(b)1 Any change in the name of the undertaking, its legal form or the address of its head office and, where appropriate, of the agency or branch which concluded the contract	(b)2 All in the information listed in points (a)(4) to (a)(12) of A in the event of a change in the policy conditions or amendment of the law the contract applicable to the contract
	(b)3 Every year, information on the state of bonuses

Annex IV

1. Professional secrecy

Until 17 November 2002, Member States may conclude cooperation agreements, providing for exchanges of information, with the competent authorities of third countries only if the information disclosed is subject to guarantees of professional secrecy at least equivalent to those referred to in Article 16 of this Directive.

2. Activities and bodies excluded from this Directive

Until 1 January 2004, this Directive shall not concern mutual associations, where:
– the articles of association contain provisions for calling up additional contributions or reducing their benefits or claiming assistance from other persons who have undertaken to provide it, and
– the annual contribution income for the activities covered by this Directive does not exceed EUR 500000 for three consecutive years. If this amount is exceeded for three consecutive years this Directive shall apply with effect from the fourth year.

3. Until 1 January 2004, Member States shall apply the following provisions:

A. Solvency margin

Each Member State shall require of every assurance undertaking whose head office is situated in its territory an adequate solvency margin in respect of its entire business.

The solvency margin shall consist of:

1. the assets of the assurance undertaking free of any foreseeable liabilities, less any intangible items. In particular the following shall be included:
– the paid-up share capital or, in the case of a mutual assurance undertaking, the effective initial fund plus any members' accounts which meet all the following criteria:

(a) the memorandum and articles of association must stipulate that payments may be made from these accounts to members only in so far as this does not cause the solvency margin to fall below the required level, or, after the dissolution of the undertaking, if all the undertaking's other debts have been settled;

(b) the memorandum and articles of association must stipulate, with respect to any such payments for reasons other than the individual termination of membership, that the competent authorities must be notified at least one month in advance and can prohibit the payment within that period;

(c) the relevant provisions of the memorandum and articles of association may be amended only after the competent authorities have declared that they have no objection to the amendment, without prejudice to the criteria stated in (a) and (b),

– one half of the unpaid share capital or initial fund, once the paid-up part amounts to 25% of that share capital or fund,
– reserves (statutory reserves and free reserves) not corresponding to underwriting liabilities,

– any profits brought forward,
– cumulative preferential share capital and subordinated loan capital may be included but, if so, only up to 50% of the margin, no more than 25% of which shall consist of subordinated loans with a fixed maturity, or fixed-term cumulative preferential share capital, if the following minimum criteria are met:

(a) in the event of the bankruptcy or liquidation of the assurance undertaking, binding agreements must exist under which the subordinated loan capital or preferential share capital ranks after the claims of all other creditors and is not to be repaid until all other debts outstanding at the time have been settled.

Subordinated loan capital must also fulfil the following conditions:

(b) only fully paid-up funds may be taken into account;

(c) for loans with a fixed maturity, the original maturity must be at least five years. No later than one year before the repayment date, the assurance undertaking must submit to the competent authorities for their approval a plan showing how the solvency margin will be kept at or brought to the required level at maturity, unless the extent to which the loan may rank as a component of the solvency margin is gradually reduced during at least the last five years before the repayment date. The competent authorities may authorise the early repayment of such loans provided application is made by the issuing assurance undertaking and its solvency margin will not fall below the required level;

(d) loans the maturity of which is not fixed must be repayable only subject to five years' notice unless the loans are no longer considered as a component of the solvency margin or unless the prior consent of the competent authorities is specifically required for early repayment. In the latter event the assurance undertaking must notify the competent authorities at least six months before the date of the proposed repayment, specifying the actual and required solvency margin both before and after that repayment. The competent authorities shall authorise repayment only if the assurance undertaking's solvency margin will not fall below the required level;

(e) the loan agreement must not include any clause providing that in specified circumstances, other than the winding-up of the assurance undertaking, the debt will become repayable before the agreed repayment dates;

(f) the loan agreement may be amended only after the competent authorities have declared that they have no objection to the amendment,

– securities with no specified maturity date and other instruments that fulfil the following conditions, including cumulative preferential shares other than those mentioned in the fifth indent, up to 50% of the margin for the total of such securities and the subordinated loan capital referred to in the fifth indent:

(a) they may not be repaid on the initiative of the bearer or without the prior consent of the competent authority;

(b) the contract of issue must enable the assurance undertaking to defer the payment of interest on the loan;

(c) the lender's claims on the assurance undertaking must rank entirely after those of all non-subordinated creditors;

(d) the documents governing the issue of the securities must provide for the loss-absorption capacity of the debt and unpaid interest, while enabling the assurance undertaking to continue its business;

(e) only fully paid-up amounts may be taken into account.

2. in so far as authorised under national law, profit reserves appearing in the balance sheet where they may be used to cover any losses which may arise and where they have not been made available for distribution to policy holders;

3. upon application, with supporting evidence, by the undertaking to the competent authority of the Member State in the territory of which its head office is situated and with the agreement of that authority:

(a) an amount equal to 50% of the undertaking's future profits; the amount of the future profits shall be obtained by multiplying the estimated annual profit by a factor which represents the average period left to run on policies; the factor used may not exceed 10; the estimated annual profit shall be the arithmetical average of the profits made over the last five years in the activities listed in Article 2 of this Directive.

The bases for calculating the factor by which the estimated annual profit is to be multiplied and the items comprising the profits made shall be defined by common agreement by the competent authorities of the Member States in collaboration with the Commission. Pending such agreement, those items shall be determined in accordance with the laws of the home Member State.

When the competent authorities have defined the concept of profits made, the Commission shall submit proposals for the harmonisation of this concept by means of a Directive on the harmonisation of the annual accounts of insurance undertakings and providing for the coordination set out in Article 1(2) of Directive 78/660/EEC;

(b) where Zillmerising is not practised or where, if practised, it is less than the loading for acquisition costs included in the premium, the difference between a non-Zillmerised or partially Zillmerised mathematical provision and a mathematical provision Zillmerised at a rate equal to the loading for acquisition costs included in the premium; this figure may not, however, exceed 3,5% of the sum of the differences between the relevant capital sums of life assurance activities and the mathematical provisions for all policies for which Zillmerising is possible; the difference shall be reduced by the amount of any undepreciated acquisition costs entered as an asset;

(c) where approval is given by the competent authorities of the Member States concerned in which the assurance undertaking is carrying on its activities any hidden reserves resulting from the underestimation of assets and overestimation of liabilities other than mathematical provisions in so far as such hidden reserves are not of an exceptional nature.

B. Minimum solvency margin

Subject to section C, the minimum solvency margin shall be determined as shown below according to the classes of assurance underwritten.

(a) For the kinds of assurance referred to in Article 2(1)(a) and (b) of this Directive other than assurance linked to investment funds and for the operations referred to in Article 2(3) of this Directive, it must be equal to the sum of the following two results:

– first result:

a 4% fraction of the mathematical provisions relating to direct business gross of reinsurance cessions and to reinsurance acceptances shall be multiplied by the ratio, for the last financial year, of the total mathematical provisions net of reinsurance cessions to the gross total mathematical provisions as specified above; that ratio may in no case be less than 85%,

– second result:

for policies on which the capital at risk is not a negative figure, a 0.3% fraction of such capital underwritten by the assurance undertaking shall be multiplied by the ratio, for the last financial year, of the total capital at risk retained as the undertaking's liability after reinsurance cessions and retrocessions to the total capital at risk gross of reinsurance; that ratio may in no case be less than 50%.

For temporary assurance on death of a maximum term of three years the above fraction shall be 0.1%; for such assurance of a term of more than three years but not more than five years the above fraction shall be 0.15%.

(b) For the supplementary insurance referred to in Article 2(1)(c) of this Directive, it shall be equal to the result of the following calculation:

– the premiums or contributions (inclusive of charges ancillary to premiums or contributions) due in respect of direct business in the last financial year in respect of all financial years shall be aggregated,

– to this aggregate there shall be added the amount of premiums accepted for all reinsurance in the last financial year,

– from this sum shall then be deducted the total amount of premiums or contributions cancelled in the last financial year as well as the total amount of taxes and levies pertaining to the premiums or contributions entering into the aggregate.

The amount so obtained shall be divided into two portions, the first extending up to EUR 10 million and the second comprising the excess; 18% and 16% of these portions respectively shall be calculated and added together.

The result shall be obtained by multiplying the sum so calculated by the ratio existing in respect of the last financial year between the amount of claims remaining to be borne by the assurance undertaking after deduction of transfers for reinsurance and the gross amount of claims; this ratio may in no case be less than 50%.

In the case of the association of underwriters known as Lloyd's, the calculation of the solvency margin shall be made on the basis of net premiums, which shall be multiplied by flat-rate percentage fixed annually by the competent authority of the head office Member State. This flat-rate percentage must be calculated on the basis of the most recent statistical data on commissions paid. The details together with the relevant calculations shall be sent to the competent authorities of the countries in whose territory Lloyd's is established.

(c) For permanent health insurance not subject to cancellation referred to in Article 2(1)(d) of this Directive, and for capital redemption operations referred to in Article 2(2)(b) thereof, it shall be equal to a 4% fraction of the mathematical provisions calculated in compliance with the conditions set out in the first result in (a) of this section.

(d) For tontines, referred to in Article 2(2)(a) of this Directive, it shall be equal to 1% of their assets.

(e) For assurance covered by Article 2(1)(a) and (b) of this Directive linked to investment funds and for the operations referred to in Article 2(2)(c), (d) and (e) of this Directive it shall be equal to:
– a 4% fraction of the mathematical provisions, calculated in compliance with the conditions set out in the first result in (a) of this section in so far as the assurance undertaking bears an investment risk, and a 1% fraction of the provisions calculated in the same way, in so far as the undertaking bears no investment risk provided that the term of the contract exceeds five years and the allocation to cover management expenses set out in the contract is fixed for a period exceeding five years, plus
– a 0.3% fraction of the capital at risk calculated in compliance with the conditions set out in the first subparagraph of the second result of (a) of this section in so far as the assurance undertaking covers a death risk.

C. Guarantee fund

1. One third of the required solvency margin as specified in section B shall constitute the guarantee fund. Subject to paragraph 2 of this section, at least 50% of this fund shall consist of the items listed in section A(1) and (2).

2. (a) The guarantee fund may not, however, be less than a minimum of EUR 800,000.

(b) Any Member State may provide for the minimum of the guarantee fund to be reduced to EUR 600,000 in the case of mutual associations and mutual-type associations and tontines.

(c) For mutual associations referred to in the second sentence of the second indent of Article 3(6) of this Directive, as soon as they come within the scope of this Directive, and for tontines, any Member State may permit the establishment of a minimum of the guarantee fund of EUR 100,000 to be increased progressively to the amount fixed in (b) of this section by successive tranches of EUR 100,000 whenever the contributions increase by EUR 500,000.

(d) The minimum of the guarantee fund referred to in (a), (b) and (c) of this section must consist of the items listed in section A(1) and (2).

3. Mutual associations wishing to extend their business within the meaning of Article 6(4) or Article 40 of this Directive may not do so unless they comply immediately with the requirements of paragraph 2(a) and (b) of this section.

Annex V

Part A

Repealed Directives together with their successive amendments (referred to in Article 72)

Council Directive 79/267/EEC

Council Directive 90/619/EEC

Council Directive 92/96/EEC

Directive 95/26/EEC of the European Parliament and of the Council (only Article 1, second indent, Article 2(2), fourth indent, and Article 3(1) as regards the references made to Directive 79/267/EEC)

Directive 2002/12/EC of the European Parliament and of the Council

Second Council Directive 90/619/EEC

Third Council Directive 92/96/EEC

Third Council Directive 92/96/EEC

Directive 95/26/EEC of the European Parliament and of the Council (only Article 1, second indent, Article 2(1), third indent, Article 4(1), (3), (5) and Article 5, third indent, as regards the references made to Directive 92/96/EEC).

Directive 2000/64/EC of the European Parliament and of the Council (Article 2, as regards the references made to Directive 92/96/EEC)

Directive 2002/12/EC of the European Parliament and of the Council (Article 2)

Part B

Deadlines for implementation

(Referred to in Article 72)

Directive	Time limits for transposition	Time limits for application
79/267/EEC (OJ L 63, 13.3.1979, 1)	15 September 1980	15 September 1981
90/619/EEC (OJ L 330, 29.11.1990, 50)	20 November 1992	20 May 1993
92/96/EEC (OJ L 360, 9.12.1992, 1)	31 December 1993	1 July 1994
95/26/EC (OJ L 168, 18.7.1995, 7)	18 July 1996	18 July 1996
2000/64/EC (OJ L 290, 17.11.2000, 27)	17 November 2002	17 November 2002
2002/12/EC (OJ L 77, 20.3.2002, 11)	20 November 2003	1 January 2004

Annex VI

Correlation table

This Directive	Directive 79/267/EEC	Directive 90/619/EEC	Directive 92/96/EEC	Directive 95/26/EC	Other Acts
Article 1(1)(a)			Article 1(a)		
Article 1(1)(b)		Article 3	Article 1(b)		
Article 1(1)(c)		Article 2(c)			
Article 1(1)(d)			Article 1(c)		
Article 1(1)(e)			Article 1(d)		
Article 1(1)(f)			Article 1(e)		
Article 1(1)(g)		Article 2(e)			
Article 1(1)(h) to (l)			Article 1(f) to (j)		
Article 1(1)(m)					New
Article 1(1)(n)			Article 1(l)		
Article 1(1)(o), (p), (q)	Article 5(b), (c) and (d)				
Article 1(1)(r)				Article 2(1)	
Article 1(2)	Article 5(a), second sentence				
Article 2	Article 1				
Article 3(1) to (4)	Article 2				
Article 3(5) and (6)	Article 3				
Article 3(7)	Article 4				
Article 3(8)					Act of Accession of Austria, Finland and Sweden, adapted by Decision 95/1/EC, Euratom, ECSC
Article 4	Article 6				
Article 5	Article 7				
Article 6(1)	Article 8(1)				
Article 6(2)	Article 8(1) last three subparagraphs				
Article 6(3)	Article 8(1)a				
Article 6(4)	Article 8(2)				
Article 6(5)	Article 8(3)				
Article 6(6)	Article 8(4)				
Article 7	Article 9				
Article 8			Article 7		
Article 9	Article 12				
Article 10	Article 15				
Article 11	Article 16				
Article 12	Article 22(1)				
Article 13	Article 23				
Article 14(1) to (5)			Article 11(2) to (6)		
Article 15			Article 14		
Article 16(1) to (5)			Article 15(1) to (5)		
Article 16(6)			Article 15(5)(a)		
Article 16(7)			Article 15(5)(b)		
Article 16(8)			Article 15(5)(c)		
Article 16(9)			Article 15(6)		
Article 17			Article 15(a)		
Article 18(1) and (2)	Article 13(1) and (2)				
Article 18(3)					New
Article 18(4) to (7)	Article 13(3) to (7)				
Article 19	Article 14				

This Directive	Directive 79/267/EEC	Directive 90/619/EEC	Directive 92/96/EEC	Directive 95/26/EC	Other Acts
Article 20	Article 17				
Article 21			Article 19		
Article 22			Article 20		
Article 23(1)			Article 21(1) first subparagraph		
Article 23(2)			Article 21(1) second subparagraph		
Article 23(3) first subparagraph			Article 21(1) third subparagraph		
Article 23(3) second subparagraph			Article 21(1) fourth subparagraph		
Article 23(4)			Article 21(2)		
Article 24			Article 22		
Article 25			Article 23		
Article 26			Article 24		
Article 27	Article 18				
Article 28	Article 19				
Article 29	Article 20				
Article 30	Article 20a				
Article 31	Article 21				
Article 32		Article 4			
Article 33			Article 28		
Article 34			Article 29		
Article 35		Article 15			
Article 36			Article 31		
Article 37	Article 24				
Article 38	Article 24a				
Article 39	Article 26				
Article 40	Article 10				
Article 41		Article 11			
Article 42		Article 14			
Article 43		Article 17			
Article 44			Article 38		
Article 45			Article 39(2)		
Article 46(1) to (9)			Article 40(2) to (10)		
Article 47			Article 41		
Article 48			Article 42(2)		
Article 49			Article 43(2)		
Article 50(1)			Article 44(2) first subparagraph		
Article 50(2)			Article 44(2) second subparagraph		
Article 50(3)			Article 44(2) third subparagraph		
Article 51(1) to (2)(f)	Article 27(1) to (2)(f)				
Article 51(2)(g)					New
Article 51(3) and (4)					New
Article 52	Article 31				
Article 53	Article 31a				
Article 54	Article 28				
Article 55	Article 29				
Article 56	Article 30				
Article 57	Article 32				
Article 58	Article 32a				
Article 59(1)	Article 32b(1)				
Article 59(2)	Article 32b(2)				
Article 59(3)	Article 32b(3)				
Article 59(4)	Article 32b(4)				

This Directive	Directive 79/267/EEC	Directive 90/619/EEC	Directive 92/96/EEC	Directive 95/26/EC	Other Acts
Article 59(5)	Article 32b(5)				
Article 59(6)	Article 32b(7)				
Article 60(1)	Article 33(4)				
Article 60(2)					New
Article 61	Article 37				
Article 62, first subparagraph	Article 38	Article 28, first subparagraph			
Article 62, second to fourth subparagraphs		Article 28, second to fourth subparagraphs			
Article 63		Article 29			
Article 64			Article 47		
Article 65			Article 47		
Article 66(1), first subparagraph					New
Article 66(1) second subparagraph			Article 48(1)		
Article 66(2)			Article 48(2)		
Article 67			Article 50		
Article 68(1)	Article 39(1)				
Article 68(2)	Article 39(3)				
Article 69(1)					New
Article 69(2)					Directive 2000/64/EC, Article 3(1), first subparagraph
Article 69(3)					Directive 2002/12/EC, Article 3(1), first subparagraph, and Directive 2000/64/EC, Article 3(2)
Article 69(4)					Directive 2000/64/EC, Article 3(1), second subparagraph, and Directive 2002/12/EC, Article 3(1), second subparagraph
Article 69(5)					Directive 2002/12/EC, Article 3(4)
Article 70	Article 41	Article 31	Article 51(2)	Article 6(2)	Directive 2000/64/EC, Article 3(2), and Directive 2002/12/EC, Article 3(3)
Article 71					Directive 2002/12/EC, Article 2
Article 72					
Article 73					
Article 74					
Annex I	Annex				
Annex II			Annex I		
Annex III			Annex II		
Annex IV					
Annex V					
Annex VI					

I. 34.

European Parliament and Council Directive 2002/92/EC of 9 December 2002 on insurance mediation[1]

THE EUROPEAN PARLIAMENT AND THE COUNCIL OF THE EUROPEAN UNION,

Having regard to the Treaty establishing the European Community, and in particular Article 47(2) and Article 55 thereof,

Having regard to the proposal from the Commission,[2]

Having regard to the opinion of the Economic and Social Committee,[3]

Acting in accordance with the procedure laid down in Article 251 of the Treaty,[4]

Whereas:

(1) Insurance and reinsurance intermediaries play a central role in the distribution of insurance and reinsurance products in the Community.

(2) A first step to facilitate the exercise of freedom of establishment and freedom to provide services for insurance agents and brokers was made by Council Directive 77/92/EEC of 13 December 1976 on measures to facilitate the effective exercise of freedom of establishment and freedom to provide services in respect of the activities of insurance agents and brokers (ex ISIC Group 630) and, in particular, transitional measures in respect of those activities.[5]

(3) Directive 77/92/EEC was to remain applicable until the entry into force of provisions coordinating national rules concerning the taking-up and pursuit of the activities of insurance agents and brokers.

(4) Commission Recommendation 92/48/EEC of 18 December 1991 on insurance intermediaries[6] was largely followed by Member States and helped to bring closer together national provisions on the professional requirements and registration of insurance intermediaries.

(5) However, there are still substantial differences between national provisions which create barriers to the taking-up and pursuit of the activities of insurance and reinsurance intermediaries in the internal market. It is therefore appropriate to replace Directive 77/92/EEC with a new directive.

(6) Insurance and reinsurance intermediaries should be able to avail themselves of the freedom of establishment and the freedom to provide services which are enshrined in the Treaty.

(7) The inability of insurance intermediaries to operate freely throughout the Community hinders the proper functioning of the single market in insurance.

(8) The coordination of national provisions on professional requirements and registration of persons taking up and pursuing the activity of insurance mediation can therefore contribute both to the completion of the single market for financial services and to the enhancement of customer protection in this field.

(9) Various types of persons or institutions, such as agents, brokers and 'bancassurance' operators, can distribute insurance products. Equality of treatment between operators and customer

---

[1] OJ L 9, 15.1.2003, 3–10.
[2] OJ C 29 E, 30.1.2001, 245.
[3] OJ C 221, 7.8.2001, 121.
[4] Opinion of the European Parliament of 14 November 2001 (OJ C 140 E, 13.6.2002, 167), Council Common Position of 18 March 2002 (OJ C 145 E, 18.6.2002, 1) and Decision of the European Parliament of 13 June 2002 (not yet published in the Official Journal). Council Decision of 28 June 2002.
[5] OJ L 26, 31.1.1977, 14, reproduced supra under no. I. 7. Directive as last amended by the Act of Accession of 1994.

[6] OJ L 19, 28.1.1992, 32.

protection requires that all these persons or institutions be covered by this Directive.

(10) This Directive contains a definition of 'tied insurance intermediary' which takes into account the characteristics of certain Member States' markets and whose purpose is to establish the conditions for registration applicable to such intermediaries. This definition is not intended to preclude Member States from having similar concepts in respect of insurance intermediaries who, while acting for and on behalf of an insurance undertaking and under the full responsibility of that undertaking, are entitled to collect premiums or amounts intended for the customer in accordance with the financial guarantees laid down by this Directive.

(11) This Directive should apply to persons whose activity consists in providing insurance mediation services to third parties for remuneration, which may be pecuniary or take some other form of agreed economic benefit tied to performance.

(12) This Directive should not apply to persons with another professional activity, such as tax experts or accountants, who provide advice on insurance cover on an incidental basis in the course of that other professional activity, neither should it apply to the mere provision of information of a general nature on insurance products, provided that the purpose of that activity is not to help the customer conclude or fulfil an insurance or reinsurance contract, nor the professional management of claims for an insurance or reinsurance undertaking, nor the loss adjusting and expert appraisal of claims.

(13) This Directive should not apply to persons practising insurance mediation as an ancillary activity under certain strict conditions.

(14) Insurance and reinsurance intermediaries should be registered with the competent authority of the Member State where they have their residence or their head office, provided that they meet strict professional requirements in relation to their competence, good repute, professional indemnity cover and financial capacity.

(15) Such registration should allow insurance and reinsurance intermediaries to operate in other Member States in accordance with the principles of freedom of establishment and freedom to provide services, provided that an appropriate notification procedure has been followed between the competent authorities.

(16) Appropriate sanctions are needed against persons exercising the activity of insurance or reinsurance mediation without being registered, against insurance or reinsurance undertakings using the services of unregistered intermediaries and against intermediaries not complying with national provisions adopted pursuant to this Directive.

(17) Cooperation and exchange of information between competent authorities are essential in order to protect customers and ensure the soundness of insurance and reinsurance business in the single market.

(18) It is essential for the customer to know whether he is dealing with an intermediary who is advising him on products from a broad range of insurance undertakings or on products provided by a specific number of insurance undertakings.

(19) This Directive should specify the obligations which insurance intermediaries should have in providing information to customers. A Member State may in this area maintain or adopt more stringent provisions which may be imposed on insurance intermediaries independently of their place of residence where they are pursuing mediation activities on its territory provided that any such more stringent provisions comply with Community law, including Directive 2000/31/EC of the European Parliament and of the Council of 8 June 2000 on certain legal aspects of information society services, in particular electronic commerce, in the Internal Market (Directive on electronic commerce).[7]

(20) If the intermediary declares that he is giving advice on products from a broad range of insurance undertakings, he should carry out a fair and

---

[7] OJ L 178, 17.7.2000, 1, reproduced supra under no. C.P. 19.

sufficiently wide-ranging analysis of the products available on the market. In addition, all intermediaries should explain the reasons underpinning their advice.

(21) There is less of a need to require that such information be disclosed when the customer is a company seeking reinsurance or insurance cover for commercial and industrial risks.

(22) There is a need for suitable and effective complaint and redress procedures in the Member States in order to settle disputes between insurance intermediaries and customers, using, where appropriate, existing procedures.

(23) Without prejudice to the right of customers to bring their action before the courts, Member States should encourage public or private bodies established with a view to settling disputes out-of-court, to cooperate in resolving cross-border disputes. Such cooperation could for example be aimed at enabling customers to contact extra-judicial bodies established in their Member State of residence about complaints concerning insurance intermediaries established in other Member States. The setting up of the FIN-NET network provides increased assistance to consumers when they use cross-border services. The provisions on procedures should take into account Commission Recommendation 98/257/EC of 30 March 1998 on the principles applicable to the bodies responsible for out-of-court settlement of consumer disputes.[8]

(24) Directive 77/92/EEC should accordingly be repealed,

HAVE ADOPTED THIS DIRECTIVE:

CHAPTER I
SCOPE AND DEFINITIONS

Article 1
Scope

1. This Directive lays down rules for the taking-up and pursuit of the activities of insurance and reinsurance mediation by natural and legal persons which are established in a Member State or which wish to become established there.

2. This Directive shall not apply to persons providing mediation services for insurance contracts if all the following conditions are met:

(a) the insurance contract only requires knowledge of the insurance cover that is provided;

(b) the insurance contract is not a life assurance contract;

(c) the insurance contract does not cover any liability risks;

(d) the principal professional activity of the person is other than insurance mediation;

(e) the insurance is complementary to the product or service supplied by any provider, where such insurance covers:
 (i) the risk of breakdown, loss of or damage to goods supplied by that provider, or
 (ii) damage to or loss of baggage and other risks linked to the travel booked with that provider, even if the insurance covers life assurance or liability risks, provided that the cover is ancillary to the main cover for the risks linked to that travel;

(f) the amount of the annual premium does not exceed EUR 500 and the total duration of the insurance contract, including any renewals, does not exceed five years.

3. This Directive shall not apply to insurance and reinsurance mediation services provided in relation to risks and commitments located outside the Community.

This Directive shall not affect a Member State's law in respect of insurance mediation business pursued by insurance and reinsurance intermediaries established in a third country and operating on its territory under the principle of freedom to provide services, provided that equal treatment is guaranteed to all persons carrying out or authorised to carry out insurance mediation activities on that market.

This Directive shall not regulate insurance mediation activities carried out in third countries nor

---

[8] OJ L 115, 17.4.1998, 31.

activities of Community insurance or reinsurance undertakings, as defined in First Council Directive 73/239/EEC of 24 July 1973 on the coordination of laws, regulations and administrative provisions relating to the taking-up and pursuit of the business of direct insurance other than life assurance[9] and First Council Directive 79/267/EEC of 5 March 1979 on the coordination of laws, regulations and administrative provisions relating to the taking-up and pursuit of the business of direct life assurance,[10] carried out through insurance intermediaries in third countries.

Article 2

Definitions

For the purpose of this Directive:

1. 'insurance undertaking' means an undertaking which has received official authorisation in accordance with Article 6 of Directive 73/239/EEC or Article 6 of Directive 79/267/EEC;

2. 'reinsurance undertaking' means an undertaking, other than an insurance undertaking or a non-member-country insurance undertaking, the main business of which consists in accepting risks ceded by an insurance undertaking, a non-member-country insurance undertaking or other reinsurance undertakings;

3. 'insurance mediation' means the activities of introducing, proposing or carrying out other work preparatory to the conclusion of contracts of insurance, or of concluding such contracts, or of assisting in the administration and performance of such contracts, in particular in the event of a claim.

These activities when undertaken by an insurance undertaking or an employee of an insurance undertaking who is acting under the responsibility of the insurance undertaking shall not be considered as insurance mediation.

The provision of information on an incidental basis in the context of another professional activity provided that the purpose of that activity is not to assist the customer in concluding or performing an insurance contract, the management of claims of an insurance undertaking on a professional basis, and loss adjusting and expert appraisal of claims shall also not be considered as insurance mediation;

4. 'reinsurance mediation' means the activities of introducing, proposing or carrying out other work preparatory to the conclusion of contracts of reinsurance, or of concluding such contracts, or of assisting in the administration and performance of such contracts, in particular in the event of a claim.

These activities when undertaken by a reinsurance undertaking or an employee of a reinsurance undertaking who is acting under the responsibility of the reinsurance undertaking are not considered as reinsurance mediation.

The provision of information on an incidental basis in the context of another professional activity provided that the purpose of that activity is not to assist the customer in concluding or performing a reinsurance contract, the management of claims of a reinsurance undertaking on a professional basis, and loss adjusting and expert appraisal of claims shall also not be considered as reinsurance mediation;

5. 'insurance intermediary' means any natural or legal person who, for remuneration, takes up or pursues insurance mediation;

6. 'reinsurance intermediary' means any natural or legal person who, for remuneration, takes up or pursues reinsurance mediation;

7. 'tied insurance intermediary' means any person who carries on the activity of insurance mediation for and on behalf of one or more insurance undertakings in the case of insurance products which are not in competition but does not collect premiums or amounts intended for the customer

---

[9] OJ L 228, 16.8.1973, 3, reproduced supra under no. I. 3. Directive as last amended by Directive 2002/13/EC of the European Parliament and of the Council (OJ L 77, 20.3.2002, 17), reproduced supra under no. I. 32.
[10] OJ L 63, 13.3.1979, 1, reproduced supra under no. I. 9. Directive as last amended by Directive 2002/12/EC of the European Parliament and of the Council (OJ L 77, 20.3.2002, 11), reproduced supra under no. I. 31.

and who acts under the full responsibility of those insurance undertakings for the products which concern them respectively.

Any person who carries on the activity of insurance mediation in addition to his principal professional activity is also considered as a tied insurance intermediary acting under the responsibility of one or several insurance undertakings for the products which concern them respectively if the insurance is complementary to the goods or services supplied in the framework of this principal professional activity and the person does not collect premiums or amounts intended for the customer;

8. 'large risks' shall be as defined by Article 5(d) of Directive 73/239/EEC;

9. 'home Member State' means:

(a) where the intermediary is a natural person, the Member State in which his residence is situated and in which he carries on business;

(b) where the intermediary is a legal person, the Member State in which its registered office is situated or, if under its national law it has no registered office, the Member State in which its head office is situated;

10. 'host Member State' means the Member State in which an insurance or reinsurance intermediary has a branch or provides services;

11. 'competent authorities' means the authorities which each Member State designates under Article 7;

12. 'durable medium' means any instrument which enables the customer to store information addressed personally to him in a way accessible for future reference for a period of time adequate to the purposes of the information and which allows the unchanged reproduction of the information stored.

In particular, durable medium covers floppy disks, CD-ROMs, DVDs and hard drives of personal computers on which electronic mail is stored, but it excludes Internet sites, unless such sites meet the criteria specified in the first paragraph.

CHAPTER II
REGISTRATION REQUIREMENTS

Article 3
Registration

1. Insurance and reinsurance intermediaries shall be registered with a competent authority as defined in Article 7(2), in their home Member State.

Without prejudice to the first subparagraph, Member States may stipulate that insurance and reinsurance undertakings and other bodies may collaborate with the competent authorities in registering insurance and reinsurance intermediaries and in the application of the requirements of Article 4 to such intermediaries. In particular, in the case of tied insurance intermediaries, they may be registered by an insurance undertaking or by an association of insurance undertakings under the supervision of a competent authority.

Member States need not apply the requirement referred to in the first and second subparagraphs to all the natural persons who work in an undertaking and pursue the activity of insurance or reinsurance mediation.

As regards legal persons, Member States shall register such persons and shall also specify in the register the names of the natural persons within the management who are responsible for the mediation business.

2. Member States may establish more than one register for insurance and reinsurance intermediaries provided that they lay down the criteria according to which intermediaries are to be registered.

Member States shall see to it that a single information point is established allowing quick and easy access to information from these various registers, which shall be compiled electronically and kept constantly updated. This information point shall also provide the identification details of the competent authorities of each Member State referred to in paragraph 1, first subparagraph. The register shall indicate further the country or countries in which the intermediary conducts business under the rules on the freedom of establishment or on the freedom to provide services.

3. Member States shall ensure that registration of insurance intermediaries—including tied ones—and reinsurance intermediaries is made subject to the fulfilment of the professional requirements laid down in Article 4.

Member States shall also ensure that insurance intermediaries—including tied ones—and reinsurance intermediaries who cease to fulfil these requirements are removed from the register. The validity of the registration shall be subject to a regular review by the competent authority. If necessary, the home Member State shall inform the host Member State of such removal, by any appropriate means.

4. The competent authorities may provide the insurance and reinsurance intermediaries with a document enabling any interested party by consultation of the register(s) referred to in paragraph 2 to verify that they are duly registered.

That document shall at least provide the information specified in Article 12(1)(a) and (b), and, in the case of a legal person, the name(s) of the natural person(s) referred to in the fourth subparagraph of paragraph 1 of this Article.

The Member State shall require the return of the document to the competent authority which issued it when the insurance or reinsurance intermediary concerned ceases to be registered.

5. Registered insurance and reinsurance intermediaries shall be allowed to take up and pursue the activity of insurance and reinsurance mediation in the Community by means of both freedom of establishment and freedom to provide services.

6. Member States shall ensure that insurance undertakings use the insurance and reinsurance mediation services only of registered insurance and reinsurance intermediaries and of the persons referred to in Article 1(2).

Article 4

Professional requirements

1. Insurance and reinsurance intermediaries shall possess appropriate knowledge and ability, as determined by the home Member State of the intermediary.

Home Member States may adjust the required conditions with regard to knowledge and ability in line with the activity of insurance or reinsurance mediation and the products distributed, particularly if the principal professional activity of the intermediary is other than insurance mediation. In such cases, that intermediary may pursue an activity of insurance mediation only if an insurance intermediary fulfilling the conditions of this Article or an insurance undertaking assumes full responsibility for his actions.

Member States may provide that for the cases referred to in the second subparagraph of Article 3(1), the insurance undertaking shall verify that the knowledge and ability of the intermediaries are in conformity with the obligations set out in the first subparagraph of this paragraph and, if need be, shall provide such intermediaries with training which corresponds to the requirements concerning the products sold by the intermediaries.

Member States need not apply the requirement referred to in the first subparagraph of this paragraph to all the natural persons working in an undertaking who pursue the activity of insurance or reinsurance mediation. Member States shall ensure that a reasonable proportion of the persons within the management structure of such undertakings who are responsible for mediation in respect of insurance products and all other persons directly involved in insurance or reinsurance mediation demonstrate the knowledge and ability necessary for the performance of their duties.

2. Insurance and reinsurance intermediaries shall be of good repute. As a minimum, they shall have a clean police record or any other national equivalent in relation to serious criminal offences linked to crimes against property or other crimes related to financial activities and they should not have previously been declared bankrupt, unless they have been rehabilitated in accordance with national law.

Member States may, in accordance with the provisions of the second subparagraph of Article 3(1), allow the insurance undertaking to check the good repute of insurance intermediaries.

Member States need not apply the requirement referred to in the first subparagraph of this paragraph to all the natural persons who work in an undertaking and who pursue the activity of insurance and reinsurance mediation.

Member States shall ensure that the management structure of such undertakings and any staff directly involved in insurance or reinsurance mediation fulfil that requirement.

3. Insurance and reinsurance intermediaries shall hold professional indemnity insurance covering the whole territory of the Community or some other comparable guarantee against liability arising from professional negligence, for at least EUR 1.000.000 applying to each claim and in aggregate EUR 1.500.000 per year for all claims, unless such insurance or comparable guarantee is already provided by an insurance undertaking, reinsurance undertaking or other undertaking on whose behalf the insurance or reinsurance intermediary is acting or for which the insurance or reinsurance intermediary is empowered to act or such undertaking has taken on full responsibility for the intermediary's actions.

4. Member States shall take all necessary measures to protect customers against the inability of the insurance intermediary to transfer the premium to the insurance undertaking or to transfer the amount of claim or return premium to the insured.

Such measures shall take any one or more of the following forms:

(a) provisions laid down by law or contract whereby monies paid by the customer to the intermediary are treated as having been paid to the undertaking, whereas monies paid by the undertaking to the intermediary are not treated as having been paid to the customer until the customer actually receives them;

(b) a requirement for insurance intermediaries to have financial capacity amounting, on a permanent basis, to 4% of the sum of annual premiums received, subject to a minimum of EUR 15.000;

(c) a requirement that customers' monies shall be transferred via strictly segregated client accounts and that these accounts shall not be used to reimburse other creditors in the event of bankruptcy;

(d) a requirement that a guarantee fund be set up.

5. Pursuit of the activities of insurance and reinsurance mediation shall require that the professional requirements set out in this Article be fulfilled on a permanent basis.

6. Member States may reinforce the requirements set out in this Article or add other requirements for insurance and reinsurance intermediaries registered within their jurisdiction.

7. The amounts referred to in paragraphs 3 and 4 shall be reviewed regularly in order to take account of changes in the European Index of Consumer Prices as published by Eurostat. The first review shall take place five years after the entry into force of this Directive and the successive reviews every five years after the previous review date.

The amounts shall be adapted automatically by increasing the base amount in euro by the percentage change in that Index over the period between the entry into force of this Directive and the first review date or between the last review date and the new review date and rounded up to the nearest euro.

Article 5

Retention of acquired rights

Member States may provide that those persons who exercised a mediation activity before 1 September 2000, who were entered in a register and who had a level of training and experience similar to that required by this Directive, shall be automatically entered in the register to be created, once the requirements set down in Article 4(3) and (4) are complied with.

Article 6

Notification of establishment and services in other Member States

1. Any insurance or reinsurance intermediary intending to carry on business for the first time in

one or more Member States under the freedom to provide services or the freedom of establishment shall inform the competent authorities of the home Member State.

Within a period of one month after such notification, those competent authorities shall inform the competent authorities of any host Member States wishing to know, of the intention of the insurance or reinsurance intermediary and shall at the same time inform the intermediary concerned.

The insurance or reinsurance intermediary may start business one month after the date on which he was informed by the competent authorities of the home Member State of the notification referred to in the second subparagraph.

However, that intermediary may start business immediately if the host Member State does not wish to be informed of the fact.

2. Member States shall notify the Commission of their wish to be informed in accordance with paragraph 1. The Commission shall in turn notify all the Member States of this.

3. The competent authorities of the host Member State may take the necessary steps to ensure appropriate publication of the conditions under which, in the interest of the general good, the business concerned must be carried on in their territories.

Article 7

Competent authorities

1. Member States shall designate the competent authorities empowered to ensure implementation of this Directive.

They shall inform the Commission thereof, indicating any division of those duties.

2. The authorities referred to in paragraph 1 shall be either public authorities or bodies recognised by national law or by public authorities expressly empowered for that purpose by national law. They shall not be insurance or reinsurance undertakings.

3. The competent authorities shall possess all the powers necessary for the performance of their duties. Where there is more than one competent authority on its territory, a Member State shall ensure that those authorities collaborate closely so that they can discharge their respective duties effectively.

Article 8

Sanctions

1. Member States shall provide for appropriate sanctions in the event that a person exercising the activity of insurance or reinsurance mediation is not registered in a Member State and is not referred to in Article 1(2).

2. Member States shall provide for appropriate sanctions against insurance or reinsurance undertakings which use the insurance or reinsurance mediation services of persons who are not registered in a Member State and who are not referred to in Article 1(2).

3. Member States shall provide for appropriate sanctions in the event of an insurance or reinsurance intermediary's failure to comply with national provisions adopted pursuant to this Directive.

4. This Directive shall not affect the power of the host Member States to take appropriate measures to prevent or to penalise irregularities committed within their territories which are contrary to legal or regulatory provisions adopted in the interest of the general good. This shall include the possibility of preventing offending insurance or reinsurance intermediaries from initiating any further activities within their territories.

5. Any measure adopted involving sanctions or restrictions on the activities of an insurance or reinsurance intermediary must be properly justified and communicated to the intermediary concerned. Every such measure shall be subject to the right to apply to the courts in the Member State which adopted it.

Article 9

Exchange of information between Member States

1. The competent authorities of the various Member States shall cooperate in order to ensure

the proper application of the provisions of this Directive.

2. The competent authorities shall exchange information on insurance and reinsurance intermediaries if they have been subject to a sanction referred to in Article 8(3) or a measure referred to in Article 8(4) and such information is likely to lead to removal from the register of such intermediaries. The competent authorities may also exchange any relevant information at the request of an authority.

3. All persons required to receive or divulge information in connection with this Directive shall be bound by professional secrecy, in the same manner as is laid down in Article 16 of Council Directive 92/49/EEC of 18 June 1992 on the coordination of laws, regulations and administrative provisions relating to direct insurance other than life assurance and amending Directives 73/239/EEC and 88/357/EEC (third non–life insurance Directive)[11] and Article 15 of Council Directive 92/96/EEC of 10 November 1992 on the coordination of laws, regulations and administrative provisions relating to direct life assurance and amending Directives 79/267/EEC and 90/619/EEC (third life assurance Directive).[12]

Article 10

Complaints

Member States shall ensure that procedures are set up which allow customers and other interested parties, especially consumer associations, to register complaints about insurance and reinsurance intermediaries. In all cases complaints shall receive replies.

Article 11

Out-of-court redress

1. Member States shall encourage the setting-up of appropriate and effective complaints and redress procedures for the out-of-court settlement of disputes between insurance intermediaries and customers, using existing bodies where appropriate.

2. Member States shall encourage these bodies to cooperate in the resolution of cross-border disputes.

Chapter III

Information Requirements for Intermediaries

Article 12

Information provided by the insurance intermediary

1. Prior to the conclusion of any initial insurance contract, and, if necessary, upon amendment or renewal thereof, an insurance intermediary shall provide the customer with at least the following information:

(a) his identity and address;

(b) the register in which he has been included and the means for verifying that he has been registered;

(c) whether he has a holding, direct or indirect, representing more than 10% of the voting rights or of the capital in a given insurance undertaking;

(d) whether a given insurance undertaking or parent undertaking of a given insurance undertaking has a holding, direct or indirect, representing more than 10% of the voting rights or of the capital in the insurance intermediary;

(e) the procedures referred to in Article 10 allowing customers and other interested parties to register complaints about insurance and reinsurance intermediaries and, if appropriate, about the out-of-court complaint and redress procedures referred to in Article 11.

In addition, an insurance intermediary shall inform the customer, concerning the contract that is provided, whether:

(i) he gives advice based on the obligation in paragraph 2 to provide a fair analysis, or

(ii) he is under a contractual obligation to conduct insurance mediation business exclusively

---

[11] OJ L 228, 11.8.1992, 1, reproduced supra under no. I. 25. Directive as last amended by Directive 2000/64/EC of the European Parliament and of the Council (OJ L 290, 17.11.2000, 27).
[12] OJ L 360, 9.12.1992, 1, reproduced supra under no. I. 26. Directive as last amended by Directive 2000/64/EC of the European Parliament and of the Council.

with one or more insurance undertakings. In that case, he shall, at the customer's request provide the names of those insurance undertakings, or

(iii) he is not under a contractual obligation to conduct insurance mediation business exclusively with one or more insurance undertakings and does not give advice based on the obligation in paragraph 2 to provide a fair analysis.

In that case, he shall, at the customer's request provide the names of the insurance undertakings with which he may and does conduct business.

In those cases where information is to be provided solely at the customer's request, the customer shall be informed that he has the right to request such information.

2. When the insurance intermediary informs the customer that he gives his advice on the basis of a fair analysis, he is obliged to give that advice on the basis of an analysis of a sufficiently large number of insurance contracts available on the market, to enable him to make a recommendation, in accordance with professional criteria, regarding which insurance contract would be adequate to meet the customer's needs.

3. Prior to the conclusion of any specific contract, the insurance intermediary shall at least specify, in particular on the basis of information provided by the customer, the demands and the needs of that customer as well as the underlying reasons for any advice given to the customer on a given insurance product. These details shall be modulated according to the complexity of the insurance contract being proposed.

4. The information referred to in paragraphs 1, 2 and 3 need not be given when the insurance intermediary mediates in the insurance of large risks, nor in the case of mediation by reinsurance intermediaries.

5. Member States may maintain or adopt stricter provisions regarding the information requirements referred to in paragraph 1, provided that such provisions comply with Community law.

Member States shall communicate to the Commission the national provisions set out in the first subparagraph.

In order to establish a high level of transparency by all appropriate means, the Commission shall ensure that the information it receives relating to national provisions is also communicated to consumers and insurance intermediaries.

Article 13
Information conditions

1. All information to be provided to customers in accordance with Article 12 shall be communicated:

(a) on paper or on any other durable medium available and accessible to the customer;

(b) in a clear and accurate manner, comprehensible to the customer;

(c) in an official language of the Member State of the commitment or in any other language agreed by the parties.

2. By way of derogation from paragraph 1(a), the information referred to in Article 12 may be provided orally where the customer requests it, or where immediate cover is necessary. In those cases, the information shall be provided to the customer in accordance with paragraph 1 immediately after the conclusion of the insurance contract.

3. In the case of telephone selling, the prior information given to the customer shall be in accordance with Community rules applicable to the distance marketing of consumer financial services. Moreover, information shall be provided to the customer in accordance with paragraph 1 immediately after the conclusion of the insurance contract.

CHAPTER IV
FINAL PROVISIONS

Article 14
Right to apply to the courts

Member States shall ensure that decisions taken in respect of an insurance intermediary, reinsurance intermediary or an insurance undertaking under the laws, regulations and administrative provisions adopted in accordance with this

Directive may be subject to the right to apply to the courts.

Article 15
Repeal

Directive 77/92/EEC is hereby repealed with effect from the date referred to in Article 16(1).

Article 16
Transposition

1. Member States shall bring into force the laws, regulations and administrative provisions necessary to comply with this Directive before 15 January 2005. They shall forthwith inform the Commission thereof.

These measures shall contain a reference to this Directive or shall be accompanied by such reference on the occasion of their official publication. The methods of making such reference shall be laid down by the Member States.

2. Member States shall communicate to the Commission the text of the laws, regulations and administrative provisions which they adopt in the field governed by this Directive. In that communication they shall provide a table indicating the national provisions corresponding to this Directive.

Article 17
Entry into force

This Directive shall enter into force on the day of its publication in the Official Journal of the European Communities.

Article 18
Addressees

This Directive is addressed to the Member States.

I. 35.

European Parliament and Council Directive 2003/41/EC of 3 June 2003 on the activities and supervision of institutions for occupational retirement provision[1]

THE EUROPEAN PARLIAMENT AND THE COUNCIL OF THE EUROPEAN UNION,

Having regard to the Treaty establishing the European Community, and in particular Article 47(2), Article 55 and Article 95(1) thereof,

Having regard to the proposal from the Commission,[2]

Having regard to the opinion of the European Economic and Social Committee,[3]

Acting in accordance with the procedure laid down in Article 251 of the Treaty,[4]

Whereas:

(1) A genuine internal market for financial services is crucial for economic growth and job creation in the Community.

(2) Major achievements have already been made in the establishment of this internal market, allowing financial institutions to operate in other Member States and ensuring a high level of protection for the consumers of financial services.

(3) The communication from the Commission 'Implementing the framework for financial markets: action plan' identifies a series of actions that are needed in order to complete the internal market for financial services, and the European Council, at its meeting in Lisbon on 23 and 24 March 2000, called for the implementation of this action plan by 2005.

(4) The action plan for financial services stresses as an urgent priority the need to draw up a directive on the prudential supervision of institutions for occupational retirement provision, as these institutions are major financial institutions which have a key role to play in ensuring the integration, efficiency and liquidity of the financial markets, but they are not subject to a coherent Community legislative framework allowing them to benefit fully from the advantages of the internal market.

(5) Since social-security systems are coming under increasing pressure, occupational retirement pensions will increasingly be relied on as a complement in future. Occupational retirement pensions should therefore be developed, without, however, calling into question the importance of social-security pension systems in terms of secure, durable and effective social protection, which should guarantee a decent standard of living in old age and should therefore be at the centre of the objective of strengthening the European social model.

(6) This Directive thus represents a first step on the way to an internal market for occupational retirement provision organised on a European scale. By setting the 'prudent person' rule as the underlying principle for capital investment and making it possible for institutions to operate across borders, the redirection of savings into the sector of occupational retirement provision is encouraged, thus contributing to economic and social progress.

(7) The prudential rules laid down in this Directive are intended both to guarantee a high degree of security for future pensioners through the imposition of stringent supervisory standards, and to clear the way for the efficient management of occupational pension schemes.

---

[1] OJ L 235, 23.9.2003, 10–21.
[2] OJ C 96 E, 27.3.2001, 136.
[3] OJ C 155, 29.5.2001, 26.
[4] Opinion of the European Parliament of 4 July 2001 (OJ C 65 E, 14.3.2002, 135), Council common position of 5 November 2002 (not yet published in the Official Journal) and decision of the European Parliament of 12 March 2003 (not yet published in the Official Journal) and decision of the Council of 13 May 2003.

(8) Institutions which are completely separated from any sponsoring undertaking and which operate on a funded basis for the sole purpose of providing retirement benefits should have freedom to provide services and freedom of investment, subject only to coordinated prudential requirements, regardless of whether these institutions are considered as legal entities.

(9) In accordance with the principle of subsidiarity, Member States should retain full responsibility for the organisation of their pension systems as well as for the decision on the role of each of the three 'pillars' of the retirement system in individual Member States. In the context of the second pillar, they should also retain full responsibility for the role and functions of the various institutions providing occupational retirement benefits, such as industry-wide pension funds, company pension funds and life-assurance companies. This Directive is not intended to call this prerogative into question.

(10) National rules concerning the participation of self-employed persons in institutions for occupational retirement provision differ. In some Member States, institutions for occupational retirement provision can operate on the basis of agreements with trade or trade groups whose members act in a self-employed capacity or directly with self-employed and employed persons. In some Member States a self-employed person can also become a member of an institution when the self-employed person acts as employer or provides his professional services to an undertaking. In some Member States self-employed persons cannot join an institution for occupational retirement provision unless certain requirements, including those imposed by social and labour law, are met.

(11) Institutions managing social-security schemes, which are already coordinated at Community level, should be excluded from the scope of this Directive. Account should nevertheless be taken of the specificity of institutions which, in a single Member State, manage both social-security schemes and occupational pension schemes.

(12) Financial institutions which already benefit from a Community legislative framework should in general be excluded from the scope of this Directive. However, as these institutions may also in some cases offer occupational pension services, it is important to ensure that this Directive does not lead to distortions of competition. Such distortions may be avoided by applying the prudential requirements of this Directive to the occupational pension business of life-assurance companies. The Commission should also carefully monitor the situation in the occupational pensions market and assess the possibility of extending the optional application of this Directive to other regulated financial institutions.

(13) When aiming at ensuring financial security in retirement, the benefits paid by institutions for occupational retirement provision should generally provide for the payment of a lifelong pension. Payments for a temporary period or a lump sum should also be possible.

(14) It is important to ensure that older and disabled people are not placed at risk of poverty and can enjoy a decent standard of living. Appropriate cover for biometrical risks in occupational pension arrangements is an important aspect of the fight against poverty and insecurity among elderly people. When setting up a pension scheme, employers and employees, or their respective representatives, should consider the possibility of the pension scheme including provisions for the coverage of the longevity risk and occupational disability risks as well as provision for surviving dependants.

(15) Giving Member States the possibility to exclude from the scope of national implementing legislation institutions managing schemes which together have less than 100 members in total can facilitate supervision in some Member States, without undermining the proper functioning of the internal market in this field. However, this should not undermine the right of such institutions to appoint for the management of their investment portfolio and the custody of their assets investment managers and custodians established in another Member State and duly authorised.

(16) Institutions such as 'Unterstützungskassen' in Germany, where the members have no legal rights to benefits of a certain amount and where their interests are protected by a compulsory statutory insolvency insurance, should be excluded from the scope of the Directive.

(17) In order to protect members and beneficiaries, institutions for occupational retirement provision should limit their activities to the activities, and those arising therefrom, referred to in this Directive.

(18) In the event of the bankruptcy of a sponsoring undertaking, a member faces the risk of losing both his/her job and his/her acquired pension rights. This makes it necessary to ensure that there is a clear separation between that undertaking and the institution and that minimum prudential standards are laid down to protect members.

(19) Institutions for occupational retirement provision operate and are supervised with significant differences in Member States. In some Member States, supervision can be exercised not only over the institution itself but also over the entities or companies which are authorised to manage these institutions. Member States should be able to take such specificity into account as long as all the requirements laid down in this Directive are effectively met. Member States should also be able to allow insurance entities and other financial entities to manage institutions for occupational retirement provision.

(20) Institutions for occupational retirement provision are financial service providers which bear a heavy responsibility for the provision of occupational retirement benefits and therefore should meet certain minimum prudential standards with respect to their activities and conditions of operation.

(21) The huge number of institutions in certain Member States means a pragmatic solution is necessary as regards prior authorisation of institutions. However, if an institution wishes to manage a scheme in another Member State, a prior authorisation granted by the competent authority of the home Member State should be required.

(22) Each Member State should require that every institution located in its territory draw up annual accounts and annual reports taking into account each pension scheme operated by the institution and, where applicable, annual accounts and annual reports for each pension scheme. The annual accounts and annual reports, reflecting a true and fair view of the institution's assets, liabilities and financial position, taking into account each pension scheme operated by an institution, and duly approved by an authorised person, are an essential source of information for members and beneficiaries of a scheme and the competent authorities. In particular, they enable the competent authorities to monitor the financial soundness of an institution and assess whether the institution is able to meet all its contractual obligations.

(23) Proper information for members and beneficiaries of a pension scheme is crucial. This is of particular relevance for requests for information concerning the financial soundness of the institution, the contractual rules, the benefits and the actual financing of accrued pension entitlements, the investment policy and the management of risks and costs.

(24) The investment policy of an institution is a decisive factor for both security and affordability of occupational pensions. The institutions should therefore draw up and, at least every three years, review a statement of investment principles. It should be made available to the competent authorities and on request also to members and beneficiaries of each pension scheme.

(25) To fulfil their statutory function, the competent authorities should be provided with adequate rights to information and powers of intervention with respect to institutions and the persons who effectively run them. Where an institution for occupational retirement provision has transferred functions of material importance such as investment management, information technology or accounting to other companies (outsourcing), it should be possible for the rights to information and powers of intervention to be enlarged so as to cover these outsourced functions in order to check whether

those activities are carried out in accordance with the supervisory rules.

(26) A prudent calculation of technical provisions is an essential condition to ensure that obligations to pay retirement benefits can be met. Technical provisions should be calculated on the basis of recognised actuarial methods and certified by qualified persons. The maximum interest rates should be chosen prudently according to any relevant national rules. The minimum amount of technical provisions should both be sufficient for benefits already in payment to beneficiaries to continue to be paid and reflect the commitments that arise out of members' accrued pension rights.

(27) Risks covered by institutions vary significantly from one Member State to another. Home Member States should therefore have the possibility of making the calculation of technical provisions subject to additional and more detailed rules than those laid down in this Directive.

(28) Sufficient and appropriate assets to cover the technical provisions protect the interests of members and beneficiaries of the pension scheme if the sponsoring undertaking becomes insolvent. In particular in cases of cross-border activity, the mutual recognition of supervisory principles applied in Member States requires that the technical provisions be fully funded at all times.

(29) If the institution does not work on a cross-border basis, Member States should be able to permit underfunding provided that a proper plan is established to restore full funding and without prejudice to the requirements of Council Directive 80/987/EEC of 20 October 1980 on the approximation of the laws of the Member States relating to the protection of employees in the event of the insolvency of their employer.[5]

(30) In many cases, it could be the sponsoring undertaking and not the institution itself that either covers any biometric risk or guarantees certain benefits or investment performance.

However, in some cases, it is the institution itself which provides such cover or guarantees and the sponsor's obligations are generally exhausted by paying the necessary contributions. In these circumstances, the products offered are similar to those of life-assurance companies and the institutions concerned should hold at least the same additional own funds as life-assurance companies.

(31) Institutions are very long-term investors. Redemption of the assets held by these institutions cannot, in general, be made for any purpose other than providing retirement benefits. Furthermore, in order to protect adequately the rights of members and beneficiaries, institutions should be able to opt for an asset allocation that suits the precise nature and duration of their liabilities. These aspects call for efficient supervision and an approach towards investment rules allowing institutions sufficient flexibility to decide on the most secure and efficient investment policy and obliging them to act prudently. Compliance with the 'prudent person' rule therefore requires an investment policy geared to the membership structure of the individual institution for occupational retirement provision.

(32) Supervisory methods and practices vary among Member States. Therefore, Member States should be given some discretion on the precise investment rules that they wish to impose on the institutions located in their territories. However, these rules must not restrict the free movement of capital, unless justified on prudential grounds.

(33) As very long-term investors with low liquidity risks, institutions for occupational retirement provision are in a position to invest in non-liquid assets such as shares as well as in risk capital markets within prudent limits. They can also benefit from the advantages of international diversification. Investments in shares, risk capital markets and currencies other than those of the liabilities should therefore not be restricted except on prudential grounds.

(34) However, if the institution works on a cross-border basis, it may be asked by the competent authorities of the host Member State to

---

[5] OJ L 283, 28.10.1980, 23, reproduced supra under no. E. 3. Directive as last amended by Directive 2002/74/EC of the European Parliament and of the Council (OJ L 270, 8.10.2002, 10), reproduced supra under no. E. 13.

apply limits for investment in shares and similar assets not admitted to trading on a regulated market, in shares and other instruments issued by the same undertaking or in assets denominated in non-matching currencies provided such rules also apply to institutions located in the host Member State.

(35) Restrictions regarding the free choice by institutions of approved asset managers and custodians limit competition in the internal market and should therefore be eliminated.

(36) Without prejudice to national social and labour legislation on the organisation of pension systems, including compulsory membership and the outcomes of collective bargaining agreements, institutions should have the possibility of providing their services in other Member States. They should be allowed to accept sponsorship from undertakings located in other Member States and to operate pension schemes with members in more than one Member State. This would potentially lead to significant economies of scale for these institutions, improve the competitiveness of the Community industry and facilitate labour mobility. This requires mutual recognition of prudential standards. Proper enforcement of these prudential standards should be supervised by the competent authorities of the home Member State, unless specified otherwise.

(37) The exercise of the right of an institution in one Member State to manage an occupational pension scheme contracted in another Member State should fully respect the provisions of the social and labour law in force in the host Member State insofar as it is relevant to occupational pensions, for example the definition and payment of retirement benefits and the conditions for transferability of pension rights.

(38) When a scheme is ring-fenced, the provisions of this Directive apply individually to that scheme.

(39) It is important to make provision for cooperation between the competent authorities of the Member States for supervisory purposes and between those authorities and the Commission for other purposes. For the purposes of carrying out their duties and of contributing to the consistent and timely implementation of this Directive, competent authorities should provide each other with the information necessary to apply the provisions of the Directive. The Commission has indicated its intention to set up a committee of supervisors in order to encourage cooperation, coordination and exchanges of views between national competent authorities, and to promote the consistent implementation of this Directive.

(40) Since the objective of the proposed action, namely to create a Community legal framework covering institutions for occupational retirement provision, cannot be sufficiently achieved by the Member States and can therefore, by reason of the scale and effects of the action, be better achieved by the Community, the Community may adopt measures, in accordance with the principle of subsidiarity as set out in Article 5 of the Treaty. In accordance with the principle of proportionality as set out in that Article, this Directive does not go beyond what is necessary in order to achieve that objective,

HAVE ADOPTED THE FOLLOWING DIRECTIVE:

Article 1
Subject

This Directive lays down rules for the taking-up and pursuit of activities carried out by institutions for occupational retirement provision.

Article 2
Scope

1. This Directive shall apply to institutions for occupational retirement provision. Where, in accordance with national law, institutions for occupational retirement provision do not have legal personality, Member States shall apply this Directive either to those institutions or, subject to paragraph 2, to those authorised entities responsible for managing them and acting on their behalf.

2. This Directive shall not apply to:

(a) institutions managing social-security schemes which are covered by Regulation (EEC)

No 1408/71[6] and Regulation (EEC) No 574/72;[7]

(b) institutions which are covered by Directive 73/239/EEC,[8] Directive 85/611/EEC,[9] Directive 93/22/EEC,[10] Directive 2000/12/EC[11] and Directive 2002/83/EC;[12]

(c) institutions which operate on a pay-as-you-go basis;

(d) institutions where employees of the sponsoring undertakings have no legal rights to benefits and where the sponsoring undertaking can redeem the assets at any time and not necessarily meet its obligations for payment of retirement benefits;

(e) companies using book-reserve schemes with a view to paying out retirement benefits to their employees.

Article 3
Application to institutions operating social-security schemes

Institutions for occupational retirement provision which also operate compulsory employment-related pension schemes which are considered to be social-security schemes covered by Regulations (EEC) No 1408/71 and (EEC) No 574/72 shall be covered by this Directive in respect of their non-compulsory occupational retirement provision business. In that case, the liabilities and the corresponding assets shall be ring-fenced and it shall not be possible to transfer them to the compulsory pension schemes which are considered as social-security schemes or vice versa.

Article 4
Optional application to institutions covered by Directive 2002/83/EC

Home Member States may choose to apply the provisions of Articles 9 to 16 and Articles 18 to 20 of this Directive to the occupational-retirement-provision business of insurance undertakings which are covered by Directive 2002/83/EC. In that case, all assets and liabilities corresponding to the said business shall be ring-fenced, managed and organised separately from the other activities of the insurance undertakings, without any possibility of transfer.

In such case, and only as far as their occupational retirement provision business is concerned, insurance undertakings shall not be subject to Articles 20 to 26, 31 and 36 of Directive 2002/83/EC.

The home Member State shall ensure that either the competent authorities, or the authorities responsible for supervision of insurance undertakings covered by Directive 2002/83/EC, as part of their supervisory work, verify the strict separation of the relevant occupational retirement provision business.

---

[6] Council Regulation (EEC) No 1408/71 of 14 June 1971 on the application of social security schemes to employed persons, to self-employed persons and to members of their families moving within the Community (OJ L 149, 5.7.1971, 2). Regulation as last amended by Regulation (EC) No 1386/2001 of the European Parliament and of the Council (OJ L 187, 10.7.2004, 1).

[7] Council Regulation (EEC) No 574/72 of 21 March 1972 fixing the procedure for implementing Regulation (EEC) No 1408/71 on the application of social-security schemes to employed persons, to self-employed persons and to members of their families moving within the Community (OJ L 74, 27.3.1972, 1). Regulation as last amended by Commission Regulation (EC) No 410/2002 (OJ L 62, 5.3.2002, 17).

[8] First Council Directive 73/239/EEC of 24 July 1973 on the coordination of laws, regulations and administrative provisions relating to the taking-up and pursuit of the business of direct insurance other than life assurance (OJ L 228, 16.8.1973, 3), reproduced supra under no. I. 3. Directive as last amended by Directive 2002/13/EC of the European Parliament and of the Council (OJ L 77, 20.3.2002, 17), reproduced supra under no. I. 32.

[9] Council Directive 85/611/EEC of 20 December 1985 on the coordination of laws, regulations and administrative provisions relating to undertakings for collective investment in transferable securities (UCITS) (OJ L 375, 31.12.1985, 3), reproduced infra under no. S. 6. Directive as last amended by Directive 2001/108/EC of the European Parliament and of the Council (OJ L 41, 13.2.2002, 35), reproduced infra under no. S. 22.

[10] Council Directive 93/22/EEC of 10 May 1993 on investment services in the securities field (OJ L 141, 11.6.1993, 27), reproduced supra under no. S. 14. Directive as last amended by Directive 2000/64/EC of the European Parliament and of the Council (OJ L 290, 17.11.2000, 27).

[11] Directive 2000/12/EC of the European Parliament and of the Council of 20 March 2000 relating to the taking-up and pursuit of the business of credit institutions (OJ L 126, 26.5.2000, 1), reproduced supra under no. B. 32. Directive as amended by Directive 2000/28/EC (OJ L 275, 27.10.2000, 37), reproduced supra under no. B. 34.

[12] Directive 2002/83/EC of the European Parliament and of the Council of 5 November 2002 concerning life assurance (OJ L 345, 19.12.2002, 1), reproduced supra under no. I. 33.

Article 5

Small pension institutions and statutory schemes

With the exception of Article 19, Member States may choose not to apply this Directive, in whole or in part, to any institution located in their territories which operates pension schemes which together have less than 100 members in total. Subject to Article 2(2), such institutions should nevertheless be given the right to apply this Directive on a voluntary basis. Article 20 may be applied only if all the other provisions of this Directive apply.

Member States may choose not to apply Articles 9 to 17 to institutions where occupational retirement provision is made under statute, pursuant to legislation, and is guaranteed by a public authority. Article 20 may be applied only if all the other provisions of this Directive apply.

Article 6

Definitions

For the purposes of this Directive:

(a) 'institution for occupational retirement provision', or 'institution', means an institution, irrespective of its legal form, operating on a funded basis, established separately from any sponsoring undertaking or trade for the purpose of providing retirement benefits in the context of an occupational activity on the basis of an agreement or a contract agreed:
- individually or collectively between the employer(s) and the employee(s) or their respective representatives, or
- with self-employed persons, in compliance with the legislation of the home and host Member States,

and which carries out activities directly arising therefrom;

(b) 'pension scheme' means a contract, an agreement, a trust deed or rules stipulating which retirement benefits are granted and under which conditions;

(c) 'sponsoring undertaking' means any undertaking or other body, regardless of whether it includes or consists of one or more legal or natural persons, which acts as an employer or in a self-employed capacity or any combination thereof and which pays contributions into an institution for occupational retirement provision;

(d) 'retirement benefits' means benefits paid by reference to reaching, or the expectation of reaching, retirement or, where they are supplementary to those benefits and provided on an ancillary basis, in the form of payments on death, disability, or cessation of employment or in the form of support payments or services in case of sickness, indigence or death. In order to facilitate financial security in retirement, these benefits usually take the form of payments for life. They may, however, also be payments made for a temporary period or as a lump sum.

(e) 'member' means a person whose occupational activities entitle or will entitle him/her to retirement benefits in accordance with the provisions of a pension scheme;

(f) 'beneficiary' means a person receiving retirement benefits;

(g) 'competent authorities' means the national authorities designated to carry out the duties provided for in this Directive;

(h) 'biometrical risks' mean risks linked to death, disability and longevity;

(i) 'home Member State' means the Member State in which the institution has its registered office and its main administration or, if it does not have a registered office, its main administration;

(j) 'host Member State' means the Member State whose social and labour law relevant to the field of occupational pension schemes is applicable to the relationship between the sponsoring undertaking and members.

Article 7

Activities of an institution

Each Member State shall require institutions located within its territory to limit their activities to retirement-benefit related operations and activities arising therefrom.

When, in accordance with Article 4, an insurance undertaking manages its occupational retirement provision business by ring-fencing its assets and liabilities, the ring-fenced assets and liabilities shall be restricted to retirement-benefit related operations and activities directly arising therefrom.

Article 8
Legal separation between sponsoring undertakings and institutions for occupational retirement provision

Each Member State shall ensure that there is a legal separation between a sponsoring undertaking and an institution for occupational retirement provision in order that the assets of the institution are safeguarded in the interests of members and beneficiaries in the event of bankruptcy of the sponsoring undertaking.

Article 9
Conditions of operation

1. Each Member State shall, in respect of every institution located in its territory, ensure that:

(a) the institution is registered in a national register by the competent supervisory authority or authorised; in the case of cross-border activities referred to in Article 20, the register shall also indicate the Member States in which the institution is operating;

(b) the institution is effectively run by persons of good repute who must themselves have appropriate professional qualifications and experience or employ advisers with appropriate professional qualifications and experience;

(c) properly constituted rules regarding the functioning of any pension scheme operated by the institution have been implemented and members have been adequately informed of these rules;

(d) all technical provisions are computed and certified by an actuary or, if not by an actuary, by another specialist in this field, including an auditor, according to national legislation, on the basis of actuarial methods recognised by the competent authorities of the home Member State;

(e) where the sponsoring undertaking guarantees the payment of the retirement benefits, it is committed to regular financing;

(f) the members are sufficiently informed of the conditions of the pension scheme, in particular concerning:
 (i) the rights and obligations of the parties involved in the pension scheme;
 (ii) the financial, technical and other risks associated with the pension scheme;
 (iii) the nature and distribution of those risks.

2. In accordance with the principle of subsidiarity and taking due account of the scale of pension benefits offered by the social-security regimes, Member States may provide that the option of longevity and disability cover, provision for surviving dependants and a guarantee of repayment of contributions as additional benefits be offered to members if employers and employees, or their respective representatives, so agree.

3. A Member State may make the conditions of operation of an institution located in its territory subject to other requirements, with a view to ensuring that the interests of members and beneficiaries are adequately protected.

4. A Member State may permit or require institutions located in its territory to entrust management of these institutions, in whole or in part, to other entities operating on behalf of those institutions.

5. In the case of cross-border activity as referred to in Article 20, the conditions of operation of the institution shall be subject to a prior authorisation by the competent authorities of the home Member State.

Article 10
Annual accounts and annual reports

Each Member State shall require that every institution located in its territory draw up annual accounts and annual reports taking into account each pension scheme operated by the institution and, where applicable, annual accounts and annual reports for each pension scheme. The annual accounts and the annual reports shall give a true and fair view of the institution's assets, liabilities and financial position. The annual accounts and information in the reports shall be consistent, comprehensive, fairly presented and duly approved by authorised persons, according to national law.

Article 11
Information to be given to the members and beneficiaries

1. Depending on the nature of the pension scheme established, each Member State shall ensure that every institution located in its territory provides at least the information set out in this Article.

2. Members and beneficiaries and/or, where applicable, their representatives shall receive:

(a) on request, the annual accounts and the annual reports referred to in Article 10, and, where an institution is responsible for more than one scheme, those relating to their particular pension scheme;

(b) within a reasonable time, any relevant information regarding changes to the pension-scheme rules.

3. The statement of investment policy principles, referred to in Article 12, shall be made available to members and beneficiaries and/or, where applicable, to their representatives on request.

4. Each member shall also receive, on request, detailed and substantial information on:

(a) the target level of the retirement benefits, if applicable;

(b) the level of benefits in case of cessation of employment;

(c) where the member bears the investment risk, the range of investment options, if applicable, and the actual investment portfolio as well as information on risk exposure and costs related to the investments;

(d) the arrangements relating to the transfer of pension rights to another institution for occupational retirement provision in the event of termination of the employment relationship.

Members shall receive every year brief particulars of the situation of the institution as well as the current level of financing of their accrued individual entitlements.

5. Each beneficiary shall receive, on retirement or when other benefits become due, the appropriate information on the benefits which are due and the corresponding payment options.

Article 12
Statement of investment policy principles

Each Member State shall ensure that every institution located in its territory prepares and, at least every three years, reviews a written statement of investment-policy principles. This statement is to be revised without delay after any significant change in the investment policy. Member States shall provide that this statement contains, at least, such matters as the investment risk measurement methods, the risk-management processes implemented and the strategic asset allocation with respect to the nature and duration of pension liabilities.

Article 13
Information to be provided to the competent authorities

Each Member State shall ensure that the competent authorities, in respect of any institution located in its territory, have the necessary powers and means:

(a) to require the institution, the members of its board of directors and other managers or directors or persons controlling the institution to supply information about all business matters or forward all business documents;

(b) to supervise relationships between the institution and other companies or between institutions, when institutions transfer functions to those other companies or institutions (outsourcing), influencing the financial situation of the institution or being in a material way relevant for effective supervision;

(c) to obtain regularly the statement of investment-policy principles, the annual accounts and the annual reports, and all the documents necessary

for the purposes of supervision. These may include documents such as:
(i) internal interim reports;
(ii) actuarial valuations and detailed assumptions;
(iii) asset-liability studies;
(iv) evidence of consistency with the investment-policy principles;
(v) evidence that contributions have been paid in as planned;
(vi) reports by the persons responsible for auditing the annual accounts referred to in Article 10;

(d) to carry out on-site inspections at the institution's premises and, where appropriate, on outsourced functions to check if activities are carried out in accordance with the supervisory rules.

Article 14

Powers of intervention and duties of the competent authorities

1. The competent authorities shall require every institution located in their territories to have sound administrative and accounting procedures and adequate internal control mechanisms.

2. The competent authorities shall have the power to take any measures including, where appropriate, those of an administrative or financial nature, either with regard to any institution located in their territories or against the persons running the institution, which are appropriate and necessary to prevent or remedy any irregularities prejudicial to the interests of the members and beneficiaries.

They may also restrict or prohibit the free disposal of the institution's assets when, in particular:

(a) the institution has failed to establish sufficient technical provisions in respect of the entire business or has insufficient assets to cover the technical provisions;

(b) the institution has failed to hold the regulatory own funds.

3. In order to safeguard the interests of members and beneficiaries, the competent authorities may transfer the powers which the persons running an institution located in their territories hold in accordance with the law of the home Member State wholly or partly to a special representative who is fit to exercise these powers.

4. The competent authorities may prohibit or restrict the activities of an institution located in their territories in particular if:

(a) the institution fails to protect adequately the interests of members and beneficiaries;

(b) the institution no longer fulfils the conditions of operation;

(c) the institution fails seriously in its obligations under the rules to which it is subject;

(d) in the case of cross-border activity, the institution does not respect the requirements of social and labour law of the host Member State relevant to the field of occupational pensions.

Any decision to prohibit the activities of an institution shall be supported by precise reasons and notified to the institution in question.

5. Member States shall ensure that decisions taken in respect of an institution under laws, regulations and administrative provisions adopted in accordance with this Directive are subject to the right to apply to the courts.

Article 15

Technical provisions

1. The home Member State shall ensure that institutions operating occupational pension schemes establish at all times in respect of the total range of their pension schemes an adequate amount of liabilities corresponding to the financial commitments which arise out of their portfolio of existing pension contracts.

2. The home Member State shall ensure that institutions operating occupational pension schemes, where they provide cover against biometric risks and/or guarantee either an investment performance or a given level of benefits, establish sufficient technical provisions in respect of the total range of these schemes.

3. The calculation of technical provisions shall take place every year. However, the home Member

State may allow a calculation once every three years if the institution provides members and/or the competent authorities with a certification or a report of adjustments for the intervening years. The certification or the report shall reflect the adjusted development of the technical provisions and changes in risks covered.

4. The calculation of the technical provisions shall be executed and certified by an actuary or, if not by an actuary, by another specialist in this field, including an auditor, according to national legislation, on the basis of actuarial methods recognised by the competent authorities of the home Member State, according to the following principles:

(a) the minimum amount of the technical provisions shall be calculated by a sufficiently prudent actuarial valuation, taking account of all commitments for benefits and for contributions in accordance with the pension arrangements of the institution. It must be sufficient both for pensions and benefits already in payment to beneficiaries to continue to be paid, and to reflect the commitments which arise out of members' accrued pension rights. The economic and actuarial assumptions chosen for the valuation of the liabilities shall also be chosen prudently taking account, if applicable, of an appropriate margin for adverse deviation;

(b) the maximum rates of interest used shall be chosen prudently and determined in accordance with any relevant rules of the home Member State. These prudent rates of interest shall be determined by taking into account:
– the yield on the corresponding assets held by the institution and the future investment returns and/or
– the market yields of high-quality or government bonds;

(c) the biometric tables used for the calculation of technical provisions shall be based on prudent principles, having regard to the main characteristics of the group of members and the pension schemes, in particular the expected changes in the relevant risks;

(d) the method and basis of calculation of technical provisions shall in general remain constant from one financial year to another. However, discontinuities may be justified by a change of legal, demographic or economic circumstances underlying the assumptions.

5. The home Member State may make the calculation of technical provisions subject to additional and more detailed requirements, with a view to ensuring that the interests of members and beneficiaries are adequately protected.

6. With a view to further harmonisation of the rules regarding the calculation of technical provisions which may be justified—in particular the interest rates and other assumptions influencing the level of technical provisions—the Commission shall, every two years or at the request of a Member State, issue a report on the situation concerning the development in cross-border activities.

The Commission shall propose any necessary measures to prevent possible distortions caused by different levels of interest rates and to protect the interest of beneficiaries and members of any scheme.

Article 16

Funding of technical provisions

1. The home Member State shall require every institution to have at all times sufficient and appropriate assets to cover the technical provisions in respect of the total range of pension schemes operated.

2. The home Member State may allow an institution, for a limited period of time, to have insufficient assets to cover the technical provisions. In this case the competent authorities shall require the institution to adopt a concrete and realisable recovery plan in order to ensure that the requirements of paragraph 1 are met again. The plan shall be subject to the following conditions:

(a) the institution shall set up a concrete and realisable plan to re-establish the required amount of assets to cover fully the technical provisions in due time. The plan shall be made available to members or, where applicable, to their representatives and/or shall be subject to approval by the competent authorities of the home Member State;

(b) in drawing up the plan, account shall be taken of the specific situation of the institution, in particular the asset/liability structure, risk profile, liquidity plan, the age profile of the members entitled to receive retirement benefits, start-up schemes and schemes changing from non-funding or partial funding to full funding;

(c) in the event of termination of a pension scheme during the period referred to above in this paragraph, the institution shall inform the competent authorities of the home Member State. The institution shall establish a procedure in order to transfer the assets and the corresponding liabilities to another financial institution or a similar body. This procedure shall be disclosed to the competent authorities of the home Member State and a general outline of the procedure shall be made available to members or, where applicable, to their representatives in accordance with the principle of confidentiality.

3. In the event of cross-border activity as referred to in Article 20, the technical provisions shall at all times be fully funded in respect of the total range of pension schemes operated. If these conditions are not met, the competent authorities of the home Member State shall intervene in accordance with Article 14. To comply with this requirement the home Member State may require ring-fencing of the assets and liabilities.

Article 17
Regulatory own funds

1. The home Member State shall ensure that institutions operating pension schemes, where the institution itself, and not the sponsoring undertaking, underwrites the liability to cover against biometric risk, or guarantees a given investment performance or a given level of benefits, hold on a permanent basis additional assets above the technical provisions to serve as a buffer. The amount thereof shall reflect the type of risk and asset base in respect of the total range of schemes operated. These assets shall be free of all foreseeable liabilities and serve as a safety capital to absorb discrepancies between the anticipated and the actual expenses and profits.

2. For the purposes of calculating the minimum amount of the additional assets, the rules laid down in Articles 27 and 28 of Directive 2002/83/EC shall apply.

3. Paragraph 1 shall, however, not prevent Member States from requiring institutions located in their territory to hold regulatory own funds or from laying down more detailed rules provided that they are prudentially justified.

Article 18
Investment rules

1. Member States shall require institutions located in their territories to invest in accordance with the 'prudent person' rule and in particular in accordance with the following rules:

(a) the assets shall be invested in the best interests of members and beneficiaries. In the case of a potential conflict of interest, the institution, or the entity which manages its portfolio, shall ensure that the investment is made in the sole interest of members and beneficiaries;

(b) the assets shall be invested in such a manner as to ensure the security, quality, liquidity and profitability of the portfolio as a whole.

Assets held to cover the technical provisions shall also be invested in a manner appropriate to the nature and duration of the expected future retirement benefits;

(c) the assets shall be predominantly invested on regulated markets. Investment in assets which are not admitted to trading on a regulated financial market must in any event be kept to prudent levels;

(d) investment in derivative instruments shall be possible insofar as they contribute to a reduction of investment risks or facilitate efficient portfolio management. They must be valued on a prudent basis, taking into account the underlying asset, and included in the valuation of the institution's assets. The institution shall also avoid excessive risk exposure to a single counterparty and to other derivative operations;

(e) the assets shall be properly diversified in such a way as to avoid excessive reliance on any particular asset, issuer or group of undertakings and accumulations of risk in the portfolio as a whole.

Investments in assets issued by the same issuer or by issuers belonging to the same group shall not expose the institution to excessive risk concentration;

(f) investment in the sponsoring undertaking shall be no more than 5% of the portfolio as a whole and, when the sponsoring undertaking belongs to a group, investment in the undertakings belonging to the same group as the sponsoring undertaking shall not be more than 10% of the portfolio.

When the institution is sponsored by a number of undertakings, investment in these sponsoring undertakings shall be made prudently, taking into account the need for proper diversification.

Member States may decide not to apply the requirements referred to in points (e) and (f) to investment in government bonds.

2. The home Member State shall prohibit the institution from borrowing or acting as a guarantor on behalf of third parties. However, Member States may authorise institutions to carry out some borrowing only for liquidity purposes and on a temporary basis.

3. Member States shall not require institutions located in their territory to invest in particular categories of assets.

4. Without prejudice to Article 12, Member States shall not subject the investment decisions of an institution located in their territory or its investment manager to any kind of prior approval or systematic notification requirements.

5. In accordance with the provisions of paragraphs 1 to 4, Member States may, for the institutions located in their territories, lay down more detailed rules, including quantitative rules, provided they are prudentially justified, to reflect the total range of pension schemes operated by these institutions.

In particular, Member States may apply investment provisions similar to those of Directive 2002/83/EC.

However, Member States shall not prevent institutions from:

(a) investing up to 70% of the assets covering the technical provisions or of the whole portfolio for schemes in which the members bear the investment risks in shares, negotiable securities treated as shares and corporate bonds admitted to trading on regulated markets and deciding on the relative weight of these securities in their investment portfolio. Provided it is prudentially justified, Member States may, however, apply a lower limit to institutions which provide retirement products with a long-term interest rate guarantee, bear the investment risk and themselves provide for the guarantee;

(b) investing up to 30% of the assets covering technical provisions in assets denominated in currencies other than those in which the liabilities are expressed;

(c) investing in risk capital markets.

6. Paragraph 5 shall not preclude the right for Member States to require the application to institutions located in their territory of more stringent investment rules also on an individual basis provided they are prudentially justified, in particular in the light of the liabilities entered into by the institution.

7. In the event of cross-border activity as referred in Article 20, the competent authorities of each host Member State may require that the rules set out in the second subparagraph apply to the institution in the home Member State. In such case, these rules shall apply only to the part of the assets of the institution that corresponds to the activities carried out in the particular host Member State. Furthermore, they shall only be applied if the same or stricter rules also apply to institutions located in the host Member State.

The rules referred to in the first subparagraph are as follows:

(a) the institution shall not invest more than 30% of these assets in shares, other securities treated as shares and debt securities which are not admitted to trading on a regulated market, or the institution shall invest at least 70% of these assets in shares, other securities treated as shares, and debt securities which are admitted to trading on a regulated market;

(b) the institution shall invest no more than 5% of these assets in shares and other securities treated as shares, bonds, debt securities and other money and capital-market instruments issued by the same undertaking and no more than 10% of these assets in shares and other securities treated as shares, bonds, debt securities and other money and capital market instruments issued by undertakings belonging to a single group;

(c) the institution shall not invest more than 30% of these assets in assets denominated in currencies other than those in which the liabilities are expressed.

To comply with these requirements, the home Member State may require ring-fencing of the assets.

Article 19
Management and custody

1. Member States shall not restrict institutions from appointing, for the management of the investment portfolio, investment managers established in another Member State and duly authorised for this activity, in accordance with Directives 85/611/EEC, 93/22/EEC, 2000/12/EC and 2002/83/EC, as well as those referred to in Article 2(1) of this Directive.

2. Member States shall not restrict institutions from appointing, for the custody of their assets, custodians established in another Member State and duly authorised in accordance with Directive 93/22/EEC or Directive 2000/12/EC, or accepted as a depositary for the purposes of Directive 85/611/EEC.

The provision referred to in this paragraph shall not prevent the home Member State from making the appointment of a depositary or a custodian compulsory.

3. Each Member State shall take the necessary steps to enable it under its national law to prohibit, in accordance with Article 14, the free disposal of assets held by a depositary or custodian located within its territory at the request of the institution's home Member State.

Article 20
Cross-border activities

1. Without prejudice to national social and labour legislation on the organisation of pension systems, including compulsory membership and the outcomes of collective bargaining agreements, Member States shall allow undertakings located within their territories to sponsor institutions for occupational retirement provision authorised in other Member States. They shall also allow institutions for occupational retirement provision authorised in their territories to accept sponsorship by undertakings located within the territories of other Member States.

2. An institution wishing to accept sponsorship from a sponsoring undertaking located within the territory of another Member State shall be subject to a prior authorisation by the competent authorities of its home Member State, as referred to in Article 9(5). It shall notify its intention to accept sponsorship from a sponsoring undertaking located within the territory of another Member State to the competent authorities of the home Member State where it is authorised.

3. Member States shall require institutions located within their territories and proposing to be sponsored by an undertaking located in the territory of another Member State to provide the following information when effecting a notification under paragraph 2:

(a) the host Member State(s);

(b) the name of the sponsoring undertaking;

(c) the main characteristics of the pension scheme to be operated for the sponsoring undertaking.

4. Where a competent authority of the home Member State is notified under paragraph 2, and unless it has reason to doubt that the administrative structure or the financial situation of the institution or the good repute and professional qualifications or experience of the persons running the institution are compatible with the operations proposed in the host Member State, it shall within three months of receiving all the information referred to in paragraph 3 communicate that information to the competent authorities of the

host Member State and inform the institution accordingly.

5. Before the institution starts to operate a pension scheme for a sponsoring undertaking in another Member State, the competent authorities of the host Member State shall, within two months of receiving the information referred to in paragraph 3, inform the competent authorities of the home Member State, if appropriate, of the requirements of social and labour law relevant to the field of occupational pensions under which the pension scheme sponsored by an undertaking in the host Member State must be operated and any rules that are to be applied in accordance with Article 18(7) and with paragraph 7 of this Article. The competent authorities of the home Member State shall communicate this information to the institution.

6. On receiving the communication referred to in paragraph 5, or if no communication is received from the competent authorities of the home Member State on expiry of the period provided for in paragraph 5, the institution may start to operate the pension scheme sponsored by an undertaking in the host Member State in accordance with the host Member State's requirements of social and labour law relevant to the field of occupational pensions, and any rules that are to be applied in accordance with Article 18(7) and with paragraph 7 of this Article.

7. In particular, an institution sponsored by an undertaking located in another Member State shall also be subject, in respect of the corresponding members, to any information requirements imposed by the competent authorities of the host Member State on institutions located in that Member State, in accordance with Article 11.

8. The competent authorities of the host Member State shall inform the competent authorities of the home Member State of any significant change in the host Member State's requirements of social and labour law relevant to the field of occupational pension schemes which may affect the characteristics of the pension scheme insofar as it concerns the operation of the pension scheme sponsored by an undertaking in the host Member State and in any rules that have to be applied in accordance with Article 18(7) and with paragraph 7 of this Article.

9. The institution shall be subject to ongoing supervision by the competent authorities of the host Member State as to the compliance of its activities with the host Member State's requirements of labour and social law relevant to the field of occupational pension schemes referred to in paragraph 5 and with the information requirements referred to in paragraph 7. Should this supervision bring irregularities to light, the competent authorities of the host Member State shall inform the competent authorities of the home Member State immediately. The competent authorities of the home Member State shall, in coordination with the competent authorities of the host Member State, take the necessary measures to ensure that the institution puts a stop to the detected breach of social and labour law.

10. If, despite the measures taken by the competent authorities of the home Member State or because appropriate measures are lacking in the home Member State, the institution persists in breaching the applicable provisions of the host Member State's requirements of social and labour law relevant to the field of occupational pension schemes, the competent authorities of the host Member State may, after informing the competent authorities of the home Member State, take appropriate measures to prevent or penalise further irregularities, including, insofar as is strictly necessary, preventing the institution from operating in the host Member State for the sponsoring undertaking.

Article 21

Cooperation between Member States and the Commission

1. Member States shall ensure, in an appropriate manner, the uniform application of this Directive through regular exchanges of information and experience with a view to developing best practices in this sphere and closer cooperation, and by so doing, preventing distortions of competition and creating the conditions required for unproblematic cross-border membership.

2. The Commission and the competent authorities of the Member States shall collaborate closely with a view to facilitating supervision of the operations of institutions for occupational retirement provision.

3. Each Member State shall inform the Commission of any major difficulties to which the application of this Directive gives rise. The Commission and the competent authorities of the Member States concerned shall examine such difficulties as quickly as possible in order to find an appropriate solution.

4. Four years after the entry into force of this Directive, the Commission shall issue a report reviewing:

(a) the application of Article 18 and the progress achieved in the adaptation of national supervisory systems, and

(b) the application of the second subparagraph of Article 19(2), in particular the situation prevailing in Member States regarding the use of depositaries and the role played by them where appropriate.

5. The competent authorities of the host Member State may ask the competent authorities of the home Member State to decide on the ring-fencing of the institution's assets and liabilities, as provided for in Article 16(3) and Article 18(7).

Article 22

Implementation

1. Member States shall bring into force the laws, regulations and administrative provisions necessary to comply with this Directive before 23 September 2005. They shall forthwith inform the Commission thereof.

When Member States adopt these measures, they shall contain a reference to this Directive or shall be accompanied by such reference on the occasion of their official publication. The methods of making such reference shall be laid down by Member States.

2. Member States shall communicate to the Commission the text of the main provisions of national law which they adopt in the field governed by this Directive.

3. Member States may postpone until 23 September 2010 the application of Article 17(1) and (2) to institutions located in their territory which at the date specified in paragraph 1 of this Article do not have the minimum level of regulatory own funds required pursuant to Article 17(1) and (2). However, institutions wishing to operate pension schemes on a cross-border basis, within the meaning of Article 20, may not do so until they comply with the rules of this Directive.

4. Member States may postpone until 23 September 2010 the application of Article 18(1)(f) to institutions located in their territory. However, institutions wishing to operate pension schemes on a cross-border basis, within the meaning of Article 20, may not do so until they comply with the rules of this Directive.

Article 23

Entry in force

This Directive shall enter into force on the day of its publication in the *Official Journal of the European Union*.

Article 24

Addressees

This Directive is addressed to the Member States.

I. 36.

II

(Acts whose publication is not obligatory)

Commission Decision 2003/564/EC
of 28 July 2003
on the application of Council Directive 72/166/EEC relating to checks on insurance against civil liability in respect of the use of motor vehicles[1]

(notified under document number C(2003) 2626)
(Text with EEA relevance)

¶ *This decision repeals as from 1 August 2003 Commission Decisions 91/323/EEC, 93/43/EEC, 97/928/EC, 99/10/EC, and 2001/160/EC. Therefore they are no longer included in this text collection.*

THE COMMISSION OF THE EUROPEAN COMMUNITIES,

Having regard to the Treaty establishing the European Community,

Having regard to Council Directive 72/166/EEC of 24 April 1972 on the approximation of the laws of the Member States relating to insurance against civil liability in respect of the use of motor vehicles and to the enforcement of the obligation to insure against such liability,[2] as last amended by Directive 90/232/EEC,[3] and in particular Articles 2(2) and 7(3) thereof,

Whereas:

(1) The relationships between the national insurers' bureaux of the Member States, as defined in Article 1(3) of Directive 72/166/EEC (hereinafter, the bureaux), and those of the Czech Republic, Hungary, Norway, Slovakia and Switzerland were governed by agreements supplementary to the Uniform Agreement on the Green Card System between national insurers' bureaux of 2 November 1951 (Supplementary Agreements). These Supplementary Agreements provided for the practical arrangements to abolish insurance checks in the case of vehicles normally based in the territories of all these countries.

(2) The Commission subsequently adopted Decisions requiring each Member State, in accordance with Directive 72/166/EEC, to refrain from making checks on insurance against civil liability in respect of vehicles which are normally based in another Member State or in the territories of the abovementioned non-member countries and which are subject of the Supplementary Agreements.

(3) The national insurers' bureaux reviewed and unified the texts of the Supplementary Agreements and replaced them by a single agreement (the Multilateral Guarantee Agreement) signed in Madrid on 15 March 1991, in accordance with the principles laid down in Article 2(2) of Directive 72/166/EEC. This Multilateral Guarantee Agreement was enclosed to the Commission Decision 91/323/EEC.[4]

(4) The Commission subsequently adopted Decisions 93/43/EEC,[5] 97/828/EC,[6] 99/103/EC[7] and 2001/160/EC[8] requiring each Member State, in accordance with Directive 72/166/EEC, to refrain from making checks on insurance

---

[1] OJ L 192, 31.7.2003, 23–39.
[2] OJ L 103, 2.5.1972, 1.
[3] OJ L 129, 19.5.1990, 33.
[4] OJ L 177, 5.7.1991, 25.
[5] OJ L 16, 25.1.1993, 1.
[6] OJ L 343, 13.12.1997, 25.
[7] OJ L 33, 6.2.1999, 25.
[8] OJ L 57, 27.2.2001, 56.

against civil liability in respect of vehicles which are normally based in another Member State or in the territories of, respectively, Iceland, Slovenia, Croatia and Cyprus.

(5) The Agreement between the National Insurers' Bureaux of the Member States of the European Economic Area and other Associate States was concluded on 30 May 2002 in Rethymno (Crete), in accordance with the principles laid down in Article 2(2) of Directive 72/166/EEC. The first Appendix of that agreement incorporates all the provisions of the Uniform Agreement between Bureaux and of the Multilateral Guarantee Agreement into a single document (the Internal Regulations). These Internal Regulations replaces these two latter agreements from 1 August 2003.

(6) Therefore Decisions 91/323/EEC, 93/43/EEC, 97/828/EC, 99/103/EC and 2001/160/EC should be repealed on 1 August 2003,

HAS ADOPTED THIS DECISION:

Article 1

As from 1 August 2003, each Member State shall refrain from making checks on insurance against civil liability in respect of vehicles which are normally based in another Member State or in the territory of the Czech Republic, Croatia, Cyprus, Hungary, Iceland, Norway, Slovakia, Slovenia and Switzerland, which are the subject of the Agreement of 30 May 2002 between the National Insurers' Bureaux of the Member States of the European Economic Area and other Associate States, attached as an appendix to the Annex to this Decision.

Article 2

Decisions 91/323/EEC, 93/43/EEC, 97/828/EC, 99/103/EC and 2001/160/EC are repealed on 1 August 2003.

Article 3

Member States shall forthwith inform the Commission of measures taken to apply this Decision.

Article 4

This Decision is addressed to the Member States.

Annex

Appendix

Agreement between the national insurers' bureaux of the Member States of the European Economic Area and other Associate States

PREAMBLE

Having regard to the 72/166/EEC Directive of the Council of 24 April 1972 (First Directive relating to motor insurance) which provides that national insurers' bureaux of the Member States shall conclude between themselves an agreement under which each national insurers' bureau shall guarantee settlement of claims occurring in its territory and caused by the use of vehicles normally based in the territory of another Member State, whether or not such vehicles are insured, in accordance with the requirements of its national law on compulsory insurance,

Having regard to the fact that the aforesaid Directive provides that vehicles normally based in a third country shall be treated as vehicles normally based in the Community if the national insurers' bureaux of all Member States severally guarantee—each in accordance with the provisions of its own national law on compulsory insurance—settlement of claims in respect of accidents occurring in their territory caused by the use of such vehicles,

Having regard to the fact that, by application of these provisions, the national insurers' bureaux of the Member States and the national insurers' bureaux of other States have concluded several agreements aiming at satisfying the prescriptions of the Directive and that these bureaux have subsequently decided to substitute for them one single agreement known as The Multilateral Guarantee Agreement between National Insurers' Bureaux signed in Madrid on 15 March 1991,

Having regard to the fact that, at the General Assembly held in Rethymno (Crete) on 30 May 2002, the Council of Bureaux decided to incorporate all provisions of the Uniform Agreement between Bureaux and of the Multilateral Guarantee Agreement between National Insurers' Bureaux governing the relations between Bureaux into a single document known as Internal Regulations,

The undersigned Bureaux have concluded the following agreement:

Article 1

The undersigned Bureaux undertake, in the context of their reciprocal relations, to abide by the mandatory provisions as well as by the optional provisions of Sections II and III of the Internal Regulations, where applicable adopted by the Council of Bureaux on 30 May 2002 a copy of which is appended to this agreement—Appendix 1.

Article 2

The undersigned Bureaux grant reciprocal authority, in their own name and in the name of their members, to other signatory Bureaux to amicably settle any claim and to accept service of any judicial or extra-judicial process likely to lead to the payment of compensation arising out of accidents within the context and purpose of these Internal Regulations.

Article 3

The undertaking referred to in Article 1 shall come into force on 1 July 2003, at which date it shall substitute for the Uniform Agreement between Bureaux and for the Multilateral Guarantee Agreement between National Insurers' Bureaux at present binding on the signatories of this Agreement.

Article 4

This Agreement is concluded for an unlimited period of time. However, each signatory Bureau may decide to withdraw from this Agreement by giving written notice of that decision to the Secretary-General of the Council of Bureaux who shall, in turn, immediately so inform the other signatory Bureaux and the Commission of the European Union. Such withdrawal shall take effect on the expiry of a 12-month period from the date of despatch of such notification. The signatory Bureau concerned shall remain liable under this Agreement and its Annexes, to satisfy all reimbursement demands relating to the settlement of claims arising from accidents occurring up to the expiry of the period defined above.

Article 5

This Agreement is concluded between the undermentioned signatory Bureaux, in respect of the territories for which each of them is competent, in the form of three specimens in each of the English and French languages.

One specimen in each of the two languages shall be lodged respectively with the Secretariat of the Council of Bureaux, the General Secretariat of the Comité Européen des Assurances and the Commission of the European Union.

The Secretary-General of the Council of Bureaux shall provide each signatory Bureau with authorised copies of this Agreement.

[...]

¶ *The list of the signatories has been cut out in article 5.*

Appendix 1

Internal Regulations of the Council of Bureaux

Preamble

(1) Whereas in 1949 the Working Party on Road Transport of the Inland Transport Committee of the Economic Commission for Europe of the United Nations sent to the Governments of Member States a recommendation[9] inviting them to ask insurers covering third party liability risks in respect of the use of vehicles to conclude agreements for the establishment of uniform and practical provisions to enable motorists to be satisfactorily insured when entering countries where insurance against such risks is compulsory.

(2) Whereas this recommendation concluded that the introduction of a uniform insurance document would be the best way to achieve that end and set out the basic principles of agreements to be concluded between insurers in the different countries.

(3) Whereas the Inter-Bureaux Agreement, the text of which was adopted in November 1951 by representatives of the insurers in States which, at the time, had responded favourably to the recommendation, formed the basis of the relationship between these insurers.

(4) Whereas:

(a) the purpose of the system, commonly known as the Green Card System, was to facilitate the international circulation of motor vehicles by enabling insurance of third party liability risks in respect of their use to fulfil the criteria imposed by the visited country and, in the case of accidents, to guarantee compensation of injured parties in accordance with the national law and regulations of that country;

(b) the international motor insurance card (Green Card), which is officially recognised by the government authorities of the States adopting the United Nations Recommendation, is proof in each visited country of compulsory civil liability insurance in respect of the use of the motor vehicle described therein;

(c) in each participating State a national bureau has been created and officially approved in order to provide a dual guarantee to:
– its government that the foreign insurer will abide by the law applicable in that country and compensate injured parties within its limits,
– the bureau of the visited country of the commitment of the member insurer covering third party liability in respect of the use of the vehicle involved in the accident;

(d) as a consequence of this non-profit-making dual mandate, each bureau is required to have its own independent financial structure based on the joint commitment of insurers authorised to transact compulsory civil liability insurance in respect of the use of motor vehicles operating in its national market which enables it to meet obligations arising out of agreements between it and other bureaux.

(5) Whereas:

(a) some States, in order to further facilitate international road traffic, have abolished Green Card inspection at their frontiers by virtue of agreements signed between their respective Bureaux, mainly based on vehicle registration;

(b) by its Directive of 24 April 1972[10] the Council of the European Union proposed to the Bureaux of Member States the conclusion of such an agreement; then known as the Supplementary

---

[9] Recommendation No 5 adopted on January 1949, superseded by Appendix 2 of the Consolidated Resolution on the Facilitation of Road Transport adopted by the Working Party on Road Transport of the Inland Transport Committee of the Economic Commission for Europe of the United Nations, the text of which is provided as Appendix I.

[10] Directive of the Council of 24 April 1972 (72/166/EEC) on the approximation of the laws of Member States relating to insurance against civil liability in respect of the use of motor vehicles and to the enforcement of the obligation to insure against such liability, the text of which is provided as Appendix II.

Inter-Bureaux Agreement, which was signed on 16 October 1972;

(c) subsequent agreements, based on the same principles, enabled the bureaux of other countries to become members; and these agreements were then collected into a single document signed on 15 March 1991 and called the Multilateral Guarantee Agreement.

(6) Whereas it is now desirable to incorporate all provisions governing the relations between bureaux into a single document, the Council of Bureaux, at its General Assembly held in Rethymno (Crete) on 30 May 2002 adopted these Internal Regulations.

Section I
General Rules
(Mandatory Provisions)

Article 1
Purpose

The purpose of these Internal Regulations is to govern the reciprocal relations between National Insurers' Bureaux thereby enforcing the provisions of Recommendation No 5 adopted on 25 January 1949 by the Working Party on Road Transport of the Inland Transport Committee of the European Economic Commission of the United Nations, superseded by Annex 2 of the Consolidated Resolution on the Facilitation of Road Transport (RE4) adopted by the Working Party at its 74th session held on 25 to 29 June 1984, in its current version (hereinafter called recommendation No 5).

Article 2
Definitions

For the purpose of these Internal Regulations the following words and expressions shall have the meanings herein assigned to them and no other:

1. 'national insurers' bureau' (hereinafter called bureau): means the professional organisation which is a Member of the Council of Bureaux and constituted in the country of its establishment pursuant to Recommendation No 5;

2. 'insurer': means any undertaking authorised to conduct the business of compulsory third party liability insurance in respect of the use of motor vehicles;

3. 'member': means any insurer who is a member of a bureau;

4. 'correspondent': means any insurer or other person appointed by one or more insurers with the approval of the Bureau of the country in which the person is established with a view to handling and settling claims arising from accidents involving vehicles for which the insurer or insurers in question have issued an insurance policy and occurring in that country;

5. 'vehicle': means any motor vehicle intended for travel on land and propelled by mechanical power but not running on rails as well as any trailer whether or not coupled but only where the motor vehicle or trailer is made subject to compulsory insurance in the country in which it is being used;

6. 'accident': means any event causing loss or injury which may, pursuant to the law of the country where it occurs, fall within the scope of compulsory third party liability insurance in respect of the use of a vehicle;

7. 'injured party': means any person entitled to claim compensation in respect of any loss or injury caused by a vehicle;

8. 'claim': means any one or more claims for compensation presented by an injured party and arising out of the same accident;

9. 'policy of insurance': means a contract of compulsory insurance issued by a member covering civil liability in respect of the use of a vehicle;

10. 'insured': means any person whose third party liability is covered by a policy of insurance;

11. 'Green Card': means the international certificate of motor insurance conforming to any of the models approved by the Council of Bureaux;

12. 'Council of Bureaux': means the body to which all Bureaux must belong and which is

responsible for the administration and the operation of the international motor civil liability insurance system (known as the Green Card System).

Article 3
Handling of claims

1. When a bureau is informed of an accident occurring in the territory of the country for which it is competent, involving a vehicle from another country it shall, without waiting for a formal claim, proceed to investigate the circumstances of the accident. It shall as soon as possible give notice of any such accident to the insurer who issued the Green Card or policy of insurance or, if appropriate, to the bureau concerned. Any omission to do so shall however not be held against it.

If, in the course of this investigation, the bureau notes that the insurer of the vehicle involved in the accident is identified and that a correspondent of this insurer has been approved in conformity with the provisions in Article 4, it shall forward this information promptly to the correspondent for further action.

2. On receipt of a claim arising out of an accident under the circumstances described above, if a correspondent of the insurer has been approved, the bureau shall forward the claim promptly to the correspondent so that it may be handled and settled in conformity with the provisions of Article 4. If there is no approved correspondent, it shall give immediate notice to the insurer who issued the Green Card or policy of insurance or, if appropriate, to the bureau concerned that it has received a claim and will handle it, or arrange for it to be handled, by an agent whose identity it shall also notify.

3. The bureau is authorised to settle any claim amicably or to accept service of any extra-judicial or judicial process likely to involve the payment of compensation.

4. All claims shall be handled by the bureau with complete autonomy in conformity with legal and regulatory provisions applicable in the country of accident relating to liability, compensation of injured parties and compulsory insurance in the best interests of the insurer who issued the Green Card or policy of insurance or, if appropriate, the bureau concerned.

The bureau shall be exclusively competent for all matters concerning the interpretation of the law applicable in the country of accident (even when it refers to the legal provisions applying in another country) and the settlement of the claim. Subject to this latter provision, the bureau shall, on express demand, inform the insurer, or the bureau concerned, before taking a final decision.

5. When the settlement envisaged is in excess of the conditions or limits applicable under the compulsory motor civil liability insurance law in force in the country of accident whilst covered under the policy of insurance, it shall consult the insurer in relation to that part of the claim which exceeds those conditions or limits. The consent of such insurer is not required if the applicable law imposes on the bureau the obligation to take account of the contractual guarantees in excess of such limits and conditions provided in the law relating to insurance against civil liability in respect of the use of motor vehicles in the country of accident.

6. A bureau may not of its own volition or without the written consent of the insurer or Bureau concerned, entrust the claim to any agent who is financially interested in it by virtue of any contractual obligation. If it does so, without such consent, its right to reimbursement shall be limited to one half of the sum otherwise recoverable.

Article 4
Correspondents

1. Subject to any agreement to the contrary binding it to other bureaux and/or to any national legal or regulatory provisions, each bureau shall set out the conditions under which it grants, refuses or withdraws its approval to correspondents established in the country for which it is competent.

However, this approval shall be granted automatically when requested in the name of a member of another Bureau for any establishment of this member in the country of the Bureau receiving the request provided that such establishment is authorised to transact insurance against civil liability in respect of the use of motor vehicles.

2. Bureaux in the Member States of the European Economic Area undertake when receiving such a request, to approve as correspondents in their country claims representatives already appointed by insurers of the other Member States pursuant to Directive 2000/26/EC. This approval cannot be withdrawn as long as the correspondent concerned retains its capacity as a claims representative under the said Directive unless it is in serious breach of its obligations under this Article.

3. Only a bureau shall have the authority, on the request of one of its members, to send to another bureau a request for approval of a correspondent established in the country of that bureau. This request shall be sent by fax or e-mail and supported by proof that the proposed correspondent accepts the requested approval.

The bureau concerned shall grant or refuse its approval within three months from the date of receipt of the request and shall notify its decision and its effective date to the bureau that made the request as well as to the correspondent concerned. In the event of no response being received, approval shall be deemed to have been granted and to have taken effect on the expiry of that period.

4. The correspondent shall handle all claims in conformity with any legal or regulatory provisions applicable in the country of accident relating to liability, compensation of injured parties and compulsory motor insurance, in the name of the bureau that has approved it and on behalf of the insurer that requested its approval, arising out of accidents occurring in that country involving vehicles insured by the insurer that requested its approval.

When any settlement envisaged exceeds the conditions or limits applicable under the compulsory motor civil liability insurance law applicable in the country of accident, whilst covered under the policy of insurance, the correspondent must comply with the provisions set out in Article 3(5).

5. The bureau that has granted its approval to a correspondent recognises it as exclusively competent to handle and settle claims in the name of the bureau and on behalf of the insurer that requested its approval. The bureau shall inform injured parties of this competence and forward to the correspondent any notifications relating to such claims. However it may, at any time and without any obligation to justify its decision, take over the handling and settlement of a claim from a correspondent.

6. If, for whatever reason, the bureau that granted the approval is required to compensate any injured party in place of the correspondent, it shall be reimbursed directly by the bureau through which the request for approval was sent, in accordance with the conditions set out in Article 5.

7. Subject to the provisions of Article 4(4), the correspondent is free to agree with the insurer that requested its approval the conditions for reimbursement of sums paid to injured parties and the method for calculating its handling fees which agreement, however, shall not be enforceable against any bureau.

If a correspondent is unable to obtain reimbursement of advance payments it has made in accordance with the conditions set out in Article 4.4 on behalf of the insurer that requested its approval, it shall be reimbursed by the bureau that approved it. The latter bureau shall subsequently be reimbursed by the bureau of which the insurer in question is a member in accordance with the conditions set out in Article 5.

8. When a bureau is informed that one of its members has decided to dismiss a correspondent, it shall immediately so inform the bureau that granted the approval. This latter bureau shall be at liberty to determine the date on which its approval will cease to have effect.

When a bureau that granted approval to a correspondent decides to withdraw it or is informed that the correspondent wishes to have its approval withdrawn, it shall immediately so inform the bureau that forwarded the request for the approval of the correspondent. It shall also inform the bureau of the date of the correspondent's effective withdrawal or the date on which its approval will cease to have effect.

Article 5
Conditions of reimbursement

1. When a bureau or the agent it has appointed for the purpose has settled all claims arising out of the same accident it shall send, within a maximum period of one year from the date of the last payment made in favour of an injured party, by fax or e-mail to the member of the bureau which issued the Green Card or policy of insurance or, if appropriate, to the bureau concerned a demand for reimbursement specifying:

1.1. the sums paid as compensation to injured parties under either an amicable settlement or a court order;

1.2. the sums disbursed for external services in the handling and settlement of each claim and all costs specifically incurred for the purposes of a legal action which would have been disbursed in similar circumstances by an insurer established in the country of the accident;

1.3. a handling fee to cover all other charges calculated under the rules approved by the Council of Bureaux.

When claims arising out of the same accident are defended and settled without any compensation being paid, such sums as provided in subparagraph (1)(2) above and the minimum fee fixed by the Council of Bureaux in conformity with subparagraph (1)(3) above may be claimed.

2. The demand for reimbursement shall specify that the amounts due are payable in the country and in the national currency of the beneficiary, free of costs, within a period of two months from the date of demand and that, on expiry of that period, late interest at 12% per annum on the amount due from the date of the demand until the date of receipt of the remittance by the bank of the beneficiary shall apply automatically.

The demand for reimbursement may also specify that amounts expressed in the national currency are payable in euro, at the official rate of exchange current in the country of the claiming bureau at the date of the demand.

3. Under no circumstances shall demands for reimbursement include payments for fines, bail bonds or other financial penalties imposed upon an insured which are not covered by insurance against civil liability in respect of the use of motor vehicles in the country of accident.

4. Supporting documents, including the objective proof that compensation due to injured parties has been paid, shall be sent promptly on demand but without delay to the reimbursement.

5. Reimbursement of all sums cited in subparagraphs (1)(1) and (1)(2) above may be claimed in accordance with the conditions set out in this Article notwithstanding that the bureau may not have settled all claims arising out of the same accident. The handling fee provided for under subparagraph (1)(3) above may also be claimed if the principal sum which is the subject of the reimbursement is in excess of the amount fixed by the Council of Bureaux.

6. If, after satisfaction of a reimbursement demand, a claim is reopened or a further claim arising out of the same accident is made, the balance of the handling fee, if any, shall be calculated in accordance with the provisions in force at the time when the demand for reimbursement in respect of the re-opened or further claim is presented.

7. Where no claim for compensation has resulted from an accident, no handling fee may be claimed.

Article 6
Obligation of guarantee

1. Each bureau shall guarantee the reimbursement by its members of any amount demanded in accordance with the provisions of Article 5 by the bureau of the country of accident or by the agent that it has appointed for the purpose.

If a member fails to make the payment demanded within the period of two months specified in Article 5, the bureau to which this member belongs shall itself make the reimbursement in accordance with the conditions described hereunder, following receipt of a guarantee call made by the bureau of the country of accident or by the agent that it has appointed for the purpose.

The bureau standing as guarantor shall make the payment within a period of one month. On expiry of that period, late interest at 12% per annum on the amount due, calculated from the date of the guarantee call to the date of receipt of the remittance by the beneficiary's bank, shall apply automatically.

The guarantee call shall be made by fax or e-mail within a period of 12 months after the date of despatch of the demand for reimbursement under Article 5. On expiry of that period and without prejudice to any late interest for which it may be liable, the liability of the bureau standing as guarantor shall be limited to the amount claimed from its member plus 12 months interest calculated at 12% per annum.

No guarantee call shall be admissible if made more than two years after the despatch of the demand for reimbursement.

2. Each bureau guarantees that its members shall instruct the correspondents whose approval they have requested to settle claims in conformity with the provisions of the first paragraph of Article 4(4) above and forward to those correspondents or to the bureau of the country of accident all documents concerning all claims entrusted to them.

Section II
Specific Rules Governing Contractual Relations Between Bureaux Based on the Green Card (Optional Provisions)

The provisions of this section apply where contractual relations between bureaux are based on the Green Card.

Article 7
Issue and delivery of green cards

1. Each bureau shall be responsible for printing its Green Cards or shall authorise its members to print them.

2. Each bureau shall authorise its members to issue Green Cards to their insurees solely for vehicles registered in any country for which it is competent.

3. Any member may be authorised by its bureau to issue Green Cards to its insurees in any country where no bureau exists provided that the member is established in that country. This option is limited to vehicles registered in the country in question.

4. All Green Cards are deemed to be valid for at least 15 days from their date of inception. In the event that a Green Card is issued for a lesser period, the bureau having authorised the issuing of the Green Card shall guarantee cover to the bureaux in the countries for which the card is valid for a period of 15 days from the date of inception of its validity.

5. Where an agreement signed between two bureaux is cancelled under Article 16(3)(5), all Green Cards delivered in their name for use in their respective territories shall be null and void as soon as the cancellation becomes effective.

6. Where an agreement is cancelled or suspended by the application of Article 16(3)(6), the residual period of validity of the Green Cards delivered in the name of the bureaux concerned for use in their respective territories shall be determined by the Council of Bureaux.

Article 8
Confirmation of the validity of a Green Card

Any request for confirmation of the validity of an identified Green Card sent by fax or e-mail to a bureau by the bureau of the country of accident or by any agent appointed for the purpose shall be given a definitive answer within three months of the request. In the event of no such response then on expiry of that period, the Green Card shall be deemed to be valid.

Article 9
False, unauthorised or illegally altered Green Cards

Any Green Card presented in a country for which it is valid, purporting to be issued under the authority of a bureau shall be guaranteed by that bureau, even if it is false, unauthorised or illegally altered.

However, the bureau's guarantee shall not apply where a Green Card relates to a vehicle which is not legally registered in that bureau's country, with the exception of the circumstances specified in Article 7(3).

Section III

Specific Rules Governing Contractual Relations Between Bureaux Based on Deemed Insurance Cover (Optional Provisions)

The provisions of this section apply when the relations between bureaux are based on deemed insurance cover, with certain exceptions.

Article 10

Obligations of the bureaux

The bureaux to which the provisions of this section apply shall guarantee, on a full reciprocity basis, the reimbursement of all amounts payable under these Regulations arising out of any accident involving a vehicle normally based in the territory of the State for which each of these bureaux is competent, whether the vehicle is insured or not.

Article 11

The normally based concept

1. The territory of the State in which the vehicle is normally based is determined on the basis of any of the following criteria:

1.1. the territory of the State of which the vehicle bears a registration plate;

1.2. where no registration is required for the type of vehicle but the vehicle bears an insurance plate, or a distinguishing sign analogous to a registration plate, the territory of the State in which the insurance plate or the sign is issued;

1.3. where neither registration plate nor insurance plate nor distinguishing sign is required for certain types of vehicles, the territory of the State in which the person who has custody of the vehicle is permanently resident.

2. If a vehicle required to bear a registration plate bears no plate or plates not or no longer legally issued to it has been involved in an accident, the territory in which the accident occurred shall, for the settlement for any resulting claim, be deemed to be the territory where the vehicle is normally based.

Article 12

Exemptions

The provisions of this section do not apply to:

1. vehicles registered in countries other than the countries of the bureaux subject to the provisions of this section and for which a Green Card has been delivered by a member of any of these bureaux. In the event of an accident involving a vehicle for which a Green Card has been issued the bureaux concerned shall act according to the rules set out in Section II;

2. vehicles belonging to certain persons, if the State in which they are registered has designated in the other States an authority or body responsible for compensating injured parties in accordance with the conditions prevailing in the country of accident;

3. certain types of vehicles or certain vehicles bearing a special plate where their use in international traffic is made conditional by the law of the country visited on their holding a valid Green Card or a frontier insurance policy.

The list of vehicles referred to under 2 and 3 as well as the list of authorities or bodies appointed in the other States shall be drawn up by each State and communicated to the Council of Bureaux by the bureau of that State.

Article 13

Confirmation of the territory in which a vehicle is normally based

Any request for confirmation of the territory in which a vehicle is normally based sent by fax or e-mail to a bureau by the bureau of the country of the accident or by any agent appointed for the purpose shall be given a definitive answer within three months of the request. In the event of no such response being received then on the expiry of that period there shall be deemed to be confirmation that the vehicle is normally based in that bureau's territory.

Article 14
Duration of the guarantee

Bureaux may limit the duration of the guarantee they extend under Article 10 in respect of:

1. vehicles with temporary registration plates, the format of which have been notified previously to the Council of bureaux. In such cases, the duration of the guarantee shall be for 12 months after the date of expiry of validity as displayed on the plate;

2. any other vehicle falling within the terms of reciprocal agreements signed with other bureaux and communicated to the Council of Bureaux.

Article 15
Unilateral application of guarantee based on a deemed insurance cover

Save legal provisions to the contrary, bureaux may agree on any unilateral application of this section within the context of their bilateral relations.

SECTION IV
RULES GOVERNING AGREEMENTS CONCLUDED BETWEEN NATIONAL INSURERS' BUREAUX (MANDATORY PROVISIONS)

Article 16
Bilateral agreements—conditions

1. Bureaux may conclude bilateral agreements between themselves whereby they undertake within the context of their reciprocal relations to abide by the mandatory provisions of these Internal Regulations, as well as the optional provisions specified herein.

2. Such agreements shall be signed in triplicate by the contracting bureaux, each of whom shall retain a copy. The third copy shall be sent to the Council of Bureaux which shall, after consultation with the concerned parties, inform them of the date commencement of their agreement.

3. Such agreements shall include clauses providing:

3.1. identification of the contracting bureaux, mentioning their status as members of the Council of Bureaux and the territories for which they are competent;

3.2. their undertaking to abide by the mandatory provisions of these Internal Regulations;

3.3. their undertaking to abide by such optional provisions as mutually chosen and agreed;

3.4. reciprocal authorities granted by these bureaux, in their own name and on behalf of their members, to settle claims amicably or to accept service of any extra-judicial or judicial process likely to lead to the payment of compensation resulting from any accident within the scope and purpose of these Internal Regulations;

3.5. unlimited duration of the agreement, subject to the right of each contracting bureau to terminate it on 12 months notice simultaneously notified to the other party and to the Council of bureaux.

3.6. automatic cancellation or suspension of the agreement if either contracting bureau ceases to be a Member of the Council of Bureaux or has its membership suspended.

4. A model of this agreement is appended (Annex III).

Article 17
Exception

1. By derogation to Article 16, the bureaux of Member States of the European Economic Area shall, in conformity with Article 2 of Directive

72/166/EEC of 24 April 1972 signify their reciprocal acceptance of these Internal Regulations by a multilateral agreement the commencement date of which is determined by the Commission of the European Union in collaboration with the Council of Bureaux.

2. The bureaux in non-member States of the European Economic Area may commit to this multilateral agreement by respecting the conditions fixed by the competent committee as acknowledged in the Constitution of the Council of Bureaux.

SECTION V

PROCEDURE FOR AMENDING THE INTERNAL REGULATIONS (MANDATORY PROVISIONS)

Article 18

Procedure

1. Any amendment to these Regulations shall fall within the exclusive competence of the General Assembly of the Council of Bureaux.

2. By derogation to the above:

(a) any amendment to the provisions set out in Section III shall fall within the exclusive competence of the committee as acknowledged in the Constitution of the Council of Bureaux. Those provisions are binding on bureaux which, although not members of this committee, have elected to apply Section III in their contractual relations with other bureaux; and

(b) any amendment to Article 4.2 shall fall within the exclusive competence of the bureaux of the European Economic Area.

SECTION VI

ARBITRATION (MANDATORY PROVISIONS)

Article 19

Arbitration clause

Any dispute arising out of these Internal Regulations or related to them shall be resolved by arbitration in accordance with the arbitration rules of Uncitral (United Nations Commission on International Trade Law) currently in force.

The Council of Bureaux shall decide upon the fees of the arbitrators and the claimable costs.

The responsibility for the nomination of arbitrators shall rest with the President of the Council of Bureaux or, if unavailable, the Chairman of the Nomination Committee.

The arbitration court shall comprise three arbitrators.

The arbitration proceedings shall be conducted in English and French.

SECTION VII

ENTRY INTO FORCE (MANDATORY PROVISION)

Article 20

Entry into force

These Regulations shall enter into force on 1 July 2003. As from this date they shall replace all uniform agreements and the Multilateral Guarantee Agreement, signed between bureaux.

Annexes

Annex I: Recommendation No 5

Annex II: Directive of 24 April 1972 (72/166/EEC)

Annex III: Model agreement between Bureaux.

The bureau ....

Member of the Council of Bureau

and

The bureau ....

Member of the Council of Bureau

Hereby undertake to abide by the mandatory provisions of the Internal Regulations adopted by the General Assembly of the Council of Bureaux on 30 May 2002 as well as to abide by the optional provisions of Section .... This undertaking shall also apply to any subsequent amendment of the said Internal Regulations.

Hereby grant reciprocal authority to accept service of any judicial or extra judicial process likely to lead to the payment of damages or to settle amicably any claim arising out of accidents within the context of the Internal Regulations.

This agreement is concluded for an unlimited period. However, either signatory may terminate it at 12 months notice. Notice of termination shall be given simultaneously to the other party to the agreement and the Secretary General of the Council of Bureaux.

It is further agreed that this agreement shall be terminated or suspended automatically if either signatory ceases to be a Member of the Council of Bureaux or is suspended from membership thereof.

The date of entry into force of this agreement will be communicated to the signatories by the Secretary General of the Council of Bureaux after receipt of a copy signed by both parties.

Appendix 2

List of Derogations

Austria

Vehicles with temporary registration plates involved in accidents occurring more than 12 months after the date of expiry displayed on the temporary registration plates.

Belgium

Vehicles with temporary registration plates involved in accidents occurring more than 12 months after the date of expiry displayed on the temporary registration plates.

Switzerland (and Liechtenstein)

Vehicles with temporary registration plates involved in accidents occurring more than 12 months after the date of expiry displayed on the temporary registration plates.

Cyprus

1. Vehicles with temporary registration plates involved in accidents occurring more than 12 months after the date of expiry displayed on the temporary registration plates.

2. Vehicles belonging to military forces and other military and civil personnel governed by international Agreements.

Czech Republic

Vehicles with temporary registration plates involved in accidents occurring more than 12 months after the date of expiry displayed on the temporary registration plates.

Germany

1. Vehicles with temporary registration plates involved in accidents occurring more than 12 months after the date of expiry displayed on the temporary registration plates.

2. Military vehicles subject to the terms of international Agreements.

Denmark (and the Faeroe Islands)

1. Vehicles with temporary registration plates involved in accidents occurring more than 12 months after the date of expiry displayed on the temporary registration plates.

2. Military vehicles subject to the terms of international Agreements.

France (and Monaco)

Military vehicles subject to the terms of international Agreements.

Finland

Vehicles with temporary registration plates involved in accidents occurring more than 12 months after the date of expiry displayed on the temporary registration plates.

United Kingdom of Great Britain and Northern Ireland (and the Channel Islands, Gibraltar and the Isle of Man)

NATO vehicles subject to the provisions of the London Convention of 19 June 1951 and the Paris Protocol of 28 August 1952.

Greece

1. Vehicles with temporary registration plates involved in accidents occurring more than 12 months after the date of expiry displayed on the temporary registration plates. (Effective for accidents occurring on or after 1 October 1993.)

2. Vehicles belonging to intergovernmental organisations (Green plates—bearing the letters 'CD' and 'ΔΣ' followed by the registration number).

3. Vehicles belonging to the armed forces and military and civil personnel of NATO (yellow plates—bearing the letters 'ΞΑ' followed by the registration number).

4. Vehicles belonging to the Greek armed forces (plates bearing the letters 'ΕΣ').

5. Vehicles belonging to allied forces in Greece (plates bearing the letters 'AFG').

6. Vehicles bearing test plates (white plates—bearing the letters 'ΔΟΚ' followed by four figures on the registration number).

Hungary

Vehicles with temporary registration plates involved in accidents occurring more than 12 months after the date of expiry displayed on the temporary registration plates.

Italy (and the Republic of San Marino and the Vatican State)

1. Vehicles with temporary registration plates involved in accidents occurring more than 12 months after the date of expiry displayed on the temporary registration plates.

2. Vehicles belonging to military forces and other military and civil personnel governed by international Agreements (as, for instance, plate 'AFI' and international organisations like NATO).

3. Vehicles with no registration plates (particularly motorised cycles).

4. Agricultural machines (such as agricultural tractors, their trailers and all other vehicles designed specifically for agricultural work).

Ireland

Vehicles with temporary registration plates involved in accidents occurring more than 12 months after the date of expiry displayed on the temporary registration plates.

Iceland

Vehicles with temporary registration plates involved in accidents occurring more than 12 months after the date of expiry displayed on the temporary registration plates.

Luxembourg

Vehicles with temporary registration plates involved in accidents occurring more than 12 months after the date of expiry displayed on the temporary registration plates.

Norway

Vehicles with temporary registration plates involved in accidents occurring more than 12 months after the date of expiry displayed on the temporary registration plates.

The Netherlands

1. Vehicles with temporary registration plates involved in accidents occurring more than 12 months after the date of expiry displayed on the temporary registration plates. (Effective for accidents occurring on or after 1 October 1993.)

2. Private vehicles belonging to Dutch military personnel and their families stationed in Germany.

3. Vehicles belonging to German military personnel stationed in The Netherlands.

4. Vehicles belonging to persons attached to Headquarters Allied Forces Central Europe.

5. Service vehicles of NATO armed forces.

Portugal

1. Agricultural machines and motorised mechanical equipment for which registration plates are not required under Portuguese Law.

2. Vehicles belonging to foreign States and to International Organisations of which Portugal is a Member State: (white plates—red figures, preceded by the letters 'CD' or 'FM').

3. Vehicles belonging to the Portuguese State— (black plates—white figures, preceded by the letters 'AM', 'AP', 'EP', 'ME', 'MG' or 'MX', according to the Government department concerned).

Sweden

Vehicles with temporary registration plates involved in accidents occurring more than 12 months after the date of expiry displayed on the temporary registration plates.

Slovakia

Vehicles with temporary registration plates involved in accidents occurring more than 12 months after the date of expiry displayed on the temporary registration plates.

Slovenia

Vehicles with temporary registration plates involved in accidents occurring more than 12 months after the date of expiry displayed on the temporary registration plates.

APPENDIX 3
SUSPENSIVE CLAUSES

France

The provision in Article 11(2) of the Internal Regulations shall not apply to the Bureau Central Français until the French regulatory provisions have been amended to ensure compliance or that an agreement enabling this application has been signed.

Italy

The provision in Article 11(2) of the Internal Regulations shall not apply to Ufficio Centrale Italiano (UCI) until the regulatory provisions applicable in this country have been amended, according to the applicable European Community law, to ensure compliance.

Portugal

The provision in Article 11(2) of the Internal Regulations shall not apply to Gabinete Português de Carta Verde until the regulatory provisions applicable in this country have been amended, according to the applicable European Community law, to ensure compliance.

Switzerland

The provision in Article 11(2) of the Internal Regulations shall not apply to the Swiss National Bureau of Insurance until the regulatory provisions applicable in this country have been amended, according to the applicable European Community law, to ensure compliance.

I. 37.

Commission Decision 2004/6/EC
of 5 November 2003
establishing the Committee of European Insurance and Occupational Pensions Supervisors[1]

(Text with EEA relevance)

THE COMMISSION OF THE EUROPEAN COMMUNITIES,

Having regard to the Treaty establishing the European Community,

Whereas:

(1) In June 2001, the Commission adopted Decisions 2001/527/EC[2] and 2001/528/EC[3] setting up the Committee of European Securities Regulators and the European Securities Committee respectively.

(2) In its Resolutions of 5 February and 21 November 2002, the European Parliament endorsed the four-level regulatory framework advocated in the report of the Committee of Wise Men and called for certain aspects of that approach to be extended to the banking and insurance sectors subject to a clear Council commitment to reform to guarantee a proper institutional balance.

(3) On 3 December 2002, the Council invited the Commission to implement such arrangements in the field of banking and insurance and occupational pensions, and to establish as soon as possible new committees in an advisory capacity in relation to those fields.

(4) A Committee of European Insurance and Occupational Pensions Supervisors (hereinafter 'the Committee') should be established to serve as an independent body for reflection, debate and advice for the Commission in the insurance, reinsurance and occupational pensions fields. However, as regards the occupational pensions field, while the Committee should consider regulatory and supervisory aspects relating to such arrangements, it should not address labour and social law aspects, such as the organisation of occupational regimes, and in particular, issues relating to compulsory membership (affiliation) or the results of collective bargaining agreements.

(5) The Committee should also contribute to the consistent and timely implementation of Community legislation in the Member States by securing more effective cooperation between national supervisory authorities, carrying out peer reviews and promoting best practices.

(6) The Committee should organise its own operational arrangements, in particular take account of the specificities of the relevant competent authorities, and maintain close operational links with the Commission and with the Committee established by Commission Decision 2004/9/EC of 5 November 2003, establishing a European Insurance and Occupational Pensions Committee.[4] It should elect its chairperson from among its members.

(7) The Committee should at an early stage consult extensively and in an open and transparent manner with market participants, consumers and end-users.

---

[1] OJ L 3, 7.1.2004, 30–31.
[2] OJ L 191, 13.7.2001, 43, reproduced infra under no. S. 19.
[3] OJ L 191, 13.7.2001, 45, reproduced infra under no. S. 20.

[4] OJ L 3, 7.1.2004, 34, reproduced infra under no. I. 38.

(8) The Committee should drawn up its own rules of procedure and fully respect the prerogatives of the institutions and the institutional balance established by the Treaty,

HAS DECIDED AS FOLLOWS:

Article 1

An independent advisory group on insurance and occupational pensions in the Community, called the 'Committee of European Insurance and Occupational Pensions Supervisors', hereinafter 'the Committee', is established.

Article 2

The role of the Committee shall be to advise the Commission, either at the Commission's request, within a time limit which the Commission may lay down according to the urgency of the matter, or on the Committee's own initiative, in particular as regards the preparation of draft implementing measures in the fields of insurance, reinsurance and occupational pensions.

The Committee shall contribute to the consistent implementation of Community Directives and to the convergence of Member States' supervisory practices throughout the Community.

The Committee shall also constitute a forum for supervisory cooperation, including the exchange of information on supervised institutions.

Article 3

The Committee shall be composed of high level representatives from the national public authorities competent in the field of supervision of insurance, reinsurance and occupational pensions. Each Member State shall designate high level representatives from its competent authorities to participate in the meetings of the Committee.

The Commission shall be present at meetings of the Committee and shall designate a high level representative to participate in all its debates. Whenever discussion of an item on the agenda entails the exchange of confidential information concerning a supervised institution, participation in such discussion may be restricted to the supervisory authorities directly involved.

The Committee shall elect a chairperson from among its members.

The Committee may invite experts and observers to attend its meetings.

The Committee shall not address labour and social law aspects such as the organisation of occupational regimes, in particular compulsory membership and the results of collective bargaining agreements.

Article 4

The Committee shall maintain close operational links with the Commission and with the Committee established by Decision 2004/9/EC.

It may set up working groups. The Commission shall be invited to participate in the working groups as observer.

Article 5

Before transmitting its opinion to the Commission, the Committee shall, at an early stage, consult extensively and in an open and transparent manner with market participants, consumers and end-users.

Article 6

The Committee shall submit an annual report to the Commission.

Article 7

The Committee shall adopt its own rules of procedure and organise its own operational arrangements.

Article 8

The Committee shall take up its duties on 24 November 2003.

I. 38.

Commission Decision 2004/9/EC
of 5 November 2003
establishing the European Insurance and Occupational Pensions Committee[1]

(Text with EEA relevance)

THE COMMISSION OF THE EUROPEAN COMMUNITIES,

Having regard to the Treaty establishing the European Community,

Whereas:

(1) In June 2001, the Commission adopted Decisions 2001/527/EC[2] and 2001/528/EC[3] setting up the Committee of European Securities Regulators and the European Securities Committee respectively.

(2) In its Resolutions of 5 February and 21 November 2002, the European Parliament endorsed the four-level approach advocated in the Final Report of the Committee of Wise Men on the regulation of European securities markets and called for certain aspects of that approach to be extended to the banking and insurance sectors subject to a clear Council commitment to reform to guarantee a proper institutional balance.

(3) On 3 December 2002, the Council invited the Commission to implement such arrangements in the fields of banking and insurance and occupational pensions and to establish as soon as possible new committees in an advisory capacity in relation to those fields.

(4) Council Directive 91/675/EEC of 19 December 1991 setting up an Insurance Committee[4] established a committee to advise the Commission in the development of legislation in the insurance field.

(5) The Commission has proposed a Directive modifying, *inter alia*, Directive 91/675/EEC, First Council Directive 73/239/EEC of 24 July 1973 on the coordination of laws, regulations and administrative provisions relating to the taking-up and pursuit of the business of direct insurance other than life assurance[5] as amended, Directive 2002/83/EC of the European Parliament and of the Council of 5 November 2002 concerning life assurance,[6] and Directive 2002/87/EC of the European Parliament and of the Council of 16 December 2002 on the supplementary supervision of credit institutions, insurance undertakings and investment firms in a financial conglomerate and amending Council Directives 73/239/EEC, 79/267/EEC, 92/49/EEC, 92/96/EEC, 93/6/EEC and 93/22/EEC, and Directives 98/78/EC and 2000/12/EC of the European Parliament and the Council,[7] to delete the advisory functions of the Insurance Committee.

(6) Such an amendment requires the corresponding and simultaneous creation of a new advisory group to advise the Commission as regards the development of Community legislation in the insurance and occupational pensions fields, hereafter called the 'European Insurance and Occupational Pensions Committee'.

---

[1] OJ L 3, 7.1.2004, 34–35.
[2] OJ L 191, 13.7.2001, 43, reproduced infra under no. S. 19.
[3] OJ L 191, 13.7.2001, 45, reproduced infra under no. S. 20.
[4] OJ L 374, 31.12.1991, 32, reproduced supra under no. I. 24.

[5] OJ L 228, 16.8.1973, 3, reproduced supra under no. I. 3.
[6] OJ L 345, 19.12.2002, 1, reproduced supra under no. I. 33.
[7] OJ L 35, 11.2.2003, 1, reproduced supra under no. B. 38.

(7) To ensure this, this Decision should only come into being at the same time as any Directive repealing the purely advisory functions of the Insurance Committee.

(8) The European Insurance and Occupational Pensions Committee should be competent to examine any question relating to the application of Community provisions concerning the fields of insurance and occupational pensions, and, in particular, should advise the Commission on new proposals for new legislation in those fields which the Commission intends to present to the European Parliament and the Council; however in the occupational pensions field, the European Insurance and Occupational Pensions Committee should not address labour and social law aspects such as the organisation of occupational regimes, in particular compulsory membership and the results of collective bargaining agreements,

HAS DECIDED AS FOLLOWS:

Article 1

An advisory group on insurance and occupational pensions in the Community, called the 'European Insurance and Occupational Pensions Committee' (hereinafter 'the Committee') is hereby established.

Article 2

1. The Committee shall advise the Commission, at the Commission's request, on policy issues relating to insurance, reinsurance and occupational pensions as well as Commission proposals in these fields. The Committee shall examine any question relating to the application of Community provisions concerning the sectors of insurance, reinsurance and occupational pensions, and in particular Directives on insurance, reinsurance and occupational pensions.

2. The Committee shall not consider specific problems relating to individual insurance or reinsurance undertakings or to occupational pensions institutions.

3. The Committee shall not address labour and social law aspects such as the organisation of occupational regimes, in particular compulsory membership and the results of collective bargaining agreements.

Article 3

1. The Committee shall be composed of high level representatives of Member States. The Committee shall be chaired by a representative of the Commission.

2. The chairperson of the Committee of European Insurance and Occupational Pensions Supervisors established by Commission Decision 2004/6/EC[8] shall participate at the meetings of the Committee as an observer.

3. The Commission may invite experts and observers to attend its meetings.

4. The secretariat of the Committee shall be provided by the Commission.

5. The Committee shall adopt its own rules of procedure.

Article 4

The Committee shall adopt its own rules of procedure. The Committee shall meet at regular intervals and whenever the situation demands. The Commission may convene an emergency meeting if it considers that the situation so requires.

Article 5

This Decision shall enter into force on the same day as the entry into force of any directive amending the purely advisory functions of the Insurance Committee.

---

[8] OJ L 3, 7.1.2004, 30, reproduced supra under no. I. 37.

I. 39.

European Parliament and Council Directive 2005/14/EC of 11 May 2005 amending Council Directives 72/166/EEC, 84/5/EEC, 88/357/EEC and 90/232/EEC and Directive 2000/26/EC of the European Parliament and of the Council relating to insurance against civil liability in respect of the use of motor vehicles[1]

(Text with EEA relevance)

THE EUROPEAN PARLIAMENT AND THE COUNCIL OF THE EUROPEAN UNION,

Having regard to the Treaty establishing the European Community, and in particular the first and third sentences of Article 47(2), Article 55 and Article 95(1) thereof,

Having regard to the proposal from the Commission,[2]

Having regard to the opinion of the European Economic and Social Committee,[3]

Acting in accordance with the procedure laid down in Article 251 of the Treaty,[4]

Whereas:

(1) Insurance against civil liability in respect of the use of motor vehicles (motor insurance) is of special importance for European citizens, whether they are policyholders or victims of an accident. It is also a major concern for insurance undertakings as it constitutes an important part of non-life insurance business in the Community. Motor insurance also has an impact on the free movement of persons and vehicles. It should therefore be a key objective of Community action in the field of financial services to reinforce and consolidate the single insurance market in motor insurance.

(2) Very significant advances in this direction have already been achieved by Council Directive 72/166/EEC of 24 April 1972 on the approximation of the laws of Member States relating to insurance against civil liability in respect of the use of motor vehicles, and to the enforcement of the obligation to insure against such liability,[5] by second Council Directive 84/5/EEC of 30 December 1983 on the approximation of the laws of the Member States relating to insurance against civil liability in respect of the use of motor vehicles,[6] by third Council Directive 90/232/EEC of 14 May 1990 on the approximation of the laws of the Member States relating to insurance against civil liability in respect of the use of motor vehicles[7] and by Directive 2000/26/EC of the European Parliament and of the Council of 16 May 2000 on the approximation of the laws of the Member States relating to insurance against civil liability in respect of the use of motor vehicles (fourth motor insurance Directive).[8]

(3) The Community system of motor insurance needs to be updated and improved. This

---

[1] OJ L 149, 11.6.2005, 14–21.
[2] OJ C 227 E, 24.9.2002, 387.
[3] OJ C 95, 23.4.2003, 45.
[4] Opinion of the European Parliament of 22 October 2003 (OJ C 82 E, 1.4.2004, 297), Council Common Position of 26 April 2004 (not yet published in the Official Journal) and Position of the European Parliament of 12 January 2005 (not yet published in the Official Journal). Council Decision of 18 April 2005.

[5] OJ L 103, 2.5.1972, 1, reproduced supra under no. I. 2. Directive as last amended by Directive 84/5/EEC (OJ L 8, 11.1.1984, 17), reproduced supra under no. I. 11.
[6] OJ L 8, 11.1.1984, 17, reproduced supra under no. I. 11. Directive as last amended by Directive 90/232/EEC (OJ L 129, 19.5.1990, 33), reproduced supra under no. I. 16.
[7] OJ L 129, 19.5.1990, 33, reproduced supra under no. I. 16.
[8] OJ L 181, 20.7.2000, 65, reproduced supra under no. I. 30.

need has been confirmed by the consultation conducted with the industry, consumers and victims' associations.

(4) In order to exclude any possible misinterpretation of the provisions of Directive 72/166/EEC and to make it easier to obtain insurance cover for vehicles bearing temporary plates, the definition of the territory in which the vehicle is normally based should refer to the territory of the State of which the vehicle bears a registration plate, irrespective of whether such a plate is permanent or temporary.

(5) In accordance with Directive 72/166/EEC, vehicles bearing false or illegal plates are considered to be normally based in the territory of the Member State that issued the original plates. This rule often means that national insurers' bureaux are obliged to deal with the economic consequences of accidents which do not have any connection with the Member State where they are established. Without altering the general criterion of the registration plate to determine the territory in which the vehicle is normally based, a special rule should be laid down for accidents caused by vehicles without a registration plate or bearing a registration plate which does not correspond or no longer corresponds to the vehicle. In this case and for the sole purpose of settling the claim, the territory in which the vehicle is normally based should be considered to be the territory in which the accident took place.

(6) In order to facilitate the interpretation and application of the term 'random checks' in Directive 72/166/EEC, the relevant provision should be clarified. The prohibition of systematic checks on motor insurance should apply to vehicles normally based in the territory of another Member State as well as to vehicles normally based in the territory of a third country but entering from the territory of another Member State. Only non-systematic checks which are not discriminatory and are carried out as part of a control not aimed exclusively at insurance verification may be permitted.

(7) Article 4(a) of Directive 72/166/EEC permits a Member State to act in derogation from the general obligation to take out compulsory insurance in respect of vehicles belonging to certain natural or public or private legal persons. For accidents caused by such vehicles, the Member State so derogating must designate an authority or body to compensate for the damage to victims of accidents caused in another Member State. In order to ensure that due compensation is paid not only to the victims of accidents caused by these vehicles abroad but also the victims of accidents occurring in the same Member State in which the vehicle is normally based, whether or not they are resident in its territory, the aforementioned Article should be amended. Furthermore, Member States should ensure that the list of persons exempt from compulsory insurance and the authorities or bodies responsible for compensation of victims of accidents caused by such vehicles is communicated to the Commission for publication.

(8) Article 4(b) of Directive 72/166/EEC permits a Member State to act in derogation from the general obligation to take out compulsory insurance in respect of certain types of vehicles or certain vehicles having a special plate. In that case, the other Member States are allowed to require, at the entry into their territory, a valid green card or a frontier insurance contract, in order to ensure the provision of compensation to victims of any accident which may be caused by those vehicles in their territories. However, since the elimination of border controls within the Community means that it is not possible to ensure that vehicles crossing frontiers are covered by insurance, compensation for victims of accidents caused abroad can no longer be guaranteed. Furthermore, it should also be ensured that due compensation is awarded not only to the victims of accidents caused by those vehicles abroad, but also in the same Member State in which the vehicle is normally based. For this purpose, Member States should treat the victims of accidents caused by those vehicles in the same way as victims of accidents caused by non-insured vehicles. Indeed, as provided for in Directive 84/5/EEC, compensation to victims of accidents caused by uninsured vehicles should be paid by the compensation body of the Member State in which the accident took place. Where payments

are made to victims of accidents caused by vehicles subject to the derogation, the compensation body should have a claim against the body of the Member State in which the vehicle is normally based. After a period of five years from the date of entry into force of this Directive, the Commission should, if appropriate, in view of the experience with the implementation and application of this derogation, submit proposals for its replacement or repeal. The corresponding provision in Directive 2000/26/EC should also be deleted.

(9) In order to clarify the scope of application of the motor insurance directives in accordance with Article 299 of the Treaty, the reference to the non-European territory of the Member States in Articles 6 and 7(1) of Directive 72/166/EEC should be deleted.

(10) Member States' obligations to guarantee insurance cover at least in respect of certain minimum amounts constitute an important element in ensuring the protection of victims. The minimum amounts provided for in Directive 84/5/EEC should not only be updated to take account of inflation, but also increased in real terms, to improve the protection of victims. The minimum amount of cover for personal injury should be calculated so as to compensate fully and fairly all victims who have suffered very serious injuries, whilst taking into account the low frequency of accidents involving several victims and the small number of accidents in which several victims suffer very serious injuries in the course of one and the same event. A minimum amount of cover of EUR 1 000 000 per victim or EUR 5 000 000 per claim, regardless of the number of victims, is a reasonable and adequate amount. With a view to facilitating the introduction of these minimum amounts, a transitional period of five years from the date of implementation of this Directive should be established. Member States should increase their amounts to at least a half of those levels within 30 months of the date of implementation.

(11) In order to ensure that the minimum amount of cover is not eroded over time, a periodic review clause should be introduced using as a benchmark the European Index of Consumer Prices (EICP) published by Eurostat, as provided for in Council Regulation (EC) No 2494/95 of 23 October 1995 concerning harmonised indices of consumer prices.[9] The procedural rules governing such a review need to be established.

(12) Directive 84/5/EEC, which allows Member States, in the interest of preventing fraud, to limit or exclude payments by the compensation body in the case of damage to property by an unidentified vehicle, may impede legitimate compensation of victims in some cases. The option of limiting or excluding compensation on the basis that the vehicle is not identified should not apply where the body has paid compensation for significant personal injuries to any victim of the same accident in which the damage to property was caused. Member States may provide for an excess up to the limit set out in the said Directive for which the victim of the damage to property may be responsible. The conditions in which personal injuries are to be considered significant should be determined by the national legislation or administrative provisions of the Member State where the accident takes place. In establishing these conditions, the Member State may take into account, *inter alia*, whether the injury has required hospital care.

(13) At present, an option contained in Directive 84/5/EEC allows Member States to authorise, up to a specified ceiling, excesses for which the victim would be responsible in the event of damage to property caused by uninsured vehicles. That option unjustly reduces the protection of victims and creates discrimination with respect to victims of other accidents. It should therefore no longer be permitted.

(14) Second Council Directive 88/357/EEC of 22 June 1988 on the coordination of laws, regulations and administrative provisions relating to direct insurance other than life assurance and laying down provisions to facilitate the effective exercise of freedom to provide services[10] should

---

[9] OJ L 257, 27.10.1995, 1. Regulation as amended by Regulation (EC) No 1882/2003 of the European Parliament and of the Council (OJ L 284, 31.10.2003, 1).

[10] OJ L 172, 4.7.1988, 1, reproduced supra under no. I. 15. Directive as last amended by Directive 2000/26/EC, reproduced supra under no. I. 30.

be amended in order to permit branches of insurance undertakings to become representatives with respect to motor insurance activities, as already happens with respect to insurance services other than motor insurance.

(15) The inclusion within the insurance cover of any passenger in the vehicle is a major achievement of the existing legislation. This objective would be placed in jeopardy if national legislation or any contractual clause contained in an insurance contract excluded passengers from insurance cover because they knew or should have known that the driver of the vehicle was under the influence of alcohol or of any other intoxicating agent at the time of the accident. The passenger is not usually in a position to assess properly the intoxication level of the driver. The objective of discouraging persons from driving whilst under the influence of intoxicating agents is not achieved by reducing the insurance cover for passengers who are victims of motor vehicle accidents. Cover of such passengers under the vehicle's compulsory motor insurance does not prejudice any liability they might incur pursuant to the applicable national legislation, nor the level of any award of damages in a specific accident.

(16) Personal injuries and damage to property suffered by pedestrians, cyclists and other non-motorised users of the road, who are usually the weakest party in an accident, should be covered by the compulsory insurance of the vehicle involved in the accident where they are entitled to compensation under national civil law. This provision does not prejudice the civil liability or the level of awards for damages in a specific accident, under national legislation.

(17) Some insurance undertakings insert into insurance policies clauses to the effect that the contract will be cancelled if the vehicle remains outside the Member State of registration for longer than a specified period. This practice is in conflict with the principle set out in Directive 90/232/EEC, according to which the compulsory motor insurance should cover, on the basis of a single premium, the entire territory of the Community. It should therefore be specified that the insurance cover is to remain valid during the whole term of the contract, irrespective of whether the vehicle remains in another Member State for a particular period, without prejudice to the obligations under Member States' national legislation with respect to the registration of vehicles.

(18) Steps should be taken to make it easier to obtain insurance cover for vehicles imported from one Member State into another, even though the vehicle is not yet registered in the Member State of destination. A temporary derogation from the general rule determining the Member State where the risk is situated should be made available. For a period of 30 days from the date when the vehicle is delivered, made available or dispatched to the purchaser, the Member State of destination should be considered to be the Member State where the risk is situated.

(19) Any person wishing to take out a new motor insurance contract with another insurer should be in a position to justify his accident and claims record under the old contract. The policyholder should have the right to request at any time a statement concerning the claims, or the absence of claims, involving the vehicle or vehicles covered by the insurance contract at least during the preceding five years of the contractual relationship. The insurance undertaking, or any body which may have been appointed by a Member State to provide compulsory insurance or to supply such statements, should provide this statement to the policyholder within 15 days of the request.

(20) In order to ensure due protection of victims of motor vehicle accidents, Member States should not permit insurance undertakings to rely on excesses against an injured party.

(21) The right to invoke the insurance contract and to claim against the insurance undertaking directly is of great importance for the protection of victims of motor vehicle accidents. Directive 2000/26/EC already provides victims of accidents occurring in a Member State other than the Member State of residence of the injured party, which are caused by the use of vehicles insured and normally based in a Member State, with a right of direct action against the insurance undertaking covering the person responsible against

civil liability. In order to facilitate an efficient and speedy settlement of claims and to avoid as far as possible costly legal proceedings, this right should be extended to victims of any motor vehicle accident.

(22) To enhance the protection of victims of motor vehicle accidents, the 'reasoned offer' procedure provided for in Directive 2000/26/EC should be extended to any kind of motor vehicle accident. This same procedure should also apply *mutatis mutandis* where the accident is settled by the system of national insurers' bureaux provided for in Directive 72/166/EEC.

(23) In order to make it easier for the injured party to seek compensation, the information centres set up in accordance with Directive 2000/26/EC should not be confined to providing information concerning the accidents covered by that Directive, but should be able to provide the same kind of information for any motor vehicle accident.

(24) Under Article 11(2) read in conjunction with Article 9(1)(b) of Council Regulation (EC) No 44/2001 of 22 December 2000 on jurisdiction and the recognition and enforcement of judgments in civil and commercial matters,[11] injured parties may bring legal proceedings against the civil liability insurance provider in the Member State in which they are domiciled.

(25) As Directive 2000/26/EC was adopted before the adoption of Regulation (EC) No 44/2001, which replaced the Brussels Convention of 27 September 1968 on the same matter for a number of Member States, the reference to that Convention in that Directive should be adapted as appropriate.

(26) Council Directives 72/166/EEC, 84/5/EEC, 88/357/EEC and 90/232/EEC and Directive 2000/26/EC of the European Parliament and of the Council should therefore be amended accordingly,

HAVE ADOPTED THIS DIRECTIVE:

---

[11] OJ L 12, 16.1.2001, 1. Regulation as last amended by Regulation (EC) No 2245/2004 (OJ L 381, 28.12.2004, 10).

Article 1
Amendments to Directive 72/166/EEC
[. . .]

¶ *This article amends article 1(4), replaces article 2(1), and amends articles 4, 6 and 7(1) of Directive 72/166/EEC, reproduced supra under no. I. 2. The modifications are directly incorporated therein.*

Article 2
Amendments to Directive 84/5/EEC
[. . .]

¶ *This article replaces article 1 of Directive 84/5/EEC, reproduced supra under no. I. 11. The modifications are directly incorporated therein.*

Article 3
Amendment to Directive 88/357/EEC
[. . .]

¶ *This article deletes the second sentence in the fourth subparagraph of Article 12a(4) of Directive 88/357/EEC, reproduced supra under no. I. 15. The modifications are directly incorporated therein.*

Article 4
Amendments to Directive 90/232/EEC
[. . .]

¶ *This article amends articles 1 and 2, inserts articles 1(a), 4(a), 4(b), 4(c), 4(d), and 4(e), and replaces article 5(1) of Directive 90/232/EEC, reproduced supra under no. I. 16. The modifications are directly incorporated therein.*

Article 5
Amendments to Directive 2000/26/EC
[. . .]

¶ *This article inserts recital 16a, replaces article 4(8), deletes article 5(1)(a), point 2(ii), and inserts article 6a in Directive 2000/26/EC, reproduced supra under no. I. 30. The modifications are directly incorporated therein.*

Article 6
Implementation

1. Member States shall bring into force the laws, regulations and administrative provisions necessary to comply with this Directive by 11 June 2007 at the latest. They shall forthwith inform the Commission thereof.

When Member States adopt those measures, they shall contain a reference to this Directive or shall be accompanied by such reference on the occasion of their official publication.

The methods of making such reference shall be laid down by Member States.

2. Member States may, in accordance with the Treaty, maintain or bring into force provisions which are more favourable to the injured party than the provisions necessary to comply with this Directive.

3. Member States shall communicate to the Commission the text of the main provisions of national law which they adopt in the field covered by this Directive.

Article 7
Entry into force

This Directive shall enter into force on the day of its publication in the *Official Journal of the European Union*.

Article 8
Addressees

This Directive is addressed to the Member States.

I. 40.

I

(Acts whose publication is obligatory)

European Parliament and Council Directive 2005/68/EC of 16 November 2005 on reinsurance and amending Council Directives 73/239/EEC, 92/49/EEC as well as Directives 98/78/EC and 2002/83/EC[1]

(Text with EEA relevance)

THE EUROPEAN PARLIAMENT AND THE COUNCIL OF THE EUROPEAN UNION,

Having regard to the Treaty establishing the European Community, and in particular Articles 47(2) and 55 thereof,

Having regard to the proposal from the Commission,

Having regard to the opinion of the European Economic and Social Committee,[2]

After consulting the Committee of the Regions,

Acting in accordance with the procedure laid down in Article 251 of the Treaty,[3]

Whereas:

(1) Council Directive 73/239/EEC of 24 July 1973 on the coordination of laws, regulations and administrative provisions relating to the taking-up and pursuit of the business of direct insurance other than life assurance,[4] Council Directive 92/49/EEC of 18 June 1992 on the coordination of laws, regulations and administrative provisions relating to direct insurance other than life assurance[5] and Directive 2002/83/EC of the European Parliament and of the Council of 5 November 2002 concerning life assurance[6] have laid down the provisions relating to the taking-up and pursuit of direct insurance in the Community.

(2) Those Directives provide for the legal framework for insurance undertakings to conduct insurance business in the internal market, from the point of view both of the right of establishment and of the freedom to provide services, in order to make it easier for insurance undertakings with head offices in the Community to cover commitments situated within the Community and to make it possible for policy holders to have recourse not only to insurers established in their own country, but also to insurers which have their head office in the Community and are established in other Member States.

(3) The regime laid down by those Directives applies to direct insurance undertakings in respect of their entire business carried on, both direct insurance activities as well as reinsurance activities by way of acceptances; however reinsurance activities conducted by specialised reinsurance undertakings are neither subject to

---

[1] OJ L 323, 9.12.2005, 1–50.
[2] OJ C 120, 20.5.2005, 1.
[3] Opinion of the European Parliament of 7 June 2005 (not yet published in the Official Journal) and Decision of the Council of 17 October 2005.
[4] OJ L 228, 16.8.1973, 3, reproduced supra under no. I. 3. Directive as last amended by Directive 2005/1/EC of the European Parliament and of the Council (OJ L 79, 24.3.2005, 9), reproduced supra under no. B. 39.
[5] OJ L 228, 11.8.1992, 1, reproduced supra under no. I. 3. Directive as last amended by Directive 2005/1/EC, reproduced supra under no. B. 39.
[6] OJ L 345, 19.12.2002, 1, reproduced supra under no. I. 33. Directive as last amended by Directive 2005/1/EC, reproduced supra under no. B. 39.

that regime nor any other regime provided for by Community law.

(4) Reinsurance is a major financial activity as it allows direct insurance undertakings, by facilitating a wider distribution of risks at worldwide level, to have a higher underwriting capacity to engage in insurance business and provide insurance cover and also to reduce their capital costs; furthermore, reinsurance plays a fundamental role in financial stability, since it is an essential element in ensuring the financial soundness and the stability of direct insurance markets as well as the financial system as a whole, because it involves major financial intermediaries and institutional investors.

(5) Council Directive 64/225/EEC of 25 February 1964 on the abolition of restrictions on freedom of establishment and freedom to provide services in respect of reinsurance and retrocession[7] has removed the restrictions on the right of establishment and the freedom to provide services related to the nationality or residence of the provider of reinsurance. It has not however removed restrictions caused by divergences between national provisions as regards prudential regulation of reinsurance. This situation has resulted in significant differences in the level of supervision of reinsurance undertakings in the Community, which create barriers to the pursuit of reinsurance business, such as the obligation for the reinsurance undertaking to pledge assets in order to cover its part of the technical provisions of the direct insurance undertaking, as well as the compliance by reinsurance undertakings with different supervisory rules in the various Member States in which they conduct business or an indirect supervision of the various aspects of a reinsurance undertaking by the competent authorities of direct insurance undertakings.

(6) The Action Plan for Financial Services has identified reinsurance as a sector which requires action at Community level in order to complete the internal market for financial services. Moreover, major financial fora, such as the International Monetary Fund and the International Association of Insurance Supervisors (IAIS) have highlighted the lack of harmonised reinsurance supervision rules at Community level as an important gap in the financial services regulatory framework that should be filled.

(7) This Directive aims at establishing a prudential regulatory framework for reinsurance activities in the Community. It forms part of the body of Community legislation in the field of insurance aimed at establishing the Internal Market in the insurance sector.

(8) This Directive is consistent with major international work carried out on reinsurance prudential rules, in particular the IAIS.

(9) This Directive follows the approach of Community legislation adopted in respect of direct insurance by carrying out the harmonisation which is essential, necessary and sufficient to ensure the mutual recognition of authorisations and prudential control systems, thereby making it possible to grant a single authorisation valid throughout the Community and apply the principle of supervision by the home Member State.

(10) As a result, the taking-up and the pursuit of the business of reinsurance are subject to the grant of a single official authorisation issued by the competent authorities of the Member State in which a reinsurance undertaking has its head office. Such authorisation enables an undertaking to carry on business throughout the Community, under the right of establishment or the freedom to provide services. The Member State of the branch or of the provision of services may not require a reinsurance undertaking which wishes to carry on reinsurance business in its territory and which has already been authorised in its home Member State to seek fresh authorisation. Furthermore a reinsurance undertaking which has already been authorised in its home Member State should not be subject to additional supervision or checks related to its financial soundness performed by the competent authorities of an insurance undertaking which is reinsured by that reinsurance undertaking. In addition, Member States should not be allowed to require a reinsurance undertaking authorised in the Community to pledge assets in order to cover its part of the

---

[7] OJ L 56, 4.4.1964, 878, reproduced supra under no. I. 1.

cedant's technical provisions. The conditions for the granting or withdrawal of such authorisation should be defined. The competent authorities should not authorise or continue the authorisation of a reinsurance undertaking which does not fulfil the conditions laid down in this Directive.

(11) This Directive should apply to reinsurance undertakings which conduct exclusively reinsurance business and do not engage in direct insurance business; it should also apply to the so-called 'captive' reinsurance undertakings created or owned by either a financial undertaking other than an insurance or reinsurance undertaking or a group of insurance or reinsurance undertakings to which Directive 98/78/EC of the European Parliament and of the Council of 27 October 1998 on the supplementary supervision of insurance undertakings in an insurance group[8] applies, or by one or several non-financial undertakings, the purpose of which is to provide reinsurance cover exclusively for the risks of the undertakings to which they belong. When in this Directive reference is made to reinsurance undertakings, it should include captive reinsurance undertakings, except where special provision is made for captive reinsurance undertakings. Captive reinsurance undertakings do not cover risks deriving from the external direct insurance or reinsurance business of an insurance or reinsurance undertaking belonging to the group. Furthermore, insurance or reinsurance undertakings belonging to a financial conglomerate may not own a captive undertaking.

(12) This Directive should however not apply to insurance undertakings which are already subject to Directives 73/239/EEC or 2002/83/EC; however, in order to ensure the financial soundness of insurance undertakings which also carry on reinsurance business and that the specific characteristics of those activities is duly taken into account by the capital requirements of those insurance undertakings, the provisions relating to the solvency margin of reinsurance undertakings contained in this Directive should apply to reinsurance business of those insurance undertakings, if the volume of their reinsurance activities represents a significant part of their entire business.

(13) This Directive should not apply to the provision of reinsurance cover carried out or fully guaranteed by a Member State for reasons of substantial public interest, in the capacity of reinsurer of last resort, in particular where because of a specific situation in a market, it is not feasible to obtain adequate commercial cover; in this regard, a lack of 'adequate commercial cover' should mainly mean a market failure which is characterised by an evident lack of a sufficient range of insurance offers, although excessive premiums should not per se imply inadequacy of that commercial cover. Article 1(2)(d) of this Directive also applies to arrangements between insurance undertakings to which Directives 73/239/EEC or 2002/83/EC apply and which aim to pool financial claims ensuing from major risks such as terrorism.

(14) Reinsurance undertakings are to limit their objects to the business of reinsurance and related operations. This requirement may allow a reinsurance undertaking to carry on, for instance, activities, such as provision of statistical or actuarial advice, risk analysis or research for its clients. It may also include a holding company function and activities with respect to financial sector activities within the meaning of Article 2, point 8, of Directive 2002/87/EC of the European Parliament and of the Council of 16 December 2002 on the supplementary supervision of credit institutions, insurance undertakings and investment firms in a financial conglomerate.[9] In any case, this requirement does not allow the carrying on of unrelated banking and financial activities.

(15) This Directive should clarify the powers and means of supervision vested in the competent authorities. The competent authorities of the reinsurance undertaking's home Member State should be responsible for monitoring the financial health of reinsurance undertakings,

---

[8] OJ L 330, 5.12.1998, 1, reproduced supra under no. I. 17. Directive as last amended by Directive 2005/1/EC, reproduced supra under no. B. 39.

[9] OJ L 35, 11.2.2003, p. 1, reproduced supra under no. B. 38. Directive as amended by Directive 2005/1/EC, reproduced supra under no. B. 39.

including their state of solvency, the establishment of adequate technical provisions and equalisation reserves and the covering of those provisions and reserves by quality assets.

(16) The competent authorities of the Member States should have at their disposal such means of supervision as are necessary to ensure the orderly pursuit of business by reinsurance undertakings throughout the Community whether carried on under the right of establishment or the freedom to provide services. In particular, they should be able to introduce appropriate safeguards or impose penalties aimed at preventing irregularities and infringements of the provisions on reinsurance supervision.

(17) The provisions governing transfers of portfolios should be in line with the single authorisation provided for in this Directive. They should apply to the various kinds of transfers of portfolios between reinsurance undertakings, such as transfers of portfolios resulting from mergers between reinsurance undertakings or other instruments of company law or transfers of portfolios of outstanding losses in run-off to another reinsurance undertaking. Moreover, the provisions governing transfers of portfolios should include provisions specifically concerning the transfer to another reinsurance undertaking of the portfolio of contracts concluded under the right of establishment or the freedom to provide services.

(18) Provision should be made for the exchange of information between the competent authorities and authorities or bodies which, by virtue of their function, help to strengthen the stability of the financial system. In order to preserve the confidential nature of the information forwarded, the list of addressees should remain within strict limits. It is therefore necessary to specify the conditions under which the above-mentioned exchanges of information are authorised; moreover, where it is laid down that information may be disclosed only with the express agreement of the competent authorities, these may, where appropriate, make their agreement subject to compliance with strict conditions. In this regard, and with a view to ensuring the proper supervision of reinsurance undertakings by the competent authorities, this Directive should provide for rules enabling Member States to conclude agreements on exchange of information with third countries provided that the information disclosed is subject to appropriate guarantees of professional secrecy.

(19) For the purposes of strengthening the prudential supervision of reinsurance undertakings, it should be laid down that an auditor has a duty to report promptly to the competent authorities, wherever, as provided for by this Directive, he/she becomes aware, while carrying out his/her tasks, of certain facts which are liable to have a serious effect on the financial situation or the administrative and accounting organisation of a reinsurance undertaking. Having regard to the aim in view, it is desirable for Member States to provide that such a duty should apply in all circumstances where such facts are discovered by an auditor during the performance of his/her tasks in an undertaking which has close links with a reinsurance undertaking. The duty of auditors to communicate, where appropriate, to the competent authorities certain facts and decisions concerning a reinsurance undertaking which they discover during the performance of their tasks in a non-reinsurance undertaking does not in itself change the nature of their tasks in that undertaking nor the manner in which they must perform those tasks in that undertaking.

(20) Provision should be made to define the application of this Directive to existing reinsurance undertakings which were already authorised or entitled to conduct reinsurance business in accordance with the provisions of the Member States before the application of this Directive.

(21) In order to allow a reinsurance undertaking to meet its commitments, the home Member State should require a reinsurance undertaking to establish adequate technical provisions. The amount of such technical provisions should be determined in accordance with Council Directive 91/674/EEC of 19 December 1991 on the annual accounts and consolidated accounts of

insurance undertakings[10] and, in respect of life reinsurance activities, the home Member State should also be allowed to lay down more specific rules in accordance with Directive 2002/83/EC.

(22) A reinsurance undertaking conducting reinsurance business in respect of credit insurance, whose credit reinsurance business amounts to more than a small proportion of its total business, should be required to set up an equalisation reserve which does not form part of the solvency margin; that reserve should be calculated according to one of the methods laid down in Directive 73/239/EEC and which are recognised as equivalent; furthermore, this Directive should allow the home Member State also to require reinsurance undertakings whose head office is situated within its territory to set up equalisation reserves for classes of risks other than credit reinsurance, following the rules laid down by that home Member State. Following the introduction of the International Financial Reporting Standards (IFRS 4), this Directive should clarify the prudential treatment of equalisation reserves established in accordance with this Directive. However, since supervision of reinsurance needs to be reassessed under the Solvency II project, this Directive does not pre-empt any future reinsurance supervision under Solvency II.

(23) A reinsurance undertaking should have assets to cover technical provisions and equalisation reserves which should take account of the type of business that it carries out in particular the nature, amount and duration of the expected claims payments, in such a way as to secure the sufficiency, liquidity, security, quality, profitability and matching of its investments, which the undertaking should ensure are diversified and adequately spread and which gives the undertaking the possibility of responding adequately to changing economic circumstances, in particular developments in the financial markets and real estate markets or major catastrophic events.

(24) It is necessary that, over and above technical provisions, reinsurance undertakings should possess a supplementary reserve, known as the solvency margin, represented by free assets and, with the agreement of the competent authority, by other implicit assets, which is to act as a buffer against adverse business fluctuations. This requirement is an important element of prudential supervision. Pending the revision of the existing solvency margin regime, which the Commission is carrying on under the so-called 'Solvency II project', in order to determine the required solvency margin of reinsurance undertakings, the rules provided for in existing legislation in the field of direct insurance should be applicable.

(25) In the light of the similarities between life reassurance covering mortality risk and non-life reinsurance, in particular the cover of insurance risks and the duration of the life reassurance contracts, the required solvency margin for life reassurance should be determined in accordance with the provisions laid down in this Directive for the calculation of the required solvency margin for non-life reinsurance; the home Member State should however be allowed to apply the rules provided for in Directive 2002/83/EC for the establishment of the required solvency margin in respect of life reassurance activities which are linked to investment funds or participating contracts.

(26) In order to take account of the particular nature of some types of reinsurance contracts or specific lines of business, provision should be made to make adjustments to the calculation of the required solvency margin; these adjustments should be made by the Commission, after consulting the European Insurance and Occupational Pensions Committee, set up by Commission Decision 2004/9/EC[11] in the exercise of its implementing powers conferred by the Treaty.

(27) These measures should be adopted by the use of the regulatory procedure provided for in Article 5 of Council Decision 1999/468/EC of 28 June 1999 laying down the procedures for the

---

[10] OJ L 374, 31.12.1991, 7, reproduced supra under no. I. 23. Directive as amended by Directive 2003/51/EC of the European Parliament and of the Council (OJ L 178, 17.7.2003, 16), reproduced supra under no. C. 23.

[11] OJ L 3, 7.1.2004, 34, reproduced supra under no. I. 37.

exercise of implementing powers conferred on the Commission.[12]

(28) The list of items eligible to represent the available solvency margin laid down by this Directive should be that provided for in Directives 73/239/EEC and 2002/83/EC.

(29) Reinsurance undertakings should also possess a guarantee fund in order to ensure that they possess adequate resources when they are set up and that in the subsequent course of business the solvency margin in no event falls below a minimum of security; however, in order to take account of the specificities of captive reinsurance undertakings, provision should be made to allow the home Member State to set the minimum guarantee fund required for captive reinsurance undertakings at a lower amount.

(30) Certain provisions of this Directive define minimum standards. A home Member State should be able to lay down stricter rules for reinsurance undertakings authorised by its own competent authorities, in particular with respect to solvency margin requirements.

(31) This Directive should be applicable to finite reinsurance activities; therefore, a definition of finite reinsurance for the purposes of this Directive is necessary; owing to the special nature of this line of reinsurance activity, the home Member State should be given the option of laying down specific provisions for the pursuit of finite reinsurance activities. These provisions could differ from the general regime laid down in this Directive on a number of specific points.

(32) This Directive should provide for rules concerning those special purpose vehicles that assume risks from insurance and reinsurance undertakings. The special nature of such special purpose vehicles, which are not insurance or reinsurance undertakings, calls for the establishment of specific provisions in Member States. Furthermore, this Directive should provide that the home Member State should lay down more detailed rules in order to set the conditions under which outstanding amounts from a special purpose vehicle can be used as assets covering technical provisions by an insurance or a reinsurance undertaking. This Directive should also provide that recoverable amounts from a special purpose vehicle may be considered as amounts deductible under reinsurance or retrocession contracts within the limits set out in this Directive, subject to an application by the insurance undertaking or reinsurance undertaking to the competent authority and after agreement by that authority.

(33) It is necessary to provide for measures in cases where the financial position of the reinsurance undertaking becomes such that it is difficult for it to meet its underwriting liabilities. In specific situations, there is also a need for the competent authorities to be empowered to intervene at a sufficiently early stage, but in the exercise of those powers, competent authorities should inform the reinsurance undertakings of the reasons motivating such supervisory action, in accordance with the principles of sound administration and due process. As long as such a situation exists, the competent authorities should be prevented from certifying that the reinsurance undertaking has a sufficient solvency margin.

(34) It is necessary to make provision for cooperation between the competent authorities of the Member States in order to ensure that a reinsurance undertaking carrying on its activities under the right of establishment and the freedom to provide services complies with the provisions applicable to it in the host Member State.

(35) Provision should be made for the right to apply to the courts should an authorisation be refused or withdrawn.

(36) It is important to provide that reinsurance undertakings whose head office is situated outside the Community and which conduct reinsurance business in the Community should not be subject to provisions which result in treatment more favourable than that provided to reinsurance undertakings having their head office in a Member State.

(37) In order to take account of the international aspects of reinsurance, provision should be made

---

[12] OJ L 184, 17.7.1999, 23.

to enable the conclusion of international agreements with a third country aimed at defining the means of supervision over reinsurance entities which conduct business in the territory of each contracting party.

(38) Provision should be made for a flexible procedure to make it possible to assess prudential equivalence with third countries on a Community basis, so as to improve liberalisation of reinsurance services in third countries, be it through establishment or cross-border provision of services. To that end, this Directive should provide for procedures for negotiating with third countries.

(39) The Commission should be empowered to adopt implementing measures provided that these do not modify the essential elements of this Directive. These implementing measures should enable the Community to take account of the future development of reinsurance. The measures necessary for implementation of this Directive should be adopted in accordance with Decision 1999/468/EC.

(40) The existing Community legal framework for insurance should be adapted in order to take account of the new supervisory regime for reinsurance undertakings laid down by this Directive and in order to ensure a consistent regulatory framework for the whole insurance sector. In particular, the existing provisions which permit 'indirect supervision' of reinsurance undertakings by the authorities competent for the supervision of direct insurance undertakings should be adapted. Furthermore, it is necessary to abolish the current provisions enabling Member States to require pledging of assets covering the technical provisions of an insurance undertaking, whatever form this requirement might take, when the insurer is reinsured by a reinsurance undertaking authorised pursuant to this Directive or by an insurance undertaking. Finally, provision should be made for the solvency margin required for insurance undertakings conducting reinsurance activities, when such activities represent asignificant part of their business, to be subject to the solvency rules provided for reinsurance undertakings in this Directive. Directives 73/239/EEC, 92/49/EEC and 2002/83/EC should therefore be amended accordingly.

(41) Directive 98/78/EC should be amended in order to guarantee that reinsurance undertakings in an insurance or a reinsurance group are subject to supplementary supervision in the same manner as insurance undertakings which are currently part of an insurance group.

(42) The Council, in accordance with paragraph 34 of the Interinstitutional agreement on better law-making,[13] should encourage Member States to draw up, for themselves and in the interest of the Community, their own tables, illustrating, as far as possible, the correlation between this Directive and the transposition measures, and to make them public.

(43) Since the objective of this Directive, namely the establishment of a legal framework for the taking up and pursuit of reinsurance activities, cannot be sufficiently achieved by the Member States and can therefore, by reason of the scale and effects of the action, be better achieved at Community level, the Community may adopt measures, in accordance with the principle of subsidiarity as set out in Article 5 of the Treaty. In accordance with the principle of proportionality, as set out in that Article, this Directive does not go beyond what is necessary in order to achieve this objective.

(44) Since this Directive defines minimum standards, Member States may lay down stricter rules,

HAVE ADOPTED THIS DIRECTIVE:

TITLE I

SCOPE AND DEFINITIONS

Article 1

Scope

1. This Directive lays down rules for the taking up and pursuit of the self-employed activity of

---

[13] OJ C 321, 31.12.2003, 1.

reinsurance carried on by reinsurance undertakings, which conduct only reinsurance activities, and which are established in a Member State or wish to become established therein.

2. This Directive shall not apply to the following:

(a) insurance undertakings to which Directives 73/239/EEC or 2002/83/EC apply;

(b) activities and bodies referred to in Articles 2 and 3 of Directive 73/239/EEC;

(c) activities and bodies referred to in Article 3 of Directive 2002/83/EC;

(d) the activity of reinsurance conducted or fully guaranteed by the government of a Member State when this is acting, for reasons of substantial public interest, in the capacity of reinsurer of last resort, including in circumstances where such a role is required by a situation in the market in which it is not feasible to obtain adequate commercial cover.

Article 2

Definitions

1. For the purposes of this Directive, the following definitions shall apply:

(a) 'reinsurance' means the activity consisting in accepting risks ceded by an insurance undertaking or by another reinsurance undertaking. In the case of the association of underwriters known as Lloyd's, reinsurance also means the activity consisting in accepting risks, ceded by any member of Lloyd's, by an insurance or reinsurance undertaking other than the association of underwriters known as Lloyd's;

(b) 'captive reinsurance undertaking' means a reinsurance undertaking owned either by a financial undertaking other than an insurance or a reinsurance undertaking or a group of insurance or reinsurance undertakings to which Directive 98/78/EC applies, or by a non-financial undertaking, the purpose of which is to provide reinsurance cover exclusively for the risks of the undertaking or undertakings to which it belongs or of an undertaking or undertakings of the group of which the captive reinsurance undertaking is a member;

(c) 'reinsurance undertaking' means an undertaking which has received official authorisation in accordance with Article 3;

(d) 'branch' means an agency or a branch of a reinsurance undertaking;

(e) 'establishment' means the head office or a branch of a reinsurance undertaking, account being taken of point (d);

(f) 'home Member State' means the Member State in which the head office of the reinsurance undertaking is situated;

(g) 'Member State of the branch' means the Member State in which the branch of a reinsurance undertaking is situated;

(h) 'host Member State' means the Member State in which a reinsurance undertaking has a branch or provides services;

(i) 'control' means the relationship between a parent undertaking and a subsidiary, as defined in Article 1 of Directive 83/349/EEC,[14] or a similar relationship between any natural or legal person and an undertaking;

(j) 'qualifying holding' means a direct or indirect holding in an undertaking which represents 10% or more of the capital or of the voting rights or which makes it possible to exercise a significant influence over the management of the undertaking in which a holding subsists;

(k) 'parent undertaking' means a parent undertaking as defined in Articles 1 and 2 of Directive 83/349/EEC;

(l) 'subsidiary' means a subsidiary undertaking as defined in Articles 1 and 2 of Directive 83/349/EEC;

(m) 'competent authorities' means the national authorities which are empowered by law or regulation to supervise reinsurance undertakings;

(n) 'close links' means a situation in which two or more natural or legal persons are linked by:
  (i) participation, which shall mean the ownership, direct or by way of control, of 20% or

---

[14] Seventh Council Directive 83/349/EEC of 13 June 1983 based on the Article 54(3)(g) of the Treaty on consolidated accounts (OJ L 193, 18.7.1983, 1), reproduced supra under no. B. 3. Directive as last amended by Directive 2003/51/EC, reproduced supra under no. C. 23.

more of the voting rights or capital of an undertaking, or

(ii) control, in all the cases referred to in Article 1(1) and (2) of Directive 83/349/EEC or a similar relationship between any natural or legal person and an undertaking;

(o) 'financial undertaking' means one of the following entities:
  (i) a credit institution, a financial institution or an ancillary banking services undertaking within the meaning of Article 1(5) and (23) of Directive 2000/12/EC,[15]
  (ii) an insurance undertaking, a reinsurance undertaking or an insurance holding company within the meaning of Article 1(i) of Directive 98/78/EC,
  (iii) an investment firm or a financial institution within the meaning of point 1 of Article 4(1) of Directive 2004/39/EC,[16]
  (iv) a mixed financial holding company within the meaning of Article 2(15) of Directive 2002/87/EC;

(p) 'special purpose vehicle' means any undertaking, whether incorporated or not, other than an existing insurance or reinsurance undertaking, which assumes risks from insurance or reinsurance undertakings and which fully funds its exposure to such risks through the proceeds of a debt issuance or some other financing mechanism where the repayment rights of the providers of such debt or other financing mechanism are subordinated to the reinsurance obligations of such a vehicle;

(q) 'finite reinsurance' means reinsurance under which the explicit maximum loss potential, expressed as the maximum economic risk transferred, arising both from a significant underwriting risk and timing risk transfer, exceeds the premium over the lifetime of the contract by a limited but significant amount, together with at least one of the following two features:
  (i) explicit and material consideration of the time value of money,
  (ii) contractual provisions to moderate the balance of economic experience between the parties over time to achieve the target risk transfer.

2. For the purposes of paragraph 1(a) of this Article, the provision of cover by a reinsurance undertaking to an institution for occupational retirement provision falling under the scope of Directive 2003/41/EC[17] where the law of the institution's home Member State permits such provision, shall also be considered as an activity falling under the scope of this Directive.

For the purposes of paragraph 1(d), any permanent presence of a reinsurance undertaking in the territory of a Member State shall be treated in the same way as an agency or branch, even if that presence does not take the form of a branch or agency, but consists merely of an office managed by the undertaking's own staff or by a person who is independent but has permanent authority to act for the undertaking as an agency would.

For the purposes of paragraph 1(j) of this Article, and in the context of Articles 12 and 19 to 23 and of the other levels of holding referred to in Article 19 to 23, the voting rights referred to in Article 92 of Directive 2001/34/EC[18] shall be taken into account.

For the purposes of paragraph 1(l), any subsidiary of a subsidiary undertaking shall also be regarded as a subsidiary of the undertaking which is those undertakings' ultimate parent undertaking.

For the purposes of paragraph 1(n):
– any subsidiary undertaking of a subsidiary undertaking shall be considered a subsidiary

---

[15] Directive 2000/12/EC of the European Parliament and of the Council of 20 March 2000 relating to the taking-up and pursuit of the business of credit institutions (OJ L 126, 26.5.2000, 1), reproduced supra under no. B. 32. Directive as last amended by Directive 2005/1/EC, reproduced supra under no. B. 39.

[16] Directive 2004/39/EC of the European Parliament and of the Council of 21 April 2004 on markets in financial instruments (OJ L 145, 30.4.2004, 1), reproduced infra under no. S. 29.

[17] Directive 2003/41/EC of the European Parliament and of the Council of 3 June 2003 on the activities and supervision of institutions for occupational retirement provision (OJ L 235, 23.9.2003, 10), reproduced supra under no. I. 35.

[18] Directive 2001/34/EC of the European Parliament and of the Council of 28 May 2001 on the admission of securities to official stock exchange listing and on information to be published on those securities (OJ L 184, 6.7.2001, 1), reproduced infra under no. S. 18. Directive as last amended by Directive 2005/1/EC, reproduced supra under no. B. 39.

of the parent undertaking which is at the head of those undertakings;
– a situation in which two or more natural or legal persons are permanently linked to one and the same person by a control relationship shall also be regarded as constituting a close link between such persons.

3. Wherever this Directive refers to the euro, the conversion value in national currency to be adopted shall, as from 31 December of each year, be that of the last day of the preceding month of October for which euro conversion values are available in all the Community currencies.

Title II

The Taking-up of the Business of Reinsurance and Authorisation of the Reinsurance Undertaking

Article 3
Principle of authorisation

The taking-up of the business of reinsurance shall be subject to prior official authorisation. Such authorisation shall be sought from the competent authorities of the home Member State by:

(a) any undertaking which establishes its head office in the territory of that State;

(b) any reinsurance undertaking which, having received the authorisation, extends its business to reinsurance activities other than those already authorised.

Article 4
Scope of authorisation

1. An authorisation pursuant to Article 3 shall be valid for the entire Community. It shall permit a reinsurance undertaking to carry on business there, under either the right of establishment or the freedom to provide services.

2. Authorisation shall be granted for non-life reinsurance activities, life reassurance activities or all kinds of reinsurance activities, according to the request made by the applicant.

It shall be considered in the light of the scheme of operations to be submitted pursuant to Articles 6(b) and 11 and the fulfilment of the conditions laid down for authorisation by the Member State from which the authorisation is sought.

Article 5
Form of the reinsurance undertaking

1. The home Member State shall require every reinsurance undertaking for which authorisation is sought to adopt one of the forms set out in Annex I.

A reinsurance undertaking may also adopt the form of a European Company (SE), as defined in Regulation (EC) No 2157/2001.[19]

2. Member States may, where appropriate, set up undertakings in any public-law form provided that such bodies have as their objects reinsurance operations under conditions equivalent to those under which private-law undertakings operate.

Article 6
Conditions

The home Member State shall require every reinsurance undertaking for which authorisation is sought to:

(a) limit its objects to the business of reinsurance and related operations; this requirement may include a holding company function and activities with respect to financial sector activities within the meaning of Article 2, point (8), of Directive 2002/87/EC;

(b) submit a scheme of operations in accordance with Article 11;

(c) possess the minimum guarantee fund provided for in Article 40(2);

(d) be effectively run by persons of good repute with appropriate professional qualifications or experience.

---

[19] Council Regulation (EC) No 2157/2001 of 8 October 2001 on the Statute for a European company (SE) (OJ L 294, 10.11.2001, 1), reproduced supra under no. C. 19. Regulation as amended by Regulation (EC) No 885/2004 (OJ L 168, 1.5.2004, 1).

Article 7
Close links

1. Where close links exist between the reinsurance undertaking and other natural or legal persons, the competent authorities shall grant authorisation only if those links do not prevent the effective exercise of their supervisory functions.

2. The competent authorities shall refuse authorisation if the laws, regulations or administrative provisions of a non-member country governing one or more natural or legal persons with which the reinsurance undertaking has close links, or difficulties involved in their enforcement, prevent the effective exercise of their supervisory functions.

3. The competent authorities shall require reinsurance undertakings to provide them with the information they require to monitor compliance with the conditions referred to in paragraph 1 on a continuous basis.

Article 8
Head office of the reinsurance undertaking

Member States shall require that the head offices of reinsurance undertakings be situated in the same Member State as their registered offices.

Article 9
Policy conditions and scales of premiums

1. This Directive shall not prevent Member States from maintaining in force or introducing laws, regulations or administrative provisions requiring approval of the memorandum and articles of association and communication of any other documents necessary for the normal exercise of supervision.

2. However, Member States may not adopt provisions requiring the prior approval or systematic notification of general and special policy conditions, scales of premiums and forms and other printed documents which a reinsurance undertaking intends to use in its dealings with ceding or retroceding undertakings.

Article 10
Economic requirements of the market

Member States may not require that any application for authorisation be considered in the light of the economic requirements of the market.

Article 11
Scheme of operations

1. The scheme of operations referred to in Article 6(b) shall include particulars or evidence of:

(a) the nature of the risks which the reinsurance undertaking proposes to cover;

(b) the kinds of reinsurance arrangements which the reinsurance undertaking proposes to make with ceding undertakings;

(c) the guiding principles as to retrocession;

(d) the items constituting the minimum guarantee fund;

(e) estimates of the costs of setting up the administrative services and the organisation for securing business and the financial resources intended to meet those costs.

2. In addition to the requirements in paragraph 1, the scheme of operations shall for the first three financial years contain:

(a) estimates of management expenses other than installation costs, in particular current general expenses and commissions;

(b) estimates of premiums or contributions and claims;

(c) a forecast balance sheet;

(d) estimates of the financial resources intended to cover underwriting liabilities and the solvency margin.

Article 12
Shareholders and members with qualifying holdings

The competent authorities of the home Member State shall not grant to an undertaking an authorisation to take up the business of reinsurance before they have been informed of the identities of the shareholders or members, direct or indirect, whether natural or legal persons, who have qualifying holdings in that undertaking and of the amounts of those holdings.

The same authorities shall refuse authorisation if, taking into account the need to ensure the sound and prudent management of a reinsurance undertaking, they are not satisfied as to the qualifications of the shareholders or members.

Article 13
Refusal of authorisation

Any decision to refuse an authorisation shall be accompanied by the precise grounds for doing so and notified to the undertaking in question.

Each Member State shall make provision for a right to apply to the courts, pursuant to Article 53, should there be any refusal.

Such provision shall also be made with regard to cases where the competent authorities have not dealt with an application for an authorisation upon the expiry of a period of six months from the date of its receipt.

Article 14
Prior consultation with the competent authorities of other Member States

1. The competent authorities of the other Member State involved shall be consulted prior to the granting of an authorisation to a reinsurance undertaking, which is:

(a) a subsidiary of an insurance or reinsurance undertaking authorised in another Member State; or

(b) a subsidiary of the parent undertaking of an insurance or reinsurance undertaking authorised in another Member State; or

(c) controlled by the same person, whether natural or legal, who controls an insurance or reinsurance undertaking authorised in another Member State.

2. The competent authority of a Member State involved, which is responsible for the supervision of credit institutions or investment firms, shall be consulted prior to the granting of an authorisation to a reinsurance undertaking which is:

(a) a subsidiary of a credit institution or investment firm authorised in the Community; or

(b) a subsidiary of the parent undertaking of a credit institution or investment firm authorised in the Community; or

(c) controlled by the same person, whether natural or legal, who controls a credit institution or investment firm authorised in the Community.

3. The relevant competent authorities referred to in paragraphs 1 and 2 shall in particular consult each other when assessing the suitability of the shareholders and the reputation and experience of directors involved in the management of another entity of the same group. They shall inform each other of any information regarding the suitability of shareholders and the reputation and experience of directors which is of relevance to the other competent authorities involved for the granting of an authorisation as well as for the ongoing assessment of compliance with operating conditions.

TITLE III
CONDITIONS GOVERNING THE BUSINESS OF REINSURANCE

CHAPTER 1
PRINCIPLES AND METHODS OF FINANCIAL SUPERVISION

SECTION 1
COMPETENT AUTHORITIES AND GENERAL RULES

Article 15
Competent authorities and object of supervision

1. The financial supervision of a reinsurance undertaking, including that of the business it carries on either through branches or under the freedom to provide services, shall be the sole responsibility of the home Member State.

If the competent authorities of the host Member State have reason to consider that the activities of a reinsurance undertaking might affect its financial soundness, they shall inform the competent authorities of the reinsurance undertaking's home Member State. The latter authorities shall determine whether the reinsurance undertaking is complying with the prudential rules laid down in this Directive.

2. The financial supervision pursuant to paragraph 1 shall include verification, with respect to the reinsurance undertaking's entire business, of its state of solvency, of the establishment of technical provisions and of the assets covering them in accordance with the rules laid down or practices followed in the home Member State under provisions adopted at Community level.

3. The home Member State of the reinsurance undertaking shall not refuse a retrocession contract concluded by the reinsurance undertaking with a reinsurance undertaking authorised in accordance with this Directive or an insurance undertaking authorised in accordance with Directives 73/239/EEC or 2002/83/EC on grounds directly related to the financial soundness of that reinsurance undertaking or that insurance undertaking.

4. The competent authorities of the home Member State shall require every reinsurance undertaking to have sound administrative and accounting procedures and adequate internal control mechanisms.

Article 16
Supervision of branches established in another Member State

The Member State of the branch shall provide that, where a reinsurance undertaking authorised in another Member State carries on business through a branch, the competent authorities of the home Member State may, after having first informed the competent authorities of the Member State of the branch, carry out themselves or through the intermediary of persons they appoint for that purpose, on-the-spot verification of the information necessary to ensure the financial supervision of the undertaking. The authorities of the Member State of the branch may participate in that verification.

Article 17
Accounting, prudential and statistical information: supervisory powers

1. Each Member State shall require every reinsurance undertaking whose head office is situated in its territory to produce an annual account, covering all types of operation, of its financial situation and of its solvency.

2. Member States shall require reinsurance undertakings with head offices within their territories to render periodically the returns, together with statistical documents, which are necessary for the purposes of supervision. The competent authorities shall provide each other with any documents and information that are useful for the purposes of supervision.

3. Every Member State shall take all steps necessary to ensure that the competent authorities have the powers and means necessary for the supervision of the business of reinsurance undertakings with head offices within their territories, including business carried on outside those territories.

4. In particular, the competent authorities shall be enabled to:

(a) make detailed enquiries regarding a reinsurance undertaking's situation and the whole of its business, inter alia, by gathering information or requiring the submission of documents concerning its reinsurance and retrocession business, and by carrying out on-the-spot investigations at the reinsurance undertaking's premises;

(b) take any measures with regard to a reinsurance undertaking, its directors or managers or the persons who control it, that are appropriate and necessary to ensure that that reinsurance undertaking's business continues to comply with the laws, regulations and administrative provisions with which the reinsurance undertaking must comply in each Member State;

(c) ensure that those measures are carried out, if need be, by enforcement and where appropriate through judicial channels.

Member States may also make provision for the competent authorities to obtain any information regarding contracts which are held by intermediaries.

Article 18
Transfer of portfolio

Under the conditions laid down by national law, each Member State shall authorise reinsurance undertakings with head offices within its territory to transfer all or part of their portfolios of contracts, including those concluded either under the right of establishment or the freedom to provide services, to an accepting office established within the Community, if the competent authorities of the home Member State of the accepting office certify that, after taking the transfer into account, the latter possesses the necessary solvency margin referred to in Chapter 3.

SECTION 2
QUALIFYING HOLDINGS

Article 19
Acquisitions

Member States shall require any natural or legal person who proposes to hold, directly or indirectly, a qualifying holding in a reinsurance undertaking first to inform the competent authorities of the home Member State, indicating the size of his intended holding. That person must likewise inform the competent authorities of the home Member State if he proposes to increase his qualifying holding so that the proportion of the voting rights or of the capital he holds would reach or exceed 20%, 33% or 50% or so that the reinsurance undertaking would become his subsidiary.

The competent authorities of the home Member State shall have up to three months from the date of the notification provided for in the first paragraph to oppose such a plan if, in view of the need to ensure sound and prudent management of the reinsurance undertaking in question, they are not satisfied as to the qualifications of the person referred to in the first paragraph. If they do not oppose the plan in question, they may fix a maximum period for its implementation.

Article 20
Acquisitions by financial undertakings

If the acquirer of the holdings referred to in Article 19 is an insurance undertaking, a reinsurance undertaking, a credit institution or an investment firm authorised in another Member State, or the parent undertaking of such an entity, or a natural or legal person controlling such an entity, and if, as a result of that acquisition, the undertaking in which the acquirer proposes to acquire such a holding would become a subsidiary or subject to the control of the acquirer, the assessment of the acquisition must be subject to the prior consultation referred to in Article 14.

Article 21
Disposals

Member States shall require any natural or legal person who proposes to dispose, directly or indirectly, of a qualifying holding in a reinsurance undertaking first to inform the competent authorities of the home Member State, indicating the size of his intended holding.

Such a person shall likewise inform the competent authorities if he proposes to reduce his qualifying holding so that the proportion of the voting rights or of the capital he holds would fall below 20%, 33% or 50% or so that the reinsurance undertaking would cease to be his subsidiary.

Article 22
Information to the competent authority by the reinsurance undertaking

On becoming aware of them, reinsurance undertakings shall inform the competent authorities of their home Member States of any acquisitions or disposals of holdings in their capital that cause holdings to exceed or fall below any of the thresholds referred to in Articles 19 and 21.

They shall also, at least once a year, inform them of the names of shareholders and members possessing qualifying holdings and the sizes of such holdings as shown, for example, by the information received at annual general meetings of shareholders or members or as a result of compliance with the regulations relating to companies listed on stock exchanges.

Article 23

Qualifying holdings: powers of the competent authority

Member States shall require that, where the influence exercised by the persons referred to in Article 19 is likely to operate against the prudent and sound management of a reinsurance undertaking, the competent authorities of the home Member State shall take appropriate measures to put an end to that situation. Such measures may consist, for example, in injunctions, penalties against directors and managers, or suspension of the exercise of the voting rights attaching to the shares held by the shareholders or members in question.

Similar measures shall apply to natural or legal persons failing to comply with the obligation to provide prior information imposed pursuant to Article 19. If a holding is acquired despite the opposition of the competent authorities, the Member States shall, regardless of any other penalties to be adopted, provide either for exercise of the corresponding voting rights to be suspended, or for the nullity of votes cast or for the possibility of their annulment.

SECTION 3

PROFESSIONAL SECRECY AND EXCHANGES OF INFORMATION

Article 24

Obligation

1. Member States shall provide that all persons working or who have worked for the competent authorities, as well as auditors and experts acting on behalf of the competent authorities, are bound by an obligation of professional secrecy.

Pursuant to that obligation, and without prejudice to cases covered by criminal law, no confidential information which they may receive while performing their duties may be divulged to any person or authority whatsoever, except in summary or aggregate form, such that individual reinsurance undertakings cannot be identified.

2. However, where a reinsurance undertaking has been declared bankrupt or is being compulsorily wound up, confidential information which does not concern third parties involved in attempts to rescue that undertaking may be divulged in civil or commercial proceedings.

Article 25

Exchange of information between competent authorities of Member States

Article 24 shall not prevent the competent authorities of different Member States from exchanging information in accordance with the Directives applicable to reinsurance undertakings. Such information shall be subject to the conditions of professional secrecy laid down in Article 24.

Article 26

Cooperation agreements with third countries

Member States may conclude cooperation agreements providing for exchange of information with the competent authorities of third countries or with authorities or bodies of third countries as defined in Article 28(1) and (2) only if the information disclosed is subject to guarantees of professional secrecy at least equivalent to those referred to in this Section. Such exchange of information shall be intended for the performance of the supervisory task of the authorities or bodies mentioned.

Where the information originates in another Member State, it may not be disclosed without the express agreement of the competent authorities which have disclosed it and, where appropriate, solely for the purposes for which those authorities gave their agreement.

Article 27
Use of confidential information

Competent authorities receiving confidential information under Articles 24 and 25 may use it only in the course of their duties:

(a) to check that the conditions governing the taking up of the business of reinsurance are met and to facilitate monitoring of the conduct of such business, especially with regard to the monitoring of technical provisions, solvency margins, administrative and accounting procedures and internal control mechanisms,

(b) to impose penalties,

(c) in administrative appeals against decisions of the competent authorities, or

(d) in court proceedings initiated under Article 53 or under special provisions provided for in this Directive and other Directives adopted in the field of insurance and reinsurance undertakings.

Article 28
Exchange of information with other authorities

1. Articles 24 and 27 shall not preclude the exchange of information within a Member State, where there are two or more competent authorities in the same Member State, or, between Member States, between competent authorities and:

(a) authorities responsible for the official supervision of credit institutions and other financial organisations and the authorities responsible for the supervision of financial markets,

(b) bodies involved in the liquidation and bankruptcy of insurance and reinsurance undertakings and in other similar procedures, and

(c) persons responsible for carrying out statutory audits of the accounts of insurance undertakings, reinsurance undertakings and other financial institutions, in the discharge of their supervisory functions, or the disclosure to bodies which administer compulsory winding-up proceedings or guarantee schemes of information necessary to the performance of their duties. The information received by those authorities, bodies and persons shall be subject to the conditions of professional secrecy laid down in Article 24.

2. Notwithstanding Articles 24 to 27, Member States may authorise exchanges of information between the competent authorities and:

(a) the authorities responsible for overseeing the bodies involved in the liquidation and bankruptcy of insurance or reinsurance undertakings and other similar procedures, or

(b) the authorities responsible for overseeing the persons charged with carrying out statutory audits of the accounts of insurance or reinsurance undertakings, credit institutions, investment firms and other financial institutions, or

(c) independent actuaries of insurance or reinsurance undertakings carrying out legal supervision of those undertakings and the bodies responsible for overseeing such actuaries.

Member States which have recourse to the option provided for in the first subparagraph shall require at least that the following conditions are met:

(a) this exchange of information shall be for the purpose of carrying out the overseeing or legal supervision referred to in the first subparagraph;

(b) information received in this context shall be subject to the conditions of professional secrecy imposed in Article 24;

(c) where the information originates in another Member State, it may not be disclosed without the express agreement of the competent authorities which have disclosed it and, where appropriate, may only be disclosed for the purposes for which those authorities gave their agreement.

Member States shall communicate to the Commission and to the other Member States the names of the authorities, persons and bodies which may receive information pursuant to this paragraph.

3. Notwithstanding Articles 24 to 27, Member States may, with the aim of strengthening the stability, including the integrity, of the financial system, authorise the exchange of information between the competent authorities and the

authorities or bodies responsible under the law for the detection and investigation of breaches of company law.

Member States which have recourse to the option provided for in the first subparagraph shall require at least that the following conditions are met:

(a) the information shall be for the purpose of performing the task referred to in the first subparagraph;

(b) information received in this context shall be subject to the conditions of professional secrecy imposed in Article 24;

(c) where the information originates in another Member State, it may not be disclosed without the express agreement of the competent authorities which have disclosed it and, where appropriate, solely for the purposes for which those authorities gave their agreement.

Where, in a Member State, the authorities or bodies referred to in the first subparagraph perform their task of detection or investigation with the aid, in view of their specific competence, of persons appointed for that purpose and not employed in the public sector, the possibility of exchanging information provided for in the first subparagraph may be extended to such persons under the conditions laid down in the second subparagraph.

In order to implement point (c) of the second subparagraph, the authorities or bodies referred to in the first subparagraph shall communicate to the competent authorities which have disclosed the information the names and precise responsibilities of the persons to whom it is to be sent.

Member States shall communicate to the Commission and to the other Member States the names of the authorities or bodies which may receive information pursuant to this paragraph.

Article 29

Transmission of information to central banks and monetary authorities

This Section shall not prevent a competent authority from transmitting to central banks and other bodies with a similar function in their capacity as monetary authorities, and where appropriate, to other public authorities responsible for overseeing payment systems, information intended for the performance of their task. Nor shall it prevent such authorities or bodies from communicating to the competent authorities such information as they may need for the purposes of Article 27.

Information received in this context shall be subject to the conditions of professional secrecy imposed in this Section.

Article 30

Disclosure of information to government administrations responsible for financial legislation

Notwithstanding Articles 24 and 27, Member States may, under provisions laid down by law, authorise the disclosure of certain information to other departments of their central government administrations responsible for legislation on the supervision of credit institutions, financial institutions, investment services and insurance or reinsurance undertakings and to inspectors acting on behalf of those departments.

However, such disclosures may be made only where necessary for reasons of prudential control.

Member States shall, however, provide that information received under Articles 25 and 28(1) and that obtained by means of the on-the-spot verification referred to in Article 16 may never be disclosed in the cases referred to in this Article except with the express consent of the competent authorities which disclosed the information or of the competent authorities of the Member State in which on-the-spot verification was carried out.

SECTION 4

DUTIES OF AUDITORS

Article 31

Duties of auditors

1. Member States shall provide at least that any person authorised in accordance with Directive

84/253/EEC,[20] performing in a reinsurance undertaking the task described in Article 51 of Directive 78/660/EEC,[21] Article 37 of Directive 83/349/EEC or Article 31 of Directive 85/611/EEC[22] or any other statutory task, shall have a duty to report promptly to the competent authorities any fact or decision concerning that undertaking of which he/she has become aware while carrying out that task which is liable to:

(a) constitute a material breach of the laws, regulations or administrative provisions which lay down the conditions governing authorisation or which specifically govern pursuit of the activities of insurance or reinsurance undertakings, or

(b) affect the continuous functioning of the reinsurance undertaking, or

(c) lead to refusal to certify the accounts or to the expression of reservations.

That person shall also have a duty to report any facts and decisions of which he/she becomes aware in the course of carrying out a task as described in the first subparagraph in an undertaking having close links resulting from a control relationship with the reinsurance undertaking within which he/she is carrying out the above-mentioned task.

2. The disclosure to the competent authorities, by persons authorised in accordance with Directive 84/253/EEC, of any relevant fact or decision referred to in paragraph 1 of this Article shall not constitute a breach of any restriction on disclosure of information imposed by contract or by any legislative, regulatory or administrative provision and shall not involve such persons in liability of any kind.

---

[20] Eighth Council Directive 84/253/EEC of 10 April 1984 based on Article 54(3)(g) of the Treaty on the approval of persons responsible for carrying out the statutory audits of accounting documents (OJ L 126, 12.5.1984, 20), reproduced supra under no. C. 7.
[21] Fourth Council Directive 78/660/EEC of 25 July 1978 based on Article 54(3)(g) of the Treaty on the annual accounts of certain types of companies (OJ L 222, 14.8.1978, 11), reproduced supra under no. C. 11. Directive as last amended by Directive 2003/51/EC, reproduced supra under no. C. 23.
[22] Council Directive 85/611/EEC of 20 December 1985 on the coordination of laws, regulations and administrative provisions relating to undertakings for collective investment in transferable securities (UCITS) (OJ L 375, 31.12.1985, 3), reproduced infra under no. S. 6. Directive as last amended by Directive 2005/1/EC, reproduced supra under no. B. 39.

CHAPTER 2

RULES RELATING TO TECHNICAL PROVISIONS

Article 32

Establishment of technical provisions

1. The home Member State shall require every reinsurance undertaking to establish adequate technical provisions in respect of its entire business.

The amount of such technical provisions shall be determined in accordance with the rules laid down in Directive 91/674/ EEC. Where applicable, the home Member State may lay down more specific rules in accordance with Article 20 of Directive 2002/83/EC.

2. Member States shall not retain or introduce a system with gross reserving which requires pledging of assets to cover unearned premiums and outstanding claims provisions if the reinsurer is a reinsurance undertaking authorised in accordance with this Directive or an insurance undertaking authorised in accordance with Directives 73/239/EEC or 2002/83/EC.

3. When the home Member State allows any technical provisions to be covered by claims against reinsurers who are not authorised in accordance with this Directive or insurance undertakings which are not authorised in accordance with Directives 73/239/EEC or 2002/83/EC, it shall set the conditions for accepting such claims.

Article 33

Equalisation reserves

1. The home Member State shall require every reinsurance undertaking which reinsures risks included in class 14 listed in point A of the Annex to Directive 73/239/EEC to set up an equalisation reserve for the purpose of offsetting any technical deficit or above-average claims ratio arising in that class in any financial year.

2. The equalisation reserve for credit reinsurance shall be calculated in accordance with the rules laid down by the home Member State in accordance with one of the four methods set out in

point D of the Annex to Directive 73/239/EEC, which shall be regarded as equivalent.

3. The home Member State may exempt reinsurance undertakings from the obligation to set up equalisation reserves for reinsurance of credit insurance business where the premiums or contributions receivable in respect of reinsurance of credit insurance are less than 4% of the total premiums or contributions receivable by them and less than EUR 2.500.000.

4. The home Member State may require every reinsurance undertaking to set up equalisation reserves for classes of risks other than credit reinsurance. The equalisation reserves shall be calculated according to the rules laid down by the home Member State.

Article 34

Assets covering technical provisions

1. The home Member State shall require every reinsurance undertaking to invest the assets covering the technical provisions and the equalisation reserve referred to in Article 33 in accordance with the following rules:

(a) the assets shall take account of the type of business carried out by a reinsurance undertaking, in particular the nature, amount and duration of the expected claims payments, in such a way as to secure the sufficiency, liquidity, security, quality, profitability and matching of its investments;

(b) the reinsurance undertaking shall ensure that the assets are diversified and adequately spread and allow the undertaking to respond adequately to changing economic circumstances, in particular developments in the financial markets and real estate markets or major catastrophic events. The undertaking shall assess the impact of irregular market circumstances on its assets and shall diversify the assets in such a way as to reduce such impact;

(c) investment in assets which are not admitted to trading on a regulated financial market shall in any event be kept to prudent levels;

(d) investment in derivative instruments shall be possible insofar as they contribute to a reduction of investment risks or facilitate efficient portfolio management. They shall be valued on a prudent basis, taking into account the underlying assets, and included in the valuation of the institution's assets. The institution shall also avoid excessive risk exposure to a single counterparty and to other derivative operations;

(e) the assets shall be properly diversified in such a way as to avoid excessive reliance on any one particular asset, issuer or group of undertakings and accumulations of risk in the portfolio as a whole. Investments in assets issued by the same issuer or by issuers belonging to the same group shall not expose the undertaking to excessive risk concentration.

Member States may decide not to apply the requirements referred to in point (e) to investment in government bonds.

2. Member States shall not require reinsurance undertakings situated in their territory to invest in particular categories of assets.

3. Member States shall not subject the investment decisions of a reinsurance undertaking situated in their territory or its investment manager to any kind of prior approval or systematic notification requirements.

4. Notwithstanding paragraphs 1 to 3, the home Member State may, for every reinsurance undertaking whose head office is situated in its territory, lay down the following quantitative rules, provided that they are prudentially justified:

(a) investments of gross technical provisions in currencies other than those in which technical provisions are set should be limited to 30%;

(b) investments of gross technical provisions in shares and other negotiable securities treated as shares, bonds and debt securities which are not admitted to trading on a regulated market should be limited to 30%;

(c) the home Member State may require every reinsurance undertaking to invest no more than 5% of its gross technical provisions in shares and other negotiable securities treated as shares, bonds, debt securities and other money and capital market instruments from the same undertaking, and no more than 10% of its total gross technical provisions in shares and other negotiable securities treated as shares, bonds, debt securities and other money and capital market instruments from undertakings which are members of the same group.

5. Furthermore, the home Member State shall lay down more detailed rules setting the conditions for the use of amounts outstanding from a special purpose vehicle as assets covering technical provisions pursuant to this Article.

Chapter 3
Rules Relating to the Solvency Margin and to the Guarantee Fund

Section 1
Available Solvency Margin

Article 35

General rule

Each Member State shall require of every reinsurance undertaking whose head office is situated in its territory an adequate available solvency margin in respect of its entire business at all times, which is at least equal to the requirements of this Directive.

Article 36

Eligible items

1. The available solvency margin shall consist of the assets of the reinsurance undertaking free of any foreseeable liabilities, less any intangible items, including:

(a) the paid-up share capital or, in the case of a mutual reinsurance undertaking, the effective initial fund plus any members' accounts which meet all the following criteria:

(i) the memorandum and articles of association shall stipulate that payments may be made from those accounts to members only in so far as this does not cause the available solvency margin to fall below the required level, or, after the dissolution of the undertaking, if all the undertaking's other debts have been settled;

(ii) the memorandum and articles of association shall stipulate, with respect to any payments referred to in point (i) for reasons other than the individual termination of membership, that the competent authorities must be notified at least one month in advance and can prohibit the payment within that period;

(iii) the relevant provisions of the memorandum and articles of association may be amended only after the competent authorities have declared that they have no objection to the amendment, without prejudice to the criteria stated in points (i) and (ii);

(b) statutory and free reserves which neither correspond to underwriting liabilities nor are classified as equalisation reserves;

(c) the profit or loss brought forward after deduction of dividends to be paid.

2. The available solvency margin shall be reduced by the amount of own shares directly held by the reinsurance undertaking.

For those reinsurance undertakings which discount or reduce their non-life technical provisions for claims outstanding to take account of investment income as permitted by Article 60 (1)(g) of Directive 91/674/EEC, the available solvency margin shall be reduced by the difference between the undiscounted technical provisions or technical provisions before deductions as disclosed in the notes on the accounts, and the discounted or technical provisions after deductions. This adjustment shall be made for all risks listed in point A of the Annex to Directive 73/239/EEC, except for risks listed under classes 1 and 2 of point A of that Annex. For classes other than 1 and 2 listed in point A of that Annex, no adjustment need be made in respect of the discounting of annuities included in technical provisions.

In addition to the deductions in the first and second subparagraphs, the available solvency margin shall be reduced by the following items:

(a) participations which the reinsurance undertaking holds in the following entities:

(i) insurance undertakings within the meaning of Article 6 of Directive 73/239/EEC, Article

4 of Directive 2002/83/EC, or Article 1(b) of Directive 98/78/EC,
(ii) reinsurance undertakings within the meaning of Article 3 of this Directive or non-member country reinsurance undertakings within the meaning of Article 1(l) of Directive 98/78/EC,
(iii) insurance holding companies within the meaning of Article 1(i) of Directive 98/78/EC,
(iv) credit institutions and financial institutions within the meaning of Article 1(1) and (5) of Directive 2000/12/EC,
(v) investment firms and financial institutions within the meaning of Article 1(2) of Directive 93/22/EEC[23] and of Article 2(4) and (7) of Directive 93/6/EEC;[24]

(b) each of the following items which the reinsurance undertaking holds in respect of the entities defined in (a) in which it holds a participation:
(i) instruments referred to in paragraph 4,
(ii) instruments referred to in Article 27(3) of Directive 2002/83/EC,
(iii) subordinated claims and instruments referred to in Article 35 and Article 36(3) of Directive 2000/12/EC.

Where shares in another credit institution, investment firm, financial institution, insurance or reinsurance undertaking or insurance holding company are held temporarily for the purposes of a financial assistance operation designed to reorganise and save that entity, the competent authority may waive the provisions on deduction referred to under (a) and (b) of the third subparagraph.

As an alternative to the deduction of the items referred to in (a) and (b) of the third subparagraph which the reinsurance undertaking holds in credit institutions, investment firms and financial institutions, Member States may allow their reinsurance undertakings to apply mutatis mutandis methods 1, 2, or 3 of Annex I to Directive 2002/87/EC. Method 1 (Accounting consolidation) shall only be applied if the competent authority is confident about the level of integrated management and internal control regarding the entities which would be included in the scope of consolidation. The method chosen shall be applied in a consistent manner over time. Member States may provide that, for the calculation of the solvency margin as provided for by this Directive, reinsurance undertakings subject to supplementary supervision in accordance with Directive 98/78/EC or to supplementary supervision in accordance with Directive 2002/87/EC need not deduct the items referred to in (a) and (b) of the third subparagraph which are held in credit institutions, investment firms, financial institutions, insurance or reinsurance undertakings or insurance holding companies which are included in the supplementary supervision.

For the purposes of the deduction of participations referred to in this paragraph, participation shall mean a participation within the meaning of Article 1(f) of Directive 98/78/EC.

3. The available solvency margin may also consist of:

(a) cumulative preferential share capital and subordinated loan capital up to 50% of the available solvency margin or the required solvency margin, whichever is the smaller, no more than 25% of which shall consist of subordinated loans with a fixed maturity, or fixed-term cumulative preferential share capital, provided that, in the event of the bankruptcy or liquidation of the reinsurance undertaking, binding agreements exist under which the subordinated loan capital or preferential share capital ranks after the claims of all other creditors and is not to be repaid until all other debts outstanding at the time have been settled.

Subordinated loan capital shall also fulfil the following conditions:
(i) only fully paid-up funds may be taken into account;

---

[23] Council Directive 93/22/EEC of 10 May 1993 on investment services in the securities field (OJ L 141, 11.6.1993, 27), reproduced infra under no. S. 14. Directive as last amended by Directive 2002/87/EC of the European Parliament and of the Council (OJ L 35, 11.2.2003, 1), reproduced supra under no. B. 38.

[24] Council Directive 93/6/EEC of 15 March 1993 on the capital adequacy of investments firms and credit institutions (OJ L 141, 11.6.1993, 1), reproduced supra under no. B. 20. Directive as last amended by Directive 2005/1/EC, reproduced supra under no. B. 39.

(ii) for loans with a fixed maturity, the original maturity shall be at least five years. No later than one year before the repayment date the reinsurance undertaking shall submit to the competent authorities for their approval a plan showing how the available solvency margin will be kept at or brought to the required level at maturity, unless the extent to which the loan may rank as a component of the available solvency margin is gradually reduced during at least the last five years before the repayment date. The competent authorities may authorise the early repayment of such loans provided that application is made by the issuing reinsurance undertaking and that its available solvency margin will not fall below the required level;

(iii) loans the maturity of which is not fixed shall be repayable only subject to five years' notice unless the loans are no longer considered as a component of the available solvency margin or unless the prior consent of the competent authorities is specifically required for early repayment. In the latter event the reinsurance undertaking shall notify the competent authorities at least six months before the date of the proposed repayment, specifying the available solvency margin and the required solvency margin both before and after that repayment. The competent authorities shall authorise repayment only if the reinsurance undertaking's available solvency margin will not fall below the required level;

(iv) the loan agreement shall not include any clause providing that in specified circumstances, other than the winding-up of the reinsurance undertaking, the debt will become repayable before the agreed repayment dates;

(v) the loan agreement may be amended only after the competent authorities have declared that they have no objection to the amendment;

(b) securities with no specified maturity date and other instruments, including cumulative preferential shares other than those referred to in point (a), up to 50% of the available solvency margin or the required solvency margin, whichever is the smaller, for the total of such securities and the subordinated loan capital referred to in point (a) provided that they fulfil the following:

(i) they may not be repaid on the initiative of the bearer or without the prior consent of the competent authority;

(ii) the contract of issue shall enable the reinsurance undertaking to defer the payment of interest on the loan;

(iii) the lender's claims on the reinsurance undertaking shall rank entirely after those of all non-subordinated creditors;

(iv) the documents governing the issue of the securities shall provide for the loss-absorption capacity of the debt and unpaid interest, while enabling the reinsurance undertaking to continue its business;

(v) only fully paid-up amounts may be taken into account.

4. Upon application, with supporting evidence, by the reinsurance undertaking to the competent authority of the home Member State and with the agreement of that competent authority, the available solvency margin may also consist of:

(a) one half of the unpaid share capital or initial fund, once the paid-up part amounts to 25% of that share capital or fund, up to 50% of the available solvency margin or the required solvency margin, whichever is the smaller;

(b) in the case of a non-life mutual or mutual-type association with variable contributions, any claim which it has against its members by way of a call for supplementary contribution, within the financial year, up to one half of the difference between the maximum contributions and the contributions actually called in, and subject to a limit of 50% of the available solvency margin or the required solvency margin, whichever is the smaller. The competent national authorities shall establish guidelines laying down the conditions under which supplementary contributions may be accepted;

(c) any hidden net reserves arising out of the valuation of assets, in so far as such hidden net reserves are not of an exceptional nature.

5. In addition, with respect to life reassurance activities, the available solvency margin may, upon application, with supporting evidence, by the reinsurance undertaking to the competent authority of the home Member State and with the agreement of that competent authority, consist of:

(a) until 31 December 2009, an amount equal to 50% of the undertaking's future profits, but not exceeding 25% of the available solvency margin or the required solvency margin, whichever is the smaller; the amount of the future profits shall be obtained by multiplying the estimated annual profit by a factor which represents the average period left to run on policies; the factor used may not exceed six; the estimated annual profit shall not exceed the arithmetical average of the profits made over the last five financial years in the activities listed in Article 2(1) of Directive 2002/83/EC.

Competent authorities may only agree to include such an amount for the available solvency margin:
(i) when an actuarial report is submitted to the competent authorities substantiating the likelihood of emergence of these profits in the future; and
(ii) insofar as that part of future profits emerging from hidden net reserves referred to in paragraph 4(c) has not already been taken into account;

(b) where Zillmerising is not practised or where, if practised, it is less than the loading for acquisition costs included in the premium, the difference between a non-Zillmerised or partially Zillmerised mathematical provision and a mathematical provision Zillmerised at a rate equal to the loading for acquisition costs included in the premium; this figure may not, however, exceed 3,5% of the sum of the differences between the relevant capital sums of life reassurance activities and the mathematical provisions for all policies for which Zillmerising is possible; the difference shall be reduced by the amount of any undepreciated acquisition costs entered as an asset.

6. Amendments to paragraphs 1 to 5 of this Article to take into account developments that justify a technical adjustment of the elements eligible for the available solvency margin shall be adopted in accordance with the procedure laid down in Article 55(2).

Section 2
Required Solvency Margin

Article 37
Required solvency margin for non-life reinsurance activities

1. The required solvency margin shall be determined on the basis either of the annual amount of premiums or contributions, or of the average burden of claims for the past three financial years.

However, in the case of reinsurance undertakings which essentially underwrite only one or more of the risks of credit, storm, hail or frost, the last seven financial years shall be taken as the reference period for the average burden of claims.

2. Subject to Article 40, the amount of the required solvency margin shall be equal to the higher of the two results as set out in paragraphs 3 and 4 of this Article.

3. The premium basis shall be calculated using the higher of gross written premiums or contributions as calculated below, and gross earned premiums or contributions.

Premiums or contributions in respect of the classes 11, 12 and 13 listed in point A of the Annex to Directive 73/239/EEC shall be increased by 50%.

Premiums or contributions in respect of classes other than classes 11, 12 and 13 listed in point A of the Annex to Directive 73/239/EEC may be increased by up to 50%, for specific reinsurance activities or contract types, in order to take account of the specificities of these activities or contracts, in accordance with the procedure referred to in Article 55(2) of this Directive. The premiums or contributions, inclusive of charges ancillary to premiums or contributions, due in respect of reinsurance business in the last financial year shall be aggregated.

From that sum there shall then be deducted the total amount of premiums or contributions cancelled in the last financial year, as well as the total amount of taxes and levies pertaining to the premiums or contributions entering into the aggregate.

The amount so obtained shall be divided into two portions, the first portion extending up to EUR 50.000.000, the second comprising the excess; 18% and 16% of these portions respectively shall be calculated and added together.

The sum so obtained shall be multiplied by the ratio existing in respect of the sum of the last three financial years between the amount of claims remaining to be borne by the reinsurance undertaking after deduction of amounts recoverable under retrocession and the gross amount of claims; that ratio may in no case be less than 50%. Upon application, with supporting evidence, by the reinsurance undertaking to the competent authority of the home Member State and with the agreement of that authority, amounts recoverable from special purpose vehicles as referred to in Article 46 may also be deducted as retrocession.

With the approval of the competent authorities, statistical methods may be used to allocate the premiums or contributions.

4. The claims basis shall be calculated, as follows, using in respect of the classes 11, 12 and 13 listed in point A of the Annex to Directive 73/239/EEC, claims, provisions and recoveries increased by 50%. Claims, provisions and recoveries in respect of classes other than classes 11, 12 and 13 listed in point A of the Annex to Directive 73/239/EEC, may be increased by up to 50%, for specific reinsurance activities or contract types, in order to take account of the specificities of those activities or contracts, in accordance with the procedure referred to in Article 55(2) of this Directive.

The amounts of claims paid, without any deduction of claims borne by retrocessionaires, in the periods specified in paragraph 1 shall be aggregated.

To that sum there shall be added the amount of provisions for claims outstanding established at the end of the last financial year.

From that sum there shall be deducted the amount of recoveries effected during the periods specified in paragraph 1.

From the sum then remaining, there shall be deducted the amount of provisions for claims outstanding established at the commencement of the second financial year preceding the last financial year for which there are accounts. If the reference period established in paragraph 1 equals seven years, the amount of provisions for claims outstanding established at the commencement of the sixth financial year preceding the last financial year for which there are accounts shall be deducted.

One third, or one seventh, of the amount so obtained, according to the reference period established in paragraph 1, shall be divided into two portions, the first extending up to EUR 35.000.000 and the second comprising the excess; 26% and 23% of these portions respectively shall be calculated and added together.

The sum so obtained shall be multiplied by the ratio existing in respect of the sum of the last three financial years between the amount of claims remaining to be borne by the undertaking after deduction of amounts recoverable under retrocession and the gross amount of claims; that ratio may in no case be less than 50%. Upon application, with supporting evidence, by the reinsurance undertaking to the competent authority of the home Member State and with the agreement of that authority, amounts recoverable from special purpose vehicles as referred to in Article 46 may also be deducted as retrocession.

With the approval of the competent authorities, statistical methods may be used to allocate claims, provisions and recoveries.

5. If the required solvency margin as calculated in paragraphs 2, 3 and 4 is lower than the required solvency margin of the year before, the required solvency margin shall be at least equal to the required solvency margin of the year before multiplied by the ratio between the amount of the technical provisions for claims outstanding at the end of the last financial year and the amount of the technical provisions for claims outstanding

at the beginning of the last financial year. In these calculations technical provisions shall be calculated net of retrocession but the ratio may in no case be higher than 1.

6. The fractions applicable to the portions referred to in the fifth subparagraph of paragraph 3 and the seventh subparagraph of paragraph 4 shall each be reduced to a third in the case of reinsurance of health insurance practised on a similar technical basis to that of life assurance, if:

(a) the premiums paid are calculated on the basis of sickness tables according to the mathematical method applied in insurance;

(b) a provision is set up for increasing age;

(c) an additional premium is collected in order to set up a safety margin of an appropriate amount;

(d) the insurance undertaking may cancel the contract before the end of the third year of insurance at the latest;

(e) the contract provides for the possibility of increasing premiums or reducing payments even for current contracts.

Article 38
Required solvency margin for life reassurance activities

1. The required solvency margin for life reassurance activities shall be determined in accordance with Article 37.

2. Notwithstanding paragraph 1 of this Article, the home Member State may provide that for reinsurance classes of assurance business covered by Article 2(1)(a) of Directive 2002/83/EC linked to investment funds or participating contracts and for the operations referred to in Article 2(1)(b), 2(2)(b), (c), (d) and (e) of Directive 2002/83/EC, the required solvency margin is to be determined in accordance with Article 28 of Directive 2002/83/EC.

Article 39
Required solvency margin for a reinsurance undertaking simultaneously conducting non-life and life reinsurance

1. The home Member State shall require every reinsurance undertaking conducting both non-life and life reinsurance business to have an available solvency margin to cover the total sum of required solvency margins in respect of both non-life and life reinsurance activities which shall be determined in accordance with Articles 37 and 38 respectively.

2. If the available solvency margin does not reach the level required in paragraph 1 of this Article, the competent authorities shall apply the measures provided for in Articles 42 and 43.

Section 3
Guarantee Fund

Article 40
Amount of the guarantee fund

1. One third of the required solvency margin as specified in Articles 37, 38 and 39 shall constitute the guarantee fund. This fund shall consist of the items listed in Article 36(1), (2) and (3) and, with the agreement of the competent authority of the home Member State, in Article 36(4)(c).

2. The guarantee fund shall not be less than a minimum of EUR 3.000.000.

Any Member State may provide that as regards captive reinsurance undertakings, the minimum guarantee fund shall be not less than EUR 1.000.000.

Article 41
Review of the amount of the guarantee fund

1. The amounts in euro as laid down in Article 40(2) shall be reviewed annually as from 10 December 2007 in order to take account of changes in the European index of consumer prices comprising all Member States as published by Eurostat.

The amounts shall be adapted automatically by increasing the base amount in euro by the percentage change in that index over the period between the entry into force of this Directive and the review date and rounded up to a multiple of EUR 100.000.

If the percentage change since the last adaptation is less than 5%, no adaptation shall take place.

2. The Commission shall inform the European Parliament and the Council annually of the review and the adapted amounts referred to in paragraph 1.

Chapter 4
Reinsurance Undertakings in Difficulty or in an Irregular Situation and Withdrawal of Authorisation

Article 42
Reinsurance undertakings in difficulty

1. If a reinsurance undertaking does not comply with Article 32, the competent authority of its home Member State may prohibit the free disposal of its assets after having communicated its intention to the competent authorities of the host Member States.

2. For the purposes of restoring the financial situation of a reinsurance undertaking the solvency margin of which has fallen below the minimum required under Articles 37, 38 and 39, the competent authority of the home Member State shall require that a plan for the restoration of a sound financial situation be submitted for its approval.

In exceptional circumstances, if the competent authority is of the opinion that the financial situation of the reinsurance undertaking will deteriorate further, it may also restrict or prohibit the free disposal of the reinsurance undertaking's assets. It shall inform the authorities of other Member States within the territories of which the reinsurance undertaking carries on business of any measures it has taken and the latter shall, at the request of the former, take the same measures.

3. If the solvency margin falls below the guarantee fund as defined in Article 40, the competent authority of the home Member State shall require the reinsurance undertaking to submit a short-term finance scheme for its approval.

It may also restrict or prohibit the free disposal of the reinsurance undertaking's assets. It shall inform the authorities of all other Member States and the latter shall, at the request of the former, take the same measures.

4. Each Member State shall take the measures necessary to be able, in accordance with its national law, to prohibit the free disposal of assets located within its territory at the request, in the cases provided for in paragraphs 1, 2 and 3, of the reinsurance undertaking's home Member State, which shall designate the assets to be covered by such measures.

Article 43
Financial recovery plan

1. Member States shall ensure that the competent authorities have the power to require a financial recovery plan for those reinsurance undertakings where competent authorities consider that their obligations arising out of reinsurance contracts are threatened.

2. The financial recovery plan shall, as a minimum, include particulars or proof for the next three financial years concerning:

(a) estimates of management expenses, in particular current general expenses and commissions;

(b) a plan setting out detailed estimates of income and expenditure in respect of reinsurance acceptances and reinsurance cessions;

(c) a forecast balance sheet;

(d) estimates of the financial resources intended to cover underwriting liabilities and the required solvency margin;

(e) the overall retrocession policy.

3. Where the financial position of the reinsurance undertaking is deteriorating and the contractual obligations of the reinsurance undertaking are threatened, Member States shall ensure that the competent authorities have the power to oblige reinsurance undertakings to have a higher required solvency margin, in order to ensure that the reinsurance undertaking is able to fulfil the solvency requirements in the near future. The level of this higher required solvency margin shall be based on a financial recovery plan referred to in paragraph 1.

4. Member States shall ensure that the competent authorities have the power to revalue downwards all elements eligible for the available

solvency margin, in particular, where there has been a significant change in the market value of those elements since the end of the last financial year.

5. Member States shall ensure that the competent authorities have the power to decrease the reduction, based on retrocession, to the solvency margin as determined in accordance with Articles 37, 38 and 39 where:

(a) the nature or quality of retrocession contracts has changed significantly since the last financial year;

(b) there is no or a limited risk transfer under the retrocession contracts.

6. If the competent authorities have required a financial recovery plan for the reinsurance undertaking in accordance with paragraph 1 of this Article, they shall refrain from issuing a certificate in accordance with Article 18, as long as they consider that its obligations arising out of reinsurance contracts are threatened within the meaning of the said paragraph 1.

Article 44
Withdrawal of authorisation

1. Authorisation granted to a reinsurance undertaking by the competent authority of its home Member State may be withdrawn by that authority if that undertaking:

(a) does not make use of that authorisation within 12 months, expressly renounces it or ceases to carry on business for more than 6 months, unless the Member State concerned has made provision for authorisation to lapse in such cases;

(b) no longer fulfils the conditions for admission;

(c) has been unable, within the time allowed, to take the measures specified in the restoration plan or finance scheme referred to in Article 42;

(d) fails seriously in its obligations under the regulations to which it is subject.

In the event of the withdrawal or lapse of authorisation, the competent authority of the home Member State shall notify the competent authorities of the other Member States accordingly, and they shall take appropriate measures to prevent the reinsurance undertaking from commencing new operations within their territories, under either the right of establishment or the freedom to provide services.

2. Any decision to withdraw an authorisation shall be supported by precise reasons and communicated to the reinsurance undertaking in question.

Title IV
Provisions Relating to Finite Reinsurance and Special Purpose Vehicles

Article 45
Finite reinsurance

1. The home Member State may lay down specific provisions concerning the pursuit of finite reinsurance activities regarding:

– mandatory conditions for inclusion in all contracts issued;

– sound administrative and accounting procedures, adequate internal control mechanisms and risk management requirements;

– accounting, prudential and statistical information requirements;

– the establishment of technical provisions to ensure that they are adequate, reliable and objective;

– investment of assets covering technical provisions in order to ensure that they take account of the type of business carried on by the reinsurance undertaking, in particular the nature, amount and duration of the expected claims payments, in such a way as to secure the sufficiency, liquidity, security, profitability and matching of its assets;

– rules relating to the available solvency margin, required solvency margin and the minimum guarantee fund that the reinsurance undertaking shall maintain in respect of finite reinsurance activities.

2. In the interests of transparency, Member States shall communicate the text of any measures laid down by their national law for the purposes of paragraph 1 to the Commission without delay.

Article 46
Special purpose vehicles

1. Where a Member State decides to allow the establishment within its territory of special purpose vehicles within the meaning of this Directive, it shall require prior official authorisation thereof.

2. The Member State where the special purpose vehicle is established shall lay down the conditions under which the activities of such an undertaking shall be carried on. In particular, that Member State shall lay down rules regarding:
– scope of authorisation;
– mandatory conditions for inclusion in all contracts issued;
– the good repute and appropriate professional qualifications of persons running the special purpose vehicle;
– fit and proper requirements for shareholders or members having a qualifying holding in the special purpose vehicle;
– sound administrative and accounting procedures, adequate internal control mechanisms and risk management requirements;
– accounting, prudential and statistical information requirements;
– the solvency requirements of special purpose vehicles.

3. In the interests of transparency, Member States shall communicate the text of any measures laid down by their national law for the purposes of paragraph 2, to the Commission without delay.

Title V
Provisions Relating to Right of Establishment and Freedom to Provide Services

Article 47
Reinsurance undertakings not complying with the legal provisions

1. If the competent authorities of the host Member State establish that a reinsurance undertaking with a branch or carrying on business under the freedom to provide services within its territory is not complying with the legal provisions applicable to it in that State, they shall require the reinsurance undertaking concerned to remedy that irregular situation. At the same time, they shall refer those findings to the competent authority of the home Member State.

If, despite the measures taken by the competent authority of the home Member State or because such measures prove inadequate, the reinsurance undertaking persists in infringing the legal provisions applicable to it in the host Member State, the latter may, after informing the competent authority of the home Member State, take appropriate measures to prevent or penalise further infringements, including, insofar as is strictly necessary, preventing that reinsurance undertaking from continuing to conclude new reinsurance contracts within its territory. Member States shall ensure that within their territories it is possible to serve the legal documents necessary for such measures on reinsurance undertakings.

2. Any measure adopted under paragraph 1 involving penalties or restrictions on the conduct of reinsurance business shall be properly reasoned and communicated to the reinsurance undertaking concerned.

Article 48
Winding-up

In the event of a reinsurance undertaking's being wound up, commitments arising out of contracts underwritten through a branch or under the freedom to provide services shall be met in the same way as those arising out of that undertaking's other reinsurance contracts.

Title VI
Reinsurance Undertakings whose Head Offices are Outside the Community and Conducting Reinsurance Activities in the Community

Article 49
Principle and conditions for conducting reinsurance business

A Member State shall not apply to reinsurance undertakings having their head offices outside the Community and commencing or carrying out reinsurance activities in its territory provisions which result in a treatment more favourable than that accorded to reinsurance undertakings having their head office in that Member State.

Article 50
Agreements with third countries

1. The Commission may submit proposals to the Council for the negotiation of agreements with one or more third countries regarding the means of exercising supervision over:

(a) reinsurance undertakings which have their head offices situated in a third country, and conduct reinsurance business in the Community,

(b) reinsurance undertakings which have their head offices in the Community and conduct reinsurance business in the territory of a third country.

2. The agreements referred to in paragraph 1 shall in particular seek to ensure under conditions of equivalence of prudential regulation, effective market access for reinsurance undertakings in the territory of each contracting party and provide for mutual recognition of supervisory rules and practices on reinsurance. They shall also seek to ensure that:

(a) the competent authorities of the Member States are able to obtain the information necessary for the supervision of reinsurance undertakings which have their head offices situated in the Community and conduct business in the territory of third countries concerned,

(b) the competent authorities of third countries are able to obtain the information necessary for the supervision of reinsurance undertakings which have their head offices situated within their territories and conduct business in the Community.

3. Without prejudice to Articles 300(1) and (2) of the Treaty, the Commission shall with the assistance of the European Insurance and Occupational Pensions Committee examine the outcome of the negotiations referred to in paragraph 1 of this Article and the resulting situation.

TITLE VII
SUBSIDIARIES OF PARENT UNDERTAKINGS GOVERNED BY THE LAWS OF A THIRD COUNTRY AND ACQUISITIONS OF HOLDINGS BY SUCH PARENT UNDERTAKINGS

Article 51
Information from Member States to the Commission

The competent authorities of the Member States shall inform the Commission and the competent authorities of the other Member States:

(a) of any authorisation of a direct or indirect subsidiary, one or more parent undertakings of which are governed by the laws of a third country;

(b) whenever such a parent undertaking acquires a holding in a Community reinsurance undertaking which would turn the latter into its subsidiary. When an authorisation as referred to in point (a) is granted to the direct or indirect subsidiary of one or more parent undertakings governed by the laws of a third country, the structure of the group shall be specified in the notification which the competent authorities shall address to the Commission.

Article 52
Third country treatment of Community reinsurance undertakings

1. Member States shall inform the Commission of any general difficulties encountered by their reinsurance undertakings in establishing themselves and operating in a third country or carrying on activities in a third country.

2. The Commission shall, periodically, draw up a report examining the treatment accorded to Community reinsurance undertakings in third countries, in the terms referred to in paragraph 3, as regards the establishment of Community reinsurance undertakings in third countries, the acquisition of holdings in third-country reinsurance undertakings, the carrying on of reinsurance

activities by such established undertakings and the cross-border provision of reinsurance activities from the Community to third countries. The Commission shall submit those reports to the Council, together with any appropriate proposals or recommendations.

3. Whenever it appears to the Commission, either on the basis of the reports referred to in paragraph 2 or on the basis of other information, that a third country is not granting Community reinsurance undertakings effective market access, the Commission may submit recommendations to the Council for the appropriate mandate for negotiation with a view to obtaining improved market access for Community reinsurance undertakings.

4. Measures taken under this Article shall comply with the Community's obligations under any international agreements, in particular in the World Trade Organisation.

Title VIII
Other Provisions

Article 53
Right to apply to the courts

Member States shall ensure that decisions taken in respect of a reinsurance undertaking under laws, regulations and administrative provisions implementing this Directive are subject to the right to apply to the courts.

Article 54
Cooperation between the Member States and the Commission

1. Member States shall cooperate with each other for the purpose of facilitating the supervision of reinsurance within the Community and the application of this Directive.

2. The Commission and the competent authorities of the Member States shall collaborate closely for the purpose of facilitating the supervision of reinsurance within the Community and of examining any difficulties which may arise in the application of this Directive.

Article 55
Committee Procedure

1. The Commission shall be assisted by the European Insurance and Occupational Pensions Committee.

2. Where reference is made to this paragraph, Articles 5 and 7 of Decision 1999/468/EC shall apply, having regard to the provisions of Article 8 thereof. The period laid down in Article 5(6) of Decision 1999/468/EC shall be set at three months.

3. The Committee shall adopt its Rules of Procedure.

Article 56
Implementing measures

The following implementing measures to this Directive shall be adopted in accordance with the procedure referred to in Article 55(2):

(a) extension of the legal forms provided for in Annex I,

(b) clarification of the items constituting the solvency margin listed in Article 36 to take account of the creation of new financial instruments,

(c) increase by up to 50% of the premiums or claims amounts used for the calculation of the required solvency margin provided for in Article 37(3) and (4), in classes other than classes 11, 12 and 13 listed in point A of the Annex to Directive 73/239/EEC, for specific reinsurance activities or contract types, to take account of the specificities of those activities or contracts,

(d) alteration of the minimum guarantee fund provided for in Article 40(2) to take account of economic and financial developments,

(e) clarification of the definitions in Article 2 in order to ensure uniform application of this Directive throughout the Community.

Title IX
Amendments to Existing Directives

Article 57
Amendments to Directive 73/239/EEC

[...]

¶ *This article amends article 12a(1) and (2), the subparagraph between brackets in article 13(2), paragraphs 2 and 3 of article 15, article 16(2), 16a, and 20(4), and inserts article 17b of Directive 73/239/EEC, reproduced supra under no. I.3. The modifications are directly incorporated therein.*

Article 58
Amendments to Directive 92/49/EEC

[...]

¶ *This article amends article 15, paragraph 1a, article 16 paragraphs 4, 5, and 6, article 21(1), and the introductory wording of article 22(1) of Directive 92/49/EEC, reproduced supra under no. I. 25. The modifications are directly incorporated therein.*

Article 59
Amendments to Directive 98/78/EC

[...]

¶ *This article amends the title, article 1, 2, 3, and 4, 5(1), 6, 7, 8, 9(3), 10, 10a, and Annexes I and II of Directive 98/78/EC, reproduced supra under no. I. 28. The modifications are directly incorporated therein.*

Article 60
Amendments to Directive 2002/83/EC

[...]

¶ *This article amends article 1(1)(s) and inserts article 9a in Directive 2002/83/EC, reproduced supra under no. I. 33. The modifications are directly incorporated therein.*

Title X
Transitional and Final Provisions

Article 61
Right acquired by existing reinsurance undertakings

1. Reinsurance undertakings subject to this Directive which were authorised or entitled to conduct reinsurance business in accordance with the provisions of the Member States in which they have their head offices before 10 December 2005 shall be deemed to be authorised in accordance with Article 3.

However, they shall be obliged to comply with the provisions of this Directive concerning the carrying on of the business of reinsurance and with the requirements set out in Article 6(a), (c), (d), Articles 7, 8 and 12 and Articles 32 to 41 as from 10 December 2007.

2. Member States may allow reinsurance undertakings referred to in paragraph 1 which at 10 December 2005 do not comply with Articles 6(a), 7, 8 and Articles 32 to 40 a period until 10 December 2008 in order to comply with such requirements.

Article 62
Reinsurance undertakings closing their activity

1. Reinsurance undertakings which by 10 December 2007 have ceased to conduct new reinsurance contracts and exclusively administer their existing portfolio in order to terminate their activity shall not be subject to this Directive.

2. Member States shall draw up the list of the reinsurance undertakings concerned and they shall communicate that list to all the other Member States.

Article 63
Transitional period for Articles 57(3) and 60(6)

A Member State may postpone the application of the provisions of Article 57(3) of this Directive amending Article 15(3) of Directive 73/239/EEC and of the provision of Article 60(6) of this Directive until 10 December 2008.

Article 64
Transposition

1. Member States shall bring into force the laws, regulations and administrative provisions necessary to comply with this Directive by 10 December

2007. They shall forthwith communicate to the Commission the texts of those measures.

When Member States adopt those measures, they shall contain a reference to this Directive or be accompanied by such a reference on the occasion of their official publication. Member States shall determine how such reference is to be made.

2. Member States shall communicate to the Commission the text of the main provisions of national law which they adopt in the field covered by this Directive.

Article 65
Entry into force

This Directive shall enter into force on the day following its publication in the Official Journal of the European Union.

Article 66
Addressees

This Directive is addressed to the Member States.

Annex I

Forms of reinsurance undertakings:
– in the case of the Kingdom of Belgium: 'société anonyme/naamloze vennootschap', 'société en commandite par actions/commanditaire vennootschap op aandelen', 'association d'assurance mutuelle/onderlinge verzekeringsvereniging', 'société coopérative/coöperatieve vennootschap';
– in the case of the Czech Republic: 'akciová společnost';
– in the case of the Kingdom of Denmark: 'aktieselskaber', 'gensidige selskaber';
– in the case of the Federal Republic of Germany: 'Aktiengesellschaft', 'Versicherungsverein auf Gegenseitigkeit', 'Öffentlich-rechtliches Wettbewerbsversicherungsunternehmen';
– in the case of the Republic of Estonia: 'aktsiaselts';
– in the case of the Hellenic Republic: 'ανώνυμη εταιρία', 'αλληλασφαλιστικός συνεταιρισμός';
– in the case of the Kingdom of Spain: 'sociedad anónima';
– in the case of the French Republic: 'société anonyme', 'société d'assurance mutuelle', 'institution de prévoyance régie par le code de la sécurité sociale', 'institution de prévoyance régie par le code rural' and 'mutuelles régies par le code de la mutualité';
– in the case of Ireland: incorporated companies limited by shares or by guarantee or unlimited;
– in the case of the Italian Republic: 'società per azioni';
– in the case of the Republic of Cyprus: 'Εταιρεία Περιορισμένης Ευθύνης με μετοχές' ή 'Εταιρεία Περιορισμένης Ευθύνης με εγγύηση';
– in the case of the Republic of Latvia: 'akciju sabiedrība', 'sabiedrība ar ierobežotu atbildību';
– in the case of the Republic of Lithuania: 'akcinė bendrovė', 'uždaroji akcinė bendrovė';
– in the case of the Grand Duchy of Luxembourg: 'société anonyme', 'société en commandite par actions', 'association d'assurances mutuelles', 'société coopérative';
– in the case of the Republic of Hungary: 'biztosító részvénytársaság', 'biztosító szövetkezet', 'harmadik országbeli biztosító magyarországi fióktelepe';
– in the case of the Republic of Malta: 'limited liability company/kumpannija tà responsabbiltà limitata';
– in the case of the Kingdom of the Netherlands: 'naamloze vennootschap', 'onderlinge waarborgmaatschappij';
– in the case of the Republic of Austria: 'Aktiengesellschaft', 'Versicherungsverein auf Gegenseitigkeit';
– in the case of the Republic of Poland: 'spółka akcyjna', 'towarzystwo ubezpieczeń wzajemnych';

- in the case of the Portuguese Republic: 'sociedade anónima', 'mútua de seguros';
- in the case of the Republic of Slovenia: 'delniška družba';
- in the case of the Slovak Republic: 'akciová spoločnost';
- in the case of the Republic of Finland: 'keskinäinen vakuutusyhtiö/ömsesidigt försäkringsbolag', 'vakuutusosakeyhtiö/försäkringsaktiebolag', 'vakuutusyhdistys/försäkringsförening';
- in the case of the Kingdom of Sweden: 'försäkringsaktiebolag', 'ömsesidigt försäkringsbolag';
- in the case of the United Kingdom: incorporated companies limited by shares or by guarantee or unlimited, societies registered under the Industrial and Provident Societies Acts, societies registered or incorporated under the Friendly Societies Acts, 'the association of underwriters known as Lloyd's'.

Annex II

[...]

¶ *Annex II replaces the annexes of Directive 98/78/EC, reproduced supra under no. I. 28. The modifications are directly incorporated therein.*

Part VII
SECURITIES REGULATION

S. 1.

Commission Recommendation 77/534/EEC
of 25 July 1977
concerning a European code of conduct relating to transactions in transferable securities[1]

Explanatory Memorandum

1. The objectives set out in Article 2 of the Treaty of Rome, particularly the harmonious development of economic activities in the Community, can only be achieved if sufficient capital is available, and the sources of capital are sufficiently diversified to enable investments in the common market to be financed as rationally as possible.

The role of the securities markets is to permit a very free interplay at all times between supply and demand for capital. Consequently, the proper working and the interpenetration of these markets must be regarded as an essential aspect of the establishment of a 'common market' in capital.

2. Although the existing differences between the various financial markets in the nine Member States have not so far constituted an insuperable barrier to a number of international transactions, the lack of full information on the securities themselves and ignorance or misunderstanding of the rules governing the various markets have certainly helped to confine the investments of the great majority of savers to the markets of the countries in which they live or to a few well-known major international securities.

A reduction in these disparities would therefore tend to encourage the interpenetration of the member countries' markets, particularly if this is accompanied by improving the safeguards available to savers.

I. The European code of conduct in the context of approximating the laws of the Member States

3. On the basis of a Decision adopted in 1968 on the provision of information to the public on securities and conditions governing transactions in them, the Commission has already carried out a certain amount of harmonisation work in this sector, covering various specific aspects such as 'the content, checking and distribution of the prospectus to be published when securities issued by companies . . . are admitted to official stock exchange quotation'[2] and co-ordination of 'the conditions for the admission of securities to official stock exchange quotation.'[3]

¶ See Directive 80/390/EEC, reproduced infra under no. S. 3, and Directive 79/279/EEC, reproduced infra under no. S. 2.

4. In parallel with the work of harmonisation by Directives, and without prejudice to this method which is the only one capable of attaining the objective of true European integration, the Commission is of the opinion that it could recommend to the Member States—in a document

---

[1] OJ L 212, 20.8.1977, 37–43.
[2] OJ C 131, 13.12.1972.
[3] OJ C 56, 10.3.1976.

covering a range of problems connected with dealing in securities—that they should ensure the observation of certain basic principles. These principles are already widely recognised in all the countries of Europe, but restating and applying them will help to create a common set of professional ethics in an ever-changing field; this, in its turn, will considerably facilitate the process of harmonisation through Directives by making clear in advance the approach the Commission will be adopting.

5. This code of conduct, to be issued in the form of a Commission recommendation, must be seen separately from the Commission's other harmonisation work in this sector:
– because the ethical approach has been given priority over the legislative approach;
– because the Commission is anxious to take full account of the dynamics of the financial market and of business life, and consciously to adopt a positive attitude which seeks to improve the machinery of the market and the effectiveness of those operating on it;
– because some of the topics dealt with in a very general way in the code may be, and in some cases already are, the subject of proposals for Directives where a strict legal framework will be appropriate.

II. Juridical scope of the Commission's recommendation

6. The purpose of the present recommendation to the Member States is that they should ensure that those who are in a position to influence the workings of securities markets comply with the principles of the code of conduct; the Commission has consulted those involved and has ascertained that there is already broad support for the principles of the code.

7. Although most States are now conscious of the need to supervise financial markets, it is only too obvious that methods of supervision still differ widely. The recommendation allows for these differences; it does not require the Member States to create special supervisory authorities, but merely to co-ordinate at national level the action of the various associations and bodies concerned.

8. It must, however, be stressed that the introduction of a code of conduct for securities transactions by means of a recommendation can in no way be an obstacle to the subsequent adoption of Directives or Regulations in one or other of the fields covered by it. A number of such instruments are in fact already under preparation.

9. In the same light, it is not impossible that certain States may feel legislation on some or all of the subjects covered by the code is necessary in order to comply with the recommendation.

III. The content of the code

10. The code sets out a fundamental objective, certain general principles and a number of supplementary principles.

11. *The general principles* are the key provisions of the code and are of overriding importance.

They take priority over and go well beyond the detailed principles which follow them, and which are merely illustrations of them.

It is the general principles which will enable the fundamental objective of the code to be complied with; the content of the code must be understood and interpreted in the light of the general principles and not only by reference to the letter of the various supplementary principles.

A. *The first general principle* emphasises the importance of this aspect of the interpretation of the code. It recalls that any transaction on the securities market must be carried out in compliance with the rules and practices in each State designed to ensure the proper working of the markets, the principles of the present code supplementing or strengthening such rules and practices.

B. *The second general principle* is that information provided to savers must be complete and accurate, since lack of knowledge is a source of imperfection in any market.

If the information is not provided, or if it is incomprehensible or wrongly interpreted by those for whom it is intended, or if it is deliberately slanted or distorted, the prices quoted may well become completely artificial and the market may cease to fulfil its role. Consequently, a large number of principles, in the second part, have been worked out to cover this problem (supplementary principles 7 to 15).

The need for properly distributed information covers a wide range of situations, as different as the issue or the negotiation of securities. Proposals for Directives have also been made in this connection (including a proposal concerning rules for admission to quotation).

C. *The third general principle* relates to equality of treatment for shareholders. Despite some criticism, the Commission has taken the view that the principle of equality of treatment should be retained, illustrating its application by two supplementary principles, with the accent mainly on a specific obligation to disclose information.

Supplementary principle 17 mentions equality of treatment for other shareholders where a controlling holding is transferred, but accepts that the protection of such shareholders could be achieved by other means; this takes account of the existence in Germany of a law limiting the powers of the dominant shareholder. It is important to realise that the fundamental principle of the equality of shareholders goes well beyond the scope of the code. It is not confined, even in the code, to the transfer of blocks of shares or to the few supplementary principles in the second part which may refer to this principle, such as the use of undisclosed information to the detriment of those not having access to it or the compartmentalisation of markets making it possible to give advantages to certain purchasers or sellers of securities over others.

Obviously, only a few of the situations in which such a principle might be relevant can be mentioned; any attempt to give a more detailed list of the cases in which the principle would involve the risk of leaving loopholes which would probably soon be exploited. This principle lays down an approach and a spirit in which certain transactions must be carried out.

D. *The fourth, fifth and sixth general principles* are more particularly concerned with certain categories of persons the importance of whose role in the realisation of the code's objectives is beyond doubt, namely the members of companies' supervisory boards, company directors and company managers (principle 4), financial intermediaries and persons concerned professionally in transactions in securities (principles 5 and 6).

The fourth general principle recalls first that the code applies in particular to the members of companies' supervisory boards, company directors and company managers and then mentions more particularly their duty to refrain from any action liable to hamper the proper working of the market in their security or to harm the other shareholders.

Objectionable action on the market in the securities of a company by directors or managers is a term to be interpreted in the broad sense, since there may well be instances of failure to act which are just as reprehensible, or more reprehensible, than positive action.

The fifth general principle recommends that persons professionally engaged in stock exchange transactions, or at least all 'persons dealing regularly on the securities markets', avoid jeopardising, by seeking immediate and unfair profit, the credibility and the effectiveness of the market which it is in their own interest to foster.

Conflicts of interest liable to arise, e.g. in the various departments of a bank, because of the diversity of the roles which a banker has to play for his various customers, led to the enunciation of the *sixth general principle*.

While conceding that it is very difficult to lay down precise limits as far as discretion is concerned, it should be emphasised that ways and means must be sought of avoiding conflicts of this nature. An example will illustrate how difficult it is to define the scope of this rule: should confidential information be kept so secret in a financial establishment that it would be wrong to advise against an investment (through without saying why the investment would be a bad one) when the aim would be not to achieve a gain but to avoid a loss? In such a case, the banker should be free to give such informed advice to the customer, and this does indeed seem to be a reasonable solution; however, only practice will show whether this interpretation of supplementary principle 8 can become the source of impropriety, and whether the Commission's recommendation will have to be strengthened on this specific point.

12. *The supplementary principles*
As their name suggests, their purpose is to supplement the general principles by making them clearer and illustrating them. They are not exhaustive; they can be supplemented through the meetings of the liaison committee responsible for applying the code, in the light of actual situations encountered on the various European markets. The supplementary principles can be divided into two parts.

A. *The first supplementary principles* indicate a number of aspects of what the expression 'fair behaviour' by financial intermediaries is to be taken to mean.

In addition to compliance with laws, regulations and current practice, supplementary principles 1 to 6 describe a number of rules of conduct specific to intermediaries.

The main rule concerns, of course, the recommendation to carry out orders on an organised market and the limits set to acting as counterparty and to offsetting orders. The Commission's recommendation does not advise formally against these operations, but it is felt that they should be brought under the supervision of the supervisory authorities where these authorities can in fact assume responsibility for them.

B. *The following supplementary principles* from rule 7 onwards until the end refer to the need for information.

It is clear that many improprieties would be avoided if accurate information were disclosed very quickly and the time during which important information was kept secret were thus cut to a minimum.

The principles relating to information can themselves be divided into several parts depending on whether they refer:

(a) to the creation of an artificial market (principle 7);

(b) to the improper use of price-sensitive information (principles 8 to 10);

(c) to information to be provided to the public by the market authorities and companies (principles 11 to 14);

(d) to equality of information to which all investors must be entitled (principles 15 and 16); and lastly,

(e) to information to be provided where there is acquisition or, where appropriate, sale of a holding conferring *de jure* or *de facto* control of a company (principles 17 and 18).

IV. Implementation of the European code of conduct

13. In recommending the European code of conduct to the Member States, the Commission is of course well aware that a recommendation does not bind the States as to the results to be achieved; the successful implementation of the code will therefore depend to a great extent on the active co-operation of those affected by it, in particular on the authority of the body or bodies which are to supervise implementation.

14. An essential feature is that, on the basis of existing structures, there should be in each Member State at least one body (supervisory authority, professional association, etc.) responsible for supervising the implementation of the code at national level.

However, the choice of the appropriate body is a matter for the Member State concerned.

The code does not require that these supervisory bodies should have the power normally vested in public authorities, since the code will not carry penal sanctions.

15. However, since the code should be complied with throughout the Community, it will be desirable that representatives of each of the supervisory bodies should come together in a liaison committee.

The committee could advise the Commission on the development of the code, in the light of the problems and practices encountered in its application.

For these reasons, under the provisions of the Treaty establishing the European Economic Community, and in particular Article [211][4] thereof, the Commission recommends the Member States, without prejudice to the

---

[4] The number between brackets has been changed as from 1 May 1999 by article 12 of the Treaty of Amsterdam.

Regulations or administrative provisions already in existence:

1. to ensure that those who operate on securities markets, or who are in a position to influence the working of these markets, respect the fundamental objective, the general principles and the supplementary provisions of the European code of conduct annexed hereto;

2. to this end, to co-ordinate the action of the professional associations and the national authorities charged, in each State, with the supervision of the proper functioning of the market and the conduct of those who operate on it;

3. to appoint one or more representatives from these associations or authorities who shall be responsible for informing the Commission each year, beginning one year after the transmission of this recommendation, of any measures adopted to implement it and of the experience in applying them, of any difficulties encountered and of any suggestions for additions or amendments to the European code of conduct;

4. to take any other measures they may consider necessary to promote the principles of the code and to supervise their application.

Annex

European code of conduct relating to transactions in transferable securities

Fundamental objective

This code of conduct is to be seen in the general context of the development and integration of securities markets within the European Community, and seeks to establish certain general principles, supported by supplementary guidelines.

The code's objective is to establish standards of ethical behaviour on a Community-wide basis, so as to promote the effective functioning of securities markets (i.e. by creating the best possible conditions for matching supply and demand for capital), and to safeguard the public interest.

Definitions

In the code, the following expressions shall have the meanings ascribed to them below:
- '*transferable securities*' shall mean all securities that are or may be the subject of dealings on an organised market;
- '*financial intermediaries*' shall mean all persons professionally concerned in transactions in transferable securities;
- '*principals*' shall mean all persons [who give orders to buy or sell transferable securities and in particular those occupying a strategic position with regard to a security and the market in it (e.g. company directors and managers, holders or acquirers of major shareholdings)];
- '*securities markets*' shall mean the official stock exchange and all the markets organised by or under the supervision of the competent authorities and also all transactions in transferable securities as defined above including privately negotiated dealings between individuals in transferable securities—the word '*market*' (in the singular) being used only for the official stock exchange and the organised markets;
- '*competent authorities*' are those who have the tasks of ensuring the proper working of the market and the proper flow of information for the market at national level—principally the stock exchange authorities and supervisory agencies.

¶ *The words between square brackets have been changed by the corrigendum published in OJ L 294, 18.11.1977, 28.*

General principles

1. The objective of this code and the general principles should be observed even in cases not expressly covered by supplementary principles. Every transaction carried out on the securities markets should be in conformity with not only

the letter but also the spirit of the laws and regulations in force in each Member State, and also the principles of good conduct already applying to these markets, or recommended by this code.

2. Information should be available to the public which is fair, accurate, clear, adequate and which is given in good time.

The information should be provided in such a way that its significance and intent can be easily understood. Any person, who by virtue of his profession or duties has the duty or the means of informing the public, is under a special obligation to ensure that it is kept properly informed, and that no particular class of persons attains a privileged position.

3. Equality of treatment should be guaranteed to all holders of securities of the same type issued by the same company; in particular, any act resulting directly or indirectly in the transfer of a holding conferring *de jure* or *de facto* control of a company whose securities are dealt in on the market, should have regard to the right of all shareholders to be treated in the same fashion.

4. When the securities of a company are dealt in on the market, the members of its supervisory board, its directors, managers, and persons exercising *de jure* or *de facto* control, should act in such manner as to ensure that the fundamental objective of this code of conduct is realised. They have a particular duty to avoid any action that would operate to the detriment of fair dealings in the securities concerned, or prejudice the rights of other shareholders.

5. Persons dealing regularly on the securities markets should act fairly in accordance with the code's objective, even if this could in certain cases result in their having to forgo short-term gains.

6. Financial intermediaries should endeavour to avoid all conflicts of interest, whether as between themselves and their clients or other persons with whom they have a fiduciary relationship, or as between these two last-mentioned categories of persons. If, however, such a conflict arises, they should not seek to gain a direct or indirect personal advantage from the situation, and should avoid any prejudice to their clients or other persons with whom they have a fiduciary relationship.

Supplementary principles

1. All persons dealing regularly on the securities markets have a duty to promote investors' confidence in the fairness of the market by observance of the best standards of commercial probity and professional conduct.

2. Financial intermediaries have a special responsibility to observe the fundamental objective and the general principles of this code of conduct.

In particular, they should not connive at any breach by other persons of the provisions and principles referred to in the second paragraph of general principle 1, and they should not engage in manipulation that could distort the normal operation of the market.

3. No person should incite another person, whether or not an intermediary, to contravene the provisions and principles referred to in the second paragraph of general principle 1, nor exert pressure to obtain:

(1) information which is not public and which cannot be divulged without contravening rules relating to such information, or

(2) the carrying out of an irregular or dishonest transaction.

4. Financial intermediaries should seek out and recommend the best conditions for their clients for the execution of orders that are given to them, while observing the fundamental objective and general principles of the code.

They should execute the orders that they are given on an organised market, unless the principal has given express instructions to the contrary. However, if the circumstances of the transaction or the nature of the securities makes it difficult even impossible to execute orders on an organised market, financial intermediaries may act as counterparties to their clients or offset orders outside the market, provided that they ensure that this does not prejudice their clients' interests, and provided that they are in a position to reply to any request on the part of the competent authorities as regards the justification for, the number of, and the conditions applying to, transactions carried out in this manner.

5. Financial intermediaries should refrain from encouraging sales or purchases with the sole object of generating commission.

6. Financial intermediaries should not disclose the identity of their principals except in cases when this is required by national regulations or the control authorities (and also in the investigation of crimes or other serious misdeeds).

7. Any attempt or manipulation by persons acting separately or in concert with others, which aims at or results in the rise or fall in the price of securities by fraudulent means, is contrary to the fundamental objective of this code.

Fraudulent means are considered in particular to be the publication or diffusion of information that is false, exaggerated or tendentious, and also the use of other devices aimed at disrupting the markets' normal operation.

Financial intermediaries and members of the supervisory board, the directors and managers of companies whose securities are dealt in on the securities markets, who become aware of any such attempt or manipulation should endeavour to take the necessary steps to thwart it. They should inform the competent authorities and the companies concerned without delay.

8. Financial intermediaries should endeavour to keep secret, even as between different departments or services of the same organisation, information which they acquire in the course of carrying out their duties which is not yet public and which is price-sensitive.

In particular, financial intermediaries should not use such information in transactions that they carry out for their own account on the securities markets, or in transactions upon which they advise their clients or carry out for their account.

9. Any person who comes into possession of information, in exercising his profession or carrying out his duties, which is not public and which relates to a company or to the market in its securities or to any event of general interest to the market, which is price-sensitive, should refrain from carrying out, directly or indirectly, any transaction in which such information is used, and should refrain from giving the information to another person so that he may profit from it before the information becomes public.

¶ *See Directive 89/592/EEC, reproduced infra under no. S. 12.*

10. Securities markets should be sufficiently open to prevent their being fragmented, whereby the same security can be dealt in at the same time on different markets at different prices.

11. When a security is dealt in on the market the public should be informed not only of the different prices at which transactions take place, but also of the volume of dealings, unless the organisation of the market makes it possible for the public to assess the liquidity of its investment by some other means.

12. Every company whose securities are dealt in on the market should publish periodically, and at least every six months, information which is clear, precise, complete and up-to-date concerning its business operations, results, and financial position. Any fact or important decision capable of having an appreciable effect on the price of securities should also be made public without delay.

¶ *See Directive 82/121/EEC, reproduced infra under no. S. 4.*

13. When a fact or important decision, referred to in the preceding provision, cannot be made public without delay, for example because certain formalities have not yet been completed or because the company would be seriously prejudiced as a result, but the company nevertheless considers that there is a risk of leaks, the company should inform the competent authorities of the position. The latter should take the necessary steps to safeguard the market's proper operation until the relevant fact or decision can be made public. In particular they may, if this step appears unavoidable, suspend transactions for the necessary period.

¶ *See Directive 79/279/EEC, Schedule C. 5, reproduced infra under no. S. 2.*

14. It is desirable that a public issue of securities should be preceded by the publication of a

prospectus. The existence of the prospectus and the place or places where it may be obtained should be indicated in any publicity concerning such issue.

¶ See Directive 89/298/EEC, reproduced infra under no. S. 11.

15. No investor or group of investors should be given more favourable treatment as regards information than other investors or the public. All investors should have free access to information.

16. On the occasion of each issue of securities of the same type that are or may be dealt in on several markets at the same time, the issuer should endeavour not to give more favourable treatment to one market than to another.

¶ See the Directive 79/279/EEC, Schedule C. 2, reproduced infra under no. S. 2.

17. Any transaction resulting in the transfer of a holding conferring control in the sense referred to in general principle 3 should not be carried out in a surreptitious fashion without informing the other shareholders and the market control authorities.

It is desirable that all the shareholders of the company whose control has changed hands should be offered the opportunity of disposing of their securities on identical conditions, unless they have the benefit of alternative safeguards which can be regarded as equivalent.

18. Any acquisition, or attempted acquisition on the market, separately or by concerted action, of a holding conferring control in the sense referred to in general principle 3, without informing the public, is against the objective of this code.

S. 2.
Council Directive 79/279/EEC
of 5 March 1979
co-ordinating the conditions for the admission of securities to official stock exchange listing[1]

This Directive has been repealed as from 26 July 2001 by article 111 of Directive 2001/34/EC (OJ L 184, 6.7.2001), reproduced infra under no. S. 18.

Correlation Table

Directive 79/279/EEC	Directive 2001/34/EC
Article 2(a), introductory phrase	Article 1(b), introductory phrase
Article 2(a), 1st and 2nd indents	Article 1(b)(i) and (ii)
Article 2(b)	Article 1(e)
Article 1(1)	Article 2(1)
Article 1(2), introductory phrase	Article 2(2), introductory phrase
Article 1(2), 1st and 2nd indents	Article 2(2)(a) and (b)
Article 3, 1st and 2nd indents	Article 5(a) and (b)
Article 4	Article 6
Article 6	Article 7
Article 5	Article 8
Article 7	Article 9
Article 8	Article 10
Article 9(1)	Article 11(1)
Article 9(3)	Article 11(2)
Article 10	Article 12
Article 18(2)	Article 13(1)
Article 18(3)	Article 13(2)
Article 11	Article 14
Article 16	Article 15
Article 13	Article 16
Article 12	Article 17
Article 14	Article 18
Article 15	Article 19
Annex—Schedule A (I) (1)	Article 42
Annex—Schedule A (I) (2)	Article 43
Annex—Schedule A (I) (3)	Article 44
Annex—Schedule A (II) (1)	Article 45
Annex—Schedule A (II) (2)	Article 46

---

[1] OJ L 66, 16.3.1979, 21–32.

Directive 79/279/EEC	Directive 2001/34/EC
Annex—Schedule A (II) (3)	Article 47
Annex—Schedule A (II) (4)	Article 48
Annex—Schedule A (II) (5)	Article 49
Annex—Schedule A (II) (6)	Article 50
Annex—Schedule A (II) (7)	Article 51
Annex—Schedule B (A) (I)	Article 52
Annex—Schedule B (A) (II) (1)	Article 53
Annex—Schedule B (A) (II) (2)	Article 54
Annex—Schedule B (A) (II) (3)	Article 55
Annex—Schedule B (A) (II) (4)	Article 56
Annex—Schedule B (A) (II) (5)	Article 57
Annex—Schedule B (A) (III) (1)	Article 58
Annex—Schedule B (A) (III) (2)	Article 59
Annex—Schedule B (B) (1)	Article 60
Annex—Schedule B (B) (2)	Article 61
Annex—Schedule B (B) (3)	Article 62
Annex—Schedule B (B) (4)	Article 63
Annex—Schedule C (1)	Article 64
Annex—Schedule C (2) (a)	Article 65(1)
Annex—Schedule C (2) (b), introductory phrase	Article 65(2) introductory phrase
Annex—Schedule C (2) (b), 1st, 2nd and 3rd indents	Article 65(2)(a), (b) and (c)
Annex—Schedule C (3)	Article 66
Annex—Schedule C (4)	Article 67
Annex—Schedule C (5)(a), (b) and (c)	Article 68
Annex—Schedule C (6)	Article 69
Annex—Schedule D (A) (1) (a)	Article 78(1)
Annex—Schedule D (A) (1) (b), introductory phrase	Article 78(2) introductory phrase
Annex—Schedule D (A) (1) (b), 1st and 2nd indents	Article 78(2)(a) and (b)
Annex—Schedule D (A) (2)	Article 79
Annex—Schedule D (A) (3)	Article 80
Annex—Schedule D (A) (4)	Article 81
Annex—Schedule D (A) (5)	Article 82
Annex—Schedule D (B) (1) (a)	Article 83(1)
Annex—Schedule D (B) (1) (b), introductory phrase	Article 83(2), introductory phrase
Annex—Schedule D (B) (1) (b), 1st and 2nd indents	Article 83(2)(a) and (b)
Annex—Schedule D (B) (2)	Article 84
Article 17(1), 1st sentence	Article 102(1), 1st subparagraph
Article 17(1), 2nd sentence	Article 102(1), 2nd subparagraph

Directive 79/279/EEC	Directive 2001/34/EC
	Article 102(2)
Article 17(2)	Article 103
Article 9(1) and (2)	Article 105(1) and (2)
Article 18(1)	Article 106
Article 19	Article 107(1) and (2)
Article 20(1), introductory phrase	Article 108(1) 1st subparagraph
Article 20(3) and (4)	Article 108(1), 2nd and 3rd subparagraphs
Article 20(1), introductory phrase and point (a)	Article 108(2), 1st subparagraph, point (a)
Article 20(1)(b)	Article 108(2), 1st subparagraph, point (c) (i)
Article 20(1)(c)	Article 108(2), 1st subparagraph, point (d)
Article 20(2)	Article 108(2), 2nd subparagraph
Article 21	Article 109
Article 22(2)	Article 110

S. 3.

Council Directive 80/390/EEC
of 17 March 1980
co-ordinating the requirements for the drawing up, scrutiny and distribution of the listing particulars to be published for the admission of securities to official stock exchange listing[1]

This Directive has been repealed as from 26 July 2001 by article 111 of Directive 2001/34/EC (OJ L 184, 6.7.2001, 1), reproduced infra under no. S. 18.

Correlation Table

Directive 80/390/EEC	Directive 2001/34/EC
Article 2(c)	Article 1(a)
Article 2(a), introductory phrase	Article 1(b), introductory phrase
Article 2(a), 1st and 2nd indents	Article 1(b)(i) and (ii)
Article 2(e)	Article 1(d)
Article 2(b)	Article 1(e)
Article 2(f)	Article 1(f)
Article 2(d)	Article 1(g)
Article 2(g)	Article 1(h)
Article 1(1)	Article 3(1)
Article 1(2), introductory phrase	Article 3(2), introductory phrase
Article 1(2), 1st and 2nd indents	Article 3(2)(a) and (b)
Article 3	Article 20
Article 4	Article 21
Article 5	Article 22
Article 6, introductory phrase	Article 23, introductory phrase
Article 6(1) and (2)	Article 23(1) and (2)
Article 6(3)(a)	Article 23(3)(a)
Article 6(3)(b), introductory phrase	Article 23(3)(b), introductory phrase
Article 6(3)(b), 1st indent	Article 23(3)(b) (i)
Article 6(3)(b), 2nd indent	Article 23(3)(b) (ii)
Article 6(3)(c), introductory phrase	Article 23(3)(c), introductory phrase
Article 6(3)(c), 1st indent	Article 23(3)(c) (i)
Article 6(3)(c), 2nd indent	Article 23(3)(c) (ii)
Article 6(3)(c), 2nd indent (i)	Article 23(3)(c) (ii), 1st indent
Article 6(3)(c), 2nd indent (ii)	Article 23(3)(c) (ii), 2nd indent

---

[1] OJ L 100, 17.4.1980, 1–26.

Directive 80/390/EEC	Directive 2001/34/EC
Article 6(3)(c), 3rd indent	Article 23(3)(c) (iii)
Article 6(3)(d) to (g)	Article 23(3)(d) to (g)
Article 6(4) and (5)	Article 23(4) and (5)
Article 7	Article 24
Article 8(1), 1st subparagraph, introductory phrase	Article 25(1), 1st subparagraph, introductory phrase
Article 8(1), 1st subparagraph, 1st to 7th indents	Article 25(1), 1st subparagraph, (a) to (g)
Article 8(1), 2nd subparagraph, introductory phrase	Article 25(1), 2nd subparagraph, introductory phrase
Article 8(1), 2nd subparagraph, 1st and 2nd indents	Article 25(1), 2nd subparagraph, (a) and (b)
Article 8(2), introductory phrase	Article 25(2), introductory phrase
Article 8(2), 1st to 4th indents	Article 25(2)(a) to (d)
Article 8(3) and (4)	Article 25(3) and (4)
Article 9(1), introductory phrase	Article 26(1), introductory phrase
Article 9(1), 1st to 7th indents	Article 26(1)(a) to (g)
Article 9(2) and (3)	Article 26(2) and (3)
Article 10	Article 27
Article 11(1), introductory phrase	Article 28(1), introductory phrase
Article 11(1), 1st and 2nd indents	Article 28(1)(a) and (b)
Article 11(2)	Article 28(2)
Article 11(3), introductory phrase	Article 28(3), introductory phrase
Article 11(3) 1st, 2nd and 3rd indent	Article 28(3)(a), (b) and (c)
Article 12 introductory phrase	Article 29 introductory phrase
Article 12, 1st and 2nd indents	Article 29(a) and (b)
Article 13(1), 1st subparagraph, introductory phrase	Article 30(1), 1st subparagraph, introductory phrase
Article 13(1), 1st subparagraph, 1st and 2nd indents	Article 30(1), 1st subparagraph, (a) and (b)
Article 13(1), 2nd subparagraph	Article 30(1), 2nd subparagraph
Article 13(2), introductory phrase	Article 30(2), introductory phrase
Article 13(2), 1st and 2nd indents	Article 30(2) (a) and (b)
Article 13(3) and (4)	Article 30(3) and (4)
Article 14(1), introductory phrase	Article 31(1), introductory phrase
Article 14(1), 1st to 4th indents	Article 31(1)(a) to (d)
Article 14(2), 1st to 4th indents	Article 31(2), 1st subparagraph (a) to (d)
Article 14(2), 2nd subparagraph	Article 31(2), 2nd subparagraph
Article 15	Article 32
Article 16(1)	Article 33(1)
Article 16(2), introductory phrase	Article 33(2), introductory phrase
Article 16(2), 1st, 2nd and 3rd indents	Article 33(2)(a), (b) and (c)

Directive 80/390/EEC	Directive 2001/34/EC
Article 16(3)	Article 33(3)
Article 17	Article 34
Article 18(2) and (3), 1st subparagraph	Article 35
Article 19	Article 36
Article 24	Article 37
Article 24a	Article 38
Article 24b	Article 39
Article 24(c) (2) and (3)	Article 40
Article 25a	Article 41
Article 20(1), introductory phrase	Article 98(1), introductory phrase
Article 20(1), 1st and 2nd indents	Article 98(1)(a) and (b)
Article 20(2)	Article 98(2)
Article 21(1),	Article 99(1)
Article 21(2), introductory phrase	Article 99(2), introductory phrase
Article 21(2), 1st and 2nd indents	Article 99(2)(a) and (b)
Article 21(3)	Article 99(3)
Article 23	Article 100
Article 22	Article 101
Article 6a	Article 104
Article 18(1) and (3), 2nd subparagraph	Article 105(1) and (2)
Article 18(4)	Article 105(3)
Article 24c(1)	Article 106
Article 25(1) and (2)	Article 107(1) and (2)
Article 25(3)	Article 107(3) 1st subparagraph
Article 26(1)(a)	Article 108(2), 1st subparagraph, point (a)
Article 26(1)(b)	Article 108(2), 1st subparagraph, point (c) (ii)
Article 26(1)(c)	Article 108(2), 1st subparagraph, point (d)
Article 26(2)	Article 108(2), 2nd subparagraph
Article 27(2)	Article 110
Annex—Schedule A, Chapter I	Annex I—Schedule A, Chapter I
Annex—Schedule A, Chapter 2—2.1 to 2.4.4	Annex I—Schedule A, Chapter 2—2.1 to 2.4.4
Annex—Schedule A, Chapter 2—2.4.5, 1st subparagraph, introductory phrase	Annex I—Schedule A, Chapter 2—2.4.5, 1st subparagraph, introductory phrase
Annex—Schedule A, Chapter 2—2.4.5, 1st subparagraph, 1st and 2nd indents	Annex I—Schedule A, Chapter 2—2.4.5, 1st subparagraph (a) and (b)
Annex—Schedule A, Chapter 2—2.4.5, 2nd subparagraph	Annex I—Schedule A, Chapter 2—2.4.5, 2nd subparagraph
Annex—Schedule A, Chapter 2—2.5	Annex I—Schedule A, Chapter 2—2.5

S. 3. Council Directive 80/390/EEC of 17 March 1980   1413

Directive 80/390/EEC	Directive 2001/34/EC
Annex—Schedule A, Chapter 3—3.1 to 3.2.0	Annex I—Schedule A, Chapter 3—3.1 to 3.2.0
Annex—Schedule A, Chapter 3—3.2.1 introductory phrase	Annex I—Schedule A, Chapter 3—3.2.1 introductory phrase
Annex—Schedule A, Chapter 3—3.2.1, 1st, 2nd and 3rd indents	Annex I—Schedule A, Chapter 3—3.2.1 (a), (b) and (c)
Annex—Schedule A, Chapter 3—3.2.2 to 3.2.9	Annex I—Schedule A, Chapter 3—3.2.2 to 3.2.9
Annex—Schedule A, Chapter 4	Annex I—Schedule A, Chapter 4
Annex—Schedule A, Chapter 5—5.1 to 5.3	Annex I—Schedule A, Chapter 5—5.1 to 5.3
Annex—Schedule A, Chapter 5—5.4 (a) and (b)	Annex I—Schedule A, Chapter 5—5.4 (a) and (b)
Annex—Schedule A, Chapter 5—5.4 (c) 1st and 2nd indents	Annex I—Schedule A, Chapter 5—5.4 (c)(i) and (ii)
Annex—Schedule A, Chapter 5—5.5 and 5.6	Annex I—Schedule A, Chapter 5—5.5 and 5.6
Annex—Schedule A, Chapter 6	Annex I—Schedule A, Chapter 6
Annex—Schedule A, Chapter 7—7.1 introductory phrase	Annex I—Schedule A, Chapter 7—7.1 introductory phrase
Annex—Schedule A, Chapter 7—7.1, 1st and 2nd indents	Annex I—Schedule A, Chapter 7—7.1 (a) and (b)
Annex—Schedule A, Chapter 7—7.2	Annex I—Schedule A, Chapter 7—7.2
Annex—Schedule B, Chapter 1—4	Annex I—Schedule B, Chapter 1—4
Annex—Schedule B, Chapter 5—5.1 to 5.1.3	Annex I—Schedule B, Chapter 5—5.1 to 5.1.3
Annex—Schedule B, Chapter 5—5.1.4, 1st subparagraph, introductory phrase	Annex I—Schedule B, Chapter 5—5.1.4, 1st subparagraph, introductory phrase
Annex—Schedule B, Chapter 5—5.1.4, 1st subparagraph, 1st, 2nd and 3rd indents	Annex I—Schedule B, Chapter 5—5.1.4, 1st subparagraph (a), (b) and (c)
Annex—Schedule B, Chapter 5—5.1.4, 2nd, 3rd and 4th subparagraphs	Annex I—Schedule B, Chapter 5—5.1.4, 2nd, 3erd and 4th subparagraphs
Annex—Schedule B, Chapter 5—5.1.5 to 5.2	Annex I—Schedule B, Chapter 5—5.1.5 to 5.2
Annex—Schedule B, Chapter 5—5.3 introductory sentence	Annex I—Schedule B, Chapter 5—5.3 introductory sentence
Annex—Schedule B, Chapter 5—5.3 (a) and (b)	Annex I—Schedule B, Chapter 5—5.3(a) and (b)
Annex—Schedule B, Chapter 5—5.3(c) 1st and 2nd indents	Annex I—Schedule B, Chapter 5—5.3(c) (i) and (ii)
Annex—Schedule B, Chapter 6	Annex I—Schedule B, Chapter 6
Annex—Schedule B, Chapter 7—7.1 introductory phrase	Annex I—Schedule B, Chapter 7—7.1 introductory phrase

Directive 80/390/EEC	Directive 2001/34/EC
Annex—Schedule B, Chapter 7—7.1, 1st and 2nd indents	Annex I—Schedule B, Chapter 7—7.1(a) and (b)
Annex—Schedule B, Chapter 7—7.2	Annex I—Schedule B, Chapter 7—7.2
Annex—Schedule C, Chapter 1	Annex I—Schedule C, Chapter 1
Annex—Schedule C, Chapter 2—2.1.2	Annex I—Schedule C, Chapter 2—2.1 to 2.1.2
Annex—Schedule C, Chapter 2—2.2 introductory phrase	Annex I—Schedule C, Chapter 2—2.2 introductory phrase
Annex—Schedule C, Chapter 2—2.2, 1st to 4th indents	Annex I—Schedule C, Chapter 2—2.2 (a) to (d)
Annex—Schedule C, Chapter 2—2.3 to 2.6	Annex I—Schedule C, Chapter 2—2.3 to 2.6

S. 4.

Council Directive 82/121/EEC
of 15 February 1982
on information to be published on a regular basis by companies the shares of which have been admitted to official stock exchange listing[1]

This Directive has been repealed as from 26 July 2001 by article 111 of Directive 2001/34/EC (OJ L 184, 6.7.2001), reproduced infra under no. S. 18.

Correlation Table

Directive 82/121/EEC	Directive 2001/34/EC
Article 1(2), 2nd subparagraph, introductory phrase	Article 1(c), introductory phrase
Article 1(2), 2nd subparagraph, 1st and 2nd indents	Article 1(c) (i) and (ii)
Article 1(1)	Article 4(1)
Article 1(2), first subparagraph	Article 4(2)
Article 1(3)	Article 4(3)
Article 2	Article 70
Article 3	Article 71
Article 4	Article 72
Article 5(1)	Article 73(1)
Article 5(2), 1st subparagraph, introductory phrase	Article 73(2), 1st subparagraph, introductory phrase
Article 5(2), 1st subparagraph, 1st and 2nd indents	Article 73(2), 1st subparagraph (a) and (b)
Article 5(2), 2nd subparagraph	Article 73(2), 2nd subparagraph
Article 5(3) to (7)	Article 73(3) to (7)
Article 6	Article 74
Article 8	Article 75
Article 9(3) to (6)	Article 76
Article 10(2)	Article 77
Article 7(1) and (3)	Article 102(2)
Article 7(2),	Article 103
Article 9(1) and (2)	Article 105(1) and (2)
Article 9(7)	Article 105(3)
Article 10(1)	Article 106

---

[1] OJ L 48, 20.2.1982, 26–29.

Directive 82/121/EEC	Directive 2001/34/EC
Article 11(1)(a)	Article 108(2), 1st subparagraph, point (a)
Article 11(1)(b)	Article 108(2), 1st subparagraph, point (c) (iii)
Article 11(1)(c)	Article 108(2), 1st subparagraph, point (d)
Article 12(3)	Article 110

S. 5.
Council Directive 82/148/EEC
of 3 March 1982
amending Directive 79/279/EEC co-ordinating the conditions for the admission of securities to official stock exchange listing and Directive 80/390/EEC co-ordinating the requirements for the drawing up, scrutiny and distribution of the listing particulars to be published for the admission of securities to official stock exchange listing[1]

This Directive has been repealed as from 26 July 2001 by article 111 of Directive 2001/34/EC (OJ L 184, 6.7.2001, 1), reproduced infra under no. S. 18.

---

[1] OJ L 62, 5.3.1982, 22–23.

S. 6.

Council Directive 85/611/EEC
of 20 December 1985
on the co-ordination of laws, regulations and administrative provisions relating to undertakings for collective investment in transferable securities (UCITS)[1]

THE COUNCIL OF THE EUROPEAN COMMUNITIES,

Having regard to the Treaty establishing the European Economic Community, and in particular Article [47(2)][2] thereof,

Having regard to the proposal from the Commission,[3]

Having regard to the opinion of the European Parliament,[4]

Having regard to the opinion of the Economic and Social Committee,[5]

Whereas the laws of the Member States relating to collective investment undertakings differ appreciably from one state to another, particularly as regards the obligations and controls which are imposed on those undertakings; whereas those differences distort the conditions of competition between those undertakings and do not ensure equivalent protection for unit-holders;

Whereas national laws governing collective investment undertakings should be co-ordinated with a view to approximating the conditions of competition between those undertakings at Community level, while at the same time ensuring more effective and more uniform protection for unit-holders; whereas such co-ordination will make it easier for a collective investment undertaking situated in one Member State to market its units in other Member States;

Whereas the attainment of these objectives will facilitate the removal of the restrictions on the free circulation of the units of collective investment undertakings in the Community, and such co-ordination will help to bring about a European capital market;

Whereas, having regard to these objectives, it is desirable that common basic rules be established for the authorisation, supervision, structure and activities of collective investment undertakings situated in the Member States and the information they must publish;

Whereas the application of these common rules is a sufficient guarantee to permit collective investment undertakings situated in Member States, subject to the applicable provisions relating to capital movements, to market their units in other Member States without those Member States being able to subject those undertakings or their units to any provisions whatsoever other than provisions which, in those states, do not fall within the field covered by this Directive; whereas, nevertheless, if a collective investment undertaking situated in one Member State markets its units in a different Member State it must take all necessary steps to ensure that unit-holders in that other Member State can exercise their financial rights there with ease and are provided with the necessary information;

Whereas the co-ordination of the laws of the Member States should be confined initially to collective investment undertakings other than of the closed-ended type which promote the sale of their units to the public in the Community and the sole object of which is investment in transferable securities (which are essentially transferable securities officially listed on stock exchanges or similar regulated markets); whereas regulation of the collective investment

---

[1] OJ L 375, 31.12.1985, 3–18.
[2] The number between brackets has been changed as from 1 May 1999 by article 12 of the Treaty of Amsterdam.
[3] OJ C 171, 26.7.1976, 1.
[4] OJ C 57, 7.3.1977, 31.
[5] OJ C 75, 26.3.1977, 10.

undertakings not covered by the Directive poses a variety of problems which must be dealt with by means of other provisions, and such undertakings will accordingly be the subject of co-ordination at a later stage; whereas pending such co-ordination any Member State may, *inter alia*, prescribe those categories of undertakings for collective investment in transferable securities (UCITS) excluded from this Directive's scope on account of their investment and borrowing policies and lay down those specific rules to which such UCITS are subject in carrying on their business within its territory;

Whereas the free marketing of the units issued by UCITS authorised to invest up to 100% of their assets in transferable securities issued by the same body (State, local authority, etc.) may not have the direct or indirect effect of disturbing the functioning of the capital market or the financing of the Member States or of creating economic situations similar to those which Article [68(3)]² of the Treaty seeks to prevent;

Whereas account should be taken of the special situations of the Hellenic Republic's and Portuguese Republic's financial markets by allowing those countries and additional period in which to implement this Directive,

HAS ADOPTED THIS DIRECTIVE:

SECTION I
GENERAL PROVISIONS AND SCOPE

Article 1

1. The Member States shall apply this Directive to undertakings for collective investment in transferable securities (hereinafter referred to as UCITS) situated within their territories.

2. For the purposes of this Directive, and subject to Article 2, UCITS shall be undertakings:
[– the sole object of which is the collective investment in transferable securities and/or in other liquid financial assets referred to in Article 19(1) of capital raised from the public and which operates on the principle of risk-spreading and]

– the units of which are, at the request of holders, repurchased or redeemed, directly or indirectly, out of those undertakings' assets. Action taken by a UCITS to ensure that the stock exchange value of its units does not significantly vary from their net asset value shall be regarded as equivalent to such repurchase or redemption.

3. Such undertakings may be constituted according to law, either under the law of contract (as common funds managed by management companies) or trust law (as unit trusts) or under statute (as investment companies).

For the purposes of this Directive 'common funds' shall also include unit trusts.

4. Investment companies the assets of which are invested through the intermediary of subsidiary companies mainly otherwise than in transferable securities shall not, however, be subject to this Directive.

5. The Member States shall prohibit UCITS that are subject to this Directive from transforming themselves into collective investment undertakings that are not covered by this Directive.

6. Subject to the provisions governing capital movements and to Articles 44, 45 and 52 (2) no Member State may apply any other provisions whatsoever in the field covered by this Directive to UCITS situated in another Member State or to the units issued by such UCITS, where they market their units within its territory.

7. Without prejudice to paragraph 6, a Member State may apply to UCITS situated within its territory requirements which are stricter than or additional to those laid down in Article 4 et seq. of this Directive, provided that they are of general application and do not conflict with the provisions of this Directive.

[8. For the purposes of this Directive, 'transferable securities' shall mean:
– shares in companies and other securities equivalent to shares in companies ('shares'),
– bonds and other forms of securitised debt ('debt securities'),
– any other negotiable securities which carry the right to acquire any such transferable securities by subscription or exchange,

excluding the techniques and instruments referred to in Article 21.

9. For the purposes of this Directive 'money market instruments' shall mean instruments normally dealt in on the money market which are liquid, and have a value which can be accurately determined at any time.]

¶ *Article 1(2) the first indent has been replaced by article 1(1) of Directive 2001/108/EC, reproduced infra under no. S. 22.*
¶ *Article 1(8) and (9) has been added by article 1(2) of Directive 2001/108/EC, reproduced infra under no. S. 22.*

[*Article 1a*
For the purposes of this Directive:

1. 'depositary' shall mean any institution entrusted with the duties mentioned in Articles 7 and 14 and subject to the other provisions laid down in Sections IIIa and IVa;

2. 'management company' shall mean any company, the regular business of which is the management of UCITS in the form of unit trusts/common funds and/or of investment companies (collective portfolio management of UCITS); this includes the functions mentioned in Annex II;

3. a 'management company's home Member State' shall mean the Member State, in which the management company's registered office is situated;

4. a 'management company's host Member State' shall mean the Member State, other than the home Member State, within the territory of which a management company has a branch or provides services;

5. a 'UCITS home Member State' shall mean:

(a) with regard to a UCITS constituted as unit trust/common fund, the Member State in which the management company's registered office is situated,

(b) with regard to a UCITS constituted as investment company, the Member State in which the investment company's registered office is situated;

6. a 'UCITS host Member State' shall mean the Member State, other than the UCITS home Member State, in which the units of the common fund/unit trust or of the investment company are marketed;

7. 'branch' shall mean a place of business which is a part of the management company, which has no legal personality and which provides the services for which the management company has been authorised; all the places of business set up in the same Member State by a management company with headquarters in another Member State shall be regarded as a single branch;

8. 'competent authorities' shall mean the authorities which each Member State designates under Article 49 of this Directive;

9. 'close links' shall mean a situation as defined in Article 2(1) of Directive 95/26/EC;[6]

10. 'qualifying holdings' shall mean any direct or indirect holding in a management company which represents 10% or more of the capital or of the voting rights or which makes it possible to exercise a significant influence over the management of the management company in which that holding subsists.

For the purpose of this definition, the voting rights referred to in Article 7 of Directive 88/627/EEC[7] shall be taken into account;

11. 'ISD' shall mean Council Directive 93/22/EEC of 10 May 1993 on investment services in the securities field;[8]

12. 'parent undertaking' shall mean a parent undertaking as defined in Articles 1 and 2 of Directive 83/349/EEC;[9]

13. 'subsidiary' shall mean a subsidiary undertaking as defined in Articles 1 and 2 of Directive 83/349/EEC; any subsidiary of a subsidiary undertaking shall also be regarded as a subsidiary of the parent undertaking which is the ultimate parent of those undertakings;

---

[6] OJ L 168, 18.7.1995, 7, reproduced supra under no. I.29.
[7] OJ L 348, 17.12.1988, 62, reproduced infra under no. S. 10.
[8] OJ L 141, 11.6.1993, 27, reproduced infra under no. S. 14. Directive as last amended by Directive 2000/64/EC (OJ L 290, 17.11.2000, 27).
[9] OJ L 193, 18.7.1983, 1, reproduced supra under no. C. 6. Directive as last amended by the 1994 Act of Accession.

14. 'initial capital' shall mean capital as defined in items 1 and 2 of Article 34(2) of Directive 2000/12/EC;[10]

15. 'own funds' shall mean own funds as defined in Title V, Chapter 2, Section 1 of Directive 2000/12/EC; this definition may, however, be amended in the circumstances described in Annex V of Directive 93/6/EEC.[11]]

¶ *Article 1a has been inserted by article 1(1) of Directive 2001/107/EC, reproduced infra under no. S. 21.*

Article 2

1. The following shall not be UCITS subject to this Directive:
– UCITS of the closed-ended type;
– UCITS that raise capital without promoting the sale of their units to the public within the Community or any part of it;
– UCITS the units of which, under the fund rules or the investment company's instruments of incorporation, may be sold only to the public in non-member countries;
– categories of UCITS prescribed by the regulations of the Member States in which such UCITS are situated, for which the rules laid down in Section V and Article 36 are inappropriate in view of their investment and borrowing policies.

2. Five years after the implementation of this Directive the Commission shall submit to the Council a report on the implementation of paragraph 1 and in particular, of its fourth indent. If necessary it shall propose suitable measures to extend the scope.

Article 3

For the purposes of this Directive, a UCITS shall be deemed to be situated in the Member State in which the investment company or the management company of the unit trust has its registered office; the Member States must require that the head office be situated in the same Member State as the registered office.

SECTION II
AUTHORISATION OF UCITS

Article 4

1. No UCITS shall carry on activities as such unless it has been authorised by the competent authorities of the Member State in which it is situated, hereinafter referred to as 'the competent authorities'.

Such authorisation shall be valid for all Member States.

2. A unit trust shall be authorised only if the competent authorities have approved the management company, the fund rules and the choice of depositary. An investment company shall be authorised only if the competent authorities have approved both its instruments of incorporation and the choice of depositary.

[3. The competent authorities may not authorise a UCITS if the management company or the investment company do not comply with the preconditions laid down in this Directive, in Sections III and IV respectively.

Moreover the competent authorities may not authorise a UCITS if the directors of the depositary are not of sufficiently good repute or are not sufficiently experienced also in relation to the type of UCITS to be managed. To that end, the names of the directors of the depositary and of every person succeeding them in office must be communicated forthwith to the competent authorities.

Directors shall mean those persons who, under the law or the instruments of incorporation, represent the depositary, or who effectively determine the policy of the depositary.

3a. The competent authorities shall not grant authorisation if the UCITS is legally prevented (e.g. through a provision in the fund rules or

---

[10] OJ L 126, 26.5.2000, 1, reproduced supra under no. B. 32. Directive as amended by Directive 2000/28/EC of the European Parliament and of the Council (OJ L 275, 27.10.2000, 37), reproduced supra under no. B. 34. Directive 2000/12/EC has been repealed as from 20 July 2007 by article 58 of Directive 2006/48/EC (OJ L 177, 30.6.2006, 1), reproduced supra under no. B. 41

[11] OJ L 141, 11.6.1993, 1, reproduced supra under no. B. 20. Directive as last amended by Directive 98/33/EC of the European Parliament and of the Council (OJ L 204, 21.7.1998, 29), reproduced supra under no. B. 30.

instruments of incorporation) from marketing its units or shares in its home Member State.]

4. Neither the management company nor the depositary may be replaced, nor may the fund rules or the investment company's instruments of incorporation be amended, without the approval of the competent authorities.

¶ *Article 4(3) has been replaced by article 1(2) of Directive 2001/107/EC, reproduced infra under no. S. 21.*

[SECTION III
OBLIGATIONS REGARDING MANAGEMENT COMPANIES

Title A
Conditions for taking up business
Article 5

1. Access to the business of management companies is subject to prior official authorisation to be granted by the home Member State's competent authorities. Authorisation granted under this Directive to a management company shall be valid for all Member States.

2. No management company may engage in activities other than the management of UCITS authorised according to this Directive except the additional management of other collective investment undertakings which are not covered by this Directive and for which the management company is subject to prudential supervision but which cannot be marketed in other Member States under this Directive.

The activity of management of unit trusts/common funds and of investment companies includes, for the purpose of this Directive, the functions mentioned in Annex II which are not exhaustive.

3. By way of derogation from paragraph 2, Member States may authorise management companies to provide, in addition to the management of unit trusts/common funds and of investment companies, the following services:

(a) management of portfolios of investments, including those owned by pension funds, in accordance with mandates given by investors on a discretionary, client-by-client basis, where such portfolios include one or more of the instruments listed in Section B of the Annex to the ISD,

(b) as non-core services:
– investment advice concerning one or more of the instruments listed in Section B of the Annex to the ISD,
– safekeeping and administration in relation to units of collective investment undertakings.

Management companies may in no case be authorised under this Directive to provide only the services mentioned in this paragraph or to provide non-core services without being authorised for the service referred to in point (a).

[4. Articles 2(2), 12, 13 and 19 of Directive 2004/39/EC of the European Parliament and of the Council of 21 April 2004 on markets in financial instruments,[12] shall apply to the provision of the services referred to in paragraph 3 of this Article by management companies.]

¶ *The fourth paragraph of this article has been replaced by article 66 of Directive 2004/39/EC, reproduced infra under no. S. 29.*

Article 5a

1. Without prejudice to other conditions of general application laid down by national law, the competent authorities shall not grant authorisation to a management company unless:

(a) the management company has an initial capital of at least EUR 125000:
– When the value of the portfolios of the management company, exceeds EUR 250000000, the management company shall be required to provide an additional amount of own funds. This additional amount of own funds shall be equal to 0,02% of the amount by which the value of the portfolios of the management company exceeds EUR 250000000. The required total of the initial capital and the additional amount shall not, however, exceed EUR 10000000.

---

[12] OJ L 145, 30.4.2004, 1, reproduced infra under no. S. 29.

- For the purpose of this paragraph, the following portfolios shall be deemed to be the portfolios of the management company:
  (i) unit trusts/common funds managed by the management company including portfolios for which it has delegated the management function but excluding portfolios that it is managing under delegation;
  (ii) investment companies for which the management company is the designated management company;
  (iii) other collective investment undertakings managed by the management company including portfolios for which it has delegated the management function but excluding portfolios that it is managing under delegation.
- Irrespective of the amount of these requirements, the own funds of the management company shall never be less than the amount prescribed in Annex IV of Directive 93/6/EEC.
- Member States may authorise management companies not to provide up to 50% of the additional amount of own funds referred to in the first indent if they benefit from a guarantee of the same amount given by a credit institution or an insurance undertaking. The credit institution or insurance undertaking must have its registered office in a Member State, or in a non-Member State provided that it is subject to prudential rules considered by the competent authorities as equivalent to those laid down in Community law.
- No later than 13 February 2005, the Commission shall present a report to the European Parliament and the Council on the application of this capital requirement, accompanied where appropriate by proposals for its revision;

(b) the persons who effectively conduct the business of a management company are of sufficiently good repute and are sufficiently experienced also in relation to the type of UCITS managed by the management company. To that end, the names of these persons and of every person succeeding them in office must be communicated forthwith to the competent authorities. The conduct of a management company's business must be decided by at least two persons meeting such conditions;

(c) the application for authorisation is accompanied by a programme of activity setting out, inter alia, the organisational structure of the management company;

(d) both its head office and its registered office are located in the same Member State.

2. Moreover where close links exist between the management company and other natural or legal persons, the competent authorities shall grant authorisation only if those do not prevent the effective exercise of their supervisory functions.

The competent authorities shall also refuse authorisation if the laws, regulations or administrative provisions of a non-member country governing one or more natural or legal persons with which the management company has close links, or difficulties involved in their enforcement, prevent the effective exercise of their supervisory functions.

The competent authorities shall require management companies to provide them with the information they require to monitor compliance with the conditions referred to in this paragraph on a continuous basis.

3. An applicant shall be informed, within six months of the submission of a complete application, whether or not authorisation has been granted. Reasons shall be given whenever an authorisation is refused.

4. A management company may start business as soon as authorisation has been granted.

5. The competent authorities may withdraw the authorisation issued to a management company subject to this Directive only where that company:

(a) does not make use of the authorisation within 12 months, expressly renounces the authorisation or has ceased the activity covered by this Directive more than six months previously unless the Member State concerned has provided for authorisation to lapse in such cases;

(b) has obtained the authorisation by making false statements or by any other irregular means;

(c) no longer fulfils the conditions under which authorisation was granted;

(d) no longer complies with Directive 93/6/EEC if its authorisation also covers the discretionary portfolio management service referred to in Article 5(3)(a) of this Directive;

(e) has seriously and/or systematically infringed the provisions adopted pursuant to this Directive; or

(f) falls within any of the cases where national law provides for withdrawal.

Article 5b

1. The competent authorities shall not grant authorisation to take up the business of management companies until they have been informed of the identities of the shareholders or members, whether direct or indirect, natural or legal persons, that have qualifying holdings and of the amounts of those holdings.

The competent authorities shall refuse authorisation if, taking into account the need to ensure the sound and prudent management of a management company, they are not satisfied as to the suitability of the aforementioned shareholders or members.

2. In the case of branches of management companies that have registered offices outside the European Union and are starting or carrying on business, the Member States shall not apply provisions that result in treatment more favourable than that accorded to branches of management companies that have registered offices in Member States.

3. The competent authorities of the other Member State involved shall be consulted beforehand on the authorisation of any management company which is:

(a) a subsidiary of another management company, an investment firm, a credit institution or an insurance undertaking authorised in another Member State,

(b) a subsidiary of the parent undertaking of another management company, an investment firm, a credit institution or an insurance undertaking authorised in another Member State, or

(c) controlled by the same natural or legal persons as control another management company, an investment firm, a credit institution or an insurance undertaking authorised in another Member State.

Title B
Relations with third countries
Article 5c

1. Relations with third countries shall be regulated in accordance with the relevant rules laid down in Article 7 of the ISD.

For the purpose of this Directive, the expressions 'firm/investment firm' and 'investment firms' contained in Article 7 of the ISD shall be construed respectively as 'management company' and 'management companies'; the expression 'providing investment services' in Article 7(2) of the ISD shall be construed as 'providing services'.

2. The Member States shall also inform the Commission of any general difficulties which UCITS encounter in marketing their units in any third country.

Title C
Operating conditions
Article 5d

1. The competent authorities of the management company's home Member State shall require that the management company which they have authorised complies at all times with the conditions laid down in Article 5 and Article 5a(1) and (2) of this Directive. The own funds of a management company may not fall below the level specified in Article 5a(1)(a). If they do, however, the competent authorities may, where the circumstances justify it, allow such firms a limited period in which to rectify their situations or cease their activities.

2. The prudential supervision of a management company shall be the responsibility of the competent authorities of the home Member State, whether the management company establishes a branch or provides services in another Member State or not, without prejudice to those provisions of this Directive which give responsibility to the authorities of the host country.

Article 5e

1. Qualifying holdings in management companies shall be subject to the same rules as those laid down in Article 9 of the ISD.

2. For the purpose of this Directive, the expressions 'firm/investment firm' and 'investment firms' contained in Article 9 of the ISD shall be construed respectively as 'management company' and 'management companies'.

Article 5f

1. Each home Member State shall draw up prudential rules which management companies, with regard to the activity of management of UCITS authorised according to this Directive, shall observe at all times.

In particular, the competent authorities of the home Member State having regard also to the nature of the UCITS managed by a management company, shall require that each such company:

(a) has sound administrative and accounting procedures, control and safeguard arrangements for electronic data processing and adequate internal control mechanisms including, in particular, rules for personal transactions by its employees or for the holding or management of investments in financial instruments in order to invest own funds and ensuring, inter alia, that each transaction involving the fund may be reconstructed according to its origin, the parties to it, its nature, and the time and place at which it was effected and that the assets of the unit trusts/common funds or of the investment companies managed by the management company are invested according to the fund rules or the instruments of incorporation and the legal provisions in force;

(b) is structured and organised in such a way as to minimise the risk of UCITS' or clients' interests being prejudiced by conflicts of interest between the company and its clients, between one of its clients and another, between one of its clients and a UCITS or between two UCITS. Nevertheless, where a branch is set up, the organisational arrangements may not conflict with the rules of conduct laid down by the host Member State to cover conflicts of interest.

2. Each management company the authorisation of which also covers the discretionary portfolio management service mentioned in Article 5(3)(a):
– shall not be permitted to invest all or a part of the investor's portfolio in units of unit trusts/common funds or of investment companies it manages, unless it receives prior general approval from the client,
– shall be subject with regard to the services referred to in Article 5(3) to the provisions laid down in Directive 97/9/EC of the European Parliament and of the Council of 3 March 1997 on investor-compensation schemes.[13]

Article 5g

1. If Member States permit management companies to delegate to third parties for the purpose of a more efficient conduct of the companies' business to carry out on their behalf one or more of their own functions the following preconditions have to be complied with:

(a) the competent authority must be informed in an appropriate manner;

(b) the mandate shall not prevent the effectiveness of supervision over the management company, and in particular it must not prevent the management company from acting, or the UCITS from being managed, in the best interests of its investors;

(c) when the delegation concerns the investment management, the mandate may only be given to undertakings which are authorised or registered for the purpose of asset management and subject to prudential supervision; the delegation must be in accordance with investment-allocation criteria periodically laid down by the management companies;

(d) where the mandate concerns the investment management and is given to a third-country undertaking, cooperation between the supervisory authorities concerned must be ensured;

(e) a mandate with regard to the core function of investment management shall not be given to the

---

[13] OJ L 84, 26.3.1997, 22, reproduced supra under no. C.P. 11.

depositary or to any other undertaking whose interests may conflict with those of the management company or the unit-holders;

(f) measures shall exist which enable the persons who conduct the business of the management company to monitor effectively at any time the activity of the undertaking to which the mandate is given;

(g) the mandate shall not prevent the persons who conduct the business of the management company to give at any time further instructions to the undertaking to which functions are delegated and to withdraw the mandate with immediate effect when this is in the interest of investors;

(h) having regard to the nature of the functions to be delegated, the undertaking to which functions will be delegated must be qualified and capable of undertaking the functions in question; and

(i) the UCITS' prospectuses list the functions which the management company has been permitted to delegate.

2. In no case shall the management company's and the depositary's liability be affected by the fact that the management company delegated any functions to third parties, nor shall the management company delegate its functions to the extent that it becomes a letter box entity.

Article 5h

Each Member State shall draw up rules of conduct which management companies authorised in that Member State shall observe at all times. Such rules must implement at least the principles set out in the following indents. These principles shall ensure that a management company:

(a) acts honestly and fairly in conducting its business activities in the best interests of the UCITS it manages and the integrity of the market;

(b) acts with due skill, care and diligence, in the best interests of the UCITS it manages and the integrity of the market;

(c) has and employs effectively the resources and procedures that are necessary for the proper performance of its business activities;

(d) tries to avoid conflicts of interests and, when they cannot be avoided, ensures that the UCITS it manages are fairly treated; and

(e) complies with all regulatory requirements applicable to the conduct of its business activities so as to promote the best interests of its investors and the integrity of the market.

Title D

The right of establishment and the freedom to provide services

Article 6

1. Member States shall ensure that a management company, authorised in accordance with this Directive by the competent authorities of another Member State, may carry on within their territories the activity for which it has been authorised, either by the establishment of a branch or under the freedom to provide services.

2. Member States may not make the establishment of a branch or the provision of the services subject to any authorisation requirement, to any requirement to provide endowment capital or to any other measure having equivalent effect.

Article 6a

1. In addition to meeting the conditions imposed in Articles 5 and 5a, any management company wishing to establish a branch within the territory of another Member State shall notify the competent authorities of its home Member State.

2. Member States shall require every management company wishing to establish a branch within the territory of another Member State to provide the following information and documents, when effecting the notification provided for in paragraph 1:

(a) the Member State within the territory of which the management company plans to establish a branch;

(b) a programme of operations setting out the activities and services according to Article 5(2) and (3) envisaged and the organisational structure of the branch;

(c) the address in the host Member State from which documents may be obtained;

(d) the names of those responsible for the management of the branch.

3. Unless the competent authorities of the home Member State have reason to doubt the adequacy of the administrative structure or the financial situation of a management company, taking into account the activities envisaged, they shall, within three months of receiving all the information referred to in paragraph 2, communicate that information to the competent authorities of the host Member State and shall inform the management company accordingly. They shall also communicate details of any compensation scheme intended to protect investors.

Where the competent authorities of the home Member State refuse to communicate the information referred to in paragraph 2 to the competent authorities of the host Member State, they shall give reasons for their refusal to the management company concerned within two months of receiving all the information. That refusal or failure to reply shall be subject to the right to apply to the courts in the home Member State.

4. Before the branch of a management company starts business, the competent authorities of the host Member State shall, within two months of receiving the information referred to in paragraph 2, prepare for the supervision of the management company and, if necessary, indicate the conditions, including the rules mentioned in Articles 44 and 45 in force in the host Member State and the rules of conduct to be respected in the case of provision of the portfolio management service mentioned in Article 5(3) and of investment advisory services and custody, under which, in the interest of the general good, that business must be carried on in the host Member State.

5. On receipt of a communication from the competent authorities of the host Member State or on the expiry of the period provided for in paragraph 4 without receipt of any communication from those authorities, the branch may be established and start business. From that moment the management company may also begin distributing the units of the unit trusts/common funds and of the investment companies subject to this Directive which it manages, unless the competent authorities of the host Member State establish, in a reasoned decision taken before the expiry of that period of two months—to be communicated to the competent authorities of the home Member State—that the arrangements made for the marketing of the units do not comply with the provisions referred to in Article 44(1) and Article 45.

6. In the event of change of any particulars communicated in accordance with paragraphs 2(b), (c) or (d), a management company shall give written notice of that change to the competent authorities of the home and host Member States at least one month before implementing the change so that the competent authorities of the home Member State may take a decision on the change under paragraph 3 and the competent authorities of the host Member State may do so under paragraph 4.

7. In the event of a change in the particulars communicated in accordance with the first subparagraph of paragraph 3, the authorities of the home Member State shall inform the authorities of the host Member State accordingly.

Article 6b

1. Any management company wishing to carry on business within the territory of another Member State for the first time under the freedom to provide services shall communicate the following information to the competent authorities of its home Member State:

(a) the Member State within the territory of which the management company intends to operate;

(b) a programme of operations stating the activities and services referred to in Article 5(2) and (3) envisaged.

2. The competent authorities of the home Member State shall, within one month of receiving the information referred to in paragraph 1, forward it to the competent authorities of the host Member State.

They shall also communicate details of any applicable compensation scheme intended to protect investors.

3. The management company may then start business in the host Member State notwithstanding the provisions of Article 46.

When appropriate, the competent authorities of the host Member State shall, on receipt of the information referred to in paragraph 1, indicate to the management company the conditions, including the rules of conduct to be respected in the case of provision of the portfolio management service mentioned in Article 5(3) and of investment advisory services and custody, with which, in the interest of the general good, the management company must comply in the host Member State.

4. Should the content of the information communicated in accordance with paragraph 1(b) be amended, the management company shall give notice of the amendment in writing to the competent authorities of the home Member State and of the host Member State before implementing the change, so that the competent authorities of the host Member State may, if necessary, inform the company of any change or addition to be made to the information communicated under paragraph 3.

5. A management company shall also be subject to the notification procedure laid down in this Article in cases where it entrusts a third party with the marketing of the units in a host Member State.

Article 6c

1. Host Member States may, for statistical purposes, require all management companies with branches within their territories to report periodically on their activities in those host Member States to the competent authorities of those host Member States.

2. In discharging their responsibilities under this Directive, host Member States may require branches of management companies to provide the same particulars as national management companies for that purpose.

Host Member States may require management companies, carrying on business within their territories under the freedom to provide services, to provide the information necessary for the monitoring of their compliance with the standards set by the host Member State that apply to them, although those requirements may not be more stringent than those which the same Member State imposes on established management companies for the monitoring of their compliance with the same standards.

3. Where the competent authorities of a host Member State ascertain that a management company that has a branch or provides services within its territory is in breach of the legal or regulatory provisions adopted in that State pursuant to those provisions of this Directive which confer powers on the host Member State's competent authorities, those authorities shall require the management company concerned to put an end to its irregular situation.

4. If the management company concerned fails to take the necessary steps, the competent authorities of the host Member State shall inform the competent authorities of the home Member State accordingly. The latter shall, at the earliest opportunity, take all appropriate measures to ensure that the management company concerned puts an end to its irregular situation. The nature of those measures shall be communicated to the competent authorities of the host Member State.

5. If, despite the measures taken by the home Member State or because such measures prove inadequate or are not available in the Member State in question, the management company persists in breaching the legal or regulatory provisions referred to in paragraph 2 in force in the host Member State, the latter may, after informing the competent authorities of the home Member State, take appropriate measures to prevent or to penalise further irregularities and, insofar as necessary, to prevent that management company from initiating any further transaction within its territory. The Member States shall ensure that within their territories it is possible to serve the legal documents necessary for those measures on management companies.

6. The foregoing provisions shall not affect the powers of host Member States to take appropriate measures to prevent or to penalise irregularities committed within their territories which are contrary to legal or regulatory provisions adopted in the interest of the general good. This shall include the possibility of preventing offending management companies from initiating any further transactions within their territories.

7. Any measure adopted pursuant to paragraphs 4, 5 or 6 involving penalties or restrictions on the activities of a management company must be properly justified and communicated to the management company concerned. Every such measure shall be subject to the right to apply to the courts in the Member State which adopted it.

8. Before following the procedure laid down in paragraphs 3, 4 or 5 the competent authorities of the host Member State may, in emergencies, take any precautionary measures necessary to protect the interests of investors and others for whom services are provided. The Commission and the competent authorities of the other Member States concerned must be informed of such measures at the earliest opportunity.

After consulting the competent authorities of the Member States concerned, the Commission may decide that the Member State in question must amend or abolish those measures.

9. In the event of the withdrawal of authorisation, the competent authorities of the host Member State shall be informed and shall take appropriate measures to prevent the management company concerned from initiating any further transactions within its territory and to safeguard investors' interests. [Every two years the Commission shall issue a report on such cases.]

10. The Member States shall inform the Commission of the number and type of cases in which there have been refusals pursuant to Article 6a or measures have been taken in accordance with paragraph 5. [Every two years the Commission shall issue a report on such cases.]

¶ *The title of Section III and articles 5 and 6 have been replaced by article 1(3) of Directive 2001/107/EC, reproduced infra under no. S. 21.*

¶ *The second sentence of paragraph 9 and the second sentence of paragraph 10 of this article have been replaced by article 9(1) of Directive 2005/1/EC, reproduced under no. B. 39.*

[SECTION IIIA

OBLIGATIONS REGARDING THE DEPOSITARY]

¶ *The title between square brackets has been inserted by article 1(4) of Directive 2001/107/EC, reproduced infra under no. S. 21.*

Article 7

1. A unit trust's assets must be entrusted to a depositary for safekeeping.

2. A depositary's liability as referred to in Article 9 shall not be affected by the fact that it has entrusted to a third party all of some of the assets in its safe-keeping.

3. A depositary must, moreover:

(a) ensure that the sale, issue, repurchase, redemption and cancellation of units effected on behalf of a unit trust or by a management company are carried out in accordance with the law and the fund rules;

(b) ensure that the value of units is calculated in accordance with the law and the fund rules;

(c) carry out the instructions of the management company, unless they conflict with the law or the fund rules;

(d) ensure that in transactions involving a unit trust's assets any consideration is remitted to it within the usual time limits;

(e) ensure that a unit trust's income is applied in accordance with the law and the fund rules.

Article 8

1. A depositary must either have its registered office in the same Member State as that of the management company or be established in that Member State if its registered office is in another Member State.

2. A depositary must be an institution that is subject to public control. It must also furnish sufficient financial and professional guarantees to be able effectively to pursue its business as depositary and meet the commitments inherent in that function.

3. The Member States shall determine which of the categories of institutions referred to in paragraph 2 shall be eligible to be depositaries.

Article 9

A depositary shall, in accordance with the national law of the State in which the management company's registered office is situated, be liable to the management company and the unit-holders for any loss suffered by them as a result of its unjustifiable failure to perform its obligations or its improper performance of them. Liability to unit-holders may be invoked either directly or indirectly through the management company, depending on the legal nature of the relationship between the depositary, the management company and the unit-holders.

Article 10

1. No single company shall act as both management company and depositary.

2. In the context of their respective roles the management company and the depositary must act independently and solely in the interest of the unit-holders.

Article 11

The law or the fund rules shall lay down the conditions for the replacement of the management company and the depositary and rules to ensure the protection of unit-holders in the event of such replacement.

[SECTION IV
OBLIGATIONS REGARDING INVESTMENT COMPANIES

Title A
Conditions for taking up business
Article 12

Access to the business of investment companies shall be subject to prior official authorisation to be granted by the home Member States competent authorities.

The Member States shall determine the legal form which an investment company must take.]

¶ *The title and article 12 have been replaced by article 1(5) of Directive 2001/107/EC, reproduced infra under no. S. 21.*

Article 13

No investment company may engage in activities other than those referred to in Article 1 (2).

[Article 13a

1. Without prejudice to other conditions of general application laid down by national law, the competent authorities shall not grant authorisation to an investment company that has not designated a management company unless the investment company has a sufficient initial capital of at least EUR 300000.

In addition, when an investment company has not designated a management company authorised pursuant to this Directive:
- the authorisation shall not be granted unless the application for authorisation is accompanied by a programme of activity setting out, inter alia, the organisational structure of the investment company;
- the directors of the investment company shall be of sufficiently good repute and be sufficiently experienced also in relation to the type of business carried out by the investment company. To that end, the names of the directors and of every person succeeding them in office must be communicated forthwith to the competent authorities. The conduct of an investment company's business must be decided by at least two persons meeting such conditions. Directors shall mean those persons who, under the law or the instruments of incorporation, represent the investment company, or who effectively determine the policy of the company;
- moreover, where close links exist between the investment company and other natural or legal persons, the competent authorities shall grant authorisation only if those do not prevent the effective exercise of their supervisory functions.

The competent authorities shall also refuse authorisation if the laws, regulations or administrative provisions of a non-member country governing one or more natural or legal persons with which the investment company has close links, or difficulties involved in their enforcement, prevent the effective exercise of their supervisory functions.

The competent authorities shall require investment companies to provide them with the information they require.

2. An applicant shall be informed, within six months of the submission of a complete application, whether or not authorisation has been granted. Reasons shall be given whenever an authorisation is refused.

3. An investment company may start business as soon as authorisation has been granted.

4. The competent authorities may withdraw the authorisation issued to an investment company subject to this Directive only where that company:

(a) does not make use of the authorisation within 12 months, expressly renounces the authorisation or has ceased the activity covered by this Directive more than 6 months previously unless the Member State concerned has provided for authorisation to lapse in such cases;

(b) has obtained the authorisation by making false statements or by any other irregular means;

(c) no longer fulfils the conditions under which authorisation was granted;

(d) has seriously and/or systematically infringed the provisions adopted pursuant to this Directive; or

(e) falls within any of the cases where national law provides for withdrawal.

Title B

Operating conditions

Article 13b

Articles 5g and 5h shall apply to investment companies that have not designated a management company authorised pursuant to this Directive. For the purpose of this Article 'management company' shall be construed as 'investment company'.

Investment companies may only manage assets of their own portfolio and may not, under any circumstances, receive any mandate to manage assets on behalf of a third party.

Article 13c

Each home Member State shall draw up prudential rules which shall be observed at all times by investment companies that have not designated a management company authorised pursuant to this Directive.

In particular, the competent authorities of the home Member State, having regard also to the nature of the investment company, shall require that the company has sound administrative and accounting procedures, control and safeguard arrangements for electronic data processing and adequate internal control mechanisms including, in particular, rules for personal transactions by its employees or for the holding or management of investments in financial instruments in order to invest its initial capital and ensuring, inter alia, that each transaction involving the company may be reconstructed according to its origin, the parties to it, its nature, and the time and place at which it was effected and that the assets of the investment company are invested according to the instruments of incorporation and the legal provisions in force.]

¶ *Articles 13a, 13b, and 13c have been inserted by article 1(6) of Directive 2001/107/EC, reproduced infra under no. S. 21.*

[SECTION IVa

OBLIGATIONS REGARDING THE DEPOSITARY]

¶ *The title of Section IVa has been inserted by article 1(7) of Directive 2001/107/EC, reproduced infra under no. S. 21.*

Article 14

1. An investment company's assets must be entrusted to a depositary for safekeeping.

2. A depositary's liability as referred to in Article 16 shall not be affected by the fact that it has entrusted to a third party all or some of the assets in its safe-keeping.

3. A depositary must, moreover:

(a) ensure that the sale, issue, repurchase, redemption and cancellation of units effected by or on behalf of a company are carried out in accordance with the law and with the company's instruments of incorporation;

(b) ensure that in transactions involving a company's assets any consideration is remitted to it within the usual time limits;

(c) ensure that a company's income is applied in accordance with the law and its instruments of incorporation.

4. A Member State may decide that investment companies situated within its territory which market their units exclusively through one or more stock exchanges on which their units are admitted to official listing shall not be required to have depositaries within the meaning of this Directive.

Articles 34, 37 and 38 shall not apply to such companies. However, the rules for the valuation of such companies' assets must be stated in law or in their instruments of incorporation.

5. A Member State may decide that investment companies situated within its territory which market at least 80% of their units through one or more stock exchanges designated in their instruments of incorporation shall not be required to have depositaries within the meaning of this Directive provided that their units are admitted to official listing on the stock exchanges of those Member States within the territories of which the units are marketed, and that any transactions which such a company may effect with stock exchanges are effected at stock exchange prices only. A company's instruments of incorporation must specify the stock exchange in the country of marketing the prices on which shall determine the prices at which that company will effect any transactions with stock exchanges in that country.

A Member State shall avail itself of the option provided for in the preceding subparagraph only if it considers that unit-holders have protection equivalent to that of unit-holders in UCITS that have depositaries within the meaning of this Directive.

In particular, such companies and the companies referred to in paragraph 4, must:

(a) in the absence of provision in law, state in their instruments of incorporation the methods of calculation of the net asset values of their units;

(b) intervene on the market to prevent the stock exchange values of their units from deviating by more than 5% from their net asset values;

(c) establish the net asset values of their units, communicate them to the competent authorities at least twice a week and publish them twice a month.

At least twice a month, an independent auditor must ensure that the calculation of the value of units is effected in accordance with the law and the company's instruments of incorporation. On such occasions, the auditor must make sure that the company's assets are invested in accordance with the rules laid down by law and the company's instruments of incorporation.

6. The Member States shall inform the Commission of the identities of the companies benefiting from the derogations provided for in paragraphs 4 and 5.

[. . .]

¶ *The second subparagraph of article 14(6) has been deleted by article 9(2) of Directive 2005/1/EC, reproduced supra under no. B. 39.*

Article 15

1. A depositary must either have its registered office in the same Member State as that of the investment company or be established in that Member State if its registered office is in another Member State.

2. A depositary must be an institution that is subject to public control. It must also furnish sufficient financial and professional guarantees to be able effectively to pursue its business as depositary and meet the commitments inherent in that function.

3. The Member States shall determine which of the categories of institutions referred to in paragraph 2 shall be eligible to be depositaries.

Article 16

A depositary shall, in accordance with the national law of the State in which the investment company's registered office is situated, be liable to the investment company and the unit-holders for any loss suffered by them as a result of its unjustifiable failure to perform its obligations, or its improper performance of them.

Article 17

1. No single company shall act as both investment company and depositary.

2. In carrying out its role as depositary, the depositary must act solely in the interests of the unit-holders.

Article 18

The law or the investment company's instruments of incorporation shall lay down the conditions for the replacement of the depositary and rules to ensure the protection of unit-holders in the event of such replacement.

SECTION V

OBLIGATIONS CONCERNING THE INVESTMENT POLICIES OF UCITS

Article 19

1. The investments of a unit trust or of an investment company must consist solely of:

[(a) transferable securities and money market instruments admitted to or dealt in on a regulated market within the meaning of Article 1(13) of the ISD, and/or]

(b) transferable securities [and money market instruments] dealt in on another regulated market in a Member State which operates regularly and is recognised and open to the public and/or;

(c) transferable securities [and money market instruments] admitted to official listing on a stock exchange in a non-member State or dealt in on another regulated market in a non-member State which operates regularly and is recognised and open to the public provided that the choice of stock exchange or market has been approved by the competent authorities or is provided for in law or the fund rules or the investment company's instruments of incorporation and/or;

(d) recently issued transferable securities, provided that:

– the terms of issue include an undertaking that application will be made for admission to official listing on a stock exchange or to another regulated market which operates regularly and is recognised and open to the public, provided that the choice of stock exchange or market has been approved by the competent authorities or is provided for in law or the fund rules or the investment company's instruments of incorporation;

– such admission is secured within a year of issue [and/or;]

[(e) units of UCITS authorised according to this Directive and/or other collective investment undertakings within the meaning of the first and second indent of Article 1(2), should they be situated in a Member State or not, provided that:

– such other collective investment undertakings are authorised under laws which provide that they are subject to supervision considered by the UCITS' competent authorities to be equivalent to that laid down in Community law, and that cooperation between authorities is sufficiently ensured,

– the level of protection for unit-holders in the other collective investment undertakings is equivalent to that provided for unit-holders in a UCITS, and in particular that the rules on assets segregation, borrowing, lending, and uncovered sales of transferable securities and money market instruments are equivalent to the requirements of this Directive,

– the business of the other collective investment undertakings is reported in half-yearly and annual reports to enable an assessment to be made of the assets and liabilities, income and operations over the reporting period,

– no more than 10% of the UCITS' or the other collective investment undertakings' assets, whose acquisition is contemplated, can, according to their fund rules or instruments of incorporation, be invested in aggregate in units of other UCITS or other collective investment undertakings, and/or;

(f) deposits with credit institutions which are repayable on demand or have the right to be withdrawn, and maturing in no more than 12 months, provided that the credit institution has its registered office in a Member State or, if the registered office of the credit institution is situated in a non-member State, provided that it is subject to prudential rules considered by the UCITS' competent authorities as equivalent to those laid down in Community law, and/or;

(g) financial derivative instruments, including equivalent cash-settled instruments, dealt in on a regulated market referred to in subparagraphs (a), (b) and (c); and/or financial derivative instruments dealt in over-the-counter ('OTC derivatives'), provided that:
– the underlying consists of instruments covered by this paragraph, financial indices, interest rates, foreign exchange rates or currencies, in which the UCITS may invest according to its investment objectives as stated in the UCITS' fund rules or instruments of incorporation,
– the counterparties to OTC derivative transactions are institutions subject to prudential supervision, and belonging to the categories approved by the UCITS' competent authorities, and
– the OTC derivatives are subject to reliable and verifiable valuation on a daily basis and can be sold, liquidated or closed by an offsetting transaction at any time at their fair value at the UCITS' initiative, and/or;

(h) money market instruments other than those dealt in on a regulated market, which fall under Article 1(9), if the issue or issuer of such instruments is itself regulated for the purpose of protecting investors and savings, and provided that they are:
– issued or guaranteed by a central, regional or local authority or central bank of a Member State, the European Central Bank, the European Union or the European Investment Bank, a non-member State or, in the case of a Federal State, by one of the members making up the federation, or by a public international body to which one or more Member States belong, or

– issued by an undertaking any securities of which are dealt in on regulated markets referred to in subparagraphs (a), (b) or (c), or
– issued or guaranteed by an establishment subject to prudential supervision, in accordance with criteria defined by Community law, or by an establishment which is subject to and complies with prudential rules considered by the competent authorities to be at least as stringent as those laid down by Community law; or
– issued by other bodies belonging to the categories approved by the UCITS' competent authorities provided that investments in such instruments are subject to investor protection equivalent to that laid down in the first, the second or the third indent and provided that the issuer is a company whose capital and reserves amount to at least EUR 10 million and which presents and publishes its annual accounts in accordance with Directive 78/660/EEC,[14] is an entity which, within a group of companies which includes one or several listed companies, is dedicated to the financing of the group or is an entity which is dedicated to the financing of securitisation vehicles which benefit from a banking liquidity line.]

2. However:

(a) a UCITS may invest no more than 10% of its assets in transferable securities [and money market instruments] other than those referred to in paragraph l;

(b) [...]

(c) an investment company may acquire movable and immovable property that is essential for the direct pursuit of its business;

(d) a UCITS may not acquire either precious metals or certificates representing them.

3. [...]

4. Unit trusts and investment companies may hold ancillary liquid assets.

---

[14] Fourth Council Directive 78/660/EEC of 25 July 1978 based on Article 54(3)(g) of the Treaty on the annual accounts of certain types of companies (OJ L 222, 14.8.1978, 11), reproduced supra under no. C. 4. Directive as last amended by Directive 1999/60/EC (OJ L 162, 26.6.1999, 65), reproduced supra under no. C. 16.

¶ *Article 19(1)(a) has been replaced by article 1(3) of Directive 2001/108/EC, reproduced infra under no. S. 22.*
¶ *The words between square brackets in article 19(1)(b) and (c) have been added by article 1(4) of Directive 2001/108/EC, reproduced infra under no. S. 22.*
¶ *Article 19(1)(e)–(h) has been added by article 1(5) of Directive 2001/108/EC, reproduced infra under no. S. 22.*
¶ *The words between square brackets in article 19(2)(a) have been added by article 1(6) of Directive 2001/108/EC, reproduced infra under no. S. 22.*
¶ *Article 19(2)(b) and (3) has been deleted by article 1(7) of Directive 2001/108/EC, reproduced infra under no. S. 22.*

Article 20

[. . .]

¶ *Article 20 has been deleted by article 1(8) of Directive 2001/108/EC, reproduced infra under no. S. 22.*

[Article 21

1. The management or investment company must employ a risk-management process which enables it to monitor and measure at any time the risk of the positions and their contribution to the overall risk profile of the portfolio; it must employ a process for accurate and independent assessment of the value of OTC derivative instruments. It must communicate to the competent authorities regularly and in accordance with the detailed rules they shall define, the types of derivative instruments, the underlying risks, the quantitative limits and the methods which are chosen in order to estimate the risks associated with transactions in derivative instruments regarding each managed UCITS.

2. The Member States may authorise UCITS to employ techniques and instruments relating to transferable securities and money market instruments under the conditions and within the limits which they lay down provided that such techniques and instruments are used for the purpose of efficient portfolio management. When these operations concern the use of derivative instruments, these conditions and limits shall conform to the provisions laid down in this Directive.

Under no circumstances shall these operations cause the UCITS to diverge from its investment objectives as laid down in the UCITS' fund rules, instruments of incorporation or prospectus.

3. A UCITS shall ensure that its global exposure relating to derivative instruments does not exceed the total net value of its portfolio.

The exposure is calculated taking into account the current value of the underlying assets, the counterparty risk, future market movements and the time available to liquidate the positions. This shall also apply to the following subparagraphs.

A UCITS may invest, as a part of its investment policy and within the limit laid down in Article 22(5), in financial derivative instruments provided that the exposure to the underlying assets does not exceed in aggregate the investment limits laid down in Article 22. The Member States may allow that, when a UCITS invests in index-based financial derivative instruments, these investments do not have to be combined to the limits laid down in Article 22.

When a transferable security or money market instrument embeds a derivative, the latter must be taken into account when complying with the requirements of this Article.

4. The Member States shall send the Commission full information and any subsequent changes in their regulation concerning the methods used to calculate the risk exposures mentioned in paragraph 3, including the risk exposure to a counterparty in OTC derivative transactions, no later than 13 February 2004. The Commission shall forward that information to the other Member States. [Such information shall be the subject of exchanges of views within the European Securities Committee.]

¶ *Article 21 has been replaced by article 1(9) of Directive 2001/108/EC, reproduced infra under no. S. 22.*
¶ *The third sentence of the fourth paragraph of article 21 has been replaced by article 9(3) of Directive 2005/1/EC, reproduced supra under no. B. 39.*

[Article 22

1. A UCITS may invest no more than 5% of its assets in transferable securities or money market instruments issued by the same body. A UCITS may not invest more than 20% of its assets in deposits made with the same body.

The risk exposure to a counterparty of the UCITS in an OTC derivative transaction may not exceed:
- 10% of its assets when the counterpart is a credit institution referred to in Article 19(1)(f), or
- 5% of its assets, in other cases.

2. Member States may raise the 5% limit laid down in the first sentence of paragraph 1 to a maximum of 10%. However, the total value of the transferable securities and the money market instruments held by the UCITS in the issuing bodies in each of which it invests more than 5% of its assets must not then exceed 40% of the value of its assets. This limitation does not apply to deposits and OTC derivative transactions made with financial institutions subject to prudential supervision.

Notwithstanding the individual limits laid down in paragraph 1, a UCITS may not combine:
- investments in transferable securities or money market instruments issued by,
- deposits made with, and/or
- exposures arising from OTC derivative transactions undertaken with a single body in excess of 20% of its assets.

3. The Member States may raise the 5% limit laid down in the first sentence of paragraph 1 to a maximum of 35% if the transferable securities or money market instruments are issued or guaranteed by a Member State, by its local authorities, by a non-member State or by public international bodies to which one or more Member States belong.

4. Member States may raise the 5% limit laid down in the first sentence of paragraph 1 to a maximum of 25% in the case of certain bonds when these are issued by a credit institution which has its registered office in a Member State and is subject by law to special public supervision designed to protect bond-holders. In particular, sums deriving from the issue of these bonds must be invested in conformity with the law in assets which, during the whole period of validity of the bonds, are capable of covering claims attaching to the bonds and which, in the event of failure of the issuer, would be used on a priority basis for the reimbursement of the principal and payment of the accrued interest.

When a UCITS invests more than 5% of its assets in the bonds referred to in the first subparagraph and issued by one issuer, the total value of these investments may not exceed 80% of the value of the assets of the UCITS.

The Member States shall send the Commission a list of the aforementioned categories of bonds together with the categories of issuers authorised, in accordance with the laws and supervisory arrangements mentioned in the first subparagraph, to issue bonds complying with the criteria set out above. A notice specifying the status of the guarantees offered shall be attached to these lists. The Commission shall immediately forward that information to the other Member States together with any comments which it considers appropriate, and shall make the information available to the public. [Such communications may be the subject of exchanges of views within the European Securities Committee.]

5. The transferable securities and money market instruments referred to in paragraphs 3 and 4 shall not be taken into account for the purpose of applying the limit of 40% referred to in paragraph 2.

The limits provided for in paragraphs 1, 2, 3 and 4 may not be combined, and thus investments in transferable securities or money market instruments issued by the same body or in deposits or derivative instruments made with this body carried out in accordance with paragraphs 1, 2, 3 and 4 shall under no circumstances exceed in total 35% of the assets of the UCITS.

Companies which are included in the same group for the purposes of consolidated accounts, as defined in accordance with Directive 83/349/EEC[15] or in accordance with recognised international accounting rules, are regarded as a single body for the purpose of calculating the limits contained in this Article.

---

[15] Seventh Council Directive 83/349/EEC of 13 June 1983 based on the Article 54(3)(g) of the Treaty on consolidated accounts (OJ L 193, 18.7.1983, 1), reproduced supra under no. C. 6. Directive as last amended by the 1994 Act of Accession.

Member States may allow cumulative investment in transferable securities and money market instruments within the same group up to a limit of 20%.]

¶ *Article 22 has been replaced by article 1(10) of Directive 2001/108/EC, reproduced infra under no. S. 22.*
¶ *The fourth sentence of the third subparagraph of article 22(4) has been amended by article 9(3) of Directive 2005/1/EC, reproduced supra under no. B. 39.*

[Article 22a

1. Without prejudice to the limits laid down in Article 25, the Member States may raise the limits laid down in Article 22 to a maximum of 20% for investment in shares and/or debt securities issued by the same body when, according to the fund rules or instruments of incorporation, the aim of the UCITS' investment policy is to replicate the composition of a certain stock or debt securities index which is recognised by the competent authorities, on the following basis:
– its composition is sufficiently diversified,
– the index represents an adequate benchmark for the market to which it refers,
– it is published in an appropriate manner.

2. Member States may raise the limit laid down in paragraph 1 to a maximum of 35% where that proves to be justified by exceptional market conditions in particular in regulated markets where certain transferable securities or money market instruments are highly dominant. The investment up to this limit is only permitted for a single issuer.]

¶ *Article 22a has been inserted by article 1(11) of Directive 2001/108/EC, reproduced infra under no. S. 22.*

Article 23

1. By way of derogation from Article 22 and without prejudice to Article [68(3)]² of the Treaty, the Member States may authorise UCITS to invest in accordance with the principle of risk-spreading up to 100% of their assets in different transferable securities [and money market instruments] issued or guaranteed by any Member State, its local authorities, a non-member State or public international bodies of which one or more Member States are members.

The competent authorities shall grant such derogation only if they consider the unit-holders in the UCITS have protection equivalent to that of unit-holders in UCITS complying with the limits laid down in Article 22.

Such a UCITS must hold securities from at least six different issues, but securities from any one issue may not account for more than 30% of its total assets.

2. The UCITS referred to in paragraph 1 must make express mention in the fund rules or in the investment company's instruments of incorporation of the States, local authorities or public international bodies issuing or guaranteeing securities in which they intend to invest more than 35% of their assets; such fund rules or instruments of incorporation must be approved by the competent authorities.

3. In addition each such UCITS referred to in paragraph 1 must include a prominent statement in its prospectus and any promotional literature drawing attention to such authorisation and indicating the States, local authorities and/or public international bodies in the securities of which it intends to invest or has invested more than 35% of its assets.

¶ *The words between square brackets in the first paragraph of article 23 have been added by article 1(12) of Directive 2001/108/EC, reproduced infra under no. S. 22.*

[Article 24

1. A UCITS may acquire the units of UCITS and/or other collective investment undertakings referred to in Article 19(1)(e), provided that no more than 10% of its assets are invested in units of a single UCITS or other collective investment undertaking. The Member States may raise the limit to a maximum of 20%.

2. Investments made in units of collective investment undertakings other than UCITS may not exceed, in aggregate, 30% of the assets of the UCITS.

The Member States may allow that, when a UCITS has acquired units of UCITS and/or other collective investment undertakings, the assets of the respective UCITS or other collective investment undertakings do not have to be combined for the purposes of the limits laid down in Article 22.

3. When a UCITS invests in the units of other UCITS and/or other collective investment undertakings that are managed, directly or by delegation, by the same management company or by any other company with which the management company is linked by common management or control, or by a substantial direct or indirect holding, that management company or other company may not charge subscription or redemption fees on account of the UCITS's investment in the units of such other UCITS and/or collective investment undertakings.

A UCITS that invests a substantial proportion of its assets in other UCITS and/or collective investment undertakings shall disclose in its prospectus the maximum level of the management fees that may be charged both to the UCITS itself and to the other UCITS and/or collective investment undertakings in which it intends to invest. In its annual report it shall indicate the maximum proportion of management fees charged both to the UCITS itself and to the UCITS and/or other collective investment undertaking in which it invests.]

¶ *Article 24 has been replaced by article 1(13) of Directive 2001/108/EC, reproduced infra under no. S. 22.*

[*Article 24a*

1. The prospectus shall indicate in which categories of assets a UCITS is authorised to invest. It shall mention if transactions in financial derivative instruments are authorised; in this event, it must include a prominent statement indicating if these operations may be carried out for the purpose of hedging or with the aim of meeting investment goals, and the possible outcome of the use of financial derivative instruments on the risk profile.

2. When a UCITS invests principally in any category of assets defined in Article 19 other than transferable securities and money market instruments or replicates a stock or debt securities index in accordance with Article 22a, its prospectus and, where necessary, any other promotional literature must include a prominent statement drawing attention to the investment policy.

3. When the net asset value of a UCITS is likely to have a high volatility due to its portfolio composition or the portfolio management techniques that may be used, its prospectus and, where necessary, any other promotional literature must include a prominent statement drawing attention to this characteristic.

4. Upon request of an investor, the management company must also provide supplementary information relating to the quantitative limits that apply in the risk management of the UCITS, to the methods chosen to this end and to the recent evolution of the main instrument categories' risks and yields.]

¶ *Article 24a has been inserted by article 1(14) of Directive 2001/108/EC, reproduced infra under no. S. 22.*

Article 25

1. An investment company or a management company acting in connection with all of the unit trusts which it manages and which fall within the scope of this Directive may not acquire any shares carrying voting rights which would enable it to exercise significant influence over the management of an issuing body.

Pending further co-ordination, the Member States shall take account of existing rules defining the principle stated in the first subparagraph under other Member States' legislation.

2. Moreover, an investment company or unit trust may acquire no more than:
- 10% of the non-voting shares of any single issuing body;
- 10% of the debt securities of any single issuing body;
- [– 25% of the units of any single UCITS and/or other collective investment undertaking within the meaning of the first and second indent of Article 1(2);]
- [– 10% of the money market instruments of any single issuing body.]

[The limits laid down in the second, third and fourth indents may be disregarded at the time of acquisition if at that time the gross amount of the debt securities or of the money market instruments, or the net amount of the securities in issue, cannot be calculated.]

3. A Member State may waive application of paragraphs 1 and 2 as regards:

(a) transferable securities [and money market instruments] issued or guaranteed by a Member State or its local authorities;

(b) transferable securities [and money market instruments] issued or guaranteed by a non-member State;

(c) transferable securities [and money market instruments] issued by public international bodies of which one or more Member States are members;

(d) shares held by a UCITS in the capital of a company incorporated in a non-member State investing its assets mainly in the securities of issuing bodies having their registered offices in that State, where under the legislation of that State such a holding represents the only way in which the UCITS can invest in the securities of issuing bodies of that State. This derogation, however, shall apply only if in its investment policy the company from the non-member State complies with the limits laid down in Articles 22, 24 and 25 (1) and (2). Where the limits set in Articles 22 and 24 are exceeded. Article 26 shall apply *mutatis mutandis*;

[(e) shares held by an investment company or investment companies in the capital of subsidiary companies carrying on only the business of management, advice or marketing in the country where the subsidiary is located, in regard to the repurchase of units at unit-holders' request exclusively on its or their behalf.]

¶ *Article 25(2), third indent has been replaced by Directive 2001/108/EC, reproduced infra under no. S. 22.*
¶ *Article 25(2), fourth indent has been added by article 1(15) of Directive 2001/108/EC, reproduced infra under no. S. 22.*
¶ *Article 25(2), second sentence has been replaced by article 1(16) of Directive 2001/108/EC, reproduced infra under no. S. 22.*
¶ *The words between square brackets in article 25(3)(a), (b), and (c), have been added by article 1(17) of Directive 2001/108/EC, reproduced infra under no. S. 22.*
¶ *Article 25(3)(e) has been replaced by article 1(18) of Directive 2001/108/EC, reproduced infra under no. S. 22.*

Article 26

[1. UCITS need not comply with the limits laid down in this section when exercising subscription rights attaching to transferable securities or money market instruments which form part of their assets.

While ensuring observance of the principle of risk spreading, the Member States may allow recently authorised UCITS to derogate from Articles 22, 22a, 23 and 24 for six months following the date of their authorisation.]

2. If the limits referred to in paragraph 1 are exceeded for reasons beyond the control of a UCITS or as a result of the exercise of subscription rights, that UCITS must adopt as a priority objective for its sales transactions the remedying of that situation, taking due account of the interests of its unit-holders.

¶ *Article 26(1) has been replaced by article 1(19) of Directive 2001/108/EC, reproduced infra under no. S. 22.*

SECTION VI

OBLIGATIONS CONCERNING INFORMATION TO BE SUPPLIED TO UNIT-HOLDERS

A. Publication of a prospectus and periodical reports

Article 27

[1. An investment company and, for each of the unit trusts and common funds it manages, a management company, must publish:
– a simplified prospectus,
– a full prospectus,
– an annual report for each financial year, and
– a half-yearly report covering the first six months of the financial year.]

2. The annual and half-yearly reports must be published within the following time limits, with effect from the ends of the periods to which they relate:
– four months in the case of the annual report,
– two months in the case of the half-yearly report.

¶ *Article 27(1) has been replaced by article 1(8) of Directive 2001/107/EC, reproduced infra under no. S. 21.*

[*Article 28*

1. Both the simplified and the full prospectuses must include the information necessary for investors to be able to make an informed judgement of the investment proposed to them, and, in particular, of the risks attached thereto. The latter shall include, independent of the instruments invested in, a clear and easily understandable explanation of the fund's risk profile.

2. The full prospectus shall contain at least the information provided for in Schedule A, Annex I to this Directive, in so far as that information does not already appear in the fund rules or instruments of incorporation annexed to the full prospectus in accordance with Article 29(1).

3. The simplified prospectus shall contain in summary form the key information provided for in Schedule C, Annex I to this Directive. It shall be structured and written in such a way that it can be easily understood by the average investor. Member States may permit that the simplified prospectus be attached to the full prospectus as a removable part of it. The simplified prospectus can be used as a marketing tool designed to be used in all Member States without alterations except translation. Member States may therefore not require any further documents or additional information to be added.

4. Both the full and the simplified prospectus may be incorporated in a written document or in any durable medium having an equivalent legal status approved by the competent authorities.

5. The annual report must include a balance-sheet or a statement of assets and liabilities, a detailed income and expenditure account for the financial year, a report on the activities of the financial year and the other information provided for in Schedule B, Annex I to this Directive, as well as any significant information which will enable investors to make an informed judgment on the development of the activities of the UCITS and its results.

6. The half-yearly report must include at least the information provided for in Chapters I to IV of Schedule B, Annex I to this Directive; where a UCITS has paid or proposes to pay an interim dividend, the figures must indicate the results after tax for the half-year concerned and the interim dividend paid or proposed.]

¶ *Article 28 has been replaced by article 1(9) of Directive 2001/107/EC, reproduced infra under no. S. 21.*

[*Article 29*

1. The fund rules or an investment company's instruments of incorporation shall form an integral part of the full prospectus and must be annexed thereto.

2. The documents referred to in paragraph 1 need not, however, be annexed to the full prospectus provided that the unit-holder is informed that on request he or she will be sent those documents or be apprised of the place where, in each Member State in which the units are placed on the market, he or she may consult them.]

¶ *Article 29 has been replaced by article 1(10) of Directive 2001/107/EC, reproduced infra under no. S. 21.*

[*Article 30*

The essential elements of the simplified and the full prospectuses must be kept up to date.]

¶ *Article 30 has been replaced by article 1(11) of Directive 2001/107/EC, reproduced infra under no. S. 21.*

Article 31

The accounting information given in the annual report must be audited by one or more persons empowered by law to audit accounts in accordance with Council Directive 84/253/EEC of 10 April 1984 based on Article [44(3)(g)]² of the EEC Treaty on the approval of persons responsible for carrying out the statutory audits of accounting documents.[16] The auditor's report, including any qualifications, shall be reproduced in full in the annual report.

[*Article 32*

UCITS must send their simplified and full prospectuses and any amendments thereto, as

---

[16] OJ L 126, 12.5.1984, 20, Eighth Company Directive, reproduced supra under no. C. 7.

well as their annual and half-yearly reports, to the competent authorities.]

¶ *Article 32 has been replaced by article 1(12) of Directive 2001/107/EC, reproduced infra under no. S. 21.*

[*Article 33*

1. The simplified prospectus must be offered to subscribers free of charge before the conclusion of the contract.

In addition, the full prospectus and the latest published annual and half-yearly reports shall be supplied to subscribers free of charge on request.

2. The annual and half-yearly reports shall be supplied to unit-holders free of charge on request.

3. The annual and half-yearly reports must be available to the public at the places, or through other means approved by the competent authorities, specified in the full and simplified prospectus.]

¶ *Article 33 has been replaced by article 1(13) of Directive 2001/107/EC, reproduced infra under no. S. 21.*

B. Publication of other information

Article 34

A UCITS must make public in an appropriate manner the issue, sale, repurchase or redemption price of its units each time it issues, sells, repurchases or redeems them, and at least twice a month. The competent authorities may, however, permit a UCITS to reduce the frequency to once a month on condition that such derogation does not prejudice the interests of the unit-holders.

[*Article 35*

All publicity comprising an invitation to purchase the units of UCITS must indicate that prospectuses exist and the places where they may be obtained by the public or how the public may have access to them.]

¶ *Article 35 has been replaced by article 1(14) of Directive 2001/107/EC, reproduced infra under no. S. 21.*

SECTION VII
THE GENERAL OBLIGATIONS OF UCITS

Article 36

1. Neither:
– an investment company, nor
– a management company or depositary acting on behalf of a unit trust, may borrow.

However, a UCITS may acquire foreign currency by means of a 'back-to-back' loan.

2. By way of derogation from paragraph 1, a Member State may authorise a UCITS to borrow:

(a) up to 10%
– of its assets, in the case of an investment company, or
– of the value of the fund, in the case of a unit trust, provided that the borrowing is on a temporary basis

(b) up to 10% of its assets, in the case of an investment company, provided that the borrowing is to make possible the acquisition of immovable property essential for the direct pursuit of its business; in this case the borrowing and that referred to in subparagraph (a) may not in any case in total exceed 15% of the borrower's assets.

Article 37

1. A UCITS must repurchase or redeem its units at the request of any unit-holder.

2. By way of derogation from paragraph 1:

(a) a UCITS may, in the cases and according to the procedures provided for by law, the fund rules or the investment company's instruments of incorporation, temporarily suspend the repurchase or redemption of its units. Suspension may be provided for only in exceptional cases where circumstances so require, and suspension is justified having regard to the interests of the unit-holders;

(b) the Member States may allow the competent authorities to require the suspension of the repurchase or redemption of units in the interest of the unit-holders or of the public.

3. In the cases mentioned in paragraph 2 (a), a UCITS must without delay communicate its decision to the competent authorities and to the authorities of all Member States in which it markets its units.

Article 38

The rules for the valuation of assets and the rules for calculating the sale or issue price and the repurchase or redemption price of the units of a UCITS must be laid down in the law, in the fund rules or in the investment company's instruments of incorporation.

Article 39

The distribution or reinvestment of the income of a unit trust or of an investment company shall be effected in accordance with the law and with the fund rules or the investment company's instruments of incorporation.

Article 40

A UCITS unit may not be issued unless the equivalent of the net issue price is paid into the assets of the UCITS within the usual time limits. This provision shall not preclude the distribution of bonus units.

Article 41

1. Without prejudice to the application of Articles 19 and 21, neither:
– an investment company, nor
– a management company or depositary acting on behalf of a unit trust

may grant loans or act as a guarantor on behalf of third parties.

[2. Paragraph 1 shall not prevent such undertakings from acquiring transferable securities, money market instruments or other financial instruments referred to in Article 19(1)(e), (g) and (h) which are not fully paid.]

¶ *Article 41, paragraph 2 has been replaced by article 1(20) of Directive 2001/108/EC, reproduced infra under no. S. 22.*

[*Article 42*

Neither:
– an investment company, nor
– a management company or depositary acting on behalf of a unit trust

may carry out uncovered sales of transferable securities, money market instruments or other financial instruments referred to in Article 19(1)(e), (g) and (h).]

¶ *Article 42 has been replaced by article 1(21) of Directive 2001/108/EC, reproduced infra under no. S. 22.*

Article 43

The law or the fund rules must prescribe the remuneration and the expenditure that a management company is empowered to charge to a unit trust and the method of calculation of such remuneration.

The law or an investment company's instruments of incorporation must prescribe the nature of the cost to be borne by the company.

SECTION VIII

SPECIAL PROVISIONS APPLICABLE TO UCITS THAT MARKET THEIR UNITS IN MEMBER STATES OTHER THAN THOSE IN WHICH THEY ARE SITUATED

Article 44

1. A UCITS that markets its units in another Member State must comply with the laws, regulations and administrative provisions in force in that State that do not fall within the field governed by this Directive.

2. Any UCITS may advertise its units in the Member State in which they are marketed. It must comply with the provisions governing advertising in that State.

3. The provisions referred to in paragraphs 1 and 2 must be applied without discrimination.

Article 45

In the case referred to in Article 44, the UCITS must, *inter alia*, in accordance with the laws, regulations and administrative provisions in force in the Member State of marketing, take the measures necessary to ensure that facilities are available in that State for making payments to unit-holders, repurchasing or redeeming units and making available the information which UCITS are obliged to provide.

[*Article 46*]

If a UCITS proposes to market its units in a Member State other than that in which it is situated, it must first inform the competent authorities of that other Member State accordingly. It must simultaneously send the latter authorities:
– an attestation by the competent authorities to the effect that it fulfils the conditions imposed by this Directive,
– its fund rules or its instruments of incorporation,
– its full and simplified prospectuses,
– where appropriate, its latest annual report and any subsequent half-yearly report, and
– details of the arrangements made of the marketing of its units in that other Member State.

An investment company or a management company may begin to market its units in that other Member State two months after such communication, unless the authorities of the Member States concerned establish, in a reasoned decision taken before the expiry of that period of two months, that the arrangements made for the marketing of units do not comply with the provisions referred to in Article 44(1) and Article 45.]

¶ *Article 46 has been replaced by article 1(15) of Directive 2001/107/EC, reproduced infra under no. S. 21.*

[*Article 47*]

If a UCITS markets its units in a Member State other than that in which it is situated, it must distribute in that other Member State, in accordance with the same procedures as those provided for in the home Member State, the full and simplified prospectuses, the annual and half-yearly reports and the other information provided for in Articles 29 and 30.

These documents shall be provided in the language or one of the official languages of the host Member State or in a language approved by the competent authorities of the host Member State.]

¶ *Article 47 has been replaced by article 1(16) of Directive 2001/107/EC, reproduced infra under no. S. 21.*

Article 48

For the purpose of carrying on its activities, a UCITS may use the same generic name (such as investment company or unit trust) in the Community as it uses in the Member State in which it is situated. In the event of any danger of confusion, the host Member State may, for the purpose of clarification, require that the name be accompanied by certain explanatory particulars.

SECTION IX

PROVISIONS CONCERNING THE AUTHORITIES RESPONSIBLE FOR AUTHORISATION AND SUPERVISION

Article 49

1. The Member States shall designate the authorities that are to carry out the duties provided for in this Directive. They shall inform the Commission thereof, indicating any division of duties.

2. The authorities referred to in paragraph 1 must be public authorities or bodies appointed by public authorities.

3. The authorities of the State in which a UCITS is situated shall be competent to supervise that UCITS. However, the authorities of the State in which a UCITS markets its units in accordance with Article 44 shall be competent to supervise compliance with Section VIII.

4. The authorities concerned must be granted all the powers necessary to carry out their task.

Article 50

1. The authorities of the Member States referred to in Article 49 shall collaborate closely in order to carry out their task and must for that purpose

alone communicate to each other all information required.

[2. Member States shall provide that all persons who work or who have worked for the competent authorities, as well as auditors and experts instructed by the competent authorities, shall be bound by the obligation of professional secrecy. Such secrecy implies that no confidential information which they may receive in the course of their duties may be divulged to any person or authority whatsoever, save in summary or aggregate form such that UCITS and management companies and depositaries (hereinafter referred to as undertakings contributing towards their business activity) cannot be individually identified, without prejudice to cases covered by criminal law.

Nevertheless, when a UCITS or an undertaking contributing towards its business activity has been declared bankrupt or is being compulsorily wound up, confidential information which does not concern third parties involved in rescue attempts may be divulged in civil or commercial proceedings.

3. Paragraph 2 shall not prevent the competent authorities of the various Member States from exchanging information in accordance with this Directive or other Directives applicable to UCITS or to undertakings contributing towards their business activity. That information shall be subject to the conditions of professional secrecy imposed in paragraph 2.

4. Member States may conclude co-operation agreements providing for exchange of information with the competent authorities of third countries or with authorities or bodies of third countries as defined in paragraphs 6 and 7 only if the information disclosed is subject to guarantees of professional secrecy at least equivalent to those referred to in this Article. Such exchange of information must be intended for the performance of the supervisory task of the authorities or bodies mentioned.

Where the information originates in another Member State, it may not be disclosed without the express agreement of the competent authorities that have disclosed it and, where appropriate, solely for the purposes for which those authorities gave their agreement.]

5. Competent authorities receiving confidential information under paragraphs 2 or 3 may use it only in the course of their duties:
– to check that the conditions governing the taking-up of the business of UCITS or of undertakings contributing towards their business activity are met and to facilitate the monitoring of the conduct of that business, administrative and accounting procedures and internal-control mechanisms,
– to impose sanctions,
– in administrative appeals against decisions by the competent authorities, or
– in court proceedings initiated under Article 51 (2).

6. Paragraphs 2 and 5 shall not preclude the exchange of information:

(a) within a Member State, where there are two or more competent authorities; or

(b) within a Member State or between Member States, between competent authorities; and
– authorities with public responsibility for the supervision of credit institutions, investment undertakings, insurance undertakings and other financial organisations and the authorities responsible for the supervision of financial markets,
– bodies involved in the liquidation or bankruptcy of UCITS and other similar procedures and of undertakings contributing towards their business activity,
– persons responsible for carrying out statutory audits of the accounts of insurance undertakings, credit institutions, investment undertakings and other financial institutions, in the performance of their supervisory functions, or the disclosure to bodies which administer compensation schemes of information necessary for the performance of their functions. Such information shall be subject to the conditions of professional secrecy imposed in paragraph 2.

7. Notwithstanding paragraphs 2 to 5, Member States may authorise exchanges of information between the competent authorities and:
– the authorities responsible for overseeing the bodies involved in the liquidation and bankruptcy of [undertaking for collective investment in transferable securities (UCITS) or

an undertaking contributing towards its business activity] and other similar procedures, or
- the authorities responsible for overseeing persons charged with carrying out statutory audits of the accounts of insurance undertakings, credit institutions, investment firms and other financial institutions.

Member States that have recourse to the option provided for in the first subparagraph shall require at least that the following conditions are met:
- the information shall be for the purpose of performing the task of overseeing referred to in the first subparagraph,
- information received in this context shall be subject to the conditions of professional secrecy imposed in paragraph 2,
- where the information originates in another Member State, it may not be disclosed without the express agreement of the competent authorities that have disclosed it and, where appropriate, solely for the purposes for which those authorities gave their agreement.

Member States shall communicate to the Commission and to the other Member States the names of the authorities that may receive information pursuant to this paragraph.

8. Notwithstanding paragraphs 2 to 5, Member States may, with the aim of strengthening the stability, including integrity, of the financial system, authorise the exchange of information between the competent authorities and the authorities or bodies responsible under the law for the detection and investigation of breaches of company law.

Member States that have recourse to the option provided for in the first subparagraph shall require at least that the following conditions are met:
- the information shall be for the purpose of performing the task referred to in the first subparagraph,—information received in this context shall be subject to the conditions of professional secrecy imposed in paragraph 2,
- where the information originates in another Member State, it may not be disclosed without the express agreement of the competent authorities that have disclosed it and, where appropriate, solely for the purposes for which those authorities gave their agreement.

Where, in a Member State, the authorities or bodies referred to in the first subparagraph perform their task of detection or investigation with the aid, in view of their specific competence, of persons appointed for that purpose and not employed in the public sector the possibility of exchanging information provided for in the first subparagraph may be extended to such persons under the conditions stipulated in the second subparagraph.

In order to implement the final indent of the second subparagraph, the authorities or bodies referred to in the first subparagraph shall communicate to the competent authorities which have disclosed the information the names and precise responsibilities of the persons to whom it is to be sent.

Member States shall communicate to the Commission and to the other Member States the names of the authorities or bodies that may receive information pursuant to this paragraph.

Before 31 December 2000, the Commission shall draw up a report on the application of this paragraph.

9. This Article shall not prevent a competent authority from transmitting to central banks and other bodies with a similar function in their capacity as monetary authorities information intended for the performance of their tasks, nor shall it prevent such authorities or bodies from communicating to the competent authorities such information as they may need for the purposes of paragraph 5. Information received in this context shall be subject to the conditions of professional secrecy imposed in this Article.

10. This Article shall not prevent the competent authorities from communicating the information referred to in paragraphs 2 to 5 to a clearing house or other similar body recognised under national law for the provision of clearing or settlement services for one of their Member State's markets if they consider that it is necessary to communicate the information in order to

ensure the proper functioning of those bodies in relation to defaults or potential defaults by market participants. The information received in this context shall be subject to the conditions of professional secrecy imposed in paragraph 2. Member States shall, however, ensure that information received under paragraph 3 may not be disclosed in the circumstances referred to in this paragraph without the express consent of the competent authorities that disclosed it.

11. In addition, notwithstanding the provisions referred to in paragraphs 2 and 5, Member States may, by virtue of provisions laid down by law, authorise the disclosure of certain information to other departments of their central government administrations responsible for legislation on the supervision of UCITS and of undertakings contributing towards their business activity, credit institutions, financial institutions, investment undertakings and insurance undertakings and to inspectors instructed by those departments.

Such disclosures may, however, be made only where necessary for reasons of prudential control.

Member States shall, however, provide that information received under paragraphs 3 and 6 may never be disclosed in the circumstances referred to in this paragraph except with the express agreement of the competent authorities which disclosed the information.]

¶ *Paragraphs 2, 3, and 4 have been replaced by article 4(7) of Directive 95/26/EC, reproduced supra under no. I. 29.*
¶ *The words 'financial undertaking' between the square brackets in the seventh paragraph of article 50 have been replaced by article 1, fourth indent of Directive 95/26/EC, reproduced supra under no. I. 29.*
¶ *Paragraph 4 has been replaced by article 1 of Directive 2000/64/EC (OJ L 290, 17.11.2000, 27).*

[*Article 50a*

1. Member States shall provide at least that:

(a) any person authorised within the meaning of Directive 84/253/EEC,[17] performing in an [undertaking for collective investment in transferable securities (UCITS) or an undertaking contributing towards its business activity]

the task described in Article 51 of Directive 78/660/EEC,[18] Article 37 of Directive 83/349/EEC or Article 31 of Directive 85/611/EEC or any other statutory task, shall have a duty to report promptly to the competent authorities any fact or decision concerning that undertaking of which he has become aware while carrying out that task which is liable to:

– constitute a material breach of the laws, regulations or administrative provisions which lay down the conditions governing authorisation or which specifically govern pursuit of the activities [undertakings for collective investment in transferable securities (UCITS) or an undertaking contributing towards its business activity], or

– affect the continuous functioning of the [undertaking for collective investment in transferable securities (UCITS) or an undertaking contributing towards its business activity], or

– lead to refusal to certify the accounts or to the expression of reservations;

(b) that person shall likewise have a duty to report any facts and decisions of which he becomes aware in the course of carrying out a task as described in (a) in an undertaking having close links resulting from a control relationship with the [undertaking for collective investment in transferable securities (UCITS) or an undertaking contributing towards its business activity] within which he is carrying out the abovementioned task.

2. The disclosure in good faith to the competent authorities, by persons authorised within the meaning of Directive 84/253/EEC, of any fact or decision referred to in paragraph 1 shall not constitute a breach of any restriction on disclosure of information imposed by contract or by any legislative, regulatory or administrative provision and shall not involve such persons in liability of any kind.]

¶ *Article 50a has been inserted by article 5 of Directive 95/26/EC, reproduced supra under no. I. 29.*

---

[17] OJ L 126, 12.5.1984, 20, Eighth Company Directive, reproduced supra under no. C. 7.

[18] OJ L 222, 14.8.1978, 11, Fourth Company Directive, reproduced supra under no. C. 4. Directive as last amended by Directive 90/605/EEC (OJ L 317, 16.11.1990, 60), reproduced supra under no. C. 12.

¶ *The words 'financial undertaking' between the square brackets in the first paragraph have been replaced by article 1, fourth indent of Directive 95/26/EC, reproduced supra under no. I. 29.*

Article 51

1. The authorities referred to in Article 49 must give reasons for any decision to refuse authorisation, and any negative decision taken in implementation of the general measures adopted in application of this Directive, and communicate them to applicants.

2. The Member States shall provide that decisions taken in respect of a UCITS pursuant to laws, regulations and administrative provisions adopted in accordance with this Directive are subject to the right to apply to the courts; the same shall apply if no decision is taken within six months of its submission on an authorisation application made by a UCITS which includes all the information required under the provisions in force.

Article 52

1. Only the authorities of the Member State in which a UCITS is situated shall have the power to take action against it if it infringes any law, regulation or administrative provision or any regulation laid down in the fund rules or in the investment company's instruments of incorporation.

2. Nevertheless, the authorities of the Member State in which the units of a UCITS are marketed may take action against it if it infringes the provisions referred to in Section VIII.

3. Any decision to withdraw authorisation, or any other serious measure taken against a UCITS, or any suspension of repurchase or redemption imposed upon it, must be communicated without delay by the authorities of the Member State in which the UCITS in question is situated to the authorities of the other Member States in which its units are marketed.

[Article 52a

1. Where, through the provision of services or by the establishment of branches, a management company operates in one or more host Member States, the competent authorities of all the Member States concerned shall collaborate closely.

They shall supply one another on request with all the information concerning the management and ownership of such management companies that is likely to facilitate their supervision and all information likely to facilitate the monitoring of such companies. In particular, the authorities of the home Member State shall cooperate to ensure that the authorities of the host Member State collect the particulars referred to in Article 6c(2).

2. Insofar as it is necessary for the purpose of exercising their powers of supervision, the competent authorities of the home Member State shall be informed by the competent authorities of the host Member State of any measures taken by the host Member State pursuant to Article 6c(6) which involve penalties imposed on a management company or restrictions on a management company's activities.

Article 52b

1. Each host Member State shall ensure that, where a management company authorised in another Member State carries on business within its territory through a branch, the competent authorities of the management company's home Member State may, after informing the competent authorities of the host Member State, themselves or through the intermediary of persons they instruct for the purpose, carry out on-the-spot verification of the information referred to in Article 52a.

2. The competent authorities of the management company's home Member State may also ask the competent authorities of the management company's host Member State to have such verification carried out. Authorities which receive such requests must, within the framework of their powers, act upon them by carrying out the verifications themselves, by allowing the authorities who have requested them to carry them out or by allowing auditors or experts to do so.

3. This Article shall not affect the right of the competent authorities of the host Member State, in discharging their responsibilities under this

Directive, to carry out on-the-spot verifications of branches established within their territory.]

¶ *Articles 52a and 52b have been inserted by article 1(17) of Directive 2001/107/EC, reproduced infra under no. S. 21.*

Section X

[European Securities Committee]

¶ *The title of section X has been replaced by article 9(5) of Directive 2005/1/EC, reproduced supra under no. B. 39.*

Article 53

[. . .]

¶ *Article 53 has been repealed by article 9(6) of Directive 2005/1/EC, reproduced supra under no. B. 39.*

[*Article 53a*

The technical amendments to be made to this Directive in the following areas shall be adopted in accordance with the procedure referred to in Article 53b(2):

(a) clarification of the definitions in order to ensure uniform application of this Directive throughout the Community;
(b) alignment of terminology and the framing of definitions in accordance with subsequent acts on UCITS and related matters.]

¶ *Article 53a has been inserted by article 1(22) of Directive 2001/108/EC, reproduced infra under no. S. 22, and has subsequently been amended by article 9(7) of Directive 2005/1/EC, reproduced supra under no. B. 39.*

[*Article 53b*

1. The Commission shall be assisted by the European Securities Committee instituted by Commission Decision 2001/528/EC,[19] hereinafter 'the Committee'.

2. Where reference is made to this paragraph, Articles 5 and 7 of Decision 1999/468/EC[20] shall apply, having regard to the provisions of Article 8 thereof.

---

[19] OJ L 191, 13.7.2001, 45, reproduced infra under no. S. 19. Decision as amended by Decision 2004/8/EC (OJ L 3, 7.1.2004, 33), reproduced supra under no. I. 41.
[20] OJ L 184, 17.7.1999, 23.

The period laid down in Article 5(6) of Decision 1999/468/EC shall be set at three months.

3. The Committee shall adopt its rules of procedure.]

¶ *Article 53b has been inserted by article 9(8) of Directive 2005/1/EC, reproduced supra under no. B. 39.*

Section XI

Transitional Provisions, Derogations and Final Provisions

Article 54

Solely for the purpose of Danish UCITS, *pantebreve* issued in Denmark shall be treated as equivalent to the transferable securities referred to in Article 19 (1) (b).

Article 55

By way of derogation from Articles 7 (1) and 14 (1), the competent authorities may authorise those UCITS which, on the date of adoption of this Directive, had two or more depositaries in accordance with their national law to maintain that number of depositaries if those authorities have guarantees that the functions to be performed under Articles 7 (3) and 14 (3) will be performed in practice.

Article 56

1. By way of derogation from Article 6, the Member States may authorise management companies to issue bearer certificates representing the registered securities of other companies.

2. The Member States may authorise those management companies which, on the date of adoption of this Directive, also carry on activities other than those provided for in Article 6 to continue those other activities for five years after that date.

Article 57

1. The Member States shall bring into force no later than 1 October 1989 the measures necessary for them to comply with this Directive. They shall forthwith inform the Commission thereof.

2. The Member States may grant UCITS existing on the date of implementation of this Directive a period of not more than 12 months from that date in order to comply with the new national legislation.

3. The Hellenic Republic and the Portuguese Republic shall be authorised to postpone the implementation of this Directive until 1 April 1992 at the latest.

One year before that date the Commission shall report to the Council on progress in implementing the Directive and on any difficulties that the Hellenic Republic or the Portuguese Republic may encounter in implementing the Directive by the date referred to in the first subparagraph.

The Commission shall, if necessary, propose that the Council extend the postponement by up to four years.

Article 58

The Member States shall ensure that the Commission is informed of the texts of the main laws, regulations and administrative provisions that they adopt in the field covered by this Directive.

Article 59

This Directive is addressed to the Member States.

Annex [I]

Schedule A

1. Information concerning the unit trust	1. Information concerning the management company	1. Information concerning the investment company
1.1. Name.	1.1. Name or style, form in law, registered office and head office if different from the registered office.	1.1. Name or style, form in law, registered office and head office if different from the registered office.
1.2. Date of establishment of the unit trust. Indication of duration, if limited.	1.2. Date of incorporation of the company. Indication of duration if limited.	1.2. Date of the incorporation of the company. Indication of duration, if limited.
	1.3. If the company manages other unit trusts, indication of those other trusts.	[1.3. In the case of investment companies having different investment compartments, the indication of the compartments.]
1.4. Statement of the place where the fund rules, if they are not annexed, and periodic reports may be obtained.		1.4. Statement of the place where the instruments of incorporation, if they are not annexed, and periodic reports may be obtained.
1.5. Brief indications relevant to unit-holders of the tax system applicable to the unit trust. Details of whether deductions are made at source from the income and capital gains paid by the trust to unit-holders.		1.5. Brief indications relevant to unit-holders of the tax system applicable to the company. Details of whether deductions are made at source from the income and capital gains paid by the company to unit-holders.
1.6. Accounting and distribution dates.		1.6. Accounting and distribution dates.
1.7. Names of the persons responsible for auditing the accounting information referred to in Article 31.		1.7. Names of the persons responsible for auditing the accounting information referred to in Article 31.

	1.8. Names and positions in the company of the members of the administrative, management and supervisory bodies. Details of their main activities outside the company where these are of significance with respect to that company.
	1.9. Amount of the subscribed capital with an indication of the capital paid-up.
1.10. Details of the types and main characteristics of the units and in particular:	1.10. Details of the types and main characteristics of the units and in particular:
– the nature of the right (real, personal or other) represented by the unit,	
– original securities or certificates providing evidence of title; entry in a register or in an account,	– original securities or certificates providing evidence of title; entry in a register or in an account,
– characteristics of the units: registered or bearer. Indication of any denominations which may be provided for,	– characteristics of the units: registered or bearer. Indication of any denominations which may be provided for,
– indication of unit-holders' voting rights if these exist,	– indication of unit-holders' voting rights,
– circumstances in which winding-up of the unit trust can be decided on and winding-up procedure, in particular as regards the rights of unit-holders.	– circumstances in which winding-up of the investment company can be decided on and winding-up procedure, in particular as regards the rights of unit-holders.
1.11. Where applicable, indication of stock exchanges or markets where the units are listed or dealt in.	1.11. Where applicable, indication of stock exchanges or markets where the units are listed or dealt in.
1.12. Procedures and conditions of issue and sale of units.	1.12. Procedures and conditions of issue and sale of units.
1.13. Procedures and conditions for re-purchase or redemption of units, and circumstances in which repurchase or redemption may be suspended.	1.13. Procedures and conditions for repurchase or redemption of units, and circumstances in which repurchase or redemption may be suspended.
	[In the case of investment companies having different investment compartments, information on how a unit-holder may pass from one compartment into another and the charges applicable in such cases.]

| | 1.8. Names and positions in the company of the members of the administrative, management and supervisory bodies. Details of their main activities outside the company where these are of significance with respect to that company. |
| | 1.9. Capital. |

| 1.14. Description of rules for determining and applying income. | 1.14. Description of rules for determining and applying income. |
| 1.15. Description of the unit trust's investment objectives, including its financial objectives (e.g. capital growth or income), investment policy (e.g. specialisation in geographical or industrial sectors), | 1.15. Description of the company's investment objectives, including its financial objectives (e.g. capital growth or income), investment policy (e.g. specialisation in geographical or industrial sectors), |

Unit trust	Investment company
any limitations on that investment policy and an indication of any techniques and instruments or borrowing powers which may be used in the management of the unit trust.	any limitations on that investment policy and an indication of any techniques and instruments or borrowing powers which may be used in the management of the company.
1.16. Rules for the valuation of assets.	1.16. Rules for the valuation of assets.
1.17. Determination of the sale or issue price and the repurchase or redemption price of units, in particular:	1.17. Determination of the sale or issue price and the repurchase or redemption price of units, in particular:
– the method and frequency of the calculation of those prices,	– the method and frequency of the calculation of those prices,
– information concerning the charges relating to the sale or issue and the repurchase or redemption of units,	– information concerning the charges relating to the sale or issue and the repurchase or redemption of units,
– the means, places and frequency of the publication of those prices.	– the means, places and frequency of the publication of those prices.[1]

1. Investment companies within the meaning of Article 14 (5) of the Directive shall also indicate:
- the method and frequency of calculation of the net asset value of units,
- the means, place and frequency of the publication of that value,
- the stock exchange in the country of marketing the price on which determines the price of transactions effected with stock exchanges in that country.

1.18. Information concerning the manner, amount and calculation of remuneration payable by the unit trust to the management company, the depositary or third parties, and reimbursement of costs by the unit trust to the management company, to the depositary or to third parties.	1.18. Information concerning the manner, amount and calculation of remuneration paid by the company to its directors, and members of the administrative, management and supervisory bodies, to the depositary, or to third parties, and reimbursement of costs by the company to its directors, to the depositary or to third parties.

2. Information concerning the depositary:

2.1. Name or style, form in law, registered office and head office if different from the registered office;

2.2. Main activity.

3. Information concerning the advisory firms or external investment advisers who give advice under contract that is paid for out of the assets of the UCITS:

3.1. Name or style of the firm or name of the adviser;

3.2. Material provisions of the contract with the management company or the investment company that may be relevant to the unit-holders, excluding those relating to remuneration;

3.3. Other significant activities.

4. Information concerning the arrangements for making payments to unit-holders, repurchasing or redeeming units and making available information concerning the UCITS. Such information must in any case be given in the Member State in which the UCITS is situated. In addition, where units are marketed in another

Member State, such information shall be given in respect of that Member State in the prospectus published there.

[5. Other investment information

5.1. Historical performance of the unit trust/common fund or of the investment company (where applicable)—such information may be either included in or attached to the prospectus;

5.2. Profile of the typical investor for whom the unit trust/common fund or the investment company is designed.

6. Economic information

6.1. Possible expenses or fees, other than the charges mentioned in paragraph 1.17, distinguishing between those to be paid by the unit-holder and those to be paid out of the unit trust's/common fund's or of the investment company's assets.]

Schedule B

I. *Statement of assets and liabilities:*
– transferable securities,
– debt instruments of the type referred to in Article 19 (2) (b),
– bank balances,
– other assets,
– total assets,
– liabilities,
– net asset value.

II. *Number of units in circulation*

III. *Net asset value per unit*

IV. *Portfolio, distinguishing between:*

(a) transferable securities admitted to official stock exchange listing;

(b) transferable securities dealt in on another regulated market;

(c) recently issued transferable securities of the type referred to in Article 19 (1) (d);

(d) other transferable securities of the type referred to in Article 19 (2) (a);

(e) debt instruments treated as equivalent in accordance with Article 19 (2) (b);

and analysed in accordance with the most appropriate criteria in the light of the investment policy of the UCITS (e.g. in accordance with economic, geographical or currency criteria) as a percentage of net assets; for each of the above investments the proportion it represents of the total assets of the UCITS should be stated.

Statement of changes in the composition of the portfolio during the reference period.

V. *Statement of the developments concerning the assets of the UCITS during the reference period including the following:*
– income from investments,
– other income,
– management charges,
– depositary's charges,
– other charges and taxes,
– net income,
– distributions and income reinvested,
– changes in capital account,
– appreciation or depreciation of investments,
– any other changes affecting the assets and liabilities of the UCITS.

VI. *A comparative table covering the last three financial years and including, for each financial year, at the end of the financial year:*
– the total net asset value,
– the net asset value per unit.

VII. *Details, by category of transaction within the meaning of Article 21 carried out by the UCITS during the reference period, of the resulting amount of commitments.*

[Schedule C
Contents of the Simplified Prospectus

Brief presentation of the UCITS
– when the unit trust/common fund or the investment company was created and indication of the Member State where the unit trust/common fund or the investment company has been registered/incorporated,

- in the case of UCITS having different investment compartments, the indication of this circumstance,
- management company (when applicable),
- expected period of existence (when applicable),
- depositary,
- auditors,
- financial group (e.g. a bank) promoting the UCITS.

Investment information
- short definition of the UCITS' objectives,
- the unit trust's/common fund's or the investment company's investment policy and a brief assessment of the fund's risk profile (including, if applicable, information according to Article 24a and by investment compartment),
- historical performance of the unit trust/common fund/investment company (where applicable) and a warning that this is not an indicator of future performance—such information may be either included in or attached to the prospectus,
- profile of the typical investor the unit trust/common fund or the investment company is designed for.

Economic information
- tax regime,
- entry and exit commissions,
- other possible expenses or fees, distinguishing between those to be paid by the unit-holder and those to be paid out of the unit trust's/common fund's or the investment company's assets.

Commercial information
- how to buy the units,
- how to sell the units,
- in the case of UCITS having different investment compartments how to pass from one investment compartment into another and the charges applicable in such cases,
- when and how dividends on units or shares of the UCITS (if applicable) are distributed,
- frequency and where/how prices are published or made available.

Additional information
- statement that, on request, the full prospectus, the annual and half-yearly reports may be obtained free of charge before the conclusion of the contract and afterwards,
- competent authority,
- indication of a contact point (person/department, timing, etc.) where additional explanations may be obtained if needed,
- publishing date of the prospectus.]

¶ *The Annex has been renumbered by article 1(18) of Directive 2001/107/EC, reproduced infra under no. S. 21.*
¶ *Schedule A has been amended by article 1(19) of Directive 2001/107/EC, reproduced infra under no. S. 21.*
¶ *Schedule C has been added by article 1(20) of Directive 2001/107/EC, reproduced infra under no. S. 21.*

[Annex II

Functions included in the activity of collective portfolio management:
- Investment management.
- Administration:

(a) legal and fund management accounting services;

(b) customer inquiries;

(c) valuation and pricing (including tax returns);

(d) regulatory compliance monitoring;

(e) maintenance of unit-holder register;

(f) distribution of income;

(g) unit issues and redemptions;

(h) contract settlements (including certificate dispatch);

(i) record keeping.
- Marketing.]

¶ *Annex II has been added by article 1(21) of Directive 2001/107/EC, reproduced infra under no. S. 21.*

S. 7.

Council Recommendation 85/612/EEC of 20 December 1985 concerning the second subparagraph of Article 25 (1) of Directive 85/611/EEC[1]

THE COUNCIL OF THE EUROPEAN COMMUNITIES,

1. HEREBY RECOMMENDS

that each time the concept of 'significant influence' for the purposes of Article 25 (1) of Directive 85/611/EEC[2] is represented in another Member State's legislation by a numerical limit, the Member State's competent authorities should ensure, if so requested by that other Member State, that such limits are observed by investment and management companies situated within its territory when they acquire shares carrying voting rights issued by a company established within the territory of a Member State where such limits apply. With a view to implementing this recommendation, the Member States in which such limits apply when that Directive is published should communicate them to the Commission, which in turn will inform the other Member States; the same applies to any subsequent relaxation of those limits.

2. HEREBY INVITES

the competent authorities to collaborate closely with each other, in accordance with Article 50 of that Directive, to implement this recommendation.

---

[1] OJ L 375, 31.12.1985, 19.
[2] OJ L 375, 31.12.1985, 3, reproduced supra under no. S. 6.

S. 8.
Council Directive 87/345/EEC
of 22 June 1987
amending Directive 80/390/EEC co-ordinating the requirements for the drawing-up, scrutiny and distribution of the listing particulars to be published for the admission of securities to official stock exchange listing

This Directive has been repealed as from 26 July 2001 by Article 111 of Directive 2001/34/EC (OJ L 184, 6.7.2001, 1), reproduced infra under no. S. 18.

S. 9.
Council Directive 88/220/EEC
of 22 March 1988
amending, as regards the investment policies of certain UCITS, Directive 85/611/EEC on the co-ordination of laws, regulations and administrative provisions relating to undertakings for collective investments in transferable securities (UCITS)[1]

THE COUNCIL OF THE EUROPEAN COMMUNITIES,

Having regard to the Treaty establishing the European Economic Community, and in particular the third sentence of Article [47(2)][2] thereof,

Having regard to the proposal from the Commission,[3]

In co-operation with the European Parliament,[4]

Having regard to the opinion of the Economic and Social Committee,[5]

Whereas Article 22 (1) and (2) of Directive 85/611/EEC[6] limits the investment of UCITS assets in transferable securities from the same issuer to 5%, a limit which may, if required, be increased to 10%;

Whereas that limit poses special problems for UCITS established in Denmark in cases where they wish to invest an appreciable proportion of their assets on the domestic bond market, since that market is dominated by mortgage credit bonds and the number of institutions issuing such bonds is very small;

Whereas those mortgage credit bonds are subject in Denmark to special rules and supervision designed to protect holders and are treated under Danish legislation as equivalent to bonds issued or guaranteed by the State;

Whereas Article 22 (3) of Directive 85/611/EEC derogates from paragraphs 1 and 2 of that Article in the case of bonds issued or guaranteed by a Member State and authorises UCITS to invest in particular up to 35% of their assets in such bonds;

Whereas a similar derogation, but of a more limited extent is justified with regard to private sector bonds which, even in the absence of a State guarantee, nevertheless offer special guarantees to the investor under the specific rules applicable thereto; whereas it is necessary therefore to extend such a derogation to the totality of such bonds which fulfil jointly fixed criteria, while leaving it to the Member States to draw up the list of bonds to which they intend, where appropriate, to grant a derogation, and providing for a procedure for informing the other Member States identical to that provided for in Article 20 of Directive 85/611/EEC,

HAS ADOPTED THIS DIRECTIVE:

[...]

¶ *This Directive modifies Directive 85/611/EEC, reproduced supra under no. S. 6. The modifications are directly incorporated therein.*

---

[1] OJ L 100, 19.4.1988, 31–32.
[2] The number between brackets has been changed as from 1 May 1999 by article 12 of the Treaty of Amsterdam.
[3] OJ C 155, 21.6.1986, 4.
[4] Opinion published in OJ C 125, 11.5.1987, 162 and OJ C 68, 14.3.1988, 54.
[5] OJ C 333, 29.12.1986, 10.
[6] OJ L 375, 31.12.1985, 3, reproduced supra under no. S. 6.

S. 10.

Council Directive 88/627/EEC
of 12 December 1988
on the information to be published when a major holding in a listed company is acquired or disposed of[1]

This Directive has been repealed as from 26 July 2001 by article 111 of Directive 2001/34/EC (OJ L 184, 6.7.2001, 1), reproduced infra under no. S. 18.

Correlation Table

Directive 88/627/EEC	Directive 2001/34/EC
Article 1(1), (2) and (3)	Article 85
Article 2	Article 86
Article 8	Article 87
Article 3	Article 88
Article 4(1), 1st subparagraph, introductory phrase	Article 89(1), 1st subparagraph, introductory phrase
Article 4(1), 1st subparagraph, 1st and 2nd indents	Article 89(1), 1st subparagraph (a) and (b)
Article 4(1), 2nd and 3rd subparagraphs	Article 89(1), 2nd and 3rd subparagraphs
Article 4(2)	Article 89(2)
Article 5	Article 90
Article 10(1)	Article 91
Article 7, 1st subparagraph, introductory phrase	Article 92, 1st subparagraph, introductory phrase
Article 7, 1st subparagraph, 1st to 8th indents	Article 92, 1st subparagraph (a) and (h)
Article 7, 2nd subparagraph	Article 92, 2nd subparagraph
Article 6	Article 93
Article 9	Article 94
Article 11	Article 95
Article 13	Article 96
Article 15	Article 97
Article 10(2), 1st subparagraph	Article 102(1), 1st subparagraph
Article 10(2), 2nd subparagraph	Article 103
Article 12(1) and (2)	Article 105(1) and (2)
Article 12(3)	Article 106
Article 14(1) and (2)	Article 107(1) and (2)

---

[1] OJ L 348, 17.12.1988, 62–65.

Directive 88/627/EEC	Directive 2001/34/EC
Article 14(3)	Article 107(3) 2nd subparagraph
Article 16(1)(a)	Article 108(2), 1st subparagraph, point (b)
Article 16(1)(b)	Article 108(2), 1st subparagraph, point (c) (iii)
Article 16(1)(c)	Article 108(2), 1st subparagraph, point (d)
Article 17(2)	Article 110

S. 11.

Council Directive 89/298/EEC
of 17 April 1989
co-ordinating the requirements for the drawing-up, scrutiny and distribution of the prospectus to be published when transferable securities are offered to the public[1]

This Directive has been repealed as from 1 July 2005 by article 28 of Directive 2003/71/EC, reproduced infra under no. S. 25.

---

[1] OJ L 124, 5.5.1989, 8–15.

S. 12.

Council Directive 89/592/EEC
of 13 November 1989
co-ordinating regulations on insider dealing[1]

This Directive has been repealed as from 12 April 2003 by article 20 of Directive 2003/6/EC, reproduced infra under no. S. 24.

---

[1] OJ L 334, 18.11.1989, 30–32.

S. 13.
Council Directive 90/211/EEC
of 23 April 1990
amending Directive 80/390/EEC in respect of the mutual recognition of public-offer prospectuses as stock exchange listing particulars

This Directive has been repealed as from 26 July 2001 by Article 111 of Directive 2001/34/EC (OJ L 184, 6.7.2001, 1), reproduced infra under no. S. 18.

S. 14.
Council Directive 93/22/EEC
of 10 May 1993
on investment services in the securities field[1]

This Directive has been repealed as from [1 November 2007] by article 69 of Directive 2004/39/EC of 21 April 2004 on markets in financial instruments, reproduced infra under no. S. 29. References to Directive 93/22/EEC shall be construed as references to Directive 2004/39/EC. References to terms defined in, or Articles of, Directive 93/22/EEC shall be construed as references to the equivalent term defined in, or Article of, Directive 2004/39/EC.

¶ *The date of repealment has been replaced by Directive 2006/31/EC, reproduced infra under no. S. 32.*

---

[1] OJ L 141, 11.6.1993, 27–46.

S. 15.

**European Parliament and Council Directive 94/18/EC
of 30 May 1994
amending Directive 80/390/EEC co-ordinating the requirements for the drawing up, scrutiny and distribution of the listing particulars to be published for the admission of securities to official stock-exchange listing, with regard to the obligation to publish listing particulars**

This Directive has been repealed as from 26 July 2001 by Article 111 of Directive 2001/34/EC (OJ L 184, 6.7.2001, 1), reproduced infra under no. S. 18.

S. 16.

European Parliament and Council Directive 97/9/EC of 3 March 1997 on investor-compensation schemes[1]

THE EUROPEAN PARLIAMENT AND THE COUNCIL OF THE EUROPEAN UNION,

Having regard to the Treaty establishing the European Community, and in particular Article [47(2)][2] thereof,

Having regard to the proposal from the Commission,[3]

Having regard to the opinion of the Economic and Social Committee,[4]

Having regard to the opinion of the European Monetary Institute,[5]

Acting in accordance with the procedure laid down in Article [251][2] of the Treaty[6] in the light of the joint text approved by the Conciliation Committee on 18 December 1996,

(1) Whereas on 10 May 1993 the Council adopted Directive 93/22/EEC on investment services in the securities field;[7] whereas that Directive is an essential instrument for the achievement of the internal market for investment firms;

(2) Whereas Directive 93/22/EEC lays down prudential rules which investment firms must observe at all times, including rules the purpose of which is to protect as far as possible investors' rights in respect of money or instruments belonging to them;

(3) Whereas, however, no system of supervision can provide complete protection, particularly where acts of fraud are committed;

(4) Whereas the protection of investors and the maintenance of confidence in the financial system are an important aspect of the completion and proper functioning of the internal market in this area; whereas to that end it is therefore essential that each Member State should have an investor-compensation scheme that guarantees a harmonised minimum level of protection at least for the small investor in the event of an investment firm being unable to meet its obligations to its investor clients;

(5) Whereas small investors will therefore be able to purchase investment services from branches of Community investment firms or on the basis of the cross-border provision of services as confidently as from domestic investment firms, in the knowledge that a harmonised minimum level of protection would be available to them in the event of an investment firm being unable to meet its obligations to its investor clients;

(6) Whereas, in the absence of such minimum harmonisation, a host Member State might consider itself justified, by considerations of investor protection, in requiring membership of its compensation scheme when a Community investment firm operating through a branch or under the freedom to provide services either belonged to no investor-compensation scheme in its home Member State or belonged to a scheme which was not regarded as offering equivalent protection; whereas such a requirement might prejudice the operation of the internal market;

---

[1] OJ L 84, 26.3.1997, 22–31.
[2] The number between brackets has been changed as from 1 May 1999 by article 12 of the Treaty of Amsterdam.
[3] OJ C 321, 27.11.1993, 15 and OJ C 382, 31.12.1994, 27.
[4] OJ C 127, 7.5.1994, 1.
[5] Opinion delivered on 28 July 1995.
[6] European Parliament opinion of 19 April 1994 (OJ C 128, 9.5.1994, 85), Council common position of 23 October 1995 (OJ C 320, 30.11.1995, 9) and European Parliament Decision of 12 March 1996 (OJ C 96, 1. 4. 1996, 28). Decision of the Council of 17 February 1997 and Decision of the European Parliament of 19 February 1997 (OJ C 85, 17.3.1997).
[7] OJ L 141, 11.6.1993, 27, reproduced supra under no. S. 14, which has been repealed by Directive 2004/39/EC, reproduced infra under no. S. 29.

(7) Whereas although most Member States currently have some investor-compensation arrangements those arrangements do not in general cover all investment firms that hold the single authorisation provided for in Directive 93/22/EEC;

(8) Whereas, therefore, every Member State should be required to have an investor-compensation scheme or schemes to which every such investment firm would belong; whereas each scheme must cover money and instruments held by an investment firm in connection with an investor's investment operations which, where an investment firm is unable to meet its obligations to its investor clients, cannot be returned to the investor; whereas this is entirely without prejudice to the rules and procedures applicable in each Member State as regards the decisions to be taken in the event of the insolvency or winding-up of an investment firm;

(9) Whereas the definition of investment firm includes credit institutions which are authorised to provide investment services; whereas every such credit institution must also be required to belong to an investor-compensation scheme to cover its investment business; whereas, however, it is not necessary to require such a credit institution to belong to two separate schemes where a single scheme meets the requirements both of this Directive and of Directive 94/19/EC of the European Parliament and of the Council of 30 May 1994 on deposit-guarantee schemes;[8] whereas, however, in the case of investment firms which are credit institutions it may in certain cases be difficult to distinguish between deposits covered by Directive 94/19/EC and money held in connection with investment business; whereas Member States should be allowed to determine which Directive shall apply to such claims;

(10) Whereas Directive 94/19/EC allows a Member State to exempt a credit institution from the obligation to belong to a deposit-guarantee scheme where that credit institution belongs to a system which protects the credit institution itself and, in particular, ensures its solvency; whereas, where a credit institution belonging to such a system is also an investment firm, a Member State should also be allowed, subject to certain conditions, to exempt it from the obligation to belong to an investor-compensation scheme;

(11) Whereas a harmonised minimum level of compensation of ECU 20 000 for each investor should be sufficient to protect the interests of the small investor where an investment firm is unable to meet its obligations to its investor clients; whereas it would therefore appear reasonable to set the harmonised minimum level of compensation at ECU 20 000; whereas, as in Directive 94/19/EC, limited transitional provisions might be required to enable compensation schemes to comply with that figure since this applies equally to Member States which, when this Directive is adopted, do not have any such scheme;

(12) Whereas the same figure was adopted in Directive 94/19/EC;

(13) Whereas in order to encourage investors to take due care in their choice of investment firms it is reasonable to allow Member States to require investors to bear a proportion of any loss; whereas, however, an investor must be covered for at least 90% of any loss as long as the compensation paid is less than the Community minimum;

(14) Whereas certain Member States' schemes offer levels of cover higher than the harmonised minimum level of protection under this Directive; whereas, however, it does not seem desirable to require any change in those schemes in that respect;

(15) Whereas the retention in the Community of schemes providing levels of cover higher than the harmonised minimum may, within the same territory, lead to disparities in compensation and unequal conditions of competition between national investment firms and branches of firms from other Member States; whereas, in order to counteract those disadvantages, branches should be authorised to join their host countries' schemes so that they may offer their investors the same cover as is provided by the schemes of the countries in which they are located; whereas it is appropriate that, in its report on the application

---

[8] OJ L 135, 31.5.1994, 5, reproduced supra under no. B. 22.

of this Directive, the Commission should indicate the extent to which branches have exercised that option and any difficulties which they or the investor-compensation schemes may have encountered in implementing those provisions; whereas the possibility that home Member States' schemes should themselves offer such supplementary cover, subject to the conditions such schemes may lay down, is not ruled out;

(16) Whereas market disturbances could be caused by branches of investment firms established in Member States other than their Member States of origin which offer levels of cover higher than those offered by investment firms authorised in their host Member States; whereas it is not appropriate that the level or scope of cover offered by compensation schemes should become an instrument of competition; whereas it is therefore necessary, at least during an initial period, to stipulate that neither the level nor the scope of cover offered by a home Member State's scheme to investors at branches located in another Member State should exceed the maximum level or scope offered by the corresponding scheme in the host Member State; whereas any market disturbances should be reviewed at an early date, on the basis of the experience acquired and in the light of developments in the financial sector;

(17) Whereas a Member State must be able to exclude certain categories of specifically listed investments or investors, if it does not consider that they need special protection, from the cover afforded by investor-compensation schemes;

(18) Whereas some Member States have investor-compensation schemes under the responsibility of professional organisations; whereas in other Member States there are schemes that have been set up and are regulated on a statutory basis; whereas that diversity of status poses a problem only with regard to compulsory membership of and exclusion from schemes; whereas it is therefore necessary to take steps to limit the powers of schemes in that area;

(19) Whereas the investor must be compensated without excessive delay once the validity of his claim has been established; whereas the compensation scheme itself must be able to fix a reasonable period for the presentation of claims; whereas, however, the fact that such a period has expired may not be invoked against an investor who for good reason has not been able to present his claim within the time allowed;

(20) Whereas informing investors of compensation arrangements is an essential element of investor protection; whereas Article 12 of Directive 93/22/EEC required investment firms to inform investors, before doing business with them, of the possible application of a compensation scheme; whereas, therefore, this Directive should lay down rules on informing such intending investors regarding the compensation schemes covering their investment business;

(21) Whereas, however, the unregulated use in advertising of references to the amount and scope of a compensation scheme could affect the stability of the financial system or investor confidence; whereas Member States should therefore lay down rules to limit such references;

(22) Whereas in principle this Directive requires every investment firm to join an investor-compensation scheme; whereas the Directives governing the admission of any investment firm the head office of which is in a non-member country, and in particular Directive 93/22/EEC, allow Member States to decide whether and subject to what conditions to permit branches of such investment firms to operate within their territories; whereas such branches will not enjoy the freedom to provide services under the second paragraph of Article [49][2] of the Treaty, or the right of establishment in Member States other than those in which they are established; whereas, accordingly, a Member State admitting such branches must decide how to apply the principles of this Directive to such branches in accordance with Article 5 of Directive 93/22/EEC and with the need to protect investors and maintain the integrity of the financial system; whereas it is essential that investors at such branches should be fully aware of the compensation arrangements applicable to them;

(23) Whereas it is not indispensable in this Directive to harmonise the ways in which investor-compensation schemes are to be financed given,

on the one hand, that the cost of financing such schemes must, in principle, be borne by investment firms themselves and, on the other hand, that the financing capacities of such schemes must be in proportion to their liabilities; whereas that must not, however, jeopardise the stability of the financial system of the Member State concerned;

(24) Whereas this Directive may not result in the Member States or their competent authorities being made liable in respect of investors if they have ensured that one or more schemes for the compensation or protection of investors under the conditions prescribed in this Directive have been introduced and officially recognised;

(25) Whereas, in conclusion, a minimum degree of harmonisation of investor-compensation arrangements is necessary for the completion of the internal market for investment firms since it will make it possible for investors to do business with such firms with greater confidence, especially firms from other Member States, and make it possible to avoid any difficulties caused by host Member States applying national investor-protection rules that are not co-ordinated at Community level; whereas a binding Community Directive is the only appropriate instrument for the achievement of the desired objective in the general absence of investor-compensation arrangements corresponding to the coverage of Directive 93/22/EEC; whereas this Directive effects only the minimum harmonisation required, allows Member States to prescribe wider or higher coverage if they desire and gives Member States the necessary latitude as regards the organisation and financing of investor-compensation schemes,

HAVE ADOPTED THIS DIRECTIVE:

Article 1

For the purposes of this Directive:

1. 'investment firm' shall mean an investment firm as defined in Article 1 (2) of Directive 93/22/EEC
 – authorised in accordance with Article 3 of Directive 93/22/EEC,
 or

 – authorised as a credit institution in accordance with Council Directive 77/780/EEC[9] and Council Directive 89/646/EEC,[10] the authorisation of which covers one or more of the investment services listed in Section A of the Annex to Directive 93/22/EEC;

2. 'investment business' shall mean any investment service as defined in Article 1 (1) of Directive 93/22/EEC and the service referred to in point 1 of Section C of the Annex to that Directive,

3. 'instruments' shall mean the instruments listed in Section B of the Annex to Directive 93/22/EEC;

4. 'investor' shall mean any person who has entrusted money or instruments to an investment firm in connection with investment business;

5. 'branch' shall mean a place of business which is a part of an investment firm, which has no legal personality and which provides investment services for which the investment firm has been authorised; all the places of business set up in the same Member State by an investment firm with headquarters in another Member State shall be regarded as a single branch;

6. 'joint investment business' shall mean investment business carried out for the account of two or more persons or over which two or more persons have rights that may be exercised by means of the signature of one or more of those persons;

7. 'competent authorities' shall mean the authorities defined in Article 22 of Directive 93/22/EEC; those authorities may, if appropriate, be

---

[9] First Council Directive 77/780/EEC of 12 December 1977 on the co-ordination of laws, regulations and administrative provisions relating to the taking up and pursuit of the business of credit institutions (OJ L 322, 17.12.1977, 30), First Banking Directive, Directive as last amended by Directive 89/646/EEC (OJ L 386, 30.12.1989, 1), Second Banking Directive, consolidated in Directive 2000/12/EC (OJ L 126, 26.5.2000, 1), reproduced supra under no. B. 32.
[10] Second Council Directive 89/646/EEC of 15 December 1989 on the co-ordination of laws, regulations and administrative provisions relating to the taking up and pursuit of the business of credit institutions and amending Directive 77/780/EEC (OJ L 386, 30.12.1989, 1), Second Banking Directive, Directive as last amended by Directive 92/30/EEC (OJ L 110, 28.4.1992, 52), consolidated in Directive 2000/12/EC, reproduced infra under no. B. 32.

those defined in Article 1 of Council Directive 92/30/EEC of 6 April 1992 on the supervision of credit institutions on a consolidated basis.[11]

Article 2

1. Each Member State shall ensure that within its territory one or more investor-compensation schemes are introduced and officially recognised. Except in the circumstances envisaged in the second subparagraph and in Article 5 (3), no investment firm authorised in that Member State may carry on investment business unless it belongs to such a scheme.

A Member State may, however, exempt a credit institution to which this Directive applies from the obligation to belong to an investor-compensation scheme where that credit institution is already exempt under Article 3 (1) of Directive 94/19/EC from the obligation to belong to a deposit-guarantee scheme, provided that the protection and information given to depositors are also given to investors on the same terms and investors thus enjoy protection at least equivalent to that afforded by an investor-compensation scheme.

Any Member State that avails itself of that option shall inform the Commission accordingly; it shall, in particular, disclose the characteristics of the protective systems in question and the credit institutions covered by them for the purposes of this Directive, as well as any subsequent changes to the information supplied. The Commission shall inform the Council thereof.

2. A scheme shall provide cover for investors in accordance with Article 4 where either:
— the competent authorities have determined that in their view an instrument firm appears, for the time being, for reasons directly related to its financial circumstances, to be unable to meet its obligations arising out of investors' claims and has no early prospect of being able to do so,
or

— a judicial authority has made a ruling, for reasons directly related to an investment firm's financial circumstances, which has the effect of suspending investors' ability to make claims against it,
whichever is the earlier.

Cover shall be provided for claims arising out of an investment firm's inability to:
— repay money owed to or belonging to investors and held on their behalf in connection with investment business,
or
— return to investors any instruments belonging to them and held, administered or managed on their behalf in connection with investment business,
in accordance with the legal and contractual conditions applicable.

3. Any claim under paragraph 2 on a credit institution which, in a given Member State, would be subject both to this Directive and to Directive 94/19/EC shall be directed by that Member State to a scheme under one or other of those Directives as that Member State shall consider appropriate. No claim shall be eligible for compensation more than once under those Directives.

4. The amount of an investor's claim shall be calculated in accordance with the legal and contractual conditions, in particular those concerning set off and counterclaims, that are applicable to the assessment, on the date of the determination or ruling referred to in paragraph 2, of the amount of the money or the value, determined where possible by reference to the market value, of the instruments belonging to the investor which the investment firm is unable to repay or return.

Article 3

Claims arising out of transactions in connection with which a criminal conviction has been obtained for money laundering, as defined in Article 1 of Council Directive 91/308/EEC of 10 June 1991 on prevention of the use of the financial system for the purpose of money laundering,[12] shall be excluded from any compensation under investor-compensation schemes.

---

[11] OJ L 110, 28.4.1992, 52, consolidated in Directive 2000/12/EC, reproduced supra under no. B. 32.

[12] OJ L 166, 28.6.1991, 77, reproduced supra under no. B. 15.

Article 4

1. Member States shall ensure that schemes provide for cover of not less than ECU 20 000 for each investor in respect of the claims referred to in Article 2 (2).

Until 31 December 1999 Member States in which, when this Directive is adopted, cover is less than ECU 20 000 may retain that lower level of cover, provided it is not less than ECU 15 000. That option shall also be available to Member States to which the transitional provisions of the second subparagraph of Article 7 (1) of Directive 94/19/EC apply.

2. A Member State may provide that certain investors shall be excluded from cover by schemes or shall be granted a lower level of cover. Those exclusions shall be as listed in Annex I.

3. This Article shall not preclude the retention or adoption of provisions which afford greater or more comprehensive cover to investors.

4. A Member State may limit the cover provided for in paragraph 1 or that referred to in paragraph 3 to a specified percentage of an investor's claim. The percentage covered must, however, be equal to or exceed 90% of the claim as long as the amount to be paid under the scheme is less than ECU 20 000.

Article 5

1. If an investment firm required by Article 2 (1) to belong to a scheme does not meet the obligations incumbent on it as a member of that scheme, the competent authorities which issued its authorisation shall be notified and, in co-operation with the compensation scheme, shall take all measures appropriate, including the imposition of penalties, to ensure that the investment firm meets its obligations.

2. If those measures fail to secure compliance on the part of the investment firm, the scheme may, where national law permits the exclusion of a member, with the express consent of the competent authorities, give not less than 12 months' notice of its intention of excluding the investment firm from membership of the scheme. The scheme shall continue to provide cover under the second subparagraph of Article 2 (2) in respect of investment business transacted during that period. If, on expiry of the period of notice, the investment firm has not met its obligations, the compensation scheme may, again having obtained the express consent of the competent authorities, exclude it.

3. Where national law permits, and with the express consent of the competent authorities which issued its authorisation, an investment firm excluded from an investor-compensation scheme may continue to provide investment services if, before its exclusion, it made alternative compensation arrangements which ensure that investors will enjoy cover that is at least equivalent to that offered by the officially recognised scheme and has characteristics equivalent to those of that scheme.

4. If an investment firm the exclusion of which is proposed under paragraph 2 is unable to make alternative arrangements which comply with the conditions imposed in paragraph 3, the competent authorities which issued its authorisation shall withdraw it forthwith.

Article 6

After the withdrawal of an investment firm's authorisation, cover under the second subparagraph of Article 2 (2) shall continue to be provided in respect of investment business transacted up to the time of that withdrawal.

Article 7

1. Investor-compensation schemes introduced and officially recognised in a Member State in accordance with Article 2 (1) shall also cover investors at branches set up by investment firms in other Member States.

Until 31 December 1999, neither the level nor the scope, including the percentage, of the cover provided for may exceed the maximum level or scope of the cover offered by the corresponding compensation scheme within the territory of the host Member State. Before that date the Commission shall draw up a report on the basis of the experience acquired in applying this subparagraph and Article 4 (1) of Directive 94/19/EC referred to above and shall consider the need to continue those provisions. If appropriate, the Commission shall submit a proposal for a Directive to the European Parliament and the Council, with a view to the extension of their validity.

Where the level or scope, including the percentage, of the cover offered by the host Member State's investor-compensation scheme exceeds the level or scope of the cover provided in the Member State in which an investment firm is authorised, the host Member State shall ensure that there is an officially recognised scheme within its territory which a branch may join voluntarily in order to supplement the cover which its investors already enjoy by virtue of its membership of its home Member State's scheme.

If a branch joins such a scheme, that scheme shall be one that covers the category of institution to which the branch belongs or most closely corresponds in its host Member State.

Member States shall ensure that objective and generally applied conditions are established concerning branches' membership of all investor-compensation schemes. Admission shall be conditional on a branch meeting the relevant membership obligations, including in particular the payment of all contributions and other charges. Member States shall follow the guiding principles set out in Annex II in implementing this paragraph.

2. If a branch which has exercised the option of voluntary membership under paragraph 1 does not meet the obligations incumbent on it as a member of an investor-compensation scheme, the competent authorities which issued its authorisation shall be notified and, in co-operation with the compensation scheme, shall take all measures necessary to ensure that the branch meets the aforementioned obligations.

If those measures fail to ensure that the branch meets the obligations referred to in this Article, after an appropriate period of notice of not less than 12 months the compensation scheme may, with the consent of the competent authorities

which issued the authorisation, exclude the branch. Investment business transacted before the date of exclusion shall continue to be covered after that date by the compensation scheme of which the branch was a voluntary member. Investors shall be informed of the withdrawal of the supplementary cover and of the date on which it takes effect.

Article 8

1. The cover provided for in Article 4 (1), (3) and (4) shall apply to the investor's aggregate claim on the same investment firm under this Directive irrespective of the number of accounts, the currency and location within the Community.

Member States may, however, provide that funds in currencies other than those of the Member States and the ecu shall be excluded from cover or be subject to lower cover. This option shall not apply to instruments.

2. Each investor's share in joint investment business shall be taken into account in calculating the cover provided for in Article 4 (1), (3) and (4).

In the absence of special provisions, claims shall be divided equally amongst investors.

Member States may provide that claims relating to joint investment business to which two or more persons are entitled as members of a business partnership, association or grouping of a similar nature which has no legal personality may, for the purpose of calculating the limits provided for in Article 4 (1), (3) and (4), be aggregated and treated as if arising from an investment made by a single investor.

3. Where an investor is not absolutely entitled to the sums or securities held, the person who is absolutely entitled shall receive the compensation, provided that that person has been or can be identified before the date of the determination or ruling referred to in Article 2 (2).

If two or more persons are absolutely entitled, the share of each under the arrangements subject to which the sums or the securities are managed shall be taken into account when the limits laid down in Article 4 (1), (3) and (4) are calculated.

This provision shall not apply to collective-investment undertakings.

Article 9

1. The compensation scheme shall take appropriate measures to inform investors of the determination or ruling referred to in Article 2 (2) and, if they are to be compensated, to compensate them as soon as possible. It may fix a period during which investors shall be required to submit their claims. That period may not be less than five months from the date of the aforementioned determination or ruling or from the date on which that determination or ruling is made public.

The fact that that period has expired may not, however, be invoked by the scheme to deny cover to an investor who has been unable to assert his right to compensation in time.

2. The scheme shall be in a position to pay an investor's claim as soon as possible and at the latest within three months of the establishment of the eligibility and the amount of the claim.

In wholly exceptional circumstances and in special cases a compensation scheme may apply to the competent authorities for an extension of the time limit. No such extension may exceed three months.

3. Notwithstanding the time limit laid down in paragraph 2, where an investor or any other person entitled to or having an interest in investment business has been charged with an offence arising out of or in relation to money laundering as defined in Article 1 of Directive 91/308/EEC, the compensation scheme may suspend any payment pending the judgment of the court.

Article 10

1. Member States shall ensure that each investment firm takes appropriate measures to make available to actual and intending investors the information necessary for the identification of the investor-compensation scheme of which the investment firm and its branches within the Community are members or any alternative arrangement provided for under the second subparagraph of Article 2 (1) or Article 5 (3).

Investors shall be informed of the provisions of the investor-compensation scheme or any alternative arrangement applicable, including the amount and scope of the cover offered by the compensation scheme and any rules laid down by the Member States pursuant to Article 2 (3). That information shall be made available in a readily comprehensible manner.

Information shall also be given on request concerning the conditions governing compensation and the formalities which must be completed to obtain compensation.

2. The information provided for in paragraph 1 shall be made available in the manner prescribed by national law in the official language or languages of the Member State in which a branch is established.

3. Member States shall establish rules limiting the use in advertising of the information referred to in paragraph 1 in order to prevent such use from affecting the stability of the financial system or investor confidence. In particular, a Member State may restrict such advertising to a factual reference to the scheme to which an investment firm belongs.

Article 11

1. Each Member State shall check whether branches established by an investment firm the head office of which is outwith the Community have cover equivalent to that prescribed in this Directive. Failing such cover, a Member State may, subject to Article 5 of Directive 93/22/EEC, stipulate that branches established by an investment firm the head office of which is outwith the Community shall join investor-compensation schemes in operation within its territory.

2. Actual and intending investors at branches established by an investment firm the head office of which is outwith the Community shall be provided by that investment firm with all relevant information concerning the compensation arrangements which cover their investments.

3. The information provided for in paragraph 2 shall be made available in the manner prescribed by national law in the official language or languages of the Member State in which a branch is

established and shall be drafted in a clear and comprehensible form.

Article 12

Without prejudice to any other rights which they may have under national law, schemes which make payments in order to compensate investors shall have the right of subrogation to the rights of those investors in liquidation proceedings for amounts equal to their payments.

Article 13

Member States shall ensure that an investor's right to compensation may be the subject of an action by the investor against the compensation scheme.

Article 14

No later than 31 December 1999 the Commission shall submit a report to the European Parliament and to the Council on the application of this Directive together, where appropriate, with proposals for its revision.

Article 15

1. The Member States shall bring into force the laws, regulations and administrative provisions necessary for them to comply with this Directive no later than 26 September 1998. They shall forthwith inform the Commission thereof.

When the Member States adopt those measures, they shall contain references to this Directive or shall be accompanied by such references on the occasion of their official publication. The methods of making such references shall be laid down by the Member States.

2. The Member States shall communicate to the Commission the texts of the main provisions of national law which they adopt in the field covered by this Directive.

Article 16

Article 12 of Directive 93/22/EEC shall be repealed with effect from the date referred to in Article 15 (1).

Article 17

This Directive shall enter into force on the day of its publication in the Official Journal of the European Communities.

Article 18

This Directive is addressed to the Member States.

Annex I

List of exclusions referred to in Article 4 (2)

1. Professional and institutional investors, including:
 – investment firms as defined in Article 1 (2) of Directive 93/22/EEC,
 – credit institutions as defined in the first indent of Article 1 of Council Directive 77/780/EEC,
 – financial institutions as defined in Article 1 (6) of Council Directive 89/646/EEC,
 – insurance undertakings,
 – collective-investment undertakings,
 – pension and retirement funds.

Other professional and institutional investors.

2. Supranational institutions, government and central administrative authorities.

3. Provincial, regional, local and municipal authorities.

4. Directors, managers and personally liable members of investment firms, persons holding 5% or more of the capital of such investment firms, persons responsible for carrying out the statutory audits of investment firms' accounting documents and investors with similar status in other firms within the same group as such a firm.

5. Close relatives and third parties acting on behalf of the investors referred to in point 4.

6. Other firms in the same group.

7. Investors who have any responsibility for or have taken advantage of certain facts relating to an investment firm which gave rise to the firm's financial difficulties or contributed to the deterioration of its financial situation.

8. Companies which are of such a size that they are not permitted to draw up abridged balance sheets under Article 11 of the Fourth Council Directive 78/660/EEC of 25 July 1978 based on Article [44(3)(g)][2] of the Treaty on the annual accounts of certain types of companies.[13]

Annex II

Guiding Principles

(referred to in the fifth subparagraph of Article 7 (1))

Where a branch applies to join a host Member State's scheme for supplementary cover, the host Member State's scheme will bilaterally establish with the home Member State's scheme appropriate rules and procedures for the payment of compensation to investors at that branch. The following principles will apply both to the drawing up of those procedures and in the framing of the membership conditions applicable to that branch (as referred to in Article 7 (1)):

(a) the host Member State's scheme will retain full rights to impose its objective and generally applied rules on participating investment firms; it will be able to require the provision of relevant information and be entitled to verify such information with the home Member State's competent authorities;

(b) the host Member State's scheme will meet claims for supplementary compensation after it has been informed by the home Member State's competent authorities of the determination or ruling referred to in Article 2 (2). The host Member State's scheme will retain full rights to verify an investor's entitlement according to its own standards and procedures before paying supplementary compensation;

(c) the host Member State's and the home Member State's schemes will co-operate fully with each other to ensure that investors receive compensation promptly and in the correct amounts. In particular, they will agree on how the existence of a counterclaim which may give rise to set-off under either scheme will affect the compensation paid to the investor by each scheme;

(d) the host Member State's scheme will be entitled to charge branches for supplementary cover on an appropriate basis which takes into account the cover funded by the home Member State's scheme. To facilitate charging, the host Member State's scheme will be entitled to assume that its liability will in all circumstances be limited to the excess of the cover it has offered over the cover offered by the home Member State regardless of whether the home Member State actually pays any compensation in respect of claims by investors within the host Member State's territory.

---

[13] Fourth Company Directive, OJ L 222, 14.8.1978, 11, reproduced supra under no. C. 4. Directive as last amended by Directive 94/8/EC (OJ L 82, 25.3.1994, 33), reproduced supra under no. C. 14.

S. 17.

European Parliament and Council Directive 98/26/EC
of 19 May 1998
on settlement finality in payment and securities settlement systems[1]

THE EUROPEAN PARLIAMENT AND THE COUNCIL OF THE EUROPEAN UNION,

Having regard to the Treaty establishing the European Community, and in particular Article [95][2] thereof,

Having regard to the proposal from the Commission,[3]

Having regard to the opinion of the European Monetary Institute,[4]

Having regard to the opinion of the Economic and Social Committee,[5]

Acting in accordance with the procedure laid down in Article [251][2] of the Treaty,[6]

(1) Whereas the Lamfalussy report of 1990 to the Governors of the central banks of the Group of Ten Countries demonstrated the important systemic risk inherent in payment systems which operate on the basis of several legal types of payment netting, in particular multilateral netting; whereas the reduction of legal risks associated with participation in real time gross settlement systems is of paramount importance, given the increasing development of these systems;

(2) Whereas it is also of the utmost importance to reduce the risk associated with participation in securities settlement systems, in particular where there is a close connection between such systems and payment systems;

(3) Whereas this Directive aims at contributing to the efficient and cost effective operation of cross-border payment and securities settlement arrangements in the Community, which reinforces the freedom of movement of capital in the internal market; whereas this Directive thereby follows up the progress made towards completion of the internal market, in particular towards the freedom to provide services and liberalisation of capital movements, with a view to the realisation of Economic and Monetary Union;

(4) Whereas it is desirable that the laws of the Member States should aim to minimise the disruption to a system caused by insolvency proceedings against a participant in that system;

(5) Whereas a proposal for a Directive on the reorganisation and winding-up of credit institutions submitted in 1985 and amended on 8 February 1988 is still pending before the Council; whereas the Convention on Insolvency Proceedings drawn up on 23 November 1995 by the Member States meeting within the Council explicitly excludes insurance undertakings, credit institutions and investment firms;

(6) Whereas this Directive is intended to cover payment and securities settlement systems of a domestic as well as of a cross-border nature; whereas the Directive is applicable to Community systems and to collateral security constituted by their participants, be they Community or third country participants, in connection with participation in these systems;

(7) Whereas Member States may apply the provisions of this Directive to their domestic institutions which participate directly in third

---

[1] OJ L 166, 11.6.1998, 45–50.
[2] The number between brackets has been changed as from 1 May 1999 by article 12 of the Treaty of Amsterdam.
[3] OJ C 207, 18.7.1996, 13, and OJ C 259, 26.8.1997, 6.
[4] Opinion delivered on 21 November 1996.
[5] OJ C 56, 24.2.1997, 1.
[6] Opinion of the European Parliament of 9 April 1997 (OJ C 132, 28.4.1997, 74), Council Common Position of 13 October 1997 (OJ C 375, 10.12.1997, 34) and Decision of the European Parliament of 29 January 1998 (OJ C 56, 23.2.1998). Council Decision of 27 April 1998.

country systems and to collateral security provided in connection with participation in such systems;

(8) Whereas Member States should be allowed to designate as a system covered by this Directive a system whose main activity is the settlement of securities even if the system to a limited extent also deals with commodity derivatives;

(9) Whereas the reduction of systemic risk requires in particular the finality of settlement and the enforceability of collateral security; whereas collateral security is meant to comprise all means provided by a participant to the other participants in the payment and/or securities settlement systems to secure rights and obligations in connection with that system, including repurchase agreements, statutory liens and fiduciary transfers; whereas regulation in national law of the kind of collateral security which can be used should not be affected by the definition of collateral security in this Directive;

(10) Whereas this Directive, by covering collateral security provided in connection with operations of the central banks of the Member States functioning as central banks, including monetary policy operations, assists the European Monetary Institute in its task of promoting the efficiency of cross-border payments with a view to the preparation of the third stage of Economic and Monetary Union and thereby contributes to developing the necessary legal framework in which the future European central bank may develop its policy;

(11) Whereas transfer orders and their netting should be legally enforceable under all Member States' jurisdictions and binding on third parties;

(12) Whereas rules on finality of netting should not prevent systems testing, before the netting takes place, whether orders that have entered the system comply with the rules of that system and allow the settlement of that system to take place;

(13) Whereas nothing in this Directive should prevent a participant or a third party from exercising any right or claim resulting from the underlying transaction which they may have in law to recovery or restitution in respect of a transfer order which has entered a system, e.g. in case of fraud or technical error, as long as this leads neither to the unwinding of netting nor to the revocation of the transfer order in the system;

(14) Whereas it is necessary to ensure that transfer orders cannot be revoked after a moment defined by the rules of the system;

(15) Whereas it is necessary that a Member State should immediately notify other Member States of the opening of insolvency proceedings against a participant in the system;

(16) Whereas insolvency proceedings should not have a retroactive effect on the rights and obligations of participants in a system;

(17) Whereas, in the event of insolvency proceedings against a participant in a system, this Directive furthermore aims at determining which insolvency law is applicable to the rights and obligations of that participant in connection with its participation in a system;

(18) Whereas collateral security should be insulated from the effects of the insolvency law applicable to the insolvent participant;

(19) Whereas the provisions of Article 9(2) should only apply to a register, account or centralised deposit system which evidences the existence of proprietary rights in or for the delivery or transfer of the securities concerned;

(20) Whereas the provisions of Article 9(2) are intended to ensure that if the participant, the central bank of a Member State or the future European central bank has a valid and effective collateral security as determined under the law of the Member State where the relevant register, account or centralised deposit system is located, then the validity and enforceability of that collateral security as against that system (and the operator thereof) and against any other person claiming directly or indirectly through it, should be determined solely under the law of that Member State;

(21) Whereas the provisions of Article 9(2) are not intended to prejudice the operation and effect of the law of the Member State under which the securities are constituted or of the law of the Member State where the securities may

otherwise be located (including, without limitation, the law concerning the creation, ownership or transfer of such securities or of rights in such securities) and should not be interpreted to mean that any such collateral security will be directly enforceable or be capable of being recognised in any such Member State otherwise than in accordance with the law of that Member State;

(22) Whereas it is desirable that Member States endeavour to establish sufficient links between all the securities settlement systems covered by this Directive with a view towards promoting maximum transparency and legal certainty of transactions relating to securities;

(23) Whereas the adoption of this Directive constitutes the most appropriate way of realising the abovementioned objectives and does not go beyond what is necessary to achieve them,

HAVE ADOPTED THIS DIRECTIVE:

SECTION I
SCOPE AND DEFINITIONS

Article 1

The provisions of this Directive shall apply to:

(a) any system as defined in Article 2(a), governed by the law of a Member State and operating in any currency, the ecu or in various currencies which the system converts one against another;

(b) any participant in such a system;

(c) collateral security provided in connection with:
– participation in a system, or
– operations of the central banks of the Member States in their functions as central banks.

Article 2

For the purpose of this Directive:

(a) 'system' shall mean a formal arrangement:
– between three or more participants, without counting a possible settlement agent, a possible central counterparty, a possible clearing house or a possible indirect participant, with common rules and standardised arrangements for the execution of transfer orders between the participants,

– governed by the law of a Member State chosen by the participants; the participants may, however, only choose the law of a Member State in which at least one of them has its head office, and

– designated, without prejudice to other more stringent conditions of general application laid down by national law, as a system and notified to the Commission by the Member State whose law is applicable, after that Member State is satisfied as to the adequacy of the rules of the system.

Subject to the conditions in the first subparagraph, a Member State may designate as a system such a formal arrangement whose business consists of the execution of transfer orders as defined in the second indent of (i) and which to a limited extent executes orders relating to other financial instruments, when that Member State considers that such a designation is warranted on grounds of systemic risk.

A Member State may also on a case-by-case basis designate as a system such a formal arrangement between two participants, without counting a possible settlement agent, a possible central counterparty, a possible clearing house or a possible indirect participant, when that Member State considers that such a designation is warranted on grounds of systemic risk;

(b) 'institution' shall mean:
– a credit institution as defined in the first indent of Article 1 of Directive 77/780/EEC[7] including the institutions set out in the list in Article 2(2) thereof, or
– an investment firm as defined in point 2 of Article 1 of Directive 93/22/EEC[8] excluding the institutions set out in the list in Article 2(2)(a) to (k) thereof, or

---

[7] First Banking Directive 77/780/EEC of 12 December 1977 on the co-ordination of the laws, regulations and administrative provisions relating to the taking up and pursuit of the business of credit institutions (OJ L 322, 17.12.1977, 30), reproduced supra under no. B.2. Directive as last amended by Directive 96/13/EC (OJ L 66, 16.3.1996, 15), consolidated in Directive 2000/12/EC, reproduced supra under no. B. 32.

[8] Council Directive 93/22/EEC of 10 May 1993 on investment services in the securities field (OJ L 141, 11.6.1993, 27), reproduced supra under no. S. 14. Directive as last amended by Directive 97/9/EC (OJ L 84, 26.3.1997, 22), reproduced supra under no. S. 16.

– public authorities and publicly guaranteed undertakings, or
– any undertaking whose head office is outside the Community and whose functions correspond to those of the Community credit institutions or investment firms as defined in the first and second indent,

which participates in a system and which is responsible for discharging the financial obligations arising from transfer orders within that system.

If a system is supervised in accordance with national legislation and only executes transfer orders as defined in the second indent of (i), as well as payments resulting from such orders, a Member State may decide that undertakings which participate in such a system and which have responsibility for discharging the financial obligations arising from transfer orders within this system, can be considered institutions, provided that at least three participants of this system are covered by the categories referred to in the first subparagraph and that such a decision is warranted on grounds of systemic risk;

(c) 'central counterparty' shall mean an entity which is interposed between the institutions in a system and which acts as the exclusive counterparty of these institutions with regard to their transfer orders;

(d) 'settlement agent' shall mean an entity providing to institutions and/or a central counterparty participating in systems, settlement accounts through which transfer orders within such systems are settled and, as the case may be, extending credit to those institutions and/or central counterparties for settlement purposes;

(e) 'clearing house' shall mean an entity responsible for the calculation of the net positions of institutions, a possible central counterparty and/or a possible settlement agent;

(f) 'participant' shall mean an institution, a central counterparty, a settlement agent or a clearing house.

According to the rules of the system, the same participant may act as a central counterparty, settlement agent or a clearing house or carry out part or all of these tasks.

A Member State may decide that for the purposes of this Directive an indirect participant may be considered a participant if it is warranted on the grounds of systemic risk and on condition that the indirect participant is known to the system;

(g) 'indirect participant' shall mean a credit institution as defined in the first indent of (b) with a contractual relationship with an institution participating in a system executing transfer orders as defined in the first indent of (i) which enables the abovementioned credit institution to pass transfer orders through the system;

(h) 'securities' shall mean all instruments referred to in section B of the Annex to Directive 93/22/EEC;

(i) 'transfer order' shall mean:
– any instruction by a participant to place at the disposal of a recipient an amount of money by means of a book entry on the accounts of a credit institution, a central bank or a settlement agent, or any instruction which results in the assumption or discharge of a payment obligation as defined by the rules of the system, or
– an instruction by a participant to transfer the title to, or interest in, a security or securities by means of a book entry on a register, or otherwise;

(j) 'insolvency proceedings' shall mean any collective measure provided for in the law of a Member State, or a third country, either to wind up the participant or to reorganise it, where such measure involves the suspending of, or imposing limitations on, transfers or payments;

(k) 'netting' shall mean the conversion into one net claim or one net obligation of claims and obligations resulting from transfer orders which a participant or participants either issue to, or receive from, one or more other participants with the result that only a net claim can be demanded or a net obligation be owed;

(l) 'settlement account' shall mean an account at a central bank, a settlement agent or a central counterparty used to hold funds and securities and to settle transactions between participants in a system;

(m) 'collateral security' shall mean all realisable assets provided under a pledge (including money provided under a pledge), a repurchase or similar agreement, or otherwise, for the purpose of securing rights and obligations potentially arising in connection with a system, or provided to central banks of the Member States or to the future European central bank.

Section II
Netting and Transfer Orders

Article 3

1. Transfer orders and netting shall be legally enforceable and, even in the event of insolvency proceedings against a participant, shall be binding on third parties, provided that transfer orders were entered into a system before the moment of opening of such insolvency proceedings as defined in Article 6(1).

Where, exceptionally, transfer orders are entered into a system after the moment of opening of insolvency proceedings and are carried out on the day of opening of such proceedings, they shall be legally enforceable and binding on third parties only if, after the time of settlement, the settlement agent, the central counterparty or the clearing house can prove that they were not aware, nor should have been aware, of the opening of such proceedings.

2. No law, regulation, rule or practice on the setting aside of contracts and transactions concluded before the moment of opening of insolvency proceedings, as defined in Article 6(1) shall lead to the unwinding of a netting.

3. The moment of entry of a transfer order into a system shall be defined by the rules of that system. If there are conditions laid down in the national law governing the system as to the moment of entry, the rules of that system must be in accordance with such conditions.

Article 4

Member States may provide that the opening of insolvency proceedings against a participant shall not prevent funds or securities available on the settlement account of that participant from being used to fulfil that participant's obligations in the system on the day of the opening of the insolvency proceedings. Furthermore, Member States may also provide that such a participant's credit facility connected to the system be used against available, existing collateral security to fulfil that participant's obligations in the system.

Article 5

A transfer order may not be revoked by a participant in a system, nor by a third party, from the moment defined by the rules of that system.

Section III
Provisions Concerning Insolvency Proceedings

Article 6

1. For the purpose of this Directive, the moment of opening of insolvency proceedings shall be the moment when the relevant judicial or administrative authority handed down its decision.

2. When a decision has been taken in accordance with paragraph 1, the relevant judicial or administrative authority shall immediately notify that decision to the appropriate authority chosen by its Member State.

3. The Member State referred to in paragraph 2 shall immediately notify other Member States.

Article 7

Insolvency proceedings shall not have retroactive effects on the rights and obligations of a participant arising from, or in connection with, its participation in a system earlier than the moment of opening of such proceedings as defined in Article 6(1).

Article 8

In the event of insolvency proceedings being opened against a participant in a system, the rights and obligations arising from, or in connection with, the participation of that participant shall be determined by the law governing that system.

Section IV

Insulation of the Rights of Holders of Collateral Security from the Effects of the Insolvency of the Provider

Article 9

1. The rights of:
- a participant to collateral security provided to it in connection with a system, and
- central banks of the Member States or the future European central bank to collateral security provided to them,

shall not be affected by insolvency proceedings against the participant or counterparty to central banks of the Member States or the future European central bank which provided the collateral security. Such collateral security may be realised for the satisfaction of these rights.

2. Where securities (including rights in securities) are provided as collateral security to participants and/or central banks of the Member States or the future European central bank as described in paragraph 1, and their right (or that of any nominee, agent or third party acting on their behalf) with respect to the securities is legally recorded on a register, account or centralised deposit system located in a Member State, the determination of the rights of such entities as holders of collateral security in relation to those securities shall be governed by the law of that Member State.

Section V

Final Provisions

Article 10

Member States shall specify the systems which are to be included in the scope of this Directive and shall notify them to the Commission and inform the Commission of the authorities they have chosen in accordance with Article 6(2).

The system shall indicate to the Member State whose law is applicable the participants in the system, including any possible indirect participants, as well as any change in them.

In addition to the indication provided for in the second subparagraph, Member States may impose supervision or authorisation requirements on systems which fall under their jurisdiction.

Anyone with a legitimate interest may require an institution to inform him of the systems in which it participates and to provide information about the main rules governing the functioning of those systems.

Article 11

1. Member States shall bring into force the laws, regulations and administrative provisions necessary to comply with this Directive before 11 December 1999. They shall forthwith inform the Commission thereof.

When Member States adopt these measures, they shall contain a reference to this Directive or shall be accompanied by such reference on the occasion of their official publication. The methods of making such a reference shall be laid down by the Member States.

2. Member States shall communicate to the Commission the text of the provisions of domestic law which they adopt in the field governed by this Directive. In this Communication, Member States shall provide a table of correspondence showing the national provisions which exist or are introduced in respect of each Article of this Directive.

Article 12

No later than three years after the date mentioned in Article 11(1), the Commission shall present a report to the European Parliament and the Council on the application of this Directive, accompanied where appropriate by proposals for its revision.

Article 13

This Directive shall enter into force on the day of its publication in the *Official Journal of the European Communities*.

Article 14

This Directive is addressed to the Member States.

S. 18.

(Acts whose publication is obligatory)

European Parliament and Council Directive 2001/34/EC of 28 May 2001 on the admission of securities to official stock exchange listing and on information to be published on those securities[1]

TABLE OF CONTENTS

Recitals	1482
TITLE I. DEFINITIONS AND SCOPE OF APPLICATION	1485
Chapter I. Definitions	1485
Article 1	1485
Chapter II. Scope of Application	1486
Article 2	1486
Article 3	1486
Article 4	1486
TITLE II. GENERAL PROVISIONS CONCERNING THE OFFICIAL LISTING OF SECURITIES	1487
Chapter I. General Conditions for Admission	1487
Article 5	1487
Article 6	1487
Article 7	1487
Chapter II. More Stringent or Additional Conditions and Obligations	1487
Article 8	1487
Chapter III. Derogations	1487
Article 9	1487
Article 10	1488
Chapter IV. Powers of the national competent authorities	1488
Section 1. Decision of Admission	1488
Article 11	1488
Article 12	1488
Article 13	1488
Article 14	1488
Article 15	1488
Section 2. Information Requested by the Competent Authorities	1488
Article 16	1488
Section 3. Actions Against an Issuer Failing to Comply with the Obligations Resulting from Admission	1489
Article 17	1489
Section 4. Suspension and Discontinuance	1489
Article 18	1489
Section 5. Right to Apply to the Courts in Case of Refusal of Admission or Discontinuance	1489
Article 19	1489
TITLE III. PARTICULAR CONDITIONS RELATING TO OFFICIAL LISTINGS OF SECURITIES	1489
Chapter I. Publication of Listing Particulars for Admission	1489
[...]	
Chapter II. Particular Conditions for the Admission of Shares	1490
Section 1. Conditions Relating to Companies for the Shares of which Admission to Official Listing is Sought	1490
Article 42	1490
Article 43	1490
Article 44	1490
Section 2. Conditions Relating to the Shares for which Admission is Sought	1490
Article 45	1490
Article 46	1490
Article 47	1491
Article 48	1491
Article 49	1491
Article 50	1491
Article 51	1491
Chapter III. Particular Conditions Relating to the Admission to the Official Listing of Debt Securities Issued by an Undertaking	1492
Section 1. Conditions Relating to Undertakings for the Debt Securities of which Admission to Official Listing is Sought	1492
Article 52	1492
Section 2. Conditions Relating to the Debt Securities for which Admission to Official Listing is Sought	1492
Article 53	1492
Article 54	1492
Article 55	1492
Article 56	1492
Article 57	1492
Section 3. Other Conditions	1492
Article 58	1492
Article 59	1493
Chapter IV. Particular Conditions Relating to the Admission to Official Listing of Debt Securities Issued by a State, its Regional or Local Authorities or a Public International Body	1493
Article 60	1493
Article 61	1493
Article 62	1493
Article 63	1493

---

[1] OJ L 184, 6.7.2001, 1–66.

Title IV. Ongoing Obligations Relating to Securities Admitted to Official Listing	1493
Chapter I. Obligations of Companies Whose Shares are Admitted to Official Listing	1493
Section 1. Listing of Newly Issued Shares of the Same Class	1493
Article 64	1493
Section 2. Treatment of Shareholders	1494
Article 65	1494
Section 3. Amendment of the Instrument of Incorporation or the Statutes	1494
Article 66	1494
Section 4. Annual Accounts and Annual Report	1494
Article 67	1494
Section 5. Additional Information	1494
Article 68	1494
Section 6. Equivalence of Information	1495
Article 69	1495
Section 7. Periodical Information to be Published	1495
Article 70	1495
Article 71	1495
Section 8. Publication and Contents of the Half-Yearly Report	1495
Article 72	1495
Article 73	1495
Article 74	1496
Article 75	1496
Article 76	1496
Article 77	1496
Chapter II. Obligation of Issuers Whose Debt Securities are Admitted to Official Listing	1497
Section 1. Debt Securities Issued by an Undertaking	1497
Article 78	1497
Article 79	1497
Article 80	1497
Article 81	1497
Article 82	1498
Section 2. Debt securities issued by a State or its Regional or Local Authorities or by a Public International Body	1498
Article 83	1498
Article 84	1498
Chapter III. Obligations Relating to the Information to be Published when a Major Holding in a Listed Company is Acquired or Disposed of	1498
Section 1. General Provisions	1498
Article 85	1498
Article 86	1499
Article 87	1499
Article 88	1499
Section 2. Information when a Major Holding is Acquired or Disposed of	1499
Article 89	1499
Article 90	1500
Article 91	1500
Section 3. Determination of the Voting Rights	1500
Article 92	1500
Section 4. Exemptions	1501
Article 93	1501
Article 94	1501
Article 95	1501
Section 5. Competent Authorities	1501
Article 96	1501
Section 6. Sanctions	1501
Article 97	1501
Title V. Publication and Communication of the Information	1502
Chapter I. Publication and Communication of Listing Particulars for the Admission of Securities to the Official Stock Exchange Listing	1502
Section 1. Procedures and Period of Publication of Listing Particulars and their Supplements [. . .]	1502
Section 2. Prior Communication to the Competent Authorities of the Means of Publication	1502
Article 101	1502
Chapter II. Publication and Communication of Information after Listing	1502
Article 102	1502
Chapter III. Languages	1502
Article 103	1502
Article 104	1502
Title VI. Competent Authorities and Co-operation between Member States	1503
Article 105	1503
Article 106	1503
Article 107	1503
Title VII. Contact Committee	1503
Chapter I. Composition, Working and Tasks of the Committee	1503
Article 108	1503
Chapter II. Adaptation of the Amount of Equity Market Capitalisation	1503
Article 109	1503
Title VIII. Final Provisions	1504
Article 110	1504
Article 111	1504
Article 112	1504
Article 113	1504
Annex I—Schedule of listing particulars for the admission of securities to the official stock exchange listing	1504
Annex II—Part A. Repealed Directives and Their Successive Amendments	1504
Annex II—Part B. Time-limits for Transposition into National Law	1505
Annex III—Correlation Table	1506

THE EUROPEAN PARLIAMENT AND THE COUNCIL OF THE EUROPEAN UNION,

Having regard to the Treaty establishing the European Economic Community, and in particular Articles 44 and 95 thereof,

Having regard to the proposal from the Commission,

Having regard to the Opinion of the Economic and Social Committee,[2]

Acting in accordance with the procedure laid down in Article 251 of the Treaty,[3]

Whereas:

(1) Council Directive 79/279/EEC of 5 March 1979 co-ordinating the conditions for the admission of securities to official stock exchange listing,[4] Council Directive 80/390/EEC of 17 March 1980 co-ordinating the requirements for the drawing up, scrutiny and distribution of the listing particulars to be published for the admission of securities to official stock exchange listing,[5] Council Directive 82/121/EEC of 15 February 1982 on information to be published on a regular basis by companies the shares of which have been admitted to official stock-exchange listing[6] and Council Directive 88/627/EEC of 12 December 1988 on the information to be published when a major holding in a listed company is acquired or disposed of[7] have been substantially amended several times. In the interests of clarity and rationality, the said Directives should therefore be codified by grouping them together in a single text.

(2) The co-ordination of the conditions for the admission of securities to official listing on stock exchanges situated or operating in the Member States is likely to provide equivalent protection for investors at Community level, because of the more uniform guarantees offered to investors in the various Member States, it will facilitate both the admission to official stock exchange listing, in each such State, of securities from other Member States and the listing of any given security on a number of stock exchanges in the Community; it will accordingly make for greater interpenetration of national securities markets by removing those obstacles that may prudently be removed and therefore contribute to the prospect of establishing a European capital market.

(3) Such co-ordination must therefore apply to securities, independently of the legal status of their issuers, and must therefore also apply to securities issued by non-member States or their regional or local authorities or international public bodies; this Directive therefore covers entities not covered by the second paragraph of Article 48 of the Treaty.

(4) There should be the possibility of a right to apply to the courts against decisions by the competent national authorities in respect of the application of this Directive, concerning the admission of securities to official listing, although such right to apply must not be allowed to restrict the discretion of these authorities.

(5) Initially, this co-ordination of the conditions for admission of securities to official listing should be sufficiently flexible to enable account to be taken of present differences in the structures of securities markets in the Member States and to enable the Member States to take account of any specific situations with which they may be confronted.

(6) For this reason, co-ordination should first be limited to the establishment of minimum conditions for the admission of securities to official listing on stock exchanges situated or operating in the Member States, without however giving issuers any right to listing.

(7) This partial co-ordination of the conditions for admission to official listing constitutes a first step towards subsequent closer alignment of the rules of Member States in this field.

---

[2] OJ C 116, 20.4.2001, 69.
[3] Opinion of the European Parliament of 14 March 2001 (OJ C 343, 5.12.2001, 152) and Council Decision of 7 May 2001.
[4] OJ L 66, 16.3.1979, 21, reproduced supra under no. S. 2. Directive as last amended by Directive 88/627/EEC (OJ L 348, 17.12.1988, 62), reproduced supra under no. S. 10.
[5] OJ L 100, 17.4.1980, 1, reproduced supra under no. S. 3. Directive as last amended by European Parliament and Council Directive 94/18/EC (OJ L 135, 31.5.1994, 1), reproduced supra under no. S. 15.
[6] OJ L 48, 20.2.1982, 26, reproduced supra under no. S. 4.
[7] OJ L 348, 17.12.1988, 62, reproduced supra under no. S. 10.

(8) The market in which undertakings operate has been enlarged to embrace the whole Community and this enlargement involves a corresponding increase in their financial requirements and extension of the capital markets on which they must call to satisfy them; admission to official listing on stock exchanges of Member States of securities issued by undertakings constitutes an important means of access to these capital markets; furthermore exchange restrictions on the purchase of securities traded on the stock exchanges of another Member State have been eliminated as part of the liberalisation of capital movements.

(9) Safeguards for the protection of the interests of actual and potential investors are required in most Member States of undertakings offering their securities to the public, either at the time of their offer or of their admission to official stock exchange listing; such safeguards require the provision of information which is sufficient and as objective as possible concerning the financial circumstances of the issuer and particulars of the securities for which admission to official listing is requested; the form under which this information is required usually consists of the publication of listing particulars.

(10) The safeguards required differ from Member State to Member State, both as regards the contents and the layout of the listing particulars and the efficacy, methods and timing of the check on the information given therein; the effect of these differences is not only to make it more difficult for undertakings to obtain admission of securities to official listing on stock exchanges of several Member States but also to hinder the acquisition by investors residing in one Member State of securities listed on stock exchanges of other Member States and thus to inhibit the financing of the undertakings and investment throughout the Community.

(11) These differences should be eliminated by co-ordinating the rules and regulations without necessarily making them completely uniform, in order to achieve an adequate degree of equivalence in the safeguards required in each Member State to ensure the provision of information which is sufficient and as objective as possible for actual or potential security holders.

(12) Such co-ordination must apply to securities independently of the legal status of the issuing undertaking; this Directive applies to entities to which no reference is made in the second paragraph of Article 48 of the Treaty.

(13) Mutual recognition of listing particulars to be published for the admission of securities to official listing represents an important step forward in the creation of the Community's internal market.

(14) In this connection, it is necessary to specify which authorities are competent to check and approve listing particulars to be published for the admission of securities to official listing in the event of simultaneous applications for admission to official listing in two or more Member States.

(15) Article 21 of Council Directive 89/298/EEC of 17 April 1989 co-ordinating the requirements for the drawing-up, scrutiny and distribution of the prospectus to be published when transferable securities are offered to the public[8] provides that where public offers are made simultaneously or within short intervals of one another in two or more Member States, a public-offer prospectus drawn up and approved in accordance with Article 7, 8 or 12 of that Directive must be recognised as a public-offer prospectus in the other Member States concerned on the basis of mutual recognition.

(16) It is also desirable to provide the recognition of a public-offer prospectus as listing particulars where admission to official stock-exchange listing is requested within a short period of the public offer.

(17) The mutual recognition of a public-offer prospectus and admission to official listings does not in itself confer a right to admissions.

(18) It is advisable to provide for the extension, by means of agreements to be concluded by the

---

[8] OJ L 124, 5.5.1989, 8, reproduced supra under no. S. 11.

Community with non-member countries, of the recognition of listing particulars for admission to official listings from those countries on a reciprocal basis.

(19) It seems appropriate to provide for the possibility for the Member State in which admission to official listing is sought in certain cases to grant partial or complete exemption from the obligation to publish listing particulars for admission to official listings to issuers the securities of which have already been admitted to official stock-exchange listing in another Member State.

(20) Companies which have already been listed in the Community for some time and are of high quality and international standing are the most likely candidates for cross-border listing. Those companies are generally well known in most Member States: information concerning them is widely circulated and available.

(21) The aim of this Directive is to ensure that sufficient information is provided for investors; therefore, when such a company seeks to have its securities admitted to listing in a host Member State, investors operating on the market in that country may be sufficiently protected by receiving only simplified information rather than full listing particulars.

(22) Member States may find it useful to establish non-discriminatory minimum quantitative criteria, such as the current equity market capitalisation, which issuers must fulfil to be eligible to benefit from the possibilities for exemption provided for in this Directive; given the increasing integration of securities markets, it should equally be open to the competent authorities to give smaller companies similar treatment.

(23) Furthermore, many stock exchanges have second-tier markets in order to deal in shares of companies not admitted to official listing; in some cases the second-tier markets are regulated and supervised by authorities recognised by public bodies that impose on companies disclosure requirements equivalent in substance to those imposed on officially listed companies; therefore, the principle underlying Article 23 of this Directive could also be applied when such companies seek to have their securities admitted to official listing.

(24) In order to protect investors the documents intended to be made available to the public must first be sent to the competent authorities in the Member State in which admission to official listing is sought; it is for that Member State to decide whether those documents should be scrutinised by its competent authorities and to determine, if necessary, the nature and the manner in which that scrutiny should be carried out.

(25) In the case of securities admitted to official stock-exchange listing, the protection of investors requires that the latter be supplied with appropriate regular information throughout the entire period during which the securities are listed; co-ordination of requirements for this regular information has similar objectives to those envisaged for the listing particulars, namely to improve such protection and to make it more equivalent, to facilitate the listing of these securities on more than one stock exchange in the Community, and in so doing to contribute towards the establishment of a genuine Community capital market by permitting a fuller interpenetration of securities markets.

(26) Under this Directive, listed companies must as soon as possible make available to investors their annual accounts and report giving information on the company for the whole of the financial year; whereas the Fourth Council Directive 78/660/EEC[9] has co-ordinated the laws, regulations and administrative provisions of the Member States concerning the annual accounts of certain types of companies.

(27) Companies should also, at least once during each financial year, make available to investors reports on their activities; this Directive can, consequently, be confined to co-ordinating the content and distribution of a single report covering the first six months of the financial year.

---

[9] OJ L 222, 14.8.1978, 11, Fourth Company Directive, reproduced supra under no. C. 4. Directive as last amended by Directive 1999/60/EC (OJ L 162, 26.6.1999, 65), reproduced supra under no. C. 16.

(28) However, in the case of ordinary debentures, because of the rights they confer on their holders, the protection of investors by means of the publication of a half-yearly report is not essential; by virtue of this Directive, convertible or exchangeable debentures and debentures with warrants may be admitted to official listing only if the related shares are already listed on the same stock exchange or on another regulated, regularly operating, recognised open market or are so admitted simultaneously; the Member States may derogate from this principle only if their competent authorities are satisfied that holders have at their disposal all the information necessary to form an opinion concerning the value of the shares to which these debentures relate; consequently, regular information needs to be co-ordinated only for companies whose shares are admitted to official stock exchange listing.

(29) The half-yearly report must enable investors to make an informed appraisal of the general development of the company's activities during the period covered by the report; however, this report need contain only the essential details on the financial position and general progress of the business of the company in question.

(30) So as to ensure the effective protection of investors and the proper operation of stock exchanges, the rules relating to regular information to be published by companies, the shares of which are admitted to official stock exchange listing within the Community, should apply not only to companies from Member States, but also to companies from non-member countries.

(31) A policy of adequate information of investors in the field of transferable securities is likely to improve investor protection, to increase investors' confidence in securities markets and thus to ensure that securities markets function correctly.

(32) By making such protection more equivalent, co-ordination of that policy at Community level is likely to make for greater inter-penetration of the Member States' transferable securities markets and therefore help to establish a true European capital market.

(33) To that end investors should be informed of major holdings and of changes in those holdings in Community companies the shares of which are officially listed on stock exchanges situated or operating within the Community.

(34) Co-ordinated rules should be laid down concerning the detailed content and the procedure for applying that requirement.

(35) Companies, the shares of which are officially listed on a Community stock exchange, can inform the public of changes in major holdings only if they have been informed of such changes by the holders of those holdings.

(36) Most Member States do not subject holders to such a requirement and where such a requirement exists there are appreciable differences in the procedures for applying it; co-ordinated rules should therefore be adopted at Community level in this field.

(37) This Directive should not affect the obligations of the Member States concerning the deadlines for transposition set out in Annex II, Part B,

HAVE ADOPTED THIS DIRECTIVE:

TITLE I
DEFINITIONS AND SCOPE OF APPLICATION

CHAPTER I
DEFINITIONS

Article 1

For the purposes of this Directive:

(a) 'issuers' shall mean companies and other legal persons and any undertaking whose securities are the subject of an application for admission to official listing on a stock exchange;

(b) 'collective investment undertakings other than the closed-end type' shall mean unit trusts and investment companies:

(i) the object of which is the collective investment of capital provided by the public, and which operate on the principle of risk spreading, and

(ii) the units of which are, at the holders' request, repurchased or redeemed, directly or indirectly, out of the assets of these undertakings. Action taken by such undertakings to ensure that the stock exchange value of its units does not significantly vary from their net asset value shall be regarded as equivalent to such repurchase or redemption;

(c) For the purposes of this Directive 'investment companies other than those of the closed-end type' shall mean investment companies:

(i) the object of which is the collective investment of capital provided by the public, and which operate on the principle of risk spreading, and

(ii) the shares of which are, at the holders' request, repurchased or redeemed, directly or indirectly, out of those companies' assets. Action taken by such companies to ensure that the stock exchange value of their shares does not significantly vary from their net asset value shall be regarded as equivalent to such repurchase or redemption;

(d) 'credit institution' shall mean an undertaking whose business is to receive deposits or other repayable funds from the public and to grant credits for its own account;

(e) 'units of a collective investment undertaking' shall mean securities issued by a collective investment undertaking as representing the rights of participants in the assets of such an undertaking;

(f) 'participating interest' shall mean rights in the capital of other undertakings, whether or not represented by certificates, which, by creating a durable link with those undertakings, are intended to contribute to the activities of the undertaking which holds these rights;

(g) ['net turnover' shall comprise the amounts derived from the sale of products and the provision of services falling within undertaking's ordinary activities, after deduction of sales rebates and of value added tax and other taxes directly linked to the turnover;]

(h) ['annual accounts' shall comprise the balance sheet, the profit and loss account and the notes on the accounts. The documents shall constitute a composite whole.]

¶ *Article 1(g) and (h) will be deleted as from 20 January 2007 by article 32(1) of Directive 2004/109/EC, reproduced infra under no. S. 31.*

Chapter II
Scope of Application

Article 2

1. Articles 5 to 19, 42 to 69, and 78 to 84 shall apply to securities which are admitted to official listing or are the subject of an application for admission to official listing on a stock exchange situated or operating within a Member State.

2. Member States may decide not to apply the provisions mentioned in paragraph 1 to:

(a) units issued by collective investment undertakings other than the closed-end type,

(b) securities issued by a Member State or its regional or local authorities.

Article 3

[. . .]

¶ *Article 3 has been repealed as from 1 July 2005 by article 27 of Directive 2003/71/EC, reproduced infra under no. S. 25.*

[Article 4

1. Articles 70 to 77 shall apply to companies the shares of which are admitted to official listing on a stock exchange situated or operating in a Member State, whether the admission is of the shares themselves or of certificates representing them, and whenever the date of this admission occurred.

2. The provisions mentioned in paragraph 1 shall not, however, apply to investment undertakings other than those of the closed-end type.

3. The Member States may exclude central banks from the scope of the provisions mentioned in paragraph 1.]

¶ *Article 4 will be deleted as from 20 January 2007 by article 32(2) of Directive 2004/109/EC, reproduced infra under no. S. 31.*

Title II
General Provisions Concerning the Official Listing of Securities

Chapter I
General Conditions for Admission

Article 5

Member States shall ensure that:

(a) securities may not be admitted to official listing on any stock exchange situated or operating within their territory unless the conditions laid down by this Directive are satisfied, and

(b) that issuers of securities admitted to such official listing, regardless of the date on which this admission takes place, are subject to the obligations provided for by this Directive.

Article 6

1. The admission of securities to official listing shall be subject to the conditions set out in Articles 42 to 51, or 52 to 63, relating to shares and debt securities respectively.

[2. The issuers of securities admitted to official listing must fulfil the obligations set out in Articles 64 to 69, or 78 to 84, relating to shares and debt securities respectively.]

3. Certificates representing shares may be admitted to official listing only if the issuer of the shares represented fulfils the conditions set out in Articles 42 to 44 and the obligations set out in Articles 64 to 69 and if the certificates fulfil the conditions set out in Articles 45 to 50.

¶ *Paragraph 2 of Article 6 will be deleted as from 20 January 2007 by article 32(3) of Directive 2004/109/EC, reproduced infra under no. S. 31.*

Article 7

Member States may not make the admission to official listing of securities issued by companies or other legal persons which are nationals of another Member State subject to the condition that the securities must already have been admitted to official listing on a stock exchange situated or operating in one of the Member States.

Chapter II
More Stringent or Additional Conditions and Obligations

Article 8

1. Subject to the prohibitions provided for in Article 7 and in Articles 42 to 63, the Member States may make the admission of securities to official listing subject to more stringent conditions than those set out in Articles 42 to 63 or to additional conditions, provided that these more stringent and additional conditions apply generally for all issuers or for individual classes of issuer and that they have been published before application for admission of such securities is made.

[2. Member States may make the issuers of securities admitted to official listing subject to more stringent obligations than those set out in Articles 64 to 69 and 78 to 84 or to additional obligations, provided that these more stringent and additional obligations apply generally for all issuers or for individual classes of issuer.]

3. Member States may, under the same conditions as those laid down in Article 9, authorise derogations from the additional or more stringent conditions and obligations referred to in paragraphs 1 and 2 hereof.

4. Member States may, in accordance with the applicable national rules require issuers of securities admitted to official listing to inform the public on a regular basis of their financial position and the general course of their business.

¶ *As from 20 January 2007 by article 32(4) of Directive 2004/109/EC reproduced infra under no. S. 31, paragraph 2 of article 8 will be amended by the following text: 'Member States may make the issuers of securities admitted to official listing subject to additional obligations, provided that those additional obligations apply generally for all issuers or for individual classes of issuer'.*

Chapter III
Derogations

Article 9

Any derogations from the conditions for the admission of securities to official listing which may be authorised in accordance with Articles 42 to 63 must apply generally for all issuers where the circumstances justifying them are similar.

Article 10

Member States may decide not to apply the conditions set out in Articles 52 to 63 and the obligations set out in Article 81(1) and (3) in respect of applications for admission to official listing of debt securities issued by companies and other legal persons which are nationals of a Member State and which are set up by, governed by or managed pursuant to a special law where repayments and interest payments in respect of those securities are guaranteed by a Member State or one of its federal states.

CHAPTER IV

POWERS OF THE NATIONAL COMPETENT AUTHORITIES

SECTION 1

DECISION OF ADMISSION

Article 11

1. The competent authorities referred to in Article 105 shall decide on the admission of securities to official listing on a stock exchange situated or operating within their territories.

2. Without prejudice to the other powers conferred upon them, the competent authorities may reject an application for the admission of a security to official listing if, in their opinion, the issuer's situation is such that admission would be detrimental to investors' interests.

Article 12

By way of derogation from Article 8, Member States may, solely in the interests of protecting the investors, give the competent authorities power to make the admission of a security to official listing subject to any special condition which the competent authorities consider appropriate and of which they have explicitly informed the applicant.

Article 13

1. Where applications are to be made simultaneously or within short intervals of one another for admission of the same securities to official listing on stock exchanges situated or operating in more than one Member State, or where an application for admission is made in respect of a security already listed on a stock exchange in another Member State, the competent authorities shall communicate with each other and make such arrangements as may be necessary to expedite the procedure and simplify as far as possible the formalities and any additional conditions required for admission of the security concerned.

2. In order to facilitate the work of the competent authorities, any application for the admission of a security to official listing on a stock exchange situated or operating in a Member State must state whether a similar application is being or has been made in another Member State, or will be made in the near future.

Article 14

The competent authorities may refuse to admit to official listing a security already officially listed in another Member State where the issuer fails to comply with the obligations resulting from admission in that Member State.

Article 15

Where an application for admission to official listing relates to certificates representing shares, the application shall be considered only if the competent authorities are of the opinion that the issuer of the certificates is offering adequate safeguards for the protection of investors.

SECTION 2

INFORMATION REQUESTED BY THE COMPETENT AUTHORITIES

Article 16

1. An issuer whose securities are admitted to official listing shall provide the competent

authorities with all the information which the latter consider appropriate in order to protect investors or ensure the smooth operation of the market.

2. Where protection of investors or the smooth operation of the market so requires, an issuer may be required by the competent authorities to publish such information in such a form and within such time limits as they consider appropriate. Should the issuer fail to comply with such requirement, the competent authorities may themselves publish such information after having heard the issuer.

Section 3
Action Against an Issuer Failing to Comply with the Obligations Resulting from Admission

Article 17

Without prejudice to any other action or penalties which they may contemplate in the event of failure on the part of the issuer to comply with the obligations resulting from admission to official listing, the competent authorities may make public the fact that an issuer is failing to comply with those obligations.

Section 4
Suspension and Discontinuance

Article 18

1. The competent authorities may decide to suspend the listing of a security where the smooth operation of the market is, or may be, temporarily jeopardised or where protection of investors so requires.

2. The competent authorities may decide that the listing of the security be discontinued where they are satisfied that, owing to special circumstances, normal regular dealings in a security are no longer possible.

Section 5
Right to Apply to the Courts in Case of Refusal of Admission or Discontinuance

Article 19

1. Member States shall ensure decisions of the competent authorities refusing the admission of a security to official listing or discontinuing such a listing shall be subject to the right to apply to the courts.

2. An applicant shall be notified of a decision regarding his application for admission to official listing within six months of receipt of the application or, should the competent authority require any further information within that period, within six months of the applicant's supplying such information.

3. Failure to give a decision within the time limit specified in paragraph 2 shall be deemed a rejection of the application. Such rejection shall give rise to the right to apply to the courts provided for in paragraph 1.

Title III
Particular Conditions Relating to Official Listings of Securities

Chapter I
Publication of Listing Particulars for Admission

Section 1
General Provisions

Articles 20–41

[. . .]

¶ *Articles 20 to 41 have been repealed as from 1 July 2005 by article 27 of Directive 2003/71/EC, reproduced infra under no. S. 25.*

Chapter II

Specific Conditions for the Admission of Shares

Section 1

Conditions Relating to Companies for the Shares of which Admission to Official Listing is Sought

Article 42

The legal position of the company must be in conformity with the laws and regulations to which it is subject, as regards both its formation and its operation under its statutes.

Article 43

1. The foreseeable market capitalisation of the shares for which admission to official listing is sought or, if this cannot be assessed, the company's capital and reserves, including profit or loss, from the last financial year, must be at least one million euro.

2. Member States may provide for admission to official listing, even when this condition is not fulfilled, provided that the competent authorities are satisfied that there will be an adequate market for the shares concerned.

3. A higher foreseeable market capitalisation or higher capital and reserves may be required by a Member State for admission to official listing only if another regulated, regularly operating, recognised open market exists in that State and the requirements for it are equal to or less than those referred to in paragraph 1.

4. The condition set out in paragraph 1 shall not be applicable for the admission to official listing of a further block of shares of the same class as those already admitted.

5. The equivalent in national currency of one million euro shall initially be the equivalent in national currency of one million European units of account that were applicable on 5 March 1979.

6. If, as a result of adjustment of the equivalent of the euro in national currency, the market capitalisation expressed in national currency remains for a period of one year at least 10% more or less than the value of one million euro the Member state must, within the 12 months following the expiry of that period, adjust its laws, regulations or administrative provisions to comply with paragraph 1.

Article 44

A company must have published or filed its annual accounts in accordance with national law for the three financial years preceding the application for official listing. By way of exception, the competent authorities may derogate from this condition where such derogation is desirable in the interests of the company or of investors and where the competent authorities are satisfied that investors have the necessary information available to be able to arrive at an informed judgement on the company and the shares for which admission to official listing is sought.

Section 2

Conditions Relating to the Shares for which Admission is Sought

Article 45

The legal position of the shares must be in conformity with the laws and regulations to which they are subject.

Article 46

1. The shares must be freely negotiable.

2. The competent authorities may treat shares which are not fully paid up as freely negotiable, if arrangements have been made to ensure that the negotiability of such shares is not restricted and that dealing is made open and proper by providing the public with all appropriate information.

3. The competent authorities may, in the case of the admission to official listing of shares which may be acquired only subject to approval, derogate from paragraph 1 only if the use of the approval clause does not disturb the market.

Article 47

Where public issue precedes admission to official listing, the first listing may be made only after the end of the period during which subscription applications may be submitted.

Article 48

1. A sufficient number of shares must be distributed to the public in one or more Member States not later than the time of admission.

2. The condition set out in paragraph 1 shall not apply where shares are to be distributed to the public through the stock exchange. In that event, admission to official listing may be granted only if the competent authorities are satisfied that a sufficient number of shares will be distributed through the stock exchange within a short period.

3. Where admission to official listing is sought for a further block of shares of the same class, the competent authorities may assess whether a sufficient number of shares has been distributed to the public in relation to all the shares issued and not only in relation to this further block.

4. By way of derogation from paragraph 1, if the shares are admitted to official listing in one or more non-member countries, the competent authorities may provide for their admission to official listing if a sufficient number of shares is distributed to the public in the non-Member State or States where they are listed.

5. A sufficient number of shares shall be deemed to have been distributed either when the shares in respect of which application for admission has been made are in the hands of the public to the extent of a least 25% of the subscribed capital represented by the class of shares concerned or when, in view of the large number of shares of the same class and the extent of their distribution to the public, the market will operate properly with a lower percentage.

Article 49

1. The application for admission to official listing must cover all the shares of the same class already issued.

2. Member States may provide that this condition shall not apply to applications for admission not covering all the shares of the same class already issued where the shares of that class for which admission is not sought belong to blocks serving to maintain control of the company or are not negotiable for a certain time under agreements, provided that the public is informed of such situations and that there is no danger of such situations prejudicing the interests of the holders of the shares for which admission to official listing is sought.

Article 50

1. For the admission to official listing of shares issued by companies which are nationals of another Member State and which shares have a physical form it is necessary and sufficient that their physical form comply with the standards laid down in that other Member State. Where the physical form does not conform to the standards in force in the Member State in which admission to official listing is applied for, the competent authorities of that state shall make that fact known to the public.

2. The physical form of shares issued by companies which are nationals of a non-member country must afford sufficient safeguard for the protection of the investors.

Article 51

If the shares issued by a company which is a national of a non-member country are not listed in either the country of origin or in the country in which the major proportion of the shares is held, they may not be admitted to official listing unless the competent authorities are satisfied that the absence of a listing in the country of origin or in the country in which the major proportion is held is not due to the need to protect investors.

Chapter III
Particular Conditions Relating to the Admission to Official Listing of Debt Securities Issued by an Undertaking

Section 1
Conditions Relating to Undertakings for the Debt Securities of which Admission to Official Listing is Sought

Article 52

The legal position of the undertaking must be in conformity with the laws and regulations to which it is subject, as regards both its formation and its operation under its statutes.

Section 2
Conditions Relating to the Debt Securities for which Admission to Official Listing is Sought

Article 53

The legal position of the debt securities must be in conformity with the laws and regulations to which they are subject.

Article 54

1. The debt securities must be freely negotiable.

2. The competent authorities may treat debt securities which are not fully paid up as freely negotiable if arrangements have been made to ensure that the negotiability of these debt securities is not restricted and that dealing is made open and proper by providing the public with all appropriate information.

Article 55

Where public issue precedes admission to official listing, the first listing may be made only after the end of the period during which subscription applications may be submitted. This provision shall not apply in the case of tap issues of debt securities when the closing date for subscription is not fixed.

Article 56

The application for admission to official listing must cover all debt securities ranking pari passu.

Article 57

1. For the admission to official listing of debt securities issued by undertakings which are nationals of another Member State and which debt securities have a physical form, it is necessary and sufficient that their physical form comply with the standards laid down in that other Member State. Where the physical form does not conform to the standards in force in the Member State in which admission to official listing is applied for, the competent authorities of that State shall make that fact known to the public.

2. The physical form of debt securities issued in a single Member State must conform to the standards in force in that State.

3. The physical form of debt securities issued by undertakings which are nationals of a non-member country must afford sufficient safeguard for the protection of the investors.

Section 3
Other Conditions

Article 58

1. The amount of the loan may not be less than EUR 200.000. This provision shall not be applicable in the case of tap issues where the amount of the loan is not fixed.

2. Member States may provide for admission to official listing even when this condition is not fulfilled, where the competent authorities are satisfied that there will be a sufficient market for the debt securities concerned.

3. The equivalent in national currency of EUR 200.000 shall initially be the equivalent in national currency of 200.000 units of account that were applicable on 5 March 1979.

4. If as a result of adjustment of the equivalent of the euro in national currency the minimum amount of the loan expressed in national currency remains, for a period of one year, at least 10% less than the value of EUR 200.000 the Member State must, within the 12 months following the expiry of that period, amend its laws, regulations and administrative provisions to comply with paragraph 1.

Article 59

1. Convertible or exchangeable debentures and debentures with warrants may be admitted to official listing only if the related shares are already listed on the same stock exchange or on another regulated, regularly operating, recognised open market or are so admitted simultaneously.

2. Member States may, by way of derogation from paragraph 1, provide for the admission to official listing of convertible or exchangeable debentures or debentures with warrants, if the competent authorities are satisfied that holders have at their disposal all the information necessary to form an opinion concerning the value of the shares to which these debt securities relate.

CHAPTER IV

PARTICULAR CONDITIONS RELATING TO THE ADMISSION TO OFFICIAL LISTING OF DEBT SECURITIES ISSUED BY A STATE, ITS REGIONAL OR LOCAL AUTHORITIES OR A PUBLIC INTERNATIONAL BODY

Article 60

The debt securities must be freely negotiable.

Article 61

Where public issue precedes admission to official listing, the first listing may be made only after the end of the period during which subscription applications may be submitted. This provision shall not apply where the closing date for subscription is not fixed.

Article 62

The application for admission to official listing must cover all the securities ranking pari passu.

Article 63

1. For the admission to official listing of debt securities which are issued by a Member State or its regional or local authorities in a physical form, it is necessary and sufficient that such physical form comply with the standards in force in that Member State. Where the physical form does not comply with the standards in force in the Member State where admission to official listing is applied for, the competent authorities of that state shall bring this situation to the attention of the public.

2. The physical form of debt securities issued by non-member countries or their regional or local authorities or by public international bodies must afford sufficient safeguard for the protection of the investors.

TITLE IV

OBLIGATIONS RELATING TO SECURITIES ADMITTED TO OFFICIAL LISTING

CHAPTER I

OBLIGATIONS OF COMPANIES WHOSE SHARES ARE ADMITTED TO OFFICIAL LISTING

SECTION 1

LISTING OF NEWLY ISSUED SHARES OF THE SAME CLASS

Article 64

Without prejudice to Article 49(2), in the case of a new public issue of shares of the same class as those already officially listed, the company shall be required, where the new shares are not automatically admitted, to apply for their admission to the same listing, either not more than a year after their issue or when they become freely negotiable.

Section 2
Treatment of Shareholders

[Article 65

1. The company shall ensure equal treatment for all shareholders who are in the same position.

2. The company must ensure, at least in each Member State in which its shares are listed, that all the necessary facilities and information are available to enable shareholders to exercise their rights. In particular, it must:

(a) inform shareholders of the holding of meetings and enable them to exercise their right to vote,

(b) publish notices or distribute circulars concerning the allocation and payment of dividends, the issue of new shares including allotment, subscription, renunciation and conversion arrangements,

(c) designate as its agent a financial institution through which shareholders may exercise their financial rights, unless the company itself provides financial services.

Section 3
Amendment of the Instrument of Incorporation or the Statutes

Article 66

1. A company planning an amendment to its instrument of incorporation or its statutes must communicate a draft thereof to the competent authorities of the Member States in which its shares are listed.

2. That draft must be communicated to the competent authorities no later than the calling of the general meeting which is to decide on the proposed amendment.

Section 4
Annual Accounts and Annual Report

Article 67

1. The company must make available to the public, as soon as possible, its most recent annual accounts and its last annual report.

2. If the company prepares both annual own and annual consolidated accounts, it must make them available to the public. In that event the competent authorities may authorise the company only to make available to the public either the own or the consolidated accounts, provided that the accounts which are not made available to the public do not contain any significant additional information.

3. If the annual accounts and reports do not comply with the provisions of Directives concerning companies' accounts and if they do not give a true and fair view of the company's assets and liabilities, financial position and profit or loss, more detailed and/or additional information must be provided.

Section 5
Additional Information

Article 68

[. . .]

2. The company must inform the public without delay of any changes in the rights attaching to the various classes of shares.

3. The company must inform the public of any changes in the structure (shareholders and breakdowns of holdings) of the major holdings in its capital as compared with information previously published on that subject as soon as such changes come to its notice.

In particular, a company which is not subject to Articles 85 to 97 must inform the public within nine calendar days whenever it comes to its notice that a person or entity has acquired or disposed of a number of shares such that his or its holding exceeds or falls below one of the thresholds laid down in Article 89.

¶ *Article 68(1) has been repealed as from 12 April 2003 by Directive 2003/6/EC, reproduced infra under no. S. 24.*

SECTION 6

EQUIVALENCE OF INFORMATION

Article 69

1. A company whose shares are officially listed on stock exchanges situated or operating in different Member States must ensure that equivalent information is made available to the market at each of these exchanges.

2. A company whose shares are officially listed on stock exchanges situated or operating in one or more Member States and in one or more non-member countries must make available to the markets of the Member State or States in which its shares are listed information which is at least equivalent to that which it makes available to the markets of the non-member country or countries in question, if such information may be of importance for the evaluation of the shares.

SECTION 7

PERIODICAL INFORMATION TO BE PUBLISHED

Article 70

Member States shall ensure that the companies referred to in Article 4 publish half-yearly reports on their activities and profits and losses during the first six months of each financial year.

Article 71

With regard to the half-yearly report, the Member States may subject companies to obligations more stringent than those provided for by Articles 70, and 72 to 76, 102(2) and Article 103 or to additional obligations, provided that they apply generally to all companies or to all companies of a given class.

SECTION 8

PUBLICATION AND CONTENTS OF THE HALF-YEARLY REPORT

Article 72

1. The half-yearly report shall be published within four months of the end of the relevant six-month period.

2. In exceptional, duly substantiated cases, the competent authorities shall be permitted to extend the time limit for publication.

Article 73

1. The half-yearly report shall consist of figures and an explanatory statement relating to the company's activities and profits and losses during the relevant six-month period.

2. The figures, presented in table form, shall indicate at least:

(a) the net turnover, and

(b) the profit or loss before or after deduction of tax.

These terms shall have the same meanings as in the Directives on company accounts.

3. The Member States may allow the competent authorities to authorise companies, exceptionally and on a case-by-case basis, to supply estimated figures for profits and losses, provided that the shares of each such company are listed officially in only one Member State. The use of this procedure must be indicated by the company in its report and must not mislead investors.

4. Where the company has paid or proposes to pay an interim dividend, the figures must indicate the profit or loss after tax for the six-month period and the interim dividend paid or proposed.

5. Against each figure there must be shown the figure for the corresponding period in the preceding financial year.

6. The explanatory statement must include any significant information enabling investors to

make an informed assessment of the trend of the company's activities and profits or losses together with an indication of any special factor which has influenced those activities and those profits or losses during the period in question, and enable a comparison to be made with the corresponding period of the preceding financial year.

It must also, as far as possible, refer to the company's likely future development in the current financial year.

7. Where the figures provided for in paragraph 2 are unsuited to the company's activities, the competent authorities shall ensure that appropriate adjustments are made.

Article 74

Where a company publishes consolidated accounts it may publish its half-yearly report in either consolidated or unconsolidated form. However, the Member States may allow the competent authorities, where the latter consider that the form not adopted would have contained additional material information, to require the company to publish such information.

Article 75

Where the accounting information has been audited by the official auditor of the company's accounts, that auditor's report and any qualifications he may have shall be reproduced in full.

Article 76

1. Where particular requirements of this Directive are unsuited to a company's activities or circumstances, the competent authorities shall ensure that suitable adaptations are made to such requirements.

2. The competent authorities may authorise the omission from the half-yearly report of certain information provided for in this Directive if they consider that disclosure of such information would be contrary to the public interest or seriously detrimental to the company, provided that, in the latter case, such omission would not be likely to mislead the public with regard to facts and circumstances knowledge of which is essential for the assessment of the shares in question.

The company or its representatives shall be responsible for the correctness and relevance of the facts on which any application for such exemption is based.

3. Paragraphs 1 and 2 shall also apply to the more stringent or additional obligations imposed pursuant to Article 71.

4. If a company governed by the law of a non-member country publishes a half-yearly report in a non-member country, the competent authorities may authorise it to publish that report instead of the half-yearly report provided for in this Directive, provided that the information given is equivalent to that which would result from the application of this Directive.

Article 77

Where a half-yearly report has to be published in more than one Member State, the competent authorities of these Member States shall, by way of derogation from Article 71, use their best endeavours to accept as a single text the text which meets the requirements of the Member State in which the company's shares were admitted to official listing for the first time or the text which most closely approximates to that text. In cases of simultaneous admission to official listing on two or more stock exchanges situated or operating in different Member States, the competent authorities of the Member States concerned shall use their best endeavours to accept as a single text the text of the report which meets the requirements of the Member State in which the company's head office is situated; if the company's head office is situated in a non-member country, the competent authorities of the Member States concerned shall use their best endeavours to accept a single version of the report.

Chapter II
Obligation of Issuers Whose Debt Securities are Admitted to Official Listing

Section 1
Debt Securities Issued by an Undertaking

Article 78

1. The undertaking must ensure that all holders of debt securities ranking pari passu are given equal treatment in respect of all the rights attaching to those debt securities.

Provided they are made in accordance with national law, this condition shall not prevent offers of early repayment of certain debt securities being made to holders by an undertaking in derogation from the conditions of issue and in particular in accordance with social priorities.

2. The undertaking must ensure that at least in each Member State where its debt securities are officially listed all the facilities and information necessary to enable holders to exercise their rights are available. In particular, it must:

(a) publish notices or distribute circulars concerning the holding of meetings of holders of debt securities, the payment of interest, the exercise of any conversion, exchange, subscription or renunciation rights, and repayment,

(b) designate as its agent a financial institution through which holders of debt securities may exercise their financial rights, unless the undertaking itself provides financial services.

Article 79

1. An undertaking planning an amendment to its instrument of incorporation or its statutes affecting the rights of holders of debt securities must forward a draft thereof to the competent authorities of the Member States in which its debt securities are listed.

2. That draft must be communicated to the competent authorities no later than the calling of the meeting of the body which is to decide on the proposed amendment.

Article 80

1. The undertaking must make available to the public as soon as possible its most recent annual accounts and its last annual report the publication of which is required by national law.

2. If the undertaking prepares both annual own and annual consolidated accounts, it must make them available to the public. In that event, however, the competent authority may authorise the undertaking only to make available to the public either the own accounts or the consolidated accounts, provided that the accounts which are not made available do not contain any significant additional information.

3. If the accounts and reports do not comply with the provisions of Directives concerning companies' accounts and if they do not give a true and fair view of the undertaking's assets and liabilities, financial position and results, more detailed and/or additional information must be provided.

Article 81

[. . .]

2. The undertaking must inform the public without delay of any change in the rights of holders of debt securities resulting in particular from a change in loan terms or in interest rates.

3. The undertaking must inform the public without delay of new loan issues and in particular of any guarantee or security in respect thereof.

4. Where the debt securities officially listed are convertible or exchangeable debentures, or debentures with warrants, the undertaking must inform the public without delay of any changes in the rights attaching to the various classes of shares to which they relate.

¶ *Article 81(1) has been repealed as from 12 April 2003 by Directive 2003/6/EC, reproduced infra under no. S. 24.*

Article 82

1. An undertaking the debt securities of which are officially listed on stock exchanges situated or operating in different Member States must ensure that equivalent information is made available to the market at each of these exchanges.

2. An undertaking the debt securities of which are officially listed on stock exchanges situated or operating in one or more Member States and in one or more non-member countries must make available to the markets of the Member State or Member States in which its debt securities are listed information which is at least equivalent to that which it makes available to the markets of the non-member country or countries in question, if such information may be of importance for the evaluation of the debt securities.

SECTION 2

DEBT SECURITIES ISSUED BY A STATE OR ITS REGIONAL OR LOCAL AUTHORITIES OR BY A PUBLIC INTERNATIONAL BODY

Article 83

1. States, their regional or local authorities and public international bodies must ensure that all holders of debt securities ranking pari passu are given equal treatment in respect of all the rights attaching to those debt securities.

Provided they are made in accordance with national law, this condition shall not prevent offers of early repayment of certain debt securities being made to holders by an issuer in derogation from the conditions of issue and in particular in accordance with social priorities.

2. States, their regional or local authorities and public international bodies must ensure that at least in each Member State in which their debt securities are officially listed all the facilities and information necessary to enable holders of debt securities to exercise their rights are available. In particular, they must:

(a) publish notices or distribute circulars concerning the holding of meetings of holders of debt securities, the payment of interest and redemption,

(b) designate as their agents financial institutions through which holders of debt securities may exercise their financial rights.

Article 84

1. States, their regional or local authorities and public international bodies the debt securities of which are officially listed on stock exchanges situated or operating in different Member States must ensure that equivalent information is made available to the market at each of these exchanges.

2. States, their regional or local authorities and public international bodies the debt securities of which are officially listed on stock exchanges situated or operating in one or more Member States and in one or more non-member countries must make available to the markets of the Member State or Member States in which their debt securities are listed information which is at least equivalent to that which they make available to the markets of the non-member country or countries in question, if such information may be of importance for the evaluation of the debt securities.

CHAPTER III

OBLIGATIONS RELATING TO THE INFORMATION TO BE PUBLISHED WHEN A MAJOR HOLDING IN A LISTED COMPANY IS ACQUIRED OR DISPOSED OF

SECTION 1

GENERAL PROVISIONS

Article 85

1. Member States shall make subject to this Chapter natural persons and legal entities in public or private law who acquire or dispose of, directly or through intermediaries, holdings meeting the criteria laid down in Article 89(1) which involve changes in the holdings of voting rights in companies incorporated under their law the shares of which are officially listed on a stock exchange or exchanges situated or operating within one or more Member States.

2. Where the acquisition or disposal of a major holding such as referred to in paragraph 1 is effected by means of certificates representing shares, this Chapter shall apply to the bearers of those certificates, and not to the issuer.

3. This Chapter shall not apply to the acquisition or disposal of major holdings in collective investment undertakings.

Article 86

For the purposes of this Chapter, 'acquiring a holding' shall mean not only purchasing a holding, but also acquisition by any other means whatsoever, including acquisition in one of the situations referred to in Article 92.

Article 87

1. For the purposes of this Chapter, 'controlled undertaking' shall mean any undertaking in which a natural person or legal entity:

(a) has a majority of the shareholders' or members' voting rights; or

(b) has the right to appoint or remove a majority of the members of the administrative, management or supervisory body and is at the same time a shareholder in, or member of, the undertaking in question; or

(c) is a shareholder or member and alone controls a majority of the shareholders' or members' voting rights pursuant to an agreement entered into with other shareholders or members of the undertaking.

2. For the purposes of paragraph 1, a parent undertaking's rights as regards voting, appointment and removal shall include the rights of any other controlled undertaking and those of any person or entity acting in his own name but on behalf of the parent undertaking or of any other controlled undertaking.

Article 88

Member States may subject the natural persons, legal entities and companies referred to in Article 85(1) to requirements stricter than those provided for in this Chapter or to additional requirements, provided that such requirements apply generally to all those acquiring or disposing of holdings and all companies or to all those falling within a particular category acquiring or disposing of holdings or of companies.

SECTION 2

INFORMATION WHEN A MAJOR HOLDING IS ACQUIRED OR DISPOSED OF

Article 89

1. Where a natural person or legal entity referred to in Article 85(1) acquires or disposes of a holding in a company referred to in Article 85(1) and where, following that acquisition or disposal, the proportion of voting rights held by that person or legal entity reaches, exceeds or falls below one of the thresholds of 10%, 20%, 1/3, 50% and 2/3, he shall notify the company and at the same time the competent authority or authorities referred to in Article 96 within seven calendar days of the proportion of voting rights he holds following that acquisition or disposal. Member States need not apply:

(a) the thresholds of 20% and 1/3 where they apply a single threshold of 25%,

(b) the threshold of 2/3 where they apply the threshold of 75%.

The period of seven calendar days shall start from the time when the owner of the major holding learns of the acquisition or disposal, or from the time when, in view of the circumstances, he should have learnt of it.

Member States may further provide that a company must also be informed in respect of the proportion of capital held by a natural person or legal entity.

2. Member States shall, if necessary, establish in their national law, and determine in accordance with it, the manner in which the voting rights to be taken into account for the purposes of applying paragraph 1 are to be brought to the notice of the natural persons and legal entities referred to in Article 85(1).

Article 90

Member States shall provide that at the first annual general meeting of a company referred to in Article 85(1), to take place, with regard to:

Belgium, as from 1 October 1993,

Denmark, as from 1 October 1991,

Germany, as from 1 April 1995,

Greece, as from 1 October 1992,

Spain, as from 15 June 1991,

France, as from 1 October 1991,

Ireland, as from 1 November 1991,

Italy, as from 1 June 1992,

Luxembourg, as from 1 June 1993,

Netherlands, as from 1 May 1992,

Austria, as from 1 April 1995,

Portugal, as from 1 August 1991,

Finland, as from 1 April 1995,

Sweden, as from 1 April 1996,

and

United Kingdom, as from 18 December 1993,

any natural person or legal entity as referred to in Article 85(1) must notify the company concerned and at the same time the competent authority or authorities where he holds 10% or more of its voting rights, specifying the proportion of voting rights actually held unless that person or entity has already made a declaration in accordance with Article 89.

Within one month of that general meeting, the public shall be informed of all holdings of 10% or more in accordance with Article 91.

Article 91

A company which has received a declaration referred to in the first subparagraph of Article 89(1) must in turn disclose it to the public in each of the Member States in which its shares are officially listed on a stock exchange as soon as possible but not more than nine calendar days after the receipt of that declaration.

A Member State may provide for the disclosure to the public, referred to in the first subparagraph, to be made not by the company concerned but by the competent authority, possibly in co-operation with that company.

SECTION 3

DETERMINATION OF THE VOTING RIGHTS

Article 92

For the purposes of determining whether a natural person or legal entity as referred to in Article 85(1) is required to make a declaration as provided for in Article 89(1) and in Article 90, the following shall be regarded as voting rights held by that person or entity:

(a) voting rights held by other persons or entities in their own names but on behalf of that person or entity,

(b) voting rights held by an undertaking controlled by that person or entity,

(c) voting rights held by a third party with whom that person or entity has concluded a written agreement which obliges them to adopt, by concerted exercise of the voting rights they hold, a lasting common policy towards the management of the company in question,

(d) voting rights held by a third party under a written agreement concluded with that person or entity or with an undertaking controlled by that person or entity providing for the temporary transfer for consideration of the voting rights in question,

(e) voting rights attaching to shares owned by that person or entity which are lodged as security, except where the person or entity holding the security controls the voting rights and declares his intention of exercising them, in which case they shall be regarded as the latter's voting rights,

(f) voting rights attaching to shares of which that person or entity has the life interest,

(g) voting rights which that person or entity or one of the other persons or entities mentioned in points (a) to (f) is entitled to acquire, on his own initiative alone, under a formal agreement; in such cases, the notification prescribed in Article 89(1) shall be effected on the date of the agreement,

(h) voting rights attaching to shares deposited with that person or entity which that person or entity can exercise at its discretion in the absence of specific instructions from the holders.

By way of derogation from Article 89(1), where a person or entity may exercise voting rights referred to in point (h) of the first paragraph in a company and where the totality of these voting rights together with the other voting rights held by that person or entity in that company reaches or exceeds one of the thresholds provided for in Article 89(1), Member States may lay down that the said person or entity is only obliged to inform the company concerned 21 calendar days before the general meeting of that company.

SECTION 4

EXEMPTIONS

Article 93

If the person or entity acquiring or disposing of a major holding as defined in Article 89 is a member of a group of undertakings required under Council Directive 83/349/EEC(9) to draw up consolidated accounts, that person or entity shall be exempt from the obligation to make the declaration provided for in Article 89[10] and in Article 90 if it is made by the parent undertaking or, where the parent undertaking is itself a subsidiary undertaking, by its own parent undertaking.

Article 94

1. The competent authorities may exempt from the declaration provided for in Article 89(1) the acquisition or disposal of a major holding, as defined in Article 89, by a professional dealer in securities, insofar as that acquisition or disposal is effected in his capacity as a professional dealer in securities and insofar as the acquisition is not used by the dealer to intervene in the management of the company concerned.

2. The competent authorities shall require the professional dealers in securities referred to in paragraph 1 to be members of a stock exchange situated or operating within a Member State or to be approved or supervised by a competent authority such as referred to in Article 105.

Article 95

The competent authorities may, exceptionally, exempt the companies referred to in Article 85(1) from the obligation to notify the public set out in Article 91 where those authorities consider that the disclosure of such information would be contrary to the public interest or seriously detrimental to the companies concerned, provided that, in the latter case, such omission would not be likely to mislead the public with regard to the facts and circumstances knowledge of which is essential for the assessment of the transferable securities in question.

SECTION 5

COMPETENT AUTHORITIES

Article 96

For the purpose of this Chapter, the competent authorities shall be those of the Member State the law of which governs the companies referred to in Article 85(1).

SECTION 6

SANCTIONS

Article 97

Member States shall provide for appropriate sanctions in cases where the natural persons or legal entities and the companies referred to in

---

[10] OJ L 193, 18.7.1983, 1, Seventh Company Directive, reproduced supra under no. C. 6. Directive as last amended by the 1994 Act of Accession.

Article 85(1) do not comply with the provisions of this Chapter.]

¶ *Articles 65 to 97 will be deleted as from 20 January 2007 by article 32(5) of Directive 2004/109/EC, reproduced infra under no. S. 31.*

Title V

Publication and Communication of the Information

Chapter I

Publication and Communication of Listing Particulars for the Admission of Securities to the Official Stock Exchange Listing

Section 1

Procedures and Period of Publication of Listing Particulars and Their Supplements

Articles 98–101

[. . .]

¶ *Articles 98 to 101 have been repealed as from 1 July 2005 by article 27 of Directive 2003/71/EC, reproduced infra under no. S. 25.*

Chapter II

Publication and Communication of Information After Listing

[Article 102

1. The information referred to in Articles 67, 68, 80, 81 and 91 which issuers of a security admitted to official listing in one or more Member States are required to make available to the public shall be published in one or more newspapers distributed throughout the Member State or States concerned or widely distributed therein or shall be made available to the public either in writing in places indicated by announcements to be published in one or more newspapers distributed throughout the Member State or States concerned or widely distributed therein, or by other equivalent means approved by the competent authorities.

The issuers must simultaneously send the information referred to in Articles 67, 68, 80 and 81 to the competent authorities.

2. The half-yearly report referred to in Article 70 must be published in the Member State or Member States where the shares are admitted to official listing by insertion in one or more newspapers distributed throughout the State or widely distributed therein or in the national gazette, or shall be made available to the public either in writing in places indicated by announcement to be published in one or more newspapers distributed throughout the State or widely distributed therein, or by other equivalent means approved by the competent authorities.

The company shall send a copy of its half-yearly report simultaneously to the competent authorities of each Member State in which its shares are admitted to official listing. It shall do so not later than the time when the half-yearly report is published for the first time in a Member State.]

¶ *Article 102 will be deleted as from 20 January 2007 by article 32(6) of Directive 2004/109/EC, reproduced infra under no. S. 31.*

Chapter III

Languages

[Article 103

The information referred to in Articles 67, 68, 80, 81 and 91, in addition to the half-yearly report referred to in Article 70, must be drawn up in the official language or languages or in one of the official languages or in another language, provided that, in the Member State concerned, such official language or languages or such other language are customary in the sphere of finance and are accepted by the competent authorities.]

¶ *Article 103 will be deleted as from 20 January 2007 by article 32(6) of Directive 2004/109/EC, reproduced infra under no. S. 31.*

Article 104

[. . .]

¶ *Article 104 has been repealed as from 1 July 2005 by article 27 of Directive 2003/71/EC, reproduced infra under no. S. 25.*

Title VI
Competent Authorities and Co-operation Between Member States

Article 105

1. Member States shall ensure that this Directive is applied and shall appoint one or more competent authorities for the purposes of the Directive. They shall notify the Commission thereof, giving details of any division of powers among them.

2. Member States shall ensure that the competent authorities have the powers necessary for them to carry out their task.

3. This Directive shall not affect the competent authorities' liability, which shall continue to be governed solely by national law.

Article 106

The competent authorities shall co-operate whenever necessary for the purpose of carrying out their duties and shall exchange any information useful for that purpose.

Article 107

1. Member States shall provide that all persons employed or formerly employed by the competent authorities shall be bound by professional secrecy. This means that any confidential information received in the course of their duties may not be divulged to any person or authority except by virtue of provisions laid down by law.

2. Paragraph 1 shall not, however, preclude the competent authorities of the various Member States from exchanging information as provided for in this Directive. Information thus exchanged shall be covered by the obligation of professional secrecy to which the persons employed or formerly employed by the competent authorities receiving the information are subject.

3. [...]

[A competent authority which, pursuant to paragraph 2, receives confidential information under Title IV, Chapter III, may use it solely for the performance of its duties.]

¶ *The first subparagraph of article 107(3) has been repealed as from 1 July 2005 by article 27(2) of Directive 2003/71/EC, reproduced infra under no. S. 25.*
¶ *The second subparagraph of article 107(3) will be deleted as from 20 January 2007 by article 32(7) of Directive 2004/109/EC, reproduced infra under no. S. 31.*

Title VII
Contact Committee

Chapter I
Composition, Working and Tasks of the Committee

Article 108

[...]

¶ *Article 108 has been deleted by article 10(1) of Directive 2005/1/EC, reproduced supra under no. B. 39.*

Chapter II
Adaptation of the Amount of Equity Market Capitalisation

[Article 109

1. For the purpose of adjusting, in the light of the requirements of the economic situation, the minimum amount of the foreseeable market capitalisation laid down in Article 43(1), the Commission shall submit to the European Securities Committee instituted by Commission Decision 2001/528/EC of 6 June 2001[11] a draft of the measures to be taken.

2. Where reference is made to this paragraph, Articles 5 and 7 of Council Decision 1999/468/EC of 28 June 1999 laying down the procedures for the exercise of implementing powers conferred on the Commission[12] shall apply, having regard to Article 8 thereof.

---

[11] OJ L 191, 13.7.2001, 45, reproduced infra under no. S. 19. Decision as amended by Decision 2004/8/EC (OJ L 3, 7.1.2004, 33), reproduced supra under no. I. 41.
[12] OJ L 184, 17.7.1999, 23.

The period laid down in Article 5(6) of Decision 1999/468/EC shall be set at three months.

3. The Committee shall adopt its rules of procedure.]

¶ *This article has been replaced by article 10(2) of Directive 2005/1/EC, reproduced supra under no. B. 39.*

Title VIII
Final Provisions

Article 110

The Member States shall communicate to the Commission the texts of the main laws, regulations and administrative provisions which they adopt in the field covered by this Directive.

Article 111

1. Directives 79/279/EEC, 80/390/EEC, 82/121/EEC and 88/627/EEC, as amended by the acts listed in Annex II Part A, are hereby repealed without prejudice to the obligations of the Member States concerning the time-limits for transposition set out in Annex II Part B.

2. References to the repealed Directives shall be construed as references to this Directive and should be read in accordance with the correlation table shown in Annex III.

Article 112

This Directive shall enter into force the twentieth day following that of its publication in the Official Journal of the European Communities.

Article 113

This Directive is addressed to the Member States.

Annex I

[. . .]

¶ *Annex I has been repealed as from 1 July 2005 by article 27(4) of Directive 2003/71/EC, reproduced infra under no. S. 25.*

Annex II

Part A
Repealed Directives and Their Successive Amendments
(referred to in Article 111)

Council Directive 79/279/EEC	(OJ L 66, 16.3.1979, p. 21)
Council Directive 82/148/EEC	(OJ L 62, 5.3.1982, p. 22)
Council Directive 88/627/EEC	(OJ L 348, 17.12.1988, p. 62)
Council Directive 80/390/EEC	(OJ L 100, 17.4.1980, p. 1)
Council Directive 82/148/EEC	(OJ L 62, 5.3.1982, p. 22)
Council Directive 87/345/EEC	(OJ L 185, 4.7.1987, p. 81)

Council Directive 90/211/EEC	(OJ L 112, 3.5.1990, p. 24)
European Parliament and Council Directive 94/18/EC	(OJ L 135, 31.5.1994, p. 1)
Council Directive 82/121/EEC	(OJ L 48, 20.2.1982, p. 26)
Council Directive 88/627/EEC	(OJ L 348, 17.12.1988, p. 62)

Annex II

Part B

TIME-LIMITS FOR TRANSPOSITION INTO NATIONAL LAW
(referred to in Article 111)

Directive	*Time-limit for transposition*
79/279/EC	8 March 1981[13]
80/390/EEC	19 September 1982[14]
82/121/EEC	
	30 June 1983[15]
82/148/EEC	
87/345/EEC	1 January 1990
	1 January 1991 for Spain
88/627/EEC	1 January 1992 for Portugal
90/211/EEC	1 January 1991
94/18/EC	17 April 1991

---

[13] 8.3.1982 for the Member States which introduce simultaneously Directives 79/279/EEC, reproduced supra under no. S. 2 and 80/390/EEC, reproduced supra under no. S. 33.

[14] 30.6.1983 for the Member States which introduce simultaneously Directives 79/279/EEC, reproduced supra under no. S. 2, 80/390/EEC, reproduced supra under no. 33 and 82/121/EEC, reproduced supra under no. 5.4.

[15] Time-limit for application: 30.6.1986.

Annex III

Correlation Table

This Directive	Dir. 79/279/EEC	Dir. 80/390/EEC	Dir. 82/121/EEC	Dir. 88/627/EEC
Article 1(a)		Article 2(c)		
Article 1(b), introductory phrase	Article 2(a), introductory phrase	Article 2(a), introductory phrase		
Article 1(b)(i) and (ii)	Article 2(a), 1st and 2nd indents	Article 2(a), 1st and 2nd indents		
Article 1(c), introductory phrase			Article 1(2), 2nd subparagraph, introductory phrase	
Article 1(c) (i) and (ii)			Article 1(2), 2nd subparagraph, 1st and 2nd indents	
Article 1(d)		Article 2(e)		
Article 1(e)	Article 2(b)	Article 2(b)		
Article 1(f)		Article 2(f)		
Article 1(g)		Article 2(d)		
Article 1(h)		Article 2(g)		
Article 2(1)	Article 1(1)			
Article 2(2), introductory phrase	Article 1(2), introductory phrase			
Article 2(2)(a) and (b)	Article 1(2), 1st and 2nd indents			
Article 3(1)		Article 1(1)		
Article 3(2), introductory phrase		Article 1(2), introductory phrase		
Article 3(2)(a) and (b)		Article 1(2), 1st and 2nd indents		
Article 4(1)			Article 1(1)	
Article 4(2)			Article 1(2), first subparagraph	
Article 4(3)			Article 1(3)	
Article 5(a) and (b)	Article 3, first and second indents			
Article 6	Article 4			
Article 7	Article 6			
Article 8	Article 5			
Article 9	Article 7			
Article 10	Article 8			
Article 11(1)	Article 9(1)			
Article 11(2)	Article 9(3)			
Article 12	Article 10			
Article 13(1)	Article 18(2)			
Article 13(2)	Article 18(3)			

This Directive	Dir. 79/279/EEC	Dir. 80/390/EEC	Dir. 82/121/EEC	Dir. 88/627/EEC
Article 14	Article 11			
Article 15	Article 16			
Article 16	Article 13			
Article 17	Article 12			
Article 18	Article 14			
Article 19	Article 15			
Article 20		Article 3		
Article 21		Article 4		
Article 22		Article 5		
Article 23, introductory phrase		Article 6, introductory phrase		
Article 23(1) and (2)		Article 6(1) and (2)		
Article 23(3)(a)		Article 6(3)(a)		
Article 23(3)(b), introductory phrase		Article 6(3)(b), introductory phrase		
Article 23(3)(b) (i)		Article 6(3)(b), 1st indent		
Article 23(3)(b) (ii)		Article 6(3)(b), 2nd indent		
Article 23(3)(c), introductory phrase		Article 6(3)(c), introductory phrase		
Article 23(3)(c) (i)		Article 6(3)(c), 1st indent		
Article 23(3)(c) (ii)		Article 6(3)(c), 2nd indent		
Article 23(3)(c) (ii), 1st indent		Article 6(3)(c), 2nd indent (i)		
Article 23(3)(c) (ii), 2nd indent		Article 6(3)(c), 2nd indent (ii)		
Article 23(3)(c) (iii)		Article 6(3)(c), 3rd indent		
Article 23(3)(d) to (g)		Article 6(3)(d) to (g)		
Article 23(4) and (5)		Article 6(4) and (5)		
Article 24		Article 7		
Article 25(1), 1st subparagraph, introductory phrase		Article 8(1), 1st subparagraph, introductory phrase		
Article 25(1), 1st subparagraph, (a) to (g)		Article 8(1), 1st subparagraph, 1st to 7th indents		
Article 25(1), 2nd subparagraph, introductory phrase		Article 8(1), 2nd subparagraph, introductory phrase		
Article 25(1), 2nd subparagraph, (a) and (b)		Article 8(1), 2nd subparagraph, 1st and 2nd indents		
Article 25(2), introductory phrase		Article 8(2), introductory phrase		

This Directive	Dir. 79/279/EEC	Dir. 80/390/EEC	Dir. 82/121/EEC	Dir. 88/627/EEC
Article 25(2)(a) to (d)		Article 8(2), 1st to 4th indents		
Article 25(3) and (4)		Article 8(3) and (4)		
Article 26(1), introductory phrase		Article 9(1), introductory phrase		
Article 26(1)(a) to (g)		Article 9(1), 1st to 7th indents		
Article 26(2) and (3)		Article 9(2) and (3)		
Article 27		Article 10		
Article 28(1), introductory phrase		Article 11(1), introductory phrase		
Article 28(1)(a) and (b)		Article 11(1), 1st and 2nd indents		
Article 28(2)		Article 11(2)		
Article 28(3), introductory phrase		Article 11(3), introductory phrase		
Article 28(3)(a), (b) and (c)		Article 11(3) 1st, 2nd and 3rd indent		
Article 29 introductory phrase		Article 12 introductory phrase		
Article 29(a) and (b)		Article 12, 1st and 2nd indents		
Article 30(1), 1st subparagraph, introductory phrase		Article 13(1), 1st subparagraph, introductory phrase		
Article 30(1), 1st subparagraph, (a) and (b)		Article 13(1), 1st subparagraph, 1st and 2nd indents		
Article 30(1), 2nd subparagraph		Article 13(1), 2nd subparagraph		
Article 30(2), introductory phrase		Article 13(2), introductory phrase		
Article 30(2) (a) and (b)		Article 13(2), 1st and 2nd indents		
Article 30(3) and (4)		Article 13(3) and (4)		
Article 31(1), introductory phrase		Article 14(1), introductory phrase		
Article 31(1)(a) to (d)		Article 14(1), 1st to 4th indents		
Article 31(2), 1st subparagraph (a) to (d)		Article 14(2), 1st to 4th indents		
Article 31(2), 2nd subparagraph		Article 14(2), 2nd subparagraph		
Article 32		Article 15		
Article 33(1)		Article 16(1)		
Article 33(2), introductory phrase		Article 16(2), introductory phrase		
Article 33(2)(a), (b) and (c)		Article 16(2), 1st, 2nd and 3rd indents		

This Directive	Dir. 79/279/EEC	Dir. 80/390/EEC	Dir. 82/121/EEC	Dir. 88/627/EEC
Article 33(3)		Article 16(3)		
Article 34		Article 17		
Article 35		Article 18(2) and (3), 1st subparagraph		
Article 36		Article 19		
Article 37		Article 24		
Article 38		Article 24a		
Article 39		Article 24b		
Article 40		Article 24(c) (2) and (3)		
Article 41		Article 25a		
Article 42	Annex—Schedule A (I) (1)			
Article 43	Annex—Schedule A (I) (2)			
Article 44	Annex—Schedule A (I) (3)			
Article 45	Annex—Schedule A (II) (1)			
Article 46	Annex—Schedule A (II) (2)			
Article 47	Annex—Schedule A (II) (3)			
Article 48	Annex—Schedule A (II) (4)			
Article 49	Annex—Schedule A (II) (5)			
Article 50	Annex—Schedule A (II) (6)			
Article 51	Annex—Schedule A (II) (7)			
Article 52	Annex—Schedule B (A) (I)			
Article 53	Annex—Schedule B (A) (II) (1)			
Article 54	Annex—Schedule B (A) (II) (2)			
Article 55	Annex—Schedule B (A) (II) (3)			
Article 56	Annex—Schedule B (A) (II) (4)			
Article 57	Annex—Schedule B (A) (II) (5)			
Article 58	Annex—Schedule B (A) (III) (1)			
Article 59	Annex—Schedule B (A) (III) (2)			
Article 60	Annex—Schedule B (B) (1)			

This Directive	Dir. 79/279/EEC	Dir. 80/390/EEC	Dir. 82/121/EEC	Dir. 88/627/EEC
Article 61	Annex—Schedule B (B) (2)			
Article 62	Annex—Schedule B (B) (3)			
Article 63	Annex—Schedule B (B) (4)			
Article 64	Annex—Schedule C (1)			
Article 65(1)	Annex—Schedule C (2) (a)			
Article 65(2) introductory phrase	Annex—Schedule C (2) (b), introductory phrase			
Article 65(2)(a), (b) and (c)	Annex—Schedule C (2) (b), 1st, 2nd and 3rd indents			
Article 66	Annex—Schedule C (3)			
Article 67	Annex—Schedule C (4)			
Article 68	Annex—Schedule C (5)(a), (b) and (c)			
Article 69	Annex—Schedule C (6)			
Article 70			Article 2	
Article 71			Article 3	
Article 72			Article 4	
Article 73(1)			Article 5(1)	
Article 73(2), 1st subparagraph, introductory phrase			Article 5(2), 1st subparagraph, introductory phrase	
Article 73(2), 1st subparagraph (a) and (b)			Article 5(2), 1st subparagraph, 1st and 2nd indents	
Article 73(2), 2nd subparagraph			Article 5(2), 2nd subparagraph	
Article 73(3) to (7)			Article 5(3) to (7)	
Article 74			Article 6	
Article 75			Article 8	
Article 76			Article 9(3) to (6)	
Article 77			Article 10(2)	
Article 78(1)	Annex—Schedule D (A) (1) (a)			
Article 78(2) introductory phrase	Annex—Schedule D (A) (1) (b), introductory phrase			
Article 78(2)(a) and (b)	Annex—Schedule D (A) (1) (b), 1st and 2nd indents			

This Directive	Dir. 79/279/EEC	Dir. 80/390/EEC	Dir. 82/121/EEC	Dir. 88/627/EEC
Article 79	Annex—Schedule D (A) (2)			
Article 80	Annex—Schedule D (A) (3)			
Article 81	Annex—Schedule D (A) (4)			
Article 82	Annex—Schedule D (A) (5)			
Article 83(1)	Annex—Schedule D (B) (1) (a)			
Article 83(2), introductory phrase	Annex—Schedule D (B) (1) (b), introductory phrase			
Article 83(2)(a) and (b)	Annex—Schedule D (B) (1) (b), 1st and 2nd indents			
Article 84	Annex—Schedule D (B) (2)			
Article 85				Article 1(1), (2) and (3)
Article 86				Article 2
Article 87				Article 8
Article 88				Article 3
Article 89(1), 1st subparagraph, introductory phrase				Article 4(1), 1st subparagraph, introductory phrase
Article 89(1), 1st subparagraph (a) and (b)				Article 4(1), 1st subparagraph, 1st and 2nd indents
Article 89(1), 2nd and 3rd subparagraphs				Article 4(1), 2nd and 3rd subparagraphs
Article 89(2)				Article 4(2)
Article 90				Article 5
Article 91				Article 10(1)
Article 92, 1st subparagraph, introductory phrase				Article 7, 1st subparagraph, introductory phrase
Article 92, 1st subparagraph (a) and (h)				Article 7, 1st subparagraph, 1st to 8th indents
Article 92, 2nd subparagraph				Article 7, 2nd subparagraph
Article 93				Article 6
Article 94				Article 9
Article 95				Article 11
Article 96				Article 13

This Directive	Dir. 79/279/EEC	Dir. 80/390/EEC	Dir. 82/121/EEC	Dir. 88/627/EEC
Article 97				Article 15
Article 98(1), introductory phrase		Article 20(1), introductory phrase		
Article 98(1)(a) and (b)		Article 20(1), 1st and 2nd indents		
Article 98(2)		Article 20(2)		
Article 99(1)		Article 21(1),		
Article 99(2), introductory phrase		Article 21(2), introductory phrase		
Article 99(2)(a) and (b)		Article 21(2), 1st and 2nd indents		
Article 99(3)		Article 21(3)		
Article 100		Article 23		
Article 101		Article 22		
Article 102(1), 1st subparagraph	Article 17(1), 1st sentence			Article 10(2), 1st subparagraph
Article 102(1), 2nd subparagraph	Article 17(1), 2nd sentence			
Article 102(2)			Article 7(1) and (3)	
Article 103	Article 17(2)		Article 7(2),	Article 10(2), 2nd subparagraph
Article 104		Article 6a		
Article 105(1) and (2)	Article 9(1) and (2)	Article 18(1) and (3), 2nd subparagraph	Article 9(1) and (2)	Article 12(1) and (2)
Article 105(3)		Article 18(4)	Article 9(7)	
Article 106	Article 18(1)	Article 24c(1)	Article 10(1)	Article 12(3)
Article 107(1) and (2)	Article 19	Article 25(1) and (2)		Article 14(1) and (2)
Article 107(3) 1st subparagraph		Article 25(3)		
Article 107(3) 2nd subparagraph				Article 14(3)
Article 108(1) 1st subparagraph	Article 20(1), introductory phrase			
Article 108(1), 2nd and 3rd subparagraphs	Article 20(3) and (4)			
Article 108(2), 1st subparagraph, point (a)	Article 20(1), introductory phrase and point (a)	Article 26(1)(a)	Article 11(1)(a)	
Article 108(2), 1st subparagraph, point (b)				Article 16(1)(a)
Article 108(2), 1st subparagraph, point (c) (i)	Article 20(1)(b)			
Article 108(2), 1st subparagraph, point (c) (ii)		Article 26(1)(b)		
Article 108(2), 1st subparagraph, point (c) (iii)			Article 11(1)(b)	Article 16(1)(b)

This Directive	Dir. 79/279/EEC	Dir. 80/390/EEC	Dir. 82/121/EEC	Dir. 88/627/EEC
Article 108(2), 1st subparagraph, point (d)	Article 20(1)(c)	Article 26(1)(c)	Article 11(1)(c)	Article 16(1)(c)
Article 108(2), 2nd subparagraph	Article 20(2)	Article 26(2)		
Article 109	Article 21			
Article 110	Article 22(2)	Article 27(2)	Article 12(3)	Article 17(2)
Article 111				
Article 112				
Article 113				
Annex I—Schedule A, Chapter I		Annex—Schedule A, Chapter I		
Annex I—Schedule A, Chapter 2—2.1 to 2.4.4		Annex—Schedule A, Chapter 2—2.1 to 2.4.4		
Annex I—Schedule A, Chapter 2—2.4.5, 1st subparagraph, introductory phrase		Annex—Schedule A, Chapter 2—2.4.5, 1st subparagraph, introductory phrase		
Annex I—Schedule A, Chapter 2—2.4.5, 1st subparagraph (a) and (b)		Annex—Schedule A, Chapter 2—2.4.5, 1st subparagraph, 1st and 2nd indents		
Annex I—Schedule A, Chapter 2—2.4.5, 2nd subparagraph		Annex—Schedule A, Chapter 2—2.4.5, 2nd subparagraph		
Annex I—Schedule A, Chapter 2—2.5		Annex—Schedule A, Chapter 2—2.5		
Annex I—Schedule A, Chapter 3—3.1 to 3.2.0		Annex—Schedule A, Chapter 3—3.1 to 3.2.0		
Annex I—Schedule A, Chapter 3—3.2.1 introductory phrase		Annex—Schedule A, Chapter 3—3.2.1 introductory phrase		
Annex I—Schedule A, Chapter 3—3.2.1 (a), (b) and (c)		Annex—Schedule A, Chapter 3—3.2.1, 1st, 2nd and 3rd indents		
Annex I—Schedule A, Chapter 3—3.2.2 to 3.2.9		Annex—Schedule A, Chapter 3—3.2.2 to 3.2.9		
Annex I—Schedule A, Chapter 4		Annex—Schedule A, Chapter 4		
Annex I—Schedule A, Chapter 5—5.1 to 5.3		Annex—Schedule A, Chapter 5—5.1 to 5.3		
Annex I—Schedule A, Chapter 5—5.4 (a) and (b)		Annex—Schedule A, Chapter 5—5.4 (a) and (b)		
Annex I—Schedule A, Chapter 5—5.4 (c)(i) and (ii)		Annex—Schedule A, Chapter 5—5.4 (c) 1st and 2nd indents		

This Directive	Dir. 79/279/EEC	Dir. 80/390/EEC	Dir. 82/121/EEC	Dir. 88/627/EEC
Annex I—Schedule A, Chapter 5—5.5 and 5.6		Annex—Schedule A, Chapter 5—5.5 and 5.6		
Annex I—Schedule A, Chapter 6		Annex—Schedule A, Chapter 6		
Annex I—Schedule A, Chapter 7—7.1 introductory phrase		Annex—Schedule A, Chapter 7—7.1 introductory phrase		
Annex I—Schedule A, Chapter 7—7.1 (a) and (b)		Annex—Schedule A, Chapter 7—7.1, 1st and 2nd indents		
Annex I—Schedule A, Chapter 7—7.2		Annex—Schedule A, Chapter 7—7.2		
Annex I—Schedule B, Chapter 1—4		Annex—Schedule B, Chapter 1—4		
Annex I—Schedule B, Chapter 5—5.1 to 5.1.3		Annex—Schedule B, Chapter 5—5.1 to 5.1.3		
Annex I—Schedule B, Chapter 5—5.1.4, 1st subparagraph, introductory phrase		Annex—Schedule B, Chapter 5—5.1.4, 1st subparagraph, introductory phrase		
Annex I—Schedule B, Chapter 5—5.1.4, 1st subparagraph (a), (b) and (c)		Annex—Schedule B, Chapter 5—5.1.4, 1st subparagraph, 1st, 2nd and 3rd indents		
Annex I—Schedule B, Chapter 5—5.1.4, 2nd, 3erd and 4th subparagraphs		Annex—Schedule B, Chapter 5—5.1.4, 2nd, 3rd and 4th subparagraphs		
Annex I—Schedule B, Chapter 5—5.1.5 to 5.2		Annex—Schedule B, Chapter 5—5.1.5 to 5.2		
Annex I—Schedule B, Chapter 5—5.3 introductory sentence		Annex—Schedule B, Chapter 5—5.3 introductory sentence		
Annex I—Schedule B, Chapter 5—5.3(a) and (b)		Annex—Schedule B, Chapter 5—5.3 (a) and (b)		
Annex I—Schedule B, Chapter 5—5.3(c) (i) and (ii)		Annex—Schedule B, Chapter 5—5.3(c) 1st and 2nd indents		
Annex I—Schedule B, Chapter 6		Annex—Schedule B, Chapter 6		
Annex I—Schedule B, Chapter 7—7.1 introductory phrase		Annex—Schedule B, Chapter 7—7.1 introductory phrase		
Annex I—Schedule B, Chapter 7—7.1(a) and (b)		Annex—Schedule B, Chapter 7—7.1, 1st and 2nd indents		

This Directive	Dir. 79/279/EEC	Dir. 80/390/EEC	Dir. 82/121/EEC	Dir. 88/627/EEC
Annex I—Schedule B, Chapter 7—7.2		Annex—Schedule B, Chapter 7—7.2		
Annex I—Schedule C, Chapter 1		Annex—Schedule C, Chapter 1		
Annex I—Schedule C, Chapter 2—2.1 to 2.1.2		Annex—Schedule C, Chapter 2—2.1.2		
Annex I—Schedule C, Chapter 2—2.2 introductory phrase		Annex—Schedule C, Chapter 2—2.2 introductory phrase		
Annex I—Schedule C, Chapter 2—2.2 (a) to (d)		Annex—Schedule C, Chapter 2—2.2, 1st to 4th indents		
Annex I—Schedule C, Chapter 2—2.3 to 2.6		Annex—Schedule C, Chapter 2—2.3 to 2.6		
Annex II				
Annex III				

S. 19.

Commission Decision 2001/527/EC
of 6 June 2001
establishing the Committee of European Securities Regulators
(notified under document number C(2001) 1501)[1]

(Text with EEA relevance)

THE COMMISSION OF THE EUROPEAN COMMUNITIES,

Having regard to the Treaty establishing the European Community,

Whereas:

(1) The freedom to provide services and the free movement of capital constitute priority objectives of the Community, as referred to in Articles 49 and 56 of the EC Treaty.

(2) Building a genuine internal market for financial services is crucial for increasing economic growth and job creation in the Community.

(3) The Commission action plan for financial services[2] identifies a series of actions that are required in order to complete the single market for financial services.

(4) At its meeting in Lisbon in March 2000, the European Council called for the implementation of this action plan by 2005.

(5) On 17 July 2000 the Council set up the Committee of Wise Men on the regulation of European securities markets.

(6) In its final report, the Committee of Wise Men called for the establishment of two committees, the European Securities Committee, comprising high-level representatives of Member States, and the Committee of European Securities Regulators, comprising senior representatives from the national public authorities competent in the field of securities in order, inter alia, to advise the Commission.

(7) In its resolution on more effective securities-market regulation in the European Union, the Stockholm European Council welcomed the Commission's intention formally to establish an independent regulators committee, as proposed in the report of the Committee of Wise Men.

(8) The Committee of European Securities Regulators should serve as an independent body for reflection, debate and advice for the Commission in the securities field.

(9) The Committee of European Securities Regulators should also contribute to the consistent and timely implementation of Community legislation in the Member States by securing more effective co-operation between national supervisory authorities, carrying out peer reviews and promoting best practice.[3]

(10) The Committee of European Securities Regulators should organise its own operational arrangements and maintain close operational links with the Commission and the European Securities Committee. It should elect its chairperson from among its members.

(11) The Committee of European Securities Regulators should consult extensively and at an early stage with market participants, consumers and end-users in an open and transparent manner.

---

[1] OJ L 191, 13.7.2001, 43–44.
[2] COM(1999) 232 final.

[3] Text taken from the third paragraph of point 6 of the Stockholm European Council resolution.

(12) The Committee of European Securities Regulators should draw up its own rules of procedure and fully respect the prerogatives of the institutions and the institutional balance established by the Treaty,[4]

HAS DECIDED AS FOLLOWS:

Article 1

An independent advisory group on securities in the Community, called the 'Committee of European Securities Regulators' (hereinafter referred to as the 'Committee'), is hereby established.

[Article 2

The role of the Committee shall be to advise the Commission, either at the Commission's request, within a time limit which the Commission may lay down according to the urgency of the matter, or on the Committee's own initiative, in particular for the preparation of draft implementing measures in the field of securities, including those relating to undertakings for collective investment in transferable securities (UCITS).]

¶ *Article 2 has been replaced by article 1 of Commission Decision 2004/7/EC of 5 November 2003 amending Decision 2001/527/EC establishing the Committee of European Securities Regulation (OJ L 3, 7.1.2004, 32).*

Article 3

[The Committee shall be composed of high-level representatives from the national public authorities competent in the field of securities, including UCITS.] Each Member State shall designate a high-level representative from its competent authority to participate in the meetings of the Committee.

The Commission shall be present at meetings of the Committee and shall designate a high-level representative to participate in all its debates.

The Committee shall elect a chairperson from among its members.

The Committee may invite experts and observers to attend its meetings.

¶ *The first sentence of article 3 has been replaced by article 1 of Commission Decision 2004/7/EC of 5 November 2003 amending Decision 2001/527/EC establishing the Committee of European Securities Regulation (OJ L 3, 7.1.2004, 32).*

Article 4

The Committee shall maintain close operational links with the Commission and the European Securities Committee.

It may set up working groups.

Article 5

Before transmitting its opinion to the Commission, the Committee shall consult extensively and at the early stage with market participants, consumers and end-users in an open and transparent manner.

Article 6

The Committee shall present an annual report to the Commission.

Article 7

The Committee shall adopt its own rules of procedure and organise its own operational arrangements.

Article 8

The Committee shall take up its duties on 7 June 2001.

---

[4] Text taken from the last paragraph of the preamble to the Stockholm European Council resolution.

S. 20.

Commission Decision 2001/528/EC of 6 June 2001 establishing the European Securities Committee (notified under document number C(2001) 1493)[1]

(Text with EEA relevance)

THE COMMISSION OF THE EUROPEAN COMMUNITIES,

Having regard to the Treaty establishing the European Community,

Whereas:

(1) The freedom to provide services and the free movement of capital constitute priority objectives of the Community, as referred to in Articles 49 and 56 of the EC Treaty.

(2) Building a genuine internal market for financial services in accordance with the principle of an open market economy with free competition is crucial for increasing economic growth and job creation in the Community.

(3) The Commission action plan for financial services[2] identifies a series of actions that are required in order to complete the single market for financial services and stresses the necessity to set up a securities committee in order to contribute to the elaboration of Community legislation in the securities field.

(4) At its meeting in Lisbon in March 2000, the European Council called for the implementation of this action plan by 2005.

(5) On 17 July 2000, the Council set up the Committee of Wise Men on the regulation of European securities markets.

(6) In its final report, the Committee of Wise Men called for the establishment of two advisory committees, the European Securities Committee, comprising high-level representatives of Member States, and the Committee of European Securities Regulators, comprising senior representatives from the national public authorities competent in the field of securities in order, inter alia, to advise the Commission.

(7) In its resolution on more effective securities market regulation in the European Union, the Stockholm European Council welcomed the intention of the Commission immediately to establish a securities committee of high-level officials from Member States, chaired by the Commission.

(8) The final report of the Committee of Wise Men emphasised the fact that implementing measures will be necessary for the application of directives or regulations in order to take account of new developments on financial markets.

(9) The European Securities Committee should serve as a body for reflection, debate and advice for the Commission in the field of securities.

(10) The European Securities Committee should adopt its own rules of procedure.

(11) This Decision establishes the European Securities Committee in its advisory capacity. Subject to specific legislative acts proposed by the Commission and adopted by the European Parliament and the Council, the Securities Committee should also function as a regulatory committee in accordance with the 1999 Decision on comitology to assist the Commission when it takes decisions on implementing measures under Article 202 of the EC Treaty,

---

[1] OJ L 191, 13.7.2001, 45–46.
[2] COM (1999) 232 final.

Article 1

A committee on securities in the Community, called the "European Securities Committee" (hereinafter referred to as the "Committee"), is hereby established.

[Article 2

The role of the Committee shall be to advise the Commission on policy issues as well as on draft proposals the Commission might adopt in the field of securities, including on undertakings for collective investment in transferable securities (UCITS).]

¶ *This article has been replaced by article 1 of Commission Decision 2004/8/EC of 5 November 2003 (OJ L 3, 7.1.2004, 33).*

Article 3

The Committee shall be composed of high-level representatives of Member States and be chaired by a representative of the Commission. The chairperson of the Committee of European Securities Regulators established by Commission Decision 2001/527/EC[3] shall participate at the meetings of the Committee as an observer.

The Committee may invite experts and observers to attend meetings.

Article 4

The Committee may set up working groups.

Article 5

The Committee shall adopt its own rules of procedure.

The secretariat of the Committee shall be provided by the Commission.

Article 6

The Committee shall take up its duties on 7 June 2001.

---

[3] See page 43 of this Official Journal.

S. 21.

European Parliament and Council Directive 2001/107/EC of 21 January 2002 amending Council Directive 85/611/EEC on the coordination of laws, regulations and administrative provisions relating to undertakings for collective investment in transferable securities (UCITS) with a view to regulating management companies and simplified prospectuses[1]

THE EUROPEAN PARLIAMENT AND THE COUNCIL OF THE EUROPEAN UNION,

Having regard to the Treaty establishing the European Community, and in particular Article 47(2) thereof,

Having regard to the proposal from the Commission,[2]

Having regard to the opinion of the Economic and Social Committee,[3]

Acting in accordance with the procedure laid down in Article 251 of the Treaty,[4]

Whereas:

(1) Council Directive 85/611/EEC of 20 December 1985 on undertakings for collective investment in transferable securities (UCITS),[5] has already contributed significantly to the achievement of the Single Market in this field, laying down—for the first time in the financial services sector—the principle of mutual recognition of authorisation and other provisions which facilitate the free circulation within the European Union of the units of the collective investment undertakings (unit trusts/common funds or as investment companies) covered by that Directive.

(2) However, Directive 85/611/EEC does not regulate to a great extent the companies which manage collective investment undertakings (so-called 'management companies'). In particular, Directive 85/611/EEC does not lay down provisions ensuring in all Member States equivalent market access rules and operating conditions for such companies. Directive 85/611/EEC does not lay down provisions regulating the establishment of branches and the free provision of services by such companies in Member States other than their home Member State.

(3) Authorisation granted in the management company's home Member State should ensure investor protection and the solvency of management companies, with a view to contributing to the stability of the financial system. The approach adopted is to ensure the essential harmonisation necessary and sufficient to secure the mutual recognition of authorisation and of prudential supervision systems, making possible the grant of a single authorisation valid throughout the European Union and the application of the home Member State supervision.

(4) It is necessary, for the protection of investors, to guarantee the internal overview of every management company in particular by means of a two-man management and by adequate internal control mechanisms.

(5) In order to ensure that the management company will be able to fulfil the obligations arising from its activities and thus to ensure its stability, initial capital and an additional amount

---

[1] OJ L 41, 13.2.2002, 20–34.
[2] OJ C 272, 1.9.1998, 7 and OJ C 311 E, 31.10.2000, 273.
[3] OJ C 116, 28.4.1999, 1.
[4] Opinion of the European Parliament of 17 February 2000 (OJ C 339, 29.11.2000, 228), Council Common Position of 5 June 2001 (OJ C 297, 23.10.2001, 10) and Decision of the European Parliament of 23 October 2001. Council Decision of 4 December 2001.
[5] OJ L 375, 31.12.1985, 3, reproduced supra under no. S. 6. Directive as last amended by Directive 2000/64/EC of the European Parliament and the Council (OJ L 290, 17.11.2000, 27).

of own funds are required. To take account of developments, particularly those pertaining to capital charges on operational risk within the European Union and other international fora, these requirements, including the use of guarantees, will have to be reviewed within three years.

(6) By virtue of mutual recognition, management companies authorised in their home Member States should be permitted to carry on the services for which they have received authorisation throughout the European Union by establishing branches or under the freedom to provide services. The approval of the fund rules of common funds/unit trusts falls within the competence of the management company's home Member State.

(7) With regard to collective portfolio management (management of unit trusts/common funds and investment companies), the authorisation granted to a management company authorised in its home Member State should permit the company to carry on in host Member States the following activities: to distribute the units of the harmonised unit trusts/common funds managed by the company in its home Member State; to distribute the shares of the harmonised investment companies, managed by such a company; to perform all the other functions and tasks included in the activity of collective portfolio management; to manage the assets of investment companies incorporated in Member States other than its home Member State; to perform, on the basis of mandates, on behalf of management companies incorporated in Member States other than its home Member State, the functions included in the activity of collective portfolio management.

(8) The principles of mutual recognition and of home Member State supervision require that the Member States' competent authorities should not grant or should withdraw authorisation where factors, such as the content of programmes of operations, the geographical distribution or the activities actually carried on indicate clearly that a management company has opted for the legal system of one Member State for the purpose of evading the stricter standards in force in another Member State within the territory of which it intends to carry on or does carry on the greater part of its activities. For the purpose of this Directive, a management company should be authorised in the Member State in which it has its registered office. In accordance with the principle of the home country control, only the Member State in which the management company has its registered office can be considered competent to approve the fund rules of unit trusts/common funds set up by such a company and the choice of the depositary. In order to prevent supervisory arbitrage and to promote confidence in the effectiveness of supervision by the home Member State authorities, a requirement for authorisation of a UCITS should be that it should not be prevented in any legal way from being marketed in its home Member State. This does not affect the free decision, once the UCITS has been authorised, to choose the Member State(s) where the units of the UCITS are to be marketed in accordance with this Directive.

(9) Directive 85/611/EEC limits the scope of management companies to the sole activity of management of unit trusts/common funds and of investment companies (collective portfolio management). In order to take into account recent developments in national legislation of Member States and to permit such companies to achieve important economies of scale, it is desirable to revise this restriction. It is therefore desirable to permit such companies to carry out also the activity of management of portfolios of investments on a client-by-client basis (individual portfolio management) including the management of pension funds as well as some specific non-core activities linked to the main business. Such an extension of the scope of the activity of the management company would not prejudge the stability of such companies. However, specific rules should be introduced preventing conflicts of interest when management companies are authorised to carry on both the business of collective and individual portfolio management.

(10) The activity of management of portfolios of investments is an investment service already covered by Council Directive 93/22/EEC of 10 May 1993 on investment services in the securities

field.[6] In order to ensure a homogeneous regulatory framework in this area, it is desirable to subject management companies, the authorisation of which also covers that service, to the operating conditions laid down in that Directive.

(11) A home Member State may, as a general rule, establish rules stricter than those laid down in this Directive, in particular as regards authorisation conditions, prudential requirements and the rules on reporting and the full prospectus.

(12) It is desirable to lay down rules defining the preconditions under which a management company may delegate, on the basis of mandates, specific tasks and functions to third parties so as to increase the efficiency of the conduct of its business. In order to ensure the correct functioning of the principles of mutual recognition of the authorisation and of the home country control, Member States permitting such delegations should ensure that the management company to which they granted an authorisation does not delegate globally its functions to one or more third parties, so as to become a letter box entity, and the existence of mandates does not hinder an effective supervision over the management company. However, the fact that the management company has delegated its own functions should in no case affect the liabilities of that company and of the depositary vis-à-vis the unit holders and the competent authorities.

(13) To safeguard shareholders' interests and to secure a level playing field in the market for harmonised collective investment undertakings, an initial capital is required for investment companies. However, investment companies which have designated a management company will be covered through the management company's additional amount of own funds.

(14) Articles 5g and 5h should always be complied with by authorised investment companies, either by the company directly according to Article 13b or indirectly, due to the fact that if an authorised investment company chooses to designate a management company, that management company should be authorised in accordance with the Directive and thus obliged to comply with Articles 5g and 5h.

(15) To take into account developments of information techniques, it is desirable to revise the current information framework provided for in Directive 85/611/EEC. In particular, it is desirable to introduce, in addition to the existing full prospectus, a new type of prospectus for UCITS (simplified prospectus). Such a new prospectus should be designed to be investor-friendly and should therefore represent a source of valuable information for the average investor. Such a prospectus should give key information about the UCITS in a clear, concise and easily understandable way. However, the investor should always be informed, by an appropriate statement to be included in the simplified prospectus, that more detailed information is contained in the full prospectus and in the UCITS' yearly and half-yearly report, which can be obtained free of charge at his/her request. The simplified prospectus should always be offered free of charge to subscribers before the conclusion of the contract. This should be a sufficient precondition to meet the legal obligation under this Directive to provide information to subscribers before the conclusion of the contract.

(16) There is a need to ensure a level playing field among intermediaries in the financial services area when providing the same services and to ensure a harmonised minimum degree of investor protection. A harmonised minimum degree of harmonisation of the conditions for taking up business and operating conditions represents the essential precondition for achieving the internal market for these operators. Therefore, only a binding Community Directive laying down agreed minimum standards in this respect can achieve the desired objectives. This Directive effects only the minimum harmonisation required, and does not go beyond what is necessary in order to achieve the objectives pursued in accordance with the third paragraph of Article 5 of the Treaty.

(17) The Commission may consider proposing codification in due time after adoption of the proposals,

---

[6] OJ L 141, 11.6.1993, 27, reproduced supra under no. S. 14. Directive as last amended by Directive 2000/64/EC.

Article 1

[...]

¶ *Article 1 inserts articles 1a and 13, the title of Section IIIa, the title of Section IV, the title of Section IVa, replaces articles 4(3), 5, 6, 12, 27(1), 28, 29, 30, 32, 33, 35, 46, and 47, the title of Section III, Schedule A of Annex I, and adds articles 52a and 52b, and the text between square brackets in Annex I and Annex II to Directive 85/611/EEC, reproduced supra under no. S. 6. The modifications are directly incorporated therein.*

Transitional and final provisions

Article 2

1. Investment firms, as defined in Article 1(2) of Directive 93/22/EEC, authorised to carry out only the services provided for in Section A(3) and in Section C(1) and (6) of the Annex to that Directive, may obtain authorisation under this Directive to manage unit trusts/common funds and investment companies and to qualify themselves as 'management companies'. In that case, such investment firms must give up the authorisation obtained under Directive 93/22/EEC.

2. Management companies already authorised before 13 February 2004 in their home Member State under Directive 85/611/EEC to manage UCITS in the form of unit trusts/common funds and investment companies shall be deemed to be authorised for the purposes of this Directive if the laws of those Member States provide that to take up such activity they must comply with conditions equivalent to those imposed in Articles 5a and 5b.

3. Management companies, already authorised before 13 February 2004, which are not included among those referred to in paragraph 2 may continue such activity provided that, no later than 13 February 2007 and pursuant to the provisions of their home Member State, they obtain authorisation to continue such activity in accordance with the provisions adopted in implementation of this Directive.

Only the grant of such authorisation shall enable such management companies to qualify under the provisions of this Directive on the right of establishment and the freedom to provide services.

Article 3

No later than 13 August 2003 Member States shall adopt the laws, regulations and administrative provisions necessary for them to comply with this Directive. They shall forthwith inform the Commission thereof.

They shall apply these measures no later than 13 February 2004.

When Member States adopt these measures they shall contain a reference to this Directive or shall be accompanied by such reference on the occasion of their official publication. The methods of making such a reference shall be laid down by the Member States.

Article 4

This Directive shall enter into force on the date of its publication in the Official Journal of the European Communities.

Article 5

This Directive is addressed to the Member States.

S. 22.

European Parliament and Council Directive 2001/108/EC of 21 January 2002 amending Council Directive 85/611/EEC on the coordination of laws, regulations and administrative provisions relating to undertakings for collective investment in transferable securities (UCITS), with regard to investments of UCITS[1]

THE EUROPEAN PARLIAMENT AND THE COUNCIL OF THE EUROPEAN UNION,

Having regard to the Treaty establishing the European Community, and in particular Article 47(2) thereof,

Having regard to the proposal from the Commission,[2]

Having regard to the opinion of the Economic and Social Committee,[3]

Acting in accordance with the procedure laid down in Article 251 of the Treaty,[4]

Whereas:

(1) The scope of Council Directive 85/611/EEC[5] was confined initially to collective investment undertakings of the open-ended type which promote the sale of their units to the public in the Community and the sole object of which is investment in transferable securities (UCITS). It was envisaged in the preamble to Directive 85/611/EEC that collective investment undertakings falling outside its scope would be the subject of coordination at a later stage.

(2) Taking into account market developments, it is desirable that the investment objective of UCITS be widened in order to permit them to invest in financial instruments, other than transferable securities, which are sufficiently liquid. The financial instruments which are eligible to be investment assets of the portfolio of the UCITS are listed in this Directive. The selection of investments for a portfolio by means of an index is a management technique.

(3) The definition of transferable securities included in this Directive is valid only for this Directive and in no way affects the various definitions used in national legislation for other purposes such as taxation. Consequently, shares and other securities equivalent to shares issued by bodies such as building societies and industrial and provident societies, the ownership of which cannot in practice be transferred except by the issuing body buying them back, are not covered by this definition.

(4) Money market instruments cover those transferable instruments which are normally not traded on regulated markets but dealt in on the money market, for example treasury and local authority bills, certificates of deposit, commercial paper, medium-term notes and bankers' acceptances.

(5) It is useful to ensure that the concept of regulated market in this Directive corresponds to that in Council Directive 93/22/EEC of 10 May 1993 on investment services in the securities field.[6]

(6) It is desirable to permit a UCITS to invest its assets in units of UCITS and/or other collective investment undertakings of the open-ended type

---

[1] OJ L 41, 13.2.2002, 35–42.
[2] OJ C 280, 9.9.1998, 6 and OJ C 311 E, 31.10.2000, 302.
[3] OJ C 116, 28.4.1999, 44.
[4] Opinion of the European Parliament of 17 February 2000 (OJ C 339, 29.11.2000, 220), Council Common Position of 5 June 2001 (OJ C 297, 23.10.2001, 35) and Decision of the European Parliament of 23 October 2001. Council Decision of 4 December 2001.
[5] OJ L 375, 31.12.1985, 3, reproduced supra under no. S. 6. Directive as last amended by Directive 2000/64/EC of the European Parliament and of the Council (OJ L 290, 17.11.2000, 27).

[6] OJ L 141, 11.6.1993, 27, reproduced supra under no. S. 14. Directive as last amended by Directive 2000/64/EC.

which also invest in liquid financial assets mentioned in this Directive and which operate on the principle of risk spreading. It is necessary that UCITS or other collective investment undertakings in which a UCITS invests be subject to effective supervision.

(7) The development of opportunities for a UCITS to invest in UCITS and in other collective investment undertakings should be facilitated. It is therefore essential to ensure that such investment activity does not diminish investor protection. Owing to the enhanced possibilities for UCITS to invest in the units of other UCITS and/or collective investment undertakings, it is necessary to lay down certain rules on quantitative limits, the disclosure of information and prevention of the cascade phenomenon.

(8) To take market developments into account and in consideration of the completion of economic and monetary union it is desirable to permit UCITS to invest in bank deposits. To ensure adequate liquidity of investments in deposits, these deposits are to be repayable on demand or have the right to be withdrawn. If the deposits are made with a credit institution the registered office of which is located in a non-Member State, the credit institution should be subject to prudential rules equivalent to those laid down in Community legislation.

(9) In addition to the case in which a UCITS invests in bank deposits according to its fund rules or instruments of incorporation, it may be necessary to allow all UCITS to hold ancillary liquid assets, such as bank deposits at sight. The holding of such ancillary liquid assets may be justified, for example, in the following cases: in order to cover current or exceptional payments; in the case of sales, for the time necessary to reinvest in transferable securities, money market instruments and/or in other financial assets provided for in this Directive; for a period of time strictly necessary when, because of unfavourable market conditions, the investment in transferable securities, money market instruments and in other financial assets must be suspended.

(10) For prudential reasons it is necessary to avoid excessive concentration by a UCITS in investments which expose them to counterparty risk to the same entity or to entities belonging to the same group.

(11) UCITS should be explicitly permitted, as part of their general investment policy and/or for hedging purposes in order to reach a set financial target or the risk profile indicated in the prospectus, to invest in financial derivative instruments. In order to ensure investor protection, it is necessary to limit the maximum potential exposure relating to derivative instruments so that it does not exceed the total net value of the UCITS's portfolio. In order to ensure constant awareness of the risks and commitments arising from derivative transactions and to check compliance with investment limits, these risks and commitments will have to be measured and monitored on an ongoing basis. Finally, in order to ensure investor protection through disclosure, UCITS should describe their strategies, techniques and investment limits governing their derivative operations.

(12) With regard to over-the-counter (OTC) derivatives, additional requirements should be set in terms of the eligibility of counterparties and instruments, liquidity and ongoing assessment of the position. The purpose of such additional requirements is to ensure an adequate level of investor protection, close to that which they obtain when they acquire derivatives dealt in on regulated markets.

(13) Operations in derivatives may never be used to circumvent the principles and rules set out in this Directive. With regard to OTC derivatives, additional risk-spreading rules should apply to exposures to a single counterparty or group of counterparties.

(14) Some portfolio management techniques for collective investment undertakings investing primarily in shares and/or debt securities are based on the replication of stock indices and/or debt-security indices. It is desirable to permit UCITS to replicate well-known and recognised stock indices and/or debt-security indices. It may therefore be necessary to introduce more flexible risk-spreading rules for UCITS investing in shares and/or debt securities to this end.

(15) Collective investment undertakings falling within the scope of this Directive should not be used for purposes other than the collective investment of the money raised from the public according to the rules laid down in this Directive. In the cases identified by this Directive a UCITS may have subsidiaries only when necessary to carry out effectively on behalf of that UCITS certain activities, also defined in this Directive. It is necessary to ensure an effective supervision of UCITS. Therefore the establishment of a subsidiary of a UCITS in a third country should be permitted only in the cases and under the conditions identified in the Directive. The general obligation to act solely in the interests of unit-holders and, in particular, the objective of increasing cost efficiencies, never justify a UCITS undertaking measures which may hinder the competent authorities from exercising effectively their supervisory functions.

(16) There is a need to ensure the free cross-border marketing of the units of a wider range of collective investment undertakings, while providing a uniform minimum level of investor protection. Therefore, only a binding Community Directive laying down agreed minimum standards can achieve the desired objectives. This Directive effects only the minimum harmonisation required and does not go beyond what is necessary in order to achieve the objectives pursued in accordance with the third paragraph of Article 5 of the Treaty.

(17) The measures necessary for the implementation of this Directive should be adopted in accordance with Council Decision 1999/468/EC of 28 June 1999 laying down the procedures for the exercise of implementing powers conferred on the Commission.[7]

(18) The Commission may consider proposing codification in due course after the adoption of the proposals,

HAVE ADOPTED THIS DIRECTIVE:

Article 1

[. . .]

---

[7] OJ L 184, 17.7.1999, 23.

¶ *Article 1 amends articles 1(2), 19(1)(b) and (c), 19(2)(a), and 23(1), adds article 1, paragraphs 8 and 9 and article 19(1)(e)–(h), replaces articles 19(1)(a), 21, 22, 24, 25(2), 25(3)(a), (b) and (c), 25(3)(e), 26(1), 41(2), and 42, deletes articles 19(2)(b) and (3) and 20, inserts article 22a, 24a, 25(2)(1) and (2), and 53a in Directive 85/611/EEC, reproduced supra under no. S. 6. The modifications are directly incorporated therein.*

Article 2

1. No later than 13 February 2005, the Commission shall forward to the European Parliament and the Council a report on the application of Directive 85/611/EEC as amended and proposals for amendments, where appropriate. The report shall in particular:

(a) analyse how to deepen and broaden the single market for UCITS, in particular with regard to cross-border marketing of UCITS (including third-party funds), the functioning of the passport for management companies, the functioning of the simplified prospectus as an information and marketing tool, the review of the scope of ancillary activities and the possibilities for improved collaboration of supervisory authorities with respect to common interpretation and application of the Directive;

(b) review the scope of the Directive in terms of how it applies to different types of products (e.g. institutional funds, real-estate funds, master-feeder funds and hedge funds); the study should in particular focus on the size of the market for such funds, the regulation, where applicable, of these funds in the Member States and an evaluation of the need for further harmonisation of these funds;

(c) evaluate the organisation of funds, including the delegation rules and practices and the relationship between fund manager and depositary;

(d) review the investment rules for UCITS, for example the use of derivatives and other instruments and techniques relating to securities, the regulation of index funds, the regulation of money market instruments, deposits, the regulation of 'fund of fund' investments, as well as the various investment limits;

(e) analyse the competitive situation between funds managed by management companies and 'self-managed' investment companies.

In preparing its report, the Commission shall consult as widely as possible with the various industries concerned and with consumer groups and supervisory bodies.

2. Member States may grant UCITS existing on the date of entry into force of this Directive a period of not more than 60 months from that date in order to comply with the new national legislation.

Article 3

No later than 13 August 2003 Member States shall adopt the laws, regulations and administrative provisions necessary for them to comply with this Directive. They shall forthwith inform the Commission thereof.

They shall apply these measures no later than 13 February 2004.

When Member States adopt these measures they shall contain a reference to this Directive or shall be accompanied by such reference on the occasion of their official publication. The methods of making such a reference shall be laid down by the Member States.

Article 4

This Directive shall enter into force on the date of its publication in the Official Journal of the European Communities.

Article 5

This Directive is addressed to the Member States.

S. 23.

European Parliament and Council Directive 2002/47/EC of 6 June 2002 on financial collateral arrangements[1]

THE EUROPEAN PARLIAMENT AND THE COUNCIL OF THE EUROPEAN UNION,

Having regard to the Treaty establishing the European Community, and in particular Article 95 thereof,

Having regard to the proposal from the Commission,[2]

Having regard to the opinion of the European Central Bank,[3]

Having regard to the opinion of the Economic and Social Committee,[4]

Acting in accordance with the procedure laid down in Article 251 of the Treaty,[5]

Whereas:

(1) Directive 98/26/EC of the European Parliament and of the Council of 19 May 1998 on settlement finality in payment and securities settlement systems[6] constituted a milestone in establishing a sound legal framework for payment and securities settlement systems. Implementation of that Directive has demonstrated the importance of limiting systemic risk inherent in such systems stemming from the different influence of several jurisdictions, and the benefits of common rules in relation to collateral constituted to such systems.

(2) In its communication of 11 May 1999 to the European Parliament and to the Council on financial services: implementing the framework for financial markets: action plan, the Commission undertook, after consultation with market experts and national authorities, to work on further proposals for legislative action on collateral urging further progress in the field of collateral, beyond Directive 98/26/EC.

(3) A Community regime should be created for the provision of securities and cash as collateral under both security interest and title transfer structures including repurchase agreements (repos). This will contribute to the integration and cost-efficiency of the financial market as well as to the stability of the financial system in the Community, thereby supporting the freedom to provide services and the free movement of capital in the single market in financial services. This Directive focuses on bilateral financial collateral arrangements.

(4) This Directive is adopted in a European legal context which consists in particular of the said Directive 98/26/EC as well as Directive 2001/24/EC of the European Parliament and of the Council of 4 April 2001 on the reorganisation and winding up of credit institutions,[7] Directive 2001/17/EC of the European Parliament and of the Council of 19 March 2001 on the reorganisation and winding-up of insurance undertakings[8] and Council Regulation 1346/2000/EC of 29 May 2000 on insolvency proceedings.[9] This Directive is in line with the general pattern of these previous legal acts and is not opposed to it. Indeed, this Directive complements these existing legal acts by dealing with further issues and going beyond them in connection with particular matters already dealt with by these legal acts.

---

[1] OJ L 168, 27.6.2002, 43–50.
[2] OJ C 180 E, 26.6.2001, 312.
[3] OJ C 196, 12.7.2001, 10.
[4] OJ C 48, 21.2.2002, 1.
[5] Opinion of the European Parliament of 13 December 2001 (OJ C 177, 25.7.2002, 287), Council Common Position of 5 March 2002 (OJ C 119, 22.5.2002, 12) and Decision of the European Parliament of 15 May 2002.
[6] OJ L 166, 11.6.1998, 45, reproduced supra under no. S. 17.

[7] OJ L 125, 5.5.2001, 15, reproduced supra under no. B. 36.
[8] OJ L 110, 20.4.2001, 28.
[9] OJ L 160, 30.6.2000, 1, reproduced supra under no. E. 9.

(5) In order to improve the legal certainty of financial collateral arrangements, Member States should ensure that certain provisions of insolvency law do not apply to such arrangements, in particular, those that would inhibit the effective realisation of financial collateral or cast doubt on the validity of current techniques such as bilateral close-out netting, the provision of additional collateral in the form of top-up collateral and substitution of collateral.

(6) This Directive does not address rights which any person may have in respect of assets provided as financial collateral, and which arise otherwise than under the terms of the financial collateral arrangement and otherwise than on the basis of any legal provision or rule of law arising by reason of the commencement or continuation of winding-up proceedings or reorganisation measures, such as restitution arising from mistake, error or lack of capacity.

(7) The principle in Directive 98/26/EC, whereby the law applicable to book entry securities provided as collateral is the law of the jurisdiction where the relevant register, account or centralised deposit system is located, should be extended in order to create legal certainty regarding the use of such securities held in a cross-border context and used as financial collateral under the scope of this Directive.

(8) The lex rei sitae rule, according to which the applicable law for determining whether a financial collateral arrangement is properly perfected and therefore good against third parties is the law of the country where the financial collateral is located, is currently recognised by all Member States. Without affecting the application of this Directive to directly-held securities, the location of book entry securities provided as financial collateral and held through one or more intermediaries should be determined. If the collateral taker has a valid and effective collateral arrangement according to the governing law of the country in which the relevant account is maintained, then the validity against any competing title or interest and the enforceability of the collateral should be governed solely by the law of that country, thus preventing legal uncertainty as a result of other unforeseen legislation.

(9) In order to limit the administrative burdens for parties using financial collateral under the scope of this Directive, the only perfection requirement which national law may impose in respect of financial collateral should be that the financial collateral is delivered, transferred, held, registered or otherwise designated so as to be in the possession or under the control of the collateral taker or of a person acting on the collateral taker's behalf while not excluding collateral techniques where the collateral provider is allowed to substitute collateral or to withdraw excess collateral.

(10) For the same reasons, the creation, validity, perfection, enforceability or admissibility in evidence of a financial collateral arrangement, or the provision of financial collateral under a financial collateral arrangement, should not be made dependent on the performance of any formal act such as the execution of any document in a specific form or in a particular manner, the making of any filing with an official or public body or registration in a public register, advertisement in a newspaper or journal, in an official register or publication or in any other matter, notification to a public officer or the provision of evidence in a particular form as to the date of execution of a document or instrument, the amount of the relevant financial obligations or any other matter. This Directive must however provide a balance between market efficiency and the safety of the parties to the arrangement and third parties, thereby avoiding inter alia the risk of fraud. This balance should be achieved through the scope of this Directive covering only those financial collateral arrangements which provide for some form of dispossession, i.e. the provision of the financial collateral, and where the provision of the financial collateral can be evidenced in writing or in a durable medium, ensuring thereby the traceability of that collateral. For the purpose of this Directive, acts required under the law of a Member State as conditions for transferring or creating a security interest on financial instruments, other than book entry securities, such as endorsement in the case of instruments to order, or recording on the issuer's register in the case of registered instruments, should not be considered as formal acts.

(11) Moreover, this Directive should protect only financial collateral arrangements which can be evidenced. Such evidence can be given in writing or in any other legally enforceable manner provided by the law which is applicable to the financial collateral arrangement.

(12) The simplification of the use of financial collateral through the limitation of administrative burdens promotes the efficiency of the cross-border operations of the European Central Bank and the national central banks of Member States participating in the economic and monetary union, necessary for the implementation of the common monetary policy. Furthermore, the provision of limited protection of financial collateral arrangements from some rules of insolvency law in addition supports the wider aspect of the common monetary policy, where the participants in the money market balance the overall amount of liquidity in the market among themselves, by cross-border transactions backed by collateral.

(13) This Directive seeks to protect the validity of financial collateral arrangements which are based upon the transfer of the full ownership of the financial collateral, such as by eliminating the so-called re-characterisation of such financial collateral arrangements (including repurchase agreements) as security interests.

(14) The enforceability of bilateral close-out netting should be protected, not only as an enforcement mechanism for title transfer financial collateral arrangements including repurchase agreements but more widely, where close-out netting forms part of a financial collateral arrangement. Sound risk management practices commonly used in the financial market should be protected by enabling participants to manage and reduce their credit exposures arising from all kinds of financial transactions on a net basis, where the credit exposure is calculated by combining the estimated current exposures under all outstanding transactions with a counterparty, setting off reciprocal items to produce a single aggregated amount that is compared with the current value of the collateral.

(15) This Directive should be without prejudice to any restrictions or requirements under national law on bringing into account claims, on obligations to set-off, or on netting, for example relating to their reciprocity or the fact that they have been concluded prior to when the collateral taker knew or ought to have known of the commencement (or of any mandatory legal act leading to the commencement) of winding-up proceedings or reorganisation measures in respect of the collateral provider.

(16) The sound market practice favoured by regulators whereby participants in the financial market use top-up financial collateral arrangements to manage and limit their credit risk to each other by mark-to-market calculations of the current market value of the credit exposure and the value of the financial collateral and accordingly ask for top-up financial collateral or return the surplus of financial collateral should be protected against certain automatic avoidance rules. The same applies to the possibility of substituting for assets provided as financial collateral other assets of the same value. The intention is merely that the provision of top-up or substitution financial collateral cannot be questioned on the sole basis that the relevant financial obligations existed before that financial collateral was provided, or that the financial collateral was provided during a prescribed period. However, this does not prejudice the possibility of questioning under national law the financial collateral arrangement and the provision of financial collateral as part of the initial provision, top-up or substitution of financial collateral, for example where this has been intentionally done to the detriment of the other creditors (this covers inter alia actions based on fraud or similar avoidance rules which may apply in a prescribed period).

(17) This Directive provides for rapid and non-formalistic enforcement procedures in order to safeguard financial stability and limit contagion effects in case of a default of a party to a financial collateral arrangement. However, this Directive balances the latter objectives with the protection of the collateral provider and third parties by explicitly confirming the possibility for Member States to keep or introduce in their national legislation an a posteriori control which

the Courts can exercise in relation to the realisation or valuation of financial collateral and the calculation of the relevant financial obligations. Such control should allow for the judicial authorities to verify that the realisation or valuation has been conducted in a commercially reasonable manner.

(18) It should be possible to provide cash as collateral under both title transfer and secured structures respectively protected by the recognition of netting or by the pledge of cash collateral. Cash refers only to money which is represented by a credit to an account, or similar claims on repayment of money (such as money market deposits), thus explicitly excluding banknotes.

(19) This Directive provides for a right of use in case of security financial collateral arrangements, which increases liquidity in the financial market stemming from such reuse of 'pledged' securities. This reuse however should be without prejudice to national legislation about separation of assets and unfair treatment of creditors.

(20) This Directive does not prejudice the operation and effect of the contractual terms of financial instruments provided as financial collateral, such as rights and obligations and other conditions contained in the terms of issue and any other rights and obligations and other conditions which apply between the issuers and holders of such instruments.

(21) This Act complies with the fundamental rights and follows the principles laid down in particular in the Charter of Fundamental Rights of the European Union.

(22) Since the objective of the proposed action, namely to create a minimum regime relating to the use of financial collateral, cannot be sufficiently achieved by the Member States and can therefore, by reason of the scale and effects of the action, be better achieved at Community level, the Community may adopt measures, in accordance with the principle of subsidiarity as set out in Article 5 of the Treaty. In accordance with the principle of proportionality, as set out in that Article, this Directive does not go beyond what is necessary in order to achieve that objective,

HAVE ADOPTED THIS DIRECTIVE:

Article 1

Subject matter and scope

1. This Directive lays down a Community regime applicable to financial collateral arrangements which satisfy the requirements set out in paragraphs 2 and 5 and to financial collateral in accordance with the conditions set out in paragraphs 4 and 5.

2. The collateral taker and the collateral provider must each belong to one of the following categories:

(a) a public authority (excluding publicly guaranteed undertakings unless they fall under points (b) to (e)) including:
 (i) public sector bodies of Member States charged with or intervening in the management of public debt, and
 (ii) public sector bodies of Member States authorised to hold accounts for customers;

(b) a central bank, the European Central Bank, the Bank for International Settlements, a multilateral development bank as defined in Article 1(19) of Directive 2000/12/EC of the European Parliament and of the Council of 20 March 2000 relating to the taking up and pursuit of the business of credit institutions,[10] the International Monetary Fund and the European Investment Bank;

(c) a financial institution subject to prudential supervision including:
 (i) a credit institution as defined in Article 1(1) of Directive 2000/12/EC, including the institutions listed in Article 2(3) of that Directive;
 (ii) an investment firm as defined in Article 1(2) of Council Directive 93/22/EEC of 10 May 1993 on investment services in the securities field;[11]

---

[10] OJ L 126, 26.5.2000, 1, reproduced supra under no. B. 32. Directive as amended by Directive 2000/28/EC (OJ L 275, 27.10.2000, 37), reproduced supra under no. B. 32. Directive 2000/12/EC has been repealed as from 20 July 2007 by article 58 of Directive 2006/48/EC (OJ L 177, 30.6.2006, 1), reproduced infra under no. B. 41.

[11] OJ L 141, 11.6.1993, 27, reproduced supra under no. S. 14. Directive as last amended by Directive 2000/64/EC of the European Parliament and of the Council (OJ L 290, 17.11.2000, 27).

(iii) a financial institution as defined in Article 1(5) of Directive 2000/12/EC;
(iv) an insurance undertaking as defined in Article 1(a) of Council Directive 92/49/EEC of 18 June 1992 on the coordination of laws, regulations and administrative provisions relating to direct insurance other than life assurance[12] and a life assurance undertaking as defined in Article 1(a) of Council Directive 92/96/EEC of 10 November 1992 on the coordination of laws, regulations and administrative provisions relating to direct life assurance;[13]
(v) an undertaking for collective investment in transferable securities (UCITS) as defined in Article 1(2) of Council Directive 85/611/EEC of 20 December 1985 on the coordination of laws, regulations and administrative provisions relating to undertakings for collective investment in transferable securities (UCITS);[14]
(vi) a management company as defined in Article 1a(2) of Directive 85/611/EEC;

(d) a central counterparty, settlement agent or clearing house, as defined respectively in Article 2(c), (d) and (e) of Directive 98/26/EC, including similar institutions regulated under national law acting in the futures, options and derivatives markets to the extent not covered by that Directive, and a person, other than a natural person, who acts in a trust or representative capacity on behalf of any one or more persons that includes any bondholders or holders of other forms of securitised debt or any institution as defined in points (a) to (d);

(e) a person other than a natural person, including unincorporated firms and partnerships, provided that the other party is an institution as defined in points (a) to (d).

3. Member States may exclude from the scope of this Directive financial collateral arrangements where one of the parties is a person mentioned in paragraph 2(e).

If they make use of this option Member States shall inform the Commission which shall inform the other Member States thereof.

4. (a) The financial collateral to be provided must consist of cash or financial instruments.

(b) Member States may exclude from the scope of this Directive financial collateral consisting of the collateral provider's own shares, shares in affiliated undertakings within the meaning of seventh Council Directive 83/349/EEC of 13 June 1983 on consolidated accounts,[15] and shares in undertakings whose exclusive purpose is to own means of production that are essential for the collateral provider's business or to own real property.

5. This Directive applies to financial collateral once it has been provided and if that provision can be evidenced in writing.

The evidencing of the provision of financial collateral must allow for the identification of the financial collateral to which it applies. For this purpose, it is sufficient to prove that the book entry securities collateral has been credited to, or forms a credit in, the relevant account and that the cash collateral has been credited to, or forms a credit in, a designated account.

This Directive applies to financial collateral arrangements if that arrangement can be evidenced in writing or in a legally equivalent manner.

Article 2

Definitions

1. For the purpose of this Directive:

(a) 'financial collateral arrangement' means a title transfer financial collateral arrangement or

---

[12] OJ L 228, 11.8.1992, 1, reproduced supra under no. I. 26. Directive as last amended by Directive 2000/64/EC of the European Parliament and of the Council.

[13] OJ L 360, 9.12.1992, 1, reproduced supra under no. I. 27. Directive as last amended by Directive 2000/64/EC of the European Parliament and of the Council.

[14] OJ L 375, 31.12.1985, 3, reproduced supra under no. S. 6. Directive as last amended by Directive 2001/108/EC of the European Parliament and of the Council. (OJ L 41, 13.2.2002, 35), reproduced supra under no. S. 22.

[15] OJ L 193, 18.7.1983, 1, reproduced supra under no. C. 6. Directive as last amended by Directive 2001/65/EC of the European Parliament and of the Council (OJ L 283, 27.10.2001, 28), reproduced supra under no. C. 18.

a security financial collateral arrangement whether or not these are covered by a master agreement or general terms and conditions;

(b) 'title transfer financial collateral arrangement' means an arrangement, including repurchase agreements, under which a collateral provider transfers full ownership of financial collateral to a collateral taker for the purpose of securing or otherwise covering the performance of relevant financial obligations;

(c) 'security financial collateral arrangement' means an arrangement under which a collateral provider provides financial collateral by way of security in favour of, or to, a collateral taker, and where the full ownership of the financial collateral remains with the collateral provider when the security right is established;

(d) 'cash' means money credited to an account in any currency, or similar claims for the repayment of money, such as money market deposits;

(e) 'financial instruments' means shares in companies and other securities equivalent to shares in companies and bonds and other forms of debt instruments if these are negotiable on the capital market, and any other securities which are normally dealt in and which give the right to acquire any such shares, bonds or other securities by subscription, purchase or exchange or which give rise to a cash settlement (excluding instruments of payment), including units in collective investment undertakings, money market instruments and claims relating to or rights in or in respect of any of the foregoing;

(f) 'relevant financial obligations' means the obligations which are secured by a financial collateral arrangement and which give a right to cash settlement and/or delivery of financial instruments.

Relevant financial obligations may consist of or include:
(i) present or future, actual or contingent or prospective obligations (including such obligations arising under a master agreement or similar arrangement);
(ii) obligations owed to the collateral taker by a person other than the collateral provider; or

(iii) obligations of a specified class or kind arising from time to time;

(g) 'book entry securities collateral' means financial collateral provided under a financial collateral arrangement which consists of financial instruments, title to which is evidenced by entries in a register or account maintained by or on behalf of an intermediary;

(h) 'relevant account' means in relation to book entry securities collateral which is subject to a financial collateral arrangement, the register or account—which may be maintained by the collateral taker—in which the entries are made by which that book entry securities collateral is provided to the collateral taker;

(i) 'equivalent collateral':
(i) in relation to cash, means a payment of the same amount and in the same currency;
(ii) in relation to financial instruments, means financial instruments of the same issuer or debtor, forming part of the same issue or class and of the same nominal amount, currency and description or, where a financial collateral arrangement provides for the transfer of other assets following the occurrence of any event relating to or affecting any financial instruments provided as financial collateral, those other assets;

(j) 'winding-up proceedings' means collective proceedings involving realisation of the assets and distribution of the proceeds among the creditors, shareholders or members as appropriate, which involve any intervention by administrative or judicial authorities, including where the collective proceedings are terminated by a composition or other analogous measure, whether or not they are founded on insolvency or are voluntary or compulsory;

(k) 'reorganisation measures' means measures which involve any intervention by administrative or judicial authorities which are intended to preserve or restore the financial situation and which affect pre-existing rights of third parties, including but not limited to measures involving a suspension of payments, suspension of enforcement measures or reduction of claims;

(l) 'enforcement event' means an event of default or any similar event as agreed between the parties on the occurrence of which, under the terms of a financial collateral arrangement or by operation of law, the collateral taker is entitled to realise or appropriate financial collateral or a close-out netting provision comes into effect;

(m) 'right of use' means the right of the collateral taker to use and dispose of financial collateral provided under a security financial collateral arrangement as the owner of it in accordance with the terms of the security financial collateral arrangement;

(n) 'close-out netting provision' means a provision of a financial collateral arrangement, or of an arrangement of which a financial collateral arrangement forms part, or, in the absence of any such provision, any statutory rule by which, on the occurrence of an enforcement event, whether through the operation of netting or set-off or otherwise:

(i) the obligations of the parties are accelerated so as to be immediately due and expressed as an obligation to pay an amount representing their estimated current value, or are terminated and replaced by an obligation to pay such an amount; and/or

(ii) an account is taken of what is due from each party to the other in respect of such obligations, and a net sum equal to the balance of the account is payable by the party from whom the larger amount is due to the other party.

2. References in this Directive to financial collateral being 'provided', or to the 'provision' of financial collateral, are to the financial collateral being delivered, transferred, held, registered or otherwise designated so as to be in the possession or under the control of the collateral taker or of a person acting on the collateral taker's behalf. Any right of substitution or to withdraw excess financial collateral in favour of the collateral provider shall not prejudice the financial collateral having been provided to the collateral taker as mentioned in this Directive.

3. References in this Directive to 'writing' include recording by electronic means and any other durable medium.

Article 3
Formal requirements

1. Member States shall not require that the creation, validity, perfection, enforceability or admissibility in evidence of a financial collateral arrangement or the provision of financial collateral under a financial collateral arrangement be dependent on the performance of any formal act.

2. Paragraph 1 is without prejudice to the application of this Directive to financial collateral only once it has been provided and if that provision can be evidenced in writing and where the financial collateral arrangement can be evidenced in writing or in a legally equivalent manner.

Article 4
Enforcement of financial collateral arrangements

1. Member States shall ensure that on the occurrence of an enforcement event, the collateral taker shall be able to realise in the following manners, any financial collateral provided under, and subject to the terms agreed in, a security financial collateral arrangement:

(a) financial instruments by sale or appropriation and by setting off their value against, or applying their value in discharge of, the relevant financial obligations;

(b) cash by setting off the amount against or applying it in discharge of the relevant financial obligations.

2. Appropriation is possible only if:

(a) this has been agreed by the parties in the security financial collateral arrangement; and

(b) the parties have agreed in the security financial collateral arrangement on the valuation of the financial instruments.

3. Member States which do not allow appropriation on 27 June 2002 are not obliged to recognise it.

If they make use of this option, Member States shall inform the Commission which in turn shall inform the other Member States thereof.

4. The manners of realising the financial collateral referred to in paragraph 1 shall, subject to the terms agreed in the security financial collateral arrangement, be without any requirement to the effect that:

(a) prior notice of the intention to realise must have been given;

(b) the terms of the realisation be approved by any court, public officer or other person;

(c) the realisation be conducted by public auction or in any other prescribed manner; or

(d) any additional time period must have elapsed.

5. Member States shall ensure that a financial collateral arrangement can take effect in accordance with its terms notwithstanding the commencement or continuation of winding-up proceedings or reorganisation measures in respect of the collateral provider or collateral taker.

6. This Article and Articles 5, 6 and 7 shall be without prejudice to any requirements under national law to the effect that the realisation or valuation of financial collateral and the calculation of the relevant financial obligations must be conducted in a commercially reasonable manner.

Article 5

Right of use of financial collateral under security financial collateral arrangements

1. If and to the extent that the terms of a security financial collateral arrangement so provide, Member States shall ensure that the collateral taker is entitled to exercise a right of use in relation to financial collateral provided under the security financial collateral arrangement.

2. Where a collateral taker exercises a right of use, he thereby incurs an obligation to transfer equivalent collateral to replace the original financial collateral at the latest on the due date for the performance of the relevant financial obligations covered by the security financial collateral arrangement.

Alternatively, the collateral taker shall, on the due date for the performance of the relevant financial obligations, either transfer equivalent collateral, or, if and to the extent that the terms of a security financial collateral arrangement so provide, set off the value of the equivalent collateral against or apply it in discharge of the relevant financial obligations.

3. The equivalent collateral transferred in discharge of an obligation as described in paragraph 2, first subparagraph, shall be subject to the same security financial collateral agreement to which the original financial collateral was subject and shall be treated as having been provided under the security financial collateral arrangement at the same time as the original financial collateral was first provided.

4. Member States shall ensure that the use of financial collateral by the collateral taker according to this Article does not render invalid or unenforceable the rights of the collateral taker under the security financial collateral arrangement in relation to the financial collateral transferred by the collateral taker in discharge of an obligation as described in paragraph 2, first subparagraph.

5. If an enforcement event occurs while an obligation as described in paragraph 2 first subparagraph remains outstanding, the obligation may be the subject of a close-out netting provision.

Article 6

Recognition of title transfer financial collateral arrangements

1. Member States shall ensure that a title transfer financial collateral arrangement can take effect in accordance with its terms.

2. If an enforcement event occurs while any obligation of the collateral taker to transfer equivalent collateral under a title transfer financial collateral arrangement remains outstanding, the obligation may be the subject of a close-out netting provision.

Article 7

Recognition of close-out netting provisions

1. Member States shall ensure that a close-out netting provision can take effect in accordance with its terms:

(a) notwithstanding the commencement or continuation of winding-up proceedings or reorganisation measures in respect of the collateral provider and/or the collateral taker; and/or

(b) notwithstanding any purported assignment, judicial or other attachment or other disposition of or in respect of such rights.

2. Member States shall ensure that the operation of a close-out netting provision may not be subject to any of the requirements that are mentioned in Article 4(4), unless otherwise agreed by the parties.

Article 8

Certain insolvency provisions disapplied

1. Member States shall ensure that a financial collateral arrangement, as well as the provision of financial collateral under such arrangement, may not be declared invalid or void or be reversed on the sole basis that the financial collateral arrangement has come into existence, or the financial collateral has been provided:

(a) on the day of the commencement of winding-up proceedings or reorganisation measures, but prior to the order or decree making that commencement; or

(b) in a prescribed period prior to, and defined by reference to, the commencement of such proceedings or measures or by reference to the making of any order or decree or the taking of any other action or occurrence of any other event in the course of such proceedings or measures.

2. Member States shall ensure that where a financial collateral arrangement or a relevant financial obligation has come into existence, or financial collateral has been provided on the day of, but after the moment of the commencement of, winding-up proceedings or reorganisation measures, it shall be legally enforceable and binding on third parties if the collateral taker can prove that he was not aware, nor should have been aware, of the commencement of such proceedings or measures.

3. Where a financial collateral arrangement contains:

(a) an obligation to provide financial collateral or additional financial collateral in order to take account of changes in the value of the financial collateral or in the amount of the relevant financial obligations, or

(b) a right to withdraw financial collateral on providing, by way of substitution or exchange, financial collateral of substantially the same value,

Member States shall ensure that the provision of financial collateral, additional financial collateral or substitute or replacement financial collateral under such an obligation or right shall not be treated as invalid or reversed or declared void on the sole basis that:

(i) such provision was made on the day of the commencement of winding-up proceedings or reorganisation measures, but prior to the order or decree making that commencement or in a prescribed period prior to, and defined by reference to, the commencement of winding-up proceedings or reorganisation measures or by reference to the making of any order or decree or the taking of any other action or occurrence of any other event in the course of such proceedings or measures; and/or

(ii) the relevant financial obligations were incurred prior to the date of the provision of the financial collateral, additional financial collateral or substitute or replacement financial collateral.

4. Without prejudice to paragraphs 1, 2 and 3, this Directive leaves unaffected the general rules of national insolvency law in relation to the voidance of transactions entered into during the prescribed period referred to in paragraph 1(b) and in paragraph 3(i).

Article 9

Conflict of laws

1. Any question with respect to any of the matters specified in paragraph 2 arising in relation to

book entry securities collateral shall be governed by the law of the country in which the relevant account is maintained. The reference to the law of a country is a reference to its domestic law, disregarding any rule under which, in deciding the relevant question, reference should be made to the law of another country.

2. The matters referred to in paragraph 1 are:

(a) the legal nature and proprietary effects of book entry securities collateral;

(b) the requirements for perfecting a financial collateral arrangement relating to book entry securities collateral and the provision of book entry securities collateral under such an arrangement, and more generally the completion of the steps necessary to render such an arrangement and provision effective against third parties;

(c) whether a person's title to or interest in such book entry securities collateral is overridden by or subordinated to a competing title or interest, or a good faith acquisition has occurred;

(d) the steps required for the realisation of book entry securities collateral following the occurrence of an enforcement event.

Article 10

Report by the Commission

Not later than 27 December 2006, the Commission shall present a report to the European Parliament and the Council on the application of this Directive, in particular on the application of Article 1(3), Article 4(3) and Article 5, accompanied where appropriate by proposals for its revision.

Article 11

Implementation

Member States shall bring into force the laws, regulations and administrative provisions necessary to comply with this Directive by 27 December 2003 at the latest. They shall forthwith inform the Commission thereof.

When Member States adopt those provisions, they shall contain a reference to this Directive or be accompanied by such reference on the occasion of their official publication. Member States shall determine how such reference is to be made.

Article 12

Entry into force

This Directive shall enter into force on the day of its publication in the Official Journal of the European Communities.

Article 13

Addressees

This Directive is addressed to the Member States.

S. 24.

European Parliament and Council Directive 2003/6/EC of 28 January 2003 on insider dealing and market manipulation (market abuse)[1]

THE EUROPEAN PARLIAMENT AND THE COUNCIL OF THE EUROPEAN UNION,

Having regard to the Treaty establishing the European Community, and in particular Article 95 thereof,

Having regard to the proposal from the Commission,[2]

Having regard to the opinion of the European Economic and Social Committee,[3]

Having regard to the opinion of the European Central Bank,[4]

Acting in accordance with the procedure laid down in Article 251,[5]

Whereas:

(1) A genuine Single Market for financial services is crucial for economic growth and job creation in the Community.

(2) An integrated and efficient financial market requires market integrity. The smooth functioning of securities markets and public confidence in markets are prerequisites for economic growth and wealth. Market abuse harms the integrity of financial markets and public confidence in securities and derivatives.

(3) The Commission Communication of 11 May 1999 entitled 'Implementing the framework for financial markets: action plan' identifies a series of actions that are needed in order to complete the single market for financial services. The Lisbon European Council of April 2000 called for the implementation of that action plan by 2005. The action plan stresses the need to draw up a Directive against market manipulation.

(4) At its meeting on 17 July 2000, the Council set up the Committee of Wise Men on the Regulation of European Securities Markets. In its final report, the Committee of Wise Men proposed the introduction of new legislative techniques based on a four-level approach, namely framework principles, implementing measures, cooperation and enforcement. Level 1, the Directive, should confine itself to broad general 'framework' principles while Level 2 should contain technical implementing measures to be adopted by the Commission with the assistance of a committee.

(5) The Resolution adopted by the Stockholm European Council of March 2001 endorsed the final report of the Committee of Wise Men and the proposed four-level approach to make the regulatory process for Community securities legislation more efficient and transparent.

(6) The Resolution of the European Parliament of 5 February 2002 on the implementation of financial services legislation also endorsed the Committee of Wise Men's report, on the basis of the solemn declaration made before Parliament the same day by the Commission and the letter of 2 October 2001 addressed by the Internal Market Commissioner to the chairman of Parliament's Committee on Economic and Monetary Affairs with regard to the safeguards for the European Parliament's role in this process.

---

[1] OJ L 96, 12.4.2003, 16–25. This Directive has been implemented by Directive 2003/124/EC, reproduced infra under no. S. 26; Directive 2003/125/EC, reproduced infra under no. S. 27 and Directive 2004/72/EC, reproduced infra under no. S. 30.
[2] OJ C 240 E, 28.8.2001, 265.
[3] OJ C 80, 3.4.2002, 61.
[4] OJ C 24, 26.1.2002, 8.
[5] Opinion of the European Parliament of 14 March 2002 (OJ C 47, 27.2.2003, 511), Council Common Position of 19 July 2002 (OJ C 228 E, 25.9.2002, 19) and Decision of the European Parliament of 24 October 2002 (not yet published in the Official Journal).

(7) The measures necessary for the implementation of this Directive should be adopted in accordance with Council Decision 1999/468/EC of 28 June 1999 laying down the procedures for the exercise of implementing powers conferred on the Commission.[6]

(8) According to the Stockholm European Council, Level 2 implementing measures should be used more frequently, to ensure that technical provisions can be kept up to date with market and supervisory developments, and deadlines should be set for all stages of Level 2 work.

(9) The European Parliament should be given a period of three months from the first transmission of draft implementing measures to allow it to examine them and to give its opinion. However, in urgent and duly justified cases, this period may be shortened. If, within that period, a resolution is passed by the European Parliament, the Commission should re-examine the draft measures.

(10) New financial and technical developments enhance the incentives, means and opportunities for market abuse: through new products, new technologies, increasing cross-border activities and the Internet.

(11) The existing Community legal framework to protect market integrity is incomplete. Legal requirements vary from one Member State to another, leaving economic actors often uncertain over concepts, definitions and enforcement. In some Member States there is no legislation addressing the issues of price manipulation and the dissemination of misleading information.

(12) Market abuse consists of insider dealing and market manipulation. The objective of legislation against insider dealing is the same as that of legislation against market manipulation: to ensure the integrity of Community financial markets and to enhance investor confidence in those markets. It is therefore advisable to adopt combined rules to combat both insider dealing and market manipulation. A single Directive will ensure throughout the Community the same framework for allocation of responsibilities, enforcement and cooperation.

(13) Given the changes in financial markets and in Community legislation since the adoption of Council Directive 89/592/EEC of 13 November 1989 coordinating regulations on insider dealing,[7] that Directive should now be replaced, to ensure consistency with legislation against market manipulation. A new Directive is also needed to avoid loopholes in Community legislation which could be used for wrongful conduct and which would undermine public confidence and therefore prejudice the smooth functioning of the markets.

(14) This Directive meets the concerns expressed by the Member States following the terrorist attacks on 11 September 2001 as regards the fight against financing terrorist activities.

(15) Insider dealing and market manipulation prevent full and proper market transparency, which is a prerequisite for trading for all economic actors in integrated financial markets.

(16) Inside information is any information of a precise nature which has not been made public, relating, directly or indirectly, to one or more issuers of financial instruments or to one or more financial instruments. Information which could have a significant effect on the evolution and forming of the prices of a regulated market as such could be considered as information which indirectly relates to one or more issuers of financial instruments or to one or more related derivative financial instruments.

(17) As regards insider dealing, account should be taken of cases where inside information originates not from a profession or function but from criminal activities, the preparation or execution of which could have a significant effect on the prices of one or more financial instruments or on price formation in the regulated market as such.

(18) Use of inside information can consist in the acquisition or disposal of financial instruments by a person who knows, or ought to have known,

---

[6] OJ L 184, 17.7.1999, 23.

[7] OJ L 334, 18.11.1989, 30, reproduced supra under no. S. 12.

that the information possessed is inside information. In this respect, the competent authorities should consider what a normal and reasonable person would know or should have known in the circumstances. Moreover, the mere fact that market-makers, bodies authorised to act as counterparties, or persons authorised to execute orders on behalf of third parties with inside information confine themselves, in the first two cases, to pursuing their legitimate business of buying or selling financial instruments or, in the last case, to carrying out an order dutifully, should not in itself be deemed to constitute use of such inside information.

(19) Member States should tackle the practice known as 'front running', including 'front running' in commodity derivatives, where it constitutes market abuse under the definitions contained in this Directive.

(20) A person who enters into transactions or issues orders to trade which are constitutive of market manipulation may be able to establish that his reasons for entering into such transactions or issuing orders to trade were legitimate and that the transactions and orders to trade were in conformity with accepted practice on the regulated market concerned. A sanction could still be imposed if the competent authority established that there was another, illegitimate, reason behind these transactions or orders to trade.

(21) The competent authority may issue guidance on matters covered by this Directive, e.g. definition of inside information in relation to derivatives on commodities or implementation of the definition of accepted market practices relating to the definition of market manipulation. This guidance should be in conformity with the provisions of the Directive and the implementing measures adopted in accordance with the comitology procedure.

(22) Member States should be able to choose the most appropriate way to regulate persons producing or disseminating research concerning financial instruments or issuers of financial instruments or persons producing or disseminating other information recommending or suggesting investment strategy, including appropriate mechanisms for self-regulation, which should be notified to the Commission.

(23) Posting of inside information by issuers on their internet sites should be in accordance with the rules on transfer of personal data to third countries as laid down in Directive 95/46/EC of the European Parliament and of the Council of 24 October 1995 on the protection of individuals with regard to the processing of personal data and on the movement of such data.[8]

(24) Prompt and fair disclosure of information to the public enhances market integrity, whereas selective disclosure by issuers can lead to a loss of investor confidence in the integrity of financial markets. Professional economic actors should contribute to market integrity by various means. Such measures could include, for instance, the creation of 'grey lists', the application of 'window trading' to sensitive categories of personnel, the application of internal codes of conduct and the establishment of 'Chinese walls'. Such preventive measures may contribute to combating market abuse only if they are enforced with determination and are dutifully controlled. Adequate enforcement control would imply for instance the designation of compliance officers within the bodies concerned and periodic checks conducted by independent auditors.

(25) Modern communication methods make it possible for financial market professionals and private investors to have more equal access to financial information, but also increase the risk of the spread of false or misleading information.

(26) Greater transparency of transactions conducted by persons discharging managerial responsibilities within issuers and, where applicable, persons closely associated with them, constitutes a preventive measure against market abuse. The publication of those transactions on at least an individual basis can also be a highly valuable source of information to investors.

(27) Market operators should contribute to the prevention of market abuse and adopt structural provisions aimed at preventing and detecting

---

[8] OJ L 281, 23.11.1995, 31.

market manipulation practices. Such provisions may include requirements concerning transparency of transactions concluded, total disclosure of price-regularisation agreements, a fair system of order pairing, introduction of an effective atypical-order detection scheme, sufficiently robust financial instrument reference price-fixing schemes and clarity of rules on the suspension of transactions.

(28) This Directive should be interpreted, and implemented by Member States, in a manner consistent with the requirements for effective regulation in order to protect the interests of holders of transferable securities carrying voting rights in a company (or which may carry such rights as a consequence of the exercise of rights or conversion) when the company is subject to a public take-over bid or other proposed change of control. In particular, this Directive does not in any way prevent a Member State from putting or having in place such measures as it sees fit for these purposes.

(29) Having access to inside information relating to another company and using it in the context of a public take-over bid for the purpose of gaining control of that company or proposing a merger with that company should not in itself be deemed to constitute insider dealing.

(30) Since the acquisition or disposal of financial instruments necessarily involves a prior decision to acquire or dispose taken by the person who undertakes one or other of these operations, the carrying out of this acquisition or disposal should not be deemed in itself to constitute the use of inside information.

(31) Research and estimates developed from publicly available data should not be regarded as inside information and, therefore, any transaction carried out on the basis of such research or estimates should not be deemed in itself to constitute insider dealing within the meaning of this Directive.

(32) Member States and the European System of Central Banks, national central banks or any other officially designated body, or any person acting on their behalf, should not be restricted in carrying out monetary, exchange-rate or public debt management policy.

(33) Stabilisation of financial instruments or trading in own shares in buy-back programmes can be legitimate, in certain circumstances, for economic reasons and should not, therefore, in themselves be regarded as market abuse. Common standards should be developed to provide practical guidance.

(34) The widening scope of financial markets, the rapid change and the range of new products and developments require a wide application of this Directive to financial instruments and techniques involved, in order to guarantee the integrity of Community financial markets.

(35) Establishing a level playing field in Community financial markets requires wide geographical application of the provisions covered by this Directive. As regards derivative instruments not admitted to trading but falling within the scope of this Directive, each Member State should be competent to sanction actions carried out on its territory or abroad which concern underlying financial instruments admitted to trading on a regulated market situated or operating within its territory or for which a request for admission to trading on such a regulated market has been made. Each Member State should also be competent to sanction actions carried out on its territory which concern underlying financial instruments admitted to trading on a regulated market in a Member State or for which a request for admission to trading on such a market has been made.

(36) A variety of competent authorities in Member States, having different responsibilities, may create confusion among economic actors. A single competent authority should be designated in each Member State to assume at least final responsibility for supervising compliance with the provisions adopted pursuant to this Directive, as well as international collaboration. Such an authority should be of an administrative nature guaranteeing its independence of economic actors and avoiding conflicts of interest. In accordance with national law, Member States should ensure appropriate financing of the competent authority. That authority should have adequate arrangements for consultation

concerning possible changes in national legislation such as a consultative committee composed of representatives of issuers, financial services providers and consumers, so as to be fully informed of their views and concerns.

(37) A common minimum set of effective tools and powers for the competent authority of each Member State will guarantee supervisory effectiveness. Market undertakings and all economic actors should also contribute at their level to market integrity. In this sense, the designation of a single competent authority for market abuse does not exclude collaboration links or delegation under the responsibility of the competent authority, between that authority and market undertakings with a view to guaranteeing efficient supervision of compliance with the provisions adopted pursuant to this Directive.

(38) In order to ensure that a Community framework against market abuse is sufficient, any infringement of the prohibitions or requirements laid down pursuant to this Directive will have to be promptly detected and sanctioned. To this end, sanctions should be sufficiently dissuasive and proportionate to the gravity of the infringement and to the gains realised and should be consistently applied.

(39) Member States should remain alert, in determining the administrative measures and sanctions, to the need to ensure a degree of uniformity of regulation from one Member State to another.

(40) Increasing cross-border activities require improved cooperation and a comprehensive set of provisions for the exchange of information between national competent authorities. The organisation of supervision and of investigatory powers in each Member State should not hinder cooperation between the competent national authorities.

(41) Since the objective of the proposed action, namely to prevent market abuse in the form of insider dealing and market manipulation, cannot be sufficiently achieved by the Member States and can therefore, by reason of the scale and effects of the measures, be better achieved at Community level, the Community may adopt measures, in accordance with the principle of subsidiarity as set out in Article 5 of the Treaty. In accordance with the principle of proportionality, as set out in that Article, this Directive does not go beyond what is necessary in order to achieve that objective.

(42) Technical guidance and implementing measures for the rules laid down in this Directive may from time to time be necessary to take account of new developments on financial markets. The Commission should accordingly be empowered to adopt implementing measures, provided that these do not modify the essential elements of this Directive and the Commission acts according to the principles set out in this Directive, after consulting the European Securities Committee established by Commission Decision 2001/528/EC.[9]

(43) In exercising its implementing powers in accordance with this Directive, the Commission should respect the following principles:
– the need to ensure confidence in financial markets among investors by promoting high standards of transparency in financial markets,
– the need to provide investors with a wide range of competing investments and a level of disclosure and protection tailored to their circumstances,
– the need to ensure that independent regulatory authorities enforce the rules consistently, especially as regards the fight against economic crime,
– the need for high levels of transparency and consultation with all market participants and with the European Parliament and the Council,
– the need to encourage innovation in financial markets if they are to be dynamic and efficient,
– the need to ensure market integrity by close and reactive monitoring of financial innovation,
– the importance of reducing the cost of, and increasing access to, capital,
– the balance of costs and benefits to market participants on a long-term basis (including small and medium-sized businesses and small investors) in any implementing measures,

---

[9] OJ L 191, 13.7.2001, 45, reproduced supra under no. S. 20.

- the need to foster the international competitiveness of EU financial markets without prejudice to a much-needed extension of international cooperation,
- the need to achieve a level playing field for all market participants by establishing EU-wide regulations every time it is appropriate,
- the need to respect differences in national markets where these do not unduly impinge on the coherence of the single market,
- the need to ensure coherence with other Community legislation in this area, as imbalances in information and a lack of transparency may jeopardise the operation of the markets and above all harm consumers and small investors.

(44) This Directive respects the fundamental rights and observes the principles recognised in particular by the Charter of Fundamental Rights of the European Union and in particular by Article 11 thereof and Article 10 of the European Convention on Human Rights. In this regard, this Directive does not in any way prevent Member States from applying their constitutional rules relating to freedom of the press and freedom of expression in the media,

HAVE ADOPTED THIS DIRECTIVE:

Article 1[10]

For the purposes of this Directive:

1. 'Inside information' shall mean information of a precise nature which has not been made public, relating, directly or indirectly, to one or more issuers of financial instruments or to one or more financial instruments and which, if it were made public, would be likely to have a significant effect on the prices of those financial instruments or on the price of related derivative financial instruments.

In relation to derivatives on commodities, 'inside information' shall mean information of a precise nature which has not been made public, relating, directly or indirectly, to one or more such derivatives and which users of markets on which such derivatives are traded would expect to receive in accordance with accepted market practices on those markets.

For persons charged with the execution of orders concerning financial instruments, 'inside information' shall also mean information conveyed by a client and related to the client's pending orders, which is of a precise nature, which relates directly or indirectly to one or more issuers of financial instruments or to one or more financial instruments, and which, if it were made public, would be likely to have a significant effect on the prices of those financial instruments or on the price of related derivative financial instruments.

2. 'Market manipulation' shall mean:

(a) transactions or orders to trade:
- which give, or are likely to give, false or misleading signals as to the supply of, demand for or price of financial instruments, or
- which secure, by a person, or persons acting in collaboration, the price of one or several financial instruments at an abnormal or artificial level,

unless the person who entered into the transactions or issued the orders to trade establishes that his reasons for so doing are legitimate and that these transactions or orders to trade conform to accepted market practices on the regulated market concerned;

(b) transactions or orders to trade which employ fictitious devices or any other form of deception or contrivance;

(c) dissemination of information through the media, including the Internet, or by any other means, which gives, or is likely to give, false or misleading signals as to financial instruments, including the dissemination of rumours and false or misleading news, where the person who made the dissemination knew, or ought to have known, that the information was false or misleading. In respect of journalists when they act in their professional capacity such dissemination of information is to be assessed, without prejudice to Article 11, taking into account the rules

---

[10] This article has been implemented by articles 1, 4 and 5 of Directive 2003/124/EC, reproduced infra under no. S. 26, and by articles 2, 3 and 4 of Directive 2004/72/EC, reproduced infra under no. S. 30.

governing their profession, unless those persons derive, directly or indirectly, an advantage or profits from the dissemination of the information in question.

In particular, the following instances are derived from the core definition given in points (a), (b) and (c) above:
– conduct by a person, or persons acting in collaboration, to secure a dominant position over the supply of or demand for a financial instrument which has the effect of fixing, directly or indirectly, purchase or sale prices or creating other unfair trading conditions,
– the buying or selling of financial instruments at the close of the market with the effect of misleading investors acting on the basis of closing prices,
– taking advantage of occasional or regular access to the traditional or electronic media by voicing an opinion about a financial instrument (or indirectly about its issuer) while having previously taken positions on that financial instrument and profiting subsequently from the impact of the opinions voiced on the price of that instrument, without having simultaneously disclosed that conflict of interest to the public in a proper and effective way.

The definitions of market manipulation shall be adapted so as to ensure that new patterns of activity that in practice constitute market manipulation can be included.

3. 'Financial instrument' shall mean:
– transferable securities as defined in Council Directive 93/22/EEC of 10 May 1993 on investment services in the securities field,[11]
– units in collective investment undertakings,
– money-market instruments,
– financial-futures contracts, including equivalent cash-settled instruments,
– forward interest-rate agreements,
– interest-rate, currency and equity swaps,
– options to acquire or dispose of any instrument falling into these categories, including equivalent cash-settled instruments. This category includes in particular options on currency and on interest rates,
– derivatives on commodities,
– any other instrument admitted to trading on a regulated market in a Member State or for which a request for admission to trading on such a market has been made.

4. 'Regulated market' shall mean a market as defined by Article 1(13) of Directive 93/22/EEC.

5. 'Accepted market practices' shall mean practices that are reasonably expected in one or more financial markets and are accepted by the competent authority in accordance with guidelines adopted by the Commission in accordance with the procedure laid down in Article 17(2).

6. 'Person' shall mean any natural or legal person.

7. 'Competent authority' shall mean the competent authority designated in accordance with Article 11.

In order to take account of developments on financial markets and to ensure uniform application of this Directive in the Community, the Commission, acting in accordance with the procedure laid down in Article 17(2), shall adopt implementing measures concerning points 1, 2 and 3 of this Article.

Article 2

1. Member States shall prohibit any person referred to in the second subparagraph who possesses inside information from using that information by acquiring or disposing of, or by trying to acquire or dispose of, for his own account or for the account of a third party, either directly or indirectly, financial instruments to which that information relates.

The first subparagraph shall apply to any person who possesses that information:

(a) by virtue of his membership of the administrative, management or supervisory bodies of the issuer; or

(b) by virtue of his holding in the capital of the issuer; or

---

[11] OJ L 141, 11.6.1993, 27, reproduced supra under no. S. 14. Directive as last amended by European Parliament and Council Directive 2000/64/EC (OJ L 290, 17.11.2000, 27).

(c) by virtue of his having access to the information through the exercise of his employment, profession or duties; or

(d) by virtue of his criminal activities.

2. Where the person referred to in paragraph 1 is a legal person, the prohibition laid down in that paragraph shall also apply to the natural persons who take part in the decision to carry out the transaction for the account of the legal person concerned.

3. This Article shall not apply to transactions conducted in the discharge of an obligation that has become due to acquire or dispose of financial instruments where that obligation results from an agreement concluded before the person concerned possessed inside information.

Article 3

Member States shall prohibit any person subject to the prohibition laid down in Article 2 from:

(a) disclosing inside information to any other person unless such disclosure is made in the normal course of the exercise of his employment, profession or duties;

(b) recommending or inducing another person, on the basis of inside information, to acquire or dispose of financial instruments to which that information relates.

> CASE
>
> **Case C-384/02 Knud Grøngaard and Allan Bang [2005] not yet reported**
>
> Article 3(a) of Council Directive 89/592/EEC precludes a person, who receives inside information in his capacity as an employees' representative on a company's board of directors or in his capacity as a member of the liaison committee of a group of undertakings, from disclosing such information to the general secretary of the professional organization which organizes those employees and which appointed that person as a member of the liaison committee, unless:
> – there is a close link between the disclosure and the exercise of his employment, profession, or duties, and
> – that disclosure is strictly necessary for the exercise of that employment, profession, or duties.

> As part of its examination, a national court must, in the light of the applicable national rules, take particular account of:
> – the fact that that exception to the prohibition of disclosure of inside information must be interpreted strictly;
> – the fact that each additional disclosure is liable to increase the risk of that information being exploited for a purpose contrary to Directive 89/592/EEC, and
> – the sensitivity of the inside information.
>
> Article 3(a) of Directive 89/592/EEC precludes disclosure of inside information by the general secretary of a professional organization to colleagues, except as mentioned above.

Article 4

Member States shall ensure that Articles 2 and 3 also apply to any person, other than the persons referred to in those Articles, who possesses inside information while that person knows, or ought to have known, that it is inside information.

> CASE
>
> **Case C-28/99 Criminal proceedings against Jean Verdonck, Ronald Everaert and Edith de Baedts [2001] ECR I-3399**
>
> 1. Article 6 of Council Directive 89/592/EEC of 13 November 1989 co-ordinating regulations on insider dealing does not preclude the application of legislative provisions of a Member State which, as regards the prohibition of use of inside information, are more stringent than those laid down by the directive, provided that the scope of the definition of inside information used for applying that legislation is the same for all natural or legal persons subject to the legislation.
>
> 2. If provisions of national law run counter to Article 6 of Directive 89/592/EEC, by reason of the fact that certain natural or legal persons are specifically exempted from a more stringent prohibition of use of inside information than that laid down by the directive, the national court must disapply those more stringent provisions with regard to all persons to whom they might otherwise apply.

Article 5

Member States shall prohibit any person from engaging in market manipulation.

Article 6[12]

1. Member States shall ensure that issuers of financial instruments inform the public as soon as possible of inside information which directly concerns the said issuers.

Without prejudice to any measures taken to comply with the provisions of the first subparagraph, Member States shall ensure that issuers, for an appropriate period, post on their Internet sites all inside information that they are required to disclose publicly.

2. An issuer may under his own responsibility delay the public disclosure of inside information, as referred to in paragraph 1, such as not to prejudice his legitimate interests provided that such omission would not be likely to mislead the public and provided that the issuer is able to ensure the confidentiality of that information. Member States may require that an issuer shall without delay inform the competent authority of the decision to delay the public disclosure of inside information.

3. Member States shall require that, whenever an issuer, or a person acting on his behalf or for his account, discloses any inside information to any third party in the normal exercise of his employment, profession or duties, as referred to in Article 3(a), he must make complete and effective public disclosure of that information, simultaneously in the case of an intentional disclosure and promptly in the case of a non-intentional disclosure.

The provisions of the first subparagraph shall not apply if the person receiving the information owes a duty of confidentiality, regardless of whether such duty is based on a law, on regulations, on articles of association or on a contract.

Member States shall require that issuers, or persons acting on their behalf or for their account, draw up a list of those persons working for them, under a contract of employment or otherwise, who have access to inside information. Issuers and persons acting on their behalf or for their account shall regularly update this list and transmit it to the competent authority whenever the latter requests it.

4. Persons discharging managerial responsibilities within an issuer of financial instruments and, where applicable, persons closely associated with them, shall, at least, notify to the competent authority the existence of transactions conducted on their own account relating to shares of the said issuer, or to derivatives or other financial instruments linked to them. Member States shall ensure that public access to information concerning such transactions, on at least an individual basis, is readily available as soon as possible.

5. Member States shall ensure that there is appropriate regulation in place to ensure that persons who produce or disseminate research concerning financial instruments or issuers of financial instruments and persons who produce or disseminate other information recommending or suggesting investment strategy, intended for distribution channels or for the public, take reasonable care to ensure that such information is fairly presented and disclose their interests or indicate conflicts of interest concerning the financial instruments to which that information relates. Details of such regulation shall be notified to the Commission.

6. Member States shall ensure that market operators adopt structural provisions aimed at preventing and detecting market manipulation practices.

7. With a view to ensuring compliance with paragraphs 1 to 5, the competent authority may take all necessary measures to ensure that the public is correctly informed.

8. Public institutions disseminating statistics liable to have a significant effect on financial markets shall disseminate them in a fair and transparent way.

9. Member States shall require that any person professionally arranging transactions in financial

---

[12] This article has been implemented by articles 2 and 3 of Directive 2003/124/EC, reproduced infra under no. S. 26, by Directive 2003/125/EC, reproduced infra under no. S. 27, and by articles 1, 5, 6 and 7 of Directive 2004/72/EC, reproduced infra under no. S. 30.

instruments who reasonably suspects that a transaction might constitute insider dealing or market manipulation shall notify the competent authority without delay.

10. In order to take account of technical developments on financial markets and to ensure uniform application of this Directive, the Commission shall adopt, in accordance with the procedure referred to in Article 17(2), implementing measures concerning:
– the technical modalities for appropriate public disclosure of inside information as referred to in paragraphs 1 and 3,
– the technical modalities for delaying the public disclosure of inside information as referred to in paragraph 2,
– the technical modalities designed to favour a common approach in the implementation of the second sentence of paragraph 2,
– the conditions under which issuers, or entities acting on their behalf, are to draw up a list of those persons working for them and having access to inside information, as referred to in paragraph 3, together with the conditions under which such lists are to be updated,
– the categories of persons who are subject to a duty of disclosure as referred to in paragraph 4 and the characteristics of a transaction, including its size, which trigger that duty, and the technical arrangements for disclosure to the competent authority,
– technical arrangements, for the various categories of person referred to in paragraph 5, for fair presentation of research and other information recommending investment strategy and for disclosure of particular interests or conflicts of interest as referred to in paragraph 5. Such arrangements shall take into account the rules, including self-regulation, governing the profession of journalist,
– technical arrangements governing notification to the competent authority by the persons referred to in paragraph 9.

Article 7

This Directive shall not apply to transactions carried out in pursuit of monetary, exchange-rate or public debt-management policy by a Member State, by the European System of Central Banks, by a national central bank or by any other officially designated body, or by any person acting on their behalf. Member States may extend this exemption to their federated States or similar local authorities in respect of the management of their public debt.

Article 8

The prohibitions provided for in this Directive shall not apply to trading in own shares in 'buyback' programmes or to the stabilisation of a financial instrument provided such trading is carried out in accordance with implementing measures adopted in accordance with the procedure laid down in Article 17(2).

Article 9

This Directive shall apply to any financial instrument admitted to trading on a regulated market in at least one Member State, or for which a request for admission to trading on such a market has been made, irrespective of whether or not the transaction itself actually takes place on that market.

Articles 2, 3 and 4 shall also apply to any financial instrument not admitted to trading on a regulated market in a Member State, but whose value depends on a financial instrument as referred to in paragraph 1.

Article 6(1) to (3) shall not apply to issuers who have not requested or approved admission of their financial instruments to trading on a regulated market in a Member State.

Article 10

Each Member State shall apply the prohibitions and requirements provided for in this Directive to:

(a) actions carried out on its territory or abroad concerning financial instruments that are admitted to trading on a regulated market situated or operating within its territory or for which a request for admission to trading on such market has been made;

(b) actions carried out on its territory concerning financial instruments that are admitted to trading on a regulated market in a Member State or for which a request for admission to trading on such market has been made.

Article 11

Without prejudice to the competences of the judicial authorities, each Member State shall designate a single administrative authority competent to ensure that the provisions adopted pursuant to this Directive are applied.

Member States shall establish effective consultative arrangements and procedures with market participants concerning possible changes in national legislation. These arrangements may include consultative committees within each competent authority, the membership of which should reflect as far as possible the diversity of market participants, be they issuers, providers of financial services or consumers.

Article 12

1. The competent authority shall be given all supervisory and investigatory powers that are necessary for the exercise of its functions. It shall exercise such powers:

(a) directly; or

(b) in collaboration with other authorities or with the market undertakings; or

(c) under its responsibility by delegation to such authorities or to the market undertakings; or

(d) by application to the competent judicial authorities.

2. Without prejudice to Article 6(7), the powers referred to in paragraph 1 of this Article shall be exercised in conformity with national law and shall include at least the right to:

(a) have access to any document in any form whatsoever, and to receive a copy of it;

(b) demand information from any person, including those who are successively involved in the transmission of orders or conduct of the operations concerned, as well as their principals, and if necessary, to summon and hear any such person;

(c) carry out on-site inspections;

(d) require existing telephone and existing data traffic records;

(e) require the cessation of any practice that is contrary to the provisions adopted in the implementation of this Directive;

(f) suspend trading of the financial instruments concerned;

(g) request the freezing and/or sequestration of assets;

(h) request temporary prohibition of professional activity.

3. This Article shall be without prejudice to national legal provisions on professional secrecy.

Article 13

The obligation of professional secrecy shall apply to all persons who work or who have worked for the competent authority or for any authority or market undertaking to whom the competent authority has delegated its powers, including auditors and experts instructed by the competent authority. Information covered by professional secrecy may not be disclosed to any other person or authority except by virtue of provisions laid down by law.

Article 14

1. Without prejudice to the right of Member States to impose criminal sanctions, Member States shall ensure, in conformity with their national law, that the appropriate administrative measures can be taken or administrative sanctions be imposed against the persons responsible where the provisions adopted in the implementation of this Directive have not been complied with. Member States shall ensure that these measures are effective, proportionate and dissuasive.

2. In accordance with the procedure laid down in Article 17(2), the Commission shall, for information, draw up a list of the administrative measures and sanctions referred to in paragraph 1.

3. Member States shall determine the sanctions to be applied for failure to cooperate in an investigation covered by Article 12.

4. Member States shall provide that the competent authority may disclose to the public every measure or sanction that will be imposed for infringement of the provisions adopted in the implementation of this Directive, unless such disclosure would seriously jeopardise the financial markets or cause disproportionate damage to the parties involved.

CASE

Case C-176/03 Commission of the European Communities v Council of the European Union [2005] not yet reported

As a general rule, neither criminal law nor the rules of criminal procedure fall within the Community's competence (see, to that effect, Case 203/80 *Casati* [1981] ECR 2595, paragraph 27, and Case C-226/97 *Lemmens* [1998] ECR I-3711, paragraph 19).

However, this finding does not prevent the Community legislature, when the application of effective, proportionate, and dissuasive criminal penalties by the competent national authorities is an essential measure for combating serious (. . .) offences, from taking measures which relate to the criminal law of the Member States which it considers necessary in order to ensure that the rules which it lays down on environmental protection are fully effective.

Article 15

Member States shall ensure that an appeal may be brought before a court against the decisions taken by the competent authority.

Article 16

1. Competent authorities shall cooperate with each other whenever necessary for the purpose of carrying out their duties, making use of their powers whether set out in this Directive or in national law. Competent authorities shall render assistance to competent authorities of other Member States. In particular, they shall exchange information and cooperate in investigation activities.

2. Competent authorities shall, on request, immediately supply any information required for the purpose referred to in paragraph 1. Where necessary, the competent authorities receiving any such request shall immediately take the necessary measures in order to gather the required information. If the requested competent authority is not able to supply the required information immediately, it shall notify the requesting competent authority of the reasons. Information thus supplied shall be covered by the obligation of professional secrecy to which the persons employed or formerly employed by the competent authorities receiving the information are subject.

The competent authorities may refuse to act on a request for information where:
– communication might adversely affect the sovereignty, security or public policy of the Member State addressed,
– judicial proceedings have already been initiated in respect of the same actions and against the same persons before the authorities of the Member State addressed, or
– where a final judgment has already been delivered in relation to such persons for the same actions in the Member State addressed.

In any such case, they shall notify the requesting competent authority accordingly, providing as detailed information as possible on those proceedings or the judgment.

Without prejudice to Article 226 of the Treaty, a competent authority whose request for information is not acted upon within a reasonable time or whose request for information is rejected may bring that non-compliance to the attention of the Committee of European Securities Regulators, where discussion will take place in order to reach a rapid and effective solution.

Without prejudice to the obligations to which they are subject in judicial proceedings under criminal law, the competent authorities which receive information pursuant to paragraph 1 may use it only for the exercise of their functions within the scope of this Directive and in the context of administrative or judicial proceedings specifically related to the exercise of those functions. However, where the competent authority communicating information consents thereto, the authority receiving the information may use it for other purposes or forward it to other States' competent authorities.

3. Where a competent authority is convinced that acts contrary to the provisions of this Directive are being, or have been, carried out on the territory of another Member State or that acts are affecting financial instruments traded on a regulated market situated in another Member State, it shall give notice of that fact in as specific a manner as possible to the competent authority of the other Member State. The competent authority of the other Member State shall take appropriate action. It shall inform the notifying competent authority of the outcome and, so far as possible, of significant interim developments. This paragraph shall not prejudice the competences of the competent authority that has forwarded the information. The competent authorities of the various Member States that are competent for the purposes of Article 10 shall consult each other on the proposed follow-up to their action.

4. A competent authority of one Member State may request that an investigation be carried out by the competent authority of another Member State, on the latter's territory.

It may further request that members of its own personnel be allowed to accompany the personnel of the competent authority of that other Member State during the course of the investigation.

The investigation shall, however, be subject throughout to the overall control of the Member State on whose territory it is conducted.

The competent authorities may refuse to act on a request for an investigation to be conducted as provided for in the first subparagraph, or on a request for its personnel to be accompanied by personnel of the competent authority of another Member State as provided for in the second subparagraph, where such an investigation might adversely affect the sovereignty, security or public policy of the State addressed, or where judicial proceedings have already been initiated in respect of the same actions and against the same persons before the authorities of the State addressed or where a final judgment has already been delivered in relation to such persons for the same actions in the State addressed. In such case, they shall notify the requesting competent authority accordingly, providing information, as detailed as possible, on those proceedings or judgment.

Without prejudice to the provisions of Article 226 of the Treaty, a competent authority whose application to open an inquiry or whose request for authorisation for its officials to accompany those of the other Member State's competent authority is not acted upon within a reasonable time or is rejected may bring that non-compliance to the attention of the Committee of European Securities Regulators, where discussion will take place in order to reach a rapid and effective solution.

5. In accordance with the procedure laid down in Article 17(2), the Commission shall adopt implementing measures on the procedures for exchange of information and cross-border inspections as referred to in this Article.

Article 17

1. The Commission shall be assisted by the European Securities Committee instituted by Decision 2001/528/EC (hereinafter referred to as the 'Committee').

2. Where reference is made to this paragraph, Articles 5 and 7 of Decision 1999/468/EC shall apply, having regard to the provisions of Article 8 thereof, provided that the implementing measures adopted according to this procedure do not modify the essential provisions of this Directive.

The period laid down in Article 5(6) of Decision 1999/468/EC shall be set at three months.

3. The Committee shall adopt its rules of procedure.

4. Without prejudice to the implementing measures already adopted, on the expiry of a four-year period following the entry into force of this Directive, the application of its provisions requiring the adoption of technical rules and decisions in accordance with paragraph 2 shall be suspended. On a proposal from the Commission,

the European Parliament and the Council may renew the provisions concerned in accordance with the procedure laid down in Article 251 of the Treaty and, to that end, they shall review them prior to the expiry of the period referred to above.

Article 18

Member States shall bring into force the laws, regulations and administrative provisions necessary to comply with this Directive not later than 12 October 2004. They shall forthwith inform the Commission thereof.

When Member States adopt those measures, they shall contain a reference to this Directive or be accompanied by such a reference on the occasion of their official publication. Member States shall determine how such reference is to be made.

Article 19

Article 11 shall not prejudge the possibility for a Member State to make separate legal and administrative arrangements for overseas European territories for whose external relations that Member State is responsible.

Article 20

Directive 89/592/EEC and Article 68(1) and Article 81(1) of Directive 2001/34/EC of the European Parliament and of the Council of 28 May 2001 on the admission of securities to official stock exchange listing and on information to be published on those securities[13] shall be repealed with effect from the date of entry into force of this Directive.

Article 21

This Directive shall enter into force on the day of its publication in the Official Journal of the European Union.

Article 22

This Directive is addressed to the Member States.

---

[13] OJ L 184, 6.7.2001, 1, reproduced supra under no. S. 18.

S. 25.

European Parliament and Council Directive 2003/71/EC of 4 November 2003 on the prospectus to be published when securities are offered to the public or admitted to trading and amending Directive 2001/34/EC[1]

(Text with EEA relevance)

THE EUROPEAN PARLIAMENT AND THE COUNCIL OF THE EUROPEAN UNION,

Having regard to the Treaty establishing the European Community, and in particular Articles 44 and 95 thereof,

Having regard to the proposal from the Commission,[2]

Having regard to the opinion of the European Economic and Social Committee,[3]

Having regard to the opinion of the European Central Bank,[4]

Acting in accordance with the procedure laid down in Article 251 of the Treaty,[5]

Whereas:

(1) Council Directives 80/390/EEC of 17 March 1980 coordinating the requirements for the drawing up, scrutiny and distribution of the listing particulars to be published for the admission of securities to official stock exchange listing[6] and 89/298/EEC of 17 April 1989 coordinating the requirements for the drawing up, scrutiny and distribution of the prospectus to be published when transferable securities are offered to the public[7] were adopted several years ago introducing a partial and complex mutual recognition mechanism which is unable to achieve the objective of the single passport provided for by this Directive. Those directives should be upgraded, updated and grouped together into a single text.

(2) Meanwhile, Directive 80/390/EEC was integrated into Directive 2001/34/EC of the European Parliament and of the Council of 28 May 2001 on the admission of securities to official stock exchange listing and on information to be published on those securities,[8] which codifies several directives in the field of listed securities.

(3) For reasons of consistency, however, it is appropriate to regroup the provisions of Directive 2001/34/EC which stem from Directive 80/390/EEC together with Directive 89/298/EEC and to amend Directive 2001/34/EC accordingly.

(4) This Directive constitutes an instrument essential to the achievement of the internal market as set out in timetable form in the Commission communications 'Risk capital action plan' and 'Implementing the framework for financial market: Action Plan' facilitating the widest possible access to investment capital on a Communitywide basis, including for small and medium-sized enterprises (SMEs) and start-ups, by granting a single passport to the issuer.

(5) On 17 July 2000, the Council set up the Committee of Wise Men on the regulation of

---

[1] OJ L 345, 31.12.2003, 64–89.
[2] OJ C 240 E, 28.8.2001, 272 and OJ C 20 E, 28.1.2003, 122.
[3] OJ C 80, 3.4.2002, 52.
[4] OJ C 344, 6.12.2001, 4.
[5] Opinion of the European Parliament of 14 March 2002 (OJ C 47 E, 27.2.2003, 417), Council Common Position of 24 March 2003 (OJ C 125 E, 27.5.2003, 21) and Position of the European Parliament of 2 July 2003 (not yet published in the Official Journal). Decision of the Council of 15 July 2003.
[6] OJ L 100, 17.4.1980, 1, reproduced supra under no. S. 3. Directive as last amended by Directive of the European Parliament and of the Council 94/18/EC (OJ L 135, 31.5.1994, 1), reproduced supra under no. S. 15.
[7] OJ L 124, 5.5.1989, 8, reproduced supra under no. S. 11.
[8] OJ L 184, 6.7.2001, 1, reproduced supra under no. S. 18.

European securities markets. In its initial report of 9 November 2000 the Committee stresses the lack of an agreed definition of public offer of securities, with the result that the same operation is regarded as a private placement in some Member States and not in others; the current system discourages firms from raising capital on a Community-wide basis and therefore from having real access to a large, liquid and integrated financial market.

(6) In its final report of 15 February 2001 the Committee of Wise Men proposed the introduction of new legislative techniques based on a four-level approach, namely framework principles, implementing measures, cooperation and enforcement. Level 1, the directive, should confine itself to broad, general 'framework' principles, while Level 2 should contain technical implementing measures to be adopted by the Commission with the assistance of a committee.

(7) The Stockholm European Council of 23 and 24 March 2001 endorsed the final report of the Committee of Wise Men and the proposed four-level approach to make the regulatory process for Community securities legislation more efficient and transparent.

(8) The resolution of the European Parliament of 5 February 2002 on the implementation of financial services legislation also endorsed the Committee of Wise Men's final report, on the basis of the solemn declaration made before Parliament the same day by the Commission and the letter of 2 October 2001 addressed by the Internal Market Commissioner to the chairman of Parliament's Committee on Economic and Monetary Affairs with regard to the safeguards for the European Parliament's role in this process.

(9) According to the Stockholm European Council, Level 2 implementing measures should be used more frequently to ensure that technical provisions can be kept up to date with market and supervisory developments and deadlines should be set for all stages of Level 2.

(10) The aim of this Directive and its implementing measures is to ensure investor protection and market efficiency, in accordance with high regulatory standards adopted in the relevant international fora.

(11) Non-equity securities issued by a Member State or by one of a Member State's regional or local authorities, by public international bodies of which one or more Member States are members, by the European Central Bank or by the central banks of the Member States are not covered by this Directive and thus remain unaffected by this Directive; the abovementioned issuers of such securities may, however, if they so choose, draw up a prospectus in accordance with this Directive.

(12) Full coverage of equity and non-equity securities offered to the public or admitted to trading on regulated markets as defined by Council Directive 93/22/EEC of 10 May 1993 on investment services in the securities field,[9] and not only securities which have been admitted to the official lists of stock exchanges, is also needed to ensure investor protection. The wide definition of securities in this Directive, which includes warrants and covered warrants and certificates, is only valid for this Directive and consequently in no way affects the various definitions of financial instruments used in national legislation for other purposes, such as taxation. Some of the securities defined in this Directive entitle the holder to acquire transferable securities or to receive a cash amount through a cash settlement determined by reference to other instruments, notably transferable securities, currencies, interest rates or yields, commodities or other indices or measures. Depositary receipts and convertible notes, e.g. securities convertible at the option of the investor, fall within the definition of non-equity securities set out in this Directive.

(13) Issuance of securities having a similar type and/or class in the case of non-equity securities issued on the basis of an offering programme, including warrants and certificates in any form, as well as the case of securities issued in a continuous or repeated manner, should be understood as

---

[9] OJ L 141, 11.6.1993, 27, reproduced supra under no. S. 14. Directive as last amended by Directive 2000/64/EC of the European Parliament and of the Council (OJ L 290, 17.11.2000, 27).

covering not only identical securities but also securities that belong in general terms to one category. These securities may include different products, such as debt securities, certificates and warrants, or the same product under the same programme, and may have different features notably in terms of seniority, types of underlying, or the basis on which to determine the redemption amount or coupon payment.

(14) The grant to the issuer of a single passport, valid throughout the Community, and the application of the country of origin principle require the identification of the home Member State as the one best placed to regulate the issuer for the purposes of this Directive.

(15) The disclosure requirements of the present Directive do not prevent a Member State or a competent authority or an exchange through its rule book to impose other particular requirements in the context of admission to trading of securities on a regulated market (notably regarding corporate governance). Such requirements may not directly or indirectly restrict the drawing up, the content and the dissemination of a prospectus approved by a competent authority.

(16) One of the objectives of this Directive is to protect investors. It is therefore appropriate to take account of the different requirements for protection of the various categories of investors and their level of expertise. Disclosure provided by the prospectus is not required for offers limited to qualified investors. In contrast, any resale to the public or public trading through admission to trading on a regulated market requires the publication of a prospectus.

(17) Issuers, offerors or persons asking for the admission to trading on a regulated market of securities which are exempted from the obligation to publish a prospectus will benefit from the single passport if they comply with this Directive.

(18) The provision of full information concerning securities and issuers of those securities promotes, together with rules on the conduct of business, the protection of investors. Moreover, such information provides an effective means of increasing confidence in securities and thus of contributing to the proper functioning and development of securities markets. The appropriate way to make this information available is to publish a prospectus.

(19) Investment in securities, like any other form of investment, involves risk. Safeguards for the protection of the interests of actual and potential investors are required in all Member States in order to enable them to make an informed assessment of such risks and thus to take investment decisions in full knowledge of the facts.

(20) Such information, which needs to be sufficient and as objective as possible as regards the financial circumstances of the issuer and the rights attaching to the securities, should be provided in an easily analysable and comprehensible form. Harmonisation of the information contained in the prospectus should provide equivalent investor protection at Community level.

(21) Information is a key factor in investor protection; a summary conveying the essential characteristics of, and risks associated with, the issuer, any guarantor and the securities should be included in the prospectus. To ensure easy access to this information, the summary should be written in non-technical language and normally should not exceed 2 500 words in the language in which the prospectus was originally drawn up.

(22) Best practices have been adopted at international level in order to allow cross-border offers of equities to be made using a single set of disclosure standards established by the International Organisation of Securities Commissions (IOSCO); the IOSCO disclosure standards[10] will upgrade information available for the markets and investors and at the same time will simplify the procedure for Community issuers wishing to raise capital in third countries. The Directive also calls for tailored disclosure standards to be adopted for other types of securities and issuers.

(23) Fast-track procedures for issuers admitted to trading on a regulated market and frequently

---

[10] International disclosure standards for cross-border offering and initial listings by foreign issuers, Part I, International Organisation of Securities Commissions, September 1998.

raising capital on these markets require the introduction at Community level of a new format of prospectuses for offering programmes or mortgage bonds and a new registration document system. Issuers may choose not to use those formats and therefore to draft the prospectus as a single document.

(24) The content of a base prospectus should, in particular, take into account the need for flexibility in relation to the information to be provided about the securities.

(25) Omission of sensitive information to be included in a prospectus should be allowed through a derogation granted by the competent authority in certain circumstances in order to avoid detrimental situations for an issuer.

(26) A clear time limit should be set for the validity of a prospectus in order to avoid outdated information.

(27) Investors should be protected by ensuring publication of reliable information. The issuers whose securities are admitted to trading on a regulated market are subject to an ongoing disclosure obligation but are not required to publish updated information regularly. Further to this obligation, issuers should, at least annually, list all relevant information published or made available to the public over the preceding 12 months, including information provided to the various reporting requirements laid down in other Community legislation. This should make it possible to ensure the publication of consistent and easily understandable information on a regular basis. To avoid excessive burdens for certain issuers, issuers of non-equity securities with high minimum denomination should not be required to meet this obligation.

(28) It is necessary for the annual information to be provided by issuers whose securities are admitted to trading on a regulated market to be appropriately monitored by Member States in accordance with their obligations under the provisions of Community and national law concerning the regulation of securities, issuers of securities and securities markets.

(29) The opportunity of allowing issuers to incorporate by reference documents containing the information to be disclosed in a prospectus— provided that the documents incorporated by reference have been previously filed with or accepted by the competent authority—should facilitate the procedure of drawing up a prospectus and lower the costs for the issuers without endangering investor protection.

(30) Differences regarding the efficiency, methods and timing of the checking of the information given in a prospectus not only make it more difficult for undertakings to raise capital or to obtain admission to trading on a regulated market in more than one Member State but also hinder the acquisition by investors established in one Member State of securities offered by an issuer established in another Member State or admitted to trading in another Member State. These differences should be eliminated by harmonising the rules and regulations in order to achieve an adequate degree of equivalence of the safeguards required in each Member State to ensure the provision of information which is sufficient and as objective as possible for actual or potential securities holders.

(31) To facilitate circulation of the various documents making up the prospectus, the use of electronic communication facilities such as the Internet should be encouraged. The prospectus should always be delivered in paper form, free of charge to investors on request.

(32) The prospectus should be filed with the relevant competent authority and be made available to the public by the issuer, the offeror or the person asking for admission to trading on a regulated market, subject to European Union provisions relating to data protection.

(33) It is also necessary, in order to avoid loopholes in Community legislation which would undermine public confidence and therefore prejudice the proper functioning of financial markets, to harmonise advertisements.

(34) Any new matter liable to influence the assessment of the investment, arising after the publication of the prospectus but before the closing of the offer or the start of trading on a regulated market, should be properly evaluated by investors and therefore requires the approval

and dissemination of a supplement to the prospectus.

(35) The obligation for an issuer to translate the full prospectus into all the relevant official languages discourages cross-border offers or multiple trading. To facilitate cross-border offers, where the prospectus is drawn up in a language that is customary in the sphere of international finance, the host or home Member State should only be entitled to require a summary in its official language(s).

(36) The competent authority of the host Member State should be entitled to receive a certificate from the competent authority of the home Member State which states that the prospectus has been drawn up in accordance with this Directive. In order to ensure that the purposes of this Directive will be fully achieved, it is also necessary to include within its scope securities issued by issuers governed by the laws of third countries.

(37) A variety of competent authorities in Member States, having different responsibilities, may create unnecessary costs and overlapping of responsibilities without providing any additional benefit. In each Member State one single competent authority should be designated to approve prospectuses and to assume responsibility for supervising compliance with this Directive. Under strict conditions, a Member State should be allowed to designate more than one competent authority, but only one will assume the duties for international cooperation. Such an authority or authorities should be established as an administrative authority and in such a form that their independence from economic actors is guaranteed and conflicts of interest are avoided. The designation of a competent authority for prospectus approval should not exclude cooperation between that authority and other entities, with a view to guaranteeing efficient scrutiny and approval of prospectuses in the interest of issuers, investors, markets participants and markets alike. Any delegation of tasks relating to the obligations provided for in this Directive and in its implementing measures should be reviewed, in accordance with Article 31, five years after the date of entry into force of this Directive and should, except for publication on the Internet of approved prospectuses, and the filing of prospectuses as mentioned in Article 14, end eight years after the entry into force of this Directive.

(38) A common minimum set of powers for the competent authorities will guarantee the effectiveness of their supervision. The flow of information to the markets required by Directive 2001/34/EC should be ensured and action against breaches should be taken by competent authorities.

(39) For the purposes of carrying out their duties, cooperation between competent authorities of the Member States is required.

(40) Technical guidance and implementing measures for the rules laid down in this Directive may from time to time be necessary to take into account developments on financial markets. The Commission should accordingly be empowered to adopt implementing measures, provided that these do not modify the essential elements of this Directive and provided that the Commission acts in accordance with the principles set out in this Directive, after consulting the European Securities Committee established by Commission Decision 2001/528/EC.[11]

(41) In exercising its implementing powers in accordance with this Directive, the Commission should respect the following principles:
– the need to ensure confidence in financial markets among small investors and small and medium-sized enterprises (SMEs) by promoting high standards of transparency in financial markets,
– the need to provide investors with a wide range of competing investment opportunities and a level of disclosure and protection tailored to their circumstances,
– the need to ensure that independent regulatory authorities enforce the rules consistently, especially as regards the fight against white-collar crime,
– the need for a high level of transparency and consultation with all market participants and with the European Parliament and the Council,

---

[11] OJ L 191, 13.7.2001, 45, reproduced supra under no. S. 20.

- the need to encourage innovation in financial markets if they are to be dynamic and efficient,
- the need to ensure systemic stability of the financial system by close and reactive monitoring of financial innovation,
- the importance of reducing the cost of, and increasing access to, capital,
- the need to balance, on a long-term basis, the costs and benefits to market participants (including SMEs and small investors) of any implementing measures,
- the need to foster the international competitiveness of the Community's financial markets without prejudice to a much-needed extension of international cooperation,
- the need to achieve a level playing field for all market participants by establishing Community legislation every time it is appropriate,
- the need to respect differences in national financial markets where these do not unduly impinge on the coherence of the single market,
- the need to ensure coherence with other Community legislation in this area, as imbalances in information and a lack of transparency may jeopardise the operation of the markets and above all harm consumers and small investors.

(42) The European Parliament should be given a period of three months from the first transmission of draft implementing measures to allow it to examine them and to give its opinion. However, in urgent and duly justified cases, this period may be shortened. If, within that period, a resolution is passed by the European Parliament, the Commission should re-examine the draft measures.

(43) Member States should lay down a system of sanctions for breaches of the national provisions adopted pursuant to this Directive and should take all the measures necessary to ensure that these sanctions are applied. The sanctions thus provided for should be effective, proportional and dissuasive.

(44) Provision should be made for the right of judicial review of decisions taken by Member States' competent authorities in respect of the application of this Directive.

(45) In accordance with the principle of proportionality, it is necessary and appropriate for the achievement of the basic objective of ensuring the completion of a single securities market to lay down rules on a single passport for issuers. This Directive does not go beyond what is necessary in order to achieve the objectives pursued in accordance with the third paragraph of Article 5 of the Treaty.

(46) The assessment made by the Commission of the application of this Directive should focus in particular on the process of approval of prospectuses by the competent authorities of the Member States, and more generally on the application of the home-country principle, and whether or not problems of investor protection and market efficiency might result from this application; the Commission should also examine the functioning of Article 10.

(47) For future developments of this Directive, consideration should be given to the matter of deciding which approval mechanism should be adopted to enhance further the uniform application of Community legislation on prospectuses, including the possible establishment of a European Securities Unit.

(48) This Directive respects the fundamental rights and observes the principles recognised in particular by the Charter of Fundamental Rights of the European Union.

(49) The measures necessary for the implementation of this Directive should be adopted in accordance with Council Decision 1999/468/EC of 28 June 1999 laying down the procedures for the exercise of implementing powers conferred on the Commission,[12]

HAVE ADOPTED THIS DIRECTIVE:

Chapter I
General Provisions

Article 1

Purpose and scope

1. The purpose of this Directive is to harmonise requirements for the drawing up, approval and distribution of the prospectus to be published

---
[12] OJ L 184, 17.7.1999, 23

when securities are offered to the public or admitted to trading on a regulated market situated or operating within a Member State.

2. This Directive shall not apply to:

(a) units issued by collective investment undertakings other than the closed-end type;

(b) non-equity securities issued by a Member State or by one of a Member State's regional or local authorities, by public international bodies of which one or more Member States are members, by the European Central Bank or by the central banks of the Member States;

(c) shares in the capital of central banks of the Member States;

(d) securities unconditionally and irrevocably guaranteed by a Member State or by one of a Member State's regional or local authorities;

(e) securities issued by associations with legal status or non-profit-making bodies, recognised by a Member State, with a view to their obtaining the means necessary to achieve their non-profit-making objectives;

(f) non-equity securities issued in a continuous or repeated manner by credit institutions provided that these securities:
(i) are not subordinated, convertible or exchangeable;
(ii) do not give a right to subscribe to or acquire other types of securities and that they are not linked to a derivative instrument;
(iii) materialise reception of repayable deposits;
(iv) are covered by a deposit guarantee scheme under Directive 94/19/EC of the European Parliament and of the Council on deposit-guarantee schemes;[13]

(g) non-fungible shares of capital whose main purpose is to provide the holder with a right to occupy an apartment, or other form of immovable property or a part thereof and where the shares cannot be sold on without this right being given up;

(h) securities included in an offer where the total consideration of the offer is less than EUR 2 500 000, which limit shall be calculated over a period of 12 months;

(i) 'bostadsobligationer' issued repeatedly by credit institutions in Sweden whose main purpose is to grant mortgage loans, provided that
(i) the 'bostadsobligationer' issued are of the same series;
(ii) the 'bostadsobligationer' are issued on tap during a specified issuing period;
(iii) the terms and conditions of the 'bostadsobligationer' are not changed during the issuing period;
(iv) the sums deriving from the issue of the said 'bostadsobligationer', in accordance with the articles of association of the issuer, are placed in assets which provide sufficient coverage for the liability deriving from securities;

(j) non-equity securities issued in a continuous or repeated manner by credit institutions where the total consideration of the offer is less than EUR 50 000 000, which limit shall be calculated over a period of 12 months, provided that these securities:
(i) are not subordinated, convertible or exchangeable;
(ii) do not give a right to subscribe to or acquire other types of securities and that they are not linked to a derivative instrument.

3. Notwithstanding paragraph 2(b), (d), (h), (i) and (j), an issuer, an offeror or a person asking for admission to trading on a regulated market shall be entitled to draw up a prospectus in accordance with this Directive when securities are offered to the public or admitted to trading.

Article 2

Definitions

1. For the purposes of this Directive, the following definitions shall apply:

(a) 'securities' means transferable securities as defined by Article 1(4) of Directive 93/22/EEC with the exception of money market instruments as defined by Article 1(5) of Directive 93/22/EEC, having a maturity of less than 12 months. For these instruments national legislation may be applicable;

---

[13] OJ L 135, 31.5.1994, 5, reproduced supra under no. B. 22.

(b) 'equity securities' means shares and other transferable securities equivalent to shares in companies, as well as any other type of transferable securities giving the right to acquire any of the aforementioned securities as a consequence of their being converted or the rights conferred by them being exercised, provided that securities of the latter type are issued by the issuer of the underlying shares or by an entity belonging to the group of the said issuer;

(c) 'non-equity securities' means all securities that are not equity securities;

(d) 'offer of securities to the public' means a communication to persons in any form and by any means, presenting sufficient information on the terms of the offer and the securities to be offered, so as to enable an investor to decide to purchase or subscribe to these securities. This definition shall also be applicable to the placing of securities through financial intermediaries;

(e) 'qualified investors' means:
(i) legal entities which are authorised or regulated to operate in the financial markets, including: credit institutions, investment firms, other authorised or regulated financial institutions, insurance companies, collective investment schemes and their management companies, pension funds and their management companies, commodity dealers, as well as entities not so authorised or regulated whose corporate purpose is solely to invest in securities;
(ii) national and regional governments, central banks, international and supranational institutions such as the International Monetary Fund, the European Central Bank, the European Investment Bank and other similar international organisations;
(iii) other legal entities which do not meet two of the three criteria set out in paragraph (f);
(iv) certain natural persons: subject to mutual recognition, a Member State may choose to authorise natural persons who are resident in the Member State and who expressly ask to be considered as qualified investors if these persons meet at least two of the criteria set out in paragraph 2;
(v) certain SMEs: subject to mutual recognition, a Member State may choose to authorise SMEs which have their registered office in that Member State and who expressly ask to be considered as qualified investors;

(f) 'small and medium-sized enterprises' means companies, which, according to their last annual or consolidated accounts, meet at least two of the following three criteria: an average number of employees during the financial year of less than 250, a total balance sheet not exceeding EUR 43 000 000 and an annual net turnover not exceeding EUR 50 000 000;

(g) 'credit institution' means an undertaking as defined by Article 1(1)(a) of Directive 2000/12/EC of the European Parliament and of the Council of 20 March 2000 relating to the taking up and pursuit of the business of credit institutions;[14]

(h) 'issuer' means a legal entity which issues or proposes to issue securities;

(i) 'person making an offer' (or 'offeror') means a legal entity or individual which offers securities to the public;

(j) 'regulated market' means a market as defined by Article 1(13) of Directive 93/22/EEC;

(k) 'offering programme' means a plan which would permit the issuance of non-equity securities, including warrants in any form, having a similar type and/or class, in a continuous or repeated manner during a specified issuing period;

(l) 'securities issued in a continuous or repeated manner' means issues on tap or at least two separate issues of securities of a similar type and/or class over a period of 12 months;

(m) 'home Member State' means:
(i) for all Community issuers of securities which are not mentioned in (ii), the Member State where the issuer has its registered office;
(ii) for any issues of non-equity securities whose denomination per unit amounts to at least EUR 1 000, and for any issues of non-equity

---

[14] OJ L 126, 26.5.2000, 1, reproduced supra under no. B. 32. Directive as last amended by Directive 2000/28/EC (OJ L 275, 27.10.2000, 37), reproduced supra under no. B. 34. Directive 2000/12/EC has been repealed as from 20 July 2007 by article 58 of Directive 2006/48/EC (OJ L 177, 30.6.2006, 1), reproduced supra under no. B. 41.

securities giving the right to acquire any transferable securities or to receive a cash amount, as a consequence of their being converted or the rights conferred by them being exercised, provided that the issuer of the non-equity securities is not the issuer of the underlying securities or an entity belonging to the group of the latter issuer, the Member State where the issuer has its registered office, or where the securities were or are to be admitted to trading on a regulated market or where the securities are offered to the public, at the choice of the issuer, the offeror or the person asking for admission, as the case may be. The same regime shall be applicable to non-equity securities in a currency other than euro, provided that the value of such minimum denomination is nearly equivalent to EUR 1 000;

(iii) for all issuers of securities incorporated in a third country, which are not mentioned in (ii), the Member State where the securities are intended to be offered to the public for the first time after the date of entry into force of this Directive or where the first application for admission to trading on a regulated market is made, at the choice of the issuer, the offeror or the person asking for admission, as the case may be, subject to a subsequent election by issuers incorporated in a third country if the home Member State was not determined by their choice;

(n) 'host Member State' means the State where an offer to the public is made or admission to trading is sought, when different from the home Member State;

(o) 'collective investment undertaking other than the closed end type' means unit trusts and investment companies:
(i) the object of which is the collective investment of capital provided by the public, and which operate on the principle of risk-spreading;
(ii) the units of which are, at the holder's request, repurchased or redeemed, directly or indirectly, out of the assets of these undertakings;

(p) 'units of a collective investment undertaking' mean securities issued by a collective investment undertaking as representing the rights of the participants in such an undertaking over its assets;

(q) 'approval' means the positive act at the outcome of the scrutiny of the completeness of the prospectus by the home Member State's competent authority including the consistency of the information given and its comprehensibility;

(r) 'base prospectus' means a prospectus containing all relevant information as specified in Articles 5, 7 and 16 in case there is a supplement, concerning the issuer and the securities to be offered to the public or admitted to trading, and, at the choice of the issuer, the final terms of the offering.

2. For the purposes of paragraph 1(e)(iv) the criteria are as follows:

(a) the investor has carried out transactions of a significant size on securities markets at an average frequency of, at least, 10 per quarter over the previous four quarters;

(b) the size of the investor's securities portfolio exceeds EUR 0.5 million;

(c) the investor works or has worked for at least one year in the financial sector in a professional position which requires knowledge of securities investment.

3. For the purposes of paragraphs 1(e)(iv) and (v) the following shall apply:

Each competent authority shall ensure that appropriate mechanisms are in place for a register of natural persons and SMEs considered as qualified investors, taking into account the need to ensure an adequate level of data protection. The register shall be available to all issuers. Each natural person or SME wishing to be considered as a qualified investor shall register and each registered investor may decide to opt out at any moment.

4. In order to take account of technical developments on financial markets and to ensure uniform application of this Directive, the Commission shall, in accordance with the procedure set out in Article 24(2), adopt implementing measures concerning the definitions referred to in paragraph 1, including adjustment of the figures used for the definition of SMEs, taking into account Community legislation and recommendations as well as economic developments and disclosure measures relating to the registration of individual qualified investors.

Article 3
Obligation to publish a prospectus

1. Member States shall not allow any offer of securities to be made to the public within their territories without prior publication of a prospectus.

2. The obligation to publish a prospectus shall not apply to the following types of offer:

(a) an offer of securities addressed solely to qualified investors; and/or

(b) an offer of securities addressed to fewer than 100 natural or legal persons per Member State, other than qualified investors; and/or

(c) an offer of securities addressed to investors who acquire securities for a total consideration of at least EUR 50 000 per investor, for each separate offer; and/or

(d) an offer of securities whose denomination per unit amounts to at least EUR 50 000; and/or

(e) an offer of securities with a total consideration of less than EUR 100 000, which limit shall be calculated over a period of 12 months.

However, any subsequent resale of securities which were previously the subject of one or more of the types of offer mentioned in this paragraph shall be regarded as a separate offer and the definition set out in Article 2(1)(d) shall apply for the purpose of deciding whether that resale is an offer of securities to the public. The placement of securities through financial intermediaries shall be subject to publication of a prospectus if none of the conditions (a) to (e) are met for the final placement.

3. Member States shall ensure that any admission of securities to trading on a regulated market situated or operating within their territories is subject to the publication of a prospectus.

Article 4
Exemptions from the obligation to publish a prospectus

1. The obligation to publish a prospectus shall not apply to offers of securities to the public of the following types of securities:

(a) shares issued in substitution for shares of the same class already issued, if the issuing of such new shares does not involve any increase in the issued capital;

(b) securities offered in connection with a takeover by means of an exchange offer, provided that a document is available containing information which is regarded by the competent authority as being equivalent to that of the prospectus, taking into account the requirements of Community legislation;

(c) securities offered, allotted or to be allotted in connection with a merger, provided that a document is available containing information which is regarded by the competent authority as being equivalent to that of the prospectus, taking into account the requirements of Community legislation;

(d) shares offered, allotted or to be allotted free of charge to existing shareholders, and dividends paid out in the form of shares of the same class as the shares in respect of which such dividends are paid, provided that a document is made available containing information on the number and nature of the shares and the reasons for and details of the offer;

(e) securities offered, allotted or to be allotted to existing or former directors or employees by their employer which has securities already admitted to trading on a regulated market or by an affiliated undertaking, provided that a document is made available containing information on the number and nature of the securities and the reasons for and details of the offer.

2. The obligation to publish a prospectus shall not apply to the admission to trading on a regulated market of the following types of securities:

(a) shares representing, over a period of 12 months, less than 10 per cent of the number of shares of the same class already admitted to trading on the same regulated market;

(b) shares issued in substitution for shares of the same class already admitted to trading on the same regulated market, if the issuing of such shares does not involve any increase in the issued capital;

(c) securities offered in connection with a takeover by means of an exchange offer, provided that a document is available containing information which is regarded by the competent authority as being equivalent to that of the prospectus, taking into account the requirements of Community legislation;

(d) securities offered, allotted or to be allotted in connection with a merger, provided that a document is available containing information which is regarded by the competent authority as being equivalent to that of the prospectus, taking into account the requirements of Community legislation;

(e) shares offered, allotted or to be allotted free of charge to existing shareholders, and dividends paid out in the form of shares of the same class as the shares in respect of which such dividends are paid, provided that the said shares are of the same class as the shares already admitted to trading on the same regulated market and that a document is made available containing information on the number and nature of the shares and the reasons for and details of the offer;

(f) securities offered, allotted or to be allotted to existing or former directors or employees by their employer or an affiliated undertaking, provided that the said securities are of the same class as the securities already admitted to trading on the same regulated market and that a document is made available containing information on the number and nature of the securities and the reasons for and detail of the offer;

(g) shares resulting from the conversion or exchange of other securities or from the exercise of the rights conferred by other securities, provided that the said shares are of the same class as the shares already admitted to trading on the same regulated market;

(h) securities already admitted to trading on another regulated market, on the following conditions:

(i) that these securities, or securities of the same class, have been admitted to trading on that other regulated market for more than 18 months;

(ii) that, for securities first admitted to trading on a regulated market after the date of entry into force of this Directive, the admission to trading on that other regulated market was associated with an approved prospectus made available to the public in conformity with Article 14;

(iii) that, except where (ii) applies, for securities first admitted to listing after 30 June 1983, listing particulars were approved in accordance with the requirements of Directive 80/390/EEC or Directive 2001/34/EC;

(iv) that the ongoing obligations for trading on that other regulated market have been fulfilled;

(v) that the person seeking the admission of a security to trading on a regulated market under this exemption makes a summary document available to the public in a language accepted by the competent authority of the Member State of the regulated market where admission is sought;

(vi) that the summary document referred to in (v) is made available to the public in the Member State of the regulated market where admission to trading is sought in the manner set out in Article 14(2); and

(vii) that the contents of the summary document shall comply with Article 5(2). Furthermore the document shall state where the most recent prospectus can be obtained and where the financial information published by the issuer pursuant to his ongoing disclosure obligations is available.

3. In order to take account of technical developments on financial markets and to ensure uniform application of this Directive, the Commission shall, in accordance with the procedure referred to in Article 24(2), adopt implementing measures concerning paragraphs 1(b), 1(c), 2(c) and 2(d), notably in relation to the meaning of equivalence.

Chapter II

Drawing Up of the Prospectus

Article 5

The prospectus

1. Without prejudice to Article 8(2), the prospectus shall contain all information which, according to the particular nature of the issuer and of the securities offered to the public or admitted to trading on a regulated market, is necessary to

enable investors to make an informed assessment of the assets and liabilities, financial position, profit and losses, and prospects of the issuer and of any guarantor, and of the rights attaching to such securities. This information shall be presented in an easily analysable and comprehensible form.

2. The prospectus shall contain information concerning the issuer and the securities to be offered to the public or to be admitted to trading on a regulated market. It shall also include a summary. The summary shall, in a brief manner and in non-technical language, convey the essential characteristics and risks associated with the issuer, any guarantor and the securities, in the language in which the prospectus was originally drawn up. The summary shall also contain a warning that:

(a) it should be read as an introduction to the prospectus;

(b) any decision to invest in the securities should be based on consideration of the prospectus as a whole by the investor;

(c) where a claim relating to the information contained in a prospectus is brought before a court, the plaintiff investor might, under the national legislation of the Member States, have to bear the costs of translating the prospectus before the legal proceedings are initiated; and

(d) civil liability attaches to those persons who have tabled the summary including any translation thereof, and applied for its notification, but only if the summary is misleading, inaccurate or inconsistent when read together with the other parts of the prospectus.

Where the prospectus relates to the admission to trading on a regulated market of non-equity securities having a denomination of at least EUR 50 000, there shall be no requirement to provide a summary except when requested by a Member State as provided for in Article 19(4).

3. Subject to paragraph 4, the issuer, offeror or person asking for the admission to trading on a regulated market may draw up the prospectus as a single document or separate documents. A prospectus composed of separate documents shall divide the required information into a registration document, a securities note and a summary note.

The registration document shall contain the information relating to the issuer. The securities note shall contain the information concerning the securities offered to the public or to be admitted to trading on a regulated market.

4. For the following types of securities, the prospectus can, at the choice of the issuer, offeror or person asking for the admission to trading on a regulated market consist of a base prospectus containing all relevant information concerning the issuer and the securities offered to the public or to be admitted to trading on a regulated market:

(a) non-equity securities, including warrants in any form, issued under an offering programme;

(b) non-equity securities issued in a continuous or repeated manner by credit institutions,

(i) where the sums deriving from the issue of the said securities, under national legislation, are placed in assets which provide sufficient coverage for the liability deriving from securities until their maturity date;

(ii) where, in the event of the insolvency of the related credit institution, the said sums are intended, as a priority, to repay the capital and interest falling due, without prejudice to the provisions of Directive 2001/24/EC of the European Parliament and of the Council of 4 April 2001 on the reorganisation and winding up of credit institutions.[15]

The information given in the base prospectus shall be supplemented, if necessary, in accordance with Article 16, with updated information on the issuer and on the securities to be offered to the public or to be admitted to trading on a regulated market.

If the final terms of the offer are not included in either the base prospectus or a supplement, the final terms shall be provided to investors and filed with the competent authority when each public offer is made as soon as practicable and if possible in advance of the beginning of the offer. The provisions of Article 8(1)(a) shall be applicable in any such case.

---

[15] OJ L 125, 5.5.2001, 15, reproduced supra under no. B. 36.

Article 6

Responsibility attaching to the prospectus

1. Member States shall ensure that responsibility for the information given in a prospectus attaches at least to the issuer or its administrative, management or supervisory bodies, the offeror, the person asking for the admission to trading on a regulated market or the guarantor, as the case may be. The persons responsible shall be clearly identified in the prospectus by their names and functions or, in the case of legal persons, their names and registered offices, as well as declarations by them that, to the best of their knowledge, the information contained in the prospectus is in accordance with the facts and that the prospectus makes no omission likely to affect its import.

2. Member States shall ensure that their laws, regulation and administrative provisions on civil liability apply to those persons responsible for the information given in a prospectus.

However, Member States shall ensure that no civil liability shall attach to any person solely on the basis of the summary, including any translation thereof, unless it is misleading, inaccurate or inconsistent when read together with the other parts of the prospectus.

Article 7

Minimum information

1. Detailed implementing measures regarding the specific information which must be included in a prospectus, avoiding duplication of information when a prospectus is composed of separate documents, shall be adopted by the Commission in accordance with the procedure referred to in Article 24(2). The first set of implementing measures shall be adopted by 1 July 2004.

2. In particular, for the elaboration of the various models of prospectuses, account shall be taken of the following:

(a) the various types of information needed by investors relating to equity securities as compared with non-equity securities; a consistent approach shall be taken with regard to information required in a prospectus for securities which have a similar economic rationale, notably derivative securities;

(b) the various types and characteristics of offers and admissions to trading on a regulated market of non-equity securities. The information required in a prospectus shall be appropriate from the point of view of the investors concerned for non-equity securities having a denomination per unit of at least EUR 50 000;

(c) the format used and the information required in prospectuses relating to non-equity securities, including warrants in any form, issued under an offering programme;

(d) the format used and the information required in prospectuses relating to non-equity securities, in so far as these securities are not subordinated, convertible, exchangeable, subject to subscription or acquisition rights or linked to derivative instruments, issued in a continuous or repeated manner by entities authorised or regulated to operate in the financial markets within the European Economic Area;

(e) the various activities and size of the issuer, in particular SMEs. For such companies the information shall be adapted to their size and, where appropriate, to their shorter track record;

(f) if applicable, the public nature of the issuer.

3. The implementing measures referred to in paragraph 1 shall be based on the standards in the field of financial and non-financial information set out by international securities commission organisations, and in particular by IOSCO and on the indicative Annexes to this Directive.

Article 8

Omission of information

1. Member States shall ensure that where the final offer price and amount of securities which

will be offered to the public cannot be included in the prospectus:

(a) the criteria, and/or the conditions in accordance with which the above elements will be determined or, in the case of price, the maximum price, are disclosed in the prospectus; or

(b) the acceptances of the purchase or subscription of securities may be withdrawn for not less than two working days after the final offer price and amount of securities which will be offered to the public have been filed.

The final offer price and amount of securities shall be filed with the competent authority of the home Member State and published in accordance with the arrangements provided for in Article 14(2).

2. The competent authority of the home Member State may authorise the omission from the prospectus of certain information provided for in this Directive or in the implementing measures referred to in Article 7(1), if it considers that:

(a) disclosure of such information would be contrary to the public interest; or

(b) disclosure of such information would be seriously detrimental to the issuer, provided that the omission would not be likely to mislead the public with regard to facts and circumstances essential for an informed assessment of the issuer, offeror or guarantor, if any, and of the rights attached to the securities to which the prospectus relates; or

(c) such information is of minor importance only for a specific offer or admission to trading on a regulated market and is not such as will influence the assessment of the financial position and prospects of the issuer, offeror or guarantor, if any.

3. Without prejudice to the adequate information of investors, where, exceptionally, certain information required by implementing measures referred to in Article 7(1) to be included in a prospectus is inappropriate to the issuer's sphere of activity or to the legal form of the issuer or to the securities to which the prospectus relates, the prospectus shall contain information equivalent to the required information. If there is no such information, this requirement shall not apply.

4. In order to take account of technical developments on financial markets and to ensure uniform application of this Directive, the Commission shall, in accordance with the procedure referred to in Article 24(2), adopt implementing measures concerning paragraph 2.

Article 9

Validity of a prospectus, base prospectus and registration document

1. A prospectus shall be valid for 12 months after its publication for offers to the public or admissions to trading on a regulated market, provided that the prospectus is completed by any supplements required pursuant to Article 16.

2. In the case of an offering programme, the base prospectus, previously filed, shall be valid for a period of up to 12 months.

3. In the case of non-equity securities referred to in Article 5(4)(b), the prospectus shall be valid until no more of the securities concerned are issued in a continuous or repeated manner.

4. A registration document, as referred to in Article 5(3), previously filed, shall be valid for a period of up to 12 months provided that it has been updated in accordance with Article 10(1). The registration document accompanied by the securities note, updated if applicable in accordance with Article 12, and the summary note shall be considered to constitute a valid prospectus.

Article 10

Information

1. Issuers whose securities are admitted to trading on a regulated market shall at least annually provide a document that contains or refers to all information that they have published or made available to the public over the preceding 12 months in one or more Member States and in third countries in compliance with their obligations under Community and national laws and rules dealing with the regulation of securities, issuers of securities and securities markets. Issuers shall refer at least to the information required pursuant to company law directives, Directive 2001/34/EC and Regulation (EC) No 1606/2002 of the European Parliament and of the

Council of 19 July 2002 on the application of international accounting standards.[16]

2. The document shall be filed with the competent authority of the home Member State after the publication of the financial statement. Where the document refers to information, it shall be stated where the information can be obtained.

3. The obligation set out in paragraph 1 shall not apply to issuers of non-equity securities whose denomination per unit amounts to at least EUR 50 000.

4. In order to take account of technical developments on financial markets and to ensure uniform application of this Directive, the Commission may, in accordance with the procedure referred to in Article 24(2), adopt implementing measures concerning paragraph 1. These measures will relate only to the method of publication of the disclosure requirements mentioned in paragraph 1 and will not entail new disclosure requirements. The first set of implementing measures shall be adopted by 1 July 2004.

Article 11

Incorporation by reference

1. Member States shall allow information to be incorporated in the prospectus by reference to one or more previously or simultaneously published documents that have been approved by the competent authority of the home Member State or filed with it in accordance with this Directive, in particular pursuant to Article 10, or with Titles IV and V of Directive 2001/34/EC. This information shall be the latest available to the issuer. The summary shall not incorporate information by reference.

2. When information is incorporated by reference, a cross-reference list must be provided in order to enable investors to identify easily specific items of information.

3. In order to take account of technical developments on financial markets and to ensure uniform application of this Directive, the Commission

---

[16] OJ L 243, 11.9.2002, 1, reproduced supra under no. C. 22.

shall, in accordance with the procedure referred to in Article 24(2), adopt implementing measures concerning the information to be incorporated by reference. The first set of implementing measures shall be adopted by 1 July 2004.

Article 12

Prospectuses consisting of separate documents

1. An issuer which already has a registration document approved by the competent authority shall be required to draw up only the securities note and the summary note when securities are offered to the public or admitted to trading on a regulated market.

2. In this case, the securities note shall provide information that would normally be provided in the registration document if there has been a material change or recent development which could affect investors' assessments since the latest updated registration document or any supplement as provided for in Article 16 was approved. The securities and summary notes shall be subject to a separate approval.

3. Where an issuer has only filed a registration document without approval, the entire documentation, including updated information, shall be subject to approval.

Chapter III

Arrangements for Approval and Publication of the Prospectus

Article 13

Approval of the prospectus

1. No prospectus shall be published until it has been approved by the competent authority of the home Member State.

2. This competent authority shall notify the issuer, the offeror or the person asking for admission to trading on a regulated market, as the case may be, of its decision regarding the approval of the prospectus within 10 working days of the submission of the draft prospectus.

If the competent authority fails to give a decision on the prospectus within the time limits laid down in this paragraph and paragraph 3, this shall not be deemed to constitute approval of the application.

3. The time limit referred to in paragraph 2 shall be extended to 20 working days if the public offer involves securities issued by an issuer which does not have any securities admitted to trading on a regulated market and who has not previously offered securities to the public.

4. If the competent authority finds, on reasonable grounds, that the documents submitted to it are incomplete or that supplementary information is needed, the time limits referred to in paragraphs 2 and 3 shall apply only from the date on which such information is provided by the issuer, the offeror or the person asking for admission to trading on a regulated market.

In the case referred to in paragraph 2 the competent authority should notify the issuer if the documents are incomplete within 10 working days of the submission of the application.

5. The competent authority of the home Member State may transfer the approval of a prospectus to the competent authority of another Member State, subject to the agreement of that authority. Furthermore, this transfer shall be notified to the issuer, the offeror or the person asking for admission to trading on a regulated market within three working days from the date of the decision taken by the competent authority of the home Member State. The time limit referred to in paragraph 2 shall apply from that date.

6. This Directive shall not affect the competent authority's liability, which shall continue to be governed solely by national law. Member States shall ensure that their national provisions on the liability of competent authorities apply only to approvals of prospectuses by their competent authority or authorities.

7. In order to take account of technical developments on financial markets and to ensure uniform application of this Directive, the Commission may, in accordance with the procedure referred to in Article 24(2), adopt implementing measures concerning the conditions in accordance with which time limits may be adjusted.

Article 14

Publication of the prospectus

1. Once approved, the prospectus shall be filed with the competent authority of the home Member State and shall be made available to the public by the issuer, offeror or person asking for admission to trading on a regulated market as soon as practicable and in any case, at a reasonable time in advance of, and at the latest at the beginning of, the offer to the public or the admission to trading of the securities involved. In addition, in the case of an initial public offer of a class of shares not already admitted to trading on a regulated market that is to be admitted to trading for the first time, the prospectus shall be available at least six working days before the end of the offer.

2. The prospectus shall be deemed available to the public when published either:

(a) by insertion in one or more newspapers circulated throughout, or widely circulated in, the Member States in which the offer to the public is made or the admission to trading is sought; or

(b) in a printed form to be made available, free of charge, to the public at the offices of the market on which the securities are being admitted to trading, or at the registered office of the issuer and at the offices of the financial intermediaries placing or selling the securities, including paying agents; or

(c) in an electronic form on the issuer's website and, if applicable, on the website of the financial intermediaries placing or selling the securities, including paying agents; or

(d) in an electronic form on the website of the regulated market where the admission to trading is sought; or

(e) in electronic form on the website of the competent authority of the home Member State if the said authority has decided to offer this service.

A home Member State may require issuers which publish their prospectus in accordance with (a) or (b) also to publish their prospectus in an electronic form in accordance with (c).

3. In addition, a home Member State may require publication of a notice stating how the prospectus has been made available and where it can be obtained by the public.

4. The competent authority of the home Member State shall publish on its website over a period of 12 months, at its choice, all the prospectuses approved, or at least the list of prospectuses approved in accordance with Article 13, including, if applicable, a hyperlink to the prospectus published on the website of the issuer, or on the website of the regulated market.

5. In the case of a prospectus comprising several documents and/or incorporating information by reference, the documents and information making up the prospectus may be published and circulated separately provided that the said documents are made available, free of charge, to the public, in accordance with the arrangements established in paragraph 2. Each document shall indicate where the other constituent documents of the full prospectus may be obtained.

6. The text and the format of the prospectus, and/or the supplements to the prospectus, published or made available to the public, shall at all times be identical to the original version approved by the competent authority of the home Member State.

7. Where the prospectus is made available by publication in electronic form, a paper copy must nevertheless be delivered to the investor, upon his request and free of charge, by the issuer, the offeror, the person asking for admission to trading or the financial intermediaries placing or selling the securities.

8. In order to take account of technical developments on financial markets and to ensure uniform application of the Directive, the Commission shall, in accordance with the procedure referred to in Article 24(2), adopt implementing measures concerning paragraphs 1, 2, 3 and 4. The first set of implementing measures shall be adopted by 1 July 2004.

Article 15
Advertisements

1. Any type of advertisements relating either to an offer to the public of securities or to an admission to trading on a regulated market shall observe the principles contained in paragraphs 2 to 5. Paragraphs 2 to 4 shall apply only to cases where the issuer, the offeror or the person applying for admission to trading is covered by the obligation to draw up a prospectus.

2. Advertisements shall state that a prospectus has been or will be published and indicate where investors are or will be able to obtain it.

3. Advertisements shall be clearly recognisable as such. The information contained in an advertisement shall not be inaccurate, or misleading. This information shall also be consistent with the information contained in the prospectus, if already published, or with the information required to be in the prospectus, if the prospectus is published afterwards.

4. In any case, all information concerning the offer to the public or the admission to trading on a regulated market disclosed in an oral or written form, even if not for advertising purposes, shall be consistent with that contained in the prospectus.

5. When according to this Directive no prospectus is required, material information provided by an issuer or an offeror and addressed to qualified investors or special categories of investors, including information disclosed in the context of meetings relating to offers of securities, shall be disclosed to all qualified investors or special categories of investors to whom the offer is exclusively addressed. Where a prospectus is required to be published, such information shall be included in the prospectus or in a supplement to the prospectus in accordance with Article 16(1).

6. The competent authority of the home Member State shall have the power to exercise control over the compliance of advertising activity, relating to a public offer of securities or an admission to trading on a regulated market, with the principles referred to in paragraphs 2 to 5.

7. In order to take account of technical developments on financial markets and to ensure uniform application of this Directive, the Commission shall, in accordance with the procedure referred to in Article 24(2), adopt implementing measures concerning the dissemination of advertisements announcing the intention to offer securities to the public or the admission to trading on a regulated market, in particular before the prospectus has been

made available to the public or before the opening of the subscription, and concerning paragraph 4. The first set of implementing measures shall be adopted by the Commission by 1 July 2004.

Article 16

Supplements to the prospectus

1. Every significant new factor, material mistake or inaccuracy relating to the information included in the prospectus which is capable of affecting the assessment of the securities and which arises or is noted between the time when the prospectus is approved and the final closing of the offer to the public or, as the case may be, the time when trading on a regulated market begins, shall be mentioned in a supplement to the prospectus. Such a supplement shall be approved in the same way in a maximum of seven working days and published in accordance with at least the same arrangements as were applied when the original prospectus was published. The summary, and any translations thereof, shall also be supplemented, if necessary to take into account the new information included in the supplement.

2. Investors who have already agreed to purchase or subscribe for the securities before the supplement is published shall have the right, exercisable within a time limit which shall not be shorter than two working days after the publication of the supplement, to withdraw their acceptances.

CHAPTER IV

CROSS-BORDER OFFERS AND ADMISSION TO TRADING

Article 17

Community scope of approvals of prospectuses

1. Without prejudice to Article 23, where an offer to the public or admission to trading on a regulated market is provided for in one or more Member States, or in a Member State other than the home Member State, the prospectus approved by the home Member State and any supplements thereto shall be valid for the public offer or the admission to trading in any number of host Member States, provided that the competent authority of each host Member State is notified in accordance with Article 18. Competent authorities of host Member States shall not undertake any approval or administrative procedures relating to prospectuses.

2. If there are significant new factors, material mistakes or inaccuracies, as referred to in Article 16, arising since the approval of the prospectus, the competent authority of the home Member State shall require the publication of a supplement to be approved as provided for in Article 13(1). The competent authority of the host Member State may draw the attention of the competent authority of the home Member State to the need for any new information.

Article 18

Notification

1. The competent authority of the home Member State shall, at the request of the issuer or the person responsible for drawing up the prospectus and within three working days following that request or, if the request is submitted together with the draft prospectus, within one working day after the approval of the prospectus provide the competent authority of the host Member State with a certificate of approval attesting that the prospectus has been drawn up in accordance with this Directive and with a copy of the said prospectus. If applicable, this notification shall be accompanied by a translation of the summary produced under the responsibility of the issuer or person responsible for drawing up the prospectus. The same procedure shall be followed for any supplement to the prospectus.

2. The application of the provisions of Article 8(2) and (3) shall be stated in the certificate, as well as its justification.

CHAPTER V

USE OF LANGUAGES AND ISSUERS INCORPORATED IN THIRD COUNTRIES

Article 19

Use of languages

1. Where an offer to the public is made or admission to trading on a regulated market is sought

only in the home Member State, the prospectus shall be drawn up in a language accepted by the competent authority of the home Member State.

2. Where an offer to the public is made or admission to trading on a regulated market is sought in one or more Member States excluding the home Member State, the prospectus shall be drawn up either in a language accepted by the competent authorities of those Member States or in a language customary in the sphere of international finance, at the choice of the issuer, offeror or person asking for admission, as the case may be. The competent authority of each host Member State may only require that the summary be translated into its official language(s).

For the purpose of the scrutiny by the competent authority of the home Member State, the prospectus shall be drawn up either in a language accepted by this authority or in a language customary in the sphere of international finance, at the choice of the issuer, offeror or person asking for admission to trading, as the case may be.

3. Where an offer to the public is made or admission to trading on a regulated market is sought in more than one Member State including the home Member State, the prospectus shall be drawn up in a language accepted by the competent authority of the home Member State and shall also be made available either in a language accepted by the competent authorities of each host Member State or in a language customary in the sphere of international finance, at the choice of the issuer, offeror, or person asking for admission to trading, as the case may be. The competent authority of each host Member State may only require that the summary referred to in Article 5(2) be translated into its official language(s).

4. Where admission to trading on a regulated market of non-equity securities whose denomination per unit amounts to at least EUR 50 000 is sought in one or more Member States, the prospectus shall be drawn up either in a language accepted by the competent authorities of the home and host Member States or in a language customary in the sphere of international finance, at the choice of the issuer, offeror or person asking for admission to trading, as the case may be. Member States may choose to require in their national legislation that a summary be drawn up in their official language(s).

Article 20
Issuers incorporated in third countries

1. The competent authority of the home Member State of issuers having their registered office in a third country may approve a prospectus for an offer to the public or for admission to trading on a regulated market, drawn up in accordance with the legislation of a third country, provided that:

(a) the prospectus has been drawn up in accordance with international standards set by international securities commission organisations, including the IOSCO disclosure standards;

(b) the information requirements, including information of a financial nature, are equivalent to the requirements under this Directive.

2. In the case of an offer to the public or admission to trading on a regulated market of securities, issued by an issuer incorporated in a third country, in a Member State other than the home Member State, the requirements set out in Articles 17, 18 and 19 shall apply.

3. In order to ensure uniform application of this Directive, the Commission may adopt implementing measures in accordance with the procedure referred to in Article 24(2), stating that a third country ensures the equivalence of prospectuses drawn up in that country with this Directive, by reason of its national law or of practices or procedures based on international standards set by international organisations, including the IOSCO disclosure standards.

Chapter VI
Competent Authorities

Article 21
Powers

1. Each Member State shall designate a central competent administrative authority responsible

for carrying out the obligations provided for in this Directive and for ensuring that the provisions adopted pursuant to this Directive are applied.

However, a Member State may, if so required by national law, designate other administrative authorities to apply Chapter III.

These competent authorities shall be completely independent from all market participants.

If an offer of securities is made to the public or admission to trading on a regulated market is sought in a Member State other than the home Member State, only the central competent administrative authority designated by each Member State shall be entitled to approve the prospectus.

2. Member States may allow their competent authority or authorities to delegate tasks. Except for delegation of the publication on the Internet of approved prospectuses and the filing of prospectuses as mentioned in Article 14, any delegation of tasks relating to the obligations provided for in this Directive and in its implementing measures shall be reviewed, in accordance with Article 31 by 31 December 2008, and shall end on 31 December 2011. Any delegation of tasks to entities other than the authorities referred to in paragraph 1 shall be made in a specific manner stating the tasks to be undertaken and the conditions under which they are to be carried out.

These conditions shall include a clause obliging the entity in question to act and be organised in such a manner as to avoid conflict of interest and so that information obtained from carrying out the delegated tasks is not used unfairly or to prevent competition. In any case, the final responsibility for supervising compliance with this Directive and with its implementing measures and for approving the prospectus shall lie with the competent authority or authorities designated in accordance with paragraph 1.

Member States shall inform the Commission and the competent authorities of other Member States of any arrangements entered into with regard to delegation of tasks, including the precise conditions regulating such delegation.

3. Each competent authority shall have all the powers necessary for the performance of its functions. A competent authority that has received an application for approving a prospectus shall be empowered at least to:

(a) require issuers, offerors or persons asking for admission to trading on a regulated market to include in the prospectus supplementary information, if necessary for investor protection;

(b) require issuers, offerors or persons asking for admission to trading on a regulated market, and the persons that control them or are controlled by them, to provide information and documents;

(c) require auditors and managers of the issuer, offeror or person asking for admission to trading on a regulated market, as well as financial intermediaries commissioned to carry out the offer to the public or ask for admission to trading, to provide information;

(d) suspend a public offer or admission to trading for a maximum of 10 consecutive working days on any single occasion if it has reasonable grounds for suspecting that the provisions of this Directive have been infringed;

(e) prohibit or suspend advertisements for a maximum of 10 consecutive working days on any single occasion if it has reasonable grounds for believing that the provisions of this Directive have been infringed;

(f) prohibit a public offer if it finds that the provisions of this Directive have been infringed or if it has reasonable grounds for suspecting that they would be infringed;

(g) suspend or ask the relevant regulated markets to suspend trading on a regulated market for a maximum of 10 consecutive working days on any single occasion if it has reasonable grounds for believing that the provisions of this Directive have been infringed;

(h) prohibit trading on a regulated market if it finds that the provisions of this Directive have been infringed;

(i) make public the fact that an issuer is failing to comply with its obligations.

Where necessary under national law, the competent authority may ask the relevant judicial authority to decide on the use of the powers referred to in points (d) to (h) above.

4. Each competent authority shall also, once the securities have been admitted to trading on a regulated market, be empowered to:

(a) require the issuer to disclose all material information which may have an effect on the assessment of the securities admitted to trading on regulated markets in order to ensure investor protection or the smooth operation of the market;

(b) suspend or ask the relevant regulated market to suspend the securities from trading if, in its opinion, the issuer's situation is such that trading would be detrimental to investors' interests;

(c) ensure that issuers whose securities are traded on regulated markets comply with the obligations provided for in Articles 102 and 103 of Directive 2001/34/EC and that equivalent information is provided to investors and equivalent treatment is granted by the issuer to all securities holders who are in the same position, in all Member States where the offer to the public is made or the securities are admitted to trading;

(d) carry out on-site inspections in its territory in accordance with national law, in order to verify compliance with the provisions of this Directive and its implementing measures. Where necessary under national law, the competent authority or authorities may use this power by applying to the relevant judicial authority and/or in cooperation with other authorities.

5. Paragraphs 1 to 4 shall be without prejudice to the possibility for a Member State to make separate legal and administrative arrangements for overseas European territories for whose external relations that Member State is responsible.

Article 22

Professional secrecy and cooperation between authorities

1. The obligation of professional secrecy shall apply to all persons who work or have worked for the competent authority and for entities to which competent authorities may have delegated certain tasks. Information covered by professional secrecy may not be disclosed to any other person or authority except in accordance with provisions laid down by law.

2. Competent authorities of Member States shall cooperate with each other whenever necessary for the purpose of carrying out their duties and making use of their powers. Competent authorities shall render assistance to competent authorities of other Member States. In particular, they shall exchange information and cooperate when an issuer has more than one home competent authority because of its various classes of securities, or where the approval of a prospectus has been transferred to the competent authority of another Member State pursuant to Article 13(5). They shall also closely cooperate when requiring suspension or prohibition of trading for securities traded in various Member States in order to ensure a level playing field between trading venues and protection of investors. Where appropriate, the competent authority of the host Member State may request the assistance of the competent authority of the home Member State from the stage at which the case is scrutinised, in particular as regards a new type or rare forms of securities. The competent authority of the home Member State may ask for information from the competent authority of the host Member State on any items specific to the relevant market.

Without prejudice to Article 21, the competent authorities of Member States may consult with operators of regulated markets as necessary and, in particular, when deciding to suspend, or to ask a regulated market to suspend or prohibit trading.

3. Paragraph 1 shall not prevent the competent authorities from exchanging confidential information. Information thus exchanged shall be covered by the obligation of professional secrecy, to which the persons employed or formerly employed by the competent authorities receiving the information are subject.

Article 23

Precautionary measures

1. Where the competent authority of the host Member State finds that irregularities have been

committed by the issuer or by the financial institutions in charge of the public offer or that breaches have been committed of the obligations attaching to the issuer by reason of the fact that the securities are admitted to trading on a regulated market, it shall refer these findings to the competent authority of the home Member State.

2. If, despite the measures taken by the competent authority of the home Member State or because such measures prove inadequate, the issuer or the financial institution in charge of the public offer persists in breaching the relevant legal or regulatory provisions, the competent authority of the host Member State, after informing the competent authority of the home Member State, shall take all the appropriate measures in order to protect investors. The Commission shall be informed of such measures at the earliest opportunity.

Chapter VII
Implementing Measures

Article 24
Committee procedure

1. The Commission shall be assisted by the European Securities Committee, instituted by Decision 2001/528/EC (hereinafter referred to as 'the Committee').

2. Where reference is made to this paragraph, Articles 5 and 7 of Decision 1999/468/EC shall apply, having regard to the provisions of Article 8 thereof and provided that the implementing measures adopted in accordance with this procedure do not modify the essential provisions of this Directive.

The period laid down in Article 5(6) of Decision 1999/468/EC shall be set at three months.

3. The Committee shall adopt its rules of procedure.

4. Without prejudice to the implementing measures already adopted, on the expiry of a four-year period following the entry into force of this Directive the application of its provisions providing for the adoption of technical rules and decisions in accordance with the procedure referred to in paragraph 2 shall be suspended. On a proposal from the Commission, the European Parliament and the Council may renew the provisions concerned in accordance with the procedure laid down in Article 251 of the Treaty and, to that end, shall review them prior to the expiry of the four-year period.

Article 25
Sanctions

1. Without prejudice to the right of Member States to impose criminal sanctions and without prejudice to their civil liability regime, Member States shall ensure, in conformity with their national law, that the appropriate administrative measures can be taken or administrative sanctions be imposed against the persons responsible, where the provisions adopted in the implementation of this Directive have not been complied with. Member States shall ensure that these measures are effective, proportionate and dissuasive.

2. Member States shall provide that the competent authority may disclose to the public every measure or sanction that has been imposed for infringement of the provisions adopted pursuant to this Directive, unless the disclosure would seriously jeopardise the financial markets or cause disproportionate damage to the parties involved.

Article 26
Right of appeal

Member States shall ensure that decisions taken pursuant to laws, regulations and administrative provisions adopted in accordance with this Directive are subject to the right to appeal to the courts.

Chapter VIII
Transitional and Final Provisions

Article 27
Amendments

[. . .]

¶ *This article modifies article 108(2)(a) and deletes articles 3, 20 to 41, 98 to 101, 104, 108(2)(c)(ii), and annex I of Directive 2001/34/EC, reproduced supra under no. S. 18. The modifications are directly incorporated therein.*

Article 28
Repeal

With effect from the date indicated in Article 29, Directive 89/298/EEC shall be repealed. References to the repealed Directive shall be construed as references to this Directive.

Article 29
Transposition

Member States shall bring into force the laws, regulations and administrative provisions necessary to comply with this Directive not later than 1 July 2005. They shall forthwith inform the Commission thereof. When Member States adopt those measures they shall contain a reference to this Directive or shall be accompanied by such a reference on the occasion of their official publication. The methods for making such reference shall be laid down by Member States.

Article 30
Transitional provision

1. Issuers which are incorporated in a third country and whose securities have already been admitted to trading on a regulated market shall choose their competent authority in accordance with Article 2(1)(m)(iii) and notify their decision to the competent authority of their chosen home Member State by 31 December 2005.

2. By way of derogation from Article 3, Member States which have used the exemption in Article 5(a) of Directive 89/298/EEC may continue to allow credit institutions or other financial institutions equivalent to credit institutions which are not covered by Article 1(2)(j) of this Directive to offer debt securities or other transferable securities equivalent to debt securities issued in a continuous or repeated manner within their territory for five years following the date of entry into force of this Directive.

3. By way of derogation from Article 29, the Federal Republic of Germany shall comply with Article 21(1) by 31 December 2008.

Article 31
Review

Five years after the date of entry into force of this Directive, the Commission shall make an assessment of the application of this Directive and present a report to the European Parliament and the Council, accompanied where appropriate by proposals for its review.

Article 32
Entry into force

This Directive shall enter into force on the day of its publication in the *Official Journal of the European Union.*

Article 33
Addressees

This Directive is addressed to the Member States.

Annex I

Prospectus

I. Summary

The summary shall provide in a few pages the most important information included in the prospectus, covering at least the following items:

A. identity of directors, senior management, advisers and auditors

B. offer statistics and expected timetable

C. key information concerning selected financial data; capitalisation and indebtedness; reasons for the offer and use of proceeds; risk factors

D. information concerning the issuer
– history and development of the issuer
– business overview

E. operating and financial review and prospects
- research and development, patents and licences, etc.
- trends

F. directors, senior management and employees

G. major shareholders and related-party transactions

H. financial information
- consolidated statement and other financial information
- significant changes

I. details of the offer and admission to trading
- offer and admission to trading
- plan for distribution
- markets
- selling shareholders
- dilution (equity securities only)
- expenses of the issue

J. additional information
- share capital
- memorandum and articles of association
- documents on display

II. Identity of Directors, Senior Management, Advisers and Auditors

The purpose is to identify the company representatives and other individuals involved in the company's offer or admission to trading; these are the persons responsible for drawing up the prospectus as required by Article 5 of the Directive and those responsible for auditing the financial statements.

III. Offer Statistics and Expected Timetable

The purpose is to provide key information regarding the conduct of any offer and the identification of important dates relating to that offer.

A. Offer statistics
B. Method and expected timetable

IV. Key Information

The purpose is to summarise key information about the company's financial condition, capitalisation and risk factors. If the financial statements included in the document are restated to reflect material changes in the company's group structure or accounting policies, the selected financial data must also be restated.

A. Selected financial data
B. Capitalisation and indebtedness
C. Reasons for the offer and use of proceeds
D. Risk factors

V. Information on the Company

The purpose is to provide information about the company's business operations, the products it makes or the services it provides, and the factors which affect the business. It is also intended to provide information regarding the adequacy and suitability of the company's properties, plant and equipment, as well as its plans for future capacity increases or decreases.

A. History and development of the company
B. Business overview
C. Organisational structure
D. Property, plant and equipment

VI. Operating and Financial Review and Prospects

The purpose is to provide the management's explanation of factors that have affected the company's financial condition and results of operations for the historical periods covered by the financial statements, and management's assessment of factors and trends which are expected to have a material effect on the company's financial condition and results of operations in future periods.

A. Operating results
B. Liquidity and capital resources

C. Research and development, patents and licences, etc.

D. Trends

VII. Directors, Senior Management and Employees

The purpose is to provide information concerning the company's directors and managers that will allow investors to assess their experience, qualifications and levels of remuneration, as well as their relationship with the company.

A. Directors and senior management
B. Remuneration
C. Board practices
D. Employees
E. Share ownership

VIII. Major Shareholders and Related-Party Transactions

The purpose is to provide information regarding the major shareholders and others that may control or have an influence on the company. It also provides information regarding transactions the company has entered into with persons affiliated with the company and whether the terms of such transactions are fair to the company.

A. Major shareholders
B. Related-party transactions
C. Interests of experts and advisers

IX. Financial Information

The purpose is to specify which financial statements must be included in the document, as well as the periods to be covered, the age of the financial statements and other information of a financial nature. The accounting and auditing principles that will be accepted for use in preparation and audit of the financial statements will be determined in accordance with international accounting and auditing standards.

A. Consolidated statements and other financial information
B. Significant changes

X. Details of the Offer and Admission to Trading Details

The purpose is to provide information regarding the offer and the admission to trading of securities, the plan for distribution of the securities and related matters.

A. Offer and admission to trading
B. Plan for distribution
C. Markets
D. Holders of securities who are selling
E. Dilution (for equity securities only)
F. Expenses of the issue

XI. Additional Information

The purpose is to provide information, most of which is of a statutory nature, that is not covered elsewhere in the prospectus.

A. Share capital
B. Memorandum and articles of association
C. Material contracts
D. Exchange controls
E. Taxation
F. Dividends and paying agents
G. Statement by experts
H. Documents on display
I. Subsidiary information

Annex II

Registration Document

I. Identity of Directors, Senior Management, Advisers and Auditors

The purpose is to identify the company representatives and other individuals involved in the company's offer or admission to trading; these are the persons responsible for drawing up the prospectus and those responsible for auditing the financial statements.

II. Key Information about the Issuer

The purpose is to summarise key information about the company's financial condition, capitalisation and risk factors. If the financial statements included in the document are restated to reflect material changes in the company's group structure or accounting policies, the selected financial data must also be restated.

A. Selected financial data
B. Capitalisation and indebtedness
C. Risk factors

III. Information on the Company

The purpose is to provide information about the company's business operations, the products it makes or the services it provides and the factors which affect the business. It is also intended to provide information regarding the adequacy and suitability of the company's properties, plants and equipment, as well as its plans for future capacity increases or decreases.

A. History and development of the company
B. Business overview
C. Organisational structure
D. Property, plants and equipment

IV. Operating and Financial Review and Prospects

The purpose is to provide the management's explanation of factors that have affected the company's financial condition and results of operations for the historical periods covered by the financial statements, and management's assessment of factors and trends which are expected to have a material effect on the company's financial condition and results of operations in future periods.

A. Operating results
B. Liquidity and capital resources
C. Research and development, patents and licences, etc.
D. Trends

V. Directors, Senior Management

The purpose is to provide information concerning the company's directors and managers that will allow investors to assess their experience, qualifications and levels of remuneration, as well as their relationship with the company.

A. Directors and senior management
B. Remuneration
C. Board practices
D. Employees
E. Share ownership

VI. Major Shareholders and Related-Party Transactions

The purpose is to provide information regarding the major shareholders and others that may control or have an influence on the company. It also provides information regarding transactions the company has entered into with persons affiliated with the company and whether the terms of such transactions are fair to the company.

A. Major shareholders
B. Related-party transactions
C. Interests of experts and advisers

VII. Financial Information

The purpose is to specify which financial statements must be included in the document, as well as the periods to be covered, the age of the financial statements and other information of a financial nature. The accounting and auditing principles that will be accepted for use in preparation and audit of the financial statements will be determined in accordance with international accounting and auditing standards.

A. Consolidated statements and other financial information
B. Significant changes

VIII. Additional Information

The purpose is to provide information, most of which is of a statutory nature, that is not covered elsewhere in the prospectus.

A. Share capital
B. Memorandum and articles of association
C. Material contracts
D. Statement by experts
E. Documents on display
F. Subsidiary information

Annex III

Securities Note

I. Identity of Directors, Senior Management, Advisers and Auditors

The purpose is to identify the company representatives and other individuals involved in the company's offer or admission to trading; these are the persons responsible for drawing up the prospectus and those responsible for auditing the financial statements.

II. Offer Statistics and Expected Timetable

The purpose is to provide key information regarding the conduct of any offer and the identification of important dates relating to that offer.

A. Offer statistics
B. Method and expected timetable

III. Key information about the User

The purpose is to summarise key information about the company's financial condition, capitalisation and risk factors. If the financial statements included in the document are restated to reflect material changes in the company's group structure or accounting policies, the selected financial data must also be restated.

A. Capitalisation and indebtedness
B. Reasons for the offer and use of proceeds
C. Risk factors

IV. Interests of Experts

The purpose is to provide information regarding transactions the company has entered into with experts or advisers employed on a contingent basis.

V. Details of the Offer and Admission to Trading

The purpose is to provide information regarding the offer and the admission to trading of securities, the plan for distribution of the securities and related matters.

A. Offer and admission to trading
B. Plan for distribution
C. Markets
D. Selling securities holders
E. Dilution (for equity securities only)
F. Expenses of the issue

VI. Additional Information

The purpose is to provide information, most of which is of a statutory nature, that is not covered elsewhere in the prospectus.

A. Exchange controls
B. Taxation
C. Dividends and paying agents
D. Statement by experts
E. Documents on display

Annex IV

Summary Note

The summary note shall provide in a few pages the most important information included in the prospectus, covering at least the following items:
- identity of directors, senior management, advisers and auditors
- offer statistics and expected timetable
- key information concerning selected financial data; capitalisation and indebtedness; reasons for the offer and use of proceeds; risk factors
- information concerning the issuer
  - history and development of the issuer
  - business overview
- operating and financial review and prospects
  - research and development, patents and licences, etc.
  - trends
- directors, senior management and employees
- major shareholders and related-party transactions
- financial information
  - consolidated statement and other financial information
  - significant changes
- details on the offer and admission to trading
  - offer and admission to trading
  - plan for distribution
  - markets
  - selling shareholders
  - dilution (for equity securities only)
  - expenses of the issue
- additional information
  - share capital
  - memorandum and articles of incorporation
  - documents available for inspection

S. 26.

Commission Directive 2003/124/EC
of 22 December 2003
implementing Directive 2003/6/EC of the European Parliament and of the Council as regards the definition and public disclosure of inside information and the definition of market manipulation[1]

(Text with EEA relevance)

THE COMMISSION OF THE EUROPEAN COMMUNITIES,

Having regard to the Treaty establishing the European Community,

Having regard to Directive 2003/6/EC of the European Parliament and of the Council of 28 January 2003 on insider dealing and market manipulation (market abuse),[2] and in particular the second paragraph of Article 1 and the first, second and third indents of Article 6(10) thereof,

After consulting the Committee of European Securities Regulators (CESR)[3] for technical advice,

Whereas:

(1) Reasonable investors base their investment decisions on information already available to them, that is to say, on ex ante available information. Therefore, the question whether, in making an investment decision, a reasonable investor would be likely to take into account a particular piece of information should be appraised on the basis of the ex ante available information. Such an assessment has to take into consideration the anticipated impact of the information in light of the totality of the related issuer's activity, the reliability of the source of information and any other market variables likely to affect the related financial instrument or derivative financial instrument related thereto in the given circumstances.

(2) Ex post information may be used to check the presumption that the ex ante information was price sensitive, but should not be used to take action against someone who drew reasonable conclusions from ex ante information available to him.

(3) Legal certainty for market participants should be enhanced through a closer definition of two of the elements essential to the definition of inside information, namely the precise nature of that information and the significance of its potential effect on the prices of financial instruments or related derivative financial instruments.

(4) Not only does the protection of investors require timely public disclosure of inside information by issuers, it also requires such disclosure to be as fast and as synchronised as possible between all categories of investors in all Member States in which the issuer has requested or approved admission of its financial instruments to trading on a regulated market, in order to guarantee at Community level equal access of investors to such information and to prevent insider dealing. To this end Member States may officially appoint mechanisms to be used for such disclosure.

(5) In order to protect the legitimate interests of issuers, it should be permissible, in closely defined specific circumstances, to delay public disclosure of inside information. However, the protection of investors requires that in such cases the information be kept confidential in order to prevent insider dealing.

---

[1] OJ L 339, 24.12.2003, 70–72.
[2] OJ L 96, 12.4.2003, 16, reproduced supra under no. S. 24.
[3] CESR was established by Commission Decision 2001/527/EC (OJ L 191,13.7.2001, 43), reproduced supra under no. S. 19.

(6) In order to guide both market participants and competent authorities, signals have to be taken into account when examining possibly manipulative behaviours.

(7) The measures provided for in this Directive are in accordance with the opinion of the European Securities Committee,

HAS ADOPTED THIS DIRECTIVE:

Article 1
Inside information

1. For the purposes of applying point 1 of Article 1 of Directive 2003/6/EC, information shall be deemed to be of a precise nature if it indicates a set of circumstances which exists or may reasonably be expected to come into existence or an event which has occurred or may reasonably be expected to do so and if it is specific enough to enable a conclusion to be drawn as to the possible effect of that set of circumstances or event on the prices of financial instruments or related derivative financial instruments.

2. For the purposes of applying point 1 of Article 1 of Directive 2003/6/EC, "information which, if it were made public, would be likely to have a significant effect on the prices of financial instruments or related derivative financial instruments" shall mean information a reasonable investor would be likely to use as part of the basis of his investment decisions.

Article 2
Means and time-limits for public disclosure of inside information

1. For the purposes of applying Article 6(1) of Directive 2003/6/EC, Articles 102(1) and Article 103 of Directive 2001/34/EC of the European Parliament and of the Council[4] shall apply.

Furthermore, Member States shall ensure that the inside information is made public by the issuer in a manner which enables fast access and complete, correct and timely assessment of the information by the public.

In addition, Member States shall ensure that the issuer does not combine, in a manner likely to be misleading, the provision of inside information to the public with the marketing of its activities.

2. Member States shall ensure that issuers are deemed to have complied with the first subparagraph of Article 6(1) of Directive 2003/6/EC where, upon the coming into existence of a set of circumstances or the occurrence of an event, albeit not yet formalised, the issuers have promptly informed the public thereof.

3. Any significant changes concerning already publicly disclosed inside information shall be publicly disclosed promptly after these changes occur, through the same channel as the one used for public disclosure of the original information.

4. Member States shall require issuers to take reasonable care to ensure that the disclosure of inside information to the public is synchronised as closely as possible between all categories of investors in all Member States in which those issuers have requested or approved the admission to trading of their financial instruments on a regulated market.

Article 3
Legitimate interests for delaying public disclosure and confidentiality

1. For the purposes of applying Article 6(2) of Directive 2003/6/EC, legitimate interests may, in particular, relate to the following non-exhaustive circumstances:

(a) negotiations in course, or related elements, where the outcome or normal pattern of those negotiations would be likely to be affected by public disclosure. In particular, in the event that the financial viability of the issuer is in grave and imminent danger, although not within the scope of the applicable insolvency law, public disclosure of information may be delayed for a limited period where such a public disclosure would seriously jeopardise the interest of existing and potential shareholders by undermining the

---
[4] OJ L 184, 6.7.2001, 1, reproduced supra under no. S. 18.

conclusion of specific negotiations designed to ensure the long-term financial recovery of the issuer;

(b) decisions taken or contracts made by the management body of an issuer which need the approval of another body of the issuer in order to become effective, where the organisation of such an issuer requires the separation between these bodies, provided that a public disclosure of the information before such approval together with the simultaneous announcement that this approval is still pending would jeopardise the correct assessment of the information by the public.

2. For the purposes of applying Article 6(2) of Directive 2003/6/EC, Member States shall require that, in order to be able to ensure the confidentiality of inside information, an issuer controls access to such information and, in particular, that:

(a) the issuer has established effective arrangements to deny access to such information to persons other than those who require it for the exercise of their functions within the issuer;

(b) the issuer has taken the necessary measures to ensure that any person with access to such information acknowledges the legal and regulatory duties entailed and is aware of the sanctions attaching to the misuse or improper circulation of such information;

(c) the issuer has in place measures which allow immediate public disclosure in case the issuer was not able to ensure the confidentiality of the relevant inside information, without prejudice to the second subparagraph of Article 6 (3) of Directive 2003/6/EC.

Article 4

Manipulative behaviour related to false or misleading signals and to price securing

For the purposes of applying point 2(a) of Article 1 of Directive 2003/6/EC, and without prejudice to the examples set out in the second paragraph of point 2 thereof, Member States shall ensure that the following non-exhaustive signals, which should not necessarily be deemed in themselves to constitute market manipulation, are taken into account when transactions or orders to trade are examined by market participants and competent authorities:

(a) the extent to which orders to trade given or transactions undertaken represent a significant proportion of the daily volume of transactions in the relevant financial instrument on the regulated market concerned, in particular when these activities lead to a significant change in the price of the financial instrument;

(b) the extent to which orders to trade given or transactions undertaken by persons with a significant buying or selling position in a financial instrument lead to significant changes in the price of the financial instrument or related derivative or underlying asset admitted to trading on a regulated market;

(c) whether transactions undertaken lead to no change in beneficial ownership of a financial instrument admitted to trading on a regulated market;

(d) the extent to which orders to trade given or transactions undertaken include position reversals in a short period and represent a significant proportion of the daily volume of transactions in the relevant financial instrument on the regulated market concerned, and might be associated with significant changes in the price of a financial instrument admitted to trading on a regulated market;

(e) the extent to which orders to trade given or transactions undertaken are concentrated within a short time span in the trading session and lead to a price change which is subsequently reversed;

(f) the extent to which orders to trade given change the representation of the best bid or offer prices in a financial instrument admitted to trading on a regulated market, or more generally the representation of the order book available to market participants, and are removed before they are executed;

(g) the extent to which orders to trade are given or transactions are undertaken at or around a specific time when reference prices, settlement prices and valuations are calculated and lead to price changes which have an effect on such prices and valuations.

Article 5

Manipulative behaviours related to the employment of fictitious devices or any other form of deception or contrivance

For the purposes of applying point 2(b) of Article 1 of Directive 2003/6/EC, and without prejudice to the examples set out in the second paragraph of point 2 thereof, Member States shall ensure that the following non-exhaustive signals, which should not necessarily be deemed in themselves to constitute market manipulation, are taken into account when transactions or orders to trade are examined by market participants and competent authorities:

(a) whether orders to trade given or transactions undertaken by persons are preceded or followed by dissemination of false or misleading information by the same persons or persons linked to them;

(b) whether orders to trade are given or transactions are undertaken by persons before or after the same persons or persons linked to them produce or disseminate research or investment recommendations which are erroneous or biased or demonstrably influenced by material interest.

Article 6

Transposition

1. Member States shall bring into force the laws, regulations and administrative provisions necessary to comply with this Directive by 12 October 2004 at the latest. They shall forthwith communicate to the Commission the text of the provisions and a correlation table between those provisions and this Directive.

When Member States adopt those provisions, they shall contain a reference to this Directive or be accompanied by such a reference on the occasion of their official publication. Member States shall determine how such reference is to be made.

2. Member States shall communicate to the Commission the text of the main provisions of national law which they adopt in the field covered by this Directive.

Article 7

Entry into force

This Directive shall enter into force on the day of its publication in the Official Journal of the European Union.

Article 8

Addressees

This Directive is addressed to the Member States.

S. 27.

Commission Directive 2003/125/EC
of 22 December 2003
implementing Directive 2003/6/EC of the European Parliament and of the Council as regards the fair presentation of investment recommendations and the disclosure of conflicts of interest[1]

(Text with EEA relevance)

THE COMMISSION OF THE EUROPEAN COMMUNITIES,

Having regard to the Treaty establishing the European Community,

Having regard to Directive 2003/6/EC of the European Parliament and of the Council of 28 January 2003 on insider dealing and market manipulation (market abuse),[2] and in particular the sixth indent of Article 6(10) thereof,

After consulting the Committee of European Securities Regulators (CESR)[3] for technical advice,

Whereas:

(1) Harmonised standards are necessary for the fair, clear and accurate presentation of information and disclosure of interests and conflicts of interest, to be complied with by persons producing or disseminating information recommending or suggesting an investment strategy, intended for distribution channels or for the public. In particular, market integrity requires high standards of fairness, probity and transparency when information recommending or suggesting an investment strategy is presented.

(2) Recommending or suggesting an investment strategy is either done explicitly (such as 'buy', 'hold' or 'sell' recommendations) or implicitly (by reference to a price target or otherwise).

(3) Investment advice, through the provision of a personal recommendation to a client in respect of one or more transactions relating to financial instruments (in particular informal short-term investment recommendations originating from inside the sales or trading departments of an investment firm or a credit institution expressed to their clients), which are not likely to become publicly available, should not be considered in themselves as recommendations within the meaning of this Directive.

(4) Investment recommendations that constitute a possible basis for investment decisions should be produced and disseminated in accordance with high standards of care in order to avoid misleading market participants.

(5) The identity of the producer of investment recommendations, his conduct of business rules and the identity of his competent authority should be disclosed, since it may be a valuable piece of information for investors to consider in relation to their investment decisions.

(6) Recommendations should be presented clearly and accurately.

(7) Own interests or conflicts of interest of persons recommending or suggesting investment strategy may influence the opinion that they express in investment recommendations. In order to ensure that the objectivity and reliability of the information can be evaluated, appropriate disclosure should be made of significant financial interests in any financial instrument which is the subject of the information recommending

---

[1] OJ L 339, 24.12.2003, 73–77.
[2] OJ L 96, 12.4.2003, 16, reproduced supra under no. S. 24.
[3] CESR was established by Commission Decision 2001/527/EC (OJ L 191, 13.7.2001, 43), reproduced supra under no. S. 19.

investment strategies, or of any conflicts of interest or control relationship with respect to the issuer to whom the information relates, directly or indirectly. However, this Directive should not require relevant persons producing investment recommendations to breach effective information barriers put in place in order to prevent and avoid conflicts of interest.

(8) Investment recommendations may be disseminated in unaltered, altered or summarised form by a person other than the producer. The way in which disseminators handle such recommendations may have an important impact on the evaluation of those recommendations by investors. In particular, the knowledge of the identity of the disseminator of investment recommendations, his conduct of business rules or the extent of alteration of the original recommendation can be a valuable piece of information for investors when considering their investment decisions.

(9) Posting of investment recommendations on internet sites should be in accordance with the rules on transfer of personal data to third countries as laid down in Directive 95/46/EC of the European Parliament and of the Council of 24 October 1995 on the protection of individuals with regard to the processing of personal data and on the movement of such data.[4]

(10) Credit rating agencies issue opinions on the creditworthiness of a particular issuer or financial instrument as of a given date. As such, these opinions do not constitute a recommendation within the meaning of this Directive. However, credit rating agencies should consider adopting internal policies and procedures designed to ensure that credit ratings published by them are fairly presented and that they appropriately disclose any significant interests or conflicts of interest concerning the financial instruments or the issuers to which their credit ratings relate.

(11) This Directive respects the fundamental rights and observes the principles recognised in particular by the Charter of Fundamental Rights of the European Union and in particular by Article 11 thereof and Article 10 of the European Convention on Human Rights. In this regard, this Directive does not in any way prevent Member States from applying their constitutional rules relating to freedom of the press and freedom of expression in the media.

(12) The measures provided for in this Directive are in accordance with the opinion of the European Securities Committee,

HAS ADOPTED THIS DIRECTIVE:

CHAPTER I
DEFINITIONS

Article 1
Definitions

For the purposes of this Directive, the following definitions shall apply in addition to those laid down in Directive 2003/6/EC:

1. 'investment firm' means any person as defined in Article 1(2) of Council Directive 93/22/EEC;[5]

2. 'credit institution' means any person as defined in Article 1(1) of Directive 2000/12/EC of the European Parliament and of the Council;[6]

3. 'recommendation' means research or other information recommending or suggesting an investment strategy, explicitly or implicitly, concerning one or several financial instruments or the issuers of financial instruments, including any opinion as to the present or future value or price of such instruments, intended for distribution channels or for the public;

4. 'research or other information recommending or suggesting investment strategy' means:

(a) information produced by an independent analyst, an investment firm, a credit institution, any other person whose main business is to

---

[4] OJ L 281, 23.11.1995, 31.

[5] OJ L 141, 11.6.1993, 27, reproduced supra under no. S. 14.
[6] OJ L 126, 26.5.2000, 1, reproduced supra under no. B. 32. Directive 2000/12/EC has been repealed as from 20 July 2007 by article 58 of Directive 2006/48/EC (OJ L 177, 30.6.2006, 1), reproduced supra under no. B. 41.

produce recommendations or a natural person working for them under a contract of employment or otherwise, that, directly or indirectly, expresses a particular investment recommendation in respect of a financial instrument or an issuer of financial instruments;

(b) information produced by persons other than the persons referred to in (a) which directly recommends a particular investment decision in respect of a financial instrument;

5. 'relevant person' means a natural or legal person producing or disseminating recommendations in the exercise of his profession or the conduct of his business;

6. 'issuer' means the issuer of a financial instrument to which a recommendation relates, directly or indirectly;

7. 'distribution channels' shall mean a channel through which information is, or is likely to become, publicly available. 'Likely to become publicly available information' shall mean information to which a large number of persons have access;

8. 'appropriate regulation' shall mean any regulation, including self-regulation, in place in Member States as referred to by Directive 2003/6/EC.

CHAPTER II
PRODUCTION OF RECOMMENDATIONS

Article 2

Identity of producers of recommendations

1. Member States shall ensure that there is appropriate regulation in place to ensure that any recommendation discloses clearly and prominently the identity of the person responsible for its production, in particular, the name and job title of the individual who prepared the recommendation and the name of the legal person responsible for its production.

2. Where the relevant person is an investment firm or a credit institution, Member States shall require that the identity of the relevant competent authority be disclosed.

Where the relevant person is neither an investment firm nor a credit institution, but is subject to self-regulatory standards or codes of conduct, Member States shall ensure that a reference to those standards or codes is disclosed.

3. Member States shall ensure that there is appropriate regulation in place to ensure that the requirements laid down in paragraphs 1 and 2 are adapted in order not to be disproportionate in the case of non-written recommendations. Such adaptation may include a reference to the place where such disclosures can be directly and easily accessed by the public, such as an appropriate internet site of the relevant person.

4. Paragraphs 1 and 2 shall not apply to journalists subject to equivalent appropriate regulation, including equivalent appropriate self regulation, in the Member States, provided that such regulation achieves similar effects as those of paragraphs 1 and 2.

Article 3

General standard for fair presentation of recommendations

1. Member States shall ensure that there is appropriate regulation in place to ensure that all relevant persons take reasonable care to ensure that:

(a) facts are clearly distinguished from interpretations, estimates, opinions and other types of non-factual information;

(b) all sources are reliable or, where there is any doubt as to whether a source is reliable, this is clearly indicated;

(c) all projections, forecasts and price targets are clearly labelled as such and that the material assumptions made in producing or using them are indicated.

2. Member States shall ensure that there is appropriate regulation in place to ensure that the requirements laid down in paragraph 1 are adapted in order not to be disproportionate in the case of non-written recommendations.

3. Member States shall require that all relevant persons take reasonable care to ensure that any

recommendation can be substantiated as reasonable, upon request by the competent authorities.

4. Paragraphs 1 and 3 shall not apply to journalists subject to equivalent appropriate regulation in the Member States, including equivalent appropriate self regulation, provided that such regulation achieves similar effects as those of paragraphs 1 and 3.

Article 4
Additional obligations in relation to fair presentation of recommendations

1. In addition to the obligations laid down in Article 3, where the relevant person is an independent analyst, an investment firm, a credit institution, any related legal person, any other relevant person whose main business is to produce recommendations, or a natural person working for them under a contract of employment or otherwise, Member States shall ensure that there is appropriate regulation in place to ensure that person to take reasonable care to ensure that at least:

(a) all substantially material sources are indicated, as appropriate, including the relevant issuer, together with the fact whether the recommendation has been disclosed to that issuer and amended following this disclosure before its dissemination;

(b) any basis of valuation or methodology used to evaluate a financial instrument or an issuer of a financial instrument, or to set a price target for a financial instrument, is adequately summarised;

(c) the meaning of any recommendation made, such as buy, sell or hold, which may include the time horizon of the investment to which the recommendation relates, is adequately explained and any appropriate risk warning, including a sensitivity analysis of the relevant assumptions, indicated;

(d) reference is made to the planned frequency, if any, of updates of the recommendation and to any major changes in the coverage policy previously announced;

(e) the date at which the recommendation was first released for distribution is indicated clearly and prominently, as well as the relevant date and time for any financial instrument price mentioned;

(f) where a recommendation differs from a recommendation concerning the same financial instrument or issuer, issued during the 12-month period immediately preceding its release, this change and the date of the earlier recommendation are indicated clearly and prominently.

2. Member States shall ensure that, where the requirements laid down in points (a), (b) or (c) of paragraph 1 would be disproportionate in relation to the length of the recommendation distributed, it shall suffice to make clear and prominent reference in the recommendation itself to the place where the required information can be directly and easily accessed by the public, such as a direct Internet link to that information on an appropriate internet site of the relevant person, provided that there has been no change in the methodology or basis of valuation used.

3. Member States shall ensure that there is appropriate regulation in place to ensure that, in the case of non-written recommendations, the requirements of paragraph 1 are adapted so that they are not disproportionate.

Article 5
General standard for disclosure of interests and conflicts of interest

1. Member States shall ensure that there is appropriate regulation in place to ensure that relevant persons disclose all relationships and circumstances that may reasonably be expected to impair the objectivity of the recommendation, in particular where relevant persons have a significant financial interest in one or more of the financial instruments which are the subject of the recommendation, or a significant conflict of interest with respect to an issuer to which the recommendation relates.

Where the relevant person is a legal person, that requirement shall apply also to any legal or natural person working for it, under a contract of employment or otherwise, who was involved in preparing the recommendation.

2. Where the relevant person is a legal person, the information to be disclosed in accordance with paragraph 1 shall at least include the following:

(a) any interests or conflicts of interest of the relevant person or of related legal persons that are accessible or reasonably expected to be accessible to the persons involved in the preparation of the recommendation;

(b) any interests or conflicts of interest of the relevant person or of related legal persons known to persons who, although not involved in the preparation of the recommendation, had or could reasonably be expected to have access to the recommendation prior to its dissemination to customers or the public.

3. Member States shall ensure that there is appropriate regulation in place to ensure that the recommendation itself shall include the disclosures provided for in paragraphs 1 and 2. Where such disclosures would be disproportionate in relation to the length of the recommendation distributed, it shall suffice to make clear and prominent reference in the recommendation itself to the place where such disclosures can be directly and easily accessed by the public, such as a direct Internet link to the disclosure on an appropriate internet site of the relevant person.

4. Member States shall ensure that there is appropriate regulation in place to ensure that the requirements laid down in paragraph 1 are adapted in order not to be disproportionate in the case of non-written recommendations.

5. Paragraphs 1 to 3 shall not apply to journalists subject to equivalent appropriate regulation, including equivalent appropriate self regulation, in the Member States, provided that such regulation achieves similar effects as those of paragraphs 1 to 3.

Article 6

Additional obligations in relation to disclosure of interests or conflicts of interest

1. In addition to the obligations laid down in Article 5, Member States shall require that any recommendation produced by an independent analyst, an investment firm, a credit institution, any related legal person, or any other relevant person whose main business is to produce recommendations, discloses clearly and prominently the following information on their interests and conflicts of interest:

(a) major shareholdings that exist between the relevant person or any related legal person on the one hand and the issuer on the other hand. These major shareholdings include at least the following instances:

– when shareholdings exceeding 5% of the total issued share capital in the issuer are held by the relevant person or any related legal person, or

– when shareholdings exceeding 5% of the total issued share capital of the relevant person or any related legal person are held by the issuer.

Member States may provide for lower thresholds than the 5% threshold as provided for in these two instances;

(b) other significant financial interests held by the relevant person or any related legal person in relation to the issuer;

(c) where applicable, a statement that the relevant person or any related legal person is a market maker or liquidity provider in the financial instruments of the issuer;

(d) where applicable, a statement that the relevant person or any related legal person has been lead manager or co-lead manager over the previous 12 months of any publicly disclosed offer of financial instruments of the issuer;

(e) where applicable, a statement that the relevant person or any related legal person is party to any other agreement with the issuer relating to the provision of investment banking services, provided that this would not entail the disclosure of any confidential commercial information and that the agreement has been in effect over the previous 12 months or has given rise during the same period to the payment of a compensation or to the promise to get a compensation paid;

(f) where applicable, a statement that the relevant person or any related legal person is party to an agreement with the issuer relating to the production of the recommendation.

2. Member States shall require disclosure, in general terms, of the effective organisational and administrative arrangements set up within the investment firm or the credit institution for the prevention and avoidance of conflicts of interest with respect to recommendations, including information barriers.

3. Member States shall require that for natural or legal persons working for an investment firm or a credit institution, under a contract of employment or otherwise, and who were involved in preparing the recommendation, the requirement under the second subparagraph of paragraph 1 of Article 5 shall include, in particular, disclosure of whether the remuneration of such persons is tied to investment banking transactions performed by the investment firm or credit institution or any related legal person.

Where those natural persons receive or purchase the shares of the issuers prior to a public offering of such shares, the price at which the shares were acquired and the date of acquisition shall also be disclosed.

4. Member States shall require that investment firms and credit institutions disclose, on a quarterly basis, the proportion of all recommendations that are 'buy', 'hold', 'sell' or equivalent terms, as well as the proportion of issuers corresponding to each of these categories to which the investment firm or the credit institution has supplied material investment banking services over the previous 12 months.

5. Member States shall ensure that the recommendation itself includes the disclosures required by paragraphs 1 to 4. Where the requirements under paragraphs 1 to 4 would be disproportionate in relation to the length of the recommendation distributed, it shall suffice to make clear and prominent reference in the recommendation itself to the place where such disclosure can be directly and easily accessed by the public, such as a direct Internet link to the disclosure on an appropriate internet site of the investment firm or credit institution.

6. Member States shall ensure that there is appropriate regulation in place to ensure that, in the case of non-written recommendations, the requirements of paragraph 1 are adapted so that they are not disproportionate.

CHAPTER III

DISSEMINATION OF RECOMMENDATIONS PRODUCED BY THIRD PARTIES

Article 7

Identity of disseminators of recommendations

Member States shall ensure that there is appropriate regulation in place to ensure that, whenever a relevant person under his own responsibility disseminates a recommendation produced by a third party, the recommendation indicates clearly and prominently the identity of that relevant person.

Article 8

General standard for dissemination of recommendations

Member States shall ensure that there is appropriate regulation in place to ensure that whenever a recommendation produced by a third party is substantially altered within disseminated information, that information clearly indicates the substantial alteration in detail. Member States shall ensure that whenever the substantial alteration consists of a change of the direction of the recommendation (such as changing a 'buy' recommendation into a 'hold' or 'sell' recommendation or vice versa), the requirements laid down in Articles 2 to 5 on producers are met by the disseminator, to the extent of the substantial alteration.

In addition, Member States shall ensure that there is appropriate regulation in place to ensure that relevant legal persons who themselves, or through natural persons, disseminate a substantially altered recommendation have a formal written policy so that the persons receiving the information may be directed to where they can have access to the identity of the producer of the recommendation, the recommendation itself and the disclosure of the producer's interests or conflicts of interest, provided that these elements are publicly available.

The first and second paragraphs do not apply to news reporting on recommendations produced by a third party where the substance of the recommendation is not altered.

In case of dissemination of a summary of a recommendation produced by a third party, the relevant persons disseminating such summary shall ensure that the summary is clear and not misleading, mentioning the source document and where the disclosures related to the source document can be directly and easily accessed by the public provided that they are publicly available.

Article 9

Additional obligations for investment firms and credit institutions

In addition to the obligations laid down in Articles 7 and 8, whenever the relevant person is an investment firm, a credit institution or a natural person working for such persons under a contract of employment or otherwise, and disseminates recommendations produced by a third party, Member States shall require that:

(a) the name of the competent authority of the investment firm or credit institution is clearly and prominently indicated;

(b) if the producer of the recommendation has not already disseminated it through a distribution channel, the requirements laid down in Article 6 on producers are met by the disseminator;

(c) if the investment firm or credit institution has substantially altered the recommendation, the requirements laid down in Articles 2 to 6 on producers are met.

Chapter IV
Final Provisions

Article 10

Transposition

1. Member States shall bring into force the laws, regulations and administrative provisions necessary to comply with this Directive by 12 October 2004 at the latest. They shall forthwith communicate to the Commission the text of those provisions and a correlation table between these provisions and this Directive.

When Member States adopt those provisions, they shall contain a reference to this Directive or be accompanied by such a reference on the occasion of their official publication. Member States shall determine how such reference is to be made.

2. Member States shall communicate to the Commission the text of the main provisions of national law which they adopt in the field covered by this Directive.

Article 11

Entry into force

This Directive shall enter into force on the day of its publication in the Official Journal of the European Union.

Article 12

Addressees

This Directive is addressed to the Member States.

S. 28.

European Parliament and Council Directive 2004/25/EC of 21 April 2004 on takeover bids[1]

(Text with EEA relevance)

THE EUROPEAN PARLIAMENT AND THE COUNCIL OF THE EUROPEAN UNION,

Having regard to the Treaty establishing the European Community, and in particular Article 44(1) thereof,

Having regard to the proposal from the Commission,[2]

Having regard to the opinion of the European Economic and Social Committee,[3]

Acting in accordance with the procedure laid down in Article 251 of the Treaty,[4]

Whereas:

(1) In accordance with Article 44(2)(g) of the Treaty, it is necessary to coordinate certain safeguards which, for the protection of the interests of members and others, Member States require of companies governed by the law of a Member State the securities of which are admitted to trading on a regulated market in a Member State, with a view to making such safeguards equivalent throughout the Community.

(2) It is necessary to protect the interests of holders of the securities of companies governed by the law of a Member State when those companies are the subject of takeover bids or of changes of control and at least some of their securities are admitted to trading on a regulated market in a Member State.

(3) It is necessary to create Community-wide clarity and transparency in respect of legal issues to be settled in the event of takeover bids and to prevent patterns of corporate restructuring within the Community from being distorted by arbitrary differences in governance and management cultures.

(4) In view of the public-interest purposes served by the central banks of the Member States, it seems inconceivable that they should be the targets of takeover bids. Since, for historical reasons, the securities of some of those central banks are listed on regulated markets in Member States, it is necessary to exclude them explicitly from the scope of this Directive.

(5) Each Member State should designate an authority or authorities to supervise those aspects of bids that are governed by this Directive and to ensure that parties to takeover bids comply with the rules made pursuant to this Directive. All those authorities should cooperate with one another.

(6) In order to be effective, takeover regulation should be flexible and capable of dealing with new circumstances as they arise and should accordingly provide for the possibility of exceptions and derogations. However, in applying any rules or exceptions laid down or in granting any derogations, supervisory authorities should respect certain general principles.

(7) Self-regulatory bodies should be able to exercise supervision.

(8) In accordance with general principles of Community law, and in particular the right to a fair hearing, decisions of a supervisory authority should in appropriate circumstances be susceptible

---

[1] OJ L 142, 30.4.2004, 12–23.
[2] OJ C 45 E, 25.2.2003, 1.
[3] OJ C 208, 3.9.2003, 55.
[4] Opinion of the European Parliament of 16 December 2003 (not yet published in the Official Journal) and Council Decision of 30 March 2004.

to review by an independent court or tribunal. However, Member States should be left to determine whether rights are to be made available which may be asserted in administrative or judicial proceedings, either in proceedings against a supervisory authority or in proceedings between parties to a bid.

(9) Member States should take the necessary steps to protect the holders of securities, in particular those with minority holdings, when control of their companies has been acquired. The Member States should ensure such protection by obliging the person who has acquired control of a company to make an offer to all the holders of that company's securities for all of their holdings at an equitable price in accordance with a common definition. Member States should be free to establish further instruments for the protection of the interests of the holders of securities, such as the obligation to make a partial bid where the offeror does not acquire control of the company or the obligation to announce a bid at the same time as control of the company is acquired.

(10) The obligation to make a bid to all the holders of securities should not apply to those controlling holdings already in existence on the date on which the national legislation transposing this Directive enters into force.

(11) The obligation to launch a bid should not apply in the case of the acquisition of securities which do not carry the right to vote at ordinary general meetings of shareholders. Member States should, however, be able to provide that the obligation to make a bid to all the holders of securities relates not only to securities carrying voting rights but also to securities which carry voting rights only in specific circumstances or which do not carry voting rights.

(12) To reduce the scope for insider dealing, an offeror should be required to announce his/her decision to launch a bid as soon as possible and to inform the supervisory authority of the bid.

(13) The holders of securities should be properly informed of the terms of a bid by means of an offer document. Appropriate information should also be given to the representatives of the company's employees or, failing that, to the employees directly.

(14) The time allowed for the acceptance of a bid should be regulated.

(15) To be able to perform their functions satisfactorily, supervisory authorities should at all times be able to require the parties to a bid to provide information concerning themselves and should cooperate and supply information in an efficient and effective manner, without delay, to other authorities supervising capital markets.

(16) In order to prevent operations which could frustrate a bid, the powers of the board of an offeree company to engage in operations of an exceptional nature should be limited, without unduly hindering the offeree company in carrying on its normal business activities.

(17) The board of an offeree company should be required to make public a document setting out its opinion of the bid and the reasons on which that opinion is based, including its views on the effects of implementation on all the company's interests, and specifically on employment.

(18) In order to reinforce the effectiveness of existing provisions concerning the freedom to deal in the securities of companies covered by this Directive and the freedom to exercise voting rights, it is essential that the defensive structures and mechanisms envisaged by such companies be transparent and that they be regularly presented in reports to general meetings of shareholders.

(19) Member States should take the necessary measures to afford any offeror the possibility of acquiring majority interests in other companies and of fully exercising control of them. To that end, restrictions on the transfer of securities, restrictions on voting rights, extraordinary appointment rights and multiple voting rights should be removed or suspended during the time allowed for the acceptance of a bid and when the general meeting of shareholders decides on defensive measures, on amendments to the articles of association or on the removal or appointment of board members at the first general meeting of shareholders following closure

of the bid. Where the holders of securities have suffered losses as a result of the removal of rights, equitable compensation should be provided for in accordance with the technical arrangements laid down by Member States.

(20) All special rights held by Member States in companies should be viewed in the framework of the free movement of capital and the relevant provisions of the Treaty. Special rights held by Member States in companies which are provided for in private or public national law should be exempted from the 'breakthrough' rule if they are compatible with the Treaty.

(21) Taking into account existing differences in Member States' company law mechanisms and structures, Member States should be allowed not to require companies established within their territories to apply the provisions of this Directive limiting the powers of the board of an offeree company during the time allowed for the acceptance of a bid and those rendering ineffective barriers, provided for in the articles of association or in specific agreements. In that event Member States should at least allow companies established within their territories to make the choice, which must be reversible, to apply those provisions. Without prejudice to international agreements to which the European Community is a party, Member States should be allowed not to require companies which apply those provisions in accordance with the optional arrangements to apply them when they become the subject of offers launched by companies which do not apply the same provisions, as a consequence of the use of those optional arrangements.

(22) Member States should lay down rules to cover the possibility of a bid's lapsing, the offeror's right to revise his/her bid, the possibility of competing bids for a company's securities, the disclosure of the result of a bid, the irrevocability of a bid and the conditions permitted.

(23) The disclosure of information to and the consultation of representatives of the employees of the offeror and the offeree company should be governed by the relevant national provisions, in particular those adopted pursuant to Council Directive 94/45/EC of 22 September 1994 on the establishment of a European Works Council or a procedure in Community-scale undertakings and Community-scale groups of undertakings for the purposes of informing and consulting employee,[5] Council Directive 98/59/EC of 20 July 1998 on the approximation of the laws of the Member States relating to collective redundancies,[6] Council Directive 2001/86/EC of 8 October 2001 supplementing the statute for a European Company with regard to the involvement of employees[7] and Directive 2002/14/EC of the European Parliament and of the Council of 11 March 2002 establishing a general framework for informing and consulting employees in the European Community—Joint declaration of the European Parliament, the Council and the Commission on employee representation.[8] The employees of the companies concerned, or their representatives, should nevertheless be given an opportunity to state their views on the foreseeable effects of the bid on employment. Without prejudice to the rules of Directive 2003/6/EC of the European Parliament and of the Council of 28 January 2003 on insider dealing and market manipulation (market abuse),[9] Member States may always apply or introduce national provisions concerning the disclosure of information to and the consultation of representatives of the employees of the offeror before an offer is launched.

(24) Member States should take the necessary measures to enable an offeror who, following a takeover bid, has acquired a certain percentage of a company's capital carrying voting rights to require the holders of the remaining securities to sell him/her their securities. Likewise, where, following a takeover bid, an offeror has acquired a certain percentage of a company's capital carrying voting rights, the holders of the remaining securities should be able to require him/her to buy their securities. These squeeze-out and sell-out procedures should apply only under specific

---

[5] OJ L 254, 30.9.1994, 64, reproduced supra under no. E. 5. Directive as amended by Directive 97/74/EC (OJ L 10, 16.1.1998, 22), reproduced supra under no. E. 6.
[6] OJ L 225, 12.8.1998, 16, reproduced supra under no. E. 8.
[7] OJ L 294, 10.11.2001, 22, reproduced supra under no. C. 20.
[8] OJ L 80, 23.3.2002, 29, reproduced supra under no. E. 12.
[9] OJ L 96, 12.4.2003, 16, reproduced supra under no. S. 24.

conditions linked to takeover bids. Member States may continue to apply national rules to squeeze-out and sell-out procedures in other circumstances.

(25) Since the objectives of the action envisaged, namely to establish minimum guidelines for the conduct of takeover bids and ensure an adequate level of protection for holders of securities throughout the Community, cannot be sufficiently achieved by the Member States because of the need for transparency and legal certainty in the case of cross-border takeovers and acquisitions of control, and can therefore, by reason of the scale and effects of the action, be better achieved at Community level, the Community may adopt measures, in accordance with the principle of subsidiarity as set out in Article 5 of the Treaty. In accordance with the principle of proportionality as set out in that Article, this Directive does not go beyond what is necessary to achieve those objectives.

(26) The adoption of a Directive is the appropriate procedure for the establishment of a framework consisting of certain common principles and a limited number of general requirements which Member States are to implement through more detailed rules in accordance with their national systems and their cultural contexts.

(27) Member States should, however, provide for sanctions for any infringement of the national measures transposing this Directive.

(28) Technical guidance and implementing measures for the rules laid down in this Directive may from time to time be necessary, to take account of new developments on financial markets. For certain provisions, the Commission should accordingly be empowered to adopt implementing measures, provided that these do not modify the essential elements of this Directive and the Commission acts in accordance with the principles set out in this Directive, after consulting the European Securities Committee established by Commission Decision 2001/528/EC.[10] The measures necessary for the implementation of this Directive should be adopted in accordance with Council Decision 1999/468/EC of 28 June 1999 laying down the procedures for the exercise of implementing powers conferred on the Commission and with due regard to the declaration made by the Commission in the European Parliament on 5 February 2002 concerning the implementation of financial services legislation. For the other provisions, it is important to entrust a contact committee with the task of assisting Member States and the supervisory authorities in the implementation of this Directive and of advising the Commission, if necessary, on additions or amendments to this Directive. In so doing, the contact committee may make use of the information which Member States are to provide on the basis of this Directive concerning takeover bids that have taken place on their regulated markets.

(29) The Commission should facilitate movement towards the fair and balanced harmonisation of rules on takeovers in the European Union. To that end, the Commission should be able to submit proposals for the timely revision of this Directive,

HAVE ADOPTED THIS DIRECTIVE:

Article 1

Scope

1. This Directive lays down measures coordinating the laws, regulations, administrative provisions, codes of practice and other arrangements of the Member States, including arrangements established by organisations officially authorised to regulate the markets (hereinafter referred to as 'rules'), relating to takeover bids for the securities of companies governed by the laws of Member States, where all or some of those securities are admitted to trading on a regulated market within the meaning of Directive 93/22/EEC[11] in one or

---

[10] OJ L 191, 13.7.2001, 45, reproduced supra under no. S. 20. Directive as amended by Decision 2004/8/EC (OJ L 3, 7.1.2004, 33).

[11] Council Directive 93/22/EEC of 10 May 1993 on investment services in the securities field (OJ L 141, 11.6.1993, 27), reproduced supra under no. S. 14. Directive as last amended by Directive 2002/87/EC of the European Parliament and of the Council (OJ L 35, 11.2.2003, 1), reproduced supra under no. B. 38.

more Member States (hereinafter referred to as a 'regulated market').

2. This Directive shall not apply to takeover bids for securities issued by companies, the object of which is the collective investment of capital provided by the public, which operate on the principle of risk-spreading and the units of which are, at the holders' request, repurchased or redeemed, directly or indirectly, out of the assets of those companies. Action taken by such companies to ensure that the stock exchange value of their units does not vary significantly from their net asset value shall be regarded as equivalent to such repurchase or redemption.

3. This Directive shall not apply to takeover bids for securities issued by the Member States' central banks.

Article 2

Definitions

1. For the purposes of this Directive:

(a) 'takeover bid' or 'bid' shall mean a public offer (other than by the offeree company itself) made to the holders of the securities of a company to acquire all or some of those securities, whether mandatory or voluntary, which follows or has as its objective the acquisition of control of the offeree company in accordance with national law;

(b) 'offeree company' shall mean a company, the securities of which are the subject of a bid;

(c) 'offeror' shall mean any natural or legal person governed by public or private law making a bid;

(d) 'persons acting in concert' shall mean natural or legal persons who cooperate with the offeror or the offeree company on the basis of an agreement, either express or tacit, either oral or written, aimed either at acquiring control of the offeree company or at frustrating the successful outcome of a bid;

(e) 'securities' shall mean transferable securities carrying voting rights in a company;

(f) 'parties to the bid' shall mean the offeror, the members of the offeror's board if the offeror is a company, the offeree company, holders of securities of the offeree company and the members of the board of the offeree company, and persons acting in concert with such parties;

(g) 'multiple-vote securities' shall mean securities included in a distinct and separate class and carrying more than one vote each.

2. For the purposes of paragraph 1(d), persons controlled by another person within the meaning of Article 87 of Directive 2001/34/EC[12] shall be deemed to be persons acting in concert with that other person and with each other.

Article 3

General principles

1. For the purpose of implementing this Directive, Member States shall ensure that the following principles are complied with:

(a) all holders of the securities of an offeree company of the same class must be afforded equivalent treatment; moreover, if a person acquires control of a company, the other holders of securities must be protected;

(b) the holders of the securities of an offeree company must have sufficient time and information to enable them to reach a properly informed decision on the bid; where it advises the holders of securities, the board of the offeree company must give its views on the effects of implementation of the bid on employment, conditions of employment and the locations of the company's places of business;

(c) the board of an offeree company must act in the interests of the company as a whole and must not deny the holders of securities the opportunity to decide on the merits of the bid;

(d) false markets must not be created in the securities of the offeree company, of the offeror company or of any other company concerned by the bid in such a way that the rise or fall of the

---

[12] Directive 2001/34/EC of the European Parliament and of the Council of 28 May 2001 on the admission of securities to official stock exchange listing and on information to be published on those securities (OJ L 184, 6.7.2001, 1), reproduced supra under no. S. 18. Directive as last amended by Directive 2003/71/EC (OJ L 345, 31.12.2003, 64), reproduced supra under no. S. 25.

prices of the securities becomes artificial and the normal functioning of the markets is distorted;

(e) an offeror must announce a bid only after ensuring that he/she can fulfil in full any cash consideration, if such is offered, and after taking all reasonable measures to secure the implementation of any other type of consideration;

(f) an offeree company must not be hindered in the conduct of its affairs for longer than is reasonable by a bid for its securities.

2. With a view to ensuring compliance with the principles laid down in paragraph 1, Member States:

(a) shall ensure that the minimum requirements set out in this Directive are observed;

(b) may lay down additional conditions and provisions more stringent than those of this Directive for the regulation of bids.

Article 4

Supervisory authority and applicable law

1. Member States shall designate the authority or authorities competent to supervise bids for the purposes of the rules which they make or introduce pursuant to this Directive. The authorities thus designated shall be either public authorities, associations or private bodies recognised by national law or by public authorities expressly empowered for that purpose by national law. Member States shall inform the Commission of those designations, specifying any divisions of functions that may be made. They shall ensure that those authorities exercise their functions impartially and independently of all parties to a bid.

2. (a) The authority competent to supervise a bid shall be that of the Member State in which the offeree company has its registered office if that company's securities are admitted to trading on a regulated market in that Member State.

(b) If the offeree company's securities are not admitted to trading on a regulated market in the Member State in which the company has its registered office, the authority competent to supervise the bid shall be that of the Member State on the regulated market of which the company's securities are admitted to trading.

If the offeree company's securities are admitted to trading on regulated markets in more than one Member State, the authority competent to supervise the bid shall be that of the Member State on the regulated market of which the securities were first admitted to trading.

(c) If the offeree company's securities were first admitted to trading on regulated markets in more than one Member State simultaneously, the offeree company shall determine which of the supervisory authorities of those Member States shall be the authority competent to supervise the bid by notifying those regulated markets and their supervisory authorities on the first day of trading.

If the offeree company's securities have already been admitted to trading on regulated markets in more than one Member State on the date laid down in Article 21(1) and were admitted simultaneously, the supervisory authorities of those Member States shall agree which one of them shall be the authority competent to supervise the bid within four weeks of the date laid down in Article 21(1). Otherwise, the offeree company shall determine which of those authorities shall be the competent authority on the first day of trading following that four-week period.

(d) Member States shall ensure that the decisions referred to in (c) are made public.

(e) In the cases referred to in (b) and (c), matters relating to the consideration offered in the case of a bid, in particular the price, and matters relating to the bid procedure, in particular the information on the offeror's decision to make a bid, the contents of the offer document and the disclosure of the bid, shall be dealt with in accordance with the rules of the Member State of the competent authority. In matters relating to the information to be provided to the employees of the offeree company and in matters relating to company law, in particular the percentage of voting rights which confers control and any derogation from the obligation to launch a bid, as well as the conditions under which the board of the offeree company may undertake any action which might result in the frustration of the bid, the applicable rules and the competent authority shall be those of the Member State in which the offeree company has its registered office.

3. Member States shall ensure that all persons employed or formerly employed by their supervisory authorities are bound by professional secrecy. No information covered by professional secrecy may be divulged to any person or authority except under provisions laid down by law.

4. The supervisory authorities of the Member States for the purposes of this Directive and other authorities supervising capital markets, in particular in accordance with Directive 93/22/EEC, Directive 2001/34/EC, Directive 2003/6/EC and Directive 2003/71/EC of the European Parliament and of the Council of 4 November 2003 on the prospectus to be published when securities are offered to the public or admitted to trading shall cooperate and supply each other with information wherever necessary for the application of the rules drawn up in accordance with this Directive and in particular in cases covered by paragraph 2(b), (c) and (e). Information thus exchanged shall be covered by the obligation of professional secrecy to which persons employed or formerly employed by the supervisory authorities receiving the information are subject. Cooperation shall include the ability to serve the legal documents necessary to enforce measures taken by the competent authorities in connection with bids, as well as such other assistance as may reasonably be requested by the supervisory authorities concerned for the purpose of investigating any actual or alleged breaches of the rules made or introduced pursuant to this Directive.

5. The supervisory authorities shall be vested with all the powers necessary for the purpose of carrying out their duties, including that of ensuring that the parties to a bid comply with the rules made or introduced pursuant to this Directive.

Provided that the general principles laid down in Article 3(1) are respected, Member States may provide in the rules that they make or introduce pursuant to this Directive for derogations from those rules:
(i) by including such derogations in their national rules, in order to take account of circumstances determined at national level and/or

(ii) by granting their supervisory authorities, where they are competent, powers to waive such national rules, to take account of the circumstances referred to in (i) or in other specific circumstances, in which case a reasoned decision must be required.

6. This Directive shall not affect the power of the Member States to designate judicial or other authorities responsible for dealing with disputes and for deciding on irregularities committed in the course of bids or the power of Member States to regulate whether and under which circumstances parties to a bid are entitled to bring administrative or judicial proceedings. In particular, this Directive shall not affect the power which courts may have in a Member State to decline to hear legal proceedings and to decide whether or not such proceedings affect the outcome of a bid. This Directive shall not affect the power of the Member States to determine the legal position concerning the liability of supervisory authorities or concerning litigation between the parties to a bid.

Article 5

Protection of minority shareholders, the mandatory bid and the equitable price

1. Where a natural or legal person, as a result of his/her own acquisition or the acquisition by persons acting in concert with him/her, holds securities of a company as referred to in Article 1(1) which, added to any existing holdings of those securities of his/hers and the holdings of those securities of persons acting in concert with him/her, directly or indirectly give him/her a specified percentage of voting rights in that company, giving him/her control of that company, Member States shall ensure that such a person is required to make a bid as a means of protecting the minority shareholders of that company. Such a bid shall be addressed at the earliest opportunity to all the holders of those securities for all their holdings at the equitable price as defined in paragraph 4.

2. Where control has been acquired following a voluntary bid made in accordance with this

Directive to all the holders of securities for all their holdings, the obligation laid down in paragraph 1 to launch a bid shall no longer apply.

3. The percentage of voting rights which confers control for the purposes of paragraph 1 and the method of its calculation shall be determined by the rules of the Member State in which the company has its registered office.

4. The highest price paid for the same securities by the offeror, or by persons acting in concert with him/her, over a period, to be determined by Member States, of not less than six months and not more than 12 before the bid referred to in paragraph 1 shall be regarded as the equitable price. If, after the bid has been made public and before the offer closes for acceptance, the offeror or any person acting in concert with him/her purchases securities at a price higher than the offer price, the offeror shall increase his/her offer so that it is not less than the highest price paid for the securities so acquired.

Provided that the general principles laid down in Article 3(1) are respected, Member States may authorise their supervisory authorities to adjust the price referred to in the first subparagraph in circumstances and in accordance with criteria that are clearly determined. To that end, they may draw up a list of circumstances in which the highest price may be adjusted either upwards or downwards, for example where the highest price was set by agreement between the purchaser and a seller, where the market prices of the securities in question have been manipulated, where market prices in general or certain market prices in particular have been affected by exceptional occurrences, or in order to enable a firm in difficulty to be rescued. They may also determine the criteria to be applied in such cases, for example the average market value over a particular period, the break-up value of the company or other objective valuation criteria generally used in financial analysis.

Any decision by a supervisory authority to adjust the equitable price shall be substantiated and made public.

5. By way of consideration the offeror may offer securities, cash or a combination of both.

However, where the consideration offered by the offeror does not consist of liquid securities admitted to trading on a regulated market, it shall include a cash alternative.

In any event, the offeror shall offer a cash consideration at least as an alternative where he/she or persons acting in concert with him/her, over a period beginning at the same time as the period determined by the Member State in accordance with paragraph 4 and ending when the offer closes for acceptance, has purchased for cash securities carrying 5% or more of the voting rights in the offeree company.

Member States may provide that a cash consideration must be offered, at least as an alternative, in all cases.

6. In addition to the protection provided for in paragraph 1, Member States may provide for further instruments intended to protect the interests of the holders of securities in so far as those instruments do not hinder the normal course of a bid.

Article 6
Information concerning bids

1. Member States shall ensure that a decision to make a bid is made public without delay and that the supervisory authority is informed of the bid. They may require that the supervisory authority must be informed before such a decision is made public. As soon as the bid has been made public, the boards of the offeree company and of the offeror shall inform the representatives of their respective employees or, where there are no such representatives, the employees themselves.

2. Member States shall ensure that an offeror is required to draw up and make public in good time an offer document containing the information necessary to enable the holders of the offeree company's securities to reach a properly informed decision on the bid. Before the offer document is made public, the offeror shall communicate it to the supervisory authority. When it is made public, the boards of the offeree company and of the offeror shall communicate it to the representatives of their respective employees or, where

there are no such representatives, to the employees themselves.

Where the offer document referred to in the first subparagraph is subject to the prior approval of the supervisory authority and has been approved, it shall be recognised, subject to any translation required, in any other Member State on the market of which the offeree company's securities are admitted to trading, without its being necessary to obtain the approval of the supervisory authorities of that Member State. Those authorities may require the inclusion of additional information in the offer document only if such information is specific to the market of a Member State or Member States on which the offeree company's securities are admitted to trading and relates to the formalities to be complied with to accept the bid and to receive the consideration due at the close of the bid as well as to the tax arrangements to which the consideration offered to the holders of the securities will be subject.

3. The offer document referred to in paragraph 2 shall state at least:

(a) the terms of the bid;

(b) the identity of the offeror and, where the offeror is a company, the type, name and registered office of that company;

(c) the securities or, where appropriate, the class or classes of securities for which the bid is made;

(d) the consideration offered for each security or class of securities and, in the case of a mandatory bid, the method employed in determining it, with particulars of the way in which that consideration is to be paid;

(e) the compensation offered for the rights which might be removed as a result of the breakthrough rule laid down in Article 11(4), with particulars of the way in which that compensation is to be paid and the method employed in determining it;

(f) the maximum and minimum percentages or quantities of securities which the offeror undertakes to acquire;

(g) details of any existing holdings of the offeror, and of persons acting in concert with him/her, in the offeree company;

(h) all the conditions to which the bid is subject;

(i) the offeror's intentions with regard to the future business of the offeree company and, in so far as it is affected by the bid, the offeror company and with regard to the safeguarding of the jobs of their employees and management, including any material change in the conditions of employment, and in particular the offeror's strategic plans for the two companies and the likely repercussions on employment and the locations of the companies' places of business;

(j) the time allowed for acceptance of the bid;

(k) where the consideration offered by the offeror includes securities of any kind, information concerning those securities;

(l) information concerning the financing for the bid;

(m) the identity of persons acting in concert with the offeror or with the offeree company and, in the case of companies, their types, names, registered offices and relationships with the offeror and, where possible, with the offeree company;

(n) the national law which will govern contracts concluded between the offeror and the holders of the offeree company's securities as a result of the bid and the competent courts.

4. The Commission shall adopt rules for the application of paragraph 3 in accordance with the procedure referred to in Article 18(2).

5. Member States shall ensure that the parties to a bid are required to provide the supervisory authorities of their Member State at any time on request with all the information in their possession concerning the bid that is necessary for the supervisory authority to discharge its functions.

Article 7

Time allowed for acceptance

1. Member States shall provide that the time allowed for the acceptance of a bid may not be less than two weeks nor more than 10 weeks from the date of publication of the offer document. Provided that the general principle laid down in Article 3(1)(f) is respected, Member States may provide that the period of 10 weeks may be

extended on condition that the offeror gives at least two weeks' notice of his/her intention of closing the bid.

2. Member States may provide for rules changing the period referred to in paragraph 1 in specific cases. A Member State may authorise a supervisory authority to grant a derogation from the period referred to in paragraph 1 in order to allow the offeree company to call a general meeting of shareholders to consider the bid.

Article 8
Disclosure

1. Member States shall ensure that a bid is made public in such a way as to ensure market transparency and integrity for the securities of the offeree company, of the offeror or of any other company affected by the bid, in particular in order to prevent the publication or dissemination of false or misleading information.

2. Member States shall provide for the disclosure of all information and documents required by Article 6 in such a manner as to ensure that they are both readily and promptly available to the holders of securities at least in those Member States on the regulated markets of which the offeree company's securities are admitted to trading and to the representatives of the employees of the offeree company and the offeror or, where there are no such representatives, to the employees themselves.

Article 9
Obligations of the board of the offeree company

1. Member States shall ensure that the rules laid down in paragraphs 2 to 5 are complied with.

2. During the period referred to in the second subparagraph, the board of the offeree company shall obtain the prior authorisation of the general meeting of shareholders given for this purpose before taking any action, other than seeking alternative bids, which may result in the frustration of the bid and in particular before issuing any shares which may result in a lasting impediment to the offeror's acquiring control of the offeree company.

Such authorisation shall be mandatory at least from the time the board of the offeree company receives the information referred to in the first sentence of Article 6(1) concerning the bid and until the result of the bid is made public or the bid lapses. Member States may require that such authorisation be obtained at an earlier stage, for example as soon as the board of the offeree company becomes aware that the bid is imminent.

3. As regards decisions taken before the beginning of the period referred to in the second subparagraph of paragraph 2 and not yet partly or fully implemented, the general meeting of shareholders shall approve or confirm any decision which does not form part of the normal course of the company's business and the implementation of which may result in the frustration of the bid.

4. For the purpose of obtaining the prior authorisation, approval or confirmation of the holders of securities referred to in paragraphs 2 and 3, Member States may adopt rules allowing a general meeting of shareholders to be called at short notice, provided that the meeting does not take place within two weeks of notification's being given.

5. The board of the offeree company shall draw up and make public a document setting out its opinion of the bid and the reasons on which it is based, including its views on the effects of implementation of the bid on all the company's interests and specifically employment, and on the offeror's strategic plans for the offeree company and their likely repercussions on employment and the locations of the company's places of business as set out in the offer document in accordance with Article 6(3)(i). The board of the offeree company shall at the same time communicate that opinion to the representatives of its employees or, where there are no such representatives, to the employees themselves. Where the board of the offeree company receives in good time a separate opinion from the representatives of its employees on the effects of the bid on employment, that opinion shall be appended to the document.

6. For the purposes of paragraph 2, where a company has a two-tier board structure 'board' shall mean both the management board and the supervisory board.

Article 10

Information on companies as referred to in Article 1(1)

1. Member States shall ensure that companies as referred to in Article 1(1) publish detailed information on the following:

(a) the structure of their capital, including securities which are not admitted to trading on a regulated market in a Member State, where appropriate with an indication of the different classes of shares and, for each class of shares, the rights and obligations attaching to it and the percentage of total share capital that it represents;

(b) any restrictions on the transfer of securities, such as limitations on the holding of securities or the need to obtain the approval of the company or other holders of securities, without prejudice to Article 46 of Directive 2001/34/EC;

(c) significant direct and indirect shareholdings (including indirect shareholdings through pyramid structures and cross-shareholdings) within the meaning of Article 85 of Directive 2001/34/EC;

(d) the holders of any securities with special control rights and a description of those rights;

(e) the system of control of any employee share scheme where the control rights are not exercised directly by the employees;

(f) any restrictions on voting rights, such as limitations of the voting rights of holders of a given percentage or number of votes, deadlines for exercising voting rights, or systems whereby, with the company's cooperation, the financial rights attaching to securities are separated from the holding of securities;

(g) any agreements between shareholders which are known to the company and may result in restrictions on the transfer of securities and/or voting rights within the meaning of Directive 2001/34/EC;

(h) the rules governing the appointment and replacement of board members and the amendment of the articles of association;

(i) the powers of board members, and in particular the power to issue or buy back shares;

(j) any significant agreements to which the company is a party and which take effect, alter or terminate upon a change of control of the company following a takeover bid, and the effects thereof, except where their nature is such that their disclosure would be seriously prejudicial to the company; this exception shall not apply where the company is specifically obliged to disclose such information on the basis of other legal requirements;

(k) any agreements between the company and its board members or employees providing for compensation if they resign or are made redundant without valid reason or if their employment ceases because of a takeover bid.

2. The information referred to in paragraph 1 shall be published in the company's annual report as provided for in Article 46 of Directive 78/660/EEC[13] and Article 36 of Directive 83/349/ EEC.[14]

3. Member States shall ensure, in the case of companies the securities of which are admitted to trading on a regulated market in a Member State, that the board presents an explanatory report to the annual general meeting of shareholders on the matters referred to in paragraph 1.

Article 11

Breakthrough

1. Without prejudice to other rights and obligations provided for in Community law for

---

[13] Fourth Council Directive 78/660/EEC of 25 July 1978 on the annual accounts of certain types of companies (OJ L 222, 14.8.1978, 11), reproduced supra under no. C. 4. Directive as last amended by Directive 2003/51/EC of the European Parliament and of the Council (OJ L 178, 17.7.2003, 16), reproduced supra under no. C. 23.

[14] Seventh Council Directive 83/349/EEC of 13 June 1983 on consolidated accounts (OJ L 193, 18.7.1983, 1), reproduced supra under no. C. 6. Directive as last amended by Directive 2003/51/EC (OJ L 178, 17.7.2003, 16), reproduced supra under no. C. 23.

the companies referred to in Article 1(1), Member States shall ensure that the provisions laid down in paragraphs 2 to 7 apply when a bid has been made public.

2. Any restrictions on the transfer of securities provided for in the articles of association of the offeree company shall not apply vis-à-vis the offeror during the time allowed for acceptance of the bid laid down in Article 7(1).

Any restrictions on the transfer of securities provided for in contractual agreements between the offeree company and holders of its securities, or in contractual agreements between holders of the offeree company's securities entered into after the adoption of this Directive, shall not apply vis-à-vis the offeror during the time allowed for acceptance of the bid laid down in Article 7(1).

3. Restrictions on voting rights provided for in the articles of association of the offeree company shall not have effect at the general meeting of shareholders which decides on any defensive measures in accordance with Article 9.

Restrictions on voting rights provided for in contractual agreements between the offeree company and holders of its securities, or in contractual agreements between holders of the offeree company's securities entered into after the adoption of this Directive, shall not have effect at the general meeting of shareholders which decides on any defensive measures in accordance with Article 9

Multiple-vote securities shall carry only one vote each at the general meeting of shareholders which decides on any defensive measures in accordance with Article 9.

4. Where, following a bid, the offeror holds 75% or more of the capital carrying voting rights, no restrictions on the transfer of securities or on voting rights referred to in paragraphs 2 and 3 nor any extraordinary rights of shareholders concerning the appointment or removal of board members provided for in the articles of association of the offeree company shall apply; multiple-vote securities shall carry only one vote each at the first general meeting of shareholders following closure of the bid, called by the offeror in order to amend the articles of association or to remove or appoint board members.

To that end, the offeror shall have the right to convene a general meeting of shareholders at short notice, provided that the meeting does not take place within two weeks of notification.

5. Where rights are removed on the basis of paragraphs 2, 3, or 4 and/or Article 12, equitable compensation shall be provided for any loss suffered by the holders of those rights. The terms for determining such compensation and the arrangements for its payment shall be set by Member States.

6. Paragraphs 3 and 4 shall not apply to securities where the restrictions on voting rights are compensated for by specific pecuniary advantages.

7. This Article shall not apply either where Member States hold securities in the offeree company which confer special rights on the Member States which are compatible with the Treaty, or to special rights provided for in national law which are compatible with the Treaty or to cooperatives.

Article 12

Optional arrangements

1. Member States may reserve the right not to require companies as referred to in Article 1(1) which have their registered offices within their territories to apply Article 9(2) and (3) and/or Article 11.

2. Where Member States make use of the option provided for in paragraph 1, they shall nevertheless grant companies which have their registered offices within their territories the option, which shall be reversible, of applying Article 9(2) and (3) and/or Article 11, without prejudice to Article 11(7).

The decision of the company shall be taken by the general meeting of shareholders, in accordance with the law of the Member State in which the company has its registered office in accordance with the rules applicable to amendment of the articles of association. The decision shall be communicated to the supervisory authority of the Member State in which the company has its registered office and to all the supervisory authorities of Member States in which its securities are admitted to trading on regulated markets or where such admission has been requested.

3. Member States may, under the conditions determined by national law, exempt companies which apply Article 9(2) and (3) and/or Article 11 from applying Article 9(2) and (3) and/or Article 11 if they become the subject of an offer launched by a company which does not apply the same Articles as they do, or by a company controlled, directly or indirectly, by the latter, pursuant to Article 1 of Directive 83/349/EEC.

4. Member States shall ensure that the provisions applicable to the respective companies are disclosed without delay.

5. Any measure applied in accordance with paragraph 3 shall be subject to the authorisation of the general meeting of shareholders of the offeree company, which must be granted no earlier than 18 months before the bid was made public in accordance with Article 6(1).

Article 13

Other rules applicable to the conduct of bids

Member States shall also lay down rules which govern the conduct of bids, at least as regards the following:

(a) the lapsing of bids;

(b) the revision of bids;

(c) competing bids;

(d) the disclosure of the results of bids;

(e) the irrevocability of bids and the conditions permitted.

Article 14

Information for and consultation of employees' representatives

This Directive shall be without prejudice to the rules relating to information and to consultation of representatives of and, if Member States so provide, co-determination with the employees of the offeror and the offeree company governed by the relevant national provisions, and in particular those adopted pursuant to Directives 94/45/EC, 98/59/EC, 2001/86/EC and 2002/14/EC.

Article 15

The right of squeeze-out

1. Member States shall ensure that, following a bid made to all the holders of the offeree company's securities for all of their securities, paragraphs 2 to 5 apply.

2. Member States shall ensure that an offeror is able to require all the holders of the remaining securities to sell him/her those securities at a fair price. Member States shall introduce that right in one of the following situations:

(a) where the offeror holds securities representing not less than 90% of the capital carrying voting rights and 90% of the voting rights in the offeree company,

or

(b) where, following acceptance of the bid, he/she has acquired or has firmly contracted to acquire securities representing not less than 90% of the offeree company's capital carrying voting rights and 90% of the voting rights comprised in the bid.

In the case referred to in (a), Member States may set a higher threshold that may not, however, be higher than 95% of the capital carrying voting rights and 95% of the voting rights.

3. Member States shall ensure that rules are in force that make it possible to calculate when the threshold is reached.

Where the offeree company has issued more than one class of securities, Member States may provide that the right of squeeze-out can be exercised only in the class in which the threshold laid down in paragraph 2 has been reached.

4. If the offeror wishes to exercise the right of squeeze-out he/she shall do so within three months of the end of the time allowed for acceptance of the bid referred to in Article 7.

5. Member States shall ensure that a fair price is guaranteed. That price shall take the same form

as the consideration offered in the bid or shall be in cash. Member States may provide that cash shall be offered at least as an alternative.

Following a voluntary bid, in both of the cases referred to in paragraph 2(a) and (b), the consideration offered in the bid shall be presumed to be fair where, through acceptance of the bid, the offeror has acquired securities representing not less than 90% of the capital carrying voting rights comprised in the bid.

Following a mandatory bid, the consideration offered in the bid shall be presumed to be fair.

Article 16
The right of sell-out

1. Member States shall ensure that, following a bid made to all the holders of the offeree company's securities for all of their securities, paragraphs 2 and 3 apply.

2. Member States shall ensure that a holder of remaining securities is able to require the offeror to buy his/her securities from him/her at a fair price under the same circumstances as provided for in Article 15(2).

3. Article 15(3) to (5) shall apply mutatis mutandis.

Article 17
Sanctions

Member States shall determine the sanctions to be imposed for infringement of the national measures adopted pursuant to this Directive and shall take all necessary steps to ensure that they are put into effect. The sanctions thus provided for shall be effective, proportionate and dissuasive. Member States shall notify the Commission of those measures no later than the date laid down in Article 21(1) and of any subsequent change thereto at the earliest opportunity.

Article 18
Committee procedure

1. The Commission shall be assisted by the European Securities Committee established by Decision 2001/528/EC (hereinafter referred to as 'the Committee').

2. Where reference is made to this paragraph, Articles 5 and 7 of Decision 1999/468/EC shall apply, having regard to Article 8 thereof, provided that the implementing measures adopted in accordance with this procedure do not modify the essential provisions of this Directive.

The period referred to in Article 5(6) of Decision 1999/468/EC shall be three months.

3. Without prejudice to the implementing measures already adopted, four years after the entry into force of this Directive, the application of those of its provisions that require the adoption of technical rules and decisions in accordance with paragraph 2 shall be suspended. On a proposal from the Commission, the European Parliament and the Council may renew the provisions concerned in accordance with the procedure laid down in Article 251 of the Treaty and, to that end, they shall review them before the end of the period referred to above.

Article 19
Contact committee

1. A contact committee shall be set up which has as its functions:

(a) to facilitate, without prejudice to Articles 226 and 227 of the Treaty, the harmonised application of this Directive through regular meetings dealing with practical problems arising in connection with its application;

(b) to advise the Commission, if necessary, on additions or amendments to this Directive.

2. It shall not be the function of the contact committee to appraise the merits of decisions taken by the supervisory authorities in individual cases.

Article 20
Revision

Five years after the date laid down in Article 21(1), the Commission shall examine this Directive in the light of the experience acquired in applying it and, if necessary, propose its revision. That examination shall include a survey of the control structures and barriers to takeover bids that are not covered by this Directive.

To that end, Member States shall provide the Commission annually with information on the takeover bids which have been launched against companies the securities of which are admitted to trading on their regulated markets. That information shall include the nationalities of the companies involved, the results of the offers and any other information relevant to the understanding of how takeover bids operate in practice.

Article 21

Transposition

1. Member States shall bring into force the laws, regulations and administrative provisions necessary to comply with this Directive no later than 20 May 2006. They shall forthwith inform the Commission thereof.

When Member States adopt those provisions, they shall contain a reference to this Directive or shall be accompanied by such reference on the occasion of their official publication. The methods of making such reference shall be laid down by the Member States.

2. Member States shall communicate to the Commission the text of the main provisions of national law that they adopt in the fields covered by this Directive.

Article 22

Entry into force

This Directive shall enter into force on the 20th day after that of its publication in the Official Journal of the European Union.

Article 23

Addressees

This Directive is addressed to the Member States.

S. 29.

I

(Acts whose publication is obligatory)

**European Parliament and Council Directive 2004/39/EC
of 21 April 2004
on markets in financial instruments amending Council Directives 85/611/EEC and
93/6/EEC and Directive 2000/12/EC of the European Parliament and of the Council
and repealing Council Directive 93/22/EEC[1]**

THE EUROPEAN PARLIAMENT AND THE COUNCIL OF THE EUROPEAN UNION,

Having regard to the Treaty establishing the European Community, and in particular Article 47(2) thereof,

Having regard to the proposal from the Commission,[2]

Having regard to the Opinion of the European Economic and Social Committee,[3]

Having regard to the opinion of the European Central Bank,[4]

Acting in accordance with the procedure laid down in Article 251 of the Treaty,[5]

Whereas:

(1) Council Directive 93/22/EEC of 10 May 1993 on investment services in the securities field[6] sought to establish the conditions under which authorised investment firms and banks could provide specified services or establish branches in other Member States on the basis of home country authorisation and supervision. To this end, that Directive aimed to harmonise the initial authorisation and operating requirements for investment firms including conduct of business rules. It also provided for the harmonisation of some conditions governing the operation of regulated markets.

(2) In recent years more investors have become active in the financial markets and are offered an even more complex wide-ranging set of services and instruments. In view of these developments the legal framework of the Community should encompass the full range of investor-oriented activities. To this end, it is necessary to provide for the degree of harmonisation needed to offer investors a high level of protection and to allow investment firms to provide services throughout the Community, being a Single Market, on the basis of home country supervision. In view of the preceding, Directive 93/22/EEC should be replaced by a new Directive.

(3) Due to the increasing dependence of investors on personal recommendations, it is appropriate to include the provision of investment advice as an investment service requiring authorisation.

(4) It is appropriate to include in the list of financial instruments certain commodity derivatives and others which are constituted and traded in such a manner as to give rise to regulatory

---

[1] OJ L 145, 30.4.2004, 1–44.
[2] OJ C 71 E, 25.3.2003, 62.
[3] OJ C 220, 16.9.2003, 1.
[4] OJ C 144, 20.6.2003, 6.
[5] Opinion of the European Parliament of 25 September 2003 (not yet published in the Official Journal), Council Common Position of 8 December 2003 (OJ C 60 E, 9.3.2004, 1), Position of the European Parliament of 30 March 2004 (not yet published in the Official Journal) and Decision of the Council of 7 April 2004.
[6] OJ L 141, 11.6.1993, 27, reproduced supra under no. S. 14. Directive as last amended by Directive 2002/87/EC of the European Parliament and of the Council (OJ L 35, 11.2.2003, 1), reproduced supra under no. B. 38.

issues comparable to traditional financial instruments.

(5) It is necessary to establish a comprehensive regulatory regime governing the execution of transactions in financial instruments irrespective of the trading methods used to conclude those transactions so as to ensure a high quality of execution of investor transactions and to uphold the integrity and overall efficiency of the financial system. A coherent and risk-sensitive framework for regulating the main types of order-execution arrangement currently active in the European financial marketplace should be provided for. It is necessary to recognise the emergence of a new generation of organised trading systems alongside regulated markets which should be subjected to obligations designed to preserve the efficient and orderly functioning of financial markets. With a view to establishing a proportionate regulatory framework provision should be made for the inclusion of a new investment service which relates to the operation of an MTF.

(6) Definitions of regulated market and MTF should be introduced and closely aligned with each other to reflect the fact that they represent the same organised trading functionality. The definitions should exclude bilateral systems where an investment firm enters into every trade on own account and not as a riskless counterparty interposed between the buyer and seller. The term 'system' encompasses all those markets that are composed of a set of rules and a trading platform as well as those that only function on the basis of a set of rules. Regulated markets and MTFs are not obliged to operate a 'technical' system for matching orders. A market which is only composed of a set of rules that governs aspects related to membership, admission of instruments to trading, trading between members, reporting and, where applicable, transparency obligations is a regulated market or an MTF within the meaning of this Directive and the transactions concluded under those rules are considered to be concluded under the systems of a regulated market or an MTF. The term 'buying and selling interests' is to be understood in a broad sense and includes orders, quotes and indications of interest. The requirement that the interests be brought together in the system by means of non-discretionary rules set by the system operator means that they are brought together under the system's rules or by means of the system's protocols or internal operating procedures (including procedures embodied in computer software). The term 'non-discretionary rules' means that these rules leave the investment firm operating an MTF with no discretion as to how interests may interact. The definitions require that interests be brought together in such a way as to result in a contract, meaning that execution takes place under the system's rules or by means of the system's protocols or internal operating procedures.

(7) The purpose of this Directive is to cover undertakings the regular occupation or business of which is to provide investment services and/or perform investment activities on a professional basis. Its scope should not therefore cover any person with a different professional activity.

(8) Persons administering their own assets and undertakings, who do not provide investment services and/or perform investment activities other than dealing on own account unless they are market makers or they deal on own account outside a regulated market or an MTF on an organised, frequent and systematic basis, by providing a system accessible to third parties in order to engage in dealings with them should not be covered by the scope of this Directive.

(9) References in the text to persons should be understood as including both natural and legal persons.

(10) Insurance or assurance undertakings the activities of which are subject to appropriate monitoring by the competent prudential-supervision authorities and which are subject to Council Directive 64/225/EEC of 25 February 1964 on the abolition of restrictions on freedom of establishment and freedom to provide services in respect of reinsurance and retrocession,[7] First Council Directive 73/239/EEC of 24 July 1973 on the coordination of laws, regulations and

---

[7] OJ L 56, 4.4. 1964, 878/64, reproduced supra under no. I. 1. Directive as amended by the 1972 Act of Accession.

administrative provisions relating to the taking up and pursuit of direct insurance other than life assurance[8] and Council Directive 2002/83/EC of 5 November 2002 concerning life assurance[9] should be excluded.

(11) Persons who do not provide services for third parties but whose business consists in providing investment services solely for their parent undertakings, for their subsidiaries, or for other subsidiaries of their parent undertakings should not be covered by this Directive.

(12) Persons who provide investment services only on an incidental basis in the course of professional activity should also be excluded from the scope of this Directive, provided that activity is regulated and the relevant rules do not prohibit the provision, on an incidental basis, of investment services.

(13) Persons who provide investment services consisting exclusively in the administration of employee-participation schemes and who therefore do not provide investment services for third parties should not be covered by this Directive.

(14) It is necessary to exclude from the scope of this Directive central banks and other bodies performing similar functions as well as public bodies charged with or intervening in the management of the public debt, which concept covers the investment thereof, with the exception of bodies that are partly or wholly State owned the role of which is commercial or linked to the acquisition of holdings.

(15) It is necessary to exclude from the scope of this Directive collective investment undertakings and pension funds whether or not coordinated at Community level, and the depositaries or managers of such undertakings, since they are subject to specific rules directly adapted to their activities.

(16) In order to benefit from the exemptions from this Directive the person concerned should comply on a continuous basis with the conditions laid down for such exemptions. In particular, if a person provides investment services or performs investment activities and is exempted from this Directive because such services or activities are ancillary to his main business, when considered on a group basis, he should no longer be covered by the exemption related to ancillary services where the provision of those services or activities ceases to be ancillary to his main business.

(17) Persons who provide the investment services and/or perform investment activities covered by this Directive should be subject to authorisation by their home Member States in order to protect investors and the stability of the financial system.

(18) Credit institutions that are authorised under Directive 2000/12/EC of the European Parliament and of the Council of 20 March 2000 relating to the taking up and pursuit of the business of credit institutions[10] should not need another authorisation under this Directive in order to provide investment services or perform investment activities. When a credit institution decides to provide investment services or perform investment activities the competent authorities, before granting an authorisation, should verify that it complies with the relevant provisions of this Directive.

(19) In cases where an investment firm provides one or more investment services not covered by its authorisation, or performs one or more investment activities not covered by its authorisation, on a non-regular basis it should not need an additional authorisation under this Directive.

(20) For the purposes of this Directive, the business of the reception and transmission of orders should also include bringing together two or more investors thereby bringing about a transaction between those investors.

---

[8] OJ L 228, 16.8.1973, 3, reproduced supra under no. I. 3. Directive as last amended by Directive 2002/87/EC, reproduced supra under no. B. 38.
[9] OJ L 345, 19.12.2002, 1, reproduced supra under no. I. 37.

[10] OJ L 126, 26.5.2000, 1, reproduced supra under no. B. 32. Directive as last amended by Directive 2002/87/EC, reproduced supra under no. B. 38. Directive 2000/12/EC has been repealed as from 20 July 2007 by article 58 of Directive 2006/48/EC (OJ L 177, 30.6.2006, 1), reproduced supra under no. B. 41

(21) In the context of the forthcoming revision of the Capital Adequacy framework in Basel II, Member States recognise the need to re-examine whether or not investment firms who execute client orders on a matched principal basis are to be regarded as acting as principals, and thereby be subject to additional regulatory capital requirements.

(22) The principles of mutual recognition and of home Member State supervision require that the Member States' competent authorities should not grant or should withdraw authorisation where factors such as the content of programmes of operations, the geographical distribution or the activities actually carried on indicate clearly that an investment firm has opted for the legal system of one Member State for the purpose of evading the stricter standards in force in another Member State within the territory of which it intends to carry on or does carry on the greater part of its activities. An investment firm which is a legal person should be authorised in the Member State in which it has its registered office. An investment firm which is not a legal person should be authorised in the Member State in which it has its head office. In addition, Member States should require that an investment firm's head office must always be situated in its home Member State and that it actually operates there.

(23) An investment firm authorised in its home Member State should be entitled to provide investment services or perform investment activities throughout the Community without the need to seek a separate authorisation from the competent authority in the Member State in which it wishes to provide such services or perform such activities.

(24) Since certain investment firms are exempted from certain obligations imposed by Council Directive 93/6/EEC of 15 March 1993 on the capital adequacy of investment firms and credit institutions,[11] they should be obliged to hold either a minimum amount of capital or professional indemnity insurance or a combination of both. The adjustments of the amounts of that insurance should take into account adjustments made in the framework of Directive 2002/92/EC of the European Parliament and of the Council of 9 December 2002 on insurance mediation.[12] This particular treatment for the purposes of capital adequacy should be without prejudice to any decisions regarding the appropriate treatment of these firms under future changes to Community legislation on capital adequacy.

(25) Since the scope of prudential regulation should be limited to those entities which, by virtue of running a trading book on a professional basis, represent a source of counterparty risk to other market participants, entities which deal on own account in financial instruments, including those commodity derivatives covered by this Directive, as well as those that provide investment services in commodity derivatives to the clients of their main business on an ancillary basis to their main business when considered on a group basis, provided that this main business is not the provision of investment services within the meaning of this Directive, should be excluded from the scope of this Directive.

(26) In order to protect an investor's ownership and other similar rights in respect of securities and his rights in respect of funds entrusted to a firm those rights should in particular be kept distinct from those of the firm. This principle should not, however, prevent a firm from doing business in its name but on behalf of the investor, where that is required by the very nature of the transaction and the investor is in agreement, for example stock lending.

(27) Where a client, in line with Community legislation and in particular Directive 2002/47/EC of the European Parliament and of the Council of 6 June 2002 on financial collateral arrangements,[13] transfers full ownership of financial instruments or funds to an investment firm for the purpose of securing or otherwise covering present or future, actual or contingent or prospective obligations, such financial

---

[11] OJ L 141, 11.6.1993, 1, reproduced supra under no. B. 20. Directive as last amended by Directive 2002/87/EC, reproduced supra under no. B. 38.

[12] OJ L 9, 15.1.2003, 3, reproduced supra under no. I. 38.
[13] OJ L 168, 27.6.2002, 43, reproduced supra under no. S. 23.

instruments or funds should likewise no longer be regarded as belonging to the client.

(28) The procedures for the authorisation, within the Community, of branches of investment firms authorised in third countries should continue to apply to such firms. Those branches should not enjoy the freedom to provide services under the second paragraph of Article 49 of the Treaty or the right of establishment in Member States other than those in which they are established. In view of cases where the Community is not bound by any bilateral or multilateral obligations it is appropriate to provide for a procedure intended to ensure that Community investment firms receive reciprocal treatment in the third countries concerned.

(29) The expanding range of activities that many investment firms undertake simultaneously has increased potential for conflicts of interest between those different activities and the interests of their clients. It is therefore necessary to provide for rules to ensure that such conflicts do not adversely affect the interests of their clients.

(30) A service should be considered to be provided at the initiative of a client unless the client demands it in response to a personalised communication from or on behalf of the firm to that particular client, which contains an invitation or is intended to influence the client in respect of a specific financial instrument or specific transaction. A service can be considered to be provided at the initiative of the client notwithstanding that the client demands it on the basis of any communication containing a promotion or offer of financial instruments made by any means that by its very nature is general and addressed to the public or a larger group or category of clients or potential clients.

(31) One of the objectives of this Directive is to protect investors. Measures to protect investors should be adapted to the particularities of each category of investors (retail, professional and counterparties).

(32) By way of derogation from the principle of home country authorisation, supervision and enforcement of obligations in respect of the operation of branches, it is appropriate for the competent authority of the host Member State to assume responsibility for enforcing certain obligations specified in this Directive in relation to business conducted through a branch within the territory where the branch is located, since that authority is closest to the branch, and is better placed to detect and intervene in respect of infringements of rules governing the operations of the branch.

(33) It is necessary to impose an effective 'best execution' obligation to ensure that investment firms execute client orders on terms that are most favourable to the client. This obligation should apply to the firm which owes contractual or agency obligations to the client.

(34) Fair competition requires that market participants and investors be able to compare the prices that trading venues (i.e. regulated markets, MTFs and intermediaries) are required to publish. To this end, it is recommended that Member States remove any obstacles which may prevent the consolidation at European level of the relevant information and its publication.

(35) When establishing the business relationship with the client the investment firm might ask the client or potential client to consent at the same time to the execution policy as well as to the possibility that his orders may be executed outside a regulated market or an MTF.

(36) Persons who provide investment services on behalf of more than one investment firm should not be considered as tied agents but as investment firms when they fall under the definition provided in this Directive, with the exception of certain persons who may be exempted.

(37) This Directive should be without prejudice to the right of tied agents to undertake activities covered by other Directives and related activities in respect of financial services or products not covered by this Directive, including on behalf of parts of the same financial group.

(38) The conditions for conducting activities outside the premises of the investment firm (door-to-door selling) should not be covered by this Directive.

(39) Member States' competent authorities should not register or should withdraw the registration where the activities actually carried on indicate clearly that a tied agent has opted for the legal system of one Member State for the purpose of evading the stricter standards in force in another Member State within the territory of which it intends to carry on or does carry on the greater part of its activities.

(40) For the purposes of this Directive eligible counterparties should be considered as acting as clients.

(41) For the purposes of ensuring that conduct of business rules (including rules on best execution and handling of client orders) are enforced in respect of those investors most in need of these protections, and to reflect well-established market practice throughout the Community, it is appropriate to clarify that conduct of business rules may be waived in the case of transactions entered into or brought about between eligible counterparties.

(42) In respect of transactions executed between eligible counterparties, the obligation to disclose client limit orders should only apply where the counter party is explicitly sending a limit order to an investment firm for its execution.

(43) Member States shall protect the right to privacy of natural persons with respect to the processing of personal data in accordance with Directive 95/46/EC of the European Parliament and of the Council of 24 October 1995 on the protection of individuals with regard to the processing of personal data and of the free movement of such data.[14]

(44) With the two-fold aim of protecting investors and ensuring the smooth operation of securities markets, it is necessary to ensure that transparency of transactions is achieved and that the rules laid down for that purpose apply to investment firms when they operate on the markets. In order to enable investors or market participants to assess at any time the terms of a transaction in shares that they are considering and to verify afterwards the conditions in which it was carried out, common rules should be established for the publication of details of completed transactions in shares and for the disclosure of details of current opportunities to trade in shares. These rules are needed to ensure the effective integration of Member State equity markets, to promote the efficiency of the overall price formation process for equity instruments, and to assist the effective operation of 'best execution' obligations. These considerations require a comprehensive transparency regime applicable to all transactions in shares irrespective of their execution by an investment firm on a bilateral basis or through regulated markets or MTFs. The obligations for investment firms under this Directive to quote a bid and offer price and to execute an order at the quoted price do not relieve investment firms of the obligation to route an order to another execution venue when such internalisation could prevent the firm from complying with 'best execution' obligations.

(45) Member States should be able to apply transaction reporting obligations of the Directive to financial instruments that are not admitted to trading on a regulated market.

(46) A Member State may decide to apply the pre- and post-trade transparency requirements laid down in this Directive to financial instruments other than shares. In that case those requirements should apply to all investment firms for which that Member State is the home Member State for their operations within the territory of that Member State and those carried out cross-border through the freedom to provide services. They should also apply to the operations carried out within the territory of that Member State by the branches established in its territory of investment firms authorised in another Member State.

(47) Investment firms should all have the same opportunities of joining or having access to regulated markets throughout the Community. Regardless of the manner in which transactions are at present organised in the Member States, it is important to abolish the technical and legal restrictions on access to regulated markets.

---

[14] OJ L 281, 23.11.1995, p. 31.

(48) In order to facilitate the finalisation of cross-border transactions, it is appropriate to provide for access to clearing and settlement systems throughout the Community by investment firms, irrespective of whether transactions have been concluded through regulated markets in the Member State concerned. Investment firms which wish to participate directly in other Member States' settlement systems should comply with the relevant operational and commercial requirements for membership and the prudential measures to uphold the smooth and orderly functioning of the financial markets.

(49) The authorisation to operate a regulated market should extend to all activities which are directly related to the display, processing, execution, confirmation and reporting of orders from the point at which such orders are received by the regulated market to the point at which they are transmitted for subsequent finalisation, and to activities related to the admission of financial instruments to trading. This should also include transactions concluded through the medium of designated market makers appointed by the regulated market which are undertaken under its systems and in accordance with the rules that govern those systems. Not all transactions concluded by members or participants of the regulated market or MTF are to be considered as concluded within the systems of a regulated market or MTF. Transactions which members or participants conclude on a bilateral basis and which do not comply with all the obligations established for a regulated market or an MTF under this Directive should be considered as transactions concluded outside a regulated market or an MTF for the purposes of the definition of systematic internaliser. In such a case the obligation for investment firms to make public firm quotes should apply if the conditions established by this Directive are met.

(50) Systematic internalisers might decide to give access to their quotes only to retail clients, only to professional clients, or to both. They should not be allowed to discriminate within those categories of clients.

(51) Article 27 does not oblige systematic internalisers to publish firm quotes in relation to transactions above standard market size.

(52) Where an investment firm is a systematic internaliser both in shares and in other financial instruments, the obligation to quote should only apply in respect of shares without prejudice to Recital 46.

(53) It is not the intention of this Directive to require the application of pre-trade transparency rules to transactions carried out on an OTC basis, the characteristics of which include that they are ad-hoc and irregular and are carried out with wholesale counterparties and are part of a business relationship which is itself characterised by dealings above standard market size, and where the deals are carried out outside the systems usually used by the firm concerned for its business as a systematic internaliser.

(54) The standard market size for any class of share should not be significantly disproportionate to any share included in that class.

(55) Revision of Directive 93/6/EEC should fix the minimum capital requirements with which regulated markets should comply in order to be authorised, and in so doing should take into account the specific nature of the risks associated with such markets.

(56) Operators of a regulated market should also be able to operate an MTF in accordance with the relevant provisions of this Directive.

(57) The provisions of this Directive concerning the admission of instruments to trading under the rules enforced by the regulated market should be without prejudice to the application of Directive 2001/34/EC of the European Parliament and of the Council of 28 May 2001 on the admission of securities to official stock exchange listing and on information to be published on those securities.[15] A regulated market should not be prevented from applying more demanding requirements in respect of the issuers of securities or instruments which it is considering for admission to trading than are imposed pursuant to this Directive.

---

[15] OJ L 184, 6.7.2001, 1, reproduced supra under no. S. 18. Directive as last amended by European Parliament and Council Directive 2003/71/EC (OJ L 345, 31.12.2003, 64.), reproduced supra under no. S. 25.

(58) Member States should be able to designate different competent authorities to enforce the wide-ranging obligations laid down in this Directive. Such authorities should be of a public nature guaranteeing their independence from economic actors and avoiding conflicts of interest. In accordance with national law, Member States should ensure appropriate financing of the competent authority. The designation of public authorities should not exclude delegation under the responsibility of the competent authority.

(59) Any confidential information received by the contact point of one Member State through the contact point of another Member State should not be regarded as purely domestic.

(60) It is necessary to enhance convergence of powers at the disposal of competent authorities so as to pave the way towards an equivalent intensity of enforcement across the integrated financial market. A common minimum set of powers coupled with adequate resources should guarantee supervisory effectiveness.

(61) With a view to protecting clients and without prejudice to the right of customers to bring their action before the courts, it is appropriate that Member States encourage public or private bodies established with a view to settling disputes out-of-court, to cooperate in resolving cross-border disputes, taking into account Commission Recommendation 98/257/EC of 30 March 1998 on the principles applicable to the bodies responsible for out-of-court settlement of consumer disputes.[16] When implementing provisions on complaints and redress procedures for out-of-court settlements, Member States should be encouraged to use existing cross-border cooperation mechanisms, notably the Financial Services Complaints Network (FIN-Net).

(62) Any exchange or transmission of information between competent authorities, other authorities, bodies or persons should be in accordance with the rules on transfer of personal data to third countries as laid down in Directive 95/46/EC.

(63) It is necessary to reinforce provisions on exchange of information between national competent authorities and to strengthen the duties of assistance and cooperation which they owe to each other. Due to increasing cross-border activity, competent authorities should provide each other with the relevant information for the exercise of their functions, so as to ensure the effective enforcement of this Directive, including in situations where infringements or suspected infringements may be of concern to authorities in two or more Member States. In the exchange of information, strict professional secrecy is needed to ensure the smooth transmission of that information and the protection of particular rights.

(64) At its meeting on 17 July 2000, the Council set up the Committee of Wise Men on the Regulation of European Securities Markets. In its final report, the Committee of Wise Men proposed the introduction of new legislative techniques based on a four-level approach, namely framework principles, implementing measures, cooperation and enforcement. Level 1, the Directive, should confine itself to broad general 'framework' principles while Level 2 should contain technical implementing measures to be adopted by the Commission with the assistance of a committee.

(65) The Resolution adopted by the Stockholm European Council of 23 March 2001 endorsed the final report of the Committee of Wise Men and the proposed four-level approach to make the regulatory process for Community securities legislation more efficient and transparent.

(66) According to the Stockholm European Council, Level 2 implementing measures should be used more frequently, to ensure that technical provisions can be kept up to date with market and supervisory developments, and deadlines should be set for all stages of Level 2 work.

(67) The Resolution of the European Parliament of 5 February 2002 on the implementation of financial services legislation also endorsed the Committee of Wise Men's report, on the basis of the solemn declaration made before Parliament the same day by the Commission and the letter of 2 October 2001 addressed by the Internal Market

---

[16] OJ L 115, 17.4.1998, 31.

Commissioner to the chairman of Parliament's Committee on Economic and Monetary Affairs with regard to the safeguards for the European Parliament's role in this process.

(68) The measures necessary for the implementation of this Directive should be adopted in accordance with Council Decision 1999/468/EC of 28 June 1999 laying down the procedures for the exercise of implementing powers conferred on the Commission.[17]

[(69) The European Parliament should be given a period of three months from the first transmission of draft amendments and implementing measures to allow it to examine them and to give its opinion. However, in urgent and duly justified cases, it should be possible to shorten that period. If, within that period, a resolution is adopted by the European Parliament, the Commission should re-examine the draft amendments or measures.]

(70) With a view to taking into account further developments in the financial markets the Commission should submit reports to the European Parliament and the Council on the application of the provisions concerning professional indemnity insurance, the scope of the transparency rules and the possible authorisation of specialised dealers in commodity derivatives as investment firms.

(71) The objective of creating an integrated financial market, in which investors are effectively protected and the efficiency and integrity of the overall market are safeguarded, requires the establishment of common regulatory requirements relating to investment firms wherever they are authorised in the Community and governing the functioning of regulated markets and other trading systems so as to prevent opacity or disruption on one market from undermining the efficient operation of the European financial system as a whole. Since this objective may be better achieved at Community level, the Community may adopt measures in accordance with the principle of subsidiarity as set out in Article 5 of the Treaty. In accordance with the principle of proportionality, as set out in that Article, this Directive does not go beyond what is necessary in order to achieve this objective,

¶ *Recital 69 has been replaced by article 1(1) of Directive 2006/31/EC, reproduced infra under no. S. 32.*

HAVE ADOPTED THIS DIRECTIVE:

TITLE I

DEFINITIONS AND SCOPE

Article 1

Scope

1. This Directive shall apply to investment firms and regulated markets.

2. The following provisions shall also apply to credit institutions authorised under Directive 2000/12/EC, when providing one or more investment services and/or performing investment activities:

– Articles 2(2), 11, 13 and 14,
– Chapter II of Title II excluding Article 23(2) second subparagraph,
– Chapter III of Title II excluding Articles 31(2) to 31(4) and 32(2) to 32(6), 32(8) and 32(9),
– Articles 48 to 53, 57, 61 and 62, and
– Article 71(1).

Article 2

Exemptions

1. This Directive shall not apply to:

(a) insurance undertakings as defined in Article 1 of Directive 73/239/EEC or assurance undertakings as defined in Article 1 of Directive 2002/83/EC or undertakings carrying on the reinsurance and retrocession activities referred to in Directive 64/225/EEC;

(b) persons which provide investment services exclusively for their parent undertakings, for their subsidiaries or for other subsidiaries of their parent undertakings;

(c) persons providing an investment service where that service is provided in an incidental manner in the course of a professional activity

---

[17] OJ L 184, 17.7.1999, 23.

and that activity is regulated by legal or regulatory provisions or a code of ethics governing the profession which do not exclude the provision of that service;

(d) persons who do not provide any investment services or activities other than dealing on own account unless they are market makers or deal on own account outside a regulated market or an MTF on an organised, frequent and systematic basis by providing a system accessible to third parties in order to engage in dealings with them;

(e) persons which provide investment services consisting exclusively in the administration of employee-participation schemes;

(f) persons which provide investment services which only involve both administration of employee-participation schemes and the provision of investment services exclusively for their parent undertakings, for their subsidiaries or for other subsidiaries of their parent undertakings;

(g) the members of the European System of Central Banks and other national bodies performing similar functions and other public bodies charged with or intervening in the management of the public debt;

(h) collective investment undertakings and pension funds whether coordinated at Community level or not and the depositaries and managers of such undertakings;

(i) persons dealing on own account in financial instruments, or providing investment services in commodity derivatives or derivative contracts included in Annex I, Section C 10 to the clients of their main business, provided this is an ancillary activity to their main business, when considered on a group basis, and that main business is not the provision of investment services within the meaning of this Directive or banking services under Directive 2000/12/EC;

(j) persons providing investment advice in the course of providing another professional activity not covered by this Directive provided that the provision of such advice is not specifically remunerated;

(k) persons whose main business consists of dealing on own account in commodities and/or commodity derivatives. This exception shall not apply where the persons that deal on own account in commodities and/or commodity derivatives are part of a group the main business of which is the provision of other investment services within the meaning of this Directive or banking services under Directive 2000/12/EC;

(l) firms which provide investment services and/or perform investment activities consisting exclusively in dealing on own account on markets in financial futures or options or other derivatives and on cash markets for the sole purpose of hedging positions on derivatives markets or which deal for the accounts of other members of those markets or make prices for them and which are guaranteed by clearing members of the same markets, where responsibility for ensuring the performance of contracts entered into by such firms is assumed by clearing members of the same markets;

(m) associations set up by Danish and Finnish pension funds with the sole aim of managing the assets of pension funds that are members of those associations;

(n) 'agenti di cambio' whose activities and functions are governed by Article 201 of Italian Legislative Decree No 58 of 24 February 1998.

2. The rights conferred by this Directive shall not extend to the provision of services as counterparty in transactions carried out by public bodies dealing with public debt or by members of the European System of Central Banks performing their tasks as provided for by the Treaty and the Statute of the European System of Central Banks and of the European Central Bank or performing equivalent functions under national provisions.

3. In order to take account of developments on financial markets, and to ensure the uniform application of this Directive, the Commission, acting in accordance with the procedure referred to in Article 64(2), may, in respect of exemptions (c) (i), and (k) define the criteria for determining when an activity is to be considered as ancillary to the main business on a group level as well as for determining when an activity is provided in an incidental manner.

Article 3
Optional exemptions

1. Member States may choose not to apply this Directive to any persons for which they are the home Member State that:
– are not allowed to hold clients' funds or securities and which for that reason are not allowed at any time to place themselves in debit with their clients, and
– are not allowed to provide any investment service except the reception and transmission of orders in transferable securities and units in collective investment undertakings and the provision of investment advice in relation to such financial instruments, and
– in the course of providing that service, are allowed to transmit orders only to:
(i) investment firms authorised in accordance with this Directive;
(ii) credit institutions authorised in accordance with Directive 2000/12/EC;
(iii) branches of investment firms or of credit institutions which are authorised in a third country and which are subject to and comply with prudential rules considered by the competent authorities to be at least as stringent as those laid down in this Directive, in Directive 2000/12/EC or in Directive 93/6/EEC;
(iv) collective investment undertakings authorised under the law of a Member State to market units to the public and to the managers of such undertakings;
(v) investment companies with fixed capital, as defined in Article 15(4) of Second Council Directive 77/91/EEC of 13 December 1976 on coordination of safeguard which, for the protection of the interests of members and others, are required by Member States of companies within the meaning of the second paragraph of Article 58 of the Treaty, in respect of the formation of public limited liability companies and the maintenance and alteration of their capital, with a view to making such safeguards equivalent,[18] the securities of which are listed or dealt in on a regulated market in a Member State;

provided that the activities of those persons are regulated at national level.

2. Persons excluded from the scope of this Directive according to paragraph 1 cannot benefit from the freedom to provide services and/or activities or to establish branches as provided for in Articles 31 and 32 respectively.

Article 4
Definitions

1. For the purposes of this Directive, the following definitions shall apply:

1) 'Investment firm' means any legal person whose regular occupation or business is the provision of one or more investment services to third parties and/or the performance of one or more investment activities on a professional basis;

Member States may include in the definition of investment firms undertakings which are not legal persons, provided that:

(a) their legal status ensures a level of protection for third parties' interests equivalent to that afforded by legal persons, and

(b) they are subject to equivalent prudential supervision appropriate to their legal form.

However, where a natural person provides services involving the holding of third parties' funds or transferable securities, he may be considered as an investment firm for the purposes of this Directive only if, without prejudice to the other requirements imposed in this Directive and in Directive 93/6/EEC, he complies with the following conditions:

(a) the ownership rights of third parties in instruments and funds must be safeguarded, especially in the event of the insolvency of the firm or of its proprietors, seizure, set-off or any other action by creditors of the firm or of its proprietors;

(b) the firm must be subject to rules designed to monitor the firm's solvency and that of its proprietors;

(c) the firm's annual accounts must be audited by one or more persons empowered, under national law, to audit accounts;

---

[18] OJ L 26, 31.1.1977, 1. Directive as last amended by the 1994 Act of Accession.

(d) where the firm has only one proprietor, he must make provision for the protection of investors in the event of the firm's cessation of business following his death, his incapacity or any other such event;

2) 'Investment services and activities' means any of the services and activities listed in Section A of Annex I relating to any of the instruments listed in Section C of Annex I;

The Commission shall determine, acting in accordance with the procedure referred to in Article 64(2):
– the derivative contracts mentioned in Section C 7 of Annex I that have the characteristics of other derivative financial instruments, having regard to whether, inter alia, they are cleared and settled through recognised clearing houses or are subject to regular margin calls
– the derivative contracts mentioned in Section C 10 of Annex I that have the characteristics of other derivative financial instruments, having regard to whether, inter alia, they are traded on a regulated market or an MTF, are cleared and settled through recognised clearing houses or are subject to regular margin calls;

¶ *See articles 38 and 39 of Commission Regulation 1287/2006/EC, reproduced infra under no. S. 33.*

3) 'Ancillary service' means any of the services listed in Section B of Annex I;

4) 'Investment advice' means the provision of personal recommendations to a client, either upon its request or at the initiative of the investment firm, in respect of one or more transactions relating to financial instruments;

¶ *See article 52 of Commission Directive 2006/73/EC, reproduced infra under no. S. 34.*

5) 'Execution of orders on behalf of clients' means acting to conclude agreements to buy or sell one or more financial instruments on behalf of clients;

6) 'Dealing on own account' means trading against proprietary capital resulting in the conclusion of transactions in one or more financial instruments;

7) 'Systematic internaliser' means an investment firm which, on an organised, frequent and systematic basis, deals on own account by executing client orders outside a regulated market or an MTF;

¶ *See article 21 of Commission Regulation 1287/2006/EC, reproduced infra under no. S. 33.*

8) 'Market maker' means a person who holds himself out on the financial markets on a continuous basis as being willing to deal on own account by buying and selling financial instruments against his proprietary capital at prices defined by him;

9) 'Portfolio management' means managing portfolios in accordance with mandates given by clients on a discretionary client-by-client basis where such portfolios include one or more financial instruments;

10) 'Client' means any natural or legal person to whom an investment firm provides investment and/or ancillary services;

11) 'Professional client' means a client meeting the criteria laid down in Annex II;

12) 'Retail client' means a client who is not a professional client;

13) 'Market operator' means a person or persons who manages and/or operates the business of a regulated market. The market operator may be the regulated market itself;

14) 'Regulated market' means a multilateral system operated and/or managed by a market operator, which brings together or facilitates the bringing together of multiple third-party buying and selling interests in financial instruments—in the system and in accordance with its nondiscretionary rules—in a way that results in a contract, in respect of the financial instruments admitted to trading under its rules and/or systems, and which is authorised and functions regularly and in accordance with the provisions of Title III;

15) 'Multilateral trading facility (MTF)' means a multilateral system, operated by an investment firm or a market operator, which brings together multiple third-party buying and selling interests in financial instruments—in the system and in accordance with non-discretionary rules—in a way that results in a contract in accordance with the provisions of Title II;

16) 'Limit order' means an order to buy or sell a financial instrument at its specified price limit or better and for a specified size;

17) 'Financial instrument' means those instruments specified in Section C of Annex I;

18) 'Transferable securities' means those classes of securities which are negotiable on the capital market, with the exception of instruments of payment, such as:

(a) shares in companies and other securities equivalent to shares in companies, partnerships or other entities, and depositary receipts in respect of shares;

(b) bonds or other forms of securitised debt, including depositary receipts in respect of such securities;

(c) any other securities giving the right to acquire or sell any such transferable securities or giving rise to a cash settlement determined by reference to transferable securities, currencies, interest rates or yields, commodities or other indices or measures;

19) 'Money-market instruments' means those classes of instruments which are normally dealt in on the money market, such as treasury bills, certificates of deposit and commercial papers and excluding instruments of payment;

20) 'Home Member State' means:

(a) in the case of investment firms:
(i) if the investment firm is a natural person, the Member State in which its head office is situated;
(ii) if the investment firm is a legal person, the Member State in which its registered office is situated;
(iii) if the investment firm has, under its national law, no registered office, the Member State in which its head office is situated;

(b) in the case of a regulated market, the Member State in which the regulated market is registered or, if under the law of that Member State it has no registered office, the Member State in which the head office of the regulated market is situated;

21) 'Host Member State' means the Member State, other than the home Member State, in which an investment firm has a branch or performs services and/or activities or the Member State in which a regulated market provides appropriate arrangements so as to facilitate access to trading on its system by remote members or participants established in that same Member State;

22) 'Competent authority' means the authority, designated by each Member State in accordance with Article 48, unless otherwise specified in this Directive;

23) 'Credit institutions' means credit institutions as defined under Directive 2000/12/EC;

24) 'UCITS management company' means a management company as defined in Council Directive 85/611/EEC of 20 December 1985, on the coordination of laws, regulations and administrative provisions relating to undertakings for collective investment in transferable securities (UCITS);[19]

25) 'Tied agent' means a natural or legal person who, under the full and unconditional responsibility of only one investment firm on whose behalf it acts, promotes investment and/or ancillary services to clients or prospective clients, receives and transmits instructions or orders from the client in respect of investment services or financial instruments, places financial instruments and/or provides advice to clients or prospective clients in respect of those financial instruments or services;

26) 'Branch' means a place of business other than the head office which is a part of an investment firm, which has no legal personality and which provides investment services and/or activities and which may also perform ancillary services for which the investment firm has been authorised; all the places of business set up in the same Member State by an investment firm with headquarters in another Member State shall be regarded as a single branch;

27) 'Qualifying holding' means any direct or indirect holding in an investment firm which represents 10% or more of the capital or of the voting rights, as set out in Article 92 of Directive 2001/34/EC, or which makes it possible to

---

[19] OJ L 375, 31.12.1985, 3, reproduced supra under no. S. 6. Directive as last amended by Directive 2001/108/EC of the European Parliament and of the Council (OJ L 41, 13.2.2002, 35), reproduced supra under no. S. 22.

exercise a significant influence over the management of the investment firm in which that holding subsists;

28) 'Parent undertaking' means a parent undertaking as defined in Articles 1 and 2 of Seventh Council Directive 83/349/EEC of 13 June 1983 on consolidated accounts;[20]

29) 'Subsidiary' means a subsidiary undertaking as defined in Articles 1 and 2 of Directive 83/349/EEC, including any subsidiary of a subsidiary undertaking of an ultimate parent undertaking;

30) 'Control' means control as defined in Article 1 of Directive 83/349/EEC;

31) 'Close links' means a situation in which two or more natural or legal persons are linked by:

(a) participation which means the ownership, direct or by way of control, of 20% or more of the voting rights or capital of an undertaking,

(b) control which means the relationship between a parent undertaking and a subsidiary, in all the cases referred to in Article 1(1) and (2) of Directive 83/349/EEC, or a similar relationship between any natural or legal person and an undertaking, any subsidiary undertaking of a subsidiary undertaking also being considered a subsidiary of the parent undertaking which is at the head of those undertakings.

A situation in which two or more natural or legal persons are permanently linked to one and the same person by a control relationship shall also be regarded as constituting a close link between such persons.

2. In order to take account of developments on financial markets, and to ensure the uniform application of this Directive, the Commission, acting in accordance with the procedure referred to in Article 64(2), may clarify the definitions laid down in paragraph 1 of this Article.

TITLE II
AUTHORISATION AND OPERATING CONDITIONS FOR INVESTMENT FIRMS

CHAPTER I
CONDITIONS AND PROCEDURES FOR AUTHORISATION

Article 5
Requirement for authorisation

1. Each Member State shall require that the performance of investment services or activities as a regular occupation or business on a professional basis be subject to prior authorisation in accordance with the provisions of this Chapter. Such authorisation shall be granted by the home Member State competent authority designated in accordance with Article 48.

2. By way of derogation from paragraph 1, Member States shall allow any market operator to operate an MTF, subject to the prior verification of their compliance with the provisions of this Chapter, excluding Articles 11 and 15.

3. Member States shall establish a register of all investment firms. This register shall be publicly accessible and shall contain information on the services and/or activities for which the investment firm is authorised. It shall be updated on a regular basis.

4. Each Member State shall require that:
– any investment firm which is a legal person have its head office in the same Member State as its registered office,
– any investment firm which is not a legal person or any investment firm which is a legal person but under its national law has no registered office have its head office in the Member State in which it actually carries on its business.

5. In the case of investment firms which provide only investment advice or the service of reception and transmission of orders under the conditions established in Article 3, Member States may allow the competent authority to delegate administrative,

---

[20] OJ L 193, 18.7.1983, 1, reproduced supra under no. C. 6. Directive as last amended by Directive 2003/51/EC of the European Parliament and of the Council (OJ L 178, 17.7.2003, 16), reproduced supra under no. C. 23.

Article 6
Scope of authorisation

1. The home Member State shall ensure that the authorisation specifies the investment services or activities which the investment firm is authorised to provide. The authorisation may cover one or more of the ancillary services set out in Section B of Annex I. Authorisation shall in no case be granted solely for the provision of ancillary services.

2. An investment firm seeking authorisation to extend its business to additional investment services or activities or ancillary services not foreseen at the time of initial authorisation shall submit a request for extension of its authorisation.

3. The authorisation shall be valid for the entire Community and shall allow an investment firm to provide the services or perform the activities, for which it has been authorised, throughout the Community, either through the establishment of a branch or the free provision of services.

Article 7
Procedures for granting and refusing requests for authorisation

1. The competent authority shall not grant authorisation unless and until such time as it is fully satisfied that the applicant complies with all requirements under the provisions adopted pursuant to this Directive.

2. The investment firm shall provide all information, including a programme of operations setting out inter alia the types of business envisaged and the organisational structure, necessary to enable the competent authority to satisfy itself that the investment firm has established, at the time of initial authorisation, all the necessary arrangements to meet its obligations under the provisions of this Chapter.

3. An applicant shall be informed, within six months of the submission of a complete application, whether or not authorisation has been granted.

Article 8
Withdrawal of authorisations

The competent authority may withdraw the authorisation issued to an investment firm where such an investment firm:

(a) does not make use of the authorisation within 12 months, expressly renounces the authorisation or has provided no investment services or performed no investment activity for the preceding six months, unless the Member State concerned has provided for authorisation to lapse in such cases;

(b) has obtained the authorisation by making false statements or by any other irregular means;

(c) no longer meets the conditions under which authorisation was granted, such as compliance with the conditions set out in Directive 93/6/EEC;

(d) has seriously and systematically infringed the provisions adopted pursuant to this Directive governing the operating conditions for investment firms;

(e) falls within any of the cases where national law, in respect of matters outside the scope of this Directive, provides for withdrawal.

Article 9
Persons who effectively direct the business

1. Member States shall require the persons who effectively direct the business of an investment firm to be of sufficiently good repute and sufficiently experienced as to ensure the sound and prudent management of the investment firm.

Where the market operator that seeks authorisation to operate an MTF and the persons that effectively direct the business of the MTF are the same as those that effectively direct the business of the regulated market, those persons are deemed to comply with the requirements laid down in the first subparagraph.

2. Member States shall require the investment firm to notify the competent authority of any

---

preparatory or ancillary tasks related to the granting of an authorisation, in accordance with the conditions laid down in Article 48(2).

changes to its management, along with all information needed to assess whether the new staff appointed to manage the firm are of sufficiently good repute and sufficiently experienced.

3. The competent authority shall refuse authorisation if it is not satisfied that the persons who will effectively direct the business of the investment firm are of sufficiently good repute or sufficiently experienced, or if there are objective and demonstrable grounds for believing that proposed changes to the management of the firm pose a threat to its sound and prudent management.

4. Member States shall require that the management of investment firms is undertaken by at least two persons meeting the requirements laid down in paragraph 1.

By way of derogation from the first subparagraph, Member States may grant authorisation to investment firms that are natural persons or to investment firms that are legal persons managed by a single natural person in accordance with their constitutive rules and national laws. Member States shall nevertheless require that alternative arrangements be in place which ensure the sound and prudent management of such investment firms.

Article 10

Shareholders and members with qualifying holdings

1. The competent authorities shall not authorise the performance of investment services or activities by an investment firm until they have been informed of the identities of the shareholders or members, whether direct or indirect, natural or legal persons, that have qualifying holdings and the amounts of those holdings.

The competent authorities shall refuse authorisation if, taking into account the need to ensure the sound and prudent management of an investment firm, they are not satisfied as to the suitability of the shareholders or members that have qualifying holdings.

Where close links exist between the investment firm and other natural or legal persons, the competent authority shall grant authorisation only if those links do not prevent the effective exercise of the supervisory functions of the competent authority.

2. The competent authority shall refuse authorisation if the laws, regulations or administrative provisions of a third country governing one or more natural or legal persons with which the undertaking has close links, or difficulties involved in their enforcement, prevent the effective exercise of its supervisory functions.

3. Member States shall require any natural or legal person that proposes to acquire or sell, directly or indirectly, a qualifying holding in an investment firm, first to notify, in accordance with the second subparagraph, the competent authority of the size of the resulting holding. Such persons shall likewise be required to notify the competent authority if they propose to increase or reduce their qualifying holding, if in consequence the proportion of the voting rights or of the capital that they hold would reach or fall below or exceed 20%, 33% or 50% or the investment firm would become or cease to be their subsidiary.

Without prejudice to paragraph 4, the competent authority shall have up to three months from the date of the notification of a proposed acquisition provided for in the first subparagraph to oppose such a plan if, in view of the need to ensure sound and prudent management of the investment firm, it is not satisfied as to the suitability of the persons referred to in the first subparagraph. If the competent authority does not oppose the plan, it may fix a deadline for its implementation.

4. If the acquirer of any holding referred to in paragraph 3 is an investment firm, a credit institution, an insurance undertaking or a UCITS management company authorised in another Member State, or the parent undertaking of an investment firm, credit institution, insurance undertaking or a UCITS management company authorised in another Member State, or a person controlling an investment firm, credit institution, insurance undertaking or a UCITS management company authorised in another Member State,

and if, as a result of that acquisition, the undertaking would become the acquirer's subsidiary or come under his control, the assessment of the acquisition shall be subject to the prior consultation provided for in Article 60.

5. Member States shall require that, if an investment firm becomes aware of any acquisitions or disposals of holdings in its capital that cause holdings to exceed or fall below any of the thresholds referred to in the first subparagraph of paragraph 3, that investment firm is to inform the competent authority without delay.

At least once a year, investment firms shall also inform the competent authority of the names of shareholders and members possessing qualifying holdings and the sizes of such holdings as shown, for example, by the information received at annual general meetings of shareholders and members or as a result of compliance with the regulations applicable to companies whose transferable securities are admitted to trading on a regulated market.

6. Member States shall require that, where the influence exercised by the persons referred to in the first subparagraph of paragraph 1 is likely to be prejudicial to the sound and prudent management of an investment firm, the competent authority take appropriate measures to put an end to that situation.

Such measures may consist in applications for judicial orders and/or the imposition of sanctions against directors and those responsible for management, or suspension of the exercise of the voting rights attaching to the shares held by the shareholders or members in question.

Similar measures shall be taken in respect of persons who fail to comply with the obligation to provide prior information in relation to the acquisition or increase of a qualifying holding. If a holding is acquired despite the opposition of the competent authorities, the Member States shall, regardless of any other sanctions to be adopted, provide either for exercise of the corresponding voting rights to be suspended, for the nullity of the votes cast or for the possibility of their annulment.

Article 11

Membership of an authorised Investor Compensation Scheme

The competent authority shall verify that any entity seeking authorisation as an investment firm meets its obligations under Directive 97/9/EC of the European Parliament and of the Council of 3 March 1997 on investor-compensation schemes[21] at the time of authorisation.

Article 12

Initial capital endowment

Member States shall ensure that the competent authorities do not grant authorisation unless the investment firm has sufficient initial capital in accordance with the requirements of Directive 93/6/EEC having regard to the nature of the investment service or activity in question.

Pending the revision of Directive 93/6/EEC, the investment firms provided for in Article 67 shall be subject to the capital requirements laid down in that Article.

Article 13

Organisational requirements

1. The home Member State shall require that investment firms comply with the organisational requirements set out in paragraphs 2 to 8.

2. An investment firm shall establish adequate policies and procedures sufficient to ensure compliance of the firm including its managers, employees and tied agents with its obligations under the provisions of this Directive as well as appropriate rules governing personal transactions by such persons.

¶ *See articles 6, 9, 10, 11, 12, 13, 14, and 15 of Commission Directive 2006/73/EC, reproduced infra under no. S. 34.*

3. An investment firm shall maintain and operate effective organisational and administrative arrangements with a view to taking all reasonable steps designed to prevent conflicts of interest as

---

[21] OJ L 84, 26.3.1997, 22, reproduced supra under no. S. 16.

defined in Article 18 from adversely affecting the interests of its clients.

¶ *See articles 21, 22, and 25 of Commission Directive 2006/73/EC, reproduced infra under no. S. 34.*

4. An investment firm shall take reasonable steps to ensure continuity and regularity in the performance of investment services and activities. To this end the investment firm shall employ appropriate and proportionate systems, resources and procedures.

5. An investment firm shall ensure, when relying on a third party for the performance of operational functions which are critical for the provision of continuous and satisfactory service to clients and the performance of investment activities on a continuous and satisfactory basis, that it takes reasonable steps to avoid undue additional operational risk. Outsourcing of important operational functions may not be undertaken in such a way as to impair materially the quality of its internal control and the ability of the supervisor to monitor the firm's compliance with all obligations.

¶ *See articles 13, 14, and 15 of Commission Directive 2006/73/EC, reproduced infra under no. S. 34.*

An investment firm shall have sound administrative and accounting procedures, internal control mechanisms, effective procedures for risk assessment, and effective control and safeguard arrangements for information processing systems.

¶ *See articles 7 and 8 of Commission Directive 2006/73/EC, reproduced infra under no. S. 34.*

6. An investment firm shall arrange for records to be kept of all services and transactions undertaken by it which shall be sufficient to enable the competent authority to monitor compliance with the requirements under this Directive, and in particular to ascertain that the investment firm has complied with all obligations with respect to clients or potential clients.

¶ *See articles 7, 8, and 23 of Commission Regulation 1287/2006/EC, reproduced infra under no. S. 33.*
¶ *See article 51 of Commission Directive 2006/73/EC, reproduced infra under no. S. 34.*

7. An investment firm shall, when holding financial instruments belonging to clients, make adequate arrangements so as to safeguard clients' ownership rights, especially in the event of the investment firm's insolvency, and to prevent the use of a client's instruments on own account except with the client's express consent.

¶ *See articles 16, 17, 19, and 20 of Commission Directive 2006/73/EC, reproduced infra under no. S. 34.*

8. An investment firm shall, when holding funds belonging to clients, make adequate arrangements to safeguard the clients' rights and, except in the case of credit institutions, prevent the use of client funds for its own account.

¶ *See articles 16, 18, and 20 of Commission Directive 2006/73/EC, reproduced infra under no. S. 34.*

9. In the case of branches of investment firms, the competent authority of the Member State in which the branch is located shall, without prejudice to the possibility of the competent authority of the home Member State of the investment firm to have direct access to those records, enforce the obligation laid down in paragraph 6 with regard to transactions undertaken by the branch.

10. In order to take account of technical developments on financial markets and to ensure the uniform application of paragraphs 2 to 9, the Commission shall adopt, in accordance with the procedure referred to in Article 64(2), implementing measures which specify the concrete organisational requirements to be imposed on investment firms performing different investment services and/or activities and ancillary services or combinations thereof.

¶ *See article 5 of Commission Directive 2006/73/EC, reproduced infra under no. S. 34.*

Article 14

Trading process and finalisation of transactions in an MTF

1. Member States shall require that investment firms or market operators operating an MTF, in addition to meeting the requirements laid down in Article 13, establish transparent and non-discretionary rules and procedures for fair and orderly trading and establish objective criteria for the efficient execution of orders.

2. Member States shall require that investment firms or market operators operating an MTF establish transparent rules regarding the criteria for determining the financial instruments that can be traded under its systems.

Member States shall require that, where applicable, investment firms or market operators operating an MTF provide, or are satisfied that there is access to, sufficient publicly available information to enable its users to form an investment judgement, taking into account both the nature of the users and the types of instruments traded.

3. Member States shall ensure that Articles 19, 21 and 22 are not applicable to the transactions concluded under the rules governing an MTF between its members or participants or between the MTF and its members or participants in relation to the use of the MTF. However, the members of or participants in the MTF shall comply with the obligations provided for in Articles 19, 21 and 22 with respect to their clients when, acting on behalf of their clients, they execute their orders through the systems of an MTF.

4. Member States shall require that investment firms or market operators operating an MTF establish and maintain transparent rules, based on objective criteria, governing access to its facility. These rules shall comply with the conditions established in Article 42(3).

5. Member States shall require that investment firms or market operators operating an MTF clearly inform its users of their respective responsibilities for the settlement of the transactions executed in that facility. Member States shall require that investment firms or market operators operating an MTF have put in place the necessary arrangements to facilitate the efficient settlement of the transactions concluded under the systems of the MTF.

6. Where a transferable security, which has been admitted to trading on a regulated market, is also traded on an MTF without the consent of the issuer, the issuer shall not be subject to any obligation relating to initial, ongoing or ad hoc financial disclosure with regard to that MTF.

7. Member States shall require that any investment firm or market operator operating an MTF comply immediately with any instruction from its competent authority pursuant to Article 50(1) to suspend or remove a financial instrument from trading.

Article 15
Relations with third countries

1. Member States shall inform the Commission of any general difficulties which their investment firms encounter in establishing themselves or providing investment services and/or performing investment activities in any third country.

2. Whenever it appears to the Commission, on the basis of information submitted to it under paragraph 1, that a third country does not grant Community investment firms effective market access comparable to that granted by the Community to investment firms from that third country, the Commission may submit proposals to the Council for an appropriate mandate for negotiation with a view to obtaining comparable competitive opportunities for Community investment firms. The Council shall act by a qualified majority.

3. Whenever it appears to the Commission, on the basis of information submitted to it under paragraph 1, that Community investment firms in a third country are not granted national treatment affording the same competitive opportunities as are available to domestic investment firms and that the conditions of effective market access are not fulfilled, the Commission may initiate negotiations in order to remedy the situation.

In the circumstances referred to in the first subparagraph, the Commission may decide, in accordance with the procedure referred to in Article 64(2), at any time and in addition to the initiation of negotiations, that the competent authorities of the Member States must limit or suspend their decisions regarding requests pending or future requests for authorisation and the acquisition of holdings by direct or indirect parent undertakings governed by the law of the third country in question. Such limitations or suspensions may not be applied to the setting-up of subsidiaries by investment firms duly authorised in the Community or by their subsidiaries, or to the acquisition of holdings in Community investment firms by such firms or subsidiaries. The duration of such measures may not exceed three months.

Before the end of the three-month period referred to in the second subparagraph and in the light of the results of the negotiations, the Commission may decide, in accordance with the procedure referred to in Article 64(2), to extend these measures.

4. Whenever it appears to the Commission that one of the situations referred to in paragraphs 2 and 3 obtains, the Member States shall inform it at its request:

(a) of any application for the authorisation of any firm which is the direct or indirect subsidiary of a parent undertaking governed by the law of the third country in question;

(b) whenever they are informed in accordance with Article 10(3) that such a parent undertaking proposes to acquire a holding in a Community investment firm, in consequence of which the latter would become its subsidiary.

That obligation to provide information shall lapse whenever agreement is reached with the third country concerned or when the measures referred to in the second and third subparagraphs of paragraph 3 cease to apply.

5. Measures taken under this Article shall comply with the Community's obligations under any international agreements, bilateral or multilateral, governing the taking-up or pursuit of the business of investment firms.

Chapter II
Operating Conditions for Investment Firms

Section 1
General Provisions

Article 16
Regular review of conditions for initial authorisation

1. Member States shall require that an investment firm authorised in their territory comply at all times with the conditions for initial authorisation established in Chapter I of this Title.

2. Member States shall require competent authorities to establish the appropriate methods to monitor that investment firms comply with their obligation under paragraph 1. They shall require investment firms to notify the competent authorities of any material changes to the conditions for initial authorisation.

3. In the case of investment firms which provide only investment advice, Member States may allow the competent authority to delegate administrative, preparatory or ancillary tasks related to the review of the conditions for initial authorisation, in accordance with the conditions laid down in Article 48(2).

Article 17
General obligation in respect of on-going supervision

1. Member States shall ensure that the competent authorities monitor the activities of investment firms so as to assess compliance with the operating conditions provided for in this Directive. Member States shall ensure that the appropriate measures are in place to enable the competent authorities to obtain the information needed to assess the compliance of investment firms with those obligations.

2. In the case of investment firms which provide only investment advice, Member States may allow the competent authority to delegate administrative, preparatory or ancillary tasks related to the regular monitoring of operational requirements, in accordance with the conditions laid down in Article 48(2).

Article 18
Conflicts of interest

1. Member States shall require investment firms to take all reasonable steps to identify conflicts of interest between themselves, including their managers, employees and tied agents, or any person directly or indirectly linked to them by control and their clients or between one client and another that arise in the course of providing

any investment and ancillary services, or combinations thereof.

¶ *See article 22 of Commission Directive 2006/73/EC, reproduced infra under no. S. 34.*

2. Where organisational or administrative arrangements made by the investment firm in accordance with Article 13(3) to manage conflicts of interest are not sufficient to ensure, with reasonable confidence, that risks of damage to client interests will be prevented, the investment firm shall clearly disclose the general nature and/or sources of conflicts of interest to the client before undertaking business on its behalf.

3. In order to take account of technical developments on financial markets and to ensure uniform application of paragraphs 1 and 2, the Commission shall adopt, in accordance with the procedure referred to in Article 64(2), implementing measures to:

(a) define the steps that investment firms might reasonably be expected to take to identify, prevent, manage and/or disclose conflicts of interest when providing various investment and ancillary services and combinations thereof;

(b) establish appropriate criteria for determining the types of conflict of interest whose existence may damage the interests of the clients or potential clients of the investment firm.

¶ *See article 21 of Commission Directive 2006/73/EC, reproduced infra under no. S. 34.*

Section 2
Provisions to Ensure Investor Protection

Article 19
Conduct of business obligations when providing investment services to clients

1. Member States shall require that, when providing investment services and/or, where appropriate, ancillary services to clients, an investment firm act honestly, fairly and professionally in accordance with the best interests of its clients and comply, in particular, with the principles set out in paragraphs 2 to 8.

¶ *See articles 26, 39, 44, 45, 47, 48, and 49 of Commission Directive 2006/73/EC, reproduced infra under no. S. 34.*

2. All information, including marketing communications, addressed by the investment firm to clients or potential clients shall be fair, clear and not misleading. Marketing communications shall be clearly identifiable as such.

¶ *See articles 24 and 27 of Commission Directive 2006/73/EC, reproduced infra under no. S. 34.*

3. Appropriate information shall be provided in a comprehensible form to clients or potential clients about:
– the investment firm and its services,

¶ *See articles 30 and 32 of Commission Directive 2006/73/EC, reproduced infra under no. S. 34.*

– financial instruments and proposed investment strategies; this should include appropriate guidance on and warnings of the risks associated with investments in those instruments or in respect of particular investment strategies,

¶ *See articles 31 and 34 of Commission Directive 2006/73/EC, reproduced infra under no. S. 34.*

– execution venues, and
– costs and associated charges

¶ *See articles 33 and 34 of Commission Directive 2006/73/EC, reproduced infra under no. S. 34.*

so that they are reasonably able to understand the nature and risks of the investment service and of the specific type of financial instrument that is being offered and, consequently, to take investment decisions on an informed basis. This information may be provided in a standardised format.

¶ *See articles 28 and 29 of Commission Directive 2006/73/EC, reproduced infra under no. S. 34.*

4. When providing investment advice or portfolio management the investment firm shall obtain the necessary information regarding the client's or potential client's knowledge and experience in the investment field relevant to the specific type of product or service, his financial situation and his investment objectives so as to enable the firm to recommend to the client or potential client the investment services and financial instruments that are suitable for him.

¶ *See articles 35 and 37 of Commission Directive 2006/73/EC, reproduced infra under no. S. 34.*

5. Member States shall ensure that investment firms, when providing investment services other than those referred to in paragraph 4, ask the client or potential client to provide information regarding his knowledge and experience in the investment field relevant to the specific type of product or service offered or demanded so as to enable the investment firm to assess whether the investment service or product envisaged is appropriate for the client.

In case the investment firm considers, on the basis of the information received under the previous subparagraph, that the product or service is not appropriate to the client or potential client, the investment firm shall warn the client or potential client. This warning may be provided in a standardised format.

In cases where the client or potential client elects not to provide the information referred to under the first subparagraph, or where he provides insufficient information regarding his knowledge and experience, the investment firm shall warn the client or potential client that such a decision will not allow the firm to determine whether the service or product envisaged is appropriate for him. This warning may be provided in a standardised format.

¶ *See article 36 and 37 of Commission Directive 2006/73/EC, reproduced infra under no. S. 34.*

6. Member States shall allow investment firms when providing investment services that only consist of execution and/or the reception and transmission of client orders with or without ancillary services to provide those investment services to their clients without the need to obtain the information or make the determination provided for in paragraph 5 where all the following conditions are met:
– the above services relate to shares admitted to trading on a regulated market or in an equivalent third country market, money market instruments, bonds or other forms of securitised debt (excluding those bonds or securitised debt that embed a derivative), UCITS and other non-complex financial instruments. A third country market shall be considered as equivalent to a regulated market if it complies with equivalent requirements to those established under Title III. The Commission shall publish a list of those markets that are to be considered as equivalent. This list shall be updated periodically,

¶ *See article 38 of Commission Directive 2006/73/EC, reproduced infra under no. S. 34.*

– the service is provided at the initiative of the client or potential client,
– the client or potential client has been clearly informed that in the provision of this service the investment firm is not required to assess the suitability of the instrument or service provided or offered and that therefore he does not benefit from the corresponding protection of the relevant conduct of business rules; this warning may be provided in a standardised format,
– the investment firm complies with its obligations under Article 18.

7. The investment firm shall establish a record that includes the document or documents agreed between the firm and the client that set out the rights and obligations of the parties, and the other terms on which the firm will provide services to the client. The rights and duties of the parties to the contract may be incorporated by reference to other documents or legal texts.

¶ *See article 39 of Commission Directive 2006/73/EC, reproduced infra under no. S. 34.*

8. The client must receive from the investment firm adequate reports on the service provided to its clients. These reports shall include, where applicable, the costs associated with the transactions and services undertaken on behalf of the client.

¶ *See articles 40, 41, 42, and 43 of Commission Directive 2006/73/EC, reproduced infra under no. S. 34.*

9. In cases where an investment service is offered as part of a financial product which is already subject to other provisions of Community legislation or common European standards related to credit institutions and consumer credits with respect to risk assessment of clients and/or information requirements, this service shall not be additionally subject to the obligations set out in this Article.

10. In order to ensure the necessary protection of investors and the uniform application of paragraphs 1 to 8, the Commission shall adopt, in accordance with the procedure referred to in Article 64(2), implementing measures to ensure that investment firms comply with the principles set out therein when providing investment or ancillary services to their clients. Those implementing measures shall take into account:

(a) the nature of the service(s) offered or provided to the client or potential client, taking into account the type, object, size and frequency of the transactions;

(b) the nature of the financial instruments being offered or considered;

(c) the retail or professional nature of the client or potential clients.

Article 20

Provision of services through the medium of another investment firm

Member States shall allow an investment firm receiving an instruction to perform investment or ancillary services on behalf of a client through the medium of another investment firm to rely on client information transmitted by the latter firm. The investment firm which mediates the instructions will remain responsible for the completeness and accuracy of the information transmitted.

The investment firm which receives an instruction to undertake services on behalf of a client in this way shall also be able to rely on any recommendations in respect of the service or transaction that have been provided to the client by another investment firm. The investment firm which mediates the instructions will remain responsible for the appropriateness for the client of the recommendations or advice provided.

The investment firm which receives client instructions or orders through the medium of another investment firm shall remain responsible for concluding the service or transaction, based on any such information or recommendations, in accordance with the relevant provisions of this Title.

Article 21

Obligation to execute orders on terms most favourable to the client

1. Member States shall require that investment firms take all reasonable steps to obtain, when executing orders, the best possible result for their clients taking into account price, costs, speed, likelihood of execution and settlement, size, nature or any other consideration relevant to the execution of the order. Nevertheless, whenever there is a specific instruction from the client the investment firm shall execute the order following the specific instruction.

¶ *See article 44 of Commission Directive 2006/73/EC, reproduced infra under no. S. 34.*

2. Member States shall require investment firms to establish and implement effective arrangements for complying with paragraph 1. In particular Member States shall require investment firms to establish and implement an order execution policy to allow them to obtain, for their client orders, the best possible result in accordance with paragraph 1.

3. The order execution policy shall include, in respect of each class of instruments, information on the different venues where the investment firm executes its client orders and the factors affecting the choice of execution venue. It shall at least include those venues that enable the investment firm to obtain on a consistent basis the best possible result for the execution of client orders.

Member States shall require that investment firms provide appropriate information to their clients on their order execution policy. Member States shall require that investment firms obtain the prior consent of their clients to the execution policy.

Member States shall require that, where the order execution policy provides for the possibility that client orders may be executed outside a regulated market or an MTF, the investment firm shall, in particular, inform its clients about this possibility. Member States shall require that investment firms obtain the prior express consent of their clients before proceeding to execute their orders outside a regulated market or an MTF. Investment firms may obtain this consent either in the form of a general agreement or in respect of individual transactions.

¶ *See article 46 of Commission Directive 2006/73/EC, reproduced infra under no. S. 34.*

4. Member States shall require investment firms to monitor the effectiveness of their order execution arrangements and execution policy in order to identify and, where appropriate, correct any deficiencies. In particular, they shall assess, on a regular basis, whether the execution venues included in the order execution policy provide for the best possible result for the client or whether they need to make changes to their execution arrangements. Member States shall require investment firms to notify clients of any material changes to their order execution arrangements or execution policy.

¶ *See article 46 of Commission Directive 2006/73/EC, reproduced infra under no. S. 34.*

5. Member States shall require investment firms to be able to demonstrate to their clients, at their request, that they have executed their orders in accordance with the firm's execution policy.

6. In order to ensure the protection necessary for investors, the fair and orderly functioning of markets, and to ensure the uniform application of paragraphs 1, 3 and 4, the Commission shall, in accordance with the procedure referred to in Article 64(2), adopt implementing measures concerning:

(a) the criteria for determining the relative importance of the different factors that, pursuant to paragraph 1, may be taken into account for determining the best possible result taking into account the size and type of order and the retail or professional nature of the client;

(b) factors that may be taken into account by an investment firm when reviewing its execution arrangements and the circumstances under which changes to such arrangements may be appropriate. In particular, the factors for determining which venues enable investment firms to obtain on a consistent basis the best possible result for executing the client orders;

(c) the nature and extent of the information to be provided to clients on their execution policies, pursuant to paragraph 3.

Article 22
Client order handling rules

1. Member States shall require that investment firms authorised to execute orders on behalf of clients implement procedures and arrangements which provide for the prompt, fair and expeditious execution of client orders, relative to other client orders or the trading interests of the investment firm.

These procedures or arrangements shall allow for the execution of otherwise comparable client orders in accordance with the time of their reception by the investment firm.

¶ *See articles 47, 48 and 49 of Commission Directive 2006/73/EC, reproduced infra under no. S. 34.*

2. Member States shall require that, in the case of a client limit order in respect of shares admitted to trading on a regulated market which are not immediately executed under prevailing market conditions, investment firms are, unless the client expressly instructs otherwise, to take measures to facilitate the earliest possible execution of that order by making public immediately that client limit order in a manner which is easily accessible to other market participants. Member States may decide that investment firms comply with this obligation by transmitting the client limit order to a regulated market and/or MTF. Member States shall provide that the competent authorities may waive the obligation to make public a limit order that is large in scale compared with normal market size as determined under Article 44(2).

¶ *See articles 31 and 32 of Commission Regulation 1287/2006/EC, reproduced infra under no. S. 33.*

3. In order to ensure that measures for the protection of investors and fair and orderly functioning of markets take account of technical developments in financial markets, and to ensure the uniform application of paragraphs 1 and 2, the Commission shall adopt, in accordance with

the procedure referred to in Article 64(2), implementing measures which define:

(a) the conditions and nature of the procedures and arrangements which result in the prompt, fair and expeditious execution of client orders and the situations in which or types of transaction for which investment firms may reasonably deviate from prompt execution so as to obtain more favourable terms for clients;

(b) the different methods through which an investment firm can be deemed to have met its obligation to disclose not immediately executable client limit orders to the market.

Article 23
Obligations of investment firms when appointing tied agents

1. Member States may decide to allow an investment firm to appoint tied agents for the purposes of promoting the services of the investment firm, soliciting business or receiving orders from clients or potential clients and transmitting them, placing financial instruments and providing advice in respect of such financial instruments and services offered by that investment firm.

2. Member States shall require that where an investment firm decides to appoint a tied agent it remains fully and unconditionally responsible for any action or omission on the part of the tied agent when acting on behalf of the firm. Member States shall require the investment firm to ensure that a tied agent discloses the capacity in which he is acting and the firm which he is representing when contacting or before dealing with any client or potential client.

Member States may allow, in accordance with Article 13(6), (7) and (8), tied agents registered in their territory to handle clients' money and/or financial instruments on behalf and under the full responsibility of the investment firm for which they are acting within their territory or, in the case of a cross-border operation, in the territory of a Member State which allows a tied agent to handle clients' money.

Member States shall require the investment firms to monitor the activities of their tied agents so as to ensure that they continue to comply with this Directive when acting through tied agents.

3. Member States that decide to allow investment firms to appoint tied agents shall establish a public register. Tied agents shall be registered in the public register in the Member State where they are established.

Where the Member State in which the tied agent is established has decided, in accordance with paragraph 1, not to allow the investment firms authorised by their competent authorities to appoint tied agents, those tied agents shall be registered with the competent authority of the home Member State of the investment firm on whose behalf it acts.

Member States shall ensure that tied agents are only admitted to the public register if it has been established that they are of sufficiently good repute and that they possess appropriate general, commercial and professional knowledge so as to be able to communicate accurately all relevant information regarding the proposed service to the client or potential client.

Member States may decide that investment firms can verify whether the tied agents which they have appointed are of sufficiently good repute and possess the knowledge as referred to in the third subparagraph.

The register shall be updated on a regular basis. It shall be publicly available for consultation.

4. Member States shall require that investment firms appointing tied agents take adequate measures in order to avoid any negative impact that the activities of the tied agent not covered by the scope of this Directive could have on the activities carried out by the tied agent on behalf of the investment firm.

Member States may allow competent authorities to collaborate with investment firms and credit institutions, their associations and other entities in registering tied agents and in monitoring compliance of tied agents with the requirements of paragraph 3. In particular, tied agents may be registered by an investment firm, credit institution or their associations and other entities under the supervision of the competent authority.

5. Member States shall require that investment firms appoint only tied agents entered in the public registers referred to in paragraph 3.

6. Member States may reinforce the requirements set out in this Article or add other requirements for tied agents registered within their jurisdiction.

Article 24
Transactions executed with eligible counterparties

1. Member States shall ensure that investment firms authorised to execute orders on behalf of clients and/or to deal on own account and/or to receive and transmit orders, may bring about or enter into transactions with eligible counterparties without being obliged to comply with the obligations under Articles 19, 21 and 22(1) in respect of those transactions or in respect of any ancillary service directly related to those transactions.

2. Member States shall recognise as eligible counterparties for the purposes of this Article investment firms, credit institutions, insurance companies, UCITS and their management companies, pension funds and their management companies, other financial institutions authorised or regulated under Community legislation or the national law of a Member State, undertakings exempted from the application of this Directive under Article 2(1)(k) and (l), national governments and their corresponding offices including public bodies that deal with public debt, central banks and supranational organisations.

Classification as an eligible counterparty under the first subparagraph shall be without prejudice to the right of such entities to request, either on a general form or on a trade-by-trade basis, treatment as clients whose business with the investment firm is subject to Articles 19, 21 and 22.

3. Member States may also recognise as eligible counterparties other undertakings meeting predetermined proportionate requirements, including quantitative thresholds. In the event of a transaction where the prospective counterparties are located in different jurisdictions, the investment firm shall defer to the status of the other undertaking as determined by the law or measures of the Member State in which that undertaking is established.

Member States shall ensure that the investment firm, when it enters into transactions in accordance with paragraph 1 with such undertakings, obtains the express confirmation from the prospective counterparty that it agrees to be treated as an eligible counterparty. Member States shall allow the investment firm to obtain this confirmation either in the form of a general agreement or in respect of each individual transaction.

¶ *See article 50 of Commission Directive 2006/73/EC, reproduced infra under no. S. 34.*

4. Member States may recognise as eligible counterparties third country entities equivalent to those categories of entities mentioned in paragraph 2.

Member States may also recognise as eligible counterparties third country undertakings such as those mentioned in paragraph 3 on the same conditions and subject to the same requirements as those laid down at paragraph 3.

5. In order to ensure the uniform application of paragraphs 2, 3 and 4 in the light of changing market practice and to facilitate the effective operation of the single market, the Commission may adopt, in accordance with the procedure referred to in Article 64(2), implementing measures which define:

(a) the procedures for requesting treatment as clients under paragraph 2;

(b) the procedures for obtaining the express confirmation from prospective counterparties under paragraph 3;

(c) the predetermined proportionate requirements, including quantitative thresholds that would allow an undertaking to be considered as an eligible counterparty under paragraph 3.

SECTION 3

MARKET TRANSPARENCY AND INTEGRITY

Article 25
Obligation to uphold integrity of markets, report transactions and maintain records

1. Without prejudice to the allocation of responsibilities for enforcing the provisions of Directive 2003/6/EC of the European Parliament and of

the Council of 28 January 2003 on insider dealing and market manipulation (market abuse),[22] Member States shall ensure that appropriate measures are in place to enable the competent authority to monitor the activities of investment firms to ensure that they act honestly, fairly and professionally and in a manner which promotes the integrity of the market.

2. Member States shall require investment firms to keep at the disposal of the competent authority, for at least five years, the relevant data relating to all transactions in financial instruments which they have carried out, whether on own account or on behalf of a client. In the case of transactions carried out on behalf of clients, the records shall contain all the information and details of the identity of the client, and the information required under Council Directive 91/308/EEC of 10 June 1991 on prevention of the use of the financial system for the purpose of money laundering.[23]

3. Member States shall require investment firms which execute transactions in any financial instruments admitted to trading on a regulated market to report details of such transactions to the competent authority as quickly as possible, and no later than the close of the following working day. This obligation shall apply whether or not such transactions were carried out on a regulated market.

The competent authorities shall, in accordance with Article 58, establish the necessary arrangements in order to ensure that the competent authority of the most relevant market in terms of liquidity for those financial instruments also receives this information.

¶ *See articles 9, 10, 11, 13, and 14 of Commission Regulation 1287/2006/EC, reproduced infra under no. S. 33.*

4. The reports shall, in particular, include details of the names and numbers of the instruments bought or sold, the quantity, the dates and times of execution and the transaction prices and means of identifying the investment firms concerned.

5. Member States shall provide for the reports to be made to the competent authority either by the investment firm itself, a third party acting on its behalf or by a trade-matching or reporting system approved by the competent authority or by the regulated market or MTF through whose systems the transaction was completed. In cases where transactions are reported directly to the competent authority by a regulated market, an MTF, or a trade-matching or reporting system approved by the competent authority, the obligation on the investment firm laid down in paragraph 3 may be waived.

¶ *See articles 12, 13, and 14 of Commission Regulation 1287/2006/EC, reproduced infra under no. S. 33.*

6. When, in accordance with Article 32(7), reports provided for under this Article are transmitted to the competent authority of the host Member State, it shall transmit this information to the competent authorities of the home Member State of the investment firm, unless they decide that they do not want to receive this information.

7. In order to ensure that measures for the protection of market integrity are modified to take account of technical developments in financial markets, and to ensure the uniform application of paragraphs 1 to 5, the Commission may adopt, in accordance with the procedure referred to in Article 64(2), implementing measures which define the methods and arrangements for reporting financial transactions, the form and content of these reports and the criteria for defining a relevant market in accordance with paragraph 3.

Article 26

Monitoring of compliance with the rules of the MTF and with other legal obligations

1. Member States shall require that investment firms and market operators operating an MTF establish and maintain effective arrangements and procedures, relevant to the MTF, for the regular monitoring of the compliance by its users

---

[22] OJ L 96, 12.4.2003, 16, reproduced supra under no. S. 24.
[23] OJ L 166, 28.6.1991, 77, reproduced supra under no. B. 15. Directive as last amended by Directive 2001/97/EC of the European Parliament and of the Council (OJ L 344, 28.12.2001, 76), reproduced supra under no. B. 37.

with its rules. Investment firms and market operators operating an MTF shall monitor the transactions undertaken by their users under their systems in order to identify breaches of those rules, disorderly trading conditions or conduct that may involve market abuse.

2. Member States shall require investment firms and market operators operating an MTF to report significant breaches of its rules or disorderly trading conditions or conduct that may involve market abuse to the competent authority. Member States shall also require investment firms and market operators operating an MTF to supply the relevant information without delay to the authority competent for the investigation and prosecution of market abuse and to provide full assistance to the latter in investigating and prosecuting market abuse occurring on or through its systems.

Article 27
Obligation for investment firms to make public firm quotes

1. Member States shall require systematic internalisers in shares to publish a firm quote in those shares admitted to trading on a regulated market for which they are systematic internalisers and for which there is a liquid market. In the case of shares for which there is not a liquid market, systematic internalisers shall disclose quotes to their clients on request.

The provisions of this Article shall be applicable to systematic internalisers when dealing for sizes up to standard market size. Systematic internalisers that only deal in sizes above standard market size shall not be subject to the provisions of this Article.

Systematic internalisers may decide the size or sizes at which they will quote. For a particular share each quote shall include a firm bid and/or offer price or prices for a size or sizes which could be up to standard market size for the class of shares to which the share belongs. The price or prices shall also reflect the prevailing market conditions for that share.

Shares shall be grouped in classes on the basis of the arithmetic average value of the orders executed in the market for that share. The standard market size for each class of shares shall be a size representative of the arithmetic average value of the orders executed in the market for the shares included in each class of shares.

¶ *See article 23 of Commission Regulation 1287/2006/EC, reproduced infra under no. S. 33.*

The market for each share shall be comprised of all orders executed in the European Union in respect of that share excluding those large in scale compared to normal market size for that share.

¶ *See articles 20 and 24 of Commission Regulation 1287/2006/EC, reproduced infra under no. S. 33.*

2. The competent authority of the most relevant market in terms of liquidity as defined in Article 25 for each share shall determine at least annually, on the basis of the arithmetic average value of the orders executed in the market in respect of that share, the class of shares to which it belongs. This information shall be made public to all market participants.

3. Systematic internalisers shall make public their quotes on a regular and continuous basis during normal trading hours. They shall be entitled to update their quotes at any time. They shall also be allowed, under exceptional market conditions, to withdraw their quotes.

The quote shall be made public in a manner which is easily accessible to other market participants on a reasonable commercial basis.

Systematic internalisers shall, while complying with the provisions set down in Article 21, execute the orders they receive from their retail clients in relation to the shares for which they are systematic internalisers at the quoted prices at the time of reception of the order.

Systematic internalisers shall execute the orders they receive from their professional clients in relation to the shares for which they are systematic internalisers at the quoted price at the time of reception of the order. However, they may execute those orders at a better price in justified cases provided that this price falls within a public range close to market conditions and provided that the orders are of a size bigger than the size customarily undertaken by a retail investor.

¶ *See article 26 of Commission Regulation 1287/2006/EC, reproduced infra under no. S. 33.*

Furthermore, systematic internalisers may execute orders they receive from their professional clients at prices different than their quoted ones without having to comply with the conditions established in the fourth subparagraph, in respect of transactions where execution in several securities is part of one transaction or in respect of orders that are subject to conditions other than the current market price.

¶ *See article 25 of Commission Regulation 1287/2006/EC, reproduced infra under no. S. 33.*

Where a systematic internaliser who quotes only one quote or whose highest quote is lower than the standard market size receives an order from a client of a size bigger than its quotation size, but lower than the standard market size, it may decide to execute that part of the order which exceeds its quotation size, provided that it is executed at the quoted price, except where otherwise permitted under the conditions of the previous two subparagraphs. Where the systematic internaliser is quoting in different sizes and receives an order between those sizes, which it chooses to execute, it shall execute the order at one of the quoted prices in compliance with the provisions of Article 22, except where otherwise permitted under the conditions of the previous two subparagraphs.

¶ *See article 29 of Commission Regulation 1287/2006/EC, reproduced infra under no. S. 33.*

4. The competent authorities shall check:

(a) that investment firms regularly update bid and/or offer prices published in accordance with paragraph 1 and maintain prices which reflect the prevailing market conditions;

(b) that investment firms comply with the conditions for price improvement laid down in the fourth subparagraph of paragraph 3.

5. Systematic internalisers shall be allowed to decide, on the basis of their commercial policy and in an objective non-discriminatory way, the investors to whom they give access to their quotes. To that end there shall be clear standards for governing access to their quotes. Systematic internalisers may refuse to enter into or discontinue business relationships with investors on the basis of commercial considerations such as the investor credit status, the counterparty risk and the final settlement of the transaction.

6. In order to limit the risk of being exposed to multiple transactions from the same client systematic internalisers shall be allowed to limit in a non-discriminatory way the number of transactions from the same client which they undertake to enter at the published conditions. They shall also be allowed, in a non-discriminatory way and in accordance with the provisions of Article 22, to limit the total number of transactions from different clients at the same time provided that this is allowable only where the number and/or volume of orders sought by clients considerably exceeds the norm.

¶ *See article 25 of Commission Regulation 1287/2006/EC, reproduced infra under no. S. 33.*

7. In order to ensure the uniform application of paragraphs 1 to 6, in a manner which supports the efficient valuation of shares and maximises the possibility of investment firms of obtaining the best deal for their clients, the Commission shall, in accordance with the procedure referred to in Article 64(2), adopt implementing measures which:

(a) specify the criteria for application of paragraphs 1 and 2;

(b) specify the criteria determining when a quote is published on a regular and continuous basis and is easily accessible as well as the means by which investment firms may comply with their obligation to make public their quotes, which shall include the following possibilities:
(i) through the facilities of any regulated market which has admitted the instrument in question to trading;
(ii) through the offices of a third party;
(iii) through proprietary arrangements;

(c) specify the general criteria for determining those transactions where execution in several securities is part of one transaction or orders that are subject to conditions other than current market price;

(d) specify the general criteria for determining what can be considered as exceptional market circumstances that allow for the withdrawal of quotes as well as conditions for updating quotes;

(e) specify the criteria for determining what is a size customarily undertaken by a retail investor;

(f) specify the criteria for determining what constitutes considerably exceeding the norm as set down in paragraph 6;

(g) specify the criteria for determining when prices fall within a public range close to market conditions.

¶ *See articles 22, 30, 32, 33, and 34 of Commission Regulation 1287/2006/EC, reproduced infra under no. S. 33.*

Article 28
Post-trade disclosure by investment firms

1. Member States shall, at least, require investment firms which, either on own account or on behalf of clients, conclude transactions in shares admitted to trading on a regulated market outside a regulated market or MTF, to make public the volume and price of those transactions and the time at which they were concluded. This information shall be made public as close to real-time as possible, on a reasonable commercial basis, and in a manner which is easily accessible to other market participants.

¶ *See article 29 of Commission Regulation 1287/2006/EC, reproduced infra under no. S. 33.*

2. Member States shall require that the information which is made public in accordance with paragraph 1 and the time-limits within which it is published comply with the requirements adopted pursuant to Article 45. Where the measures adopted pursuant to Article 45 provide for deferred reporting for certain categories of transaction in shares, this possibility shall apply mutatis mutandis to those transactions when undertaken outside regulated markets or MTFs.

3. In order to ensure the transparent and orderly functioning of markets and the uniform application of paragraph 1, the Commission shall adopt, in accordance with the procedure referred to in Article 64(2), implementing measures which:

(a) specify the means by which investment firms may comply with their obligations under paragraph 1 including the following possibilities:

(i) through the facilities of any regulated market which has admitted the instrument in question to trading or through the facilities of an MTF in which the share in question is traded;

(ii) through the offices of a third party;

(iii) through proprietary arrangements;

(b) clarify the application of the obligation under paragraph 1 to transactions involving the use of shares for collateral, lending or other purposes where the exchange of shares is determined by factors other than the current market valuation of the share.

¶ *See articles 27, 28, 30, 32, 33, and 34 of Commission Regulation 1287/2006/EC, reproduced infra under no. S. 33.*

Article 29
Pre-trade transparency requirements for MTFs

1. Member States shall, at least, require that investment firms and market operators operating an MTF make public current bid and offer prices and the depth of trading interests at these prices which are advertised through their systems in respect of shares admitted to trading on a regulated market. Member States shall provide for this information to be made available to the public on reasonable commercial terms and on a continuous basis during normal trading hours.

¶ *See article 29 of Commission Regulation 1287/2006/EC, reproduced infra under no. S. 33.*

2. Member States shall provide for the competent authorities to be able to waive the obligation for investment firms or market operators operating an MTF to make public the information referred to in paragraph 1 based on the market model or the type and size of orders in the cases defined in accordance with paragraph 3. In particular, the competent authorities shall be able to waive the obligation in respect of transactions that are large in scale compared with normal market size for the share or type of share in question.

¶ *See articles 18, 19, and 20 of Commission Regulation 1287/2006/EC, reproduced infra under no. S. 33.*

3. In order to ensure the uniform application of paragraphs 1 and 2, the Commission shall, in

accordance with the procedure referred to in Article 64(2) adopt implementing measures as regards:

(a) the range of bid and offers or designated market-maker quotes, and the depth of trading interest at those prices, to be made public;

(b) the size or type of orders for which pre-trade disclosure may be waived under paragraph 2;

(c) the market model for which pre-trade disclosure may be waived under paragraph 2 and in particular, the applicability of the obligation to trading methods operated by an MTF which conclude transactions under their rules by reference to prices established outside the systems of the MTF or by periodic auction.

Except where justified by the specific nature of the MTF, the content of these implementing measures shall be equal to that of the implementing measures provided for in Article 44 for regulated markets.

¶ *See articles 17, 30, 32, 33, and 34 of Commission Regulation 1287/2006/EC, reproduced infra under no. S. 33.*

Article 30
Post-trade transparency requirements for MTFs

1. Member States shall, at least, require that investment firms and market operators operating an MTF make public the price, volume and time of the transactions executed under its systems in respect of shares which are admitted to trading on a regulated market. Member States shall require that details of all such transactions be made public, on a reasonable commercial basis, as close to real-time as possible. This requirement shall not apply to details of trades executed on an MTF that are made public under the systems of a regulated market.

2. Member States shall provide that the competent authority may authorise investment firms or market operators operating an MTF to provide for deferred publication of the details of transactions based on their type or size. In particular, the competent authorities may authorise the deferred publication in respect of transactions that are large in scale compared with the normal market size for that share or that class of shares. Member States shall require MTFs to obtain the competent authority's prior approval to proposed arrangements for deferred trade-publication, and shall require that these arrangements be clearly disclosed to market participants and the investing public.

3. In order to provide for the efficient and orderly functioning of financial markets, and to ensure the uniform application of paragraphs 1 and 2, the Commission shall, in accordance with the procedure referred to in Article 64(2) adopt implementing measures in respect of:

(a) the scope and content of the information to be made available to the public;

(b) the conditions under which investment firms or market operators operating an MTF may provide for deferred publication of trades and the criteria to be applied when deciding the transactions for which, due to their size or the type of share involved, deferred publication is allowed.

Except where justified by the specific nature of the MTF, the content of these implementing measures shall be equal to that of the implementing measures provided for in Article 45 for regulated markets.

¶ *See articles 27, 28, 30, 32, 33, and 34 of Commission Regulation 1287/2006/EC, reproduced infra under no. S. 33.*

CHAPTER III
RIGHTS OF INVESTMENT FIRMS

Article 31
Freedom to provide investment services and activities

1. Member States shall ensure that any investment firm authorised and supervised by the competent authorities of another Member State in accordance with this Directive, and in respect of credit institutions in accordance with Directive 2000/12/EC, may freely perform investment services and/or activities as well as ancillary services within their territories, provided that such services and activities are covered by its authorisation. Ancillary services may only be provided together with an investment service and/or activity.

Member States shall not impose any additional requirements on such an investment firm or credit institution in respect of the matters covered by this Directive.

2. Any investment firm wishing to provide services or activities within the territory of another Member State for the first time, or which wishes to change the range of services or activities so provided, shall communicate the following information to the competent authorities of its home Member State:

(a) the Member State in which it intends to operate;

(b) a programme of operations stating in particular the investment services and/or activities as well as ancillary services which it intends to perform and whether it intends to use tied agents in the territory of the Member States in which it intends to provide services.

In cases where the investment firm intends to use tied agents, the competent authority of the home Member State of the investment firm shall, at the request of the competent authority of the host Member State and within a reasonable time, communicate the identity of the tied agents that the investment firm intends to use in that Member State. The host Member State may make public such information.

3. The competent authority of the home Member State shall, within one month of receiving the information, forward it to the competent authority of the host Member State designated as contact point in accordance with Article 56(1). The investment firm may then start to provide the investment service or services concerned in the host Member State.

4. In the event of a change in any of the particulars communicated in accordance with paragraph 2, an investment firm shall give written notice of that change to the competent authority of the home Member State at least one month before implementing the change. The competent authority of the home Member State shall inform the competent authority of the host Member State of those changes.

5. Member States shall, without further legal or administrative requirement, allow investment firms and market operators operating MTFs from other Member States to provide appropriate arrangements on their territory so as to facilitate access to and use of their systems by remote users or participants established in their territory.

6. The investment firm or the market operator that operates an MTF shall communicate to the competent authority of its home Member State the Member State in which it intends to provide such arrangements. The competent authority of the home Member State of the MTF shall communicate, within one month, this information to the Member State in which the MTF intends to provide such arrangements.

The competent authority of the home Member State of the MTF shall, on the request of the competent authority of the host Member State of the MTF and within a reasonable delay, communicate the identity of the members or participants of the MTF established in that Member State.

Article 32
Establishment of a branch

1. Member States shall ensure that investment services and/or activities as well as ancillary services may be provided within their territories in accordance with this Directive and Directive 2000/12/EC through the establishment of a branch provided that those services and activities are covered by the authorisation granted to the investment firm or the credit institution in the home Member State. Ancillary services may only be provided together with an investment service and/or activity.

Member States shall not impose any additional requirements save those allowed under paragraph 7, on the organisation and operation of the branch in respect of the matters covered by this Directive.

2. Member States shall require any investment firm wishing to establish a branch within the territory of another Member State first to notify the competent authority of its home Member State and to provide it with the following information:

(a) the Member States within the territory of which it plans to establish a branch;

(b) a programme of operations setting out inter alia the investment services and/or activities as well as the ancillary services to be offered and the organisational structure of the branch and indicating whether the branch intends to use tied agents;

(c) the address in the host Member State from which documents may be obtained;

(d) the names of those responsible for the management of the branch.

In cases where an investment firm uses a tied agent established in a Member State outside its home Member State, such tied agent shall be assimilated to the branch and shall be subject to the provisions of this Directive relating to branches.

3. Unless the competent authority of the home Member State has reason to doubt the adequacy of the administrative structure or the financial situation of an investment firm, taking into account the activities envisaged, it shall, within three months of receiving all the information, communicate that information to the competent authority of the host Member State designated as contact point in accordance with Article 56(1) and inform the investment firm concerned accordingly.

4. In addition to the information referred to in paragraph 2, the competent authority of the home Member State shall communicate details of the accredited compensation scheme of which the investment firm is a member in accordance with Directive 97/9/EC to the competent authority of the host Member State. In the event of a change in the particulars, the competent authority of the home Member State shall inform the competent authority of the host Member State accordingly.

5. Where the competent authority of the home Member State refuses to communicate the information to the competent authority of the host Member State, it shall give reasons for its refusal to the investment firm concerned within three months of receiving all the information.

6. On receipt of a communication from the competent authority of the host Member State, or failing such communication from the latter at the latest after two months from the date of transmission of the communication by the competent authority of the home Member State, the branch may be established and commence business.

7. The competent authority of the Member State in which the branch is located shall assume responsibility for ensuring that the services provided by the branch within its territory comply with the obligations laid down in Articles 19, 21, 22, 25, 27 and 28 and in measures adopted pursuant thereto.

The competent authority of the Member State in which the branch is located shall have the right to examine branch arrangements and to request such changes as are strictly needed to enable the competent authority to enforce the obligations under Articles 19, 21, 22, 25, 27 and 28 and measures adopted pursuant thereto with respect to the services and/or activities provided by the branch within its territory.

8. Each Member State shall provide that, where an investment firm authorised in another Member State has established a branch within its territory, the competent authority of the home Member State of the investment firm, in the exercise of its responsibilities and after informing the competent authority of the host Member State, may carry out on-site inspections in that branch.

9. In the event of a change in any of the information communicated in accordance with paragraph 2, an investment firm shall give written notice of that change to the competent authority of the home Member State at least one month before implementing the change. The competent authority of the host Member State shall also be informed of that change by the competent authority of the home Member State.

Article 33

Access to regulated markets

1. Member States shall require that investment firms from other Member States which are authorised to execute client orders or to deal on own account have the right of membership or have access to regulated markets established in their

territory by means of any of the following arrangements:

(a) directly, by setting up branches in the host Member States;

(b) by becoming remote members of or having remote access to the regulated market without having to be established in the home Member State of the regulated market, where the trading procedures and systems of the market in question do not require a physical presence for conclusion of transactions on the market.

2. Member States shall not impose any additional regulatory or administrative requirements, in respect of matters covered by this Directive, on investment firms exercising the right conferred by paragraph 1.

Article 34

Access to central counterparty, clearing and settlement facilities and right to designate settlement system

1. Member States shall require that investment firms from other Member States have the right of access to central counterparty, clearing and settlement systems in their territory for the purposes of finalising or arranging the finalisation of transactions in financial instruments.

Member States shall require that access of those investment firms to such facilities be subject to the same non-discriminatory, transparent and objective criteria as apply to local participants. Member States shall not restrict the use of those facilities to the clearing and settlement of transactions in financial instruments undertaken on a regulated market or MTF in their territory.

2. Member States shall require that regulated markets in their territory offer all their members or participants the right to designate the system for the settlement of transactions in financial instruments undertaken on that regulated market, subject to:

(a) such links and arrangements between the designated settlement system and any other system or facility as are necessary to ensure the efficient and economic settlement of the transaction in question; and

(b) agreement by the competent authority responsible for the supervision of the regulated market that technical conditions for settlement of transactions concluded on the regulated market through a settlement system other than that designated by the regulated market are such as to allow the smooth and orderly functioning of financial markets.

This assessment of the competent authority of the regulated market shall be without prejudice to the competencies of the national central banks as overseers of settlement systems or other supervisory authorities on such systems. The competent authority shall take into account the oversight/supervision already exercised by those institutions in order to avoid undue duplication of control.

3. The rights of investment firms under paragraphs 1 and 2 shall be without prejudice to the right of operators of central counterparty, clearing or securities settlement systems to refuse on legitimate commercial grounds to make the requested services available.

Article 35

Provisions regarding central counterparty, clearing and settlement arrangements in respect of MTFs

1. Member States shall not prevent investment firms and market operators operating an MTF from entering into appropriate arrangements with a central counterparty or clearing house and a settlement system of another Member State with a view to providing for the clearing and/or settlement of some or all trades concluded by market participants under their systems.

2. The competent authority of investment firms and market operators operating an MTF may not oppose the use of central counterparty, clearing houses and/or settlement systems in another Member State except where this is demonstrably necessary in order to maintain the orderly functioning of that MTF and taking into account the conditions for settlement systems established in Article 34(2).

In order to avoid undue duplication of control, the competent authority shall take into account the oversight/supervision of the clearing and settlement system already exercised by the national central banks as overseers of clearing and settlement systems or by other supervisory authorities with a competence in such systems.

Title III
Regulated Markets

Article 36
Authorisation and applicable law

1. Member States shall reserve authorisation as a regulated market to those systems which comply with the provisions of this Title.

Authorisation as a regulated market shall be granted only where the competent authority is satisfied that both the market operator and the systems of the regulated market comply at least with the requirements laid down in this Title.

In the case of a regulated market that is a legal person and that is managed or operated by a market operator other than the regulated market itself, Member States shall establish how the different obligations imposed on the market operator under this Directive are to be allocated between the regulated market and the market operator.

The operator of the regulated market shall provide all information, including a programme of operations setting out inter alia the types of business envisaged and the organisational structure, necessary to enable the competent authority to satisfy itself that the regulated market has established, at the time of initial authorisation, all the necessary arrangements to meet its obligations under the provisions of this Title.

2. Member States shall require the operator of the regulated market to perform tasks relating to the organisation and operation of the regulated market under the supervision of the competent authority. Member States shall ensure that competent authorities keep under regular review the compliance of regulated markets with the provisions of this Title. They shall also ensure that competent authorities monitor that regulated markets comply at all times with the conditions for initial authorisation established under this Title.

3. Member States shall ensure that the market operator is responsible for ensuring that the regulated market that he manages complies with all requirements under this Title.

Member States shall also ensure that the market operator is entitled to exercise the rights that correspond to the regulated market that he manages by virtue of this Directive.

4. Without prejudice to any relevant provisions of Directive 2003/6/EC, the public law governing the trading conducted under the systems of the regulated market shall be that of the home Member State of the regulated market.

5. The competent authority may withdraw the authorisation issued to a regulated market where it:

(a) does not make use of the authorisation within 12 months, expressly renounces the authorisation or has not operated for the preceding six months, unless the Member State concerned has provided for authorisation to lapse in such cases;

(b) has obtained the authorisation by making false statements or by any other irregular means;

(c) no longer meets the conditions under which authorisation was granted;

(d) has seriously and systematically infringed the provisions adopted pursuant to this Directive;

(e) falls within any of the cases where national law provides for withdrawal.

Article 37
Requirements for the management of the regulated market

1. Member States shall require the persons who effectively direct the business and the operations of the regulated market to be of sufficiently good repute and sufficiently experienced as to ensure the sound and prudent management and operation of the regulated market. Member States shall also require the operator of the regulated market to inform the competent authority of the identity and any other subsequent changes of the

persons who effectively direct the business and the operations of the regulated market.

The competent authority shall refuse to approve proposed changes where there are objective and demonstrable grounds for believing that they pose a material threat to the sound and prudent management and operation of the regulated market.

2. Member States shall ensure that, in the process of authorisation of a regulated market, the person or persons who effectively direct the business and the operations of an already authorised regulated market in accordance with the conditions of this Directive are deemed to comply with the requirements laid down in paragraph 1.

Article 38
Requirements relating to persons exercising significant influence over the management of the regulated market

1. Member States shall require the persons who are in a position to exercise, directly or indirectly, significant influence over the management of the regulated market to be suitable.

2. Member States shall require the operator of the regulated market:

(a) to provide the competent authority with, and to make public, information regarding the ownership of the regulated market and/or the market operator, and in particular, the identity and scale of interests of any parties in a position to exercise significant influence over the management;

(b) to inform the competent authority of and to make public any transfer of ownership which gives rise to a change in the identity of the persons exercising significant influence over the operation of the regulated market.

3. The competent authority shall refuse to approve proposed changes to the controlling interests of the regulated market and/or the market operator where there are objective and demonstrable grounds for believing that they would pose a threat to the sound and prudent management of the regulated market.

Article 39
Organisational requirements

Member States shall require the regulated market:

(a) to have arrangements to identify clearly and manage the potential adverse consequences, for the operation of the regulated market or for its participants, of any conflict of interest between the interest of the regulated market, its owners or its operator and the sound functioning of the regulated market, and in particular where such conflicts of interest might prove prejudicial to the accomplishment of any functions delegated to the regulated market by the competent authority;

(b) to be adequately equipped to manage the risks to which it is exposed, to implement appropriate arrangements and systems to identify all significant risks to its operation, and to put in place effective measures to mitigate those risks;

(c) to have arrangements for the sound management of the technical operations of the system, including the establishment of effective contingency arrangements to cope with risks of systems disruptions;

(d) to have transparent and non-discretionary rules and procedures that provide for fair and orderly trading and establish objective criteria for the efficient execution of orders;

(e) to have effective arrangements to facilitate the efficient and timely finalisation of the transactions executed under its systems;

(f) to have available, at the time of authorisation and on an ongoing basis, sufficient financial resources to facilitate its orderly functioning, having regard to the nature and extent of the transactions concluded on the market and the range and degree of the risks to which it is exposed.

Article 40
Admission of financial instruments to trading

1. Member States shall require that regulated markets have clear and transparent rules regarding the admission of financial instruments to trading.

Those rules shall ensure that any financial instruments admitted to trading in a regulated market are capable of being traded in a fair, orderly and efficient manner and, in the case of transferable securities, are freely negotiable.

¶ *See articles 35, 36, and 37 of Commission Regulation 1287/2006/EC, reproduced infra under no. S. 33.*

2. In the case of derivatives, the rules shall ensure in particular that the design of the derivative contract allows for its orderly pricing as well as for the existence of effective settlement conditions.

¶ *See article 37 of Commission Regulation 1287/2006/EC, reproduced infra under no. S. 33.*

3. In addition to the obligations set out in paragraphs 1 and 2, Member States shall require the regulated market to establish and maintain effective arrangements to verify that issuers of transferable securities that are admitted to trading on the regulated market comply with their obligations under Community law in respect of initial, ongoing or ad hoc disclosure obligations.

Member States shall ensure that the regulated market establishes arrangements which facilitate its members or participants in obtaining access to information which has been made public under Community law.

4. Member States shall ensure that regulated markets have established the necessary arrangements to review regularly the compliance with the admission requirements of the financial instruments which they admit to trading.

5. A transferable security that has been admitted to trading on a regulated market can subsequently be admitted to trading on other regulated markets, even without the consent of the issuer and in compliance with the relevant provisions of Directive 2003/71/EC of the European Parliament and of the Council of 4 November 2003 on the prospectus to be published when securities are offered to the public or admitted to trading and amending Directive 2001/34/EC.[24] The issuer shall be informed by the regulated market of the fact that its securities are traded on that regulated market. The issuer shall not be subject to any obligation to provide information required under paragraph 3 directly to any regulated market which has admitted the issuer's securities to trading without its consent.

6. In order to ensure the uniform application of paragraphs 1 to 5, the Commission shall, in accordance with the procedure referred to in Article 64(2) adopt implementing measures which:

(a) specify the characteristics of different classes of instruments to be taken into account by the regulated market when assessing whether an instrument is issued in a manner consistent with the conditions laid down in the second subparagraph of paragraph 1 for admission to trading on the different market segments which it operates;

(b) clarify the arrangements that the regulated market is to implement so as to be considered to have fulfilled its obligation to verify that the issuer of a transferable security complies with its obligations under Community law in respect of initial, ongoing or ad hoc disclosure obligations;

(c) clarify the arrangements that the regulated market has to establish pursuant to paragraph 3 in order to facilitate its members or participants in obtaining access to information which has been made public under the conditions established by Community law.

Article 41

Suspension and removal of instruments from trading

1. Without prejudice to the right of the competent authority under Article 50(2)(j) and (k) to demand suspension or removal of an instrument from trading, the operator of the regulated market may suspend or remove from trading a financial instrument which no longer complies with the rules of the regulated market unless such a step would be likely to cause significant damage to the investors' interests or the orderly functioning of the market.

Notwithstanding the possibility for the operators of regulated markets to inform directly the operators of other regulated markets, Member States shall require that an operator of a regulated market that suspends or removes from trading a

---

[24] OJ L 345, 31.12.2003, 64, reproduced supra under no. S. 25.

financial instrument make public this decision and communicates relevant information to the competent authority. The competent authority shall inform the competent authorities of the other Member States.

2. A competent authority which demands the suspension or removal of a financial instrument from trading on one or more regulated markets shall immediately make public its decision and inform the competent authorities of the other Member States. Except where it could cause significant damage to the investors' interests or the orderly functioning of the market the competent authorities of the other Member States shall demand the suspension or removal of that financial instrument from trading on the regulated markets and MTFs that operate under their authority.

Article 42
Access to the regulated market

1. Member States shall require the regulated market to establish and maintain transparent and non-discriminatory rules, based on objective criteria, governing access to or membership of the regulated market.

2. Those rules shall specify any obligations for the members or participants arising from:

(a) the constitution and administration of the regulated market;

(b) rules relating to transactions on the market;

(c) professional standards imposed on the staff of the investment firms or credit institutions that are operating on the market;

(d) the conditions established, for members or participants other than investment firms and credit institutions, under paragraph 3;

(e) the rules and procedures for the clearing and settlement of transactions concluded on the regulated market.

3. Regulated markets may admit as members or participants investment firms, credit institutions authorised under Directive 2000/12/EC and other persons who:

(a) are fit and proper;

(b) have a sufficient level of trading ability and competence;

(c) have, where applicable, adequate organisational arrangements;

(d) have sufficient resources for the role they are to perform, taking into account the different financial arrangements that the regulated market may have established in order to guarantee the adequate settlement of transactions.

4. Member States shall ensure that, for the transactions concluded on a regulated market, members and participants are not obliged to apply to each other the obligations laid down in Articles 19, 21 and 22. However, the members or participants of the regulated market shall apply the obligations provided for in Articles 19, 21 and 22 with respect to their clients when they, acting on behalf of their clients, execute their orders on a regulated market.

5. Member States shall ensure that the rules on access to or membership of the regulated market provide for the direct or remote participation of investment firms and credit institutions.

6. Member States shall, without further legal or administrative requirements, allow regulated markets from other Member States to provide appropriate arrangements on their territory so as to facilitate access to and trading on those markets by remote members or participants established in their territory.

The regulated market shall communicate to the competent authority of its home Member State the Member State in which it intends to provide such arrangements. The competent authority of the home Member State shall communicate, within one month, this information to the Member State in which the regulated market intends to provide such arrangements.

The competent authority of the home Member State of the regulated market shall, on the request of the competent authority of the host Member State and within a reasonable time, communicate the identity of the members or participants of the regulated market established in that Member State.

7. Member States shall require the operator of the regulated market to communicate, on a regular basis, the list of the members and participants of the regulated market to the competent authority of the regulated market.

Article 43
Monitoring of compliance with the rules of the regulated market and with other legal obligations

1. Member States shall require that regulated markets establish and maintain effective arrangements and procedures for the regular monitoring of the compliance by their members or participants with their rules. Regulated markets shall monitor the transactions undertaken by their members or participants under their systems in order to identify breaches of those rules, disorderly trading conditions or conduct that may involve market abuse.

2. Member States shall require the operators of the regulated markets to report significant breaches of their rules or disorderly trading conditions or conduct that may involve market abuse to the competent authority of the regulated market. Member States shall also require the operator of the regulated market to supply the relevant information without delay to the authority competent for the investigation and prosecution of market abuse on the regulated market and to provide full assistance to the latter in investigating and prosecuting market abuse occurring on or through the systems of the regulated market.

Article 44
Pre-trade transparency requirements for regulated markets

1. Member States shall, at least, require regulated markets to make public current bid and offer prices and the depth of trading interests at those prices which are advertised through their systems for shares admitted to trading. Member States shall require this information to be made available to the public on reasonable commercial terms and on a continuous basis during normal trading hours.

Regulated markets may give access, on reasonable commercial terms and on a non-discriminatory basis, to the arrangements they employ for making public the information under the first subparagraph to investment firms which are obliged to publish their quotes in shares pursuant to Article 27.

¶ *See article 29 of Commission Regulation 1287/2006/EC, reproduced infra under no. S. 33.*

2. Member States shall provide that the competent authorities are to be able to waive the obligation for regulated markets to make public the information referred to in paragraph 1 based on the market model or the type and size of orders in the cases defined in accordance with paragraph 3. In particular, the competent authorities shall be able to waive the obligation in respect of transactions that are large in scale compared with normal market size for the share or type of share in question.

¶ *See articles 18, 19, and 20 of Commission Regulation 1287/2006/EC, reproduced infra under no. S. 33.*

3. In order to ensure the uniform application of paragraphs 1 and 2, the Commission shall, in accordance with the procedure referred to in Article 64(2) adopt implementing measures as regards:

(a) the range of bid and offers or designated market-maker quotes, and the depth of trading interest at those prices, to be made public;

(b) the size or type of orders for which pre-trade disclosure may be waived under paragraph 2;

(c) the market model for which pre-trade disclosure may be waived under paragraph 2, and in particular, the applicability of the obligation to trading methods operated by regulated markets which conclude transactions under their rules by reference to prices established outside the regulated market or by periodic auction.

¶ *See articles 17, 30, 32, 33, and 34 of Commission Regulation 1287/2006/EC, reproduced infra under no. S. 33.*

Article 45
Post-trade transparency requirements for regulated markets

1. Member States shall, at least, require regulated markets to make public the price, volume and time of the transactions executed in respect of shares admitted to trading. Member States shall require details of all such transactions to be made public, on a reasonable commercial basis and as close to real-time as possible.

Regulated markets may give access, on reasonable commercial terms and on a non-discriminatory basis, to the arrangements they employ for making public the information under the first subparagraph to investment firms which are obliged to publish the details of their transactions in shares pursuant to Article 28.

¶ *See article 29 of Commission Regulation 1287/2006/EC, reproduced infra under no. S. 33.*

2. Member States shall provide that the competent authority may authorise regulated markets to provide for deferred publication of the details of transactions based on their type or size. In particular, the competent authorities may authorise the deferred publication in respect of transactions that are large in scale compared with the normal market size for that share or that class of shares. Member States shall require regulated markets to obtain the competent authority's prior approval of proposed arrangements for deferred trade-publication, and shall require that these arrangements be clearly disclosed to market participants and the investing public.

3. In order to provide for the efficient and orderly functioning of financial markets, and to ensure the uniform application of paragraphs 1 and 2, the Commission shall, in accordance with the procedure referred to in Article 64(2) adopt implementing measures in respect of:

(a) the scope and content of the information to be made available to the public;

(b) the conditions under which a regulated market may provide for deferred publication of trades and the criteria to be applied when deciding the transactions for which, due to their size or the type of share involved, deferred publication is allowed.

¶ *See articles 27, 28, 30, 32, 33, and 34 of Commission Regulation 1287/2006/EC, reproduced infra under no. S. 33.*

Article 46
Provisions regarding central counterparty and clearing and settlement arrangements

1. Member States shall not prevent regulated markets from entering into appropriate arrangements with a central counterparty or clearing house and a settlement system of another Member State with a view to providing for the clearing and/or settlement of some or all trades concluded by market participants under their systems.

2. The competent authority of a regulated market may not oppose the use of central counterparty, clearing houses and/or settlement systems in another Member State except where this is demonstrably necessary in order to maintain the orderly functioning of that regulated market and taking into account the conditions for settlement systems established in Article 34(2).

In order to avoid undue duplication of control, the competent authority shall take into account the oversight/supervision of the clearing and settlement system already exercised by the national central banks as overseers of clearing and settlement systems or by other supervisory authorities with competence in relation to such systems.

Article 47
List of regulated markets

Each Member State shall draw up a list of the regulated markets for which it is the home Member State and shall forward that list to the other Member States and the Commission. A similar communication shall be effected in respect of each change to that list. The Commission shall publish a list of all regulated markets in the *Official Journal of the European Union* and update it at least once a year. The Commission shall also publish and update the list at its website, each time the Member States communicate changes to their lists.

Title IV
Competent Authorities

Chapter I
Designation, Powers and Redress Procedures

Article 48
Designation of competent authorities

1. Each Member State shall designate the competent authorities which are to carry out each of the duties provided for under the different

provisions of this Directive. Member States shall inform the Commission and the competent authorities of other Member States of the identity of the competent authorities responsible for enforcement of each of those duties, and of any division of those duties.

2. The competent authorities referred to in paragraph 1 shall be public authorities, without prejudice to the possibility of delegating tasks to other entities where that is expressly provided for in Articles 5(5), 16(3), 17(2) and 23(4).

Any delegation of tasks to entities other than the authorities referred to in paragraph 1 may not involve either the exercise of public authority or the use of discretionary powers of judgement. Member States shall require that, prior to delegation, competent authorities take all reasonable steps to ensure that the entity to which tasks are to be delegated has the capacity and resources to effectively execute all tasks and that the delegation takes place only if a clearly defined and documented framework for the exercise of any delegated tasks has been established stating the tasks to be undertaken and the conditions under which they are to be carried out. These conditions shall include a clause obliging the entity in question to act and be organised in such a manner as to avoid conflict of interest and so that information obtained from carrying out the delegated tasks is not used unfairly or to prevent competition. In any case, the final responsibility for supervising compliance with this Directive and with its implementing measures shall lie with the competent authority or authorities designated in accordance with paragraph 1.

Member States shall inform the Commission and the competent authorities of other Member States of any arrangements entered into with regard to delegation of tasks, including the precise conditions regulating such delegation.

3. The Commission shall publish a list of the competent authorities referred to in paragraphs 1 and 2 in the *Official Journal of the European Union* at least once a year and update it continuously on its website.

Article 49

Cooperation between authorities in the same Member State

If a Member State designates more than one competent authority to enforce a provision of this Directive, their respective roles shall be clearly defined and they shall cooperate closely.

Each Member State shall require that such cooperation also take place between the competent authorities for the purposes of this Directive and the competent authorities responsible in that Member State for the supervision of credit and other financial institutions, pension funds, UCITS, insurance and reinsurance intermediaries and insurance undertakings.

Member States shall require that competent authorities exchange any information which is essential or relevant to the exercise of their functions and duties.

Article 50

Powers to be made available to competent authorities

1. Competent authorities shall be given all supervisory and investigatory powers that are necessary for the exercise of their functions. Within the limits provided for in their national legal frameworks they shall exercise such powers:

(a) directly; or

(b) in collaboration with other authorities; or

(c) under their responsibility by delegation to entities to which tasks have been delegated according to Article 48(2); or

(d) by application to the competent judicial authorities.

2. The powers referred to in paragraph 1 shall be exercised in conformity with national law and shall include, at least, the rights to:

(a) have access to any document in any form whatsoever and to receive a copy of it;

(b) demand information from any person and if necessary to summon and question a person with a view to obtaining information;

(c) carry out on-site inspections;

(d) require existing telephone and existing data traffic records;

(e) require the cessation of any practice that is contrary to the provisions adopted in the implementation of this Directive;

(f) request the freezing and/or the sequestration of assets;

(g) request temporary prohibition of professional activity;

(h) require authorised investment firms and regulated markets' auditors to provide information;

(i) adopt any type of measure to ensure that investment firms and regulated markets continue to comply with legal requirements;

(j) require the suspension of trading in a financial instrument;

(k) require the removal of a financial instrument from trading, whether on a regulated market or under other trading arrangements;

(l) refer matters for criminal prosecution;

(m) allow auditors or experts to carry out verifications or investigations.

Article 51
Administrative sanctions

1. Without prejudice to the procedures for the withdrawal of authorisation or to the right of Member States to impose criminal sanctions, Member States shall ensure, in conformity with their national law, that the appropriate administrative measures can be taken or administrative sanctions be imposed against the persons responsible where the provisions adopted in the implementation of this Directive have not been complied with. Member States shall ensure that these measures are effective, proportionate and dissuasive.

2. Member States shall determine the sanctions to be applied for failure to cooperate in an investigation covered by Article 50.

3. Member States shall provide that the competent authority may disclose to the public any measure or sanction that will be imposed for infringement of the provisions adopted in the implementation of this Directive, unless such disclosure would seriously jeopardise the financial markets or cause disproportionate damage to the parties involved.

Article 52
Right of appeal

1. Member States shall ensure that any decision taken under laws, regulations or administrative provisions adopted in accordance with this Directive is properly reasoned and is subject to the right to apply to the courts. The right to apply to the courts shall also apply where, in respect of an application for authorisation which provides all the information required, no decision is taken within six months of its submission.

2. Member States shall provide that one or more of the following bodies, as determined by national law, may, in the interests of consumers and in accordance with national law, take action before the courts or competent administrative bodies to ensure that the national provisions for the implementation of this Directive are applied:

(a) public bodies or their representatives;

(b) consumer organisations having a legitimate interest in protecting consumers;

(c) professional organisations having a legitimate interest in acting to protect their members.

Article 53
Extra-judicial mechanism for investors' complaints

1. Member States shall encourage the setting-up of efficient and effective complaints and redress procedures for the out-of-court settlement of consumer disputes concerning the provision of investment and ancillary services provided by investment firms, using existing bodies where appropriate.

2. Member States shall ensure that those bodies are not prevented by legal or regulatory provisions from cooperating effectively in the resolution of cross-border disputes.

Article 54
Professional secrecy

1. Member States shall ensure that competent authorities, all persons who work or who have worked for the competent authorities or entities to whom tasks are delegated pursuant to Article 48(2), as well as auditors and experts instructed by the competent authorities, are bound by the obligation of professional secrecy. No confidential information which they may receive in the course of their duties may be divulged to any person or authority whatsoever, save in summary or aggregate form such that individual investment firms, market operators, regulated markets or any other person cannot be identified, without prejudice to cases covered by criminal law or the other provisions of this Directive.

2. Where an investment firm, market operator or regulated market has been declared bankrupt or is being compulsorily wound up, confidential information which does not concern third parties may be divulged in civil or commercial proceedings if necessary for carrying out the proceeding.

3. Without prejudice to cases covered by criminal law, the competent authorities, bodies or natural or legal persons other than competent authorities which receive confidential information pursuant to this Directive may use it only in the performance of their duties and for the exercise of their functions, in the case of the competent authorities, within the scope of this Directive or, in the case of other authorities, bodies or natural or legal persons, for the purpose for which such information was provided to them and/or in the context of administrative or judicial proceedings specifically related to the exercise of those functions. However, where the competent authority or other authority, body or person communicating information consents thereto, the authority receiving the information may use it for other purposes.

4. Any confidential information received, exchanged or transmitted pursuant to this Directive shall be subject to the conditions of professional secrecy laid down in this Article. Nevertheless, this Article shall not prevent the competent authorities from exchanging or transmitting confidential information in accordance with this Directive and with other Directives applicable to investment firms, credit institutions, pension funds, UCITS, insurance and reinsurance intermediaries, insurance undertakings regulated markets or market operators or otherwise with the consent of the competent authority or other authority or body or natural or legal person that communicated the information.

5. This Article shall not prevent the competent authorities from exchanging or transmitting in accordance with national law, confidential information that has not been received from a competent authority of another Member State.

Article 55
Relations with auditors

1. Member States shall provide, at least, that any person authorised within the meaning of Eighth Council Directive 84/253/EEC of 10 April 1984 on the approval of persons responsible for carrying out the statutory audits of accounting documents,[25] performing in an investment firm the task described in Article 51 of Fourth Council Directive 78/660/EEC of 25 July 1978 on the annual accounts of certain types of companies,[26] Article 37 of Directive 83/349/EEC or Article 31 of Directive 85/611/EEC or any other task prescribed by law, shall have a duty to report promptly to the competent authorities any fact or decision concerning that undertaking of which that person has become aware while carrying out that task and which is liable to:

(a) constitute a material breach of the laws, regulations or administrative provisions which lay down the conditions governing authorisation or which specifically govern pursuit of the activities of investment firms;

(b) affect the continuous functioning of the investment firm;

---

[25] OJ L 126, 12.5.1984, 20, reproduced supra under no. C. 7.
[26] OJ L 222, 14.8.1978, 11, reproduced supra under no. C. 4. Directive as last amended by Directive 2003/51/EC of the European Parliament and of the Council (OJ L 178, 17.7.2003, 16), reproduced supra under no. C. 23.

(c) lead to refusal to certify the accounts or to the expression of reservations.

That person shall also have a duty to report any facts and decisions of which the person becomes aware in the course of carrying out one of the tasks referred to in the first subparagraph in an undertaking having close links with the investment firm within which he is carrying out that task.

2. The disclosure in good faith to the competent authorities, by persons authorised within the meaning of Directive 84/253/EEC, of any fact or decision referred to in paragraph 1 shall not constitute a breach of any contractual or legal restriction on disclosure of information and shall not involve such persons in liability of any kind.

Chapter II
Cooperation Between Competent Authorities of Different Member States

Article 56

Obligation to cooperate

1. Competent authorities of different Member States shall cooperate with each other whenever necessary for the purpose of carrying out their duties under this Directive, making use of their powers whether set out in this Directive or in national law.

Competent authorities shall render assistance to competent authorities of the other Member States. In particular, they shall exchange information and cooperate in any investigation or supervisory activities.

In order to facilitate and accelerate cooperation, and more particularly exchange of information, Member States shall designate one single competent authority as a contact point for the purposes of this Directive. Member States shall communicate to the Commission and to the other Member States the names of the authorities which are designated to receive requests for exchange of information or cooperation pursuant to this paragraph.

2. When, taking into account the situation of the securities markets in the host Member State, the operations of a regulated market that has established arrangements in a host Member State have become of substantial importance for the functioning of the securities markets and the protection of the investors in that host Member State, the home and host competent authorities of the regulated market shall establish proportionate cooperation arrangements.

¶ *See article 16 of Commission Regulation 1287/2006/EC, reproduced infra under no. S. 33.*

3. Member States shall take the necessary administrative and organisational measures to facilitate the assistance provided for in paragraph 1.

Competent authorities may use their powers for the purpose of cooperation, even in cases where the conduct under investigation does not constitute an infringement of any regulation in force in that Member State.

4. Where a competent authority has good reasons to suspect that acts contrary to the provisions of this Directive, carried out by entities not subject to its supervision, are being or have been carried out on the territory of another Member State, it shall notify this in as specific a manner as possible to the competent authority of the other Member State. The latter authority shall take appropriate action. It shall inform the notifying competent authority of the outcome of the action and, to the extent possible, of significant interim developments. This paragraph shall be without prejudice to the competences of the competent authority that has forwarded the information.

5. In order to ensure the uniform application of paragraph 2 the Commission may adopt, in accordance with the procedure referred to in Article 64(2), implementing measures to establish the criteria under which the operations of a regulated market in a host Member State could be considered as of substantial importance for the functioning of the securities markets and the protection of the investors in that host Member State.

Article 57

Cooperation in supervisory activities, on-the-spot verifications or in investigations

A competent authority of one Member State may request the cooperation of the competent authority of another Member State in a supervisory activity or for an on-the-spot verification or in an investigation. In the case of investment firms that are remote members of a regulated market the competent authority of the regulated market may choose to address them directly, in which case it shall inform the competent authority of the home Member State of the remote member accordingly.

Where a competent authority receives a request with respect to an on-the-spot verification or an investigation, it shall, within the framework of its powers:

(a) carry out the verifications or investigations itself; or

(b) allow the requesting authority to carry out the verification or investigation; or

(c) allow auditors or experts to carry out the verification or investigation.

Article 58

Exchange of information

1. Competent authorities of Member States having been designated as contact points for the purposes of this Directive in accordance with Article 56(1) shall immediately supply one another with the information required for the purposes of carrying out the duties of the competent authorities, designated in accordance to Article 48(1), set out in the provisions adopted pursuant to this Directive.

Competent authorities exchanging information with other competent authorities under this Directive may indicate at the time of communication that such information must not be disclosed without their express agreement, in which case such information may be exchanged solely for the purposes for which those authorities gave their agreement.

¶ *See article 15 of Commission Regulation 1287/2006/EC, reproduced infra under no. S. 33.*

2. The competent authority having been designated as the contact point may transmit the information received under paragraph 1 and Articles 55 and 63 to the authorities referred to in Article 49. They shall not transmit it to other bodies or natural or legal persons without the express agreement of the competent authorities which disclosed it and solely for the purposes for which those authorities gave their agreement, except in duly justified circumstances. In this last case, the contact point shall immediately inform the contact point that sent the information.

3. Authorities as referred to in Article 49 as well as other bodies or natural and legal persons receiving confidential information under paragraph 1 of this Article or under Articles 55 and 63 may use it only in the course of their duties, in particular:

(a) to check that the conditions governing the taking-up of the business of investment firms are met and to facilitate the monitoring, on a non-consolidated or consolidated basis, of the conduct of that business, especially with regard to the capital adequacy requirements imposed by Directive 93/6/EEC, administrative and accounting procedures and internal-control mechanisms;

(b) to monitor the proper functioning of trading venues;

(c) to impose sanctions;

(d) in administrative appeals against decisions by the competent authorities;

(e) in court proceedings initiated under Article 52; or

(f) in the extra-judicial mechanism for investors' complaints provided for in Article 53.

4. The Commission may adopt, in accordance with the procedure referred to in Article 64(2), implementing measures concerning procedures for the exchange of information between competent authorities.

5. Articles 54, 58 and 63 shall not prevent a competent authority from transmitting to central banks, the European System of Central Banks and the European Central Bank, in their capacity as monetary authorities, and, where appropriate, to other public authorities responsible for overseeing payment and settlement systems, confidential

information intended for the performance of their tasks; likewise such authorities or bodies shall not be prevented from communicating to the competent authorities such information as they may need for the purpose of performing their functions provided for in this Directive.

Article 59
Refusal to cooperate

A competent authority may refuse to act on a request for cooperation in carrying out an investigation, on-the-spot verification or supervisory activity as provided for in Article 57 or to exchange information as provided for in Article 58 only where:

(a) such an investigation, on-the-spot verification, supervisory activity or exchange of information might adversely affect the sovereignty, security or public policy of the State addressed;

(b) judicial proceedings have already been initiated in respect of the same actions and the same persons before the authorities of the Member State addressed;

(c) final judgment has already been delivered in the Member State addressed in respect of the same persons and the same actions.

In the case of such a refusal, the competent authority shall notify the requesting competent authority accordingly, providing as detailed information as possible.

Article 60
Inter-authority consultation prior to authorisation

1. The competent authorities of the other Member State involved shall be consulted prior to granting authorisation to an investment firm which is:

(a) a subsidiary of an investment firm or credit institution authorised in another Member State; or

(b) a subsidiary of the parent undertaking of an investment firm or credit institution authorised in another Member State; or

(c) controlled by the same natural or legal persons as control an investment firm or credit institution authorised in another Member State.

2. The competent authority of the Member State responsible for the supervision of credit institutions or insurance undertaking shall be consulted prior to granting an authorisation to an investment firm which is:

(a) a subsidiary of a credit institution or insurance undertaking authorised in the Community; or

(b) a subsidiary of the parent undertaking of a credit institution or insurance undertaking authorised in the Community; or

(c) controlled by the same person, whether natural or legal, who controls a credit institution or insurance undertaking authorised in the Community.

3. The relevant competent authorities referred to in paragraphs 1 and 2 shall in particular consult each other when assessing the suitability of the shareholders or members and the reputation and experience of persons who effectively direct the business involved in the management of another entity of the same group. They shall exchange all information regarding the suitability of shareholders or members and the reputation and experience of persons who effectively direct the business that is of relevance to the other competent authorities involved, for the granting of an authorisation as well as for the ongoing assessment of compliance with operating conditions.

Article 61
Powers for host Member States

1. Host Member States may, for statistical purposes, require all investment firms with branches within their territories to report to them periodically on the activities of those branches.

2. In discharging their responsibilities under this Directive, host Member States may require branches of investment firms to provide the information necessary for the monitoring of their compliance with the standards set by the host Member State that apply to them for the cases provided for in Article 32(7). Those requirements may not be more stringent than those which the same Member State imposes on established firms

Article 62
Precautionary measures to be taken by host Member States

1. Where the competent authority of the host Member State has clear and demonstrable grounds for believing that an investment firm acting within its territory under the freedom to provide services is in breach of the obligations arising from the provisions adopted pursuant to this Directive or that an investment firm that has a branch within its territory is in breach of the obligations arising from the provisions adopted pursuant to this Directive which do not confer powers on the competent authority of the host Member State, it shall refer those findings to the competent authority of the home Member State.

If, despite the measures taken by the competent authority of the home Member State or because such measures prove inadequate, the investment firm persists in acting in a manner that is clearly prejudicial to the interests of host Member State investors or the orderly functioning of markets, the competent authority of the host Member State, after informing the competent authority of the home Member State shall take all the appropriate measures needed in order to protect investors and the proper functioning of the markets. This shall include the possibility of preventing offending investment firms from initiating any further transactions within their territories. The Commission shall be informed of such measures without delay.

2. Where the competent authorities of a host Member State ascertain that an investment firm that has a branch within its territory is in breach of the legal or regulatory provisions adopted in that State pursuant to those provisions of this Directive which confer powers on the host Member State's competent authorities, those authorities shall require the investment firm concerned to put an end to its irregular situation.

If the investment firm concerned fails to take the necessary steps, the competent authorities of the host Member State shall take all appropriate measures to ensure that the investment firm concerned puts an end to its irregular situation. The nature of those measures shall be communicated to the competent authorities of the home Member State.

If, despite the measures taken by the host Member State, the investment firm persists in breaching the legal or regulatory provisions referred to in the first subparagraph in force in the host Member State, the latter may, after informing the competent authorities of the home Member State, take appropriate measures to prevent or to penalise further irregularities and, in so far as necessary, to prevent that investment firm from initiating any further transactions within its territory. The Commission shall be informed of such measures without delay.

3. Where the competent authority of the host Member State of a regulated market or an MTF has clear and demonstrable grounds for believing that such regulated market or MTF is in breach of the obligations arising from the provisions adopted pursuant to this Directive, it shall refer those findings to the competent authority of the home Member State of the regulated market or the MTF.

If, despite the measures taken by the competent authority of the home Member State or because such measures prove inadequate, the said regulated market or the MTF persists in acting in a manner that is clearly prejudicial to the interests of host Member State investors or the orderly functioning of markets, the competent authority of the host Member State, after informing the competent authority of the home Member State, shall take all the appropriate measures needed in order to protect investors and the proper functioning of the markets. This shall include the possibility of preventing the said regulated market or the MTF from making their arrangements available to remote members or participants established in the host Member State. The Commission shall be informed of such measures without delay.

4. Any measure adopted pursuant to paragraphs 1, 2 or 3 involving sanctions or restrictions on the

activities of an investment firm or of a regulated market shall be properly justified and communicated to the investment firm or to the regulated market concerned.

Chapter III
Cooperation with Third Countries

Article 63
Exchange of information with third countries

1. Member States may conclude cooperation agreements providing for the exchange of information with the competent authorities of third countries only if the information disclosed is subject to guarantees of professional secrecy at least equivalent to those required under Article 54. Such exchange of information must be intended for the performance of the tasks of those competent authorities.

Member States may transfer personal data to a third country in accordance to Chapter IV of Directive 95/46/EC.

Member States may also conclude cooperation agreements providing for the exchange of information with third country authorities, bodies and natural or legal persons responsible for:
  (i) the supervision of credit institutions, other financial organisations, insurance undertakings and the supervision of financial markets;
  (ii) the liquidation and bankruptcy of investment firms and other similar procedures;
  (iii) carrying out statutory audits of the accounts of investment firms and other financial institutions, credit institutions and insurance undertakings, in the performance of their supervisory functions, or which administer compensation schemes, in the performance of their functions;
  (iv) overseeing the bodies involved in the liquidation and bankruptcy of investment firms and other similar procedures;
  (v) overseeing persons charged with carrying out statutory audits of the accounts of insurance undertakings, credit institutions, investment firms and other financial institutions,

only if the information disclosed is subject to guarantees of professional secrecy at least equivalent to those required under Article 54. Such exchange of information must be intended for the performance of the tasks of those authorities or bodies or natural or legal persons.

2. Where the information originates in another Member State, it may not be disclosed without the express agreement of the competent authorities which have transmitted it and, where appropriate, solely for the purposes for which those authorities gave their agreement. The same provision applies to information provided by third country competent authorities.

Title V
Final Provisions

Article 64
Committee procedure

1. The Commission shall be assisted by the European Securities Committee established by Commission Decision 2001/528/EC[27] (hereinafter referred to as 'the Committee').

2. Where reference is made to this paragraph, Articles 5 and 7 of Decision 1999/468/EC shall apply, having regard to the provisions of Article 8 thereof, provided that the implementing measures adopted in accordance with that procedure do not modify the essential provisions of this Directive.

The period laid down in Article 5(6) of Decision 1999/468/EC shall be set at three months.

[2a. None of the implementing measures enacted may change the essential provisions of this Directive.]

[3. Without prejudice to the implementing measures already adopted, on 1 April 2008 at the latest, the application of this Directive's provisions requiring the adoption of technical rules, amendments and decisions in accordance with paragraph 2 shall be suspended. Acting on a

---

[27] OJ L 191, 13.7.2001, 45, reproduced supra under no. S. 20.

proposal from the Commission, the European Parliament and the Council may renew the provisions concerned in accordance with the procedure laid down in Article 251 of the Treaty and, to that end, they shall review them prior to the date referred to above.]

¶ *Paragraph 2a has been inserted and paragraph 3 has been replaced by article 1(2) of Directive 2006/31/EC, reproduced infra under no. S. 32.*

[*Article 65*
Reports and review

1. By 31 October 2007, the Commission shall, on the basis of public consultation and in the light of discussions with competent authorities, report to the European Parliament and to the Council on the possible extension of the scope of the provisions of this Directive concerning pre- and post-trade transparency obligations to transactions in classes of financial instruments other than shares.

2. By 31 October 2008, the Commission shall present the European Parliament and the Council with a report on the application of Article 27.

3. By 30 April 2008, the Commission shall, on the basis of public consultations and in the light of discussions with competent authorities, report to the European Parliament and to the Council on:

(a) the continued appropriateness of the exemption provided for in Article 2(1)(k) for undertakings whose main business is dealing on own account in commodity derivatives;

(b) the content and form of proportionate requirements for the authorisation and supervision of such undertakings as investment firms within the meaning of this Directive;

(c) the appropriateness of rules concerning the appointment of tied agents in performing investment services and/or activities, in particular with respect to the supervision of them;

(d) the continued appropriateness of the exemption provided for in Article 2(1)(i).

4. By 30 April 2008, the Commission shall present the European Parliament and the Council with a report on the state of the removal of the obstacles which may prevent the consolidation at European level of the information that trading venues are required to publish.

5. On the basis of the reports referred to in paragraphs 1 to 4, the Commission may submit proposals for related amendments to this Directive.

6. By 31 October 2006, the Commission shall, in the light of discussions with competent authorities, report to the European Parliament and to the Council on the continued appropriateness of the requirements for professional indemnity insurance imposed on intermediaries under Community law.]

¶ *Article 65 has been replaced by article 1(3) of Directive 2006/31/EC, reproduced infra under no. S. 32.*

Article 66
Amendment of Directive 85/611/EEC

[. . .]

¶ *This article modifies article 5, paragraph 4 of Directive 85/611/EEC, reproduced supra under no. S. 6. The modifications are directly incorporated therein.*

Article 67
Amendment of Directive 93/6/EEC

[. . .]

¶ *This article modifies articles 2(2) and 3(4) and inserts paragraphs 4(a) and 4(b) to article 3 of Directive 93/6/EEC, reproduced supra under no. B. 20. This Directive has been repealed as from 20 July 2006 by article 52 of Directive 2006/49/EC (OJ L 177, 30.6.2006, 201), reproduced supra under no. B. 42.*

Correlation Table

Directive 2004/39/EC	Directive 2006/49/EC
Article 67(1)	Article 3(1)(b)
Article 67(2)	Article 6
Article 67(3)	Article 7
Article 67(3)	Article 8

Article 68
Amendment of Directive 2000/12/EC

[. . .]

¶ *This article modifies Annex I of Directive 2000/12/EC, reproduced supra under no. B. 32. Directive 2000/12/EC has been repealed as from 20 July 2007 by article 58 of Directive 2006/48/EC (OJ L 177, 30.6.2006, 1), reproduced supra under no. B. 41.*

Correlation Table

Directive 2004/39/EC	Directive 2006/48/EC
Article 68	Annex I, final paragraph

[*Article 69*

Repeal of Directive 93/22/EEC

Directive 93/22/EEC shall be repealed with effect from 1 November 2007. References to Directive 93/22/EEC shall be construed as references to this Directive. References to terms defined in, or Articles of, Directive 93/22/EEC shall be construed as references to the equivalent term defined in, or Article of, this Directive.]

¶ *Article 69 has been replaced by article 1(4) of Directive 2006/31/EC, reproduced infra under no. S. 32.*

Article 70

Transposition

[Member States shall adopt the laws, regulations and administrative provisions necessary to comply with this Directive by 31 January 2007. They shall forthwith inform the Commission thereof.

They shall apply these measures from 1 November 2007.]

When Member States adopt these measures, they shall contain a reference to this Directive or shall be accompanied by such reference on the occasion of their official publication. The methods of making such reference shall be laid down by the Member States.

¶ *The first paragraph of article 70 has been replaced by article 1(5) of Directive 2006/31/EC, reproduced infra under no. S. 32.*

Article 71

Transitional provisions

[1. Investment firms already authorised in their home Member State to provide investment services before 1 November 2007 shall be deemed to be so authorised for the purposes of this Directive if the laws of that Member State provide that to take up such activities they must comply with conditions comparable to those provided for in Articles 9 to 14.

2. A regulated market or a market operator already authorised in its home Member State before 1 November 2007 shall be deemed to be so authorised for the purposes of this Directive if the laws of that Member State provide that the regulated market or market operator, as the case may be, must comply with conditions comparable to those provided for in Title III.

3. Tied agents already entered in a public register before 1 November 2007 shall be deemed to be so registered for the purposes of this Directive if the laws of Member States concerned provide that tied agents must comply with conditions comparable to those provided for in Article 23.

4. Information communicated before 1 November 2007 for the purposes of Articles 17, 18 or 30 of Directive 93/22/EEC shall be deemed to have been communicated for the purposes of Articles 31 and 32 of this Directive.

5. Any existing system falling under the definition of an MTF operated by a market operator of a regulated market shall, at the request of the market operator of the regulated market, be authorised as an MTF, provided that it complies with rules equivalent to those required by this Directive for the authorisation and operation of MTFs and that the request concerned is made within eighteen months following 1 November 2007.]

6. Investment firms shall be authorised to continue considering existing professional clients as such provided that this categorisation has been granted by the investment firm on the basis of an adequate assessment of the expertise, experience and knowledge of the client which gives reasonable assurance, in light of the nature of the transactions or services envisaged, that the client is capable of making his own investment decisions and understands the risks involved. Those investment firms shall inform their clients about the conditions established in the Directive for the categorisation of clients.

¶ *Paragraphs 1 to 5 have been replaced by article 1(6) of Directive 2006/31/EC, reproduced infra under no. S. 32.*

Article 72
Entry into force

This Directive shall enter into force on the day of its publication in the *Official Journal of the European Union*.

Article 73
Addressees

This Directive is addressed to the Member States.

Annex I

List of Services and Activities and Financial Instruments

SECTION A

INVESTMENT SERVICES AND ACTIVITIES

(1) Reception and transmission of orders in relation to one or more financial instruments.

(2) Execution of orders on behalf of clients.

(3) Dealing on own account.

(4) Portfolio management.

(5) Investment advice.

(6) Underwriting of financial instruments and/or placing of financial instruments on a firm commitment basis.

(7) Placing of financial instruments without a firm commitment basis.

(8) Operation of Multilateral Trading Facilities.

SECTION B

ANCILLARY SERVICES

(1) Safekeeping and administration of financial instruments for the account of clients, including custodianship and related services such as cash/collateral management;

(2) Granting credits or loans to an investor to allow him to carry out a transaction in one or more financial instruments, where the firm granting the credit or loan is involved in the transaction;

(3) Advice to undertakings on capital structure, industrial strategy and related matters and advice and services relating to mergers and the purchase of undertakings;

CASE

Case C-356/00 Antonio Testa and Lido Lazzeri v Commissione Nazionale per la Società e la Borsa (Consob) [2002] ECR I-10797

Point [4] of Section A of the Annex to Council Directive 93/22/EEC of 10 May 1993 on investment services in the securities field, which defines managing portfolios of investments, precludes national legislation which departs from that definition by not requiring, for the purposes of the implementation of that directive, that the management of portfolios of investments should be 'on a discriminatory, client-by-client basis' and 'in accordance with mandates given by investors'. However, there is nothing to prevent a Member State from extending by national legislation the applicability of the provisions of that directive to operations not covered by it, provided that it is made clear that the national legislation in question does not constitute the transposition of the directive, but arises from the independent will of the legislature.

---

(4) Foreign exchange services where these are connected to the provision of investment services;

(5) Investment research and financial analysis or other forms of general recommendation relating to transactions in financial instruments;

(6) Services related to underwriting;

(7) Investment services and activities as well as ancillary services of the type included under Section A or B of Annex 1 related to the underlying of the derivatives included under Section C—5, 6, 7 and 10—where these are

connected to the provision of investment or ancillary services.

Section C
Financial Instruments

(1) Transferable securities;

(2) Money-market instruments;

(3) Units in collective investment undertakings;

(4) Options, futures, swaps, forward rate agreements and any other derivative contracts relating to securities, currencies, interest rates or yields, or other derivatives instruments, financial indices or financial measures which may be settled physically or in cash;

(5) Options, futures, swaps, forward rate agreements and any other derivative contracts relating to commodities that must be settled in cash or may be settled in cash at the option of one of the parties (otherwise than by reason of a default or other termination event);

(6) Options, futures, swaps, and any other derivative contract relating to commodities that can be physically settled provided that they are traded on a regulated market and/or an MTF;

(7) Options, futures, swaps, forwards and any other derivative contracts relating to commodities, that can be physically settled not otherwise mentioned in C.6 and not being for commercial purposes, which have the characteristics of other derivative financial instruments, having regard to whether, inter alia, they are cleared and settled through recognised clearing houses or are subject to regular margin calls;

(8) Derivative instruments for the transfer of credit risk;

(9) Financial contracts for differences;

(10) Options, futures, swaps, forward rate agreements and any other derivative contracts relating to climatic variables, freight rates, emission allowances or inflation rates or other official economic statistics that must be settled in cash or may be settled in cash at the option of one of the parties (otherwise than by reason of a default or other termination event), as well as any other derivative contracts relating to assets, rights, obligations, indices and measures not otherwise mentioned in this Section, which have the characteristics of other derivative financial instruments, having regard to whether, inter alia, they are traded on a regulated market or an MTF, are cleared and settled through recognised clearing houses or are subject to regular margin calls.

Annex II
Professional Clients for the Purpose of this Directive

Professional client is a client who possesses the experience, knowledge and expertise to make its own investment decisions and properly assess the risks that it incurs. In order to be considered a professional client, the client must comply with the following criteria:

I. Categories of Client Who are Considered to be Professionals

The following should all be regarded as professionals in all investment services and activities and financial instruments for the purposes of the Directive.

(1) Entities which are required to be authorised or regulated to operate in the financial markets. The list below should be understood as including all authorised entities carrying out the characteristic activities of the entities mentioned: entities authorised by a Member State under a Directive, entities authorised or regulated by a Member State without reference to a Directive, and entities authorised or regulated by a non-Member State:

(a) Credit institutions

(b) Investment firms

(c) Other authorised or regulated financial institutions

(d) Insurance companies

(e) Collective investment schemes and management companies of such schemes

(f) Pension funds and management companies of such funds

(g) Commodity and commodity derivatives dealers

(h) Locals

(i) Other institutional investors

(2) Large undertakings meeting two of the following size requirements on a company basis:
– balance sheet total: EUR 20 000 000,
– net turnover: EUR 40 000 000,
– own funds: EUR 2 000 000.

(3) National and regional governments, public bodies that manage public debt, Central Banks, international and supranational institutions such as the World Bank, the IMF, the ECB, the EIB and other similar international organisations.

(4) Other institutional investors whose main activity is to invest in financial instruments, including entities dedicated to the securitisation of assets or other financing transactions.

The entities mentioned above are considered to be professionals. They must however be allowed to request non-professional treatment and investment firms may agree to provide a higher level of protection. Where the client of an investment firm is an undertaking referred to above, the investment firm must inform it prior to any provision of services that, on the basis of the information available to the firm, the client is deemed to be a professional client, and will be treated as such unless the firm and the client agree otherwise. The firm must also inform the customer that he can request a variation of the terms of the agreement in order to secure a higher degree of protection.

It is the responsibility of the client, considered to be a professional client, to ask for a higher level of protection when it deems it is unable to properly assess or manage the risks involved.

This higher level of protection will be provided when a client who is considered to be a professional enters into a written agreement with the investment firm to the effect that it shall not be treated as a professional for the purposes of the applicable conduct of business regime. Such agreement should specify whether this applies to one or more particular services or transactions, or to one or more types of product or transaction.

II. Clients Who May be Treated as Professionals on Request

II.1. Identification criteria

Clients other than those mentioned in section I, including public sector bodies and private individual investors, may also be allowed to waive some of the protections afforded by the conduct of business rules.

Investment firms should therefore be allowed to treat any of the above clients as professionals provided the relevant criteria and procedure mentioned below are fulfilled. These clients should not, however, be presumed to possess market knowledge and experience comparable to that of the categories listed in section I.

Any such waiver of the protection afforded by the standard conduct of business regime shall be considered valid only if an adequate assessment of the expertise, experience and knowledge of the client, undertaken by the investment firm, gives reasonable assurance, in light of the nature of the transactions or services envisaged, that the client is capable of making his own investment decisions and understanding the risks involved.

The fitness test applied to managers and directors of entities licensed under Directives in the financial field could be regarded as an example of the assessment of expertise and knowledge. In the case of small entities, the person subject to the above assessment should be the person authorised to carry out transactions on behalf of the entity.

In the course of the above assessment, as a minimum, two of the following criteria should be satisfied:
– the client has carried out transactions, in significant size, on the relevant market at an

average frequency of 10 per quarter over the previous four quarters,
- the size of the client's financial instrument portfolio, defined as including cash deposits and financial instruments exceeds EUR 500 000,
- the client works or has worked in the financial sector for at least one year in a professional position, which requires knowledge of the transactions or services envisaged.

II.2. Procedure

The clients defined above may waive the benefit of the detailed rules of conduct only where the following procedure is followed:
- they must state in writing to the investment firm that they wish to be treated as a professional client, either generally or in respect of a particular investment service or transaction, or type of transaction or product,
- the investment firm must give them a clear written warning of the protections and investor compensation rights they may lose,
- they must state in writing, in a separate document from the contract, that they are aware of the consequences of losing such protections.

Before deciding to accept any request for waiver, investment firms must be required to take all reasonable steps to ensure that the client requesting to be treated as a professional client meets the relevant requirements stated in Section II.1 above.

However, if clients have already been categorised as professionals under parameters and procedures similar to those above, it is not intended that their relationships with investment firms should be affected by any new rules adopted pursuant to this Annex.

Firms must implement appropriate written internal policies and procedures to categorise clients. Professional clients are responsible for keeping the firm informed about any change, which could affect their current categorisation. Should the investment firm become aware however that the client no longer fulfils the initial conditions, which made him eligible for a professional treatment, the investment firm must take appropriate action.

S. 30.

Commission Directive 2004/72/EC
of 29 April 2004
implementing Directive 2003/6/EC of the European Parliament and of the Council as regards accepted market practices, the definition of inside information in relation to derivatives on commodities, the drawing up of lists of insiders, the notification of managers' transactions and the notification of suspicious transactions[1]

(Text with EEA relevance)

THE COMMISSION OF THE EUROPEAN COMMUNITIES,

Having regard to the Treaty establishing the European Community,

Having regard to Directive 2003/6/EC of the European Parliament and of the Council of 28 January 2003 on insider dealing and market manipulation (market abuse),[2] and in particular the second paragraph of point 1 and point 2(a) of Article 1 and the fourth, fifth and seventh indents of Article 6(10) thereof,

After consulting the Committee of European Securities Regulators (CESR)[3] for technical advice,

Whereas:

(1) Practising fairness and efficiency by market participants is required in order not to create prejudice to normal market activity and market integrity. In particular, market practices inhibiting the interaction of supply and demand by limiting the opportunities for other market participants to respond to transactions can create higher risks for market integrity and are, therefore, less likely to be accepted by competent authorities. On the other hand, market practices which enhance liquidity are more likely to be accepted than those practices reducing them. Market practices breaching rules and regulations designed to prevent market abuse, or codes of conduct, are less likely to be accepted by competent authorities. Since market practices change rapidly in order to meet investors' needs, competent authorities need to be alert to new and emerging market practice.

(2) Transparency of market practices by market participants is crucial for considering whether a particular market practice can be accepted by competent authorities. The less transparent a practice is, the more likely it is not to be accepted. However, practices on non regulated markets might for structural reasons be less transparent than similar practices on regulated markets. Such practices should not be in themselves considered as unacceptable by competent authorities.

(3) Particular market practices in a given market should not put at risk market integrity of other, directly or indirectly, related markets throughout the Community, whether those markets be regulated or not. Therefore, the higher the risk for market integrity on such a related market within the Community, the less those practices are likely to be accepted by competent authorities.

(4) Competent authorities, while considering the acceptance of a particular market practice, should consult other competent authorities, particularly for cases where there exist comparable markets to the one under scrutiny. However, there might be circumstances in which a market practice can be deemed to be acceptable on one

---

[1] OJ L 162, 30.4.2004, 70–75.
[2] OJ L 96, 12.4.2003, 16, reproduced supra under no. S. 24.
[3] CESR was established by Commission Decision 2001/527/EC of 6 June 2001 (OJ L 191, 13.7.2001, 34), reproduced supra under no. S. 19.

particular market and unacceptable on another comparable market within the Community. In case of discrepancies between market practices which are accepted in one Member State and not in another one, discussion could take place in the Committee of European Securities Regulators in order to find a solution. With regard to their decisions about such acceptance, competent authorities should ensure a high degree of consultation and transparency vis-à-vis market participants and end-users.

(5) It is essential for market participants on derivative markets the underlying of which is not a financial instrument, to get greater legal certainty on what constitutes inside information.

(6) The establishment, by issuers or persons acting on their behalf or for their account, of lists of persons working for them under a contract of employment or otherwise and having access to inside information relating, directly or indirectly, to the issuer, is a valuable measure for protecting market integrity. These lists may serve issuers or such persons to control the flow of such inside information and thereby manage their confidentiality duties. Moreover, these lists may also constitute a useful tool for competent authorities when monitoring the application of market abuse legislation. Identifying inside information to which any insider has access and the date on which it gained access thereto is necessary for issuers and competent authorities. Access to inside information relating, directly or indirectly, to the issuer by persons included on such a list is without prejudice to their duty to refrain from insider dealing on the basis of any inside information as defined in Directive 2003/6/EC.

(7) The notification of transactions conducted by persons discharging managerial responsibilities within an issuer on their own account, or by persons closely associated with them, is not only a valuable information for market participants, but also constitutes an additional means for competent authorities to supervise markets. The obligation by senior executives to notify transactions is without prejudice to their duty to refrain from insider dealing on the basis of any inside information as defined in Directive 2003/6/EC.

(8) Notification of transactions should be in accordance with the rules on transfer of personal data laid down in Directive 95/46/EC[4] of the European Parliament and of the Council of 24 October 1995 on the protection of individuals with regard to the processing of personal data and on the movement of such data.

(9) Notification of suspicious transactions by persons professionally arranging transactions in financial instruments to the competent authority requires sufficient indications that the transactions might constitute market abuse, i.e. transactions which give reasonable ground for suspecting that insider dealing or market manipulation is involved. Certain transactions by themselves may seem completely void of anything suspicious, but might deliver such indications of possible market abuse, when seen in perspective with other transactions, certain behaviour or other information.

(10) This Directive respects the fundamental rights and observes the principles recognised in particular by the Charter of Fundamental Rights of the European Union and in particular by Article 8 of the European Convention on Human Rights.

(11) The measures provided for in this Directive are in accordance with the opinion of the European Securities Committee,

HAS ADOPTED THIS DIRECTIVE:

Article 1

Definitions

For the purpose of applying Article 6(10) of Directive 2003/6/EC:

1. 'Person discharging managerial responsibilities within an issuer' shall mean a person who is

(a) a member of the administrative, management or supervisory bodies of the issuer:

(b) a senior executive, who is not a member of the bodies as referred to in point (a), having regular access to inside information relating, directly or indirectly, to the issuer, and the power to make

---

[4] OJ L 281, 23.11.1995, 31.

managerial decisions affecting the future developments and business prospects of this issuer.

2. 'Person closely associated with a person discharging managerial responsibilities within an issuer of financial instruments' shall mean:

(a) the spouse of the person discharging managerial responsibilities, or any partner of that person considered by national law as equivalent to the spouse;

(b) according to national law, dependent children of the person discharging managerial responsibilities;

(c) other relatives of the person discharging managerial responsibilities, who have shared the same household as that person for at least one year on the date of the transaction concerned;

(d) any legal person, trust or partnership, whose managerial responsibilities are discharged by a person referred to in point 1 of this Article or in letters (a), (b) and (c) of this point, or which is directly or indirectly controlled by such a person, or that is set up for the benefit of such a person, or whose economic interests are substantially equivalent to those of such person.

3. 'Person professionally arranging transactions' shall mean at least an investment firm or a credit institution.

4. 'Investment firm' shall mean any person as defined in Article 1(2) of Council Directive 93/22/EEC.[5]

5. 'Credit institution' shall mean any person as defined in Article 1(1) of Directive 2000/12/EC of the European Parliament and of the Council.[6]

6. 'Competent authority' shall mean the competent authority as defined in Article 1(7) of Directive 2003/6/EC.

Article 2

Factors to be taken into account when considering market practices

1. For the purposes of applying paragraph 2 of point 1 and point 2(a) of Article 1 of Directive 2003/6/EC, Member States shall ensure that the following non exhaustive factors are taken into account by competent authorities, without prejudice to collaboration with other authorities, when assessing whether they can accept a particular market practice:

(a) the level of transparency of the relevant market practice to the whole market;

(b) the need to safeguard the operation of market forces and the proper interplay of the forces of supply and demand;

(c) the degree to which the relevant market practice has an impact on market liquidity and efficiency;

(d) the degree to which the relevant practice takes into account the trading mechanism of the relevant market and enables market participants to react properly and in a timely manner to the new market situation created by that practice;

(e) the risk inherent in the relevant practice for the integrity of, directly or indirectly, related markets, whether regulated or not, in the relevant financial instrument within the whole Community;

(f) the outcome of any investigation of the relevant market practice by any competent authority or other authority mentioned in Article 12(1) of Directive 2003/6/EC, in particular whether the relevant market practice breached rules or regulations designed to prevent market abuse, or codes of conduct, be it on the market in question or on directly or indirectly related markets within the Community;

(g) the structural characteristics of the relevant market including whether it is regulated or not, the types of financial instruments traded and the type of market participants, including the extent of retail investors participation in the relevant market.

Member States shall ensure that competent authorities shall, when considering the need for safeguard referred to in point (b) of the first subparagraph, in particular analyse the impact of the relevant market practice against the main market parameters, such as the specific market conditions before carrying out the relevant market

---

[5] OJ L 141, 11.6.1993, 27, reproduced supra under no. S. 14.
[6] OJ L 126, 26.5.2000, 1, reproduced supra under no. B. 32.

practice, the weighted average price of a single session or the daily closing price.

2. Member States shall ensure that practices, in particular new or emerging market practices are not assumed to be unacceptable by the competent authority simply because they have not been previously accepted by it.

3. Member States shall ensure that competent authorities review regularly the market practices they have accepted, in particular taking into account significant changes to the relevant market environment, such as changes to trading rules or to market infrastructure.

Article 3

Consultation procedures and disclosure of decisions

1. For the purposes of applying paragraph 2 of point 1 and point 2(a) of Article 1 of Directive 2003/6/EC, Member States shall ensure that the procedures set out in paragraphs 2 and 3 of this Article are observed by competent authorities when considering whether to accept or continue to accept a particular market practice.

2. Without prejudice to Article 11(2) of Directive 2003/6/EC, Member States shall ensure that competent authorities, before accepting or not the market practice concerned, consult as appropriate relevant bodies such as representatives of issuers, financial services providers, consumers, other authorities and market operators.

The consultation procedure shall include consultation of other competent authorities, in particular where there exist comparable markets, i.e. in structures, volume, type of transactions.

3. Member States shall ensure that competent authorities publicly disclose their decisions regarding the acceptability of the market practice concerned, including appropriate descriptions of such practices. Member States shall further ensure that competent authorities transmit their decisions as soon as possible to the Committee of European Securities Regulators which shall make them immediately available on its website.

The disclosure shall include a description of the factors taken into account in determining whether the relevant practice is regarded as acceptable, in particular where different conclusions have been reached regarding the acceptability of the same practice on different Member States markets.

4. When investigatory actions on specific cases have already started, the consultation procedures set out in paragraphs 1 to 3 may be delayed until the end of such investigation and possible related sanctions.

5. A market practice which was accepted following the consultation procedures set out in paragraphs 1 to 3 shall not be changed without using the same consultation procedures.

Article 4

Inside information in relation to derivatives on commodities

For the purposes of applying the second paragraph of point 1 of Article 1 of Directive 2003/6/EC, users of markets on which derivatives on commodities are traded, are deemed to expect to receive information relating, directly or indirectly, to one or more such derivatives which is:

(a) routinely made available to the users of those markets, or

(b) required to be disclosed in accordance with legal or regulatory provisions, market rules, contracts or customs on the relevant underlying commodity market or commodity derivatives market.

Article 5

Lists of insiders

1. For the purposes of applying the third subparagraph of Article 6(3) of Directive 2003/6/EC, Member States shall ensure that lists of insiders include all persons covered by that Article who have access to inside information relating, directly or indirectly, to the issuer, whether on a regular or occasional basis.

2. Lists of insiders shall state at least:

(a) the identity of any person having access to inside information;

(b) the reason why any such person is on the list;

(c) the date at which the list of insiders was created and updated.

3. Lists of insiders shall be promptly updated

(a) whenever there is a change in the reason why any person is already on the list;

(b) whenever any new person has to be added to the list;

(c) by mentioning whether and when any person already on the list has no longer access to inside information.

4. Member States shall ensure that lists of insiders will be kept for at least five years after being drawn up or updated.

5. Member States shall ensure that the persons required to draw up lists of insiders take the necessary measures to ensure that any person on such a list that has access to inside information acknowledges the legal and regulatory duties entailed and is aware of the sanctions attaching to the misuse or improper circulation of such information.

Article 6

Managers' Transactions

1. For the purposes of applying Article 6(4) of Directive 2003/6/EC, and without prejudice to the right of Member States to provide for other notification obligations than those covered by that Article, Member States shall ensure that all transactions related to shares admitted to trading on a regulated market, or to derivatives or other financial instruments linked to them, conducted on the own account of persons referred to in Article 1 points 1 and 2 above, are notified to the competent authorities. The rules of notification to which those persons have to comply with shall be those of the Member State where the issuer is registered. The notification shall be made within five working days of the transaction date to the competent authority of that Member State. When the issuer is not registered in a Member State, this notification shall be made to the competent authority of the Member State in which it is required to file the annual information in relation to the shares in accordance with Article 10 of Directive 2003/71/EC.

2. Member States may decide that, until the total amount of transactions has reached five thousand Euros at the end of a calendar year, no notification is required or notification may be delayed until the 31 January of the following year. The total amount of transactions shall be computed by summing up the transactions conducted on the own account of persons referred to in Article 1 point 1 with the transactions conducted on the own account of persons referred to in Article 1 point 2.

3. The notification shall contain the following information:

(a) name of the person discharging managerial responsibilities within the issuer, or, where applicable, name of the person closely associated with such a person,

(b) reason for responsibility to notify,

(c) name of the relevant issuer,

(d) description of the financial instrument,

(e) nature of the transaction (e.g. acquisition or disposal),

(f) date and place of the transaction,

(g) price and volume of the transaction.

Article 7

Suspicious transactions to be notified

For the purposes of applying Article 6(9) of Directive 2003/6/EC, Member States shall ensure that persons referred to in Article 1 point 3 above shall decide on a case-by-case basis whether there are reasonable grounds for suspecting that a transaction involves insider dealing or market manipulation, taking into account the elements constituting insider dealing or market manipulation, referred to in Articles 1 to 5 of Directive 2003/6/EC, in Commission Directive 2003/124/EC[7] implementing Directive 2003/6/EC as regards the definition and public disclosure of inside information and the definition of market manipulation, and in Article 4 of this Directive. Without prejudice to Article 10 of Directive 2003/6/EC, persons professionally arranging

---

[7] OJ L 339, 24.12.2003, 70, reproduced supra under no. S. 26.

transactions shall be subject to the rules of notification of the Member State in which they are registered or have their head office, or in the case of a branch, the Member State where the branch is situated. The notification shall be addressed to the competent authority of this Member State.

Member States shall ensure that competent authorities receiving the notification of suspicious transactions transmit such information immediately to the competent authorities of the regulated markets concerned.

Article 8
Timeframe for notification

Member States shall ensure that in the event that persons, as referred to in Article 1 point 3, become aware of a fact or information that gives reasonable ground for suspicion concerning the relevant transaction, make a notification without delay.

Article 9
Content of notification

1. Member States shall ensure that persons subject to the notification obligation transmit to the competent authority the following information:

(a) description of the transactions, including the type of order (such as limit order, market order or other characteristics of the order) and the type of trading market (such as block trade);

(b) reasons for suspicion that the transactions might constitute market abuse;

(c) means for identification of the persons on behalf of whom the transactions have been carried out, and of other persons involved in the relevant transactions;

(d) capacity in which the person subject to the notification obligation operates (such as for own account or on behalf of third parties);

(e) any information which may have significance in reviewing the suspicious transactions.

2. Where that information is not available at the time of notification, the notification shall include at least the reasons why the notifying persons suspect that the transactions might constitute insider dealing or market manipulation. All remaining information shall be provided to the competent authority as soon as it becomes available.

Article 10
Means of notification

Member States shall ensure that notification to the competent authority can be done by mail, electronic mail, telecopy or telephone, provided that in the latter case confirmation is notified by any written form upon request by the competent authority.

Article 11
Liability and professional secrecy

1. Member States shall ensure that the person notifying to the competent authority as referred to in Articles 7 to 10 shall not inform any other person, in particular the persons on behalf of whom the transactions have been carried out or parties related to those persons, of this notification, except by virtue of provisions laid down by law. The fulfilment of this requirement shall not involve the notifying person in liability of any kind, providing the notifying person acts in good faith.

2. Member States shall ensure that competent authorities do not disclose to any person the identity of the person having notified these transactions, if disclosure would, or would be likely to harm the person having notified the transactions. This provision is without prejudice to the requirements of the enforcement and the sanctioning regimes under Directive 2003/6/EC and to the rules on transfer of personal data laid down in Directive 95/46/EC.

3. The notification in good faith to the competent authority as referred to in Articles 7 to 10 shall not constitute a breach of any restriction on disclosure of information imposed by contract or by any legislative, regulatory or administrative provision, and shall not involve the person notifying in liability of any kind related to such notification.

Article 12

Transposition

1. Member States shall bring into force the laws, regulations and administrative provisions necessary to comply with this Directive by 12 October 2004 at the latest. They shall forthwith communicate to the Commission the text of the provisions and a correlation table between those provisions and this Directive.

When Member States adopt those provisions, they shall contain a reference to this Directive or be accompanied by such a reference on the occasion of their official publication. Member States shall determine how such reference is to be made.

2. Member States shall communicate to the Commission the text of the main provisions of national law which they adopt in the field covered by this Directive.

Article 13

Entry into force

This Directive shall enter into force on the day of its publication in the Official Journal of the European Union.

Article 14

Addressees

This Directive is addressed to the Member States.

S. 31.

**European Parliament and Council Directive 2004/109/EC
of 15 December 2004
on the harmonization of transparency requirements in relation to information about issuers whose securities are admitted to trading on a regulated market and amending Directive 2001/34/EC[1]**

THE EUROPEAN PARLIAMENT AND THE COUNCIL OF THE EUROPEAN UNION,

Having regard to the Treaty establishing the European Community, and in particular Articles 44 and 95 thereof,

Having regard to the proposal from the Commission,

Having regard to the opinion of the European Economic and Social Committee,[2]

Having regard to the opinion of the European Central Bank,[3]

Acting in accordance with the procedure laid down in Article 251 of the Treaty,[4]

Whereas:

(1) Efficient, transparent and integrated securities markets contribute to a genuine single market in the Community and foster growth and job creation by better allocation of capital and by reducing costs. The disclosure of accurate, comprehensive and timely information about security issuers builds sustained investor confidence and allows an informed assessment of their business performance and assets. This enhances both investor protection and market efficiency.

(2) To that end, security issuers should ensure appropriate transparency for investors through a regular flow of information. To the same end, shareholders, or natural persons or legal entities holding voting rights or financial instruments that result in an entitlement to acquire existing shares with voting rights, should also inform issuers of the acquisition of or other changes in major holdings in companies so that the latter are in a position to keep the public informed.

(3) The Commission Communication of 11 May 1999, entitled 'Implementing the framework for financial markets: Action Plan', identifies a series of actions that are needed in order to complete the single market for financial services. The Lisbon European Council of March 2000 calls for the implementation of that Action Plan by 2005. The Action Plan stresses the need to draw up a Directive upgrading transparency requirements. That need was confirmed by the Barcelona European Council of March 2002.

(4) This Directive should be compatible with the tasks and duties conferred upon the European System of Central Banks (ESCB) and the Member States' central banks by the Treaty and the Statute of the European System of Central Banks and of the European Central Bank; particular attention in this regard needs to be given to the Member States' central banks whose shares are currently admitted to trading on a regulated market, in order to guarantee the pursuit of primary Community law objectives.

(5) Greater harmonisation of provisions of national law on periodic and ongoing information requirements for security issuers should lead to a high level of investor protection throughout the Community. However, this Directive does not affect existing Community legislation on units issued by collective investment undertakings other than the closed-end type, or on units acquired or disposed of in such undertakings.

---

[1] OJ L 390, 31.12.2004, 38–57.
[2] OJ C 80, 30.3.2004, 128.
[3] OJ C 242, 9.10.2003, 6.
[4] Opinion of the European Parliament of 30 March 2004 (not yet published in the Official Journal) and Council Decision of 2 December 2004.

(6) Supervision of an issuer of shares, or of debt securities the denomination per unit of which is less than EUR 1 000, for the purposes of this Directive, would be best effected by the Member State in which the issuer has its registered office. In that respect, it is vital to ensure consistency with Directive 2003/71/EC of the European Parliament and of the Council of 4 November 2003 on the prospectus to be published when securities are offered to the public or admitted to trading.[5] Along the same lines, some flexibility should be introduced allowing third country issuers and Community companies issuing only securities other than those mentioned above a choice of home Member State.

(7) A high level of investor protection throughout the Community would enable barriers to the admission of securities to regulated markets situated or operating within a Member State to be removed. Member States other than the home Member State should no longer be allowed to restrict admission of securities to their regulated markets by imposing more stringent requirements on periodic and ongoing information about issuers whose securities are admitted to trading on a regulated market.

(8) The removal of barriers on the basis of the home Member State principle under this Directive should not affect areas not covered by this Directive, such as rights of shareholders to intervene in the management of an issuer. Nor should it affect the home Member State's right to request the issuer to publish, in addition, parts of or all regulated information through newspapers.

(9) Regulation (EC) No 1606/2002 of the European Parliament and of the Council of 19 July 2002 on the application of international accounting standards[6] has already paved the way for a convergence of financial reporting standards throughout the Community for issuers whose securities are admitted to trading on a regulated market and who are required to prepare consolidated accounts. Thus, a specific regime for security issuers beyond the general system for all companies, as laid down in the Company Law Directives, is already established. This Directive builds on this approach with regard to annual and interim financial reporting, including the principle of providing a true and fair view of an issuer's assets, liabilities, financial position and profit or loss. A condensed set of financial statements, as part of a half-yearly financial report, also represents a sufficient basis for giving such a true and fair view of the first six months of an issuer's financial year.

(10) An annual financial report should ensure information over the years once the issuer's securities have been admitted to a regulated market. Making it easier to compare annual financial reports is only of use to investors in securities markets if they can be sure that this information will be published within a certain time after the end of the financial year. As regards debt securities admitted to trading on a regulated market prior to 1 January 2005 and issued by issuers incorporated in a third country, the home Member State may under certain conditions allow issuers not to prepare annual financial reports in accordance with the standards required under this Directive.

(11) This Directive introduces more comprehensive half yearly financial reports for issuers of shares admitted to trading on a regulated market. This should allow investors to make a more informed assessment of the issuer's situation.

(12) A home Member State may provide for exemptions from half-yearly reporting by issuers of debt securities in the case of:
- credit institutions acting as small-size issuers of debt securities, or
- issuers already existing on the date of the entry into force of this Directive who exclusively issue debt securities unconditionally and irrevocably guaranteed by the home Member State or by one of its regional or local authorities, or
- during a transitional period of ten years, only in respect of those debt securities admitted to trading on a regulated market prior to 1 January 2005 which may be purchased by professional investors only. If such an exemption is given by the home Member State, it may not

---

[5] OJ L 345, 31.12.2003, 64.
[6] OJ L 243, 11.9.2002, 1, reproduced supra under no. C. 22.

be extended in respect of any debt securities admitted to a regulated market thereafter.

(13) The European Parliament and the Council welcome the Commission's commitment rapidly to consider enhancing the transparency of the remuneration policies, total remuneration paid, including any contingent or deferred compensation, and benefits in kind granted to each member of administrative, management or supervisory bodies under its Action Plan for 'Modernising Company Law and Enhancing Corporate Governance in the European Union' of 21 May 2003 and the Commission's intention to make a Recommendation on this topic in the near future.

(14) The home Member State should encourage issuers whose shares are admitted to trading on a regulated market and whose principal activities lie in the extractive industry to disclose payments to governments in their annual financial report. The home Member State should also encourage an increase in the transparency of such payments within the framework established at various international financial fora.

(15) This Directive will also make half-yearly reporting mandatory for issuers of only debt securities on regulated markets. Exemptions should only be provided for wholesale markets on the basis of a denomination per unit starting at EUR 50 000, as under Directive 2003/71/EC. Where debt securities are issued in another currency, exemptions should only be possible where the denomination per unit in such a currency is, at the date of the issue, at least equivalent to EUR 50 000.

(16) More timely and more reliable information about the share issuer's performance over the financial year also requires a higher frequency of interim information. A requirement should therefore be introduced to publish an interim management statement during the first six months and a second interim management statement during the second six months of a financial year. Share issuers who already publish quarterly financial reports should not be required to publish interim management statements.

(17) Appropriate liability rules, as laid down by each Member State under its national law or regulations, should be applicable to the issuer, its administrative, management or supervisory bodies, or persons responsible within the issuer. Member States should remain free to determine the extent of the liability.

(18) The public should be informed of changes to major holdings in issuers whose shares are traded on a regulated market situated or operating within the Community. This information should enable investors to acquire or dispose of shares in full knowledge of changes in the voting structure; it should also enhance effective control of share issuers and overall market transparency of important capital movements. Information about shares or financial instruments as determined by Article 13, lodged as collateral, should be provided in certain circumstances.

(19) Articles 9 and 10(c) should not apply to shares provided to or by the members of the ESCB in carrying out their functions as monetary authorities provided that the voting rights attached to such shares are not exercised; the reference to a 'short period' in Article 11 should be understood with reference to credit operations carried out in accordance with the Treaty and the European Central Bank (ECB) legal acts, in particular the ECB Guidelines on monetary policy instruments and procedures and TARGET, and to credit operations for the purpose of performing equivalent functions in accordance with national provisions.

(20) In order to avoid unnecessary burdens for certain market participants and to clarify who actually exercises influence over an issuer, there is no need to require notification of major holdings of shares, or other financial instruments as determined by Article 13 that result in an entitlement to acquire shares with regard to market makers or custodians, or of holdings of shares or such financial instruments acquired solely for clearing and settlement purposes, within limits and guarantees to be applied throughout the Community. The home Member State should be allowed to provide limited exemptions as regards holdings of

shares in trading books of credit institutions and investment firms.

(21) In order to clarify who is actually a major holder of shares or other financial instruments in the same issuer throughout the Community, parent undertakings should not be required to aggregate their own holdings with those managed by undertakings for collective investment in transferable securities (UCITS) or investment firms, provided that such undertakings or firms exercise voting rights independently from their parent undertakings and fulfil certain further conditions.

(22) Ongoing information to holders of securities admitted to trading on a regulated market should continue to be based on the principle of equal treatment. Such equal treatment only relates to shareholders in the same position and does not therefore prejudice the issue of how many voting rights may be attached to a particular share. By the same token, holders of debt securities ranking *pari passu* should continue to benefit from equal treatment, even in the case of sovereign debt. Information to holders of shares and/or debt securities in general meetings should be facilitated. In particular, holders of shares and/or debt securities situated abroad should be more actively involved in that they should be able to mandate proxies to act on their behalf. For the same reasons, it should be decided in a general meeting of holders of shares and/or debt securities whether the use of modern information and communication technologies should become a reality. In that case, issuers should put in place arrangements in order effectively to inform holders of their shares and/or debt securities, insofar as it is possible for them to identify those holders.

(23) Removal of barriers and effective enforcement of new Community information requirements also require adequate control by the competent authority of the home Member State. This Directive should at least provide for a minimum guarantee for the timely availability of such information. For this reason, at least one filing and storage system should exist in each Member State.

(24) Any obligation for an issuer to translate all ongoing and periodic information into all the relevant languages in all the Member States where its securities are admitted to trading does not foster integration of securities markets, but has deterrent effects on cross-border admission of securities to trading on regulated markets. Therefore, the issuer should in certain cases be entitled to provide information drawn up in a language that is customary in the sphere of international finance. Since a particular effort is needed to attract investors from other Member States and third countries, Member States should no longer prevent shareholders, persons exercising voting rights, or holders of financial instruments, from making the required notifications to the issuer in a language that is customary in the sphere of international finance.

(25) Access for investors to information about issuers should be more organised at a Community level in order to actively promote integration of European capital markets. Investors who are not situated in the issuer's home Member State should be put on an equal footing with investors situated in the issuer's home Member State, when seeking access to such information. This could be achieved if the home Member State ensures compliance with minimum quality standards for disseminating information throughout the Community, in a fast manner on a non-discriminatory basis and depending on the type of regulated information in question. In addition, information which has been disseminated should be available in the home Member State in a centralised way allowing a European network to be built up, accessible at affordable prices for retail investors, while not leading to unnecessary duplication of filing requirements for issuers. Issuers should benefit from free competition when choosing the media or operators for disseminating information under this Directive.

(26) In order to further simplify investor access to corporate information across Member States, it should be left to the national supervisory authorities to formulate guidelines for setting up electronic networks, in close consultation with the other parties concerned, in particular security

issuers, investors, market participants, operators of regulated markets and financial information providers.

(27) So as to ensure the effective protection of investors and the proper operation of regulated markets, the rules relating to information to be published by issuers whose securities are admitted to trading on a regulated market should also apply to issuers which do not have a registered office in a Member State and which do not fall within the scope of Article 48 of the Treaty. It should also be ensured that any additional relevant information about Community issuers or third country issuers, disclosure of which is required in a third country but not in a Member State, is made available to the public in the Community.

(28) A single competent authority should be designated in each Member State to assume final responsibility for supervising compliance with the provisions adopted pursuant to this Directive, as well as for international cooperation. Such an authority should be of an administrative nature, and its independence from economic players should be ensured in order to avoid conflicts of interest. Member States may however designate another competent authority for examining that information referred to in this Directive is drawn up in accordance with the relevant reporting framework and taking appropriate measures in case of discovered infringements; such an authority need not be of an administrative nature.

(29) Increasing cross-border activities require improved cooperation between national competent authorities, including a comprehensive set of provisions for the exchange of information and for precautionary measures. The organisation of the regulatory and supervisory tasks in each Member State should not hinder efficient cooperation between the competent national authorities.

(30) At its meeting on 17 July 2000, the Council set up the Committee of Wise Men on the Regulation of European securities markets. In its final report, that Committee proposed the introduction of new legislative techniques based on a four-level approach, namely essential principles, technical implementing measures, cooperation amongst national securities regulators, and enforcement of Community law. This Directive should confine itself to broad 'framework' principles, while implementing measures to be adopted by the Commission with the assistance of the European Securities Committee established by Commission Decision 2001/528/EC[7] should lay down the technical details.

(31) The Resolution adopted by the Stockholm European Council of March 2001 endorsed the final report of the Committee of Wise Men and the proposed four-level approach to make the regulatory process for Community securities legislation more efficient and transparent.

(32) According to that Resolution, implementing measures should be used more frequently, to ensure that technical provisions can be kept up to date with market and supervisory developments, and deadlines should be set for all stages of implementing rules.

(33) The Resolution of the European Parliament of 5 February 2002 on the implementation of financial services legislation also endorsed the Committee of Wise Men's report, on the basis of the solemn declaration made before the European Parliament the same day by the President of the Commission and the letter of 2 October 2001 addressed by the Internal Market Commissioner to the Chairman of the Parliament's Committee on Economic and Monetary Affairs with regard to safeguards for the European Parliament's role in this process.

(34) The European Parliament should be given a period of three months from the first transmission of draft implementing measures to allow it to examine them and to give its opinion. However, in urgent and duly justified cases, that period may be shortened. If, within that period, a Resolution is passed by the European Parliament, the Commission should re-examine the draft measures.

---

[7] OJ L 191, 13.7.2001, 45, reproduced supra under no. S. 20. Decision as amended by Decision 2004/8/EC (OJ L 3, 7.1.2004, 33), reproduced supra under no. I. 41.

(35) Technical implementing measures for the rules laid down in this Directive may be necessary to take account of new developments on securities markets. The Commission should accordingly be empowered to adopt implementing measures, provided that they do not modify the essential elements of this Directive and provided that the Commission acts in accordance with the principles set out therein, after consulting the European Securities Committee.

(36) In exercising its implementing powers in accordance with this Directive, the Commission should respect the following principles:
– the need to ensure confidence in financial markets among investors by promoting high standards of transparency in financial markets;
– the need to provide investors with a wide range of competing investments and a level of disclosure and protection tailored to their circumstances;
– the need to ensure that independent regulatory authorities enforce the rules consistently, especially as regards the fight against economic crime;
– the need for high levels of transparency and consultation with all market participants and with the European Parliament and the Council;
– the need to encourage innovation in financial markets if they are to be dynamic and efficient;
– the need to ensure market integrity by close and reactive monitoring of financial innovation;
– the importance of reducing the cost of, and increasing access to, capital;
– the balance of costs and benefits to market participants on a long-term basis, including small and medium-sized businesses and small investors, in any implementing measures;
– the need to foster the international competitiveness of Community financial markets without prejudice to a much-needed extension of international cooperation;
– the need to achieve a level playing field for all market participants by establishing Community-wide regulations wherever appropriate;
– the need to respect differences in national markets where these do not unduly impinge on the coherence of the single market;
– the need to ensure coherence with other Community legislation in this area, as imbalances in information and a lack of transparency may jeopardise the operation of the markets and above all harm consumers and small investors.

(37) In order to ensure that the requirements set out in this Directive or the measures implementing this Directive are fulfilled, any infringement of those requirements or measures should be promptly detected and, if necessary, subject to penalties. To that end, measures and penalties should be sufficiently dissuasive, proportionate and consistently enforced. Member States should ensure that decisions taken by the competent national authorities are subject to the right of appeal to the courts.

(38) This Directive aims to upgrade the current transparency requirements for security issuers and investors acquiring or disposing of major holdings in issuers whose shares are admitted to trading on a regulated market. This Directive replaces some of the requirements set out in Directive 2001/34/EC of the European Parliament and of the Council of 28 May 2001 on the admission of securities to official stock exchange listing and on information to be published on those securities.[8] In order to gather transparency requirements in a single act it is necessary to amend it accordingly. Such an amendment however should not affect the ability of Member States to impose additional requirements under Articles 42 to 63 of Directive 2001/34/EC, which remain valid.

(39) This Directive is in line with Directive 95/46/EC of the European Parliament and of the Council of 24 October 1995 on the protection of individuals with regard to the processing of personal data and on the free movement of such data.[9]

(40) This Directive respects fundamental rights and observes the principles recognised in

---

[8] OJ L 184, 6.7.2001, 1, reproduced supra under no. S. 18. Directive as last amended by Directive 2003/71/EC, reproduced supra under no. S. 25.

[9] OJ L 281, 23.11.1995, 31. Directive as amended by Regulation (EC) No 1882/2003 (OJ L 284, 31.10.2003, 1).

particular by the Charter of the Fundamental Rights of the European Union.

(41) Since the objectives of this Directive, namely to ensure investor confidence through equivalent transparency throughout the Community and thereby to complete the internal market, cannot be sufficiently achieved by the Member States on the basis of the existing Community legislation and can therefore be better achieved at Community level, the Community may adopt measures, in accordance with the principle of subsidiarity as set out in Article 5 of the Treaty. In accordance with the principle of proportionality, as set out in that Article, this Directive does not go beyond what is necessary in order to achieve these objectives.

(42) The measures necessary for implementing this Directive should be adopted in accordance with Council Decision 1999/468/EC of 28 June 1999 laying down the procedures for the exercise of implementing powers conferred on the Commission,[10]

HAVE ADOPTED THIS DIRECTIVE:

Chapter I
General Provisions

Article 1
Subject matter and scope

1. This Directive establishes requirements in relation to the disclosure of periodic and ongoing information about issuers whose securities are already admitted to trading on a regulated market situated or operating within a Member State.

2. This Directive shall not apply to units issued by collective investment undertakings other than the closed-end type, or to units acquired or disposed of in such collective investment undertakings.

3. Member States may decide not to apply the provisions mentioned in Article 16(3) and in paragraphs 2, 3 and 4 of Article 18 to securities which are admitted to trading on a regulated market issued by them or their regional or local authorities.

4. Member States may decide not to apply Article 17 to their national central banks in their capacity as issuers of shares admitted to trading on a regulated market if this admission took place before 20 January 2005.

Article 2
Definitions

1. For the purposes of this Directive the following definitions shall apply:

(a) 'securities' means transferable securities as defined in Article 4(1), point 18, of Directive 2004/39/EC of the European Parliament and of the Council of 21 April 2004 on markets in financial instruments[11] with the exception of money-market instruments, as defined in Article 4(1), point 19, of that Directive having a maturity of less than 12 months, for which national legislation may be applicable;

(b) 'debt securities' means bonds or other forms of transferable securitised debts, with the exception of securities which are equivalent to shares in companies or which, if converted or if the rights conferred by them are exercised, give rise to a right to acquire shares or securities equivalent to shares;

(c) 'regulated market' means a market as defined in Article 4(1), point 14, of Directive 2004/39/EC;

(d) 'issuer' means a legal entity governed by private or public law, including a State, whose securities are admitted to trading on a regulated market, the issuer being, in the case of depository receipts representing securities, the issuer of the securities represented;

(e) 'shareholder' means any natural person or legal entity governed by private or public law, who holds, directly or indirectly:

(i) shares of the issuer in its own name and on its own account;

---

[10] OJ L 184, 17.7.1999, 23.

[11] OJ L 145, 30.4.2004, 1, reproduced supra under no. S. 29.

(ii) shares of the issuer in its own name, but on behalf of another natural person or legal entity;

(iii) depository receipts, in which case the holder of the depository receipt shall be considered as the shareholder of the underlying shares represented by the depository receipts;

(f) 'controlled undertaking' means any undertaking
  (i) in which a natural person or legal entity has a majority of the voting rights; or
  (ii) of which a natural person or legal entity has the right to appoint or remove a majority of the members of the administrative, management or supervisory body and is at the same time a shareholder in, or member of, the undertaking in question; or
  (iii) of which a natural person or legal entity is a shareholder or member and alone controls a majority of the shareholders' or members' voting rights, respectively, pursuant to an agreement entered into with other shareholders or members of the undertaking in question; or
  (iv) over which a natural person or legal entity has the power to exercise, or actually exercises, dominant influence or control;

(g) 'collective investment undertaking other than the closed-end type' means unit trusts and investment companies:
  (i) the object of which is the collective investment of capital provided by the public, and which operate on the principle of risk spreading; and
  (ii) the units of which are, at the request of the holder of such units, repurchased or redeemed, directly or indirectly, out of the assets of those undertakings;

(h) 'units of a collective investment undertaking' means securities issued by a collective investment undertaking and representing rights of the participants in such an undertaking over its assets;

(i) 'home Member State' means
  (i) in the case of an issuer of debt securities the denomination per unit of which is less than EUR 1 000 or an issuer of shares:
    – where the issuer is incorporated in the Community, the Member State in which it has its registered office;
    – where the issuer is incorporated in a third country, the Member State in which it is required to file the annual information with the competent authority in accordance with Article 10 of Directive 2003/71/EC.

    The definition of 'home' Member State shall be applicable to debt securities in a currency other than Euro, provided that the value of such denomination per unit is, at the date of the issue, less than EUR 1 000, unless it is nearly equivalent to EUR 1 000;
  (ii) for any issuer not covered by (i), the Member State chosen by the issuer from among the Member State in which the issuer has its registered office and those Member States which have admitted its securities to trading on a regulated market on their territory. The issuer may choose only one Member State as its home Member State. Its choice shall remain valid for at least three years unless its securities are no longer admitted to trading on any regulated market in the Community;

(j) 'host Member State' means a Member State in which securities are admitted to trading on a regulated market, if different from the home Member State;

(k) 'regulated information' means all information which the issuer, or any other person who has applied for the admission of securities to trading on a regulated market without the issuer's consent, is required to disclose under this Directive, under Article 6 of Directive 2003/6/EC of the European Parliament and of the Council of 28 January 2003 on insider dealing and market manipulation (market abuse),[12] or under the laws, regulations or administrative provisions of a Member State adopted under Article 3(1) of this Directive;

(l) 'electronic means' are means of electronic equipment for the processing (including digital compression), storage and transmission of data, employing wires, radio, optical technologies, or any other electromagnetic means;

---

[12] OJ L 96, 12.4.2003, 16, reproduced supra under no. S. 24.

(m) 'management company' means a company as defined in Article 1a(2) of Council Directive 85/611/EEC of 20 December 1985 on the coordination of laws, regulations and administrative provisions relating to undertakings for collective investment in transferable securities (UCITS);[13]

(n) 'market maker' means a person who holds himself out on the financial markets on a continuous basis as being willing to deal on own account by buying and selling financial instruments against his proprietary capital at prices defined by him;

(o) 'credit institution' means an undertaking as defined in Article 1(1)(a) of Directive 2000/12/EC of the European Parliament and of the Council of 20 March 2000 relating to the taking up and pursuit of the business of credit institutions;[14]

(p) 'securities issued in a continuous or repeated manner' means debt securities of the same issuer on tap or at least two separate issues of securities of a similar type and/or class.

2. For the purposes of the definition of 'controlled undertaking' in paragraph 1(f)(ii), the holder's rights in relation to voting, appointment and removal shall include the rights of any other undertaking controlled by the shareholder and those of any natural person or legal entity acting, albeit in its own name, on behalf of the shareholder or of any other undertaking controlled by the shareholder.

3. In order to take account of technical developments on financial markets and to ensure the uniform application of paragraph 1, the Commission shall, in accordance with the procedure referred to in Article 27(2), adopt implementing measures concerning the definitions set out in paragraph 1.

The Commission shall, in particular:

(a) establish, for the purposes of paragraph 1(i)(ii), the procedural arrangements in accordance with which an issuer may make the choice of the home Member State;

(b) adjust, where appropriate for the purposes of the choice of the home Member State referred to in paragraph 1(i)(ii), the three-year period in relation to the issuer's track record in the light of any new requirement under Community law concerning admission to trading on a regulated market;

(c) establish, for the purposes of paragraph 1(l), an indicative list of means which are not to be considered as electronic means, thereby taking into account Annex V to Directive 98/34/EC of the European Parliament and of the Council of 22 June 1998 laying down a procedure for the provision of information in the field of technical standards and regulations.[15]

Article 3
Integration of securities markets

1. The home Member State may make an issuer subject to requirements more stringent than those laid down in this Directive.

The home Member State may also make a holder of shares, or a natural person or legal entity referred to in Articles 10 or 13, subject to requirements more stringent than those laid down in this Directive.

2. A host Member State may not:

(a) as regards the admission of securities to a regulated market in its territory, impose disclosure requirements more stringent than those laid down in this Directive or in Article 6 of Directive 2003/6/EC;

(b) as regards the notification of information, make a holder of shares, or a natural person or legal entity referred to in Articles 10 or 13, subject to requirements more stringent than those laid down in this Directive.

---

[13] OJ L 375, 31.12.1985, 3, reproduced supra under no. S. 6. Directive as last amended by Directive 2004/39/EC, reproduced supra under no. S. 26.

[14] OJ L 126, 26.5.2000, 1, reproduced supra under no. B. 32. Directive as last amended by Commission Directive 2004/69/EC (OJ L 125, 28.4.2004, 44).

[15] OJ L 204, 21.7.1998, 37, reproduced supra under no. B. 30. Directive as last amended by the 2003 Act of Accession.

Chapter II
Periodic Information

Article 4
Annual financial reports

1. The issuer shall make public its annual financial report at the latest four months after the end of each financial year and shall ensure that it remains publicly available for at least five years.

2. The annual financial report shall comprise:

(a) the audited financial statements;

(b) the management report; and

(c) statements made by the persons responsible within the issuer, whose names and functions shall be clearly indicated, to the effect that, to the best of their knowledge, the financial statements prepared in accordance with the applicable set of accounting standards give a true and fair view of the assets, liabilities, financial position and profit or loss of the issuer and the undertakings included in the consolidation taken as a whole and that the management report includes a fair review of the development and performance of the business and the position of the issuer and the undertakings included in the consolidation taken as a whole, together with a description of the principal risks and uncertainties that they face.

3. Where the issuer is required to prepare consolidated accounts according to the Seventh Council Directive 83/349/EEC of 13 June 1983 on consolidated accounts,[16] the audited financial statements shall comprise such consolidated accounts drawn up in accordance with Regulation (EC) No 1606/2002 and the annual accounts of the parent company drawn up in accordance with the national law of the Member State in which the parent company is incorporated.

Where the issuer is not required to prepare consolidated accounts, the audited financial statements shall comprise the accounts prepared in accordance with the national law of the Member State in which the company is incorporated.

4. The financial statements shall be audited in accordance with Articles 51 and 51a of the Fourth Council Directive 78/660/EEC of 25 July 1978 on the annual accounts of certain types of companies[17] and, if the issuer is required to prepare consolidated accounts, in accordance with Article 37 of Directive 83/349/EEC.

The audit report, signed by the person or persons responsible for auditing the financial statements, shall be disclosed in full to the public together with the annual financial report.

5. The management report shall be drawn up in accordance with Article 46 of Directive 78/660/EEC and, if the issuer is required to prepare consolidated accounts, in accordance with Article 36 of Directive 83/349/EEC.

6. The Commission shall, in accordance with the procedure referred to in Article 27(2), adopt implementing measures in order to take account of technical developments in financial markets and to ensure the uniform application of paragraph 1. The Commission shall in particular specify the technical conditions under which a published annual financial report, including the audit report, is to remain available to the public. Where appropriate, the Commission may also adapt the five-year period referred to in paragraph 1.

Article 5
Half-yearly financial reports

1. The issuer of shares or debt securities shall make public a half-yearly financial report covering the first six months of the financial year as soon as possible after the end of the relevant period, but at the latest two months thereafter. The issuer shall ensure that the half-yearly financial report remains available to the public for at least five years.

---

[16] OJ L 193, 18.7.1983, 1, reproduced supra under no. C. 6. Directive as last amended by Directive 2003/51/EC of the European Parliament and of the Council (OJ L 178, 17.7.2003, 16), reproduced supra under no. C.P. 19.

[17] OJ L 222, 14.8.1978, reproduced supra under no. C. 4. Directive as last amended by Directive 2003/51/EC, reproduced supra under no. C. 23.

2. The half-yearly financial report shall comprise:

(a) the condensed set of financial statements;

(b) an interim management report; and

(c) statements made by the persons responsible within the issuer, whose names and functions shall be clearly indicated, to the effect that, to the best of their knowledge, the condensed set of financial statements which has been prepared in accordance with the applicable set of accounting standards gives a true and fair view of the assets, liabilities, financial position and profit or loss of the issuer, or the undertakings included in the consolidation as a whole as required under paragraph 3, and that the interim management report includes a fair review of the information required under paragraph 4.

3. Where the issuer is required to prepare consolidated accounts, the condensed set of financial statements shall be prepared in accordance with the international accounting standard applicable to the interim financial reporting adopted pursuant to the procedure provided for under Article 6 of Regulation (EC) No 1606/2002.

Where the issuer is not required to prepare consolidated accounts, the condensed set of financial statements shall at least contain a condensed balance sheet, a condensed profit and loss account and explanatory notes on these accounts. In preparing the condensed balance sheet and the condensed profit and loss account, the issuer shall follow the same principles for recognising and measuring as when preparing annual financial reports.

4. The interim management report shall include at least an indication of important events that have occurred during the first six months of the financial year, and their impact on the condensed set of financial statements, together with a description of the principal risks and uncertainties for the remaining six months of the financial year. For issuers of shares, the interim management report shall also include major related parties transactions.

5. If the half-yearly financial report has been audited, the audit report shall be reproduced in full. The same shall apply in the case of an auditors' review. If the half-yearly financial report has not been audited or reviewed by auditors, the issuer shall make a statement to that effect in its report.

6. The Commission shall, in accordance with the procedure referred to in Article 27(2), adopt implementing measures in order to take account of technical developments on financial markets and to ensure the uniform application of paragraphs 1 to 5 of this Article.

The Commission shall, in particular:

(a) specify the technical conditions under which a published half-yearly financial report, including the auditors' review, is to remain available to the public;

(b) clarify the nature of the auditors' review;

(c) specify the minimum content of the condensed balance sheet and profit and loss accounts and explanatory notes on these accounts, where they are not prepared in accordance with the international accounting standards adopted pursuant to the procedure provided for under Article 6 of Regulation (EC) No 1606/2002.

Where appropriate, the Commission may also adapt the five-year period referred to in paragraph 1.

Article 6
Interim management statements

1. Without prejudice to Article 6 of Directive 2003/6/EC, an issuer whose shares are admitted to trading on a regulated market shall make public a statement by its management during the first six-month period of the financial year and another statement by its management during the second six-month period of the financial year. Such statement shall be made in a period between ten weeks after the beginning and six weeks before the end of the relevant six-month period. It shall contain information covering the period between the beginning of the relevant six-month period and the date of publication of the statement. Such a statement shall provide:

– an explanation of material events and transactions that have taken place during the relevant period and their impact on the financial

position of the issuer and its controlled undertakings, and
- a general description of the financial position and performance of the issuer and its controlled undertakings during the relevant period.

2. Issuers which, under either national legislation or the rules of the regulated market or of their own initiative, publish quarterly financial reports in accordance with such legislation or rules shall not be required to make public statements by the management provided for in paragraph 1.

3. The Commission shall provide a report to the European Parliament and the Council by 20 January 2010 on the transparency of quarterly financial reporting and statements by the management of issuers to examine whether the information provided meets the objective of allowing investors to make an informed assessment of the financial position of the issuer. Such a report shall include an impact assessment on areas where the Commission considers proposing amendments to this Article.

Article 7
Responsibility and liability

Member States shall ensure that responsibility for the information to be drawn up and made public in accordance with Articles 4, 5, 6 and 16 lies at least with the issuer or its administrative, management or supervisory bodies and shall ensure that their laws, regulations and administrative provisions on liability apply to the issuers, the bodies referred to in this Article or the persons responsible within the issuers.

Article 8
Exemptions

1. Articles 4, 5 and 6 shall not apply to the following issuers:

(a) a State, a regional or local authority of a State, a public international body of which at least one Member State is a member, the ECB, and Member States' national central banks whether or not they issue shares or other securities; and

(b) an issuer exclusively of debt securities admitted to trading on a regulated market, the denomination per unit of which is at least EUR 50 000 or, in the case of debt securities denominated in a currency other than Euro, the value of such denomination per unit is, at the date of the issue, equivalent to at least EUR 50 000.

2. The home Member State may choose not to apply Article 5 to credit institutions whose shares are not admitted to trading on a regulated market and which have, in a continuous or repeated manner, only issued debt securities provided that the total nominal amount of all such debt securities remains below EUR 100 000 000 and that they have not published a prospectus under Directive 2003/71/EC.

3. The home Member State may choose not to apply Article 5 to issuers already existing at the date of the entry into force of Directive 2003/71/EC which exclusively issue debt securities unconditionally and irrevocably guaranteed by the home Member State or by one of its regional or local authorities, on a regulated market.

CHAPTER III
ONGOING INFORMATION
SECTION I
INFORMATION ABOUT MAJOR HOLDINGS

Article 9
Notification of the acquisition or disposal of major holdings

1. The home Member State shall ensure that, where a shareholder acquires or disposes of shares of an issuer whose shares are admitted to trading on a regulated market and to which voting rights are attached, such shareholder notifies the issuer of the proportion of voting rights of the issuer held by the shareholder as a result of the acquisition or disposal where that proportion reaches, exceeds or falls below the thresholds of 5%, 10%, 15%, 20%, 25%, 30%, 50% and 75%.

The voting rights shall be calculated on the basis of all the shares to which voting rights are attached even if the exercise thereof is suspended.

Moreover this information shall also be given in respect of all the shares which are in the same class and to which voting rights are attached.

2. The home Member States shall ensure that the shareholders notify the issuer of the proportion of voting rights, where that proportion reaches, exceeds or falls below the thresholds provided for in paragraph 1, as a result of events changing the breakdown of voting rights, and on the basis of the information disclosed pursuant to Article 15. Where the issuer is incorporated in a third country, the notification shall be made for equivalent events.

3. The home Member State need not apply:

(a) the 30% threshold, where it applies a threshold of one-third;

(b) the 75% threshold, where it applies a threshold of two-thirds.

4. This Article shall not apply to shares acquired for the sole purpose of clearing and settling within the usual short settlement cycle, or to custodians holding shares in their custodian capacity provided such custodians can only exercise the voting rights attached to such shares under instructions given in writing or by electronic means.

5. This Article shall not apply to the acquisition or disposal of a major holding reaching or crossing the 5% threshold by a market maker acting in its capacity of a market maker, provided that:

(a) it is authorised by its home Member State under Directive 2004/39/EC; and

(b) it neither intervenes in the management of the issuer concerned nor exerts any influence on the issuer to buy such shares or back the share price.

6. Home Member States under Article 2(1)(i) may provide that voting rights held in the trading book, as defined in Article 2(6) of Council Directive 93/6/EEC of 15 March 1993 on the capital adequacy of investment firms and credit institutions,[18] of a credit institution or investment firm shall not be counted for the purposes of this Article provided that:

(a) the voting rights held in the trading book do not exceed 5%, and

(b) the credit institution or investment firm ensures that the voting rights attaching to shares held in the trading book are not exercised nor otherwise used to intervene in the management of the issuer.

7. The Commission shall, in accordance with the procedure referred to in Article 27(2), adopt implementing measures in order to take account of technical developments on financial markets and to ensure the uniform application of paragraphs 2, 4 and 5 of this Article.

The Commission shall in particular specify the maximum length of the 'short settlement cycle' referred to in paragraph 4, as well as the appropriate control mechanisms by the competent authority of the home Member State. In addition, the Commission may draw up a list of the events referred to in paragraph 2.

Article 10
Acquisition or disposal of major proportions of voting rights

The notification requirements defined in paragraphs 1 and 2 of Article 9 shall also apply to a natural person or legal entity to the extent it is entitled to acquire, to dispose of, or to exercise voting rights in any of the following cases or a combination of them:

(a) voting rights held by a third party with whom that person or entity has concluded an agreement, which obliges them to adopt, by concerted exercise of the voting rights they hold, a lasting common policy towards the management of the issuer in question;

(b) voting rights held by a third party under an agreement concluded with that person or entity providing for the temporary transfer for consideration of the voting rights in question;

(c) voting rights attaching to shares which are lodged as collateral with that person or entity, provided the person or entity controls the voting rights and declares its intention of exercising them;

---

[18] OJ L 141, 11.6.1993, 1, reproduced supra under no. B. 20. Directive as last amended by Directive 2004/39/EC, reproduced supra under S. 29.

(d) voting rights attaching to shares in which that person or entity has the life interest;

(e) voting rights which are held, or may be exercised within the meaning of points (a) to (d), by an undertaking controlled by that person or entity;

(f) voting rights attaching to shares deposited with that person or entity which the person or entity can exercise at its discretion in the absence of specific instructions from the shareholders;

(g) voting rights held by a third party in its own name on behalf of that person or entity;

(h) voting rights which that person or entity may exercise as a proxy where the person or entity can exercise the voting rights at its discretion in the absence of specific instructions from the shareholders.

Article 11

1. Articles 9 and 10(c) shall not apply to shares provided to or by the members of the ESCB in carrying out their functions as monetary authorities, including shares provided to or by members of the ESCB under a pledge or repurchase or similar agreement for liquidity granted for monetary policy purposes or within a payment system.

2. The exemption shall apply to the above transactions lasting for a short period and provided that the voting rights attaching to such shares are not exercised.

Article 12

Procedures on the notification and disclosure of major holdings

1. The notification required under Articles 9 and 10 shall include the following information:

(a) the resulting situation in terms of voting rights;

(b) the chain of controlled undertakings through which voting rights are effectively held, if applicable;

(c) the date on which the threshold was reached or crossed; and

(d) the identity of the shareholder, even if that shareholder is not entitled to exercise voting rights under the conditions laid down in Article 10, and of the natural person or legal entity entitled to exercise voting rights on behalf of that shareholder.

2. The notification to the issuer shall be effected as soon as possible, but not later than four trading days, the first of which shall be the day after the date on which the shareholder, or the natural person or legal entity referred to in Article 10,

(a) learns of the acquisition or disposal or of the possibility of exercising voting rights, or on which, having regard to the circumstances, should have learned of it, regardless of the date on which the acquisition, disposal or possibility of exercising voting rights takes effect; or

(b) is informed about the event mentioned in Article 9(2).

3. An undertaking shall be exempted from making the required notification in accordance with paragraph 1 if the notification is made by the parent undertaking or, where the parent undertaking is itself a controlled undertaking, by its own parent undertaking.

4. The parent undertaking of a management company shall not be required to aggregate its holdings under Articles 9 and 10 with the holdings managed by the management company under the conditions laid down in Directive 85/611/EEC, provided such management company exercises its voting rights independently from the parent undertaking.

However, Articles 9 and 10 shall apply where the parent undertaking, or another controlled undertaking of the parent undertaking, has invested in holdings managed by such management company and the management company has no discretion to exercise the voting rights attached to such holdings and may only exercise such voting rights under direct or indirect instructions from the parent or another controlled undertaking of the parent undertaking.

5. The parent undertaking of an investment firm authorised under Directive 2004/39/EC shall not be required to aggregate its holdings under Articles 9 and 10 with the holdings which such investment firm manages on a client-by-client

basis within the meaning of Article 4(1), point 9, of Directive 2004/39/EC, provided that:
- the investment firm is authorised to provide such portfolio management under point 4 of Section A of Annex I to Directive 2004/39/EC;
- it may only exercise the voting rights attached to such shares under instructions given in writing or by electronic means or it ensures that individual portfolio management services are conducted independently of any other services under conditions equivalent to those provided for under Directive 85/611/EEC by putting into place appropriate mechanisms; and
- the investment firm exercises its voting rights independently from the parent undertaking.

However, Articles 9 and 10 shall apply where the parent undertaking, or another controlled undertaking of the parent undertaking, has invested in holdings managed by such investment firm and the investment firm has no discretion to exercise the voting rights attached to such holdings and may only exercise such voting rights under direct or indirect instructions from the parent or another controlled undertaking of the parent undertaking.

6. Upon receipt of the notification under paragraph 1, but no later than three trading days thereafter, the issuer shall make public all the information contained in the notification.

7. A home Member State may exempt issuers from the requirement in paragraph 6 if the information contained in the notification is made public by its competent authority, under the conditions laid down in Article 21, upon receipt of the notification, but no later than three trading days thereafter.

8. In order to take account of technical developments on financial markets and to ensure the uniform application of paragraphs 1, 2, 4, 5 and 6 of this Article, the Commission shall, in accordance with the procedure referred to in Article 27(2), adopt implementing measures:

(a) to establish a standard form to be used throughout the Community when notifying the required information to the issuer under paragraph 1 or when filing information under Article 19(3);

(b) to determine a calendar of 'trading days' for all Member States;

(c) to establish in which cases the shareholder, or the natural person or legal entity referred to in Article 10, or both, shall effect the necessary notification to the issuer;

(d) to clarify the circumstances under which the shareholder, or the natural person or legal entity referred to in Article 10, should have learned of the acquisition or disposal;

(e) to clarify the conditions of independence to be complied with by management companies and their parent undertakings or by investment firms and their parent undertakings to benefit from the exemptions in paragraphs 4 and 5.

Article 13

1. The notification requirements laid down in Article 9 shall also apply to a natural person or legal entity who holds, directly or indirectly, financial instruments that result in an entitlement to acquire, on such holder's own initiative alone, under a formal agreement, shares to which voting rights are attached, already issued, of an issuer whose shares are admitted to trading on a regulated market.

2. The Commission shall, in accordance with the procedure referred to in Article 27(2), adopt implementing measures in order to take account of technical developments in financial markets and to ensure the uniform application of paragraph 1. It shall in particular determine:

(a) the types of financial instruments referred to in paragraph 1 and their aggregation;

(b) the nature of the formal agreement referred to in paragraph 1;

(c) the contents of the notification to be made, establishing a standard form to be used throughout the Community for that purpose;

(d) the notification period;

(e) to whom the notification is to be made.

Article 14

1. Where an issuer of shares admitted to trading on a regulated market acquires or disposes of its own shares, either itself or through a person acting in his own name but on the issuer's behalf, the home Member State shall ensure that the issuer makes public the proportion of its own shares as soon as possible, but not later than four trading days following such acquisition or disposal where that proportion reaches, exceeds or falls below the thresholds of 5% or 10% of the voting rights. The proportion shall be calculated on the basis of the total number of shares to which voting rights are attached.

2. The Commission shall, in accordance with the procedure referred to in Article 27(2), adopt implementing measures in order to take account of technical developments in financial markets and to ensure the uniform application of paragraph 1.

Article 15

For the purpose of calculating the thresholds provided for in Article 9, the home Member State shall at least require the disclosure to the public by the issuer of the total number of voting rights and capital at the end of each calendar month during which an increase or decrease of such total number has occurred.

Article 16

Additional information

1. The issuer of shares admitted to trading on a regulated market shall make public without delay any change in the rights attaching to the various classes of shares, including changes in the rights attaching to derivative securities issued by the issuer itself and giving access to the shares of that issuer.

2. The issuer of securities, other than shares admitted to trading on a regulated market, shall make public without delay any changes in the rights of holders of securities other than shares, including changes in the terms and conditions of these securities which could indirectly affect those rights, resulting in particular from a change in loan terms or in interest rates.

3. The issuer of securities admitted to trading on a regulated market shall make public without delay of new loan issues and in particular of any guarantee or security in respect thereof. Without prejudice to Directive 2003/6/EC, this paragraph shall not apply to a public international body of which at least one Member State is member.

Section II

Information for Holders of Securities Admitted to Trading on a Regulated Market

Article 17

Information requirements for issuers whose shares are admitted to trading on a regulated market

1. The issuer of shares admitted to trading on a regulated market shall ensure equal treatment for all holders of shares who are in the same position.

2. The issuer shall ensure that all the facilities and information necessary to enable holders of shares to exercise their rights are available in the home Member State and that the integrity of data is preserved. Shareholders shall not be prevented from exercising their rights by proxy, subject to the law of the country in which the issuer is incorporated. In particular, the issuer shall:

(a) provide information on the place, time and agenda of meetings, the total number of shares and voting rights and the rights of holders to participate in meetings;

(b) make available a proxy form, on paper or, where applicable, by electronic means, to each person entitled to vote at a shareholders' meeting, together with the notice concerning the meeting or, on request, after an announcement of the meeting;

(c) designate as its agent a financial institution through which shareholders may exercise their financial rights; and

(d) publish notices or distribute circulars concerning the allocation and payment of dividends and the issue of new shares, including information on any arrangements for allotment, subscription, cancellation or conversion.

3. For the purposes of conveying information to shareholders, the home Member State shall allow issuers the use of electronic means, provided such a decision is taken in a general meeting and meets at least the following conditions:

(a) the use of electronic means shall in no way depend upon the location of the seat or residence of the shareholder or, in the cases referred to in Article 10(a) to (h), of the natural persons or legal entities;

(b) identification arrangements shall be put in place so that the shareholders, or the natural persons or legal entities entitled to exercise or to direct the exercise of voting rights, are effectively informed;

(c) shareholders, or in the cases referred to in Article 10(a) to (e) the natural persons or legal entities entitled to acquire, dispose of or exercise voting rights, shall be contacted in writing to request their consent for the use of electronic means for conveying information and, if they do not object within a reasonable period of time, their consent shall be deemed to be given. They shall be able to request, at any time in the future, that information be conveyed in writing, and

(d) any apportionment of the costs entailed in the conveyance of such information by electronic means shall be determined by the issuer in compliance with the principle of equal treatment laid down in paragraph 1.

4. The Commission shall, in accordance with the procedure provided for in Article 27(2), adopt implementing measures in order to take account of technical developments in financial markets, to take account of developments in information and communication technology and to ensure the uniform application of paragraphs 1, 2 and 3. It shall, in particular, specify the types of financial institution through which a shareholder may exercise the financial rights provided for in paragraph 2(c).

Article 18

Information requirements for issuers whose debt securities are admitted to trading on a regulated market

1. The issuer of debt securities admitted to trading on a regulated market shall ensure that all holders of debt securities ranking *pari passu* are given equal treatment in respect of all the rights attaching to those debt securities.

2. The issuer shall ensure that all the facilities and information necessary to enable debt securities holders to exercise their rights are publicly available in the home Member State and that the integrity of data is preserved. Debt securities holders shall not be prevented from exercising their rights by proxy, subject to the law of country in which the issuer is incorporated. In particular, the issuer shall:

(a) publish notices, or distribute circulars, concerning the place, time and agenda of meetings of debt securities holders, the payment of interest, the exercise of any conversion, exchange, subscription or cancellation rights, and repayment, as well as the right of those holders to participate therein;

(b) make available a proxy form on paper or, where applicable, by electronic means, to each person entitled to vote at a meeting of debt securities holders, together with the notice concerning the meeting or, on request, after an announcement of the meeting; and

(c) designate as its agent a financial institution through which debt securities holders may exercise their financial rights.

3. If only holders of debt securities whose denomination per unit amounts to at least EUR 50 000 or, in the case of debt securities denominated in a currency other than Euro whose denomination per unit is, at the date of the issue, equivalent to at least EUR 50 000, are to be invited to a meeting, the issuer may choose as venue any Member State, provided that all the facilities and information necessary to enable such holders to exercise their rights are made available in that Member State.

4. For the purposes of conveying information to debt securities holders, the home Member State, or the Member State chosen by the issuer pursuant to paragraph 3, shall allow issuers the use of electronic means, provided such a decision is taken in a general meeting and meets at least the following conditions:

(a) the use of electronic means shall in no way depend upon the location of the seat or residence of the debt security holder or of a proxy representing that holder;

(b) identification arrangements shall be put in place so that debt securities holders are effectively informed;

(c) debt securities holders shall be contacted in writing to request their consent for the use of electronic means for conveying information and if they do not object within a reasonable period of time, their consent shall be deemed to be given. They shall be able to request, at any time in the future, that information be conveyed in writing; and

(d) any apportionment of the costs entailed in the conveyance of information by electronic means shall be determined by the issuer in compliance with the principle of equal treatment laid down in paragraph 1.

5. The Commission shall, in accordance with the procedure provided for in Article 27(2), adopt implementing measures in order to take account of technical developments in financial markets, to take account of developments in information and communication technology and to ensure the uniform application of paragraphs 1 to 4. It shall, in particular, specify the types of financial institution through which a debt security holder may exercise the financial rights provided for in paragraph 2(c).

CHAPTER IV
GENERAL OBLIGATIONS

Article 19
Home Member State control

1. Whenever the issuer, or any person having requested, without the issuer's consent, the admission of its securities to trading on a regulated market, discloses regulated information, it shall at the same time file that information with the competent authority of its home Member State. That competent authority may decide to publish such filed information on its Internet site.

Where an issuer proposes to amend its instrument of incorporation or statutes, it shall communicate the draft amendment to the competent authority of the home Member State and to the regulated market to which its securities have been admitted to trading. Such communication shall be effected without delay, but at the latest on the date of calling the general meeting which is to vote on, or be informed of, the amendment.

2. The home Member State may exempt an issuer from the requirement under paragraph 1 in respect of information disclosed in accordance with Article 6 of Directive 2003/6/EC or Article 12(6) of this Directive.

3. Information to be notified to the issuer in accordance with Articles 9, 10, 12 and 13 shall at the same time be filed with the competent authority of the home Member State.

4. In order to ensure the uniform application of paragraphs 1, 2 and 3, the Commission shall, in accordance with the procedure referred to in Article 27(2), adopt implementing measures.

The Commission shall, in particular, specify the procedure in accordance with which an issuer, a holder of shares or other financial instruments, or a person or entity referred to in Article 10, is to file information with the competent authority of the home Member State under paragraphs 1 or 3, respectively, in order to:

(a) enable filing by electronic means in the home Member State;

(b) coordinate the filing of the annual financial report referred to in Article 4 of this Directive with the filing of the annual information referred to in Article 10 of Directive 2003/71/EC.

Article 20
Languages

1. Where securities are admitted to trading on a regulated market only in the home Member

State, regulated information shall be disclosed in a language accepted by the competent authority in the home Member State.

2. Where securities are admitted to trading on a regulated market both in the home Member State and in one or more host Member States, regulated information shall be disclosed:

(a) in a language accepted by the competent authority in the home Member State; and

(b) depending on the choice of the issuer, either in a language accepted by the competent authorities of those host Member States or in a language customary in the sphere of international finance.

3. Where securities are admitted to trading on a regulated market in one or more host Member States, but not in the home Member State, regulated information shall, depending on the choice of the issuer, be disclosed either in a language accepted by the competent authorities of those host Member States or in a language customary in the sphere of international finance.

In addition, the home Member State may lay down in its law, regulations or administrative provisions that the regulated information shall, depending on the choice of the issuer, be disclosed either in a language accepted by its competent authority or in a language customary in the sphere of international finance.

4. Where securities are admitted to trading on a regulated market without the issuer's consent, the obligations under paragraphs 1, 2 and 3 shall be incumbent not upon the issuer, but upon the person who, without the issuer's consent, has requested such admission.

5. Member States shall allow shareholders and the natural person or legal entity referred to in Articles 9, 10 and 13 to notify information to an issuer under this Directive only in a language customary in the sphere of international finance. If the issuer receives such a notification, Member States may not require the issuer to provide a translation into a language accepted by the competent authorities.

6. By way of derogation from paragraphs 1 to 4, where securities whose denomination per unit amounts to at least EUR 50 000 or, in the case of debt securities denominated in a currency other than Euro equivalent to at least EUR 50 000 at the date of the issue, are admitted to trading on a regulated market in one or more Member States, regulated information shall be disclosed to the public either in a language accepted by the competent authorities of the home and host Member States or in a language customary in the sphere of international finance, at the choice of the issuer or of the person who, without the issuer's consent, has requested such admission.

7. If an action concerning the content of regulated information is brought before a court or tribunal in a Member State, responsibility for the payment of costs incurred in the translation of that information for the purposes of the proceedings shall be decided in accordance with the law of that Member State.

Article 21
Access to regulated information

1. The home Member State shall ensure that the issuer, or the person who has applied for admission to trading on a regulated market without the issuer's consent, discloses regulated information in a manner ensuring fast access to such information on a non-discriminatory basis and makes it available to the officially appointed mechanism referred to in paragraph 2. The issuer, or the person who has applied for admission to trading on a regulated market without the issuer's consent, may not charge investors any specific cost for providing the information. The home Member State shall require the issuer to use such media as may reasonably be relied upon for the effective dissemination of information to the public throughout the Community. The home Member State may not impose an obligation to use only media whose operators are established on its territory.

2. The home Member State shall ensure that there is at least one officially appointed mechanism for the central storage of regulated information. These mechanisms should comply with minimum quality standards of security, certainty as to the information source, time recording and

easy access by end users and shall be aligned with the filing procedure under Article 19(1).

3. Where securities are admitted to trading on a regulated market in only one host Member State and not in the home Member State, the host Member State shall ensure disclosure of regulated information in accordance with the requirements referred to in paragraph 1.

4. In order to take account of technical developments in financial markets, to take account of developments in information and communication technology and to ensure the uniform application of paragraphs 1, 2 and 3, the Commission shall adopt implementing measures in accordance with the procedure referred to in Article 27(2).

The Commission shall in particular specify:

(a) minimum standards for the dissemination of regulated information, as referred to in paragraph 1;

(b) minimum standards for the central storage mechanism as referred to in paragraph 2.

The Commission may also specify and update a list of media for the dissemination of information to the public.

Article 22
Guidelines

1. The competent authorities of the Member States shall draw up appropriate guidelines with a view to further facilitating public access to information to be disclosed under Directive 2003/6/EC, Directive 2003/71/EC and this Directive.

The aim of those guidelines shall be the creation of:

(a) an electronic network to be set up at national level between national securities regulators, operators of regulated markets and national company registers covered by the First Council Directive 68/151/EEC of 9 March 1968 on coordination of safeguards which, for the protection of the interests of members and others, are required by Member States of companies within the meaning of the second paragraph of Article 48[19] of the Treaty, with a view to making such safeguards equivalent throughout the Community;[20] and

(b) a single electronic network, or a platform of electronic networks across Member States.

2. The Commission shall review the results achieved under paragraph 1 by 31 December 2006 and may, in accordance with the procedure referred to in Article 27(2), adopt implementing measures to facilitate compliance with Articles 19 and 21.

Article 23
Third countries

1. Where the registered office of an issuer is in a third country, the competent authority of the home Member State may exempt that issuer from requirements under Articles 4 to 7 and Articles 12(6), 14, 15 and 16 to 18, provided that the law of the third country in question lays down equivalent requirements or such an issuer complies with requirements of the law of a third country that the competent authority of the home Member State considers as equivalent.

However, the information covered by the requirements laid down in the third country shall be filed in accordance with Article 19 and disclosed in accordance with Articles 20 and 21.

2. By way of derogation from paragraph 1, an issuer whose registered office is in a third country shall be exempted from preparing its financial statement in accordance with Article 4 or Article 5 prior to the financial year starting on or after 1 January 2007, provided such issuer prepares its financial statements in accordance with internationally accepted standards referred to in Article 9 of Regulation (EC) No 1606/2002.

3. The competent authority of the home Member State shall ensure that information

---

[19] The title has been adjusted to take account of the renumbering of the Articles of the Treaty establishing the European Community in accordance with Article 12 of the Treaty of Amsterdam; the original reference was to Article 58 of the Treaty.

[20] OJ L 65, 14.3.1968, 8, reproduced supra under no. C. 1. Directive as last amended by Directive 2003/58/EC of the European Parliament and of the Council (OJ L 221, 4.9.2003, 13), reproduced supra under no. C. 24.

disclosed in a third country which may be of importance for the public in the Community is disclosed in accordance with Articles 20 and 21, even if such information is not regulated information within the meaning of Article 2(1)(k).

4. In order to ensure the uniform application of paragraph 1, the Commission shall, in accordance with the procedure referred to in Article 27(2), adopt implementing measures
 (i) setting up a mechanism ensuring the establishment of equivalence of information required under this Directive, including financial statements and information, including financial statements, required under the law, regulations or administrative provisions of a third country;
 (ii) stating that, by reason of its domestic law, regulations, administrative provisions, or of the practices or procedures based on the international standards set by international organisations, the third country where the issuer is registered ensures the equivalence of the information requirements provided for in this Directive.

The Commission shall, in accordance with the procedure referred to in Article 27(2), take the necessary decisions on the equivalence of accounting standards which are used by third country issuers under the conditions set out in Article 30(3) at the latest five years following the date referred to in Article 31. If the Commission decides that the accounting standards of a third country are not equivalent, it may allow the issuers concerned to continue using such accounting standards during an appropriate transitional period.

5. In order to ensure uniform application of paragraph 2, the Commission may, in accordance with the procedure referred to in Article 27(2), adopt implementing measures defining the type of information disclosed in a third country that is of importance to the public in the Community.

6. Undertakings whose registered office is in a third country which would have required an authorisation in accordance with Article 5(1) of Directive 85/611/EEC or, with regard to portfolio management under point 4 of section A of Annex I to Directive 2004/39/EC if it had its registered office or, only in the case of an investment firm, its head office within the Community, shall also be exempted from aggregating holdings with the holdings of its parent undertaking under the requirements laid down in Article 12(4) and (5) provided that they comply with equivalent conditions of independence as management companies or investment firms.

7. In order to take account of technical developments in financial markets and to ensure the uniform application of paragraph 6, the Commission shall, in accordance with the procedure referred to in Article 27(2), adopt implementing measures stating that, by reason of its domestic law, regulations, or administrative provisions, a third country ensures the equivalence of the independence requirements provided for under this Directive and its implementing measures.

Chapter V

Competent Authorities

Article 24

Competent authorities and their powers

1. Each Member State shall designate the central authority referred to in Article 21(1) of Directive 2003/71/EC as central competent administrative authority responsible for carrying out the obligations provided for in this Directive and for ensuring that the provisions adopted pursuant to this Directive are applied. Member States shall inform the Commission accordingly.

However, for the purpose of paragraph 4(h) Member States may designate a competent authority other than the central competent authority referred to in the first subparagraph.

2. Member States may allow their central competent authority to delegate tasks. Except for the tasks referred to in paragraph 4(h), any delegation of tasks relating to the obligations provided for in this Directive and in its implementing measures shall be reviewed five years after the entry into force of this Directive and shall end eight years after the entry into force of this

Directive. Any delegation of tasks shall be made in a specific manner stating the tasks to be undertaken and the conditions under which they are to be carried out.

Those conditions shall include a clause requiring the entity in question to be organised in a manner such that conflicts of interest are avoided and information obtained from carrying out the delegated tasks is not used unfairly or to prevent competition. In any case, the final responsibility for supervising compliance with the provisions of this Directive and implementing measures adopted pursuant thereto shall lie with the competent authority designated in accordance with paragraph 1.

3. Member States shall inform the Commission and competent authorities of other Member States of any arrangements entered into with regard to the delegation of tasks, including the precise conditions for regulating the delegations.

4. Each competent authority shall have all the powers necessary for the performance of its functions. It shall at least be empowered to:

(a) require auditors, issuers, holders of shares or other financial instruments, or persons or entities referred to in Articles 10 or 13, and the persons that control them or are controlled by them, to provide information and documents;

(b) require the issuer to disclose the information required under point (a) to the public by the means and within the time limits the authority considers necessary. It may publish such information on its own initiative in the event that the issuer, or the persons that control it or are controlled by it, fail to do so and after having heard the issuer;

(c) require managers of the issuers and of the holders of shares or other financial instruments, or of persons or entities referred to in Articles 10 or 13, to notify the information required under this Directive, or under national law adopted in accordance with this Directive, and, if necessary, to provide further information and documents;

(d) suspend, or request the relevant regulated market to suspend, trading in securities for a maximum of ten days at a time if it has reasonable grounds for suspecting that the provisions of this Directive, or of national law adopted in accordance with this Directive, have been infringed by the issuer;

(e) prohibit trading on a regulated market if it finds that the provisions of this Directive, or of national law adopted in accordance with this Directive, have been infringed, or if it has reasonable grounds for suspecting that the provisions of this Directive have been infringed;

(f) monitor that the issuer discloses timely information with the objective of ensuring effective and equal access to the public in all Member States where the securities are traded and take appropriate action if that is not the case;

(g) make public the fact that an issuer, or a holder of shares or other financial instruments, or a person or entity referred to in Articles 10 or 13, is failing to comply with its obligations;

(h) examine that information referred to in this Directive is drawn up in accordance with the relevant reporting framework and take appropriate measures in case of discovered infringements; and

(i) carry out on-site inspections in its territory in accordance with national law, in order to verify compliance with the provisions of this Directive and its implementing measures. Where necessary under national law, the competent authority or authorities may use this power by applying to the relevant judicial authority and/or in cooperation with other authorities.

5. Paragraphs 1 to 4 shall be without prejudice to the possibility for a Member State to make separate legal and administrative arrangements for overseas European territories for whose external relations that Member State is responsible.

6. The disclosure to competent authorities by the auditors of any fact or decision related to the requests made by the competent authority under paragraph (4)(a) shall not constitute a breach of any restriction on disclosure of information imposed by contract or by any law, regulation or administrative provision and shall not involve such auditors in liability of any kind.

Article 25
Professional secrecy and cooperation between Member States

1. The obligation of professional secrecy shall apply to all persons who work or who have worked for the competent authority and for entities to which competent authorities may have delegated certain tasks. Information covered by professional secrecy may not be disclosed to any other person or authority except by virtue of the laws, regulations or administrative provisions of a Member State.

2. Competent authorities of the Member States shall cooperate with each other, whenever necessary, for the purpose of carrying out their duties and making use of their powers, whether set out in this Directive or in national law adopted pursuant to this Directive. Competent authorities shall render assistance to competent authorities of other Member States.

3. Paragraph 1 shall not prevent the competent authorities from exchanging confidential information. Information thus exchanged shall be covered by the obligation of professional secrecy to which the persons employed or formerly employed by the competent authorities receiving the information are subject.

4. Member States may conclude cooperation agreements providing for the exchange of information with the competent authorities or bodies of third countries enabled by their respective legislation to carry out any of the tasks assigned by this Directive to the competent authorities in accordance with Article 24. Such an exchange of information is subject to guarantees of professional secrecy at least equivalent to those referred to in this Article. Such exchange of information shall be intended for the performance of the supervisory task of the authorities or bodies mentioned. Where the information originates in another Member State, it may not be disclosed without the express agreement of the competent authorities which have disclosed it and, where appropriate, solely for the purposes for which those authorities gave their agreement.

Article 26
Precautionary measures

1. Where the competent authority of a host Member State finds that the issuer or the holder of shares or other financial instruments, or the person or entity referred to in Article 10, has committed irregularities or infringed its obligations, it shall refer its findings to the competent authority of the home Member State.

2. If, despite the measures taken by the competent authority of the home Member State, or because such measures prove inadequate, the issuer or the security holder persists in infringing the relevant legal or regulatory provisions, the competent authority of the host Member State shall, after informing the competent authority of the home Member State, take, in accordance with Article 3(2), all the appropriate measures in order to protect investors. The Commission shall be informed of such measures at the earliest opportunity.

CHAPTER VI
IMPLEMENTING MEASURES

Article 27
Committee procedure

1. The Commission shall be assisted by the European Securities Committee, instituted by Article 1 of Decision 2001/528/EC.

2. Where reference is made to this paragraph, Articles 5 and 7 of Decision 1999/468/EC shall apply, having regard to the provisions of Article 8 thereof, provided that the implementing measures adopted in accordance with that procedure do not modify the essential provisions of this Directive. The period laid down in Article 5(6) of Decision 1999/468/EC shall be set at three months.

3. The Committee shall adopt its Rules of Procedure.

4. Without prejudice to the implementing measures already adopted by 20 January 2009 the application of the provisions of this Directive

concerning the adoption of technical rules and decisions in accordance with the procedure referred to in paragraph 2 shall be suspended. On a proposal from the Commission, the European Parliament and the Council may renew the provisions concerned in accordance with the procedure laid down in Article 251 of the Treaty and, to that end, shall review them prior to the expiry of the four-year period.

Article 28

Penalties

1. Without prejudice to the right of Member States to impose criminal penalties, Member States shall ensure, in conformity with their national law, that at least the appropriate administrative measures may be taken or civil and/or administrative penalties imposed in respect of the persons responsible, where the provisions adopted in accordance with this Directive have not been complied with. Member States shall ensure that those measures are effective, proportionate and dissuasive.

2. Member States shall provide that the competent authority may disclose to the public every measure taken or penalty imposed for infringement of the provisions adopted in accordance with this Directive, save where such disclosure would seriously jeopardise the financial markets or cause disproportionate damage to the parties involved.

Article 29

Right of appeal

Member States shall ensure that decisions taken under laws, regulations, and administrative provisions adopted in accordance with this Directive are subject to the right of appeal to the courts.

Chapter VII

Transitional and Final Provisions

Article 30

Transitional provisions

1. By way of derogation from Article 5(3) of this Directive, the home Member State may exempt from disclosing financial statements in accordance with Regulation (EC) No 1606/2002 issuers referred to in Article 9 of that Regulation for the financial year starting on or after 1 January 2006.

2. Notwithstanding Article 12(2), a shareholder shall notify the issuer at the latest two months after the date in Article 31(1) of the proportion of voting rights and capital it holds, in accordance with Articles 9, 10 and 13, with issuers at that date, unless it has already made a notification containing equivalent information before that date.

Notwithstanding Article 12(6), an issuer shall in turn disclose the information received in those notifications no later than three months after the date in Article 31(1).

3. Where an issuer is incorporated in a third country, the home Member State may exempt such issuer only in respect of those debt securities which have already been admitted to trading on a regulated market in the Community prior to 1 January 2005 from drawing up its financial statements in accordance with Article 4(3) and its management report in accordance with Article 4(5) as long as

(a) the competent authority of the home Member State acknowledges that annual financial statements prepared by issuers from such a third country give a true and fair view of the issuer's assets and liabilities, financial position and results;

(b) the third country where the issuer is incorporated has not made mandatory the application of international accounting standards referred to in Article 2 of Regulation (EC) No 1606/2002; and

(c) the Commission has not taken any decision in accordance with Article 23(4)(ii) as to whether there is an equivalence between the abovementioned accounting standards and

– the accounting standards laid down in the law, regulations or administrative provisions of the third country where the issuer is incorporated, or

– the accounting standards of a third country such an issuer has elected to comply with.

4. The home Member State may exempt issuers only in respect of those debt securities which have already been admitted to trading on a regulated market in the Community prior to 1 January 2005 from disclosing half-yearly financial reports in accordance with Article 5 for 10 years following 1 January 2005, provided that the home Member State had decided to allow such issuers to benefit from the provisions of Article 27 of Directive 2001/34/EC at the point of admission of those debt securities.

Article 31
Transposition

1. Member States shall take the necessary measures to comply with this Directive by 20 January 2007. They shall forthwith inform the Commission thereof. When Member States adopt these measures, they shall contain a reference to this Directive or shall be accompanied by such reference on the occasion of their official publication. The methods of making such reference shall be laid down by Member States.

2. Where Member States adopt measures pursuant to Articles 3(1), 8(2), 8(3), 9(6) or 30, they shall immediately communicate those measures to the Commission and to the other Member States.

Article 32
Amendments

[. . .]

¶ *This article modifies articles 1, 6, 8, 107, and 108 and deletes articles 4, 65 to 97, 102, and 103 of Directive 2001/34/EC, reproduced supra under no. S. 18. The modifications are directly incorporated therein.*

Article 33
Review

The Commission shall by 30 June 2009 report on the operation of this Directive to the European Parliament and to the Council including the appropriateness of ending the exemption for existing debt securities after the 10-year period as provided for by Article 30(4) and its potential impact on the European financial markets.

Article 34
Entry into force

This Directive shall enter into force on the twentieth day following that of its publication in the *Official Journal of the European Union*.

Article 35
Addressees

This Directive is addressed to the Member States.

S. 32.

European Parliament and Council Directive 2006/31/EC
of 5 April 2006
amending directive on markets in financial instruments, as regards certain deadlines[1]

(Text with EEA relevance)

THE EUROPEAN PARLIAMENT AND THE COUNCIL OF THE EUROPEAN UNION,

Having regard to the Treaty establishing the European Community, and in particular Article 47(2) thereof,

Having regard to the proposal from the Commission,

After consulting the European Economic and Social Committee,

Having regard to the opinion of the European Central Bank,[2]

Acting in accordance with the procedure laid down in Article 251 of the Treaty,[3]

Whereas:

(1) Directive 2004/39/EC of the European Parliament and of the Council of 21 April 2004 on markets in financial instruments[4] introduces a comprehensive regulatory regime to ensure a high quality of execution of investor transactions.

(2) Directive 2004/39/EC provides that Member States are to adopt the laws, regulations and administrative provisions necessary to comply with it by 30 April 2006. In order to ensure uniform application in the Member States, a significant number of complex provisions of that Directive need to be supplemented by implementing measures, to be adopted by the Commission during the period for transposition by Member States. Because Member States cannot fully prepare and finalise their national laws until the content of the implementing measures is clear, they may have difficulty in meeting the current transposition deadline.

(3) In order to comply with the requirements of Directive 2004/39/EC and national implementing legislation, investment firms and other regulated entities may have to introduce new information technology systems, new organisational structures, and reporting and record-keeping procedures, or to make significant modifications to existing systems and practices. This can only be done once the contents of the implementing measures to be adopted by the Commission and of the national legislation transposing the Directive are settled.

(4) It is also necessary that Directive 2004/39/EC and its implementing measures be transposed into national law or apply directly in Member States simultaneously for the Directive to produce its full effect.

(5) It is therefore appropriate to extend the deadline for Member States to transpose Directive 2004/39/EC into national law. Similarly, the deadline for investment firms and credit institutions to comply with the new requirements should be postponed for a period after the transposition into national law has been completed by the Member States.

(6) Given the interaction between the different provisions of Directive 2004/39/EC, it is appropriate that any extension of those deadlines apply to all the provisions of that Directive. Any extension of the transposition and application deadlines should be proportionate to, and not exceed,

---

[1] OJ L 114, 27.4.2006, 60–63.
[2] OJ C 323, 20.12.2005, 31.
[3] Opinion of the European Parliament of 13 December 2005 (not yet published in the Official Journal) and Council Decision of 10 March 2006.
[4] OJ L 145, 30.4.2004, 1, reproduced supra under no. S. 29.

the needs of the Member States and regulated entities. In order to avoid fragmentation that could hamper the functioning of the internal market in securities, Member States should apply the provisions of Directive 2004/39/EC at the same time.

(7) In its Resolution of 5 February 2002 on the implementation of financial services legislation,[5] the European Parliament requested that it and the Council should have an equal role in supervising the way in which the Commission exercises its executive role in order to reflect the legislative powers of the European Parliament under Article 251 of the Treaty. In the solemn declaration made before the European Parliament the same day by its President, the Commission supported that request. On 11 December 2002, the Commission proposed amendments to Council Decision 1999/468/EC of 28 June 1999 laying down the procedures for the exercise of implementing powers conferred on the Commission,[6] and then submitted an amended proposal on 22 April 2004. The European Parliament does not consider that this proposal preserves its legislative prerogatives. In the view of the European Parliament, it and the Council should have the opportunity of evaluating the conferral of implementing powers on the Commission within a determined period. It is therefore appropriate to limit the period during which the Commission may adopt implementing measures.

(8) The European Parliament should be given a period of three months from the first transmission of draft amendments and implementing measures to allow it to examine them and to give its opinion. However, in urgent and duly justified cases, it should be possible to shorten that period. If, within that period, a resolution is adopted by the European Parliament, the Commission should re-examine the draft amendments or measures.

(9) Further consequential amendments are necessary to postpone the dates for the repeal of Council Directive 93/22/EEC of 10 May 1993 on investment services in the securities field[7] and for the transitional provisions laid down in Directive 2004/39/EC, and to extend the timetable for the Commission's reporting obligations.

(10) Given the postponed deadline between the obligation for Member States to transpose Directive 2004/39/EC into national law and the deadline for investment firms and credit institutions to comply with the new requirements, the provisions of Directive 2004/39/EC will remain ineffective until 1 November 2007; it is therefore appropriate to repeal Directive 93/22/EEC with effect from 1 November 2007.

(11) Directive 2004/39/EC should therefore be amended accordingly,

HAVE ADOPTED THIS DIRECTIVE:

Article 1

[. . .]

¶ *Article 1 amends recital 69, paragraphs 2a and 3 of article 64, article 65, article 69, the first paragraph of article 70, and paragraphs 1 to 5 of article 71 of Directive 2004/39/EC, reproduced supra under no. S. 29. The modifications are directly incorporated therein.*

Article 2

1. Member States shall adopt the laws, regulations and administrative provisions necessary to comply with this Directive by 31 January 2007. They shall forthwith inform the Commission thereof.

They shall apply these measures from 1 November 2007.

2. When Member States adopt these measures, they shall contain a reference to this Directive or shall be accompanied by such reference on the

---

[5] OJ C 284 E, 21.11.2002, 115.
[6] OJ L 184, 17.7.1999, 23.

[7] OJ L 141, 11.6.1993, 27, reproduced supra under no. S. 14. Directive as last amended by Directive 2002/87/EC of the European Parliament and of the Council (OJ L 35, 11.2.2003, 1), reproduced supra under no. B. 38.

occasion of their official publication. The methods of making such reference shall be laid down by Member States.

Article 3

This Directive shall enter into force on the day following that of its publication in the Official Journal of the European Union.

Article 4

This Directive is addressed to the Member States.

S. 33.

Commission Regulation 1287/2006/EC
of 10 August 2006
implementing Directive 2004/39/EC of the European Parliament and of the Council as regards record-keeping obligations for investment firms, transaction reporting, market transparency, admission of financial instruments to trading, and defined terms for the purposes of that Directive[1]

(Text with EEA relevance)

THE COMMISSION OF THE EUROPEAN COMMUNITIES,

Having regard to the Treaty establishing the European Community,

Having regard to Directive 2004/39/EC of the European Parliament and of the Council of 21 April 2004 on markets in financial instruments amending Council Directives 85/611/EEC and 93/6/EEC and Directive 2000/12/EC of the European Parliament and of the Council and repealing Council Directive 93/22/EEC,[2] and in particular Articles 4(1)(2), 4(1)(7) and 4(2), Article 13(10), Article 25(7), Article 27(7), Article 28(3), Article 29(3), Article 30(3), Article 40(6), Article 44(3), Article 45(3), Article 56(5), and Article 58(4) thereof,

Whereas:

(1) Directive 2004/39/EC establishes the general framework for a regulatory regime for financial markets in the Community, setting out, among other matters: operating conditions relating to the performance by investment firms of investment and ancillary services, and investment activities; organisational requirements (including record-keeping obligations) for investment firms performing such services and activities on a professional basis, and for regulated markets; transaction reporting requirements in respect of transactions in financial instruments, and transparency requirements in respect of transactions in shares.

(2) It is appropriate that the provisions of this Regulation take that legislative form in order to ensure a harmonised regime in all Member States, to promote market integration and the cross-border provision of investment and ancillary services, and to facilitate the further consolidation of the single market. Provisions relating to certain aspects of record-keeping, and to transaction reporting, transparency and commodity derivatives have few interfaces with national law and with detailed laws governing client relationships.

(3) Detailed and fully harmonised transparency requirements and rules regulating transaction reporting are appropriate so as to ensure equivalent market conditions and the smooth operation of securities markets throughout the Community, and to facilitate the effective integration of those markets. Certain aspects of record-keeping are closely allied as they make use of the same concepts as are defined for transaction reporting and transparency purposes.

(4) The regime established by Directive 2004/39/EC governing transaction reporting requirements in respect of transactions in financial instruments aims to ensure that relevant competent authorities are properly informed about transactions in which they have a supervisory interest. For those purposes it is necessary to ensure that a single data set is collected from all

---

[1] OJ L 241, 2.9.2006, 1–25.
[2] OJ L 145, 30.4.2004, 1, reproduced supra under no. S. 29. Directive as amended by Directive 2006/31/EC (OJ L 114, 27.4.2006, 60), reproduced supra under no. S. 32.

investment firms with a minimum of variation between Member States, so as to minimise the extent to which businesses operating across borders are subject to different reporting obligations, and so as to maximise the proportion of data held by a competent authority that can be shared with other competent authorities. The measures are also designed to ensure that competent authorities are in a position to carry out their obligations under that Directive as expeditiously and efficiently as possible.

(5) The regime established by Directive 2004/39/EC governing transparency requirements in respect of transactions in shares admitted to trading on a regulated market aims to ensure that investors are adequately informed as to the true level of actual and potential transactions in such shares, whether those transactions take place on regulated markets, multilateral trading facilities, hereinafter 'MTFs', systematic internalisers, or outside those trading venues. Those requirements are part of a broader framework of rules designed to promote competition between trading venues for execution services so as to increase investor choice, encourage innovation, lower transaction costs, and increase the efficiency of the price formation process on a pan-Community basis. A high degree of transparency is an essential part of this framework, so as to ensure a level playing field between trading venues so that the price discovery mechanism in respect of particular shares is not impaired by the fragmentation of liquidity, and investors are not thereby penalised. On the other hand, that Directive recognises that there may be circumstances where exemptions from pre-trade transparency obligations, or deferral of post-trade transparency obligations, may be necessary. This Regulation sets out details of those circumstances, bearing in mind the need both to ensure a high level of transparency, and to ensure that liquidity on trading venues and elsewhere is not impaired as an unintended consequence of obligations to disclose transactions and thereby to make public risk positions.

(6) For the purposes of the provisions on record-keeping, a reference to the type of the order should be understood as referring to its status as a limit order, market order, or other specific type of order. For the purposes of the provisions on record-keeping, a reference to the nature of the order or transaction should be understood as referring to orders to subscribe for securities or the subscription of securities, or to exercise an option or the exercise of an option, or similar client orders or transactions.

(7) It is not necessary at this stage to specify or prescribe in detail the type, nature and sophistication of the arrangements for the exchange of information between competent authorities.

(8) Where a notification made by a competent authority relating to the alternative determination of the most relevant market in terms of liquidity is not acted upon within a reasonable time, or where a competent authority does not agree with the calculation made by the other authority, the competent authorities concerned should seek to find a solution. It is open to the competent authorities, where appropriate, to discuss the matter in the Committee of European Securities Regulators.

(9) The competent authorities should coordinate the design and establishment of arrangements for the exchange of transaction information between themselves. Again it is open to the competent authorities to discuss those matters in the Committee of European Securities Regulators. Competent authorities should report to the Commission which should inform the European Securities Committee of those arrangements. In carrying out the coordination, competent authorities should consider the need to monitor the activities of investment firms effectively, so as to ensure that they act honestly, fairly and professionally and in a manner which promotes the integrity of the market in the Community, the need for decisions to be based on a thorough cost-benefit analysis, the need to ensure that transaction information is used only for the proper discharge of the functions of competent authorities and finally the need to have effective and accountable governance arrangements for any common system that might be considered necessary.

(10) It is appropriate to set the criteria for determining when the operations of a regulated market are of substantial importance in a host Member State and the consequences of that status in such a way as to avoid creating an obligation on a regulated market to deal with or be made subject to more than one competent authority where otherwise there would be no such obligation.

(11) ISO 10962 (Classification of financial instruments code) is an example of a uniform internationally accepted standard for financial instrument classification.

(12) If granting waivers in relation to pre-trade transparency requirements, or authorising the deferral of post-trade transparency obligations, competent authorities should treat all regulated markets and MTFs equally and in a non-discriminatory manner, so that a waiver or deferral is granted either to all regulated markets and MTFs that they authorise under Directive 2004/39/EC, or to none. Competent authorities which grant the waivers or deferrals should not impose additional requirements.

(13) It is appropriate to consider that a trading algorithm operated by a regulated market or MTF usually should seek to maximise the volume traded, but other trading algorithms should be possible.

(14) A waiver from pre-trade transparency obligations arising under Articles 29 or 44 of Directive 2004/39/EC conferred by a competent authority should not enable investment firms to avoid such obligations in respect of those transactions in liquid shares which they conclude on a bilateral basis under the rules of a regulated market or an MTF where, if carried out outside the rules of the regulated market or MTF, those transactions would be subject to the requirements to publish quotes set out in Article 27 of that Directive.

(15) An activity should be considered as having a material commercial role for an investment firm if the activity is a significant source of revenue, or a significant source of cost. An assessment of significance for these purposes should, in every case, take into account the extent to which the activity is conducted or organised separately, the monetary value of the activity, and its comparative significance by reference both to the overall business of the firm and to its overall activity in the market for the share concerned in which the firm operates. It should be possible to consider an activity to be a significant source of revenue for a firm even if only one or two of the factors mentioned is relevant in a particular case.

(16) Shares not traded daily should not be considered as having a liquid market for the purposes of Directive 2004/39/EC. However, if, for exceptional reasons, trading in a share is suspended for reasons related to the preservation of an orderly market or force majeure and therefore a share is not traded during some trading days, this should not mean that the share cannot be considered to have a liquid market.

(17) The requirement to make certain quotes, orders or transactions public pursuant to Articles 27, 28, 29, 30, 44 and 45 of Directive 2004/39/EC and this Regulation should not prevent regulated markets and MTFs from requiring their members or participants to make public other such information.

(18) Information which is required to be made available as close to real time as possible should be made available as close to instantaneously as technically possible, assuming a reasonable level of efficiency and of expenditure on systems on the part of the person concerned. The information should only be published close to the three minute maximum limit in exceptional cases where the systems available do not allow for a publication in a shorter period of time.

(19) For the purposes of the provisions of this Regulation as to the admission to trading on a regulated market of a transferable security as defined in Article 4(1)(18)(c) of Directive 2004/39/EC, in the case of a security within the meaning of Directive 2003/71/EC of the European Parliament and of the Council of 4 November 2003 on the prospectus to be published when securities are offered to the public or admitted to trading and amending Directive

2001/34/EC,[3] there should be considered to be sufficient information publicly available of a kind needed to value that financial instrument.

(20) The admission to trading on a regulated market of units issued by undertakings for collective investment in transferable securities should not allow the avoidance of the relevant provisions of Council Directive 85/611/EEC of 20 December 1985 on the coordination of laws, regulations and administrative provisions relating to undertakings for collective investment in transferable securities (UCITS),[4] and in particular Articles 44 to 48 of that Directive.

(21) A derivative contract should only be considered to be a financial instrument under Section C(7) of Annex I to Directive 2004/39/EC if it relates to a commodity and meets the criteria in this Regulation for determining whether a contract should be considered as having the characteristics of other derivative financial instruments and as not being for commercial purposes. A derivative contract should only be considered to be a financial instrument under Section C(10) of that Annex if it relates to an underlying specified in Section C(10) or in this Regulation and meets the criteria in this Regulation for determining whether it should be considered as having the characteristics of other derivative financial instruments.

(22) The exemptions in Directive 2004/39/EC that relate to dealing on own account or to dealing or providing other investment services in relation to commodity derivatives covered by Sections C(5), C(6) and C(7) of Annex I to that Directive or derivatives covered by Section C(10) of that Annex I could be expected to exclude significant numbers of commercial producers and consumers of energy and other commodities, including energy suppliers, commodity merchants and their subsidiaries from the scope of that Directive, and therefore such participants will not be required to apply the tests in this Regulation to determine if the contracts they deal in are financial instruments.

(23) In accordance with Section B(7) of Annex I to Directive 2004/39/EC, investment firms may exercise the freedom to provide ancillary services in a Member State other than their home Member State, by performing investment services and activities and ancillary services of the type included under Section A or B of that Annex related to the underlying of the derivatives included under Sections C(5), (6), (7) and (10) of that Annex, where these are connected to the provision of investment or ancillary services. On this basis, a firm performing investment services or activities, and connected trading in spot contracts, should be capable to take advantage of the freedom to provide ancillary services in respect of that connected trading.

(24) The definition of a commodity should not affect any other definition of that term in national legislation and other community legislation. The tests for determining whether a contract should be considered as having the characteristics of other derivative financial instruments and not being for commercial purposes are only intended to be used for the purposes of determining whether contracts fall within Section C(7) or C(10) of Annex I to Directive 2004/39/EC.

(25) A derivative contract should be understood as relating to a commodity or to another factor where there is a direct link between that contract and the relevant underlying commodity or factor. A derivative contract on the price of a commodity should therefore be regarded as a derivative contract relating to the commodity, while a derivative contract on the transportation costs for the commodity should not be regarded as a derivative contract relating to the commodity. A derivative that relates to a commodity derivative, such as an option on a commodity future (a derivative relating to a derivative) would constitute an indirect investment in commodities and should therefore still be regarded as a commodity derivative for the purposes of Directive 2004/39/EC.

(26) The concept of commodity should not include services or other items that are not goods,

---

[3] OJ L 345, 31.12.2003, 64, reproduced supra under no. S. 25.
[4] OJ L 375, 31.12.1985, 3, reproduced supra under no. S. 6. Directive as last amended by Directive 2005/1/EC of the European Parliament and of the Council (OJ L 79, 24.3.2005, 9), reproduced supra under no. B. 39.

such as currencies or rights in real estate, or that are entirely intangible.

(27) The Committee of European Securities Regulators, established by Commission Decision 2001/527/EC[5] has been consulted for technical advice.

(28) The measures provided for in this Regulation are in accordance with the opinion of the European Securities Committee,

HAS ADOPTED THIS REGULATION:

CHAPTER I

GENERAL

Article 1

Subject-matter and scope

1. This Regulation lays down the detailed rules for the implementation of Articles 4(1)(2), 4(1)(7), 13(6), 25, 27, 28, 29, 30, 40, 44, 45, 56 and 58 of Directive 2004/39/EC.

2. Articles 7 and 8 shall apply to management companies in accordance with Article 5(4) of Directive 85/611/EEC.

Article 2

Definitions

For the purposes of this Regulation, the following definitions shall apply:

(1) 'commodity' means any goods of a fungible nature that are capable of being delivered, including metals and their ores and alloys, agricultural products, and energy such as electricity;

(2) 'issuer' means an entity which issues transferable securities and, where appropriate, other financial instruments;

(3) 'Community issuer' means an issuer which has its registered office in the Community;

(4) 'third country issuer' means an issuer which is not a Community issuer;

(5) 'normal trading hours' for a trading venue or an investment firm means those hours which the trading venue or investment firm establishes in advance and makes public as its trading hours;

(6) 'portfolio trade' means a transaction in more than one security where those securities are grouped and traded as a single lot against a specific reference price;

(7) 'relevant competent authority' for a financial instrument means the competent authority of the most relevant market in terms of liquidity for that financial instrument;

(8) 'trading venue' means a regulated market, MTF or systematic internaliser acting in its capacity as such, and, where appropriate, a system outside the Community with similar functions to a regulated market or MTF;

(9) 'turnover', in relation to a financial instrument, means the sum of the results of multiplying the number of units of that instrument exchanged between buyers and sellers in a defined period of time, pursuant to transactions taking place on a trading venue or otherwise, by the unit price applicable to each such transaction;

(10) 'securities financing transaction' means an instance of stock lending or stock borrowing or the lending or borrowing of other financial instruments, a repurchase or reverse repurchase transaction, or a buy-sell back or sell-buy back transaction.

Article 3

Transactions related to an individual share in a portfolio trade and volume weighted average price transactions

1. A transaction related to an individual share in a portfolio trade shall be considered, for the purposes of Article 18(1)(b)(ii), as a transaction subject to conditions other than the current market price.

It shall also be considered, for the purposes of Article 27(1)(b), as a transaction where the exchange of shares is determined by factors other than the current market valuation of the share.

2. A volume weighted average price transaction shall be considered, for the purposes of Article 18(1)(b)(ii), as a transaction subject to conditions

---

[5] OJ L 191, 13.7.2001, 43, reproduced supra under no. S. 19.

other than the current market price and, for the purposes of Article 25, as an order subject to conditions other than the current market price.

It shall also be considered, for the purposes of Article 27(1)(b), as a transaction where the exchange of shares is determined by factors other than the current market valuation of the share.

Article 4
References to trading day

1. A reference to a trading day in relation to a trading venue, or in relation to post-trade information to be made public under Article 30 or 45 of Directive 2004/39/EC in relation to a share, shall be a reference to any day during which the trading venue concerned is open for trading.

A reference to the opening of the trading day shall be a reference to the commencement of the normal trading hours of the trading venue.

A reference to noon on the trading day shall be a reference to noon in the time zone where the trading venue is established.

A reference to the end of the trading day shall be a reference to the end of its normal trading hours.

2. A reference to a trading day in relation to the most relevant market in terms of liquidity for a share, or in relation to post-trade information to be made public under Article 28 of Directive 2004/39/EC in relation to a share, shall be a reference to any day of normal trading on trading venues in that market.

A reference to the opening of the trading day shall be a reference to the earliest commencement of normal trading in that share on trading venues in that market.

A reference to noon on the trading day shall be a reference to noon in the time zone of that market.

A reference to the end of the trading day shall be a reference to the latest cessation of normal trading in that share on trading venues in that market.

3. A reference to a trading day in relation to a spot contract, within the meaning of Article 38(2), shall be a reference to any day of normal trading of that contract on trading venues.

Article 5
References to transaction

For the purposes of this Regulation, a reference to a transaction is a reference only to the purchase and sale of a financial instrument. For the purposes of this Regulation, other than Chapter II, the purchase and sale of a financial instrument does not include any of the following:

(a) securities financing transactions;

(b) the exercise of options or of covered warrants;

(c) primary market transactions (such as issuance, allotment or subscription) in financial instruments falling within Article 4(1)(18)(a) and (b) of Directive 2004/39/EC.

Article 6
First admission to trading of a share on a regulated market

For the purposes of this Regulation, the first admission to trading of a share on a regulated market referred to in Article 40 of Directive 2004/39/EC shall be considered to take place at a time when one of the following conditions applies:

(a) the share has not previously been admitted to trading on a regulated market;

(b) the share has previously been admitted to trading on a regulated market but the share is removed from trading on every regulated market which has so admitted it.

Chapter II
Record-keeping: Client Orders and Transactions

Article 7
(Article 13(6) of Directive 2004/39/EC)
Record-keeping of client orders and decisions to deal

An investment firm shall, in relation to every order received from a client, and in relation to every decision to deal taken in providing the service of portfolio management, immediately make a record of the following details, to the extent they are applicable to the order or decision to deal in question:

(a) the name or other designation of the client;

(b) the name or other designation of any relevant person acting on behalf of the client;

(c) the details specified in points 4, 6 and 16 to 19, of Table 1 of Annex I;

(d) the nature of the order if other than buy or sell;

(e) the type of the order;

(f) any other details, conditions and particular instructions from the client that specify how the order must be carried out;

(g) the date and exact time of the receipt of the order, or of the decision to deal, by the investment firm.

Article 8

(Article 13(6) of Directive 2004/39/EC)

Record-keeping of transactions

1. Immediately after executing a client order, or, in the case of investment firms that transmit orders to another person for execution, immediately after receiving confirmation that an order has been executed, investment firms shall record the following details of the transaction in question:

(a) the name or other designation of the client;

(b) the details specified in points 2, 3, 4, 6 and 16 to 21, of Table 1 of Annex I;

(c) the total price, being the product of the unit price and the quantity;

(d) the nature of the transaction if other than buy or sell;

(e) the natural person who executed the transaction or who is responsible for the execution.

2. If an investment firm transmits an order to another person for execution, the investment firm shall immediately record the following details after making the transmission:

(a) the name or other designation of the client whose order has been transmitted;

(b) the name or other designation of the person to whom the order was transmitted;

(c) the terms of the order transmitted;

(d) the date and exact time of transmission.

CHAPTER III

TRANSACTION REPORTING

Article 9

(Second subparagraph of Article 25(3) of Directive 2004/39/EC)

Determination of the most relevant market in terms of liquidity

1. The most relevant market in terms of liquidity for a financial instrument which is admitted to trading on a regulated market, hereinafter 'the most relevant market', shall be determined in accordance with paragraphs 2 to 8.

2. In the case of a share or other transferable security covered by Article 4(1)(18)(a) of Directive 2004/39/EC or of a unit in a collective investment undertaking, the most relevant market shall be the Member State where the share or the unit was first admitted to trading on a regulated market.

3. In the case of a bond or other transferable security covered by Article 4(1)(18)(b) of Directive 2004/39/EC or of a money market instrument which, in either case, is issued by a subsidiary, within the meaning of Seventh Council Directive 83/349/EEC of 13 June 1983 on consolidated accounts,[6] of an entity which has its registered office in a Member State, the most relevant market shall be the Member State where the registered office of the parent entity is situated.

4. In the case of a bond or other transferable security covered by Article 4(1)(18)(b) of Directive 2004/39/EC or of a money market instrument which, in either case, is issued by a Community issuer and which is not covered by paragraph 3 of this Article, the most relevant market shall be the Member State where the registered office of the issuer is situated.

5. In the case of a bond or other transferable security covered by Article 4(1)(18)(b) of Directive

---

[6] OJ L 193, 18. 7.1983, 1, reproduced supra under no. C. 6.

2004/39/EC or a money market instrument which, in either case, is issued by a third country issuer and which is not covered by paragraph 3 of this Article, the most relevant market shall be the Member State where that security was first admitted to trading on a regulated market.

6. In the case of a derivative contract or a financial contract for differences or a transferable security covered by Article 4(1)(18)(c) of Directive 2004/39/EC, the most relevant market shall be:

(a) where the underlying security is a share or other transferable security covered by Article 4(1)(18)(a) of Directive 2004/39/EC which is admitted to trading on a regulated market, the Member State deemed to be the most relevant market in terms of liquidity for the underlying security, in accordance with paragraph 2;

(b) where the underlying security is a bond or other transferable security covered by Article 4(1)(18)(b) of Directive 2004/39/EC or a money market instrument which is admitted to trading on a regulated market, the Member State deemed to be the most relevant market in terms of liquidity for that underlying security, in accordance with paragraphs 3, 4 or 5;

(c) where the underlying is an index composed of shares all of which are traded on a particular regulated market, the Member State where that regulated market is situated.

7. In any case not covered by paragraphs 2 to 6, the most relevant market shall be the Member State where the regulated market that first admitted the transferable security or derivative contract or financial contract for differences to trading is located.

8. Where a financial instrument covered by paragraphs 2, 5 or 7, or the underlying financial instrument of a financial instrument covered by paragraph 6 to which one of paragraphs 2, 5 or 7 is relevant, was first admitted to trading on more than one regulated market simultaneously, and all those regulated markets share the same home Member State, that Member State shall be the most relevant market.

Where the regulated markets concerned do not share the same home Member State, the most relevant market in terms of liquidity for that instrument shall be the market where the turnover of that instrument is highest.

For the purposes of determining the most relevant market where the turnover of the instrument is highest, each competent authority that has authorised one of the regulated markets concerned shall calculate the turnover for that instrument in its respective market for the previous calendar year, provided that the instrument was admitted to trading at the beginning of that year.

Where the turnover for the relevant financial instrument cannot be calculated by reason of insufficient or non-existent data and the issuer has its registered office in a Member State, the most relevant market shall be the market of the Member State where the registered office of the issuer is situated.

However, where issuer does not have its registered office in a Member State, the most relevant market for that instrument shall be the market where the turnover of the relevant instrument class is the highest. For the purposes of determining that market, each competent authority that has authorised one of the regulated markets concerned shall calculate the turnover for the instruments of the same class in its respective market for the preceding calendar year.

The relevant classes of financial instrument are the following:

(a) shares;

(b) bonds or other forms of securitised debt;

(c) any other financial instruments.

Article 10

(Second subparagraph of Article 25(3) of Directive 2004/39/EC)

Alternative determination of most relevant market in terms of liquidity

1. A competent authority may, in January every year, notify the relevant competent authority for a particular financial instrument that it intends to contest the determination, made in accordance with Article 9, of the most relevant market for that instrument.

2. Within four weeks of the sending of the notification, both authorities shall calculate the turnover for that financial instrument in their respective markets over the period of the previous calendar year.

If the results of that calculation indicate that the turnover is higher in the market of the contesting competent authority, that market shall be the most relevant market for that financial instrument. Where that financial instrument is of a type specified in Article 9(6)(a) or (b), that market shall also be the most relevant market for any derivative contract or financial contract for differences or transferable security which is covered by Article 4(1)(18)(c) of Directive 2004/39/EC and in respect of which that financial instrument is the underlying.

Article 11
(Article 25(3) of Directive 2004/39/EC)
List of financial instruments

The relevant competent authority for one or more financial instruments shall ensure that there is established and maintained an updated list of those financial instruments. That list shall be made available to the single competent authority designated as a contact point by each Member State in accordance with Article 56 of Directive 2004/39/EC. That list shall be made available for the first time on the first trading day in June 2007.

In order to assist competent authorities to comply with the first subparagraph, each regulated market shall submit identifying reference data on each financial instrument admitted to trading in an electronic and standardised format to its home competent authority. This information shall be submitted for each financial instrument before trading commences in that particular instrument. The home competent authority shall ensure the data is transmitted to the relevant competent authority for the financial instrument concerned. The reference data shall be updated whenever there are changes to the data with respect to an instrument. The requirements in this subparagraph may be waived if the relevant competent authority for that financial instrument obtains the relevant reference data by other means.

Article 12
(Article 25(5) of Directive 2004/39/EC)
Reporting channels

1. The reports of transactions in financial instruments shall be made in an electronic form except under exceptional circumstances, when they may be made in a medium which allows for the storing of the information in a way accessible for future reference by the competent authorities other than an electronic form, and the methods by which those reports are made shall satisfy the following conditions:

(a) they ensure the security and confidentiality of the data reported;

(b) they incorporate mechanisms for identifying and correcting errors in a transaction report;

(c) they incorporate mechanisms for authenticating the source of the transaction report;

(d) they include appropriate precautionary measures to enable the timely resumption of reporting in the case of system failure;

(e) they are capable of reporting the information required under Article 13 in the format required by the competent authority and in accordance with this paragraph, within the time limits set out in Article 25(3) of Directive 2004/39/EC.

2. A trade-matching or reporting system shall be approved by the competent authority for the purposes of Article 25(5) of Directive 2004/39/EC if the arrangements for reporting transactions established by that system comply with paragraph 1 of this Article and are subject to monitoring by a competent authority in respect of their continuing compliance.

Article 13
(Article 25(3) and (5) of Directive 2004/39/EC)
Content of the transaction report

1. The reports of transactions referred to in Article 25(3) and (5) of Directive 2004/39/EC shall contain the information specified in Table 1

of Annex I to this Regulation which is relevant to the type of financial instrument in question and which the competent authority declares is not already in its possession or is not available to it by other means.

2. For the purposes of the identification of a counterparty to the transaction which is a regulated market, an MTF or other central counterparty, as specified in Table 1 of Annex I, each competent authority shall make publicly available a list of identification codes of the regulated markets and MTFs for which, in each case, it is the competent authority of the home Member State, and of any entities which act as central counterparties for such regulated markets and MTFs.

3. Member States may require reports made in accordance with Article 25(3) and (5) of Directive 2004/39/EC to contain information related to the transactions in question which is additional to that specified in Table 1 of Annex I where that information is necessary to enable the competent authority to monitor the activities of investment firms to ensure that they act honestly, fairly and professionally and in a manner that promotes the integrity of the market, and provided that one of the following criteria is met:

(a) the financial instrument which is the subject of the report has characteristics which are specific to an instrument of that kind and which are not covered by the information items specified in that table;

(b) trading methods which are specific to the trading venue where the transaction took place involve features which are not covered by the information items specified in that table.

4. Member States may also require a report of a transaction made in accordance with Article 25(3) and (5) of Directive 2004/39/EC to identify the clients on whose behalf the investment firm has executed that transaction.

Article 14

(Article 25(3) and (5) of Directive 2004/39/EC)

Exchange of information on transactions

1. The competent authorities shall establish arrangements designed to ensure that the information received in accordance with Article 25(3) and (5) of Directive 2004/39/EC is made available to the following:

(a) the relevant competent authority for the financial instrument in question;

(b) in the case of branches, the competent authority that has authorised the investment firm providing the information, without prejudice to its right not to receive this information in accordance with Article 25(6) of Directive 2004/39/EC;

(c) any other competent authority that requests the information for the proper discharge of its supervisory duties under Article 25(1) of Directive 2004/39/EC.

2. The information to be made available in accordance with paragraph 1 shall contain the information items described in Tables 1 and 2 of Annex I.

3. The information referred to in paragraph 1 shall be made available as soon as possible.

With effect from 1 November 2008 that information shall be made available no later than the close of the next working day of the competent authority that received the information or the request following the day on which the competent authority has received the information or the request.

4. The competent authorities shall coordinate the following:

(a) the design and establishment of arrangements for the exchange of transaction information between the competent authorities as required by Directive 2004/39/EC and this Regulation;

(b) any future upgrading of the arrangements.

5. Before 1 February 2007, the competent authorities shall report to the Commission, which shall inform the European Securities Committee, on the design of the arrangements to be established in accordance with paragraph 1.

They shall also report to the Commission, which shall inform the European Securities Committee, whenever significant changes to those arrangements are proposed.

Article 15
(Article 58(1) of Directive 2004/39/EC)
Request for cooperation and exchange of information

1. Where a competent authority wishes another competent authority to supply or exchange information in accordance with Article 58(1) of Directive 2004/39/EC, it shall submit a written request to that competent authority containing sufficient detail to enable it to provide the information requested.

However, in a case of urgency, the request may be transmitted orally provided that it is confirmed in writing.

The competent authority which receives a request shall acknowledge receipt as soon as practicable.

2. Where the information requested under paragraph 1 is internally available to the competent authority that receives the request, that authority shall transmit the requested information without delay to the competent authority which made the request.

However, if the competent authority that receives the request does not possess or control the information requested, it shall immediately take the necessary steps to obtain that information and to comply fully with the request. That competent authority shall also inform the competent authority that made the request of the reasons for not sending immediately the information requested.

Article 16
(Article 56(2) of Directive 2004/39/EC)
Determination of the substantial importance of a regulated market's operations in a host Member State

The operations of a regulated market in a host Member State shall be considered to be of substantial importance for the functioning of the securities markets and the protection of investors in that host State where one of the following criteria is met:

(a) the host Member State has formerly been the home Member State of the regulated market in question;

(b) the regulated market in question has acquired through merger, takeover, or any other form of transfer the business of a regulated market which had its registered office or head office in the host Member State.

CHAPTER IV
MARKET TRANSPARENCY

SECTION 1
PRE-TRADE TRANSPARENCY FOR REGULATED MARKETS AND MTFs

Article 17
(Articles 29 and 44 of Directive 2004/39/EC)
Pre-trade transparency obligations

1. An investment firm or market operator operating an MTF or a regulated market shall, in respect of each share admitted to trading on a regulated market that is traded within a system operated by it and specified in Table 1 of Annex II, make public the information set out in paragraphs 2 to 6.

2. Where one of the entities referred to in paragraph 1 operates a continuous auction order book trading system, it shall, for each share as specified in paragraph 1, make public continuously throughout its normal trading hours the aggregate number of orders and of the shares those orders represent at each price level, for the five best bid and offer price levels.

3. Where one of the entities referred to in paragraph 1 operates a quote-driven trading system, it shall, for each share as specified in paragraph 1, make public continuously throughout its normal trading hours the best bid and offer by price of each market maker in that share, together with the volumes attaching to those prices.

The quotes made public shall be those that represent binding commitments to buy and sell the shares and which indicate the price and volume of shares in which the registered market makers are prepared to buy or sell.

In exceptional market conditions, however, indicative or one-way prices may be allowed for a limited time.

4. Where one of the entities referred to in paragraph 1 operates a periodic auction trading system, it shall, for each share specified in paragraph 1, make public continuously throughout its normal trading hours the price that would best satisfy the system's trading algorithm and the volume that would potentially be executable at that price by participants in that system.

5. Where one of the entities referred to in paragraph 1 operates a trading system which is not wholly covered by paragraph 2 or 3 or 4, either because it is a hybrid system falling under more than one of those paragraphs or because the price determination process is of a different nature, it shall maintain a standard of pre-trade transparency that ensures that adequate information is made public as to the price level of orders or quotes for each share specified in paragraph 1, as well as the level of trading interest in that share.

In particular, the five best bid and offer price levels and/or two-way quotes of each market maker in that share shall be made public, if the characteristics of the price discovery mechanism permit it.

6. A summary of the information to be made public in accordance with paragraphs 2 to 5 is specified in Table 1 of Annex II.

Article 18

(Articles 29(2) and 44(2) of Directive 2004/39/EC)

Waivers based on market model and type of order or transaction

1. Waivers in accordance with Article 29(2) and 44(2) of Directive 2004/39/EC may be granted by the competent authorities for systems operated by an MTF or a regulated market, if those systems satisfy one of the following criteria:

(a) they must be based on a trading methodology by which the price is determined in accordance with a reference price generated by another system, where that reference price is widely published and is regarded generally by market participants as a reliable reference price;

(b) they formalise negotiated transactions, each of which meets one of the following criteria:
(i) it is made at or within the current volume weighted spread reflected on the order book or the quotes of the market makers of the regulated market or MTF operating that system or, where the share is not traded continuously, within a percentage of a suitable reference price, being a percentage and a reference price set in advance by the system operator;
(ii) it is subject to conditions other than the current market price of the share.

For the purposes of point (b), the other conditions specified in the rules of the regulated market or MTF for a transaction of this kind must also have been fulfilled.

In the case of systems having functionality other than as described in points (a) or (b), the waiver shall not apply to that other functionality.

2. Waivers in accordance with Articles 29(2) and 44(2) of Directive 2004/39/EC based on the type of orders may be granted only in relation to orders held in an order management facility maintained by the regulated market or the MTF pending their being disclosed to the market.

Article 19

(Articles 29(2) and 44(2) of Directive 2004/39/EC)

References to negotiated transaction

For the purpose of Article 18(1)(b) a negotiated transaction shall mean a transaction involving members or participants of a regulated market or an MTF which is negotiated privately but executed within the regulated market or MTF and where that member or participant in doing so undertakes one of the following tasks:

(a) dealing on own account with another member or participant who acts for the account of a client;

(b) dealing with another member or participant, where both are executing orders on own account;

(c) acting for the account of both the buyer and seller;

(d) acting for the account of the buyer, where another member or participant acts for the account of the seller;

(e) trading for own account against a client order.

Article 20
(Articles 29(2) and 44(2), and fifth subparagraph of Article 27(1) of Directive 2004/39/EC)
Waivers in relation to transactions which are large in scale

An order shall be considered to be large in scale compared with normal market size if it is equal to or larger than the minimum size of order specified in Table 2 in Annex II. For the purposes of determining whether an order is large in scale compared to normal market size, all shares admitted to trading on a regulated market shall be classified in accordance with their average daily turnover, which shall be calculated in accordance with the procedure set out in Article 33.

Section 2
Pre-trade Transparency for Systematic Internalisers

Article 21
(Article 4(1)(7) of Directive 2004/39/EC)
Criteria for determining whether an investment firm is a systematic internaliser

1. Where an investment firm deals on own account by executing client orders outside a regulated market or an MTF, it shall be treated as a systematic internaliser if it meets the following criteria indicating that it performs that activity on an organised, frequent and systematic basis:

(a) the activity has a material commercial role for the firm, and is carried on in accordance with non-discretionary rules and procedures;

(b) the activity is carried on by personnel, or by means of an automated technical system, assigned to that purpose, irrespective of whether those personnel or that system are used exclusively for that purpose;

(c) the activity is available to clients on a regular or continuous basis.

2. An investment firm shall cease to be a systematic internaliser in one or more shares if it ceases to carry on the activity specified in paragraph 1 in respect of those shares, provided that it has announced in advance that it intends to cease that activity using the same publication channels for that announcement as it uses to publish its quotes or, where that is not possible, using a channel which is equally accessible to its clients and other market participants.

3. The activity of dealing on own account by executing client orders shall not be treated as performed on an organised, frequent and systematic basis where the following conditions apply:

(a) the activity is performed on an ad hoc and irregular bilateral basis with wholesale counterparties as part of business relationships which are themselves characterised by dealings above standard market size;

(b) the transactions are carried out outside the systems habitually used by the firm concerned for any business that it carries out in the capacity of a systematic internaliser.

4. Each competent authority shall ensure the maintenance and publication of a list of all systematic internalisers, in respect of shares admitted to trading on a regulated market, which it has authorised as investment firms.

It shall ensure that the list is current by reviewing it at least annually.

The list shall be made available to the Committee of European Securities Regulators. It shall be considered as published when it is published by the Committee of European Securities Regulators in accordance with Article 34(5).

Article 22
(Article 27 of Directive 2004/39/EC)
Determination of liquid shares

1. A share admitted to trading on a regulated market shall be considered to have a liquid

market if the share is traded daily, with a free float not less than EUR 500 million, and one of the following conditions is satisfied:

(a) the average daily number of transactions in the share is not less than 500;

(b) the average daily turnover for the share is not less than EUR 2 million.

However, a Member State may, in respect of shares for which it is the most relevant market, specify by notice that both of those conditions are to apply. That notice shall be made public.

2. A Member State may specify the minimum number of liquid shares for that Member State. The minimum number shall be no greater than five. The specification shall be made public.

3. Where, pursuant to paragraph 1, a Member State would be the most relevant market for fewer liquid shares than the minimum number specified in accordance with paragraph 2, the competent authority for that Member State may designate one or more additional liquid shares, provided that the total number of shares which are considered in consequence to be liquid shares for which that Member State is the most relevant market does not exceed the minimum number specified by that Member State.

The competent authority shall designate the additional liquid shares successively in decreasing order of average daily turnover from among the shares for which it is the relevant competent authority that are admitted to trading on a regulated market and are traded daily.

4. For the purposes of the first subparagraph of paragraph 1, the calculation of the free float of a share shall exclude holdings exceeding 5% of the total voting rights of the issuer, unless such a holding is held by a collective investment undertaking or a pension fund.

Voting rights shall be calculated on the basis of all the shares to which voting rights are attached, even if the exercise of such a right is suspended.

5. A share shall not be considered to have a liquid market for the purposes of Article 27 of Directive 2004/39/EC until six weeks after its first admission to trading on a regulated market, if the estimate of the total market capitalisation for that share at the start of the first day's trading after that admission, provided in accordance with Article 33(3), is less than EUR 500 million.

6. Each competent authority shall ensure the maintenance and publication of a list of all liquid shares for which it is the relevant competent authority.

It shall ensure that the list is current by reviewing it at least annually.

The list shall be made available to the Committee of European Securities Regulators. It shall be considered as published when it is published by the Committee of European Securities Regulators in accordance with Article 34(5).

Article 23
(Fourth subparagraph of Article 27(1) of Directive 2004/39/EC)
Standard market size

In order to determine the standard market size for liquid shares, those shares shall be grouped into classes in terms of the average value of orders executed in accordance with Table 3 in Annex II.

Article 24
(Article 27(1) of Directive 2004/39/EC)
Quotes reflecting prevailing market conditions

A systematic internaliser shall, for each liquid share for which it is a systematic internaliser, maintain the following:

(a) a quote or quotes which are close in price to comparable quotes for the same share in other trading venues;

(b) a record of its quoted prices, which it shall retain for a period of 12 months or such longer period as it considers appropriate.

The obligation laid down in point (b) is without prejudice to the obligation of the investment firm under Article 25(2) of Directive 2004/39/EC to keep at the disposal of the competent authority for at least five years the relevant data relating to all transactions it has carried out.

Article 25

(Fifth subparagraph of Article 27(3) and Article 27(6) of Directive 2004/39/EC)

Execution of orders by systematic internalisers

1. For the purposes of the fifth subparagraph of Article 27(3) of Directive 2004/39/EC, execution in several securities shall be regarded as part of one transaction if that one transaction is a portfolio trade that involves 10 or more securities.

For the same purposes, an order subject to conditions other than the current market price means any order which is neither an order for the execution of a transaction in shares at the prevailing market price, nor a limit order.

2. For the purposes of Article 27(6) of Directive 2004/39/EC, the number or volume of orders shall be regarded as considerably exceeding the norm if a systematic internaliser cannot execute those orders without exposing itself to undue risk.

In order to identify the number and volume of orders that it can execute without exposing itself to undue risk, a systematic internaliser shall maintain and implement as part of its risk management policy under Article 7 of Commission Directive 2006/73/EC[7] a non-discriminatory policy which takes into account the volume of the transactions, the capital that the firm has available to cover the risk for that type of trade, and the prevailing conditions in the market in which the firm is operating.

3. Where, in accordance with Article 27(6) of Directive 2004/39/EC, an investment firm limits the number or volume of orders it undertakes to execute, it shall set out in writing, and make available to clients and potential clients, the arrangements designed to ensure that such a limitation does not result in the discriminatory treatment of clients.

---

[7] See page 26 of this Official Journal.

Article 26

(Fourth subparagraph of Article 27(3) of Directive 2004/39/EC)

Retail size

For the purposes of the fourth subparagraph of Article 27(3) of Directive 2004/39/EC, an order shall be regarded as being of a size bigger than the size customarily undertaken by a retail investor if it exceeds EUR 7 500.

SECTION 3

POST-TRADE TRANSPARENCY FOR REGULATED MARKETS, MTFs AND INVESTMENT FIRMS

Article 27

(Articles 28, 30 and 45 of Directive 2004/39/EC)

Post-trade transparency obligation

1. Investment firms, regulated markets, and investment firms and market operators operating an MTF shall, with regard to transactions in respect of shares admitted to trading on regulated markets concluded by them or, in the case of regulated markets or MTFs, within their systems, make public the following details:

(a) the details specified in points 2, 3, 6, 16, 17, 18, and 21 of Table 1 in Annex I;

(b) an indication that the exchange of shares is determined by factors other than the current market valuation of the share, where applicable;

(c) an indication that the trade was a negotiated trade, where applicable;

(d) any amendments to previously disclosed information, where applicable.

Those details shall be made public either by reference to each transaction or in a form aggregating the volume and price of all transactions in the same share taking place at the same price at the same time.

2. By way of exception, a systematic internaliser shall be entitled to use the acronym 'SI' instead of the venue identification referred to in paragraph

1(a) in respect of a transaction in a share that is executed in its capacity as a systematic internaliser in respect of that share.

The systematic internaliser may exercise that right only as long as it makes available to the public aggregate quarterly data as to the transactions executed in its capacity as a systematic internaliser in respect of that share relating to the most recent calendar quarter, or part of a calendar quarter, during which the firm acted as a systematic internaliser in respect of that share. That data shall be made available no later than one month after the end of each calendar quarter.

It may also exercise that right during the period between the date specified in Article 41(2), or the date on which the firm commences to be a systematic internaliser in relation to a share, whichever is the later, and the date that aggregate quarterly data in relation to a share is first due to be published.

3. The aggregated quarterly data referred to in the second subparagraph of paragraph 2 shall contain the following information for the share in respect of each trading day of the calendar quarter concerned:

(a) the highest price;

(b) the lowest price;

(c) the average price;

(d) the total number of shares traded;

(e) the total number of transactions;

(f) such other information as the systematic internaliser decides to make available.

4. Where the transaction is executed outside the rules of a regulated market or an MTF, one of the following investment firms shall, by agreement between the parties, arrange to make the information public:

(a) the investment firm that sells the share concerned;

(b) the investment firm that acts on behalf of or arranges the transaction for the seller;

(c) the investment firm that acts on behalf of or arranges the transaction for the buyer;

(d) the investment firm that buys the share concerned.

In the absence of such an agreement, the information shall be made public by the investment firm determined by proceeding sequentially from point (a) to point (d) until the first point that applies to the case in question.

The parties shall take all reasonable steps to ensure that the transaction is made public as a single transaction. For those purposes two matching trades entered at the same time and price with a single party interposed shall be considered to be a single transaction.

Article 28

(Articles 28, 30 and 45 of Directive 2004/39/EC)

Deferred publication of large transactions

The deferred publication of information in respect of transactions may be authorised, for a period no longer than the period specified in Table 4 in Annex II for the class of share and transaction concerned, provided that the following criteria are satisfied:

(a) the transaction is between an investment firm dealing on own account and a client of that firm;

(b) the size of the transaction is equal to or exceeds the relevant minimum qualifying size, as specified in Table 4 in Annex II.

In order to determine the relevant minimum qualifying size for the purposes of point (b), all shares admitted to trading on a regulated market shall be classified in accordance with their average daily turnover to be calculated in accordance with Article 33.

SECTION 4

PROVISIONS COMMON TO PRE- AND POST-TRADE TRANSPARENCY

Article 29

(Articles 27(3), 28(1), 29(1), 44(1) and 45(1) of Directive 2004/39/EC)

Publication and availability of pre- and post-trade transparency data

1. A regulated market, MTF or systematic internaliser shall be considered to publish pre-trade

information on a continuous basis during normal trading hours if that information is published as soon as it becomes available during the normal trading hours of the regulated market, MTF or systematic internaliser concerned, and remains available until it is updated.

2. Pre-trade information, and post-trade information relating to transactions taking place on trading venues and within normal trading hours, shall be made available as close to real time as possible. Post-trade information relating to such transactions shall be made available in any case within three minutes of the relevant transaction.

3. Information relating to a portfolio trade shall be made available with respect to each constituent transaction as close to real time as possible, having regard to the need to allocate prices to particular shares. Each constituent transaction shall be assessed separately for the purposes of determining whether deferred publication in respect of that transaction is available under Article 28.

4. Post-trade information relating to transactions taking place on a trading venue but outside its normal trading hours shall be made public before the opening of the next trading day of the trading venue on which the transaction took place.

5. For transactions that take place outside a trading venue, post-trade information shall be made public:

(a) if the transaction takes place during a trading day of the most relevant market for the share concerned, or during the investment firm's normal trading hours, as close to real time as possible. Post-trade information relating to such transactions shall be made available in any case within three minutes of the relevant transaction;

(b) in a case not covered by point (a), immediately upon the commencement of the investment firm's normal trading hours or at the latest before the opening of the next trading day in the most relevant market for that share.

Article 30
(Articles 27, 28, 29, 30, 44 and 45 of Directive 2004/39/EC)
Public availability of pre- and post-trade information

For the purposes of Articles 27, 28, 29, 30, 44 and 45 of Directive 2004/39/EC and of this Regulation, pre- and post-trade information shall be considered to be made public or available to the public if it is made available generally through one of the following to investors located in the Community:

(a) the facilities of a regulated market or an MTF;

(b) the facilities of a third party;

(c) proprietary arrangements.

Article 31
(Article 22(2) of Directive 2004/39/EC)
Disclosure of client limit orders

An investment firm shall be considered to disclose client limit orders that are not immediately executable if it transmits the order to a regulated market or MTF that operates an order book trading system, or ensures that the order is made public and can be easily executed as soon as market conditions allow.

Article 32
(Article 22(2), 27, 28, 29, 30, 44 and 45 of Directive 2004/39/EC)
Arrangements for making information public

Any arrangement to make information public, adopted for the purposes of Articles 30 and 31, shall satisfy the following conditions:

(a) it must include all reasonable steps necessary to ensure that the information to be published is reliable, monitored continuously for errors, and corrected as soon as errors are detected;

(b) it must facilitate the consolidation of the data with similar data from other sources;

(c) it must make the information available to the public on a non-discriminatory commercial basis at a reasonable cost.

Article 33
(Articles 27, 28, 29, 30, 44 and 45 of Directive 2004/39/EC)
Calculations and estimates for shares admitted to trading on a regulated market

1. In respect of each share that is admitted to trading on a regulated market, the relevant competent authority for that share shall ensure that the following calculations are made in respect of that share promptly after the end of each calendar year:

(a) the average daily turnover;

(b) the average daily number of transactions;

(c) for those shares which satisfy the conditions laid down in Article 22(1)(a) or (b) (as applicable), the free float as at 31 December;

(d) if the share is a liquid share, the average value of the orders executed.

This paragraph and paragraph 2 shall not apply to a share which is first admitted to trading on a regulated market four weeks or less before the end of the calendar year.

2. The calculation of the average daily turnover, average value of the orders executed and average daily number of transactions shall take into account all the orders executed in the Community in respect of the share in question between 1 January and 31 December of the preceding year, or, where applicable, that part of the year during which the share was admitted to trading on a regulated market and was not suspended from trading on a regulated market.

In the calculations of the average daily turnover, average value of the orders executed and average daily number of transactions of a share, non-trading days in the Member State of the relevant competent authority for that share shall be excluded.

3. Before the first admission of a share to trading on a regulated market, the relevant competent authority for that share shall ensure that estimates are provided, in respect of that share, of the average daily turnover, the market capitalisation as it will stand at the start of the first day of trading and, where the estimate of the market capitalisation is EUR 500 million or more:

(a) the average daily number of transactions and, for those shares which satisfy the conditions laid down in Article 22(1)(a) or (b) (as applicable), the free float;

(b) in the case of a share that is estimated to be a liquid share, the average value of the orders executed.

The estimates shall relate to the six-week period following admission to trading, or the end of that period, as applicable, and shall take account of any previous trading history of the share, as well as that of shares that are considered to have similar characteristics.

4. After the first admission of a share to trading on a regulated market, the relevant competent authority for that share shall ensure that, in respect of that share, the figures referred to in points (a) to (d) of paragraph 1 are calculated, using data relating to the first four weeks' trading, as if a reference in point (c) of paragraph 1 to 31 December were a reference to the end of the first four weeks' trading, as soon as practicable after those data are available, and in any case before the end of the six-week period referred to in Article 22(5).

5. During the course of a calendar year, the relevant competent authorities shall ensure the review and where necessary the recalculation of the average daily turnover, average value of the orders executed, average daily number of transactions executed and the free float whenever there is a change in relation to the share or the issuer which significantly affects the previous calculations on an ongoing basis.

6. The calculations referred to in paragraphs 1 to 5 which are to be published on or before the first trading day in March 2009 shall be made on the basis of the data relating to the regulated market or markets of the Member State which is the most relevant market in terms of liquidity for the share in question. For those purposes, negotiated transactions within the meaning of Article 19 shall be excluded from the calculations.

Article 34

(Articles 27, 28, 29, 30, 44 and 45 of Directive 2004/39/EC)

Publication and effect of results of required calculations and estimates

1. On the first trading day of March of each year, each competent authority shall, in relation to each share for which it is the relevant competent authority that was admitted to trading on a regulated market at the end of the preceding calendar year, ensure the publication of the following information:

(a) the average daily turnover and average daily number of transactions, as calculated in accordance with Article 33(1) and (2);

(b) the free float and average value of the orders executed, where calculated in accordance with Article 33(1) and (2).

This paragraph shall not apply to shares to which the second subparagraph of Article 33(1) applies.

2. The results of the estimates and calculations required under Article 33(3), (4) or (5) shall be published as soon as practicable after the calculation or estimate is completed.

3. The information referred to in paragraphs 1 or 2 shall be considered as published when it is published by the Committee of European Securities Regulators in accordance with paragraph 5.

4. For the purposes of this Regulation, the following shall apply:

(a) the classification based on the publication referred to in paragraph 1 shall apply for the 12-month period starting on 1 April following publication and ending on the following 31 March;

(b) the classification based on the estimates provided for in Article 33(3) shall apply from the relevant first admission to trading until the end of the six-week period referred to in Article 22(5);

(c) the classification based on the calculations specified in Article 33(4) shall apply from the end of the six-week period referred to in Article 22(5), until:

(i) where the end of that six-week period falls between 15 January and 31 March (both inclusive) in a given year, 31 March of the following year;

(ii) otherwise, the following 31 March after the end of that period.

However, the classification based on the recalculations specified in Article 33(5) shall apply from the date of publication and, unless further recalculated under Article 33(5), until the following 31 March.

5. The Committee of European Securities Regulators shall, on the basis of data supplied to it by or on behalf of competent authorities, publish on its website consolidated and regularly updated lists of:

(a) every systematic internaliser in respect of a share admitted to trading on a regulated market;

(b) every share admitted to trading on a regulated market, specifying:

(i) the average daily turnover, average daily number of transactions and, for those shares which satisfy the conditions laid down in Article 22(1)(a) or (b) (as applicable), the free float;

(ii) in the case of a liquid share, the average value of the orders executed and the standard market size for that share;

(iii) in the case of a liquid share which has been designated as an additional liquid share in accordance with Article 22(3), the name of the competent authority that so designated it; and

(iv) the relevant competent authority.

6. Each competent authority shall ensure the first publication of the details referred to in points (a) and (b) of paragraph 1 on the first trading day in July 2007, based on the reference period 1 April 2006 to 31 March 2007. By way of derogation from paragraph 4, the classification based on that publication shall apply for the five-month period starting on 1 November 2007 and ending on 31 March 2008.

Chapter V
Admission of Financial Instruments to Trading

Article 35
(Article 40(1) of Directive 2004/39/EC)
Transferable securities

1. Transferable securities shall be considered freely negotiable for the purposes of Article 40(1) of Directive 2004/39/EC if they can be traded between the parties to a transaction, and subsequently transferred without restriction, and if all securities within the same class as the security in question are fungible.

2. Transferable securities which are subject to a restriction on transfer shall not be considered as freely negotiable unless that restriction is not likely to disturb the market.

3. Transferable securities that are not fully paid may be considered as freely negotiable if arrangements have been made to ensure that the negotiability of such securities is not restricted and that adequate information concerning the fact that the securities are not fully paid, and the implications of that fact for shareholders, is publicly available.

4. When exercising its discretion whether to admit a share to trading, a regulated market shall, in assessing whether the share is capable of being traded in a fair, orderly and efficient manner, take into account the following:

(a) the distribution of those shares to the public;

(b) such historical financial information, information about the issuer, and information providing a business overview as is required to be prepared under Directive 2003/71/EC, or is or will be otherwise publicly available.

5. A transferable security that is officially listed in accordance with Directive 2001/34/EC of the European Parliament and of the Council,[8] and the listing of which is not suspended, shall be deemed to be freely negotiable and capable of being traded in a fair, orderly and efficient manner.

6. For the purposes of Article 40(1) of Directive 2004/39/EC, when assessing whether a transferable security referred to in Article 4(1)(18)(c) of that Directive is capable of being traded in a fair, orderly and efficient manner, the regulated market shall take into account, depending on the nature of the security being admitted, whether the following criteria are satisfied:

(a) the terms of the security are clear and unambiguous and allow for a correlation between the price of the security and the price or other value measure of the underlying;

(b) the price or other value measure of the underlying is reliable and publicly available;

(c) there is sufficient information publicly available of a kind needed to value the security;

(d) the arrangements for determining the settlement price of the security ensure that this price properly reflects the price or other value measure of the underlying;

(e) where the settlement of the security requires or provides for the possibility of the delivery of an underlying security or asset rather than cash settlement, there are adequate settlement and delivery procedures for that underlying as well as adequate arrangements to obtain relevant information about that underlying.

Article 36
(Article 40(1) of Directive 2004/39/EC)
Units in collective investment undertakings

1. A regulated market shall, when admitting to trading units in a collective investment undertaking, whether or not that undertaking is constituted in accordance with Directive 85/611/EEC, satisfy itself that the collective investment undertaking complies or has complied with the registration, notification or other procedures which are a necessary precondition for the marketing of the collective investment undertaking in the jurisdiction of the regulated market.

---

[8] OJ L 184, 6.7.2001, 1, reproduced supra under no. S. 18. Directive as last amended by Directive 2005/1/EC, reproduced supra under no. B. 39.

2. Without prejudice to Directive 85/611/EEC or any other Community legislation or national law relating to collective investment undertakings, Member States may provide that compliance with the requirements referred to in paragraph 1 is not a necessary precondition for the admission of units in a collective investment undertaking to trading on a regulated market.

3. When assessing whether units in an open-ended collective investment undertaking are capable of being traded in a fair, orderly and efficient manner in accordance with Article 40(1) of Directive 2004/39/EC, the regulated market shall take the following aspects into account:

(a) the distribution of those units to the public;

(b) whether there are appropriate market-making arrangements, or whether the management company of the scheme provides appropriate alternative arrangements for investors to redeem the units;

(c) whether the value of the units is made sufficiently transparent to investors by means of the periodic publication of the net asset value.

4. When assessing whether units in a closed-end collective investment undertaking are capable of being traded in a fair, orderly and efficient manner in accordance with Article 40(1) of Directive 2004/39/EC, the regulated market shall take the following aspects into account:

(a) the distribution of those units to the public;

(b) whether the value of the units is made sufficiently transparent to investors, either by publication of information on the fund's investment strategy or by the periodic publication of net asset value.

Article 37
(Article 40(1) and (2) of Directive 2004/39/EC)

Derivatives

1. When admitting to trading a financial instrument of a kind listed in points of Sections C(4) to (10) of Annex I to Directive 2004/39/EC, regulated markets shall verify that the following conditions are satisfied:

(a) the terms of the contract establishing the financial instrument must be clear and unambiguous, and enable a correlation between the price of the financial instrument and the price or other value measure of the underlying;

(b) the price or other value measure of the underlying must be reliable and publicly available;

(c) sufficient information of a kind needed to value the derivative must be publicly available;

(d) the arrangements for determining the settlement price of the contract must be such that the price properly reflects the price or other value measure of the underlying;

(e) where the settlement of the derivative requires or provides for the possibility of the delivery of an underlying security or asset rather than cash settlement, there must be adequate arrangements to enable market participants to obtain relevant information about that underlying as well as adequate settlement and delivery procedures for the underlying.

2. Where the financial instruments concerned are of a kind listed in Sections C (5), (6), (7) or (10) of Annex I to Directive 2004/39/EC, point (b) of paragraph 1 shall not apply if the following conditions are satisfied:

(a) the contract establishing that instrument must be likely to provide a means of disclosing to the market, or enabling the market to assess, the price or other value measure of the underlying, where the price or value measure is not otherwise publicly available;

(b) the regulated market must ensure that appropriate supervisory arrangements are in place to monitor trading and settlement in such financial instruments;

(c) the regulated market must ensure that settlement and delivery, whether physical delivery or by cash settlement, can be effected in accordance with the contract terms and conditions of those financial instruments.

CHAPTER VI
DERIVATIVE FINANCIAL INSTRUMENTS

Article 38
(Article 4(1)(2) of Directive 2004/39/EC)

Characteristics of other derivative financial instruments

1. For the purposes of Section C(7) of Annex I to Directive 2004/39/EC, a contract which is not a spot contract within the meaning of paragraph 2 of this Article and which is not covered by paragraph 4 shall be considered as having the characteristics of other derivative financial instruments and not being for commercial purposes if it satisfies the following conditions:

(a) it meets one of the following sets of criteria:
(i) it is traded on a third country trading facility that performs a similar function to a regulated market or an MTF;
(ii) it is expressly stated to be traded on, or is subject to the rules of, a regulated market, an MTF or such a third country trading facility;
(iii) it is expressly stated to be equivalent to a contract traded on a regulated market, MTF or such a third country trading facility;

(b) it is cleared by a clearing house or other entity carrying out the same functions as a central counterparty, or there are arrangements for the payment or provision of margin in relation to the contract;

(c) it is standardised so that, in particular, the price, the lot, the delivery date or other terms are determined principally by reference to regularly published prices, standard lots or standard delivery dates.

2. A spot contract for the purposes of paragraph 1 means a contract for the sale of a commodity, asset or right, under the terms of which delivery is scheduled to be made within the longer of the following periods:

(a) two trading days;

(b) the period generally accepted in the market for that commodity, asset or right as the standard delivery period.

However, a contract is not a spot contract if, irrespective of its explicit terms, there is an understanding between the parties to the contract that delivery of the underlying is to be postponed and not to be performed within the period mentioned in the first subparagraph.

3. For the purposes of Section C(10) of Annex I to Directive 2004/39/EC, a derivative contract relating to an underlying referred to in that Section or in Article 39 shall be considered to have the characteristics of other derivative financial instruments if one of the following conditions is satisfied:

(a) that contract is settled in cash or may be settled in cash at the option of one or more of the parties, otherwise than by reason of a default or other termination event;

(b) that contract is traded on a regulated market or an MTF;

(c) the conditions laid down in paragraph 1 are satisfied in relation to that contract.

4. A contract shall be considered to be for commercial purposes for the purposes of Section C(7) of Annex I to Directive 2004/39/EC, and as not having the characteristics of other derivative financial instruments for the purposes of Sections C(7) and (10) of that Annex, if it is entered into with or by an operator or administrator of an energy transmission grid, energy balancing mechanism or pipeline network, and it is necessary to keep in balance the supplies and uses of energy at a given time.

Article 39
(Article 4(1)(2) of Directive 2004/39/EC)

Derivatives within Section C(10) of Annex I to Directive 2004/39/EC

In addition to derivative contracts of a kind referred to in Section C(10) of Annex I to Directive 2004/39/EC, a derivative contract relating to any of the following shall fall within that Section if it meets the criteria set out in that Section and in Article 38(3):

(a) telecommunications bandwidth;

(b) commodity storage capacity;

(c) transmission or transportation capacity relating to commodities, whether cable, pipeline or other means;

(d) an allowance, credit, permit, right or similar asset which is directly linked to the supply, distribution or consumption of energy derived from renewable resources;

(e) a geological, environmental or other physical variable;

(f) any other asset or right of a fungible nature, other than a right to receive a service, that is capable of being transferred;

(g) an index or measure related to the price or value of, or volume of transactions in any asset, right, service or obligation.

CHAPTER VII

FINAL PROVISIONS

Article 40

Re-examinations

1. At least once every two years, and after consulting the Committee of European Securities Regulators, the Commission shall re-examine the definition of 'transaction' for the purposes of this Regulation, the Tables included in Annex II, as well as the criteria for determination of liquid shares contained in Article 22.

2. The Commission shall, after consulting the Committee of European Securities Regulators, re-examine the provisions of Articles 38 and 39 relating to criteria for determining which instruments are to be treated as having the characteristics of other derivative financial instruments, or as being for commercial purposes, or which fall within Section C(10) of Annex I to Directive 2004/39/EC if the other criteria set out in that Section are satisfied in relation to them.

The Commission shall report to the European Parliament and to the Council at the same time that it makes its reports under Article 65(3)(a) and (d) of Directive 2004/39/EC.

3. The Commission shall, no later than two years after the date of application of this Regulation, after consulting the Committee of European Securities Regulators, re-examine Table 4 of Annex II and report on the results of this re-examination to the European Parliament and the Council.

Article 41

Entry into force

This Regulation shall enter into force on the 20th day following its publication in the Official Journal of the European Union.

This Regulation shall apply from 1 November 2007, except Article 11 and Article 34(5) and (6), which shall apply from 1 June 2007.

This Regulation shall be binding in its entirety and directly applicable in all Member States.

Annex I

Table 1

List of fields for reporting purposes

Field Identifier	Description
1. Reporting firm identification	A unique code to identify the firm which executed the transaction.
2. Trading day	The trading day on which the transaction was executed.
3. Trading time	The time at which the transaction was executed, reported in the local time of the competent authority to which the transaction will be reported, and the basis in which the transaction is reported expressed as Coordinated Universal Time (UTC) +/− hours.

Field Identifier	Description
4. Buy/sell indicator	Identifies whether the transaction was a buy or sell from the perspective of the reporting investment firm or, in the case of a report to a client, of the client.
5. Trading capacity	Identifies whether the firm executed the transaction: — on its own account (either on its own behalf or on behalf of a client), — for the account, and on behalf, of a client.
6. Instrument identification	This shall consist of: — a unique code, to be decided by the competent authority (if any) to which the report is made identifying the financial instrument which is the subject of the transaction, — if the financial instrument in question does not have a unique identification code, the report must include the name of the instrument or, in the case of a derivative contract, the characteristics of the contract.
7. Instrument code type	The code type used to report the instrument.
8. Underlying instrument	The instrument identification applicable to the security that is identification of the underlying asset in a derivative contract as well as the transferable security falling within Article 4(1)(18)(c) of Directive 2004/39/EC.
9. Underlying instrument identification code type	The code type used to report the underlying instrument.
10. Instrument type	The harmonised classification of the financial instrument that is the subject of the transaction. The description must at least indicate whether the instrument belongs to one of the top level categories as provided by a uniform internationally accepted standard for financial instrument classification.
11. Maturity date	The maturity date of a bond or other form of securitised debt, or the exercise date/maturity date of a derivative contract.
12. Derivative type	The harmonised description of the derivative type should be done according to one of the top level categories as provided by a uniform internationally accepted standard for financial instrument classification.
13. Put/call	Specification whether an option or any other financial instrument is a put or a call.
14. Strike price	The strike price of an option or other financial instrument.
15. Price multiplier	The number of units of the financial instrument in question which are contained in a trading lot; for example, the number of derivatives or securities represented by one contract.
16. Unit price	The price per security or derivative contract excluding commission and (where relevant) accrued interest. In the case of a debt instrument, the price may be expressed either in terms of currency or as a percentage.
17. Price notation	The currency in which the price is expressed. If, in the case of a bond or other form of securitised debt, the price is expressed as a percentage, that percentage shall be included.
19. Quantity notation	The number of units of the financial instruments, the nominal value of bonds, or the number of derivative contracts included in the transaction.
20. Counterparty	An indication as to whether the quantity is the number of units of financial instruments, the nominal value of bonds or the number of derivative contracts.

Field Identifier	Description
	Identification of the counterparty to the transaction. That identification shall consist of: – where the counterparty is an investment firm, a unique code for that firm, to be determined by the competent authority (if any) to which the report is made, – where the counterparty is a regulated market or MTF or an entity acting as its central counterparty, the unique harmonised identification code for that market, MTF or entity acting as central counterparty, as specified in the list published by the competent authority of the home Member State of that entity in accordance with Article 13(2), – where the counterparty is not an investment firm, a regulated market, an MTF or an entity acting as central counterparty, it should be identified as 'customer/client' of the investment firm which executed the transaction.
21. Venue identification	Identification of the venue where the transaction was executed. That identification shall consist in: – where the venue is a trading venue: its unique harmonized identification code, – otherwise: the code 'OTC'.
22. Transaction reference number	A unique identification number for the transaction provided by the investment firm or a third party reporting on its behalf.
23. Cancellation flag	An indication as to whether the transaction was cancelled.

Table 2

Further details for use of competent authorities

Field Identifier	Description
1. Reporting firm identification	If a unique code as referred to in Table 1 of Annex I is not sufficient to identify the counterparty, competent authorities should develop adequate measures that ensure the identification of the counterparty.
6. Instrument identification	The unique code, agreed between all the competent authorities, applicable to the financial instrument in question shall be used.
20. Counterparty	If a unique code, or unique harmonised identification code as referred to in Table 1 of Annex 1 is not sufficient to identify the counterparty, competent authorities should develop adequate measures that ensure the identification of the counterparty.

Annex II

Table 1

Information to be made public in accordance with Article 17

Type of system	Description of system	Summary of information to be made public, in accordance with Article 17
Continuous auction order book trading system	A system that by means of an order book and a trading algorithm operated without human intervention matches sell orders with matching buy orders on the basis of the best available price on a continuous basis.	The aggregate number of orders and the shares they represent at each price level, for at least the five best bid and offer price levels.
Quote-driven trading system	A system where transactions are concluded on the basis of firm quotes that are continuously made available to participants, which requires the market makers to maintain quotes in a size that balances the needs of members and participants to deal in a commercial size and the risk to which the market maker exposes itself.	The best bid and offer by price of each market maker in that share, together with the volumes attaching to those prices.
Periodic auction trading system	A system that matches orders on the basis of a periodic auction and a trading algorithm operated without human intervention.	The price at which the auction trading system would best satisfy its trading algorithm and the volume that would potentially be executable at that price.
Trading system not covered by first three rows	A hybrid system falling into two or more of the first three rows or a system where the price determination process is of a different nature than that applicable to the types of system covered by first three rows.	Adequate information as to the level of orders or quotes and of trading interest; in particular, the five best bid and offer price levels and/or two-way quotes of each market maker in the share, if the characteristics of the price discovery mechanism so permit.

Table 2

Orders large in scale compared with normal market size

(in EUR)

Class in terms of average daily turnover (ADT)	ADT < 500 000	500 000 ≤ ADT < 1 000 000	1 000 000 ≤ ADT < 25 000 000	25 000 000 ≤ ADT < 50 000 000	ADT ≥ 50 000 000
Minimum size of order qualifying as large in scale compared with normal market size	50 000	100 000	250 000	400 000	500 000

Table 3
Standard market sizes

(in EUR)

Class in terms of average value of transactions (AVT)	AVT < 10 000	10 000 ≤ AVT < 20 000	20 000 ≤ AVT < 30 000	30 000 ≤ AVT < 40 000	40 000 ≤ AVT < 50 000	50 000 ≤ AVT < 70 000	70 000 ≤ AVT < 90 000	Etc.
Standard market size	7 500	15 000	25 000	35 000	45 000	60 000	80 000	Etc.

Table 4
Deferred publication thresholds and delays

The table below shows, for each permitted delay for publication and each class of shares in terms of average daily turnover (ADT), the minimum qualifying size of transaction that will qualify for that delay in respect of a share of that type.

		Class of shares in terms of average daily turnover (ADT)			
		ADT < EUR 100 000	EUR 100 000 ≤ ADT < EUR 1 000 000	EUR 1 000 000 ≤ ADT < EUR 50 000 000	ADT ≥ EUR 50 000 000
		Minimum qualifying size of transaction for permitted delay			
Permitted delay for publication	60 minutes	EUR 10 000	Greater of 5% of ADT and EUR 25 000	Lower of 10% of ADT and EUR 3 500 000	Lower of 10% of ADT and EUR 7 500 000
	180 minutes	EUR 25 000	Greater of 15% of ADT and EUR 75 000	Lower of 15% of ADT and EUR 5 000 000	Lower of 20% of ADT and EUR 15 000 000
	Until end of trading day (or roll-over to noon of next trading day if trade undertaken in final two hours of trading day)	EUR 45 000	Greater of 25% of ADT and EUR 100 000 000	Lower of 25% of ADT and EUR 10 000	Lower of 30% of ADT and EUR 30 000 000
	Until end of trading day next after trade	EUR 60 000	Greater of 50% of ADT and EUR 100 000	Greater of 50% of ADT and EUR 1 000 000	100% of ADT
	Until end of second trading day next after trade	EUR 80 000	100% of ADT	100% of ADT	250% of ADT
	Until end of third trading day next after trade		250% of ADT	250% of ADT	

S. 34.

Commission Directive 2006/73/EC
of 10 August 2006
implementing Directive 2004/39/EC of the European Parliament and of the Council as regards organisational requirements and operating conditions for investment firms and defined terms for the purposes of that Directive[1]

(Text with EEA relevance)

THE COMMISSION OF THE EUROPEAN COMMUNITIES,

Having regard to the Treaty establishing the European Community,

Having regard to Directive 2004/39/EC of the European Parliament and of the Council of 21 April 2004 on markets in financial instruments amending Council Directives 85/611/EEC and 93/6/EEC and Directive 2000/12/EC of the European Parliament and of the Council and repealing Council Directive 93/22/EEC,[2] and in particular Article 4(2), Article 13(10), Article 18(3), Article 19(10), Article 21(6), Article 22(3) and Article 24(5) thereof,

Whereas:

(1) Directive 2004/39/EC establishes the framework for a regulatory regime for financial markets in the Community, governing, among other matters, operating conditions relating to the performance by investment firms of investment services and, where appropriate, ancillary services and investment activities; organisational requirements for investment firms performing such services and activities, and for regulated markets; reporting requirements in respect of transactions in financial instruments; and transparency requirements in respect of transactions in shares admitted to trading on a regulated market.

(2) The rules for the implementation of the regime governing organisational requirements for investment firms performing investment services and, where appropriate, ancillary services and investment activities on a professional basis, and for regulated markets, should be consistent with the aim of Directive 2004/39/EC. They should be designed to ensure a high level of integrity, competence and soundness among investment firms and entities that operate regulated markets or MTFs, and to be applied in a uniform manner.

(3) It is necessary to specify concrete organisational requirements and procedures for investment firms performing such services or activities. In particular, rigorous procedures should be provided for with regard to matters such as compliance, risk management, complaints handling, personal transactions, outsourcing and the identification, management and disclosure of conflicts of interest.

(4) The organisational requirements and conditions for authorisation for investment firms should be set out in the form of a set of rules that ensures the uniform application of the relevant provisions of Directive 2004/39/EC. This is necessary in order to ensure that investment firms have equal access on equivalent terms to all markets in the Community and to eliminate obstacles, linked to authorisation procedures, to cross-border activities in the field of investment services.

(5) The rules for the implementation of the regime governing operating conditions for the

---

[1] OJ L 241, 2.9.2006, 26–58.
[2] OJ L 145, 30.4.2004, 1, reproduced supra under no. S. 29. Directive as amended by Directive 2006/31/EC (OJ L 114, 27.4.2006, 60), reproduced supra under no. S. 32.

performance of investment and ancillary services and investment activities should reflect the aim underlying that regime. That is to say, they should be designed to ensure a high level of investor protection to be applied in a uniform manner through the introduction of clear standards and requirements governing the relationship between an investment firm and its client. On the other hand, as regards investor protection, and in particular the provision of investors with information or the seeking of information from investors, the retail or professional nature of the client or potential client concerned should be taken into account.

(6) The form of a Directive is necessary in order to enable the implementing provisions to be adjusted to the specificities of the particular market and legal system in each Member State.

(7) In order to ensure the uniform application of the various provisions of Directive 2004/39/EC, it is necessary to establish a harmonised set of organisational requirements and operating conditions for investment firms. Consequently, Member States and competent authorities should not add supplementary binding rules when transposing and applying the rules specified in this Directive, save where this Directive makes express provision to this effect.

(8) However, in exceptional circumstances, it should be possible for Member States to impose requirements on investment firms additional to those laid down in the implementing rules. However, such intervention should be restricted to those cases where specific risks to investor protection or to market integrity including those related to the stability of the financial system have not been adequately addressed by the Community legislation, and it should be strictly proportionate.

(9) Any additional requirements retained or imposed by Member States in conformity with this Directive must not restrict or otherwise affect the rights of investment firms under Articles 31 and 32 of Directive 2004/39/EC.

(10) The specific risks addressed by any additional requirements retained by Member States at the date of application of this Directive should be of particular importance to the market structure of the State in question, including the behaviour of firms and consumers in that market. The assessment of those specific risks should be made in the context of the regulatory regime put in place by Directive 2004/39/EC and its detailed implementing rules. Any decision to retain additional requirements should be made with proper regard to the objectives of that Directive to remove barriers to the cross-border provision of investment service by harmonising the initial authorisation and operating requirements for investment firms.

(11) Investment firms vary widely in their size, their structure and the nature of their business. A regulatory regime should be adapted to that diversity while imposing certain fundamental regulatory requirements which are appropriate for all firms. Regulated entities should comply with their high level obligations and design and adopt measures that are best suited to their particular nature and circumstances.

(12) However, a regulatory regime which entails too much uncertainty for investment firms may reduce efficiency. Competent authorities are expected to issue interpretative guidance on provisions on this Directive, with a view in particular to clarifying the practical application of the requirements of this Directive to particular kinds of firms and circumstances. Non-binding guidance of this kind might, among other things, clarify how the provisions of this Directive and Directive 2004/39/EC apply in the light of market developments. To ensure a uniform application of this Directive and Directive 2004/39/EC, the Commission may issue guidance by way of interpretative communications or other means. Furthermore, the Committee of European Securities Regulators may issue guidance in order to secure convergent application of this Directive and Directive 2004/39/EC by competent authorities.

(13) The organisational requirements established under Directive 2004/39/EC are without prejudice to systems established by national law for the registration of individuals working within investment firms.

(14) For the purposes of the provisions of this Directive requiring an investment firm to establish, implement and maintain an adequate risk management policy, the risks relating to the firm's activities, processes and systems should include the risks associated with the outsourcing of critical or important functions or of investment services or activities. Such risks should include those associated with the firm's relationship with the service provider, and the potential risks posed where the outsourced activities of multiple investment firms or other regulated entities are concentrated within a limited number of service providers.

(15) The fact that risk management and compliance functions are performed by the same person does not necessarily jeopardise the independent functioning of each function. The conditions that persons involved in the compliance function should not also be involved in the performance of the functions that they monitor, and that the method of determining the remuneration of such persons should not be likely to compromise their objectivity, may not be proportionate in the case of small investment firms. However, they would only be disproportionate for larger firms in exceptional circumstances.

(16) A number of the provisions of Directive 2004/39/EC require investment firms to collect and maintain information relating to clients and services provided to clients. Where those requirements involve the collection and processing of personal data, firms should ensure that they comply with national measures implementing Directive 95/46/EC of the European Parliament and of the Council of 24 October 1995[3] on the protection of individuals with regard to the processing of personal data and on the free movement of such data.

(17) Where successive personal transactions are carried out on behalf of a person in accordance with prior instructions given by that person, the obligations under the provisions of this Directive relating to personal transactions should not apply separately to each such successive transaction if those instructions remain in force and unchanged. Similarly, those obligations should not apply to the termination or withdrawal of such instructions, provided that any financial instruments which had previously been acquired pursuant to the instructions are not disposed of at the same time as the instructions terminate or are withdrawn. However, those obligations should apply in relation to a personal transaction, or the commencement of successive personal transactions, carried out on behalf of the same person if those instructions are changed or if new instructions are issued.

(18) Competent authorities should not make the authorisation to provide investment services or activities subject to a general prohibition on the outsourcing of one or more critical or important functions or investment services or activities. Investment firms should be allowed to outsource such activities if the outsourcing arrangements established by the firm comply with certain conditions.

(19) For the purposes of the provisions of this Directive setting out conditions for outsourcing critical or important operational functions or investment services or activities, an outsourcing that would involve the delegation of functions to the extent that the firm becomes a letter box entity should be considered to undermine the conditions with which the investment firm must comply in order to be and remain authorised in accordance with Article 5 of Directive 2004/39/EC.

(20) The outsourcing of investment services or activities or critical and important functions is capable of constituting a material change of the conditions for the authorisation of the investment firm, as referred to in Article 16(2) of Directive 2004/39/EC. If such outsourcing arrangements are to be put in place after the investment firm has obtained an authorisation according to the provisions included in Chapter I of Title II of Directive 2004/39/EC, those arrangements should be notified to the competent authority where required by Article 16(2) of Directive 2004/39/EC.

---

[3] OJ L 281, 23.11.1995, 31. Directive as amended by Regulation (EC) No 1882/2003 (OJ L 284, 31.10.2003, 1).

(21) Investment firms are required by this Directive to give the responsible competent authority prior notification of any arrangement for the outsourcing of the management of retail client portfolios that it proposes to enter into with a service provider located in a third country, where certain specified conditions are not met. However, competent authorities are not expected to authorise or otherwise approve any such arrangement or its terms. The purpose of the notification, rather, is to ensure that the competent authority has the opportunity to intervene in appropriate cases. It is the responsibility of the investment firm to negotiate the terms of any outsourcing arrangement, and to ensure that those terms are consistent with the obligations of the firm under this Directive and Directive 2004/39/EC, without the formal intervention of the competent authority.

(22) For the purposes of regulatory transparency, and in order to ensure an appropriate level of certainty for investment firms, this Directive requires each competent authority to publish a statement of its policy in relation to the outsourcing of retail portfolio management to service providers located in third countries. That statement must set out examples of cases where the competent authority is unlikely to object to such outsourcing, and must include an explanation of why outsourcing in such cases is unlikely to impair the ability of the firm to comply with the general conditions for outsourcing under this Directive. In providing that explanation, a competent authority should always indicate the reasons why outsourcing in the cases in question would not impede the effectiveness of its access to all the information relating to the outsourced service that is necessary for the authority to carry out its regulatory functions in respect of the investment firm.

(23) Where an investment firm deposits funds it holds on behalf of a client with a qualifying money market fund, the units in that money market fund should be held in accordance with the requirements for holding financial instruments belonging to clients.

(24) The circumstances which should be treated as giving rise to a conflict of interest should cover cases where there is a conflict between the interests of the firm or certain persons connected to the firm or the firm's group and the duty the firm owes to a client; or between the differing interests of two or more of its clients, to whom the firm owes in each case a duty. It is not enough that the firm may gain a benefit if there is not also a possible disadvantage to a client, or that one client to whom the firm owes a duty may make a gain or avoid a loss without there being a concomitant possible loss to another such client.

(25) Conflicts of interest should be regulated only where an investment service or ancillary service is provided by an investment firm. The status of the client to whom the service is provided—as either retail, professional or eligible counterparty—is irrelevant for this purpose.

(26) In complying with its obligation to draw up a conflict of interest policy under Directive 2004/39/EC which identifies circumstances which constitute or may give rise to a conflict of interest, the investment firm should pay special attention to the activities of investment research and advice, proprietary trading, portfolio management and corporate finance business, including underwriting or selling in an offering of securities and advising on mergers and acquisitions. In particular, such special attention is appropriate where the firm or a person directly or indirectly linked by control to the firm performs a combination of two or more of those activities.

(27) Investment firms should aim to identify and manage the conflicts of interest arising in relation to their various business lines and their group's activities under a comprehensive conflicts of interest policy. In particular, the disclosure of conflicts of interest by an investment firm should not exempt it from the obligation to maintain and operate the effective organisational and administrative arrangements required under Article 13(3) of Directive 2004/39/EC. While disclosure of specific conflicts of interest is required by Article 18(2) of Directive 2004/39/EC, an over-reliance on disclosure without adequate consideration as to how conflicts may appropriately be managed is not permitted.

(28) Investment research should be a subcategory of the type of information defined as a recommendation in Commission Directive 2003/125/EC of 22 December 2003 implementing Directive 2003/6/EC of the European Parliament and of the Council as regards the fair presentation of investment recommendations and the disclosure of conflicts of interest,[4] but it applies to financial instruments as defined in Directive 2004/39/EC. Recommendations, of the type so defined, which do not constitute investment research as defined in this Directive are nevertheless subject to the provisions of Directive 2003/125/EC as to the fair presentation of investment recommendations and the disclosure of conflicts of interest.

(29) The measures and arrangements adopted by an investment firm to manage the conflicts of interests that might arise from the production and dissemination of material that is presented as investment research should be appropriate to protect the objectivity and independence of financial analysts and of the investment research they produce. Those measures and arrangements should ensure that financial analysts enjoy an adequate degree of independence from the interests of persons whose responsibilities or business interests may reasonably be considered to conflict with the interests of the persons to whom the investment research is disseminated.

(30) Persons whose responsibilities or business interests may reasonably be considered to conflict with the interests of the persons to whom investment research is disseminated should include corporate finance personnel and persons involved in sales and trading on behalf of clients or the firm.

(31) Exceptional circumstances in which financial analysts and other persons connected with the investment firm who are involved in the production of investment research may, with prior written approval, undertake personal transactions in instruments to which the research relates should include those circumstances where, for personal reasons relating to financial hardship, the financial analyst or other person is required to liquidate a position.

(32) Small gifts or minor hospitality below a level specified in the firm's conflicts of interest policy and mentioned in the summary description of that policy that is made available to clients should not be considered as inducements for the purposes of the provisions relating to investment research.

(33) The concept of dissemination of investment research to clients or the public should not include dissemination exclusively to persons within the group of the investment firm.

(34) Current recommendations should be considered to be those recommendations contained in investment research which have not been withdrawn and which have not lapsed.

(35) The same requirements should apply to the substantial alteration of investment research produced by a third party as apply to the production of research.

(36) Financial analysts should not become involved in activities other than the preparation of investment research where such involvement is inconsistent with the maintenance of that person's objectivity. The following involvements should ordinarily be considered as inconsistent with the maintenance of that person's objectivity: participating in investment banking activities such as corporate finance business and underwriting, participating in 'pitches' for new business or 'road shows' for new issues of financial instruments; or being otherwise involved in the preparation of issuer marketing.

(37) Without prejudice to the provisions of this Directive relating to the production or dissemination of investment research, it is recommended that producers of investment research that are not investment firms should consider adopting internal policies and procedures designed to ensure that they also comply with the principles set out in this Directive as to the protection of the independence and objectivity of that research.

(38) Requirements imposed by this Directive, including those relating to personal transactions,

---

[4] OJ L 339, 24.12.2003, 73, reproduced supra under no. S. 27.

to dealing with knowledge of investment research and to the production or dissemination of investment research, apply without prejudice to other requirements of Directive 2004/39/EC and Directive 2003/6/EC of the European parliament and of the Council of 28 January 2003 on insider dealing and market manipulation (market abuse)[5] and their respective implementing measures.

(39) For the purposes of the provisions of this Directive concerning inducements, the receipt by an investment firm of a commission in connection with investment advice or general recommendations, in circumstances where the advice or recommendations are not biased as a result of the receipt of commission, should be considered as designed to enhance the quality of the investment advice to the client.

(40) This Directive permits investment firms to give or receive certain inducements only subject to specific conditions, and provided they are disclosed to the client, or are given to or by the client or a person on behalf of the client.

(41) This Directive requires investment firms that provide investment services other than investment advice to new retail clients to enter into a written basic agreement with the client, setting out the essential rights and obligations of the firm and the client. However, it imposes no other obligations as to the form, content and performance of contracts for the provisions of investment or ancillary services.

(42) This Directive sets out requirements for marketing communications only with respect to the obligation in Article 19(2) of Directive 2004/39/EC that information addressed to clients, including marketing communications, should be fair, clear and not misleading.

(43) Nothing in this Directive requires competent authorities to approve the content and form of marketing communications. However, neither does it prevent them from doing so, insofar as any such pre-approval is based only on compliance with the obligation in Directive 2004/39/EC that information to clients, including marketing communications, should be fair, clear and not misleading.

(44) Appropriate and proportionate information requirements should be established which take account of the status of a client as either retail or professional. An objective of Directive 2004/39/EC is to ensure a proportionate balance between investor protection and the disclosure obligations which apply to investment firms. To this end, it is appropriate that less stringent specific information requirements be included in this Directive with respect to professional clients than apply to retail clients. Professional clients should, subject to limited exceptions, be able to identify for themselves the information that is necessary for them to make an informed decision, and to ask the investment firm to provide that information. Where such information requests are reasonable and proportionate investment firms should provide additional information.

(45) Investment firms should provide clients or potential clients with adequate information on the nature of financial instruments and the risks associated with investing in them so that their clients can take each investment decision on a properly informed basis. The level of detail of this information may vary according to the client's categorisation as either a retail client or a professional client and the nature and risk profile of the financial instruments that are being offered, but should never be so general as to omit any essential elements. It is possible that for some financial instruments only the information referring to the type of an instrument will be sufficient whereas for some others the information will need to be product-specific.

(46) The conditions with which information addressed by investment firms to clients and potential clients must comply in order to be fair, clear and not misleading should apply to communications intended for retail clients in a way that is appropriate and proportionate, taking into account, for example, the means of communication, and the information that the communication is intended to convey to the clients or potential clients. In particular, it would

---

[5] OJ L 96, 12.4.2003, 16, reproduced supra under no. S. 24.

not be appropriate to apply such conditions to marketing communications which consist only of one or more of the following: the name of the firm, a logo or other image associated with the firm, a contact point, a reference to the types of investment services provided by the firm, or to its fees or commissions.

(47) For the purposes of Directive 2004/39/EC and of this Directive, information should be considered to be misleading if it has a tendency to mislead the person or persons to whom it is addressed or by whom it is likely to be received, whether or not the person who provides the information considers or intends it to be misleading.

(48) In determining what constitutes the provision of information in good time before a time specified in this Directive, an investment firm should take into account, having regard to the urgency of the situation and the time necessary for the client to absorb and react to the specific information provided, the client's need for sufficient time to read and understand it before taking an investment decision. A client is likely to require less time to review information about a simple or standardised product or service, or a product or service of a kind he has purchased previously, than he would require for a more complex or unfamiliar product or service.

(49) Nothing in this Directive obliges investment firms to provide all required information about the investment firm, financial instruments, costs and associated charges, or concerning the safeguarding of client financial instruments or client funds immediately and at the same time, provided that they comply with the general obligation to provide the relevant information in good time before the time specified in this Directive. Provided that the information is communicated to the client in good time before the provision of the service, nothing in this Directive obliges firms to provide it either separately, as part of a marketing communication, or by incorporating the information in a client agreement.

(50) In cases where an investment firm is required to provide information to a client before the provision of a service, each transaction in respect of the same type of financial instrument should not be considered as the provision of a new or different service.

(51) In cases where an investment firm providing portfolio management services is required to provide to retail clients or potential retail clients information on the types of financial instruments that may be included in the client portfolio and the types of transactions that may be carried out in such instruments, such information should state separately whether the investment firm will be mandated to invest in financial instruments not admitted to trading on a regulated market, in derivatives, or in illiquid or highly volatile instruments; or to undertake short sales, purchases with borrowed funds, securities financing transactions, or any transactions involving margin payments, deposit of collateral or foreign exchange risk.

(52) The provision by an investment firm to a client of a copy of a prospectus that has been drawn up and published in accordance with Directive 2003/71/EC of the European Parliament and of the Council of 4 November 2003 on the prospectus to be published when securities are offered to the public or admitted to trading[6] should not be treated as the provision by the firm of information to a client for the purposes of the operating conditions under Directive 2004/39/EC which relate to the quality and contents of such information, if the firm is not responsible under that directive for the information given in the prospectus.

(53) The information which an investment firm is required to give to a retail client concerning costs and associated charges includes information about the arrangements for payment or performance of the agreement for the provision of investment services and any other agreement relating to a financial instrument that is being offered. For this purpose, arrangements for payment will generally be relevant where a financial instrument contract is terminated by cash settlement. Arrangements for performance will generally be

---

[6] OJ L 345, 31.12.2003, 64, reproduced supra under no. S. 25.

relevant where, upon termination, a financial instrument requires the delivery of shares, bonds, a warrant, bullion or another instrument or commodity.

(54) As regards collective investment undertakings covered by Council Directive 85/611/EEC of 20 December 1985 on the coordination of laws, regulations and administrative provisions relating to undertakings for collective investment in transferable securities (UCITS),[7] it is not the purpose of this Directive to regulate the content of the simplified prospectus as defined by Article 28 of Directive 85/611/EEC. No information should be added to the simplified prospectus as a result of the implementation of this Directive.

(55) The simplified prospectus provides, notably, sufficient information in relation to the costs and associated charges in respect to the UCITS itself. However, investment firms distributing units in UCITS should additionally inform their clients about all the other costs and associated charges related to their provision of investment services in relation to units in UCITS.

(56) It is necessary to make different provision for the application of the suitability test in Article 19(4) of Directive 2004/39/EC and the appropriateness test in Article 19(5) of that Directive. These tests have different scope with regards to the investment services to which they relate, and have different functions and characteristics.

(57) For the purposes of Article 19(4) of Directive 2004/39/EC, a transaction may be unsuitable for the client or potential client because of the risks of the financial instruments involved, the type of transaction, the characteristics of the order or the frequency of the trading. A series of transactions that are each suitable when viewed in isolation may be unsuitable if the recommendation or the decisions to trade are made with a frequency that is not in the best interests of the client. In the case of portfolio management, a transaction might also be unsuitable if it would result in an unsuitable portfolio.

(58) In accordance with Article 19(4) of Directive 2004/39/EC, a firm is required to assess the suitability of investment services and financial instruments to a client only when it is providing investment advice or portfolio management to that client. In the case of other investment services, the firm is required by Article 19(5) of that Directive to assess the appropriateness of an investment service or product for a client, and then only if the product is not offered on an execution-only basis under Article 19(6) of that Directive (which applies to non-complex products).

(59) For the purposes of the provisions of this Directive requiring investment firms to assess the appropriateness of investment services or products offered or demanded, a client who has engaged in a course of dealings involving a specific type of product or service beginning before the date of application of Directive 2004/39/EC should be presumed to have the necessary experience and knowledge in order to understand the risks involved in relation to that product or investment service. Where a client engages in a course of dealings of that kind through the services of an investment firm, beginning after the date of application of that Directive, the firm is not required to make a new assessment on the occasion of each separate transaction. It complies with its duty under Article 19(5) of that Directive provided that it makes the necessary assessment of appropriateness before beginning that service.

(60) A recommendation or request made, or advice given, by a portfolio manager to a client to the effect that the client should give or alter a mandate to the portfolio manager that defines the limits of the portfolio manager's discretion should be considered a recommendation within the meaning of Article 19(4) of Directive 2004/39/EC.

(61) For the purposes of determining whether a unit in a collective investment undertaking which does not comply with the requirements of Directive 85/611/EC, that has been authorised for marketing to the public, should be considered as non-complex, the circumstances in which valuation systems will be independent of the issuer

---

[7] OJ L 375, 31.12.1985, 3, reproduced supra under no. S. 6. Directive as last amended by Directive 2005/1/EC of the European Parliament and of the Council (OJ L 79, 24.3.2005, 9), reproduced supra under no. B. 39.

should include where they are overseen by a depositary that is regulated as a provider of depositary services in a Member State.

(62) Nothing in this Directive requires competent authorities to approve the content of the basic agreement between an investment firm and its retail clients. However, neither does it prevent them from doing so, insofar as any such approval is based only on the firm's compliance with its obligations under Directive 2004/39/EC to act honestly, fairly and professionally in accordance with the best interests of its clients, and to establish a record that sets out the rights and obligations of investment firms and their clients, and the other terms on which firms will provide services to their clients.

(63) The records an investment firm is required to keep should be adapted to the type of business and the range of investment services and activities performed, provided that the record-keeping obligations set out in Directive 2004/39/EC and this Directive are fulfilled. For the purposes of the reporting obligations in respect of portfolio management, a contingent liability transaction is one that involves any actual or potential liability for the client that exceeds the cost of acquiring the instrument.

(64) For the purposes of the provisions on reporting to clients, a reference to the type of the order should be understood as referring to its status as a limit order, market order, or other specific type of order.

(65) For the purposes of the provisions on reporting to clients, a reference to the nature of the order should be understood as referring to orders to subscribe for securities, or to exercise an option, or similar client order.

(66) When establishing its execution policy in accordance with Article 21(2) of Directive 2004/39/EC, an investment firm should determine the relative importance of the factors mentioned in Article 21(1) of that Directive, or at least establish the process by which it determines the relative importance of these factors, so that it can deliver the best possible result to its clients. In order to give effect to that policy, an investment firm should select the execution venues that enable it to obtain on a consistent basis the best possible result for the execution of client orders. An investment firm should apply its execution policy to each client order that it executes with a view to obtaining the best possible result for the client in accordance with that policy. The obligation under Directive 2004/39/EC to take all reasonable steps to obtain the best possible result for the client should not be treated as requiring an investment firm to include in its execution policy all available execution venues.

(67) For the purposes of ensuring that an investment firm obtains the best possible result for the client when executing a retail client order in the absence of specific client instructions, the firm should take into consideration all factors that will allow it to deliver the best possible result in terms of the total consideration, representing the price of the financial instrument and the costs related to execution. Speed, likelihood of execution and settlement, the size and nature of the order, market impact and any other implicit transaction costs may be given precedence over the immediate price and cost consideration only insofar as they are instrumental in delivering the best possible result in terms of the total consideration to the retail client.

(68) When an investment firm executes an order following specific instructions from the client, it should be treated as having satisfied its best execution obligations only in respect of the part or aspect of the order to which the client instructions relate. The fact that the client has given specific instructions which cover one part or aspect of the order should not be treated as releasing the investment firm from its best execution obligations in respect of any other parts or aspects of the client order that are not covered by such instructions. An investment firm should not induce a client to instruct it to execute an order in a particular way, by expressly indicating or implicitly suggesting the content of the instruction to the client, when the firm ought reasonably to know that an instruction to that effect is likely to prevent it from obtaining the best possible result for that client. However, this should not prevent a firm inviting a client to choose between two or

more specified trading venues, provided that those venues are consistent with the execution policy of the firm.

(69) Dealing on own account with clients by an investment firm should be considered as the execution of client orders, and therefore subject to the requirements under Directive 2004/39/EC and this Directive and, in particular, those obligations in relation to best execution. However, if an investment firm provides a quote to a client and that quote would meet the investment firm's obligations under Article 21(1) of Directive 2004/39/EC if the firm executed that quote at the time the quote was provided, then the firm will meet those same obligations if it executes its quote after the client accepts it, provided that, taking into account the changing market conditions and the time elapsed between the offer and acceptance of the quote, the quote is not manifestly out of date.

(70) The obligation to deliver the best possible result when executing client orders applies in relation to all types of financial instruments. However, given the differences in market structures or the structure of financial instruments, it may be difficult to identify and apply a uniform standard of and procedure for best execution that would be valid and effective for all classes of instrument. Best execution obligations should therefore be applied in a manner that takes into account the different circumstances associated with the execution of orders related to particular types of financial instruments. For example, transactions involving a customised OTC financial instrument that involve a unique contractual relationship tailored to the circumstances of the client and the investment firm may not be comparable for best execution purposes with transactions involving shares traded on centralised execution venues.

(71) For the purposes of determining best execution when executing retail client orders, the costs related to execution should include an investment firm's own commissions or fees charged to the client for limited purposes, in cases where more than one venue listed in the firm's execution policy is capable of executing a particular order.

In such cases, the firm's own commissions and costs for executing the order on each of the eligible execution venues should be taken into account in order to assess and compare the results for the client that would be achieved by executing the order on each such venue. However, it is not intended to require a firm to compare the results that would be achieved for its client on the basis of its own execution policy and its own commissions and fees, with results that might be achieved for the same client by any other investment firm on the basis of a different execution policy or a different structure of commissions or fees. Nor is it intended to require a firm to compare the differences in its own commissions which are attributable to differences in the nature of the services that the firm provides to clients.

(72) The provisions of this Directive that provide that costs of execution should include an investment firm's own commissions or fees charged to the client for the provision of an investment service should not apply for the purpose of determining what execution venues must be included in the firm's execution policy for the purposes of Article 21(3) of Directive 2004/39/EC.

(73) It should be considered that an investment firm structures or charges its commissions in a way which discriminates unfairly between execution venues if it charges a different commission or spread to clients for execution on different execution venues and that difference does not reflect actual differences in the cost to the firm of executing on those venues.

(74) The provisions of this Directive as to execution policy are without prejudice to the general obligation of an investment firm under Article 21(4) of Directive 2004/39/EC to monitor the effectiveness of its order execution arrangements and policy and assess the venues in its execution policy on a regular basis.

(75) This Directive is not intended to require a duplication of effort as to best execution between an investment firm which provides the service of reception and transmission of order or portfolio management and any investment firm to which that investment firm transmits its orders for execution.

(76) The best execution obligation under Directive 2004/39/EC requires investment firms to take all reasonable steps to obtain the best possible result for their clients. The quality of execution, which includes aspects such as the speed and likelihood of execution (fill rate) and the availability and incidence of price improvement, is an important factor in the delivery of best execution. Availability, comparability and consolidation of data related to execution quality provided by the various execution venues is crucial in enabling investment firms and investors to identify those execution venues that deliver the highest quality of execution for their clients. This Directive does not mandate the publication by execution venues of their execution quality data, as execution venues and data providers should be permitted to develop solutions concerning the provision of execution quality data. The Commission should submit a report by 1 November 2008 on the market-led developments in this area with a view to assessing availability, comparability and consolidation at a European level of information concerning execution quality.

(77) For the purposes of the provisions of this Directive concerning client order handling, the reallocation of transactions should be considered as detrimental to a client if, as an effect of that reallocation, unfair precedence is given to the investment firm or to any particular client.

(78) Without prejudice to Directive 2003/6/EC, for the purposes of the provisions of this Directive concerning client order handling, client orders should not be treated as otherwise comparable if they are received by different media and it would not be practicable for them to be treated sequentially. For the further purposes of those provisions, any use by an investment firm of information relating to a pending client order in order to deal on own account in the financial instruments to which the client order relates, or in related financial instruments, should be considered a misuse of that information. However, the mere fact that market makers or bodies authorised to act as counterparties confine themselves to pursuing their legitimate business of buying and selling financial instruments, or that persons authorised to execute orders on behalf of third parties confine themselves to carrying out an order dutifully, should not in itself be deemed to constitute a misuse of information.

(79) Advice about financial instruments given in a newspaper, journal, magazine or any other publication addressed to the general public (including by means of the internet), or in any television or radio broadcast, should not be considered as a personal recommendation for the purposes of the definition of 'investment advice' in Directive 2004/39/EC.

(80) This Directive respects the fundamental rights and observes the principles recognised in particular by the Charter of Fundamental Rights of the European Union and in particular by Article 11 thereof and Article 10 of the European Convention on Human Rights. In this regard, this Directive does not in any way prevent Member States from applying their constitutional rules relating to freedom of the press and freedom of expression in the media.

(81) Generic advice about a type of financial instrument is not investment advice for the purposes of Directive 2004/39/EC, because this Directive specifies that, for the purposes of Directive 2004/39/EC, investment advice is restricted to advice on particular financial instruments. However, if an investment firm provides generic advice to a client about a type of financial instrument which it presents as suitable for, or based on a consideration of the circumstances of, that client, and that advice is not in fact suitable for the client, or is not based on a consideration of his circumstances, depending on the circumstances of the particular case, the firm is likely to be acting in contravention of Article 19(1) or (2) of Directive 2004/39/EC. In particular, a firm which gives a client such advice would be likely to contravene the requirement of Article 19(1) to act honestly, fairly and professionally in accordance with the best interests of its clients. Similarly or alternatively, such advice would be likely to contravene the requirement of Article 19(2) that information addressed by a firm to a client should be fair, clear and not misleading.

(82) Acts carried out by an investment firm that are preparatory to the provision of an investment

service or carrying out an investment activity should be considered as an integral part of that service or activity. This would include, for example, the provision of generic advice by an investment firm to clients or potential clients prior to or in the course of the provision of investment advice or any other investment service or activity.

(83) The provision of a general recommendation (that is, one which is intended for distribution channels or the public) about a transaction in a financial instrument or a type of financial instrument constitutes the provision of an ancillary service within Section B(5) of Annex I of Directive 2004/39/EC, and consequently Directive 2004/39/EC and its protections apply to the provision of that recommendation.

(84) The Committee of European Securities Regulators, established by Commission Decision 2001/527/EC[8] has been consulted for technical advice.

(85) The measures provided for in this Directive are in accordance with the opinion of the European Securities Committee,

HAS ADOPTED THIS DIRECTIVE:

Chapter I
Scope and Definitions

Article 1
Subject-matter and scope

1. This Directive lays down the detailed rules for the implementation of Article 4(1)(4) and 4(2), Article 13(2) to (8), Article 18, Article 19(1) to (6), Article 19(8), and Articles 21, 22 and 24 of Directive 2004/39/EC.

2. Chapter II and Sections 1 to 4, Article 45 and Sections 6 and 8 of Chapter III and, to the extent they relate to those provisions, Chapter I and Section 9 of Chapter III and Chapter IV of this Directive shall apply to management companies in accordance with Article 5(4) of Directive 85/611/EEC.

Article 2
Definitions

For the purposes of this Directive, the following definitions shall apply:

(1) 'distribution channels' means distribution channels within the meaning of Article 1(7) of Commission Directive 2003/125/EC;

(2) 'durable medium' means any instrument which enables a client to store information addressed personally to that client in a way accessible for future reference for a period of time adequate for the purposes of the information and which allows the unchanged reproduction of the information stored;

(3) 'relevant person' in relation to an investment firm, means any of the following:

(a) a director, partner or equivalent, manager or tied agent of the firm;

(b) a director, partner or equivalent, or manager of any tied agent of the firm;

(c) an employee of the firm or of a tied agent of the firm, as well as any other natural person whose services are placed at the disposal and under the control of the firm or a tied agent of the firm and who is involved in the provision by the firm of investment services and activities;

(d) a natural person who is directly involved in the provision of services to the investment firm or to its tied agent under an outsourcing arrangement for the purpose of the provision by the firm of investment services and activities;

(4) 'financial analyst' means a relevant person who produces the substance of investment research;

(5) 'group', in relation to an investment firm, means the group of which that firm forms a part, consisting of a parent undertaking, its subsidiaries and the entities in which the parent undertaking or its subsidiaries hold a participation, as well as undertakings linked to each other by a relationship within the meaning of Article 12(1) of Council Directive 83/349/EEC on consolidated accounts;[9]

---

[8] OJ L 191, 13.7.2001, 43, reproduced supra under no. S. 19.

[9] OJ No L 193, 18.7.1983, 1, reproduced supra under no. C. 6.

(6) 'outsourcing' means an arrangement of any form between an investment firm and a service provider by which that service provider performs a process, a service or an activity which would otherwise be undertaken by the investment firm itself;

(7) 'person with whom a relevant person has a family relationship' means any of the following:

(a) the spouse of the relevant person or any partner of that person considered by national law as equivalent to a spouse;

(b) a dependent child or stepchild of the relevant person;

(c) any other relative of the relevant person who has shared the same household as that person for at least one year on the date of the personal transaction concerned;

(8) 'securities financing transaction' has the meaning given in Commission Regulation (EC) No 1287/2006;[10]

(9) 'senior management' means the person or persons who effectively direct the business of the investment firm as referred to in Article 9(1) of Directive 2004/39/EC.

Article 3

Conditions applying to the provision of information

1. Where, for the purposes of this Directive, information is required to be provided in a durable medium, Member States shall permit investment firms to provide that information in a durable medium other than on paper only if:

(a) the provision of that information in that medium is appropriate to the context in which the business between the firm and the client is, or is to be, carried on; and

(b) the person to whom the information is to be provided, when offered the choice between information on paper or in that other durable medium, specifically chooses the provision of the information in that other medium.

---

[10] See page 1 of this Official Journal.

2. Where, pursuant to Article 29, 30, 31, 32, 33 or 46(2) of this Directive, an investment firm provides information to a client by means of a website and that information is not addressed personally to the client, Member States shall ensure that the following conditions are satisfied:

(a) the provision of that information in that medium is appropriate to the context in which the business between the firm and the client is, or is to be, carried on;

(b) the client must specifically consent to the provision of that information in that form;

(c) the client must be notified electronically of the address of the website, and the place on the website where the information may be accessed;

(d) the information must be up to date;

(e) the information must be accessible continuously by means of that website for such period of time as the client may reasonably need to inspect it.

3. For the purposes of this Article, the provision of information by means of electronic communications shall be treated as appropriate to the context in which the business between the firm and the client is, or is to be, carried on if there is evidence that the client has regular access to the internet. The provision by the client of an e-mail address for the purposes of the carrying on of that business shall be treated as such evidence.

Article 4

Additional requirements on investment firms in certain cases

1. Member States may retain or impose requirements additional to those in this Directive only in those exceptional cases where such requirements are objectively justified and proportionate so as to address specific risks to investor protection or to market integrity that are not adequately addressed by this Directive, and provided that one of the following conditions is met:

(a) the specific risks addressed by the requirements are of particular importance in the circumstances of the market structure of that Member State;

(b) the requirement addresses risks or issues that emerge or become evident after the date of application of this Directive and that are not otherwise regulated by or under Community measures.

2. Any requirements imposed under paragraph 1 shall not restrict or otherwise affect the rights of investment firms under Articles 31 and 32 of Directive 2004/39/EC.

3. Member States shall notify to the Commission:

(a) any requirement which it intends to retain in accordance with paragraph 1 before the date of transposition of this Directive; and

(b) any requirement which it intends to impose in accordance with paragraph 1 at least one month before the date appointed for that requirement to come into force.

In each case, the notification shall include a justification for that requirement.

The Commission shall communicate to Member States and make public on its website the notifications it receives in accordance with this paragraph.

4. By 31 December 2009 the Commission shall report to the European Parliament and the Council on the application of this Article.

Chapter II
Organisational Requirements
Section 1
Organisation

Article 5
(Article 13(2) to (8) of Directive 2004/39/EC)

General organisational requirements

1. Member States shall require investment firms to comply with the following requirements:

(a) to establish, implement and maintain decision-making procedures and an organisational structure which clearly and in documented manner specifies reporting lines and allocates functions and responsibilities;

(b) to ensure that their relevant persons are aware of the procedures which must be followed for the proper discharge of their responsibilities;

(c) to establish, implement and maintain adequate internal control mechanisms designed to secure compliance with decisions and procedures at all levels of the investment firm;

(d) to employ personnel with the skills, knowledge and expertise necessary for the discharge of the responsibilities allocated to them;

(e) to establish, implement and maintain effective internal reporting and communication of information at all relevant levels of the investment firm;

(f) to maintain adequate and orderly records of their business and internal organisation;

(g) to ensure that the performance of multiple functions by their relevant persons does not and is not likely to prevent those persons from discharging any particular function soundly, honestly, and professionally.

Member States shall ensure that, for those purposes, investment firms take into account the nature, scale and complexity of the business of the firm, and the nature and range of investment services and activities undertaken in the course of that business.

2. Member States shall require investment firms to establish, implement and maintain systems and procedures that are adequate to safeguard the security, integrity and confidentiality of information, taking into account the nature of the information in question.

3. Member States shall require investment firms to establish, implement and maintain an adequate business continuity policy aimed at ensuring, in the case of an interruption to their systems and procedures, the preservation of essential data and functions, and the maintenance of investment services and activities, or, where that is not possible, the timely recovery of such data and functions and the timely resumption of their investment services and activities.

4. Member States shall require investment firms to establish, implement and maintain accounting

policies and procedures that enable them, at the request of the competent authority, to deliver in a timely manner to the competent authority financial reports which reflect a true and fair view of their financial position and which comply with all applicable accounting standards and rules.

5. Member States shall require investment firms to monitor and, on a regular basis, to evaluate the adequacy and effectiveness of their systems, internal control mechanisms and arrangements established in accordance with paragraphs 1 to 4, and to take appropriate measures to address any deficiencies.

Article 6

(Article 13(2) of Directive 2004/39/EC)

Compliance

1. Member States shall ensure that investment firms establish, implement and maintain adequate policies and procedures designed to detect any risk of failure by the firm to comply with its obligations under Directive 2004/39/EC, as well as the associated risks, and put in place adequate measures and procedures designed to minimise such risk and to enable the competent authorities to exercise their powers effectively under that Directive.

Member States shall ensure that, for those purposes, investment firms take into account the nature, scale and complexity of the business of the firm, and the nature and range of investment services and activities undertaken in the course of that business.

2. Member States shall require investment firms to establish and maintain a permanent and effective compliance function which operates independently and which has the following responsibilities:

(a) to monitor and, on a regular basis, to assess the adequacy and effectiveness of the measures and procedures put in place in accordance with the first subparagraph of paragraph 1, and the actions taken to address any deficiencies in the firm's compliance with its obligations;

(b) to advise and assist the relevant persons responsible for carrying out investment services and activities to comply with the firm's obligations under Directive 2004/39/EC.

3. In order to enable the compliance function to discharge its responsibilities properly and independently, Member States shall require investment firms to ensure that the following conditions are satisfied:

(a) the compliance function must have the necessary authority, resources, expertise and access to all relevant information;

(b) a compliance officer must be appointed and must be responsible for the compliance function and for any reporting as to compliance required by Article 9(2);

(c) the relevant persons involved in the compliance function must not be involved in the performance of services or activities they monitor;

(d) the method of determining the remuneration of the relevant persons involved in the compliance function must not compromise their objectivity and must not be likely to do so.

However, an investment firm shall not be required to comply with point (c) or point (d) if it is able to demonstrate that in view of the nature, scale and complexity of its business, and the nature and range of investment services and activities, the requirement under that point is not proportionate and that its compliance function continues to be effective.

Article 7

(Second subparagraph of Article 13(5) of Directive 2004/39/EC)

Risk management

1. Member States shall require investment firms to take the following actions:

(a) to establish, implement and maintain adequate risk management policies and procedures which identify the risks relating to the firm's activities, processes and systems, and where appropriate, set the level of risk tolerated by the firm;

(b) to adopt effective arrangements, processes and mechanisms to manage the risks relating to the firm's activities, processes and systems, in light of that level of risk tolerance;

(c) to monitor the following:
(i) the adequacy and effectiveness of the investment firm's risk management policies and procedures;
(ii) the level of compliance by the investment firm and its relevant persons with the arrangements, processes and mechanisms adopted in accordance with point (b);
(iii) the adequacy and effectiveness of measures taken to address any deficiencies in those policies, procedures, arrangements, processes and mechanisms, including failures by the relevant persons to comply with such arrangements, processes and mechanisms or follow such policies and procedures.

2. Member States shall require investment firms, where appropriate and proportionate in view of the nature, scale and complexity of their business and the nature and range of the investment services and activities undertaken in the course of that business, to establish and maintain a risk management function that operates independently and carries out the following tasks:

(a) implementation of the policy and procedures referred to in paragraph 1;

(b) provision of reports and advice to senior management in accordance with Article 9(2).

Where an investment firm is not required under the first sub-paragraph to establish and maintain a risk management function that functions independently, it must nevertheless be able to demonstrate that the policies and procedures which it has adopted in accordance with paragraph 1 satisfy the requirements of that paragraph and are consistently effective.

Article 8
(Second subparagraph of Article 13(5) of Directive 2004/39/EC)
Internal audit

Member States shall require investment firms, where appropriate and proportionate in view of the nature, scale and complexity of their business and the nature and range of investment services and activities undertaken in the course of that business, to establish and maintain an internal audit function which is separate and independent from the other functions and activities of the investment firm and which has the following responsibilities:

(a) to establish, implement and maintain an audit plan to examine and evaluate the adequacy and effectiveness of the investment firm's systems, internal control mechanisms and arrangements;

(b) to issue recommendations based on the result of work carried out in accordance with point (a);

(c) to verify compliance with those recommendations;

(d) to report in relation to internal audit matters in accordance with Article 9(2).

Article 9
(Article 13(2) of Directive 2004/39/EC)
Responsibility of senior management

1. Member States shall require investment firms, when allocating functions internally, to ensure that senior management, and, where appropriate, the supervisory function, are responsible for ensuring that the firm complies with its obligations under Directive 2004/39/EC.

In particular, senior management and, where appropriate, the supervisory function shall be required to assess and periodically to review the effectiveness of the policies, arrangements and procedures put in place to comply with the obligations under Directive 2004/39/EC and to take appropriate measures to address any deficiencies.

2. Member States shall require investment firms to ensure that their senior management receive on a frequent basis, and at least annually, written reports on the matters covered by Articles 6, 7 and 8 indicating in particular whether the appropriate remedial measures have been taken in the event of any deficiencies.

3. Member States shall require investment firms to ensure that the supervisory function, if any,

receives on a regular basis written reports on the same matters.

4. For the purposes of this Article, 'supervisory function' means the function within an investment firm responsible for the supervision of its senior management.

Article 10
(Article 13(2) of Directive 2004/39/EC)
Complaints handling

Member States shall require investment firms to establish, implement and maintain effective and transparent procedures for the reasonable and prompt handling of complaints received from retail clients or potential retail clients, and to keep a record of each complaint and the measures taken for its resolution.

Article 11
(Article 13(2) of Directive 2004/39/EC)
Meaning of personal transaction

For the purposes of Article 12 and Article 25, personal transaction means a trade in a financial instrument effected by or on behalf of a relevant person, where at least one of the following criteria are met:

(a) that relevant person is acting outside the scope of the activities he carries out in that capacity;

(b) the trade is carried out for the account of any of the following persons:
(i) the relevant person;
(ii) any person with whom he has a family relationship, or with whom he has close links;
(iii) a person whose relationship with the relevant person is such that the relevant person has a direct or indirect material interest in the outcome of the trade, other than a fee or commission for the execution of the trade.

Article 12
(Article 13(2) of Directive 2004/39/EC)
Personal transactions

1. Member States shall require investment firms to establish, implement and maintain adequate arrangements aimed at preventing the following activities in the case of any relevant person who is involved in activities that may give rise to a conflict of interest, or who has access to inside information within the meaning of Article 1(1) of Directive 2003/6/EC or to other confidential information relating to clients or transactions with or for clients by virtue of an activity carried out by him on behalf of the firm:

(a) entering into a personal transaction which meets at least one of the following criteria:
(i) that person is prohibited from entering into it under Directive 2003/6/EC;
(ii) it involves the misuse or improper disclosure of that confidential information;
(iii) it conflicts or is likely to conflict with an obligation of the investment firm under Directive 2004/39/EC;

(b) advising or procuring, other than in the proper course of his employment or contract for services, any other person to enter into a transaction in financial instruments which, if a personal transaction of the relevant person, would be covered by point (a) or Article 25(2)(a) or (b) or Article 47(3);

(c) without prejudice to Article 3(a) of Directive 2003/6/EC, disclosing, other than in the normal course of his employment or contract for services, any information or opinion to any other person if the relevant person knows, or reasonably ought to know, that as a result of that disclosure that other person will or would be likely to take either of the following steps:
(i) to enter into a transaction in financial instruments which, if a personal transaction of the relevant person, would be covered by point (a) or Article 25(2)(a) or (b) or Article 47(3);
(ii) to advise or procure another person to enter into such a transaction.

2. The arrangements required under paragraph 1 must in particular be designed to ensure that:

(a) each relevant person covered by paragraph 1 is aware of the restrictions on personal transactions, and of the measures established by the investment firm in connection with personal transactions and disclosure, in accordance with paragraph 1;

(b) the firm is informed promptly of any personal transaction entered into by a relevant person, either by notification of that transaction or by other procedures enabling the firm to identify such transactions;

In the case of outsourcing arrangements the investment firm must ensure that the firm to which the activity is outsourced maintains a record of personal transactions entered into by any relevant person and provides that information to the investment firm promptly on request.

(c) a record is kept of the personal transaction notified to the firm or identified by it, including any authorisation or prohibition in connection with such a transaction.

3. Paragraphs 1 and 2 shall not apply to the following kinds of personal transaction:

(a) personal transactions effected under a discretionary portfolio management service where there is no prior communication in connection with the transaction between the portfolio manager and the relevant person or other person for whose account the transaction is executed;

(b) personal transactions in units in collective undertakings that comply with the conditions necessary to enjoy the rights conferred by Directive 85/611/EEC or are subject to supervision under the law of a Member State which requires an equivalent level of risk spreading in their assets, where the relevant person and any other person for whose account the transactions are effected are not involved in the management of that undertaking.

SECTION 2

OUTSOURCING

Article 13

(Article 13(2) and first subparagraph of Article 13(5) of Directive 2004/39/EC)

Meaning of critical and important operational functions

1. For the purposes of the first subparagraph of Article 13(5) of Directive 2004/39/EC, an operational function shall be regarded as critical or important if a defect or failure in its performance would materially impair the continuing compliance of an investment firm with the conditions and obligations of its authorisation or its other obligations under Directive 2004/39/EC, or its financial performance, or the soundness or the continuity of its investment services and activities.

2. Without prejudice to the status of any other function, the following functions shall not be considered as critical or important for the purposes of paragraph 1:

(a) the provision to the firm of advisory services, and other services which do not form part of the investment business of the firm, including the provision of legal advice to the firm, the training of personnel of the firm, billing services and the security of the firm's premises and personnel;

(b) the purchase of standardised services, including market information services and the provision of price feeds.

Article 14

(Article 13(2) and first subparagraph of Article 13(5) of Directive 2004/39/EC)

Conditions for outsourcing critical or important operational functions or investment services or activities

1. Member States shall ensure that, when investment firms outsource critical or important operational functions or any investment services or activities, the firms remain fully responsible for discharging all of their obligations under Directive 2004/39/EC and comply, in particular, with the following conditions:

(a) the outsourcing must not result in the delegation by senior management of its responsibility;

(b) the relationship and obligations of the investment firm towards its clients under the terms of Directive 2004/39/EC must not be altered;

(c) the conditions with which the investment firm must comply in order to be authorised in accordance with Article 5 of Directive

2004/39/EC, and to remain so, must not be undermined;

(d) none of the other conditions subject to which the firm's authorisation was granted must be removed or modified.

2. Member States shall require investment firms to exercise due skill, care and diligence when entering into, managing or terminating any arrangement for the outsourcing to a service provider of critical or important operational functions or of any investment services or activities.

Investment firms shall in particular take the necessary steps to ensure that the following conditions are satisfied:

(a) the service provider must have the ability, capacity, and any authorisation required by law to perform the outsourced functions, services or activities reliably and professionally;

(b) the service provider must carry out the outsourced services effectively, and to this end the firm must establish methods for assessing the standard of performance of the service provider;

(c) the service provider must properly supervise the carrying out of the outsourced functions, and adequately manage the risks associated with the outsourcing;

(d) appropriate action must be taken if it appears that the service provider may not be carrying out the functions effectively and in compliance with applicable laws and regulatory requirements;

(e) the investment firm must retain the necessary expertise to supervise the outsourced functions effectively and manage the risks associated with the outsourcing and must supervise those functions and manage those risks;

(f) the service provider must disclose to the investment firm any development that may have a material impact on its ability to carry out the outsourced functions effectively and in compliance with applicable laws and regulatory requirements;

(g) the investment firm must be able to terminate the arrangement for outsourcing where necessary without detriment to the continuity and quality of its provision of services to clients;

(h) the service provider must cooperate with the competent authorities of the investment firm in connection with the outsourced activities;

(i) the investment firm, its auditors and the relevant competent authorities must have effective access to data related to the outsourced activities, as well as to the business premises of the service provider; and the competent authorities must be able to exercise those rights of access;

(j) the service provider must protect any confidential information relating to the investment firm and its clients;

(k) the investment firm and the service provider must establish, implement and maintain a contingency plan for disaster recovery and periodic testing of backup facilities, where that is necessary having regard to the function, service or activity that has been outsourced.

3. Member States shall require the respective rights and obligations of the investment firms and of the service provider to be clearly allocated and set out in a written agreement.

4. Member States shall provide that, where the investment firm and the service provider are members of the same group, the investment firm may, for the purposes of complying with this Article and Article 15, take into account the extent to which the firm controls the service provider or has the ability to influence its actions.

5. Member States shall require investment firms to make available on request to the competent authority all information necessary to enable the authority to supervise the compliance of the performance of the outsourced activities with the requirements of this Directive.

Article 15

(Article 13(2) and first subparagraph of Article 13(5) of Directive 2004/39/EC)

Service providers located in third countries

1. In addition to the requirements set out in Article 14, Member States shall require that, where an investment firm outsources the investment service of portfolio management provided

to retail clients to a service provider located in a third country, that investment firm ensures that the following conditions are satisfied:

(a) the service provider must be authorised or registered in its home country to provide that service and must be subject to prudential supervision;

(b) there must be an appropriate cooperation agreement between the competent authority of the investment firm and the supervisory authority of the service provider.

2. Where one or both of those conditions mentioned in paragraph 1 are not satisfied, an investment firm may outsource investment services to a service provider located in a third country only if the firm gives prior notification to its competent authority about the outsourcing arrangement and the competent authority does not object to that arrangement within a reasonable time following receipt of that notification.

3. Without prejudice to paragraph 2, Member States shall publish or require competent authorities to publish a statement of policy in relation to outsourcing covered by paragraph 2. That statement shall set out examples of cases where the competent authority would not, or would be likely not to, object to an outsourcing under paragraph 2 where one or both of the conditions in points (a) and (b) of paragraph 1 are not met. It shall include a clear explanation as to why the competent authority considers that in such cases outsourcing would not impair the ability of investment firms to fulfil their obligations under Article 14.

4. Nothing in this article limits the obligations on investment firms to comply with the requirements in Article 14.

5. Competent authorities shall publish a list of the supervisory authorities in third countries with which they have cooperation agreements that are appropriate for the purposes of point (b) of paragraph 1.

SECTION 3

SAFEGUARDING OF CLIENT ASSETS

Article 16

(Article 13(7) and (8) of Directive 2004/39/EC)

Safeguarding of client financial instruments and funds

1. Member States shall require that, for the purposes of safeguarding clients' rights in relation to financial instruments and funds belonging to them, investment firms comply with the following requirements:

(a) they must keep such records and accounts as are necessary to enable them at any time and without delay to distinguish assets held for one client from assets held for any other client, and from their own assets;

(b) they must maintain their records and accounts in a way that ensures their accuracy, and in particular their correspondence to the financial instruments and funds held for clients;

(c) they must conduct, on a regular basis, reconciliations between their internal accounts and records and those of any third parties by whom those assets are held;

(d) they must take the necessary steps to ensure that any client financial instruments deposited with a third party, in accordance with Article 17, are identifiable separately from the financial instruments belonging to the investment firm and from financial instruments belonging to that third party, by means of differently titled accounts on the books of the third party or other equivalent measures that achieve the same level of protection;

(e) they must take the necessary steps to ensure that client funds deposited, in accordance with Article 18, in a central bank, a credit institution or a bank authorised in a third country or a qualifying money market fund are held in an account or accounts identified separately from any accounts used to hold funds belonging to the investment firm;

(f) they must introduce adequate organisational arrangements to minimise the risk of the loss or diminution of client assets, or of rights in connection with those assets, as a result of misuse of the assets, fraud, poor administration, inadequate record-keeping or negligence.

2. If, for reasons of the applicable law, including in particular the law relating to property or insolvency, the arrangements made by investment firms in compliance with paragraph 1 to safeguard clients' rights are not sufficient to satisfy the requirements of Article 13(7) and (8) of Directive 2004/39/EC, Member States shall prescribe the measures that investment firms must take in order to comply with those obligations.

3. If the applicable law of the jurisdiction in which the client funds or financial instruments are held prevents investment firms from complying with points (d) or (e) of paragraph 1, Member States shall prescribe requirements which have an equivalent effect in terms of safeguarding clients' rights.

Article 17
(Article 13(7) of Directive 2004/39/EC)
Depositing client financial instruments

1. Member States shall permit investment firms to deposit financial instruments held by them on behalf of their clients into an account or accounts opened with a third party provided that the firms exercise all due skill, care and diligence in the selection, appointment and periodic review of the third party and of the arrangements for the holding and safekeeping of those financial instruments.

In particular, Member States shall require investment firms to take into account the expertise and market reputation of the third party as well as any legal requirements or market practices related to the holding of those financial instruments that could adversely affect clients' rights.

2. Member States shall ensure that, if the safekeeping of financial instruments for the account of another person is subject to specific regulation and supervision in a jurisdiction where an investment firm proposes to deposit client financial instruments with a third party, the investment firm does not deposit those financial instruments in that jurisdiction with a third party which is not subject to such regulation and supervision.

3. Member States shall ensure that investment firms do not deposit financial instruments held on behalf of clients with a third party in a third country that does not regulate the holding and safekeeping of financial instruments for the account of another person unless one of the following conditions is met:

(a) the nature of the financial instruments or of the investment services connected with those instruments requires them to be deposited with a third party in that third country;

(b) where the financial instruments are held on behalf of a professional client, that client requests the firm in writing to deposit them with a third party in that third country.

Article 18
(Article 13(8) of Directive 2004/39/EC)
Depositing client funds

1. Member States shall require investment firms, on receiving any client funds, promptly to place those funds into one or more accounts opened with any of the following:

(a) a central bank;

(b) a credit institution authorised in accordance with Directive 2000/12/EC;

(c) a bank authorised in a third country;

(d) a qualifying money market fund.

The first subparagraph shall not apply to a credit institution authorised under Directive 2006/48/EC of the European Parliament and of the Council of 14 June 2006 relating to the taking up and pursuit of the business of credit institutions (recast)[11] in relation to deposits within the meaning of that Directive held by that institution.

---

[11] OJ L 177, 30.6.2006, 1, reproduced supra under no. B. 41.

2. For the purposes of point (d) of paragraph 1, and of Article 16(1)(e), a 'qualifying money market fund' means a collective investment undertaking authorised under Directive 85/611/EEC, or which is subject to supervision and, if applicable, authorised by an authority under the national law of a Member State, and which satisfies the following conditions:

(a) its primary investment objective must be to maintain the net asset value of the undertaking either constant at par (net of earnings), or at the value of the investors' initial capital plus earnings;

(b) it must, with a view to achieving that primary investment objective, invest exclusively in high quality money market instruments with a maturity or residual maturity of no more than 397 days, or regular yield adjustments consistent with such a maturity, and with a weighted average maturity of 60 days. It may also achieve this objective by investing on an ancillary basis in deposits with credit institutions;

(c) it must provide liquidity through same day or next day settlement.

For the purposes of point (b), a money market instrument shall be considered to be of high quality if it has been awarded the highest available credit rating by each competent rating agency which has rated that instrument. An instrument that is not rated by any competent rating agency shall not be considered to be of high quality.

For the purposes of the second subparagraph, a rating agency shall be considered to be competent if it issues credit ratings in respect of money market funds regularly and on a professional basis and is an eligible ECAI within the meaning of Article 81(1) of Directive 2006/48/EC.

3. Member States shall require that, where investment firms do not deposit client funds with a central bank, they exercise all due skill, care and diligence in the selection, appointment and periodic review of the credit institution, bank or money market fund where the funds are placed and the arrangements for the holding of those funds.

Member States shall ensure, in particular, that investment firms take into account the expertise and market reputation of such institutions or money market funds with a view to ensuring the protection of clients' rights, as well as any legal or regulatory requirements or market practices related to the holding of client funds that could adversely affect clients' rights.

Member States shall ensure that clients have the right to oppose the placement of their funds in a qualifying money market fund.

Article 19
(Article 13(7) of Directive 2004/39/EC)
Use of client financial instruments

1. Member States shall not allow investment firms to enter into arrangements for securities financing transactions in respect of financial instruments held by them on behalf of a client, or otherwise use such financial instruments for their own account or the account of another client of the firm, unless the following conditions are met:

(a) the client must have given his prior express consent to the use of the instruments on specified terms, as evidenced, in the case of a retail client, by his signature or equivalent alternative mechanism;

(b) the use of that client's financial instruments must be restricted to the specified terms to which the client consents.

2. Member States may not allow investment firms to enter into arrangements for securities financing transactions in respect of financial instruments which are held on behalf of a client in an omnibus account maintained by a third party, or otherwise use financial instruments held in such an account for their own account or for the account of another client unless, in addition to the conditions set out in paragraph 1, at least one of the following conditions is met:

(a) each client whose financial instruments are held together in an omnibus account must have given prior express consent in accordance with point (a) of paragraph 1;

(b) the investment firm must have in place systems and controls which ensure that only financial instruments belonging to clients who have given prior express consent in accordance with point (a) of paragraph 1 are so used.

The records of the investment firm shall include details of the client on whose instructions the use of the financial instruments has been effected, as well as the number of financial instruments used belonging to each client who has given his consent, so as to enable the correct allocation of any loss.

Article 20

(Article 13(7) and (8) of Directive 2004/39/EC)

Reports by external auditors

Member States shall require investment firms to ensure that their external auditors report at least annually to the competent authority of the home Member State of the firm on the adequacy of the firm's arrangements under Articles 13(7) and (8) of Directive 2004/39/EC and this Section.

SECTION 4

CONFLICTS OF INTEREST

Article 21

(Articles 13(3) and 18 of Directive 2004/39/EC)

Conflicts of interest potentially detrimental to a client

Member States shall ensure that, for the purposes of identifying the types of conflict of interest that arise in the course of providing investment and ancillary services or a combination thereof and whose existence may damage the interests of a client, investment firms take into account, by way of minimum criteria, the question of whether the investment firm or a relevant person, or a person directly or indirectly linked by control to the firm, is in any of the following situations, whether as a result of providing investment or ancillary services or investment activities or otherwise:

(a) the firm or that person is likely to make a financial gain, or avoid a financial loss, at the expense of the client;

(b) the firm or that person has an interest in the outcome of a service provided to the client or of a transaction carried out on behalf of the client, which is distinct from the client's interest in that outcome;

(c) the firm or that person has a financial or other incentive to favour the interest of another client or group of clients over the interests of the client;

(d) the firm or that person carries on the same business as the client;

(e) the firm or that person receives or will receive from a person other than the client an inducement in relation to a service provided to the client, in the form of monies, goods or services, other than the standard commission or fee for that service.

Article 22

(Articles 13(3) and 18(1) of Directive 2004/39/EC)

Conflicts of interest policy

1. Member States shall require investment firms to establish, implement and maintain an effective conflicts of interest policy set out in writing and appropriate to the size and organisation of the firm and the nature, scale and complexity of its business.

Where the firm is a member of a group, the policy must also take into account any circumstances, of which the firm is or should be aware, which may give rise to a conflict of interest arising as a result of the structure and business activities of other members of the group.

2. The conflicts of interest policy established in accordance with paragraph 1 shall include the following content:

(a) it must identify, with reference to the specific investment services and activities and ancillary services carried out by or on behalf of the investment firm, the circumstances which constitute or may give rise to a conflict of interest entailing a material risk of damage to the interests of one or more clients;

(b) it must specify procedures to be followed and measures to be adopted in order to manage such conflicts.

3. Member States shall ensure that the procedures and measures provided for in paragraph 2(b) are designed to ensure that relevant persons engaged in different business activities involving a conflict of interest of the kind specified in paragraph 2(a) carry on those activities at a level of independence appropriate to the size and activities of the investment firm and of the group to which it belongs, and to the materiality of the risk of damage to the interests of clients.

For the purposes of paragraph 2(b), the procedures to be followed and measures to be adopted shall include such of the following as are necessary and appropriate for the firm to ensure the requisite degree of independence:

(a) effective procedures to prevent or control the exchange of information between relevant persons engaged in activities involving a risk of a conflict of interest where the exchange of that information may harm the interests of one or more clients;

(b) the separate supervision of relevant persons whose principal functions involve carrying out activities on behalf of, or providing services to, clients whose interests may conflict, or who otherwise represent different interests that may conflict, including those of the firm;

(c) the removal of any direct link between the remuneration of relevant persons principally engaged in one activity and the remuneration of, or revenues generated by, different relevant persons principally engaged in another activity, where a conflict of interest may arise in relation to those activities;

(d) measures to prevent or limit any person from exercising inappropriate influence over the way in which a relevant person carries out investment or ancillary services or activities;

(e) measures to prevent or control the simultaneous or sequential involvement of a relevant person in separate investment or ancillary services or activities where such involvement may impair the proper management of conflicts of interest.

If the adoption or the practice of one or more of those measures and procedures does not ensure the requisite degree of independence, Member States shall require investment firms to adopt such alternative or additional measures and procedures as are necessary and appropriate for those purposes.

4. Member States shall ensure that disclosure to clients, pursuant to Article 18(2) of Directive 2004/39/EC, is made in a durable medium and includes sufficient detail, taking into account the nature of the client, to enable that client to take an informed decision with respect to the investment or ancillary service in the context of which the conflict of interest arises.

Article 23
(Article 13(6) of Directive 2004/39/EC)
Record of services or activities giving rise to detrimental conflict of interest

Member States shall require investment firms to keep and regularly to update a record of the kinds of investment or ancillary service or investment activity carried out by or on behalf of the firm in which a conflict of interest entailing a material risk of damage to the interests of one or more clients has arisen or, in the case of an ongoing service or activity, may arise.

Article 24
(Article 19(2) of Directive 2004/39/EC)
Investment research

1. For the purposes of Article 25, 'investment research' means research or other information recommending or suggesting an investment strategy, explicitly or implicitly, concerning one or several financial instruments or the issuers of financial instruments, including any opinion as to the present or future value or price of such instruments, intended for distribution channels or for the public, and in relation to which the following conditions are met:

(a) it is labelled or described as investment research or in similar terms, or is otherwise presented as an objective or independent explanation of the matters contained in the recommendation;

(b) if the recommendation in question were made by an investment firm to a client, it would not constitute the provision of investment advice for the purposes of Directive 2004/39/EC.

2. A recommendation of the type covered by Article 1(3) of Directive 2003/125/EC but relating to financial instruments as defined in Directive 2004/39/EC that does not meet the conditions set out in paragraph 1 shall be treated as a marketing communication for the purposes of Directive 2004/39/EC and Member States shall require any investment firm that produces or disseminates the recommendation to ensure that it is clearly identified as such.

Additionally, Member States shall require those firms to ensure that any such recommendation contains a clear and prominent statement that (or, in the case of an oral recommendation, to the effect that) it has not been prepared in accordance with legal requirements designed to promote the independence of investment research, and that it is not subject to any prohibition on dealing ahead of the dissemination of investment research.

Article 25
(Article 13(3) of Directive 2004/39/EC)
Additional organisational requirements where a firm produces and disseminates investment research

1. Member States shall require investment firms which produce, or arrange for the production of, investment research that is intended or likely to be subsequently disseminated to clients of the firm or to the public, under their own responsibility or that of a member of their group, to ensure the implementation of all the measures set out in Article 22(3) in relation to the financial analysts involved in the production of the investment research and other relevant persons whose responsibilities or business interests may conflict with the interests of the persons to whom the investment research is disseminated.

2. Member States shall require investment firms covered by paragraph 1 to have in place arrangements designed to ensure that the following conditions are satisfied:

(a) financial analysts and other relevant persons must not undertake personal transactions or trade, other than as market makers acting in good faith and in the ordinary course of market making or in the execution of an unsolicited client order, on behalf of any other person, including the investment firm, in financial instruments to which investment research relates, or in any related financial instruments, with knowledge of the likely timing or content of that investment research which is not publicly available or available to clients and cannot readily be inferred from information that is so available, until the recipients of the investment research have had a reasonable opportunity to act on it;

(b) in circumstances not covered by point (a), financial analysts and any other relevant persons involved in the production of investment research must not undertake personal transactions in financial instruments to which the investment research relates, or in any related financial instruments, contrary to current recommendations, except in exceptional circumstances and with the prior approval of a member of the firm's legal or compliance function;

(c) the investment firms themselves, financial analysts, and other relevant persons involved in the production of the investment research must not accept inducements from those with a material interest in the subject-matter of the investment research;

(d) the investment firms themselves, financial analysts, and other relevant persons involved in the production of the investment research must not promise issuers favourable research coverage;

(e) issuers, relevant persons other than financial analysts, and any other persons must not before the dissemination of investment research be permitted to review a draft of the investment research for the purpose of verifying the accuracy of factual statements made in that research, or for any other purpose other than verifying compliance with the firm's legal obligations, if the draft includes a recommendation or a target price.

For the purposes of this paragraph, 'related financial instrument' means a financial instrument the price of which is closely affected by price movements in another financial instrument which is the subject of investment research, and includes a derivative on that other financial instrument.

3. Member States shall exempt investment firms which disseminate investment research produced by another person to the public or to clients from complying with paragraph 1 if the following criteria are met:

(a) the person that produces the investment research is not a member of the group to which the investment firm belongs;

(b) the investment firm does not substantially alter the recommendations within the investment research;

(c) the investment firm does not present the investment research as having been produced by it;

(d) the investment firm verifies that the producer of the research is subject to requirements equivalent to the requirements under this Directive in relation to the production of that research, or has established a policy setting such requirements.

Chapter III
Operating Conditions for Investment Firms

Section 1
Inducements

Article 26
(Article 19(1) of Directive 2004/39/EC)
Inducements

Member States shall ensure that investment firms are not regarded as acting honestly, fairly and professionally in accordance with the best interests of a client if, in relation to the provision of an investment or ancillary service to the client, they pay or are paid any fee or commission, or provide or are provided with any non-monetary benefit, other than the following:

(a) a fee, commission or non-monetary benefit paid or provided to or by the client or a person on behalf of the client;

(b) a fee, commission or non-monetary benefit paid or provided to or by a third party or a person acting on behalf of a third party, where the following conditions are satisfied:

(i) the existence, nature and amount of the fee, commission or benefit, or, where the amount cannot be ascertained, the method of calculating that amount, must be clearly disclosed to the client, in a manner that is comprehensive, accurate and understandable, prior to the provision of the relevant investment or ancillary service;

(ii) the payment of the fee or commission, or the provision of the non-monetary benefit must be designed to enhance the quality of the relevant service to the client and not impair compliance with the firm's duty to act in the best interests of the client;

(c) proper fees which enable or are necessary for the provision of investment services, such as custody costs, settlement and exchange fees, regulatory levies or legal fees, and which, by their nature, cannot give rise to conflicts with the firm's duties to act honestly, fairly and professionally in accordance with the best interests of its clients.

Member States shall permit an investment firm, for the purposes of point (b)(i), to disclose the essential terms of the arrangements relating to the fee, commission or non-monetary benefit in summary form, provided that it undertakes to disclose further details at the request of the client and provided that it honours that undertaking.

Section 2
Information to Clients and Potential Clients

Article 27
(Article 19(2) of Directive 2004/39/EC)
Conditions with which information must comply in order to be fair, clear and not misleading

1. Member States shall require investment firms to ensure that all information they address to, or disseminate in such a way that it is likely to be received by, retail clients or potential retail

clients, including marketing communications, satisfies the conditions laid down in paragraphs 2 to 8.

2. The information referred to in paragraph 1 shall include the name of the investment firm.

It shall be accurate and in particular shall not emphasise any potential benefits of an investment service or financial instrument without also giving a fair and prominent indication of any relevant risks.

It shall be sufficient for, and presented in a way that is likely to be understood by, the average member of the group to whom it is directed, or by whom it is likely to be received.

It shall not disguise, diminish or obscure important items, statements or warnings.

3. Where the information compares investment or ancillary services, financial instruments, or persons providing investment or ancillary services, the following conditions shall be satisfied:

(a) the comparison must be meaningful and presented in a fair and balanced way;

(b) the sources of the information used for the comparison must be specified;

(c) the key facts and assumptions used to make the comparison must be included.

4. Where the information contains an indication of past performance of a financial instrument, a financial index or an investment service, the following conditions shall be satisfied:

(a) that indication must not be the most prominent feature of the communication;

(b) the information must include appropriate performance information which covers the immediately preceding 5 years, or the whole period for which the financial instrument has been offered, the financial index has been established, or the investment service has been provided if less than five years, or such longer period as the firm may decide, and in every case that performance information must be based on complete 12-month periods;

(c) the reference period and the source of information must be clearly stated;

(d) the information must contain a prominent warning that the figures refer to the past and that past performance is not a reliable indicator of future results;

(e) where the indication relies on figures denominated in a currency other than that of the Member State in which the retail client or potential retail client is resident, the currency must be clearly stated, together with a warning that the return may increase or decrease as a result of currency fluctuations;

(f) where the indication is based on gross performance, the effect of commissions, fees or other charges must be disclosed.

5. Where the information includes or refers to simulated past performance, it must relate to a financial instrument or a financial index, and the following conditions shall be satisfied:

(a) the simulated past performance must be based on the actual past performance of one or more financial instruments or financial indices which are the same as, or underlie, the financial instrument concerned;

(b) in respect of the actual past performance referred to in point (a), the conditions set out in points (a) to (c), (e) and (f) of paragraph 4 must be complied with;

(c) the information must contain a prominent warning that the figures refer to simulated past performance and that past performance is not a reliable indicator of future performance.

6. Where the information contains information on future performance, the following conditions shall be satisfied:

(a) the information must not be based on or refer to simulated past performance;

(b) it must be based on reasonable assumptions supported by objective data;

(c) where the information is based on gross performance, the effect of commissions, fees or other charges must be disclosed;

(d) it must contain a prominent warning that such forecasts are not a reliable indicator of future performance.

7. Where the information refers to a particular tax treatment, it shall prominently state that the

tax treatment depends on the individual circumstances of each client and may be subject to change in the future.

8. The information shall not use the name of any competent authority in such a way that would indicate or suggest endorsement or approval by that authority of the products or services of the investment firm.

Article 28
(Article 19(3) of Directive 2004/39/EC)
Information concerning client categorisation

1. Member States shall ensure that investment firms notify new clients, and existing clients that the investment firm has newly categorised as required by Directive 2004/39/EC, of their categorisation as a retail client, a professional client or an eligible counterparty in accordance with that Directive.

2. Member States shall ensure that investment firms inform clients in a durable medium about any right that client has to request a different categorisation and about any limitations to the level of client protection that it would entail.

3. Member States shall permit investment firms, either on their own initiative or at the request of the client concerned:

(a) to treat as a professional or retail client a client that might otherwise be classified as an eligible counterparty pursuant to Article 24(2) of Directive 2004/39/EC;

(b) to treat as a retail client a client that is considered as a professional client pursuant to Section I of Annex II to Directive 2004/39/EC.

Article 29
(Article 19(3) of Directive 2004/39/EC)
General requirements for information to clients

1. Member States shall require investment firms, in good time before a retail client or potential retail client is bound by any agreement for the provision of investment services or ancillary services or before the provision of those services, whichever is the earlier, to provide that client or potential client with the following information:

(a) the terms of any such agreement;

(b) the information required by Article 30 relating to that agreement or to those investment or ancillary services.

2. Member States shall require investment firms, in good time before the provision of investment services or ancillary services to retail clients or potential retail clients, to provide the information required under Articles 30 to 33.

3. Member States shall require investment firms to provide professional clients with the information referred to in Article 32(5) and (6) in good time before the provision of the service concerned.

4. The information referred to in paragraphs 1 to 3 shall be provided in a durable medium or by means of a website (where that does not constitute a durable medium) provided that the conditions specified in Article 3(2) are satisfied.

5. By way of exception to paragraphs 1 and 2, Member States shall permit investment firms, in the following circumstances, to provide the information required under paragraph 1 to a retail client immediately after that client is bound by any agreement for the provision of investment services or ancillary services, and the information required under paragraph 2 immediately after starting to provide the service:

(a) the firm was unable to comply with the time limits specified in paragraphs 1 and 2 because, at the request of the client, the agreement was concluded using a means of distance communication which prevents the firm from providing the information in accordance with paragraph 1 or 2;

(b) in any case where Article 3(3) of Directive 2002/65/EC of the European Parliament and of the Council of 23 September 2002 concerning the distance marketing of consumer financial services and amending Council Directive 90/619/EEC and Directives 97/7/EC and

98/27/EC[12] does not otherwise apply, the investment firm complies with the requirements of that Article in relation to the retail client or potential retail client, as if that client or potential client were a 'consumer' and the investment firm were a 'supplier' within the meaning of that Directive.

6. Member State shall ensure that investment firms notify a client in good time about any material change to the information provided under Articles 30 to 33 which is relevant to a service that the firm is providing to that client. That notification shall be given in a durable medium if the information to which it relates is given in a durable medium.

7. Member States shall require investment firms to ensure that information contained in a marketing communication is consistent with any information the firm provides to clients in the course of carrying on investment and ancillary services.

8. Member States shall ensure that, where a marketing communication contains an offer or invitation of the following nature and specifies the manner of response or includes a form by which any response may be made, it includes such of the information referred to in Articles 30 to 33 as is relevant to that offer or invitation:

(a) an offer to enter into an agreement in relation to a financial instrument or investment service or ancillary service with any person who responds to the communication;

(b) an invitation to any person who responds to the communication to make an offer to enter into an agreement in relation to a financial instrument or investment service or ancillary service.

However, the first subparagraph shall not apply if, in order to respond to an offer or invitation contained in the marketing communication, the potential retail client must refer to another document or documents, which, alone or in combination, contain that information.

---

[12] OJ L 271, 9.10.2002, 16, reproduced supra under no. C.P. 22.

Article 30
(first indent of Article 19(3) of Directive 2004/39/EC)
Information about the investment firm and its services for retail clients and potential retail clients

1. Member States shall require investment firms to provide retail clients or potential retail clients with the following general information, where relevant:

(a) the name and address of the investment firm, and the contact details necessary to enable clients to communicate effectively with the firm;

(b) the languages in which the client may communicate with the investment firm, and receive documents and other information from the firm;

(c) the methods of communication to be used between the investment firm and the client including, where relevant, those for the sending and reception of orders;

(d) a statement of the fact that the investment firm is authorised and the name and contact address of the competent authority that has authorised it;

(e) where the investment firm is acting through a tied agent, a statement of this fact specifying the Member State in which that agent is registered;

(f) the nature, frequency and timing of the reports on the performance of the service to be provided by the investment firm to the client in accordance with Article 19(8) of Directive 2004/39/EC;

(g) if the investment firm holds client financial instruments or client funds, a summary description of the steps which it takes to ensure their protection, including summary details of any relevant investor compensation or deposit guarantee scheme which applies to the firm by virtue of its activities in a Member State;

(h) a description, which may be provided in summary form, of the conflicts of interest policy maintained by the firm in accordance with Article 22;

(i) at any time that the client requests it, further details of that conflicts of interest policy in a durable medium or by means of a website (where that does not constitute a durable medium) provided that the conditions specified in Article 3(2) are satisfied.

2. Member States shall ensure that, when providing the service of portfolio management, investment firms establish an appropriate method of evaluation and comparison such as a meaningful benchmark, based on the investment objectives of the client and the types of financial instruments included in the client portfolio, so as to enable the client for whom the service is provided to assess the firm's performance.

3. Member States shall require that where investment firms propose to provide portfolio management services to a retail client or potential retail client, they provide the client, in addition to the information required under paragraph 1, with such of the following information as is applicable:

(a) information on the method and frequency of valuation of the financial instruments in the client portfolio;

(b) details of any delegation of the discretionary management of all or part of the financial instruments or funds in the client portfolio;

(c) a specification of any benchmark against which the performance of the client portfolio will be compared;

(d) the types of financial instrument that may be included in the client portfolio and types of transaction that may be carried out in such instruments, including any limits;

(e) the management objectives, the level of risk to be reflected in the manager's exercise of discretion, and any specific constraints on that discretion.

Article 31

(Second indent of Article 19(3) of Directive 2004/39/EC)

Information about financial instruments

1. Member States shall require investment firms to provide clients or potential clients with a general description of the nature and risks of financial instruments, taking into account, in particular, the client's categorisation as either a retail client or a professional client. That description must explain the nature of the specific type of instrument concerned, as well as the risks particular to that specific type of instrument in sufficient detail to enable the client to take investment decisions on an informed basis.

2. The description of risks shall include, where relevant to the specific type of instrument concerned and the status and level of knowledge of the client, the following elements:

(a) the risks associated with that type of financial instrument including an explanation of leverage and its effects and the risk of losing the entire investment;

(b) the volatility of the price of such instruments and any limitations on the available market for such instruments;

(c) the fact that an investor might assume, as a result of transactions in such instruments, financial commitments and other additional obligations, including contingent liabilities, additional to the cost of acquiring the instruments;

(d) any margin requirements or similar obligations, applicable to instruments of that type.

Member States may specify the precise terms, or the contents, of the description of risks required under this paragraph.

3. If an investment firm provides a retail client or potential retail client with information about a financial instrument that is the subject of a current offer to the public and a prospectus has been published in connection with that offer in accordance with Directive 2003/71/EC, that firm shall inform the client or potential client where that prospectus is made available to the public.

4. Where the risks associated with a financial instrument composed of two or more different financial instruments or services are likely to be greater than the risks associated with any of the components, the investment firm shall provide an adequate description of the components of that instrument and the way in which its interaction increases the risks.

5. In the case of financial instruments that incorporate a guarantee by a third party, the information about the guarantee shall include sufficient detail about the guarantor and the guarantee to enable the retail client or potential retail client to make a fair assessment of the guarantee.

Article 32
(First indent of Article 19(3) of Directive 2004/39/EC)
Information requirements concerning safeguarding of client financial instruments or client funds

1. Member States shall ensure that, where investment firms hold financial instruments or funds belonging to retail clients, they provide those retail clients or potential retail clients with such of the information specified in paragraphs 2 to 7 as is relevant.

2. The investment firm shall inform the retail client or potential retail client where the financial instruments or funds of that client may be held by a third party on behalf of the investment firm and of the responsibility of the investment firm under the applicable national law for any acts or omissions of the third party and the consequences for the client of the insolvency of the third party.

3. Where financial instruments of the retail client or potential retail client may, if permitted by national law, be held in an omnibus account by a third party, the investment firm shall inform the client of this fact and shall provide a prominent warning of the resulting risks.

4. The investment firm shall inform the retail client or potential retail client where it is not possible under national law for client financial instruments held with a third party to be separately identifiable from the proprietary financial instruments of that third party or of the investment firm and shall provide a prominent warning of the resulting risks.

5. The investment firm shall inform the client or potential client where accounts that contain financial instruments or funds belonging to that client or potential client are or will be subject to the law of a jurisdiction other than that of a Member State and shall indicate that the rights of the client or potential client relating to those financial instruments or funds may differ accordingly.

6. An investment firm shall inform the client about the existence and the terms of any security interest or lien which the firm has or may have over the client's financial instruments or funds, or any right of set-off it holds in relation to those instruments or funds. Where applicable, it shall also inform the client of the fact that a depository may have a security interest or lien over, or right of set-off in relation to those instruments or funds.

7. An investment firm, before entering into securities financing transactions in relation to financial instruments held by it on behalf of a retail client, or before otherwise using such financial instruments for its own account or the account of another client, shall in good time before the use of those instruments provide the retail client, in a durable medium, with clear, full and accurate information on the obligations and responsibilities of the investment firm with respect to the use of those financial instruments, including the terms for their restitution, and on the risks involved.

Article 33
(Fourth indent of Article 19(3) of Directive 2004/39/EC)
Information about costs and associated charges

Member States shall require investment firms to provide their retail clients and potential retail clients with information on costs and associated charges that includes such of the following elements as are relevant:

(a) the total price to be paid by the client in connection with the financial instrument or the investment service or ancillary service, including all related fees, commissions, charges and expenses, and all taxes payable via the investment firm or, if an exact price cannot be indicated, the basis for the calculation of the total price so that the client can verify it;

(b) where any part of the total price referred to in point (a) is to be paid in or represents an amount of foreign currency, an indication of the currency involved and the applicable currency conversion rates and costs;

(c) notice of the possibility that other costs, including taxes, related to transactions in connection with the financial instrument or the investment service may arise for the client that are not paid via the investment firm or imposed by it;

(d) the arrangements for payment or other performance.

For the purposes of point (a), the commissions charged by the firm shall be itemised separately in every case.

Article 34

(Second and Fourth indent of Article 19(3) of Directive 2004/39/EC)

Information drawn up in accordance with Directive 85/611/EEC

1. Member States shall ensure that in respect of units in a collective investment undertaking covered by Directive 85/611/EEC, a simplified prospectus complying with Article 28 of that Directive is regarded as appropriate information for the purposes of the second indent of Article 19(3) of Directive 2004/39/EC.

2. Member States shall ensure that in respect of units in a collective investment undertaking covered by Directive 85/611/EEC, a simplified prospectus complying with Article 28 of that Directive is regarded as appropriate information for the purposes of the fourth indent of Article 19(3) of Directive 2004/39/EC with respect to the costs and associated charges related to the UCITS itself, including the exit and entry commissions.

Section 3
Assessment of Suitability and Appropriateness

Article 35

(Article 19(4) of Directive 2004/39/EC)

Assessment of suitability

1. Member States shall ensure that investment firms obtain from clients or potential clients such information as is necessary for the firm to understand the essential facts about the client and to have a reasonable basis for believing, giving due consideration to the nature and extent of the service provided, that the specific transaction to be recommended, or entered into in the course of providing a portfolio management service, satisfies the following criteria:

(a) it meets the investment objectives of the client in question;

(b) it is such that the client is able financially to bear any related investment risks consistent with his investment objectives;

(c) it is such that the client has the necessary experience and knowledge in order to understand the risks involved in the transaction or in the management of his portfolio.

2. Where an investment firm provides an investment service to a professional client it shall be entitled to assume that, in relation to the products, transactions and services for which it is so classified, the client has the necessary level of experience and knowledge for the purposes of paragraph 1(c).

Where that investment service consists in the provision of investment advice to a professional client covered by Section 1 of Annex II to Directive 2004/39/EC, the investment firm shall be entitled to assume for the purposes of paragraph 1(b) that the client is able financially to bear any related investment risks consistent with the investment objectives of that client.

3. The information regarding the financial situation of the client or potential client shall include, where relevant, information on the source and extent of his regular income, his assets, including liquid assets, investments and real property, and his regular financial commitments.

4. The information regarding the investment objectives of the client or potential client shall include, where relevant, information on the length of time for which the client wishes to hold the investment, his preferences regarding risk taking, his risk profile, and the purposes of the investment.

5. Where, when providing the investment service of investment advice or portfolio management,

an investment firm does not obtain the information required under Article 19(4) of Directive 2004/39/EC, the firm shall not recommend investment services or financial instruments to the client or potential client.

Article 36
(Article 19(5) of Directive 2004/39/EC)
Assessment of appropriateness

Member States shall require investment firms, when assessing whether an investment service as referred to in Article 19(5) of Directive 2004/39/EC is appropriate for a client, to determine whether that client has the necessary experience and knowledge in order to understand the risks involved in relation to the product or investment service offered or demanded.

For those purposes, an investment firm shall be entitled to assume that a professional client has the necessary experience and knowledge in order to understand the risks involved in relation to those particular investment services or transactions, or types of transaction or product, for which the client is classified as a professional client.

Article 37
(Article 19(4) and (5) of Directive 2004/39/EC)
Provisions common to the assessment of suitability or appropriateness

1. Member States shall ensure that the information regarding a client's or potential client's knowledge and experience in the investment field includes the following, to the extent appropriate to the nature of the client, the nature and extent of the service to be provided and the type of product or transaction envisaged, including their complexity and the risks involved:

(a) the types of service, transaction and financial instrument with which the client is familiar;

(b) the nature, volume, and frequency of the client's transactions in financial instruments and the period over which they have been carried out;

(c) the level of education, and profession or relevant former profession of the client or potential client.

2. An investment firm shall not encourage a client or potential client not to provide information required for the purposes of Article 19(4) and (5) of Directive 2004/39/EC.

3. An investment firm shall be entitled to rely on the information provided by its clients or potential clients unless it is aware or ought to be aware that the information is manifestly out of date, inaccurate or incomplete.

Article 38
(First indent of Article 19(6) of Directive 2004/39/EC)
Provision of services in non-complex instruments

A financial instrument which is not specified in the first indent of Article 19(6) of Directive 2004/39/EC shall be considered as non-complex if it satisfies the following criteria:

(a) it does not fall within Article 4(1)(18)(c) of, or points (4) to (10) of Section C of Annex I to, Directive 2004/39/EC;

(b) there are frequent opportunities to dispose of, redeem, or otherwise realise that instrument at prices that are publicly available to market participants and that are either market prices or prices made available, or validated, by valuation systems independent of the issuer;

(c) it does not involve any actual or potential liability for the client that exceeds the cost of acquiring the instrument;

(d) adequately comprehensive information on its characteristics is publicly available and is likely to be readily understood so as to enable the average retail client to make an informed judgment as to whether to enter into a transaction in that instrument.

Article 39
(Article 19(1) and (7) of Directive 2004/39/EC)
Retail client agreement

Member States shall require an investment firm that provides an investment service other than investment advice to a new retail client for the first time after the date of application of this Directive to enter into a written basic agreement, in paper or another durable medium, with the client setting out the essential rights and obligations of the firm and the client.

The rights and duties of the parties to the agreement may be incorporated by reference to other documents or legal texts.

SECTION 4

REPORTING TO CLIENTS

Article 40

(Article 19(8) of Directive 2004/39/EC)

Reporting obligations in respect of execution of orders other than for portfolio management

1. Member States shall ensure that where investment firms have carried out an order, other than for portfolio management, on behalf of a client, they take the following action in respect of that order:

(a) the investment firm must promptly provide the client, in a durable medium, with the essential information concerning the execution of that order;

(b) in the case of a retail client, the investment firm must send the client a notice in a durable medium confirming execution of the order as soon as possible and no later than the first business day following execution or, if the confirmation is received by the investment firm from a third party, no later than the first business day following receipt of the confirmation from the third party.

Point (b) shall not apply where the confirmation would contain the same information as a confirmation that is to be promptly dispatched to the retail client by another person.

Points (a) and (b) shall not apply where orders executed on behalf of clients relate to bonds funding mortgage loan agreements with the said clients, in which case the report on the transaction shall be made at the same time as the terms of the mortgage loan are communicated, but no later than one month after the execution of the order.

2. In addition to the requirements under paragraph 1, Member States shall require investment firms to supply the client, on request, with information about the status of his order.

3. Member States shall ensure that, in the case of orders for a retail clients relating to units or shares in a collective investment undertaking which are executed periodically, investment firms either take the action specified in point (b) of paragraph 1 or provide the retail client, at least once every six months, with the information listed in paragraph 4 in respect of those transactions.

4. The notice referred to in point (b) of paragraph 1 shall include such of the following information as is applicable and, where relevant, in accordance with Table 1 of Annex I to Regulation (EC) No 1287/2006:

(a) the reporting firm identification;

(b) the name or other designation of the client;

(c) the trading day;

(d) the trading time;

(e) the type of the order;

(f) the venue identification;

(g) the instrument identification;

(h) the buy/sell indicator;

(i) the nature of the order if other than buy/sell;

(j) the quantity;

(k) the unit price;

(l) the total consideration;

(m) a total sum of the commissions and expenses charged and, where the retail client so requests, an itemised breakdown;

(n) the client's responsibilities in relation to the settlement of the transaction, including the time limit for payment or delivery as well as the appropriate account details where these details and responsibilities have not previously been notified to the client;

(o) if the client's counterparty was the investment firm itself or any person in the investment firm's group or another client of the investment firm, the fact that this was the case unless the order was executed through a trading system that facilitates anonymous trading.

For the purposes of point (k), where the order is executed in tranches, the investment firm may supply the client with information about the price of each tranche or the average price. Where the average price is provided, the investment firm shall supply the retail client with information about the price of each tranche upon request.

5. The investment firm may provide the client with the information referred to in paragraph 4 using standard codes if it also provides an explanation of the codes used.

Article 41
(Article 19(8) of Directive 2004/39/EC)
Reporting obligations in respect of portfolio management

1. Member States shall require investments firms which provide the service of portfolio management to clients to provide each such client with a periodic statement in a durable medium of the portfolio management activities carried out on behalf of that client unless such a statement is provided by another person.

2. In the case of retail clients, the periodic statement required under paragraph 1 shall include, where relevant, the following information:

(a) the name of the investment firm;

(b) the name or other designation of the retail client's account;

(c) a statement of the contents and the valuation of the portfolio, including details of each financial instrument held, its market value, or fair value if market value is unavailable and the cash balance at the beginning and at the end of the reporting period, and the performance of the portfolio during the reporting period;

(d) the total amount of fees and charges incurred during the reporting period, itemising at least total management fees and total costs associated with execution, and including, where relevant, a statement that a more detailed breakdown will be provided on request;

(e) a comparison of performance during the period covered by the statement with the investment performance benchmark (if any) agreed between the investment firm and the client;

(f) the total amount of dividends, interest and other payments received during the reporting period in relation to the client's portfolio;

(g) information about other corporate actions giving rights in relation to financial instruments held in the portfolio;

(h) for each transaction executed during the period, the information referred to in Article 40(4)(c) to (l) where relevant, unless the client elects to receive information about executed transactions on a transaction-by-transaction basis, in which case paragraph 4 of this Article shall apply.

3. In the case of retail clients, the periodic statement referred to in paragraph 1 shall be provided once every six months, except in the following cases:

(a) where the client so requests, the periodic statement must be provided every three months;

(b) in cases where paragraph 4 applies, the periodic statement must be provided at least once every 12 months;

(c) where the agreement between an investment firm and a retail client for a portfolio management service authorises a leveraged portfolio, the periodic statement must be provided at least once a month.

Investment firms shall inform retail clients that they have the right to make requests for the purposes of point (a).

However, the exception provided for in point (b) shall not apply in the case of transactions in financial instruments covered by Article 4(1)(18)(c) of, or any of points 4 to 10 of Section C in Annex I to, Directive 2004/39/EC.

4. Member States shall require investment firms, in cases where the client elects to receive information about executed transactions on a transaction-by-transaction basis, to provide promptly to the client, on the execution of a transaction by the portfolio manager, the essential information concerning that transaction in a durable medium.

Where the client concerned is a retail client, the investment firm must send him a notice confirming the transaction and containing the information referred to in Article 40(4) no later than the first business day following that execution or, if the confirmation is received by the investment firm from a third party, no later than the first business day following receipt of the confirmation from the third party.

The second subparagraph shall not apply where the confirmation would contain the same information as a confirmation that is to be promptly dispatched to the retail client by another person.

Article 42
(Article 19(8) of Directive 2004/39/EC)
Additional reporting obligations for portfolio management or contingent liability transactions

Member States shall ensure that where investment firms provide portfolio management transactions for retail clients or operate retail client accounts that include an uncovered open position in a contingent liability transaction, they also report to the retail client any losses exceeding any predetermined threshold, agreed between the firm and the client, no later than the end of the business day in which the threshold is exceeded or, in a case where the threshold is exceeded on a non-business day, the close of the next business day.

Article 43
(Article 19(8) of Directive 2004/39/EC)
Statements of client financial instruments or client funds

1. Member States shall require investment firms that hold client financial instruments or client funds to send at least once a year, to each client for whom they hold financial instruments or funds, a statement in a durable medium of those financial instruments or funds unless such a statement has been provided in any other periodic statement.

The first subparagraph shall not apply to a credit institution authorised under Directive 2000/12/EC in respect of deposits within the meaning of that Directive held by that institution.

2. The statement of client assets referred to in paragraph 1 shall include the following information:

(a) details of all the financial instruments or funds held by the investment firm for the client at the end of the period covered by the statement;

(b) the extent to which any client financial instruments or client funds have been the subject of securities financing transactions;

(c) the extent of any benefit that has accrued to the client by virtue of participation in any securities financing transactions, and the basis on which that benefit has accrued.

In cases where the portfolio of a client includes the proceeds of one or more unsettled transactions, the information referred to in point (a) may be based either on the trade date or the settlement date, provided that the same basis is applied consistently to all such information in the statement.

3. Member States shall permit investment firms which hold financial instruments or funds and which carry out the service of portfolio management for a client to include the statement of client assets referred to in paragraph 1 in the periodic statement it provides to that client pursuant to Article 41(1).

SECTION 5
BEST EXECUTION

Article 44
(Articles 21(1) and 19(1) of Directive 2004/39/EC)
Best execution criteria

1. Member States shall ensure that, when executing client orders, investment firms take into

account the following criteria for determining the relative importance of the factors referred to in Article 21(1) of Directive 2004/39/EC:

(a) the characteristics of the client including the categorisation of the client as retail or professional;

(b) the characteristics of the client order;

(c) the characteristics of financial instruments that are the subject of that order;

(d) the characteristics of the execution venues to which that order can be directed.

For the purposes of this Article and Article 46, 'execution venue' means a regulated market, an MTF, a systematic internaliser, or a market maker or other liquidity provider or an entity that performs a similar function in a third country to the functions performed by any of the foregoing.

2. An investment firm satisfies its obligation under Article 21(1) of Directive 2004/39/EC to take all reasonable steps to obtain the best possible result for a client to the extent that it executes an order or a specific aspect of an order following specific instructions from the client relating to the order or the specific aspect of the order.

3. Where an investment firm executes an order on behalf of a retail client, the best possible result shall be determined in terms of the total consideration, representing the price of the financial instrument and the costs related to execution, which shall include all expenses incurred by the client which are directly related to the execution of the order, including execution venue fees, clearing and settlement fees and any other fees paid to third parties involved in the execution of the order.

For the purposes of delivering best execution where there is more than one competing venue to execute an order for a financial instrument, in order to assess and compare the results for the client that would be achieved by executing the order on each of the execution venues listed in the firm's order execution policy that is capable of executing that order, the firm's own commissions and costs for executing the order on each of the eligible execution venues shall be taken into account in that assessment.

4. Member States shall require that investment firms do not structure or charge their commissions in such a way as to discriminate unfairly between execution venues.

5. Before 1 November 2008 the Commission shall present a report to the European Parliament and to the Council on the availability, comparability and consolidation of information concerning the quality of execution of various execution venues.

Article 45
(Article 19(1) of Directive 2004/39/EC)
Duty of investment firms carrying out portfolio management and reception and transmission of orders to act in the best interests of the client

1. Member States shall require investment firms, when providing the service of portfolio management, to comply with the obligation under Article 19(1) of Directive 2004/39/EC to act in accordance with the best interests of their clients when placing orders with other entities for execution that result from decisions by the investment firm to deal in financial instruments on behalf of its client.

2. Member States shall require investment firms, when providing the service of reception and transmission of orders, to comply with the obligation under Article 19(1) of Directive 2004/39/EC to act in accordance with the best interests of their clients when transmitting client orders to other entities for execution.

3. Member States shall ensure that, in order to comply with paragraphs 1 or 2, investment firms take the actions mentioned in paragraphs 4 to 6.

4. Investment firms shall take all reasonable steps to obtain the best possible result for their clients taking into account the factors referred to

in Article 21(1) of Directive 2004/39/EC. The relative importance of these factors shall be determined by reference to the criteria set out in Article 44(1)and, for retail clients, to the requirement under Article 44(3).

An investment firm satisfies its obligations under paragraph 1 or 2, and is not required to take the steps mentioned in this paragraph, to the extent that it follows specific instructions from its client when placing an order with, or transmitting an order to, another entity for execution.

5. Investment firms shall establish and implement a policy to enable them to comply with the obligation in paragraph 4. The policy shall identify, in respect of each class of instruments, the entities with which the orders are placed or to which the investment firm transmits orders for execution. The entities identified must have execution arrangements that enable the investment firm to comply with its obligations under this Article when it places or transmits orders to that entity for execution.

Investment firms shall provide appropriate information to their clients on the policy established in accordance with this paragraph.

6. Investment firms shall monitor on a regular basis the effectiveness of the policy established in accordance with paragraph 5 and, in particular, the execution quality of the entities identified in that policy and, where appropriate, correct any deficiencies.

In addition, investment firms shall review the policy annually. Such a review shall also be carried out whenever a material change occurs that affects the firm's ability to continue to obtain the best possible result for their clients.

7. This Article shall not apply when the investment firm that provides the service of portfolio management and/or reception and transmission of orders also executes the orders received or the decisions to deal on behalf of its client's portfolio. In those cases Article 21 of Directive 2004/39/EC applies.

Article 46
(Article 21(3) and (4) of Directive 2004/39/EC)
Execution policy

1. Member States shall ensure that investment firms review annually the execution policy established pursuant to Article 21(2) of Directive 2004/39/EC, as well as their order execution arrangements.

Such a review shall also be carried out whenever a material change occurs that affects the firm's ability to continue to obtain the best possible result for the execution of its client orders on a consistent basis using the venues included in its execution policy.

2. Investment firms shall provide retail clients with the following details on their execution policy in good time prior to the provision of the service:

(a) an account of the relative importance the investment firm assigns, in accordance with the criteria specified in Article 44(1), to the factors referred to in Article 21(1) of Directive 2004/39/EC, or the process by which the firm determines the relative importance of those factors;

(b) a list of the execution venues on which the firm places significant reliance in meeting its obligation to take all reasonable steps to obtain on a consistent basis the best possible result for the execution of client orders;

(c) a clear and prominent warning that any specific instructions from a client may prevent the firm from taking the steps that it has designed and implemented in its execution policy to obtain the best possible result for the execution of those orders in respect of the elements covered by those instructions.

That information shall be provided in a durable medium, or by means of a website (where that does not constitute a durable medium) provided that the conditions specified in Article 3(2) are satisfied.

Section 6
Client Order Handling

Article 47
(Articles 22(1) and 19(1) of Directive 2004/39/EC)

General principles

1. Member States shall require investment firms to satisfy the following conditions when carrying out client orders:

(a) they must ensure that orders executed on behalf of clients are promptly and accurately recorded and allocated;

(b) they must carry out otherwise comparable client orders sequentially and promptly unless the characteristics of the order or prevailing market conditions make this impracticable, or the interests of the client require otherwise;

(c) they must inform a retail client about any material difficulty relevant to the proper carrying out of orders promptly upon becoming aware of the difficulty.

2. Where an investment firm is responsible for overseeing or arranging the settlement of an executed order, it shall take all reasonable steps to ensure that any client financial instruments or client funds received in settlement of that executed order are promptly and correctly delivered to the account of the appropriate client.

3. An investment firm shall not misuse information relating to pending client orders, and shall take all reasonable steps to prevent the misuse of such information by any of its relevant persons.

Article 48
(Articles 22(1) and 19(1) of Directive 2004/39/EC)

Aggregation and allocation of orders

1. Member States shall not permit investment firms to carry out a client order or a transaction for own account in aggregation with another client order unless the following conditions are met:

(a) it must be unlikely that the aggregation of orders and transactions will work overall to the disadvantage of any client whose order is to be aggregated;

(b) it must be disclosed to each client whose order is to be aggregated that the effect of aggregation may work to its disadvantage in relation to a particular order;

(c) an order allocation policy must be established and effectively implemented, providing in sufficiently precise terms for the fair allocation of aggregated orders and transactions, including how the volume and price of orders determines allocations and the treatment of partial executions.

2. Member States shall ensure that where an investment firm aggregates an order with one or more other client orders and the aggregated order is partially executed, it allocates the related trades in accordance with its order allocation policy.

Article 49
(Articles 22(1) and 19(1) of Directive 2004/39/EC)

Aggregation and allocation of transactions for own account

1. Member States shall ensure that investment firms which have aggregated transactions for own account with one or more client orders do not allocate the related trades in a way that is detrimental to a client.

2. Member States shall require that, where an investment firm aggregates a client order with a transaction for own account and the aggregated order is partially executed, it allocates the related trades to the client in priority to the firm.

However, if the firm is able to demonstrate on reasonable grounds that without the combination it would not have been able to carry out the order on such advantageous terms, or at all, it may allocate the transaction for own account proportionally, in accordance with its order allocation policy referred to in Article 48(1)(c).

3. Member States shall require investment firms, as part of the order allocation policy referred to in Article 48(1)(c), to put in place procedures designed to prevent the reallocation, in a way that is detrimental to the client, of transactions for own account which are executed in combination with client orders.

SECTION 7

ELIGIBLE COUNTERPARTIES

Article 50
(Article 24(3) of Directive 2004/39/EC)

Eligible counterparties

1. Member States may recognise an undertaking as an eligible counterparty if that undertaking falls within a category of clients who are to be considered professional clients in accordance with paragraphs 1, 2 and 3 of Section I of Annex II to Directive 2004/39/EC, excluding any category which is explicitly mentioned in Article 24(2) of that Directive.

On request, Member States may also recognise as eligible counterparties undertakings which fall within a category of clients who are to be considered professional clients in accordance with Section II of Annex II to Directive 2004/39/EC. In such cases, however, the undertaking concerned shall be recognised as an eligible counterparty only in respect of the services or transactions for which it could be treated as a professional client.

2. Where, pursuant to the second subparagraph of Article 24(2) of Directive 2004/39/EC, an eligible counterparty requests treatment as a client whose business with an investment firm is subject to Articles 19, 21 and 22 of that Directive, but does not expressly request treatment as a retail client, and the investment firm agrees to that request, the firm shall treat that eligible counterparty as a professional client.

However, where that eligible counterparty expressly requests treatment as a retail client, the provisions in respect of requests of non-professional treatment specified in the second, third and fourth sub-paragraphs of Section I of Annex II to Directive 2004/39/EC shall apply.

SECTION 8

RECORD-KEEPING

Article 51
(Article 13(6) of Directive 2004/39/EC)

Retention of records

1. Member States shall require investment firms to retain all the records required under Directive 2004/39/EC and its implementing measures for a period of at least five years.

Additionally, records which set out the respective rights and obligations of the investment firm and the client under an agreement to provide services, or the terms on which the firm provides services to the client, shall be retained for at least the duration of the relationship with the client.

However, competent authorities may, in exceptional circumstances, require investment firms to retain any or all of those records for such longer period as is justified by the nature of the instrument or transaction, if that is necessary to enable the authority to exercise its supervisory functions under Directive 2004/39/EC.

Following the termination of the authorisation of an investment firm, Member States or competent authorities may require the firm to retain records for the outstanding term of the five year period required under the first subparagraph.

2. The records shall be retained in a medium that allows the storage of information in a way

accessible for future reference by the competent authority, and in such a form and manner that the following conditions are met:

(a) the competent authority must be able to access them readily and to reconstitute each key stage of the processing of each transaction;

(b) it must be possible for any corrections or other amendments, and the contents of the records prior to such corrections or amendments, to be easily ascertained;

(c) it must not be possible for the records otherwise to be manipulated or altered.

3. The competent authority of each Member State shall draw up and maintain a list of the minimum records investment firms are required to keep under Directive 2004/39/EC and its implementing measures.

4. Record-keeping obligations under Directive 2004/39/EC and in this Directive are without prejudice to the right of Member States to impose obligations on investment firms relating to the recording of telephone conversations or electronic communications involving client orders.

5. Before 31 December 2009 the Commission shall, in the light of discussions with the Committee of European Securities Regulators, report to the European Parliament and the Council on the continued appropriateness of the provisions of paragraph 4.

Section 9

Defined Terms for the Purposes of Directive 2004/39/EC

Article 52

(Article 4(1)(4) of Directive 2004/39/EC)

Investment advice

For the purposes of the definition of 'investment advice' in Article 4(1)(4) of Directive 2004/39/EC, a personal recommendation is a recommendation that is made to a person in his capacity as an investor or potential investor, or in his capacity as an agent for an investor or potential investor.

That recommendation must be presented as suitable for that person, or must be based on a consideration of the circumstances of that person, and must constitute a recommendation to take one of the following sets of steps:

(a) to buy, sell, subscribe for, exchange, redeem, hold or underwrite a particular financial instrument;

(b) to exercise or not to exercise any right conferred by a particular financial instrument to buy, sell, subscribe for, exchange, or redeem a financial instrument.

A recommendation is not a personal recommendation if it is issued exclusively through distribution channels or to the public.

Chapter IV

Final Provisions

Article 53

Transposition

1. Member States shall adopt and publish, by 31 January 2007 at the latest, the laws, regulations and administrative provisions necessary to comply with this Directive. They shall forthwith communicate to the Commission the text of those provisions and a correlation table between those provisions and this Directive.

2. Member States shall apply those provisions from 1 November 2007.

3. When Member States adopt those provisions, they shall contain a reference to this Directive or be accompanied by such a reference on the occasion of their official publication. Member States shall determine how such reference is to be made.

4. Member States shall communicate to the Commission the text of the main provisions of national law which they adopt in the field covered by this Directive.

Article 54

Entry into force

This Directive shall enter into force on the 20th day following its publication in the Official Journal of the European Union.

Article 55

Addressees

This Directive is addressed to the Member States.

CHRONOLOGICAL LIST OF DIRECTIVES

Date	Number	Name	OJ	Reproduced in	Page
25 February 1964	64/225/EEC	Council Directive on the abolition of restrictions on freedom of establishment and freedom to provide services in respect of reinsurance and retrocession	OJ L 56, 4 April 1964, 878–880	I. 1.	1049
9 March 1968	68/151/EEC	First Council Directive on co-ordination of safeguards which, for the protection of the interests of members and others, are required by Member States of companies within the meaning of the second paragraph of Article [48]* of the Treaty, with a view to making such safeguards equivalent throughout the Community	OJ L 65, 14 March 1968, 8–12	C. 1.	445
24 April 1972	72/166/EEC	Council Directive on the approximation of the laws of Member States relating to insurance against civil liability in respect of the use of motor vehicles, and to the enforcement of the obligation to insure against such liability	OJ L 103, 2 May 1972, 1–4	I. 2.	1052
28 June 1973	73/183/EEC	Council Directive on the abolition of restrictions on freedom of establishment and freedom to provide services in respect of self-employed activities of banks and other financial institutions	OJ L 194, 16 July 1973, 1–10	B. 1.	1
24 July 1973	73/239/EEC	Council Directive on the co-ordination of laws, regulations and administrative provisions relating to the taking-up and pursuit of the business of direct insurance other than life assurance	OJ L 228, 16 August 1973, 3–19	I. 3.	1059
24 July 1973	73/240/EEC	Council Directive abolishing restrictions on freedom of establishment in the business of direct insurance other than life assurance	OJ L 228, 16 August 1973, 20–22	I. 4.	1092
6 February 1974	74/165/EEC	Commission recommendation to the Member States concerning the application of the Council Directive of 24 April 1972 on the approximation of the laws of the Member States relating to the use of motor vehicles, and to the enforcement of the obligation to insure against such liability	OJ L 87, 30 March 1974, 12	I. 5.	1095

* The number between brackets has been changed as from 1 May 1999 by article 12 of the Treaty of Amsterdam.

Date	Number	Name	OJ	Reproduced in	Page
17 February 1975	75/129/EEC	Council Directive on the approximation of the laws of the Member States relating to collective redundancies	OJ L 48, 22 February 1975, 29–30	E. 1.	961
29 June 1976	76/580/EEC	Council Directive amending Directive 73/239/EEC on the co-ordination of laws, regulations and administrative provisions relating to the taking-up and pursuit of the business of direct insurance other than life assurance	OJ L 189, 13 July 1976, 13–14	I. 6.	1096
13 December 1976	77/91/EEC	Second Council Directive on co-ordination of safeguards which, for the protection of the interests of members and others, are required by Member States of companies within the meaning of the second paragraph of Article [48]* of the Treaty, in respect of the formation of public limited liability companies and the maintenance and alteration of their capital, with a view to making such safeguards equivalent	OJ L 26, 31 January 1977, 1–13	C. 2.	454
13 December 1976	77/92/EEC	Council Directive on measures to facilitate the effective exercise of freedom of establishment and freedom to provide services in respect of the activities of insurance agents and brokers (ex ISIC Group 630) and, in particular, transitional measures in respect of those activities	OJ L 26, 31 January 1977, 14–19	I. 7.	1097
14 February 1977	77/187/EEC	Council Directive on the approximation of the laws of the Member States relating to the safeguarding of employees' rights in the event of transfers of undertakings, businesses or parts of undertakings or businesses	OJ L 61, 5 March 1977, 26	E. 2.	962
25 July 1977	77/534/EEC	Commission Recommendation concerning a European code of conduct relating to transactions in transferable securities	OJ L 212, 20 August 1977, 37–43	S. 1.	1399
12 December 1977	77/780/EEC	First Council Directive on the co-ordination of laws, regulations and administrative provisions relating to the taking-up and pursuit of the business of credit institutions	OJ L 322, 17 December 1977, 30	B. 2.	2
30 May 1978	78/473/EEC	Council Directive on the co-ordination of laws, regulations and administrative provisions relating to Community co-insurance	OJ L 151, 7 June 1978, 25–28	I. 8.	1098
25 July 1978	78/660/EEC	Fourth Council Directive based on Article [44(3)(g)]* of the Treaty on the annual accounts of certain types of companies	OJ L 222, 14 August 1978, 11–31	C. 4.	486

Date	Number	Name	OJ	Reproduced in	Page
9 October 1978	78/855/EEC	Third Council Directive based on Article [44(3)(g)]* of the Treaty concerning mergers of public limited liability companies	OJ L 295, 20 October 1978, 36–43	C. 3.	476
5 March 1979	79/267/EEC	Council Directive on the co-ordination of laws, regulations and administrative provisions relating to the taking-up and pursuit of the business of direct life assurance	OJ L 63, 13 March 1979, 1–18	I. 9.	1102
5 March 1979	79/279/EEC	Council Directive co-ordinating the conditions for the admission of securities to official stock exchange listing	OJ L 66, 16 March 1979, 21–32	S. 2.	1407
17 March 1980	80/390/EEC	Council Directive co-ordinating the requirements for the drawing up, scrutiny and distribution of the listing particulars to be published for the admission of securities to official stock exchange listing	OJ L 100, 17 April 1980, 1–26	S. 3.	1410
20 October 1980	80/987/EEC	Council Directive to the protection of employees in the event of the insolvency of their employer	OJ L 283, 28 November 1980, 23–27	E. 3.	963
8 January 1981	81/76/EEC	Commission recommendation on accelerated settlement of claims under insurance against civil liability in respect of the use of motor vehicles	OJ L 57, 4 March 1981, 27	I. 10.	1104
15 February 1982	82/121/EEC	Council Directive on information to be published on a regular basis by companies the shares of which have been admitted to official stock-exchange listing	OJ L 48, 20 February 1982, 26–29	S. 4.	1415
3 March 1982	82/148/EEC	Council Directive amending Directive 79/279/EEC co-ordinating the conditions for the admission of securities to official stock exchange listing and Directive 80/390/EEC co-ordinating the requirements for the drawing up, scrutiny and distribution of the listing particulars to be published for the admission of securities to official stock exchange listing	OJ L 62, 5 March 1982, 22–23	S. 5.	1417
17 December 1982	82/891/EEC	Sixth Council Directive based on Article [44(3)(g)]* of the Treaty, concerning the division of public limited liability companies	OJ L 378, 31 December 1982, 47–54	C. 5.	520
13 June 1983	83/350/EEC	Council Directive on the supervision of credit institutions on consolidated basis	OJ L 193, 18 July 1983, 18–20	B. 3.	3

Date	Number	Name	OJ	Reproduced in	Page
13 June 1983	83/349/EEC	Seventh Council Directive based on Article [44(3)(g)]* of the Treaty on consolidated accounts	OJ L 193, 18 July 1983, 1–17	C. 6.	529
30 December 1983	84/5/EEC	Council Directive on the approximation of the laws of the Member States relating to insurance against civil liability in respect of the use of motor vehicles	OJ L 8, 11 January 1984, 17–20	I. 11.	1105
10 April 1984	84/253/EEC	Eighth Council Directive based on Article [44(3)(g)]* of the Treaty on the approval of persons responsible for carrying out the statutory audits of accounting documents	OJ L 126, 12 May 1984, 20–26	C. 7.	550
10 September 1984	84/450/EEC	Council Directive concerning misleading and comparative advertising	OJ L 250, 19 September 1984, 17–20	C.P. 1.	789
10 December 1984	84/641/EEC	Council Directive amending, particularly as regards tourist assistance, the First Directive 73/239/EEC on the co-ordination of laws, regulations and administrative provisions relating to the taking-up and pursuit of the business of direct insurance other than life assurance	OJ L 339, 27 December 1984, 21–25	I. 12.	1111
8 July 1985	85/345/EEC	Council Directive amending Directive 77/780/EEC on the co-ordination of laws, regulations and administrative provisions relating to the taking-up and pursuit of the business of credit institutions	OJ L 183, 16 July 1985, 19–20	B. 4.	4
25 July 1985	2137/85/EEC	Council Regulation on the European Economic Interest Grouping (EEIG)	OJ L 199, 31 July 1985, 1–9	C. 8.	551
25 July 1985	85/374/EEC	Council Directive on the approximation of the laws, regulations and administrative provisions of the Member States concerning liability for defective products	OJ L 210, 7 August 1985, 29–33	C.P. 2.	796
20 December 1985	85/577/EEC	Council Directive to protect the consumer in respect of contracts negotiated away from business premises	OJ L 372, 31 December 1985, 31–33	C.P. 3.	803
20 December 1985	85/611/EEC	Council Directive on the co-ordination of laws, regulations and administrative provisions relating to undertakings for collective investment in transferable securities (UCITS)	OJ L 375, 31 December 1985, 3–18	S. 6.	1418
20 December 1985	85/612/EEC	Council Recommendation concerning the second subparagraph of Article 25(1) of Directive 85/611/EEC	OJ L 375, 31 December 1985, 19	S. 7.	1454

Date	Number	Name	OJ	Reproduced in	Page
17 April 1986	86/137/EEC	Council Directive authorising certain Member States to defer further application of Directive 77/780/EEC as regards certain credit institutions	OJ L 106, 23 April 1986, 35	B. 5.	5
27 October 1986	86/524/EEC	Council Directive amending Directive 77/780/EEC in respect of the list of permanent exclusions of certain credit institutions	OJ L 309, 4 November 1986, 15–16	B. 6.	6
8 December 1986	86/635/EEC	Council Directive on the annual accounts and consolidated accounts of banks and other financial institutions	OJ L 372, 31 December 1986, 1–17	B. 7.	7
22 December 1986	87/62/EEC	Commission Recommendation on monitoring and controlling large exposures of credit institutions	OJ L 33, 4 February 1987, 10–15	B. 8.	26
22 December 1986	87/63/EEC	Commission Recommendation concerning the introduction of deposit-guarantee schemes in the Community	OJ L 33, 4 February 1986, 16–17	B. 9.	27
22 December 1986	87/102/EEC	Council Directive for the approximation of the laws, regulations and administrative provisions of the Member States concerning consumer credit	OJ L 42, 12 February 1987, 48–53	C.P. 4.	811
22 June 1987	87/343/EEC	Council Directive amending, as regards credit insurance and suretyship insurance, First Directive 73/239/EEC on the co-ordination of laws, regulations and administrative provisions relating to the taking-up and pursuit of the business of direct insurance other than life assurance	OJ L 185, 4 July 1987, 72–76	I. 13.	1114
22 June 1987	87/344/EEC	Council Directive on the co-ordination of laws, regulations and administrative provisions relating to legal expenses insurance	OJ L 185, 4 July 1987, 77–80	I. 14.	1116
22 June 1987	87/345/EEC	Council Directive amending Directive 80/390/EEC co-ordinating the requirements for the drawing-up, scrutiny and distribution of the listing particulars to be published for the admission of securities to official stock exchange listing	OJ L 185, 4 July 1987, 81–83	S. 8.	1455
8 December 1987	87/598/EEC	Commission Recommendation on a European Code of Conduct relating to electronic payment	OJ L 365, 24 December 1987, 72–76	C.P. 5.	822
22 March 1988	88/220/EEC	Council Directive amending, as regards the investment policies of certain UCITS, Directive 85/611/EEC on the co-ordination of laws, regulations and administrative provisions relating to undertakings for collective investments in transferable securities (UCITS)	OJ L 100, 19 April 1988, 31–32	S. 9.	1456

Date	Number	Name	OJ	Reproduced in	Page
22 June 1988	88/357/EEC	Council Directive on the co-ordination of laws, regulations and administrative provisions relating to direct insurance other than life assurance and laying down provisions to facilitate the effective exercise of freedom to provide services and amending Directive 73/239/EEC	OJ L 172, 4 July 1988, 1–14	I. 15.	1120
24 June 1988	88/361/EEC	Council Directive for the implementation of Article [67]** of the Treaty	OJ L 178, 8 July 1988, 5–18	C.M. 2.	431
17 November 1988	88/590/EEC	Commission Recommendation concerning payment systems, and in particular the relationship between cardholder and card issuer	OJ L 317, 24 November 1988, 55–58	C.P. 6.	825
12 December 1988	88/627/EEC	Council Directive on the information to be published when a major holding in a listed company is acquired or disposed of	OJ L 348, 17 December 1988, 62–65	S. 10.	1457
13 February 1989	89/117/EEC	Council Directive on the obligations of branches established in a Member State of credit institutions and financial institutions having their head offices outside that Member State regarding the publication of annual accounting documents	OJ L 44, 16 February 1989, 40–42	B. 10.	28
17 April 1989	89/298/EEC	Council Directive co-ordinating the requirements for the drawing-up, scrutiny and distribution of the prospectus to be published when transferable securities are offered to the public	OJ L 124, 5 May 1989, 8–15	S. 11.	1459
17 April 1989	89/299/EEC	Council Directive on the own funds of credit institutions	OJ L 124, 5 May 1989, 16–20	B. 11.	32
13 November 1989	89/592/EEC	Council Directive co-ordinating regulations on insider dealing	OJ L 334, 18 November 1989, 30–32	S. 12.	1460
15 December 1989	89/646/EEC	Second Council Directive on the co-ordination of laws, regulations and administrative provisions relating to the taking-up and pursuit of the business of credit institutions and amending Directive 77/780/EEC	OJ L 386, 30 December 1989, 1–13	B. 12.	33
18 December 1989	89/647/EEC	Council Directive on a solvency ratio for credit institutions	OJ L 386, 30 December 1989, 14–22	B. 13.	34
21 December 1989	89/666/EEC	Eleventh Council Directive concerning disclosure requirements in respect of branches opened in a Member State by certain types of company governed by the law of another State	OJ L 395, 30 December 1989, 36–39	C. 9.	562

** The number between brackets has been repeated as from 1 May 1999 by article 12 of the Treaty of Amsterdam.

Date	Number	Name	OJ	Reproduced in	Page
21 December 1989	89/667/EEC	Twelfth Council Directive on single-member private limited-liability companies	OJ L 395, 30 December 1989, 40–42	C. 10.	567
14 February 1990	90/109/EEC	Commission Recommendation on the transparency of banking conditions relating to cross-border financial transactions	OJ L 67, 15 March 1990, 39–42	C.P. 7.	830
22 February 1990	90/88/EEC	Council Directive amending Directive 87/102/EEC for the approximation of the laws, regulations and administrative provisions of the Member States concerning consumer credit	OJ L 61, 10 March 1990, 14–18	C.P. 8.	835
23 April 1990	90/211/EEC	Council Directive amending Directive 80/390/EEC in respect of the mutual recognition of public-offer prospectuses as stock-exchange listing particulars	OJ L 112, 3 May 1990, 24–25	S. 13.	1461
14 May 1990	90/232/EEC	Council Directive on the approximation of the laws of the Member States relating to insurance against civil liability in respect of the use of motor vehicles	OJ L 129, 19 May 1990, 33–36	I. 16.	1131
8 November 1990	90/604/EEC	Council Directive amending Directive 78/660/EEC on annual accounts and Directive 83/349/EEC on consolidated accounts as concerns the exemptions for small and medium-sized companies and the publication of accounts in ecus	OJ L 317, 16 November 1990, 57–59	C. 11.	570
8 November 1990	90/605/EEC	Council Directive amending Directive 78/660/EEC on annual accounts and Directive 83/349/EEC on consolidated accounts as regards the scope of those Directives	OJ L 317, 16 November 1990, 60–62	C. 12.	572
8 November 1990	90/618/EEC	Council Directive amending, particularly as regards motor vehicle liability insurance, Directive 73/239/EEC and Directive 88/357/EEC which concern the co-ordination of laws, regulations and administrative provisions relating to direct insurance other than life assurance	OJ L 330, 29 November 1990, 44–49	I. 17.	1135
8 November 1990	90/619/EEC	Council Directive on the co-ordination of laws, regulations and administrative provisions relating to direct life assurance, laying down provisions to facilitate the effective exercise of freedom to provide services and amending Directive 79/267	OJ L 330, 29 November 1990, 50–61	I. 18.	1139
19 December 1990	91/31/EEC	Commission Directive adapting the technical definition of 'multilateral development banks' in Council Directive 89/647/EEC of 18 December 1989 on a solvency ratio for credit institutions	OJ L 17, 23 January 1991, 20	B. 14.	35

Date	Number	Name	OJ	Reproduced in	Page
31 May 1991	1534/91/EEC	Council Regulation on the application of Article [81(3)]* of the Treaty to certain categories of agreements, decisions and concerted practices in the insurance sector	OJ L 143, 7 June 1991, 1–3	I. 19.	1140
10 June 1991	91/308/EEC	Council Directive on prevention of the use of the financial system for the purpose of money laundering	OJ L 166, 28 June 1991, 77–83	B. 15.	36
20 June 1991	2155/91/EEC	Council Regulation laying down particular provisions for the application of Articles 37, 39 and 40 of the Agreement between the European Economic Community and the Swiss Confederation on direct insurance other than life insurance	OJ L 205, 27 July 1991, 1	I. 20.	1143
20 June 1991	91/371/EEC	Council Directive on the implementation of the Agreement between the European Economic Community and the Swiss Confederation concerning direct insurance other than life insurance	OJ L 205, 27 July 1991, 48	I. 21.	1144
3 December 1991	91/633/EEC	Council Directive implementing Directive 89/299/EEC on the own funds of credit institutions	OJ L 339, 11 December 1991, 33–34	B. 16.	38
18 December 1991	92/48/EEC	Commission Recommendation on insurance intermediaries	OJ L 19, 28 January 1992, 32–33	I. 22.	1145
19 December 1991	91/674/EEC	Council Directive on the annual accounts and consolidated accounts of insurance undertakings	OJ L 374, 3 1 December 1991, 7–31	I. 23.	1148
19 December 1991	91/675/EEC	Council Directive 91/675/EEC of 19 December 1991 setting up a European Insurance and Occupational Pensions Committee	OJ L 374, 31 December 1991, 32–33	I. 24.	1172
16 March 1992	92/16/EEC	Council Directive amending Directive 89/299/EEC on the own funds of credit institutions	OJ L 75, 21 March 1992, 48–50	B. 17.	39
6 April 1992	92/30/EEC	Council Directive on the supervision of credit institutions on a consolidated basis	OJ L 110, 28 April 1992, 52–58	B. 18.	40
18 June 1992	92/49/EEC	Council Directive on the co-ordination of laws, regulations and administrative provisions relating to direct insurance other than life assurance and amending Directives 73/239/EEC and 88/357/EEC	OJ L 228, 11 August 1992, 1–23	I. 25.	1174
24 June 1992	92/56/EEC	Council Directive amending Directive 75/129/EEC on the approximation of the laws of the Member States relating to collective redundancies	OJ L 245, 26 August 1992, 3–5	E. 4.	973

Date	Number	Name	OJ	Reproduced in	Page
10 November 1992	92/96/EEC	Council Directive on the co-ordination of laws, regulations and administrative provisions relating to direct life assurance and amending Directives 79/267/EEC and 90/619/EEC	OJ L 360, 9 December 1992, 1–27	I. 26.	1196
23 November 1992	92/101/EEC	Council Directive for a Council Directive amending Directive 77/91/EEC on the formation of public limited-liability companies and the maintenance and the alteration of their capital	OJ L 347, 28 November 1992, 64–66	C. 13.	574
21 December 1992	92/121/EEC	Council Directive on the monitoring and control of large exposures of credit institutions	OJ L 29, 5 February 1993, 1–8	B. 19.	41
15 March 1993	93/6/EEC	Council Directive on the capital adequacy of investments firms and credit institutions	OJ L 141, 11 June 1993, 1–26	B. 20.	42
5 April 1993	93/13/EEC	Council Directive on unfair terms in consumer contracts	OJ L 95, 21 April 1993, 29–34	C.P. 9.	835
10 May 1993	93/22/EEC	Council Directive on investment services in the securities field	OJ L 141, 11 June 1993, 27–46	S. 14.	1462
15 March 1994	94/7/EC	Commission Directive adapting Council Directive 89/647/EEC on a solvency ratio for credit institutions as regards the technical definition of 'multilateral development banks'	OJ L 89, 6 April 1994, 17	B. 21.	45
21 March 1994	94/8/EC	Council Directive amending Directive 78/660/EEC as regards the revision of amounts expressed in ecus	OJ L 82, 25 March 1994, 33–34	C. 14.	576
30 May 1994	94/18/EC	European Parliament and Council Directive amending Directive 80/390/EEC co-ordinating the requirements for the drawing up, scrutiny and distribution of the listing particulars to be published for the admission of securities to official stock-exchange listing, with regard to the obligation to publish listing particulars	OJ L 135, 31 May 1994, 1–4	S. 15.	1463
30 May 1994	94/19/EC	European Parliament and Council Directive on deposit-guarantee schemes	OJ L 135, 31 May 1994, 5–14	B. 22.	46
22 September 1994	94/45/EC	Council Directive on the establishment of a European Works Council or a procedure in Community-scale undertakings and Community-scale groups of undertakings for the purposes of informing and consulting employees	OJ L 254, 30 September 1994, 64–72	E. 5.	974

Date	Number	Name	OJ	Reproduced in	Page
31 May 1995	95/15/EC	Commission Directive adapting Council Directive 89/647/EEC on a solvency ratio for credit institutions, as regards the technical definition of 'Zone A' and in respect of the weighting of asset items constituting claims carrying the explicit guarantee of the European Communities	OJ L 125, 8 June 1995, 23–24	B. 23.	59
29 June 1995	95/26/EC	European Parliament and Council Directive amending Directives 77/780/EEC and 89/646/EEC in the field of credit institutions, Directives 73/239/EEC and 92/49/EEC in the field of non-life insurance, Directives 79/267/EEC and 92/96/EEC in the field of life assurance, Directive 93/22/EEC in the field of investment firms and Directive 85/611/EEC in the field of undertakings for collective investment in transferable securities (UCITS), with a view to reinforcing prudential supervision	OJ L 168, 18 July 1995, 7–13	I. 27.	1198
15 December 1995	95/67/EC	Commission Directive making a technical amendment to Council Directive 89/647/EEC on a solvency ratio for credit institutions as regards the definition of 'multilateral development banks'	OJ L 314, 28 December 1995, 72	B. 24.	60
11 March 1996	96/13/EC	Council Directive amending Article 2(2) of Directive 77/780/EEC in respect of the list of permanent exclusions of certain credit institutions	OJ L 66, 16 March 1996, 15–16	B. 25.	61
21 March 1996	96/10/EC	European Parliament and Council Directive amending Directive 89/647/EEC as regards recognition of contractual netting by the competent authorities	OJ L 85, 3 April 1996, 17–21	B. 26.	62
27 January 1997	97/5/EC	European Parliament and Council Directive on cross-border credit transfers	OJ L 43, 14 February 1997, 25–31	C.P. 10.	842
3 March 1997	97/9/EC	European Parliament and Council Directive on investor-compensation schemes	OJ L 84, 26 March 1997, 22–31	S. 16.	1464
20 May 1997	97/7/EC	European Parliament and Council Directive on the protection of consumers in respect of distance contracts—Statement by the Council and the Parliament re Article 6 (1)—Statement by the Commission re Article 3 (1), first indent	OJ L 144, 4 June 1997, 19–28	C.P. 11.	849

Date	Number	Name	OJ	Reproduced in	Page
10 July 1997	97/C 209/04	Commission Interpretative Communication on freedom to provide services and the interest of the general good in the Second Banking Directive	OJ C 209, 10 July 1997, 6–22	B. 27.	63
30 July 1997	97/489/EC	Commission Recommendation concerning transactions by electronic payment instruments and in particular the relationship between issuer and holder	OJ L 208, 2 August 1997, 52–58	C.P. 12.	858
6 October 1997	97/55/EC	European Parliament and Council Directive amending Directive 84/450/EEC concerning misleading advertising so as to include comparative advertising	OJ L 290, 23 October 1997, 18–23	C.P. 13.	864
—	97/C 285/10	Communication from the Commission. Participation of European Economic Interest Groupings (EEIGs) in public contracts and programmes financed by public funds	OJ C 285, 20 September 1997, 17–24	C. 15.	577
15 December 1997	97/74/EC	Council Directive extending, to the United Kingdom of Great Britain and Northern Ireland, Directive 94/45/EC on the establishment of a European Works Council or a procedure in Community-scale undertakings and Community-scale groups of undertakings for the purposes of informing and consulting employees	OJ L 10, 16 January 1998, 22–23	E. 6.	985
16 February 1998	98/7/EC	European Parliament and Council Directive amending Directive 87/102/EEC for the approximation of the laws, regulations and administrative provisions of the Member States concerning consumer credit	OJ L 101, 1 April 1998, 17–23	C.P. 14.	868
19 May 1998	98/26/EC	European Parliament and Council Directive on settlement finality in payment and securities settlement systems	OJ L 166, 11 June 1998, 45–50	S. 17.	1474
19 May 1998	98/27/EC	European Parliament and Council Directive on injunctions for the protection of consumers' interests	OJ L 166, 11 June 1998, 51–55	C.P. 15.	870
22 June 1998	98/31/EC	European Parliament and Council Directive amending Council Directive 93/6/EEC on the capital adequacy of investment firms and credit institutions	OJ L 204, 21 July 1998, 13–25	B. 28.	82
22 June 1998	98/32/EC	European Parliament and Council Directive amending, as regards in particular mortgages, Council Directive 89/647/EEC on a solvency ratio for credit institutions	OJ L 204, 21 July 1998, 26–28	B. 29.	85

Date	Number	Name	OJ	Reproduced in	Page
22 June 1998	98/33/EC	European Parliament and Council Directive amending Article 12 of Council Directive 77/780/EEC on the taking-up and pursuit of the business of credit institutions, Articles 2, 5, 6, 7, 8 of and Annexes II and III to Council Directive 89/647/EEC on a solvency ratio for credit institutions and Article 2 of and Annex II to Council Directive 93/6/EEC on the capital adequacy of investment firms and credit institutions	OJ L 204, 21 July 1998, 29–36	B. 30.	86
29 June 1998	98/50/EC	Council Directive amending Directive 77/187/EEC on the approximation of the laws of the Member States relating to the safeguarding of employees' rights in the event of transfers of undertakings, businesses or parts of businesses	OJ L 201, 17 July 1998, 88–92	E. 7.	987
20 July 1998	98/59/EC	Council Directive on the approximation of the laws of the Member States relating to collective redundancies	OJ L 225, 12 August 1998, 16–21	E. 8.	989
27 October 1998	98/78/EC	European Parliament and Council Directive 98/78/EC of 27 October 1998 on the supplementary supervision of insurance and reinsurance undertakings in an insurance or reinsurance group	OJ L 330, 5 December 1998, 1–12	I. 28.	1199
3 December 1998	98/699/JHA	Joint Action adopted by the Council on the basis of Article [31]* of the Treaty on European Union, on money laundering, the identification, tracing, freezing, seizing and confiscation of instrumentalities and the proceeds from crime	OJ L 333, 9 December 1998, 1–3	B. 31.	87
10 May 1999	1999/34/EC	European Parliament and Council Directive amending Council Directive 85/374/EEC on the approximation of the laws, regulations and administrative provisions of the Member States concerning liability for defective products	OJ L 141, 4 June 1999, 20–21	C.P. 16.	875
25 May 1999	1999/44/EC	European Parliament and Council Directive on certain aspects of the sale of consumer goods and associated guarantees	OJ L 171, 7 July 1999, 12–16	C.P. 17.	877
17 June 1999	1999/60/EC	Council Directive amending Directive 78/660/EEC as regards amounts expressed in ecus	OJ L 162, 26 June 1999, 65–66	C. 16.	586
13 December 1999	1999/93/EC	European Parliament and Council Directive on a Community framework for electronic signatures	OJ L 13, 19 January 2000, 12–20	C.P. 18.	884
—	2000/C 43/03	Commission Interpretative Communication on freedom to provide services and the general good in the insurance sector	OJ C 43, 16 February 2000, 5–27	I. 29.	1213

Date	Number	Name	OJ	Reproduced in	Page
20 March 2000	2000/12/EC	European Parliament and Council Directive relating to the taking-up and pursuit of the business of credit institutions	OJ L 126, 26 May 2000, 1–59	B. 32.	91
16 May 2000	2000/26/EC	European Parliament and Council Directive on the approximation of the laws of the Member States relating to insurance against civil liability in respect of the use of motor vehicles and amending Council Directives 73/239/EEC and 88/357/EEC	OJ L 181, 20 July 2000, 65–74	I. 30.	1241
29 May 2000	1346/2000/EC	Council regulation on insolvency proceedings	OJ L 160, 30 June 2000, 1–18	E. 9.	997
8 June 2000	2000/31/EC	European Parliament and Council Directive on certain legal aspects of information society services, in particular electronic commerce, in the Internal Market	OJ L 178, 17 July 2000, 1–16	C.P. 19.	894
23 June 2000	2000/408/EC	Commission Recommendation concerning disclosure of information on financial instruments and other items complementing the disclosure required according to Council Directive 86/635/EEC on the annual accounts and consolidated accounts of banks and other financial institutions	OJ L 154, 27 June 2000, 36–41	B. 33.	95
29 June 2000	2000/35/EC	European Parliament and Council Directive on combating late payment in commercial transactions	OJ L 200, 8 August 2000, 35–38	E. 10.	1016
18 September 2000	2000/28/EC	European Parliament and Council Directive amending Directive 2000/12/EC relating to the taking-up and pursuit of the business of credit institutions	OJ L 275, 27 October 2000, 37–38	B. 34.	101
18 September 2000	2000/46/EC	European Parliament and Council Directive on the taking-up, pursuit of and prudential supervision of the business of electronic money institutions	OJ L 275, 27 October 2000, 39–43	B. 35.	102
1 March 2001	2001/193/EC	Commission Recommendation on pre-contractual information to be given to consumers by lenders offering home loans	OJ L 69, 10 March 2001, 25–29	C.P. 20.	912
12 March 2001	2001/23/EC	Council Directive on the approximation of the laws of the Member States relating to the safeguarding of employees' rights in the event of transfers of undertakings, businesses or parts of undertakings or businesses	OJ L 82, 22 March 2001, 16–20	E. 11.	1022

Date	Number	Name	OJ	Reproduced in	Page
4 April 2001	2001/24/EC	European Parliament and Council Directive on the reorganisation and winding up of credit institutions	OJ L 125, 5 May 2001, 15–23	B. 36.	108
28 May 2001	2001/34/EC	European Parliament and Council Directive on the admission of securities to official stock exchange listing and on information to be published on those securities	OJ L 184, 6 July 2001, 1–66	S. 18.	1480
30 May 2001	2001/453/EC	Commission recommendation on the recognition, measurement and disclosure of environmental issues in the annual accounts and annual reports of companies	OJ L 156, 13 June 2001, 33–42	C. 17.	588
6 June 2001	2001/527/EC	Commission Decision establishing the Committee of European Securities Regulators	OJ L 191, 13 July 2001, 43–44	S. 19.	1516
6 June 2001	2001/528/EC	Commission Decision establishing the European Securities Committee	OJ L 191, 13 July 2001, 45–46	S. 20.	1518
27 September 2001	2001/65/EC	European Parliament and Council Directive amending 78/660/EEC, 83/349/EEC and 86/635/EEC as regards the valuation rules for the annual and consolidated accounts of certain types of companies as well as of banks and other financial institutions	OJ L 283, 27 October 2001, 28	C. 18.	600
8 October 2001	2157/2001/EC	Council Regulation on the statute for a European Company (SE)	OJ L 294, 10 November 2001, 1–21	C. 19.	603
8 October 2001	2001/86/EC	Council Directive supplementing the Statute for a European company with regard to the involvement of employees	OJ L 294, 10 November 2001, 22–32	C. 20.	625
4 December 2001	2001/97/EC	European Parliament and Council Directive amending Council Directive 91/308/EEC on prevention of the use of the financial system for the purpose of money laundering	OJ L 344, 28 December 2001, 76–81	B. 37.	120
19 December 2001	2560/2001/EC	European Parliament and Council Regulation on cross-border payments in euro	OJ L 344, 28 December 2001, 13–16	C.P. 21.	917
21 January 2002	2001/107/EC	European Parliament and Council Directive amending Council Directive 85/611/EEC on the coordination of laws, regulations and administrative provisions relating to undertakings for collective investment in transferable securities (UCITS) with a view to regulating management companies and simplified prospectuses	OJ L 41, 13 February 2002, 20–34	S. 21.	1520

Date	Number	Name	OJ	Reproduced in	Page
21 January 2002	2001/108/EC	European Parliament and Council Directive amending Council Directive 85/611/EEC on the coordination of laws, regulations and administrative provisions relating to undertakings for collective investment in transferable securities (UCITS), with regard to investments of UCITS	OJ L 41, 13 February 2002, 35–42	S. 22.	1524
5 March 2002	2002/12/EC	European Parliament and Council Directive amending Council Directive 79/267/EEC as regards the solvency margin requirements for life assurance undertakings	OJ L 77, 20 March 2002, 11–16	I. 31.	1251
5 March 2002	2002/13/EC	European Parliament and Council Directive of amending Council Directive 73/239/EEC as regards the solvency margin requirements for non-life insurance undertakings	OJ L 77, 20 March 2002, 17–22	I. 32.	1252
11 March 2002	2002/14/EC	European Parliament and Council Directive establishing a general framework for informing and consulting employees in the European Community	OJ L 80, 23 March 2002, 29–33	E. 12.	1040
16 May 2002	2002/590/EC	Commission Recommendation, Statutory Auditors' Independence in the EU: A Set of Fundamental Principles	OJ L 191, 19 July 2002, 22–57	C. 21.	637
6 June 2002	2002/47/EC	European Parliament and Council Directive on financial collateral arrangements	OJ L 168, 27 June 2002, 43–50	S. 23.	1528
19 July 2002	1606/2002/EC	European Parliament and Council Regulation on the application of international accounting standards	OJ L 243, 11 September 2002, 1–4	C. 22.	677
23 September 2002	2002/74/EC	European Parliament and Council Directive amending Council Directive 80/987/EEC on the approximation of of the Member States relating to the protection of employees in the event of the insolvency of their employer	OJ L 270, 8 October 2002, 10–13.	E. 13.	1046
23 September 2002	2002/65/EC	European Parliament and Council Directive concerning the distance marketing of consumer financial services and amending Council Directive 90/619/EEC and Directives 97/7/EC and 98/27/EC	OJ L 271, 9 October 2002, 16–24	C.P. 22.	922
5 November 2002	2002/83/EC	European Parliament and Council Directive concerning life assurance	OJ L 345, 19 December 2002, 1–51	I. 33.	1255
9 December 2002	2002/92/EC	European Parliament and Council Directive on insurance mediation	OJ L 9, 15 January 2003, 3–10	I. 34.	1314

Date	Number	Name	OJ	Reproduced in	Page
16 December 2002	2002/87/EC	European Parliament and Council Directive on the supplementary supervision of credit institutions, insurance undertakings and investment firms in a financial conglomerate and amending Council Directives 73/239/EEC, 79/267/EEC, 92/49/EEC, 92/96/EEC, 93/6/EEC and 93/22/EEC, and Directives 98/78/EC and 2000/12/EC of the European Parliament and of the Council	OJ L 35, 11 February 2003, 1–27	B. 38.	123
28 January 2003	2003/6/EC	European Parliament and Council Directive on insider dealing and market manipulation (market abuse)	OJ L 96, 12 April 2003, 16–25	S. 24.	1538
3 June 2003	2003/41/EC	European Parliament and Council Directive on the activities of institutions for occupational retirement provision	OJ L 235, 23 September 2003, 10–21	I. 35.	1325
18 June 2003	2003/51/EC	European Parliament and Council Directive amending Directives 78/660/EEC, 83/349/EEC, 86/635/EEC and 91/674/EEC on the annual and consolidated accounts of certain types of companies, banks and other financial institutions and insurance undertakings	OJ L 178, 17 July 2003, 16–22	C. 23.	683
15 July 2003	2003/58/EC	European Parliament and Council Directive amending Council Directive 68/151/EC, as regards disclosure requirements in respect of certain types of companies	OJ L 221, 4 September 2003, 13–16	C. 24.	686
22 July 2003	1435/2003/EC	Council Regulation on the Statute for a European Cooperative Society (SCE)	OJ L 207, 18 August 2003, 1–24	C. 25.	688
22 July 2003	2003/72/EC	Council Directive supplementing the Statute for a European Cooperative Society with regard to the involvement of employees	OJ L 207, 18 August 2003, 25–36	C. 26.	715
28 July 2003	2003/564/EC	Commission Decision on the application of Council Directive 72/166/EEC relating to checks on insurance against civil liability in respect of the use of motor vehicles	OJ L 192, 31 July 2003, 23–39	I. 36.	1341
4 November 2003	2003/71/EC	European Parliament and Council Directive on the prospectus to be published when securities are offered to the public or admitted to trading and amending Directive 2001/34/EC	OJ L 345, 31 December 2003, 64–89	S. 25.	1552
5 November 2003	2004/6/EC	Commission Decision establishing the Committee of European Insurance and Occupational Supervisors	OJ L 3, 7 January 2004, 30–31	I. 37.	1356

Date	Number	Name	OJ	Reproduced in	Page
5 November 2003	2004/9/EC	Commission Decision establishing the Committee of European Insurance and Occupational Pensions Supervisors	OJ L 3, 7 January 2004, 34–35	I. 38.	1358
22 December 2003	2003/124/EC	Commission Directive implementing Directive 2003/6/EC of the European Parliament and of the Council as regards the definition and public disclosure of inside information and the definition of market manipulation	OJ L 339, 24 December 2003, 70–72	S. 26.	1580
22 December 2003	2003/125/EC	Commission Directive implementing Directive 2003/6/EC of the European Parliament and of the Council as regards the fair presentation of investment recommendations and the disclosure of conflicts of interest	OJ L 339, 24 December 2003, 73–77	S. 27.	1584
21 April 2004	2004/25/EC	European Parliament and Council Directive on takeover bids	OJ L 142, 30 April 2004, 12–23	S. 28.	1591
21 April 2004	2004/39/EC	European Parliament and Council Directive on markets in financial instruments amending Council Directives 85/611/EC and 93/6/EEC and Directive 2000/12/EC of the European Parliament and of the Council and repealing Council Directive 93/22/EEC	OJ L 145, 30 April 2004, 1–44	S. 29.	1606
29 April 2004	2004/72/EC	Commission Directive implementing Directive 2003/6/EC of the European Parliament and of the Council as regards accepted market practices, the definition of inside information in relation to derivatives on commodities, the drawing up of lists of insiders, the notification of managers' transactions and the notification of suspicious transactions	OJ L 162, 30 April 2004, 70–75	S. 30.	1660
27 October 2004	2006/2004/EC	European Parliament and Council Regulation on cooperation between national authorities responsible for the enforcement of consumer protection laws	OJ L 364, 9 December 2004, 1–11	C.P. 23.	933
14 December 2004	2004/913/EC	Commission Recommendation fostering an appropriate regime for the remuneration of directors of listed companies	OJ L 385, 29 December 2004, 55–59	C. 27.	728
15 December 2004	2004/109/EC	European Parliament and Council Directive on the harmonisation of transparency requirements in relation to information about issuers whose securities are admitted to trading on a regulated market and amending Directive 2001/34/EC	OJ L 390, 31 December 2004, 38–57	S. 31.	1667

Chronological List of Directives

Date	Number	Name	OJ	Reproduced in	Page
15 February 2005	2005/162/EC	Commission Recommendation on the role of non-executive or supervisory directors of listed companies and on the committees of the (supervisory) board	*OJ L 52*, 25 February 2005, 51–63	C. 28.	734
9 March 2005	2005/1/EC	European Parliament and Council Directive amending Council Directives 73/239/EEC, 85/611/EEC, 91/675/EEC, 92/49/EEC and 93/6/EEC and Directives 94/19/EC, 98/78/EC, 2000/12/EC, 2001/34/EC, 2002/83/EC and 2002/87/EC in order to establish a new organisational structure for financial services committee	*OJ L 79*, 24 March 2005, 9–17	B. 39.	145
11 May 2005	2005/14/EC	European Parliament and Council Directive amending Council Directives 72/166/EEC, 84/5/EEC, 88/357/EEC and 90/232/EEC and Directive 2000/26/EC of the European Parliament and of the Council relating to insurance against civil liability in respect of the use of motor vehicles	*OJ L 149*, 11 June 2005, 14–21. 14–21	I. 39.	1360
11 May 2005	2005/29/EC	European Parliament and of the Council Directive concerning unfair business-to-consumer commercial practices in the internal market and amending Council Directive 84/450/EEC, Directives 97/7/EC, 98/27/EC and 2002/65/EC of the European Parliament and of the Council and Regulation (EC) No 2006/2004 of the European Parliament and of the Council (Unfair Commercial Practices Directive)	*OJ L 149*, 11 June 2005, 22–39	C.P. 24.	946
26 October 2005	2005/60/EC	European Parliament and of the Council Directive on the prevention of the use of the financial system for the purpose of money laundering and terrorist financing	*OJ L 309*, 25 November 2005, 15–36	B. 40.	151
26 October 2005	2005/56/EC	European Parliament and Council Directive on cross-border mergers of limited liability companies	*OJ L 310*, 25 November 2005, 1–9	C. 29.	747
16 November 2005	2005/68/EC	European Parliament and Council Directive on reinsurance and amending Council Directives 73/239/EEC, 92/49/EEC as well as Directives 98/78/EC and 2002/83/EC	*OJ L 323*, 9 December 2005, 1–50	I. 40.	1366
5 April 2006	2006/31/EC	European Parliament and Council Directive amending Directive on markets in financial instruments, as regards certain deadlines	*OJ L 114*, 27 April 2006, 60–63	S. 32.	1692

Date	Number	Name	OJ	Repro-duced in	Page
17 May 2006	2006/43/EC	European Parliament and Council Directive on statutory audits of annual accounts and consolidated accounts, amending Council Directives 78/660/EEC and 83/349/EEC and repealing Council Directive 84/253/EEC	OJ L 157, 9 June 2006, 87–107	C. 30.	757
14 June 2006	2006/46/EC	European Parliament and Council Directive amending Council Directives 78/660/EEC on the annual accounts of certain types of companies, 83/349/EEC on consolidated accounts, 86/635/EEC on the annual accounts and consolidated accounts of banks and other financial institutions and 91/674/EEC on the annual accounts and consolidated accounts of insurance undertakings	OJ L 224, 16 August 2006, 1–7	C. 31.	783
14 June 2006	2006/48/EC	European Parliament and Council Directive relating to the taking up and pursuit of the business of credit institutions (recast)	OJ L 177, 30 June 2006, 1–200	B. 41.	175
14 June 2006	2006/49/EC	European Parliament and Council Directive on the capital adequacy of investment firms and credit institutions (recast)	OJ L 177, 30 June 2006, 201–255	B. 42.	369
10 August 2006	1287/2006/EC	Commission Regulation implementing Directive 2004/39/EC of the European Parliament and of the Council as regards record-keeping obligations for investment firms, transaction reporting, market transparency, admission of financial instruments to trading, and defined terms for the purposes of that Directive	OJ L 241, 2 September 2006, 1–25	S. 33.	1695
10 August 2006	2006/73/EC	Commission Directive implementing Directive 2004/39/EC of the European Parliament and of the Council as regards organisational requirements and operating conditions for investment firms and defined terms for the purposes of that Directive	OJ L 241, 2 September 2006, 26–58	S. 34.	1722
9 September 2006	2006/68/EC	European Parliament and Council Directive amending Council Directive 77/91/EEC as regards the formation of public limited liability companies and the maintenance and alteration of their capital	OJ L 264, 25 September 2006, 32–36	C. 32.	787

ALPHABETICAL LIST OF CASES

Name	Case number	Date	ECR	Reproduced in	Page
A.G.R. Regeling v Bestuur van de Bedrijfsvereniging voor de Metaalnijverheid	C-125/97	14.07.1998	[1998] I-4493	E. 3	970
AGS Assedic Pas-de-Calais v Dumon, F. and Froment, liquidator and representative of Établissements Pierre Gilson					
Allen, G. C. and others v Amalgamated Construction Co. Ltd.	C-234/98	02.12.1999	[1999] I-8643	E. 11	1025
Alpine Investments BV v Minister van Financiën	C-384/93	10.05.1995	[1995] I-1141	C.P. 3	803
Association basco-béarnaise des opticiens indépendants v Préfet des Pyrénées-Atlantiques	C-109/99	21.09.2000	[2000] I-7247	I. 3	1068
Association Eglise de scientologie de Paris and Scientology International Reserves Trust v The Prime Minister	C-54/99	14.03.2000	[2000] I-1335	C.M. 1	430
Axa Royale Belge SA v Georges Ochoa and Stratégie Finance SPRL	C-386/00	05.03.2002	[2002] I-2209	I. 33	1290
Banque internationale pour l'Afrique occidentale SA (BIAO) v Finanzamt für Großunternehmen in Hamburg	C-306/99	07.01.2003	[2003] I-1	C. 4	495
Bayerische Hypotheken- und Wechselbank AG v Dietzinger, E.	C-45/96	17.03.1998	[1998] I-1199	C.P. 3	803, 806
Beckmann, K. v Dynamco Whichloe Macfarlane Ltd	C-164/00	04.06.2002	[2002] I-4893	E. 11	1030
Berg, H. and Busschers, J. T. M. v Besselsen, I. M.	144/87 145/87	05.05.1988	[1988] 2559	E. 11	1027, 1032
Berliner Kindl Brauerei AG v Siepert, A.	C-208/98	23.03.2000	[2000] I-1741	C.P. 4	811
Betriebsrat der bofrost* Josef H. Boquoi Deutschland West GmbH & Co. KG v Bofrost* Josef H. Boquoi Deutschland West GmbH & Co. KG.	C-62/99	29.03.2001	[2001] I-2579	E. 5	981
Betriebsrat der Firma ADS Anker GmbH v ADS Anker GmbH	C-349/01	15.07.2004	[2004] I-6803	E. 5	978
Bonifaci, D. and others (C-94/95) and Berto, W. and others (C-95/95) v Istituto nazionale della previdenza sociale (INPS)	C-94/95 C-95/95	10.07.1997	[1997] I-3969	E. 3	968
Botzen, A. and others v Rotterdamsche Droogdok Maatschappij BV	186/83	07.02.1985	[1985] 519	E. 11	1033

Name	Case number	Date	ECR	Reproduced in	Page
Brugnoni, L. and Ruffinengo R. v. Cassa di risparmio di Genova e Imperia	157/85	24.06.1986	[1986] 2013	C.M. 1	428
Burdalo Trevejo, P. and others v Fondo Garantía Salarial	C-336/95	17.04.1997	[1997] I-2115	E. 11	1038
Bureau Belge des Assureurs Automobiles Asbl v Fantozzi, A. and SA Les Assurances populaires	116/83	21.06.1984	[1984] 2481	I. 2	1056
Bureau Central Français v Fonds de Garantie Automobile and others	64/83	09.02.1984	[1984] 689	I. 2	1056
Caballero, A.R. v Fondo de Garantía Salarial (Fogasa)	C-442/00	12.12.2002	[2002] I-11915	E. 3	965
Candolin, K., Viljaniemi, J.-A. and Paananen, V.-M. v Pohjola, V. and Ruokoranta, J.	C-537/03	30.06.2005	[2005] I-5745	I. 2	1056
Cape Snc v Idealservice Srl (C-541/99) and Idealservice MN RE Sas v OMAI Srl	C-541/99 (C-542/99) C-542/99	22.11.2001	[2001] I-9049	C.P. 9	838
Card Protection Plan Ltd (CPP) v Commissioners of Customs & Excise	C-349/96	25.02.1999	[1999] I-973	I. 3	1091
Celtec Ltd v Astley, J. and others	C-478/03	26.05.2005	[2005] I-4389	E. 11	1030
Centros Ltd v Erhvervs- og Selskabsstyrelsen	C-212/97	09.03.1999	[1999] I-1459	C. 2	458
Cofidis SA v Fredout, J.-L.	C-473/00	21.11.2002	[2002] I-10875	C.P. 9	835
Cofinoga Mérignac SA v Sachithanathan, S.	C-264/02	04.03.2004	[2004] I-2157	C.P. 4	816
Collino, R. and Chiappero, L. v Telecom Italia SpA	C-343/98	14.09.2000	[2000] I-6659	E. 11	1025, 1031
Comité Central d'Entreprise de la Société Anonyme Vittel and Comité d'Etablissement de Pierval and Fédération Générale Agroalimentaire v Commission of the European Communities	T-12/93	27.04.1995	[1995] II-1247	E. 11	1028, 1037
Commission of the European Communities v Council of the European Union	C-176/03	13.09.2005	[2005] I-07879	S. 24	1549
Commission of the European Communities v Federal Republic of Germany	205/84	04.12.1986	[1986] 3755	I. 3 I. 8 I. 33	1059 1058 1255
Commission of the European Communities v French Republic	C-483/99	04.07.2002	[2002] I-4781	C.M. 1	423
Commission of the European Communities v French Republic	C-52/00	25.04.2002	[2002] I-3827	C.P. 1 C.P. 3	809, 810
Commission of the European Communities v French Republic	220/83	04.12.1986	[1986] 3663	I. 8	1098
Commission of the European Communities v Grand Duchy of Luxemburg	C-346/02	07.09.2004	[2004] I-7517	I. 25	1174

Name	Case number	Date	ECR	Reproduced in	Page
Commission of the European Communities v Hellenic Republic	53/88	08.11.1990	[1990] I-3917	E. 3	965
Commission of the European Communities v Ireland	206/84	04.12.1986	[1986] 3817	I. 3 I. 8 I. 33	1059 1098 1255
Commission of the European Communities v Italian Republic	300/81	01.03.1983	[1983] 449	B. 41	176
Commission of the European Communities v Italian Republic	C-174/04	02.06.2005	[2005] I-4933	C.M. 1	423
Commission of the European Communities v Italian Republic	22/87	02.02.1989	[1989] 143	E. 3	964
Commission of the European Communities v Italian Republic	91/81	08.06.1982	[1982] 2133	E. 8	994
Commission of the European Communities v Italian Republic	235/84	10.07.1986	[1986] 2291	E. 11	1038
Commission of the European Communities v Italian Republic	C-59/01	25.02.2003	[2003] I-1759	I. 25	1189
Commission of the European Communities v Kingdom of Belgium	C-503/99	04.07.2002	[2002] I-4809	C.M. 1	429
Commission of the European Communities v Kingdom of Belgium	237/84	15.04.1986	[1986] 1247	E. 11	1034
Commission of the European Communities v Kingdom of Denmark	252/83	04.12.1986	[1986] 3713	I. 3	1059
Commission of the European Communities v Kingdom of Sweden	C-478/99	07.05.2002	[2002] I-4147	C.P. 9	838
Commission of the European Communities v Portuguese Republic	C-367/98	04.07.2002	[2002] I-4731	C.M. 1	423
Commission of the European Communities v United Kingdom of Great Britain and Northern Ireland	C-300/95	29.05.1997	[1997] I-2649	C.P. 2	799
Commission of the European Communities v United Kingdom of Great Britain and Northern Ireland	C-383/92	08.06.1994	[1994] I-2479	E. 8	989
Commune de Hillegom v Hillenius, C.	110/84	11.12.1985	[1985] 3947	B. 41	202
Conradsen, P. A/S v Ministeriet for Skatter og Afgifter	161/78	27.06.1979	[1979] 2221	C. 4	497
Coöperatieve Rabobank "Vecht en Plassengebied" BA v Minderhoud, E. A., liquidator of Mediasafe BV	C-104/96	16.12.1997	[1997] I-7211	C. 1	451
Crailsheimer Volksbank eG v Conrads, K., Schulzke F. and Schulzke-Lösche, P.	C-229/04	25.10.2005	[2005] I-9273	C.P. 3	805, 808
Criminal proceedings against Aldo Bordessa and Vicente Marí Mellado and Concepción Barbero Maestre	C-358/93 C-416/93	23.02.1995	[1995] I-361	C.M. 1	427, 430

Name	Case number	Date	ECR	Reproduced in	Page
Criminal proceedings against André Ambry	C-410/96	01.12.1998	[1998] I-7875	B. 32 I. 25 C.M. 1	175 1174 426
Criminal proceedings against Berlusconi, S., Adelchi, S. and Dell'Utri, M. and others	C-387/02 C-391/02 C-403/02	03.05.2005	[2005] I-3565	C. 1	450
Criminal proceedings against Italo Bullo and Francesco Bonivento	166/85	07.04.1987	[1987] 1583	B. 41	176
Criminal proceedings against Jean Verdonck, Ronald Everaert and Edith de Baedts	C-28/99	03.05.2001	[2001] I-3399	S. 24	1545
Criminal proceedings against Lucas Emilio Sanz de Lera, Raimundo Díaz Jiménez and Figen Kapanoglu	C-163/94 C-165/94 C-250/94	14.12.1995	[1995] I-4821	C.M. 1	426, 430
Criminal proceedings against Massimo Romanelli and Paolo Romanelli	C-366/97	11.02.1999	[1999] I-855	B. 32	191
Criminal proceedings against Patrice Di Pinto	C-361/89	14.03.1991	[1991] I-1189	C.P. 3	806
Criminal proceedings against R. Lambert	308/86	14.07.1988	[1988] 4369	C.M. 1	428
Criminal proceedings against Rafael Ruiz Bernáldez	C-129/94	28.03.1996	[1996] I-1829	I. 2 I. 11	1056 1109
Criminal proceedings against X	C-373/90	16.01.1992	[1992] I-131	C.P. 1	792
Cura Anlagen GmbH v Auto Service Leasing GmbH (ASL)	C-451/99	21.03.2002	[2002] I-3193	I. 2	1052
Danmarks Aktive Handelsrejsende, acting on behalf of Carina Mosbæk v Lønmodtagernes Garantifond	C-117/96	17.09.1997	[1997] I-5017	E. 3	966
Dansk Metalarbejderforbund acting on behalf of John Lauge and others v Lønmodtagernes Garantifond	C-250/97	17.12.1998	[1998] I-8737	E. 8	993
Dansk Metalarbejderforbund and Specialarbejderforbundet i Danmark v Nielsen, H. & Søn, Maskinfabrik A/S. in liquidation	284/83	12.02.1985	[1985] 553	E. 8	994
DE + ES Bauunternehmung GmbH v Finanzamt Bergheim	C-275/97	14.09.1999	[1999] I-5331	C. 4	497
Delahaye, J. M., née Delahaye v Ministre de la Fonction publique et de la Réforme administrative	C-425/02	11.11.2004	[2004] I-10823	E. 11	1030
Demouche, M. and others v Fonds de garantie automobile and Bureau central français	152/83	06.10.1987	[1987] 3833	I. 2	1052
Diamantis, D. v Elliniko Dimosio (Greek State) and Organismos Ikonomikis Anasygkrotisis Epicheiriseon AE (OAE)	C-373/97	23.03.2000	[2000] I-1705	C. 2	467
Dr. Sophie Redmond Stichting v Bartol, H. and others	C-29/91	19.05.1992	[1992] I-3189	E. 11	1026

Name	Case number	Date	ECR	Reproduced in	Page
d'Urso. Adriana Ventadori, G. and others v Ercole Marelli Elettromeccanica Generale SpA and others	C-362/89	25.07.1991	[1991] I-4105	E. 11	1032, 1035
EasyCar (UK) Ltd v Office of Fair Trading	C-336/03	10.03.2005	[2005] I-1947	C.P. 11	852
ED Srl v Italo Fenocchio ECR	C-412/97	22.06.1999	[1999] I-3845	C.M. 1	424
European Information Technology Observatory, Europäische Wirtschaftliche Interessenvereinigung	C-402/96	18.12.1997	[1997] I-7515	C. 8	554
Europièces SA v Sanders, W. and Automotive Industries Holding Company SA	C-399/96	12.11.1998	[1998] I-6965	E. 11	1031, 1034, 1035
Evans, S. S. v The Secretary of State for the Environment, Transport and the Regions and The Motor Insurers' Bureau	C-63/01	04.12.2003	[2003] I-14447	I. 11	1107
Everson, G. and Barrass, T.J. v Secretary of State for Trade and Industry and Bell Lines Ltd	C-198/98	16.12.1999	[1999] I-8903	E. 3	967
Faccini Dori, P. v Recreb Srl	C-91/92	14.07.1994	[1994] I-3325	C.P. 3	805, 806, 809, 810
Federal Republic of Germany v European Parliament and Council of the European Union	C-233/94	13.05.1997	[1997] I-2405	B. 22	51, 52
Foreningen af Arbejdsledere i Danmark v A/S Danmols Inventar, in liquidation	105/84	11.07.1985	[1985] 2639	E. 11	1027, 1029, 1033
Foreningen af Arbejdsledere i Danmark v Daddy's Dance Hall A/S	324/86	10.02.1988	[1988] 739	E. 11	1027, 1033
Försäkringsaktiebolaget Skandia (publ).	C-241/97	20.04.1999	[1999] I-1879	I. 3 I. 33	1078 1289
Fournier, A. and others v Van Werven, V., Bureau central français and others	C-73/89	12.11.1992	[1992] I-5621	I. 2	1055
Francisco Hernández Vidal SA v Gómez Pérez, P., Gómez Pérez, M. and Contratas y Limpiezas SL (C-127/96), Santner, F. v Hoechst AG (C-229/96), Gómez Montaña, M. v Claro Sol SA and Red Nacional de Ferrocarriles Españoles (Renfe) (C-74/97)	C-127/96 C-229/96 C-74/97	10.12.1998	[1998] I-8179	E. 11	1025
Francovich, A. and Bonifaci, D. and others v Italian Republic	C-6/90 C-9/90	19.11.1991	[1991] I-5357	E. 3	963
Gambetta Auto SA v Bureau Central Français and Fonds de Garantie Automobile	344/82	09.02.1984	[1984] 591	I. 2	1053
García, J. and others v Mutuelle de Prévoyance Sociale d'Aquitaine and others	C-238/94	26.03.1996	[1996] I-1673	I. 25	1180
Gómez Montaña, M. v Claro Sol SA and Red Nacional de Ferrocarriles Españoles (Renfe)	C-74/97	10.12.1998	[1998] I-8179	E. 11	1025
González Sánchez, M.V. v Medicina Asturiana SA	C-183/00	25.04.2002	[2002] I-3901	C.P. 2	801

Name	Case number	Date	ECR	Reproduced in	Page
Grøngaard, K. and Bang, A.	C-384/02	22.11.2005	[2005] I-09939	S. 24	1545
Güney-Görres, N. and Demir, G. v Securicor Aviation (Germany) Ltd and Kötter Aviation Security GmbH & Co. KG	C-232/04 C-233/04	15.12.2005	[2005] I-11237	E. 11	1024
Henke A. v Gemeinde Schierke and Verwaltungsgemeinschaft Brocken	C-298/94	15.10.1996	[1996] I-4989	E. 11	1025
Heininger, G. et Heininger, H. v Bayerische Hypo- und Vereinsbank AG	C-481/99	13.12.2001	[2001] I-9945	C.P. 3	803, 809
Henning Veedfald v Århus Amtskommune	C-203/99	10.05.2001	[2001] I-3569	C.P. 2	799, 800
Industriebond FNV and Federatie Nederlandse Vakbeweging (FNV) v The Netherlands State	179/83	07.02.1985	[1985] 511	E. 11	1036
Istituto nazionale della previdenza sociale (INPS) v Barsotti, A. and others	C-19/01 C-50/01 C-84/01	04.03.2004	[2004] I-2005	E. 3	967
Jules Dethier Équipement SA v Dassy, J. and Sovam SPRL	C-319/94	12.03.1998	[1998] I-1061	E. 11	1034, 1035
Junk, I. v Kühnel, W.	C-188/03	27.01.2005	[2005] I-885	E. 8	992
Kamer van Koophandel en Fabrieken voor Amsterdam v Inspire Art Ltd	C-167/01	30.09.2003	[2003] I-10155	C. 2 C. 9	457 564
Karella M. and Karellas N. v Minister for Industry, Energy and Technology and Organismos Anasygkrotiseos Epicheiriseon AE	C-19/90 C-20/90	30.05.1991	[1991] I-2691	C. 2	469
Katsikas, G. v Konstantinidis, A. and Skreb, U. and Schroll, G. v PCO Stauereibetrieb Paetz & Co. Nachfolger GmbH	C-132/91 C-138/91 C-139/91	16.12.1992	[1992] I-6577	E. 11	1031, 1038
Kefalaio, E. v Anaptyxis, Y.	C-28/03	16.09.2004	[2004] I-8533	I. 33	1072, 1075, 1271
Kefalas, A. and others v Dimosio Elliniko (Greek State) and Organismos Oikonomikis Anasygkrotisis Epicheiriseon AE (OAE)	C-367/96	12.05.1998	[1998] I-2843	C. 2	468
Kerafina-Keramische-und Finanz Holding AG and Vioktimatiki AEVE v Hellenic Republic and Organismos Oikonomikis Anasygkrotissis Epicheirisseon AE	C-134/91 C-135/91	12.11.1992	[1992] I-5699	C. 2	
Kingdom of Spain v Commission of the European Communities	C-342/96	29.04.1999	[1999] I-2459	E. 3	963
Konle, K. v Republik Österreich	C-302/97	01.06.1999	[1999] I-3099	C.M. 1	425
Konsumentombudsmannen (KO) v De Agostini (Svenska) Förlag AB (C-34/95) and TV-Shop i Sverige AB (C-35/95 and C-36/95)	C-34/95 C-35/95 C-36/95	02.12.1999	[1997] I-3843	C.P. 1	794
Kvaerner plc v Staatssecretaris van Financiën	C-191/99	14.06.2001	[2001] I-4447	I. 15	1122

Alphabetical List of Cases 1789

Name	Case number	Date	ECR	Reproduced in	Page
Landsorganisationen i Danmark for Tjenerforbundet i Danmark v Ny Mølle Kro	287/86	17.12.1987	[1987] 5465	E. 11	1027, 1033
Ledernes Hovedorganisation, acting for Ole Rygaard v Dansk Arbejdsgiverforening, acting for Strø Mølle Akustik A/S	C-48/94	19.09.1995	[1995] I-2745	E. 11	1026
Les Assurances du Crédit SA and Compagnie Belge d'Assurance Crédit SA v Council of the European Communities and Commission of the European Communities	C-63/89	18.04.1991	[1991] I-1799	I. 3 I. 13	1059 1114
Luisi, G. and Carbone, G. v Ministero del Tesoro	286/82 26/83	31.01.1984	[1984] 377	C.M. 1	428
Manninen, P.	C-319/02	07.09.2004	[2004] I-7477	C.M. 2	423
Markopoulos, P. and others v Anaptyxis, Y. and Elegkton, S. O.	C-255/01	07.10.2004	[2004] I-9077	C. 30	767
Marleasing SA v La Comercial Internacional de Alimentacion SA	C-106/89	13.11.1990	[1990] I-4135	C. 1	452
Maso, F. and others and Gazzetta, G. and others v Istituto nazionale della previdenza sociale (INPS) and Repubblica italiana	C-373/95	10.07.1997	[1997] I-4051	E. 3	963
Mau, K. v Bundesanstalt für Arbeit	C-160/01	15.05.2003	[2003] I-4791	E. 3	967
Mayeur, D. v Association Promotion de l'information messine (APIM)	C-175/99	26.09.2000	[2000] I-7755	E. 11	1024
Mendes Ferreira, V. M. and Delgado Correia Ferreira M. C. v Companhia de Seguros Mundial Confiança SA	C-348/98	14.09.2000	[2000] I-6711	I. 11	1108, 1109, 1110
Merckx, A. and Neuhuys, P. v Ford Motors Company Belgium SA	C-171/94 C-172/94	07.03.1996	[1996] I-1253	E. 11	1026, 1031, 1034
O'Byrne, D. v Sanofi Pasteur MSD Ltd and Sanofi Pasteur SA	C-127/04	09.02.2006	[2006] I-1313	C.P. 2	800
Océano Grupo Editorial SA v Murciano Quintero, R. (C-240/98) and Salvat Editores SA v Sánchez Alcón Prades, J. M. (C-241/98), Copano Badillo, J. L. (C-242/98), Berroane, M. (C-243/98) and Viñas Feliú, E. (C-244/98)	C-240/98 to C-244/98	27.06.2000	[2000] I-4941	C.P. 9	835
Olaso Valero, J. V. v Fondo de Garantía Salarial (Fogasa)	C-520/03	16.12.2004	[2004] I-12065	E. 3	967
Oy Liikenne Ab v Liskojärvi, P. and Juntunen, P.	C-172/99	25.01.2001	[2001] I-745	E. 11	1024
Pafitis, P. and others v Trapeza Kentrikis Ellados A.E. and others	C-441/93	12.03.1996	[1996] I-1347	C. 2	468
Parodi, Société civile immobilière v Banque H. Albert de Bary et Cie	C-222/95	09.07.1997	[1997] I-3899	B. 41	176

Name	Case number	Date	ECR	Reproduced in	Page
P. Bork International A/S, in liquidation v Foreningen af Arbejdsledere I Danmark, acting on behalf of Birger E. Petersen and Jens E. Olsen and others v Junckers Industrier A/S	101/87	15.06.1988	[1988] 3057	E. 11	1027, 1032
Pippig Augenoptik GmbH & Co. KG v Hartlauer Handelsgesellschaft mbH en Verlassenschaft nach dem verstorbenen Franz Josef Hartlauer	C-44/01	08.04.2003	[2003] I-3095	C.P. 1	791, 795
QDQ Media SA v Lecha, A. O.	C-235/03	10.03.2005	[2005] I-1937	E. 10	1016
Ramrath, C. v Ministre de la Justice and l'Institut des réviseurs d'entreprises	C-106/91	20.05.1992	[1992] I-3351	C. 30	757
R. Comité Central d'Entreprise de la Société Générale des Grandes Sources and others v Commission of the European Communities	T-96/92	27.04.1995	[1995] II-1213	E. 11	1022
Regina v Ernest George Thompson, Brian Albert Johnson and Colin Alex Norman Woodiwiss	7/78	23.11.1978	[1978] 2247	C.M. 1	428
Riksskatteverket v Soghra Gharehveran	C-441/99	18.10.2001	[2001] I-7687	E. 3	972
Rockfon A/S v Specialarbejderforbundet i Danmark	C-449/93	07.12.1995	[1995] I-4291	E. 8	991
Rotsart de Hertaing, C. v J. Benoidt SA in liquidation and IGC Housing Service SA	C-305/94	14.11.1996	[1996] I-5927	E. 11	1031
Safir, J. v Skattemyndigheten i Dalarnas Län, formerly Skattemyndigheten i Kopparbergs Län	C-118/96	28.04.1998	[1998] I-1897	C.M. 1	430
Sánchez Hidalgo, F. and others v Asociación de Servicios Aser and Sociedad Cooperativa Minerva	C-173/96	10.12.1998	[1998] I-8237	E. 11	1025
Sandoz GmbH v Finanzlandesdirektion für Wien, Niederösterreich und Burgenland	C-439/97	14.10.1999	[1999] I-7041	C.M. 1	425
Santner, F. v Hoechst AG	C-229/96	10.12.1998	[1998] I-8179	E. 11	1025
Schmidt, C. v Spar- und Leihkasse der früheren Ämter Bordesholm, Kiel und Cronshagen	C-392/92	14.04.1994	[1994] I-1311	E. 11	1026
Schulte, E. and Schulte, W. v Deutsche Bausparkasse Badenia AG	C-350/03	25.10.2005	[2005] I-9215	C.P. 3	807, 808, 809
Sevic Systems AG	C-411/03	13.12.2005	[2005] I-10805	C. 3	476
Siemens AG v Nold, H.	C-42/95	19.11.1996	[1996] I-6017	C. 2	471
Siemens AG v VIPA Gesellschaft für Visualisierung und Prozeßautomatisierung mbH	C-59/05	23.02.2006	[2006] I-2147	C.P. 1	791
Skov Æg v Bilka Lavprisvarehus A/S and Bilka Lavprisvarehus A/S v Jette Mikkelsen, J. and Due Nielsen, M.	C-402/03	10.01.2006	[2006] I-199	C.P. 2	798

Name	Case number	Date	ECR	Reproduced in	Page
Sonnen-Lütte, P. P. C. and Mörkens, C. v Bundesrepublik Deutschland	C-222/02	12.10.2004	[2004] I-9425	B. 22 B. 41	46 175
Spano, L. and others v Fiat Geotech SpA and Fiat Hitachi Excavators SpA	C-472/93	07.12.1995	[1995] I-4321	E. 11	1035
Spijkers, J. M. A. v Gebroeders Benedik Abattoir CV et Alfred Benedik en Zonen BV	24/85	18.03.1986	[1986] 1119	E. 11	1027
Staatssecretaris van Financiën v B.G.M. Verkooijen	C-35/98	06.06.2000	[2000] I-4071	C.M. 1	424
Süzen, A. v Zehnacker Gebäudereinigung GmbH Krankenhausservice	C-13/95	11.03.1997	[1997] I-1259	E. 11	1028
Svensson, P. et Gustavsson, L. v Ministre du Logement et de l'Urbanisme	C-484/93	14.11.1995	[1995] I-3955	C.M. 1	427
Syndesmos Melon tis Eleftheras Evangelikis Ekklissias and others v Greek State and others	C-381/89	24.03.1992	[1992] I-2111	C. 2	469
Temco Service Industries SA v Imzilyen, S. and others	C-51/00	24.01.2002	[2002] I-969	E. 11	1024, 1030
Testa, A. and Lazzeri, L. v Commissione Nazionale per la Società e la Borsa (Consob)	C-356/00	21.11.2002	[2002] I-10797	S. 14	1659
The Administrative Board of the Bedrijfsvereniging voor de Metaalindustrie en de Electrotechnische Industrie	135/83	07.02.1985	[1985] 469	E. 11	1033, 1036
The Queen v H. M. Treasury and Commissioners of Inland Revenue, ex parte Daily Mail and General Trust plc	81/87	27.09.1988	[1988] 5483	C. 2	458
Tomberger, W. v Gebrüder von der Wettern GmbH	C-234/94	27.06.1996	[1996] I-3133	C. 4	502
Toshiba Europe GmbH v Katun Germany GmbH	C-112/99	25.10.2001	[2001] I-7945	C.P. 1	792
Travel Vac SL v José Antelm Sanchis, M.	C-423/97	22.04.1999	[1999] I-2195	C.P. 3	805, 807, 809
Trummer, M. and Mayer P.	C-222/97	16.03.1999	[1999] I-1661	C.M. 1	424
Ubbink Isolatie BV v Dak- en Wandtechniek BV	136/87	20.09.1988	[1988] 4665	C. 1	451
Überseering BV v Nordic Construction Company Baumanagement GmbH (NCC)	C-208/00	05.11.2002	[2002] I-9919	C. 2	457
Ufficio Henry van Ameyde S.r.l. v Ufficio centrale italiano di assistenza assicurativa automobilisti in circolazione internazionale (UCI) S.r.l.	90/76	09.06.1977	[1977] 1091	I. 2	1053
Verband deutscher Daihatsu-Händler eV v Daihatsu Deutschland GmbH	C-97/96	04.12.1997	[1997] I-6843	C. 1	450
Wagner Miret, T. v Fondo de Garantía Salarial	C-334/92	16.12.1993	[1993] I-6911	E. 3	965

Name	Case number	Date	ECR	Reproduced in	Page
Walcher, M. v Bundesamt für Soziales und Behindertenwesen Steiermark	C-201/01	11.09.2003	[2003] I-8827	E. 3	969
Watson Rask, A. and Christensen, K. v Iss Kantineservice A/S	C-209/91	12.11.1992	[1992] I-5755	E. 11	1026, 1032
Wendelboe, K. and others v L.J. Music ApS., in liquidation	19/83	07.02.1985	[1985] 457	E. 11	1033
Westdeutsche Landesbank Girozentrale v Friedrich Stefan and Republik Österreich	C-464/98	11.01.2001	[2001] I-173	C.M. 1	424
Ziemann, H. v Ziemann Sicherheit GmbH and Horst Bohn Sicherheitsdienst	C-247/96	10.12.1998	[1998] I-8237	E. 11	1025

CHRONOLOGICAL LIST OF CASES

Date	Case number	Name	ECR	Reproduced in	Page
09.06.1977	90/76	Ufficio Henry van Ameyde S.r.l. v Ufficio centrale italiano di assistenza assicurativa automobilisti in circolazione internazionale (UCI) S.r.l.	[1977] 1091	I. 2	1053
23.11.1978	7/78	Regina v Ernest George Thompson, Brian Albert Johnson and Colin Alex Norman Woodiwiss	[1978] 2247	C.M. 1	428
27.06.1979	161/78	Conradsen, P. A/S v Ministeriet for Skatter og Afgifter	[1979] 2221	C. 4	497
08.06.1982	91/81	Commission of the European Communities v Italian Republic	[1982] 2133	E. 8	994
01.03.1983	300/81	Commission of the European Communities v Italian Republic	[1983] 449	B. 41	176
31.01.1984	286/82 26/83	Luisi, G. and Carbone, G. v Ministero del Tesoro	[1984] 377	C.M. 1	428
09.02.1984	344/82	Gambetta Auto SA v Bureau Central Français and Fonds de Garantie Automobile	[1984] 591	I. 2	1053
09.02.1984	64/83	Bureau Central Français v Fonds de Garantie Automobile and others	[1984] 689	I. 2	1056
21.06.1984	116/83	Bureau Belge des Assureurs Automobiles Asbl v Fantozzi, A. and SA Les Assurances populaires	[1984] 2481	I. 2	1056
07.02.1985	19/83	Wendelboe, K. and others v L.J. Music ApS., in liquidation	[1985] 457	E. 11	1033
07.02.1985	135/83	The Administrative Board of the Bedrijfsvereniging voor de Metaalindustrie en de Electrotechnische Industrie	[1985] 469	E. 11	1033, 1036
07.02.1985	179/83	Industriebond FNV and Federatie Nederlandse Vakbeweging (FNV) v The Netherlands State	[1985] 511	E. 11	1036
07.02.1985	186/83	Botzen, A. and others v Rotterdamsche Droogdok Maatschappij BV	[1985] 519	E. 11	1033
12.02.1985	284/83	Dansk Metalarbejderforbund and Specialarbejderforbundet i Danmark v Nielsen, H. & Søn, Maskinfabrik A/S in liquidation	[1985] 553	E. 8	994
11.07.1985	105/84	Foreningen af Arbejdsledere i Danmark v A/S Danmols Inventar, in liquidation	[1985] 2639	E. 11	1027, 1029, 1033

Date	Case Number	Name	OJ	Reproduced in	Page
11.12.1985	110/84	Commune de Hillegom v Hillenius, C.	[1985] 3947	B. 41	202
18.03.1986	24/85	Spijkers, J. M. A. v Gebroeders Benedik Abattoir CV et Alfred Benedik en Zonen BV	[1986] 1119	E. 11	1027
15.04.1986	237/84	Commission of the European Communities v Kingdom of Belgium	[1986] 1247	E. 11	1034
24.06.1986	157/85	Brugnoni, L. and Ruffinengo R. v. Cassa di risparmio di Genova e Imperia	[1986] 2013	C.M. 1	428
10.07.1986	235/84	Commission of the European Communities v Italian Republic	[1986] 2291	E. 11	1038
04.12.1986	205/84	Commission of the European Communities v Federal Republic of Germany	[1986] 3755	I. 3 I. 8 I. 33	1059 1098 1255
04.12.1986	220/83	Commission of the European Communities v French Republic	[1986] 3663	I. 8	1098
04.12.1986	206/84	Commission of the European Communities v Ireland	[1986] 3817	I. 3 I. 8 I. 33	1059 1098 1255
04.12.1986	252/83	Commission of the European Communities v Kingdom of Denmark	[1986] 3713	I. 3	1059
07.04.1987	166/85	Criminal proceedings against Italo Bullo and Francesco Bonivento	[1987] 1583	B. 41	176
06.10.1987	152/83	Demouche, M. and others v Fonds de garantie automobile and Bureau central français	[1987] 3833	I. 2	1052
17.12.1987	287/86	Landsorganisationen i Danmark for Tjenerforbundet i Danmark v Ny Mølle Kro	[1987] 5465	E. 11	1027, 1033
10.02.1988	324/86	Foreningen af Arbejdsledere i Danmark v Daddy's Dance Hall A/S	[1988] 739	E. 11	1027, 1033
05.05.1988	144/87 145/87	Berg, H. and Busschers, J. T. M. v Besselsen, I. M.	[1988] 2559	E. 11	1027, 1032
15.06.1988	101/87	P. Bork International A/S, in liquidation v Foreningen af Arbejdsledere I Danmark, acting on behalf of Birger E. Petersen. and Jens E. Olsen and others v Junckers Industrier A/S	[1988] 3057	E. 11	1027, 1032
14.07.1988	308/86	Criminal proceedings against R. Lambert	[1988] 4369	C.M. 1	428
20.09.1988	136/87	Ubbink Isolatie BV v Dak- en Wandtechniek BV	[1988] 4665	C. 1	451
27.09.1988	81/87	The Queen v H. M. Treasury and Commissioners of Inland Revenue, ex parte Daily Mail and General Trust plc	[1988] 5483	C. 2	458
02.02.1989	22/87	Commission of the European Communities v Italian Republic	[1989] 143	E. 3	964
08.11.1990	53/88	Commission of the European Communities v Hellenic Republic	[1990] I-3917	E. 3	965

Date	Case number	Name	ECR	Reproduced in	Page
13.11.1990	C-106/89	Marleasing SA v La Comercial Internacional de Alimentacion SA	[1990] I-4135	C. 1	452
14.03.1991	C-361/89	Criminal proceedings against Patrice Di Pinto	[1991] I-1189	C.P. 3	806
18.04.1991	C-63/89	Les Assurances du Crédit SA and Compagnie Belge d'Assurance Crédit SA v Council of the European Communities and Commission of the European Communities	[1991] I-1799	I. 3 I. 13	1059 1114
30.05.1991	C-19/90 C-20/90	Karella M. and Karellas N. v Minister for Industry, Energy and Technology and Organismos Anasygkrotiseos Epicheiriseon AE	[1991] I-2691	C. 2	469
25.07.1991	C-362/89	d'Urso. Adriana Ventadori, G. and others v Ercole Marelli Elettromeccanica Generale SpA and others	[1991] I-4105	E. 11	1032, 1035
19.11.1991	C-6/90 C-9/90	Francovich, A. and Bonifaci, D. and others v Italian Republic	[1991] I-5357	E. 3	963
16.01.1992	C-373/90	Criminal proceedings against X	[1992] I-131	C.P. 1	792
24.03.1992	C-381/89	Syndesmos Melon tis Eleftheras Evangelikis Ekklissias and others v Greek State and others	[1992] I-2111	C. 2	469
19.05.1992	C-29/91	Dr. Sophie Redmond Stichting v Bartol, H. and others	[1992] I-3189	E. 11	1026
20.05.1992	C-106/91	Ramrath, C. v Ministre de la Justice and l'Institut des réviseurs d'entreprises	[1992] I-3351	C. 30	757
12.11.1992	C-73/89	Fournier, A. and others v Van Werven, V., Bureau central français and others	[1992] I-5621	I. 2	1055
12.11.1992	C-134/91 C-135/91	Kerafina-Keramische-und Finanz Holding AG and Vioktimatiki AEVE v Hellenic Republic and Organismos Oikonomikis Anasygkrotissis Epicheirisseon AE	[1992] I-5699	C. 2	469
12.11.1992	C-209/91	Watson Rask, A. and Christensen, K. v Iss Kantineservice A/S	[1992] I-5755	E. 11	1026, 1032
16.12.1992	C-132/91 C-138/91 C-139/91	Katsikas, G. v Konstantinidis, A. and Skreb, U. and Schroll, G. v PCO Stauereibetrieb Paetz & Co. Nachfolger GmbH	[1992] I-6577	E. 11	1031, 1038
16.12.1993	C-334/92	Wagner Miret, T. v Fondo de Garantía Salarial	[1993] I-6911	E. 3	965
14.04.1994	C-392/92	Schmidt, C. v Spar- und Leihkasse der früheren Ämter Bordesholm, Kiel und Cronshagen	[1994] I-1311	E. 11	1026
08.06.1994	C-383/92	Commission of the European Communities v United Kingdom of Great Britain and Northern Ireland	[1994] I-2479	E. 8	989
14.07.1994	C-91/92	Faccini Dori, P. v Recreb Srl	[1994] I-3325	C.P. 3	805, 806, 809, 810

Date	Case number	Name	ECR	Reproduced in	Page
23.02.1995	C-358/93 C-416/93	Criminal proceedings against Aldo Bordessa and Vicente Marí Mellado and Concepción Barbero Maestre	[1995] I-361	C.M. 1	427, 430
27.04.1995	T-96/92	R. Comité Central d'Entreprise de la Société Générale des Grandes Sources and others v Commission of the European Communities	[1995] II-1213	E. 11	1022
27.04.1995	T-12/93	Comité Central d'Entreprise de la Société Anonyme Vittel and Comité d'Etablissement de Pierval and Fédération Générale Agroalimentaire v Commission of the European Communities	[1995] II-1247	E. 11	1028, 1037
10.05.1995	C-384/93	Alpine Investments BV v Minister van Financiën	[1995] I-1141	C.P. 3	803
19.09.1995	C-48/94	Ledernes Hovedorganisation, acting for Ole Rygaard v Dansk Arbejdsgiverforening, acting for Strø Mølle Akustik A/S	[1995] I-2745	E. 11	1026
14.11.1995	C-484/93	Svensson, P. et Gustavsson, L. v Ministre du Logement et de l'Urbanisme	[1995] I-3955	C.M. 1	427
07.12.1995	C-449/93	Rockfon A/S v Specialarbejderforbundet i Danmark	[1995] I-4291	E. 8	991
07.12.1995	C-472/93	Spano, L. and others v Fiat Geotech SpA and Fiat Hitachi Excavators SpA	[1995] I-4321	E. 11	1035
14.12.1995	C-163/94 C-165/94 C-250/94	Criminal proceedings against Lucas Emilio Sanz de Lera, Raimundo Díaz Jiménez and Figen Kapanoglu	[1995] I-4821	C.M. 1	426, 430
07.03.1996	C-171/94 C-172/94	Merckx, A. and Neuhuys, P. v Ford Motor Company Belgium SA	[1996] I-1253	E. 11	1026, 1031, 1034
12.03.1996	C-441/93	Pafitis, P. and others v Trapeza Kentrikis Ellados A.E. and others	[1996] I-1347	C. 2	468
26.03.1996	C-238/94	García, J. and others v Mutuelle de Prévoyance Sociale d'Aquitaine and others	[1996] I-1673	I. 25	1180
28.03.1996	C-129/94	Criminal proceedings against Rafael Ruiz Bernáldez	[1996] I-1829	I. 2 I. 11	1056 1109
27.06.1996	C-234/94	Tomberger, W. v Gebrüder von der Wettern GmbH	[1996] I-3133	C. 4	502
15.10.1996	C-298/94	Henke A. v Gemeinde Schierke and Verwaltungsgemeinschaft Brocken	[1996] I-4989	E. 11	1025
14.11.1996	C-305/94	Rotsart de Hertaing, C. v J. Benoidt SA in liquidation and IGC Housing Service SA	[1996] I-5927	E. 11	1031
19.11.1996	C-42/95	Siemens AG v Nold, H.	[1996] I-6017	C. 2	471
11.03.1997	C-13/95	Süzen, A. v Zehnacker Gebäudereinigung GmbH Krankenhausservice	[1997] I-1259	E. 11	1028
17.04.1997	C-336/95	Burdalo Trevejo, P. and others v Fondo Garantía Salarial	[1997] I-2115	E. 11	1038

Date	Case number	Name	ECR	Reproduced in	Page
13.05.1997	C-233/94	Federal Republic of Germany v European Parliament and Council of the European Union	[1997] I-2405	B. 22	51, 52
29.05.1997	C-300/95	Commission of the European Communities v United Kingdom of Great Britain and Northern Ireland	[1997] I-2649	C.P. 2	799
09.07.1997	C-222/95	Parodi, Société civile immobilière v Banque H. Albert de Bary et Cie	[1997] I-3899	B. 41	176
10.07.1997	C-94/95 C-95/95	Bonifaci, D. and others (C-94/95) and Berto, W. and others (C-95/95) v Istituto nazionale della previdenza sociale (INPS)	[1997] I-3969	E. 3	968
10.07.1997	C-373/95	Maso, F. and others and Gazzetta, G. and others v Istituto nazionale della previdenza sociale (INPS) and Repubblica italiana	[1997] I-4051	E. 3	963
17.09.1997	C-117/96	Danmarks Aktive Handelsrejsende, acting on behalf of Carina Mosbæk v Lønmodtagernes Garantifond	[1997] I-5017	E. 3	966
04.12.1997	C-97/96	Verband deutscher Daihatsu-Händler eV v Daihatsu Deutschland GmbH	[1997] I-6843	C. 1	450
16.12.1997	C-104/96	Coöperatieve Rabobank "Vecht en Plassengebied" BA v Minderhoud, E. A., liquidator of Mediasafe BV	[1997] I-7211	C. 1	451
18.12.1997	C-402/96	European Information Technology Observatory, Europäische Wirtschaftliche Interessenvereinigung	[1997] I-7515	C. 8	554
12.03.1998	C-319/94	Jules Dethier Équipement SA v Dassy, J. and Sovam SPRL	[1998] I-1061	E. 11	1034, 1035
17.03.1998	C-45/96	Bayerische Hypotheken- und Wechselbank AG v Edgard Dietzinger	[1998] I-1199	C.P. 3	803, 806
28.04.1998	C-118/96	Safir, J. v Skattemyndigheten i Dalarnas Län, formerly Skattemyndigheten i Kopparbergs Län	[1998] I-1897	C.M. 1	430
12.05.1998	C-367/96	Kefalas, A. and others v Dimosio Elliniko (Greek State) and Organismos Oikonomikis Anasygkrotisis Epicheiriseon AE (OAE)	[1998] I-2843	C. 2	468
14.07.1998	C-125/97	A.G.R. Regeling v Bestuur van de Bedrijfsvereniging voor de Metaalnijverheid	[1998] I-4493	E. 3	970
16.07.1998	C-235/95	AGS Assedic Pas-de-Calais v Dumon, F. and Froment, liquidator and representative of Établissements Pierre Gilson	[1998] I-4531	E. 3	969
12.11.1998	C-399/96	Europièces SA v Sanders, W. and Automotive Industries Holding Company SA	[1998] I-6965	E. 11	1031, 1034, 1035
01.12.1998	C-410/96	Criminal proceedings against André Ambry	[1998] I-7875	B. 41 I. 25 C.M. 1	175 1174 426

Date	Case number	Name	ECR	Reproduced in	Page
10.12.1998	C-127/96 C-229/96 C-74/97	Francisco Hernández Vidal SA v Gómez Pérez, P., Gómez Pérez, M. and Contratas y Limpiezas SL (C-127/96), Santner, F. v Hoechst AG (C-229/96), Gómez Montaña, M. v Claro Sol SA and Red Nacional de Ferrocarriles Españoles (Renfe) (C-74/97)	[1998] I-8179	E. 11	1025
10.12.1998	C-173/96 C-247/96	Sánchez Hidalgo, F. and others v Asociación de Servicios Aser and Sociedad Cooperativa Minerva (C-173/96), Ziemann, H. v Ziemann Sicherheit GmbH and Horst Bohn Sicherheitsdienst (C-247/96)	[1998] I-8237	E. 11	1025
17.12.1998	C-250/97	Dansk Metalarbejderforbund acting on behalf of John Lauge and others v Lønmodtagernes Garantifond	[1998] I-8737	E. 8	993
11.02.1999	C-366/97	Criminal proceedings against Massimo Romanelli and Paolo Romanelli	[1999] I-855	B. 41	191
25.02.1999	C-349/96	Card Protection Plan Ltd (CPP) v Commissioners of Customs & Excise	[1999] I-973	I. 3	1091
09.03.1999	C-212/97	Centros Ltd v Erhvervs- og Selskabsstyrelsen	[1999] I-1459	C. 2	458
16.03.1999	C-222/97	Trummer, M. and Mayer P.	[1999] I-1661	C.M. 1	424
20.04.1999	C-241/97	Försäkringsaktiebolaget Skandia (publ)	[1999] I-1879	I. 3 I. 33	1078 1289
22.04.1999	C-423/97	Travel Vac SL v José Antelm Sanchis, M.	[1999] I-2195	C.P. 3	805, 807, 809
29.04.1999	C-342/96	Kingdom of Spain v Commission of the European Communities	[1999] I-2459	E. 3	963
01.06.1999	C-302/97	Konle, K. v Republik Österreich	[1999] I-3099	C.M. 1	425
22.06.1999	C-412/97	ED Srl v Italo Fenocchio ECR	[1999] I-3845	C.M. 1	424
14.09.1999	C-275/97	DE + ES Bauunternehmung GmbH v Finanzamt Bergheim	[1999] I-5331	C. 4	497
14.10.1999	C-439/97	Sandoz GmbH v Finanzlandesdirektion für Wien, Niederösterreich und Burgenland	[1999] I-7041	C.M. 1	425
02.12.1999	C-34/95 C-35/95 C-36/95	Konsumentombudsmannen (KO) v De Agostini (Svenska) Förlag AB (C-34/95) and TV-Shop i Sverige AB (C-35/95 and C-36/95)	[1997] I-3843	C.P. 1	794
02.12.1999	C-234/98	Allen, G. C. and others v Amalgamated Construction Co. Ltd.	[1999] I-8643	E. 11	1025
16.12.1999	C-198/98	Everson, G. and Barrass, T.J. v Secretary of State for Trade and Industry and Bell Lines Ltd	[1999] I-8903	E. 3	967
14.03.2000	C-54/99	Association Eglise de scientologie de Paris and Scientology International Reserves Trust v The Prime Minister	[2000] I-1335	C.M. 1	430

Date	Case number	Name	ECR	Reproduced in	Page
23.03.2000	C-373/97	Diamantis, D. v Elliniko Dimosio (Greek State) and Organismos Ikonomikis Anasygkrotisis Epicheiriseon AE (OAE)	[2000] I-1705	C. 2	467
23.03.2000	C-208/98	Berliner Kindl Brauerei AG v Siepert, A.	[2000] I-1741	C.P. 4	811
06.06.2000	C-35/98	Staatssecretaris van Financiën v B.G.M. Verkooijen	[2000] I-4071	C.M. 1	424
27.06.2000	C-240/98 to C-244/98	Océano Grupo Editorial SA v Murciano Quintero, R. (C-240/98) and Salvat Editores SA v Sánchez Alcón Prades, J. M. (C-241/98), Copano Badillo, J. L. (C-242/98), Berroane, M. (C-243/98) and Viñas Feliú, E. (C-244/98)	[2000] I-4941	C.P. 9	835
14.09.2000	C-343/98	Collino, R. and Chiappero, L. v Telecom Italia SpA	[2000] I-6659	E. 11	1025, 1031
14.09.2000	C-348/98	Mendes Ferreira, V. M. and Delgado Correia Ferreira M. C. v Companhia de Seguros Mundial Confiança SA	[2000] I-6711	I. 11	1108, 1109, 1110
21.09.2000	C-109/99	Association basco-béarnaise des opticiens indépendants v Préfet des Pyrénées-Atlantiques	[2000] I-7247	I. 3	1068
26.09.2000	C-175/99	Mayeur, D. v Association Promotion de l'information messine (APIM)	[2000] I-7755	E. 11	1024
11.01.2001	C-464/98	Westdeutsche Landesbank Girozentrale v Friedrich Stefan and Republik Österreich	[2001] I-173	C.M. 1	424
25.01.2001	C-172/99	Oy Liikenne Ab v Liskojärvi, P. and Juntunen, P.	[2001] I-745	E. 11	1024
29.03.2001	C-62/99	Betriebsrat der bofrost* Josef H. Boquoi Deutschland West GmbH & Co. KG v Bofrost* Josef H. Boquoi Deutschland West GmbH & Co. KG	[2001] I-2579	E. 5	981
03.05.2001	C-28/99	Criminal proceedings against Jean Verdonck, Ronald Everaert and Edith de Baedts	[2001] I-3399	S. 24	1545
10.05.2001	C-203/99	Henning Veedfald v Århus Amtskommune	[2001] I-3569	C.P. 2	799, 800
14.06.2001	C-191/99	Kvaerner plc v Staatssecretaris van Financiën	[2001] I-4447	I. 15	1122
18.10.2001	C-441/99	Riksskatteverket v Soghra Gharehveran	[2001] I-7687	E. 3	972
25.10.2001	C-112/99	Toshiba Europe GmbH v Katun Germany GmbH	[2001] I-7945	C.P. 1	792
22.11.2001	C-541/99 C-542/99	Cape Snc v Idealservice Srl (C-541/99) and Idealservice MN RE Sas v OMAI Srl (C-542/99)	[2001] I-9049	C.P. 9	838
13.12.2001	C-481/99	Heininger, G. et Heininger, H. v Bayerische Hypo- und Vereinsbank AG	[2001] I-9945	C.P. 3	803, 809

Date	Case number	Name	ECR	Reproduced in	Page
24.01.2002	C-51/00	Temco Service Industries SA v Imzilyen, S. and others	[2002] I-969	E. 11	1024, 1030
05.03.2002	C-386/00	Axa Royale Belge SA v Georges Ochoa and Stratégie Finance SPRL	[2002] I-2209	I. 33	1290
21.03.2002	C-451/99	Cura Anlagen GmbH v Auto Service Leasing GmbH (ASL)	[2002] I-3193	I. 2	1052
25.04.2002	C-52/00	Commission of the European Communities v French Republic	[2002] I-3827	C.P. 1	809, 810
25.04.2002	C-183/00	González Sánchez, M.V. v Medicina Asturiana SA	[2002] I-3901	C.P. 2	801
07.05.2002	C-478/99	Commission of the European Communities v Kingdom of Sweden	[2002] I-4147	C.P. 9	838
04.06.2002	C-164/00	Beckmann, K. v Dynamco Whichloe Macfarlane Ltd	[2002] I-4893	E. 11	1030
04.07.2002	C-483/99	Commission of the European Communities v French Republic	[2002] I-4781	C.M. 1	423
04.07.2002	C-367/98	Commission of the European Communities v Portuguese Republic	[2002] I-4731	C.M. 1	423
04.07.2002	C-503/99	Commission of the European Communities v Kingdom of Belgium	[2002] I-4809	C.M. 1	429
05.11.2002	C-208/00	Überseering BV v Nordic Construction Company Baumanagement GmbH (NCC)	[2002] I-9919	C. 2	457
21.11.2002	C-356/00	Testa, A. and Lazzeri, L. v Commissione Nazionale per la Società e la Borsa (Consob)	[2002] I-10797	S. 14	1659
21.11.2002	C-473/00	Cofidis SA v Fredout, J.-L.	[2002] I-10875	C.P. 9	835
12.12.2002	C-442/00	Caballero, A.R. v Fondo de Garantía Salarial (Fogasa)	[2002] I-11915	E. 3	965
07.01.2003	C-306/99	Banque internationale pour l'Afrique occidentale SA (BIAO) v Finanzamt für Großunternehmen in Hamburg	[2003] I-1	C. 4	495
25.02.2003	C-59/01	Commission of the European Communities v Italian Republic	[2003] I-1759	I. 25	1189
08.04.2003	C-44/01	Pippig Augenoptik GmbH & Co. KG v Hartlauer Handelsgesellschaft mbH en Verlassenschaft nach dem verstorbenen Franz Josef Hartlauer	[2003] I-3095	C.P. 1	791, 795
15.05.2003	C-160/01	Karen Mau v Bundesanstalt für Arbeit	[2003] I-4791	E. 3	967
11.09.2003	C-201/01	Maria Walcher v Bundesamt für Soziales und Behindertenwesen Steiermark	[2003] I-8827	E. 3	969
30.09.2003	C-167/01	Kamer van Koophandel en Fabrieken voor Amsterdam v Inspire Art Ltd	[2003] I-10155	C. 2 C. 9	457 564

Date	Case number	Name	ECR	Reproduced in	Page
04.12.2003	C-63/01	Samuel Sidney Evans v The Secretary of State for the Environment, Transport and the Regions and The Motor Insurers' Bureau	[2003] I-14447	I. 11	1107
04.03.2004	C-19/01 C-50/01 C-84/01	Istituto nazionale della previdenza sociale (INPS) v Alberto Barsotti and others	[2004] I-2005	E. 3	967
04.03.2004	C-264/02	Cofinoga Mérignac SA v Sylvain Sachithanathan	[2004] I-2157	C.P. 4	816
15.07.2004	C-349/01	Betriebsrat der Firma ADS Anker GmbH v ADS Anker GmbH	[2004] I-6803	E. 5	978
07.09.2004	C-319/02	Petri Manninen	[2004] I-7477	C.M. 2	423
07.09.2004	C-346/02	Commission of the European Communities v Grand Duchy of Luxemburg	[2004] I-7517	I. 25	1174
16.09.2004	C-28/03	Epikouriko kefalaio v Ypourgos Anaptyxis	[2004] I-8533	I. 33	1072, 1075, 1271
07.10.2004	C-255/01	Panagiotis Markopoulos and others v Ypourgos Anaptyxis and Soma Orkoton Elegkton	[2004] I-9077	C. 30	767
12.10.2004	C-222/02	Peter Paul, Cornelia Sonnen-Lütte and Christel Mörkens v Bundesrepublik Deutschland	[2004] I-9425	B. 22 B. 41	46 175
11.11.2004	C-425/02	Johanna Maria Delahaye, née Delahaye v Ministre de la Fonction publique et de la Réforme administrative	[2004] I-10823	E. 11	1030
16.12.2004	C-520/03	José Vicente Olaso Valero v Fondo de Garantía Salarial (Fogasa)	[2004] I-12065	E. 3	967
27.01.2005	C-188/03	Irmtraud Junk v Wolfgang Kühnel	[2005] I-885	E. 8	992
10.03.2005	C-235/03	QDQ Media SA v Alejandro Omedas Lecha	[2005] I-1937	E. 10	1016
10.03.2005	C-336/03	EasyCar (UK) Ltd v Office of Fair Trading	[2005] I-1947	C.P. 11	852
03.05.2005	C-387/02 C-391/02 C-403/02	Criminal proceedings against Silvio Berlusconi, Sergio Adelchi and Marcello Dell'Utri and others	[2005] I-3565	C. 1	450
26.05.2005	C-478/03	Celtec Ltd v John Astley and others	[2005] I-4389	E. 11	1030
02.06.2005	C-174/04	Commission of the European Communities v Italian Republic	[2005] I-4933	C.M. 2	423
30.06.2005	C-537/03	Katja Candolin, Jari-Antero Viljaniemi and Veli-Matti Paananen v Vahinkovakuutusosakeyhtiö Pohjola and Jarno Ruokoranta	[2005] I-5745	I. 2	1056
13.09.2005	C-176/03	Commission of the European Communities v Council of the European Union	[2005] I-07879	S. 24	1549
25.10.2005	C-229/04	Crailsheimer Volksbank eG v Klaus Conrads, Frank Schulzke and Petra Schulzke-Lösche	[2005] I-9273	C.P. 3	805, 808

Date	Case number	Name	ECR	Reproduced in	Page
25.10.2005	C-350/03	Elisabeth Schulte and Wolfgang Schulte v Deutsche Bausparkasse Badenia AG	[2005] I-9215	C.P. 3	807, 808, 809
22.11.2005	C-384/02	Knud Grøngaard and Allan Bang	[2005] I-09939	S. 24	1545
13.12.2005	C-411/03	Sevic Systems AG	[2005] I-10805	C. 3	476
15.12.2005	C-232/04 C-233/04	Nurten Güney-Görres and Gul Demir v Securicor Aviation (Germany) Ltd and Kötter Aviation Security GmbH & Co. KG	[2005] I-11237	E. 11	1024
10.01.2006	C-402/03	Skov Æg v Bilka Lavprisvarehus A/S and Bilka Lavprisvarehus A/S v Jette Mikkelsen and Michael Due Nielsen	[2006] I-199	C.P. 2	798
09.02.2006	C-127/04	Declan O'Byrne v Sanofi Pasteur MSD Ltd and Sanofi Pasteur SA	[2006] I-1313	C.P. 2	800
23.02.2006	C-59/05	Siemens AG v VIPA Gesellschaft für Visualisierung und Prozeßautomatisierung mbH	[2006] I-02147	C.P. 1	791

CORRELATION TABLE
EU-TREATY—TREATY OF AMSTERDAM

A. TREATY ON EUROPEAN UNION

Previous numbering	New numbering
Title I	Title I
Article A	Article 1
Article B	Article 2
Article C	Article 3
Article D	Article 4
Article E	Article 5
Article F	Article 6
Article F.1	Article 7
Title II	Title II
Article G	Article 8
Title III	Title III
Article H	Article 9
Title IV	Title IV
Article I	Article 10
Title V (***)	Title V
Article J.1	Article 11
Article J.2	Article 12
Article J.3	Article 13
Article J.4	Article 14
Article J.5	Article 15
Article J.6	Article 16
Article J.7	Article 17
Article J.8	Article 18
Article J.9	Article 19
Article J.10	Article 20
Article J.11	Article 21

Previous numbering	New numbering
Article J.12	Article 22
Article J.13	Article 23
Article J.14	Article 24
Article J.15	Article 25
Article J.16	Article 26
Article J.17	Article 27
Article J.18	Article 28
Title VI (***)	Title VI
Article K.1	Article 29
Article K.2	Article 30
Article K.3	Article 31
Article K.4	Article 32
Article K.5	Article 33
Article K.6	Article 34
Article K.7	Article 35
Article K.8	Article 36
Article K.9	Article 37
Article K.10	Article 38
Article K.11	Article 39
Article K.12	Article 40
Article K.13	Article 41
Article K.14	Article 42
Title VIa (**)	Title VII
Article K.15	Article 43
Article K.16 (*)	Article 44
Article K.17 (*)	Article 45
Title VII	Title VIII
Article L	Article 46
Article M	Article 47
Article N	Article 48
Article O	Article 49
Article P	Article 50
Article Q	Article 51
Article R	Article 52
Article S	Article 53

B. TREATY ESTABLISHING THE EUROPEAN COMMUNITY

Previous numbering	New numbering
Part One	*Part One*
Article 1	Article 1
Article 2	Article 2
Article 3	Article 3
Article 3a	Article 4
Article 3b	Article 5
Article 3c	Article 6
Article 4	Article 7
Article 4a	Article 8
Article 4b	Article 9
Article 5	Article 10
Article 5a (*)	Article 11
Article 6	Article 12
Article 6a (*)	Article 13
Article 7 (repealed)	—
Article 7a	Article 14
Article 7b (repealed)	—
Article 7c	Article 15
Article 7d (*)	Article 16
Part Two	*Part Two*
Article 8	Article 17
Article 8a	Article 18
Article 8b	Article 19
Article 8c	Article 20
Article 8d	Article 21
Article 8e	Article 22
Part Three	*Part Three*
Title I	*Title I*
Article 9	Article 23
Article 10	Article 24
Article 11 (repealed)	—
Chapter 1	*Chapter 1*
Section 1 (deleted)	—
Article 12	Article 25

Previous numbering	New numbering
Article 13 (repealed)	—
Article 14 (repealed)	—
Article 15 (repealed)	—
Article 16 (repealed)	—
Article 17 (repealed)	—
Section 2 (deleted)	—
Article 18 (repealed)	—
Article 19 (repealed)	—
Article 20 (repealed)	—
Article 21 (repealed)	—
Article 22 (repealed)	—
Article 23 (repealed)	—
Article 24 (repealed)	—
Article 25 (repealed)	—
Article 26 (repealed)	—
Article 27 (repealed)	—
Article 28	Article 26
Article 29	Article 27
Chapter 2	*Chapter 2*
Article 30	Article 28
Article 31 (repealed)	—
Article 32 (repealed)	—
Article 33 (repealed)	—
Article 34	Article 29
Article 35 (repealed)	—
Article 36	Article 30
Article 37	Article 31
Title II	Title II
Article 38	Article 32
Article 39	Article 33
Article 40	Article 34
Article 41	Article 35
Article 42	Article 36
Article 43	Article 37
Article 44 (repealed)	—
Article 45 (repealed)	—
Article 46	Article 38
Article 47 (repealed)	—

Previous numbering	New numbering
Title III	Title III
Chapter 1	*Chapter 1*
Article 48	Article 39
Article 49	Article 40
Article 50	Article 41
Article 51	Article 42
Chapter 2	*Chapter 2*
Article 52	Article 43
Article 53 (repealed)	—
Article 54	Article 44
Article 55	Article 45
Article 56	Article 46
Article 57	Article 47
Article 58	Article 48
Chapter 3	*Chapter 3*
Article 59	Article 49
Article 60	Article 50
Article 61	Article 51
Article 62 (repealed)	—
Article 63	Article 52
Article 64	Article 53
Article 65	Article 54
Article 66	Article 55
Chapter 4	*Chapter 4*
Article 67 (repealed)	—
Article 68 (repealed)	—
Article 69 (repealed)	—
Article 70 (repealed)	—
Article 71 (repealed)	—
Article 72 (repealed)	—
Article 73 (repealed)	—
Article 73a (repealed)	—
Article 73b	Article 56
Article 73c	Article 57
Article 73d	Article 58
Article 73e (repealed)	—
Article 73f	Article 59

Previous numbering	New numbering
Article 73g	Article 60
Article 73h (repealed)	—
Title IIIa (**)	*Title IV*
Article 73i	Article 61
Article 73j (*)	Article 62
Article 73k (*)	Article 63
Article 73l (*)	Article 64
Article 73m	Article 65
Article 73n (*)	Article 66
Article 73o (*)	Article 67
Article 73p (*)	Article 68
Article 73q (*)	Article 69
Title IV	*Title V*
Article 74	Article 70
Article 75	Article 71
Article 76	Article 72
Article 77	Article 73
Article 78	Article 74
Article 79	Article 75
Article 80	Article 76
Article 81	Article 77
Article 82	Article 78
Article 83	Article 79
Article 84	Article 80
Title V	*Title VI*
Chapter 1	*Chapter 1*
Section 1	*Section 1*
Article 85	Article 81
Article 86	Article 82
Article 87	Article 83
Article 88	Article 84
Article 89	Article 85
Article 90	Article 86
Section 2 (deleted)	—
Article 91 (repealed)	—

Previous numbering	New numbering
Section 3	*Section 2*
Article 92	Article 87
Article 93	Article 88
Article 94	Article 89
Chapter 2	*Chapter 2*
Article 95	Article 90
Article 96	Article 91
Article 97 (repealed)	—
Article 98	Article 92
Article 99	Article 93
Chapter 3	*Chapter 3*
Article 100	Article 94
Article 100a	Article 95
Article 100b (repealed)	—
Article 100c (repealed)	—
Article 100d (repealed)	—
Article 101	Article 96
Article 102	Article 97
Title VI	Title VII
Chapter 1	*Chapter 1*
Article 102a	Article 98
Article 103	Article 99
Article 103a	Article 100
Article 104	Article 101
Article 104a	Article 102
Article 104b	Article 103
Article 104c	Article 104
Chapter 2	*Chapter 2*
Article 105	Article 105
Article 105a	Article 106
Article 106	Article 107
Article 107	Article 108
Article 108	Article 109
Article 108a	Article 110
Article 109	Article 111

Previous numbering	New numbering
Chapter 3	*Chapter 3*
Article 109a	Article 112
Article 109b	Article 113
Article 109c	Article 114
Article 109d	Article 115
Chapter 4	*Chapter 4*
Article 109e	Article 116
Article 109f	Article 117
Article 109g	Article 118
Article 109h	Article 119
Article 109i	Article 120
Article 109j	Article 121
Article 109k	Article 122
Article 109l	Article 123
Article 109m	Article 124
Title VIa (**)	Title VIII
Article 109n	Article 125
Article 109o (*)	Article 126
Article 109p (*)	Article 127
Article 109q (*)	Article 128
Article 109r (*)	Article 129
Article 109s (*)	Article 130
Title VII	Title IX
Article 110	Article 131
Article 111 (repealed)	—
Article 112	Article 132
Article 113	Article 133
Article 114 (repealed)	—
Article 115	Article 134
Article 116 (repealed)	—
Title VIIa (**)	Title X
Article 116a	Article 135
Title VIII	Title XI
Chapter 1 (***)	*Chapter 1*
Article 117	Article 136
Article 118	Article 137

Previous numbering	New numbering
Article 118a	Article 138
Article 118b	Article 139
Article 118c	Article 140
Article 119	Article 141
Article 119a	Article 142
Article 120	Article 143
Article 121	Article 144
Article 122	Article 145
Chapter 2	*Chapter 2*
Article 123	Article 146
Article 124	Article 147
Article 125	Article 148
Chapter 3	*Chapter 3*
Article 126	Article 149
Article 127	Article 150
Title IX	Title XII
Article 128	Article 151
Title X	Title XIII
Article 129	Article 152
Title XI	Title XIV
Article 129a	Article 153
Title XII	Title XV
Article 129b	Article 154
Article 129c	Article 155
Article 129d	Article 156
Title XIII	Title XVI
Article 130	Article 157
Title XIV	Title XVII
Article 130a	Article 158
Article 130b	Article 159
Article 130c	Article 160
Article 130d	Article 161
Article 130e	Article 162

Previous numbering	New numbering
Title XV	Title XVIII
Article 130f	Article 163
Article 130g	Article 164
Article 130h	Article 165
Article 130i	Article 166
Article 130j	Article 167
Article 130k	Article 168
Article 130l	Article 169
Article 130m	Article 170
Article 130n	Article 171
Article 130o	Article 172
Article 130p	Article 173
Article 130q (repealed)	—
Title XVI	Title XIX
Article 130r	Article 174
Article 130s	Article 175
Article 130t	Article 176
Title XVII	Title XX
Article 130u	Article 177
Article 130v	Article 178
Article 130w	Article 179
Article 130x	Article 180
Article 130y	Article 181
Part Four	*Part Four*
Article 131	Article 182
Article 132	Article 183
Article 133	Article 184
Article 134	Article 185
Article 135	Article 186
Article 136	Article 187
Article 136a	Article 188
Part Five	*Part Five*
Title I	*Title I*
Chapter 1	*Chapter 1*
Section 1	*Section 1*
Article 137	Article 189

Previous numbering	New numbering
Article 138	Article 190
Article 138a	Article 191
Article 138b	Article 192
Article 138c	Article 193
Article 138d	Article 194
Article 138e	Article 195
Article 139	Article 196
Article 140	Article 197
Article 141	Article 198
Article 142	Article 199
Article 143	Article 200
Article 144	Article 201
Section 2	*Section 2*
Article 145	Article 202
Article 146	Article 203
Article 147	Article 204
Article 148	Article 205
Article 149 (repealed)	—
Article 150	Article 206
Article 151	Article 207
Article 152	Article 208
Article 153	Article 209
Article 154	Article 210
Section 3	*Section 3*
Article 155	Article 211
Article 156	Article 212
Article 157	Article 213
Article 158	Article 214
Article 159	Article 215
Article 160	Article 216
Article 161	Article 217
Article 162	Article 218
Article 163	Article 219
Section 4	*Section 4*
Article 164	Article 220
Article 165	Article 221
Article 166	Article 222

Previous numbering	New numbering
Article 167	Article 223
Article 168	Article 224
Article 168a	Article 225
Article 169	Article 226
Article 170	Article 227
Article 171	Article 228
Article 172	Article 229
Article 173	Article 230
Article 174	Article 231
Article 175	Article 232
Article 176	Article 233
Article 177	Article 234
Article 178	Article 235
Article 179	Article 236
Article 180	Article 237
Article 181	Article 238
Article 182	Article 239
Article 183	Article 240
Article 184	Article 241
Article 185	Article 242
Article 186	Article 243
Article 187	Article 244
Article 188	Article 245
Section 5	*Section 5*
Article 188a	Article 246
Article 188b	Article 247
Article 188c	Article 248
Chapter 2	*Chapter 2*
Article 189	Article 249
Article 189a	Article 250
Article 189b	Article 251
Article 189c	Article 252
Article 190	Article 253
Article 191	Article 254
Article 191a	Article 255
Article 192	Article 256

Previous numbering	New numbering
Chapter 3	*Chapter 3*
Article 193	Article 257
Article 194	Article 258
Article 195	Article 259
Article 196	Article 260
Article 197	Article 261
Article 198	Article 262
Chapter 4	*Chapter 4*
Article 198a	Article 263
Article 198b	Article 264
Article 198c	Article 265
Chapter 5	*Chapter 5*
Article 198d	Article 266
Article 198e	Article 267
Title II	Title II
Article 199	Article 268
Article 200 (repealed)	—
Article 201	Article 269
Article 201a	Article 270
Article 202	Article 271
Article 203	Article 272
Article 204	Article 273
Article 205	Article 274
Article 205a	Article 275
Article 206	Article 276
Article 206a (repealed)	—
Article 207	Article 277
Article 208	Article 278
Article 209	Article 279
Article 209a	Article 280
Part Six	*Part Six*
Article 210	Article 281
Article 211	Article 282
Article 212 (*)	Article 283
Article 213	Article 284
Article 213a	Article 285

Previous numbering	New numbering
Article 213b	Article 286
Article 214	Article 287
Article 215	Article 288
Article 216	Article 289
Article 217	Article 290
Article 218 (*)	Article 291
Article 219	Article 292
Article 220	Article 293
Article 221	Article 294
Article 222	Article 295
Article 223	Article 296
Article 224	Article 297
Article 225	Article 298
Article 226 (repealed)	—
Article 227	Article 299
Article 228	Article 300
Article 228a	Article 301
Article 229	Article 302
Article 230	Article 303
Article 231	Article 304
Article 232	Article 305
Article 233	Article 306
Article 234	Article 307
Article 235	Article 308
Article 236 (*)	Article 309
Article 237 (repealed)	—
Article 238	Article 310
Article 239	Article 311
Article 240	Article 312
Article 241 (repealed)	—
Article 242 (repealed)	—
Article 243 (repealed)	—
Article 244 (repealed)	—
Article 245 (repealed)	—
Article 246 (repealed)	—
Final Provisions	*Final Provisions*
Article 247	Article 313
Article 248	Article 314